■ United States Holocaust Memorial Museum
Center for Advanced Holocaust Studies

Documenting Life and Destruction
Holocaust Sources in Context

SERIES EDITOR

JÜRGEN MATTHÄUS

DOCUMENTING LIFE AND DESTRUCTION

HOLOCAUST SOURCES IN CONTEXT

This groundbreaking series provides a new perspective on history using first-hand accounts of the lives of those who suffered through the Holocaust, those who perpetrated it, and those who witnessed it as bystanders. The United States Holocaust Memorial Museum's Center for Advanced Holocaust Studies presents a wide range of documents from different archival holdings, expanding knowledge about the lives and fates of Holocaust victims and making those resources broadly available to the general public and scholarly communities for the first time.

SERIES EDITOR:
Jürgen Matthäus is the research director at the United States Holocaust Memorial Museum's Center for Advanced Holocaust Studies.

BOOKS IN THE SERIES

1. *Jewish Responses to Persecution, 1933–1946, Volume I, 1933–1938*, Jürgen Matthäus and Mark Roseman (2009)
2. *Children during the Holocaust*, Patricia Heberer (2011)

with major support from

The Gilbert and Eleanor Kraus Fund
for the Study of the Fate and Rescue
of Children in the Holocaust
and
The Blum Family Foundation

The authors have worked to provide clear information about the provenance of each document and illustration included here. In some instances we have been unable to verify the existence or identity of any present copyright owners. If notified of any item inadvertently credited wrongly, we will include updated credit information in reprints of this work. In the same vein, if a reader has verifiable information about a person's fate that remains incomplete in this volume, it would be greatly appreciated if that data were shared with the authors.

Documenting Life and Destruction
Holocaust Sources in Context

CHILDREN DURING THE HOLOCAUST

Patricia Heberer

Introduction by Nechama Tec

Advisory Committee:

Christopher R. Browning
David Engel
Sara Horowitz
Steven T. Katz
Aaron Rodrigue
Alvin H. Rosenfeld
Nechama Tec

AltaMira Press
in association with the United States Holocaust Memorial Museum
2011

For USHMM:
Project Manager: Mel Hecker
Contributing Editor: Jan Lambertz
Researchers: Ryan Farrell, Greg Wilkowski
Translators: Ania Borejsza-Wysocka, Pavel Ilyin, Louise Lawrence-Israels, Jolanta Kraemer, Kathleen Luft, Margit Meissner, Anya Nowakowski, Steven Sage, Veronika Szabó

Published by AltaMira Press
A division of Rowman & Littlefield Publishers, Inc.
A wholly owned subsidary of The Rowman & Littlefield Publishing Group, Inc.
4501 Forbes Boulevard, Suite 200, Lanham, Maryland 20706
http://www.altamirapress.com

Estover Road, Plymouth PL6 7PY, United Kingdom

Copyright © 2011 by AltaMira Press

British Library Cataloguing in Publication Information Available

Library of Congress Cataloging-in-Publication Data

Heberer, Patricia.
    Children during the Holocaust / Patricia Heberer.
        p. cm. — (Documenting life and destruction)
    Includes bibliographical references.
    ISBN 978-0-7591-1984-0 (cloth : alk. paper) — ISBN 978-0-7591-1986-4 (ebook)
    1. Jewish children in the Holocaust. 2. Jewish children in the Holocaust—Sources.
    3. Holocaust, Jewish (1939-1945) 4. Holocaust, Jewish (1939-1945)—Sources.
    5. World War, 1939-1945—Children. 6. World War, 1939-1945—Children—Sources.
    7. Jews—Persecutions—Europe—History—20th century. 8. Jews—Persecutions—
    Europe—History—20th century—Sources. I. Title.
    D804.48.H43 2011
    940.53'18083—dc22   2010047167

∞™ The paper used in this publication meets the minimum requirements of American National Standard for Information Sciences—Permanence of Paper for Printed Library Materials, ANSI/NISO Z39.48-1992.

Printed in the United States of America

"I think that possibly the greatest tragedy the Jewish people underwent was the tragedy of the children. The children in the ghetto also used to play and laugh, and in their games the tragedy of the Jewish people was reflected."

— From Document 8-8. Testimony of Dr. Aharon Peretz, May 4, 1961, in *The Trial of Adolf Eichmann: Record of Proceedings in the District Court of Jerusalem* (Jerusalem: Trust for the Publication of the Proceedings of the Eichmann Trial in cooperation with the Israel State Archives and Yad Vashem, the Holocaust Martyrs' and Heroes' Remembrance Authority, 1992–1995), 1:478–479.

CONTENTS

Author's Introduction

KRYSTYNA ŻYWULSKA (born Sonia Landau) was a survivor of Auschwitz. Born in September 1914, she and her family fled to the Polish capital to escape Nazi persecution in their native city of Łódź and were resettled in the Warsaw ghetto in 1941. In late August 1942, Żywulska and her mother escaped to Warsaw's "Aryan side," where the young woman assumed a Christian identity and joined the Polish resistance. Arrested and interrogated by the Gestapo in August 1943, "Blond Zosia," as she was known, was incarcerated in Auschwitz as a political prisoner. Creating poems to endure the endless *Appells* (roll calls) at Auschwitz II–Birkenau, Żywulska established herself after the war as an author and songwriter, retaining her Polish gentile identity. Compelled in the early 1960s to reveal her Jewish ethnicity, Żywulska wrote *Empty Water* (*Pusta Woda*, 1963), which detailed her life as a young woman in the Warsaw ghetto.[1] Within its pages, she recalls observing the play of her young neighbors, six-year-old Szymus and Anulka, aged five. Szymus was constructing forms with a set of building blocks, which Anulka always angrily destroyed. The young boy explained his playmate's actions to Żywulska.

---

1. See Barbara Milewski, "Krystyna Żywulska: The Making of a Satirist and Songwriter in Auschwitz-Birkenau As Discovered through Camp Mementos," *Swarthmore College Bulletin* (July 2009): 30. Most famous for her memoir *Przeżyłam Oświęcim* (1946), Żywulska married a prominent official in the Polish communist secret police. In 1970, she emigrated to join her son in Düsseldorf, Germany, and died there in 1992.

[She acts so] because I am building a forest. And I say to her: this is the green tree named the oak. The oak is a tree with leaves. And there is a tree named a pine, and it has needles. And then she destroys the blocks and says that there are not any trees anywhere in the world. But my Mom told me that there are many trees because she saw them herself. And these trees smell and when I am big we will go to see them.

"There are no trees, you are lying!" said Anulka.

"You see, she doesn't believe me," said Szymus. "She never believes me but anyway my Mom doesn't lie. Yesterday she didn't believe there was water named a river. With this river, water is flowing and together this is called the Vistula River.[2] So tell her that the Vistula exists; you saw it, didn't you? Did you see the Vistula or not?"

"There is no river," said Anulka, scowling and stamping her feet. "There is no river at all. [. . .]"

"Leave her in peace, Szymus," Krystyna intervened. "You can play other games. Perhaps Anulka would like to build something from the blocks herself. Let her do it and don't quarrel anymore."

"She wants to play only 'The Wall and the Gendarme,'" replied Szymus. "She always builds the wall. Then she shouts at me, 'Stop smuggling!' or 'I'm the gendarme and now I will kill you!' But I don't want to play such a game. I don't want to be a smuggler."[3]

Approximately 1.1 million Jewish children were murdered in the Holocaust.[4] Millions of youngsters—Jews and non-Jews—suffered persecution, deprivation, and resettlement at the hands of the National Socialists and their wartime allies. Like Szymus and Anulka in the Warsaw ghetto, a generation of young people lost their childhoods in the conventional sense. Like them, many European children of the period knew less about meadows, flowers, pets, and toys than they did about violence, hunger, and death.

This volume is, in essence, a narrative in microcosm: it is the story of the Holocaust as seen through the eyes, and fates, of its youngest victims. With notable exceptions, the contours and chronology of Nazi racial policy were par-

2. The Vistula is one of Poland's longest and most important waterways.

3. Krystyna Żylwulska, *Pusta Wodo*, quoted in Barbara Engelking-Boni, "Childhood in the Warsaw Ghetto," in *Children and the Holocaust: Symposium Presentations of the Center for Advanced Holocaust Studies* (Washington, DC: U.S. Holocaust Memorial Museum, 2004), 34.

4. Nicholas Stargardt, *Witnesses of War: Children's Lives under the Nazis* (New York: Alfred A. Knopf, 2006), 9.

allel for children, throughout defined as youths under the age of eighteen, and adults.[5] Jewish youngsters, just like their parents, were victims of discrimination, ghettoization, deportation, and mass murder. Yet, children encountered and contended with the persecutory policies of the Nazis in markedly different ways. This study portrays the experiences of children during the Nazi era and explores their reactions and responses to war and persecution in the schoolroom, on the playground, at home, and in the camps and ghettos of Nazi-occupied Europe.

To depict the lives and circumstances of children during the Holocaust, this volume embeds contemporary documentation within an explanatory narrative. The documents represented in each chapter have been selected to reflect the full range of experiences of children during the Nazi period in terms of region, age, and ethnic identity. I have also endeavored to capture a diversity of voices and viewpoints in this volume. As a result, this story of child witnesses and victims of the Holocaust is told not only through the accounts of young persons themselves but in the words of their parents and caregivers, teachers and rescuers, liberators and persecutors. Wherever possible, the documents in this collection stem from an in situ source—that is to say, they were written or recorded at the time in which the events portrayed occurred. It is true that today there is no shortage of excellent memoirs authored by child survivors of the Holocaust. Yet, to freely juxtapose contemporary and latter-day sources (produced after the Holocaust) creates a kind of tension within the text in which the immediacy of events inherent in the former contends with the teleology and circumspection of the latter. Thus, every effort has been made to limit the use of memoir material in this volume. Sometimes the nature of the event in question or the age of the child involved has made it impossible to use in situ documentation. In these instances, the closest available primary source, such as postwar trial testimony or the accounts of witnesses made in the immediate postwar period, have been used in their stead.

These considerations pose a number of difficulties to the collector of sources concerning children during the Holocaust. This volume represents a very small selection from among the wealth of materials concerning the fate of children during the Nazi era; yet, a close examination of such documentation reveals that

---

5. Significant exceptions include, at least in its initial stages, the child "euthanasia" program, which, unlike its adult corollary, also targeted disabled infants and toddlers outside institutional settings. Another notable exception includes aspects of Germanization policy associated with the *Lebensborn* program, which sought out Slavic children in German areas of occupation who possessed German racial characteristics and, often removing them from their parents by force, settled them with adoptive parents in Germany; see chapter 6 of this volume.

only a fraction of these contemporary sources were actually created by children. In part, the physical circumstances of persecutees and victims of war are responsible for this dearth of materials. Resettlement, deportation, and incarceration in concentration or forced labor camp settings imposed formidable obstacles for both adults and children who wished to record accounts of their experiences. The lack of writing instruments and especially paper hampered children's efforts to depict what happened to them and their parents. Other reasons for the lack of children's sources lies in the very nature of childhood and young adolescence. Children generally did not, and do not, generate as much written material as their adult contemporaries. With certain exceptions, children do not engage in the same amount of private and public correspondence as their parents do; they do not, in the main, write studies, monographs, or letters to newspaper editors or author administrative files or legal documents. Furthermore, persecutory polices in German- and Axis-occupied countries often prevented school-age youngsters from acquiring the education necessary to read and write, thus depriving them of the intellectual capacity to record their experiences. There is a marked imbalance between sources created by young children and those stemming from older youngsters and adolescents, which this volume reflects. Most of the childhood diaries, letters, and drawings available to us from the Holocaust period came from young people in their preteen or teenaged years. Of course, very young children without the appropriate skill sets to write or draw had no chance to document their thoughts and feelings. Particularly for these youngsters, accounts by adult parents, relatives, or caretakers are the only sources we have to testify to their young lives. These voices often restrict our insight, for not even the most sensitive or perceptive adult can capture the full range of a child's experiences, hopes, and anxieties.[6]

Using the varied sources available to us, this volume forms a narrative weaving historical documentation with contextualization by the author. Its chapters have been developed thematically to articulate the wide variety of children's experiences during the Holocaust. The majority of these deal with young Jewish victims and follow the chronological arc of persecution from discrimination to deportation, ghettoization, and incarceration and murder in the vast Nazi concentration camp system. The last two chapters of the book cover issues of resistance and rescue of Jewish youngsters and the experiences of surviving young Jewish victims at liberation and in the immediate postwar period. Chapters 2 and 7 examine Jewish and non-Jewish children as victims of war and as targets of racial hygiene (eugenic) policy, respectively. Chapter 7, "The Lives of Others," stands

---

6. See, e.g., Bela Weicherz, *In Her Father's Eyes: A Childhood Extinguished by the Holocaust*, ed. and trans. Daniel Magilow (New Brunswick, NJ: Rutgers University Press, 2008).

out in this collection in that it addresses the experiences of youngsters growing up as "Aryans" in Nazi Germany. Chapter 8, "The World of the Child," also deviates from the chronological progression of the work in order to explore the ways in which youngsters coped with their menacing world through study, play, and creative endeavors. In each chapter, the historical documents have been printed in a distinct format to distinguish them from the explanatory text. They have been reproduced, and translated where necessary, to correspond as faithfully as possible to their original version both in form and content. Emphasis on words or phrases by the original author or authors of the document has been highlighted here by underlining the relevant portion. In places where the document could not be printed in its entirety, ellipses ([. . .]) have been inserted to mark omissions in the text. In some places, always clearly delineated by footnotes in the text, the surnames of victims and their families have been anonymized or replaced by pseudonyms to protect the privacy of these individuals.

A number of names, places, events, and organizations appear in boldface throughout this volume when they are mentioned for the first time in a chapter. This indicates that readers can find further information on these highlighted terms in the glossary at the end of the volume. Using the rich resources of the United States Holocaust Memorial Museum's library and archives, I have attempted to provide brief information concerning the lives and fates of individuals discussed in this book. Some of this data appears in the glossary and some of it in the footnotes to the documents and explanatory texts. Regrettably, it was not always possible to find biographical information on every individual named in these pages. A bibliography at the end of the volume offers readers the opportunity to explore the topics discussed in this book in greater depth.

Finally, it gives me great pleasure to thank the many individuals who made this volume possible. I am grateful to our donors, the Blum Family Foundation and the Gilbert and Eleanor Kraus Fund for the Study of the Fate and Rescue of Children in the Holocaust, for their generous support, which proved crucial to the fruition of this project. Series editor Jürgen Matthäus offered scholarly direction and was a voice of calm reason during the vicissitudes of production and publication. He and project manager Mel Hecker provided careful and conscientious editing and saw that the transition from draft to publication went smoothly and efficiently. Researcher Greg Wilkowski helped me enormously with reference work for this volume, while Ryan Farrell undertook the thorny task of securing rights with patience and tenacity. Jan Lambertz continuously plied me with new source materials and bibliographical references. Doris Bergen (Toronto), Jochen Böhler (Jena), and Beate Meyer (Hamburg) provided me with many useful suggestions and references to documents that are reprinted in this book. Sara Horowitz (Toronto) and Judy Gerson (New Brunswick) reviewed an early version of the manuscript, providing helpful insights for revision and commentary on its use as a source edition for classroom teaching. Nechama Tec (Connecticut), in addition to authoring the volume's introduction, shared valuable advice and suggestions at every stage of writing. I am profoundly grateful to Louise Lawrence-Israels, Rabbi Jacob Weiner, and Robert Ehrenreich for sharing with me materials and firsthand accounts concerning their experiences or those of their family members during the Holocaust. At AltaMira Press, thanks are in order to Marissa Parks, Elaine McGarraugh, Jennifer Kelland, and Kim Lyons for their dedication to this project.

I am indebted to so many of my wonderful colleagues at the United States Holocaust Memorial Museum. Paul A. Shapiro, director of the Center for Advanced Holocaust Studies, has provided unwavering support for the staff's scholarly endeavors, including the production of this volume. The personnel of the museum's library; film, photo, and textual records archives; and its collections division have been enormously helpful in securing documents, photographs, and other sources. Special thanks are due to my colleagues Michlean Amir, Vadim Altskan, Bill Connelly, Judy Cohen, Radu Ioanid, Marc Masurovsky, Nancy Hartman, Teresa Pollin, Vincent Slatt, and Anatol Steck for making me aware of an interesting collection, an important artifact, or a fascinating document that I might have otherwise overlooked. Within the Center for Advanced Holocaust Studies, staff historians Martin Dean, Emil Kerenji, Geoffrey Megargee, and Leah Wolfson shared with me their knowledge and experiences gleaned from their efforts for the center's *Encyclopedia of Camps and Ghettos* and *Jewish Responses to Persecution*. I am also grateful to my supervisor, Senior Historian Peter Black, for the breadth of his historical knowledge and for his enduring support of this project; thanks also to our interns Elissa Frankle, Johannes Breit, Lukas Lang, Philipp Selim, Emily Utzerath, and Anna Ullrich, who, when deadlines loomed, generously undertook some of my usual tasks to free my time for writing.

I owe a very personal debt of gratitude to my family: to Jim Rice, who endured long-winded descriptions of each new find I made in the library or archive and who read several iterations of this manuscript; and to Diane Heberer: may every child have such a kind and loving parent. My very last thanks go to our museum's survivor volunteers, many whom of were child survivors of the Holocaust and who have been a daily source of inspiration to me as I wrote this volume. This work is dedicated to them.

Patricia Heberer
Washington, DC, 2010

ABBREVIATIONS

AJDC, AJJDC, JDC, the Joint	**American Jewish Joint Distribution Committee**
BDM	**Bund Deutscher Mädel** (League of German Girls)
BdS	*Befehlshaber der Sicherheitspolizei und des SD* (commander of the Security Police and SD)
DP	**displaced person(s)**
Gestapo	Geheime Staatspolizei (Secret State Police)
HIAS	Hebrew Immigrant Aid Society
HJ	Hitlerjugend (Hitler Youth)
ICRC	**International Committee of the Red Cross**
ITS	International Tracing Service
KLV	*Kinderlandverschickung* (literally, "transfer of children to the countryside")
KZ	*Konzentrationslager* (concentration camp)
NARA	National Archives and Records Administration
NSDAP	Nationalsozialistische Deutsche Arbeiter Partei (National Socialist German Workers' Party, or Nazi Party)
NSV	Nationalsozialistische Volkswohlfahrt (National Socialist People's Welfare Organization)

ORT	**Obshestvo Remeslenofo zemledelcheskofo Truda** (Society for Trades and Agricultural Labor)
OSE	**Oeuvre de Secours aux Enfants** (Children's Aid Society)
Pg.	*Parteigenosse* (party comrade)
POW	prisoner of war
RKFDV	Reichskommissariat für die Festigung deutschen Volkstums (Reich Commissariat for the Strengthening of German Ethnicity)
RM	**Reichsmark**
RSHA	**Reichssicherheitshauptamt** (Reich Security Main Office)
RuSHA	**Rasse- und Siedlungshauptamt**
SA	Sturmabteilung (Storm Division or Storm Troopers)
SD	**Sicherheitsdienst** (Security Service)
SS	Schutzstaffel (Protective Squadron)
UNRRA	**United Nations Relief and Rehabilitation Administration**
USHMM	United States Holocaust Memorial Museum, Washington, D.C.
USHMMA	USHMM Archives
USHMMPA	USHMM Photo Archive
YIVO	Yidisher Visnshaftlekher Institut (Jewish Scientific Institute)

INTRODUCTION

BY NECHAMA TEC

A S A HOLOCAUST scholar and child survivor, I welcome Dr. Patricia Heberer's essential publication about children during the Holocaust. I am convinced that the crimes committed against children are the most shocking and least understood injustices against humanity. As we try to unravel the mysteries of these crimes, we inevitably turn to Poland, the largest Jewish community in Europe and the prewar home of roughly 1 million Jewish children. In part because of my personal experiences, I concentrate in this introduction on the Holocaust in Poland and its effects on the fate of Jewish children in order to highlight some specific features of this book's intriguing topic.[1]

My Holocaust research is guided by the assumption that a concentration on the extreme inevitably promotes our understandings of less acute circumstances. From the perspective of the Third Reich, what did the presence of Jewish children mean? It appears that there was a dual and contradictory perception of Jewish children as they were seen as at once useless and potentially threatening. They were useless because children could not contribute to the German economy. They were threatening because, as future adults, these children would inevitably undermine the purity of the "**Aryan**" race. Eventually, and more certainly, as adults, these former children would want to avenge the

---

1. This text draws on my earlier publications, particularly Nechama Tec, *Dry Tears: The Story of a Lost Childhood* (Oxford: Oxford University Press, 1984).

crimes committed against their ancestors. Even in cases where Jewish children were considered useful for exploitation, their ultimate fate seldom differed. Historical evidence consistently shows that when the Germans faced decisions that required choosing between racial and economic advantages, racial calculations usually trumped considerations of economic utility.[2]

Historical documentation concerning the fate of Jewish children during the Holocaust is at the same time extensive and limited. German perpetrators generated many of the sources that survived the war, but these often offer dry statistics or general references to the execution of what came to be called the "Final Solution of the Jewish Question." These documents shed at best a pale light on the suffering of victims, and clearly they show no empathy even for the most innocent and vulnerable among them. But even the most cursory reference in German documents to underaged targets of mass annihilation is historically important. In the course of events that formed the Holocaust, the systematic murder of Jewish children marked the passing of the threshold toward genocide. In the summer of 1941, just weeks after the Third Reich commenced its war of annihilation against the Soviet Union, traces of the "Final Solution" began to appear in reports and letters written by Germans who were involved in or witnessed the wave of mass executions sweeping across the occupied area. A member of a German police battalion wrote home to his family in the Reich, "The Jews are free game. [. . .] One can only give the Jews some well-intentioned advice: bring no more children into the world. They no longer have a future." In early August 1941 he noted, "Last night 150 Jews from this village were shot, men, women, and children, all killed. The Jews are being totally eradicated."[3] In perpetrator documents, Jewish children, like adult Jews, appear only as logical targets in a process of "cleansing" German-dominated territory; yet, as the murders of the children in Byelaya Tserkov (Documents 3-9 through 3-11) demonstrate, what transpired in the ghettos and at the killing sites in eastern Europe depended as much on local conditions and decisions on the ground as on directions from Berlin.

What do we learn from listening to the voice of a child attesting in the early postwar period to the criminality of the German regime? The time is 1945 to 1946. The name of the child survivor is Ala Openheim; she is from Poland. What she shares she calls "A Horrible Experience," recollections of her escape

---

2. See Saul Friedländer, *Nazi Germany and the Jews*, Vol. 1: *The Years of Persecution, 1933–1939*; Vol. 2: *The Years of Extermination, 1939–1945* (New York: HarperCollins, 1997, 2007).

3. Quoted from Christopher R. Browning with Jürgen Matthäus, *The Origins of the Final Solution: The Evolution of Nazi Jewish Policy, September 1939–March 1942* (Lincoln/Jerusalem: University of Nebraska Press/Yad Vashem, 2004), 260–61.

from persecution as an eight-year-old. She wrote these lines in an orphanage in Pieszyce (formerly called Pietrolesie, located in Lower Silesia):

> With the approaching New Year, my past returns to haunt me. This past forces me to revisit portions of my wartime experiences. These are memories which I cannot forget. They had penetrated into the depths of my existence, towering over my entire soul. They cannot and ought not to be forgotten! Horrible, horrible . . . !
>
> A dark night. The city is engrossed in a deep sleep. The city is in a state of complete silence. Here and there, desperate people fly by, actually already not people but shadows of people. They run to hiding places to become invisible to the SS men. This means that I, my mother and my sister were among them. Nevertheless, nothing helped us. We fell into the hands of the oppressors. The hands of these bandits were beating us in a horrible way. They were pushing us into the prison. They forced us into a cell in which there were many people like us. Many who resembled us, in darkness, in dampness, in horrible hygienic conditions of cleanliness. We sat there for two weeks. Patience was bursting with impatience. Our fate was anyway predetermined. This fate was hanging over us. In the same camp I stayed in were my father and my brother. They were not locked up. Here and there, they would approach our barred windows.
>
> One time, in the middle of the night I asked my astonished father for a hammer. Father refused to grant my request, but my brother, exposing himself to death, brought me a large German hammer. It was very dark. The prison was surrounded by SS men. Without giving it much thought, I banged the bars, everything hit the ground with a big crash. I, an eight-year-old child jumped out in a nightgown through the opening in the window. The Germans shot after me, but I escaped. Bullets were whizzing past my head, but I did not stop. I imagined that someone was calling me, screaming, "Escape, escape!" Behind me I heard steps. Someone was running, but no one could have guessed who. My little sister ran after me. It was terribly cold. This was December. We were barefoot and in nightgowns. We ran in an unknown direction, petrified, unconscious through the streets of the little town. Where to? We had no idea.
>
> Here we were: two little orphans! We sat down next to a gate. Our frozen feet refused to obey. Sitting like that, we realized that we were all alone. Our mother had not succeeded in running away with us. Remembering that we had abandoned our mother, we forgot about the freezing cold. We forgot that we were almost naked. The snow kept falling,

covering us. Exhausted, leaning on the gate of the house, we wondered if happy children, in clean beds, had lived and slept there. Also wondering if such children had mothers, we fell asleep.[4]

Postwar recollections by child survivors are crucial because they open a window onto a past otherwise closed to us. At the same time, a combination of factors—children's lack of perspective at the time of persecution, the impact of trauma, and later transformations in memory—may blur our comprehension of the concrete circumstances and causal connections of events that are remembered. No doubt, postwar accounts by child survivors are indispensable to our understanding of what happened to children, their families, and their communities. At the same time, we must acknowledge especially the limits—or, rather, the complexities—of young children's recollections in our attempt to reconstruct the harrowing history of the Holocaust.

More than half a century after the end of the war, this is what Charlene Schiff remembers about the loss of her mother and her struggle to stay alive:

I was in the water up to my neck. The water was cold. We were hiding in the bulrushes and I knew we could not move. It was very quiet and any sound would give us away. Mama gave me some soggy bread. It tasted awful, but she insisted I had to eat it to keep strong. I was tired and wet. The night was dark and dawn came suddenly. In the light of day we saw that many other people from the ghetto had made their way to the river. Shots, which had been sporadic during the night, became more regular now. The Ukrainian guards kept yelling, "Come out, Jew. I can see you," and most of the people were doing just that.

Mama kept whispering to me to stay put and not to make any sound. Days passed in confusion. Shots kept coming, seemingly from every direction. It was hard to remain quiet while listening to screams and cries and watching fire and smoke coming from the ghetto.

"When are we going to cross the river, Mama?" I wanted to know.

Mama tried to keep me calm and assured me that we could cross the river as soon as the Ukrainians and Germans left.

"When will that be?" I asked rather impatiently. After all I was only eleven years old.

"Soon, my sweet child, soon," Mama replied.

"At that time we will make our way to the farm of the K. family," Mama explained.

---

4. Testimony by Ada Openheim, 1945/46, ŻIH 301/2215 (my translation from Polish).

Farmer K. had promised to hide Mama and me. We knew his family. We used to buy dairy products from them before the war.

It was very tiring to stand in the river and at times I dozed off leaning on the bulrushes. One horrible moment I woke up and Mama was nowhere in sight. I was terrified, all alone, lost. I felt betrayed and guilty for falling asleep. I felt like screaming and crying for Mama, but could do neither. By evening, all had become quiet.

I thought Mama had not been able to wake me and had made her way to the farm where she would be waiting for me. I crossed the river and walked until I reached the farmer's place. He greeted me in the barn like a stranger who was not welcome at all. He would not even let me in the house. I noticed Papa's gold pocket watch and chain dangling from his dirty coveralls. He told me my Mama was not there.

I never saw my mother again.

In search of her mother, Charlene began a forest journey that lasted two years.[5]

In countries under the German occupation, the survival rate of Jewish children was consistently lower than that of the general Jewish population. By war's end, the Germans had succeeded in murdering at least 1.1 million Jewish children. In France, out of 350,000 French Jews, an estimated 75 percent survived; among them, the number of child survivors ranges from 5,000 to 15,000, or about 2 to 4 percent. After the war in **Łódź**, social workers collected evidence about the fates of 1,246 children under the age of fourteen who had registered with different Jewish committees, offering some information about the history of their survival. The distribution in the following table shows how these Jewish children endured the Holocaust.[6]

---

5. See Charlene Schiff's wartime recollections in *Echoes of Memory: Stories of the Memory Project* (Washington, DC: U.S. Holocaust Memorial Museum [USHMM], 2003), 2:59–60. Over many years, as a member of the USHMM Speaker's Bureau, Charlene has lectured to a wide range of audiences, including college and high school students. She was married to Brigadier General Edward Schiff, who had shared his wife's interest in the Holocaust. Charlene is the sole survivor of her family of four. Her father, Professor Perlmutter, was a distinguished Professor of Philosophy at Lvov University. As most Jewish elites he was murdered during the early stages of the German occupation. The circumstances under which her mother and sister perished are unknown.

6. Lucjan Dobroszycki, "Redemption of the Children," in "An Inventory to the Rescue Children Inc. Collection, 1946–1985," Yeshiva University Archives, 1986, http://libfindaids. yu.edu:8082/xtf/view?query=redemption+of+the+children&docId=ead%2Frescue%2Frescue. xml&chunk.id= (accessed November 20, 2010).

	Number	*Percentage*
On the Aryan side	742	59
In concentration camps	280	22
In the forests	125	10
In the Łódź ghetto	61	5
In partisan units	38	3

These figures point to certain patterns. The fact that about 60 percent of the children survived on the "Aryan side" suggests that most of them were protected by Christians. Moreover, additional evidence shows that in countries under the German occupation, the survival rate of Jewish children was consistently lower than that of the general Jewish population. With time, the Germans succeeded in murdering 1.1 million Jewish children. Also, right after the war, according to lists compiled by ad hoc committees, five thousand Jewish children were left alive in Poland.[7]

As an eight-year-old Jewish child, how did I fit into German-occupied Poland? At the time, I heard my parents say over and over again that childhood was a luxury Jewish children could not afford. They elaborated this idea in a variety of ways. Clearly it meant that if I wanted to live, I had to grow up fast. But what did growing up fast mean? It called for my willingness to learn, to follow directions. Most significantly, it required keeping secrets. Time and the changes around us had inevitably taught me that some things could not be mentioned to anyone associated with Germans—or even to anyone I was unfamiliar with. My parents were watchful, ready to explain, to clarify any of the changes that continued to evolve. Gradually for me, to be silent, to deny knowledge of things, became second nature. Explanations that came with examples helped me grasp all kinds of situations. When we were forced to move to less desirable quarters and lost valuable possessions, I heard my parents say, "You cry for people, not for things."

Indeed, my father, owner of a candle factory and co-owner of a large chemical plant in the city of Lublin, never complained about the loss of both. The candle factory he fictitiously transferred to one of his friendly employees, Mr. P.

---

7. These figures are discussed in Nechama Tec, "Jewish Children: Between Protectors and Murderers," *Occasional Paper of the Center for Advanced Holocaust Studies* (Washington, D.C.: U.S. Holocaust Memorial Museum, 2005), 2–3; see also Nechama Tec, "Between Two Worlds," *Journal of Literature & Belief* 18, no. 1 (1998): 16–17.

The Germans had confiscated his chemical plant and installed in it a German director, known as a commissioner, who offered my father a job. Father hardly talked about this switch of roles. As we relocated to a modest part of this plant, my parents and my sister worked all day. I was too young to be given any kind of responsibility—a fact that I resented. I would have liked to visit my family during the day, but my father felt that the workers might object to a child's presence, and he advised me to stay away.

The factory consisted of a cluster of simple structures, some of them one and others two stories high, arranged in a half circle. In the back of the half circle, stairs led to an upper level, on which there was a house divided into a few apartments and a garden surrounded by a wall. Beyond the wall was a convent that an order of teaching nuns ran as a boarding school for girls. I found a small opening in the wall from which, unobserved, I could watch the girls at play. To me they seemed so content, so carefree, and I envied them their fun. Did they know that a war was on? At times, as I watched them, I too became engrossed in their games and almost forgot about the war. But the bell, which called them back to class, called me back to reality, and at such moments I became more acutely aware of my loneliness. In the end, these small excursions made me feel more miserable than ever. The girls in the boarding school were so near and yet so far. The wall that separated us was thick indeed, and eventually I could not bear to go near it.

My parents were aware of my loneliness and depression, but there was little they could do to comfort me. Then, one day in 1942, I heard that many young Jewish women would be coming to work and live in this factory. Sure enough, about fifty of them moved onto the same floor, a portion of which had served as our old living quarters. They were young, between fifteen and twenty. They came from the ghetto, in the Majdan Tatarski suburb on the outskirts of Lublin.[8] Most of them had lost their families. Each was given a bed with curtains around it for privacy so that all of us had an illusion of small separate rooms within the huge space. These newcomers made a fuss over me, and for a while I felt less lonely. But with time the novelty wore off, and even though it was lively and pleasant after working hours, I still had to be alone during the entire day. My depression returned more strongly than before. I lost my appetite, as well as all interest in my surroundings, and when it became obvious that

---

8. See "Lublin Ghetto," in *U.S. Holocaust Memorial Museum Encyclopedia of Camps and Ghettos, 1933–1945*, Vol. 2: *Ghettos in German-Occupied Eastern Europe*, ed. Martin Dean (Bloomington: Indiana University Press in association with the U.S. Holocaust Memorial Museum, 2011), 30.

I was losing weight day by day, my parents began to worry. Because at that time it was peaceful in the ghetto, to improve my state of mind, mother took me there for visits. I could see Czuczka, the teacher I loved, and I would visit other children. Each time I went, my urge to stay grew stronger. I found it harder and harder to leave.

One day, casually, Czuczka said to my mother, referring to me by my pet name, "I wish I could keep Helka with me. This would make the two of us happy." "And what if there should be a new **deportation**, and we lost her?" my mother asked sadly. Her fears, after all, were justified. One never knew what the Germans would do or when they would do it. But as my depression grew and I lost more weight, my parents became increasingly concerned about my health. After much hesitation, and despite serious reservations, they agreed that I should move to the ghetto and stay with Czuczka for a while. I was delighted. It did not matter that Czuczka worked in an office during the day. I knew that she would be happy to devote all her free time to me. I had no doubt that for her I was special, just as she was special for me. Welcoming me with a hug, she said, "Helka, this time there will be no regular lessons—we will only enjoy each other's company."

On its surface the ghetto looked tranquil, but it was vibrating with anticipation and anxiety. It was a community predominantly of young people, most between eighteen and thirty, most of them unattached, and they appeared to be throwing off all social restraints. The breakup of families, the Nazi restrictions, and the imminent danger all led to an emphasis on the now. The few older members of this community were neither willing nor able to impose their authority. After all, why should they try? These were perilous times: why should the young not feel free to enjoy themselves for as long as they could? Furthermore, what claim to authority did older people have when their traditional roles had been completely undermined: men had lost their ability to provide for their wives and families; women lacked the means to care for their children.

As a matter of policy, the Nazis had concentrated on the extermination of Jewish children. Because we were in special danger, adults looked upon us as a precious commodity. No Jew would have thought of mistreating a child, and almost all of them refrained from even the mildest form of discipline. In the Lublin ghetto, children like me formed a tiny minority. We came to expect our elders to treat us with indulgence, and they did. It was the summer of 1942. Because few of us were left, we felt close to each other and relied on one another for support, for entertainment, and for enlightenment. We children managed to enjoy ourselves as we roamed about the ghetto. We spent our days outdoors. In the evenings we took turns visiting each other's homes. One house in particular we enjoyed—the home where our friend Hanka lived. Hanka was an accomplished pianist, as the Germans knew, and sometimes they would summon her to entertain them and their guests. They even provided her with a piano of her own, the only one in the ghetto. We loved to gather at Hanka's. She would play both popular and classical music, and we would join her in singing. We were all aware of the special value of these gatherings. Although unable to express the presentiment in words, we felt that our carefree existence could not last much longer.

We knew that we lived in a dangerous and unstable world, but we preferred not to talk about it. Did we think that the danger would go away if nobody mentioned it? Or was the situation simply too frightening for discussion? In the crowded house in which I lived with Czuczka and her family, there also lived the agronomist Stach. He was a tall, good-looking man, with dark hair and intelligent black eyes. There was an overall sadness that never left him, even when he smiled. Mixed with his sadness was a touch of resignation. I learned that during the last deportation, his wife, who was eight months pregnant, had been beaten to death by a German right in front of his eyes. According to Czuczka, the image of his dying wife was always with him. Yet he was not bitter but kind, eager to help in whatever way he could. When he was doing someone a favor, when he worked in our garden—that was when he smiled. During the day he had a laborer's job outside the ghetto. His evenings he devoted to our garden. His love for gardening, coupled with his great fund of agricultural knowledge, transformed our garden into a showpiece.

Frequently, as we worked and chatted, Czuczka would join us. Sometimes Stach, Czuczka, and I would go for a walk. I walked between them, holding each one's hand. They both spoke softly, including me in their conversation, trying to make it interesting for me. They never talked down to me. They gave me a feeling of importance. Those were precious moments; I was acutely conscious of their value, knowing they would not last. The friendship they felt for me and for each other I valued highly. I observed them, and I understood enough to know that they cared for each other in two different ways. Quietly and tenderly, Czuczka was in love with Stach, but she never made her love known. Stach respected Czuczka and appreciated her as a friend. He talked to her, confided in her more than in anyone else, wanted her support and her understanding, and needed her comfort. I was impressed by the depth of their friendship. I was also aware that other women tried to press their attentions on Stach. Sometimes they interrupted our work in the garden, and I got angry with them—angry that they dared to intrude, that they were trying to spoil something so precious to me. I was glad that Stach did not encourage them. Interpreting his lack of interest as an act of faithfulness to Czuczka, I was grateful that our friendship could continue untouched by the distractions of our surroundings.

For a while, the summer of 1942 continued without any major disasters. Then one afternoon my mother came to Czuczka's house, very upset. She had heard disturbing rumors and wanted to take me back to the factory. She insisted that I would be safer there. The prospect of leaving all my friends and Czuczka as well was unbearable, and I pleaded with my mother to let me stay at least until the next day so I would have time to say good-bye to everyone. I cried until she agreed, saying she would stay with me at Czuczka's until the morning. That night I lay silently beside my mother, feeling angry and sorry for myself. I had been having such a good time. What did she want from me? Why didn't she leave me alone? My questions were soon answered. At about 4 a.m., mother shook me violently out of my sleep. "Hurry, Helka, hurry. There is no time. We must hide." Someone had come to warn us that there would be an *Aktion* in the ghetto. Children and the elderly were, as always, in particular danger. I did not need to ask questions, and in no time I was ready.

My mother grabbed me by the hand and ran across the street to the house of friends who had a special hiding place, a skillfully camouflaged cellar. Breathless, we knocked, and my mother begged for admittance. But there was no room there. They were crowded, sitting virtually on top of each other. They could not take us. "Save at least the child, please," my mother entreated. They refused, suggesting another place. Frantically my mother ran, dragging me along. I could not keep up with her. Twice I fell and got up again, not daring to complain. We knocked at a number of doors, all in vain. But my mother had courage. She did not give up easily. She ran—she almost flew. She knew many people, and she was convinced that someone would help. On our way we passed a few baby carriages in full view, babies inside. There was no place for them. No one would allow them into a hiding place for fear that they would cry and lead to discovery. At last mother's pleas were heard, and I found myself squeezed into a cramped cellar, where I almost had to sit on someone's head. There was no place for my mother, so she left me there. I learned later that only at the last minute did she find shelter.

Loudspeakers blared that all Jews were to come out of their houses and into the square. Farmers were needed in recently reclaimed lands, and those selected would work them and lead good lives. A thorough search of every house followed this announcement, and many people were removed. When the *Aktion* was over, the population was reduced to a fraction of what it had been. Again, an unusually large proportion of those taken were older people, women, and children. Many were killed immediately. All the babies in carriages were shot, and so were some adults who desperately attempted to run away. A friend of my mother's tried to escape through an opening in the barbed wire, holding a child in her arms. A Ukrainian guard shot at her, and the child, a boy, was killed. Half crazed, she was pushed into the group for deportation, clinging to the dead child. She was taken away, still holding him in her arms.

Only after some hours did the people with whom I was hidden allow me to leave. I walked out into a deserted, lifeless street. When I looked into the baby carriage, I saw an unrecognizable, bloody mass that seemed strangely alive. I felt weak and dizzy. All curiosity left me and all courage as well. I began to run, trying to avoid the bloodstained baby carriages and the bodies scattered in every direction on the ground. I felt all the dead were trying to keep me there with some terrifying, inexplicable power. I had to get away. I burst into Czuczka's home, straight into my mother's outstretched arms. Only so close to her was I able to let myself cry. Then, relieved, I noted that Stach, Czuczka, and her family were all there too. I stopped crying. But there was no happiness in our reunion. Without asking questions, I began to pack. This time I knew that my departure was inevitable, and I felt numb with guilt for having caused my mother so much pain and anxiety.

I expected her to reproach me. Instead she said tenderly, almost in a whisper, "Helka, I am so grateful that you are alive. Maybe there is a God after all!" I felt too miserable and ashamed of myself to answer. A few people stopped by for a brief moment to see if we had been spared and to tell us of the disasters that had befallen so many others. Almost all of those I cared about were gone; there would be no point in looking for them. Czuczka and Stach watched as I silently got ready to go. I could not bear the idea of saying good-bye to them at that public ghetto gate, and it was as if Czuczka had read my mind. "Let us part here," she said, "not at the gate." First I embraced Czuczka's parents and brother. Then I turned to Stach. After a strong, almost desperate hug, he took my face into his hands, looked straight into my eyes, and said seriously, "Promise me always to be brave. Don't ever give up. Ever!" I nodded, feeling a lump in my throat, and turned to Czuczka. I held on to her with all my strength. If I hurt her, she did not show it. I lost control and began to cry bitterly. I could not let go of her. I felt her body tremble, and she too began to cry openly—Czuczka, whom I had never seen weep before.

My mother's hand was on my shoulder: "We must go. Surely you will see them again soon." I did not believe her. I felt my mother did not believe herself. Inside me was a void, and with it came the strong conviction that I would never see any of them again. Still crying, I followed my mother into the street. When I turned, Czuczka and Stach were standing just as I had left them. Blinded by my tears and unable to make out their faces, I quickly wiped my eyes with the palms of both my hands, but just as quickly, before I had a chance to see them one last time, I turned away. My mother, with her shoulders stooped, walked in front of me. As we neared the ghetto gate, she lovingly reached for my hand. I was overcome by a wave of sad tenderness. Oh, Mama, how good it is to have you! I thought.

Majdan Tatarski, the Lublin ghetto, was behind me. I had spent less than two months there, but the time seemed longer. I had learned so much, made so many friends, received so much attention and love. It had been a period packed with meaningful impressions and events, and everything that had happened had touched me deeply. Perhaps it was the significance and fullness of life that made those few months seem to stretch out in memory as if they had been years.

Back in Lublin, no one worried about my well-being. Survival was the only consideration, and my parents were convinced that the factory was a good place to work. Everybody had enough food, and the treatment was humane. But we were not making the decisions; nor was the seemingly powerful and humane German director of the plant. I became friendly with a Polish chemist named Bronek and his wife, Genia, who lived in the house in the garden. Genia, in particular, enjoyed having me around. She liked to hug me and would say, "You are such a lovely child, not Jewish at all, not at all." As I did not "look Jewish" and spoke Polish very well, I had a good chance of passing as a "hidden child" on the "Aryan side"; in addition, my parents had the means to facilitate our evading the German's escalating anti-Jewish measures. In the early part of November 1942, Lublin was declared free of Jews (*judenrein*). Majdan Tatarski ceased to exist. Some of the ghetto inmates were murdered. Others were deported to concentration camps. Only a handful escaped. After my parents had acquired false papers, we moved to Warsaw in stages. There, we spent much of our energy on eluding the relentless Jewish persecutions. For safety we moved separately from place to place. In Warsaw the life-threatening situations prevented us from staying together for long. As most Jews, we had to change locations frequently to elude capture.

Because I could more easily pass for a Polish Catholic than the rest of my family, I often had to be separated from my parents and sister. I found these separations painful and refused to recognize that they were supposed to improve my chances of survival. Most Jews who tried to pass for Christian Poles were forced to change their living quarters often. By placing me with Poles who were willing to protect me, my parents felt that they were improving my chances of eluding the Nazis. Fortunately, after a number of life-threatening efforts, my father and mother found Polish rescuers who, for payment, offered them a more permanent place to reside. Officially my parents ceased to exist. For two years they never left their living quarters. My sister moved in with us. Protected by my "Aryan" looks and command of the Polish language, I had often stayed behind alone. For the final two years of the war, we did reconnect as a family in Kielce. My parents remained invisible. My sister and I appeared as nieces of the Polish family of laborers who protected us for payment. We were, in effect, supporting this Polish family.

Publications about the Holocaust refer to children who tried to survive by pretending to be Christian as "hidden children." Two basic demands dominated our lives: relinquishing our Jewish identity and remaining silent. Complying with both, even temporarily, implied a rejection of our pasts. In part, this was also a denial of our religion. Most of us came from secular homes—Jewish Orthodox children hardly ever made it to the Christian world. And yet, religion assumed an important place in our lives. We knew that being Jewish had deprived us of our right to live. Being Jewish meant something bad, something for which we could be killed. Being Christian meant being protected. The difference between being Christian and being Jewish hinged on the approval of different kinds of Gods. Invariably, the question had to come up about the differences between these Gods. A God who could not even protect his children did not seem very trustworthy. Undoubtedly, the extent to which children followed this kind of reasoning depended on many factors: age, Christian protectors, and contact with both parents and other Jews.

We were disappointed in our God. We felt abandoned by Him. Yet, we needed consolation from a God, from a religion. Comforted by a new God who promised us acceptance and safety, we were in fact ready for that God. By saving us, this new God protected us from evil, and so we equated Him with goodness. Of the different Christian religions, Catholicism was particularly influential in the lives of the hidden children, partly for the simple reason that the vast majority of Poles are Catholic. Those of us old enough to realize what was happening welcomed Catholicism; those who were very young embraced it blindly. From the perspective of the Jewish child, baptism and Catholicism were positive forces. Each shielded him or her from danger. Each offered a feeling of security and comfort. However, this security required a certain proficiency and ability to learn the kind of behaviors required by the Catholic religion. We had to become well versed in the new religion. We had to know principles, prayers, and how to behave in church. We had to know which behavior was appropriate for each religious and nonreligious setting.

Inevitably, the influence of religion spilled over into the postwar lives of the hidden children. For them, their very survival proved that they had adjusted well to their roles as Christians. But at the end of the war, they were often asked to switch again. For many of us, the return to Jewish identity was a drawn-out process. Some never returned. Acceptance, hostility, ambivalence, resentment, shame, and regret were only some of the emotions we hidden children shared. Some of us may continue to harbor such feelings about our Jewishness, about our religion. At times mixed together, appearing and disappearing, these emotions are not surprising. We could not easily give up that which had helped us to survive. If being Jewish brought danger and disapproval, if it was something one could be killed for, why would a child want to take it back? Most of us felt conflicted about these issues. For a while, we were suspended between two worlds. Some of us could not reconcile them. Still others took a definite step toward Christianity or Judaism. Did becoming a part of two different worlds give us a broader, less prejudiced perspective on life, on people? Perhaps.[9]

Children represent the future. In the ghettos, women, bound by their special ties to children, continued to gravitate toward activities related to the young. But precisely because ghetto children promised a Jewish future, the Germans targeted them for annihilation, most visibly by prohibiting births. Under German rule, the laws and expectations regarding procreation and motherhood were diametrically opposed when applied to the Jewish women and to the "Aryan" German women. As chapter 6 of this volume, devoted to German racial hygiene policies, demonstrates, for "Aryan" German women, childbearing and child care were highly valued, promising imaginary and actual rewards. In sharp contrast, Jewish procreation and motherhood were defined as political threats. The severity of German opposition to Jewish children and to Jewish procreation varied with time and place. Humiliation, starvation, and the accompanying oppressions themselves diminished the chances of successful births. When occasionally pregnancies happened, to avert punishment, Jews often relied on abortions.

Dobka Freund-Waldhorn was one of the women caught in a web of conflicting orders and wishes: prohibitions against Jewish motherhood and a desire to give birth to a baby. Dobka came from a wealthy, Orthodox family of nine children. Her father, in particular, saw Dobka as an independent rebel. Even in her 1939 marriage to Julek Frohlich, a man she loved deeply, this father saw a form of resistance. Handsome, intelligent, and from a respectable family, Julek was deemed unsuitable because he was not Orthodox. The war and the opposition to Dobka's marriage pushed the young couple to Vilna and from there into the Vilna ghetto. In Israel, in 1995, in Dobka's comfortable home, at the end of a long interview, she invited me to come again because she wanted to share with me a secret she never talked about: a wartime pregnancy. Since I was leaving Israel the next day,

9. See also Nechama Tec, "Conflicts of Identity," *The Hidden Child Newsletter* 7, no. 1 (1997): 1–2.

the interview took place a year later. At that time I heard that when Dobka was transferred from the Vilna ghetto to a nearby estate, she realized that she was pregnant. By then Jewish women in Vilna were prohibited from having babies. Dobka's husband and a Polish doctor at the estate pleaded with her to discontinue the pregnancy. She refused. In love with Julek, she wanted his child.

When she was seven months pregnant, as a concession to her husband, Dobka went to the ghetto hospital to learn firsthand about her options. Although sympathetic, the doctor in the ghetto hospital urged her to give birth and "to dispose" of the baby. Under the existing rules, unless she followed that advice, both she and her baby would die. The doctor accepted Dobka into the ghetto hospital and tried to induce delivery. In a restrained, almost artificial voice, Dobka said,

> I stayed in the hospital, for a long time, maybe a month. They gave me medication to have the water move, but there was no birth. They increased the dosage. They did all kinds of things, but the child refused to be born. Eventually, I got a fever, high fever. I think that it was already the eighth month. Only then it happened. She was alive. They showed me the little girl. She was so beautiful. She looked just like my husband, and we were so much in love! Then, they took her away. . . . The doctor tried to console me, that I was young, that I will have other children, that this had to be. . . . My husband came to the hospital. He knelt next to my bed. . . . He took my hands into his, and he cried . . . terribly, terribly. "You will see, we will have children, there will be children."[10]

With Julek Frohlich, there were no more children. He died in the Klooga concentration camp (in Estonia). After the war, Dobka remarried and gave birth to two sons. In the same, constrained voice, Dobka continued: "After the birth of my second son, with my second husband, I dreamt that my first husband, Julek, came to me. He looked very neglected, not shaved. 'Where were you?' I asked, 'so many years? I have a husband and children.' He answered, 'Yes, but you will come back to me.' In the dream I thought how could I go back to him? But to him I said, 'I will come back to you.' I woke up and found my pillow soaking wet from my tears."[11]

---

10. Dobka Freund-Waldhorn, personal interviews conducted by the author, Kvar Shmariahu, Israel, 1995, 1996. See also Nechama Tec, *Resilience and Courage: Women, Men and the Holocaust* (New Haven, CT: Yale University Press, 2003), 67–69.

11. See Nechama Tec, "Historical Perspective: Tracing the History of the Hidden Child Experience," in *The Hidden Children: The Secret Survivors of the Holocaust*, ed. Jane Marks (New York: Ballantine Books, 1993), 273–91. Marks's book is a collection of memoirs written by Jewish child survivors.

Childbearing and child rearing are universally cherished traditions. Hence these anti-childbearing German prohibitions created havoc within Jewish communities, especially among potential and actual parents. Significantly, the intricately close mother-child connections, by themselves, took a heavy toll upon potential and actual mothers of young children. In the end, these German measures resulted in startling differences between young single women and mothers. Beyond the direct German killing of Jewish mothers and their young offspring, Jewish mothers often experienced the terrible pain of watching their children starve to death or witnessing their brutal murder. Many reports about parents, and more particularly mothers, marvel at the ingenuity and courage with which they tried to protect their young, born and unborn.

Pregnancy as a prelude to life compelled some Jewish women toward life-threatening decisions. At one time, when Zwia Rechtman roamed the Polish countryside alone, searching for a resting place, she heard that her mother had been denounced and murdered. This intelligent and resourceful woman was arrested in the office of a Polish gynecologist to whom she had turned for help. Zwia was convinced that this physician had betrayed her mother when she asked him to abort her pregnancy. Jewish mothers with children often faced insurmountable obstacles. Even though most of them preferred to stay with their children, they were willing to separate if doing so promised the child's survival. Sometimes Gentile rescuers agreed to keep a child but not the mother.

Indeed, ten at the time, Zwia Rechtman recalls in an interview conducted in 1995 how she and her mother had to move from one place to another begging for shelter. Rarely were they kept for more than a few days. Then, one winter night, when the two were resting in a cold attic, the peasant giving them shelter asked them to leave. This daughter recalled with pain how her intelligent and proud mother begged the peasant to let Zwia stay. In the end, the woman agreed to keep the starved and half-frozen girl. Zwia was not sure whether her acquiescence was promoted by pity, money, or both. When I asked how she felt about staying there, I heard Zwia say, "I don't know if I wanted to stay or not. The situation was such that if she wanted to keep me, I should have stayed. Of course, I didn't know that I will never see my mother again. . . . Till the present, I cannot say good-bye to anyone! [Zwia cries]. . . . When mother left, the woman asked me to come into the house. [. . .] There was only one small room in the entire place. I don't even remember who else was there. I wasn't even thinking if that peasant was nice or not. She was very, very poor. [. . .] But this arrangement did not last." In a little while, Zwia had to leave.[12] She received sporadic help from a variety of Poles. Eventually exhausted by the many changes, with the help of one of her protectors, Zwia decided to volunteer, pretending to be a Pole, for work in Germany. She survived the war as a Polish laborer in the German countryside.

In trying to understand the Holocaust as it relates to Jewish children, the meaning of motherhood, and death, we cannot ignore the diversity of findings. The assaults upon Jewish children and their parents varied with time and place. As the war drew to a close, persecution against Jews and their rescuers became more stringent. In eastern European countries, more so than western ones, German opposition to motherhood and Jewish children had perilous implications. As the Germans lost the war at the front, they seemingly became more obsessed with winning the war against the Jews. Concretely, this meant that the attacks against all and any Jews became more severe.

Margot Draenger was one of the rare women who did not take into consideration the hardships associated with motherhood. Born in 1922 in Berlin, Margot was deported to Poland with her Polish-born parents in 1938. The family relocated to Kraków, then was forced into the Kraków ghetto. There, Margot met and married Jurek Draenger. At the end of 1943, the young couple was in hiding in a bunker in Bochnia, near Kraków. Jurek Draenger, familiar with this area and its many forests, was very resourceful. He knew who among the local peasants had sheltered Jews. For a while, the young Draengers stayed at a farm owned by a widow, Hanka Berota, who protected them without pay. The couple shared a small, damp, dark hiding place with Margot's father and uncle. They were denounced twice. Each time the police failed to find their hideout. Food and money were scarce. At night, Jurek would sneak out to steal whatever he could find in fields and unguarded barns. Their protector was barely able to feed her two young children.

Soon Margot realized that she was pregnant, which she took for granted. When she felt the baby's movements, the couple began to collect rags, cotton, and scissors. Shortly before Easter, in 1944, Margot's birth pains began. She knew the danger of screaming; she kept silent. Only her hands forcefully gripped the ladder next to her bunk. Her husband helped with the delivery. He cut the umbilical cord with scissors. It was a little girl. But the infant lived only a few hours.

---

12. Zwia Rechtman, personal interview conducted by the author, Tel Aviv, Israel, 1995. Born in 1927 in Niedrzwica Duża in the Lublin district of Poland, of her five-member family only Zwia survived. Her interview was permeated with admiration for and pain about her mother, whom Zwia continues to miss. She had a family of her own that she valued and loved. A capable and fine individual—for Zwia the loss of her mother is a painful reminder that she continues to deplore deeply.

Margot thought that a poorly tied umbilical cord had caused the baby's death. She suffered from serious postpartum complications, yet had no time to dwell on them. Two days after the delivery, the farm was raided. This time, the Germans came instead of the Polish police. Once more they found no trace of the fugitives. But the Draengers' protector had had enough. Fearing for her own two children's lives, she asked her charges to look for another place. Three days later, the Draengers left and entered a bunker, prepared by another peasant. They were fortunate. Somehow during the entire war, they managed to find Christians who were willing to protect them.[13]

Fathers also devoted themselves to saving their children. After his wife was shot by Ukrainians in July 1941, one such man, Dr. Richard Aptowicz, protected his son, Adam, born in 1933, for three years in the Kraków ghetto. Father and son had a challenging journey ahead of them. They passed through more than eight concentration camps, each seriously threatening their lives.[14] As chapter 5 of this volume explains, a child in a concentration camp was a rare and unexpected presence—not surprisingly, one welcomed by some and opposed by others. Among the individuals whom this father remembered warmly was Mrs. Wolf, who devoted much attention to Adam, particularly when father and son were prisoners in the Skarzysko Kamienna munitions factory,[15] in its notorious Department C, widely known for its cruel mistreatment of workers and very high death rate from toxic materials.[16] Fortunately, this father and son were, in time, transferred to other camps. Among the various moves, the most effective one had to do with their arrival at **Buchenwald**, known for its long-lasting, well-organized underground, directed and run by political prisoners, some of whom were Jewish communists, while others were

13. Yad Vashem testimony, 03/1686, recorded in September 1960 in Tel Aviv, Israel, 30–31. After the war the doctors advised Margot against pregnancy as they felt that giving birth to another child would endanger her life. Margot disregarded the physician's warnings and in 1949 gave birth to a son. The problem predicted by the physicians did not materialize.

14. Ryszard Aptowicz, Yad Vashem testimony, 03/2712; Eugene Weinstock, *Beyond the Last Path* (New York: Boni & Gaer, 1947), 127, 191–93.

15. See Felicja Karay, *Death Comes in Yellow: Skarzysko Kamienna Slave Labor Camp* (Amsterdam: Harwood Academic, 1996). The word "yellow" refers to the color that those prisoners who worked in Section C acquired from the poisonous substance trotyl. Not only did exposure to this chemical turn the workers' skin yellow, but trotyl attacked various parts of the body, which led to deterioration and death.

16. For additional sources describing the deadly effects of trotyl, see Ida Buszmicz, Yad Vashem testimony, 03/2798. For testimony by a former prisoner in Skarzysko Kamienna, Section C, who escaped from this camp, thanks to the help extended by Dr. Aptowicz, see: ŻIH 301/1322.

affiliated with a range of political parties. The prisoners came from a variety of countries, including Germany. In charge of the second block was an old-time underground member, German Jewish communist Emil Karlebach, a prisoner since 1939. One of the earliest initiators of the underground child rescue program, he personally accepted Adam into the children's block (***Kinderblock***).[17]

At Buchenwald, children were protected in a variety of ways. First, they were shielded from heavy work, which was potentially lethal for young forced laborers. Second, many prisoners attempted to safeguard children in every way that they could and sacrificed their own rations so that youngsters could have access to larger portions and more nourishing food. Third, the well-established Buchenwald underground organization did everything in its power to prevent children of all ages from being removed from this camp. Adam was assigned to one of the children's blocks, where he was prevented from overwork and received adequate nourishment and, very significantly, where he stayed until liberation. On the initiative of the camp elders, two separate *Kinderblocks* were established that included Jewish children belonging to a variety of groups. In effect, because of these efforts, 904 children were saved in Buchenwald.[18] The youngest among them was Stefan Jerzy Zweig, featured in Document 5-13. The son of a Polish Jewish lawyer, Zacharias Zweig, Stefan was three and a half years old when he was liberated from Buchenwald.

One particular source of help for young Adam came from Motel, a prisoner who had recently come to Buchenwald from Skarzysko Kamienna, where he had earlier benefited from Dr. Aptowicz's care. Now he was eager to reciprocate and thank the doctor for his past help. Motel was also familiar with Buchenwald's underground members and willing to use his influence to promote Dr. Aptowicz and his son. At Motel's initiative the Buchenwald underground investigated Dr. Aptowicz's past. Impressed by his credentials and particularly by the help he had been extending to camp inmates, they arranged for Dr. Aptowicz to stay in the children's block and hide there for the duration of any future *Aktion*. The blocks for the young were very well protected by the resistance members. American troops liberated Buchenwald in April 1945. Father and son moved to Kraków; in 1950, the pair moved with the doctor's new wife to Israel.

---

17. Yad Vashem testimony, 03/2712, 23–24.

18. See *U.S. Holocaust Memorial Museum Encyclopedia of Camps and Ghettos, 1933–1945*, Vol. 1: *Early Camps, Youth Camps, and Concentration Camps and Subcamps under the SS–Business Administration Main Office* (WVHA), ed., Geoffrey Megargee (Bloomington: Indiana University Press in association with the U.S. Holocaust Memorial Museum, 2009), 293.

As with Jewish fathers, the wartime experiences of mothers varied greatly; thus, so did the fates of their children. Cyla Fast, born in 1907, was married to an engineer who, at the start of the German invasion of Lvov, was arrested with a group of prominent Jewish men. His wife was never officially informed of her husband's fate. Expecting the birth of their first baby, Cyla had waited in vain for his return. Most probably, exposed first to degrading experiences, her husband, a gifted engineer, was murdered with a large group of Jewish men, all of whom had shared their elitist class affiliation. Cyla had a hard time accepting the circulating rumors about the killing of this entire group of men. In the fall of 1941, still missing and waiting for him, Cyla gave birth to their daughter. Now the mother and baby experienced a series of forced moves from one place to another, each entailing the loss of property, of freedoms, and of people. Soon, Cyla and the baby ended up in the Lvov ghetto.

During one of the ghetto deportations, mother and baby were pushed outside their home and into a group of ghetto inmates. At that point Cyla was approached by a Ukrainian, who asked her what she, a Christian, was doing there in a group of Jews. Noticing that the baby must have pushed her Jewish armband down, making it invisible, she told the Ukrainian that she had been passing by and was simply pushed into the group of waiting ghetto inmates. She went along with his suggestion that she was not Jewish, knowing that her looks and her knowledge of both the Russian and Polish languages denied her Jewishness. In a sense, this Ukrainian was giving her a chance to live. And so, on his own, he turned to one of his superiors, explaining why Cyla should be free to return to her home.

This is how mother and baby moved into the Christian world. When the two reached the outskirts of town with its high grass, they sat down to rest. She was at a loss as to what to do next. At that point, a woman came by and invited mother and child to her nearby cottage. Later on, thanking her for the hospitality, Cyla left to seek out some of her Polish friends for help. In fact, one of these friends helped her buy false papers. She stayed for two weeks in the homes of two other Polish friends. Then yet another Polish friend located a young, unmarried Polish woman who was willing to adopt the six-month-old baby. This required a birth certificate, which the local priest supplied, together with other needed documents. Again, the unexpected happened. At the moment of parting, the baby clung to her mother, crying loudly. There was something so disheartening and sorrowful in the infant's crying that the Polish woman who came for her could not take her. The baby stayed with Cyla, who soon found a job as a cook on an estate. She welcomed the work and the peace that came with it. In her free time she befriended a teacher, a woman who was out of work, and a Polish woman who was helping Jews who lived in a nearby forest. Cyla supplied food to these new friends.

All ran smoothly until a new law was passed requiring Poles to get special working papers. As a result, the estate manager discovered that Cyla's birth certificate was fake, and he asked her to leave immediately. She was glad that he did not denounce her to the authorities. Several Christian friends helped by keeping her for a day or two. This sporadic aid, together with her strong will to protect her baby, kept her going. Her prospects improved drastically when one of her friends found her a job with a German officer who was looking for a cook. There she worked practically until the 1944 takeover by the Red Army. In fact, this officer wanted to take her and the baby with him to protect them from the "barbarian Russians." Cyla had a hard time explaining to him why she had to stay behind. At the end of the war, she wrote, "My little daughter has been the sunshine of my life. Till this day she continues to bring me good luck. At dangerous times this child would distract a murderer's attention from me to herself. Occasionally, too, the compassion people felt for her made them invite us both into their homes during our horrible wanderings."[19]

Such happy endings were extremely rare. The effects of war and persecution often left their mark upon mother-child relationships and continued to exert an enduring pressure upon the surviving parties that sometimes reached beyond the grave. This volume provides only a glimpse of the universe of loss that defines the history of children during the Holocaust: the loss of childhood and innocence and, for many hundreds of thousands of Jewish children, the loss of life and loved ones. My most painful experiences had to do with temporary and permanent losses of those I loved. High on this list was Czuczka. My parents made all the necessary arrangements to save her—but failed. When our trusted Pole went to the designated place to pick Czuczka up, he found her murdered body on the ground. Throughout Poland, the devastation of Jewish communities and families was almost complete. In 1939, Lublin had a Jewish population of forty thousand. When the war was over in 1945, about 150 Jews came back to this city. Among these, there were only three intact families. My parents, my sister, and I were one of them.

---

19. See Yad Vashem testimony, 033/634, in which Cyla describes her gratitude to the Catholic priest who was most generous with his help. She also expressed appreciation to the various Polish friends who offered her protection. After the war, only gradually did she identify herself as a Jew. After locating some relatives in Israel, she and her daughter settled in that country, where she worked as a librarian.

CHAPTER 1

CHILDREN IN THE EARLY YEARS OF ANTISEMITIC PERSECUTION

O N NOVEMBER 27, 1938, the family of **Elisabeth Block**, Bavarian Jews from the small village of Niedernburg, made an outing in the surrounding countryside. "At around 11:30 we all made ourselves ready to drive with the car," wrote fifteen-year-old Elisabeth, "because the whole week we have had such lovely weather. [. . .] At Chiemsee we got out and hunted for shells. The lake mirrored the splendid blue of the mountains; it was a wonderful sight. We also got out in Traunstein [. . . and] drove along the German Alpine Road, where we also looked out upon the glacier garden. [. . .] Only at quarter to six did we finally turn for home."[1]

As elsewhere in her diary, Elisabeth Block devoted her energies that autumn day in 1938 to describing those things that absorbed her most: the intimacies of family life, the familiar pastimes enjoyed with relatives and friends, and the splendor and beauty of nature. Elisabeth does not, however, mention in her journal entries concerning her trip to Chiemsee a development that must have troubled each family member: the excursion would be the Blocks' last outing together in their own automobile. Beginning on December 3, 1938, German Jews would be forced to surrender their drivers' licenses and registration papers. Also omitted in the text are allusions to the lingering effects that the family continued to experience in the wake of the nationwide **pogrom** against Jews on

---

1. Elisabeth Block, *Erinnerungszeichen: Die Tagebücher der Elisabeth Block*, ed. Haus der Bayerischen Geschichte/Historischer Verein Rosenheim (Rosenheim: Wendelstein-Druck, 1993), 163–64.

Reichskristallnacht (Night of the Broken Glass) on November 9 and 10, 1938. Although the well-assimilated Blocks had been spared the worst of the antisemitic excesses in their insulated hamlet of Niedernburg, local **Sturmabteilung** (**SA**) and Nazi Party activists had plundered and vandalized Jewish-owned shops and businesses in nearby Rosenheim. More significantly, Elisabeth's uncle, Dr. Leo Levy of Bad Polzin,[2] had been murdered in his apartment by SA men in the midst of the pogrom, an event Elisabeth references only in passing in her journal.[3] Further disturbing developments—the exclusion of Jewish pupils from "German" schools and the economic and social dislocation caused by the stringent antisemitic decrees issued in the wake of *Kristallnacht*—receive similarly short shrift. Worse trials lay ahead, although, as always, the maturing teenager was loathe to record them: the loss of the family home[4] and business; the **compulsory sterilization** of Elisabeth's father; the 1941 forced labor provisions for all able-bodied German Jews. Until the family's transfer to Munich-Milbertshofen, a **collection camp** (*Sammellager*) for Jews pending **deportation**, Block remained largely silent in the face of such ominous developments.

Elisabeth Block's reticence concerning the difficulties she and her family encountered as a result of National Socialist anti-Jewish policy was perhaps an atypical response to persecution. For a generation of Jewish children like Elisabeth, the 1930s in Nazi Germany was a time of danger, anguish, and uncertainty. Nazi antisemitic measures isolated Jewish youngsters from their "**Aryan**" friends and classmates, deprived them of physical and financial security, and subjected them to scorn and humiliation. How did these children respond to such difficult circumstances? How did they view the discriminatory practices aimed at themselves and their loved ones? What strategies did they employ in order to cope with the emotional and psychological trauma they experienced?[5] This chapter follows the arc of persecutory policies against Jews in Nazi Germany and their impact and consequences for Jewish children.

---

2. Formerly a German spa town in Pomerania, today this is the Polish city of Połczyn-Zdrój.

3. Block, *Erinnerungszeichen*, 162.

4. In October 1939, the Blocks learned that they must relinquish their family home to other owners, but were allowed to inhabit one of its upper rooms.

5. For a discussion of German Jewish reactions to persecution in general, see Jürgen Matthäus and Mark Roseman, *Jewish Responses to Persecution*, Vol. 1: *1933–1938* (Lanham, MD: AltaMira Press in association with the U.S. Holocaust Memorial Museum, 2010).

FROM ASSIMILATION TO MARGINALIZATION

Some 523,000 Jews lived in Germany in January 1933.[6] Comprising less than 1 percent of the total population, German Jewry had throughout the nineteenth century waged a hard-fought battle for emancipation and gained full civil rights with the unification of the German state in 1871. Although tacit—and open—anti-Jewish sentiment persisted and received added impetus with the formation of antisemitic political parties and the development of new "racially based" antisemitic theories at the turn of the century, the establishment of the democratic **Weimar Republic** (1918–1933) marked an era of unprecedented integration of Jewish citizens into German social, cultural, and economic life.[7] The process of assimilation, manifested by soaring rates of intermarriage[8] and a rise in conversions to Christianity, facilitated Jewry's tenacious and thorough-going participation in nearly all aspects of German society. At the same time, German Jews cultivated a diverse, yet distinct, identity ranging in scope from the mainstream assimilationists to more marginal Orthodox and Zionist circles. An overwhelmingly middle-class community as a result of the economic opportunities that came with industrialization, a majority of Jews lived in Germany's great cities: Berlin, Frankfurt, Breslau,[9] Cologne. Just the same, in 1933, one in five German Jews still lived in a small town. Wherever they lived, most Jews thought of themselves as Germans, as inherently a part of the country and society in which they lived.[10]

---

6. Of these, approximately four hundred thousand were German citizens; the remaining number represented chiefly eastern European Jews, many of whom had been born in Germany and held permanent residence status.

7. Karl Schleunes, *The Twisted Road to Auschwitz: Nazi Policy toward German Jews, 1933–1939* (London: André Deutsch, 1970), 36ff.

8. In 1927, for example, 54 percent of all German Jews who wed contracted their marriage with a non-Jewish partner.

9. Today this is the Polish city of Wrocław.

10. Marion Kaplan, *Between Dignity and Despair: Jewish Life in Nazi Germany* (Oxford: Oxford University Press, 1998), esp. 5ff. See also Edward Timms and Andrea Hammel, eds., *The German-Jewish Dilemma: From the Enlightenment to the Shoah* (Lewiston, NY: Edwin Mellen Press, 1999); Hermann Levin Goldschmidt, *The Legacy of German Jewry*, trans. David Suchoff (New York: Fordham University Press, 2007); George Mosse, *German Jews beyond Judaism* (Bloomington: University of Indiana Press, 1985); Paul Mendes-Flohr, *German Jews: A Dual Identity* (New Haven, CT: Yale University Press, 1999); Marion Kaplan and Beate Meyer, eds., *Jüdische Welten: Juden in Deutschland vom 18. Jahrhundert bis in die Gegenwart* (Göttingen: Wallstein Verlag, 2005); Arnold Paucker et al., eds., *The Jews in Nazi Germany, 1933–1945* (Tübingen: Mohr, 1986).

Bertel Kugelmann[11] was nine years old when the National Socialists came to power in January 1933. Her family of grain merchants lived in the small municipality of Fritzlar, one hundred miles north of Frankfurt am Main. For most of her young life, she had lived a secure existence in rural Hessen. Yet, within weeks of Adolf Hitler's becoming chancellor of Germany, the unexpected responses of her neighbors and playmates had shaken much of this sense of security and rootedness. Bertel Kugelmann, who like many of her coreligionists had never before encountered overt antisemitism, was now made to feel the brunt of that prejudice often lying just beneath the surface of German village life. For children and adults alike, the profound integration of German Jews within German society and their deep roots in their own local communities made the dislocation and marginalization that accompanied early Nazi antisemitic policy all the more disconcerting and incomprehensible.

DOCUMENT 1-1. **Bertel Kugelmann, "My Story," quoted in Paulgerhard Lohmann,** *"Hier waren wir zu Hause": Die Geschichte der Juden vom Fritzlar, 1096–2000, vor dem Hintergrund der allgemeinen Geschichte der deutschen Juden* **(Norderstedt: Books on Demand, 2002), 257–58 (translated from the German).**

We were Jews and our neighbors Catholics, and during my early childhood that was unexceptional. But soon after Hitler came to power in 1933, things slowly began to change. The non-Jewish children from the neighborhood harassed us. Many of them said, "You are a Jew, and you killed Jesus. I can't play with you any more." I went home crying and asked my parents what was meant by this accusation. My parents tried to comfort me and told me that we weren't to blame for the death of Jesus. [. . .] As the persecution of the Jews began to intensify, and one heard from Jews in nearby towns and villages that they had been beaten, that gravestones had been overturned, and that windowpanes had been shattered, Jewish families and some of the [single] adult Jews left their homes and the place of their birth, and emigrated. . . .

---

11. Bertel Kugelmann lived with her family in Fritzlar until 1939, when she moved to be near a sister in Hamburg. On June 25, 1943, she was deported to the Mauthausen concentration camp; she was interned there for almost two years and liberated at Lenzing-Oberdonau, a subcamp of Mauthausen, by American troops on May 5, 1945. In June 1946, Kugelmann immigrated to the United States, where she pursued a career in nursing. In 1956, she married Dr. Melvin Borowsky.

My father, Josef Kugelmann,[12] was a grain dealer, highly respected in the community and also among the farmers in the nearby villages with whom he did business. Everyone knew him and came to him when they needed help. Once, when he gave a surety for one of the farmers, he had to put out a good deal of money in order to free him from his debt. He had served in the German army and fought at the front in France throughout all four years of World War I. His father, my grandfather, had served during the Franco-Prussian War. Both felt themselves Germans, like all the other veterans. With their wartime comrades, they were members of veterans' associations and organizations. When my mother pressed my father to leave Germany, he would not listen to her. "Don't get yourself worked up," he said. "Nothing will happen to us. After a little while, Hitler will go away again."

My brother Max, twelve years older than I, was an enthusiastic soccer player and belonged to the local soccer league. One day he came home after a soccer game to my room—I remember it as if it were yesterday. His face was black and blue, his lips swollen. He told me that he had been beaten up by some of the spectators; they didn't like it that a Jewish boy was playing with the rest of the team members. After this incident, my father agreed that my brother should go to my father's two sisters in the United States, where my older sister Irene had already emigrated in 1929.[13] This is what happened to Jewish children already in April of 1933; nevertheless most people voted for Adolf Hitler and the Nazi Party in November 1933.[14]

---

12. Josef Kugelmann (1877–1942) was incarcerated in the Buchenwald concentration camp in the immediate aftermath of *Kristallnacht*. In May 1941, he was again detained, in the Breitenau camp near Kassel. On December 16, 1941, Kugelmann was transferred to Dachau, where he died on June 16, 1942. His wife, Betty Kugelmann (née Plaut), perished in the Ravensbrück concentration camp on October 11, 1942. Three of their four children, including Bertel Kugelmann, survived the war. Their second daughter, Brunhilde, born 1916, was deported to the Łódź ghetto in 1942 and later perished at the Izbica transit camp near Lublin.

13. Max Kugelmann served in the U.S. Army from 1943 to 1945 and returned to Germany in the immediate postwar period in order to locate surviving family members.

14. On November 13, 1933, German voters went to the polls to vote in an election to the Reichstag; the ballot also contained a referendum asking German citizens to sanction Germany's withdrawal from the League of Nations. The electorate voted overwhelmingly for the National Socialists; however, the ballot for the Reichstag election contained no other party lists beside the Nazi roster.

National Socialist ideology declared that Jews exerted an undue and pernicious influence upon the German and world economies, an influence promoted, Nazi dogma suggested, by the growth of "international Jewry" and its "conspiracy" for world domination. When the Hitler regime came to power in late January 1933, Nazi authorities proclaimed their intention to eliminate Jews from German economic life. When the American Jewish Congress and allied Jewish organizations held a rally in New York's Madison Square Garden[15] on March 27, 1933, to protest early Nazi discriminatory measures and to exhort fellow American Jews not to buy German-manufactured products, the Nazi government used the occasion as a pretext to launch its first centrally directed economic measure against German Jewry. On March 28, 1933, the Nazi Party leadership announced a boycott effort against Jewish-owned shops and businesses to begin on April 1. The rationale behind the endeavor was twofold: the campaign would at once represent an initial effort to marginalize Jews in their own communities and might also consolidate public opinion in favor of Nazi antisemitic policy. On the morning of the boycott, local party action committees stationed SA or **Schutzstaffel** (**SS**) men outside Jewish-owned stores and enterprises, often holding placards encouraging passersby to purchase their wares only in German stores. Officially, sentries were posted only to "warn the population against entering Jewish businesses"; in practice, "Aryan" shoppers attempting to cross the picket line were often verbally or physically harassed, and in some places, demonstrations turned to violence against Jewish shop owners and spectators. Nevertheless, despite the best intention of central planners like **Der Stürmer** publisher **Julius Streicher**, the boycott ultimately failed to win the public support the Nazis had wished for, and international condemnation of the measure ensured that the centralized boycott campaign would be confined to a one-day affair.[16] However, depending on the degree of local antisemitic sentiment, so-called wild boycotts, or **Einzelaktionen** (uncoordinated individual acts against Jews), continued well into the late 1930s, inevitably forcing Jewish-owned businesses in many localities into insolvency or liquidation.[17]

---

15. In addition to the event at Madison Square Garden, similar protest rallies took place in Boston, Cleveland, Philadelphia, Chicago, Baltimore, and several other American cities.

16. Schleunes, *The Twisted Road to Auschwitz*, 84–89.

17. See Avraham Barkai, *From Boycott to Annihilation: The Economic Struggle of German Jews, 1933–1943*, trans. William Templer (Hanover, NH: University Press of New England, 1989).

Irmgard Marx lived in Höchst, today a municipal district of Frankfurt am Main, where her father owned a grain and feed business. She was ten years old on the day of the **boycott of April 1, 1933**. In contrast to the campaign's unsuccessful engagement in Berlin, the national capital, the boycott movement in Frankfurt experienced a measure of success, and the young Marx witnessed, perhaps without fully comprehending, the earliest efforts of the Nazi government to displace Jews from German economic life. From a financial standpoint, the stream of antisemitic measures aimed at Jewish-owned businesses had grave repercussions for Marx's family, who lost their business in 1937 and emigrated to the United States after *Kristallnacht* in 1938. For both ten-year-old Irmgard Marx and her parents, the loss of familiar customers and the gradual erosion of community support in a place where they had once felt at home would take an emotional toll.

DOCUMENT 1-2. Irmgard Marx, "Everyday Terror," in Elfi Pracht, ed., *Frankfurter jüdische Erinnerungen: Ein Lesebuch zur Sozialgeschichte* (Sigmaringen: Jan Thorbecke Verlag, 1997), 227–32 (translated from the German).

On the day of the boycott, on April 1, 1933, an SA man stood in uniform before our store and hindered customers from coming inside. A few brave souls came in through the courtyard[18] in order to buy their goods, but the largest share of our customers stayed away. In one case a man, very agitated, came to us in our apartments after he had an exchange of words with the SA man. But this was an exception, and I cannot remember his name. My parents had told us children nothing about the boycott. I myself was shocked when I saw the SA man, but had no inkling of what all this meant for the future. After the boycott, the business went on. The circle of customers had grown smaller, but there was still enough to do. No, in any event, Christian businesses did not shut down for the day out of solidarity [with us]. Things like that just didn't happen in those days. Later one could see certain Christian-owned stores with signage that said "German" or "Aryan." Many were businesses that had formerly belonged to Jewish owners. I can still remember very well the signs which appeared on the restaurants, cafes, and movie theaters—when this was I can't remember any more—which said that Jews were not desired there or that entry was forbidden to Jews. These signs were also posted for swimming pools. In one bakery in our neighborhood, there was once a sign that read,

---

18. That is, through the back entrance.

"We do not say *Grüss Gott*[19] any more, but *Heil Hitler!*"[20] Even as young as I was, I was horrified. Now I couldn't even say "Good day" when I entered a shop or store in order to buy bread or rolls. There was a steady stream of new discriminatory laws which made the daily lives of Jews more difficult. Even my parents and their business were affected.

Yes, there were several "faithful customers" who came to buy from us long after the boycott, but that circle—especially after 1936—became smaller and smaller. My parents closed their business either in late 1937 or early 1938. How high their losses were I can't say. [. . .] After the store was empty, my parents rented the space to the "Boha" shoe store.[21]

DOCUMENT 1-3. The antisemitic *Der Stürmer* newspaper portrays Jewish children ejected from a public swimming pool in Bad Herweck, near Mannheim, 1935, USHMMPA WS# 11196, courtesy of the Wiener Library Institute of Contemporary History.

19. This was the customary greeting, meaning "good day," used throughout most of southern Germany and Austria.

20. This was the so-called German greeting introduced by the Nazis as a standard salutation.

21. Following the *Kristallnacht* pogrom, the Marx family emigrated to the United States, where Irmgard Marx pursued a career as a textile artist in New York City.

IN THE SCHOOLROOM

Many of the Nazi discriminatory measures of the 1930s aimed to marginalize Jews within their own communities. For adults, marginalization meant removal from professional life, the loss of livelihood and property, and restrictions on their movements and actions in communal spaces. For children, a prominent aspect of segregation was the limitation on numbers and eventual dismissal of Jewish youngsters from German schools. The April 25, 1933, **Law against the Overcrowding of German Schools and Universities** had introduced a *numerus clausus*[22] for Jewish pupils and students, stipulating that enrollment of Jewish youth in schools and universities be limited to 1.5 percent of those registered at any given institution. The expulsion process concluded on November 15, 1938, with a decree definitively banning Jewish pupils from state and public schools.[23] Until then, as German law prescribed mandatory education for youngsters under the age of fourteen, significant numbers of Jewish children remained in school beside their "Aryan" classmates. The experiences of these pupils differed appreciably. Elisabeth Block, introduced in the chapter's introduction, remained at her desk in her rural Bavarian schoolhouse until November 1938, cherishing the time she spent among her sympathetic instructors and close-knit school friends. Yet, many other children were not so lucky and faced mounting discrimination in the public school environment throughout the 1930s. Treated as pariahs and the objects of harassment and ridicule, Jewish students were often subjected to public humiliation and punitive measures by politically zealous teachers and experienced both scorn and neglect at the hands of their peers. Because Nazi authorities also sought to win the hearts and minds of society's youngest members, Jewish children, beside their "Aryan" colleagues, also endured the endless homilies dedicated to Nazi political, racial, and antisemitic ideology, distilled in class lectures, assembly addresses, and daily songs and rituals.

Gerd Zwienicki[24] was a high school student[25] in the northern German city-state of Bremen. The eldest of four children, he was the son of Jewish parents

---

22. Literally, this means "closed number"; in normal usage, it is a method to limit the number of students at universities where the number of applicants greatly exceeds the places available. Before 1945, such limitations were often used as a racial quota in order to limit the number of students of a given minority, especially Jews.

23. See Document 1-11.

24. Gerd Zwienicki, later Rabbi Jacob Wiener (1917–2011), earned a PhD in human development and social relations from New York University and became a social worker for the New York City Department of Human Resource Administration after World War II. In 1948, he married Trudel Farntrog, a fellow survivor. Rabbi Wiener was a longtime volunteer at the U.S. Holocaust Memorial Museum.

25. That is, he was a pupil in an *Oberrealschule*.

who ran a bicycle shop in the Hanseatic port city. After his graduation in the mid-1930s, Zwienicki began rabbinical studies in Frankfurt and enrolled at the Jewish Teachers' Seminary in Würzburg. In the course of *Kristallnacht* in Bremen in November 1938, his mother, Selma, was murdered by SA men. The following year, the remaining Zwienicki family members emigrated to Canada, and in 1944 Gerd was ordained as a rabbi, taking up a position at the Hebrew National Orphan's Home in Yonkers, New York. But in 1934, Gerd Zwienicki was a seventeen-year-old teenager with a class composition to write. The topic assigned to him for the essay—"Does history show that racial mixing leads to the decline of a people?"—forced the young Jewish student to reflect and reiterate Nazi racial theories concerning the purity of the Nordic "Aryan" race and the danger of assimilation with "inferior peoples."

DOCUMENT 1-4. A class essay by Gerd Zwienicki, "Does History Show that Racial Mixing Leads to the Decline of a People," c. 1934, USHMMA, Acc. 2055.122.1 (translated from the German).

Does History Show That Racial Mixing Leads to the
Decline of a People[?]

It is the most significant merit of the National Socialist movement that it clearly recognizes—and that it time and again points out to all racial comrades [*Volksgenossen*][26]—that a great people [*Volk*] can only endure for the long term when it concerns itself with maintaining the purity of its race. To support the assertion that a mixing of races unquestionably leads to the decline of a people, history delivers several striking examples.

First, let us think of the fate of the great world empires of antiquity: the Persian, the Macedonian, and the Roman empires, to summon forth the most conspicuous examples. From the peasant stock of the Iranians came the establishment of the Persian Empire that was sustained by the spectacular religious movement of Zarathustra. This religion has a very Nordic composition in that all world events are connected to the battle between good and evil, of light against darkness. The idea of world empire

---

26. The term *Volksgenosse* (*Volk* comrade) first appeared in usage in German-speaking countries in the early nineteenth century; it had a meaning similar to the German term *Landsmann* (compatriot). The term was adopted and widely used by National Socialists to impart a feeling of inclusivity to those persons of "German blood" who belonged to the *Volksgemeinschaft*, the German racial community.

was originally foreign to the Aryan[27] peoples of Persia. Only after the final conquest of Babylon did they adopt the idea from vanquished Semitic peoples and follow this course to its highest realization. But the borders [of the empire] were spread too far; and the upper stratum of peasant and chivalric peoples of Nordic ancestry and upbringing were not of sufficient number in such a multiracial world empire, and they dissolved into racial chaos. The Persian Empire grew ever more frail and irresolute. With ease it could be overwhelmed by such a powerful people as the Macedonians. Even Alexander [the Great] fell victim to the dream of world empire, which he came so close to accomplishing. Here we witness the terrible tragedy, unparalleled in history. Just so, the Führer, as the willing servant of his people, in accordance with their nature, willfully rejects the notion of the fusion of races, so that he might establish a world empire of eternal peace, God's kingdom upon earth. This mixing of races and peoples, however, transpired at the cost of the Macedonian-Greek conquerors and naturally led within the briefest of periods to the decline of this people and to the disintegration of their world empire. Nevertheless, the vision of world empire experienced such a renewal and intensification through Alexander that this ideal has never again disappeared.

The history of the Roman Empire is the history of Rome. Its march of destiny leads from the Latin patrician state to the national state and climaxed with world empire. The founders of the Roman state [were] the Indo-Germanic and Nordic peasant peoples. The healthy growth from city-state to national state advanced mainly through the constant foundation of farming settlements, which was first made possible by the great reproductive capacity [*Kinderreichtum*] of the peasant families and the gens.[28] For centuries, the vitality of the Roman people, built upon peasant foundations, maintained its ascendancy. With the further expansion of the empire beyond the borders of Italy, friction slowly developed between

---

27. The word "Aryan" derives from Sanskrit. Since ancient times, Persians (the peoples of modern-day Iran) have used the term *Aryan* as a racial and ethnic designation to describe their lineage, language, and culture. Indeed, the name "Iran" is a cognate of "Aryan" and means "land of the Aryans." In linguistic terminology, "Aryan" refers to a subfamily of the Indo-European languages, and before the term's adoption and perversion by National Socialist ideologues, it was employed to describe the parent language of the Indo-European language family. In the late nineteenth and early twentieth centuries, linguists and ethnologists began to argue that speakers of the Indo-European languages constituted a distinct race, separated in the racial hierarchy from the Semitic peoples (i.e., Jews).

28. These were Roman patrilineal clans comprising families with the same stock in the male line, sharing a common family name and worshipping a common ancestor.

those peoples who, no longer tied to the soil, followed the advance of expansion—together with nonfarming peoples engaged in trade—and those of a Nordic hereditary disposition whose innate drive for expansion of ethnic territory functioned through a strategy of colonization. These two opposing impulses, which developed side by side contemporaneously, we can clearly perceive in Rome's political actions, but to explore specific examples would take us too far afield from our subject matter. After the greatest and most difficult wars which Rome had to fight, after the war against Carthage, the foundation of the state, its peasant class, was almost completely [decimated][29]; the racial core of the population was most gravely affected. Now the greatly enervated foundation of peasant stock succumbed to the geopolitical laws of a world power, with all of the consequences inherent in racial transformation. With the riches from every land streamed into Rome also masses of peoples of foreign race. A mercantile spirit and a dissolute culture, introduced from other religious practices, also permeated deeply into political life. The newly established class of great landholders adopted from Carthage the plantation farming economy, with thousands of slaves. The peasantry was completely undermined, both racially and economically. While the Romans' hereditary character, as well as their political forms and prototypical works, would have great impact for hundreds of years to come, the old vitality of the Roman *Volk*, with its origins in the race, began slowly to erode, until their world empire was overrun by Germanic tribes. [. . .]In conclusion, let us look within the confines of contemporary history and the present. Can we not here clearly see the results and consequences of racial mixing? We have only to compare North and South America. While in South America, the predominantly Latin European settlers have for the most part mingled with the aboriginal inhabitants, the largely Nordic population of North America has interbred very little with the lowly colored peoples.[30] The results that must arise from these circumstances we see before us. The racial makeup and culture of South America are clearly different from that in North America; the racially pure Germanic has become the lord of the American continent, and will remain so as long as he does not degenerate by defiling his blood.

In September 1935, in the midst of the seventh annual Nuremberg party rally, Nazi leaders promulgated the so-called Nuremberg racial laws, which

---

29. This word is obscured in the original.
30. Today this reference would be viewed as pejorative.

historians view as a central feature of the acceleration of legislated discriminatory measures in Nazi Germany. The first, the **Law for the Protection of German Blood and German Honor** (Blood Protection Law) (*Gesetz zum Schutze des deutschen Blutes und der deutschen Ehre*, or *Blutschutzgesetz*), imposed bans upon marriage and extramarital relations between German Jews and German "Aryans," thus providing a legal basis for the punishment of *Rassenschande* ("race defilement"), or miscegenation. The second piece of legislation, the **Reich Citizenship Law** (*Reichsbürgergesetz*), created a new status for "Aryan" Germans, "Reich citizen," upon which all political and civil rights in Germany would be based. Jews were denied most integral civil rights, possessing only *Staatsbürgerschaft* (state citizenship), a status that suggested they were now subjects, not citizens. Ancillary ordinances provided a legal definition for "Jewishness" based on confessional, as well as biological, terms.[31]

Artist Irene Spicker Awret lives today in Falls Church, Virginia. In the summer months of 1935, fourteen-year-old Irene lived with her parents in a comfortable middle-class district of Berlin, where she dreamed of becoming a painter. Although the escalating discriminatory legislation had persuaded the secular teenager to take increased pride in her Jewish heritage, the regime's antisemitic measures had had limited practical impact upon the young girl's life: the demeanor of her teachers and classmates had not yet altered, and best friend Tutti Mahlow "did not care that [she] was Jewish."[32] The two girls spent hours together, playing, studying, and reciting the plays of Goethe and Schiller. With the promulgation of the **Nuremberg Laws**, however, Irene's world changed dramatically. Lifelong friendships extinguished overnight, and the girl who had once hidden her childhood illnesses from her parents in her eagerness to go to school now hated the classroom lectures in history and ethnology (*Volkskunde*), which were punctuated with antisemitic rhetoric and Nazi propaganda. With the Nuremberg Laws came a heightened sense of discomfort and anxiety for Germany's Jews, both young and old. For young Irene Spicker, in those difficult

---

31. See Uwe Dietrich Adam, *Judenpolitik im Dritten Reich* (Düsseldorf: Droste, 2003); Cornelia Essner, *"Die Nürnberger Gesetze" oder die Verwaltung des Rassenwahns, 1933–1945* (Paderborn: F. Schöningh, 2002); Lothar Gruchmann, "Blutschutzgesetz und Justiz: Zur Entstehung und Auswirkung des Nürnberger Gesetzes vom 15. September 1935," *Vierteljahrshefte für Zeitgeschichte* 31 (1983): 418–42; Otto Dov Kulka, "Die Nürnberger Rassengesetze und die deutsche Bevölkerung im Lichte geheimer Stimmungs- und Lageberichte," *Vierteljahrshefte für Zeitgeschichte* 32 (1984): 582–624; Abraham Margaliot, "The Reaction of the Jewish Public in Germany to the Nuremberg Laws," *Yad Vashem Studies* 12 (1977): 75–107.

32. Irene Spicker Awret, *They'll Have to Catch Me First: An Artist's Coming of Age in the Third Reich* (Madison: University of Wisconsin Press, 2004), 78.

days before her family left Germany for Belgium in 1939, art seemed her only stable refuge.[33]

DOCUMENT 1-5. Irene Spicker Awret, *They'll Have to Catch Me First: An Artist's Coming of Age in the Third Reich* (Madison, WI/Takoma Park, MD: University of Wisconsin Press/Dryad Press, 2004), 88.

Shortly after returning from my vacation trip, the Nuremberg Laws were published, making mixed marriages unlawful and punishing sexual intercourse between Jews and "Aryans" with hard labor.[34] At the same time we were demoted from citizens to subjects. To top it all, my friend Tutti Mahlow dropped me like the proverbial hot potato. I should try to understand, she said, sounding very considerate—her father was a magistrate, her sister had to think of her fiancé's career. In the space of a day, we went from being good friends to classmates who politely greeted each other from a distance. It was more humiliating than having to sit through one of Doctor Kadner's ethnology courses. Though he was a good teacher of French and geography, and had a doctorate from the Sorbonne, the Nazi bacillus seemed to have softened his brain. More and more often he arrived in class wearing his brown S.A. uniform, giving the "*Heil Hitler*" salute as if from a grandstand, and proclaiming the planned geography lesson had been changed to ethnology. For forty-five minutes I would try to concentrate on a drawing so as not to have to listen to Doctor Kadner's description of the characteristics of sub-species such as Negroes and Jews, mainly of Jews. On the blackboard, he wrote in neat rows: "kinky hair," "flat feet," "receding forehead," "obesity." Then he strode to my bench at the back of the class, praising my drawing. My teacher's conduct toward me remained correct and friendly, the unspoken agreement of my dispen-

---

33. Irene Spicker (1921–) fled from Berlin to Belgium in 1939, where she remained in hiding for several years. Arrested in 1943, she continued to draw while confined to a Gestapo prison in Brussels. Her artwork attracted the attention of Gestapo officials, who ordered her transfer to an art workshop at the Mechelen (Malines) transit camp. There Spicker avoided deportation and fell in love with fellow prisoner-artist Azriel Awret. The couple married soon after their liberation from Mechelen in September 1944.

34. Persons convicted of *Rassenschande* ("race defilement") typically received a prison sentence; during the war years, such a crime might warrant the death sentence or internment in a concentration camp without trial.

sation from the "German greeting,"[35] extending to ethnology. While he taught his revolting antisemitic drivel, I continued to sit in the back of the class drawing.

"I DECIDE WHO IS A JEW"[36]

On March 12, 1938, German troops marched into Austria. A long tradition of sentiment in both countries favored a unification of the two German-speaking lands, particularly in truncated Austria after World War I. Although the **Treaty of Versailles** and that of St. Germaine[37] specifically forbade such a union, a pan-German nation represented a political goal of many disparate interest groups in both states, including the National Socialist Party. Supported by the Hitler government, the Austrian Nazi Party, which had been illegal since 1933, staged a coup on March 11, 1938, the eve of the German invasion, in part to preclude a national referendum on Austro-German unification. The so-called **Anschluss**, the incorporation of Austria into Germany, proceeded formally on March 13, 1938, and received the enthusiastic support of most of the Austrian population.[38] In the days and weeks following these events, German anti-Jewish legislation was extended to what came to be called the **Ostmark**, and Vienna and other centers of Jewish life in Austria became sites of brutal and spontaneous antisemitic violence.[39] For Austria's 192,000 Jews, some 4 percent of the general population, the spring and summer months of 1938 played out in nightmarish scenes of physical violence, appropriation of private property, and public

---

35. This was *Heil Hitler*, the Nazi salutation that often replaced such greetings as "good day" in common conversation.

36. This saying, later attributed to various Nazi leaders, was first spoken by Karl Lueger (1844–1910), the antisemitic Christian Socialist mayor of Vienna.

37. The Versailles Treaty officially ended the state of war between Germany and the Allied powers in World War I, while the Treaty of St. Germaine-en-Laye represented peace terms between the Allies and the new Republic of Austria.

38. See Evan Burr Bukey, *Hitler's Austria: Popular Sentiment in the Nazi Era, 1938–1945* Chapel Hill: University of North Carolina Press, 2000).

39. See Hans Safrian and Hans Witek, *Und keiner war dabei: Dokumente des alltäglichen Antisemitismus in Wien*, 2nd ed. (1938; Vienna: Picus Verlag, 2008); Evan Burr Bukey and F. Parkinson, eds., *Conquering the Past: Austrian Nazism Yesterday and Today* (Detroit, MI: Wayne State University Press, 1989; Hans Safrian, *Eichmann's Men*, trans. Uta Stargardt (Cambridge: Cambridge University Press in association with the U.S. Holocaust Memorial Museum, 2010).

humiliation. Eighteen-year-old Walter Grab,[40] from a Viennese middle-class family, learned two valuable lessons from his own encounter with local Nazi zealots in this context. For him, the events of the spring of 1938 demonstrated what many Jews in Germany did not yet comprehend and would first grasp in the wake of *Kristallnacht*: that Jews could no longer count themselves safe from the escalating anti-Jewish measures of regional and national authorities or from the sometimes violent wrath of the local antisemitic population, many of whom were their neighbors. Second, Grab began to understand that grassroots antisemitism was neither logical nor rational and that familiarity could breed both contempt and salvation.

DOCUMENT 1-6. **Walter Grab, "The Jews are Vermin Except for My Jewish Schoolmate Grab,"[41] in** *"Niemand war dabei, und keiner hat's gewußt": Die deutsche Öffentlichkeit und die Judenverfolgung, 1933–1945,* **ed. Jörg Wollenberg (Munich: Piper, 1989), 45–50 (translated from the German).**

On the afternoon of April 25, 1938, after six weeks of Nazi rule in Austria, I was on my way home. Not far from our apartment there was a Jewish gymnasium [*Turnheim*] in the basement of the house at 20 Liechtensteinstrasse. As a child of seven or eight, I had often exercised there. As I neared this building, I was halted by a number of Nazis who had formed a column and were wearing armbands and swastikas. One of them called to me, "Are you a Jew?" As I answered in the affirmative, he dragged me to the building where the gym hall was and ordered me down the cellar stairs. [. . .] In this anteroom of the gymnasium, I saw some twenty to twenty-five Jews, whom the Nazis had assembled and forced into a corner of the room. A Nazi sent me over there as well. The large gymnasium and also this antechamber were—you must pardon the expression—completely covered in shit. The floors and even the walls were completely plastered with excrement. It stank to high heaven. Here, in my estimation, an entire regiment of SA or SS or some other kind of Nazis had relieved themselves, and clearly right before they began to gather Jews

40. Walter Grab (1919–2000) emigrated to Palestine in 1938. He became a prominent historian of Germany, researching the democratic trends prevalent before German unification in 1870 and writing extensively on the history of German-Jewish emancipation. As a professor of history at the University of Tel Aviv, Grab founded that university's Institute for German History in 1971.

41. In German, "Die Juden sind Ungeziefer, ausgenommen mein jüdischer Schulkamerad Grab."

together here; the excrement was still very fresh and moist. Apart from the Jews, there were fifteen or twenty Nazis in the changing room. Behind me there were more Jews being forced down the cellar steps, so that there were thirty-five or forty of us in all—only males. For the Nazis, this was enormous fun. They amused themselves tremendously because they could vent their anger on these helpless and perplexed Jews whom they had chased into this excrement-covered gymnasium. They laughed and shouted at us for ten or fifteen minutes, and mocked us because we were afraid. Finally, one of them stepped forward and said, "You Jews have left us this filthy gymnasium. Jewish gyms are so dirty! Once again one can see how filthy Jews are! And now you have to lick it up!" What does one say when one is delivered into the hands of such barbarians, who seem to have human faces? Nothing. We stood there silently. We had been delivered up to them and imagined now that anything could happen. But they were just making a joke. They had devised a way to humiliate and humble the Jews. This was not an ordered action, like the pogrom of November 9 [*Kristallnacht*], in which Jewish businesses were plundered and the homes of Jewish citizens demolished. No, this was mob amusement. I am not sure if such "fun" took place in other cities, but in Vienna it did. We were completely at the mercy of the arbitrary whims of these Nazis. And they found it so hilarious that we huddled together in terror. How could one lick up this Nazi excrement?

And then one of them shouted, "Okay, let's get started. To work!" And several Jews actually tried to scrape together the excrement with their hands and to throw it in the bathroom toilets. But it was impossible. At the best one could only smear the excrement around. It wasn't possible to clean the dressing room and gymnasium in this way. The Nazis laughed and jeered at us, but finally one of them brought us a shovel, a broom, a waste can, and a couple of towels, and we turned the water faucet on. But for this type of cleaning one needed a fire hose. I took one of the towels— had a burning fear of being beaten in this cellar by these Nazis and tried to crawl after the other Jews and throw the excrement into the toilets. The whole thing lasted a quarter of an hour or twenty minutes, during which time we tried to obey the Nazi orders. We were not very successful. And while I squatted and bent, so that in my terror, I would hide my fright as much as possible, I lift my eyes, and my glance meets unequivocally the glance of one of these laughing Nazis, standing around with the swastika armband on his brown shirt. And I recognized him immediately. It was a [former] schoolmate of mine from the *Volksschule*. [. . .] He had even once

DOCUMENT 1-7. **A crowd of Viennese children look on as an Austrian Nazi forces a youth to paint the word *Jud* (Jew) on the facade of his father's store, 1938, USHMMPA WS# 01510, courtesy of the Österreichische Gesellschaft für Zeitgeschichte.**

TRAINING YOUTH FOR JOBS ABROAD

As antisemitic policies escalated in the mid-1930s, thousands of German Jews chose to emigrate from their native land. By the outbreak of war in September 1939, some 282,000 Jews—nearly half of the Jewish population as it had existed in 1933—had fled Nazi Germany.[42] But emigration was difficult: it required sufficient funds and flexibility to resettle in a foreign land. The worldwide Great Depression and pervasive antisemitism presented added obstacles to immigration. Moreover, in order to obtain the necessary visas for entry and residence, most countries demanded that each new immigrant provide the name of a guarantor, who might pledge financial support for the new arrival in the event of illness or unemployment. Most also required that the refugees possess the skills and ability to find work in their new homeland.

German Jewish youth faced particular difficulties both in gaining professional skills and in facilitating their emigration abroad. Limited educational opportunities and the decrease in the number of businesses that might take in Jewish employees or apprentices prevented many youngsters from garnering the knowledge and proficiency required for professional placement. Those who had gained the necessary expertise or experience were "not unemployed," as Jewish educator Heinemann Stern noted; rather "they [were] without a profession."[43] As one solution, Jewish self-help organizations promoted occupational training centers, where young people could acquire the skills they needed to find a job overseas. Most of these training centers were sponsored and directed by Zionist associations, which offered their students vocational training as well as Hebrew-language instruction in the hope that they might immigrate to **Palestine**.

In 1936, the **Reichsvertretung der Juden in Deutschland** (Reich Association of Jews in Germany) established an emigration-training farm (*Auswandererlehrgut*) at Gross-Breesen in Silesia, one of the only non-Zionist centers of its kind.[44] Organized by the Hamburg-born pedagogue Curt Bondy (1894–1972), Gross-Breesen began its efforts with 135 boys and girls, aged fifteen to seventeen.[45] This initial cadre learned farming and animal husbandry techniques, housekeeping, and artisan skills, as well as carpentry and metalworking. In tandem with the technical curriculum, students received foreign-language training, courses in history and civics, and in-depth instruction in the Jewish religion, with an emphasis on their common cultural heritage. Although

42. That is, Germany's 1937 borders; 117,000 Jews had also emigrated from annexed Austria by September 1939.

43. Heinemann Stern, *Warum hassen sie uns eigentlich? Jüdisches Leben zwischen den Kriegen: Erinnerungen*, ed. Hans Christian Meyer (Düsseldorf: Droste Verlag, 1970), 194.

44. For a definitive account of the *Auswandererlehrgut* Gross-Breesen, see Werner T. Angress, *Between Fear and Hope: Jewish Youth in the Third Reich*, trans. Werner T. Angress and Christine Granger (New York: Columbia University Press, 1985).

45. Despite Bondy's repeated efforts to recruit more female candidates for the training farm, the overwhelming majority of Gross-Breesen's student population consisted of teenage males.

early conditions at the center proved primitive, Bondy's two-year training program would ultimately attract 240 students to the 567-acre estate at Gross-Breesen. Candidates for the training farm were usually recruited from the Bund Deutsch-Jüdischer Jugend (League of German Jewish Youth),[46] while the youngsters' parents or guardians undertook the costs for schooling and board.

The leaders of the Reichsvertretung had conceived of their emigration-training farm as a basis for a number of Gross-Breesen settlements abroad. Preliminary efforts focused on the establishment of a coffee plantation in the Paraná province of Brazil, but negotiations foundered, and although new opportunities for satellite farms presented themselves to Bondy and his colleagues, their painstaking efforts yielded few results. Their only successful overseas endeavor materialized in the Virginia Plan. In 1938, William Thalhimer Sr., owner of a Southern-based department store chain headquartered in Richmond, donated a tract of land in nearby Burkeville, Virginia, as the foundation for a communal farm on American soil. Thirty-seven young trainees would immigrate to Virginia in an effort to establish Thalhimer's Hyde Farm as an outpost of the Breesen experiment; each young person, including Ernst Löwensberg,[47] author of the correspondence below, received joint stock in the farm from Thalhimer so that he or she could fulfill residency requirements through the ownership of property.[48] While Löwensberg toiled in Burkeville, many of his male colleagues and the staff at the Gross-Breesen training center were arrested by Nazi authorities in the aftermath of *Kristallnacht* and imprisoned at the **Buchenwald** concentration camp, while the farm itself suffered extensive damage as a result of the pogrom. Thereafter, several students emigrated; in the following years, thirty-one additional students made their way to England, Argentina, Australia, Kenya, and Palestine. Curt Bondy himself ultimately escaped Nazi Germany through the Netherlands and found a post teaching psychology in the United States at the College of William and Mary. On August 31, 1941, **Gestapo** officials ordered the dissolution of the Gross-

46. The League of German Jewish Youth was established in 1933 as a union of several Jewish youth organizations. In 1936, under pressure from Nazi authorities, the association changed its name to the Ring Bund Jüdische Jugend; in January of the following year, the association was banned.

47. Ernst Moritz Löwensberg (later Ernest Loew) served in the U.S. Army during World War II. Following the war, he purchased a farm near Norwich, Connecticut, which he managed until his death in January 1986.

48. Virginia Historical Society Archive, Manuscripts Mss1 T3275 a FA1, William Blum Thalhimer Papers, 1914–2005.

Breesen farm and deployed remaining faculty and trainees as forced laborers.[49] Many of the last generation of Gross-Bresseners perished during the Holocaust.

DOCUMENT 1-8. Letter of Ernst Löwensberg, Burkeville, Virginia, to students of the emigration-training farm at Gross-Breesen, Silesia, June 16, 1938, USHMMA, Acc. 2000.227, Herbert Cohn Gross-Breesen Collection (translated from the German).

Dear Friends!

It is eight days that I have been here on the farm, where we will all be gathered together in the near future in order primarily to advance what we started in Breesen: working and learning. Concerning what comes after that, we don't want to discuss right now. I will try to report briefly to you all that I have done and experienced and seen since I have been here.

From Richmond it is about sixty miles to Burkeville, and then another six miles beyond that. [Curt] Bondy has told us that the landscape here is like that of the Black Forest, and this is true. [. . .] The road leading here is very curvy and hilly, and also much varied in appearance. The fields on either side are always surrounded by forest. People's houses lie quite aloof from the roadway. That somewhere in the distance there must be a house, one determines in the following way. At the edge of the road stand posts on which a kind of pipe has been mounted (it almost looks like a drainage pipe), and on this there is a name. This is the mailbox for the *U.S. Mail*,*[50] which comes once a day by automobile. [. . .] Some six miles beyond Burkeville there is also such a mailbox. The lettering reads "R. J. Barron," and next to it a pretty sign announces Hyde Farmlands, and here the road forks. Then one drives another five minutes with the car, and then one does not see a cottage but a massively built manor house. [. . .] I won't write much about it. I can only say to you that it is excellently suited to our purposes. Twenty-two rooms are at our disposal—bigger ones and smaller ones. They are only waiting for a painter to spruce them up a bit. [. . .] There is a lovely balcony on the second floor, and I can imagine that we will put our musicians up there, while we sit and listen on the lawn below.[51] The former owner of the grounds is living here—a man who like

---

49. Angress, *Between Fear and Hope*, 73.

50. All phrases marked in italics with an asterisk (*) in this document were written in English by Löwensberg within the original German-language text.

51. The Gross-Breesen students held nightly musical performances at their training farm.

other people in the area only farmed a portion of the entire property. He'll remain here on the site principally as an "expert." Since the farm property has been purchased by Mr. Thalhimer, he is working now with two young hands who live here and with a neighbor family. [. . .] Tuesday we harrowed with the new machine for *cowpeas*,* and at the same time we spread phosphorus fertilizer. Then I separated and hoed the *cucumbers** (*Gurken*). When each of you hears that from me, I can imagine that many of you cannot resist letting a smile cross your lips. Yes, indeed, Ernst Löwensberg does the weeding, and he will do much, much more. Here hoeing is more difficult than in Breesen because there is only one *hoe*,* and you cannot change blades on it. One cannot always be running to the blacksmith to sharpen it all the time. What sort of tool do you all imagine I used over and over, one and the same, for all the hoeing I have done? It is dull on every side. But in any case, we keep going. In Breesen I would have said that I couldn't work with such a tool. But one gets used to many things! On Wednesday, we hoed *cucumbers** the whole day. This morning hoeing watermelons.* Then *butter beans*.* This afternoon we hoed the *corn** (*Mais*). In between we planted more butter beans. But what soil! In Gr[oss] Breesen, it would be sifted, plowed, cleared of roots and stumps, and harrowed beforehand. I can't describe to all of you how much stubborn quack grass there was, in addition to all the other weeds. The hoeing work proceeds like this: the weeds are hoed out of the rows [and fall] into the furrow. They are left there. One rain is all it takes, and they are [striking root and] growing again to beat the band. There are not enough people to clear them away and then burn them. I'll say it again: through intensive effort and supported only by our brief experience at Gr[oss]-Breesen, we will cultivate the soil here and will then succeed in bringing in a full harvest. The chief crop here is tobacco. [. . .]

I could write about much more. But for now this is enough. I hope that you have at least an impression of what it looks like here from what I've told you. There are many special things of which I have not written. I have resumed the connection with you all after the four weeks of silence while I was underway on my journey here. I will gladly answer your questions as best I can. You only need to write to me. There are certainly things that would interest each of you.

Now I have written you all! Now I expect that you will write me!
Greetings to you all,
Ernst Löwensberg

DOCUMENT 1-9. **Jewish teenagers unload a cart of hay at the Gross-Breesen's emigration-training farm, Germany, c. 1936, USHMMPA WS# 68299, courtesy of George Landecker.**

REICHSKRISTALLNACHT

On the night of November 9 and 10, 1938, a nationwide pogrom against German Jews erupted throughout Germany and annexed Austria and in areas of the **Sudetenland** and Czechoslovakia recently occupied by German troops. *Kristallnacht*, or Night of the Broken Glass, as the event came to be known, had its roots in the murder of Ernst vom Rath, a German embassy official stationed in Paris, on November 7, 1938. Herschel Grynszpan, a seventeen-year-old Polish Jew living in Paris, had shot the diplomat in response to the German authorities' recent expulsion of several thousand resident Polish Jews from the Reich.[52] Vom Rath's death two days later happened to coincide with the anniversary of the Nazi's 1923 Beer Hall Putsch, the most significant date in the National Socialist calendar. The Nazi Party leadership, assembled in Munich for the commemoration, chose to use the occasion as a pretext to launch a night of antisemitic excesses.

---

52. See Gerald Schwab, *The Day the Holocaust Began: The Odyssey of Herschel Gynszpan* (New York: Praeger, 1990). Grynszpan's family numbered among the deportees.

In its aftermath, German officials would contend that *Kristallnacht* had begun as a spontaneous outburst of public sentiment; in reality, the pogrom was initiated primarily by Nazi Party officials and conducted by members of the Nazi Party, the SA, and the **Hitler Youth**. The "rioters" destroyed 267 synagogues throughout Greater Germany. Many synagogues burned throughout the night, in full view of the public and local firefighters, who had received orders to intervene only to prevent flames from spreading to nearby buildings. SA and Hitler Youth members smashed windows, plundered homes, and looted Jewish-owned shops and businesses. The pogrom proved especially destructive in Berlin and Vienna, home to the two largest German Jewish communities. Mobs of SA men roamed the streets, attacking Jews they encountered and forcing them to submit to acts of public humiliation. Although Nazi authorities had not specifically ordered aggravated violence against individuals, *Kristallnacht* claimed the lives of at least ninety-one Jews between November 9 and 10. As the pogrom spread, units of the SS and Gestapo arrested some thirty thousand Jewish males, ultimately transferring most to **Dachau**, Buchenwald, Sachsenhausen, and other concentration camps until each prisoner could produce the requisite papers for emigration abroad. Significantly, *Kristallnacht* marked the first instance in which the Nazi regime incarcerated Jews on a massive scale on the basis of their ethnicity. The events of *Kristallnacht* represented an important turning point in Nazi antisemitic policy. After the pogrom, anti-Jewish measures radicalized dramatically, with a concentration of powers for antisemitic policy resting more and more concretely in the hands of the SS.[53]

Twelve-year-old Marguerite Strasser experienced the events of November 9 and 10, 1938, in Munich, the cradle of the National Socialist movement. Strasser's mother had died shortly after her birth, and her father had recently fled to Strasbourg, so Marguerite lived until her own flight to France in the care of her elderly grandmother. The events of November 10 made a powerful impression upon the young girl. Many of the pogrom's central features—the burning synagogues, the mistreatment of Jews in the streets, the ransacking and destruction of houses and businesses, and the arrest of Jewish men en masse in the wake of the action—figure as Strasser's fundamental images of the event. Her latter-day recollections also make it clear that Strasser internalized much of

---

53. For a more detailed account of the *Kristallnacht* pogrom, see Hermann Graml, *Reichskristallnacht: Antisemitismus und Judenverfolgung im Dritten Reich* (Munich: Deutscher Taschenbuch Verlag, 1988); Walter Pehle, ed., *November 1938: From "Reichskristallnacht" to Genocide*, trans. William Templer (New York: Berg, 1991); Alan E. Steinweis, *Kristallnacht, 1938* (Cambridge, MA: Belknap Press, 2009).

the rejection and trauma she and other Jews experienced at the hands of their fellow Germans in the wake of *Kristallnacht*.[54]

DOCUMENT 1-10. **Marguerite Strasser, "Then I Felt Like a Subhuman . . . ," in Friedrich Kraft, ed., *Kristallnacht in Bayern: Judenpogrom am 9. November 1938: Eine Dokumentation* (Ingolstadt: Claudius Verlag, 1988), 109–10 (translated from the German).**

On this day [November 10, 1938], I didn't want to go to school, because I already had the feeling that something was up. In my class, it was doubly difficult, because I was already a complete outsider there. And on this day the atmosphere was worse still. I was harassed more often, and the looks were even more hateful. In the first period we had calisthenics, and the teacher humiliated me on this day more than usual. Then my schoolmates hid all of my clothes, and I, completely dissolved in tears, had to search for them in every nook and cranny.

It was a very wicked prank, and of course as a result I came much too late to the math hour which followed. And, because I had also not done my homework, I promptly received an extra homework assignment.

In the middle of class, a pupil came in with an order from the director that the Jewish pupils had to leave the school immediately. I packed up my things. My classmates made very merry: they clapped and shrieked as I crept towards the door. But the mathematics teacher called after me, "And don't forget your extra assignment!" With this he showed that he didn't approve of this expulsion. It was very nice of him—until today I have not forgotten that. I was afraid to go straight home and went first to the home of a friend, who lived close by. She was half Jewish. She was not home yet, however, and her parents were in complete despair. She came home a half an hour later, sobbing, with torn clothing and covered with bruises. She was treated so cruelly by her fellow classmates. Her parents were so distressed that they sent me home immediately.

I was able to sneak past the synagogue in the Kanalstrasse.[55] The building was still giving off clouds of smoke. The windowpanes were shat-

---

54. Marguerite Strasser (b. 1926) emigrated in May 1939 to France, where she worked for several years as a social worker. In 1951 she returned to Munich, where she worked as a translator and raised a family.

55. This is today Munich's Herzog-Rudolf-Strasse.

tered. On the street among the shards of glass lay singed books and burnt religious objects.

Many people were standing before the synagogue, most of them in uniform, yelling "*Juda, verrecke*"[56] or something of that nature. Others walked by shyly—it was embarrassing to them. I went away then, with tears in my eyes. I did not dare take the tram.

When I arrived home crying, my grandmother said to me that I should save my tears until I knew everything. That is to say that my uncle, like all Jewish men over the age of eighteen, had been taken to Dachau. The Gestapo had been to the house, had ransacked the place, and ordered that we had to leave the apartment immediately.

Our loyal housekeeper, Afra, was indignant that an old lady and a little girl should simply be thrown out of their apartment. So she went in the afternoon to the Gestapo headquarters and carried on like a madwoman, asking what the big idea was and declaring how inhumane they were. In any case, we were allowed to remain in the apartment.

My grandmother had always said I must be proud that I am Jewish, but that was completely incomprehensible to me. I had always been terribly ashamed that I belonged to this horrible people with their terrible Jewish grimaces, as they were pictured in *Der Stürmer*. In my family certainly no one looked like that, but somehow it had still made an impression on me, and I felt like an inferior *Untermensch*.[57] And in school I was treated in exactly this manner, and at some point came to accept that I was of lesser value than the others.

THE DISMISSAL OF JEWISH CHILDREN FROM "GERMAN" SCHOOLS

In 1933, some sixty thousand Jewish children were of school age in Nazi Germany.[58] Especially in the earliest days of anti-Jewish legislation, parents and family members may have been able to shield youngsters from the worst aspects of antisemitic persecution: financial difficulties, the diminution within the circles of customers and business associates, the attenuation of social and community support, the likelihood of the loss of livelihood and property. But no one could protect Jewish children from the unconcealed prejudice and

56. This invective, used often in Nazi parlance, translates roughly as "Die, Jews!" or "Jews, drop dead!"
57. This means "inferior being."
58. See Kaplan, *Between Dignity and Despair*, 103.

discrimination that they encountered in their classrooms. Long before comprehensive efforts were undertaken to displace Jewish pupils from German public schools, Jewish boys and girls often experienced brutal treatment and painful rejection at the hands of their teachers and fellow students. In many schoolroom settings, they were held up to public ridicule by instructors and endured both taunting and bullying from their peers. Jewish children often had to sit on separate benches from their "Aryan" schoolmates, and in some schools, Jewish and German pupils were physically segregated. Spurned by classmates with whom they had been friendly for years, they could not join in many student events and were often excluded from school festivities and outings. The curriculum itself was alienating, with its emphasis on "Aryan" superiority, **racial hygiene**, and Nazi themes such as antisemitism and the subordination of so-called inferior peoples. In the midst of these indignities, Jewish pupils had few alternatives. As German law prescribed that school attendance was mandatory until age fourteen, many Jewish teenagers simply dropped out of school. Others—some 52 percent by 1936—enrolled in Jewish schools supported by the Reichsvertretung or other private organizations. Although this was a substantial leap from the 14 percent of students attending Jewish schools in 1932, a significant percentage of Jewish children nevertheless remained in public school classrooms until a decree in November 1938 definitively banned them from attending German schools.[59]

Nazi efforts to expel Jewish pupils from German public schools began with the April 25, 1933 Law against the Overcrowding of German Schools and Universities. This legislation imposed a quota for Jewish students, stipulating that enrollment of Jewish youth in schools and universities be limited to 1.5 percent of the students registered. The decree looked imposing, but in practice, its bark was worse than its bite, for exemptions were granted to all students whose fathers had fought in World War I; and in many areas, the Jewish population was such that resident Jewish children in a given district fit within the prescribed quota. In the years that followed, regional ordinances further limited Jewish school attendance in certain areas, but a comprehensive national ban came only in the wake of *Kristallnacht*. Among the multitude of regulations marginalizing Jews in German social and economic spheres in the aftermath of the pogrom came a November 15, 1938, decree from the Reich Minister of Education, dismissing all Jewish pupils from German (i.e., public) schools.[60]

59. Kaplan, *Between Dignity and Despair*, 103.
60. See Saul Friedländer, *Nazi Germany and the Jews*, Vol. 1: *The Years of Persecution, 1933–1939* (New York: Harper Collins, 1997); Monika Kingreen, ed., *"Nach der Kristallnacht": Jüdisches Leben und antijüdische Politik in Frankfurt am Main, 1938–1945* (Frankfurt am Main: Campus Verlag, 1999).

DOCUMENT 1-11. Decree of the Reich Minister of Science, Education, and Adult Education re the schooling of Jews, November 15, 1938 (translated from the German).

The City President
of the Reich Capital, Berlin
Dept. of Higher Education

Berlin, C.2., November 22, 1938
Burgstrasse 20
Tel. no. 52 0021

III Gen 1952/38

Copy

The Reich Minister for Science,
Education, and Adult Education

Berlin, W 8, November 15, 1938
Postal Box

E I b 745 (b)

Re: Schooling for Jews

After the infamous act of murder in Paris, no German schoolteacher can further be expected to give instruction to Jewish schoolchildren. It also goes without saying that it is intolerable for German school pupils to sit in the same classroom with Jews. The segregation of races in schools has already been generally accomplished in the last several years; but there is still a residual number of Jewish students in German schools, for whom school attendance with German boys and girls can no longer be permitted.

Subject to further legal regulations, I hereby order the following, effective immediately:

1. Jews are not permitted to attend German schools. They may only attend Jewish schools. As far as this has not occurred already, all Jewish male and female pupils now attending German schools are to be immediately dismissed.

2. Jews are defined by §5 of the First Decree of November 14, 1935, of the Reich Citizenship Law (*German Law Gazette*, I.P. 1333).

3. This regulation extends to all schools falling under my jurisdiction, inclusive of compulsory education establishments.

Signed for
(L. S.)

Zschintzsch

Elisabeth Block, a fifteen-year-old Jewish girl from Niedernburg, Bavaria, had remained in her unsegregated classroom until the late fall of 1938.

Although she lived in a rural community, where the abuse of Jewish pupils often proved harshest, Elisabeth thrived, surrounded by friendly schoolmates and buoyed by frequent outings with her class to the beautiful Alpine countryside. Elisabeth, who was introduced earlier, kept a diary in which, even during this dark period, she was loathe to record unpleasant developments. On November 17, 1938, she noted her expulsion and that of her siblings, Trudi and Arno, from their small Bavarian school. Just a week after the murder of her uncle, killed by SA men during *Kristallnacht*, Elisabeth remained cautiously optimistic about the new state of affairs. Although resolved to make the most of her new homeschooling, her entry makes plain the pain of isolation and separation from her friends and old life that lay just beneath the surface.

DOCUMENT 1-12. Diary for Elisabeth Block, entry for November 17, 1938, in Elisabeth Block, *Erinnerungszeichen: Die Tagebücher der Elisabeth Block*, ed. Haus der Bayerischen Geschichte/Historischer Verein Rosenheim (Rosenheim: Wendelstein-Druck, 1993), 162–63 (translated from the German).

<u>November 17, 1938</u>

Now what Mama has feared for so long has come to pass. Trudi, Arno, and I may not go to school any longer. With a terribly heavy heart, I took leave of my dear schoolmates.

My Schedule:
6:30: wake up; make the beds after breakfast. Around 8:00 a.m.: go to "school" in Papa's room, which will last till 10:00 a.m. We have German, mathematics, geography, history, drawing, and geometry. Tuesdays and Fridays from 1:00 p.m. to 3:15 p.m.: stenography and English with Mama. Between 10:00 and 1:00: cooking and washing dishes. Afternoons: digging in the garden, homework, etc. Mondays: help Kathi with the wash, which is very much fun, because in the shed we've had a very nice, spacious laundry set up. In the evenings, *Gabriele von Bülow's Daughters*[61] and *An Artist's Life* by F. Wasmann will be read aloud while we sew.

---

61. This was *Gabriele von Bülow's Töchter*, a book coauthored by Anna von Sydow and Gabriele von Bülow, daughter of the famous German scholar, philosopher, and linguist Wilhelm von Humboldt.

I am now completely preoccupied with this schedule and with preparations for Christmas[62] and feel exactly as content again as if I were going to school.

DOCUMENT 1-13. **A young girl reads her classroom lesson in Hebrew to her fellow classmates at a school sponsored by the Jewish Community of Berlin, c. 1935, USHMMPA WS# 32505, courtesy of the Bildarchiv Preussischer Kulturbesitz.**

WHAT'S IN A NAME? ISRAEL AND SARA

In the wake of *Reichskristallnacht*, Nazi authorities accelerated legislation aimed at the "**Aryanization**" of Jewish-owned property and businesses and intensified efforts to isolate and segregate Jews from their fellow Germans. Jews were barred from all public schools and universities, as well as from cinemas, theaters, and sports facilities. In many municipalities, Jews were forbidden to enter designated "Aryan" zones. In order to further marginalize members of the Jewish community, German officials required Jews to identify themselves in ways that

---

62. Like many German Jews, the secular Blocks celebrated Christmas and other Christian holidays, not from religious conviction but to participate in the holiday's outer trappings. The Blocks had a Christmas tree and joined in local public festivals; Elisabeth's diary is full of holiday drawings and references to religious events and periods, such as Lent.

would separate them from the rest of the population. All German Jews were required to carry identity cards that indicated their "racial" heritage, and in the autumn of 1938, all Jewish passports bore the identifying letter *J*. In August 1938, German authorities had already decreed that Jews could employ as a forename only those "Jewish names" from an official list maintained by the Reich Interior Ministry. This Second Decree for the Implementation of the Law for the Changing of Family Names and First Names[63] went into effect on January 1, 1939. Thereafter, Jews whose given names did not correspond to those on the authorized register had to add the name "Sara" after their first name if female, and "Israel" if male. On September 1, 1941, Nazi officials took this marginalization effort to an ominous conclusion, ordering all Jews over the age of six resident in the German Reich to wear a yellow star on their outer garments when in public.

In the summer of 1939, lawyer **Gilbert Kraus** and his wife, Eleanor, traveled to Europe to bring refugee Jewish children back with them to the United States. Under the aegis of the Brith Sholom lodge, a Jewish fraternal organization headquartered in Philadelphia, the Krauses, with the help of Vienna's Jewish Community (*Israelitische Kultusgemeinde*) chose fifty Viennese youngsters who already possessed affidavits and stood on the U.S. quota list. The Krauses and their lodge personally vouched for the financial security of the children and arranged foster homes for them in the Philadelphia area.[64] While procuring visas for the youngsters at the American consulate in Berlin, Eleanor Kraus witnessed the disquieting effects of recent Nazi policy upon a young Jewish girl in her charge.

DOCUMENT 1-14. **Eleanor Kraus, "Don't Wave Good-bye" (unpublished manuscript, private collection, c. 1940), 144–46 (© Liz Perle and Steven Kraus, reprinted with permission).**

> The children looked terrible. They were so weary and most of the little ones were still crying. The more we tried to stop them, the more they seemed to cry. Finally, I saw Gil.[65] I went up to him. "What about the visas? What about the visas?" I said. He leaned over and whispered to me, "There are fifty-seven visas here and waiting. All our worries are over."

63. The German is *Zweite Verordnung zur Durchführung des Gesetzes über die Änderung von Familiennamen und Vornamen.*

64. For a more comprehensive discussion of the Krauses' rescue efforts on behalf of Brith Sholom, see chapter 9.

65. This refers to Eleanor's husband, Gilbert Kraus.

I went to Bob[66] and gave him the news. None of us made any comments. After all, no one else but the three of us knew what a gamble we had taken. Now we had to settle down to clearing the children's papers. The Embassy had put on about fifteen extra clerks to help with the paper work. Each child had to be interviewed separately and had to fill out a form and each child would have to have a physical examination by the doctor at the Embassy.

Gil went into Mr. Volmer's office and I went into Mr. Rose's office. We decided to bring one child in at a time for the interview. The child would enter and sit at the desk and Mr. Volmer and his German secretary would ask the questions of the child in German. He would give his name, address and all the other information. He would also have to sign, if he could write. Mr. Volmer was sweet with each and every child. I tried to make the child feel at home. The secretary kept typing all the information as it was given. The Vice Consuls were most considerate—had worked out every detail to make things go as quickly as possible for all of us. It was tedious, it took time, but on the whole it was going quickly. Some of the children were only four years old and these interviews naturally consumed more time than the older children.

There was one little girl I will never forget. I think she was about six or seven years old. She came in for her interview and sat in the big office chair across from Mr. Volmer. She looked like an Alice in Wonderland figure sitting in the chair with her long blond hair and her bright blue eyes. Mr. Volmer smiled. "Can you write?" "*Ya*" [*sic*], she said. We put the pen in her hand. "Write your name here," said he, showing her the place on the paper. At this she seemed to freeze with fear. She grabbed the pen, lowered her head, and began to sob hysterically. She mumbled something over and over again which we could not hear. "What's the matter? Don't cry. Raise your head. We can't hear you."

Still she kept her head lowered, still she kept mumbling the same words over and over. She naturally spoke in German. I said to Mr. Volmer, "Can you understand her? What is she saying? I can't make it out." [. . .]

She was so overcome with terror I did not know how to pacify her. Finally she raised her head and said for all to hear, "*Muss ich Sarah schreiben?*" ["Must I write 'Sarah'?"]

---

66. This refers to Dr. Robert Reuss, who accompanied the Krauses to Germany to make arrangements for the emigration of the children.

It took a moment for the implication of this question to hit all of us. We were too stunned to answer. Even the German clerk stood with her mouth open. Mr. Volmer lowered his head into his hands for a moment. My German was so limited, but I answered, "*Nein, nein. Schreibe Charlotta. Schreibe Charlotta*" [*sic*].

Mr. Volmer took over. "Write Charlotta. Write Charlotta," said he. "Your name is Charlotta. You will always keep your name where you are going. You need never write Sarah again."

CHAPTER 2

CHILDREN AND THE WAR

WORLD WAR II was the most destructive conflict in modern history. Beginning in Europe on September 1, 1939, with the German invasion of Poland and later extending into the Pacific sphere, the war prompted the mobilization of 100 million military personnel. Although accurate casualty statistics are difficult to ascertain, scholars estimate that the number of total dead as a result of hostilities ranges from 50 to 70 million, including some 20 to 25 million combatants.[1] Even as it exceeded the aggregate military deaths from the Great War which preceded it,[2] World War II also marked an early manifestation of a new trend in modern warfare: it claimed far more civilian lives than military casualties. Within the parameters of "Total War" which blurred the distinction between military and civilian targets, it is believed that at least 40 million noncombatants fell victim to strategic bombing, war crimes, persecution, famine, and epidemic in the course of World War II.

This chapter covers World War II in the European context and examines the effect of German and Axis aggression upon civilian families and their children, viewing the hardships and tragedies of warfare through the eyes of youngsters. In this context, children often witnessed death for the first time and experienced hunger and deprivation. The German occupation of nations in eastern and western Europe meant that Jewish children and adults in lands under Axis control became subject to stringent anti-Jewish measures. Other

---

1. This number includes some 5 million military personnel who died in captivity.
2. That is, World War I.

young people found themselves caught up in the midst of **partisan** warfare or fell victim to bitter reprisal actions. The following documentation demonstrates how children confronted the realities of conflict as World War II came home to them.

THE FIRST TASTE OF CONFLICT

Julien Hequembourg Bryan (1899–1974) was a well-known American photographer, filmmaker, and author, widely respected as the founder of the International Film Foundation, established in 1945. Bryan had gained fame in the 1930s for his vivid depiction of life in the Soviet Union under Joseph Stalin and for the extensive lecture tours he undertook in the wake of his visits there. In September 1939, Bryan found himself the sole photojournalist from a neutral country left in Warsaw when German forces began their *Blitzkrieg* invasion of Poland. Fortunately still in possession of several thousand feet of film left over from a recent tour of western Europe, Bryan remained in the Polish capital throughout the three-week-long siege, witnessing the German army's brutal attacks on military and civilian targets and documenting the anguish and courage of the Polish population. Bryan managed to evacuate the war zone along with other citizens of neutral countries during a brief truce on September 21, 1939. His film footage of the German assault on Warsaw would figure as America's first cinematic glimpse of the European conflict that became World War II and would earn the filmmaker an Academy Award nomination in 1940.[3]

One of Bryan's most famous and moving images of the Polish campaign portrays ten-year-old Kazimiera Kostewicz,[4] who, in the presence of the photographer and his Polish guides, discovered the body of her elder sister, killed in a strafing run by German pilots. Bryan's photograph and accompanying postwar commentary capture the cruelty of a war waged against civilians and of a child's first experience of death.

---

3. Bryan's film Siege (Pathé Films, 1940) lost the Oscar that year for short subjects on a technicality: the film had not been released to general audiences at the time of its nomination. For a discussion of Bryan's contributions to photojournalism and documentary cinematography, see "Everyone Would Believe My Pictures: The Legacy of Julien Bryan," U.S. Holocaust Memorial Museum, www.ushmm.org/research/collections/highlights/bryan (accessed November 20, 2010).

4. Kazimiera Mika (née Kostewicz, 1929–) survived the war and was reunited with Julian Bryan when he returned to Warsaw in 1959. Mika recently joined the cinematographer's son Sam Bryan at the seventieth-anniversary screening of Siege in Poland in 2009.

DOCUMENT 2-1. **Ten-year-old Kazimiera Kostewicz (Mika) discovers the body of her sister Anna, killed in a strafing run by German pilots on Polish civilians near Warsaw, September 1939, USHMMPA WS# 50898, courtesy of Julien Bryan.**

DOCUMENT 2-2. **Julien Bryan,** *Warsaw: 1939 Siege, 1959 Warsaw Revisited* **(Warsaw: Polonia Publishing House, 1959), 20–21.**

Bodies are not pleasant sights under any circumstances, and when they are of young women, torn to pieces by bombs and sometimes without heads or arms or legs, they are horrible to behold. In photography we ordinarily think of beauty of composition. There was no beauty here. But it was true: women and children had been killed by enemy bombs. I was not making a travelogue. I was in Warsaw, whether I liked it or not, making a historical record on film of what happens in modern war. People might not believe my story if I told it in words when I returned to America. Everyone would believe my pictures. [. . .]

As we drove by a small field at the edge of town, we were just a few minutes too late to witness a tragic event, the most incredible of all. Seven women had been digging potatoes in a field. There was no flour in their district, and they were desperate for food. Suddenly two German planes appeared from nowhere and dropped two bombs only two hundred yards away on a small home. Two women in the house were killed. The potato diggers dropped flat upon the ground, hoping to be unnoticed. After the bombers had gone, the women returned to their work. They had to have food. But the Nazi fliers were not satisfied with their work. In a few minutes they came back and swooped down to within two hundred feet of the ground, this time raking the field with machine-gun fire. Two of the seven women were killed. The other five escaped somehow.

While I was photographing the bodies, a little ten-year-old girl came running up and stood transfixed by one of the dead. The woman was her older sister. The child had never before seen death and couldn't understand why her sister would not speak to her.

"What has happened?" she cried. Then she leaned down and touched the dead girl's face, and drew back in horror.

"Oh, my beautiful sister!" she wailed. "What have they done to you? You are so ugly!" Then, after a few seconds: "Please talk to me! Please, oh, please! What will become of me without you!"

The child looked at us in bewilderment. I threw my arm about her and held her tightly, trying to comfort her. She cried. So did I and the two Polish officers who were with me.

What could we, or anyone else, say to this child?

As the first battles of World War II raged in Poland, German citizens too were coming to terms with the early ramifications of the new conflict. German Jews, already marginalized and persecuted in the early years of the Third Reich, now found living in Nazi Germany even more precarious. Among them was seventeen-year-old Inge Deutschkron. An award-winning writer and journalist in the postwar, she survived the war years in Berlin as a "U-boat,"[5] a Jew living

---

5. The German is *U-Boot*, meaning "submarine." For a discussion of Jews living underground in Berlin during the war years, see Leonard Gross, *The Last Jews in Berlin* (New York: Simon & Schuster, 1982); Inge Deutschkron, *Berlin Jews Underground*, trans. Hanna Silver (Berlin: Gedenkstätte Deutscher Widerstand, 1990).

"underground," often under a fictive name or on false papers. Her father, a *Gymnasium*[6] teacher and staunch Social Democrat, lost his post in 1933, when the Nazi **Law for the Restoration of the Professional Civil Service** banned both Jews and "politically unreliable" elements from civil service posts. In 1939, Martin Deutschkron managed to flee to London, but Inge and her mother were prevented from joining him when World War II in Europe commenced on September 1 of that year. A flurry of anti-Jewish legislation in the wake of *Kristallnacht* had already curtailed Jewish life in social and economic spheres. With the outbreak of war, a new rash of decrees and regulations further limited Jews' ability to function within German society.[7] Jewish citizens were severely limited in their movements, especially in public places. Food and clothing were strictly rationed. Inge Deutschkron recalled the anxiety and frustration of Jewish existence in those early war days, before Nazi antisemitic policies drove her and her mother "underground."[8]

DOCUMENT 2-3. Inge Deutschkron, *Ich trug den gelben Stern*, 4th ed. (1975; Cologne: Verlag Wissenschaft und Politik, 1983), 60–67 (translated from the German).

In the months following [the outbreak of war], Jews were the subjects of a multitude of decrees and ordinances, in order, so it was said, to hinder "subversive activities." Jews had to give up their radios. Their telephone lines were disconnected. Between 8:00 p.m. (9:00 p.m. in summer) and 5:00 a.m., Jews were not allowed to leave their residences. They had to remain in their air raid bunkers until the all-clear signal was blown, so that they could not give any lighted signals to the enemy. All protections for Jewish renters were lifted. Jews had to give up their furs, binoculars, cameras, electrical appliances. [. . .] In the end, Jews were not allowed to visit theaters or concert halls or cinemas. Parks and public spaces were closed to them. Even sitting on a bench once meant for Jews and marked with a yellow star was forbidden. Certain areas of Berlin were declared off-limits to Jews: the government district was one of them.[9]

---

6. This is a German school providing secondary education in preparation for college study, much like college-preparatory high schools in the United States.

7. See Schleunes, *The Twisted Road to Auschwitz*, esp. 245ff.

8. Deutschkron (1922–) began writing as the German correspondent for the Israeli newspaper *Ma'ariv* in 1958 and in 1966 became an Israeli citizen. She later settled in Berlin, where she remained active as a writer; in 2008, Deutschkron won the prestigious Carl von Ossietzky Prize for contemporary history and politics.

9. This refers to the traditional district encompassing government buildings, most lining the Wilhelm-Strasse below Unter den Linden in the central Tiergarten district of Berlin.

Naturally, it can be ascribed to my youth that, unruffled, I declared to my mother that I would not even think of adhering to these regulations. I needed to visit the theater once in a while; I needed music or a walk in the Grunewald.[10] I couldn't endure the narrowness of Jewish society, which had now been turned in upon itself. Their conversations now revolved around all the aggravating things that the Nazis had already decreed or those things that we could expect from them in the future. Fear and depressive foreboding resonated from these discussions. People tormented themselves: "I have heard from a reliable friend who has it directly from the propaganda ministry that the Nazis are planning this and that." Then this passed [. . .] from house to house and frightened and plagued the people, who were already so anxious. [. . .]

The Jewish population of Berlin had almost without exception all that they needed that their limited ration cards deprived them of. Their fellow citizens in Berlin saw to that. First of all there were the owners of the grocery stores who put aside their "extras" for their faithful old customers. My mother and I went once each week to Richard Junghans, a former Social Democrat and friend of my father's, who opened a grocery store at the "Knie" (today Ernst-Reuter-Platz) after he lost his post with the union in 1933. He furnished us with fruits and vegetables as if it were the most natural thing in the world to do so. It was the same with our butcher Krachudel, who had his stand at the weekly market on the Wittenbergplatz, where my mother had shopped for the last fifteen years. Now he gave my mother the same amount of meat that our family had requested for years, without our having to give up one single ration card. [. . .]

On April 1, 1939, my school years ended. That did not happen voluntarily. The Nazis closed the Jewish schools.[11] [. . .] We girls celebrated our "graduation" in our own way, by dancing with each other. [. . .] Dance class, which at this time was customary for well-bred girls, was of course not available for Jewish students. Even meeting with young people of the same age was rarely possible. The fear of being recognized by some Nazi in a café or park and abused deprived these moments of flirtation of any pleasure. [. . .]

Shortly after the outbreak of war, the Nazis blocked my father's pension fund with the justification that he lived in an enemy country, and so

---

10. This large and picturesque forest in the Charlottenburg-Wilhelmsdorfer neighborhood of Berlin later became a deportation site for the Jews of Berlin.

11. Most segregated Jewish schools were officially closed on July 7, 1942.

we had no right to the money. We had to cut back our spending, although at that time we couldn't spend much money. The sale of food supplies was restricted. Jews didn't receive ration cards for textiles. We moved into a more modest room in the Hansaviertel.[12] [. . .] Constantly the radio intoned, "Because we're marching, because we're marching, because we're marching on England," and "Today Germany belongs to us, and tomorrow, the world."[13] For us Jews it was eerie. We were filled with fear. What would happen if Hitler, against expectations, won the war? Little Frau Oppenheimer, whose husband was once a lawyer and was a friend of my father, said to my mother in a conversation on the street, "We will not live through that. For us there would be no survival." It is difficult to say where she got the courage to say out loud what none of us knew, what we did not want to believe. Shortly before the outbreak of war, she had sent her thirteen-year-old son to England. Later, in the midst of the deportations, the Oppenheimers took their own lives—true to their motto, "*Us* they won't get."

As **Wehrmacht** forces expanded the boundaries of the German Reich and those regions under its military and civilian control, German authorities transferred various tenets of antisemitic legislation to areas under their jurisdiction. In Austria (the *Ostmark*) and in German-annexed areas of Czechoslovakia (the so-called **Protectorate of Bohemia and Moravia**) and Poland, German officials simply extended those regulations concerning racial policy to these territories as they were incorporated into the Greater German Reich. In the *Generalgouvernement* (**General Government**)—those parts of occupied Poland not directly annexed to Germany—Governor General **Hans Frank** issued a string of anti-Jewish ordinances in the late autumn of 1939, ordering the clear designation of Jewish persons and Jewish-owned property and businesses, prohibiting Jews from moving their residences, restricting freedom of movement and travel without permit, and introducing forced labor. In most cases, those antisemitic regulations put in place in German-occupied Poland represented harsher and more repressive measures than those imposed in Germany or its annexed territories at the time. In other nations that Germany had defeated and in which it installed occupation administrations or quasi-independent puppet governments—as in France, the Netherlands, Luxembourg, Norway, Yugoslavia, and Greece—German authorities or their

---

12. This refers to a small quarter in central Berlin near the Tiergarten.
13. Both phrases are lines from Nazi wartime propaganda songs.

indigenous collaborators introduced legislation defining who within the population would be regarded as Jewish, usually based on Nazi Germany's **Nuremberg
Laws**. Parallel laws circumscribed Jews from that nation's social, cultural, and
economic life.[14] This phenomenon also occurred in Axis countries allied to
Germany, such as Hungary, Romania, and Italy, although Nazi German leaders could not control the internal policies of these nations and needed to exert
varying degrees of pressure to persuade their allies to accede to their demands.

One of the most ubiquitous antisemitic measures employed in German-
and Axis-controlled Europe was the mandatory wearing of the **Jewish badge**
(yellow star). This effort to impose a distinctive mark upon the Jewish population marginalized its members and made them more vulnerable to official
and spontaneous discriminatory actions. The measure affected both children
and adults and varied in its essentials from region to region. The first such
decrees requiring Jews to wear the Jewish badge appeared in occupied Poland
in November 1939, where Hans Frank ordered that all Jews above the age of
twelve living in the General Government must wear on the right sleeve of their
outermost garment a white armband affixed with a blue Jewish star. Similar
regulations, with various discrepancies in the badge's appearance and the age
of the wearer, materialized in other districts of Poland and in areas occupied
by German forces following the invasion of the Soviet Union in June 1941.[15]

Twelve-year-old Idel Kozłowski experienced firsthand the series of restric-
tive decrees and regulations imposed by German authorities following the occupation of western Belorussia. Shortly after the arrival of German forces in June
1941, Jews in his hometown of Golshany were compelled to wear the Jewish
star and confined to an enclosed area of the town that formed a small ghetto.
To the youngster, it was immediately clear that the new measures rendered him
and his fellow Jews vulnerable to the aggressions of their antisemitic neighbors
and helpless in the face of Nazi persecution.

---

14. An exception to this pattern was Denmark, whose government steadfastly resisted the
implementation of most antisemitic measures, including the imposition of the Jewish badge.

15. For a discussion of the designation of Jews in Germany and in German-occupied
Europe, see Diemut Majer, *"Non-Germans under the Third Reich": The Nazi Judicial and
Administrative System in Germany and Occupied Eastern Europe, with Special Regard to
Occupied Poland, 1939–1945*, trans. Peter Thomas Hill, Edward Vance Humphrey, and Brian
Levin (Baltimore: Johns Hopkins University Press in association with the U.S. Holocaust
Memorial Museum, 2003).

DOCUMENT 2-4. **Interview of Idel Kozłowski (Kozlovskij) by the Central Jewish Historical Commission, February 14, 1947, USHMM, RG-15.084, Holocaust Survivor Testimonies, Łódź, 301/3626 (translated from the Russian).**

Autobiography:

I, Idel Abramovič Kozlovskij,[16] was born in 1929 in the small town of Golshany [Polish: Holszany; Yiddish: Olshan] in the Vilno oblast to a family of merchants. My father traded in linen cloth. Our family consisted of six persons. My father Abram Kozlovskij, my mother Masha Kozlovskaja. Two brothers: Ėlia and Isaak. My sister Chasia. From 1937 until 1939, I went to a Jewish school. In 1939, when the Germans conquered Poland, the Red Army took over our oblast, western Belorussia, as well as the western Ukraine and transferred it to the jurisdiction of the Soviet Union. With the beginning of Soviet control [in the area], I went to the Jewish N.E.Š. [Novaja Evreskaja Škola, or New Jewish School]. These were the last happy days of my young and promising life. So my life went before 1941. [. . .]

On June 23, 1941, the German marauders, in a breach of trust,[17] invaded the USSR, and by June 24, 1941, they were already in our village. Already in those first days the Germans commenced their predatory and bloody deeds. From the scoundrels [*Psy*] within the Polish population, they assembled a police force that helped them to accomplish their rapacious deeds. Immediately, the Germans issued the order that from now on Jews would not be considered equal citizens [under the law]. The Jews had to wear a white band with a large six-pointed star in the middle upon the arm.

Jews were forbidden to walk on the sidewalk, only in the gutter. The police went to all the Jewish houses [and] beat, robbed and ridiculed everyone. Two months later, we were chased from our houses and driven into the "GHETTO"[18]—that is, into a section of the village that was fenced in with planks—and in that they drove all of us Jews. With our move to the ghetto, a new order decreed that Jews were forbidden to go outside the ghetto. The Jews had to wear a new kind of marking: a large, six-pointed star on the chest and back. Circumvention of this order was

---

16. The child's name is spelled in two different ways in the interview protocol.

17. The German army's invasion of the Soviet Union on June 22, 1941, violated the German-Soviet Non-Aggression Pact of August 23, 1939.

18. Capitals and quotation marks are present in the original.

punished with shooting. [. . .] So we lived in this difficult, bloody situation and witnessed how these dogs—our enemies—lived in our houses, how they walked untroubled in the streets [while] we sat fenced in like cattle in the ghetto, awaiting death every day and without the possibility to [save] ourselves.

German Jews were finally forced to wear the Jewish badge on September 15, 1941,[19] shortly before the first **deportations** of Jews from the Reich began in October 1941. The Police Decree Concerning the Designation of Jews (*Polizeiverordnung über die Kennzeichnung der Juden*) required all Jews over the age of six to attach to the left side of their outer garment a six-pointed yellow star, inscribed with the word *Jude* (Jew) in black lettering. The decree further applied to Jews in Austria and the Protectorate; it was also officially introduced at this time in German-annexed territories of Poland, although in many areas such policies had already been in place since the autumn of 1939.

Legislation mandating the Jewish badge was soon adopted in western lands occupied by Germany and in German satellite states. Belgian and Dutch Jews, for example, began to wear the yellow star in the spring months of 1942. In occupied France, such an ordinance was issued on June 7, 1942, although bureaucratic resistance on the part of French officials meant that a similar measure was never applied in **Vichy France**, even when German forces occupied those regions of France in November 1942.[20]

---

19. The decree appeared on September 1, 1941, and went into effect two weeks later.

20. See Michael R. Marrus and Robert O. Paxton, *Vichy France and the Jews* (New York: Basic Books, 1981), esp. 234ff.

DOCUMENT 2-5. **A Jewish child in occupied France wears the yellow star, USHMMPA WS# 63042, courtesy of Michael O'Hara.**

CAUGHT IN THE CROSSFIRE: THE WAR ON CIVILIANS

The sustained bombing of London and other British cities between September 7, 1940, and May 10, 1941, known colloquially as the Blitz,[21] figures as one of the most well-known events of World War II. At its height, German bombs rained down on London for fifty-seven consecutive nights, causing extensive damage and loss of life among the civilian population.

What many historians call the Battle of Britain began in July 1940. Prior to the planned invasion of the British Isles (Operation Sea Lion), the German Luftwaffe (air force) began to bomb strategic targets such as military airfields

---

21. This is a shortening of the German word *Blitzkrieg* (lightning war).

and key manufacturing areas in an effort to achieve air superiority over the Royal Air Force and to facilitate a possible German invasion across the English Channel. The first deliberate air raids on civilian London began on September 7.[22] In that initial attack, launched in late afternoon, the Luftwaffe struck the city's port and Docklands, where bombs, falling in nearby residential districts, killed more than 430 Londoners. In the days that followed, some one to two hundred German aircraft bombarded the city nightly, dropping an estimated thirteen thousand tons of explosives on the British capital. Perhaps the most devastating raid came shortly after Christmas, on the evening of December 29, when Luftwaffe planes dropped incendiary and high-explosive bombs on the city center. The resulting firestorm destroyed the largest contiguous area of urban land witnessed in any German raid of its kind, rivaling the devastation of the Great Fire of London in 1666.[23]

London was not the only target of German bombing. From November 1940 through February 1941, the Luftwaffe attacked British port cities, such as Liverpool, Cardiff, Plymouth, and Southampton, as well as military and industrial centers, such as Manchester, Hull,[24] Belfast, and Coventry. Although in the campaign's later stages bombers increasingly concentrated on strategic, rather than civilian, targets, the principle objective of the Blitz remained the same: to shatter the morale of the British people. British citizens, however, responded to the destructive raids with great courage and determination. London's civilian population contributed enormously to the defense of their city, volunteering with the Home Guard, as air raid wardens, and as the intrepid "Blitz scouts," who aided local fire brigades in their rescue efforts. By night, thousands of Londoners descended into the safety of London's Tube, or subway system, or crowded into public bunkers; others huddled with family members in so-called Anderson shelters, small self-constructed bomb shelters made of corrugated steel, sunk in the backyards and gardens of homes throughout the country. Youngsters endured long separations from their parents and family members, as British authorities

---

22. When an initial German foray over residential London prompted a retaliatory British raid upon Berlin, an enraged Hitler called for a "disruptive attack upon the population and air defenses of major British cities, including London, by day and night" (quoted in Klaus Maier et al., *Germany and the Second World War: Germany's Initial Conquests in Europe* [Oxford: Oxford University Press, 1991], 387). Controversy has long existed over whether this earliest bombing of London's East End on August 24, 1940, was accidental or German pilots were acting on a loosely worded order from Reichsmarschall Hermann Göring.

23. See Peter Stansky, *The First Day of the Blitz* (New Haven, CT: Yale University Press, 2007); Richard Overy, *The Battle of Britain: Myth and Reality* (London: Penguin, 2000).

24. After London, Hull was the most severely bombed British city during World War II, with 95 percent of its housing damaged or destroyed.

evacuated nearly one hundred thousand children and adolescents from their homes in London and other urban areas to the safety of the countryside.[25]

The bravery and resilience of British citizens paid off. By May 1941, with no British surrender forthcoming, most Luftwaffe units had redeployed to the East for the coming invasion of the Soviet Union. Although the German air force would never again attack British targets with such intensity, smaller raids upon British cities would claim the lives of some eight thousand more civilians, while the infamous V-1 and V-2[26] flying bombs, early forms of cruise missiles, killed an almost equal number of Britons in the last stages of World War II. But the sustained bombing experienced throughout the Blitz was over. From early September 1940 until late May 1941, forty-three thousand British citizens had died in air raids, half of them in London, while 1 million housing units had been damaged or destroyed.

Olive McNeil was fourteen years old on "Black Saturday," September 7, 1940, when German bombs pounded the residential neighborhoods bordering the Docklands on London's East Side. The family had just installed a private shelter, and she, her mother, and her younger brothers had just enough time to reach the bunker before the first shells fell. Olive recollected that, on that first day of the Blitz, an air of unreality mingled with the terror of the moment.

DOCUMENT 2-6. **Olive McNeil, London, England, undated testimony, quoted in Jane Waller and Michael Vaughan-Rees, *Blitz: The Civilian War, 1940–1945* (London: McDonald Optima, 1990), 12–13.**

> I was in the backyard watching my two little brothers play—although most of our yard was taken up by the Anderson [shelter] that the council workmen had put in—and I could hear this strange droning sound. Looking up I could see lots of planes very small and very high. I called the boys to look. We said how pretty they looked with the sun glinting on them, they looked like stars. But there were so many of them and they were coming over us in lines. Suddenly everything changed, the planes that were high up started to swoop down and down and the air was filled with screaming whistling sounds. The siren was blowing and Mum came running out and pushed us down the shelter. But the screaming whistlings

---

25. The bulk of these evacuations occurred in and after June 1940; many children returned over the course of 1941 as urban areas became safer. Another evacuation of women and children from London began in June 1944, when German forces deployed V-1 and V-2 rockets on British civilian targets. See Carleton Jackson, *Who Will Take Our Children: The British Evacuation Program of World War II* (Jefferson, NC: McFarland Press, 2008).

26. In each case, the V stood for *Vergeltungswaffe* (revenge weapon).

didn't stop, they got louder and louder[;] I could feel the thudding of the ground around me. Some of the screaming whistlings were making the earth floor in the shelter jump. I could feel the dirt and dust was coming through the cracks in the shelter. I could hardly see, it was covering my hair and was getting in our eyes. Mum told us to lie down and she lay on top of us and she kept saying her prayers, and I said, "Please Jesus, don't let the screaming whistlings come too close." Mum told me to shut up and not frighten the boys. But the screaming whistlings went on and on, and one got so close that the shelter nearly got lifted out of the ground. We all screamed and we heard glass breaking and things flying around.

Suddenly everything went quiet, and we clung together in the blessed silence until the all clear went and we thanked God we were all right. I was out first. By now it was getting dark. I remember standing by the shelter and looking around me, it was as though I was in a dream. The sky as far as I could see all around me was orange and pink. It glowed, making everything look like fairyland.

World War II fits within the paradigm that defines an increasingly more common pattern in warfare: it claimed more civilian lives than military casualties. Noncombatants on both the Allied and Axis sides fell victim to strategic bombing and mining, war crimes, persecution, population transfers, famine, and disease. In many countries, hapless civilians were caught in the veritable crossfire of partisan warfare.

Perhaps no region saw a more vicious partisan struggle than the former Yugoslavia, where resistance against the Axis occupiers combined with internecine warfare. On April 6, 1941, the Axis powers invaded the Kingdom of Yugoslavia from all sides. The country was quickly overrun by, and partitioned among, the aggressors: Germany, Italy, Hungary, and Bulgaria. German forces occupied northern Slovenia and the truncated Serbian state; in the regions representing the modern nations of Croatia and Bosnia-Herzegovina, German authorities created the Independent State of Croatia (Nezavisna Drzava Hrvatska), a puppet state over which Germany exerted considerable influence. A strong Yugoslav resistance emerged, in two distinct manifestations. The Chetniks, a conservative royalist and nationalist force whose support came largely from the Serbian population, initially gained recognition from the Western Allies, but they compromised their position through increasing collaboration with Axis forces.[27] In July 1941, the communist resistance formed

---

27. After the Teheran Conference in late 1943, the Allies and the Yugoslavian government in exile recognized the Yugoslav Partisan Movement as the country's legitimate liberation force.

the People's Liberation Army and Partisan Detachments of Yugoslavia, known simply as the Partisans, led by future Yugoslav leader Josip Broz Tito (1892–1980). At the outset, Partisan forces were poorly armed and lacked an efficient infrastructure, but they possessed two important assets that they would use to advantage. First, their units formed around a small central cadre of men who had gained combat experience in the recent Spanish Civil War and could share with their comrades important strategies and tactics employed in modern guerrilla warfare. Second, the Partisan movement united under an antifascist ideology that embraced factions from the republican, socialist, and communist Left but transcended the boundaries of ethnicity in a multiethnic state. The Partisans fought an increasingly successful guerrilla campaign against the Axis occupiers and the fascist Croatian **Ustaše** regime. The occupying forces and their local collaborators administered the region with such brutality that the Partisans gained widespread support and assistance from the local populations. In the end, the government of the Independent State of Croatia found itself unable to control its territory, resulting in a number of anti-insurgency campaigns undertaken by the Germany army and the Ustaše militia.[28]

The Partisans were ultimately successful in cooperating with Allied forces to liberate Yugoslavia, but the ensuing partisan warfare came at a tremendous cost. Throughout the period of insurgency, law and order effectively broke down in many regions, and guerrilla groups combed the countryside, terrorizing the populace. Both the Ustaše militias and the Chetniks committed wide-ranging atrocities against the local populations. The German occupiers carried out massive reprisals for guerrilla activity against German troops and murdered thousands of civilians in retaliation for resistance activity. The Yugoslav Partisans also engaged in reprisal actions, although the most egregious of these occurred in the immediate postwar period.

In July 1942, Milovan Đjilas, a guerrilla commander with the Yugoslav Partisans, wrote an entry in the diary of his closest associate, Vladimir Dedijer. Both men would play vital roles in the founding of the communist Federal People's Republic of Yugoslavia in the immediate postwar.[29] Visiting his com-

28. See John Lampe, *Yugoslavia As History: Twice There Was a Country* (Cambridge: Cambridge University Press, 1996); Sabrina Ramet, ed., *The Independent State of Croatia* (London: Routledge Press, 2007).

29. Milovan Đjilas (1911–1995) was groomed as Tito's eventual successor until his calls for greater democratization in both party and state led to his downfall in 1954. Vladimir Dedijer was Tito's official biographer but lost influence with Đjilas's fall from power. Thereafter, he devoted himself to writing and teaching history at a number of universities in the former Yugoslavia, Great Britain, and the United States. Among his well-known works is *The Yugoslav Auschwitz and the Vatican: The Croatian Massacre of the Serbs during World War II*, trans. Harvey Kendall (Buffalo, NY: Prometheus, 1992).

rade after a month's absence, the battle-hardened Đjilas described with horror the Ustaše massacre of women and children he had witnessed in Urije, in
present-day Bosnia-Herzegovina. "When he had finished," wrote Dedijer, "I
gave him my diary and said, 'Note for me all of this so nothing is lost.'"[30]

**DOCUMENT 2-7. Addendum of Milovan Đjilas to the July 28, 1942, diary entry of
Vladimir Dedijer, in Vladimir Dedijer, *The War Diaries of Vladimir Dedijer*, Vol. 1: *From
April 6, 1941, to November 27, 1942* (Ann Arbor: University of Michigan Press, 1990),
269–70.**

I was following an ordinary village road, and it was an ordinary summer
morning, rather clean because of the gentle rain which had fallen during
the night. . . . I was so depressed I wanted to cry, because I could not drive
from my mind the picture of those wonderful comrades who had died in
yesterday's skirmish with the Ustaše, there somewhere in front of me, in
the lush meadows. But what I saw yesterday [. . .] so filled me with disgust
that it totally erased all the pain I felt for my dear comrades. [. . .]

We went on our way a little further, on both sides of the road, hazel
hedges and ferns, and suddenly, in the middle of the road, I do not recall
the exact number, ten or twelve corpses. I think there were two middle-
aged men—the remainder were women, girls, children, babies. Three or
four paces from this heap of blood and flesh—an empty cradle, without
swaddling, without a child, with straw dampened by a child's urine. This
straw seemed as if it was still warm from the child's body. The child was
lying in the heap of corpses, but its head was completely smashed. [. . .]

The remaining corpses too were disfigured. The face of a ten-year-old
had knife wounds on its forehead and cheeks. Some boy, also with an
empty skull, like that infant, lay twisted around the bush at the side of
the road, his bare legs and thin arms bent. Because rigor mortis had set in,
the skin was gathered and the sharp white bones peered out at the temple.
If the boy had not been so disfigured, one would have thought he was
sleeping in the shade, by the road, a little hidden so the farmers wouldn't
see him and scold him for sleeping, not keeping an eye on the livestock so
they wouldn't get into the farmer's fields and meadows. [. . .]

The road at this point is broad and there is a lot of room, as there should
be on the outskirts of a town, where the peasants can sit in the evening, to rest

---

30. Vladimir Dedijer, *The War Diaries of Vladimir Dedijer*, Vol. 1: *From April 6, 1941, to
November 27, 1942* (Ann Arbor: University of Michigan Press, 1990), 269.

and admire the town. But the corpses were all slaughtered on the edge of the road, up against the fence, as if a storm had swept them there.

Among them were two mothers with their infants. If at the earlier group, one could not tell who the mothers of the children were, here it could easily be seen. One mother, young and dark, held her child in her arms. [. . .] The other mother had not held her child so firmly. She lay on her back, and the child, abandoned by her side, lay in a heap, its blouse torn from its chest. The first mother, with dark eyebrows, gave the impression of those old-fashioned, false romantic pictures of murdered or drowned mothers with children, but this was nothing old-fashioned or false, or romantic, but an actual mother killed with her child, a mother whom death had frozen, holding her infant to her breast.

DOCUMENT 2-8. **Body of a young boy killed in an antipartisan campaign on the slopes of Petrova Gora, a stronghold of communist resistance activity in Yugoslavia, 1942, USHMMPA WS# 01138, courtesy of Lydia Chagoll.**

As for most civilians in war-torn Europe, privation was the central experience of children's wartime existence. For a significant number of Europe's young population, it was neither exploding shells nor encroaching invaders but hunger that proved the greatest enemy. One scene of unparalleled deprivation in the midst of World War II was the Soviet city of Leningrad (today Saint Petersburg), the site of a devastating 872-day siege by German forces, which began on September 8, 1941, when an advance of German troops to the shores of Lake Lagoda on Leningrad's eastern edge effectively completed the encirclement of the city. On September 19, Red Army soldiers and civilians from the town halted the Germans before hastily dug defense lines in a 10-kilometer (6.2-mile) perimeter about the city. While Adolf Hitler announced that his forces had no interest in saving the lives of the civilian population, German army units settled in for a protracted siege. Early in the conflict, German bombs had destroyed the city's major supply depot, and with only a trickle of provisions reaching the metropolis, the city's 3.5 million inhabitants—400,000 of them children—knew the most extreme deprivation.[31] Without sufficient foodstuffs, water, or fuel, the death rate that winter soared. In January 1942, rations dropped to their lowest point: just 125 grams (4.4 ounces) of bread per person per day. City dwellers ate paper, wallpaper paste, their pets. Furniture, books, and floorboards were burned for warmth. In January and February 1942, amid the coldest winter in recent memory, some two hundred thousand Leningraders died from starvation, disease, and the incessant bombing and shelling by German forces.[32] Despite the grim conditions, the city did not surrender. In January 1943, a Soviet offensive opened a narrow corridor near Lake Lagoda that would prove a vital artery for goods and supplies and an urgently needed evacuation route for the city's thousands of starving inhabitants. On January 27, 1944, Soviet forces dislodged German troops from the city's southern outskirts, breaking the nearly nine-hundred-day siege. Leningrad had survived one of the most devastating blockades in modern history, one that claimed the lives of at least eight hundred thousand of its citizens.[33]

Twelve-year-old Tanya Savicheva is perhaps Russia's most famous chronicler of the Leningrad siege. Tanya began keeping her brief "journal" during roughly the same period that **Anne Frank** commenced writing to her "Dear Kitty," in

---

31. Lynn Nicholas, *Cruel World: The Children of Europe in the Nazi Web* (New York: Alfred A. Knopf, 2005), 313.

32. Nicholas, *Cruel World*, 313.

33. Reinhard Rürup, ed., *Der Krieg gegen die Sowjetunion, 1941–1945: Eine Dokumentation zum 50. Jahrestag des Überfalls auf die Sowjetunion* (Berlin: Argon-Verlag, 1991), 67. For a detailed discussion of the Leningrad siege, see Harrison Salisbury, *The 900 Days: The Siege of Leningrad* (New York: Harper & Row, 1969); Lisa A. Kirschenbaum, *Legacy of the Siege of Leningrad, 1941–1995: Myth, Memories, and Monuments* (Cambridge: Cambridge University Press, 2006).

early 1942. While the Russian youngster's entries lack the length, elegance, and intricate detail of Frank's more famous diary, they succeed by terse intensity in conveying the desperateness of the times. Tanya was born on January 25, 1930, the youngest child of a Leningrad baker, Nicolai Rodionovich Savichev, and his wife, Mariya Ignatievna, a seamstress. Savichev died when Tanya was six, leaving his wife to support their five children. When the siege began in September 1941, all family members but Mikhail, an elder son who had left Leningrad months earlier, helped to promote the city's survival. Mariya Ignatievna sewed uniforms. Her son Leka worked as a planner in the admiralty office. Tanya's elder sister Nina was enlisted to help in constructing and stabilizing the city's defense lines, while sister Zhenya labored in a munitions factory. Uncles Vasily (Vasya) and Alexander (Lesha) manned antiaircraft defenses. Tanya herself, then only eleven, was put to work digging ditches.

In the late fall of 1941, as the siege tightened, Nina Savicheva was evacuated with other defense workers. Unaware of the measure, her family believed her dead. It was in memory of Nina that Tanya received her sister's small address book in which to record her thoughts. Tanya had long kept a real diary, a thick leaf volume, but along with all the other books in the house, it had long ago been burned for fuel. Because it had once belonged to the "dead" girl, Nina's address book was spared and would now serve as the basis for Tanya's unusual journal.

Tanya Savicheva began making entries in her diminutive "diary" shortly after December 28, 1941, the day on which her sister Zhenya succumbed to severe malnutrition during her shift at the munitions plant. Thereafter the youngster noted the deaths of each family member throughout the terrible Leningrad winter and spring of 1942. On May 13, the day her mother died, Tanya presumably made the final three entries in her journal, noting that she was the last living member of her family. In August 1943, a students' nursing brigade rescued Tanya, weak with hunger, from the family apartment. The young girl was then evacuated with other Leningrad children along the narrow lifeline carved out by the Soviet army that summer, to an orphanage in Krasny Bor, 20 kilometers (12.4 miles) away. Despite the best efforts of physicians and nursing staff, Tanya Savicheva died in the hospital on July 1, 1944, probably of chronic dysentery. At war's end in 1945, Nina Savicheva, evacuated in 1941, returned to the family home in Leningrad and discovered Tanya's writings. The diary contains only nine lines; the child was too weak to write more. The terse pages bear witness to the harrowing world of deprivation and death that children inhabited during the Leningrad siege.

DOCUMENT 2-9. Diary of Tanya Savicheva, Leningrad, December 1941 to May 1942, courtesy of the Saint Petersburg Museum of History, Saint Petersburg, Russia (translated from the Russian).

> Sheet 1: Zhenya died on December 28, 1941, at twelve noon.
> Sheet 2: Grandma died on January 25, 1942, at three in the afternoon.
> Sheet 3. Leka died on March 17, 1942, at five o'clock in the morning.
> Sheet 4: Uncle Vasya died on April 13, 1942, at two o'clock at night.
> Sheet 5: Uncle Lesha died on May 10, 1942, at four o'clock in the afternoon.
> Sheet 6: Mama died on May 13, 1942, at 7:30 in the morning.
> Sheet 7: The Savichevs are dead.
> Sheet 8: Everyone is dead.
> Sheet 9: The only one left is Tanya. [See sample page below.]

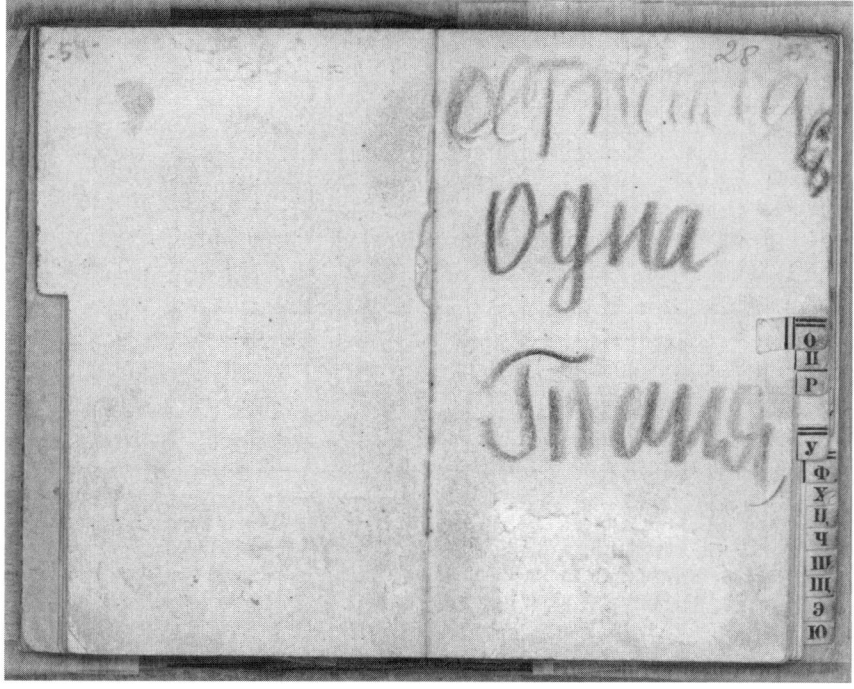

In territories controlled by German military or civilian administrations, indigenous resistance, in both organized and spontaneous forms, attempted to break the hold of the Nazi occupiers. German authorities reacted to the killing of German soldiers and occupation officials by guerrilla forces with brutal reprisals, often directed against innocent civilians. In the spring of 1942, trained volunteers of the Czech army in exile, aided by British armed forces, planned the assassination of **Reinhard Heydrich**, acting Reich Protector of German-annexed Bohemia and Moravia. On May 27, 1942, Czech parachutist Jan Kubiš and his Slovakian counterpart, Jozef Gabčík,[34] succeeded in hurling a bomb at the passing motorcade as Heydrich made his way from his living quarters at the villa Panenské Břežany to his headquarters in Prague. Heydrich, best known for his seminal role in planning the "Final Solution," survived the attack but succumbed to infection on June 4, 1942. In the days immediately following the attempt on Heydrich's life, **Gestapo** intelligence in the Protectorate erroneously linked the small Czech town of **Lidice** with the assassins.

On June 9, the day of Heydrich's state funeral in Berlin, Hitler ordered retaliatory measures against the Czech population. Services for the fallen Protector had scarcely ended when SS-Gruppenführer Karl Hermann Frank,[35] who held the positions of German state secretary (*Staatssekretär*) and higher SS and Police Leader of the Protectorate of Bohemia and Moravia, ordered units under SS-Standartenführer Horst Böhme[36] to raze the small village of Lidice to the ground and to take a number of prescribed actions against its citizens.[37]

That very evening, German police and **Schutzstaffel** (**SS**) officials surrounded Lidice. Near midnight, the town's five hundred residents learned that they must pack warm clothing, valuables, and food for three days and appear in the village square. Once the people had assembled, SS-men separated males over the age of fifteen from the townswomen and children. On the following morning, the village's 173 men and boys were shot by firing squad on

---

34. SS and police discovered Jan Kubiš (1913–1942) and Jozef Gabčík (1912–1942) with several other resistance fighters on June 18, 1942, in the Church of St. Cyril and St. Methodious in Prague. Kubiš died of wounds incurred in the firefight with police officials, while Gabčík and his comrades committed suicide in order to evade capture.

35. Czech authorities convicted and executed Karl Hermann Frank (1898–1946) in May 1946 for his role in organizing the massacres of the citizens of Lidice and Ležáky.

36. Following the retaliatory measures at Lidice, Horst Böhme (1909–1945) was transferred as a police attaché to Bucharest. From January 1943 through August 1944, he undertook the leadership of *Einsatzgruppen B* and *C*. He was last seen on April 1945 in the area of Königsberg; in 1954, a German court in Kiel officially declared him dead.

37. Less famously, the small Bohemian town of Ležáky (pop. forty-seven) was also included in the retaliatory actions. Most of the village's adult inhabitants were shot to death, and the town, like Lidice, was razed to its foundations.

a farmstead on the outskirts of Lidice.[38] Later that day, the women and children, who had spent the night in the local schoolhouse, were transferred to the nearby town of Kladno. "You know what has happened in Lidice," a Gestapo official told the group, "and that is why you will spend some time in a camp. You women will travel by train; the children will be sent to you by bus because it will be more comfortable for them."[39] With few exceptions, the women of Lidice found themselves deported to the **Ravensbrück** concentration camp, where most spent the balance of the war years. Of the 203 women, 60 died in the Nazi camp system prior to the end of World War II.

Before the forcible separation of the townswomen from their children, the youngsters of Lidice endured a racial screening carried out by SS personnel. On the orders of **Heinrich Himmler**, officials of the organization *Lebensborn* (Fount of Life)[40] ultimately chose nine children[41] who possessed sufficient Germanic background or "appropriate racial features" to make them candidates for **Germanization** and placed them with adoptive German parents.[42] At war's end, Allied humanitarian agencies returned these children to their mothers or to other surviving family members in Czechoslovakia. Under the auspices of the **SS Race and Settlement Main Office (SS Rasse- und Siedlungshauptamt)**, the remaining children of Lidice traveled by train to Łódź in occupied Poland. There they found themselves interned at a camp in the city's Gneisenaustrasse, while German authorities awaited further instructions. Confined in an abandoned textile factory, the group, which included many small children, lived for several weeks, ill clothed, lice ridden, sleeping on the bare floor, and surviving on a bare minimum of black bread and water. On July 2, 1942, **Security Police** officials in Łódź took formal possession of the children, sealing their fates. It was presumably on this day or the next that German authorities asked the children

---

38. In all, 192 men and boys from the village were murdered in this and later shootings in the vicinity of Lidice.

39. Unidentified female survivor of Lidice, quoted in Jolana Macková and Ivan Ulrych, eds., *Fates of the Children of Lidice: Memories, Testimonies, Documents*, trans. Elias Khelil (Nymburk: Lidice Memorial, 2004), 15.

40. For a detailed discussion of the Nazi organization *Lebensborn* and its part in Nazi racial policies, see chapter 6.

41. Ten children were initially chosen from racial selections for "Germanization," three in Kladno and a further seven when the remainder of the children arrived at the camp at Łódź. One of the children, Dagmar Veselá, who had been selected and later rejected for inclusion in the *Lebensborn* program, was sent to Łódź on a later transport and shared the fate of the other Lidice children.

42. NARA, RG 238, Office of U.S. Chief of Counsel for War Crimes, Doc, NO-4173, Heinrich Himmler to Max Sollmann (*Lebensborn*), re Lidice children, June 21, 1943.

to compose letters to surviving relatives in the Protectorate, instructing them to request that food, clothing, and other provisions be sent to them in Łódź. On July 3, 1942, the camp register noted the transfer of the children to an undisclosed location. At this point, they vanished without a trace. Historians strongly suspect that the eighty-two remaining youngsters from Lidice—including fifteen-year-old Marie Šroubková and her eight-year-old brother Josef—perished in the mobile gas chambers of **Chełmno**, the first killing center of the "Final Solution."[43]

DOCUMENT 2-10. **Letter of Marie (Maruška) Šroubková, c. July 2, 1942, in Jolana Macková and Ivan Ulrych, eds.,** *Fates of the Children of Lidice: Memories, Testimonies, Documents,* **trans. Elias Khelil (Nymburk: Lidice Memorial, 2004), 36.**

Dear Uncle and Auntie!

Regards and memories from Poland from Pepoušek[44] and Maruška. We are all children here. Do you know of Daddy's whereabouts?[45] Do you know about Mommy?[46] We would like to ask you to send us something. We have nothing but what we are dressed in. We need a lot. Please if you could send something for Pepoušek and me as well. Besides, I would need a couple of needles and a reel of w[hite] thread and a reel of b[lack] thread. We have got only one pair of shoes and one pair of stockings each here. On Saturday it will have been three weeks since we came here, and we have not changed clothes yet. And if you could send us also some German money—coins would be best—also notepaper, envelopes—and German stamps. Please speak to the Čičovskýs [and see] whether they could send us something too. I have sent them a letter too. We do not know how long we will stay here [. . .] but it is likely that we will stay

---

43. See Macková and Ulrych, *Fates of the Children of Lidice,* 41; Isabel Heinemann, *"Rasse, Siedlung, deutsches Blut": Die Rasse- und Siedlungshauptamt der SS und die rassenpolitische Neuordnung Europas* (Göttingen: Wallstein Verlag, 2003).

44. This is the Czech diminutive for Josef, the name of Marie Šroubková's younger brother.

45. Josef Šroubek Sr. (1894–1942) was murdered in the Lidice massacre on June 10, 1942.

46. The elder Marie Šroubková (née Chalupová, b. 1914) was transferred to the Ravensbrück concentration camp on June 12, 1942; there she was subjected to medical experimentation and murdered in September 1942. See Bärbel Schindler-Saefkow, *Gedenkbuch für die Opfer des Konzentrationslagers Ravensbrück* (Berlin: Metropol, 2005).

long. Reply soon, with a detailed letter. If you would, also send us something to eat, we would appreciate it.

Please, I have just been told that I am allowed to write only one letter;
could you show this letter to Grandpa and Grandma in Chýně? I know
they will feel sorry about it, but I cannot help it.

Yours,
Pepoušek and Maruška

[On reverse of postcard]
To Chýně: Dear Grandpa and Grandma!

First, accept please the warmest regards and memories from Poland.
Can you answer any of the questions on the other side? Please, if you
could send Pepoušek a pair of stockings. And if you could send us two
spoons, a comb, a towel, a pencil, and maybe some food. God bless you
for this.

Yours,
Pepoušek and Maruška

THE WAR'S LONG SHADOW:
THE LAST YEARS OF CONFLICT

In the winter months of 1944 to 1945, the population of the German-occupied
Netherlands experienced a devastating famine. Following their successful landing on the coast of Normandy on D-day (June 6, 1944), Allied forces were able
to drive into the Dutch interior, liberating the country's southern provinces.
The failure of Operation Market Garden,[47] which halted western troops at the
Rhine, effectively thwarted further Allied efforts to wrest northern and western
regions of the Netherlands from German control until the very last days of
the European conflict. A national railway strike, called by the Dutch government in exile in support of the Allied offensive, triggered a retaliatory German
embargo on food provisions to the Dutch western provinces. By November,
even as German administrators had lifted certain terms of the embargo, food
resources in occupied areas were in short supply. A particularly harsh winter set
in, further compounding the crisis, as frozen canals impeded barge traffic. As

---

47. This was an Allied offensive of September 17–25, 1944, whose strategic purpose was
to facilitate the crossing of the Rhine River, the last major natural barrier to an advance into
Germany and into that nation's industrial stronghold in the Ruhr Valley. The operation's
failure to capture the bridge at Arnhem formed the basis for the popular epic film *A Bridge
Too Far* (1977).

the deadly winter wore on, fierce fighting, now on Dutch soil, contributed to a further dislocation of the transport system; the destruction of agricultural lands, as well as German sabotage of locks and dams, which flooded arable areas, exacerbated the shortages. As the nutritional intake of the Dutch population plummeted to less than one thousand calories per day, city dwellers fanned out into the countryside to forage for fuel and foodstuff. In desperation, Dutch citizens ate tulip bulbs and sugar beets and destroyed vacant lodgings for firewood. Relief finally came in late April and early May of 1945, when Canadian, British, and American troops liberated the remnant of the Netherlands still in German hands. In the end, the Dutch Hunger Winter of 1944 to 1945 claimed the lives of eighteen thousand citizens.[48]

The well-known Dutch poet Bert Voeten (1918–1992) chronicled the months before Allied liberation in his only prose work, *Doortocht: Een Oorlagsdagboek* (*Passage: A War Diary*), published in 1946. Linked with the Dutch Resistance, Voeten was living on false papers in Heemstede, near Amsterdam, in 1944. Joining him in hiding was the writer and journalist Marga Minco (1920–), whose Orthodox Jewish parents had already been deported to the **Auschwitz** or **Sobibór** concentration camps. The only member of her family to survive the Holocaust, Minco would use her wartime experiences to transform her approach to writing, establishing herself as one of the Netherlands' most important postwar authors with such powerful and laconic works as *Bitter Herbs* (*Het bittere Kruid*, 1957) and *An Empty House* (*Een leeg huis*, 1966). Minco and Voeten, a non-Jew, were able to legally marry at war's end in 1945. In December 1944, their first daughter, Bettie, was born amid the catastrophic first months of the Hunger Winter. In his diary entry for December 12, Voeten contemplated the birth of a child in such harrowing and uncertain times.

DOCUMENT 2-11. Bert Voeten, *Doortocht: Een Oorlogsdagboek, 1940–1945*, 4th ed. (Amsterdam: Uitgeverij Contact, 1947), 198–99 (translated from the Dutch).

December 12, 1944

Our child was born on this night. The surroundings were quite primitive with a stove which consumed our entire supply of heating oil, a clandestine gas jet,[49] and a smoldering oil lamp. The sky was full of thundering

---

48. See Henri A. van der Zee, *The Hunger Winter: Occupied Holland, 1944–1945* (Lincoln: University of Nebraska Press, 1998), esp. 304ff.

49. The German occupying force ordered a general blackout in the Netherlands after dark.

aircraft. There was a dark and heavy atmosphere over the city, over the house, over the small room in which this new life gave its first cries. How fragile yet how resilient, this life which emerged in the midst of this reign of terror.

<u>December 18, 1944</u>

The famine is inevitable.

Tens of thousands make their way to the outlying areas, to Haarlemmermeer and Wieringermeer,[50] to the east, and even to Friesland, in order to get whatever [food] there is still to be had. An unusually heavy rainfall has flooded the roads and open fields. The flooding[51] has turned the fields into lakes. All this makes it even more difficult to reach the far-away sources of plenty.

Today the temperature hovered around the freezing point. One cannot bear the cold any longer. People collapse in the street. Empty houses are stripped bare in broad daylight, trees are chopped down, fences and poles uprooted. Bakers' carts are overturned and plundered by packs of local women. A policeman standing guard near a bread cart is no longer a rare sight. Yesterday a crowd ransacked a grocery store in Zuid.[52] Desperation breaks down the boundaries of bourgeois respectability.

Under these circumstances our child was brought into the world. In this misery it must grow, must be fed, and kept as warm as a tender hothouse plant. Fortunately, our friends from the "Movement"[53] generously support us. They have even provided a legal document with false names. Our little creature is already in hiding.

---

50. Haarlemmermeer and Wieringermeer are both polders (low-lying land reclaimed from lakes) located in the province of North Holland to the west and north of Amsterdam, respectively.

51. These floods were caused in part by German forces sabotaging Dutch locks and dams.

52. This is the southern district of Amsterdam.

53. This refers to the Dutch underground resistance.

DOCUMENT 2-12. **Malnourished Dutch children in the German-occupied Netherlands, 1944, USHMMPA WS# 89175, courtesy of David Briggs.**

The German conquest of Poland in September 1939 and the invasion of the Soviet Union in June 1941 brought a massive influx of civilian laborers into Germany from the East, most forcibly deported from their homelands to augment the Reich's critical labor shortage in agriculture, manufacturing, and the armaments industries. By 1944, 7.5 million foreign laborers, including prisoners of war, remained on German soil, among them 2.2 million Soviet and 1.65 million Polish civilians. Laboring and subsisting under deplorable conditions, these Eastern workers (*Ostarbeiter*) fell victim in large number to serious illnesses, injuries, or debilitating psychiatric disorders.

Before mid-1943, Eastern workers incapacitated by illness or injury for more than three weeks were simply returned to their countries of origin.[54] Initially included among these *Arbeitsunfähigen*[55] were pregnant foreign workers. In August 1941, the Reich Labor Ministry ordered that participating agencies and work installations immediately report female laborers for transfer as soon as the fact of their pregnancy became known in order to obviate unnecessary costs in medical care and maintenance to their employers or local labor offices.[56]

From the beginning, German authorities found themselves torn between two conflicting facets of National Socialist policy with regard to the problem of pregnant Eastern workers: aspects of race and ideology, of primary relevance to Himmler's **Reich Security Main Office (Reichssicherheitshauptamt)**, and the economic aspects that underpinned the use of forced labor, a significant concern to Germany's labor administration. Reaching a compromise in September 1942, Fritz Sauckel, the general plenipotentiary for labor allocation (*Generalbevollmächtiger für den Arbeitseinsatz*), made plans to retain "racially valuable" children of foreign laborers. From December 12 until March 31, 1943, German authorities excluded pregnant workers from transports returning ailing civilian forced laborers to their native lands. On March 20, 1943, this directive was extended until the end of the war, and on July 27, 1943, a further SS decree removed all exemptions for the repatriation of pregnant Eastern workers. By the spring of 1943, a string of ordinances had lifted existing abortion restrictions in Germany for all female Eastern workers, provided they were not expecting "racially valuable" children.[57]

At this time, German administrators opened the first so-called *Säuglingslager* (infant camps) and *Ausländerkinderpflegestätten* (so-called nursery care facilities)

54. By mid-1943, this policy had begun to change. As the successful advance of the Soviet army and the pressing need for all available resources in support of retreating German lines made such repatriations impossible, mentally ill "Eastern workers" were assembled at specially designated mental health facilities throughout Germany and Austria; in the course of 1944 and 1945, many of these people fell victim to the Nazi "euthanasia" program (see chapter 6). Physically incapacitated Eastern workers were confined in so-called infirmary camps (*Krankenlager*), where thousands perished under deplorable conditions. For further reading, see Matthias Hamann, "Die Morde an polnischen und sowjetischen Zwangsarbeitern in deutschen Anstalten," in *Aussonderung und Tod: Die klinische Hinrichtung der Unbrauchbaren. Beiträge zur Nationalsozialistischen Gesundheits- und Sozialpolitik* (Berlin: Rotbuch Verlag, 1985), 160–67; Holker Kaufmann and Klaus Schulmeyer, "Die polnischen und sowjetischen Zwangsarbeiter in Hadamar," in *Psychiatrie im Faschismus: Die Anstalt Hadamar, 1933–1945,* ed. Dorothee Roer and Dieter Henkel (Bonn: Psychiatrie-Verlag, 1986), 256–82.

55. This was the Nazi German term for "individuals unable to work."

56. Hamann, "Die Morde," 122.

57. Abortion was illegal for most "racially valuable" Germans.

for foreign laborers. Although initial plans for such establishments did not clearly specify which groups of laborers such institutions were to serve, subsequent decrees from Sauckel's office and from the Reichssicherheitshauptamt made it plain that these facilities were meant to house the offspring of female Eastern workers—primarily women from Poland and the Soviet Union, who made up the largest percentage within the female forced labor population. Such installations ostensibly provided a place where female workers could give birth and where they and their infants might receive postnatal care.

Viktor Klemperer, in his incisive work *LTI—Lingua Tertian Imperii* (*The Language of the Third Reich*),[58] asserts that National Socialist authorities were skillful and consistent manipulators of the German language for purposes of public consumption. In precisely this vein, the notion that Germany's *Ausländerkinderpflegestätten* were infant-care facilities was pure metaphor. These establishments existed purely to ensure that pregnant laborers returned to their work sites as quickly as possible, unencumbered by their newborns. Labor officials were completely disinterested in the fate of the children inhabiting these facilities. Local authorities often divided sharply over which agencies bore actual responsibility for managing and funding the makeshift institutions, with the result that foodstuffs and supplies were often in woefully short supply, and appalling conditions prevailed.[59] Fellow female Eastern workers served as untrained nurses and caretakers for the mothers and their offspring. Under fortunate circumstances, German authorities might enlist Soviet medics from nearby prisoner of war camps to serve as physicians but even these functioned under the most primitive conditions, usually without appropriate medicine or equipment. Records pertaining to the *Ausländerkinderpflegestätten* are sparse and incomplete, and these institutions often provided fictive mortality statistics for official records, so we may never know definitively how many of these facilities existed in the last years of the war or how many lives they claimed. We do know concretely from postwar adjudication of these crimes, in such proceedings as the

---

58. Viktor Klemperer, *The Language of the Third Reich: LTI—Lingua Tertii Imperii: A Philologist's Notebook*, trans. Martin Brady (London: Continuum, 2002).

59. For a closer examination of Germany's *Ausländerkinderpflegestätten* and their conditions, see Gisela Schwarze, *Kinder, die nicht zählten: Ostarbeiterinnen und ihre Kinder im Zweiten Weltkrieg* (Essen: Klartext Verlag, 1997); Raymond Raiter, *Tötungsstätten für Ausländische Kinder im Zweiten Weltkrieg* (Hanover: Hansche Buchhandlung, 2003); Evelyn Zegenhagen, "Facilities for Pregnant Forced Laborers and Their Infants in Germany, 1943–1945," in *Children and the Holocaust: Symposium Presentations of the Center for Advanced Holocaust Studies* (Washington DC: U.S. Holocaust Memorial Museum, 2004), 65–76.

Velpke and Rühen trials,[60] that the death rates at most of these establishments were extremely high. In a work focusing on institutions for infants of Eastern workers in northern Germany, Raymond Raiter estimates that at "care centers" serving large-scale industrial or agricultural concerns, mortality among infants neared 90 percent.[61]

In the following testimony, Ernst Wirtz,[62] a defendant in the Nuremberg proceeding against German industrialist Alfried Krupp[63] and his associates, describes the conditions of a "care facility" for the infants of forced laborers in Voerde, near Essen.

DOCUMENT 2-13. **Testimony of Ernst Wirtz, 1948,** *United States of America v. Alfried Krupp, et al.* (Case 10: "Krupp Case"), in *Trials of War Criminals before the Nürnberg Military Tribunals under Control Council Law No. 10*, 14 vols. (Buffalo, NY: William S. Hein & Co., 1997), 9:1113–17.

Q: Where were you in January 1945?

A: In January 1945, I was in Kulmbach in Oberfranken [Upper Franconia, Germany].

Q: What was the order that Director Hupe gave you in Kulmbach regarding the transport of eastern workers from Voerde?

A: In January 1945, I had to go to Essen—the beginning of January—and I had to pick up a consignment of eastern workers. In Essen I was told by Mr. Dollwein that I had to go to Voerde in order to set up the transport of eastern workers.

---

60. George Brand, ed., *Trial of Heinrich Gerike, Gustav Claus, Georg Hessling, Richard Demmerlich, Werner Noth, Fritz Flint, Hermann Müller, Valentina Bilien (The Velpke Baby Home Trial)* (London: W. Hodge, 1950); Rühen Baby Farm Case, British Public Record Office, WO 235/263–277 and WO 235/674, Judge Advocate General's Office, War Crimes Case Files, Second World War.

61. Raiter, *Tötungsstätten*, 201.

62. Ernst Wirtz supervised foreign forced laborers for the Krupp concern beginning in the autumn of 1942. A denazification tribunal in Kulmbach sentenced Wirtz to eight years in prison for his mistreatment of forced laborers in the areas of Essen, Kulmbach, and Mulhouse.

63. Alfried Krupp von Bohlen und Halbach (1907–1967) was a member of Krupp family of industrialists headquartered in Germany's Ruhr Valley. Famous for its steel and armaments manufacture, Friedrich Krupp AG Hoesch-Krupp was Europe's largest company in the early twentieth century. During World War II, the Krupp concern was an important supplier of arms to the Third Reich and utilized foreign forced laborers and concentration camp prisoners in various plants and factories. As head of the conglomerate from 1943, Krupp, together with eleven other associates, was tried by American military authorities in the tenth Subsequent Nuremberg Trial (known as the Krupp Trial); in 1948, Krupp was convicted and sentenced to twelve years in prison. He was released from Landsberg Prison in 1951.

Q: What was in Voerde?

A: In Voerde we have a former camp of the Organisation Todt. [. . .][64]

Q: How many people were in this camp?

A: I assume about 4,000.

Q: Were these men and women?

A: Mixed, men, women, and children.

Q: From among these women and children, did you pick the people for Kulmbach?

A: Yes.

Q: What did you see in the barracks in which the children lived?

A: The children were undernourished. There was no child at all whose arms or hands were thicker than my thumb.

Q: How old were those children?

A: From babies up to the age of two years.

Q: Were these the children of eastern workers?

A: Yes, they had been born in the camp.

Q: How were these babies housed in the Voerde camp when you saw them?

A: In sort of prison bunks. They had paillasses [straw-filled mattresses] with rubber sheets, and the children were there quite naked.

Q: Could you see definite signs of undernourishment in these children?

A: Yes, many of them had swollen heads. [. . .][65]

Q: Mr. Witness, were you surprised about this pitiable state of the children?

A: Yes.

Q: What did you tell the camp leader?

A: I told the girls in charge of the children—I asked them how it came about that these children were so undernourished, and I was told that these children had very little to eat.

Q: Were these female eastern workers?

A: Yes.

Q: And they told you that these children didn't get enough food?

A: Yes.

---

64. The Organisation Todt was a civil and military engineering group named for its founder, Fritz Todt, a German engineer and senior Nazi official. The organization was responsible for a large range of engineering projects both in Germany and in German-occupied territories, deploying hundreds of thousands of forced laborers.

65. Presumably this was caused by edema, a sign of acute malnourishment.

Q: Did these female eastern workers also tell you how many children died every day?

A: Yes. Fifty or sixty children died every day, and as many were born every day, because there was a constant influx of eastern female workers with children.

Q: You said fifty to sixty children died every day.

A: Yes.

Q: And there was a steady influx of new ones?

A: Yes.

Q: Were these eastern female workers who had children married for the greater part?

A: Yes.

Q: What happened to the children of the female eastern workers— did they tell you what happened with the children who died?

A: I asked the interpreter to ask them how it came about that so many children died, and if the children were buried; and the interpreter told me the children were cremated inside the camp. [. . .]

Q: Do you know how long—do you know during which time, how long a time it was during which Krupp administered the camp at Voerde?

A: I can't tell you in detail, but I assume since 1943.

Q: Since 1943?

A: Yes.

Q: But if you say that the female workers told you fifty or sixty children died every day, you didn't mean that this number of children died over the whole period?

A: No.

Q: This only referred to a short period?

A: Yes.

Q: Could you give us an estimate concerning which period approximately?

A: There was January 1945—it may have been for one year.

Q: At the most for one year?

A: Yes [. . .]

Q: [. . .] Witness, do you know what happened to the children of a female worker who worked for Krupp?

A: As soon as the eastern worker had given birth to the child, she was allowed six weeks; and after this six weeks, she went back to work; and the child was kept in the camp so that the female workers could go to work again. She saw that child only after work.

Q: Was this child separated from the mother?

A: Yes. [. . .]

CHAPTER 3

Lives in the Balance
ESCAPE AND DEPORTATION

NATIONAL SOCIALIST policies directed at "cleansing" those territories under their control of their Jewish populations hinged on the twin dynamic of emigration and **deportation**. In their early efforts to remove Jews from German economic, political, and cultural life, Nazi authorities promoted measures that encouraged a mass emigration of Jews from the Reich. Discriminatory laws and the hardships these engendered prompted thousands of German Jews to relocate abroad. The first part of this chapter examines the efforts of Jewish families to flee persecution and the impact these actions had upon affected children and adolescents. Both children and adults faced an uncertain future in a new land. While affording escape from Nazi persecution, emigration imposed financial and emotional hardships upon refugees. The need to adapt to a new language and culture added to the anxieties of would-be emigrants, as did the very real threat of detention by German authorities. The absence of friends and family members weighed heavily upon youngsters who emigrated, as did their anxiety for loved ones left behind. How did the loss of homeland and familiar surroundings impact the lives of such children? The documentation below explores the challenges these young refugees faced in adjusting to new environments and new circumstances.

The opposite extreme of emigration was deportation—and death. Those Jews who did not escape persecution by fleeing abroad Nazi authorities aimed to "cleanse" from their territories by murdering them in their own communities or deporting them from lands under German and Axis control to ghettos, concentration camps, and killing centers in the East. The mobile killing units of the *Einsatzgruppen* followed **Wehrmacht** forces deep into Soviet territory, murdering over 1 million Jews, as well as thousands of **Roma**, disabled patients, and Soviet political officials. Even children, not spared from these shooting actions, were murdered beside their family members on the killing fields of the Soviet Union. For Jews in other areas of Europe under Axis occupation, deportation was an integral mechanism in the implementation of the "Final Solution." In this volume, deportation carries two meanings. First, it refers to the process of uprooting Jews from their home communities and transporting them to ghettos, camps, or extermination centers. Second, deportation was a method of transferring Jews from ghettoized communities, such as Warsaw or Łódź, to killing centers for "liquidation." In most instances, Nazi policy dictated that whole families be deported together, although, as we shall see in the case of Felicitas Gumpel (Document 3-14), French officials initially opted to dispatch only adult Jews to the East, a decision that rent families apart and hampered deportation efforts. Germany's Axis allies developed diverse strategies for ridding their territories of Jewish populations. Here, too, children's voices documented the harrowing circumstances of their dislocation.

STRANGERS IN A STRANGE LAND: EMIGRATION

The antisemitic policies pursued by the National Socialist government in the 1930s drove more than half of Germany's Jewish population into exile. From the time of the Nazi rise to power in January 1933 until October 23, 1941, when Reichsführer-SS **Heinrich Himmler** imposed a ban on further Jewish emigration from Reich territory, some 340,000 Jews left Germany and German-annexed Austria.[1] The impetus to flee Nazi Germany began with the first major discriminatory measures imposed by Nazi authorities in the spring of 1933. Pressure to leave mounted with the introduction of the **Nuremberg Laws** in September 1935 and reached its climax with the *Kristallnacht* **pogrom** of November 1938. Desperate to find a safe haven from Nazi persecution, many

---

1. For further discussion of German-Jewish emigration during the Nazi period, see Stiftung Jüdisches Museum Berlin and Stiftung Haus der Geschichte der Bundesrepublik Deutschland, *Heimat und Exil: Emigration der Deutschen Juden nach 1933* (Frankfurt am Main: Suhrkamp Verlag, 2006); Marion Berghahn, *Continental Britons: German-Jewish Refugees from Nazi Germany* (Oxford: Berghahn, 2006); Herbert Strauss, ed., *Jewish Immigrants of the Nazi Period in the USA* (New York: Saur, 1978); Jim Tobias, *"Und wir waren Deutsche!": Jüdische Emigranten erinnern sich* (Nuremberg: Antogo, 2009).

German Jews hoped to emigrate overseas—to the United States, Great Britain, or **Palestine**.[2]

DOCUMENT 3-1. **Youth Aliyah immigrants pose for photographer Dr. Franz Ziss upon their arrival at Kibbutz Ben Shemen agricultural school in Palestine, 1940, USHMMPA WS# 07152, courtesy of the Keren Kayemet Archives.**

Thea Gersten was thirteen years old when she left her home in Leipzig in eastern Germany. Her father, Chaim Lazar Gersten, a Polish Jew, had settled in Berlin before World War I. He and his German-born wife, Rosa, owned a successful fur business; they were prosperous and devoutly Orthodox and shared a comfortable home with their two young children, Thea and Adi. But the events of *Kristallnacht* shattered the family's quiet existence. On the night of November 9, 1938, local Nazi activists plundered and destroyed their residence and store. Fleeing arrest, Thea's father, still a Polish citizen, perhaps unwisely made his way to Warsaw, where he worked to establish a new furrier trade and to make preparations for his family's immigration to America. While her

---

2. Palestine, then under a British mandate, was a favored destination of many European Jews, but British authorities sharply curtailed Jewish immigration in the mid-1930s. In 1939, the famous White Paper further restricted such immigration and the purchase of land in Palestine by Jews.

fortunate brother had secured emigration papers and settled with a host family in England, Thea, with Rosa, joined her father in Warsaw in July 1939. On the eve of World War II, mother and daughter traveled to London to visit Adi and to set up temporary quarters until the family's quota number came up, allowing the Gerstens entry into the United States. Waiting for a shipment of furs with which he could finance his family's voyage to America, Chaim Gersten remained behind in Warsaw to settle his business affairs.

In the chaotic months before her emigration, Thea Gersten began to keep a diary. Deprived of her closest friend, Lolo, who had recently left Germany, she found in her journal a tool to restructure her perplexing circumstances and a confidante for her disquieting thoughts and memories. After a first unsettling month in London, Thea wrote her first diary entry since her arrival in Britain. In it she reflected upon the sudden loss of her childhood. "For what does childhood mean?" she later wrote. "Is it not the sensation of being rooted and safe, sheltered and needed?"[3] Thea's reflections mirrored the feelings and concerns of thousands of children in similar circumstances: the isolation and loneliness, the loss of familiar surroundings and native language, the uncertainty of life in a new land, the absence of friends and family members. Shortly before leaving Germany, she had had her first kiss; now, despite the crises of war and fears for her young Jewish associates back home, the future of her new romance dominated her thoughts. The safety of her father was another source of abiding anxiety and concern, one that would only grow as the war progressed. Unable to join his family in Poland when war broke out in September 1939, Chaim Lazar Gersten was swept up in the Nazi dragnet. Interned in the **Warsaw ghetto**, he was deported on January 20, 1943, to the **Treblinka** killing center, where he perished.[4]

DOCUMENT 3-2. **Thea Gersten Hurst,** *Das Tagebuch der Thea Gersten: Aufzeichnungen aus Leipzig, Warschau und London, 1939–1947* **(Leipzig: Evangelische Verlagsanstalt, 2001), 58 (translated from the German).**

London, August 21, 1939

It has been so long since I've written in my beloved diary. But these four weeks were such a difficult time for me that I had no patience for

---

3. Thea Gersten Hurst, *Das Tagebuch der Thea Gersten: Aufzeichnungen aus Leipzig, Warschau und London, 1939–1947* (Leipzig: Evangelische Verlagsanstalt, 2001), 11.
4. Gita Conn, "Thea's Diary," *Manchester Guardian*, January 27, 2003. Thea, her mother, and her brother survived the war in Great Britain.

anything. But I don't even want to mention it, don't want to think of it. Now everything has improved a bit. But it is still not entirely better. It can only be better when I have my Lolo again. And there is no prospect of seeing her. Oh, how will I be able to stand it? I miss her more and more each day. I am frantic about her, and [we've received] no mail.

The day is too short for me. I have so much to think about and so much to do that I will never be finished. I don't stop until 12:30 at night. And still! I have just been reading, and then such a terrible longing for Philipp came over me. But now that has all passed. It always comes in waves. I have even kissed his picture. He would be the only one to completely understand me. But what should I do? I would really like to know if he is still in Grimma.[5] He wrote me, "You really cared for me. I still care for you!" But does he still think that?

We have been living here for almost four weeks. I thought that here I could find contentment. But just the opposite. I am so discontented. I need a friend. But I don't want to form any new friendships here. I only want to be together with Lolo. Every acquaintance that I make here is only superficial. During the day, all this doesn't really enter my consciousness, but at nighttime, just like now, one feels it all so keenly. I am so discontented. I look forward to tomorrow afternoon. Most probably I will be all alone here. Then at least I can daydream. Oh, how wonderful! I wish that I could give free reign to my thoughts. But I never have time for this. I am so dissatisfied with myself, and exactly that is the worst thing of all. But what shall I do? I reproach myself that I think so seldom about my father. But then when I do think of him, I do it with my whole heart. I am also displeased that I have not yet accomplished everything I have undertaken. But these are all things that I cannot change.

For refugees escaping Nazi Germany, the flight from one's homeland represented a traumatic experience on many levels. The labyrinthine bureaucratic arrangements, the harrowing wait for visas and travel documents, and the financial hardships imposed by emigration all combined to create a limitless number of worries and headaches for adults organizing asylum for their families in a

5. This is a town in Germany about 25 kilometers (15.5 miles) from Leipzig. Philipp had been trying to leave Germany aboard a *Kindertransport* and succeeded in acquiring a place on the last one, on September 1, 1939, the day on which Germany invaded Poland, initiating World War II. Philipp would locate Thea in England, and the childhood romance would develop into a lasting friendship, which continued until Philipp's death in 2002. See Conn, "Thea's Diary."

foreign country. Beyond the planning and preparation, prospects for a new life abroad also presented a formidable set of difficulties. Would the family manage to adapt to its new surroundings? Would the household's breadwinner be able to find work in a new land and in a new language? What would become of friends and family left behind?

While emigrating abroad may have been a distressing and unsettling time for adults, it could also represent an adventure for young children, especially those who had been shielded from the direst aspects of Nazi persecution. Fritz Freudenheim was twelve years old when his family left Germany in October 1938. In order to document his family's flight into exile, young Fritz endeavored to make a colored pencil drawing of their long voyage overseas to their new quarters in South America. He began his sketch, "From Our Old Home to Our New Home" (*"Von der alten Heimat zu der neuen Heimat"*), in Berlin's Levetzowstrasse, where the Freudenheims lived at the time of Fritz's birth. In 1927, the household moved to Mühlhausen in Thuringia. The whimsical map illustrates how the family traveled by train to Berlin in March 1938, presumably to arrange the appropriate documents, and then on to the German port at Hamburg, where the Freudenheims boarded the SS *Jamaïque* on October 23, 1938. Fritz recalls the liner's many ports of call in Europe and northern Africa before the Freudenheim family arrived at its destination in Montevideo, Uruguay, on November 30, 1938.[6]

6. Fritz, later Frederico, Freudenheim grew up in South America and settled in São Paulo, Brazil, with his wife, Irene (née Gebhardt). He died there on March 15, 2008.

DOCUMENT 3-3. **Crayon drawing by Fritz Freudenheim, "*From Our Old Home to Our New Home*," c. 1938, in Stiftung Jüdisches Museum Berlin and Stiftung Haus der Geschichte der Bundesrepublik Deutschland, *Heimat und Exil: Emigration der deutschen Juden nach 1933* (Frankfurt am Main: Suhrkamp Verlag, 2006), 155.**

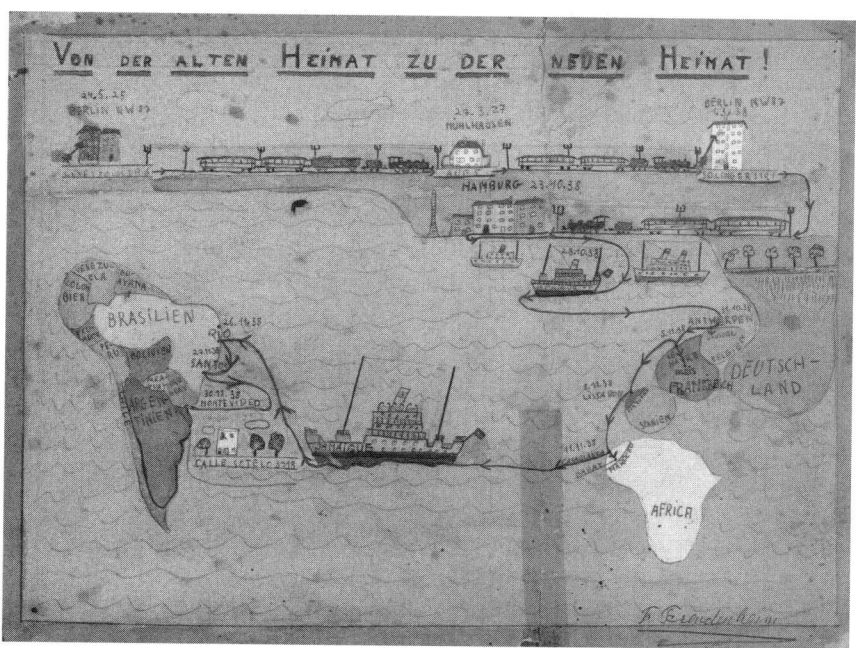

The violent events of *Kristallnacht* accelerated the emigration of Jews from the Third Reich. The rescue of children became a paramount concern among refugee and children's aid organizations, both in Germany and abroad. Following the November pogrom, the British government agreed to permit an unspecified number of children under the age of seventeen to enter the United Kingdom from Germany and German-annexed territories. Many public and private organizations, most significantly the Movement for the Care of Children from Germany, worked to bring refugee children to Great Britain. These efforts, collectively known as the ***Kindertransport*** (children's transports), rescued some nine to ten thousand children, seventy-five hundred of them Jewish, from Nazi Germany, Austria, and German-occupied Czechoslovakia and Poland.[7]

The first *Kindertransport* from Germany arrived in Harwich, England, on December 2, 1938. Children chosen for a *Kindertransport* convoy typically

---

7. For a more comprehensive description of the *Kindertransporte*, also see chapter 9.

traveled by train to ports in the Netherlands, where they sailed for Great Britain. Private citizens or organizations had to guarantee to pay for each child's care, education, and eventual emigration from Britain. In return for this guarantee, the British government agreed to allow these unaccompanied refugee children to enter the country on temporary travel visas. It was understood that when the crisis was over, the children would return to their families. Parents or guardians could not accompany them. The few infants included in the program were tended by other children on their transport.

Cilia Jutta Horwitz, nicknamed Cilly, and her elder brother Max sailed with the first *Kindertransport* to England. Born in 1926, Cilly had enjoyed a comfortable middle-class existence with her family in Harburg, near Hamburg. Her Jewish father, Walter Horwitz, owned a local department store. Although her husband was not deeply religious, Cilly's Christian mother, Margarete, had converted to Judaism upon her marriage. The Nazi's rise to power brought the Horwitzes' happy family life to an end. According to the Nuremberg Laws, Margarete Horwitz was still legally an "**Aryan**," but the children of her mixed marriage had been raised in the Jewish faith and were thus regarded as Jews (*Geltungsjuden*),[8] subject to the full range of antisemitic persecution. In 1936, the family moved to Hamburg. Soon thereafter, Cilly's father lost his business; shattered that he could not find employment, he attempted suicide. In the wake of this incident, Max and Cilly were removed from their home and placed in an orphanage. Desperate to regain their children, the Horwitzes decided to divorce so that Margarete might work.[9] Fortunately, after *Reichskristallnacht* the Horwitz children were chosen to travel with the first *Kindertransport* to Britain. They lived apart, with different host families, and hoped for a time when their father and his new Jewish wife might join them in England.[10]

A letter from Walter Horwitz to his daughter in February 1939, three months after twelve-year-old Cilly arrived in England, reflects the hardships that both child and parent endured as a result of such a difficult separation. Refugee children found themselves alone in a strange land, far away from family

---

8. According to the First Supplementary Decree to the Nuremberg Laws from November 14, 1935, children of a mixed marriage who were *Mischlinge* of the first degree and had been raised in the Jewish religion counted as "full Jews" in the context of Nazi racial laws.

9. Enormous pressure brought to bear on "Aryan" partners in mixed marriages to divorce their Jewish spouses included restrictions on civil service employment and limited opportunities for private employment.

10. See "Der Kindertransport nach England," *Hamburger Abendblatt*, September 1, 2007.

and friends. Although many such children found an affectionate home among English host parents, some foster families found it difficult to integrate the new arrivals into their households, and many youngsters, like Cilly, spent most of the war years in a children's home, an environment that often intensified feelings of isolation, abandonment, and rootlessness. As time went on, it was often difficult for parents to disguise their increasingly desperate circumstances back in Germany, which added to the children's anxiety. Cilly and Max Horwitz remained in England for the duration of the war. On November 8, 1941, Walter Horwitz and his second wife, Sophie (née de Vries), were deported from Hamburg to Minsk; both perished in the Holocaust. Although Cilly often visited her mother, who survived in Hamburg, after the war, she herself married an Englishman and as Celia Jane Lee made her home in Great Britain.[11]

DOCUMENT 3-4. **Letter of Walter Horwitz to his daughter Cilia (Cilly) Horwitz, February 15, 1939, in Reiner Lehberger and Ursula Randt, eds., "Aus Kindern werden Briefe": Dokumente zum Schicksal jüdischer Kinder und Jugendlicher in der NS-Zeit (Hamburg: Freie und Hansestadt Hamburg Behörde für Schule, Jugend und Berufsbildung, 1999), 39–40 (translated from the German).**

Air Mail

Hamburg 13, February 15, 1939
Grindelallee 79, 3rd floor
My dear, sweet Cilly!
Very many thanks for your dear card, which made me very happy. And so too for the kind words and greetings from your dear [host] parents, Mr. and Mrs. Watts. I return them with all my heart and send them my very best greetings. In the next few days I will write them personally; please let them know that. Now you are in good hands, my child, and are being properly spoiled. I am delighted for your sake. Do you often meet with Max? What is he up to? Children, I am so happy that everything has come together so well for you. My thoughts linger often with you. My fiancée sent a package with chocolates for you to Selsey, but it came back, "delivery refused"; customs probably should have been paid on it. Tonight I'm eating the last piece and thinking of you, Cilly. Be good and nice to

---

11. See Reiner Lehberger and Ursula Randt, eds., *"Aus Kindern werden Briefe"*: *Dokumente zum Schicksal jüdischer Kinder und Jugendlicher in der NS-Zeit* (Hamburg: Freie und Hansestadt Hamburg Behörde für Schule, Jugend und Berufsbildung, 1999), 39–44.

your host parents, but don't completely forget your Papa. You asked me in your last letter how things are going with my emigration. Right now, very badly. I don't know what to do. My fiancée has a sponsorship for the U.S.[12] and will try through relatives who hold an influential position in New York to arrange for me also to have a sponsor. [One of them] is a patent lawyer. However, [my fiancée] falls under the Polish quota, which comes up only in July, and probably has to wait until the end of the year. She wants to go to England to work as a housemaid in the interim; she is already in communication with a family, who has already requested a permit for her from the Home Office.[13] [She] would like to have me out along with her, even wants to put her income at my disposal. You know why. Think of the time before your departure. I don't have any salary or income anymore. We have written Max at length about this; read the letter that we wrote to him. Perhaps your [host] family can do something for me. You two must get in touch with Aunt Johanna. She must get involved now and help, together with Robert. Today I heard that [even] if one has a guarantor there, one can end up in a camp.[14] Perhaps, dear children, you can do a favor for me. I want to come to England only for the short-term and from there go on to the United States. I don't want to become a burden or exploit anyone. I would like to move forward, but I want to have my peace of mind again. My intended bride is very sweet and nice and has grown so fond of you, has heard so many good things about you, and I am very happy. She has become good friends with Mommy, which would also interest you. I hope now to get a detailed answer from Max concerning my last letter. Be good, my child, work very hard in school. Just this Friday, an acquaintance of mine will be in London, just a day before his departure for America. A Mr. Behr from Hamburg, the brother of my landlord, will bring you both greetings from me. You can reach the gentleman in London under the name Martin Behr from Hamburg, Endsleigh Hotel, Endsleigh Garden, London. Perhaps Mr. Watts will drive you and Max to see the gentlemen if you ask very nicely, and then write me about it. You could also call ahead to the hotel and make an appointment with him, because the gentleman has much to do. He can tell you all

---

12. That is, Sophie de Vries had a guarantor who was willing to vouch for her financial security in the United States.

13. This refers to the British government ministry administering security, public order, and immigration issues.

14. German citizens living in Britain following the outbreak of hostilities, including German-Jewish refugees, were often interned as enemy aliens.

about Papa, also knows my fiancée, and will also meet our relatives in New York. I am hoping for the best. I have also written to my cousin Waldemar Horwitz in New York. Well, now my child, I have related to you everything that's worth knowing. I hope that you are doing very well. Continue to stay healthy and cheerful. Hold me dear. Greet the Watts family and their daughter Betty for me. For you, my child, I am sending a thousand tender greetings and kisses.

Always,

Your devoted, fat Papa!

[P.S.] My intended, Ms. Sophie de Vries, sends her warm greetings. She will write you soon. I'll write too. Papa.

On May 13, 1939, the Hamburg-America transatlantic liner MS *St. Louis* left the German port of Hamburg bound for Havana, Cuba. The vast majority of her 938 passengers were refugees, fleeing persecution in Nazi Germany. Most were Jews who had applied for visas to reside in the United States and purchased transit visas that would allow them to remain in Cuba until their quota number came up, granting them U.S. entry. The ship's passengers were not aware that, even before they sailed, Cuban president Federico Laredo Bru (1875–1950) had invalidated all recently issued landing certificates, in part because the director of Cuba's immigration office had come under scrutiny for selling such certificates illegally. When the *St. Louis* docked in Havana harbor, immigration officials admitted twenty-eight passengers with legitimate landing cards. Cuban authorities, however, refused to honor the landing certificates of the remaining 908 passengers[15] and denied them entry into the country. Thus began the drama of the *St. Louis*, played out in the international press before millions of readers in Europe and the Americas.[16] Representatives of the **American Jewish Joint Distribution Committee** (Joint, or JDC) at once began desperate negotiations with President Bru to convince him to take in the refugees, without success. Aboard the *St. Louis*, German attorney Josef Joseph and several of his fellow passengers formed an onboard committee

---

15. Concerning the fate of the two remaining individuals from the original passenger list, one desperate immigrant aboard the *St. Louis* was evacuated to a hospital in Havana after attempting suicide when the ship anchored in Cuba; another passenger died of natural causes during the voyage.

16. For further discussion of the *St. Louis* incident, see Sarah A. Ogilvie and Scott Miller, *Refuge Denied: The St. Louis Passengers and the Holocaust* (Madison: University of Wisconsin Press, in association with the U.S. Holocaust Memorial Museum, 2006); Diane Afoumado, *Exil impossible: l'errance des Juifs du paquebot St-Louis* (Paris: Harmattan, 2005).

to help aid the Joint in their efforts and to lift the morale of the refugees. Sailing so close to the U.S. mainland that they could see the coast of Florida, the passenger committee cabled President Franklin Roosevelt, appealing for refuge in the United States. The U.S. State Department, however, declined to undertake special measures that might allow the refugees admittance to a U.S. port, informing the passenger committee that "refugees must wait their turns on the waiting list and qualify for and obtain immigration visas" before they could enter the United States.[17]

Barred from safe haven in the Americas, the *St. Louis* was forced to sail back to Europe. Of course the terrified passengers did not wish to return to Nazi Germany. In the end, several Jewish organizations, most significantly the Joint under its European director, Morris C. Troper (1892–1962), secured entry for the refugees into four European countries: France, Belgium, Great Britain, and the Netherlands. This *St. Louis* story did not end, however, when the steamship docked in Antwerp, Belgium, on June 17, 1939. While all but one of the refugees admitted to Great Britain survived the war,[18] 532 *St. Louis* passengers who remained in France and the Low Countries following the German invasion of May 1940 fell again within the Nazi dragnet. Just over half of these people lived through the war years, while 254 of their number perished in the Holocaust.

On June 17, 1939, the day on which the *St. Louis* arrived in Antwerp, Liesel Joseph, the daughter of passenger committee chairman Josef Joseph, was celebrating her eleventh birthday.[19] Upon learning that she and her parents would find refuge in England, Liesel wrote a note thanking Morris C. Troper on behalf of all the children aboard the vessel. In the following month, Troper received dozens of letters from young passengers recounting their adventures aboard the MS *St. Louis*.

---

17. A. M. Warren, State Department Visa Division, quoted in the *Congressional Record*, Senate Resolution 111, "Seventieth Anniversary of the Tragedy of the MS *Saint Louis*," May 19, 2009, S5646; Ogilvie and Miller, *Refuge Denied*, 25.

18. One of the former St. Louis passengers admitted to Britain died in an air raid in 1940.

19. Liesel Joseph, later Loeb (1928–), spent the first year of the war in England. The youngster lived with her mother in London during this time, while her father, Josef, was interned as an enemy alien on the Isle of Man. In September 1940, the family reunited and emigrated to the United States. In 1947, Liesel married fellow German-Jewish refugee Hans Loeb, who had served with the American army during World War II.

DOCUMENT 3-5. **Letter of Liesel Joseph to Morris C. Troper, European director of the American Jewish Joint Distribution Committee, June 17, 1939, USHMMA, Acc. 1997.36.12, Betty Troper Yaeger Collection (translated from the German).**

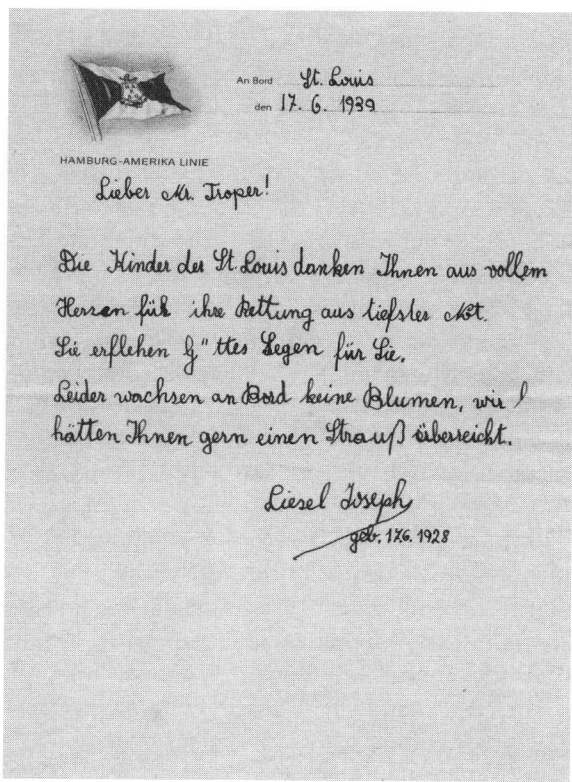

(Insignia of the Hamburg-America Line)

On Board: The *St. Louis*

Date: June 17, 1939

Dear Mr. Troper!

The children of the *St. Louis* thank you with their whole heart for rescuing us from deepest despair. We entreat G-d's blessing upon you. Unfortunately, no flowers grow here on shipboard; we would have liked to have sent you a bouquet.

Liesel Joseph, born June 17, 1928

DOCUMENT 3-6. **Letter of unidentified young *St. Louis* passenger to Morris C. Troper, July 1939, USHMMA, Acc. 1997.36.12, Betty Troper Yaeger Collection (translated from the German).**

(Boy, fifteen years old)   July 1939

<u>My Experiences aboard the *St. Louis*</u>

When, on May 13, 1939, the MS *St. Louis* lifted anchor in Hamburg, a thousand passengers breathed more easily to be leaving Germany, land of unhappiness and oppression. Everyone said that now we would finally come to a free land, Cuba.

When I came onto the ship, I first went to the cabin, and then I explored the whole ship.

After two days, we arrived at the French harbor at Cherbourg in order to take on passengers from France and Holland.

Everyone was happy. During the day, we played on the sports deck. In the evening there was the cinema, dancing, or some type of party. The captain and the entire crew treated the people very well, and the service was first-rate.

After a merry voyage of fourteen days, we landed in Havana. Then a physician and a commission came on board. The physician examined us, and the commission looked at our passports. All at once, we heard that negotiations about our landing were still in progress. We waited a few days; the boats with relatives, parents, and children who were already in Havana sailed in circles around our steamer and yelled to us that we would soon be coming ashore. Fifty men from the harbor police came on board. After five days some of the people had already lost their nerve. One man slit his wrists and jumped into the water. A sailor rescued him, and he was taken to a hospital in Havana, where his life was saved.

After eight days the captain was forced to leave Havana with his ship, and us. After a few days we sailed by Florida, saw Miami, and then the ship set course towards Europe. We thought at first that we would come back to Havana; once we were supposed to be able to land on the island of Pinosa, but the ship sailed on an unaltered course towards Europe.

One day there came a telegram from Paris from Mr. Troper, the head of the European [wing of the] American Joint Distribution Committee, telling us that our landing outside of Germany was secured and that in thirty-six hours we would learn something more definite. The telegram of salvation came punctually. Mr. Troper had secured us landings in England, Holland, France, and Belgium.

The last days brought us happiness and contentment. Finally the ship landed in Antwerp on June 17, 1939. There we were divided into groups for the four countries. The people who were going to Belgium were taken from the ship, then those going to Holland. Those going to France and England were to sail with the HAPAG[20] ship MS *Rhakotis*. On June 18, we left Antwerp, and on June 19 we arrived in Boulogne, France. We disembarked and were driven to a hotel for immigrants. From there we were

---

20. This is an acronym for the Hamburg-American Passenger Line.

divided among all the regions of France. Thus we have happily landed outside Germany after all.

DOCUMENT 3-7. **German émigré scientist Albert Einstein welcomes a group of Jewish children newly immigrated to the United States from Germany, c. 1945, USHMMPA WS# 71763, courtesy of the Hebrew Immigrant Aid Society.**

VICTIMS OF *EINSATZGRUPPEN* ACTIVITY

The infamous *Einsatzgruppen* operated in Soviet territory as mobile killing units composed primarily of German **Schutzstaffel (SS)** and police personnel. Under the command of the German **Security Police (Sicherheitspolizei, or Sipo)** and **Security Service (Sicherheitsdienst, or SD)**, the *Einsatzgruppen* had among their tasks the murder of perceived racial or political enemies found behind German combat lines in the occupied Soviet Union. These "enemies" included Jewish civilians, **Roma** (Gypsies), and officials of the Soviet Communist Party. The *Einsatzgruppen* also murdered thousands of residents of institutions for the

mentally and physically disabled. Many scholars believe that the systematic killing of Jews by these forces represented the first step of the "Final Solution," the
Nazi policy to murder all European Jews.[21]

During the invasion of the Soviet Union in June 1941, the *Einsatzgruppen*
followed the German army as it advanced deep into Soviet territory. The
mobile units, often drawing on indigenous auxiliary support, carried out
mass killing operations. In contrast to the methods employed later, in which
Jews were deported from their towns and cities to ghettos and killing centers,
Einsatzgruppen came directly to the home communities of Jews and murdered
them there. With the aid of local informants, Jews in a given locality were identified and received instructions to report to collection points. Thereafter they
were marched or transported by truck to the execution site, where trenches had
been prepared; in some cases the captive victims had to dig their own graves.
After the victims had surrendered their valuables and undressed, men, women,
and children were shot, either "military style," standing before an open trench,
or lying face down in a prepared pit, in a manner that came to be known
irreverently as "sardine packing." Shooting was the most common form of
killing used by the *Einsatzgruppen*. Yet, in the late summer of 1941, Heinrich
Himmler, noting the psychological burden that mass shootings produced on
his men, requested that a more convenient mode of killing be developed. The
result was the **gas van**, a mobile gas chamber mounted on the chassis of a cargo
truck that employed carbon monoxide from the truck's exhaust to kill its victims. Gas vans made their first appearance on the eastern front in late fall 1941
and were eventually used, along with shooting, to murder Jews and other targets in most areas where the *Einsatzgruppen* operated.[22] By the spring of 1943,
Einsatzgruppen and Order Police battalions had killed over 1 million Soviet
Jews and tens of thousands of Soviet political commissars, **partisans,** Roma,
and institutionalized disabled patients. The mobile killing methods, particularly
shooting, proved inefficient and psychologically burdensome to the killers. Even
as *Einsatzgruppen* units carried out their operations, the German authorities

---

21. See Christopher Browning, "A Reply to Martin Broszat Regarding the Origins of the
Final Solution," *Simon Wiesenthal Center Annual* 1 (1984), 113–29.

22. See Mathias Beer, "Die Entwicklung der Gaswagen beim Mord an den Juden,"
Vierteljahrshefte für Zeitgeschichte 35 (1987): 403–17.

planned and began construction of special stationary gassing facilities at central-ized killing centers in order to murder vast numbers of Jews.[23]

Eyewitness accounts by victims of these massacres are rare because very few survived to tell their stories. Rivka Yoselewska lived with her extended family in the small town of Zagrodski, near Pinsk (in modern Belarus). On the morning of August 15, 1942, mobile killing units attached to Einsatzgruppe B rounded up several hundred Jewish families from the Zagrodski ghetto and marched them to a series of prepared trenches on the outskirts of the village. On that day, unit forces murdered Yoselewska's entire family before her eyes, including her young daughter, Marka. The young mother herself received a head wound during the shooting, which propelled her into the burial pit. Regaining consciousness, she was able to extricate herself from the tangled bodies of her friends and neighbors and pull herself from the trench. Rivka Yoselewska survived her horrifying ordeal and lived in hiding until the end of the war. Her testimony at the **Eichmann Trial** in Jerusalem in 1961 presents us with indelible images of that August day and is a poignant reminder of the terrible fate that awaited children on the killing fields of the Soviet Union.

DOCUMENT 3-8. **Testimony of Rivka Yoselewska, May 8, 1961, in *The Trial of Adolf Eichmann: Record of Proceedings in the District Court of Jerusalem* (Jerusalem: Trust for the Publication of the Proceedings of the Eichmann Trial in cooperation with the Israel State Archives and Yad Vashem, the Holocaust Martyrs' and Heroes' Remembrance Authority, 1992–1995), 1:516–17.**

Witness Yoselewska: [. . .] Children began screaming [at the assembly point]. They couldn't help it. They wanted to eat and drink. We were left standing all day. We were used to such things, because more than once they chased us out of the ghetto. [. . .] Then the gate of the ghetto opened and a truck moved in. Those who were strong enough climbed up by

23. For further discussion of the activities of the *Einsatzgruppen*, see Christopher Browning with Jürgen Matthäus, *The Origins of the Final Solution: The Evolution of Nazi Jewish Policy, September 1939–March 1942* (Lincoln/Jerusalem: University of Nebraska Press/Yad Vashem, 2004); Helmut Krausnick, *Hitlers Einsatzgruppen: Die Truppe des Weltanschauungskrieges, 1938–1942* (Frankfurt am Main: Fischer Taschenbuch Verlag, 1985); Edward B. Westermann, *Hitler's Police Battalions: Enforcing Racial War in the East* (Lawrence: University of Kansas, 2005); Ronald Headland, *Messages of Murder: A Study of the Reports of the Einsatzgruppen of the Security Police and the Security Service, 1941–1943* (London: Associated University Presses, 1992).

themselves, but the weak ones were thrown in. They were piled into the truck like cattle.

Attorney General: Did they count the Jews beforehand?

Witness Yoselewska: They counted all of us. Some were missing. They went back into the ghetto and searched. They tormented us this way until afternoon.

Q: They filled up the truck. What happened to those who had no room on the truck?

A: The rest they made run after the truck.

Q: And you were running with your little girl?

A: I was holding my little girl and running after the truck, too. Many mothers had two or three children. All the way we had to run. When somebody fell down, they wouldn't let him get up; they shot him on the spot. All my family was there. We arrived at the place. Those who had been on the truck had already got down, undressed and stood in a row. [. . .]

Q: What did you see when you came there?

A: When we arrived at this place, we saw naked people standing there already, so we thought maybe they are being tormented, perhaps there was still hope we would remain alive. To get away was impossible. I was curious to see whether anybody was below that hill where the people had to stand and I made a quick turn. I saw three or four rows, twelve people already killed.

I wish to add that when they lined us up in the ghetto, my little daughter asked, "Mother, why are you wearing your Sabbath dress? They are going to kill us." Even when we stood near the ditch she said, "What are we waiting for, come, let's escape." Some of the younger ones tried to run away. They hardly managed a few steps, they were caught and shot. Then came our turn. It was difficult to hold the children, they were shaking. We took turns. Parents took the children, took other people's children. This was to help us to get through it all; to get it over with, and not see the children suffer. Mothers took leave of their children, the mothers, the parents.

Presiding Judge: How did you survive all this killing?

Attorney General: She will tell it all in her own words.

Presiding Judge: Very well, only please lead her somewhat.

Witness Yoselewska: We were lined up in fours. We stood there naked. Our clothing was taken away. My father didn't want to undress completely and kept on his underwear. When he was lined up for the shooting and was told to undress, he refused; he was beaten. We begged him, "Take off your clothes. Enough of suffering." No. He insisted on dying in his underwear.

Q: And then the Germans tore it off?

A: They tore his things off and shot him.

Q: And he fell into the pit?

A: I saw it. Then they took Mother. She didn't want to go, but wanted us to go first. Yet we made her go first. They grabbed her and shot her. There was my father's mother, who was eighty, with two grandchildren in her arms. My father's sister was also there. She, too, was shot with children in her arms.

Q: Then your turn came?

A: Then my turn came. My younger sister also. She had suffered so much in the ghetto, and yet at the last moment, she wanted to stay alive, and begged the German to let her live. She was standing there naked holding on to her girlfriend. So he looked at her and shot them both. Both of them fell, my sister and her girlfriend. My other sister was next. Then he got ready to shoot me.

Q: Did he ask for something?

A: We stood there facing the ditch. I turned my head. He asked, "Whom do I shoot first?" I didn't answer. He tore the child away from me. I heard her last cry and he shot her. Then he got ready to kill me, grabbed my hair, and turned my head about. I remained standing and heard a shot, but I didn't move. He turned me around, loaded his pistol, so that I could see what he was doing. Then he again turned me around and shot me. I fell down.

Q: And then you fell into the pit?

A: I felt nothing. At that moment I felt that something was weighing me down. I thought that I was dead, but that I could feel something even though I was dead. I couldn't believe that I was alive. I felt I was suffocating, bodies had fallen on me. I felt I was drowning. But still I could move and felt I was alive and tried to get up. I was choking, I heard shots, and again somebody falling down. I twisted and turned, but I could not. I felt I was going to suffocate. I had no strength left. But then I felt that somehow I was crawling upwards. As I climbed up, people grabbed me, hit me, dragged me downwards, but I pulled myself up with the last bit of strength. When I reached the top I looked around, but I couldn't recognize the place. Corpses strewn all over, there was no end to the bodies. You could hear people moaning in their death agony. Some children were running around naked and screaming, "Mama, Papa." I couldn't get up.

Presiding Judge: The Germans were still there at that time?

Witness Yoselewska: No. The Germans were not there. No one was there.

Attorney General: You were naked and covered with blood.

Witness Yoselewska: I got out naked, covered with blood from the corpses whose bellies had burst.

Q: What did you have on your head?

A: When he shot me I was wounded in the head. I still have a big scar on my head, where I was wounded by the Germans. [The witness shows the scar.] I got to my feet to see that horrible scene. The screaming was unbearable, the children shouting, "Mama, Papa." I ran over to the children, maybe my daughter was there. I called out, "Markele."[24] I didn't see her. The children shouted, "Mama," "Papa." I didn't recognize the children either. All of them were covered with blood.

Q: There were three other women?

A: Further off I saw two women standing up. I walked over to them. I didn't know them, and they didn't know me. We asked each other for our names. Then they said, "You're alive, too. You also survived?" "What should we do?" [. . .]

Q: Please let us be brief, Mrs. Yoselewska. It is difficult to recount and difficult to listen to. Tell us, did you hide?

A: We struggled all night long and all day screaming and shouting. Looking around, we saw Germans again and people with horses and shovels. The Germans ordered the gentiles[25] to pile all the corpses together in one place. So they did. A lot were still alive. The children were all running around in the field. As I was walking, I saw them and went over to them. The children were running after me and wouldn't leave. I sat down in the field and remained there.

Q: The Germans came back and rounded up the children?

A: Germans came and helped round up the children. They left me alone. I just sat and looked. There was no need for much shooting at the children. They fired some shots and children fell down. [. . .]

In August 1941, the mobile killing units of the *Einsatzgruppen* had been operating in German-occupied Soviet territory for less than two months. From August 8 to 19, units of the **Sonderkommando** 4a (SK 4a), under the

---

24. This is the Yiddish diminutive for Marka.
25. Presumably this refers to farmers living in the area of the shooting site.

command of SS-Standartenführer Paul Blobel[26] (1894–1951), murdered several hundred Jewish inhabitants in the Ukrainian town of Byelaya Tserkov (today Bela Tserkva). Initially, the *Einsatzgruppen*, following in the wake of Wehrmacht forces, focused primarily on the killing of Jewish males of military age as well as other racial and political targets. However, by late July, with larger deployments of SS and police auxiliaries in place, *Einsatzgruppen* practice shifted to the destruction of whole Jewish communities, including women and children. This extension of killing actions to entire populations followed an uneven chronological and regional pattern and evidently led to initial confusion among mobile killing units. Thus, while the **Waffen-SS** platoon and local Ukrainian auxiliaries attached to SK 4a carried out the murders of hundreds of adult males and females belonging to Byelaya Tserkov's sizable Jewish community, they neglected to shoot the children.

The offspring of the murdered Jews were assembled in an abandoned building at the edge of town. On August 19, perhaps realizing for the first time the infeasibility of maintaining hundreds of unsupervised children without provisions in such a locale, mobile-unit commanders ordered their troops to collect three truckloads of youngsters and shoot them at a nearby rifle range. Ninety young children remained behind. Languishing in deplorable conditions without food or water, the children, and their predicament, soon came to the attention of Wehrmacht troops quartered in the vicinity. Outraged noncommissioned officers appealed to military chaplains Ernst Tewes and Gerhard Wilczik[27] to intercede on behalf of the children. Tewes and Wilczik alerted the chaplains attached to the 295th Infantry Division, Dr. Joseph Maria Reuss (1906–1985), later bishop of Mainz after the war, and his Protestant colleague Pastor Kornmann, who visited the children and reported their findings to Lieutenant Colonel Helmuth Groscurth (1898–1943), the division's first general staff officer.

The incident put local military leaders at loggerheads with those SS officers responsible for the massacre in Byelaya Tserkov. At the core of the conflict was

---

26. Paul Blobel's Sonderkommando 4a was attached to Einsatzgruppe C in the Ukraine. He and his unit organized the killing of Jews and other Soviet citizens in cities such as Lutsk, Zhitomir, and Berdichev, and they were responsible for the murder of over thirty-three thousand Kiev Jews at Babi Yar on September 29 and 30, 1941. In June 1942 he was tasked with *Aktion* 1005 (Operation 1005), the effort to destroy evidence of Nazi atrocities in eastern Europe. Following the war, Blobel was tried and convicted by an American military tribunal in the *Einsatzgruppen* Trial in Nuremberg and hanged at Landsberg Prison on June 7, 1951.

27. Ernst Tewes (1908–1998) survived the war and became an auxiliary bishop of Munich and Freising in 1968. Gerhard Wilczek returned to his duties as a parish pastor in 1945.

Groscurth, a former member of military intelligence (Abwehr) and an early active opponent of the Nazi regime.[28] Groscurth's protest to senior officials reflected traditional conceptions of correct military conduct toward civilian populations and echoed the sentiments of many conservative career military officers who had grown increasingly uneasy with Germany's "racial war" in the East. His attitudes stood in stark contrast to the ideologically driven positions of SK 4a commander Blobel and the unit's field commander, General Walther von Reichenau,[29] who "considered the extermination of Jewish women and children to be pressingly urgent and should be carried out in whatever form it took."[30] Groscurth's efforts to forestall the murders of the Jewish youngsters ultimately ended in failure. Nevertheless, the ensuing conflict among commanders concerning which unit would carry out the shootings suggests that even among those inured to the brutal realities of German racial policy, the taboo against the killing of children still initially remained intact.

---

28. In 1938, Helmuth Groscurth joined in the so-called September Conspiracy, an aborted attempt among military and Abwehr officials to overthrow Hitler's regime. In October 1939, with Hasso von Etzdorf and Erich Kordt, Groscurth penned the memorandum "Das drohende Unheil" ("The Threatening Calamity"), exhorting military officers to resist. In April 1943, Groscurth died in Soviet captivity following the battle of Stalingrad. See Browning, *The Origins of the Final Solution*, 73ff.

29. Walther von Reichenau (1882–1942) commanded the Tenth Army during the invasion of Poland; this army group was renamed the Sixth Army, which Reichenau commanded in Belgium and France in 1940. In the same year, Reichenau was promoted to field marshal, the German army's highest military rank. In 1941, he led the Sixth Army in the invasion of the Soviet Union, becoming the commander of Army Group South in November 1941. Reichenau is best known for his October 10, 1941, order (*Tagesbefehl*), which encouraged Wehrmacht troops under his command to cooperate with *Einsatzgruppen* forces in murdering indigenous Jewish populations; many of the most famous massacres conducted by mobile killing units, including the September 29–30, 1941, murders of thirty-three thousand Jews at Babi Yar, occurred in areas under the jurisdiction of the Sixth Army. In January 1942, Reichenau suffered a massive cerebral hemorrhage and died on January 17, 1942, of a subsequent heart attack when the plane flying him back to Germany for medical care made an emergency landing near Poltava.

30. Helmut Groscurth, quoted in Ernst Klee, Willi Dressen, and Volker Riess, eds., *The Good Old Days: The Holocaust As Seen by Its Perpetrators and Bystanders*, trans. Deborah Burnstone (New York: The Free Press, 1988), 148.

DOCUMENT 3-9. **Report of military chaplain Dr. Joseph Maria Reuss, Catholic divisional chaplain, to Lieutenant Colonel Helmuth Groscurth, First Generalstabsoffizier, 295th Infantry Division, August 20, 1941, in Ernst Klee, Willi Dressen, and Volker Riess, eds., *"Schöne Zeiten": Judenmord aus der Sicht der Täter und Gaffer* (Frankfurt: S. Fischer Verlag, 1988), 135–36 (translated from the German).**

I submit the following report to 295th Infantry Division:

This afternoon around 14:30 hours Military Chaplains Tewes and Wilczek of the reserve military hospital 4/607 came to the Protestant divisional chaplain and myself and reported the following:

German soldiers had drawn their attention to the fact that Jewish children, aged between a few months and five and six years, whose parents are said to have been executed, are locked up in a house under intolerable conditions and are under guard by Ukrainian militiamen. In the vicinity of this house, the children can be heard whimpering continuously. They went there themselves in order to confirm this fact, but did not see any member of the Wehrmacht or any other authority responsible for keeping order there or carrying out guard duty. Only a few German soldiers were present as spectators, and these men had expressed indignation at this state of affairs. They asked us to report this issue to our headquarters.

Their description of these incidents made it reasonable to suspect that this was an arbitrary action on the part of the Ukrainian militia. In order to be able to report the matter accurately, I myself, accompanied by the two military chaplains and the Protestant Divisional Chaplain Kornmann, paid a visit to the house, where we discovered the following:

In the courtyard in front of the house the crying and whimpering of children could be heard very audibly. Outside there were a Ukrainian militiaman keeping guard with a rifle, a number of German soldiers, and several young Ukrainian girls. We immediately entered the house unhindered and found in two rooms some ninety (I counted) children aged from a few months to five, six or seven years old. There was no kind of supervision by the Wehrmacht or other German authorities. [. . .]

The two rooms where the children were accommodated [. . .] were in a filthy state. The children lay or sat on the floor, which was covered in their excrement. There were flies on the legs and abdomens of most of the children, some of whom were only half dressed. Some of the bigger children (two, three, four years old) were scratching the mortar from the wall and eating it. [. . .] The stench was terrible; the small children, especially those who were only a few months old, cried and whimpered continuously. The visiting soldiers were shaken, as we were, by these unbelievable conditions and expressed their outrage over them. [. . .] German soldiers who were present in the courtyard told me that they had their quarters there (in the house in the immediate proximity) and that since the afternoon of the previous day, they had heard the children, who had been there for such a long time, crying constantly. Sometime on the evening of the previous day, three lorry loads of children had already been taken away. An official from the SD[31] had been present. The lorry driver had told them that these were children of Jews and Jewesses who had already been shot, and the children were now going to be taken to be shot. The shooting of the children was to be carried out by Ukrainian militia. The children still in the house were also to be shot. The soldiers expressed extreme indignation over the conditions in which the children were being kept; in addition, one of them pointed out that he too had children back home. [. . .]

Because there is no German watch or supervision over this house and these children and because German soldiers can observe the present circumstances at any time—which has already happened and provoked declarations of indignation and criticism, I am herewith reporting this incident to my immediate superiors.

Dr. Reuss,
Military Chaplain[32]

DOCUMENT 3-10. Lieutenant Colonel Helmuth Groscurth to commander in chief of the Sixth Army, Field Marshall Walther von Reichenau in re report on events in Byelaya Tserkov on August 20, 1941, August 21, 1941, in Ernst Klee, Willi Dressen, and Volker Riess, eds., *"Schöne Zeiten": Judenmord aus der Sicht der Täter und Gaffer* (Frankfurt: S. Fischer Verlag, 1988), 140–42 (translated from the German).

On August 21 at 11:00 a.m., Captain Luley [Abwehr officer AOK 6] appeared together with Standartenführer Blobel and Obersturmführer [August] Häfner[33] to a meeting called by the army. This meeting took

---

31. That is, the German Sicherheitsdienst (Security Service).

32. This document and those that accompany it are available in complete English translation in Klee, Dressen, and Riess, *The Good Old Days*, 137–54.

33. August Häfner, born 1912, was an officer with Blobel's unit, Sonderkommando 4a. In 1968, he was a defendant in the Callsen Trial in Darmstadt for the murder of thirty-three thousand Jews at Babi Yar on September 29–30, 1941, but charges against him were eventually dismissed. In 1973, another Darmstadt court sentenced him to eight years in prison.

place at the field commander's office. [. . .] I conveyed the views of the division and made it very clear that the division had only intervened because of the way in which the action was being carried out. The Standartenführer and the Obersturmführer admitted there had been shortcomings in the way things had been run and stated that a way had to be found to settle the matter quickly on the basis of the prevailing conditions. [Häfner] said he did not now see himself as still in a position to be able to carry out the shooting. [. . .]

Concluding remarks

1. The troops have been trained by their officers to have a decent, soldierly attitude and to avoid violence and brutality against a defenseless population. They have complete understanding for the need for the most stringent intervention against [partisans]. In the case in question, however, the measures are undertaken against women and children. These in no way differ from those atrocities being carried out by the enemy, about which the troops are continually being informed. It is unavoidable that these events will be reported back home, where they will be compared to the Lemberg atrocities.[34] The troops expect their officers to intervene. This is particularly true for the older, married men. An officer is therefore forced to intervene out of consideration for his troops when such things take place in a public setting. In the interest of maintaining military discipline, all similar measures should be carried out, out of the sight of the troops.

2. The shootings might have been carried out without any sensation if the field commander and also the local commander had taken the necessary steps to keep the troops away from the scene. [. . .] Following the shooting of the town's entire Jewish population, it became per force necessary to eliminate the Jewish children, particularly the infants. This should have transpired together with the elimination of the adults in order to prevent this inhuman agony. The field commander and the Obersturmführer declared that it was not possible to provide an alternative accommodation for the children, whereby the field commander declared several times that this brood was to be exterminated.

Signed,

Groscurth

---

34. This refers to a report of Soviet atrocities against the civilian population of Lvov (German: Lemberg; today: Lviv), used extensively in German propaganda.

Following the discussion of Groscurth with members of Sonderkommando 4a, SS-Obersturmführer August Häfner was instructed to arrange for the killing of the remaining children. In 1965, he described his actions to German postwar investigators.

DOCUMENT 3-11. Testimony of August Häfner, May 31, 1965, in Ernst Klee, Willi Dressen, and Volker Riess, eds., *"Schöne Zeiten": Judenmord aus der Sicht der Täter und Gaffer* (Frankfurt: S. Fischer Verlag, 1988), 145 (translated from the German).

Then Blobel ordered me to have the children shot. I asked him, "Who should carry out the shooting?" He answered, "The Waffen SS." I objected. I said to him, "These are all young men. How are we going to answer to them if we make them shoot small children?" To this, he said, "Then take your men." Again I said to him, "How can they do that? They also have little children." This tug-of-war lasted about ten minutes. . . . I suggested that the field commander's Ukrainian militia should shoot the children. There were no objections from either side to this suggestion . . . ;

I went out to the woods all alone. The Wehrmacht had already dug a pit. The children were brought along in an all-terrain military vehicle. I had nothing to do with these technical arrangements. The Ukrainians stood around trembling. The children were taken down from the [vehicle]. They were lined up along the edge of the pit and shot so that they fell into it. They were hit wherever they were hit.[35] They fell into the pit. The wailing was indescribable. This scene I will never forget as long as I live. I [still] find it very hard to bear. I particularly remember an experience I had with a small blond-haired girl who took me by the hand. She was shot later too. [. . .] Some of the children were hit four or five times before they died.

---

35. By this, Häfner means that the Ukrainian commando, apparently intimidated by the age of the children, did not aim carefully at their victims.

DOCUMENT 3-12. A young mother with her two young children waits with other Jews from Lubny at an assembly point before their murder, c. April 1942, USHMMPA WS# 83014, courtesy of the Hamburger Institut für Sozialforschung.

"WE'VE BEEN PICKED UP": ROUNDUPS AND DEPORTATIONS

The note was written hastily on a small slip of paper. Several months after Nazi authorities began deporting German Jews from the Reich to ghettos and concentration camps in the East, agents of the Berlin **Gestapo** had come to collect young Klaus Scheurenberg and his mother, Lucie. Sixteen-year-old Klaus left a quickly scrawled message for his father on the kitchen table, notifying him that the pair had been rounded up and could be found at the **collection camp** (*Sammellager*) for Jews awaiting deportation in Berlin's Grosse-Hamburger-Strasse. This was not the first time that Klaus and Lucie Scheurenberg had been picked up by the Gestapo or that the family patriarch, Paul Scheurenberg, would be able to wrest his family members from the grasp of deportation officials.

The elder Scheurenberg had served the Jewish community through their social welfare agency, the Jewish Winterhilfe (Winter Relief Organization), throughout the late 1930s. As Gestapo authorities regularly compelled officials of the Reich Association of Jews in Germany to assist in deportation measures, Paul Scheurenberg received a summons in November 1942 to help organize transports of Berlin Jews at a collection point in the Levetzowstrasse. There he worked distributing food to hapless deportees as they awaited processing and stored their baggage for the journey east. His forced service in the deportation of his own community weighed heavily upon him. Scheurenberg's one consolation was that his loathsome responsibilities granted his immediate family a stay from deportation. Several times he had freed his wife and son from internment in the Grosse-Hamburger-Strasse, and although he had not been able to prevent initial measures against his newly wed daughter, Lisa, and her husband, technically a separate household, he had, with the help of a sympathetic SS officer, been able to retain them at the collection camp indefinitely, staving off the threat of immediate deportation.[36]

Luck ran out for the family in May 1943, when Gestapo agents came at last for the Scheurenbergs at their home in the Elsässer Strasse. As Paul Scheurenberg had been a veteran of World War I, the family was deported to **Theresienstadt**, where young Klaus Scheurenberg became so proficient in carpentry that, in August 1944, he was transferred to a detachment of Jewish artisans assigned to build evacuation headquarters for the **Reich Security Main Office** (**Reichssicherheitshauptamt**) 60 kilometers (37.3 miles) outside Berlin.

---

36. The couple was eventually transferred in 1943 to Theresienstadt and in 1944 to Auschwitz, where both perished in the gas chambers immediately upon arrival.

Camp officials promised that the Jewish workmen and their immediate households would be spared from deportation to killing centers. Although tendered in order to reduce the chance of flight among workmen at the thinly guarded worksite, this measure meant that sixteen-year-old Klaus effectively replaced his father as the family's benefactor. Klaus Scheurenberg and his parents survived the war. From 1981 until his death in 1990, Scheurenberg served as chairman of the Berlin Society for Christian-Jewish Relations.[37]

DOCUMENT 3-13. Note of Klaus Scheurenberg to his father, Paul Scheurenberg, c. 1942, Scheurenberg collection, Stiftung Neue Synagoge Berlin–Centrum Judaicum, CJA 614 Nr. 8.

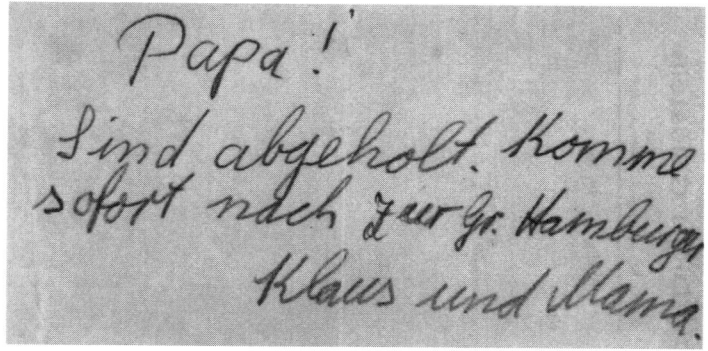

Papa!
Have been picked up. Come to the Gr.[oss]-Hamburger[-Strasse] immediately.
Klaus and Mama.

Following the **Wannsee Conference** of January 20, 1942, Nazi authorities began to prepare the deportation of Jews in France and other western European countries occupied by Germany. Securing the cooperation of the French government in **Vichy**, German officials aided by French police conducted round-ups of Jews in both occupied and unoccupied zones of France throughout the summer of 1942. As regional policy dictated that these initial deportation convoys from France carry only adult Jews to the East, these **razzias** literally rent

37. For a complete discussion of the Scheurenberg family, see Christian Dirks, "'Traurige Erlebnisse aus der Nazi-Hölle Deutschland': Zum Schicksal der Familie Scheurenberg," in *Juden in Berlin, 1938–1945: Begleitband zur gleichnamigen Ausstellung in der Stiftung Neue Synagoge Berlin*, ed. Beate Meyer and Hermann Simon (Berlin: Philo Verlagsgesellschaft, 2000), 204–13.

families apart, as parents, grandparents, and elder siblings were separated from younger children at collection points and at French or German assembly camps. By the autumn of 1942, some forty-two thousand Jews had passed through the **Drancy** transit camp on the outskirts of Paris. Nearly one-third of these individuals came from unoccupied France. A significant percentage of these were foreign or stateless Jews, sacrificed by the Vichy government in a vain attempt to spare France's indigenous Jewish population. The final destination of these deportees was **Auschwitz**, where the vast majority was gassed upon arrival.[38]

Among those caught in the roundups in Vichy were members of the Gumpel family from northern Germany. In August 1937 Gertrud Gumpel had left Hamburg with her young children, Felicitas and Thomas, to join her husband and eldest son, Kurt, in Antwerp. In the months before the German invasion of Belgium and the Netherlands, businessman Berthold Gumpel succeeded in emigrating to the United States, but as his prospective employer had issued the visa to him alone, he had had to leave his family, now settled in Brussels, behind. With the German occupation of Belgium in May 1940, Gumpel, in New York, frantically sought to secure the necessary travel papers for his wife and children, without success. As the Nazi persecution of Belgian Jews escalated, Gertrud Gumpel decided to undertake a dangerous venture: to journey with her children across southern France in an attempt to reach Portugal, where her husband's business associates might help her arrange a passage to America. The desperate gamble failed, and the small family fell into the hands of Nazi authorities, who interned them.

On July 14, 1942, thirteen-year-old Felicitas Gumpel, nicknamed Fee, wrote a letter to her grandmother from Drancy advising her that her mother, Gertrud, and eighteen-year-old brother, Kurt, had been taken away to another camp. Writing awkwardly in German, for she had only had a few years of formal schooling in Hamburg before fleeing to Belgium, Fee attempted to calm the elderly woman's fears about the fate of her daughter and grandchildren. The brief lines added by her eleven-year-old brother, Tommy, as a postscript reveals the children's true sense of loss and despair. On July 20, 1942, Gertrud and Kurt Gumpel departed France on a convoy to Auschwitz, where they perished. By late summer, local exigencies had convinced French authorities to alter their

---

38. See Serge Klarsfeld, *Memorial to the Jews Deported from France, 1942–1944: Documentation of the Deportation of the Victims of the Final Solution in France* (New York: Beate Klarsfeld Foundation, 1983); Michael Marrus and Robert Paxton, *Vichy France and the Jews* (New York: Basic Books, 1981); Renée Poznanski, *Jews in France during World War II*, trans. Nathan Bracher (Hanover, NH: Brandeis University Press in association with University Press of New England and the U.S. Holocaust Memorial Museum, 2001).

policy in favor of including juveniles in deportations to the East. On September 23, 1942, Felicitas and Thomas boarded Convoy 36 from Drancy to Auschwitz, where they shared the fate of their mother and brother.[39]

DOCUMENT 3-14. **Letter of Felicitas and Thomas Gumpel, July 14, 1942, in Reiner Lehberger and Ursula Randt, eds.,** *"Aus Kindern werden Briefe": Dokumente zum Schicksal jüdischer Kinder und Jugendlicher in der NS-Zeit* **(Hamburg: Freie und Hansestadt Hamburg Behörde für Schule, Jugend und Berufsbildung, 1999), 52–53 (translated from the German).**

July 14, 1942

Dear Grandma,

Now don't be shocked about the newest thing that I have to tell you: this morning Mama and Kurt were taken away with others to work. But they are staying in France, they are still in Tours in order that they will be examined [by a doctor]. Those that are sick[40] will come back here. We children all remained here and are in good hands; they are taking good care of us. We have good things to eat, better than normal anyway: cookies, bread with butter, etc. We even sleep at night with a family that Mama had befriended before; they are very kind to us. At nine-thirty we must all assemble again in our barracks, and then we will get to hear news; I hope good news. Just don't excite yourself too much; this is all only for the time being. Share this letter with the entire family, because I cannot write to everyone. It is very sad in the camp, because only the old men and women are here. They each have a suitcase a piece and 200 francs and a comforter, a thick one from us. This evening we haven't heard any more [news]. I must close for today. Many, many greetings and kisses,

Your Fee

Dear Grandma,

With this news I think I have cried as never before, but this is how it is, so [many] fathers gone from their children, mothers gone from their children. I write these lines with tears in my eyes. Many greetings and kisses,

Your Tommy

---

39. See Gert Koppel, *Untergetaucht: Eine Flucht aus Deutschland* (Westermann: Braunschweig, 1999).

40. The translator has attempted to reflect Fee Gumpel's imperfect German in the text.

DOCUMENT 3-15. Lissy Asser, a young girl from Göttingen, waits with other German Jews at a deportation point in Hildesheim, c. March 1942. Lissy, her parents, and a younger brother are believed to have been murdered in Treblinka, USHMMPA WS# 69635, courtesy of the Stadtarchiv Hildesheim.

While Nazi authorities and their indigenous collaborators carried on their efforts to deport Jews from German-occupied central and western Europe, the fate of Romanian Jewry lay in the hands of Germany's Axis allies. Approximately one-half of Romania's prewar Jewish population of 756,000 perished in the Holocaust. As a result of territorial changes realized during the course of World War II, 150,000 Romanian Jews living in northern Transylvania fell under Hungarian jurisdiction. In 1944, Hungarian authorities deported this population, along with other Hungarian Jews, to Nazi concentration camps and killing centers, where 135,000 were murdered. Some forty-five to sixty thousand Jews living within wartime Romanian borders were killed by Romanian and German forces in the regions of Bessarabia and Bukovina in the summer and fall months of 1941.[41] Most remaining Jews from these areas were deported in 1941 to the so-called Transnistrian Reservation, within a newly created Romanian military district established from recently acquired Soviet territory between the Bug and Dniester rivers. Terrible atrocities often preceded these deportations, such as the infamous Iasi Pogrom (June 28 to July 2, 1941), in which as many as thirteen thousand Jews were murdered in cold blood or died of starvation, dehydration, or suffocation aboard the infamous "Death Trains" that carried the surviving Jews of Iasi to other parts of the province.

Transnistria was a deathtrap for the 155,000 Jews and 25,000 Roma driven to remote areas by Romanian authorities. Thousands died en route of hunger, thirst, exposure, and maltreatment. Once the deportees reached their destination, Romanian officials took little responsibility for feeding and sheltering them. Interned in ghettos and camps, thousands fell victim to mass shootings and epidemics of **typhus** and other diseases. Starvation, forced labor, and abuse shaped deportees' daily lives. Between 105,000 and 120,000 Romanian Jews and 11,000 Roma died as a result of the expulsions to Transnistria.[42]

Among those Jews deported from Bessarabia were ten-year-old Iser Franghieru and his family. Placed in a Hehalutz[43] orphanage after the war, the teenager shared his wartime experiences in the Transnistria with a social worker from the American Jewish Joint Distribution Committee.

---

41. See Radu Ioanid, *The Holocaust in Romania: The Destruction of Jews and Gypsies under the Antonescu Regime, 1940–1944* (Chicago: Ivan R. Dee in association with the U.S. Holocaust Memorial Museum, 2000); *"Executive Summary" in Final Report of the International Commission on the Holocaust in Romania* (Bucharest: International Commission on the Holocaust in Romania, 2004).

42. *Final Report*, 3. The reservation was also a killing site for indigenous Jews. Scholars estimate that between 115,000 and 180,000 Jews living in the area of the newly formed Transnistria were murdered, especially in Odessa and in the counties of Golta and Berezovka.

43. This international youth organization was founded in 1921 in Warsaw. Dedicated to the Zionist ideal of reestablishing a Jewish homestead, the Hehalutz organized professional training courses for European Jews as they prepared to leave for Palestine and create kibbutz settlements there. In the ghettos of German-occupied eastern Europe, Hehalutz cells maintained their structure, and the organization's members formed the activist core of fighters in ghetto uprisings and the Jewish partisan units. In the postwar period, it was instrumental in encouraging Jewish emigration to Palestine.

DOCUMENT 3-16. Vita of Iser Franghieru, Hehalutz Orphanage, September 12, 1947, American Jewish Joint Distribution Committee, USHMMA RG 25.001, American Joint Distribution Committee, Case Files of Romanian Orphans.

Iser Franghieru

Among the crowd of children, inmates of the Hehalutz, Bucharest, home for Transnistrian orphans, it is rather easy to discern the tall figure of this young fellow, and the warm smile permanently fluttering on his face.

Iser Franghieru is a boy of Hertza, where he was born on February 12, 1931. His father, Haim Leib, the shoemaker, died when Iser was only a baby.

In 1941 the ten-year-old child followed his mother and a married sister with her husband and two children over the Dniester into deportation, in a convoy formed at Edinetz.

"We marched whole days and nights, through rain and knee-deep mud as far as Casauti forest. There we halted for the night. I was terribly cold and shivering. The first snow flakes of winter were falling and the next dawn revealed among the trees in the snow several hundred dead hard frozen by the frost."

The others resumed their trudge, eyes fixed on the ground. All moaned with pain, many fell. Of these some died immediately as they fell, others were helped to death by the gendarmes.

"All the road was strewn with corpses. I saw many children fall with little streams of blood oozing from their mouths. Mother covered my eyes to stop me from seeing so many dead."

The convoy crossed the Dniester, then marched through Jampol and towards evening halted one kilometer [0.6 miles] off Obodowka.

"The whole night was spent in a stable, but only after the first hour you stepped[44] on the dead bodies of those who succumbed to hunger and weariness. Dead and alive were robbed by those who drove us."

The next day in a crowd of 283, they were sent to labor on a farm at Dubina. All were huddled for the night in a stable.

Before long the continual hunger began to tell on the mother. She suffered, and the child ran out one afternoon to beg by all means some food for his mother. On his return towards evening, it was too late. She

---

44. This word is misspelled as "stipped" in the original. The author of the document, typing for Joint records, made many similar typographical errors in the text. To aid the reader, they have been corrected in this manuscript.

had died. Transportation of the dead was allowed for full cartloads only. So the dead body lay for three days with the living until twelve corpses were completed [collected]. The deportees worked hard and long hours and were too scantily fed, so mortality was great. The boy's brother-in-law died, a child of his died, and out of the 238 which [*sic*] set out, only seventy-six were left in the end.

The dead were buried under the dung heap and covered with snow. But in spring the pigs unearthed heads and limbs from the rotten bodies.

Left alone with his married sister and one of her children, the boy did all he could to get them some food. He toiled in the fields, sold off the remnants of the rags they had left, begged, and at last watched a herd of swine. Of the food for his charge he too could have his fill, and when he managed to save some for his relatives there was jubilation in the stable.

But one day, new hope surged in the weakened hearts of the survivors. Iser had sighted a group of partisans.

He was repatriated in 1944. For three months in Iasi, then at Baarlad, now in Bucharest. Here the Hehalutz movement supervises a home exclusively supported by JDC [the American Jewish Joint Distribution Committee] for Transnistrian orphans. Iser enjoys young life in it and attends the ORT[45] technical courses, likewise supported by JDC. He does very well and is particularly good at draughtsmanship. His plans for the near future are to become an efficient mechanic and then emigrate.

---

45. Established in Russia in 1880, the Jewish self-help organization Obshestvo Remeslenofo zemledelcheskofo Truda (The Society for Trades and Agricultural Labor) still provides occupational training to Jewish communities around the world.

DOCUMENT 3-17. Iser Franghieru in a Bucharest orphanage, c. 1947, USHMMPA WS# 01827, courtesy of the American Jewish Joint Distribution Committee.

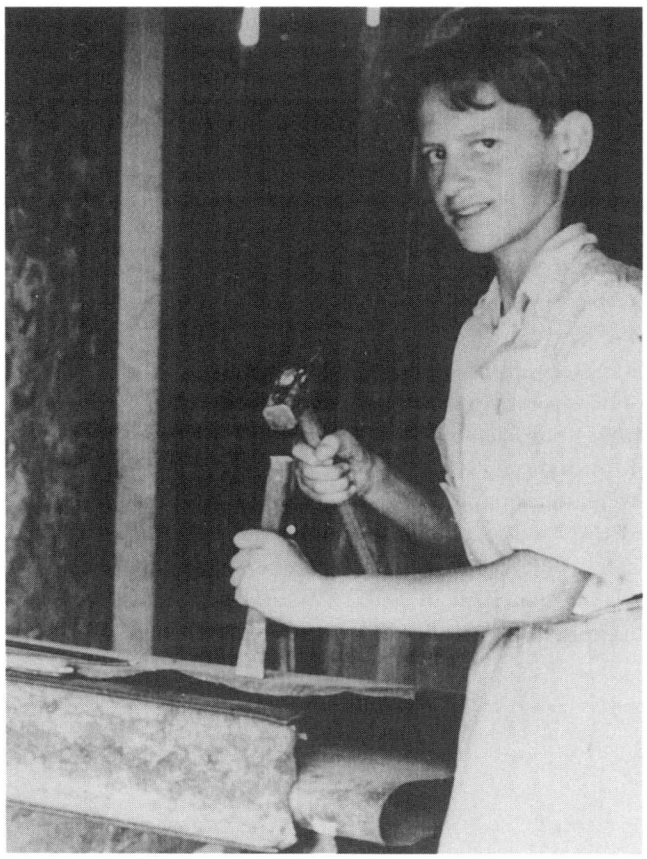

Throughout the early 1940s, the National Socialist regime and its allies succeeded in destroying most of the Jewish communities within their jurisdictions. Yet, incredibly, in 1944 in the heart of central Europe, one large national community of Jews remained largely intact. Hungary's Jewish population numbered approximately 825,000. Four hundred thousand of these individuals lived in Trianon Hungary,[46] together with several hundred thousand Jews living in regions acquired by the regime of Admiral **Miklós Horthy** after 1938. A

---

46. This refers to the traditional Hungarian borders minus those crown lands ceded in the Treaty of Trianon following World War I.

further one hundred thousand people in these areas were classified as Jews by the Hungarian racial laws. Hungary's Jews faced harsh discriminatory measures beginning in 1938. After 1940, further legislation compelled all able-bodied Jewish males of draft age to perform forced labor. Working under brutal conditions without adequate food, shelter, or medical care, at least twenty-seven thousand perished before the German forces occupied Hungary in March 1944.

And yet, even as their coreligionists all over Europe perished in the Holocaust, members of Hungary's Jewish community continued to survive. Most Hungarian Jews had been spared deportation prior to the German occupation because Nazi German leaders were unable to control the internal policies of their Hungarian allies. Confident after the German defeat of Stalingrad in 1943 that Nazi Germany would ultimately lose the war, Hungarian prime minister Miklós Kállay,[47] with the tacit approval of Admiral Horthy, sought to negotiate a separate armistice with the Western powers. In order to preclude these events, German troops moved to occupy Hungary on March 19, 1944. Dismissing Kállay, who had so far resisted German demands to deport Hungarian Jewry, Nazi leaders installed the pro-German Döme Sztójay as premier.[48] Sztójay proved committed to Hungary's continued participation in the war effort and yielded to German pressure to allow the deportation process to begin. In April 1944, German authorities ordered Jews living outside Budapest to concentrate in certain regional centers; Hungarian gendarmes enforced this ghettoization of Jews from rural areas. Beginning in mid-May, German authorities under the personal direction of **Adolf Eichmann** worked with Hungarian officials to deport Jews from these districts. By July 1944, some 440,000 Jewish

---

47. Miklós Kállay (1887–1967) was a member of the Upper House of the Hungarian Parliament when he replaced the pro-German Lászlo Bárdossy as prime minister of Hungary. Following the arrest of Admiral Miklós Horthy in October 1944, Kállay surrendered to Arrow Cross officials and was deported to Mauthausen and then Dachau, where he was imprisoned with other prominent political prisoners. Kállay survived the war and settled in New York City, where he served on the Executive Committee of the Hungarian National Council in Exile. He died in New York on January 14, 1967.

48. Döme Sztójay (1883–1946) was a member of the Hungarian General Staff; from 1925 to 1933, he was a military attaché in Berlin, and from 1935 until March 1944, he served as Hungary's chief diplomat to Nazi Germany. Replacing Kállay as prime minister, Sztójay introduced extensive anti-Jewish legislation and allowed the deportation of Hungarian Jews to killing centers. Following his removal as prime minister on August 29, 1944, Sztójay, already in failing health, retired to a sanatorium. Sztójay fled Hungary before the arrival of Soviet troops in January 1945, but he was arrested by American military authorities and tried by a Budapest court for war crimes in March 1946. He was sentenced to death and executed by firing squad on August 24, 1946.

men, women, and children had been removed from Hungarian soil, primarily to Auschwitz; only the Jews of Budapest remained.

Faced with Allied threats and a worsening military situation, Miklós Horthy called a halt to these deportations on July 7, 1944. While the admiral negotiated with Soviet leaders, whose troops were nearing the Hungarian frontier, and prepared to announce an armistice, German officials staged a coup d'état. On October 15, 1944, they arrested Horthy and installed a new government under Ferenc Szalasi, leader of the fascist and radically antisemitic **Arrow Cross**. During its brief time in power, the Arrow Cross initiated a reign of terror, torturing and murdering Budapest Jews in the streets and reinitiating deportations from the capital.[49]

Caught up in the initial wave of Arrow Cross violence against Jews was seventeen-year-old Pinchas Eisner. Fearing his family would soon be deported or share the fate of neighbors murdered in their own homes, the youth wrote a letter of farewell to his elder brother Mordechai, who was serving in a Hungarian forced labor camp. Five days later, the young man was seized by an Arrow Cross militia and transferred to the village of Csomád outside Budapest. On November 3, 1944, Eisner and seventy other Jews were marched to a nearby forest, instructed to dig a large trench, and shot to death before their self-made grave. Mordechai Eisner received his brother's letter when he returned home upon liberation.

DOCUMENT 3-18. Letter of Pinchas Eisner to his brother Mordechai Eisner, Budapest, October 16, 1944, in Reuvan Dafni and Yehudit Keliman, eds., *Final Letters* (London: Weidenfeld & Nicholas 1991), 454–57.

Budapest, October 16, 1944, 6:15 p.m.

My Dear Brother:
Good-bye! Think of our talk that night. I felt as one with you. I knew that, if it were you whose life would end, I would go on living as if I had lost half of my body and soul. You said that if I die, you will kill yourself.

---

49. See Randolph Braham and Brewster Chamberlin, eds., *The Holocaust in Hungary: Sixty Years Later* (New York: Rosenthal Institute for Holocaust Studies, 2006); Randolph Braham, *Eichmann and the Destruction of Hungarian Jewry* (New York: World Federation of Hungarian Jews, 1961); Randolph Braham and Scott Miller, eds., *The Nazis' Last Victims: The Holocaust in Hungary* (Detroit, MI: Wayne State University Press in association with the U.S. Holocaust Memorial Museum, 1998); Hans Safrian, *Eichmann's Men*, trans. Uta Stargardt (Cambridge: Cambridge University Press in association with the U.S. Holocaust Memorial Museum, 2010).

Think of what I told you, that if you stay alive, I will live on within you. I would have liked to continue my life with you and with our family. Plans, desires, hopes were before me. I longed for the unknown. I would have liked to know, to live, to see, to do, to love. . . . But now it is all over. In the city, Jews were exterminated from entire streets. There is no escape. Tonight or at the latest tomorrow it will be our turn. At seventeen I have to face certain death. There is no escape. We thought that we would be exceptions, but fate made no exceptions. [. . .] It seems like fate put a curse on each of us. After Jisreal[50] it is now my turn together with my father, mother, and Sorele. I hope you will survive us. Farewell and forgive me if ever I have offended you. [. . .]

The calamity started last evening. By nightfall, the Jews of [house numbers] 64 and 54 had already been taken away. There was a pool of blood on the pavement, but by morning it was washed away. I was awake the whole night. R. J. and K. S. [friends of the boys] were here. Poor R. J. could hardly stand on his feet he was so full of fright. At first we hoped that the police and the army would protect us, but after a phone call we learned everything. Slowly morning arrived, but the events of the day made our situation hopeless. K. S. came at 6:00. He was about to faint after he fought with four Nazis who beat him terribly. He barely escaped with his life. He was stumbling and trembling, and could not start talking because of what he had seen and been through. I write fast, who knows if I will have time to finish? K. S. offered to take Sorele to a safe place. She promptly jumped at the suggestion and wanted to go immediately. But Mummy stepped in front of her and with a completely calm voice said that she would not let her go, because the Nazis might catch them on the street. Sorele was crying and hysterical. She wanted to go, she wants to live. Finally Mother proposed that if I go too then she will give her consent. You should have heard the way she said that. Sorele wanted to go, I stayed. . . . I could not leave our mother and father. [. . .] Father was praying the whole night. He still has some hope left, but he is talking about this world being like a vestibule to prepare ourselves [for] the real world to come.

Mother and Father are telling religious parables to K. S. about the inevitability of destiny. Mathild [an aunt] is sitting next to us and listens. Sorele is outside and I am writing. I am relatively calm, facing death, my

---

50. This was the Eisners' brother, who died at nineteen. Sorele, mentioned in the next line, is their sister.

CHAPTER 4

CHILDREN IN THE WORLD OF THE GHETTO

DURING WORLD WAR II, German policy aimed to isolate Jewish communities from non-Jewish populations, particularly in the occupied eastern territories. Shortly after the German invasion of Poland in September 1939, German authorities began a systematic concentration of Jews in so-called ghettos in many Polish metropolitan areas. Confined within an enclosed municipal district, Jewish populations were often incarcerated behind makeshift walls and barbed wire fences and forced to live under deplorable conditions. Nazi officials often compelled Jews from surrounding communities and adjacent rural districts to resettle in urban ghettos so that many ghettoized populations suffered from severe overcrowding and acute shortages of food and essential goods.

German authorities established over one thousand ghettos in German-annexed Poland, the **General Government**,[1] and the occupied Soviet territories alone. The first ghettoization effort took place in the small city of Piotrków Trybunalski, in central Poland in October 1939. Other major ghettos were established in Łódź, Vilna (today Vilnius), Kovno (today Kaunas), Białystok, Kraków, Riga, Lvov (today Lviv), Czestochowa, Minsk, and **Theresienstadt** (**Terezin**). The largest of these concentrated communities was the **Warsaw ghetto** with four hundred thousand Jews crowded into a total area of 1.3 square miles. Although each community differed appreciably in terms of composition and structure, most ghettos in eastern Europe shared some characteristics in common. Communal life within the ghetto was administered by

---

1. That is, German-occupied Poland.

a German-appointed **Jewish Council** (*Judenrat*), responsible for the internal organization of the community and the management of its goods and services. A ghetto police force, the **Jewish Order Service**, imposed public order and enforced the decrees of German authorities and ordinances promulgated by the Jewish Council. Jews within the ghettos were required to wear distinguishing badges or armbands, often bearing the **Jewish star**, in order to further differentiate them from the population outside the ghetto. Many ghetto inhabitants were subjected to forced labor, either outside the parameters of the ghetto itself or within the community's workshops and industries. Finally, many ghettos in the German-occupied East were the destinations of Jews deported from western Europe, especially from the Third Reich itself. In ghettos such as Riga, Łódź, Minsk, Kovno, and Theresienstadt, these deportees blended with Jews from indigenous communities and contributed to even more drastic overcrowding.[2]

Most scholars believe that German authorities viewed ghettoization as a provisional measure that allowed Nazi officials to segregate and control Jewish populations while planners in Berlin deliberated the ultimate objectives of their anti-Jewish policy. With the implementation of the "Final Solution," Nazi officials targeted ghetto populations for **deportation** and mass murder. In occupied Soviet territories, units of the *Einsatzgruppen* and their auxiliaries murdered thousands of Jews at killing sites in the vicinity of ghettos, such as Riga, Vilna, Kovno, and Minsk. In Poland, many larger ghettos, such as that in Łódź, maintained their own industries, which supported the German war effort. In these cases, ghetto populations were gradually decimated by a series of "actions" (*Aktionen*) in which **Schutzstaffel (SS)** authorities, often with the aid of the Jewish Order Police, rounded up thousands of ghetto residents for transfer to killing centers. In 1943 and 1944, these larger communities were liquidated through large-scale deportations to extermination camps. The destruction of the Jewish community in Warsaw in April 1943 initiated the Warsaw Ghetto Uprising, one of the most ambitious insurgencies by Jewish resistance fighters against Nazi authorities.

This chapter explores the roles and reactions of children within the wider context of Nazi ghettoization policy. Children often played unique roles in the ghetto communities. As adept and nimble smugglers, they helped to sustain their fellow ghetto inhabitants with black market goods and contraband from the "**Aryan** side." As forced laborers, those youngsters fit enough to work

---

2. In some cases, as in the instance of the Riga ghetto, a significant segment of the local population of Jews was murdered in order to make room for deportees from Germany or western Europe. See Gertrude Schneider, *Reise in den Tod: Deutsche Juden in Riga, 1941–1944* (Berlin: Hentrich, 2006).

helped their families survive in a perilous climate of starvation and deportation. Children were manifestly recipients of the ghettos' extensive self-help and social welfare organizations. Yet, for children the ghetto also represented a particularly dangerous environment. Youngsters figured as the likeliest victims of starvation, illness, and destitution. Along with the elderly and sick, children also numbered among the first deported from ghetto settings to killing centers. **Łódź ghetto** elder **Mordechai Chaim Rumkowski** famously appealed to parents under his jurisdiction to "give me your children" in order to avert wider deportation measures during that ghetto's notorious *Gehsperre*. So-called **children's actions** (*Kinderaktionen*), like the one associated with the *Gehsperre*, occurred in many major ghettos, as Nazi authorities targeted these "useless eaters" for early deportation measures. Likewise, German ordinances strictly forbade pregnancies or live births in many ghettos, forcing parents to make agonizing decisions concerning their future offspring. The following documentation explores these complex experiences of children and adolescents in the world of the ghetto.

INTO THE GHETTO

Beginning in 1939 with the occupation of Poland, German authorities began a systematic concentration of Jewish populations within specially designated sectors of Polish metropolitan areas. The first large-scale efforts at ghettoization began in Łódź, Poland's second-largest city: the Łódź ghetto was created in April 1940 and eventually held 164,000 inhabitants. The largest ghetto of its kind, the Warsaw ghetto, established in October 1940, incarcerated 390,000 Jews. Following the invasion of the Soviet Union in June 1941, German administrators in Soviet territories altered their strategy of ghettoization, initially creating ghettos in order to concentrate Jews for shooting actions as the *Einsatzgruppen* followed **Wehrmacht** forces into the Soviet interior. An illustrative example of such a practice was the formation of the Vilna ghetto in Lithuania in September 1941.

In July 1941, shortly after the German occupation of Vilna, units of the *Einsatzgruppen*, together with local collaborators, rounded up some five thousand Jewish men in the Lithuanian capital and murdered them in the **Ponary** (or Paneriai) woods, some eleven kilometers (seven miles) from Vilna. In early August, Lithuania passed from German military governance to German civilian administration. From August 31 until September 3, mobile killing units attached to Einsatzkommando 9 carried out a more ambitious shooting action, murdering eight thousand Jews at Ponary, including members of Vilna's recently appointed Jewish Council. In the following days, German authorities fenced off the enclosure that had been used to detain assembled Jews prior to their murder in the recent massacre and created from this space two ghettos, separated from each other by a municipal thoroughfare.[3] On September 6, 1941, all surviving Jewish inhabitants of the city of Vilna were ordered into the two areas, which together comprised the Vilna ghetto. Each component ghetto had its own Jewish Council, appointed the following day, and maintained its own Jewish Order Police force and welfare and social services.[4]

We know much about what that tumultuous day in September 1941 looked and sounded like from the diary of **Yitskhok Rudashevski**, an only child born in Vilna on December 10, 1927. Rudashevski lived in the Lithuanian capital with his parents and maternal grandmother. His father was a typesetter for the city's most prominent Yiddish newspaper, *Vilner Tog*, and perhaps this proximity to the world of journalism spurred Yitskhok's interest in writing. He attended high school at the city's prestigious *Realgymnasium*, where he excelled in languages, history, and literature. On September 6, 1941, his small household, like so many others in the city's Jewish community, received orders to move into the Vilna ghetto. Not yet fourteen, Rudashevski recorded the chaos and pathos of that day in his journal. The youngster's poignant account reveals how acutely he felt his sudden loss of freedom, as well as a strong presentiment of tragedy. Once settled, Yitskhok filled his diary with vivid descriptions of the ghetto and the individuals who inhabited it. Prominent in his narrative is a discussion of the vibrant intellectual and cultural world that he and other like-minded youths nurtured there.[5]

That world came to an abrupt end with the ghetto's liquidation in early autumn of 1943. Like many ghetto inhabitants, Yitskhok and his family went into hiding when deportations from Vilna began, but SS officials or their auxiliaries discovered them two weeks later. In early October 1943, Yitskhok Rudashevski, together with all those concealed with him, were transported to Ponary, where they were shot to death.[6]

---

3. This refers to Niemiecka (German) Street.

4. See Yitzhak Arad, *Ghetto in Flames: The Struggle and Destruction of the Jews in Vilna in the Holocaust* (New York: Holocaust Library, 1982).

5. For a discussion of Yitskhok Rudashevski's interest in literary and cultural events in the Vilna ghetto, see Document 8-4.

6. See Isaac (Yitskhok) Rudashevski, *The Diary of the Vilna Ghetto, June 1941–April 1943* (Tel Aviv: Ghetto Fighters' House, 1973); Alexandra Zapruder, ed., *Salvaged Pages: Young Writers' Diaries of the Holocaust* (New Haven, CT: Yale University Press, 2002), 190ff.

DOCUMENT 4-1. **Diary of Yitskhok Rudashevski, Vilna ghetto, entry for September 6, 1941, in Alexandra Zapruder, ed.,** *Salvaged Pages: Young Writers' Diaries of the Holocaust* **(New Haven, CT: Yale University Press, 2002), 199–201.**

A beautiful sunny day has risen. The streets are closed off by Lithuanians. The streets are turbulent. Jewish workers are permitted to enter. A ghetto is being created for Vilna Jews.

People are packing in the house. The women go back and forth. They wring their hands when they see the house looking as if after a pogrom. I go around with bleary eyes among the bundles, see how we are being uprooted overnight from our home. Soon we have our first view of the move to the ghetto, a picture of the Middle Ages—a gray black mass of people goes harnessed to large bundles. We understand that soon our turn will come. I look at the house in disarray, at the bundles, at the perplexed, desperate people. I see things scattered that were dear to me, that I was accustomed to use.

We carry the bundles to the courtyard. On our street a new mass of Jews streams continually to the ghetto. The small number of Jews of our courtyard begins to drag the bundles to the gate. Gentiles are standing and taking part in our sorrow. Some Jews hire gentile boys to help carry the bundles. A bundle was suddenly stolen from a neighbor. The woman stands in despair among her bundles and does not know how to cope with them, weeps and wrings her hands. Suddenly everything around me begins to weep. Everything weeps. [. . .]

The street streamed with Jews carrying bundles. The first great tragedy. People are harnessed to bundles, which they drag across the pavement. People fall, bundles scatter. [. . .] I walk burdened and irritated. The Lithuanians drive us on, do not let us rest. I think of nothing: not what I am losing, not what I have just lost, not what is in store for me. I do not see the streets before me, the people passing by. I only feel that I am terribly weary, I feel that an insult, a hurt is burning inside me. Here is the ghetto gate. I feel that I have been robbed, my freedom is being robbed from me, my home, and the familiar Vilna streets I love so much. I have been cut off from all that is dear and precious to me.

People crowd at the gate. Finally I am on the other side of the gate. The stream of people flings me into a gate blocked with bundles. I throw down the bundles that cut my shoulders. I find my parents and here we are in the ghetto house. It is dusk, rather dark and rainy. The little streets, Rudnitsker, Shavler, Yatkever, Shpitalne, and Disner, which constitute the [first] ghetto, look like anthills. It swarms with people. The newcomers begin to settle down, each in his tiny bit of space, on his bundles. Additional Jews keep streaming in constantly. We settle down in our place. Besides the four of us, there are eleven persons in the room. The room is a dirty and stuffy one. It is crowded. The first ghetto night. We lie three together on two doors. I do not sleep. In my ears resound the lamentation of this day. I hear the restless breathing of the people with whom I have been suddenly thrown together, people who just like me have suddenly been uprooted from their homes.

The first ghetto day begins. I run right out into the street. The little streets are still full of a restless mass of people. It is hard to push your way through. I feel as if I were in a box. There is no air to breathe. Wherever you go, you encounter a gate that hems you in. [. . .]

I decide to hunt up my friends in the courtyard. I have an idea that all of us will be there. I soon find Benkye Nayer, Gabik, and several others. The first day is spent in settling down, hunting up one another. The second evening in the ghetto, people feel a little more at home, calmer. My chums are figuring out how many weeks we shall be sitting here.

While teenagers like Yitskhok Rudashevski lamented the loss of freedom and autonomy that incarceration in the ghetto imposed, very small children, such as Seweryn Dobrecki, found resettlement away from familiar surroundings and cherished possessions confusing and frightening. Born January 26, 1936, in Łódź to the prosperous industrialist Zygmunt Dobrecki and his wife, Róża, young Seweryn was three years old when German troops invaded Poland in September 1939. One of his earliest memories of the war was the loss of his collection of toys when German troops appropriated the Dobreckis' apartment upon their arrival in Łódź. The family attempted to flee with other refugees to unoccupied Warsaw but was turned back by a German advance on the capital. Despite Poland's defeat, Seweryn viewed the ensuing weeks as halcyon days because he had returned to his grandmother's familiar apartment and could play with his toys as if there were no "such thing as Germans."

In November 1939, following the annexation of the Wartheland, the western part of German-occupied Poland, to the Reich, German authorities demanded the evacuation of at least thirty thousand Jews from Łódź, either through voluntary resettlement or forced expulsions.[7] The Dobreckis presumably traveled to Warsaw

---

7. This order preceded the establishment of the Łódź ghetto in February 1940 and corresponded with a massive expulsion of Jews and Poles from the Wartheland. See Lucjan Dobroszycki, ed., *The Chronicle of the Łódź Ghetto*, 1941–1944, trans. Richard Lourie et al. (New Haven, NJ: Yale University Press, 1984), xxxiv–xxxvi.

in early 1940 and were interned in the Warsaw ghetto. Four-year-old Seweryn found the family's relocation disconcerting. Yet, he discovered to his surprise that he lacked neither companions nor amusements in his new environment—although the games he and his ghetto playmates engaged in differed appreciably from the diversions the youngster had pursued in his nursery in Łódź.[8]

DOCUMENT 4-2. **Interview of Seweryn Dobrecki by the Central Jewish Historical Commission, c. 1946, USHMMA, RG-15.084, Holocaust Survivor Testimonies, 301/3611/4-5 (translated from the Polish).**

We had scarcely left Łódź when the Germans broke through the Polish front and we had to turn back to Łódź. The whole way was paved with human corpses; I turned my head away and didn't want to look. After three days and nights we returned to Łódź, looked for Mama, and went back to grandmother's apartment. As soon as I was back home, I immediately collected all of my belongings and my toys, fetched a playmate from downstairs, and began to play. I was enormously happy that I was back at home and that I had found all my toys; my playmate from the apartment building came to me, I played and forgot that there was such a thing as Germans.

This domestic tranquility lasted only two months. One day I went with Mama to visit my friend. On the way we saw a large white sign; I asked Mama to read it to me. She didn't want to do it, but I begged and my mother let herself be persuaded and read to me that a resettlement was coming: that all Jews from Łódź had to move to Warsaw. I was sad and I was afraid that I would have to see again the human misery that I had witnessed when we sat in our buggy,[9] and I burst into tears. I was very sad; I wouldn't even speak to my playmate anymore. I asked Mama to take me back home.

After several days we had to move away. I took my [toy] pony with me, hid it under my coat, and played the whole way with my pony and did not even look at the Germans. So it was the whole way to Warsaw.

In Warsaw we lived in the Jewish quarter [i.e., the Warsaw ghetto]. Mama and Papa went to work, and I stayed at home and played alone; I longed for Łódź and for my old great grandmother, who was 101 years old and who had remained behind in Łódź. I begged Mama to put me in a school where there were a lot of children. I was very happy when Mama

8. For a detailed discussion of children at play during the Holocaust, see chapter 8.
9. That is, on their drive back to Łódź, described at the outset of this document.

agreed to this and brought me to a kindergarten in Chmielna Street. I was very happy; I let my toys lie and played war with the [other] children. (We made rifles and revolvers for ourselves out of sticks and string.) One camp had its headquarters behind a desk, the other behind [a number of] chairs (Germans [against] Jews and Poles). I did not want to play the Germans because I hated them, but the other boys wanted me to be the commander. Every dead person had to lie on the ground and remain lying there until the game was over. Twice the Germans won, and once the Poles and the Jews. Later the two opposing sides asked the other's pardon, each shook the other's hand,[10] and harmony reigned, but the teacher did not let us play that for a long time as we wanted, because we had to eat, wash our hands, converse with each other, and go home.

DOCUMENT 4-3. **Two children beg on the streets of the Warsaw ghetto, September 1941, USHMMPA WS# 32327, courtesy of Günther Schwarberg.**

---

10. That is, each boy.

"THE GARDEN OF EDEN": EDUCATION IN THE ŁÓDŹ GHETTO

When German forces occupied the city of Łódź in early September 1939, among the initial measures taken by occupation officials was the dissolution of all Jewish community organizations. In their place, they appointed a *Judenrat*, which in the newly created ghetto of Litzmannstadt (Łódź),[11] established in February 1940, came to be known as the ***Ältestenrat*** (Council of Elders). At its head German authorities placed Mordechai Chaim Rumkowski, a former director of the Helenowek Jewish Orphanage in Łódź and a member of the banned Jewish community board. Directly accountable to the German ghetto administration under **Hans Biebow**, Rumkowski wielded extraordinary authority over the internal management of the ghetto, including the appointment of officials, the enforcement of public order, and the administration of goods and services. Rumkowski displayed enormous organizational skill in overseeing the ghettos' workshops and social agencies, but he governed in an autocratic fashion, and contemporaries, like scholars today, viewed him as a controversial and divisive figure.

It remains indisputable, however, that under Rumkowski's leadership, the Łódź ghetto fostered an impressive array of social services. Subordinated under Biebow's jurisdiction, the *Judenrat* controlled the distribution of food, the appropriation of housing, and the management of a functioning postal system, which tied the ghetto to the outside world. Despite a shortage of medical equipment and supplies, the council founded twelve hospitals and clinics and five pharmacies that served ghetto inhabitants until the summer of 1942. Perhaps because of his extensive career as the director of an orphanage, Rumkowski in particular showed a consuming interest in the education and welfare of the ghetto's children. Under his administration, the Jewish Council established some forty-three elementary schools, two high schools, and one vocational-training facility, serving some 63 percent of the ghetto's school-age youngsters. Marysin, the ghetto's "green lung" located in its northeastern corner, was the site of the so-called *Kinderkolonie* (children's colony), which housed sixteen hundred orphans and children of parents with exceptionally limited means. This oasis in the ghetto hosted a library, a cultural center, and a convalescent

---

11. When the Germans occupied Łódź, they renamed the municipality Litzmannstadt, for long-time Nazi Party supporter Karl Litzmann, the German general who had taken the city during World War I.

home for children. Here, away from the urban misery and despair, children could play in Marysin's open fields, surrounded by trees and wildflowers.[12]

On the eve of the Jewish New Year in September 1941, the students and teachers of the Łódź ghetto presented chairman Rumkowski with an album of Rosh Hashanah greetings. Bound in wood and leather, the album contained the signatures of some fourteen thousand pupils and 715 educators who studied or taught in the ghetto's elementary, secondary, or vocational schools. Students from each school created their own distinctive New Year's greeting, like the one below from the pupils of Marysin, to honor the man who had so tirelessly worked to create an autonomous and functioning educational system in the Łódź ghetto.

---

12. See Andrea Löw, *Juden in Getto Litzmannstadt: Lebensbedingungen, Selbstwahrnehmung, Verhalten* (Göttingen: Wallstein Verlag, 2006), esp. 189–91.

DOCUMENT 4-4. **Album page of a New Year's greeting from the children of School No. 25, to Ghetto Elder Mordechai Chaim Rumkowski, Łódź ghetto, September 1941, USHMMPA WS# 22473, courtesy of YIVO Institute (translated from the Hebrew).**

May You Be Written Down and Sealed,[13] School 25, Marysin

To you, our dear father, the good angel of children, we the children of School No. 25 wish you a year of happiness and blessing. Our hearts are filled with thanks for the food for the body and the soul which you satisfy us with day by day. And for the wonderful vision, a Garden of Eden, which you grant us.

Ghetto chronicler Josef Zelkowicz was less enthusiastic about the self-sufficiency of the Łódź ghetto as expressed through its social and welfare institutions.

---

13. This traditional Rosh Hashanah greeting suggests that the names of the righteous are inscribed in the Book of Life and therefore "sealed" to live.

A scholar of ethnography and history and a contributor to efforts to record the lives and fates of ghetto inhabitants, Zelkowicz often laced detailed descriptions of ghetto life with biting satire and an underlying criticism of ghetto leaders and their policies.[14] In his poignant 1941 essay "The Breadwinner," he pondered the efficacy of an "autonomous" Łódź ghetto whose inhabitants were reduced to such miserable and degrading circumstances. Concerned with the ubiquitous manifestations of child labor, Zelkowicz seized upon the figure of the young "coal miners," youngsters who rummaged abandoned buildings and fields in the ghetto for materials that might be sold for heating fuel on the black market. These soot-covered children were a common site in Łódź and grew in number as more and more young people found in "mining" an outlet to provide an income for their families. In a ghetto that prided itself on its educational system, Zelkowicz made it plain that not every child was going to school.

DOCUMENT 4-5. **Diary essay of Josef Zelkowicz, "The Breadwinner (The Seventh Apartment)," 1941, in Josef Zelkowicz, *In Those Terrible Days: Writings from the Lodz Ghetto*, ed. Michal Unger, trans. Naftali Greenwood (Jerusalem: Yad Vashem, 2002), 63–69.**

Do you remember, Ryva Bramson,[15] attending a public rally in the ghetto where a "senior" ghetto official appeared and described in his speech how the "ghetto kingdom" was organized? Surely you also remember how enthusiastic he was when he spoke about "our" police, "our" postal service, "our" factories, and—the main thing, "our" currency. [. . .][16]

Today you know: if the ghetto is a "kingdom" with "our" police, "our" offices, and "our" high-ranking officials, some higher and others highest, if the ghetto is a "kingdom" whose borders are patrolled

14. See Josef Zelkowicz, *In Those Terrible Days: Writings from the Lodz Ghetto*, ed. Michal Unger, trans. Naftali Greenwood (Jerusalem: Yad Vashem, 2002).

15. In September 1940, German authorities granted a loan of 3 million Reichsmark for ghetto welfare services. Many ghetto inhabitants applied for relief based on the loan, including dozens who falsified their claims. In order to prevent corruption, Chaim Rumkowski ordered inspectors to interview potential applicants for relief in their homes. Josef Zelkowicz numbered among these inspectors, as did his colleague Ryva Bramson. Zelkowicz wrote a number of vignettes in 1940 and 1941 based on his visits to ghetto residents in this capacity in which Bramson served as a foil for his observations.

16. The Łódź ghetto maintained its own currency, which residents dubbed the "chaimke" or "rumki," after Chairman Chaim Rumkowski.

and guarded against any trespasser, then the ghetto also has the natural resources that back "our currency" . . .

In the bowels of the ghetto . . . yellow sand is buried, with which housewives cover the splendid abjection of [their] floors. In the bowels of the ghetto is . . . clay, with which they plug the cracks in the walls and ceilings of the apartments and crypts that they inhabit, and . . . in the bowels of the ghetto, one even finds . . . coal!

The "coal mines" in the ghetto are fly-infested heaps of trash. From dawn to dusk the shafts are filled to overflowing with people large and small, elderly and children—burrowing in the muddy soil, plumbing its innards, rummaging, sifting, sorting. . . .

The "coal" that they mine is offered later on to the homes of citizens and sold for forty pfennigs, fifty pfennigs, or even more per kilogram, depending on its quality and size, and, mainly, demand.

The "coal" is excavated in vacant lots and places where buildings, fences or other structures once stood. It is really just the sooty residue of firewood, bones, stones, or rags. This "coal "doesn't burn at all, but when you lay it on the stove over firewood, it makes the wood burn less quickly: it burns slowly along with the coal. After you stand for a few hours, blowing uninterruptedly into the opening of the stove to keep the fire from dying, the pot with the food inside comes to life. [. . .]

A boy or girl sets out from home in the morning, clutching a carefully weighed, rationed slice of bread—the meal—in one hand and schoolbooks in the other hand. Instead of heading for school, the children head for the "coal mines." They're not miners yet, but they keep their eyes open, and slowly but steadily they learn the technique. [. . .] From now on, Moshe, Chaim, or Mendel are recognized "coal miners" who go about this work with their mothers' and fathers' permission.

Such a "miner," officially recognized, finds an old baking pan or some other old container, pokes holes in it with a nail to use as a sieve, and becomes a contractor himself. As this Chaim, Moshe, or Mendel sinks into the mud up to his neck on a summer day and delivers the results of his labor at dusk, he gradually brings into the business his younger or older brother; sometimes the father too—who in any case has nothing more lucrative to do—or even his mother, who would rather rummage through the trash or carry a load on her stooped back than run a household on nothing.

When this Moshe, Chaim, or Mendel becomes an official "coal miner," his upbringing in Jewish values comes to an end. [. . .] Here in the "coal mine" sit girls who own nothing but the dresses they wear and cannot bear to wear them as they sit in the mud. So they take off their dresses and lay them on the heap. Their unclad bodies are immediately clad with mud and dust. This dusty nakedness, however, is even more alluring. Here, in the "coal mine," boys aged eleven and twelve and girls aged thirteen and fourteen discover mommy's and daddy's secrets. Here, in the coal mine, everyone is equal and everyone sees to nature's demands under each other's noses. Why waste time? [. . .]

Where's Lipa? Twelve-year-old Lipa, does he go to school? [. . .]

No, he doesn't go to school.

Lipa, why don't you go to school?

Because I don't have shoes.

And in the summer, when you could have gone barefoot? Why not?

I didn't go then either! What for? What did they give me in school that I should run to them barefoot?

Reading, writing, and other things: don't you think they're important?

If I knew how to read and write, wouldn't I still be hungry . . . ?

And when you stayed home from school, were you well fed?

Better than in school. I dug coal!

How much did you make from digging coal?

Well, sometimes, a mark, or a mark and a few pfennigs. You gotta be lucky [. . .]!

Lipa, the twelve-year-old "coal miner."

DOCUMENT 4-6. **Children digging for "coal" in the Łódź ghetto, 1941, USHMMPA WS# 61900, courtesy of the YIVO Institute.**

"GIVE ME YOUR CHILDREN": THE "CHILDREN'S ACTIONS"

The Łódź, or Litzmannstadt, ghetto was the longest-lasting entity of its kind in German-occupied Poland. The process of ghettoizing the Jewish communities of Łódź and its surrounding territories began on September 8, 1939, shortly after the German conquest of the city.[17] On April 30, 1940, German civilian authorities under Hans Biebow ordered the enclosure of the ghetto, effectively incarcerating some 164,000 individuals within its walls. Its population experienced a number of harrowing roundups, or **razzias**, in which thousands of Jews and **Roma** were deported to their deaths at the **Chełmno** extermination camp. Yet, even as ghettos in occupied Poland were liquidated one by one—including the largest, the Warsaw ghetto in May 1943—the Łódź ghetto endured

---

17. See Jochen Boehler, *Auftakt zum Vernichtungskrieg: Die Wehrmacht in Polen, 1939* (Frankfurt: Fischer Taschenbuch Verlag, 2006).

as a working entity, until its last inhabitants were deported to the **Auschwitz** concentration camp in August 1944.[18]

The longevity of the Łódź ghetto must be attributed at least in part to the policies of Mordechai Chaim Rumkowski, chairman of its *Judenrat*. A controversial figure who wielded almost dictatorial power over his fellow Jews, Rumkowski believed from the start that the ghetto's best chance for survival lay in cooperating fully with the German officials. As elder of the Jews, he reported directly to the Nazi administration under Hans Biebow. In return, Biebow allowed Rumkowski almost unlimited authority in shaping the Łódź ghetto into a viable working community. Given the enormous obstacles encountered by Jewish communities in German-occupied Poland, "Rumkowski's ghetto" boasted an impressive array of welfare institutions and social services. Under the chairman's auspices, Łódź flourished in its early stages, with workshops, schools, hospitals, a postal system, and a broad range of self-help organizations. Nevertheless, many Jews saw in Rumkowski not a benevolent administrator of the public trust but a collaborator and an "incomparable tyrant"[19] who used German authority to crush all existing opposition and sacrificed the welfare of his fellow Jews in order to maintain his personal power.[20]

From the beginning, Rumkowski felt that providing a labor force in ghetto industries and workshops would make the Łódź ghetto indispensable to German authorities. Under the motto "Labor is our only way," Rumkowski argued that only ghetto industry could stave off liquidation of the ghetto population by the

18. For a detailed discussion of the Łódź ghetto, see Isaiah Trunk, *Łódź Ghetto: A History*, ed. and trans. Robert Moses Shapiro (Bloomington: University of Indiana Press in association with the U.S. Holocaust Memorial Museum, 2006); Lucjan Dobroszycki, ed., *The Chronicle of the Łódź Ghetto, 1941–1944*, trans. Richard Lourie et al. (New Haven, CT: Yale University Press, 1984); Alan Adelson and Robert Lapides, eds., *Łódź Ghetto: Inside a Community under Siege* (New York: Viking, 1989); Peter Klein, *Die "Gettoverwaltung Litzmannstadt," 1940–1944: Eine Dienststelle im Spannungsfeld von Kommunalbürokratie und staatlicher Verfolgungspolitik* (Hamburg: Hamburger Edition, 2009); Löw, Juden in Getto Litzmannstadt.

19. This phrase comes from Łódź ghetto survivor Yehuda Leib Gerst in his *From the Straits* (Jerusalem: Safra Fund, 1949), 26.

20. For a discussion of the debate surrounding Rumkowski's role as chairman of the Łódź ghetto, see Michal Unger, *Reassessment of the Image of Mordechai Chaim Rumkowski* (Jerusalem: Yad Vashem, 2004); Richard Rubenstein, "Gray into Black: The Case of Mordecai Chaim Rumkowski," in *Gray Zones: Ambiguity and Compromise in the Holocaust and Its Aftermath*, ed. Jonathan Petropoulos and John K. Roth (New York: Berghahn Books, 2005), 299–310.

German civilian administration.[21] In early December 1941, as the Chełmno extermination camp began gassing operations, the first deportations to that killing center took place. By May of 1942, some fifty thousand Jews and five thousand Roma[22] from Łódź had been deported to their deaths there. In time, word reached the ghetto's *Judenrat* concerning the true significance of this Nazi "resettlement" policy. In similar circumstances, the chairman of Warsaw's *Judenrat,* Adam Czerniakow, took his own life rather than participate in the preparation of deportation lists.[23] In stark contrast, Rumkowski cooperated, stressing even more vehemently the necessity for compliance with Nazi policies and emphasizing the imperative of maintaining a viable forced labor workforce to ensure the ghetto's long-term survival.

Following these initial roundups, the ghetto experienced a brief period of calm. In the late summer of 1942, however, German authorities approached Rumkowski with demands for an additional twenty thousand deportees from Łódź. Following unsuccessful efforts on the part of the *Judenrat* to reverse these orders, Rumkowski seized upon a desperate and terrible solution; he would fill the required quota with the ghetto's least productive members: the ailing, the aged, and children under ten. On September 4, 1942, Mordechai Chaim Rumkowski, a man who had spent much of his career advancing the welfare of youngsters, addressed the ghetto's parents in a now infamous speech. "Give me your children!" he pleaded, in order to avert a communitywide deportation.

Rumkowski's appeal preceded the *Gehsperre* (curfew) in Łódź. In the days between September 5 and 12, German forces entered the ghetto and proceeded block by block, brutally seizing those unfit for labor from their homes and from the community's streets. The *Gehsperre* began with the liquidation of the ghetto hospitals, where SS officials apprehended ailing patients in their beds. In the days that followed, police units, with great violence, cleared schoolrooms and orphanages, many of them in Marysin, once a haven for Łódź's youngsters. Of the approximately 15,500 individuals rounded up for deportation, the vast majority were young children and adults over the age of sixty-five. Those attempting to evade arrest were summarily shot. Heartrending scenes

---

21. See Hanno Loewy et al., eds., "*Unser einziger Weg ist Arbeit*": *Das Getto in Łódź, 1940–1944* (Vienna: Löcker Verlag, 1990).

22. From September 5 to 9, 1941, some five thousand Roma were deported to Łódź and concentrated in their own area of the ghetto, known as the *Zigeunerlager* (Gypsy camp). These individuals were among the first to be included in the initial deportation actions to Chełmno.

23. See Adam Czerniakow, *The Warsaw Diary of Adam Czerniakow,* ed. Raul Hilberg et al. (New York: Ivan R. Dee, 1979.)

took place along the length of wire fence at the ghetto's central prison, where family members bid farewell to their loved ones awaiting deportation to their deaths at Chełmno.

Following the bloody week of the *Gehsperre*, no further deportations from Łódź to the extermination camps occurred for the next year and a half. For Rumkowski, the cessation of roundups within the ghetto vindicated his policy of compliance with German demands. However, in the late spring of 1944, Nazi authorities decided to liquidate this last large ghetto existing in German-occupied Poland. From June 23 to July 15, 1944, seven thousand Jews from the Łódź ghetto were deported to Chełmno, which Nazi authorities had reactivated as a killing center in order to support the action. Then, in August, transports carrying the ghetto's remaining seventy-four thousand inhabitants turned toward Auschwitz. Among these deportees was Mordechai Chaim Rumkowski, whose moral ambiguity as chairman of the Łódź ghetto continues to engage scholars in the debate concerning collaboration. Rumkowski died, together with his family, in **Auschwitz II–Birkenau** on August 28, 1944.

DOCUMENT 4-7. **Speech of Mordechai Chaim Rumkowski, Łódź ghetto, September 4, 1942, in Isaiah Trunk,** *Łódź Ghetto: A History*, **ed. and trans. Robert Moses Shapiro (Bloomington: University of Indiana Press in association with the U.S. Holocaust Memorial Museum, 2006), 272–75.**

A severe blow has befallen the ghetto. They are asking from it the best that it possesses—children and old people. I have not had the privilege to have a child of my own, and therefore I devoted the best of my years to children. I lived and breathed together with the children. I never imagined that my own hands would have to deliver the sacrifice to the altar. In my old age, I must stretch out my hands and beg: Brothers and sisters, give them to me! Fathers and mothers, give me your children! (Tremendous and dreadful weeping among the assembled crowd.)

I had the premonition that something was descending upon us. I anticipated "something" and I stood constantly on alert like a guard, in order to avoid that "something." But I could not do it, because I did not know what was menacing us. I did not know what is awaiting us.

That the sick were taken away from the hospitals, this was for me totally unanticipated. You have the best sign: I had my own kin and near ones there and I could not do anything for them. I thought that it would end with this, that after that we would be left in peace. This is the peace for which I yearn so strongly, for which I have always worked and striven, but it turned out that something different was predestined for us. The luck of Jews is of course thus: always to suffer more and worse, particularly in wartime.

Yesterday during the day, I was given a command to send twenty-odd thousand Jews out from the ghetto; if not—"We will do it." And the question arose, "Should we take it over and do it ourselves, or leave it for others to carry out?" But being dominated not by the thought, "How many will be lost," but by the thought, "How many can be saved," we, i.e., I and my closest co-workers, came to the conclusion that as difficult as this will be for us, we must take into our own hands the carrying out of the decree. I have to carry out this difficult and bloody operation. I must cut off limbs in order to save the body! I must take children because, if not, others could also, God forbid, be taken . . . (Frightful wailing).

I have not come today to console you. Nor have I come today to calm you, but to uncover all your sorrow and pain. I have come like a robber to take away from you the best from under your hearts! I tried with all my abilities to get the decree revoked. After trying to get it revoked was impossible, I attempted to moderate it. Just yesterday, I arranged a registration of all nine-year-old children. I wanted to rescue at least that single year, from nine to ten years old. But they did not want to grant this to me. One thing I succeeded [in]—to save the children from ten years and up. Let this be our comfort in our great sorrow. [. . .]

I understand you, mothers. I see your tears quite well. I also feel your hearts, fathers, that tomorrow, immediately after your child will have been taken away from you, you will have to go to work, while just yesterday you still played with your dear kids. I know all of this and I feel it. Since four o'clock yesterday, since I found out about the decree, I am entirely broken down. I am living with your grief and your pain torments me and I don't know how and with what strength I will be able to survive it. I must disclose to you a secret: twenty-four thousand victims were demanded. Through eight days of three thousand people each day, but I succeeded in pushing the number down to twenty thousand, even less than twenty thousand, but on condition that there will be children up to ten years old. Children from ten years and up are secure. Since the children together with the elderly give only a number of approximately thirteen thousand souls, it will be necessary to fill the gap with sick people too.

It is difficult for me to speak. I don't have any strength, I only want to say to you my request: Help me carry out the action! I am trembling. I fear that others will, God forbid, take over the implementation into their hands. . . .

A broken Jew is standing before you. Don't envy me. It is the most difficult decree that I have ever had to carry out. I extend to you my broken, trembling arms and I beg: give the victims into my hands, in order through them to avoid additional victims, in order to protect a congregation of a hundred thousand Jews. They promised me so: if we ourselves will deliver our victims, there will be calm. . . . (Yells are heard: "We'll all go"; "Mr. Chairman, not only-children should be taken—individual children should be taken away from those who have several!" . . .) These are empty phrases! I don't have any strength to conduct discussions with you! If someone will come from the authorities, no one [would] yell. . . .

I understand what it means to tear off a limb from the body. Yesterday, I pleaded on my knees, but it was no use. From small towns that possessed seven thousand to eight thousand Jews, barely a thousand have arrived here. What then is better? What are you asking for? To leave eighty thousand to ninety thousand Jews or, God forbid, to annihilate everybody? . . . Judge as you wish; my obligation is to take care of the remnant of Jews. I am not talking to hotheads—I am speaking to your reason and conscience. I have done everything and will also continue to do everything to prevent weapons being brought into the streets and that blood be shed. . . . The decree did not permit us to get it revoked; it only allowed itself to be reduced.

One needs the heart of a bandit in order to ask for what I am asking of you. But put yourself in my position and think logically and you yourself will come to the conclusion that you cannot act differently, because the number of the portion that can be saved is much larger than the part that must be surrendered.

DOCUMENT 4-8. **Children selected for deportation bid farewell to their families through the wire fence of the central prison during the *Gehsperre* action in the Łódź ghetto, September 1942, USHMMPA WS# 30057, courtesy of Beit Lohamei Haghetaot.**

A large percentage of the 15,500 persons deported to Chełmno from the Łódź ghetto in September 1942 were young inhabitants under the age of ten. Because young children were not usually utilized for forced labor, Nazi authorities viewed them as "useless eaters" and targeted them for early deportation measures. So-called children's actions like the one associated with the *Gehsperre* occurred in many of the major ghettos in German-occupied eastern Europe. In two shooting operations known collectively as the Dünamünde Action, for example, Latvian auxiliaries attached to the *Einsatzgruppen* removed thirty-eight hundred Jews from the Riga ghetto and massacred them in the nearby Bikernieke Forest on March 15 and 26, 1942.[24] Young children, the ailing, and the aged represented a majority of these victims. In Vilna and Kovno, large-scale actions against inhabitants and their family members who did not possess work certificates (*Scheine*) radically reduced the number of young persons in each ghetto. In addition a children's action directed against Kovno's still significant

---

24. For a discussion of deportations from the Riga ghetto, see Andrej Angrick and Peter Klein, *Final Solution in Riga: Exploitation and Annihilation*, trans. Ray Brandon (New York: Berghahn Books, 2009).

number of young residents took place on March 27 and 28, 1944.[25] On those days, German forces and their auxiliaries sent at least thirteen hundred children to the Auschwitz concentration camp and to the nearby massacre site at the infamous **Fort IX**, where these victims were shot to death. In the Warsaw ghetto, the largest such community in German-occupied eastern Europe, the first large-scale deportation efforts targeted the most defenseless members of that population. Beginning on July 22, 1942, SS troops rounded up thousands of the ghetto's young children and sent them to their deaths at the **Treblinka** extermination camp some eighty kilometers (fifty miles) northwest of Warsaw.[26] Many of these first young deportees were homeless and abandoned children or youngsters living with their families in the so-called death houses, where the very poorest strata of Warsaw's Jewish community found shelter. Approximately one week later, the director of the ghetto's **CENTOS** relief agency, Adolf Avraham Berman,[27] received word that all orphanage officials under his administration were to prepare their charges to join in the next wave of deportations. The CENTOS organization represented an arm of the **American Jewish Joint Distribution Committee** founded specifically to address the needs of Jewish orphans and children living in impoverished circumstances. Within the context of the Warsaw ghetto, CENTOS operatives, with the aid and good will of *Judenrat* officials, developed a broad network of institutions that provided relief to the ghetto's poorest youngsters. Under its auspices, CENTOS founded soup kitchens, homes, and dormitories for the many hundreds of destitute children who begged, and starved, in the ghetto's city streets. CENTOS also supported educational programs and youth clubs for young people.[28]

---

25. See Dennis Klein et al., *A Hidden History of the Kovno Ghetto* (Boston: Little, Brown & Co., 1997).

26. For a discussion of the Treblinka killing center, see Alexander Donat, ed., *The Death Camp Treblinka: A Documentary* (New York: Holocaust Library, 1979); Richard Glazar: *Trap with a Green Fence*, trans. Roslyn Theobald (Evanston, IL: Northwestern University Press, 1995); and Yizhak Arad, *Belzec, Sobibor, Treblinka: The Operation Reinhard Death Camps* (Bloomington: Indiana University Press, 1987).

27. Adolf Avraham Berman (1906–1978) was a Zionist activist and politician active in the Warsaw ghetto underground. A psychologist by training, Berman served as the director of CENTOS until September 1942. In the midst of the mass deportations of Jews from the ghetto, Berman and his wife succeeded in fleeing to Warsaw's "Aryan side." Passing as a gentile, he survived the war, functioning as a general secretary with the Żegota, the Polish Council to Aid Jews. In 1950, he emigrated to Israel, where he served briefly as a member of the Knesset. In 1961, Berman testified at the Eichmann Trial in Jerusalem.

28. See Barbara Engelking and Jacek Leociak, *The Warsaw Ghetto: A Guide to a Perished City*, trans. Emma Harris (New Haven, CT: Yale University Press, 2009).

After receiving notification that SS officials would begin clearing the ghetto's orphanages, Berman attempted to mobilize ghetto authorities in defense of the children, in vain. Each day Berman witnessed SS troops leading columns of young orphans under his charge to the *Umschlagplatz*, the loading area where deportees boarded freight trains bound for Treblinka.

One of the orphanages under Berman's jurisdiction stood under the management of the famous **Janusz Korczak**, pen name of eminent pediatrician, pedagogue, and children's author Henryk Goldszmit. Korczak was born in Warsaw to assimilated Jewish parents on July 22, 1878. After studying medicine at the University of Warsaw, he set up a pediatric practice at the Berson-Baumann Children's Hospital in the Polish capital in 1904. While working for the Polish Orphan's Society in 1909, he met Stefania Wilczyńska (1886–1942), a gifted pedagogue who would become his closest associate. In 1911, Korczak came to direct his own orphanage, Dom Seriot, which incorporated his innovative approaches to child care. By the 1930s, Korczak was a celebrity in his native Poland. Over the course of his career, he had founded Poland's first national children's newspaper, written influential books on parenting and child psychology, and worked within the juvenile court system to defend the rights of children and adolescents. His most famous children's book, *King Matt the First*, had become a beloved classic in many languages, and Korczak himself hosted a syndicated radio program in which he dispensed advice on child rearing and family matters.[29]

As director of a Jewish and a Catholic orphanage, Korczak witnessed the occupation of Warsaw by German forces. In 1940 when German authorities established the Warsaw ghetto, Korczak moved with his young Jewish charges inside the ghetto's walls. His many Gentile friends offered to hide him on the "Aryan side," but Korczak refused. "You do not leave a sick child in the night," he said, "and you do not leave children at a time like this."[30] Korczak's orphanage within the ghetto remained a model of progressive reform. Even in the midst of the terrible deprivations imposed by ghetto life, Korczak provided a safe haven for hundreds of orphans, protecting them from disease and starvation. In August 1942, however, he could no longer shield his charges from the brutal effects of Nazi policy. On August 5, 1942, SS officials ordered

---

29. For further discussion of the life and works of Janusz Korczak, see Betty Jean Lifton, *The King of Children: A Biography of Janusz Korczak* (New York: Farrar, Straus & Giroux, 1988); Janusz Korczak, *Ghetto Diary* (New Haven, CT: Yale University Press, 2003); Janusz Korczak, *King Matt the First*, trans. Richard Lourie (New York: Farrar, Straus & Giroux, 1986).

30. Lifton, *The King of Children*, 3.

the 192 children living at the orphanage to appear with their caregivers for deportation.[31] Aides cautioned Janusz Korczak that, as director of the facility, he did not have to join the children, but he and his chief associate, Stefania Wilczyńska, prepared the young children as best they could, ensuring that each had a favorite stuffed animal, book, or toy, and emerged from the building with the youngsters. Many eyewitnesses, including Warsaw CENTOS director Adolf Berman, who recalled the event in testimony at the **Eichmann Trial** in 1961, observed a dignified Korczak, leading with Wilczyńska the solemn procession of children through the ghetto streets to the roundup point, some two miles away. When the group reached the *Umschlagplatz*, Jewish, and by some accounts also German, policemen on the scene attempted to intervene to save the celebrated educator. Korczak refused to abandon the children and, with Wilczyńska, boarded the train with his charges. The group was gassed upon arrival at Treblinka.

DOCUMENT 4-9. **Testimony of Adolf Avraham Berman, May 3, 1961, in *The Trial of Adolf Eichmann: Record of Proceedings in the District Court of Jerusalem* (Jerusalem: Trust for the Publication of the Proceedings of the Eichmann Trial in cooperation with the Israel State Archives and Yad Vashem, the Holocaust Martyrs' and Heroes' Remembrance Authority, 1992–1995), 1:425–26.**

Presiding Judge: What is your full name?

Witness: Adolf Avraham Berman. [. . .]

Q: After the outbreak of the Second World War, you were one of the directors of "CENTOS" in Warsaw?

A: Yes. [. . .]

Q: Tell us what the position was of children in the Warsaw ghetto in those years in which you served as director of the institution?

A: The tragedy of the Jewish children began on 8 September 1939, on the day Hitler's forces entered Warsaw, the capital of Poland. Then the position was such that the authorities conducted a policy of systematic and planned starvation, they conducted a policy which led to epidemics, first of all to typhus and also to the spread of tuberculosis.

Q: Is it true that the incidence of death amongst the Jewish children reached thousands per month?

---

31. Eyewitness sources differ as to whether the date of this particular deportation action was August 5 or 6; likewise, some contemporary records suggest that 196, not 192, children were affected.

A: Yes. This process of pauperization, of continually increasing poverty of the masses, cast a multitude of children onto the streets. What did they turn into? To street children and little beggars. [. . .]

Q: How many of them needed the help and care of "CENTOS"?

A: Generally speaking, it may be said that within the Jewish population of the Warsaw ghetto, which at its peak period reached almost half a million Jews [. . .]—here were more than 100,000 children. Of these 100,000 children, at least seventy-five percent were in need of aid.

Q: To how many of these did you manage to extend help in the institutions of "CENTOS"?

A: As soon as we saw that a huge disaster was coming, we decided to mobilize ourselves for an extensive operation for the rescue of children, thanks to a great effort on the part of the organized Jewish community in the Warsaw ghetto, thanks to the unity in this matter of all those involved, from the left to the right, we managed to set up a large network of institutions for the aid of children. We had about one hundred institutions and we succeeded in giving help to 25,000 Jewish children.

Q: Amongst these institutions there was one headed by the well-known pedagogue Janusz Korczak—is that right?

A: Yes.

Q: You established tens of dormitories and kitchens for children and day shelters and kitchens for children and youths?

A: We set up thirty orphanages and dormitories also for the street children. In these dormitories and orphanages there were about 4,000 children. Amongst these institutions there was also the well-known orphanage headed by that genius educator and distinguished writer, children's writer, Janusz Korczak, whose name used to be Dr. Henryk Goldszmit, whose books and whose methods were both exceedingly famous in Poland. Apart from this, we established about twenty day shelters, especially for the small children. In addition to this, we set up about twenty kitchens for children. We also established about thirty children's and youth clubs for the children of the refugee houses. We wanted to take advantage of every corner of vegetation for the children who had never known what greenery was, what a forest was, what a flower was.

Q: You maintained a widespread education network in the underground, since education was forbidden?

A: Yes.

Presiding Judge: Was all education forbidden?

Witness Berman: Vocational education was possible to some extent, but general education was banned. Under cover of the children's kitchens and other institutions, we maintained a large network of secret underground schools, of all trends—from the secular to the religious, from the left to the right, in complete unity.[32]

Attorney General: You observed children's festivals under the slogan "Give the child a little joy." Is that correct?

Witness Berman: Yes. I would like to say a few words about this. We saw what the situation was, and we wanted to make the melancholy and terrible life of tens of thousands of children easier. We then decided to organize a Month of the Jewish Child in the ghetto and also a Jewish children's festival in the ghetto. The last festival before the awful "action" which commenced on 22 July 1942, we had already celebrated on 5 May. And on that day—I remember this well—in all our institutions, in all the orphanages, in all the dormitories, in all the kitchens, there were celebrations. There were performances of children, on that day the children were given slightly more food, some sweets. And our slogan was "Give our children a little joy."

Q: But all this was in vain, Dr. Berman. You kept the children busy, [but they were to] be the victims of the "actions," isn't that so? And the children were the first victims of the "actions," is that correct?

A: Correct. I would like to say that almost from the outset the tragic race began between the efforts of the Jewish community in the Warsaw ghetto and the policy of mass impoverishment and general decline—the race between social aid and starvation. Our watchword was naturally to save our children from hunger and from death. We did not save them. We did not succeed in saving them.

Q: Do you recall attacks especially directed against children, on the part of German units?

A: Yes.

Q: Which units?

A: First of all, SS units. This I would like to describe somewhat in detail. As is known, the first large "action" of the extermination of Jews [in the ghetto] began on 22 July 1942. On that day, the first victims of the "action" were the Jewish children and I shall never forget the shocking, the frightful scenes, when SS men together with their collaborators cruelly fell

---

32. For a discussion of clandestine learning in the ghettos of German-occupied Europe, see chapter 8.

upon the children, on the street children, and dragged them onto carts. And I remember how these children defended themselves. To this day I can hear the crying of the children—I hear the screams "Mama, Mama! *Rette, rette!*" ["Save us! Save us!"] They put up a struggle.

Q: Did they burst into your institutions?

A: On the same day also the expulsion from the refugee homes commenced and especially from the death houses, as they called them then, where there was the greatest mortality rate. And amongst them they deported many, many thousands of children to Treblinka. The inferno lasted thus for about a week.

Q: What happened to your institutions, those of "CENTOS?"

A: After one week the SS men and their collaborators began to attack our institutions as well, including the orphanages and the dormitories. We then informed all the institutions in the name of the "CENTOS" management—all the institutions in the ghetto and also Police Headquarters in the ghetto—that the orphans must be saved, the children must be saved. No entreaties on our part, no requests of ours, saved them, and during these days long columns of the children of our institutions, institution after institution, together with their tutors, with their teachers, began to march through the streets of Warsaw.

Q: Where were they marching to?

A: To the *Umschlagplatz*, to the death [cars], and from there to Treblinka.

Q: Do you remember Janusz Korczak marching at the head of the procession?

A: Yes, I remember that well. One of those institutions which they were leading off to the *Umschlagplatz* was this outstanding and exemplary institution, the orphanage of Janusz Korczak. It was a shocking procession.

Presiding Judge: You saw this with your own eyes?

Witness Berman: Yes. He walked at the head of the procession, and next to him there were two small children. Behind him was the chief woman tutor, Stefania Wilczyńska, together with little children. They marched together with the huge crowd of Jews who had been caught in this blockade, in this terrible siege in this quarter. When they reached the *Umschlagplatz*, there were certain policemen there who ran to free Janusz Korczak. He was very well known and beloved.

Attorney General: Polish policemen?

Witness Berman: Jewish. But then he said that he didn't want to be separated from the children whom he had taught. The sole worry of Janusz

Korczak then was that the children who were forced to [come out] . . . at the shouts I remember to this day: "*Alle herunter, alle herunter, schneller, heraus*" ["Everybody out, everybody out, faster, out!"]—this I shall never forget, the "*alle herunter*"; at that time Janusz Korczak's concern was that the children did not have enough time to get dressed—they were bare-footed. Stefania Wilczyńska told the small children that they were going on an outing, that at long last they would see the fields and the forests, and the flowers that they had never seen in the ghetto. And there was a smile, a faint smile on her lips. Of course, after he refused, after several hours, they made them enter the death wagons, and this was the last journey of this great educator.

DEATH AND SURVIVAL IN THE GHETTO

One of the cardinal features of ghetto life in German-occupied eastern Europe was hunger. The general policy of German administrators was to provide ghettoized communities with only a modicum of resources necessary to fulfill their basic needs. Warsaw ghetto inhabitants in 1941, for example, typically received a maximum allocation of 2.5 kilograms (5.5 pounds) of bread each month.[33] The minuscule allotments available through the ration card system meant that residents had to acquire additional food by other means: through legitimate channels, such as soup kitchens, schools, and welfare associations, or illegally, through the omnipresent black market. As the war progressed, ration allowances diminished consistently, with terrible consequences for the captive population. In most ghettos, moreover, the number of ration cards available to each individual was invariably tied to participation in the forced labor pool, so persons unable to work and their dependents soon succumbed to severe malnutrition. Children suffered particularly under these conditions, especially those youngsters who had been orphaned or abandoned by their parents. Hundreds of children begged or sold improvised wares in the streets of ghettos such as Warsaw and Łódź in order to survive or to help subsidize their family's meager rations. Many died on those streets too, of starvation and neglect.

While malnutrition played an outward and visible role in undermining the ghetto community, it also represented a destabilizing and divisive element in the homes and kitchens of ghetto inhabitants. "The hunger grows stronger," Łódź ghetto chronicler Oskar Rosenfeld reported in his diary in 1942. "One person becomes the enemy of the other. The son takes the [last] bite away from

---

33. Engelking and Leociak, *The Warsaw Ghetto*, 417.

his father. Everyone has lost their feeling for how to live normally."[34] In March 1942, an anonymous diarist captured an image of a family divided by hunger. We know little about the young writer, except that she lived in the Łódź ghetto with her parents and two elder siblings. She was called either Esther or Minia because a passage in her diary cites a letter addressed to herself and her sister using these names. As the only person in her household who did not work, the teenager[35] remained home alone for much of the day. In two entries in her journal, dated March 10 and 11, she records her daylong and often futile struggle to refrain from eating the entirety of her daily rations in one sitting—and those of her absent family as well. The teenager's shame at devouring provisions meant for her entire household was compounded by the perceived restraint and self-sacrifice manifested by her parents. It is unknown whether this young diarist survived hunger and disease in Łódź or perished in the deportations that decimated the ghetto's population. A fragment of her diary detailing the winter and spring months of 1942 was found in the ruins of the Łódź ghetto in July 1945.

DOCUMENT 4-10. **Diary of an anonymous girl, Łódź ghetto, entries for March 10 and 11, 1942, in Alexandra Zapruder, ed.,** *Salvaged Pages: Young Writers' Diaries of the Holocaust* **(New Haven, CT: Yale University Press, 2002), 236–38.**

Tuesday, March 10, 1942

My mom, brother, and sister leave for work at seven-thirty in the morning. My father leaves at 8:00. Lying in bed, I noticed that my sister had forgotten her bread. I got dressed very quickly and brought it to her. [. . .] I have no idea why I don't live more harmoniously with my sister. We fight all the time and scream at each other. I must cause my parents a lot of worry. My sister doesn't look well. She is like a stranger to me.

The hunger is getting worse. In the morning I want my father to leave as soon as possible. Then I jump up from my bed and consume all the bread my mom has left me for the entire day. My God, what has happened to me? I [don't] know how to restrain myself. Then I starve all day. I wish I were different. God, take pity on me. During the day I drink tap water and vinegar left from the pickled beets. Eating only this I wait until seven o'clock. I have a stomachache frequently.

---

34. Diary of Oskar Rosenfeld, quoted in Loewy et al., *Unser einziger Weg*, 235.

35. The diarist had a sister aged seventeen in 1942 and a brother aged sixteen. As the youngest child, the girl in question must have been fifteen years old or younger.

Today they are distributing bread. I stood three hours in the line and got three loaves. When I came back, I just had to take a piece. In the evening I promised myself not to eat, even if my mom offered me some, because I can't have someone else's bread. [. . .]

Everybody is home, except my father. He came back at seven in the evening. We could hardly wait for him. He showed up with his two co-workers. They put two rutabagas on the table and divided each of them into three. It worked out at 70 decagrams (24.7 ounces) each.[36] When they left, my father took out [a few] pieces of rutabaga from his pocket. Two rutabagas had been swiped from the kitchen, but some other scraps were given to my father by the women working there. He knew that there was nothing to eat at home, so he didn't eat them on the spot, although he was very hungry. The soup has been thrown out by one of the apprentices. I can't write anymore, my eyes are filled with tears.

<u>Wednesday March 11, 1942</u>

[. . .] When I went out to the street, I heard that there was a food ration for those who were not getting any food in the kitchen. This ration could be eaten only on the sixteenth.[37] [. . .]

This ration is much worse than the previous one. Terrible hunger is awaiting us again. I got the vegetable ration right away. There is only vinegar and ice in the beets. There is no food, we are going to starve to death. All my teeth ache and I am very hungry. My left leg is frostbitten. I ate almost all the honey. What have I done? I'm so selfish. What are they going to put on their bread now, what will they say? Mom, I'm unworthy of you. You work so hard. Besides working in the workshop, she also moonlights by working for a woman who sells clothes in the street. My mom looks awful, like a shadow. She works very hard. When I wake up at twelve or one o'clock at night, I see her exhaustedly struggling to keep working at the sewing machine. And she gets up at six in the morning. I must have a heart of stone. I'm ruthless. I eat everything I can lay my hands on.

Today I had a fight with my father. I swore at him, even cursed him. It happened because yesterday I weighed twenty decagrams [7 ounces] of *zacierki*[38] and then sneaked a spoonful. When my father came back, he

---

36. A decagram is 1/1,000 of a kilogram, or 10 grams.
37. That is, on March 16.
38. This is a kind of noodle used in Polish cuisine, usually in soup.

immediately noticed that some *zacierki* were missing. My father started yelling at me and he was right. But since the chairman[39] gave out these *zacierki* to be cooked, why can't I have some? I became very upset and cursed my father. What have I done? I regret so much, but it can't be undone. My father is not going to forgive me. How will I ever look him in the eyes? He stood by the window and cried like a baby. Not even a stranger has ever insulted him before [like this]. The whole family witnessed this incident. I went to bed as soon as possible, without dinner. I thought I would die of hunger, because we have our meal only in the evening. I fell asleep and woke up at twelve. My mom was still working at the sewing machine. I couldn't stand the hunger, so I got up and took a piece of meal. We would be a happy family, if I didn't fight with everybody. All the fights are started by me. I must be manipulated by an evil force. I would like to be different, but I don't have a strong enough will. Why isn't there anybody who would guide me, why can't anybody teach me? I hate my sister. She is a stranger to me. God show me what is right.

Starvation was a daily reality of life in the Łódź ghetto and in other communities of its kind. Because the German administration essentially intended to sustain only the ghetto's labor force over the long term, the rationing system favored "productive" members of the community at the expense of the "unproductive." Those who worked in ghetto workshops, industries, or services received a larger allocation of food than those who had no employment. Thus, a place in the ghetto's labor pool often meant more than a stay from deportation, as it literally did for carriers of work certificates (*Scheine*) in ghettos like Kovno or Vilna; a work position, however humble or low paying, also represented a vital lifeline, providing the ghetto's working community with the very sustenance its members needed to survive.

A significant amount of the forced labor carried out in the ghettos of German-occupied eastern Europe was performed by children. Of course such labor provided youngsters with their most basic nutritional needs and helped to lessen the burden on impoverished households. Likewise, in the upside-down world of the ghetto, older children and juveniles often shouldered tremendous responsibilities for the upkeep of their families. In such an environment, these young people might represent their household's sole source of income. In July

---

39. That is, Ghetto Elder Rumkowski.

1942, writer Oskar Singer[40] chronicled the life of such a youngster, sixteen-year-old Alfred B. from Prague.[41] Following his deportation from the Czech capital to Łódź in October 1941, Singer joined fellow writers, such as Julian Cukier,[42] **Josef Zelkowicz**, and Oskar Rosenfeld, in assembling material for their *Ghetto Chronicle*,[43] which would collect pertinent data and statistics concerning the Łódź ghetto and portray the lives and deaths of its inhabitants. In one of his most poignant entries, Singer traces the story of a young Czech Jew arriving in the Łódź ghetto in the early winter of 1941 to 1942. Alfred B. is a likeable and capable young man, who immediately finds work with a construction battalion in order to bolster his family's precarious circumstances. All goes well until a minor accident at the worksite causes the teenager to lose his position. Alfred's fate is a tragic example of how Nazi ghettoization policy cost a generation of Jewish youth their lives.

DOCUMENT 4-11. Diary of Oskar Singer, entry for July 28, 1942, in Hanno Loewy et al., eds., *"Unser einziger Weg ist Arbeit": Das Getto in Łódź, 1940–1944* (Vienna: Löcker Verlag, 1990), 221–22 (translated from the German).

With his parents and a sister, Alfred B. came from Prague to the Litzmannstadt [Łódź] ghetto. Just sixteen years old, Alfred has graduated from an agricultural *Hachscharah*[44] as a member of the Maccabi Hazair.[45] His comrades loved him for his kindly, helpful ways. Arriving in the ghetto, he is the first in the family immediately to seek work and receives a place in a construction battalion. After him his mother succeeds in getting work in a straw shoe workshop. She puts in honest labor in order to share her soup with her husband and daughter. She comes from a wealthy, respectable family in Prague. Alfred's father was an attorney in Prague. Shortly before the journey here he had a serious operation upon his stom-

---

40. Born in 1883 in Prague, Oskar Singer was an author and journalist, writing for such Czech and Jewish newspapers as the *Prager Tagblatt* (*Czech Daily*) and the *Jüdische Nachrichten* (*Jewish News*). In August 1944, Singer was deported to Auschwitz where he perished.

41. Singer abbreviated his subject's surname to protect the young man's privacy.

42. Julian Cukier (1900–1943) is better known by his pen name, Stanisław Cerski.

43. See Dobroszycki, *The Chronicle of the Łódź Ghetto*.

44. This refers to a vocational-training program aimed at training Jewish youths for emigration to Palestine.

45. This refers to a Zionist youth organization.

ach, and came, so to speak, with half a stomach to the ghetto. He dared not undertake physical labor. [. . .]

Alfred carries heavy burdens. But he is still aided by the reserves of strength he has stored up before his arrival. In a good mood he goes early in the morning to his daily work. Alfred is a strong youth; he will survive this ghetto adventure. The same cannot be guaranteed of his father. He is visibly falling apart, although he only has half a stomach. Alfred suffers from hunger, but he does not complain very much. But his parents observe with deep concern that he is losing so much weight. But everyone in the ghetto is losing weight. Everyone will lose several pounds, but Alfred will survive all that. [. . .]

One day Alfred comes home with a slight injury to his leg. Mother treats the insignificant wound carefully. Nevertheless it becomes infected. In the ghetto no wound will heal properly, and an infection not at all. The body does not have any defenses; the cells are helplessly abandoned to decay. Alfred cannot work for several weeks. Whoever does not work receives no soup, and later when an additional piece of bread replaces the soup ration, receives no bread. That lack is felt acutely. Father searches frantically for work. [. . .]

Alfred suffers terribly from his unemployment. He sees how his mother is overworked and then gives her worker's rations to the children and his father. He pulls himself together and looks for work. Perhaps he can find something easier in one of the many workshops. No, he finds nothing, because now the sixteen-year-olds have to arrange things through the school department. A little patronage helps a bit. Someone puts in a good word for this upstanding young man. Because in Prague he attended the school of the Youth Aliyah and learned metalworking, he finally succeeds in getting a place in a metal workshop. It pays almost nothing, but the main thing is the bread and sausage! Every worker gets that now because there is no longer any soup. That works for a few days. But the department director is no do-gooder. He expects production. Even in the ghetto one wants to get ahead. Alfred cannot get lighter work. He wishes himself back at the lathe in Prague where he learned his trade and where one could just stand and work and did not have to carry heavy pieces of metal up and down the stairs.

It doesn't work. He has to give up all the walking, has to stay at home again, must lie down. In the meantime he loses a frightening amount of weight. The skin clings like a transparent membrane to his forehead and nose. The young man is simply not recognizable anymore. At least he wants to help with the housework, while Mother works so hard in the workshop and Father looks for work without ceasing. He carries the heaviest water buckets from the courtyard up two flights of stairs to the miserable apartment, stands in the long line before the stores; sometimes he still has enough energy to contend with those behind him in line, who would like to drive him from the queue.

Then at home he must lie quietly. The physician thinks that his heart is not working quite right. Certainly better nutrition would help, but there is nothing to be done about that. Alfred knows for certain. Whoever does not work here must die. He does not want to die! Again he seeks out a benefactor. He manages this with certain difficulty, and obtains a place in a carpentry shop. The director is already well informed. He has seen the young man and will manage to give him very light tasks. The school department does not make any difficulties. Alfred can start already tomorrow morning. But tomorrow . . . tomorrow, that means that today there will be no bread with sausage. And yesterday already he had nothing to eat. That is already two days. But things can't be hurried along. Introduced yesterday and starting tomorrow—what more can one ask? How many in the ghetto are that lucky? Alfred is certainly a rare exception. All right, we will have to wait till morning, then there will be light work and bread with sausage. Good, says Albert, we'll wait, starve until morning, that is only one more night.

But in the morning, he cannot go to work, he cannot begin his easy tasks, and cannot eat his bread with sausage. Tomorrow—there will be no tomorrow for him. Alfred did not wake up. Today he will already lie in Marysin.[46] Perhaps this would not have happened if yesterday he had just had his bread and sausage.

---

46. This was the ghetto's "green lung," where the cemetery was located.

DOCUMENT 4-12. **Jewish children work at a box-making factory in the Glubokoye ghetto, Belorussia, c. early 1942, USHMMPA WS# 08059, courtesy of Karl Katz.**

In ghettos across German-occupied Europe, Nazi persecutory policies decimated a generation of young people, through starvation, disease, deportation, and murder. In many ghettoized communities, German administrators employed an additional measure to ensure the eventual extinction of the "Jewish race": a ban on Jewish births. The cruel realities of ghetto life surely discouraged couples from reproducing and from forming large families. Moreover, malnutrition and heavy labor caused the onset of amenorrhea[47] in a large proportion of women of reproductive age. For these reasons, birthrates in most ghettos were already extremely low; in Łódź, only 2,306 babies were born in the ghetto in the four years of its existence (1940–1944), relative to an initial population of 164,000.[48] Nevertheless, in 1942 German authorities

47. This refers to the temporary cessation of menstruation in women of child-bearing age. Deficits in caloric and protein intake often caused this condition, which was also widely reported among women prisoners of reproductive age in the Nazi concentration camp system. Most women with this disorder who survived to liberation found that their normal menstrual cycles were restored on return to a balanced and nutritious diet.

48. Leah Preiss, "Women's Health in the Ghettoes of Eastern Europe," *Jewish Women's Archive*, http://jwa.org/encyclopedia/author/preiss-leah (accessed January 22, 2010).

in Lithuania issued a number of decrees prohibiting Jewish births in the ghettos of Vilna, Kovno, and Shavli (Sauliai). In Kovno, a July 1942 edict forbade
both pregnancies and births in that ghetto. Gynecologists such as Dr. Aharon
Peretz,[49] whose chief occupation had been the delivery of babies, now found
that his major work consisted in terminating pregnancies. Initially, Peretz
reported, the decree, viewed as a propaganda maneuver, had not been taken
seriously; thus, a large part of the physician's efforts lay in informing women
of the dire consequences that resulted from disobeying the order. The ghetto
health administration arranged the medical services for most abortions; ghetto
policemen escorted women in advanced stages of pregnancy to the hospital to
enforce the procedure. As the prohibition went into effect, German authorities
announced that women then in their eighth and ninth months of pregnancy
would be permitted to carry their babies to term; all other pregnancies were
to be terminated. Peretz suddenly found himself confronted with complicated
surgeries for those women who required late-term abortions. In all cases, the
ghetto's crowded and unhygienic conditions and the lack of medicine and
other supplies compounded his moral and material difficulties. Many women
tried to defy the ban and delivered their infants in secret, often with terrible
consequences for both mother and child. In May 1961, Peretz testified at the
Eichmann Trial in Jerusalem concerning the effects of this policy on the Kovno
ghetto population.

DOCUMENT 4-13. **Testimony of Dr. Aharon Peretz, May 4, 1961, in *The Trial of
Adolf Eichmann: Record of Proceedings in the District Court of Jerusalem* (Jerusalem:
Trust for the Publication of the Proceedings of the Eichmann Trial in cooperation
with the Israel State Archives and Yad Vashem, the Holocaust Martyrs' and Heroes'
Remembrance Authority, 1992–1995), 1:478.**

Presiding Judge: [. . .] Dr. Peretz, you are a gynaecologist. Were there
births in the ghetto during the occupation?

Aharon Peretz: There were births, obviously, for pregnant women had
entered the ghetto—in all the months of pregnancy.

Q: What were the orders regarding pregnant women?

A: In July 1942 an order was issued forbidding women to become
pregnant and to give birth.

---

49. In the postwar period, Dr. Aharon Peretz (b. 1910) became director of the gynecological and obstetrics department at Rambam Hospital and a professor in the medical faculty
of the Institute of Technology (Technion) in Haifa.

Q: What women?

A: The women in the ghetto, the Jewish women. And we—I must tell the truth—both the *Ältestenrat* [the Council of Elders] and the doctors, did not take this order too seriously. For each time we received a new blow, some time had to pass for us to believe and get used to this blow. But once, when a woman came to me in the advanced months of pregnancy and told me that an SS man had encountered her in the street, in one of the lanes of the ghetto, had recorded her address and said that he would come in two weeks' time and if she were still pregnant he would kill her—the matter became clear.

And, as the gynaecologist in the ghetto, I received an instruction from the *Ältestenrat* to end each and every pregnancy that came our way. We then made arrangements and received confirmation from the Germans that only those who were in the eighth and ninth months would be permitted to give birth, and up to the eighth month the pregnancy would be terminated. Naturally, as a doctor, I was confronted with very serious medical problems, because to end a pregnancy in the sixth and seventh months involved a difficult operation. The conditions were very bad, for when we left the small ghetto they burned the hospital, and we did not have one. All the operations were performed under difficult conditions—in kitchens, in small attics, amidst terrible congestion, and understandably there were fatalities. But the head of the Jewish Council was at the same time a very well-known physician of Kovno, an internist; he understood these problems, and he told me that we were permitted to end a pregnancy on the grounds of danger to the woman's life, because anyhow the life of the woman was in danger and consequently, "You have to terminate the pregnancy."

We terminated every pregnancy. There were women, I would say, who displayed signs of heroism and who, under no circumstances, wanted to end their pregnancy. And it goes without saying that, in such cases, we encouraged them, although I now feel myself to be guilty. For I, too, would encourage her—I would give her further strength. All kinds of outside events or news items, which described a setback for Hitler, would encourage the women to continue their pregnancy. [. . .]

With every political event women would come and ask, "Perhaps I should wait some while longer before having the abortion." There were also those who took the risk and did not put an end to it. Needless to say their fate was very bitter, afterwards, when the babies were put to death. Women who were forbidden to give birth would cover themselves beneath the pillows, they didn't cry out, they would not utter a sound, so that nobody would hear any cries. I was also requested only to come to a birth when I was sent for by the midwife or nurse, when there was some complication, and not to go to a normal birth, for by doing so I could arouse the suspicions of the neighbourhood. [. . .]

Eva Ginzová was born in Prague on February 21, 1930, the daughter of a mixed marriage. Her father, Otto Ginz, came from a liberal Jewish family and worked as a manager at a large textile concern in Prague. His wife, Maria, had been raised a Catholic but left the church in her early twenties. The Ginzes maintained a traditional Jewish home, observing the Sabbath and major holidays and keeping a kosher household, while Eva and her brother, Petr, attended a Jewish school. Eva adored her elder brother and had strong bonds with her large extended family, especially her father's brother Miloš and his two children, Pavel and Hanka.

The fate of Eva Ginzová and her family closely followed the course of Nazi policy in the Czech lands. During the Munich Crisis of September 1938, Great Britain and France forced the Czechoslovak republic to cede the German-speaking borderlands (e.g., the **Sudetenland**) to Nazi Germany. On March 15, 1939, the German army occupied the remainder of rump Czechoslovakia. The region of Slovakia became the quasi-independent Slovak State,[50] a puppet republic allied to Nazi Germany. German authorities annexed to the Reich the territory roughly encompassing the modern Czech Republic, creating the **Protectorate of Bohemia and Moravia**. With its incorporation by National Socialist Germany, the new Protectorate adopted Nazi antisemitic legislation. As children of a mixed marriage and themselves practicing Jews, the Ginzes were categorized as *Geltungsjuden* according to the tenets of the **Nuremberg Laws** and therefore subject to a number of restrictions. Beginning in September 1941, when all Jews in the Reich had to wear distinguishing badges on their outer garments, Petr and Eva, too, were forced to wear the yellow star.

In December 1941, deportations of Jews from Prague to **Theresienstadt** began. Two months earlier, as planners of the "Final Solution" began to organize the first transports of German Jews to the East, **Reinhard Heydrich**—who once served as chief of the **Reich Security Main Office** (**Reichssicherheitshauptamt**) and as governor general of the Protectorate[51]—

50. This is sometimes known as the First Slovak Republic.
51. On September 27, 1941, Reinhard Heydrich was appointed deputy Reich Protector (Stellvertretender Reichsprotektor) in the Protectorate of Bohemia and Moravia, assuming the effective government of the territory. Konstantin von Neurath, Heydrich's immediate predecessor in this post, held the official title of Protector until August 20, 1943, but, as Hitler believed him ineffectual in the position, he retained very little power.

suggested that the Theresienstadt site act as the primary way station for Jews in the Czech lands being deported to the camps and ghettos. On November 24, 1941, the first one thousand Czech Jews arrived at Theresienstadt, whose old fortress works, built in the era of Empress Maria Theresa, served as an ideal infrastructure for the new ghetto. Following the **Wannsee Conference** of January 20, 1942, Theresienstadt also became a "settlement area" for German and Austrian Jews over the age of sixty-five and for Jewish war veterans who had been decorated or disabled in combat, those categories of German Jews initially exempted from deportation. Later the ghetto also came to hold prominent Jewish artists, musicians, and other cultural figures whose disappearance might evoke adverse public reaction at home and abroad.

Thus, from the beginning, Theresienstadt served a dual purpose. First, it functioned as a device to help allay criticism of Nazi racial policy at home. Nazi propagandists portrayed Theresienstadt as a kind of model ghetto community for Jews deported from the Reich. This fiction helped to solve a dilemma inherent in Nazi claims that Jews "resettled in the East" were being relocated to labor colonies. Why then, many German citizens wondered, were elderly and disabled Jews included in such transports when they might no longer be deployed as forced labor? The Theresienstadt ghetto helped to put an end to such questions. German authorities also employed the "model Jewish city" to manipulate foreign governments and agencies, as when concentration camp administration officials permitted the **International Committee of the Red Cross** (**ICRC**) to visit a highly sanitized Theresienstadt in June 1944.[52] The reality of Theresienstadt was quite different from the impressions foreign dignitaries gathered on carefully choreographed visits and from those images captured on film, just before the ICRC's inspection, in the Nazi propaganda piece *Der Führer schenkt den Juden eine Stadt* (*The Führer Gives a City to the Jews*). Theresienstadt was a complex amalgam of Nazi concentration camp, forced labor camp, and ghetto. Of the more than 140,000 Jews transferred to Terezin, 33,500 died there, victims of starvation, disease, and ill treatment. More significantly, Theresienstadt, in its second essential role, functioned as a way station for deported Czech Jews and eventually for Jews deported from the Reich to the **Auschwitz II–Birkenau**, **Majdanek**, and Treblinka extermination camps. Between December 1941 and the end of war in the spring of 1945, eighty-eight

---

52. See Birgitt Morgenbrod and Stephanie Merkenich, *Das Rote Kreuz unter der NS-Diktatur, 1933–1945* (Paderborn: Ferdinand Schöningh, 2008), 374–91.

thousand individuals passed through Theresienstadt on their way to the East and to almost certain death.[53]

At least fifteen thousand Jewish children came to Terezin. One of them was Eva Ginzová, who arrived at the ghetto in May 1944, when she was fourteen. Her beloved brother, Petr, had already been transferred to Theresienstadt in October 1942; her paternal grandmother, uncle Miloš, and cousins Pavel and Hanka had preceded her there as well. Eva began keeping a diary on June 24, after spending approximately six weeks in the ghetto. Her father did not arrive at Terezin until the very end of the war, so Eva's central experience at Theresienstadt was one of homesickness and the pain of separation from her parents. Her loneliness intensified in the fall of 1944, when both her brother and cousin Pavel were deported to Auschwitz. Eva's diary entries from this period underscore an elemental feature in the lives of many ghetto inhabitants: the grief, uncertainty, and anxiety felt by those whose loved ones had been deported to an unknown fate. Eva's despondency over the loss of her brother grew with each passing week and increased in the last days of the war as trainloads of Auschwitz prisoners passed through Theresienstadt, telling stories about the horror of death camps in the East.

Units of the Soviet army liberated Eva and her father at Theresienstadt in May 1945. The pair returned home to Prague in order to reunite with Eva's mother and to await news of Petr. Eva Ginzová closed her Theresienstadt diary with the notation "When Petr comes back, I'll write it here." Almost two years later she added a final note: "Petr hasn't come back."[54] He would not. Petr Ginz perished in the gas chambers at Auschwitz shortly after his arrival.[55]

---

53. For a more detailed discussion of the Theresienstadt ghetto, see H. G. Adler, *Theresienstadt, 1941–1945: Antlitz einer Zwangsgemeinschaft* (Tübingen: Mohr, 1960); Vojtěch Blodig, *Terezin in the "Final Solution to the Jewish Question," 1941–1945*, trans. Jan Valěska and Lewis Paines (Prague: Památník Terezín/Oswald, 2003).

54. Zapruder, *Salvaged Pages*, 167.

55. Petr Ginz also left a diary to posterity; see Petr Ginz, *The Diary of Petr Ginz, 1941–1942*, ed. Chava Pressburger, trans. Eva Lappin (New York: Atlantic Monthly Press, 2007).

DOCUMENT 4-14. Diary of Eva Ginzová, entries for September 28, 1944, and April 23, 1945, Theresienstadt, in Alexandra Zapruder, ed., *Salvaged Pages: Young Writers' Diaries of the Holocaust* (New Haven, CT: Yale University Press, 2002), 180, 187–88.

September 28, [1944]

The train's already here and both boys have already got on it. Petr's number [is] 2392 and Pavel 2626. They're together in the same car. Petr's terribly calm and Uncle is full of admiration for him. I hoped to the last minute that the train wouldn't come, even though I knew it would. But what can be done? Just this morning Hanka and I were with them at the *slojska.*[56] It was a horrible sight that will stay with me forever. A crowd of women, children, and old men were pressed around the barracks to get a last look at their son, husband, father, or brother. The men leaning out of the windows were pressed one against the other to catch a glimpse of their dearest ones. But the barracks were guarded by police guards so that no one would escape. The *Ghettowachmanns* [ghetto guards] stood by the building and drove back people who came too close to it. The men from the windows waved and said good-bye to their relatives with looks. The sound of crying came from all around. We quickly ran home and brought the boys two slices of bread each so that they wouldn't be hungry. I pressed through the crowd, crawled under the rope that separated the crowd from the barracks, and passed Petr the bread through the window. I had enough time to hold his hand through the bars before a guard drove me away. At least it worked out all right. Now the boys are gone and the only thing left from them here is their empty beds.

April 23, [1945]

[. . .] My God, the things that are happening here now, it's difficult to describe. One afternoon (on Friday, April 20), I was at work when we saw a freight train go past. There were people sticking their heads out of the window. They looked awful. They were pale, completely yellow and green in the face, unshaven, emaciated, with sunken cheeks and shaven heads, dressed in prison clothes . . . and with a strange shine in their eyes . . . from hunger.

---

56. This is the Czech variant of the German *Schleuse* (sluice), a slang word used in Theresienstadt for the collection point for prisoners arriving and departing upon transports. Here, incoming and outgoing baggage was examined and "contraband" confiscated.

I ran to the ghetto straightaway (we're working outside at the moment), to the railway station. They were just getting off the train, if one can call it getting off. Very few could stand on their feet (bones, covered in nothing but skin), others lay on the floor completely exhausted. They'd been traveling for two weeks with hardly anything to eat. They came from Buchenwald and Auschwitz (Oświęcim). Most of them were Hungarians and Poles. I was so upset I thought I would collapse. I was still looking for our Petr among them since some of those who arrived now were those who had left from here. But our Petr wasn't there.

One transport after another started to arrive now. Hungarians, Frenchmen, Slovaks, Poles (they had spent seven years in concentration camps), Czechs, too. No one from our family. And the number of dead among them! A whole pile in every car. Dressed in rags, barefoot or in broken clogs. It was such a terrible sight that hardly anyone had seen before. I wish I could express on paper all the things that are happening inside me. But I'm not talented enough to do that.

And how the poor people threw themselves at any food they were given, whatever it was. How they fought over it—awful! A woman gave a lump of sugar to a sick boy, he was about seventeen. He burst out crying. He was sobbing terribly, kept looking at the piece of sugar and the bread the woman had given him and kept on crying, "Sugar, sugar, sugar, *weissbrot, weissbrot* [white bread]." Then he ate it. God knows how long it had been since he had seen any. Some have spotted fever [presumably typhus] and many other nasty diseases.

And those who arrived from Litzmannstadt [Łódź] and from Birkenau told us awful things. They said Oświęcim [Auschwitz] and Birkenau were made into one. They used to be two concentration camps right next to each other. Now it has been liberated. Every transport that had arrived in Birkenau had had everything taken away and been divided immediately. Children under fourteen, people over fifty, went straight into the gas chambers and were then burned. Moreover, they always selected some more to be gassed from those who remained. And the food was lousy. Coffee, soup, coffee, and so on. I wouldn't believe any of it if I wasn't told about it by those who themselves experienced it. I'm so worried about Petr and whether he's still alive.

CHAPTER 5

CHILDREN IN THE CONCENTRATION CAMP UNIVERSE

IN NATIONAL SOCIALIST Germany, the concentration camp (*Konzentrationslager,* or KZ) system was an integral feature of the regime. The very first concentration camps were established soon after the appointment of Adolf Hitler as German chancellor in January 1933. Nazi authorities founded the first regular camp of its kind, **Dachau**, near Munich, in March of that same year to incarcerate political prisoners and ideological opponents. Before World War II, concentration camps served primarily as detention centers for real and perceived enemies of the Reich. One deviation from this policy was the arrest and imprisonment in camps of some thirty thousand German Jewish men, entirely on racial grounds, following the ***Kristallnacht* pogrom** of November 9 and 10, 1938. At the time of the German invasion of Poland in September 1939, six major concentration camps were operating in the Greater German Reich: Dachau (founded 1933); Sachsenhausen, near Berlin (1936); **Buchenwald**, near Weimar (1937); Flossenbürg, in northeastern Bavaria near the former Czech border (1938); **Mauthausen**, near Linz, in Austria (the *Ostmark*) (1938); and **Ravensbrück**, a women's camp established in the province of Brandenburg (1939).

Following the outbreak of World War II, Germany's vast territorial conquests prompted an expansion of the concentration camp system, primarily to its eastern annexed and occupied territories. At first the war did not alter the original function of these camps as detention centers for political prisoners, resistance figures, and dissidents of belief and conscience. Gradually, however, such sites began to serve as reservoirs for an expanding population of forced laborers deployed in construction and industrial enterprises in support of the German war effort. Nazi policy with regard to the use of concentration camp labor evolved in three discrete phases. In the period between 1933 and 1937, prison labor served a punitive purpose and was limited primarily to the construction and maintenance of the camps themselves. With the coming of war, forced laborers were deployed on large-scale construction projects and in the raw materials industry, largely under the auspices of the **Schutzstaffel (SS)**. After 1942, with the war in full swing, prison labor was utilized extensively in the armaments industry and in weapons manufacture; dozens of subcamps were established for each major concentration camp, often located near production facilities or sites for the extraction of raw materials.[1] Despite a pressing need for forced labor, SS officials and guards deliberately malnourished and mistreated their prisoners so that hundreds of thousands of their number died in camps throughout Europe of hunger, illness, and maltreatment.

The exploitation of prison labor was a significant factor in the expansion of the Nazi concentration camp system. But with the invasion of the Soviet Union and the escalation of Nazi racial policy, a new category of camps emerged, sites designated to facilitate the "Final Solution" and the mass murder of groups and individuals deemed inferior by Nazi ideology and racial theory. German authorities established the first of these killing centers, **Chełmno**, in December 1941. SS officials murdered at least 152,000 individuals, primarily Jews and **Roma**, there between December 1941 and March 1943 and in June and July of 1944. In 1942, the planners of genocide founded the **Bełżec, Sobibór,** and **Treblinka** killing centers, known collectively as the **Operation Reinhard** (*Aktion* **Reinhard**) camps, to murder the Jews of the *Generalgouvernement* (**General Government**). At these extermination camps (*Vernichtungslager*), the SS and their auxiliaries killed approximately 1,526,500 Jews between March 1942 and November 1943. The largest killing center was **Auschwitz**, which by the spring of 1943 deployed four massive gas chambers, known as **crematoria**. At the height of the **deportations** to Auschwitz, up to six thousand Jews were gassed each day in its killing center, **Birkenau**. By November 1944, over 1 mil-

---

1. See Franciszek Piper, "The System of Prisoner Exploitation," in *Anatomy of the Auschwitz Death Camp*, ed. Yisrael Gutman and Michael Berenbaum (Bloomington: University of Indiana Press in association with the U.S. Holocaust Memorial Museum, 1994); Paul Jaskot, *The Architecture of Oppression: The SS, Forced Labor, and the Nazi Monumental Building Economy* (London: Routledge, 2000).

lion Jews and tens of thousands of Roma, Poles, and Soviet prisoners of war had been murdered at the Auschwitz complex.

Young children had almost no chance to survive in the Nazi system of concentration camps and killing centers. In camps where **selections** took place, German officials almost always dispatched Jewish children directly to the gas chambers. Infants and toddlers who arrived in the arms of their mothers or another relative went immediately to their deaths, often dooming the adults who accompanied them. The very young likewise rarely survived labor and concentration camps settings. When they did so, it was usually with the aid of relatives, adult prisoners, or members of the camp underground, who protected them and shared food and other essentials. Juveniles, particularly those over the age of twelve, often managed to mix in with the camp's adult population because of their fitness and ability to work. The following documentation examines the fates of children and adolescents who lived and died in the concentration camp universe and explores the ways in which the experiences of child detainees paralleled and diverged from those of their adult counterparts.

AT THE EDGE OF THE ABYSS

Janina Hescheles[2] was born in Lvov (then in Polish Galicia; today Lviv in Ukraine) on January 2, 1931. Her father, Henryk Hescheles, a respected journalist with Zionist credentials, served as the editor in chief of the Polish-language daily newspaper *Chwila* (*The Moment*) and was murdered shortly after German forces occupied Lvov in June 1941. Her mother worked as a nurse and administrator at a local hospital.[3] As a young child, Janina had already been drawn to writing, especially to poetry, a form in which she would preserve many of her wartime memories and experiences. After a number of unsuccessful attempts to place the young girl with a Christian aunt on Lvov's "**Aryan** side," Janina and her mother found themselves incarcerated in the Janowska concentration camp.[4] This complex was established in the autumn of 1941 to intern forced laborers working in a network of factories belonging to the German Armaments Works (Deutsche Rüstungswerke, or DAW); the first of

---

2. She is also cited as Jania, or Janka, Hescheles.

3. Janina Hescheles, "Mit den Augen eines zwölfjähriges Mädchen," in *Im Feuer vergangen: Tagebücher aus dem Ghetto*, ed. Johann Christoph Hampe (Munich: Chr. Kaiser Verlag, 1963), 151–89.

4. See Nechama Tec, *When Light Pierced the Darkness: Christian Rescue of Jews in Nazi-Occupied Poland* (Oxford: Oxford University Press, 1986), 131.

these factories stood along the Janowska Road in Lvov's suburbs.[5] Owned and operated by the SS, the DAW works deployed thousands of Jewish prisoners as well as Jewish inhabitants of the Lvov ghetto, founded by German authorities in November 1941. In addition to its role as a forced labor camp, Janowska also served as a transit camp for the mass deportation of Jews from the region to killing centers in the context of the "Final Solution." Jews arriving in Janowska on transports, or more commonly from the adjacent ghetto, underwent selections much as they might have experienced upon arrival at Auschwitz. Those found fit to work were absorbed into Janowska's prisoner population. The rest were deported to the Bełżec killing center or shot at the Piaski ravine, a massacre site north of the camp.

By August 1942, some sixty-five thousand Jews from Lvov had been deported to their deaths from Janowska. At this time, the camp was rife with rumors of what awaited these transports at Bełżec, an extermination camp on the Lvov-Lublin axis—one of three facilities, with Sobibór and Treblinka, comprising the camps of Operation Reinhard. These killing centers, which together claimed the lives of some 1.5 million Jews and thousands of Poles, Roma, and Soviet prisoners of war, were tasked principally with the murder of the Jewish population of the General Government.[6] In 1943, young Janina, who often composed and recited poems for her fellow inmates, turned her thoughts to the deportees bound for Bełżec and the terrible fate that awaited them.[7]

Janina herself did not share the destiny of those Jews who passed through Janowska to their destruction. After the death of her mother, who committed suicide before her eyes, the young girl was spirited out of the camp by Josefa Rysinska (alias "Ziutka"),[8] an operative of the Polish underground organization

5. See Leon Weliczker Wells, *The Janowska Road* (Washington DC: U.S. Holocaust Memorial Museum, 1999).

6. See Yitzhak Arad, *Belžec, Sobibor, Treblinka: The Operation Reinhard Death Camps* (Bloomington: University of Indiana Press, 1987); Bogdan Musial, ed., *"Aktion Reinhardt": Der Völkermord an den Juden im Generalgouvernement, 1941–1944* (Osnabrück: Fibre Verlag, 2004).

7. Robert Kuwalek, *From Lublin to Bełżec: Traces of Jewish Presence and the Holocaust in South-Eastern Part of the Lublin Region*, trans. Adam Janiszewski (Lublin: Ad Rem, 2005); Arad, *Belzec, Sobibor, Treblinka*.

8. Josefa Rysinska (b. 1922) served as a liaison officer in the Kraków branch of the underground Żegota organization. Among other rescue missions, she helped Jews to escape from the Pustkow and Szebnie forced labor camps and provided them with "Aryan" papers. Rysinska was arrested and interrogated by the Gestapo during a rescue attempt and sent to the Płaszów concentration camp in 1943. She was liberated from Płaszów in January 1945. In September 1979, Josefa Rysinska was recognized by Yad Vashem as "Righteous Among the Nations."

Żegota, which aided in the rescue of Jewish children. Traveling with Ziutka to Kraków in 1943, Janina Hescheles survived the war in hiding. To the vexation of her rescuers, who feared her journal might fall into German hands, she used every available scrap of paper to record her wartime experiences. In 1946, the Jewish Historical Commission of Kraków published her diary under the title *Through the Eyes of a Twelve-Year-Old Girl.*

DOCUMENT 5-1. Janina Hescheles, "Bełżec," Janowska, 1943, published in Michał Borwicz, ed., *Pieśń ujdzie cało: Antologia wierszy o żydach pod okupacją niemiecką* (Warsaw/Łódź/Kraków: Centralna Żydowska Komisja Historyczna w Polsce, 1947), 270–71 (translated from the Polish).

Bełżec

How terrible the sight:
A cattle car filled with people
And corpses in the corner.
Naked they stand;
Their moans roll down in the clatter of the wheels.
Only the condemned knows
What the wheel says to him:
To Bełżec!—to Bełżec!—to Bełżec!
To death!—To death!—To death!

If you want to live,
then jump! run! rush! but remember
The train guards lie in wait
And whisper to the other condemned,
"Nevermore will you see your mother.
Useless to cry, useless to sob,
Your father, never more shall you see.
Because the wheel drives you to Bełżec!"
To Bełżec!—to Bełżec!—to Bełżec!
To death!—To death!—To death!

The train goes more slowly, ends its travels.
From a thousand breasts wells up one moan.
The train has reached its goal,
the locomotive whistles:
Here is Bełżec! Here is Bełżec! Here is Bełżec!

DEATH AT AUSCHWITZ

The Auschwitz complex was the largest camp of its kind established by the National Socialist regime. Located near Oświęcim, Poland, some forty miles west of Kraków, the complex comprised three camps: Auschwitz I, established in May 1940; Birkenau (Auschwitz II), built in early 1942; and **Monowitz**, or **Buna** (Auschwitz III), established in May 1942. Auschwitz I, the main camp, was similar to most German concentration camps in that its primary aim was to incarcerate real and perceived enemies of the German Reich; like Monowitz, it also deployed a significant number of forced laborers both on-site and in SS-owned construction and war-related enterprises. Auschwitz II–Birkenau, with sections for men and women and temporary family camps for Roma (Gypsies) and for Jewish deportees from **Theresienstadt**, housed the largest prisoner population and accommodated the complex's killing center. It was Birkenau, with its four massive crematoria, which played a central role in the genocide of European Jewry.[9]

From 1942 through the late summer of 1944, trains carrying transports of Jews arrived at Auschwitz II–Birkenau from every corner of Axis-occupied Europe. In all, some 1.1 million Jews were deported there.[10] Depending upon their point of origin, Jewish transports often traveled many days before they reached their destination. Occasionally, deportees from western European countries came to Auschwitz aboard regular passenger trains so as not to alert unsuspecting individuals to the fate that awaited them. For Jews from eastern Europe, many of whom had experienced years of brutal treatment in ghettos or labor camps, such subterfuge was unnecessary; these individuals reached Birkenau in freight cars. Eighty to one hundred people often crowded into each car, with little or no provisions for a journey of several days. Such neglect was strategic, for exhausted prisoners, driven by extreme hunger and thirst, were more likely to cooperate in the offloading and sorting procedures when promised a shower and refreshment after their long ordeal.

New arrivals on the Birkenau ramp underwent the process of selection. Amid the chaos of disembarkation, Auschwitz prisoner-workers and SS guards separated the deportees by gender and ordered them to form short ranks. SS

---

9. For a discussion of the Auschwitz complex, see Wacław Długoborski and Franciszek Piper, eds., *Auschwitz: 1940–1945*, trans. William Brand, 5 vols. (Oświęcim: Auschwitz-Birkenau State Museum, 2000); Danuta Czech, *Auschwitz Chronicle, 1939–1945* (New York: Henry Holt, 1990); Yisrael Gutman and Michael Berenbaum, *Anatomy of the Auschwitz Death Camp* (Bloomington: University of Indiana Press in association with the U.S. Holocaust Memorial Museum, 1994).

10. See Franciszek Piper, *Auschwitz: How Many Perished There?* (Kraków: Polygraphia ITS, 1992).

medical staff then performed selections of Jewish prisoners, determining from among the mass of humanity who would be retained for work and who would perish immediately in the gas chambers. Young and able-bodied Jews were often chosen for labor and registered as prisoners at the camp. The sick, the weak, and the aged were murdered upon arrival. Young children generally shared the fate of the elderly and unfit in going directly to the gas chamber, often dooming their mothers or other adults who accompanied them.

DOCUMENT 5-2. **Jewish women and children from Transcarpathian Rus who have been selected for the death walk to the gas chamber, Auschwitz, May 1944, USHMMPA WS# 77342, courtesy of Yad Vashem.**

Magda Szabo[11] was a young schoolteacher when she arrived at Auschwitz with her mother, sister-in-law, and two-year-old niece from Udvárhely, then in Hungary, in the late spring of 1944. She was holding the toddler on the ramp when a prisoner approached her and entreated her to hand the child to her own mother. Hoping that such an action would spare the older woman from hard labor and provide supervision for her niece, Szabo unwittingly sealed her mother's fate.

11. Magda Szabo (née Guttmann, b. 1919) survived the Auschwitz and Bergen Belsen concentration camps. Following the war she became a teacher in Sighişoara, Romania. In August 1964, she became a key witness at the Frankfurt Auschwitz Trial.

DOCUMENT 5-3. **Testimony of Magda Szabo, August 24, 1964, Frankfurt Auschwitz Trial, in Fritz Bauer Institute and the State Museum of Auschwitz-Birkenau, eds.,** *Der Auschwitz-Prozess: Tonbandmitschnitte, Protokolle, Dokumente* **(DVD) (Berlin: Directmedia Publishing, 2004) (translated from the German).**

Presiding Judge: Ms. Szabo, you lived with your parents where, before you were arrested?

Witness Magda Szabo: In Odorhei, Udvárhely. [. . .]

Judge: Did you have a profession at that time?

Magda Szabo: Yes, I was employed as a teacher.

Judge: Employed as a teacher. And when were you arrested?

Magda Szabo: Early May, around May 5, we were taken from Vásárhely into the ghetto at Tîrgu Mures, everyone from the area of Odorhei, together with my parents. And in the ghetto I also met my brother, his wife and children, and her parents; and we were transported after about three weeks with the first transport to Auschwitz.

Judge: Then you were first assembled in a ghetto—

Magda Szabo: [interrupting] Yes.

Judge: Near Tîrgu Mures, yes?

Magda Szabo: In the brick factory, yes.

Judge: And there you were together with your family?

Magda Szabo: Yes, yes.

Judge: Who belonged to your family?

Magda Szabo: Father, mother, sister-in-law and her children and her sister, the sister-in-law of her sister, and her parents. . . .

Judge: And did you have children? Did you already have at this time—

Magda Szabo: [Interrupting] Myself, no, no. I was still unmarried. [. . .]

Judge: Now when were you sent to Auschwitz?

Magda Szabo: At the end of May. I think it was May 29th, 30th, 1st of June or so. My sister-in-law had a little child, two years old: she had her birthday in the cattle car. It was—I don't know—the last day in the car or so.

Judge: So you think the end of May?

Magda Szabo: In any case at the end of May, early June, to the 1st of June. I can't remember exactly any more. [. . .]

Judge: Do you know approximately how many people were in your transport? Naturally you didn't count them, but . . .

Magda Szabo: I didn't count, but we were eighty people in that car, and that was a very long . . .

Judge: Very long train.

Magda Szabo: Transport. Forty, fifty cars there were at least.

Judge: Tell me, please, during this transport, did you receive any provisions?

Magda Szabo: No. As we got into the car, we got a small piece of bread, every person, no water, nothing. We climbed in. We brought some food with us, but we ate it sparingly—we thought that we were going somewhere to work, [and] the children should have some of it.

Judge: Did you at least receive anything to drink?

Magda Szabo: No. Once it rained, I remember very well, and we caught the water in a glass.

Judge: Some rainwater.

Magda Szabo: A little water so that we could give the children in the car at least a little water.

Judge: When you arrived in Auschwitz, do you know who opened your cars and had you get out?

Magda Szabo: There were prisoners there who helped us. And they said we should leave our baggage there. We should get out. And then immediately five to a row . . .

Judge: They lined you up?

Magda Szabo: Women separately, yes, lined us up. And I was with my sister-in-law; she had a small child, two years old. I took it in my arms because she was still younger and weaker [than I was]. And as we stood there in the row, a prisoner came to me and asked me if the child belonged to me. "No," I said. He said, "Give it to the mother." And I understood that I should give the child to my mother. Perhaps she would get lighter work. And so I gave it to her. Probably he meant that I should give it to an older . . .

Judge: Woman.

Magda Szabo: [An older woman], yes. And I also said to my mother, "Mother, say that you are old. Perhaps you can stay there, if you are older, so you could care for the children when my sister-in-law goes to work."

Judge: Yes.

Magda Szabo: And because this officer, the SS officer who was there, spoke so nicely to me and even spoke in Hungarian,[12] I said, "Oh

---

12. The individual in question was pharmacist Victor Capesius, a Transylvanian ethnic German (*Volksdeutsche*) who was a defendant in the Frankfurt Auschwitz Trial.

Mama, how good it would be if you could be with the children. Say that you are old."

Judge: Yes.

Magda Szabo: And I was taken out of the row, and I never saw her again. [. . .]

Fifteen-year-old Helga Weissová faced selection at Auschwitz with her own mother. In December 1941, shortly after her twelfth birthday, Helga and her parents, Otto and Irena Weiss, arrived with one of the first transports of Czech Jews to **Theresienstadt**. The girl would remain in the **Terezin** ghetto for three years, during which time she honed an early talent for drawing and painting. Enjoined by her father to paint what she observed around her, Helga completed over one hundred drawings and illustrations during her tenure at Theresienstadt, most of them portraying the bleak and often surreal aspects of ghetto existence.

In late 1944, Helga and her mother were deported to Auschwitz. Helga was fifteen, an age at which Birkenau camp officials often selected adolescents for forced labor. Moreover, mother and daughter arrived at Auschwitz shortly before the camp's liquidation and, amid the chaotic conditions, were transported almost immediately to camps in the German interior. In the last days of the war, the pair found themselves in the Mauthausen concentration camp, where American forces liberated them and their fellow prisoners on May 5, 1945.

Helga and her mother returned to Prague, where they learned of the death of Otto Weiss and of most of their family members and friends. At this time, Helga began to draw again, eager to capture images of her experiences, which, after her deportation to Auschwitz, she had had no opportunity to put down on paper. In late 1945 or early 1946, Helga Weissová depicted her vision of the ramp at Birkenau, where many of her fellow deportees had met their end. Wrote Weissová of her illustration, "Selection," "Prisoners were classified immediately on arrival to Auschwitz and subsequently from time to time. It was determined that the young and the strong should work, while the old, the weak, and the children were sent to the gas chambers. Children under fifteen had no chance of survival."[13]

---

13. Helga Weissová, *Zeichne, was Du siehst! Zeichnungen eines Kindes aus Theresienstadt/ Terezin*, ed. Niedersächsischer Verein zur Förderung von Theresienstadt/Terezin, e.V. (Göttingen: Wallstein Verlag, 1998), 138.

DOCUMENT 5-4. Ink drawing by Helga Weissová, "Selection," 1945–1946, in Helga Weissová, *Zeichne, was Du siehst! Zeichnungen eines Kindes aus Theresienstadt/Terezin*, ed. Niedersächsischer Verein zur Förderung von Theresienstadt/Terezin, e.V. (Göttingen: Wallstein Verlag, 1998), 139.

Although historians have long understood the process of gassing human beings at killing centers such as Auschwitz, we know little of the anguish these victims experienced in those terrifying minutes before they perished in the gas chamber. Survival of such an ordeal, either at stationary facilities or in **gas vans**, miraculously did occur, but it was extremely rare; in the majority of cases, attending guards subsequently murdered any surviving victims. Thus, few eyewitnesses have been left to recount what they endured.[14]

14. Survival in the less technologically complex gas vans did occasionally occur. Drivers often halted the gassing procedure as soon as the screams of the victims had ceased, which did not necessarily guarantee that all individuals within the van were dead. Eyewitness testimony indicates that SS guards routinely shot those victims who survived the gas vans at Chełmno. Famously, a Soviet civilian survived a gassing of mental patients in a gas van at Krasnodar on the Kuban River in present-day Russia and testified concerning his experience at the 1943 Krasnodar Trial, the first war crimes proceedings against Axis criminals and their accomplices.

In his 1946 memoir, *Auschwitz: A Doctor's Eyewitness Account*, Hungarian prisoner-physician **Miklós Nyiszli** gives us an idea of how such a gassing must have seemed to a child in Auschwitz in 1944. In June of that year, Nyiszli was deported with his wife and young daughter from Oradea, in present day Romania,[15] to Auschwitz. Volunteering to work as a physician in the prisoner barracks, Nyiszli came to the attention of Birkenau camp physician **Josef Mengele**, who commandeered the young doctor to aid in his own "research." Forced to assist Mengele with his experimentation, Nyiszli was quartered in Birkenau's Crematorium III, which he shared with the Jewish *Sonderkommando* responsible for the removal and disposal of corpses after gassing. In this context Nyiszli encountered a young girl who emerged alive from the gas chambers at Auschwitz.

DOCUMENT 5-5. Miklós Nyiszli, *Auschwitz: A Doctor's Eyewitness Account,* trans. Tibère Kremer and Richard Seaver (Hungarian ed., 1946; New York: Frederick Fell Publishers, 1960), 114–20.

In Number One Crematorium's gas chamber 3,000 dead were piled up. The *Sonderkommando* had already begun to untangle the lattice of flesh. The noise of the elevators and the sound of their clanging doors reached my room. The work moved ahead double time. The gas chambers had to be cleared, for the arrival of a new convoy had been announced.

The chief of the gas chamber [commando] almost tore the hinges off the door to my room as he arrived out of breath, his eyes wide with fear or surprise.

"Doctor," he said, "come quickly. We just found a girl alive at the bottom of the pile of corpses."

I grabbed my instrument case, which was always ready, and dashed to the gas chamber. Against the wall, near the entrance of the immense room, half covered with other bodies, I saw a girl in the throes of a death-rattle, her body seized with convulsions. The gas *Kommando* men around me were in a state of panic. Nothing like this had ever happened in the course of their horrible career.

We removed the still-living body from the corpses pressing against it. I gathered the tiny adolescent body into my arms and carried it back into

---

15. Oradea had, along with northern Transylvania, been ceded by Hungary to Romania in the 1919 Treaty of Trianon. Hungary regained the territory in 1940 but was forced to return it to Romania in 1947.

the room adjoining the gas chamber, where normally the gas *Kommando* men change clothes for work. I laid the body on a bench. A frail young girl, almost a child, she could have been no more than fifteen. I took out my syringe and, taking her arm—she had not yet recovered consciousness and was breathing with difficulty—I administered three intravenous injections. My companions covered her body which was as cold as ice with a heavy overcoat. One ran to the kitchen to fetch some tea and warm broth. Everybody wanted to help, as if she were his own child. [. . .]

She looked around her with astonishment, and glanced at us. She still did not realize what was happening to her, and was still incapable of distinguishing the present, of knowing whether she was dreaming or really awake. A veil of mist clouded her consciousness. Perhaps she vaguely remembered a train, a long line of boxcars which had brought her here. Then she had lined up for selection and, before she knew what was happening, been swept along by the current of the mass into a large, brilliantly lighted underground room. Everything had happened so quickly. Perhaps she remembered that everyone had had to undress. The impression had been disagreeable, but everybody had yielded resignedly to the order. And so, naked, she had been swept along into another room. The second room had also been lighted by powerful lamps. Completely bewildered, she had let her gaze wander over the mass huddled there, but found none of her family. Pressed close against the wall, she had waited, her heart frozen, for what was going to happen. All of a sudden, the lights had gone out, leaving her enveloped in total darkness. Something had stung her eyes, seized her throat, suffocated her. She had fainted. There her memories ceased.

Her movements were becoming more and more animated; she tried to move her hands, her feet, to turn her head left and right. [. . .] I received the first reply to my questions. Not wanting to tire her, I asked only a few. I learned that she was sixteen years old, and that she had come with her parents in a convoy from Transylvania. [. . .]

What could one do with a young girl in the crematorium's *Sonderkommando*? I knew the past history of the place: no one had ever come out of here alive, either from the convoys or the *Sonderkommando*.[16]

Little time remained for reflection. [Oberscharführer] Mussfeld arrived to supervise the work, as was his wont. [. . .] I calmly related

---

16. After several months at their ghastly labor, members of the *Sonderkommando* were routinely murdered and replaced in their duties by a fresh detachment of prisoners.

the terrible case we found ourselves confronted with. I described for his benefit what pains the child must have suffered in the undressing room, and the horrible scenes that preceded death in the gas chamber. When the room had been plunged into darkness, she had breathed in a few lungfuls of [Zyklon B] gas. Only a few, though, for her fragile body had given way under the pushing and shoving of the mass as they fought against death. By chance she had fallen with her face against the wet concrete floor. That bit of humidity had kept her from being asphyxiated, for [Zyklon B] gas does not react under humid conditions.

These were my arguments, and I asked him to do something for the child. He listened to me attentively, then asked me exactly what I proposed doing. [. . .] One solution would have been to put her in front of the crematorium gate. A *Kommando* of women always worked there. She could have slipped in among them and accompanied them back to the camp barracks after they had finished work. She would never relate what had happened to her. The presence of one new face among so many thousands would never be detected, for no one in the camp knew all the other inmates.

If she had been three or four years older that might have worked. A girl of twenty would have been able to understand clearly the miraculous circumstances of her survival, and have enough foresight not to tell anyone about them. She would wait for better times, like so many other thousands were waiting, to recount what she had lived through. But Mussfeld thought that a young girl of sixteen would in all naiveté tell the first person she met where she had just come from, what she had seen and what she had lived through. The news would spread like wildfire, and we would all be forced to pay for it with our lives.

"There's no way of getting round it," he said, "the child will have to die."

Half an hour later the young girl was led, or rather carried into the furnace room hallway, and there Mussfeld sent another in his place to do the job. A bullet in the back of the neck.

IN A LIVING HELL: SURVIVAL IN CAMPS

Beginning in the autumn months of 1943, prisoners resident in Birkenau, the camp that housed Auschwitz's killing center, were privy to a strange and puzzling sight. Those venturing near the area of the camp designated "B II b" could see young children—hundreds of them—playing, performing calisthenics, and engaging in study in the company of their teachers and guardians. With the exception of those youngsters—many of them twins—whom camp physician Dr. Josef Mengele had selected for medical experimentation and housed in Block 10, there were, practically speaking, no Jewish children in Birkenau.[17] The vast majority of young persons arriving at Auschwitz perished immediately in the gas chambers. To Auschwitz prisoners, the image was jarring: unshorn and relatively well-fed youngsters gamboling about their blocks in civilian clothes. Where had these children come from, and what were they doing in Birkenau?

The children in question belonged to a unique group of prisoners from the Terezin ghetto who for nearly a year formed the **Theresienstadt family camp**. In September 1943, five thousand Czech Jews, among them over one thousand youngsters and adolescents,[18] arrived at Auschwitz from Theresienstadt. Spared the customary selection, they were brought directly to a special part of the Birkenau quarantine area close to the main entrance gate. Placed within a separate barracks network, designated "B II b," these Jews were processed as special prisoners with the designation "SB6." Although they received tattooed prisoner numbers upon their arms, their hair remained unshorn, and they were allowed to retain their civilian clothing. Men and women were housed in separate blocks, but prisoners could move freely within the small camp, and children could remain with their parents.[19] These Jews were not assigned to labor brigades and were allowed, even encouraged, to write letters as well as to receive correspondence and parcels from outside Auschwitz.

At the time, no one understood the purpose of the family camp or why its inhabitants received such preferential treatment. When a further transport of five thousand Jews from Theresienstadt arrived at Birkenau that December and were added to their ranks, residents of the little camp could only infer from their privileged existence that they had been spared for a reason and that their fate would be essentially different from that of other prisoners. However, on the night of March 7, 1944, exactly six months after their arrival from Theresienstadt to the family camp, prisoners from the first transport of Jews were assembled and taken to the gas chamber without a selection. Gradually,

---

17. Nili Keren, "The Family Camp," in *Anatomy of the Auschwitz Death Camp*, ed. Yisrael Gutman and Michael Berenbaum (Bloomington: University of Indiana Press, in association with the U.S. Holocaust Memorial Museum, 1994), 431.

18. See Helena Kubica, "Children," in *Anatomy of the Auschwitz Death Camp*, ed. Yisrael Gutman and Michael Berenbaum (Bloomington: University of Indiana Press, in association with the U.S. Holocaust Memorial Museum, 1994), 415.

19. In the late spring of 1944, shortly before the liquidation of the family camp, a separate block was designated for children so that they no longer slept in their parents' barracks.

the significance of the notation "SB6" in the Czech Jews' prisoner records became clear. The code implied *Sonderbehandlung* (special treatment)[20] in six months, suggesting that six months after their arrival, surviving Jews from the December transport would share the fate of earlier family camp members.

But what could explain the curious delay between the arrival and gassing of these deportees, and why were those ultimately doomed to perish in the crematoria detained under such privileged circumstances? Most historians believe that the answer to this question lies in the correspondence between Nazi authorities and officials of the **International Committee of the Red Cross** (**ICRC**). Succumbing to pressure following the deportation of Danish Jews to Theresienstadt, German administrators arranged to allow representatives of the ICRC to inspect the Theresienstadt ghetto on June 23, 1944. Originally Nazi officials had planned to include a Red Cross visit to Birkenau in the ICRC's itinerary in order to deflect allegations that camps like Auschwitz represented industrialized killing centers that were claiming the lives of thousands of Jews and other persecutees. Just as Theresienstadt became a sanitized "model ghetto" for ICRC visitors, the Theresienstadt family camp would "give the lie" to rumors of the mass murder of European Jewry. International Red Cross members, however, were satisfied after their visit to Theresienstadt that Jews transferred there remained in the ghetto and were relatively well cared for. Correspondence from Birkenau to relatives and friends in Theresienstadt, relating the satisfactory conditions at the camp, furnished further evidence that speculation about the systematic murder of Jews in Auschwitz was "unfounded." After ten months, the family camp in Birkenau had served its purpose. In July 1944, survivors of the camp's December transports were put to a selection. The majority was gassed, while the camp itself was liquidated.

Thirteen-year-old **Michal Kraus** arrived at Auschwitz with his parents from Theresienstadt in December 1943. The teenager had been raised in the Bohemian town of Nachod, where his father, Karl Kraus, was a physician. In December 1942, the Krauses, like many Czech Jews, were deported to Theresienstadt. One year later, the small family came with a transport of five thousand Jews from the Terezin ghetto to Birkenau and was absorbed within the family camp. For six months the Krauses lived there in relative safety. Then, in June 1944, Kraus's mother, Lotte, was transferred to the Stutthof concentration camp near Danzig (Gdańsk), where she perished in January 1945. In early July, camp officials moved to eliminate the family camp and subjected its residents to the selection process. Michal numbered among the eighty-nine young boys, aged fourteen to sixteen, spared by Auschwitz camp physician Josef Mengele for

---

20. This was a Nazi euphemism for execution or killing.

reasons that remain unclear. These "Birkenau Boys," as they came to be known, were removed to the men's camp (*Männerlager*) and initially settled in the punishment block there. From this vantage point, the young Kraus could observe the gassing and incineration of friends and loved ones in the family camp, including his father, who was killed on July 11. Michal eventually lodged in the *Unterkunft-Verwaltung*, the housing administration. He survived Auschwitz as a runner (*Läufer*), a messenger assigned to convey communications and supplies among officials in the heart of the extermination camp.

In the early months of 1945, the fourteen-year-old endured a series of forced marches from Auschwitz to Gleiwitz and then to several camps and subcamps of the Mauthausen concentration camp system. On May 5, 1945, he was liberated by American forces at the Gunskirchen *Lager* in Upper Austria. Returning orphaned to Czechoslovakia, the teenager reconstructed his Holocaust experiences in a three-volume chronicle, completed in 1947. Michal's postwar diary, which he dedicated to his slain parents, yields unique insight into the experiences and viewpoints of children during the Holocaust. Punctuated by remarkable illustrations, such as the images included here of the blazing crematoria, the journal is an extraordinary story of survival in the charnel world of the death camp.

DOCUMENT 5-6. **Diary of Michal (Michael) Kraus, handwritten with illustrations, 1945–1947, 54–60, USHMMA, Acc. 2006.51, Michael Kraus Collection (translated from the Czech).**

At that time—in the summer of 1944, at the beginning of July, I saw my dearest parents for the last time. It is hard for me to describe how I felt at the time.

Generally speaking, with every transport, new names appeared: [Blechhammer], Belsen, Buchenwald. Mother left on the 5th or the 8th to Stutthof from the *Frauenlager* [women's camp] together with Vera Loewenbach, with whom she has been together since the first.

I did not know that we would never, never see each other again. Maybe it was better. And then they selected us, eighty-nine boys. The others had to stay behind and . . . it is a horror to think about it. Leaving father was terrible. I see him in front of me, emaciated, sick. How he cried, he who had always been so good to everyone, and now I left him behind, left him to die. I can't think about this because it was the most horrible moment of my life.

They led us to the gate, in the direction of the Sauna[21]—the crematorium lay nearby. We were surprised that they took us to the Sauna in the Gypsy Camp and then to Block 13, the men's camp.

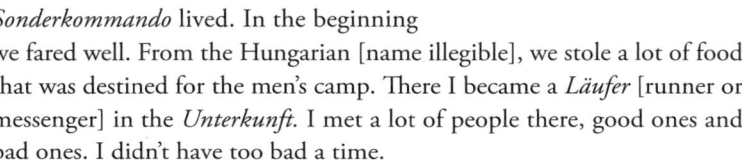

It is painful to remember all those who at that time remained in B II b, so that they could be gassed later on—hundreds of acquaintances and comrades, those who never returned from the transports. [. . .]

We came to a block where the *Sonderkommando* lived. In the beginning we fared well. From the Hungarian [name illegible], we stole a lot of food that was destined for the men's camp. There I became a *Läufer* [runner or messenger] in the *Unterkunft*. I met a lot of people there, good ones and bad ones. I didn't have too bad a time.

On July 11, I did not sleep. The night was bright, the sky red. Of that—I cannot talk about it. On July 11, they killed my father. I balled my fists, I cried, and I promised to avenge him. Many of us lost their loved ones that day. [. . .]

The sky was burning!

Yes, it really was! At night the windows of the block were completely red. All the crematoria worked in full swing. The gas chambers continuously choked their victims. It was a slaughterhouse such as the world had never seen. Tens of thousands went daily to the gas. They hounded them out of the cattle cars directly to their deaths. And sometimes directly into the flames. And that was what we were supposed to see in the camp!

21. In Birkenau, this building housed shower and steam rooms for the disinfection of registered prisoners.

In its brief months of existence, the Theresienstadt family camp at Birkenau was a haven for children who might otherwise have gone directly to the gas. Among the first arrivals to the family camp from Theresienstadt in September 1943 was **Fredy Hirsch**, a well-known educator and a youth leader in the Terezin ghetto. Hirsch used his privileged circumstances at the camp to improve the lot of hundreds of children assigned there. He arranged with camp officials to create a separate children's block (Block 31) where youngsters might receive educational instruction, engage in structured play, and obtain more appropriate and nutritious meals.

The *Kinderblock* was the "one oasis in our camp," recalled Hanna Hoffmann, a young and idealistic instructor in the children's block. The children spent most of their waking hours in this area of the camp. Here they took their meals and washed themselves, even in the coldest weather. Prisoners in the family camp were not exempt from the monotonous roll calls conducted twice daily in Auschwitz, but Hirsch arranged for his charges to report to *Appell* inside their block, a relative luxury, especially in inclement weather. Calisthenics were generally held before instruction began, and children were also allowed time for games, sport, and recreation. Youngsters spent the evening hours with their parents and slept in the barracks of their father or mother, depending on their gender.[22] The difficult conditions that prevailed in the family camp created special challenges for the young educators who sought to improve the lot of their pupils. Yet, as instructor Avi Fischer later recounted, when the children came together to play or sing in the afternoon, "the barracks became a safe ship sailing through the vast spaces,"[23] even in the heart of Birkenau.

DOCUMENT 5-7. Personal testimony of Hanna Hoffmann-Fischel, c. 1960, in Inge Deutschkron, *Denn ihrer war die Hölle: Kinder in Gettos und Lagern* (Cologne: Verlag Wissenschaft und Politik, 1965), 49–52 (translated from the German).

There was one oasis in our camp, a place in which one could forget the present, in which one was still a human being. That was the children's home [*Kinderheim*], an undertaking of Fredy Hirsch. Fredy, whose demeanor and bearing the Germans approved of and were even impressed by right from the start, was at the first *Lagerkapo* [camp **kapo**]. From the SS *Lagerleiter* he had succeeded in obtaining an area of the block in

---

22. Keren, "*The Family Camp*," 431–33.
23. Avi Fischer, quoted in Keren, "*The Family Camp*," 435.

which could be set up a day care home for children between eight and fourteen years of age. Before this time, children had been divided among the various blocks, among the old and sick, and no one had taken care of them. Their only activity was roll call [*Appell*]; anything else would have destroyed the "discipline" of the camp.

Fredy then looked for several young people among the prisoners who had already worked as educators in Theresienstadt. With their help he assembled, according to age and language, 700 children who up till this time were only "numbers." He managed to acquire better food for them and was even successful in requisitioning for the *Kinderblock* a portion of the parcels which came to the concentration camp and whose recipients were no longer alive. (These parcels came only for "Aryan" Germans and Poles.) The caregivers for the various groups of children were above all responsible for the cleanliness of their charges. Daily, all articles of clothing were searched for lice; care was taken that hands, fingernails, ears, eating utensils, and so on were clean. Fredy even made spot-checks himself. And when a child was not completely clean, the whole group lost its special rations.

Each day there were five hours of lessons. Most of the children could not speak German. Fredy had convinced the SS that lessons in the German language would be in their best interest. Naturally, these German lessons were limited to drilling the children in a few phrases, to be used in the event that a German guest would visit the home.[24] The classroom lessons took place under difficult conditions. The tables of the various groups stood close together, so that it was difficult for the children to concentrate. They were noisy, and it was difficult to keep them in their seats; the nagging hunger troubled both the children and their caregivers. Then we had neither paper nor pencils, not to mention any books. Few of us were trained as teachers, who might at least have some special skills at our disposal. Nevertheless, we attempted to teach the children, many of whom had not yet had any schooling, the fundamental basics.

The distribution of food at noon and in the evenings demanded a great deal of moral fortitude on the part of the caregivers. The children received better food than we did and got extra rations in addition; and

---

24. Auschwitz authorities were expecting a visit of officials from the International Committee of the Red Cross, as had been organized at Theresienstadt, an event that never transpired.

they kept a sharp lookout because they knew that we should not keep anything back for ourselves. The caregivers were placed in an especially difficult position when the children, out of compassion, offered them something from their own rations. Fredy had also strictly forbidden this, and we would also have lost the respect of the children. Some who could not resist the temptation—especially the young men, who already suffered edema[25] from hunger—were barred without leniency from the home.

Because we came from the Zionist movement, we tried as hard as we could to give the children some understanding of the things which we wanted to live for. We assembled everything we knew about Israel, portrayed to them life on a kibbutz, tried to get them enthused about collectives in Israel. But this was very difficult. The children, stemming mostly from assimilated Czech families were, in experience, as old as we were, and therefore more skeptical, even cynical. They certainly had had very little opportunity in their short lives to learn about goodness and beauty. They couldn't believe in anything; no, there was one thing in which they believed: the omnipotent power of the crematorium chimney, which they saw smoking before them. When it spewed forth flames, they only remarked drily that another transport must have come in. And if we sometimes believed to have ignited a spark in them, then it came time to distribute the food again, and the youth leader was once again a poor sucker and the [Israeli] collective forgotten.

Of the 231,640 children deported to Auschwitz, some 650 young persons under the age of seventeen remained at the camp to witness its liberation by Soviet forces on January 27, 1945.[26] Hundreds more of their number survived brutal forced marches from Auschwitz to an array of camps in the German interior in the weeks proceeding the liquidation of that complex. As meager as these survival rates appear, they are significant when compared to

---

25. Edema is the abnormal accumulation of fluid beneath the skin or in one or more cavities of the body. Edema caused by severe malnourishment (hunger edema) often appears in the extremities, especially the lower legs.

26. See Helena Kubica, "Children and Adolescents in Auschwitz," in *Auschwitz, 1940–1945: Central Issues in the History of the Camp*, ed. Tadeusz Iwasko et al., trans. William Brand (Oświęcim: Auschwitz-Birkenau State Museum, 2000), 2:201–90. Jewish children represented a majority (93 percent) of this figure, but the statistic also includes Roma and other non-Jewish children, especially from Poland, the Soviet Union, and Yugoslavia.

corresponding figures for the remainder of the National Socialist extermination camps. Unlike Auschwitz, these killing centers did not have genuine selections. The overwhelming majority of Jews and other deportees arriving at these centers went directly to their deaths in the gas chambers. Only a few hundred individuals among the 1.5 million Jews deported to the Operation Reinhard camps of Bełżec, Sobibór, and Treblinka survived the war, and even this survival rate resulted largely from prisoner revolts at the latter two facilities. Four prisoners survived to tell of their experiences at Chełmno, the first extermination camp of the "Final Solution." In each of these instances, only a tiny fraction of the surviving prisoners were children.

Berel Dov Freiberg (or Fraiberg)[27] was one of the very few youngsters to survive the Sobibór killing center. The small village of Sobibór lies five kilometers (three miles) west of the Bug River, near Włodawa, on the eastern border of today's Poland. During World War II, the town fell within occupied Poland's Lublin District; due to its location in a wooded and thinly populated region at a point along the Chelm-Włodawa railroad line, Sobibór was chosen as a site for the second of those extermination camps operating under the auspices of Operation Reinhard, the campaign to murder the Jews of the General Government.[28]

The camp personnel at Sobibór comprised twenty to thirty German SS and police officials, as well as some one hundred Ukrainian and Polish civilians recruited as auxiliary guards. Although each German functionary nominally belonged to the SS, the core of the German staff formally remained personnel of **Operation T4**, the mass-murder program that targeted disabled patients in killing centers on German soil. The directors of this "**euthanasia**" program had loaned these operatives to the planners of the "Final Solution" during the halt in their killing operations beginning in the summer of 1941. Sobibór's first commandant, Franz Stangl, had been a former T4 administrator at the Hartheim "euthanasia" facility before his transfer to the East in the spring of 1942. In August of that year, Stangl was transferred to the Treblinka camp to replace

---

27. Berel Dov Freiberg wrote a memoir of his experiences at Sobibór; see Dov Fraiberg, *To Survive Sobibor* (Jerusalem: Gefen, 2007).

28. For a discussion of the Sobibór killing center, see Jules Schelvis, *Sobibor: A History of a Nazi Death Camp*, trans. Karin Dixon (Oxford: Berg in association with the U.S. Holocaust Memorial Museum, 2007); Arad, *Belzec, Sobibor, Treblinka*; Miriam Novitch, ed., *Sobibor, Martyrdom and Revolt: Documents and Testimonies* (New York: Holocaust Library, 1980).

its ineffectual commandant, Dr. Irmfried Eberl,[29] and Stangl's deputy, Franz Reichleitner,[30] succeeded him at Sobibór.[31]

The Sobibór killing center comprised three separate camps consisting of an administrative area for camp offices, another area for guard residences, and a third area containing barracks for the small prison labor force. Camp II accommodated a receiving area, adjacent to the railroad siding. Beginning in May 1942, when regular gassing operations began at the killing center, transports consisting of forty to sixty freight cars arrived at the Sobibór railway station, several hundred yards away. Twenty cars at a time approached the siding, where camp guards ordered deportees to descend from the train to the platform, enjoining them to leave their luggage behind. The camp's reception area held barracks where the new arrivals were forced to undress and surrender any last valuables and other possessions. Now guards forced their victims down a narrow enclosed footpath, known as the "Tube" (*Schlauch*), which connected the receiving area to Camp III, the part of the complex that housed the gas chambers. In a special barracks inside the Tube, a handful of veteran prisoners sheared the hair of the Jewish women. Thereafter, the victims were driven, often with brutal

---

29. Graduating with a degree in medicine from the University of Innsbruck, Austrian psychiatrist Irmfried Eberl (1910–1948) was the director of the Brandenburg and Bernburg "euthanasia" (T4) facilities. Following a temporary halt in T4 operations, Eberl served as the first commandant of the Treblinka killing center. At the end of August 1942, gross disorganization at the complex resulted in Eberl's replacement by Franz Stangl (1908–1971). Eberl was arrested by American authorities in early 1948 and committed suicide in custody on February 16, 1948.

30. Franz Reichleitner (1906–1944), like Franz Stangl, was a member of the Austrian criminal police and served with his colleague as an official at the Hartheim "euthanasia" (T4) facility. When Stangl became commandant at the Treblinka killing center in September 1942, Reichleitner, his deputy, assumed his role as commandant at Sobibór. Following the liquidation of the Reinhard camps in November 1943, Reichleitner joined other T4 personnel for the so-called *Aktion* R (Operation R) on the Adriatic coast, where at least a portion of the group's responsibility was to carry out the deportation and murder of Italian Jewry. Reichleitner was killed by partisans near Fiume in January 1944.

31. In the immediate postwar period, Franz Stangl procured a fictive Red Cross passport and fled abroad. He lived hidden in Syria for three years and in 1951 joined his wife in São Paulo, Brazil, where he found work in a Volkswagen automobile plant. Although he had registered with consular officials under his own name and his crimes were known to Austrian justice officials, Stangl continued to live unencumbered in Brazil. Spurred by Nazi hunter Simon Wiesenthal, Brazilian police arrested him in 1967. In 1970, a Düsseldorf court sentenced Stangl to life imprisonment in proceedings against former officials of the Treblinka killing center. Stangl died of heart failure while incarcerated on June 28, 1971. For an intensive discussion of Stangl's activities in the T4 and Operation Reinhard programs, see Gitta Sereny, *Into That Darkness: An Examination of Conscience* (New York: Vintage Books, 1983).

force, into gas chambers disguised as shower facilities. Once the doors were sealed, powerful engines from adjacent rooms pumped deadly carbon monoxide gas into the chambers, killing all inside. This process was repeated until the entire transport had been murdered.

German SS and police officials conducted gassing operations at Sobibór from May 1942 until the fall of 1943, when revolts by Jewish prisoners here and at Treblinka spurred the liquidation of both killing centers.[32] In all, at least 167,000 individuals perished at the Sobibór extermination camp.

On the ramp of Sobibór, no elaborate selection process separated individuals physically fit for labor from the bulk of deportees destined for immediate gassing. Often whole transports were sent directly to their deaths in the gas chambers. Occasionally, as the need arose, guards in the reception area chose from among the new arrivals a handful of prisoners who seemed physically robust or possessed specific skills to round out the camp's prison labor force. A number of these individuals worked as tailors or cobblers, serving the needs of the German or auxiliary guards. This force also typically included several women who cooked, cleaned, and laundered for camp personnel. Most of the prisoners, however, served in so-called *Sonderkommandos* (special detachments). As at Auschwitz and other extermination camps, these forced laborers worked in the reception area to facilitate the processing of each transport to the camp; others worked in Camp III, hurrying the victims along the Tube or shearing the hair of female prisoners. After each transport, these veteran Jewish prisoners were forced to burn or bury the corpses of murdered victims, to sort and store their abandoned possessions, and to clean the freight cars for the next round of deportations. Camp officials regularly murdered members of these labor brigades and filled their ranks with prisoners from newly arriving transports.

Berel Dov Freiberg was fourteen when he arrived at Sobibór. When he was a young child, he and his family had left their native Łódź for the **Warsaw ghetto**. In 1942, he and other family members had escaped the ghetto but were caught in a roundup in the town of Turobin, near Lublin in eastern Poland. Berel and his uncle were deported to Sobibór in May 1942. From his long experience as a youth in the ghetto, Berel immediately recognized an opportunity for survival when camp officials announced that they were looking for artisans and skilled laborers. Although he had neither training nor experience, the young boy was chosen from among the prisoners and soon found himself a member of the camp's *Sonderkommando*. Freiberg endured brutal treatment, hunger, and disease in his first months at Sobibór. Hard physical labor and

---

32. For a discussion of the Sobibór prisoner uprising, see chapter 9.

the heart-wrenching nature of his new tasks quickly took their toll. Suicide was common among *Sonderkommando* units, and the teenager tried to hang himself on at least one occasion.[33] Memories of his loved ones helped steel his resilience, as did his decision to join the growing underground resistance movement among veteran Jewish prisoners at the camp. Freiberg participated in the Sobibór Uprising on October 14, 1943, and was one of nearly seventy Sobibór prisoners to survive the war.[34] In 1945, he gave an account of his arrival at the killing center to former **Oneg Shabbat** chronicler **Bluma Wasser**, herself a survivor of the Warsaw ghetto.

DOCUMENT 5-8. **Oral history of Berel Dov Freiberg, recorded by Bluma Wasser, 1945, in Isaiah Trunk, ed.,** *Jewish Responses to Nazi Persecution: Collective and Individual Behavior in Extremis* **(New York: Stein and Day, 1982), 268–78.**

After traveling on the train for a few hours, we suddenly stopped—we'd arrived in Sobibór. A platform on both sides of the tracks in the middle of a forest, with a tower ahead of us covered by barbed wire and vines through which the tracks led deeper into the woods. [. . .]

After our train moved in, the doors were thrown open and armed Germans and Ukrainians, cracking whips, drove us out of the wagons. We had bloody welts all over our bodies. The day we came to Sobibór was May 5, in the year [19]42. We were led through a second tower to an assembly point which was ringed by barbed wire fences, with posts on the wire perimeters capped by some sort of metal hoods. They split us up here—men to one side, and women and children to the other. Soon, SS squads came in and led the women with the children away. Where they were being taken to we didn't know, but off in the distance we heard screams of people being beaten and stripped and then we heard the rumblings of motors being started. It was the women and children being killed. We could sense in the air that, locked up like this between the wires, we'd be slaughtered right here. Night fell and we fell into a panic. We'd been told that in Bełżec, people were burned alive in pits. We wouldn't believe this while we were in the ghetto, but here, when we saw

---

33. See Berel Dov Freiberg's complete account in Isaiah Trunk, ed., *Jewish Responses to Nazi Persecution: Collective and Individual Behavior in Extremis* (New York: Stein and Day, 1982), 268–87.

34. For an account of Berel Dov Freiberg's actions in the Sobibór prisoner revolt, see chapter 9.

a fire in the distance, we were sure they were burning people. We were overcome with fear and started saying our *viduyim.*[35]

It was a nightmare. The Ukrainians beat us and wouldn't let us out to relieve ourselves. People evacuated on the spot. Later, they told us they wouldn't do anything to us, that the women had only been taken off to work. In the morning, SS men came and selected craftsmen and artisans to work as shoemakers, carpenters, locksmiths. I felt they'd let these people live. I also wanted to join these *baleymlukhe* [artisans], but I'd never been a worker and was afraid that if they ordered me to saw off a small piece of wood even, I'd bungle it and then would be worse off. So I sat and wondered—what can I do? Then the SS man pointed out all the healthy young men and ordered them to step forward, so I jumped up and squeezed in among these towering youths and sturdy craftsmen. I pleaded with my uncle to come with me, but he wouldn't move and I went alone. He was afraid, and something in my heart told me he wouldn't survive anyway. It took a long time to carry out this [selection]. We were led through still another tower, again to an assembly area, but there were no barracks here yet, only lean-tos and frames. The others were immediately sent away and we never saw them again.

There were thirty men in our group. They divided us up right away. Some [of us] were used to sort our belongings. The bundles were lying in ditches surrounded by wires and vines, with the same metal-hooded perimeter posts. The whole camp looked like this. I was taken into the second group and set to work digging a latrine. I never held a shovel in my life and a German who guarded us at work noticed my "skill" and let fly such a blow over my head that he nearly split my skull. That was when I learned how to work.

We worked from daybreak till nine, then they gave us breakfast. Bread and fingerbowls of fat [were] all we got and afterwards, they put us to work till late evening. As night fell, we were all lined up and an SS man informed us nothing would happen to us if we behaved well. If we didn't—they'd "make us a gift" of a bullet to the head. For the time being, they say, we work here, and in a week they'll take us to where the women are working. They'd already reached their destination and we'll be able to correspond with them soon. Their belongings which [were] still lying in the ditch were left behind because [they had been given] new work clothes at the labor site, so we could go ahead and help ourselves to their

---

35. In the Jewish liturgy, these are public prayers of confession.

coats and cover ourselves up and even sleep in the work shacks nearby. Then, simply, because he had the urge, he picked two men out—one who had stomach pains and the other who just wasn't to his liking—and led them off into the woods where he shot them. Most of the time the men returned from work beaten, bloodied, and injured all over the body. We knew what was in store for us now and everyone just limped off to go to sleep. [. . .]

Wagner[36]—he was the worst murderer—[once] broke a shovel over my head. My face was completely disfigured. The eyes were pulp. No matter on which side I tried to lie down, I couldn't. I stayed up whole nights and howled and wept in pain. They tortured us unbelievably. I looked like death itself. Everyone said I was a candidate for the *Lazarett*[37] because, in the beginning, I was never completely conscious. I was young, so they kept beating me. We had to keep working like this for two weeks without stop, because what seemed like an endless number of transports were arriving then from Czechoslovakia, Austria, and Germany, and afterwards, from Poland. [. . .]

While we cut their hair, we stole some conversation with the women—as long as no German was watching, of course. They asked, "Tell us, can you? Will this death be painless? Does it last long?"

They asked us how we were still able to work for "them" while everyone else was dead. We answered, "You have it better. You're going to die soon—but we have to keep working, getting beaten all the time, till we're finally exterminated too."

Many told us where they hid their gold and jewels so that we could save ourselves, and they begged us to take revenge against the murderers. They couldn't part with their children—if to die, then together, together till the last moment. While we cut their hair, they clutched their children to their bodies to be together like this till the end. And many women wouldn't let their hair be cut! They were shot at and beaten, but it was no use. They sat down and refused to move, not letting the barbers cut their

---

36. SS-Oberscharführer Gustav Wagner (1911–1980) served as an official at the Hartheim T4 facility and as deputy camp commandant at the Sobibór killing center. In the postwar years, Wagner fled to Brazil with T4 colleague Franz Stangl. A survivor of Sobibór identified Wagner in 1978, and German justice authorities applied for his extradition, a request Brazilian authorities denied in June 1979. Wagner committed suicide in São Paulo on October 3, 1980.

37. At Sobibór, this was a site disguised as an infirmary, where guards shot prisoners too elderly or weak to walk to the gas chambers under their own power.

hair, and refusing to walk on into the "bath" [i.e., the gas chamber]. They were either shot on the spot, or such a hail of blows rained down on them that they were driven [alive] into the furnaces. . . .

Many times, we planned dropping poison into the soup kettles so we'd die—but what would it have accomplished? We wanted to achieve a death that would take some of "them" along with us. But some of us must survive so the world would learn of us. There were countless times we planned rebelling and sabotaging the work. Enough! But then what? They'd shoot us and get others. It was senseless. We had to do something which would really change things and hit at them: arson, assassinations. As long as one person survived to tell the world!

Thousands of children survived the war years in concentration and forced labor camps throughout German- and Axis-controlled Europe. While young Jewish children were almost inevitably sent immediately to the gas chambers upon their arrival at killing centers such as Auschwitz, some adolescents, particularly those in their late teens, did survive such selections. Life for young people in concentration camp settings was fraught with danger, particularly if those youngsters were separated from their parents. Young prisoners suffered the same deprivation, overcrowding, and unsanitary conditions as adult detainees did, but children often proved less resourceful than their grown-up counterparts and were more vulnerable to duplicity and abuse both from their guards and from their fellow prisoners. In many camps, such as Auschwitz, children under the age of fourteen could not officially be assigned to forced labor details, although in practice this regulation was seldom observed.[38] Those who did not or could not work found themselves continually at risk of deportation to a killing center in the frequent selections that took place in forced labor and concentration camps. Children proved especially vulnerable to these *selektsyes*, as prisoners called them, and several camps experienced genuine "children's actions" aimed at culling very young prisoners from the camp population.

Youngsters who survived such hellish conditions needed an equal share of courage, stamina, and good fortune. Adolescents often did manage to mix in with the camps' adult populations because of their fitness or ability to work, and many succeeded in enduring the harsh conditions and grueling labor through the help of adult prisoners. One such lucky youngster was Janka Avram.[39] Born in Kraków in 1931, she was just ten years old when Nazi authorities estab-

---

38. Kubica, "Children and Adolescents in Auschwitz," 249.

39. The name of the interviewee cannot be established with certainty; a pseudonym has been used instead.

lished a ghetto for Jews in her native city in March 1941. In June 1942, Janka hid amid rubbish in a garbage can near the local *Judenrat* headquarters as SS officials and members of the **Jewish Order Police** searched nearby buildings, rounding up children for deportation. Nearly half of the Kraków ghetto's population—four thousand Jews—was transported to the Bełżec extermination camp as a result of this deportation action, including most of the ghetto's remaining children.[40] In the aftermath of the **razzia**, Janka's mother paid *Judenrat* officials to supply her young daughter with a fictive birth certificate so that she might be spared in any future children's actions. "I was eleven, looked like I was five, and was passing for a sixteen-year-old," recalled Janka, who worked for the next year in a ghetto factory.[41]

On March 13 and 14, 1943, SS units under SS-Untersturmführer Amon Göth liquidated the Kraków ghetto. Some three thousand Jews were deported to Auschwitz, while two thousand other residents were murdered directly within the ghetto walls in the course of the roundups themselves. Janka, along with her mother and father, numbered among the remaining two thousand Jews who were deemed fit to work and transferred to the nearby Płaszów forced labor camp. Separated from her parents, Janka again survived an extensive culling of the camp's children by sheer pluck and determination. Ultimately spared by Göth, Płaszów's universally feared commandant, twelve-year-old Janka was restored to her mother and survived the war at her side.[42] In February 1955, the twenty-four-year-old university student recounted her remarkable escape from Płaszów guards—immortalized in the Academy Award–winning film *Schindler's List*—to oral historian Icek Shmulewitz.

DOCUMENT 5-9. **Testimony of anonymous girl (Janka Avram), interviewed by Icek Shmulewitz, New York, 1955, in Isaiah Trunk, ed.,** *Jewish Responses to Nazi Persecution: Collective and Individual Behavior in Extremis* **(New York: Stein and Day, 1982), 117–19.**

The Kraków Ghetto was liquidated at the start of 1943. Most of the people still left inside the ghetto were taken to the death camps. Those who could still work were interned in the Płaszów concentration camp. [. . .]

40. An initial deportation action in the Kraków ghetto, on May 30, 1942, claimed seven thousand inhabitants.

41. J. A., quoted in Trunk, *Jewish Responses*, 117.

42. Avram and her mother survived a brief stay at Auschwitz and a series of forced marches into the German interior. In the midst of one such "death march," American units liberated the women near the village of Husinec on the Czech border.

There, my mother and I were put in the women's camp and my father was separated from us along with the men.[43] The 100 of us were taken to work at the factory from Płaszów just like we'd been taken from the Kraków Ghetto. After two months in Płaszów, I was no longer allowed to work at the factory because the Germans said my strength was failing and I could no longer do the work right. They had me work at the brush factory in Płaszów for the time. I could no longer see my parents, either, because the 100 Jews who worked at the factory were locked up inside and never let out—they were no longer part of Płaszów as they had been till now. [. . .]

Selektsyes [selections] took place all the time now, and the people were sent either to other labor camps or to Auschwitz. The most tragic [selection] was the one in August 1943. Children, sick people, and the aged were hunted down, herded together, and packed off to Auschwitz.

There was a children's home in Płaszów where the workers left their children for the day. The children of the Jüdischer Ordnungsdienst [Jewish Order Service] were also kept there. I was put inside this home with many other children while the big [selection] I just mentioned was going on.

The head of the Jewish police in Płaszów had been a suspected informer, but said he'd only been a milkman in Kraków. His name was Chilewicz. He knew I was going by a false birth certificate, that I was still a child. His wife was the head inmate of the women's camp. Soon, during an [*Appell*], Chilewicz's wife took me out of line and sent me to the children's home where all the other children were being gathered for deportation. She said I was also a child and belonged with them.

There were about 500 to 600 of us inside the children's home. The building was sealed behind barbed wire and guarded by Gestapo agents and not the sentries of the Ordnungsdienst. I spent only one night inside this children's home. The following morning, they started loading the children into trucks headed for Auschwitz. I felt sure they were leading us away to die and I decided to escape. As they were pushing me toward a truck with the other children, a German guard stopped a moment to light his cigarette. He stood [with his legs apart]. In a second, me [*sic*] and three other children—a boy and two girls—dropped out of line and, running low on the ground, we shot through the German's spread long legs. We

---

43. After a brutal beating by the commandant of the Płaszów concentration camp, Amon Göth (1908–1946), Avram's father was transferred to the Mauthausen concentration camp, where he died in the summer of 1944. Infamous today, partly because of his portrayal by Ralph Fiennes in the movie *Schindler's List*, Göth was found guilty of war crimes by a Polish court in Kraków and executed in 1946.

broke for the latrine. The German whirled around and fired, but he didn't hit anyone because we dropped to the ground as soon as we heard the first of his many shots. He couldn't come after us because he was afraid if he left the other children, they'd break away too.

The camp latrine in which the three children and I hid was exposed. As we stood there, we could be seen from all sides and we were afraid they'd spot us. So I quickly ripped out one of the boards covering the pit and jumped right into the hole, into all the excrement. The children jumped down after me. The last child dragged down the board I had ripped out with him, and this saved us. The latrine ditch was very deep because they dug the waste out every few days. We edged the board in between the two walls of the pit and sat over the feces on it for six long hours, not knowing what to do or how to get out.

When the [action] had finished, after the children and the old people were gone, the Jewish women started coming into the latrine to relieve themselves in the ditch we were in. The excrement was dropping all over us. We screamed and yelled to them for help, but no one could hear us because we were down so deep. So we dug our feet into the pit wall, and holding each other up, we used the board to bang on the floor above our heads. The Jewish women finally heard our screams and knocking; they yanked the boards out of the floor and pulled us up. Two children were half-faint from the stench they'd breathed in during the long hours at the bottom of the pit and collapsed. There were now no other children left in the camp—we were the last four Jewish children of Płaszów.

The women brought us inside their barracks and hid us in the top bunks. We were separated—each one of us to a different barrack. The women got one of the Jewish doctors in the camp to come see us, and he gave us shots against cholera—this was all done secretly, of course. We were hidden inside the four separate barracks for a week. The women took very good care of us and brought us food. Finally, the head of the women's camp—Chilewicz's wife—found out about us and informed the camp commandant, Göth. This German said to her that if we four children had the guts to jump into the waste to save ourselves, then we should be spared and not deported like the other children. This is how we were able to remain in the camp legally. We were the only children there and were really well taken care of—this was because the thousands of Jewish women who lost their children to the death camps treated us like their own.

My mother no longer believed I was alive—she again thought I'd been taken away with the other children when they cleared out the children's home. Someone who took food to the factory where my mother was locked up let her know I was alive and that I was still inside the camp. When my mother heard I'd survived, she went straight to the factory supervisor and begged him to let me come to her, to let me work by her side. The supervisor was a German, Captain Fischer—a decent man. This German gave in to my mother's pleas and went to the Płaszów Gestapo chief himself to take out a permit that would let me work in the factory with my mother. Captain Fischer then sent his adjutant, Hilbig, also a German, to bring me to my mother by auto. My mother had no idea this would happen—she didn't even believe they had really listened to her at all. But Captain Fischer and his aide were kind—it's because of them that I'm alive. [As the witness recounts this episode, she's noticeably moved when speaking of the two Hitlerite officers.—I. S.] From then on, I stayed at the plant with my mother and the others—we worked together past the summer of 1943.

DOCUMENT 5-10. **Following the liberation of Auschwitz, child survivors display their tattooed arms, January 1945, USHMMPA WS# 12110C, courtesy Wytwornia Filmow Dokumentalnych i Fabularnych.**

In late 1941, the National Socialist regime established the first stationary killing center to murder Jews within the context of the "Final Solution." German SS and police authorities chose the small village of Chełmno (German: Kulmhof) on the Ner River because of its location along a central road linking the nearby town of Koło to the city of Łódź. An abandoned manorial estate (the *Schloss*, or "palace") and an adjacent forest formed the nexus of the camp, which was planned as a killing site for the Jewish population of the **Wartheland**,[44] including the inhabitants of the **Łódź ghetto**.

Mass-murder operations began at Chełmno on December 8, 1941.[45] From that time until the spring of 1943, almost daily transports of Jews arrived at the "palace," where SS officials informed the deportees that they were to be

---

44. This region in Poland was annexed by the Third Reich.

45. For a discussion of the Chełmno killing center, see Shmuel Krakowski, *Chełmno, A Small Village in Europe: The First Nazi Mass Extermination Camp*, trans. Ralph Mandel (Jerusalem: Yad Vashem, 2009); Łucja Pawlicka-Nowak, ed., *The Extermination Center for Jews in Chełmno-on-Ner in the Light of the Latest Research*, trans. Arkadiusz Kamiński and Katarzyna Krawczyk (Konin: District Museum, 2004).

transferred as foreign laborers to Germany but must first undergo disinfection. After the unsuspecting Jews had undressed and surrendered their valuables, SS and police personnel led them to the well-lit cellar; there they forced the naked prisoners down a sloping ramp that led into the rear of a large cargo van parked outside. The vehicle in question was a gas van, like those already used successfully by the ***Einsatzgruppen*** (mobile killing units) to murder Jews and other victims on the killing fields of the Soviet Union. Once the cargo room was filled to capacity, the doors of the van were closed and sealed, and an SS driver diverted the carbon monoxide fumes from the exhaust into the interior of the van, asphyxiating those inside. Once the victims were believed dead, the van drove from the so-called *Schlosslager* (palace camp) to the seclusion of the *Waldlager* (forest camp), where any surviving Jews in the van were shot and the bodies buried in mass graves by a handful of Jews forming a special labor detachment, or *Sonderkommando*.[46] In the summer of 1942, when the smell of decomposing bodies could be detected in the surrounding villages, the *Sonderkommando* was enlisted to burn freshly murdered and buried bodies in crematory pits, while a smaller Jewish unit, the so-called *Hauskommando* (housework detail), sorted the victims' clothes and belongings and catered to the needs of camp officials. As at other killing centers, camp guards periodically murdered the members of each *Sonderkommando* and replaced them with a new detail selected from the incoming transports.

At the camp's inception, the small number of SS and police functionaries united under the command of SS-Standartenführer Herbert Lange; although his tenure was brief, the detachment would ever after be described in German documents as "Sonderkommando Lange"[47] even after SS-Standartenführer Hans Bothmann[48] replaced Lange in the spring of 1942. By this time, Chełmno had already claimed the lives of five thousand Roma from Austria, among the first transports arriving at the killing center from the Łódź (or Litzmannstadt)

---

46. Note that the term *Sonderkommando*, literally meaning "special detail or detachment," was applied equally to certain special SS units, such as the Sonderkommando Lange above, and to those details of Jewish prisoners who disposed of victims' bodies and belongings in Nazi killing centers.

47. In 1939 and 1940, before his tenure at Chełmno, Herbert Lange (1909–1945) had been responsible for the deaths of thousands of institutionalized disabled patients in the Wartheland. His unit, already styled as the Sonderkommando Lange, employed an early, ad hoc version of the gas vans used at Chełmno; see Volker Riess, *Die Anfänge der Vernichtung "lebensunwerten Lebens" in den Reichsgauen Danzig, Westpreussen und Wartheland, 1939–1940* (Frankfurt am Main: Peter Lang, 1995). Lange is believed to have died in Berlin on April 20, 1945.

48. Hans Bothmann (1911–1946) committed suicide in British custody in 1946.

ghetto. From mid-January 1942 until March 1943, thousands of Jewish ghetto inhabitants, as well as indigenous Jews from the surrounding districts, were murdered at Chełmno. In the spring of 1943, these deportation actions ceased, and SS personnel dismantled the camp, demolishing the so-called palace and shooting the last detachment of Jewish workers. In the spring of 1944, however, German authorities decided at last to liquidate the Łódź ghetto. Thus, for a brief period, trains again rolled along the Koło-Łódź line from Litzmannstadt, bringing Jewish transports to Chełmno until mid-July 1944, when the last Łódź ghetto inhabitants were deported to Auschwitz.

In all, at least 152,000 persons, the vast majority of them Jews, were murdered at Chełmno. Only four people are known to have survived the killing center,[49] one of them a teenage boy. Szymon Srebrnik (Simon Srebnik) was thirteen when he arrived at the camp from Łódź. His father had recently been shot before his eyes in the ghetto; his mother perished in Chełmno's gas vans. Once at the killing center, he was assigned to the *Hauskommando*. Nicknamed "*Spinnefix*"[50] for his swiftness and agility, the boy became something of a mascot among the German camp personnel, especially for gas van driver Walter Burmeister,[51] who insisted he would take the youth home with him after the war. Prized for his beautiful voice, Srebnik endured frequent beatings and humiliations at the camp, but he was continually spared in the numerous selections, during which other *Sonderkommando* Jews were put to death.[52] On January 17, 1945, two days before the arrival of Soviet troops, Bothmann ordered Chełmno's liquidation and, with it, the shooting of the Jewish *Sonderkommando*. Among the first to be shot, Srebnik miraculously

---

49. Like Simon Srebnik, Max Żurawski survived the second phase of gassings at Chełmno and gave testimony to Polish authorities in June 1945. Mordechai (Michael) Podchlebnik, from a village near Koło, arrived at Chełmno in January 1942, during the first killing phase, and as a member of the *Sonderkommando* managed to escape the camp, spending the rest of the war in hiding. He was a witness at the Eichmann Trial in 1961. A fourth individual, Szlamek Bajler, served in the so-called *Waldkommando* with Podchlebnik and escaped some two weeks after his arrival at Chełmno. He made his way to the Warsaw ghetto, where Emmanuel Ringelblum, director of the secret ghetto archive Oneg Shabbat, encouraged Bajler to write an account of Chełmno. Bajler was later deported to Bełzec and murdered there.

50. Literally meaning "quick little spider," this German term of endearment usually applies to slim, nimble youngsters.

51. Walter Burmeister was sentenced to thirteen years in prison at the 1962–1965 West German Chełmno Trial.

52. U.S. Holocaust Memorial Museum Steven Spielberg Film and Video Archive, RG 60.5024 (Claude Lanzmann Shoah Collection), Outtakes, Interview with Simon Srebnik, Tape 3279, Transcript, 8.

survived, as the bullet missed both spine and skull, instead propelling through the oral cavity and exiting through the nose. Quickly regaining consciousness, the youngster made his way to a nearby farmhouse, where he hid until the arrival of Soviet forces. Treated by a Red Army physician, Srebnik gave testimony concerning his experiences to Polish authorities in June 1945, as did fellow prisoner Max (Mordechai or Mordka) Żurawski, the only other known survivor of Chełmno from this period. In the early 1980s, Srebnik, then in his forties, appeared in the haunting opening sequence of Claude Lanzmann's epic documentary film *Shoah*. Simon Srebnik died in September 2006 in Ness Ziona, Israel, aged seventy-six.

DOCUMENT 5-11. **Testimony of Szymon (Simon) Srebrnik before the examining judge of the district court in Łódź, Władysław Bednarz, June 29, 1945, in Archives of the District Museum in Konin, *Chełmno Witnesses Speak*, ed., Łucja Pawlicka-Nowak, trans. Juliet D. Golden (Konin: Council for the Protection of Memory of Combat and Martyrdom in Warsaw/District Museum in Konin, 2004), 125–29.**

Up to March 1944, I had been in the Łódź ghetto, from where I was then driven off to Chełmno. In Łódź, I worked in the ghetto in the so-called "metal department." In March 1944, the Germans organized a roundup. They caught me while I was on a streetcar and led me to Bałucki Square where there were some cars from Chełmno. We were loaded inside and driven off. Besides me, there were fifty other Jews on the truck. [. . .] The Germans took us to a granary on the grounds of the Chełmno palace. There were no other Jews. We found out that we were in the *Sonderkommando* camp. An hour later the prisoners were divided into two groups. The stronger and better workers were sent to the woods; they formed the so-called "*Waldkommando*." Weaker and younger ones, I was among them, were left to work in the so-called "*Hauskommando*." The *Waldkommando* chief was Lenz. Other Germans employed in the woods were Runge and [Kretschmer].[53] The *Hauskommando* chief was [Häfele]. The *Waldkommando* consisted of about forty Jews; the remainder was assigned to the *Hauskommando*. We were all shackled. The shackles prevented us from walking in a normal way. We had to take very short steps. The shackles on our ankles were also chained to our waists. We slept in the granary on a cement floor. It was very cold. The members of the *Waldkommando* told us that they were building two furnaces in the woods.

---

53. Misspelled in original text; names in brackets are the correct spellings.

They did not know what purpose they would serve, but they expected the furnaces might be used to make charcoal. The furnaces were very primitive. [. . .] Jews building the furnaces were sometimes killed for entertainment. Lenz and *Sonderkommando* chief commissioner Bothmann showed extreme cruelty. At times, out of thirty workers sent to the woods, only fourteen returned. The groups of workers were constantly supplied with new men brought from Łódź. [. . .] The workers were given 200 grams (7 ounces) of bread a day, some coffee in the morning, and one-half liter (one pint) of soup for dinner. Only after the first transport had arrived did we get any blankets. We were constantly beaten during work. They hit us with their hands or spades. Obviously, blows from a spade resulted in death or mutilation, which actually equaled death, as those unable to work were finished off. [. . .]

The first transport came at the beginning of April from Łódź. In the morning Bothmann ordered the *Hauskommando* out of the granary. We were ordered to move baggage that had been unloaded near the narrow-gauge railroad track, in the place where it met the road. The prisoners were already locked in the church. We carried their belongings to the park, where two barracks had been built, one larger than the other. The confiscated clothes were sorted in the smaller building. Suitcases were put on one side and the sorted items on the other. The belongings were sorted by the *Hauskommando*. The most valuable items, new suits, etc., were kept in the smaller building. Valuables were given to Burmeister. The transported prisoners were taken to the woods by trucks at six in the morning. But before that the *Waldkommando*, consisting of about thirty people, had already left for the woods. The Jews did not expect any danger on the way. Three trucks transported prisoners to the woods. They were not allowed to take any baggage. In the evening fellow prisoners from the *Waldkommando* told us what had happened in the woods. After the trucks arrived the Jews were ordered to go to one of the barracks in the woods. The Germans told them to take off their clothes and put them in a separate pile, because they would put them back on after bathing. The underwear also had to be removed. Women could leave their panties on. Signs on the walls of the barracks read: "to the bathhouse" and "to the doctor." The Jews were driven out of the barracks and loaded into a van of a special type. If they refused to get in, the Germans used force. There were three vans: [a] larger one and two smaller ones. The larger van could hold up to 170 people, while the smaller ones, 100–120. The van doors were locked with a bolt and a padlock. Then the engine was started. The exhaust fumes entered the interior of the van and suffocated those inside. [. . .] Shouting and banging on the door lasted about four minutes. The van was not moving at that time. After the shouting faded, the vehicle started moving in the direction of the crematoriums. When the van reached its destination, its door was unlocked to let the fumes out. Then two Jews went inside and threw out the bodies. The gas coming out had all the characteristics of exhaust fumes (color and smell). I cannot be mistaken here. The corpses, having been searched through, were placed in the furnace. [. . .] It took approximately one hour for the corpses to burn. Then a new pile of bodies was added. There were a few instances of unintended self-incineration: a Jew trying to set fire to a pile of bodies died in the flames himself. The bones were ground with the use of a hand-operated grinder on a cement surface near the woods. [. . .]

[Srebnik reports that transports arrived in Chełmno every second day for two months, until July 1944.]

The camp was liquidated and the barracks dismantled. Machines for shredding clothes and underwear were sent back. The furnaces were also dismantled. In the granary there were still eighty-seven Jewish workers. Those were tailors and shoemakers. They lived upstairs. The number of workers decreased and finally there were forty-seven of them left—twenty-two tailors and twenty-five courtyard workers. Bothmann wanted to kill me several times, but [Häfele] liked me and this partly helped save my life. [. . .] When the Soviet army was advancing quickly, one night we were ordered to leave the granary in groups of five. I cannot remember the date. The area was lit with car headlights. I went outside in the first group of five. Lenz ordered us to lie down on the ground. He shot everybody in the back of the head. I lost consciousness and regained it when there was no one around. All the SS-men were shooting inside the granary. I crawled to the car lighting the spot and broke both headlights. Under the cover of darkness, I managed to run away. The wound was not deadly. The bullet went through the neck and mouth and pierced the nose and then went out. I hid in Wieczorek's barn (he knew about it). They did not find me. Later I learned that while killing the Jews, Lenz and [Haase] also died (I saw their bodies). When the two went inside, the Jews hung one of them and shot the other one with his own weapon. Apart from me, one other person managed to save his life that night. It was Max Żurawski, who pushed his way past the gendarmes and escaped.

Unlike the teenage survivors we have encountered, very young children had almost no chance to survive in the Nazi system of concentration camps and killing centers. In camps where selections took place, the very young shared the fate of the elderly and unfit in going directly to the gas chambers. Small children likewise rarely survived labor and concentration camp settings, although some succeeded in doing so, usually with the complicity and aid of adult prisoners or the camp underground. This was certainly the case with young Stefan Jerzy Zweig, whose rescue by members of the socialist and communist underground resistance movement at Buchenwald formed the basis for the celebrated East German novel *Nackt unter Wölfen*, written by Bruno Apitz in 1958.[54]

Stefan Jerzy Zweig, born in Kraków, Poland, on January 28, 1941, was the second child of Zacharias Zweig, a prominent young attorney, and his wife, Helena.[55] Less than one month after Stefan's birth, the family went into hiding to escape deportation to Lublin.

Moving into the newly created Kraków ghetto, Zacharias Zweig promised his small family that he would do his utmost to see that they all remained together. Miraculously surviving the liquidation of the Kraków ghetto and several work camps, the Zweig family, still intact, learned in July 1944 that they would all be sent to a HASAG[56] armaments factory camp in Leipzig, in the German interior. Upon their arrival in Leipzig, Zacharias and his son were separated from Helena and Stefan's eleven-year-old sister, Sylvia. Zacharias never saw his wife or daughter again; their train was bound for Auschwitz, where the two were murdered upon arrival. Zacharias, concealing his three-year-old son from German guards, reached the Buchenwald concentration camp, near Weimar, Germany, on August 5, 1944. Once at Buchenwald, the elder Zweig explained to camp authorities that he had received permission to bring the toddler along on the transport, and Stefan was officially registered as a camp prisoner. His personal information index card, shown in Document 5-12, indicates that camp authorities recorded the grounds for the three-year-old's incarceration as "Political [Prisoner], Pole—Jew" and gave him the prisoner number 67509.

---

54. A successful German film by the same name premiered in 1961.

55. Biographical information concerning Stefan Jerzy Zweig and his family is drawn from Zacharias Zweig's, *"Mein Vater, was machst Du hier?" Zwischen Buchenwald und Auschwitz: Der Bericht des Zacharias Zweig* (Frankfurt: Dipa-Verlag, 1987).

56. This is an acronym for Hugo Schneider Aktiengesellschaft–Metallwarenfabrik, Leipzig, one of the largest privately owned German industrial companies, which utilized concentration camp prisoners for armaments manufacture.

Buchenwald had existed as a concentration camp complex since 1937, and over the years, a strong underground resistance movement flourished there. A large percentage of its detainees were German political prisoners: communists and socialists arrested in the early 1930s and long established among the prisoner population. Many held influential positions as the heads of forced labor brigades or played vital roles within the camp prisoner administration. A circle of these prisoners, led by Willi Bleicher[57] and Robert Siewert,[58] decided that protecting the small boy would represent an act of resistance to camp authorities. These political prisoners worked to record the toddler in official records as a regular inmate and settled him in their barracks, providing him with food, clothing, and toys. In the fall of 1944, Zweig's prisoner guardians averted the young boy's deportation to Auschwitz by hiding him in the camp infirmary and replacing his name on the transport list with that of a sixteen-year-old Roma boy, Willy Blum, who tragically died in the gas chambers upon arrival at Birkenau.

Stefan Jerzy Zweig and his father were liberated by American troops at Buchenwald on April 11, 1945. The toddler was one of several hundred "Buchenwald Boys"[59] who survived the camp, although at four years of age, he was certainly one of the youngest of their number. Father and son were reunited with their chief benefactor, Willi Bleicher in 1963. Stefan Jerzy Zweig settled in Vienna, where he worked as a cameraman for Austrian public television (ORF).

---

57. Arrested by the Gestapo in 1934 for endangering state security, young trade unionist Willi Bleicher (1907–1981) was sentenced to two and a half years in prison. After serving his full sentence, he was transferred in 1938 directly to the Buchenwald concentration camp, where he was liberated in April 1945. After the war he continued his efforts as a trade unionist in West Germany. From 1959 until his retirement in 1972, he served as regional director of the trade union IG Metall in northern Baden and northern Württemberg. In 1977, Bleicher was awarded the Carl von Ossietzky prize for achievements in human rights.

58. Following the war, Robert Siewert (1887–1973) rejoined the Communist Party in East Germany, becoming the first vice president of the East German state of Saxony and later minister of the interior of Saxony-Anhalt. In 1950, the official Socialist Unity Party (Sozialistische Einheitspartei) of the German Democratic Republic (GDR) fostered a series of campaigns to discredit its more moderate members, and Siewert's career suffered as a consequence. Following Stalin's death in 1953, Siewert was rehabilitated. Until the end of his life, he was an important voice within the GDR's Union of Persecutees of the Nazi Regime.

59. For a discussion of the "Buchenwald Boys" in the postwar period, see chapter 10 of this volume.

DOCUMENT 5-12. **Prisoner personal information card of Stefan Jerzy Zweig, Buchenwald, August 5, 1944, USHMMA ITS Digital Collection, Buchenwald—Individual Documents, Male Section, R. 1.1.5.3, 7503616 1.**

Concentration Camp: Buchenwald   [handwritten:] Jew and Juvenile

Prisoner Personal Information Card

Family name: Zweig	Transferred	Personal description:
First name: Stefan Jerzy	[blank]	Height: 97 centimeters (3 ft., 1 in.)
Born on: January 18, 1941, in Kraków	Figure: slender	
Civil status: single	Children? No	Face: oval
Residence: Kraków, Burgstr. 4	Eyes: brown	
Street:	Nose: gen[eral]	
Religion: [Jewish]	Citizenship: Pole	Mouth: gen[eral]
Address of relatives: mother	Teeth: complete	
Helena Z., Schönewald near Leipzig	Ears: ———	
Concentration camp, H. Schneider AG[60]	Hair: blond	
Admitted: August 5, 1944	Language: Polish	
Through: RSHA[61]	Distinguishing features: none	
Admitted to: Buchenwald		
Grounds: Political Pole—Jew		

---

60. This refers to Hugo Schneider, Aktiengesellschaft (HASAG).
61. The Reichssicherheitshauptamt (Reich Main Security Office).

DOCUMENT 5-13. Survivors of Buchenwald walk through the liberated camp with Stefan Jerzy Zweig, a four-year-old Jewish boy protected by the camp's underground resistance, between April and June 1945, USHMMPA WS# 19041, courtesy of the Fédération Nationale des Déportés et Internés Résistants et Patriotes.

CHAPTER 6

CHILDREN IN THE WEB OF RACIAL HYGIENE POLICY

A SIGNIFICANT SEGMENT of Nazi persecutory policies stemmed from **racial hygiene** or **eugenic** theories prevalent among the international scientific community in the first decades of the twentieth century. The movement's leading American advocate, Charles B. Davenport, described eugenics as the "science devoted to the improvement of the human race through better breeding."[1] Eugenicists believed that the ravaging social ills that attended modern society—mental illness, alcoholism, sexually transmitted diseases, tuberculosis, criminality, and even poverty—derived from hereditary factors. Eugenics proponents championed three primary objectives: to discover and enumerate "hereditary" characteristics that contributed to societal ills, to develop biological solutions for these dilemmas, and to campaign actively for public measures that might combat these dangers. Throughout western Europe and the United States, where the movement was eagerly embraced in the 1910s and 1920s, adherents lobbied for "positive" eugenic efforts: public policy that aimed to maintain physically, racially, and hereditarily "healthy" individuals through social welfare for "deserving" families, marriage counseling, and motherhood training. Through these efforts, proponents hoped to encourage "better" families to reproduce. Dovetailing with these endeavors to support the "productive," however, followed negative eugenic measures: initiatives to exclude and hinder society's "unproductive" elements and to redirect social and economic resources from these "less valuable" to the "worthy." Many members of the

---

1. Charles Davenport, quoted in Henry Friedlander, *The Origins of Nazi Genocide: From Euthanasia to the Final Solution* (Chapel Hill: University of North Carolina Press, 1995), 4.

eugenics community, in Germany as well as in the United States, promoted strategies that sought to marginalize segments of society with limited mental or social capacity—the "feebleminded," the mentally ill, and persons with disabilities—and to limit their reproduction through voluntary or **compulsory sterilization**. Eugenicists targeted the mentally ill and cognitively impaired, arguing a direct link between diminished capacity and depravity, promiscuity, and criminality. They viewed as a menace the racially "inferior" and "shiftless poor" who transmitted their dependency on the public through the modus of heredity. Tainted through inherited deficiencies, these groups endangered the national hereditary community, eugenicists maintained, and placed a financial burden on the society that sustained them. More often than not, eugenicists' "scientifically" drawn conclusions about disabled individuals or ethnic and racial minorities did little more than incorporate popular prejudice. Yet, by employing "research" and "theory" in their efforts, they could assert their own notions of human inferiority and superiority as scientific fact.[2]

German eugenics pursued a terrible and separate course after 1933, but before 1914, the German racial hygiene movement did not differ appreciably from its British and American counterparts.[3] A genuine radicalization of the German eugenics community began shortly after World War I. Here, the conflict's unprecedented carnage, coupled with the economic dislocation of the interwar years, underscored in popular discourse the division between hereditarily "valuable" Germans who had died on the battlefield and the "unproductive" Germans institutionalized in prisons, hospitals, and welfare facilities, who had remained behind to reproduce and to draw their sustenance from the slender resources of the state. An allegory of the "stab-in-the-back" legend, such argumentation resurfaced consistently in the Weimar and early Nazi eras to justify eugenic sterilization and an abrogation of social services for the disabled and institutionalized. By 1933, the theories of racial hygiene had embedded themselves into professional and public conception and influenced the thinking of Adolf Hitler and many of his supporters and followers. Embracing an ideology that blended racial antisemitism with eugenic theory, the Hitler regime provided both the context and the latitude for the realization of eugenic measures in their most concrete and radical manifestations.

---

2. See Patricia Heberer, "Science," in *The Oxford Handbook of Holocaust Studies*, ed. John Roth and Peter Hayes (Oxford: Oxford University Press, 2011), 39–53.

3. See Sheila Faith Weiss, "Die rassenhygienische Bewegung in Deutschland, 1904–1933," in *Der Wert des Menschen: Medizin in Deutschland, 1918–1945*, ed. Christian Pross and Götz Aly (Berlin: Edition Hentrich, 1989), 153–73.

Children and adults of diverse backgrounds became victims of Nazi racial hygiene policy. This chapter discusses the compulsory sterilization of youngsters on the basis of presumed hereditary disorders, and—in the case of the so-called "Rhineland Bastards" ("*Rheinland-Bastarde*") (see Document 6-2)—of "mixed" and "inferior" blood. It examines the much understudied German policy of **Lebensborn** (Fount of Life), an organization that in Germany worked to sustain unwed mothers and their children but in occupied countries, particularly in Poland, located and abducted "racially valuable" indigenous children for **Germanization** and adoption by German families. It explores the National Socialists' only killing campaign that specifically targeted children: the child **"euthanasia" program**, which claimed the lives of five to seven thousand disabled German infants, toddlers, and juveniles. The following documentation also traces Nazi policies directed against European **Roma and Sinti** (**Gypsies**), targeting both settled and nomadic Romani populations for mass murder. Finally, it considers children as victims of medical "research," deployed in agonizing and often lethal experimentation to further the careers of unethical researchers or to underpin the racialist and ideological tenets of the Nazi worldview.

COMPULSORY STERILIZATION

One of the first racial hygiene measures employed by the National Socialist government when it came to power in 1933 was compulsory sterilization—an effort that stood at the core of broad-based plans to forge a new and utopian population policy in Nazi Germany. Such a strategy proved a double-edged sword. In a positive vein, German authorities would soon implement several complementary pronatal strategies, such as marriage loans (*Ehestandsdarlehen*), expanded marital and prenatal counseling, and child-support allowances (*Kindergeld*), meant to reverse Germany's dwindling birthrate[4] and to promote the increase of racially "valuable" children.

Compulsory sterilization was the other edge of the sword—an antinatal measure aimed at proscribing the propagation of "hereditarily compromised" Germans. Nazi ideologues portrayed individuals with mental, physical, or social disabilities as a "fifth column" within their "racial community"

---

4. The birthrate in Germany had been on the decline since 1870 but hit an all-time low in 1932. This was in part a consequence of the heavy losses among young men in World War I, but it also resulted from the demographic changes that came with urbanization in German lands and with women's efforts at enfranchisement and emancipation.

(***Volksgemeinschaft***), corrupting Germany's national gene pool and burdening its social welfare network.[5]

Nazi authorities resolved to intervene in the reproductive capacities of such persons. On July 14, 1933, at the injunction of Germany's leading eugenicists and racial theorists, the Hitler cabinet promulgated the **Law for the Prevention of Progeny with Hereditary Diseases** (*Gesetz zur Verhütung erbkranken Nachwuchses*). Also known as the **Hereditary Health Law** (Erbgesundheitsgesetz), the new legislation ordered the compulsory sterilization of persons suffering from specific diseases or impairments. Five of the disabilities designated in the ordinance represented psychiatric or neurological disorders, including schizophrenia, manic-depressive (bipolar) disorder, hereditary epilepsy, Huntington's chorea,[6] and "hereditary feeblemindedness."[7] Four physical conditions also warranted sterilization under the new law: hereditary deafness, hereditary blindness, serious hereditary physical deformity, and severe alcoholism, which many physicians and scientists believed to have a genetic component. Medical professionals, including doctors and midwives, were now obliged to report patients with these illnesses or disabilities in the exercise of their duties. Directors of hospitals, mental institutions, schools, prisons, workhouses, and concentration camps also proposed candidates for sterilization, as did teachers, social workers, and public welfare agencies. Denunciation by ordinary citizens—by employers, employees, neighbors, and even family members—was not uncommon.

After a petition to sterilize an individual had been proposed and processed, the suit came before a special hereditary health court (*Erbgesundheitsgericht*), a Nazi legal innovation superimposed on the existing German juridical structure. By 1936, there were approximately 230 hereditary health tribunals throughout Germany, each constituting two physicians and one jurist. If a particular court ruled for sterilization, the individual in question had four weeks in which to appeal the verdict, for it was a legal process. In the absence of an appeal—or if a

5. See Gisela Bock, "Racism and Sexism in Nazi Germany: Motherhood, Compulsory Sterilization, and the State," in *When Biology Became Destiny: Women in Weimar and Nazi Germany*, ed. Renate Bridenthal, Atina Grossmann, and Marion Kaplan (New York: Monthly Review Press, 1984), 271–96.

6. This incurable neurodegenerative disease causes a cumulative decline in mental and physical abilities, often leading to institutionalization. The disease results from a dominant mutation; any offspring of an affected parent incurs a 50 percent risk of inheriting the malady.

7. This ambiguous diagnosis today might include a wide spectrum of disorders, ranging in scope from various learning disabilities to mild and severe forms of cognitive and developmental impairment.

higher court turned down a standing appeal—the implementing decree for the 1933 law demanded execution of the sterilization procedure within two weeks' time at the hospital or clinic designated in the verdict. Paragraph 12 of the legislation sanctioned the use of force on unwilling victims. Those attempting to circumvent the procedure might be escorted by police guard to the facility in question. Gisela Bock, whose work still represents the seminal study of the topic, suggests that from January 1, 1934, when the legislation took effect, until the end of World War II, some four hundred thousand Germans were forcibly sterilized under the auspices of the Hereditary Health Law.[8]

The terms of the law allowed for sterilization of children as young as ten with parental consent and compulsory sterilization, mandated by hereditary health courts, for adolescents aged fourteen and older.[9] One youngster subjected to the procedure was Gerda E.,[10] a teenager from Freienwalde, a village 50 kilometers (31 miles) northeast of Berlin. Gerda was deaf and, like many hearing-impaired children at the time, had been institutionalized in order to receive a special education. In this period, school authorities made little effort to integrate blind or deaf pupils with their seeing and hearing classmates. Moreover, some medical professionals associated the inability (or unwillingness) to speak—then labeled "deaf-mutism"—with mental retardation, and many profoundly deaf children and adults who lacked oral development found themselves confined to a mental health facility or institution for the deaf.[11] Gerda E. was sterilized in early August 1936. The following correspondence, written by the director of the State Institute for the Deaf and Mute to Gerda's mother, speaks to the thoroughness of this process.

---

8. Gisela Bock, *Zwangssterilisation im Nationalsozialismus: Studien zur Rassenpolitik und Frauenpolitik* (Opladen: Westdeutscher Verlag, 1986). See also Paul Weindling, "Compulsory Sterilization in National Socialist Germany," *German History* 5 (1987): 10–24. This figure does not include individuals sterilized extralegally, either experimentally in the Nazi concentration camp system during the war or as a result of anti-Roma regulations surrounding the December 1942 Auschwitz Decree, by which German Roma and Sinti exempted from deportation to Auschwitz were subject to compulsory sterilization.

9. Martin Rudnick, *Aussondern, Sterilisieren, Liquidieren: Die Verfolgung Behinderte im Nationalsozialismus* (Berlin: Edition Marhold, 1990), 97.

10. This individual's surname has been abbreviated in order to protect her privacy and that of her family.

11. For a discussion of the German deaf community in this period, see Donna F. Ryan and John S. Schuchman, eds., *Deaf People in Hitler's Europe* (Washington, DC: Gallaudet University Press, 2002); Horst Biesold, *Crying Hands: Eugenics and Deaf People in Nazi Germany*, trans. William Sayers (Washington, DC: Gallaudet University Press, 1999).

DOCUMENT 6-1A. **Letter of Dr. Gotthold Lehmann, director of the State Institute for the Deaf and Mute and Teaching Institute for Teachers of the Deaf and Mute, to Frau E., Freienwalde, c. July 1936, USHMMA, RG-10.320, Horst Biesold Collection (translated from the German).**

On the basis of the Law for the Prevention of Progeny with Hereditary Diseases, your child Gerda was required to be registered with the local district physician [*Kreisarzt*] because it is suspected that she suffers from hereditary deafness. As you are certainly aware, hereditarily ill persons must, according to law, be sterilized in order to hinder the further spread of hereditary diseases.

I attach a leaflet containing instructions concerning the sterilization procedure for your information. You are asked to seek out your physician as soon as possible in order to discuss with him, in presentation of this letter, the case of your child and to ask him for oral clarification concerning the nature and consequences of sterilization. You will then ask him to confirm with his signature on the attached form that this instruction [concerning the sterilization procedure] has taken place.

I encourage you yourself to put in an application for the sterilization of your child. A form for the same is attached. The application does not imply that your child will be sterilized. It should serve instead to lead to an accurate examination of the case before the Hereditary Health Court. Sterilization will only occur when the Hereditary Health Court reaches the conclusion that your child is hereditarily ill.

You will lessen the work of the court appreciably and at the same time serve the interests of your child if you give accurate information concerning any cases of deafness or other illnesses among your family members. We attach a chart for a family tree, and ask you to fill in the details as fully as possible.

Heil Hitler!
[signed Lehmann]

DOCUMENT 6-1B. **Letter of Dr. Gotthold Lehmann, director of the State Institute for the Deaf and Mute and Teaching Institute for Teachers of the Deaf and Mute, to Frau E., Freienwalde, July 31, 1936, USHMMA, RG-10.320, Horst Biesold Collection (translated from the German).**

To Frau E., Freienwalde on the Oder

[address obscured]

By order of the Public Health Officer [*Amtsarzt*] of [Berlin-]Neukölln, your daughter Gerda, now resident at the State Women's Clinic Neukölln, Mariendorfer Weg, must be transferred for sterilization. Because Gerda is over fourteen years of age, a special declaration of consent from you is not necessary. Any objection would not alter this course.

Gerda will be transferred on Monday.

Heil Hitler!

[Signed Dr. Lehmann]

The Law for the Prevention of Progeny with Hereditary Diseases targeted Germans who suffered from certain mental, physical, or social disabilities. Yet even as the measure represented an endeavor to purify the German racial community by curtailing the reproductive capacity of its "hereditarily compromised" members, racism ensured that persons whom Nazi authorities considered outsiders to that community were also incorporated in the measure. For the most part, German Jews sterilized legally under the Hereditary Health Law tended to be included under the legislation because of perceived biological deficiencies, not solely on the grounds of racial antisemitism. **Sterilizations** of Jewish citizens were most common in large Jewish communities like Berlin, particularly where there was a concentration of poorer, eastern European Jews. As with German working-class victims, the grounds for sterilization in these cases lay predominantly in socioeconomic factors rather than in overt racism.[12] So-called Gypsies (Roma and Sinti), African Germans, and a segment of the Polish minority in Upper Silesia, however, figured as targets for sterilization on purely racial bases.[13] This was especially true for the so-called "Rhineland Bastards," the children of German women and French colonial troops who had occupied the left and right banks of the Rhine directly following World War I and again when Germany defaulted on its foreign loans in the 1920s.

---

12. Bock, "Racism and Sexism," 283. In the case of both Jews and "Aryans," the sterilization law tended to affect the lower economic strata of society.

13. Bock, "Racism and Sexism," 283.

By the early 1930s, there were approximately five hundred of these children between the ages of four and fifteen, many of them living in such Rhenish urban areas as Cologne, Koblenz, and Mainz. The Allied occupation of the German Rhineland was a source of national humiliation during the Weimar and Nazi periods, and these youngsters—some the offspring of consensual relations with occupying soldiers but also, in considerable numbers, the product of rape—had emerged as a living symbol of Germany's disgrace. Many of the children bore the physical features of their French African[14] and Indochinese fathers and were marginalized by the local populace. Police and medical officials had registered a large percentage of these "Rhineland Bastards" in the Weimar era, and several German public health administrators had urged their sterilization in the 1920s. By July 1933, with compulsory sterilization now a legally sanctioned measure, Nazi authorities refocused their attention on this tiny racial minority. On February 28, 1934, the Prussian Interior Ministry underscored the danger that these "mixed breeds" (*Mischlinge*) represented to the German population and recommended their sterilization. This 1934 memorandum warned officials in Germany's Foreign Office of the difficulty of sterilizing the children under the terms of the current legislation, for, with few exceptions, they did not suffer from the mental or physical ailments mentioned in the regulation. Ultimately, because the 1933 Hereditary Health Law contained no provisions for implementation of the procedure on racial bases, Hitler authorized the **Gestapo** and certain hereditary health court officials to carry out sterilization of these juveniles in a secret action in 1937.[15] This clandestine effort applied only in the Rhineland. Other African Germans, although marginalized as second-class citizens throughout the Nazi period, remained unaffected by the measure.[16] The wider fate of the "Rhineland Bastards" remains largely unknown: scholars researching this particular topic were unable to locate more than a few members of this minority still alive in the last decades of the twentieth century.[17]

---

14. The French Republic at the time had colonies in North Africa, including Algeria, Morocco, and Tunisia; French Equatorial Africa, including Chad, Gabon, Middle Congo (now the Republic of the Congo), and Ubangi-Chari (now the Central African Republic); and French West Africa, including Côte d'Ivoire (Ivory Coast), Dahomey (now Benin), French Guinea (now Guinea), French Sudan (now Mali), Mauritania, and Upper Volta (now Burkina Faso).

15. See Reiner Pommerin, *Sterilisierung der Rheinlandbastarde: Schicksal einer farbigen deutschen Minderheit* (Düsseldorf: Droste Verlag, 1979).

16. See, for example, Hans Massaquoi, *Destined to Witness: Growing Up Black in Nazi Germany* (New York: Harper Perennial, 2001).

17. Christian Pross and Götz Aly, *Der Wert des Menschen: Medizin in Deutschland, 1918–1945* (Berlin: Edition Hentrich, 1989), 196.

DOCUMENT 6-2. **Memorandum of the Prussian Minister of the Interior to the German Foreign Office, March 28, 1934, Political Office of the German Foreign Office, R99166, Partei, 84/4 (translated from the German).**

<u>Copy</u>

The Prussian Minister of the Interior   Berlin, February 28, 1934

III a II 714/34

As a result of the assertions repeatedly raised in the press, as well as in the petitions to the Minister President and the Ministry of the Interior, that a serious danger in the form of racial degeneration of the German population is to be expected from the mixed-breeds [*Mischlinge*] produced by colored[18] occupying troops and German women and girls, I requested in April 1933 an inquiry and a report from the appropriate *Regierungspräsidenten*[19] (Koblenz, Cologne, Aachen, Trier, Wiesbaden, Düsseldorf) concerning the resident mixed-breeds resident in their areas of jurisdiction. According to the information reported to me, a total of 145 authenticated cases of children produced by colored troops were discovered (administrative district of Koblenz: twenty-four; Cologne: six; Aachen: six; Trier: sixteen; Wiesbaden: eighty-nine; Düsseldorf: four). These were born in the years between 1919 and 1930, and are therefore today between the ages of four and fifteen. This figure may, however, be considerably lower than the actual number because, for obvious reasons, the mothers keep silent about their racially foreign [*fremdrassig*] offspring or deny that they are such, and therefore an exact figure remains elusive. Further, in my experience the mixed-breeds often appear to be of a pure European type, and therefore cannot be distinguished from the rest of the German population, even by racial experts. This is especially true for those mixed-breeds produced by white Frenchmen who themselves derive from African blood; these are represented even today in a significant number among the French people. If, therefore, all of the children produced by these soldiers could be surveyed, then even the figure of 500 to 600 estimated by experts in the field may not be too high.

In order to ascertain an unimpeachable judgment regarding the physical and mental state of the bastard children and concerning the racial

---

18. This term was used at the time to designate persons of color—above all, in this context, black Germans. The term is seen as pejorative today.

19. These were the local chiefs of administration.

significance of this intermingling of foreign blood in our western borderlands, I have, with the consent of the Director of the Kaiser Wilhelm
Institute for Anthropology, Human Heredity, and Eugenics in Berlin-
Dahlem, Eugen Fischer,[20] tasked his assistant, Dr. Abel—a recognized
expert in the field of racial studies—with a thorough investigation of an
easily recognizable segment of the bastard children. Dr. Abel[21] undertook
this assignment in July 1933, and with the help of state and communal
authorities, as well as schoolteachers, examined all known mixed-breeds in
the cities of Wiesbaden and [Biberach], in total thirty-eight persons. These
results, briefly summarized, are as follows:

The fathers of the thirty-eight children produced for inspection were
twenty-six Moroccans, six Vietnamese,[22] presumably two Turks, one Scot,
and one Frenchman. A further father is a cross between an Englishman
and an Indian; the latter, unknown, was in any case not of colored origin.

In outward appearance, the children of the Moroccans and the
Vietnamese—the others are irrelevant to these comments—were mostly
readily distinguishable as such. It must, however, be stated that the children produced by Moroccan fathers often display a completely European
appearance: a fact which has the natural explanation that many Moroccans
possess no negro blood, but on the contrary in a racial sense are fully

---

20. A prominent German anthropologist and physician, Eugen Fischer (1874–1967)
made his name in 1913 with the publication of research concerning the so-called Rehoboth
Bastards, the offspring of unions between Dutch colonizers and Hottentot tribeswomen in
southwestern Africa. His contribution to the seminal two-volume work *Grundriss der men-
schlichen Erblichkeitslehre und Rassenhygiene* (*The Foundations of the Study of Human Heredity
and Racial Hygiene*), coauthored with Fritz Lenz and Erwin Baur in 1921, established
Fischer as a preeminent German eugenicist. Fischer directed the Kaiser Wilhelm Institute
of Anthropology, Human Heredity, and Eugenics from 1927 to 1942. In this capacity,
he strongly influenced Nazi racial and eugenic policies. Fischer retired from his academic
appointments in 1942.

21. Wolfgang Abel (1905–1997), an Austrian anthropologist and racial hygienist, served
at the Kaiser Wilhelm Institute of Anthropology, Human Heredity, and Eugenics, beginning
in 1931. In 1942, Abel succeeded his mentor, Eugen Fischer, as chair of racial biology at the
University of Berlin. In conjunction with Fischer, Abel was involved in efforts to Germanize,
expel, and liquidate segments of the Soviet population in conjunction with the *Generalplan
Ost* (General Plan East). Following the war, he lived as a private citizen in Austria until his
death in 1997.

22. The original German texts refers to "Annamites," indicating a mountain chain in
the former French region of Indochina, including areas of Laos, Vietnam, and Cambodia.
Annam itself was a former kingdom and French protectorate in central Vietnam on the
South China Sea.

comparable to certain members of the southern Italian, Spanish, and Portuguese populations.

However, a large number of Moroccan mixed-breeds displayed a pronounced negroid appearance. The physical development of these mixed-breeds can in certain cases be designated as quite poor. Much more striking, however, was the inferior mental and emotional predisposition of these children, as was established through the examinations of Dr. Abel and through the questioning of teachers and social workers. With few exceptions, they show themselves to be possessed of an insolent temperament, exhibited through disobedience, slovenliness, a predilection for street life, and an inclination for pilfering. Great excitability, rising to the point of violence, makes education extremely difficult or fully impossible.

The children of Vietnamese extraction are to be categorized very differently. Even when the Mongoloid traits are clearly in evidence, they showed very satisfactory physical development, were easy to rear, and learned well in school. [. . .]

While the estimated number of 500 to 600 mixed-breeds within a population of 60,000 is not very large in itself, it must still be stated that these mixed-breeds now resident in the western borderlands, and the anticipated offspring, represent a racially foreign element among the local population. It must certainly be made clear from a social standpoint that the native population avoids contact with these mixed-breeds, that these individuals are held back from gainful employment, and that as a result, they will decline to a socially inferior segment of the population which feels no sense of belonging to the German people. In France there are already today half a million colored persons, and with the low birthrate among the French people, the mixed-breeds will make up half of the population within four to five generations. Therefore there is the obvious danger that, with the passage of time, the racial differences in the Franco-German border areas will increasingly be obscured through the propagation of the Moroccan descendants, and that the present racially predicated wall of protection will be leveled.

Certainly this danger has an excellent chance of being counteracted with a systematic population policy. Such efforts, however, must also be carried out with all energy because at this time they appear to be the only measures which can be undertaken. Because voices from many sides suggest a sterilization of the upper-age cohorts of those mixed-breeds soon to reach reproductive age, it must be countered that, according to the provisions of the Law for the Prevention of Progeny with Hereditary Diseases, only those mixed-breeds can be sterilized who are hereditarily ill in the sense of the law. If one were to deviate from this standpoint or adopt a special law allowing the possibility of sterilizing all mixed-breeds, then there may be the danger of highly unwelcome international implications. The French would probably view such a measure as directed against their colored French citizens, as the Japanese would view the sterilization of the Vietnamese offspring as directed against the Mongol race. Furthermore, a special law would have to encompass all of the numerous progeny of Negroes, Chinese, and members of other races produced through legitimate marriages with German women, and who are not present in large numbers in Germany. Such a measure on the part of Germany could then provide a pretext for other peoples, for example, the Japanese, to sterilize half-Germans living among them through legal measures. One must also reflect upon the fact that over half of the women made pregnant by colored soldiers during the time of the occupation are today married to German men and through these marriages have legitimated their mixed-breed children. [. . .]

Nevertheless, one must reason on the basis of the results of recent research that among the mixed-breeds of Moroccan origins there are certainly a large number who are of inferior material, to whom the Law of July 14, 1933,[23] is applicable without further question. If the pertinent agencies were to be advised in the implementation of this law, to direct especial attention to these mixed-breeds, then it may be expected that a not inconsiderable number of these carriers of unwelcome hereditary traits [*unerwünschte Keimträger*] can be eliminated from the reproductive pool within the framework of the existing law. Perhaps at some later date the Reich government will approach the idea of a law forbidding marriage between Germans and those of foreign [*artfremd*] races, as the United States of America has already considered, so that further legal grounds are available to protect us from the indubitably degenerative impact of racially foreign blood.

THE MANY FACES OF LEBENSBORN

Lebensborn (Fount of Life) was a Nazi organization established on December 10, 1935, in an effort to reverse Germany's dwindling birthrate and to increase the number of racially valuable offspring according to National Socialist

---

23. That is, the compulsory sterilization law.

principles.[24] Instigated by Reichsführer-SS **Heinrich Himmler**, Lebensborn represented an office of the **Race and Settlement Main Office (RuSHA)** until 1938, when it became part of the Main Office of the Personal Staff of the Reichsführer-SS.

In part, Lebensborn extended the 1932 **Schutzstaffel (SS)** Marriage Ordinance, through which the *Reichsführer-*SS granted SS members permission to marry based on the racial and hereditary health of potential couples. In September 1936 a further Lebensborn statute enjoined every SS man to produce at least four children, whether in or out of wedlock. Partly as a result of this injunction, Lebensborn gained notoriety in the postwar based on the false assumption that it represented a "breeding program" that forced unmarried German women into sexual unions with selected SS men. Lebensborn was nothing of the sort. The organization did function within the context of Nazi pronatal policy in that it carefully screened its participants according to strict racial and eugenic criteria and furnished advanced health care to the select mothers and children in its charge. In simple terms, the effort provided financial assistance and maternity care to the wives of SS men and also to unmarried mothers, a group that concerned Nazi racial hygienists and population planners. Illegitimacy still carried a strong social stigma in Nazi Germany, but to National Socialist ideologues, the reproduction of racially valuable children trumped traditional mores and religious values. Under the motto "Bear a Child for the Führer," such policy makers hoped to encourage racially "pure" German women to reproduce regardless of their marital status and undertook serious efforts to make single motherhood appear more respectable. Furthermore, as the termination of pregnancies was generally prohibited for "**Aryan**" women,[25] Lebensborn was seen as a measure to reduce the significant number of illegal abortions. Lebensborn homes, the first of which opened in 1935, provided a safe environment in which unwed mothers could spend the time of their

---

24. For a comprehensive discussion of the Lebensborn program in all its aspects, see Georg Lilienthal, *Lebensborn, e. V.: Ein Instrument nationalsozialistischer Rassenpolitik: Forschungen zur neueren Medizin- und Biologiegeschichte* (Stuttgart: Gustav Fischer Verlag, 1985); Dorothee Schmitz-Köster, *Deutsche Mutter, bist du bereit? Alltag im Lebensborn* (Berlin: Aufbau-Verlag, 1997).

25. A May 1933 German law prohibited the availability of abortion facilities and services and effected a stricter enforcement of existing antiabortion laws. Nazi anti-abortion policies forbade medical abortions even to women who had experienced two Caesarean sections, but they allowed eugenic abortions for women whom hereditary health courts had ruled must be sterilized and who were pregnant at the time of the decision. See Bock, "Racism and Sexism," 277; Lothar Gruchmann, "Euthanasie und Justiz im Dritten Reich," *Vierteljahrshefte für Zeitgeschichte* 20 (1972): 239.

confinement and delivery away from the prying eyes of neighbors and family members. Here they might receive excellent pre- and postnatal care and gain a chance to rebuild their lives after childbirth. The Lebensborn organization constructed a sophisticated support system, offering the mothers secrecy, aid in finding employment, and assistance in altering their civil status to that of divorcée or widow in public records if they wished to retain their child.[26] Lebensborn administrators encouraged unwed mothers to give up their infants after birth, and the organization managed both orphanages and adoption services that placed Lebensborn children in "good German homes." In the end, the organization established nine such homes on German soil and several more in German-occupied Europe. Many of the latter flourished in Norway, where local women who had conceived children with German occupying troops faced severe social ostracism. Georg Lilienthal, an authority on the Lebensborn effort, estimates that some seven thousand children were born in the organization's homes in Germany between 1936 and 1945[27]; 60 percent of these were the offspring of unwed mothers.

DOCUMENT 6-3. Letter of Frau A.[28] to Lebensborn, e.V., October 7, 1938, Bundesarchiv Berlin, NS 19/1064 (translated from the German).

Copy

October 7, 1938

T.B. 58, Straubing

Poste Restante

I read your address in the newspaper and now turn to you in confidence in my great desperation. I am expecting a child from a man I cannot marry. Because I don't know where I should go for the delivery—the matter must not be known either within my household nor here in Straubing (I am a social worker)—I would like to ask if you have a home where one can go long before the delivery date. The father of the child and I are both healthy "Aryan" individuals, and I would look forward to the birth of my child in a quiet place, away from the turmoil of my professional

---

26. See Michelle Mouton, *From Nurturing the Nation to Purifying the Volk: Women and Nazi Family Policy, 1918–1945* (Cambridge/Washington, DC: Cambridge University Press/German Historical Institute, 2007), 212–32.

27. See Lilienthal, 242ff. This statistic revises an earlier figure of twelve thousand children, introduced at the 1947–1948 Nuremberg Greifelt (RuSHA) Trial, whose data have in the last two decades become a matter of dispute.

28. This individual's surname has been abbreviated to protect her identity.

responsibilities. Do you guarantee secrecy? What are conditions like at your home; how high are the costs? I am a member of the Barmen private insurance benefits program: could this insurance company pay for my costs without all of this becoming known? Please send me your reply quickly. Because I do not know if I copied your address down correctly and the letter might come back as undeliverable, I'm asking that you send your response poste restante.[29] I am now in my third month and would like to go into a home in December or January, because by that time my condition will be apparent.

Heil Hitler!

P. S. Does your institution also help with the accommodation of a child after birth?

The Lebensborn program represented a positive eugenic strategy, even as the measure confined itself to a small number of racially "valuable" mothers and their children and excluded those deemed unfit or undesirable. But the effort also had a much darker side. With the German invasion of Poland, Heinrich Himmler added to his already formidable number of domains the Reich Commissariat for the Strengthening of German Ethnicity (Reichskommissariat für die Festigung deutschen Volkstums, or RKFDV).[30] The RKFDV had as its mission the Germanization of "racially desirable populations" in territories occupied by German forces. In part its task was to discover ethnic Germans (*Volksdeutsche*) among the indigenous Slavic populations and to relocate, or "repatriate," them. Under the auspices of Germanization, administrators from the Race and Settlement Main Office also conducted broad-based racial screenings of children in Slavic territories, searching for "racially valuable" children from among the local populace.[31] German authorities seized those youngsters whom they believed possessed sufficient Germanic background or "appropriate racial features" and passed them on to Lebensborn officials. These administrators in turn processed the children and placed them for adoption with German

29. This refers to a postal service in which a piece of mail is held at a locality's central post office until the recipient retrieves it; in the United States, the terms poste restante and general delivery are employed for international and domestic mail, respectively.

30. See Robert L. Koehl, *RKFDV: German Resettlement and Population Policy, 1939–1945: History of the Reich Commission for the Strengthening of Germandom* (Cambridge, MA: Harvard University Press, 1957).

31. See Isabel Heinemann, *"Rasse, Siedlung, deutsches Blut": Die Rasse- und Siedlungshauptamt der SS und die rassenpolitische Neuordnung Europas* (Göttingen: Wallstein Verlag, 2003).

families. As seen in the case of the children of **Lidice**,[32] those young persons rejected for Germanization were generally not returned to their homes and families but instead murdered or sent to labor or reeducation camps.

DOCUMENT 6-4. **German medical personnel examine Polish children at an intern-ment camp set up by the Reich Commissariat for the Strengthening of German Ethnicity in Łódź to select youngsters "acceptable" for Germanization and adoption by German families, 1941, USHMMPA WS# 90416, courtesy of the Instytut Pamieci Narodowej.**

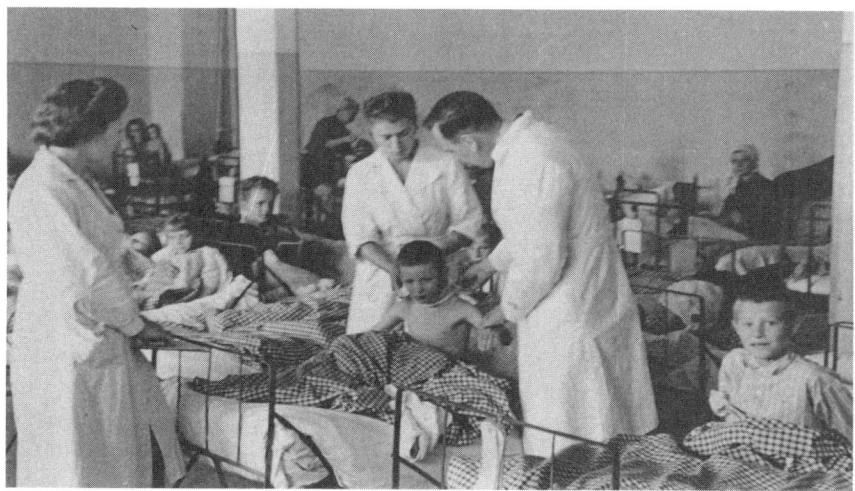

Because of the destruction of Lebensborn records during the war years, it is difficult to establish where the responsibility of agencies like the RuSHA or RKFDV ended and where Lebensborn's accountability began with regard to these crimes. In the eighth Subsequent Nuremberg Trial—the so-called RuSHA, or Greifelt, Case—Lebensborn officials succeeded in shifting culpabil-ity for the abduction of several thousand non-German children onto the various organs of the SS. Yet, as the following testimony from that trial makes clear, the collaboration of Lebensborn in the Germanization effort left a considerable number of victims: the children abducted from their homes, the bereft parents and relatives left behind, and, in many cases, the unsuspecting German families who adopted the youngsters.

---

32. For a discussion of the children of Lidice, see chapter 2.

DOCUMENT 6-5. **Testimony of Otto Uebe, November 4, 1947,** *United States of America v. Ulrich Greifelt et al.* **(Subsequent Nuremberg Case No. 8, RuSHA Trial), in** *Trials of War Criminals before the Nürnberg Military Tribunals under Control Council Law No. 10*, **14 vols. (Buffalo, NY: William S. Hein & Co., 1997), 4:1060–62.**

Q: When did you first think of adopting a child?

A: In 1942, before my son was killed in combat, he requested that if he were to be killed in the war, I was to adopt a child and that I was to bring him up [in remembrance of] him and devote myself again to living with my wife.

Q: When did you first apply to Lebensborn for an orphan child?

A: As far as I know, early November 1943.

Q: With whom—

A: Just a minute, please. I must correct myself. It was 1942. [. . .]

Q: Did you continue to correspond with Lebensborn after this?

A: Yes, I repeatedly requested that a child be assigned to me. Later on I asked an acquaintance in Munich to personally speak to [the] Lebensborn [organization] and thereupon both he and Lebensborn informed me that I was again to go to Kohren-Sahlis,[33] and there were two children available there, not two years of age yet, one a boy and one a girl. My wife and I, therefore, on the 7th of June [1942] went there because just on this day I was anxious to take over the child, this being my son's birthday, and there together with my wife I took the boy.

Q: Witness, what were you told about those two children and about their parents and what nationality they were?

A: I was told that those children came from South Carniola.[34] I wasn't interested any further in the girl, but I was told about the boy that his parents had probably been murdered by Serbian bands; that this was a full orphan.

Q: Witness, is the child sitting at the prosecution table the child you selected?

A: Yes.

Q: Witness, would you have taken this child if there would have been any doubt in your mind that the parents of this child were living?

A: No, I desired to adopt the child and this could only be done if it was a full orphan.

---

33. This was a Lebensborn home and adoption center in Saxony.
34. This is currently part of the country of Slovenia.

Q: Witness, did you ask Lebensborn to have the name of the child changed?

A: Yes. I was asked whether I was anxious that the child bear my name immediately. This could be done, I was told, and then I replied in the affirmative, and in Kohren-Sahlis the child was signed out under the name of Wolfgang Uebe, and registered again in that name in Bayreuth.

Q: Did you have any further correspondence with Lebensborn after that?

A: All I did was to request Lebensborn to confirm for me that I was taking care of the child myself, so that I could get a tax deduction and furthermore that I would get a child's allowance from the place where I worked.[35] I received another letter thereupon in which it was confirmed that the child Mathias Potucnik, now called Wolfgang Uebe, had been taken into my family and that I alone was responsible for the welfare of the child, as there were no other people alive responsible for taking care of it.

Q: After that did Lebensborn ever let you know that anyone else or the parents of this child were living?

A: Yes. At the end of 1944, I was notified that the father had been found and wanted the child returned to him. I was informed about it, and asked if and when I was willing to turn over the child to him. On that point I replied that I loved the child, that it was in our family and had become used to us, and would they kindly give me the address of the father so that I could contact him personally. In answer to this, I received a letter that I was to do nothing whatsoever; the matter would be submitted to The Reich Leader SS [Reichsführer-SS Heinrich Himmler] personally for his decision. Thereupon I heard nothing further from Lebensborn on the subject.

Q: Witness, after the war did you register this child as a foreign child adopted by you?

A: Yes. When the order was issued that children were to be registered, I made the notification that I had such a child which was actually not adopted; it is a foster child still in the care of my family, but the adoption had not formally taken place.

---

35. During the Nazi era, individuals received a financial lump sum annually for each child (*Kindergeld*) and a possible percentage reduction of any existing marriage loans (*Ehestandsdarlehen*) contracted by the parents; the former practice continues to the present day in the Federal Republic of Germany.

Q: Did you later hear from Mr. Mathias Potucnik?

A: Yes, I was told by the municipal administration at Oberhausen, where I live, that UNRRA[36] by order of Mr. Potucnik at Klagenfurt, St. Veiterstrasse 77, was inquiring as to the welfare of the child, and thereupon knowing that Potucnik was the father, I wrote to him; months passed before a Mr. Fahrenberger notified me that Mr. Potucnik was the father and he demanded that the child should be returned to him; as a matter of fact the letter was very nice. The father himself did not know German well and therefore the gentleman, an uncle and relative, was taking up negotiations with me; [the child's] father and mother had been in a concentration camp and the mother had died there, while the father had come back and now wished to have the child.

Q: Witness, where are you taking the child from here?

A: I am going to take the child to the German-Austrian frontier and there I will hand it over to Mr. Fahrenberger, who will turn it over to the father.

"EUTHANASIA"

The "euthanasia" program was one of many radical racial hygiene measures that aimed to restore the racial "integrity" of the German nation. The effort was National Socialist Germany's first program of mass murder predating the "Final Solution," or the genocide of European Jewry, by approximately two years. It endeavored to eliminate what Nazi authorities considered "life unworthy of life"—those individuals who, because of their severe psychiatric, neurological, or physical disabilities, were seen to represent both a genetic and a financial burden upon German society and the state. Hitler's authorization of the policy, signed on his personal stationery in the autumn of 1939, decreed that those judged incurably ill by medical science "could be granted a mercy death."[37] But "euthanasia" was a euphemism. The program systematically targeted disabled children as well as disabled adults living in institutions in Germany and in German-annexed territories. Historians estimate that two hundred thousand

---

36. This acronym stands for the United Nations Relief and Rehabilitation Agency.

37. This was Hitler's authorization for the "euthanasia" program; reprinted in Ernst Klee, *Dokumente zur Euthanasie* (Frankfurt am Main: Fischer Taschenbuch Verlag, 1985), 85.

patients, some 60 percent of Germany's institutionalized population, perished as a result of the "euthanasia" program.[38]

In the spring and summer months of 1939, a number of planners, led by Philipp Bouhler,[39] director of the Führer Chancellery,[40] and **Karl Brandt**, Hitler's attending physician, began to organize a secret killing operation targeting disabled children. Bouhler's trusted subordinates Viktor Brack[41] and Hans Hefelmann[42] joined them in this endeavor, as did Dr. Herbert Linden[43] from the Reich Interior Ministry's Department IV, which enforced public health policy. The group enlisted the aid of four physicians: Hellmuth Unger,[44] Ernst Wentzler, Hans Heinze, and Werner Catel. The latter three men were

---

38. Hans-Ludwig Siemen, *Menschen blieben auf der Strecke: Psychiatrie zwischen Reform und Nationalsozialismus* (Gütersloh: Jan van Hoddis Verlag, 1987), 214. For a detailed discussion of the "euthanasia" (T4) program, see H. Friedlander, The Origins of Nazi Genocide; Michael Burleigh, *Death and Deliverance: Euthanasia in Germany, 1900–1945* (Cambridge: Cambridge University Press, 1994); Winfried Suess, *Der Volkskörper im Krieg: Gesundheitspolitik, Gesundheitsverhältnisse und Krankenmord im nationalsozialistischen Deutschland, 1939–1945* (Munich: R. Oldenbourg Verlag, 2003); Ernst Klee, *"Euthanasie" im NS-Staat: Die "Vernichtung lebensunwerten Lebens"* (Frankfurt am Main: Fischer Taschenbuch Verlag, 1985.

39. Philipp Bouhler (1899–1945), the director of the Führer Chancellery, was one of the earliest members of the Nazi Party: he held NSDAP membership number twelve and participated in the Beer Hall Putsch. With Karl Brandt, he was a leading planner of the "euthanasia," or T4, program. Bouhler and his wife committed suicide on May 19, 1945, shortly after their capture by American authorities.

40. This was Hitler's private chancellery, a small office that managed his private affairs as head of state and responded to correspondence and petitions directed to the Führer personally.

41. Viktor Brack (1904–1948) ran the Führer Chancellery's Main Office II and, in this capacity, became involved in the clandestine "euthanasia" program. Until 1942, when he transferred to the front with his Waffen-SS unit, Brack served as T4's chief administrator, managing its daily organizational operations. Convicted by an American military commission in August 1947 as a defendant in the Nuremberg Medical Trial, Brack was executed at Landsberg Prison on June 2, 1948.

42. Hans Hefelmann (1906–1986) was the administrative director of the child "euthanasia" program. Although he was originally included in the indictment of several major T4 perpetrators in February 1964, the Limburg court ruled that Hefelmann was physically unable to stand trial and closed proceedings against him definitively in 1972; he died in 1986.

43. Herbert Linden (1899–1945) directed the Reich Interior Ministry's section responsible for state sanatoria and nursing homes and, as such, played an essential planning role in the "euthanasia" program. Linden committed suicide on April 27, 1945.

44. An ophthalmologist by profession, Hellmuth Unger (1891–1953) penned the novel *Sendung und Gewissen* (*Mission and Conscience*), which, adapted as a feature film, appeared as the 1941 "euthanasia" propaganda vehicle *Ich klage an* (*I Accuse*).

pediatricians with excellent credentials; Heinze had established a practice at Brandenburg-Görden, a pediatric clinic renowned for its modern facilities and advanced therapies, while Wentzler was the inventor of an incubator for premature infants ubiquitously known as the Wentzler Warmer. A fundamental concern of the planners was to develop a mechanism by which disabled youngsters—who often were not institutionalized until they reached school age—might come to the attention of public health authorities. On the basis of their recommendations, the Reich Ministry of the Interior on August 18, 1939, circulated a decree compelling all physicians and midwives to report newborn infants and children under the age of three who showed signs of severe mental or physical disability. Under the auspices of a front organization, the Reich Committee for the Scientific Registration of Severe Hereditary and Congenital Disorders (Reichsausschuss zur wissenschaftlichen Erfassung von erb- und anlagebedingten schweren Leiden), "euthanasia" operatives convinced or cajoled parents to surrender their severely disabled youngsters to one of the committee's many "special pediatric units" (*Kinderfachabteilungen*) throughout Germany and Austria. The clinics were in reality children's killing wards where specially recruited medical staff murdered their young charges by administering lethal overdoses of medication or by starving them.

At first, medical professionals and clinic administrators incorporated only infants and toddlers in the operation, but as the scope of the measure widened, they included juveniles up to seventeen years of age. Conservative estimates suggest that at least five to seven thousand physically and mentally disabled German children perished as a result of the child "euthanasia" program during the war years.

DOCUMENT 6-6. Circular decree of the Reich Minister of the Interior, re obligatory registration for "Deformed, etc., Newborns," etc., August 18, 1939 (Bundesarchiv Berlin, R 1501/5586, Reichsinnenministerium) (translated from the German).

The Reich Minister of the Interior	Berlin, August 18, 1939
IV b 3088/39	NW, 40 Königsplatz 6.
1079 Mi	Telephone: Depts.
	Z, I, II, V, III 12 00 34
	III, IV, VI (Unter den
	Linden 72) 12 00 34
	Top Secret

Re: Obligatory Registration for Deformed etc., Newborns

1. For the clarification of scientific questions in the area of hereditary deformity and of mental underdevelopment, a registration of relevant cases is necessary at the earliest possible instance.

2. I therefore order that the midwife who has rendered assistance in the birth of a child—even in the case in which a physician is present at the delivery—must submit a registration to the public health office within whose jurisdiction the birthplace of the child lies, upon the attached form, available at the individual public health offices, if it is suspected that the newborn child is afflicted with the following serious hereditary ailments:

1) Idiocy, as well as Mongoloidism[45] (especially in cases combined with blindness or deafness);

2) Microcephaly;

3) Hydrocephaly in severe or progressive stages;

4) Deformation of every kind, especially the absence of limbs, severe malformation of the head and the spine, etc.

5) Paralysis, including Little's Disease [cerebral palsy].

In the case of birthing centers and maternity wards of hospitals, the midwife has the obligation to register only when a chief physician (para. 5) is not available or is unable to complete the registration.

3. Furthermore, all physicians are to register children who are afflicted with one of the conditions named in para. 2, items 1–5 and have not yet reached their third year in those instances where physicians discover such cases in the practice of their profession.

---

45. Considered pejorative today, this term refers to Down's syndrome.

4. The midwife will receive a compensation of 2 RM [Reichsmark] for her efforts. The payment of this sum is to proceed through the public health office. In addition, she will be reimbursed for any postal fees she has incurred.

5. On the basis of §46, para. 2, items 3 and 4 of the Reich Physicians' Order of December 13, 1935 (*Reich Law Gazette* I, p. 1433), the Reich Health Leader [*Reichsgesundheitsführer*] requires all chief physicians of birthing centers and maternity wards to give the required notification for those children born in their institution or ward to the public health office in whose jurisdiction the child's place of birth lies.

All physicians are further required to send notification of registration to the responsible public health officer [*Amtsarzt*] at the child's place of residence in those cases in which children fall under para. 2 of this circular decree and have not yet reached their third year, and who have come to the attention of the physician in the exercise of his duties. In the possible event of a prolonged stay in an institution, the notification of registration is to be sent to the public health office in whose jurisdiction the institution lies.

6. For the filer of the registration suit (physician, midwife), the obligation to report, in accordance with article 3, para. 4 of the First Ordinance for the Implementation of the Law for the Prevention of Progeny with Hereditary Diseases[46] of December 5, 1933 (*Reich Law Gazette* I, p. 1021), is fulfilled with this registration. Further obligatory registrations, especially according to the Prussian Law for the Welfare of Cripples[47] of May 6, 1920 (Law. S., p. 280), remains, as before, in effect.

7. For each incoming registration, the public health officer is personally required promptly to satisfy himself as to the accuracy of the registration form presented to him. In the event that he is unable to do so personally, the public health officer may appoint a physician with a full-time or part-time appointment to the public health office as his proxy.

8. The public health officer must confirm the completeness of the data in the registration forms which he receives and, after supplying any requisite supplementary information, is to send the form, together with an accompanying findings report from him or his representative, promptly to the Reich Committee for the Scientific Registration of Severe Hereditary and Congenital Disorders [Reichsausschuss zur wissenschaftlichen

---

46. This refers to the compulsory sterilization law; see a discussion of the law and its ramifications in the first section of this chapter.

47. In German, the law was called *Krüppelfürsorgegesetz*.

Erfassung von erb- und anlagenbedingten schweren Leiden] in Berlin
W 9, Post Office Box 101.

9. The funds (compensation for special registrations, waiver of fees) paid out by the public health offices (including the communal offices) are to be requisitioned monthly from the Government Central Treasuries [Regierungshauptkassen] [. . .] On January 2 and July 1 of each year, the sums of funds paid out by the Government Central Treasuries [. . .] are to be reported to me in accordance with the appended example. The sums will be reimbursed by me through Reich funds. Negative data reports [*Fehlanzeigen*][48]are required.

10. A copy of this decree is to be prepared for the public health officer of each district. From these, a copy of this decree with the enclosed example is to be prepared together with a certificate of receipt for all midwives [and] chief physicians of birthing centers and maternity wards of hospitals in the district of the public health office. A corresponding number of carbon copies of the decree abstract will be sent to you by separate cover. With reference to the licensing of new midwives and the establishment of new installations of the aforementioned institutions, the same procedures should be followed.

At every opportunity, the public health officers should make midwives cognizant of the registration procedure.

11. The necessary registration forms are to be requested by the public health offices from the higher administration offices, whose needs will be covered by the Reich Printing Office. The forms will be dispensed from this source at no cost. A larger number of carbon copies for the first instance of usage will be sent to the higher administration offices by the Reich Printing Office by order of this decree. The shipping costs will be paid from this office in advance, and accounts of the same should be sent to me with the calculated balances as discussed in para. 9.

By Proxy,
[Signed W. Stuckart[49]]

---

48. Such a statement, usually from a regular recording post, indicates that there is no data to convey within a given time frame.

49. Wilhelm Stuckart (1902–1953), state secretary in the Reich Ministry of the Interior, was a legal advisor for the fledgling Nazi Party. Stuckart was heavily involved in the early persecution of Jews, cowriting the Nuremberg race laws imposed in 1935. A representative for the Interior Ministry at the Wannsee Conference on January 20, 1942, Stuckart supported forced sterilization for *Mischlinge* instead of deportation. Stuckart was convicted by an American military commission at the Nuremberg Ministries Trial, but his sentence was reduced to time served, and he was released in April 1949.

DOCUMENT 6-7. **Annamarie R., a young disabled girl born in Kassel, Germany, on January 30, 1935. She was murdered, likely by an overdose of medication, in the Eichberg "euthanasia" facility c. June 27, 1941, USHMMPA WS# 58297/HHStAW Abt. 3008 Picture collection, courtesy of the Hessisches Hauptstaatsarchiv Wiesbaden.**

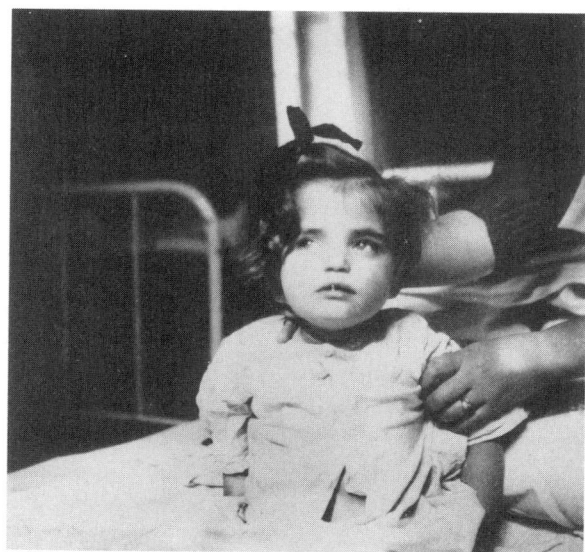

"Euthanasia" planners quickly envisioned extending the killing program from young children to adult disabled patients living in institutional settings. In the autumn of 1939, Adolf Hitler signed a secret authorization in order to protect participating physicians, medical staff, and administrators from prosecution; this authorization was backdated to September 1, 1939, to suggest that the effort was related to wartime measures.[50] "Euthanasia" functionaries called their

---

50. "Euthanasia" functionaries differ in their testimony concerning the exact dating of the Hitler authorization. T4 plenipotentiary Karl Brandt suggested that Hitler signed the document in late October 1939; see testimony of Karl Brandt, *Trials of War Criminals before Nuremberg Military Tribunals under Control Council Law No. 10* (Washington, DC: Government Printing Office, 1951–1952), 1:893. According to "euthanasia" physician Horst Schumann, the document was signed in mid-October. The most reliable evidence may come from Viktor Brack, perhaps the person most clearly in a position to know, as the text was written and transcribed in his office. Brack placed the time of Hitler's written authorization at late 1939 or early 1940, when the first killings began. In this way the authorization clearly laid an extralegal basis for the measure that protected participating doctors and administrators; see Ernst Klee, *"Euthanasie" im NS-Staat: Die "Vernichtung lebensunwerten Lebens"* (Frankfurt am Main: Fischer Taschenbuch Verlag, 1985), 100.

secret enterprise T4. The operation took its code name from the street address of the program's coordinating office in Berlin at Tiergartenstrasse 4. According to Hitler's directive, Philipp Bouhler, the director of Hitler's private chancellery, and Karl Brandt, Hitler's attending physician, undertook leadership of the killing operation. Under their auspices, T4 operatives established six gassing installations for adults as part of the "euthanasia" action: Brandenburg, on the Havel River near Berlin; Grafeneck in southwestern Germany; Bernburg and Sonnenstein, both in Saxony; Hartheim, near Linz on the Danube in Austria (then the **Ostmark**); and Hadamar in Hessen.[51]

Utilizing a practice developed for the child "euthanasia" program, T4 planners began in the autumn of 1939 to distribute carefully formulated questionnaires to all public health officials, public and private hospitals, mental institutions, and nursing homes for the chronically ill and aged. The limited space and wording on the forms, as well as the instructions in the accompanying cover letter, combined to convey the impression that the survey was intended to gather statistical data. The form's sinister purpose was suggested only by the emphasis that the questionnaire placed on the individual patient's capacity to work and by the categories of patients that the inquiry required health authorities to identify: those suffering from severe psychiatric disorders or physical disabilities, those not of German or "related" blood, those committed to a mental health facility on criminal grounds, and those who had been confined to the institution in question for more than five years. Secretly recruited physicians and psychiatrists—many of them of significant reputation—worked in teams of three to select patients for the program, often without seeing the individuals in question. On the basis of their decisions, T4 functionaries began in January 1940 to remove designated patients from their home institutions and to transport them by bus or rail to one of the central gassing installations for killing. Within hours of their arrival at such centers, the victims were murdered in specially designed gas chambers, disguised as shower facilities, utilizing chemically produced pure carbon monoxide gas. Thereafter, "euthanasia" personnel burned the bodies in crematoria adjacent to the gassing facilities. Other workers took the ashes of cremated victims from a common pile and placed them in urns to send to the relatives of the victims. The families or guardians of the victims received such an urn, along with a death certificate and other documentation, listing a fictive cause and date of death.

---

51. Only four centralized gassing installations operated at any one time from January 1940 until August 1941. In late 1940 the Brandenburg and Grafeneck T4 facilities were closed down and replaced with killing centers at Bernburg and Hadamar.

Because of the program's clandestine nature, T4 planners and functionaries took elaborate measures to conceal its deadly designs. Even though, in every case, physicians and institutional administrators falsified official records to indicate that the victims had died of natural causes, the "euthanasia" program quickly become an open secret. In view of widespread public knowledge of the measure at a critical juncture in the war effort, Hitler ordered a halt to the "euthanasia" operation in late August 1941. According to T4's own internal calculations, the "euthanasia" effort claimed the lives of 70,273 mentally and physically disabled adult patients at the six gassing facilities between January 1940 and August 1941.

Hitler's call for a halt to the T4 action did not mean an end to the "euthanasia" effort. The child "euthanasia" program continued throughout the year-long pause in T4 killing operations. Moreover, in the late summer of 1942, German medical professionals and health-care workers resumed the killing of adults, albeit in a more carefully concealed manner than before. More decentralized than the initial gassing phase, the renewed effort relied closely on regional exigencies, with local authorities determining the pace of the killing. T4 functionaries now employed drug overdose and starvation, methods already successfully utilized in child "euthanasia," as a more covert means of killing. Resuming at a broad range of custodial institutions throughout the Reich, the "euthanasia" program continued until the last days of World War II. Historians estimate that Operation T4 and its ancillary operations claimed the lives of two hundred thousand individuals, among them five to seven thousand children.

During the second phase of "euthanasia" operations, T4 facilities often participated in the murder of both juvenile and adult patients. Institutions such as Eichberg in Hessen, Langenhorn in Hamburg, Stadtroda in Thuringia, and Kaufbeuren, near the Bavarian city of Augsburg, housed adult killing wards as well as the "special pediatric units"[52] of the child "euthanasia" program. At each of these facilities, "euthanasia" operatives, functioning through a fictive organization, the Reich Committee for the Scientific Registration of Severe Hereditary and Congenital Disorders, arranged the transfer of disabled children from the parental home or from another pediatric institution to a participating T4 facility for killing. One of their victims was four-year-old Anita Hart.[53]

---

52. The German *Kinderfachabteilungen*, literally meaning "children's wards," is translated in this context as "special pediatric units" to denote a killing center of the child "euthanasia" program.

53. This individual's surname has been changed to protect her privacy and that of her family.

Anita Rosemarie Hart was born into a Catholic family in Ludwigsburg, near Stuttgart in southwestern Germany, on September 1, 1938. The infant girl was healthy, and Albert Hart, a skilled metalworker, and his wife, Erika, happily welcomed their first child. In early childhood, however, Anita contracted meningitis, a life-threatening infection that causes an inflammation of the protective membranes surrounding the brain and spinal cord. The toddler recovered from the disease, but the resulting encephalitis[54] had caused blindness and permanent brain damage.

As the child grew, medical professionals advised the Harts that severe cognitive impairment would likely leave her uneducable and that the youngster would probably require institutionalization. Yet, as with many young children with disabilities, Anita remained with her parents until she approached school age. At this time, Albert Hart had been drafted into military service and was serving with **Wehrmacht** forces at the front. Erika Hart was in the early stages of a new pregnancy. Alarmed by the prospect of caring as a single parent for a newborn and a severely disabled child, she yielded to the pressure of local public health authorities and agreed to place Anita in a pediatric institution. Representatives of the Reich Committee for the Scientific Registration of Severe Hereditary and Congenital Disorders—in reality operatives of the child "euthanasia" program—arranged Anita Hart's committal to the Kaufbeuren Sanatorium and Nursing Home (Heil- und Pflegeanstalt Kaufbeuren) on March 30, 1943. The facility's chief medical director, Valentin Faltlhauser,[55] informed the Harts that their daughter's prognosis for recovery was "extraordinarily bleak" but indicated that the child was "trusting and good-natured" and presented few difficulties for the nurses who managed her care. Anita lived at the facility for three months, during which time her mother, despite wartime travel restrictions, journeyed the 140 kilometers (89 miles) from Ludwigsburg to visit her child. Abruptly, on June 22, 1943, Erika Hart received a telegram that her daughter had died of pneumonia. In reality, Anita Hart, aged four years and nine months, had been murdered with a lethal overdose of medication. She

---

54. This is an acute inflammation of the brain.

55. Valentin Faltlhauser (1876–1961) served as the medical director for the Kaufbeuren institution from 1929. He not only directed both the adult and child "euthanasia" programs at the facility but also served as a consultant who selected adult patients for the "euthanasia" effort. Arrested in 1945 and tried by an Augsburg court in 1949, Faltlhauser was convicted on the relatively minor charge of abetting manslaughter and sentenced to three years in prison. For the fate of "euthanasia" perpetrators in the postwar period, see Ernst Klee, *Was sie taten—was sie wurden: Ärzte, Juristen und andere Beteiligte am Kranken- und Judenmord* (Frankfurt am Main: Fischer Taschenbuch Verlag, 1986), 198–99.

is one of 209 infants, toddlers, and juveniles who perished at the Kaufbeuren "euthanasia" facility between December 1941 and May 1945.[56]

DOCUMENT 6-8. Excerpts from the patient file of Anita Hart, March 30, 1943, to June 22, 1943, File No. 13029, USHMMA, RG-14.030M, Bezirkskrankenhaus Kaufbeuren (translated from the German).

Kreis Association Ludwigsburg (Württemberg)   Mathildenstrasse 8
                                                Telefon 4857–4859
                                                February 12, 1943
Juvenile Office
Re: Accommodations for the child Anita Hart, born September 1, 1938, from Ludwigsburg, Wernerstrasse 62.

The Reich Committee for the Scientific Registration of Severe Hereditary and Congenital Disorders in Berlin W9 reported to me in a letter of October 19, 1942, that admittance of the above mentioned child to your institution has come into question. Because her mother is five months pregnant, time is of an essence in placing this child.

I therefore ask a response at your earliest convenience as to when and under what conditions this child can be admitted there. What must be sent with [the child] in terms of clothing? The cost of care and lodging will be undertaken by the City Office for Family Support in Ludwigsburg, as the father at this time has been inducted into the army.

[signature]

Mr. Albert Hart
Ludwigsburg/Württemberg

Dear Mr. Hart!   April 8, 1943
Your child Anita has adjusted very well to the pediatric unit. She is causing no trouble. The condition of the child remains the same as before, as you are already aware.

The planned eye examination here has shown that at least in the right eye, some vision has been retained. In the left eye, the optic nerve has

---

56. Michael von Cranach, Martin Schmidt, and Robert Kuhlmann, "Heil- und Pflegeanstalt Kaufbeuren," in *Psychiatrie im Nationalsozialismus: Die Bayerischen Heil- und Pflegeanstalten zwischen 1933 und 1945*, ed. Michael von Cranach and Hans-Ludwig Siemen (Munich: R. Oldenbourg Verlag, 1999), 295. Approximately 1,350 adult patients were also murdered at the facility during the war years.

completely disappeared, while in the case of the right eye, some of the nerve has been left intact.

When the child is assisted in time, she does not soil her bed. The child is for the most part very trusting and good-natured; only on occasion is she temperamental for a short while and somewhat more difficult.

Given the nature of the illness, frankly there is unfortunately very little hope for the future.

Heil Hitler!
Signed Faltlhauser
Director

Dear Mr. Hart!   May 15, 1943
In the case of your child Anita, she suffers from blindness caused by encephalitis and meningitis contracted in early childhood. The blindness is caused by an atrophy of the optic nerve, which is in any case the consequence of the aforementioned illness. The brain damage resulting from a swelling of the brain during this illness unfortunately cannot be reversed. As regrettable as it is, the prospects for the future of your child are extraordinarily bleak. Here the physician's arts are at an end.

Heil Hitler!
Signed Faltlhauser
Director of Kaufbeuren

Telegram

Erika Hart   Wernerstrasse 62
                                                        Ludwigsburg/Württemberg
       Anita dead. Burial, unless other arrangements are indicated by you, on Friday, 11:00 a.m. at Kaufbeuren.
       Mental Health Facility
       June 22, 1943.

Death Certificate

Copy 1
Register No. 86   Month: June   Year: 1943
Place of Death: Kaufbeuren   District Police: Kaufbeuren
                           Street: Kermatherstrasse House No.: 16
                           Parish: Kaufbeuren   County Registry

District: <u>Kaufbeuren</u>
Place of Residence: District Police: <u>Ludwigsburg</u>
<u>Ludwigsburg</u>   Street: <u>Wernerstrasse</u>   House No.: <u>62</u>
Surname: <u>Hart</u>   First Name: <u>Anita Rosemarie</u>
Rank or Occupation: <u>Child</u>
Age: <u>4 Yrs. 9 Months</u>   Civil Status: <u>Single</u>
For children under the age of 15, it is to be specified whether legitimate or illegitimate: <u>Legitimate</u>
Religion: <u>Catholic</u>
Date and Hour of Death: <u>June 22, 1943</u>   <u>11:45 a.m.</u>
Duration of Illness: <u>Since early childhood</u>
Name of Illness (Main Cause): <u>Consequences of early childhood meningitis-encephalitis</u>
Secondary Conditions: <u>Idiocy,</u>[57] <u>atrophy of the optic nerve</u>
    Complications: <u>Pneumonia</u>
    Cause of Death: <u>Pneumonia as a result of influenza (33a)</u>
    According to Whose Diagnosis: <u>Dr. med. Faltlhauser</u>
    If Suicide, by What Means: _____
    Probable Cause: _____
    By Deadly Accident, Cause of Accident: [. . .]
    Labor or Industrial Accident: _____
    Probable Burial Time: <u>June 24–25, 1943, 11:45 a.m.</u>
    Notations: <u>Autopsy June 25, 1943</u>

THE DANGER OF "GYPSY BLOOD": ROMA AND SINTI

Without question, Jews represented the most significant "enemy" within the National Socialist worldview and the chief target of their racial policy. Roma and Sinti (Gypsies) figured as another group of "biological enemies" singled out by Nazi authorities for persecution. Although the scope, dimension, and course of the two campaigns differed appreciably, the convergence of eugenic and racialist motivations formed a common link between anti-Jewish and anti-Roma policies.[58] The proposed solution to the "Gypsy problem" varied not only among administrators in different regions but among top Nazi policy makers

---

57. In the German- and English-language contexts, "feeblemindedness," that is cognitive impairment, was defined medically in three grades: *Schwachsinn* (moronism), its mildest form; *Imbezilität* (imbecility); and *Idiotie* (idiocy), the severest degree.

58. See H. Friedlander, *The Origins of Nazi Genocide.*

themselves, who divided sharply into those who saw Roma in unequivocally racial terms and those who believed Gypsies represented a criminal element best left to police officials.[59]

The year 1936 marked a turning point in the Nazi persecution of Roma and Sinti. By this time, German officials had begun to concentrate German Sinti and Roma in so-called Gypsy camps. Furthermore, in November of that year, psychologist Dr. Robert Ritter assumed directorship of the newly established Eugenic and Population Biological Research Station attached to the Reich Public Health Office in Berlin. Ritter's primary task was to register persons of "Gypsy blood" in the German Reich and to classify them in terms of their racial makeup and "purity." In one sense, this was not a new phenomenon. Roma and Sinti had been registered in Germany since 1899, when the Bavarian State's Ministry of the Interior created an Information Service for the **Security Police** in Reference to Gypsies. Certainly in pre-Nazi times, there had been ethnographical study of Roma and Sinti language, culture, and traditions that predated, however subtly, the racial concepts of the Nazi era. The innovative nature of Ritter's efforts lay in categorizing Sinti and Roma according to a specifically eugenic worldview; in doing so, medical professionals and scientists could provide "evidence" of each individual's racial inferiority through the lens of "science."[60] Ritter employed a team of trusted researchers, among them the nurse Eva Justin, who served as Ritter's right hand and profited from her work with the Research Station by including a portion of its findings in her 1943 dissertation.

As Ritter's work increasingly became the basis for implementing a radicalizing Nazi policy toward Gypsies, his office was absorbed into the Reich Office of the Criminal Police (Reichskriminalpolizeiamt, or RKPA),[61] and in 1941, Ritter came to direct the Criminal Biological Institute of the Security Police. Ritter and his researchers continued to register and classify Roma and Sinti by charting genealogical data, tracing members of extended families, documenting marriages to "outsiders," and recording information on physical health, education, criminal activity, and social interaction. In the field, the researchers exploited their knowledge of Sinti culture, speaking fluent Romani, distributing candy

59. See Michael Zimmermann, *Rassenutopie und Genozid: Die nationalsozialistische "Lösung der Zigeunerfrage"* (Hamburg: Hans Christians Verlag, 1996).

60. See Patricia Heberer, "Roma and Sinti in Light of Nazi Medical and Eugenic Policy," in *The Genocide of Roma during World War II*, ed. Jana Horváthová (Prague: Office of the President of the Czech Republic and the International Task Force for Holocaust Education, Remembrance, and Research, 2004), 132–38.

61. This was Office V of the Reich Security Main Office, or Reichssicherheitshauptamt.

and trinkets to youngsters, and coaxing information from suspicious adults and guileless children. When their subjects arrived at the Research Station for blood samples, assessment of body features, and anthropometric measurement, team members were often less genial, using humiliation and threats to elicit responses to their numerous questions.[62]

In the end, the findings of Ritter and his team were a matter of life and death. On December 16, 1942, Reichsführer-SS Heinrich Himmler issued his infamous Auschwitz Decree, ordering the **deportation** of all German "Gypsy mixed-breeds" (*Zigeunermischlinge*) to **Auschwitz**. There were, of course, exceptions to Himmler's directive: "racially pure" Gypsies were exempt from the decree, as were Roma and Sinti who could show consistent employment and fixed residence,[63] those serving in the German army,[64] and those laborers whose employers could demonstrate that they were essential to the war effort. The decree provided specifically that all those individuals above the age of twelve who remained in Germany should be immediately sterilized. Most of the deportation lists for the twenty-three thousand German Sinti and Roma transferred to Auschwitz were compiled on the basis of Ritter's "scientific" efforts. Ritter and his team were conscientious in their task until the end: in the days before deportation of Sinti from Magdeburg began, Ritter and Eva Justin were seen at the Gross Silberberg and Sülze Gypsy camps, dutifully verifying their classification against transport rosters. Justin also spent the busy month of March 1943 doing similar work at the Feldberg and Marzahn camps, in southwestern Germany and outside Berlin, respectively.[65]

Because, in the course of his research, Ritter had concluded that most of the Roma and Sinti he had categorized did not represent "racially pure" Gypsies but "mixed-breeds" who continued to intermarry among themselves, the vast majority of German Sinti registered by the Ritter team were deported to Auschwitz, where nineteen thousand perished from starvation, disease, or gassing during the liquidation of the Gypsy family camp in **Auschwitz II–**

---

62. See Reimar Gilsenbach, "Wie Lolitschai zur Doktorwürde kam," in *Feinderklärung und Prävention: Kriminalbiologie, Zigeunerforschung und Asozialpolitik*, ed. Götz Aly et al. *Beiträge zur nationalsozialistischen Gesundheits- und Sozialpolitik* 6 (Berlin: Rotbuch Verlag, 1988), 101–34.

63. The overwhelming majority of Sinti and Roma did not meet this criterion, even if they once could have, for by the time of the deportations, most were already in collection camps, which did not count as a form of permanent or fixed residence.

64. Veterans and decorated individuals were also exempted.

65. Gilsenbach, "Wie Lolitschai," 110.

Birkenau on August 2, 1944.[66] One group of *Mischlinge*, however, was spared the 1943 deportations: forty "Gypsy hybrid" children housed at the Catholic orphanage Sankt Josefspflege in Mulfingen in southwestern Germany. These youngsters figured as the subject of Eva Justin's dissertation research and so were carefully shielded from transfer. By safeguarding them at the orphanage, Justin meant to preserve her living test subjects while she defended her doctoral thesis at the University of Berlin. In May 1944, shortly following the publication of her dissertation—the juncture at which a German doctoral title is officially awarded—the children were registered by local officials and likewise deported to Auschwitz.[67] Three of the older children were retained and sterilized as a condition of their deferment. All but four of those transferred to Auschwitz met their deaths in the gas chamber in Birkenau.

DOCUMENT 6-9. **ITO/ITS Report of Johannes Meister, children's search officer, regarding Gypsy children of Sankt Josefspflege in Mulfingen, c. 1948, USHMMA, RG-07.004*01, Zigeunerkinder aus der Sankt Josefspflege in Mulfingen (translated from the German).**

Inventory

The following children, examined by Dr. Ritter of Racial Hygiene Institute Berlin, in association with Dr. Eyrich, were transferred from St. Josefspflege to the camp at Auschwitz.[68]

On January 20, [19]44:

Steck, Siegfried	b. 01/19/1929	in Wiesbaden
Steck, Luana	b. 05/04/1934	in Wiesbaden
	(Parents: Franz Leonard and Johanna Dorf)	
Dorf, Rudolf	b. 08/12/1935	in Wiesbaden
Dorf, Maria	b. 11/12/1937	in Wiesbaden
	(Mother: Johanna Dorf)	

66. H. Friedlander, *The Origins of Nazi Genocide*, 252; Reimar Gilsenbach, "Die Verfolgung der Sinti—ein Weg, der nach Auschwitz führte," in *Feinderklärung und Prävention: Kriminalbiologie, Zigeunerforschung und Asozialenpolitik*, ed. Götz Aly et al. *Beiträge zur nationalsozialistischen Gesundheits- und Sozialpolitik 6* (Berlin: Rotbuch Verlag, 1988), 32. After the war both Ritter and Eva Justin were employed by the Frankfurt Public Health Office. In 1948, the Frankfurt prosecutor's office opened an inquiry into Ritter's Nazi-era activities but closed the case on the grounds of insufficient evidence in 1950. Ritter died in 1951. Eva Justin died of cancer in Offenbach, near Frankfurt, in 1966.

67. Gilsenbach, "Wie Lolitschai," 110–17.

68. The surnames of these individuals have been replaced by pseudonyms to preserve their privacy.

On May 9, [19]44:

Engel, Fritz	b. 08/14/1928	in Schmalfelden
Engel, Martin	b. 10/14/1931	in Odenheim
Engel, Amandus	b. 07/11/1933	in Busenbach
		near Ettlingen

(Parents: Johann Engel and
Beate Pfeiffer)

Gross, Rosa	b. 10/28/1927	in Weiler in
		den Bergen
Gross, Sofie	b. 07/04/1934	in Wilsingen
Gross, Ferdinand	b. 09/11/1935	in Gigen

(Parents: Ferdinand Reiner and
Friderike Gross)

Kolb, Johanna	b. 05/22/1928	in ?
Kolb, Franz	b. 04/30/1930	in ?
Kolb, Olga	b. 11/06/1933	in ?
Kolb, Anton	b. 09/19/1932	in ?
Kolb, Elis	b. 05/28/1935	in ?
Kolb, Johann	b. 07/12/1936	in ?

(Parents: Josef and Hilda Kolb)

Kolb, Anton	b. 12/07/1934	in Ravensburg
Kolb, Josef	b. 01/03/1936	in ?

(Mother: Elisabeth Kolb, tradeswoman)

Kern, Otto	b. 06/06/1934	in Stuttgart
Kern, Sonia	b. 10/02/1935	in Stuttgart
Kern, Thomas	b. 02/21/1937	in Stuttgart

(Parents: Otto and Franziska,
née Pfeiffer)

Mann, Luise	b. 08/20/1929	in Baltringen
Mann, Martha	b. 11/08/1932	in Dorndorf
Mann, Karl	b. 1933	in ?
Mann, Elisabeth	b. 07/29/1936	in Ittenhausen

(Mother: Ludwina Mann)

Reiner, Amalie	b. 01/18/1929	in ?
Reiner, Scholastika	b. 08/02/1933	in ?
Reiner, Anton	b. 04/04/1931	in ?
Reiner, Adolf	b. 03/10/1936	in Kirchdorf/Iller

(Parents: Josef and Amalie Reiner)

Reiner, Ottilie	b. 12/16/1930	in ?
Reiner, Klara	b. 08/11/1933	in ?

(Parents: Paul Reiner and Christine, née Gut)

Wand, Karl	b. 01/03/1933

(Mother: Katharina Wand)

Walther, Rosina	b. 03/11/1933	in Oberndorf
Walther Maria	b. 07/24/1932	in Hohentengen
Walther, Josef	b. 10/30/1936	Reinstetten

(Parents: Franz Walther and Maria, née Kolb)

Gross, Wilhelm	b. 02/28/1929	in ?
Reiner, Andreas	b. 08/16/1929	in ?
Gross, Patriska	b. 06/26/1925	in Baldern

Came to the Braun family in Markelsheim on June 5, 1941, and were collected from there and sent to Auschwitz.

Of these, the following children returned [from Auschwitz]:

Reiner, Amalie	b. 01/13/1929
	[here or above a mistake in the orignal]
Mann, Luise	b. 08/20/1929
Gross, Rosa	b. 10/28/1927

The following were sterilized:

Gross, Josef	b. 03/09/1922
Pfleger, Alfons	b. 08/24/1930
Pfleger, Mathilde	b. 10/28/1927

DOCUMENT 6-10. **Sinti children pose with a nun at the St. Josefspflege home at Mulfingen, ca.1943–1944. The children, spared as "research material" from immediate deportation, were later transferred to Auschwitz, USHMMPA WS# 08632, courtesy of the Zentralrat Deutscher Sinti und Roma.**

   In Germany, Roma policy followed a meandering, but ultimately, deadly course. In contrast to within Nazi Germany proper, Roma policy in German-occupied and Axis Europe varied from country to country and depended largely on local conditions. For example, authorities in Romania, a German ally, did not undertake a systematic killing of its Roma inhabitants per se. Instead, they deported some twenty-five thousand Roma to the Transnistrian Reservation, a section of southwestern Ukraine placed under Romanian administration, where eleven thousand Gypsies perished due to starvation, disease, and ill treatment beside deported Romanian Jews. Conversely, the Independent State of Croatia, an Axis satellite of Nazi Germany, virtually annihilated its national Roma population, murdering some twenty-six to twenty-eight thousand Gypsies, many at the infamous Jasenovac concentration camp complex.[69] In the occupied Soviet Union, including the Baltic States, the mobile killing units of the **Einsatzgruppen**, together with German police, SS units, and indigenous auxiliaries, shot members of local Gypsy communities beside Jews and political commissars, claiming the lives of at least thirty thousand Soviet and Baltic Roma. It is not known precisely how many Roma were killed in the Holocaust. While exact figures cannot be ascertained, historians estimate that the Germans and their Axis allies murdered 195,000 to 225,000 Gypsies, or some 25 percent of Europe's Roma and Sinti population.

On the eve of the German invasion of the Soviet Union, some nine hundred Roma lived in the small Baltic nation of Estonia.[70] In the first months of German occupation, no clear policy existed regarding this largely assimilated community, and the few Roma murdered in that period died at the hands of indigenous collaborators. This situation changed throughout 1942 as nomadic Gypsies fell prey to mobile killing units. In early 1943, all remaining Roma, without distinction to assimilation, were concentrated in camps in and around Tallinn, the Estonian capital. Here, Roma fit for work were mobilized for forced labor. In March 1943, a transport of "unfit" Roma—mainly the elderly, the ailing, and young children—found themselves transferred to the Jägala camp, 30 kilometers (18.6 miles) from Tallinn. Upon their arrival, Ain-Ervin Mere,[71] chief of the Security Police in Estonia, supervised a further **selection**, as he had recently done in the case of two previous transports of German and Czech Jews from the **Theresienstadt ghetto**. As in the case of the Jewish deportees, Mere and three colleagues—Jägala camp commandant Aleksander Laak, deputy commandant Ralf Gerrets, and camp guard Jaan Viik—drove the fifty Roma

---

69. See Marc Biondich, "Persecution of Roma-Sinti in Croatia, 1941–1945," in *Roma and Sinti: Understudied Victims of Nazism. Symposium Proceedings of the Center for Advanced Holocaust Studies* (Washington, DC: U.S. Holocaust Memorial Museum, 2002).

70. For an examination of the fate of Estonian Roma during the Holocaust, see Anton Weiss Wendt, *Murder without Hatred: Estonians and the Holocaust* (Syracuse, NY: Syracuse University Press, 2009); Ruth Bettina Birn, *Die Sicherheitspolizei in Estland, 1941–1944: Eine Studie zur Kollaboration im Osten* (Paderborn: Schöningh, 2006).

71. Following the war, Ain-Ervin Mere (1903–1969) fled to Great Britain. In 1961, the Estonian Soviet Socialist Republic tried several Estonian collaborators in Nazi crimes in the Baltic countries. Mere was tried in absentia and sentenced to death for his actions, but British officials refused to extradite him, and he died a free man in Leicester, England, in 1969.

prisoners by bus to nearby Kalevi-Liiva.[72] Here camp authorities had dug a large burial pit, now filled with an early spring snow. Half of the captives were Roma women; the remainder were children under the age of five. In proceedings before the Supreme Court of the Estonian Soviet Socialist Republic in March 1961, Ralf Gerrets described to the state prosecutor the murder of the Roma children. Prominent in Gerret's recollection of that day is the hesitancy of his commander, the bloodthirsty Lieutenant Laak, to shoot the youngsters.

DOCUMENT 6-11. Trial proceedings of *Supreme Court of the Estonian Soviet Socialist Republic v. Ain-Ervin Mere (in absentia), Ralf Gerrets, and Jaan Viik (Mere Trial)*, USHMMA, RG-06.026.12, Estonian State Archives of the former Estonian KGB State Security Committee, Records Relating to War Crimes Investigations and Trials in Estonia, 1940–1987.

> Prosecutor: By whom were [the Roma] shot?
>
> Gerrets: By Lieutenant Laak.
>
> Prosecutor: All alone?
>
> Gerrets: Yes, all alone. The last to be slain was an invalid, an old woman who had no legs. The warders were drunk; they seized her and dragged her, like a sack, along the ground. It was only when she gave them her gold ring and some money that they lifted her up and threw her "gently" into the pit. [. . .] When Gerrets opened the door of the second car, it turned out that there were small children there.
>
> Prosecutor: How old were they?
>
> Gerrets: Something between three and five, not more. They were crying.
>
> Prosecutor: What was done with them?
>
> Gerrets: The warders came and took them away.
>
> Prosecutor: Where?
>
> Gerrets: To the pit. There were seven men, each of them carrying two children. Two children were left in the bus. I took them. I was about five or six meters [sixteen to twenty feet] from the pit when the warder Purka ran to meet me and took the children from me. I myself did not get quite near to the pit.

---

72. Following his stint as commandant at the Jägala camp, Aleksander Laak served as commandant of the Tallinn central prison until September 1944. He ultimately fled to Canada after the war, where all evidence suggests he committed suicide in Winnipeg in 1960. His colleagues Ralf Gerrets and Jan Viik received death sentences in the Mere Trial in 1961 and were executed. See Birn, *Die Sicherheitspolizei in Estland*, 232ff.

Prosecutor: But you took the children out of the car?

Gerrets: Yes. A warder wanted to help me, but I said it was not necessary, I'd manage by myself.

Prosecutor: Who shot the children?

Gerrets: When I took a glance at the pit, I saw that Laak was standing on the right, Viik on the left, both with automatic guns in their hands. When we got back to the camp, we sat down to dinner and the commandant brought a bottle of vodka. Viik, too, came there, having already emptied his bottle. Laak praised him: "You were a brave man, Viik, to be the first to shoot!"

CHILDREN AS "RESEARCH MATERIAL"

As we have seen in the case of Eva Justin, Romani (Gypsy) children figured not only as the objects of racial discrimination and persecution but also as "research material," gathered and studied in order to further the career of a woman who had played such a vital role in the enforcement of anti-Gypsy policy. German medical professionals and scientists performing human experimentation under the Nazi aegis felt little compunction about utilizing "inferior" individuals of every category to develop pharmaceuticals and treatment methods, to promote Nazi racial goals, or to advance their own academic or professional standings, even when the "test subjects" for that research were children. SS physician Kurt Heissmeyer, whose consuming ambition was to find a cure for tuberculosis, serves as a case in point.

Born in 1905, Heissmeyer received his physician's license in 1933 and shortly thereafter took up a position at the Hohenlychen sanatorium, 120 kilometers (about 75 miles) north of Berlin.[73] By 1944, after nearly ten years at this post, he still aspired to become a professor of medicine, a goal supported by his superior, Dr. Karl Gebhardt, Hohenlychen's head clinician and the author of a series of grisly medical experiments conducted on female prisoners at the nearby **Ravensbrück** concentration camp. As a topic of research

---

73. During the war years, the Hohenlychen clinic for tubercular patients acquired an unsavory reputation in light of its designation as a health resort for SS officers in 1942 and as a result of the grisly experimentation by its director, Karl Gebhardt (1897–1948), at the sanatorium and at the nearby Ravensbrück concentration camp. In August 1947, Gebhardt was convicted and sentenced to death by an American military tribunal in the Nuremberg Doctors' Trial; he was executed on June 2, 1948. See Birgitt Morgenbrod and Stephanie, *Merkenich, Das Deutsche Rote Kreuz unter der NS-Diktatur, 1933–1945* (Paderborn: Ferdinand Schöningh, 2008), 139ff.

for his *Habilitation*, Heissmeyer proposed to combat primary tuberculosis (tuberculosis of the lung) by the artificial introduction of cutaneous tuberculosis (tuberculosis of the skin) in an ailing patient. As the nephew of influential SS general August Heissmeyer,[74] the thirty-eight-year-old physician gained entrée into the highest SS circles and, with Gebhardt's intervention, obtained permission from Reich Physician Leader (Reichsärzteführer) Leonardo Conti[75] and from Reichsführer-SS Heinrich Himmler to test his hypothesis on concentration camp prisoners. Unfortunately, pulmonologists had long rejected Heissmeyer's theory, first suggested by Austrian physicians a decade earlier; it says much about Heissmeyer's professional competence that he was not sufficiently acquainted with his own field to be aware of these earlier findings. In early June 1944, Heissmeyer began experimentation with several dozen Russian and Polish prisoners at the Neuengamme concentration camp near Hamburg. In the autumn of that year, he himself came to the conclusion that the theory was erroneous when the condition of the adult male prisoners manifestly worsened as a result of his treatments. Desperate to fulfill the requirements for his *Habilitation*, however, Heissmeyer decided to press on with his last cohort of "test subjects," juveniles, and ordered the transfer of twenty Jewish children from the Auschwitz concentration camp.[76]

On November 27, 1944, the youngsters, ten girls and ten boys, arrived at Neuengamme. They were mainly Polish, Dutch, and French Jews, entrusted to the care of French prisoner-physicians René Quenouille and Gabriel Florence

---

74. August Heissmeyer (1897–1979) served provisionally as Theodor Eiche's successor as inspector of concentration camps in November 1939. With the outbreak of war, Heissmeyer received his own bureau (Dienststelle Obergruppenführer Heissmeyer) through which he was responsible for the military training of students of the National Political Education Institutes (Nationalpolitische Erziehungsanstalten). In 1940, he married Reich Women's Leader (Reichsfrauenführer) Gertrud Scholtz-Klink. After the war he received a three-year prison sentence from a denazification court in the French zone of occupation.

75. Replacing his rival Gerhard Wagner as Reich Physician Leader in 1939, Leonardo Conti (1900–1945) was initially involved in the T4 "euthanasia" program, although Hitler's choice of Karl Brandt and Philipp Bouhler to spearhead the clandestine operation meant that Conti would ultimately play an auxiliary role in the measure. Conti committed suicide while in Allied custody in 1945.

76. Michael Kater, "Criminal Physicians in the Third Reich: Toward a Group Portrait," in *Medicine and Medical Ethics in Nazi Germany: Origins, Practices, Legacies*, ed. Francis Nicosia and Jonathan Huener (Oxford: Berghahn Books, 2002), 84–85; Günther Schwarberg, *Der SS-Arzt und die Kinder: Bericht über den Mord von Bullenhuser Damm* (Hamburg: Stern Verlag, 1979), 11–15, 30–34.

and two Dutch male nurses, Anton Hölzel and Dirk Deutekom.[77] The eldest
children of the group were twelve years old, the youngest just five. Shortly after
their appearance at the camp, Heissmeyer made incisions in the skin of each
child and infected him or her with tubercular bacillus cultures. By Christmas
1944, the children were severely ill with tuberculosis, but their ordeal was not
over. In mid-January, Heissmeyer, himself not a surgeon, ordered a Czech
prisoner-physician to remove the youngsters' axillary lymph nodes, located in
the underarm area, in order to determine how each child's lymphatic system
reacted to tubercular infection. Throughout the winter, the children remained
bedridden. They quickly attracted the sympathy and solidarity of their fellow
prisoners, who, in violation of regulations, came in significant numbers to visit
the young patients and to supplement their diet from their own meager rations.

By mid-April 1944, British troops stood only a few miles from Hamburg.
Everyone knew that occupation was close at hand, and Heissmeyer, still based
at Hohenlychen, had not dared to visit Neuengamme or his test subjects for
several weeks. On April 20, guards of the Neuengamme camp received orders
to murder the children before the arrival of Allied forces. At ten that evening,
prisoner-physicians Florence and Quenouille and male nurses Deutekom and
Hölzel were instructed to wake their young charges and dress them. Shortly
thereafter, SS physician Alfred Trzebinkski and a handful of Neuengamme
guards drove with the prisoners to the Rothenburgsort district of Hamburg, to
a large school building on the Bullenhuser Damm. The area had been bombed
out since 1943, and the ruins of the facility had since served as a Neuengamme
satellite camp. Improvising, because he did not have a sufficient supply of seda-
tives to murder the children, Trzebinkski injected the children with morphine.
While they slept, Obersturmführer Arnold Strippel and SS men Johann Frahm
and Ewald Jauch hanged the children from coat hooks in the school's abandoned cloakroom. The group also murdered their four adult attendants, as
well as several other Soviet detainees newly transferred to the satellite camp. In
October 1946, British authorities executed Trzebinkski, Jauch, and Frahm for
their part in crimes at the Neuengamme complex. Imprisoned for other crimes,
Strippel was charged in 1983 by the Hamburg prosecutors' office for his role
in the deaths of the twenty children, but after several years of legal wrangling,
Strippel was finally adjudged unfit to stand trial. Kurt Heissmeyer, author of
the tuberculosis experiments, eluded arrest for nearly twenty years, working as a
lung specialist in Magdeburg. In 1966, an East German court finally sentenced

---

77. The four men had been arrested for resistance activities in their native countries.
The four female Polish nurses who had accompanied the children on the transport from
Auschwitz were murdered in Neuengamme shortly after their arrival.

the physician to life imprisonment.[78] In 1980, the city of Hamburg established a memorial in the former schoolhouse to the Children of Bullenhuser Damm.

DOCUMENT 6-12. **Testimony of Johann Frahm, March 3 to June 18, 1946, *UK v. Max Pauly, et al.* (Curio-Haus Case) March 29, 1946, USHMMA, RG-59.016M, Reel 4, Judge Advocate General's Office, United Kingdom, War Crimes Case Files, Second World War, 1945–1953, Public Record Office.**

Defense Counsel Dr. Lappenberg: I must ask you whether you have not withheld something from the court?

Johann Frahm: Not that I know of.

Lappenberg: You said that the children fell asleep. What happened after that?

Frahm: They were all bedded down in one room.

Lappenberg: Did you see them lying in the room?

Frahm: Yes, they slept and did not wake up again.

Lappenberg: How did you know that those children were dead?

Frahm: One could see that.

Lappenberg: What kind of an injection did they get?

Frahm: I cannot say.

Lappenberg: Did those children die as a result of those injections, or did they die because of anything else?

Frahm: They died as a cause of the injections. Some of the children were hanged on top of that.

Lappenberg: And when did that hanging happen?

Frahm: Immediately afterwards.

Lappenberg: Who was taking part in that?

Frahm: Dr. Trzebinkski and I myself helped.

Lappenberg: You said immediately afterwards. What do you mean by that?

Frahm: I mean if they had still a breath of life in them after a quarter of an hour, but I cannot say for certain about a quarter of an hour, whether it was shorter or longer.

President of the Commission: Do you mean that after about a quarter of an hour, if they had any life in them, they were hanged?

Frahm: Yes.

Lappenberg: Who put the rope around the neck of the children?

---

78. Kurt Heissmeyer died in custody fourteen months later of a heart attack.

Frahm: I [did]. [. . .]

Lappenberg: Where did you get your orders from to go into the cellar with these children?

Frahm: From Oberscharführer Jauch.

Judge Advocate[79]: Was he the senior of the SS personnel in this out-station or was there an SS officer in charge of this outstation?

Frahm: He was responsible for that working party or for that detach-ment, but there was an officer responsible for several detachments, and he was of course senior.

Judge Advocate: Do you know the name of that officer?

Frahm: Obersturmführer [Strippel].[80]

Judge Advocate: [. . .] How long did this hanging of the children take?

Frahm: They were left hanging for about ten minutes, but I am not sure about the time.

Judge Advocate: Did anybody explain to you why it was necessary first of all to inject these children and then afterwards to hang them?

Frahm: No. [. . .]

President: You said just now that [the children] were injected one by one; if that was so, were the rest who were waiting to be injected all in one room in the cellar or not?

Frahm: Yes, that is correct.

President: Were the children in your opinion ill and all lying down in this room and waiting to be injected or did they appear to be fairly healthy?

Frahm: I believe that the great majority were slightly sickly—not ill and not healthy.

President: Were they able to walk?

Frahm: Yes.

President: Who brought each child in to be injected in this one room?

Frahm: They were called in.

President: Did each child walk in?

Frahm: Yes; some of them were fetched.

President: Who fetched them?

Frahm: I fetched them also. [. . .]

---

79. This was the chief prosecutor in British and American military proceedings.

80. Throughout the transcript of this very early postwar crimes trial, Obersturmführer Arnold Strippel is incorrectly identified as Strible.

President: Am I right in saying that only those who were still alive after the injections, after a certain period had elapsed, only this certain number were hung?

Frahm: That is correct.

President: Is it correct that you said about ten were hung?

Frahm: I am not quite sure about the number.

President: Is it correct to say that only one was hung at a time?

Frahm: Sometimes two at a time.

President: You mentioned just now the pipe over which the rope had been put to hang these children. Do you say there were two?

Frahm: It is correct [that] the grown-ups[81] were hung with this rope over the pipe. The children were hung at a wall where some ropes were passing over some [coat] hooks.

President: What was the largest number of children hanging at any one time?

Frahm: There were two hooks and two children were hanging at a time. [. . .]

During World War II, German physicians and scientists engaged in unethical and often deadly human medical experimentation upon thousands of concentration camp prisoners. Within the context of Nazi policy, physicians and scientists received full license to perform painful and dangerous experimentation upon prisoner populations without their consent. Test subjects often died as a result of the experiments or were murdered in order to facilitate postmortem examination.

Unlike the Nazi sterilization and "euthanasia" programs—crimes also perpetrated by members of the German medical community—human experimentation using concentration camp prisoners was not a matter of state policy. It was, rather, with few exceptions, a crime of opportunity carried out by various agencies for the enhancement of the war effort or by individual physicians and scientists for personal gain, either through pursuit of research interests or for the attainment of university degrees, career positions, or higher civil service status. Generally speaking, inhumane medical experimentation under Nazism may be divided into three categories. The first consists of experiments aimed at facilitating the survival of German military personnel in the field. In **Dachau**, for instance, physicians and scientists of the German air force (Luftwaffe)

---

81. This refers to the two prisoner-physicians, Renè Quenouille and Gabriel Florence, and two Dutch male nurses, Anton Hötzel and Dirk Deutekom, who served as caretakers for the children.

conducted high-altitude (low-pressure) experiments in order to determine the maximum altitude from which crews of damaged aircraft might parachute to safety. At the same camp, German scientists conducted so-called freezing experiments to develop an effective treatment for hypothermia and tested various protocols for making seawater potable. The second category of experimentation embraced similar aims in the testing and production of pharmaceuticals and treatment methods to combat or prevent diseases and injuries German military and occupation personnel encountered in the field. In this context German scientists and physicians tested immunization compounds and sera for the prevention and treatment of diseases such as **typhus**, tuberculosis, malaria, typhoid fever, and infectious hepatitis. Karl Gebhardt, director of the famed Hohenlychen clinic, conducted grisly sulfa drug and bone-grafting experiments using female prisoners at the Ravensbrück concentration camp, while scientists at the Natzweiler and Sachsenhausen concentration camps subjected detainees to poisonous gasses in order to test possible antidotes.

The third category of experimentation, however, elicits the greatest attention and abhorrence from contemporary audiences. To this group belong those medical experiments that sought to advance National Socialist racial policy or to underpin the racialist and ideological tenets of the Nazi worldview. For example, Carl Clauberg[82] and Horst Schumann[83] undertook experimentation, primarily at Auschwitz, to develop effective and inexpensive methods of mass sterilization that might in time be used to limit the reproductive capacities of "racially inferior" populations. The most infamous experiments founded on ide-

---

82. Carl Clauberg (1898–1957), a gynecologist by training, began experimentation in Auschwitz in 1942 at the suggestion of Reichsführer-SS Heinrich Himmler. As the Soviet army approached the complex, Clauberg fled to Ravensbrück concentration camp, where he briefly continued his "research." Soviet troops captured him there at the war's end, and Clauberg received a twenty-three-year sentence for war crimes from a Soviet court in 1948. The physician returned to Germany as a result of a prisoner exchange in 1955. West German prosecutors immediately filed criminal charges against him for crimes committed during the Nazi period, but Clauberg died of a heart attack in confinement before proceedings could commence.

83. Horst Schumann (1906–1983) participated in the "euthanasia" program as a physician at the Grafeneck and Sonnenstein T4 killing centers. Following the halt in the "euthanasia" program, he transferred to Auschwitz, where he conducted sterilization experiments upon male and female prisoners from July 1941 until September 1944. Although arrested by American troops in January 1945, Schumann was released and gradually made his way to Sudan, where he functioned as a hospital director. From 1962 to 1966 he lived in Ghana under the protection of the country's dictator, Kwame Nkrumah. Following his extradition to Germany in 1966, West German prosecutors attempted to open murder proceedings against Schumann, but these were ultimately put aside in 1972; Schumann died on May 5, 1983.

ological bases, however, were those conducted by **Josef Mengele** at Auschwitz after his arrival in the spring of 1943. Mengele had a variety of research interests, including investigation of the disease Noma, a type of gangrene that destroys the mucous membrane of the mouth and other tissues, most common in malnourished children. As there were plenty of these at Auschwitz, the physician was never without interesting "research material." Mengele also had a fascination with heterochromia, a condition in which a person's two irises differ in coloration, and pursued the topic with a passion, collecting the eyes of hundreds of dead subjects in the hope that he could unlock the secret of changing eye color. Mengele is most notorious for his research on twins at Auschwitz. The young physician had become interested in this field through Otmar von Verschuer, a leading figure in twin research. Verschuer experimented with identical and fraternal twins in order to trace the genetic origins of diseases.[84] At the time, twin research was seen as an ideal tool in weighing the variant factors of human heredity and environment. Mengele, with his mentor, had performed a number of legitimate research protocols using twins as test subjects throughout the 1930s. Now, at Auschwitz, with full license to maim or kill his subjects, Mengele performed a broad range of agonizing and often lethal experiments with Jewish and Roma twins, most of them children.

---

84. A leading German eugenicist, Otmar von Verschuer (1896–1969) directed the newly founded Institute for Hereditary Biology and Racial Hygiene at the University of Frankfurt am Main beginning in 1935 and succeeded Eugen Fischer as director of the prestigious Kaiser Wilhelm Institute for Anthropology in 1942. An advocate of compulsory sterilization and the inclusion of racial hygiene instruction in German medical school curricula, he wrote extensively on the "Jewish issue," calling in 1941 for a "complete solution to the Jewish Question." Adjudged lightly by a denazification court in the postwar period, Verschuer assumed a coveted position as professor of genetics at Münster, which he succeeded in making a leading center for genetic research in the new Federal Republic of Germany.

DOCUMENT 6-13. Relief workers lead child survivors from Birkenau following the liberation of Auschwitz by Soviet forces. Leading the ranks (beside the nurse) are Miriam and Eva Mozes, survivors of Josef Mengele's infamous experimentation with twins, January 1945, USHMMPA WS# 88591, courtesy of the Instytut Pamieci Narodowej.

Mengele firmly endorsed National Socialist racial theory and engaged in a wide spectrum of experiments that aimed to illustrate the lack of resilience among Jews or Roma to various diseases. He also attempted to demonstrate the "degeneration" of Jewish and Gypsy blood through the documentation of physical oddities and the collection and harvesting of tissue samples and body parts. Many of his test subjects died as a result of the experimentation or were murdered in order to facilitate postmortem examination. Like most scientists at work in the concentration camp setting, Mengele enlisted the aid of trained medical professionals among the prisoner population to perform the more grisly or mundane tasks and to carry out autopsies on his dead victims. We owe much of our early knowledge of Mengele's activities at Auschwitz to Dr. **Miklós Nyiszli**, a prisoner-physician who assisted Mengele under duress and published his experiences, initially in his native Hungarian, in 1946. In Document 6-14, Nyiszli tells the story of a Jewish father and son from the **Łódź ghetto** whom Mengele had targeted for his research purposes.

DOCUMENT 6-14. Miklós Nyiszli, *Auschwitz: A Doctor's Eyewitness Account*, trans. Tibère Kremer and Richard Seaver (Hungarian ed., 1946; New York: Fell, 1960), 175–78.

When the convoys arrived, Dr. Mengele espied, among those lined up for selection, a hunchbacked man about fifty years old. He was not alone; standing beside him was a tall, handsome boy of fifteen or sixteen. The latter, however, had a deformed right foot, which had been corrected by an apparatus made of a metal plate and an orthopedic, thick-soled shoe. They were father and son. Dr. Mengele thought he had discovered, in the person of the hunchback father and his lame son, a sovereign example to demonstrate his theory of the Jewish race's degeneracy. He had them fall out of ranks immediately. Taking his notebook, he inscribed something in it and entrusted the two wretches to the care of an SS trooper, who took them to number one crematorium.

It was around noon. [. . .] The SS soldier on duty came in and asked me to report to the gate. The father and son, accompanied by the SS guard, were already there. I took the message sent me, which read, "Dissecting room, number one crematorium: that these two men be examined from a clinical point of view; that exact measurements of the two men be made; that clinical records be set up including all interesting details, and most especially those relative to the causes which provoked the bodily deformities."

A second note was enclosed for Oberscharführer[85] Mussfeld. Even without reading it, I knew what it said. I entrusted it for transmission to a *Sonder* man.[86]

Father and son—their faces wan from their miserable years in the Litzmannstadt [Łódź] ghetto—were filled with forebodings. They looked at me questioningly. I took them across the courtyard, which at this hour of the day was filled with sunlight. On our way to the dissecting room I reassured them with a few well-chosen words. Luckily there were no corpses on the dissecting table; it would have indeed been a horrible sight for them to come upon.

---

85. This German word is misspelled in the English translation.

86. That is, to a member of the *Sonderkommando*, meaning, literally, "special commando" but in this context referring to a specially selected group of prisoners tasked with processing and cremating victims murdered in the gas chambers at Auschwitz.

To spare them I decided not to conduct the examination in the austere dissecting room, which reeked with the odor of formaldehyde, but in the pleasant, well-lighted study hall. From our conversation, I learned that the father had been a respected citizen of Litzmannstadt [Łódź], a wholesaler in cloth. During the years of peace between wars he had often taken his son with him on his business trips to Vienna, to have him examined and treated by the most famous specialists.

I first examined the father in detail, omitting nothing. The deviation of his spinal column was the result of retarded rickets. In spite of a most thorough examination, I discovered no symptom of any other illness.

I tried to console him by saying that he would probably be sent to a work camp.

Before proceeding to the examination of the boy I conversed with him at some length. He had a pleasant face, an intelligent look, but his morale was badly shaken. Trembling with fear, he related in an expressionless voice the sad, painful, sometimes terrible events which had marked his five years in the ghetto. His mother, a frail and sensitive creature, had not been able to long endure the ordeals which had befallen her. She had become melancholic and depressed. For weeks on end she had eaten almost nothing, so that her son and husband might have a little more food. A true wife and Jewish mother, who had loved her own to the point of madness, she had died a martyr during the first year of her life in the ghetto. So it was that they had lived in the ghetto, the father without his wife, the son without his mother.

And now they were in number one crematorium. Once again I was struck by the horrible irony of the situation. I, a Jewish doctor, had to examine them with exact clinical methods before they died, and then perform the dissection on their still warm bodies. [. . .]

By an immense effort of self-control, I got ahold of myself and examined the boy. On his right foot I noticed a congenital deformity: some of the muscles were lacking.

The medical term used to describe this deformity is hypomyelia. I could see that extremely expert hands had practiced several operations on him, but as a result one foot was shorter than the other. With a bandage and orthopedic socks, however, he could walk perfectly well. I saw no other deformity to be indicated.

I asked them if they wanted something to eat. "We haven't had anything to eat for some time," they told me.

I called a man from the *Sonderkommando* and had some food brought for them: a plate of stewed beef and macaroni, a dish not to be found outside the confines of the *Sonderkommando*.[87] They began to eat ravenously, unaware that this was their "Last Supper."

Scarcely half an hour later Oberscharführer Mussfeld appeared with four *Sonderkommando* men. They took the two prisoners into the furnace room and had them undress. Then the *Ober*'s revolver cracked twice. Father and son were stretched out on the concrete, covered with blood, dead. Oberscharführer Mussfeld had faithfully executed Dr. Mengele's orders.

Now it was my turn again. The two bodies were brought back into the dissecting room. So sickened was I by what had just happened that I entrusted the dissection to my associates and confined myself to recording the data. The dissection revealed nothing more than I had previously ascertained in my in vivo examination. The cases were banal but could nevertheless very easily be utilized as propaganda in support of the Third Reich's theory concerning the degeneracy of the Jewish race.

During his nefarious tenure at Auschwitz, Josef Mengele was not the only physician at the Auschwitz complex. Nor was he, as common wisdom often maintains, the highest-ranking physician at the camp; this distinction belonged to SS-Hauptsturmführer Dr. Eduard Wirths,[88] whose position as garrison physician made him responsible in all medical matters for the entire camp complex. Mengele began his career at Auschwitz in the spring of 1943 as the medical officer responsible for Birkenau's Gypsy camp; several weeks after its liquidation, he undertook a new position as chief camp physician of Auschwitz II–Birkenau, in November 1943, still under Wirths's jurisdiction. Even after his arrival at Auschwitz, he kept in close contact with his mentor Otmar von Verschuer, a prominent German scientist in the field of hereditary pathology. Since September 1937, Mengele had served as Verschuer's assistant in Frankfurt, and even at his new post in Birkenau, he continued to serve his old professor in singular

---

87. Because of the particularly grisly tasks assigned their members, *Sonderkommando* units at Auschwitz regularly received food of good quality and sufficient quantity.

88. Eduard Wirths (1909–1945) was the chief SS physician (SS-Standortarzt) at the Auschwitz concentration camp complex from September 1942 to January 1945. At Auschwitz, Wirths was involved in medical experimentation, particularly in gynecological and typhus-related experimental tests. Historians believe that Wirths never directly participated in such experiments but rather delegated these procedures to subordinates. Captured by the Allied forces at the war's end, Wirths committed suicide in British custody on September 20, 1945.

fashion. In 1944, with a deteriorating war effort, Verschuer was encountering difficulties in obtaining biological materials for his pathological research, but he discovered an unlikely solution in the form of his former graduate student. On March 20, 1944, Verschuer wrote the German Research Society (Deutsche Forschungsgemeinschaft, or DFG), "My assistant Dr. Mengele . . . has joined me in this branch of research. He is at present assigned as SS-*Hauptsturmführer* and camp physician at the Auschwitz concentration camp. With the permission of SS-Reichsführer [Heinrich Himmler,] anthropological investigations of the most diverse racial groups are being conducted, and the blood samples sent for processing to my lab." Mengele's notorious human experimentation at Auschwitz was funded in part by the DFG, while the young and ambitious physician sent his mentor a vast variety of "research material," including the skeletons of murdered Jews, the internal organs of Roma (Gypsy) victims, the severed heads of Roma children, and blood samples of various prisoners, including twins that Mengele had infected with typhus. There is no question that Verschuer, in Berlin, knew the origin of this "genetic material" and the circumstances of its procurement.

DOCUMENT 6-15. **Hygiene-Bacteriological Research Station of the Waffen SS, Southeast, delivery slip for the head of a corpse, signed by Dr. Josef Mengele, June 29, 1944, USHMMPA WS# 00592, courtesy of the Auschwitz Memorial Museum (Państwowe Muzeum w Oświęcim-Brzezinka) (translated from the German).**

Hygiene-Bacteriological Research Station of the Waffen SS, Southeast
Auschwitz, Upper Silesia, June 29, 1944
The following accompanies this document:
Material: <u>Head of a corpse   (12-year-old child)</u>
Taken on: _____
To be examined as: <u>microscopic tissue samples histological slices</u>
Surname, first name: _____
Rank, unit: <u>see attached</u>
Clinical diagnosis: _____
Address of the transmitting agency: <u>(C)entral infirmary, Gypsy camp, Auschwitz II [Birkenau] B II e</u>
Notations_____
    Senior SS Physician
    Concentration Camp Auschwitz II
    [signed] Dr. Mengele
    SS-Hauptsturmführer

CHAPTER 7

THE LIVES OF OTHERS
"ARYAN" CHILDREN AND
THE NAZI REGIME

T HE BULK OF documentation featured in this book focuses on the lives and fates of children who fell victim to the policies of the National Socialists or their European Axis allies. This chapter reflects on the experiences and viewpoints of "**Aryan**" children growing up in Nazi Germany. The National Socialist government hoped to capture the imagination and loyalty of Germany's younger generation. Accordingly, Nazi strategists shaped their youth policy in a way calculated to win young people to their principles and policies. Quite early in its development, the Nazi Party had initiated official organizations for the young, the **Hitler Youth** and the League of German Girls, which served as conduits to ideological indoctrination and political mobilization. Both formal education and structured extracurricular activities were designed to cultivate the new "civic" virtues of obedience, self-sacrifice, and race consciousness. Nazi propagandists also hoped to win the hearts and minds of German youngsters. In an effort to inculcate an unreflecting political loyalty among the German public, young people became a particular focus of ideological instruction. Nazi propaganda confronted German children everywhere: in the classroom, on the playground, in their bedtime reading. And yet, even as Nazi authorities demanded subservience and allegiance from their youngest citizens, a segment of German youth clearly rejected their complete integration into the Nazi state. The nonconformity of many teens, such as the Edelweiss Pirates (Documents 7-4 through 7-6), suggests that the history of German children and adolescents under the swastika is less a story of uniformity than one of divergence and

243

contradiction. The following documentation illustrates that German youth were at once the benefactors of Nazism and the heirs to its terrible legacy. Young Germans engaged in the daily activities of a country at war: they were its combatants and its targets. They were perpetrators and victims. German "Aryan" children experienced a radically different aspect of National Socialism than did young persecutees of its racialist policies; yet, as witnesses to its national transformation, its conquests, and its defeat, their views and perspectives have much to tell us about life under the Nazi dictatorship.

YOUTH ORGANIZATIONS IN THE THIRD REICH

From the movement's inception, leaders of the National Socialist Party placed a high priority on winning the hearts and minds of German youth, whom they viewed as the future of the nation and hoped to mold to their purposes. The Hitler Youth (Hitlerjugend, or HJ) represented the party's second oldest paramilitary organ, after its adult counterpart, the Storm Division (**Sturmabteilung,** or **SA**), upon which it was modeled. The organization began its existence as the Youth League of the Nazi Party (Jugendbund der NSDAP) in March 1922; it was restructured as the Greater German Youth Movement (Grossdeutsche Jugendbewegung) in 1924. In July 1926, this now official youth organization of the Nazi Party became the Hitler Youth, League of German Worker Youth (Hitler-Jugend, Bund Deutscher Arbeiterjugend), and was officially incorporated into the SA.

By 1930, the Hitler Youth had already recruited twenty-five thousand members. Following the Nazi assumption of power, the new Reich youth leader (*Reichsjugendführer*), **Baldur von Schirach**,[1] assumed control of the HJ and began to promote the program in earnest, organizing a general membership of boys from fourteen to eighteen and a corresponding junior branch, the German Young Volk (**Deutsches Jungvolk**). Hitler Youth members received both physical and paramilitary training and ideological indoctrination. A key component of Schirach's strategy was to create from the Hitler Youth's ranks competent and loyal soldiers for future wars and citizens ideologically committed to the Third Reich and its policies. On December 1, 1936, the Law Concerning the Hitler Youth (Gesetz über die Hitlerjugend) called for the assimilation of all German youth into the appropriate youth organizations. Although the law made membership obligatory, compliance was not universal, and two ancillary decrees issued in March 1939, making youth service compulsory and nonmembership

---

1. In 1940, Artur Axmann replaced Baldur von Schirach as Reich youth leader; Schirach himself became *Gauleiter* of the Reichsgau Vienna from 1940 until war's end.

a punishable offense, were ultimately necessary to ensure thoroughgoing conformity with the initial legislation.²

DOCUMENT 7-1. **A young boy leaps into the clasped arms of his schoolmates during
outdoor physical education exercises at the Hilter Youth training facility in Memmingen,
Germany, USHMMPA WS# 30590, courtesy of the Holocaust Museum Houston.**

Concerned with the conspicuous lack of compliance with the December
1936 law in the Reich capital region, the director of Berlin's Deaf Athletes'
Association used the popular youth supplement to the association's monthly
newsletter to cajole young athletes belonging to his organization to join the now
obligatory Hitler Youth. "The highest achievement in sports does not shield you
from the fact that service to Hitler's Reich is the highest service of all," Director
Werner Thomas³ reminded his young charges.

2. For a discussion of the Hitler Youth organization, see Michael Kater, *Hitler Youth*
(Cambridge, MA: Harvard University Press, 2006).
3. Werner Thomas (b. 1908) joined the Nazi Party in May 1930. No information is available on his postwar fate.

Thomas's enthusiasm for the Nazi movement contained an element of irony. As deaf individuals, members of his athletic organization, both young and old, already represented potential targets of the regime's thoroughgoing **eugenic** policies.[4] Since January 1934, they had been subject to the **Law for the Prevention of Progeny with Hereditary Diseases**,[5] legislation mandating **compulsory sterilization** for specific disorders and disabilities, including hereditary deafness. In October 1935, the Marital Hygiene Law (Ehegesundheitsgesetz) further prohibited the marriage of "Aryans" with persons possessing "diseased, inferior or dangerous genetic material,"[6] among them the hereditarily deaf. A staunch National Socialist, Director Thomas may have felt that he and his associates belonged intrinsically to Germany's *Volksgemeinschaft*, but a segment of Nazi policy makers certainly thought otherwise.

DOCUMENT 7-2. **Editorial of W. Thomas, director of the Berlin Deaf Athletes' Association,** *Youth Supplement of the Newsletter of the Berlin Deaf Athletes' Association*, **May 1, 1937, USHMMA, RG-10.320, Horst Biesold Collection (translated from the German).**

My dear young comrades!
A sorry circumstance compels me to express my opinion on the Hitler Youth question. [I understand that] nearly 100 percent of the youth from the Leipzig and Dresden sports associations render their services in the Hitler Youth with a joyful heart. It is simply humiliating that so many young athletes from the Berlin community are still opposed to joining. As an old SA man of many years standing, I have early on been able to have many valuable experiences which demonstrated to me that the education afforded by the Hitler Youth and SA is very useful: because there our youth will learn iron discipline, comradeship, and the will to sacrifice. There they will ripen into splendid and proper men—better said, into the best National Socialists.

---

4. See Horst Biesold, *Crying Hands: Eugenics and Deaf People in Nazi Germany*, trans. William Sayers (Washington, DC: Gallaudet University Press, 1999); Donna Ryan and John Schuchman, eds., *Deaf People in Hitler's Europe* (Washington, DC: Gallaudet University Press, 2002).

5. For a broader discussion of the Nazi sterilization law and its ramifications, see chapter 6.

6. Robert Proctor, *Racial Hygiene: Medicine under the Nazis* (Cambridge, MA: Harvard University Press, 1988), 175.

As deaf persons, we will never be called into the Labor Service, into the Wehrmacht, and so on, and service in the Hitler Youth offers you your last opportunity to go through a rigorous training.

The highest achievement in sports does not shield you from the fact that service to Adolf Hitler's Reich is the highest service of all!!!

In accordance with the proclamation of our Reich Sports Leader von Tschammer u. Osten[7] and that of the leader of our association, Pg. [Party Comrade] Siepmann, I enjoin you for the last time, dear comrades: those of you who are not yet eighteen should report to the leader of Troop G/2, Scharführer Müller, before May 12. Otherwise you will be excluded from our excellent sports association.

At this opportunity, I would like to make all Hitler Youth members cognizant that when one of you is dishonorably discharged from your troop, you will also automatically forfeit your membership in this sports association.

In conclusion I appeal to all the esteemed parents and also to my association comrades to show their complete understanding for my actions, which are necessary for the future of our nation.

Everything for Germany!

For many youngsters in the regime's early years, membership in the Nazi youth associations proved neither an irksome obligation nor a burdensome chore. In many ways, the HJ extended to adolescents many of the same leisure and outdoor activities formerly afforded by earlier exponents of the German youth movement, such as the **Scout Movement** (Pfadfinder) and the Youth Leagues (Bündische Jugend), both banned after 1933. Likewise, the well-appointed uniforms, the carefully orchestrated pageantry and ritual, and the ubiquitous competition among units for sport and service awards combined to give youngsters a sense of belonging, unity, and purpose. For youths in remote or rural areas, moreover, the Hitler Youth often provided an initial opportunity to come into contact with children from diverse regions, to erect an official

---

7. Hans von Tschammer und Osten (1887–1943) had held the position of Reich Sport Leader (Reichssportführer) since 1933. As such he played a major role in the planning and organization of the 1936 Winter and Summer Olympic Games, held in Garmisch-Partenkirchen and Berlin, Germany, respectively; during these competitions he supported a ban of non-Aryan competitors on Germany's Olympic team, a policy widely condemned in the international press. Von Tschammer died of pneumonia in 1943 and was succeeded as Reichssportführer by Arno Breitmeyer.

clubhouse or sporting field in their small hamlets, or to visit new places on weekend or camping expeditions.

The emancipatory possibilities that came with the Nazi youth movement were potentially even greater for German girls and young women. Through the League of German Girls (**Bund Deutscher Mädel**, or BDM), girls could escape from the narrow confines of home and family and participate in the kinds of activities and outings usually reserved for boys. Although its ideological aim was to prepare German females for their future roles as wives, mothers, and home-makers, the BDM also offered young women an outlet for experiences outside the spheres of school and the parental home and presented further educational and vocational opportunities that they were unlikely to derive elsewhere. The organization also afforded its paid and unpaid functionaries a conduit to par-ticipation in political activity, albeit within a limited context.

Like the Hitler Youth, the BDM had its origins in the 1920s, first as the Mädchenschaften (Girls' Organizations), then as the Schwesternschaften (Sisterhood Organizations) of the HJ. In 1930, the **Bund Deutscher Mädel** in der Hitler-Jugend (League of German Girls within the Hitler Youth) was founded as the official female branch of the Hitler Youth organization. Before the Nazi rise to power in January 1933, the BDM did not attract a mass follow-ing, but membership expanded rapidly throughout the 1930s, until participa-tion for eligible girls became compulsory in 1936. The BDM's core constituency consisted of girls from fourteen to eighteen years of age, with a correspond-ing junior branch, the Jungmädel (Young Girls' League), for girls aged ten to fourteen. In 1938, a third component, the BDM Union for Belief and Beauty (BDM-Werk Glaube und Schönheit), offered a voluntary association for young women aged seventeen to twenty-one that served as a bridge to membership in the National Socialist Women's League (NS-Frauenschaft, or NSF).[8]

Anecdotal evidence suggests that, especially before World War II, the BDM enjoyed a great deal of popularity among German girls and elicited far more eager participation among its young female cohorts than did the Hitler Youth among boys, not least because of the latter's rigorous paramilitary training. For some, no doubt, the League of German Girls exerted an unsettling influence, as when its ideological indoctrination or stance on religion and traditional author-ity figures clashed with deeply held values. Enthusiasm for the league likewise declined during the war years as public service duties increasingly replaced outings and recreational activities. BDM members ran charity and collection

---

8. See Gisela Miller-Kipp, ed., *"Auch Du gehörst dem Führer": Die Geschichte des Bundes Deutscher Mädel (BDM)* in *Quellen und Dokumenten. Forschungsreihe Materialien zur Historischen Jugendforschung* (Weinheim: Juventa Verlag, 2001).

drives, volunteered as nurse's aides, and organized care packages for troops at the front. After 1943, older members might be conscripted to work in armaments factories or other industries or to aid in the war effort as auxiliaries in civilian air defense. Whatever their role, for many young women the League of German Girls presented both difficult challenges and rewarding experiences, as three long-term members recalled in 1946.

DOCUMENT 7-3. **Young women remember the League of German Girls, 1946, in Gisela Miller-Kipp, ed., *"Auch Du gehörst dem Führer": Die Geschichte des Bundes Deutscher Mädel (BDM) in Quellen und Dokumenten. Forschungsreihe Materialien zur Historischen Jugendforschung* (Weinheim: Juventa Verlag, 2001), 315–16 (translated from the German).**

Ursula G., 19 years old

I have, perhaps because I am an only child, always sought the companionship of persons my own age, and always felt drawn to my circle of schoolmates as well as to those of the National Socialist youth movement. I participated in many camping trips and outings, as well as several training courses. Each time I had the good fortune to have genuine "leaders" [to follow]. Never did I have the feeling that I was being "educated" or directed towards certain thought processes. More often than not, I encountered people who guided me in a very subtle manner really to reflect upon things that up to that time had remained a mystery to me. Those were people who—as far as I may judge—had a real understanding for us girls and were truly examples to us. I didn't just take pleasure in earnest discussions with my comrades, but also enjoyed taking part in play, sports, camp life, and in both solemn and festive ceremonies. Often in these instances I had the task of writing reports concerning the experiences in our young circles for school and camp journals as well as for newspapers and magazines; and this always made me so happy that for a long time it was my wish to build my later career on such activities.

During the year 1944 our school was almost completely closed because we were so often utilized for wartime public service. I helped in agricultural work, in our canning factory, was a temporary mail delivery girl for two months and from time to time dug trenches. [. . .] After three months in the Erzgebirge,[9] we came to E. Here I witnessed Germany's col-

---

9. This refers to a small mountain chain in eastern Germany.

lapse, and with it, the collapse of everything I lived for in terms of belief, enthusiasm, ideals. [. . .]

<u>Karin K., 20 years old</u>

Besides school there came to us a new form of social interaction: at ten years of age there began the compulsory membership in the Young Girls' League [Jungmädelbund]. I will not lie when I say that we all greeted this at first with a great deal of enthusiasm. They appealed to us with those things that gave us pleasure. We played together, learned songs, or our leader read fairy tales to us which we acted out on parents' nights. Everything ideological was still quite foreign to us. Certainly, we each received a uniform, but this appealed to our pride, and all that marching was certainly not at odds with our disposition—belonged to that part of us that was young, anyway as I imagine it. Perhaps it was wrong to make this urge stronger in us, instead of instilling maidenly virtues in us. They also knew how to goad our ambition. Wasn't it tempting to be a pennant bearer or a leader [*Führerin*[10]] oneself? We could not recognize at the time that the truly good thing—namely the sincere striving and the readiness to give one's complete effort—would be misused. For us Berliners there was so much enthusiasm! What we all saw, what we experienced! The Hitler Youth was always on hand.

<u>Elisabeth K., 19 years old</u>

My home is East Prussia. I was born in L., a small town nestled between clear lakes and dark forests in Masuria.[11] In 1937, at the same time that I was transferred to a secondary school [*Oberschule*] for girls, I was accepted into the Jungmädelbund. This new environment overwhelmed me, and I changed much as a result, became more self-sufficient, more self-confident. I was motivated by all the playing, singing, and sports, and at first I took pleasure in the strict discipline and order. This time brought me many wonderful hours in the company of people of my own age, and I never thought of the work in political terms. But with all this came the first serious conflict in my life. I grew up in a strict Christian household and had never encountered other kinds of beliefs or convictions. Now there was this thing which brought me great pleasure, but which clearly stood in complete contrast to my earlier way of life. I suffered very much

10. That is, a low-level leader of the BDM.
11. This area of East Prussia, famed for its lakes, was ceded to Poland in 1945.

from this dichotomy, and always tried to unite the two opposites until I realized that this was not possible if I did not wish to deceive myself. Later, when my father was drafted into the military and my mother experienced difficulties in running our store, I withdrew completely, except for the demands which school imposed.

NONCONFORMITY AND DISSIDENCE: THE EDELWEISS PIRATES

As the late German historian Detlev Peukert ably demonstrated, Nazi leaders' assertions that their organizations successfully assimilated and mobilized German youth portrayed only one facet of the Third Reich's social reality. The more readily the Nazi Party exerted coercion to bring German adolescents into its ranks, the more conspicuous became the pattern of nonconformity.[12] By the late 1930s, a surprising number of German teenagers, chiefly males, were rejecting the discipline and regimentation of party youth organizations in favor of the free and spontaneous lifestyle of informal clubs and gangs. Growing in numbers during the war years, these youths, aged fourteen to eighteen, particularly vexed Nazi authorities, for most belonged to precisely that age cohort whose chief socialization had taken place under the all-pervasive influence of the Nazi state. Some of these teens stemmed from the upper middle classes, such as the well-documented "Swing Kids" (*Swingjugend*), youths of both sexes who doffed their Hitler Youth and BDM uniforms for English-cut suits and defied the ban on public assembly to gather in illegal clubs and at the homes of consenting (or absent) parents to listen to jazz and swing numbers and dance the jitterbug.[13] Perhaps more numerous and unconventional, at least in Nazi eyes, however, were those working-class youths from western Germany who styled themselves as "Edelweiss[14] Pirates." Throughout the industrial Rhine and Ruhr regions, teenage boys gathered in loose associations to spend their evenings and

---

12. See Detlev Peukert, *Inside Nazi Germany: Conformity, Opposition, and Racism in Everyday Life*, trans. Richard Deveson (New Haven, CT: Yale University Press, 1987); also Detlev Peukert, "Youth in the Third Reich," in *Life in the Third Reich*, ed. Richard Bessel (Oxford: Oxford University Press, 1987), 30–37.

13. This term used to describe a number of swing dances popular in the United States in the late 1930s. Jitterbugging first made its appearance in African American clubs and, like the musical forms of jazz and swing that inspired it, was viewed as "degenerate" by Nazi authorities.

14. Edelweiss is a woolly white perennial flower common to alpine regions of German-speaking Europe.

weekends together, away from the probing gaze and controlling grasp of the Hitler Youth. Although they organized in small groups of a dozen or more under various epithets—the Kittelbach Pirates from Düsseldorf, the Cologne Navajos, or the Essen Roving Dudes—each group identified itself as belonging to the network of Edelweiss Pirates, recognizable to each other and to the experienced observer by their costume: the invariable checkered shirt, neck scarf, short trousers, white socks, and clogs. Many of these young men had once been members of the Scout Movement (Pfadfinder)or the Youth Leagues (Bündische Jugend[15]), now banned in Nazi Germany, and many of their activities—camping, hiking, singing ballads—mirrored the activities of the Weimar-era German youth movement.[16] Unlike these organized associations, however, the Edelweiss Pirates came together spontaneously because they knew each other: as neighbors, schoolmates, teammates in local sports associations, or coworkers. Most had finished their formal schooling[17] but were not yet of draft age; many were apprentices or, during the war years with their shortage of manpower, already earning a steady wage as unskilled laborers. In eschewing the activities organized by Nazi Party associations, these young people had sufficient free time to meet at a nearby street corner, bar, or park and venture weekend outings in the surrounding countryside, despite wartime restrictions on travel and tight police controls. Teenaged girls often accompanied the group on excursions, a factor that distinguished Pirate bands from the gender-segregated Nazi youth organizations. Female companionship also afforded young members an opportunity for uninhibited romantic and sexual encounters eagerly embraced by developing teens but associated with indecency and delinquency by Nazi officials.

Historians often locate the Edelweiss Pirates within that gray area between nonconformity and dissidence. That these adolescents did not adhere to the image of German youth envisioned by the Nazi regime is clear. Moreover, nonfascist sentiments stood out clearly in the groups' words and deeds. For Edelweiss Pirates, the Hitler Youth embodied the visible enemy. More often than not, the HJ was the object of their invective and the target of their

---

15. Bündische Jugend was a German youth movement of the interwar years that combined elements of the *Wandervögel* (romanticism, a desire to return to pristine nature, and a culture of hiking and touring) with those of the International Scouting movement. Like all other competing youth movements, the youth leagues of the Bündische Jugend were banned by the Nazis in the summer of 1933 in order to facilitate the integration of German youth into the Hitler Youth and its auxiliary organizations.

16. See Peter Statura, *The German Youth Movement, 1900–1945: An Interpretative and Documentary History* (London: MacMillan, 1981).

17. This happened at age fourteen, provided the individual in question did not intend to go to university or vocational school.

aggression: assaults on individual Hitler Youth members and attacks on HJ street patrols proved an enduring group pastime. But the Pirates' motives for dissent were complex. Clearly most members of this loose confederation came from working-class milieus and stemmed from neighborhoods and communities where, before 1933, the German Communist and Social Democratic parties maintained traditional strongholds. But unlike their cousins, the *Leipziger Meuten* (Leipzig Gangs), groups who shared many of the Pirates' characteristics but manifested a clear class consciousness and harbored communist and socialist sympathies, the Edelweiss Pirates demonstrated no clearly politicized identity. Rather, these Rhenish teenagers seemed principally determined to flout the norms of conventional working life and to enjoy an independent and autonomous existence away from the state's ever-present interference. The endless training and mindless drilling experienced in the Hitler Youth organization did not appeal to them, and as the war progressed, more and more of these young men feared, as doubtless their more traditional colleagues did, that they might end as cannon fodder in an increasingly ruinous conflict. It is difficult to classify the Edelweiss Pirates as an unambiguous resistance group. Yet several bands certainly did perform acts of outright resistance, such as rescuing downed Allied fliers,[18] aiding German deserters, and surreptitiously distributing Allied propaganda leaflets. Moreover, many youths also involved themselves in more organized resistance efforts. The **Gestapo**, police, and Hitler Youth employed a number of strategies to disperse and suppress the Edelweiss Pirates, with limited success. In November 1944, thirteen anti-Nazi activists, among them six young ringleaders of the Cologne Navajos, were publicly hanged without trial in Cologne-Ehrenfeld.[19]

---

18. Allied pilots who crash-landed in Germany were in particular danger. Toward war's end, the Nazi regime encouraged the population to assault or murder downed airmen, whom they held responsible for the mounting death toll from Allied bombings.

19. The six included Bartholomäus Schink, sixteen; Günther Schwarz, sixteen; Gustav Bermel, seventeen; Johann Müller, sixteen; Franz Rheinberger, seventeen, and Adolf Schütz, eighteen.

DOCUMENT 7-4. **Report of the Gestapo, Düsseldorf, December 10, 1937, in Detlev Peukert, *Die Edelweisspiraten: Protestbewegungen jugendlicher Arbeiter im Dritten Reich. Eine Dokumentation*, 2nd ed. (Cologne: Bund-Verlag, 1983), 28–30 (translated from the German).**

In the last few years a generally loose confederation of youths has been detected in most western regions and particularly in the Ruhrgebiet,[20] whose activities exceed the usual parameters (standing around on street corners during the evening hours, etc.). The development of these groups in a political and moral context can no longer be viewed as a so-called local incident. It is expanding ever more strongly in a direction which demands not only that we observe it, but also that we combat it.

In most cases the issue concerns youths who earlier were in the HJ and were expelled or, because they did not like the strict discipline there, withdrew their membership. These expulsions resulted in almost every case from discipline violations or from a lack of enthusiasm for service. In our experience, the latter case can be traced to the fact that various members of the HJ—who perhaps because of their earlier upbringing or because they naturally find it difficult to subordinate themselves to others—observe that their comrades of the same age who do not belong to the Hitler Youth lead an independent lifestyle. It can also be determined in many cases that these individuals meet with nonmembers of the HJ in the various places where youths congregate or join them on their outings. Here of course they learn a lifestyle that has nothing in common with the discipline and order that must necessarily hold sway in the HJ. One must add to this the fact that in isolated instances, the leaders of the HJ do not know how to reach out to young people. The disinterest in service which emanates from these circumstances is further compounded by those who have never fostered an interest in the current state. The result then is that these youths are ever more firmly bound to the circles in question. Even if these [groups] can rarely be considered organizationally cohesive, there still exists the potential that they will bond more closely together and thus constitute an instrument that would become, in the hands of enemies of the state, a danger to the youth and thus to the nation.

Throughout the entire time frame—from the seizure of power [*Machtergreifung*] to the present—there is among the majority of groups

---

20. This refers to a large metropolitan area in western Germany bordered by the Ruhr, Rhine, and Lippe rivers and encompassing the industrial cities of Duisburg, Bochum, Essen, Gelsenkirchen, Dortmund, and Hamm.

an unmistakably negative attitude toward the HJ. They see their "freedom" infringed upon if they are once detained by the patrols of the HJ or even by the police. This finds expression in their conversations concerning the HJ or concerning the Movement,[21] in songs, and in actual attacks upon individual members of the HJ. They have parodied many [popular or party] songs. They now sing, among other things, "Break the Youth League Free," "Rend the Hitler Youth in Two," "The Wickinger [sic] Flag Belongs under the KP,"[22] "The Kittelbach Pirates' Flag Must Not Perish," "We Remain True to the Polar Bears," etc.[23]

At the various gatherings, the spirit of the former members of the banned Youth Leagues [Bündische Jugend] shows through more and more. It is sometimes true today that he who can say that he was a former member of a Youth League is "seen with different eyes." It often happens that young people claim to have been members of the banned Youth Leagues even when they have not. They want to "be someone" among like-minded youths.

As an outward sign, and in order to contrast themselves with the Hitler Youth, the so-called outing costumes are worn, which for the most part look similar to the uniform of the banned Youth Leagues or have been adopted from the latter. The preferred modes of dress are the plaid (tartan) shirt—also called ski shirts—short pants, boots with turned down socks, clogs, neck scarves, and string ties on which are to be found every possible ornamentation. This outfit ensures that like-minded individuals on outings or in other places can recognize each other, and although unknown to each other, may strike up a friendship. In most instances, it is the case that the youths do not know each other by a surname at all, but only by first name or nickname. The universal greeting, used when these youths meet each other underway, and even if they do not know each other but recognize their camaraderie from their similar outfits, is "Ahoy." On other occasions, [they use] the greeting "Heidewitzka,"[24] which, according to the experiences we have had, represents a substitute for "*Heil Hitler*."

The youths in question prefer to call themselves Kittelbach Pirates [KP]. This association has existed since 1933 in Düsseldorf and its

21. That is, the Nazi movement.
22. That is, the Kittelbach Pirates.
23. All are lines from Nazi Party songs or slogans that have been altered, sometimes to humorous effect.
24. This is a nonsense word, based on a popular song.

environs. Even when these members became conspicuous in general through their boorish conduct, there was nothing about them to object to within a political context. After the seizure of power, this association certainly gathered a large influx of those elements who did not wish to assimilate with the National Socialist front. When even at this time no cohesive organization can be established, a good number wear the attire of the KP, sing their songs, and greet each other with the KP greeting, "Ahoy." Besides this, the badge of the KP—a death's head—is commonly worn. One finds the death's head motif on tie clasps, pocket books, rings, and even gym equipment. The majority of these youths have never belonged to this association. For those reasons already mentioned, these persons happily boast that they do belong to the KP.

While in past years the youths were generally given a warning, recent developments show that stricter measures must be undertaken to curb the danger that this group poses to the young.

DOCUMENT 7-5. **Handwritten flyer distributed by the Wuppertal troop of the Edelweiss Pirates, "To the Subjugated German Youth," c. 1942, in Detlev Peukert,** *Die Edelweisspiraten: Protestbewegungen jugendlicher Arbeiter im Dritten Reich. Eine Dokumentation,* **2nd ed. (Cologne: Bund-Verlag, 1983), 81 (translated from the German).**

To the Subjugated German Youth

German Youth:
Think of the old, golden age of the Boy Scouts, think back to the sunny days of outings and camping. All of this is denied to us today. Why? Because today's Nazi Germany wants to stick you all in the "Hitler Youth." Where you will be trained militarily and technically in marching, shooting, map reading, and topography, etc. The goal of all that leads back to this: cannon fodder for Hitler's insatiable greed for power![25]

German youth, rise up to fight for freedom and right, for your children and your children's children, for if Hitler wins this war, Europe will be in chaos; the world will be subjugated unto the Judgment Day. Make an end of this slavery before it is too late.

Lord, make us free!

25. Emphasis is in the original.

DOCUMENT 7-6. The "Cologne Navajos' Fight Song," c. 1944, in Detlev Peukert, *Die Edelweisspiraten: Protestbewegungen jugendlicher Arbeiter im Dritten Reich. Eine Dokumentation*, 2nd ed. (Cologne: Bund-Verlag, 1983), 51 (translated from the German).

Hitler's power makes us small.	*Des Hitlers Zwang, der macht uns klein.*
We still lie in chains.	*Noch liegen wir in Ketten.*
But one day we'll be free again.	*Doch einmal werden wir wieder frei,*
We will break our chains.	*Wir werden die Ketten schon brechen.*
Because our fists, they are strong,	*Denn unsere Fäuste, die sind hart,*
And our knives hang by our sides.	*Ja, und die Messer sitzen los.*
For the freedom of our youth,	*Für die Freiheit der Jugend*
We're the fighting Navajos.	*Kämpfen Navajos.*

HEARTS AND MINDS: NAZI PROPAGANDA

Children, perhaps more than their parents, were particularly susceptible to the appeal of National Socialist propaganda. Already in the 1920s, the fledgling Nazi Party viewed young people as an important target for ideological indoctrination. Nazism portrayed itself as a young and dynamic movement, and its ideologues saw particularly in German youth a malleable audience for its messages. The content of Nazi propaganda varied over time. During the party's early years—in its so-called Time of Struggle and its first years in power—much emphasis was placed on the iniquitous peace that followed World War I and the need to revise the **Versailles Treaty**, which had forced Germany to concede territory in Europe and abroad, imposed an ignominious "war-guilt clause," and saddled Germany with ruinous reparation payments. Propagandists railed against the political Left—communists and the still influential Social Democratic Party in Germany—which had, in Nazi estimation, "stabbed Germany in the back" by accepting the "shameful" peace terms and ostensibly aligned with the powers in the newly formed Soviet Union, exposing Germany to the dangers of bolshevism. National Socialist ideologues promised a better Germany: a nation restored to full sovereignty, economic security, and political stability. Following German rearmament and the remilitarization of the Rhineland, Nazi propaganda stressed even more consistently the National Socialists' goal of expansion and *Lebensraum*, the German *Volk*'s claim to "living room" in eastern Europe. Their messages invariably struck a martial tone, extolling the virtues of a disciplined and militaristic society. They portrayed the

German armed forces as the defenders of Western culture and its purveyors to the "uncivilized" East, underscoring the military's fundamental role as a bulwark against the Soviet threat. Virulent antisemitism and an aggressive racism remained enduring themes of Nazi propaganda, which sought to marginalize Jews and other "racial" enemies and to prepare the public for persecutory measures against them.

Nazi propagandists hoped to foster in the German population, as well as in **ethnic Germans (*Volksdeutsche*)** living in the occupied territories, an unreflecting political loyalty and a strong "race consciousness." They aimed to groom their populace to be obedient and self-sacrificing citizens and to be active or passive participants in Germany's war for "race and space."[26] Naturally, Nazi ideologues did not confine their efforts to adults but also sought to win the hearts and minds of German youngsters. Much of the propaganda to which young people were exposed came through structured events and settings. Children and adolescents received ideological training as a result of their participation in youth organizations, such as the Hitler Youth or the League of German Girls. Yet, by far the largest arena for the indoctrination of German youth was the classroom. In April 1933, the **Law for the Restoration of the Professional Civil Service** purged the public school system, as well as other civil service posts, of Jews and "politically unreliable elements." The majority of instructors who remained—some 97 percent of educators—joined the National Socialist Teachers' League in the regime's early years. Indeed, teachers also joined the Nazi Party in greater numbers than did members of any other professions. Instructors inducted their pupils into the cult of Adolf Hitler and imparted to them the tenets of Nazi doctrine. While Nazi authorities burned the books of "un-German" and "degenerate" authors and removed "unreliable" texts from the classroom, German educators introduced new textbooks that subtly or transparently instilled the party values of militarism, antisemitism, and racism.[27]

Document 7-7 provides two examples of this phenomenon, both in support of the ongoing National Socialist eugenics policy. In 1933, the Hitler cabinet had promulgated the Law for the Prevention of Progeny with Hereditary

---

26. This phrase succinctly defining Nazi Germany's political mission was coined by Gerhard Weinberg; see, for example, Gerhard Weinberg, *Germany, Hitler, and World War II: Essays in Modern German and World History* (New York: Cambridge University Press, 1995), 36.

27. See Jeffrey Herf, *Jewish Enemy: Nazi Propaganda during World War II and the Holocaust* (Cambridge, MA: Belknap Press, 2006); David Welch, *Politics and Propaganda*, 2nd ed. (London: Routledge Press, 2002); David Welch, ed., *Nazi Propaganda: The Power and the Limitations* (London: Barnes & Noble, 1983).

Diseases, which mandated **sterilization** of individuals with specific psychiatric, neurological, or physical disorders and disabilities.[28]

Some four hundred thousand Germans were forcibly sterilized under this legislation between January 1934, when the law went into effect, and the war's end in May 1945. The measure proved genuinely unpopular, especially in Catholic regions where it clashed with traditional church doctrine. By the mid-1930s, Nazi medical and racial hygiene authorities headed by Walter Gross,[29] director of the Information Office for Population Policy and Race Cultivation (Aufklärungsamt für Bevölkerungspolitik und Rassenpflege), had initiated a full-scale propaganda campaign to shore up support for the effort. "Documentary" films—usually shorts shown to cinema audiences before feature films—such as *Das Erbe* (*The Inheritance*) (1935), *Erbkrank* (*Hereditarily Ill*) (1936), and *Opfer der Vergangenheit* (*Victims of the Past*) (1937) sought to dehumanize and marginalize the severely mentally and physically disabled in the eyes of their fellow Germans.[30] In the same instance, complementary material began to appear in children's textbooks and teaching materials. In Jakob Graf's *Biology for Secondary Schools*, published in 1943, the illustration "*Hier trägst Du mit!*" taught students that German taxpayers shouldered the financial responsibility for the hereditarily ill and disabled. The inset depicts a "racially valuable" and healthy German standing before the silhouette of an asylum or mental health facility. Upon his back the man balances two "degenerate" and impaired individuals. The caption reads, "A hereditarily ill individual who has reached his sixtieth year costs 50,000 **Reichsmark**." "You are carrying the load," the text enjoins, reminding its young readers that they will ultimately bear the burden of society's "ballast existences," its "useless eaters." A mathematics primer for seventh and eighth graders takes a similar tack, employing the familiar story-problem construction to drive home an ominous message. "How many homesteads or farms could be financed with the funds now dedicated to the upkeep of the hereditarily ill and institutionalized?" the textbook asks. While such propaganda clearly aimed to garner grassroots support for the Nazi sterilization campaign, these messages also represented an effort to undergird the foundation for more

---

28. For a closer examination of Nazi sterilization policy, see chapter 6.

29. Walter Gross (1904–1945) died in combat during the Battle of Berlin on April 25, 1945.

30. For a thoroughgoing discussion of Nazi films in support of sterilization, "euthanasia," and other eugenic measures, see "Killing Films of the Third Reich," in Burleigh, *Death and Deliverance*, 183–219; Ulf Schmidt, *Medical Films, Ethics, and Euthanasia in Nazi Germany: The History of Medical Research and Teaching Films of the Reich Office for Educational Films, Reich Institute for Films in Science and Education, 1933–1945* (Husum, Germany: Matthiesen, 2002).

radical eugenics policies and to prepare the public, including young children, for such measures.

DOCUMENT 7-7A. **Excerpt from a children's textbook in the Third Reich: "You Are Carrying the Load!" ("Hier trägst Du mit!"), in Jacob Graf,** *Biologie für höhere Schulen (Biology for Secondary Schools)* **(Munich: Lehmann Verlag, 1943), table 25.**

DOCUMENT 7-7B. **Excerpt from a children's textbook in the Third Reich: A story problem in** *Arithmetic for Volksschulen: Governing District Cologne and Aachen, School Years in Seven and Eight*, **1941, quoted in Ute Hoffmann,** *Todesursache "Angina": Zwangssterilisation und "Euthanasie" in der Landes-Heil- und Pflegeanstalt Bernburg* **(Magdeburg: Eigenverlag des Ministeriums des Innern des Landes Sachsen-Anhalt, 1996), 24 (translated from the German).**

The costs for one hereditarily ill patient today amount to 4.5–6 RM per day. Calculate the total sum of the cost per day, per month, per year. In the year 1930, approximately 1 billion RM were spent for the hereditarily ill. In contrast, only 730 million RM were spent for the German army in 1930 and only 713 million RM for the whole Reich administration. How many farm settlements, of which each should cost 32,000 RM, could have been constructed with the amount used for the hereditarily ill? How many homesteads could have been erected with this sum, if the aggregate building cost was 6,000 RM per house?

Few facets of German life remained free of the propagandists' gloss. Reich Minister **Josef Goebbels** and his propaganda ministry used every available venue—the news media, film, radio, and the popular press—to convey the party's ideological message. Even the arts and sciences were harnessed to help proclaim the virtues and principles of the National Socialist state. To reach young audiences, Nazi propagandists employed particular means to convey their ideological agenda. Children's books served as a ready conduit to distill the Nazi worldview for young people. Story books such as *Der Giftpilz* (*The Poisonous Mushroom*) and *Trau keinem Fuchs auf grüner Heid und keinem Jud bei seinem Eid* (*Trust No Fox in a Green Meadow Nor a Jew by His Oath*), both distributed by **Julius Streicher**'s *Der Stürmer* publishing house, elaborated the regime's antisemitic tenets in such a way that young minds might accept and adopt them.

DOCUMENT 7-8. **German school children read the antisemitic children's story** *Der Giftpilz* (*The Poisonous Mushroom*), **c. 1938, USHMMPA WS# 69561/E 39 Nr. 2381/7, courtesy of the Stadtarchiv Nürnberg.**

Another successful vehicle that Nazi propagandists employed to direct their ideological values to young people included children's toys and games. Toy figurine enterprise OM Hausser Elastolin experienced a burgeoning business not only in its traditional production line of toy soldiers and military paraphernalia but also in figurines from every major Nazi Party paramilitary organization, including the **Schutzstaffel** (**SS**), SA, and Hitler Youth. Figurines representing personalities of the Third Reich, such as Adolf Hitler, **Heinrich Himmler**, and **Hermann Göring**, also proved popular items. One German stuffed animal manufacturer created a version of its Teddy Bear dressed in full Nazi regalia.[31] In 1936, the Dresden-based concern Günther & Co. produced and distributed a board game called *"Juden raus!"* ("Jews, Get Out!"). Based on the classic game Parcheesi and representing a variant of today's American versions, "Sorry!" and "Trouble," *"Juden raus!"* clearly intended to instill in young children the basest tenets of Nazi antisemitism. According to the roll of the dice, children moved their play pieces the designated number of spaces along the game board, illustrated to depict the walls and streets of a medieval city. The wooden game pieces themselves represented highly caricatured "Jewish" figures with exaggerated features. The first person to drive all six of his or her "Jews" from the city and to the area ominously termed the "collection point" was the winner. "Show skill in rolling the dice," the instructions enjoined, "so that you collect many Jews!" In most editions, the game board bore the caption *"Auf nach Palästina"* ("Off to **Palestine**!"), reflecting the Nazis' then current policy of encouraging Jewish emigration from Germany. The game reportedly sold well in 1938, the year in which an accelerated antisemitic policy ended in ***Kristallnacht***.

---

31. German toy manufacturers are credited with popularizing the world-famous "Teddy Bear," named for Theodore Roosevelt, in 1902.

DOCUMENT 7-9. Game board "Juden raus!" ("Jews, Get Out!"), Günther & Co., 1938, USHMMPA WS# 11894, courtesy of the Leo Baeck Institute.

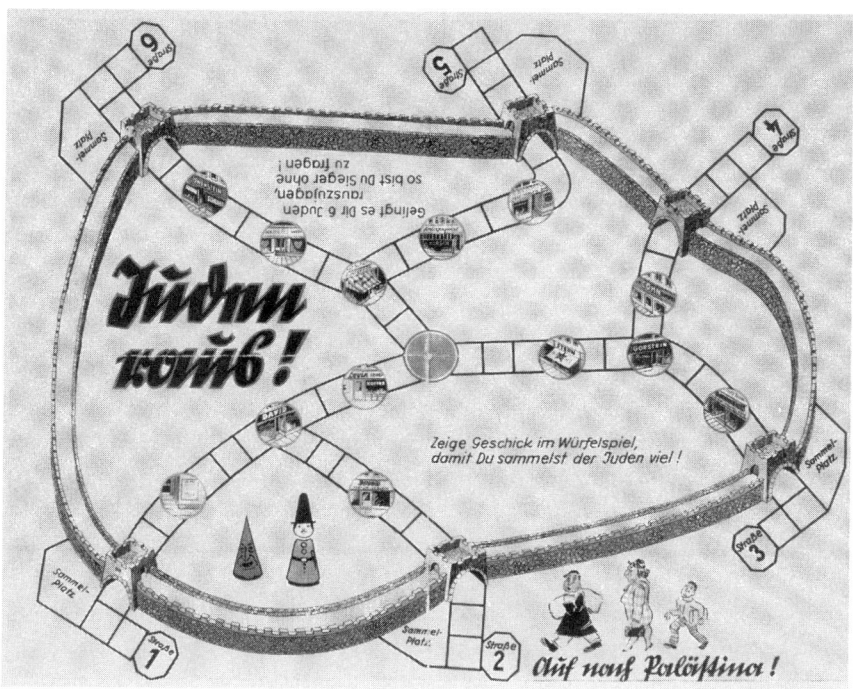

PERPETRATORS AND VICTIMS

Through propaganda, Nazi leaders attempted to capture the imagination and loyalty of Germany's younger generation. Fully exposed to the suggestive force of Nazi ideology, young people were highly susceptible to Nazism and its message and accepted its influence perhaps more uncritically than did their adult counterparts. Early antisemitic propaganda efforts often aimed at the marginalization of Jews in their own communities and regularly stressed popular participation in circumscribing their participation in economic, professional, and social spheres. Especially in the early years of the regime, local leaders of the Nazi Party and its auxiliary organizations, such as the SA and the Hitler Youth, instigated acts of violence and aggression against Jewish citizens and Jewish-owned property. Sometimes, too, "wild" boycotts of Jewish-owned stores and businesses, vandalism of Jewish cemeteries, and other antisemitic excesses sprang from individual initiative, spurred on by deep-seated personal or professional antagonisms or fanned by concentrated regional or national propaganda campaigns. Children often followed where adults led, introducing themes of exclusion and prejudice within their own milieus. Before legislation in November 1938 definitively banned them from attending "German" schools, Jewish pupils endured public humiliation, scorn, and bullying from many of their classmates. Adults too could figure as the objects of children's malice. At a trade and vocational school for boys in Frankfurt, one Jewish instructor, exempted from the civil service purge by dint of his military service in World War I, remained among the faculty in the autumn of 1935. Heightened antisemitic rhetoric had flooded the media since the promulgation of the **Nuremberg Laws** the month before, reminding German citizens of the need to root out Jewish influence from public life. When the school's administration seemed oblivious to this imperative, members of the student body decided to take matters into their own hands.

DOCUMENT 7-10. **Letter from the director of the Trade and Vocational School for Boys to the Department of Education, Frankfurt am Main, October 1, 1935, in Kommission zur Erforschung der Geschichte der Frankfurter Juden, eds.,** *Dokumente zur Geschichte der Frankfurter Juden, 1933–1945* **(Frankfurt am Main: Verlag Waldemar Kramer, 1963), 111 (translated from the German).**

Yesterday, September 30, [1935,] Herr Fröhlich alerted me that in the classroom of Herr Kromer, in which he has been assigned to teach shorthand, someone had hung a sign with the inscription, "Jews are not wanted here" ["*Juden sind hier unerwünscht*"]. So I went alone to the class, explained to the students that the swiftest solution to the "Jewish Question" for our school would emanate from school officials and until then, unauthorized actions must remain prohibited. Then I had the sign with the aforementioned slogan removed.

Today, on October 1, many pupils appeared conspicuously in uniform, and I learned that "something was planned." "When the school director takes Jews under his protection, then we'll proceed against him as well!" After recess the boys did not go back to their classrooms. A large throng collected in the hallways, and one could see that a demonstration was underway. I had already spoken with the municipal councilor, Mr. Beiling, and school inspector Müller on the telephone and received permission from the latter to suspend Mr. Fröhlich immediately if necessary. Mr. Fröhlich had already told me yesterday that he would rather be pensioned off. He promised, on my counsel, to put in a request for retirement today, as well as a suspension with pay in the meantime, upon which I released him provisionally from his duties.

I announced this measure to the pupils who had gathered in the gymnasium, reminded them of the dangers that may arise in our foreign policy when we undertake such arbitrary and unauthorized actions, and admonished them to abide by order and discipline. I succeeded in restoring calm to the situation, and the instruction could go forward until the end of the day as planned.

When properly motivated, children could prove a formidable force for National Socialist agitation. Such was the case with a group of Deutsches Jungvolk (German Young Volk), the division of the Hitler Youth created for ten- to fourteen-year-old boys, ubiquitously known as ***Pimpfe***.[32] When a handful of *Pimpfe* became involved in an altercation with a Jewish shop owner in Schivelbein, a small city in Pomerania, the youths in question used the incident to ignite public sentiment against the town's Jewish residents. Enlisting the aid of their Hitler Youth cell and the local citizenry, the boys succeeded in precipitating the arrest of the "offending" shopkeeper and the closure of the municipality's Jewish businesses. In a report to the Berlin office of the Centralverein (Central Association of German Citizens of the Jewish Faith, or CV),[33] a local CV administrator gave an account of the proceedings.

---

32. The word "*Pimpf*" (pl. *Pimpfe*) has an interesting etymology. It actually derives from an onomatopoetic device for audible flatulence. Just as English speakers might use the colloquial expression "little fart" for a young child, German speakers used "*Pimpf*" humorously to describe a prepubescent boy. In the 1920s, the word came to denote the youngest members of the German Youth Movement. The term migrated to the Hitler Youth organization in the 1930s and was used semiofficially to describe members of the Deutsches Jungvolk.

33. The CV was founded in 1893 to defend the rights of German Jews while fostering the "cultivation of German sentiment" among its members. The radicalization of the German political landscape in the final years of the Weimar Republic prompted the use of more aggressive means for combating the Nazi threat, an effort coordinated from the CV head office in Berlin. The CV spearheaded the formation of the Reichsvertretung der Juden in Deutschland in September 1933 and played a leading role in that organization's practical work. Renamed in September 1935 as Centralverein der Juden in Deutschland and one year later as Jüdischer Centralverein, the organization was abolished by the Gestapo in the wake of *Reichskristallnacht*.

DOCUMENT 7-11. **Report of the Centralverein Landesverband Pommern (Pomerania), signed Michelsohn, to the Central Office of the Centralverein, in re Schivelbein, August 16, 1935, USHMMA, RG-11.00, Osobyi Archive Moscow, 721-1-3019, Centralverein Records, 91 (translated from the German).**

Central Association of German Citizens of the Jewish Faith, e.V.[34]
Provincial Association [*Landesverband*] Pomerania
Stettin, August 15, 1935
Re: Schivelbein
To the Central Office Berlin
The recently reported occurrences in Schivelbein may be reported as follows:

On Sunday the 10th (August) a *Pimpf* purchased a pound of flour from the store owner Kronheim in Schivelbein. The *Pimpf* was in uniform. As he left the store, he was accosted by five *Pimpfe* who had ascended the three steps to the store; these boys demanded to know why he was buying goods at a Jewish-owned store. Kronheim saw this through the windowpane and yelled to the boys, "Get out of here!" ["*Macht, dass Ihr hier wegkommt!*"]. A member of the SA Sports School in Schivelbein, who was coincidently standing on the other side of the street, yelled something at Kronheim and threatened him. K[ronheim] as a consequence immediately shut the door.

As a result of the menacing tone which Kronheim had taken with the boys, an enormous agitation immediately manifested itself among Schivelbein's local cell of the Jungvolk (*Pimpfenschaft*). Approximately forty *Pimpfe* assembled outside Kronheim's store. The police came. The crowd pushed its way into the building, took hold of Kronheim, who had hidden himself, dragged him out, hung a placard around his neck which read, "The Jew Kronheim wanted to strike a *Pimpf*," and took him off to the police station. In the end the gang of *Pimpfe* forced the closure of all the Jewish businesses [in town]. A unit of *Pimpfe* came into the store of Mr. Fritz Jacobus, intending to provoke him, and one of them yelled to him, "Come on and hit me, come on and hit me!" But Fritz Jacobus restrained himself.

The forced closure of Jewish-owned businesses occurred in full view of the police.

---

34. The abbreviation "e.V." indicates a registered (nonprofit) society.

Towards evening a large protest demonstration was called. Large posters were hung with the announcement "Gathering of *Pimpfe* and Jungvolk. Protest demonstration against the Jew Kronheim, who wanted to strike a *Pimpf*. All residents are invited."

The assembly then took place with significant participation from among the local population. A high school student [*Unterpriminar*[35]], a local leader of the Hitler Youth, addressed the crowd. That night several windowpanes were shattered at the homes of Jewish residents.

Kronheim spent the night in protective custody.[36] On the next day he was sent for a physical examination to the Johanniter Hospital in Bad Polzin. On Wednesday he was again brought from there under policy custody to Schivelbein, interrogated, and released early on Thursday. His business is closed; a large placard has been nailed to the metal blinds of the store window so that it cannot be opened. The family has gone to stay with relatives in the area.

Early yesterday I reported the incident to the State Police[37] in Köslin. They were already informed there from the interrogation protocol taken by the police department in Schivelbein. I shared with them the inside facts of the matter. Because neither the mayor of Schivelbein nor the incumbent district magistrate [*Landrat*] will extend permission for the business to be reopened and for Kronheim to return to Schivelbein, it was my goal to secure this permission, which I succeeded in doing. Since yesterday morning the shop was open again; Kronheim may return to Schivelbein on the evening of the 18th. It remains to be seen whether a renewal of such incidents will occur.

During its twelve years in power, the Nazi dictatorship targeted individuals whom its ideology defined as biological enemies—most significantly Jews but also **Roma and Sinti** (Gypsies)—for discrimination, for

---

35. This denotes a high school student, usually sixteen to eighteen years of age, equivalent to a pupil in the sixth form in British secondary schools or a senior in high school in the United States.

36. In German, the term is *Schutzhaft*; it is by definition a type of police custody used to protect an individual from harm, either from outside sources or, if the individual is already in custody, from other prisoners. In Nazi Germany, the term was increasingly employed euphemistically to describe the practice of extralegal arrest and confinement of Jews and other real or perceived "enemies" of the Reich. Here the legal fiction suggested that the custody was necessary to protect the individual in question from the "righteous anger" of the German population.

37. This is the *Staatspolizeistelle*, or *Stapostelle*, the local branch of the Gestapo.

disenfranchisement, and finally for systematic destruction. Yet, even within their own *Volksgemeinschaft*—the German racial community envisioned by Nazi ideologues—National Socialist authorities identified real and perceived enemies of the regime whom they singled out for persecution. Among these were Jehovah's Witnesses, a religious group whose members, from religious conviction, refused to swear loyalty to any temporal government, to participate in its civic activities, or to serve in its armed forces. Founded in Pittsburgh, Pennsylvania, by American religious leader Charles Taze Russell (1852–1916) in 1872, the International Bible Study Society began missionary work in Europe in the 1890s. A first German branch of the group's Watch Tower Society was established in Elbersfeld in Westphalia in 1902. In 1931, the international association changed its name to Jehovah's Witnesses. By 1933, when the Nazis came to power, some thirty thousand Germans were Witnesses.[38]

Even before the establishment of the Third Reich, Jehovah's Witnesses figured as objects of prejudice. Germany's mainstream Catholic and Protestant churches disparaged the movement as a cult, while many ordinary citizens found the Witnesses' house-to-house proselytizing intrusive. Individual German state jurisdictions often enforced strict bans on such solicitation and prohibited the distribution of Witness literature, such as the movement's official journal, *The Watchtower*. While the Weimar period brought broader official acceptance of religious minorities, the National Socialist regime revived old prejudices and intensified persecution of the Earnest Bible Students (*Ernste Bibelforscher*), as the group was known in Germany. The international tenor of the Witness movement inspired immediate distrust among Nazi authorities. The Witnesses' reliance on Old Testament texts suggested to them a connection to international Jewry, the bête noire of Nazi ideology. National Socialist officials perceived as treasonous the Witnesses' refusal to swear allegiance to the Nazi regime or to demonstrate the outward manifestations of that loyalty through the Hitler salute (the so-called German greeting) or through the singing of the national anthem. When the Nazi state reintroduced conscription in 1935, most Jehovah's Witnesses refused to enlist or serve. German authorities prosecuted all Witnesses failing to report for the draft or declining to join the German Labor Front (Deutsche Arbeitsfront, or DAF) whose membership became mandatory

---

38. For a broader discussion of Jehovah's Witnesses under National Socialism, see Detlef Garbe, *Between Resistance and Martyrdom: Jehovah's Witnesses in the Third Reich*, trans. Dagmar G. Grimm (Madison: University of Wisconsin Press in association with the U.S. Holocaust Memorial Museum, 2008).

for all salaried employees following the Nazi ban on trade unions. Nazi authorities often incarcerated Jehovah's Witnesses in concentration camps following service of their prison terms. The vast majority of Witnesses refused to abandon their faith, despite persecution, the imposition of prison sentences, and confinement in the Nazi concentration camp system. Of thirty thousand members of the sect in Germany in 1933, some 10 percent languished in camps during the war years. Approximately one thousand of their number perished during their imprisonment, as did four hundred Witnesses from other nations. In addition, some 250 German Witnesses were executed, most under the authority of military tribunals, for refusing to serve in the German armed forces.

The children of committed Jehovah's Witnesses also faced persecution under the Nazi regime. Refusing, like their parents, to give the "German greeting" or to participate in patriotic or school ceremonies, young Witnesses often found themselves expelled from school. During the Nazi era, 850 Witness children were removed from their parental homes and placed in reformatory schools or foster homes. One of these youngsters was Willi Seitz, a young follower of the movement born in Karlsruhe on March 11, 1923. At age fourteen, school authorities expelled him from the local *Volksschule* for repeatedly failing to give the Hitler salute and refusing to take part in Nazi-inspired classroom activities. His father, Franz Josef Seitz, was a devout and active Witness. His fervent belief had come at a price, for in 1936 he was removed from his civil service post with the municipal waterworks administration; in July of that year he received a four-month sentence from a Mannheim court for his continued religious activities. Wishing to make an example of Seitz, local officials sued him in juvenile court in January 1937, shortly after his release from prison, in order to remove fourteen-year-old Willi Seitz from parental custody. On April 6, the district court ruled that the young boy should be transferred to a reformatory school and eventually placed with a German family that might inculcate in the youngster the proper respect for his country and its principles. Franz Josef Seitz appealed this decision, but on April 15, 1937, a superior court in Karlsruhe upheld the earlier judgment. The Seitz family ultimately succeeded in removing Willi from the reformatory school and sending him to Strasbourg in Alsace, beyond the reach of local authorities. Through the help of Swiss Witnesses, the youth settled with a family in Bern, in neutral Switzerland, where he remained until the end of the war. Shortly after his appeal to the juvenile court in Karlsruhe, Franz Josef Seitz refused to appear for a physical examination conditional for military service and was arrested shortly thereafter for distributing "subversive" literature. After he had served an eighteen-month sentence,

Gestapo officials transferred Seitz to **Buchenwald**, where he was incarcerated until the liberation of that camp in April 1945. He and Willi were reunited after the war, having been apart for eight years.[39]

DOCUMENT 7-12. Decision of the State Court, Karlsruhe, concerning the appeal of Franz Josef Seitz against the removal of parental custody, Karlsruhe, April 15, 1937, USHMMA, RG-32.008*01, Willi Seitz Collection (translated from the German).

State Court [Landgericht]   Karlsruhe, April 15, 1937
Civil Court I
1 ZFH 33/37 Parental authority concerning Willi Josef Seitz, born March 11, 1923

Decree

The appeal of the stoker Franz Josef Seitz in Karlsruhe, Kriegsstrasse 171, against the decision of the District Court [*Amtsgericht*] B III Karlsruhe of April 6, 1937 is dismissed with costs [to plaintiff].

Grounds

On April 6, 1937, the District Court B III Karlsruhe removed from the stoker Franz Josef Seitz parental custody of his son Willi Josef and ordered in the same instance that the boy be removed temporarily to the observation station of the Schloss Flehingen reformatory school. Concerning the circumstances which led to this measure, a detailed statement of the district court is appended to this decree.

The father appealed against this ruling with the petition that the judgment be reversed. He disputes that the criteria for an infraction according to §1666 of the Civil Code [Bürgerliches Gesetzbuch] are not met. He insists that he has not endangered the emotional or physical well-being of his son or abused the rights of parental custody vested in him. The son had a strict upbringing and is deeply religious. Since his expulsion from school, he has taken up an apprenticeship. There have been no complaints against his son either during his schooling or during his apprenticeship. He does not deny that his son refused to take part in patriotic school festivals, refuses to give the "German greeting," and refuses to salute the flag. But this purportedly does not stem from [the father's] influence.

---

39. Franz Josef Seitz, "Meine Erlebnisse im Dritten Reich," U.S. Holocaust Memorial Museum, RG-32.008*01 (Willi Seitz Collection).

He says he did not prevail upon his son in any manner and left it up to him as to how he should behave. He himself formerly belonged to the Association of Earnest Bible Students and still belongs today to the confession of Jehovah's Witnesses. Reference to the circumstances of the case and the charge made by the complainant will be made in detail in the file.

According to the findings, whose correctness is not disputed by the father, the boy refused to participate in patriotic ceremonies at school, [refused] to salute the flag, to give the "German greeting," and to sing the national anthems.[40] He explained to the school director that he would not become a soldier and, besides this, set down in two essays his opinion of current events. Consistent with his entire manner of behavior and according to opinions expressed in his school essays, the minor is not able to feel himself a German or even to evince respect for the great German men and their deeds or consciously to dedicate himself to his duties to his people [*Volk*] and his country. It is the specific duty of the parents to bring their children up in a way which does not alienate them from their German nature, to raise their children according to German customs and precepts, and to educate them spiritually and morally in the spirit of National Socialism in the service of the people [*Volk*] and the *Volksgemeinschaft* (Preamble and §2, Law Concerning the Hitler Youth of December 1, 1936, *Reich Law Gazette* I, p. 993). An offense against this duty must be seen as a subjective failure of the parents in the interpretation of §1666 of the Civil Code. Contrary to the statements of the father, the court is convinced that the attitude of the son can be traced to the influence of the parents. The father is still a member of the Jehovah's Witnesses. He was released from his post because of his activities as a Jehovah's Witness and also served a jail term for this [offense]. The mother holds the same opinions as the father. It is obvious that a youth at this age does not think for himself but adopts the convictions of his parents. In consideration of his behavior, he has additionally been expelled from school. [Because of this] it would therefore be impossible for him to receive the necessary further education in order to attain any career position. For all of this, [the court] acknowledges and rules with the district court that there exist the necessary preconditions to take legal measures according to §1666 of the Civil Code. Because those measures ordered by the district court do not

---

40. This refers to the official German national anthem, the so-called "*Deutschlandlied*" ("*Deutschland, Deutschland, über alles*"), followed by the "Horst Wessel Song" ("*Horst-Wessel-Lied*"), a song composed by early Nazi Party martyr Horst Wessel and embraced as the Party anthem.

exceed the requisite mandated by the unusual circumstances, the appeal must be rejected.

GERMAN CHILDREN AND THE WAR

Marion Lubien[41] was one of many young Germans who kept a wartime diary. Like most of her adult contemporaries, the fourteen-year-old seemed fascinated by firsthand accounts of distant battles and intoxicated by the string of early victories. For Marion and her generation, the war was a source of genuine excitement. While grown-ups may not have shared their enthusiasm, youngsters often relished the exciting novelties that the new conflict ushered in: blackouts, gas mask and civil defense drills, letters and presents from absent fathers postmarked from Poland and France. Besides the sense of sacrifice that rationing and conservation engendered in young patriots, wartime privation also produced its own small dividends. As school buildings began to perform double duty as first aid stations, military registration centers, and distribution points for ration coupons, school hours were altered or curtailed, while early shortages in coal and fuel products produced lengthy "coal holidays" for school children in the coldest winter months. Wartime infused the structured activities of the Nazi youth organizations with a greater sense of purpose. Young people did their part for the Fatherland by participating in scrap-metal and rubber recycling campaigns and collecting clothing and donations for the National Socialist Winter Relief (Winterhilfe) association. Young boys felt connected to troops in the field through their own paramilitary training and drilling with the Hitler Youth. Under the auspices of the League of German Girls, teenage girls ran charity drives, wrote letters to convalescent soldiers, and assembled care packages for frontline troops.

---

41. Marion Lubien (a pseudoynm to protect the child diarist's privacy) was born in 1928 in Essen. In 1943, she was evacuated with her Realschule class to Bad-Bohdanetsch (today Lázně Bohdaneč), near Prague, in order to escape Allied bombing. She returned home to Essen in February 1945 and survived the war.

DOCUMENT 7-13. **Members of the Hitler Youth practice donning gas masks during an air raid drill, c. 1937, USHMMPA WS# 31512, courtesy of Bildarchiv Preussischer Kulturbesitz.**

Although many youngsters felt themselves engaged in some manner in the war effort, from their vantage point on the home front, the war—at least in its initial stages—still seemed so far away. Marion Lubien dutifully recorded in her diary the stream of military developments and ringing victories as these played out in the early years of the conflict. Her journal entries often emulated the news accounts of the day with their terse and authoritative prose. Lubien's tone remained neutral and unemotional, and she made little reference to her personal experiences—until British Royal Air Force (RAF) bombs began to rain down on the teenager's home city of Essen.[42]

For most German youngsters, the Allied bombing of German urban centers and industrial sectors often represented their first genuine encounter with

---

42. See Nicholas Stargardt, *Witnesses of War: Children's Lives under the Nazis* (New York: Knopf, 2006).

the realities of warfare. With the vital exception of those children who had lost fathers, brothers, or other male relatives in the Polish or western campaigns, many young people faced for the first time the immediate possibility of loss of home and family as the aerial raids literally brought the war home to them.

The RAF implemented the first significant strategic bombing of a German city, Berlin, on September 24, 1940. As was the case in Great Britain, the Nazi regime responded to the threat of future air raids with a plan to evacuate school-age children from areas potentially threatened by Allied bombardment. Since the late nineteenth century, various German governments had promoted the transfer of youngsters from urban centers for extended recreational stays in rural settings (*Kinderlandverschickung*, or KLV). The purpose of these endeavors— to provide youths from Germany's polluted industrial areas the opportunity to spend their school and summer holidays in the fresh air and wholesome environment of the countryside—was immediately adopted as a policy by the National Socialist People's Welfare Organization (Nationalsozialistische Volkswohlfahrt, or NSV[43]) shortly after the Nazis came to power in 1933. On September 27, 1940, three days after the first intensive bombing of the capital, Reichsleiter Martin Bormann,[44] head of the Nazi Party Chancellery, issued a confidential circular decree ordering that children resident in regions threat-ened by Allied air raids might be temporarily relocated to safer areas within Reich territory.[45] In its initial stages, this measure was completely voluntary and scheduled to continue for a period of only six months. To allay public fears of a potential prolonged assault by Allied air forces on German population centers, Bormann specifically forbade mention of an "evacuation" of German children. Rather officials were to couch the action in terms of an "expanded transfer of children to the countryside" (*Erweiterte Kinderlandverschickung*), suggesting an extension of the earlier social welfare program.

---

43. The NSV became the official welfare organization of the Nazi Party in 1933. Absorbing all non-Nazi charity organizations, it became the second-largest Nazi group orga-nization by 1939, after the German Labor Front (Deutsche Arbeitsfront, or DAF).

44. Martin Bormann (1900–1945) served as head of the Party Chancellery (Parteikanzlei) and Hitler's private secretary. As the Führer's closest aide, he gained enormous bureaucratic power and influence through Hitler's implicit trust and by controlling access to the German leader. On May 1, 1945, the day following Hitler's suicide, Bormann, with other German personnel, fled the Führerbunker during the Battle of Berlin; he was never seen alive again. The International Military Tribunal at Nuremberg convicted Bormann in absentia and sen-tenced him to death. In 1972, remains thought to be Bormann's were uncovered in Berlin; these findings were confirmed by DNA testing in 1998.

45. By 1941, German children were also being relocated to German-occupied territo-ries, such as Denmark, and to territories controlled by German allies, such as Slovakia and Hungary.

The former leader of the Hitler Youth, Baldur von Schirach, in his capacity as Reich Leader of Youth and Education of the Nazi Party, undertook the coordination of state, public, and party agencies participating in the effort. The NSV assumed responsibility for youngsters under the age of ten. Mothers generally accompanied infants and toddlers in these relocations[46]; together with elder siblings, they were usually housed with host families, who received a subsidy from the state. The NSV also settled children aged six to ten with foster families in locations where they might continue their elementary school education. Young people aged ten to fourteen fell under the jurisdiction of the Hitler Youth organization. Divided by gender, pupils in this age cohort traveled with their teachers from target cities such as Berlin, Essen, and Düsseldorf to rural areas in Bavaria, Austria, Saxony, and East Prussia. A majority of these children lodged in so-called KLV camps, which integrated classroom instruction and structured play with ideological indoctrination. The measure formally remained voluntary, although as the air war intensified, many students were compulsorily relocated to KLV camps to compensate for the closure of schools in bombed-out neighborhoods. Despite the hardship of separation, many German parents welcomed the chance to remove their children from harm's way. The KLV effort did ensure its participants a safe environment, uninterrupted schooling, and access to better nutrition. The state absorbed all substantial costs for the program and, particularly in the last difficult years of the war, relieved hard-pressed families from the responsibility of child care. From October 1940 until war's end, the Reich Office (Reichsdienststelle) KLV evacuated 2 million German children to safety and accommodated 850,000 school-age pupils between ten and fourteen in its nine thousand camps. In a class essay written in 1946, an eleven-year-old girl remembered her evacuation from her home city of Nuremberg to the Bavarian countryside.[47]

---

46. So-called mother-and-child transfers (*Mutter-und-Kind-Verschickungen*) were initially intended for small children aged three and younger; in later years, however, they encompassed children up to age six.

47. See Gerhard Kock, *Der Führer sorgt für unsere Kinder: Die Kinderlandverschickung im Zweiten Weltkrieg* (Paderborn: F. Schöningh, 1997); Stargardt, *Witnesses of War*, esp. 229–88.

DOCUMENT 7-14. **School essay of an eleven-year-old girl, Nuremberg, 1946, in Emmy E. Werner, *Through the Eyes of Innocents: Children Witness World War II* (Boulder, CO: Westview Press, 2000), 49.**

> We suffered several devastating air raids. My parents made up their minds to send me (aged 9) and my brother to the countryside. My mother packed our belongings. Then [. . .] on September 1, 1943, we departed. There were thirty of us, varying in age from six to fourteen, from the first to eighth grade. We were accompanied by a teacher from our school. We travelled by train to Weissenburg. There we were picked up by a bus and travelled to the village of Bergen. There we all stood around, waiting to get a number. That was the number of [the] house. When it was called, someone from the family came to meet us. My brother and I ended up on a large farm, with strangers. But they were very friendly to us. They fed us frequently and well. We helped on the farm and stayed nearly one and a half years in the village. Then our parents brought us back home.

On June 7, 1944, the German public awoke to read a terse dispatch from the Military High Command in their morning papers: "In the night just past," it announced, "the enemy began their long-planned invasion of western Europe, an attack which we have been expecting."[48]

It was D-day. In the early-morning hours of June 6, 1944, some 175,000 Allied troops stormed ashore on the beaches of Normandy in northern France. Thousands of British, American, Canadian, and Free French reinforcements would follow in the coming weeks. By late summer, Allied troops had liberated Paris and reached the Siegfried Line, the so-called Western Wall (*Westwall*) of Germany's fortified defense system. Their armies now pressed toward the German frontier, while in the East, Soviet forces pushed to the borders of East Prussia.

In the context of these mounting military defeats, Hitler decreed the creation of the Volkssturm, a home guard consisting of previously unconscripted men between the ages of sixteen and sixty.[49] Individual *Gauleiters* were responsible for the organization and command of local units, while Reichsführer-SS

---

48. This announcement of the D-day invasion is quoted in Emmy E. Werner, *Through the Eyes of Innocents: Children Witness World War II* (Boulder, CO: Westview Press, 2000), 120.

49. The Führer decree establishing the Volkssturm proceeded on September 25, 1944, but was first made public on October 18, 1944, the anniversary of the Battle of Nations (*Völkerschlacht*), fought near Leipzig, in which Napoleon was decisively routed in 1813.

Heinrich Himmler and Reichsleiter Martin Bormann undertook military and political leadership of the troops, respectively. Tasked with the defense of the immediate homeland, nearly 6 million men were drafted into this service. Three separate age cohorts were affected: those born between the years 1884 and 1924, who had previously been excluded for reasons of age or health; those men currently eligible for conscription but whose occupations had exempted them as essential to the war effort (*Unabkömmlichstellung*, or *UK-Stellung*); and those teenagers born between 1925 and 1928, who were not yet of draft age. In the last desperate months of World War II, young boys in their early teens were drawn into action as well.

Lacking necessary materiel and qualified instructors, Volkssturm formations were poorly trained and inadequately armed. Germany had a long tradition of compulsory military service, so most older members of the Volkssturm would at least have received some military training when they previously served with the army. This was not true of conscripted teenagers, who received minimal basic training from the Hitler Youth organization or from the Reich Labor Service (Reicharbeitsdienst).[50] Actual weapons training was often so deficient that Volkssturm members had to familiarize themselves with their firearms in the field. Chronically short of arms and ammunition, Volkssturm units fought with captured weapons, as well as with portable antitank rocket launchers (bazookas) and improvised light rifles, such as the *Volksgewehr* (people's rifle); often they were armed with little more than picks and shovels. It was common to deploy such forces in digging antitank ditches and entrenchments and in building makeshift shelters and dugouts, but many units saw heavy combat. Although individual regiments were initially intended to operate in their home districts, numerous divisions were sent directly to the front. These ragtag forces were used extensively in the Battle of Königsberg (today Kaliningrad) (April 6 to 9, 1945) and in the Battle for Berlin (April 20 to May 2, 1945), one of the war's bloodiest battles. Ill-equipped and inadequately provisioned, they suffered enormous casualties. Tens of thousands died in action. Nearly 1 million Volkssturm soldiers were prisoners of war at war's end, while 175,000 were officially listed as missing.

Volkssturm formations often fought with desperate courage, but the military value of their deployment remained insignificant. The Nazi leadership believed that the formation and presence of a home guard would bolster plummeting public morale, but the sight of ragged boys and graybeards marching

---

50. For further discussion of the Volkssturm, see David K. Yelton, *Hitler's Volkssturm: The Nazi Militia and the Fall of Germany, 1944–1945* (Lawrence: University Press of Kansas, 2002).

into combat presumably did little to restore citizens' belief in ultimate victory. Nevertheless, *Völkischer Beobachter*, the official newspaper of the Nazi Party, often carried stories heralding the valor and tenacity of young boys dispatched to the defense of their embattled Fatherland. In early 1945, it printed an interview with fifteen-year-old Harry Bahrmann, whose courage and quick action halted the entry of a Soviet tank into a village in eastern Germany.

DOCUMENT 7-15. Interview with Harry Bahrmann, *Völkischer Beobachter*, c. March 1945, in Franz Seidler, *Deutsche Volkssturm: Das letzte Aufgebot, 1944–1945*, 2nd ed. (Berlin: Herbig, 1991), 322.

Harry Bahrmann, Hitler Youth member, fifteen years old:

I lie in the roadside ditch in the middle of the village. In the area before me, the street comes to an end to my right. I lie where the road makes a sharp bend. The ditch is not deep, but I duck down. I can see for about fifty meters [164 feet] down the street, then the corner of the adjacent house cuts off my view. I hear the tank coming and duck down even lower. He must not see me first. He shoots and [the shots] resound in my ear, but I think, "He cannot see me and is shooting over me." I want to let him come up very close. I'm almost lying completely on my stomach on the embankment, releasing the safety catch of the bazooka and pressing it against me. I try to decide how I will do it. The roar of the turret gun almost knocks me over. Then I see [the tank] and quickly duck my head away. I didn't think any more, except that it was almost directly upon me. I see it suddenly, although I keep my head low. It is no more than six meters [twenty feet] away. I really wanted to shoot from a prone position, but I spring up halfway and discharge the weapon, and I cannot miss. There was immediately a dense cloud of smoke about the tank, from which a cascade of bright lights appeared as if someone were doing welding. The tank half turned, blocked the street, and burned out. I was completely dirty and wet from the culvert. I thought, "Now you can really come out of the ditch." From the entryway of a nearby house, someone ran out to me and said, "You shot the tank."

"Yes," I said.

On January 12, 1945, the Red Army launched its last major offensive against German forces, beginning from its start positions on the Vistula River in Poland and fanning out along a broad front. On the fourth day of the endeavor,

Soviet army groups broke German lines and advanced rapidly westward at the rate of approximately thirty to forty kilometers (twenty-five miles) per day. In swift succession, Soviet forces captured the German territories of East Prussia, East Pomerania, Upper Silesia, and Posen (today Posnań) before halting on a line along the Oder River some seventy kilometers (forty-four miles) from Berlin. The German **Wehrmacht** had lost more than 1 million troops since the Allied invasion of western Europe in June 1944, and it lacked sufficient men and material to adequately defend the capital. As the Soviets pushed toward the gates of Berlin, the U.S. Army Air Force launched a number of devastating daytime air raids upon the city, while the RAF rained bombs on the capital for thirty-six consecutive nights before the arrival of Red Army forces. Soviet artillery units began shelling the metropolitan area on April 20, 1945, and did not halt their efforts until the city's surrender.

The Battle for Berlin had begun. By April 24, units of the First Belorussian Front[51] and the First Ukrainian Front completed an encirclement of the capital. The German defenses consisted of some forty-five thousand disorganized and ill-equipped Wehrmacht and **Waffen-SS** troops, as well as police, Volkssturm, and Hitler Youth units. Following one of the most fiercely fought battles of World War II, Soviet troops reached the Reichstag and the adjoining government district at the city's center on April 30. That afternoon Germany's Führer, Adolf Hitler, committed suicide in his subterranean bunker beneath the New Reich Chancellery building on the nearby Voßstrasse. On May 2, Berlin capitulated, although fighting continued on the city's outskirts until Germany's official surrender on May 8, 1945. While precise mortality statistics are difficult to attain, scholars estimate that as many as 125,000 civilians perished in the Battle for Berlin.[52]

Seventeen-year-old Lili G. experienced the collapse of the Third Reich in Germany's capital. From her home in the Kaiserallee in Berlin's Tempelhof district, the teenager recorded in terse journal entries the arrival of Soviet forces and the intense aerial and artillery bombardment that confined her and her family to their cellar as fighting raged through the streets. As the Red Army took possession of the city, vengeful Soviet troops spread terror throughout the capital, looting homes, arresting anyone in uniform, and sometimes murdering civilians in cold blood. As in Vienna, which had fallen to the Soviet army on February 13, some 10 to 20 percent of Berlin's female population was raped in

---

51. The term front described a major military organization in the Soviet army during World War II; it was roughly equivalent to an Allied army group.

52. See Earl Ziemke, *Stalingrad to Berlin: The German Defeat in the East* (Washington, DC: Center for Military History, United States Army, 1968).

the first days of occupation,[53] among them Lili's mother. On May 1, the family fled to Lichterfelde in the city's southern suburbs to escape the chaos of the battle's final days and the excesses of Soviet soldiers. Following the city's capitulation on May 2, Lili, her mother, and her younger sister, Margit, returned to their shell-ravaged neighborhood to await the war's end and to begin picking up the pieces of their shattered lives.

DOCUMENT 7-16. Journal of Lili G., entries for April 15 through May 9, 1945, in Reinhard Rürup, ed., *Der Krieg gegen die Sowjetunion, 1941–1945: Eine Dokumentation zum 50. Jahrestag des Überfalls auf die Sowjetunion* (Berlin: Argon-Verlag, 1991), 257–58 (translated from the German).

April 15, [1945]: Air raid siren! The British are in Magdeburg, the Russians have reached Frankfurt [an der Oder].

April 16: Air raid siren! Digging around for things [in the old house] in the Jagowstrasse.

April 17: Air raid siren! Was paying off accounts with our ration coupons.

April 18: Air raid siren! Retrieving things in the Jagowstrasse.

April 19: Air raid siren! Retrieving things in the Jagowstrasse. Can already hear shooting.

April 20: Air raid siren! Little water, no electricity. The siren no longer sounds during air raids.

April 21: The train doesn't go out to the Jagowstrasse anymore.

April 22: We are now sleeping in the cellar. The Russians have reached Berlin. Uncle Willi is now a refugee and has come to stay with us.

April 23: Went out to the Jagowstrasse with Uncle Willi. Visited Papa. He had got drunk from his alcohol rations.

April 24: Five people dead through a grenade blast in the Trautenaustrasse.

April 25: No water! No gas! No light!

April 26: Artillery fire!

April 27: The enemy is at the Kaiserplatz.

April 28: Our house was hit for the fourth time by artillery!

April 29: Our house was struck about twenty times [by artillery fire]. It is very difficult to cook anything because of the constant danger to life and limb when one leaves the cellar.

---

53. See Stargardt, *Witnesses of War*, 316–20.

April 30: I was standing up on the stairs of the cellar with Mrs. Behrendt during a bombing raid. The Russians are here. They are completely drunk. There are rapes at night. Not me. Mama yes. Some five to twenty times.

May 1: The Russians go in and out [of our house]. All of our clocks and watches are gone. Their horses lie in the courtyard on our bedding. They have broken into the cellar. We have all fled to Stubenrauchstrasse 33.[54]

May 2: The first night of quiet. We have moved from hell to heaven. We cried when we discovered the lilacs blooming in the courtyard. Everyone must give up their radios.

May 3: Still in the Stubenrauchstrasse. Can't go to the window, lest you are seen by the Russians. We've heard that there are rapes everywhere.

May 4: No news from Father in the Derfflinger Strasse.

May 5: Back to the Kaiserallee. Complete chaos!

May 6: Our building took twenty-one hits! Cleared things away and packed all day. Attack at night. Crept under the bed for fear the Russians were coming. But the building was just rattling because of the shelling.

May 7: The street has been cleared of rubble. I got numbers for our bread ration, cleaned things up, washed up.

May 8: Cleared rubble in the street. Stood in line for bread. Got news that Father is alive.

May 9: Armistice. There is milk for Margit.

---

54. This refers to a street in Lichterfelde, a quiet, affluent neighborhood in southern Berlin and thus away from the chaos of the city center.

DOCUMENT 7-17. A German mother shields the eyes of her young son as American troops force her and other townspeople to view the bodies of Soviet civilians from a mass grave near Suttrop, Germany, May 3, 1945, USHMMPA WS# 08197, courtesy of the National Archives and Records Administration.

CHAPTER 8

THE WORLD OF THE CHILD

U NDERSTANDABLY, children and adults contended with the persecutory policies of the Nazi period in markedly different ways. Child victims and survivors of genocide were, after all, still children. This chapter reflects the events of the Shoah, or Holocaust, through their eyes and explores the ways in which youngsters coped with the menacing world in which they found themselves.

Learning and play are two elemental activities associated with childhood. During the Holocaust, children used both to adapt to their difficult circumstances and to restore a sense of normalcy to their disordered lives. In many ghettos throughout eastern Europe, Nazi authorities forbade formal educational instruction for Jewish children. Yet, thousands of school-age children defied such bans by attending a network of clandestine schools organized by education and welfare agencies in many ghetto communities. For young people, such secret study was a means of transcending the narrow walls of the ghetto and fulfilling important intellectual and emotional needs. Teenagers also took pleasure in participating in extracurricular educational and cultural events, such as literary circles, exhibitions, and musical recitals, which offered an important conduit for creativity and artistic collaboration within a captive community.

Play provided children with another powerful outlet to give the terrifying world about them safer contours. Entering a realm of daydream and imagination allowed youngsters to escape their harrowing and uncertain existence and eschew the fear and hunger that tormented them. With a creativity and ingenuity that surprised adult observers, youngsters invented new toys and games with the very limited resources available to them. Often children incorporated the macabre realities of their camp or ghetto surroundings. Integrating the horrors and tragedies that they witnessed into their play may have helped young children to absorb and assimilate the traumatic events that punctuated their everyday existence.

Like learning and play, innocence is another element closely associated with childhood. But were children in Nazi camps and ghettos innocent of the dangers that awaited them? Could children comprehend the malignant forces that they faced? Documentation concerning innocence and knowledge examines the degree to which children lived aware or unaware of their perilous circumstances. In most cases, youngsters matured quickly, gaining experience beyond their years, witnessing unimaginable horrors, and shouldering grown-up responsibilities. With a flexibility that many adults lacked, children often found highly creative ways to cope with the difficulties they confronted. Through imagination, play, and their dreams for the future, young people managed to transcend the physical and emotional traumas they experienced and cling to their hopes for survival.

ESCAPE INTO LEARNING

Learning is an essential and indispensable feature of childhood, the school years being part of a youngster's evolution to adulthood. Yet, during the war years in German-occupied Europe, a majority of Jewish children were denied the possibility of a formal education. In November 1939, just weeks after the Polish army capitulated, German officials in the **General Government** banned Jewish children from all public and private schools. In the Polish capital alone, forty thousand Jewish youngsters of school age were barred from attending classes.[1] With very few exceptions, as in the case of the **Łódź ghetto**, which boasted an impressive array of officially sanctioned educational institutions,[2] prohibitions or severe restrictions upon formal instruction for Jewish children remained in effect when Jewish populations were ghettoized in Poland and other German-occupied territories in eastern Europe. When the largest of these communities, the **Warsaw ghetto**, was enclosed in November 1940, German authorities imposed a ban on the establishment of schools, citing the threat of contagion.

---

1. Barbara Engelking and Jacek Leociak, *The Warsaw Ghetto: A Guide to a Perished City*, trans. Emma Harris (New Haven, CT: Yale University Press, 2009), 343.
2. For a discussion of education in the Łódź ghetto, see chapter 4.

Only a select number of vocational-training courses were permitted in August 1940, and only in September 1941 did German officials countenance the opening of a number of elementary schools for ghetto pupils.[3]

According to available statistics, some 48,207 school-age children between the ages of seven and fourteen lived in the Warsaw ghetto[4]; to this figure we must add thousands of adolescents who, under normal circumstances, would have attended secondary or college-preparatory schools (*Gymnasia*). Yet, only a small fraction of their number had access to formal instruction. In such a setting, how was it possible to provide an education to the youth of the Warsaw ghetto? Clearly, a certain number of children were educated within their own homes, by parents, older siblings, or relatives. Several thousand orphaned or severely disadvantaged youths who lived in **CENTOS** homes or orphanages presumably also received at least limited informal instruction from caregivers. Yet, already in the summer and autumn of 1940, representatives of Jewish educational and welfare organizations had begun working to construct a network of clandestine schools for youngsters and adolescents. Many underground classrooms gathered in soup kitchens and care institutions for young people. In these instances, instructors and administrators pursued the dual goal of feeding hungry children and providing them a basic educational foundation. Other less formally organized "schools" met secretly in the private homes of instructors or their pupils. From the autumn of 1940 until the summer of 1942, a wide range of underground centers offered educational instruction to ghetto youths. In addition to kindergartens and elementary schools, there existed a number of high schools, *Gymnasia*, vocational-training institutions, and *cheder* schools for religious instruction.

Clandestine classes for very young children incorporated lessons through stories, songs, and games. Parents and educators often described such gatherings as "play groups" in order to conceal covert learning activities and to prevent youngsters from inadvertently revealing their illicit schooling to others. Teachers stressed the importance of *Beschäftigung* (engagement in useful activity) as a way to combat boredom and delinquency among young children and

---

3. Barbara Engelking-Boni, "Childhood in the Warsaw Ghetto," in *Children and the Holocaust: Symposium Presentations of the Center for Advanced Holocaust Studies* (Washington DC: U.S. Holocaust Memorial Museum, 2004), 34–35.

4. Engelking-Boni, "Childhood in the Warsaw Ghetto," 34.

to prepare them for the proficiency necessary from primary education.[5] For elementary school children, educators stressed reading and writing, fearing that such skill sets might be lost to a generation of Jewish youth. For older children, clandestine *Gymnasia* and secondary schools also thrived in ghetto communities. The first underground *Gymnasium* in Warsaw, established under the auspices of the Dror youth organization, sheltered seventy-two pupils in its first year and employed as its teachers intellectuals such as the famed Jewish writer Isaac Katzenelson.[6] Because many instructors and sponsoring organizations were Zionist in political orientation, curricula often stressed Judaic and Zionist themes and offered theoretical and practical preparation for a new Jewish future in **Palestine**. Covert secondary schools in the ghetto maintained high standards, devising enrollment criteria for prospective pupils, offering advanced courses in literature, the arts, and the sciences, and issuing degrees. As secrecy was an important issue, students did not receive certificates on graduation; examination records were preserved in hiding and legitimized by a special education commission after the war.[7]

According to calculations made by chroniclers of the **Oneg Shabbat** archive, some ten thousand children and adolescents attended clandestine classes in the Warsaw ghetto between 1940 and 1942.[8] One of those students was fifteen-year-old Miriam Wattenberg, whose family had fled Łódź in late 1939. Mary's mother was an American citizen, a connection that provided some security to Mary and her fellow pupils who engaged in a series of

---

5. See Lisa Anne Plante, "Transition and Resistance: Schooling Efforts for Jewish Children and Youth in Hiding, Ghettos, and Camps," in *Children and the Holocaust: Symposium Presentations of the Center for Advanced Holocaust Studies* (Washington, DC: U.S. Holocaust Memorial Museum, 2004), 45ff.

6. Engelking and Leociak, *The Warsaw Ghetto*, 346. Isaac Katzenelson (1886–1944) was born in Korelichi in Belorussia (now Belarus) and moved to Warsaw as a small boy. For many years he directed a Hebrew-Polish school in Łódź; writing in Hebrew, he produced many well-received plays, including *The Prophet* and *The White Life*. When German forces invaded Poland, Katzenelson began to write his works in Yiddish. In November 1939, he fled to Warsaw, where he was active as a writer and educator until 1943. In April 1943, during the Warsaw Ghetto Uprising, Katzenelson escaped and succeeded in making his way to France on false papers; he was interned, however, in the Vittel detention camp and in 1944 deported to Auschwitz, where he perished. After the war his manuscript titled *The Song of the Slaughtered Jewish People* was discovered at Vittel and published in several languages.

7. Engelking and Leociak, *The Warsaw Ghetto*, 349.

8. Engelking and Leociak, *The Warsaw Ghetto*, 344.

Gymnasium-level courses in the Wattenberg home.[9] In her diary/memoir, published in February 1945, Wattenberg described how the clandestine nature of the instruction inspired a "strange earnestness" in pursuing an education among like-minded teachers and classmates.

DOCUMENT 8-1. Diary/memoir of Miriam Wattenberg, entry for July 12, 1940, in Mary Berg, *Warsaw Ghetto: A Diary by Mary Berg*, ed. S. L. Shneiderman, trans. Norbert Guterman and Sylvia Glass (New York: L. B. Fischer, 1945), 32–33.

There are now a great number of illegal schools, and they are multiplying every day. People are studying in attics and cellars, and every subject is included in the curriculum, even Latin and Greek. Two such schools were discovered by the Germans some time in June [1940]; later we heard that the teachers were shot on the spot, and that the pupils had been sent to a concentration camp near Lublin.

Our Łódź *Gymnasium* too has started its classes.[10] The majority of the teachers are in Warsaw, and twice a week the courses are given at our home, which is a relatively safe spot because of my mother's American citizenship. We study all the regular subjects, and have even organized a chemical and physics laboratory using glasses and pots from our kitchen, instead of test tubes and retorts.[11] Special attention is paid to the study of foreign languages, chiefly English and Hebrew. Our discussions of Polish

---

9. Miriam Wattenberg was born in Łódź on October 10, 1924. She began a wartime diary in October 1939; in November 1940, Miriam, with her parents and younger sister, was compelled to live in the Warsaw ghetto. The Wattenbergs held a privileged position there because Miriam's mother, Lena Wattenberg, was an American citizen. On July 17, 1942, shortly before the first large deportation of Warsaw Jews to Treblinka, German authorities detained the Wattenbergs and other residents with foreign passports in Warsaw's infamous Pawiak Prison. In January 1943, the family was transferred to the Vittel internment camp, then one year later was allowed to emigrate to the United States. Wattenberg's diary was published in English in February 1945, three months before the end of World War II in Europe; to protect friends and relatives still in Nazi hands, the author employed the pen name "Mary Berg." The resulting volume, *The Diary of Mary Berg*, was one of the very few eyewitness accounts of the Warsaw ghetto available to American audiences before the end of World War II. See Susan Lee Pentlin, ed., *The Diary of Mary Berg: Growing Up in the Warsaw Ghetto*, ed. S. L. Shneiderman, trans. Norbert Guterman and Sylvia Glass (Oxford: Oneworld Publishers, 2006).

10. Many of Mary Wattenberg's classmates and teachers from Łódź had also gone to Warsaw. A portion of this class now reassembled for clandestine schooling in Mary's house.

11. These are vessels often used in chemistry to distill or decompose substances over heat.

literature have a peculiarly passionate character. The teachers try to show that the great Polish poets Mickiewicz, Slowacki, and Wyspianski prophesied the present disaster. [. . .]

The teachers put their whole heart and soul into their teaching, and all the pupils study with exemplary diligence. There are no bad pupils. The illegal character of the teaching, the danger that threatens us every minute, fills us all with a strange earnestness. The old distance between teachers and pupils has vanished, we feel like comrades-in-arms responsible to each other.

For Warsaw ghetto teenager Pola Rotszyld, meeting with her clandestine study group gave her a sense of identity and purpose. "From this moment the most beautiful period of my life began," she later recalled, "which lasted for more than a year. It was a time when I was really alive. I knew why and what I lived for."[12]

Teenagers like Pola came to feel that emotional and intellectual survival was integral to their physical survival. Clandestine learning provided a sense of fellowship and camaraderie, which had evaporated elsewhere among a desperate community, and allowed young students, at least temporarily, to transcend the deprivation and misery of ghetto life. Such secret study was quite literally an escape into learning. For sixteen-year-old Pola and her circle of fellow pupils,[13] these clandestine classes represented a central and transforming experience, as she recounted in 1945.

DOCUMENT 8-2. Diary entry of Pola Rotszyld (Yad Vashem Archives, sign. 03/438) in Barbara Engelking-Boni, "Childhood in the Warsaw Ghetto," in *Children and the Holocaust: Symposium Presentations of the Center for Advanced Holocaust Studies* (Washington DC: USHMM, 2004), 35.

These lessons were our happiness, our oblivion. Outside there was a war-storm[;] the groans of people dying of hunger, and the animal-like screams of Germans beating up people on the street were heard. And somewhere in

---

12. Pola Rotszyld, quoted in Engelking-Boni, *Childhood in the Warsaw Ghetto*, 35. Born in 1926, Rotszyld survived the Warsaw ghetto and the final deportations and emigrated to Palestine in 1945.

13. This circle included Andzia Adler, Luba Bursztyn, Sara Fajfer, Estera Gutgold, Dorka Jelén, Henia Majzlic, Gucia Rozenstrauch, and Guta Wołowicz. With the exception of Pola Rotszyld, none of these young girls survived the Holocaust. See Engelking-Boni, *Childhood in the Warsaw Ghetto*, 34–35.

the corner of the room on Pawia or Nowolipki Street, some girls between thirteen to fifteen years of age were sitting around the table with a teacher, engaged in studying. They all forgot about the whole world, even about the fact that they were a bit hungry, maybe more than a bit.

DOCUMENT 8-3. Three girls study at a clandestine Jewish school in Prague, c. 1942, USHMMPA WS# 37424, courtesy of the Jewish Museum of Prague Photo Archive.

Particularly for older children and adolescents, the chance to engage in educational and cultural activities was a means to regain the normal opportunities of intellectual enrichment and advancement available to most school-age youths but inaccessible to those living within the finite borders of the ghetto. In many ghettoized communities, child-welfare associations attempted to provide youngsters with academic and vocational training, as well as a variety of organized educational and leisure activities. Sometimes, too, the impetus for creative and cultural endeavors sprang from young people themselves.

Yitskhok Rudashevski lived in the Vilna ghetto from the time of its inception until its final liquidation in the autumn of 1943. His father was a typesetter for Vilna's most prominent prewar Yiddish daily newspaper, *Vilner Tog*, and from a young age, young Yitskhok showed a pronounced gift for writing. In

September 1941, when he and his family were forced to settle in Vilna's newly established ghetto, the fourteen-year-old began to keep a diary.[14] The teenager filled his journal with vignettes of ghetto life, penning sketches of its teeming streets and its diverse and colorful inhabitants. Yet, the young man's chronicle focused primarily on his own efforts and those of like-minded individuals to forge an intellectual life for the youth of the Vilna ghetto. In addition to his studies, at which he excelled, Rudashevski dedicated himself to the activities of two youth organizations, the first of which endeavored to compile a history of the ghetto and its residents in order to leave a record for future generations. The second club collected ghetto folklore: its stories and tall tales, jokes and curses, songs and literature. "Our youth works and does not perish,"[15] Rudashevski wrote on October 22, 1942, suggesting that his activities and those of his colleagues represented a means to transcend the narrow limitations of their confinement and to defy both the physical and spiritual repression that persecution embodied. For the young Rudashevski, efforts such as those to create an exhibition honoring the Yiddish poet Yehoash[16] provided a way to escape the moral and material barrenness of the ghetto and to create a space and time in which beauty and enlightenment could continue to exist.[17]

DOCUMENT 8-4. Diary of Yitskhok Rudashevski, Vilna ghetto, entry for March 14, 1943, in Alexandra Zapruder, ed., *Salvaged Pages: Young Writers' Diaries of the Holocaust* (New Haven, CT: Yale University Press, 2002), 223.

Today the Yehoash celebration as well as the opening of the Yehoash exhibition took place in the club. The exhibition is exceptionally beautiful. The entire reading room in the club is filled with material. The room is bright and clean. It is a delight to come into it. We are indebted for the exhibition to Friend Sutzkever, who smuggled into the ghetto from

14. See Yitskhok Rudashevski's description of his family's relocation to the Vilna ghetto in Document 4-1.

15. Yitskhok Rudashevski, quoted in Alexandra Zapruder, ed., *Salvaged Pages: Young Writers' Diaries of the Holocaust* (New Haven, CT: Yale University Press, 2002), 192.

16. This is the pen name of Lithuanian-born Solomon Blumgarten (1870–1927), one of the most celebrated Yiddish poets of the early twentieth century. Immigrating to the United States in 1890, Blumgarten was responsible for translating many of the classics of world literature into Yiddish; his two-volume translation of the Bible is widely regarded as one of the great masterpieces in that language.

17. Yitskhok Rudashevski was shot to death with members of his family in the Ponary Woods in October 1943, during the dissolution of the Vilna ghetto.

the YIVO where he works a great deal of material for the Yehoash exhibition. [. . .]

People entering here forgot that this is the ghetto. Here in the Yehoash exhibition we have many valuable documents that now are treasures: manuscripts from Peretz to Yehoash, Yehoash's original letters. We have rare newspaper clippings. In the section—Bible translations into Yiddish—we have old Bible translations into Yiddish from the seventeenth century. Looking at the exhibition, at our work, our hearts swell with enthusiasm. We actually forget that we are in a dark ghetto. The celebration today was also carried out in a grand manner. The dramatic circle presented Yehoash's tableau *Saul*. The members read essays on the writings of Yehoash, on Yehoash the poet, on beauty, sound, and color.

The mood of the celebration was an exalted one. It was indeed a holiday, a demonstration on behalf of Yiddish literature and culture.

AT PLAY DURING THE HOLOCAUST

The juxtaposition of child's play with the tragic events of the Holocaust presents the reader with a striking contradiction. Popular imagination associates play with the carefree world of merriment and simple delights. Instinctively, we balk at the suggestion that mass murder and the games and amusements of youth could exist side by side. And yet, scores of contemporary documents and the vivid recollections of survivors and bystanders make it plain that they did.[18]

What can account for the existence of such activities in the midst of such catastrophic circumstances—in the desolate streets of the ghetto, in the bleak and dangerous world of the concentration camp? The most logical explanation for such a phenomenon is that play in every place and time is an instinct of childhood. Child survivor Nechama Tec recalled that her stay in the Majdan Tatarski ghetto in Lublin in 1942, though fraught with danger, was a happy time for her, for after a long period of isolation, she at last had the opportunity to play with other children.

> The children formed a small minority. As a matter of policy, the Nazis were concentrating on the extermination of Jewish children. Because we were thus in special danger, adults looked upon us as a special commodity.

---

18. See George Eisen, *Children and Play in the Holocaust: Games among the Shadows* (Amherst: University of Massachusetts Press, 1988); Yad Vashem, *No Child's Play* (Jerusalem: Yad Vashem, 2004).

We came to expect our elders to treat us with special indulgence, and they did. No Jew would have thought of mistreating a child, and almost all of them refrained from even the mildest form of discipline.

And so we were free of adult supervision. We had no special duties. It was summer. Because there were few of us left, we felt close to each other. We relied on each other for entertainment, and for enlightenment. [. . .] We children managed to be happy as we roamed the little dirt roads in search of adventure. We spent our days outdoors, constantly on the move. In the evenings we took turns visiting each other's houses. In the process, we made many exciting adventures about life, love, and our fellow mortals.[19]

To run and frolic with their playmates, to act out their fantasies, and to explore the world about them gave children a powerful way to escape the harsh realities that surrounded them. Play also represented a way for youngsters to adapt to the difficulties and traumatic circumstances they confronted and to reshape their environment through daydream and imagination. As in the pre-Holocaust world, children also used such activities in order to develop needed skill sets and to socialize themselves for future mature roles and responsibilities.[20]

---

19. Nechama Tec, *Dry Tears: The Story of a Lost Childhood* (Oxford: Oxford University Press, 1982), 22–23.

20. See Catherine Wheeler, *Representing Children at Play in the Literature of the Shoah* (PhD diss., University of Massachusetts, Amherst, 2003).

DOCUMENT 8-5. Children at play in a field in Marysin, Łódź ghetto, c. 1941, USHMMPA WS# 33844, courtesy of the Archiwum Panstowe w Łódźi, sygn. 1120, fot. 27-832-6.

For many adults, the sight of children at play in the camp barracks or among the rubble of the ghetto alley was a heartening sight. While the misery and deprivation of their surroundings told a story of destruction and loss, child's play prefigured life, continuity, and collective survival. One such encouraged individual was Oskar Rosenfeld (1884–1944),[21] a Czech-born writer and

---

21. Living in Vienna in the interwar period, Moravian-born Oskar Rosenfeld worked as a journalist and author, publishing a series of novels under the title *Tage und Nächte* (*Days and Nights*); from 1929 he was the editor in chief of the Viennese illustrated weekly *Die Neue Welt* (*The New World*). Following the *Anschluss*, Rosenfeld and his wife moved to Prague. Unable to emigrate to England, the couple was deported to the Łódź ghetto in November 1941, where Rosenfeld became active in writing for *The Chronicle of the Łódź Ghetto*. Upon the liquidation of the ghetto, Rosenfeld was deported to Auschwitz in August 1944, where he perished. See Oskar Rosenfeld, *In the Beginning There Was the Ghetto: Notebooks of Łódź* (Evanston, IL: Northwestern University Press, 2002).

novelist who had been active in Vienna until the *Anschluss*. Deported to the Łódź ghetto from Prague in November 1941, Rosenfeld soon numbered among the authors who contributed essays and commentaries for *The Chronicle of the Łódź Ghetto*,[22] an effort to document the history of the incarcerated community. In July 1943, Rosenfeld captured ghetto youngsters' enduring love of play and pastimes in an essay for the official chronicle titled "The Ghetto Children's Toys." A month later, Rosenfeld took up this theme again, announcing to his readers that the children of the Łódź ghetto had invented a new plaything.

DOCUMENT 8-6. Oskar Rosenfeld, entry in *The Chronicle of the Łódź Ghetto*, August 25, 1943, in Lucjan Dobroszycki, ed., *The Chronicle of the Łódź Ghetto, 1941–1944*, trans. Richard Lourie et al. (New Haven, CT: Yale University Press, 1987), 373–74.

For several days now, the streets and courtyards of the ghetto have been filled with a noise like the clatter of wooden shoes. The noise is disturbing at first, but one gradually gets used to it and says to oneself: this is as much a part of the ghetto as are cesspools. The observer soon discovers that this "clattering" is produced by boys who have invented a pastime, an entertainment. More precisely, the children of the ghetto have invented a new toy.

All the various amusing toys and noisemakers—harmonicas, hobby horses, rattles, building blocks, decals, etc.—are things our youngsters must, of course, do without. In other ways as well, as ghetto dwellers, they are excluded from all the enchantments of the child's world. And so, on their own, they invent toys to replace all the things that delight children everywhere and are unavailable here.

The ghetto toy in the summer of 1943: two small slabs of wood—hardwood if possible! One slab is held between the forefinger and the middle finger, the other between the middle finger and the ring finger. The little finger presses against the other fingers, squeezing them so hard that the slabs are rigidly fixed in position and can thus be struck against one another by means of a skillful motion. The resulting noise resembles the clattering of storks or, to use musical terms, the clicking of castanets. The harder the wood, the more piercing and precise the clicking, the more successful the toy, and the greater the enjoyment. Naturally, the artistic talents of the toy carver and performer can be refined to a very high level.

22. Lucjan Dobroszycki, ed., *The Chronicle of the Łódź Ghetto, 1941–1944*, trans. Richard Lourie et al. (New Haven, CT: Yale University Press, 1987).

The instrument imposes no limit on the individual's musical ability. There are children who are content to use the primitive clicking of the slabs to produce something like the sounds of a Morse code transmitter. Other children imitate the beating of a drum, improvising marches out of banging sounds as they parade with their playmates like soldiers.

The streets of the Litzmannstadt ghetto are filled with clicking, drumming, banging. . . . Barefoot boys scurry past you, performing their music right under your nose, with great earnestness, as though their lives depended on it. Here the musical instinct of eastern European Jews is cultivated to the full. An area that has given the world so many musicians, chiefly violinists—just think of Hubermann, Heifetz, Elman, Milstein, Menuhin[23]—now presents a new line of artists.

A conversation with a virtuoso: "We get the wood from the Wood Works Department, but only the hardest wood is good enough."—"What is the toy called?"—"It's called a castanet. . . . I don't know why. Never heard the name before. We paint the toy to make it look nicer. That guy over there," he pointed to a barefoot boy who was sitting in the street dust, ragged and dirty, "doesn't know how to do it. You have to swing your whole hand if you want to get a good tune out. Hard wood and a hefty swing—those are the main things." A few boys gathered, clicked their castanets, and all hell let loose. It was the first castanet concert I had ever attended.

The chronicler assumes that the clicker music will vanish "after it's run its course" and be replaced by some other sort of music. But he may be wrong.

O[skar] R[osenfeld]

Youngsters in camp and ghetto settings lived in a kind of exile from childhood. With the loss of their homes and belongings, young children felt the absence of their favorite playthings acutely. With forced ghettoization, families brought to their cramped quarters only what they could carry; personal items, among them children's toys and games, were necessarily limited. Possession of material goods became even more severely circumscribed with an individual's transfer to concentration and forced labor camps, and where young children survived in these circumstances, as in the so-called **Theresienstadt family camp** in **Auschwitz**, playthings were a rare commodity. With a creativity and ingenuity that often impressed their adult contemporaries, young people forged new

23. All are famous contemporary Jewish violinists.

toys from cardboard, bits of wood, scraps of metal and cloth—the refuse of the captive society that surrounded them. Children played with what was at hand. When her interviewer expressed incredulity that she had been able to entertain herself at Auschwitz, a young survivor from Kielce exclaimed adamantly, "But I played! I played there with nothing! With the snow. With balls of snow."[24]

For those children fortunate enough to retain a cherished toy or childhood possession, a doll or stuffed animal might figure as the center of the young-ster's existence. Playthings were rare and precious, and their young owners often clung to them with a fierce possessiveness. Such toys offered not only an oppor-tunity for amusement but also a source of emotional stability and security. In a menacing world of upheaval and change, material items remained steadfast and unchanging. Toys were good listeners in the way that harried and exhausted adults were not. Even broken and damaged playthings retained their currency; they did not wither away from hunger or face **deportation** as parents or siblings did. A toy might also transport its small owner into an imaginary world, far away from the miserable surroundings of the camp or ghetto.

In the formative years of the **Theresienstadt ghetto**, a prisoner employed as a carpenter in a joiner's workshop in the Small Fortress created the remark-able pull toy in the shape of a butterfly shown in Document 8-7. Affixed to a wheeled base, the brightly painted butterfly "takes flight," fluttering its wooden wings, when it is rolled across a floor or flat surface. The butterfly motif has long been associated with the children of Theresienstadt, thanks largely to the discovery and widespread publication of Pavel Friedman's poem "I Never Saw Another Butterfly," written shortly after the young man's arrival in the Theresienstadt ghetto in April 1942. Friedman died at age twenty-three in the gas chambers at **Birkenau** in late September 1944, but his poem is one of the most famous in the genre of Holocaust poetry:

> The last, the very last,
> So richly, brightly, dazzlingly yellow.
> Perhaps if the sun's tears sing
> against a white stone [. . .]
> For seven weeks I've lived in here,
> Penned up inside this ghetto,
> But I have found my people here.
> The dandelions call to me,
> And the white chestnut candles in the court.

---

24. Quoted in Eisen, *Children and Play in the Holocaust*, 72.

Only I never saw another butterfly.
That butterfly was the last one.
Butterflies don't live here in the ghetto.[25]

The butterfly was an evocative symbol not only because it represented an element of natural beauty long inaccessible to Theresienstadt's incarcerated community but also because the winged creature had the ability literally to transcend the confining walls of the ghetto and to escape the barrenness and despair of the prisoners' existence. Of course, the craftsman who constructed the pull toy in question is unlikely to have been aware of Friedman's poem, and it is doubtful that a concrete connection lies between the artifact and the young writer's famous verse. The maker of the small wooden toy is unknown, as are the identity and fate of its young recipient. But the object is a poignant reminder of children's need for the tangible vestiges of childhood in the harrowing world of the Holocaust.

---

25. Pavel Friedman, "I Never Saw Another Butterfly," in *I Never Saw Another Butterfly: Children's Drawings and Poems from Terezin Concentration Camp, 1942–44*, ed. Hana Volavková, exp. 2nd ed. (New York: Schocken Books and the U.S. Holocaust Memorial Museum, 1993), 39.

DOCUMENT 8-7. **Painted wooden butterfly toy, Small Fortress, Theresienstadt ghetto, 1941–1945, USHMMPA WS# N00049, original reposited in Pamatnik Terezin Narodni Kulturni Pamatka.**

As we have seen, children often invented new modes of play in order to accommodate their difficult circumstances and the limited resources available to them. Sometimes, too, youngsters adapted traditional children's games to incorporate their radically altered environment.[26] To the horror of many adult witnesses, who had experienced normal childhoods, youngsters modified such conventional children's games as tag and hide-and-seek with the macabre trappings of their camp or ghetto existence. At the 1961 **Eichmann Trial**, Dr. Aharon Peretz, a physician who survived the Kovno ghetto, recounted how the play of ghetto children came to reflect the frightening reality of the Holocaust.

---

26. See Eisen, *Children and Play in the Holocaust*, esp. 76–80.

DOCUMENT 8-8. Testimony of Dr. Aharon Peretz, May 4, 1961, in *The Trial of Adolf Eichmann: Record of Proceedings in the District Court of Jerusalem* **(Jerusalem: Trust for the Publication of the Proceedings of the Eichmann Trial in cooperation with the Israel State Archives and Yad Vashem, the Holocaust Martyrs' and Heroes' Remembrance Authority, 1992–1995), 1:478–79.**

Witness Peretz: I think that possibly the greatest tragedy the Jewish people underwent was the tragedy of the children. The children in the ghetto also used to play and laugh, and in their games the tragedy of the Jewish people was reflected. They used to play at graves, they would dig a pit, place a child in it, and call him Hitler. They used to play as if they were at the gate of the ghetto, some would be Germans and others Jews. The Germans would shout and strike the Jews. They used to play at funerals, and all such games.

Children's "new" games accurately depicted the dramas and tragedies of ghetto life. Many Jewish youngsters had never known a park or a playground, had never owned a doll or stuffed animal, had never frolicked amid trees and flowery meadows. Thus, they constructed their make-believe worlds from the only existence they knew. Starvation and deprivation were a part of their quotidian lives. Words from the ghetto vernacular, such as *Aktion*, "deportation," and "transport," became a part of their daily vocabulary. While play that incorporated camp or ghetto life was unconventional and shocked adult observers, such activities presumably helped young children to process the perplexing circumstances in which they found themselves and offered them a kind of "buffered learning," as George Eisen suggests—a way to rehearse a dangerous situation within a secure sphere, as within the parameters of a game or play activity.[27] Into their imaginary world, children integrated the cruelty, irony, and pathos that they observed around them. In personal testimony given in the 1960s, Hanna Hoffmann-Fischel, a young and idealistic educator, recalled the unsettling games played by her young charges at the Theresienstadt family camp in Birkenau.

---

27. Eisen, *Children and Play in the Holocaust*, 79.

DOCUMENT 8-9. **Personal testimony of Hanna Hoffmann-Fischel, c. 1960, in Inge Deutschkron,** *Denn ihrer war die Hölle: Kinder in Gettos und Lagern* **(Cologne: Verlag Wissenschaft und Politik, 1965), 52–55 (translated from the German).**

Even in the next block, with the smaller children, we had enormous difficulties. We could not teach them according to a lesson plan, but we told them of the kind of life that we wished for ourselves. But if we were not careful, they played the kind of life's games that they had experienced themselves. They played "Camp Elder and Block Elder," "Roll Call," with "caps off!"[28] They played the ailing prisoners who would faint during roll call and receive a thrashing, or the "Doctor" who took away patients' rations and who refused to give treatment if they could not give him anything in return. Once they even played the game "Gas Chamber." They made a trench into which they pushed in one stone after another. These were supposed to be people who went into the crematorium, and they imitated their cries. They came to me for advice, asking me to show them where they should put the crematorium chimney.

Children's games incorporated the harrowing reality of the camp or ghetto environment. This kind of play was not an escape into fantasy or imagination but a way of assimilating the dangerous world that surrounded youngsters during the Holocaust. Role-playing in particular represented a creative means of accommodating and coping with the tremendous challenges youngsters confronted. Naturally, such play grew in part from children's natural impulse to emulate the actions of adults. As in the normal realm of childhood, the enactment of adult behaviors often followed gender lines. Predictably, as in other places and times, young boys' play frequently took the shape of war games. Ghetto lads of six or seven engaged in make-believe combat as Germans and Russians or pretended to join in the adventures of the **partisans** of whom they had heard so much. Closer to their own experience, preteenage boys in Vilna or Warsaw played "Going through the Gate" in which young "**Gestapo** men" searched returning "forced laborers" for smuggled food and contraband.[29] Girls could and did participate in such games, but their play more often embraced

---

28. In German, *"Mützen ab!"* is the command SS guards inevitably gave prisoners at roll call.

29. Testimony of Dr. Aharon Peretz, May 4, 1961, in *The Trial of Adolf Eichmann: Record of Proceedings in the District Court of Jerusalem* (Jerusalem: Trust for the Publication of the Proceedings of the Eichmann Trial in cooperation with the Israel State Archives and Yad Vashem, the Holocaust Martyrs' and Heroes' Remembrance Authority, 1992–1995), 1:478.

female roles in the ghetto. Small girls who had perhaps once nursed their dolls now imitated their mothers in an eerily realistic form of playing house. Standing in queues before an imaginary shop window, little girls clutched make-believe ration cards, jostling their neighbors and bickering with the shopkeeper over goods and wares. The young housewives could be heard to wonder aloud where their next piece of bread would come from or how, with their few rotten potatoes, they might manage to feed their families.[30]

One activity that perhaps best exemplifies the tragedy of Jews during the Holocaust was a favorite of both genders. The game "Jews and Germans" wed aspects of cops and robbers with the traditional hide-and-seek. In Document 8-10, an eight-year-old inhabitant of the Vilna ghetto explains how youngsters masqueraded as members of the **Schutzstaffel (SS)** or **Jewish Order Police** and sought to round up their playmates for deportation. Document 8-11, a photograph capturing children at play in the Łódź ghetto, illustrates that the game Jews and Germans was popular in almost every ghetto in German-occupied eastern Europe.

DOCUMENT 8-10. An eight-year-old resident of the Vilna ghetto describes the game "Jews and Germans" (Genia Silkes Collection, YIVO Institute), quoted in George Eisen, *Children and Play in the Holocaust: Games among the Shadows* (Amherst: University of Massachusetts Press, 1988), 72.

> Part of the children became "policemen" and part "German." The third group was comprised of "Jews" who were to hide in make-believe bunkers; that is under chairs, tables, in barrels and garbage cans. The highest distinction went to the child who played Kommandant [Kittel], the head of the Gestapo [*sic*].[31] He was always the strongest boy or girl. If a dressed-up "policeman" happened to find "Jewish" children, he handed them over to the "Germans."

---

30. Eisen, *Children and Play in the Holocaust*, 77.

31. Oberscharführer Bruno Kittel, a member of the Security Police, was later responsible for the liquidation of Vilna ghetto.

DOCUMENT 8-11. In the Łódź ghetto, children, one dressed as a ghetto policeman, play a peculiar version of cops and robbers, 1943, USHMMPA WS# 80401, courtesy of Beit Lohamei Haghetaot.

INNOCENCE AND KNOWLEDGE

Innocence is a characteristic closely associated with childhood. And yet, as the testimony of Aharon Peretz and the anecdotes of Hanna Hoffmann-Fischel show, most Jewish children did not long remain in ignorance of the perilous circumstances in which they found themselves during the Holocaust. As a rule, innocence suggests a kind of purity that stems from the ignorance of evil and an absence of worldliness and guile. Yet, living in the upside-down world of the ghetto or in the charnel atmosphere of the concentration camps, many children had become well acquainted with evil and understood from their own limited experience that guilelessness and naiveté could prove a deadly combination. Here youngsters grew up quickly. At a tender age, many had witnessed unimaginable horrors and shouldered adult responsibilities. Łódź ghetto chronicler **Josef Zelkowicz** noted this premature maturation during that ghetto's notorious *Gehsperre*. In the late summer of 1942, German authorities approached ghetto elder **Mordechai Chaim Rumkowski** demanding twenty thousand deportees. Faced with an ultimatum, Rumkowski settled upon a desperate and terrible solution; he would fill the prescribed quota with the least productive members of the community: the severely ill, the aged, and all children up to the age of ten. From September 5 through 12, 1942, German forces entered the ghetto, seizing those unfit for labor from their homes and from the community's streets. The *Gehsperre* began with the liquidation of the ghetto hospitals, where SS officials apprehended patients in their beds. In the days that followed, police units cleared schoolrooms and orphanages, many of them in Marysin, once a haven for Łódź's youngsters. Approximately 15,500 individuals were rounded up for deportation; the vast majority of these victims were young children and adults over the age of sixty-five.[32]

Josef Zelkowicz recorded the events of the *Gehsperre* in a 1942 anthology of essays he called *In Those Terrible Days*.[33] Amid the chaos of the September roundups, Zelkowicz noted that most youngsters were well aware of the terrifying implications of the **razzias**, although parents often chose not to share the news of the upcoming tragedy with their youngsters.

> Some children [. . .] have caught on. And that is because ten-year-olds in the ghetto are already adults. They know and understand the fate that awaits them. They may not, for now, know why they are being torn from their parents; this may not have been explained to them. For now it suffices to know that they are being separated from their trusted guardians, their devoted mothers and fathers. [. . .] They already rove alone in the street. They already cry their own tears, and these tears are so bitter and stinging that they pierce the heart like poisoned arrows. . . . The ghetto hearts, however, have ossified. They wish to break but cannot. This may be the cruelest curse of all.[34]

Of course very young children could not fathom—as their parents might— the terrible significance of the roundups or the fate that awaited them at the **Chełmno** killing center. As Zelkowicz observed that autumn, some youngsters stood in carts bound for the collection point, bemused by the cacophony and the laments of adult bystanders, eager for the "game" to continue.

---

32. See Isaiah Trunk, *Łódź Ghetto: A History*, ed. and trans., Robert Moses Shapiro (Bloomington: University of Indiana Press in association with the U.S. Holocaust Memorial Museum, 2006).

33. See the essay in its entirety in Josef Zelkowitz, *In Those Terrible Days: Writings from the Lodz Ghetto*, ed. Michal Unger, trans. Naftali Greenwood (Jerusalem: Yad Vashem, 2002), 249–381.

34. Zelkowitz, *In Those Terrible Days*, 265–67.

DOCUMENT 8-12. **Excerpt from Josef Zelkowicz's essay "The Optimist in the Potato Queue," Łódź ghetto, September 5, 1942, in Josef Zelkowicz,** *In Those Terrible Days: Writings from the Lodz Ghetto*, **ed. Michal Unger, trans. Naftali Greenwood (Jerusalem: Yad Vashem, 2002), 306–7.**

A cart stands on Rybna Street. Several children are standing in the cart, their eyes wide, as if they were lost. They have already been "nabbed"— *gekhapped.* They do not know what all these people want from them. Why are all these people standing around them and gazing at them sadly? Why are they crying? Why are they pounding their chests in despair?

These children see no reason to cry. They are quite content: they have been placed on a wagon and they are going for a ride! Since when have children in the ghetto had such an opportunity? If it were not for all those wailing people, if their mothers and fathers had not screamed so as they placed them in the cart, they would have danced to the cart. After all, they are going for a wagon ride. But all that shouting, noise, and crying upset them and disrupted their joy. They jostle in the elongated wagon bed with its high barriers, as if lost, and their bulging eyes ask: What's going on? What do these people want from us? Why won't they let us take a little ride?

DOCUMENT 8-13. **Young children from the Marysin colony wait to be conveyed to the deportation assembly point during the** *Gehsperre*, **Łódź ghetto, September 1942, USHMMPA WS# 50334, courtesy of the Instytut Pamięci Narodowej.**

"Draw what you see!" Inspired by her father's injunction, Helga Weissová began to sketch her observations of ghetto life shortly after her arrival in Theresienstadt in December 1941.[35] Helga was born on November 10, 1929, to Otto Weiss, a state bank official, and his wife, Irena. The family led a comfortable middle-class existence in the Czech capital, and from an early age young Helga occupied much of her free time with drawing and painting. Exactly one month after her twelfth birthday, Helga arrived with her parents on one of the first transports of Czech Jews to Theresienstadt. The youngster would remain at **Terezin** for almost three years, during which time she completed over one hundred drawings and illustrations. In late 1944, Helga and Irena Weissová were deported to the Auschwitz concentration camp. Due to the continuing advance

35. For a more extensive view of Helga Weissová's life and Holocaust-era drawings, see Helga Weissová, *Zeichne, was Du siehst! Zeichnungen eines Kindes aus Theresienstadt/Terezin*, ed., Niedersächsischen Verein zur Förderung von Theresienstadt/Terezin, e.V. (Göttingen: Wallstein Verlag, 1998).

of the Soviet army, the two women were transported almost immediately to a series of camps in the German interior. In the last days of the war, the pair found themselves in the **Mauthausen** concentration camp, where American forces liberated them and their fellow prisoners on May 5, 1945. Mother and daughter returned to Prague, where they learned of the deaths of Otto Weiss and most of their nearest relatives and acquaintances. Helga Weissová pursued a career in graphic arts at the National Academy of the Arts and in 1954 married Czech musician Jiři Hošek. She became an internationally celebrated artist, settling in her native Prague.

Helga began to ply her artistic talents in Terezin shortly after settling into *Mädchenheim* L-410, one of the ghetto's homes for young girls, in December 1941. Using art supplies that she had packed with her at the time of her deportation, Weissová initially sought to ease her loneliness by drawing upon the happy images of her girlhood in Prague. After painting a nostalgic winter scene in which small children built a snowman, she persuaded fellow prisoners to smuggle the picture to her father in the men's barracks. Otto Weiss, who had constantly championed his daughter's artistic endeavors, admonished Helga instead to draw what she observed around her. "That snowman was actually my last genuine drawing as a child," Weissová later recalled. "Through this sentence of my father's, and through my own inner motivation, I felt called from now on to capture in my drawings the everyday life of the ghetto. The impressions that from this point in time would affect me, ended my childhood."[36]

Twelve-year-old Helga clearly comprehended the dangers of her new environment in Theresienstadt and resolved to record them on paper and canvas. For the next several years, she created paintings and illustrations that captured the quotidian incidents and tragedies of ghetto life. "We all did the same things, with the exception of Helga—who, when she was not working, used to sit on her bed and draw and paint constantly," Charlotta Verešová,[37] a child diarist of Theresienstadt, remembered of her friend and bunkmate. "We all admired her because she was able to depict our plight."[38] With an unsettling candidness, the young teenager faithfully portrayed the wrenching arrivals and departures of

---

36. Weissová, *Zeichne, was Du siehst!* 13.

37. Charlotta Verešová was born on December 13, 1928, in Litoměřice, Czechoslovakia, the daughter of a mixed marriage. At age fourteen she was separated from her family and deported to Theresienstadt, where she kept a diary of her time in confinement. Verešová survived the war in the Terezin ghetto and worked as a librarian and technical designer after the war; see Laurel Holliday, *Children in the Holocaust and World War II: Their Secret Diaries* (New York: Washington Square Press, 1995), 201–7.

38. Holliday, *Children in the Holocaust and World War II*, 16.

transports at Terezin, the unending lines to receive meager rations, the colonies of workers going to forced labor. Helga had an eye for the ironic, depicting with unvarnished candor the macabre and surreal aspects of ghetto culture. We feel for the aged German Jews who arrive at the "rest community for the elderly," promised them by the Nazi government, only to encounter the ugly and deadly reality of Theresienstadt. We are likewise amused by the farcical efforts of camp authorities to create from Terezin a "model ghetto" for the visit of officials from the **International Committee of the Red Cross** in 1944. Other illustrations capture the pathos and suffering of Helga's fellow prisoners: the faces of deportees waiting for days in the cold or heat of the ghetto's dreaded "Sluice"[39] before their transport to Auschwitz or ghetto residents' solemn farewells to their dead comrades, who were daily carried on sledges to a crematorium outside the ghetto.

Sometimes Helga deployed her artistic gifts in a more traditional vein: to create a birthday greeting or a holiday card for friends and loved ones. In *Birthday Wish I (Přání k narozeninám I)*, she transcends the hunger and deprivation of the ghetto by conjuring a delicious torte for the birthday honoree. Here a childish yearning is fulfilled as a young boy and girl, clad in their summer best, wheel an enormous birthday cake from Prague to Theresienstadt. The fourteen-year-old artist gave her native city gauzy contours; one can make out the prominent features of Prague Castle—the Hradschin—in its outlines. The well-dressed youngsters push the gigantic confection through the green landscape and up to the fortress walls of Terezin. On the surface, the composition is a dreamlike, innocent vision, like a fairytale from childhood. But the idyllic scene bristles with dark humor. The cart that carries the mighty cake is a hearse, a conveyance often used in Theresienstadt to transport items. In another stroke of wit, the wagon seems to bear the inscription *"Entsorgung"* (waste disposal). Perhaps the young artist meant to suggest that her diminutive helpers have cleared the ghetto of its debris and brought back in its place a wonderful cake?

---

39. *Slojska* is a Czech variant of the German *Schleuse*, a slang term used in Theresienstadt for the collection point that held deportees arriving and departing on transports.

DOCUMENT 8-14. **Watercolor by Helga Weissová, Birthday Wish I (Přání k narozen-inám I), Theresienstadt ghetto, December 1941, USHMMPA WS# 60926, courtesy Helga Weissová.**

A third document concerning innocence and knowledge strikes out into different territory. The opening pages of this book introduce the reader to **Elisabeth Block**, a Jewish teenager living in rural Bavaria. As Peter Miesbeck, the historian who helped to publish Block's journal in 1993, noted, Elisabeth was "no Bavarian **Anne Frank**,"[40] who described her experiences explicitly and in vivid detail. Indeed, her diary is interesting to scholars because, even in the blackest moments of her personal history, she appears almost pathologically unable to record unpleasant developments. It is certainly true that in the village of Niedernburg, near Rosenheim, Elisabeth and her family felt closely integrated into the small community in which they lived and endured little discrimination at the hands of their neighbors, even as Nazi anti-Jewish policy escalated in the late 1930s. Elisabeth was loath to record those encroachments that the government's antisemitic measures made on her family's economic and social circumstances during these years. During *Kristallnacht*, for example,

40. Elisabeth Block, *Erinnerungszeichen: Die Tagebücher der Elisabeth Block*, ed. Haus der Bayerischen Geschichte/Historischer Verein Rosenheim (Rosenheim: Wendelstein-Druck, 1993), 17.

rampaging **Sturmabteilung** (**SA**) men had murdered Elisabeth's uncle, Dr. Leo Levy in his apartment in Bad Polzin, an event the teenager referenced only in passing in her journal. Further disturbing developments—the exclusion of Jewish pupils from public schools, the loss of the family home and business, and the **compulsory sterilization** of Elisabeth's father, Fritz Block—received similarly short shrift. It was as if the young girl failed to see herself and her family within the wider framework of Nazi persecution. In her diary, coincidentally begun in 1933, Block uses the phrase "we Jews" just once, in the context of the September 1941 decree requiring German Jews to wear the yellow star.[41]

On March 8, 1942, Elisabeth Block wrote the last entry in her journal. As usual, she focused on her daily activities, on her interactions with friends and family members, on the weather, and on events that had transpired in her community. In this instance, the latest excitement was the birth and baptism of little Friedi, the newborn daughter of Elisabeth's friend Regina Zielke, in Benning, a little town two kilometers from Niedernburg. Elisabeth had been deployed to a farm in the vicinity in compliance with a March 1941 decree compelling all able-bodied Jews to undertake compulsory labor assignments. It is clear from the teenager's own descriptions of her experiences and from contemporary eyewitnesses that she was well treated on the farmstead and that she and her employers felt she was part of the family there. This may explain in part why she makes so little mention of the summons by the local labor office (*Arbeitsamt*) dispatching her to agricultural work or of the fact that her service there, however agreeable, was essentially forced labor.[42] Elisabeth pays little attention to her father's more strenuous compulsory service laying tracks for railway and commuter transit lines. In her March 1942 account, she mentions only that the frostbite that Fritz Block contracted from his heavy work in freezing weather had fortunately occasioned him leave at a time when the family could spend the weekend together.

Most notably missing from Elisabeth's March 1943 entry is mention of the Blocks' fear of imminent deportation "to the East." The exact date on which they received their summons to assemble at the collection point (*Sammelstelle*) in Munich-Milbertshofen is unknown, but in the early weeks of March, when the teenager wrote of Friedi's baptism and her winter sleigh ride, the family had clearly already begun packing up their household, gathering those few possessions they might be allowed to carry with them and storing furniture and

---

41. Block, *Erinnerungszeichen*, 25.

42. German Jews performing compulsory labor in accordance with the 1941 decree were not entitled to compensation, paid leave, or benefits, which German "Aryan" workers received.

valuables with trusted friends and neighbors.[43] Eighteen years old when she wrote the last passage in her diary, Elisabeth could scarcely have been ignorant of the mass deportation of Jews from Germany and the policy's significance for herself and her family. Was her silence on this point a matter of discretion or circumspection? Did her refusal to acknowledge these menacing developments spring from denial or a naive belief that the charmed existence she and her loved ones enjoyed in Niedernburg would continue, even as the rest of her coreligionists were sent to their deaths? We will never know. On April 3, 1942, the Blocks were deported with 989 fellow Bavarian Jews to the Piaski ghetto, near Lublin, in German-occupied Poland. On an unknown date, Elisabeth and her family were transferred to a killing center, presumably **Bełżec** or **Sobibór**, and murdered there.

DOCUMENT 8-15. **Diary of Elisabeth Block, entry for March 8, 1943, in Elisabeth Block,** *Erinnerungszeichen: Die Tagebücher der Elisabeth Block,* **ed. Haus der Bayerischen Geschichte/Historischer Verein Rosenheim (Rosenheim: Wendelstein-Druck, 1993), 265–66.**

<u>Sunday, March 8, 1942</u>

It has already been seven weeks now that I have not written in my diary, a long time, and what has happened in the meantime! The most important and greatest event would be the birth of the little Friedi on Wednesday, January 28.[44] That was a terribly exciting day. The hard struggle lasted from ten a.m. until four in the afternoon, then finally there was a black-haired, healthy girl there. On Friday, amidst a terrible snowstorm and deep snow, the little tot [*Butzerl*] was carried, heavily bundled, to the baptism. Christl stood up as the godmother. To everyone's great surprise and joy, Mama came in the afternoon, just in time to attend the christening luncheon and to inquire after the mother and child. The farmer's wife was very touched that Mama dared to come in such weather and walked two hours, but I was very happy to be able to speak my piece on the subject again.

The whole time until February 22, it snowed practically every day, so that we had three-quarters of a meter [2.5 feet] of snow, and with it minus 16 to 20 degrees (Celsius) [3.2 to –4 degrees Fahrenheit] and even a week of 35 degrees below zero [–31 degrees Fahrenheit]. My daily work now consists of laundering, mending, and darning. In the mornings the

43. See Block, *Erinnerungszeichen*, 46.
44. Emphasis is in the original.

farmer's wife (and I) get up at quarter to seven and milk our nine cows—recently I even milked seven of them by myself—and are finished cleaning the stalls by 8:30. We have just had three calves and now have twenty-four head of cattle. After breakfast at 10:00, when the living room, foyer, and kitchen have been cleaned, I do the wash; after the midday meal at 12:30, I go back to the stalls to clean the stable and water the animals. After this there is the mending, and at 6:00 p.m. back out to the stall. That is the daily flow of things, to which is added the washing of the cows and calves and scouring of the house on Saturday.

From January 18 till February 2, I was not at home; but it was so convenient that I could go ride along for a few hours by sleigh by riding with Christl and Gina-Maus because [their trip] coincided with a farmer's holiday.[45] That was really fun, and it appeared to me as if [the scene] came out of a novel or a winter's tale, riding in a charming horse-drawn sleigh through the winter landscape, bundled warmly. And when home, what a surprise, Papa was home; he had frostbite on his fingers and had leave—the timing was perfect. We all drank coffee together, and then they were off once more, but I was happy when I came again into the warm living room, because I was completely frozen when I arrived.

IN HOPES AND DREAMS: COPING WITH THE HOLOCAUST

Perhaps Elisabeth Block's aversion to recording unpleasant developments represented a strategy to cope with the increasingly difficult circumstances in which she found herself. It is possible that the teenager used her diary to rewrite events: to reshape painful experiences, giving them gentler and less threatening contours. In recasting each day without its uncertainties and adversities, she may have discovered a way to regain a sense of control over her situation and to replace disagreeable memories with those thoughts of home, nature, and family that she treasured most.

Children adopted many strategies to help them adapt to the horrors and deprivations of the Holocaust. Youngsters matured quickly and beyond their years under such conditions, and many of their responses to persecution were practical and pragmatic. Often powerless to shape their individual circumstances in the way that adults could, however, children frequently found highly creative ways to cope with the terrors they faced. Through imagination, play, and their dreams

---

45. February 2 is Candlemas in the Christian calendar.

for the future, young people were able to transcend the physical and emotional traumas they experienced and cling to their hopes for survival.

Where possible, adults contributed to this process. Through educational activities and structured play, teachers and caregivers worked to create a world in which children could thrive and feel secure, if only temporarily. In the Theresienstadt family camp in Auschwitz, dedicated instructors like Hanna Hoffmann (later Hanna Hoffmann-Fischel) constructed a safe haven for youngsters in the so-called ***Kinderblock*** (children's block) located in the midst of the killing center in Birkenau. Under the aegis of **Fredy Hirsch**, a popular youth leader in the Theresienstadt ghetto, teachers in the children's home organized craft workshops and cultural events for their young charges. A high point for the youngsters was the staging of a play adapted from the beloved Walt Disney film *Snow White*, produced in 1937.

DOCUMENT 8-16. **Personal testimony of Hanna Hoffmann-Fischel, c. 1960, in Inge Deutschkron,** *Denn ihrer war die Hölle: Kinder in Gettos und Lagern* **(Cologne: Verlag Wissenschaft und Politik, 1965), 52–55 (translated from the German).**

We taught lessons in sociology, Jewish history, etc. When the SS men came for inspection, the children had to recite poems in the German language while standing at attention. It was thanks to Fredy's exemplary leadership that the SS were pleased with the *Kinderblock* and often showed it off as a curiosity to the commandants of other camps. They also provided us with further favors. Thus, for example, we could even establish a sewing room in the block.

For the home, one of our comrades painted pictures from Walt Disney's *Snow White*. At the German's request, as they were very impressed by the pictures, Fredy produced a play of the fairy tale with the children in the German language and performed it for the dignitaries at Auschwitz. From tables, stools, and straw sacks, we constructed the stage, the backdrop, and the costumes. Because of the language difficulties which had to be overcome, the rehearsals lasted three months. We practiced dances and choruses with the children, rewrote the script, and adapted it to our circumstances. Thus the dwarves appeared as representatives of order and cleanliness. The demoralization to which they were opposed was embodied by the wicked stepmother. It was a truly lovely performance, and for the children it was the grandest experience of their lives—for many of them unfortunately also their last.

It was thanks not least to this performance that the SS-*Lagerführer* put aside a second block, as a day care center for children from three to eight years old and into whose living quarters mothers with children up to the age of ten could move. In this way, we could also look after the children at night, and prevent the exchange of children's food for other goods and services. [. . .]

After a while, we succeeded in translating the harmony which existed among us youth leaders unto the children themselves. We initiated a boy scout system, with challenges that had to be undergone; the children composed slogans and songs. The groups competed with each other to see if each one in the group could do a good deed each day for fourteen days straight. We organized scouting games, made playthings from clay, colored woven straw, and paper, which we later displayed in an exhibition where they were very much admired by the Germans.

This world, into which we had fled from reality, was suddenly shaken to its foundations in early March 1944. We had already spent the three winter months in Birkenau; those from the September transport had even been there for six months. And nothing had happened up until then. Of course many had perished, dead of starvation, and there were more and more *Muselmänner.* But the roll calls were shorter and occurred less frequently. Block curfew [*Blocksperre*] was seldom declared. Those of us who did not suffer from "chimney fever"[46] had new cause for hope. But one day the camp elder announced that those from the September transport would be going as a unit to work in Heidebrück in Germany—men, women and children; only the very ill would be exempted. There began a wild guessing game as to where this Heidebrück would be and if it was also a concentration camp. The pessimists maintained that this time certainly they would go to the gas: saying that the chimneys had not been smoking for many days now and they needed new material for burning. The optimists saw this very fact as proof that the gas chambers would be shut down for good.

The pessimists maintained correctly: the September transport, to which nearly all of these children belonged, was within a short time sent to the gas chamber.

---

46. That is, fear of being gassed.

DOCUMENT 8-17. Just as youngsters at Birkenau reenacted *Snow White*, children in the Novaky labor camp perform a play about another popular Disney character, Mickey Mouse, Slovakia, 1944, USHMMPA WS# 40080, courtesy of Mira Frenkel.

Separation from loved ones was a central experience for many young perse-cutees during the Holocaust. Whether divided by long distances or isolated in hiding, youngsters often bore the pain of separation in silence, either because they lacked a sympathetic environment in which to express their emotions or because doing so might endanger themselves or their rescuers. Very young children, such as hidden child Ilona Goldman (later Alona Frankel), suffered doubly, for they had very few practical avenues to communicate with parents or family members or to convey their feelings of loneliness and abandonment. Born in Kraków on July 27, 1937,[47] Ilona was two years old when German forces invaded her native Poland in September 1939. Like many Jewish families, the Goldmans decided to escape German-occupied Poland and fled to Lvov (now Lviv), then in Soviet territory.

Her father, Salomon (1900–1958), a Communist Party member from nearby Bochnia, owned a wholesale materials business. Her mother, Gusta

---

47. Concerning the story of Ilona Goldman and her family, see Alona Frankel, *A Girl*, trans. Sondra Silverston (Ramat Gan: Institute for the Translation of Hebrew Literature, 2009).

(b. 1904), a Ha-Shomer Ha-Za'ir[48] youth group member who had spent her teenage years in Palestine, came from the Silesian town of Oświęcim, a city better known by its German name, Auschwitz. Following the German invasion of the Soviet Union in June 1941, the Goldman family found itself incarcerated in the Lvov ghetto. In the spring of 1942, fearing the upcoming liquidation of the ghetto, Salomon Goldman managed to escape with his family to the "**Aryan** side" of Lvov, where a former employee, Josef Jozak, agreed to hide the Goldmans on one condition: that they find another place of concealment for their lively and voluble four-year-old daughter.[49] In the end, Salomon and Gusta found a hiding place for young Ilona with a Polish peasant family in the small village of Marcinkowice. Ilona spent some six months there posing as a Christian child with the family of Hania Seremet, whom the Goldmans paid handsomely each week for the care and concealment of their daughter. In Ilona's last months with her foster family, Gusta Goldman sacrificed a gold dental crown every week for her only child's continued safety, with Salomon prying each tooth from her mouth with the help of his Swiss Army knife.[50] The Goldmans were careful to pay Seremet on schedule, for they had learned that the rescuer had abandoned an earlier charge, a very young boy, to his death when his parents were killed in a ghetto action and relatives were unable to pay for his continued upkeep.[51]

Ilona Goldman spent several months separated from her parents. Because the four-year-old had not yet learned to write, she could not converse with her parents through notes or letters. Instead she communicated with them through a series of drawings sketched on the reverse side of Seremet's weekly correspondence with the Goldmans. Besides the connection they established between parents and child, Ilona's drawings served another important purpose: the pictures assured the Goldmans on a weekly basis that their daughter was still alive.

Now in the collection of the United States Holocaust Memorial Museum, Ilona Goldman's childhood drawings capture the themes of village life: the work of peasants in the fields, animals ambling across green meadows, passenger

---

48. Ha-Shomer Ha-Za'ir (also Hashomer Hatzair, youth organization of socialist Zionism) was founded in 1918, merging two groups, Hashomer, a Zionist scouting group, and Ze'irei Zion, an ideological group committed to the study of Zionism, socialism, and Jewish history. The oldest existing Zionist youth movement, Ha-Shomer Ha-Za'ir encouraged *Aliyah* to Palestine and the establishment of kibbutzim; it counted among its members Mordecai Anielewicz, leader of the Warsaw Ghetto Uprising.

49. Frankel, *A Girl*, 18.

50. Frankel, *A Girl*, 2.

51. Frankel, *A Girl*, 16.

DOCUMENT 8-18. Drawing of Ilona Goldman (Alona Frankel) for her parents in hiding, Marcinkowice, Poland, 1942, USHMM Collections, gift of Alona Goldman Frankel (note: writing showing through from other side).

Ilona Goldman's drawings served both as a mode of communication with absent parents and as a means of entertaining herself during her long and lonely time in hiding. For many children during the Holocaust, escape into a world of imagination proved an efficacious way to eschew the harsh realities that surrounded them. Whether through drawing, painting, poetry, or play, imagination provided an important avenue for eluding the miseries of hunger, fear, and deprivation. For young Abram (Avraham) Koplowicz, writing became a way to reassert a sense of control over his environment and to banish feelings of pain and helplessness. Born in Łódź on February 18, 1930, the only child of Mendel and Yochet Koplowicz (née Gittel),[52] Abram was just nine years old when German troops entered his native city and forced its Jewish inhabitants to reside in the Łódź ghetto. Even in his preteen years, he showed a precocious talent for writing, and within the ghetto walls, the young boy turned to poetry to transcend the physical and spiritual barrenness of his surroundings. His poem

---

52. Institute of Tolerance/State Archives in Łódź (in cooperation with the Centre de Civilization Française and the Embassy of France in Poland), eds., *The Children of the Łódź Ghetto* (Łódź: Bilbo, 2004), n.p.

"When I Am Twenty" is a literal flight into fancy, a magical journey into a space and time where the horrors of the ghetto could not reach him.

Abram Koplowicz was deported with the transport from the Łódź ghetto to Auschwitz in August 1944 and perished in the Birkenau gas chambers in September of that year. Mendel Koplowicz succeeded in surviving the war and, on returning to Łódź, discovered his son's illustrated volume of poetry among the ruins of the ghetto. Abram Koplowicz's original copybook is now reposited in the archives of **Yad Vashem**. Several selections of the young boy's poetry were published in their original Polish in 1993.[53]

DOCUMENT 8-19. **Abram Koplowicz, "When I Am Twenty," Łódź ghetto, c. 1943, in Institute of Tolerance/State Archives in Łódź (in cooperation with the Centre de Civilization Française and the Embassy of France in Poland), eds.,** *The Children of the Łódź Ghetto* **(Łódź: Bilbo, 2004).**

When I Am Twenty

When I am twenty,
I will start admiring our beautiful world
I will sit down in a huge motor-bird
And I will rise heavenward
I will sail, I will fly over rivers, seas and skies
Clouds will be my sisters, winds will be my brothers
I'll be watching rivers: Nile, Euphrates and others
I'll see the sphinxes and the pyramids
In the old country of divine [Isis].
I'll conquer the huge water of Niagara
And I'll be sunbathing in the heat of the Sahara
Over Tibetan mountains which reach for the sky
Over wonderful and mysterious land of the magicians
And when I finally leave the kingdom of heat
I'll rush flying to see the ice of the North
I'll fly over the great kangaroo island
And over the ruins of the Pompeian walls
Over the Holy Land of Orthodox Order
And over famous Homer's mother country
I'll be stunned by our beautiful world
Clouds will be my sister, wind will be my brother.

53. Abramka Koplowicz, *Utwory własne: Niezwykłe świadectwo trzynastoletniego poety z łódzkiego getta* (Łódź: Oficyna Bibliofilów, 1993).

Lvov ghetto survivor Nelly Toll used her interest in painting to transcend the dangerous world in which she lived. She was born Nelly Landau in 1933, the only daughter of Sygmunt and Rose Landau.[54] With her parents and her younger brother, Janek (b. 1937), Nelly resided in Lvov,[55] where her father was an affluent businessman who owned several apartment buildings. When Lvov came under Soviet occupation in the early months of World War II, Sygmunt Landau went into hiding, fearing arrest by the Soviets as a "wealthy capitalist." The family was therefore initially relieved when German troops arrived in the region on June 30, 1941, and Sygmunt could leave his hiding place and rejoin his loved ones. The Landaus' enthusiasm for the new Nazi occupiers was short-lived, however, as German authorities quickly initiated draconian legislation against the large local Jewish population.

On November 8, 1941, the Germans established a ghetto in the city's northern districts and, by December 15, had forced all Jews in the municipal area into the sealed "Jewish quarter." The Landaus' initial strategy was to place Nelly with a Catholic family outside the ghetto until the war's end. In hiding, the eight-year-old began to use the world of fantasy to cope with the intense loneliness and confusion she experienced. While the young girl lived clandestinely on Lvov's "Aryan side," she imagined that she was journeying on a long trip without her parents. During her later time in hiding, she would capture the sense of isolation she felt during these weeks in a wartime self-portrait that she titled *All Alone*.

Nelly tried to make the best of her time with her kindly Polish guardians, but a few short months later, tragedy struck. Nelly's younger brother, Janek, together with his aunt and young cousin, was caught up in a wave of deportations from Lvov and murdered, presumably in the Bełżec killing center. After Janek's death, Nelly returned to her parents in the ghetto. Sygmunt Landau was now more desperate than ever to rescue his remaining family from the Nazi dragnet. After an ill-fated attempt to escape to Hungary, Landau succeeded in finding a hiding place for his wife and daughter. Drawing on earlier loyalties and proffering a handsome sum as compensation, he convinced his former Polish tenants Michaj and Krysia Wojtek to conceal Nelly and her mother in a hidden room in their apartment. Sygmunt planned to join them there as soon

---

54. For information concerning Nelly Landau Toll and her Holocaust experiences, see Nelly S. Toll, *Behind the Secret Window: A Memoir of Hidden Childhood during World War Two* (New York: Dial Books, 1993).

55. Before World War II, Lvov had the third-largest Jewish population in Poland, numbering nearly one hundred thousand individuals; this number nearly doubled during the period of Soviet occupation with a rapid influx of Jewish refugees from German-occupied Poland.

as he had found places for members of his extended family. Yet, a short time after his wife and daughter went into hiding, Sygmunt Landau disappeared without a trace; Nelly and Rose Landau never saw him again.[56]

For the next thirteen months, Nelly and her mother lived in their tiny room with its boarded window, their quarters sealed off from the Wojteks' flat by a door concealed behind a hanging tapestry. After a few long weeks in hiding, Rose Landau arranged for a Polish friend to procure a set of watercolors for her daughter. Over the next several months, ten-year-old Nelly amused herself by painting images on small note cards and writing in her diary. The youngster drew many of her miniature scenes from imagination: from her readings in Leo Tolstoy and Jules Verne, from stories her mother told her to pass the time, or from memories of her happy childhood before the war. Looking through her "secret window," Nelly Landau often blended the reality of what she saw with her own fantasies and hopes for the future. In *Teacher with Children Wearing Black Uniforms*, Nelly painted children she glimpsed on their way to class, imagining the time when she too could be out of doors and go to school. "I walked with them. I silently talked with them,"[57] Nelly Landau Toll recalled in a 1998 interview.[58] Young Nelly's watercolors enabled her to reshape the perilous world around her into gentle tones and tranquil scenes. "My art was done in very dangerous times," Toll explained. "It gave me pleasure, it let me forget."

Nelly and Rose Landau were liberated in July 1944, when Soviet forces arrived in Lvov. After Rose's remarriage, seventeen-year-old Nelly joined her mother and stepfather in immigrating to the United States in 1951. There she married Ervin Toll in 1954 and went on to pursue studies in English and art, gaining a doctorate from the University of Pennsylvania. She has authored three books, as well as a play based on her wartime experiences. Nelly Toll's contemporary paintings continue to transform her observations and experiences into works of art.

---

56. After Soviet authorities liberated Lvov, Rose Landau tried, without success, to learn the fates of her husband and other family members still incarcerated in the Lvov ghetto at the time of their concealment. Sygmunt Landau likely perished at Bełżec.

57. Bruce Frankel, "Nelly's Secret," *People* 49, no. 27 (July 13, 1998).

58. Frankel, "Nelly's Secret."

DOCUMENT 8-20. Watercolor by Nelly Toll, Teacher with Children Wearing Black Uniforms, Lvov, Poland, c.1943–1944, USHMMPA WS# 94466, courtesy of Nelly Landau Toll.

CHAPTER 9

CHILDREN AND RESISTANCE AND RESCUE

THIS CHAPTER addresses a theme traditionally important to Holocaust discourse: resistance. In this case, the subject is children's resistance, a theme often overlooked in monographs dedicated to active opposition to Nazi rule. Boys and girls in their teens participated in armed resistance, their tender ages belying their achievements as **partisans**, ghetto fighters, and members of organized resistance groups. Youngsters struck at Nazi genocidal policy in uprisings at concentration camps and killing centers, such as the prisoner revolt at **Sobibór** in 1943 (Document 9-2). Children lived in family units protected by partisan bands in the forests of eastern Europe (Document 9-4). Young people formed the core of insurgents who battled Nazi forces in the Warsaw Ghetto Uprising (Document 9-1) and in other armed struggles in ghettoized communities under Nazi occupation. More often, however, children engaged in acts of unarmed resistance, as with the publication of clandestine youth newspapers in the Warsaw ghetto (Document 9-5) or through the provision of aid and intelligence to armed opposition movements (Documents 9-8 and 9-9). Even young children practiced solitary acts of defiance against Nazi authorities, often as smugglers risking their lives to bring food and essential goods to fellow ghetto inhabitants from outside the ghetto boundaries.

Rescue is the mirror image of resistance. Hundreds of organizations and thousands of committed individuals worked to save persecutees in Axis-occupied Europe. Many of these focused principally or solely on the rescue of children. In Allied countries, refugee organizations sought to bring children to the safety of their shores. In England, associations such as the British Committee for the Jews of Germany and the Movement for the Care of Children from Germany organized the famous *Kindertransporte*, which carried Jewish and refugee children to Great Britain (Document 9-13), an effort that many private benefactors worked to emulate (Documents 9-14 and 9-15). Within Nazi-occupied territories, children's aid organizations such as the **Oeuvre de Secours aux Enfants** in France and the **Żegota**, an auxiliary branch of the Polish Home Army (*Armia Krajowa*), proved particularly successful in removing young children from concentration and internment camps and concealing them from Nazi authorities in a series of safe houses and children's homes. Finally, thousands of young Jewish children spent the war in hiding, either alone or with their families, shielded by a network of rescuers and protectors. These so-called hidden children (Documents 9-10 through 9-12) have become an iconic symbol of rescue efforts during the Holocaust, but the following documentation demonstrates that a dense nexus of individuals, aid organizations, and child-welfare agencies worked tirelessly and with singular ingenuity to save Jewish and non-Jewish children from harm in Nazi Europe.

YOUTH AND ARMED RESISTANCE

One of the most ambitious and fiercely contended insurgencies against Nazi genocidal policy, the Warsaw Ghetto Uprising had its origins in the perceived defenselessness of Warsaw's incarcerated Jewish population during the time of the Great **Deportation** Action, a period between July 22 and September 21, 1942, when German authorities dispatched three hundred thousand ghetto inhabitants to the **Treblinka** killing center. On July 23, the day the first massive deportation effort from Warsaw began, members of the ghetto's underground movement met to discuss a plan of action that might save the endangered community. Representatives of Warsaw's Jewish youth organizations, which had thus far played a vital role in ghetto resistance, favored the formation of a defense force that might resist further deportation measures through armed intervention. On July 28, 1942, members of the Ha-Shomer, Dror, Ha-Za'ir, and Akiva movements founded the Jewish Fighting Organization (Żydowska Organizacja Bojowa, or ŻOB) under the command of twenty-three-year-old Ha-Shomer Ha-Za'ir[1] organizer Mordechai Anielewicz.[2]

---

1. See note 48, chapter 8.

2. Mordechai Anielewicz (1919–1943) was born in the small town of Wyszków, near Warsaw, Poland. In his late teenage years, he joined, and became a local leader of, the Zionist youth movement Ha-Shomer Ha-Za'ir. In early 1943, Anielewicz was instrumental in organizing the first clashes with German forces during the brief January deportation action in the Warsaw ghetto. As the leader of the ŻOB, he played a chief role in the Warsaw Ghetto Uprising of April 1943. It is believed that Anielewicz committed suicide with other leading resistance figures when German forces captured ŻOB headquarters on May 8, 1943. See Norah Levin, *Mordechai Anielewicz: Leader of the Warsaw Ghetto Uprising* (Philadelphia: Association of Jewish Holocaust Survivors in Philadelphia, 1988).

In the coming months, activists from the ŻOB distributed leaflets to the ghetto populace informing them of the significance of the Treblinka camp and the fate of persons deported there. More significantly, its leaders made overtures to the Polish Home Army and the Polish communist underground in an attempt to acquire arms, with limited success. In the autumn, another resistance organization, the Jewish Military Union (Żydowski Związek Wojskowy, or ŻZW) formed under the auspices of the Revisionist Zionist associations. For a time the two defense forces vied for men and material, but in the face of renewed deportations from the ghetto, the ŻZW accepted the ŻOB's authority, and the two bodies worked to coordinate their activities.

On January 18, 1943, a second wave of deportations to Treblinka began. This time, members of the ŻOB engaged German forces in combat. Encouraged by the resistance fighters, thousands of ghetto inhabitants refused to show in response to German deportation summons in the days that followed. Nazi officials succeeded in rounding up five to six thousand Jews and halted the action after a few days. Jews and "**Aryan**" Poles alike interpreted the brevity of the deportation action as a victory for the ghetto's defense organizations. The heroism of the ghetto fighters, together with the realization that any further deportation efforts would mean the final liquidation of the ghetto unit, worked to undercut the authority of the **Jewish Order Police** and the *Judenrat*, which had counseled against armed resistance. The ŻOB had given ghetto inhabitants a measure of hope, and the population gave its allegiance to the ghetto resistance leaders in the days to come. In the winter months of 1943, the preparation of bunkers and subterranean hiding places (malines) proceeded on a massive scale, while ghetto defense forces worked to consolidate their strategies and to arm and equip themselves for the coming battle. The commanders of these units were under no illusion that their resistance efforts would lead to rescue: most viewed the upcoming revolt as a last protest against Nazi Germany's murderous policies and an attempt to live and die with their honor intact.

The resistance campaign known as the Warsaw Ghetto Uprising began on the evening of Passover on April 19, 1943.[3] The ŻOB had received advanced warning of this final deportation action and prepared assiduously for the coming attack. From their experiences in January, German authorities likewise had knowledge of the ghetto's defense organizations and, on the eve of the action, replaced the chief of the **Schutzstaffel (SS)** and police in Warsaw,

---

3. For a discussion of the Warsaw Ghetto Uprising, see Israel Gutman, *The Jews of Warsaw, 1939–1943: Ghetto, Underground, Revolt*, trans. Ina Friedman (Bloomington: University of Indiana Press, 1982); Barbara Engelking and Jacek Leociak, *The Warsaw Ghetto: A Guide to a Perished City*, trans. Emma Harris (New Haven, CT: Yale University Press, 2009).

Obergruppenführer Ferdinand von Sammern-Frankenegg,[4] with SS and Police Leader (SS- und Polizeiführer) Jürgen Stroop,[5] a man with considerable experience in partisan warfare. The uprising lasted twenty-seven days. Stroop had committed a considerable force, some 2,054 soldiers and police, reinforced with artillery and tanks. Clashing with them, sometimes in hand-to-hand combat, were some seven hundred young Jewish fighters, poorly equipped and lacking in military training and experience. The ŻOB did have the advantage of waging a guerrilla war, striking and then retreating to the safety of ghetto buildings and rooftops. The general population likewise thwarted German deportation efforts, refusing to assemble at collection points and burrowing in malines and underground bunkers. In the end, German troops were obliged to burn the ghetto down block by block in order to smoke out their quarry. The ghetto fighters and the population that supported them held out for nearly a month. On May 8, 1943, German forces succeeded in seizing ŻOB headquarters at 18 Mila Street; Anielewicz and many of his staff commanders are thought to have committed suicide in order to avoid capture. On May 16, Stroop announced in his daily report to Berlin that "the former Jewish Quarter in Warsaw is no more."[6] Some thirteen thousand Jews had died in the uprising, while the remaining fifty thousand Warsaw ghetto residents were deported to Treblinka. Only a handful of ghetto inhabitants survived the final *Aktion* in Warsaw, subsisting in their subterranean hiding places or escaping through the city's labyrinthine sewer system to the "Aryan side."

The first major revolt of an urban population in German-occupied Europe, the Warsaw Ghetto Uprising combined the valiant efforts of ghetto fighters

---

4. SS-Oberführer Ferdinand von Sammern-Frankenegg (1897–1944) was the Police Leader (Polizeiführer) of the Warsaw district on the eve of the Warsaw Ghetto Uprising. Transferred to Croatia following his replacement by Jürgen Stroop in Warsaw, he was killed by Yugoslav partisans on September 20, 1944.

5. Jürgen Stroop (1895–1952) joined the Nazi Party and SS in 1932 and saw combat during the invasion of the Soviet Union in 1941. In 1942, as SS-Brigadeführer, Stroop commanded an SS garrison at Kherson before becoming the SS and Police Leader for Lemberg (now Lviv) in February 1943. Following his suppression of the Warsaw Ghetto Uprising in April 1943, he was dispatched to Greece as Higher SS and Police Leader. After difficulties with German civilian authorities there, he ended the war as commander of SS-Oberabschnitt Rhein-Westmark in the Rhineland. An American military court condemned Stroop to death in March 1947 for his role in the murder of downed Allied fliers within his jurisdiction but allowed him to be extradited to Poland to face trial for his crimes there, including the liquidation of the Warsaw ghetto. Jürgen Stroop was convicted of war crimes and executed in Warsaw on March 6, 1952.

6. See Jürgen Stroop, *The Stroop Report, The Jewish Quarter of Warsaw Is No More!* ed. and trans. Sybil Milton (New York: Pantheon Books, 1979).

with the dogged resistance of the general population. Many of those who engaged in armed resistance in Warsaw were adolescents in their teens; a majority of these came from the city's active underground Jewish youth movements. Writing at the height of the insurgency, **Oneg Shabbat** chronicler **Emmanuel Ringelblum** noted that many of the bravest fighters were not men but young girls, who matched their male counterparts in courage, daring, and commitment. In his essay "Little Stalingrad Defends Itself," Ringelblum reports that a Jewish teenager in Świętojerska Street had captured the public's imagination as the Jewish Joan of Arc.

DOCUMENT 9-1. **Emmanuel Ringelblum, "Little Stalingrad Defends Itself," c. April 1943, in Joseph Kermish, ed., *"To Live with Honor and Die with Honor": Selected Documents from the Warsaw Ghetto Underground Archives "O.S." (Oneg Shabbath)* (Jerusalem: Yad Vashem, 1986), 601–3.**

On the "Aryan side" there was intense interest in what was happening in the ghetto. It was related that the Germans were afraid to show themselves in the ghetto, and that they operated on burnt ground [i.e., scorched earth policy] only, moving forward by burning down block after block. The Germans were spoken of with contempt because of their atrocities. They were laughed at for not being able to put down a handful of Jews fighting for their honour. [. . .] There were rumours about Jews reconquering the Pawiak[7] and releasing the prisoners there, who then joined the fighting. A story was spread in town about a handful of Jews who had captured a tank, got into it, and left the ghetto area. Popular fantasy also created a Jewish Joan of Arc. At 28 Świętojerska Street, the bristle workshop, a beautiful eighteen-year-old girl dressed in white had been seen firing a machine gun at the Germans with extraordinary accuracy, while she herself was invulnerable. [. . .] Among the rumours being spread on the "Aryan side" at that time there was a good deal of fantasy, but there were also authentic facts, if somewhat altered. The legend about the Jewish Maid of Orleans[8] had its origin in the fact that Jewish girls took part in combat alongside the men. I knew these heroic girls from the period preceding the "action." Most of them belonged to the Ha-Shomer Ha-Za'ir

---

7. During the German occupation of Warsaw, Pawiak Prison served as the Gestapo's largest political prison in occupied Poland and became synonymous with Nazi terror.

8. This is an appellation of Joan of Arc, whose greatest military success was the lifting of the Siege of Orleans against English forces in April 1429 during the Hundred Years' War.

and Hechalutz [youth] movements. Throughout the war, they had carried on welfare work all the time with great devotion and extraordinary self-sacrifice. Disguised as "Aryan" women, they had carried illegal literature around the country, managed to get everywhere with instructions from the Jewish National Committee; they bought and transported arms, executed O.B.[9] death sentences, and shot gendarmes and SS-men during the January "action." Altogether they completely outdid the men in courage, alertness, and daring. I myself saw Jewish women firing a machine gun from a roof. Clearly one of these heroic girls must have distinguished herself in the heavy fighting waged by the O.B. at Świętojerska Street, and that was probably the origin of the story of the Jewish Maid of Orleans.

The 1943 Warsaw Ghetto Uprising was the largest show of Jewish armed resistance in the course of World War II. The ŻOB and ŻZW, which instigated the insurgency, were two of the most successful manifestations of organized resistance, but they represented just the tip of the iceberg. Jewish underground organizations existed in over one hundred ghettos in German-occupied eastern Europe. Incredibly, under the most adverse conditions, Jewish prisoners also succeeded in forming resistance cells within the Nazi concentration camp system. During the late war years, surviving Jewish *Sonderkommando* units initiated uprisings at several extermination camps. On August 2, 1943, for example, Jewish prisoners rebelled at Treblinka, seizing firearms from their captors and setting fire to the camp. Some two hundred individuals escaped; half their number were soon recaptured and executed. Likewise, on October 7, 1944, **Auschwitz** prisoners assigned to maintain **Crematorium** IV in the **Auschwitz II–Birkenau** concentration camp rebelled when they learned that their unit was slated for killing. German guards and their auxiliaries brutally crushed the revolt, murdering several hundred prisoners, but not before the *Sonderkommando* succeeded in destroying Crematorium IV with homemade explosives, rendering it inoperable for the duration of the war.[10]

---

9. This is a common abbreviation of the Żydowska Organizacja Bojowa (Jewish Fighting Organization, or ŻOB). The ŻOB issued "death sentences" against those within the ghetto who collaborated with the Germans, including certain members of the Jewish Order Police.

10. See Hermann Langbein, "The Auschwitz Underground," and Nathan Cohen, "Diaries of the *Sonderkommando*," both in *Anatomy of the Auschwitz Death Camp*, ed. Yisrael Gutman and Michael Berenbaum (Bloomington: University of Indiana Press in association with the U.S. Holocaust Memorial Museum, 1994), 485–502 and 522–34; Gideon Graif, *We Wept without Tears: Testimonies of the Jewish Sonderkommando from Auschwitz* (New Haven, CT: Yale University Press, 2005).

The most successful uprising of its kind, however, took place at the Sobibór extermination camp. In the summer of 1943, transports of Jews from the **General Government** to the killing center grew fewer in number. Sensing that they might be murdered along with the last groups of deportees, the veteran Jewish *Sonderkommando* laboring at the extermination camp formed an underground resistance cell, led by Leon Feldhendler, a former *Judenrat* member from the nearby village of Zolkiewka. Feldhendler believed that the group's best chance of survival was to escape the camp. He and his followers had witnessed many individual flight attempts, but experience had taught them that these invariably ended in the capture of the escaping prisoners and fierce retaliation on the rest of the camp population. Feldhendler convinced his colleagues that the solution lay in a mass escape from Sobibór. But how to organize a breakout that could provide all prisoners a chance to escape? In September 1943, a transport of Jews from Minsk brought to the camp first lieutenant Aleksandr ("Sasha") Pechersky, a trained Soviet officer with combat experience. The resistance cell recruited Pechersky, asking him to mastermind an uprising that might free Sobibór's six hundred prisoners.

On October 14, 1943, Pechersky's plan came to fruition. At 4:00 p.m., Thomas (Tuvia) Blatt and a handful of his fellow prisoners cornered their first adversary, SS-Unterscharführer Josef Wolf, murdering him with an axe. Wolf was the first of eleven German and Ukrainian guards killed in the uprising. Other conspirators seized weapons and explosives. The facility's electricity and phone wires were cut. Under a hale of SS fire, prisoners cut through the camp's dense net of barbed wire and made a perilous dash through the minefields that encircled the camp.

By evening, half of the camp's population, three hundred prisoners, had escaped. About one-third of these individuals were eventually recaptured and murdered. Those inmates who had remained behind during the uprising were also killed shortly before the liquidation of the camp some weeks later.[11] Many of those still at liberty joined partisan units or received shelter and aid from sympathetic Poles. Nearly seventy prisoners who escaped Sobibór survived the war.[12]

---

11. Many of these were prisoners in Camp III, where, isolated from the main camp, they remained unaware of the uprising.

12. Among these individuals were Sasha Pechersky (1909–1990), Thomas (Tuvia) Blatt (1927–), and Leon Feldhendler (1909–1945). Feldhendler survived to see the July 1944 liberation of Lublin, where he and his wife had lived in hiding, but was murdered by members of an antisemitic Polish paramilitary group on April 2, 1945. For a discussion of the Sobibór revolt by eyewitnesses, see Dov Freiberg, *To Survive Sobibor* (Jerusalem: Gefen, 2007); Thomas Blatt, *From the Ashes of Sobibor: A Story of Survival* (Evanston, IL: Northwestern University Press, 1997).

One of those survivors was **Berel Dov Freiberg**, just fourteen years of age when he was selected from a transport of Jews from Krasnystaw to labor in a *Sonderkommando* unit at Sobibór.[13] A year later the teenage Freiberg served as a courier during the Sobibór uprising, keeping the individual actors in the revolt abreast of developments occurring in other parts of the camp. With his fellow prisoners, the fifteen-year-old participated in the killing of several German and Ukrainian guards before making his escape. In 1945, the youngster gave a dramatic account of the prisoner rebellion to **Bluma Wasser**, herself a survivor of the Warsaw ghetto and, with her husband, **Hersh Wasser**, a chronicler for the underground archival organization Oneg Shabbat.

DOCUMENT 9-2. **Oral history of Berel Dov Freiberg, recorded by Bluma Wasser, 1945, in Isaiah Trunk, ed.,** *Jewish Responses to Nazi Persecution: Collective and Individual Behavior in Extremis* **(New York: Stein and Day, 1982), 283–87.**

At exactly four p.m. Untersturmführer Neumann came to the tailors to have a uniform measured. He was received very warmly, told to sit down, and from behind, his head was split into two pieces with an axe and the halves were swept under the bunks. [. . .] At the exact same time, [Oberscharführer] Greshits, a Ukrainian, arrived at the shoemaker workshop, and in a second, he was turned into a corpse. Any German caught by the Jews was assassinated. If they came into the barrack to force us off to the labor sites, we thought to ourselves: "*Briederke* [brother], this won't take long—you'll be dead in no time." We let them into the barracks and they never left again.

I ran from battle station to battle station as a courier, informing the units of our progress. We broke into the German compound and took all their arms, then headed for the administration office. [Scharführer] Beckmann was at his desk. He knew right away something was up because he'd just come from our barrack and found no one there, not even the [*Oberscharführer*], so he went straight back to the administration office, where we cut him off. He reached for his revolver, but there wasn't a chance—all of us jumped him without guns and beat him dead because we didn't want to shoot. The longer we kept things quiet the better off we'd be. It was hard to keep him down because he jerked around in wild death spasms. [. . .]

---

13. For a more detailed discussion of the experiences of Berel Dov Freiberg and his arrival at Sobibór, see chapter 5.

When everyone was already assembled inside the camp and we were getting ready to attack the arsenal, *Zugwachmann Rel*—how many times he'd beaten me!—suddenly appeared and realized something was happening when he saw the cut wires. The electricity and telephones were all put out of order by one of us who had access to the generators and smashed them. Rel asked us nervously: "*Was gibt es Neues?*" ["What's up?"]. He just happened to be walking right in front of me, so I raised my axe and, along with two friends, chopped him up into little pieces.

Now everyone knew what was about to happen and a deafening cheer went up, shouts of "*Vperyod!*" "*Vorverts!*" "*Foros!*" ["Forward!"]. Our targets were now ahead of us, not behind us—the arms stockpiles! We stormed the arsenal, killed two Germans where they stood, and brought out the guns. All this time we could see nothing but bullet after bullet ripping at us from all sides—from the guard towers, from the Germans and the *Volksdeutsche* and the 300 Ukrainians who were shooting at us from all around, especially from the fourth camp. They were soon reinforced by another 150 Ukrainians who assaulted us with heavy automatic weapon fire. We returned fire with the few guns we had. But we didn't keep static positions—we ran from station to station shooting in all directions, and defying the risk, broke out of camp. We were still at the wire perimeter when a youth beside me took a bullet and was left hanging on the wires. I was using a rifle I had gotten from the stockpile and kept on running. There were explosions all around—the mines went off, the bullets struck and flashed everywhere we went. The sound of men being torn to pieces, bullets shattering, and mines detonating thundered all through the area. Later, all we could do was laugh as we heard the rattling of the machine guns trailing off behind us. The shooting kept up all night and we got farther and farther away from the camp. We threw off everything along the way. [. . .]

After we ran several hours and were far from the camp by now, we counted ourselves up because everyone had run off in a different direction. There were twenty-four in our group. We kissed and embraced and couldn't believe we were really outside the camp. We walked all night through the forest and found a good spot in a gorge grown over with thicket, and that's where we rested. We didn't eat all day because what we'd accomplished put us into such a state that we were all flushed from exhilaration and our blood was feverish and made us tremble. We couldn't eat a bite and there was nothing to eat in the forest anyway. Someone had a piece of bread, a lump of sugar, so we shared it later.

The prisoner uprisings at Sobibór and subsequently at Treblinka were remarkable in that the rebellions struck at the very heart of the genocidal apparatus. Many escapees joined the ranks of partisan units, where they continued to defy Nazi military and occupation authorities. Jewish partisan bands operated extensively throughout Nazi-occupied Europe. Some twenty to thirty thousand Jewish fighters engaged in guerrilla warfare and sabotage against German forces and those who collaborated with them. These units faced tremendous obstacles in acquiring weapons, food, and shelter and were in constant danger of capture or denunciation by hostile elements within the local population. In eastern Europe, many Jews merged with the Soviet partisan movement, although they often faced discrimination or betrayal by antisemitic comrades in arms. As a result, many Jewish fighters preferred to maintain their own fighting organizations. One of the most successful of these partisan units combined traditional guerrilla activity with extensive rescue efforts. These were the Bielski partisans.[14]

Following the German invasion of the Soviet Union, units of the *Einsatzgruppen* killed thousands of Jews in western Belorussia (now Belarus).[15] Surviving Jews in the Nowogrodek District were confined in ghettos, principally in the towns of Nowogrodek and Lida. In 1942 and early 1943, German authorities liquidated these ghettos, murdering most of the region's remaining Jewish population.

The Bielskis were a family of millers and grocers residing in a farming region near the town of Stankiewicze. After a ghetto action in December 1941 in which their parents and other family members were murdered, the four surviving brothers—Tuvia, Alexander (Zus), Asael, and Aron—fled the Nowogrodek ghetto to the nearby forest and, with a handful of fellow escapees, formed the nucleus of a fledging Jewish partisan band. Familiar with the surrounding district, the brothers received arms and supplies from local non-Jewish friends and acquaintances. As their unit expanded, the Bielskis were able to augment their arsenal with captured German weapons and guns supplied by Soviet partisans.

Armed in this manner, the small band began to target and harass German troops and their collaborators operating in the region. Although paramilitary

---

14. See Nechama Tec, *Defiance: The Bielski Partisans* (Oxford: Oxford University Press, 1993).

15. Western Belorussia had been Polish territory before World War II, but it had been annexed by the Soviet Union following the invasion of Poland by German and Soviet forces in September 1939.

objectives were a major focus, the unit's recognized leader, Tuvia Bielski,[16] began to view as the group's primary mission the rescue of Jews from the surrounding community. The Bielskis helped Jewish inhabitants of nearby ghettos to escape. Many Jews hiding in small family units also joined their ranks so that, by late 1942, the group had grown to over three hundred members.

Such a large partisan group eventually attracted the attention of German authorities, and in the summer of 1943, occupation officials offered a bounty of one hundred thousand Reichsmark for information leading to the capture of Tuvia Bielski. Some twenty thousand German military and local auxiliary units were deployed to locate the Bielski band and to curb the growing partisan movement, composed of Soviet, Polish, and Jewish units, in the Belorussian forests.

In order to escape the German dragnet, the Bielski group, now seven hundred strong, moved in December 1943 to a new base in the swampy marshes of the Naliboki Forest, on the right bank of Nieman River. Here the band established an unlikely and remarkable community. A core group of 150 men—and a handful of women—engaged in armed operations on behalf of the group. Despite dissension within their own ranks from those who insisted that their unit should accept only armed and able-bodied fighters, Tuvia Bielski proved adamant in accepting all Jews who appealed to the group for aid. "To save a Jew is much more important than to kill Germans," Tuvia told his men.[17] As the armed fighters engaged German forces in defense of the unit, other members of the band cultivated arable land in the vicinity and foraged for food and supplies. The community ultimately established a bakery, laundry, and infirmary and set up an improvised synagogue, a tribunal to adjudicate disputes, and a makeshift jail. Some thirty children lived within the Bielski family group.[18] The Naliboki base housed a school for adolescents, while a group of female members organized to supervise the youngest children.

In the summer of 1944, the Soviet army staged an offensive that swept the German Army Group Center back to the banks of the Vistula and liberated the greater part of Belorussia. Through the efforts of Tuvia Bielski and his comrades, an astonishing 1,236 Jews from the family camp had survived the war. At liberation, 70 percent of the group consisted of women, children, and the elderly, those individuals most likely to have perished during the German occupation.

---

16. Tuvia Bielski (1906–1987) emigrated with his third wife, Lilka (née Titkin), to Israel after the war, where he participated in the 1948 Israeli War of Independence. He and his family moved to Brooklyn, New York, in 1956. Bielski died in the United States in 1987; in 1988, his body was reburied with full military honors in Haar Hmnuchot in Jerusalem.

17. Tec, *Defiance*, 82.

18. Tec, *Defiance*, 165.

DOCUMENT 9-3. **Members of the Bielski partisan family camp, including several small children, shortly before liberation, Naliboki Forest, Belorussia, 1944, USHMMPA WS# 77654, courtesy of the Yad Vashem Photo Archives.**

    The Bielski partisan movement represented the most successful rescue effort of its kind, but it was not the only instance in which Jewish partisans accepted and protected family units within their ranks. Rachmiel Łozowski was nine years old when he witnessed the killing of the Jews of Zhetl (Zdzięcioł), near Grodno in what is today Belarus in August 1942. As he and his family tried to flee the massacre, police officials apprehended his mother, two younger brothers, and sister, whom he never saw again. Rachmiel, his twelve-year-old brother, and his father were reunited after the raid and found their way to shelter in the Lipiczanska Puszcza forest. There they joined local partisans and lived in their family group for the next two years, surviving the war. In 1947 in Tel Aviv, Łozowski shared with historian A. Yerushalmi his experiences of a childhood spent among the partisan resistance.

DOCUMENT 9-4. Oral history of Rachmiel Łozowski, Tel Aviv, 1947, USHMMA RG 15.084, Holocaust Survivor Testimonies, 301/540 (translated from the Yiddish).

The forest we were in was at Lipiczanska Puszcza. We stayed together as a family group. There were large partisan units all around us and they didn't bother us. There were fifty people in our family unit, including five children. We would get food from peasants we knew. A teacher, Lazar Meir, used to take care of the children. He was also able to buy guns for the group. One time he left for the Lida [Ghetto] and came back with five Jews.

In the winter of 1943, fifteen other Jews and two children came to us. After that, still more and more people joined us. [. . .]

In the summer of 1944, the forests were put under siege by 32,000 Germans and Ukrainians. Partisan units pulled back. We hid out in underground bunkers. The starvation during that time was horrible. We used to get a few beans a day to eat. This went on for fourteen days. There was room for five people in our bunker—fourteen people lay down there during the siege. As a camouflage, we dragged two dead horses over to cover the entrance. When the Germans moved through with their hounds, the dogs bolted back from the stench. But we suffered terribly from those worm-eaten carcasses. The worms crawled all over us and we choked on the stink of death. We fainted from the putrid air.

Another time, we heard cavalry riding past followed by infantry. We thought they were Germans. We crawled out and started to run. My father was the only one to stay behind in the bunker. The "Germans" got him out and wanted to know who he was and what he was doing here. He told them he was part of a partisan family unit. All they did was yell at him for keeping a fire lit, then they left. They were partisans too, just like us. [. . .]

Sometimes the children would wander around outside the bunker. Once, two boys—Yosif and Srulik, aged seven and eight—and two little girls, aged four and five, fell into the hands of the Ukrainians. They shot the little girls dead right away and took the boys into the village gendarmes. The boys pleaded with the Ukrainians to let them go, but in vain. At that moment, grown-ups from our group passed by, and the boys started shouting: "See?! There go the adults!" The Ukrainians let go of the children and chased the grown-ups. The children got away and ran down into the bunker. Malke Shmulovitch fell into the Ukrainians' hands. They led her into the village, raped her, cut out strips of her flesh, and poured salt into her wounds. She betrayed no one, though, and died heroically.

This is the way we suffered for such a long time. We always had knives ready at our sides, to take our own lives if we fell into the hands of the Ukrainians.

One day, Captain "Severny," the Jewish Avreyml Shereshevski, came to see us to tell us the good news that the Red Army was near. I was the first one he met. I ran to tell the glad news to my people. I searched for them all day and finally found them. When I told them the news, they came back to life.

UNARMED RESISTANCE: THE CHILDREN'S WAR

Acts of armed resistance against Nazi and Axis oppression make up an integral chapter in the history of the Holocaust. Large-scale uprisings undertaken by Jewish underground organizations, such as those in the Warsaw and Białystok ghettos or in the Auschwitz, Sobibór, and Treblinka killing centers, demonstrated that Jewish populations did not go meekly like lambs to the slaughter, as some analysts have claimed, but openly defied German authorities and those who collaborated with them. For many Jewish communities in Nazi-occupied Europe, however, the constraints of captivity and the threat of brutal reprisals made armed resistance difficult and dangerous. Under such extreme conditions, most sectors of the Jewish population that wished to oppose Nazi persecution engaged in unarmed resistance. Such efforts included organized escapes of individuals to partisan units or to safe havens outside ghettos or camps, as well as the noncompliance of ghetto administrators, officials, and residents with Nazi decrees and the organization of educational, religious, and cultural activities prohibited by German authorities. While such actions posed no physical threat to their antagonists, they struck at the core of Nazi discriminatory policy.

In German-occupied Poland, the constellation of political and cultural organizations that had existed before the outbreak of World War II continued to function within the world of the ghetto. Because of the draconian measures imposed on ghettoized communities, many of these associations were driven underground, where they worked assiduously to counteract the effects of Nazi oppression. In the Warsaw ghetto, political parties and organizations were particularly active, and the clandestine publications they generated "multiplied like mushrooms in the rain," noted Emmanuel Ringelblum, chief archivist of the Oneg Shabbat archive.[19] The numerous youth organizations, a significant force in ghetto resistance activity, played an active part in these endeavors.

---

19. Joseph Kermish, "On the Underground Press in the Warsaw Ghetto," *Yad Vashem Studies* 1 (1957): 85.

Those clandestine newspapers[20] produced in the ghetto certainly did not match the standards of their organizations' prewar publications. With printing materials in short supply, most news sheets were printed on carbon paper or lightweight flimsy paper.[21] Many associations produced hectographed[22] or type-written editions, while others circulated handwritten copies. Few of the newspapers were very large. The majority was limited to a handful of pages—a dozen at most. Despite a perennial shortage of resources, these underground publications played an important role in the politics and civic life of the Warsaw ghetto. Their most essential task was to lift the flagging spirits of their readers and to strengthen their morale and will to resist Nazi oppression. Another unequivocal mission of the illegal press was to keep residents informed of events inside and outside the ghetto. Appearing in Polish, Yiddish, or Hebrew, underground newspapers and periodicals kept their readers abreast of wartime developments and the unparalleled atrocities leveled against Europe's Jewish communities. In 1941 and 1942, many columns were devoted to speculation concerning the evolution of Nazi policy and to the acts of terror perpetrated by German officials against Warsaw's incarcerated Jews. The clandestine press also focused on various aspects of ghetto life: economic conditions, employment issues, the activities of cultural and welfare institutions, and the policies of the *Judenrat*, about which most editors of the illegal press had little good to say. Largely socialist in orientation, underground newspapers were also sharply critical of the genuine social and class disparities that existed in the ghetto and railed against the measures of the *Judenrat* and other agencies that unfairly burdened the most impoverished sectors of the community.[23]

Among the underground publishing organizations in the Warsaw ghetto, the clandestine youth press fulfilled a special need, encouraging young people to hold fast to their ideals in the face of Nazi persecution and offering spiritual and intellectual direction. The struggle against apathy, despair, and spiritual degeneracy proved a common goal among these newspapers and periodicals. Appropriate to their readers' age and outlook, the underground youth press urged opposition to Nazi oppression and preparation for a Jewish future. Thus, publications such as the Polish-language *El Al* (*Upwards*) encouraged young

20. See Kermish, "On the Underground Press," 85–123; Engelking and Leociak, *The Warsaw Ghetto*, 685–94.

21. This refers to an inferior-grade paper traditionally used for making multiple copies.

22. Hectography is a low-technology printing process involving the transfer of an original, prepared with special aniline inks, to a pan of gelatin or a gelatin pad pulled over a frame. Virtually obsolete in modern printing, the process is still used to produce temporary tattoos on human skin.

23. Kermish, "On the Underground Press," 116ff.

audiences to take an active part in their community and to "look ahead to what the future may bring,"[24] while others, such as *Yunge Gwardie* (*Young Guard*), a Yiddish news sheet, reminded youth active in resistance activities not to neglect their education and self-improvement. Dozens of underground newspapers were produced by young people for young people in the years 1941 and 1942, including *Jungtruf* (*The Call of Youth*), *Di Yugent Stimme* (*The Voice of Youth*), *Avangarda Młodzieży* (*Youth Avant-Garde*), and *Płomienie* (*The Flame*), the latter a publication of the Jewish defense organization Ha-Shomer Ha-Za'ir.

The Gordonia youth organization sponsored three clandestine papers in the Warsaw ghetto: *Oisdoier* (*Endurance*), *Z Problematyki ruchu w chwili obecnej* (*On the Present Problems of the Movement*), and *Słowo Młodych* (*Young People's Voice*). Before November 1941, when editor Eliezer Geller[25] began to focus his attentions on older audiences, the latter publication targeted primarily youths in their middle and late teens. A Polish-language biweekly, *Słowo Młodych* was Gordonia's mouthpiece, espousing the sentiments of that pioneering youth movement founded in Poland in 1925. Named for Aaron David Gordon (1856–1922), a proponent of Labor Zionism, Gordonia became an international movement in the late 1930s, promoting the creation of a Jewish homeland, the revival of Hebrew culture, and the preparation of youth for **Aliyah** to **Palestine** through education and vocational training. In the Warsaw ghetto, the Gordonia movement gained many adherents by promoting underground educational activities for its young members, comprising several age groups. *Słowo Młodych* spoke to the heart of its young readers, urging them to courageous action and to hopes for a brighter future. In an undated edition from the fall of 1941, *Słowo Młodych* urged its readers to ensure that they would not be the last generation of Jewish youth but rather "the first generation reborn to the Jewish nation." The newspaper's publishers invoked the Bible's Eighty-third Psalm, "Keep Not Thou Silence, O God," a lament for the nation of Israel traditionally interpreted as a prayer for the destruction of its enemies. As the Jewish people faced a new and terrible oppressor, the paper exhorted its young audience to courage.

---

24. *El Al*, quoted in Kermish, "Underground Press," 86.

25. Eliezer Geller (b. 1918) was a Gordonia activist and member of the ŻOB underground resistance in Warsaw. Geller led a unit of armed resistors during the Warsaw Ghetto Uprising; on April 29, 1943, he succeeded in fleeing through the sewer system to the "Aryan side" of Warsaw. Taking refuge at the Hotel Polski, where German authorities interned Jews with foreign passports, Geller was discovered and ultimately transferred to Auschwitz, where he perished.

DOCUMENT 9-5. **"Let the Jewish Youth Remember,"** *Słowo Młodych* (*Young People's Voice*), Warsaw ghetto, spring, 1942, USHMMA, RG-15.070M, Zespół podziemie–prasa konspiracyjna [Clandestine Publications], 230/13/1.

Słowo Młodych .

Niechaj pamięta młodzież żydowska
że albo jest ostatnim pokoleniem
wymierających wędrowców pustyni ,
albo pierwszym pokoleniem Odrodzo-
nego Narodu Żydowskiego w Erec
Izrael .

Psalm 83 .

Pieśń psalmowa Asafa.

Boże nie Tobie milczyć ,

Nie zachowuj ciszy ni spokoju .

Bo oto wrogowie Twoi szumią ,

Nieprzyjaciele Twoi podnieśli głowę .

Przeciw ludowi Twemu chytrze knują ,

Zmawiają się przeciw Twym umiłowanym .

Powiadają : Nuże , wytraćmy ich , by nie byli narodem ,

By nie wspominano,więcej imienia Izrael .

O Boże , uczyń ich jako ten kurz wirujący ,

Jako sieczka pędzona przed wiatrem !

Jak ogień spala las ,

Jak płomień pożera drzewa gór ,

Tak goń ich swoją burzą ,

Orkanem swym wpraw ich w zamieszanie .

Niech się wiecznie wstydzą i lękają ,

Niech będą hańbieni i traceni .

A wiedzieć będą żeś Ty – Imię Twe Jehowa –

Ponad wszystkie światy .

Spolszczył .

<u>Young People's Voice</u>
Let the Jewish youth remember that it is either the last generation of the dying wanderers of the desert, or the first generation of the Reborn Jewish Nation in Eretz Israel.

Psalm 83
    Keep not Thou silence, O God: hold not Thy peace, and be not still, O God.
    For, lo, Thine enemies make a tumult: and they that hate Thee have lifted up
        their heads.
    They have taken crafty counsel against Thy people, and consulted against Thy
        hidden ones.
    They have said, "Come and let us cut them off from being a nation; that the
        name of Israel may be no more in remembrance."
    O my God, make them like a wheel; as the stubble before the wind.
    As the fire burneth a wood, and as the flame setteth the mountains on fire;
    So persecute them with Thy tempest, and make them afraid with Thy storm.
    Fill their faces with shame; that they may seek Thy name, O Lord.
    Let them be confounded and troubled forever; yea, let them be put to shame,
        and perish:
    That men may know that Thou, whose name alone is Jehovah, art the most high
        over all the earth.

Involvement in the clandestine youth press required a certain set of intellectual skills and abilities and remained the sphere of young people in their late
teens and early twenties. Young children, by contrast, were of course limited in
the kinds of resistance in which they could engage. In the ghettos of German-
occupied Europe, however, there remained one kind of resistance activity for
which their size and agility particularly suited them. The smuggling of foodstuffs and other essentials from the "Aryan side" was an illegal, but indispensable, component of ghetto life. It represented a vital source of food and supplies
for the captive community, and many families lived on the resources that their
members brought into the ghetto illicitly or the proceeds generated from selling
smuggled goods. Very young children were especially well adapted for this perilous enterprise. Their diminutive forms enabled them to slip through small gaps
and holes in the ghetto walls and to escape to municipal districts from which
Jews had been proscribed. Once outside the ghetto, their youth often shielded
them from the suspicion of German officials and local citizens so that they
might safely beg, steal, barter, or purchase provisions for consumption in their
incarcerated communities. Enterprising young smugglers often wore clothing
with concealed inner pockets in order to return laden with half their weight in
potatoes, bread, and other commodities.

Smuggling provided the sole means of survival for many families, and discouraging ghetto youngsters from such endeavors proved a difficult challenge, despite the best effort of child-welfare organizations. In his 1943 essay "Jewish Children on the Aryan Side,"[26] Oneg Shabbat's chief archivist, Emmanuel Ringelblum, recalled the case of a **CENTOS** administrator who tried to intercede on behalf of a group of orphaned smugglers who lodged together in the Warsaw ghetto. The youths earned up to fifty **złoty** per day through their exploits and had sufficient reserves of cash to set up in an apartment in the ghetto's Mila Street. "When the CENTOS worker proposed that they move into a boarding school," Ringelblum reported, "the children refused, declaring that they were managing very well by themselves. They said that the CENTOS should put starving children in the boarding schools."[27]

Ringelblum noted that the child smugglers he had seen possessed "the most extraordinary and fantastic courage."[28] The work was manifestly dangerous. Returning to the ghetto weighted down with contraband, the youths had little chance to escape potential captors, and many young "entrepreneurs" were intercepted with their heavy loads at ghetto exits or checkpoints. At the very least German officials or Jewish Order Police beat the youngsters mercilessly and seized their hard-won provisions. Many young smugglers paid with their lives for their efforts to bring food and necessities back to their starving community.

---

26. Emmanuel Ringelblum, *Polish-Jewish Relations during the Second World War*, ed. Joseph Kermish and Shmuel Krakowski (Jerusalem: Yad Vashem, 1974), 140–51.

27. Ringelblum, *Polish-Jewish Relations*, 149.

28. Ringelblum, *Polish-Jewish Relations*, 147.

DOCUMENT 9-6. Arrested at a checkpoint, a Jewish boy holds a bag of smuggled goods, Warsaw ghetto, c. 1941, USHMMPA WS# 60611B, courtesy of the YIVO Institute.

One of Ringelblum's Oneg Shabbat colleagues, Henryka Łazowertówna, helped to immortalize these everyday heroes who risked life and limb to convey food and supplies to the Warsaw ghetto. During the "Great Deportation" action of July 1942, Łazowertówna voluntarily joined her mother at the **Umschlagplatz** and was deported to her death at Treblinka.[29] In the preceding year, however, her poem "The Little Smuggler" had already been set to music and become a popular ballad among ghetto inhabitants.

29. Samuel D. Kassow, *Who Will Write Our History? Emmanuel Ringelblum, the Warsaw Ghetto, and the Oyneg Shabes Archive* (Bloomington: Indiana University Press, 2007), 182.

DOCUMENT 9-7. Henryka Łazowertówna (Lazowert), "The Little Smuggler," Warsaw ghetto, c. 1941, in Michał Borwicz, ed., *Pieśń ujdzie cało: Antologia wierszy o żydach pod okupacją niemiecką* (Warsaw: Centralna Żydowska Komisja Historyczna w Polsce, 1947), 115–16 (translated from the Polish).

The Little Smuggler (a Song)

Through walls, through holes, though sentry points,
Through wires, through rubble, through fences:
Hungry, daring, stubborn
I flee, dart like a cat.
At noon, at night, in dawning hours,
In blizzards, in the heat,
A hundred times I risk my life,
I risk my childish neck.

Under my arm a burlap sack,
On my back a tattered rag;
Running on my swift, young legs
With fear ever in my heart.
Yet everything must be suffered;
And all must be endured,
So that tomorrow you can all
Eat your fill of bread.

Through walls, through holes, through brickwork,
At night, at dawn, at day,
Hungry, daring, cunning,
Quiet as a shadow I move.
And if the hand of sudden fate
Seizes me at some point in this game,
It's only the common snare of life.
Mama, don't wait for me.

I won't return to you,
Your far-off voice won't reach.
The dust of the street will bury
The lost youngster's fate.
And only one grim thought,
A grimace on your lips:
Who, my dear Mama, who
Will bring you bread tomorrow?

The following photographs (Documents 9-8 and 9-9) are wrenching and arrest the eye instantly. Well known to students of World War II, the images portray one of the first public executions of resistance members by **Wehrmacht** soldiers following the German invasion of the Soviet Union. On October 26, 1941, members of the German 707th Infantry Division hanged twelve members of the communist underground near or on the grounds of a yeast factory in Minsk, Belorussia. The condemned were executed in groups of three. The Lithuanian collaborator tasked with recording these events presumably photographed only one of the proceedings in its entirety, near the gates of the old factory works. The first in the series of images he captured that day shows German and Lithuanian troops of the 707th parading three of the captive resistance figures through the streets of Minsk to the execution site. One of the prisoners, a young woman, commands attention. Around her neck she wears a placard reading in German and Russian, "We are partisans and have shot at German soldiers."

DOCUMENT 9-8. **Historians believe the girl in the center of the photograph to be teenage resistance member Masha Bruskina, being marched with her comrades Kiril Trus and Volodya Shcherbatsevich to their place of execution by German soldiers, Minsk, October 26, 1941, USHMMPA WS# 14101, courtesy of the Bundesarchiv, Bild 146-1972-026-43.**

The young girl is believed to be seventeen-year-old Masha Bruskina,[30] born in Minsk in 1924 to a Jewish family. Shortly after the German occupation of the Belorussian capital in late June 1941, she moved with her mother into the Minsk ghetto. The teenage Masha was, however, a communist and soon escaped to the city's "Aryan side," lightened her hair, and took on her mother's maiden name, Bugakova, to avoid detection. The young woman volunteered as a nurse at the hospital attached to the city's polytechnical institute, which occupying German forces had requisitioned as an infirmary for wounded Soviet prisoners of war. Perhaps at this juncture Masha joined a local resistance cell organized by Kiril Trus and Olga Shcherbatsevicha. The teenager used her post at the hospital to smuggle to the Soviet underground medical supplies and photographic equipment, the latter instrumental in creating false identity papers and other forged documentation. With her aid, other resistance members were able to remove Soviet prisoners of war to safety and to redeploy captured Soviet officers with significant combat experience to the ranks of the growing partisan movement. Despite the inscription on the placard she wore on the day of her death, Masha was not involved in armed resistance. At this time, such efforts were almost wholly the province of male members of the fledgling Belorussian resistance, while females functioned principally as couriers of supplies and information.

In early October 1941, a Soviet prisoner-patient denounced the resistance group to German authorities. Masha and several members of her cell, including leaders Kiril Trus and Olga Shcherbatsevicha, as well as the latter's sixteen-year-old son, Volodya Shcherbatsevich, were arrested. All, including Masha, were brutally beaten and tortured, but none would give the names of fellow resistance members.

On October 26, 1941, Masha, with Kiril and Volodya, walked together with their German and Lithuanian captors to the gates of the yeast factory near Karl Marx Street, the chosen place of execution. Those citizens who observed her that day remarked upon the calmness of the three condemned and the quiet courage and self-possession of the teenage girl.[31] Masha was chosen as the first victim. With her hands tightly bound, the young girl stepped onto a chair, aided by one of the soldiers, while a German officer adjusted the noose about her neck. In one of the extant photographs of the event, the teenager turned her

---

30. See Nechama Tec and Daniel Weiss, "A Historical Injustice: The Case of Masha Bruskina," *Holocaust and Genocide Studies* 11, no. 3 (winter 1997): 366–77.

31. See the testimony of Nina Antonovna Zhevzhik, reprinted in Tec and Weiss, "A Historical Injustice," 367–68.

back to the crowd. "When they put her on the stool," recalled eyewitnesses Petr
Pavlovich Borisenko, "the girl turned her face towards the fence. The executioners wanted her to stand with her face to the crowd, but she turned away and
that was that. No matter how much they pushed her and tried to turn her, she
remained standing with her back to the crowd. Only then did they kick away
the stool from under her."[32]

Document 9-9 portrays the young girl directly after her hanging. Her comrade, sixteen-year-old Volodya Shcherbatsevich, weeps at the sight of his dead
friend, as a German officer tightens the noose about his neck.

DOCUMENT 9-9. **The hanging of teenage resistance figures, believed to be Masha
Bruskina and Volodya Shcherbatsevich, by an officer of the German 707th Infantry
Division, Minsk, October 26, 1941, USHMMPA WS# 25136, courtesy of Ada Dekhtyar.**

The photographs became public in the immediate postwar period and soon
became iconic images of the Great Patriotic War, as the Soviet partisan resistance
movement came to be known. The two men in the photos were quickly identified, but the identity of the "unknown girl" remained a mystery for years to
come. Many historians now believe the teenage female in the photographs to be

---

32. Petr Pavlovich Borisenko, quoted in Lev Arkadiev and Ada Dekhtyar, "The Unknown
Girl: A Documentary Story," *Yiddish Writers' Almanac* 1 (1987): 187.

Masha Bruskina, based on extensive documentary evidence and identification by contemporary eyewitnesses, family members, and friends.

IN HIDING

When war began in Europe in September 1939, some 1.6 million Jewish children lived in those areas that would fall under the control of Nazi Germany and its allies. Historians estimate that as many as 1.1 million youngsters died in the Holocaust. The small percentage of young people who survived the genocide did so in part because they were the focus of rescue efforts by individuals, religious institutions, welfare agencies, and resistance organizations that sought to save Jews—especially Jewish children—from Nazi persecution. Many thousands survived because their rescuers concealed them in their own homes or because a dense network of supporters protected and sustained them.[33]

Jewish children faced exceptional challenges when they went into hiding. Some youngsters could pass as non-Jews and lived openly with their rescuers. In these circumstances, obtaining falsified identity papers, often purchased on the black market or provided by members of the underground resistance, was crucial. By acquiring forged papers, such children might have access to legitimate documentation from local authorities as well as to food and clothing ration coupons, essential for survival in Nazi Germany or its occupied territories. A hidden child's safety depended on strict secrecy. Rescuers often needed to invent elaborate fictions in order to justify the child's presence in their household, explaining to neighbors that the youngster was a distant relative or a refugee from a distant town or village. It was essential that the child adapt swiftly and completely to his new identity and environment. Young people learned to answer by their fictive name without fail and to avoid any language or mannerisms that might be considered "Jewish" or foreign. As most Jewish children were hidden by individuals or religious institutions that embraced faiths different from their own, youngsters carefully learned to recite the prayers and catechism of their "adopted" religion in order to avert the suspicions of both adults and

---

33. For a discussion of hidden children, see Howard Greenfeld, *The Hidden Children* (New York: Ticknor & Fields, 1993); Andre Stein, *Hidden Children: Forgotten Survivors of the Holocaust* (Toronto: Penguin Books, 1994); Ewa Kurek, *Your Life Is Worth Mine: How Polish Nuns Saved Hundreds of Jewish Children in German-Occupied Poland, 1939–1945* (New York: Hippocrene Books, 1997); Mordecai Paldiel, "Fear and Comfort: The Plight of Hidden Children in Wartime-Poland," *Holocaust and Genocide Studies* 6, no. 4 (1992): 397–413.

peers. One false word or gesture was sufficient to place both the child and his or her rescuers in jeopardy.

Of course, there were children who could not pass as "Aryans" or live openly with their protectors. Many youngsters had classical "Jewish features" or had spoken only Yiddish at home, and thus spoke the local language imperfectly or with a telltale accent. Others had lived in the immediate area before ghettoization or deportation had taken place and feared that former neighbors and acquaintances might recognize them. These children remained physically concealed for a significant portion, or for the entirety, of their time in hiding. In rural settings, such youngsters might live out the war in barns, root cellars, or farm outbuildings. In urban areas the risks were greater, so rescuers might conceal their young charges in attics, cellars, closets, or wardrobes, away from prying eyes. Youngsters often had to remain silent or even motionless in their hiding places for hours at a time. Both children and their protectors lived in constant fear lest a raised voice or a footfall should arouse the suspicion of their neighbors. While children with an "Aryan appearance" might continue their education and find companionship among school-age friends, children in complete concealment had no such options and spent interminable hours alone, often in uncomfortable quarters, without occupation or human interaction. Like their coreligionists living openly with foster families, clandestinely concealed children often moved from one hiding place to another to ensure the safety of both the rescuers and their charges. Some hidden children lived with their families; for others, life in hiding meant long separation from loved ones, a division that tormented both children and their parents.

Through his work as the chief archivist of the underground archive Oneg Shabbat, Emmanuel Ringelblum observed the minute workings of the Warsaw ghetto. In an essay in 1943, he chronicled the daily challenges faced by children hiding with family members or rescuers on Warsaw's "Aryan side."

DOCUMENT 9-10. Emmanuel Ringelblum, "Jewish Children on the Aryan Side," 1943, in Emmanuel Ringelblum, *Polish-Jewish Relations during the Second World War*, ed. Joseph Kermish and Shmuel Krakowski (Jerusalem: Yad Vashem, 1974), 140–45.

Jewish families rarely crossed to the Aryan side together. First the children went, while the parents stayed on in the ghetto in order to mobilize the necessary funds for staying on the Aryan side. Very often the parents gave up the idea of going across to the Aryan side, as they did not have the money to fix up the whole family. The cost of keeping a child on the Aryan side in the summer of 1942, when the number of children being sent over was at its peak, was very high, about 100 złoty a day. A sum was demanded for six months or a year in advance, for fear that the parents might be deported in the interim. Thus, a sum of several tens of thousands of złoty was required to fix up a child on the Aryan side and only very wealthy people could afford to do so. Parents of limited means and especially working intellectuals were forced to see their children taken as the first victims in the various "selections" and "actions." Not all Jewish parents wanted to send their children to the Aryan side. There were those who weighed the question of survival for the children, especially the youngest ones, when no one knew what would happen to the parents at the next "selection." Some parents argued that a child deprived of its parents' care will wither like a flower without the sun. There were children who strongly opposed being sent to the Aryan side. They did not want to go to the other side alone, but preferred to die together with their parents. [. . .]

The majority of children, however, agreed to go across to the Aryan side, as living conditions in the ghetto were terrible. They were not allowed to leave their flats, they stayed for whole weeks in stuffy, uncomfortable hide-outs, they did not see daylight for long months. No wonder then that they let themselves be tempted by the promise of going out into the street, of walking in a garden, etc., and agreed to go to the Aryan side by themselves.

I know an eight-year-old boy who stayed for eight months on the Aryan side without his parents. The boy was hiding with friends of his father's, who treated him like their own child. The child spoke in whispers and moved as silently as a cat, so that the neighbors should not become aware of the presence of a Jewish child. He often had to listen to the anti-Semitic talk of young Poles who came to visit the landlord's daughters. Then he would pretend not to listen to the conversation and become engrossed in reading one of the books which he devoured in quantities. On one occasion he was present when the young visitors boasted that Hitler had taught the Poles how to deal with the Jews and that the remnant that survived the Nazi slaughter would be dealt with likewise. The boy was choking with tears; so that no one would notice he was upset, he hid in the kitchen and there burst out crying. He is now staying in a narrow, stuffy hideout, but he is happy because he is with his parents.

The situation is much worse for the children who have lost their parents, who were taken away to Treblinka. Some of their Aryan protectors have meanwhile taken a liking to the children and keep them and look after them. But these are only a small percentage of the protectors, generally people of limited means in whom Mammon has not yet killed all human feeling. People like these have to suffer on account of the Jewish children, but they do not throw them out into the street. The more energetic among them know how to fix themselves up and receive money subsidies from suitable social organizations. We know of cases where the governesses of wealthy children took care of them after their parents had been taken away to Treblinka. They keep these children out of their beggarly wages and don't want to leave them to their fate. Some of these Jewish orphans were fixed up in institutions, registered as having come from places affected by the displacement of the Polish population (Zamość, Hrubieszów, Poznań, Lublin, etc.). A considerable percentage of the orphans returned to the ghetto, where the Jewish Council fixed them up in boarding schools; they were taken away in the "resettlement actions." There were frequent instances, when the "protectors," having received a large sum of money, simply turned the child out into the street. There were even worse cases where the "protectors" turned Jewish children over to the uniformed police or the Germans, who sent them back to the ghetto while it was still in existence.

There were also cases of Jewish children, especially very small children, who were adopted by childless couples, or by noble individuals who wanted to manifest their attitude to the tragedy of the Jews. A few Jewish children were rescued by being placed in foundling homes, where they arrive as Christian children; they are brought by Polish Police, who, for remuneration of course, report them as having been found in staircase wells, inside the entrances to blocks of flats, etc.

There were no problems with Jewish children as far as the need for keeping their Jewish origin secret. In the ghetto Jewish children went through stern schooling for life. [. . .] They ceased to be children and grew up fast, surpassing their elders in many things. So when they were sent to the Aryan side, their parents could assure their Aryan friends and acquaintances that their little daughter or son would never breathe a word about his Jewish origin and would keep the secret to the grave. I know of a young girl who was dying in an Aryan hospital, far from her parents. She kept the secret of her origin till her death. Even in those moments of the death agony, when earthly ties are loosed and people no longer master themselves, she did not betray herself by a word or the least movement.

When the nurse who was present at her death bed called her by her Jewish name, Dorka, she would not reply, for she remembered that she was only allowed to respond to the sound of the Aryan name, Ewa.

Even the youngest children were able to carry out their parents' instructions and conceal their Jewish origin expertly. I remember a four-year-old tot who replied to my asking him treacherously what he was called before—a question often put to children by police agents—by giving his Aryan name and surname and declaring emphatically that he never had any other name.

Hidden children often spent anguished weeks and months away from their parents. Szepsel Griner, born shortly before the outbreak of World War II, became separated from his family in the early years of the German occupation of Poland. Presumably because Szepsel was the youngest child, his father placed the toddler with a Polish farmer before relocating his wife and remaining children to a hiding place in the home of an acquaintance. Szepzel's father visited him daily, bringing his son toys and provisions, and it was from him that the small boy learned of the deportation and murder of his mother and siblings. After a time, the elder Griner stopped coming to the farm, and Szepzel came to understand that his father had been killed. Following the liberation of Zamość by Soviet forces, the youngster spent a year in a Polish orphanage. Discovered at the home by his nineteen-year-old cousin, Szepsel was adopted by an aunt who had been living in Russia. In the immediate postwar period, the young boy related his experiences in hiding to an official of the Jewish Historical Commission in Warsaw.

DOCUMENT 9-11. Oral history of Szepsel Griner by the Central Jewish Historical Commission in Poland, c. 1947, USHMMA RG 15.084, Holocaust Survivor Testimonies, 301/2284 (translated from the Polish).

Statement 35

Szepsel Griner, eight years old, born in Zamość. Before the war he lived in Zamość. During the occupation in Zamość. Currently he lives in Wałbrzych 1-Maja 4:

When the German marched into our area, a man knocked on our window and called to Papa to flee. Papa took some clothes with him and fled to a German acquaintance. We—that is, I, Mama, my sister and two brothers, as well as my uncle—were supposed to follow.

Once, as we sat in our hiding place, the Germans came to take us away, but our German defended us. He said he would not deliver us up, and they had to go away empty-handed. We stayed there hidden for ten days.

Papa lodged me with a Polish woman, and he himself went to find another hiding place. He found an empty room at someone's home. He prepared a lot to eat there and brought Mama, my sister, and my brothers there. After four weeks they were discovered by the Germans and brought to a camp. Mama was sick. The Germans came to the camp, and Papa understood that they wanted to kill all the Jews, so he fled, but my sister and my brothers didn't manage to get away. The Germans took them, deported them, and killed them. Papa came to me and told me all of that. At first he didn't want to tell me any of this, but I saw that he was so sad, and I cried constantly that I wanted to go to Mama. So he told me everything. Papa came to me daily. Every time he brought vodka for the Pole and other things with him. He said to me that I should be good, mind the Pole, and not wander out upon the farm.

Papa brought me a revolver (a play one), a harmonica, and other toys. The whole day I played the harmonica.

In the shed next to me the farmer kept rabbits, which I liked to play with.

At night I cried often. I was so sad, I wanted so badly to have someone from among my relatives with me.

I had completely lost my appetite and I got very bad food to eat besides. For a long time, Papa didn't come anymore to me. This is when I understood that the Germans had killed Papa too.

Once I sat in the house and looked out the window. I saw that many Jews with children were being led away. Some of them didn't have any hands. Where they were brought to, I don't know.

I always felt as if I were going to burst into tears, but I only cried when no one was in the house, or at nights.

Later, the Russians started throwing bombs, and soon they also came to us.

During World War II, thousands of Jewish children were concealed by conscientious individuals, by religious and resistance groups, and by various aid and relief organizations dedicated to helping Jews and other persecutees escape from harm in areas controlled by Nazi Germany and its allies. In most cases, hidden children lived with their rescuers or in a series of safe houses, isolated from friends and loved ones. Yet the Shoah's most famous hidden child did not suffer her long ordeal alone but lived in concealment with her family, aided and insulated from deportation by a network of friends and supporters. That youngster was, of course, **Anne Frank**, whose diary has captured the imagination of generations of young readers and personalized the fate of hundreds of thousands of children murdered in the Holocaust.

Annelies (Anne) Frank was born in Frankfurt am Main, Germany, on June 12, 1929, the second daughter of prosperous businessman Otto Frank, and his wife, Edith. Immediately after Hitler's rise to power, Anne fled with her parents and elder sister, Margot, to Amsterdam in the Netherlands. The Franks had hoped to escape antisemitic persecution in their native Germany, but when German forces invaded Dutch territory, the family once again figured as targets of Nazi anti-Jewish policy. When Margot Frank received a summons for deportation on July 5, 1942, Otto Frank convinced his family to go into hiding. On the following day, the family entered a narrow, three-story annex attached to Frank's Opetka office building at 263 Prinsengracht[34]; the family would not leave it again until their arrests two years later. The vivacious Anne had just received a plaid-covered autograph book for her twelfth birthday and now began to use the volume as her diary, keeping a faithful and detailed account of events as they took place in the "secret annex." Addressing her entries to "Dear Kitty," a favorite character in a book series that she had been reading, the young Anne captured a portrait of a family in hiding; she also vividly portrayed a young girl growing up under desperate circumstances. Among the individuals introduced in her journal were the van Pels family and Fritz Pfeffer, friends or acquaintances who eventually joined the Frank family in their hiding space,[35] and the groups' rescuers, including Miep Gies and Viktor Kugler, Otto Frank's former employees, who brought food, supplies, and information and ensured the hidden Jews' safety during their confinement. In March 1944, while listening to Radio Oranje, a Dutch resistance radio station, Anne heard a broadcast by Gerrit Bolkestein, education minister within the Dutch government in exile. Bolkestein announced that he would make a public record of the Dutch population's experiences during World War II and asked his countrymen

---

34. Otto Frank had owned two businesses in Amsterdam that produced and sold pectin and other food preservatives and spices. After Nazi German forces overran the Netherlands, Frank was forced to liquidate his assets. He transferred the ownership of the businesses, including Opetka, to trusted colleagues so that he could continue to make sufficient income for his family and might recover his assets in the postwar period.

35. Anne Frank gave pseudonyms to fellow dwellers in the annex who were not members of her immediate family. The van Pelses received the fictive name "van Daan," while the dentist Fritz Pfeffer became "Albert Dussel."

to save their letters and journals for collection in the postwar. At this point, Anne began composing and editing her diary with future publication in mind. She continued writing until August 1, 1944.

This diary entry would be her last. Three days later, on August 4, 1944, members of the SS and Dutch Green Police discovered the Franks' hiding place and arrested its inhabitants. Anne, her family, and the friends who had been concealed with them were transferred to the Dutch transit camp Westerbork, then on September 3 to Auschwitz. Sometime in October 1944, Anne and Margot arrived on a transport from Auschwitz to the **Bergen Belsen concentration camp**. Both succumbed to **typhus** there in late February or early March 1945, just weeks before the liberation of the camp by British forces. The sole survivor of the group in hiding, Otto Frank,[36] returned to Amsterdam in the summer of 1945. There he recovered his daughter's diary and papers, which had been retained by Miep Gies. Anne's diary appeared in print for the first time in Dutch in 1947 and has been in publication ever since.[37]

Two days before Anne Frank wrote the last lines in her journal, another young girl in Amsterdam, Louise Israels, was celebrating her second birthday in hiding. She had been born on July 30, 1942, in the Dutch city of Haarlem, where she lived with her parents, grandparents, and elder brother. The Israelses were a secular and assimilated Jewish family. Louise's father, a reserve officer with the Dutch army, worked in the family business selling women's lingerie and accessories. Although the Nazi occupation of the Netherlands had imposed a number of antisemitic measures and restrictions upon the Jewish population, the Israelses, like many Dutch Jews, hoped that their little family might emerge from the war years intact. Two events shook their confidence. In early March 1943, in a bold and imaginative move, the Dutch national resistance bombed the central population registry office in Amsterdam, effectively hindering German authorities from comparing forged personal documents held by Jews and other persecutees in Holland against authentic public records. Nazi officials countered this measure with a series of brutal reprisals. In Haarlem, Nazi occupiers arrested the Israelses'

---

36. Hermann van Pels was gassed shortly after arrival at Auschwitz, where Edith Frank died of starvation in January 1945. Fritz Pfeffer perished in Neuengamme concentration camp in December 1944. Peter van Pels, Anne's love interest, survived until the last days of the war, dying of exhaustion at Mauthausen on May 5, 1945. Mrs. van Pels joined Margot and Anne briefly at Bergen Belsen and probably died shortly thereafter on a transport bound for Theresienstadt.

37. For a further discussion of Anne Frank and the influence of her diary, see Anne Frank, *The Diary of Anne Frank: The Revised Critical Edition*, ed. David Barouw and Gerrold van der Stroom, trans. Arnold J. Pomerans, B. M. Mooyaart-Doubleday, and Susan Massotty (New York: Doubleday, 2001); Hyman Aaron Enzer and Sandra Solotaroff-Enzer, eds., *Anne Frank: Reflections on Her Life and Legacy* (Urbana: University of Illinois Press, 2000).

neighbor, the president of the city's Jewish community, and shot him and nine other prominent Jews before the eyes of their fellow citizens. At the same time, the Jews of Haarlem received a summons to concentrate in Amsterdam as a prelude to deportation. Spurred by these events, Louise's father devised a daring plan to save his family. First, he secured false papers for his wife and children from the Dutch underground. Then, liquidating all available assets, Israels located a small apartment near the city's famous Vondelpark and paid the leasing agent funds sufficient for ten years' rent.

Sometime in the spring months of 1943, the young family slipped quietly inside the doors of their new residence. They would not emerge again until the arrival of Allied forces in Amsterdam two years later. Joining the Israelses in hiding was a young woman named Selma, the daughter of the president of Haarlem's Jewish community who had been murdered just weeks before. Her family had been deported following her father's death, and the young woman now became an integral part of the Israels family. She would prove a valuable source of information when a maturing Louise Israels began to piece together her wartime experiences.

Unlike the more famous Frank family, who lived in a secret annex, the Israelses literally hid in plain sight, lodged in a residential apartment building amid dozens of neighbors. It was a perilous existence in which the threat of denunciation was an ever-present reality. The family lived in a silent world, isolated from the vibrant city outside. After dark, Louise's father risked a night-time curfew to provide his family with food and firewood. Israels' army reserve comrades represented a vital lifeline for the little household, regularly bringing them provisions and news from the outside world.

In the summer of 1944, the family had been living in hiding for more than one year. Although their situation was certainly preferable to that of thousands of Dutch Jews awaiting deportation in transit camps such as Westerbork and Vught, the family knew hunger and privation and lived in constant fear lest a raised voice or obtrusive noise should rouse the suspicion of their neighbors. So, when little Louise's second birthday arrived on July 30, 1944, her parents decided to use the event to lift the family's morale. In a photograph from that day, Louise wears a new dress for her party, which her mother made from an old blouse. She is perched on a rattan doll's chair that her father purchased through Dutch friends "on the outside." Her nurse, Selma, cobbled together old scraps to make a rag doll, which Louise clutches wistfully. For the occasion, her elder brother has lent her his favorite pull-toy horse, a special treat—but just for the day![38]

---

38. Information concerning the story of the Israelses' years in hiding is provided courtesy of Louise Lawrence-Israels.

DOCUMENT 9-12. **Louise Israels celebrates her second birthday in hiding, Amsterdam, July 30, 1944, USHMMPA WS# 16427, courtesy of Louise Lawrence-Israels.**

Louise and her family would remain in hiding for almost ten more months before Canadian forces liberated the city of Amsterdam on May 5, 1945. In the Netherlands Louise Israels would eventually earn a degree in physical education; in 1967 she married American physician Sidney Lawrence and immigrated to the United States. She later became a volunteer at the U.S. Holocaust Memorial Museum, where her small rattan doll's chair is displayed in the museum's "Permanent Exhibition."

The stories of two young girls in Amsterdam, Louise Israels and Anne Frank, present us with two very different pictures of children in hiding and represent dramatically different fates.

CHILDREN AND AID ORGANIZATIONS: THE POLITICS OF RESCUE

Among the myriad attempts to rescue children from persecution during the Holocaust, none is more celebrated than the efforts of public and private refugee and child-welfare organizations to bring children from Germany to Great Britain, collectively known as the *Kindertransporte* (children's transports). Following the violent *Kristallnacht* **pogrom** staged by the Nazi authorities on Jews in Germany on November 9 and 10, 1938, the British government eased immigration restrictions for certain categories of Jewish refugees. Spurred by British public opinion and the persistent efforts of refugee aid committees, most notably the British Committee for the Jews of Germany and the Movement for the Care of Children from Germany, British authorities agreed to permit an unspecified number of children under the age of seventeen to enter Great Britain from Germany and German-annexed territories in what had formerly been Austria and the Czech lands.[39]

Private citizens or organizations had to guarantee to pay for each child's care, education, and eventual emigration from Britain. In return, the British government agreed to allow unaccompanied refugee children to enter the country on temporary travel visas. It was understood at the time that when the crisis was over, the youngsters would return to their families. Parents or guardians could not travel with their children.

The first *Kindertransport* arrived in Harwich, Great Britain, on December 2, 1938, bringing some two hundred children, many from a Jewish orphanage in Berlin that had been destroyed during *Kristallnacht*. Like this convoy, most transports left by train from Berlin, Vienna, Prague, and other major cities in central Europe. Children from smaller towns and villages traveled from their homes to these collection points in order to join the transports. Jewish organizations inside the Greater German Reich—specifically the **Reichsvereinigung der Juden in Deutschland** (Reich Association of Jews in Germany),[40] headquartered in Berlin, as well as the Jewish Community Organization

---

39. For a discussion of the *Kindertransporte*, see Mark Jonathan Harris and Deborah Oppenheimer, *Into the Arms of Strangers: Stories of the Kindertransport* (New York: Bloomsbury Publishers of St. Martin's Press, 2000); Rebekka Göpfert, *Der jüdische Kindertransport von Deutschland nach England, 1938–1939: Geschichte und Erinnerung* (Frankfurt: Campus Verlag, 1999); Anne L. Fox and Eva Abraham-Podietz, *Ten Thousand Children: True Stories Told by Children who Escaped the Holocaust on the Kindertransport* (West Orange, NJ: Behrman House, 1999).

40. In early 1939, this organization replaced the Reichsvertretung der deutschen Juden (Reich Representation of German Jewry), founded in September 1933.

(Kultusgemeinde) in Vienna—planned the transports. These associations generally favored children whose emigration was urgent because their parents were in concentration camps or no longer able to support them. They also gave priority to homeless children and orphans.

Children chosen for a *Kindertransport* convoy traveled by train to ports in Belgium and the Netherlands, then by ship to Harwich. At least one of the early transports left from the port of Hamburg in Germany, while some children from Czechoslovakia flew by plane directly to Britain. The last transport from Germany left on September 1, 1939, just as World War II began, while the very last *Kindertransport* sailed from the Netherlands for Britain on May 14, 1940, the day on which the Dutch army surrendered to German forces. In all, the rescue operation brought about nine to ten thousand children, some seventy-five hundred of them Jewish, from Germany, Austria, Czechoslovakia, and Poland to Great Britain.

After the children's transports arrived in Harwich, those children with sponsors went to London to meet their host families. Those children without sponsors were housed in a summer camp in Dovercourt Bay and in other facilities until individual families agreed to care for them or until hostels could be organized to accept larger groups of children. About half the children lived with foster families. The others stayed in boarding houses, at schools, or on farms throughout Great Britain. In 1940, British authorities interned about one thousand adolescents from the children's transport program as enemy aliens on the Isle of Man and in other internment camps in Canada and Australia. Despite their classification as German aliens, some of the young men from the children's transport program later joined the British army and fought in the war against Germany. After the war, many children from the children's transport program became citizens of Great Britain or emigrated to Israel, the United States, Canada, or Australia. Most of these children would never again see their parents, who were murdered in the Holocaust.

Helmuth Ehrenreich was one of thousands of German children fortunate enough to gain a place aboard a *Kindertransport* headed for Britain. Born in Frankfurt am Main on May 11, 1928, Helmuth was the son of Nathan Ehrenreich, a prominent pianist, choral director, and music critic, and his wife, Frieda. In the early summer of 1939, a distant cousin had gained a berth on a children's transport, but then decided to remain behind with his family. Frieda Ehrenreich accepted her relatives' offer to send young Helmuth in his cousin's place, a decision that saved her son's life. Eleven-year-old Helmuth traveled with a *Kindertransport* on June 20, 1939, arriving in Harwich the following day. In the following weeks, he was housed at a refugee camp in Margate, before being lodged with a host family in the heart of London. Helmuth enjoyed exploring the city and practicing his newly gained English skills, but when London became the target of German bombs during the Blitz, he, like many British children, was evacuated to the English countryside. There Helmuth settled with a foster family that harbored antisemitic sympathies, and they mistreated him. Fortunately, in August 1939, his mother had succeeded in obtaining an entry visa for Britain and fled Germany on one of the last airplane flights from Frankfurt to London before hostilities began. She found work as a housekeeper in Ditchling, in East Sussex, and was able to relocate her son to a nearby home so that they could visit each other more easily. That winter the family's U.S. visas were finally issued, and Nathan Ehrenreich, who had spent the last year in a Dutch refugee camp following his arrest on *Kristallnacht*, arrived in New York City. In March 1940, nine months after Helmuth's voyage to Britain aboard a *Kindertransport*, the entire family was reunited in the United States. Adopting the more American name "Henry," the young man thrived in the United States, excelling in high school and attending Cornell and Columbia universities. In 1963 he became a professor of engineering and applied physics at Harvard University, a post he retained, finally as emeritus professor, until his death in 2008.

DOCUMENT 9-13. **Child identification card of Helmuth Ehrenreich, Police Presidium of Frankfurt am Main, June 16, 1939, USHMMA, Acc. 2006.396, Ehrenreich Family Papers (translated from the German).**

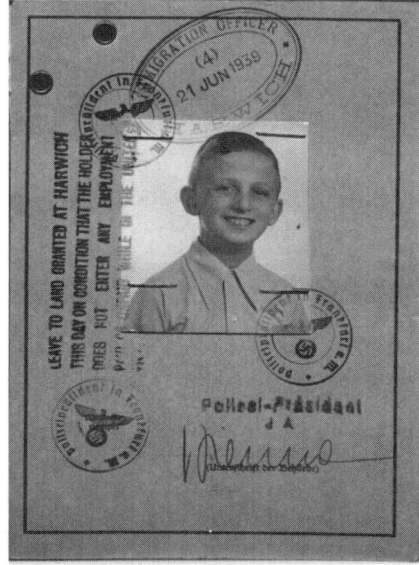
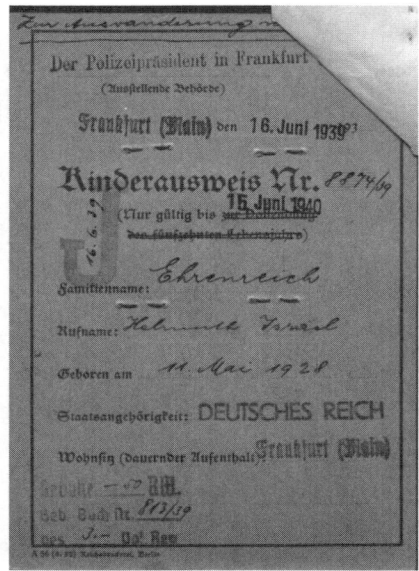

[Handwritten] For emigration to [England]
The Police Presidium in Frankfurt am Main
(Issuing Authority)
Frankfurt am Main, June 16, 1939
Child Identification Number 8874/39
[Only valid until June 15, 1940]
Family name: Ehrenreich
First Name: Helmuth Israel[41]
Born on: May 11, 1928
Nationality: German Reich
Residence (permanent): Frankfurt am Main
Fee 50 RM
[Administrative remarks]

---

41. Beginning in January 1939, all Jews whose given names did not correspond to those on an authorized register of "Jewish" names had to add the name "Sara" after their first name if female and "Israel" if male. The letter J stamped on the identification card indicates that Helmuth Ehrenreich is a Jew.

Many aid agencies worked to ensure the success of the *Kindertransport* endeavor. The effort of British child-welfare societies to rescue children from Nazi Germany inspired Jewish and refugee organizations in the United States to emulate the English example. In the early 1930s a small number of German Jewish children arrived as unaccompanied minors on U.S. shores. They came largely through the sponsorship of private citizens or under the auspices of local Jewish congregations who undertook the costs of their immigration and provided foster homes for the youngsters. Such efforts increased as Nazi anti-semitic policy radicalized in the wake of the November 1938 *Kristallnacht* pogrom. Even in this time of sorest need, refugee organizations faced major obstacles in bringing young children to the United States. The effects of the Great Depression had sparked hostility to foreigners entering the United States, and American internal and foreign policy continued to place limits on immi-gration.[42] The Wagner-Rogers Bill, cosponsored by Senator Robert Wagner (D-NY) and Representative Edith Rogers (R-MA), proposed to admit twenty thousand Jewish refugee children under the age of fourteen from National Socialist Germany but failed to garner congressional approval in February 1939. Although many welfare organizations were daunted by this decision, one young American couple refused to abandon their plans to rescue Jewish youngsters from Nazi oppression.

The mission to bring fifty children to safety in the United States was the brainchild of Philadelphia lawyer **Gilbert Kraus** and his wife, **Eleanor**.[43] Kraus's father had been a founding member of the Independent Order Brith Sholom, a Jewish fraternal organization that, particularly in the first decades of the twentieth century, supported many charitable and educational programs for Jewish immigrants. Kraus's local chapter had recently erected a new residence center just outside Philadelphia. Faced with the mounting crisis in Europe, Brith Sholom's grand master, Louis Levine, suggested to Kraus that the complex be used to house refugee Jewish children from Germany.

Both Levine and Kraus were aware that many efforts on the part of wel-fare and religious organizations to arrange a kind of *Kindertransport* to America had met with failure. Hampering such efforts was an otherwise reasonable U.S. Labor Department guideline making it unlawful for any organization to bring unaccompanied children into the United States. A capable lawyer, Kraus now

---

42. See David Wyman, *Paper Walls: America and the Refugee Crisis, 1938–1941* (New York: Pantheon, 1985); Richard Breitman and Alan Kraut, *American Refugee Policy and European Jewry, 1933–1945* (Bloomington: University of Indiana Press, 1987).

43. The rescue efforts of Gilbert and Eleanor Kraus are documented in Eleanor Kraus, "Don't Wave Good-bye" (unpublished manuscript, private collection, c. 1940).

suggested locating fifty members within his local Brith Sholom lodge who would be willing to serve as individual sponsors for the children. Each would have to pledge to support a young person and to guarantee that he or she would not become a public charge. On February 3, 1939, Kraus laid out his plans to Assistant Secretary of State George Messerschmidt.

DOCUMENT 9-14. Letter of Gilbert Kraus to George Messerschmidt, assistant secretary of state, February 3, 1939 (National Archives and Records Administration, RG-59, General Records of the Department of State, Decimal File 150.6265/610).

Law Offices

Kraus & Weyl

Gilbert J. Kraus	Bell Telephone
Edward S. Weyl	Kingsley-4416

_____ Bankers Securities Building _____

Philadelphia

H. J. Seman	Cable Addres
Milton Brooks	"Kreyl"
Jerome L. Markovitz	
	February 3, 1939

Hon. George Messerschmidt
Assistant Secretary of State
Washington, D.C.

Dear Mr. Messerschmidt:

Following our recent interviews and as suggested by you, I wish to submit a general outline of our plan.

The members of the Independent Order Brith Sholom are extremely eager to bring fifty refugee children from Germany to the United States. They are ready to provide a home and education for them. The Society was founded in 1905 as a Jewish fraternal institution, to provide a refuge for immigrant Jews in America. Brith Sholom has become an organization of large size and substantial wealth, with membership in fifty-three cities, in twenty States of the Union. Mr. Louis Levine, who attended our conferences with you, is the present Grand Master. He is a substantial citizen of New York City.

The Society has just completed a home in Collegeville, Pa., at a cost of $250,000. It has eighty-five acres of beautiful farm country ground and is twenty-eight miles from Philadelphia. Due to the anxiety and distress of the members over the pressing need for aid for German refugees, the

Order wishes to turn over this new home for the housing of the refugee children. Last summer, the grounds were used as a summer camp for one hundred and fifteen children. The home has complete modern equipment, tile swimming pool, recreation hall, infirmary, solarium, large spacious bedrooms, kitchens, dining hall and other necessary facilities.

We will supply satisfactory affidavits and guarantees from individuals of good standing and character to fulfill the public charge requirements. Each child shall have his own affidavit. There are ample private funds to provide transportation of the children from Germany to Philadelphia and for their support, maintenance, and education.

The children are to be selected from those within the quota regulations whose numbers have been reached or are about to be reached and have met all other essential requirements except that relating to the public charge clause. For these, we will be prepared to supply satisfactory affidavits and guarantees from the United States, executed by private individuals.

To accomplish our purposes as promptly as possible, Mrs. Kraus and I are prepared to go to Germany to arrange with the proper Governmental authorities for the selection of eligible children, the filing of the affidavits, and the transportation of the children.

We should like, if possible, to get under way immediately, since there is still the better part of three months of this year's quota left for emigration from Germany to the United States. Before planning any further, we await word from your Department concerning the feasibility of our plan and news from Germany.

Hoping to hear from you as promptly and conveniently as possible, and with sincere thanks for all the assistance you have given us, I remain,

Respectfully yours,

[signature]

Gilbert J. Kraus

GJK/B

Shortly after posting this letter, Kraus journeyed to Washington, DC, to discuss his proposal with Messerschmidt. During the interview, the assistant secretary suggested that the real difficulty lodge members would likely encounter in sponsoring the children lay in the current U.S. quota system, which set strict limits on immigration from foreign countries. In the early months of 1939, the number of German emigrants registering with U.S. consulates had already filled the German quota for the entire year. There would be no exceptions, Messerschmidt noted; each youngster would have to wait until his or her quota number came up in order to obtain a visa.

Returning to Philadelphia, Kraus tried to discover a legal way to work within the existing quota system in order to secure the appropriate paperwork for the children. He seized upon the idea of using so-called dead-number visas—visas that for various reasons had gone unused in the previous year and might be carried over and applied to the next year's quota. Uncertain that such a strategy would prove successful, the Krauses resolved to go to Germany themselves and to work with consular officials to bring a group of children back to the United States.

Their efforts met with stiff opposition from many local and national aid agencies. Representatives of several established Jewish refugee and charitable organizations wrote to the Krauses and to their State Department contacts, suggesting that they abandon their plans.[44] The Krauses "should be [. . .] stopped from this undertaking at all costs," wrote one director of an American Jewish aid agency to George Messerschmidt:

> They could be harmful and a hindrance to those agencies which are properly qualified to do this work. We are certain they could not possibly be successful in this endeavor. [. . .] As you know, we are sincerely engaged in trying to bring children to this country and we feel that personal and sensational publicity on the part of outsiders would make trouble for all. We must discredit these people in every way and I urge you to give this matter your serious consideration. You must be fully aware that the only thing they seek is private publicity.[45]

In the face of intense criticism, Gilbert and Eleanor Kraus set sail for Europe in the early spring of 1939. Despite the danger the Jewish Krauses faced in traveling to Nazi Germany, the couple journeyed from Berlin to Vienna, where representatives of that city's Jewish Community Organization (Israelitische Kultusgemeinde) helped to interview potential young candidates for emigration, together with their parents. On May 21, the Krauses left the former Austrian capital with fifty children, aged four to fourteen, whom they had chosen for sponsorship by Brith Sholom members. The Krauses traveled with their young charges by train to Berlin in order to apply for formal visas from the American consulate. In the end, Gilbert Kraus's gamble to make a claim for dead-number visas paid off, and all fifty Austrian youngsters received the necessary papers for entry to the United States. On June 3, 1939, the

---

44. See "Fifty German-Jewish Refugee Children," *The Jewish Exponent*, June 9, 1939.
45. Kraus, "Don't Wave Good-bye," 17–18.

Krauses and their wards sailed into New York Harbor aboard the SS *President Harding*. The children were bussed directly to "Sholomville," Brith Sholom's residence outside Philadelphia, which had been equipped to house the youngsters. Despite the excellent facilities available there, community leaders quickly resolved that the young refugees would thrive best in private homes rather than in an institutional setting, and by Labor Day of 1939, Brith Sholom members had found foster families for each of the fifty children. Eleanor and Gilbert Kraus themselves took in a pair of siblings from Vienna, Robert and Johanna Braun. These children remained with their benefactors until the end of the war and were ultimately reunited with their parents.

DOCUMENT 9-15. **Aided by philanthropists Gilbert and Eleanor Kraus, a group of Austrian Jewish children finds safe haven in the United States, June 3, 1939, USHMMPA WS# 96464, courtesy of Anita Willens.**

An oft-cited African proverb suggests that it takes a village to raise a child. The same may also be said of saving the lives of children during the Holocaust. The Krauses' successful rescue of fifty Austrian children in 1939 demonstrates that, with community support, a few committed individuals could overcome enormous odds in order to bring Jewish youngsters to the safety of American shores. But often it took a veritable network of agencies to protect Jewish children from the threat of deportation. In the years immediately preceding World War II, the Committee to Assist Jewish Refugee Children (Comité d'Assistance aux Enfants Juif Refugiés, or CAEJR) had worked to shelter Jewish refugee youths in Belgium. The organization had been founded by Marguerite Goldschmidt-Brodsky, whose husband, Alfred, served as treasurer of the Belgian Red Cross. In response to the thousands of German and stateless refugees fleeing persecution in Nazi Germany, Goldschmidt-Brodsky and a handful of determined society matrons, among them Lily Felddegen, worked to persuade the Belgian government to grant asylum to Jewish children until they could safely emigrate to other countries. Many of the children under their protection had entered Belgium illegally or come as a part of organized transports from the German city of Cologne, adjacent to the Belgian border. The CAEJR arranged foster families for many of the children; over one hundred of their charges lived in homes in the Brussels suburbs organized under their auspices, Home Speyer for boys and Home General Bernheim for girls. Following the German invasion of Belgium, most of these youngsters escaped on one of the many refugee trains to southern France. For nearly a year they lived in primitive conditions on a large farm in Seyre, near the city of Toulouse; there many of the older youths aided in agricultural work on-site or on the neighboring estates.

In the meanwhile, Marguerite Goldschmidt-Brodsky had also fled to southern France, where her husband and his Red Cross colleagues were working to settle hundreds of Belgian Jewish refugees. From their home in Cahors, she used her husband's connections with the Swiss Red Cross, persuading members of its auxiliary organization, the Secours Suisse aux Enfants (Swiss Children's Aid) to rescue "her" children. Local members of the Secours Suisse were able to furnish the youngsters and their caretakers, Elka and Alexander Frank, with much-needed food and supplies, and in the early spring of 1941, they succeeded in moving the young people to an abandoned castle, the Château de la Hille, in a rural area of the Pyrenees near the Spanish border. During the children's tenure at La Hille, an unknown youth created the drawing shown in Document 9-16, capturing the arrival of his companions and rescuers at the old château. Although the castle was located near the French town of Pamiers, the young artist placed a Swiss flag upon its ramparts in honor of the welfare organization that had done so much to support them.

DOCUMENT 9-16. **Child's drawing of Château de la Hille, La Hille, France, c. 1942, USHMMPA WS# 45699, courtesy of Vera Friedlander.**

Nearly all of La Hille's young occupants survived the Holocaust. Through the intervention of Lily Felddegen, one of the children's Belgian benefactors now working through the Hebrew Immigrant Aid Society (HIAS)[46] in New York, the U.S. Committee for the Care of European Children and the American

---

46. An international organization established in 1881 in New York City to assist the emigration of Jews fleeing czarist Russia, HIAS offered important immigration and resettlement services to Jewish populations fleeing the persecution of Nazi Germany. After the Nazis came to power in early 1933, the most urgent mission of HIAS became the emigration of Germany's Jewish population. By providing an emigration route through France, Spain, and Portugal to North and South America during wartime, HIAS (joining with two other immigration services under the name HICEM) continued to provide emigration assistance to Jews who escaped the occupied territories. In the postwar period, HIAS joined with an arm of the American Jewish Joint Distribution Committee to form the Displaced Persons Coordinating Committee and administer emigration and family reunification services in hundreds of displaced persons camps.

Friends Service Committee,[47] a Quaker organization, furnished seventeen of the youngest children at La Hille with visas to enter the United States in the summer of 1941. A year later, in August 1942, French police conducted a raid upon the château, arresting forty teenagers from the group aged fifteen or older and incarcerating them in LeVernet internment camp to await deportation. Desperate to rescue them, Rösli Näf,[48] the educator who had inherited the directorship of the La Hille colony, immediately contacted their benefactors in the Secours Suisse. At her instigation, chief Secours Suisse administrator Maurice Dubois[49] successfully negotiated with Rene Bousquet,[50] secretary general of the **Vichy** police, for the release of the children. After this narrow escape, Näf initiated efforts to smuggle the remaining children into neutral Switzerland or nearby Spain. A handful of these youngsters were apprehended by border police and perished at the Auschwitz and **Majdanek**

47. The American Friends Service Committee (AFSC) is a Quaker organization founded in 1917 to provide an alternative to military service in the pacifist tradition and to furnish humanitarian aid to civilians overseas. Headquartered in Philadelphia, Pennsylvania, the refugee section of the AFSC worked during World War II with Jewish welfare organizations to provide relief for those persecuted in Germany and in Nazi-occupied Europe. Operating chiefly out of its Geneva, Berlin, and Rome offices in continental Europe, the AFSC also worked to procure travel visas for refugees of German persecution, particularly those residing in North Africa and in neutral countries. Following the cessation of hostilities in 1945, the AFSC engaged in relief and reconstruction work in postwar Europe. See Howard Wriggins, *Picking Up the Pieces from Portugal to Palestine: Quaker Refugee Relief in World War II* (New York: University Press of America, 2004).

48. Swiss-born Rosa (Rösli) Näf (1911–1996) had worked for Dr. Albert Schweitzer in Africa for three years before undertaking the responsibility for the castle of La Hille. After the war, Näf settled in Denmark. In 1986, Yad Vashem named her "Righteous Among the Nations."

49. After the military defeat of France, Maurice Dubois (1905–1998) provided aid to hundreds of refugees in southern France. He soon became responsible for the Swiss Aid Cartel for Child War Victims in unoccupied France and, after this organization became affiliated with the Red Cross, for Swiss Children's Aid. He worked for the employment of Swiss nurses in the internment camps of Gurs and Rivesaltes and helped to develop a network of children's homes for refugee children. He was declared "Righteous Among the Nations" in 1985.

50. René Bousquet (1909–1993) was a high-ranking member of the collaborationist Vichy regime who was instrumental in the infamous roundup of Parisian Jews at the Vélodrome d'Hiver in July 1942. This action resulted in the arrest and deportation of thirteen thousand Jews. Bousquet remained influential in French politics until serious allegations about his Vichy past resurfaced in the late 1980s. After initial efforts by political allies to prevent Bousquet's prosecution, French justice officials indicted the aging civil servant in 1991, accusing him of crimes against humanity in the deportation of 194 children. Bousquet was assassinated on June 8, 1993, shortly before his trial was to take place.

concentration camps.[51] Ninety of the original La Hille children survived the war. In the 1980s, the **Yad Vashem** remembrance authorities declared Maurice Dubois and Rösli Näf "**Righteous Among the Nations.**"

WHEN RESCUE FAILS

For every successful rescue of a child during the Holocaust, many such efforts undoubtedly ended in tragedy. The fate of the children of Izieu is a case in point. Their would-be rescuers, Sabine and Miron Zlatin, were eastern European Jews who made their home in northern France, obtaining French citizenship in 1939.[52] At the outbreak of World War II, Sabine Zlatin trained as a Red Cross nurse. After the couple fled occupied France, Sabine became involved with the Oeuvre de Secours aux Enfants (Children's Aid Society, or OSE), through which she assisted in the release of several youngsters from the Rivesaltes and Agde internment camps. When German forces occupied Vichy France in 1943, Zlatin and her husband received permission to take possession of an empty farmhouse in the remote mountain village of Izieu in southeastern France. There the couple established a refugee children's home, La Maison d'Izieu, some sixty miles from Lyon in the Rhone Valley. The local subprefect of Belley (Ain), Pierre-Marcel Witzler, who had offered the retreat to the Zlatins, perfectly understood that the small home would provide Jewish youngsters safe haven from deportation. The first arrivals to the refuge came from Lodève in the Herault department in the Languedoc; others came from internment camps in the south of France. Ranging in age from three to eighteen, the children lived, by wartime standards, an idyllic existence, enjoying their school lessons as well as varied and nutritious meals, weekly hikes in the beautiful countryside, and abundant time for games, drawing, and play. The Jewish identities of the youngsters and their caretakers were a closely guarded secret, and official records identified the young persons only as refugee children. Surrounded by the Zlatins and five other staff, the children felt safe and secure.

---

51. Just one of those deported, Werner Epstein succeeded in surviving Auschwitz and a death march before liberation in the spring of 1945.

52. Sabine Zlatin (née Chwast, 1907–1996) was born in Warsaw and emigrated as a young woman to France; she met Russian-born Miron Zlatin (1904–1944), an agronomy student in Nancy, where the couple married in 1927.

DOCUMENT 9-17. Jewish refugee children pose at a children's home in Izieu, France, summer 1943, USHMMPA WS# 15513, courtesy of Serge Klarsfeld.

That security was shattered on the morning of April 6, 1944, when SS-Hauptsturmführer Klaus Barbie (1913–1991), chief of the Lyon **Gestapo**, led a raid upon the children's colony at Izieu. SS and police authorities found the youngsters and the staff in the refectory eating breakfast. As Barbie indicated in his now infamous telex, he and his men seized the forty-four children resident in the home (the original document states forty-one children, as three of the teenagers were counted as adults) and seven grown-ups, including Miron Zlatin. His wife, Sabine, had gone to Montpellier to collect supplies and thus escaped the dragnet. Only one youngster, Leon Reifman, managed to leap from one of the home's windows and escape.

The captive children and their adult attendants spent the night in Lyon's Fort Montluc prison. Fearing that local authorities might intervene on the children's behalf, Barbie arranged for their immediate transfer to the **Drancy** transit camp, near Paris. Miron Zlatin and two of the oldest youngsters were ultimately transferred from there to Tallinn, Estonia, where they were shot to death. The rest of the children traveled on the next available transport to Auschwitz, where they were gassed immediately upon arrival. Of the adults who accompanied them to the killing center, only one, twenty-four-year-old Léa Feldblum, was spared at **selection** and survived Auschwitz.[53] Together with Sabine Zlatin, by then eighty, a sixty-nine-year-old Feldblum testified against Klaus Barbie at his trial in Lyon in 1987. The tragic fate of the Izieu children played a pivotal role in Barbie's indictment and conviction. The so-called Butcher of Lyon died in prison in 1991.[54]

---

53. Léa (Laja) Feldblum (1918–) was born July 1, 1918, in Warsaw. By 1929, her family had emigrated to Antwerp, but after the German occupation of Belgium, the Feldblums fled to southern France. Léa Feldblum worked at several OSE facilities before her employment at the Izieu children's home. Here, like the Zlatins, she lived under false papers, assuming the name Marie-Louise Decoste. Arriving at the Drancy transit camp following the Barbie raid on Izieu, she revealed her true identity so that she might be deported with the children to Auschwitz. Feldblum was liberated at the Auschwitz complex in January 1945 and emigrated the following year to Palestine.

54. For a discussion of the trials of Klaus Barbie and René Bousquet, mentioned previously, see Richard J. Golsan, "Crimes-against-Humanity Trials in France and Their Historical and Legal Contexts," in *Atrocities on Trial: Historical Perspectives on the Politics of Prosecuting War Crimes*, ed. Patricia Heberer and Jürgen Matthäus (Lincoln: University of Nebraska Press in association with the U.S. Holocaust Memorial Museum, 2008), 247–61.

DOCUMENT 9-18. Telex from Klaus Barbie, commanding officer of the Security Police and Security Service IV B, Lyon, to Department IV B 4, Paris (Barbie Telex), April 6, 1944, in Serge Klarsfeld, *The Children of Izieu: A Human Tragedy*, trans. Kenneth Jacobsen (New York: Harry N. Abrams, 1985), 95 (translated from the German).

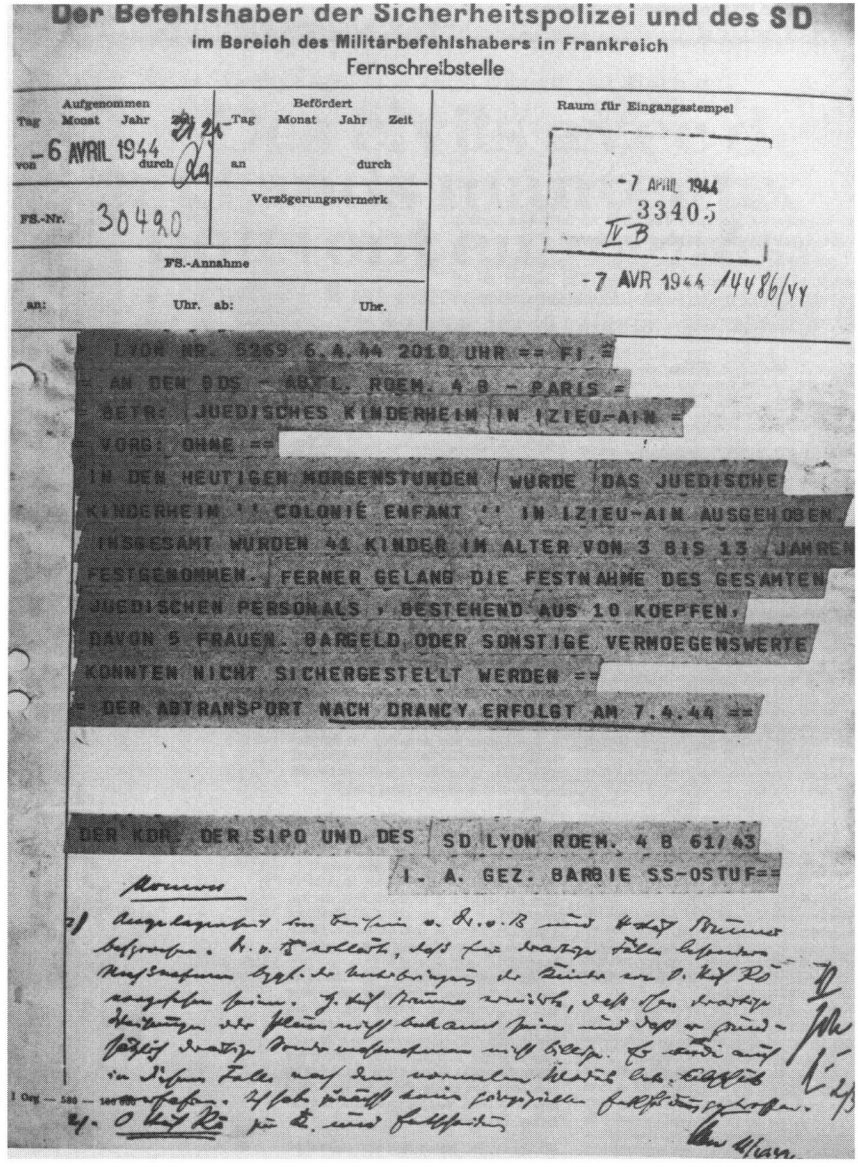

The Commander of the Security Police and the SD [Sicherheitsdienst, or Security Service] in the area of the Military Commander in France

[Telegraph Office]

Lyon No 5,269 4/6/44 8:10 p.m. Fl.

To the BdS Dept. IV B Paris

Re: Jewish children's home in Izieu/Ain

Prev[ious]: none

This morning the Jewish children's home "Colonie Enfant" in Izieu/Ain was raided. In total, forty-one children aged from three to thirteen were taken into custody. In addition, officials succeeded in arresting the entire Jewish staff, consisting of ten persons, five of them women. Neither cash nor other valuables could be secured.

The transport to Drancy is to take place on April 7, 1944.

The commanding officer of the Sipo [Sicherheitspolizei, or Security Police] and the SD Lyon, IV B 61/43 [Dr. Werner Knab]

As authorized, signed [Klaus] Barbie, SS[-Obersturmführer]

[Handwritten]

1. Affair discussed in the presence of Dr. v. B.[55] and Hauptsturmführer [Alois] Brunner.[56] Dr. v. B. stated that in such cases, special measures regarding the lodging of the children had been provided for by Obersturmführer Röthke. Hauptsturmführer Brunner replied that he had no knowledge of such instructions or plans, and that as a matter of principle, he would not consent to such special measures. In these cases also he would proceed in the normal manner as regards deportation. For the time being I have made no decision in principle.

[Obersturmführer] Röthke for information and decision.

---

55. Dr. von Behr, director of the Einsatzstab Rosenberg in Paris, was responsible for the confiscation of the valuables of deported Jews.

56. Alois Brunner (1912–?) was one of Adolf Eichmann's most trusted associates in the deportation of European Jews to killing centers and ghettos in the East. As commander of the Drancy internment camp outside Paris from June 1943 to August 1944, Brunner was responsible for sending thousands of Jews to their deaths. After the war, Brunner escaped abroad and is believed to have resided in Syria. He was condemned to death in absentia by French courts in 1954 and again in March 2002. It is unclear whether Brunner is alive and at large. See Hans Safrian, *Eichmann's Men*, trans. Uta Stargardt (Cambridge: Cambridge University Press in association with the U.S. Holocaust Memorial Museum, 2009).

CHAPTER 10

ELSEWHERE, PERHAPS?
CHILDREN AND THE END OF THE HOLOCAUST

O N MAY 8, 1945, World War II, the most destructive conflict in modern history, came to an end in Europe. Between 7 and 9 million people had been uprooted from their homes as a result of hostilities. Between 2 and 3 million of these individuals were former prisoners—Jews and non-Jews—who had survived the war in concentration camps, forced labor camps, and killing centers throughout Axis-controlled Europe.[1] Ill and exhausted from years of malnourishment and maltreatment, many child and adult survivors greeted their liberation with jubilation and set about making plans for a new future. Particularly for adolescents who had witnessed the deaths of parents and family members, however, a sense of overwhelming loss and uncertainty tempered the joy of this newfound freedom. Where would they go now? What would the future hold in a world without family love and support?

For survivors, the end of World War II marked a rupture between past and present. The immediate postwar period was a time to reconstruct their lives and reestablish homes and households dissolved during the war years. Separation from loved ones was a central experience of Jewish families during the Holocaust, and already in the late spring of 1945, surviving Jews and other victims of Axis policy began the complex process of locating family members

---

1. Hagit Lavsky, "The Role of Children in the Rehabilitation Process of Survivors: The Case of Bergen Belsen," *Children and the Holocaust: Symposium Presentations of the Center for Advanced Holocaust Studies* (Washington, DC: U.S. Holocaust Memorial Museum, 2004), 103.

scattered during the years of persecution. Parents sought their missing children in orphanages, children's homes, and religious institutions throughout Europe. Such searches often became protracted, as hidden children had often moved from safe house to safe house during the war years, and many were still listed in official records under assumed names. Even those children fortunate enough to be reunited with their parents or other relatives often found rejoining their family units traumatic. For many young children, leaving the safety of their rescuers' homes for parents they scarcely remembered was a distressing experience. Likewise, hidden children who had spent years living under false identities discovered that returning to the family fold meant a difficult period of readjustment, as youngsters struggled to reconcile their past and present selves.

And then, child and adult Holocaust survivors alike faced the most daunting dilemma of all: where should they call home? Was it a viable option to return to one's homeland, where the memories of persecution were still fresh? Could one begin a new life in old surroundings? Would they discover missing friends and relatives when they returned, or would they find only the ghosts of the past? Many children, both with and without parents, waited, sometimes for years, in **displaced persons (DP) camps** throughout the Allied occupation zones of Germany and Austria for the chance to settle elsewhere, to emigrate abroad, perhaps to the United States or British-controlled **Palestine**. And there these surviving children began again, pursing the education denied to them under Nazi occupation. Slowly and tenaciously, they made lives for themselves in the shadow of the Shoah. Many later shared their experiences, filtering the memories of their extraordinary childhoods with the perspectives they had gained as adults. Their testimonies are essential, for sixty-five years after those harrowing years of war and genocide, these individuals are our last living witnesses to the events of the Holocaust.

"OVER THIS FIELD OF DEATH, PEACE BREAKS OUT": LIBERATION

It is impossible to ascertain with precision the number of young people who survived persecution by the Nazi regime or its allies in concentration camps and ghettos or in hiding. Yet, in the winter and spring months of 1945, thousands of children experienced liberation, as Allied armies made their way through Axis-controlled Europe and into the German Reich itself. In the last months of the war, as German military and occupation forces retreated, they evacuated hundreds of camps in eastern Europe before the advance of the Soviet army, driving their prisoner populations to camps deep in the German interior.

Schutzstaffel (**SS**) personnel forced these prisoners to march hundreds of miles on foot in brutal winter conditions without adequate food, shelter, or clothing. Their SS guards summarily shot those too ill or exhausted to keep pace on these death marches. Concentration camps on German soil were often unprepared for the vast numbers of incoming prisoners from the east. Burgeoning camp populations outstripped the food and water supplies; extreme overcrowding spread epidemics of **typhus**, tuberculosis, and dysentery. In many camps the last weeks of the war witnessed catastrophic losses among Jewish and non-Jewish prisoners due to starvation, exposure, and disease.[2]

On April 11, 1945, units of the U.S. Ninth Armored Infantry Battalion liberated the **Buchenwald** concentration camp near Weimar, Germany. On that day, the camp's underground prisoner resistance movement seized control of Buchenwald in order to prevent atrocities by retreating camp guards. It was the first major Nazi concentration camp uncovered by U.S. forces,[3] and American soldiers were horrified when they encountered more than twenty thousand starving and emaciated prisoners.[4]

Gert Silberbart was sixteen when he learned that American troops were approaching the perimeter of the Buchenwald camp. A young Jew from Berlin, Silberbart had lived in the German capital until February 1943, when **Gestapo** agents arrested him and his family and transported them to Berlin's **collection camp** (*Sammellager*) for Jews at Grosse-Hamburger-Strasse. The Silberbarts were deported directly to the **Auschwitz** concentration camp. His parents and eight-year-old sister went directly to the gas chambers, but Gert, then fourteen, had an athletic build and was selected for forced labor. He spent several months in the **Buna** camp (Auschwitz III–Monowitz), before civilian contractors from the Siemens concern recruited him as a skilled worker in an electronics factory attached to the Bobrek[5] subcamp of Auschwitz. There the youth worked under comparatively good conditions until the last months of the war. In early January

---

2. See, for example, a discussion of the final days of the Bergen Belsen camp in Suzanne Bardgett and David Cesarani, eds., *Belsen 1945: New Historical Perspectives* (London: Imperial War Museum, 2006).

3. On April 4, 1945, units of the U.S. 89th Infantry Division overran Ohrdruf, a Buchenwald subcamp. It was the first Nazi concentration camp liberated by U.S. forces.

4. See Robert Abzug, *Inside the Vicious Heart: Americans and the Liberation of Nazi Concentration Camps* (Oxford: Oxford University Press, 1985).

5. See "Bobrek" in *The U.S. Holocaust Memorial Museum Encyclopedia of Camps and Ghettos, 1933–1945*, Vol. 1: *Early Camps, Youth Camps, and Concentration Camps and Subcamps under the SS–Business Administration Main Office (WVHA)*, ed. Geoffrey Megargee (Bloomington: Indiana University Press in association with the U.S. Holocaust Memorial Museum, 2009), 228–30.

1945, he and several of his fellow prisoners from Bobrek endured a forced march to Buchenwald. In the last days of the camp's existence, SS guards oversaw almost daily transports of prisoners to other camps in Germany's interior. Fearing that he would have to undergo another death march, a starving and exhausted Silberbart hid in the camp's cellars and sewage holes, hoping to survive a potential liquidation of Buchenwald's prisoner population. The teenager's first indication that Allied forces had arrived at the complex was the sound of American music playing from the camp's loudspeakers. Silberbart emerged from his hiding place and embraced his fellow prisoners with joy.

Gert Silberbart responded to his liberation at Buchenwald with jubilation. Although weak and malnourished, he walked out to greet his American rescuers and to share the happiness and relief of the moment with his fellow survivors. In an August 1946 interview with American psychologist Dr. **David Boder**,[6] Silberbart expressed his satisfaction at the arrest of his former SS tormentors. His rejection of retribution against SS guards held temporarily at the Buchenwald camp after liberation indicates that the young man had emerged from the years of persecution with his humanity intact. Now almost eighteen, Gert Silberbart looked ahead to a brighter future; he envisioned reuniting with his extended family and studying dentistry.

DOCUMENT 10-1. **David P. Boder, interview with Gert Silberbart, Geneva, August 27, 1946, USHMMA RG-50.472, spool 9-82 and 83 (translated from the German).**

> Gert Silberbart: [. . .] I stayed hidden for about a week. Constantly there was the call "*Juden raus, Juden raus*," ["Jews out, Jews out!"] and when the largest part of the Jews were gone, they went after the Christians. There were daily transports from the camp, so that in the camp that had held 100,000 people a week before, at the point of liberation by the Americans on April 11, there were only 22,000 people left. [. . .]
>
> David Boder: Well? And so?
>
> Gert Silberbart: And so the Americans came on the 11th, on April 11 at four o'clock in the afternoon, and liberated us.

---

6. See David Boder, *The Displaced People of Europe: Preliminary Notes on a Psychological and Anthropological Study* (Chicago: Illinois Institute of Technology and the Psychological Museum, 1947), and David Boder, *I Did Not Interview the Dead* (Urbana: University of Illinois Press, 1949), as well as the online site for Boder interviews, "Voices of the Holocaust" (http://voices.iit.edu), a project of the Paul V. Galvin Library, Illinois Institute of Technology.

David Boder: Now, and how was that? Do you want to tell us about the last three days? [. . .]

Gert Silberbart: Well, so, during these . . . during these last three days I hid in cellars and sewage holes. I did not eat or drink during these days, just always listened anxiously to the cry of "*Juden raus*"; and when somebody, something moved close to me, when I heard any sound, I immediately grew terrified.

David Boder: So you say you did not really eat anything during those three days?

Gert Silberbart: Yes. That was not . . . that was not the first time. I had already starved for seven days. Nothing to eat and nothing to drink. [. . .] [I hid] until I heard the cries of jubilation on the afternoon of April 11, and heard American music from the loud speakers, and then I immediately crawled out, completely exhausted, and we embraced each other, crying . . .

David Boder: So American music from the radios . . .

Gert Silberbart: It was like this. In the room of the camp commandant, which was outside the camp, there was a big . . . a microphone [. . .] and this radio in the commandant's room played American music. The inmates stood immediately. [. . .]

David Boder: Tuned in and one heard American music?

Gert Silberbart: . . . immediately heard American music. And then the first Americans immediately talked over the loudspeakers. We were . . . we just [knew] we were free.

David Boder: And?

Gert Silberbart: We just could not grasp it in the first hours. Yes, and then we embraced crying. It is really hard to describe the last—the first hours after the liberation.

David Boder: Try it!

Gert Silberbart: Yes, when I crawled out, I saw some comrades again whom I had known for a long time, and we embraced and we almost could not fathom that we were free. We were so exhausted from the last days that we had not eaten—in short, we were exhausted. The bad thing was also that the Germans in their retreat had destroyed the water pipeline, so that there was no water in the whole camp, and we almost died of thirst.

David Boder: [Interviewer David Boder changes the recording spool and identifies the interviewee, date, and time.] So you said you heard American music, now go on.

Gert Silberbart: Yes, so we just crawled out of our hiding places and were happy about our newly regained freedom; many actually collapsed from the thought, at this occasion . . .

David Boder: Did you immediately see some Americans, too?

Gert Silberbart: Yes, we immediately saw American tanks that drove through the barbed wire and the electrical fences. At once you saw white flags on all the roofs, and—to make a long story short—there was jubilation and laughter all over the camp.

David Boder: Who put out the white flags?

Gert Silberbart: Those were simple bed sheets. [. . .]

David Boder: Now, the prisoners did not have to surrender. What did the white flags mean?

Gert Silberbart: No, the white flags meant simply that we were together with the Americans. [. . .]

David Boder: Yes, and what happened to the kapos?

Gert Silberbart: The kapos were—a part of the kapos who had a bad conscience, who had collaborated with the SS men during all these times, fled with the SS men who fled at the last minute. [. . .] The kapos who had a good conscience, who had been behaving fairly towards their fellow prisoners, they stayed with us and also celebrated their freedom.

David Boder: Yes. Now. Eh—did they catch some SS men? Did they . . . ?

Gert Silberbart: Very many were still caught on the way because . . . many inmates took, eh, plundered right away these weapons arsenals, the arsenals of the SS . . .

David Boder: Yes . . .

Gert Silberbart: . . . and armed themselves, and those who were strong enough ran after the SS, together with the Americans. Quite a few were still arrested.

David Boder: And what was done with them?

Gert Silberbart: They were first brought into the camp and held in a block. They were disarmed and everything taken from them. Then, several days later, they were transported by the Americans, by the military, further into Germany. [. . .]

David Boder: Did you have an opportunity to talk to the SS?

Gert Silberbart: I did not have an opportunity myself because the whole time I was too weak to just go a few steps. [. . .] I just rested. Others had the opportunity to talk to the SS men. Many also took revenge on them.

David Boder: In what form?

Gert Silberbart: Simply by harassing them.

David Boder: Yes. Did the Americans defend or protect the SS in any form?

Gert Silberbart: Neither defended nor protected them. They took— in the first . . . in the first days you saw rather few Americans in our camp because the camp was still on the front lines, that whole area. Only later, when the front had moved further into Germany, there came a special camp commando of the U.S. Army, a great number of personnel who took over the running of the camp. Also many tankers came that brought water into the camp. Because it took about a week and a half after our liberation until the water pipeline was restored.

David Boder: Aha. Now tell me, there were so many inmates, how come the SS was even left alive?

Gert Silberbart: They were left alive. Because if we would not have let them live, then we would—we would not have been much different than the Germans. So we had to—we wanted, after all, to set a good example. If not a good example . . . but we should not act as they acted towards us: then we would have been just like them in the end.

David Boder: That was the philosophy of the matter?

Gert Silberbart: That was not the philosophy of the matter. That is my opinion. Surely many others had a different opinion. But overall that was the mind set in the camp. [. . .]

David Boder: Now, and how did it go with the food and care?

Gert Silberbart: Of course the food improved immediately and immensely. Many were not used to the good fare of the American military, in fact, no one was. [. . .] [Many] suffered right away from diarrhea, gastritis, stomach cramps. Nobody took well to it. The whole camp suffered from diarrhea. And only later, slowly, slowly, did we get used to the normal diet.

David Boder: Now, and how long were you then in Buchenwald?

Gert Silberbart: I was then in Buchenwald until the beginning of June 1945, when many youths had to sign up through the UN,[7] and the

---

7. Gert Silberbart is referring to the United Nations Relief and Rehabilitation Administration, which undertook the provision of food, clothing, and essentials for displaced persons and victims of war and persecution following World War II. Among the administration's tasks were documenting orphaned or unaccompanied minors and assisting in their reunion with relatives or relocation.

transports went to Switzerland, and I was among them. And so I came to Switzerland. [. . .]

David Boder: And how old are you now?

Gert Silberbart: I will be eighteen.

David Boder: And what are your plans? What do you want to do in the future?

Gert Silberbart: I am intending to finish the dental technician course and the [evening] course at the trade school, and then go to my relatives in Chile and work there as a dental technician.

DOCUMENT 10-2. **Young boys join adult survivors in cheering their U.S. Army liberators at Dachau, April 29, 1945, USHMMPA WS# 45075, courtesy of the National Archives and Records Administration, College Park.**

Fourteen-year-old P. H.[8] experienced his liberation from the **Dachau** concentration camp in a markedly different way. At the age of nine, the young boy had been forced to move into the **Łódź ghetto** with his family. There, in

---

8. Editor Isaiah Trunk chose to anonymize all sources of oral testimony published in his 1982 anthology *Jewish Responses to Nazi Persecution*.

September 1942, he and his younger brother had evaded the children's action (***Kinderaktion***) associated with the ghetto's notorious ***Gehsperre*** by hiding in the attic of their small apartment. The family remained in Łódź until the final liquidation of that ghetto in August 1944. At the time, P. H. reflected, he did not understand that his intact family had provided an invaluable source of stability and support. "I didn't value as a young child what it means to have a family with a father and mother. I only really appreciate it now that it's too late . . . "[9] During the final **deportation** action, thirteen-year-old P. H. was separated from his mother and little brother and arrived with his father on a transport to Auschwitz. Flushed with crying and wearing several sets of clothing in the warm summer heat, the young H. appeared robust to SS officers performing **selections** on the ramp, and he and his father were chosen for labor. Two days after disembarking at **Birkenau**, father and son reboarded a transport for the Kaufbeuren concentration camp,[10] a subcamp of Dachau near Augsburg. In the last weeks of the war, young H. was transferred with other ill and exhausted Jews to the Dachau concentration camp.

Unlike Gert Silberbart, P. H. did not experience a sense of joy when U.S. forces liberated Dachau on April 28, 1945. While Silberbart had lost his parents and other family members at the outset of his Holocaust odyssey, H.'s father had died just weeks before the arrival of American troops, deepening his son's sense of loss. Bereft of family members and close friends, H. felt a profound sense of loneliness and abandonment at liberation. Isolated from his fellow survivors, with whom, as a new arrival at Dachau, he felt very little connection, H. could not understand the elation that other prisoners demonstrated when their hour of freedom finally came. In this moment of celebration, the fourteen-year-old felt only apathy and despair. In a February 1946 interview, he confided to oral historian David Rum that only the injunction of his dying father enabled him to face his future alone.

---

9. P. H., quoted in Isaiah Trunk, ed., *Jewish Responses to Nazi Persecution: Collective and Individual Behavior in Extremis* (New York: Stein and Day, 1982), 326.

10. The Bavarian city of Kaufbeuren was also the location of the "euthanasia" facility mentioned in chapter 6.

DOCUMENT 10-3. Oral history testimony of P. H. by the Canadian Jewish Congress, Montreal, February 1946, in Isaiah Trunk, ed., *Jewish Responses to Nazi Persecution: Collective and Individual Behavior in Extremis* (New York: Stein and Day, 1982), 326–28.

We were 600 men. On the first morning, we were sent out to the sites. My father worked in the forest for two days and caught pneumonia. I tried to muster all my strength for this work and was beaten hard all the time. After eight days, my father got better, but he was still too weak for the labor gangs. They put him in the infirmary—which was very bad. He died in two days. I was left all alone, without anyone or any hope for tomorrow. The number of dead grew from day to day. Of 600 Jews, only 320 were left. The camp went on operating for another week, and by then, the last exhausted remnant of 125 people was transferred to Dachau. I looked like a corpse, with no strength left at all. We were put into the infirmary, but forty other people had died in the train on the way there—they couldn't have held out for another moment. Since I was the youngest here, the others gave me more food and I only started coming back to life after two long weeks. The doctor, who was French, felt sorry for me and didn't discharge me from the infirmary right away. He gave me light work to do inside the clinic. On April 25, all the Jews were packed into a transport that was headed for the Tyrol. This doctor tried to save me and write out a false diagnosis which confined me to bed, though I was already better. Both of us risked our lives doing this. But luckily, they crossed me off the transport list and I stayed behind in the infirmary.

On April 28, the Americans walked in. Thousands of people "rose from the dead" to come out on the grounds and stare at the liberators. The SS were marched past us with their hands stuck high in the air. I reacted coldly to all these signs of liberation—I had no reason to be glad. I fell into complete apathy. I watched the people sing and dance with joy, and they seemed to me as if they'd lost their minds. I looked at myself and couldn't recognize who I was. I lost all sense of what had happened to me. After a long time, I began to understand. I was left all alone, without help or protection, without a living soul I could call my own. There were [times] I regretted having been left alive among these last survivors and handful of Jews. This was how the two months at Dachau passed. Many people died and many recovered. [. . .] I only live today for the words my father said to me on his deathbed: "I'm already forty-three—I won't be able to survive this hell. But you—you're young, see to it our name isn't torn out from the pages of the world."

This keeps alive my spirit and I live with the hope for a better tomorrow.

One of the most extraordinary accounts of the last days of the **Theresienstadt ghetto** comes to us from the diary of eighteen-year-old Alice Ehrmann (later Alisa[11] Shek), born in Prague, Czechoslovakia, on May 5, 1927. Her Czech Jewish father, Rudolf Ehrmann, was a successful civil engineer; her Catholic mother, Pavla, was from Vienna. As children of a mixed marriage, Alice and her siblings became subject to Nazi antisemitic legislation when the Czech lands were annexed by the German Reich in March 1939.

Like many other Czech *Mischling* children, sixteen-year-old Alice and her sister Ruth, nineteen, were deported to Theresienstadt in July 1943 without their parents. While their "**Aryan**" mother continued to live in Prague until the end of the war, Rudolf Ehrmann was arrested and held in Theresienstadt's Small Fortress in the spring of 1944. He was ultimately deported to Auschwitz, which he survived.

Alice Ehrmann began her diary in October 1944. In the ghetto she had met twenty-four-year-old Ze'ev Shek (then Scheck), a leading figure in the Czech Zionist youth movement. Soon after his arrival in the ghetto in October 1943, Shek began to assemble a small archive in order to document the true state of Theresienstadt, which Nazi authorities showcased to outsiders as a model ghetto. The young couple fell in love. After Shek was deported to Auschwitz in October 1944, Alice took over his task, concealing his trunk of documents within the workings of the **Terezin** fortress. When Shek returned to Prague after the war, Ehrmann retrieved the trunk from its hiding place, and the couple presented the collection to the new Czech director of the Jewish Agency.[12]

Through her diary, the teenage Alice performed another important service. Her descriptions of the ghetto's last months provide us with a detailed eye-witness account of those turbulent days after the arrival of the Russian forces

---

11. This is also transliterated as Alisah in some sources.

12. In 1947, Ze'ev Shek received permission to emigrate to Palestine, where he studied at the Hebrew University in Jerusalem. That same year he returned to Prague as a member of a delegation to a youth conference and married Alice Ehrmann. The couple emigrated to Israel in July 1948, and Ze'ev entered the diplomatic service. From 1950 to 1953, he was the first secretary of the Israeli embassy in Prague. His diplomatic career included postings in London and Paris. From 1967 until 1971, he served as Israeli ambassador to Austria. From 1977 he functioned as ambassador to Italy until his death in Rome on October 2, 1978. Alisa Shek was instrumental in founding and sustaining Israel's Beit Theresienstadt, a memorial to the survivors of the Terezin ghetto. She died in 2007.

that liberated Prague and, with it, Theresienstadt. Particularly poignant are her impressions of the first days of peace, in which the celebratory mood of the local population contrasted starkly with the ongoing suffering of the liberated ghetto inhabitants. As she and her sister Ruth, a nurse, stayed behind to aid in the general evacuation, they could not fail to notice the mounting mortality rates among ghetto survivors. Amid the chaos, young Alice Ehrmann portrayed the experiences of many concentration camp and ghetto inmates for whom the first days of liberation appeared an incongruous juxtaposition of death and salvation.

DOCUMENT 10-4. Diary of Alice Ehrmann (Alisah Shek), entries for May 10, 11, and 18, 1945, in Alisah Shek, "Tagebuch," in *Theresienstädter Studien und Dokumente*, ed. Miroslav Kárný, Raimund Kemper, and Margita Kárná (Prague: Verlag Academica, 1994), 196–99 (translated from the German).

May 10, 1945

Russians in the ghetto. They came to pick up the Russian [prisoners of war]. They broke through to the "Hamburg" [barracks], were halfway pushed out again. The Russians have disarmed the gendarmes; the chaos grows exponentially. The racially "Aryan" prisoners are registering; people are running away, they are going with the Russians. The Soviet flag flies over headquarters. Everywhere else, Czechoslovakian and Red Cross flags. [. . .] In the afternoon two cars with German wounded. Boys with red armbands and weapons in front of headquarters. Rioting. In the back sit two girls; a soldier holds a thin blonde, and around them the crowd howls. They threaten them with their fists. I know that they have done all this, but really, it wasn't just them. What does it help to beat them? Everything is always the same; people are always the same; no, they are always malicious. I am so unhappy. [. . .]

Evenings: the Russians drive all about, young girls ride on their tanks. The modern woman. People fill the city. Shaven heads and women's hairstyles, painted backs and summer clothes; stripes and bright clothing.[13] [. . .] What are we to them? For the Russians a hospital city. And here there is no nurse besides Ruth and another girl. South barracks: we drove over two cars with beds and mattresses for twelve "Aryan" nurses.

---

13. Here the author means to indicate the mix of concentration camp prisoners and members of the local population.

Night. Down below the barracks with half-lit windows, barbed wire, and everywhere the death's head: typhus, rags, blankets full of lice, and shoes lie everywhere. And the smell, the eternal stench of cattle cars and assembly areas [*Schleusen*]. Here and there a bent figure hobbles from one barracks to another. The shaved head next to the signboard. . . . The first barracks, No. 11, almost everyone dead. Only a few moan, whimper, and wail. And over this field of death, peace breaks out. In the distances you can see rockets. The people are celebrating peace—peace, happiness. They build from the unhappiness they have caused a joy and are happy, and now everyone is supposed to go home.

May 11, 1945

Relative order, the ghetto is functioning, more or less. Many are leaving. [. . .] South barracks: the promised transfer [of the sick] to a field hospital does not materialize. The doctor does not dare to go inside; he[14] promised to transfer them. All who can walk have been disinfected and moved to the Bodenbacher barracks. Two hundred and fifty who cannot move must face a gruesome death in the barracks, surrounded by their own excrement and the corpses. It is terrible, terrible. My sister is there; she cannot pull herself away. I understand her. The decision to leave the barracks behind, knowing that 250 living, young people are gasping their last—and how, who could do that? And even when one knows that, he cannot help. I am unendingly tired of everything. I think it must be wonderful not to have to do anything anymore. Ever.

May 18, 1945

In the evening Mařka Pick, Honza Meissner [visited]. Father in Slovakia,[15] I believe. Everything is spinning round me. All the compressed thoughts of horror concerning him fly before my eyes. It is like a storm that breaks out, terrible and yet harmless, all dark spirits and ghosts of night—I extinguish them with one gesture. No, the light is too bright, and I am blind [from it]. And around me the darkness is so thick. A letter this evening. I have my mother again.

---

14. That is, the physician; emphasis is in the original.
15. Emphasis is in the original.

THE SEARCH FOR FAMILY MEMBERS

One of the most universal experiences of the Holocaust was the separation from loved ones. The division of family members tormented both children and their parents. Each lived in fear for the others' safety, yet remained in ignorance of their circumstances and felt powerless to aid them in extremity. Hidden children in particular learned to bear this burden in silence, for any mention of an absent mother or father might endanger their own safety or jeopardize the lives of their rescuers or loved ones. Thousands of young people spent most of the war years divided from their families. For many youngsters, the long separation in wartime would become a permanent reality.

As the war in Europe ended in May 1945, surviving Jews and other victims of Axis policy began the arduous process of locating family members scattered during the years of persecution. Parents searched for their children in foster families, orphanages, and religious institutions. Such quests were often grueling and protracted, for the war and Nazi policies of deportation and population transfer had produced massive relocation, a ceaseless stream of refugees from devastated regions, and millions of displaced persons. Tracing services, most notably the International Tracing Service of the Red Cross,[16] together with many other relief organizations and Jewish agencies, aided in locating missing persons, but these searches were often fraught with difficulty. Many hidden children had passed through several safe houses during the war years and thus no longer remained with the original foster families in which their parents had left them. Others had relocated with their rescuers from war-torn areas and now lived far from their native communities. Still others languished, ill and exhausted, among other concentration camp survivors in relief camps or hospitals or lived in DP camps hundreds of miles from home. Psychologist and child survivor Peter Suedfeld, quartered in a Red Cross children's home in Budapest after World War II, remembers that he thought he might be lost forever. "I was passing as a Christian, under a false name unknown to my family, and my current orphanage was only the latest in a series of bombed-out shelters, far from the original address where they had left me."[17] Parents, siblings, grandparents, and other family members often spent months looking for their young ones. In many instances, such searches ended in tragedy, as parents learned that their

16. International Tracing Service, *An Introduction to the International Tracing Service* (Bad Arolsen: International Tracing Service, 2009).

17. Peter Suedfeld, "Life after the Ashes: The Postwar Pain, and Resilience, of Young Holocaust Survivors," *Occasional Paper of the Center for Advanced Holocaust Studies* (Washington, DC: U.S. Holocaust Memorial Museum, 2002), 5.

youngsters had perished. Children too came face to face with the devastating knowledge that none of their family had survived. Thousands spent their childhoods in orphanages or were placed with foster families by state or municipal authorities when no family members stepped forward to reclaim them.

DOCUMENT 10-5. Hedvig Dydyna holds a name card intended to help surviving family members locate her at the Kloster Indersdorf DP camp, Germany, c. May 1945, USHMMPA WS# 06677, courtesy of Lilo Plaschkes.

Maria Straucher was one of the more fortunate ones. Born on May 4, 1938, in Bochnia, a town near Kraków in southern Poland, Maria remembered little about her parents, who perished in the Holocaust, or about life before her concealment with peasants in the Polish countryside. Like many hidden children, Maria stayed with several rescuers before settling with her newly married guardian, Tadeusz Polowiec, in the last stages of the war. There the youngster, made to work long hours, was often beaten by Polowiec, a man with a violent temper who did not spare his own infant child. Maria was precisely seven years old when the war ended in May 1945. After several months of searching, Maria's aunt, now her closest living relative, succeeded in locating and reclaiming the youngster, showing her perhaps the first tenderness the child had experienced for some years.

DOCUMENT 10-6. Interview with Maria Straucher by the Central Jewish Historical Commission, Kraków, December 2, 1947, USHMMA, RG-15.084, Holocaust Survivor Testimonies, 301/3292/1-2 (translated from the Polish).

<u>Maria Straucher, born in Bochnia, May 4, 1938, reports:</u>

I don't remember anything about things before the war. I remember that I lived with an old woman in the area of Bochnia. There I was very hungry; it was already war. Day after day I was locked in the house. I was never permitted to go outside. Then Tadeusz Polowiec, who had taken charge of me, took me away from there and housed me with another old woman. There were many Germans there at the farmyard who came there with wagons. I always situated myself in the area of the wagons and got something to eat from the Germans, who did not know that I was Jewish. I didn't know it either. There I looked after a cow or goats. I was often struck when I was not obedient. After a year Polowiec took me to peasants in the countryside. There I went to school. After school I tended the cows. There were no children in the house. I don't remember anymore how long I stayed there—maybe the whole summer? Then the man took me back and put me with a younger woman who had had a little baby. There I washed diapers, cleaned, and brought water from the cellar; I had a lot of work to do. This woman had married my guardian, Polowiec. I was often beaten there. My guardian in his rage even beat his little eight-month-old child. Because of this, his mother had to call the physician in order to bandage up the child, who had a wound on its buttocks. Once he kicked me with so much force that I fell down and dislocated a bone in my throat. I became unconscious. They poured cold water on me. When I came to, Polowiec had me wipe up and mop up the water that they had poured on me. I liked the little child very much. They always swore at me, calling me "Jewess," which I didn't understand, because nobody explained it to me. Polowiec never called me by name, always only "little girl." He never petted or hugged me. The first time in my life someone kissed me was an aunt, whom I call mother. She had located me and come to me. She kissed me, and burst into tears. I didn't know and couldn't understand why she was crying. She told me that she was my aunt. I went back to work on this day as usual and did not interrupt my chores. Only in the evening did I sleep by my aunt; she stayed the night with us. My aunt explained to me that she was a sister of my mother and how she had finally found me in Bochnia after searching a long time; and she promised me to take me with her to Kraków. I wasn't afraid and immediately agreed to go with her. My guardian asked me if I would file a complaint against him. Later I was taken before a judge and asked if I wanted to go with my aunt. All the neighbors knew how hard and how much I had worked and wondered how I had held out, because I had been beaten so often there.

I went with my aunt to Kraków, where she placed me in the children's home. I have been there a month, that is, since October. My aunt I call "Mama," and I am doing so well, oh so well!

Maria S.

Kraków, December 2, 1947

Protocol by Janina Masłowska

The effort to reunite as a family unit was not confined to the task of locating missing members. For many young people, the search for parents and other loved ones was often a search for their own identity. Hidden children in particular had spent years concealing their true origins, their religion, and even their own names. Children whose parents had placed them with rescuers in their infancy or young childhood had little or no memory of their families or their lives before the war. Many remained unaware that they were Jewish. For these youngsters, reunion with family members initiated a long and often painful process of reconciling their past and present selves.[18]

On the other hand, a parent's recovery of a missing child did not necessarily guarantee the successful reconstruction of the family circle. Throughout Europe, thousands of rescuers refused to return their charges to parents, family members, or Jewish or public organizations. Sometimes their motives were pecuniary: former foster families demanded that parents compensate them for their care of the child and for incurring tremendous risks in their safekeeping. Other individuals had exploited the labor of their wards in households and on family farms and were reluctant to lose the child's services. More commonly, however, rescuers had grown genuinely attached to their young charges and

---

18. See Robert Krell, *Child Holocaust Survivors: Memories and Reflections* (Victoria: Trafford Publishing, 2007).

did not wish to part with them. Sometimes it was the child who resisted such a reunion. Many youngsters had endured such traumatic upheaval in their young lives that they proved profoundly averse to yet another change. Many, through experience, had grown distrustful of adults and were reluctant to put their faith in family members who had "reappeared" to claim them after the war, particularly if these were distant relatives with whom the child had had little contact before hostilities began. Children often felt betrayed by parents who had "abandoned" them during their long years in hiding. Others had learned to renounce their Jewish heritage and were reluctant to discard their new Christian identity, which had offered them such security, in order to return to the Jewish roots that had been the source of their persecution. Very young children could remember no other home than that of their rescuers and fiercely resisted leaving the only family they had known for the arms of strangers—in this case, their parents.

DOCUMENT 10-7. Renée Pallarés (right) and her family helped save Diane Popowski, an infant who had been with her mother at the Agde internment camp in France. In 1949, nine-year-old Diane reluctantly returned to her widowed father. She reunited with the Pallarés family some years later. USHMMPA WS# 13346, courtesy of Diane Popowski Fenster.

Gizela Szulberg was five years old when her parents left her with relatives of their gardener in the village of Włoska Wola. Michał and Necha Szulberg were fleeing a roundup of Jews in the area of Dubeczno, near Lublin, Poland, and had packed a small suitcase for their only child, believing they would be reunited with her soon. The Szulbergs' gardener had received handsome compensation for hiding the youngster and advised his relations to kill the girl so that they might pocket the money. The Wajdziks, a fiercely antisemitic peasant family, had nevertheless refused to harm Gizela and reluctantly hid the child. Gizela settled with them for the remainder of the war. For much of her stay, the family concealed the youngster in a wardrobe, away from the prying eyes of farmhands and neighbors. In time, Gizela learned that her parents had been murdered on their way to reclaim her. Her foster family, who had presumably expected a lucrative payment from the Szulbergs for the safe return of their daughter, decided to continue concealing the child, but only if the youngster signed over her property to her rescuers. Gizela's father had been a prosperous engineer and part owner of a glass factory in Warsaw before the invasion of Poland, and it is possible that the Wajdziks hoped to acquire these assets as payment for their troubles at the end of the war. Following the cessation of hostilities, Gizela, like many hidden children, continued to live with her foster family. Although she had been sorely mistreated and exploited by her rescuers, the eleven-year-old felt enduring gratitude to the Wajdziks and had herself baptized in 1946 in order to "give them my soul as a gift." Although they had created a hostile environment for the child, the family represented the only stability that Gizela had known for seven years. Strongly identifying with the Wajdziks and their beliefs, she was violently opposed to returning to Warsaw with a surviving family member when her distant cousin came to claim her.

DOCUMENT 10-8. Interview with Gizela Szulberg by the Central Jewish Historical Commission, Bytom, September 3, 1947, USHMMA RG 15.084, Holocaust Survivor Testimonies, 301/2731/2-3 (translated from the Polish).

Deposition: Szulberg, Gizela, born October 23, 1934, in Warsaw
Father: Michał   Mother: Necha, née Bernstein
Resident: Bytom, ul. Prusa 23, Jewish orphanage.

[. . .] At this time I found out what had happened to my parents. They had been in hiding, but later they had nothing to live on because this woman [with whom they had stored their possessions] did not want to give them their things back. They were on their way to me, to pick me up, when the Germans caught them, killed them, and buried their bodies into a ditch. My host wanted to keep me, but I should sign all of my property over to him. They talked for days on end of nothing else but this property, only of this property. I wanted to ingratiate myself with them and promised to give them everything. Despite this, they once threw me out of the house. I set myself out by the barn because I didn't have anywhere else to go. Later they found me there and allowed me to return to the house. I was already so resigned that I didn't really care what happened to me. In the spring I watched after the cows and was already much happier, because I did not have to cower locked up in the wardrobe. I am even still a little humped over from sitting like that so much. After this I came down with the measles, and my hostess laid me on top of the stove, where it was very dusty, and at the end of my illness I lay up in the attic. How much I have had to suffer from them! They hated me because I was a Jew. I was treated like Cinderella, truly. At dawn I rose and tended the cattle, together with the sheep there were eighteen [animals]. My legs were covered in sores—it was so frightening.

Then the Soviets came and the people said to me, "Now the Germans won't kill you anymore; now you are free." But I didn't believe in my good fortune. In spring 1946, I had myself baptized, because I wanted to show [my rescuers] that I appreciated it that they had taken me in. I simply wanted to give them my soul. After this I went to the grave of my parents, that is to the ditch [where they were buried], and lay [a bouquet of] violets there and cried a good deal. Today I don't cry anymore, so hardened is my heart from all the fear through which I have lived. After this the people from the AK [*Armia Krajowa*, or Polish Home Army] wanted to kill me. They said to my host, "If you don't hide us, we will kill this *Chaja*[19] of yours." My hosts still often called me "Bejlis!"[20] After all this, one of my cousins found me and wanted to take me away from them. But they said, "Either a half a million or the child." He didn't have that much money because he was in the military, and he went away. I didn't even want to say good-bye to him, I was so dumb. I wanted to stay with them and be a Pole, so used had I grown to this way of life. But my cousin had told the Jews[21] about me and they took me away from the Wajdziks. While on

---

19. "Chaja" or "Chaya," the Hebrew form of "Eva," is used here to designate a female Jew.

20. Menahem Mendel Bejilis (also transliterated as Beilis or Beiliss) was a Ukrainian Jew tried for ritual murder in a notorious trial in Kiev in 1913. The proceedings sparked international criticism of antisemitic sentiment and practice in Imperial Russia. Szulberg suggests that her foster family repeatedly confronted her with Bejilis's "crimes," although Bejilis was ultimately acquitted of murder charges.

21. That is, to officials of the Jewish Committee.

the way I ran away from them, ran seven kilometers [almost 4.5 miles] on foot, and went back to my host family. The police came to get me, but they had to drag me by my hands and feet because I always broke free. Then the Jews put me in an orphanage and now I am really doing well.

Protocol taken by Ida Gliksztejn [signature]

Bytom, September 3, 1947

Witness: Gizela Szulberg

WHERE IS HOME?

At the end of World War II in Europe, the Allied powers discovered that some 7 to 9 million persons remained displaced by the conflict. This number included 2 to 3 million former camp inmates—Jews and non-Jews—who had survived concentration and forced labor camps, killing centers, and death marches from the east into the German interior in the last months of the war.[22] Many thousands of former prisoners, exhausted and ill from years of malnourishment and mistreatment, perished in the weeks directly following their liberation. Those who survived joined the hundreds of thousands seeking repatriation through Allied efforts or migration to European ports in the hopes of settling abroad. By the end of 1945, more than 6 million individuals had returned to their countries of origin or succeeded in immigrating to non-European countries, such as the United States, Canada, and Australia or in a trickle to British-controlled Palestine. Remaining behind, mainly on German and Austrian soil, were some 2 million refugees and displaced persons, among them 250,000 Jews.

Three kinds of Jewish DPs lived in the Allied zones of occupation by early 1946. The first included those who had remained in western Europe, hoping for a British settlement to the "Palestine Question" so that they might legally emigrate to today's Israel. The second category included those who had refused to return to their homelands directly after the war, either because they chose not to reside in an eastern Europe haunted by memories of the Holocaust or because they feared a resurgence of antisemitism in these regions. Finally, a third set of Jewish refugees had remained in, or returned to, their homelands in the early postwar period but now migrated west to the safety of the Allied zones in Germany and Austria. In this so-called *Beriha* (flight, migration, or exodus), tens of thousands of Holocaust survivors fled eastern Europe in order to evade economic ruin or renewed anti-Jewish persecution from local populations.

22. Lavksy, "The Role of Children," 103.

Approximately three hundred thousand Jewish survivors resided in German and Austrian territory between late 1945 and 1950.[23]

To deal with the massive postwar refugee crisis, a series of DP camps had been established in Allied zones throughout Germany and Austria and in occupied areas of Italy.[24] Originally these camps were run by Allied authorities within their zones of occupation. Initial conditions at such facilities were dismal. Rations were meager, and residents lived under imposed curfews in fenced enclosures, often within the same confines as Nazi perpetrators and collaborators. As relations between Jewish DPs and Allied officials became strained, the **United Nations Relief and Rehabilitation Administration** (**UNRRA**), established in 1943 to aid victims of war and to facilitate the repatriation of refugees, undertook the management of the DP camps, aided by voluntary relief agencies and Jewish organizations. Jewish DPs, known in Hebrew as the *Sh'erit ha Pletah* (Surviving Remnant), would prove long-term charges of the UNRRA camps, whose last displaced persons facility, Föhrenwald, near Munich, closed in 1957.[25]

By the summer of 1945, most Jewish DP camps had begun to exercise internal autonomy within their complexes, fostering the creation of a Jewish society within the camp structure. Once Jewish displaced persons had won the right to separate from the general DP population, each camp elected a central committee, which managed the facility's internal administration and promoted cultural and religious activities. Camp committees also established an elaborate school system, at least within the American and British zones, which provided youngsters and adolescents with nursery schools, elementary education, religious schools and yeshivas, high schools, teacher-training academies, and vocational-training facilities organized by the ORT. As the Jewish Agency for Palestine[26] sponsored many school systems, education in the DP camps had a

---

23. Lavksy, "The Role of Children," 104.

24. Concerning the topic of displaced persons camps following World War II, see Angelika Königseder and Juliane Wetzel, *Waiting for Hope: Jewish Displaced Persons in Post–World War II Germany*, trans. John Broadwin (Evanston, IL: Northwestern University Press, 2001); Michael Marrus, *The Unwanted: European Refugees from the First World War through the Cold War* (Philadelphia: Temple University Press, 2002); Mark Wyman, *DPs: Europe's Displaced Persons, 1945–1951* (Ithaca, NY: Cornell University Press, 1998.)

25. Joachim Schröder, "Politische und kulturelle Geschichte der jüdischen Displaced Persons anhand des von den USA verwalteten Lagers Föhrenwald in der amerikanischen Besatzungszone" (master's thesis, Ludwig-Maximilians Universitat, 1990).

26. The Jewish Agency for Palestine was established by the World Zionist Organization in 1922. Its offices in Jerusalem, London, and Geneva facilitated emigration to Palestine and provided representation to those Jews already in the British Mandate of Palestine until the founding of the state of Israel in 1948.

decidedly Zionist orientation; course work and curricula inculcated in young students the ambition to make *Aliyah* and provided extensive language training and instruction in those disciplines useful for immigration to Palestine. Despite the tremendous obstacles they faced, teachers and administrators worked to aid in the emotional, physical, and intellectual rehabilitation of child survivors, many of whom had had little or no formal instruction during the war years.

DOCUMENT 10-9. **An exercise class for preschoolers in the Bergen-Belsen DP Camp, Germany, 1947, USHMMPA WS# 11811, courtesy of the American Jewish Joint Distribution Committee.**

Regina Laks (later Regina Gelb) was a bright young student at the Hebrew Public School sponsored by UNRRA at the Schlachtensee Displaced Persons Camp in Berlin. Regina, often called Renia, was born in Wierzbnik, Poland, on December 16, 1929, the youngest daughter of Isaac and Pola Laks. The Laks were a secular Jewish family but maintained a kosher household at the behest of Pola Laks, an activist in local Zionist organizations. Like her elder sisters, Hania and Rozalia Krysia (later Chris), Regina attended Polish public school, as well as Hebrew school in the afternoon. The girls were excellent pupils, and when, following the German occupation, Jewish students were prohibited from attending school, Pola Laks organized an ad hoc classroom in her own home. Eager to expand their knowledge and education, Regina and her friends organized an informal lending library, pooling the reading resources of many local Jewish families.[27]

On October 27, 1942, German authorities rounded up Jews in the Wierzbnik-Starachowice region. Pola Laks, who had assisted an elderly woman as they approached the assembly point, was deported directly to the **Treblinka** extermination camp. Regina, her father, and her sisters survived for the next two years in a series of labor camps, sustained by a gentile Polish family whom the Lakses had entrusted with their possessions and who, at great risk, smuggled money to the family to purchase food on the camps' black markets. In the early autumn of 1944, the girls and their father were deported to Auschwitz, where Isaac Laks perished in October. Regina and her sisters did not face a selection on the ramp at Birkenau but were processed and confined to the quarantine camp. In October or November 1944, an acquaintance among the prisoner staff arranged for the girls to work with a special labor detail in the *Effektenkammer*, a separate warehouse that held the confiscated effects of non-Jewish prisoners. In this indoor environment, the Laks sisters survived the cold autumn and winter months before the liquidation of the Auschwitz camp in January 1945. Preparing for a forced march to the Gleiwitz concentration camp, Hania, Rozalia, and Regina helped themselves to the piles of warm clothing and shoes in the warehouse, an act of foresight that may have saved their lives. Escaping from a death march near Retzow, an auxiliary camp of the **Ravensbrück** concentration camp near Mecklenburg, Germany, Regina and her sisters spent the last days of the war at an abandoned German estate.

At war's end the Laks sisters took a train to Poland, where they were reunited with members of their father's family in Łódź. Yet, as they attempted to return to their native village of Wierzbnik, they narrowly evaded an attack by angry Poles who wished to keep them from regaining their family's property. In the spring of 1946, Regina traveled with her sister Rozalia—who had recently wed Jewish resistance fighter Shmuel Milek (Miles) Lerman[28]—to Berlin in

---

27. Information concerning the Laks sisters stems from "Interview with Regina Gelb," February 20, 2001, and "Interview with Rosalie (Chris) Lerman," January 13, 1999, both of the Holocaust Museum Oral History Project, U.S. Holocaust Memorial Museum.

28. Miles Lerman (1920–2008) was a founding member of the U.S. Holocaust Memorial Museum. Born in Tomaszów Lubelski, Poland, Lerman grew up with Zionist convictions and hoped to emigrate to Palestine. With the German invasion of Poland, he was arrested and sent to the Viniki forced labor camp. Lerman escaped and spent the rest of the war years as a Jewish partisan. Following his emigration to the United States, Lerman became a successful businessman, active in the real estate, gasoline, and heating trades. In 1979, U.S. President Jimmy Carter named him to the advisory board of the President's Commission on the Holocaust. Lerman served as chairman of the U.S. Holocaust Memorial Museum's governing board from the time of its opening in 1993 until his retirement from the museum in 2000.

order to escape rising antisemitic violence in Poland. There they settled in the Schlachtensee DP Camp, where Regina proved an excellent student at the Hebrew public high school sponsored by UNRRA. In the winter of 1947, the teenager joined the Lermans in immigrating to the United States.

DOCUMENT 10-10. **Report card of Regina Laks from the Herzel Hebrew Public School, Schlachtensee DP Camp, Berlin, January 18, 1947, USHMMPA WS# 96426, courtesy of Regina Laks Gelb.**

Hebrew Public School
"Herzel"
UNRRA Camp "Düppel Center"
Berlin Schlachtensee
Certificate
Pupil: <u>Regina Laks</u>   Born: <u>December 16, 1929</u>
City: <u>Starachowice</u>   Country: <u>[Poland]</u>
Attended the <u>Fifth class</u> from <u>September 18, 1946</u> to <u>January 18, 1947</u>
And graded as follows

Behavior:	Excellent	Mathematics:	Excellent
Bible:	Excellent	Algebra:	Excellent
Hebrew Language:	Excellent	Geometry:	Excellent
Hebrew Literature	Excellent	Physics:	Excellent
English Language:	Excellent	Botanics:	Excellent
Hebrew History:	Excellent	Drawing:	Excellent
Palestine Geography:	Excellent	Music:	Excellent
Geography:	Excellent	Physical Training:	Excellent

Decision of the pedagogical body
Day: <u>January 18th</u>   Year: <u>1947</u>
Class teacher   [signature]   School director

Both Jewish and non-Jewish survivors faced the daunting challenge of rebuilding their lives in the aftermath of the Holocaust. After liberation, Jewish displaced persons often feared returning to their homes in view of the antisemitism that persisted in many regions of Europe. Particularly in postwar Poland, many Jewish refugees encountered violence as they attempted to return to their old residences and reclaim their former possessions.[29] For others, the inability to locate or discover the fate of family members or loved ones made the journey home a distressing prospect. Children who had lost or become separated from their parents in the course of the war faced a number of difficult dilemmas. Should they attempt to make the arduous journey back to their place of origin, or should they remain in an orphanage or DP camp that could provide them with food and shelter? How was such a journey possible without resources or provisions? Would missing parents, siblings, or relatives be waiting for them on their return? Who would care for them if their relatives were dead? Could one

---

29. In early July 1946, a pogrom initiated by Polish rioters in Kielce claimed the lives of forty-two Jewish Poles and a Polish gentile who attempted to help wounded victims to safety. See Monika Adamczyk-Garbowska, "Patterns of Return: Survivors' Postwar Journeys to Poland," *Occasional Paper of the Center for Advanced Holocaust Studies* (Washington, DC: U.S. Holocaust Memorial Museum, 2007).

build a new life and a new future beside one's old roots, in a place where one had perhaps been forgotten or forsaken by one's neighbors?

In the late spring of 1945, fifteen-year-old **Michal Kraus** returned to his native Czechoslovakia. Michal (later Michael) had been raised in the Bohemian town of Nachod, where his father, Karl Kraus, was a physician. In December 1942, the Krauses, like many Czech Jews, were deported to Theresienstadt. The following year the small family arrived on a transport to Auschwitz II–Birkenau. There the Krauses joined other deportees of the Terezin ghetto in the so-called **Theresienstadt family camp** in Birkenau.[30] When this camp was liquidated in July 1944, an emaciated Karl Kraus perished in the gas chambers, while camp physician Dr. **Josef Mengele** selected young Michal and eighty-eight other young boys from the family camp to serve as *Läufer* (runners), couriers who carried information and goods among guards and officials within the Birkenau camp. In the early months of 1945, the fourteen-year-old endured a series of forced marches from Auschwitz to Gleiwitz and then to several camps and subcamps of the **Mauthausen** concentration camp system. He was severely ill with typhus when liberated by American forces at Gunskirchen Lager on May 5, 1945.

After recovering in an American military hospital, Michal and several other young Czech friends decided to make their way back to Prague. The journey to Czechoslovakia was arduous; without sufficient funds, the boys made their way along the Danube by boat and train, then walked nearly 100 kilometers (62 miles) to reach Bratislava (in today's Slovakia) when local rail lines fell into disrepair. The group reached Prague on June 28, 1945. There Michal Kraus remained briefly with a family friend, Vera Loewenbach. Loewenbach had been with Lotte Kraus on a transport from Auschwitz, and it was she who told the young boy of his mother's death in Stutthof in January 1945.

Michal lodged with a number of family friends and acquaintances in his hometown of Nachod, where he returned to school. At this time he began a retrospective "diary" of his Holocaust experiences, which he finished in 1947 and dedicated to his parents. In the summer of 1948, Michal's guardian arranged for him to join an **American Jewish Joint Distribution Committee** orphans' transport to Canada. In 1951, the youth emigrated to the United States, where he enrolled in Columbia University's School of Architecture. After positions with architectural firms in London and Geneva, he settled with his new wife, Ilana Eppenstein, in the Boston area. Of Michael Kraus's extended family, only one aunt and one cousin survived the Holocaust.

---

30. For a broader discussion of the Krauses and the Theresienstadt family camp, see chapter 5.

DOCUMENT 10-11. Memoir/Diary of Michal (Michael) Kraus, handwritten with illustrations, 1945–1947, 2, 23–28, USHMMA, Acc. 2006.51, Michael Kraus Collection (translated from the Czech).

Thousands of people returned to their homes. You see the repatriated everywhere. Everyone hurries home. What kind of upheaval were you able to create, Hitler! And those are just the few who are left: those who endured, and they will not forget! [. . .]

We were all at the end of our strength. It was evening as we walked along the Bratislava streets. People turned around to stare at us. We looked terrible. They led us to a new building that was supposed to have been a department store; but now many refugees are sleeping there on the floor. On the third story, we settled down on the floor of a small room. Last night we were able to get a piece of bread and some coffee; and a man on the street gave us about 20 KC [Czechoslovak crowns].

We went to sleep early and fell asleep immediately after the exhausting trip. We were still not completely recuperated, and walking the whole distance was terribly taxing. We spent several days in Bratislava. At the Jewish Community office, we received 400 KC after a considerable wait, which we used to purchase food in a soup kitchen. The food was not anything special, but better than that usually given to refugees. We even went to the movies there for the first time: *Ivan the Terrible*.

Daily we waited in the repatriation offices for our turn to come. They issued us identity cards. We went to the public baths to bathe, and the next day set off for Prague. A lady gave us a loaf of bread. We hopped on a streetcar, went along to the railroad station, and without tickets got on the express train.

Our group dispersed. Herz and Goldberger got out in Brno. Here the train emptied out a bit, so that we were able to sit down instead of standing in the corridor. A man joined us in our compartment; he gave us a sweet pastry, which for us was an incredible delight. In Pardubice Pavel Werner got out; and at two in the morning only three of us stood at the Wilson Railway Station[31]: Fink, Skoba and I.

First we looked for the repatriation office. It was closed, it opened at eight a.m. So we went to the Masaryk Railway Station, and I slept under a desk.

---

31. From 1945 until 1953, this was the name of the central railway station in Prague.

In the morning Harry left us and we went to the repatriation office, across from the Representative House in the Hybernska. There we met Mr. Berger, an acquaintance from Terezin. They sent us to some sort of shelter on Peter Square. [. . .] At Peter Square I asked about my relatives, but nobody knew anything. I still hoped that Mother was alive, but I began to have my doubts. It was a terrible uncertainty.

They sent us to the Milicova[32] house where they received us cordially and told us that we had to get examined for lice and only then could we go to the convalescent center. [. . .] They found that I had some scabs, so that I had to go to the disinfection station, and only late at night they came to get us again. In the morning I went to the Milicova again and then immediately went to the convalescent center by car with Director Pitter.

The car in which we were traveling stopped in Olesovice. [. . .] We got out there and walked through the beautiful countryside to Kamenice. It was June 19. Yesterday was my birthday. There in Prague, in the disinfection station, it was my fifteenth birthday. But now I feel good. I go with Skoba and a lady teacher to a pretty castle in a large garden. There for the first time I ate again at a table with knife and fork, slept in a bed, went on outings and enjoyed my freedom.

I began to correspond. With the Horaceks, the Bazelovs. Then Vera [Loewenbach] told me the sad news of my mother's fate. One day we drove to Pardubice and then to Skalice. Vera said that she will keep me there for the time being.

---

32. This refers to a street in central Prague.

DOCUMENT 10-12. "Where are our parents, you murderers?" a young survivor of Buchenwald writes on the side of the train car that will take him and other "Buchenwald Boys" from Germany to an orphanage in France, June 1945, USHMMPA WS# 44251, courtesy of Willy Fogel.

While the teenage Michal Kraus was able to travel with his comrades back to his Czech homeland in the hopes of finding his mother, many young Holocaust survivors had no home to which they could return. Many had no surviving family. Others were too young to travel on their own or to make an informed choice about where to go. What to do with youngsters such as these?

This dilemma confronted U.S. authorities shortly after the liberation of Buchenwald in April 1945. American soldiers of the U.S. Ninth Armored Infantry Battalion, arriving at the concentration camp complex on April 11, were astonished to discover among the twenty thousand starving and emaciated prisoners over one thousand children, most of them Jewish youngsters from Poland, Romania, and Hungary. The bewildered U.S. commander immediately cabled officials of the **Children's Aid Society (Oeuvre de Secours aux Enfants, or OSE)**, the French Jewish humanitarian organization with offices in Geneva: "Have found a thousand Jewish children in Buchenwald," the commander wrote. "Take immediate measures to evacuate them."[33]

---

33. Judith Hemmendinger and Robert Krell, *The Children of Buchenwald: Child Survivors of the Holocaust and Their Post-War Lives* (Jerusalem: Gefen Press, 2000), 21.

DOCUMENT 10-13. Page of convoy list of Buchenwald's orphaned children taken from Germany to Écouis, France, June 8, 1945, in Judith Hemmendinger and Robert Krell, *The Children of Buchenwald: Child Survivors of the Holocaust and Their Post-War Lives* (Jerusalem: Gefen Press, 2000), 180.

```
                              - 2 -
            ORPHAN CHILDREN FROM BUCHENWALD NOW IN PARIS

            ENFANTS VENUS D'ALLEMAGNE - CONVOI DU 8 JUIN 1945
                          A ECOUIS (Eure)

                                            Paris List N° 1162 .

   49    ENGLANDER     Matton     II/II/28.   Szatmar         Hongr.
   50    ERNST         Miklos     19/5/29     Typest             "
   51    FACHLER       Joseph     6/2/29      Bodzotyr        Pol.
   52    FARKAS        Chaim      3/8/28      Borsa           Roum.
   53    FARKAS        Erwin      5/6/31      Oradéa            "
   54    FARKAS        Mendel     10/1/28     Karynesavj        "
   55    FARKOWTZ      Martin     8/5/23                        "
   56    FEIG          Lamar      5/5/29      Visent            "
   57    FEIN          Idel       I/1/30      Kowno           Lith.
   58    FELD          Chrsz      18/1/28     Krakow          Pol.
   59    FELDBERG      Aron       15/4/28     Bedzin
   60    FEUERBERG     Abraham    15/1/28     Bacau           Hongr.
   61    FINKERLSTEIN-Salek      9/7/31       Movikaroczyn    Pol.
   62    FINKERLSTAJN-Chaim      13/8/29      Strsemioszyce     "
   63        "         Jakob      I/2/32           "            "
   64    FISCHMAN      Zoltan     4/6/28      Kaletele        Roum.
   65        "         Hersch     1/5/28      Sighet            "
   66    FISCHMAN      Mendel     22/8/29          "            "
   67    FLUGELMANN    Abraham    II/7/23     Opatiew         Pol.
   38    FOGEL         Perec      23/8/28     Ronadejos       Roum.
   69    FOGEL         Izcak      4/4/29           "            "
   70    FOGEL         Jeno       8/5/28      Satmar            "
   71    FOJGEL        Wolf       15/8/28     Dziatoszuce     Pol.
   72    FREILICH      Moritz     25/10/28    Pjotskow          "
   73    FREIMAN       Mozek      29/9/28     Chorzáb           "
   74    FRENKEL       Samuel     I2/3/27                     Tché.
   75    FRIEDMAN      Herman     5/5/29      Rachow
   76    FRIEDMAN      Leb        28/5/29     Viseul de Sus   Roum.
   77    FROM          Natan      17,7/27     Sosnowiec       Pol.
   78    FROMAN        Zysman     8/II/29     Bedzin            "
   79    FRUCHTER      Zalel      24/4/29     Féliste         Roum.
   80    FRUCHTER      Major      6/10/29     Creesunest        "
   81    FRYDMAN       Léon       30/12/30    Lodz            Pol.
   82    FUCHS         Mor        20/I/28     Oradéa          Roum.
   83    FULOP         Marton     2/2/29      Ilenda            "
   84    FULOP         Simon      19/9/28          "            "
   85    FUSYNSKI      Abram      27/9/29                     Pol.
   86    FULOP         Abraham    7/4/28      Surduc          Roum.
   87    GANC          Chaim      26/I/29     Maramosos         "
   88    GEMUTH        Sandor     24/8/29     Viseul de Sus     "
   89    GERSON        Gerszon    I/I/29      Kasimiers       Pol.
   90    GERTRUCZ      Mozès      15/4/28                       "
   91    GLIKSMAN      Moniek     15/10/29    Pabianice         "
   92    GLUCK         Jakob      15/3/30     Viseul de Sus   Roum.
   93    GLUCK         Miklos     2/5/29      Tarkal          Hongr.
   94    GODINGER Rafael          25/6/29     Lopusno         Tché.
   95    GOLDBERG      Berek      8/II/34     Lodz            Pol.
   96    GOLDBERG      Abram      15/2/28     Zdunska-Wola      "
   97    GOLDBLUM      Idel       9/8/29      Lodz              "
   98    GOLBERGER     Lipot      4/10/29     Barochovo       Tché.
```

Two American army chaplains, Rabbis Herschel Schacter and Robert Marcus, coordinated the evacuation of the children with OSE representatives. Most of the children wanted to go to Palestine, but the British Mandate there had placed strict limitations on Jewish immigration. In the end, it was arranged that English organizations would take in 250 boys, while OSE homes and orphanages in France and Switzerland would accommodate the remaining children. On June 2, 1945, 426 boys boarded a train bound for the French town of Écouis (Eure) in Normandy. Incongruously, many of the youngsters wore **Hitler Youth** uniforms, the only age-appropriate clothing that American officials could find; thus, the appearance of the boys in their compartment windows initiated a full-blown riot among local observers when the train crossed the French frontier at Metz. When the boys reached Écouis, their instructors realized that their new pupils faced a formidable array of obstacles. Most of the children, both young and old, had experienced Auschwitz and the horrors of the death marches, as well as the last terrible months of the war in Buchenwald. Starved and brutalized, the boys now grappled with the physical and emotional trauma of their recent past, as well as the very present grief for their murdered loved ones. Besides the psychological devastation, there were intellectual hurdles as well. Many of these young charges had not undertaken formal schooling since the beginning of the war; all had missed several years of instruction and lagged behind their age cohort in terms of academic development. Teachers and administrators understood that the boys' rehabilitation would pose difficult challenges, but they were quite unprepared for what they found as the boys moved into Écouis. The youngsters were sullen and intractable. Years spent in the concentration camp universe had left them distinctly distrustful of adults and utterly free of many moral scruples. Polite and correct comportment was conducive to the classroom setting, but such behavior might mean certain death in a place like Auschwitz. Committed instructors, among them twenty-two-year-old social worker Judith Feist, saw that they had their work cut out for them. Feist was a German Jewish refugee working in the Geneva OSE offices when she heard of the now-famous Buchenwald Boys and decided to visit some of the youngsters at the OSE home of Ambloy.[34] Deeply moved by what she found, Feist agreed to take over directorship of the facility and remained until 1947, when the last boy was settled elsewhere. In 1984, Feist, by then Judith

---

34. In August 1945, the Écouis home was closed down and the children redistributed among more suitable facilities, such as Ambloy, Le Vesinet, and Taverny; 173 of the youngsters with relatives in Palestine were permitted to immigrate to the mandate by British officials and departed Marseilles for Palestine aboard the RMS *Mataroa* in July 1945.

Hemmendinger,[35] recalled the first challenging months with "her children of Buchenwald."

DOCUMENT 10-14. Judith Feist Hemmendinger remembers the "Buchenwald Boys," 1984, in Judith Hemmendinger and Robert Krell, *The Children of Buchenwald: Child Survivors of the Holocaust and Their Post-War Lives* (Jerusalem: Gefen Press, 2000, 27–31).

When the special French train arrived at Buchenwald on June 2, 1945, children stormed it for fear that it would leave without them. Dr. Revel, who accompanied the children, described that "dressed in their striped pyjamas or in uniforms of the Hitler Youth (the only clothes available), they looked like young savages." Many had suffered a total loss of identity. They did not remember their names, having been addressed only by their numbers or nicknames.

Each time the train stopped, the boys jumped out to pillage the countryside, but once in France, the vandalism stopped. A new problem presented itself when the French spotted the German uniforms and attacked the train. The child survivors, now perceived as the enemy, were in such great danger that the train had to be diverted to a sidetrack overnight at the Metz railroad station. [. . .]

Écouis was an abandoned sanatorium placed at the disposal of the OSE by the French government. The OSE had prepared 500 beds for little children, unaware that nearly 400 were aged twelve to twenty-one and only thirty were between eight and twelve years old. They looked like bandits, suspicious and mute. Their heads were shorn; all dressed the same, with faces still swollen from hunger and not a smile to be seen. Their eyes bespoke sadness and suspicion. They were apathetic towards the outside world. They likened the supervisors to guards and were terror stricken at the sight of doctors who reminded them of Mengele, the man who, upon their arrival in Auschwitz, had sent the weak ones to gas chambers, the able-bodied to slave labour.

It was clear that Écouis would not function in the manner of more traditional institutions. The youngsters felt entitled to everything that they

---

35. Judith Feist Hemmendinger was born in 1923 in Bad Homburg, Germany. In the late 1920s, her family moved to France; in 1943, her father, Phillip Feist, was deported and murdered in Auschwitz. During World War II, Feist worked extensively for Oeuvre de Secours aux Enfants. In 1948 she married Claude Hemmendinger and emigrated to Israel.

had been deprived of for so many years. The food they had received from American soldiers was of better quality than what postwar France could offer during the first year. So they bartered in the neighboring farms for extra food by trading blankets, sheets, and dishes and pots from the home. One of them stole puppies that he sold in Paris.

Écouis was a collection of houses surrounding a common yard where all the youngsters were gathered on various occasions. It was at Écouis [that] they vented their anger, their rage. Their rebelliousness led to factions splitting off into groups, by age, by degree of [religious] observance, and by nationality. The older boys in their late teens and even early twenties were sent to Paris, to a big home on Rue Rollin and to Fontenay-aux-Roses, another place on the outskirts of Paris. They were about ten to fifteen percent of the total group.

Unfortunately, the architecture of Écouis reminded the children of the camps. In addition the Director spoke only French and German and could communicate, barely, only with the [Romanians] who knew a little French. All the other boys would not respond when addressed in German. When pieces of bread were handed out, this too reminded them of the camps and they requested that bread be put on the table so that they could help themselves. At the end of each meal the leftovers disappeared into their rooms since one could never know when the next meal would be served.

For these young people, all adults were potential enemies who were not to be trusted. One day they were served Camembert cheese for dessert. The strong smell convinced them that it was poison. They threw the cheese at the adults who were supervising dinner. [. . .]

There were many visitors who came to Écouis to talk with the young survivors of Buchenwald. There were journalists and rabbis and numerous officials who came to meet with these earliest arrivals from Germany. As a matter of fact, visitors <u>did</u>[36] want to hear [their] experiences but the boys refused to speak of them. The children listened silently to the beautiful and affectionate words, noted that it was well meant, but did not react for they were totally disillusioned about human nature.

One day Chaplain Marcus of the American army came to Écouis. He had met the boys before in Buchenwald. They sat in a circle around him on the lawn. The Chaplain stood in front of them unable to utter a word, overcome by his emotions, tears streamed down his cheeks. It had

---

36. Emphasis is in the original.

been a long time since the children had seen an adult cry. Something in them thawed and they too began to cry. One of them described later, "The Chaplain returned to us our souls. He reawakened the feeling we had buried within us."

THE PROCESS OF REMEMBERING

When Judith Feist Hemmendinger decided to publish her compelling account of her years with the Buchenwald Boys in 1984, she received a letter from a former student, in 1945 a fifteen-year-old youngster from Romania.

> I read your book and I remember. I see us back in 1945. Écouis, Ambloy, Taverny. The dumbfounded instructors, the disoriented children. [. . .] Did you know, Judith, that we pitied you? We felt sorry for you. I hope you are not angry that I speak so openly? You thought you could educate us, and yet the younger of us knew more than the oldest among you, about what existed in the world, of the futility of life, the brutal triumph of death. We were not impressed with your age, or your authority. We observed you with amusement and mistrust. We felt ourselves stronger than you. How did you succeed to tame us, Judith? [. . .] Reasonably, Judith, we were doomed to live cloistered lives on the other side of the wall. And yet we succeeded in a short time to find ourselves on the same side. To whom can we attribute the miracle? How can one explain it? To our belief? To yours?[37]

The author of this letter, soon to receive the Nobel Peace Prize, was Elie Wiesel. By then an internationally recognized writer and chairman of the U.S. Presidential Commission on the Holocaust,[38] Wiesel had certainly fulfilled the promise of integrity and intellectual achievement that Hemmendinger had seen in that band of sullen, mistrustful boys from Buchenwald in 1945. Wiesel was born on September 30, 1928, in Sighet, Transylvania, then part of the Kingdom of Romania. His father, Shlomo, an Orthodox Jew of Hungarian descent, was a shopkeeper who owned a grocery store in Sighet and figured as a respected and influential man in his community. His mother, Sarah (née Feig), was the daughter of a prominent Hassidic family from the next village. Wiesel often

---

37. Elie Wiesel, quoted in Hemmendinger and Krell, *The Children of Buchenwald*, 10–11.
38. Later, this became the U.S. Holocaust Memorial Council, the founding and governing body of the U.S. Holocaust Memorial Museum.

claimed that within his household circle, his father had represented reason and his mother belief and faith. Shlomo Wiesel had always encouraged young Elie to improve his intellect, urging him to study literature, history, and modern Hebrew. It was Sarah who convinced her young son to read the Torah and other religious works.[39]

Romania ceded northern and eastern Transylvania to Hungary in 1940, and as Hungarian authorities instituted an array of antisemitic legislation, Transylvanian Jews like the Wiesels became subject to these measures. In April 1944, thirteen thousand Jews from Sighet and the surrounding rural communities were ghettoized. In the following month the Hungarian authorities, in coordination with the German **Security Police**, began systematically to deport Hungarian Jews. Between May 16 and 22, 1944, the Wiesels and their fellow residents of the Sighet ghetto were dispatched to Auschwitz. In the chaos of selection at Birkenau, Wiesel's elder sisters were separated from the family and survived the war. Sarah Wiesel and her youngest daughter, Tzipora, perished in the gas chamber immediately upon arrival at the camp. Spared on the ramp, Elie and his father found themselves attached to a labor detail in Buna (Auschwitz III–Monowitz). Father and son endured appalling conditions there and at three subsequent forced labor camps, and survived the "death march" that brought them to Buchenwald. There, in the last weeks of the war, Shlomo Wiesel died of dysentery, starvation, and exhaustion. On April 11, 1945, Elie Wiesel, just fifteen years old, witnessed the liberation of Buchenwald by American forces.

Following World War II, Wiesel, as we have seen, traveled with other young former prisoners of Buchenwald to France, where he convalesced and received formal educational instruction at OSE children's homes at Écouis, Ambloy, and Taverny. At this time, he learned that his sisters Hilda and Beatrice had survived the war and was reunited with them. Wiesel remained in France after leaving the OSE home and began studies at the Sorbonne in literature and philosophy. Although he supported himself by working as a journalist for French and Israeli newspapers, Wiesel initially refused to write or speak about his Holocaust experiences. In 1954, however, he broke his self-imposed silence, penning an 862-page manuscript that he called *Un di Velt Hot Geshvign* (*And the World Remained Silent*). The manuscript, published in Yiddish in Argentina, failed to attract literary interest, and Wiesel shelved the project until an interview he hoped to carry out for a Tel Aviv daily with French prime minister Pierre

---

39. See Ellen S. Fine, *The Legacy of Night: The Literary Universe of Elie Wiesel* (Albany, NY: State University of New York Press, 1982).

Mendes-France brought the young man into contact with French novelist and Nobel laureate François Mauriac. Mauriac persuaded Wiesel to translate and shorten his text. The result was a spare, 109-page volume published in 1958 in French and retitled *La Nuit,* or in English, *Night* (1960). With **Anne Frank**'s *Diary of a Young Girl* and Primo Levi's *If This Is a Man,*[40] *Night* remains one of the seminal memoirs in Holocaust literature.[41]

The following selection, a pivotal scene in Wiesel's original Yiddish manuscript as well as in *Night,*[42] differs strikingly from most sources presented in this volume. With few exceptions, this edition has attempted to reconstruct the experiences of children during the Holocaust through sources produced at the time or through oral testimony or trial depositions provided in the early postwar years. The last section of this chapter, however, examines how adult survivors have framed their memories of childhood during the Holocaust. It is not uncommon for a survivor's in situ accounts or recollections articulated in the immediate aftermath of the Shoah to differ appreciably from testimonies given decades later, if not in detail, then in emphasis and perspective. This is particularly true of the testimonies of child survivors, for whom the passage into adulthood may fundamentally alter perceptions of persons and events. The passing of time obscures certain aspects of the past, while others stand out in sharp relief. Intellectual understanding and emotional maturity sharpen the lens and bring once inexplicable incidents into clearer focus. The middle-aged man connects more cogently the kaleidoscope of events that facilitated his survival. A child may have felt only anger and bitterness toward parents who "abandoned" her to utter strangers during the war years; now grown with children of her own, the adult survivor may at last comprehend the deed that saved her life and the tremendous personal sacrifice made by her parents in such an undertaking. For Wiesel, writing a decade after his arrival at Auschwitz, the intervening years had accentuated the caesura between past and future, which had emerged in that first terrible night in the camp: that break which separated the author from his childhood and his faith.

---

40. The American title of this work by Primo Levi is *Survival in Auschwitz.*

41. Scholars have had difficulty classifying Elie Wiesel's masterpiece specifically as a memoir; some call it an autobiographical novel and others as a semifictional memoir. See Harold Bloom, ed., *Modern Critical Interpretations: Elie Wiesel's Night* (Philadelphia: Chelsea House Publishers, 2001). Wiesel himself disputes that his work has any aspects of a novel, calling it instead his "deposition"; see Elie Wiesel, *All Rivers Run to the Sea* (New York: Schocken Books, 1996).

42. Compare Document 10-15 with the depiction of this scene in Elie Wiesel, *Night,* trans. Stella Rodway (New York: Bantam Books, 1980), 31–32.

DOCUMENT 10-15. Elie Wiesel, *Un di Velt hot Geshvign*, trans. Vera Szabó (Buenos Aires: Tsentral-Farband fun Poylishe Yidn in Argentine, 1956), 66–71 (translated from the Yiddish).

At that point we did not yet know which was the good direction—left or right; which way led to work, and which to the crematorium. Nevertheless, I felt lucky—I was going with my father.

A new inmate came up to us:

"Satisfied?"

"Yes," someone replied.

"Idiots," he said, "you're going straight to the chimney."

They are taking us to the chimney. . . .

Could this be true? Or is he just trying to scare us? Is he just a sadist, who takes pleasure in seeing others' fear? No, it looks like he was telling the truth. Sixty meters [almost 200 feet] from us, flames are leaping up from a pit, gigantic flames. They are burning something there. What can it be? A truck drives up to the pit and drops its load automatically. Suddenly, I catch a glimpse of what it was delivering and pouring into the pit—little children! Infants! Newborn babies! Yes, I saw it with my own eyes. . . . I saw that they threw children into the flames alive!

(Is it surprising, dear Reader, that I have not been able to sleep ever since? Is it surprising, that I stopped believing in the holiness of fire? And in the *shkhine*[43] that is supposed to be present when babies are born?)

The blood froze in my veins. Suddenly, an icy wind blew through my entire body. So it's true, we are really going to the chimney. To the burning pit. There must be another pit farther down, a bigger one, for adults. For us. For me.

I pinch my cheek instinctively. Am I still alive? Am I awake? Or is this just a dream of a hypersensitive child? Maybe it's a nightmare? Or a feverish vision? The fruit of my sick fantasy?

I pinched my cheek, I felt the pain, but I still couldn't believe that this was really happening. One thought kept hammering away at my brain: how is it possible that they are burning people, and the world remains silent? How is it possible that they are throwing children into burning pits alive, just like coal; and the civilized world, our educated, progressive world is not voicing its fury and not protesting. "Impossible . . . impossible," I murmured to myself. The world would not remain silent. People would say something. They would revolt, or at least react somehow. After all, we are not living in the Middle Ages! We are more advanced; this is

---

43. That is, "Divine Presence."

the twentieth century! Once upon a time there was wanton disregard for human life ["amol iz take dem mentshns lebn hefker geven"], but today? No, none of this is true; it can't be true. It was a dream. Just a dream. I am dreaming. A nightmare . . . I will wake up soon, with a pounding heart, and I will see again the home where I grew up, the bookshelf. . . .

My father's voice ripped me out of the quarrel that was going on in my head:

"It's a pity . . . a pity that you didn't go with your mother. . . . I saw several boys your age going with their mothers . . ."

His voice was terribly sad. I realized that he did not want to see what they were going to do to me. He did not want to see how they burned his only son alive. . . .

You have to know: at that point we did not yet know about the perfection of the German death factory, about the elegant gas chambers. We thought that they simply burned people alive. . . . And we were even wondering—how come we can't hear the agonizing moans of the dying, their painful outcries.

A cold sweat ran down my forehead. Death by fire! The most horrible way to die. No, I don't want to die like this. No way!

But why cause pain to my father? I tell him that I don't believe they would burn people in our modern world. Humanity would never let this happen. . . .

"Humanity?" answered my father. "Humanity is not concerned with us. They wouldn't move a finger for us. Our age is the age of possibilities, endless possibilities. . . . Today anything is possible. Anything is permitted, even these chimneys."

His voice was choking on the tears he held back.

"Father," I said, "if that is so, I will commit suicide. I am going to run to the electric wire. Let them shoot me. And if they won't, I will be electrocuted. I would rather die quickly than after a long agony . . . after fighting with the flames for hours. If I have to die, Father, I would rather die like a human being, not a piece of wood."

He did not answer. He was weeping. My father's entire body, his whole self, was shaking convulsively. Everyone was weeping.

Someone began to say kaddish.[44] Another person said the *vide*.[45] I do not know if it has ever happened before, in the long history of the Jewish people's sufferings, that Jews would say kaddish for themselves.

---

44. This is a prayer for the dead.
45. This prayer confessing sins is said on Yom Kippur and before dying.

"*Yisgadal . . . veyiskadash shmey rabo. . . .*[46] I hear my father whisper it too.

This was the first time that I revolted against God, against the One whose name is blessed.

Why should I sanctify His name? Does He deserve it? How did He earn our blessings? If humanity is silent, I won't sanctify its name. But the Lord of the Universe, the great, mighty and awesome God—He was silent too. So why should I thank Him? Why should I sanctify His name? Why praise Him?

Meanwhile, we continue walking and come closer to the pit, the flames. An infernal heat was rising from it. [. . .] In the depths of my heart, I bid farewell to my father and to the whole world. Words are forming themselves in my mind involuntarily, without crossing the threshold of my lips: *Yisgadal veyiskadash shmey rabo.* And I still thought of Him, of God. I was still too close to my past, to my illusions back then. My heart is about to burst from too much excitement. That's it! Soon . . . a rendezvous with the Angel of Death. . . .

No. All the fear was in vain. Two steps from the pit we were ordered to turn to the left, toward the bath barracks. [. . .] I will never forget that night either. The first night in the camp, which turned my entire life into one long night.

I will never forget the smoke that took my mother and Tsipoyrele,[47] like sacrifices, up to heaven.

I will never forget the little faceless children, whose tiny bodies and souls I saw turned into clouds in a clear, sinfully silent sky.

I will never forget the fire that consumed my faith in everything that is beautiful, in everything that is true, and in everything that is holy, forever. I will never forget that nocturnal silence which deprived me of the desire to live and the possibility to make peace with the future.

I will never forget those moments which murdered my God and my soul and turned my dreams into a desert.

I will never forget these things, even if I am condemned to live longer than God himself. Never.

Historians often prefer in situ testimony because of its immediacy to events: there is no time for embellishment or outside influence to cloud or to

---

46. From the Hebrew, "Magnified and sanctified be His great name," the opening line of the Kaddish prayer.

47. This is the Yiddish diminutive of Tzipora, the name of Wiesel's sister.

intrude upon the "truth" of the matter. Yet, scholars must also be grateful for postwar accounts of Holocaust survivors. Time allows for the contemplation and recollection of details perhaps omitted in initial testimonies and facilitates the interweaving of historical and factual knowledge with personal experiences. In some cases, the lack of immediacy to events also allows for the candidness that comes with distance. While former persecutees generally do not hesitate to come forward with memories of shootings, roundups, and deportations, many survivors are loathe to discuss incidents of a sensitive nature connected with the war years—family conflict, betrayal of personal principles, issues of child abuse and sexual violence—and feel safer in including such topics in their history only with the passage of time.

Child survivors who write about their experiences face an extraordinary challenge in untangling the confusing web of childhood memories. In his memoir *A Story of a Life*, Israeli novelist Aharon Appelfeld suggests that his recollection of six perilous years of war are, for the most part, fragmented images that "fade away quickly, as if refusing to reveal themselves."[48]

Appelfeld was born in 1932 in Czernowicz (Ukrainian: Chernitvsi; Romanian: Cernăuți), a city occupied by Romanian forces following the German invasion of the Soviet Union in the summer of 1941. He was eight when his mother was murdered by Romanian fascists. Deported with his father to a camp in the Transnistrian Reservation, in Romanian-occupied Ukraine, the young Appelfeld escaped and spent three years in hiding before joining the Soviet army as a kitchen boy. He came to Palestine via Italy in 1946 and is widely regarded today as one of the most prominent Hebrew-language authors.[49]

In his series of essays titled *Beyond Despair*, Appelfeld records his fascination with the manner in which child survivors like himself absorbed and processed the tragedies that they had witnessed and experienced. While adults had known another life before the Holocaust and toiled to rebuild their lives in the postwar years on the memory of those former times, the children of the Shoah had no other chronology. The Holocaust was the indestructible present that shaped their lives, while their adult contemporaries could and often chose to exorcise such memories from their histories.

---

48. See Aharon Appelfeld, *The Story of a Life*, trans. Aloma Halter (New York: Schocken Books, 2004), vii.

49. From his prolific oeuvre, see Appelfeld, *The Story of a Life*, and Aharon Appelfeld, *Beyond Despair: Three Lectures and a Conversation with Philip Roth*, trans. Jeffrey M. Green (New York: Fromm, 1994).

DOCUMENT 10-16. Aharon Appelfeld, *Beyond Despair: Three Lectures and a Conversation with Philip Roth*, trans. Jeffrey M. Green (New York: Fromm International Publishing Corporation, 1994), 36–37.

There were child acrobats who walked tightropes with marvelous skill. In the woods they had learned how to climb in the highest, thinnest branches. Among them was a set of twins, boys of about ten, who juggled wooden balls fantastically. There were also child mimics who would imitate animals and birds. Dozens of children like that wandered around the camps. While the adults tried to forget what had happened and to forget themselves, to get back into the fabric of life, the children refined their sufferings as, perhaps, can be done only in a folk song.

I have discussed the children because it was from them, in the course of time, that artistic expression arose. I shall try to explain myself. Ultimately the children did not absorb the full horror, only that portion of it which children could take in. Children lack a sense of chronology, of comparison with the past. While the adults spoke about what had been, for the children the Holocaust was the present, their childhood and youth. They knew no other childhood. Or happiness. They grew up in dread. They knew no other life.

While the adults fled from themselves and from their memories, repressing them and building up a new life in the place of the previous one, the children had no previous life or, if they had, it was now effaced. The Holocaust was the black milk, as the poet said, that they sucked morning, noon, and night. [. . .]⁵⁰

The Holocaust as life, as life in its most dreadfully concentrated form from both the existential and social point of view—that approach was rejected by the [adult] victim. The numerous books of testimony that were written about the Holocaust are, if you will, a desperate effort to force the Holocaust into a remote recess of madness, to cut it off from life, and in other cases, to envelop it in a kind of mystical aura, intangible, which must be discussed as a kind of experience that cannot be expressed in words, but rather in prolonged silence. In the case of children who grew up in the Holocaust, life during the Holocaust was something they could understand, for they had absorbed it with their blood.

---

50. This line refers to a recurring line in the celebrated 1948 poem "*Todesfuge*" ("Death Fugue") by Romanian Holocaust survivor Paul Celan.

While some individuals prefer not to discuss their memories of the Holocaust, many survivors, including child survivors, feel the need to share their experiences with others, either through oral or written testimonies. Many hope that their stories will have historical or pedagogical value, or they feel compelled to bear witness to the tragedy, lest the world forget. For others, the process of remembering has become an artistic endeavor. For those already gifted at writing, drawing, or sculpting, creativity and memory can combine in a lasting testament to their Holocaust experience. Visual arts and literature also provide an innovative way for former persecutees to process their experiences and convey the deep emotions attached to them. For child survivors like Halina Birenbaum, poetry is a means to articulate childhood recollections in an adult voice.

Halina was born in Warsaw in 1929.[51] At the age of ten, she was interned with her family in the **Warsaw ghetto**. In April 1943, the thirteen-year-old, along with her mother, brother, and sister-in-law, were deported from the *Umschlagplatz* in Warsaw to the **Majdanek** concentration camp on the outskirts of Lublin. Halina's mother died in the gas chambers directly upon arrival.[52] Two months later, Halina and her sister-in-law, Hela, found themselves on a transport to Auschwitz. There, the twenty-year-old Hela assumed the role of the young girl's mother and protector; when Hela died of tuberculosis in the Auschwitz infirmary, a heartbroken Halina was left to face the horrors of the killing center alone. Struck by a sentry's bullet on New Year's Day 1945, the youngster was convalescing when she learned that the camp was being liquidated on January 27, 1945. Still weak from her injuries, Hadina endured a series of forced marches to Ravensbrück and Neustadt-Glewe, where on May 2, she and her fellow prisoners were liberated by Soviet army forces.

In 1947, Halina Birenbaum emigrated to Israel and worked on a **kibbutz** until her marriage in 1950. She remembers that in the chaotic early days of Israeli independence, she found little time to contemplate her recent past. "When I arrived in Israel, at the beginning of the War of Independence in 1947, everyone was struggling for his very existence and that of the State which had just been established. There was no time to talk about still fresh memories. There was also no one interested in listening. There was no lack of burn-

---

51. See Halina Birenbaum, *Hope Is the Last to Die: A Coming of Age under Nazi Terror*, trans. David Welsh (Armonk, NY: M. E. Sharpe, 1996).

52. See Halina Birenbaum's poem "She Was Waiting There" describing her first visit to the Majdanek memorial site in 1986, in Halina Birenbaum, *Sounds of a Guilty Silence: Selected Poems*, trans. June Friedman (Kraków: Centrum Dialogu, 1997), 50–52.

ing issues of the moment, and a great desire to provide [ourselves] with new experiences and values—different ones, the ones of Israel."[53]

The **Eichmann Trial**, played out in a Jerusalem courtroom from 1961 to 1962, galvanized Birenbaum to reflect upon her childhood and to express her recollections in writing. In 1967, she published a memoir, *Hope Is the Last to Die*, and spent much of the next three decades recounting her history to young listeners and pressing, particularly in her native Poland, for Jewish-Christian reconciliation. In the early 1980s, Birenbaum turned to poetry to give voice to the powerful memories that linked her harrowing past with her workaday present. Many of her poems turn on the contemplation of a common activity or object that holds a deeper significance in her traumatic childhood. Other works arose as a result of visits she made to the Auschwitz and Majdanek concentration camp memorials in the 1980s and 1990s. In "There Is My Soul," the poet is aware that she sees more vividly than her fellow visitors as she walks through a deserted Auschwitz in spring. She is haunted. She sees ghosts in the ruins, in the dust, in the sky where once there was smoke. Her experiences and memories hold her here, as if she were bound. Whatever her future, her fate is here, where so many of her friends and loved ones have died. In "My Life Started from the End," however, Birenbaum sees resurrection in the miracle of her survival. The nightmare years have done their work, but they have not destroyed her or her belief in the essential good in human nature. Painful memories remain, but they cannot eclipse the present or bar her egress to the living world.

DOCUMENTS 10-17 AND 10-18. Halina Birenbaum, "There Is My Soul" (1994) and "My Life Started from the End" (1983), in Halina Birenbaum, *Sounds of a Guilty Silence: Selected Poems*, trans. June Friedman (Kraków: Centrum Dialogu, 1997), 5, 35–36.

There Is My Soul

> There among the ghosts
> between the barracks,
> crematorium's ruins,
> silence full of murmurs
> audible, visible, but
> only to me
> faces, figures
> between present greenery
> or whiteness of snow
> futile moans, prayers

---

53. Birenbaum, *Hope*, ix–x.

Dead and gone, suspended forever
in the clouds over Auschwitz
on the ground, in the earth
in every pebble, speck of sand
speck of dust,
over there among ashes and bones
crushed, mixed
crowds of souls in space
lost for eternity
also mine
it's not important where I live
when, how or where I will die
or wherever in the world
they will bury my body
marked number 48693
tattooed here

My Life Started from the End

My life started from the end
first I have known death,
then—birth
I was growing amidst hatred,
in the kingdom of destruction
only to learn later about creation
breathing bleakness, fires, deterioration of feeling
this was the atmosphere of my childhood
only then I have seen the light;
only then I have flourished.
I have always known love
even when it was terrible or worse!
love was there even in hell
I have encountered it!
my life began from the end and just then
everything returned to the beginning,
I was resurrected.
it was all not in vain, not in vain,
because goodness is not less powerful then evil
in me is strength too
I am the proof.

DOCUMENT 10-19. A boy displays his Auschwitz tattoo as other children from the Neu Freimann DP camp look on, USHMMPA WS# 29314, courtesy of Jack Sutin.

LIST OF DOCUMENTS

1 Children in the Early Years of Antisemitic Persecution

From Assimilation to Marginalization

Document 1-1. Bertel Kugelmann, "My Story," 1996, quoted in Paulgerhard Lohmann, *"Hier waren wir zu Hause": Die Geschichte der Juden vom Fritzlar, 1096–2000, vor dem Hintergrund der allgemeinen Geschichte der deutschen Juden* (Norderstedt: Books on Demand, 2002), 257–58 (translated from the German).

Document 1-2. Irmgard Marx, "Everyday Terror," 1989, in Elfi Pracht, ed., *Frankfurter jüdische Erinnerungen: Ein Lesebuch zur Sozialgeschichte* (Sigmaringen: Jan Thorbecke Verlag, 1997), 227–32 (translated from the German).

Document 1-3. The antisemitic *Der Stürmer* newspaper portrays Jewish children ejected from a public swimming pool in Bad Herweck, near Mannheim, 1935, USHMMPA WS# 11196, courtesy of the Wiener Library Institute of Contemporary History.

In the Schoolroom

Document 1-4. A class essay by Gerd Zwienicki, "Does History Show That Racial Mixing Leads to the Decline of a People," c. 1934, USHMMA, Acc. 2005.122.1 (translated from the German).

Document 1-5. Irene Spicker Awret, *They'll Have to Catch Me First: An Artist's Coming of Age in the Third Reich* (Madison, WI/Takoma Park, MD: University of Wisconsin Press/Dryad Press, 2004), 88.

"I Decide Who Is a Jew"

Document 1-6. Walter Grab, "The Jews are Vermin Except for my Jewish Schoolmate Grab," in *"Niemand war dabei, und keiner hat's gewußt": Die deutsche Öffentlichkeit und die Judenverfolgung, 1933–1945*, ed. Jörg Wollenberg (Munich: Piper, 1989), 45–50 (translated from the German).

Document 1-7. A crowd of Viennese children look on as an Austrian Nazi forces a youth to paint the word *Jud* (Jew) on the facade of his father's store, 1938, USHMMPA WS# 01510, courtesy of the Österreichische Gesellschaft für Zeitgeschichte.

Training Youth for Jobs Abroad

Document 1-8. Letter of Ernst Löwensberg, Burkeville, Virginia, to students of the emigration-training farm at Gross-Breesen, Silesia, June 16, 1938, USHMMA, Acc. 2000.227, Herbert Cohn Gross-Breesen Collection (translated from the German).

Document 1-9. Jewish teenagers unload a cart of hay at the Gross-Breesen's emigration-training farm, Germany, c. 1936, USHMMPA WS# 68299, courtesy of George Landecker.

Reichskristallnacht

Document 1-10. Marguerite Strasser, "Then I Felt Like a Subhuman . . . ," in Friedrich Kraft, ed., *Kristallnacht in Bayern: Judenpogrom am 9. November 1938: Eine Dokumentation* (Ingolstadt: Claudius Verlag, 1988), 109–10 (translated from the German).

The Dismissal of Jewish Children from "German" Schools

Document 1-11. Decree of the Reich Minister of Science, Education, and Adult Education re the Schooling of Jews, November 15, 1938 (translated from the German).

Document 1-12. Diary of Elisabeth Block, entry for November 17, 1938, in Elisabeth Block, *Erinnerungszeichen: Die Tagebücher der Elisabeth Block*, ed. Haus der Bayerischen Geschichte/ Historischer Verein Rosenheim (Rosenheim: Wendelstein-Druck, 1993), 162–63 (translated from the German).

Document 1-13. A young girl reads her classroom lesson in Hebrew to her fellow classmates at a school sponsored by the Jewish Community of Berlin, c. 1935, USHMMPA WS# 32505, courtesy of the Bildarchiv Preussischer Kulturbesitz.

What's in a Name? Israel and Sara

Document 1-14. Eleanor Kraus, "Don't Wave Good-bye" (unpublished manuscript, private collection, c. 1940), 144–46 (© Liz Perle and Steven Kraus, reprinted with permission).

2 Children and the War

The First Taste of Conflict

Document 2-1. Ten-year-old Kazimiera Kostewicz (Mika) discovers the body of her sister Anna, killed in a strafing run by German pilots on Polish civilians near Warsaw, September 1939, USHMMPA WS# 50898, courtesy of Julien Bryan.

Document 2-2. Julien Bryan, *Warsaw: 1939 Siege, 1959 Warsaw Revisited* (Warsaw: Polonia Publishing House, 1959), 20–21.

Document 2-3. Inge Deutschkron, *Ich trug den gelben Stern*, 4th ed. (1975; Cologne: Verlag Wissenschaft und Politik, 1983), 60–67 (translated from the German).

Document 2-4. Interview of Idel Kozłowski (Kozlovskij) by the Central Jewish Historical Commission, February 14, 1947, USHMMA, RG-15.084, Holocaust Survivor Testimonies, Lódź, 301/3626 (translated from the Russian).

Document 2-5. A Jewish child in occupied France wears the yellow star, USHMMPA WS# 63042, courtesy of Michael O'Hara.

Caught in the Crossfire: The War on Civilians

Document 2-6. Olive McNeil, London, England, undated testimony, quoted in Jane Waller and Michael Vaughan-Rees, *Blitz: The Civilian War, 1940–1945* (London: McDonald Optima, 1990), 12–13.

Document 2-7. Addendum of Milovan Đjilas to the July 28, 1942, diary entry of Vladimir Dedijer, in Vladimir Dedijer, *The War Diaries of Vladimir Dedijer*, Vol. 1: *From April 6, 1941, to November 27, 1942* (Ann Arbor: University of Michigan Press, 1990), 269–70.

Document 2-8. Body of a young boy killed in an antipartisan campaign on the slopes of Petrova Gora, a stronghold of communist resistance activity in Yugoslavia, 1942, USHMMPA WS# 01138, courtesy of Lydia Chagoll.

Document 2-9. Diary of Tanya Savicheva, Leningrad, December 1941 to May 1942, courtesy of the Saint Petersburg Museum of History, Saint Petersburg, Russia (translated from the Russian).

Document 2-10. Letter of Marie (Maruška) Šroubková, c. July 2, 1942, in Jolana Macková and Ivan Ulrych, eds., *Fates of the Children of Lidice: Memories, Testimonies, Documents,* trans. Elias Khelil (Nymburk: Lidice Memorial, 2004), 36.

The War's Long Shadow: The Last Years of Conflict

Document 2-11. Bert Voeten, *Doortocht: Een Oorlogsdagboek, 1940–1945*, 4th ed. (Amsterdam: Uitgeverij Contact, 1947), 198–99 (translated from the Dutch).

3 Lives in the Balance

Strangers in a Strange Land: Emigration

Victims of *Einsatzgruppen* Activity

Yad Vashem, the Holocaust Martyrs' and Heroes' Remembrance Authority, 1992–1995), 1:516–17.

Document 3-9. Report of military chaplain Dr. Joseph Maria Reuss, Catholic divisional chaplain, to Lieutenant Colonel Helmuth Groscurth, First Generalstabsoffizier, 295th Infantry Division, August 20, 1941, in Ernst Klee, Willi Dressen, and Volker Riess, eds., *"Schöne Zeiten": Judenmord aus der Sicht der Täter und Gaffer* (Frankfurt: S. Fischer Verlag, 1988), 135–36 (translated from the German).

Document 3-10. Lieutenant Colonel Helmuth Groscurth to commander in chief of the Sixth Army, Field Marshall Walther von Reichenau in re report on events in Byelaya Tserkov on August 20, 1941, August 21, 1941, in Ernst Klee, Willi Dressen, and Volker Riess, eds., *"Schöne Zeiten": Judenmord aus der Sicht der Täter und Gaffer* (Frankfurt: S. Fischer Verlag, 1988), 140–42 (translated from the German).

Document 3-11. Testimony of August Häfner, May 31, 1965, in Ernst Klee, Willi Dressen, and Volker Riess, eds., *"Schöne Zeiten": Judenmord aus der Sicht der Täter und Gaffer* (Frankfurt: S. Fischer Verlag, 1988), 145 (translated from the German).

Document 3-12. A young mother with her two young children waits with other Jews from Lubny at an assembly point before their murder, c. April 1942, USHMMPA WS# 83014, courtesy of the Hamburger Institut für Sozialforschung.

"We've Been Picked Up": Roundups and Deportations

Document 3-13. Note of Klaus Scheurenberg to his father, Paul Scheurenberg, c. 1942, Scheurenberg collection, Stiftung Neue Synagoge Berlin—Centrum Judaicum, CJA 614 Nr. 8.

Document 3-14. Letter of Felicitas and Thomas Gumpel, July 14, 1942, in Reiner Lehberger and Ursula Randt, eds., *"Aus Kindern werden Briefe": Dokumente zum Schicksal jüdischer Kinder und Jugendlicher in der NS-Zeit* (Hamburg: Freie und Hansestadt Hamburg Behörde für Schule, Jugend und Berufsbildung, 1999), 52–53 (translated from the German).

Document 3-15. Lissy Asser, a young girl from Göttingen, waits with other German Jews at a deportation point in Hildesheim, c. March 1942. Lissy, her parents, and a younger brother are believed to have been murdered in Treblinka, USHMMPA WS# 69635, courtesy of the Stadtarchiv Hildesheim.

Document 3-16. Vita of Iser Franghieru, Hehalutz Orphanage, September 12, 1947, American Jewish Joint Distribution Committee Archive, RG 25.001, American Joint Distribution Committee, Case Files of Romanian Orphans.

Document 3-17. Iser Franghieru in a Bucharest orphanage, c. 1947, USHMMPA WS# 01827, courtesy of the American Jewish Joint Distribution Committee.

Document 3-18. Letter of Pinchas Eisner to his brother Mordechai Eisner, Budapest, October 16, 1944, in Reuvan Dafni and Yehudit Keliman, eds., *Final Letters* (London: Weidenfeld & Nicholas 1991), 454–57.

4 Children in the World of the Ghetto

Into the Ghetto

Document 4-1. Diary of Yitskhok Rudashevski, Vilna ghetto, entry for September 6, 1941, in Alexandra Zapruder, ed., *Salvaged Pages: Young Writers' Diaries of the Holocaust* (New Haven, CT: Yale University Press, 2002), 199–201.

Document 4-2. Interview of Seweryn Dobrecki by the Central Jewish Historical Commission, c. 1946, USHMMA, RG-15.084, Holocaust Survivor Testimonies, 301/3611/4-5 (translated from the Polish).

Document 4-3. Two children beg on the streets of the Warsaw ghetto, September 1941, USHMMPA WS# 32327, courtesy of Günther Schwarberg.

"The Garden of Eden": Education in the Łódź Ghetto

Document 4-4. Album page of a New Year's greeting from the children of School No. 25, to Ghetto Elder Mordechai Chaim Rumkowski, Łódź ghetto, September 1941, USHMMPA WS# 22473, courtesy of YIVO Institute (translated from the Hebrew)

Document 4-5. Diary essay of Josef Zelkowicz, "The Breadwinner (The Seventh Apartment)," 1941, in Josef Zelkowicz, *In Those Terrible Days: Writings from the Lodz Ghetto*, ed. Michal Unger, trans. Naftali Greenwood (Jerusalem: Yad Vashem, 2002), 63–69.

Document 4-6. Children digging for "coal" in the Łódź ghetto, 1941, USHMMPA WS# 61900, courtesy of the YIVO Institute.

"Give Me Your Children": The "Children's Actions"

Document 4-7. Speech of Mordechai Chaim Rumkowski, Łódź ghetto, September 4, 1942, in Isaiah Trunk, *Łódź Ghetto: A History*, ed. and trans. Robert Moses Shapiro (Bloomington: University of Indiana Press in association with the U.S. Holocaust Memorial Museum, 2006), 272–75.

Document 4-8. Children selected for deportation bid farewell to their families through the wire fence of the central prison during the *Gehsperre* action in the Łódź ghetto, September 1942, USHMMPA WS# 30057, courtesy of Beit Lohamei Haghetaot.

Document 4-9. Testimony of Adolf Avraham Berman, May 3, 1961, in *The Trial of Adolf Eichmann: Record of Proceedings in the District Court of Jerusalem* (Jerusalem: Trust for the Publication of the Proceedings of the Eichmann Trial in cooperation with the Israel State Archives and Yad Vashem, the Holocaust Martyrs' and Heroes' Remembrance Authority, 1992–1995), 1:425–26.

Death and Survival in the Ghetto

Document 4-10. Diary of an anonymous girl, Łódź ghetto, entries for March 10 and 11, 1942, in Alexandra Zapruder, ed., *Salvaged Pages: Young Writers' Diaries of the Holocaust* (New Haven, CT: Yale University Press, 2002), 236–38.

Document 4-11. Diary of Oskar Singer, entry for July 28, 1942, in Hanno Loewy et al., eds., *"Unser einziger Weg ist Arbeit": Das Getto in Łódź, 1940–1944* (Vienna: Löcker Verlag, 1990), 221–22 (translated from the German).

Document 4-12. Jewish children work at a box-making factory in the Glubokoye ghetto, Belorussia, c. early 1942, USHMMPA WS# 08059, courtesy of Karl Katz.

Document 4-13. Testimony of Dr. Aharon Peretz, May 4, 1961, in *The Trial of Adolf Eichmann: Record of Proceedings in the District Court of Jerusalem* (Jerusalem: Trust for the Publication of the Proceedings of the Eichmann Trial in cooperation with the Israel State Archives and Yad Vashem, the Holocaust Martyrs' and Heroes' Remembrance Authority, 1992–1995), 1:478.

Document 4-14. Diary of Eva Ginzová, entries for September 28, 1944, and April 23, 1945, Theresienstadt, in Alexandra Zapruder, ed., *Salvaged Pages: Young Writers' Diaries of the Holocaust* (New Haven, CT: Yale University Press, 2002), 180, 187–88.

5 Children in the Concentration Camp Universe

At the Edge of the Abyss

Document 5-1. Janina Hescheles, "Bełżec," Janowska, 1943, published in Michał Borwicz, ed., *Pieśń ujdzie cało: Antologia wierszy o żydach pod okupacją niemiecką* (Warsaw/Łódź/Kraków: Centralna Żydowska Komisja Historyczna w Polsce, 1947), 270–71 (translated from the Polish).

Death at Auschwitz

Document 5-2. Jewish women and children from Transcarpathian Rus who have been selected for the death walk to the gas chamber, Auschwitz, May 1944, USHMMPA WS# 77342, courtesy of Yad Vashem.

Document 5-3. Testimony of Magda Szabo, August 24, 1964, Frankfurt Auschwitz Trial, in Fritz Bauer Institute and the State Museum of Auschwitz-Birkenau, eds., *Der Auschwitz-Prozess: Tonbandmitschnitte, Protokolle, Dokumente* (DVD) (Berlin: Directmedia Publishing, 2004) (translated from the German).

Document 5-4. Ink drawing by Helga Weissová, "Selection," 1945–1946, in Helga Weissová, *Zeichne, was Du siehst! Zeichnungen eines Kindes aus Theresienstadt/Terezin*, ed. Niedersächsischen Verein zur Förderung von Theresienstadt/Terezin, e.V. (Göttingen: Wallstein Verlag, 1998), 139.

Document 5-5. Miklós Nyiszli, *Auschwitz: A Doctor's Eyewitness Account*, trans. Tibère Kremer and Richard Seaver (Hungarian ed., 1946; New York: Frederick Fell Publishers, 1960), 114–20.

In a Living Hell: Survival in Camps

Document 5-6. Diary of Michal (Michael) Kraus, handwritten with illustrations, 1945–1947, 54–60, USHMMA, Acc. 2006.51, Michael Kraus Collection (translated from the Czech).

Document 5-7. Personal testimony of Hanna Hoffmann-Fischel, c. 1960, in Inge Deutschkron, *Denn ihrer war die Hölle: Kinder in Gettos und Lagern* (Cologne: Verlag Wissenschaft und Politik, 1965), 49–52 (translated from the German).

Document 5-8. Oral history of Berel Dov Freiberg, recorded by Bluma Wasser, 1945, in Isaiah Trunk, ed., *Jewish Responses to Nazi Persecution: Collective and Individual Behavior in Extremis* (New York: Stein and Day, 1982), 268–78.

Document 5-9. Testimony of anonymous girl (Janka Avram), interviewed by Icek Shmulewitz, New York, 1955, in Isaiah Trunk, ed., *Jewish Responses to Nazi Persecution: Collective and Individual Behavior in Extremis* (New York: Stein and Day, 1982), 117–19.

Document 5-10. Following the liberation of Auschwitz, child survivors display their tattooed arms, January 1945, USHMMPA WS# 12110C, courtesy Wytwornia Filmow Dokumentalnych i Fabularnych.

Document 5-11. Testimony of Szymon (Simon) Srebrnik before the examining judge of the district court in Łódź, Władysław Bednarz, June 29, 1945, in Archives of the District Museum in Konin, *Chełmno Witnesses Speak*, ed., Łucja Pawlicka-Nowak, trans. Juliet D. Golden (Konin: Council for the Protection of Memory of Combat and Martyrdom in Warsaw/District Museum in Konin, 2004), 125–29.

Document 5-12. Prisoner personal information card of Stefan Jerzy Zweig, Buchenwald, August 5, 1944, USHMMA ITS Digital Collections, Buchenwald—Individual Documents, Male Section, R. 1.1.5.3, 7503616 1.

Document 5-13. Survivors of Buchenwald walk through the liberated camp with Stefan Jerzy Zweig, a four-year-old Jewish boy protected by the camp's underground resistance, April and June 1945, USHMMPA WS# 19041, courtesy of the Fédération Nationale des Déportés et Internés Résistants et Patriotes.

6 Children in the Web of Racial Hygiene Policy

Compulsory Sterilization

Document 6-1A. Letter of Dr. Gotthold Lehmann, director of the State Institute for the Deaf and Mute and Teaching Institute for Teachers of the Deaf and Mute, to Frau E., Freienwalde, c. July 1936, USHMMA, RG-10.320, Horst Biesold Collection (translated from the German).

Document 6-1B. Letter of Dr. Gotthold Lehmann, director of the State Institute for the Deaf and Mute and Teaching Institute for Teachers of the Deaf and Mute, to Frau E., Freienwalde, July 31, 1936, USHMMA, RG-10.320, Horst Biesold Collection (translated from the German).

Document 6-2. Memorandum of the Prussian Minister of the Interior to the German Foreign Office, March 28, 1934, Political Office of the German Foreign Office, R 99166, Partei, 84/4 (translated from the German).

The Many Faces of Lebensborn

Document 6-3. Letter of Frau A. to Lebensborn, e.V., October 7, 1938, Bundesarchiv Berlin, NS 19/1064 (translated from the German).

Document 6-4. German medical personnel examine Polish children at an internment camp set up by the Reich Commissariat for the Strengthening of German Ethnicity in Łódź to select youngsters "acceptable" for Germanization and adoption by German families, 1941, USHMMPA WS# 90416, courtesy of the Instytut Pamięci Narodowej.

Document 6-5. Testimony of Otto Uebe, November 4, 1947, *United States of America v. Ulrich Greifelt et al.* (Subsequent Nuremberg Case No. 8, RuSHA Trial), in *Trials of War Criminals before the Nürnberg Military Tribunals under Control Council Law No. 10*, 14 vols. (Buffalo, NY: William S. Hein & Co., 1997), 4:1060–62.

"Euthanasia"

Document 6-6. Circular decree of the Reich Minister of the Interior, re obligatory registration for "Deformed, etc., Newborns," etc., August 18, 1939 (Bundesarchiv Berlin, R 1501/5586, Reichsinnenministerium) (translated from the German).

Document 6-7. Annamarie R., a young disabled girl born in Kassel, Germany, on January 30, 1935. She was murdered, likely by an overdose of medication, in the Eichberg "euthanasia" facility c. June 27, 1941, USHMMPA WS# 58297 HHStAW Abt 3008-Picture Collection, courtesy of the Hessisches Hauptstaatsarchiv Wiesbaden.

Document 6-8. Excerpts from the patient file of Anita Hart, March 30, 1943, to June 22, 1943, File No. 13029, USHMMA, RG-14.030M, Bezirkskrankenhaus Kaufbeuren (translated from the German).

The Danger of "Gypsy Blood": Roma and Sinti

Document 6-9. ITO/ITS Report of Johannes Meister, children's search officer, regarding Gypsy children of Sankt Josefspflege in Mulfingen, c. 1948, USHMMA, RG-07.004*01, Zigeunerkinder aus der Sankt Josefspflege in Mulfingen (translated from the German).

Document 6-10. Sinti children pose with a nun at the St. Josefspflege home at Mulfingen, ca.1943–1944. The children, spared as "research material" from immediate deportation, were later transferred to Auschwitz, USHMMPA WS# 08632, courtesy of the Zentralrat Deutscher Sinti und Roma.

Document 6-11. Trial proceedings of *Supreme Court of the Estonian Soviet Socialist Republic v. Ain-Ervin Mere (in absentia), Ralf Gerrets, and Jaan Viik* (Mere Trial), USHMMA, RG-06.026.12, Estonian State Archives of the former Estonian KGB State Security Committee, Records Relating to War Crimes Investigations and Trials in Estonia, 1940–1987.

Children As "Research Material"

Document 6-12. Testimony of Johann Frahm, March 3 to June 18, 1946, *UK v. Max Pauly, et al.* (Curio-Haus Case), March 29, 1946, USHMMA, RG-59.016M, Reel 4, Judge Advocate General's Office, United Kingdom, War Crimes Case Files, Second World War, 1945–1953, Public Record Office.

Document 6-13. Relief workers lead child survivors from Birkenau following the liberation of Auschwitz by Soviet forces. Leading the ranks (beside the nurse) are Miriam and Eva Mozes, survivors of Josef Mengele's infamous experimentation with twins, January 1945, USHMMPA WS# 88591, courtesy of the Instytut Pamieci Narodowej.

Document 6-14. Miklós Nyiszli, *Auschwitz: A Doctor's Eyewitness Account*, trans. Tibère Kremer and Richard Seaver (Hungarian ed., 1946; New York: Fell, 1960), 175–78.

Document 6-15. Hygiene-Bacteriological Research Station of the Waffen SS, Southeast, delivery slip for the head of a corpse, signed by Dr. Josef Mengele, June 29, 1944, USHMMPA WS# 00592, courtesy of the Auschwitz Memorial Museum (Państwowe Muzeum w Oświęcim-Brzezinka) (translated from the German).

7 The Lives of Others

Youth Organizations in the Third Reich

Document 7-1. A young boy leaps into the clasped arms of his schoolmates during outdoor physical education exercises at the Hitler Youth training facility in Memmingen, Germany, USHMMPA WS# 30590, courtesy of the Holocaust Museum Houston.

Document 7-2. Editorial of W. Thomas, director of the Berlin Deaf Athletes' Association, *Youth Supplement of the Newsletter of the Berlin Deaf Athletes' Association*, May 1, 1937, USHMMA, RG-10.320, Horst Biesold Collection (translated from the German).

Document 7-3. Young women remember the League of German Girls, 1946, in Gisela Miller-Kipp, ed., *"Auch Du gehörst dem Führer": Die Geschichte des Bundes Deutscher Mädel (BDM) in Quellen und Dokumenten. Forschungsreihe Materialien zur Historischen Jugendforschung* (Weinheim: Juventa Verlag, 2001), 315–16 (translated from the German).

Nonconformity and Dissidence: The Edelweiss Pirates

Document 7-4. Report of the Gestapo, Düsseldorf, December 10, 1937, in Detlev Peukert, *Die Edelweisspiraten: Protestbewegungen jugendlicher Arbeiter im Dritten Reich. Eine Dokumentation*, 2nd ed. (Cologne: Bund-Verlag, 1983), 28–30 (translated from the German).

Document 7-5. Handwritten flyer distributed by the Wuppertal troop of the Edelweiss Pirates, "To the Subjugated German Youth," c. 1942, in Detlev Peukert, *Die Edelweisspiraten: Protestbewegungen jugendlicher Arbeiter im Dritten Reich. Eine Dokumentation*, 2nd ed. (Cologne: Bund-Verlag, 1983), 81 (translated from the German).

Document 7-6. The "Cologne Navajos' Fight Song," c. 1944, in Detlev Peukert, *Die Edelweisspiraten: Protestbewegungen jugendlicher Arbeiter im Dritten Reich. Eine Dokumentation*, 2nd ed. (Cologne: Bund-Verlag, 1983), 51 (translated from the German).

Hearts and Minds: Nazi Propaganda

Document 7-7A. Excerpt from a children's textbook in the Third Reich: "You Are Carrying the Load!" ("Hier trägst Du mit!"), in Jacob Graf, *Biologie für höhere Schulen (Biology for Secondary Schools)* (Munich: Lehmann Verlag, 1943), table 25.

Document 7-7B. Excerpt from a children's textbook in the Third Reich: A story problem in *Arithmetic for Volksschulen: Governing District Cologne and Aachen, School Years in Seven and Eight*, 1941, quoted in Ute Hoffmann, *Todesursache "Angina": Zwangssterilisation und "Euthanasie" in der Landes-Heil- und Pflegeanstalt Bernburg* (Magdeburg: Eigenverlag des Ministeriums des Innern des Landes Sachsen-Anhalt, 1996), 24 (translated from the German).

Document 7-8. German school children read the antisemitic children's story *Der Giftpilz* (*The Poisonous Mushroom*), c. 1938, USHMMPA WS# 69561, E39 No. 2381/7, courtesy of the Stadtarchiv Nürnberg.

Document 7-9. Game board *"Juden raus!"* ("Jews, Get Out!"), Günther & Co., 1938, USHMMPA WS# 11894, courtesy of the Leo Baeck Institute.

Perpetrators and Victims

Document 7-10. Letter from the director of the Trade and Vocational School for Boys to the Department of Education, Frankfurt am Main, October 1, 1935, in Kommission zur Erforschung der Geschichte der Frankfurter Juden, eds., *Dokumente zur Geschichte der Frankfurter Juden, 1933–1945* (Frankfurt am Main: Verlag Waldemar Kramer, 1963), 111 (translated from the German).

Document 7-11. Report of the Centralverein Landesverband Pommern (Pomerania), signed Michelsohn, to the Central Office of the Centralverein, in re Schivelbein, August 16, 1935, USHMMA, RG-11.00, Osobyi Archive Moscow, 721-1-3019, Centralverein Records, 91 (translated from the German).

Document 7-12. Decision of the State Court, Karlsruhe, concerning the appeal of Franz Josef Seitz against the removal of parental custody, Karlsruhe, April 15, 1937, USHMMA, RG-32.008*01, Willi Seitz Collection (translated from the German).

German Children and the War

Document 7-13. Members of the Hitler Youth practice donning gas masks during an air raid drill, c. 1937, USHMMPA WS# 31512, courtesy of Bildarchiv Preussischer Kulturbesitz.

Document 7-14. School essay of an eleven-year-old girl, Nuremberg, 1946, in Emmy E. Werner, *Through the Eyes of Innocents: Children Witness World War II* (Boulder, CO: Westview Press, 2000), 49.

Document 7-15. Interview with Harry Bahrmann, *Völkischer Beobachter*, c. March 1945, in Franz Seidler, *Deutsche Volkssturm: Das letzte Aufgebot, 1944–1945*, 2nd ed. (Berlin: Herbig, 1991), 322.

Document 7-16. Journal of Lili G., entries for April 15 through May 9, 1945, in Reinhard Rürup, ed., *Der Krieg gegen die Sowjetunion, 1941–1945: Eine Dokumentation zum 50. Jahrestag des Überfalls auf die Sowjetunion* (Berlin: Argon-Verlag, 1991), 257–58 (translated from the German).

Document 7-17. A German mother shields the eyes of her young son as American troops force her and other townspeople to view the bodies of Soviet civilians from a mass grave near Suttrop, Germany, May 3, 1945, USHMMPA WS# 08197, courtesy of the National Archives and Records Administration.

8 The World of the Child

Escape into Learning

Document 8-1. Diary/memoir of Miriam Wattenberg, entry for July 12, 1940, in Mary Berg, *Warsaw Ghetto: A Diary by Mary Berg*, ed. S. L. Shneiderman, trans. Norbert Guterman and Sylvia Glass (New York: L. B. Fischer, 1945), 32–33.

Document 8-2. Diary entry of Pola Rotszyld (Yad Vashem Archives, sign. 03/438) in Barbara Engelking-Boni, "Childhood in the Warsaw Ghetto," in *Children and the Holocaust: Symposium Presentations of the Center for Advanced Holocaust Studies* (Washington DC: USHMM, 2004), 35.

Document 8-3. Three girls study at a clandestine Jewish school in Prague, c. 1942, USHMMPA WS# 37424, courtesy of the Jewish Museum of Prague Photo Archive.

Document 8-4. Diary of Yitskhok Rudashevski, Vilna ghetto, entry for March 14, 1943, in Alexandra Zapruder, ed., *Salvaged Pages: Young Writers' Diaries of the Holocaust* (New Haven, CT: Yale University Press, 2002), 223.

At Play during the Holocaust

Document 8-5. Children at play in a field in Marysin, Łódź ghetto, c. 1941, USHMMPA WS# 33844, courtesy of the Archiwum Panstowe w Łódźi, sygn. 1120, fot. 27-832-6.

Document 8-6. Oskar Rosenfeld, entry in *The Chronicle of the Łódź Ghetto*, August 25, 1943, in Lucjan Dobroszycki, ed., *The Chronicle of the Łódź Ghetto, 1941–1944*, trans. Richard Lourie et al. (New Haven, CT: Yale University Press, 1987), 373–74.

Document 8-7. Painted wooden butterfly toy, Small Fortress, Theresienstadt ghetto, 1941–1945, USHMMPA WS# N00049, original reposited in Pamatnik Terezin Narodni Kulturni Pamatka.

Document 8-8. Testimony of Dr. Aharon Peretz, May 4, 1961, in *The Trial of Adolf Eichmann: Record of Proceedings in the District Court of Jerusalem* (Jerusalem: Trust for the

Publication of the Proceedings of the Eichmann Trial in cooperation with the Israel State Archives and Yad Vashem, the Holocaust Martyrs' and Heroes' Remembrance Authority, 1992–1995), 1:478–79.

Document 8-9. Personal testimony of Hanna Hoffmann-Fischel, c. 1960, in Inge Deutschkron, *Denn ihrer war die Hölle: Kinder in Gettos und Lagern* (Cologne: Verlag Wissenschaft und Politik, 1965), 52–55 (translated from the German).

Document 8-10. An eight-year-old resident of the Vilna ghetto describes the game "Jews and Germans" (Genia Silkes Collection, YIVO Institute), quoted in George Eisen, *Children and Play in the Holocaust: Games among the Shadows* (Amherst: University of Massachusetts Press, 1988), 72.

Document 8-11. In the Łódź ghetto, children, one dressed as a ghetto policeman, play a peculiar version of cops and robbers, 1943, USHMMPA WS# 80401, courtesy of Beit Lohamei Haghetaot.

Innocence and Knowledge

Document 8-12. Excerpt from Josef Zelkowicz's essay "The Optimist in the Potato Queue," Łódź ghetto, September 5, 1942, in Josef Zelkowicz, *In Those Terrible Days: Writings from the Lodz Ghetto*, ed. Michal Unger, trans. Naftali Greenwood (Jerusalem: Yad Vashem, 2002), 306–7.

Document 8-13. Young children from the Marysin colony wait to be conveyed to the deportation assembly point during the *Gehsperre*, Łódź ghetto, September 1942, USHMMPA WS# 50334, courtesy of the Instytut Pamięci Narodowej.

Document 8-14. Watercolor by Helga Weissová, *Birthday Wish I* (*Přání k narozeninám I*), Theresienstadt ghetto, December 1941, USHMMPA WS# 60926, courtesy Helga Weissová.

Document 8-15. Diary of Elisabeth Block, entry for March 8, 1943, in Elisabeth Block, *Erinnerungszeichen: Die Tagebücher der Elisabeth Block*, ed. Haus der Bayerischen Geschichte/ Historischer Verein Rosenheim (Rosenheim: Wendelstein-Druck, 1993), 265–66.

In Hopes and Dreams: Coping with the Holocaust

Document 8-16. Personal testimony of Hanna Hoffmann-Fischel, c. 1960, in Inge Deutschkron, *Denn ihrer war die Hölle: Kinder in Gettos und Lagern* (Cologne: Verlag Wissenschaft und Politik, 1965), 52–55 (translated from the German).

Document 8-17. Just as youngsters at Birkenau reenacted *Snow White,* children in the Novaky labor camp perform a play about another popular Disney character, Mickey Mouse, Slovakia, 1944, USHMMPA WS# 40080, courtesy of Mira Frenkel.

Document 8-18. Drawing of Ilona Goldman (Alona Frankel) for her parents in hiding, Marcinkowice, Poland, 1942, USHMM Collections, gift of Alona Goldman Frankel.

Document 8-19. Abram Koplowicz, "When I Am Twenty," Łódź ghetto, c. 1943, in Institute of Tolerance/State Archives in Łódź (in cooperation with the Centre de Civilization Française and the Embassy of France in Poland), eds., *The Children of the Łódź Ghetto* (Łódź: Bilbo, 2004).

Document 8-20. Watercolor by Nelly Toll, *Teacher with Children Wearing Black Uniforms*, Lvov, Poland, c. 1943–1944, USHMMPA WS# 94466, courtesy of Nelly Landau Toll.

9 Children and Resistance and Rescue

Youth and Armed Resistance

Document 9-1. Emmanuel Ringelblum, "Little Stalingrad Defends Itself," c. April 1943, in Joseph Kermish, ed., *"To Live with Honor and Die with Honor": Selected Documents from the Warsaw Ghetto Underground Archives "O.S." (Oneg Shabbath)* (Jerusalem: Yad Vashem, 1986), 601–3.

Document 9-2. Oral history of Berel Dov Freiberg, recorded by Bluma Wasser, 1945, in Isaiah Trunk, ed., *Jewish Responses to Nazi Persecution: Collective and Individual Behavior in Extremis* (New York: Stein and Day, 1982), 283–87.

Document 9-3. Members of the Bielski partisan family camp, including several small children, shortly before liberation, Naliboki Forest, Belorussia, 1944, USHMMPA WS# 77654, courtesy of the Yad Vashem Photo Archives.

Document 9-4. Oral history of Rachmiel Łozowski, Tel Aviv, 1947, USHMMA RG 15.084, Holocaust Survivor Testimonies, 301/540 (translated from the Yiddish).

Unarmed Resistance: The Children's War

Document 9-5. "Let the Jewish Youth Remember," *Słowo Młodych* (*Young People's Voice*), Warsaw ghetto, spring, 1942, USHMMA, RG-15.070M, Zespół podziemie–prasa konspiracyjna [Clandestine Publications], 230/13/1.

Document 9-6. Arrested at a checkpoint, a Jewish boy holds a bag of smuggled goods, Warsaw ghetto, c. 1941, USHMMPA WS# 60611B, courtesy of the YIVO Institute.

Document 9-7. Henryka Łazowertówna (Lazowert), "The Little Smuggler," Warsaw ghetto, c. 1941, in Michał Borwicz, ed., *Pieśń ujdzie cało: Antologia wierszy o Żydach pod okupacją niemiecką* (Warsaw: Centralna Żydowska Komisja Historyczna w Polsce, 1947), 115–16 (translated from the Polish).

Document 9-8. Historians believe the girl in the center of the photograph to be teenage resistance member Masha Bruskina, being marched with her comrades Kiril Trus and Volodya Shcherbatsevich to their place of execution by German soldiers, Minsk, October 26, 1941, USHMMPA WS# 14101, courtesy of the Bundesarchiv, Bild 146-197-026-43.

Document 9-9. The hanging of teenage resistance figures, believed to be Masha Bruskina and Volodya Shcherbatsevich, by an officer of the German 707th Infantry Division, Minsk, October 26, 1941, USHMMPA WS# 25136, courtesy of Ada Dekhtyar.

In Hiding

Document 9-10. Emmanuel Ringelblum, "Jewish Children on the Aryan Side," 1943, in Emmanuel Ringelblum, *Polish-Jewish Relations during the Second World War*, ed. Joseph Kermish and Shmuel Krakowski (Jerusalem: Yad Vashem, 1974), 140–45.

Document 9-11. Oral history of Szepsel Griner by the Central Jewish Historical Commission in Poland, c. 1947, USHMMA RG 15.084, Holocaust Survivor Testimonies, 301/2284 (translated from the Polish).

Document 9-12. Louise Israels celebrates her second birthday in hiding, Amsterdam, July 30, 1944, USHMMPA WS# 16427, courtesy of Louise Lawrence-Israels.

Children and Aid Organizations: The Politics of Rescue

Document 9-13. Child identification card of Helmuth Ehrenreich, Police Presidium of Frankfurt am Main, June 16, 1939, USHMMA, Acc. 2006.396, Ehrenreich Family Papers (translated from the German).

Document 9-14. Letter of Gilbert Kraus to George Messerschmidt, assistant secretary of state, February 3, 1939 (National Archives and Records Administration, RG-59, General Records of the Department of State, Decimal File 150.6265/610).

Document 9-15. Aided by philanthropists Gilbert and Eleanor Kraus, a group of Austrian Jewish children finds safe haven in the United States, June 3, 1939, USHMMPA WS# 96464, courtesy of Anita Willens.

Document 9-16. Child's drawing of Château de la Hille, La Hille, France, c. 1942, USHMMPA WS# 45699, courtesy of Vera Friedlander.

When Rescue Fails

Document 9-17. Jewish refugee children pose at a children's home in Izieu, France, summer 1943, USHMMPA WS# 15513, courtesy of Serge Klarsfeld.

Document 9-18. Telex from Klaus Barbie, commanding officer of the Security Police and Security Service IV B, Lyon, to Department IV B 4, Paris (Barbie Telex), April 6, 1944, in Serge Klarsfeld, *The Children of Izieu: A Human Tragedy*, trans. Kenneth Jacobsen (New York: Harry N. Abrams, 1985), 95 (translated from the German).

10 Elsewhere, Perhaps?

"Over This Field of Death, Peace Breaks Out": Liberation

Document 10-1. David P. Boder, interview with Gert Silberbart, Geneva, August 27, 1946, USHMMA RG-50.472, spool 9-82 and 83 (translated from the German).

Document 10-2. Young boys join adult survivors in cheering their U.S. Army liberators at Dachau, April 29, 1945, USHMMPA WS# 45075, courtesy of the National Archives and Records Administration, College Park.

Document 10-3. Oral history testimony of P. H. by the Canadian Jewish Congress, Montreal, February 1946, in Isaiah Trunk, ed., *Jewish Responses to Nazi Persecution: Collective and Individual Behavior in Extremis* (New York: Stein and Day, 1982), 326–28.

Document 10-4. Diary of Alice Ehrmann (Alisah Shek), entries for May 10, 11, and 18, 1945, in Alisah Shek, "Tagebuch," in *Theresienstädter Studien und Dokumente, 1994*, ed. Miroslav Kárný, Raimund Kemper, and Margita Kárná (Prague: Verlag Academica, 1994), 196–99 (translated from the German).

The Search for Family Members

Document 10-5. Hedvig Dydyna holds a name card intended to help surviving family members locate her at the Kloster Indersdorf DP camp, Germany, c. May 1945, USHMMPA WS# 06677, courtesy of Lilo Plaschkes.

Document 10-6. Interview with Maria Straucher by the Central Jewish Historical Commission, Kraków, December 2, 1947, USHMMA, RG-15.084, Holocaust Survivor Testimonies, 301/3292/1-2, 1949 (translated from the Polish).

Document 10-7. Renée Pallarés (right) and her family helped save Diane Popowski, an infant who had been with her mother at the Agde internment camp in France. In 1949, nine-year-old Diane reluctantly returned to her widowed father. She reunited with the Pallarés family some years later. USHMMPA WS# 13346, courtesy of Diane Popowski Fenster.

Document 10-8. Interview with Gizela Szulberg by the Central Jewish Historical Commission, Bytom, September 3, 1947, USHMMA RG 15.084, Holocaust Survivor Testimonies, 301/2731/2-3 (translated from the Polish).

Where Is Home?

Document 10-9. An exercise class for preschoolers in the Bergen-Belsen DP Camp, Germany, 1947, USHMMPA WS# 11811, courtesy of the American Jewish Joint Distribution Committee.

Document 10-10. Report card of Regina Laks from the Herzel Hebrew Public School, Schlachtensee DP Camp, Berlin, January 18, 1947, USHMMPA WS# 96426, courtesy of Regina Laks Gelb.

Document 10-11. Diary of Michal (Michael) Kraus, handwritten with illustrations, 1945–1947, 2, 23–28, USHMMA, Acc. 2006.51, Michael Kraus Collection (translated from the Czech).

Document 10-12. "Where are our parents, you murderers?" a young survivor of Buchenwald writes on the side of the train car that will take him and other "Buchenwald Boys" from

Germany to an orphanage in France, June 1945, USHMMPA WS# 44251, courtesy of Willy Fogel.

Document 10-13. Page of convoy list of Buchenwald's orphaned children taken from Germany to Écouis, France, June 8, 1945, in Judith Hemmendinger and Robert Krell, *The Children of Buchenwald: Child Survivors of the Holocaust and Their Post-War Lives* (Jerusalem: Gefen Press, 2000), 180.

Document 10-14. Judith Feist Hemmendinger remembers the "Buchenwald Boys," 1984, in Judith Hemmendinger and Robert Krell, *The Children of Buchenwald: Child Survivors of the Holocaust and Their Post-War Lives* (Jerusalem: Gefen Press, 2000, 27–31).

The Process of Remembering

Document 10-15. Elie Wiesel, *Un di Velt hot Geshvign*, trans. Vera Szabó (Buenos Aires: Tsentral-Farband fun Poylishe Yidn in Argentine, 1956), 66–71 (translated from the Yiddish).

Document 10-16. Aharon Appelfeld, *Beyond Despair: Three Lectures and a Conversation with Philip Roth*, trans. Jeffrey M. Green (New York: Fromm International Publishing Corporation, 1994), 36–37.

Documents 10-17 and 10-18. Halina Birenbaum, "There Is My Soul" (1994) and "My Life Started from the End" (1983), in Halina Birenbaum, *Sounds of a Guilty Silence: Selected Poems*, trans. June Friedman (Kraków: Centrum Dialogu, 1997), 5, 35–36.

Document 10-19. A boy displays his Auschwitz tattoo as other children from the Neu Freimann DP camp look on, USHMMPA WS# 29314, courtesy of Jack Sutin.

BIBLIOGRAPHY

PUBLISHED PRIMARY SOURCES

Adelson, Alan, and Robert Lapides, eds. *Łódź Ghetto: Inside a Community under Siege*. New York: Viking, 1989.

Archives of the District Museum in Konin. *Chełmno Witnesses Speak*, edited by Łucja Pawlicka-Nowak, translated by Juliet Golden. Konin: Council for the Protection of Memory of Combat and Martyrdom in Warsaw/District Museum in Konin, 2004.

Berg, Mary. *Warsaw Ghetto: A Diary by Mary Berg*, edited by S. L. Shneiderman, translated by Norbert Guterman and Sylvia Glass. New York: L. B. Fischer, 1945.

Block, Elisabeth. *Erinnerungszeichen: Die Tagebücher der Elisabeth Block*, edited by Haus der Bayerischen Geschichte/Historischer Verein Rosenheim. Rosenheim: Wendelstein-Druck, 1993.

Czerniakow, Adam. *The Warsaw Diary of Adam Czerniakow*, edited by Raul Hilberg et al. New York: Ivan R. Dee, 1979.

Dedijer, Vladimir. *From April 6, 1941 to November 27, 1942*. Vol. 1 of *The War Diaries of Vladimir Dedijer*. Ann Arbor: University of Michigan Press, 1990.

Deutschkron, Inge. *Denn ihrer war die Hölle: Kinder in Gettos und Lagern*. Cologne: Verlag Wissenschaft und Politik, 1965.

Dobroszycki, Lucjan, ed. *The Chronicle of the Łódź Ghetto, 1941–1944*, translated by Richard Lourie et al. New Haven, CT: Yale University Press, 1984.

Frank, Anne. *The Diary of Anne Frank: The Revised Critical Edition*, edited by David Barouw and Gerrold van der Stroom, translated by Arnold J. Pomerans, B. M. Mooyaart-Doubleday, and Susan Massotty. New York: Doubleday, 2001.

Fritz Bauer Institute and the State Museum of Auschwitz-Birkenau, eds. *Der Auschwitz-Prozess: Tonbandmitschnitte, Protokolle, Dokumente* (DVD). Berlin: Directmedia Publishing, 2004.

Ginz, Petr. *The Diary of Petr Ginz, 1941–1942*, edited by Chava Pressburger, translated by Eva Lappin. New York: Atlantic Monthly Press, 2007.

Gutman, Yisrael, and Michael Berenbaum, eds. *Anatomy of the Auschwitz Death Camp*. Bloomington: Indiana University Press in association with the U.S. Holocaust Memorial Museum, 1994.

Hescheles, Janina. "Mit den Augen eines zwölfjähriges Mädchen." In *Im Feuer vergangen: Tagebücher aus dem Ghetto*, edited by Johann Christoph Hampe, 151–89. Munich: Chr. Kaiser Verlag, 1963.

Hurst, Thea Gersten. *Das Tagebuch der Thea Gersten: Aufzeichnungen aus Leipzig, Warschau und London, 1939–1947*. Leipzig: Evangelische Verlagsanstalt, 2001.

Kermish, Joseph. *To Live with Honor and Die with Honor: Selected Documents from the Warsaw Ghetto Underground Archives "O.S." (Oneg Shabbath)*. Jerusalem: Yad Vashem, 1986.

Klarsfeld, Serge. *Memorial to the Jews Deported from France, 1942–1944: Documentation of the Deportation of the Victims of the Final Solution in France*. New York: Beate Klarsfeld Foundation, 1983.

Klee, Ernst. *Dokumente zur "Euthanasie."* Frankfurt am Main: Fischer Taschenbuch Verlag, 1985.

Klee, Ernst, Willi Dressen, and Volker Riess, eds. *"The Good Old Days": The Holocaust As Seen by Its Perpetrators and Bystanders*, translated by Deborah Burnstone. New York: Free Press, 1988.

Kommission zur Erforschung der Geschichte der Frankfurter Juden, eds. *Dokumente zur Geschichte der Frankfurter Juden, 1933–1945*. Frankfurt am Main: Verlag Waldemar Kramer, 1963.

Korczak, Janusz. *Ghetto Diary*. New Haven, CT: Yale University Press, 2003.

Kraft, Friedrich, ed. *Kristallnacht in Bayern: Judenpogrom am 9. November 1938: Eine Dokumentation*. Ingolstadt: Claudius Verlag, 1988.

Lehberger, Reiner, and Ursula Randt, eds. *"Aus Kindern werden Briefe": Dokumente zum Schicksal jüdischer Kinder und Jugendlicher in der NS-Zeit*. Hamburg: Freie und Hansestadt Hamburg Behörde für Schule, Jugend und Berufsbildung, 1999.

Macková, Jolana, and Ivan Ulrych, eds. *Fates of the Children of Lidice: Memories, Testimonies, Documents*, translated by Elias Khelil. Nymburk: Lidice Memorial, 2004.

Pentlin, Susan Lee, ed. *The Diary of Mary Berg: Growing Up in the Warsaw Ghetto*, edited by S. L. Shneiderman, translated by Norbert Guterman and Sylvia Glass. Oxford: Oneworld Publishers, 2006.

Reichsgesetzblatt. 42 vols. Berlin: Reichsverlagsamt, 1916–1942.

Ringelblum, Emmanuel. *Polish-Jewish Relations during the Second World War*, edited by Joseph Kermish and Shmuel Krakowski. Jerusalem: Yad Vashem, 1974.

Rosenfeld, Oskar. *In the Beginning There Was the Ghetto: Notebooks of Łódź*. Evanston, IL: Northwestern University Press, 2002.

Rudashevski, Isaac. *The Diary of the Vilna Ghetto, June 1941–April 1943*. Tel Aviv: Ghetto Fighters' House, 1973.

Sierakowiak, Dawid. *The Diary of Dawid Sierakowiak: Five Notebooks from the Łódź Ghetto*, edited by Alan Adelson, translated by Kamil Turowski. Oxford: Oxford University Press, 1996.

Stroop, Jürgen. *The Stroop Report: "The Jewish Quarter of Warsaw Is No More!"* edited and translated by Sybil Milton. New York: Pantheon Books, 1979.

The Trial of Adolf Eichmann: Record of Proceedings in the District Court of Jerusalem. 8 vols. Jerusalem: Trust for the Publication of the Proceedings of the Eichmann Trial in cooperation with the Israel State Archives and Yad Vashem, the Holocaust Martyrs' and Heroes' Remembrance Authority, 1992–1995.

Trials of War Criminals before the Nürnberg Military Tribunals under Control Council Law No. 10 (Green Series). 15 vols. Buffalo, NY: William S. Hein, 1997.

Trunk, Isaiah, ed. *Jewish Responses to Nazi Persecution: Collective and Individual Behavior in Extremis.* New York: Stein and Day, 1982.

Tych, Feliks, et al., eds. *Kinder über den Holocaust. Frühe Zeugnisse: Interviewprotokolle der Zentralen Jüdischen Historischen Kommission in Polen,* translated by Jürgen Hensel et al. Berlin: Metropol, 2008.

Voeten, Bert. *Doortocht: Een Oorlagsdagboek, 1940–1945.* 4th ed. Amsterdam: Uitgeverij Contact, 1947.

Volavková, Hana, ed. *I Never Saw Another Butterfly: Children's Drawings and Poems from Terezin Concentration Camp, 1942–44.* 2nd ed. New York: Schocken Books in association with the U.S. Holocaust Memorial Museum, 1993.

Weicherz, Bela. *In Her Father's Eyes: A Childhood Extinguished by the Holocaust,* edited and translated by Daniel Magilow. New Brunswick, NJ: Rutgers University Press, 2008.

Zapruder, Alexandra, ed. *Salvaged Pages: Young Writers' Diaries of the Holocaust.* New Haven, CT: Yale University Press, 2002.

Zelkowicz, Josef. *"In Those Terrible Days": Writings from the Lodz Ghetto,* edited by Michal Unger, translated by Naftali Greenwood. Jerusalem: Yad Vashem, 2002.

MEMOIRS

Appelfeld, Aharon. *The Story of a Life,* translated by Aloma Halter. New York: Schocken Books, 2004.

Awret, Irene Spicker. *They'll Have to Catch Me First: An Artist's Coming of Age in the Third Reich.* Madison: University of Wisconsin Press, 2004.

Blatt, Thomas (Tuvia). *From the Ashes of Sobibor: A Story of Survival.* Evanston, IL: Northwestern University Press, 1997.

Bryan, Julien. *Warsaw: 1939 Siege, 1959 Warsaw Revisited.* Warsaw: Polonia Publishing House, 1959.

Deutschkron, Inge. *Ich trug den gelben Stern.* 4th ed. Cologne: Verlag Wissenschaft und Politik, 1983.

Freiberg, Dov. *To Survive Sobibor.* Jerusalem: Gefen, 2007.

Klüger, Ruth. *Weiter leben: Eine Jugend.* Göttingen: Wallstein Verlag, 1992.

Massaquoi, Hans. *Destined to Witness: Growing Up Black in Nazi Germany.* New York: Harper Perennial, 2001.

Nyiszli, Miklós. *Auschwitz: A Doctor's Eyewitness Account,* translated by Tibére Kremer and Richard Seaver. New York: Fell, 1960.

Tec, Nechama. *Dry Tears: The Story of a Lost Childhood.* Oxford: Oxford University Press, 1984.

Toll, Nelly S. *Behind the Secret Window: A Memoir of a Hidden Childhood during World War Two.* New York: Dial Books, 1993.

Weissová, Helga. *"Zeichne, was Du siehst! Zeichnungen eines Kindes aus Theresienstadt,* ed. Niedersächsischen Verein zur Förderung von Theresienstadt/Terezin, e.V. Göttingen: Wallstein Verlag, 1998.

Wiesel, Elie. *All Rivers Run to the Sea.* New York: Schocken Books, 1996.

———. *Night,* translated by Stella Rodway. New York: Bantam Books, 1980.

MONOGRAPH STUDIES, EDITED VOLUMES, AND ARTICLES

Abzug, Robert. *Inside the Vicious Heart: Americans and the Liberation of Nazi Concentration Camps.* Oxford: Oxford University Press, 1985.

Adam, Uwe Dietrich. *Judenpolitik im Dritten Reich.* Düsseldorf: Droste, 2003.

Adamczyk-Garbowska, Monika. "Patterns of Return: Survivors' Postwar Journeys to Poland." *Occasional Papers of the Center for Advanced Holocaust Studies.* Washington, DC: U.S. Holocaust Memorial Museum, 2007.

Adler, H. G. *Theresienstadt, 1941–1945: Das Antlitz einer Zwangsgemeinschaft.* 2nd ed. Tübingen: J. C. B. Mohr, 1960.

Afoumado, Diane. *Exil impossible: L'errance des Juifs du paquebot* St-Louis. Paris: Harmattan, 2005.

Angress, Werner. *Between Fear and Hope: Jewish Youth in the Third Reich,* translated by Werner Angress and Christine Granger. New York: Columbia University Press, 1985.

Angrick, Andrej, and Peter Klein. *Final Solution in Riga: Exploitation and Annihilation,* translated by Ray Brandon. New York: Berghahn Books, 2009.

Appelfeld, Aharon. *Beyond Despair: Three Lectures and Conversation with Philip Roth,* translated by Jeffrey Green. New York: Fromm International, 1994.

Arad, Yitzhak. *Belzec, Sobibor, Treblinka: The Operation Reinhard Death Camps.* Bloomington: Indiana University Press, 1987.

———. *Ghetto in Flames: The Struggle and Destruction of the Jews in Vilna in the Holocaust.* New York: Holocaust Library, 1982.

Baer, Elizabeth R., and Myrna Goldenberg, eds. *Experience and Expression: Women, the Nazis, and the Holocaust.* Detroit, MI: Wayne State University Press, 2003.

Barkai, Avraham. *From Boycott to Annihilation: The Economic Struggle of German Jews, 1933–1943,* translated by William Templer. Hanover, NH: University Press of New England, 1989.

Bauer, Barbara, and Waltraud Strickhausen, eds. *"Für ein Kind war das anders:" Traumatische Erfahrungen jüdischer Kinder und Jugendlicher im nationalsozialistischen Deutschland.* Berlin: Metropol, 1999.

Beer, Mathias. "Die Entwicklung der Gaswagen beim Mord an den Juden," *Vierteljahrshefte für Zeitgeschichte* 35 (1987): 403–17.

Biesold, Horst. *Crying Hands: Eugenics and Deaf People in Nazi Germany,* translated by William Sayers. Washington, DC: Gallaudet University Press, 1999.

Birenbaum, Halina. *Sounds of a Guilty Silence: Selected Poems,* translated by June Friedman. Kraków: Centrum Dialogu, 1997.

Birn, Ruth Bettina. *Die Sicherheitspolizei in Estland, 1941–1944: Eine Studie zur Kollaboration im Osten.* Paderborn: Schöningh, 2006.

Blodig, Vojtěch. *Terezin in the "Final Solution to the Jewish Question," 1941–1945*, translated by Jan Valěska and Lewis Paines. Prague: Památník Terezín/Oswald, 2003.

Bock, Gisela. "Racism and Sexism in Nazi Germany: Motherhood, Compulsory Sterilization, and the State." In *When Biology Became Destiny: Women in Weimar and Nazi Germany*, edited by Renate Bridenthal, Atina Grossmann, and Marion Kaplan, 271–87. New York: Monthly Review Press, 1984.

———. *Zwangssterilisation im Nationalsozialismus: Studien zur Rassenpolitik und Frauenpolitik.* Opladen: Westdeutscher Verlag, 1986.

Boder, David. *The Displaced People of Europe: Preliminary Notes on a Psychological and Anthropological Study.* Chicago: Illinois Institute of Technology and the Psychological Museum, 1947.

Boehler, Jochen. *Auftakt zum Vernichtungskrieg: Die Wehrmacht in Polen, 1939.* Frankfurt: Fischer Taschenbuch Verlag, 2006.

Braham, Randolph. *Eichmann and the Destruction of Hungarian Jewry.* New York: World Federation of Hungarian Jews, 1961.

Braham, Randolph, and Scott Miller, eds. *The Nazis' Last Victims: The Holocaust in Hungary.* Detroit, MI: Wayne State University Press in association with the U.S. Holocaust Memorial Museum, 1998.

Breitman, Richard, and Alan Kraut. *American Refugee Policy and European Jewry, 1933–1945.* Bloomington: Indiana University Press, 1987.

Browning, Christopher. "A Reply to Martin Broszat Regarding the Origins of the Final Solution," *Simon Wiesenthal Center Annual* 1 (1984): 113–29.

Browning, Christopher, with contributions by Jürgen Matthäus. *The Origins of the Final Solution: The Evolution of Nazi Jewish Policy, September 1939–March 1942.* Lincoln: University of Nebraska Press, 2004.

Bukey, Evan Burr. *Hitler's Austria: Popular Sentiment in the Nazi Era, 1938–1945.* Chapel Hill: University of North Carolina Press, 2000.

Burleigh, Michael. *Death and Deliverance: Euthanasia in Germany, 1900–1945.* Cambridge: Cambridge University Press, 1994.

Burleigh, Michael, and Wolfgang Wippermann. *The Racial State: Germany, 1933–1945.* Cambridge: Cambridge University Press, 1991.

Curio, Claudia. *Verfolgung, Flucht, Rettung. Die Kindertransporte 1938–1939 nach Grossbritanien.* Berlin: Metropol, 2006.

Czech, Danuta. *Auschwitz Chronicle, 1939–1945.* New York: Henry Holt, 1990.

Deutschkron, Inge. *Berlin Jews Underground*, translated by Hanna Silver. Berlin: Gedenkstätte Deutscher Widerstand, 1990.

Długoborski, Wacław, and Franciszek Piper, eds. *Auschwitz: 1940–1945*, translated by William Brand. 5 vols. Oświęcim: Auschwitz-Birkenau State Museum, 2000.

Donat, Alexander, ed. *The Death Camp Treblinka: A Documentary.* New York: Holocaust Library, 1979.

Eisen, George. *Children and Play in the Holocaust: Games among the Shadows.* Amherst: University of Massachusetts Press, 1988.

Engelking, Barbara, and Jacek Leociak. *The Warsaw Ghetto: A Guide to a Perished City*, translated by Emma Harris. New Haven, CT: Yale University Press, 2009.

Engelking-Boni, Barbara. "Childhood in the Warsaw Ghetto." In *Children and the Holocaust: Symposium Presentations of the Center for Advanced Holocaust Studies.* Washington, DC: U.S. Holocaust Memorial Museum, 2004, 33–42.

Final Report of the International Commission on the Holocaust in Romania. Bucharest: International Commission on the Holocaust in Romania, 2004.

Friedlander, Henry. *The Origins of Nazi Genocide: From Euthanasia to the Final Solution.* Chapel Hill: University of North Carolina Press, 1995.

Friedländer, Saul. *The Years of Persecution, 1933–1939.* Vol. 1, *Nazi Germany and the Jews.* New York: Harper Collins, 1997.

Garbe, Detlef. *Between Resistance and Martyrdom: Jehovah's Witnesses in the Third Reich,* translated by Dagmar G. Grimm. Madison: University of Wisconsin Press in association with the U.S. Holocaust Memorial Museum, 2008.

Gilsenbach, Reimar. "Wie Lolitschai zur Doktorwürde kam." In *Feinderklärung und Prävention: Kriminalbiologie, Zigeunerforschung und Asozialenpolitik. Beiträge zur nationalsozialistischen Gesundheits- und Sozialpolitik,* Band VI, edited by Götz Aly et al., 101–34. Berlin: Rotbuch Verlag, 1988.

Glassner, Martin Ira, and Robert Krell. *And Life Is Changed Forever: Holocaust Childhoods Remembered.* Detroit, MI: Wayne State University Press, 2006.

Greenfeld, Howard. *The Hidden Children.* New York: Ticknor & Fields, 1993.

Gross, Leonard. *The Last Jews in Berlin.* New York: Simon & Schuster, 1982.

Gutman, Israel. *The Jews of Warsaw, 1939–1943: Ghetto, Underground, Revolt,* translated by Ina Friedman. Bloomington: Indiana University Press, 1982.

Hamann, Matthias. "Die Morde an polnischen und sowjetischen Zwangsarbeitern in deutschen Anstalten." In *Aussonderung und Tod: Die klinische Hinrichtung der Unbrauchbaren. Beiträge zur Nationalsozialistischen Gesundheits- und Sozialpolitik,* Vol. 1, edited by Götz Aly et al., 160–67. Berlin: Rotbuch Verlag, 1985.

Harris, Mark Jonathan, and Deborah Oppenheimer. *Into the Arms of Strangers: Stories of the Kindertransport.* New York: Bloomsbury Publishers of St. Martin's Press, 2000.

Headland, Ronald. *Messages of Murder: A Study of the Reports of the Einsatzgruppen of the Security Police and the Security Service, 1941–1943.* London: Associated University Presses, 1992.

Heberer, Patricia. "Roma and Sinti in Light of Nazi Medical and Eugenic Policy." In *The Genocide of Roma during World War II,* edited by Jana Horváthová, 132–38. Prague: Office of the President of the Czech Republic and the International Task Force for Holocaust Education, Remembrance, and Research, 2004.

———. "Science." In *The Oxford Handbook of Holocaust Studies,* edited by John Roth and Peter Hayes, 39–53. Oxford: Oxford University Press, 2011.

Heinemann, Isabel. *"Rasse, Siedlung, deutsches Blut": Das Rasse- und Siedlungshauptamt der SS und die rassenpolitische Neuordnung Europas.* Göttingen: Wallstein Verlag, 2003.

Hemmendinger, Judith, and Robert Krell. *The Children of Buchenwald: Child Survivors of the Holocaust and Their Post-War Lives.* Jerusalem: Gefen, 2000.

Herf, Jeffrey. *Jewish Enemy: Nazi Propaganda during World War II and the Holocaust.* Cambridge, MA: Belknap Press of Harvard University Press, 2006.

Hoffmann, Ute. *Todesursache "Angina": Zwangssterilisation und "Euthanasie" in der Landes-Heil- und Pflegeanstalt Bernburg.* Magdeburg: Eigenverlag des Ministeriums des Innern des Landes Sachsen-Anhalt, 1996.

Institute of Tolerance/State Archives in Łódź (in cooperation with the Centre de Civilisation Française and the Embassy of France in Poland). *The Children of the Łódź Ghetto.* Łódź: Bilbo, 2004.

Ioanid, Radu. *The Holocaust in Romania: The Destruction of Jews and Gypsies under the Antonescu Regime, 1940–1944.* Chicago: Ivan R. Dee in association with the U.S. Holocaust Memorial Museum, 2000.

Jaskot, Paul. *The Architecture of Oppression: The SS, Forced Labor, and the Nazi Monumental Building Economy.* London: Routledge, 2000.

Kaplan, Marion. *Between Dignity and Despair: Jewish Life in Nazi Germany.* Oxford: Oxford University Press, 1998.

Kaplan, Marion, and Beate Meyer, eds. *Jüdische Welten: Juden in Deutschland vom 18. Jahrhundert bis in die Gegenwart.* Göttingen: Wallstein Verlag, 2005.

Kárný, Miroslav, Raimund Kemper, and Margita Kárná. *Theresienstädter Studien und Dokumente, 1994.* Prague: Verlag Academica, 1994.

Kassow, Samuel D. *Who Will Write Our History? Emmanuel Ringelblum, the Warsaw Ghetto, and the Oyneg Shabes Archive.* Bloomington: Indiana University Press, 2007.

Kater, Michael. *Hitler Youth.* Cambridge, MA: Harvard University Press, 2006.

Keren, Nili. "The Family Camp." In *Anatomy of the Auschwitz Death Camp*, edited by Yisrael Gutman and Michael Berenbaum, 428–40. Bloomington: University of Indiana Press, in association with the U.S. Holocaust Memorial Museum, 1994.

Kingreen, Monika, ed. *"Nach der Kristallnacht": Jüdisches Leben und antijüdische Politik in Frankfurt am Main 1938–1945.* Frankfurt am Main: Campus Verlag, 1999.

Klarsfeld, Serge. *The Children of Izieu: A Human Tragedy*, translated by Kenneth Jacobsen. New York: Harry N. Abrams, 1985.

Klee, Ernst. *Auschwitz: Die NS-Medizin und ihre Opfer.* Frankfurt am Main: Fischer Verlag, 1997.
———. *"Euthanasie" im NS-Staat: Die "Vernichtung lebensunwerten Lebens."* Frankfurt am Main: Fischer Taschenbuch Verlag, 1985.

Klein, Peter. *Die "Gettoverwaltung Litzmannstadt," 1940–1944: Eine Dienststelle im Spannungsfeld von Kommunalbürokratie und staatlicher Verfolgungspolitik.* Hamburg: Hamburger Edition, 2009.

Klemperer, Viktor. *The Language of the Third Reich: LTI—Lingua Tertii Imperii: A Philologist's Notebook*, translated by Martin Brady. London: Continuum, 2002.

Kock, Gerhard. *Der Führer sorgt für unsere Kinder: Die Kinderlandverschickung im Zweiten Weltkrieg.* Paderborn: Schöningh, 1997.

Koehl, Robert L. *RKFDV, German Resettlement and Population Policy, 1939–1945: History of the Reich Commission for the Strengthening of Germandom.* Cambridge, MA: Harvard University Press, 1957.

Königseder, Angelika, and Juliane Wetzel. *Waiting for Hope: Jewish Displaced Persons in Post–World War II Germany*, translated by John Broadwin. Evanston, IL: Northwestern University Press, 2001.

Krakowski, Shmuel. *Chełmno, a Small Village in Europe: The First Nazi Mass Extermination Camp*, translated by Ralph Mandel. Jerusalem: Yad Vashem, 2009.

Krausnick, Helmut. *Hitlers Einsatzgruppen: Die Truppe des Weltanschauungskrieges, 1938–1942.* Frankfurt am Main: Fischer Taschenbuch Verlag, 1985.

Krell, Robert. *Child Holocaust Survivors: Memories and Reflections.* Victoria: Trafford Publishing, 2007.

Kubica, Helena. "Children." In *Anatomy of the Auschwitz Death Camp*, edited by Yisrael Gutman and Michael Berenbaum, 412–27. Bloomington: Indiana University Press, in association with the U.S. Holocaust Memorial Museum, 1994.

———. "Children and Adolescents in Auschwitz." In *Auschwitz, 1940–1945: Central Issues in the History of the Camp*, Vol. 2, edited by Tadeusz Iwasko et al., translated by William Brand, 201–90. Oświęcim: Auschwitz-Birkenau State Museum, 2000.

Kurek, Ewa. *Your Life Is Worth Mine: How Polish Nuns Saved Hundreds of Jewish Children in German-Occupied Poland, 1939–1945*. New York: Hippocrene Books, 1997.

Kuwalek, Robert. *From Lublin to Bełżec: Traces of Jewish Presence and the Holocaust in the South-Eastern Part of the Lublin Region*, translated by Adam Janiszewski. Lublin: Ad Rem, 2005.

Lampe, John. *Yugoslavia As History: Twice There Was a Country*. Cambridge: Cambridge University Press, 1996.

Lavsky, Hagit. "The Role of Children in the Rehabilitation Process of Survivors: The Case of Bergen Belsen." In *Children in the Holocaust: Center for Advanced Holocaust Studies Symposium Presentations*, 103–16. Washington, DC: U.S. Holocaust Memorial Museum, 2004.

Lifton, Betty Jean. *The King of Children: A Biography of Janusz Korczak*. New York: Farrar, Straus & Giroux, 1988.

Lilienthal, Georg. *Lebensborn, e. V.: Ein Instrument nationalsozialistischer Rassenpolitik: Forschungen zur neueren Medizin- und Biologiegeschichte*, Vol. 1. Stuttgart: Gustav Fischer Verlag, 1985.

Loewy, Hanno, et al., eds. *"Unser einziger Weg ist Arbeit": Das Getto in Łódź, 1940–1944*. Vienna: Löcker Verlag, 1990.

Lohmann, Paulgerhard. *"Hier waren wir zu Hause": Die Geschichte der Juden vom Fritzlar, 1096–2000, vor dem Hintergrund der allgemeinen Geschichte der deutschen Juden*. Norderstedt: Books on Demand, 2002.

Löw, Andrea. *Juden in Getto Litzmannstadt: Lebensbedingungen, Selbstwahrnehmung, Verhalten*. Göttingen: Wallstein Verlag, 2006.

Maier, Klaus, et al. *Germany and the Second World War: Germany's Initial Conquests in Europe*. Oxford: Oxford University Press, 1991.

Margaliot, Abraham. "The Reaction of the Jewish Public in Germany to the Nuremberg Laws," *Yad Vashem Studies* 12 (1977): 75–107.

Marrus, Michael. *The Unwanted: European Refugees from the First World War through the Cold War*. Philadelphia: Temple University Press, 2002.

Marrus, Michael, and Robert Paxton. *Vichy France and the Jews*. New York: Basic Books, 1981.

Matthäus, Jürgen, and Mark Roseman. *Jewish Responses to Persecution*, Vol. 1, *1933–1938*. Lanham, MD: AltaMira Press in association with the U.S. Holocaust Memorial Museum, 2010.

Megargee, Geoffrey, ed. *Early Camps, Youth Camps, and Concentration Camps and Subcamps under the SS-Business Administration Main Office (WVHA)*. Vol. 1 of *The United States Holocaust Memorial Museum Encyclopedia of Camps and Ghettos, 1933–1945*. Bloomington: Indiana University Press in association with the U.S. Holocaust Memorial Museum, 2009.

Meijer, Daphne. *Onbekende Kinder: De laatste Trein uit Westerbork*. Amsterdam: Mets & Schilt, 2001.

Meyer, Beate, and Hermann Simon, eds. *Juden in Berlin, 1938–1945. Begleitband zur gleichnamigen Ausstellung in der Stiftung 'Neue Synagoge Berlin—Centrum Judaicum.'* Berlin: Philo Verlagsgesellschaft mbH., 2000.

Miller-Kipp, Gisela, ed. *"Auch Du gehörst dem Führer": Die Geschichte des Bundes Deutscher Mädel (BDM) in Quellen und Dokumenten. Forschungsreihe Materialien zur Historischen Jugendforschung*. Weinheim: Juventa Verlag, 2001.

Moore, Bob. *Victims and Survivors: The Nazi Persecution of Jews in the Netherlands, 1940–1945*. London: Arnold, 1997.

Morgenbrod, Birgitt, and Stephanie Merkenich. *Das Deutsche Rote Kreuz unter der NS-Diktatur, 1933–1945*. Paderborn: Schöningh, 2008.

Mouton, Michelle. *From Nurturing the Nation to Purifying the Volk: Women and Nazi Family Policy, 1918–1945*. Cambridge/Washington, DC: Cambridge University Press/German Historical Institute, 2007.

Musial, Bogdan, ed. *"Aktion Reinhardt": Der Völkermord an den Juden im Generalgouvernement, 1941–1944*. Osnabrück: Fibre Verlag, 2004.

Nicholas, Lynn. *Cruel World: The Children of Europe in the Nazi Web*. New York: Alfred A. Knopf, 2005.

Ogilvie, Sarah A., and Scott Miller. *Refuge Denied: The* St. Louis *Passengers and the Holocaust*. Madison: University of Wisconsin Press, 2006.

Oppenheimer, Walter W. Jacob. *Jüdische Jugend in Deutschland*. Munich: Juventa Verlag, 1967.

Paldiel, Mordecai. "Fear and Comfort: The Plight of Hidden Children in Wartime-Poland," *Holocaust and Genocide Studies* 6, no. 4 (1992): 397–413.

Paucker, Arnold, et al., eds. *The Jews in Nazi Germany 1933–1945*. Tübingen: Mohr, 1986.

Pehle, Walter, ed. *November 1938: From "Reichskristallnacht" to Genocide*, translated by William Templer. New York: Berg, 1991.

Petropoulos, Jonathan, and John K. Roth, eds. *Gray Zones: Ambiguity and Compromise in the Holocaust and Its Aftermath*. New York: Berghahn Books, 2005.

Peukert, Detlev. *Die Edelweisspiraten: Protestbewegungen jugendlicher Arbeiter im Dritten Reich. Eine Dokumentation*. 2nd ed. Cologne: Bund-Verlag, 1983.

———. *Inside Nazi Germany: Conformity, Opposition, and Racism in Everyday Life*, translated by Richard Deveson. New Haven, CT: Yale University Press, 1987.

———. "Youth in the Third Reich." In *Life in the Third Reich*, edited by Richard Bessel, 30–37. Oxford: Oxford University Press, 1987.

Piper, Franciszek. *Auschwitz: How Many Perished There?* Kraków: Polygraphia ITS, 1992.

Plante, Lisa Anne. "Transition and Resistance: Schooling Efforts for Jewish Children and Youth in Hiding, Ghettos, and Camps." In *Children and the Holocaust: Symposium Presentations of the Center for Advanced Holocaust Studies*, 43–64. Washington, DC: U.S. Holocaust Memorial Museum, 2004.

Pommerin, Reiner. *Sterilisierung der "Rheinlandbastarde": Das Schicksal einer farbigen deutschen Minderheit, 1918–1937*. Düsseldorf: Droste, 1979.

Poznanski, Renée. *Jews in France during World War II*, translated by Nathan Bracher. Hanover: Brandeis University Press in association with University Press of New England and the U.S. Holocaust Memorial Museum, 2001.

Pracht, Elfi, ed. *Frankfurter jüdische Erinrungen: Ein Lesebuch zur Sozialgeschichte.* Sigmaringen: Jan Thorbecke Verlag, 1997.

Proctor, Robert. *Racial Hygiene: Medicine under the Nazis.* Cambridge, MA: Harvard University Press, 1988.

Pross, Christian, and Götz Aly. *Der Wert des Menschen: Medizin in Deutschland, 1918–1945.* Berlin: Edition Hentrich, 1989.

Rürup, Reinhard, ed. *Der Krieg gegen die Sowjetunion, 1941–1945: Eine Dokumentation zum 50. Jahrestag des Überfalls auf die Sowjetunion.* Berlin: Argon-Verlag, 1991.

Ryan, Donna F., and John S. Schuchman, eds. *Deaf People in Hitler's Europe.* Washington, DC: Gallaudet University Press, 2002.

Safrian, Hans. *Eichmann's Men,* translated by Uta Stargardt. Cambridge: Cambridge University Press in association with the U.S. Holocaust Memorial Museum, 2010.

Safrian, Hans, and Hans Witek. *Und keiner war dabei: Dokumente des alltäglichen Antisemitismus in Wien.* 2nd ed. Vienna: Picus Verlag, 2008.

Salisbury, Harrison. *The 900 Days: The Siege of Leningrad.* New York: Harper & Row, 1969.

Schelvis, Jules. *Sobibor: A History of a Nazi Death Camp,* translated by Karin Dixon. Oxford: Berg in association with the U.S. Holocaust Memorial Museum, 2007.

Schleunes, Karl A. *The Twisted Road to Auschwitz: Nazi Policy toward German Jews, 1933–1939.* London: Andre Deutsch, 1970.

Schmitz-Köster, Dorothee. *"Deutsche Mutter, bist du bereit . . . ?" Alltag im Lebensborn.* Berlin: Aufbau-Verlag, 1997.

Schneider, Gertrude. *Reise in den Tod: Deutsche Juden in Riga, 1941–1944.* Berlin: Hentrich, 2006.

Schwab, Gerald. *The Day the Holocaust Began: The Odyssey of Herschel Gynszpan.* New York: Praeger, 1990.

Schwarberg, Günther. *Der SS-Arzt und die Kinder: Bericht über den Mord vom Bullenhuser Damm.* Hamburg: Stern Verlag, 1979.

Schwarze, Gisela. *Kinder, die nicht zählten: Ostarbeiterinnen und ihre Kinder im Zweiten Weltkrieg.* Essen: Klartext Verlag, 1997.

Seidler, Franz. *Deutsche Volkssturm: Das letzte Aufgebot, 1944–1945.* 2nd ed. Berlin: Herbig, 1991.

Sereny, Gitta. *Into That Darkness: An Examination of Conscience.* New York: Vintage Books, 1983.

Stargardt, Nicholas. *Witnesses of War: Children's Lives under the Nazis.* New York: Alfred A. Knopf, 2006.

Statura, Peter. *The German Youth Movement, 1900–1945: An Interpretative and Documentary History.* London: MacMillan, 1981.

Stein, Andre. *Hidden Children: Forgotten Survivors of the Holocaust.* Toronto: Penguin Books, 1994.

Steinweis, Alan E. *Kristallnacht, 1938.* Cambridge, MA: Belknap Press, 2009.

Stiftung Jüdisches Museum Berlin and Stiftung Haus der Geschichte der Bundesrepublik Deutschland, *Heimat und Exil: Emigration der deutschen Juden nach 1933.* Frankfurt am Main: Suhrkamp Verlag, 2006.

Strauss, Herbert, ed. *Jewish Immigrants of the Nazi Period in the USA.* New York: Saur, 1978.

Suedfeld, Peter. "Life after the Ashes: The Postwar Pain, and Resilience, of Young Holocaust Survivors." *Occasional Papers of the Center for Advanced Holocaust Studies.* Washington, DC: U.S. Holocaust Memorial Museum, 2002.

Suess, Winfried. *Der "Volkskörper" im Krieg: Gesundheitspolitik, Gesundheitsverhältnisse und Krankenmord im nationalsozialistischen Deutschland, 1939–1945.* Munich: R. Oldenbourg Verlag, 2003.

Tec, Nechama. *Defiance: The Bielski Partisans.* Oxford: Oxford University Press, 1993.

———. *When Light Pierced the Darkness: Christian Rescue of Jews in Nazi-Occupied Poland.* Oxford: Oxford University Press, 1986.

Tec, Nechama, and Daniel Weiss. "A Historical Injustice: The Case of Masha Bruskina." *Holocaust and Genocide Studies* 11, no. 3 (winter 1997): 366–77.

Tobias, Jim. *"Und wir waren Deutsche!" Jüdische Emigranten erinnern sich.* Nuremberg: Antogo, 2009.

Trial of Heinrich Gerike, Gustav Claus, Georg Hessling, Richard Demmerlich, Werner Noth, Fritz Flint, Hermann Müller, Valentina Bilien (The Velpke Baby Home Trial), edited by George Brand. London: W. Hodge, 1950.

Trunk, Isaiah. *Łódź Ghetto: A History*, edited and translated by Robert Moses Shapiro. Bloomington: Indiana University Press in association with the U.S. Holocaust Memorial Museum, 2006.

Unger, Michal. *Reassessment of the Image of Mordechai Chaim Rumkowski.* Jerusalem: Yad Vashem, 2004.

Valent, Paul. *Child Survivors of the Holocaust.* London: Routledge, 2002.

van der Zee, Henri A. *The Hunger Winter: Occupied Holland, 1944–1945.* Lincoln: University of Nebraska Press, 1998.

Waller, Jane, and Michael Vaughan-Rees. *Blitz: The Civilian War, 1940–1945.* London: McDonald Optima, 1990.

Weinberg, Gerhard. *Germany, Hitler, and World War II: Essays in Modern German and World History.* New York: Cambridge University Press, 1995.

Weiss-Wendt, Anton. *Murder without Hatred: Estonians and the Holocaust.* Syracuse, NY: Syracuse University Press, 2009.

Welch, David. *Politics and Propaganda.* 2nd ed. London: Routledge Press, 2002.

Wells, Leon Weliczker. *The Janowska Road.* Washington, DC: U.S. Holocaust Memorial Museum, 1999.

Werner, Emmy. *Through the Eyes of Innocents: Children Witnesses of World War II.* Boulder, CO: Westview Press, 2000.

Westermann, Edward B. *Hitler's Police Battalions: Enforcing Racial War in the East.* Lawrence: University of Kansas, 2005.

Wollenberg, Jörg, ed. *"Niemand war dabei, und keiner hat's gewußt": Die deutsche Öffentlichkeit und die Judenverfolgung, 1933–1945.* Munich: Piper, 1989.

Wyman, Mark. *DPs: Europe's Displaced Persons, 1945–1951.* Ithaca, NY: Cornell University Press, 1998.

———. *Paper Walls: America and the Refugee Crisis, 1938–1941.* New York: Pantheon, 1985.

Yelton, David K. *Hitler's Volkssturm: The Nazi Militia and the Fall of Germany, 1944–1945.* Lawrence: University Press of Kansas, 2002.

Zegenhagen, Evelyn. "Facilities for Pregnant Forced Laborers and Their Infants in Germany, 1943–1945." In *Children and the Holocaust: Symposium Presentations of the Center for Advanced Holocaust Studies*, 65–76. Washington, DC: U.S. Holocaust Memorial Museum, 2004.

Zimmermann, Michael. *Rassenutopie und Genozid: Die nationalsozialistische "Lösung der Zigeunerfrage."* Hamburg: Hans Christians Verlag, 1996.

GLOSSARY

Note: Terms below are defined in reference to the period covered in the text, 1933–1946.

Aktion (operation or action): In the National Socialist context, German authorities often employed this term to mean a campaign to further Nazi racial goals, such as *Aktion* T4 (the **"euthanasia"** program) or *Aktion* Reinhard, the killing of the Jews of the **General Government**.

Aliyah (Hebrew: "ascent"): In the context of the Zionist movement, this term describes the mass settlement of Diaspora Jews in **Palestine** to establish a Jewish homeland. In the period between 1933 and 1941, more than fifty-two hundred Jews left the German Reich for Palestine. The Youth Aliyah movement organized by German-Jewish educator Recha Freier and others in 1933 helped more than five thousand Jewish youths to emigrate before September 1939. As British restrictions on Jewish settlements in Palestine increased in the mid-1930s, the illegal *Aliyah* (*Aliyah Bet*) gained in significance; the movement continued until the founding of the state of Israel in 1948.

See Brian Amkraut, *Between Home and Homeland: Youth Aliyah from Nazi Germany* (Tuscaloosa: University of Alabama Press, 2006); Recha Freier, *Let the Children Come: The Early History of the Youth Aliyah* (London: Weidenfeld and Nicolson, 1961).

American Jewish Joint Distribution Committee (AJJDC, AJDC, Joint, or JDC): Founded in 1914, the Joint provided assistance to Jews around the world, particularly in eastern Europe. During the Nazi era, this umbrella agency for aid organizations in the United States was involved in emigration planning and relief work in Germany, until

1939 providing an increasing share of the budget for German Jewish organizations, such as the **Reichsvertretung**. The Joint's efforts continued after the war began and extended beyond the Reich into countries occupied or controlled by Germany.

See Yehuda Bauer, *American Jewry and the Holocaust: The American Jewish Joint Distribution Committee, 1939–45* (Detroit, MI: Wayne State University Press, 1981).

Anschluss (literally, "connection" or "joining"): Nazi officials employed this euphemism to describe the German annexation of Austria in March 1938. Although it constituted an act of aggression on the part of Germany against its independent neighbor and resulted in mass arrests and anti-Jewish violence, the *Anschluss* met with widespread popular support in both Austria and Germany. Austria, renamed the *Ostmark*, remained a part of the German Reich until the end of World War II.

See Evan Burr Bukey, *Hitler's Austria: Popular Sentiment in the Nazi Era, 1938–1945* (Chapel Hill: University of North Carolina Press, 2000).

Appell (roll call): A practice followed at least twice a day in the vast Nazi concentration camp system, *Appell* was usually performed in the early morning and again in the evening on the *Appellplatz* (roll call yard). Camp officials forced emaciated and exhausted prisoners to stand at attention for hours on end, even in inclement weather, while **SS** guards, assisted by prisoners, counted and inspected the inmates and distributed daily punishment for real or invented infractions. The *Appell* functioned both as a means of furnishing a prisoner head count and as a punitive measure.

Arrow Cross: The Arrow Cross Party was a fascist political movement in Hungary during the 1930s and 1940s, modeled after Germany's National Socialist Party. Led by Ferenc Szálasi (1897–1946), the Arrow Cross promoted an ideology that fused Hungarian nationalism with a virulent antisemitism. In October 1944, with German support, Szálasi launched a successful coup to dislodge Hungarian regent **Miklós Horthy**. During their brief time in power, the Arrow Cross initiated a reign of terror, torturing and murdering Budapest Jews in the streets and reinitiating **deportations** of Jews from the capital. In the immediate postwar, Hungarian authorities tried and executed Szálasi and other leaders of the Arrow Cross Party.

See Randolph L. Braham, *The Politics of Genocide* (Detroit, MI: Wayne State University Press, 2000).

"**Aryan**": The word "Aryan" derives from Sanskrit. Since ancient times, the peoples of modern-day Iran have used the term to describe their lineage, language, and culture. In linguistic terminology, "Aryan" refers to a subfamily of the Indo-European languages, and before the term's adoption and perversion by National Socialist ideologues, it was the name employed to describe the parent language of the Indo-European language family. In the late nineteenth and early twentieth centuries, linguists and ethnologists began to argue that speakers of the Indo-European languages constituted a distinct race, separated in the racial hierarchy from the Semitic peoples (i.e., Jews). Nazi ideology used the construct of an "Aryan" ideal type to denigrate "non-Aryans," particularly Jews, in the attempt to create a racially homogenous *Volksgemeinschaft*. In German-occupied Europe, Jews described the municipal district beyond the ghetto walls, inhabited by non-Jews, as the "Aryan side."

See Michael Burleigh and Wolfgang Wippermann, *The Racial State: Germany, 1933–1945* (Cambridge: Cambridge University Press, 1991).

"**Aryanization**": Derived from the vocabulary of Nazi antisemitism, this term denotes the process of expropriating Jews and excluding them from German economic life. Beginning in early 1933, the process gathered pace over time. The events surrounding the *Anschluss* of Austria and the **pogrom** of *Kristallnacht* in 1938 triggered a wave of exclusionary measures that culminated in the forced "Aryanization" of the remaining Jewish-owned businesses later that year. German allies and satellites, such as Hungary and **Vichy France**, often adopted such "Aryanization" policies.

See Avraham Barkai, *From Boycott to Annihilation: The Economic Struggle of German Jews, 1933–1943* (Hanover, NH: University of New England Press, 1989).

Auschwitz: The Auschwitz complex was the largest camp of its kind established by the Nazi regime. Located outside Oświęcim, Poland, near Kraków, the complex comprised three camps: Auschwitz I, established in May 1940; **Birkenau** (Auschwitz II), built in early 1942; and **Monowitz**, or **Buna** (Auschwitz III), established in October 1942. Auschwitz I, the main camp, resembled most German concentration camps in that its primary aim was to incarcerate real and perceived enemies of the German Reich; like Monowitz, it also deployed a significant number of forced laborers both on-site and in **SS**-owned construction and war-related enterprises. Birkenau, with sections for men and women and temporary family camps for **Roma** (Gypsies) and for Jewish deportees from **Theresienstadt**, housed the largest prisoner population and accommodated the complex's killing center. From 1942 through the late summer of 1944, trains carrying transports of Jews arrived at Birkenau from every corner of Axis-occupied Europe. It is estimated that the SS and police deported more than 1.3 million people to Auschwitz. Of these, camp authorities gassed about 1.1 million. In mid-January 1945, as Soviet forces approached the complex, officials began evacuating Auschwitz and its subcamps. Soviet troops liberated the Auschwitz complex on January 27, 1945, freeing some seven thousand ailing prisoners who had remained at the camp following its evacuation.

See Wacław Długoborski and Franciszek Piper, eds., *Auschwitz: 1940–1945*, trans. William Brand, 5 vols. (Oświęcim: Auschwitz-Birkenau State Museum, 2000); Danuta Czech, *Auschwitz Chronicle, 1939–1945* (New York: Henry Holt, 1990); Yisrael Gutman and Michael Berenbaum, *Anatomy of the Auschwitz Death Camp* (Bloomington: University of Indiana Press in association with the U.S. Holocaust Memorial Museum, 1994).

Bełżec: Bełżec, **Sobibór**, and **Treblinka** comprised the killing centers of **Operation Reinhard** (*Aktion* Reinhard). Located directly on the Lublin-Zamość-Rava Russkaya railroad line, the spot was chosen by Reinhard planners in order to tap the municipalities of Lublin, Kraków, and Lvov, all cities with a large Jewish population. Christian Wirth served as Bełżec's first commander, succeeded by former **Operation T4** administrator Gottlieb Hering in June 1942. Operations began at Bełżec on March 17, 1942. Initial gassings still employed the pure bottled carbon monoxide utilized at "**euthanasia**" installations; later, carbon monoxide gas generated by diesel engine became the standard mode of killing here and at all Reinhard extermination centers. Between March and December 1942, approximately 434,500 Jews and an undetermined number of Poles and **Roma** were deported and murdered at Bełżec.

See Bogdan Musial, ed., *"Aktion Reinhardt": Der Völkermord an den Juden im Generalgouvernement, 1941–1944* (Osnabrück: Fibre Verlag, 2004).

Bergen-Belsen: A concentration camp established by German authorities near Celle in northwestern Germany in 1940, Bergen-Belsen first served as a POW camp, first for French and Belgian soldiers and then for Soviet POWs until 1943. Converted into a concentration camp in that year, Bergen-Belsen also served as a holding camp (*Aufenthaltslager*) for privileged Jews whom German authorities hoped to exchange for German civilians interned abroad. In the war's last stages, Bergen-Belsen became a reservoir for thousands of Jewish prisoners evacuated from concentration camps in the East. Overcrowding, insufficient provisions, and poor sanitation led to deplorable conditions in the camp, and tens of thousands perished of disease and malnutrition in Bergen-Belsen's last months. Between May 1943 and April 1945, some thirty-seven thousand prisoners died at Bergen-Belsen. British forces liberated the camp on April 15, 1945, freeing some fifty-five thousand ailing and emaciated prisoners. More than thirteen thousand former prisoners, too ill to recover, perished in the weeks following liberation.

See Suzanne Bardgett and David Cesarani, eds., *Belsen 1945: New Historical Perspectives* (Portland, OR: Vallentine Mitchell, 2006).

Biebow, Hans (1902–1947): Born in Bremen, German businessman and Nazi official Hans Biebow headed the German administration of the **Łódź ghetto** from October 1940 until August 1944. Biebow encouraged the establishment of ghetto factories and workshops and gleaned enormous profits both from these forced labor enterprises and from the stolen property of the incarcerated community. Eager to maintain this flow of proceeds, he helped to ensure the ghetto's continued existence until the summer of 1944. Following the decision to liquidate the Łódź ghetto, Biebow helped to organize the final **deportations** of ghetto residents to the **Chełmno** and **Auschwitz** killing centers. He was tried and sentenced to death by a Polish court in Łódź in April 1947 and executed.

Birkenau (Auschwitz II–Birkenau): Birkenau, with its sections for men and women and its temporary family camps for **Roma** and for Jewish deportees from **Theresienstadt**, housed the largest prisoner population within **Auschwitz** and accommodated its killing center. In all, some 1.1 million Jews were transported there. New arrivals underwent the process of **selection**. Young and able-bodied Jews were often chosen for labor and registered as prisoners at the camp. The sick, the weak, young children, and the aged were murdered upon arrival. Gassing operations continued at Birkenau until November 1944.]

See Wacław Długoborski and Franciszek Piper, eds., *Auschwitz: 1940–1945*, trans. William Brand, 5 vols. (Oświęcim: Auschwitz-Birkenau State Museum, 2000); Danuta Czech, *Auschwitz Chronicle, 1939–1945* (New York: Henry Holt, 1990); Yisrael Gutman and Michael Berenbaum, *Anatomy of the Auschwitz Death Camp* (Bloomington: University of Indiana Press in association with the U.S. Holocaust Memorial Museum, 1994).

Block, Elisabeth (1923–1942): Living with her parents and two siblings in rural Bavaria, Elisabeth Block began a diary in 1933 in which she made few direct references to the persecution of her fellow German Jews. In the spring of 1942, she was deported with her family via Munich-Milbertshofen to Piaski in the Lublin district. On an unknown date, Elisabeth and her family were transferred to a killing center, presumably **Bełżec** or **Sobibór**, and murdered there.

See Elisabeth Block, *Erinnerungszeichen: Die Tagebücher der Elisabeth Block*, ed. Haus der Bayerischen Geschichte (Rosenheim: Bayerische Staatskanzlei, 1993).

Boder, David (1886–1961): Born in Latvia, David Boder was a professor of psychology at the Illinois Institute of Technology. In 1946, he headed a pioneering project to interview Holocaust survivors. Boder recorded over 120 hours of oral testimony, a significant source of primary documentation concerning the Holocaust.

See Alan Rosen, *The Wonder of Their Voices: The 1946 Holocaust Interviews of David Boder* (Oxford: Oxford University Press, 2010).

Boycott of April 1, 1933: When Adolf Hitler's regime came to power in late January 1933, Nazi authorities proclaimed their intention to eliminate Jews from German economic life. On March 28, 1933, the Nazi Party leadership announced a boycott effort against Jewish-owned shops and businesses to begin on April 1. On the morning of the boycott, local party action committees stationed **SA** or **SS** men outside Jewish-owned stores and enterprises, encouraging passersby to buy their wares only in "German" stores. Despite the best efforts of central planners such as *Der Stürmer* publisher **Julius Streicher**, the boycott failed to win the public support the Nazis hoped for, and international condemnation of the measure ensured that the centralized boycott campaign would be confined to a one-day affair. However, depending on the degree of local antisemitic sentiment, so-called wild boycotts continued throughout the 1930s, forcing many Jewish-owned businesses into insolvency or liquidation.

See Karl Schleunes, *The Twisted Road to Auschwitz: Nazi Policy toward German Jews, 1933–1939* (London: André Deutsch, 1970).

Brandt, Karl (1904–1948): Born in Alsace, Karl Brandt was from 1934 Adolf Hitler's attending physician. Along with Philipp Bouhler, director of the Führer Chancellery, Brandt headed the planning and implementation of the **"euthanasia"** program, beginning in 1939. In July 1942, Hitler appointed him General Commissioner for Sanitation and Health (*Generalkommissar für das Sanitäts- und Gesundheitswesen*) and, later, Reich commissioner, which placed Brandt in control of all German military and civilian medical institutions. In 1946, Brandt served as chief defendant at the Nuremberg Doctors' Trial, in which an American military tribunal sentenced him to death. He was executed on June 2, 1948.

See Ulf Schmidt, *Karl Brandt, the Nazi Doctor: Medicine and Power in the Third Reich* (London: Hambledon Continuum, 2007).

Buchenwald: Together with its over 130 satellite camps, Buchenwald, near Weimar in eastern Germany, was one of the largest concentration camps within the Reich proper. Established in July 1937, most of its early inmates were political prisoners, who played an important role in the camp's prisoner infrastructure and its underground resistance. In the aftermath of *Kristallnacht*, German **SS** and police sent about ten thousand Jews to Buchenwald. Between July 1937 and April 1945, the camp held some 250,000 persons from all countries of Europe; recidivist criminals, Jehovah's Witnesses, **Roma and Sinti** (Gypsies), and German military deserters numbered among its prisoner population. In the camp's later stages, the SS also incarcerated prisoners of war, resistance fighters, prominent former government officials of German-occupied countries, and foreign forced laborers there. At least fifty-six thousand prisoners were murdered in the Buchenwald camp system, over eighteen thousand of them Jews. On April 11, 1945, as U.S. troops neared the camp, Buchenwald prisoners stormed the watchtowers, seizing control of the camp. Later that afternoon, U.S. forces arrived at Buchenwald, liberating more than twenty thousand prisoners, among them over nine hundred young children.

See David A. Hackett, ed. and trans., *The Buchenwald Report* (Boulder, CO: Westview Press, 1995).

Buna (Auschwitz III–Monowitz): Auschwitz III–Monowitz, also known also as the Buna labor camp, was the first and largest Auschwitz satellite camp for forced labor and later operated as the administrative headquarters for all Auschwitz satellite camps employing prison labor in factories. Construction of the camp began in April 1941. The great majority of forced laborers at Monowitz worked at the IG Farben Buna Werke, a large synthetic rubber plant located only 300 meters (984 feet) from the camp. Due to IG Farben's continual need for forced labor, Buna held as many as eleven thousand prisoners in 1944. With the approach of the Soviet army, German authorities evacuated Buna on January 18, 1945. From Gleiwitz, a subcamp of Auschwitz, most of these prisoners were transferred to **Buchenwald** and Mittelbau. More than eight hundred ill and exhausted prisoners remained at the camp following evacuation and were liberated by Soviet forces on January 27, 1945.

See Wacław Długoborski and Franciszek Piper, eds., *Auschwitz 1940–1945: Central Issues in the History of the Camp*, trans. William Brand (Oświęcim: Auschwitz-Birkenau State Museum, 2000), 1:108–15.

Bund Deutscher Mädel (BDM, or League of German Girls): In 1930, the Bund Deutscher Mädel in der Hitler-Jugend (League of German Girls within the **Hitler Youth**) was founded as the official female branch of the Hitler Youth organization. Before the Nazi rise to power in January 1933, the BDM did not attract a mass following, but membership expanded rapidly throughout the 1930s, until participation for eligible girls became compulsory in 1936. The BDM's core constituency consisted of girls from fourteen to eighteen years of age, with a corresponding junior branch, the Jungmädel (Young Girls' League), for girls aged ten to fourteen. In 1938, a third component, the BDM Union for Belief and Beauty (BDM-Werk Glaube und Schönheit), offered a voluntary association for young women aged seventeen to twenty-one.

See Gisela Miller-Kipp, *"Auch Du gehörst dem Führer": Die Geschichte des Bundes Deutscher Mädel (BDM) in Quellen und Dokumenten* (Weinheim/Munich: Juventa Verlag, 2001).

CENTOS (Central Organization for Orphan Care): Founded in 1924 to unite voluntary child-care organizations throughout Poland under one agency, CENTOS operated aid organizations for children and youth, including orphanages, boarding and trade schools, day-care centers, food- and clothing-distribution centers, and children's camps. It also provided funding to foster families. Prior to the German invasion of Poland, CENTOS functioned in more than two hundred Polish cities and cared for tens of thousands of children. CENTOS was very active in the **Warsaw ghetto**, operating over one hundred care institutions for forty-five thousand children, among them **Janusz Korczak**'s well-known Orphans' Home. Dr. Adolf Berman and Józef Barski assumed the directorship of CENTOS in the Warsaw ghetto in January 1940.

See Barbara Engelking and Lacek Leociak, *The Warsaw Ghetto: A Guide to the Perished City* (New Haven, CT: Yale University Press, 2009).

Chełmno (Kulmhof): In late 1941, the National Socialist regime established the first stationary killing center to murder Jews within the context of the "Final Solution" at Chełmno. German authorities chose the site because of its location along a central road that linked it to the city of Łódź. An abandoned manorial estate and adjacent forest formed the nexus of the camp, which was planned as a killing site for the Jewish population of the **Wartheland**, including the inhabitants of the **Łódź ghetto**. Mass-murder operations began at Chełmno on December 8, 1941. The killing center employed **gas vans** to murder its victims. Herbert Lange initially commanded the small number of **SS** and police functionaries at the site until his replacement by Hans Bothmann in the spring of 1942. From mid-January 1942 until March 1943, thousands of Łódź ghetto inhabitants, as well as Jews from the surrounding districts, were murdered at Chełmno. In the spring of 1943, these **deportations** actions ceased, and SS personnel dismantled the camp. In the spring of 1944, however, German authorities decided to liquidate the Łódź ghetto, and for a brief period, Chełmno was again the site of killing operations, until mid-July 1944 when the last Łódź ghetto inhabitants were deported to **Auschwitz**. In all, at least 152,000 persons, the vast majority of them Jews, were murdered at Chełmno.

See Archives of the District Museum in Konin, *Chełmno Witnesses Speak,* ed. Łucja Pawlicka-Nowak, trans. Juliet D. Golden (Konin: Council for the Protection of Memory of Combat and Martyrdom in Warsaw/District Museum in Konin, 2004).

Collection camp (*Sammellager*): These were holding locations where regional Jewish populations were detained before their **deportation** from Germany. Under the supervision of the **Gestapo**, collections camps served as assembly points where deportees were ordered to appear and register themselves and their property before their transport to ghettos, concentration camps, or killing centers in the East.

Compulsory sterilization: see **Law for the Prevention of Progeny with Hereditary Diseases**.

Crematorium (*Krematorium*, Auschwitz): Five crematoria complexes with adjoining gas chambers were the primary means of murdering European Jews in **Auschwitz II– Birkenau**. Crematorium I, housing three large furnaces, was first used in September 1940 to incinerate the bodies of prisoners who had died or been murdered in Auschwitz and its satellite camps. Concealed behind large hedges, Crematoria II through V and their connected gas chambers were operational in Birkenau by the summer of 1943. After **selection**, victims were assembled in the crematoria yards. Under the guise of delousing, the victims undressed in a room connected to the gassing chamber. The **Zyklon B** gas used generally killed its victims within thirty minutes. *Sonderkommando* units then sorted the victims' clothing and valuables in the anterooms of the crematoria, while others of their number incinerated the corpses of the gassing victims. In the summer of 1944, the crematoria reached a burning capacity of twenty thousand corpses per day. Following the *Sonderkommando* revolt in October 7, 1944, in which Crematorium IV was severely damaged, **Heinrich Himmler** ordered the destruction of the Auschwitz gassing apparatus.

See Franciszek Piper, "Gas Chambers and Crematoria," in *Anatomy of the Auschwitz Death Camp*, ed. Yisrael Gutman and Michael Berenbaum (Bloomington: Indiana University Press in association with the U.S. Holocaust Memorial Museum, 1994), 157–182.

Dachau: Established in March 1933, the Dachau concentration camp was the first regular concentration camp established by the National Socialist government. Located near Munich, Germany, the early prisoner population consisted chiefly of political prisoners and other ideological opponents of the Nazi regime. In time, Jehovah's Witnesses, **Roma**, homosexuals, "asocials," and recidivist criminals were also interned there; in the wake of *Kristallnacht*, more than eleven thousand Jewish men were briefly incarcerated at Dachau as well. The Dachau camp was a training center for **SS** concentration camp guards and became the model for all Nazi concentration camps. Prisoners at Dachau engaged in forced labor, both at the main camp and in over 160 subcamps. The total number of prisoners incarcerated at Dachau between 1933 and 1945 exceeded 188,000. Over forty thousand died at the camp between January 1940 and May 1945, as did an unknown number of unregistered prisoners. American forces liberated Dachau on April 29, 1945.

See Harold Marcuse, *Legacies of Dachau: The Uses and Abuses of a Concentration Camp, 1933–2001* (Cambridge: Cambridge University Press, 2001).

Deportation: Deportation was an integral mechanism in the implementation of the "Final Solution." In this volume, the word has two contexts. First, it was the process of uprooting individuals, most notably Jews, from their home communities and transporting them to ghettos, camps, or extermination centers in the East. Second, deportation was a method of transferring Jews from ghettoized communities, such as the **Warsaw** and **Łódź ghettos**, to killing centers for "liquidation."

Der Stürmer: see **Julius Streicher**.

Deutsches Jungvolk: see **Hitler Youth**.

Displaced persons (DPs) and **Displaced persons camps**: At the end of World War II in Europe, some 7 to 9 million people had been displaced by the conflict. This number included 2 to 3 million former camp inmates—Jews and non-Jews—who had survived concentration and forced labor camps, killing centers, and forced death marches into the German interior in the last months of the war. By the end of 1945, more than 6 million individuals had returned to their countries of origin or succeeded in immigrating to other countries. Remaining behind were some 2 million refugees and displaced persons, among them 250,000 Jews. In order to deal with the massive postwar refugee crisis, a series of DP camps were established in Allied zones throughout Germany and Austria and in occupied areas of Italy. Originally run by Allied authorities within their zones of occupation, responsibility for the camps eventually devolved to the **United Nations Relief and Rehabilitation Administration**.

See Angelika Königseder and Juliane Wetzel, *Waiting for Hope: Jewish Displaced Persons in Post–World War II Germany*, trans. John Broadwin (Evanston, IL: Northwestern University Press, 2001); Michael Marrus, *The Unwanted: European Refugees from the First World War through the Cold War* (Philadelphia: Temple University Press, 2002); Mark Wyman, *DPs: Europe's Displaced Persons, 1945–1951* (Ithaca, NY: Cornell University Press, 1998).

Drancy: Located 20 kilometers (almost 12.5 miles) southeast of Paris, a former housing complex served as a transit and internment camp for the German occupiers and their

French collaborators after the invasion of France in May 1940. On August 21, 1941, Drancy became an internment camp for Jews. Although **SS** captain Theodor Dannecker, leader of the *Judenreferat* in Paris and **Adolf Eichmann**'s representative in France, had ultimate authority over the camp (he was succeeded by Heinz Röthke as of July 1942), its direct administration was originally entrusted to French officials. The first **deportation** left Drancy on March 27, 1942. Of a total seventy-five thousand Jews deported from French soil, predominantly to **Auschwitz** and **Sobibór**, some sixty-five thousand passed through Drancy.

See Michael Marrus and Robert Paxton, *Vichy France and the Jews* (New York: Basic Books, 1981); Renée Poznanski, *Jews in France during World War II* (Hanover, NH : University Press of New England for Brandeis University Press in association with the U.S. Holocaust Memorial Museum, 2001).

Eichmann, Adolf (1906–1962): Raised in the Austrian city of Linz, Adolf Eichmann joined the Nazi Party and the **SS** in 1932 in Austria before moving to Germany, where he joined **Reinhard Heydrich**'s **Security Service**. Following the *Anschluss* of Austria, Eichmann began to serve a key function among German officials as an expert for "Jewish affairs." With the coming of war, he became one of the chief agents of Nazi anti-Jewish policy and played a pivotal role in the **deportation** of European Jews to the killing centers of the "Final Solution." In hiding after the war, he was abducted by the Israeli secret service in Argentina in May 1960 and put on trial in Jerusalem. Sentenced to death by the court, he was hanged in June 1962.

See Hans Safrian, *Eichmann's Men,* trans. Uta Stargardt (Cambridge: Cambridge University Press in association with the U.S. Holocaust Memorial Museum, 2010).

Eichmann Trial: The trial of **Adolf Eichmann** began on April 10, 1961, following his arrest in Argentina in May 1960. Israeli officials brought Eichmann to trial on the basis of Israel's Nazi and Nazi Collaborators' Punishment Law of 1950. Eichmann was found guilty and sentenced to death on December 11, 1961. Hanged on May 31, 1962, Eichmann remains the only person executed by the state of Israel. Prime Minister David Ben Gurion expressed the wish that the televised trial might educate audiences concerning the genocide of European Jewry. The depositions of survivors at the trial have contributed greatly to the wealth of eyewitness testimony concerning the Holocaust.

See State of Israel Ministry of Justice, *The Trial of Adolf Eichmann: Record of Proceedings of the District Court of Jerusalem*, 9 vols. (Jerusalem: Trust for the Publication of the Proceedings of the Eichmann Trial in cooperation with the Israel State Archives and Yad Vashem, the Holocaust Martyrs' and Heroes' Remembrance Authority, 1992–1995).

Einsatzgruppen (literally, "task forces"): In the context of the Holocaust, this word refers to mobile killing units composed primarily of German **SS** and police personnel operating in Soviet territory. Under the command of the German **Security Police** and **Security Service**, the *Einsatzgruppen* had among their tasks the murder of perceived racial or political enemies found behind German combat lines in the occupied Soviet Union. Many scholars believe that the systematic killing of Jews by these forces represented the first step of the "Final Solution." During the invasion of the Soviet Union in June 1941, the *Einsatzgruppen* followed the German army into Soviet territory, carrying out mass killing operations, often with the aid of indigenous auxiliary support. By the spring of 1943, the *Einsatzgruppen* and Order Police battalions had killed over 1 million Soviet Jews and tens of thousands of Soviet political commissars, partisans, **Roma**, and institutionalized disabled patients.

See Christopher Browning with contributions by Jürgen Matthäus, *The Origins of the Final Solution: The Evolution of Nazi Jewish Policy, September 1939–March 1942* (Lincoln: University of Nebraska Press, 2004); Ronald Headland, *Messages of Murder: A Study of the Reports of the Einsatzgruppen of the Security Police and the Security Service, 1941–1943* (London: Associated University Presses, 1992).

Einzelaktion: This was an individual or spontaneous action against Jews.

Eugenics (also **racial hygiene**): Together with virulent antisemitism, eugenics, or racial hygiene, formed a governing tenet in the development of Nazi ideology and helped to inspire some of the Nazi regime's most radical and deadly policies. An international movement of the late nineteenth and early twentieth centuries, it endorsed "selective breeding" as a way to build a better society. Eugenicists sought to define "valuable" members of their community and encourage them to reproduce. They also aimed to discourage society's "unworthy" from reproducing, often through proposed voluntary or **compulsory sterilization** measures. Many eugenicists concerned themselves with the "problem" of the mixing of races. Finally, eugenicists wished to divert vital resources from the "unworthy" to society's "valuable" members. During the era of the Third Reich, Nazi authorities implemented policies that applied the concepts of racial hygiene in its most concrete and radical forms. In 1933, Adolf Hitler's cabinet promulgated the **Law for the Prevention of Progeny with Hereditary Diseases**, which mandated the compulsory sterilization of four hundred thousand "hereditarily ill" Germans. With the coming of war, German authorities inaugurated a clandestine "**euthanasia**," or T4, program which claimed the lives of some two hundred thousand mentally and physically disabled patients during the war years. Finally, the genocide of 6 million European Jews and hundreds of thousands of **Roma and Sinti** (Gypsies) may be interpreted as the Nazis' most radical application of racial hygiene.

See Robert Proctor, *Racial Hygiene: Medicine under the Nazis* (Cambridge, MA: Harvard University Press, 1988).

"Euthanasia" program (Operation T4): "Euthanasia" was a euphemism for the National Socialist state's first program of mass murder, a radical eugenic measure targeting disabled children and disabled adult patients living in institutional settings in Germany and German-annexed territories. In the autumn of 1939, Adolf Hitler signed an authorization vesting Philipp Bouhler, director of the Führer Chancellery, and **Karl Brandt**, Hitler's attending physician, to spearhead the killing operation. Bouhler and Brandt initiated a child "euthanasia" program through which at least five thousand physically and mentally disabled children were murdered during the war years. By 1940, Brandt and Bouhler had commenced an adult killing campaign known as **Operation T4** (*Aktion T4*). At least 70,273 institutionalized mentally and physically disabled adults were murdered at the "euthanasia" gassing installations between January 1940 and August 1941. In August 1941 Hitler ordered a halt to the adult "euthanasia" gassing measure. At this time, many T4 functionaries were recruited as German personnel for the **Operation Reinhard** extermination camps of **Bełżec**, **Sobibór**, and **Treblinka**. In the summer of 1942, the adult "euthanasia" killing program resumed in a decentralized format. In all, historians estimate that some two hundred thousand institutionalized mentally and physically disabled people were murdered as a result of Operation T4 and its corollary programs between 1939 and 1945.

See Henry Friedlander, *The Origins of Nazi Genocide: From Euthanasia to the Final Solution* (Chapel Hill: University of North Carolina Press, 1995).

Fort IX: Located outside the city of Kovno (today Kaunas) in Lithuania, Fort IX served as the primary killing site for the Jews of the Kovno ghetto and for Jews deported from western Europe to Kovno during the German occupation from 1941 to 1944. The largest mass shooting at Fort IX took place on October 28 and 29, 1941, during the *Grosse Aktion* in the Kovno ghetto, which claimed the lives of ninety-two hundred Jews.

See U.S. Holocaust Memorial Museum, *Hidden History of the Kovno Ghetto* (Boston: Little, Brown & Co., 1997).

Frank, Anne (1929–1945): Annelies Frank was born in Frankfurt, Germany, on June 12, 1929, the second daughter of businessman Otto Frank and his wife, Edith. Upon Adolf Hitler's rise to power, the Franks fled to Amsterdam in order to evade the Nazis' anti-Jewish measures; when German troops invaded the Netherlands in May 1940, the family again faced Nazi persecution. On July 5, 1942, Anne's sister, Margot, was summoned for **deportation**; on the following day, the family went into hiding in an annex attached to Otto Frank's office building. During their time in hiding, Anne kept a diary, detailing the events that took place in the "secret annex." On August 4, 1944, the Franks' hiding place was discovered. The inhabitants of the annex were transferred to **Westerbork** and on September 3 to **Auschwitz**. Sometime the following month, Anne and her sister Margot arrived at **Bergen Belsen**, where both succumbed to **typhus** in late February or early March 1945. Otto Frank, the sole survivor of the group, returned to Amsterdam in the summer of 1945, where he recovered Anne's journal. Published in English in 1952, the work has become one of the world's most widely read books and transformed its author into a symbol of the hundreds of thousands of Jewish children murdered in the Holocaust.

See Anne Frank, *The Diary of Anne Frank: The Revised Critical Edition*, eds. David Barouw and Gerrold van der Stroom, trans. Arnold J. Pomerans, B. M. Mooyaart-Doubleday, and Susan Massotty (New York: Doubleday, 2001).

Frank, Hans (1900–1946): Receiving his law degree in 1926, Hans Frank became an early legal adviser for the fledgling Nazi Party and founded the National Socialists' Lawyers League (NS-Rechtswahrerbund) in 1928. In October 1939, Adolf Hitler appointed Frank to administer the *Generalgouvernement* (**General Government**), the unincorporated portion of German-controlled Poland. In his role as the powerful chief civilian administrator of this region, Frank issued persecutory decrees for the region's Polish and Jewish populations and ordered forced labor for its residents. In the immediate postwar, the International Military Tribunal found Frank guilty of war crimes and crimes against humanity at the trial of the major Nazi criminals at Nuremberg and sentenced him to death. Frank was hanged on October 16, 1946.

See Chris Klessman, "Hans Frank: Party Jurist and Governor General of Poland," in *The Brown Elite*, ed. Ronald Smelser and Rainer Zitelmann, trans. Mary Fischer (New York: New York University Press, 1993), 39–47.

Freiberg, Berel Dov (also Fraiberg, 1927–): Born in 1927, Berel Dov Freiberg was one of the very few youngsters to survive the **Sobibór** killing center. In 1942, he and other family members escaped the **Warsaw ghetto** but were caught in a roundup near Lublin in eastern Poland. Freiberg was deported to Sobibór in May 1942, aged fourteen. Surviving as a member of a *Sonderkommando* unit, he participated in the Sobibór Uprising on October 14, 1943, and was one of nearly seventy Sobibór prisoners to survive the war. The only member of his family to survive the Holocaust, Freiberg emigrated to Israel, where he testified at the **Eichmann Trial** in Jerusalem in 1961.

See Dov Freiberg, *To Survive Sobibor* (Jerusalem: Gefen, 2007).

Gas van: Shooting was the most common form of killing used by the *Einsatzgruppen*. Yet, in the late summer of 1941, **Heinrich Himmler** requested that a more convenient mode of killing be developed. The result was the gas van, a mobile gas chamber mounted on the chassis of a cargo truck that employed carbon monoxide from the truck's exhaust to kill its victims. Gas vans made their first appearance on the eastern front in the late fall of 1941 and were eventually utilized, along with shooting, to murder Jews and other targets in most areas where the *Einsatzgruppen* operated. They were also employed at **Chełmno**, the first extermination center of the "Final Solution."

See Mathias Beer, "Die Entwicklung der Gaswagen beim Mord an den Juden," *Vierteljahrshefte für Zeitgeschichte* 35 (1987): 403–417.

Gauleiter: Resulting from the stratification of the Nazi Party after 1925, a man serving as *Gauleiter* acted as the regional party head in a *Gau*, or region, and maintained a strong personal connection to Adolf Hitler in his capacity as Party leader. In acting as a kind of regional governor, the *Gauleiter*'s functions as a Party official increasingly became intertwined with state functions at the regional level.

Gehsperre: In early September 1942, German officials announced an *Allgemeine Gehsperre* (general curfew) in the **Łódź ghetto**. From September 5 to 12, 1942, German forces brutally seized all those unfit for labor for **deportation**. Ghetto elder **Mordechai Chaim Rumkowski** had famously pled with ghetto inhabitants to "give me your children" to fill the German-imposed quota, thereby averting a communitywide deportation. Approximately 15,500 individuals were transported to their deaths at **Chełmno**; the vast majority of these victims were young children and adults over the age of sixty-five.

See Isaiah Trunk, *Łódź Ghetto: A History*, ed. and trans. Robert Moses Shapiro (Bloomington: University of Indiana Press in association with the U.S. Holocaust Memorial Museum, 2006).

Geltungsjude: A term used based on the First Ordinance to the **Reich Citizenship Law** of November 14, 1935, to describe a "**Mischling**" of the first degree (with two Jewish grandparents) who was legally treated as a "full Jew" based on his/her marriage to a Jewish spouse or practice of the Jewish faith.

See Raul Hilberg, *The Destruction of the European Jews* (New Haven, CT: Yale University Press, 2003).

Generalgouvernement (**General Government**): The *Generalgouvernement* was the unincorporated portion of German-occupied Poland, governed by the civil administration of Governor General **Hans Frank**. After the German invasion and defeat of Poland in the autumn of 1939, Adolf Hitler ordered the creation of the General Government as a territory in which to concentrate Jews and other undesirable racial elements resettled from the Polish territories incorporated into the Reich, including Danzig, West Prussia, Eastern Upper Silesia, and Posen (Poznań).

Germanization: Implemented under the rubric of such efforts as the *Generalplan Ost* (General Plan East), Germanization aimed to homogenize ethnically the eastern annexed and occupied territories with Germans by deporting or killing the local Slavic and Jewish populations, settling ***Volksdeutsche*** (**ethnic Germans**) in their place, and allowing a small proportion of the local population to remain as forced laborers. Implementing Germanization involved multiple agencies, including the **Reich Security Main Office**, the **Race and Settlement Main Office**, and the office of the Reich Commissar for the Strengthening of Germandom (Reichskommissar für die Festigung deutschen Volkstums, or RKFDV).

See Isabel Heinemann, *"Rasse, Siedlung, Deutsches Blut": Das Rasse- und Siedlungshauptamt der SS und die rassenpolitische Neuordnung Europas* (Göttingen: Wallstein Verlag, 2003).

Gestapo (acronym for Geheime Staatspolizei, or Secret State Police): As the chief executive agency charged with fighting internal "enemies of the state," the Gestapo functioned as the Third Reich's main surveillance and terror instrument, first within Germany and later in the territories occupied by Germany. After 1933, the Gestapo became part of a complex apparatus of state and party police agencies and maintained special administrative offices to supervise anti-Jewish policies. After 1934, the Gestapo was placed under **SS** chief **Heinrich Himmler**, then became part of **Reinhard Heydrich**'s **Security Police** apparatus in mid-1936; in September 1939 the Gestapo was merged with the **Security Service** (SD) into the **Reich Security Main Office**.

See George C. Browder, *Foundations of the Nazi Police State: The Formation of Sipo and SD* (Lexington: Kentucky University Press, 1990).

Goebbels, Josef (1897–1945): Serving from 1926 as *Gauleiter* of Berlin, Josef Goebbels became the architect of the Nazi propaganda machine, with its radical anti-semitism and mystification of Adolf Hitler as Führer. In March 1933, Hitler appointed him Reich Minister for Public Enlightenment and Propaganda (*Reichsminister für Volksaufklärung und Propaganda*). Goebbels also directed the policies of the Reich Chamber of Culture (Reichskulturkammer), particularly in matters of race, and played a key role in the instigation of *Kristallnacht* and subsequent anti-Jewish measures, including the **deportation** of Jews from Berlin to ghettos, concentration camps, and extermination centers.

See Jeffrey Herf, *The Jewish Enemy: Nazi Propaganda during World War II and the Holocaust* (Cambridge, MA: Belknap Press, 2006).

Göring, Hermann (1893–1946): A World War I flight commander and participant in the 1923 Nazi putsch attempt in Munich, Hermann Göring provided an important link for Adolf Hitler's movement with Germany's conservative elite. Göring amassed an array of functions, particularly in the area of rearmament and economic policy; for instance, he was named Plenipotentiary for the Four-Year Plan in October 1936 and Hitler's official successor in September 1939. In 1941, Göring charged **Reinhard Heydrich** with development of a "total solution to the Jewish Question." The highest-ranking Nazi in the dock at the International Military Tribunal in Nuremberg, Göring was convicted and sentenced to death in 1946.

See Richard J. Overy, *Göring: The "Iron Man"* (London: Routledge & Keagan Paul, 1984).

Gymnasium: This is a German school providing secondary education in preparation for college study, much like college-preparatory high schools in the United States.

Hereditary Health Law (Erbgesundheitsgesetz): see **Law for the Prevention of Progeny with Hereditary Diseases**.

Heydrich, Reinhard (1904–1942): After his dismissal from the German navy in 1931, Reinhard Heydrich received a commission from **SS** chief **Heinrich Himmler** to create a secret service for the Nazi Party, the **Sicherheitsdienst (SD)**, or **Security Service**, which Heydrich headed until his death. In 1936, he became head of the **Security Police** main office that combined the **Gestapo** and the Criminal Police. The Security Police, together with the SD, increasingly controlled the Third Reich's anti-Jewish policy. In the autumn of 1939, Heydrich merged the two agencies into the newly created **Reich Security Main Office,** which became the single most important agency for the implementation of the Holocaust through **deportation,** and mass murder. Attempting to bring the "Final Solution" under his closer control, Heydrich invited leading officials from state and party agencies to the **Wannsee Conference** held on January 20, 1942. Heydrich died as the result of an assassination attempt by Czechoslovak partisans in Prague; as a reprisal for his death, the Czech city of **Lidice** was destroyed and its inhabitants murdered or deported to concentration camps.

See Mark Roseman, *The Wannsee Conference and the Final Solution: A Reconsideration* (New York: Metropolitan Books, 2002).

Himmler, Heinrich (1900–1945): An early Nazi Party member and a participant in the November 1923 Beer Hall Putsch in Munich, Heinrich Himmler was appointed by Adolf Hitler in early 1929 to become the leader of the **SS** (*Reichsführer* SS) . After 1933, Himmler advanced rapidly from his initially small power base in Bavaria as police president in Munich to become head of the **Gestapo** in Prussia in 1934 and chief of the German police in mid-1936. During the war, Himmler further expanded his SS and police apparatus to uphold Nazi control in the Reich and in German-controlled countries and to play the key role in executing the genocide of European Jewry.

See Richard Breitman, *The Architect of Genocide: Himmler and the Final Solution* (New York: Alfred A. Knopf, 1991).

Hirsch, Fredy (Alfred) (1916–1944): Aboard one of the first transports to **Theresienstadt** in the winter of 1941, popular Jewish youth leader Fredy Hirsch became deputy director for youth services in the ghetto. In September 1943, Hirsch was deported from Theresienstadt to **Auschwitz** and absorbed into the **Theresienstadt family camp** in **Birkenau**. There, Hirsch and a staff of counselors and teachers organized educational and social activities for the camp's youngsters and sought to improve their physical welfare. On March 8, 1944, the family camp was liquidated, and most of the children, along with their family members and teachers, were murdered. On March 7, Hirsch apparently committed suicide in his quarters.

See Nili Keren, "The Family Camp," in *Anatomy of the Auschwitz Death Camp*, ed. Yisrael Gutman and Michael Berenbaum (Bloomington: University of Indiana Press in association with the U.S. Holocaust Memorial Museum, 1994), 428–40.

Hitler Youth (Hitlerjugend): In July 1926, this official youth organization of the Nazi Party was officially incorporated into the **SA**. Following the Nazi assumption of power, **Baldur von Schirach** assumed the leadership of the Hitlerjugend, organizing a general membership of boys from fourteen to eighteen and a corresponding junior branch, the German Young Volk (**Deutsches Jungvolk,** or *Pimpfe*). Hitler Youth members received both physical and paramilitary training and ideological indoctrination. On December 1, 1936, the Law Concerning the Hitler Youth (Gesetz über die Hitlerjugend) called for the assimilation of all German youth into the appropriate youth organizations and made membership obligatory.

Horthy, Miklós (1868–1957): In 1920, Miklós Horthy was declared regent and head of the Hungarian state, a position he held until October 1944. A political conservative, Horthy forged an alliance with Nazi Germany in an effort to regain Hungarian crown lands ceded following World War I. The Horthy regime imposed harsh antisemitic measures against Hungarian Jews beginning in 1938. German troops moved to occupy Hungary on March 19, 1944, and began to deport Hungarian Jews in May of that year. Faced with a worsening military situation, Horthy called a halt to these **deportations** on July 7, 1944. When Horthy negotiated with Soviet authorities and prepared to announce an armistice, German officials arrested him on October 15, 1944, and installed a new government under the fascist and radically antisemitic **Arrow Cross**. Following Hungarian defeat and his release by the Allies, Horthy emigrated to Portugal, where he died in 1957.

International Committee of the Red Cross (**ICRC**): This humanitarian organization was begun in the mid-nineteenth century to aid victims of international conflict. The ICRC has often been criticized for failing to make the rescue of Jews and political victims of Nazi persecution a priority during the war years. Under pressure from Danish authorities, German officials allowed a rare and highly choreographed visit of ICRC representatives to a sanitized **Theresienstadt** in June 1944.

See Jean-Claude Favez, *The Red Cross and the Holocaust* (Cambridge: Cambridge University Press, 1999).

Jewish Badge (also **Jewish Star** or Yellow Star): One of the most ubiquitous antisemitic measures employed in German- and Axis-controlled Europe was the mandatory wearing of the Jewish badge. The effort to impose a distinctive mark on the Jewish population marginalized Jews and rendered them more vulnerable to official and spontaneous discriminatory actions. **Hans Frank** issued the first decree imposing the Jewish badge in occupied Poland in November 1939, ordering all Jews over the age of twelve living in the **General Government** to wear an armband affixed with a blue Jewish star on the right sleeve of their outer garment. Similar regulations, with various discrepancies regarding the badge's appearance and the age of the wearer, were enacted in other districts of Poland and in areas occupied by German forces following the invasion of the Soviet Union in June 1941. German Jews were forced to wear the Jewish badge on September 15, 1941, shortly before the first **deportations** of Jews from the Reich. Legislation mandating the Jewish badge was soon adopted in western lands occupied by Germany and in German satellite states.

See Diemut Majer, *"Non-Germans under the Third Reich": The Nazi Judicial and Administrative System in Germany and Occupied Eastern Europe, with Special Regard to Occupied Poland, 1939–1945*, trans. Peter Thomas Hill, Edward Vance Humphrey, and Brian Levin (Baltimore: Johns Hopkins University Press in association with the U.S. Holocaust Memorial Museum, 2003).

Jewish Order Service (also Jewish Order Police): This refers to the Jewish police force in the ghettos of eastern Europe created by local **Jewish Councils** on the order of the German authorities to police the ghettos and enforce German commands and decrees. When **deportations** began and German authorities compelled the Jewish Order Police to assist in the operations, aversion to the Jewish Order Police among ghetto residents turned to hostility and fanned resistance among underground organizations.

Judenrat (**Jewish Council**; pl.: *Judenräte*): During World War II, German authorities established Jewish Councils among Jewish communities in areas under their jurisdiction. These Jewish municipal administrations were required to ensure that Nazi orders and regulations were implemented. In ghettoized communities, Jewish Councils also worked to provide community services for their incarcerated population. Used as a tool to implement Nazi anti-Jewish policy, Jewish Councils often incurred the distrust and odium of their communities, and they remain a controversial feature of the Holocaust among survivors and postwar scholars.

See Isaiah Trunk, *Judenrat: The Jewish Councils in Eastern Europe under Nazi Occupation* (New York: Macmillan, 1972).

Kapo (also capo): In the Nazi concentration camp system, *Kapos* were prisoner functionaries selected by, and under the command of, the **SS** *Kommandoführer*. Most often chosen from among the criminal and political prisoner population in the camps, *Kapos* oversaw the work production of their units, accounted for the prisoners under their supervision, and distributed punishment to those under their command. In the latter capacity, many *Kapos* earned a reputation for extreme cruelty and mistreatment of other prisoners.

Kibbutz (Hebrew: "gathering"): In the early twentieth century, the kibbutz was a form of collective settlement instigated by the Zionist movement in **Palestine** and based on ideas about shared forms of production, education, and ownership popular among reformist circles since the late nineteenth century.

See Michael Brenner, *Zionism: A Brief History* (Princeton, NJ: Markus Wiener, 2003).

Kinderaktion (children's action): This refers to the roundup and **deportation** of children from a ghetto or concentration camp. Because very young children were not usually utilized for forced labor, Nazi authorities viewed them as "useless eaters" and targeted them for early deportation measures. A large percentage of the 15,500 people deported during the *Gehsperre* from the **Łódź ghetto** to **Chełmno** in September 1942 were children under the age of ten. Children figured as a large proportion of victims in the Dünamünde Aktion, in which thirty-eight hundred Jews from the Riga ghetto were massacred in March 1942. In addition, children's actions took place in Kovno on March 27 and 28, 1944, and in the context of the first great deportation from the **Warsaw ghetto** to **Treblinka** in July 1942.

Kinderblock (Children's Block, Auschwitz)): In the brief months of its existence, the **Theresienstadt family camp** at **Birkenau** was a haven for children who might otherwise have been murdered directly upon arrival at Auschwitz. **Fredy Hirsch**, earlier deputy director for youth services in the **Theresienstadt** ghetto, arranged with Birkenau camp officials to create a separate children's block (Block 31) where youngsters might receive educational instruction, engage in structured play, and obtain more appropriate and nutritious meals. The *Kinderblock* was dissolved with the liquidation of the Theresienstadt family camp in early July 1944.

See Nili Keren, "The Family Camp," in *Anatomy of the Auschwitz Death Camp*, ed. Yisrael Gutman and Michael Berenbaum (Bloomington: University of Indiana Press in association with the U.S. Holocaust Memorial Museum, 1994), 428–40.

Kindertransport (children's transport): Following *Kristallnacht*, the British government agreed to permit an unspecified number of children under the age of seventeen to enter Great Britain from Germany and German-annexed territories. Private citizens or organizations had to guarantee to pay for each child's care, education, and eventual emigration from Britain. The first *Kindertransport* arrived in Harwich, Great Britain, on December 2, 1938, bringing some two hundred children; the very last *Kindertransport* sailed from the Netherlands for Britain on May 14, 1940, the day on which the Dutch army surrendered to German forces. In all, the rescue operation brought about nine to ten thousand children from Germany, Austria, Czechoslovakia, and Poland to Great Britain.

See Mark Jonathan Harris and Deborah Oppenheimer, *Into the Arms of Strangers: Stories of the Kindertransport* (New York: St. Martin's Press, 2000).

Korczak, Janusz (1878–1942): This was the pen name of Henryk Goldszmit, an eminent Polish pediatrician, pedagogue, and children's author, born in Warsaw on July 22, 1878. In 1911, Korczak came to direct the Dom Seriot orphanage, which incorporated his innovative approaches to child care. Over the course of his career, he founded Poland's first national children's newspaper, wrote influential books on parenting and child psychology, and worked within the juvenile court system to defend the rights of children. In 1940, when German authorities established the **Warsaw ghetto**, Korczak resettled there with his young Jewish charges. On August 5, 1942, **SS** officials ordered the children living at the orphanage to appear for **deportation**. Refusing to abandon his charges, Korczak led a column of children to the *Umschlagplatz* and boarded the train with his wards. The group was gassed upon arrival at **Treblinka**.

See Janusz Korczak, *Ghetto Diary* (New Haven, CT: Yale University Press, 2003); Janusz Korczak, *King Matt the First*, trans. Richard Lourie (New York: Farrar, Straus & Giroux, 1986); Betty Jean Lifton, *The King of Children: A Biography of Janusz Korczak* (New York: Farrar, Straus & Giroux, 1988).

Kraus, Gilbert and Eleanor: Inspired by the *Kindertransport* campaign that brought young Austrian and German refugees to Great Britain, Philadelphia attorney Gilbert

Kraus and his wife, Eleanor, led a successful effort in the summer of 1939 to bring a group of Jewish refugee children to the United States. Under the aegis of the Brith Sholom lodge, a Jewish fraternal organization headquartered in Philadelphia, the Krauses visited Nazi Germany, choosing fifty Jewish children from Vienna and securing visas for the youngsters to travel to the United States. The Krauses and their lodge personally vouched for the financial maintenance of the children and arranged foster homes for them in the Philadelphia area.

Kraus, Michal (Michael) (1930–): Michal Kraus grew up in the town of Nachod (today in the Czech Republic), where his father, Karl, was a physician. In December 1942, the Krauses were deported to **Theresienstadt**. In December 1943, the family was transported to **Auschwitz II–Birkenau** and absorbed within the **Theresienstadt family camp**. In June 1944, Michal's mother, Lotte, was transferred to the Stutthof concentration camp, where she perished in January 1945. In early July, Auschwitz camp officials liquidated the family camp; Karl Kraus was gassed on July 11, 1944. Michal numbered among eighty-nine young boys spared by physician **Josef Mengele** and survived Auschwitz as a "runner," assigned to convey communications and supplies among officials in Birkenau. In early 1945, Kraus endured a series of forced marches from Auschwitz; on May 5, 1945, he was liberated by American forces at Gunskirchen in Upper Austria. Returning to Czechoslovakia, the teenager reconstructed his Holocaust experiences in an extraordinary three-volume chronicle, completed in 1947.

Kristallnacht or *Reichskristallnacht* (Crystal Night or Night of the Broken Glass): On the night of November 9 to 10, 1938, a nationwide **pogrom** against German Jews erupted throughout Germany and annexed Austria, as well as in areas of Czechoslovakia recently occupied by German troops. *Kristallnacht* had its roots in the shooting of Ernst vom Rath, a German official stationed in Paris, by a young Polish Jew, Herschel Grynszpan, on November 7, 1938. Vom Rath's death two days later coincided with the anniversary of the 1923 Beer Hall Putsch; the Nazi Party leadership used the occasion to launch a night of antisemitic excesses. The pogrom was initiated primarily by Nazi Party officials and conducted by members of the Nazi Party, the **SA**, and the **Hitler Youth**. The violence destroyed 267 synagogues throughout Greater Germany. Rioters smashed windows, plundered homes, and looted Jewish-owned shops and businesses. *Kristallnacht* claimed the lives of at least ninety-one Jews. In its aftermath, **SS** and police units arrested some thirty thousand Jewish males, incarcerating them in concentration camps until each prisoner could produce papers for emigration abroad. The events of *Kristallnacht* represented an important turning point in Nazi antisemitic policy. After the pogrom, anti-Jewish measures radicalized dramatically, with a concentration of powers for their implementation resting more and more concretely in the hands of the SS.

See Walter Pehle, ed., *November 1938: From "Reichskristallnacht" to Genocide*, trans. William Templer (New York: Berg, 1991); Alan E. Steinweis, *Kristallnacht, 1938* (Cambridge, MA: Belknap Press, 2009).

Law against the Overcrowding of German Schools and Universities (Gesetz gegen die Überfüllung deutscher Schulen und Hochschulen): Nazi efforts to expel Jewish pupils from German public schools began with the April 25, 1933, Law against the Overcrowding of German Schools. In the years that followed, regional ordinances further limited Jewish school attendance in certain areas, but a comprehensive national ban came only with the Decree on Schooling of Jews of November 15, 1938, which dismissed all Jewish pupils from German schools.

See Saul Friedländer, *Nazi Germany and the Jews.* Vol. 1: *The Years of Persecution, 1933–1939* (New York: Harper Collins, 1997).

Law for the Prevention of Progeny with Hereditary Diseases (Gesetz zur Verhütung erbkranken Nachwuchses): Also known as the Hereditary Health Law (Erbgesundheitsgesetz) of July 1933, this legislation ordered the **compulsory sterilization** of persons suffering from specific diseases or impairments. Five of the disabilities designated in the ordinance represented psychiatric or neurological disorders, including schizophrenia, manic-depressive (bipolar) disorder, hereditary epilepsy, Huntington's chorea, and "hereditary feeblemindedness." Four physical conditions also warranted sterilization under the new law: hereditary deafness, hereditary blindness, serious hereditary physical deformity, and severe alcoholism. From January 1, 1934, until the end of World War II, some four hundred thousand Germans were forcibly sterilized under the auspices of the Hereditary Health Law.

See Gisela Bock, *Zwangssterilisation im Nationalsozialismus: Studien zur Rassenpolitik und Frauenpolitik* (Opladen: Westdeutscher Verlag, 1986); Paul Weindling, "Compulsory Sterilization in National Socialist Germany," *German History* 5 (1987): 10–24.

Law for the Protection of German Blood and German Honor (Gesetz zum Schutze des deutschen Blutes und der deutschen Ehre, or Blutschutzgesetz): see **Nuremberg Laws**.

Law for the Restoration of the Professional Civil Service: (Gesetz zur Wiederherstellung des Berufsbeamtentums): The Civil Service Law decreed the enforced retirement of Jews and "politically unreliable elements" from the German civil service. Signed by Adolf Hitler on April 7, 1933, the measure marked the National Socialists' first major piece of anti-Jewish legislation.

See Karl Schleunes, *The Twisted Road to Auschwitz: Nazi Policy toward German Jews, 1933–1939* (London: André Deutsch, 1970).

Lebensborn (Fount of Life): This Nazi organization was established in 1935 in an effort to reverse Germany's dwindling birthrate and to increase the number of "racially valuable" offspring. Instigated by Reichsführer **Heinrich Himmler**, the effort provided financial assistance and maternity care to the wives of SS men and also to unmarried mothers, a group that concerned Nazi racial hygienists and population planners. Lebensborn administrators encouraged unwed mothers to give up their infants after birth, and the organization managed both orphanages and adoption services that placed

Lebensborn children with "deserving" German families. Some seven thousand children were born in the organization's homes in Germany between 1936 and 1945. Lebensborn officials played a more insidious role in placing children from eastern Europe chosen for **Germanization** with adoptive families in Germany.

Lidice: On May 27, 1942, Czechoslovak parachutists Jan Kubiš and Jozef Gabčík succeeded in fatally injuring **Reinhard Heydrich**, a key planner of the "Final Solution" and the governor of the **Protectorate of Bohemia and Moravia**. Following the assassination attempt, **Gestapo** intelligence erroneously linked the Czech village of Lidice with the assassins. On June 10, 1942, German **SS** and police shot the village's 173 men and boys on the outskirts of Lidice. The town itself was razed to the ground. With few exceptions, the female adult population of Lidice was deported to Ravensbrück concentration camp. Forcibly separated from their mothers, the children of Lidice received a racial screening by SS personnel. Nine children who possessed sufficient "Germanic" background to make them candidates for **Germanization** were placed with adoptive German parents. The remaining children of Lidice were transported to Łódź and are believed to have been gassed at **Chełmno** in early July 1942.

See Jolana Macková and Ivan Ulrych, eds., *Fates of the Children of Lidice: Memories, Testimonies, Documents,* trans. Elias Khelil (Nymburk: Lidice Memorial, 2004).

Łódź ghetto (also Litzmannstadt ghetto): The Łódź ghetto was established in February 1940 and initially held 164,000 inhabitants. Appointed head of its *Judenrat* by German authorities, **Mordechai Chaim Rumkowski** displayed energy and organizational skill in overseeing the ghetto's workshops and social agencies, but he was viewed as a controversial and divisive figure. The ghetto boasted an impressive array of social services, including schools, hospitals, and a postal system. Living conditions there were deplorable, however, and some 20 percent of the ghetto's population died as a result of starvation and disease. From January to September 1942, German authorities deported over seventy thousand Jews and five thousand **Roma** to **Chełmno**. In the spring of 1944, the Nazis decided to liquidate the Łódź ghetto, then the last remaining ghetto in Poland. In June and July 1944, the Germans deported thousands of Jews to Chełmno; in August 1944, the surviving population of the ghetto was deported to Auschwitz.

See Isaiah Trunk, *Łódź Ghetto: A History*, ed. and trans. Robert Moses Shapiro (Bloomington: Indiana University Press in association with the U.S. Holocaust Memorial Museum, 2006).

Majdanek (Lublin/Majdanek): This was a vast forced labor and concentration camp near Lublin. Constructed in October 1941, it incarcerated Jews temporarily spared from **Operation Reinhard** killing operations in order to serve as forced labor in the Lublin District. Tens of thousands of Jewish forced laborers too weak to work were murdered in the Majdanek gas chambers and in shooting operations or died through mistreatment and starvation. After uprisings at **Sobibór** and **Treblinka**, **Heinrich Himmler** ordered **SS** and police forces to shoot over forty thousand Jewish prisoners in the Lublin

District, including eight thousand from Majdanek, at the camp under the auspices of Operation Harvest Festival (*Erntefest*) on November 3, 1943. Soviet forces liberated an intact Majdanek on July 24, 1944.

Mauthausen: After the incorporation of Austria in the *Anschluss* in March 1938, German authorities established the Mauthausen concentration camp near Linz, Austria. The camp held recidivist criminals and asocials in the first years of its existence. After World War II began, the number of prisoners in Mauthausen increased greatly, including more than seven thousand Spanish republicans turned over by **Vichy** authorities in France. Of more than two hundred thousand prisoners who passed through the Mauthausen camp system between August 1938 and May 1945, over one hundred thousand died there, including fourteen thousand Jewish prisoners. U.S. forces liberated Mauthausen on May 5, 1945.

See Hans Marsalek, *The History of Mauthausen Concentration Camp,* trans. Max Garcia (Vienna: Austrian Society of Mauthausen Concentration Camp, 1995).

Mengele, Josef (1911–1979): In 1937 Josef Mengele joined the Nazi Party; the following year, the same year in which he received his medical degree, he joined the **SS**. After service with the **Waffen-SS**, Mengele was transferred to **Auschwitz**, on May 30, 1943. He began as the medical officer responsible for **Birkenau**'s Gypsy camp; several weeks after the Gypsy camp's liquidation, Mengele became chief camp physician of Auschwitz II (Birkenau) in November 1943. Associated more closely with **selection** duty than any other medical officer at Auschwitz, Mengele also became infamous for his deadly medical experimentation, particularly with twins. With the aid of his prosperous family, Mengele evaded postwar prosecution and fled to South America; in declining health, he drowned while swimming near Bertioga, Brazil, on February 7, 1979.

See Sven Keller, *Günzburg und der Fall Josef Mengele: Die Heimatstadt und die Jagd nach dem NS-Verbrecher* (Munich: Oldenbourg, 2003); Office of Special Investigations, *In the Matter of Josef Mengele: A Report to the Attorney General of the United States* (Washington, DC: Office of Special Investigations, 1992).

Mischling (mixed-breed, hybrid; pl.: *Mischlinge*): This was a racial category formally introduced into the Third Reich's anti-Jewish politics following the promulgation of the **Nuremberg Laws**. This term also applied to children of other mixed "races."

See Jeremy Noakes, "The Development of Nazi Policy towards the German-Jewish 'Mischlinge,' 1933–1945," *Leo Baeck Institute Year Book* 34 (1989): 291–354.

Monowitz (Auschwitz III): see **Buna**.

Muselmann (pl.: *Muselmänner*): Concentration camp inmates used this term to describe ailing or exhausted fellow prisoners who had lost the will to live. Given their inability to work or stand for roll call (*Appell*) for significant lengths of time, *Muselmänner* might survive for only a short while. The origin of the term is uncertain but is believed to stem from the German word for "Muslim," as many Europeans at the time believed Islam to have a fatalistic element.

Mussfeld, Erich (also recorded as Mussfeldt) (1913–1948): A baker by profession, Erich Mussfeld joined the Nazi Party in 1939. He first served as a guard at the **Majdanek** concentration camp and was transferred to **Auschwitz** in May 1944. There he supervised the *Sonderkommando* at the **Birkenau** crematoria. In January 1947, an American military tribunal sentenced Mussfeld to a life term; shortly thereafter, he was extradited to Poland where he was sentenced to death and executed on January 24, 1948, in Kraków for crimes committed at Auschwitz.

Nuremberg Laws: This phrase is frequently used to describe the two basic pillars of Nazi antisemitic legislation: the **Reich Citizenship Law** (Reichsbürgergesetz) and the **Law for the Protection of German Blood and German Honor** (Gesetz zum Schutze des deutschen Blutes und der deutschen Ehre). This legislation was promulgated, together with the Reich Flag Law, on September 15, 1935, during the annual Nazi Party rally and at a specially convened session of the Reichstag in Nuremberg, Franconia. The first law restricted citizenship, and thus full protection under the law, to those of "German or related blood." The Law for Protection of German Blood and German Honor proscribed marriage and sexual contact between German "**Aryans**" and Jews. Subsequent regulations defined a "Jew" as someone with at least three Jewish grandparents (according to their religious affiliation) or as someone descended from two Jewish grandparents who him- or herself practiced the Jewish religion or was married to a Jew. Persons with two Jewish grandparents, but without Jewish religious affiliation or a Jewish spouse, came to be defined as "*Mischlinge* of the first degree" (*Mischlinge ersten Grades*). Persons with one Jewish grandfather or grandmother were labeled "*Mischlinge* of the second degree" (*Mischlinge zweiten Grades*). With later clauses added, the Nuremberg Laws formed one of the basic laws of the Third Reich that facilitated the **deportation**, murder, and expropriation of German Jews.

See Raul Hilberg, *The Destruction of the European Jews* (New Haven, CT: Yale University Press, 2003), 61–78; Karl A. Schleunes, ed., *Legislating the Holocaust: The Bernhard Loesener Memoirs and Supporting Documents* (Boulder, CO: Westview Press, 2001).

Nyiszli, Miklós (1901–1956): A Hungarian physician, Miklós Nyiszli was deported in June 1944 with his wife and young daughter to **Auschwitz**. Volunteering to work as a physician in the prisoner barracks, Nyiszli came to the attention of **Birkenau** camp physician **Josef Mengele**, who forced the doctor to aid in his medical experimentation upon Auschwitz prisoners. In 1946, Nyiszli published a harrowing account of his experiences as a prisoner-physician in *Dr. Mengele boncoló orvosa voltam az Auschwitzi krematóriumban.*

See Miklós Nyiszli, *Auschwitz: A Doctor's Eyewitness Account,* trans. Tibère Kremer and Richard Seaver (Hungarian ed., 1946; New York: Frederick Fell Publishers, 1960).

Obshestvo Remeslenofo zemledelcheskofo Truda (ORT, or **Society for Trades and Agricultural Labor)**: This was a Jewish self-help organization founded in 1880 in Russia to provide Jews with occupational training in agriculture and trade. The organization expanded in the interwar years to nearly every country of eastern and central Europe with a significant Jewish population, often in cooperation with the **American Jewish Joint Distribution Committee**. During World War II, ORT continued vocational training in many ghettos in eastern Europe. With the Jewish **displaced persons** crisis after the war, ORT, in cooperation with the **United Nations Relief and Rehabilitation Administration**, trained forty to forty-five thousand individuals, providing Jewish displaced persons with skills often critical to securing an immigration visa.

Oeuvre de Secours aux Enfants (**OSE**, or **Children's Aid Society**): Begun by physicians in Russia in 1912 as Obshchestvo Zdravookhraneniya Yevreyev (Society for the Protection of the Health of Jews), the organization expanded into many European countries with significant Jewish populations and focused increasingly on the welfare of children in its care. Relocating to Paris in 1933, the organization assumed the name Oeuvre de Secours aux Enfants. OSE ran a number of orphanages in France for Jewish refugee children and, when the **deportations** of Jews in France began in 1942, organized an underground effort to smuggle many of the children from OSE orphanages to the safety of neutral countries.

Oneg Shabbat (In Celebration of the Sabbath; also Oneg Shabbas and Oneg Shabes): Established by Warsaw historian and social worker **Emmanuel Ringelblum**, Oneg Shabbat was a clandestine archive that documented the history of the **Warsaw ghetto** and its inhabitants. With the aid of his assistant, Rabbi Simon Huberband, archive secretary **Hersh Wasser**, and a core of other professionals and volunteers, Ringelblum collected diaries, letters, and testimonies of ghetto residents, compiled hundreds of documents concerning the German occupation, and commissioned studies of the ghetto by experts. The activities of Oneg Shabbat continued until the first large-scale **deportation** action, when Ringelblum directed that the underground archive's material be buried in milk cans and metal boxes within the ghetto. After the war, Hersh Wasser helped to recover much of the archive's materials, which are reposited in the Jewish Historical Institute in Warsaw.

See Joseph Kermish, *To Live with Honor and Die with Honor: Selected Documents from the Warsaw Ghetto Underground Archives "O.S." (Oneg Shabbath)* (Jerusalem: Yad Vashem, 1986); Samuel D. Kassow, *Who Will Write Our History? Emmanuel Ringelblum, the Warsaw Ghetto, and the Oyneg Shabes Archive* (Bloomington: Indiana University Press, 2007).

Operation Reinhard (Aktion Reinhard or Aktion Reinhardt): In late 1941 and spring 1942, the planners of the "Final Solution" founded the **Bełżec**, **Sobibór**, and **Treblinka** killing centers, known collectively as the Operation Reinhard camps, to facilitate the murder of the Jews of the **General Government**. These killing centers claimed the lives of some 1.5 million Jews and thousands of Poles, **Roma**, and Soviet prisoners of war. In November 1943, after prisoner revolts at Sobibór and Treblinka, **SS** and police units shot the Jewish labor forces still incarcerated at Trawniki, Poniatowa, and **Majdanek** during Operation Harvest Festival (*Erntefest*). Forty-two thousand prisoners were murdered through this shooting action on November 3 and 4, 1943, bringing Operation Reinhard to a close.

See Yitzhak Arad, *Belzec, Sobibor, Treblinka: The Operation Reinhard Camps* (Bloomington: Indiana University Press, 1987).

Operation T4: see **"euthanasia"** program.

Ostmark: This was the Nazi name for annexed Austria after the **Anschluss**; it derives from the medieval designation for what was then the Austrian March.

Palestine (or Palestinian Mandate): This was a territory under British mandate beginning in 1920. Zionists had advocated a return to the Jewish "ancestral homeland" for Jews since the late nineteenth century, and Jewish immigration to Palestine began in earnest in 1882. Increased Jewish immigration and native Arab resistance to its manifestation induced the British government to place a strict quota on Jews immigrating to Palestine; the British White Paper of 1939 tightened these restrictions, limiting the ability of Jewish refugees from Nazi persecution to find a safe haven there. After the war, the growing number of Holocaust survivors and refugees hoping to reach Palestine led to massive illegal immigration. The British government announced that it would vacate the Palestinian Mandate by August 1948; on May 14, 1948, the Jewish leadership under future prime minister David Ben-Gurion declared an independent state of Israel.

Partisan: In the context of this volume, "partisan" refers to a unit or detachment of irregular troops waging guerilla warfare and sabotage against German forces and those who collaborated with them. Some twenty to thirty thousand Jewish fighters joined partisan bands that operated extensively throughout Nazi-occupied Europe, often cooperating with the broad-based Soviet partisan movement.

Pimpf: This refers to a member of the **Deutsches Jungvolk**; see **Hitler Youth**.

Pogrom (from Russian: "destruction"): A localized violent assault on a group of individuals and their property, often instigated by state or local authorities. The term is usually ascribed to antisemitic violence. The events of ***Kristallnacht*** are often characterized as a pogrom.

Police Decree Concerning the Designation of Jews (Polizeiverordnung über die Kennzeichnung der Juden): This police decree of September 15, 1941, compelled German Jews to wear the **Jewish badge**, shortly before the first systematic **deportations** of Jews from the Reich began in October 1941. The measure required all Jews over the age of six to attach to the left side of their outermost garment a six-pointed yellow star, inscribed with the word *Jude* (Jew) in black lettering. The decree also applied to Jews in Austria and the **Protectorate of Bohemia and Moravia**.

Ponary: The Ponary Woods, located eight miles from the city of Vilna (today Vilnius, Lithuania), served as the primary killing site for the Jewish population in the Vilna ghetto. From July 4, 1941, to July 1944, German ***Einsatzgruppen*** and Lithuanian auxiliary units systematically massacred around one hundred thousand Jews at Ponary.

Protectorate of Bohemia and Moravia: During the Munich crisis of September 1938, Great Britain and France forced the Czechoslovak Republic to cede its German-speaking borderlands (e.g., the Sudetenland) to Nazi Germany. On March 15, 1939, the German army occupied the remainder of rump Czechoslovakia. German authorities annexed to the Reich the territory roughly encompassing the modern Czech Republic, creating the Protectorate of Bohemia and Moravia. With its incorporation by Nazi Germany, the new Protectorate adopted the bulk of Nazi antisemitic legislation. On September 27, 1941, **Reinhard Heydrich** assumed the effective government of the territory until his death following an assassination attempt in June 1942.

Race and Settlement Main Office SS (Rasse- und Siedlungshauptamt, or RuSHA): The Race and Resettlement Office was originally established in 1931 to maintain the "racial purity" of the **SS** organization. Initially tasked with vetting the ancestry of SS recruits and their existing or intended spouses, RuSHA officials eventually helped to implement Nazi race and settlement policies in the eastern occupied and annexed territories during World War II. Their racial "experts" helped to determine *Volksdeutsche* (ethnic Germans) fit for assimilation in the German Reich and chose "racially suitable" children in Slavic lands for inclusion in the **Lebensborn** program.

See Isabel Heinemann, *"Rasse, Siedlung, Deutsches Blut": Das Rasse- und Siedlungshauptamt der SS und die rassenpolitische Neuordnung Europas* (Göttingen: Wallstein Verlag, 2003).

Racial hygiene: see **eugenics**.

Rassenschande ("race defilement"): This term describes real or purported sexual contact between "**Aryans**" and "non-Aryans" (especially Jews). The **Nuremberg Laws** provided the apparatus to make such relations punishable by law.

Ravensbrück: This, following the women's camp at Auschwitz, was the largest concentration camp for women in the German Reich. German authorities began construction of the camp in November 1938 at a site in northern Germany some eighty kilometers (fifty miles) north of Berlin. In April 1941, **SS** officials established a small men's camp adjacent to the main camp. Beginning in the summer of 1942, SS physicians subjected many prisoners at Ravensbrück to grisly medical experimentation. In January 1945, Ravensbrück and its subcamps held more than fifty thousand, mostly female, prisoners; among the inmates were political prisoners, "asocials," **Roma and Sinti**, Jews, Jehovah's Witnesses, and "race defilers" (see *Rassenschande*). Soviet troops liberated Ravensbrück in April 1945.

Razzia: This refers to a roundup, as for **deportation** to a concentration camp or killing center.

Realschule: This refers to a type of secondary school in German-speaking lands, generally catering to pupils between the ages of eleven and seventeen.

Reich Citizenship Law: see **Nuremberg Laws**.

Reichsmark (RM): This was the currency used in Germany from 1924 until June 20, 1948. The Reichsmark was subdivided into one hundred (Reichs)pfennigs.

Reichssicherheitshauptamt (**RSHA**, or **Reich Security Main Office**): This agency combined with the **Security Police** and the **Security Service** under the authority of Reichsführer-SS **Heinrich Himmler** and was directed by **Reinhard Heydrich**; after Heydrich's death, Ernst Kaltenbrunner eventually undertook leadership of the organization. The RSHA was the central mechanism for extrajudicial terror and repression in Germany and the occupied territories and a key agency in the implementation of the "Final Solution."

Reichsvereinigung der Juden in Deutschland (Reich Association of Jews in Germany): This successor organization to the **Reichsvertretung der Juden in Deutschland** was formally installed in July 1939. In the hands of the *Gestapo*, the Reichsvereinigung became a tool for the administration and control of Jews remaining in Germany. Having served the purpose set by the regime, it was dissolved in 1943 and its staff deported.

See Beate Meyer, "The Inevitable Dilemma: The Reich Association (*Reichsvereinigung*) of Jews in Germany, the Deportations, and the Jews Who Went Underground," in *On Germans and Jews under the Nazi Regime*, ed. Moshe Zimmermann (Jerusalem: Hebrew University Magnes Press, 2006), 297–312.

Reichsvertretung der deutschen Juden (Reich Representation of German Jews, or RV); also **Reichsvertretung der Juden in Deutschland** (Reich Representation of Jews in Germany): The Reichsvertretung was founded in September 1933 by a coalition of leading German Jewish functionaries, most prominently Leo Baeck, who subsequently served as the organization's president. Intended as a coordinating umbrella organization for the many German Jewish organizations in the Third Reich, the Reichsvertretung cooperated closely with the Jewish agencies and associations inside and outside Germany. The **Nuremberg Laws** had an immediate effect on the organization's ability to protect Jews in Germany from persecution and resulted in the organization's extended efforts to encourage emigration; the organization also changed its name to Reichsvertretung der Juden in Deutschland at this time. By the spring of 1939, the hitherto largely autonomous Reichsvertretung had transformed into the **Gestapo**-controlled Reichsvereinigung.

See Otto Dov Kulka and Esriel Hildesheimer, "The Central Organization of Jews in the Third Reich and Its Archives," *Leo Baeck Institute Year Book* 34 (1989): 187–201.

Righteous Among the Nations: **Yad Vashem** bestows this title on non-Jewish individuals who risked their lives to save Jews during the Holocaust. In German-occupied eastern Europe, the punishment for sheltering or assisting Jews was often death. In 1962, Yad Vashem formed a thirty-five-member Commission for the Designation of the Righteous to award the title "Righteous Among the Nations." As of January 2010, 23,226 people from forty-four countries have been recognized as "Righteous Gentiles."

See Israel Gutman and Sara Bender, eds., *The Encyclopedia of the Righteous among the Nations: Rescuers of Jews during the Holocaust*, 5 vols. (Jerusalem: Yad Vashem, 2003).

Ringelblum, Emmanuel (1900–1944): A historian by training, Emmanuel Ringelblum established **Oneg Shabbat**, a clandestine archive that documented the history of the **Warsaw ghetto** and its inhabitants. Ringelblum himself contributed to the documentation effort, with writings such as the monograph *Polish-Jewish Relations during the Second World War*. During the first great **deportation** action from the Warsaw ghetto in the summer of 1942, Ringelblum ordered that the archive be buried in a series of milk cans and metal boxes in order to preserve the work of the organization. In March 1943, Ringelblum and his family succeeded in escaping to the "**Aryan** side" of Warsaw, where they were discovered in their hideout in March 1944 and murdered.

See Emmanuel Ringelblum, *Polish-Jewish Relations during the Second World War*, eds. Joseph Kermish and Shmuel Krakowski (Jerusalem: Yad Vashem, 1974); Samuel D. Kassow, *Who Will Write Our History? Emmanuel Ringelblum, the Warsaw Ghetto, and the Oyneg Shabes Archive* (Bloomington: Indiana University Press, 2007).

Roma and Sinti (Gypsies; also Romani): Among the groups the Nazi regime and its Axis partners singled out for persecution on racial grounds were the Roma and Sinti. Roma were affected in great numbers by several acts of Nazi legislation, including the **Law for the Prevention of Progeny with Hereditary Diseases** and the **Law for the Protection of German Blood and German Honor**, whose ancillary legislation was extended to Roma and other "racially inferior" minorities. In the mid-1930s, German authorities established Gypsy camps (*Zigeunerlager*) throughout the Reich. Roma were deported to concentration camps including **Buchenwald**, **Dachau**, Sachsenhausen, **Mauthausen, Auschwitz, Chełmno**, and **Ravensbrück**. In addition they were interned in the Lublin, **Łódź**, and **Warsaw ghettos**. Members of the *Einsatzgruppen* undertook killing actions that included Roma victims in the Soviet Union and Serbia. The Croatian **Ustaša** killed and interned thousands of Roma along with Serbs and Jews. In 1941, thousands of Romanian Roma and Jews were deported to Transnistria. Historians estimate that the Germans and their allies killed 25 percent of all European Roma, or some 220,000 Roma individuals.

See Michael Zimmermann, *Verfolgt, Vertrieben, Vernichtet: Die nationalsozialistische Vernichtungspolitik gegen Roma and Sinti* (Essen: Klartext, 1989).

Rudashevski, Yitskhok (1927–1943): On September 6, 1941, Yitskhok Rudashevski and his family received orders to move into the Vilna ghetto. Shortly thereafter, the fourteen-year-old began to write a diary, which he filled with vivid descriptions of the ghetto and the individuals who inhabited it. Rudashevski was also active in forging an intellectual life for the youth of the Vilna ghetto. He and his family went into hiding when **deportations** from Vilna began, but **SS** officials discovered them in early October 1943 and murdered them at **Ponary**. A cousin who had escaped deportation located the family's hiding place immediately after the war and found Rudashevski's diary, which was first published in Yiddish in 1953.

See Isaac Rudashevski, *The Diary of the Vilna Ghetto, June 1941–April 1943* (Tel Aviv: Ghetto Fighters' House, 1973).

Rumkowski, Mordechai Chaim (1887–1944): Russian-born Chaim Rumkowski served as the director of the Helenowek Jewish orphanage in Łódź until October 1939. Following the German invasion of Poland, German authorities established the **Łódź ghetto** and appointed a *Judenrat* with Rumkowski at its head. Directly accountable to German administrator **Hans Biebow**, Rumkowski wielded extraordinary authority over the internal management of the ghetto. He displayed enormous organizational skill in overseeing the ghetto's workshops and social agencies, but he governed in an autocratic fashion and was viewed by contemporaries, as by scholars today, as a controversial and divisive figure. Rumkowski believed from the start that the ghetto's best chance for survival lay in cooperating fully with the German officials. Thus, he acceded in December 1941 to German demands for **deportations** of ghetto residents to **Treblinka**. On September 4, 1942, faced with a further call for twenty thousand deportees, Rumkowski decided he would fill the required quota with the ghetto's least productive members: the ailing, the aged, and children under ten. Rumkowski was deported with his family to **Auschwitz** during the liquidation of the Łódź ghetto and died there on August 28, 1944.

See Michal Unger, *Reassessment of the Image of Mordechai Chaim Rumkowski* (Jerusalem: Yad Vashem, 2004).

Schirach, Baldur von (1907–1974): The son of Berlin theater director Rittmeister Carl Baily Norris von Schirach and his American wife, Baldur von Schirach was an early leader of the National Socialist German Students' League. Acting as the first Reich Youth Leader (*Reichsjugendführer*), he headed the **Hitler Youth** from 1933 until 1940. At this time, he became *Gauleiter* of the *Reichsgau* Vienna until the war's end; in this capacity he helped to oversee the **deportation** of Viennese Jews to the camps and ghettos in the East. Von Schirach was a defendant before the International Military Tribunal in Nuremburg, which found him guilty of crimes against humanity and gave him a twenty-year prison sentence.

Schutzstaffel (**SS**, or **Protective Squadron**): Established in 1925 as a protective service for prominent Nazi Party functionaries, the SS grew under the stewardship of **Heinrich Himmler** into one of the most important tools for maintaining the regime's grip on political power through suppression and terror directed against real or imagined internal "enemies of the Reich." Many of these enemies were incarcerated in concentration camps run by the SS. Through its party branch, the SS increasingly overlapped with state agencies such as the **Gestapo** and other parts of the police subordinated to Himmler. In 1940 it added a military wing, the **Waffen-SS**. Himmler's apparatus, which by the war's end comprised more than 1 million men in a range of different agencies, played a key role in planning and implementing the genocide of European Jewry.

See Heinz Höhne, *The Order of the Death's Head: The Story of Hitler's SS* (New York: Coward-McCann, 1970).

Scout Movement: Founded in England in 1907 by Robert Baden Powell, scouting is an international youth movement that offers youngsters practical training in outdoor activities, sports, and crafts. A German scouting movement began in 1910 and attracted thousands of members. The group was banned by the Nazis in the 1933 and 1934 in order to facilitate the integration of German youth into the **Hitler Youth** and its auxiliary organizations.

Security Police (Sicherheitspolizei, or Sipo): This branch of the German police comprised the **Gestapo** (Secret State Police), the Criminal Police (Kriminalpolizei, or Kripo), and the Border Police (Grenzpolizei). As chief of the Security Police as well as the **Security Service, Reinhard Heydrich** merged the two organizations by establishing the **Reich Security Main Office** in September 1939. The Security Police helped to supply the forces of the *Einsatzgruppen*, which served as both security police and mobile killing units in German-occupied territories.

Security Service (Sicherheitsdienst, or SD): This intelligence and surveillance organization was established in 1931 under **Reinhard Heydrich**. Among its major tasks were monitoring real or imagined enemies of national socialism and reporting on the state of opinion among the German public. As chief of the Security Service as well as of the **Security Police**, Reinhard Heydrich merged the two organizations, establishing the **Reich Security Main Office** in September 1939.

Selection: New arrivals to **Auschwitz II–Birkenau** underwent the process of "selection." Amid the chaos of disembarkation, Auschwitz prisoner-workers and **SS** guards separated the deportees by gender and ordered them to form short ranks. SS medical staff performed selections of Jewish prisoners, determining who would be retained for work and who would perish immediately in the gas chambers. Young and able-bodied Jews were often chosen for labor and registered as prisoners at the camp. Along with the sick, weak, and aged, children were generally murdered upon arrival. Selections took place on a regular basis at many other camps in the Nazi concentration camp system to cull children and ailing prisoners for gassing.

Sobibór: Located in a wooded and thinly populated region, the village of Sobibór was chosen as a site for the second of three extermination camps operating under the auspices of the **Operation Reinhard**. Sobibór's first commandant was Franz Stangl; in August 1942, Stangl was transferred to **Treblinka** and succeeded by his deputy, Franz Reichleitner. German **SS** and police officials conducted gassing operations at Sobibór from May 1942 until autumn 1943, when Jewish prisoner revolts there and at Treblinka spurred the liquidation of both killing centers. In all, at least 167,000 individuals perished at the Sobibór extermination camp.

See Jules Schelvis, *Sobibor: A History of a Nazi Death Camp*, trans. Karin Dixon (Oxford: Berg Publishers in association with the U.S. Holocaust Memorial Museum, 2007);

Miriam Novitch, ed., *Sobibór, Martyrdom and Revolt: Documents and Testimonies* (New York: Holocaust Library, 1980).

Sonderkommando (literally, "special detail or detachment"): The word *Sonderkommando* had two meanings in the context of the Holocaust. First, it applied to certain **SS** units, such as special units of the **Einsatzgruppen** and to unit commands like that of Sonderkommando Lange, which ran the **Chełmno** killing center. Second, it applied to details of Jewish prisoners compelled to dispose of victims' bodies and belongings in National Socialist killing centers.

Sterilization: see **Law for the Prevention of Progeny with Hereditary Diseases**.

Streicher, Julius (1885–1946): One of the Nazi Party's earliest members, Streicher established his virulently antisemitic newspaper, **Der Stürmer** (*The Storm Trooper*), in 1923; in the same year, he took part in the abortive Beer Hall Putsch. Following Adolf Hitler's release from prison, the Nazi leader named Streicher **Gauleiter** of Middle Franconia (later Franconia). In the first months of the Nazi regime, Streicher helped to organize the **Boycott of April 1, 1933**, of Jewish-owned businesses. In 1938, Streicher's *Stürmer* reached its highpoint in terms of circulation; his successful publishing house of the same name produced, among other works, a host of antisemitic children's literature, including the infamous *Der Giftpilz* (*The Poisonous Mushroom*). Despite his strong personal association with Hitler, Streicher was viewed as mercurial by leading officials and, in 1939, stripped of his party posts. Streicher was convicted of crimes against humanity in a trial of major war criminals before the International Military Tribunal. He was hanged in Nuremberg, his former stronghold, on October 16, 1946.

See Dennis Showalter, *Little Man, What Now?* Der Stürmer *in the Weimar Republic* (Hamden, CT: Archon, 1982).

Sturmabteilung (Storm Division, or **SA**; also Storm Troopers): As the paramilitary wing of the Nazi Party, the SA, formed in 1921, initially comprised mainly German World War I veterans, militia members, and others opposed to both the democratic **Weimar Republic** and to the Communist Party. Its terror tactics against opponents increased the public visibility of the Nazi movement, both before and after Adolf Hitler's rise to power. Once the Nazi regime was established, it began to perceive the disruptive tactics of the SA as a threat. Hitler agreed to the murder of the SA's top leadership in the Röhm Purge," or "The Night of the Long Knives," in June 1934, carried out primarily by the **SS**. The SS, previously a part of the SA, relegated that organization to a Nazi Party agency of secondary importance.

See Richard Bessel, *Political Violence and the Rise of Nazism: The Stormtroopers in Eastern Germany, 1925–1934* (New Haven, CT: Yale University Press, 1984).

Sudetenland: Adolf Hitler demanded this borderland of western Czechoslovakia because of its majority ethnic German population; it was annexed to the German Reich at the conclusion of the Munich Conference in September 1938. Like their coreligionists in Germany proper, Jews in the Sudetenland experienced **Kristallnacht** on November 9 to 10, 1938.

Theresienstadt (Terezin): In autumn 1941, **Reinhard Heydrich**, governor general of the **Protectorate of Bohemia and Moravia**, suggested that the former imperial fortress of Theresienstadt near Prague act as the holding station for Jews in the Czech lands on their way to the camps and ghettos in the East. Following the **Wannsee Conference** of January 20, 1942, Theresienstadt also became a "settlement area" for German Jews over the age of sixty-five and for Jewish war veterans who had been decorated or disabled in combat, those categories of German Jews initially exempted from **deportation**. Nazi propagandists portrayed Theresienstadt as a kind of model ghetto community for Jews, employing the "Jewish city" to deceive foreign governments and agencies, as when the **International Committee of the Red Cross (ICRC)** visited a highly sanitized Theresienstadt in June 1944. In reality, Theresienstadt amalgamated Nazi concentration camp and ghetto. Of the more than 140,000 Jews transferred to Terezin, 33,500 died there, victims of starvation, disease, and ill treatment. More significantly, Theresienstadt functioned as a way station for deported Czech Jews and eventually for Jews deported from the Reich to the **Auschwitz, Majdanek**, and **Treblinka** extermination camps. Between December 1941 and the end of the war in the spring of 1945, eighty-eight thousand individuals passed through Theresienstadt on the way to almost certain death in the East.

See H. G. Adler, *Theresienstadt, 1941–1945: Antlitz einer Zwangsgemeinschaft* (Tübingen: Mohr, 1960); Vojtěch Blodig, *Terezin in the "Final Solution to the Jewish Question," 1941– 1945*, trans. Jan Valěska and Lewis Paines (Prague: Památník Terezín/Oswald, 2003).

Theresienstadt Family Camp (Auschwitz II–Birkenau): In September 1943, five thousand Jews, among them over one thousand children, arrived at Auschwitz from **Theresienstadt**. Spared the customary **selection**, they were brought directly to a separate barracks network in Birkenau, designated the Theresienstadt Family Camp. A second transport from Theresienstadt joined their ranks in December 1943. Its inmates were processed as special prisoners; their hair was not shorn, and they were allowed to retain their civilian clothing. Men and women were housed in separate blocks, but prisoners could move freely within the small camp, and children could remain with their parents. Historians believe that the family camp was allowed its short, privileged existence in order to deceive representatives of the **International Committee of the Red Cross**, who had visited Theresienstadt and planned to make a similar visit to Auschwitz. In early July 1944, survivors of the camp's December 1943 transports were put to a selection. The majority of these prisoners were gassed, while the camp itself was liquidated.

See Nili Keren, "The Family Camp," in *Anatomy of the Auschwitz Death Camp*, ed. Yisrael Gutman and Michael Berenbaum (Bloomington: Indiana University Press in association with the U.S. Holocaust Memorial Museum, 1994), 428–40.

Treblinka: Planners of the "Final Solution" chose the site for this third **Operation Reinhard** killing center in an isolated area some eighty kilometers (fifty miles) northeast of Warsaw. The most fully developed and deadly of the Reinhard camps, Treblinka began killing operations in late July 1942. Commandants of the Treblinka killing center were Dr. Irmfried Eberl (July–August 1942), Franz Stangl (August 1942–August

1943), and Kurt Franz (August 1943–November 1943). **Deportations** to Treblinka came mainly from the **Warsaw ghetto** and from smaller ghettos in the Warsaw and Radom districts of the **General Government**. Jews from Germany, Austria, France, Slovakia, Thrace, and Macedonia were also murdered there, as were thousands of **Roma** and Poles. On August 2, 1943, Treblinka inmates organized a prisoner revolt at the camp, spurring liquidation of the site in the autumn of 1943. From July 1942 through November 1943, camp authorities killed 870,000 to 925,000 Jews at the killing center.

Typhus: This acute, contagious disease is caused by rickettsial microorganisms and usually transmitted by an animal vector, such as fleas or lice. It should not be confused with typhoid, an unrelated disease. Typhus epidemics claimed thousands of lives in ghettos and concentration camps in German-occupied Europe.

Umschlagplatz (transfer point): Located on the corner of Zamenhof and Niska streets, the *Umschlagplatz* was an area separating the **Warsaw ghetto** from the Polish, or "**Aryan**," side of the city. Originally the official transit point through which manufactured goods from the outside were transported into the ghetto, the site, with its adjacent railroad siding, became the assembly point for the thousands of Jews deported from the Warsaw ghetto, predominantly to the **Treblinka** killing center, between July 1942 and May 1943.

United Nations Relief and Rehabilitation Administration (**UNRRA**): The UNRRA agency was established in November 1943 in response to the unfolding **displaced persons** crisis in Europe. Subject to the authority of the Supreme Headquarters of the Allied Expeditionary Forces (SHAEF) in Europe, UNRRA facilitated repatriation of non-German refugees under Allied control, administering hundreds of displaced persons camps in Germany, Italy, and Austria. Twenty-three volunteer relief agencies worked through the UNRRA, including the **American Jewish Joint Distribution Committee**, **ORT**, and the Hebrew Immigrant Aid Society (HIAS). The International Refugee Organization succeeded UNRRA in 1947 in caring for some 650,000 remaining displaced persons.

Ustaša/Ustaše (also anglicized: Ustasha): This Croatian fascist party controlled the Independent State of Croatia, as a puppet state of Nazi Germany, from 1941 to 1945 and helped to implement the Holocaust in Croatia. Under leader Ante Pavelić, the Croatian state persecuted its Serb, Jewish, and **Roma** populations. Thirty thousand Jews and 325,000 to 333,000 Serbs were murdered in the territory of the Independent State of Croatia under the Ustaša government.

Versailles Treaty: Drafted by the victors in World War I and signed by Reich officials amid widespread German protests in June 1919, the Versailles Treaty laid out the conditions of the German defeat. The treaty imposed harsh financial sanctions, territorial demands, and military limitations on Germany, undermining the troubled democratic **Weimar Republic**. Many blamed the treaty's provisions for having provided the essential precondition for the Nazi Party's success, but other domestic factors also proved critical in contributing to the demise of Germany's Weimar democracy.

See Conan Fisher and Alan Sharp, *After the Versailles Treaty: Enforcement, Compliance, Contested Identities* (London: Routledge, 2008).

Vichy France: Following the German defeat of France in May 1940, French and German officials signed an armistice on June 22 of that year. Under its terms, northern France came under direct German occupation. Southern France remained unoccupied and was governed by a French administration, headquartered in the city of Vichy. In July the French National Assembly voted to suspend the constitution of the Third Republic and placed the new "Vichy regime" under the leadership of the aging Marshal Henri Philippe Pétain. Officially neutral, Vichy France collaborated closely with Germany. In the autumn of 1940, Vichy administrators began to promulgate antisemitic legislation closely patterned on that of German anti-Jewish decrees and ordinances in place in the German-occupied zone. In March 1941, a central agency, the General Commissariat for Jewish Affairs (Commissariat Général aux Questions Juives), was established to coordinate anti-Jewish legislation and policy. Thousands of Jews were interned under deplorable conditions in French-administered detention camps, where at least three thousand individuals died during the war years. As **deportation** of Jews from western Europe began, German officials, aided by French police, conducted roundups of Jews in both occupied and unoccupied zones of France throughout the summer of 1942. In November 1942, German troops occupied Vichy's formerly "free" zone.

See Michael Marrus and Robert Paxton, *Vichy France and the Jews* (New York: Basic Books, 1981); Renée Poznanski, *Jews in France during World War II* (Hanover, NH : University Press of New England for Brandeis University Press in association with the U.S. Holocaust Memorial Museum, 2001).

Volk: Acquiring currency from romantic writers in the nineteenth century, the German word *Volk*, meaning "folk" or "people," became a catchword used by National Socialists to define a nation or people united by culture, language, and ethnicity. For Nazi ideologues, it suggested a "community of the blood" in racial terms.

Volksdeutsche (ethnic Germans): This National Socialist term included people of German ethnic origin who lived outside the borders of the German Reich and were not Reich citizens. Large communities of ethnic Germans lived in the Baltic countries and in southeastern and eastern Europe. Nazi ideologues were particularly eager to integrate these individuals into the *Volksgemeinschaft*. Following the invasion of Poland, German authorities established a central registration bureau, the German People's List (Deutsche Volksliste, or DVL), to register ethnic Germans. The Ethnic Germans' Central Agency (Volksdeutsche Mittelstelle, or VoMi) organized the spoliation of property from Jews and Poles and its redistribution to ethnic Germans. In line with Reich policy of **Germanization**, thousands of ethnic Germans were resettled in German-annexed territories of the Reich, either voluntarily or under compulsion.

See Doris Bergen, "The Nazi Concept of 'Volksdeutsche' and the Exacerbation of Anti-Semitism in Eastern Europe, 1939–45," *Journal of Contemporary History* 29, no. 4 (October 1994): 569–82.

Volksgemeinschaft: This was the Nazi term for the German ethnic and racial community, as defined by National Socialist ideology.

Volksschule: This is a primary school in German-speaking lands.

Waffen-SS: The Waffen-SS represented the military wing of the **SS**, itself a Nazi Party organ. In accordance with Adolf Hitler's wishes, the Waffen-SS was never incorporated into the regular German army. Its thirty-eight divisions fought beside the regular army (**Wehrmacht**). It was also a multiethnic force, as nearly 60 percent of its troops were foreign recruits and volunteers by war's end. Waffen-SS divisions were implicated in numerous war crimes, including the Malmedy, Ardeatine, and Oradour-sur-Glane massacres.

Wannsee Conference: On January 20, 1942, fifteen high-ranking Nazi Party and German government officials met at a villa in the Wannsee suburb of Berlin to discuss and coordinate the implementation of the "Final Solution." **Reinhard Heydrich**, the head of the **Reichssicherheitshauptamt**, convened the Wannsee Conference to secure support from government ministries and other interested agencies. The participants did not deliberate whether such a plan should be undertaken but instead discussed the implementation of a policy decision already made at the highest level of the Nazi regime.

See Mark Roseman, *The Wannsee Conference and the Final Solution* (New York: Metropolitan Books, 2002).

Warsaw ghetto: On October 12, 1940, the Germans decreed the establishment of the Warsaw ghetto. Containing over four hundred thousand inhabitants, the ghetto was sealed off from the rest of the city in November 1940. Food allotments rationed to the ghetto by the German civilian authorities were not sufficient to sustain life; between 1940 and mid-1942, eighty-three thousand Jews died of starvation and disease. From July 22 until September 12, 1942, German **SS** and police units carried out mass **deportations** from the Warsaw ghetto, sending 265,000 Jews to the **Treblinka** killing center. On April 19, 1943, German authorities commenced finally to liquidate the ghetto. Led by the Jewish Fighting Organization (Żydowska Organizacja Bojowa), ghetto fighters and residents resisted for nearly a month, mounting the Warsaw Ghetto Uprising. German troops overcame the insurgency on May 16, 1943, deporting forty-two thousand Warsaw Jews to forced labor camps and killing centers. Perhaps as many as several thousand Warsaw Jews continued to live in hiding on the "**Aryan** side" of Warsaw after the liquidation of the ghetto.

See Barbara Engelking and Lacek Leociak, *The Warsaw Ghetto: A Guide to the Perished City* (New Haven, CT: Yale University Press, 2009).

Wartheland/Warthegau: The *Reichsgau* of **Wartheland** (*Reichsgau* of Posen until 1940) was one of four incorporated territories of the Reich that were part of prewar Poland but annexed by the Nazi state following the Polish defeat in 1939. German authorities marked the Warthegau for **Germanization**. The native Polish and Jewish populations were forcibly resettled in the non-incorporated territory of the Reich known as the

General Government, while ethnic Germans were resettled in the Warthegau territory in order to restructure the region ethnically.

Wasser, Hersh and Bluma (1912–1980 and 1912–1990): Hersh Wasser played an important leadership role in the **Warsaw ghetto** and was active as secretary of the **Oneg Shabbat** archive. After the war, Wasser helped to recover much of the archive's materials, which had been buried in milk cans and other containers within the Warsaw ghetto. Along with his wife, Bluma, a teacher and contributor to the archive, Wasser emigrated to Israel, where he served as director of the J. L. Peretz Publishing House See Hersh Wasser, "Daily Entries of Hersh Wasser," ed. and trans. Joseph Kermish, in *Yad Vashem Studies* 15 (1983): 201–82.

Wehrmacht: The Wehrmacht (defense force) included the combined German armed forces from 1935 until 1945. It comprised the *Heer* (army), the *Kriegsmarine* (navy), and the *Luftwaffe* (air force).

Weimar Republic: This German democracy formed at the end of World War I was named after the city in which its national constitution was adopted in February 1919. Following a phase of relative internal stability, the Weimar Republic underwent a massive crisis, triggered by the worldwide economic downturn in 1929. Elite manipulation of the republic's constitution, combined with the economic crisis, produced the rapid erosion of political support for democratic parties. Against this backdrop, conservative elites negotiated Adolf Hitler's appointment as chancellor on January 30, 1933.

See Detlev J. K. Peukert, *The Weimar Republic: The Crisis of Classical Modernity* (New York: Hill & Wang, 1993).

Westerbork: The Dutch government established Westerbork in the Dutch province of Drenthe in October 1939 to intern Jewish refugees who had entered the Netherlands illegally. The camp continued to function after the German invasion of the Netherlands in May 1940. In 1941, it had a population of eleven hundred Jewish refugees, mainly from Germany. From 1942 to 1944, Westerbork served as a transit camp for Dutch Jews before their **deportation** to concentration camps and killing centers in German-occupied Poland. Westerbork was liberated on April 12, 1945, by Canadian forces.

Yad Vashem: Located on the Mount of Remembrance (Har Hazikaron) in Jerusalem, Yad Vashem is Israel's official remembrance authority to commemorate, document, research, and educate concerning the Holocaust. In 1953, the Israeli Knesset enacted the Law of the Martyrs' and Heroes' Remembrance Authority proposed by Education Minister Ben-Zion Dinur. Among its activities, the institution is responsible for awarding the title **"Righteous Among the Nations"** to non-Jewish individuals who, at personal risk to themselves, aided Jews during the Holocaust.

See Bella Gutterman and Avner Shalev, *To Bear Witness: Holocaust Remembrance at Yad Vashem* (Jerusalem: Yad Vashem, 2005); James E. Young, *The Texture of Memory: Holocaust Memorials and Meaning* (New Haven, CT: Yale University Press, 1993).

YIVO (Yiddisher Visnshaftlekher Institut, or Jewish Scientific Institute): The YIVO Institute was founded in Vilna, Poland (today Vilnius, Lithuania), in 1925 to document and research the language, literature, history, and culture of eastern European Jewry. In 1940, YIVO moved its headquarters to New York City. Today its library holds over 385,000 books and periodicals in twelve major languages.

Żegota (Council for the Aid to Jews; *Rada Pomocy Żydom,* or RPŻ): This secret organization was created in the fall of 1942 by the Bureau for Jewish Affairs of the Polish government in exile to assist Jews in hiding in occupied Poland with financial support, housing, employment, medical care, forged documentation, and child welfare. The organization predominantly comprised non-Jewish social and political activists. At least four thousand Jews received direct assistance from Żegota, and tens of thousands more benefited under its auspices.

See Irene Tomaszewski and Tecia Werbowski, *Żegota: The Council for Aid to Jews in Occupied Poland, 1942–1945* (Montreal: Price-Patterson Ltd., 1994) and David Engel, *Facing a Holocaust: The Polish Government-in-Exile and the Jews, 1943–1945* (Chapel Hill: University of North Carolina Press, 1993).

Zelkowicz, Josef (1897–1944): Born in Konstantynow, near Łódź, Josef Zelkowicz began to write for Yiddish newspapers and publications in the 1920s. In 1929 he became a member of the board and staff of the YIVO Institute branch in Łódź. Incarcerated in the **Łódź ghetto**, he became a teacher of Yiddish and a leading writer and archivist of *The Chronicle of the Łódź Ghetto*. Zelkowicz also kept a personal diary, twenty-seven notebooks of which are now reposited in the Jewish Historical Institute in Warsaw. In August 1944, Zelkowicz was deported to **Auschwitz** during the liquidation of the Łódź ghetto and was murdered there.

See Josef Zelkowicz, *In Those Terrible Days: Writings from the Lodz Ghetto,* ed. Michal Unger, trans. Naftali Greenwood (Jerusalem: Yad Vashem, 2002).

Złoty: This unit of Polish currency comprises one hundred *groszy*. During the German occupation of Poland in World War II, the złoty was the official currency of the **General Government** and was pegged at a fixed exchange rate to the German **Reichsmark**.

Zyklon B: The Nazi authorities used this lethal hydrogen cyanide (prussic acid) gas as a method of mass killing in the Nazi concentration camp system. First used on September 3, 1941, in a test gassing of 650 Soviet prisoners of war and 200 ailing prisoners at **Auschwitz**, Zyklon B, in pellet form, was procured from private chemical firms that employed the acid as a pesticide for fumigation. Nazi authorities had previously used carbon monoxide gas as a means of gas killing and continued to do so at the camps of **Operation Reinhard**. Zyklon B was utilized to kill predominantly Jewish prisoners at **Auschwitz II–Birkenau** and **Majdanek**.

INDEX

Entries which appear in boldface can be found in the Glossary. Cities and countries are listed according to 1933 borders; references to variations on place names in other languages are also included. References to notes are included when unique (otherwise page references are used). Italicized page numbers refer to photographs.

ABOUT THE AUTHORS

Patricia Heberer has served as an historian with the Center for Advanced Holocaust Studies at the United States Holocaust Memorial Museum in Washington, DC, since 1994. She is the Museum's in-house specialist on medical crimes and eugenics policies in Nazi Germany. Dr. Heberer received her PhD in history from the University of Maryland in 2001. A contributor and consultant for two United States Holocaust Memorial Museum publications, *1945: The Year of Liberation* and *In Pursuit of Justice: Examining Evidence of the Holocaust,* she published *Atrocities on Trial: The Politics of Prosecuting War Crimes in Historical Perspective,* co-edited with Jürgen Matthäus, in 2008 with the University of Nebraska Press. Two recent articles by Dr. Heberer, "Science," in John Roth and Peter Hayes, ed., *The Oxford Handbook of Holocaust Studies* and "The 'Euthanasia' Program," in Jonathan Friedman, ed., *Routledge History of the Holocaust,* appeared in 2011.

Nechama Tec is professor emerita of sociology at the University of Connecticut at Stamford. She holds honorary degrees from Lafayette College, Seton Hall University, and Hebrew Union College and is a member of the United States Holocaust Memorial Museum's Academic Advisory Committee. Her publications include *Every Day Lasts a Year: A Jewish Family's Correspondence from Poland,* with Christopher R. Browning and Richard S. Hollander (2007); *Resilience and Courage: Women, Men, and the Holocaust* (2003); and *Defiance: The Bielski Partisans* (1993; adapted for a motion picture directed by Edward Zwick). Her books have been translated into Dutch, French, Hebrew, German, Italian, Polish, Portuguese, and Japanese. She is currently working on a book titled "Resistance" to be published by Oxford University Press.

I thank my God every time I remember you,

constantly praying with joy

in every one of my prayers for all of you.

Philippians 1.3–4

Presented to

_____

By

_____

On

_____

PRAY IT!

This book can change your life.
The Bible's essential message is this: God **LOVES** us and wants to be in a lifelong **friendship** with us. The Bible tells the story of God's love, revealed most perfectly in Jesus' **life**, **death**, and **RESURRECTION**. Through Christ, God offers us forgiveness, freedom, companionship, and **new** life. It is a wonderful gift, but we must choose to **ACCEPT** it. How will you **respond** to that invitation?

Lord God, here I am!

You created me and know me completely.

You know all about my life—my joys and my
     sufferings, my questions and my dreams.

I know you love me, even when I feel my sins
     and mistakes make me unlovable.

Help me to love you, God, with all my heart,
     mind, and soul, and to love all people,
     even as I love myself.

Jesus, thank you for showing me how to live.

I know you want only the best for my life,
     and I believe following you is the way to a
     full and abundant life.

Holy Spirit, give me the courage and wisdom
     to be Jesus' follower, even when it isn't easy.

Fill me with the joy and peace that comes
     from doing your will.

     Amen.

THE Catholic Youth Bible

For the text of the articles and introductions
Nihil Obstat: Rev. Jack L. Krough
           Censor Librorum
           15 December 1998
Imprimatur: †Most Rev. Bernard J. Harrington, DD
           Bishop of Winona
           7 January 1999

The nihil obstat and imprimatur are official declarations that a book or pamphlet is free of doctrinal or moral error. No implication is contained therein that those who have granted the nihil obstat or imprimatur agree with the contents, opinions, or statements expressed.

For the text of the New Revised Standard Version (NRSV): Catholic Edition
Imprimatur: †Most Rev. Daniel E. Pilarczyk
           President, National Conference of Catholic Bishops
           Washington, D.C., 12 September 1991
Imprimatur: Canadian Conference of Catholic Bishops
           Ottawa, 15 October 1991

Writers: Eduardo Arnouil; Lisa-Marie Calderone-Stewart; Carmen María Cervantes; Catherine Cory; Gary Dreier; Karen Emmerich; Carole Goodwin; Ron Kenney; Edward P. Kunzman; Judi Lanciotti; Joseph A. Morris, CM; Daniel Ponsetto; Rosa Sanchez; Larry Schatz, FSC; Valerie Shields; Brian Singer-Towns; and Michael Theisen

The acknowledgments continue on page 1525.

ISBN 0-88489-489-4, paper
ISBN 0-88489-667-6, hardcover

Catholic
THE
Youth
Bible

New Revised Standard Version:
Catholic Edition

Saint Mary's Press
Christian Brothers Publications
Winona, Minnesota

Contents

The New Testament

Welcome!

THIS UNIQUE BIBLE IS FOR YOU.

The Catholic Youth Bible (CYB) is filled with things that will make it easier for you to understand the Bible's message. The authors, editors, designers, and artists involved in creating its special features were focused on you—a young person seeking answers to life's important questions. The CYB can be a true companion, helping you find the answers you seek and perhaps raising new questions along the way. It will help you see yourself in God's image and likeness, A VITAL PART OF GOD'S SAVING WORK IN THE WORLD.

WHAT MAKES THIS YOUTH BIBLE *CATHOLIC*? For starters, its introductions and articles reflect Catholic interpretation of the Bible and make connections to Catholic beliefs and traditions. In addition, this Bible contains all seventy-three books and letters that form a complete Catholic Bible, seven more than most other Bibles (see "The Case of the Missing Books," near Tob 1.16). Does this mean that other Christians cannot use *The Catholic Youth Bible*? Not at all. When it comes to the Scriptures, Christians from all cultures and denominations have more in common than we have differences.

AS YOU USE THIS BIBLE, keep in mind two important points. The first is that the Bible is for everyone. Wherever you are in your relationship with God, *the Bible can speak to you.* The articles in the *CYB* invite you to consider what the church teaches about God's message in the Bible whether you are a committed Christian or a searcher with lots of questions.

The second point is that all the special features in *The Catholic Youth Bible* are designed to encourage you *to read the Bible itself.* It is the Bible's stories, poems, prophecies, and letters that carry this central message: *God desires a loving relationship with us.* The special features of this Bible can help you understand God's message. *BUT IT IS GOD'S WORD IN THE BIBLE THAT CAN CHANGE YOUR LIFE.*

Love one another

SPECIAL FEATURES

The Catholic Youth Bible is loaded with special features to help make it easier for you to read and understand the Bible. Here is a list of some of those features and where to find them.

HOW TO READ AND STUDY THE BIBLE

The chapter that follows this general introduction gives advice for interpreting the Bible and a process for studying the Bible alone or with a group.

SUGGESTED READING PLANS

This chapter offers some great reading plans to get you started in studying the Bible.

SECTION INTRODUCTIONS

Each major section of the Bible (the Pentateuch, the historical books, the wisdom books, the prophetic books, the Gospels and the Acts of the Apostles, and the Letters and Revelation) begins with background on the books in that section.

BOOK INTRODUCTIONS

Introductions at the beginning of most books (sometimes two or three books share a single introduction) give insight into each book's central message and an overview of its contents.

LIVE IT!

The "Live It!" articles apply the Bible's messages to situations you may be facing now or will face in the future.

PRAY IT!

The "Pray It!" articles can help you use the Bible for personal prayer. They show the biblical basis for the prayer and sacramental life of the Catholic church.

DID YOU KNOW?

The "Did You Know?" articles provide background from biblical scholars to help you understand the culture and traditions of biblical times, or the church's interpretation of certain passages.

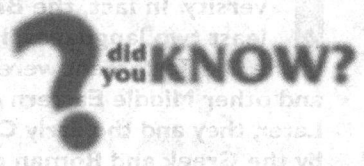

INTRODUCING . . .

The "Introducing . . ." articles give a quick introduction to the lives of important biblical people.

CATHOLIC CONNECTIONS

The "Catholic Connections" articles show the biblical basis for many Catholic Christian beliefs and practices.

WHERE DO I FIND IT?

Several indexes are located at the back of the Bible, before the maps. The first index contains several lists that can help you locate Bible passages on events, people, and teachings of Jesus. The second index helps you find Bible passages related to each sacrament. The third index helps you find Bible passages related to specific life and faith issues. The fourth index leads you to articles on specific topics throughout *The Catholic Youth Bible*. The first three indexes generally use Bible citations to guide you, and the fourth index uses page numbers.

STUDY AIDS

Color maps, a timeline, and pictures are found at the back of the Bible. The timeline and maps will help you locate where and when different biblical events occurred.

The Bible Is MULTICULTURAL

THE BIBLE developed in the midst of great cultural diversity. In fact, the Bible was originally written in at least two languages, Hebrew and Greek. The people of the Old Testament were influenced by Arabic, Egyptian, and other Middle Eastern cultures that surrounded them. Later, they and the early Christian church were influenced by the Greek and Roman cultures. In the Bible, God is revealed as the God of *all* nations and *all* cultures.

Christians believe that the Bible's core message of God's love for human beings speaks to people of any culture. That is one reason the Bible has been translated into more languages than any other book in the world. Christians also believe that God is at work in the lives of people of every culture, whether or not they have been formally introduced to the Christian message. Listening to other cultures' experience of God can deepen Christian people's appreciation of God's message present in the Bible.

We also live in a multicultural world. *The Catholic Youth Bible* responds to this reality in two main ways. First, all the articles attempt to speak in a way that people of all cultures can appreciate and understand. Second, some articles have been specially written to represent one of four distinct cultural perspectives: African American, Asian American, Hispanic and Latino, and Native American. These articles share cultural experiences and traditions, religious symbols, prayers, and poetry, and they connect all these elements to the Bible. The article subject index at the back of this book lists the location of the articles for each of these cultural perspectives.

The four major cultural perspectives represented in *The Catholic Youth Bible* are actually a small sampling of the many unique cultures in the world. Because of space restrictions, most of these cultures are not included. Despite these limitations, the multicultural articles can deepen your appreciation of the Bible's message and the rich ways different cultures live that message.

NAVIGATING *The Catholic Youth Bible*

THE CATHOLIC YOUTH BIBLE has several aids to help you locate references to Bible books and the Bible's special features. The contents on pages iv–v will be your main guide in locating the different books and features. However, the last page in the color section (facing the back cover) lists all the Bible books alphabetically and gives their abbreviations and beginning page numbers. You will find this a useful and easy-to-locate guide. Also, as mentioned previously, the section "Where Do I Find It?" offers several types of indexes to help you locate specific passages and articles.

Throughout *The Catholic Youth Bible,* there are many references to specific Bible passages. These references are given in shorthand form, such as Jn 3.16–17. The initial letters are the abbreviation for (or, in a few cases, the full name of) the Bible book. The number before the period stands for the chapter and the number(s) after the period stands for the verse(s). So Jn 3.16–17 refers to the Gospel According to John, chapter 3, verses 16 to 17.

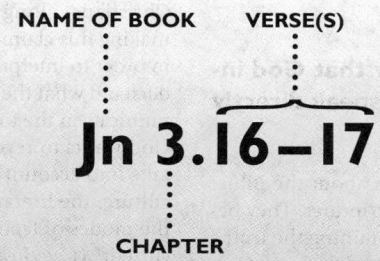

NAME OF BOOK   VERSE(S)

Jn 3.16–17

CHAPTER

Most of the articles end with a citation identifying the Bible passage the article is based on. It is important to read the passage before reading the article.

QUESTIONS AND ANSWERS About the Bible

THE BIBLE—which is also called the sacred Scriptures—tells the story of the loving relationship between God and humankind. It brings people to a deeper relationship with God, teaches important truths about Christian faith, and challenges how we live our life and relate with other people. However, studying the Bible raises questions for many people. This section gives some answers to key questions from Catholic Christian teaching. Because these are brief answers to important questions, you may want to talk more about them with someone in your family, church, or school.

What does it mean to say that God inspired the Bible? Did God speak directly to the Bible's authors?

Christians make a fantastic claim about the Bible: God is the author of the sacred Scriptures. They believe the Bible is God's word, containing the truths that God wishes to reveal to humankind for our salvation. Through the Holy Spirit, God inspired the human authors of the Bible's books to reveal these truths in their writings. These two concepts—God's **inspiration** of the biblical authors and God's **revelation** in their writings of the truths about God and God's will for us—are two important Christian beliefs about the Bible.

To say that biblical authors were inspired by God does not mean that they took dictation directly from God. They were true authors using creative literary forms to communicate the people's experience of God. In fact, many of the books had more than one author. Some books went through several decades of development in which the stories were told and retold, written down, combined, and edited. The church believes the Holy Spirit was guiding the many people involved throughout this whole process.

How do I know that what is in the Bible is true? Aren't there mistakes in the Bible?

Christians believe that the Bible is true and without errors when it teaches the things God wishes to reveal for the sake of our salvation. This is called the inerrancy of the Bible.

Some Christians also believe that the Bible is without error in every respect, including all references to scientific and historical facts. But Catholic Christians, along with others, are cautious about making this claim. The Catholic church teaches that in order to interpret the Bible correctly, we must understand what the human authors intended to communicate at the time of their writing. To know what God wants to reveal through their words, we must take into account "the conditions of their time and culture, the literary genres in use at that time, and the modes of feeling, speaking, and narrating then current" (*Catechism of the Catholic Church*, no. 110).

In other words, from our modern viewpoint, some statements in the Bible may seem like mistakes. But these "mistakes" may be due to the difference between a biblical author's cultural perspective and our cultural perspective. Or they may be due to our misunderstanding of a biblical author's use of literary devices such as metaphors, fiction, and poetry. Or perhaps they are due to a biblical author's different understanding of science or history. In its introductions and articles, *The Catholic Youth Bible* will help you understand the biblical authors' intentions and the church's teaching about what God is revealing through them.

Why do Catholics believe that the Bible alone isn't enough to teach all the truths about the Christian faith?

All Christians believe that God's complete revelation—all that people need to know about God and about their relation to God—is expressed in Jesus Christ. They believe that Jesus is the living Word of God, "the image of the invisible God" (Col 1.15). All Christians believe that the Bible is a primary way of communicating God's revelation, which has its ultimate source in Christ.

But Catholic Christians believe that God's revelation is also communicated through **sacred Tradition.** Sacred Tradition, which is sometimes simply called Tradition, is all that the first Apostles learned from Jesus and the Holy Spirit. Under the guidance of the Holy Spirit, it is preserved, taught, and reinterpreted for each new generation by the Apostles' successors—the pope and bishops. Scripture and Tradition are closely related and support each other, having their common source in Jesus Christ. Some of the articles in *The Catholic Youth Bible* expand on the Bible's message with teaching from sacred Tradition.

Why does the Bible have two testaments?

The Bible reveals God's plan for humanity. It is divided into two parts. The Old Testament records the relationship between God and the descendants of Abraham, particularly the descendants of Abraham's grandson Jacob. At different times in their history, these descendants are called the Hebrews, the Israelites, and the Jews. The Old Testament contains their religious history, laws, and sacred stories. Because the Old Testament contains the sacred Scriptures of the Jewish people, many Christians also call the Old Testament the Hebrew Scriptures.

The New Testament presents Jesus as the full revelation of God. Jesus was a Jew, and he affirmed the core beliefs of the Jewish faith. He knew and cherished the Hebrew Scriptures. But he also revealed new insights into God's desired relationship with human beings. After his Resurrection, as his followers lived out the implications of his teachings, they eventually formed a new religious faith that came to be called Christianity. The books and letters in the New Testament record their central teachings and beliefs about Jesus.

The church teaches that there is a profound unity to the Old and New Testaments in relation to God's revelation. "The Old Testament prepares for the New and the New Testament fulfills the Old; the two shed light on each other; both are true Word of God" (*Catechism*, no. 140).

The Bible was written a long time ago. What does it have to do with my life today?

Christians believe the Bible's core message of God's desire to be in a loving relationship with human beings is greater than the difficulties caused by the passing of time and by cultural differences between the biblical era and our time. They believe that the more people read, reflect on, and study the Bible, the more they can discover what God is saying to people today. The Bible's message does not wear out or become obsolete. However, the Bible was originally written by and for people who lived in different historical circumstances. In order to make the Bible relevant to our time, people need to interpret it in its proper context (see the next chapter, "How to Read and Study the Bible," for help with this). This process of making the Bible's message current for our time is called **actualization.**

Each person, community, and culture brings its life experiences to interact with God's revelation in the Bible. God's word sheds light on our hopes and struggles and in so doing becomes a source of new life for us. Knowing that God forgives our sins, liberates us from the things that oppress and enslave us, and rejoices in our successes gives us the inner peace we all seek. The Bible tells us that we are entrusted with Jesus' mission to share God's peace, justice, and love—a mission that gives true meaning to our life.

Of course, the best way to discover what the Bible has to do with your life is to read and study it yourself. The same Holy Spirit who inspired the original authors will also be your companion as you spend time with the Bible—comforting, exciting, challenging, and encouraging you along your way.

How to Read AND Study THE BIBLE

MAKING SENSE OF THE BIBLE

> "The Word became flesh and lived among us" (Jn 1.14).

God's Word came to earth as a person, Jesus Christ. Jesus was fully human so that people could experience God's love firsthand. He was also fully God so that through him death is overcome and new life is breathed into sinful humanity.

The Bible is called God's word because it is closely linked to Jesus. Like Jesus, it can be said to be both human and divine. It is divine because it reveals to us God and God's plan. But it is also the work of human authors and reflects their knowledge, culture, and biases. It is through their words that the Bible reveals God's nature, God's saving work in the world (often called salvation history), and God's purpose for humanity—including our lives. It follows that an important part of understanding the Bible is understanding the human authors' intentions.

However, understanding the authors' intentions isn't enough either. We must also look at the message of any individual book or passage within the bigger picture of the entire Bible's message and the church's interpretation of it. Here are some suggestions for considering these different contexts when you read the Bible.

Consider the Book's Central Themes

The Bible's authors usually had a central theme or themes in mind when writing their particular book or letter. So when you are confused about the meaning of a particular verse or passage, it often helps to go back and read the whole chapter or even check out the introduction to the book. For example, you may wonder what Jesus is trying to teach us in the story of the prodigal son, Lk 15.11–32. You might try reading from the beginning of chapter 15. You'll find that Jesus told the story in response to people who criticized him for welcoming sinners. This helps us understand that the prodigal son story teaches that we are supposed to welcome sinners too.

Consider the Historical Situation and the Audience

Certain Bible passages do not make sense unless we understand the historical situation the author was trying to address. The introductions to each of the books in *The Catholic Youth Bible* help you with this. For example, in Am 5.21,23 God tells the people: "I hate, I despise your festivals. . . . / Take away from me the noise of your songs." Doesn't God like worship? In the introduction to Amos, we learn that God sent Amos to speak against the rich people who exploited the poor and then attended elaborate religious festivals to worship God. The hypocrisy was what God hated.

Consider the Teaching of the Whole Bible

An old saying calls us to "use the Bible to interpret the Bible." Some people focus on a single verse from the Bible and ignore other passages on the same subject. For example, some churches will not allow women in any position of leadership. They base this on 1 Cor 14.34, which says, "Women should be silent in the churches." But in doing this, they ignore other passages, such as those in which Paul pays respect to women who were deacons and leaders in the church.

Consider the Church's Interpretation

Most Christian churches have traditions and teachings for interpreting the Bible and applying its message. For Roman Catholics, bishops ultimately have the responsibility for properly interpreting God's revelation in the Bible, although many people (Scripture scholars, priests, parish ministers, and teachers, for example) share this responsibility with them. *The Catholic Youth Bible* points out the Catholic church's established teaching for important passages, especially in the "Catholic Connections" articles. When in doubt, ask a priest, minister, parish leader, teacher, or parent for help in looking for the correct interpretation of a confusing passage.

HEAD AND HEART

Sometimes when you pick up the Bible, you want to study and learn. Maybe you want to learn some Bible history or understand more about Baptism. Maybe you want to know why the Gospel of John is so different from the other Gospels. These are things of the head, the intellect.

Sometimes when you pick up the Bible, you are hungry to grow closer to God. You want to experience God's presence in your life or receive guidance about a problem. These are things of the heart, the soul.

Ask God to touch both your head and heart when you read the Bible. It's important to be open to both because we were created to be whole people. *The Catholic Youth Bible* can help. Some of the articles, particularly the introductions to the books, the "Did You Know?" articles, and the "Catholic Connections" articles, give background to help your understanding for head reading. The "Live It!" and "Pray It!" articles are more for your heart reading.

THE PRIMA PROCESS

Prima is the Latin word for "first." In the PRIMA process, each letter of the word stands for a step in reading and studying the Bible individually or with a group. Using the PRIMA process helps you remember to keep God first in your life!

Pray. Begin with a prayer that your time with the Bible will draw you closer to God.

Read attentively, trusting that God will give you what you need to learn or grow.

Imagine what was going on when the passage was first written. What is its cultural and historical context? Try to put yourself into the story. What was the author trying to get across?

Meditate on what you have read. How does this fit in the context of the rest of the Bible's teaching? with the church's teaching? What do you think God is teaching you?

Apply what you have read to your life. God may be calling you to address a particular issue or relationship. Or you may find words of comfort and support you need at this particular time. Carry God's word into the rest of your day, the rest of your life!

PERSONAL AND GROUP STUDY

Personal Reading and Study

Faith is personal. Reading the Bible by yourself can help you grow in both your head and heart relationships with God. Choose a time that fits for you and make a commitment to read *The Catholic Youth Bible* regularly, at least once a week if not every day. The PRIMA process and the Bible reading plans in the

next chapter will give you a structure for your personal reading.

Group Reading and Study

Your faith is personal, but it is not private. The Bible itself teaches that God calls us to be part of a Christian community. Reading and studying the Bible with a group can feed you and teach you in an exciting way. Consider starting a group Bible study by inviting some friends or family members to meet with you. Or check at your parish to see what Bible studies might already be going on.

Again, the PRIMA process and the Bible reading plans in this book can provide a structure for reading the Bible with a group. Check with your parish or school for other resources you can use with a group.

MAKING A PLAN

Note: All the reading plans described in this section are found in the next chapter, "Suggested Reading Plans."

The Catholic church has an excellent plan for reading and studying the Bible, called the lectionary. The lectionary includes a cycle of Scripture passages read at Sunday Eucharist in the liturgy of the word. It is inspiring to know that other Catholics all over the world are hearing and reflecting on the same Scriptures at the same time. Studying the Sunday lectionary readings can make a big difference in your appreciation of the Eucharist. You can use reading plan 1, "Reading the Bible with the Church," to help you do this for part of the year. It lists the Sunday lectionary readings for the seasons of Advent, Christmas, Lent, and Easter.

Reading whole books of the Bible is important to fully understanding the Bible in context. But it rarely works to say, "I'm going to read the whole Bible cover to cover." Most people quit when they hit the detailed laws in the Book of Exodus. So as a start, you can use reading plan 2, "A Walk Through the Bible," which gives a four-week overview of the important events in the Bible. After that you might read one of the four Gospels—Mark is good because it is short and filled with action. Then try the Acts of the Apostles. Follow this by one of the letters from the New Testament—1 Corinthians is a good one to start with. Eventually, move on to Genesis and Exodus from the Old Testament to see how their themes are connected to the New Testament books you have read.

You could also make a plan to study themes in the Bible. To get started, pick from reading plans 3 to 8, which cover topics such as sin and salvation, suffering, God's call, and women in the Bible. Or use the article subject index in the back of *The Catholic Youth Bible* to create your own reading plan on a topic that interests you.

Suggested Reading Plans

READING PLAN 1: Reading the Bible with the Church

This reading plan lists the Sunday readings for the liturgical seasons of Advent, Christmas, Lent, and Easter.

ADVENT AND CHRISTMAS

Cycle A (2001, 2004, 2007)	Cycle B (2002, 2005, 2008)	Cycle C (2000, 2003, 2006)
The First Sunday of Advent		
Isa 2.1–5	Isa 63.16–17; 64.1–8	Jer 33.14–16
Rom 13.11–14	1 Cor 1.3–9	1 Thess 3.12—4.2
Mt 24.37–44	Mk 13.33–37	Lk 21.25–28,34–36
The Second Sunday of Advent		
Isa 11.1–10	Isa 40.1–5,9–11	Bar 5.1–9
Rom 15.4–9	2 Pet 3.8–14	Phil 1.4–6,8–11
Mt 3.1–12	Mk 1.1–8	Lk 3.1–6
The Third Sunday of Advent		
Isa 35.1–6,10	Isa 61.1–2,10–11	Zeph 3.14–18
Jas 5.7–10	1 Thess 5.16–24	Phil 4.4–7
Mt 11.2–11	Jn 1.6–8,19–28	Lk 3.10–18
The Fourth Sunday of Advent		
Isa 7.10–14	2 Sam 7.1–5,8–11,16	Mic 5.2–4
Rom 1.1–7	Rom 16.25–27	Heb 10.5–10
Mt 1.18–24	Lk 1.26–38	Lk 1.39–45
Midnight Mass *(25 December, every year, readings are the same for all cycles)*		
Isa 9.2–7	Isa 9.2–7	Isa 9.2–7
Titus 2.11–14	Titus 2.11–14	Titus 2.11–14
Lk 2.1–14	Lk 2.1–14	Lk 2.1–14
Feast of the Holy Family		
Sir 3.2–6,12–14	Sir 3.2–6,12–14	Sir 3.2–6,12–14
Col 3.12–21	Col 3.12–21	Col 3.12–21
Mt 2.13–15,19–23	Lk 2.22–40	Lk 2.41–52
Solemnity of Mary, Mother of God *(1 January, every year, readings are the same for all cycles)*		
Num 6.22–27	Num 6.22–27	Num 6.22–27
Gal 4.4–7	Gal 4.4–7	Gal 4.4–7
Lk 2.16–21	Lk 2.16–21	Lk 2.16–21
Epiphany *(readings are the same for all cycles)*		
Isa 60.1–6	Isa 60.1–6	Isa 60.1–6
Eph 3.2–3,5–6	Eph 3.2–3,5–6	Eph 3.2–3,5–6
Mt 2.1–12	Mt 2.1–12	Mt 2.1–12
Baptism of the Lord		
Isa 42.1–4,6–7	Isa 42.1–4,6–7	Isa 42.1–4,6–7
Acts 10.34–38	Acts 10.34–38	Acts 10.34–38
Mt 3.13–17	Mk 1.7–11	Lk 3.15–16,21–22

LENT AND EASTER

Cycle A (2002, 2005, 2008)	Cycle B (2000, 2003, 2006)	Cycle C (2001, 2004, 2007)
Ash Wednesday *(readings are the same for all cycles)*		
Joel 2.12–18	Joel 2.12–18	Joel 2.12–18
2 Cor 5.20—6.2	2 Cor 5.20—6.2	2 Cor 5.20—6.2
Mt 6.1–6,16–18	Mt 6.1–6,16–18	Mt 6.1–6,16–18
The First Sunday of Lent		
Gen 2.7–9; 3.1–7	Gen 9.8–15	Deut 26.4–10
Rom 5.12–19	1 Pet 3.18–22	Rom 10.8–13
Mt 4.1–11	Mk 1.12–15	Lk 4.1–13

	Cycle A (2002, 2005, 2008)	Cycle B (2000, 2003, 2006)	Cycle C (2001, 2004, 2007)
The Second Sunday of Lent	Gen 12.1–4 2 Tim 1.8–10 Mt 17.1–9	Gen 22.1–2,9,10–13,15–18 Rom 8.31–34 Mk 9.2–10	Gen 15.5–12,17–18 Phil 3.17—4.1 Lk 9.28–36
The Third Sunday of Lent	Ex 17.3–7 Rom 5.1–2,5–8 Jn 4.5–42	Ex 20.1–17 1 Cor 1.22–25 Jn 2.13–25	Ex 3.1–8,13–15 1 Cor 10.1–6,10–12 Lk 13.1–9
The Fourth Sunday of Lent	1 Sam 16.1,6–7,10–13 Eph 5.8–14 Jn 9.1–41	2 Chr 36.14–17,19–23 Eph 2.4–10 Jn 3.14–21	Josh 5.9,10–12 2 Cor 5.17–21 Lk 15.1–3,11–32
The Fifth Sunday of Lent	Ezek 37.12–14 Rom 8.8–11 Jn 11.1–45	Jer 31.31–34 Heb 5.7–9 Jn 12.20–33	Isa 43.16–21 Phil 3.8–14 Jn 8.1–11
Passion Sunday (Palm Sunday)	Isa 50.4–7 Phil 2.6–11 Mt 26.14—27.66	Isa 50.4–7 Phil 2.6–11 Mk 14.1—15.47	Isa 50.4–7 Phil 2.6–11 Lk 22.14—23.56
Holy Thursday *(readings are the same for all cycles)*	Ex 12.1–8,11–14 1 Cor 11.23–26 Jn 13.1–15	Ex 12.1–8,11–14 1 Cor 11.23–26 Jn 13.1–15	Ex 12.1–8,11–14 1 Cor 11.23–26 Jn 13.1–15
Good Friday *(readings are the same for all cycles)*	Isa 52.13—53.12 Heb 4.14–16; 5.7–9 Jn 18.1—19.42	Isa 52.13—53.12 Heb 4.14–16; 5.7–9 Jn 18.1—19.42	Isa 52.13—53.12 Heb 4.14–16; 5.7–9 Jn 18.1—19.42
Easter Sunday *(readings are the same for all cycles)*	Acts 10.34,37–43 Col 3.1–4 or 1 Cor 5.6–8 Jn 20.1–9	Acts 10.34,37–43 Col 3.1–4 or 1 Cor 5.6–8 Jn 20.1–9	Acts 10.34,37–43 Col 3.1–4 or 1 Cor 5.6–8 Jn 20.1–9
Second Sunday of Easter	Acts 2.42–47 1 Pet 1.3–9 Jn 20.19–31	Acts 4.32–35 1 Jn 5.1–6 Jn 20.19–31	Acts 5.12–16 Rev 1.9–19 Jn 20.19–31
Third Sunday of Easter	Acts 2.14,22–28 1 Pet 1.17–21 Lk 24.13–35	Acts 3.13–19 1 Jn 2.1–5 Lk 24.35–48	Acts 5.27–32,40–41 Rev 5.11–14 Jn 21.1–19
Fourth Sunday of Easter	Acts 2.14,36–41 1 Pet 2.20–25 Jn 10.1–10	Acts 4.8–12 1 Jn 3.1–2 Jn 10.11–18	Acts 13.14,43–52 Rev 7.9,14–17 Jn 10.27–30
Fifth Sunday of Easter	Acts 6.1–7 1 Pet 2.4–9 Jn 14.1–12	Acts 9.26–31 1 Jn 3.18–24 Jn 15.1–8	Acts 14.21–27 Rev 21.1–5 Jn 13.31–35
Sixth Sunday of Easter	Acts 8.5–8,14–17 1 Pet 3.15–18 Jn 14.15–21	Acts 10.25–26,34–35,44–48 1 Jn 4.7–10 Jn 15.9–17	Acts 15.1–2,22–29 Rev 21.10–14,22–23 Jn 14.23–29
Seventh Sunday of Easter	Acts 1.12–14 1 Pet 4.13–16 Jn 17.1–11	Acts 1.15–17,20–26 1 Jn 4.11–16 Jn 17.11–19	Acts 7.55–60 Rev 22.12–14,16–17,20 Jn 17.20–26
Pentecost Sunday *(readings are the same for all cycles)*	Acts 2.1–11 1 Cor 12.3–7,12–13 Jn 20.19–23	Acts 2.1–11 1 Cor 12.3–7,12–13 Jn 20.19–23	Acts 2.1–11 1 Cor 12.3–7,12–13 Jn 20.19–23

READING PLAN 2:
A Walk Through the Bible

In four weeks, you can visit some of the highlights of the Bible in chronological order.

Day	Bible Reading	Story	Day	Bible Reading	Story
☐ 1	Gen, chs 1–2	Creation	☐ 15	Wis, chs 7–9	God's wisdom
☐ 2	Gen, ch 3	the first sin	☐ 16	Mic, chs 1–3	the sins of Judah and Israel
☐ 3	Gen 6.9—9.17	the Flood	☐ 17	Isa, chs 11–12	promises of hope
☐ 4	Gen 17.1—18.15	God's covenant with Abraham	☐ 18	Mal, chs 3–4	the day of the Lord
☐ 5	Gen, chs 37, 42–45	Joseph and his brothers	☐ 19	Lk, ch 2	the birth and childhood of Jesus
☐ 6	Ex, chs 2–4	the call of Moses	☐ 20	Mt, chs 5–7	Jesus' Sermon on the Mount
☐ 7	Ex, chs 12–14	God's victory over Pharaoh	☐ 21	Lk, chs 15–16	Jesus' parables
☐ 8	Ex, chs 19–20	the Covenant at Sinai and the Ten Commandments	☐ 22	Mk, ch 15	the death of Jesus
☐ 9	Judg, chs 13–16	Sampson	☐ 23	Jn, ch 20	the Resurrection of Jesus
☐ 10	1 Sam, ch 17	David and Goliath	☐ 24	Acts 9.1–22	the conversion of Saul (Paul)
☐ 11	2 Sam, chs 6–7	God's promise to David			
☐ 12	2 Chr, chs 1–3	King Solomon	☐ 25	1 Cor, chs 12–14	Christian community
☐ 13	2 Chr, chs 34–36	from King Josiah to the fall of Jerusalem	☐ 26	Gal, chs 1–3	faith and the Law
			☐ 27	Jas	Christian living
☐ 14	Ps 51, 139	David's repentance and God's presence	☐ 28	Rev, chs 21–22	the new heaven and the new earth

---

READING PLAN 5:
The Justice of God

God, it seems, has a preference for the poor. Spend a week reading about God's justice in the Old Testament, and a week in the New Testament.

Day	Bible Reading	Theme
☐ 1	Gen 1.1—2.3	God's Creation is good.
☐ 2	Gen, ch 45	God sides with the youngest.
☐ 3	Ex 3.7–10	God sides with the oppressed.
☐ 4	Lev, ch 25	the Jubilee year
☐ 5	Deut 24.10–21	God is with the least.
☐ 6	Ps 82	justice to the needy
☐ 7	Am 5.21–24; 8.4–8	Let justice roll down.
☐ 8	Mt 5.43–48	Love your enemies.
☐ 9	Mt 19.13–15	Jesus welcomes little children.
☐ 10	Mt 25.31–46	Jesus identifies with the least.
☐ 11	Lk 1.46–56; 6.20–26	God reverses the world's order.
☐ 12	Lk 16.19–31	a rich man and poor Lazarus
☐ 13	Lk 22.24–27	Who is the greatest?
☐ 14	Jas 2.1–13	showing favorites?

READING PLAN 6:
Sin and Salvation

The truth is, none of us is perfect—we are all sinners. But God has a plan to save us. Take a two-week journey as you walk from sin to salvation.

Day	Bible Reading	Theme
☐ 1	Gen, ch 3	the first sin
☐ 2	Gen, ch 6	evil everywhere
☐ 3	Gen 12.1–9	God starts a relationship.
☐ 4	Ex 6.1–8	God rescues God's people.
☐ 5	Lev, ch 4	a sacrifice for sin
☐ 6	Jn 3.1–21	for God so loved the world
☐ 7	Mk 8.31–38	a new sacrifice
☐ 8	Rom 7.14–25	the predicament
☐ 9	Rom 6.1–8, 20–23	the promise
☐ 10	Gal 3.23–29	children of God
☐ 11	Joel 2.12–13; 1 Jn 1.8—2.2	return, repent, and confess
☐ 12	Ps 53	confession prayer
☐ 13	Heb 10.8–15	the only sacrifice
☐ 14	Mt 26.26–28	the Eucharist

READING PLAN 3:
Images of God

God has revealed the divine self to us in many wonderful ways. Enjoy two weeks of "seeing" the different pictures of our God.

Day	Bible Reading	Picture of God
☐ 1	Gen 1.26—3.24	Creator
☐ 2	Ex 3.13–15; 6.2–3	"I AM"
☐ 3	Lev 11.44–45; Mt 25.31–46	holy one and judge
☐ 4	Deut, ch 20	warrior and defender
☐ 5	Ps 12.5	advocate of the poor
☐ 6	Ps 23	great shepherd
☐ 7	Job 42.1–6; Jer 18.1–11	mysterious awesome one
☐ 8	Wis 6.12–20	feminine, wise
☐ 9	Isa 49.14–15	faithful mother
☐ 10	Jon 1.1–2; 3.5–10	universal God of all
☐ 11	Lk 11.1–4	father
☐ 12	Lk, ch 15	domestic God
☐ 13	Jn 1.1–18; Col 1.15–20	Jesus, the Word made flesh
☐ 14	1 Cor, ch 13; 1 Jn 4.7–8	love

READING PLAN 4:
Called by God

Throughout the Bible, God calls people to serve. You too are called to be a disciple. Take two weeks and pray about your call.

Day	Bible Reading	The One Called
☐ 1	Gen 12.1–9	Abram (Abraham)
☐ 2	Ex 3.1—4.17	Moses
☐ 3	Ruth	Ruth
☐ 4	1 Sam, ch 3	Samuel
☐ 5	1 Sam, ch 16	David
☐ 6	Isa 43.1–7	Isaiah
☐ 7	Jer 1.4–10	Jeremiah
☐ 8	Mt 4.18–22	the first disciples
☐ 9	Mk 8.31–38	any disciple
☐ 10	Lk 9.1–6	any disciple
☐ 11	Lk 18.18–30	a rich ruler
☐ 12	Acts 9.1–19	Saul (Paul)
☐ 13	Eph 5.1–20	any disciple
☐ 14	1 Pet 2.9–17	you!

READING PLAN 7:
Why Do We Suffer?

Why God allows suffering has been a question for many of the Bible's authors. During this two-week study, look for the growing awareness that God is with us in our suffering.

Day	Bible Reading	Theme or Article Title
☐ 1	introduction to Tob	God rescues the suffering?
☐ 2	Tob, ch 3	suffering and suicide
☐ 3	Job 1.13–21	suffering and faith
☐ 4	the article near Job 24.1	"A Long Debate"
☐ 5	the article near Job 38.1—42.6	"Why?"
☐ 6	Ps 6	praying for deliverance
☐ 7	the article near Lam 5.22	"Growing Through Loss"
☐ 8	Isa 52.13—53.12	the suffering servant
☐ 9	Jn 12.24–26	the paschal mystery
☐ 10	the article near Mk 15.16–20	"Facing the Hard Times"
☐ 11	the article near Mt 27.27–44	"Suffering Prayer"
☐ 12	2 Cor 1.3–11	God's presence
☐ 13	2 Cor 11.16–30	Paul's suffering
☐ 14	1 Pet 3.13—4.19	suffering as a Christian

READING PLAN 8:
Women in the Bible

In the ancient world, many people considered women to be inferior to men. But throughout the Bible, God shows otherwise. Here is a two-week look at women who have served God and the church.

Day	Bible Reading	Woman or Women
☐ 1	Gen 2.18—3.20	Eve
☐ 2	Gen 17.15–16; 21.1–7	Sarai (Sarah)
☐ 3	Ex 15.19–21	Miriam
☐ 4	Judg, chs 4–5	Deborah
☐ 5	Ruth	Ruth
☐ 6	1 Sam 1.1—2.11	Hannah
☐ 7	Esth, ch 8	Esther
☐ 8	Lk 1.5–25,57–66	Elizabeth
☐ 9	Lk 1.26—2.20	Mary, the mother of our Lord
☐ 10	Lk 2.36–38	Anna
☐ 11	Jn 20.1–18	Mary Magdalene
☐ 12	Jn 11.1–44; 12.1–8	Mary and Martha
☐ 13	Acts 16.11–15; ch 18	Lydia and Priscilla
☐ 14	Rom 16.1–7	Phoebe and Junia

Preface to the NRSV: Catholic Edition

This Catholic edition of the New Revised Standard Version of the Bible has been authorized by the National Conference of Catholic Bishops in the U.S.A. and by the National Council of the Churches of Christ in the U.S.A. It has received the ecclesiastical approval of the Catholic Bishops of both the United States and Canada. The undersigned, who prepared this edition, is a member of the Revised Standard Version Bible Translation Committee as well as an active member and past president of the Catholic Biblical Association of America.

Roman Catholics are already familiar with the accuracy and elegance of the New Revised Standard Version, first published in 1990. It has previously appeared in two major types of edition: an edition of the Old and New Testaments alone, the Bible of most Protestants; and an edition of the Old and New Testaments with the Apocryphal/Deuterocanonical Books placed between the two Testaments. The text of the latter edition received the Imprimatur (official approbation) of the United States and Canadian Catholic Bishops. The New Revised Standard Version is truly an ecumenical translation, for it was produced by Roman Catholic, Eastern Orthodox, Protestant, and Jewish scholars. Because of this Catholic presence no change in the translation was requested for this edition. The only exceptions are the Book of Esther, which exists in two different forms that are explained below, and the Book of Daniel, which includes the deuterocanonical portions that are listed below.

Regarding the number of the books of the Old Testament canon and their arrangement, however, Protestants and Jews on the one hand, and Roman Catholics and Orthodox Christians on the other, hold different beliefs. From the time of the Reformation in the sixteenth century, Protestants have adopted the Jewish canon of the Old Testament, which was established by the rabbis at the end of the first century of the Common Era. This canon includes only those books that were written in Hebrew and Aramaic. In addition to these books, however, Roman Catholics, following the ancient tradition of the Christian church, also hold the Deuterocanonical Books of the Old Testament to be sacred and inspired, and therefore canonical. Protestants and Jews call these books Apocrypha, a word that means "hidden or concealed," an inappropriate title for works that were part of the Greek Old Testament (the Septuagint) from pre-Christian times. The Roman Catholic canon, which was fixed by the time of the Council of Hippo in 393 and reaffirmed by the two Councils of Carthage in 397 and 419, was formally defined by the Council of Trent in 1546. This canon contains seven Deuterocanonical Books: Tobit, Judith, the Wisdom of Solomon, Sirach (the Wisdom of Ben Sira, also known as Ecclesiasticus), Baruch including the Letter of Jeremiah as chapter 6, and 1 and 2 Maccabees; and extra portions of two other books: the Additions to Esther; and the Prayer of Azariah and the Song of the Three Jews inserted between verses 23 and 24 of Daniel 3, Susanna as Daniel 13, and Bel and the Dragon as Daniel 14. Over and above these books and extra portions, the Bible of Greek and Slavonic Orthodox Christians includes 1 Esdras, the Prayer of Manasseh, Psalm 151, and 3 Maccabees. The Slavonic Bible also contains 2 Esdras, and an appendix to the Greek Bible includes 4 Maccabees.

Several of the Deuterocanonical Books were written originally in Hebrew or Aramaic, the rest in Greek. More than two-thirds of the Book of Sirach is now extant in Hebrew, and four fragments of the Book of Tobit in Hebrew and Aramaic were recovered from Qumran Cave IV. It seems certain that Judith and the additions to Daniel were also written originally in Hebrew. Hebrew is the original language of the prose parts of Baruch; the poetic parts were composed in Greek. The Wisdom of Solomon was written completely in Greek. The original language of 1 Maccabees was Hebrew while 2 Maccabees was composed in Greek.

The Book of Esther has two different forms: the short Hebrew original; and the longer Greek version that contains one hundred and seven additional verses comprising six distinct portions, A through F. It is the translation of the entire Greek version that appears in the Deuterocanonical section of the New Revised Standard Version. In this Catholic edition, however, the translation of the Greek portions has been inserted at the appropriate places of the translation of the Hebrew form of the book. Some of the Greek portions apparently had a Hebrew origin; the others were written in Greek.

What is distinctive about this Catholic edition—as well as every other edition published by Roman Catholics—is that the Deuterocanonical Books and portions are placed in their proper order among the other books of the Old Testament. Thus, Tobit, Judith, the long form of Esther, and 1 and 2 Maccabees are found among the so-called historical books directly after Nehemiah. The Wisdom of Solomon and the Book of Sirach follow after the Song of Solomon among the wisdom books. Because Baruch, the well-known secretary of Jeremiah, is said to be the author of the work that bears his name, the book is placed after Jeremiah and Lamentations. This order of books comes from the Latin Vulgate translated by St. Jerome in the late fourth and early fifth centuries. It is essentially the same order as that found in the fourth-century Codex Vaticanus, one of the oldest extant manuscripts of the Septuagint.

Roman Catholics will welcome this edition of the New Revised Standard Version of the Bible for personal reading and study as well as liturgical usage. Based on the latest manuscript discoveries and critical editions, it offers the fruits of the best biblical scholarship in the idiom of today while being sensitive to the contemporary concern for inclusive language when referring to human beings.

ALEXANDER A. DI LELLA, O.F.M.
Andrews-Kelly-Ryan Distinguished Professor of Biblical Studies
The Catholic University of America

September 30, 1992
Feast of St. Jerome

To the Reader

This preface is addressed to you by the Committee of translators, who wish to explain, as briefly as possible, the origin and character of our work. The publication of our revision is yet another step in the long, continual process of making the Bible available in the form of the English language that is most widely current in our day. To summarize in a single sentence: the New Revised Standard Version of the Bible is an authorized revision of the Revised Standard Version, published in 1952, which was a revision of the American Standard Version, published in 1901, which, in turn, embodied earlier revisions of the King James Version, published in 1611.

In the course of time, the King James Version came to be regarded as "the Authorized Version." With good reason it has been termed "the noblest monument of English prose," and it has entered, as no other book has, into the making of the personal character and the public institutions of the English-speaking peoples. We owe to it an incalculable debt.

Yet the King James Version has serious defects. By the middle of the nineteenth century, the development of biblical studies and the discovery of many biblical manuscripts more ancient than those on which the King James Version was based made it apparent that these defects were so many as to call for revision. The task was begun, by authority of the Church of England, in 1870. The (British) Revised Version of the Bible was published in 1881–1885; and the American Standard Version, its variant embodying the preferences of the American scholars associated with the work, was published, as was mentioned above, in 1901. In 1928 the copyright of the latter was acquired by the International Council of Religious Education and thus passed into the ownership of the churches of the United States and Canada that were associated in this Council through their boards of education and publication.

The Council appointed a committee of scholars to have charge of the text of the American Standard Version and to undertake inquiry concerning the need for further revision. After studying the questions whether or not revision should be undertaken, and if so, what its nature and extent should be, in 1937 the Council authorized a revision. The scholars who served as members of the Committee worked in two sections, one dealing with the Old Testament and one with the New Testament. In 1946 the Revised Standard Version of the New Testament was published. The publication of the Revised Standard Version of the Bible, containing the Old and New Testaments, took place on September 30, 1952. A translation of the Apocryphal/Deuterocanonical Books of the Old Testament followed in 1957. In 1977 this collection was issued in an expanded edition, containing three additional texts received by Eastern Orthodox communions (3 and 4 Maccabees and Psalm 151). Thereafter the Revised Standard Version gained the distinction of being officially authorized for use by all major Christian churches: Protestant, Anglican, Roman Catholic, and Eastern Orthodox.

The Revised Standard Version Bible Committee is a continuing body, comprising about thirty members, both men and women. Ecumenical in representation, it includes scholars affiliated with various Protestant denominations, as well as several Roman Catholic members, an Eastern Orthodox member, and a Jewish member who serves in the Old Testament section. For a period of time the Committee included several members from Canada and from England.

Because no translation of the Bible is perfect or is acceptable to all groups of readers, and because discoveries of older manuscripts and further investigation of linguistic features of the text continue to become available, renderings of the Bible have proliferated. During the years following the publication of the Revised Standard Version, twenty-six other English translations and revisions of the Bible were produced by committees and by individual scholars—not to mention twenty-five other translations and revisions of the New Testament alone. One of the latter was the second edition of the RSV New Testament, issued in 1971, twenty-five years after its initial publication.

Following the publication of the RSV Old Testament in 1952, significant advances were made in the discovery and interpretation of documents in Semitic languages related to Hebrew. In addition to the information that had become available in the late 1940s from the Dead Sea texts of Isaiah and Habakkuk, subsequent acquisitions from the same area brought to light many other early copies of all the books of the Hebrew Scriptures (except Esther), though most of these copies are fragmentary. During the same period early Greek manuscript copies of books of the New Testament also became available.

In order to take these discoveries into account, along with recent studies of documents in Semitic languages related to Hebrew, in 1974 the Policies Committee of the Revised Standard Version, which is a standing committee of the National Council of the Churches of Christ in the U.S.A., authorized the preparation of a revision of the entire RSV Bible.

For the Old Testament the Committee has made use of the *Biblia Hebraica Stuttgartensia* (1977; ed. sec. emendata, 1983). This is an edition of the Hebrew and Aramaic text as current early in the Christian era and fixed by Jewish scholars (the "Masoretes") of the sixth to the ninth centuries. The vowel signs, which were added by the Masoretes, are accepted in the main, but where a more probable and convincing reading can be obtained by assuming different vowels this has been done. No notes are given in such cases, because the vowel points are less ancient and reliable than the consonants. When an alternative reading given by the Masoretes is translated in a footnote, this is identified by the words "Another reading is."

Departures from the consonantal text of the best manuscripts have been made only where it seems clear that errors in copying had been made before the text was standardized. Most of the corrections adopted are based on the ancient versions (translations into Greek, Aramaic, Syriac, and Latin), which were made prior to the time of the work of the Masoretes and which therefore may reflect earlier forms of the Hebrew text. In such instances a footnote specifies the version or versions from which the correction has been derived and also gives a translation of the Masoretic Text. Where it was deemed appropriate to do so, information is supplied in footnotes from subsidiary Jewish traditions concerning other textual readings (the *Tiqqune Sopherim*, "emendations of the scribes"). These are identified in the footnotes as "Ancient Heb tradition."

Occasionally it is evident that the text has suffered in transmission and that none of the versions provides a satisfactory restoration. Here we can only follow the best judgment of competent scholars as to the most probable reconstruction of the original text. Such reconstructions are indicated in footnotes by the abbreviation Cn ("Correction"), and a translation of the Masoretic Text is added.

For the Apocryphal/Deuterocanonical Books of the Old Testament the Committee has made use of a number of texts. For most of these books the basic Greek text from which the present translation was made is the edition of the Septuagint prepared by Alfred Rahlfs and published by the Württemberg Bible Society (Stuttgart, 1935). For several of the books the more recently published individual volumes of the Göttingen Septuagint project were utilized. For the Book of Tobit it was decided to follow the form of the Greek text found in codex Sinaiticus (supported as it is by evidence from Qumran); where this text is defective, it was supplemented and corrected by other Greek manuscripts. For the three Additions to Daniel (namely, Susanna, the Prayer of Azariah and the Song of the Three Jews, and Bel and the Dragon) the Committee continued to use the Greek version attributed to Theodotion (the so-called "Theodotion-Daniel"). In translating Ecclesiasticus (Sirach), while constant reference was made to the Hebrew fragments of a large portion of this book (those discovered at Qumran and Masada as well as those recovered from the Cairo Geniza), the Committee generally followed the Greek text (including verse numbers) published by Joseph Ziegler in the Göttingen Septuagint (1965). But in many places the Committee has translated the Hebrew text when this provides a reading that is clearly superior to the Greek; the Syriac and Latin versions were also consulted throughout and occasionally adopted. Finally, in the Book of Esther we have placed the deuterocanonical portions, translated from Robert Hanhart's Göttingen edition of the Greek (1983), in their original context within the translation of the Hebrew text.

For the New Testament the Committee has based its work on the most recent edition of *The Greek New Testament*, prepared by an interconfessional and international committee and published by the United Bible Societies (1966, 3rd ed. corrected, 1983; information concerning changes to be introduced into the critical apparatus of the forthcoming 4th edition was available to the Committee). As in that edition, double brackets are used to enclose a few passages that are generally regarded to be later additions to the text, but which we have retained because of their evident antiquity and their importance in the textual tradition. Only in very rare instances have we replaced the text or the punctuation of the Bible Societies' edition by an alternative that seemed to us to be superior. Here and there in the footnotes the phrase, "Other ancient authorities read," identifies alternative readings preserved by Greek manuscripts and early versions. In both Testaments, alternative renderings of the text are indicated by the word "Or."

As for the style of English adopted for the present revision, among the mandates given to the Committee in 1980 by the Division of Education and Ministry of the National Council of the Churches of Christ (which now holds the copyright of the RSV Bible) was the directive to continue in the tradition of the King James Bible, but to introduce such changes as are warranted on the basis of accuracy, clarity, euphony, and current English usage. Within the constraints set by the original texts and by the mandates of the Division, the Committee has followed the maxim, "As literal as possible, as free as necessary." As a consequence, the New Revised Standard Version (NRSV) remains essentially a literal translation. Paraphrastic renderings have been adopted only sparingly, and then chiefly to compensate for a deficiency in the English language—the lack of a common gender third person singular pronoun.

During the almost half a century since the publication of the RSV, many in the churches have become sensitive to the danger of linguistic sexism arising from the inherent bias of the English language towards the masculine gender, a bias that in the case of the Bible has often restricted or obscured the meaning of the original text. The mandates from the Division specified that, in references to men and women, masculine-oriented language should be eliminated as far as this can be done without altering passages that reflect the historical situation of ancient patriarchal culture. As can be appreciated, more than once the Committee found that the several mandates stood in tension and even in conflict. The various concerns had to be balanced case by case in order to provide a faithful and acceptable rendering without using contrived English. Only very occasionally has the pronoun "he" or "him" been retained in passages where the reference may have been to a woman as well as to a man; for example, in several legal texts in Leviticus and Deuteronomy. In such instances of formal, legal language, the options of either putting the passage in the plural or of introducing additional nouns to avoid masculine pronouns in English seemed to the Committee to obscure the historic structure and literary character of the original. In the vast majority of cases, however, inclusiveness has been attained by simple rephrasing or by introducing plural forms when this does not distort the meaning of the passage. Of course, in narrative and in parable no attempt was made to generalize the sex of individual persons.

Another aspect of style will be detected by readers who compare the more stately English rendering of the Old Testament with the less formal rendering adopted for the New Testament. For example, the traditional distinction between *shall* and *will* in English has been retained in the Old Testament as appropriate in rendering a document that embodies what may be termed the classic form of Hebrew, while in the New Testament the abandonment of such distinctions in the usage of the future tense in English reflects the more colloquial nature of the koine Greek used by most New Testament authors except when they are quoting the Old Testament.

Careful readers will notice that here and there in the Old Testament the word LORD (or in certain cases GOD) is printed in capital letters. This represents the traditional manner in English versions of rendering the Divine Name, the "Tetragrammaton" (see the notes on Exodus 3.14, 15), following the precedent of the ancient Greek and Latin translators and the long established practice in the reading of the Hebrew Scriptures in the synagogue. While it is almost if not quite certain that the Name was originally pronounced "Yahweh," this pronunciation was not indicated when the Masoretes added vowel sounds to the consonantal Hebrew text. To the four consonants YHWH of the Name, which had come to be regarded as too sacred to be pronounced, they attached vowel signs indicating that in its place should be read the Hebrew word *Adonai* meaning "Lord" (or *Elohim* meaning "God"). Ancient Greek translators employed the word *Kyrios* ("Lord") for the Name. The Vulgate likewise used the Latin word *Dominus* ("Lord"). The form "Jehovah" is of late medieval origin; it is a combination of the consonants of the Divine Name and the vowels attached to it by the Masoretes but belonging to an entirely different word. Although the American Standard Version (1901) had used "Jehovah" to render the Tetragrammaton (the sound of Y being represented by J and the sound of W by V, as in Latin), for two reasons the Committees that produced the RSV and the NRSV returned to the more familiar usage of the King James Version. (1) The word "Jehovah" does not accurately represent any form of the Name ever used in Hebrew. (2) The use of any proper name for the one and only God, as though there were other gods from whom the true God had to be distinguished, began to be discontinued in Judaism before the Christian era and is inappropriate for the universal faith of the Christian Church.

It will be seen that in the Psalms and in other prayers addressed to God the archaic second person singular pronouns (*thee, thou, thine*) and verb forms (*art, hast, hadst*) are no longer used. Although some readers may regret this change, it should be pointed out that in the original languages neither the Old Testament nor the New makes any linguistic distinction between addressing a human being and addressing the Deity. Furthermore, in the tradition of the King James Version one will not expect to find the use of capital letters for pronouns that refer to the Deity—such capitalization is an unnecessary innovation that has only recently been introduced into a few English translations of the Bible. Finally, we have left to the discretion of the licensed publishers such matters as section headings, cross-references, and clues to the pronunciation of proper names.

This new version seeks to preserve all that is best in the English Bible as it has been known and used through the years. It is intended for use in public reading and congregational worship, as well as in private study, instruction, and meditation. We have resisted the temptation to introduce terms and phrases that merely reflect current moods, and have tried to put the message of the Scriptures in simple, enduring words and expressions that are worthy to stand in the great tradition of the King James Bible and its predecessors.

In traditional Judaism and Christianity, the Bible has been more than a historical document to be preserved or a classic of literature to be cherished and admired; it is recognized as the unique record of God's dealings with people over the ages. The Old Testament sets forth the call of a special people to enter into covenant relation with the God of justice and steadfast love and to bring God's law to the nations. The New Testament records the life and work of Jesus Christ, the one in whom "the Word became flesh," as well as describes the rise and spread of the early Christian Church. The Bible carries its full message, not to those who regard it simply as a noble literary heritage of the past or who wish to use it to enhance political purposes and advance otherwise desirable goals, but to all persons and communities who read it so that they may discern and understand what God is saying to them. That message must not be disguised in phrases that are no longer clear, or hidden under words that have changed or lost their meaning; it must be presented in language that is direct and plain and meaningful to people today. It is the hope and prayer of the translators that this version of the Bible may continue to hold a large place in congregational life and to speak to all readers, young and old alike, helping them to understand and believe and respond to its message.

For the Committee,
BRUCE M. METZGER

Guide to the Pronunciation of Proper Names

This edition of the New Revised Standard Version includes a simplified self-pronunciation system for proper names. The system is designed to provide assistance to the reader without filling the text with a complicated variety of symbols, many of which provide unneeded pronunciation clues.

Well-known proper names such as Moses, Nazareth, and Timothy are printed without pronunciation marks of any kind. Such names are a familiar part of our cultural heritage, and they are instantly recognizable to most readers .

More difficult proper names (as well as certain transliterated non-English words) are shown in the text with simplified pronunciation markings. (Two notes of caution: The anglicized pronunciation of a name differs at times from that of the ancient language. Also, there are differences of opinion among speakers of English concerning the most desirable pronunciation of certain names.)

Three kinds of marks are used:

- ´ The acute accent mark: shows which syllable of a name is to be stressed. A compound name—with parts separated by a hyphen—has an accent mark in each part having more than one syllable.

- · The centered dot: shows where an unaccented syllable ends and another syllable begins.

- ¯ The macron: printed over a vowel that has a "long" sound. The macron is shown over the following vowels when they are sounded as indicated:

  a as in g*a*te
  e as in k*e*y
  i as in *i*ce
  o as in h*o*pe
  u as in *u*se or r*u*le
  y as in t*y*pe

The macron also indicates the pronunciation of certain diphthongs, or vowel combinations:

  over the *a* in *ai* as in p*ai*l
  over the *i* in *ai* as in *ai*sle

A vowel that does not have a "long" sound is printed with no pronunciation mark. In most cases the sound of such a vowel can be determined closely enough by observing how the name is spelled, divided into syllables, and accented.

Abbreviations Used in the Notes

In the notes to the books of the Old Testament the following abbreviations are used:

Ant.	Josephus, *Antiquities of the Jews*
Aram	Aramaic
Ch, chs	Chapter, chapters
Cn	Correction; made where the text has suffered in transmission and the versions provide no satisfactory restoration but where the Standard Bible Committee agrees with the judgment of competent scholars as to the most probable reconstruction of the original text
Gk	Septuagint, Greek version of the Old Testament
Heb	Hebrew of the consonantal Masoretic Text of the Old Testament
Josephus	Flavius Josephus (Jewish historian, about A.D. 37 to about 95)
Macc.	The book(s) of the Maccabees
Ms(s)	Manuscript(s)
MT	The Hebrew of the pointed Masoretic Text of the Old Testament
OL	Old Latin
Q Ms(s)	Manuscript(s) found at Qumran by the Dead Sea
Sam	Samaritan Hebrew text of the Old Testament
Syr	Syriac Version of the Old Testament
Syr H	Syriac Version of Origen's Hexapla
Tg	Targum
Vg	Vulgate, Latin Version of the Old Testament

THE *Old Testament*

Introduction to the

Pentateuch

Did you ever get to a movie late? Did you end up bothering your friends who got there on time by asking: "What's happening? Why did he do that? What did she mean by that?" Like the first crucial minutes of a movie, the five books of the Pentateuch set the stage for much of what happens in the rest of the Bible. If you are not familiar with their wonderful stories, you might find yourself asking: "What's happening? Why is he doing that? Why did she say that?" when reading later books.

In-depth

THE NAME PENTATEUCH LITERALLY MEANS A "five-part writing." Thus, the Pentateuch is the first five books of the Old Testament: Genesis, Exodus, Leviticus, Numbers, and Deuteronomy. These books are special to Jewish and Christian believers because they tell of the origins of God's people and their unique relationship with God—sometimes called salvation history. They are the blueprint needed for properly understanding the rest of the Bible. The Pentateuch introduces the idea of a single God who is responsible for all creation. It also tells that this God is active in the world and in the lives of its people, and that the Israelites have been called into a special relationship with this God.

One of the central elements of the special relationship between God and the Israelites described in the Pentateuch is the Sinai Covenant. A covenant is a solemn promise between two parties, where both parties agree to fulfill certain obligations. The Sinai Covenant is the most famous one between God and Israel, with Moses as the mediator, which you will read about in Exodus. In Genesis, you will read about the covenants God makes with Noah, Abraham, and Jacob, which lead to the Sinai Covenant.

Reading the Pentateuch is like appreciating a fine tapestry. When you view a tapestry from the front, all the threads combine to make a beautiful, coherent image. In the same way, an overall look at the covenants, stories, and laws in the Pentateuch combine to form a picture of the love relationship between God and the people of Israel. A close look at the back of a tapestry shows a more chaotic mix of colors and yarn. So too a closer look at the writings in the Pentateuch reveals not one story but many.

Biblical scholars speak of four primary sources for the stories and traditions in the Pentateuch. The sources reflect four different schools of thought about Israel's relationship with God. For convenience, each source is referred to as an individual author.

- The Yahwist used Yahweh as God's name. This writer focused on the southern kingdom of Judah, used lots of stories, emphasized God's closeness to humanity, and portrayed God acting as a human person.
- The Elohist referred to God as Elohim or Lord. The Elohist wrote about the northern kingdom of Israel and was concerned about idolatry and morality. The writings of the Elohist present God speaking through symbols such as a burning bush.
- The Deuteronomist emphasized the Law as the foundation of the kingdom of Judah. The Deuteronomist emerged toward the end of the monarchy (the time of the Israelite kings), when the Covenant Law seemed to have been forgotten.
- Finally, the Priestly writer emphasized religious rituals and the role of the priesthood. This writer portrayed God as more distant and used a more formal style. This source was written after the Babylonian Exile.

Knowing that these four sources contributed to the final form of the Pentateuch can help us understand that the Pentateuch books are not simply records of events as they occurred, but rather faith accounts about the Israelites' growing relationship with God, inspired by God and told from different perspectives.

In the Pentateuch, God reveals how much God loves the human race collectively and how much God loves us personally. God wishes to be in a relationship with us today just as much as God did back then. The Pentateuch reminds us that we are all children of God.

Other Background

- **Some of the most familiar stories and people of the Old Testament are found in Genesis and Exodus. Genesis includes the stories of Creation, Adam and Eve, Noah and the Flood, Abraham and Sarah, and Joseph and his brothers. Exodus contains the stories of Moses and the burning bush, Pharaoh and the ten plagues, the parting of the Red Sea, and the Ten Commandments.**

- **The Jews also refer to the five books of the Pentateuch as the Torah, meaning "teaching" or "instruction."**

- **An ancient tradition named Moses as the author of the Pentateuch. This was no doubt due to Moses' importance in the Pentateuch itself. But evidence suggests that most of the Pentateuch was written hundreds of years after Moses' death.**

- **The two types of writing in the Pentateuch are stories and laws. Genesis is all stories, Leviticus and Deuteronomy are mostly laws, and Exodus and Numbers are about half stories and half laws.**

Displays of awesome cosmic power, tender love stories, tearful family reunions, and tales of deceit, rape, murder, and worldwide destruction. Does this sound like the script for next summer's blockbuster movie? No, it's the Book of Genesis! It is the story of how a world created for love and harmony goes astray because of human sin. Through it all, God is at work, forming a people to restore what was lost.

At a Glance

- **1.1—11.32.** the creation of the world and human beings by God
- **12.1—50.26.** stories of the ancestors (matriarchs and patriarchs) of Israel

In-depth

Genesis gathers together inspired stories and traditions that reveal God's nature and purpose, and the beginning of the Israelites' special relationship with God. Genesis has two main sections. The first section, chapters 1–11, contains some of the Bible's most memorable stories about Creation and the effect of sin. Chapters 1–2 tell two stories of Creation that portray the beauty and wonder of the natural world and emphasize the goodness and harmony that God intended in Creation. Creation culminates in human beings, made in God's own image. Those first human beings, Adam and Eve, live in a wonderful garden in harmony with God, Creation, and each other. But in chapter 3, sin enters the world, and as a result, Adam and Eve will experience separation, suffering, and ultimately death.

And sin spreads, first to the family (Cain and Abel in chapter 4), then to all society (Noah and the Flood in chapters 6–9). Even after the Flood and God's promise to Noah, the story of the tower of Babel demonstrates that sin pits nation against nation. As you read these chapters, remember that they were written not as historical accounts or scientific explanations but as symbolic stories that shared faith experiences and taught important religious truths.

The second section of Genesis, chapters 12–50, tells the story of the origins of the Israelite people. It begins with Abraham and Sarah (originally called Abram and Sarai) and continues with Ishmael and Isaac and with Isaac and Rebekah's children, Esau and Jacob. Genesis ends with Joseph, one of Jacob's twelve sons, cleverly saving Egypt and Israel from famine. This section introduces the covenant God makes with Abraham and Sarah and reminds the reader that God's plans will overcome human sin and weakness.

Quick Facts

Period Covered

The stories in the first eleven chapters are prehistory. Chapters 12–15 cover the period of the ancestors, or patriarchs and matriarchs (from 1900 to 1500 B.C.).

Author

An unknown author gathered oral traditions and stories from tribal peoples sometime from 1225 to 1000 B.C.

Themes

the goodness of Creation, human responsibility, the effects of sin, covenant, God's bringing good out of evil

4

Genesis

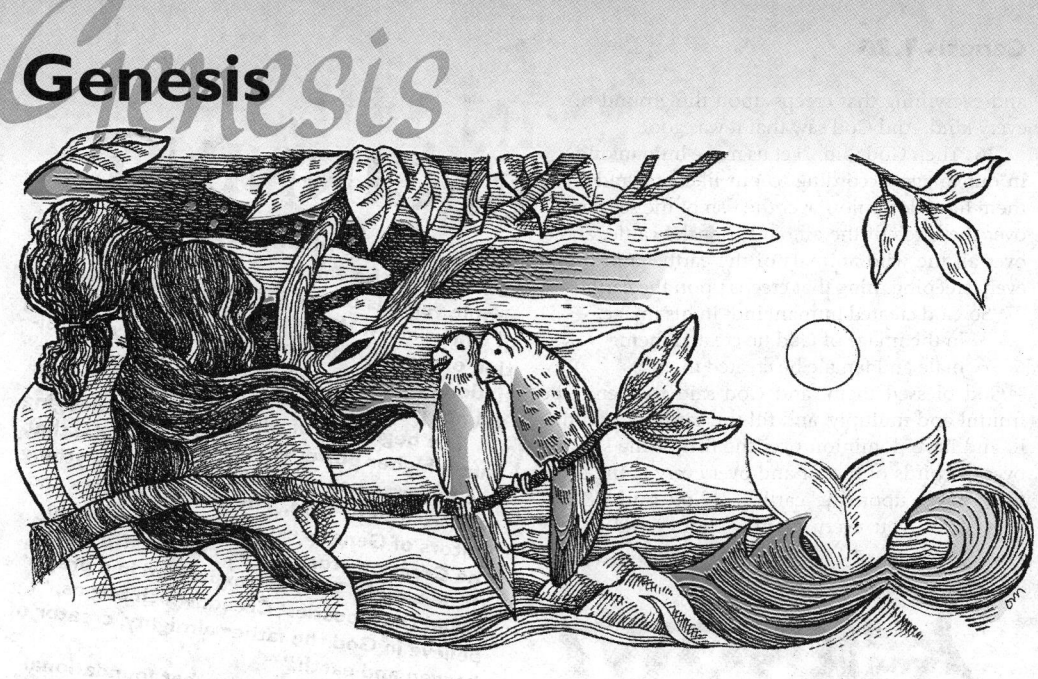

Six Days of Creation and the Sabbath
(Gen 2.4b–9; Job 38.4–11; Jn 1.1–5)

In the beginning when God created[a] the heavens and the earth, 2 the earth was a formless void and darkness covered the face of the deep, while a wind from God[b] swept over the face of the waters. 3 Then God said, "Let there be light"; and there was light. 4 And God saw that the light was good; and God separated the light from the darkness. 5 God called the light Day, and the darkness he called Night. And there was evening and there was morning, the first day.

6 And God said, "Let there be a dome in the midst of the waters, and let it separate the waters from the waters." 7 So God made the dome and separated the waters that were under the dome from the waters that were above the dome. And it was so. 8 God called the dome Sky. And there was evening and there was morning, the second day.

9 And God said, "Let the waters under the sky be gathered together into one place, and let the dry land appear." And it was so. 10 God called the dry land Earth, and the waters that were gathered together he called Seas. And God saw that it was good. 11 Then God said, "Let the earth put forth vegetation: plants yielding seed, and fruit trees of every kind on earth that bear fruit with the seed in it." And it was so. 12 The earth brought forth vegetation: plants yielding seed of every kind, and trees of every kind bearing fruit with the seed in it. And God saw that it was good. 13 And there was evening and there was morning, the third day.

14 And God said, "Let there be lights in the dome of the sky to separate the day from the night; and let them be for signs and for seasons and for days and years, 15 and let them be lights in the dome of the sky to give light upon the earth." And it was so. 16 God made the two great lights— the greater light to rule the day and the lesser light to rule the night—and the stars. 17 God set them in the dome of the sky to give light upon the earth, 18 to rule over the day and over the night, and to separate the light from the darkness. And God saw that it was good. 19 And there was evening and there was morning, the fourth day.

20 And God said, "Let the waters bring forth swarms of living creatures, and let birds fly above the earth across the dome of the sky." 21 So God created the great sea monsters and every living creature that moves, of every kind, with which the waters swarm, and every winged bird of every kind. And God saw that it was good. 22 God blessed them, saying, "Be fruitful and multiply and fill the waters in the seas, and let birds multiply on the earth." 23 And there was evening and there was morning, the fifth day.

24 And God said, "Let the earth bring forth living creatures of every kind: cattle and creeping things and wild animals of the earth of every kind." And it was so. 25 God made the wild animals of the earth of every kind, and the cattle of every kind,

---

a Or *when God began to create* or *In the beginning God created*   *b* Or *while the spirit of God* or *while a mighty wind*

and everything that creeps upon the ground of every kind. And God saw that it was good.

26 Then God said, "Let us make humankind*c* in our image, according to our likeness; and let them have dominion over the fish of the sea, and over the birds of the air, and over the cattle, and over all the wild animals of the earth,*d* and over every creeping thing that creeps upon the earth."
²⁷ So God created humankind*c* in his image,
   in the image of God he created them;*e*
   male and female he created them.
²⁸ God blessed them, and God said to them, "Be fruitful and multiply, and fill the earth and subdue it; and have dominion over the fish of the sea and over the birds of the air and over every living thing that moves upon the earth." ²⁹ God said, "See, I have given you every plant yielding seed that is

did you KNOW?

Literary Genres

Some Christians believe that God actually created the world in seven twenty-four-hour days. Such a belief comes from a literal reading of the first chapter of Genesis, as though it were a scientific textbook. However, Genesis was written not as a science article but as symbolic stories, sometimes called mythic stories, that convey great moral and spiritual truths. We should not try to come to any scientific conclusions about the creation of the world from reading these stories.

Mythic stories are one literary type, or genre. You just have to look in a newspaper to see examples of different literary genres: news stories, advice columns, editorials, and comics. Each genre has different rules for interpreting its meaning. The Bible also contains many types of literary genres, including hero stories, poetry, laws, legends, fictional satire, debates, and letters. To properly understand the Bible, pay attention to the literary genre—otherwise, you might believe the Bible is saying something God doesn't intend.

▶ Gen 1.1—2.4

IN THE BEGINNING

"In the beginning when God created the heavens and the earth . . ." (Gen 1.1). This simple verse is one of the foundational beliefs of Christianity. We are not a random collection of atoms. The world is not a lucky combination of cosmic circumstances. The universe did not just accidentally happen.

The beginning of wisdom is acknowledging that a higher power is at work in our life, that the universe has purpose, and that everything was created by God. The ancient writers and editors of Genesis expressed these ideas in the Creation stories. The church affirms these beliefs. They are expressed in a prayer called the Apostles' Creed, which begins, "I believe in God the father almighty, creator of heaven and earth."

Genesis expresses another foundational belief: God created everything good! Read the story in chapter 1 and see how this belief is constantly repeated: And humankind is "very good," created in God's own image. This is God's message to you in the first chapter of the Bible: You carry God's image within you. You are very good! Don't let anyone ever convince you otherwise.

▶ Gen 1.1—2.4

upon the face of all the earth, and every tree with seed in its fruit; you shall have them for food. ³⁰ And to every beast of the earth, and to every bird of the air, and to everything that creeps on the earth, everything that has the breath of life, I have given every green plant for food." And it was so. ³¹ God saw everything that he had made, and indeed, it was very good. And there was evening and there was morning, the sixth day.

Thus the heavens and the earth were finished, and all their multitude. ² And on the seventh day God finished the work that he had done, and he rested on the seventh day from all the work that he had done. ³ So God blessed the seventh day and hallowed it, because on it God rested from all the work that he had done in creation.

4 These are the generations of the heavens and the earth when they were created.

---

c Heb *adam*   *d* Syr: Heb *and over all the earth*
e Heb *him*

PRAY IT!
The Sabbath

Even God needed to take a rest. The writer of Genesis makes this point to remind readers to set aside a day for rest and prayer, which Jewish people call the Sabbath. Honoring the Sabbath is an act of trust in God. It means we believe that the world will not fall apart if we stop our activity. The world is in God's hands. We can hear this truth echoed in Jesus' words:

Consider the lilies, how they grow: they neither toil nor spin; yet I tell you, even Solomon in all his glory was not clothed like one of these. But if God so clothes the grass of the field, which is alive today and tomorrow is thrown into the oven, how much more will he clothe you. (Lk 12.27–28)

Traditionally, Christians have honored the Sabbath on Sunday because it is the day Jesus was resurrected. In our culture today, it seems that many people are losing the practice of honoring the Sabbath. What could we gain if we recommitted ourselves to a day of rest, celebration, and prayer? What can you do personally to more fully honor the Sabbath?

▶ Gen 2.1–3

Another Account of the Creation
(Gen 1.26–30)

In the day that the LORD*f* God made the earth and the heavens, ⁵when no plant of the field was yet in the earth and no herb of the field had yet sprung up—for the LORD God had not caused it to rain upon the earth, and there was no one to till the ground; ⁶but a stream would rise from the earth, and water the whole face of the ground— ⁷then the LORD God formed man from the dust of the ground,*g* and breathed into his nostrils the breath of life; and the man became a living being. ⁸And the LORD God planted a garden in Eden, in the east; and there he put the man whom he had formed. ⁹Out of the ground the LORD God made to grow every tree that is pleasant to the sight and good for food, the tree of life also in the midst of

the garden, and the tree of the knowledge of good and evil.

10 A river flows out of Eden to water the garden, and from there it divides and becomes four branches. ¹¹The name of the first is Pī′shon; it is the one that flows around the whole land of Hav′-i•lah, where there is gold; ¹²and the gold of that land is good; bdellium and onyx stone are there. ¹³The name of the second river is Gī′hon; it is the one that flows around the whole land of Cush. ¹⁴The name of the third river is Tigris, which flows east of Assyria. And the fourth river is the Euphrates.

15 The LORD God took the man and put him in the garden of Eden to till it and keep it. ¹⁶And the LORD God commanded the man, "You may freely eat of every tree of the garden; ¹⁷but of the tree of the knowledge of good and evil you shall not eat, for in the day that you eat of it you shall die."

f Heb YHWH, as in other places where "LORD" is spelled with capital letters (see also Exod 3.14–15 with notes). *g* Or *formed a man* (Heb *adam*) *of dust from the ground* (Heb *adamah*)

AFRICAN AMERICAN
In God's Image

God does not make mistakes; people do. Some African Americans might be tempted to deny their African heritage, to forget their roots, to even change their physical appearance in order to fit into Anglo culture. We must remember that physical features— African American or otherwise—are not accidents. God planned for them—we are all made in God's image.

If we are to authentically love ourselves, we must love our whole selves. For African Americans, this includes a love for ebony-hued skin, tight curly hair, thick lips, and wide noses. Whatever our racial descent, we are all blessed of God (see also Song 1.5, "Black and Beautiful").

Dear God, I praise you for who I am on the inside and on the outside. Amen.

▶ Gen 1.26–27

GOD IS OUR CREATOR!

HISPANIC

¡Dios es nuestro Creador!

According to Genesis, chapters 1–2, God created the universe and is the source of order in all creation. Creation is good, and its goodness is reflected in the harmony, peace, and love between the Creator and its creatures, and among the creatures themselves. In Hispanic theological traditions, this ideal relationship—symbolized by the way God and Adam and Eve relate in the Garden of Eden—is considered the foundation in which salvation history is rooted.

- How are your relationships with God, your friends, your family, and nature characterized by harmony, peace, and love?
- Reflect on how you can improve some of your strained relationships, and ask God's help to do it.

Human beings are created in God's image and likeness and share God's attributes: freedom, love, knowledge, and the ability to create. With these gifts comes the responsibility of caring for all creation.

- Give thanks and praise to God for creation, especially for your own life and the lives of the people around you.
- Think of how you, your family, and your community can take better care of all creation. Pray that you fully develop your capacity to love, to know the truth, and to use your freedom wisely.

God established a covenant with us at the moment of our creation, and we keep this covenant by freely placing ourselves in God's hands and being responsive to God's invitation to live in communion with God and people.

- How do you use your freedom to respond to God's invitation?
- Think about the aspects of your life for which you most need God's wisdom to live in harmony and love. Put yourself in God's hands, and let God help and direct you.

▶ Genesis, chapters 1–2

18 Then the LORD God said, "It is not good that the man should be alone; I will make him a helper as his partner." 19 So out of the ground the LORD God formed every animal of the field and every bird of the air, and brought them to the man to see what he would call them; and whatever the man called every living creature, that was its name. 20 The man gave names to all cattle, and to the birds of the air, and to every animal of the field; but for the man*g* there was not found a helper as his partner. 21 So the LORD God caused a deep sleep to fall upon the man, and he slept; then he took one of his ribs and closed up its place with flesh. 22 And the rib that the LORD God had taken from the man he made into a woman and brought her to the man. 23 Then the man said,

"This at last is bone of my bones
and flesh of my flesh;
this one shall be called Woman,*h*
for out of Man*i* this one was taken."

24 Therefore a man leaves his father and his mother and clings to his wife, and they become one flesh.

25 And the man and his wife were both naked, and were not ashamed.

The First Sin and Its Punishment
(Rom 5.12–21)

Now the serpent was more crafty than any other wild animal that the LORD God had made. He said to the woman, "Did God say, 'You shall not eat from any tree in the garden'?" 2 The woman said to the serpent, "We may eat of the fruit of the trees in the garden; 3 but God said, 'You shall not eat of the fruit of the tree that is in the middle of the garden, nor shall you touch it, or you shall die.' " 4 But the serpent said to the woman, "You will not die; 5 for God knows that when you eat of it your eyes will be opened, and you will be like God,*j* knowing good and evil." 6 So when the woman saw that the tree was good for food, and that it was a delight to the eyes, and that the tree was to be desired to make one wise, she took of its fruit and

g Or *for Adam*   *h* Heb *ishshah*   *i* Heb *ish*   *j* Or *gods* ate; and she also gave some to her husband, who was with her, and he ate. 7 Then the eyes of both were opened, and they knew that they were naked; and they sewed fig leaves together and made loincloths for themselves.

8 They heard the sound of the LORD God walking in the garden at the time of the evening breeze, and the man and his wife hid themselves from the presence of the LORD God among the trees of the garden. 9 But the LORD God called to the man, and said to him, "Where are you?" 10 He said, "I heard the sound of you in the garden, and I was afraid, because I was naked; and I hid myself." 11 He said, "Who told you that you were naked? Have you eaten from the tree of which I commanded you not to eat?" 12 The man said, "The woman whom you gave to be with me, she gave me fruit from the tree, and I ate." 13 Then the LORD God said to the woman, "What is this that you have done?" The woman said, "The serpent tricked me, and I ate." 14 The LORD God said to the serpent,

"Because you have done this,
    cursed are you among all animals
    and among all wild creatures;
upon your belly you shall go,
    and dust you shall eat
    all the days of your life.
15 I will put enmity between you and the
        woman,
    and between your offspring and hers;
he will strike your head,
    and you will strike his heel."
16 To the woman he said,
"I will greatly increase your pangs in
        childbearing;
    in pain you shall bring forth children,
yet your desire shall be for your husband,
    and he shall rule over you."
17 And to the man[k] he said,
"Because you have listened to the voice of
        your wife,
    and have eaten of the tree
about which I commanded you,
    'You shall not eat of it,'
cursed is the ground because of you;
    in toil you shall eat of it all the days of
        your life;
18 thorns and thistles it shall bring forth for
        you;
    and you shall eat the plants of the field.
19 By the sweat of your face
    you shall eat bread
until you return to the ground,
    for out of it you were taken;
you are dust,
    and to dust you shall return."

20 The man named his wife Eve,[l] because she was the mother of all living. 21 And the LORD God made garments of skins for the man[m] and for his wife, and clothed them.

Catholic Connections

ORIGINAL SIN BREAKS OUR RELATIONSHIP WITH GOD

The story of Adam and Eve is about the human weakness for sinning and disobeying God. The serpent tells Adam and Eve they can be like God, and know good and evil. After disobeying God, they recognize that they are naked and feel shame. Their relationship of trust with God is broken. This story teaches that soon after men and women were created, sin entered human history and led to pain and suffering.

This reality—that every human person, beginning with our first ancestors, chooses to disobey God—the Catholic church calls original sin. Original sin is another way of saying that every person makes choices that separate him or her from God. We are born into this condition, which has been passed on from the beginning of the human race.

▸ Gen 3.1–24

22 Then the LORD God said, "See, the man has become like one of us, knowing good and evil; and now, he might reach out his hand and take also from the tree of life, and eat, and live forever"— 23 therefore the LORD God sent him forth from the garden of Eden, to till the ground from which he was taken. 24 He drove out the man; and at the east of the garden of Eden he placed the cherubim, and a sword flaming and turning to guard the way to the tree of life.

k Or to Adam   l In Heb Eve resembles the word for living
m Or for Adam

Brothers and Sisters

"Am I my brother's keeper?" (Gen 4.9). With that famous question, Cain pretends that he does not know where his brother is. God does not answer Cain's question directly, but each of us knows the response. We are—each of us and all of us—responsible for one another: family, friends, and strangers. We are brothers and sisters because God has created us that way. We cannot avoid our obligation to watch out for one another.

Are there people in your life who need you to be a brother or sister to them? If so, commit yourself right now to reach out to them.

▶ Gen 4.9

Cain Murders Abel
(Lk 11.51; Heb 11.4; 12.24)

Now the man knew his wife Eve, and she conceived and bore Cain, saying, "I have produced[n] a man with the help of the LORD." 2 Next she bore his brother Abel. Now Abel was a keeper of sheep, and Cain a tiller of the ground. 3 In the course of time Cain brought to the LORD an offering of the fruit of the ground, 4 and Abel for his part brought of the firstlings of his flock, their fat portions. And the LORD had regard for Abel and his offering, 5 but for Cain and his offering he had no regard. So Cain was very angry, and his countenance fell. 6 The LORD said to Cain, "Why are you angry, and why has your countenance fallen? 7 If you do well, will you not be accepted? And if you do not do well, sin is lurking at the door; its desire is for you, but you must master it."

8 Cain said to his brother Abel, "Let us go out to the field."[o] And when they were in the field, Cain rose up against his brother Abel, and killed him. 9 Then the LORD said to Cain, "Where is your brother Abel?" He said, "I do not know; am I my brother's keeper?" 10 And the LORD said, "What have you done? Listen; your brother's blood is crying out to me from the ground! 11 And now you are cursed from the ground, which has opened its mouth to receive your brother's blood from your hand. 12 When you till the ground, it will no longer yield to you its strength; you will be a fugitive and a wanderer on the earth." 13 Cain said to the LORD, "My punishment is greater than I can bear! 14 Today you have driven me away from the soil, and I shall be hidden from your face; I shall be a fugitive and a wanderer on the earth, and anyone who meets me may kill me." 15 Then the LORD said to him, "Not so![p] Whoever kills Cain will suffer a sevenfold vengeance." And the LORD put a mark on Cain, so that no one who came upon him would kill him. 16 Then Cain went away from the presence of the LORD, and settled in the land of Nod,[q] east of Eden.

THE CYCLE OF VIOLENCE

Cain was a murderer. Some might say he deserved the death penalty. But in Gen 4.15, God marks Cain so that he is protected from being killed. God seeks to stop the cycle of violence. Why kill someone to show that it is wrong to kill someone?

Think of a television show or movie with violent sequences that you have seen recently. What attitude did it portray toward violence? Often, violence in revenge is shown as justified, even satisfying. How does violence on television or in the movies affect your own attitude toward it? How might you respond to God's call to stop the cycle of violence?

▶ Gen 4.15

Beginnings of Civilization

17 Cain knew his wife, and she conceived and bore Ē'noch; and he built a city, and named it Ē'noch after his son Ē'noch. 18 To Ē'noch was born Ī'rad; and Ī'rad was the father of Me•hū'ja•el, and Me•hū'ja•el the father of Me•thū'sha•el, and Me-

---

n The verb in Heb resembles the word for *Cain*
o Sam Gk Syr Compare Vg: MT lacks *Let us go out to the field*   p Gk Syr Vg: Heb *Therefore*   q That is *Wandering*

thū'sha•el the father of Lā'mech. 19Lā'mech took two wives; the name of the one was Ā'dah, and the name of the other Zil'lah. 20Ā'dah bore Jā'bal; he was the ancestor of those who live in tents and have livestock. 21His brother's name was Jū'bal; he was the ancestor of all those who play the lyre and pipe. 22Zil'lah bore Tū'bal-cāin, who made all kinds of bronze and iron tools. The sister of Tū'-bal-cāin was Nā'a•mah.

23 Lā'mech said to his wives:

"Ā'dah and Zil'lah, hear my voice;
    you wives of Lā'mech, listen to what I
        say:
I have killed a man for wounding me,
    a young man for striking me.
24 If Cain is avenged sevenfold,
    truly Lā'mech seventy-sevenfold."

25 Adam knew his wife again, and she bore a son and named him Seth, for she said, "God has appointed[r] for me another child instead of Abel, because Cain killed him." 26To Seth also a son was born, and he named him Ē'nosh. At that time people began to invoke the name of the LORD.

Adam's Descendants to Noah and His Sons
(1 Chr 1.1–4; Lk 3.36–38)

This is the list of the descendants of Adam. When God created humankind,[s] he made them[t] in the likeness of God. 2Male and female he created them, and he blessed them and named them "Humankind"[s] when they were created.

3 When Adam had lived one hundred thirty years, he became the father of a son in his likeness, according to his image, and named him Seth. 4The days of Adam after he became the father of Seth were eight hundred years; and he had other sons and daughters. 5Thus all the days that Adam lived were nine hundred thirty years; and he died.

6 When Seth had lived one hundred five years, he became the father of Ē'nosh. 7Seth lived after the birth of Ē'nosh eight hundred seven years, and had other sons and daughters. 8Thus all the days of Seth were nine hundred twelve years; and he died.

9 When Ē'nosh had lived ninety years, he became the father of Kē'nan. 10Ē'nosh lived after the birth of Kē'nan eight hundred fifteen years, and had other sons and daughters. 11Thus all the days of Ē'nosh were nine hundred five years; and he died.

12 When Kē'nan had lived seventy years, he became the father of Ma•hal'a•lel. 13Kē'nan lived after the birth of Ma•hal'a•lel eight hundred and forty years, and had other sons and daughters. 14Thus all the days of Kē'nan were nine hundred and ten years; and he died.

15 When Ma•hal'a•lel had lived sixty-five years, he became the father of Jar'ed. 16Ma•hal'a•lel lived after the birth of Jar'ed eight hundred thirty years, and had other sons and daughters. 17Thus all the days of Ma•hal'a•lel were eight hundred ninety-five years; and he died.

18 When Jar'ed had lived one hundred sixty-two years he became the father of Ē'noch. 19Jar'ed lived after the birth of Ē'noch eight hundred years, and had other sons and daughters. 20Thus all the days of Jar'ed were nine hundred sixty-two years; and he died.

21 When Ē'noch had lived sixty-five years, he became the father of Me•thū'se•lah. 22Ē'noch walked with God after the birth of Me•thū'se•lah three hundred years, and had other sons and daughters. 23Thus all the days of Ē'noch were three hundred sixty-five years. 24Ē'noch walked with God; then he was no more, because God took him.

25 When Me•thū'se•lah had lived one hundred eighty-seven years, he became the father of Lā'-mech. 26Me•thū'se•lah lived after the birth of Lā'-mech seven hundred eighty-two years, and had other sons and daughters. 27Thus all the days of Me•thū'se•lah were nine hundred sixty-nine years; and he died.

28 When Lā'mech had lived one hundred eighty-two years, he became the father of a son; 29he named him Noah, saying, "Out of the ground that the LORD has cursed this one shall bring us relief from our work and from the toil of our hands." 30Lā'mech lived after the birth of Noah five hundred ninety-five years, and had other sons and daughters. 31Thus all the days of Lā'mech were seven hundred seventy-seven years; and he died.

32 After Noah was five hundred years old, Noah became the father of Shem, Ham, and Jā'-pheth.

The Wickedness of Humankind

When people began to multiply on the face of the ground, and daughters were born to them, 2the sons of God saw that they were fair; and they took wives for themselves of all that they chose. 3Then the LORD said, "My spirit shall not abide[u] in mortals forever, for they are flesh; their days shall be one hundred twenty years." 4The Neph'i•lim were on the earth in those days—and also afterward—when the sons of God went in to the daughters of humans, who bore children to them. These were the heroes that were of old, warriors of renown.

---

r The verb in Heb resembles the word for *Seth*
s Heb *adam*   t Heb *him*   u Meaning of Heb uncertain

GEN

5 The LORD saw that the wickedness of humankind was great in the earth, and that every inclination of the thoughts of their hearts was only evil continually. 6 And the LORD was sorry that he had made humankind on the earth, and it grieved him to his heart. 7 So the LORD said, "I will blot out from the earth the human beings I have created— people together with animals and creeping things and birds of the air, for I am sorry that I have made them." 8 But Noah found favor in the sight of the LORD.

the earth, to destroy from under heaven all flesh in which is the breath of life; everything that is on the earth shall die. 18 But I will establish my covenant with you; and you shall come into the ark, you, your sons, your wife, and your sons' wives with you. 19 And of every living thing, of all flesh, you shall bring two of every kind into the ark, to keep them alive with you; they shall be male and fe-

Sin Has Social Consequences

At the beginning of the Noah story, sin has continued to spread so that it has become an accepted part of society. The Great Flood, which wipes out a whole civilization, symbolizes the consequences of widespread sin. Later in Genesis, the story of the tower of Babel (11.1–9) symbolizes another consequence of the institutionalized sin of disobedience and pride.

When sin becomes part of our social systems and our institutions, the church calls it social sin. Social sin is a result of personal sin, but it is bigger than any one person's choice. Examples of social sin are the unequal distribution of the world's wealth, the exploitation of workers by corporations, and discrimination based on race or gender. The good news is that God's saving power is greater than social sin! What are the effects of social sin in your community? in your country? in the world? How are Christians in your church or community organizing to stand against social sin?

▸ Gen 6.1—9.17

Noah Pleases God
(Heb 11.7; 1 Pet 3.20)

9 These are the descendants of Noah. Noah was a righteous man, blameless in his generation; Noah walked with God. 10 And Noah had three sons, Shem, Ham, and Ja'pheth.

11 Now the earth was corrupt in God's sight, and the earth was filled with violence. 12 And God saw that the earth was corrupt; for all flesh had corrupted its ways upon the earth. 13 And God said to Noah, "I have determined to make an end of all flesh, for the earth is filled with violence because of them; now I am going to destroy them along with the earth. 14 Make yourself an ark of cypress*v* wood; make rooms in the ark, and cover it inside and out with pitch. 15 This is how you are to make it: the length of the ark three hundred cubits, its width fifty cubits, and its height thirty cubits. 16 Make a roof*w* for the ark, and finish it to a cubit above; and put the door of the ark in its side; make it with lower, second, and third decks. 17 For my part, I am going to bring a flood of waters on

male. 20 Of the birds according to their kinds, and of the animals according to their kinds, of every creeping thing of the ground according to its kind, two of every kind shall come in to you, to keep them alive. 21 Also take with you every kind of food that is eaten, and store it up; and it shall serve as food for you and for them." 22 Noah did this; he did all that God commanded him.

The Great Flood
(Lk 17.26–27)

Then the LORD said to Noah, "Go into the ark, you and all your household, for I have seen that you alone are righteous before me in this generation. 2 Take with you seven pairs of all clean animals, the male and its mate; and a pair of the animals that are not clean, the male and its mate; 3 and seven pairs of the birds of the air also, male and female, to keep their kind alive on the face of all the earth. 4 For in seven days I will send rain on the earth for forty days and forty nights; and every living thing that I have made I will blot out from the face of the ground." 5 And Noah did all that the LORD had commanded him.

---

v Meaning of Heb uncertain   *w* Or *window*

? did you KNOW?

The Flood

The sin of Adam and Eve in the garden starts a disastrous trend in which each generation adds to sin in the world. This sin leads to the corruption of the world and the destruction of human beings. The Great Flood illustrates the ancient belief that God washed the world clean of this sinfulness and gave another chance to those who were faithful to God.

Other ancient cultures had stories about great floods. But in those stories, vindictive gods caused the floods for petty reasons. These gods had no real love for humanity. The Bible's Flood story is unique because it insists that God acted out of justice and in response to great evil.

God takes great care to save Noah and his family because they are faithful to God. After the Flood, God makes a covenant with Noah, promising never to destroy the earth by flood again—another unique element not found in the stories of other cultures.

▶ Gen 6.1—9.17

6 Noah was six hundred years old when the flood of waters came on the earth. 7 And Noah with his sons and his wife and his sons' wives went into the ark to escape the waters of the flood. 8 Of clean animals, and of animals that are not clean, and of birds, and of everything that creeps on the ground, 9 two and two, male and female, went into the ark with Noah, as God had commanded Noah. 10 And after seven days the waters of the flood came on the earth.

11 In the six hundredth year of Noah's life, in the second month, on the seventeenth day of the month, on that day all the fountains of the great deep burst forth, and the windows of the heavens were opened. 12 The rain fell on the earth forty days and forty nights. 13 On the very same day Noah with his sons, Shem and Ham and Ja′pheth, and Noah's wife and the three wives of his sons entered the ark, 14 they and every wild animal of every kind, and all domestic animals of every kind, and every creeping thing that creeps on the earth,

and every bird of every kind—every bird, every winged creature. 15 They went into the ark with Noah, two and two of all flesh in which there was the breath of life. 16 And those that entered, male and female of all flesh, went in as God had commanded him; and the LORD shut him in.

17 The flood continued forty days on the earth; and the waters increased, and bore up the ark, and it rose high above the earth. 18 The waters swelled and increased greatly on the earth; and the ark floated on the face of the waters. 19 The waters swelled so mightily on the earth that all the high mountains under the whole heaven were covered; 20 the waters swelled above the mountains, covering them fifteen cubits deep. 21 And all flesh died that moved on the earth, birds, domestic animals, wild animals, all swarming creatures that swarm on the earth, and all human beings; 22 everything on dry land in whose nostrils was the breath of life died. 23 He blotted out every living thing that was on the face of the ground, human beings and animals and creeping things and birds of the air; they were blotted out from the earth. Only Noah was left, and those that were with him in the ark. 24 And the waters swelled on the earth for one hundred fifty days.

The Flood Subsides

But God remembered Noah and all the wild animals and all the domestic animals that were with him in the ark. And God made a wind blow over the earth, and the waters subsided; 2 the fountains of the deep and the windows of the heavens were closed, the rain from the heavens was restrained, 3 and the waters gradually receded from the earth. At the end of one hundred fifty days the waters had abated; 4 and in the seventh month, on the seventeenth day of the month, the ark came to rest on the mountains of Ar′a•rat. 5 The waters continued to abate until the tenth month; in the tenth month, on the first day of the month, the tops of the mountains appeared.

6 At the end of forty days Noah opened the window of the ark that he had made 7 and sent out the raven; and it went to and fro until the waters were dried up from the earth. 8 Then he sent out the dove from him, to see if the waters had subsided from the face of the ground; 9 but the dove found no place to set its foot, and it returned to him to the ark, for the waters were still on the face of the whole earth. So he put out his hand and took it and brought it into the ark with him. 10 He waited another seven days, and again he sent out the dove from the ark; 11 and the dove came back to him in the evening, and there in its beak was a freshly plucked olive leaf; so Noah knew that the

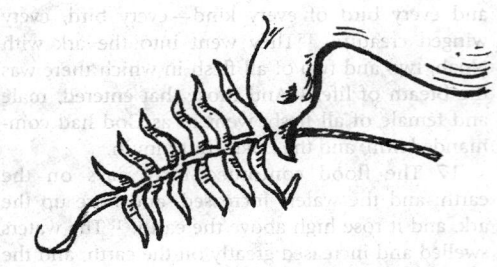

8.11

waters had subsided from the earth. 12 Then he waited another seven days, and sent out the dove; and it did not return to him any more.

13 In the six hundred first year, in the first month, on the first day of the month, the waters were dried up from the earth; and Noah removed the covering of the ark, and looked, and saw that the face of the ground was drying. 14 In the second month, on the twenty-seventh day of the month, the earth was dry. 15 Then God said to Noah, 16 "Go out of the ark, you and your wife, and your sons and your sons' wives with you. 17 Bring out with you every living thing that is with you of all flesh—birds and animals and every creeping thing that creeps on the earth—so that they may abound on the earth, and be fruitful and multiply on the earth." 18 So Noah went out with his sons and his wife and his sons' wives. 19 And every animal, every creeping thing, and every bird, everything that moves on the earth, went out of the ark by families.

God's Promise to Noah

20 Then Noah built an altar to the LORD, and took of every clean animal and of every clean bird, and offered burnt offerings on the altar. 21 And when the LORD smelled the pleasing odor, the LORD said in his heart, "I will never again curse the ground because of humankind, for the inclination of the human heart is evil from youth; nor will I ever again destroy every living creature as I have done.
22 As long as the earth endures,
seedtime and harvest, cold and heat,
summer and winter, day and night,
shall not cease."

The Covenant with Noah

God blessed Noah and his sons, and said to them, "Be fruitful and multiply, and fill the earth. 2 The fear and dread of you shall rest on every animal of the earth, and on every bird of the air, on everything that creeps on the ground, and on all the fish of the sea; into your hand they are delivered. 3 Every moving thing that lives shall be food for you; and just as I gave you the green plants, I give you everything. 4 Only, you shall not eat flesh with its life, that is, its blood. 5 For your own lifeblood I will surely require a reckoning: from every animal I will require it and from human beings, each one for the blood of another, I will require a reckoning for human life.

6 Whoever sheds the blood of a human,
    by a human shall that person's blood be
      shed;
  for in his own image
      God made humankind.

7 And you, be fruitful and multiply, abound on the earth and multiply in it."

did you KNOW?

Water in the Bible

For the ancient Hebrews, water was considered the wellspring of life: from the waters of chaos, God created the world (Gen 1.1–2); from the waters of the Great Flood, God re-created the world (8.13–19). In the semiarid land of Israel, water symbolized both life and death: a good rainfall ensured that people would eat and life would go on; too much or too little rainfall meant that people would starve and death would open its hungry jaws. In the New Testament, water becomes a symbol of spiritual life and renewal, particularly through baptism.

8 Then God said to Noah and to his sons with him, 9 "As for me, I am establishing my covenant with you and your descendants after you, 10 and with every living creature that is with you, the birds, the domestic animals, and every animal of the earth with you, as many as came out of the ark.ˣ 11 I establish my covenant with you, that never again shall all flesh be cut off by the waters

---

x Gk: Heb adds *every animal of the earth*

of a flood, and never again shall there be a flood to destroy the earth." 12 God said, "This is the sign of the covenant that I make between me and you and every living creature that is with you, for all future generations: 13 I have set my bow in the clouds, and it shall be a sign of the covenant be-

PRAY IT!
The Rainbow

What do you see when you see a rainbow? Do you see a multicolored
arc caused by the refraction of sunlight
through droplets of water? Or do you
see a wonder of nature that causes you
to stop and stare in awe? Something as
remarkable as a rainbow can never be
reduced to a scientific explanation. It's no
wonder that the writer of Genesis used it
as a symbol of God's covenant promise.
When God and Israel see the rainbow in
the clouds, they will recall their covenant
together.

*God of imagination and color, only you
could come up with the idea of a rainbow!
Rainstorm and sunshine, harmony and
diversity, mercy and hope, promise and joy,
wonder and awe. Are these inside me, the
wondrous creation you delight in? Guide
me to the rainbows in my life!*

▶ **Gen 9.8–17**

tween me and the earth. 14 When I bring clouds over the earth and the bow is seen in the clouds, 15 I will remember my covenant that is between me and you and every living creature of all flesh; and the waters shall never again become a flood to destroy all flesh. 16 When the bow is in the clouds, I will see it and remember the everlasting covenant between God and every living creature of all flesh that is on the earth." 17 God said to Noah, "This is the sign of the covenant that I have established between me and all flesh that is on the earth."

Noah and His Sons

18 The sons of Noah who went out of the ark were Shem, Ham, and Ja′pheth. Ham was the father of Cā′naan. 19 These three were the sons of Noah; and from these the whole earth was peopled.

20 Noah, a man of the soil, was the first to plant a vineyard. 21 He drank some of the wine and became drunk, and he lay uncovered in his tent. 22 And Ham, the father of Cā′naan, saw the nakedness of his father, and told his two brothers outside. 23 Then Shem and Ja′pheth took a garment, laid it on both their shoulders, and walked backward and covered the nakedness of their father; their faces were turned away, and they did not see their father's nakedness. 24 When Noah awoke from his wine and knew what his youngest son had done to him, 25 he said,

"Cursed be Cā′naan;
    lowest of slaves shall he be to his
        brothers."
26 He also said,
"Blessed by the LORD my God be Shem;
    and let Cā′naan be his slave.
27 May God make space for*y* Ja′pheth,
    and let him live in the tents of Shem;
    and let Cā′naan be his slave."

28 After the flood Noah lived three hundred fifty years. 29 All the days of Noah were nine hundred fifty years; and he died.

Nations Descended from Noah
(1 Chr 1.5–27)

These are the descendants of Noah's sons, Shem, Ham, and Ja′pheth; children were born to them after the flood.

2 The descendants of Ja′pheth: Gō′mer, Mā′-gog, Mā′dai, Ja′van, Tū′bal, Mē′shech, and Tī′ras. 3 The descendants of Gō′mer: Ash′ke•naz, Rī′phath, and Tō•gar′mah. 4 The descendants of Ja′van: E•li′-shah, Tar′shish, Kit′tim, and Rod′a•nim.*z* 5 From these the descendants of Ja′pheth*a* in their lands, with their own language, by their families, in their nations.

6 The descendants of Ham: Cush, Egypt, Put, and Cā′naan. 7 The descendants of Cush: Sē′ba, Hav′i•lah, Sab′tah, Rā′a•mah, and Sab′te•ca. The descendants of Rā′a•mah: Shē′ba and Dē′dan. 8 Cush became the father of Nim′rod; he was the first on earth to become a mighty warrior. 9 He was a mighty hunter before the LORD; therefore it is said, "Like Nim′rod a mighty hunter before the LORD." 10 The beginning of his kingdom was Bā′bel, Ē′rech, and Ac′cad, all of them in the land of Shī′-nar. 11 From that land he went into Assyria, and built Nin′e•veh, Re•hō′both-ir, Cā′lah, and 12 Rē′-sen between Nin′e•veh and Cā′lah; that is the great city. 13 Egypt became the father of Lū′dim,

---

y Heb *yapht,* a play on *Japheth*   *z* Heb Mss Sam Gk See
1 Chr 1.7: MT *Dodanim*   *a* Compare verses 20, 31. Heb
lacks *These are the descendants of Japheth*

A Barrier or a Bridge?

Language can be either a barrier or a bridge. Through our speech, we connect with other people. And we often hear it expressed that love, music, and a smile are universal languages. Yet, languages also separate, symbolizing differences between cultures and nations that can erupt in wars and other atrocities.

The story of the tower of Babel is an ancient explanation of why the separation between people, symbolized by different languages, occurs. The people ignore God's command to "fill the earth" (Gen 1.28). Instead, they gather in one place to try to build a tower reaching to heaven, a sin of pride and arrogance. God confuses their language to foil their plan. It is not language but pride that separates us.

In the Acts of the Apostles, chapter 2, language serves as a bridge. The Holy Spirit enables the people from many different lands to hear the Apostles speaking in their own languages. The Spirit serves to unify us, no matter what earthly language we speak. Anyone who has attended a World Youth Day knows that when we live by the Spirit, we can rise above the differences of language and culture. The Good News is universal and unites us!

▶ Gen 11.1–9

An'a•mim, Le•hā'bim, Naph'tū•him, ¹⁴ Path•rū'sim, Cas•lū'him, and Caph'to•rim, from which the Phi•lis'tines come.ᵇ

15 Cā'naan became the father of Sī'don his firstborn, and Heth, ¹⁶ and the Jeb'ū•sītes, the Am'o•rītes, the Gir'ga•shītes, ¹⁷ the Hī'vītes, the Ar'kītes, the Sī'nītes, ¹⁸ the Ar'vad•ītes, the Zem'a•rītes, and the Hā'math•ītes. Afterward the families of the Cā'naan•ītes spread abroad. ¹⁹ And the territory of the Cā'naan•ītes extended from Sī'don, in the direction of Gē'rar, as far as Gā'za, and in the direction of Sod'om, Go•mor'rah, Ad'mah, and Ze•boi'im, as far as Lā'sha. ²⁰ These are the descendants of Ham, by their families, their languages, their lands, and their nations.

21 To Shem also, the father of all the children of Ē'ber, the elder brother of Jā'pheth, children were born. ²² The descendants of Shem: Ē'lam, As'shur, Ar•pach'shad, Lud, and Ar'am. ²³ The descendants of Ar'am: Uz, Hul, Gē'ther, and Mash. ²⁴ Ar•pach'shad became the father of Shē'lah; and Shē'lah became the father of Ē'ber. ²⁵ To Ē'ber were born two sons: the name of the one was Pē'leg,ᶜ for in his days the earth was divided, and his brother's name was Jok'tan. ²⁶ Jok'tan became the father of Al•mō'dad, Shē'leph, Hā•zar•mā'veth, Jē'rah, ²⁷ Ha•dor'am, U'zal, Dik'lah, ²⁸ Ō'bal, A•bim'a•el, Shē'ba, ²⁹ Ō'phir, Hav'i•lah, and Jō'bab; all these were the descendants of Jok'tan. ³⁰ The territory in which they lived extended from Mē'sha in the direction of Sē'phar, the hill country of the east. ³¹ These are the descendants of Shem, by their families, their languages, their lands, and their nations.

32 These are the families of Noah's sons, according to their genealogies, in their nations; and from these the nations spread abroad on the earth after the flood.

The Tower of Babel

Now the whole earth had one language and the same words. ² And as they migrated from the east,ᵈ they came upon a plain in the land of Shī'nar and settled there. ³ And they said to one another, "Come, let us make bricks, and burn them thoroughly." And they had brick for stone, and bitumen for mortar. ⁴ Then they said, "Come, let us build ourselves a city, and a tower with its top in the heavens, and let us make a name for ourselves; otherwise we shall be scattered abroad upon the face of the whole earth." ⁵ The LORD came down to see the city and the tower, which mortals had built. ⁶ And the LORD said, "Look, they are one people, and they have all one language; and this is only the beginning of what they will do; nothing that they propose to do will now be impossible for them. ⁷ Come, let us go down, and confuse their language there, so that they will not understand one another's speech." ⁸ So the LORD scattered them abroad from there over the face of all the earth, and they left off building the city. ⁹ Therefore it was called Bā'bel, because there the LORD con-

---

ᵇ Cn: Heb *Casluhim, from which the Philistines come, and Caphtorim*   ᶜ That is *Division*   ᵈ Or *migrated eastward*

fused[e] the language of all the earth; and from there the LORD scattered them abroad over the face of all the earth.

Descendants of Shem
(1 Chr 1.17–27; Lk 3.34–36)

10 These are the descendants of Shem. When Shem was one hundred years old, he became the father of Ar•pach'shad two years after the flood; [11] and Shem lived after the birth of Ar•pach'shad five hundred years, and had other sons and daughters.

12 When Ar•pach'shad had lived thirty-five years, he became the father of She'lah; [13] and Ar•pach'shad lived after the birth of She'lah four hundred three years, and had other sons and daughters.

14 When She'lah had lived thirty years, he became the father of E'ber; [15] and She'lah lived after the birth of E'ber four hundred three years, and had other sons and daughters.

16 When E'ber had lived thirty-four years, he became the father of Pe'leg; [17] and E'ber lived after the birth of Pe'leg four hundred thirty years, and had other sons and daughters.

18 When Pe'leg had lived thirty years, he became the father of Re'ū; [19] and Pe'leg lived after the birth of Re'ū two hundred nine years, and had other sons and daughters.

20 When Re'ū had lived thirty-two years, he became the father of Se'rug; [21] and Re'ū lived after the birth of Se'rug two hundred seven years, and had other sons and daughters.

22 When Se'rug had lived thirty years, he became the father of Na'hor; [23] and Se'rug lived after the birth of Na'hor two hundred years, and had other sons and daughters.

24 When Na'hor had lived twenty-nine years, he became the father of Te'rah; [25] and Na'hor lived after the birth of Te'rah one hundred nineteen years, and had other sons and daughters.

26 When Te'rah had lived seventy years, he became the father of Abram, Na'hor, and Har'an.

Descendants of Terah

27 Now these are the descendants of Te'rah. Te'rah was the father of Abram, Na'hor, and Har'an; and Har'an was the father of Lot. [28] Har'an died before his father Te'rah in the land of his birth, in Ūr of the Chal•de'ans. [29] Abram and Na'hor took wives; the name of Abram's wife was Sar'ai, and the name of Na'hor's wife was Mil'cah. She was the daughter of Har'an the father of Mil'cah and Is'cah. [30] Now Sar'ai was barren; she had no child.

31 Te'rah took his son Abram and his grandson Lot son of Har'an, and his daughter-in-law Sar'ai, his son Abram's wife, and they went out together from Ūr of the Chal•de'ans to go into the land of Cā'naan; but when they came to Har'an, they settled there. [32] The days of Te'rah were two hundred five years; and Te'rah died in Har'an.

The Call of Abram
(Acts 7.2–5)

Now the LORD said to Abram, "Go from your country and your kindred and your father's house to the land that I will show you. [2] I will make of you a great nation, and I will bless you, and make your name great, so that you will be a blessing. [3] I will bless those who bless you, and the one who curses you I will curse; and in you all the families of the earth shall be blessed."[f]

4 So Abram went, as the LORD had told him; and Lot went with him. Abram was seventy-five years old when he departed from Har'an. [5] Abram took his wife Sar'ai and his brother's son Lot, and all the possessions that they had gathered, and the persons whom they had acquired in Har'an; and they set forth to go to the land of Cā'naan. When they had come to the land of Cā'naan, [6] Abram passed through the land to the place at She'chem, to the oak[g] of Mō'reh. At that time the Cā'naan-ites were in the land. [7] Then the LORD appeared to Abram, and said, "To your offspring[h] I will give this land." So he built there an altar to the LORD, who had appeared to him. [8] From there he moved on to the hill country on the east of Beth'el, and pitched his tent, with Beth'el on the west and Ai on the east; and there he built an altar to the LORD and invoked the name of the LORD. [9] And Abram journeyed on by stages toward the Neg'eb.

Abram and Sarai in Egypt

10 Now there was a famine in the land. So Abram went down to Egypt to reside there as an alien, for the famine was severe in the land. [11] When he was about to enter Egypt, he said to his wife Sar'ai, "I know well that you are a woman beautiful in appearance; [12] and when the Egyptians see you, they will say, 'This is his wife'; then they will kill me, but they will let you live. [13] Say you are my sister, so that it may go well with me because of you, and that my life may be spared on your account." [14] When Abram entered Egypt the Egyptians saw that the woman was very beautiful. [15] When the officials of Pharaoh saw her, they

---

e Heb *balal, meaning to confuse*   *f* Or *by you all the families of the earth shall bless themselves*   *g* Or *terebinth*   *h* Heb *seed*

praised her to Pharaoh. And the woman was taken into Pharaoh's house. 16 And for her sake he dealt well with Abram; and he had sheep, oxen, male donkeys, male and female slaves, female donkeys, and camels.

17 But the LORD afflicted Pharaoh and his house with great plagues because of Sar'ai, Abram's wife. 18 So Pharaoh called Abram, and said, "What is this you have done to me? Why did you not tell me that she was your wife? 19 Why did you say, 'She is my sister,' so that I took her for my

had flocks and herds and tents, 6 so that the land could not support both of them living together; for their possessions were so great that they could not live together, 7 and there was strife between the herders of Abram's livestock and the herders of Lot's livestock. At that time the Cā'naan•ītes and the Per'iz•zītes lived in the land.

8 Then Abram said to Lot, "Let there be no strife between you and me, and between your herders and my herders; for we are kindred. 9 Is not the whole land before you? Separate yourself

Introducing
▶ ABRAHAM AND SARAH

Abraham, whose name was originally Abram, is an important figure for three major world religions: Judaism, Christianity, and Islam. Abraham is regarded as the great example of faith in God. He first appears in Gen 11.26. For many years, Abram lives in Haran in northern Mesopotamia (see map 1, "The World of the Patriarchs") with his wife, Sarai. God calls Abram and Sarai to leave their home, seals a covenant with them, and changes their names to Abraham and Sarah. God's covenant promises that they will be the parents "of a multitude of nations" (17.5) and their descendants will be as numerous as the "stars of heaven" (22.17).

Later, God requests that Abraham sacrifice his son Isaac. God stops him from going through with it, but Abraham's willingness to cooperate with God and his complete trust in God become the foundation for Israel's faith. Not surprisingly, in the Old Testament, when a prophet or teacher needed an example of someone with unwavering trust in God, Abraham was often cited.

In the New Testament, Abraham is revered as the first patriarch to enter into a covenant with God (see Mt 1.1; Lk 16.19–31) and the great pioneer of Israel's faith (Acts 7.2–50; Rom 4.1–25; Heb 7.1–10).

▶ **Gen 12.1—25.11**

wife? Now then, here is your wife, take her, and be gone." 20 And Pharaoh gave his men orders concerning him; and they set him on the way, with his wife and all that he had.

Abram and Lot Separate

So Abram went up from Egypt, he and his wife, and all that he had, and Lot with him, into the Neg'eb. 2 Now Abram was very rich in livestock, in silver, and in gold. 3 He journeyed on by stages from the Neg'eb as far as Beth'el, to the place where his tent had been at the beginning, between Beth'el and Aī, 4 to the place where he had made an altar at the first; and there Abram called on the name of the LORD. 5 Now Lot, who went with Abram, also

from me. If you take the left hand, then I will go to the right; or if you take the right hand, then I will go to the left." 10 Lot looked about him, and saw that the plain of the Jordan was well watered everywhere like the garden of the LORD, like the land of Egypt, in the direction of Zō'ar; this was before the LORD had destroyed Sod'om and Go•mor'rah. 11 So Lot chose for himself all the plain of the Jordan, and Lot journeyed eastward; thus they separated from each other. 12 Abram settled in the land of Cā'naan, while Lot settled among the cities of the Plain and moved his tent as far as Sod'om. 13 Now the people of Sod'om were wicked, great sinners against the LORD.

14 The LORD said to Abram, after Lot had separated from him, "Raise your eyes now, and look

from the place where you are, northward and southward and eastward and westward; 15 for all the land that you see I will give to you and to your offspring[i] forever. 16 I will make your offspring like the dust of the earth; so that if one can count the dust of the earth, your offspring also can be counted. 17 Rise up, walk through the length and the breadth of the land, for I will give it to you." 18 So Abram moved his tent, and came and settled by the oaks[j] of Mam′re, which are at He′bron; and there he built an altar to the LORD.

Lot's Captivity and Rescue

In the days of King Am′ra•phel of Shi′nar, King Ar′i•och of El•la′sar, King Ched•or•la•o′mer of E′lam, and King Ti′dal of Goi′im, 2 these kings made war with King Be′ra of Sod′om, King Bir′sha of Go•mor′rah, King Shi′nab of Ad′mah, King Shem•e′ber of Ze•boi′im, and the king of Be′la (that is, Zo′ar). 3 All these joined forces in the Valley of Sid′dim (that is, the Dead Sea).[k] 4 Twelve years they had served Ched•or•la•o′mer, but in the thirteenth year they rebelled. 5 In the fourteenth year Ched•or•la•o′mer and the kings who were with him came and subdued the Reph′a•im in Ash′te•roth-kar•na′im, the Zu′zim in Ham, the E′mim in Sha′veh-kir•i•a•tha′im, 6 and the Hor′ites in the hill country of Se′ir as far as El-par′an on the edge of the wilderness; 7 then they turned back and came to En-mish′pat (that is, Ka′desh), and subdued all the country of the A•mal′e•kites, and also the Am′o•rites who lived in Haz′a•zon-ta′mar. 8 Then the king of Sod′om, the king of Go•mor′rah, the king of Ad′-mah, the king of Ze•boi′im, and the king of Be′la (that is, Zo′ar) went out, and they joined battle in the Valley of Sid′dim 9 with King Ched•or•la•o′mer of E′lam, King Ti′dal of Goi′im, King Am′ra•phel of Shi′nar, and King Ar′i•och of El•la′sar, four kings against five. 10 Now the Valley of Sid′dim was full of bitumen pits; and as the kings of Sod′om and Go•mor′rah fled, some fell into them, and the rest fled to the hill country. 11 So the enemy took all the goods of Sod′om and Go•mor′rah, and all their provisions, and went their way; 12 they also took Lot, the son of Abram′s brother, who lived in Sod′om, and his goods, and departed.

13 Then one who had escaped came and told Abram the Hebrew, who was living by the oaks[j] of Mam′re the Am′o•rite, brother of Esh′col and of A′ner; these were allies of Abram. 14 When Abram heard that his nephew had been taken captive, he led forth his trained men, born in his house, three hundred eighteen of them, and went in pursuit as far as Dan. 15 He divided his forces against them by night, he and his servants, and routed them and pursued them to Ho′bah, north of Damascus.

16 Then he brought back all the goods, and also brought back his nephew Lot with his goods, and the women and the people.

Abram Blessed by Melchizedek
(Heb 7.1–2)

17 After his return from the defeat of Ched•or•la•o′mer and the kings who were with him, the king of Sod′om went out to meet him at the Valley of Sha′veh (that is, the King′s Valley). 18 And King Mel•chiz′e•dek of Salem brought out bread and

Catholic Connections

BREAD AND WINE

Melchizedek, a king and priest, uses bread and wine in a ritual to bless Abram. Bread and wine served as an ancient symbol of nourishment and celebration. The sacrament of the Eucharist has its roots in rituals such as this one. See Heb 7.1–10 for a New Testament interpretation of Melchizedek's importance.

▶ Gen 14.17–20

wine; he was priest of God Most High.[l] 19 He blessed him and said,

"Blessed be Abram by God Most High,[l]
　maker of heaven and earth;
20　and blessed be God Most High,[l]
　who has delivered your enemies into
　　　your hand!"

And Abram gave him one-tenth of everything. 21 Then the king of Sod′om said to Abram, "Give me the persons, but take the goods for yourself." 22 But Abram said to the king of Sod′om, "I have sworn to the LORD, God Most High,[l] maker of heaven and earth, 23 that I would not take a thread or a sandal-thong or anything that is yours, so that you might not say, 'I have made Abram rich.' 24 I

---

i Heb *seed*　j Or *terebinths*　k Heb *Salt Sea*　l Heb *El Elyon* will take nothing but what the young men have eaten, and the share of the men who went with me—Ā'ner, Esh'col, and Mam're. Let them take their share."

God's Covenant with Abram
(Heb 11.8–10)

After these things the word of the LORD came to Abram in a vision, "Do not be afraid, Abram, I am your shield; your reward shall be very great." [2] But Abram said, "O Lord GOD, what will you give me, for I continue childless, and the heir of my house is El•i•ē'zer of Damascus?"[m] [3] And Abram said, "You have given me no offspring, and so a slave born in

Fire

Fire appears frequently throughout the Old Testament, symbolizing two aspects of God: presence and holiness. Fire symbolizes a special presence of God in the sealing of the covenant with Abraham (Gen 15.17), in the burning bush (Ex 3.2), and in the pillar of fire leading Israel through the desert (Ex 13.21). Fire also symbolizes God's holiness appearing to purge and purify those who deviate from God's ways, as in Sodom and Gomorrah (Gen 19.24) and the seventh plague against Egypt (Ex 9.23).

▶ **Gen 15.17**

my house is to be my heir." [4] But the word of the LORD came to him, "This man shall not be your heir; no one but your very own issue shall be your heir." [5] He brought him outside and said, "Look toward heaven and count the stars, if you are able to count them." Then he said to him, "So shall your descendants be." [6] And he believed the LORD; and the LORD[n] reckoned it to him as righteousness.

[7] Then he said to him, "I am the LORD who brought you from Ūr of the Chal•dē'ans, to give you this land to possess." [8] But he said, "O Lord GOD, how am I to know that I shall possess it?" [9] He said to him, "Bring me a heifer three years old, a

female goat three years old, a ram three years old, a turtledove, and a young pigeon." [10] He brought him all these and cut them in two, laying each half over against the other; but he did not cut the birds in two. [11] And when birds of prey came down on the carcasses, Abram drove them away.

[12] As the sun was going down, a deep sleep fell upon Abram, and a deep and terrifying darkness descended upon him. [13] Then the LORD[n] said to Abram, "Know this for certain, that your offspring shall be aliens in a land that is not theirs, and shall be slaves there, and they shall be oppressed for four hundred years; [14] but I will bring judgment on the nation that they serve, and afterward they shall come out with great possessions. [15] As for yourself, you shall go to your ancestors in peace; you shall be buried in a good old age. [16] And they shall come back here in the fourth generation; for the iniquity of the Am'o•rītes is not yet complete."

[17] When the sun had gone down and it was dark, a smoking fire pot and a flaming torch passed between these pieces. [18] On that day the LORD made a covenant with Abram, saying, "To your descendants I give this land, from the river of Egypt to the great river, the river Euphrates, [19] the land of the Ken'ītes, the Ken'iz•zītes, the Kad'mon-ītes, [20] the Hit'tītes, the Per'iz•zītes, the Reph'a•im, [21] the Am'o•rītes, the Cā'naan•ītes, the Gir'ga•shītes, and the Jeb'ū•sītes."

The Birth of Ishmael

Now Sar'aī, Abram's wife, bore him no children. She had an Egyptian slave-girl whose name was Hā'gar, [2] and Sar'aī said to Abram, "You see that the LORD has prevented me from bearing children; go in to my slave-girl; it may be that I shall obtain children by her." And Abram listened to the voice of Sar'aī. [3] So, after Abram had lived ten years in the land of Cā'naan, Sar'aī, Abram's wife, took Hā'gar the Egyptian, her slave-girl, and gave her to her husband Abram as a wife. [4] He went in to Hā'-gar, and she conceived; and when she saw that she had conceived, she looked with contempt on her mistress. [5] Then Sar'aī said to Abram, "May the wrong done to me be on you! I gave my slave-girl to your embrace, and when she saw that she had conceived, she looked on me with contempt. May the LORD judge between you and me!" [6] But Abram said to Sar'aī, "Your slave-girl is in your power; do to her as you please." Then Sar'aī dealt harshly with her, and she ran away from her.

---

[m] Meaning of Heb uncertain   [n] Heb *he*

7 The angel of the LORD found her by a spring
of water in the wilderness, the spring on the way
to Shur. 8 And he said, "Hā'gar, slave-girl of Sar'aī,
where have you come from and where are you going?" She said, "I am running away from my mistress Sar'aī." 9 The angel of the LORD said to her,
"Return to your mistress, and submit to her." 10 The
angel of the LORD also said to her, "I will so greatly
multiply your offspring that they cannot be
counted for multitude." 11 And the angel of the LORD
said to her,

"Now you have conceived and shall bear a
son;
you shall call him Ish'ma•el,[o]
for the LORD has given heed to your
affliction.
12 He shall be a wild ass of a man,
with his hand against everyone,
and everyone's hand against him;
and he shall live at odds with all his
kin."

13 So she named the LORD who spoke to her, "You
are El-roi";[p] for she said, "Have I really seen God
and remained alive after seeing him?"[q] 14 Therefore
the well was called Bē'er-la'haī-roi;[r] it lies between Kā'desh and Bē'red.

15 Hā'gar bore Abram a son; and Abram
named his son, whom Hā'gar bore, Ish'ma•el.
16 Abram was eighty-six years old when Hā'gar
bore him[s] Ish'ma•el.

The Sign of the Covenant

(Ex 12.43—13.2)

17 When Abram was ninety-nine years old, the LORD
appeared to Abram, and said to him, "I am God
Almighty;[t] walk before me, and be blameless.
2 And I will make my covenant between me and
you, and will make you exceedingly numerous."
3 Then Abram fell on his face; and God said to
him, 4 "As for me, this is my covenant with you:
You shall be the ancestor of a multitude of nations. 5 No longer shall your name be Abram,[u] but
your name shall be Abraham;[v] for I have made
you the ancestor of a multitude of nations. 6 I will
make you exceedingly fruitful; and I will make nations of you, and kings shall come from you. 7 I
will establish my covenant between me and you,
and your offspring after you throughout their generations, for an everlasting covenant, to be God to
you and to your offspring[w] after you. 8 And I will
give to you, and to your offspring after you, the
land where you are now an alien, all the land of
Cā'naan, for a perpetual holding; and I will be
their God."

9 God said to Abraham, "As for you, you shall
keep my covenant, you and your offspring after

[o] That is *God hears* [p] Perhaps *God of seeing* or *God who sees* [q] Meaning of Heb uncertain [r] That is *the Well of the Living One who sees me* [s] Heb *Abram* [t] Traditional rendering of Heb *El Shaddai* [u] That is *exalted ancestor* [v] Here taken to mean *ancestor of a multitude* [w] Heb *seed*

LIVE IT!

Love and Jealousy

A love triangle in the Bible! The relationship between Abram, Sarai, and Hagar is shocking by Christian moral standards but would not have been unusual in their time. A patriarch like Abram would often have children by several wives, slaves, and concubines (something like mistresses who lived with the household). It's not surprising that such relationships would have fostered jealousy and tension. The conflict between Hagar and Sarai must have been fierce for Hagar to leave the security of Abram's household.

So, why does God's angel seek out Hagar and ask her to return to a place where she is likely to be mistreated? To answer this, we have to remember that the writer of Genesis was concerned more with explaining the rise of nations than with teaching a moral lesson. Hagar must return to bear her son, Ishmael, so that the Ishmaelites (descendants of Ishmael) have a clear connection to Abraham as their ancestor.

Today, we encourage victims of abuse and harassment to speak out and take action. When we encounter people who have been abused or harassed, we need to help them seek justice and set things right. Remember the larger message in Genesis—that every person is created in God's image and is to be treated with the utmost dignity and respect. Carrying out this message is our responsibility as brothers and sisters to one another.

▸ **Gen 16.1–16**

Covenant

Covenant is a powerful word in the Bible, with deep religious significance because it expresses the intimate relationship between God and God's people. At its most basic level, a covenant is a promise by both parties involved to do certain things.

In the covenant God makes with Noah, God promises never to destroy the earth again, and Noah's family promises to fill the earth and subdue it (Gen 9.1–17). In the covenant with Abraham, God promises that Abram's descendants will be numerous and become a great nation. In return, Abram and all the male members of his household and their male descendants must practice circumcision to mark that they belong to God (17.1–27). In the Covenant made at Mount Sinai with Moses (Ex 19.1–9) and the Hebrew people, God promises to give them the Promised Land. In return, they promise to follow the laws God gives to them.

As told by the author of Genesis, these covenants are always initiated by God, who wants to lead the people to a better way of life. But the people must respond to God's offer as a sign of their faith in God. The New Testament tells of a new and lasting Covenant for all people and for all time (2 Cor 3.3; Gal 4.21–31).

And so we, each of us, are part of these ancient promises. Like the many faithful people who have gone before us, we too are the descendants of Abraham and Sarah, believers in the one God and members of God's family. We too are heirs to a special, intimate relationship with the Holy One of Israel.

▶ Gen 17.1–27

you throughout their generations. ¹⁰ This is my covenant, which you shall keep, between me and you and your offspring after you: Every male among you shall be circumcised. ¹¹ You shall circumcise the flesh of your foreskins, and it shall be a sign of the covenant between me and you. ¹² Throughout your generations every male among you shall be circumcised when he is eight days old, including the slave born in your house and the one bought with your money from any foreigner who is not of your offspring. ¹³ Both the slave born in your house and the one bought with your money must be circumcised. So shall my covenant be in your flesh an everlasting covenant. ¹⁴ Any uncircumcised male who is not circumcised in the flesh of his foreskin shall be cut off from his people; he has broken my covenant."

¹⁵ God said to Abraham, "As for Sar′aī your wife, you shall not call her Sar′aī, but Sarah shall be her name. ¹⁶ I will bless her, and moreover I will give you a son by her. I will bless her, and she shall give rise to nations; kings of peoples shall come from her." ¹⁷ Then Abraham fell on his face and laughed, and said to himself, "Can a child be born to a man who is a hundred years old? Can Sarah, who is ninety years old, bear a child?" ¹⁸ And Abraham said to God, "O that Ish′ma•el might live

in your sight!" ¹⁹ God said, "No, but your wife Sarah shall bear you a son, and you shall name him Isaac.ˣ I will establish my covenant with him as an everlasting covenant for his offspring after him. ²⁰ As for Ish′ma•el, I have heard you; I will bless him and make him fruitful and exceedingly numerous; he shall be the father of twelve princes, and I will make him a great nation. ²¹ But my covenant I will establish with Isaac, whom Sarah shall bear to you at this season next year." ²² And when he had finished talking with him, God went up from Abraham.

23 Then Abraham took his son Ish′ma•el and all the slaves born in his house or bought with his money, every male among the men of Abraham's house, and he circumcised the flesh of their foreskins that very day, as God had said to him. ²⁴ Abraham was ninety-nine years old when he was circumcised in the flesh of his foreskin. ²⁵ And his son Ish′ma•el was thirteen years old when he was circumcised in the flesh of his foreskin. ²⁶ That very day Abraham and his son Ish′ma•el were circumcised; ²⁷ and all the men of his house, slaves born in the house and those bought with money from a foreigner, were circumcised with him.

ˣ That is *he laughs*

did you KNOW?

Circumcision

Circumcision, the removal of the fore-skin of the penis, was practiced by many peoples in the ancient world. In Israel, circumcision was performed shortly after birth. It symbolized that this person belonged to the people of God, and was required by the covenant that God made first with Abraham, then with Moses and all Israel. Today, most Jews continue circumcision as a religious practice, and other people may be circumcised for personal reasons.

In the early church, circumcision became the center of a controversy about whether Gentiles who wanted to become Christians had to first become Jews (Acts of the Apostles, chapter 15; Phil 3.9).

▶ Gen 17.9–14

A Son Promised to Abraham and Sarah
(Heb 13.2)

The LORD appeared to Abraham*y* by the oaks*z* of Mam're, as he sat at the entrance of his tent in the heat of the day. 2 He looked up and saw three men standing near him. When he saw them, he ran from the tent entrance to meet them, and bowed down to the ground. 3 He said, "My lord, if I find favor with you, do not pass by your servant. 4 Let a little water be brought, and wash your feet, and rest yourselves under the tree. 5 Let me bring a little bread, that you may refresh yourselves, and after that you may pass on—since you have come to your servant." So they said, "Do as you have said." 6 And Abraham hastened into the tent to Sarah, and said, "Make ready quickly three measures*a* of choice flour, knead it, and make cakes." 7 Abraham ran to the herd, and took a calf, tender and good, and gave it to the servant, who hastened to prepare it. 8 Then he took curds and milk and the calf that he had prepared, and set it before them; and he stood by them under the tree while they ate.

9 They said to him, "Where is your wife Sarah?" And he said, "There, in the tent." 10 Then one said, "I will surely return to you in due season, and your wife Sarah shall have a son." And Sarah was listening at the tent entrance behind him. 11 Now Abraham and Sarah were old, advanced in age; it had ceased to be with Sarah after the manner of women. 12 So Sarah laughed to herself, saying, "After I have grown old, and my husband is old, shall I have pleasure?" 13 The LORD said to Abraham, "Why did Sarah laugh, and say, 'Shall I indeed bear a child, now that I am old?' 14 Is anything too wonderful for the LORD? At the set time I will return to you, in due season, and Sarah shall have a son." 15 But Sarah denied, saying, "I did not laugh"; for she was afraid. He said, "Oh yes, you did laugh."

---

y Heb *him*   *z* Or *terebinths*   *a* Heb *seahs*

What's So Funny?

LIVE IT!

Laughter is not a word we usually associate with the Bible, and certainly not with the Old Testament. Most of the stories are serious, filled with accounts of sacrifice, battles, and the Covenant. But here is Sarah, an old woman, long past child-bearing age. She overhears one of Abraham's mysterious guests tell him that in a year, he and Sarah will have a son (Gen 18.10). How can she help but laugh? She and Abraham do produce, of course, a son called Isaac, whose Hebrew name, Yishaq, means "laughed." Sarah's cynical chuckles must have turned to joyful laughs at the birth of her beloved son. Laughter is a wonderful response to the gift of life and is a natural and often spontaneous response to God's presence within us and around us.

"Is anything too wonderful for the LORD?" (verse 14). We are all tempted to laugh at the notion that miracles can happen to us. As we grow in faith and open ourselves to God's goodness, our laughter will change from cynical laughter to joyful laughter.

▶ Gen 18.9–15

PRAY IT!
Get Close to God

Our prayers reveal what we believe about God and what we value. Abraham's bargaining for the inhabitants of Sodom and Gomorrah shows his faith, his care for others, and his closeness with God. Although he is humble, he deals with God as a friend whom he is not afraid to be honest with.

We too must be honest with God in our prayer. Too many Christians simply do not trust God enough to be completely themselves with God. They are afraid to share their doubts, anger, grief, and frustrations. But God is big enough to handle it all. Find a way in your prayer to share your innermost thoughts and feelings with God. For some people, journaling helps; others yell and shout aloud at the Lord. Remember that God's healing touch cannot enter our life until we are willing to share our deepest feelings.

▸ Gen 18.22–33

Judgment Pronounced on Sodom

16 Then the men set out from there, and they looked toward Sod'om; and Abraham went with them to set them on their way. 17 The LORD said, "Shall I hide from Abraham what I am about to do, 18 seeing that Abraham shall become a great and mighty nation, and all the nations of the earth shall be blessed in him?*b* 19 No, for I have chosen*c* him, that he may charge his children and his household after him to keep the way of the LORD by doing righteousness and justice; so that the LORD may bring about for Abraham what he has promised him." 20 Then the LORD said, "How great is the outcry against Sod'om and Go•mor'rah and how very grave their sin! 21 I must go down and see whether they have done altogether according to the outcry that has come to me; and if not, I will know."

22 So the men turned from there, and went toward Sod'om, while Abraham remained standing before the LORD.*d* 23 Then Abraham came near and said, "Will you indeed sweep away the righteous with the wicked? 24 Suppose there are fifty righteous within the city; will you then sweep away the place and not forgive it for the fifty righ-

teous who are in it? 25 Far be it from you to do such a thing, to slay the righteous with the wicked, so that the righteous fare as the wicked! Far be that from you! Shall not the Judge of all the earth do what is just?" 26 And the LORD said, "If I find at Sod'om fifty righteous in the city, I will forgive the whole place for their sake." 27 Abraham answered, "Let me take it upon myself to speak to the Lord, I who am but dust and ashes. 28 Suppose five of the fifty righteous are lacking. Will you destroy the whole city for lack of five?" And he said, "I will not destroy it if I find forty-five there." 29 Again he spoke to him, "Suppose forty are found there." He answered, "For the sake of forty I will not do it." 30 Then he said, "Oh do not let the Lord be angry if I speak. Suppose thirty are found there." He answered, "I will not do it, if I find thirty there." 31 He said, "Let me take it upon myself to speak to the Lord. Suppose twenty are found there." He answered, "For the sake of twenty I will not destroy it." 32 Then he said, "Oh do not let the Lord be angry if I speak just once more. Suppose ten are found there." He answered, "For the sake of ten I will not destroy it." 33 And the LORD went his way, when he had finished speaking to Abraham; and Abraham returned to his place.

The Depravity of Sodom

The two angels came to Sod'om in the evening, and Lot was sitting in the gateway of Sod'om. When Lot saw them, he rose to meet them, and bowed down with his face to the ground. 2 He said, "Please, my lords, turn aside to your servant's house and spend the night, and wash your feet; then you can rise early and go on your way." They said, "No; we will spend the night in the square." 3 But he urged them strongly; so they turned aside to him and entered his house; and he made them a feast, and baked unleavened bread, and they ate. 4 But before they lay down, the men of the city, the men of Sod'om, both young and old, all the people to the last man, surrounded the house; 5 and they called to Lot, "Where are the men who came to you tonight? Bring them out to us, so that we may know them." 6 Lot went out of the door to the men, shut the door after him, 7 and said, "I beg you, my brothers, do not act so wickedly. 8 Look, I have two daughters who have not known a man; let me bring them out to you, and do to them as you please; only do nothing to these men, for they have come under the shelter of my roof." 9 But they replied, "Stand back!" And they said, "This fellow came here as an alien, and he would play the

b Or and all the nations of the earth shall bless themselves by him   c Heb known   d Another ancient tradition reads while the LORD remained standing before Abraham

Be Kind to Strangers

LIVE IT!

If our first gesture to outsiders were one of respect, kindness, and gracious hospitality, what might our world be like? The story of Sodom and Gomorrah shows us the results of disrespect, inhospitality, and the attempted abuse of strangers. Like Abraham, Lot is a wonderful host. But the people of Sodom want Lot's visitors for their own sexual pleasure (to "know" someone is often biblical language for sexual intercourse). For the author of Genesis, this horrendous crime calls for the most severe punishment.

As children of God, it is our responsibility to extend our kindness to stranger and friend alike. So how are visitors or new students treated in your school? How are visitors treated in your home?

▸ Gen 19.1–11

judge! Now we will deal worse with you than with them." Then they pressed hard against the man Lot, and came near the door to break it down. 10 But the men inside reached out their hands and brought Lot into the house with them, and shut the door. 11 And they struck with blindness the men who were at the door of the house, both small and great, so that they were unable to find the door.

Sodom and Gomorrah Destroyed
(Mt 11.23–24; Lk 17.28–32)

12 Then the men said to Lot, "Have you anyone else here? Sons-in-law, sons, daughters, or anyone you have in the city—bring them out of the place. 13 For we are about to destroy this place, because the outcry against its people has become great before the LORD, and the LORD has sent us to destroy it." 14 So Lot went out and said to his sons-in-law, who were to marry his daughters, "Up, get out of this place; for the LORD is about to destroy the city." But he seemed to his sons-in-law to be jesting.

15 When morning dawned, the angels urged Lot, saying, "Get up, take your wife and your two daughters who are here, or else you will be consumed in the punishment of the city." 16 But he lingered; so the men seized him and his wife and his two daughters by the hand, the LORD being merciful to him, and they brought him out and left him outside the city. 17 When they had brought them outside, they^e said, "Flee for your life; do not look back or stop anywhere in the Plain; flee to the hills, or else you will be consumed." 18 And Lot said to them, "Oh, no, my lords; 19 your servant has found favor with you, and you have shown me great kindness in saving my life; but I cannot flee

to the hills, for fear the disaster will overtake me and I die. 20 Look, that city is near enough to flee to, and it is a little one. Let me escape there—is it not a little one?—and my life will be saved!" 21 He said to him, "Very well, I grant you this favor too, and will not overthrow the city of which you have spoken. 22 Hurry, escape there, for I can do nothing until you arrive there." Therefore the city was called Zō'ar.^f 23 The sun had risen on the earth when Lot came to Zō'ar.

24 Then the LORD rained on Sod'om and Go-mor'rah sulfur and fire from the LORD out of heaven; 25 and he overthrew those cities, and all the Plain, and all the inhabitants of the cities, and what grew on the ground. 26 But Lot's wife, behind him, looked back, and she became a pillar of salt.

27 Abraham went early in the morning to the place where he had stood before the LORD; 28 and he looked down toward Sod'om and Go•mor'rah and toward all the land of the Plain and saw the smoke of the land going up like the smoke of a furnace.

29 So it was that, when God destroyed the cities of the Plain, God remembered Abraham, and sent Lot out of the midst of the overthrow, when he overthrew the cities in which Lot had settled.

The Shameful Origin of Moab and Ammon

30 Now Lot went up out of Zō'ar and settled in the hills with his two daughters, for he was afraid to stay in Zō'ar; so he lived in a cave with his two daughters. 31 And the firstborn said to the younger, "Our father is old, and there is not a man on earth to come in to us after the manner of all the world. 32 Come, let us make our father drink wine, and we will lie with him, so that we

e Gk Syr Vg: Heb *he*   f That is *Little*

may preserve offspring through our father." [33] So they made their father drink wine that night; and the firstborn went in, and lay with her father; he did not know when she lay down or when she rose. [34] On the next day, the firstborn said to the younger, "Look, I lay last night with my father; let us make him drink wine tonight also; then you go in and lie with him, so that we may preserve offspring through our father." [35] So they made their father drink wine that night also; and the younger rose, and lay with him; and he did not know when she lay down or when she rose. [36] Thus both the daughters of Lot became pregnant by their father. [37] The firstborn bore a son, and named him Mō'ab; he is the ancestor of the Mō'ab·ītes to this day. [38] The younger also bore a son and named him Ben-am'mī; he is the ancestor of the Am'-mon·ites to this day.

Abraham and Sarah at Gerar

From there Abraham journeyed toward the region of the Neg'eb, and settled between Kā'desh and Shur. While residing in Gē'rar as an alien, [2] Abraham said of his wife Sarah, "She is my sister." And King A·bim'e·lech of Gē'rar sent and took Sarah. [3] But God came to A·bim'e·lech in a dream by night, and said to him, "You are about to die because of the woman whom you have taken; for she is a married woman." [4] Now A·bim'e·lech had not approached her; so he said, "Lord, will you destroy an innocent people? [5] Did he not himself say to me, 'She is my sister'? And she herself said, 'He is my brother.' I did this in the integrity of my heart and the innocence of my hands." [6] Then God said to him in the dream, "Yes, I know that you did this in the integrity of your heart; furthermore it was I who kept you from sinning against me. Therefore I did not let you touch her. [7] Now then, return the man's wife; for he is a prophet, and he will pray for you and you shall live. But if you do not restore her, know that you shall surely die, you and all that are yours."

[8] So A·bim'e·lech rose early in the morning, and called all his servants and told them all these things; and the men were very much afraid. [9] Then A·bim'e·lech called Abraham, and said to him, "What have you done to us? How have I sinned against you, that you have brought such great guilt on me and my kingdom? You have done things to me that ought not to be done." [10] And A·bim'e·lech said to Abraham, "What were you thinking of, that you did this thing?" [11] Abraham said, "I did it because I thought, There is no fear of God at all in this place, and they will kill me because of my wife. [12] Besides, she is indeed my sister, the daughter of my father but not the daughter of my

mother; and she became my wife. [13] And when God caused me to wander from my father's house, I said to her, 'This is the kindness you must do me: at every place to which we come, say of me, He is my brother.' " [14] Then A·bim'e·lech took sheep and oxen, and male and female slaves, and gave them to Abraham, and restored his wife Sarah to him. [15] A·bim'e·lech said, "My land is before you; settle where it pleases you." [16] To Sarah he said, "Look, I have given your brother a thousand pieces of silver; it is your exoneration before all who are with you; you are completely vindicated." [17] Then Abraham prayed to God; and God healed A·bim'e·lech, and also healed his wife and female slaves so that they bore children. [18] For the LORD had closed fast all the wombs of the house of A·bim'e·lech because of Sarah, Abraham's wife.

The Birth of Isaac
(Heb 11.11)

The LORD dealt with Sarah as he had said, and the LORD did for Sarah as he had promised. [2] Sarah conceived and bore Abraham a son in his old age, at the time of which God had spoken to him. [3] Abraham gave the name Isaac to his son whom Sarah bore him. [4] And Abraham circumcised his son Isaac when he was eight days old, as God had commanded him. [5] Abraham was a hundred years old when his son Isaac was born to him. [6] Now Sarah said, "God has brought laughter for me; everyone who hears will laugh with me." [7] And she said, "Who would ever have said to Abraham that Sarah would nurse children? Yet I have borne him a son in his old age."

Hagar and Ishmael Sent Away
(Gal 4.21–30)

[8] The child grew, and was weaned; and Abraham made a great feast on the day that Isaac was weaned. [9] But Sarah saw the son of Hā'gar the Egyptian, whom she had borne to Abraham, playing with her son Isaac.[8] [10] So she said to Abraham, "Cast out this slave woman with her son; for the son of this slave woman shall not inherit along with my son Isaac." [11] The matter was very distressing to Abraham on account of his son. [12] But God said to Abraham, "Do not be distressed because of the boy and because of your slave woman; whatever Sarah says to you, do as she tells you, for it is through Isaac that offspring shall be named for you. [13] As for the son of the slave woman, I will make a nation of him also, because he is your offspring." [14] So Abraham rose early in the morning, and took bread and a skin of water, and gave it to

---

8 Gk Vg: Heb lacks *with her son Isaac*

Hā′gar, putting it on her shoulder, along with the child, and sent her away. And she departed, and wandered about in the wilderness of Bē′er-she′ba.

15 When the water in the skin was gone, she cast the child under one of the bushes. 16 Then she went and sat down opposite him a good way off, about the distance of a bowshot; for she said, "Do not let me look on the death of the child." And as she sat opposite him, she lifted up her voice and

PRAY IT!
Hagar's Rescue

Genesis 21.8–21 is part 2 of the Hagar and Ishmael story begun in 16.1–16. Once again, Hagar is the victim of Sarah's jealousy. But this time God does not send her back. Seemingly facing certain death, Hagar receives from God the ability to see the opportunity for life in front of her. This time the writer of Genesis makes the point that God rescues the abused and abandoned. Hagar and Ishmael survive, and from their descendants, a great people emerges.

Hagar's story reminds us that God wants to rescue us from oppression, injustice, and abuse. Often, we want to ask God to magically take these things away. But because God has given human beings free will, we cannot always be spared from the abuse and injustice of others. In your prayer, you can always ask God to rescue you, to give you the vision to see the healthy choices you can make to improve your situation. Do that right now if you are in an unjust or abusive situation.

▶ Gen 21.8–21

wept. 17 And God heard the voice of the boy; and the angel of God called to Hā′gar from heaven, and said to her, "What troubles you, Hā′gar? Do not be afraid; for God has heard the voice of the boy where he is. 18 Come, lift up the boy and hold him fast with your hand, for I will make a great nation of him." 19 Then God opened her eyes and she saw a well of water. She went, and filled the skin with water, and gave the boy a drink.

20 God was with the boy, and he grew up; he lived in the wilderness, and became an expert with the bow. 21 He lived in the wilderness of Par′an; and his mother got a wife for him from the land of Egypt.

Abraham and Abimelech Make a Covenant

22 At that time A•bim′e•lech, with Phi′col the commander of his army, said to Abraham, "God is with you in all that you do; 23 now therefore swear to me here by God that you will not deal falsely with me or with my offspring or with my posterity, but as I have dealt loyally with you, you will deal with me and with the land where you have resided as an alien." 24 And Abraham said, "I swear it."

25 When Abraham complained to A•bim′e•lech about a well of water that A•bim′e•lech's servants had seized, 26 A•bim′e•lech said, "I do not know who has done this; you did not tell me, and I have not heard of it until today." 27 So Abraham took sheep and oxen and gave them to A•bim′e•lech, and the two men made a covenant. 28 Abraham set apart seven ewe lambs of the flock. 29 And A•bim′e•lech said to Abraham, "What is the meaning of these seven ewe lambs that you have set apart?" 30 He said, "These seven ewe lambs you shall accept from my hand, in order that you may be a witness for me that I dug this well." 31 Therefore that place was called Bē′er-she′ba;*h* because there both of them swore an oath. 32 When they had made a covenant at Bē′er-she′ba, A•bim′e•lech, with Phi′col the commander of his army, left and returned to the land of the Phi•lis′tines. 33 Abraham*i* planted a tamarisk tree in Bē′er-she′ba, and called there on the name of the LORD, the Everlasting God.*j* 34 And Abraham resided as an alien many days in the land of the Phi•lis′tines.

The Command to Sacrifice Isaac
(Heb 11.17–19)

After these things God tested Abraham. He said to him, "Abraham!" And he said, "Here I am." 2 He said, "Take your son, your only son Isaac, whom you love, and go to the land of Mō•rī′ah, and offer him there as a burnt offering on one of the mountains that I shall show you." 3 So Abraham rose early in the morning, saddled his donkey, and took two of his young men with him, and his son Isaac; he cut the wood for the burnt offering, and set out and went to the place in the distance that God had shown him. 4 On the third day Abraham looked up and saw the place far away. 5 Then Abraham said to his young men, "Stay here with the donkey; the boy and I will go over there; we will worship, and then we will come back to you."

h That is *Well of seven* or *Well of the oath*   *i* Heb *He*
j Or *the* LORD, *El Olam*

⁶Abraham took the wood of the burnt offering and laid it on his son Isaac, and he himself carried the fire and the knife. So the two of them walked on together. ⁷Isaac said to his father Abraham, "Father!" And he said, "Here I am, my son." He said, "The fire and the wood are here, but where is the lamb for a burnt offering?" ⁸Abraham said, "God himself will provide the lamb for a burnt offering, my son." So the two of them walked on together.

PRAY IT!
Ultimate Trust in God!

To us it seems horrible that God would ask Abraham to sacrifice his son Isaac. But this story is meant to be a sign of Abraham's complete trust in God. Ultimately, God prevented the sacrifice because God wanted not Isaac's death but Abraham's faith. Because of his willingness to respond to God's demand, Abraham is recognized as the father of our faith. Our trust in God should be as total as Abraham's trust was.

We probably won't ever be faced with the test of Abraham, but the story shows us the power of faith. Because of Abraham's faith in God's promise, Isaac lived and became the father of Jacob, whose twelve sons became the twelve tribes of Israel. In your prayer, reflect or journal on the following questions:

- Because of your beliefs, have you ever had to give up someone or something that was precious to you?
- How has your life been enriched as a result of your trust in God in a difficult situation?

▸ Gen 22.1–19

9 When they came to the place that God had shown him, Abraham built an altar there and laid the wood in order. He bound his son Isaac, and laid him on the altar, on top of the wood. ¹⁰Then Abraham reached out his hand and took the knife to kill[k] his son. ¹¹But the angel of the LORD called to him from heaven, and said, "Abraham, Abraham!" And he said, "Here I am." ¹²He said, "Do not lay your hand on the boy or do anything to him; for now I know that you fear God, since you

have not withheld your son, your only son, from me." ¹³And Abraham looked up and saw a ram, caught in a thicket by its horns. Abraham went and took the ram and offered it up as a burnt offering instead of his son. ¹⁴So Abraham called that place "The LORD will provide";[l] as it is said to this day, "On the mount of the LORD it shall be provided."[m]

15 The angel of the LORD called to Abraham a second time from heaven, ¹⁶and said, "By myself I have sworn, says the LORD: Because you have done this, and have not withheld your son, your only son, ¹⁷I will indeed bless you, and I will make your offspring as numerous as the stars of heaven and as the sand that is on the seashore. And your offspring shall possess the gate of their enemies, ¹⁸and by your offspring shall all the nations of the earth gain blessing for themselves, because you have obeyed my voice." ¹⁹So Abraham returned to his young men, and they arose and went together to Bē′er-shē′ba; and Abraham lived at Bē′er-shē′ba.

Chap. 22

The Children of Nahor

20 Now after these things it was told Abraham, "Mil′cah also has borne children, to your brother Nā′hor: ²¹Uz the firstborn, Buz his brother, Ke-mū′el the father of Ar′am, ²²Chē′sed, Hā′zō, Pil′-dash, Jid′laph, and Be•thū′el." ²³Be•thū′el became the father of Rebekah. These eight Mil′cah bore to Nā′hor, Abraham's brother. ²⁴Moreover, his con-

---

k Or *to slaughter* l Or *will see;* Heb traditionally transliterated *Jehovah Jireh* m Or *he shall be seen*

cubine, whose name was Re•ū′mah, bore Tē′bah, Gā′ham, Tā′hash, and Mā′a•cah.

Sarah's Death and Burial

Sarah lived one hundred twenty-seven years; this was the length of Sarah's life. 2 And Sarah died at Kir′i•ath-ar′ba (that is, Hē′bron) in the land of Cā′naan; and Abraham went in to mourn for Sarah and to weep for her. 3 Abraham rose up from beside his dead, and said to the Hit′tites, 4 "I am a stranger and an alien residing among you; give me property among you for a burying place, so that I may bury my dead out of my sight." 5 The Hit′tites answered Abraham, 6 "Hear us, my lord; you are a mighty prince among us. Bury your dead in the choicest of our burial places; none of us will withhold from you any burial ground for burying your dead." 7 Abraham rose and bowed to the Hit′tites, the people of the land. 8 He said to them, "If you are willing that I should bury my dead out of my sight, hear me, and entreat for me Ē′phron son of Zō′har, 9 so that he may give me the cave of Mach-pē′lah, which he owns; it is at the end of his field. For the full price let him give it to me in your presence as a possession for a burying place." 10 Now Ē′phron was sitting among the Hit′tites; and Ē′phron the Hit′tite answered Abraham in the hearing of the Hit′tites, of all who went in at the gate of his city, 11 "No, my lord, hear me; I give you the field, and I give you the cave that is in it; in the presence of my people I give it to you; bury your dead." 12 Then Abraham bowed down before the people of the land. 13 He said to Ē′phron in the hearing of the people of the land, "If you only will listen to me! I will give the price of the field; accept it from me, so that I may bury my dead there." 14 Ē′phron answered Abraham, 15 "My lord, listen to me; a piece of land worth four hundred shekels of silver—what is that between you and me? Bury your dead." 16 Abraham agreed with Ē′phron; and Abraham weighed out for Ē′phron the silver that he had named in the hearing of the Hit′tites, four hundred shekels of silver, according to the weights current among the merchants.

17 So the field of Ē′phron in Mach•pē′lah, which was to the east of Mam′re, the field with the cave that was in it and all the trees that were in the field, throughout its whole area, passed 18 to Abraham as a possession in the presence of the Hit′tites, in the presence of all who went in at the gate of his city. 19 After this, Abraham buried Sarah his wife in the cave of the field of Mach•pē′lah facing Mam′re (that is, Hē′bron) in the land of Cā′naan. 20 The field and the cave that is in it passed from the Hit′tites into Abraham's possession as a burying place.

The Marriage of Isaac and Rebekah

Now Abraham was old, well advanced in years; and the LORD had blessed Abraham in all things. 2 Abraham said to his servant, the oldest of his house, who had charge of all that he had, "Put your hand under my thigh 3 and I will make you swear by the LORD, the God of heaven and earth, that you will not get a wife for my son from the daughters of the Cā′naan•ites, among whom I live, 4 but will go to my country and to my kindred and get a wife for my son Isaac." 5 The servant said to him, "Perhaps the woman may not be willing to follow me to this land; must I then take your son back to the land from which you came?" 6 Abraham said to him, "See to it that you do not take my son back there. 7 The LORD, the God of heaven, who took me from my father's house and from the land of my birth, and who spoke to me and swore to me, 'To your offspring I will give this land,' he will send his angel before you, and you shall take a wife for my son from there. 8 But if the woman is not willing to follow you, then you will be free from this oath of mine; only you must not take my son back there." 9 So the servant put his hand under the thigh of Abraham his master and swore to him concerning this matter.

10 Then the servant took ten of his master's camels and departed, taking all kinds of choice gifts from his master; and he set out and went to Ar′am-nā•ha•rā′im, to the city of Nā′hor. 11 He made the camels kneel down outside the city by the well of water; it was toward evening, the time when women go out to draw water. 12 And he said, "O LORD, God of my master Abraham, please grant me success today and show steadfast love to my master Abraham. 13 I am standing here by the spring of water, and the daughters of the townspeople are coming out to draw water. 14 Let the girl to whom I shall say, 'Please offer your jar that I may drink,' and who shall say, 'Drink, and I will water your camels'—let her be the one whom you have appointed for your servant Isaac. By this I shall know that you have shown steadfast love to my master."

15 Before he had finished speaking, there was Rebekah, who was born to Be•thū′el son of Mil′-cah, the wife of Nā′hor, Abraham's brother, coming out with her water jar on her shoulder. 16 The girl was very fair to look upon, a virgin, whom no man had known. She went down to the spring, filled her jar, and came up. 17 Then the servant ran to meet her and said, "Please let me sip a little water from your jar." 18 "Drink, my lord," she said, and quickly lowered her jar upon her hand and gave him a drink. 19 When she had finished giving

him a drink, she said, "I will draw for your camels also, until they have finished drinking." 20 So she quickly emptied her jar into the trough and ran again to the well to draw, and she drew for all his camels. 21 The man gazed at her in silence to learn whether or not the LORD had made his journey successful.

22 When the camels had finished drinking, the man took a gold nose-ring weighing a half shekel, and two bracelets for her arms weighing ten gold shekels, 23 and said, "Tell me whose daughter you are. Is there room in your father's house for us to spend the night?" 24 She said to him, "I am the daughter of Be•thū'el son of Mil'cah, whom she bore to Nā'hor." 25 She added, "We have plenty of straw and fodder and a place to spend the night." 26 The man bowed his head and worshiped the LORD 27 and said, "Blessed be the LORD, the God of my master Abraham, who has not forsaken his steadfast love and his faithfulness toward my master. As for me, the LORD has led me on the way to the house of my master's kin."

28 Then the girl ran and told her mother's household about these things. 29 Rebekah had a brother whose name was Lā'ban; and Lā'ban ran out to the man, to the spring. 30 As soon as he had seen the nose-ring, and the bracelets on his sister's arms, and when he heard the words of his sister Rebekah, "Thus the man spoke to me," he went to the man; and there he was, standing by the camels at the spring. 31 He said, "Come in, O blessed of the LORD. Why do you stand outside when I have prepared the house and a place for the camels?" 32 So the man came into the house; and Lā'ban unloaded the camels, and gave him straw and fodder for the camels, and water to wash his feet and the feet of the men who were with him. 33 Then food was set before him to eat; but he said, "I will not eat until I have told my errand." He said, "Speak on."

34 So he said, "I am Abraham's servant. 35 The LORD has greatly blessed my master, and he has become wealthy; he has given him flocks and herds, silver and gold, male and female slaves, camels and donkeys. 36 And Sarah my master's wife bore a son to my master when she was old; and he has given him all that he has. 37 My master made me swear, saying, 'You shall not take a wife for my son from the daughters of the Cā'naan•ites, in whose land I live; 38 but you shall go to my father's house, to my kindred, and get a wife for my son.' 39 I said to my master, 'Perhaps the woman will not follow me.' 40 But he said to me, 'The LORD, before whom I walk, will send his angel with you and make your way successful. You shall get a wife for my son from my kindred, from my

father's house. 41 Then you will be free from my oath, when you come to my kindred; even if they will not give her to you, you will be free from my oath.'

42 "I came today to the spring, and said, 'O LORD, the God of my master Abraham, if now you will only make successful the way I am going! 43 I am standing here by the spring of water; let the young woman who comes out to draw, to whom I shall say, "Please give me a little water from your jar to drink," 44 and who will say to me, "Drink, and I will draw for your camels also"—let her be the woman whom the LORD has appointed for my master's son.'

45 "Before I had finished speaking in my heart, there was Rebekah coming out with her water jar on her shoulder; and she went down to the spring, and drew. I said to her, 'Please let me drink.' 46 She quickly let down her jar from her shoulder, and said, 'Drink, and I will also water your camels.' So I drank, and she also watered the camels. 47 Then I asked her, 'Whose daughter are you?' She said, 'The daughter of Be•thū'el, Nā'hor's son, whom Mil'cah bore to him.' So I put the ring on her nose, and the bracelets on her arms. 48 Then I bowed my head and worshiped the LORD, and blessed the LORD, the God of my master Abraham, who had led me by the right way to obtain the daughter of my master's kinsman for his son. 49 Now then, if you will deal loyally and truly with my master, tell me; and if not, tell me, so that I may turn either to the right hand or to the left."

50 Then Lā'ban and Be•thū'el answered, "The thing comes from the LORD; we cannot speak to you anything bad or good. 51 Look, Rebekah is before you, take her and go, and let her be the wife of your master's son, as the LORD has spoken."

52 When Abraham's servant heard their words, he bowed himself to the ground before the LORD. 53 And the servant brought out jewelry of silver and of gold, and garments, and gave them to Rebekah; he also gave to her brother and to her mother costly ornaments. 54 Then he and the men who were with him ate and drank, and they spent the night there. When they rose in the morning, he said, "Send me back to my master." 55 Her brother and her mother said, "Let the girl remain with us a while, at least ten days; after that she may go." 56 But he said to them, "Do not delay me, since the LORD has made my journey successful; let me go that I may go to my master." 57 They said, "We will call the girl, and ask her." 58 And they called Rebekah, and said to her, "Will you go with this man?" She said, "I will." 59 So they sent away their sister Rebekah and her nurse along with Abra-

ham's servant and his men. 60 And they blessed Rebekah and said to her,

> "May you, our sister, become
>   thousands of myriads;
> may your offspring gain possession
>   of the gates of their foes."

61 Then Rebekah and her maids rose up, mounted the camels, and followed the man; thus the servant took Rebekah, and went his way.

62 Now Isaac had come from*n* Bē′er-la-haī-roi, and was settled in the Neg′eb. 63 Isaac went out in the evening to walk*o* in the field; and looking up, he saw camels coming. 64 And Rebekah looked up, and when she saw Isaac, she slipped quickly from the camel, 65 and said to the servant, "Who is the man over there, walking in the field to meet us?" The servant said, "It is my master." So she took her veil and covered herself. 66 And the servant told Isaac all the things that he had done. 67 Then Isaac brought her into his mother Sarah's tent. He took Rebekah, and she became his wife; and he loved her. So Isaac was comforted after his mother's death.

Abraham Marries Keturah
(1 Chr 1.32–33)

Abraham took another wife, whose name was Ke-tū′rah. 2 She bore him Zim′ran, Jok′shan, Mē′dan, Mid′i-an, Ish′bak, and Shū′ah. 3 Jok′shan was the father of Shē′ba and Dē′dan. The sons of Dē′dan were As-shū′rim, Le-tū′shim, and Le-um′mim. 4 The sons of Mid′i-an were Ē′phah, Ē′pher, Hā′noch, A-bī′da, and El-dā′ah. All these were the children of Ke-tū′rah. 5 Abraham gave all he had to Isaac. 6 But to the sons of his concubines Abraham gave gifts, while he was still living, and he sent them away from his son Isaac, eastward to the east country.

The Death of Abraham

7 This is the length of Abraham's life, one hundred seventy-five years. 8 Abraham breathed his last and died in a good old age, an old man and full of years, and was gathered to his people. 9 His sons Isaac and Ish′ma-el buried him in the cave of Mach-pē′lah, in the field of Ē′phron son of Zō′har the Hit′tīte, east of Mam′re, 10 the field that Abraham purchased from the Hit′tītes. There Abraham was buried, with his wife Sarah. 11 After the death of Abraham God blessed his son Isaac. And Isaac settled at Bē′er-la-haī-roi.

Ishmael's Descendants
(1 Chr 1.29–31)

12 These are the descendants of Ish′ma-el, Abraham's son, whom Hā′gar the Egyptian, Sarah's slave-girl, bore to Abraham. 13 These are the names of the sons of Ish′ma-el, named in the order of their birth: Ne-bā′i-oth, the firstborn of Ish′ma-el; and Kē′dar, Ad′bē-el, Mib′sam, 14 Mish′ma, Dū′mah, Mas′sa, 15 Hā′dad, Tē′ma, Jē′tur, Nā′phish, and Ked′e-mah. 16 These are the sons of Ish′ma-el and these are their names, by their villages and by their encampments, twelve princes according to their tribes. 17 (This is the length of the life of Ish′ma-el, one hundred thirty-seven years; he breathed his last and died, and was gathered to his people.) 18 They settled from Hav′i-lah to Shur, which is opposite Egypt in the direction of Assyria; he settled down*p* alongside of*q* all his people.

The Birth and Youth of Esau and Jacob
(Rom 9.10–12)

19 These are the descendants of Isaac, Abraham's son: Abraham was the father of Isaac, 20 and Isaac was forty years old when he married Rebekah, daughter of Be-thū′el the Ar-a-mē′an of Pad′dan-ar′am, sister of Lā′ban the Ar-a-mē′an. 21 Isaac

---

n Syr Tg: Heb *from coming to*   *o* Meaning of Heb word is uncertain   *p* Heb *he fell*   *q* Or *down in opposition to*

prayed to the LORD for his wife, because she was barren; and the LORD granted his prayer, and his wife Rebekah conceived. 22 The children struggled together within her; and she said, "If it is to be this way, why do I live?"r So she went to inquire of the LORD. 23 And the LORD said to her,

"Two nations are in your womb,
     and two peoples born of you shall be
          divided;
the one shall be stronger than the other,
     the elder shall serve the younger."

PRAY IT!
Sibling Rivalry

I t is common for siblings to have conflict in their relationship, but with Jacob and Esau, the conflict becomes extreme. Follow their story in Genesis, chapters 27–28, 33.

For another story of extreme sibling rivalry, see 37.12–36. Joseph's brothers (all sons of Jacob) are so jealous of him that they plot to kill him. But instead, he gets sold as a slave—and that turns out to be a great career move for him.

The story of the prodigal son in Lk 15.11–32 is yet another example of sibling rivalry.

Do you have any brothers or sisters? If so, how do you treat them? Do you ever pray for them? Do you ever tell them that you care about them—even if they drive you crazy at times?

If you don't have any brothers or sisters, how about cousins, neighbors, or friends? All relationships get better with prayer and care.

▶ Gen 25.19–34

24 When her time to give birth was at hand, there were twins in her womb. 25 The first came out red, all his body like a hairy mantle; so they named him Esau. 26 Afterward his brother came out, with his hand gripping Esau's heel; so he was named Jacob.s Isaac was sixty years old when she bore them.

27 When the boys grew up, Esau was a skillful hunter, a man of the field, while Jacob was a quiet

man, living in tents. 28 Isaac loved Esau, because he was fond of game; but Rebekah loved Jacob.

Esau Sells His Birthright
(Heb 12.16)

29 Once when Jacob was cooking a stew, Esau came in from the field, and he was famished. 30 Esau said to Jacob, "Let me eat some of that red stuff, for I am famished!" (Therefore he was called E´dom.t) 31 Jacob said, "First sell me your birthright." 32 Esau said, "I am about to die; of what use is a birthright to me?" 33 Jacob said, "Swear to me first."u So he swore to him, and sold his birthright to Jacob. 34 Then Jacob gave Esau bread and lentil stew, and he ate and drank, and rose and went his way. Thus Esau despised his birthright.

Isaac and Abimelech

Now there was a famine in the land, besides the former famine that had occurred in the days of Abraham. And Isaac went to Ge´rar, to King A·bim´e·lech of the Phi·lis´tines. 2 The LORD appeared to Isaacv and said, "Do not go down to Egypt; settle in the land that I shall show you. 3 Reside in this land as an alien, and I will be with you, and will bless you; for to you and to your descendants I will give all these lands, and I will fulfill the oath that I swore to your father Abraham. 4 I will make your offspring as numerous as the stars of heaven, and will give to your offspring all these lands; and all the nations of the earth shall gain blessing for themselves through your offspring, 5 because Abraham obeyed my voice and kept my charge, my commandments, my statutes, and my laws."

6 So Isaac settled in Ge´rar. 7 When the men of the place asked him about his wife, he said, "She is my sister"; for he was afraid to say, "My wife," thinking, "or else the men of the place might kill me for the sake of Rebekah, because she is attractive in appearance." 8 When Isaac had been there a long time, King A·bim´e·lech of the Phi·lis´tines looked out of a window and saw him fondling his wife Rebekah. 9 So A·bim´e·lech called for Isaac, and said, "So she is your wife! Why then did you say, 'She is my sister'?" Isaac said to him, "Because I thought I might die because of her." 10 A·bim´e·lech said, "What is this you have done to us? One of the people might easily have lain with your wife, and you would have brought guilt upon us." 11 So A·bim´e·lech warned all the people, saying, "Whoever touches this man or his wife shall be put to death."

---

r Syr: Meaning of Heb uncertain   s That is *He takes by the heel* or *He supplants*   t That is *Red*   u Heb *today*
v Heb *him*

12 Isaac sowed seed in that land, and in the same year reaped a hundredfold. The Lord blessed him, 13 and the man became rich; he prospered more and more until he became very wealthy. 14 He had possessions of flocks and herds, and a great household, so that the Phi•lis′tines envied him. 15 (Now the Phi•lis′tines had stopped up and filled with earth all the wells that his father's servants had dug in the days of his father Abraham.) 16 And A•bim′e•lech said to Isaac, "Go away from us; you have become too powerful for us."

17 So Isaac departed from there and camped in the valley of Gē′rar and settled there. 18 Isaac dug again the wells of water that had been dug in the days of his father Abraham; for the Phi•lis′tines had stopped them up after the death of Abraham; and he gave them the names that his father had given them. 19 But when Isaac's servants dug in the valley and found there a well of spring water, 20 the herders of Gē′rar quarreled with Isaac's herders, saying, "The water is ours." So he called the well Ē′sek,ʷ because they contended with him. 21 Then they dug another well, and they quarreled over that one also; so he called it Sit′nah.ˣ 22 He moved from there and dug another well, and they did not quarrel over it; so he called it Re•hō′both,ʸ saying, "Now the Lord has made room for us, and we shall be fruitful in the land."

23 From there he went up to Bē′er-shē′ba. 24 And that very night the Lord appeared to him and said, "I am the God of your father Abraham; do not be afraid, for I am with you and will bless you and make your offspring numerous for my servant Abraham's sake." 25 So he built an altar there, called on the name of the Lord, and pitched his tent there. And there Isaac's servants dug a well.

26 Then A•bim′e•lech went to him from Gē′rar, with A•huz′zath his adviser and Phī′col the commander of his army. 27 Isaac said to them, "Why have you come to me, seeing that you hate me and have sent me away from you?" 28 They said, "We see plainly that the Lord has been with you; so we say, let there be an oath between you and us, and let us make a covenant with you 29 so that you will do us no harm, just as we have not touched you and have done to you nothing but good and have sent you away in peace. You are now the blessed of the Lord." 30 So he made them a feast, and they ate and drank. 31 In the morning they rose early and exchanged oaths; and Isaac set them on their way, and they departed from him in peace. 32 That same day Isaac's servants came and told him about the well that they had dug, and said to him, "We have found water!" 33 He called it Shī′bah;ᶻ there-

fore the name of the city is Bē′er-shē′baᵃ to this day.

Esau's Hittite Wives

34 When Esau was forty years old, he married Judith daughter of Be•ē′rī the Hit′tite, and Bas′emath daughter of Ē′lon the Hit′tite; 35 and they made life bitter for Isaac and Rebekah.

Isaac Blesses Jacob

When Isaac was old and his eyes were dim so that he could not see, he called his elder son Esau and said to him, "My son"; and he answered, "Here I am." 2 He said, "See, I am old; I do not know the day of my death. 3 Now then, take your weapons, your quiver and your bow, and go out to the field, and hunt game for me. 4 Then prepare for me savory food, such as I like, and bring it to me to eat, so that I may bless you before I die."

5 Now Rebekah was listening when Isaac spoke to his son Esau. So when Esau went to the field to hunt for game and bring it, 6 Rebekah said to her son Jacob, "I heard your father say to your brother Esau, 7 'Bring me game, and prepare for me savory food to eat, that I may bless you before the Lord before I die.' 8 Now therefore, my son, obey my word as I command you. 9 Go to the flock, and get me two choice kids, so that I may prepare from them savory food for your father, such as he likes; 10 and you shall take it to your father to eat, so that he may bless you before he dies." 11 But Jacob said to his mother Rebekah, "Look, my brother Esau is a hairy man, and I am a man of smooth skin. 12 Perhaps my father will feel me, and I shall seem to be mocking him, and bring a curse on myself and not a blessing." 13 His mother said to him, "Let your curse be on me, my son; only obey my word, and go, get them for me." 14 So he went and got them and brought them to his mother; and his mother prepared savory food, such as his father loved. 15 Then Rebekah took the best garments of her elder son Esau, which were with her in the house, and put them on her younger son Jacob; 16 and she put the skins of the kids on his hands and on the smooth part of his neck. 17 Then she handed the savory food, and the bread that she had prepared, to her son Jacob.

18 So he went in to his father, and said, "My father"; and he said, "Here I am; who are you, my son?" 19 Jacob said to his father, "I am Esau your firstborn. I have done as you told me; now sit up

ʷ That is *Contention*   ˣ That is *Enmity*   ʸ That is *Broad places* or *Room*   ᶻ A word resembling the word for *oath*   ᵃ That is *Well of the oath* or *Well of seven*

GEN

and eat of my game, so that you may bless me." 20 But Isaac said to his son, "How is it that you have found it so quickly, my son?" He answered, "Because the LORD your God granted me success." 21 Then Isaac said to Jacob, "Come near, that I may feel you, my son, to know whether you are really my son Esau or not." 22 So Jacob went up to his father Isaac, who felt him and said, "The voice is Jacob's voice, but the hands are the hands of Esau." 23 He did not recognize him, because his hands were hairy like his brother Esau's hands; so he blessed him. 24 He said, "Are you really my son Esau?" He answered, "I am." 25 Then he said, "Bring it to me, that I may eat of my son's game and bless you." So he brought it to him, and he ate; and he brought him wine, and he drank. 26 Then his father Isaac said to him, "Come near and kiss me, my son." 27 So he came near and kissed him; and he smelled the smell of his garments, and blessed him, and said,

"Ah, the smell of my son
   is like the smell of a field that the LORD
      has blessed.
28 May God give you of the dew
      of heaven,
   and of the fatness of the earth,
      and plenty of grain and wine.
29 Let peoples serve you,
      and nations bow down to you.
   Be lord over your brothers,
      and may your mother's sons bow down
         to you.

Cursed be everyone who curses you,
   and blessed be everyone who blesses
      you!"

Esau's Lost Blessing
(Heb 12.17)

30 As soon as Isaac had finished blessing Jacob, when Jacob had scarcely gone out from the presence of his father Isaac, his brother Esau came in from his hunting. 31 He also prepared savory food, and brought it to his father. And he said to his father, "Let my father sit up and eat of his son's game, so that you may bless me." 32 His father Isaac said to him, "Who are you?" He answered, "I am your firstborn son, Esau." 33 Then Isaac trembled violently, and said, "Who was it then that hunted game and brought it to me, and I ate it all[b] before you came, and I have blessed him?—yes, and blessed he shall be!" 34 When Esau heard his father's words, he cried out with an exceedingly great and bitter cry, and said to his father, "Bless me, me also, father!" 35 But he said, "Your brother came deceitfully, and he has taken away your blessing." 36 Esau said, "Is he not rightly named Jacob?[c] For he has supplanted me these two times. He took away my birthright; and look, now he has taken away my blessing." Then he said, "Have you not reserved a blessing for me?" 37 Isaac answered Esau, "I have already made him your lord, and I have given him all his brothers as servants, and

---

b Cn: Heb *of all*   *c* That is *He supplants* or *He takes by the heel*

Introducing ▶ JACOB

According to the Bible, Abraham was the father of Isaac, and Isaac was the father of Jacob, and Jacob was the father of twelve sons who became the leaders of the twelve tribes of Israel. Jacob, like his ancestors, participated in the covenant with God that promised a great land and many descendants. He is portrayed as a very human character with a wide range of emotions and actions, both good and bad. Jacob is a repentant brother, a kind father, and a successful herder, but he is also a trickster who steals his brother Esau's birthright and his father's blessing (Gen 25.29–34; 27.1–29). It is no wonder that Jacob's name means "supplanter" or "heel grabber."

In a dream, God renews the covenant promises to Jacob (28.10–17), and in another dream (35.9–15), God changes Jacob's name to Israel (Gen 32.24–32; 33.4). Jacob's descendants become known as the Israelites. His story reveals that God's blessing continues to work even through flawed human beings.

▶ Gen 25.19—50.14

with grain and wine I have sustained him. What then can I do for you, my son?" ³⁸ Esau said to his father, "Have you only one blessing, father? Bless me, me also, father!" And Esau lifted up his voice and wept.

did you KNOW?

God's Surprising Choice

In most ancient cultures, including Israel's, the oldest son of the family was expected to inherit his father's property (the birthright) and authority (the blessing). In the story of Esau and Jacob, Jacob tricks Esau (the oldest son) out of his birthright (Gen 25.29–34) and deceives his blind father into giving him the blessing (27.1–29).

It is surprising that Genesis makes no comment on the morality of Jacob's actions. However, the story is not about morality but about God's justice: God is not bound by human expectations. Again and again in the Old Testament, God defies human rules by choosing the "little ones" for big responsibilities: Jacob, Joseph, Ruth, David, and Esther, for example. Even the Israelites themselves were an unlikely choice on God's part. Why didn't God choose a nation of great wealth and power instead of a group that was enslaved?

The story of Jacob and Esau reminds us that God does not bow to human rules, expectations, or plans. God's ways are often surprising! (For more on God's surprising choices, see reading plan 5, "The Justice of God.")

▶ Gen 27.1–40

39 Then his father Isaac answered him:
  "See, away from^d the fatness of the earth
      shall your home be,
  and away from^e the dew of heaven on
      high.
40 By your sword you shall live,
    and you shall serve your brother;
  but when you break loose,^f
    you shall break his yoke from your neck."

Jacob Escapes Esau's Fury

41 Now Esau hated Jacob because of the blessing with which his father had blessed him, and Esau said to himself, "The days of mourning for my father are approaching; then I will kill my brother Jacob." ⁴² But the words of her elder son Esau were told to Rebekah; so she sent and called her younger son Jacob and said to him, "Your brother Esau is consoling himself by planning to kill you. ⁴³ Now therefore, my son, obey my voice; flee at once to my brother La'ban in Har'an, ⁴⁴ and stay with him a while, until your brother's fury turns away— ⁴⁵ until your brother's anger against you turns away, and he forgets what you have done to him; then I will send, and bring you back from there. Why should I lose both of you in one day?"

46 Then Rebekah said to Isaac, "I am weary of my life because of the Hit'tite women. If Jacob marries one of the Hit'tite women such as these, one of the women of the land, what good will my life be to me?"

Then Isaac called Jacob and blessed him, and charged him, "You shall not marry one of the Ca'naan•ite women. ² Go at once to Pad'dan-ar'am to the house of Be•thu'el, your mother's father; and take as wife from there one of the daughters of La'ban, your mother's brother. ³ May God Almighty^g bless you and make you fruitful and numerous, that you may become a company of peoples. ⁴ May he give to you the blessing of Abraham, to you and to your offspring with you, so that you may take possession of the land where you now live as an alien—land that God gave to Abraham." ⁵ Thus Isaac sent Jacob away; and he went to Pad'dan-ar'am, to La'ban son of Be•thu'el the Ar•a•me'an, the brother of Rebekah, Jacob's and Esau's mother.

Esau Marries Ishmael's Daughter

6 Now Esau saw that Isaac had blessed Jacob and sent him away to Pad'dan-ar'am to take a wife from there, and that as he blessed him he charged him, "You shall not marry one of the Ca'naan•ite women," ⁷ and that Jacob had obeyed his father and his mother and gone to Pad'dan-ar'am. ⁸ So when Esau saw that the Ca'naan•ite women did not please his father Isaac, ⁹ Esau went to Ish'ma•el and took Ma'ha•lath daughter of Abraham's son Ish'ma•el, and sister of Ne•ba'i•oth, to be his wife in addition to the wives he had.

---

^d Or *See, of*   ^e Or *and of*   ^f Meaning of Heb uncertain
^g Traditional rendering of Heb *El Shaddai*

GEN

Jacob's Dream at Bethel

10 Jacob left Bē′er-shē′ba and went toward Har′an. 11 He came to a certain place and stayed there for the night, because the sun had set. Taking one of the stones of the place, he put it under

Friendship with God

Just as Jacob is leaving his home and everything he knows, God establishes a personal relationship with him through a dream. In this relationship, God and Jacob interact personally, are accountable to each other, and trust each other. Jacob will need this relationship to help him through the tough times ahead. See Gen 32.22–32 for further developments in Jacob's relationship with God.

God, I want to know your presence. Use my dreams and my waking thoughts, use my family, friends, and neighbors, use your holy word. Use them all to reach me. For I know your presence will sustain me on my most difficult journeys, as it did Jacob.

▶ Gen 28.10–22

his head and lay down in that place. 12 And he dreamed that there was a ladder*h* set up on the earth, the top of it reaching to heaven; and the angels of God were ascending and descending on it. 13 And the LORD stood beside him*i* and said, "I am the LORD, the God of Abraham your father and the God of Isaac; the land on which you lie I will give to you and to your offspring; 14 and your offspring shall be like the dust of the earth, and you shall spread abroad to the west and to the east and to the north and to the south; and all the families of the earth shall be blessed*j* in you and in your offspring. 15 Know that I am with you and will keep you wherever you go, and will bring you back to this land; for I will not leave you until I have done what I have promised you." 16 Then Jacob woke from his sleep and said, "Surely the LORD is in this place—and I did not know it!" 17 And he was afraid, and said, "How awesome is this place! This is none other than the house of God, and this is the gate of heaven."

18 So Jacob rose early in the morning, and he took the stone that he had put under his head and

set it up for a pillar and poured oil on the top of it. 19 He called that place Beth′el;*k* but the name of the city was Luz at the first. 20 Then Jacob made a vow, saying, "If God will be with me, and will keep me in this way that I go, and will give me bread to eat and clothing to wear, 21 so that I come again to my father's house in peace, then the LORD shall be my God, 22 and this stone, which I have set up for a pillar, shall be God's house; and of all that you give me I will surely give one-tenth to you."

Jacob Meets Rachel

Then Jacob went on his journey, and came to the land of the people of the east. 2 As he looked, he saw a well in the field and three flocks of sheep lying there beside it; for out of that well the flocks were watered. The stone on the well's mouth was large, 3 and when all the flocks were gathered there, the shepherds would roll the stone from the mouth of the well, and water the sheep, and put the stone back in its place on the mouth of the well.

4 Jacob said to them, "My brothers, where do you come from?" They said, "We are from Har′an." 5 He said to them, "Do you know Lā′ban son of Nā′hor?" They said, "We do." 6 He said to them, "Is it well with him?" "Yes," they replied, "and here is his daughter Rachel, coming with the sheep." 7 He said, "Look, it is still broad daylight; it is not time for the animals to be gathered together. Water the sheep, and go, pasture them." 8 But they said, "We cannot until all the flocks are gathered together, and the stone is rolled from the mouth of the well; then we water the sheep."

9 While he was still speaking with them, Rachel came with her father's sheep; for she kept them. 10 Now when Jacob saw Rachel, the daughter of his mother's brother Lā′ban, and the sheep of his mother's brother Lā′ban, Jacob went up and rolled the stone from the well's mouth, and watered the flock of his mother's brother Lā′ban. 11 Then Jacob kissed Rachel, and wept aloud. 12 And Jacob told Rachel that he was her father's kinsman, and that he was Rebekah's son; and she ran and told her father.

13 When Lā′ban heard the news about his sister's son Jacob, he ran to meet him; he embraced him and kissed him, and brought him to his house. Jacob*l* told Lā′ban all these things, 14 and Lā′ban said to him, "Surely you are my bone and my flesh!" And he stayed with him a month.

h Or *stairway* or *ramp*   *i* Or *stood above it*   *j* Or *shall bless themselves*   *k* That is *House of God*   *l* Heb *He*

Jacob Marries Laban's Daughters

15 Then Lā'ban said to Jacob, "Because you are my kinsman, should you therefore serve me for nothing? Tell me, what shall your wages be?" ¹⁶ Now Lā'ban had two daughters; the name of the elder was Leah, and the name of the younger was Rachel. ¹⁷ Leah's eyes were lovely,^m and Rachel was graceful and beautiful. ¹⁸ Jacob loved Rachel; so he said, "I will serve you seven years for your younger daughter Rachel." ¹⁹ Lā'ban said, "It is better that I give her to you than that I should give her to any other man; stay with me." ²⁰ So Jacob served seven years for Rachel, and they seemed to him but a few days because of the love he had for her.

21 Then Jacob said to Lā'ban, "Give me my wife that I may go in to her, for my time is completed." ²² So Lā'ban gathered together all the people of the place, and made a feast. ²³ But in the evening he took his daughter Leah and brought her to Jacob; and he went in to her. ²⁴ (Lā'ban gave his maid Zil'pah to his daughter Leah to be her maid.) ²⁵ When morning came, it was Leah! And Jacob said to Lā'ban, "What is this you have done to me? Did I not serve with you for Rachel? Why then have you deceived me?" ²⁶ Lā'ban said, "This is not done in our country—giving the younger before the firstborn. ²⁷ Complete the week of this one, and we will give you the other also in return for serving me another seven years." ²⁸ Jacob did so, and completed her week; then Lā'ban gave him his daughter Rachel as a wife. ²⁹ (Lā'ban gave his maid Bil'hah to his daughter Rachel to be her

will love me." ³³ She conceived again and bore a son, and said, "Because the LORD has heard^p that I am hated, he has given me this son also"; and she named him Sim'e·on. ³⁴ Again she conceived and bore a son, and said, "Now this time my husband will be joined^q to me, because I have borne him three sons"; therefore he was named Levi. ³⁵ She conceived again and bore a son, and said, "This time I will praise^r the LORD"; therefore she named him Judah; then she ceased bearing.

When Rachel saw that she bore Jacob no children, she envied her sister; and she said to Jacob, "Give me children, or I shall die!" ² Jacob became very angry with Rachel and said, "Am I in the place of God, who has withheld from you the fruit of the womb?" ³ Then she said, "Here is my maid Bil'hah; go in to her, that she may bear upon my knees and that I too may have children through her." ⁴ So she gave him her maid Bil'hah as a wife; and Jacob went in to her. ⁵ And Bil'hah conceived and bore Jacob a son. ⁶ Then Rachel said, "God has judged me, and has also heard my voice and given me a son"; therefore she named him Dan.^s ⁷ Rachel's maid Bil'hah conceived again and bore Jacob a second son. ⁸ Then Rachel said, "With mighty wrestlings I have wrestled^t with my sister, and have prevailed"; so she named him Naph'ta·lī.

9 When Leah saw that she had ceased bearing children, she took her maid Zil'pah and gave her to Jacob as a wife. ¹⁰ Then Leah's maid Zil'pah bore Jacob a son. ¹¹ And Leah said, "Good for-

LIVE IT!

When Lies Boomerang

Predictably, Jacob becomes upset when he finds out that he has been deceived by Laban (Gen 29.25). Yet, the very reason Jacob is working for his uncle Laban is that he has fled from his brother Esau, whom he deceived several years ago (27.1–40). Jacob's lies and deceit have boomeranged, so now he is the victim.

Somehow, our lies, gossip, and manipulation of others often come back to haunt us. So it was with Jacob. So it will be with us if we follow his example.

▶ Gen 29.15–30

maid.) ³⁰ So Jacob went in to Rachel also, and he loved Rachel more than Leah. He served Lā'ban^n for another seven years.

31 When the LORD saw that Leah was unloved, he opened her womb; but Rachel was barren. ³² Leah conceived and bore a son, and she named him Reuben;^o for she said, "Because the LORD has looked on my affliction; surely now my husband

tune!" so she named him Gad.^u ¹² Leah's maid Zil'pah bore Jacob a second son. ¹³ And Leah said, "Happy am I! For the women will call me happy"; so she named him Ash'er.^v

---

^m Meaning of Heb uncertain   ^n Heb *him*   ^o That is *See, a son*   ^p Heb *shama*   ^q Heb *lawah*   ^r Heb *hodah*   ^s That is *He judged*   ^t Heb *niphtal*   ^u That is *Fortune*   ^v That is *Happy*

GEN

14 In the days of wheat harvest Reuben went and found mandrakes in the field, and brought them to his mother Leah. Then Rachel said to Leah, "Please give me some of your son's mandrakes." 15 But she said to her, "Is it a small matter that you have taken away my husband? Would you take away my son's mandrakes also?" Rachel said, "Then he may lie with you tonight for your son's mandrakes." 16 When Jacob came from the field in the evening, Leah went out to meet him, and said, "You must come in to me; for I have hired you with my son's mandrakes." So he lay with her that night. 17 And God heeded Leah, and she conceived and bore Jacob a fifth son. 18 Leah said, "God has given me my hire*w* because I gave my maid to my husband"; so she named him Is'sachar. 19 And Leah conceived again, and she bore Jacob a sixth son. 20 Then Leah said, "God has endowed me with a good dowry; now my husband will honor*x* me, because I have borne him six sons"; so she named him Zeb'ū•lun. 21 Afterwards she bore a daughter, and named her Dī'nah.

22 Then God remembered Rachel, and God heeded her and opened her womb. 23 She conceived and bore a son, and said, "God has taken away my reproach"; 24 and she named him Joseph,*y* saying, "May the LORD add to me another son!"

Jacob Prospers at Laban's Expense

25 When Rachel had borne Joseph, Jacob said to Lā'ban, "Send me away, that I may go to my own home and country. 26 Give me my wives and my children for whom I have served you, and let me go; for you know very well the service I have given you." 27 But Lā'ban said to him, "If you will allow me to say so, I have learned by divination that the LORD has blessed me because of you; 28 name your wages, and I will give it." 29 Jacob said to him, "You yourself know how I have served you, and how your cattle have fared with me. 30 For you had little before I came, and it has increased abundantly; and the LORD has blessed you wherever I turned. But now when shall I provide for my own household also?" 31 He said, "What shall I give you?" Jacob said, "You shall not give me anything; if you will do this for me, I will again feed your flock and keep it: 32 let me pass through all your flock today, removing from it every speckled and spotted sheep and every black lamb, and the spotted and speckled among the goats; and such shall be my wages. 33 So my honesty will answer for me later, when you come to look into my wages with you. Every one that is not speckled and spotted among the goats and black among the lambs, if found with me, shall be counted stolen." 34 Lā'ban said, "Good! Let it be as you have said."

35 But that day Lā'ban removed the male goats that were striped and spotted, and all the female goats that were speckled and spotted, every one that had white on it, and every lamb that was black, and put them in charge of his sons; 36 and he set a distance of three days' journey between himself and Jacob, while Jacob was pasturing the rest of Lā'ban's flock.

37 Then Jacob took fresh rods of poplar and almond and plane, and peeled white streaks in them, exposing the white of the rods. 38 He set the rods that he had peeled in front of the flocks in the troughs, that is, the watering places, where the flocks came to drink. And since they bred when they came to drink, 39 the flocks bred in front of the rods, and so the flocks produced young that were striped, speckled, and spotted. 40 Jacob separated the lambs, and set the faces of the flocks toward the striped and the completely black animals in the flock of Lā'ban; and he put his own droves apart, and did not put them with Lā'ban's flock. 41 Whenever the stronger of the flock were breeding, Jacob laid the rods in the troughs before the eyes of the flock, that they might breed among the rods, 42 but for the feebler of the flock he did not lay them there; so the feebler were Lā'ban's, and the stronger Jacob's. 43 Thus the man grew exceedingly rich, and had large flocks, and male and female slaves, and camels and donkeys.

Jacob Flees with Family and Flocks

Now Jacob heard that the sons of Lā'ban were saying, "Jacob has taken all that was our father's; he has gained all this wealth from what belonged to our father." 2 And Jacob saw that Lā'ban did not regard him as favorably as he did before. 3 Then the LORD said to Jacob, "Return to the land of your ancestors and to your kindred, and I will be with you." 4 So Jacob sent and called Rachel and Leah into the field where his flock was, 5 and said to them, "I see that your father does not regard me as favorably as he did before. But the God of my father has been with me. 6 You know that I have served your father with all my strength; 7 yet your father has cheated me and changed my wages ten times, but God did not permit him to harm me. 8 If he said, 'The speckled shall be your wages,' then all the flock bore speckled; and if he said, 'The striped shall be your wages,' then all the flock bore striped. 9 Thus God has taken away the livestock of your father, and given them to me.

10 "During the mating of the flock I once had a dream in which I looked up and saw that the male goats that leaped upon the flock were striped,

---

w Heb *sakar*   *x* Heb *zabal*   *y* That is *He adds*

speckled, and mottled. 11 Then the angel of God said to me in the dream, 'Jacob,' and I said, 'Here I am!' 12 And he said, 'Look up and see that all the goats that leap on the flock are striped, speckled, and mottled; for I have seen all that Lā'ban is doing to you. 13 I am the God of Beth'el,*z* where you anointed a pillar and made a vow to me. Now leave this land at once and return to the land of your birth.' " 14 Then Rachel and Leah answered him, "Is there any portion or inheritance left to us in our father's house? 15 Are we not regarded by him as foreigners? For he has sold us, and he has been using up the money given for us. 16 All the property that God has taken away from our father belongs to us and to our children; now then, do whatever God has said to you."

17 So Jacob arose, and set his children and his wives on camels; 18 and he drove away all his livestock, all the property that he had gained, the livestock in his possession that he had acquired in Pad'dan-ar'am, to go to his father Isaac in the land of Cā'naan.

19 Now Lā'ban had gone to shear his sheep, and Rachel stole her father's household gods. 20 And Jacob deceived Lā'ban the Ar•a•mē'an, in that he did not tell him that he intended to flee. 21 So he fled with all that he had; starting out he crossed the Euphrates,*a* and set his face toward the hill country of Gil'e•ad.

Laban Overtakes Jacob

22 On the third day Lā'ban was told that Jacob had fled. 23 So he took his kinsfolk with him and pursued him for seven days until he caught up with him in the hill country of Gil'e•ad. 24 But God came to Lā'ban the Ar•a•mē'an in a dream by night, and said to him, "Take heed that you say not a word to Jacob, either good or bad."

25 Lā'ban overtook Jacob. Now Jacob had pitched his tent in the hill country, and Lā'ban with his kinsfolk camped in the hill country of Gil'e•ad. 26 Lā'ban said to Jacob, "What have you done? You have deceived me, and carried away my daughters like captives of the sword. 27 Why did you flee secretly and deceive me and not tell me? I would have sent you away with mirth and songs, with tambourine and lyre. 28 And why did you not permit me to kiss my sons and my daughters farewell? What you have done is foolish. 29 It is in my power to do you harm; but the God of your father spoke to me last night, saying, 'Take heed that you speak to Jacob neither good nor bad.' 30 Even though you had to go because you longed greatly for your father's house, why did you steal my gods?" 31 Jacob answered Lā'ban, "Because I was afraid, for I thought that you would take your

daughters from me by force. 32 But anyone with whom you find your gods shall not live. In the presence of our kinsfolk, point out what I have that is yours, and take it." Now Jacob did not know that Rachel had stolen the gods.*b*

33 So Lā'ban went into Jacob's tent, and into Leah's tent, and into the tent of the two maids, but he did not find them. And he went out of Leah's tent, and entered Rachel's. 34 Now Rachel had taken the household gods and put them in the camel's saddle, and sat on them. Lā'ban felt all about in the tent, but did not find them. 35 And she said to her father, "Let not my lord be angry that I cannot rise before you, for the way of women is upon me." So he searched, but did not find the household gods.

36 Then Jacob became angry, and upbraided Lā'ban. Jacob said to Lā'ban, "What is my offense? What is my sin, that you have hotly pursued me? 37 Although you have felt about through all my goods, what have you found of all your household goods? Set it here before my kinsfolk and your kinsfolk, so that they may decide between us two. 38 These twenty years I have been with you; your ewes and your female goats have not miscarried, and I have not eaten the rams of your flocks. 39 That which was torn by wild beasts I did not bring to you; I bore the loss of it myself; of my hand you required it, whether stolen by day or stolen by night. 40 It was like this with me: by day the heat consumed me, and the cold by night, and my sleep fled from my eyes. 41 These twenty years I have been in your house; I served you fourteen years for your two daughters, and six years for your flock, and you have changed my wages ten times. 42 If the God of my father, the God of Abraham and the Fear*c* of Isaac, had not been on my side, surely now you would have sent me away emptyhanded. God saw my affliction and the labor of my hands, and rebuked you last night."

Laban and Jacob Make a Covenant

43 Then Lā'ban answered and said to Jacob, "The daughters are my daughters, the children are my children, the flocks are my flocks, and all that you see is mine. But what can I do today about these daughters of mine, or about their children whom they have borne? 44 Come now, let us make a covenant, you and I; and let it be a witness between you and me." 45 So Jacob took a stone, and set it up as a pillar. 46 And Jacob said to his kinsfolk, "Gather stones," and they took stones, and made a heap; and they ate there by the heap.

---

z Cn: Meaning of Heb uncertain   *a* Heb *the river*
b Heb *them*   *c* Meaning of Heb uncertain

47 Lā'ban called it Jē·gar-sā·ha·dū'tha:*d* but Jacob called it Gal'e·ed.*e* 48 Lā'ban said, "This heap is a witness between you and me today." Therefore he called it Gal'e·ed, 49 and the pillar*f* Miz'pah,*g* for he said, "The LORD watch between you and me, when we are absent one from the other. 50 If you ill-treat my daughters, or if you take wives in addition to my daughters, though no one else is with us, remember that God is witness between you and me."

51 Then Lā'ban said to Jacob, "See this heap and see the pillar, which I have set between you and me. 52 This heap is a witness, and the pillar is a witness, that I will not pass beyond this heap to you, and you will not pass beyond this heap and this pillar to me, for harm. 53 May the God of Abraham and the God of Nā'hor"—the God of their father—"judge between us." So Jacob swore by the Fear*h* of his father Isaac, 54 and Jacob offered a sacrifice on the height and called his kinsfolk to eat bread; and they ate bread and tarried all night in the hill country.

55*i* Early in the morning Lā'ban rose up, and kissed his grandchildren and his daughters and blessed them; then he departed and returned home.
Jacob went on his way and the angels of God met him; 2 and when Jacob saw them he said, "This is God's camp!" So he called that place Mā·ha·nā'im.*j*

Jacob Sends Presents to Appease Esau

3 Jacob sent messengers before him to his brother Esau in the land of Sē'ir, the country of É'dom, 4 instructing them, "Thus you shall say to my lord Esau: Thus says your servant Jacob, 'I have lived with Lā'ban as an alien, and stayed until now; 5 and I have oxen, donkeys, flocks, male and female slaves; and I have sent to tell my lord, in order that I may find favor in your sight.' "

6 The messengers returned to Jacob, saying, "We came to your brother Esau, and he is coming to meet you, and four hundred men are with him." 7 Then Jacob was greatly afraid and distressed; and he divided the people that were with him, and the flocks and herds and camels, into two companies, 8 thinking, "If Esau comes to the one company and destroys it, then the company that is left will escape."

9 And Jacob said, "O God of my father Abraham and God of my father Isaac, O LORD who said to me, 'Return to your country and to your kindred, and I will do you good,' 10 I am not worthy of the least of all the steadfast love and all the faithfulness that you have shown to your servant, for with only my staff I crossed this Jordan; and now I have become two companies. 11 Deliver me,

PRAY IT
Wrestling with God

Even after twenty years, Jacob is anxious about meeting Esau again. This time, Jacob uses his craftiness not to deceive Esau but to gain Esau's good graces. Then while on the way home, he has an amazing religious experience. Many Scripture scholars believe that the strange wrestling encounter is a symbol that Jacob has become a changed person. He finally realizes that in all his troubles, God was his true opponent.

Perhaps at times you have wrestled with yourself or with God. It is not so much that God is your opponent or that you are in a contest. It is the wrestling itself that matters. When you face the challenges, especially the big ones, you wrestle between the person you are now and the person God is calling you to be.

In your prayer, reflect or journal on the following questions:
- When does it seem like God is trying to wrestle with you? What does it feel like?
- Is God challenging you about something in your life right now?
- What blessings might you gain in accepting God's challenge and changing your life?

▸ Gen 32.22–32

please, from the hand of my brother, from the hand of Esau, for I am afraid of him; he may come and kill us all, the mothers with the children. 12 Yet you have said, 'I will surely do you good, and make your offspring as the sand of the sea, which cannot be counted because of their number.' "

13 So he spent that night there, and from what he had with him he took a present for his brother Esau, 14 two hundred female goats and twenty male goats, two hundred ewes and twenty rams, 15 thirty milch camels and their colts, forty cows and ten bulls, twenty female donkeys and ten male donkeys. 16 These he delivered into the hand of his

---

d In Aramaic *The heap of witness*   *e* In Hebrew *The heap of witness*   *f* Compare Sam: MT lacks *the pillar*   *g* That is *Watchpost*   *h* Meaning of Heb uncertain   *i* Ch 32.1 in Heb   *j* Here taken to mean *Two camps*

servants, every drove by itself, and said to his servants, "Pass on ahead of me, and put a space between drove and drove." [17] He instructed the foremost, "When Esau my brother meets you, and asks you, 'To whom do you belong? Where are you going? And whose are these ahead of you?' [18] then you shall say, 'They belong to your servant Jacob; they are a present sent to my lord Esau; and moreover he is behind us.' " [19] He likewise instructed the second and the third and all who followed the droves, "You shall say the same thing to Esau when you meet him, [20] and you shall say, 'Moreover your servant Jacob is behind us.' " For he thought, "I may appease him with the present that goes ahead of me, and afterwards I shall see his face; perhaps he will accept me." [21] So the present passed on ahead of him; and he himself spent that night in the camp.

Jacob Wrestles at Peniel

22 The same night he got up and took his two wives, his two maids, and his eleven children, and crossed the ford of the Jab'bok. [23] He took them and sent them across the stream, and likewise everything that he had. [24] Jacob was left alone; and a man wrestled with him until daybreak. [25] When the man saw that he did not prevail against Jacob, he struck him on the hip socket; and Jacob's hip was put out of joint as he wrestled with him. [26] Then he said, "Let me go, for the day is breaking." But Jacob said, "I will not let you go, unless you bless me." [27] So he said to him, "What is your name?" And he said, "Jacob." [28] Then the man[k] said,

"You shall no longer be called Jacob, but Israel,[l] for you have striven with God and with humans,[m] and have prevailed." [29] Then Jacob asked him, "Please tell me your name." But he said, "Why is it that you ask my name?" And there he blessed him. [30] So Jacob called the place Pe·ni'el,[n] saying, "For I have seen God face to face, and yet my life is preserved." [31] The sun rose upon him as he passed Pe·nu'el, limping because of his hip. [32] Therefore to this day the Israelites do not eat the thigh muscle that is on the hip socket, because he struck Jacob on the hip socket at the thigh muscle.

Jacob and Esau Meet

Now Jacob looked up and saw Esau coming, and four hundred men with him. So he divided the children among Leah and Rachel and the two maids. [2] He put the maids with their children in front, then Leah with her children, and Rachel and Joseph last of all. [3] He himself went on ahead of them, bowing himself to the ground seven times, until he came near his brother.

4 But Esau ran to meet him, and embraced him, and fell on his neck and kissed him, and they wept. [5] When Esau looked up and saw the women and children, he said, "Who are these with you?" Jacob said, "The children whom God has graciously given your servant." [6] Then the maids drew near, they and their children, and bowed down;

---

k Heb *he*   l That is *The one who strives with God* or *God strives*   m Or *with divine and human beings*   n That is *The face of God*

Letting Go of the Past

LIVE IT!

Jacob is understandably apprehensive as he approaches his long-estranged twin brother. How will Esau react? But Esau, who was wronged by Jacob, runs to meet him and gives him a hug. All is forgiven, and the two are reconciled at last. This story is like the parable of the prodigal son in Lk 15.11–32.

All of us have wronged others, especially the people we care about most. All of us have also experienced forgiveness. Nothing is quite like the freedom that comes with genuine forgiveness and reconciliation. A burden is lifted. A heavy heart is made lighter. A vengeful attitude is transformed into a feeling of inner peace and harmony. This is the work of God's grace. Forgiveness and reconciliation are powerful signs of the presence of God. We can almost feel the enormous sense of relief experienced by Jacob as he realizes his brother holds no grudge.

Does a relationship in your life need forgiveness and reconciliation? If so, what can you do to bring about healing in this relationship?

▶ Gen 33.1–17

7 Leah likewise and her children drew near and bowed down; and finally Joseph and Rachel drew near, and they bowed down. 8 Esau said, "What do you mean by all this company that I met?" Jacob answered, "To find favor with my lord." 9 But Esau said, "I have enough, my brother; keep what you have for yourself." 10 Jacob said, "No, please; if I find favor with you, then accept my present from my hand; for truly to see your face is like seeing the face of God—since you have received me with such favor. 11 Please accept my gift that is brought to you, because God has dealt graciously with me, and because I have everything I want." So he urged him, and he took it.

12 Then Esau said, "Let us journey on our way, and I will go alongside you." 13 But Jacob said to him, "My lord knows that the children are frail and that the flocks and herds, which are nursing, are a care to me; and if they are overdriven for one day, all the flocks will die. 14 Let my lord pass on ahead of his servant, and I will lead on slowly, according to the pace of the cattle that are before me and according to the pace of the children, until I come to my lord in Sē'ir."

15 So Esau said, "Let me leave with you some of the people who are with me." But he said, "Why should my lord be so kind to me?" 16 So Esau returned that day on his way to Sē'ir. 17 But Jacob journeyed to Suc'coth,*o* and built himself a house, and made booths for his cattle; therefore the place is called Suc'coth.

Jacob Reaches Shechem

18 Jacob came safely to the city of Shē'chem, which is in the land of Cā'naan, on his way from Pad'dan-ar'am; and he camped before the city. 19 And from the sons of Hā'mor, Shē'chem's father, he bought for one hundred pieces of money*p* the plot of land on which he had pitched his tent. 20 There he erected an altar and called it El-Ē-lō'he-Is'rā-el.*q*

The Rape of Dinah

Now Dī'nah the daughter of Leah, whom she had borne to Jacob, went out to visit the women of the region. 2 When Shē'chem son of Hā'mor the Hī'vite, prince of the region, saw her, he seized her and lay with her by force. 3 And his soul was drawn to Dī'nah daughter of Jacob; he loved the girl, and spoke tenderly to her. 4 So Shē'chem spoke to his father Hā'mor, saying, "Get me this girl to be my wife."

5 Now Jacob heard that Shē'chem*r* had defiled his daughter Dī'nah; but his sons were with his cattle in the field, so Jacob held his peace until they came. 6 And Hā'mor the father of Shē'chem went out to Jacob to speak with him, 7 just as the sons of Jacob came in from the field. When they heard of it, the men were indignant and very angry, because he had committed an outrage in Israel by lying with Jacob's daughter, for such a thing ought not to be done.

8 But Hā'mor spoke with them, saying, "The heart of my son Shē'chem longs for your daughter; please give her to him in marriage. 9 Make marriages with us; give your daughters to us, and take our daughters for yourselves. 10 You shall live with us; and the land shall be open to you; live and trade in it, and get property in it." 11 Shē'chem also said to her father and to her brothers, "Let me find favor with you, and whatever you say to me I will give. 12 Put the marriage present and gift as high as you like, and I will give whatever you ask me; only give me the girl to be my wife."

13 The sons of Jacob answered Shē'chem and his father Hā'mor deceitfully, because he had defiled their sister Dī'nah. 14 They said to them, "We cannot do this thing, to give our sister to one who is uncircumcised, for that would be a disgrace to us. 15 Only on this condition will we consent to you: that you will become as we are and every male among you be circumcised. 16 Then we will give our daughters to you, and we will take your daughters for ourselves, and we will live among you and become one people. 17 But if you will not listen to us and be circumcised, then we will take our daughter and be gone."

18 Their words pleased Hā'mor and Hā'mor's son Shē'chem. 19 And the young man did not delay to do the thing, because he was delighted with Jacob's daughter. Now he was the most honored of all his family. 20 So Hā'mor and his son Shē'chem came to the gate of their city and spoke to the men of their city, saying, 21 "These people are friendly with us; let them live in the land and trade in it, for the land is large enough for them; let us take their daughters in marriage, and let us give them our daughters. 22 Only on this condition will they agree to live among us, to become one people: that every male among us be circumcised as they are circumcised. 23 Will not their livestock, their property, and all their animals be ours? Only let us agree with them, and they will live among us." 24 And all who went out of the city gate heeded Hā'mor and his son Shē'chem; and every male was circumcised, all who went out of the gate of his city.

---

o That is *Booths* *p* Heb *one hundred qesitah* *q* That is *God, the God of Israel* *r* Heb *he*

Dinah's Brothers Avenge Their Sister

25 On the third day, when they were still in pain, two of the sons of Jacob, Sim'ē•on and Levi, Dī'nah's brothers, took their swords and came against the city unawares, and killed all the males. 26 They killed Hā'mor and his son Shē'chem with the sword, and took Dī'nah out of Shē'chem's house, and went away. 27 And the other sons of Jacob came upon the slain, and plundered the city, because their sister had been defiled. 28 They took their flocks and their herds, their donkeys, and whatever was in the city and in the field. 29 All their wealth, all their little ones and their wives, all that was in the houses, they captured and made their prey. 30 Then Jacob said to Sim'ē•on and Levi, "You have brought trouble on me by making me odious to the inhabitants of the land, the Cā'naan-ītes and the Per'iz•zītes; my numbers are few, and if they gather themselves against me and attack me, I shall be destroyed, both I and my household." 31 But they said, "Should our sister be treated like a whore?"

Jacob Returns to Bethel

God said to Jacob, "Arise, go up to Beth'el, and settle there. Make an altar there to the God who appeared to you when you fled from your brother Esau." 2 So Jacob said to his household and to all who were with him, "Put away the foreign gods that are among you, and purify yourselves, and change your clothes; 3 then come, let us go up to Beth'el, that I may make an altar there to the God who answered me in the day of my distress and has been with me wherever I have gone." 4 So they gave to Jacob all the foreign gods that they had, and the rings that were in their ears; and Jacob hid them under the oak that was near Shē'chem.

5 As they journeyed, a terror from God fell upon the cities all around them, so that no one pursued them. 6 Jacob came to Luz (that is, Beth'el), which is in the land of Cā'naan, he and all the people who were with him, 7 and there he built an altar and called the place El-beth'el,ˢ because it was there that God had revealed himself to him when he fled from his brother. 8 And Deb'-or•ah, Rebekah's nurse, died, and she was buried under an oak below Beth'el. So it was called Al'-lon-bac'uth.ᵗ

9 God appeared to Jacob again when he came from Pad'dan-ar'am, and he blessed him. 10 God said to him, "Your name is Jacob; no longer shall you be called Jacob, but Israel shall be your name." So he was called Israel. 11 God said to him, "I am God Almighty:ᵘ be fruitful and multiply; a nation and a company of nations shall come from you, and kings shall spring from you. 12 The land that I gave to Abraham and Isaac I will give to you, and I will give the land to your offspring after you." 13 Then God went up from him at the place where he had spoken with him. 14 Jacob set up a pillar in the place where he had spoken with him, a pillar of stone; and he poured out a drink offering on it, and poured oil on it. 15 So Jacob called the place where God had spoken with him Beth'el.

ˢ That is *God of Bethel*   ᵗ That is *Oak of weeping*
ᵘ Traditional rendering of Heb *El Shaddai*

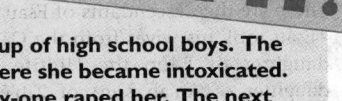

No Way, Shechem!

A news article reported on the rape of a girl by a group of high school boys. The girl was dating one of the boys and went to a party where she became intoxicated. The boys decided to take advantage of her and one-by-one raped her. The next day, she told her parents what had happened, the police were contacted, and the boys were arrested. Many people were left wondering how this could have happened in their little town.

Rape is more about power than it is about sex. The story in Genesis, chapter 34, tells us of Shechem, a local prince, who rapes Dinah. Because of his power, he figured he could do what he wanted to her. But in the end, his life is taken.

The boys in the story above felt that they had the power to do what they wanted, but in the end, they were arrested and sentenced to serve time in a juvenile facility. We are to respect one another. Position or power does not give us the right to commit sexual violence. Rape and any other sexual abuse is an outrage to God.

▶ Gen 34.1–31

The Birth of Benjamin and the Death of Rachel

16 Then they journeyed from Beth'el; and when they were still some distance from Eph'rath, Rachel was in childbirth, and she had hard labor. 17 When she was in her hard labor, the midwife said to her, "Do not be afraid; for now you will have another son." 18 As her soul was departing (for she died), she named him Ben-o′ni;*v* but his father called him Benjamin.*w* 19 So Rachel died, and she was buried on the way to Eph'rath (that is, Bethlehem), 20 and Jacob set up a pillar at her grave; it is the pillar of Rachel's tomb, which is there to this day. 21 Israel journeyed on, and pitched his tent beyond the tower of E′der.

22 While Israel lived in that land, Reuben went and lay with Bil'hah his father's concubine; and Israel heard of it.

Now the sons of Jacob were twelve. 23 The sons of Leah: Reuben (Jacob's firstborn), Sim′e·on, Levi, Judah, Is′sa·char, and Zeb′u·lun. 24 The sons of Rachel: Joseph and Benjamin. 25 The sons of Bil'hah, Rachel's maid: Dan and Naph′ta·li. 26 The sons of Zil'pah, Leah's maid: Gad and Ash′er. These were the sons of Jacob who were born to him in Pad′-dan-ar′am.

The Death of Isaac

27 Jacob came to his father Isaac at Mam′re, or Kir′i·ath-ar′ba (that is, He′bron), where Abraham and Isaac had resided as aliens. 28 Now the days of Isaac were one hundred eighty years. 29 And Isaac breathed his last; he died and was gathered to his people, old and full of days; and his sons Esau and Jacob buried him.

Esau's Descendants
(1 Chr 1.35–42)

These are the descendants of Esau (that is, E′dom). 2 Esau took his wives from the Ca·naan·ites: A′dah daughter of E′lon the Hit′tite, O·hol·i·ba′mah daughter of An′ah son*x* of Zib′e·on the Hi′vite, 3 and Bas′e·math, Ish′ma·el's daughter, sister of Ne-ba′i·oth. 4 A′dah bore E·li′phaz to Esau; Bas′e·math bore Reü′el; 5 and O·hol·i·ba′mah bore Je′ush, Ja′-lam, and Ko′rah. These are the sons of Esau who were born to him in the land of Ca′naan.

6 Then Esau took his wives, his sons, his daughters, and all the members of his household, his cattle, all his livestock, and all the property he had acquired in the land of Ca′naan; and he moved to a land some distance from his brother Jacob. 7 For their possessions were too great for them to live together; the land where they were staying could not support them because of their livestock. 8 So Esau settled in the hill country of Se′ir; Esau is E′dom.

9 These are the descendants of Esau, ancestor of the E′dom·ites, in the hill country of Se′ir. 10 These are the names of Esau's sons: E·li′phaz son of A′dah the wife of Esau; Reü′el, the son of Esau's wife Bas′e·math. 11 The sons of E·li′phaz were Te′man, O′mar, Ze′pho, Ga′tam, and Ke′naz. 12 (Tim′na was a concubine of E·li′phaz, Esau's son; she bore Am′a·lek to E·li′phaz.) These were the sons of A′dah, Esau's wife. 13 These were the sons of Reü′el: Na′hath, Ze′rah, Sham′mah, and Miz′-zah. These were the sons of Esau's wife, Bas′e·math. 14 These were the sons of Esau's wife O·hol·i·ba′mah, daughter of An′ah son*y* of Zib′e·on: she bore to Esau Je′ush, Ja′lam, and Ko′rah.

Clans and Kings of Edom

15 These are the clans*z* of the sons of Esau. The sons of E·li′phaz the firstborn of Esau: the clans*z* Te′man, O′mar, Ze′pho, Ke′naz, 16 Ko′rah, Ga′tam, and Am′a·lek; these are the clans*z* of E·li′-phaz in the land of E′dom; they are the sons of A′dah. 17 These are the sons of Esau's son Reü′el: the clans*z* Na′hath, Ze′rah, Sham′mah, and Miz′-zah; these are the clans*z* of Reü′el in the land of E′dom; they are the sons of Esau's wife Bas′e·math. 18 These are the sons of Esau's wife O·hol·i·ba′mah: the clans*z* Je′ush, Ja′lam, and Ko′rah; these are the clans*z* born of Esau's wife O·hol·i·ba′mah, the daughter of An′ah. 19 These are the sons of Esau (that is, E′dom), and these are their clans.*z*

20 These are the sons of Se′ir the Hor′ite, the inhabitants of the land: Lo′tan, Sho′bal, Zib′e·on, An′ah, 21 Di′shon, E′zer, and Di′shan; these are the clans*z* of the Hor′ites, the sons of Se′ir in the land of E′dom. 22 The sons of Lo′tan were Ho′ri and He′man; and Lo′tan's sister was Tim′na. 23 These are the sons of Sho′bal: Al′van, Man′a-hath, E′bal, She′pho, and O′nam. 24 These are the sons of Zib′e·on: A′i·ah and An′ah; he is the An′ah who found the springs*a* in the wilderness, as he pastured the donkeys of his father Zib′e·on. 25 These are the children of An′ah: Di′shon and O·hol·i·ba′mah daughter of An′ah. 26 These are the sons of Di′shon: Hem′dan, Esh′ban, Ith′ran, and Che′ran. 27 These are the sons of E′zer: Bil′han, Za′a·van, and A′kan. 28 These are the sons of Di′shan: Uz and Ar′an. 29 These are the clans*z* of the Hor′ites: the clans*z* Lo′tan, Sho′bal, Zib′e·on,

---

v That is *Son of my sorrow*   *w* That is *Son of the right hand* or *Son of the South*   *x* Sam Gk Syr: Heb *daughter*   *y* Gk Syr: Heb *daughter*   *z* Or *chiefs*   *a* Meaning of Heb uncertain

An'ah, 30 Dī'shon, Ē'zer, and Dī'shan; these are the clans[b] of the Hor'ītes, clan by clan[c] in the land of Sē'ir.

31 These are the kings who reigned in the land of Ē'dom, before any king reigned over the Israelites. 32 Bē'la son of Bē'or reigned in Ē'dom, the name of his city being Din'ha•bah. 33 Bē'la died, and Jō'bab son of Zē'rah of Boz'rah succeeded him as king. 34 Jō'bab died, and Hū'sham of the land of the Tē'man•ītes succeeded him as king. 35 Hū'sham died, and Hā'dad son of Bē'dad, who defeated Mid'i•an in the country of Mō'ab, succeeded him as king, the name of his city being Ā'vith. 36 Hā'dad died, and Sam'lah of Mas•rē'kah succeeded him as king. 37 Sam'lah died, and Shā'ūl of Re•hō'both on the Euphrates succeeded him as king. 38 Shā'ūl died, and Bā'al-hā'nan son of Ach'bor succeeded him as king. 39 Bā'al-hā'nan son of Ach'bor died, and Hā'dar succeeded him as king, the name of his city being Pā'ū; his wife's name was Me•het'a•bel, the daughter of Mā'tred, daughter of Me-za•hab'.

40 These are the names of the clans[b] of Esau, according to their families and their localities by their names: the clans[b] Tim'na, Al'vah, Jē'theth, 41 Ō•hol•i•bā'mah, Ē'lah, Pī'non, 42 Kē'naz, Tē'man, Mib'zar, 43 Mag'di•el, and I'ram; these are the clans[b] of Ē'dom (that is, Esau, the father of Ē'dom), according to their settlements in the land that they held.

Joseph Dreams of Greatness

Jacob settled in the land where his father had lived as an alien, the land of Cā'naan. 2 This is the story of the family of Jacob.

Joseph, being seventeen years old, was shepherding the flock with his brothers; he was a helper to the sons of Bil'hah and Zil'pah, his father's wives; and Joseph brought a bad report of them to their father. 3 Now Israel loved Joseph more than any other of his children, because he was the son of his old age; and he had made him a long robe with sleeves.[d] 4 But when his brothers saw that their father loved him more than all his brothers, they hated him, and could not speak peaceably to him.

5 Once Joseph had a dream, and when he told it to his brothers, they hated him even more. 6 He said to them, "Listen to this dream that I dreamed. 7 There we were, binding sheaves in the field. Suddenly my sheaf rose and stood upright; then your sheaves gathered around it, and bowed down to my sheaf." 8 His brothers said to him, "Are you indeed to reign over us? Are you indeed to have dominion over us?" So they hated him even more because of his dreams and his words.

9 He had another dream, and told it to his brothers, saying, "Look, I have had another

---

b Or chiefs   c Or chief by chief   d Traditional rendering (compare Gk): *a coat of many colors*; meaning of Heb uncertain

Introducing ▶ JOSEPH

The timeless power of Joseph's story is reaffirmed by the long and successful run of the Broadway play *Joseph and the Amazing Technicolor Dreamcoat.* (In other Bible versions, the "long robe with sleeves" in Gen 37.3 is translated as a "coat of many colors.") The play is based on chapters 37–50 of Genesis, which contains one of the world's greatest stories of family, jealousy, betrayal, and forgiveness.

A son of Jacob and Rachel, Joseph carries to Egypt the divine promises of land and descendants, and eventually becomes the link with the story of Moses and the Exodus. As Jacob's favorite son, Joseph experiences the jealousy of his brothers, who sell him to Egyptian merchants. In Egypt, Joseph rises to power, becoming second in command to the pharaoh. Later, when Joseph's brothers come to Egypt looking for food, he forgives them and becomes reconciled with them.

Joseph's story encourages us to forgive others, even when we have been unjustly treated by them. Whenever we have been greatly wronged, remembering Joseph will offer us hope and courage.

▶ Gen 37.1—50.26

dream: the sun, the moon, and eleven stars were bowing down to me." 10 But when he told it to his father and to his brothers, his father rebuked him, and said to him, "What kind of dream is this that you have had? Shall we indeed come, I and your mother and your brothers, and bow to the ground before you?" 11 So his brothers were jealous of him, but his father kept the matter in mind.

Joseph Is Sold by His Brothers

12 Now his brothers went to pasture their father's flock near Shě'chem. 13 And Israel said to Joseph, "Are not your brothers pasturing the flock at Shě'chem? Come, I will send you to them." He answered, "Here I am." 14 So he said to him, "Go now, see if it is well with your brothers and with the flock; and bring word back to me." So he sent him from the valley of Hě'bron.

He came to Shě'chem, 15 and a man found him wandering in the fields; the man asked him, "What are you seeking?" 16 "I am seeking my brothers," he said; "tell me, please, where they are pasturing the flock." 17 The man said, "They have gone away, for I heard them say, 'Let us go to Dō'than.' " So Joseph went after his brothers, and found them at Dō'than. 18 They saw him from a distance, and before he came near to them, they conspired to kill him. 19 They said to one another, "Here comes this dreamer. 20 Come now, let us kill him and throw him into one of the pits; then we shall say that a wild animal has devoured him, and we shall see what will become of his dreams." 21 But when Reuben heard it, he delivered him out of their hands, saying, "Let us not take his life." 22 Reuben said to them, "Shed no blood; throw him into this pit here in the wilderness, but lay no hand on him"—that he might rescue him out of their hand and restore him to his father. 23 So when Joseph came to his brothers, they stripped him of his robe, the long robe with sleeves*e* that he wore; 24 and they took him and threw him into a pit. The pit was empty; there was no water in it.

25 Then they sat down to eat; and looking up they saw a caravan of Ish'ma·el·ites coming from Gil'e·ad, with their camels carrying gum, balm, and resin, on their way to carry it down to Egypt. 26 Then Judah said to his brothers, "What profit is it if we kill our brother and conceal his blood? 27 Come, let us sell him to the Ish'ma·el·ites, and not lay our hands on him, for he is our brother, our own flesh." And his brothers agreed. 28 When some Mid'i·an·ite traders passed by, they drew Joseph up, lifting him out of the pit, and sold Joseph to the Ish'ma·el·ites for twenty pieces of silver. And they took Joseph to Egypt.

29 When Reuben returned to the pit and saw that Joseph was not in the pit, he tore his clothes. 30 He returned to his brothers, and said, "The boy is gone; and I, where can I turn?" 31 Then they took Joseph's robe, slaughtered a goat, and dipped the robe in the blood. 32 They had the long robe with sleeves*e* taken to their father, and they said, "This we have found; see now whether it is your son's robe or not." 33 He recognized it, and said, "It is my son's robe! A wild animal has devoured him; Joseph is without doubt torn to pieces." 34 Then Jacob tore his garments, and put sackcloth on his loins, and mourned for his son many days. 35 All his sons and all his daughters sought to comfort him; but he refused to be comforted, and said, "No, I shall go down to Shě'ōl to my son, mourning." Thus his father bewailed him. 36 Meanwhile the Mid'i·an·ites had sold him in Egypt to Pot'i·phar, one of Pharaoh's officials, the captain of the guard.

Judah and Tamar

It happened at that time that Judah went down from his brothers and settled near a certain A·dul'lam·ite whose name was Hī'rah. 2 There Judah saw the daughter of a certain Cā'naan·ite whose name was Shū'a; he married her and went in to her. 3 She conceived and bore a son; and he named him Er. 4 Again she conceived and bore a son whom she named Ō'nan. 5 Yet again she bore a son, and she named him Shě'lah. She*f* was in Chě'zib when she bore him. 6 Judah took a wife for Er his firstborn; her name was Tā'mar. 7 But Er, Judah's firstborn, was wicked in the sight of the LORD, and the LORD put him to death. 8 Then Judah said to Ō'nan, "Go in to your brother's wife and perform the duty of a brother-in-law to her; raise up offspring for your brother." 9 But since Ō'nan knew that the offspring would not be his, he spilled his semen on the ground whenever he went in to his brother's wife, so that he would not give offspring to his brother. 10 What he did was displeasing in the sight of the LORD, and he put him to death also. 11 Then Judah said to his daughter-in-law Tā'mar, "Remain a widow in your father's house until my son Shě'lah grows up"—for he feared that he too would die, like his brothers. So Tā'mar went to live in her father's house.

12 In course of time the wife of Judah, Shū'a's daughter, died; when Judah's time of mourning was over,*g* he went up to Tim'nah to his sheepshearers, he and his friend Hī'rah the A·dul'lam·ite. 13 When Tā'mar was told, "Your father-in-law is going up to Tim'nah to shear his sheep," 14 she put

---

e See note on 37.3   *f* Gk: Heb He   *g* Heb when Judah was comforted

did you KNOW?

Levirate Marriage

Why does Onan have to marry his dead brother's wife and have a son by her? One of the laws specified in Deut 25.5–10 regulates what is called levirate marriage. *Levirate* means "brother-in-law." When a man's married brother dies without a son, that man is obligated to marry the wife who was left, and the first son whom she bears shall "succeed to the name of the deceased" (verse 6). This marriage practice seems to have developed in Israel for several reasons:

- A male child was needed to be heir to the dead man's property because women generally did not own property.
- The dead man's widow needed support and protection.
- A male heir ensured that the family property was kept within the immediate family.

▶ **Gen 38.8**

off her widow's garments, put on a veil, wrapped herself up, and sat down at the entrance to E•na′im, which is on the road to Tim′nah. She saw that She′lah was grown up, yet she had not been given to him in marriage. 15 When Judah saw her, he thought her to be a prostitute, for she had covered her face. 16 He went over to her at the roadside, and said, "Come, let me come in to you," for he did not know that she was his daughter-in-law. She said, "What will you give me, that you may come in to me?" 17 He answered, "I will send you a kid from the flock." And she said, "Only if you give me a pledge, until you send it." 18 He said, "What pledge shall I give you?" She replied, "Your signet and your cord, and the staff that is in your hand." So he gave them to her, and went in to her, and she conceived by him. 19 Then she got up and went away, and taking off her veil she put on the garments of her widowhood.

20 When Judah sent the kid by his friend the A•dul′lam•ite, to recover the pledge from the woman, he could not find her. 21 He asked the townspeople, "Where is the temple prostitute who was at E•na′im by the wayside?" But they said, "No prostitute has been here." 22 So he returned to Ju-

dah, and said, "I have not found her; moreover the townspeople said, 'No prostitute has been here.' " 23 Judah replied, "Let her keep the things as her own, otherwise we will be laughed at; you see, I sent this kid, and you could not find her."

24 About three months later Judah was told, "Your daughter-in-law Ta′mar has played the whore; moreover she is pregnant as a result of whoredom." And Judah said, "Bring her out, and let her be burned." 25 As she was being brought out, she sent word to her father-in-law, "It was the owner of these who made me pregnant." And she said, "Take note, please, whose these are, the signet and the cord and the staff." 26 Then Judah acknowledged them and said, "She is more in the right than I, since I did not give her to my son She′lah." And he did not lie with her again.

27 When the time of her delivery came, there were twins in her womb. 28 While she was in labor, one put out a hand; and the midwife took and bound on his hand a crimson thread, saying, "This one came out first." 29 But just then he drew back his hand, and out came his brother; and she said, "What a breach you have made for yourself!" Therefore he was named Per′ez.[h] 30 Afterward his brother came out with the crimson thread on his hand; and he was named Ze′rah.[i]

Joseph and Potiphar's Wife

Now Joseph was taken down to Egypt, and Pot′i-phar, an officer of Pharaoh, the captain of the guard, an Egyptian, bought him from the Ish′ma-el•ites who had brought him down there. 2 The LORD was with Joseph, and he became a successful man; he was in the house of his Egyptian master. 3 His master saw that the LORD was with him, and that the LORD caused all that he did to prosper in his hands. 4 So Joseph found favor in his sight and attended him; he made him overseer of his house and put him in charge of all that he had. 5 From the time that he made him overseer in his house and over all that he had, the LORD blessed the Egyptian's house for Joseph's sake; the blessing of the LORD was on all that he had, in house and field. 6 So he left all that he had in Joseph's charge; and, with him there, he had no concern for anything but the food that he ate.

Now Joseph was handsome and good-looking. 7 And after a time his master's wife cast her eyes on Joseph and said, "Lie with me." 8 But he refused and said to his master's wife, "Look, with me here, my master has no concern about anything in the

---

h That is *A breach*　i That is *Brightness;* perhaps alluding to the crimson thread

house, and he has put everything that he has in my hand. 9 He is not greater in this house than I am, nor has he kept back anything from me except yourself, because you are his wife. How then could I do this great wickedness, and sin against God?" 10 And although she spoke to Joseph day after day, he would not consent to lie beside her or to be with her. 11 One day, however, when he went into the house to do his work, and while no one else was in the house, 12 she caught hold of his garment, saying, "Lie with me!" But he left his garment in her hand, and fled and ran outside. 13 When she saw that he had left his garment in her hand and had fled outside, 14 she called out to the members of her household and said to them, "See, my husband*j* has brought among us a Hebrew to insult us! He came in to me to lie with me, and I cried out with a loud voice; 15 and when he heard me raise my voice and cry out, he left his garment beside me, and fled outside." 16 Then she kept his garment by her until his master came home, 17 and she told him the same story, saying, "The Hebrew servant, whom you have brought among us, came in to me to insult me; 18 but as soon as I raised my voice and cried out, he left his garment beside me, and fled outside."

19 When his master heard the words that his wife spoke to him, saying, "This is the way your servant treated me," he became enraged. 20 And Joseph's master took him and put him into the prison, the place where the king's prisoners were confined; he remained there in prison. 21 But the LORD was with Joseph and showed him steadfast love; he gave him favor in the sight of the chief jailer. 22 The chief jailer committed to Joseph's care all the prisoners who were in the prison, and whatever was done there, he was the one who did it. 23 The chief jailer paid no heed to anything that was in Joseph's care, because the LORD was with him; and whatever he did, the LORD made it prosper.

The Dreams of Two Prisoners

Some time after this, the cupbearer of the king of Egypt and his baker offended their lord the king of Egypt. 2 Pharaoh was angry with his two officers, the chief cupbearer and the chief baker, 3 and he put them in custody in the house of the captain of the guard, in the prison where Joseph was confined. 4 The captain of the guard charged Joseph with them, and he waited on them; and they continued for some time in custody. 5 One night they both dreamed—the cupbearer and the baker of the king of Egypt, who were confined in the prison— each his own dream, and each dream with its own meaning. 6 When Joseph came to them in the morning, he saw that they were troubled. 7 So he asked Pharaoh's officers, who were with him in custody in his master's house, "Why are your faces downcast today?" 8 They said to him, "We have had dreams, and there is no one to interpret them." And Joseph said to them, "Do not interpretations belong to God? Please tell them to me."

9 So the chief cupbearer told his dream to Joseph, and said to him, "In my dream there was a vine before me, 10 and on the vine there were three branches. As soon as it budded, its blossoms came out and the clusters ripened into grapes. 11 Pharaoh's cup was in my hand; and I took the grapes and pressed them into Pharaoh's cup, and placed the cup in Pharaoh's hand." 12 Then Joseph said to him, "This is its interpretation: the three branches are three days; 13 within three days Pharaoh will lift up your head and restore you to your office; and you shall place Pharaoh's cup in his hand, just as you used to do when you were his cupbearer. 14 But remember me when it is well with you; please do me the kindness to make mention of me to Pharaoh, and so get me out of this place. 15 For in fact I was stolen out of the land of the Hebrews; and here also I have done nothing that they should have put me into the dungeon."

16 When the chief baker saw that the interpretation was favorable, he said to Joseph, "I also had a dream: there were three cake baskets on my head, 17 and in the uppermost basket there were all sorts of baked food for Pharaoh, but the birds were eating it out of the basket on my head." 18 And Joseph answered, "This is its interpretation: the three baskets are three days; 19 within three days Pharaoh will lift up your head—from you!—and hang you on a pole; and the birds will eat the flesh from you."

20 On the third day, which was Pharaoh's birthday, he made a feast for all his servants, and lifted up the head of the chief cupbearer and the head of the chief baker among his servants. 21 He restored the chief cupbearer to his cupbearing, and he placed the cup in Pharaoh's hand; 22 but the chief baker he hanged, just as Joseph had interpreted to them. 23 Yet the chief cupbearer did not remember Joseph, but forgot him.

Joseph Interprets Pharaoh's Dream

After two whole years, Pharaoh dreamed that he was standing by the Nile, 2 and there came up out of the Nile seven sleek and fat cows, and they grazed in the reed grass. 3 Then seven other cows, ugly and thin, came up out of the Nile after them, and stood by the other cows on the bank of the

j Heb *he*

Nile. ⁴The ugly and thin cows ate up the seven sleek and fat cows. And Pharaoh awoke. ⁵Then he fell asleep and dreamed a second time; seven ears of grain, plump and good, were growing on one stalk. ⁶Then seven ears, thin and blighted by the east wind, sprouted after them. ⁷The thin ears swallowed up the seven plump and full ears. Pharaoh awoke, and it was a dream. ⁸In the morning his spirit was troubled; so he sent and called for all the magicians of Egypt and all its wise men. Pharaoh told them his dreams, but there was no one who could interpret them to Pharaoh.

did you KNOW?

Dreams

In the ancient world, belief in the reality and significance of dreams was widespread. The ancients believed that dreams and visions revealed messages, prophecies, and healing from their gods. Israel shared this view of the importance of dreams. Joseph is described as an interpreter of dreams, and this skill earns him Pharaoh's respect (Gen 41.37–45), as well as his brothers' jealousy (37.5–11).

In the Old Testament, the prophets are often referred to as seers because the word of God so often comes to them through dreams and visions. The focus, however, is always on the word of God and its meaning, not on the dream itself. In fact, God usually gives a character in the story the interpretation of the dream, which aims to lead the people to more faithful observance of the covenant. If the dream does not do this, it is to be considered a false dream. (See other references to dreams in Gen 28.10–22; Deut 13.2–6; Sir 34.1–4; Jer 27.9–10; 29.8–9; Joel 2.28; Zech 1.8; Mt 1.20; 2.13.)

▶ Gen 37.1–11; 40.1—41.36

9 Then the chief cupbearer said to Pharaoh, "I remember my faults today. ¹⁰Once Pharaoh was angry with his servants, and put me and the chief baker in custody in the house of the captain of the guard. ¹¹We dreamed on the same night, he and I, each having a dream with its own meaning. ¹²A

young Hebrew was there with us, a servant of the captain of the guard. When we told him, he interpreted our dreams to us, giving an interpretation to each according to his dream. ¹³As he interpreted to us, so it turned out; I was restored to my office, and the baker was hanged."

14 Then Pharaoh sent for Joseph, and he was hurriedly brought out of the dungeon. When he had shaved himself and changed his clothes, he came in before Pharaoh. ¹⁵And Pharaoh said to Joseph, "I have had a dream, and there is no one who can interpret it. I have heard it said of you that when you hear a dream you can interpret it." ¹⁶Joseph answered Pharaoh, "It is not I; God will give Pharaoh a favorable answer." ¹⁷Then Pharaoh said to Joseph, "In my dream I was standing on the banks of the Nile; ¹⁸and seven cows, fat and sleek, came up out of the Nile and fed in the reed grass. ¹⁹Then seven other cows came up after them, poor, very ugly, and thin. Never had I seen such ugly ones in all the land of Egypt. ²⁰The thin and ugly cows ate up the first seven fat cows, ²¹but when they had eaten them no one would have known that they had done so, for they were still as ugly as before. Then I awoke. ²²I fell asleep a second timeᵏ and I saw in my dream seven ears of grain, full and good, growing on one stalk, ²³and seven ears, withered, thin, and blighted by the east wind, sprouting after them; ²⁴and the thin ears swallowed up the seven good ears. But when I told it to the magicians, there was no one who could explain it to me."

25 Then Joseph said to Pharaoh, "Pharaoh's dreams are one and the same; God has revealed to Pharaoh what he is about to do. ²⁶The seven good cows are seven years, and the seven good ears are seven years; the dreams are one. ²⁷The seven lean and ugly cows that came up after them are seven years, as are the seven empty ears blighted by the east wind. They are seven years of famine. ²⁸It is as I told Pharaoh; God has shown to Pharaoh what he is about to do. ²⁹There will come seven years of great plenty throughout all the land of Egypt. ³⁰After them there will arise seven years of famine, and all the plenty will be forgotten in the land of Egypt; the famine will consume the land. ³¹The plenty will no longer be known in the land because of the famine that will follow, for it will be very grievous. ³²And the doubling of Pharaoh's dream means that the thing is fixed by God, and God will shortly bring it about. ³³Now therefore let Pharaoh select a man who is discerning and wise, and set him over the land of Egypt. ³⁴Let Pharaoh proceed to appoint overseers over the

ᵏ Gk Syr Vg: Heb lacks *I fell asleep a second time*

G
E
N

land, and take one-fifth of the produce of the land of Egypt during the seven plenteous years. 35 Let them gather all the food of these good years that are coming, and lay up grain under the authority of Pharaoh for food in the cities, and let them keep it. 36 That food shall be a reserve for the land against the seven years of famine that are to befall the land of Egypt, so that the land may not perish through the famine."

Joseph's Rise to Power

37 The proposal pleased Pharaoh and all his servants. 38 Pharaoh said to his servants, "Can we find anyone else like this—one in whom is the spirit of God?" 39 So Pharaoh said to Joseph, "Since God has shown you all this, there is no one so discerning and wise as you. 40 You shall be over my house, and all my people shall order themselves as you command; only with regard to the throne will I be greater than you." 41 And Pharaoh said to Joseph, "See, I have set you over all the land of Egypt." 42 Removing his signet ring from his hand, Pharaoh put it on Joseph's hand; he arrayed him in garments of fine linen, and put a gold chain around his neck. 43 He had him ride in the chariot of his second-in-command; and they cried out in front of him, "Bow the knee!"*l* Thus he set him over all the land of Egypt. 44 Moreover Pharaoh said to Joseph, "I am Pharaoh, and without your consent no one shall lift up hand or foot in all the land of Egypt." 45 Pharaoh gave Joseph the name Zaph'e·nath-pa·nē'ah; and he gave him As'e-nath daughter of Pō·ti'phe·ra, priest of On, as his wife. Thus Joseph gained authority over the land of Egypt.

46 Joseph was thirty years old when he entered the service of Pharaoh king of Egypt. And Joseph went out from the presence of Pharaoh, and went through all the land of Egypt. 47 During the seven plenteous years the earth produced abundantly. 48 He gathered up all the food of the seven years when there was plenty*m* in the land of Egypt, and stored up food in the cities; he stored up in every city the food from the fields around it. 49 So Joseph stored up grain in such abundance—like the sand of the sea—that he stopped measuring it; it was beyond measure.

50 Before the years of famine came, Joseph had two sons, whom As'e·nath daughter of Pō·ti'-phe·ra, priest of On, bore to him. 51 Joseph named the firstborn Ma·nas'seh,*n* "For," he said, "God has made me forget all my hardship and all my father's house." 52 The second he named Ē'phra·im,*o* "For God has made me fruitful in the land of my misfortunes."

53 The seven years of plenty that prevailed in the land of Egypt came to an end; 54 and the seven years of famine began to come, just as Joseph had said. There was famine in every country, but throughout the land of Egypt there was bread. 55 When all the land of Egypt was famished, the people cried to Pharaoh for bread. Pharaoh said to all the Egyptians, "Go to Joseph; what he says to you, do." 56 And since the famine had spread over all the land, Joseph opened all the storehouses,*p* and sold to the Egyptians, for the famine was severe in the land of Egypt. 57 Moreover, all the world came to Joseph in Egypt to buy grain, because the famine became severe throughout the world.

Joseph's Brothers Go to Egypt

When Jacob learned that there was grain in Egypt, he said to his sons, "Why do you keep looking at one another? 2 I have heard," he said, "that there is grain in Egypt; go down and buy grain for us there, that we may live and not die." 3 So ten of Joseph's brothers went down to buy grain in Egypt. 4 But Jacob did not send Joseph's brother Benjamin with his brothers, for he feared that harm might come to him. 5 Thus the sons of Israel were among the other people who came to buy grain, for the famine had reached the land of Cā'naan.

6 Now Joseph was governor over the land; it was he who sold to all the people of the land. And Joseph's brothers came and bowed themselves before him with their faces to the ground. 7 When Joseph saw his brothers, he recognized them, but he treated them like strangers and spoke harshly to them. "Where do you come from?" he said. They said, "From the land of Cā'naan, to buy food." 8 Although Joseph had recognized his brothers, they did not recognize him. 9 Joseph also remembered the dreams that he had dreamed about them. He said to them, "You are spies; you have come to see the nakedness of the land!" 10 They said to him, "No, my lord; your servants have come to buy food. 11 We are all sons of one man; we are honest men; your servants have never been spies." 12 But he said to them, "No, you have come to see the nakedness of the land!" 13 They said, "We, your servants, are twelve brothers, the sons of a certain man in the land of Cā'naan; the youngest, however, is now with our father, and one is no more." 14 But Joseph said to them, "It is just as I have said to you; you are spies! 15 Here is how you shall be

---

l *Abrek,* apparently an Egyptian word similar in sound to the Hebrew word meaning *to kneel*   *m* Sam Gk: MT *the seven years that were*   *n* That is *Making to forget*   *o* From a Hebrew word meaning *to be fruitful*   *p* Gk Vg Compare Syr: Heb *opened all that was in* (or, *among*) *them*

tested: as Pharaoh lives, you shall not leave this place unless your youngest brother comes here! 16 Let one of you go and bring your brother, while the rest of you remain in prison, in order that your words may be tested, whether there is truth in you; or else, as Pharaoh lives, surely you are spies." 17 And he put them all together in prison for three days.

18 On the third day Joseph said to them, "Do this and you will live, for I fear God: 19 if you are honest men, let one of your brothers stay here where you are imprisoned. The rest of you shall go and carry grain for the famine of your households, 20 and bring your youngest brother to me. Thus your words will be verified, and you shall not die." And they agreed to do so. 21 They said to one another, "Alas, we are paying the penalty for what we did to our brother; we saw his anguish when he pleaded with us, but we would not listen. That is why this anguish has come upon us." 22 Then Reuben answered them, "Did I not tell you not to wrong the boy? But you would not listen. So now there comes a reckoning for his blood." 23 They did not know that Joseph understood them, since he spoke with them through an interpreter. 24 He turned away from them and wept; then he returned and spoke to them. And he picked out Sim′e•on and had him bound before their eyes. 25 Joseph then gave orders to fill their bags with grain, to return every man's money to his sack, and to give them provisions for their journey. This was done for them.

Joseph's Brothers Return to Canaan

26 They loaded their donkeys with their grain, and departed. 27 When one of them opened his sack to give his donkey fodder at the lodging place, he saw his money at the top of the sack. 28 He said to his brothers, "My money has been put back; here it is in my sack!" At this they lost heart and turned trembling to one another, saying, "What is this that God has done to us?"

29 When they came to their father Jacob in the land of Ca′naan, they told him all that had happened to them, saying, 30 "The man, the lord of the land, spoke harshly to us, and charged us with spying on the land. 31 But we said to him, 'We are honest men, we are not spies. 32 We are twelve brothers, sons of our father; one is no more, and the youngest is now with our father in the land of Ca′naan.' 33 Then the man, the lord of the land, said to us, 'By this I shall know that you are honest men: leave one of your brothers with me, take grain for the famine of your households, and go your way. 34 Bring your youngest brother to me, and I shall know that you are not spies but honest

men. Then I will release your brother to you, and you may trade in the land.' "

35 As they were emptying their sacks, there in each one's sack was his bag of money. When they and their father saw their bundles of money, they were dismayed. 36 And their father Jacob said to them, "I am the one you have bereaved of children: Joseph is no more, and Sim′e•on is no more, and now you would take Benjamin. All this has happened to me!" 37 Then Reuben said to his father, "You may kill my two sons if I do not bring him back to you. Put him in my hands, and I will bring him back to you." 38 But he said, "My son shall not go down with you, for his brother is dead, and he alone is left. If harm should come to him on the journey that you are to make, you would bring down my gray hairs with sorrow to She′ol."

The Brothers Come Again, Bringing Benjamin

Now the famine was severe in the land. 2 And when they had eaten up the grain that they had brought from Egypt, their father said to them, "Go again, buy us a little more food." 3 But Judah said to him, "The man solemnly warned us, saying, 'You shall not see my face unless your brother is with you.' 4 If you will send our brother with us, we will go down and buy you food; 5 but if you will not send him, we will not go down, for the man said to us, 'You shall not see my face, unless your brother is with you.' " 6 Israel said, "Why did you treat me so badly as to tell the man that you had another brother?" 7 They replied, "The man questioned us carefully about ourselves and our kindred, saying, 'Is your father still alive? Have you another brother?' What we told him was in answer to these questions. Could we in any way know that he would say, 'Bring your brother down'?" 8 Then Judah said to his father Israel, "Send the boy with me, and let us be on our way, so that we may live and not die—you and we and also our little ones. 9 I myself will be surety for him; you can hold me accountable for him. If I do not bring him back to you and set him before you, then let me bear the blame forever. 10 If we had not delayed, we would now have returned twice."

11 Then their father Israel said to them, "If it must be so, then do this: take some of the choice fruits of the land in your bags, and carry them down as a present to the man—a little balm and a little honey, gum, resin, pistachio nuts, and almonds. 12 Take double the money with you. Carry back with you the money that was returned in the top of your sacks; perhaps it was an oversight. 13 Take your brother also, and be on your way

again to the man; 14 may God Almighty*q* grant you mercy before the man, so that he may send back your other brother and Benjamin. As for me, if I am bereaved of my children, I am bereaved." 15 So the men took the present, and they took double the money with them, as well as Benjamin. Then they went on their way down to Egypt, and stood before Joseph.

16 When Joseph saw Benjamin with them, he said to the steward of his house, "Bring the men into the house, and slaughter an animal and make ready, for the men are to dine with me at noon." 17 The man did as Joseph said, and brought the men to Joseph's house. 18 Now the men were afraid because they were brought to Joseph's house, and they said, "It is because of the money, replaced in our sacks the first time, that we have been brought in, so that he may have an opportunity to fall upon us, to make slaves of us and take our donkeys." 19 So they went up to the steward of Joseph's house and spoke with him at the entrance to the house. 20 They said, "Oh, my lord, we came down the first time to buy food; 21 and when we came to the lodging place we opened our sacks, and there was each one's money in the top of his sack, our money in full weight. So we have brought it back with us. 22 Moreover we have brought down with us additional money to buy food. We do not know who put our money in our sacks." 23 He replied, "Rest assured, do not be afraid; your God and the God of your father must have put treasure in your sacks for you; I received your money." Then he brought Sim'e•on out to them. 24 When the steward*r* had brought the men into Joseph's house, and given them water, and they had washed their feet, and when he had given their donkeys fodder, 25 they made the present ready for Joseph's coming at noon, for they had heard that they would dine there.

26 When Joseph came home, they brought him the present that they had carried into the house, and bowed to the ground before him. 27 He inquired about their welfare, and said, "Is your father well, the old man of whom you spoke? Is he still alive?" 28 They said, "Your servant our father is well; he is still alive." And they bowed their heads and did obeisance. 29 Then he looked up and saw his brother Benjamin, his mother's son, and said, "Is this your youngest brother, of whom you spoke to me? God be gracious to you, my son!" 30 With that, Joseph hurried out, because he was overcome with affection for his brother, and he was about to weep. So he went into a private room and wept there. 31 Then he washed his face and came out; and controlling himself he said, "Serve the meal." 32 They served him by himself, and them

by themselves, and the Egyptians who ate with him by themselves, because the Egyptians could not eat with the Hebrews, for that is an abomination to the Egyptians. 33 When they were seated before him, the firstborn according to his birthright and the youngest according to his youth, the men looked at one another in amazement. 34 Portions were taken to them from Joseph's table, but Benjamin's portion was five times as much as any of theirs. So they drank and were merry with him.

Joseph Detains Benjamin

Then he commanded the steward of his house, "Fill the men's sacks with food, as much as they can carry, and put each man's money in the top of his sack. 2 Put my cup, the silver cup, in the top of the sack of the youngest, with his money for the grain." And he did as Joseph told him. 3 As soon as the morning was light, the men were sent away with their donkeys. 4 When they had gone only a short distance from the city, Joseph said to his steward, "Go, follow after the men; and when you overtake them, say to them, 'Why have you returned evil for good? Why have you stolen my silver cup?*s* 5 Is it not from this that my lord drinks? Does he not indeed use it for divination? You have done wrong in doing this.'"

6 When he overtook them, he repeated these words to them. 7 They said to him, "Why does my lord speak such words as these? Far be it from your servants that they should do such a thing! 8 Look, the money that we found at the top of our sacks, we brought back to you from the land of Ca'naan; why then would we steal silver or gold from your lord's house? 9 Should it be found with any one of your servants, let him die; moreover the rest of us will become my lord's slaves." 10 He said, "Even so; in accordance with your words, let it be: he with whom it is found shall become my slave, but the rest of you shall go free." 11 Then each one quickly lowered his sack to the ground, and each opened his sack. 12 He searched, beginning with the eldest and ending with the youngest; and the cup was found in Benjamin's sack. 13 At this they tore their clothes. Then each one loaded his donkey, and they returned to the city.

14 Judah and his brothers came to Joseph's house while he was still there; and they fell to the ground before him. 15 Joseph said to them, "What deed is this that you have done? Do you not know that one such as I can practice divination?" 16 And Judah said, "What can we say to my lord? What

---

q Traditional rendering of Heb *El Shaddai*   *r* Heb *the man*
s Gk Compare Vg: Heb lacks *Why have you stolen my silver cup?*

can we speak? How can we clear ourselves? God has found out the guilt of your servants; here we are then, my lord's slaves, both we and also the one in whose possession the cup has been found." [17] But he said, "Far be it from me that I should do so! Only the one in whose possession the cup was found shall be my slave; but as for you, go up in peace to your father."

Judah Pleads for Benjamin's Release

18 Then Judah stepped up to him and said, "O my lord, let your servant please speak a word in my lord's ears, and do not be angry with your servant; for you are like Pharaoh himself. [19] My lord asked his servants, saying, 'Have you a father or a brother?' [20] And we said to my lord, 'We have a father, an old man, and a young brother, the child of his old age. His brother is dead; he alone is left of his mother's children, and his father loves him.' [21] Then you said to your servants, 'Bring him down to me, so that I may set my eyes on him.' [22] We said to my lord, 'The boy cannot leave his father, for if he should leave his father, his father would die.' [23] Then you said to your servants, 'Unless your youngest brother comes down with you, you shall see my face no more.' [24] When we went back to your servant my father we told him the words of my lord. [25] And when our father said, 'Go again, buy us a little food,' [26] we said, 'We cannot go down. Only if our youngest brother goes with us, will we go down; for we cannot see the man's face unless our youngest brother is with us.' [27] Then your servant my father said to us, 'You know that my wife bore me two sons; [28] one left me, and I said, Surely he has been torn to pieces; and I have never seen him since. [29] If you take this one also from me, and harm comes to him, you will bring down my gray hairs in sorrow to Shē'ōl.' [30] Now therefore, when I come to your servant my father and the boy is not with us, then, as his life is bound up in the boy's life, [31] when he sees that the boy is not with us, he will die; and your servants will bring down the gray hairs of your servant our father with sorrow to Shē'ōl. [32] For your servant became surety for the boy to my father, saying, 'If I do not bring him back to you, then I will bear the blame in the sight of my father all my life.' [33] Now therefore, please let your servant remain as a slave to my lord in place of the boy; and let the boy go back with his brothers. [34] For how can I go back to my father if the boy is not with me? I fear to see the suffering that would come upon my father."

Joseph Reveals Himself to His Brothers

Then Joseph could no longer control himself before all those who stood by him, and he cried out, "Send everyone away from me." So no one stayed with him when Joseph made himself known to his brothers. [2] And he wept so loudly that the Egyptians heard it, and the household of Pharaoh heard it. [3] Joseph said to his brothers, "I am Joseph. Is my father still alive?" But his brothers could not answer him, so dismayed were they at his presence.

4 Then Joseph said to his brothers, "Come closer to me." And they came closer. He said, "I am your brother, Joseph, whom you sold into Egypt. [5] And now do not be distressed, or angry with yourselves, because you sold me here; for God sent me before you to preserve life. [6] For the famine has been in the land these two years; and there are five more years in which there will be neither plowing nor harvest. [7] God sent me before you to preserve for you a remnant on earth, and to keep alive for you many survivors. [8] So it was not you who sent me here, but God; he has made me a father to Pharaoh, and lord of all his house and ruler over all the land of Egypt. [9] Hurry and go up to my father and say to him, 'Thus says your son Joseph, God has made me lord of all Egypt; come down to me, do not delay. [10] You shall settle in the land of Gō'shen, and you shall be near me, you and your children and your children's children, as well as your flocks, your herds, and all that you have. [11] I will provide for you there—since there are five more years of famine to come—so that you and your household, and all that you have, will not come to poverty.' [12] And now your eyes and the eyes of my brother Benjamin see that it is my own mouth that speaks to you. [13] You must tell my father how greatly I am honored in Egypt, and all that you have seen. Hurry and bring my father down here." [14] Then he fell upon his brother Benjamin's neck and wept, while Benjamin wept upon his neck. [15] And he kissed all his brothers and wept upon them; and after that his brothers talked with him.

16 When the report was heard in Pharaoh's house, "Joseph's brothers have come," Pharaoh and his servants were pleased. [17] Pharaoh said to Joseph, "Say to your brothers, 'Do this: load your animals and go back to the land of Cā'naan. [18] Take your father and your households and come to me, so that I may give you the best of the land of Egypt, and you may enjoy the fat of the land.' [19] You are further charged to say, 'Do this: take wagons from the land of Egypt for your little ones and for your wives, and bring your father, and

God's Master Plan

After Joseph's tearful reconciliation with his brothers, he tells them that their past treatment of him enabled him to save them from the famine. Because he ended up in Egypt and rose to power, he can now invite them to stay as guests of the pharaoh.

Joseph realizes that good has come out of an evil act. He sees the events of his family's life as part of God's plan to preserve life and to make sure that the covenant continues. Joseph's insight does not justify what his brothers did, but it does help us realize that good can come out of a tragic event. It is often hard for us to understand why something bad is happening, but as time passes, we often gain perspective and insight. These are the rewards of trust and faith. Joseph remained faithful, despite many difficulties. Let us strive to do the same, assured that not even human sinfulness can thwart God's saving plans.

When have you experienced good things coming out of a bad situation? Has it ever seemed like God has upset part of your life, only to result in something better than you expected?

▸ **Gen 45.5–8**

come. ²⁰Give no thought to your possessions, for the best of all the land of Egypt is yours.' "

21 The sons of Israel did so. Joseph gave them wagons according to the instruction of Pharaoh, and he gave them provisions for the journey. ²²To each one of them he gave a set of garments; but to Benjamin he gave three hundred pieces of silver and five sets of garments. ²³To his father he sent the following: ten donkeys loaded with the good things of Egypt, and ten female donkeys loaded with grain, bread, and provision for his father on the journey. ²⁴Then he sent his brothers on their way, and as they were leaving he said to them, "Do not quarrel*t* along the way."

25 So they went up out of Egypt and came to their father Jacob in the land of Cā'naan. ²⁶And they told him, "Joseph is still alive! He is even ruler over all the land of Egypt." He was stunned; he could not believe them. ²⁷But when they told him all the words of Joseph that he had said to them, and when he saw the wagons that Joseph had sent to carry him, the spirit of their father Jacob revived. ²⁸Israel said, "Enough! My son Joseph is still alive. I must go and see him before I die."

Jacob Brings His Whole Family to Egypt
(Ex 6.14–25)

When Israel set out on his journey with all that he had and came to Bē'er-shē'ba, he offered sacrifices to the God of his father Isaac. ²God spoke to Israel in visions of the night, and said, "Jacob, Jacob." And he said, "Here I am." ³Then he said, "I am God,*u* the God of your father; do not be afraid to

go down to Egypt, for I will make of you a great nation there. ⁴I myself will go down with you to Egypt, and I will also bring you up again; and Joseph's own hand shall close your eyes."

5 Then Jacob set out from Bē'er-shē'ba; and the sons of Israel carried their father Jacob, their little ones, and their wives, in the wagons that Pharaoh had sent to carry him. ⁶They also took their livestock and the goods that they had acquired in the land of Cā'naan, and they came into Egypt, Jacob and all his offspring with him, ⁷his sons, and his sons' sons with him, his daughters, and his sons' daughters; all his offspring he brought with him into Egypt.

8 Now these are the names of the Israelites, Jacob and his offspring, who came to Egypt. Reuben, Jacob's firstborn, ⁹and the children of Reuben: Hā'noch, Pal'lū, Hez'ron, and Car'mī. ¹⁰The children of Sim'ē·on: Je·mū'el, Jā'min, Ō'had, Jā'chin, Zō'har, and Shā'ūl,*v* the son of a Cā'naan·ite woman. ¹¹The children of Levi: Ger'shon, Kō'-hath, and Me·rar'ī. ¹²The children of Judah: Er, O'nan, Shē'lah, Per'ez, and Zē'rah (but Er and O'nan died in the land of Cā'naan); and the children of Per'ez were Hez'ron and Hā'mul. ¹³The children of Is'sa·char: Tō'la, Pū'vah, Jash'ub,*w* and Shim'ron. ¹⁴The children of Zeb'ū·lun: Sē'red, E'lon, and Jah'lē·el ¹⁵(these are the sons of Leah, whom she bore to Jacob in Pad'dan-ar'am, together with his daughter Dī'nah; in all his sons and his daughters numbered thirty-three). ¹⁶The children of Gad: Ziph'i·on, Hag'gī, Shū'nī, Ez'bon,

---

t Or *be agitated*   *u* Heb *the God*   *v* Or *Saul*
w Compare Sam Gk Num 26.24; 1 Chr 7.1: MT *Iob*

Ē′rī, A•rō′dī, and A•rē′lī. 17The children of Ash′er: Im′nah, Ish′vah, Ish′vī, Bē•rī′ah, and their sister Sē′rah. The children of Bē•rī′ah: Hē′ber and Mal′chi•el 18 (these are the children of Zil′pah, whom Lā′ban gave to his daughter Leah; and these she bore to Jacob—sixteen persons). 19The children of Jacob's wife Rachel: Joseph and Benjamin. 20To Joseph in the land of Egypt were born Ma•nas′seh and Ē′phra•im, whom As′e•nath daughter of Pō•ti′phe•ra, priest of On, bore to him. 21The children of Benjamin: Bē′la, Bē′cher, Ash′bel, Gē′ra, Nā′aman, Ē′hī, Rosh, Mup′pim, Hup′pim, and Ard 22 (these are the children of Rachel, who were born to Jacob—fourteen persons in all). 23The children of Dan: Hā′shum.*x* 24The children of Naph′ta•lī: Jah′zē•el, Gū′nī, Jē′zer, and Shil′lem 25 (these are the children of Bil′hah, whom Lā′ban gave to his daughter Rachel, and these she bore to Jacob—seven persons in all). 26All the persons belonging to Jacob who came into Egypt, who were his own offspring, not including the wives of his sons, were sixty-six persons in all. 27The children of Joseph, who were born to him in Egypt, were two; all the persons of the house of Jacob who came into Egypt were seventy.

Jacob Settles in Goshen

28 Israel*y* sent Judah ahead to Joseph to lead the way before him into Gō′shen. When they came to the land of Gō′shen, 29Joseph made ready his chariot and went up to meet his father Israel in Gō′shen. He presented himself to him, fell on his neck, and wept on his neck a good while. 30 Israel said to Joseph, "I can die now, having seen for myself that you are still alive." 31Joseph said to his brothers and to his father's household, "I will go up and tell Pharaoh, and will say to him, 'My brothers and my father's household, who were in the land of Cā′naan, have come to me. 32The men are shepherds, for they have been keepers of livestock; and they have brought their flocks, and their herds, and all that they have.' 33When Pharaoh calls you, and says, 'What is your occupation?' 34you shall say, 'Your servants have been keepers of livestock from our youth even until now, both we and our ancestors'—in order that you may settle in the land of Gō′shen, because all shepherds are abhorrent to the Egyptians."

So Joseph went and told Pharaoh, "My father and my brothers, with their flocks and herds and all that they possess, have come from the land of Cā′naan; they are now in the land of Gō′shen." 2From among his brothers he took five men and presented them to Pharaoh. 3Pharaoh said to his brothers, "What is your occupation?" And they said to Pharaoh, "Your servants are shepherds, as our

ancestors were." 4They said to Pharaoh, "We have come to reside as aliens in the land; for there is no pasture for your servants' flocks because the famine is severe in the land of Cā′naan. Now, we ask you, let your servants settle in the land of Gō′shen." 5Then Pharaoh said to Joseph, "Your father and your brothers have come to you. 6The land of Egypt is before you; settle your father and your brothers in the best part of the land; let them live in the land of Gō′shen; and if you know that there are capable men among them, put them in charge of my livestock."

7 Then Joseph brought in his father Jacob, and presented him before Pharaoh, and Jacob blessed Pharaoh. 8Pharaoh said to Jacob, "How many are the years of your life?" 9Jacob said to Pharaoh, "The years of my earthly sojourn are one hundred thirty; few and hard have been the years of my life. They do not compare with the years of the life of my ancestors during their long sojourn." 10Then Jacob blessed Pharaoh, and went out from the presence of Pharaoh. 11Joseph settled his father and his brothers, and granted them a holding in the land of Egypt, in the best part of the land, in the land of Ram′e•sēs, as Pharaoh had instructed. 12And Joseph provided his father, his brothers, and all his father's household with food, according to the number of their dependents.

The Famine in Egypt

13 Now there was no food in all the land, for the famine was very severe. The land of Egypt and the land of Cā′naan languished because of the famine. 14Joseph collected all the money to be found in the land of Egypt and in the land of Cā′naan, in exchange for the grain that they bought; and Joseph brought the money into Pharaoh's house. 15When the money from the land of Egypt and from the land of Cā′naan was spent, all the Egyptians came to Joseph, and said, "Give us food! Why should we die before your eyes? For our money is gone." 16And Joseph answered, "Give me your livestock, and I will give you food in exchange for your livestock, if your money is gone." 17So they brought their livestock to Joseph; and Joseph gave them food in exchange for the horses, the flocks, the herds, and the donkeys. That year he supplied them with food in exchange for all their livestock. 18When that year was ended, they came to him the following year, and said to him, "We can not hide from my lord that our money is all spent; and the herds of cattle are my lord's. There is nothing left in the sight of my lord but our bodies and our lands. 19Shall we die before

x Gk: Heb *Hushim*   *y* Heb *He*

GEN

your eyes, both we and our land? Buy us and our land in exchange for food. We with our land will become slaves to Pharaoh; just give us seed, so that we may live and not die, and that the land may not become desolate."

20 So Joseph bought all the land of Egypt for Pharaoh. All the Egyptians sold their fields, because the famine was severe upon them; and the land became Pharaoh's. 21 As for the people, he made slaves of them[z] from one end of Egypt to the other. 22 Only the land of the priests he did not buy; for the priests had a fixed allowance from Pharaoh, and lived on the allowance that Pharaoh gave them; therefore they did not sell their land. 23 Then Joseph said to the people, "Now that I have this day bought you and your land for Pharaoh, here is seed for you; sow the land. 24 And at the harvests you shall give one-fifth to Pharaoh, and four-fifths shall be your own, as seed for the field and as food for yourselves and your households, and as food for your little ones." 25 They said, "You have saved our lives; may it please my lord, we will be slaves to Pharaoh." 26 So Joseph made it a statute concerning the land of Egypt, and it stands to this day, that Pharaoh should have the fifth. The land of the priests alone did not become Pharaoh's.

The Last Days of Jacob

27 Thus Israel settled in the land of Egypt, in the region of Gō'shen; and they gained possessions in it, and were fruitful and multiplied exceedingly. 28 Jacob lived in the land of Egypt seventeen years; so the days of Jacob, the years of his life, were one hundred forty-seven years.

29 When the time of Israel's death drew near, he called his son Joseph and said to him, "If I have found favor with you, put your hand under my thigh and promise to deal loyally and truly with me. Do not bury me in Egypt. 30 When I lie down with my ancestors, carry me out of Egypt and bury me in their burial place." He answered, "I will do as you have said." 31 And he said, "Swear to me"; and he swore to him. Then Israel bowed himself on the head of his bed.

Jacob Blesses Joseph's Sons
(Heb 11.21)

After this Joseph was told, "Your father is ill." So he took with him his two sons, Ma•nas'seh and Ē'phra•im. 2 When Jacob was told, "Your son Joseph has come to you," he[a] summoned his strength and sat up in bed. 3 And Jacob said to Joseph, "God Almighty[b] appeared to me at Luz in the land of Cā'naan, and he blessed me, 4 and said to me, 'I am going to make you fruitful and increase

your numbers; I will make of you a company of peoples, and will give this land to your offspring after you for a perpetual holding.' 5 Therefore your two sons, who were born to you in the land of Egypt before I came to you in Egypt, are now mine; Ē'phra•im and Ma•nas'seh shall be mine, just as Reuben and Sim'ē•on are. 6 As for the offspring born to you after them, they shall be yours. They shall be recorded under the names of their brothers with regard to their inheritance. 7 For when I came from Pad'dan, Rachel, alas, died in the land of Cā'naan on the way, while there was still some distance to go to Eph'rath; and I buried her there on the way to Eph'rath" (that is, Bethlehem).

8 When Israel saw Joseph's sons, he said, "Who are these?" 9 Joseph said to his father, "They are my sons, whom God has given me here." And he said, "Bring them to me, please, that I may bless them." 10 Now the eyes of Israel were dim with age, and he could not see well. So Joseph brought them near him; and he kissed them and embraced them. 11 Israel said to Joseph, "I did not expect to see your face; and here God has let me see your children also." 12 Then Joseph removed them from his father's knees,[c] and he bowed himself with his face to the earth. 13 Joseph took them both, Ē'phra•im in his right hand toward Israel's left, and Ma•nas'seh in his left hand toward Israel's right, and brought them near him. 14 But Israel stretched out his right hand and laid it on the head of Ē'phra•im, who was the younger, and his left hand on the head of Ma•nas'seh, crossing his hands, for Ma•nas'seh was the firstborn. 15 He blessed Joseph, and said,

"The God before whom my ancestors
    Abraham and Isaac walked,
the God who has been my shepherd all my
    life to this day,
16 the angel who has redeemed me from all
    harm, bless the boys;
and in them let my name be perpetuated,
    and the name of my ancestors
    Abraham and Isaac;
and let them grow into a multitude on the
    earth."

17 When Joseph saw that his father laid his right hand on the head of Ē'phra•im, it displeased him; so he took his father's hand, to remove it from Ē'phra•im's head to Ma•nas'seh's head. 18 Joseph said to his father, "Not so, my father! Since this one is the firstborn, put your right hand on his head." 19 But his father refused, and said, "I

---

z Sam Gk Compare Vg: MT *He removed them to the cities*
a Heb *Israel*   b Traditional rendering of Heb *El Shaddai*
c Heb *from his knees*

Asian American

Assemble and Hear!

Genesis 49.1–2 is the first reading at Mass on the ninth day before Christmas. This is an important day for Filipino Catholics because it marks the beginning of Simbang Gabi, or Dawn Worship.

On the nine days before Christmas, people gather to celebrate Mass in the dark of the predawn—usually between four and five o'clock in the morning. Mass ends with chocolate and buns and socializing. In fact, this is such a popular custom that even people who don't come to Mass all year will make it for the nine Masses of Simbang Gabi! It is a special celebration of thankfulness for the gift of their Catholic faith.

This Philippine tradition is an example of a Catholic custom called a novena. A novena is a public or private prayer repeated nine times. It can be a prayer said every day for nine days, one day a week for nine weeks, one day a month for nine months, or in any other pattern of nine. Why not make up your own personal novena? Just think of a prayer in a form you find meaningful (journaling, singing, reading the Scriptures, or even praying silently), and repeat it once a day for nine days or once a week for nine weeks. Happy praying!

▶ **Gen 49.1–2**

know, my son, I know; he also shall become a people, and he also shall be great. Nevertheless his younger brother shall be greater than he, and his offspring shall become a multitude of nations." 20 So he blessed them that day, saying,

"By you[d] Israel will invoke blessings,
saying,
'God make you[d] like E'phra·im and like Ma·nas'seh.' "

So he put E'phra·im ahead of Ma·nas'seh. 21 Then Israel said to Joseph, "I am about to die, but God will be with you and will bring you again to the land of your ancestors. 22 I now give to you one

portion[e] more than to your brothers, the portion[e] that I took from the hand of the Am'o·rītes with my sword and with my bow."

Jacob's Last Words to His Sons

Then Jacob called his sons, and said: "Gather around, that I may tell you what will happen to you in days to come.
2 Assemble and hear, O sons of Jacob;
listen to Israel your father.

3 Reuben, you are my firstborn,
my might and the first fruits of my vigor,
excelling in rank and excelling in power.
4 Unstable as water, you shall no longer excel
because you went up onto your father's bed;
then you defiled it—you[f] went up onto my couch!

5 Sim'ē·on and Levi are brothers;
weapons of violence are their swords.
6 May I never come into their council;
may I not be joined to their company—
for in their anger they killed men,
and at their whim they hamstrung oxen.
7 Cursed be their anger, for it is fierce,
and their wrath, for it is cruel!
I will divide them in Jacob,
and scatter them in Israel.

8 Judah, your brothers shall praise you;
your hand shall be on the neck of your enemies;
your father's sons shall bow down before you.
9 Judah is a lion's whelp;
from the prey, my son, you have gone up.
He crouches down, he stretches out like a lion,
like a lioness—who dares rouse him up?
10 The scepter shall not depart from Judah,
nor the ruler's staff from between his feet,
until tribute comes to him;[g]
and the obedience of the peoples is his.
11 Binding his foal to the vine
and his donkey's colt to the choice vine,
he washes his garments in wine
and his robe in the blood of grapes;
12 his eyes are darker than wine,
and his teeth whiter than milk.

[d] you here is singular in Heb   [e] Or mountain slope (Heb shekem, a play on the name of the town and district of Shechem)   [f] Gk Syr Tg: Heb he   [g] Or until Shiloh comes or until he comes to Shiloh or (with Syr) until he comes to whom it belongs

GEN

13 Zeb′u·lun shall settle at the shore of the sea;
     he shall be a haven for ships,
         and his border shall be at Sī′don.

14 Is′sa·char is a strong donkey,
     lying down between the sheepfolds;
15 he saw that a resting place was good,
     and that the land was pleasant;
so he bowed his shoulder to the burden,
     and became a slave at forced labor.

16 Dan shall judge his people
     as one of the tribes of Israel.
17 Dan shall be a snake by the roadside,
     a viper along the path,
that bites the horse's heels
     so that its rider falls backward.

18 I wait for your salvation, O LORD.

19 Gad shall be raided by raiders,
     but he shall raid at their heels.

20 Ash′er's[h] food shall be rich,
     and he shall provide royal delicacies.

21 Naph′ta·lī is a doe let loose
     that bears lovely fawns.[i]

22 Joseph is a fruitful bough,
     a fruitful bough by a spring;
     his branches run over the wall.[j]
23 The archers fiercely attacked him;
     they shot at him and pressed him hard.
24 Yet his bow remained taut,
     and his arms[k] were made agile
by the hands of the Mighty One of Jacob,
     by the name of the Shepherd, the Rock
         of Israel,
25 by the God of your father, who will help
         you,
     by the Almighty[l] who will bless you
with blessings of heaven above,
blessings of the deep that lies beneath,
     blessings of the breasts and of the womb.
26 The blessings of your father
     are stronger than the blessings of the
         eternal mountains,
     the bounties[m] of the everlasting hills;
may they be on the head of Joseph,
     on the brow of him who was set apart
         from his brothers.

27 Benjamin is a ravenous wolf,
     in the morning devouring the prey,
     and at evening dividing the spoil."

28 All these are the twelve tribes of Israel, and this is what their father said to them when he blessed them, blessing each one of them with a suitable blessing.

Jacob's Death and Burial

29 Then he charged them, saying to them, "I am about to be gathered to my people. Bury me with my ancestors—in the cave in the field of Ē′phron the Hit′tīte, 30 in the cave in the field at Mach·pē′lah, near Mam′re, in the land of Cā′naan, in the field that Abraham bought from Ē′phron the Hit′tīte as a burial site. 31 There Abraham and his wife Sarah were buried; there Isaac and his wife Rebekah were buried; and there I buried Leah— 32 the field and the cave that is in it were purchased from the Hit′tītes." 33 When Jacob ended his charge to his sons, he drew up his feet into the bed, breathed his last, and was gathered to his people.

Then Joseph threw himself on his father's face and wept over him and kissed him. 2 Joseph commanded the physicians in his service to embalm his father. So the physicians embalmed Israel; 3 they spent forty days in doing this, for that is the time required for embalming. And the Egyptians wept for him seventy days.

4 When the days of weeping for him were past, Joseph addressed the household of Pharaoh, "If now I have found favor with you, please speak to Pharaoh as follows: 5 My father made me swear an oath; he said, 'I am about to die. In the tomb that I hewed out for myself in the land of Cā′naan, there you shall bury me.' Now therefore let me go up, so that I may bury my father; then I will return." 6 Pharaoh answered, "Go up, and bury your father, as he made you swear to do."

7 So Joseph went up to bury his father. With him went up all the servants of Pharaoh, the elders of his household, and all the elders of the land of Egypt, 8 as well as all the household of Joseph, his brothers, and his father's household. Only their children, their flocks, and their herds were left in the land of Gō′shen. 9 Both chariots and charioteers went up with him. It was a very great company. 10 When they came to the threshing floor of Ā′tad, which is beyond the Jordan, they held there a very great and sorrowful lamentation; and he observed a time of mourning for his father seven days. 11 When the Cā′naan·ite inhabitants of the land saw the mourning on the threshing floor of Ā′tad, they said, "This is a grievous mourning on the part of the Egyptians." Therefore the place was

---

h Gk Vg Syr: Heb *From Asher*   i Or *that gives beautiful words*   j Meaning of Heb uncertain   k Heb *the arms of his hands*   l Traditional rendering of Heb *Shaddai*   m Cn Compare Gk: Heb *of my progenitors to the boundaries*

named Ā'bel-miz'ra•im;[n] it is beyond the Jordan.
[12]Thus his sons did for him as he had instructed
them. [13]They carried him to the land of Cā'naan
and buried him in the cave of the field at Mach•pē'-
lah, the field near Mam're, which Abraham
bought as a burial site from Ē'phron the Hit'tite.
[14]After he had buried his father, Joseph returned
to Egypt with his brothers and all who had gone
up with him to bury his father.

Joseph Forgives His Brothers

15 Realizing that their father was dead, Joseph's brothers said, "What if Joseph still bears a
grudge against us and pays us back in full for all
the wrong that we did to him?" [16]So they approached[o] Joseph, saying, "Your father gave this
instruction before he died, [17]'Say to Joseph: I beg
you, forgive the crime of your brothers and the
wrong they did in harming you.' Now therefore
please forgive the crime of the servants of the God
of your father." Joseph wept when they spoke to
him. [18]Then his brothers also wept,[p] fell down before him, and said, "We are here as your slaves."
[19]But Joseph said to them, "Do not be afraid! Am
I in the place of God? [20]Even though you intended
to do harm to me, God intended it for good, in
order to preserve a numerous people, as he is doing today. [21]So have no fear; I myself will provide
for you and your little ones." In this way he reassured them, speaking kindly to them.

Joseph's Last Days and Death
(Heb 11.22)

22 So Joseph remained in Egypt, he and his
father's household; and Joseph lived one hundred
ten years. [23]Joseph saw Ē'phra•im's children of the
third generation; the children of Mā'chir son of
Ma•nas'seh were also born on Joseph's knees.
24 Then Joseph said to his brothers, "I am
about to die; but God will surely come to you, and
bring you up out of this land to the land that he
swore to Abraham, to Isaac, and to Jacob." [25]So
Joseph made the Israelites swear, saying, "When
God comes to you, you shall carry up my bones
from here." [26]And Joseph died, being one hundred
ten years old; he was embalmed and placed in a
coffin in Egypt.

---

[n] That is *mourning* (or *meadow*) *of Egypt*   [o] Gk Syr: Heb
they commanded   [p] Cn: Heb *also came*

? did you KNOW?

Israel's Ancestry

**Although the Israelites descended from
many different kin, the Book of Genesis
traces their origins back to a series of
common ancestors, which served to unite
them as a people. Genesis tells the stories
of those great ancestors, men and women
called patriarchs and matriarchs, who
were the founders of what later became
the people of Israel. The twelve tribes of
Israel are understood to be descendants
from Jacob's twelve sons (see Jacob's last
words in Genesis, chapter 49, for a description of those tribes). Twelve becomes
an important number that comes up
again and again in the Bible. For example,
the twelve Apostles are Jesus' closest
followers in the New Testament.**

**It can be confusing to remember who
is related to whom, so here's a chart to
keep everyone straight:**

Abraham

Hagar ——— Ishmael
(Sarah's slave)

Sarah ——— Isaac

  Rebekah ——— Esau (Edom)

  Jacob (Israel)

  Leah ——— Reuben
   — Simeon
   — Levi
   — Judah
   — Issachar
   — Zebulun
   — Dinah
    (only daughter)

Bilhah ——— Dan
(Rachel's maid) — Naphtali

Zilpah ——— Gad
(Leah's maid) — Asher

Rachel ——— Joseph
   — Benjamin

   — Ephraim
   — Manasseh

- **Levi's tribe was set aside as priests and
  was not assigned land after the conquest of Canaan.**
- **Because Jacob adopted Joseph's sons
  Ephraim and Manasseh, Joseph is the
  father of two tribes.**

Click! Chains snap shut around your ankles. Crack! The tip of a whip whistles past your head. Bang! A door shuts, leaving you in darkness. These are the sounds of slavery, and they come as a surprise at the beginning of the Book of Exodus. What happened after the happy ending in Genesis? Like an action-packed drama, Exodus tells a story of deceit and broken promises, and of how God's miraculous interventions delivered the Israelites from their slavery in Egypt.

At a Glance

- **Chapters 1–10.** Pharaoh's oppression, the call of Moses, the plagues

- **11.1—15.21.** the Passover, deliverance at the Red Sea

- **15.22—18.27.** the journey through the wilderness

- **19.1—35.3.** the Covenant at Mount Sinai, difficulty living the Covenant

- **35.4—40.38.** construction of the tabernacle

In-depth

The Book of Exodus is the story of Israel's liberation. Exodus literally means "going out," and this book's central story is of how God liberates the people from slavery in Egypt (an event called the Exodus). Its central character is Moses, who is chosen by God to become God's voice and the instrument of God's power. Exodus was written hundreds of years after these events, using oral traditions that described the origin of many of the Israelite's beliefs and religious rituals.

Exodus is divided into two major sections. The first section, chapters 1–18, begins with the Israelites enslaved in Egypt and prohibited from worshiping their God. Israel cries out to God, and God answers by sending Moses. When Pharaoh refuses to let the Israelites go, God sends ten devastating plagues, and Pharaoh finally gives in. Later, Pharaoh changes his mind and chases the Israelites, only to have his army destroyed after the Israelites' escape through the Red Sea. This section ends with the people wandering through the wilderness, sustained by food and water miraculously provided by God.

Quick Facts

Period Covered
sometime from 1500 to 1250 B.C.

Author
unknown author gathering oral traditions and stories from various tribal peoples

Themes
God liberates people from slavery and oppression. God sustains the Israelites in the wilderness. God forms a covenant marked by laws and rituals.

The second section of Exodus, chapters 19–40, occurs at Mount Sinai. There, God enters into a covenant with all the people. God's part of the Sinai Covenant is to guarantee continued protection. Israel's part is to be faithful to God alone, a faithfulness marked by special laws (chapters 20–23) and special worship (chapters 24–31) that unite them as a people. Exodus ends with Israel still encamped at Mount Sinai, struggling to become a people of the Covenant.

The stories and laws in Exodus are at the heart of both Jewish and Christian belief in a God who saves, a God of freedom. You cannot fully appreciate the meaning of Jesus' life, death, and Resurrection without knowing these stories.

The Book of *Exodus*

Exodus

These are the names of the sons of Israel who came to Egypt with Jacob, each with his household: [2] Reuben, Sim'e•on, Levi, and Judah, [3] Is'sa-char, Zeb'ū•lun, and Benjamin, [4] Dan and Naph'ta•lī, Gad and Ash'er. [5] The total number of people born to Jacob was seventy. Joseph was already in Egypt. [6] Then Joseph died, and all his brothers, and that whole generation. [7] But the Israelites were fruitful and prolific; they multiplied and grew exceedingly strong, so that the land was filled with them.

The Israelites Are Oppressed

[8] Now a new king arose over Egypt, who did not know Joseph. [9] He said to his people, "Look, the Israelite people are more numerous and more powerful than we. [10] Come, let us deal shrewdly with them, or they will increase and, in the event of war, join our enemies and fight against us and escape from the land." [11] Therefore they set task-masters over them to oppress them with forced labor. They built supply cities, Pī'thom and Ram'e•sēs, for Pharaoh. [12] But the more they were oppressed, the more they multiplied and spread, so that the Egyptians came to dread the Israelites. [13] The Egyptians became ruthless in imposing tasks on the Israelites, [14] and made their lives bitter with hard service in mortar and brick and in every kind of field labor. They were ruthless in all the tasks that they imposed on them.

[15] The king of Egypt said to the Hebrew mid-wives, one of whom was named Shiph'rah and the other Pū'ah, [16] "When you act as midwives to the Hebrew women, and see them on the birthstool, if it is a boy, kill him; but if it is a girl, she shall live." [17] But the midwives feared God; they did not do as the king of Egypt commanded them, but they let the boys live. [18] So the king of Egypt summoned the midwives and said to them, "Why have you done this, and allowed the boys to live?" [19] The midwives said to Pharaoh, "Because the Hebrew women are not like the Egyptian women; for they are vigorous and give birth before the midwife comes to them." [20] So God dealt well with the mid-wives; and the people multiplied and became very strong. [21] And because the midwives feared God, he gave them families. [22] Then Pharaoh com-manded all his people, "Every boy that is born to the Hebrews[a] you shall throw into the Nile, but you shall let every girl live."

Birth and Youth of Moses
(Heb 11.23)

Now a man from the house of Levi went and mar-ried a Lē'vīte woman. [2] The woman conceived and bore a son; and when she saw that he was a fine baby, she hid him three months. [3] When she could hide him no longer she got a papyrus basket for him, and plastered it with bitumen and pitch; she put the child in it and placed it among the reeds on the bank of the river. [4] His sister stood at a distance, to see what would happen to him.

---

a Sam Gk Tg: Heb lacks *to the Hebrews*

Saving Lives

In the story of the birth of Moses, Pharaoh ordered the Egyptian midwives to kill all the male Israelite babies at birth. The midwives recognized such killing as an atrocity and refused to obey Pharaoh. Their actions might be considered civil disobedience against unjust laws.

Some people claim that the right to have an abortion is a just law. Aren't they right? Consider this incident: At a youth group gathering, abortion was discussed and a video was shown on how abortions are performed. One young man shared that although he did not believe in abortion, he used to believe exceptions could be made, such as in the case of rape or incest. After watching the video, he said he no longer believed such exceptions could be morally justified. A young woman said the video had convinced her that abortion was in the same moral category as serial murder. These young people, like the midwives in Exodus, recognized that all human life is sacred.

▶ Ex 1.15–22

5 The daughter of Pharaoh came down to bathe at the river, while her attendants walked beside the river. She saw the basket among the reeds and sent her maid to bring it. ⁶When she opened it, she saw the child. He was crying, and she took pity on him. "This must be one of the Hebrews' children," she said. ⁷Then his sister said to Pharaoh's daughter, "Shall I go and get you a nurse from the Hebrew women to nurse the child for you?" ⁸Pharaoh's daughter said to her, "Yes." So the girl went and called the child's mother. ⁹Pharaoh's daughter said to her, "Take this child and nurse it for me, and I will give you your wages." So the woman took the child and nursed it. ¹⁰When the child grew up, she brought him to Pharaoh's daughter, and she took him as her son. She named him Moses,ᵇ "because," she said, "I drew him outᶜ of the water."

Moses Flees to Midian
(Heb 11.24–25)

11 One day, after Moses had grown up, he went out to his people and saw their forced labor.

b Heb *Mosheh*   *c* Heb *mashah*

Introducing ▶ MOSES

Moses is, without doubt, the most important character in the Pentateuch, if not the entire Old Testament. Struggling to find language to describe his greatness, Deut 34.10 says, "Never since has there arisen a prophet in Israel like Moses, whom the LORD knew face to face." Born to an unnamed couple from the tribe of Levi and raised as an Egyptian by the Pharaoh's daughter, Moses was perfectly suited to negotiate Israel's freedom from slavery in Egypt. In event after event, the author of Exodus shows us Moses' wonder-working power, his prophetic skill, and his intimacy with God.

Despite all of Moses' great accomplishments, he never loses his humanness. He lacks confidence in his ability to speak (Ex 4.10), he is angry and frustrated with his people (17.4), and he bargains with God out of love for his people (32.11–14). Moses, noble but also knowing sadness, is elegantly portrayed in the passage where he dies within sight of the Promised Land (Deuteronomy, chapter 34). These qualities paint a picture of someone whose perseverance and trust allowed God to work through him.

A prophet is literally God's voice, and Moses was indeed God's voice, which shaped Israel to be a people of the Covenant. All other leaders and figures in the Old Testament are compared with Moses. In the New Testament, even Jesus is compared with Moses.

He saw an Egyptian beating a Hebrew, one of his kinsfolk. 12 He looked this way and that, and seeing no one he killed the Egyptian and hid him in the sand. 13 When he went out the next day, he saw two Hebrews fighting; and he said to the one who was in the wrong, "Why do you strike your fellow Hebrew?" 14 He answered, "Who made you a ruler and judge over us? Do you mean to kill me as you killed the Egyptian?" Then Moses was afraid and thought, "Surely the thing is known." 15 When Pharaoh heard of it, he sought to kill Moses.

But Moses fled from Pharaoh. He settled in the land of Mid′i•an, and sat down by a well. 16 The priest of Mid′i•an had seven daughters. They came to draw water, and filled the troughs to water their father's flock. 17 But some shepherds came and drove them away. Moses got up and came to their defense and watered their flock. 18 When they returned to their father Reŭ′el, he said, "How is it that you have come back so soon today?" 19 They said, "An Egyptian helped us against the shepherds; he even drew water for us and watered the flock." 20 He said to his daughters, "Where is he? Why did you leave the man? Invite him to break bread." 21 Moses agreed to stay with the man, and he gave Moses his daughter Zip•pō′rah in marriage. 22 She bore a son, and he named him Ger′shom; for he said, "I have been an alien[d] residing in a foreign land."

23 After a long time the king of Egypt died. The Israelites groaned under their slavery, and cried out. Out of the slavery their cry for help rose up to God. 24 God heard their groaning, and God remembered his covenant with Abraham, Isaac, and Jacob. 25 God looked upon the Israelites, and God took notice of them.

Moses at the Burning Bush
(Ex 6.2—7.7; 11.1–4; 12.35–36)

Moses was keeping the flock of his father-in-law Jeth′rō, the priest of Mid′i•an; he led his flock beyond the wilderness, and came to Hō′reb, the mountain of God. 2 There the angel of the LORD appeared to him in a flame of fire out of a bush; he looked, and the bush was blazing, yet it was not consumed. 3 Then Moses said, "I must turn aside and look at this great sight, and see why the bush is not burned up." 4 When the LORD saw that he had turned aside to see, God called to him out of the bush, "Moses, Moses!" And he said, "Here I am." 5 Then he said, "Come no closer! Remove the sandals from your feet, for the place on which you are standing is holy ground." 6 He said further, "I am the God of your father, the God of Abra-

Asian American

Holy Ground

In many Asian cultures, before people enter a home, they remove their shoes. People do this before entering a mosque too. Perhaps you remove your shoes before entering your home as well. Removing one's shoes is a common sign of respect. Moses is commanded to remove his sandals in Ex 3.5. Why? Because he is standing on holy ground. Why is the ground holy? Because God is present.

Moses is awestruck and humbled by his experience of God's presence. In today's multimedia culture, we are rarely awed by anything. Even the burning bush would be just another special effect. How can we regain our sense of awe at God's majesty? Some people experience it in nature, looking at a star-filled sky or the waves rolling in on the ocean. Others experience it in getting to know other people deeply. Still others find it in the amazing patterns that science reveals. The one common element to experiencing awe seems to be the ability to slow down, look closely, and appreciate what you discover.

So slow down, find your own holy ground, take your shoes off, and let God fill you with awe!

▶ Ex 3.1–6

ham, the God of Isaac, and the God of Jacob." And Moses hid his face, for he was afraid to look at God.

7 Then the LORD said, "I have observed the misery of my people who are in Egypt; I have heard their cry on account of their taskmasters. Indeed, I know their sufferings, 8 and I have come down to deliver them from the Egyptians, and to bring them up out of that land to a good and broad land, a land flowing with milk and honey, to the country of the Cā′naan•ites, the Hit′tītes, the

---

d Heb *ger*

NATIVE AMERICAN

The Name of God

Many Native American peoples, such as the Lakota and the Sioux, have several names for God. Wakan-Tanka and Tun-ka-shi-la are still commonly used today. These words for God are often translated as Great Spirit.

This is a good translation because Wakan is a word that brings together the concepts of mystery, sacredness, holiness, awe, and inspiration. Tanka describes something that is great.

Tun-ka-shi-la is often used the same way as Wakan-Tanka, but its meaning is slightly different. Tun-ka-shi-la is often translated as Grandfather or Great Grandfather, but it means the "one who is the oldest, so old that nothing or no one is older." Tun-ka-shi-la is a name that reflects the Great Spirit as the source of all things, the one who has existed from the beginning.

▶ Ex 3.13–15

Am'o•rītes, the Per'iz•zītes, the Hī'vītes, and the Jeb'ū•sītes. 9 The cry of the Israelites has now come to me; I have also seen how the Egyptians oppress them. 10 So come, I will send you to Pharaoh to bring my people, the Israelites, out of Egypt." 11 But Moses said to God, "Who am I that I should go to Pharaoh, and bring the Israelites out of Egypt?" 12 He said, "I will be with you; and this shall be the sign for you that it is I who sent you: when you have brought the people out of Egypt, you shall worship God on this mountain."

The Divine Name Revealed

13 But Moses said to God, "If I come to the Israelites and say to them, 'The God of your ancestors has sent me to you,' and they ask me, 'What is his name?' what shall I say to them?" 14 God said to Moses, "I AM WHO I AM."*e* He said further, "Thus you shall say to the Israelites, 'I AM has sent me to

you.' " 15 God also said to Moses, "Thus you shall say to the Israelites, 'The LORD,*f* the God of your ancestors, the God of Abraham, the God of Isaac, and the God of Jacob, has sent me to you':

This is my name forever,
and this my title for all generations.
16 Go and assemble the elders of Israel, and say to them, 'The LORD, the God of your ancestors, the God of Abraham, of Isaac, and of Jacob, has appeared to me, saying: I have given heed to you and to what has been done to you in Egypt. 17 I declare that I will bring you up out of the misery of Egypt, to the land of the Cā'naan•ītes, the Hit'tītes, the Am'o•rītes, the Per'iz•zītes, the Hī'vītes, and the Jeb'ū•sītes, a land flowing with milk and honey.' 18 They will listen to your voice; and you and the elders of Israel shall go to the king of Egypt and say to him, 'The LORD, the God of the Hebrews, has met with us; let us now go a three days' journey into the wilderness, so that we may sacrifice to the LORD our God.' 19 I know, however, that the king of

---

e Or *I AM WHAT I AM* or *I WILL BE WHAT I WILL BE*   *f* The word "LORD" when spelled with capital letters stands for the divine name, *YHWH,* which is here connected with the verb *hayah,* "to be"

did you KNOW?

God's Mysterious Name

"I AM WHO I AM"—one possible translation of Yahweh from Ex 3.14—seems more like a definition than a name. Some scholars have suggested Yahweh might be better translated "he causes to be what exists." In any case, the four Hebrew letters *YHWH* (or Yahweh in English) are difficult to translate. Over the centuries, the Jewish people stopped pronouncing the four letters out of reverence for God and replaced them with the word Adonai, meaning "my Lord." Most English translations of the Bible respect this long-standing tradition, translating the original *YHWH* as LORD. This mysterious name of God reminds us that no name or symbol can fully express who God is.

▶ Ex 3.13–15

HISPANIC

¡Dios envía profetas para liberar a su pueblo!

GOD SENDS PROPHETS TO LIBERATE HIS PEOPLE!

God responded to the cry of his people, choosing Moses as a prophet and commissioning him to lead the Israelites to freedom. Despite Moses' first doubts, with God's assistance, Moses became an effective and powerful leader. God would not let Moses' excuses stand in the way of God's mission of liberation.

Christians share in Jesus Christ's prophetic work as well. We too need to speak out against injustice and help the victims of oppression. Like the prophets before us, we can only succeed with God's help.

In our time, great spiritual leaders have risen up to lead people to freedom: Mohandas Gandhi, Martin Luther King Jr., Dorothy Day, Archbishop Oscar Romero, and Cesar Chavez are just a few. As in the case of Moses, God inspired these leaders to see their people experiencing injustice and to seek to liberate them from oppressive powers. You can be sure that these people also had their doubts and relied on God for their strength and hope.

- Are you aware of any group that is being oppressed today? How might God be calling you to help?
- Ask God for wisdom, strength, and help in your mission.

▶ Ex 4.1–17

EX

Egypt will not let you go unless compelled by a mighty hand.*g* 20 So I will stretch out my hand and strike Egypt with all my wonders that I will perform in it; after that he will let you go. 21 I will bring this people into such favor with the Egyptians that, when you go, you will not go empty-handed; 22 each woman shall ask her neighbor and any woman living in the neighbor's house for jewelry of silver and of gold, and clothing, and you shall put them on your sons and on your daughters; and so you shall plunder the Egyptians."

Moses' Miraculous Power

Then Moses answered, "But suppose they do not believe me or listen to me, but say, 'The LORD did not appear to you.' " 2 The LORD said to him, "What is that in your hand?" He said, "A staff." 3 And he said, "Throw it on the ground." So he threw the staff on the ground, and it became a snake; and Moses drew back from it. 4 Then the LORD said to Moses, "Reach out your hand, and seize it by the tail"—so he reached out his hand and grasped it, and it became a staff in his hand— 5 "so that they may believe that the LORD, the God of their ancestors, the God of Abraham, the God of Isaac, and the God of Jacob, has appeared to you."

6 Again, the LORD said to him, "Put your hand inside your cloak." He put his hand into his cloak; and when he took it out, his hand was leprous,*h* as white as snow. 7 Then God said, "Put your hand

back into your cloak"—so he put his hand back into his cloak, and when he took it out, it was restored like the rest of his body— 8 "If they will not believe you or heed the first sign, they may believe the second sign. 9 If they will not believe even these two signs or heed you, you shall take some water from the Nile and pour it on the dry ground; and the water that you shall take from the Nile will become blood on the dry ground."

10 But Moses said to the LORD, "O my Lord, I have never been eloquent, neither in the past nor even now that you have spoken to your servant; but I am slow of speech and slow of tongue." 11 Then the LORD said to him, "Who gives speech to mortals? Who makes them mute or deaf, seeing or blind? Is it not I, the LORD? 12 Now go, and I will be with your mouth and teach you what you are to speak." 13 But he said, "O my Lord, please send someone else." 14 Then the anger of the LORD was kindled against Moses and he said, "What of your brother Aaron the Lē′vīte? I know that he can speak fluently; even now he is coming out to meet you, and when he sees you his heart will be glad. 15 You shall speak to him and put the words in his mouth; and I will be with your mouth and with his mouth, and will teach you what you shall do. 16 He indeed shall speak for you to the people; he shall serve as a mouth for you, and you shall serve

---

g Gk Vg: Heb *no, not by a mighty hand*   *h* A term for several skin diseases; precise meaning uncertain

as God for him. [17] Take in your hand this staff, with which you shall perform the signs."

Moses Returns to Egypt

18 Moses went back to his father-in-law Jeth'rō and said to him, "Please let me go back to my kindred in Egypt and see whether they are still living." And Jeth'rō said to Moses, "Go in peace." [19] The LORD said to Moses in Mid'i·an, "Go back to Egypt; for all those who were seeking your life are dead." [20] So Moses took his wife and his sons, put them on a donkey, and went back to the land of Egypt; and Moses carried the staff of God in his hand.

21 And the LORD said to Moses, "When you go back to Egypt, see that you perform before Pharaoh all the wonders that I have put in your power; but I will harden his heart, so that he will not let the people go. [22] Then you shall say to Pharaoh, 'Thus says the LORD: Israel is my firstborn son. [23] I said to you, "Let my son go that he may worship me." But you refused to let him go; now I will kill your firstborn son.' "

24 On the way, at a place where they spent the night, the LORD met him and tried to kill him. [25] But Zip·pō'rah took a flint and cut off her son's foreskin, and touched Moses'[i] feet with it, and said, "Truly you are a bridegroom of blood to me!" [26] So he let him alone. It was then she said, "A bridegroom of blood by circumcision."

27 The LORD said to Aaron, "Go into the wilderness to meet Moses." So he went; and he met him at the mountain of God and kissed him. [28] Moses told Aaron all the words of the LORD with which he had sent him, and all the signs with which he had charged him. [29] Then Moses and Aaron went and assembled all the elders of the Israelites. [30] Aaron spoke all the words that the LORD had spoken to Moses, and performed the signs in the sight of the people. [31] The people believed; and when they heard that the LORD had given heed to the Israelites and that he had seen their misery, they bowed down and worshiped.

Bricks without Straw

Afterward Moses and Aaron went to Pharaoh and said, "Thus says the LORD, the God of Israel, 'Let my people go, so that they may celebrate a festival to me in the wilderness.' " [2] But Pharaoh said, "Who is the LORD, that I should heed him and let Israel go? I do not know the LORD, and I will not let Israel go." [3] Then they said, "The God of the Hebrews has revealed himself to us; let us go a three days' journey into the wilderness to sacrifice to the LORD our God, or he will fall upon us with pestilence or sword." [4] But the king of Egypt said to

PRAY IT!
Why Me?

Read Ex 5.22–23. Can you imagine how Moses must have felt? He did what God told him to do, and things only got worse for the Israelites. But Moses was still able to talk to God, even if only to say, "Why did you ever send me?"

Thomas Merton, a famous Trappist monk and spiritual writer, knew that Christians sometimes feel like Moses did:

> The Christian
> must have the courage
> to follow Christ.
> The Christian
> who is risen in Christ
> must dare
> to be like Christ:
> he must dare
> to follow conscience
> even in unpopular causes.
> He must, if necessary,
> be able to disagree with the majority
> and make decisions
> that he knows
> to be according to the Gospel
> and teaching of Christ,
> even when others
> do not understand
> why he is acting this way.
> (*He Is Risen*, p. 22)

The next time you are feeling a little like Moses and wondering, Why me? try this prayer:

Faithful God, help me to trust in you during times of disappointment and disillusion. I want to believe you are working in ways I cannot see. Please help my disbelief. For I know that you will honor my best efforts and make things come out right in the end. Amen.

▶ Ex 5.22–23

them, "Moses and Aaron, why are you taking the people away from their work? Get to your labors!" [5] Pharaoh continued, "Now they are more numerous than the people of the land[j] and yet you want them to stop working!" [6] That same day Pharaoh

---

i Heb *his*   *j* Sam: Heb *The people of the land are now many*

commanded the taskmasters of the people, as well as their supervisors, 7 "You shall no longer give the people straw to make bricks, as before; let them go and gather straw for themselves. 8 But you shall require of them the same quantity of bricks as they have made previously; do not diminish it, for they are lazy; that is why they cry, 'Let us go and offer sacrifice to our God.' 9 Let heavier work be laid on them; then they will labor at it and pay no attention to deceptive words."

10 So the taskmasters and the supervisors of the people went out and said to the people, "Thus says Pharaoh, 'I will not give you straw. 11 Go and get straw yourselves, wherever you can find it; but your work will not be lessened in the least.' " 12 So the people scattered throughout the land of Egypt, to gather stubble for straw. 13 The taskmasters were urgent, saying, "Complete your work, the same daily assignment as when you were given straw." 14 And the supervisors of the Israelites, whom Pharaoh's taskmasters had set over them, were beaten, and were asked, "Why did you not finish the required quantity of bricks yesterday and today, as you did before?"

15 Then the Israelite supervisors came to Pharaoh and cried, "Why do you treat your servants like this? 16 No straw is given to your servants, yet they say to us, 'Make bricks!' Look how your servants are beaten! You are unjust to your own people."k 17 He said, "You are lazy, lazy; that is why you say, 'Let us go and sacrifice to the LORD.' 18 Go now, and work; for no straw shall be given you, but you shall still deliver the same number of bricks." 19 The Israelite supervisors saw that they were in trouble when they were told, "You shall not lessen your daily number of bricks." 20 As they left Pharaoh, they came upon Moses and Aaron who were waiting to meet them. 21 They said to them, "The LORD look upon you and judge! You have brought us into bad odor with Pharaoh and his officials, and have put a sword in their hand to kill us."

22 Then Moses turned again to the LORD and said, "O LORD, why have you mistreated this people? Why did you ever send me? 23 Since I first came to Pharaoh to speak in your name, he has mistreated this people, and you have done nothing at all to deliver your people."

Israel's Deliverance Assured
(Ex 3.1—4.17)

Then the LORD said to Moses, "Now you shall see what I will do to Pharaoh: Indeed, by a mighty hand he will let them go; by a mighty hand he will drive them out of his land."

PRAY IT?
You Promised, God

The Israelite people had been slaves for so long, they were discouraged and did not believe Moses' liberating message in Ex 6.1–9. Moses probably sounded crazy to them. The writer of Exodus reminds us of God's faithfulness to God's promises and that God's plans cannot be stopped by human weakness. We too may find it hard to believe in God's power in our life when we feel burdened and oppressed, especially over a long time.

In your prayer, reflect or journal on the following questions and suggestion:
- When do you find it hard to believe in God's promises?
- What people do you know who find it hard to accept God's power in their life?
- What barriers are keeping them from accepting God?
- Make up your own prayer expressing your desire to count on God's promises.

▶ Ex 6.1–9

2 God also spoke to Moses and said to him: "I am the LORD. 3 I appeared to Abraham, Isaac, and Jacob as God Almighty,l but by my name 'The LORD'm I did not make myself known to them. 4 I also established my covenant with them, to give them the land of Cā'naan, the land in which they resided as aliens. 5 I have also heard the groaning of the Israelites whom the Egyptians are holding as slaves, and I have remembered my covenant. 6 Say therefore to the Israelites, 'I am the LORD, and I will free you from the burdens of the Egyptians and deliver you from slavery to them. I will redeem you with an outstretched arm and with mighty acts of judgment. 7 I will take you as my people, and I will be your God. You shall know that I am the LORD your God, who has freed you from the burdens of the Egyptians. 8 I will bring you into the land that I swore to give to Abraham, Isaac, and Jacob; I will give it to you for a possession. I am the LORD.' " 9 Moses told this to the Israelites;

k Gk Compare Syr Vg: Heb *beaten, and the sin of your people*
l Traditional rendering of Heb *El Shaddai*   m Heb *YHWH*; see note at 3.15

but they would not listen to Moses, because of their broken spirit and their cruel slavery.

10 Then the LORD spoke to Moses, 11 "Go and tell Pharaoh king of Egypt to let the Israelites go out of his land." 12 But Moses spoke to the LORD, "The Israelites have not listened to me; how then shall Pharaoh listen to me, poor speaker that I am?"[n] 13 Thus the LORD spoke to Moses and Aaron, and gave them orders regarding the Israelites and Pharaoh king of Egypt, charging them to free the Israelites from the land of Egypt.

The Genealogy of Moses and Aaron
(Gen 46.8–27)

14 The following are the heads of their ancestral houses: the sons of Reuben, the firstborn of Israel: Hā′noch, Pal′lū, Hez′ron, and Car′mī; these are the families of Reuben. 15 The sons of Sim′ē•on: Je•mū′el, Jā′min, Ō′had, Jā′chin, Zō′har, and Shā′ūl,[o] the son of a Cā′naan•ite woman; these are the families of Sim′ē•on. 16 The following are the names of the sons of Levi according to their genealogies: Ger′shon,[p] Kō′hath, and Me•rar′ī, and the length of Levi's life was one hundred thirty-seven years. 17 The sons of Ger′shon:[p] Lib′nī and Shim′ē•ī, by their families. 18 The sons of Kō′hath: Am′ram, Iz′har, Hē′bron, and Uz′zi•el, and the length of Kō′hath's life was one hundred thirty-three years. 19 The sons of Me•rar′ī: Mah′lī and Mū′shī. These are the families of the Lē′vītes according to their genealogies. 20 Am′ram married Joch′e•bed his father's sister and she bore him Aaron and Moses, and the length of Am′ram's life was one hundred thirty-seven years. 21 The sons of Iz′har: Kō′rah, Nē′pheg, and Zich′rī. 22 The sons of Uz′zi•el: Mish′a•el, El′za•phan, and Sith′rī. 23 Aaron married E•lish′e•ba, daughter of Am•min′a•dab and sister of Nah′shon, and she bore him Nā′dab, A•bī′hū, El•ē•ā′zar, and Ith′a•mar. 24 The sons of Kō′rah: As′sir, El•kā′nah, and A•bī′a•saph; these are the families of the Kō′ra•hites. 25 Aaron's son El•ē•ā′zar married one of the daughters of Pū′ti•el, and she bore him Phin′e•has. These are the heads of the ancestral houses of the Lē′vītes by their families.

26 It was this same Aaron and Moses to whom the LORD said, "Bring the Israelites out of the land of Egypt, company by company." 27 It was they who spoke to Pharaoh king of Egypt to bring the Israelites out of Egypt, the same Moses and Aaron.

Moses and Aaron Obey God's Commands

28 On the day when the LORD spoke to Moses in the land of Egypt, 29 he said to him, "I am the LORD; tell Pharaoh king of Egypt all that I am speaking to you." 30 But Moses said in the LORD's presence, "Since I am a poor speaker,[q] why would Pharaoh listen to me?"

The LORD said to Moses, "See, I have made you like God to Pharaoh, and your brother Aaron shall be your prophet. 2 You shall speak all that I command you, and your brother Aaron shall tell Pharaoh to let the Israelites go out of his land. 3 But I will harden Pharaoh's heart, and I will multiply my signs and wonders in the land of Egypt. 4 When Pharaoh does not listen to you, I will lay my hand upon Egypt and bring my people the Israelites, company by company, out of the land of Egypt by great acts of judgment. 5 The Egyptians shall know that I am the LORD, when I stretch out my hand against Egypt and bring the Israelites out from among them." 6 Moses and Aaron did so; they did just as the LORD commanded them. 7 Moses was eighty years old and Aaron eighty-three when they spoke to Pharaoh.

Aaron's Miraculous Rod
(Ex 4.1–5)

8 The LORD said to Moses and Aaron, 9 "When Pharaoh says to you, 'Perform a wonder,' then you shall say to Aaron, 'Take your staff and throw it down before Pharaoh, and it will become a snake.' " 10 So Moses and Aaron went to Pharaoh and did as the LORD had commanded; Aaron threw down his staff before Pharaoh and his officials, and it became a snake. 11 Then Pharaoh summoned the wise men and the sorcerers; and they also, the magicians of Egypt, did the same by their secret arts. 12 Each one threw down his staff, and they became snakes; but Aaron's staff swallowed up theirs. 13 Still Pharaoh's heart was hardened, and he would not listen to them, as the LORD had said.

The First Plague: Water Turned to Blood

14 Then the LORD said to Moses, "Pharaoh's heart is hardened; he refuses to let the people go. 15 Go to Pharaoh in the morning, as he is going out to the water; stand by at the river bank to meet him, and take in your hand the staff that was turned into a snake. 16 Say to him, 'The LORD, the God of the Hebrews, sent me to you to say, "Let my people go, so that they may worship me in the wilderness." But until now you have not listened. 17 Thus says the LORD, "By this you shall know that I am the LORD." See, with the staff that is in my hand I will strike the water that is in the Nile, and it shall be turned to blood. 18 The fish in the river shall die, the river itself shall stink, and the Egyp-

---

n Heb *me? I am uncircumcised of lips*   o Or *Saul*   p Also spelled *Gershom*; see 2.22   q Heb *am uncircumcised of lips*; see 6.12

did you KNOW?

Plagues and the Crossing of the Red Sea

The writer of Exodus combines several versions of what happened in describing the ten plagues and the crossing of the Red Sea. Like in a fine tapestry, the different strands are carefully woven together to produce a suspenseful story. When Pharaoh refuses to let the Israelites go, God sends ten plagues to convince Pharaoh to cooperate. The first nine plagues are exaggerations of naturally occurring events. For example, Exodus says the first plague is the water of the Nile turning to blood. At times, silt and microbes pollute and redden the Nile, making the water undrinkable. The Israelite people see God at work in the timing of these natural events.

Finally, God must resort to drastic measures. For the tenth plague, God sends the angel of death to kill the first-born children of the Egyptians. Moses has the Israelites mark their doorposts with the blood of a lamb so that the angel of death "passes over" their homes. Pharaoh is now eager to get rid of the Israelites and releases them from service. They gladly begin their journey to God's Promised Land.

After the Israelites leave, Pharaoh regrets his decision and sends his army after them. As the Egyptians close in, the Israelites seem to be trapped at the marshlands by the Red Sea (see map 2, "The Exodus from Egypt"). Although the prose version of this situation in Exodus, chapter 14, and the poetic version in chapter 15 differ in many details, both stress that the Israelites are able to pass through a section of wetlands that were made nearly dry by a strong east wind. The chariot wheels of the Egyptians get stuck in the mud, and as the water returns, they drown. Again, it is the timing of God's help that enables the miraculous escape. God hears God's people and sets them free!

▶ Ex 7.1—14.31

tians shall be unable to drink water from the Nile.' " [19] The LORD said to Moses, "Say to Aaron, 'Take your staff and stretch out your hand over the waters of Egypt—over its rivers, its canals, and its ponds, and all its pools of water—so that they may become blood; and there shall be blood throughout the whole land of Egypt, even in vessels of wood and in vessels of stone.' "

20 Moses and Aaron did just as the LORD commanded. In the sight of Pharaoh and of his officials he lifted up the staff and struck the water in the river, and all the water in the river was turned into blood, [21] and the fish in the river died. The river stank so that the Egyptians could not drink its water, and there was blood throughout the whole land of Egypt. [22] But the magicians of Egypt did the same by their secret arts; so Pharaoh's heart remained hardened, and he would not listen to them, as the LORD had said. [23] Pharaoh turned and went into his house, and he did not take even this to heart. [24] And all the Egyptians had to dig along the Nile for water to drink, for they could not drink the water of the river.

25 Seven days passed after the LORD had struck the Nile.

The Second Plague: Frogs

[r] Then the LORD said to Moses, "Go to Pharaoh and say to him, 'Thus says the LORD: Let my people go, so that they may worship me. [2] If you refuse to let them go, I will plague your whole country with frogs. [3] The river shall swarm with frogs; they shall come up into your palace, into your bedchamber and your bed, and into the houses of your officials and of your people,[s] and into your ovens and your kneading bowls. [4] The frogs shall come up on you and on your people and on all your officials.' "

[5t] And the LORD said to Moses, "Say to Aaron, 'Stretch out your hand with your staff over the rivers, the canals, and the pools, and make frogs come up on the land of Egypt.' " [6] So Aaron stretched out his hand over the waters of Egypt; and the frogs came up and covered the land of Egypt. [7] But the magicians did the same by their secret arts, and brought frogs up on the land of Egypt.

8 Then Pharaoh called Moses and Aaron, and said, "Pray to the LORD to take away the frogs from me and my people, and I will let the people go to sacrifice to the LORD." [9] Moses said to Pharaoh, "Kindly tell me when I am to pray for you and for your officials and for your people, that the frogs may be removed from you and your houses and

---

r Ch 7.26 in Heb   s Gk: Heb *upon your people*   t Ch 8.1 in Heb

be left only in the Nile." [10] And he said, "Tomorrow." Moses said, "As you say! So that you may know that there is no one like the LORD our God, [11] the frogs shall leave you and your houses and your officials and your people; they shall be left only in the Nile." [12] Then Moses and Aaron went out from Pharaoh; and Moses cried out to the LORD concerning the frogs that he had brought upon Pharaoh.[u] [13] And the LORD did as Moses requested: the frogs died in the houses, the courtyards, and the fields. [14] And they gathered them together in heaps, and the land stank. [15] But when Pharaoh saw that there was a respite, he hardened his heart, and would not listen to them, just as the LORD had said.

The Third Plague: Gnats

16 Then the LORD said to Moses, "Say to Aaron, 'Stretch out your staff and strike the dust of the earth, so that it may become gnats throughout the whole land of Egypt.'" [17] And they did so; Aaron stretched out his hand with his staff and struck the dust of the earth, and gnats came on humans and animals alike; all the dust of the earth turned into gnats throughout the whole land of Egypt. [18] The magicians tried to produce gnats by their secret arts, but they could not. There were gnats on both humans and animals. [19] And the magicians said to Pharaoh, "This is the finger of God!" But Pharaoh's heart was hardened, and he would not listen to them, just as the LORD had said.

The Fourth Plague: Flies

20 Then the LORD said to Moses, "Rise early in the morning and present yourself before Pharaoh, as he goes out to the water, and say to him, 'Thus says the LORD: Let my people go, so that they may worship me. [21] For if you will not let my people go, I will send swarms of flies on you, your officials, and your people, and into your houses; and the houses of the Egyptians shall be filled with swarms of flies; so also the land where they live. [22] But on that day I will set apart the land of Gō'-shen, where my people live, so that no swarms of flies shall be there, that you may know that I the LORD am in this land. [23] Thus I will make a distinction[v] between my people and your people. This sign shall appear tomorrow.'" [24] The LORD did so, and great swarms of flies came into the house of Pharaoh and into his officials' houses; in all of Egypt the land was ruined because of the flies.

25 Then Pharaoh summoned Moses and Aaron, and said, "Go, sacrifice to your God within the land." [26] But Moses said, "It would not be right to do so; for the sacrifices that we offer to the LORD our God are offensive to the Egyptians. If we offer in the sight of the Egyptians sacrifices that are offensive to them, will they not stone us? [27] We must go a three days' journey into the wilderness and sacrifice to the LORD our God as he commands us." [28] So Pharaoh said, "I will let you go to sacrifice to the LORD your God in the wilderness, provided you do not go very far away. Pray for me." [29] Then Moses said, "As soon as I leave you, I will pray to the LORD that the swarms of flies may depart tomorrow from Pharaoh, from his officials, and from his people; only do not let Pharaoh again deal falsely by not letting the people go to sacrifice to the LORD."

30 So Moses went out from Pharaoh and prayed to the LORD. [31] And the LORD did as Moses asked: he removed the swarms of flies from Pharaoh, from his officials, and from his people; not one remained. [32] But Pharaoh hardened his heart this time also, and would not let the people go.

The Fifth Plague: Livestock Diseased

Then the LORD said to Moses, "Go to Pharaoh, and say to him, 'Thus says the LORD, the God of the Hebrews: Let my people go, so that they may worship me. [2] For if you refuse to let them go and still hold them, [3] the hand of the LORD will strike with a deadly pestilence your livestock in the field: the horses, the donkeys, the camels, the herds, and the flocks. [4] But the LORD will make a distinction between the livestock of Israel and the livestock of Egypt, so that nothing shall die of all that belongs to the Israelites.'" [5] The LORD set a time, saying, "Tomorrow the LORD will do this thing in the land." [6] And on the next day the LORD did so; all the livestock of the Egyptians died, but of the livestock of the Israelites not one died. [7] Pharaoh inquired and found that not one of the livestock of the Israelites was dead. But the heart of Pharaoh was hardened, and he would not let the people go.

The Sixth Plague: Boils
(Deut 28.27)

8 Then the LORD said to Moses and Aaron, "Take handfuls of soot from the kiln, and let Moses throw it in the air in the sight of Pharaoh. [9] It shall become fine dust all over the land of Egypt, and shall cause festering boils on humans and animals throughout the whole land of Egypt." [10] So they took soot from the kiln, and stood before Pharaoh, and Moses threw it in the air, and it caused festering boils on humans and animals. [11] The magicians could not stand before Moses because of the boils, for the boils afflicted the magi-

---

u Or frogs, as he had agreed with Pharaoh   v Gk Vg: Heb will set redemption cians as well as all the Egyptians. 12 But the LORD hardened the heart of Pharaoh, and he would not listen to them, just as the LORD had spoken to Moses.

The Seventh Plague: Thunder and Hail

13 Then the LORD said to Moses, "Rise up early in the morning and present yourself before Pharaoh, and say to him, 'Thus says the LORD, the God of the Hebrews: Let my people go, so that they may worship me. 14 For this time I will send all my plagues upon you yourself, and upon your officials, and upon your people, so that you may know that there is no one like me in all the earth. 15 For by now I could have stretched out my hand and struck you and your people with pestilence, and you would have been cut off from the earth. 16 But this is why I have let you live: to show you my power, and to make my name resound through all the earth. 17 You are still exalting yourself against my people, and will not let them go. 18 Tomorrow at this time I will cause the heaviest hail to fall that has ever fallen in Egypt from the day it was founded until now. 19 Send, therefore, and have your livestock and everything that you have in the open field brought to a secure place; every human or animal that is in the open field and is not brought under shelter will die when the hail comes down upon them.' " 20 Those officials of Pharaoh who feared the word of the LORD hurried their slaves and livestock off to a secure place. 21 Those who did not regard the word of the LORD left their slaves and livestock in the open field.

22 The LORD said to Moses, "Stretch out your hand toward heaven so that hail may fall on the whole land of Egypt, on humans and animals and all the plants of the field in the land of Egypt." 23 Then Moses stretched out his staff toward heaven, and the LORD sent thunder and hail, and fire came down on the earth. And the LORD rained hail on the land of Egypt; 24 there was hail with fire flashing continually in the midst of it, such heavy hail as had never fallen in all the land of Egypt since it became a nation. 25 The hail struck down everything that was in the open field throughout all the land of Egypt, both human and animal; the hail also struck down all the plants of the field, and shattered every tree in the field. 26 Only in the land of Go'shen, where the Israelites were, there was no hail.

27 Then Pharaoh summoned Moses and Aaron, and said to them, "This time I have sinned; the LORD is in the right, and I and my people are in the wrong. 28 Pray to the LORD! Enough of God's thunder and hail! I will let you go; you need stay no longer." 29 Moses said to him, "As soon as I have gone out of the city, I will stretch out my hands to the LORD; the thunder will cease, and there will be no more hail, so that you may know that the earth is the LORD's. 30 But as for you and your officials, I know that you do not yet fear the LORD God." 31 (Now the flax and the barley were ruined, for the barley was in the ear and the flax was in bud. 32 But the wheat and the spelt were not ruined, for they are late in coming up.) 33 So Moses left Pharaoh, went out of the city, and stretched out his hands to the LORD; then the thunder and the hail ceased, and the rain no longer poured down on the earth. 34 But when Pharaoh saw that the rain and the hail and the thunder had ceased, he sinned once more and hardened his heart, he and his officials. 35 So the heart of Pharaoh was hardened, and he would not let the Israelites go, just as the LORD had spoken through Moses.

The Eighth Plague: Locusts
(Joel 1.2–4)

Then the LORD said to Moses, "Go to Pharaoh; for I have hardened his heart and the heart of his officials, in order that I may show these signs of mine among them, 2 and that you may tell your children and grandchildren how I have made fools of the Egyptians and what signs I have done among them—so that you may know that I am the LORD."

3 So Moses and Aaron went to Pharaoh, and said to him, "Thus says the LORD, the God of the Hebrews, 'How long will you refuse to humble yourself before me? Let my people go, so that they may worship me. 4 For if you refuse to let my people go, tomorrow I will bring locusts into your country. 5 They shall cover the surface of the land, so that no one will be able to see the land. They shall devour the last remnant left you after the hail, and they shall devour every tree of yours that grows in the field. 6 They shall fill your houses, and the houses of all your officials and of all the Egyptians—something that neither your parents nor your grandparents have seen, from the day they came on earth to this day.' " Then he turned and went out from Pharaoh.

7 Pharaoh's officials said to him, "How long shall this fellow be a snare to us? Let the people go, so that they may worship the LORD their God; do you not yet understand that Egypt is ruined?" 8 So Moses and Aaron were brought back to Pharaoh, and he said to them, "Go, worship the LORD your God! But which ones are to go?" 9 Moses said, "We will go with our young and our old; we will go with our sons and daughters and with our flocks and herds, because we have the LORD's festival to celebrate." 10 He said to them, "The LORD indeed will be with you, if ever I let your little ones

go with you! Plainly, you have some evil purpose in mind. ¹¹ No, never! Your men may go and worship the LORD, for that is what you are asking." And they were driven out from Pharaoh's presence.

12 Then the LORD said to Moses, "Stretch out your hand over the land of Egypt, so that the locusts may come upon it and eat every plant in the land, all that the hail has left." ¹³ So Moses stretched out his staff over the land of Egypt, and the LORD brought an east wind upon the land all that day and all that night; when morning came, the east wind had brought the locusts. ¹⁴ The locusts came upon all the land of Egypt and settled on the whole country of Egypt, such a dense swarm of locusts as had never been before, nor ever shall be again. ¹⁵ They covered the surface of the whole land, so that the land was black; and they ate all the plants in the land and all the fruit of the trees that the hail had left; nothing green was left, no tree, no plant in the field, in all the land of Egypt. ¹⁶ Pharaoh hurriedly summoned Moses and Aaron and said, "I have sinned against the LORD your God, and against you. ¹⁷ Do forgive my sin just this once, and pray to the LORD your God that at the least he remove this deadly thing from me." ¹⁸ So he went out from Pharaoh and prayed to the LORD. ¹⁹ The LORD changed the wind into a very strong west wind, which lifted the locusts and drove them into the Red Sea;ʷ not a single locust was left in all the country of Egypt. ²⁰ But the LORD hardened Pharaoh's heart, and he would not let the Israelites go.

The Ninth Plague: Darkness

21 Then the LORD said to Moses, "Stretch out your hand toward heaven so that there may be darkness over the land of Egypt, a darkness that can be felt." ²² So Moses stretched out his hand toward heaven, and there was dense darkness in all the land of Egypt for three days. ²³ People could not see one another, and for three days they could not move from where they were; but all the Israelites had light where they lived. ²⁴ Then Pharaoh summoned Moses, and said, "Go, worship the LORD. Only your flocks and your herds shall remain behind. Even your children may go with you." ²⁵ But Moses said, "You must also let us have sacrifices and burnt offerings to sacrifice to the LORD our God. ²⁶ Our livestock also must go with us; not a hoof shall be left behind, for we must choose some of them for the worship of the LORD our God, and we will not know what to use to worship the LORD until we arrive there." ²⁷ But the LORD hardened Pharaoh's heart, and he was unwilling to let them go. ²⁸ Then Pharaoh said to him, "Get away from me! Take care that you do not see

my face again, for on the day you see my face you shall die." ²⁹ Moses said, "Just as you say! I will never see your face again."

Warning of the Final Plague
(Ex 3.21–22; 12.35–36)

The LORD said to Moses, "I will bring one more plague upon Pharaoh and upon Egypt; afterwards he will let you go from here; indeed, when he lets you go, he will drive you away. ² Tell the people that every man is to ask his neighbor and every woman is to ask her neighbor for objects of silver and gold." ³ The LORD gave the people favor in the sight of the Egyptians. Moreover, Moses himself was a man of great importance in the land of Egypt, in the sight of Pharaoh's officials and in the sight of the people.

4 Moses said, "Thus says the LORD: About midnight I will go out through Egypt. ⁵ Every firstborn in the land of Egypt shall die, from the firstborn of Pharaoh who sits on his throne to the firstborn of the female slave who is behind the handmill, and all the firstborn of the livestock. ⁶ Then there will be a loud cry throughout the whole land of Egypt, such as has never been or will ever be again. ⁷ But not a dog shall growl at any of the Israelites—not at people, not at animals—so that you may know that the LORD makes a distinction between Egypt and Israel. ⁸ Then all these officials of yours shall come down to me, and bow low to me, saying, 'Leave us, you and all the people who follow you.' After that I will leave." And in hot anger he left Pharaoh.

9 The LORD said to Moses, "Pharaoh will not listen to you, in order that my wonders may be multiplied in the land of Egypt." ¹⁰ Moses and Aaron performed all these wonders before Pharaoh; but the LORD hardened Pharaoh's heart, and he did not let the people of Israel go out of his land.

The First Passover Instituted
(Num 9.1–14; Deut 16.1–8; Ezek 45.21–25)

The LORD said to Moses and Aaron in the land of Egypt: ² This month shall mark for you the beginning of months; it shall be the first month of the year for you. ³ Tell the whole congregation of Israel that on the tenth of this month they are to take a lamb for each family, a lamb for each household. ⁴ If a household is too small for a whole lamb, it shall join its closest neighbor in obtaining one; the lamb shall be divided in proportion to the number of people who eat of it. ⁵ Your lamb shall be without blemish, a year-old male; you may take it from the sheep or from the goats. ⁶ You shall keep it

---

ʷ Or *Sea of Reeds*

until the fourteenth day of this month; then the whole assembled congregation of Israel shall slaughter it at twilight. 7They shall take some of the blood and put it on the two doorposts and the lintel of the houses in which they eat it. 8They shall eat the lamb that same night; they shall eat it roasted over the fire with unleavened bread and bitter herbs. 9Do not eat any of it raw or boiled in water, but roasted over the fire, with its head, legs, and inner organs. 10You shall let none of it remain until the morning; anything that remains until the morning you shall burn. 11This is how you shall eat it: your loins girded, your sandals on your feet, and your staff in your hand; and you shall eat it hurriedly. It is the passover of the LORD. 12For I will pass through the land of Egypt that night, and I will strike down every firstborn in the land of Egypt, both human beings and animals; on all the gods of Egypt I will execute judgments: I am the LORD. 13The blood shall be a sign for you on the houses where you live: when I see the blood, I will pass over you, and no plague shall destroy you when I strike the land of Egypt.

14 This day shall be a day of remembrance for you. You shall celebrate it as a festival to the LORD; throughout your generations you shall observe it as a perpetual ordinance. 15Seven days you shall eat unleavened bread; on the first day you shall remove leaven from your houses, for whoever eats leavened bread from the first day until the seventh day shall be cut off from Israel. 16On the first day you shall hold a solemn assembly, and on the seventh day a solemn assembly; no work shall be done on those days; only what everyone must eat, that alone may be prepared by you. 17You shall observe the festival of unleavened bread, for on this very day I brought your companies out of the land of Egypt: you shall observe this day throughout your generations as a perpetual ordinance. 18In the first month, from the evening of the fourteenth day until the evening of the twenty-first day, you shall eat unleavened bread. 19For seven days no leaven shall be found in your houses; for whoever eats what is leavened shall be cut off from the congregation of Israel, whether an alien or a native of the land. 20You shall eat nothing leavened; in all your settlements you shall eat unleavened bread.

21 Then Moses called all the elders of Israel and said to them, "Go, select lambs for your families, and slaughter the passover lamb. 22Take a bunch of hyssop, dip it in the blood that is in the basin, and touch the lintel and the two doorposts with the blood in the basin. None of you shall go outside the door of your house until morning. 23For the LORD will pass through to strike down

the Egyptians; when he sees the blood on the lintel and on the two doorposts, the LORD will pass over that door and will not allow the destroyer to enter your houses to strike you down. 24You shall observe this rite as a perpetual ordinance for you and

did you KNOW?
The Passover

"Why is this night so different from all other nights?" This question, asked by the youngest member of the family, is part of the Jewish celebration of the Passover celebration. Jewish people continue to celebrate the Passover today in fulfillment of Moses' command, "You shall observe this rite as a perpetual ordinance for you and your children" (Ex 12.24).

The Passover is celebrated around a meal including lamb and unleavened bread. The lamb recalls the Passover lamb whose blood was placed on the doorpost to protect the firstborn from the angel of death. The unleavened bread recalls the haste in which the people prepared to depart. Retelling the ancient story, generations of Jews have remembered that "night of nights" when the angel of death passed over the Israelites' houses and struck down the firstborn of the Egyptians. On that night, the people of God were finally released from slavery. Thus, Passover is a celebration of God's gift of freedom—a religious Independence Day, so to speak.

It was during the Passover celebration that Jesus had his farewell dinner (see Jn 13.1), placing himself as the paschal sacrifice. Christians see Jesus as the new Passover; through his death and Resurrection, we are finally liberated from all bondage, including sin and death.

▸ Ex 12.14–28

your children. 25When you come to the land that the LORD will give you, as he has promised, you shall keep this observance. 26And when your children ask you, 'What do you mean by this observance?' 27you shall say, 'It is the passover sacrifice to the LORD, for he passed over the houses of the Israelites in Egypt, when he struck down the Egyptians but spared our houses.' " And the people bowed down and worshiped.

28 The Israelites went and did just as the LORD had commanded Moses and Aaron.

The Tenth Plague: Death of the Firstborn
(Ex 11.1–10)

29 At midnight the LORD struck down all the firstborn in the land of Egypt, from the firstborn of Pharaoh who sat on his throne to the firstborn of the prisoner who was in the dungeon, and all the firstborn of the livestock. 30 Pharaoh arose in the night, he and all his officials and all the Egyptians; and there was a loud cry in Egypt, for there was not a house without someone dead. 31 Then he summoned Moses and Aaron in the night, and said, "Rise up, go away from my people, both you and the Israelites! Go, worship the LORD, as you said. 32 Take your flocks and your herds, as you said, and be gone. And bring a blessing on me too!"

The Exodus: From Rameses to Succoth

33 The Egyptians urged the people to hasten their departure from the land, for they said, "We shall all be dead." 34 So the people took their dough before it was leavened, with their kneading bowls wrapped up in their cloaks on their shoulders. 35 The Israelites had done as Moses told them; they had asked the Egyptians for jewelry of silver and gold, and for clothing, 36 and the LORD had given the people favor in the sight of the Egyptians, so that they let them have what they asked. And so they plundered the Egyptians.

37 The Israelites journeyed from Ram'e•sēs to Suc'coth, about six hundred thousand men on foot, besides children. 38 A mixed crowd also went up with them, and livestock in great numbers, both flocks and herds. 39 They baked unleavened cakes of the dough that they had brought out of Egypt; it was not leavened, because they were driven out of Egypt and could not wait, nor had they prepared any provisions for themselves.

40 The time that the Israelites had lived in Egypt was four hundred thirty years. 41 At the end of four hundred thirty years, on that very day, all the companies of the LORD went out from the land of Egypt. 42 That was for the LORD a night of vigil, to bring them out of the land of Egypt. That same night is a vigil to be kept for the LORD by all the Israelites throughout their generations.

Directions for the Passover
(Gen 17.9–14; Ex 12.1–13)

43 The LORD said to Moses and Aaron: This is the ordinance for the passover: no foreigner shall eat of it, 44 but any slave who has been purchased may eat of it after he has been circumcised; 45 no bound or hired servant may eat of it. 46 It shall be eaten in one house; you shall not take any of the animal outside the house, and you shall not break any of its bones. 47 The whole congregation of Israel shall celebrate it. 48 If an alien who resides with you wants to celebrate the passover to the LORD, all his males shall be circumcised; then he may draw near to celebrate it; he shall be regarded as a native of the land. But no uncircumcised person shall eat of it; 49 there shall be one law for the native and for the alien who resides among you.

50 All the Israelites did just as the LORD had commanded Moses and Aaron. 51 That very day the LORD brought the Israelites out of the land of Egypt, company by company.

The LORD said to Moses: 2 Consecrate to me all the firstborn; whatever is the first to open the womb among the Israelites, of human beings and animals, is mine.

The Festival of Unleavened Bread
(Ex 12.14–20)

3 Moses said to the people, "Remember this day on which you came out of Egypt, out of the house of slavery, because the LORD brought you out from there by strength of hand; no leavened bread shall be eaten. 4 Today, in the month of Ā'bib, you are going out. 5 When the LORD brings you into the land of the Cā'naan•ites, the Hit'tītes, the Am'orītes, the Hi'vītes, and the Jeb'ū•sītes, which he swore to your ancestors to give you, a land flowing with milk and honey, you shall keep this observance in this month. 6 Seven days you shall eat unleavened bread, and on the seventh day there shall be a festival to the LORD. 7 Unleavened bread shall be eaten for seven days; no leavened bread shall be seen in your possession, and no leaven shall be seen among you in all your territory. 8 You shall tell your child on that day, 'It is because of what the LORD did for me when I came out of Egypt.' 9 It shall serve for you as a sign on your hand and as a reminder on your forehead, so that the teaching of the LORD may be on your lips; for with a strong hand the LORD brought you out of Egypt. 10 You shall keep this ordinance at its proper time from year to year.

The Consecration of the Firstborn

11 "When the LORD has brought you into the land of the Cā'naan•ites, as he swore to you and your ancestors, and has given it to you, 12 you shall set apart to the LORD all that first opens the womb. All the firstborn of your livestock that are males shall be the LORD's. 13 But every firstborn donkey you shall redeem with a sheep; if you do not redeem it, you must break its neck. Every firstborn male among your children you shall redeem. 14 When in the future your child asks you, 'What does this mean?' you shall answer, 'By strength of

AFRICAN AMERICAN
Look to the Hills

A black theology professor tells a story about two Israelites who, while crossing the Red Sea, kept looking down at their feet. One said: "Look at my feet. They're covered with mud. This is some fine mess that Moses led us into." They crossed the sea without ever looking up. They never saw the sea parted on either side. As they wiped the mud from their feet and garments, they completely missed the sea closing and the Egyptians being swallowed up at God's command!

So many of us—perhaps especially young African Americans—spend too much of our life with our eyes looking down. We see only the oppressions, rejections, denials, and struggles, and miss seeing the power of God. We waste a lot of time looking down at life's struggles and not looking up.

People of all races and cultures, the resurrected Christ has won the victory for all, so look up! Keep your eyes on the prize of the high calling of God in Christ Jesus. Remember Ps 121.1–2:

**I lift up my eyes to the hills—
  from where will my help come?
My help comes from the LORD,
  who made heaven and earth.**

Let's encourage one another as we work toward the same goals and keep looking up!

▶ Ex 14.1–31

hand the LORD brought us out of Egypt, from the house of slavery. 15 When Pharaoh stubbornly refused to let us go, the LORD killed all the firstborn in the land of Egypt, from human firstborn to the firstborn of animals. Therefore I sacrifice to the LORD every male that first opens the womb, but every firstborn of my sons I redeem.' 16 It shall serve as a sign on your hand and as an emblem[x] on your forehead that by strength of hand the LORD brought us out of Egypt."

The Pillars of Cloud and Fire
(Ex 40.34–38; Num 9.15–23; 1 Kings 8.10–11)

17 When Pharaoh let the people go, God did not lead them by way of the land of the Phi•lis'-tines, although that was nearer; for God thought, "If the people face war, they may change their minds and return to Egypt." 18 So God led the people by the roundabout way of the wilderness toward the Red Sea.[y] The Israelites went up out of the land of Egypt prepared for battle. 19 And Moses took with him the bones of Joseph who had required a solemn oath of the Israelites, saying, "God will surely take notice of you, and then you must carry my bones with you from here." 20 They set out from Suc'coth, and camped at Ē'tham, on the edge of the wilderness. 21 The LORD went in front of them in a pillar of cloud by day, to lead them along the way, and in a pillar of fire by night, to give them light, so that they might travel by day and by night. 22 Neither the pillar of cloud by day nor the pillar of fire by night left its place in front of the people.

Crossing the Red Sea

Then the LORD said to Moses: 2 Tell the Israelites to turn back and camp in front of Pī-ha•hī'roth, between Mig'dōl and the sea, in front of Bā'al-zē'-phon; you shall camp opposite it, by the sea. 3 Pharaoh will say of the Israelites, "They are wandering aimlessly in the land; the wilderness has closed in on them." 4 I will harden Pharaoh's heart, and he will pursue them, so that I will gain glory for myself over Pharaoh and all his army; and the Egyptians shall know that I am the LORD. And they did so.

5 When the king of Egypt was told that the people had fled, the minds of Pharaoh and his officials were changed toward the people, and they said, "What have we done, letting Israel leave our service?" 6 So he had his chariot made ready, and took his army with him; 7 he took six hundred

---

x Or *as a frontlet*; meaning of Heb uncertain   y Or *Sea of Reeds*

picked chariots and all the other chariots of Egypt with officers over all of them. ⁸ The LORD hardened the heart of Pharaoh king of Egypt and he pursued the Israelites, who were going out boldly. ⁹ The Egyptians pursued them, all Pharaoh's horses and chariots, his chariot drivers and his army; they overtook them camped by the sea, by Pī-ha·hī′roth, in front of Bā′al-zē′phon.

10 As Pharaoh drew near, the Israelites looked back, and there were the Egyptians advancing on them. In great fear the Israelites cried out to the LORD. ¹¹ They said to Moses, "Was it because there were no graves in Egypt that you have taken us away to die in the wilderness? What have you done to us, bringing us out of Egypt? ¹² Is this not the very thing we told you in Egypt, 'Let us alone and let us serve the Egyptians'? For it would have been better for us to serve the Egyptians than to die in the wilderness." ¹³ But Moses said to the people, "Do not be afraid, stand firm, and see the deliverance that the LORD will accomplish for you today; for the Egyptians whom you see today you shall never see again. ¹⁴ The LORD will fight for you, and you have only to keep still."

15 Then the LORD said to Moses, "Why do you cry out to me? Tell the Israelites to go forward. ¹⁶ But you lift up your staff, and stretch out your hand over the sea and divide it, that the Israelites may go into the sea on dry ground. ¹⁷ Then I will harden the hearts of the Egyptians so that they will go in after them; and so I will gain glory for myself over Pharaoh and all his army, his chariots, and his chariot drivers. ¹⁸ And the Egyptians shall know that I am the LORD, when I have gained glory for myself over Pharaoh, his chariots, and his chariot drivers."

19 The angel of God who was going before the Israelite army moved and went behind them; and the pillar of cloud moved from in front of them and took its place behind them. ²⁰ It came between the army of Egypt and the army of Israel. And so the cloud was there with the darkness, and it lit up the night; one did not come near the other all night.

GOD LIBERATES US FROM OPPRESSION!

Many centuries before Christ, the Israelites migrated to Egypt from Canaan, seeking food because of an extreme drought in their land. The Egyptians, taking advantage of the Israelites' need for food and shelter, set taskmasters to rule over them and made their lives bitter with hard service.

- **Have you, your family, or your people ever experienced oppression through forced labor?**
- **Are you aware of situations in which people are being oppressed or exploited because of their immigrant status, their educational level, or their need for food and shelter?**
- **Pray for God's liberating power, and ask God to give you the strength to fight unjust situations and oppression.**

The Israelite people groaned under their slavery and asked God for help. God responded to their plight and sent Moses to lead them into freedom. But they needed to overcome their fear of the unknown future and step out in trust. Their liberation was accomplished when they responded to God's initiative to free themselves from a life of bondage. To be free, we must first be willing to admit that we are enslaved to something.

- **What types of oppression or pressures have taken away your freedom to live according to God's will?**
- **How can your community help young people to recognize when they are enslaved by social and peer pressures?**
- **Pray with Psalm 54 to ask for God's help in your struggle. Or pray with Psalm 146 to praise and thank God for liberation that you have experienced.**

▶ Ex 14.1–31

21 Then Moses stretched out his hand over the sea. The LORD drove the sea back by a strong east wind all night, and turned the sea into dry land; and the waters were divided. 22 The Israelites went into the sea on dry ground, the waters forming a wall for them on their right and on their left. 23 The Egyptians pursued, and went into the sea after them, all of Pharaoh's horses, chariots, and chariot drivers. 24 At the morning watch the LORD in the pillar of fire and cloud looked down upon the Egyptian army, and threw the Egyptian army into panic. 25 He clogged[z] their chariot wheels so that they turned with difficulty. The Egyptians said, "Let us flee from the Israelites, for the LORD is fighting for them against Egypt."

The Pursuers Drowned

26 Then the LORD said to Moses, "Stretch out your hand over the sea, so that the water may come back upon the Egyptians, upon their chariots and chariot drivers." 27 So Moses stretched out his hand over the sea, and at dawn the sea returned to its normal depth. As the Egyptians fled before it, the LORD tossed the Egyptians into the sea. 28 The waters returned and covered the chariots and the chariot drivers, the entire army of Pharaoh that had followed them into the sea; not one of them remained. 29 But the Israelites walked on dry ground through the sea, the waters forming a wall for them on their right and on their left.

30 Thus the LORD saved Israel that day from the Egyptians; and Israel saw the Egyptians dead on the seashore. 31 Israel saw the great work that the LORD did against the Egyptians. So the people feared the LORD and believed in the LORD and in his servant Moses.

The Song of Moses
(Ex 14.13–14; Ps 78.12–14)

Then Moses and the Israelites sang this song to the LORD:
"I will sing to the LORD, for he has
        triumphed gloriously;
    horse and rider he has thrown into the
        sea.
2   The LORD is my strength and my might,[a]
        and he has become my salvation;
    this is my God, and I will praise him,
        my father's God, and I will exalt him.
3   The LORD is a warrior;
        the LORD is his name.

4   "Pharaoh's chariots and his army he cast
        into the sea;
    his picked officers were sunk in the Red
        Sea.[b]

5   The floods covered them;
        they went down into the depths like a
        stone.
6   Your right hand, O LORD, glorious in
        power—
    your right hand, O LORD, shattered the
        enemy.
7   In the greatness of your majesty you
        overthrew your adversaries;
    you sent out your fury, it consumed them
        like stubble.
8   At the blast of your nostrils the waters piled
        up,
    the floods stood up in a heap;
    the deeps congealed in the heart of the
        sea.
9   The enemy said, 'I will pursue, I will
        overtake,
    I will divide the spoil, my desire shall
        have its fill of them.
    I will draw my sword, my hand shall
        destroy them.'
10 You blew with your wind, the sea covered
        them;
    they sank like lead in the mighty waters.

11 "Who is like you, O LORD, among the gods?
    Who is like you, majestic in holiness,
        awesome in splendor, doing wonders?
12 You stretched out your right hand,
        the earth swallowed them.

13 "In your steadfast love you led the people
        whom you redeemed;
    you guided them by your strength to
        your holy abode.
14 The peoples heard, they trembled;
        pangs seized the inhabitants of Phi•lis′ti•a.
15 Then the chiefs of E′dom were dismayed;
        trembling seized the leaders of Mō′ab;
    all the inhabitants of Cā′naan melted
        away.
16 Terror and dread fell upon them;
        by the might of your arm, they became
        still as a stone
    until your people, O LORD, passed by,
        until the people whom you acquired
        passed by.
17 You brought them in and planted them on
        the mountain of your own
        possession,
    the place, O LORD, that you made your
        abode,

---

z Sam Gk Syr: MT *removed*   a Or *song*   b Or *Sea of Reeds*

the sanctuary, O LORD, that your hands
have established.
18 The LORD will reign forever and ever."

19 When the horses of Pharaoh with his chariots and his chariot drivers went into the sea, the
LORD brought back the waters of the sea upon
them; but the Israelites walked through the sea on
dry ground.

PRAY IT?

Miriam Leads
the People in Praise

The Song at the Sea in Ex 15.1–21 is
probably the oldest writing in the
Bible. It is an example of how the Israelite
people put stories of God's mighty deeds
into song so that they could be remembered and passed on from generation to
generation.

Verses 20–21 tell us the prophet
Miriam led the prayer-singing and dancing. Miriam was Moses and Aaron's sister.
The three of them formed a leadership
team. Many biblical scholars believe that
she may be the author of the song. This is
one of the few biblical stories that clearly
show a woman serving as a prayer leader.

▸ Ex 15.1–21

The Song of Miriam
(Num 26.59)

20 Then the prophet Miriam, Aaron's sister,
took a tambourine in her hand; and all the
women went out after her with tambourines and
with dancing. 21 And Miriam sang to them:
"Sing to the LORD, for he has triumphed
gloriously;
horse and rider he has thrown into the sea."

Bitter Water Made Sweet

22 Then Moses ordered Israel to set out from
the Red Sea,*c* and they went into the wilderness of
Shur. They went three days in the wilderness and
found no water. 23 When they came to Mar'ah,
they could not drink the water of Mar'ah because
it was bitter. That is why it was called Mar'ah.*d*
24 And the people complained against Moses, saying, "What shall we drink?" 25 He cried out to the
LORD; and the LORD showed him a piece of wood;*e*

he threw it into the water, and the water became
sweet.

There the LORD *f* made for them a statute and an
ordinance and there he put them to the test. 26 He
said, "If you will listen carefully to the voice of the
LORD your God, and do what is right in his sight,
and give heed to his commandments and keep all
his statutes, I will not bring upon you any of the
diseases that I brought upon the Egyptians; for I
am the LORD who heals you."

27 Then they came to E'lim, where there were
twelve springs of water and seventy palm trees;
and they camped there by the water.

Bread from Heaven

The whole congregation of the Israelites set out
from E'lim; and Israel came to the wilderness of
Sin, which is between E'lim and Sinai, on the fifteenth day of the second month after they had
departed from the land of Egypt. 2 The whole
congregation of the Israelites complained against
Moses and Aaron in the wilderness. 3 The Israelites
said to them, "If only we had died by the hand of
the LORD in the land of Egypt, when we sat by the
fleshpots and ate our fill of bread; for you have
brought us out into this wilderness to kill this
whole assembly with hunger."

4 Then the LORD said to Moses, "I am going to
rain bread from heaven for you, and each day the
people shall go out and gather enough for that
day. In that way I will test them, whether they will
follow my instruction or not. 5 On the sixth day,
when they prepare what they bring in, it will be
twice as much as they gather on other days." 6 So
Moses and Aaron said to all the Israelites, "In the
evening you shall know that it was the LORD who
brought you out of the land of Egypt, 7 and in the
morning you shall see the glory of the LORD, because he has heard your complaining against the
LORD. For what are we, that you complain against
us?" 8 And Moses said, "When the LORD gives you
meat to eat in the evening and your fill of bread in
the morning, because the LORD has heard the complaining that you utter against him—what are we?
Your complaining is not against us but against the
LORD."

9 Then Moses said to Aaron, "Say to the whole
congregation of the Israelites, 'Draw near to the
LORD, for he has heard your complaining.' " 10 And
as Aaron spoke to the whole congregation of the
Israelites, they looked toward the wilderness, and
the glory of the LORD appeared in the cloud. 11 The
LORD spoke to Moses and said, 12 "I have heard the

---

c Or *Sea of Reeds*   *d* That is *Bitterness*   *e* Or *a tree*
f Heb *he*

LIVE IT!

Those Whiny Israelites

It's so easy to complain, isn't it? As soon as things aren't quite the way we would like, we start fussing and whining and grumbling. We have all done it. We are no different from the Israelites who, despite having just been miraculously delivered from slavery, start complaining after a few days in the wilderness. "Why," they ask, "would God lead us through the Red Sea only to let us die of hunger?"

Perspective. Faith. That's what it takes. Once we have been through a crisis or spent time in a place where people are truly poor and hungry, we gain a perspective on our own culture, on our own tendency to want everything just the way we like it and as soon as possible. The next time we hear ourselves complaining about something, let's pause and try to see a bigger picture, perhaps the one that God sees. Then we can ask ourselves, Is this really worth complaining about?

▶ Ex 16.1–3

E
X

complaining of the Israelites; say to them, 'At twilight you shall eat meat, and in the morning you shall have your fill of bread; then you shall know that I am the LORD your God.' "

13 In the evening quails came up and covered the camp; and in the morning there was a layer of dew around the camp. 14 When the layer of dew lifted, there on the surface of the wilderness was a fine flaky substance, as fine as frost on the ground. 15 When the Israelites saw it, they said to one another, "What is it?" g For they did not know what it was. Moses said to them, "It is the bread that the LORD has given you to eat. 16 This is what the LORD has commanded: 'Gather as much of it as each of you needs, an omer to a person according to the number of persons, all providing for those in their own tents.' " 17 The Israelites did so, some gathering more, some less. 18 But when they measured it with an omer, those who gathered much had nothing over, and those who gathered little had no shortage; they gathered as much as each of them needed. 19 And Moses said to them, "Let no one leave any of it over until morning." 20 But they did not listen to Moses; some left part of it until morning, and it bred worms and became foul. And Moses was angry with them. 21 Morning by morning they gathered it, as much as each needed; but when the sun grew hot, it melted.

22 On the sixth day they gathered twice as much food, two omers apiece. When all the leaders of the congregation came and told Moses, 23 he said to them, "This is what the LORD has commanded: 'Tomorrow is a day of solemn rest, a holy sabbath to the LORD; bake what you want to bake and boil what you want to boil, and all that is left over put aside to be kept until morning.' "

24 So they put it aside until morning, as Moses commanded them; and it did not become foul, and there were no worms in it. 25 Moses said, "Eat it today, for today is a sabbath to the LORD; today you will not find it in the field. 26 Six days you shall gather it; but on the seventh day, which is a sabbath, there will be none."

27 On the seventh day some of the people went out to gather, and they found none. 28 The LORD said to Moses, "How long will you refuse to keep my commandments and instructions? 29 See! The LORD has given you the sabbath, therefore on the sixth day he gives you food for two days; each of you stay where you are; do not leave your place on the seventh day." 30 So the people rested on the seventh day.

31 The house of Israel called it manna; it was like coriander seed, white, and the taste of it was like wafers made with honey. 32 Moses said, "This is what the LORD has commanded: 'Let an omer of it be kept throughout your generations, in order that they may see the food with which I fed you in the wilderness, when I brought you out of the land of Egypt.' " 33 And Moses said to Aaron, "Take a jar, and put an omer of manna in it, and place it before the LORD, to be kept throughout your generations." 34 As the LORD commanded Moses, so Aaron placed it before the covenant, h for safekeeping. 35 The Israelites ate manna forty years, until they came to a habitable land; they ate manna, until they came to the border of the land of Cā'naan. 36 An omer is a tenth of an ephah.

g Or "It is manna" (Heb man hu, see verse 31)   h Or treaty or testimony; Heb eduth

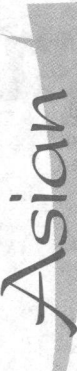

Manna and Rice

Rice is the symbol of our life
We eat rice daily
There are different kinds of rice
But we are one
as the rice-eating community
Rice is the symbol of celebration
We express our joy of harvest with it
There are many sufferings in Asia
but we anticipate the time of cosmic
    celebration.

(From Maren C. Tirabassi and
Kathy Wonson Eddy, editors,
Gifts of Many Cultures, p. 186)

This poem from Japan by Masao and Fumiko Takenaka expresses their appreciation for rice, the most basic food of the Japanese. It unites them as a people and reminds them to be joyful. In a similar way, Exodus tells how the gift of manna united the Israelites and gave them a reason for celebration despite their many trials. What foods unite you and your friends? family? culture? What connections do you see between manna, rice, and the Eucharist?

▶ Ex 16.1–36

Water from the Rock
(Num 20.1–13)

From the wilderness of Sin the whole congregation of the Israelites journeyed by stages, as the LORD commanded. They camped at Reph'i•dim, but there was no water for the people to drink. ² The people quarreled with Moses, and said, "Give us water to drink." Moses said to them, "Why do you quarrel with me? Why do you test the LORD?" ³ But the people thirsted there for water; and the people complained against Moses and said, "Why did you bring us out of Egypt, to kill us and our children and livestock with thirst?" ⁴ So Moses cried out to the LORD, "What shall I do with this people? They are almost ready to stone me." ⁵ The LORD said to Moses, "Go on ahead of the people, and take some of the elders of Israel with you; take in your hand the staff with which you struck the Nile, and go. ⁶ I will be standing there in front of you on the rock at Hō'reb. Strike the rock, and water will come out of it, so that the people may drink." Moses did so, in the sight of the elders of Israel. ⁷ He called the place Mas'sah*ⁱ* and Mer'i•bah,*ʲ* because the Israelites quarreled and tested the LORD, saying, "Is the LORD among us or not?"

Amalek Attacks Israel and Is Defeated
(Gen 14.7; Num 13.29; 14.25)

8 Then Am'a•lek came and fought with Israel at Reph'i•dim. ⁹ Moses said to Joshua, "Choose some men for us and go out, fight with Am'a•lek. Tomorrow I will stand on the top of the hill with the staff of God in my hand." ¹⁰ So Joshua did as Moses told him, and fought with Am'a•lek, while Moses, Aaron, and Hur went up to the top of the hill. ¹¹ Whenever Moses held up his hand, Israel prevailed; and whenever he lowered his hand, Am'a•lek prevailed. ¹² But Moses' hands grew weary; so they took a stone and put it under him, and he sat on it. Aaron and Hur held up his hands, one on one side, and the other on the other side; so his hands were steady until the sun set. ¹³ And Joshua

---

ⁱ That is *Test*　　*ʲ* That is *Quarrel*

PRAY IT!

Prayer in Support of Others

During the battle against Amalek, Moses' outstretched arms could be understood as a prayer of support for the Israelites. It was an effective prayer, too, because as long as he was able to maintain it, the Israelites were winning. When he could not maintain the prayer by himself, Aaron and Hur helped.

Prayer makes a difference. Research has shown that prayer helps people's emotional and physical health and healing, though it cannot explain why. Spiritual energy is a proven, powerful force.

Prayer doesn't even need words. To hold someone in prayer, just think of them and quietly take their pain or joy into your heart.

▶ Ex 17.8–15

defeated Am′a•lek and his people with the sword.

14 Then the LORD said to Moses, "Write this as a reminder in a book and recite it in the hearing of Joshua: I will utterly blot out the remembrance of Am′a•lek from under heaven." 15 And Moses built an altar and called it, The LORD is my banner. 16 He said, "A hand upon the banner of the LORD!*k* The LORD will have war with Am′a•lek from generation to generation."

Jethro's Advice
(Deut 1.9–18)

Jeth′rō, the priest of Mid′i•an, Moses' father-in-law, heard of all that God had done for Moses and for his people Israel, how the LORD had brought Israel out of Egypt. 2 After Moses had sent away his wife Zip•pō′rah, his father-in-law Jeth′rō took her back,

had beset them on the way, and how the LORD had delivered them. 9 Jeth′rō rejoiced for all the good that the LORD had done to Israel, in delivering them from the Egyptians.

10 Jeth′rō said, "Blessed be the LORD, who has delivered you from the Egyptians and from Pharaoh. 11 Now I know that the LORD is greater than all gods, because he delivered the people from the Egyptians,*n* when they dealt arrogantly with them." 12 And Jeth′rō, Moses' father-in-law, brought a burnt offering and sacrifices to God; and Aaron came with all the elders of Israel to eat bread with Moses' father-in-law in the presence of God.

13 The next day Moses sat as judge for the people, while the people stood around him from morning until evening. 14 When Moses' father-in-law saw all that he was doing for the people, he

E
X

Sharing Responsibility

Was Moses a workaholic (see Ex 18.18)? Maybe he just found himself suddenly overwhelmed with too many responsibilities. Fortunately for Moses, he had a wise father-in-law who could see an alternative that Moses could not see—or maybe did not want to see.

Who in this story do you feel most like?
- Moses, surrounded by people clamoring for your attention
- Jethro, concerned about Moses but able to offer some advice
- one of the people, hoping that Moses has a few minutes to listen to your problem
- one of the trustworthy judges, chosen by Moses to make sure that the Israelites experience justice in all their day-to-day business

When leaders share responsibility, they are saying to other people, "I trust you, we're in this together, and you are needed." When you are in a leadership position, remember Jethro's advice to Moses and don't be a lone ranger; ask others to help!

▶ Ex 18.13–26

3 along with her two sons. The name of the one was Ger′shom (for he said, "I have been an alien*l* in a foreign land"), 4 and the name of the other, El•i•ē′zer*m* (for he said, "The God of my father was my help, and delivered me from the sword of Pharaoh"). 5 Jeth′rō, Moses' father-in-law, came into the wilderness where Moses was encamped at the mountain of God, bringing Moses' sons and wife to him. 6 He sent word to Moses, "I, your father-in-law Jeth′rō, am coming to you, with your wife and her two sons." 7 Moses went out to meet his father-in-law; he bowed down and kissed him; each asked after the other's welfare, and they went into the tent. 8 Then Moses told his father-in-law all that the LORD had done to Pharaoh and to the Egyptians for Israel's sake, all the hardship that

said, "What is this that you are doing for the people? Why do you sit alone, while all the people stand around you from morning until evening?" 15 Moses said to his father-in-law, "Because the people come to me to inquire of God. 16 When they have a dispute, they come to me and I decide between one person and another, and I make known to them the statutes and instructions of God." 17 Moses' father-in-law said to him, "What you are doing is not good. 18 You will surely wear yourself out, both you and these people with you. For the task is too heavy for you; you cannot do it

---

k Cn: Meaning of Heb uncertain   *l* Heb *ger*   *m* Heb *Eli,* my God; *ezer*, help   *n* The clause *because . . . Egyptians* has been transposed from verse 10

alone. 19 Now listen to me. I will give you counsel, and God be with you! You should represent the people before God, and you should bring their cases before God; 20 teach them the statutes and instructions and make known to them the way they are to go and the things they are to do. 21 You should also look for able men among all the people, men who fear God, are trustworthy, and hate dishonest gain; set such men over them as officers over thousands, hundreds, fifties, and tens. 22 Let them sit as judges for the people at all times; let them bring every important case to you, but decide every minor case themselves. So it will be easier for you, and they will bear the burden with you. 23 If you do this, and God so commands you, then you will be able to endure, and all these people will go to their home in peace."

24 So Moses listened to his father-in-law and did all that he had said. 25 Moses chose able men from all Israel and appointed them as heads over the people, as officers over thousands, hundreds, fifties, and tens. 26 And they judged the people at all times; hard cases they brought to Moses, but any minor case they decided themselves. 27 Then Moses let his father-in-law depart, and he went off to his own country.

The Israelites Reach Mount Sinai

On the third new moon after the Israelites had gone out of the land of Egypt, on that very day, they came into the wilderness of Sinai. 2 They had journeyed from Reph'i•dim, entered the wilderness of Sinai, and camped in the wilderness; Israel camped there in front of the mountain. 3 Then Moses went up to God; the LORD called to him from the mountain, saying, "Thus you shall say to the house of Jacob, and tell the Israelites: 4 You have seen what I did to the Egyptians, and how I bore you on eagles' wings and brought you to myself. 5 Now therefore, if you obey my voice and keep my covenant, you shall be my treasured possession out of all the peoples. Indeed, the whole earth is mine, 6 but you shall be for me a priestly kingdom and a holy nation. These are the words that you shall speak to the Israelites."

7 So Moses came, summoned the elders of the people, and set before them all these words that the LORD had commanded him. 8 The people all answered as one: "Everything that the LORD has spoken we will do." Moses reported the words of the people to the LORD. 9 Then the LORD said to Moses, "I am going to come to you in a dense cloud, in order that the people may hear when I speak with you and so trust you ever after."

The People Consecrated

When Moses had told the words of the people to the LORD, 10 the LORD said to Moses: "Go to the people and consecrate them today and tomorrow. Have them wash their clothes 11 and prepare for the third day, because on the third day the LORD will come down upon Mount Sinai in the sight of all the people. 12 You shall set limits for the people all around, saying, 'Be careful not to go up the mountain or to touch the edge of it. Any who touch the mountain shall be put to death. 13 No hand shall touch them, but they shall be stoned or shot with arrows;*o* whether animal or human being, they shall not live.' When the trumpet sounds a long blast, they may go up on the mountain." 14 So Moses went down from the mountain to the people. He consecrated the people, and they washed their clothes. 15 And he said to the people, "Prepare for the third day; do not go near a woman."

16 On the morning of the third day there was thunder and lightning, as well as a thick cloud on the mountain, and a blast of a trumpet so loud that all the people who were in the camp trembled. 17 Moses brought the people out of the camp to meet God. They took their stand at the foot of the mountain. 18 Now Mount Sinai was wrapped in smoke, because the LORD had descended upon it in fire; the smoke went up like the smoke of a kiln, while the whole mountain shook violently. 19 As the blast of the trumpet grew louder and louder, Moses would speak and God would answer him in thunder. 20 When the LORD descended upon Mount Sinai, to the top of the mountain, the LORD summoned Moses to the top of the mountain, and Moses went up. 21 Then the LORD said to Moses, "Go down and warn the people not to break through to the LORD to look; otherwise many of them will perish. 22 Even the priests who approach the LORD must consecrate themselves or the LORD will break out against them." 23 Moses said to the LORD, "The people are not permitted to come up to Mount Sinai; for you yourself warned us, saying, 'Set limits around the mountain and keep it holy.' " 24 The LORD said to him, "Go down, and come up bringing Aaron with you; but do not let either the priests or the people break through to come up to the LORD; otherwise he will break out against them." 25 So Moses went down to the people and told them.

---

o Heb lacks *with arrows*

The Ten Commandments
(Deut 5.1–22)

Then God spoke all these words:

2 I am the LORD your God, who brought you out of the land of Egypt, out of the house of slavery; 3 you shall have no other gods before*p* me.

4 You shall not make for yourself an idol, whether in the form of anything that is in heaven

did you KNOW?
The Ten Commandments

The Covenant God made with the Israelites is often called the Sinai Covenant. The Ten Commandments are a handy summary of the Sinai Covenant—literally handy because they can be counted off on one's fingers. Because the Commandments are short (so short that they are sometimes called the Ten Words) and most of them begin with a similar phrase ("You shall not"), they are easily committed to memory. The ancient Israelites believed that everyone had to know and observe these basic rules if God's people were to live together in peace and security. Today, three major world religions—Jewish, Christian, and Islamic—continue to revere the Ten Commandments as basic building blocks of human community.

For the ancient Israelites, the Ten Commandments covered specific behaviors that made them different from the neighboring cultures. Over the centuries, Christians have applied the moral principles of the Ten Commandments to many other moral questions. In fact, the *Catechism of the Catholic Church* presents the Ten Commandments as the structure for teaching about many moral issues. For Jesus' teaching on the Commandments, see Mt 5.1—7.29; 22.34–40; Mk 12.28–34.

▶ Ex 20.1–17

above, or that is on the earth beneath, or that is in the water under the earth. 5 You shall not bow down to them or worship them; for I the LORD your God am a jealous God, punishing children for the iniquity of parents, to the third and the fourth generation of those who reject me, 6 but showing steadfast love to the thousandth generation*q* of those who love me and keep my commandments.

7 You shall not make wrongful use of the name of the LORD your God, for the LORD will not acquit anyone who misuses his name.

8 Remember the sabbath day, and keep it holy. 9 Six days you shall labor and do all your work. 10 But the seventh day is a sabbath to the LORD your God; you shall not do any work—you, your son or your daughter, your male or female slave, your livestock, or the alien resident in your towns. 11 For in six days the LORD made heaven and earth, the sea, and all that is in them, but rested the seventh day; therefore the LORD blessed the sabbath day and consecrated it.

12 Honor your father and your mother, so that your days may be long in the land that the LORD your God is giving you.

13 You shall not murder.*r*

14 You shall not commit adultery.

15 You shall not steal.

16 You shall not bear false witness against your neighbor.

17 You shall not covet your neighbor's house; you shall not covet your neighbor's wife, or male or female slave, or ox, or donkey, or anything that belongs to your neighbor.

18 When all the people witnessed the thunder and lightning, the sound of the trumpet, and the mountain smoking, they were afraid*s* and trembled and stood at a distance, 19 and said to Moses, "You speak to us, and we will listen; but do not let God speak to us, or we will die." 20 Moses said to the people, "Do not be afraid; for God has come only to test you and to put the fear of him upon you so that you do not sin." 21 Then the people stood at a distance, while Moses drew near to the thick darkness where God was.

The Law concerning the Altar

22 The LORD said to Moses: Thus you shall say to the Israelites: "You have seen for yourselves that I spoke with you from heaven. 23 You shall not make gods of silver alongside me, nor shall you make for yourselves gods of gold. 24 You need make for me only an altar of earth and sacrifice on it your burnt offerings and your offerings of well-being, your sheep and your oxen; in every place where I cause my name to be remembered I will come to you and bless you. 25 But if you make for me an altar of stone, do not build it of hewn

p Or *besides*   *q* Or *to thousands*   *r* Or *kill*   *s* Sam Gk Syr Vg: MT *they saw*

The TEN Commandments

1 I am the LORD your God . . . you shall have no other gods before me. **2** You shall not make wrongful use of the name of the LORD your God. **3** Remember the sabbath day, and keep it holy. **4** Honor your father and your mother. **5** You shall not murder. **6** You shall not commit adultery. **7** You shall not steal. **8** You shall not bear false witness against your neighbor. **9 & 10** You shall not covet your neighbor's house; you shall not covet your neighbor's wife . . . or anything that belongs to your neighbor.

20.2–17

stones; for if you use a chisel upon it you profane it. 26 You shall not go up by steps to my altar, so that your nakedness may not be exposed on it."

The Law concerning Slaves
(Deut 15.12–18)

These are the ordinances that you shall set before them:

2 When you buy a male Hebrew slave, he shall serve six years, but in the seventh he shall go out a free person, without debt. 3 If he comes in single, he shall go out single; if he comes in married, then his wife shall go out with him. 4 If his master gives him a wife and she bears him sons or daughters, the wife and her children shall be her master's and he shall go out alone. 5 But if the slave declares, "I love my master, my wife, and my children; I will not go out a free person," 6 then his master shall bring him before God.[t] He shall be brought to the door or the doorpost; and his master shall pierce his ear with an awl; and he shall serve him for life.

7 When a man sells his daughter as a slave, she shall not go out as the male slaves do. 8 If she does not please her master, who designated her for himself, then he shall let her be redeemed; he shall have no right to sell her to a foreign people, since he has dealt unfairly with her. 9 If he designates her for his son, he shall deal with her as with a daughter. 10 If he takes another wife to himself, he shall not diminish the food, clothing, or marital

---

[t] Or *to the judges*

rights of the first wife.*ᵘ* ¹¹And if he does not do these three things for her, she shall go out without debt, without payment of money.

The Law concerning Violence

12 Whoever strikes a person mortally shall be put to death. ¹³If it was not premeditated, but came about by an act of God, then I will appoint for you a place to which the killer may flee. ¹⁴But if someone willfully attacks and kills another by treachery, you shall take the killer from my altar for execution.

15 Whoever strikes father or mother shall be put to death.

16 Whoever kidnaps a person, whether that person has been sold or is still held in possession, shall be put to death.

17 Whoever curses father or mother shall be put to death.

18 When individuals quarrel and one strikes the other with a stone or fist so that the injured party, though not dead, is confined to bed, ¹⁹but recovers and walks around outside with the help of a staff, then the assailant shall be free of liability, except to pay for the loss of time, and to arrange for full recovery.

20 When a slaveowner strikes a male or female slave with a rod and the slave dies immediately, the owner shall be punished. ²¹But if the slave survives a day or two, there is no punishment; for the slave is the owner's property.

22 When people who are fighting injure a pregnant woman so that there is a miscarriage, and yet no further harm follows, the one responsible shall be fined what the woman's husband demands, paying as much as the judges determine. ²³If any harm follows, then you shall give life for life, ²⁴eye for eye, tooth for tooth, hand for hand, foot for foot, ²⁵burn for burn, wound for wound, stripe for stripe.

26 When a slaveowner strikes the eye of a male or female slave, destroying it, the owner shall let the slave go, a free person, to compensate for the eye. ²⁷If the owner knocks out a tooth of a male or female slave, the slave shall be let go, a free person, to compensate for the tooth.

Laws concerning Property

28 When an ox gores a man or a woman to death, the ox shall be stoned, and its flesh shall not be eaten; but the owner of the ox shall not be liable. ²⁹If the ox has been accustomed to gore in the past, and its owner has been warned but has not restrained it, and it kills a man or a woman, the ox shall be stoned, and its owner also shall be put to death. ³⁰If a ransom is imposed on the owner, then the owner shall pay whatever is imposed for the redemption of the victim's life. ³¹If it gores a boy or a girl, the owner shall be dealt with according to this same rule. ³²If the ox gores a male or female slave, the owner shall pay to the slaveowner thirty shekels of silver, and the ox shall be stoned.

33 If someone leaves a pit open, or digs a pit and does not cover it, and an ox or a donkey falls into it, ³⁴the owner of the pit shall make restitution, giving money to its owner, but keeping the dead animal.

35 If someone's ox hurts the ox of another, so that it dies, then they shall sell the live ox and divide the price of it; and the dead animal they shall also divide. ³⁶But if it was known that the ox

---

ᵘ Heb *of her*

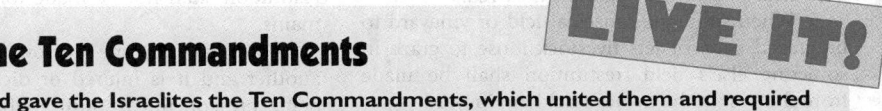

Living the Ten Commandments

God gave the Israelites the Ten Commandments, which united them and required from them certain attitudes and behaviors toward God and their fellow Israelites. Obedience to the Commandments became the sign of faithfulness to the Covenant with God. Later, the prophets again and again held the Israelites accountable for this Covenant, calling them to repent and reconcile with God when they disobeyed God's Law.

The Ten Commandments continue to be the moral foundation for Jews and Christians today. How do you use them in making your moral decisions? How familiar are you with church teaching that applies the Ten Commandments today? Ask God for the understanding and the strength to keep God's Commandments, especially those that are the most difficult for you.

▶ Ex 20.1–17

was accustomed to gore in the past, and its owner has not restrained it, the owner shall restore ox for ox, but keep the dead animal.

Laws of Restitution

v When someone steals an ox or a sheep, and slaughters it or sells it, the thief shall pay five oxen for an ox, and four sheep for a sheep.*w* The thief shall make restitution, but if unable to do so, shall be sold for the theft. 4 When the animal, whether ox or donkey or sheep, is found alive in the thief's possession, the thief shall pay double.

which one party says, "This is mine," the case of both parties shall come before God;*y* the one whom God condemns*z* shall pay double to the other.

10 When someone delivers to another a donkey, ox, sheep, or any other animal for safekeeping, and it dies or is injured or is carried off, without anyone seeing it, 11 an oath before the LORD shall decide between the two of them that the one has not laid hands on the property of the other; the owner shall accept the oath, and no restitution shall be made. 12 But if it was stolen, resti-

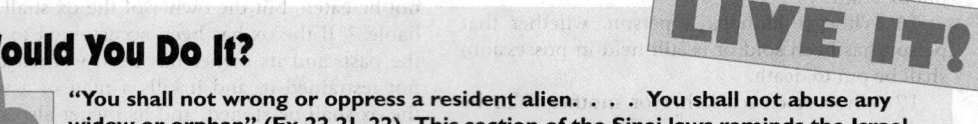

Would You Do It?

LIVE IT!

"You shall not wrong or oppress a resident alien. . . . You shall not abuse any widow or orphan" (Ex 22.21–22). This section of the Sinai laws reminds the Israelites to take care of the poor and vulnerable in their midst. It reminds the Israelites not to become abusive like the Egyptians.

How can we care for poor people? Consider this story: Mike and Dave were spending some time in New York City. During a walk, they went by the train station, a place where many runaways and homeless people found refuge. They came across a young man hunched over with his back to the wall. His clothes were wet, and he was shivering. He was holding a cup, panhandling. Dave took out some change and threw it into the cup. Mike just stood and stared. Dave motioned to Mike to keep on moving, but Mike didn't move. Then, Mike did something that amazed Dave. He sat down and took off his shoes, an almost brand-new pair of insulated leather hiking boots he had received for Christmas. He motioned to the young homeless man to do the same. He took his boots and socks and put them on the young man. Mike put on the young man's old canvas sneakers, stood up, and walked away. Dave followed in silence.

▶ Ex 22.21–27

2*x* If a thief is found breaking in, and is beaten to death, no bloodguilt is incurred; 3 but if it happens after sunrise, bloodguilt is incurred.

5 When someone causes a field or vineyard to be grazed over, or lets livestock loose to graze in someone else's field, restitution shall be made from the best in the owner's field or vineyard.

6 When fire breaks out and catches in thorns so that the stacked grain or the standing grain or the field is consumed, the one who started the fire shall make full restitution.

7 When someone delivers to a neighbor money or goods for safekeeping, and they are stolen from the neighbor's house, then the thief, if caught, shall pay double. 8 If the thief is not caught, the owner of the house shall be brought before God,*y* to determine whether or not the owner had laid hands on the neighbor's goods.

9 In any case of disputed ownership involving ox, donkey, sheep, clothing, or any other loss, of

tution shall be made to its owner. 13 If it was mangled by beasts, let it be brought as evidence; restitution shall not be made for the mangled remains.

14 When someone borrows an animal from another and it is injured or dies, the owner not being present, full restitution shall be made. 15 If the owner was present, there shall be no restitution; if it was hired, only the hiring fee is due.

Social and Religious Laws

16 When a man seduces a virgin who is not engaged to be married, and lies with her, he shall give the bride-price for her and make her his wife. 17 But if her father refuses to give her to him, he

---

v Ch 21.37 in Heb   *w* Verses 2, 3, and 4 rearranged thus: 3b, 4, 2, 3a   *x* Ch 22.1 in Heb   *y* Or *before the judges*   *z* Or *the judges condemn*

shall pay an amount equal to the bride-price for virgins.

18 You shall not permit a female sorcerer to live.

19 Whoever lies with an animal shall be put to death.

20 Whoever sacrifices to any god, other than the LORD alone, shall be devoted to destruction.

21 You shall not wrong or oppress a resident alien, for you were aliens in the land of Egypt. 22 You shall not abuse any widow or orphan. 23 If you do abuse them, when they cry out to me, I will surely heed their cry; 24 my wrath will burn, and I will kill you with the sword, and your wives shall become widows and your children orphans.

25 If you lend money to my people, to the poor among you, you shall not deal with them as a creditor; you shall not exact interest from them. 26 If you take your neighbor's cloak in pawn, you shall restore it before the sun goes down; 27 for it may be your neighbor's only clothing to use as cover; in what else shall that person sleep? And if your neighbor cries out to me, I will listen, for I am compassionate.

28 You shall not revile God, or curse a leader of your people.

29 You shall not delay to make offerings from the fullness of your harvest and from the outflow of your presses.*a*

The firstborn of your sons you shall give to me. 30 You shall do the same with your oxen and with your sheep: seven days it shall remain with its mother; on the eighth day you shall give it to me.

31 You shall be people consecrated to me; therefore you shall not eat any meat that is mangled by beasts in the field; you shall throw it to the dogs.

Justice for All

You shall not spread a false report. You shall not join hands with the wicked to act as a malicious witness. 2 You shall not follow a majority in wrongdoing; when you bear witness in a lawsuit, you shall not side with the majority so as to pervert justice; 3 nor shall you be partial to the poor in a lawsuit.

4 When you come upon your enemy's ox or donkey going astray, you shall bring it back.

5 When you see the donkey of one who hates you lying under its burden and you would hold back from setting it free, you must help to set it free.*a*

6 You shall not pervert the justice due to your poor in their lawsuits. 7 Keep far from a false charge, and do not kill the innocent and those in the right, for I will not acquit the guilty. 8 You shall

take no bribe, for a bribe blinds the officials, and subverts the cause of those who are in the right.

9 You shall not oppress a resident alien; you know the heart of an alien, for you were aliens in the land of Egypt.

Sabbatical Year and Sabbath

10 For six years you shall sow your land and gather in its yield; 11 but the seventh year you shall let it rest and lie fallow, so that the poor of your people may eat; and what they leave the wild animals may eat. You shall do the same with your vineyard, and with your olive orchard.

12 Six days you shall do your work, but on the seventh day you shall rest, so that your ox and your donkey may have relief, and your homeborn slave and the resident alien may be refreshed. 13 Be attentive to all that I have said to you. Do not invoke the names of other gods; do not let them be heard on your lips.

The Annual Festivals
(Ex 34.18–26; Deut 16.1–17)

14 Three times in the year you shall hold a festival for me. 15 You shall observe the festival of unleavened bread; as I commanded you, you shall eat unleavened bread for seven days at the appointed time in the month of A'bib, for in it you came out of Egypt.

No one shall appear before me empty-handed.

16 You shall observe the festival of harvest, of the first fruits of your labor, of what you sow in the field. You shall observe the festival of ingathering at the end of the year, when you gather in from the field the fruit of your labor. 17 Three times in the year all your males shall appear before the Lord GOD.

18 You shall not offer the blood of my sacrifice with anything leavened, or let the fat of my festival remain until the morning.

19 The choicest of the first fruits of your ground you shall bring into the house of the LORD your God.

You shall not boil a kid in its mother's milk.

The Conquest of Canaan Promised

20 I am going to send an angel in front of you, to guard you on the way and to bring you to the place that I have prepared. 21 Be attentive to him and listen to his voice; do not rebel against him, for he will not pardon your transgression; for my name is in him.

---

a Meaning of Heb uncertain

22 But if you listen attentively to his voice and do all that I say, then I will be an enemy to your enemies and a foe to your foes.

23 When my angel goes in front of you, and brings you to the Am′o•rītes, the Hit′tītes, the Per′-iz•zītes, the Cā′naan•ites, the Hī′vītes, and the Jeb′-ū•sītes, and I blot them out, 24 you shall not bow down to their gods, or worship them, or follow their practices, but you shall utterly demolish them and break their pillars in pieces. 25 You shall worship the LORD your God, and I[b] will bless your bread and your water; and I will take sickness away from among you. 26 No one shall miscarry or be barren in your land; I will fulfill the number of your days. 27 I will send my terror in front of you, and will throw into confusion all the people against whom you shall come, and I will make all your enemies turn their backs to you. 28 And I will send the pestilence[c] in front of you, which shall drive out the Hī′vītes, the Cā′naan•ites, and the Hit′tītes from before you. 29 I will not drive them out from before you in one year, or the land would become desolate and the wild animals would multiply against you. 30 Little by little I will drive them out from before you, until you have increased and possess the land. 31 I will set your borders from the Red Sea[d] to the sea of the Phi•lis′-tines, and from the wilderness to the Euphrates; for I will hand over to you the inhabitants of the land, and you shall drive them out before you. 32 You shall make no covenant with them and their gods. 33 They shall not live in your land, or they will make you sin against me; for if you worship their gods, it will surely be a snare to you.

The Blood of the Covenant

Then he said to Moses, "Come up to the LORD, you and Aaron, Nā′dab, and A•bī′hū, and seventy of the elders of Israel, and worship at a distance. 2 Moses alone shall come near the LORD; but the others shall not come near, and the people shall not come up with him."

3 Moses came and told the people all the words of the LORD and all the ordinances; and all the people answered with one voice, and said, "All the words that the LORD has spoken we will do." 4 And Moses wrote down all the words of the LORD. He rose early in the morning, and built an altar at the foot of the mountain, and set up twelve pillars, corresponding to the twelve tribes of Israel. 5 He sent young men of the people of Israel, who offered burnt offerings and sacrificed oxen as offerings of well-being to the LORD. 6 Moses took half of the blood and put it in basins, and half of the blood he dashed against the altar. 7 Then he took the book of the covenant, and read it in the hearing of the people; and they said, "All that the LORD has spoken we will do, and we will be obedient." 8 Moses took the blood and dashed it on the people, and said, "See the blood of the covenant that the LORD has made with you in accordance with all these words."

---

b Gk Vg: Heb *he*   c Or *hornets*: Meaning of Heb uncertain
d Or *Sea of Reeds*

did you KNOW?

Sacrifice and the Eucharist

Sacrifice is defined as an offering made to God that becomes holy by being set apart, blessed, and burned or consumed. Just as food and gifts were brought to a king as a form of tribute and worship, so too in Israel animals were brought to God and sacrificed, their blood splattered on the altar, and their meat cooked and eaten as a form of worship that brought communion with God. The blood symbolized God's gift of life, and when the blessed sacrifice was eaten, communion occurred between God and people. In Exodus, chapter 24, when Israel is about to ratify the Covenant with God, Moses smears the blood of the animal on the altar to assert the Israelites' union with God through the observance of the Covenant.

In the New Testament, the language Jesus uses at his Last Supper seems to reflect this sacrificial understanding. Jesus shares bread and wine as his body and blood and speaks about a New Covenant that will be ratified by the giving of his body and the shedding of his blood. Even today, Catholics celebrating the Eucharist in Jesus' memory encounter the real presence of Jesus in the sacred food of bread and wine, recalling the New Covenant of love he established through giving his body and shedding his blood.

▶ **Ex 24.1–8**

On the Mountain with God

9 Then Moses and Aaron, Nā′dab, and A•bī′hū, and seventy of the elders of Israel went up, 10 and they saw the God of Israel. Under his feet there was something like a pavement of sapphire stone, like the very heaven for clearness. 11 God*ᵉ* did not lay his hand on the chief men of the people of Israel; also they beheld God, and they ate and drank.

12 The LORD said to Moses, "Come up to me on the mountain, and wait there; and I will give you the tablets of stone, with the law and the commandment, which I have written for their instruction." 13 So Moses set out with his assistant Joshua, and Moses went up into the mountain of God. 14 To the elders he had said, "Wait here for us, until we come to you again; for Aaron and Hur are with you; whoever has a dispute may go to them."

15 Then Moses went up on the mountain, and the cloud covered the mountain. 16 The glory of the LORD settled on Mount Sinai, and the cloud covered it for six days; on the seventh day he called to Moses out of the cloud. 17 Now the appearance of the glory of the LORD was like a devouring fire on the top of the mountain in the sight of the people of Israel. 18 Moses entered the cloud, and went up on the mountain. Moses was on the mountain for forty days and forty nights.

25.10–22

Offerings for the Tabernacle
(Ex 35.4–9)

The LORD said to Moses: 2 Tell the Israelites to take for me an offering; from all whose hearts prompt them to give you shall receive the offering for me. 3 This is the offering that you shall receive from them: gold, silver, and bronze, 4 blue, purple, and crimson yarns and fine linen, goats' hair, 5 tanned rams' skins, fine leather, *f* acacia wood, 6 oil for the lamps, spices for the anointing oil and for the fragrant incense, 7 onyx stones and gems to be set in the ephod and for the breastpiece. 8 And have them make me a sanctuary, so that I may dwell among them. 9 In accordance with all that I show you concerning the pattern of the tabernacle and of all its furniture, so you shall make it.

The Ark of the Covenant
(Ex 37.1–9)

10 They shall make an ark of acacia wood; it shall be two and a half cubits long, a cubit and a half wide, and a cubit and a half high. 11 You shall overlay it with pure gold, inside and outside you shall overlay it, and you shall make a molding of gold upon it all around. 12 You shall cast four rings of gold for it and put them on its four feet, two rings on the one side of it, and two rings on the other side. 13 You shall make poles of acacia wood, and overlay them with gold. 14 And you shall put the poles into the rings on the sides of the ark, by which to carry the ark. 15 The poles shall remain in the rings of the ark; they shall not be taken from it. 16 You shall put into the ark the covenant *g* that I shall give you.

17 Then you shall make a mercy seat *h* of pure gold; two cubits and a half shall be its length, and a cubit and a half its width. 18 You shall make two cherubim of gold; you shall make them of hammered work, at the two ends of the mercy seat. *i* 19 Make one cherub at the one end, and one cherub at the other; of one piece with the mercy seat *i* you shall make the cherubim at its two ends. 20 The cherubim shall spread out their wings above, overshadowing the mercy seat *i* with their wings. They shall face one another; the faces of the cherubim shall be turned toward the mercy seat. *i* 21 You shall put the mercy seat *i* on the top of the ark; and in the ark you shall put the covenant *g* that I shall give you. 22 There I will meet with you, and from above the mercy seat, *i* from between the two cherubim that are on the ark of the covenant, *g* I will deliver to you all my commands for the Israelites.

The Table for the Bread of the Presence
(Ex 37.10–16)

23 You shall make a table of acacia wood, two cubits long, one cubit wide, and a cubit and a half high. 24 You shall overlay it with pure gold, and make a molding of gold around it. 25 You shall

---

e Heb *He*   *f* Meaning of Heb uncertain   *g* Or *treaty*, or *testimony*; Heb *eduth*   *h* Or *a cover*   *i* Or *the cover*

make around it a rim a handbreadth wide, and a molding of gold around the rim. 26 You shall make for it four rings of gold, and fasten the rings to the four corners at its four legs. 27 The rings that hold the poles used for carrying the table shall be close to the rim. 28 You shall make the poles of acacia wood, and overlay them with gold, and the table shall be carried with these. 29 You shall make its plates and dishes for incense, and its flagons and bowls with which to pour drink offerings; you shall make them of pure gold. 30 And you shall set the bread of the Presence on the table before me always.

The Lampstand
(Ex 37.17–24)

31 You shall make a lampstand of pure gold. The base and the shaft of the lampstand shall be made of hammered work; its cups, its calyxes, and its petals shall be of one piece with it; 32 and there shall be six branches going out of its sides, three branches of the lampstand out of one side of it and three branches of the lampstand out of the other side of it; 33 three cups shaped like almond blossoms, each with calyx and petals, on one branch, and three cups shaped like almond blossoms, each with calyx and petals, on the other branch—so for the six branches going out of the lampstand. 34 On the lampstand itself there shall be four cups shaped like almond blossoms, each with its calyxes and petals. 35 There shall be a calyx of one piece with it under the first pair of branches, a calyx of one piece with it under the next pair of branches, and a calyx of one piece with it under the last pair of branches—so for the six branches that go out of the lampstand. 36 Their calyxes and their branches shall be of one piece with it, the whole of it one hammered piece of pure gold. 37 You shall make the seven lamps for it; and the lamps shall be set up so as to give light on the space in front of it. 38 Its snuffers and trays shall be of pure gold. 39 It, and all these utensils, shall be made from a talent of pure gold. 40 And see that you make them according to the pattern for them, which is being shown you on the mountain.

The Tabernacle
(Ex 36.8–38)

Moreover you shall make the tabernacle with ten curtains of fine twisted linen, and blue, purple, and crimson yarns; you shall make them with cherubim skillfully worked into them. 2 The length of each curtain shall be twenty-eight cubits, and the width of each curtain four cubits; all the curtains shall be of the same size. 3 Five curtains shall be joined to one another; and the other five curtains shall be joined to one another. 4 You shall make loops of blue on the edge of the outermost curtain in the first set; and likewise you shall make loops on the edge of the outermost curtain in the second set. 5 You shall make fifty loops on the one curtain, and you shall make fifty loops on the edge of the curtain that is in the second set; the loops shall be opposite one another. 6 You shall make fifty clasps of gold, and join the curtains to one another with the clasps, so that the tabernacle may be one whole.

7 You shall also make curtains of goats' hair for a tent over the tabernacle; you shall make eleven curtains. 8 The length of each curtain shall be thirty cubits, and the width of each curtain four cubits; the eleven curtains shall be of the same size. 9 You shall join five curtains by themselves, and six curtains by themselves, and the sixth curtain you shall double over at the front of the tent. 10 You shall make fifty loops on the edge of the curtain that is outermost in one set, and fifty loops on the edge of the curtain that is outermost in the second set.

11 You shall make fifty clasps of bronze, and put the clasps into the loops, and join the tent together, so that it may be one whole. 12 The part that remains of the curtains of the tent, the half curtain that remains, shall hang over the back of the tabernacle. 13 The cubit on the one side, and the cubit on the other side, of what remains in the length of the curtains of the tent, shall hang over the sides of the tabernacle, on this side and that side, to cover it. 14 You shall make for the tent a covering of tanned rams' skins and an outer covering of fine leather.*j*

The Framework

15 You shall make upright frames of acacia wood for the tabernacle. 16 Ten cubits shall be the length of a frame, and a cubit and a half the width of each frame. 17 There shall be two pegs in each frame to fit the frames together; you shall make these for all the frames of the tabernacle. 18 You shall make the frames for the tabernacle: twenty frames for the south side; 19 and you shall make forty bases of silver under the twenty frames, two bases under the first frame for its two pegs, and two bases under the next frame for its two pegs; 20 and for the second side of the tabernacle, on the north side twenty frames, 21 and their forty bases of silver, two bases under the first frame, and two bases under the next frame; 22 and for the rear of the tabernacle westward you shall make six frames.

---

j Meaning of Heb uncertain

23 You shall make two frames for corners of the tabernacle in the rear; 24 they shall be separate beneath, but joined at the top, at the first ring; it shall be the same with both of them; they shall form the two corners. 25 And so there shall be eight frames, with their bases of silver, sixteen bases; two bases under the first frame, and two bases under the next frame.

26 You shall make bars of acacia wood, five for the frames of the one side of the tabernacle, 27 and five bars for the frames of the other side of the tabernacle, and five bars for the frames of the side of the tabernacle at the rear westward. 28 The middle bar, halfway up the frames, shall pass through from end to end. 29 You shall overlay the frames with gold, and shall make their rings of gold to hold the bars; and you shall overlay the bars with gold. 30 Then you shall erect the tabernacle according to the plan for it that you were shown on the mountain.

The Curtain

31 You shall make a curtain of blue, purple, and crimson yarns, and of fine twisted linen; it shall be made with cherubim skillfully worked into it. 32 You shall hang it on four pillars of acacia overlaid with gold, which have hooks of gold and rest on four bases of silver. 33 You shall hang the curtain under the clasps, and bring the ark of the covenant *k* in there, within the curtain; and the curtain shall separate for you the holy place from the most holy. 34 You shall put the mercy seat *l* on the ark of the covenant *k* in the most holy place. 35 You shall set the table outside the curtain, and the lampstand on the south side of the tabernacle opposite the table; and you shall put the table on the north side.

36 You shall make a screen for the entrance of the tent, of blue, purple, and crimson yarns, and of fine twisted linen, embroidered with needlework. 37 You shall make for the screen five pillars of acacia, and overlay them with gold; their hooks shall be of gold, and you shall cast five bases of bronze for them.

The Altar of Burnt Offering
(Ex 38.1–7)

You shall make the altar of acacia wood, five cubits long and five cubits wide; the altar shall be square, and it shall be three cubits high. 2 You shall make horns for it on its four corners; its horns shall be of one piece with it, and you shall overlay it with bronze. 3 You shall make pots for it to receive its ashes, and shovels and basins and forks and firepans; you shall make all its utensils of bronze. 4 You shall also make for it a grating, a

network of bronze; and on the net you shall make four bronze rings at its four corners. 5 You shall set it under the ledge of the altar so that the net shall extend halfway down the altar. 6 You shall make poles for the altar, poles of acacia wood, and overlay them with bronze; 7 the poles shall be put through the rings, so that the poles shall be on the two sides of the altar when it is carried. 8 You shall make it hollow, with boards. They shall be made just as you were shown on the mountain.

The Court and Its Hangings
(Ex 38.9–20)

9 You shall make the court of the tabernacle. On the south side the court shall have hangings of fine twisted linen one hundred cubits long for that side; 10 its twenty pillars and their twenty bases shall be of bronze, but the hooks of the pillars and their bands shall be of silver. 11 Likewise for its length on the north side there shall be hangings one hundred cubits long, their pillars twenty and their bases twenty, of bronze, but the hooks of the pillars and their bands shall be of silver. 12 For the width of the court on the west side there shall be fifty cubits of hangings, with ten pillars and ten bases. 13 The width of the court on the front to the east shall be fifty cubits. 14 There shall be fifteen cubits of hangings on the one side, with three pillars and three bases. 15 There shall be fifteen cubits of hangings on the other side, with three pillars and three bases. 16 For the gate of the court there shall be a screen twenty cubits long, of blue, purple, and crimson yarns, and of fine twisted linen, embroidered with needlework; it shall have four pillars and with them four bases. 17 All the pillars around the court shall be banded with silver; their hooks shall be of silver, and their bases of bronze. 18 The length of the court shall be one hundred cubits, the width fifty, and the height five cubits, with hangings of fine twisted linen and bases of bronze. 19 All the utensils of the tabernacle for every use, and all its pegs and all the pegs of the court, shall be of bronze.

The Oil for the Lamp
(Lev 24.1–4)

20 You shall further command the Israelites to bring you pure oil of beaten olives for the light, so that a lamp may be set up to burn regularly. 21 In the tent of meeting, outside the curtain that is before the covenant, *k* Aaron and his sons shall tend it from evening to morning before the LORD. It shall be a perpetual ordinance to be observed throughout their generations by the Israelites.

---

k Or *treaty,* or *testimony;* Heb *eduth*   *l* Or *the cover*

Vestments for the Priesthood
(Ex 39.1–7)

Then bring near to you your brother Aaron, and his sons with him, from among the Israelites, to serve me as priests—Aaron and Aaron's sons, Nā′dab and A•bī′hū, El•ē•ā′zar and Ith′a•mar. ² You shall make sacred vestments for the glorious adornment of your brother Aaron. ³ And you shall speak to all who have ability, whom I have endowed with skill, that they make Aaron's vestments to consecrate him for my priesthood. ⁴ These are the vestments that they shall make: a breastpiece, an ephod, a robe, a checkered tunic, a turban, and a sash. When they make these sacred vestments for your brother Aaron and his sons to serve me as priests, ⁵ they shall use gold, blue, purple, and crimson yarns, and fine linen.

The Ephod

6 They shall make the ephod of gold, of blue, purple, and crimson yarns, and of fine twisted linen, skillfully worked. ⁷ It shall have two shoulder-pieces attached to its two edges, so that it may be joined together. ⁸ The decorated band on it shall be of the same workmanship and materials, of gold, of blue, purple, and crimson yarns, and of fine twisted linen. ⁹ You shall take two onyx stones, and engrave on them the names of the sons of Israel, ¹⁰ six of their names on the one stone, and the names of the remaining six on the other stone, in the order of their birth. ¹¹ As a gem-cutter engraves signets, so you shall engrave the two stones with the names of the sons of Israel; you shall mount them in settings of gold filigree. ¹² You shall set the two stones on the shoulder-pieces of the ephod, as stones of remembrance for the sons of Israel; and Aaron shall bear their names before the LORD on his two shoulders for remembrance. ¹³ You shall make settings of gold filigree, ¹⁴ and two chains of pure gold, twisted like cords; and you shall attach the corded chains to the settings.

The Breastplate
(Ex 39.8–21)

15 You shall make a breastpiece of judgment, in skilled work; you shall make it in the style of the ephod; of gold, of blue and purple and crimson yarns, and of fine twisted linen you shall make it. ¹⁶ It shall be square and doubled, a span in length and a span in width. ¹⁷ You shall set in it four rows of stones. A row of carnelian,ᵐ chrysolite, and emerald shall be the first row; ¹⁸ and the second row a turquoise, a sapphire,ⁿ and a moonstone; ¹⁹ and the third row a jacinth, an agate, and

an amethyst; ²⁰ and the fourth row a beryl, an onyx, and a jasper; they shall be set in gold filigree. ²¹ There shall be twelve stones with names corresponding to the names of the sons of Israel; they shall be like signets, each engraved with its name, for the twelve tribes. ²² You shall make for the breastpiece chains of pure gold, twisted like cords; ²³ and you shall make for the breastpiece two rings of gold, and put the two rings on the two edges of the breastpiece. ²⁴ You shall put the two cords of gold in the two rings at the edges of the breastpiece; ²⁵ the two ends of the two cords you shall attach to the two settings, and so attach it in front to the shoulder-pieces of the ephod. ²⁶ You shall make two rings of gold, and put them at the two ends of the breastpiece, on its inside edge next to the ephod. ²⁷ You shall make two rings of gold, and attach them in front to the lower part of the two shoulder-pieces of the ephod, at its joining above the decorated band of the ephod. ²⁸ The breastpiece shall be bound by its rings to the rings of the ephod with a blue cord, so that it may lie on the decorated band of the ephod, and so that the breastpiece shall not come loose from the ephod. ²⁹ So Aaron shall bear the names of the sons of Israel in the breastpiece of judgment on his heart when he goes into the holy place, for a continual remembrance before the LORD. ³⁰ In the breastpiece of judgment you shall put the Ū′rim and the Thum′mim, and they shall be on Aaron's heart when he goes in before the LORD; thus Aaron shall bear the judgment of the Israelites on his heart before the LORD continually.

Other Priestly Vestments
(Ex 39.22–31)

31 You shall make the robe of the ephod all of blue. ³² It shall have an opening for the head in the middle of it, with a woven binding around the opening, like the opening in a coat of mail,ᵒ so that it may not be torn. ³³ On its lower hem you shall make pomegranates of blue, purple, and crimson yarns, all around the lower hem, with bells of gold between them all around— ³⁴ a golden bell and a pomegranate alternating all around the lower hem of the robe. ³⁵ Aaron shall wear it when he ministers, and its sound shall be heard when he goes into the holy place before the LORD, and when he comes out, so that he may not die.

36 You shall make a rosette of pure gold, and engrave on it, like the engraving of a signet, "Holy to the LORD." ³⁷ You shall fasten it on the turban with a blue cord; it shall be on the front of the

---

ᵐ The identity of several of these stones is uncertain
ⁿ Or *lapis lazuli*   ᵒ Meaning of Heb uncertain

turban. ³⁸ It shall be on Aaron's forehead, and Aaron shall take on himself any guilt incurred in the holy offering that the Israelites consecrate as their sacred donations; it shall always be on his forehead, in order that they may find favor before the LORD.

39 You shall make the checkered tunic of fine linen, and you shall make a turban of fine linen, and you shall make a sash embroidered with needlework.

40 For Aaron's sons you shall make tunics and sashes and headdresses; you shall make them for their glorious adornment. ⁴¹ You shall put them on your brother Aaron, and on his sons with him, and shall anoint them and ordain them and consecrate them, so that they may serve me as priests. ⁴² You shall make for them linen undergarments to cover their naked flesh; they shall reach from the hips to the thighs; ⁴³ Aaron and his sons shall wear them when they go into the tent of meeting, or when they come near the altar to minister in the holy place; or they will bring guilt on themselves and die. This shall be a perpetual ordinance for him and for his descendants after him.

The Ordination of the Priests
(Lev 8.1–36)

Now this is what you shall do to them to consecrate them, so that they may serve me as priests. Take one young bull and two rams without blemish, ² and unleavened bread, unleavened cakes mixed with oil, and unleavened wafers spread with oil. You shall make them of choice wheat flour. ³ You shall put them in one basket and bring them in the basket, and bring the bull and the two rams. ⁴ You shall bring Aaron and his sons to the entrance of the tent of meeting, and wash them with water. ⁵ Then you shall take the vestments, and put on Aaron the tunic and the robe of the ephod, and the ephod, and the breastpiece, and gird him with the decorated band of the ephod; ⁶ and you shall set the turban on his head, and put the holy diadem on the turban. ⁷ You shall take the anointing oil, and pour it on his head and anoint him. ⁸ Then you shall bring his sons, and put tunics on them, ⁹ and you shall gird them with sashes*ᵖ* and tie headdresses on them; and the priesthood shall be theirs by a perpetual ordinance. You shall then ordain Aaron and his sons.

10 You shall bring the bull in front of the tent of meeting. Aaron and his sons shall lay their hands on the head of the bull, ¹¹ and you shall slaughter the bull before the LORD, at the entrance of the tent of meeting, ¹² and shall take some of the blood of the bull and put it on the horns of the altar with your finger, and all the rest of the blood you shall pour out at the base of the altar. ¹³ You shall take all the fat that covers the entrails, and the appendage of the liver, and the two kidneys with the fat that is on them, and turn them into smoke on the altar. ¹⁴ But the flesh of the bull, and its skin, and its dung, you shall burn with fire outside the camp; it is a sin offering.

15 Then you shall take one of the rams, and Aaron and his sons shall lay their hands on the head of the ram, ¹⁶ and you shall slaughter the ram, and shall take its blood and dash it against all sides of the altar. ¹⁷ Then you shall cut the ram into its parts, and wash its entrails and its legs, and put them with its parts and its head, ¹⁸ and turn the whole ram into smoke on the altar; it is a burnt offering to the LORD; it is a pleasing odor, an offering by fire to the LORD.

19 You shall take the other ram; and Aaron and his sons shall lay their hands on the head of the ram, ²⁰ and you shall slaughter the ram, and take some of its blood and put it on the lobe of Aaron's right ear and on the lobes of the right ears of his sons, and on the thumbs of their right hands, and on the big toes of their right feet, and dash the rest of the blood against all sides of the altar. ²¹ Then you shall take some of the blood that is on the altar, and some of the anointing oil, and sprinkle it on Aaron and his vestments and on his sons and his sons' vestments with him; then he and his vestments shall be holy, as well as his sons and his sons' vestments.

22 You shall also take the fat of the ram, the fat tail, the fat that covers the entrails, the appendage of the liver, the two kidneys with the fat that is on them, and the right thigh (for it is a ram of ordination), ²³ and one loaf of bread, one cake of bread made with oil, and one wafer, out of the basket of unleavened bread that is before the LORD; ²⁴ and you shall place all these on the palms of Aaron and on the palms of his sons, and raise them as an elevation offering before the LORD. ²⁵ Then you shall take them from their hands, and turn them into smoke on the altar on top of the burnt offering of pleasing odor before the LORD; it is an offering by fire to the LORD.

26 You shall take the breast of the ram of Aaron's ordination and raise it as an elevation offering before the LORD; and it shall be your portion. ²⁷ You shall consecrate the breast that was raised as an elevation offering and the thigh that was raised as an elevation offering from the ram of ordination, from that which belonged to Aaron and his sons. ²⁸ These things shall be a perpetual

---

ᵖ Gk: Heb *sashes, Aaron and his sons*

ordinance for Aaron and his sons from the Israel-ites, for this is an offering; and it shall be an offer-ing by the Israelites from their sacrifice of offerings of well-being, their offering to the LORD.

29 The sacred vestments of Aaron shall be passed on to his sons after him; they shall be anointed in them and ordained in them. 30 The son who is priest in his place shall wear them seven days, when he comes into the tent of meet-ing to minister in the holy place.

31 You shall take the ram of ordination, and boil its flesh in a holy place; 32 and Aaron and his sons shall eat the flesh of the ram and the bread that is in the basket, at the entrance of the tent of meeting. 33 They themselves shall eat the food by which atonement is made, to ordain and conse-crate them, but no one else shall eat of them, be-cause they are holy. 34 If any of the flesh for the ordination, or of the bread, remains until the morning, then you shall burn the remainder with fire; it shall not be eaten, because it is holy.

35 Thus you shall do to Aaron and to his sons, just as I have commanded you; through seven days you shall ordain them. 36 Also every day you shall offer a bull as a sin offering for atonement. Also you shall offer a sin offering for the altar, when you make atonement for it, and shall anoint it, to consecrate it. 37 Seven days you shall make atone-ment for the altar, and consecrate it, and the altar shall be most holy; whatever touches the altar shall become holy.

The Daily Offerings
(Num 28.1–8)

38 Now this is what you shall offer on the al-tar: two lambs a year old regularly each day. 39 One lamb you shall offer in the morning, and the other lamb you shall offer in the evening; 40 and with the first lamb one-tenth of a measure of choice flour mixed with one-fourth of a hin of beaten oil, and one-fourth of a hin of wine for a drink offer-ing. 41 And the other lamb you shall offer in the evening, and shall offer with it a grain offering and its drink offering, as in the morning, for a pleasing odor, an offering by fire to the LORD. 42 It shall be a regular burnt offering throughout your generations at the entrance of the tent of meeting before the LORD, where I will meet with you, to speak to you there. 43 I will meet with the Israelites there, and it shall be sanctified by my glory; 44 I will consecrate the tent of meeting and the altar; Aaron also and his sons I will consecrate, to serve me as priests. 45 I will dwell among the Israelites, and I will be their God. 46 And they shall know that I am the LORD their God, who brought them out of the land

of Egypt that I might dwell among them; I am the LORD their God.

The Altar of Incense
(Ex 37.25–28)

You shall make an altar on which to offer incense; you shall make it of acacia wood. 2 It shall be one cubit long, and one cubit wide; it shall be square, and shall be two cubits high; its horns shall be of one piece with it. 3 You shall overlay it with pure gold, its top, and its sides all around and its horns; and you shall make for it a molding of gold all around. 4 And you shall make two golden rings for it; under its molding on two opposite sides of it you shall make them, and they shall hold the poles with which to carry it. 5 You shall make the poles of acacia wood, and overlay them with gold. 6 You shall place it in front of the curtain that is above the ark of the covenant,q in front of the mercy seatr that is over the covenant,q where I will meet with you. 7 Aaron shall offer fragrant incense on it; every morning when he dresses the lamps he shall offer it, 8 and when Aaron sets up the lamps in the evening, he shall offer it, a regular incense offering before the LORD throughout your genera-tions. 9 You shall not offer unholy incense on it, or a burnt offering, or a grain offering; and you shall not pour a drink offering on it. 10 Once a year Aaron shall perform the rite of atonement on its horns. Throughout your generations he shall per-form the atonement for it once a year with the blood of the atoning sin offering. It is most holy to the LORD.

The Half Shekel for the Sanctuary

11 The LORD spoke to Moses: 12 When you take a census of the Israelites to register them, at regis-tration all of them shall give a ransom for their lives to the LORD, so that no plague may come upon them for being registered. 13 This is what each one who is registered shall give: half a shekel according to the shekel of the sanctuary (the shekel is twenty gerahs), half a shekel as an offer-ing to the LORD. 14 Each one who is registered, from twenty years old and upward, shall give the LORD's offering. 15 The rich shall not give more, and the poor shall not give less, than the half shekel, when you bring this offering to the LORD to make atone-ment for your lives. 16 You shall take the atone-ment money from the Israelites and shall designate it for the service of the tent of meeting; before the LORD it will be a reminder to the Israel-ites of the ransom given for your lives.

q Or *treaty*, or *testimony*; Heb *eduth*   r Or *the cover*

The Bronze Basin

17 The LORD spoke to Moses: 18 You shall make a bronze basin with a bronze stand for washing. You shall put it between the tent of meeting and the altar, and you shall put water in it; 19 with the water[s] Aaron and his sons shall wash their hands and their feet. 20 When they go into the tent of meeting, or when they come near the altar to minister, to make an offering by fire to the LORD, they shall wash with water, so that they may not die. 21 They shall wash their hands and their feet, so that they may not die: it shall be a perpetual ordinance for them, for him and for his descendants throughout their generations.

The Anointing Oil and Incense
(Ex 37.29)

22 The LORD spoke to Moses: 23 Take the finest spices: of liquid myrrh five hundred shekels, and of sweet-smelling cinnamon half as much, that is, two hundred fifty, and two hundred fifty of aromatic cane, 24 and five hundred of cassia—measured by the sanctuary shekel—and a hin of olive oil; 25 and you shall make of these a sacred anointing oil blended as by the perfumer; it shall be a holy anointing oil. 26 With it you shall anoint the tent of meeting and the ark of the covenant,[t] 27 and the table and all its utensils, and the lampstand and its utensils, and the altar of incense, 28 and the altar of burnt offering with all its utensils, and the basin with its stand; 29 you shall consecrate them, so that they may be most holy; whatever touches them will become holy. 30 You shall anoint Aaron and his sons, and consecrate them, in order that they may serve me as priests. 31 You shall say to the Israelites, "This shall be my holy anointing oil throughout your generations. 32 It shall not be used in any ordinary anointing of the body, and you shall make no other like it in composition; it is holy, and it shall be holy to you. 33 Whoever compounds any like it or whoever puts any of it on an unqualified person shall be cut off from the people."

34 The LORD said to Moses: Take sweet spices, stacte, and onycha, and galbanum, sweet spices with pure frankincense (an equal part of each), 35 and make an incense blended as by the perfumer, seasoned with salt, pure and holy; 36 and you shall beat some of it into powder, and put part of it before the covenant[t] in the tent of meeting where I shall meet with you; it shall be for you most holy. 37 When you make incense according to this composition, you shall not make it for yourselves; it shall be regarded by you as holy to the LORD. 38 Whoever makes any like it to use as perfume shall be cut off from the people.

Bezalel and Oholiab
(Ex 35.30—36.1)

The LORD spoke to Moses: 2 See, I have called by name Bez'a•lel son of U'ri son of Hur, of the tribe of Judah: 3 and I have filled him with divine spirit,[u] with ability, intelligence, and knowledge in every kind of craft, 4 to devise artistic designs, to work in gold, silver, and bronze, 5 in cutting stones for setting, and in carving wood, in every kind of craft. 6 Moreover, I have appointed with him O•ho'-li•ab son of A•his'a•mach, of the tribe of Dan; and I have given skill to all the skillful, so that they may make all that I have commanded you: 7 the tent of meeting, and the ark of the covenant,[t] and the mercy seat[v] that is on it, and all the furnishings of the tent, 8 the table and its utensils, and the pure lampstand with all its utensils, and the altar of incense, 9 and the altar of burnt offering with all its utensils, and the basin with its stand, 10 and the finely worked vestments, the holy vestments for the priest Aaron and the vestments of his sons, for their service as priests, 11 and the anointing oil and the fragrant incense for the holy place. They shall do just as I have commanded you.

The Sabbath Law

12 The LORD said to Moses: 13 You yourself are to speak to the Israelites: "You shall keep my sabbaths, for this is a sign between me and you throughout your generations, given in order that you may know that I, the LORD, sanctify you. 14 You shall keep the sabbath, because it is holy for you; everyone who profanes it shall be put to death; whoever does any work on it shall be cut off from among the people. 15 Six days shall work be done, but the seventh day is a sabbath of solemn rest, holy to the LORD; whoever does any work on the sabbath day shall be put to death. 16 Therefore the Israelites shall keep the sabbath, observing the sabbath throughout their generations, as a perpetual covenant. 17 It is a sign forever between me and the people of Israel that in six days the LORD made heaven and earth, and on the seventh day he rested, and was refreshed."

The Two Tablets of the Covenant

18 When God[w] finished speaking with Moses on Mount Sinai, he gave him the two tablets of the covenant,[t] tablets of stone, written with the finger of God.

---

[s] Heb it   [t] Or treaty, or testimony; Heb eduth   [u] Or with the spirit of God   [v] Or the cover   [w] Heb he

The Golden Calf
(Deut 9.6–29)

When the people saw that Moses delayed to come down from the mountain, the people gathered around Aaron, and said to him, "Come, make gods for us, who shall go before us; as for this Moses, the man who brought us up out of the land of Egypt, we do not know what has become of him." 2 Aaron said to them, "Take off the gold rings that are on the ears of your wives, your sons, and your daughters, and bring them to me." 3 So all the people took off the gold rings from their ears, and brought them to Aaron. 4 He took the gold from them, formed it in a mold,ˣ and cast an image of a calf; and they said, "These are your gods, O Israel, who brought you up out of the land of Egypt!" 5 When Aaron saw this, he built an altar before it; and Aaron made proclamation and said, "Tomorrow shall be a festival to the LORD." 6 They rose early the next day, and offered burnt offerings and brought sacrifices of well-being; and the people sat down to eat and drink, and rose up to revel.

7 The LORD said to Moses, "Go down at once! Your people, whom you brought up out of the land of Egypt, have acted perversely; 8 they have been quick to turn aside from the way that I commanded them; they have cast for themselves an image of a calf, and have worshiped it and sacrificed to it, and said, 'These are your gods, O Israel, who brought you up out of the land of Egypt!' " 9 The LORD said to Moses, "I have seen this people, how stiff-necked they are. 10 Now let me alone, so that my wrath may burn hot against them and I may consume them; and of you I will make a great nation."

11 But Moses implored the LORD his God, and said, "O LORD, why does your wrath burn hot against your people, whom you brought out of the land of Egypt with great power and with a mighty hand? 12 Why should the Egyptians say, 'It was with evil intent that he brought them out to kill them in the mountains, and to consume them from the face of the earth'? Turn from your fierce wrath; change your mind and do not bring disaster on your people. 13 Remember Abraham, Isaac, and Israel, your servants, how you swore to them by your own self, saying to them, 'I will multiply your descendants like the stars of heaven, and all this land that I have promised I will give to your descendants, and they shall inherit it forever.' " 14 And the LORD changed his mind about the disaster that he planned to bring on his people.

15 Then Moses turned and went down from the mountain, carrying the two tablets of the covenantʸ in his hands, tablets that were written on both sides, written on the front and on the back. 16 The tablets were the work of God, and the writing was the writing of God, engraved upon the tablets. 17 When Joshua heard the noise of the people as they shouted, he said to Moses, "There is a noise of war in the camp." 18 But he said,

"It is not the sound made by victors,
    or the sound made by losers;
it is the sound of revelers that I hear."

19 As soon as he came near the camp and saw the calf and the dancing, Moses' anger burned hot, and he threw the tablets from his hands and broke them at the foot of the mountain. 20 He took the calf that they had made, burned it with fire, ground it to powder, scattered it on the water, and made the Israelites drink it.

21 Moses said to Aaron, "What did this people do to you that you have brought so great a sin upon them?" 22 And Aaron said, "Do not let the anger of my lord burn hot; you know the people, that they are bent on evil. 23 They said to me, 'Make us gods, who shall go before us; as for this Moses, the man who brought us up out of the land of Egypt, we do not know what has become of him.' 24 So I said to them, 'Whoever has gold, take it off'; so they gave it to me, and I threw it into the fire, and out came this calf!"

25 When Moses saw that the people were running wild (for Aaron had let them run wild, to the derision of their enemies), 26 then Moses stood in the gate of the camp, and said, "Who is on the LORD's side? Come to me!" And all the sons of Levi gathered around him. 27 He said to them, "Thus says the LORD, the God of Israel, 'Put your sword on your side, each of you! Go back and forth from gate to gate throughout the camp, and each of you kill your brother, your friend, and your neighbor.' " 28 The sons of Levi did as Moses commanded, and about three thousand of the people fell on that day. 29 Moses said, "Today you have ordained yourselvesᶻ for the service of the LORD, each one at the cost of a son or a brother, and so have brought a blessing on yourselves this day."

30 On the next day Moses said to the people, "You have sinned a great sin. But now I will go up to the LORD; perhaps I can make atonement for your sin." 31 So Moses returned to the LORD and said, "Alas, this people has sinned a great sin; they have made for themselves gods of gold. 32 But now, if you will only forgive their sin—but if not, blot me out of the book that you have written." 33 But the LORD said to Moses, "Whoever has

---

ˣ Or *fashioned it with a graving tool*; Meaning of Heb uncertain   ʸ Or *treaty*, or *testimony*; Heb *eduth*   ᶻ Gk Vg Compare Tg: Heb *Today ordain yourselves*

Caught Up in the Moment

Now that I think about it, it was a stupid thing to do. But it is so hard to be objective when you are caught up in the excitement of the moment. We had been waiting a long time for Moses—too long, it seems. We got bored and restless.

You know how it is. Someone came up with the idea of the golden calf. It sounded like fun, something to pass the time and remind us of the old gods. And I have to admit, that calf did look pretty good!

I do feel sorry for Aaron. Moses saw what we had done and hurled the stone tablets to the ground in a fit of rage. Aaron tried to explain how it was, but Moses would hear none of it. He was upset. He had a right to be. There is no valid excuse for what we did. Aaron tried to pretend that the calf sort of formed itself, but it was a feeble excuse. We all knew it. And when we learned what was on the stone tablets, we knew we had done wrong. Moses had those tablets from the hands of God. This was to have been a solemn moment, followed by a great celebration. But instead, we had to face the wrath of Moses and pick up the shattered pieces of stone.

It is so easy to lose sight of what we are all about. It is so easy to do something stupid when we are bored and tired of waiting. And then, we wonder how we could have let ourselves get so far off track. It is too easy, isn't it? We are all too human at times.

No, I don't blame Moses for losing his temper. He had every right. We let him down. We let ourselves down. But most of all, we let God down.

▶ Ex 32.1–35

---

sinned against me I will blot out of my book. ³⁴ But now go, lead the people to the place about which I have spoken to you; see, my angel shall go in front of you. Nevertheless, when the day comes for punishment, I will punish them for their sin."

35 Then the LORD sent a plague on the people, because they made the calf—the one that Aaron made.

The Command to Leave Sinai

The LORD said to Moses, "Go, leave this place, you and the people whom you have brought up out of the land of Egypt, and go to the land of which I swore to Abraham, Isaac, and Jacob, saying, 'To your descendants I will give it.' ² I will send an angel before you, and I will drive out the Cā′naan-ites, the Am′o•rītes, the Hit′tītes, the Per′iz•zītes, the Hī′vītes, and the Jeb′ū•sītes. ³ Go up to a land flowing with milk and honey; but I will not go up among you, or I would consume you on the way, for you are a stiff-necked people."

4 When the people heard these harsh words, they mourned, and no one put on ornaments. ⁵ For the LORD had said to Moses, "Say to the Israelites, 'You are a stiff-necked people; if for a single moment I should go up among you, I would consume you. So now take off your ornaments, and I will decide what to do to you.' " ⁶ Therefore the

Israelites stripped themselves of their ornaments, from Mount Hō′reb onward.

The Tent outside the Camp

7 Now Moses used to take the tent and pitch it outside the camp, far off from the camp; he called it the tent of meeting. And everyone who sought the LORD would go out to the tent of meeting, which was outside the camp. ⁸ Whenever Moses went out to the tent, all the people would rise and stand, each of them, at the entrance of their tents and watch Moses until he had gone into the tent. ⁹ When Moses entered the tent, the pillar of cloud would descend and stand at the entrance of the tent, and the LORD would speak with Moses. ¹⁰ When all the people saw the pillar of cloud standing at the entrance of the tent, all the people would rise and bow down, all of them, at the entrance of their tent. ¹¹ Thus the LORD used to speak to Moses face to face, as one speaks to a friend. Then he would return to the camp; but his young assistant, Joshua son of Nun, would not leave the tent.

Moses' Intercession

12 Moses said to the LORD, "See, you have said to me, 'Bring up this people'; but you have not let me know whom you will send with me. Yet you have said, 'I know you by name, and you have

EX

also found favor in my sight." 13 Now if I have found favor in your sight, show me your ways, so that I may know you and find favor in your sight. Consider too that this nation is your people." 14 He said, "My presence will go with you, and I will give you rest." 15 And he said to him, "If your presence will not go, do not carry us up from here. 16 For how shall it be known that I have found favor in your sight, I and your people, unless you go with us? In this way, we shall be distinct, I and your people, from every people on the face of the earth."

17 The LORD said to Moses, "I will do the very thing that you have asked; for you have found favor in my sight, and I know you by name." 18 Moses said, "Show me your glory, I pray." 19 And he said, "I will make all my goodness pass before you, and will proclaim before you the name, 'The LORD';*a* and I will be gracious to whom I will be gracious, and will show mercy on whom I will show mercy. 20 But," he said, "you cannot see my face; for no one shall see me and live." 21 And the LORD continued, "See, there is a place by me where you shall stand on the rock; 22 and while my glory passes by I will put you in a cleft of the rock, and I will cover you with my hand until I have passed by; 23 then I will take away my hand, and you shall see my back; but my face shall not be seen."

Moses Makes New Tablets
(Deut 10.1–5)

The LORD said to Moses, "Cut two tablets of stone like the former ones, and I will write on the tablets the words that were on the former tablets, which you broke. 2 Be ready in the morning, and come up in the morning to Mount Sinai and present yourself there to me, on the top of the mountain. 3 No one shall come up with you, and do not let anyone be seen throughout all the mountain; and do not let flocks or herds graze in front of that mountain." 4 So Moses cut two tablets of stone like the former ones; and he rose early in the morning and went up on Mount Sinai, as the LORD had commanded him, and took in his hand the two tablets of stone. 5 The LORD descended in the cloud and stood with him there, and proclaimed the name, "The LORD."*a* 6 The LORD passed before him, and proclaimed,

"The LORD, the LORD,
a God merciful and gracious,
slow to anger,
and abounding in steadfast love and
    faithfulness,
7 keeping steadfast love for the thousandth
    generation,*b*
forgiving iniquity and transgression and sin,

yet by no means clearing the guilty,
but visiting the iniquity of the parents
upon the children
and the children's children,
to the third and the fourth generation."
8 And Moses quickly bowed his head toward the earth, and worshiped. 9 He said, "If now I have found favor in your sight, O Lord, I pray, let the Lord go with us. Although this is a stiff-necked people, pardon our iniquity and our sin, and take us for your inheritance."

The Covenant Renewed
(Ex 23.14–19; Deut 7.1–6; 16.1–17)

10 He said: I hereby make a covenant. Before all your people I will perform marvels, such as have not been performed in all the earth or in any nation; and all the people among whom you live

---

PRAY IT

God Passing By

How close can we get to God without actually seeing God's face? If anyone would know, it is Moses. His rather amazing encounter with God is recorded in Ex 33.17–23.

We too can experience, as many saints and mystics have, a deep intimacy with God. It is significant that God and Moses most often met in nature. If you are lucky, you have a favorite outdoor spot. Perhaps it is a place where you can simply sit and ponder as you gaze at the scenery before you. Perhaps during a sunset on a lovely summer evening or while gazing at the sea or a flowing stream, you somehow connect with God. You may not actually see or feel the hand of God, but somehow you know that God is with you and you are catching a glimpse of God's glory. You feel yourself held in the palm of God's gracious hand. And sometimes, like Moses (see 34.29), you are transformed by the power of God's presence.

Where do you most fully experience the presence of God?

▸ Ex 33.17–23

---

a Heb *YHWH*; see note at 3.15   *b* Or *for thousands*

shall see the work of the LORD; for it is an awesome thing that I will do with you.

11 Observe what I command you today. See, I will drive out before you the Am′o•rītes, the Cā′-naan•ītes, the Hit′tītes, the Per′iz•zītes, the Hī′vītes, and the Jeb′ū•sītes. 12 Take care not to make a covenant with the inhabitants of the land to which you are going, or it will become a snare among you. 13 You shall tear down their altars, break their pillars, and cut down their sacred poles[c] 14 (for you shall worship no other god, because the LORD, whose name is Jealous, is a jealous God). 15 You shall not make a covenant with the inhabitants of the land, for when they prostitute themselves to their gods and sacrifice to their gods, someone among them will invite you, and you will eat of the sacrifice. 16 And you will take wives from among their daughters for your sons, and their daughters who prostitute themselves to their gods will make your sons also prostitute themselves to their gods.

17 You shall not make cast idols.

18 You shall keep the festival of unleavened bread. Seven days you shall eat unleavened bread, as I commanded you, at the time appointed in the month of Ā′bib; for in the month of Ā′bib you came out from Egypt.

19 All that first opens the womb is mine, all your male[d] livestock, the firstborn of cow and sheep. 20 The firstborn of a donkey you shall redeem with a lamb, or if you will not redeem it you shall break its neck. All the firstborn of your sons you shall redeem.

No one shall appear before me empty-handed.

21 Six days you shall work, but on the seventh day you shall rest; even in plowing time and in harvest time you shall rest. 22 You shall observe the festival of weeks, the first fruits of wheat harvest, and the festival of ingathering at the turn of the year. 23 Three times in the year all your males shall appear before the LORD God, the God of Israel. 24 For I will cast out nations before you, and enlarge your borders; no one shall covet your land when you go up to appear before the LORD your God three times in the year.

25 You shall not offer the blood of my sacrifice with leaven, and the sacrifice of the festival of the passover shall not be left until the morning.

26 The best of the first fruits of your ground you shall bring to the house of the LORD your God.

You shall not boil a kid in its mother's milk.

27 The LORD said to Moses: Write these words; in accordance with these words I have made a covenant with you and with Israel. 28 He was there

[c] Heb *Asherim*   [d] Gk Theodotion Vg Tg: Meaning of Heb uncertain

did you KNOW?

Major Jewish Feasts

The joyful anticipation that we feel before a major holiday seems to be shared by people of all cultures and religious traditions. Certainly, the Israelites had that feeling before the three festivals described in Ex 34.18–26 (and in 23.14–17). They looked forward to them the way we might look forward to Christmas or Easter. These three feasts were called pilgrimage feasts because they required males to travel to the Temple in Jerusalem.

The *feast of unleavened bread*, which began on the day after Passover and lasted a week, marked the beginning of the barley harvest. This feast probably originated in a pre-Passover agricultural holiday. Originally, unleavened bread—bread made without yeast—was eaten during this week to symbolize a fresh start. Later, the feast was connected to the Passover celebration, and the custom of eating unleavened bread came to be seen as a reminder of the haste with which the people had left Egypt—before having time to leaven their bread.

The *feast of weeks*, or Pentecost, began seven weeks after the barley harvest, to celebrate the start of the wheat harvest. Later, the feast of weeks took on added significance. Because the Israelites had arrived at Mount Sinai in the third month after their departure from Egypt (19.1), this weeklong feast came to be seen as a celebration of God's Covenant with Israel.

The third weeklong festival, *the feast of booths*, was celebrated as the produce of the land was gathered. Much like our own Thanksgiving Day, it was a time set aside to thank God for the bounty of the earth. It is the most popular of the pilgrimage feasts. In Exodus, it is called the festival of ingathering, and in other places, simply the festival (1 Kings 8.2).

▶ Ex 34.18–26

with the LORD forty days and forty nights; he neither ate bread nor drank water. And he wrote on
the tablets the words of the covenant, the ten commandments.*e*

The Shining Face of Moses

29 Moses came down from Mount Sinai. As he
came down from the mountain with the two tablets of the covenant*f* in his hand, Moses did not
know that the skin of his face shone because he
had been talking with God. 30 When Aaron and all
the Israelites saw Moses, the skin of his face was
shining, and they were afraid to come near him.
31 But Moses called to them; and Aaron and all the
leaders of the congregation returned to him, and
Moses spoke with them. 32 Afterward all the Israelites came near, and he gave them in commandment all that the LORD had spoken with him on
Mount Sinai. 33 When Moses had finished speaking with them, he put a veil on his face; 34 but
whenever Moses went in before the LORD to speak
with him, he would take the veil off, until he came
out; and when he came out, and told the Israelites
what he had been commanded, 35 the Israelites
would see the face of Moses, that the skin of his
face was shining; and Moses would put the veil on
his face again, until he went in to speak with him.

Sabbath Regulations

Moses assembled all the congregation of the Israelites and said to them: These are the things that
the LORD has commanded you to do:
2 Six days shall work be done, but on the seventh day you shall have a holy sabbath of solemn
rest to the LORD; whoever does any work on it shall
be put to death. 3 You shall kindle no fire in all
your dwellings on the sabbath day.

Preparations for Making the Tabernacle
(Ex 25.1–9; 39.32–43)

4 Moses said to all the congregation of the Israelites: This is the thing that the LORD has commanded: 5 Take from among you an offering to the
LORD; let whoever is of a generous heart bring the
LORD's offering: gold, silver, and bronze; 6 blue,
purple, and crimson yarns, and fine linen; goats'
hair, 7 tanned rams' skins, and fine leather;*g* acacia
wood, 8 oil for the light, spices for the anointing
oil and for the fragrant incense, 9 and onyx stones
and gems to be set in the ephod and the breastpiece.
10 All who are skillful among you shall come
and make all that the LORD has commanded: the
tabernacle, 11 its tent and its covering, its clasps
and its frames, its bars, its pillars, and its bases;
12 the ark with its poles, the mercy seat,*h* and the

curtain for the screen; 13 the table with its poles
and all its utensils, and the bread of the Presence;
14 the lampstand also for the light, with its utensils
and its lamps, and the oil for the light; 15 and the
altar of incense, with its poles, and the anointing
oil and the fragrant incense, and the screen for the
entrance, the entrance of the tabernacle; 16 the altar
of burnt offering, with its grating of bronze, its
poles, and all its utensils, the basin with its stand;
17 the hangings of the court, its pillars and its
bases, and the screen for the gate of the court;
18 the pegs of the tabernacle and the pegs of the
court, and their cords; 19 the finely worked vestments for ministering in the holy place, the holy
vestments for the priest Aaron, and the vestments
of his sons, for their service as priests.

Offerings for the Tabernacle

20 Then all the congregation of the Israelites
withdrew from the presence of Moses. 21 And they
came, everyone whose heart was stirred, and everyone whose spirit was willing, and brought the
LORD's offering to be used for the tent of meeting,
and for all its service, and for the sacred vestments.
22 So they came, both men and women; all who
were of a willing heart brought brooches and earrings and signet rings and pendants, all sorts of
gold objects, everyone bringing an offering of gold
to the LORD. 23 And everyone who possessed blue
or purple or crimson yarn or fine linen or goats'
hair or tanned rams' skins or fine leather,*i* brought
them. 24 Everyone who could make an offering of
silver or bronze brought it as the LORD's offering;
and everyone who possessed acacia wood of any
use in the work, brought it. 25 All the skillful
women spun with their hands, and brought what
they had spun in blue and purple and crimson
yarns and fine linen; 26 all the women whose
hearts moved them to use their skill spun the
goats' hair. 27 And the leaders brought onyx stones
and gems to be set in the ephod and the breastpiece, 28 and spices and oil for the light, and for
the anointing oil, and for the fragrant incense.
29 All the Israelite men and women whose hearts
made them willing to bring anything for the work
that the LORD had commanded by Moses to be
done, brought it as a freewill offering to the LORD.

Bezalel and Oholiab
(Ex 31.1–11)

30 Then Moses said to the Israelites: See, the
LORD has called by name Bez′a·lel son of U′rī son

---

e Heb *words*   *f* Or *treaty*, or *testimony*; Heb *eduth*
g Meaning of Heb uncertain   *h* Or *the cover*   *i* Meaning
of Heb uncertain

of Hur, of the tribe of Judah; ³¹ he has filled him with divine spirit,*ʲ* with skill, intelligence, and knowledge in every kind of craft, ³² to devise artistic designs, to work in gold, silver, and bronze, ³³ in cutting stones for setting, and in carving wood, in every kind of craft. ³⁴ And he has inspired him to teach, both him and Ō•hŏ′li•ab son of A•his′-a•mach, of the tribe of Dan. ³⁵ He has filled them with skill to do every kind of work done by an artisan or by a designer or by an embroiderer in blue, purple, and crimson yarns, and in fine linen, or by a weaver—by any sort of artisan or skilled designer.

Bez′a•lel and Ō•hŏ′li•ab and every skillful one to whom the LORD has given skill and understanding to know how to do any work in the construction of the sanctuary shall work in accordance with all that the LORD has commanded.

2 Moses then called Bez′a•lel and Ō•hŏ′li•ab and every skillful one to whom the LORD had given skill, everyone whose heart was stirred to come to do the work; ³ and they received from Moses all the freewill offerings that the Israelites had brought for doing the work on the sanctuary. They still kept bringing him freewill offerings every morning, ⁴ so that all the artisans who were doing every sort of task on the sanctuary came, each from the task being performed, ⁵ and said to Moses, "The people are bringing much more than enough for doing the work that the LORD has commanded us to do." ⁶ So Moses gave command, and word was proclaimed throughout the camp: "No man or woman is to make anything else as an offering for the sanctuary." So the people were restrained from bringing; ⁷ for what they had already brought was more than enough to do all the work.

Construction of the Tabernacle
(Ex 26.1–37)

8 All those with skill among the workers made the tabernacle with ten curtains; they were made of fine twisted linen, and blue, purple, and crimson yarns, with cherubim skillfully worked into them. ⁹ The length of each curtain was twenty-eight cubits, and the width of each curtain four cubits; all the curtains were of the same size.

10 He joined five curtains to one another, and the other five curtains he joined to one another. ¹¹ He made loops of blue on the edge of the outermost curtain of the first set; likewise he made them on the edge of the outermost curtain of the second set; ¹² he made fifty loops on the one curtain, and he made fifty loops on the edge of the curtain that was in the second set; the loops were opposite one another. ¹³ And he made fifty clasps of gold, and joined the curtains one to the other with clasps; so the tabernacle was one whole.

14 He also made curtains of goats' hair for a tent over the tabernacle; he made eleven curtains. ¹⁵ The length of each curtain was thirty cubits, and the width of each curtain four cubits; the eleven curtains were of the same size. ¹⁶ He joined five curtains by themselves, and six curtains by themselves. ¹⁷ He made fifty loops on the edge of the outermost curtain of the one set, and fifty loops on the edge of the other connecting curtain. ¹⁸ He made fifty clasps of bronze to join the tent together so that it might be one whole. ¹⁹ And he made for the tent a covering of tanned rams' skins and an outer covering of fine leather.*ᵏ*

20 Then he made the upright frames for the tabernacle of acacia wood. ²¹ Ten cubits was the length of a frame, and a cubit and a half the width of each frame. ²² Each frame had two pegs for fitting together; he did this for all the frames of the tabernacle. ²³ The frames for the tabernacle he made in this way: twenty frames for the south side; ²⁴ and he made forty bases of silver under the twenty frames, two bases under the first frame for its two pegs, and two bases under the next frame for its two pegs. ²⁵ For the second side of the tabernacle, on the north side, he made twenty frames ²⁶ and their forty bases of silver, two bases under the first frame and two bases under the next frame. ²⁷ For the rear of the tabernacle westward he made six frames. ²⁸ He made two frames for corners of the tabernacle in the rear. ²⁹ They were separate beneath, but joined at the top, at the first ring; he made two of them in this way, for the two corners. ³⁰ There were eight frames with their bases of silver: sixteen bases, under every frame two bases.

31 He made bars of acacia wood, five for the frames of the one side of the tabernacle, ³² and five bars for the frames of the other side of the tabernacle, and five bars for the frames of the tabernacle at the rear westward. ³³ He made the middle bar to pass through from end to end halfway up the frames. ³⁴ And he overlaid the frames with gold, and made rings of gold for them to hold the bars, and overlaid the bars with gold.

35 He made the curtain of blue, purple, and crimson yarns, and fine twisted linen, with cherubim skillfully worked into it. ³⁶ For it he made four pillars of acacia, and overlaid them with gold; their hooks were of gold, and he cast for them four bases of silver. ³⁷ He also made a screen for the entrance to the tent, of blue, purple, and crimson yarns, and fine twisted linen, embroidered with needlework; ³⁸ and its five pillars with their hooks.

ʲ Or *the spirit of God*　　*ᵏ* Meaning of Heb uncertain

He overlaid their capitals and their bases with gold, but their five bases were of bronze.

Making the Ark of the Covenant
(Ex 25.10–22)

Bez'a•lel made the ark of acacia wood; it was two and a half cubits long, a cubit and a half wide, and a cubit and a half high. 2 He overlaid it with pure gold inside and outside, and made a molding of gold around it. 3 He cast for it four rings of gold for its four feet, two rings on its one side and two rings on its other side. 4 He made poles of acacia wood, and overlaid them with gold, 5 and put the poles into the rings on the sides of the ark, to carry the ark. 6 He made a mercy seat *l* of pure gold; two cubits and a half was its length, and a cubit and a half its width. 7 He made two cherubim of hammered gold; at the two ends of the mercy seat *m* he made them, 8 one cherub at the one end, and one cherub at the other end; of one piece with the mercy seat *m* he made the cherubim at its two ends. 9 The cherubim spread out their wings above, overshadowing the mercy seat *m* with their wings. They faced one another; the faces of the cherubim were turned toward the mercy seat. *m*

Making the Table for the Bread of the Presence
(Ex 25.23–30)

10 He also made the table of acacia wood, two cubits long, one cubit wide, and a cubit and a half high. 11 He overlaid it with pure gold, and made a molding of gold around it. 12 He made around it a rim a handbreadth wide, and made a molding of gold around the rim. 13 He cast for it four rings of gold, and fastened the rings to the four corners at its four legs. 14 The rings that held the poles used for carrying the table were close to the rim. 15 He made the poles of acacia wood to carry the table, and overlaid them with gold. 16 And he made the vessels of pure gold that were to be on the table, its plates and dishes for incense, and its bowls and flagons with which to pour drink offerings.

Making the Lampstand
(Ex 25.31–40)

17 He also made the lampstand of pure gold. The base and the shaft of the lampstand were made of hammered work; its cups, its calyxes, and its petals were of one piece with it. 18 There were six branches going out of its sides, three branches of the lampstand out of one side of it and three branches of the lampstand out of the other side of it; 19 three cups shaped like almond blossoms, each with calyx and petals, on one branch, and three cups shaped like almond blossoms, each with calyx and petals, on the other branch—so for

the six branches going out of the lampstand. 20 On the lampstand itself there were four cups shaped like almond blossoms, each with its calyxes and petals. 21 There was a calyx of one piece with it under the first pair of branches, a calyx of one piece with it under the next pair of branches, and a calyx of one piece with it under the last pair of branches. 22 Their calyxes and their branches were of one piece with it, the whole of it one hammered piece of pure gold. 23 He made its seven lamps and its snuffers and its trays of pure gold. 24 He made it and all its utensils of a talent of pure gold.

l Or *a cover*   *m* Or *the cover*

Making the Altar of Incense
(Ex 30.1–5)

25 He made the altar of incense of acacia wood, one cubit long, and one cubit wide; it was square, and was two cubits high; its horns were of one piece with it. 26 He overlaid it with pure gold, its top, and its sides all around, and its horns; and he made for it a molding of gold all around, 27 and made two golden rings for it under its molding, on two opposite sides of it, to hold the poles with which to carry it. 28 And he made the poles of acacia wood, and overlaid them with gold.

Making the Anointing Oil and the Incense
(Ex 30.22–38)

29 He made the holy anointing oil also, and the pure fragrant incense, blended as by the perfumer.

Making the Altar of Burnt Offering
(Ex 27.1–8)

He made the altar of burnt offering also of acacia wood; it was five cubits long, and five cubits wide; it was square, and three cubits high. 2 He made horns for it on its four corners; its horns were of one piece with it, and he overlaid it with bronze. 3 He made all the utensils of the altar, the pots, the shovels, the basins, the forks, and the firepans: all its utensils he made of bronze. 4 He made for the altar a grating, a network of bronze, under its ledge, extending halfway down. 5 He cast four rings on the four corners of the bronze grating to hold the poles; 6 he made the poles of acacia wood, and overlaid them with bronze. 7 And he put the poles through the rings on the sides of the altar, to carry it with them; he made it hollow, with boards.

8 He made the basin of bronze with its stand of bronze, from the mirrors of the women who served at the entrance to the tent of meeting.

Making the Court of the Tabernacle
(Ex 27.9–19)

9 He made the court; for the south side the hangings of the court were of fine twisted linen, one hundred cubits long; 10 its twenty pillars and their twenty bases were of bronze, but the hooks of the pillars and their bands were of silver. 11 For the north side there were hangings one hundred cubits long; its twenty pillars and their twenty bases were of bronze, but the hooks of the pillars and their bands were of silver. 12 For the west side there were hangings fifty cubits long, with ten pillars and ten bases; the hooks of the pillars and their bands were of silver. 13 And for the front to the east, fifty cubits. 14 The hangings for one side of the gate were fifteen cubits, with three pillars and three bases. 15 And so for the other side; on each side of the gate of the court were hangings of fifteen cubits, with three pillars and three bases. 16 All the hangings around the court were of fine twisted linen. 17 The bases for the pillars were of bronze, but the hooks of the pillars and their bands were of silver; the overlaying of their capitals was also of silver, and all the pillars of the court were banded with silver. 18 The screen for the entrance to the court was embroidered with needlework in blue, purple, and crimson yarns and fine twisted linen. It was twenty cubits long and, along the width of it, five cubits high, corresponding to the hangings of the court. 19 There were four pillars; their four bases were of bronze, their hooks of silver, and the overlaying of their capitals and their bands of silver. 20 All the pegs for the tabernacle and for the court all around were of bronze.

Materials of the Tabernacle

21 These are the records of the tabernacle, the tabernacle of the covenant,[n] which were drawn up at the commandment of Moses, the work of the Lēʹvites being under the direction of Ithʹa·mar son of the priest Aaron. 22 Bezʹa·lel son of Uʹrī son of Hur, of the tribe of Judah, made all that the LORD commanded Moses; 23 and with him was O·hōʹli·ab son of A·hisʹa·mach, of the tribe of Dan, engraver, designer, and embroiderer in blue, purple, and crimson yarns, and in fine linen.

24 All the gold that was used for the work, in all the construction of the sanctuary, the gold from the offering, was twenty-nine talents and seven hundred thirty shekels, measured by the sanctuary shekel. 25 The silver from those of the congregation who were counted was one hundred talents and one thousand seven hundred seventy-five shekels, measured by the sanctuary shekel; 26 a beka a head (that is, half a shekel, measured by the sanctuary shekel), for everyone who was counted in the census, from twenty years old and upward, for six hundred three thousand, five hundred fifty men. 27 The hundred talents of silver were for casting the bases of the sanctuary, and the bases of the curtain; one hundred bases for the hundred talents, a talent for a base. 28 Of the thousand seven hundred seventy-five shekels he made hooks for the pillars, and overlaid their capitals and made bands for them. 29 The bronze that was contributed was seventy talents, and two thousand four hundred shekels; 30 with it he made the bases for the

---

n Or *treaty,* or *testimony;* Heb *eduth*

entrance of the tent of meeting, the bronze altar and the bronze grating for it and all the utensils of the altar, 31 the bases all around the court, and the bases of the gate of the court, all the pegs of the tabernacle, and all the pegs around the court.

Making the Vestments for the Priesthood
(Ex 28.1–43)

Of the blue, purple, and crimson yarns they made finely worked vestments, for ministering in the holy place; they made the sacred vestments for Aaron; as the LORD had commanded Moses. 2 He made the ephod of gold, of blue, purple, and crimson yarns, and of fine twisted linen. 3 Gold leaf was hammered out and cut into threads to work into the blue, purple, and crimson yarns and into the fine twisted linen, in skilled design. 4 They made for the ephod shoulder-pieces, joined to it at its two edges. 5 The decorated band on it was of the same materials and workmanship, of gold, of blue, purple, and crimson yarns, and of fine twisted linen; as the LORD had commanded Moses.

6 The onyx stones were prepared, enclosed in settings of gold filigree and engraved like the engravings of a signet, according to the names of the sons of Israel. 7 He set them on the shoulder-pieces of the ephod, to be stones of remembrance for the sons of Israel; as the LORD had commanded Moses. 8 He made the breastpiece, in skilled work, like the work of the ephod, of gold, of blue, purple, and crimson yarns, and of fine twisted linen. 9 It was square; the breastpiece was made double, a span in length and a span in width when doubled. 10 They set in it four rows of stones. A row of carnelian,*o* chrysolite, and emerald was the first row; 11 and the second row, a turquoise, a sapphire,*p* and a moonstone; 12 and the third row, a jacinth, an agate, and an amethyst; 13 and the fourth row, a beryl, an onyx, and a jasper; they were enclosed in settings of gold filigree. 14 There were twelve stones with names corresponding to the names of the sons of Israel; they were like signets, each engraved with its name, for the twelve tribes. 15 They made on the breastpiece chains of pure gold, twisted like cords; 16 and they made two settings of gold filigree and two gold rings, and put the two rings on the two edges of the breastpiece; 17 and they put the two cords of gold in the two rings at the edges of the breastpiece. 18 Two ends of the two cords they had attached to the two settings of filigree; in this way they attached it in front to the shoulder-pieces of the ephod. 19 Then they made two rings of gold, and put them at the two ends of the breastpiece, on its inside edge next to the ephod. 20 They made two rings of gold, and attached them

in front to the lower part of the two shoulder-pieces of the ephod, at its joining above the decorated band of the ephod. 21 They bound the breastpiece by its rings to the rings of the ephod with a blue cord, so that it should lie on the decorated band of the ephod, and that the breastpiece should not come loose from the ephod; as the LORD had commanded Moses.

22 He also made the robe of the ephod woven all of blue yarn; 23 and the opening of the robe in the middle of it was like the opening in a coat of mail,*q* with a binding around the opening, so that it might not be torn. 24 On the lower hem of the robe they made pomegranates of blue, purple, and crimson yarns, and of fine twisted linen. 25 They also made bells of pure gold, and put the bells between the pomegranates on the lower hem of the robe all around, between the pomegranates; 26 a bell and a pomegranate, a bell and a pomegranate all around on the lower hem of the robe for ministering; as the LORD had commanded Moses.

27 They also made the tunics, woven of fine linen, for Aaron and his sons, 28 and the turban of fine linen, and the headdresses of fine linen, and the linen undergarments of fine twisted linen, 29 and the sash of fine twisted linen, and of blue, purple, and crimson yarns, embroidered with needlework; as the LORD had commanded Moses.

30 They made the rosette of the holy diadem of pure gold, and wrote on it an inscription, like the engraving of a signet, "Holy to the LORD." 31 They tied to it a blue cord, to fasten it on the turban above; as the LORD had commanded Moses.

The Work Completed
(Ex 35.10–19)

32 In this way all the work of the tabernacle of the tent of meeting was finished; the Israelites had done everything just as the LORD had commanded Moses. 33 Then they brought the tabernacle to Moses, the tent and all its utensils, its hooks, its frames, its bars, its pillars, and its bases; 34 the covering of tanned rams' skins and the covering of fine leather,*q* and the curtain for the screen; 35 the ark of the covenant*r* with its poles and the mercy seat;*s* 36 the table with all its utensils, and the bread of the Presence; 37 the pure lampstand with its lamps set on it and all its utensils, and the oil for the light; 38 the golden altar, the anointing oil and the fragrant incense, and the screen for the entrance of the tent; 39 the bronze altar, and its

---

o The identification of several of these stones is uncertain
p Or *lapis lazuli*   *q* Meaning of Heb uncertain
r Or *treaty,* or *testimony;* Heb *eduth*   *s* Or *the cover*

grating of bronze, its poles, and all its utensils; the basin with its stand; ⁴⁰the hangings of the court, its pillars, and its bases, and the screen for the gate of the court, its cords, and its pegs; and all the utensils for the service of the tabernacle, for the tent of meeting; ⁴¹the finely worked vestments for ministering in the holy place, the sacred vestments for the priest Aaron, and the vestments of his sons to serve as priests. ⁴²The Israelites had done all of the work just as the LORD had commanded Moses. ⁴³When Moses saw that they had done all the work just as the LORD had commanded, he blessed them.

The Tabernacle Erected and Its Equipment Installed

The LORD spoke to Moses: ²On the first day of the first month you shall set up the tabernacle of the tent of meeting. ³You shall put in it the ark of the covenant,ᵗ and you shall screen the ark with the curtain. ⁴You shall bring in the table, and arrange its setting; and you shall bring in the lampstand, and set up its lamps. ⁵You shall put the golden altar for incense before the ark of the covenant,ᵗ and set up the screen for the entrance of the tabernacle. ⁶You shall set the altar of burnt offering before the entrance of the tabernacle of the tent of meeting, ⁷and place the basin between the tent of meeting and the altar, and put water in it. ⁸You shall set up the court all around, and hang up the screen for the gate of the court. ⁹Then you shall take the anointing oil, and anoint the tabernacle and all that is in it, and consecrate it and all its furniture, so that it shall become holy. ¹⁰You shall also anoint the altar of burnt offering and all its utensils, and consecrate the altar, so that the altar shall be most holy. ¹¹You shall also anoint the basin with its stand, and consecrate it. ¹²Then you shall bring Aaron and his sons to the entrance of the tent of meeting, and shall wash them with water, ¹³and put on Aaron the sacred vestments, and you shall anoint him and consecrate him, so that he may serve me as priest. ¹⁴You shall bring his sons also and put tunics on them, ¹⁵and anoint them, as you anointed their father, that they may serve me as priests: and their anointing shall admit them to a perpetual priesthood throughout all generations to come.

16 Moses did everything just as the LORD had commanded him. ¹⁷In the first month in the second year, on the first day of the month, the tabernacle was set up. ¹⁸Moses set up the tabernacle; he laid its bases, and set up its frames, and put in its poles, and raised up its pillars; ¹⁹and he spread the tent over the tabernacle, and put the covering of the tent over it; as the LORD had commanded

Asian American

Umbrellas, Arks, and Tents

Umbrellas offer protection from the sun or rain. In Asian cultures, servants would hold umbrellas over emperors and kings. Catholics in Indonesia have adapted this custom for their worship. Often, an umbrella is set up over the tabernacle. Umbrellas are held over a priest when he carries the Blessed Sacrament or over the statue of Jesus' Sacred Heart when it is carried in a procession. The umbrella has become a sign of reverence for something that symbolizes God's presence.

The ark of the Covenant was built to act like an umbrella, to protect and reverence the tablets of the Law (the Commandments). When the ark was not being carried, it rested in the tabernacle in the holy of holies, which was a special tent at the center of the Israelites' camp. The ark and the tent served the same practical purpose as an umbrella and had the same deeper meaning of reverencing God's presence.

The next time you use an umbrella, remember how umbrellas are used to show respect for that which is holy: the body of Christ, the Ten Commandments, and one of God's greatest creations, *you!*

▶ **Ex 40.1–15**

Moses. ²⁰He took the covenantᵗ and put it into the ark, and put the poles on the ark, and set the mercy seatᵘ above the ark; ²¹and he brought the ark into the tabernacle, and set up the curtain for screening, and screened the ark of the covenant;ᵗ as the LORD had commanded Moses. ²²He put the table in the tent of meeting, on the north side of the tabernacle, outside the curtain, ²³and set the bread in order on it before the LORD; as the LORD had commanded Moses. ²⁴He put the lampstand in the tent of meeting, opposite the table on the south side of the tabernacle, ²⁵and set up the

---

ᵗ Or *treaty*, or *testimony*; Heb *eduth*   ᵘ Or *the cover*

lamps before the LORD; as the LORD had commanded Moses. 26 He put the golden altar in the tent of meeting before the curtain, 27 and offered fragrant incense on it; as the LORD had commanded Moses. 28 He also put in place the screen for the entrance of the tabernacle. 29 He set the altar of burnt offering at the entrance of the tabernacle of the tent of meeting, and offered on it the burnt offering and the grain offering as the LORD had commanded Moses. 30 He set the basin between the tent of meeting and the altar, and put water in it for washing, 31 with which Moses and Aaron and his sons washed their hands and their feet. 32 When they went into the tent of meeting, and when they approached the altar, they washed; as the LORD had commanded Moses. 33 He set up the court around the tabernacle and the altar, and put up the screen at the gate of the court. So Moses finished the work.

The Cloud and the Glory
(Ex 13.21–22; Num 9.15–23)

34 Then the cloud covered the tent of meeting, and the glory of the LORD filled the tabernacle. 35 Moses was not able to enter the tent of meeting because the cloud settled upon it, and the glory of the LORD filled the tabernacle. 36 Whenever the cloud was taken up from the tabernacle, the Israelites would set out on each stage of their journey; 37 but if the cloud was not taken up, then they did not set out until the day that it was taken up. 38 For the cloud of the LORD was on the tabernacle by day, and fire was in the cloud[v] by night, before the eyes of all the house of Israel at each stage of their journey.

v Heb it

When approaching a stop sign, come to a complete stop before proceeding." "You are not allowed to pass when a yellow line is on your side of the road." Sometime soon you will be given a book to learn these rules of driving—unless you have already had the pleasure! These laws may be a pain to memorize, but without them driving would be chaos. The Book of Leviticus has a similar function. It is primarily a list of laws, rules, and instructions to ensure holiness and order in worship and the people's way of life.

At a Glance

- **Chapters 1–7.** laws regulating various sacrifices
- **Chapters 8–10.** the ordination ceremony of Aaron and his sons
- **Chapters 11–16.** purity laws and the celebration of Yom Kippur
- **Chapters 17–26.** holiness laws
- **Chapters 27–34.** the re-dedication of holy things

In-depth

Leviticus, the third book of the Pentateuch, or Torah, is named after the tribe of Levi, whose male members were designated priests in Israel. It was their responsibility to conduct appropriate worship of God. For that reason, the book has often been referred to as the Torah (Law) of the Priests.

Most Scripture scholars believe that the laws and regulations in Leviticus developed over hundreds of years after the people entered the Promised Land. The book was composed at a time when the priests were struggling to unify Israel as it lay in ruins from its Babylonian conquerers. They wished to gather the various traditions and regulations that governed Israel's way of life. The author of Leviticus, referred to as the Priestly writer, writes as if these gathered traditions and regulations were given by God to Moses at Mount Sinai as part of the original Law. The author wishes to show that these laws are an extension of the Sinai Covenant.

If the goal of Israel's existence is to "be holy, for I [the Lord] am holy" (Lev 11.44), then the Book of Leviticus records how holiness becomes part of every aspect of Israel's existence. Chapters 17–26 are described as the Holiness Code. The words on love of neighbor in 19.18 are quoted several times in the New Testament. The purpose of Leviticus is to call Israel to follow the Law, and thus become a holy people and make its land a suitable place for God to dwell.

The customs and rites in Jesus' time are observances of the laws in Leviticus. Many of those customs and rites were left behind as Christianity emerged as a distinct religion.

Quick Facts

Period Covered
after the Exodus, during the Israelites' encampment at Mount Sinai

Author
the Priestly writer writing after the Babylonian Exile

Theme
to teach the way of holiness through observance of the Law and religious ritual

Leviticus

The Burnt Offering

The LORD summoned Moses and spoke to him from the tent of meeting, saying: 2 Speak to the people of Israel and say to them: When any of you bring an offering of livestock to the LORD, you shall bring your offering from the herd or from the flock.

3 If the offering is a burnt offering from the herd, you shall offer a male without blemish; you shall bring it to the entrance of the tent of meeting, for acceptance in your behalf before the LORD. 4 You shall lay your hand on the head of the burnt offering, and it shall be acceptable in your behalf as atonement for you. 5 The bull shall be slaughtered before the LORD; and Aaron's sons the priests shall offer the blood, dashing the blood against all sides of the altar that is at the entrance of the tent of meeting. 6 The burnt offering shall be flayed and cut up into its parts. 7 The sons of the priest Aaron shall put fire on the altar and arrange wood on the fire. 8 Aaron's sons the priests shall arrange the parts, with the head and the suet, on the wood that is on the fire on the altar; 9 but its entrails and its legs shall be washed with water. Then the priest shall turn the whole into smoke on the altar as a burnt offering, an offering by fire of pleasing odor to the LORD.

10 If your gift for a burnt offering is from the flock, from the sheep or goats, your offering shall be a male without blemish. 11 It shall be slaughtered on the north side of the altar before the LORD, and Aaron's sons the priests shall dash its blood against all sides of the altar. 12 It shall be cut up into its parts, with its head and its suet, and the priest shall arrange them on the wood that is on the fire on the altar; 13 but the entrails and the legs shall be washed with water. Then the priest shall offer the whole and turn it into smoke on the altar; it is a burnt offering, an offering by fire of pleasing odor to the LORD.

14 If your offering to the LORD is a burnt offering of birds, you shall choose your offering from turtledoves or pigeons. 15 The priest shall bring it to the altar and wring off its head, and turn it into smoke on the altar; and its blood shall be drained out against the side of the altar. 16 He shall remove its crop with its contents[a] and throw it at the east side of the altar, in the place for ashes. 17 He shall tear it open by its wings without severing it. Then the priest shall turn it into smoke on the altar, on the wood that is on the fire; it is a burnt offering, an offering by fire of pleasing odor to the LORD.

Grain Offerings

When anyone presents a grain offering to the LORD, the offering shall be of choice flour; the worshiper shall pour oil on it, and put frankincense on it, 2 and bring it to Aaron's sons the priests. After taking from it a handful of the choice flour and oil,

---

a Meaning of Heb uncertain

with all its frankincense, the priest shall turn this token portion into smoke on the altar, an offering by fire of pleasing odor to the LORD. ³And what is left of the grain offering shall be for Aaron and his sons, a most holy part of the offerings by fire to the LORD.

?did you KNOW?
The Covenant Laws

Even though Christians are not bound by the Jewish religion—see the Letters to the Hebrews and to the Romans—the laws in Leviticus help us understand the meaning of life for the Israelites. These laws developed out of their experience of striving to be faithful to God and were interpreted and taught by the priests of the tribe of Levi.

The purity laws may seem the strangest to us today. They defined who or what was pure—that is, free from contamination—and therefore acceptable to God. They included laws on sickness, especially leprosy, because physical disease was understood as a symptom of sin or spiritual contamination. Purity laws also covered food, animals, bodily discharges, and corpses.

Other laws described proper relationships between people. These laws reflected more the intentions of the heart. Later, the prophets and Jesus would emphasize that impurity comes from the heart, not from something outside the person (Mk 7.1–23). Other laws regulated priestly ministry, and still others regulated social institutions. Nothing was left to chance. The laws of the Covenant made it clear that God was present in every aspect of the people's lives.

4 When you present a grain offering baked in the oven, it shall be of choice flour: unleavened cakes mixed with oil, or unleavened wafers spread with oil. ⁵If your offering is grain prepared on a griddle, it shall be of choice flour mixed with oil, unleavened; ⁶break it in pieces, and pour oil on it; it is a grain offering. ⁷If your offering is grain prepared in a pan, it shall be made of choice flour in

oil. ⁸You shall bring to the LORD the grain offering that is prepared in any of these ways; and when it is presented to the priest, he shall take it to the altar. ⁹The priest shall remove from the grain offering its token portion and turn this into smoke on the altar, an offering by fire of pleasing odor to the LORD. ¹⁰And what is left of the grain offering shall be for Aaron and his sons; it is a most holy part of the offerings by fire to the LORD.

11 No grain offering that you bring to the LORD shall be made with leaven, for you must not turn any leaven or honey into smoke as an offering by fire to the LORD. ¹²You may bring them to the LORD as an offering of choice products, but they shall not be offered on the altar for a pleasing odor. ¹³You shall not omit from your grain offerings the salt of the covenant with your God; with all your offerings you shall offer salt.

14 If you bring a grain offering of first fruits to the LORD, you shall bring as the grain offering of your first fruits coarse new grain from fresh ears, parched with fire. ¹⁵You shall add oil to it and lay frankincense on it; it is a grain offering. ¹⁶And the priest shall turn a token portion of it into smoke— some of the coarse grain and oil with all its frankincense; it is an offering by fire to the LORD.

Offerings of Well-Being

If the offering is a sacrifice of well-being, if you offer an animal of the herd, whether male or female, you shall offer one without blemish before the LORD. ²You shall lay your hand on the head of the offering and slaughter it at the entrance of the tent of meeting; and Aaron's sons the priests shall dash the blood against all sides of the altar. ³You shall offer from the sacrifice of well-being, as an offering by fire to the LORD, the fat that covers the entrails and all the fat that is around the entrails; ⁴the two kidneys with the fat that is on them at the loins, and the appendage of the liver, which he shall remove with the kidneys. ⁵Then Aaron's sons shall turn these into smoke on the altar, with the burnt offering that is on the wood on the fire, as an offering by fire of pleasing odor to the LORD.

6 If your offering for a sacrifice of well-being to the LORD is from the flock, male or female, you shall offer one without blemish. ⁷If you present a sheep as your offering, you shall bring it before the LORD ⁸and lay your hand on the head of the offering. It shall be slaughtered before the tent of meeting, and Aaron's sons shall dash its blood against all sides of the altar. ⁹You shall present its fat from the sacrifice of well-being, as an offering by fire to the LORD: the whole broad tail, which shall be removed close to the backbone, the fat that covers the entrails, and all the fat that is around the

entrails; [10] the two kidneys with the fat that is on them at the loins, and the appendage of the liver, which you shall remove with the kidneys. [11] Then the priest shall turn these into smoke on the altar as a food offering by fire to the LORD.

12 If your offering is a goat, you shall bring it before the LORD [13] and lay your hand on its head; it shall be slaughtered before the tent of meeting; and the sons of Aaron shall dash its blood against all sides of the altar. [14] You shall present as your offering from it, as an offering by fire to the LORD, the fat that covers the entrails, and all the fat that is around the entrails; [15] the two kidneys with the fat that is on them at the loins, and the appendage of the liver, which you shall remove with the kidneys. [16] Then the priest shall turn these into smoke on the altar as a food offering by fire for a pleasing odor.

All fat is the LORD's. [17] It shall be a perpetual statute throughout your generations, in all your settlements: you must not eat any fat or any blood.

Sin Offerings

The LORD spoke to Moses, saying, [2] Speak to the people of Israel, saying: When anyone sins unintentionally in any of the LORD's commandments about things not to be done, and does any one of them:

3 If it is the anointed priest who sins, thus bringing guilt on the people, he shall offer for the sin that he has committed a bull of the herd without blemish as a sin offering to the LORD. [4] He shall bring the bull to the entrance of the tent of meeting before the LORD and lay his hand on the head of the bull; the bull shall be slaughtered before the LORD. [5] The anointed priest shall take some of the blood of the bull and bring it into the tent of meeting. [6] The priest shall dip his finger in the blood and sprinkle some of the blood seven times before the LORD in front of the curtain of the sanctuary. [7] The priest shall put some of the blood on the horns of the altar of fragrant incense that is in the tent of meeting before the LORD; and the rest of the blood of the bull he shall pour out at the base of the altar of burnt offering, which is at the entrance of the tent of meeting. [8] He shall remove all the fat from the bull of sin offering: the fat that covers the entrails and all the fat that is around the entrails; [9] the two kidneys with the fat that is on them at the loins; and the appendage of the liver, which he shall remove with the kidneys, [10] just as these are removed from the ox of the sacrifice of well-being. The priest shall turn them into smoke upon the altar of burnt offering. [11] But the skin of the bull and all its flesh, as well as its head, its legs, its entrails, and its dung— [12] all the rest of the

bull—he shall carry out to a clean place outside the camp, to the ash heap, and shall burn it on a wood fire; at the ash heap it shall be burned.

13 If the whole congregation of Israel errs unintentionally and the matter escapes the notice of the assembly, and they do any one of the things that by the LORD's commandments ought not to be done and incur guilt; [14] when the sin that they have committed becomes known, the assembly shall offer a bull of the herd for a sin offering and bring it before the tent of meeting. [15] The elders of the congregation shall lay their hands on the head of the bull before the LORD, and the bull shall be slaughtered before the LORD. [16] The anointed priest shall bring some of the blood of the bull into the tent of meeting, [17] and the priest shall dip his finger in the blood and sprinkle it seven times before the LORD, in front of the curtain. [18] He shall put some of the blood on the horns of the altar that is before the LORD in the tent of meeting; and the rest of the blood he shall pour out at the base of the altar of burnt offering that is at the entrance of the

PRAY IT!

Sin Offering

The sin-offering laws probably seem strange to you. Because of Jesus' sacrifice, Christians have never had to make sin offerings. But they do serve an important role in understanding what Jesus' death and Resurrection mean for our own sin and salvation.

The Israelites understood that sin affects not only the sinner but also those whose lives the sinner touches. They understood sin as incurring a debt that must be repaid. The sinner made a guilt offering to atone for the sin.

Isaiah said that God made the life of the suffering servant a guilt offering for those who were too far into debt to repay (Isa 53.10). At the Last Supper, Jesus told the Apostles, "This is my blood . . . , which is poured out for many for the forgiveness of sins" (Mt 26.27–28). Jesus became our sin offering to take on the debt of our sin. In prayerful thanks for this great gift, read Eph 1.3–14.

▶ Lev 4.1—6.7

tent of meeting. ¹⁹ He shall remove all its fat and turn it into smoke on the altar. ²⁰ He shall do with the bull just as is done with the bull of sin offering; he shall do the same with this. The priest shall make atonement for them, and they shall be forgiven. ²¹ He shall carry the bull outside the camp, and burn it as he burned the first bull; it is the sin offering for the assembly.

22 When a ruler sins, doing unintentionally any one of all the things that by commandments of the LORD his God ought not to be done and incurs guilt, ²³ once the sin that he has committed is made known to him, he shall bring as his offering a male goat without blemish. ²⁴ He shall lay his hand on the head of the goat; it shall be slaughtered at the spot where the burnt offering is slaughtered before the LORD; it is a sin offering. ²⁵ The priest shall take some of the blood of the sin offering with his finger and put it on the horns of the altar of burnt offering, and pour out the rest of its blood at the base of the altar of burnt offering. ²⁶ All its fat he shall turn into smoke on the altar, like the fat of the sacrifice of well-being. Thus the priest shall make atonement on his behalf for his sin, and he shall be forgiven.

27 If anyone of the ordinary people among you sins unintentionally in doing any one of the things that by the LORD's commandments ought not to be done and incurs guilt, ²⁸ when the sin that you have committed is made known to you, you shall bring a female goat without blemish as your offering, for the sin that you have committed. ²⁹ You shall lay your hand on the head of the sin offering; and the sin offering shall be slaughtered at the place of the burnt offering. ³⁰ The priest shall take some of its blood with his finger and put it on the horns of the altar of burnt offering, and he shall pour out the rest of its blood at the base of the altar. ³¹ He shall remove all its fat, as the fat is removed from the offering of well-being, and the priest shall turn it into smoke on the altar for a pleasing odor to the LORD. Thus the priest shall make atonement on your behalf, and you shall be forgiven.

32 If the offering you bring as a sin offering is a sheep, you shall bring a female without blemish. ³³ You shall lay your hand on the head of the sin offering; and it shall be slaughtered as a sin offering at the spot where the burnt offering is slaughtered. ³⁴ The priest shall take some of the blood of the sin offering with his finger and put it on the horns of the altar of burnt offering, and pour out the rest of its blood at the base of the altar. ³⁵ You shall remove all its fat, as the fat of the sheep is removed from the sacrifice of well-being, and the priest shall turn it into smoke on the altar, with

the offerings by fire to the LORD. Thus the priest shall make atonement on your behalf for the sin that you have committed, and you shall be forgiven.

5 When any of you sin in that you have heard a public adjuration to testify and—though able to testify as one who has seen or learned of the matter—do not speak up, you are subject to punishment. ² Or when any of you touch any unclean thing—whether the carcass of an unclean beast or the carcass of unclean livestock or the carcass of an unclean swarming thing—and are unaware of it, you have become unclean, and are guilty. ³ Or when you touch human uncleanness—any uncleanness by which one can become unclean—and are unaware of it, when you come to know it, you shall be guilty. ⁴ Or when any of you utter aloud a rash oath for a bad or a good purpose, whatever people utter in an oath, and are unaware of it, when you come to know it, you shall in any of these be guilty. ⁵ When you realize your guilt in any of these, you shall confess the sin that you have committed. ⁶ And you shall bring to the LORD, as your penalty for the sin that you have committed, a female from the flock, a sheep or a goat, as a sin offering; and the priest shall make atonement on your behalf for your sin.

7 But if you cannot afford a sheep, you shall bring to the LORD, as your penalty for the sin that you have committed, two turtledoves or two pigeons, one for a sin offering and the other for a burnt offering. ⁸ You shall bring them to the priest, who shall offer first the one for the sin offering, wringing its head at the nape without severing it. ⁹ He shall sprinkle some of the blood of the sin offering on the side of the altar, while the rest of the blood shall be drained out at the base of the altar; it is a sin offering. ¹⁰ And the second he shall offer for a burnt offering according to the regulation. Thus the priest shall make atonement on your behalf for the sin that you have committed, and you shall be forgiven.

11 But if you cannot afford two turtledoves or two pigeons, you shall bring as your offering for the sin that you have committed one-tenth of an ephah of choice flour for a sin offering; you shall not put oil on it or lay frankincense on it, for it is a sin offering. ¹² You shall bring it to the priest, and the priest shall scoop up a handful of it as its memorial portion, and turn this into smoke on the altar, with the offerings by fire to the LORD; it is a sin offering. ¹³ Thus the priest shall make atonement on your behalf for whichever of these sins you have committed, and you shall be forgiven. Like the grain offering, the rest shall be for the priest.

Offerings with Restitution

14 The LORD spoke to Moses, saying: 15 When any of you commit a trespass and sin unintentionally in any of the holy things of the LORD, you shall bring, as your guilt offering to the LORD, a ram without blemish from the flock, convertible into silver by the sanctuary shekel; it is a guilt offering. 16 And you shall make restitution for the holy thing in which you were remiss, and shall add one-fifth to it and give it to the priest. The priest shall make atonement on your behalf with the ram of the guilt offering, and you shall be forgiven.

17 If any of you sin without knowing it, doing any of the things that by the LORD's commandments ought not to be done, you have incurred guilt, and are subject to punishment. 18 You shall bring to the priest a ram without blemish from the flock, or the equivalent, as a guilt offering; and the priest shall make atonement on your behalf for the error that you committed unintentionally, and you shall be forgiven. 19 It is a guilt offering; you have incurred guilt before the LORD.

b The LORD spoke to Moses, saying: 2 When any of you sin and commit a trespass against the LORD by deceiving a neighbor in a matter of a deposit or a pledge, or by robbery, or if you have defrauded a neighbor, 3 or have found something lost and lied about it—if you swear falsely regarding any of the various things that one may do and sin thereby— 4 when you have sinned and realize your guilt, and would restore what you took by robbery or by fraud or the deposit that was committed to you, or the lost thing that you found, 5 or anything else about which you have sworn falsely, you shall repay the principal amount and shall add one-fifth to it. You shall pay it to its owner when you realize your guilt. 6 And you shall bring to the priest, as your guilt offering to the LORD, a ram without blemish from the flock, or its equivalent, for a guilt offering. 7 The priest shall make atonement on your behalf before the LORD, and you shall be forgiven for any of the things that one may do and incur guilt thereby.

Instructions concerning Sacrifices

8 *c* The LORD spoke to Moses, saying: 9 Command Aaron and his sons, saying: This is the ritual of the burnt offering. The burnt offering itself shall remain on the hearth upon the altar all night until the morning, while the fire on the altar shall be kept burning. 10 The priest shall put on his linen vestments after putting on his linen undergarments next to his body; and he shall take up the ashes to which the fire has reduced the burnt offering on the altar, and place them beside the altar. 11 Then he shall take off his vestments and put on other garments, and carry the ashes out to a clean place outside the camp. 12 The fire on the altar shall be kept burning; it shall not go out. Every morning the priest shall add wood to it, lay out the burnt offering on it, and turn into smoke the fat pieces of the offerings of well-being. 13 A perpetual fire shall be kept burning on the altar; it shall not go out.

14 This is the ritual of the grain offering: The sons of Aaron shall offer it before the LORD, in front of the altar. 15 They shall take from it a handful of the choice flour and oil of the grain offering, with all the frankincense that is on the offering, and they shall turn its memorial portion into smoke on the altar as a pleasing odor to the LORD. 16 Aaron and his sons shall eat what is left of it; it shall be eaten as unleavened cakes in a holy place; in the court of the tent of meeting they shall eat it. 17 It shall not be baked with leaven. I have given it as their portion of my offerings by fire; it is most holy, like the sin offering and the guilt offering. 18 Every male among the descendants of Aaron shall eat of it, as their perpetual due throughout your generations, from the LORD's offerings by fire; anything that touches them shall become holy.

19 The LORD spoke to Moses, saying: 20 This is the offering that Aaron and his sons shall offer to the LORD on the day when he is anointed: one-tenth of an ephah of choice flour as a regular offering, half of it in the morning and half in the evening. 21 It shall be made with oil on a griddle; you shall bring it well soaked, as a grain offering of baked *d* pieces, and you shall present it as a pleasing odor to the LORD. 22 And so the priest, anointed from among Aaron's descendants as a successor, shall prepare it; it is the LORD's—a perpetual due—to be turned entirely into smoke. 23 Every grain offering of a priest shall be wholly burned; it shall not be eaten.

24 The LORD spoke to Moses, saying: 25 Speak to Aaron and his sons, saying: This is the ritual of the sin offering. The sin offering shall be slaughtered before the LORD at the spot where the burnt offering is slaughtered; it is most holy. 26 The priest who offers it as a sin offering shall eat of it; it shall be eaten in a holy place, in the court of the tent of meeting. 27 Whatever touches its flesh shall become holy; and when any of its blood is spattered on a garment, you shall wash the bespattered part in a holy place. 28 An earthen vessel in which it was boiled shall be broken; but if it is boiled in a

---

b Ch 5.20 in Heb   *c* Ch 6.1 in Heb   *d* Meaning of Heb uncertain

bronze vessel, that shall be scoured and rinsed in water. [29] Every male among the priests shall eat of it; it is most holy. [30] But no sin offering shall be eaten from which any blood is brought into the tent of meeting for atonement in the holy place; it shall be burned with fire.

This is the ritual of the guilt offering. It is most holy; [2] at the spot where the burnt offering is slaughtered, they shall slaughter the guilt offering, and its blood shall be dashed against all sides of the altar. [3] All its fat shall be offered: the broad tail, the fat that covers the entrails, [4] the two kidneys with the fat that is on them at the loins, and the appendage of the liver, which shall be removed with the kidneys. [5] The priest shall turn them into smoke on the altar as an offering by fire to the LORD; it is a guilt offering. [6] Every male among the priests shall eat of it; it shall be eaten in a holy place; it is most holy.

7 The guilt offering is like the sin offering, there is the same ritual for them; the priest who makes atonement with it shall have it. [8] So, too, the priest who offers anyone's burnt offering shall keep the skin of the burnt offering that he has offered. [9] And every grain offering baked in the oven, and all that is prepared in a pan or on a griddle, shall belong to the priest who offers it. [10] But every other grain offering, mixed with oil or dry, shall belong to all the sons of Aaron equally.

Further Instructions

11 This is the ritual of the sacrifice of the offering of well-being that one may offer to the LORD. [12] If you offer it for thanksgiving, you shall offer with the thank offering unleavened cakes mixed with oil, unleavened wafers spread with oil, and cakes of choice flour well soaked in oil. [13] With your thanksgiving sacrifice of well-being you shall bring your offering with cakes of leavened bread. [14] From this you shall offer one cake from each offering, as a gift to the LORD; it shall belong to the priest who dashes the blood of the offering of well-being. [15] And the flesh of your thanksgiving sacrifice of well-being shall be eaten on the day it is offered; you shall not leave any of it until morning. [16] But if the sacrifice you offer is a votive offering or a freewill offering, it shall be eaten on the day that you offer your sacrifice, and what is left of it shall be eaten the next day; [17] but what is left of the flesh of the sacrifice shall be burned up on the third day. [18] If any of the flesh of your sacrifice of well-being is eaten on the third day, it shall not be acceptable, nor shall it be credited to the one who offers it; it shall be an abomination, and the one who eats of it shall incur guilt.

19 Flesh that touches any unclean thing shall not be eaten; it shall be burned up. As for other flesh, all who are clean may eat such flesh. [20] But those who eat flesh from the LORD's sacrifice of well-being while in a state of uncleanness shall be cut off from their kin. [21] When any one of you touches any unclean thing—human uncleanness or an unclean animal or any unclean creature—and then eats flesh from the LORD's sacrifice of well-being, you shall be cut off from your kin.

22 The LORD spoke to Moses, saying: [23] Speak to the people of Israel, saying: You shall eat no fat of ox or sheep or goat. [24] The fat of an animal that died or was torn by wild animals may be put to any other use, but you must not eat it. [25] If any one of you eats the fat from an animal of which an offering by fire may be made to the LORD, you who eat it shall be cut off from your kin. [26] You must not eat any blood whatever, either of bird or of animal, in any of your settlements. [27] Any one of you who eats any blood shall be cut off from your kin.

28 The LORD spoke to Moses, saying: [29] Speak to the people of Israel, saying: Any one of you who would offer to the LORD your sacrifice of well-being must yourself bring to the LORD your offering from your sacrifice of well-being. [30] Your own hands shall bring the LORD's offering by fire; you shall bring the fat with the breast, so that the breast may be raised as an elevation offering before the LORD. [31] The priest shall turn the fat into smoke on the altar, but the breast shall belong to Aaron and his sons. [32] And the right thigh from your sacrifices of well-being you shall give to the priest as an offering; [33] the one among the sons of Aaron who offers the blood and fat of the offering of well-being shall have the right thigh for a portion. [34] For I have taken the breast of the elevation offering, and the thigh that is offered, from the people of Israel, from their sacrifices of well-being, and have given them to Aaron the priest and to his sons, as a perpetual due from the people of Israel. [35] This is the portion allotted to Aaron and to his sons from the offerings made by fire to the LORD, once they have been brought forward to serve the LORD as priests; [36] these the LORD commanded to be given them, when he anointed them, as a perpetual due from the people of Israel throughout their generations.

37 This is the ritual of the burnt offering, the grain offering, the sin offering, the guilt offering, the offering of ordination, and the sacrifice of well-being, [38] which the LORD commanded Moses on Mount Sinai, when he commanded the people of Israel to bring their offerings to the LORD, in the wilderness of Sinai.

The Rites of Ordination

(Ex 29.1–37)

The LORD spoke to Moses, saying: 2 Take Aaron and his sons with him, the vestments, the anointing oil, the bull of sin offering, the two rams, and the basket of unleavened bread; 3 and assemble the whole congregation at the entrance of the tent of meeting. 4 And Moses did as the LORD commanded him. When the congregation was assembled at the entrance of the tent of meeting, 5 Moses said to the congregation, "This is what the LORD has commanded to be done."

6 Then Moses brought Aaron and his sons forward, and washed them with water. 7 He put the tunic on him, fastened the sash around him, clothed him with the robe, and put the ephod on him. He then put the decorated band of the ephod around him, tying the ephod to him with it. 8 He placed the breastpiece on him, and in the breastpiece he put the U'rim and the Thum'mim. 9 And he set the turban on his head, and on the turban, in front, he set the golden ornament, the holy crown, as the LORD commanded Moses.

10 Then Moses took the anointing oil and anointed the tabernacle and all that was in it, and consecrated them. 11 He sprinkled some of it on the altar seven times, and anointed the altar and all its utensils, and the basin and its base, to consecrate them. 12 He poured some of the anointing oil on Aaron's head and anointed him, to consecrate him. 13 And Moses brought forward Aaron's sons, and clothed them with tunics, and fastened sashes around them, and tied headdresses on them, as the LORD commanded Moses.

14 He led forward the bull of sin offering; and Aaron and his sons laid their hands upon the head of the bull of sin offering, 15 and it was slaughtered. Moses took the blood and with his finger put some on each of the horns of the altar, purifying the altar; then he poured out the blood at the base of the altar. Thus he consecrated it, to make atonement for it. 16 Moses took all the fat that was around the entrails, and the appendage of the liver, and the two kidneys with their fat, and turned them into smoke on the altar. 17 But the bull itself, its skin and flesh and its dung, he burned with fire outside the camp, as the LORD commanded Moses.

18 Then he brought forward the ram of burnt offering. Aaron and his sons laid their hands on the head of the ram, 19 and it was slaughtered. Moses dashed the blood against all sides of the altar. 20 The ram was cut into its parts, and Moses turned into smoke the head and the parts and the suet. 21 And after the entrails and the legs were washed with water, Moses turned into smoke the whole ram on the altar; it was a burnt offering for a pleasing odor, an offering by fire to the LORD, as the LORD commanded Moses.

22 Then he brought forward the second ram, the ram of ordination. Aaron and his sons laid their hands on the head of the ram, 23 and it was slaughtered. Moses took some of its blood and put it on the lobe of Aaron's right ear and on the thumb of his right hand and on the big toe of his right foot. 24 After Aaron's sons were brought forward, Moses put some of the blood on the lobes of their right ears and on the thumbs of their right hands and on the big toes of their right feet; and Moses dashed the rest of the blood against all sides of the altar. 25 He took the fat—the broad tail, all the fat that was around the entrails, the appendage of the liver, and the two kidneys with their fat—and the right thigh. 26 From the basket of unleavened bread that was before the LORD, he took one cake of unleavened bread, one cake of bread with oil, and one wafer, and placed them on the fat and on the right thigh. 27 He placed all these on the palms of Aaron and on the palms of his sons, and raised them as an elevation offering before the LORD. 28 Then Moses took them from their hands and turned them into smoke on the altar with the burnt offering. This was an ordination offering for a pleasing odor, an offering by fire to the LORD. 29 Moses took the breast and raised it as an elevation offering before the LORD; it was Moses' portion of the ram of ordination, as the LORD commanded Moses.

30 Then Moses took some of the anointing oil and some of the blood that was on the altar and sprinkled them on Aaron and his vestments, and also on his sons and their vestments. Thus he consecrated Aaron and his vestments, and also his sons and their vestments.

31 And Moses said to Aaron and his sons, "Boil the flesh at the entrance of the tent of meeting, and eat it there with the bread that is in the basket of ordination offerings, as I was commanded, 'Aaron and his sons shall eat it'; 32 and what remains of the flesh and the bread you shall burn with fire. 33 You shall not go outside the entrance of the tent of meeting for seven days, until the day when your period of ordination is completed. For it will take seven days to ordain you; 34 as has been done today, the LORD has commanded to be done to make atonement for you. 35 You shall remain at the entrance of the tent of meeting day and night for seven days, keeping the LORD's charge so that you do not die; for so I am commanded." 36 Aaron and his sons did all the things that the LORD commanded through Moses.

Aaron's Priesthood Inaugurated

On the eighth day Moses summoned Aaron and his sons and the elders of Israel. 2 He said to Aaron, "Take a bull calf for a sin offering and a ram for a burnt offering, without blemish, and offer them before the LORD. 3 And say to the people of Israel, 'Take a male goat for a sin offering; a calf and a lamb, yearlings without blemish, for a burnt offering; 4 and an ox and a ram for an offering of well-being to sacrifice before the LORD; and a grain offering mixed with oil. For today the LORD will appear to you.' " 5 They brought what Moses commanded to the front of the tent of meeting; and the whole congregation drew near and stood before the LORD. 6 And Moses said, "This is the thing that the LORD commanded you to do, so that the glory of the LORD may appear to you." 7 Then Moses said to Aaron, "Draw near to the altar and sacrifice your sin offering and your burnt offering, and make atonement for yourself and for the people; and sacrifice the offering of the people, and make atonement for them; as the LORD has commanded."

8 Aaron drew near to the altar, and slaughtered the calf of the sin offering, which was for himself. 9 The sons of Aaron presented the blood to him, and he dipped his finger in the blood and put it on the horns of the altar; and the rest of the blood he poured out at the base of the altar. 10 But the fat, the kidneys, and the appendage of the liver from the sin offering he turned into smoke on the altar, as the LORD commanded Moses; 11 and the flesh and the skin he burned with fire outside the camp.

12 Then he slaughtered the burnt offering. Aaron's sons brought him the blood, and he dashed it against all sides of the altar. 13 And they brought him the burnt offering piece by piece, and the head, which he turned into smoke on the altar. 14 He washed the entrails and the legs and, with the burnt offering, turned them into smoke on the altar.

15 Next he presented the people's offering. He took the goat of the sin offering that was for the people, and slaughtered it, and presented it as a sin offering like the first one. 16 He presented the burnt offering, and sacrificed it according to regulation. 17 He presented the grain offering, and, taking a handful of it, he turned it into smoke on the altar, in addition to the burnt offering of the morning.

18 He slaughtered the ox and the ram as a sacrifice of well-being for the people. Aaron's sons brought him the blood, which he dashed against all sides of the altar, 19 and the fat of the ox and of the ram—the broad tail, the fat that covers the entrails, the two kidneys and the fat on them,[e] and the appendage of the liver. 20 They first laid the fat on the breasts, and the fat was turned into smoke on the altar; 21 and the breasts and the right thigh Aaron raised as an elevation offering before the LORD, as Moses had commanded.

22 Aaron lifted his hands toward the people and blessed them; and he came down after sacrificing the sin offering, the burnt offering, and the offering of well-being. 23 Moses and Aaron entered the tent of meeting, and then came out and blessed the people; and the glory of the LORD appeared to all the people. 24 Fire came out from the LORD and consumed the burnt offering and the fat on the altar; and when all the people saw it, they shouted and fell on their faces.

Nadab and Abihu

Now Aaron's sons, Nā′dab and A•bī′hū, each took his censer, put fire in it, and laid incense on it; and they offered unholy fire before the LORD, such as he had not commanded them. 2 And fire came out from the presence of the LORD and consumed them, and they died before the LORD. 3 Then Moses said to Aaron, "This is what the LORD meant when he said,

'Through those who are near me
I will show myself holy,
and before all the people
I will be glorified.' "

And Aaron was silent.

4 Moses summoned Mish′a•el and El′za•phan, sons of Uz′zi•el the uncle of Aaron, and said to them, "Come forward, and carry your kinsmen away from the front of the sanctuary to a place outside the camp." 5 They came forward and carried them by their tunics out of the camp, as Moses had ordered. 6 And Moses said to Aaron and to his sons El•ē•ā′zar and Ith′a•mar, "Do not dishevel your hair, and do not tear your vestments, or you will die and wrath will strike all the congregation; but your kindred, the whole house of Israel, may mourn the burning that the LORD has sent. 7 You shall not go outside the entrance of the tent of meeting, or you will die; for the anointing oil of the LORD is on you." And they did as Moses had ordered.

8 And the LORD spoke to Aaron: 9 Drink no wine or strong drink, neither you nor your sons, when you enter the tent of meeting, that you may not die; it is a statute forever throughout your generations. 10 You are to distinguish between the holy and the common, and between the unclean

---

e Gk: Heb *the broad tail, and that which covers, and the kidneys*

and the clean; ¹¹ and you are to teach the people of Israel all the statutes that the LORD has spoken to them through Moses.

12 Moses spoke to Aaron and to his remaining sons, El•ē•ā′zar and Ith′a•mar: Take the grain offering that is left from the LORD's offerings by fire, and eat it unleavened beside the altar, for it is most holy; ¹³ you shall eat it in a holy place, because it is your due and your sons' due, from the offerings by fire to the LORD; for so I am commanded. ¹⁴ But the breast that is elevated and the thigh that is raised, you and your sons and daughters as well may eat in any clean place; for they have been assigned to you and your children from the sacrifices of the offerings of well-being of the people of Israel. ¹⁵ The thigh that is raised and the breast that is elevated they shall bring, together with the offerings by fire of the fat, to raise for an elevation offering before the LORD; they are to be your due and that of your children forever, as the LORD has commanded.

16 Then Moses made inquiry about the goat of the sin offering, and—it had already been burned! He was angry with El•ē•ā′zar and Ith′a•mar, Aaron's remaining sons, and said, ¹⁷ "Why did you not eat the sin offering in the sacred area? For it is most holy, and God*f* has given it to you that you may remove the guilt of the congregation, to make atonement on their behalf before the LORD. ¹⁸ Its blood was not brought into the inner part of the sanctuary. You should certainly have eaten it in the sanctuary, as I commanded." ¹⁹ And Aaron spoke to Moses, "See, today they offered their sin offering and their burnt offering before the LORD; and yet such things as these have befallen me! If I had eaten the sin offering today, would it have been agreeable to the LORD?" ²⁰ And when Moses heard that, he agreed.

Clean and Unclean Foods
(Deut 14.3–21)

The LORD spoke to Moses and Aaron, saying to them: ² Speak to the people of Israel, saying:

From among all the land animals, these are the creatures that you may eat. ³ Any animal that has divided hoofs and is cleft-footed and chews the cud—such you may eat. ⁴ But among those that chew the cud or have divided hoofs, you shall not eat the following: the camel, for even though it chews the cud, it does not have divided hoofs; it is unclean for you. ⁵ The rock badger, for even though it chews the cud, it does not have divided hoofs; it is unclean for you. ⁶ The hare, for even though it chews the cud, it does not have divided hoofs; it is unclean for you. ⁷ The pig, for even

though it has divided hoofs and is cleft-footed, it does not chew the cud; it is unclean for you. ⁸ Of their flesh you shall not eat, and their carcasses you shall not touch; they are unclean for you.

9 These you may eat, of all that are in the waters. Everything in the waters that has fins and scales, whether in the seas or in the streams—such you may eat. ¹⁰ But anything in the seas or the streams that does not have fins and scales, of the swarming creatures in the waters and among all the other living creatures that are in the waters—they are detestable to you ¹¹ and detestable they shall remain. Of their flesh you shall not eat, and their carcasses you shall regard as detestable. ¹² Everything in the waters that does not have fins and scales is detestable to you.

13 These you shall regard as detestable among the birds. They shall not be eaten; they are an abomination: the eagle, the vulture, the osprey, ¹⁴ the buzzard, the kite of any kind; ¹⁵ every raven of any kind; ¹⁶ the ostrich, the nighthawk, the sea gull, the hawk of any kind; ¹⁷ the little owl, the cormorant, the great owl, ¹⁸ the water hen, the desert owl,*g* the carrion vulture, ¹⁹ the stork, the heron of any kind, the hoopoe, and the bat.*h*

20 All winged insects that walk upon all fours are detestable to you. ²¹ But among the winged insects that walk on all fours you may eat those that have jointed legs above their feet, with which to leap on the ground. ²² Of them you may eat: the locust according to its kind, the bald locust according to its kind, the cricket according to its kind, and the grasshopper according to its kind. ²³ But all other winged insects that have four feet are detestable to you.

Unclean Animals

24 By these you shall become unclean; whoever touches the carcass of any of them shall be unclean until the evening, ²⁵ and whoever carries any part of the carcass of any of them shall wash his clothes and be unclean until the evening. ²⁶ Every animal that has divided hoofs but is not cleft-footed or does not chew the cud is unclean for you; everyone who touches one of them shall be unclean. ²⁷ All that walk on their paws, among the animals that walk on all fours, are unclean for you; whoever touches the carcass of any of them shall be unclean until the evening, ²⁸ and the one who carries the carcass shall wash his clothes and be unclean until the evening; they are unclean for you.

f Heb *he*   *g* Or *pelican*   *h* Identification of several of the birds in verses 13-19 is uncertain

?did you KNOW?

The Israelite Diet

The diet of the ancient Israelites consisted mainly of breads, cereals, fruits, vegetables, and dairy products. Meat was served only on special occasions because it was expensive. A typical family meal was made up of barley or wheat bread, grapes, figs, olive oil, beans, cucumbers, onions, and cheese. On festive occasions, beef or lamb might grace the table as well.

The laws in Leviticus, chapter 11, contain many restrictions regarding the eating of animals. The reasons for these restrictions are not clear, although many scholars believe that one purpose was to keep the Israelites from consuming animals used in pagan worship (for example, the pig offered in Babylonian services). Hygiene was likely another consideration.

The basic "meat laws" were as follows:

- Of the larger animals, those that chewed their cud and had split hooves could be eaten. Therefore, lamb was acceptable, but pork was not.
- Sea creatures only with both fins and scales could be eaten. Thus, catfish and eels were to be avoided.
- Eagles, vultures, buzzards, and many other birds were excluded from the table.
- Rodents, reptiles, and insects (except locusts and grasshoppers) were spurned altogether.

The blood from all animals had to be drained completely before cooking because blood was seen as the life force and therefore as belonging to God alone. In addition, it was unlawful to touch or eat any animal found dead; contact with any dead body made one impure.

▶ Lev 11.1–47

29 These are unclean for you among the creatures that swarm upon the earth: the weasel, the mouse, the great lizard according to its kind, 30 the gecko, the land crocodile, the lizard, the sand liz-

ard, and the chameleon. 31 These are unclean for you among all that swarm; whoever touches one of them when they are dead shall be unclean until the evening. 32 And anything upon which any of them falls when they are dead shall be unclean, whether an article of wood or cloth or skin or sacking, any article that is used for any purpose; it shall be dipped into water, and it shall be unclean until the evening, and then it shall be clean. 33 And if any of them falls into any earthen vessel, all that is in it shall be unclean, and you shall break the vessel. 34 Any food that could be eaten shall be unclean if water from any such vessel comes upon it; and any liquid that could be drunk shall be unclean if it was in any such vessel. 35 Everything on which any part of the carcass falls shall be unclean; whether an oven or stove, it shall be broken in pieces; they are unclean, and shall remain unclean for you. 36 But a spring or a cistern holding water shall be clean, while whatever touches the carcass in it shall be unclean. 37 If any part of their carcass falls upon any seed set aside for sowing, it is clean; 38 but if water is put on the seed and any part of their carcass falls on it, it is unclean for you.

39 If an animal of which you may eat dies, anyone who touches its carcass shall be unclean until the evening. 40 Those who eat of its carcass shall wash their clothes and be unclean until the evening; and those who carry the carcass shall wash their clothes and be unclean until the evening.

41 All creatures that swarm upon the earth are detestable; they shall not be eaten. 42 Whatever moves on its belly, and whatever moves on all fours, or whatever has many feet, all the creatures that swarm upon the earth, you shall not eat; for they are detestable. 43 You shall not make yourselves detestable with any creature that swarms; you shall not defile yourselves with them, and so become unclean. 44 For I am the LORD your God; sanctify yourselves therefore, and be holy, for I am holy. You shall not defile yourselves with any swarming creature that moves on the earth. 45 For I am the LORD who brought you up from the land of Egypt, to be your God; you shall be holy, for I am holy.

46 This is the law pertaining to land animal and bird and every living creature that moves through the waters and every creature that swarms upon the earth, 47 to make a distinction between the unclean and the clean, and between the living creature that may be eaten and the living creature that may not be eaten.

LEV

Purification of Women after Childbirth
(Cp Lk 2.22–24).

The LORD spoke to Moses, saying: ²Speak to the people of Israel, saying:

If a woman conceives and bears a male child, she shall be ceremonially unclean seven days; as at the time of her menstruation, she shall be unclean. ³On the eighth day the flesh of his foreskin

time of blood purification shall be sixty-six days.

6 When the days of her purification are completed, whether for a son or for a daughter, she shall bring to the priest at the entrance of the tent of meeting a lamb in its first year for a burnt offering, and a pigeon or a turtledove for a sin offering. ⁷He shall offer it before the LORD, and make atonement on her behalf; then she shall be clean from

NATIVE AMERICAN

A Mother's Prayer at Childbirth

Sun, moon, stars,
you that move in the heavens,
hear this mother!
A new life has come among you.
Make its path smooth that it may reach
the brow of the first hill.

Winds, clouds, rain, mist,
all that move in the air,
hear this mother!
A new life has come among you.
Make its path smooth that it may reach
the brow of the second hill.

Hills, valleys, rivers, lakes, trees, grasses,
all of the earth,
hear this mother!
A new life has come among you.
Make its path smooth that it may reach
the brow of the third hill.

Birds that fly in the air,
animals that dwell in the forest,
insects that creep in the grasses and burrow
*   in the ground,*
hear this mother!
A new life has come among you.
Make its path smooth that it may reach
the brow of the fourth hill.

All the heavens, air and earth,
hear this mother!
A new life has come among you.
Make its path smooth—then shall it travel
*   beyond the four hills!*

(From Suzanne Slesin and
Emily Gwathmey, compilers, Amen, n.p.)

Like the Israelites, with their purification ritual described in Leviticus, chapter 12, most cultures have rituals and prayers associated with childbirth. In this mother's prayer of the Omaha tribe, the four hills refer to the four parts of human life—childhood, youth, adulthood, and old age. What a wonderful reminder that life is a journey and that all creation is invited to celebrate new life.

▶ **Lev 12.1–8**

shall be circumcised. ⁴Her time of blood purification shall be thirty-three days; she shall not touch any holy thing, or come into the sanctuary, until the days of her purification are completed. ⁵If she bears a female child, she shall be unclean two weeks, as in her menstruation; her

her flow of blood. This is the law for her who bears a child, male or female. ⁸If she cannot afford a sheep, she shall take two turtledoves or two pigeons, one for a burnt offering and the other for a sin offering; and the priest shall make atonement on her behalf, and she shall be clean.

Leprosy, Varieties and Symptoms

The LORD spoke to Moses and Aaron, saying:
2 When a person has on the skin of his body a swelling or an eruption or a spot, and it turns into a leprous[i] disease on the skin of his body, he shall be brought to Aaron the priest or to one of his sons the priests. 3 The priest shall examine the disease on the skin of his body, and if the hair in the diseased area has turned white and the disease appears to be deeper than the skin of his body, it is a leprous[i] disease; after the priest has examined him he shall pronounce him ceremonially unclean. 4 But if the spot is white in the skin of his body, and appears no deeper than the skin, and the hair in it has not turned white, the priest shall confine the diseased person for seven days. 5 The priest shall examine him on the seventh day, and if he sees that the disease is checked and the disease has not spread in the skin, then the priest shall confine him seven days more. 6 The priest shall examine him again on the seventh day, and if the disease has abated and the disease has not spread in the skin, the priest shall pronounce him clean; it is only an eruption; and he shall wash his clothes, and be clean. 7 But if the eruption spreads in the skin after he has shown himself to the priest for his cleansing, he shall appear again before the priest. 8 The priest shall make an examination, and if the eruption has spread in the skin, the priest shall pronounce him unclean; it is a leprous[i] disease.

9 When a person contracts a leprous[i] disease, he shall be brought to the priest. 10 The priest shall make an examination, and if there is a white swelling in the skin that has turned the hair white, and there is quick raw flesh in the swelling, 11 it is a chronic leprous[i] disease in the skin of his body. The priest shall pronounce him unclean; he shall not confine him, for he is unclean. 12 But if the disease breaks out in the skin, so that it covers all the skin of the diseased person from head to foot, so far as the priest can see, 13 then the priest shall make an examination, and if the disease has covered all his body, he shall pronounce him clean of the disease; since it has all turned white, he is clean. 14 But if raw flesh ever appears on him, he shall be unclean; 15 the priest shall examine the raw flesh and pronounce him unclean. Raw flesh is unclean, for it is a leprous[i] disease. 16 But if the raw flesh again turns white, he shall come to the priest; 17 the priest shall examine him, and if the disease has turned white, the priest shall pronounce the diseased person clean. He is clean.

18 When there is on the skin of one's body a boil that has healed, 19 and in the place of the boil there appears a white swelling or a reddish-white spot, it shall be shown to the priest. 20 The priest shall make an examination, and if it appears deeper than the skin and its hair has turned white, the priest shall pronounce him unclean; this is a leprous[i] disease, broken out in the boil. 21 But if the priest examines it and the hair on it is not white, nor is it deeper than the skin but has abated, the priest shall confine him seven days. 22 If it spreads in the skin, the priest shall pronounce him unclean; it is diseased. 23 But if the spot remains in one place and does not spread, it is the scar of the boil; the priest shall pronounce him clean.

24 Or, when the body has a burn on the skin and the raw flesh of the burn becomes a spot, reddish-white or white, 25 the priest shall examine it. If the hair in the spot has turned white and it appears deeper than the skin, it is a leprous[i] disease; it has broken out in the burn, and the priest shall pronounce him unclean. This is a leprous[i] disease. 26 But if the priest examines it and the hair in the spot is not white, and it is no deeper than the skin but has abated, the priest shall confine him seven days. 27 The priest shall examine him the seventh day; if it is spreading in the skin, the priest shall pronounce him unclean. This is a leprous[i] disease. 28 But if the spot remains in one place and does not spread in the skin but has abated, it is a swelling from the burn, and the priest shall pronounce him clean; for it is the scar of the burn.

29 When a man or woman has a disease on the head or in the beard, 30 the priest shall examine the disease. If it appears deeper than the skin and the hair in it is yellow and thin, the priest shall pronounce him unclean; it is an itch, a leprous[i] disease of the head or the beard. 31 If the priest examines the itching disease, and it appears no deeper than the skin and there is no black hair in it, the priest shall confine the person with the itching disease for seven days. 32 On the seventh day the priest shall examine the itch; if the itch has not spread, and there is no yellow hair in it, and the itch appears to be no deeper than the skin, 33 he shall shave, but the itch he shall not shave. The priest shall confine the person with the itch for seven days more. 34 On the seventh day the priest shall examine the itch; if the itch has not spread in the skin and it appears to be no deeper than the skin, the priest shall pronounce him clean. He shall wash his clothes and be clean. 35 But if the itch spreads in the skin after he was

i A term for several skin diseases; precise meaning uncertain

pronounced clean, 36 the priest shall examine him. If the itch has spread in the skin, the priest need not seek for the yellow hair; he is unclean. 37 But if in his eyes the itch is checked, and black hair has grown in it, the itch is healed, he is clean; and the priest shall pronounce him clean.

38 When a man or a woman has spots on the skin of the body, white spots, 39 the priest shall make an examination, and if the spots on the skin of the body are of a dull white, it is a rash that has broken out on the skin; he is clean.

40 If anyone loses the hair from his head, he is bald but he is clean. 41 If he loses the hair from his forehead and temples, he has baldness of the forehead but he is clean. 42 But if there is on the bald head or the bald forehead a reddish-white diseased spot, it is a leprousʲ disease breaking out on his bald head or his bald forehead. 43 The priest shall examine him; if the diseased swelling is reddish-white on his bald head or on his bald forehead, which resembles a leprousʲ disease in the skin of the body, 44 he is leprous,ʲ he is unclean. The priest shall pronounce him unclean; the disease is on his head.

45 The person who has the leprousʲ disease shall wear torn clothes and let the hair of his head be disheveled; and he shall cover his upper lip and cry out, "Unclean, unclean." 46 He shall remain unclean as long as he has the disease; he is unclean. He shall live alone; his dwelling shall be outside the camp.

47 Concerning clothing: when a leprousʲ disease appears in it, in woolen or linen cloth, 48 in warp or woof of linen or wool, or in a skin or in anything made of skin, 49 if the disease shows greenish or reddish in the garment, whether in warp or woof or in skin or in anything made of skin, it is a leprousʲ disease and shall be shown to the priest. 50 The priest shall examine the disease, and put the diseased article aside for seven days. 51 He shall examine the disease on the seventh day. If the disease has spread in the cloth, in warp or woof, or in the skin, whatever be the use of the skin, this is a spreading leprousʲ disease; it is unclean. 52 He shall burn the clothing, whether diseased in warp or woof, woolen or linen, or anything of skin, for it is a spreading leprousʲ disease; it shall be burned in fire.

53 If the priest makes an examination, and the disease has not spread in the clothing, in warp or woof or in anything of skin, 54 the priest shall command them to wash the article in which the disease appears, and he shall put it aside seven days more. 55 The priest shall examine the diseased article after it has been washed. If the diseased spot has not changed color, though the disease has

not spread, it is unclean; you shall burn it in fire, whether the leprousʲ spot is on the inside or on the outside.

56 If the priest makes an examination, and the disease has abated after it is washed, he shall tear the spot out of the cloth, in warp or woof, or out of skin. 57 If it appears again in the garment, in warp or woof, or in anything of skin, it is spreading; you shall burn with fire that in which the disease appears. 58 But the cloth, warp or woof, or anything of skin from which the disease disappears when you have washed it, shall then be washed a second time, and it shall be clean.

59 This is the ritual for a leprousʲ disease in a cloth of wool or linen, either in warp or woof, or in anything of skin, to decide whether it is clean or unclean.

Purification of Lepers and Leprous Houses
(Cp Mt 8.1–4; Lk 5.12–14)

The LORD spoke to Moses, saying: 2 This shall be the ritual for the leprousʲ person at the time of his cleansing:

He shall be brought to the priest; 3 the priest shall go out of the camp, and the priest shall make an examination. If the disease is healed in the leprousʲ person, 4 the priest shall command that two living clean birds and cedarwood and crimson yarn and hyssop be brought for the one who is to be cleansed. 5 The priest shall command that one of the birds be slaughtered over fresh water in an earthen vessel. 6 He shall take the living bird with the cedarwood and the crimson yarn and the hyssop, and dip them and the living bird in the blood of the bird that was slaughtered over the fresh water. 7 He shall sprinkle it seven times upon the one who is to be cleansed of the leprousʲ disease; then he shall pronounce him clean, and he shall let the living bird go into the open field. 8 The one who is to be cleansed shall wash his clothes, and shave off all his hair, and bathe himself in water, and he shall be clean. After that he shall come into the camp, but shall live outside his tent seven days. 9 On the seventh day he shall shave all his hair: of head, beard, eyebrows; he shall shave all his hair. Then he shall wash his clothes, and bathe his body in water, and he shall be clean.

10 On the eighth day he shall take two male lambs without blemish, and one ewe lamb in its first year without blemish, and a grain offering of three-tenths of an ephah of choice flour mixed with oil, and one logᵏ of oil. 11 The priest who cleanses shall set the person to be cleansed, along

ʲ A term for several skin diseases; precise meaning uncertain   ᵏ A liquid measure

with these things, before the Lord, at the entrance of the tent of meeting. 12 The priest shall take one of the lambs, and offer it as a guilt offering, along with the log[l] of oil, and raise them as an elevation offering before the Lord. 13 He shall slaughter the lamb in the place where the sin offering and the burnt offering are slaughtered in the holy place; for the guilt offering, like the sin offering, belongs to the priest: it is most holy. 14 The priest shall take some of the blood of the guilt offering and put it on the lobe of the right ear of the one to be cleansed, and on the thumb of the right hand, and on the big toe of the right foot. 15 The priest shall take some of the log[l] of oil and pour it into the palm of his own left hand, 16 and dip his right finger in the oil that is in his left hand and sprinkle some oil with his finger seven times before the Lord. 17 Some of the oil that remains in his hand the priest shall put on the lobe of the right ear of the one to be cleansed, and on the thumb of the right hand, and on the big toe of the right foot, on top of the blood of the guilt offering. 18 The rest of the oil that is in the priest's hand he shall put on the head of the one to be cleansed. Then the priest shall make atonement on his behalf before the Lord: 19 the priest shall offer the sin offering, to make atonement for the one to be cleansed from his uncleanness. Afterward he shall slaughter the burnt offering; 20 and the priest shall offer the burnt offering and the grain offering on the altar. Thus the priest shall make atonement on his behalf and he shall be clean.

21 But if he is poor and cannot afford so much, he shall take one male lamb for a guilt offering to be elevated, to make atonement on his behalf, and one-tenth of an ephah of choice flour mixed with oil for a grain offering and a log[l] of oil; 22 also two turtledoves or two pigeons, such as he can afford, one for a sin offering and the other for a burnt offering. 23 On the eighth day he shall bring them for his cleansing to the priest, to the entrance of the tent of meeting, before the Lord; 24 and the priest shall take the lamb of the guilt offering and the log[l] of oil, and the priest shall raise them as an elevation offering before the Lord. 25 The priest shall slaughter the lamb of the guilt offering and shall take some of the blood of the guilt offering, and put it on the lobe of the right ear of the one to be cleansed, and on the thumb of the right hand, and on the big toe of the right foot. 26 The priest shall pour some of the oil into the palm of his own left hand, 27 and shall sprinkle with his right finger some of the oil that is in his left hand seven times before the Lord. 28 The priest shall put some of the oil that is in his hand on the lobe of the right ear of the one to be cleansed, and

on the thumb of the right hand, and the big toe of the right foot, where the blood of the guilt offering was placed. 29 The rest of the oil that is in the priest's hand he shall put on the head of the one to be cleansed, to make atonement on his behalf before the Lord. 30 And he shall offer, of the turtledoves or pigeons such as he can afford, 31 one[m] for a sin offering and the other for a burnt offering, along with a grain offering; and the priest shall make atonement before the Lord on behalf of the one being cleansed. 32 This is the ritual for the one who has a leprous[n] disease, who cannot afford the offerings for his cleansing.

33 The Lord spoke to Moses and Aaron, saying: 34 When you come into the land of Cā′naan, which I give you for a possession, and I put a leprous[n] disease in a house in the land of your possession, 35 the owner of the house shall come and tell the priest, saying, "There seems to me to be some sort of disease in my house." 36 The priest shall command that they empty the house before the priest goes to examine the disease, or all that is in the house will become unclean; and afterward the priest shall go in to inspect the house. 37 He shall examine the disease; if the disease is in the walls of the house with greenish or reddish spots, and if it appears to be deeper than the surface, 38 the priest shall go outside to the door of the house and shut up the house seven days. 39 The priest shall come again on the seventh day and make an inspection; if the disease has spread in the walls of the house, 40 the priest shall command that the stones in which the disease appears be taken out and thrown into an unclean place outside the city. 41 He shall have the inside of the house scraped thoroughly, and the plaster that is scraped off shall be dumped in an unclean place outside the city. 42 They shall take other stones and put them in the place of those stones, and take other plaster and plaster the house.

43 If the disease breaks out again in the house, after he has taken out the stones and scraped the house and plastered it, 44 the priest shall go and make inspection; if the disease has spread in the house, it is a spreading leprous[n] disease in the house; it is unclean. 45 He shall have the house torn down, its stones and timber and all the plaster of the house, and taken outside the city to an unclean place. 46 All who enter the house while it is shut up shall be unclean until the evening; 47 and all who sleep in the house shall wash their

---

[l] A liquid measure   [m] Gk Syr: Heb afford, 31 such as he can afford, one   [n] A term for several skin diseases; precise meaning uncertain

clothes; and all who eat in the house shall wash their clothes.

48 If the priest comes and makes an inspection, and the disease has not spread in the house after the house was plastered, the priest shall pronounce the house clean; the disease is healed. ⁴⁹For the cleansing of the house he shall take two birds, with cedarwood and crimson yarn and hyssop, ⁵⁰and shall slaughter one of the birds over fresh water in an earthen vessel, ⁵¹and shall take the cedarwood and the hyssop and the crimson yarn, along with the living bird, and dip them in the blood of the slaughtered bird and the fresh water, and sprinkle the house seven times. ⁵²Thus he shall cleanse the house with the blood of the bird, and with the fresh water, and with the living bird, and with the cedarwood and hyssop and crimson yarn; ⁵³and he shall let the living bird go out of the city into the open field; so he shall make atonement for the house, and it shall be clean.

54 This is the ritual for any leprousᵒ disease: for an itch, ⁵⁵for leprousᵒ diseases in clothing and houses, ⁵⁶and for a swelling or an eruption or a spot, ⁵⁷to determine when it is unclean and when it is clean. This is the ritual for leprousᵒ diseases.

Concerning Bodily Discharges

The LORD spoke to Moses and Aaron, saying: ²Speak to the people of Israel and say to them:

When any man has a discharge from his member,ᵖ his discharge makes him ceremonially unclean. ³The uncleanness of his discharge is this: whether his memberᵖ flows with his discharge, or his memberᵖ is stopped from discharging, it is uncleanness for him. ⁴Every bed on which the one with the discharge lies shall be unclean; and everything on which he sits shall be unclean. ⁵Anyone who touches his bed shall wash his clothes, and bathe in water, and be unclean until the evening. ⁶All who sit on anything on which the one with the discharge has sat shall wash their clothes, and bathe in water, and be unclean until the evening. ⁷All who touch the body of the one with the discharge shall wash their clothes, and bathe in water, and be unclean until the evening. ⁸If the one with the discharge spits on persons who are clean, then they shall wash their clothes, and bathe in water, and be unclean until the evening. ⁹Any saddle on which the one with the discharge rides shall be unclean. ¹⁰All who touch anything that was under him shall be unclean until the evening, and all who carry such a thing shall wash their clothes, and bathe in water, and be unclean until the evening. ¹¹All those whom the one with the discharge touches without his having rinsed his hands in wa-

ter shall wash their clothes, and bathe in water, and be unclean until the evening. ¹²Any earthen vessel that the one with the discharge touches shall be broken; and every vessel of wood shall be rinsed in water.

13 When the one with a discharge is cleansed of his discharge, he shall count seven days for his cleansing; he shall wash his clothes and bathe his body in fresh water, and he shall be clean. ¹⁴On the eighth day he shall take two turtledoves or two pigeons and come before the LORD to the entrance of the tent of meeting and give them to the priest. ¹⁵The priest shall offer them, one for a sin offering and the other for a burnt offering; and the priest shall make atonement on his behalf before the LORD for his discharge.

16 If a man has an emission of semen, he shall bathe his whole body in water, and be unclean until the evening. ¹⁷Everything made of cloth or of skin on which the semen falls shall be washed with water, and be unclean until the evening. ¹⁸If a man lies with a woman and has an emission of semen, both of them shall bathe in water, and be unclean until the evening.

19 When a woman has a discharge of blood that is her regular discharge from her body, she shall be in her impurity for seven days, and whoever touches her shall be unclean until the evening. ²⁰Everything upon which she lies during her impurity shall be unclean; everything also upon which she sits shall be unclean. ²¹Whoever touches her bed shall wash his clothes, and bathe in water, and be unclean until the evening. ²²Whoever touches anything upon which she sits shall wash his clothes, and bathe in water, and be unclean until the evening; ²³whether it is the bed or anything upon which she sits, when he touches it he shall be unclean until the evening. ²⁴If any man lies with her, and her impurity falls on him, he shall be unclean seven days; and every bed on which he lies shall be unclean.

25 If a woman has a discharge of blood for many days, not at the time of her impurity, or if she has a discharge beyond the time of her impurity, all the days of the discharge she shall continue in uncleanness; as in the days of her impurity, she shall be unclean. ²⁶Every bed on which she lies during all the days of her discharge shall be treated as the bed of her impurity; and everything on which she sits shall be unclean, as in the uncleanness of her impurity. ²⁷Whoever touches these things shall be unclean, and shall wash his clothes, and bathe in water, and be un-

---

ᵒ A term for several skin diseases; precise meaning uncertain   ᵖ Heb *flesh*

clean until the evening. 28 If she is cleansed of her discharge, she shall count seven days, and after that she shall be clean. 29 On the eighth day she shall take two turtledoves or two pigeons and bring them to the priest at the entrance of the tent of meeting. 30 The priest shall offer one for a sin offering and the other for a burnt offering; and the priest shall make atonement on her behalf before the LORD for her unclean discharge.

31 Thus you shall keep the people of Israel separate from their uncleanness, so that they do not die in their uncleanness by defiling my tabernacle that is in their midst.

32 This is the ritual for those who have a discharge: for him who has an emission of semen, becoming unclean thereby, 33 for her who is in the infirmity of her period, for anyone, male or female, who has a discharge, and for the man who lies with a woman who is unclean.

The Day of Atonement

16 The LORD spoke to Moses after the death of the two sons of Aaron, when they drew near before the LORD and died. 2 The LORD said to Moses:

Tell your brother Aaron not to come just at any time into the sanctuary inside the curtain before the mercy seat*q* that is upon the ark, or he will die; for I appear in the cloud upon the mercy seat.*q* 3 Thus shall Aaron come into the holy place: with a young bull for a sin offering and a ram for a burnt offering. 4 He shall put on the holy linen tunic, and shall have the linen undergarments next to his body, fasten the linen sash, and wear the linen turban; these are the holy vestments. He shall bathe his body in water, and then put them on. 5 He shall take from the congregation of the people of Israel two male goats for a sin offering, and one ram for a burnt offering.

6 Aaron shall offer the bull as a sin offering for himself, and shall make atonement for himself and for his house. 7 He shall take the two goats and set them before the LORD at the entrance of the tent of meeting; 8 and Aaron shall cast lots on the two goats, one lot for the LORD and the other lot for Az′a•zel.*r* 9 Aaron shall present the goat on which the lot fell for the LORD, and offer it as a sin offering; 10 but the goat on which the lot fell for Az′a•zel*r* shall be presented alive before the LORD to make atonement over it, that it may be sent away into the wilderness to Az′a•zel.*r*

11 Aaron shall present the bull as a sin offering for himself, and shall make atonement for himself and for his house; he shall slaughter the bull as a sin offering for himself. 12 He shall take a censer full of coals of fire from the altar before the LORD, and two handfuls of crushed sweet incense, and he shall bring it inside the curtain 13 and put the incense on the fire before the LORD, that the cloud of the incense may cover the mercy seat*q* that is upon the covenant,*s* or he will die. 14 He shall take some of the blood of the bull, and sprinkle it with his finger on the front of the mercy seat,*q* and before the mercy seat*q* he shall sprinkle the blood with his finger seven times.

15 He shall slaughter the goat of the sin offering that is for the people and bring its blood inside the curtain, and do with its blood as he did with the blood of the bull, sprinkling it upon the mercy seat*q* and before the mercy seat.*q* 16 Thus he shall make atonement for the sanctuary, because of the uncleannesses of the people of Israel, and because of their transgressions, all their sins; and so he shall do for the tent of meeting, which

q Or *the cover*　　*r* Traditionally rendered *a scapegoat*
s Or *treaty*, or *testament*; Heb *eduth*

The Scapegoat

What an interesting tradition! In the Israelite ritual described in Lev 16.20–21, the leader symbolically transfers all the people's sins onto a goat and drives it away. It is a liberating act that allows a fresh start.

But today, the idea of a scapegoat conveys oppression rather than freedom. A person becomes the scapegoat when other people blame him or her for their problems. Here is an example:

Suppose you are on a soccer team that expects this week's game to be easy, so no one works hard at practice. On game day, the score is tied near the end of the game. Your team is already thinking about going home when the other team scores a goal and wins the game. Everyone gets mad at the goalie for not preventing the goal. The goalie is the scapegoat, but everyone should share in the fault for the loss because they did not practice well or play their best.

- **Have you ever been the scapegoat for someone else's problems? If so, how did that feel? What did you do?**
- **Have you ever scapegoated someone else when you were partly to blame for some situation? What happened? How will you prevent scapegoating in the future?**

▶ Lev 16.20–21

---

remains with them in the midst of their uncleannesses. ¹⁷No one shall be in the tent of meeting from the time he enters to make atonement in the sanctuary until he comes out and has made atonement for himself and for his house and for all the assembly of Israel. ¹⁸Then he shall go out to the altar that is before the LORD and make atonement on its behalf, and shall take some of the blood of the bull and of the blood of the goat, and put it on each of the horns of the altar. ¹⁹He shall sprinkle some of the blood on it with his finger seven times, and cleanse it and hallow it from the uncleannesses of the people of Israel.

20 When he has finished atoning for the holy place and the tent of meeting and the altar, he shall present the live goat. ²¹Then Aaron shall lay both his hands on the head of the live goat, and confess over it all the iniquities of the people of Israel, and all their transgressions, all their sins, putting them on the head of the goat, and sending it away into the wilderness by means of someone designated for the task.ᵗ ²²The goat shall bear on itself all their iniquities to a barren region; and the goat shall be set free in the wilderness.

23 Then Aaron shall enter the tent of meeting, and shall take off the linen vestments that he put on when he went into the holy place, and shall leave them there. ²⁴He shall bathe his body in water in a holy place, and put on his vestments; then he shall come out and offer his burnt offering and the burnt offering of the people, making atonement for himself and for the people. ²⁵The fat of

the sin offering he shall turn into smoke on the altar. ²⁶The one who sets the goat free for Az'a·zelᵘ shall wash his clothes and bathe his body in water, and afterward may come into the camp. ²⁷The bull of the sin offering and the goat of the sin offering, whose blood was brought in to make atonement in the holy place, shall be taken outside the camp; their skin and their flesh and their dung shall be consumed in fire. ²⁸The one who burns them shall wash his clothes and bathe his body in water, and afterward may come into the camp.

29 This shall be a statute to you forever: In the seventh month, on the tenth day of the month, you shall deny yourselves,ᵛ and shall do no work, neither the citizen nor the alien who resides among you. ³⁰For on this day atonement shall be made for you, to cleanse you; from all your sins you shall be clean before the LORD. ³¹It is a sabbath of complete rest to you, and you shall deny yourselves;ᵛ it is a statute forever. ³²The priest who is anointed and consecrated as priest in his father's place shall make atonement, wearing the linen vestments, the holy vestments. ³³He shall make atonement for the sanctuary, and he shall make atonement for the tent of meeting and for the altar, and he shall make atonement for the priests and for all the people of the assembly. ³⁴This shall be an everlasting statute for you, to make atonement for the people of Israel once in the year for

---

ᵗ Meaning of Heb uncertain   ᵘ Traditionally rendered *a scapegoat*   ᵛ Or *shall fast*

all their sins. And Moses did as the LORD had commanded him.

The Slaughtering of Animals

The LORD spoke to Moses:

2 Speak to Aaron and his sons and to all the people of Israel and say to them: This is what the LORD has commanded. 3 If anyone of the house of Israel slaughters an ox or a lamb or a goat in the camp, or slaughters it outside the camp, 4 and does not bring it to the entrance of the tent of meeting, to present it as an offering to the LORD before the tabernacle of the LORD, he shall be held guilty of bloodshed; he has shed blood, and he shall be cut off from the people. 5 This is in order that the people of Israel may bring their sacrifices that they offer in the open field, that they may bring them to the LORD, to the priest at the entrance of the tent of meeting, and offer them as sacrifices of well-being to the LORD. 6 The priest shall dash the blood against the altar of the LORD at the entrance of the tent of meeting, and turn the fat into smoke as a pleasing odor to the LORD, 7 so that they may no longer offer their sacrifices for goat-demons, to whom they prostitute themselves. This shall be a statute forever to them throughout their generations.

8 And say to them further: Anyone of the house of Israel or of the aliens who reside among them who offers a burnt offering or sacrifice, 9 and does not bring it to the entrance of the tent of meeting, to sacrifice it to the LORD, shall be cut off from the people.

Eating Blood Prohibited

10 If anyone of the house of Israel or of the aliens who reside among them eats any blood, I will set my face against that person who eats blood, and will cut that person off from the people. 11 For the life of the flesh is in the blood; and I have given it to you for making atonement for your lives on the altar; for, as life, it is the blood that makes atonement. 12 Therefore I have said to the people of Israel: No person among you shall eat blood, nor shall any alien who resides among you eat blood. 13 And anyone of the people of Israel, or of the aliens who reside among them, who hunts down an animal or bird that may be eaten shall pour out its blood and cover it with earth. 14 For the life of every creature—its blood is its life; therefore I have said to the people of Israel: You shall not eat the blood of any creature, for the life of every creature is its blood; whoever eats it shall be cut off. 15 All persons, citizens or aliens, who eat what dies of itself or what has been torn by wild animals, shall wash their clothes, and bathe themselves in water, and be unclean until the evening; then they shall be clean. 16 But if they do not wash themselves or bathe their body, they shall bear their guilt.

Sexual Relations

The LORD spoke to Moses, saying:

2 Speak to the people of Israel and say to them: I am the LORD your God. 3 You shall not do as they do in the land of Egypt, where you lived, and you shall not do as they do in the land of Cā'naan, to which I am bringing you. You shall not follow their statutes. 4 My ordinances you shall observe and my statutes you shall keep, following them: I am the LORD your God. 5 You shall keep my statutes and my ordinances; by doing so one shall live: I am the LORD.

6 None of you shall approach anyone near of kin to uncover nakedness: I am the LORD. 7 You shall not uncover the nakedness of your father, which is the nakedness of your mother; she is your mother, you shall not uncover her nakedness. 8 You shall not uncover the nakedness of your father's wife; it is the nakedness of your father. 9 You shall not uncover the nakedness of your sister, your father's daughter or your mother's daughter, whether born at home or born abroad. 10 You shall not uncover the nakedness of your son's daughter or of your daughter's daughter, for their nakedness is your own nakedness. 11 You shall not uncover the nakedness of your father's wife's daughter, begotten by your father, since she is your sister. 12 You shall not uncover the nakedness of your father's sister; she is your father's flesh. 13 You shall not uncover the nakedness of your mother's sister, for she is your mother's flesh. 14 You shall not uncover the nakedness of your father's brother, that is, you shall not approach his wife; she is your aunt. 15 You shall not uncover the nakedness of your daughter-in-law: she is your son's wife; you shall not uncover her nakedness. 16 You shall not uncover the nakedness of your brother's wife; it is your brother's nakedness. 17 You shall not uncover the nakedness of a woman and her daughter, and you shall not take[w] her son's daughter or her daughter's daughter to uncover her nakedness; they are your[x] flesh; it is depravity. 18 And you shall not take[w] a woman as a rival to her sister, uncovering her nakedness while her sister is still alive.

19 You shall not approach a woman to uncover her nakedness while she is in her menstrual

---

w Or *marry*　x Gk: Heb lacks *your*

uncleanness. 20 You shall not have sexual relations with your kinsman's wife, and defile yourself with her. 21 You shall not give any of your offspring to sacrifice them*y* to Mō′lech, and so profane the name of your God: I am the LORD. 22 You shall not lie with a male as with a woman; it is an abomination. 23 You shall not have sexual relations with any animal and defile yourself with it, nor shall any woman give herself to an animal to have sexual relations with it: it is perversion.

24 Do not defile yourselves in any of these ways, for by all these practices the nations I am casting out before you have defiled themselves. 25 Thus the land became defiled; and I punished it for its iniquity, and the land vomited out its inhabitants. 26 But you shall keep my statutes and my ordinances and commit none of these abominations, either the citizen or the alien who resides among you 27 (for the inhabitants of the land, who were before you, committed all of these abominations, and the land became defiled); 28 otherwise the land will vomit you out for defiling it, as it

Ritual and Moral Holiness

The LORD spoke to Moses, saying: 2 Speak to all the congregation of the people of Israel and say to them: You shall be holy, for I the LORD your God am holy. 3 You shall each revere your mother and father, and you shall keep my sabbaths: I am the LORD your God. 4 Do not turn to idols or make cast images for yourselves: I am the LORD your God.

5 When you offer a sacrifice of well-being to the LORD, offer it in such a way that it is acceptable in your behalf. 6 It shall be eaten on the same day you offer it, or on the next day; and anything left over until the third day shall be consumed in fire. 7 If it is eaten at all on the third day, it is an abomination; it will not be acceptable. 8 All who eat it shall be subject to punishment, because they have profaned what is holy to the LORD; and any such person shall be cut off from the people.

9 When you reap the harvest of your land, you shall not reap to the very edges of your field, or

LIVE IT!

A Very Special Gift

The laws about sexual relations in Leviticus, chapter 18, are another example of how holiness extended to all aspects of life for the Israelites. The people had experienced the sexual promiscuity of other cultures (see Genesis, chapter 19). To become a great nation, the children of God, they had to abandon unhealthy and unholy sexual practices and follow God's way.

Young people today also receive many confusing cultural messages about when it is okay to have sex. In movies, television, and music, sex happens all the time between unmarried people, with no consequences. But the church, parents, and teachers are saying to wait until marriage. What is a person to believe?

Think about this: Suppose you are receiving a special gift for Christmas. The gift has been wrapped up and then hidden until Christmas Day. How would it feel if you discovered the present and opened it before Christmas? You probably would initially feel some excitement and pleasure in opening the gift. But the special meaning of opening it on the right day would be lost—for both you and the one presenting it to you.

Sex is a wonderful gift from God, meant for that day when you say, "I do," to someone you are committed to for life. You can only appreciate the full beauty of the gift when it is shared in marriage. God wants us to wait, so it will be as special as it is meant to be.

▶ Lev 18.1–30

vomited out the nation that was before you. 29 For whoever commits any of these abominations shall be cut off from their people. 30 So keep my charge not to commit any of these abominations that were done before you, and not to defile yourselves by them: I am the LORD your God.

gather the gleanings of your harvest. 10 You shall not strip your vineyard bare, or gather the fallen grapes of your vineyard; you shall leave them for the poor and the alien: I am the LORD your God.

y Heb *to pass them over*

LEV

11 You shall not steal; you shall not deal falsely; and you shall not lie to one another. ¹²And you shall not swear falsely by my name, profaning the name of your God: I am the LORD.

13 You shall not defraud your neighbor; you shall not steal; and you shall not keep for yourself the wages of a laborer until morning. ¹⁴You shall not revile the deaf or put a stumbling block before the blind; you shall fear your God: I am the LORD.

15 You shall not render an unjust judgment; you shall not be partial to the poor or defer to the great: with justice you shall judge your neighbor. ¹⁶You shall not go around as a slandererᶻ among your people, and you shall not profit by the bloodᵈ of your neighbor: I am the LORD.

17 You shall not hate in your heart anyone of your kin; you shall reprove your neighbor, or you will incur guilt yourself. ¹⁸You shall not take vengeance or bear a grudge against any of your people, but you shall love your neighbor as yourself: I am the LORD.

19 You shall keep my statutes. You shall not let your animals breed with a different kind; you shall not sow your field with two kinds of seed; nor shall you put on a garment made of two different materials.

20 If a man has sexual relations with a woman who is a slave, designated for another man but not ransomed or given her freedom, an inquiry shall be held. They shall not be put to death, since she has not been freed; ²¹but he shall bring a guilt offering for himself to the LORD, at the entrance of the tent of meeting, a ram as guilt offering. ²²And the priest shall make atonement for him with the ram of guilt offering before the LORD for his sin that he committed; and the sin he committed shall be forgiven him.

23 When you come into the land and plant all kinds of trees for food, then you shall regard their fruit as forbidden;ᵇ three years it shall be forbiddenᶜ to you, it must not be eaten. ²⁴In the fourth year all their fruit shall be set apart for rejoicing in the LORD. ²⁵But in the fifth year you may eat of their fruit, that their yield may be increased for you: I am the LORD your God.

26 You shall not eat anything with its blood. You shall not practice augury or witchcraft. ²⁷You shall not round off the hair on your temples or mar the edges of your beard. ²⁸You shall not make any gashes in your flesh for the dead or tattoo any marks upon you: I am the LORD.

29 Do not profane your daughter by making her a prostitute, that the land not become prostituted and full of depravity. ³⁰You shall keep my sabbaths and reverence my sanctuary: I am the LORD.

31 Do not turn to mediums or wizards; do not seek them out, to be defiled by them: I am the LORD your God.

32 You shall rise before the aged, and defer to the old; and you shall fear your God: I am the LORD.

33 When an alien resides with you in your land, you shall not oppress the alien. ³⁴The alien who resides with you shall be to you as the citizen among you; you shall love the alien as yourself, for you were aliens in the land of Egypt: I am the LORD your God.

35 You shall not cheat in measuring length, weight, or quantity. ³⁶You shall have honest balances, honest weights, an honest ephah, and an honest hin: I am the LORD your God, who brought you out of the land of Egypt. ³⁷You shall keep all my statutes and all my ordinances, and observe them: I am the LORD.

Penalties for Violations of Holiness

The LORD spoke to Moses, saying: ²Say further to the people of Israel:

Any of the people of Israel, or of the aliens who reside in Israel, who give any of their offspring to Mŏ′lech shall be put to death; the people of the land shall stone them to death. ³I myself will set my face against them, and will cut them off from the people, because they have given of their offspring to Mŏ′lech, defiling my sanctuary and profaning my holy name. ⁴And if the people of the land should ever close their eyes to them, when they give of their offspring to Mŏ′lech, and do not put them to death, ⁵I myself will set my face against them and against their family, and will cut them off from among their people, them and all who follow them in prostituting themselves to Mŏ′lech.

6 If any turn to mediums and wizards, prostituting themselves to them, I will set my face against them, and will cut them off from the people. ⁷Consecrate yourselves therefore, and be holy; for I am the LORD your God. ⁸Keep my statutes, and observe them; I am the LORD; I sanctify you. ⁹All who curse father or mother shall be put to death; having cursed father or mother, their blood is upon them.

10 If a man commits adultery with the wife ofᵈ his neighbor, both the adulterer and the adulteress shall be put to death. ¹¹The man who lies with his father's wife has uncovered his father's nakedness;

ᶻ Meaning of Heb uncertain   ᵃ Heb *stand against the blood*   ᵇ Heb *as their uncircumcision*
ᶜ Heb *uncircumcision*   ᵈ Heb repeats *if a man commits adultery with the wife of*

Leviticus 20.12   128

both of them shall be put to death; their blood is upon them. ¹²If a man lies with his daughter-in-law, both of them shall be put to death; they have committed perversion, their blood is upon them. ¹³If a man lies with a male as with a woman, both of them have committed an abomination; they shall be put to death; their blood is upon them. ¹⁴If a man takes a wife and her mother also, it is depravity; they shall be burned to death, both he and they, that there may be no depravity among you. ¹⁵If a man has sexual relations with an animal, he shall be put to death; and you shall kill the animal. ¹⁶If a woman approaches any animal and has sexual relations with it, you shall kill the woman and the animal; they shall be put to death, their blood is upon them.

17 If a man takes his sister, a daughter of his father or a daughter of his mother, and sees her nakedness, and she sees his nakedness, it is a disgrace, and they shall be cut off in the sight of their people; he has uncovered his sister's nakedness, he shall be subject to punishment. ¹⁸If a man lies with a woman having her sickness and uncovers her nakedness, he has laid bare her flow and she has laid bare her flow of blood; both of them shall be cut off from their people. ¹⁹You shall not uncover the nakedness of your mother's sister or of your father's sister, for that is to lay bare one's own flesh; they shall be subject to punishment. ²⁰If a man lies with his uncle's wife, he has uncovered his uncle's nakedness; they shall be subject to punishment; they shall die childless. ²¹If a man takes his brother's wife, it is impurity; he has uncovered his brother's nakedness; they shall be childless.

22 You shall keep all my statutes and all my ordinances, and observe them, so that the land to which I bring you to settle in may not vomit you out. ²³You shall not follow the practices of the nation that I am driving out before you. Because they did all these things, I abhorred them. ²⁴But I have said to you: You shall inherit their land, and I will give it to you to possess, a land flowing with milk and honey. I am the LORD your God; I have separated you from the peoples. ²⁵You shall therefore make a distinction between the clean animal and the unclean, and between the unclean bird and the clean; you shall not bring abomination on yourselves by animal or by bird or by anything with which the ground teems, which I have set apart for you to hold unclean. ²⁶You shall be holy to me; for I the LORD am holy, and I have separated you from the other peoples to be mine.

27 A man or a woman who is a medium or a wizard shall be put to death; they shall be stoned to death, their blood is upon them.

You Shall Be Holy

As the Israelites' image of God developed, so did their sense of how they needed to live as God's people. As God's chosen people, they felt called to behave according to God's plan for them by keeping themselves pure as individuals and as a community. The laws in the Book of Leviticus are examples of how they lived out the call to be holy. For them, holiness was not just for the Sabbath or the Temple, but for every day and everything.

Think about the choices you make in the following areas. How do your choices help you to be holy as God is holy?

- what you eat
- what you watch
- what you wear
- what you buy
- what you listen to
- how you relate to other people

▸ Leviticus, chapters 19–20

The Holiness of Priests
(Cp Ezek 44.15–31)

21 The LORD said to Moses: Speak to the priests, the sons of Aaron, and say to them:

No one shall defile himself for a dead person among his relatives, ²except for his nearest kin: his mother, his father, his son, his daughter, his brother; ³likewise, for a virgin sister, close to him because she has had no husband, he may defile himself for her. ⁴But he shall not defile himself as a husband among his people and so profane himself. ⁵They shall not make bald spots upon their heads, or shave off the edges of their beards, or make any gashes in their flesh. ⁶They shall be holy to their God, and not profane the name of their God; for they offer the LORD's offerings by fire, the food of their God; therefore they shall be holy. ⁷They shall not marry a prostitute or a woman who has been defiled; neither shall they marry a woman divorced from her husband. For they are holy to their God, ⁸and you shall treat them as holy, since they offer the food of your God; they shall be holy to you, for I the LORD, I who sanctify you, am holy. ⁹When the daughter of a priest profanes herself through prostitution, she profanes her father; she shall be burned to death.

10 The priest who is exalted above his fellows, on whose head the anointing oil has been poured and who has been consecrated to wear the vestments, shall not dishevel his hair, nor tear his vestments. 11 He shall not go where there is a dead body; he shall not defile himself even for his father or mother. 12 He shall not go outside the sanctuary and thus profane the sanctuary of his God; for the consecration of the anointing oil of his God is upon him: I am the LORD. 13 He shall marry only a woman who is a virgin. 14 A widow, or a divorced woman, or a woman who has been defiled, a prostitute, these he shall not marry. He shall marry a virgin of his own kin, 15 that he may not profane his offspring among his kin; for I am the LORD; I sanctify him.

16 The LORD spoke to Moses, saying: 17 Speak to Aaron and say: No one of your offspring throughout their generations who has a blemish may approach to offer the food of his God. 18 For no one who has a blemish shall draw near, one who is blind or lame, or one who has a mutilated face or a limb too long, 19 or one who has a broken foot or a broken hand, 20 or a hunchback, or a dwarf, or a man with a blemish in his eyes or an itching disease or scabs or crushed testicles. 21 No descendant of Aaron the priest who has a blemish shall come near to offer the LORD's offerings by fire; since he has a blemish, he shall not come near to offer the food of his God. 22 He may eat the food of his God, of the most holy as well as of the holy. 23 But he shall not come near the curtain or approach the altar, because he has a blemish, that he may not profane my sanctuaries; for I am the LORD; I sanctify them. 24 Thus Moses spoke to Aaron and to his sons and to all the people of Israel.

The Use of Holy Offerings

The LORD spoke to Moses, saying: 2 Direct Aaron and his sons to deal carefully with the sacred donations of the people of Israel, which they dedicate to me, so that they may not profane my holy name; I am the LORD. 3 Say to them: If anyone among all your offspring throughout your generations comes near the sacred donations, which the people of Israel dedicate to the LORD, while he is in a state of uncleanness, that person shall be cut off from my presence: I am the LORD. 4 No one of Aaron's offspring who has a leprous*e* disease or suffers a discharge may eat of the sacred donations until he is clean. Whoever touches anything made unclean by a corpse or a man who has had an emission of semen, 5 and whoever touches any swarming thing by which he may be made unclean or any human being by whom he may be made unclean—whatever his uncleanness may be—

6 the person who touches any such shall be unclean until evening and shall not eat of the sacred donations unless he has washed his body in water. 7 When the sun sets he shall be clean; and afterward he may eat of the sacred donations, for they are his food. 8 That which died or was torn by wild animals he shall not eat, becoming unclean by it: I am the LORD. 9 They shall keep my charge, so that they may not incur guilt and die in the sanctuary*f* for having profaned it: I am the LORD; I sanctify them.

10 No lay person shall eat of the sacred donations. No bound or hired servant of the priest shall eat of the sacred donations; 11 but if a priest acquires anyone by purchase, the person may eat of them; and those that are born in his house may eat of his food. 12 If a priest's daughter marries a layman, she shall not eat of the offering of the sacred donations; 13 but if a priest's daughter is widowed or divorced, without offspring, and returns to her father's house, as in her youth, she may eat of her father's food. No lay person shall eat of it. 14 If a man eats of the sacred donation unintentionally, he shall add one-fifth of its value to it, and give the sacred donation to the priest. 15 No one shall profane the sacred donations of the people of Israel, which they offer to the LORD, 16 causing them to bear guilt requiring a guilt offering, by eating their sacred donations: for I am the LORD; I sanctify them.

Acceptable Offerings

17 The LORD spoke to Moses, saying: 18 Speak to Aaron and his sons and all the people of Israel and say to them: When anyone of the house of Israel or of the aliens residing in Israel presents an offering, whether in payment of a vow or as a freewill offering that is offered to the LORD as a burnt offering, 19 to be acceptable in your behalf it shall be a male without blemish, of the cattle or the sheep or the goats. 20 You shall not offer anything that has a blemish, for it will not be acceptable in your behalf.

21 When anyone offers a sacrifice of wellbeing to the LORD, in fulfillment of a vow or as a freewill offering, from the herd or from the flock, to be acceptable it must be perfect; there shall be no blemish in it. 22 Anything blind, or injured, or maimed, or having a discharge or an itch or scabs—these you shall not offer to the LORD or put any of them on the altar as offerings by fire to the LORD. 23 An ox or a lamb that has a limb too long or too short you may present for a freewill offering; but it

---

e A term for several skin diseases; precise meaning uncertain *f* Vg: Heb *incur guilt for it and die in it*

will not be accepted for a vow. 24 Any animal that has its testicles bruised or crushed or torn or cut, you shall not offer to the LORD; such you shall not do within your land, 25 nor shall you accept any such animals from a foreigner to offer as food to your God; since they are mutilated, with a blemish in them, they shall not be accepted in your behalf.

26 The LORD spoke to Moses, saying: 27 When an ox or a sheep or a goat is born, it shall remain seven days with its mother, and from the eighth day on it shall be acceptable as the LORD's offering by fire. 28 But you shall not slaughter, from the herd or the flock, an animal with its young on the same day. 29 When you sacrifice a thanksgiving offering to the LORD, you shall sacrifice it so that it may be acceptable in your behalf. 30 It shall be eaten on the same day; you shall not leave any of it until morning: I am the LORD.

31 Thus you shall keep my commandments and observe them: I am the LORD. 32 You shall not profane my holy name, that I may be sanctified among the people of Israel: I am the LORD; I sanctify you, 33 I who brought you out of the land of Egypt to be your God: I am the LORD.

Appointed Festivals

The LORD spoke to Moses, saying: 2 Speak to the people of Israel and say to them: These are the appointed festivals of the LORD that you shall proclaim as holy convocations, my appointed festivals.

The Sabbath, Passover, and Unleavened Bread
(Num 28.16–25)

3 Six days shall work be done; but the seventh day is a sabbath of complete rest, a holy convocation; you shall do no work: it is a sabbath to the LORD throughout your settlements.

4 These are the appointed festivals of the LORD, the holy convocations, which you shall celebrate at the time appointed for them. 5 In the first month, on the fourteenth day of the month, at twilight, g there shall be a passover offering to the LORD, 6 and on the fifteenth day of the same month is the festival of unleavened bread to the LORD; seven days you shall eat unleavened bread. 7 On the first day you shall have a holy convocation; you shall not work at your occupations. 8 For seven days you shall present the LORD's offerings by fire; on the seventh day there shall be a holy convocation: you shall not work at your occupations.

The Offering of First Fruits

9 The LORD spoke to Moses, saying: 10 Speak to the people of Israel and say to them: When you enter the land that I am giving you and you reap its harvest, you shall bring the sheaf of the first fruits of your harvest to the priest. 11 He shall raise the sheaf before the LORD, that you may find acceptance; on the day after the sabbath the priest shall raise it. 12 On the day when you raise the sheaf, you shall offer a lamb a year old, without blemish, as a burnt offering to the LORD. 13 And the grain offering with it shall be two-tenths of an ephah of choice flour mixed with oil, an offering by fire of pleasing odor to the LORD; and the drink offering with it shall be of wine, one-fourth of a hin. 14 You shall eat no bread or parched grain or fresh ears until that very day, until you have brought the offering of your God: it is a statute forever throughout your generations in all your settlements.

The Festival of Weeks
(Ex 34.22; Num 28.26–31; Deut 16.9–10)

15 And from the day after the sabbath, from the day on which you bring the sheaf of the elevation offering, you shall count off seven weeks; they shall be complete. 16 You shall count until the day after the seventh sabbath, fifty days; then you shall present an offering of new grain to the LORD. 17 You shall bring from your settlements two loaves of bread as an elevation offering, each made of two-tenths of an ephah; they shall be of choice flour, baked with leaven, as first fruits to the LORD. 18 You shall present with the bread seven lambs a year old without blemish, one young bull, and two rams; they shall be a burnt offering to the LORD, along with their grain offering and their drink offerings, an offering by fire of pleasing odor to the LORD. 19 You shall also offer one male goat for a sin offering, and two male lambs a year old as a sacrifice of well-being. 20 The priest shall raise them with the bread of the first fruits as an elevation offering before the LORD, together with the two lambs; they shall be holy to the LORD for the priest. 21 On that same day you shall make proclamation; you shall hold a holy convocation; you shall not work at your occupations. This is a statute forever in all your settlements throughout your generations.

22 When you reap the harvest of your land, you shall not reap to the very edges of your field, or gather the gleanings of your harvest; you shall leave them for the poor and for the alien: I am the LORD your God.

The Festival of Trumpets
(Num 29.1–6)

23 The LORD spoke to Moses, saying: 24 Speak to the people of Israel, saying: In the seventh

---

g Heb *between the two evenings*

month, on the first day of the month, you shall observe a day of complete rest, a holy convocation commemorated with trumpet blasts. 25 You shall not work at your occupations; and you shall present the LORD's offering by fire.

The Day of Atonement
(Num 29.7–11)

26 The LORD spoke to Moses, saying: 27 Now, the tenth day of this seventh month is the day of atonement; it shall be a holy convocation for you: you shall deny yourselves[h] and present the LORD's offering by fire; 28 and you shall do no work during that entire day; for it is a day of atonement, to make atonement on your behalf before the LORD your God. 29 For anyone who does not practice self-denial[i] during that entire day shall be cut off from the people. 30 And anyone who does any work during that entire day, such a one I will destroy from the midst of the people. 31 You shall do no work: it is a statute forever throughout your generations in all your settlements. 32 It shall be to you a sabbath of complete rest, and you shall deny yourselves;[h] on the ninth day of the month at evening, from evening to evening you shall keep your sabbath.

The Festival of Booths
(Num 29.12–40; Deut 16.13–17)

33 The LORD spoke to Moses, saying: 34 Speak to the people of Israel, saying: On the fifteenth day of this seventh month, and lasting seven days, there shall be the festival of booths[j] to the LORD. 35 The first day shall be a holy convocation; you shall not work at your occupations. 36 Seven days you shall present the LORD's offerings by fire; on the eighth day you shall observe a holy convocation and present the LORD's offerings by fire; it is a solemn assembly; you shall not work at your occupations.

37 These are the appointed festivals of the LORD, which you shall celebrate as times of holy convocation, for presenting to the LORD offerings by fire—burnt offerings and grain offerings, sacrifices and drink offerings, each on its proper day—38 apart from the sabbaths of the LORD, and apart from your gifts, and apart from all your votive offerings, and apart from all your freewill offerings, which you give to the LORD.

39 Now, the fifteenth day of the seventh month, when you have gathered in the produce of the land, you shall keep the festival of the LORD, lasting seven days; a complete rest on the first day, and a complete rest on the eighth day. 40 On the first day you shall take the fruit of majestic[k] trees, branches of palm trees, boughs of leafy trees, and

Asian American

Korean Festival Customs

In preparation for the Lunar New Year (in January or February) and for the Moon Festival (a feast of thanksgiving in August), Korean families follow some traditional customs. These customs are similar to those of the Israelite festivals described in Leviticus, chapter 23.

In Korea, the day before each feast is used for purification. People take ceremonial baths symbolizing the total cleansing of their body, their spirit, and their attitudes. The baths wash away meanness, carelessness, and other faults. The people also wear new clothes and often get a new haircut.

Before sunrise on the day of the feast, the people bow before a table holding name cards of their ancestors. They use incense, pour out wine, and pray to their ancestors, asking for their intercession and help. Family members pray silently for all their individual and family needs. During the day, families visit the homes of their extended family. During these visits, prayer ritual is often repeated.

After a day of visiting, families return home for a feast of the best food and drink possible. The sharing of food is the most significant part of the meal. Neighbors exchange portions of food with one another and bring food to poor families. Families set food on a small table near the door as an offering of thanks to the Creator and sprinkle rice on the ground around their house in gratitude for the crops.

▶ Lev 23.9–44

willows of the brook; and you shall rejoice before the LORD your God for seven days. 41 You shall keep it as a festival to the LORD seven days in the year; you shall keep it in the seventh month as a

---

h Or *shall fast*   i Or *does not fast*   j Or *tabernacles*: Heb *succoth*   k Meaning of Heb uncertain

statute forever throughout your generations. [42]You shall live in booths for seven days; all that are citizens in Israel shall live in booths, [43]so that your generations may know that I made the people of Israel live in booths when I brought them out of the land of Egypt: I am the LORD your God.

44 Thus Moses declared to the people of Israel the appointed festivals of the LORD.

The Lamp
(Ex 27.20–21)

The LORD spoke to Moses, saying: [2]Command the people of Israel to bring you pure oil of beaten olives for the lamp, that a light may be kept burning regularly. [3]Aaron shall set it up in the tent of meeting, outside the curtain of the covenant,[l] to burn from evening to morning before the LORD regularly; it shall be a statute forever throughout your generations. [4]He shall set up the lamps on the lampstand of pure gold[m] before the LORD regularly.

The Bread for the Tabernacle

5 You shall take choice flour, and bake twelve loaves of it; two-tenths of an ephah shall be in each loaf. [6]You shall place them in two rows, six in a row, on the table of pure gold.[n] [7]You shall put pure frankincense with each row, to be a token offering for the bread, as an offering by fire to the LORD. [8]Every sabbath day Aaron shall set them in order before the LORD regularly as a commitment of the people of Israel, as a covenant forever. [9]They shall be for Aaron and his descendants, who shall eat them in a holy place, for they are most holy portions for him from the offerings by fire to the LORD, a perpetual due.

Blasphemy and Its Punishment

10 A man whose mother was an Israelite and whose father was an Egyptian came out among the people of Israel; and the Israelite woman's son and a certain Israelite began fighting in the camp. [11]The Israelite woman's son blasphemed the Name in a curse. And they brought him to Moses— now his mother's name was She•lō'mith, daughter of Dib'ri, of the tribe of Dan— [12]and they put him in custody, until the decision of the LORD should be made clear to them.

13 The LORD said to Moses, saying: [14]Take the blasphemer outside the camp; and let all who were within hearing lay their hands on his head, and let the whole congregation stone him. [15]And speak to the people of Israel, saying: Anyone who curses God shall bear the sin. [16]One who blasphemes the name of the LORD shall be put to death; the whole congregation shall stone the blasphemer. Aliens as well as citizens, when they blas-

pheme the Name, shall be put to death. [17]Anyone who kills a human being shall be put to death. [18]Anyone who kills an animal shall make restitution for it, life for life. [19]Anyone who maims another shall suffer the same injury in return: [20]fracture for fracture, eye for eye, tooth for tooth; the injury inflicted is the injury to be suffered. [21]One who kills an animal shall make restitution for it; but one who kills a human being shall be put to death. [22]You shall have one law for the alien and for the citizen: for I am the LORD your God. [23]Moses spoke thus to the people of Israel; and they took the blasphemer outside the camp, and stoned him to death. The people of Israel did as the LORD had commanded Moses.

The Sabbatical Year
(Deut 15.1–11)

The LORD spoke to Moses on Mount Sinai, saying: [2]Speak to the people of Israel and say to them: When you enter the land that I am giving you, the land shall observe a sabbath for the LORD. [3]Six years you shall sow your field, and six years you shall prune your vineyard, and gather in their yield; [4]but in the seventh year there shall be a sabbath of complete rest for the land, a sabbath for the LORD: you shall not sow your field or prune your vineyard. [5]You shall not reap the aftergrowth of your harvest or gather the grapes of your unpruned vine: it shall be a year of complete rest for the land. [6]You may eat what the land yields during its sabbath—you, your male and female slaves, your hired and your bound laborers who live with you; [7]for your livestock also, and for the wild animals in your land all its yield shall be for food.

The Year of Jubilee

8 You shall count off seven weeks[o] of years, seven times seven years, so that the period of seven weeks of years gives forty-nine years. [9]Then you shall have the trumpet sounded loud; on the tenth day of the seventh month—on the day of atonement—you shall have the trumpet sounded throughout all your land. [10]And you shall hallow the fiftieth year and you shall proclaim liberty throughout the land to all its inhabitants. It shall be a jubilee for you: you shall return, every one of you, to your property and every one of you to your family. [11]That fiftieth year shall be a jubilee for you: you shall not sow, or reap the aftergrowth, or harvest the unpruned vines. [12]For it is a jubilee; it shall be holy to you: you shall eat only what the field itself produces.

---

l Or *treaty,* or *testament;* Heb *eduth*   m Heb *pure lampstand*
n Heb *pure table*   o Or *sabbaths*

?did you KNOW?

7 x 7 + 1 = Jubilee!

In the Bible, seven is a special number. Just as the seventh day of the week was set aside as a day of rest in ancient Israel, so the seventh year was set aside as a year of rest for the land. Fields were to remain uncultivated during the seventh year; whatever fruits or grains grew on their own were to be left for the poor. The "sabbatical year" was a reminder to the people that the land actually belonged to God, not to them.

Seven may be a special number, but seven times seven plus one is very special. The fiftieth year—the year after seven times seven years—was declared the Jubilee year, and God's Law demanded some very special things to happen. The people were to take a year of vacation from their normal routine. This meant no planting for a farmer, no lending for a banker, and no big sales for a merchant. Why this break? Because God wanted the Jubilee year to be a time when everyone started over with a clean slate. During the Jubilee, all land was to be returned to its original owners, and all Israelite slaves were to be set free. Debts were to be forgiven and justly settled. The year of Jubilee was like the reset button on a computer, stopping everything and returning it to its original setting. It was a check against the unjust distribution of property and wealth.

The Catholic church has continued the custom of celebrating the fiftieth year, especially when it marks the end of a century. Faithful to its Jewish roots, the church sees the Jubilee year as a special time for renewal. In preparation for a Jubilee year, it asks individuals and communities to commit themselves to following Jesus more faithfully.

▸ Leviticus, chapter 25

13 In this year of jubilee you shall return, every one of you, to your property. 14 When you make a sale to your neighbor or buy from your neighbor,

you shall not cheat one another. 15 When you buy from your neighbor, you shall pay only for the number of years since the jubilee; the seller shall charge you only for the remaining crop years. 16 If the years are more, you shall increase the price, and if the years are fewer, you shall diminish the price; for it is a certain number of harvests that are being sold to you. 17 You shall not cheat one another, but you shall fear your God; for I am the LORD your God.

18 You shall observe my statutes and faithfully keep my ordinances, so that you may live on the land securely. 19 The land will yield its fruit, and you will eat your fill and live on it securely. 20 Should you ask, "What shall we eat in the seventh year, if we may not sow or gather in our crop?" 21 I will order my blessing for you in the sixth year, so that it will yield a crop for three years. 22 When you sow in the eighth year, you will be eating from the old crop; until the ninth year, when its produce comes in, you shall eat the old. 23 The land shall not be sold in perpetuity, for the land is mine; with me you are but aliens and tenants. 24 Throughout the land that you hold, you shall provide for the redemption of the land.

25 If anyone of your kin falls into difficulty and sells a piece of property, then the next of kin shall come and redeem what the relative has sold. 26 If the person has no one to redeem it, but then prospers and finds sufficient means to do so, 27 the years since its sale shall be computed and the difference shall be refunded to the person to whom it was sold, and the property shall be returned. 28 But if there are not sufficient means to recover it, what was sold shall remain with the purchaser until the year of jubilee; in the jubilee it shall be released, and the property shall be returned.

29 If anyone sells a dwelling house in a walled city, it may be redeemed until a year has elapsed since its sale; the right of redemption shall be one year. 30 If it is not redeemed before a full year has elapsed, a house that is in a walled city shall pass in perpetuity to the purchaser, throughout the generations; it shall not be released in the jubilee. 31 But houses in villages that have no walls around them shall be classed as open country; they may be redeemed, and they shall be released in the jubilee. 32 As for the cities of the Lē'vītes, the Lē'vītes shall forever have the right of redemption of the houses in the cities belonging to them. 33 Such property as may be redeemed from the Lē'vītes— houses sold in a city belonging to them—shall be released in the jubilee; because the houses in the cities of the Lē'vītes are their possession among the people of Israel. 34 But the open land around

their cities may not be sold; for that is their possession for all time.

35 If any of your kin fall into difficulty and become dependent on you, *p* you shall support them; they shall live with you as though resident aliens. 36 Do not take interest in advance or otherwise make a profit from them, but fear your God; let them live with you. 37 You shall not lend them your money at interest taken in advance, or provide them food at a profit. 38 I am the LORD your God, who brought you out of the land of Egypt, to give you the land of Ca'naan, to be your God.

39 If any who are dependent on you become so impoverished that they sell themselves to you, you shall not make them serve as slaves. 40 They shall remain with you as hired or bound laborers. They shall serve with you until the year of the jubilee. 41 Then they and their children with them shall be free from your authority; they shall go back to their own family and return to their ancestral property. 42 For they are my servants, whom I brought out of the land of Egypt; they shall not be sold as slaves are sold. 43 You shall not rule over them with harshness, but shall fear your God. 44 As for the male and female slaves whom you may have, it is from the nations around you that you may acquire male and female slaves. 45 You may also acquire them from among the aliens residing with you, and from their families that are with you, who have been born in your land; and they may be your property. 46 You may keep them as a possession for your children after you, for them to inherit as property. These you may treat as slaves, but as for your fellow Israelites, no one shall rule over the other with harshness.

47 If resident aliens among you prosper, and if any of your kin fall into difficulty with one of them and sell themselves to an alien, or to a branch of the alien's family, 48 after they have sold themselves they shall have the right of redemption; one of their brothers may redeem them, 49 or their uncle or their uncle's son may redeem them, or anyone of their family who is of their own flesh may redeem them; or if they prosper they may redeem themselves. 50 They shall compute with the purchaser the total from the year when they sold themselves to the alien until the jubilee year; the price of the sale shall be applied to the number of years: the time they were with the owner shall be rated as the time of a hired laborer. 51 If many years remain, they shall pay for their redemption in proportion to the purchase price; 52 and if few years remain until the jubilee year, they shall compute thus: according to the years involved they shall make payment for their redemption. 53 As a laborer hired by the year they shall be under the alien's authority, who shall not, however, rule with harshness over them in your sight. 54 And if they have not been redeemed in any of these ways, they and their children with them shall go free in the jubilee year. 55 For to me the people of Israel are servants; they are my servants whom I brought out from the land of Egypt: I am the LORD your God.

Rewards for Obedience
(Deut 7.12–24; 28.1–14)

You shall make for yourselves no idols and erect no carved images or pillars, and you shall not place figured stones in your land, to worship at them; for I am the LORD your God. 2 You shall keep my sabbaths and reverence my sanctuary: I am the LORD.

3 If you follow my statutes and keep my commandments and observe them faithfully, 4 I will give you your rains in their season, and the land shall yield its produce, and the trees of the field shall yield their fruit. 5 Your threshing shall overtake the vintage, and the vintage shall overtake the sowing; you shall eat your bread to the full, and live securely in your land. 6 And I will grant peace in the land, and you shall lie down, and no one shall make you afraid; I will remove dangerous animals from the land, and no sword shall go through your land. 7 You shall give chase to your enemies, and they shall fall before you by the sword. 8 Five of you shall give chase to a hundred, and a hundred of you shall give chase to ten thousand; your enemies shall fall before you by the sword. 9 I will look with favor upon you and make you fruitful and multiply you; and I will maintain my covenant with you. 10 You shall eat old grain long stored, and you shall have to clear out the old to make way for the new. 11 I will place my dwelling in your midst, and I shall not abhor you. 12 And I will walk among you, and will be your God, and you shall be my people. 13 I am the LORD your God who brought you out of the land of Egypt, to be their slaves no more; I have broken the bars of your yoke and made you walk erect.

Penalties for Disobedience
(Deut 28.15–68)

14 But if you will not obey me, and do not observe all these commandments, 15 if you spurn my statutes, and abhor my ordinances, so that you will not observe all my commandments, and you break my covenant, 16 I in turn will do this to you: I will bring terror on you; consumption and fever that waste the eyes and cause life to pine away.

p Meaning of Heb uncertain

You shall sow your seed in vain, for your enemies shall eat it. 17 I will set my face against you, and you shall be struck down by your enemies; your foes shall rule over you, and you shall flee though no one pursues you. 18 And if in spite of this you will not obey me, I will continue to punish you sevenfold for your sins. 19 I will break your proud glory, and I will make your sky like iron and your earth like copper. 20 Your strength shall be spent to no purpose: your land shall not yield its produce, and the trees of the land shall not yield their fruit.

21 If you continue hostile to me, and will not obey me, I will continue to plague you sevenfold for your sins. 22 I will let loose wild animals against you, and they shall bereave you of your children and destroy your livestock; they shall make you few in number, and your roads shall be deserted.

23 If in spite of these punishments you have not turned back to me, but continue hostile to me, 24 then I too will continue hostile to you: I myself will strike you sevenfold for your sins. 25 I will bring the sword against you, executing vengeance for the covenant; and if you withdraw within your cities, I will send pestilence among you, and you shall be delivered into enemy hands. 26 When I break your staff of bread, ten women shall bake your bread in a single oven, and they shall dole out your bread by weight; and though you eat, you shall not be satisfied.

27 But if, despite this, you disobey me, and continue hostile to me, 28 I will continue hostile to you in fury; I in turn will punish you myself sevenfold for your sins. 29 You shall eat the flesh of your sons, and you shall eat the flesh of your daughters. 30 I will destroy your high places and cut down your incense altars; I will heap your carcasses on the carcasses of your idols. I will abhor you. 31 I will lay your cities waste, will make your sanctuaries desolate, and I will not smell your pleasing odors. 32 I will devastate the land, so that your enemies who come to settle in it shall be appalled at it. 33 And you I will scatter among the nations, and I will unsheathe the sword against you; your land shall be a desolation, and your cities a waste.

34 Then the land shall enjoy*q* its sabbath years as long as it lies desolate, while you are in the land of your enemies; then the land shall rest, and enjoy*q* its sabbath years. 35 As long as it lies desolate, it shall have the rest it did not have on your sabbaths when you were living on it. 36 And as for those of you who survive, I will send faintness into their hearts in the lands of their enemies; the sound of a driven leaf shall put them to flight, and they shall flee as one flees from the sword, and they shall fall though no one pursues. 37 They shall

stumble over one another, as if to escape a sword, though no one pursues; and you shall have no power to stand against your enemies. 38 You shall perish among the nations, and the land of your enemies shall devour you. 39 And those of you who survive shall languish in the land of your enemies because of their iniquities; also they shall languish because of the iniquities of their ancestors.

40 But if they confess their iniquity and the iniquity of their ancestors, in that they committed treachery against me and, moreover, that they continued hostile to me— 41 so that I, in turn, continued hostile to them and brought them into the land of their enemies; if then their uncircumcised heart is humbled and they make amends for their iniquity, 42 then will I remember my covenant with Jacob; I will remember also my covenant with Isaac and also my covenant with Abraham, and I will remember the land. 43 For the land shall be deserted by them, and enjoy*q* its sabbath years by lying desolate without them, while they shall make amends for their iniquity, because they dared to spurn my ordinances, and they abhorred my statutes. 44 Yet for all that, when they are in the land of their enemies, I will not spurn them, or abhor them so as to destroy them utterly and break my covenant with them; for I am the LORD their God; 45 but I will remember in their favor the covenant with their ancestors whom I brought out of the land of Egypt in the sight of the nations, to be their God: I am the LORD.

46 These are the statutes and ordinances and laws that the LORD established between himself and the people of Israel on Mount Sinai through Moses.

Votive Offerings

The LORD spoke to Moses, saying: 2 Speak to the people of Israel and say to them: When a person makes an explicit vow to the LORD concerning the equivalent for a human being, 3 the equivalent for a male shall be: from twenty to sixty years of age the equivalent shall be fifty shekels of silver by the sanctuary shekel. 4 If the person is a female, the equivalent is thirty shekels. 5 If the age is from five to twenty years of age, the equivalent is twenty shekels for a male and ten shekels for a female. 6 If the age is from one month to five years, the equivalent for a male is five shekels of silver, and for a female the equivalent is three shekels of silver. 7 And if the person is sixty years old or over, then the equivalent for a male is fifteen shekels, and for a female ten shekels. 8 If any cannot afford the

q Or make up for

equivalent, they shall be brought before the priest and the priest shall assess them; the priest shall assess them according to what each one making a vow can afford.

9 If it concerns an animal that may be brought as an offering to the LORD, any such that may be given to the LORD shall be holy. 10 Another shall not be exchanged or substituted for it, either good for bad or bad for good; and if one animal is substituted for another, both that one and its substitute shall be holy. 11 If it concerns any unclean animal that may not be brought as an offering to the LORD, the animal shall be presented before the priest. 12 The priest shall assess it: whether good or bad, according to the assessment of the priest, so it shall be. 13 But if it is to be redeemed, one-fifth must be added to the assessment.

14 If a person consecrates a house to the LORD, the priest shall assess it: whether good or bad, as the priest assesses it, so it shall stand. 15 And if the one who consecrates the house wishes to redeem it, one-fifth shall be added to its assessed value, and it shall revert to the original owner.

16 If a person consecrates to the LORD any inherited landholding, its assessment shall be in accordance with its seed requirements: fifty shekels of silver to a homer of barley seed. 17 If the person consecrates the field as of the year of jubilee, that assessment shall stand; 18 but if the field is consecrated after the jubilee, the priest shall compute the price for it according to the years that remain until the year of jubilee, and the assessment shall be reduced. 19 And if the one who consecrates the field wishes to redeem it, then one-fifth shall be added to its assessed value, and it shall revert to the original owner; 20 but if the field is not redeemed, or if it has been sold to someone else, it shall no longer be redeemable. 21 But when the field is released in the jubilee, it shall be holy to the LORD as a devoted field; it becomes the priest's holding. 22 If someone consecrates to the LORD a field that has been purchased, which is not a part of the inherited landholding, 23 the priest shall compute for it the proportionate assessment up to the year of jubilee, and the assessment shall be paid as of that day, a sacred donation to the LORD. 24 In the year of jubilee the field shall return to the one from whom it was bought, whose holding the land is. 25 All assessments shall be by the sanctuary shekel: twenty gerahs shall make a shekel.

26 A firstling of animals, however, which as a firstling belongs to the LORD, cannot be consecrated by anyone; whether ox or sheep, it is the LORD's. 27 If it is an unclean animal, it shall be ransomed at its assessment, with one-fifth added; if it is not redeemed, it shall be sold at its assessment.

28 Nothing that a person owns that has been devoted to destruction for the LORD, be it human or animal, or inherited landholding, may be sold or redeemed; every devoted thing is most holy to the LORD. 29 No human beings who have been devoted to destruction can be ransomed; they shall be put to death.

30 All tithes from the land, whether the seed from the ground or the fruit from the tree, are the LORD's; they are holy to the LORD. 31 If persons wish to redeem any of their tithes, they must add one-fifth to them. 32 All tithes of herd and flock, every tenth one that passes under the shepherd's staff, shall be holy to the LORD. 33 Let no one inquire whether it is good or bad, or make substitution for it; if one makes substitution for it, then both it and the substitute shall be holy and cannot be redeemed.

34 These are the commandments that the LORD gave to Moses for the people of Israel on Mount Sinai.

Sound the trumpet, beat the drum, we are going to war! The call to arms brings out the best and the worst in people—courage and cowardice, love and hate, hope and fear. The Book of Numbers records the varied experiences of the Israelites as they prepare for the armed conquest of the Promised Land. But most important, it tells of God's insistence that they maintain their purity and holiness to be worthy recipients of God's promises.

At a Glance

- **1.1—10.10.** preparation at Mount Sinai for conquest of the Promised Land

- **10.11—25.18.** the desert journey and the death of the older generation

- **Chapters 26–36.** the birth of a new generation ready to enter the Promised Land

In-depth

Although the Book of Numbers is named for the census mentioned in it, the book's original Hebrew name, meaning "in the desert," describes it better. Numbers picks up the story of the Israelites where Exodus leaves off. The first section begins with a census at Mount Sinai to determine who is eligible for military service. As the people prepare to enter the Promised Land, their leaders review the laws and regulations with them.

In the second section, the Israelites begin their journey to the Promised Land. Unfortunately, they have not learned to put their faith in God, and their journey is marked by grumbling, rebellion, and even idolatry. When the first army refuses to enter the Promised Land because of reports that it is inhabited by fierce giants (Num 13.32), God decrees that none of the older generation who left Egypt shall enter the Promised Land. So, the Israelites begin their desert wandering, which lasts thirty-nine years (see map 2, "The Exodus from Egypt").

The third section of Numbers paints a more hopeful picture. The people of the new generation are faithful and obedient as they prepare to enter the Land. They experience victory against the Midianites (chapter 31) and conquer the land east of the Jordan (chapter 32). The God who liberated their ancestors from Egypt, sustained and led them through the wilderness with Moses, is the same God who now makes ready to fulfill the promise of the Land to Israel.

Numbers was written by priestly scribes hundreds of years after these events, after the people had lost the Promised Land to the Babylonians. They fully appreciated the gift of the Land only after they had lost it. For the Israelites in the Babylonian Exile, Numbers portrayed the hopeful, grateful, and faithful hearts required of those whom God blesses.

Quick Facts

Period Covered
the thirty-nine years of wandering in the desert after the Exodus

Authors
priestly scribes writing during the Babylonian Exile (587–538 B.C.)

Theme
Faithfulness and gratefulness to God are necessary for Israel to obtain the Promised Land.

The Book of Numbers

Numbers

Chap. 31

The First Census of Israel
(Cp 2 Sam 24.1–9; 1 Chr 21.1–6)

The LORD spoke to Moses in the wilderness of Sinai, in the tent of meeting, on the first day of the second month, in the second year after they had come out of the land of Egypt, saying: ²Take a census of the whole congregation of Israelites, in their clans, by ancestral houses, according to the number of names, every male individually; ³from twenty years old and upward, everyone in Israel able to go to war. You and Aaron shall enroll them, company by company. ⁴A man from each tribe shall be with you, each man the head of his ancestral house. ⁵These are the names of the men who shall assist you:

From Reuben, E·lī′zur son of Shed′ē·ur.

6 From Sim′ē·on, She·lū′mi·el son of
     Zū·ri·shad′daī.
7 From Judah, Nah′shon son of Am·min′a·dab.
8 From Is′sa·char, Ne·than′el son of Zū′ar.
9 From Zeb′ū·lun, E·lī′ab son of Hē′lon.
10 From the sons of Joseph:
     from Ē′phra·im, E·lish′a·ma son of
       Am·mī′hud;
     from Ma·nas′seh, Ga·mā′li·el son of
       Pe·dah′zur.
11 From Benjamin, A·bī′dan son of Gid·ē·ō′ni.
12 From Dan, Ā·hī·ē′zer son of Am·mi·shad′daī.
13 From Ash′er, Pā′gi·el son of Och′ran.

14 From Gad, E·lī′a·saph son of Deū′el.
15 From Naph′ta·lī, A·hī′ra son of E′nan.
16 These were the ones chosen from the congregation, the leaders of their ancestral tribes, the heads of the divisions of Israel.

17 Moses and Aaron took these men who had been designated by name, 18 and on the first day of the second month they assembled the whole congregation together. They registered themselves in their clans, by their ancestral houses, according to the number of names from twenty years old and upward, individually, 19 as the LORD commanded Moses. So he enrolled them in the wilderness of Sinai.

20 The descendants of Reuben, Israel's firstborn, their lineage, in their clans, by their ancestral houses, according to the number of names, individually, every male from twenty years old and upward, everyone able to go to war: 21 those enrolled of the tribe of Reuben were forty-six thousand five hundred.

22 The descendants of Sim′ē·on, their lineage, in their clans, by their ancestral houses, those of them that were numbered, according to the number of names, individually, every male from twenty years old and upward, everyone able to go to war: 23 those enrolled of the tribe of Sim′ē·on were fifty-nine thousand three hundred.

24 The descendants of Gad, their lineage, in their clans, by their ancestral houses, according to

the number of the names, from twenty years old and upward, everyone able to go to war: 25 those enrolled of the tribe of Gad were forty-five thousand six hundred fifty.

26 The descendants of Judah, their lineage, in their clans, by their ancestral houses, according to the number of names, from twenty years old and upward, everyone able to go to war: 27 those enrolled of the tribe of Judah were seventy-four thousand six hundred.

28 The descendants of Is'sa·char, their lineage, in their clans, by their ancestral houses, according to the number of names, from twenty years old and upward, everyone able to go to war: 29 those enrolled of the tribe of Is'sa·char were fifty-four thousand four hundred.

30 The descendants of Zeb'u·lun, their lineage, in their clans, by their ancestral houses, according to the number of names, from twenty years old and upward, everyone able to go to war: 31 those enrolled of the tribe of Zeb'u·lun were fifty-seven thousand four hundred.

32 The descendants of Joseph, namely, the descendants of E'phra·im, their lineage, in their clans, by their ancestral houses, according to the number of names, from twenty years old and upward, everyone able to go to war: 33 those enrolled of the tribe of E'phra·im were forty thousand five hundred.

34 The descendants of Ma·nas'seh, their lineage, in their clans, by their ancestral houses, according to the number of names, from twenty years old and upward, everyone able to go to war: 35 those enrolled of the tribe of Ma·nas'seh were thirty-two thousand two hundred.

36 The descendants of Benjamin, their lineage, in their clans, by their ancestral houses, according to the number of names, from twenty years old and upward, everyone able to go to war: 37 those enrolled of the tribe of Benjamin were thirty-five thousand four hundred.

38 The descendants of Dan, their lineage, in their clans, by their ancestral houses, according to the number of names, from twenty years old and upward, everyone able to go to war: 39 those enrolled of the tribe of Dan were sixty-two thousand seven hundred.

40 The descendants of Ash'er, their lineage, in their clans, by their ancestral houses, according to the number of names, from twenty years old and upward, everyone able to go to war: 41 those enrolled of the tribe of Ash'er were forty-one thousand five hundred.

42 The descendants of Naph'ta·li, their lineage, in their clans, by their ancestral houses, according to the number of names, from twenty years old and upward, everyone able to go to war: 43 those enrolled of the tribe of Naph'ta·li were fifty-three thousand four hundred.

44 These are those who were enrolled, whom Moses and Aaron enrolled with the help of the leaders of Israel, twelve men, each representing his ancestral house. 45 So the whole number of the Israelites, by their ancestral houses, from twenty years old and upward, everyone able to go to war in Israel— 46 their whole number was six hundred three thousand five hundred fifty. 47 The Le'vites, however, were not numbered by their ancestral tribe along with them.

48 The LORD had said to Moses: 49 Only the tribe of Levi you shall not enroll, and you shall not take a census of them with the other Israelites. 50 Rather you shall appoint the Le'vites over the tabernacle of the covenant,[a] and over all its equipment, and over all that belongs to it; they are to carry the tabernacle and all its equipment, and they shall tend it, and shall camp around the tabernacle. 51 When the tabernacle is to set out, the Le'vites shall take it down; and when the tabernacle is to be pitched, the Le'vites shall set it up. And any outsider who comes near shall be put to death. 52 The other Israelites shall camp in their respective regimental camps, by companies; 53 but the Le'vites shall camp around the tabernacle of the covenant,[a] that there may be no wrath on the congregation of the Israelites; and the Le'vites shall perform the guard duty of the tabernacle of the covenant.[a] 54 The Israelites did so; they did just as the LORD commanded Moses.

The Order of Encampment and Marching

The LORD spoke to Moses and Aaron, saying: 2 The Israelites shall camp each in their respective regiments, under ensigns by their ancestral houses; they shall camp facing the tent of meeting on every side. 3 Those to camp on the east side toward the sunrise shall be of the regimental encampment of Judah by companies. The leader of the people of Judah shall be Nah'shon son of Am·min'a·dab, 4 with a company as enrolled of seventy-four thousand six hundred. 5 Those to camp next to him shall be the tribe of Is'sa·char. The leader of the Is'sa·char·ites shall be Ne·than'el son of Zu'ar, 6 with a company as enrolled of fifty-four thousand four hundred. 7 Then the tribe of Zeb'u·lun: The leader of the Zeb'u·lun·ites shall be E·li'ab son of He'lon, 8 with a company as enrolled of fifty-seven thousand four hundred. 9 The total enrollment of the camp of Judah, by companies, is one hundred

---

a Or treaty, or testimony; Heb eduth

did you KNOW?

Holy War

The Book of Numbers begins with a census of "everyone in Israel able to go to war" (1.3). The people of Israel are preparing to take over the land God had promised to them, the Chosen People. This is no ordinary war but a holy war, a war that they believe is divinely inspired, even a war God commands. In 31.2, God says to Moses, "Avenge the Israelites on the Midianites." The Israelites go on to kill every Midianite except for the young girls who are virgins.

How are we to understand this? Does God really order the killing of innocent people? To answer this, let's first remember that the writers of the Bible were influenced by their own cultural background and understanding of God. Three main things were probably on the mind of the writer of Numbers. First, the early Israelites viewed God as a warrior god fighting for them. Second, they believed the Canaanites were a wicked and idolatrous people who deserved punishment. And finally, they believed the Midianites deserved special punishment because they had led the Israelites into idolatry and sin at Shittim (see 25.1–3).

Holy wars are dangerous. Throughout history, people have committed atrocities in the name of God. Christians must interpret the Old Testament in the light of Jesus' teachings in the New Testament. And Jesus clearly taught about a God of mercy and love, not a God of war and vengeance. This is one area where the New Testament teaching replaces an earlier Old Testament understanding. Holy wars have no place in the lives of Christians.

eighty-six thousand four hundred. They shall set out first on the march.

10 On the south side shall be the regimental encampment of Reuben by companies. The leader of the Reū'ben·ītes shall be E·lī'zur son of Shed'ē·ur, [11] with a company as enrolled of forty-six thousand five hundred. [12] And those to camp next to him shall be the tribe of Sim'ē·on. The leader of the Sim'ē·on·ītes shall be She·lū'mi·el son of Zū·ri·shad'daī, [13] with a company as enrolled of fifty-nine thousand three hundred. [14] Then the tribe of Gad: The leader of the Gad'ītes shall be E·lī'a·saph son of Reū'el, [15] with a company as enrolled of forty-five thousand six hundred fifty. [16] The total enrollment of the camp of Reuben, by companies, is one hundred fifty-one thousand four hundred fifty. They shall set out second.

17 The tent of meeting, with the camp of the Lē'vītes, shall set out in the center of the camps; they shall set out just as they camp, each in position, by their regiments.

18 On the west side shall be the regimental encampment of Ē'phra·im by companies. The leader of the people of Ē'phra·im shall be E·lish'a·ma son of Am·mī'hud, [19] with a company as enrolled of forty thousand five hundred. [20] Next to him shall be the tribe of Ma·nas'seh. The leader of the people of Ma·nas'seh shall be Ga·mā'li·el son of Pe·dah'zur, [21] with a company as enrolled of thirty-two thousand two hundred. [22] Then the tribe of Benjamin: The leader of the Ben'ja·min·ītes shall be A·bī'dan son of Gid·ē·ō'ni, [23] with a company as enrolled of thirty-five thousand four hundred. [24] The total enrollment of the camp of Ē'phra·im, by companies, is one hundred eight thousand one hundred. They shall set out third on the march.

25 On the north side shall be the regimental encampment of Dan by companies. The leader of the Dan'ītes shall be Ā·hī·e'zer son of Am·mi·shad'daī, [26] with a company as enrolled of sixty-two thousand seven hundred. [27] Those to camp next to him shall be the tribe of Ash'er. The leader of the Ash'er·ītes shall be Pā'gi·el son of Ōch'ran, [28] with a company as enrolled of forty-one thousand five hundred. [29] Then the tribe of Naph'ta·lī: The leader of the Naph'ta·lītes shall be A·hī'ra son of Ē'nan, [30] with a company as enrolled of fifty-three thousand four hundred. [31] The total enrollment of the camp of Dan is one hundred fifty-seven thousand six hundred. They shall set out last, by companies.[b]

32 This was the enrollment of the Israelites by their ancestral houses; the total enrollment in the camps by their companies was six hundred three thousand five hundred fifty. [33] Just as the LORD had commanded Moses, the Lē'vītes were not enrolled among the other Israelites.

34 The Israelites did just as the LORD had commanded Moses: They camped by regiments, and they set out the same way, everyone by clans, according to ancestral houses.

---

b Compare verses 9, 16, 24: Heb *by their regiments*

The Sons of Aaron
(Lev 10.1–7)

This is the lineage of Aaron and Moses at the time when the LORD spoke with Moses on Mount Sinai. ²These are the names of the sons of Aaron: Nā′dab the firstborn, and A•bī′hū, El•ē•ā′zar, and Ith′a•mar; ³these are the names of the sons of Aaron, the anointed priests, whom he ordained to minister as priests. ⁴Nā′dab and A•bī′hū died before the LORD when they offered unholy fire before the LORD in the wilderness of Sinai, and they had no children. El•ē•ā′zar and Ith′a•mar served as priests in the lifetime of their father Aaron.

The Duties of the Levites

5 Then the LORD spoke to Moses, saying: ⁶Bring the tribe of Levi near, and set them before Aaron the priest, so that they may assist him. ⁷They shall perform duties for him and for the whole congregation in front of the tent of meeting, doing service at the tabernacle; ⁸they shall be in charge of all the furnishings of the tent of meeting, and attend to the duties for the Israelites as they do service at the tabernacle. ⁹You shall give the Lē′vites to Aaron and his descendants; they are unreservedly given to him from among the Israelites. ¹⁰But you shall make a register of Aaron and his descendants; it is they who shall attend to the priesthood, and any outsider who comes near shall be put to death.

11 Then the LORD spoke to Moses, saying: ¹²I hereby accept the Lē′vites from among the Israelites as substitutes for all the firstborn that open the womb among the Israelites. The Lē′vites shall be mine, ¹³for all the firstborn are mine; when I killed all the firstborn in the land of Egypt, I consecrated for my own all the firstborn in Israel, both human and animal; they shall be mine. I am the LORD.

A Census of the Levites
(Cp Num 1.47–54)

14 Then the LORD spoke to Moses in the wilderness of Sinai, saying: ¹⁵Enroll the Lē′vites by ancestral houses and by clans. You shall enroll every male from a month old and upward. ¹⁶So Moses enrolled them according to the word of the LORD, as he was commanded. ¹⁷The following were the sons of Levi, by their names: Ger′shon, Kō′hath, and Me•rar′ī. ¹⁸These are the names of the sons of Ger′shon by their clans: Lib′nī and Shim′ē•ī. ¹⁹The sons of Kō′hath by their clans: Am′ram, Iz′har, Hē′bron, and Uz′zi•el. ²⁰The sons of Me•rar′ī by their clans: Mah′lī and Mū′shī. These are the clans of the Lē′vites, by their ancestral houses.

21 To Ger′shon belonged the clan of the Lib′nites and the clan of the Shim′ē•ites; these were the clans of the Ger′shon•ites. ²²Their enrollment, counting all the males from a month old and upward, was seven thousand five hundred. ²³The clans of the Ger′shon•ites were to camp behind the tabernacle on the west, ²⁴with E•lī′a•saph son of Lā′el as head of the ancestral house of the Ger′shon•ites. ²⁵The responsibility of the sons of Ger′shon in the tent of meeting was to be the tabernacle, the tent with its covering, the screen for the entrance of the tent of meeting, ²⁶the hangings of the court, the screen for the entrance of the court that is around the tabernacle and the altar, and its cords—all the service pertaining to these.

27 To Kō′hath belonged the clan of the Am′ram•ites, the clan of the Iz′har•ites, the clan of the Hē′bron•ites, and the clan of the Uz′zi•el•ites; these are the clans of the Kō′hath•ites. ²⁸Counting all the males, from a month old and upward, there were eight thousand six hundred, attending to the duties of the sanctuary. ²⁹The clans of the Kō′hath•ites were to camp on the south side of the tabernacle, ³⁰with E•li•zā′phan son of Uz′zi•el as head of the ancestral house of the clans of the Kō′hath•ites. ³¹Their responsibility was to be the ark, the table, the lampstand, the altars, the vessels of the sanctuary with which the priests minister, and the screen—all the service pertaining to these. ³²El•ē•ā′zar son of Aaron the priest was to be chief over the leaders of the Lē′vites, and to have oversight of those who had charge of the sanctuary.

33 To Me•rar′ī belonged the clan of the Mah′lites and the clan of the Mū′shites: these are the clans of Me•rar′ī. ³⁴Their enrollment, counting all the males from a month old and upward, was six thousand two hundred. ³⁵The head of the ancestral house of the clans of Me•rar′ī was Zū′ri•el son of Ab•i•hā′il; they were to camp on the north side of the tabernacle. ³⁶The responsibility assigned to the sons of Me•rar′ī was to be the frames of the tabernacle, the bars, the pillars, the bases, and all their accessories—all the service pertaining to these; ³⁷also the pillars of the court all around, with their bases and pegs and cords.

38 Those who were to camp in front of the tabernacle on the east—in front of the tent of meeting toward the east—were Moses and Aaron and Aaron's sons, having charge of the rites within the sanctuary, whatever had to be done for the Israelites; and any outsider who came near was to be put to death. ³⁹The total enrollment of the Lē′vites whom Moses and Aaron enrolled at the commandment of the LORD, by their clans, all the males from a month old and upward, was twenty-two thousand.

N
U
M

The Redemption of the Firstborn

40 Then the LORD said to Moses: Enroll all the firstborn males of the Israelites, from a month old and upward, and count their names. 41 But you shall accept the Lē′vītes for me—I am the LORD—as substitutes for all the firstborn among the Israelites, and the livestock of the Lē′vītes as substitutes for all the firstborn among the livestock of the Israelites. 42 So Moses enrolled all the firstborn among the Israelites, as the LORD commanded him. 43 The total enrollment, all the firstborn males from a month old and upward, counting the number of names, was twenty-two thousand two hundred seventy-three.

44 Then the LORD spoke to Moses, saying: 45 Accept the Lē′vītes as substitutes for all the firstborn among the Israelites, and the livestock of the Lē′vītes as substitutes for their livestock; and the Lē′vītes shall be mine. I am the LORD. 46 As the price of redemption of the two hundred seventy-three of the firstborn of the Israelites, over and above the number of the Lē′vītes, 47 you shall accept five shekels apiece, reckoning by the shekel of the sanctuary, a shekel of twenty gerahs. 48 Give to Aaron and his sons the money by which the excess number of them is redeemed. 49 So Moses took the redemption money from those who were over and above those redeemed by the Lē′vītes; 50 from the firstborn of the Israelites he took the money, one thousand three hundred sixty-five shekels, reckoned by the shekel of the sanctuary; 51 and Moses gave the redemption money to Aaron and his sons, according to the word of the LORD, as the LORD had commanded Moses.

The Kohathites

The LORD spoke to Moses and Aaron, saying: 2 Take a census of the Kō′hath‧ites separate from the other Lē′vītes, by their clans and their ancestral houses, 3 from thirty years old up to fifty years old, all who qualify to do work relating to the tent of meeting. 4 The service of the Kō′hath‧ites relating to the tent of meeting concerns the most holy things.

5 When the camp is to set out, Aaron and his sons shall go in and take down the screening curtain, and cover the ark of the covenant[c] with it; 6 then they shall put on it a covering of fine leather,[d] and spread over that a cloth all of blue, and shall put its poles in place. 7 Over the table of the bread of the Presence they shall spread a blue cloth, and put on it the plates, the dishes for incense, the bowls, and the flagons for the drink offering; the regular bread also shall be on it; 8 then they shall spread over them a crimson cloth, and cover it with a covering of fine leather,[d] and

shall put its poles in place. 9 They shall take a blue cloth, and cover the lampstand for the light, with its lamps, its snuffers, its trays, and all the vessels for oil with which it is supplied; 10 and they shall put it with all its utensils in a covering of fine leather,[d] and put it on the carrying frame. 11 Over the golden altar they shall spread a blue cloth, and cover it with a covering of fine leather,[d] and shall put its poles in place; 12 and they shall take all the utensils of the service that are used in the sanctuary, and put them in a blue cloth, and cover them with a covering of fine leather,[d] and put them on the carrying frame. 13 They shall take away the ashes from the altar, and spread a purple cloth over it; 14 and they shall put on it all the utensils of the altar, which are used for the service there, the firepans, the forks, the shovels, and the basins, all the utensils of the altar; and they shall spread on it a covering of fine leather,[d] and shall put its poles in place. 15 When Aaron and his sons have finished covering the sanctuary and all the furnishings of the sanctuary, as the camp sets out, after that the Kō′hath‧ites shall come to carry these, but they must not touch the holy things, or they will die. These are the things of the tent of meeting that the Kō′hath‧ites are to carry.

16 El‧ē‧ā′zar son of Aaron the priest shall have charge of the oil for the light, the fragrant incense, the regular grain offering, and the anointing oil, the oversight of all the tabernacle and all that is in it, in the sanctuary and in its utensils.

17 Then the LORD spoke to Moses and Aaron, saying: 18 You must not let the tribe of the clans of the Kō′hath‧ites be destroyed from among the Lē′vītes. 19 This is how you must deal with them in order that they may live and not die when they come near to the most holy things: Aaron and his sons shall go in and assign each to a particular task or burden. 20 But the Kō′hath‧ites[e] must not go in to look on the holy things even for a moment; otherwise they will die.

The Gershonites and Merarites

21 Then the LORD spoke to Moses, saying: 22 Take a census of the Ger′shon‧ites also, by their ancestral houses and by their clans; 23 from thirty years old up to fifty you shall enroll them, all who qualify to do work in the tent of meeting. 24 This is the service of the clans of the Ger′shon‧ites, in serving and bearing burdens: 25 They shall carry the curtains of the tabernacle, and the tent of meeting with its covering, and the outer covering of fine leather[d] that is on top of it,

---

c Or *treaty,* or *testimony;* Heb *eduth*   d Meaning of Heb uncertain   e Heb *they*

and the screen for the entrance of the tent of meeting, 26 and the hangings of the court, and the screen for the entrance of the gate of the court that is around the tabernacle and the altar, and their cords, and all the equipment for their service; and they shall do all that needs to be done with regard to them. 27 All the service of the Ger'shon·ites shall be at the command of Aaron and his sons, in all that they are to carry, and in all that they have to do; and you shall assign to their charge all that they are to carry. 28 This is the service of the clans of the Ger'shon·ites relating to the tent of meeting, and their responsibilities are to be under the oversight of Ith'a·mar son of Aaron the priest.

29 As for the Me·rar'ites, you shall enroll them by their clans and their ancestral houses; 30 from thirty years old up to fifty years old you shall enroll them, everyone who qualifies to do the work of the tent of meeting. 31 This is what they are charged to carry, as the whole of their service in the tent of meeting: the frames of the tabernacle, with its bars, pillars, and bases, 32 and the pillars of the court all around with their bases, pegs, and cords, with all their equipment and all their related service; and you shall assign by name the objects that they are required to carry. 33 This is the service of the clans of the Me·rar'ites, the whole of their service relating to the tent of meeting, under the hand of Ith'a·mar son of Aaron the priest.

Census of the Levites

34 So Moses and Aaron and the leaders of the congregation enrolled the Kō'hath·ites, by their clans and their ancestral houses, 35 from thirty years old up to fifty years old, everyone who qualified for work relating to the tent of meeting; 36 and their enrollment by clans was two thousand seven hundred fifty. 37 This was the enrollment of the clans of the Kō'hath·ites, all who served at the tent of meeting, whom Moses and Aaron enrolled according to the commandment of the LORD by Moses.

38 The enrollment of the Ger'shon·ites, by their clans and their ancestral houses, 39 from thirty years old up to fifty years old, everyone who qualified for work relating to the tent of meeting— 40 their enrollment by their clans and their ancestral houses was two thousand six hundred thirty. 41 This was the enrollment of the clans of the Ger'shon·ites, all who served at the tent of meeting, whom Moses and Aaron enrolled according to the commandment of the LORD.

42 The enrollment of the clans of the Me·rar'ites, by their clans and their ancestral houses, 43 from thirty years old up to fifty years old, everyone who qualified for work relating to the tent of

meeting— 44 their enrollment by their clans was three thousand two hundred. 45 This is the enrollment of the clans of the Me·rar'ites, whom Moses and Aaron enrolled according to the commandment of the LORD by Moses.

46 All those who were enrolled of the Lé'vites, whom Moses and Aaron and the leaders of Israel enrolled, by their clans and their ancestral houses, 47 from thirty years old up to fifty years old, everyone who qualified to do the work of service and the work of bearing burdens relating to the tent of meeting, 48 their enrollment was eight thousand five hundred eighty. 49 According to the commandment of the LORD through Moses they were appointed to their several tasks of serving or carrying; thus they were enrolled by him, as the LORD commanded Moses.

Unclean Persons
(Cp Lev 15.1–33)

The LORD spoke to Moses, saying: 2 Command the Israelites to put out of the camp everyone who is leprous,*f* or has a discharge, and everyone who is unclean through contact with a corpse; 3 you shall put out both male and female, putting them outside the camp; they must not defile their camp, where I dwell among them. 4 The Israelites did so, putting them outside the camp; as the LORD had spoken to Moses, so the Israelites did.

Confession and Restitution
(Lev 6.1–7)

5 The LORD spoke to Moses, saying: 6 Speak to the Israelites: When a man or a woman wrongs another, breaking faith with the LORD, that person incurs guilt 7 and shall confess the sin that has been committed. The person shall make full restitution for the wrong, adding one-fifth to it, and giving it to the one who was wronged. 8 If the injured party has no next of kin to whom restitution may be made for the wrong, the restitution for wrong shall go to the LORD for the priest, in addition to the ram of atonement with which atonement is made for the guilty party. 9 Among all the sacred donations of the Israelites, every gift that they bring to the priest shall be his. 10 The sacred donations of all are their own; whatever anyone gives to the priest shall be his.

Concerning an Unfaithful Wife

11 The LORD spoke to Moses, saying: 12 Speak to the Israelites and say to them: If any man's wife goes astray and is unfaithful to him, 13 if a man

---

f A term for several skin diseases; precise meaning uncertain

has had intercourse with her but it is hidden from her husband, so that she is undetected though she has defiled herself, and there is no witness against her since she was not caught in the act; 14 if a spirit of jealousy comes on him, and he is jealous of his wife who has defiled herself; or if a spirit of jealousy comes on him, and he is jealous of his wife, though she has not defiled herself; 15 then the man shall bring his wife to the priest. And he shall bring the offering required for her, one-tenth of an ephah of barley flour. He shall pour no oil on it and put no frankincense on it, for it is a grain offering of jealousy, a grain offering of remembrance, bringing iniquity to remembrance.

16 Then the priest shall bring her near, and set her before the LORD; 17 the priest shall take holy water in an earthen vessel, and take some of the dust that is on the floor of the tabernacle and put it into the water. 18 The priest shall set the woman before the LORD, dishevel the woman's hair, and place in her hands the grain offering of remembrance, which is the grain offering of jealousy. In his own hand the priest shall have the water of bitterness that brings the curse. 19 Then the priest shall make her take an oath, saying, "If no man has lain with you, if you have not turned aside to uncleanness while under your husband's authority, be immune to this water of bitterness that brings the curse. 20 But if you have gone astray while under your husband's authority, if you have defiled yourself and some man other than your husband has had intercourse with you," 21 —let the priest make the woman take the oath of the curse and say to the woman—"the LORD make you an execration and an oath among your people, when the LORD makes your uterus drop, your womb discharge; 22 now may this water that brings the curse enter your bowels and make your womb discharge, your uterus drop!" And the woman shall say, "Amen. Amen."

23 Then the priest shall put these curses in writing, and wash them off into the water of bitterness. 24 He shall make the woman drink the water of bitterness that brings the curse, and the water that brings the curse shall enter her and cause bitter pain. 25 The priest shall take the grain offering of jealousy out of the woman's hand, and shall elevate the grain offering before the LORD and bring it to the altar; 26 and the priest shall take a handful of the grain offering, as its memorial portion, and turn it into smoke on the altar, and afterward shall make the woman drink the water. 27 When he has made her drink the water, then, if she has defiled herself and has been unfaithful to her husband, the water that brings the curse shall enter into her and cause bitter pain, and her womb shall dis-charge, her uterus drop, and the woman shall become an execration among her people. 28 But if the woman has not defiled herself and is clean, then she shall be immune and be able to conceive children.

29 This is the law in cases of jealousy, when a wife, while under her husband's authority, goes astray and defiles herself, 30 or when a spirit of jealousy comes on a man and he is jealous of his wife; then he shall set the woman before the LORD, and the priest shall apply this entire law to her. 31 The man shall be free from iniquity, but the woman shall bear her iniquity.

The Nazirites

The LORD spoke to Moses, saying: 2 Speak to the Israelites and say to them: When either men or women make a special vow, the vow of a nazirite,g to separate themselves to the LORD, 3 they shall separate themselves from wine and strong drink; they shall drink no wine vinegar or other vinegar, and shall not drink any grape juice or eat grapes, fresh or dried. 4 All their days as nazirites h they shall eat nothing that is produced by the grapevine, not even the seeds or the skins.

5 All the days of their nazirite vow no razor shall come upon the head; until the time is completed for which they separate themselves to the LORD, they shall be holy; they shall let the locks of the head grow long.

6 All the days that they separate themselves to the LORD they shall not go near a corpse. 7 Even if their father or mother, brother or sister, should die, they may not defile themselves; because their consecration to God is upon the head. 8 All their days as nazirites h they are holy to the LORD.

9 If someone dies very suddenly nearby, defiling the consecrated head, then they shall shave the head on the day of their cleansing; on the seventh day they shall shave it. 10 On the eighth day they shall bring two turtledoves or two young pigeons to the priest at the entrance of the tent of meeting, 11 and the priest shall offer one as a sin offering and the other as a burnt offering, and make atonement for them, because they incurred guilt by reason of the corpse. They shall sanctify the head that same day, 12 and separate themselves to the LORD for their days as nazirites,h and bring a male lamb a year old as a guilt offering. The former time shall be void, because the consecrated head was defiled.

13 This is the law for the nazirites h when the time of their consecration has been completed:

---

g That is *one separated* or *one consecrated*   h That is *those separated* or *those consecrated*

PRAY IT!
God Bless You

A very old blessing in Num 6.22–27 (some of which is repeated in Ps 4.6 and 67.1) was not originally a Christian blessing, but its three parts remind us of Christian blessings calling on the Trinity.

This blessing is a good one for special occasions. You could write it on a card for a birthday, Mother's Day or Father's Day, a wedding anniversary, or any other special event. Or you could use it to make a poster or an engraving for a first Communion, a wedding, or a confirmation.

If this blessing sounds familiar, maybe it's because on New Year's Day (the feast of Mary, mother of God), we hear it as the first reading. It's the perfect way to start the new year.

▸ Num 6.22–27

they shall be brought to the entrance of the tent of meeting, 14 and they shall offer their gift to the LORD, one male lamb a year old without blemish as a burnt offering, one ewe lamb a year old without blemish as a sin offering, one ram without blemish as an offering of well-being, 15 and a basket of unleavened bread, cakes of choice flour mixed with oil and unleavened wafers spread with oil, with their grain offering and their drink offerings. 16 The priest shall present them before the LORD and offer their sin offering and burnt offering, 17 and shall offer the ram as a sacrifice of well-being to the LORD, with the basket of unleavened bread; the priest also shall make the accompanying grain offering and drink offering. 18 Then the nazirites[i] shall shave the consecrated head at the entrance of the tent of meeting, and shall take the hair from the consecrated head and put it on the fire under the sacrifice of well-being. 19 The priest shall take the shoulder of the ram, when it is boiled, and one unleavened cake out of the basket, and one unleavened wafer, and shall put them in the palms of the nazirites,[i] after they have shaved the consecrated head. 20 Then the priest shall elevate them as an elevation offering before the LORD; they are a holy portion for the priest, together with the breast that is elevated and the thigh that is offered. After that the nazirites[i] may drink wine.

21 This is the law for the nazirites[i] who take a vow. Their offering to the LORD must be in accordance with the nazirite[j] vow, apart from what else they can afford. In accordance with whatever vow they take, so they shall do, following the law for their consecration.

The Priestly Benediction

22 The LORD spoke to Moses, saying: 23 Speak to Aaron and his sons, saying, Thus you shall bless the Israelites: You shall say to them,
24 The LORD bless you and keep you;
25 the LORD make his face to shine upon you,
    and be gracious to you;
26 the LORD lift up his countenance upon you,
    and give you peace.
27 So they shall put my name on the Israelites, and I will bless them.

Offerings of the Leaders

On the day when Moses had finished setting up the tabernacle, and had anointed and consecrated it with all its furnishings, and had anointed and consecrated the altar with all its utensils, 2 the leaders of Israel, heads of their ancestral houses, the leaders of the tribes, who were over those who were enrolled, made offerings. 3 They brought their offerings before the LORD, six covered wagons and twelve oxen, a wagon for every two of the leaders, and for each one an ox; they presented them before the tabernacle. 4 Then the LORD said to Moses: 5 Accept these from them, that they may be used in doing the service of the tent of meeting, and give them to the Lēʹvites, to each according to his service. 6 So Moses took the wagons and the oxen, and gave them to the Lēʹvites. 7 Two wagons and four oxen he gave to the Gerʹshon•ites, according to their service; 8 and four wagons and eight oxen he gave to the Me•rarʹites, according to their service, under the direction of Ithʹa•mar son of Aaron the priest. 9 But to the Kōʹhath•ites he gave none, because they were charged with the care of the holy things that had to be carried on the shoulders.

10 The leaders also presented offerings for the dedication of the altar at the time when it was anointed; the leaders presented their offering before the altar. 11 The LORD said to Moses: They shall present their offerings, one leader each day, for the dedication of the altar.

12 The one who presented his offering the first day was Nahʹshon son of Am•minʹa•dab, of the tribe of Judah; 13 his offering was one silver plate

i That is those separated or those consecrated   j That is one separated or one consecrated

NUM

weighing one hundred thirty shekels, one silver basin weighing seventy shekels, according to the shekel of the sanctuary, both of them full of choice flour mixed with oil for a grain offering; 14 one golden dish weighing ten shekels, full of incense; 15 one young bull, one ram, one male lamb a year old, for a burnt offering; 16 one male goat for a sin offering; 17 and for the sacrifice of well-being, two oxen, five rams, five male goats, and five male lambs a year old. This was the offering of Nah′-shon son of Am·min′a·dab.

18 On the second day Ne·than′el son of Zū′ar, the leader of Is′sa·char, presented an offering; 19 he presented for his offering one silver plate weighing one hundred thirty shekels, one silver basin weighing seventy shekels, according to the shekel of the sanctuary, both of them full of choice flour mixed with oil for a grain offering; 20 one golden dish weighing ten shekels, full of incense; 21 one young bull, one ram, one male lamb a year old, as a burnt offering; 22 one male goat as a sin offering; 23 and for the sacrifice of well-being, two oxen, five rams, five male goats, and five male lambs a year old. This was the offering of Ne·than′el son of Zū′ar.

24 On the third day E·li′ab son of Hē′lon, the leader of the Zeb′u·lun·ites: 25 his offering was one silver plate weighing one hundred thirty shekels, one silver basin weighing seventy shekels, according to the shekel of the sanctuary, both of them full of choice flour mixed with oil for a grain offering; 26 one golden dish weighing ten shekels, full of incense; 27 one young bull, one ram, one male lamb a year old, for a burnt offering; 28 one male goat for a sin offering; 29 and for the sacrifice of well-being, two oxen, five rams, five male goats, and five male lambs a year old. This was the offering of E·li′ab son of Hē′lon.

30 On the fourth day E·li′zur son of Shed′ē·ur, the leader of the Reū′ben·ites: 31 his offering was one silver plate weighing one hundred thirty shekels, one silver basin weighing seventy shekels, according to the shekel of the sanctuary, both of them full of choice flour mixed with oil for a grain offering; 32 one golden dish weighing ten shekels, full of incense; 33 one young bull, one ram, one male lamb a year old, for a burnt offering; 34 one male goat for a sin offering; 35 and for the sacrifice of well-being, two oxen, five rams, five male goats, and five male lambs a year old. This was the offering of E·li′zur son of Shed′ē·ur.

36 On the fifth day She·lū′mi·el son of Zū·ri-shad′daī, the leader of the Sim′ē·on·ites: 37 his offering was one silver plate weighing one hundred thirty shekels, one silver basin weighing seventy shekels, according to the shekel of the sanctuary,

both of them full of choice flour mixed with oil for a grain offering; 38 one golden dish weighing ten shekels, full of incense; 39 one young bull, one ram, one male lamb a year old, for a burnt offering; 40 one male goat for a sin offering; 41 and for the sacrifice of well-being, two oxen, five rams, five male goats, and five male lambs a year old. This was the offering of She·lū′mi·el son of Zū·ri·shad′daī.

42 On the sixth day E·li′a·saph son of Deū′el, the leader of the Gad′ites: 43 his offering was one silver plate weighing one hundred thirty shekels, one silver basin weighing seventy shekels, according to the shekel of the sanctuary, both of them full of choice flour mixed with oil for a grain offering; 44 one golden dish weighing ten shekels, full of incense; 45 one young bull, one ram, one male lamb a year old, for a burnt offering; 46 one male goat for a sin offering; 47 and for the sacrifice of well-being, two oxen, five rams, five male goats, and five male lambs a year old. This was the offering of E·li′a·saph son of Deū′el.

48 On the seventh day E·lish′a·ma son of Am-mi′hud, the leader of the Ē′phra·im·ites: 49 his offering was one silver plate weighing one hundred thirty shekels, one silver basin weighing seventy shekels, according to the shekel of the sanctuary, both of them full of choice flour mixed with oil for a grain offering; 50 one golden dish weighing ten shekels, full of incense; 51 one young bull, one ram, one male lamb a year old, for a burnt offering; 52 one male goat for a sin offering; 53 and for the sacrifice of well-being, two oxen, five rams, five male goats, and five male lambs a year old. This was the offering of E·lish′a·ma son of Am·mi′hud.

54 On the eighth day Ga·mā′li·el son of Pe·dah′-zur, the leader of the Ma·nas′sites: 55 his offering was one silver plate weighing one hundred thirty shekels, one silver basin weighing seventy shekels, according to the shekel of the sanctuary, both of them full of choice flour mixed with oil for a grain offering; 56 one golden dish weighing ten shekels, full of incense; 57 one young bull, one ram, one male lamb a year old, for a burnt offering; 58 one male goat for a sin offering; 59 and for the sacrifice of well-being, two oxen, five rams, five male goats, and five male lambs a year old. This was the offering of Ga·mā′li·el son of Pe·dah′zur.

60 On the ninth day A·bī′dan son of Gid·ē·ō′ni, the leader of the Ben′ja·min·ites: 61 his offering was one silver plate weighing one hundred thirty shekels, one silver basin weighing seventy shekels, according to the shekel of the sanctuary, both of them full of choice flour mixed with oil for a grain offering; 62 one golden dish weighing ten shekels, full of incense; 63 one young bull, one ram, one male lamb a year old, for a burnt offering; 64 one

male goat for a sin offering; [65] and for the sacrifice of well-being, two oxen, five rams, five male goats, and five male lambs a year old. This was the offering of A•bĭ′dan son of Gid•e•ō′ni.

66 On the tenth day Ă•hĭ•ē′zer son of Am•mi-shad′daī, the leader of the Dan′ites: [67] his offering was one silver plate weighing one hundred thirty shekels, one silver basin weighing seventy shekels, according to the shekel of the sanctuary, both of them full of choice flour mixed with oil for a grain offering; [68] one golden dish weighing ten shekels, full of incense; [69] one young bull, one ram, one male lamb a year old, for a burnt offering; [70] one male goat for a sin offering; [71] and for the sacrifice of well-being, two oxen, five rams, five male goats, and five male lambs a year old. This was the offering of Ă•hĭ•ē′zer son of Am•mi•shad′daī.

72 On the eleventh day Pā′gi•el son of Ŏch′ran, the leader of the Ash′er•ites: [73] his offering was one silver plate weighing one hundred thirty shekels, one silver basin weighing seventy shekels, according to the shekel of the sanctuary, both of them full of choice flour mixed with oil for a grain offering; [74] one golden dish weighing ten shekels, full of incense; [75] one young bull, one ram, one male lamb a year old, for a burnt offering; [76] one male goat for a sin offering; [77] and for the sacrifice of well-being, two oxen, five rams, five male goats, and five male lambs a year old. This was the offering of Pā′gi•el son of Ŏch′ran.

78 On the twelfth day A•hĭ′ra son of Ē′nan, the leader of the Naph′ta•lites: [79] his offering was one silver plate weighing one hundred thirty shekels, one silver basin weighing seventy shekels, according to the shekel of the sanctuary, both of them full of choice flour mixed with oil for a grain offering; [80] one golden dish weighing ten shekels, full of incense; [81] one young bull, one ram, one male lamb a year old, for a burnt offering; [82] one male goat for a sin offering; [83] and for the sacrifice of well-being, two oxen, five rams, five male goats, and five male lambs a year old. This was the offering of A•hĭ′ra son of Ē′nan.

84 This was the dedication offering for the altar, at the time when it was anointed, from the leaders of Israel: twelve silver plates, twelve silver basins, twelve golden dishes, [85] each silver plate weighing one hundred thirty shekels and each basin seventy, all the silver of the vessels two thousand four hundred shekels according to the shekel of the sanctuary, [86] the twelve golden dishes, full of incense, weighing ten shekels apiece according to the shekel of the sanctuary, all the gold of the dishes being one hundred twenty shekels; [87] all the livestock for the burnt offering twelve bulls, twelve rams, twelve male lambs a year old, with their grain offering; and twelve male goats for a sin offering; [88] and all the livestock for the sacrifice of well-being twenty-four bulls, the rams sixty, the male goats sixty, the male lambs a year old sixty. This was the dedication offering for the altar, after it was anointed.

89 When Moses went into the tent of meeting to speak with the LORD,[k] he would hear the voice speaking to him from above the mercy seat[l] that was on the ark of the covenant[m] from between the two cherubim; thus it spoke to him.

The Seven Lamps
(Ex 25.31–40)

The LORD spoke to Moses, saying: [2] Speak to Aaron and say to him: When you set up the lamps, the seven lamps shall give light in front of the lampstand. [3] Aaron did so; he set up its lamps to give light in front of the lampstand, as the LORD had commanded Moses. [4] Now this was how the lampstand was made, out of hammered work of gold. From its base to its flowers, it was hammered work; according to the pattern that the LORD had shown Moses, so he made the lampstand.

Consecration and Service of the Levites

5 The LORD spoke to Moses, saying: [6] Take the Lĕ′vites from among the Israelites and cleanse them. [7] Thus you shall do to them, to cleanse them: sprinkle the water of purification on them, have them shave their whole body with a razor and wash their clothes, and so cleanse themselves. [8] Then let them take a young bull and its grain offering of choice flour mixed with oil, and you shall take another young bull for a sin offering. [9] You shall bring the Lĕ′vites before the tent of meeting, and assemble the whole congregation of the Israelites. [10] When you bring the Lĕ′vites before the LORD, the Israelites shall lay their hands on the Lĕ′vites, [11] and Aaron shall present the Lĕ′vites before the LORD as an elevation offering from the Israelites, that they may do the service of the LORD. [12] The Lĕ′vites shall lay their hands on the heads of the bulls, and he shall offer the one for a sin offering and the other for a burnt offering to the LORD, to make atonement for the Lĕ′vites. [13] Then you shall have the Lĕ′vites stand before Aaron and his sons, and you shall present them as an elevation offering to the LORD.

14 Thus you shall separate the Lĕ′vites from among the other Israelites, and the Lĕ′vites shall be mine. [15] Thereafter the Lĕ′vites may go in to do service at the tent of meeting, once you have

N
U
M

---

[k] Heb *him*   [l] Or *the cover*   [m] Or *treaty,* or *testimony;* Heb *eduth*

cleansed them and presented them as an elevation offering. 16 For they are unreservedly given to me from among the Israelites; I have taken them for myself, in place of all that open the womb, the firstborn of all the Israelites. 17 For all the firstborn among the Israelites are mine, both human and animal. On the day that I struck down all the first-born in the land of Egypt I consecrated them for myself, 18 but I have taken the Lē'vītes in place of all the firstborn among the Israelites. 19 Moreover, I have given the Lē'vītes as a gift to Aaron and his sons from among the Israelites, to do the service for the Israelites at the tent of meeting, and to make atonement for the Israelites, in order that there may be no plague among the Israelites for coming too close to the sanctuary.

20 Moses and Aaron and the whole congregation of the Israelites did with the Lē'vītes accordingly; the Israelites did with the Lē'vītes just as the LORD had commanded Moses concerning them. 21 The Lē'vītes purified themselves from sin and washed their clothes; then Aaron presented them as an elevation offering before the LORD, and Aaron made atonement for them to cleanse them. 22 Thereafter the Lē'vītes went in to do their service in the tent of meeting in attendance on Aaron and his sons. As the LORD had commanded Moses concerning the Lē'vītes, so they did with them.

23 The LORD spoke to Moses, saying: 24 This applies to the Lē'vītes: from twenty-five years old and upward they shall begin to do duty in the service of the tent of meeting; 25 and from the age of fifty years they shall retire from the duty of the service and serve no more. 26 They may assist their brothers in the tent of meeting in carrying out their duties, but they shall perform no service. Thus you shall do with the Lē'vītes in assigning their duties.

The Passover at Sinai
(Ex 12.1–20)

The LORD spoke to Moses in the wilderness of Sinai, in the first month of the second year after they had come out of the land of Egypt, saying: 2 Let the Israelites keep the passover at its appointed time. 3 On the fourteenth day of this month, at twilight,[n] you shall keep it at its appointed time; according to all its statutes and all its regulations you shall keep it. 4 So Moses told the Israelites that they should keep the passover. 5 They kept the passover in the first month, on the fourteenth day of the month, at twilight,[n] in the wilderness of Sinai. Just as the LORD had commanded Moses, so the Israelites did. 6 Now there were certain people who were unclean through touching a corpse, so that they could not keep the passover on that day. They

came before Moses and Aaron on that day, 7 and said to him, "Although we are unclean through touching a corpse, why must we be kept from presenting the LORD's offering at its appointed time among the Israelites?" 8 Moses spoke to them, "Wait, so that I may hear what the LORD will command concerning you."

9 The LORD spoke to Moses, saying: 10 Speak to the Israelites, saying: Anyone of you or your descendants who is unclean through touching a corpse, or is away on a journey, shall still keep the passover to the LORD. 11 In the second month on the fourteenth day, at twilight,[n] they shall keep it; they shall eat it with unleavened bread and bitter herbs. 12 They shall leave none of it until morning, nor break a bone of it; according to all the statute for the passover they shall keep it. 13 But anyone who is clean and is not on a journey, and yet refrains from keeping the passover, shall be cut off from the people for not presenting the LORD's offering at its appointed time; such a one shall bear the consequences for the sin. 14 Any alien residing among you who wishes to keep the passover to the LORD shall do so according to the statute of the passover and according to its regulation; you shall have one statute for both the resident alien and the native.

The Cloud and the Fire
(Ex 13.21–22; 40.34–38)

15 On the day the tabernacle was set up, the cloud covered the tabernacle, the tent of the covenant;[o] and from evening until morning it was over the tabernacle, having the appearance of fire. 16 It was always so: the cloud covered it by day[p] and the appearance of fire by night. 17 Whenever the cloud lifted from over the tent, then the Israelites would set out; and in the place where the cloud settled down, there the Israelites would camp. 18 At the command of the LORD the Israelites would set out, and at the command of the LORD they would camp. As long as the cloud rested over the tabernacle, they would remain in camp. 19 Even when the cloud continued over the tabernacle many days, the Israelites would keep the charge of the LORD, and would not set out. 20 Sometimes the cloud would remain a few days over the tabernacle, and according to the command of the LORD they would remain in camp; then according to the command of the LORD they would set out. 21 Sometimes the cloud would remain from evening until morning; and when the cloud lifted in the morning, they would set out, or if it continued for a day and a

---

n Heb *between the two evenings*   o Or *treaty*, or *testimony*; Heb *eduth*   p Gk Syr Vg: Heb lacks *by day*

night, when the cloud lifted they would set out. 22 Whether it was two days, or a month, or a longer time, that the cloud continued over the tabernacle, resting upon it, the Israelites would remain in camp and would not set out; but when it lifted they would set out. 23 At the command of the LORD they would camp, and at the command of the LORD they would set out. They kept the charge of the LORD, at the command of the LORD by Moses.

The Silver Trumpets

The LORD spoke to Moses, saying: 2 Make two silver trumpets; you shall make them of hammered work; and you shall use them for summoning the congregation, and for breaking camp. 3 When both are blown, the whole congregation shall assemble before you at the entrance of the tent of meeting. 4 But if only one is blown, then the leaders, the heads of the tribes of Israel, shall assemble before you. 5 When you blow an alarm, the camps on the east side shall set out; 6 when you blow a second alarm, the camps on the south side shall set out. An alarm is to be blown whenever they are to set out. 7 But when the assembly is to be gathered, you shall blow, but you shall not sound an alarm. 8 The sons of Aaron, the priests, shall blow the trumpets; this shall be a perpetual institution for you throughout your generations. 9 When you go to war in your land against the adversary who oppresses you, you shall sound an alarm with the trumpets, so that you may be remembered before the LORD your God and be saved from your enemies. 10 Also on your days of rejoicing, at your appointed festivals, and at the beginnings of your months, you shall blow the trumpets over your burnt offerings and over your sacrifices of well-being; they shall serve as a reminder on your behalf before the LORD your God: I am the LORD your God.

Departure from Sinai

11 In the second year, in the second month, on the twentieth day of the month, the cloud lifted from over the tabernacle of the covenant. 12 Then the Israelites set out by stages from the wilderness of Sinai, and the cloud settled down in the wilderness of Par'an. 13 They set out for the first time at the command of the LORD by Moses. 14 The standard of the camp of Judah set out first, company by company, and over the whole company was Nah'shon son of Am·min'a·dab. 15 Over the company of the tribe of Is'sa·char was Ne·than'el son of Zū'ar; 16 and over the company of the tribe of Zeb'ū·lun was E·lī'ab son of Hē'lon. 17 Then the tabernacle was taken down, and the Ger'shon·ites and the Me·rar'ites, who carried

the tabernacle, set out. 18 Next the standard of the camp of Reuben set out, company by company; and over the whole company was E·lī'zur son of Shed'ē·ur. 19 Over the company of the tribe of Sim'ē·on was She·lū'mi·el son of Zū·ri·shad'dai, 20 and over the company of the tribe of Gad was E·lī'a·saph son of Deū'el.

21 Then the Kō'hath·ites, who carried the holy things, set out; and the tabernacle was set up before their arrival. 22 Next the standard of the E'phra·im·ite camp set out, company by company, and over the whole company was E·lish'a·ma son of Am·mī'hud. 23 Over the company of the tribe of Ma·nas'seh was Ga·mā'li·el son of Pe·dah'zur, 24 and over the company of the tribe of Benjamin was A·bī'dan son of Gid·ē·ō'ni.

25 Then the standard of the camp of Dan, acting as the rear guard of all the camps, set out, company by company, and over the whole company was Ā·hī·ē'zer son of Am·mi·shad'dai. 26 Over the company of the tribe of Ash'er was Pā'gi·el son of Ōch'ran, 27 and over the company of the tribe of Naph'ta·lī was A·hī'ra son of Ē'nan. 28 This was the order of march of the Israelites, company by company, when they set out.

29 Moses said to Hō'bab son of Reū'el the Mid'i·an·ite, Moses' father-in-law, "We are setting out for the place of which the LORD said, 'I will give it to you'; come with us, and we will treat you well; for the LORD has promised good to Israel." 30 But he said to him, "I will not go, but I will go back to my own land and to my kindred." 31 He said, "Do not leave us, for you know where we should camp in the wilderness, and you will serve as eyes for us. 32 Moreover, if you go with us, whatever good the LORD does for us, the same we will do for you."

33 So they set out from the mount of the LORD three days' journey with the ark of the covenant of the LORD going before them three days' journey, to seek out a resting place for them, 34 the cloud of the LORD being over them by day when they set out from the camp.

35 Whenever the ark set out, Moses would say,
> "Arise, O LORD, let your enemies be
>   scattered,
>   and your foes flee before you."
36 And whenever it came to rest, he would say,
> "Return, O LORD of the ten thousand
>   thousands of Israel."r

---

q Or *treaty*, or *testimony*; Heb *eduth*   r Meaning of Heb uncertain

Complaining in the Desert

Now when the people complained in the hearing of the LORD about their misfortunes, the LORD heard it and his anger was kindled. Then the fire of the LORD burned against them, and consumed some outlying parts of the camp. 2 But the people cried out to Moses; and Moses prayed to the LORD, and the fire abated. 3 So that place was called Tab′-e·rah,[s] because the fire of the LORD burned against them.

4 The rabble among them had a strong craving; and the Israelites also wept again, and said, "If only we had meat to eat! 5 We remember the fish we used to eat in Egypt for nothing, the cucumbers, the melons, the leeks, the onions, and the garlic; 6 but now our strength is dried up, and there is nothing at all but this manna to look at."

7 Now the manna was like coriander seed, and its color was like the color of gum resin. 8 The people went around and gathered it, ground it in mills or beat it in mortars, then boiled it in pots and made cakes of it; and the taste of it was like the taste of cakes baked with oil. 9 When the dew fell on the camp in the night, the manna would fall with it.

10 Moses heard the people weeping throughout their families, all at the entrances of their tents. Then the LORD became very angry, and Moses was displeased. 11 So Moses said to the LORD, "Why have you treated your servant so badly? Why have I not found favor in your sight, that you lay the burden of all this people on me? 12 Did I conceive all this people? Did I give birth to them, that you should say to me, 'Carry them in your bosom, as a nurse carries a sucking child,' to the land that you promised on oath to their ancestors? 13 Where am I to get meat to give to all this people? For they come weeping to me and say, 'Give us meat to eat!' 14 I am not able to carry all this people alone, for they are too heavy for me. 15 If this is the way you are going to treat me, put me to death at once—if I have found favor in your sight—and do not let me see my misery."

The Seventy Elders

16 So the LORD said to Moses, "Gather for me seventy of the elders of Israel, whom you know to be the elders of the people and officers over them; bring them to the tent of meeting, and have them take their place there with you. 17 I will come down and talk with you there; and I will take some of the spirit that is on you and put it on them; and they shall bear the burden of the people along with you so that you will not bear it all by yourself. 18 And say to the people: Consecrate yourselves for tomorrow, and you shall eat meat; for you have wailed in the hearing of the LORD,

saying, 'If only we had meat to eat! Surely it was better for us in Egypt.' Therefore the LORD will give you meat, and you shall eat. 19 You shall eat not only one day, or two days, or five days, or ten days, or twenty days, 20 but for a whole month—until it comes out of your nostrils and becomes loathsome to you—because you have rejected the LORD who is among you, and have wailed before him, saying, 'Why did we ever leave Egypt?' " 21 But Moses said, "The people I am with number six hundred thousand on foot; and you say, 'I will give them meat, that they may eat for a whole month'! 22 Are there enough flocks and herds to slaughter for them? Are there enough fish in the sea to catch for them?" 23 The LORD said to Moses, "Is the LORD's power limited?[t] Now you shall see whether my word will come true for you or not."

24 So Moses went out and told the people the words of the LORD; and he gathered seventy elders of the people, and placed them all around the tent. 25 Then the LORD came down in the cloud and spoke to him, and took some of the spirit that was on him and put it on the seventy elders; and when the spirit rested upon them, they prophesied. But they did not do so again.

26 Two men remained in the camp, one named El′dad, and the other named Mē′dad, and the spirit rested on them; they were among those registered, but they had not gone out to the tent, and so they prophesied in the camp. 27 And a young man ran and told Moses, "El′dad and Mē′-dad are prophesying in the camp." 28 And Joshua son of Nun, the assistant of Moses, one of his chosen men,[u] said, "My lord Moses, stop them!" 29 But Moses said to him, "Are you jealous for my sake? Would that all the LORD's people were prophets, and that the LORD would put his spirit on them!" 30 And Moses and the elders of Israel returned to the camp.

The Quails

31 Then a wind went out from the LORD, and it brought quails from the sea and let them fall beside the camp, about a day's journey on this side and a day's journey on the other side, all around the camp, about two cubits deep on the ground. 32 So the people worked all that day and night and all the next day, gathering the quails; the least anyone gathered was ten homers; and they spread them out for themselves all around the camp. 33 But while the meat was still between their teeth, before it was consumed, the anger of the LORD was kindled against the people, and the LORD struck the people with a very great plague. 34 So that place was called Kib′roth-hat·tā′a·vah,[v] because there

---

[s] That is Burning   [t] Heb LORD's hand too short?   [u] Or of Moses from his youth   [v] That is Graves of craving

they buried the people who had the craving. 35 From Kib'roth-hat•tā'a•vah the people journeyed to Ha•zē'roth.

Aaron and Miriam Jealous of Moses

While they were at Ha•zē'roth, Miriam and Aaron spoke against Moses because of the Cū'shīte woman whom he had married (for he had indeed married a Cū'shīte woman); 2 and they said, "Has the LORD spoken only through Moses? Has he not spoken through us also?" And the LORD heard it. 3 Now the man Moses was very humble,ʷ more so than anyone else on the face of the earth. 4 Suddenly the LORD said to Moses, Aaron, and Miriam, "Come out, you three, to the tent of meeting." So the three of them came out. 5 Then the LORD came down in a pillar of cloud, and stood at the entrance of the tent, and called Aaron and Miriam; and they both came forward. 6 And he said, "Hear my words:

When there are prophets among you,
I the LORD make myself known to them
    in visions;
I speak to them in dreams.
7 Not so with my servant Moses;
    he is entrusted with all my house.
8 With him I speak face to face—clearly, not in
    riddles;
and he beholds the form of the LORD.

Why then were you not afraid to speak against my servant Moses?" 9 And the anger of the LORD was kindled against them, and he departed.

10 When the cloud went away from over the tent, Miriam had become leprous,ˣ as white as snow. And Aaron turned towards Miriam and saw that she was leprous. 11 Then Aaron said to Moses, "Oh, my lord, do not punish usʸ for a sin that we have so foolishly committed. 12 Do not let her be like one stillborn, whose flesh is half consumed when it comes out of its mother's womb." 13 And Moses cried to the LORD, "O God, please heal her." 14 But the LORD said to Moses, "If her father had but spit in her face, would she not bear her shame for seven days? Let her be shut out of the camp for seven days, and after that she may be brought in again." 15 So Miriam was shut out of the camp for seven days; and the people did not set out on the march until Miriam had been brought in again. 16 After that the people set out from Ha•zē'roth, and camped in the wilderness of Par'an.

Spies Sent into Canaan
(Deut 1.19–33)

The LORD said to Moses, 2 "Send men to spy out the land of Cā'naan, which I am giving to the Israelites; from each of their ancestral tribes you shall send a man, every one a leader among them." 3 So

---

ʷ Or *devout*   ˣ A term for several skin diseases; precise meaning uncertain   ʸ Heb *do not lay sin upon us*

The Jealousy of Miriam and Aaron

Miriam. I don't know, Aaron. Sometimes Moses really gets to me. He seems to forget that we're all in this together.

Aaron. Yes, we are God's chosen people. All of us, not just Moses. And, of course, he married outside the fold. A Cushite, of all people.

Miriam. It really is a scandal. He is the self-appointed leader of our people, and yet he is not even married to an Israelite woman. That just doesn't sit well with our people.

Aaron. And he can be so aloof. I know he has a special connection with God, and I know it isn't easy being a leader. But he always seems to set himself apart, acting like he's better than the rest of us.

Miriam. What bothers me most is that Moses assumes that God speaks only through him.

Aaron. Yes, it's as if the rest of us have no role to play. What if I receive a revelation from God? Will Moses respond the same way we are expected to whenever he speaks? I doubt it!

Miriam. So do I. He pretends to be humble and to speak for God. I'm tired of it. We need to have a voice also.

Jealousy is like a dangerous cancer, growing until it affects your whole outlook on life (see what happens to Miriam in Num 12.10). What happens inside of you when you feel jealous? How does jealousy affect your attitudes toward other people?

▶ Numbers, chapter 12

Moses sent them from the wilderness of Par'an, according to the command of the LORD, all of them leading men among the Israelites. 4 These were their names: From the tribe of Reuben, Sham'mu·a son of Zac'cur; 5 from the tribe of Sim'e·on, Shā'phat son of Hō'rī; 6 from the tribe of Judah, Caleb son of Je·phūn'neh; 7 from the tribe of Is'sa·char, Ī'gal son of Joseph; 8 from the tribe of Ē'phra·im, Hō·shē'a son of Nun; 9 from the tribe of Benjamin, Pal'tī son of Rā'phū; 10 from the tribe of Zeb'ū·lun, Gad'di·el son of Sō'dī; 11 from the tribe of Joseph (that is, from the tribe of Ma·nas'seh), Gad'dī son of Sū'sī; 12 from the tribe of Dan, Am'mi·el son of Ge·mal'lī; 13 from the tribe of Ash'er, Seth'ur son of Michael; 14 from the tribe of Naph'ta·lī, Nah'bī son of Voph'sī; 15 from the tribe of Gad, Ge·ū'el son of Mā'chī. 16 These were the names of the men whom Moses sent to spy out the land. And Moses changed the name of Hō·shē'a son of Nun to Joshua.

17 Moses sent them to spy out the land of Cā'naan, and said to them, "Go up there into the Neg'eb, and go up into the hill country, 18 and see what the land is like, and whether the people who live in it are strong or weak, whether they are few or many, 19 and whether the land they live in is good or bad, and whether the towns that they live in are unwalled or fortified, 20 and whether the land is rich or poor, and whether there are trees in it or not. Be bold, and bring some of the fruit of the land." Now it was the season of the first ripe grapes.

21 So they went up and spied out the land from the wilderness of Zin to Rē'hob, near Lē'bō-hā'math. 22 They went up into the Neg'eb, and came to Hē'bron; and A·hī'man, Shē'shaī, and Tal'maī, the An'a·kītes, were there. (Hē'bron was built seven years before Zō'an in Egypt.) 23 And they came to the Wadi Esh'col, and cut down from there a branch with a single cluster of grapes, and they carried it on a pole between two of them. They also brought some pomegranates and figs. 24 That place was called the Wadi Esh'col,z because of the cluster that the Israelites cut down from there.

The Report of the Spies

25 At the end of forty days they returned from spying out the land. 26 And they came to Moses and Aaron and to all the congregation of the Israelites in the wilderness of Par'an, at Kā'desh; they brought back word to them and to all the congregation, and showed them the fruit of the land. 27 And they told him, "We came to the land to which you sent us; it flows with milk and honey, and this is its fruit. 28 Yet the people who live in the land are strong, and the towns are fortified and very large; and besides, we saw the descendants of Ā'nak there. 29 The A·mal'e·kītes live in the land of the Neg'eb; the Hit'tītes, the Jeb'ū·sītes, and the Am'o·rītes live in the hill country; and the Cā'naan·ītes live by the sea, and along the Jordan."

30 But Caleb quieted the people before Moses, and said, "Let us go up at once and occupy it, for we are well able to overcome it." 31 Then the men who had gone up with him said, "We are not able to go up against this people, for they are stronger than we." 32 So they brought to the Israelites an unfavorable report of the land that they had spied out, saying, "The land that we have gone through as spies is a land that devours its inhabitants; and all the people that we saw in it are of great size. 33 There we saw the Neph'i·lim (the An'a·kītes come from the Neph'i·lim); and to ourselves we seemed like grasshoppers, and so we seemed to them."

The People Rebel

Then all the congregation raised a loud cry, and the people wept that night. 2 And all the Israelites complained against Moses and Aaron; the whole congregation said to them, "Would that we had died in the land of Egypt! Or would that we had died in this wilderness! 3 Why is the LORD bringing us into this land to fall by the sword? Our wives and our little ones will become booty; would it not be better for us to go back to Egypt?" 4 So they said to one another, "Let us choose a captain, and go back to Egypt."

5 Then Moses and Aaron fell on their faces before all the assembly of the congregation of the Israelites. 6 And Joshua son of Nun and Caleb son of Je·phūn'neh, who were among those who had spied out the land, tore their clothes 7 and said to all the congregation of the Israelites, "The land that we went through as spies is an exceedingly good land. 8 If the LORD is pleased with us, he will bring us into this land and give it to us, a land that flows with milk and honey. 9 Only, do not rebel against the LORD; and do not fear the people of the land, for they are no more than bread for us; their protection is removed from them, and the LORD is with us; do not fear them." 10 But the whole congregation threatened to stone them.

z That is *Cluster*

Then the glory of the LORD appeared at the tent of meeting to all the Israelites. 11 And the LORD said to Moses, "How long will this people despise me? And how long will they refuse to believe in me, in spite of all the signs that I have done among them? 12 I will strike them with pestilence and disinherit them, and I will make of you a nation greater and mightier than they."

Moses Intercedes for the People

13 But Moses said to the LORD, "Then the Egyptians will hear of it, for in your might you brought up this people from among them, 14 and they will tell the inhabitants of this land. They have heard that you, O LORD, are in the midst of this people; for you, O LORD, are seen face to face, and your cloud stands over them and you go in front of them, in a pillar of cloud by day and in a pillar of fire by night. 15 Now if you kill this people all at one time, then the nations who have heard about you will say, 16 'It is because the LORD was not able to bring this people into the land he swore to give them that he has slaughtered them in the wilderness.' 17 And now, therefore, let the power of the LORD be great in the way that you promised when you spoke, saying,

18 'The LORD is slow to anger,
and abounding in steadfast love,
forgiving iniquity and transgression,
but by no means clearing the guilty,
visiting the iniquity of the parents
upon the children
to the third and the fourth generation.'

19 Forgive the iniquity of this people according to the greatness of your steadfast love, just as you have pardoned this people, from Egypt even until now."

20 Then the LORD said, "I do forgive, just as you have asked; 21 nevertheless—as I live, and as all the earth shall be filled with the glory of the LORD— 22 none of the people who have seen my glory and the signs that I did in Egypt and in the wilderness, and yet have tested me these ten times and have not obeyed my voice, 23 shall see the land that I swore to give to their ancestors; none of those who despised me shall see it. 24 But my servant Caleb, because he has a different spirit and has followed me wholeheartedly, I will bring into the land into which he went, and his descendants shall possess it. 25 Now, since the A·mal'e·kites and the Cā'naanītes live in the valleys, turn tomorrow and set out for the wilderness by the way to the Red Sea."*a*

An Attempted Invasion is Repulsed
(Deut 1.41–45)

26 And the LORD spoke to Moses and to Aaron, saying: 27 How long shall this wicked congregation complain against me? I have heard the complaints of the Israelites, which they complain against me. 28 Say to them, "As I live," says the LORD, "I will do to you the very things I heard you say: 29 your dead bodies shall fall in this very wilderness; and of all your number, included in the census, from twenty years old and upward, who have complained against me, 30 not one of you shall come into the land in which I swore to settle you, except Caleb son of Je·phūn'neh and Joshua son of Nun. 31 But your little ones, who you said would become booty, I will bring in, and they shall know the land that you have despised. 32 But as for you, your dead bodies shall fall in this wilderness. 33 And your children shall be shepherds in the wilderness for forty years, and shall suffer for your faithlessness, until the last of your dead bodies lies in the wilderness. 34 According to the number of the days in which you spied out the land, forty days, for every day a year, you shall bear your iniquity, forty years, and you shall know my displeasure." 35 I the LORD have spoken; surely I will do thus to all this wicked congregation gathered together against me: in this wilderness they shall come to a full end, and there they shall die.

36 And the men whom Moses sent to spy out the land, who returned and made all the congregation complain against him by bringing a bad report about the land— 37 the men who brought an unfavorable report about the land died by a plague before the LORD. 38 But Joshua son of Nun and Caleb son of Je·phūn'neh alone remained alive, of those men who went to spy out the land.

39 When Moses told these words to all the Israelites, the people mourned greatly. 40 They rose early in the morning and went up to the heights of the hill country, saying, "Here we are. We will go up to the place that the LORD has promised, for we have sinned." 41 But Moses said, "Why do you continue to transgress the command of the LORD? That will not succeed. 42 Do not go up, for the LORD is not with you; do not let yourselves be struck down before your enemies. 43 For the A·mal'e·kites and the Cā'naan·ītes will confront you there, and you shall fall by the sword; because you have turned back from following the LORD, the LORD will not be with you." 44 But they presumed to go up to the heights of the hill country, even though the ark of the covenant of the LORD, and Moses, had not left the camp. 45 Then the A·mal'e·kites and the

a Or *Sea of Reeds*

Cā′naan•ītes who lived in that hill country came down and defeated them, pursuing them as far as Hor′mah.

Various Offerings

The LORD spoke to Moses, saying: 2 Speak to the Israelites and say to them: When you come into the land you are to inhabit, which I am giving you, 3 and you make an offering by fire to the LORD from the herd or from the flock—whether a burnt offering or a sacrifice, to fulfill a vow or as a free-will offering or at your appointed festivals—to make a pleasing odor for the LORD, 4 then whoever presents such an offering to the LORD shall present also a grain offering, one-tenth of an ephah of choice flour, mixed with one-fourth of a hin of oil. 5 Moreover, you shall offer one-fourth of a hin of wine as a drink offering with the burnt offering or the sacrifice, for each lamb. 6 For a ram, you shall offer a grain offering, two-tenths of an ephah of choice flour mixed with one-third of a hin of oil; 7 and as a drink offering you shall offer one-third of a hin of wine, a pleasing odor to the LORD. 8 When you offer a bull as a burnt offering or a sacrifice, to fulfill a vow or as an offering of well-being to the LORD, 9 then you shall present with the bull a grain offering, three-tenths of an ephah of choice flour, mixed with half a hin of oil, 10 and you shall present as a drink offering half a hin of wine, as an offering by fire, a pleasing odor to the LORD.

11 Thus it shall be done for each ox or ram, or for each of the male lambs or the kids. 12 According to the number that you offer, so you shall do with each and every one. 13 Every native Israelite shall do these things in this way, in presenting an offering by fire, a pleasing odor to the LORD. 14 An alien who lives with you, or who takes up permanent residence among you, and wishes to offer an offering by fire, a pleasing odor to the LORD, shall do as you do. 15 As for the assembly, there shall be for both you and the resident alien a single statute, a perpetual statute throughout your generations; you and the alien shall be alike before the LORD. 16 You and the alien who resides with you shall have the same law and the same ordinance.

17 The LORD spoke to Moses, saying: 18 Speak to the Israelites and say to them: After you come into the land to which I am bringing you, 19 whenever you eat of the bread of the land, you shall present a donation to the LORD. 20 From your first batch of dough you shall present a loaf as a donation; you shall present it just as you present a donation from the threshing floor. 21 Throughout your generations you shall give to the LORD a donation from the first of your batch of dough.

22 But if you unintentionally fail to observe all these commandments that the LORD has spoken to Moses— 23 everything that the LORD has commanded you by Moses, from the day the LORD gave commandment and thereafter, throughout your generations— 24 then if it was done unintentionally without the knowledge of the congregation, the whole congregation shall offer one young bull for a burnt offering, a pleasing odor to the LORD, together with its grain offering and its drink offering, according to the ordinance, and one male goat for a sin offering. 25 The priest shall make atonement for all the congregation of the Israelites, and they shall be forgiven; it was unintentional, and they have brought their offering, an offering by fire to the LORD, and their sin offering before the LORD, for their error. 26 All the congregation of the Israelites shall be forgiven, as well as the aliens residing among them, because the whole people was involved in the error.

27 An individual who sins unintentionally shall present a female goat a year old for a sin offering. 28 And the priest shall make atonement before the LORD for the one who commits an error, when it is unintentional, to make atonement for the person, who then shall be forgiven. 29 For both the native among the Israelites and the alien residing among them—you shall have the same law for anyone who acts in error. 30 But whoever acts high-handedly, whether a native or an alien, affronts the LORD, and shall be cut off from among the people. 31 Because of having despised the word of the LORD and broken his commandment, such a person shall be utterly cut off and bear the guilt.

Penalty for Violating the Sabbath
(Ex 31.12–17)

32 When the Israelites were in the wilderness, they found a man gathering sticks on the sabbath day. 33 Those who found him gathering sticks brought him to Moses, Aaron, and to the whole congregation. 34 They put him in custody, because it was not clear what should be done to him. 35 Then the LORD said to Moses, "The man shall be put to death; all the congregation shall stone him outside the camp." 36 The whole congregation brought him outside the camp and stoned him to death, just as the LORD had commanded Moses.

Fringes on Garments

37 The LORD said to Moses: 38 Speak to the Israelites, and tell them to make fringes on the corners of their garments throughout their generations and to put a blue cord on the fringe at each corner. 39 You have the fringe so that, when you see it, you will remember all the commandments of the LORD

and do them, and not follow the lust of your own heart and your own eyes. 40 So you shall remember and do all my commandments, and you shall be holy to your God. 41 I am the LORD your God, who brought you out of the land of Egypt, to be your God: I am the LORD your God.

Revolt of Korah, Dathan, and Abiram

Now Kōʹrah son of Izʹhar son of Kōʹhath son of Levi, along with Dāʹthan and Aˑbiʹram sons of Eˑliʹab, and On son of Pēʹleth—descendants of Reuben—took 2 two hundred fifty Israelite men, leaders of the congregation, chosen from the assembly, well-known men,[b] and they confronted Moses. 3 They assembled against Moses and against Aaron, and said to them, "You have gone too far! All the congregation are holy, every one of them, and the LORD is among them. So why then do you exalt yourselves above the assembly of the LORD?" 4 When Moses heard it, he fell on his face. 5 Then he said to Kōʹrah and all his company, "In the morning the LORD will make known who is his, and who is holy, and who will be allowed to approach him; the one whom he will choose he will allow to approach him. 6 Do this: take censers, Kōʹrah and all your[c] company, 7 and tomorrow put fire in them, and lay incense on them before the LORD; and the man whom the LORD chooses shall be the holy one. You Lēʹvites have gone too far!" 8 Then Moses said to Kōʹrah, "Hear now, you Lēʹvites! 9 Is it too little for you that the God of Israel has separated you from the congregation of Israel, to allow you to approach him in order to perform the duties of the LORD's tabernacle, and to stand before the congregation and serve them? 10 He has allowed you to approach him, and all your brother Lēʹvites with you; yet you seek the priesthood as well! 11 Therefore you and all your company have gathered together against the LORD. What is Aaron that you rail against him?"

12 Moses sent for Dāʹthan and Aˑbiʹram sons of Eˑliʹab; but they said, "We will not come! 13 Is it too little that you have brought us up out of a land flowing with milk and honey to kill us in the wilderness, that you must also lord it over us? 14 It is clear you have not brought us into a land flowing with milk and honey, or given us an inheritance of fields and vineyards. Would you put out the eyes of these men? We will not come!"

15 Moses was very angry and said to the LORD, "Pay no attention to their offering. I have not taken one donkey from them, and I have not harmed any one of them." 16 And Moses said to Kōʹrah, "As for you and all your company, be present tomorrow before the LORD, you and they and Aaron; 17 and let each one of you take his cen-

ser, and put incense on it, and each one of you present his censer before the LORD, two hundred fifty censers; you also, and Aaron, each his censer." 18 So each man took his censer, and they put fire in the censers and laid incense on them, and they stood at the entrance of the tent of meeting with Moses and Aaron. 19 Then Kōʹrah assembled the whole congregation against them at the entrance of the tent of meeting. And the glory of the LORD appeared to the whole congregation.

20 Then the LORD spoke to Moses and to Aaron, saying: 21 Separate yourselves from this congregation, so that I may consume them in a moment. 22 They fell on their faces, and said, "O God, the God of the spirits of all flesh, shall one person sin and you become angry with the whole congregation?"

23 And the LORD spoke to Moses, saying: 24 Say to the congregation: Get away from the dwellings of Kōʹrah, Dāʹthan, and Aˑbiʹram. 25 So Moses got up and went to Dāʹthan and Aˑbiʹram; the elders of Israel followed him. 26 He said to the congregation, "Turn away from the tents of these wicked men, and touch nothing of theirs, or you will be swept away for all their sins." 27 So they got away from the dwellings of Kōʹrah, Dāʹthan, and Aˑbiʹram; and Dāʹthan and Aˑbiʹram came out and stood at the entrance of their tents, together with their wives, their children, and their little ones. 28 And Moses said, "This is how you shall know that the LORD has sent me to do all these works; it has not been of my own accord: 29 If these people die a natural death, or if a natural fate comes on them, then the LORD has not sent me. 30 But if the LORD creates something new, and the ground opens its mouth and swallows them up, with all that belongs to them, and they go down alive into Shēʹōl, then you shall know that these men have despised the LORD."

31 As soon as he finished speaking all these words, the ground under them was split apart. 32 The earth opened its mouth and swallowed them up, along with their households—everyone who belonged to Kōʹrah and all their goods. 33 So they with all that belonged to them went down alive into Shēʹōl; the earth closed over them, and they perished from the midst of the assembly. 34 All Israel around them fled at their outcry, for they said, "The earth will swallow us too!" 35 And fire came out from the LORD and consumed the two hundred fifty men offering the incense.

36[d] Then the LORD spoke to Moses, saying: 37 Tell Elˑēˑaʹzar son of Aaron the priest to take the

---

b Cn: Heb *and they confronted Moses, and two hundred fifty men . . . well-known men*   *c* Heb *his*   *d* Ch 17.1 in Heb

censers out of the blaze; then scatter the fire far and wide. ³⁸ For the censers of these sinners have become holy at the cost of their lives. Make them into hammered plates as a covering for the altar, for they presented them before the LORD and they became holy. Thus they shall be a sign to the Israelites. ³⁹ So El·e·ā′zar the priest took the bronze censers that had been presented by those who were burned; and they were hammered out as a covering for the altar— ⁴⁰ a reminder to the Israelites that no outsider, who is not of the descendants of Aaron, shall approach to offer incense before the LORD, so as not to become like Kō′rah and his company—just as the LORD had said to him through Moses.

41 On the next day, however, the whole congregation of the Israelites rebelled against Moses and against Aaron, saying, "You have killed the people of the LORD." ⁴² And when the congregation had assembled against them, Moses and Aaron turned toward the tent of meeting; the cloud had covered it and the glory of the LORD appeared. ⁴³ Then Moses and Aaron came to the front of the tent of meeting, ⁴⁴ and the LORD spoke to Moses, saying, ⁴⁵ "Get away from this congregation, so that I may consume them in a moment." And they fell on their faces. ⁴⁶ Moses said to Aaron, "Take your censer, put fire on it from the altar and lay incense on it, and carry it quickly to the congregation and make atonement for them. For wrath has gone out from the LORD; the plague has begun." ⁴⁷ So Aaron took it as Moses had ordered, and ran into the middle of the assembly, where the plague had already begun among the people. He put on the incense, and made atonement for the people. ⁴⁸ He stood between the dead and the living; and the plague was stopped. ⁴⁹ Those who died by the plague were fourteen thousand seven hundred, besides those who died in the affair of Kō′rah. ⁵⁰ When the plague was stopped, Aaron returned to Moses at the entrance of the tent of meeting.

The Budding of Aaron's Rod

^e The LORD spoke to Moses, saying: ² Speak to the Israelites, and get twelve staffs from them, one for each ancestral house, from all the leaders of their ancestral houses. Write each man's name on his staff, ³ and write Aaron's name on the staff of Levi. For there shall be one staff for the head of each ancestral house. ⁴ Place them in the tent of meeting before the covenant,^f where I meet with you. ⁵ And the staff of the man whom I choose shall sprout; thus I will put a stop to the complaints of the Israelites that they continually make against

you. ⁶ Moses spoke to the Israelites; and all their leaders gave him staffs, one for each leader, according to their ancestral houses, twelve staffs; and the staff of Aaron was among theirs. ⁷ So Moses placed the staffs before the LORD in the tent of the covenant.^f

8 When Moses went into the tent of the covenant^f on the next day, the staff of Aaron for the house of Levi had sprouted. It put forth buds, produced blossoms, and bore ripe almonds. ⁹ Then Moses brought out all the staffs from before the LORD to all the Israelites; and they looked, and each man took his staff. ¹⁰ And the LORD said to Moses, "Put back the staff of Aaron before the covenant,^f to be kept as a warning to rebels, so that you may make an end of their complaints against me, or else they will die." ¹¹ Moses did so; just as the LORD commanded him, so he did.

12 The Israelites said to Moses, "We are perishing; we are lost, all of us are lost! ¹³ Everyone who approaches the tabernacle of the LORD will die. Are we all to perish?"

Responsibility of Priests and Levites

The LORD said to Aaron: You and your sons and your ancestral house with you shall bear responsibility for offenses connected with the sanctuary, while you and your sons alone shall bear responsibility for offenses connected with the priesthood. ² So bring with you also your brothers of the tribe of Levi, your ancestral tribe, in order that they may be joined to you, and serve you while you and your sons with you are in front of the tent of the covenant.^f ³ They shall perform duties for you and for the whole tent. But they must not approach either the utensils of the sanctuary or the altar, otherwise both they and you will die. ⁴ They are attached to you in order to perform the duties of the tent of meeting, for all the service of the tent; no outsider shall approach you. ⁵ You yourselves shall perform the duties of the sanctuary and the duties of the altar, so that wrath may never again come upon the Israelites. ⁶ It is I who now take your brother Lē′vites from among the Israelites; they are now yours as a gift, dedicated to the LORD, to perform the service of the tent of meeting. ⁷ But you and your sons with you shall diligently perform your priestly duties in all that concerns the altar and the area behind the curtain. I give your priesthood as a gift; ^g any outsider who approaches shall be put to death.

---

^e Ch 17.16 in Heb   ^f Or *treaty*, or *testimony*; Heb *eduth*
^g Heb *as a service of gift*

The Priests' Portion

8 The LORD spoke to Aaron: I have given you charge of the offerings made to me, all the holy gifts of the Israelites; I have given them to you and your sons as a priestly portion due you in perpetuity. 9 This shall be yours from the most holy things, reserved from the fire: every offering of theirs that they render to me as a most holy thing, whether grain offering, sin offering, or guilt offering, shall belong to you and your sons. 10 As a most holy thing you shall eat it; every male may eat it; it shall be holy to you. 11 This also is yours: I have given to you, together with your sons and daughters, as a perpetual due, whatever is set aside from the gifts of all the elevation offerings of the Israelites; everyone who is clean in your house may eat them. 12 All the best of the oil and all the best of the wine and of the grain, the choice produce that they give to the LORD, I have given to you. 13 The first fruits of all that is in their land, which they bring to the LORD, shall be yours; everyone who is clean in your house may eat of it. 14 Every devoted thing in Israel shall be yours. 15 The first issue of the womb of all creatures, human and animal, which is offered to the LORD, shall be yours; but the firstborn of human beings you shall redeem, and the firstborn of unclean animals you shall redeem. 16 Their redemption price, reckoned from one month of age, you shall fix at five shekels of silver, according to the shekel of the sanctuary (that is, twenty gerahs). 17 But the firstborn of a cow, or the firstborn of a sheep, or the firstborn of a goat, you shall not redeem; they are holy. You shall dash their blood on the altar, and shall turn their fat into smoke as an offering by fire for a pleasing odor to the LORD; 18 but their flesh shall be yours, just as the breast that is elevated and as the right thigh are yours. 19 All the holy offerings that the Israelites present to the LORD I have given to you, together with your sons and daughters, as a perpetual due; it is a covenant of salt forever before the LORD for you and your descendants as well. 20 Then the LORD said to Aaron: You shall have no allotment in their land, nor shall you have any share among them; I am your share and your possession among the Israelites.

21 To the Lēʹvītes I have given every tithe in Israel for a possession in return for the service that they perform, the service in the tent of meeting. 22 From now on the Israelites shall no longer approach the tent of meeting, or else they will incur guilt and die. 23 But the Lēʹvītes shall perform the service of the tent of meeting, and they shall bear responsibility for their own offenses; it shall be a perpetual statute throughout your generations. But among the Israelites they shall have no allotment, 24 because I have given to the Lēʹvītes as their portion the tithe of the Israelites, which they set apart as an offering to the LORD. Therefore I have said of them that they shall have no allotment among the Israelites.

25 Then the LORD spoke to Moses, saying: 26 You shall speak to the Lēʹvītes, saying: When you receive from the Israelites the tithe that I have given you from them for your portion, you shall set apart an offering from it to the LORD, a tithe of the tithe. 27 It shall be reckoned to you as your gift, the same as the grain of the threshing floor and the fullness of the wine press. 28 Thus you also shall set apart an offering to the LORD from all the tithes that you receive from the Israelites; and from them you shall give the LORD's offering to the priest Aaron. 29 Out of all the gifts to you, you shall set apart every offering due to the LORD; the best of all of them is the part to be consecrated. 30 Say also to them: When you have set apart the best of it, then the rest shall be reckoned to the Lēʹvītes as produce of the threshing floor, and as produce of the wine press. 31 You may eat it in any place, you and your households; for it is your payment for your service in the tent of meeting. 32 You shall incur no guilt by reason of it, when you have offered the best of it. But you shall not profane the holy gifts of the Israelites, on pain of death.

Ceremony of the Red Heifer

The LORD spoke to Moses and Aaron, saying: 2 This is a statute of the law that the LORD has commanded: Tell the Israelites to bring you a red heifer without defect, in which there is no blemish and on which no yoke has been laid. 3 You shall give it to the priest El·ē·aʹzar, and it shall be taken outside the camp and slaughtered in his presence. 4 The priest El·ē·aʹzar shall take some of its blood with his finger and sprinkle it seven times towards the front of the tent of meeting. 5 Then the heifer shall be burned in his sight; its skin, its flesh, and its blood, with its dung, shall be burned. 6 The priest shall take cedarwood, hyssop, and crimson material, and throw them into the fire in which the heifer is burning. 7 Then the priest shall wash his clothes and bathe his body in water, and afterwards he may come into the camp; but the priest shall remain unclean until evening. 8 The one who burns the heifer[h] shall wash his clothes in water

---

h Heb it

NUM

NUM

and bathe his body in water; he shall remain unclean until evening. 9 Then someone who is clean shall gather up the ashes of the heifer, and deposit them outside the camp in a clean place; and they shall be kept for the congregation of the Israelites for the water for cleansing. It is a purification offering. 10 The one who gathers the ashes of the heifer shall wash his clothes and be unclean until evening.

This shall be a perpetual statute for the Israelites and for the alien residing among them. 11 Those who touch the dead body of any human being shall be unclean seven days. 12 They shall purify themselves with the water on the third day and on the seventh day, and so be clean; but if they do not purify themselves on the third day and on the seventh day, they will not become clean. 13 All who touch a corpse, the body of a human being who has died, and do not purify themselves, defile the tabernacle of the LORD; such persons shall be cut off from Israel. Since water for cleansing was not dashed on them, they remain unclean; their uncleanness is still on them.

14 This is the law when someone dies in a tent: everyone who comes into the tent, and everyone who is in the tent, shall be unclean seven days. 15 And every open vessel with no cover fastened on it is unclean. 16 Whoever in the open field touches one who has been killed by a sword, or who has died naturally,[i] or a human bone, or a grave, shall be unclean seven days. 17 For the unclean they shall take some ashes of the burnt purification offering, and running water shall be added in a vessel; 18 then a clean person shall take hyssop, dip it in the water, and sprinkle it on the tent, on all the furnishings, on the persons who were there, and on whoever touched the bone, the slain, the corpse, or the grave. 19 The clean person shall sprinkle the unclean ones on the third day and on the seventh day, thus purifying them on the seventh day. Then they shall wash their clothes and bathe themselves in water, and at evening they shall be clean. 20 Any who are unclean but do not purify themselves, those persons shall be cut off from the assembly, for they have defiled the sanctuary of the LORD. Since the water for cleansing has not been dashed on them, they are unclean.

21 It shall be a perpetual statute for them. The one who sprinkles the water for cleansing shall wash his clothes, and whoever touches the water for cleansing shall be unclean until evening. 22 Whatever the unclean person touches shall be unclean, and anyone who touches it shall be unclean until evening.

The Waters of Meribah
(Ex 17.1–7)

The Israelites, the whole congregation, came into the wilderness of Zin in the first month, and the people stayed in Ka′desh. Miriam died there, and was buried there.

2 Now there was no water for the congregation; so they gathered together against Moses and against Aaron. 3 The people quarreled with Moses and said, "Would that we had died when our kindred died before the LORD! 4 Why have you brought the assembly of the LORD into this wilderness for us and our livestock to die here? 5 Why have you brought us up out of Egypt, to bring us to this wretched place? It is no place for grain, or figs, or vines, or pomegranates; and there is no water to drink." 6 Then Moses and Aaron went away from the assembly to the entrance of the tent of meeting; they fell on their faces, and the glory of the LORD appeared to them. 7 The LORD spoke to Moses, saying: 8 Take the staff, and assemble the congregation, you and your brother Aaron, and command the rock before their eyes to yield its water. Thus you shall bring water out of the rock for them; thus you shall provide drink for the congregation and their livestock.

9 So Moses took the staff from before the LORD, as he had commanded him. 10 Moses and Aaron gathered the assembly together before the rock, and he said to them, "Listen, you rebels, shall we bring water for you out of this rock?" 11 Then Moses lifted up his hand and struck the rock twice with his staff; water came out abundantly, and the congregation and their livestock drank. 12 But the LORD said to Moses and Aaron, "Because you did not trust in me, to show my holiness before the eyes of the Israelites, therefore you shall not bring this assembly into the land that I have given them." 13 These are the waters of Mer′i•bah,[j] where the people of Israel quarreled with the LORD, and by which he showed his holiness.

Passage through Edom Refused

14 Moses sent messengers from Ka′desh to the king of E′dom, "Thus says your brother Israel: You know all the adversity that has befallen us: 15 how our ancestors went down to Egypt, and we lived in Egypt a long time; and the Egyptians oppressed us and our ancestors; 16 and when we cried to the LORD, he heard our voice, and sent an angel and brought us out of Egypt; and here we are in Ka′desh, a town on the edge of your territory. 17 Now let us pass through your land. We will not pass through field or vineyard, or drink water from any

---

i Heb lacks *naturally*   j That is *Quarrel*

well; we will go along the King's Highway, not turning aside to the right hand or to the left until we have passed through your territory."

18 But Ē′dom said to him, "You shall not pass through, or we will come out with the sword against you." 19 The Israelites said to him, "We will stay on the highway; and if we drink of your water, we and our livestock, then we will pay for it. It is only a small matter; just let us pass through on foot." 20 But he said, "You shall not pass through." And Ē′dom came out against them with a large force, heavily armed. 21 Thus Ē′dom refused to give Israel passage through their territory; so Israel turned away from them.

The Death of Aaron

22 They set out from Kā′desh, and the Israelites, the whole congregation, came to Mount Hor. 23 Then the LORD said to Moses and Aaron at Mount Hor, on the border of the land of Ē′dom, 24 "Let Aaron be gathered to his people. For he shall not enter the land that I have given to the Israelites, because you rebelled against my command at the waters of Mer′i·bah. 25 Take Aaron and his son El·e·ā′zar, and bring them up Mount Hor; 26 strip Aaron of his vestments, and put them on his son El·e·ā′zar. But Aaron shall be gathered to his people,[k] and shall die there." 27 Moses did as the LORD had commanded; they went up Mount Hor in the sight of the whole congregation. 28 Moses stripped Aaron of his vestments, and put them on his son El·e·ā′zar; and Aaron died there on the top of the mountain. Moses and El·e·ā′zar came down from the mountain. 29 When all the congregation saw that Aaron had died, all the house of Israel mourned for Aaron thirty days.

The Bronze Serpent

When the Cā′naan·ite, the king of Ar′ad, who lived in the Neg′eb, heard that Israel was coming by the way of Ath′a·rim, he fought against Israel and took some of them captive. 2 Then Israel made a vow to the LORD and said, "If you will indeed give this people into our hands, then we will utterly destroy their towns." 3 The LORD listened to the voice of Israel, and handed over the Cā′naan·ites; and they utterly destroyed them and their towns; so the place was called Hor′mah.[l]

4 From Mount Hor they set out by the way to the Red Sea,[m] to go around the land of Ē′dom; but the people became impatient on the way. 5 The people spoke against God and against Moses, "Why have you brought us up out of Egypt to die in the wilderness? For there is no food and no water, and we detest this miserable food." 6 Then the LORD sent poisonous[n] serpents among the people,

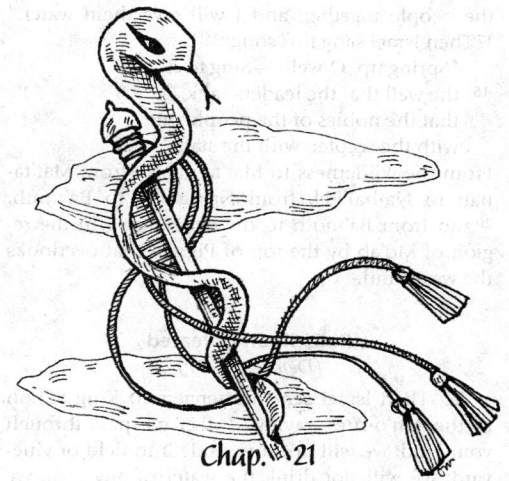

Chap. 21

and they bit the people, so that many Israelites died. 7 The people came to Moses and said, "We have sinned by speaking against the LORD and against you; pray to the LORD to take away the serpents from us." So Moses prayed for the people. 8 And the LORD said to Moses, "Make a poisonous[o] serpent, and set it on a pole; and everyone who is bitten shall look at it and live." 9 So Moses made a serpent of bronze, and put it upon a pole; and whenever a serpent bit someone, that person would look at the serpent of bronze and live.

The Journey to Moab

10 The Israelites set out, and camped in Ō′both. 11 They set out from Ō′both, and camped at I′ye-ab′a·rim, in the wilderness bordering Mō′ab toward the sunrise. 12 From there they set out, and camped in the Wadi Zē′red. 13 From there they set out, and camped on the other side of the Ar′non, in[p] the wilderness that extends from the boundary of the Am′o·rītes; for the Ar′non is the boundary of Mō′ab, between Mō′ab and the Am′o·rītes. 14 Wherefore it is said in the Book of the Wars of the LORD,

"Wa′heb in Sū′phah and the wadis.
The Ar′non 15 and the slopes of the
        wadis
that extend to the seat of Ar,
and lie along the border of Mō′ab."[q]

16 From there they continued to Bē′er;[r] that is the well of which the LORD said to Moses, "Gather

---

[k] Heb lacks *to his people*   [l] Heb *Destruction*   [m] Or *Sea of Reeds*   [n] Or *fiery;* Heb *seraphim*   [o] Or *fiery;* Heb *seraph*   [p] Gk: Heb *which is in*   [q] Meaning of Heb uncertain   [r] That is *Well*

the people together, and I will give them water."
[17] Then Israel sang this song:

"Spring up, O well! — Sing to it! —
[18] the well that the leaders sank,
  that the nobles of the people dug,
  with the scepter, with the staff."

From the wilderness to Mat′ta·nah, [19] from Mat′ta-nah to Na·hal′i·el, from Na·hal′i·el to Bā′moth, [20] and from Bā′moth to the valley lying in the region of Mō′ab by the top of Pis′gah that overlooks the wasteland.[s]

King Sihon Defeated
(Deut 2.26–37)

21 Then Israel sent messengers to King Sī′hon of the Am′o·rites, saying, [22] "Let me pass through your land; we will not turn aside into field or vineyard; we will not drink the water of any well; we will go by the King's Highway until we have passed through your territory." [23] But Sī′hon would not allow Israel to pass through his territory. Sī′hon gathered all his people together, and went out against Israel to the wilderness; he came to Jā′haz, and fought against Israel. [24] Israel put him to the sword, and took possession of his land from the Ar′non to the Jab′bok, as far as to the Am′mon·ites; for the boundary of the Am′mon·ites was strong. [25] Israel took all these towns, and Israel settled in all the towns of the Am′o·rites, in Hesh′-bon, and in all its villages. [26] For Hesh′bon was the city of King Sī′hon of the Am′o·rites, who had fought against the former king of Mō′ab and captured all his land as far as the Ar′non. [27] Therefore the ballad singers say,

"Come to Hesh′bon, let it be built;
  let the city of Sī′hon be established.
[28] For fire came out from Hesh′bon,
  flame from the city of Sī′hon.
 It devoured Ar of Mō′ab,
  and swallowed up[t] the heights of the
    Ar′non.
[29] Woe to you, O Mō′ab!
  You are undone, O people of
    Chē′mosh!
 He has made his sons fugitives,
  and his daughters captives,
   to an Am′o·rite king, Sī′hon.
[30] So their posterity perished
   from Hesh′bon[u] to Dī′bon,
  and we laid waste until fire spread to
    Med′e·ba."[v]

31 Thus Israel settled in the land of the Am′o-rites. [32] Moses sent to spy out Jā′zer; and they captured its villages, and dispossessed the Am′o·rites who were there.

King Og Defeated
(Deut 3.1–22)

33 Then they turned and went up the road to Bā′shan; and King Og of Bā′shan came out against them, he and all his people, to battle at Ed′re·ī. [34] But the LORD said to Moses, "Do not be afraid of him; for I have given him into your hand, with all his people, and all his land. You shall do to him as you did to King Sī′hon of the Am′o·rites, who ruled in Hesh′bon." [35] So they killed him, his sons, and all his people, until there was no survivor left; and they took possession of his land.

Balak Summons Balaam to Curse Israel

22 The Israelites set out, and camped in the plains of Mō′ab across the Jordan from Jericho. [2] Now Bā′-lak son of Zip′por saw all that Israel had done to the Am′o·rites. [3] Mō′ab was in great dread of the people, because they were so numerous; Mō′ab was overcome with fear of the people of Israel. [4] And Mō′ab said to the elders of Mid′i·an, "This horde will now lick up all that is around us, as an ox licks up the grass of the field." Now Bā′lak son of Zip′por was king of Mō′ab at that time. [5] He sent messengers to Bā′laam son of Bē′or at Pē′-thor, which is on the Euphrates, in the land of Ā′maw,[w] to summon him, saying, "A people has come out of Egypt; they have spread over the face of the earth, and they have settled next to me. [6] Come now, curse this people for me, since they are stronger than I; perhaps I shall be able to defeat them and drive them from the land; for I know that whomever you bless is blessed, and whomever you curse is cursed."

7 So the elders of Mō′ab and the elders of Mid′i·an departed with the fees for divination in their hand; and they came to Bā′laam, and gave him Bā′lak's message. [8] He said to them, "Stay here tonight, and I will bring back word to you, just as the LORD speaks to me"; so the officials of Mō′ab stayed with Bā′laam. [9] God came to Bā′-laam and said, "Who are these men with you?" [10] Bā′laam said to God, "King Bā′lak son of Zip′-por of Mō′ab, has sent me this message: [11] 'A people has come out of Egypt and has spread over the face of the earth; now come, curse them for me; perhaps I shall be able to fight against them and drive them out.' " [12] God said to Bā′laam, "You shall not go with them; you shall not curse the people, for they are blessed." [13] So Bā′laam rose in the morning, and said to the officials of Bā′lak, "Go to your own land, for the LORD has refused to

---

[s] Or *Jeshimon*   [t] Gk: Heb *and the lords of*   [u] Gk: Heb *we have shot at them; Heshbon has perished*   [v] Compare Sam Gk: Meaning of MT uncertain   [w] Or *land of his kinsfolk*

let me go with you." [14] So the officials of Mō'ab rose and went to Bā'lak, and said, "Bā'laam refuses to come with us."

15 Once again Bā'lak sent officials, more numerous and more distinguished than these. [16] They came to Bā'laam and said to him, "Thus says Bā'lak son of Zip'por: 'Do not let anything hinder you from coming to me; [17] for I will surely do you great honor, and whatever you say to me I will do; come, curse this people for me.' " [18] But Bā'laam replied to the servants of Bā'lak, "Although Bā'lak were to give me his house full of silver and gold, I could not go beyond the command of the LORD my God, to do less or more. [19] You remain here, as the others did, so that I may learn what more the LORD may say to me." [20] That night God came to Bā'laam and said to him, "If the men have come to summon you, get up and go with them; but do only what I tell you to do." [21] So Bā'laam got up in the morning, saddled his donkey, and went with the officials of Mō'ab.

Balaam, the Donkey, and the Angel

22 God's anger was kindled because he was going, and the angel of the LORD took his stand in the road as his adversary. Now he was riding on the donkey, and his two servants were with him. [23] The donkey saw the angel of the LORD standing in the road, with a drawn sword in his hand; so the donkey turned off the road, and went into the field; and Bā'laam struck the donkey, to turn it back onto the road. [24] Then the angel of the LORD stood in a narrow path between the vineyards, with a wall on either side. [25] When the donkey saw the angel of the LORD, it scraped against the wall, and scraped Bā'laam's foot against the wall; so he struck it again. [26] Then the angel of the LORD went ahead, and stood in a narrow place, where there was no way to turn either to the right or to the left. [27] When the donkey saw the angel of the LORD, it lay down under Bā'laam; and Bā'laam's anger was kindled, and he struck the donkey with his staff. [28] Then the LORD opened the mouth of the donkey, and it said to Bā'laam, "What have I done to you, that you have struck me these three times?" [29] Bā'laam said to the donkey, "Because you have made a fool of me! I wish I had a sword in my hand! I would kill you right now!" [30] But the donkey said to Bā'laam, "Am I not your donkey, which you have ridden all your life to this day? Have I been in the habit of treating you this way?" And he said, "No."

31 Then the LORD opened the eyes of Bā'laam, and he saw the angel of the LORD standing in the road, with his drawn sword in his hand; and he bowed down, falling on his face. [32] The angel of

PRAY IT

The Talking Donkey

Balaam is an interesting biblical character. He is not an Israelite and seems to be a sort of prophet for hire. Balak, the king of Moab, hires him to prophesy against Israel. But Balaam, hearing a message from God through his donkey, instead of cursing the Israelites, blesses them four times. Even though the Israelites were unfaithful, God continues to be with them, to bless them.

Balaam is a sign of the universal character of God's call, and the donkey is a symbol of the poor and oppressed. The complaining and whining donkey represents those who usually are not heard but are given a voice through the prophets.

This story gives us two insights into prayer. First, if God can use a donkey to talk to Balaam, God can use anything to talk to us. God speaks to us in many ways—through our experiences, the Scriptures, poetry and music, our relationship with nature, and more. Are we paying attention? Second, God wants us to hear the often unheard voice of the poor and oppressed. Do you hear God's voice expressed through them?

▶ **Num 22.22–35**

the LORD said to him, "Why have you struck your donkey these three times? I have come out as an adversary, because your way is perverse[x] before me. [33] The donkey saw me, and turned away from me these three times. If it had not turned away from me, surely just now I would have killed you and let it live." [34] Then Bā'laam said to the angel of the LORD, "I have sinned, for I did not know that you were standing in the road to oppose me. Now therefore, if it is displeasing to you, I will return home." [35] The angel of the LORD said to Bā'laam, "Go with the men; but speak only what I tell you to speak." So Bā'laam went on with the officials of Bā'lak.

36 When Bā'lak heard that Bā'laam had come, he went out to meet him at Ir-mō'ab, on the boundary formed by the Ar'non, at the farthest point of the boundary. [37] Bā'lak said to Bā'laam,

---

[x] Meaning of Heb uncertain

"Did I not send to summon you? Why did you not come to me? Am I not able to honor you?" 38 Bā′laam said to Bā′lak, "I have come to you now, but do I have power to say just anything? The word God puts in my mouth, that is what I must say." 39 Then Bā′laam went with Bā′lak, and they came to Kir′i•ath-hū′zoth. 40 Bā′lak sacrificed oxen and sheep, and sent them to Bā′laam and to the officials who were with him.

Balaam's First Oracle

41 On the next day Bā′lak took Bā′laam and brought him up to Bā′moth-ba′al; and from there he could see part of the people of Israel.y 1 Then Bā′laam said to Bā′lak, "Build me seven altars here, and prepare seven bulls and seven rams for me." 2 Bā′lak did as Bā′laam had said; and Bā′lak and Bā′laam offered a bull and a ram on each altar. 3 Then Bā′laam said to Bā′lak, "Stay here beside your burnt offerings while I go aside. Perhaps the LORD will come to meet me. Whatever he shows me I will tell you." And he went to a bare height.

4 Then God met Bā′laam; and Bā′laam said to him, "I have arranged the seven altars, and have offered a bull and a ram on each altar." 5 The LORD put a word in Bā′laam's mouth, and said, "Return to Bā′lak, and this is what you must say." 6 So he returned to Bā′lak,z who was standing beside his burnt offerings with all the officials of Mō′ab. 7 Then Bā′laama uttered his oracle, saying:

"Bā′lak has brought me from Ar′am,
　the king of Mō′ab from the eastern
　　mountains:
'Come, curse Jacob for me;
　Come, denounce Israel!'
8 How can I curse whom God has not cursed?
　How can I denounce those whom the
　　LORD has not denounced?
9 For from the top of the crags I see him,
　from the hills I behold him.
Here is a people living alone,
　and not reckoning itself among the
　　nations!
10 Who can count the dust of Jacob,
　or number the dust-cloudb of Israel?
Let me die the death of the upright,
　and let my end be like his!"

11 Then Bā′lak said to Bā′laam, "What have you done to me? I brought you to curse my enemies, but now you have done nothing but bless them." 12 He answered, "Must I not take care to say what the LORD puts into my mouth?"

Balaam's Second Oracle

13 So Bā′lak said to him, "Come with me to another place from which you may see them; you shall see only part of them, and shall not see them all; then curse them for me from there." 14 So he took him to the field of Zō′phim, to the top of Pis′gah. He built seven altars, and offered a bull and a ram on each altar. 15 Bā′laam said to Bā′lak, "Stand here beside your burnt offerings, while I meet the LORD over there." 16 The LORD met Bā′laam, put a word into his mouth, and said, "Return to Bā′lak, and this is what you shall say." 17 When he came to him, he was standing beside his burnt offerings with the officials of Mō′ab. Bā′lak said to him, "What has the LORD said?" 18 Then Bā′laam uttered his oracle, saying:

"Rise, Bā′lak, and hear;
　listen to me, O son of Zip′por:
19 God is not a human being, that he should
　　lie,
　or a mortal, that he should change his
　　mind.
Has he promised, and will he not do it?
　Has he spoken, and will he not fulfill it?
20 See, I received a command to bless;
　he has blessed, and I cannot revoke it.
21 He has not beheld misfortune in Jacob;
　nor has he seen trouble in Israel.
The LORD their God is with them,
　acclaimed as a king among them.
22 God, who brings them out of Egypt,
　is like the horns of a wild ox for them.
23 Surely there is no enchantment against
　　Jacob,
　no divination against Israel;
now it shall be said of Jacob and Israel,
　'See what God has done!'
24 Look, a people rising up like a lioness,
　and rousing itself like a lion!
It does not lie down until it has eaten the
　　prey
　and drunk the blood of the slain."

25 Then Bā′lak said to Bā′laam, "Do not curse them at all, and do not bless them at all." 26 But Bā′laam answered Bā′lak, "Did I not tell you, 'Whatever the LORD says, that is what I must do'?"

27 So Bā′lak said to Bā′laam, "Come now, I will take you to another place; perhaps it will please God that you may curse them for me from there." 28 So Bā′lak took Bā′laam to the top of Pē′or, which overlooks the wasteland.c 29 Bā′laam said to Bā′lak, "Build me seven altars here, and prepare seven bulls and seven rams for me." 30 So

---

y Heb lacks *of Israel*   z Heb *him*   a Heb *he*.
b Or *fourth part*   c Or *overlooks Jeshimon*

Bā′lak did as Bā′laam had said, and offered a bull and a ram on each altar.

Balaam's Third Oracle

Now Bā′laam saw that it pleased the LORD to bless Israel, so he did not go, as at other times, to look for omens, but set his face toward the wilderness. ² Bā′laam looked up and saw Israel camping tribe by tribe. Then the spirit of God came upon him, ³ and he uttered his oracle, saying:

"The oracle of Bā′laam son of Bē′or,
 the oracle of the man whose eye is clear,ᵈ
 ⁴ the oracle of one who hears the words of
  God,
 who sees the vision of the Almighty,ᵉ
 who falls down, but with eyes uncovered:
⁵ how fair are your tents, O Jacob,
 your encampments, O Israel!
⁶ Like palm groves that stretch far away,
 like gardens beside a river,
like aloes that the LORD has planted,
 like cedar trees beside the waters.
⁷ Water shall flow from his buckets,
 and his seed shall have abundant water,
his king shall be higher than Ā′gag,
 and his kingdom shall be exalted.
⁸ God who brings him out of Egypt,
 is like the horns of a wild ox for him;
he shall devour the nations that are his foes
 and break their bones.
He shall strike with his arrows.ᶠ
⁹ He crouched, he lay down like a lion,
 and like a lioness; who will rouse him
  up?
Blessed is everyone who blesses you,
 and cursed is everyone who curses you."

10 Then Bā′lak's anger was kindled against Bā′laam, and he struck his hands together. Bā′lak said to Bā′laam, "I summoned you to curse my enemies, but instead you have blessed them these three times. ¹¹ Now be off with you! Go home! I said, 'I will reward you richly,' but the LORD has denied you any reward." ¹² And Bā′laam said to Bā′lak, "Did I not tell your messengers whom you sent to me, ¹³ 'If Bā′lak should give me his house full of silver and gold, I would not be able to go beyond the word of the LORD, to do either good or bad of my own will; what the LORD says, that is what I will say'? ¹⁴ So now, I am going to my people; let me advise you what this people will do to your people in days to come."

Balaam's Fourth Oracle

15 So he uttered his oracle, saying:
"The oracle of Bā′laam son of Bē′or,
 the oracle of the man whose eye is clear,ᵈ
¹⁶ the oracle of one who hears the words of
 God,
 and knows the knowledge of the Most
  High,ᵍ
who sees the vision of the Almighty,ᵉ
 who falls down, but with his eyes
  uncovered:
¹⁷ I see him, but not now;
 I behold him, but not near—
a star shall come out of Jacob,
 and a scepter shall rise out of Israel;
it shall crush the borderlandsʰ of Mō′ab,
 and the territoryⁱ of all the Sheth′ites.
¹⁸ Ē′dom will become a possession,
 Sē′ir a possession of its enemies,ʲ
 while Israel does valiantly.
¹⁹ One out of Jacob shall rule,
 and destroy the survivors of Ir."

20 Then he looked on Am′a·lek, and uttered his oracle, saying:
"First among the nations was Am′a·lek,
 but its end is to perish forever."
21 Then he looked on the Ken′ite, and uttered his oracle, saying:
"Enduring is your dwelling place,
 and your nest is set in the rock;
²² yet Kāin is destined for burning.
 How long shall As′shur take you away
  captive?"
23 Again he uttered his oracle, saying:
"Alas, who shall live when God does this?
²⁴ But ships shall come from Kit′tim
and shall afflict As′shur and Ē′ber;
 and he also shall perish forever."
25 Then Bā′laam got up and went back to his place, and Bā′lak also went his way.

Worship of Baal of Peor

While Israel was staying at Shit′tim, the people began to have sexual relations with the women of Mō′ab. ² These invited the people to the sacrifices of their gods, and the people ate and bowed down to their gods. ³ Thus Israel yoked itself to the Bā′al of Pē′or, and the LORD's anger was kindled against Israel. ⁴ The LORD said to Moses, "Take all the chiefs of the people, and impale them in the sun before the LORD, in order that the fierce anger of the LORD may turn away from Israel." ⁵ And Moses said to the judges of Israel, "Each of you shall kill any of your people who have yoked themselves to the Bā′al of Pē′or."

ᵈ Or closed or open ᵉ Traditional rendering of Heb Shaddai ᶠ Meaning of Heb uncertain ᵍ Or of Elyon ʰ Or forehead ⁱ Some Mss read skull ʲ Heb Seir, its enemies, a possession

6 Just then one of the Israelites came and brought a Mid′i•an•īte woman into his family, in the sight of Moses and in the sight of the whole congregation of the Israelites, while they were weeping at the entrance of the tent of meeting. 7 When Phin′e•has son of El•ē•ā′zar, son of Aaron the priest, saw it, he got up and left the congregation. Taking a spear in his hand, 8 he went after the Israelite man into the tent, and pierced the two of them, the Israelite and the woman, through the belly. So the plague was stopped among the people of Israel. 9 Nevertheless those that died by the plague were twenty-four thousand.

10 The LORD spoke to Moses, saying: 11 "Phin′-e•has son of El•ē•ā′zar, son of Aaron the priest, has turned back my wrath from the Israelites by manifesting such zeal among them on my behalf that in my jealousy I did not consume the Israelites. 12 Therefore say, 'I hereby grant him my covenant of peace. 13 It shall be for him and for his descendants after him a covenant of perpetual priesthood, because he was zealous for his God, and made atonement for the Israelites.' "

14 The name of the slain Israelite man, who was killed with the Mid′i•an•īte woman, was Zim′rī son of Sa′lū, head of an ancestral house belonging to the Sim′ē•on•ītes. 15 The name of the Mid′i•an•īte woman who was killed was Cōz′bī daughter of Zur, who was the head of a clan, an ancestral house in Mid′i•an.

16 The LORD said to Moses, 17 "Harass the Mid′i•an•ītes, and defeat them; 18 for they have harassed you by the trickery with which they deceived you in the affair of Pē′or, and in the affair of Cōz′bī, the daughter of a leader of Mid′i•an, their sister; she was killed on the day of the plague that resulted from Pē′or."

A Census of the New Generation

After the plague the LORD said to Moses and to El•ē•ā′zar son of Aaron the priest, 2 "Take a census of the whole congregation of the Israelites, from twenty years old and upward, by their ancestral houses, everyone in Israel able to go to war." 3 Moses and El•ē•ā′zar the priest spoke with them in the plains of Mō′ab by the Jordan opposite Jericho, saying, 4 "Take a census of the people,^k from twenty years old and upward," as the LORD commanded Moses.

The Israelites, who came out of the land of Egypt, were:

5 Reuben, the firstborn of Israel. The descendants of Reuben: of Hā′noch, the clan of the Hā′-noch•ītes; of Pal′lū, the clan of the Pal′lū•ītes; 6 of Hez′ron, the clan of the Hez′ron•ītes; of Car′mī, the clan of the Car′mītes. 7 These are the clans of the Reū′ben•ītes; the number of those enrolled was forty-three thousand seven hundred thirty. 8 And the descendants of Pal′lū: E•lī′ab. 9 The descendants of E•lī′ab: Nem′ū•el, Dā′than, and A•bī′ram. These are the same Dā′than and A•bī′ram, chosen from the congregation, who rebelled against Moses and Aaron in the company of Kō′rah, when they rebelled against the LORD, 10 and the earth opened its mouth and swallowed them up along with Kō′rah, when that company died, when the fire devoured two hundred fifty men; and they became a warning. 11 Notwithstanding, the sons of Kō′rah did not die.

12 The descendants of Sim′ē•on by their clans: of Nem′ū•el, the clan of the Nem′ū•el•ītes; of Jā′min, the clan of the Jā′min•ītes; of Jā′chin, the clan of the Jā′chin•ītes; 13 of Zē′rah, the clan of the Zē′ra-hītes; of Shā′ūl, the clan of the Shā′u•lītes.^l 14 These are the clans of the Sim′ē•on•ītes, twenty-two thousand two hundred.

15 The children of Gad by their clans: of Zē′-phon, the clan of the Zē′phon•ītes; of Hag′gī, the clan of the Hag′gītes; of Shū′nī, the clan of the Shū′nītes; 16 of Oz′nī, the clan of the Oz′nītes; of Ē′rī, the clan of the Ē′rītes; 17 of Ar′od, the clan of the Ar′o•dītes; of A•rē′lī, the clan of the A•rē′lītes. 18 These are the clans of the Gad′ītes: the number of those enrolled was forty thousand five hundred.

19 The sons of Judah: Er and Ō′nan; Er and Ō′nan died in the land of Cā′naan. 20 The descendants of Judah by their clans were: of Shē′lah, the clan of the Shē′la•nītes; of Per′ez, the clan of the Per′e•zītes; of Zē′rah, the clan of the Zē′ra•hītes. 21 The descendants of Per′ez were: of Hez′ron, the clan of the Hez′ron•ītes; of Hā′mul, the clan of the Hā′mul•ītes. 22 These are the clans of Judah: the number of those enrolled was seventy-six thousand five hundred.

23 The descendants of Is′sa•char by their clans: of Tō′la, the clan of the Tō′la•ītes; of Pū′vah, the clan of the Pū′nītes; 24 of Jash′ub, the clan of the Jash′ub•ītes; of Shim′ron, the clan of the Shim′ron-ītes. 25 These are the clans of Is′sa•char: sixty-four thousand three hundred enrolled.

26 The descendants of Zeb′ū•lun by their clans: of Sē′red, the clan of the Sē′red•ītes; of Ē′lon, the clan of the Ē′lon•ītes; of Jah′lē•el, the clan of the Jah′lē•el•ītes. 27 These are the clans of the Zeb′ū•lun-ītes; the number of those enrolled was sixty thousand five hundred.

28 The sons of Joseph by their clans: Ma•nas′-seh and Ē′phra•im. 29 The descendants of Ma•nas′-seh: of Mā′chir, the clan of the Mā′chir•ītes; and

---

k Heb lacks *take a census of the people*: Compare verse 2
l Or *Saul . . . Saulites*

Mā'chir was the father of Gil'e·ad; of Gil'e·ad, the clan of the Gil'e·ad·ites. 30These are the descendants of Gil'e·ad: of Ī'ē'zer, the clan of the Ī'ē'zer·ites; of Hē'lek, the clan of the Hē'lek·ites; 31and of As'ri·el, the clan of the As'ri·el·ites; and of Shē'chem, the clan of the Shē'chem·ites; 32and of She·mi'da, the clan of the She·mi'da·ites; and of Hē'pher, the clan of the Hē'pher·ites. 33Now Ze·loph'e·had son of Hē'pher had no sons, but daughters: and the names of the daughters of Ze·loph'e·had were Mah'lah, Noah, Hog'lah, Mil'cah, and Tir'zah. 34These are the clans of Ma·nas'seh; the number of those enrolled was fifty-two thousand seven hundred.

35 These are the descendants of Ē'phra·im according to their clans: of Shū·thē'lah, the clan of the Shū·thē·lā'hites; of Bē'cher, the clan of the Bē'cher·ites; of Tā'han, the clan of the Tā'ha·nites. 36And these are the descendants of Shū·thē'lah: of Ē'ran, the clan of the Ē'ran·ites. 37These are the clans of the Ē'phra·im·ites: the number of those enrolled was thirty-two thousand five hundred. These are the descendants of Joseph by their clans.

38 The descendants of Benjamin by their clans: of Bē'la, the clan of the Bē'la·ites; of Ash'bel, the clan of the Ash'bel·ites; of A·hī'ram, the clan of the A·hī'ram·ites; 39of She·phū'pham, the clan of the Shū'pham·ites; of Hū'pham, the clan of the Hū'pham·ites. 40And the sons of Bē'la were Ard and Nā'a·man: of Ard, the clan of the Ard'ites; of Nā'a·man, the clan of the Nā'a·mites. 41These are the descendants of Benjamin by their clans; the number of those enrolled was forty-five thousand six hundred.

42 These are the descendants of Dan by their clans: of Shū'ham, the clan of the Shū'ham·ites. These are the clans of Dan by their clans. 43All the clans of the Shū'ham·ites: sixty-four thousand four hundred enrolled.

44 The descendants of Ash'er by their families: of Im'nah, the clan of the Im'nites; of Ish'vī, the clan of the Ish'vites; of Bē·rī'ah, the clan of the Bē·rī'ites. 45Of the descendants of Bē·rī'ah: of Hē'ber, the clan of the Hē'ber·ites; of Mal'chi·el, the clan of the Mal'chi·el·ites. 46And the name of the daughter of Ash'er was Sē'rah. 47These are the clans of the Ash'er·ites: the number of those enrolled was fifty-three thousand four hundred.

48 The descendants of Naph'ta·lī by their clans: of Jah'zē·el, the clan of the Jah'zē·el·ites; of Gū'nī, the clan of the Gū'nites; 49of Jē'zer, the clan of the Jē'zer·ites; of Shil'lem, the clan of the Shil'lem·ites. 50These are the Naph'ta·lites^m by their clans: the number of those enrolled was forty-five thousand four hundred.

51 This was the number of the Israelites enrolled: six hundred and one thousand seven hundred thirty.

52 The LORD spoke to Moses, saying: 53To these the land shall be apportioned for inheritance according to the number of names. 54To a large tribe you shall give a large inheritance, and to a small tribe you shall give a small inheritance; every tribe shall be given its inheritance according to its enrollment. 55But the land shall be apportioned by lot; according to the names of their ancestral tribes they shall inherit. 56Their inheritance shall be apportioned according to lot between the larger and the smaller.

57 This is the enrollment of the Lē'vites by their clans: of Ger'shon, the clan of the Ger'shon·ites; of Kō'hath, the clan of the Kō'hath·ites; of Me·rar'ī, the clan of the Me·rar'ites. 58These are the clans of Levi: the clan of the Lib'nites, the clan of the Hē'bron·ites, the clan of the Mah'lites, the clan of the Mū'shites, the clan of the Kō'ra·hites. Now Kō'hath was the father of Am'ram. 59The name of Am'ram's wife was Joch'e·bed daughter of Levi, who was born to Levi in Egypt; and she bore to Am'ram: Aaron, Moses, and their sister Miriam. 60To Aaron were born Nā'dab, A·bī'hū, El·ē·ā'zar, and Ith'a·mar. 61But Nā'dab and A·bī'hū died when they offered unholy fire before the LORD. 62The number of those enrolled was twenty-three thousand, every male one month old and upward; for they were not enrolled among the Israelites because there was no allotment given to them among the Israelites.

63 These were those enrolled by Moses and El·ē·ā'zar the priest, who enrolled the Israelites in the plains of Mō'ab by the Jordan opposite Jericho. 64Among these there was not one of those enrolled by Moses and Aaron the priest, who had enrolled the Israelites in the wilderness of Sinai. 65For the LORD had said of them, "They shall die in the wilderness." Not one of them was left, except Caleb son of Je·phŭn'neh and Joshua son of Nun.

The Daughters of Zelophehad

Then the daughters of Ze·loph'e·had came forward. Ze·loph'e·had was son of Hē'pher son of Gil'e·ad son of Mā'chir son of Ma·nas'seh son of Joseph, a member of the Ma·nas'site clans. The names of his daughters were: Mah'lah, Noah, Hog'lah, Mil'cah, and Tir'zah. 2They stood before Moses, El·ē·ā'zar the priest, the leaders, and all the congregation, at the entrance of the tent of meeting, and they said, 3"Our father died in the wilderness; he was not among the company of those who gathered

^m Heb *clans of Naphtali*

themselves together against the LORD in the company of Kō'rah, but died for his own sin; and he had no sons. 4 Why should the name of our father be taken away from his clan because he had no son? Give to us a possession among our father's brothers."

5 Moses brought their case before the LORD. 6 And the LORD spoke to Moses, saying: 7 The daughters of Ze·loph'e·had are right in what they are saying; you shall indeed let them possess an inheritance among their father's brothers and pass the inheritance of their father on to them. 8 You shall also say to the Israelites, "If a man dies, and has no son, then you shall pass his inheritance on to his daughter. 9 If he has no daughter, then you shall give his inheritance to his brothers. 10 If he has no brothers, then you shall give his inheritance to his father's brothers. 11 And if his father has no brothers, then you shall give his inheritance to the nearest kinsman of his clan, and he shall possess it. It shall be for the Israelites a statute and ordinance, as the LORD commanded Moses."

Joshua Appointed Moses' Successor
(Deut 31.1–8)

12 The LORD said to Moses, "Go up this mountain of the Ab'a·rim range, and see the land that I have given to the Israelites. 13 When you have seen it, you also shall be gathered to your people, as your brother Aaron was, 14 because you rebelled against my word in the wilderness of Zin when the congregation quarreled with me.*n* You did not show my holiness before their eyes at the waters." (These are the waters of Mer'i·bath-ka'desh in the wilderness of Zin.) 15 Moses spoke to the LORD, saying, 16 "Let the LORD, the God of the spirits of all flesh, appoint someone over the congregation 17 who shall go out before them and come in before them, who shall lead them out and bring them in, so that the congregation of the LORD may not be like sheep without a shepherd." 18 So the LORD said to Moses, "Take Joshua son of Nun, a man in whom is the spirit, and lay your hand upon him; 19 have him stand before El·e·a'zar the priest and all the congregation, and commission him in their sight. 20 You shall give him some of your authority, so that all the congregation of the Israelites may obey. 21 But he shall stand before El·e·a'zar the priest, who shall inquire for him by the decision of the U'rim before the LORD; at his word they shall go out, and at his word they shall come in, both he and all the Israelites with him, the whole congregation." 22 So Moses did as the LORD commanded him. He took Joshua and had him stand before El·e·a'zar the priest and the whole

congregation; 23 he laid his hands on him and commissioned him—as the LORD had directed through Moses.

Daily Offerings
(Ex 29.38–46)

28 The LORD spoke to Moses, saying: 2 Command the Israelites, and say to them: My offering, the food for my offerings by fire, my pleasing odor, you shall take care to offer to me at its appointed time. 3 And you shall say to them, This is the offering by fire that you shall offer to the LORD: two male lambs a year old without blemish, daily, as a regular offering. 4 One lamb you shall offer in the morning, and the other lamb you shall offer at twilight;*o* 5 also one-tenth of an ephah of choice flour for a grain offering, mixed with one-fourth of a hin of beaten oil. 6 It is a regular burnt offering, ordained at Mount Sinai for a pleasing odor, an offering by fire to the LORD. 7 Its drink offering shall be one-fourth of a hin for each lamb; in the sanctuary you shall pour out a drink offering of strong drink to the LORD. 8 The other lamb you shall offer at twilight*o* with a grain offering and a drink offering like the one in the morning; you shall offer it as an offering by fire, a pleasing odor to the LORD.

Sabbath Offerings

9 On the sabbath day: two male lambs a year old without blemish, and two-tenths of an ephah of choice flour for a grain offering, mixed with oil, and its drink offering— 10 this is the burnt offering for every sabbath, in addition to the regular burnt offering and its drink offering.

Monthly Offerings

11 At the beginnings of your months you shall offer a burnt offering to the LORD: two young bulls, one ram, seven male lambs a year old without blemish; 12 also three-tenths of an ephah of choice flour for a grain offering, mixed with oil, for each bull; and two-tenths of choice flour for a grain offering, mixed with oil, for the one ram; 13 and one-tenth of choice flour mixed with oil as a grain offering for every lamb—a burnt offering of pleasing odor, an offering by fire to the LORD. 14 Their drink offerings shall be half a hin of wine for a bull, one-third of a hin for a ram, and one-fourth of a hin for a lamb. This is the burnt offering of every month throughout the months of the year. 15 And there shall be one male goat for a sin offering to the LORD; it shall be offered in addition to the regular burnt offering and its drink offering.

---

n Heb lacks *with me*   *o* Heb *between the two evenings*

Offerings at Passover
(Lev 23.5–14)

16 On the fourteenth day of the first month there shall be a passover offering to the LORD. [17] And on the fifteenth day of this month is a festival; seven days shall unleavened bread be eaten. [18] On the first day there shall be a holy convocation. You shall not work at your occupations. [19] You shall offer an offering by fire, a burnt offering to the LORD: two young bulls, one ram, and seven male lambs a year old; see that they are without blemish. [20] Their grain offering shall be of choice flour mixed with oil: three-tenths of an ephah shall you offer for a bull, and two-tenths for a ram; [21] one-tenth shall you offer for each of the seven lambs; [22] also one male goat for a sin offering, to make atonement for you. [23] You shall offer these in addition to the burnt offering of the morning, which belongs to the regular burnt offering. [24] In the same way you shall offer daily, for seven days, the food of an offering by fire, a pleasing odor to the LORD; it shall be offered in addition to the regular burnt offering and its drink offering. [25] And on the seventh day you shall have a holy convocation; you shall not work at your occupations.

Offerings at the Festival of Weeks
(Lev 23.15–22)

26 On the day of the first fruits, when you offer a grain offering of new grain to the LORD at your festival of weeks, you shall have a holy convocation; you shall not work at your occupations. [27] You shall offer a burnt offering, a pleasing odor to the LORD: two young bulls, one ram, seven male lambs a year old. [28] Their grain offering shall be of choice flour mixed with oil, three-tenths of an ephah for each bull, two-tenths for one ram, [29] one-tenth for each of the seven lambs; [30] with one male goat, to make atonement for you. [31] In addition to the regular burnt offering with its grain offering, you shall offer them and their drink offering. They shall be without blemish.

Offerings at the Festival of Trumpets
(Lev 23.23–25)

29 On the first day of the seventh month you shall have a holy convocation; you shall not work at your occupations. It is a day for you to blow the trumpets, [2] and you shall offer a burnt offering, a pleasing odor to the LORD: one young bull, one ram, seven male lambs a year old without blemish. [3] Their grain offering shall be of choice flour mixed with oil, three-tenths of one ephah for the bull, two-tenths for the ram, [4] and one-tenth for

each of the seven lambs; [5] with one male goat for a sin offering, to make atonement for you. [6] These are in addition to the burnt offering of the new moon and its grain offering, and the regular burnt offering and its grain offering, and their drink offerings, according to the ordinance for them, a pleasing odor, an offering by fire to the LORD.

did you KNOW?

Other Jewish Feasts

In chapter 29 of Numbers, we find the instructions for two more Jewish festivals. (For other Jewish festivals, see Ex 34.18–26.) The festival of trumpets is a fall celebration prescribed for "the first day of the seventh month" (Num 29.1). This day of rest, marked by trumpet blasts and sacrifices, came to be called Rosh Hashanah (head of the year), the beginning of the Jewish New Year.

On the tenth day of the seventh month, the Israelites celebrated the Day of Atonement (Yom Kippur). On this solemn day of penance and fasting, the high priest laid the sins of the people on a so-called scapegoat (see Lev 16.20–21), then ran the beast into the wilderness, thus symbolically purifying the nation.

▶ **Num 29.1–11**

Offerings on the Day of Atonement
(Lev 23.26–32)

7 On the tenth day of this seventh month you shall have a holy convocation, and deny yourselves;[p] you shall do no work. [8] You shall offer a burnt offering to the LORD, a pleasing odor: one young bull, one ram, seven male lambs a year old. They shall be without blemish. [9] Their grain offering shall be of choice flour mixed with oil, three-tenths of an ephah for the bull, two-tenths for the one ram, [10] one-tenth for each of the seven lambs; [11] with one male goat for a sin offering, in addition to the sin offering of atonement, and the regular burnt offering and its grain offering, and their drink offerings.

p Or and fast

N U M

Offerings at the Festival of Booths
(Lev 23.33–44)

12 On the fifteenth day of the seventh month you shall have a holy convocation; you shall not work at your occupations. You shall celebrate a festival to the LORD seven days. 13 You shall offer a burnt offering, an offering by fire, a pleasing odor to the LORD: thirteen young bulls, two rams, fourteen male lambs a year old. They shall be without blemish. 14 Their grain offering shall be of choice flour mixed with oil, three-tenths of an ephah for each of the thirteen bulls, two-tenths for each of the two rams, 15 and one-tenth for each of the fourteen lambs; 16 also one male goat for a sin offering, in addition to the regular burnt offering, its grain offering and its drink offering.

17 On the second day: twelve young bulls, two rams, fourteen male lambs a year old without blemish, 18 with the grain offering and the drink offerings for the bulls, for the rams, and for the lambs, as prescribed in accordance with their number; 19 also one male goat for a sin offering, in addition to the regular burnt offering and its grain offering, and their drink offerings.

20 On the third day: eleven bulls, two rams, fourteen male lambs a year old without blemish, 21 with the grain offering and the drink offerings for the bulls, for the rams, and for the lambs, as prescribed in accordance with their number; 22 also one male goat for a sin offering, in addition to the regular burnt offering and its grain offering and its drink offering.

23 On the fourth day: ten bulls, two rams, fourteen male lambs a year old without blemish, 24 with the grain offering and the drink offerings for the bulls, for the rams, and for the lambs, as prescribed in accordance with their number; 25 also one male goat for a sin offering, in addition to the regular burnt offering, its grain offering and its drink offering.

26 On the fifth day: nine bulls, two rams, fourteen male lambs a year old without blemish, 27 with the grain offering and the drink offerings for the bulls, for the rams, and for the lambs, as prescribed in accordance with their number; 28 also one male goat for a sin offering, in addition to the regular burnt offering and its grain offering and its drink offering.

29 On the sixth day: eight bulls, two rams, fourteen male lambs a year old without blemish, 30 with the grain offering and the drink offerings for the bulls, for the rams, and for the lambs, as prescribed in accordance with their number; 31 also one male goat for a sin offering, in addition to the regular burnt offering, its grain offering, and its drink offerings.

32 On the seventh day: seven bulls, two rams, fourteen male lambs a year old without blemish, 33 with the grain offering and the drink offerings for the bulls, for the rams, and for the lambs, as prescribed in accordance with their number; 34 also one male goat for a sin offering, besides the regular burnt offering, its grain offering, and its drink offering.

35 On the eighth day you shall have a solemn assembly; you shall not work at your occupations. 36 You shall offer a burnt offering, an offering by fire, a pleasing odor to the LORD: one bull, one ram, seven male lambs a year old without blemish, 37 and the grain offering and the drink offerings for the bull, for the ram, and for the lambs, as prescribed in accordance with their number; 38 also one male goat for a sin offering, in addition to the regular burnt offering and its grain offering and its drink offering.

39 These you shall offer to the LORD at your appointed festivals, in addition to your votive offerings and your freewill offerings, as your burnt offerings, your grain offerings, your drink offerings, and your offerings of well-being.

40*q* So Moses told the Israelites everything just as the LORD had commanded Moses.

Vows Made by Women

Then Moses said to the heads of the tribes of the Israelites: This is what the LORD has commanded. 2 When a man makes a vow to the LORD, or swears an oath to bind himself by a pledge, he shall not break his word; he shall do according to all that proceeds out of his mouth.

3 When a woman makes a vow to the LORD, or binds herself by a pledge, while within her father's house, in her youth, 4 and her father hears of her vow or her pledge by which she has bound herself, and says nothing to her; then all her vows shall stand, and any pledge by which she has bound herself shall stand. 5 But if her father expresses disapproval to her at the time that he hears of it, no vow of hers, and no pledge by which she has bound herself, shall stand; and the LORD will forgive her, because her father had expressed to her his disapproval.

6 If she marries, while obligated by her vows or any thoughtless utterance of her lips by which she has bound herself, 7 and her husband hears of it and says nothing to her at the time that he hears, then her vows shall stand, and her pledges by which she has bound herself shall stand. 8 But if, at

---

q Ch 30.1 in Heb

did you KNOW?

Making a Vow

Vow.

Such a simple word, really. Three letters. One syllable. But its simplicity masks its meaning. If a word's length were directly related to its significance, then vow would have to become a long word indeed. It is a heavy word, one that we use sparingly. We associate it with marriage or the life commitment of priests and religious sisters and brothers. Then we speak of solemn vows.

From a faith perspective, a person making a vow is making a deep, binding promise before witnesses and, most especially, before God. A vow cannot really be captured on paper. A vow must be lived out. It must be internalized. It is the foundation for a life choice. For we know, deep in our heart, that God is part of our vows.

The Israelites also took vows seriously. Numbers, chapter 30, is devoted to laws about vows. The laws were sexist by our standards. For example, a father or a husband could veto a woman's vows. Such laws were deemed acceptable in the Israelites' patriarchal society, but they are not in ours.

▸ **Num 30.2–4**

the time that her husband hears of it, he expresses disapproval to her, then he shall nullify the vow by which she was obligated, or the thoughtless utterance of her lips, by which she bound herself; and the LORD will forgive her. 9 (But every vow of a widow or of a divorced woman, by which she has bound herself, shall be binding upon her.) 10 And if she made a vow in her husband's house, or bound herself by a pledge with an oath, 11 and her husband heard it and said nothing to her, and did not express disapproval to her, then all her vows shall stand, and any pledge by which she bound herself shall stand. 12 But if her husband nullifies them at the time that he hears them, then whatever proceeds out of her lips concerning her vows, or concerning her pledge of herself, shall not stand. Her husband has nullified them, and the LORD will forgive her. 13 Any vow or any binding

oath to deny herself,ʳ her husband may allow to stand, or her husband may nullify. 14 But if her husband says nothing to her from day to day,ˢ then he validates all her vows, or all her pledges, by which she is obligated; he has validated them, because he said nothing to her at the time that he heard of them. 15 But if he nullifies them some time after he has heard of them, then he shall bear her guilt.

16 These are the statutes that the LORD commanded Moses concerning a husband and his wife, and a father and his daughter while she is still young and in her father's house.

War against Midian

The LORD spoke to Moses, saying, 2 "Avenge the Israelites on the Mid′i·an·ītes; afterward you shall be gathered to your people." 3 So Moses said to the people, "Arm some of your number for the war, so that they may go against Mid′i·an, to execute the LORD's vengeance on Mid′i·an. 4 You shall send a thousand from each of the tribes of Israel to the war." 5 So out of the thousands of Israel, a thousand from each tribe were conscripted, twelve thousand armed for battle. 6 Moses sent them to the war, a thousand from each tribe, along with Phin′e·has son of El·e·ā′zar the priest,ᵗ with the vessels of the sanctuary and the trumpets for sounding the alarm in his hand. 7 They did battle against Mid′i·an, as the LORD had commanded Moses, and killed every male. 8 They killed the kings of Mid′i·an: Ē′vī, Rē′kem, Zur, Hur, and Rē′ba, the five kings of Mid′i·an, in addition to others who were slain by them; and they also killed Bā′laam son of Bē′or with the sword. 9 The Israelites took the women of Mid′i·an and their little ones captive; and they took all their cattle, their flocks, and all their goods as booty. 10 All their towns where they had settled, and all their encampments, they burned, 11 but they took all the spoil and all the booty, both people and animals. 12 Then they brought the captives and the booty and the spoil to Moses, to El·e·ā′zar the priest, and to the congregation of the Israelites, at the camp on the plains of Mō′ab by the Jordan at Jericho.

Return from the War

13 Moses, El·e·ā′zar the priest, and all the leaders of the congregation went to meet them outside the camp. 14 Moses became angry with the officers of the army, the commanders of thousands and the commanders of hundreds, who had come from service in the war. 15 Moses said to them,

ʳ Or to fast   ˢ Or from that day to the next   ᵗ Gk: Heb adds to the war

NUM

"Have you allowed all the women to live? 16 These women here, on Bā'laam's advice, made the Israelites act treacherously against the LORD in the affair of Pē'or, so that the plague came among the congregation of the LORD. 17 Now therefore, kill every male among the little ones, and kill every woman who has known a man by sleeping with him. 18 But all the young girls who have not known a man by sleeping with him, keep alive for yourselves. 19 Camp outside the camp seven days; whoever of you has killed any person or touched a corpse, purify yourselves and your captives on the third and on the seventh day. 20 You shall purify every garment, every article of skin, everything made of goats' hair, and every article of wood."

21 El·e·ā'zar the priest said to the troops who had gone to battle: "This is the statute of the law that the LORD has commanded Moses: 22 gold, silver, bronze, iron, tin, and lead— 23 everything that can withstand fire, shall be passed through fire, and it shall be clean. Nevertheless it shall also be purified with the water for purification; and whatever cannot withstand fire, shall be passed through the water. 24 You must wash your clothes on the seventh day, and you shall be clean; afterward you may come into the camp."

Disposition of Captives and Booty

25 The LORD spoke to Moses, saying, 26 "You and El·e·ā'zar the priest and the heads of the ancestral houses of the congregation make an inventory of the booty captured, both human and animal. 27 Divide the booty into two parts, between the warriors who went out to battle and all the congregation. 28 From the share of the warriors who went out to battle, set aside as tribute for the LORD, one item out of every five hundred, whether persons, oxen, donkeys, sheep, or goats. 29 Take it from their half and give it to El·e·ā'zar the priest as an offering to the LORD. 30 But from the Israelites' half you shall take one out of every fifty, whether persons, oxen, donkeys, sheep, or goats—all the animals—and give them to the Lē'vites who have charge of the tabernacle of the LORD."

31 Then Moses and El·e·ā'zar the priest did as the LORD had commanded Moses:

32 The booty remaining from the spoil that the troops had taken totaled six hundred seventy-five thousand sheep, 33 seventy-two thousand oxen, 34 sixty-one thousand donkeys, 35 and thirty-two thousand persons in all, women who had not known a man by sleeping with him.

36 The half-share, the portion of those who had gone out to war, was in number three hundred thirty-seven thousand five hundred sheep and goats, 37 and the LORD's tribute of sheep and goats was six hundred seventy-five. 38 The oxen were thirty-six thousand, of which the LORD's tribute was seventy-two. 39 The donkeys were thirty thousand five hundred, of which the LORD's tribute was sixty-one. 40 The persons were sixteen thousand, of which the LORD's tribute was thirty-two persons. 41 Moses gave the tribute, the offering for the LORD, to El·e·ā'zar the priest, as the LORD had commanded Moses.

42 As for the Israelites' half, which Moses separated from that of the troops, 43 the congregation's half was three hundred thirty-seven thousand five hundred sheep and goats, 44 thirty-six thousand oxen, 45 thirty thousand five hundred donkeys, 46 and sixteen thousand persons. 47 From the Israelites' half Moses took one of every fifty, both of persons and of animals, and gave them to the Lē'vites who had charge of the tabernacle of the LORD; as the LORD had commanded Moses.

48 Then the officers who were over the thousands of the army, the commanders of thousands and the commanders of hundreds, approached Moses, 49 and said to Moses, "Your servants have counted the warriors who are under our command, and not one of us is missing. 50 And we have brought the LORD's offering, what each of us found, articles of gold, armlets and bracelets, signet rings, earrings, and pendants, to make atonement for ourselves before the LORD." 51 Moses and El·e·ā'zar the priest received the gold from them, all in the form of crafted articles. 52 And all the gold of the offering that they offered to the LORD, from the commanders of thousands and the commanders of hundreds, was sixteen thousand seven hundred fifty shekels. 53 (The troops had all taken plunder for themselves.) 54 So Moses and El·e·ā'zar the priest received the gold from the commanders of thousands and of hundreds, and brought it into the tent of meeting as a memorial for the Israelites before the LORD.

Conquest and Division of Transjordan
(Deut 3.12–22)

Now the Reū'ben·ites and the Gad'ites owned a very great number of cattle. When they saw that the land of Jā'zer and the land of Gil'e·ad was a good place for cattle, 2 the Gad'ites and the Reū'ben·ites came and spoke to Moses, to El·e·ā'zar the priest, and to the leaders of the congregation, saying, 3 "At'a·roth, Dī'bon, Jā'zer, Nim'rah, Hesh'bon, Ē·le·ā'leh, Sē'bam, Nē'bō, and Bē'on— 4 the land that the LORD subdued before the congregation of Israel—is a land for cattle; and your servants have cattle." 5 They continued, "If we have found favor in your sight, let this land be given to your servants for a possession; do not make us cross the Jordan."

6 But Moses said to the Gad'ites and to the Reū'ben·ites, "Shall your brothers go to war while you sit here? 7 Why will you discourage the hearts of the Israelites from going over into the land that the LORD has given them? 8 Your fathers did this, when I sent them from Kā'desh-bar'nē·a to see the land. 9 When they went up to the Wadi Esh'col and saw the land, they discouraged the hearts of the Israelites from going into the land that the LORD had given them. 10 The LORD's anger was kindled on that day and he swore, saying, 11 'Surely none of the people who came up out of Egypt, from twenty years old and upward, shall see the land that I swore to give to Abraham, to Isaac, and to Jacob, because they have not unreservedly followed me— 12 none except Caleb son of Je·phūn'-neh the Ken'iz·zīte and Joshua son of Nun, for they have unreservedly followed the LORD.' 13 And the LORD's anger was kindled against Israel, and he made them wander in the wilderness for forty years, until all the generation that had done evil in the sight of the LORD had disappeared. 14 And now you, a brood of sinners, have risen in place of your fathers, to increase the LORD's fierce anger against Israel! 15 If you turn away from following him, he will again abandon them in the wilderness; and you will destroy all this people."

16 Then they came up to him and said, "We will build sheepfolds here for our flocks, and towns for our little ones, 17 but we will take up arms as a vanguard*u* before the Israelites, until we have brought them to their place. Meanwhile our little ones will stay in the fortified towns because of the inhabitants of the land. 18 We will not return to our homes until all the Israelites have obtained their inheritance. 19 We will not inherit with them on the other side of the Jordan and beyond, because our inheritance has come to us on this side of the Jordan to the east."

20 So Moses said to them, "If you do this—if you take up arms to go before the LORD for the war, 21 and all those of you who bear arms cross the Jordan before the LORD, until he has driven out his enemies from before him 22 and the land is subdued before the LORD—then after that you may return and be free of obligation to the LORD and to Israel, and this land shall be your possession before the LORD. 23 But if you do not do this, you have sinned against the LORD; and be sure your sin will find you out. 24 Build towns for your little ones, and folds for your flocks; but do what you have promised."

25 Then the Gad'ites and the Reū'ben·ites said to Moses, "Your servants will do as my lord commands. 26 Our little ones, our wives, our flocks, and all our livestock shall remain there in the towns of Gil'e·ad; 27 but your servants will cross over, everyone armed for war, to do battle for the LORD, just as my lord orders."

28 So Moses gave command concerning them to El·ē·ā'zar the priest, to Joshua son of Nun, and to the heads of the ancestral houses of the Israelite tribes. 29 And Moses said to them, "If the Gad'ites and the Reū'ben·ites, everyone armed for battle before the LORD, will cross over the Jordan with you and the land shall be subdued before you, then you shall give them the land of Gil'e·ad for a possession; 30 but if they will not cross over with you armed, they shall have possessions among you in the land of Cā'naan." 31 The Gad'ites and the Reū'-ben·ites answered, "As the LORD has spoken to your servants, so we will do. 32 We will cross over armed before the LORD into the land of Cā'naan, but the possession of our inheritance shall remain with us on this side of*v* the Jordan."

33 Moses gave to them—to the Gad'ites and to the Reū'ben·ites and to the half-tribe of Ma·nas'seh son of Joseph—the kingdom of King Sī'hon of the Am'o·rītes and the kingdom of King Og of Bā'-shan, the land and its towns, with the territories of the surrounding towns. 34 And the Gad'ites rebuilt Dī'bon, At'a·roth, A·rō'er, 35 At'roth-shō'phan, Jā'-zer, Jog'be·hah, 36 Beth-nim'rah, and Beth-har'an, fortified cities, and folds for sheep. 37 And the Reū'ben·ites rebuilt Hesh'bon, Ê·le·ā'leh, Kir·i·a-thā'im, 38 Nē'bō, and Bā'al-mē'on (some names being changed), and Sib'mah; and they gave names to the towns that they rebuilt. 39 The descendants of Mā'chir son of Ma·nas'seh went to Gil'e·ad, captured it, and dispossessed the Am'o-rītes who were there; 40 so Moses gave Gil'e·ad to Mā'chir son of Ma·nas'seh, and he settled there. 41 Jā'ir son of Ma·nas'seh went and captured their villages, and renamed them Hav'voth-jā'ir.*w* 42 And Nō'bah went and captured Kē'nath and its villages, and renamed it Nō'bah after himself.

The Stages of Israel's Journey from Egypt

These are the stages by which the Israelites went out of the land of Egypt in military formation under the leadership of Moses and Aaron. 2 Moses wrote down their starting points, stage by stage, by command of the LORD; and these are their stages according to their starting places. 3 They set out from Ram'e·sēs in the first month, on the fifteenth day of the first month; on the day after the passover the Israelites went out boldly in the sight of

---

u Cn: Heb *hurrying*   *v* Heb *beyond*   *w* That is *the villages of Jair*

all the Egyptians, 4 while the Egyptians were burying all their firstborn, whom the LORD had struck down among them. The LORD executed judgments even against their gods.

5 So the Israelites set out from Ram′e•sēs, and camped at Suc′coth. 6 They set out from Suc′coth, and camped at Ē′tham, which is on the edge of the wilderness. 7 They set out from Ē′tham, and turned back to Pī-ha•hī′roth, which faces Bā′al-zē′phon; and they camped before Mig′dol. 8 They set out from Pī-ha•hī′roth, passed through the sea into the wilderness, went a three days' journey in the wilderness of Ē′tham, and camped at Mar′ah. 9 They set out from Mar′ah and came to Ē′lim; at Ē′lim there were twelve springs of water and seventy palm trees, and they camped there. 10 They set out from Ē′lim and camped by the Red Sea.x 11 They set out from the Red Seax and camped in the wilderness of Sin. 12 They set out from the wilderness of Sin and camped at Doph′kah. 13 They set out from Doph′kah and camped at Ā′lush. 14 They set out from Ā′lush and camped at Reph′i•dim, where there was no water for the people to drink. 15 They set out from Reph′i•dim and camped in the wilderness of Sinai. 16 They set out from the wilderness of Sinai and camped at Kib′roth-hat•tā′a•vah. 17 They set out from Kib′roth-hat•tā•a•vah and camped at Ha•zē′roth. 18 They set out from Ha•zē′-roth and camped at Rith′mah. 19 They set out from Rith′mah and camped at Rim′mon-per′ez. 20 They set out from Rim′mon-per′ez and camped at Lib′-nah. 21 They set out from Lib′nah and camped at Ris′sah. 22 They set out from Ris′sah and camped at Kē•he•lā′thah. 23 They set out from Kē•he•lā′thah and camped at Mount Shē′pher. 24 They set out from Mount Shē′pher and camped at Ha•rā′dah. 25 They set out from Ha•rā′dah and camped at Mak-hē′loth. 26 They set out from Mak•hē′loth and camped at Tā′hath. 27 They set out from Tā′hath and camped at Tē′rah. 28 They set out from Tē′rah and camped at Mith′kah. 29 They set out from Mith′kah and camped at Hash•mō′nah. 30 They set out from Hash•mō′nah and camped at Mō•sē′roth. 31 They set out from Mō•sē′roth and camped at Ben′ē-ja′a•kan. 32 They set out from Ben′ē-ja′a•kan and camped at Hor-hag•gid′gad. 33 They set out from Hor-hag•gid′gad and camped at Jot′ba•thah. 34 They set out from Jot′ba•thah and camped at A•brō′nah. 35 They set out from A•brō′nah and camped at Ē′zi•on-gē′ber. 36 They set out from Ē′zi-on-gē′ber and camped in the wilderness of Zin (that is, Kā′desh). 37 They set out from Kā′desh and camped at Mount Hor, on the edge of the land of Ē′dom.

38 Aaron the priest went up Mount Hor at the command of the LORD and died there in the forti-eth year after the Israelites had come out of the land of Egypt, on the first day of the fifth month. 39 Aaron was one hundred twenty-three years old when he died on Mount Hor.

40 The Cā′naan•īte, the king of Ar′ad, who lived in the Neg′eb in the land of Cā′naan, heard of the coming of the Israelites.

41 They set out from Mount Hor and camped at Zal′mō′nah. 42 They set out from Zal•mō′nah and camped at Pū′non. 43 They set out from Pū′non and camped at Ō′both. 44 They set out from Ō′both and camped at Ī′ye-ab′a•rim, in the territory of Mō′ab. 45 They set out from Ī′yim and camped at Dī′bon-gad. 46 They set out from Dī′bon-gad and camped at Al′mon-dib•la•thā′im. 47 They set out from Al′mon-dib•la•thā′im and camped in the mountains of Ab′a•rim, before Nē′bō. 48 They set out from the mountains of Ab′-a•rim and camped in the plains of Mō′ab by the Jordan at Jericho; 49 they camped by the Jordan from Beth-jesh′i•moth as far as Ā′bel-shit′tim in the plains of Mō′ab.

Directions for the Conquest of Canaan

50 In the plains of Mō′ab by the Jordan at Jericho, the LORD spoke to Moses, saying: 51 Speak to the Israelites, and say to them: When you cross over the Jordan into the land of Cā′naan, 52 you shall drive out all the inhabitants of the land from before you, destroy all their figured stones, destroy all their cast images, and demolish all their high places. 53 You shall take possession of the land and settle in it, for I have given you the land to possess. 54 You shall apportion the land by lot according to your clans; to a large one you shall give a large inheritance, and to a small one you shall give a small inheritance; the inheritance shall belong to the person on whom the lot falls; according to your ancestral tribes you shall inherit. 55 But if you do not drive out the inhabitants of the land from before you, then those whom you let remain shall be as barbs in your eyes and thorns in your sides; they shall trouble you in the land where you are settling. 56 And I will do to you as I thought to do to them.

The Boundaries of the Land

The LORD spoke to Moses, saying: 2 Command the Israelites, and say to them: When you enter the land of Cā′naan (this is the land that shall fall to you for an inheritance, the land of Cā′naan, defined by its boundaries), 3 your south sector shall extend from the wilderness of Zin along the side of Ē′dom. Your southern boundary shall begin from

x Or *Sea of Reeds*

the end of the Dead Sea^y on the east; 4 your
boundary shall turn south of the ascent of Ak•rab′-
bim, and cross to Zin, and its outer limit shall be
south of Kā′desh-bar′nē•a; then it shall go on to
Hā′zar-ad′dar, and cross to Az′mon; 5 the boundary shall turn from Az′mon to the Wadi of Egypt,
and its termination shall be at the Sea.

6 For the western boundary, you shall have the
Great Sea and its^z coast; this shall be your western
boundary.

7 This shall be your northern boundary: from
the Great Sea you shall mark out your line to
Mount Hor; 8 from Mount Hor you shall mark it
out to Lē′bō-hā′math, and the outer limit of the
boundary shall be at Zē′dad; 9 then the boundary shall extend to Ziph′ron, and its end shall
be at Hā′zar-ē′nan; this shall be your northern
boundary.

10 You shall mark out your eastern boundary from Hā′zar-ē′nan to Shē′pham; 11 and the
boundary shall continue down from Shē′pham to
Rib′lah on the east side of Ā′in; and the boundary
shall go down, and reach the eastern slope of the
sea of Chin′ne•reth; 12 and the boundary shall go
down to the Jordan, and its end shall be at the
Dead Sea.^y This shall be your land with its boundaries all around.

13 Moses commanded the Israelites, saying:
This is the land that you shall inherit by lot, which
the LORD has commanded to give to the nine tribes
and to the half-tribe; 14 for the tribe of the Reū′-
ben•ites by their ancestral houses and the tribe of
the Gad′ītes by their ancestral houses have taken
their inheritance, and also the half-tribe of Ma-
nas′seh; 15 the two tribes and the half-tribe have
taken their inheritance beyond the Jordan at Jericho eastward, toward the sunrise.

Tribal Leaders

16 The LORD spoke to Moses, saying: 17 These
are the names of the men who shall apportion the
land to you for inheritance: the priest El•e•ā′zar and
Joshua son of Nun. 18 You shall take one leader of
every tribe to apportion the land for inheritance.
19 These are the names of the men: Of the tribe of
Judah, Caleb son of Je•phūn′neh. 20 Of the tribe
of the Sim′ē•on•ites, She•mū′el son of Am•mī′hud.
21 Of the tribe of Benjamin, Ē•lī′dad son of Chis′-
lon. 22 Of the tribe of the Dan′ites a leader, Buk′kī
son of Jog′lī. 23 Of the tribe of the Jō′seph•ites: of the tribe of
the Ma•nas′sītes a leader, Han′ni•el son of Ē′phod,
24 and of the tribe of the Ē′phra•im•ites a leader, Ke-
mū′el son of Shiph′tan. 25 Of the tribe of the Zeb′-
ū•lun•ites a leader, Ē′lī-zā′phan son of Par′nach.
26 Of the tribe of the Is′sa•char•ites a leader, Pal′ti•el
son of Az′zan. 27 And of the tribe of the Ash′er•ites

a leader, A•hī′hud son of She•lō′mī. 28 Of the tribe
of the Naph′ta•lites a leader, Pe•dah′el son of Am-
mi′hud. 29 These were the ones whom the LORD
commanded to apportion the inheritance for the
Israelites in the land of Cā′naan.

Cities for the Levites

In the plains of Mō′ab by the Jordan at Jericho,
the LORD spoke to Moses, saying: 2 Command the
Israelites to give, from the inheritance that they
possess, towns for the Lē′vītes to live in; you shall
also give to the Lē′vītes pasture lands surrounding
the towns. 3 The towns shall be theirs to live in,
and their pasture lands shall be for their cattle, for
their livestock, and for all their animals. 4 The pasture lands of the towns, which you shall give to
the Lē′vītes, shall reach from the wall of the town
outward a thousand cubits all around. 5 You shall
measure, outside the town, for the east side two
thousand cubits, for the south side two thousand
cubits, for the west side two thousand cubits, and
for the north side two thousand cubits, with the
town in the middle; this shall belong to them as
pasture land for their towns.

6 The towns that you give to the Lē′vītes shall
include the six cities of refuge, where you shall
permit a slayer to flee, and in addition to them
you shall give forty-two towns. 7 The towns that
you give to the Lē′vītes shall total forty-eight, with
their pasture lands. 8 And as for the towns that you
shall give from the possession of the Israelites,
from the larger tribes you shall take many, and
from the smaller tribes you shall take few; each, in
proportion to the inheritance that it obtains, shall
give of its towns to the Lē′vītes.

Cities of Refuge
(Deut 19.1–13; Josh 20.1–9)

9 The LORD spoke to Moses, saying: 10 Speak to
the Israelites, and say to them: When you cross the
Jordan into the land of Cā′naan, 11 then you shall
select cities to be cities of refuge for you, so that a
slayer who kills a person without intent may flee
there. 12 The cities shall be for you a refuge from
the avenger, so that the slayer may not die until
there is a trial before the congregation.

13 The cities that you designate shall be six cities of refuge for you: 14 you shall designate three
cities beyond the Jordan, and three cities in the
land of Cā′naan, to be cities of refuge. 15 These six
cities shall serve as refuge for the Israelites, for the
resident or transient alien among them, so that
anyone who kills a person without intent may flee
there.

---

^y Heb *Salt Sea*   ^z Syr: Heb lacks *its*

Concerning Murder and Blood Revenge

16 But anyone who strikes another with an iron object, and death ensues, is a murderer; the murderer shall be put to death. 17 Or anyone who strikes another with a stone in hand that could cause death, and death ensues, is a murderer; the murderer shall be put to death. 18 Or anyone who strikes another with a weapon of wood in hand that could cause death, and death ensues, is a murderer; the murderer shall be put to death. 19 The avenger of blood is the one who shall put the murderer to death; when they meet, the avenger of blood shall execute the sentence. 20 Likewise, if someone pushes another from hatred, or hurls something at another, lying in wait, and death ensues, 21 or in enmity strikes another with the hand, and death ensues, then the one who struck the blow shall be put to death; that person is a murderer; the avenger of blood shall put the murderer to death, when they meet.

22 But if someone pushes another suddenly without enmity, or hurls any object without lying in wait, 23 or, while handling any stone that could cause death, unintentionally[a] drops it on another and death ensues, though they were not enemies, and no harm was intended, 24 then the congregation shall judge between the slayer and the avenger of blood, in accordance with these ordinances; 25 and the congregation shall rescue the slayer from the avenger of blood. Then the congregation shall send the slayer back to the original city of refuge. The slayer shall live in it until the death of the high priest who was anointed with the holy oil. 26 But if the slayer shall at any time go outside the bounds of the original city of refuge, 27 and is found by the avenger of blood outside the bounds of the city of refuge, and is killed by the avenger, no bloodguilt shall be incurred. 28 For the slayer must remain in the city of refuge until the death of the high priest; but after the death of the high priest the slayer may return home.

29 These things shall be a statute and ordinance for you throughout your generations wherever you live.

30 If anyone kills another, the murderer shall be put to death on the evidence of witnesses; but no one shall be put to death on the testimony of a single witness. 31 Moreover you shall accept no ransom for the life of a murderer who is subject to the death penalty; a murderer must be put to death. 32 Nor shall you accept ransom for one who has fled to a city of refuge, enabling the fugitive to return to live in the land before the death of the high priest. 33 You shall not pollute the land in which you live; for blood pollutes the land, and no expiation can be made for the land, for the blood that is shed in it, except by the blood of the one who shed it. 34 You shall not defile the land in which you live, in which I also dwell; for I the LORD dwell among the Israelites.

Marriage of Female Heirs

The heads of the ancestral houses of the clans of the descendants of Gil·e·ad son of Ma′chir son of Ma·nas′seh, of the Jo′seph·ite clans, came forward and spoke in the presence of Moses and the leaders, the heads of the ancestral houses of the Israelites; 2 they said, "The LORD commanded my lord to give the land for inheritance by lot to the Israelites; and my lord was commanded by the LORD to give the inheritance of our brother Ze·loph′e·had to his daughters. 3 But if they are married into another Israelite tribe, then their inheritance will be taken from the inheritance of our ancestors and added to the inheritance of the tribe into which they marry; so it will be taken away from the allotted portion of our inheritance. 4 And when the jubilee of the Israelites comes, then their inheritance will be added to the inheritance of the tribe into which they have married; and their inheritance will be taken from the inheritance of our ancestral tribe."

5 Then Moses commanded the Israelites according to the word of the LORD, saying, "The descendants of the tribe of Joseph are right in what they are saying. 6 This is what the LORD commands concerning the daughters of Ze·loph′e·had, 'Let them marry whom they think best; only it must be into a clan of their father's tribe that they are married, 7 so that no inheritance of the Israelites shall be transferred from one tribe to another; for all Israelites shall retain the inheritance of their ancestral tribes. 8 Every daughter who possesses an inheritance in any tribe of the Israelites shall marry one from the clan of her father's tribe, so that all Israelites may continue to possess their ancestral inheritance. 9 No inheritance shall be transferred from one tribe to another; for each of the tribes of the Israelites shall retain its own inheritance.' "

10 The daughters of Ze·loph′e·had did as the LORD had commanded Moses. 11 Mah′lah, Tir′zah, Hog′lah, Mil′cah, and Noah, the daughters of Ze·loph′e·had, married sons of their father's brothers. 12 They were married into the clans of the descendants of Ma·nas′seh son of Joseph, and their inheritance remained in the tribe of their father's clan.

13 These are the commandments and the ordinances that the LORD commanded through Moses to the Israelites in the plains of Mo′ab by the Jordan at Jericho.

---

a Heb *without seeing*

I magine this touching scene: You are standing at the bedside of your aging grandparent with all your cousins and family members. Your grandfather or grandmother begins to speak, sharing stories about the lessons he or she has learned from life. You listen to the familiar stories as if for the first time, and you are awed by the wisdom and love they contain. This is the scene Deuteronomy sets up—Moses is like the wise, aging grandparent, sharing his instructions and encouragement before dying.

At a Glance

- **1.1—4.43.** Moses reviews Israel's history.

- **4.44—11.32.** Moses proclaims obedience to the Torah.

- **Chapters 12–26.** Moses adapts the Covenant for settlement in the Land.

- **Chapters 27–34.** Moses gives a farewell address and dies.

In-depth

The word Deuteronomy means "second law" in Greek. The first Law given on Mount Sinai was proposed by God to guide Israel in its wilderness journey. Written at a time when Israel was settled in the Promised Land and in need of religious reformation, Deuteronomy is a "second Law," adapted to the new situation of a people that needs to be reminded of its Covenant with God.

Deuteronomy has four divisions:

- In the first part (1.1–4.43), Moses addresses Israel by reviewing its history since Mount Horeb (Deuteronomy's term for Mount Sinai). Moses calls Israel to faithfulness and loyalty.

- In part 2 (4.44–11.32), Moses reviews the Ten Commandments and the essence of the Law. He reminds the Israelites of the rewards for obeying and the consequences of disobeying the Law.

- In part 3 (chapters12–26), the most important section of Deuteronomy, Moses spells out a law to shape and govern the Israelites' new life as they settle in the Land.

- Finally, in part 4 (chapters 27–34), Moses gives his last will and testament, offers a final blessing, and dies. His death is portrayed as the "sealing" of the second Law.

More than anything else, Deuteronomy stresses Israel as one people, with one God, one sanctuary, and now one land. These elements not only make Israel a unique people but bind it together in unity and solidarity. The Land of Promise now becomes a symbol of God's blessing and favor, the fulfillment of God's promises in the Covenant.

Quick Facts

Period Covered
just before the Israelites enter the Promised Land

Authors
scribes from the eighth century B.C. adapting the earlier Covenant Law to Israel's changing situation

Theme
the importance of the Covenant, the total commitment required by God's law

The Book of *Deuteronomy*

Deuteronomy

Events at Horeb Recalled

These are the words that Moses spoke to all Israel beyond the Jordan—in the wilderness, on the plain opposite Sūph, between Par'an and Tō'phel, Lā'ban, Ha·zē'roth, and Di-za·hab'. 2 (By the way of Mount Sē'ir it takes eleven days to reach Ka'desh-bar'nē·a from Hō'reb.) 3 In the fortieth year, on the first day of the eleventh month, Moses spoke to the Israelites just as the LORD had commanded him to speak to them. 4 This was after he had defeated King Sī'hon of the Am'o·rītes, who reigned in Hesh'bon, and King Og of Bā'shan, who reigned in Ash'ta·roth and*a* in Ed'rē·ī. 5 Beyond the Jordan in the land of Mō'ab, Moses undertook to expound this law as follows:

6 The LORD our God spoke to us at Hō'reb, saying, "You have stayed long enough at this mountain. 7 Resume your journey, and go into the hill country of the Am'o·rītes as well as into the neighboring regions—the Ar'a·bah, the hill country, the She·phē'lah, the Neg'eb, and the seacoast—the land of the Cā'naan·ītes and the Lebanon, as far as the great river, the river Euphrates. 8 See, I have set the land before you; go in and take possession of the land that I*b* swore to your ancestors, to Abraham, to Isaac, and to Jacob, to give to them and to their descendants after them."

Appointment of Tribal Leaders
(Ex 18.13–27)

9 At that time I said to you, "I am unable by myself to bear you. 10 The LORD your God has multiplied you, so that today you are as numerous as the stars of heaven. 11 May the LORD, the God of your ancestors, increase you a thousand times more and bless you, as he has promised you! 12 But how can I bear the heavy burden of your disputes all by myself? 13 Choose for each of your tribes individuals who are wise, discerning, and reputable to be your leaders." 14 You answered me, "The plan you have proposed is a good one." 15 So I took the leaders of your tribes, wise and reputable individuals, and installed them as leaders over you, commanders of thousands, commanders of hundreds, commanders of fifties, commanders of tens, and officials, throughout your tribes. 16 I charged your judges at that time: "Give the members of your community a fair hearing, and judge rightly between one person and another, whether citizen or resident alien. 17 You must not be partial in judging: hear out the small and the great alike; you shall not be intimidated by anyone, for the judgment is God's. Any case that is too hard for

a Gk Syr Vg Compare Josh 12.4: Heb lacks *and*
b Sam Gk: MT *the LORD*

you, bring to me, and I will hear it." [18] So I charged you at that time with all the things that you should do.

Israel's Refusal to Enter the Land
(Num 13.1–33)

19 Then, just as the LORD our God had ordered us, we set out from Hō'reb and went through all that great and terrible wilderness that you saw, on the way to the hill country of the Am'o•rītes, until we reached Kā'desh-bar'nē•a. [20] I said to you, "You have reached the hill country of the Am'o•rītes, which the LORD our God is giving us. [21] See, the LORD your God has given the land to you; go up, take possession, as the LORD, the God of your ancestors, has promised you; do not fear or be dismayed."

22 All of you came to me and said, "Let us send men ahead of us to explore the land for us and bring back a report to us regarding the route by which we should go up and the cities we will come to." [23] The plan seemed good to me, and I selected twelve of you, one from each tribe. [24] They set out and went up into the hill country, and when they reached the Valley of Esh'col they spied it out [25] and gathered some of the land's produce, which they brought down to us. They brought back a report to us, and said, "It is a good land that the LORD our God is giving us."

26 But you were unwilling to go up. You rebelled against the command of the LORD your God; [27] you grumbled in your tents and said, "It is because the LORD hates us that he has brought us out of the land of Egypt, to hand us over to the Am'o•rītes to destroy us. [28] Where are we headed? Our kindred have made our hearts melt by reporting, 'The people are stronger and taller than we; the cities are large and fortified up to heaven! We actually saw there the offspring of the An'a•kim!' " [29] I said to you, "Have no dread or fear of them. [30] The LORD your God, who goes before you, is the one who will fight for you, just as he did for you in Egypt before your very eyes, [31] and in the wilderness, where you saw how the LORD your God carried you, just as one carries a child, all the way that you traveled until you reached this place. [32] But in spite of this, you have no trust in the LORD your God, [33] who goes before you on the way to seek out a place for you to camp, in fire by night, and in the cloud by day, to show you the route you should take."

The Penalty for Israel's Rebellion
(Num 14.20–45)

34 When the LORD heard your words, he was wrathful and swore: [35] "Not one of these—not one

of this evil generation—shall see the good land that I swore to give to your ancestors, [36] except Caleb son of Je•phūn'neh. He shall see it, and to him and to his descendants I will give the land on which he set foot, because of his complete fidelity to the LORD." [37] Even with me the LORD was angry on your account, saying, "You also shall not enter there. [38] Joshua son of Nun, your assistant, shall enter there; encourage him, for he is the one who will secure Israel's possession of it. [39] And as for your little ones, who you thought would become booty, your children, who today do not yet know right from wrong, they shall enter there; to them I will give it, and they shall take possession of it. [40] But as for you, journey back into the wilderness, in the direction of the Red Sea."[c]

41 You answered me, "We have sinned against the LORD! We are ready to go up and fight, just as the LORD our God commanded us." So all of you strapped on your battle gear, and thought it easy to go up into the hill country. [42] The LORD said to me, "Say to them, 'Do not go up and do not fight, for I am not in the midst of you; otherwise you will be defeated by your enemies.' " [43] Although I told you, you would not listen. You rebelled against the command of the LORD and presumptuously went up into the hill country. [44] The Am'o•rītes who lived in that hill country then came out against you and chased you as bees do. They beat you down in Sē'ir as far as Hor'mah. [45] When you returned and wept before the LORD, the LORD would neither heed your voice nor pay you any attention.

The Desert Years

46 After you had stayed at Kā'desh as many days as you did, [1] we journeyed back into the wilderness, in the direction of the Red Sea,[c] as the LORD had told me and skirted Mount Sē'ir for many days. [2] Then the LORD said to me: [3] "You have been skirting this hill country long enough. Head north, [4] and charge the people as follows: You are about to pass through the territory of your kindred, the descendants of Esau, who live in Sē'ir. They will be afraid of you, so, be very careful [5] not to engage in battle with them, for I will not give you even so much as a foot's length of their land, since I have given Mount Sē'ir to Esau as a possession. [6] You shall purchase food from them for money, so that you may eat; and you shall also buy water from them for money, so that you may drink. [7] Surely the LORD your God has blessed you in all your undertakings; he knows your going through this great wilderness. These forty years the LORD your God has been with you; you have lacked

---

c Or *Sea of Reeds*

nothing." 8 So we passed by our kin, the descendants of Esau who live in Sē'ir, leaving behind the route of the Ar'a•bah, and leaving behind Ē'lath and Ē'zi•on-gē'ber.

When we had headed out along the route of the wilderness of Mō'ab, 9 the LORD said to me: "Do not harass Mō'ab or engage them in battle, for I will not give you any of its land as a possession, since I have given Ar as a possession to the descendants of Lot." 10 (The Ē'mim—a large and numerous people, as tall as the An'a•kim—had formerly inhabited it. 11 Like the An'a•kim, they are usually reckoned as Reph'a•im, though the Mō'ab•ites call them Ē'mim. 12 Moreover, the Hō'rim had formerly inhabited Sē'ir, but the descendants of Esau dispossessed them, destroying them and settling in their place, as Israel has done in the land that the LORD gave them as a possession.) 13 "Now then, proceed to cross over the Wadi Zē'red."

So we crossed over the Wadi Zē'red. 14 And the length of time we had traveled from Kā'desh-bar'nē•a until we crossed the Wadi Zē'red was thirty-eight years, until the entire generation of warriors had perished from the camp, as the LORD had sworn concerning them. 15 Indeed, the LORD's own hand was against them, to root them out from the camp, until all had perished.

16 Just as soon as all the warriors had died off from among the people, 17 the LORD spoke to me, saying, 18 "Today you are going to cross the boundary of Mō'ab at Ar. 19 When you approach the frontier of the Am'mon•ites, do not harass them or engage them in battle, for I will not give the land of the Am'mon•ites to you as a possession, because I have given it to the descendants of Lot." 20 (It also is usually reckoned as a land of Reph'a•im. Reph'a•im formerly inhabited it, though the Am'mon•ites call them Zam•zum'mim, 21 a strong and numerous people, as tall as the An'a•kim. But the LORD destroyed them from before the Am'mon•ites so that they could dispossess them and settle in their place. 22 He did the same for the descendants of Esau, who live in Sē'ir, by destroying the Hō'rim before them so that they could dispossess them and settle in their place even to this day. 23 As for the Av'vim, who had lived in settlements in the vicinity of Gā'za, the Caph'to•rim, who came from Caph'tor, destroyed them and settled in their place.) 24 "Proceed on your journey and cross the Wadi Ar'non. See, I have handed over to you King Sī'hon the Am'o•rite of Hesh'bon, and his land. Begin to take possession by engaging him in battle. 25 This day I will begin to put the dread and fear of you upon the peoples everywhere under heaven; when they hear report of you, they will tremble and be in anguish because of you."

Defeat of King Sihon
(Num 21.21–32)

26 So I sent messengers from the wilderness of Ked'e•moth to King Sī'hon of Hesh'bon with the following terms of peace: 27 "If you let me pass through your land, I will travel only along the road; I will turn aside neither to the right nor to the left. 28 You shall sell me food for money, so that I may eat, and supply me water for money, so that I may drink. Only allow me to pass through on foot— 29 just as the descendants of Esau who live in Sē'ir have done for me and likewise the Mō'ab•ites who live in Ar—until I cross the Jordan into the land that the LORD our God is giving us." 30 But King Sī'hon of Hesh'bon was not willing to let us pass through, for the LORD your God had hardened his spirit and made his heart defiant in order to hand him over to you, as he has now done.

31 The LORD said to me, "See, I have begun to give Sī'hon and his land over to you. Begin now to take possession of his land." 32 So when Sī'hon came out against us, he and all his people for battle at Jā'haz, 33 the LORD our God gave him over to us; and we struck him down, along with his offspring and all his people. 34 At that time we captured all his towns, and in each town we utterly destroyed men, women, and children. We left not a single survivor. 35 Only the livestock we kept as spoil for ourselves, as well as the plunder of the towns that we had captured. 36 From A•rō'er on the edge of the Wadi Ar'non (including the town that is in the wadi itself) as far as Gil'e•ad, there was no citadel too high for us. The LORD our God gave everything to us. 37 You did not encroach, however, on the land of the Am'mon•ites, avoiding the whole upper region of the Wadi Jab'bok as well as the towns of the hill country, just as[d] the LORD our God had charged.

Defeat of King Og
(Num 21.33–35)

When we headed up the road to Bā'shan, King Og of Bā'shan came out against us, he and all his people, for battle at Ed'rē•i. 2 The LORD said to me, "Do not fear him, for I have handed him over to you, along with his people and his land. Do to him as you did to King Sī'hon of the Am'o•rites, who reigned in Hesh'bon." 3 So the LORD our God also handed over to us King Og of Bā'shan and all his people. We struck him down until not a single survivor was left. 4 At that time we captured all his towns; there was no citadel that we did not take from them—sixty towns, the whole region of Ar'-

---

d Gk Tg: Heb and all

gob, the kingdom of Og in Bā'shan. [5] All these were fortress towns with high walls, double gates, and bars, besides a great many villages. [6] And we utterly destroyed them, as we had done to King Sī'hon of Hesh'bon, in each city utterly destroying men, women, and children. [7] But all the livestock and the plunder of the towns we kept as spoil for ourselves.

8 So at that time we took from the two kings of the Am'o•rītes the land beyond the Jordan, from the Wadi Ar'non to Mount Hermon [9] (the Sī•dō'ni-ans call Hermon Sir'i•on, while the Am'o•rītes call it Sē'nir), [10] all the towns of the tableland, the whole of Gil'e•ad, and all of Bā'shan, as far as Sal'e•cah and Ed'rē•ī, towns of Og's kingdom in Bā'shan. [11] (Now only King Og of Bā'shan was left of the remnant of the Reph'a•im. In fact his bed, an iron bed, can still be seen in Rab'bah of the Am'mon-ītes. By the common cubit it is nine cubits long and four cubits wide.) [12] As for the land that we took possession of at that time, I gave to the Reū'-ben•ītes and Gad'ītes the territory north of A•rō'er,[e] that is on the edge of the Wadi Ar'non, as well as half the hill country of Gil'e•ad with its towns, [13] and I gave to the half-tribe of Ma•nas'seh the rest of Gil'e•ad and all of Bā'shan, Og's kingdom. (The whole region of Ar'gob: all that portion of Bā'shan used to be called a land of Reph'a•im; [14] Jā'ir the Ma•nas'sīte acquired the whole region of Ar'gob as far as the border of the Gesh'ū•rītes and the Mā'a-ca•thītes, and he named them—that is, Bā'shan—after himself, Hav'voth-jā'ir,[f] as it is to this day.) [15] To Mā'chir I gave Gil'e•ad. [16] And to the Reū'-ben•ītes and the Gad'ītes I gave the territory from Gil'e•ad as far as the Wadi Ar'non, with the middle of the wadi as a boundary, and up to the Jab'bok, the wadi being boundary of the Am'mon•ītes; [17] the Ar'a•bah also, with the Jordan and its banks, from Chin'ne•reth down to the sea of the Ar'a•bah, the Dead Sea,[g] with the lower slopes of Pis'gah on the east.

18 At that time, I charged you as follows: "Al-though the LORD your God has given you this land to occupy, all your troops shall cross over armed as the vanguard of your Israelite kin. [19] Only your wives, your children, and your livestock—I know that you have much livestock—shall stay behind in the towns that I have given to you. [20] When the LORD gives rest to your kindred, as to you, and they too have occupied the land that the LORD your God is giving them beyond the Jordan, then each of you may return to the property that I have given to you." [21] And I charged Joshua as well at that time, saying: "Your own eyes have seen everything that the LORD your God has done to these two kings; so the LORD will do to all the kingdoms into which

you are about to cross. [22] Do not fear them, for it is the LORD your God who fights for you."

Moses Views Canaan from Pisgah

23 At that time, too, I entreated the LORD, say-ing: [24] "O Lord GOD, you have only begun to show your servant your greatness and your might; what god in heaven or on earth can perform deeds and mighty acts like yours! [25] Let me cross over to see the good land beyond the Jordan, that good hill country and the Lebanon." [26] But the LORD was an-gry with me on your account and would not heed me. The LORD said to me, "Enough from you! Never speak to me of this matter again! [27] Go up to the top of Pis'gah and look around you to the west, to the north, to the south, and to the east. Look well, for you shall not cross over this Jor-dan. [28] But charge Joshua, and encourage and strengthen him, because it is he who shall cross over at the head of this people and who shall se-cure their possession of the land that you will see." [29] So we remained in the valley opposite Beth-pe'or.

Moses Commands Obedience

So now, Israel, give heed to the statutes and ordi-nances that I am teaching you to observe, so that you may live to enter and occupy the land that the LORD, the God of your ancestors, is giving you. [2] You must neither add anything to what I com-mand you nor take away anything from it, but keep the commandments of the LORD your God with which I am charging you. [3] You have seen for yourselves what the LORD did with regard to the Bā'al of Pē'or—how the LORD your God destroyed from among you everyone who followed the Bā'al of Pē'or, [4] while those of you who held fast to the LORD your God are all alive today.

5 See, just as the LORD my God has charged me, I now teach you statutes and ordinances for you to observe in the land that you are about to enter and occupy. [6] You must observe them diligently, for this will show your wisdom and discernment to the peoples, who, when they hear all these stat-utes, will say, "Surely this great nation is a wise and discerning people!" [7] For what other great na-tion has a god so near to it as the LORD our God is whenever we call to him? [8] And what other great nation has statutes and ordinances as just as this entire law that I am setting before you today?

9 But take care and watch yourselves closely, so as neither to forget the things that your eyes have seen nor to let them slip from your mind all the

---

e Heb *territory from Aroer*　f That is *Settlement of Jair*
g Heb *Salt Sea*

days of your life; make them known to your children and your children's children— 10 how you once stood before the LORD your God at Hō'reb, when the LORD said to me, "Assemble the people for me, and I will let them hear my words, so that they may learn to fear me as long as they live on the earth, and may teach their children so"; 11 you approached and stood at the foot of the mountain while the mountain was blazing up to the very heavens, shrouded in dark clouds. 12 Then the LORD spoke to you out of the fire. You heard the sound of words but saw no form; there was only a voice. 13 He declared to you his covenant, which he charged you to observe, that is, the ten commandments;h and he wrote them on two stone tablets. 14 And the LORD charged me at that time to teach you statutes and ordinances for you to observe in the land that you are about to cross into and occupy.

15 Since you saw no form when the LORD spoke to you at Hō'reb out of the fire, take care and watch yourselves closely, 16 so that you do not act corruptly by making an idol for yourselves, in the form of any figure—the likeness of male or female, 17 the likeness of any animal that is on the earth, the likeness of any winged bird that flies in the air, 18 the likeness of anything that creeps on the ground, the likeness of any fish that is in the water under the earth. 19 And when you look up to the heavens and see the sun, the moon, and the stars, all the host of heaven, do not be led astray and bow down to them and serve them, things that the LORD your God has allotted to all the peoples everywhere under heaven. 20 But the LORD has taken you and brought you out of the iron-smelter, out of Egypt, to become a people of his very own possession, as you are now.

21 The LORD was angry with me because of you, and he vowed that I should not cross the Jordan and that I should not enter the good land that the LORD your God is giving for your possession. 22 For I am going to die in this land without crossing over the Jordan, but you are going to cross over to take possession of that good land. 23 So be careful not to forget the covenant that the LORD your God made with you, and not to make for yourselves an idol in the form of anything that the LORD your God has forbidden you. 24 For the LORD your God is a devouring fire, a jealous God.

25 When you have had children and children's children, and become complacent in the land, if you act corruptly by making an idol in the form of anything, thus doing what is evil in the sight of the LORD your God, and provoking him to anger, 26 I call heaven and earth to witness against you today that you will soon utterly perish from the land that

you are crossing the Jordan to occupy; you will not live long on it, but will be utterly destroyed. 27 The LORD will scatter you among the peoples; only a few of you will be left among the nations where the LORD will lead you. 28 There you will serve other gods made by human hands, objects of wood and stone that neither see, nor hear, nor eat, nor smell. 29 From there you will seek the LORD your God, and you will find him if you search after him with all your heart and soul. 30 In your distress, when all these things have happened to you in time to come, you will return to the LORD your God and heed him. 31 Because the LORD your God is a merciful God, he will neither abandon you nor destroy you; he will not forget the covenant with your ancestors that he swore to them.

32 For ask now about former ages, long before your own, ever since the day that God created human beings on the earth; ask from one end of heaven to the other: has anything so great as this ever happened or has its like ever been heard of? 33 Has any people ever heard the voice of a god speaking out of a fire, as you have heard, and lived? 34 Or has any god ever attempted to go and take a nation for himself from the midst of another nation, by trials, by signs and wonders, by war, by a mighty hand and an outstretched arm, and by terrifying displays of power, as the LORD your God did for you in Egypt before your very eyes? 35 To you it was shown so that you would acknowledge that the LORD is God; there is no other besides him. 36 From heaven he made you hear his voice to discipline you. On earth he showed you his great fire, while you heard his words coming out of the fire. 37 And because he loved your ancestors, he chose their descendants after them. He brought you out of Egypt with his own presence, by his great power, 38 driving out before you nations greater and mightier than yourselves, to bring you in, giving you their land for a possession, as it is still today. 39 So acknowledge today and take to heart that the LORD is God in heaven above and on the earth beneath; there is no other. 40 Keep his statutes and his commandments, which I am commanding you today for your own well-being and that of your descendants after you, so that you may long remain in the land that the LORD your God is giving you for all time.

Cities of Refuge East of the Jordan

41 Then Moses set apart on the east side of the Jordan three cities 42 to which a homicide could flee, someone who unintentionally kills another person, the two not having been at enmity before;

---

h Heb the ten words

the homicide could flee to one of these cities and live: 43 Bĕ′zer in the wilderness on the tableland belonging to the Reū′ben•ītes, Rā′moth in Gil′e•ad belonging to the Gad′ītes, and Gō′lan in Bā′shan belonging to the Ma•nas′sītes.

Transition to the Second Address

44 This is the law that Moses set before the Israelites. 45 These are the decrees and the statutes and ordinances that Moses spoke to the Israelites when they had come out of Egypt, 46 beyond the Jordan in the valley opposite Beth-pĕ′or, in the land of King Sī′hon of the Am′o•rītes, who reigned at Hesh′bon, whom Moses and the Israelites defeated when they came out of Egypt. 47 They occupied his land and the land of King Og of Bā′shan, the two kings of the Am′o•rītes on the eastern side of the Jordan: 48 from A•rō′er, which is on the edge of the Wadi Ar′non, as far as Mount Sir′i•on^j (that is, Hermon), 49 together with all the Ar′a•bah on the east side of the Jordan as far as the Sea of the Ar′a•bah, under the slopes of Pis′gah.

The Ten Commandments
(Ex 20.1–17)

Moses convened all Israel, and said to them:

Hear, O Israel, the statutes and ordinances that I am addressing to you today; you shall learn them and observe them diligently. 2 The LORD our God made a covenant with us at Hō′reb. 3 Not with our ancestors did the LORD make this covenant, but with us, who are all of us here alive today. 4 The LORD spoke with you face to face at the mountain, out of the fire. 5 (At that time I was standing between the LORD and you to declare to you the words^j of the LORD; for you were afraid because of the fire and did not go up the mountain.) And he said:

6 I am the LORD your God, who brought you out of the land of Egypt, out of the house of slavery; 7 you shall have no other gods before^k me.

8 You shall not make for yourself an idol, whether in the form of anything that is in heaven above, or that is on the earth beneath, or that is in the water under the earth. 9 You shall not bow down to them or worship them; for I the LORD your God am a jealous God, punishing children for the iniquity of parents, to the third and fourth generation of those who reject me, 10 but showing steadfast love to the thousandth generation^l of those who love me and keep my commandments.

11 You shall not make wrongful use of the name of the LORD your God, for the LORD will not acquit anyone who misuses his name.

12 Observe the sabbath day and keep it holy, as the LORD your God commanded you. 13 Six days

▶▶▶▶▶▶▶▶▶▶▶

NATIVE AMERICAN

The Lakota Code

See how similar these guidelines from a Native American tribal code are to the Ten Commandments (Deut 5.1–21), not to mention our own civil laws, school policies, and even family rules. What can we learn from them?

- Love one another.
- Pity orphan children. Be kind to them because they are poor; feed them and clothe them.
- Do not kill one another.
- Do not steal anything from anyone, especially from your own people.
- Do not tell lies to anyone, or lie about anyone.
- Respect your brothers and sisters. Do not marry in your own family.
- The ability to make good speech is a great gift from their maker, owner of all things, to the people. This is why you should not talk badly about anyone. Bad talk can hurt one's family or everyday life.
- Never quarrel among one another. Be good to others and always be friendly to whomever you meet, wherever you meet them.
- Do not brag about yourself, or try to hurt another's feelings. The generous person is the one who is respected.

(Ron Zeilinger, *Sacred Ground*, pp. 74–75)

▶ Deut 5.1–21

you shall labor and do all your work. 14 But the seventh day is a sabbath to the LORD your God; you shall not do any work—you, or your son or your daughter, or your male or female slave, or your ox or your donkey, or any of your livestock, or the resident alien in your towns, so that your male and female slave may rest as well as you.

---

i Syr: Heb *Sion* j Q Mss Sam Gk Syr Vg Tg: MT *word*
k Or *besides* l Or *to thousands*

DEUT

15 Remember that you were a slave in the land of Egypt, and the LORD your God brought you out from there with a mighty hand and an outstretched arm; therefore the LORD your God commanded you to keep the sabbath day.

16 Honor your father and your mother, as the LORD your God commanded you, so that your days may be long and that it may go well with you in the land that the LORD your God is giving you.

17 You shall not murder.*m*

18 Neither shall you commit adultery.

19 Neither shall you steal.

20 Neither shall you bear false witness against your neighbor.

21 Neither shall you covet your neighbor's wife.

Neither shall you desire your neighbor's house, or field, or male or female slave, or ox, or donkey, or anything that belongs to your neighbor.

Moses the Mediator of God's Will
(Ex 20.18–21)

22 These words the LORD spoke with a loud voice to your whole assembly at the mountain, out of the fire, the cloud, and the thick darkness, and he added no more. He wrote them on two stone tablets, and gave them to me. 23 When you heard the voice out of the darkness, while the mountain was burning with fire, you approached me, all the heads of your tribes and your elders; 24 and you said, "Look, the LORD our God has shown us his glory and greatness, and we have heard his voice out of the fire. Today we have seen that God may speak to someone and the person may still live. 25 So now why should we die? For this great fire will consume us; if we hear the voice of the LORD our God any longer, we shall die. 26 For who is there of all flesh that has heard the voice of the living God speaking out of fire, as we have, and remained alive? 27 Go near, you yourself, and hear all that the LORD our God will say. Then tell us everything that the LORD our God tells you, and we will listen and do it."

28 The LORD heard your words when you spoke to me, and the LORD said to me: "I have heard the words of this people, which they have spoken to you; they are right in all that they have spoken. 29 If only they had such a mind as this, to fear me and to keep all my commandments always, so that it might go well with them and with their children forever! 30 Go say to them, 'Return to your tents.' 31 But you, stand here by me, and I will tell you all the commandments, the statutes and the ordinances, that you shall teach them, so that they may do them in the land that I am giving them to

possess." 32 You must therefore be careful to do as the LORD your God has commanded you; you shall not turn to the right or to the left. 33 You must follow exactly the path that the LORD your God has commanded you, so that you may live, and that it may go well with you, and that you may live long in the land that you are to possess.

The Great Commandment

Now this is the commandment—the statutes and the ordinances—that the LORD your God charged me to teach you to observe in the land that you are about to cross into and occupy, 2 so that you and your children and your children's children may fear the LORD your God all the days of your life, and keep all his decrees and his commandments that I am commanding you, so that your days may be long. 3 Hear therefore, O Israel, and observe them diligently, so that it may go well with you, and so that you may multiply greatly in a land flowing with milk and honey, as the LORD, the God of your ancestors, has promised you.

4 Hear, O Israel: The LORD is our God, the LORD alone.*n* 5 You shall love the LORD your God with all your heart, and with all your soul, and with all your might. 6 Keep these words that I am commanding you today in your heart. 7 Recite them to your children and talk about them when you are at home and when you are away, when you lie down and when you rise. 8 Bind them as a sign on your hand, fix them as an emblem*o* on your forehead, 9 and write them on the doorposts of your house and on your gates.

Caution against Disobedience

10 When the LORD your God has brought you into the land that he swore to your ancestors, to Abraham, to Isaac, and to Jacob, to give you—a land with fine, large cities that you did not build, 11 houses filled with all sorts of goods that you did not fill, hewn cisterns that you did not hew, vineyards and olive groves that you did not plant—and when you have eaten your fill, 12 take care that you do not forget the LORD, who brought you out of the land of Egypt, out of the house of slavery. 13 The LORD your God you shall fear; him you shall serve, and by his name alone you shall swear. 14 Do not follow other gods, any of the gods of the peoples who are all around you, 15 because the LORD your God, who is present with you, is a jeal-

---

m Or *kill*   *n* Or *The LORD our God is one LORD*, or *The LORD our God, the LORD is one*, or *The LORD is our God, the LORD is one*   *o* Or *as a frontlet*

PRAY IT!

The Shema: Putting God First

Deuteronomy 6.4 is the most famous declaration of faith in the Old Testament: "Hear, O Israel: The LORD is our God, the LORD alone." This short verse, part of a prayer called the Shema, is uttered daily by faithful Jews. It has been so important that the commands of verses 8–9 often have been interpreted literally. The Pharisees of Jesus' day, for example, wore miniature copies of the prayer on their bodies and attached other copies to their doorposts. Orthodox Jews today continue this tradition. Keeping the law of God is a privilege—something to be "worn" with pride!

The Shema reminds Jewish people to put God first and to love God with all their heart, soul, and might. Think about someone who seems to carry God in their heart all the time. Are they lost and frustrated? Do they seem angry and hate filled? Chances are they seem more relaxed and sure of themselves than most people do. Having God in your sights at all times will help in more ways than you could ever imagine!

▸ **Deut 6.4–9**

ous God. The anger of the LORD your God would be kindled against you and he would destroy you from the face of the earth.

16 Do not put the LORD your God to the test, as you tested him at Mas′sah. 17 You must diligently keep the commandments of the LORD your God, and his decrees, and his statutes that he has commanded you. 18 Do what is right and good in the sight of the LORD, so that it may go well with you, and so that you may go in and occupy the good land that the LORD swore to your ancestors to give you, 19 thrusting out all your enemies from before you, as the LORD has promised.

20 When your children ask you in time to come, "What is the meaning of the decrees and the statutes and the ordinances that the LORD our God has commanded you?" 21 then you shall say to your children, "We were Pharaoh's slaves in Egypt,

but the LORD brought us out of Egypt with a mighty hand. 22 The LORD displayed before our eyes great and awesome signs and wonders against Egypt, against Pharaoh and all his household. 23 He brought us out from there in order to bring us in, to give us the land that he promised on oath to our ancestors. 24 Then the LORD commanded us to observe all these statutes, to fear the LORD our God, for our lasting good, so as to keep us alive, as is now the case. 25 If we diligently observe this entire commandment before the LORD our God, as he has commanded us, we will be in the right."

A Chosen People
(Ex 34.10–16)

When the LORD your God brings you into the land that you are about to enter and occupy, and he clears away many nations before you—the Hit′tītes, the Gir′ga•shītes, the Am′o•rītes, the Cā′naan•ītes, the Per′iz•zītes, the Hī′vītes, and the Jeb′ū•sītes, seven nations mightier and more numerous than you— 2 and when the LORD your God gives them over to you and you defeat them, then you must utterly destroy them. Make no covenant with them and show them no mercy. 3 Do not intermarry with them, giving your daughters to their sons or taking their daughters for your sons, 4 for that would turn away your children from following me, to serve other gods. Then the anger of the LORD would be kindled against you, and he would destroy you quickly. 5 But this is how you must deal with them: break down their altars, smash their pillars, hew down their sacred poles,*p* and burn their idols with fire. 6 For you are a people holy to the LORD your God; the LORD your God has chosen you out of all the peoples on earth to be his people, his treasured possession.

7 It was not because you were more numerous than any other people that the LORD set his heart on you and chose you—for you were the fewest of all peoples. 8 It was because the LORD loved you and kept the oath that he swore to your ancestors, that the LORD has brought you out with a mighty hand, and redeemed you from the house of slavery, from the hand of Pharaoh king of Egypt. 9 Know therefore that the LORD your God is God, the faithful God who maintains covenant loyalty with those who love him and keep his commandments, to a thousand generations, 10 and who repays in their own person those who reject him. He does not delay but repays in their own person

p Heb *Asherim*

DEUT

those who reject him. ¹¹ Therefore, observe diligently the commandment—the statutes and the ordinances—that I am commanding you today.

Blessings for Obedience
(Lev 26.1–13; Deut 28.1–14)

12 If you heed these ordinances, by diligently observing them, the LORD your God will maintain with you the covenant loyalty that he swore to your ancestors; ¹³ he will love you, bless you, and multiply you; he will bless the fruit of your womb and the fruit of your ground, your grain and your wine and your oil, the increase of your cattle and the issue of your flock, in the land that he swore to your ancestors to give you. ¹⁴ You shall be the most blessed of peoples, with neither sterility nor barrenness among you or your livestock. ¹⁵ The LORD will turn away from you every illness; all the dread diseases of Egypt that you experienced, he will not inflict on you, but he will lay them on all who hate you. ¹⁶ You shall devour all the peoples that the LORD your God is giving over to you, showing them no pity; you shall not serve their gods, for that would be a snare to you.

17 If you say to yourself, "These nations are more numerous than I; how can I dispossess them?" ¹⁸ do not be afraid of them. Just remember what the LORD your God did to Pharaoh and to all Egypt, ¹⁹ the great trials that your eyes saw, the signs and wonders, the mighty hand and the outstretched arm by which the LORD your God brought you out. The LORD your God will do the same to all the peoples of whom you are afraid. ²⁰ Moreover, the LORD your God will send the pestilence*q* against them, until even the survivors and the fugitives are destroyed. ²¹ Have no dread of them, for the LORD your God, who is present with you, is a great and awesome God. ²² The LORD your God will clear away these nations before you little by little; you will not be able to make a quick end of them, otherwise the wild animals would become too numerous for you. ²³ But the LORD your God will give them over to you, and throw them into great panic, until they are destroyed. ²⁴ He will hand their kings over to you and you shall blot out their name from under heaven; no one will be able to stand against you, until you have destroyed them. ²⁵ The images of their gods you shall burn with fire. Do not covet the silver or the gold that is on them and take it for yourself, because you could be ensnared by it; for it is abhorrent to the LORD your God. ²⁶ Do not bring an abhorrent thing into your house, or you will be set apart for destruction like it. You must utterly detest and abhor it, for it is set apart for destruction.

A Warning Not to Forget God in Prosperity

This entire commandment that I command you today you must diligently observe, so that you may live and increase, and go in and occupy the land that the LORD promised on oath to your ancestors. ² Remember the long way that the LORD your God has led you these forty years in the wilderness, in order to humble you, testing you to know what was in your heart, whether or not you would keep his commandments. ³ He humbled you by letting you hunger, then by feeding you with manna, with which neither you nor your ancestors were acquainted, in order to make you understand that one does not live by bread alone, but by every word that comes from the mouth of the LORD.*r* ⁴ The clothes on your back did not wear out and your feet did not swell these forty years. ⁵ Know then in your heart that as a parent disciplines a child so the LORD your God disciplines you. ⁶ Therefore keep the commandments of the LORD your God, by walking in his ways and by fearing him. ⁷ For the LORD your God is bringing you into a good land, a land with flowing streams, with springs and underground waters welling up in valleys and hills, ⁸ a land of wheat and barley, of vines and fig trees and pomegranates, a land of olive trees and honey, ⁹ a land where you may eat bread without scarcity, where you will lack nothing, a land whose stones are iron and from whose hills you may mine copper. ¹⁰ You shall eat your fill and bless the LORD your God for the good land that he has given you.

11 Take care that you do not forget the LORD your God, by failing to keep his commandments, his ordinances, and his statutes, which I am commanding you today. ¹² When you have eaten your fill and have built fine houses and live in them, ¹³ and when your herds and flocks have multiplied, and your silver and gold is multiplied, and all that you have is multiplied, ¹⁴ then do not exalt yourself, forgetting the LORD your God, who brought you out of the land of Egypt, out of the house of slavery, ¹⁵ who led you through the great and terrible wilderness, an arid wasteland with poisonous*s* snakes and scorpions. He made water flow for you from flint rock, ¹⁶ and fed you in the wilderness with manna that your ancestors did not know, to humble you and to test you, and in the end to do you good. ¹⁷ Do not say to yourself, "My power and the might of my own hand have gotten me this wealth." ¹⁸ But remember the LORD your God, for it is he who gives you power to get wealth, so that he may confirm his covenant that

---

q Or *hornets*: Meaning of Heb uncertain   *r* Or *by anything that the* LORD *decrees*   *s* Or *fiery*; Heb *seraph*

AFRICAN AMERICAN
The Principle of *Ujima*

Picture in your mind the Pyramids of Egypt. Think about the hundreds of years it took to build them and the thousands of years that they have been standing. Think about the complexity of their architectural design. Some of the stones weigh as much as 2.5 tons, and all of them were aligned perfectly without cement. Modern teams of architects, scientists, mathematicians, and builders have studied the Pyramids and still not been able to fathom re-creating this feat.

The Pyramids are just one example of what can be accomplished through the Kwanzaa principle of *ujima* (see "Kwanzaa as a Way of Life," Deut 10.12–22), which is collective work and responsibility. Long ago, Africans (Egyptians) worked together diligently to accomplish this task. Some had to begin the task knowing that they would never see the finished product. Today, we need young people who are willing to work on the foundation of a structure that may not be completed for many years.

Martin Luther King Jr. did this. In his last speech, he said to you and me: "I've been to the Mountain top and I've seen the Promised Land. I may not get there with you, but I want you to know that we as a people will get to the Promised Land." He knew that he would not live to see his people freed from prejudice and discrimination. But he spent his whole life working with others toward that goal.

The author of Deuteronomy wrote long after Moses' time. Many of the Chosen People had indeed become wealthy, so he used Moses' authority to remind them of how they had gotten to where they were. Their ancestors—escaped, impoverished slaves—trusted in God and worked together over a long time to bring prosperity to the nation. This is the mentality we too must cultivate in order to bring success to ourselves and our people.

▶ **Deut 8.11–18**

---

he swore to your ancestors, as he is doing today. ¹⁹ If you do forget the LORD your God and follow other gods to serve and worship them, I solemnly warn you today that you shall surely perish. ²⁰ Like the nations that the LORD is destroying before you, so shall you perish, because you would not obey the voice of the LORD your God.

The Consequences of Rebelling against God
(Ex 32.1–35)

Hear, O Israel! You are about to cross the Jordan today, to go in and dispossess nations larger and mightier than you, great cities, fortified to the heavens, ² a strong and tall people, the offspring of the An'a•kim, whom you know. You have heard it said of them, "Who can stand up to the An'a•kim?" ³ Know then today that the LORD your God is the one who crosses over before you as a devouring fire; he will defeat them and subdue them before you, so that you may dispossess and destroy them quickly, as the LORD has promised you.

4 When the LORD your God thrusts them out before you, do not say to yourself, "It is because of my righteousness that the LORD has brought me in to occupy this land"; it is rather because of the wickedness of these nations that the LORD is dispossessing them before you. ⁵ It is not because of your righteousness or the uprightness of your heart that you are going in to occupy their land; but because of the wickedness of these nations the LORD your God is dispossessing them before you, in order to fulfill the promise that the LORD made on oath to your ancestors, to Abraham, to Isaac, and to Jacob.

6 Know, then, that the LORD your God is not giving you this good land to occupy because of your righteousness; for you are a stubborn people. ⁷ Remember and do not forget how you provoked the LORD your God to wrath in the wilderness; you have been rebellious against the LORD from the day you came out of the land of Egypt until you came to this place.

8 Even at Hō'reb you provoked the LORD to wrath, and the LORD was so angry with you that he was ready to destroy you. ⁹ When I went up the mountain to receive the stone tablets, the tablets

D
E
U
T

of the covenant that the LORD made with you, I remained on the mountain forty days and forty nights; I neither ate bread nor drank water. 10 And the LORD gave me the two stone tablets written with the finger of God; on them were all the words that the LORD had spoken to you at the mountain out of the fire on the day of the assembly. 11 At the end of forty days and forty nights the LORD gave me the two stone tablets, the tablets of the covenant. 12 Then the LORD said to me, "Get up, go down quickly from here, for your people whom you have brought from Egypt have acted corruptly. They have been quick to turn from the way that I commanded them; they have cast an image for themselves." 13 Furthermore the LORD said to me, "I have seen that this people is indeed a stubborn people. 14 Let me alone that I may destroy them and blot out their name from under heaven; and I will make of you a nation mightier and more numerous than they."

15 So I turned and went down from the mountain, while the mountain was ablaze; the two tablets of the covenant were in my two hands. 16 Then I saw that you had indeed sinned against the LORD your God, by casting for yourselves an image of a calf; you had been quick to turn from the way that the LORD had commanded you. 17 So I took hold of the two tablets and flung them from my two hands, smashing them before your eyes. 18 Then I lay prostrate before the LORD as before, forty days and forty nights; I neither ate bread nor drank water, because of all the sin you had committed, provoking the LORD by doing what was evil in his sight. 19 For I was afraid that the anger that the LORD bore against you was so fierce that he would destroy you. But the LORD listened to me that time also. 20 The LORD was so angry with Aaron that he was ready to destroy him, but I interceded also on behalf of Aaron at that same time. 21 Then I took the sinful thing you had made, the calf, and burned it with fire and crushed it, grinding it thoroughly, until it was reduced to dust; and I threw the dust of it into the stream that runs down the mountain.

22 At Tab'e•rah also, and at Mas'sah, and at Kib'roth-hat•ta'a•vah, you provoked the LORD to wrath. 23 And when the LORD sent you from Kā'-desh-bar'nē•a, saying, "Go up and occupy the land that I have given you," you rebelled against the command of the LORD your God, neither trusting him nor obeying him. 24 You have been rebellious against the LORD as long as he hasᵗ known you.

25 Throughout the forty days and forty nights that I lay prostrate before the LORD when the LORD intended to destroy you, 26 I prayed to the LORD and said, "Lord GOD, do not destroy the people

who are your very own possession, whom you redeemed in your greatness, whom you brought out of Egypt with a mighty hand. 27 Remember your servants, Abraham, Isaac, and Jacob; pay no attention to the stubbornness of this people, their wickedness and their sin, 28 otherwise the land from which you have brought us might say, 'Because the LORD was not able to bring them into the land that he promised them, and because he hated them, he has brought them out to let them die in the wilderness.' 29 For they are the people of your very own possession, whom you brought out by your great power and by your outstretched arm."

The Second Pair of Tablets
(Ex 34.1–9)

At that time the LORD said to me, "Carve out two tablets of stone like the former ones, and come up to me on the mountain, and make an ark of wood. 2 I will write on the tablets the words that were on the former tablets, which you smashed, and you shall put them in the ark." 3 So I made an ark of acacia wood, cut two tablets of stone like the former ones, and went up the mountain with the two tablets in my hand. 4 Then he wrote on the tablets the same words as before, the ten commandmentsᵘ that the LORD had spoken to you on the mountain out of the fire on the day of the assembly; and the LORD gave them to me. 5 So I turned and came down from the mountain, and put the tablets in the ark that I had made; and there they are, as the LORD commanded me.

6 (The Israelites journeyed from Be•er'oth-ben'-ē-ja'a•kanᵛ to Mō•se'rah. There Aaron died, and there he was buried; his son El•e•a'zar succeeded him as priest. 7 From there they journeyed to Gud'-gō•dah, and from Gud'gō•dah to Jot'ba•thah, a land with flowing streams. 8 At that time the LORD set apart the tribe of Levi to carry the ark of the covenant of the LORD, to stand before the LORD to minister to him, and to bless in his name, to this day. 9 Therefore Levi has no allotment or inheritance with his kindred; the LORD is his inheritance, as the LORD your God promised him.)

10 I stayed on the mountain forty days and forty nights, as I had done the first time. And once again the LORD listened to me. The LORD was unwilling to destroy you. 11 The LORD said to me, "Get up, go on your journey at the head of the people, that they may go in and occupy the land that I swore to their ancestors to give them."

ᵗ Sam Gk: MT *I have*   ᵘ Heb *the ten words*   ᵛ Or *the wells of the Bene-jaakan*

The Essence of the Law

12 So now, O Israel, what does the LORD your God require of you? Only to fear the LORD your God, to walk in all his ways, to love him, to serve the LORD your God with all your heart and with all your soul, 13 and to keep the commandments of the LORD your God[w] and his decrees that I am commanding you today, for your own well-being.

great God, mighty and awesome, who is not partial and takes no bribe, 18 who executes justice for the orphan and the widow, and who loves the strangers, providing them food and clothing. 19 You shall also love the stranger, for you were strangers in the land of Egypt. 20 You shall fear the LORD your God; him alone you shall worship; to him you shall hold fast, and by his name you shall

AFRICAN AMERICAN Kwanzaa as a Way of Life

The heart of the Law is love, our love for God and God's love for us. We express that love through the values we live out. Conflicts occur when the way we rank our values comes into conflict with the way someone else ranks their values.

For example: You may place a value on completing all your schoolwork, studying, and excelling in school. Another person sitting near you in class may not place the same high value on school. The two of you may come into conflict because this person disrupts the class and makes it difficult for you to understand what the teacher is explaining.

This is why a universal value system is important. It is why the Book of Deuteronomy has laws on everything from worship to sanitation. These laws gave the Israelites a common value system.

Kwanzaa is the name of a value system accepted by many African peoples. It was developed by Maulana Karenga after studying many different cultures throughout Africa. In 1965, he codified the unifying aspects of each of these cultures into the seven principles of Kwanzaa (also known as the Nguzo Saba). The seven principles are written in Swahili (an African trade and business language) and speak to the holistic development of the individual, family, community, nation, and race. Kwanzaa is celebrated from 26 December to 1 January. It is good that more and more African Americans are celebrating it each year, but these principles must be fully put into practice year-round as a way of life.

Kwanzaa is not a religion or a religious holiday, but it can strengthen the faith that you already practice. Look up the Bible passages listed with the following Kwanzaa principles to learn more about each one:

1. *umoja* (unity): Psalm 133; 1 Cor 12.12–26
2. *kujichagulia* (self-determination): Jdt 8.9
3. *ujima* (collective work and responsibility): Deut 8.11–18
4. *ujamaa* (cooperative economics): Mt 16.25
5. *nia* (purpose): Rom 8.28
6. *kuumba* (creativity): Mt 25.14–30
7. *imani* (faith): Gal 6.9

▶ Deut 10.12–22

14 Although heaven and the heaven of heavens belong to the LORD your God, the earth with all that is in it, 15 yet the LORD set his heart in love on your ancestors alone and chose you, their descendants after them, out of all the peoples, as it is today. 16 Circumcise, then, the foreskin of your heart, and do not be stubborn any longer. 17 For the LORD your God is God of gods and Lord of lords, the

swear. 21 He is your praise; he is your God, who has done for you these great and awesome things that your own eyes have seen. 22 Your ancestors went down to Egypt seventy persons; and now the LORD your God has made you as numerous as the stars in heaven.

w Q Ms Gk Syr: MT lacks *your God*

Rewards for Obedience

You shall love the LORD your God, therefore, and keep his charge, his decrees, his ordinances, and his commandments always. 2 Remember today that it was not your children (who have not known or seen the discipline of the LORD your God), but it is you who must acknowledge his greatness, his mighty hand and his outstretched arm, 3 his signs and his deeds that he did in Egypt to Pharaoh, the king of Egypt, and to all his land; 4 what he did to the Egyptian army, to their horses and chariots, how he made the water of the Red Sea*x* flow over them as they pursued you, so that the LORD has destroyed them to this day; 5 what he did to you in the wilderness, until you came to this place; 6 and what he did to Dā'than and A•bī'-ram, sons of E•lī'ab son of Reuben, how in the midst of all Israel the earth opened its mouth and swallowed them up, along with their households, their tents, and every living being in their company; 7 for it is your own eyes that have seen every great deed that the LORD did.

8 Keep, then, this entire commandment that I am commanding you today, so that you may have strength to go in and occupy the land that you are crossing over to occupy, 9 and so that you may live long in the land that the LORD swore to your ancestors to give them and to their descendants, a land flowing with milk and honey. 10 For the land that you are about to enter to occupy is not like the land of Egypt, from which you have come, where you sow your seed and irrigate by foot like a vegetable garden. 11 But the land that you are crossing over to occupy is a land of hills and valleys, watered by rain from the sky, 12 a land that the LORD your God looks after. The eyes of the LORD your God are always on it, from the beginning of the year to the end of the year.

13 If you will only heed his every commandment*y* that I am commanding you today—loving the LORD your God, and serving him with all your heart and with all your soul— 14 then he*z* will give the rain for your land in its season, the early rain and the later rain, and you will gather in your grain, your wine, and your oil; 15 and he*z* will give grass in your fields for your livestock, and you will eat your fill. 16 Take care, or you will be seduced into turning away, serving other gods and worshiping them, 17 for then the anger of the LORD will be kindled against you and he will shut up the heavens, so that there will be no rain and the land will yield no fruit; then you will perish quickly off the good land that the LORD is giving you.

18 You shall put these words of mine in your heart and soul, and you shall bind them as a sign on your hand, and fix them as an emblem*a* on your forehead. 19 Teach them to your children, talking about them when you are at home and when you are away, when you lie down and when you rise. 20 Write them on the doorposts of your house and on your gates, 21 so that your days and the days of your children may be multiplied in the land that the LORD swore to your ancestors to give them, as long as the heavens are above the earth.

22 If you will diligently observe this entire commandment that I am commanding you, loving the LORD your God, walking in all his ways, and holding fast to him, 23 then the LORD will drive out all these nations before you, and you will dispossess nations larger and mightier than yourselves. 24 Every place on which you set foot shall be yours; your territory shall extend from the wilderness to the Lebanon and from the River, the river Euphrates, to the Western Sea. 25 No one will be able to stand against you; the LORD your God will put the fear and dread of you on all the land on which you set foot, as he promised you.

26 See, I am setting before you today a blessing and a curse: 27 the blessing, if you obey the commandments of the LORD your God that I am commanding you today; 28 and the curse, if you do not obey the commandments of the LORD your God, but turn from the way that I am commanding you today, to follow other gods that you have not known.

29 When the LORD your God has brought you into the land that you are entering to occupy, you shall set the blessing on Mount Ger'i•zim and the curse on Mount Ē'bal. 30 As you know, they are beyond the Jordan, some distance to the west, in the land of the Cā'naan•ites who live in the Ar'a-bah, opposite Gil'gal, beside the oak*b* of Mō'reh.

31 When you cross the Jordan to go in to occupy the land that the LORD your God is giving you, and when you occupy it and live in it, 32 you must diligently observe all the statutes and ordinances that I am setting before you today.

Pagan Shrines to Be Destroyed

These are the statutes and ordinances that you must diligently observe in the land that the LORD, the God of your ancestors, has given you to occupy all the days that you live on the earth.

2 You must demolish completely all the places where the nations whom you are about to dispossess served their gods, on the mountain heights, on the hills, and under every leafy tree. 3 Break

---

x Or *Sea of Reeds*   *y* Compare Gk: Heb *my commandments*
z Sam Gk Vg: MT *I*   *a* Or *as a frontlet*   *b* Gk Syr:
Compare Gen 12.6; Heb *oaks* or *terebinths*

down their altars, smash their pillars, burn their sacred poles[c] with fire, and hew down the idols of their gods, and thus blot out their name from their places. [4] You shall not worship the LORD your God in such ways. [5] But you shall seek the place that the LORD your God will choose out of all your tribes as his habitation to put his name there. You shall go there, [6] bringing there your burnt offerings and your sacrifices, your tithes and your donations, your votive gifts, your freewill offerings, and the firstlings of your herds and flocks. [7] And you shall eat there in the presence of the LORD your God, you and your households together, rejoicing in all the undertakings in which the LORD your God has blessed you.

[8] You shall not act as we are acting here today, all of us according to our own desires, [9] for you have not yet come into the rest and the possession that the LORD your God is giving you. [10] When you cross over the Jordan and live in the land that the LORD your God is allotting to you, and when he gives you rest from your enemies all around so that you live in safety, [11] then you shall bring everything that I command you to the place that the LORD your God will choose as a dwelling for his name: your burnt offerings and your sacrifices, your tithes and your donations, and all your choice votive gifts that you vow to the LORD. [12] And you shall rejoice before the LORD your God, you together with your sons and your daughters, your male and female slaves, and the Lĕʹvites who reside in your towns (since they have no allotment or inheritance with you).

A Prescribed Place of Worship

[13] Take care that you do not offer your burnt offerings at any place you happen to see. [14] But only at the place that the LORD will choose in one of your tribes—there you shall offer your burnt offerings and there you shall do everything I command you.

[15] Yet whenever you desire you may slaughter and eat meat within any of your towns, according to the blessing that the LORD your God has given you; the unclean and the clean may eat of it, as they would of gazelle or deer. [16] The blood, however, you must not eat; you shall pour it out on the ground like water. [17] Nor may you eat within your towns the tithe of your grain, your wine, and your oil, the firstlings of your herds and your flocks, any of your votive gifts that you vow, your freewill offerings, or your donations; [18] these you shall eat in the presence of the LORD your God at the place that the LORD your God will choose, you together with your son and your daughter, your male and female slaves, and the Lĕʹvites resident in your towns, rejoicing in the presence of the LORD your God in all your undertakings. [19] Take care that you do not neglect the Lĕʹvite as long as you live in your land.

[20] When the LORD your God enlarges your territory, as he has promised you, and you say, "I am going to eat some meat," because you wish to eat meat, you may eat meat whenever you have the desire. [21] If the place where the LORD your God will choose to put his name is too far from you, and you slaughter as I have commanded you any of your herd or flock that the LORD has given you, then you may eat within your towns whenever you desire. [22] Indeed, just as gazelle or deer is eaten, so you may eat it; the unclean and the clean alike may eat it. [23] Only be sure that you do not eat the blood; for the blood is the life, and you shall not eat the life with the meat. [24] Do not eat it; you shall pour it out on the ground like water. [25] Do not eat it, so that all may go well with you and your children after you, because you do what is right in the sight of the LORD. [26] But the sacred donations that are due from you, and your votive gifts, you shall bring to the place that the LORD will choose. [27] You shall present your burnt offerings, both the meat and the blood, on the altar of the LORD your God; the blood of your other sacrifices shall be poured out beside[d] the altar of the LORD your God, but the meat you may eat.

[28] Be careful to obey all these words that I command you today,[e] so that it may go well with you and with your children after you forever, because you will be doing what is good and right in the sight of the LORD your God.

Warning against Idolatry

[29] When the LORD your God has cut off before you the nations whom you are about to enter to dispossess them, when you have dispossessed them and live in their land, [30] take care that you are not snared into imitating them, after they have been destroyed before you: do not inquire concerning their gods, saying, "How did these nations worship their gods? I also want to do the same." [31] You must not do the same for the LORD your God, because every abhorrent thing that the LORD hates they have done for their gods. They would even burn their sons and their daughters in the fire to their gods. [32] [f] You must diligently observe everything that I command you; do not add to it or take anything from it.

---

[c] Heb *Asherim*   [d] Or *on*   [e] Gk Sam Syr: MT lacks *today*
[f] Ch 13.1 in Heb

[8] If prophets or those who divine by dreams appear among you and promise you omens or portents, [2] and the omens or the portents declared by them take place, and they say, "Let us follow other gods" (whom you have not known) "and let us serve them," [3] you must not heed the words of those prophets or those who divine by dreams; for the LORD your God is testing you, to know whether you indeed love the LORD your God with all your heart and soul. [4] The LORD your God you shall follow, him alone you shall fear, his commandments you shall keep, his voice you shall obey, him you shall serve, and to him you shall hold fast. [5] But those prophets or those who divine by dreams shall be put to death for having spoken treason against the LORD your God—who brought you out of the land of Egypt and redeemed you from the house of slavery—to turn you from the way in which the LORD your God commanded you to walk. So you shall purge the evil from your midst.

[6] If anyone secretly entices you—even if it is your brother, your father's son or[h] your mother's son, or your own son or daughter, or the wife you embrace, or your most intimate friend—saying, "Let us go worship other gods," whom neither you nor your ancestors have known, [7] any of the gods of the peoples that are around you, whether near you or far away from you, from one end of the earth to the other, [8] you must not yield to or heed any such persons. Show them no pity or compassion and do not shield them. [9] But you shall surely kill them; your own hand shall be first against them to execute them, and afterwards the hand of all the people. [10] Stone them to death for trying to turn you away from the LORD your God, who brought you out of the land of Egypt, out of the house of slavery. [11] Then all Israel shall hear and be afraid, and never again do any such wickedness.

[12] If you hear it said about one of the towns that the LORD your God is giving you to live in, [13] that scoundrels from among you have gone out and led the inhabitants of the town astray, saying, "Let us go and worship other gods," whom you have not known, [14] then you shall inquire and make a thorough investigation. If the charge is established that such an abhorrent thing has been done among you, [15] you shall put the inhabitants of that town to the sword, utterly destroying it and everything in it—even putting its livestock to the sword. [16] All of its spoil you shall gather into its public square; then burn the town and all its spoil with fire, as a whole burnt offering to the LORD your God. It shall remain a perpetual ruin, never

to be rebuilt. [17] Do not let anything devoted to destruction stick to your hand, so that the LORD may turn from his fierce anger and show you compassion, and in his compassion multiply you, as he swore to your ancestors, [18] if you obey the voice of the LORD your God by keeping all his commandments that I am commanding you today, doing what is right in the sight of the LORD your God.

Pagan Practices Forbidden

You are children of the LORD your God. You must not lacerate yourselves or shave your forelocks for the dead. [2] For you are a people holy to the LORD your God; it is you the LORD has chosen out of all the peoples on earth to be his people, his treasured possession.

Clean and Unclean Foods
(Lev 11.1–47)

[3] You shall not eat any abhorrent thing. [4] These are the animals you may eat: the ox, the sheep, the goat, [5] the deer, the gazelle, the roebuck, the wild goat, the ibex, the antelope, and the mountain-sheep. [6] Any animal that divides the hoof and has the hoof cleft in two, and chews the cud, among the animals, you may eat. [7] Yet of those that chew the cud or have the hoof cleft you shall not eat these: the camel, the hare, and the rock badger, because they chew the cud but do not divide the hoof; they are unclean for you. [8] And the pig, because it divides the hoof but does not chew the cud, is unclean for you. You shall not eat their meat, and you shall not touch their carcasses.

[9] Of all that live in water you may eat these: whatever has fins and scales you may eat. [10] And whatever does not have fins and scales you shall not eat; it is unclean for you.

[11] You may eat any clean birds. [12] But these are the ones that you shall not eat: the eagle, the vulture, the osprey, [13] the buzzard, the kite of any kind; [14] every raven of any kind; [15] the ostrich, the nighthawk, the sea gull, the hawk of any kind; [16] the little owl and the great owl, the water hen [17] and the desert owl,[i] the carrion vulture and the cormorant, [18] the stork, the heron of any kind; the hoopoe and the bat.[j] [19] And all winged insects are unclean for you; they shall not be eaten. [20] You may eat any clean winged creature.

[21] You shall not eat anything that dies of itself; you may give it to aliens residing in your towns for them to eat, or you may sell it to a for-

---

g Ch 13.2 in Heb   h Sam Gk Compare Tg: MT lacks *your father's son* or   i Or *pelican*   j Identification of several of the birds in verses 12–18 is uncertain

eigner. For you are a people holy to the LORD your God.

You shall not boil a kid in its mother's milk.

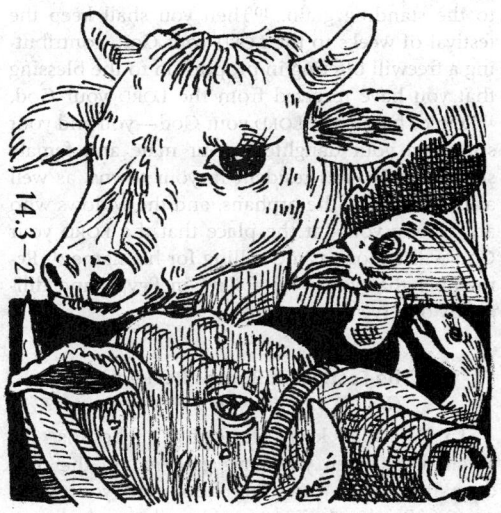

Regulations concerning Tithes

22 Set apart a tithe of all the yield of your seed that is brought in yearly from the field. 23 In the presence of the LORD your God, in the place that he will choose as a dwelling for his name, you shall eat the tithe of your grain, your wine, and your oil, as well as the firstlings of your herd and flock, so that you may learn to fear the LORD your God always. 24 But if, when the LORD your God has blessed you, the distance is so great that you are unable to transport it, because the place where the LORD your God will choose to set his name is too far away from you, 25 then you may turn it into money. With the money secure in hand, go to the place that the LORD your God will choose; 26 spend the money for whatever you wish—oxen, sheep, wine, strong drink, or whatever you desire. And you shall eat there in the presence of the LORD your God, you and your household rejoicing together. 27 As for the Lē'vītes resident in your towns, do not neglect them, because they have no allotment or inheritance with you.

28 Every third year you shall bring out the full tithe of your produce for that year, and store it within your towns; 29 the Lē'vītes, because they have no allotment or inheritance with you, as well as the resident aliens, the orphans, and the widows in your towns, may come and eat their fill so that the LORD your God may bless you in all the work that you undertake.

Laws concerning the Sabbatical Year
(Ex 21.1–11; Lev 25.1–7)

Every seventh year you shall grant a remission of debts. 2 And this is the manner of the remission: every creditor shall remit the claim that is held against a neighbor, not exacting it of a neighbor who is a member of the community, because the LORD's remission has been proclaimed. 3 Of a foreigner you may exact it, but you must remit your claim on whatever any member of your community owes you. 4 There will, however, be no one in need among you, because the LORD is sure to bless you in the land that the LORD your God is giving you as a possession to occupy, 5 if only you will obey the LORD your God by diligently observing this entire commandment that I command you today. 6 When the LORD your God has blessed you, as he promised you, you will lend to many nations, but you will not borrow; you will rule over many nations, but they will not rule over you.

7 If there is among you anyone in need, a member of your community in any of your towns within the land that the LORD your God is giving you, do not be hard-hearted or tight-fisted toward your needy neighbor. 8 You should rather open your hand, willingly lending enough to meet the need, whatever it may be. 9 Be careful that you do not entertain a mean thought, thinking, "The seventh year, the year of remission, is near," and therefore view your needy neighbor with hostility and give nothing; your neighbor might cry to the LORD against you, and you would incur guilt. 10 Give liberally and be ungrudging when you do so, for on this account the LORD your God will bless you in all your work and in all that you undertake. 11 Since there will never cease to be some in need on the earth, I therefore command you, "Open your hand to the poor and needy neighbor in your land."

12 If a member of your community, whether a Hebrew man or a Hebrew woman, is sold[k] to you and works for you six years, in the seventh year you shall set that person free. 13 And when you send a male slave[l] out from you a free person, you shall not send him out empty-handed. 14 Provide liberally out of your flock, your threshing floor, and your wine press, thus giving to him some of the bounty with which the LORD your God has blessed you. 15 Remember that you were a slave in the land of Egypt, and the LORD your God redeemed you; for this reason I lay this command upon you today. 16 But if he says to you, "I will not go out from you," because he loves you and your household, since he is well off with you,

---

k Or sells himself or herself   l Heb him

17 then you shall take an awl and thrust it through his earlobe into the door, and he shall be your slave[m] forever.

You shall do the same with regard to your female slave.[n]

18 Do not consider it a hardship when you send them out from you free persons, because for six years they have given you services worth the wages of hired laborers; and the LORD your God will bless you in all that you do.

The Firstborn of Livestock

19 Every firstling male born of your herd and flock you shall consecrate to the LORD your God; you shall not do work with your firstling ox nor shear the firstling of your flock. 20 You shall eat it, you together with your household, in the presence of the LORD your God year by year at the place that the LORD will choose. 21 But if it has any defect—any serious defect, such as lameness or blindness—you shall not sacrifice it to the LORD your God; 22 within your towns you may eat it, the unclean and the clean alike, as you would a gazelle or deer. 23 Its blood, however, you must not eat; you shall pour it out on the ground like water.

The Passover Reviewed
(Ex 12.1–20; 23.14–19; 34.18–26)

Observe the month[o] of A'bib by keeping the passover to the LORD your God, for in the month of A'bib the LORD your God brought you out of Egypt by night. 2 You shall offer the passover sacrifice to the LORD your God, from the flock and the herd, at the place that the LORD will choose as a dwelling for his name. 3 You must not eat with it anything leavened. For seven days you shall eat unleavened bread with it—the bread of affliction—because you came out of the land of Egypt in great haste, so that all the days of your life you may remember the day of your departure from the land of Egypt. 4 No leaven shall be seen with you in all your territory for seven days; and none of the meat of what you slaughter on the evening of the first day shall remain until morning. 5 You are not permitted to offer the passover sacrifice within any of your towns that the LORD your God is giving you. 6 But at the place that the LORD your God will choose as a dwelling for his name, only there shall you offer the passover sacrifice, in the evening at sunset, the time of day when you departed from Egypt. 7 You shall cook it and eat it at the place that the LORD your God will choose; the next morning you may go back to your tents. 8 For six days you shall continue to eat unleavened bread, and on the seventh day there shall be a solemn assembly for the LORD your God, when you shall do no work.

The Festival of Weeks Reviewed
(Ex 34.22; Lev 23.15–21; Num 28.26–31)

9 You shall count seven weeks; begin to count the seven weeks from the time the sickle is first put to the standing grain. 10 Then you shall keep the festival of weeks to the LORD your God, contributing a freewill offering in proportion to the blessing that you have received from the LORD your God. 11 Rejoice before the LORD your God—you and your sons and your daughters, your male and female slaves, the Le'vites resident in your towns, as well as the strangers, the orphans, and the widows who are among you—at the place that the LORD your God will choose as a dwelling for his name. 12 Remember that you were a slave in Egypt, and diligently observe these statutes.

The Festival of Booths Reviewed
(Lev 23.33–43; Num 29.12–40)

13 You shall keep the festival of booths[p] for seven days, when you have gathered in the produce from your threshing floor and your wine press. 14 Rejoice during your festival, you and your sons and your daughters, your male and female slaves, as well as the Le'vites, the strangers, the orphans, and the widows resident in your towns. 15 Seven days you shall keep the festival to the LORD your God at the place that the LORD will choose; for the LORD your God will bless you in all your produce and in all your undertakings, and you shall surely celebrate.

16 Three times a year all your males shall appear before the LORD your God at the place that he will choose: at the festival of unleavened bread, at the festival of weeks, and at the festival of booths.[p] They shall not appear before the LORD empty-handed; 17 all shall give as they are able, according to the blessing of the LORD your God that he has given you.

Municipal Judges and Officers

18 You shall appoint judges and officials throughout your tribes, in all your towns that the LORD your God is giving you, and they shall render just decisions for the people. 19 You must not distort justice; you must not show partiality; and you must not accept bribes, for a bribe blinds the eyes of the wise and subverts the cause of those who are in the right. 20 Justice, and only justice, you shall pursue, so that you may live and occupy the land that the LORD your God is giving you.

---

m Or *bondman*   n Or *bondwoman*   o Or *new moon*
p Or *tabernacles*; Heb *succoth*

Forbidden Forms of Worship

21 You shall not plant any tree as a sacred pole[q] beside the altar that you make for the LORD your God; 22 nor shall you set up a stone pillar— things that the LORD your God hates. You must not sacrifice to the LORD your God an ox or a sheep that has a defect, anything seriously wrong; for that is abhorrent to the LORD your God.

2 If there is found among you, in one of your towns that the LORD your God is giving you, a man or woman who does what is evil in the sight of the LORD your God, and transgresses his covenant 3 by going to serve other gods and worshiping them— whether the sun or the moon or any of the host of heaven, which I have forbidden— 4 and if it is reported to you or you hear of it, and you make a thorough inquiry, and the charge is proved true that such an abhorrent thing has occurred in Israel, 5 then you shall bring out to your gates that man or that woman who has committed this crime and you shall stone the man or woman to death. 6 On the evidence of two or three witnesses the death sentence shall be executed; a person must not be put to death on the evidence of only one witness. 7 The hands of the witnesses shall be the first raised against the person to execute the death penalty, and afterward the hands of all the people. So you shall purge the evil from your midst.

Legal Decisions by Priests and Judges

8 If a judicial decision is too difficult for you to make between one kind of bloodshed and another, one kind of legal right and another, or one kind of assault and another—any such matters of dispute in your towns—then you shall immediately go up to the place that the LORD your God will choose, 9 where you shall consult with the levitical priests and the judge who is in office in those days; they shall announce to you the decision in the case. 10 Carry out exactly the decision that they announce to you from the place that the LORD will choose, diligently observing everything they instruct you. 11 You must carry out fully the law that they interpret for you or the ruling that they announce to you; do not turn aside from the decision that they announce to you, either to the right or to the left. 12 As for anyone who presumes to disobey the priest appointed to minister there to the LORD your God, or the judge, that person shall die. So you shall purge the evil from Israel. 13 All the people will hear and be afraid, and will not act presumptuously again.

Limitations of Royal Authority

14 When you have come into the land that the LORD your God is giving you, and have taken possession of it and settled in it, and you say, "I will

did you KNOW?

The Torah

The Hebrew word Torah means "instruction" or "teaching," and only over time has come to mean "the Law." Torah refers most fundamentally to the Law that was recorded as given by God to Moses on Mount Sinai. As the people of Israel lived the Torah, it became equated with their very life and existence. It was the key for their organization as a people and gave consistency to their struggle to live their Covenant with God.

Jewish people refer to the first five books of the Bible (the Pentateuch) as the Torah because those books contain the Law and instruction on how to live it. The other books of the Hebrew Scriptures (Old Testament) are also strongly connected to the Torah. The historical books record how the people and their kings kept the Torah or disobeyed it. When they obeyed, they were blessed with happiness, health, and prosperity. When they disobeyed, they were punished with barrenness, destruction, and death. The prophets in the prophetic books call the people to faithfulness to the Law. They condemn idolatry and injustice and call the people to live the spirit of the Torah.

What law are Christians called to live by? For a hint, see the Letter of Paul to the Galatians and the Letter of James.

▶ **Deut 17.8–11**

set a king over me, like all the nations that are around me," 15 you may indeed set over you a king whom the LORD your God will choose. One of your own community you may set as king over you; you are not permitted to put a foreigner over you,

q Heb *Asherah*

who is not of your own community. 16 Even so, he must not acquire many horses for himself, or return the people to Egypt in order to acquire more horses, since the LORD has said to you, "You must never return that way again." 17 And he must not acquire many wives for himself, or else his heart will turn away; also silver and gold he must not acquire in great quantity for himself. 18 When he has taken the throne of his kingdom, he shall have a copy of this law written for him in the presence of the levitical priests. 19 It shall remain with him and he shall read in it all the days of his life, so that he may learn to fear the LORD his God, diligently observing all the words of this law and these statutes, 20 neither exalting himself above other members of the community nor turning aside from the commandment, either to the right or to the left, so that he and his descendants may reign long over his kingdom in Israel.

Privileges of Priests and Levites

The levitical priests, the whole tribe of Levi, shall have no allotment or inheritance within Israel. They may eat the sacrifices that are the LORD's portion[r] 2 but they shall have no inheritance among the other members of the community; the LORD is their inheritance, as he promised them.

3 This shall be the priests' due from the people, from those offering a sacrifice, whether an ox or a sheep: they shall give to the priest the shoulder, the two jowls, and the stomach. 4 The first fruits of your grain, your wine, and your oil, as well as the first of the fleece of your sheep, you shall give him. 5 For the LORD your God has chosen Levi[s] out of all your tribes, to stand and minister in the name of the LORD, him and his sons for all time.

6 If a Lē'vite leaves any of your towns, from wherever he has been residing in Israel, and comes to the place that the LORD will choose (and he may come whenever he wishes), 7 then he may minister in the name of the LORD his God, like all his fellow-Lē'vītes who stand to minister there before the LORD. 8 They shall have equal portions to eat, even though they have income from the sale of family possessions.[r]

Child-Sacrifice, Divination, and Magic Prohibited

9 When you come into the land that the LORD your God is giving you, you must not learn to imitate the abhorrent practices of those nations. 10 No one shall be found among you who makes a son or daughter pass through fire, or who practices divination, or is a soothsayer, or an augur, or a sorcerer, 11 or one who casts spells, or who consults ghosts or spirits, or who seeks oracles from the dead. 12 For whoever does these things is abhorrent to the LORD; it is because of such abhorrent practices that the LORD your God is driving them out before you. 13 You must remain completely loyal to the LORD your God. 14 Although these nations that you are about to dispossess do give heed to soothsayers and diviners, as for you, the LORD your God does not permit you to do so.

A New Prophet Like Moses

15 The LORD your God will raise up for you a prophet[t] like me from among your own people; you shall heed such a prophet.[u] 16 This is what you requested of the LORD your God at Hō'reb on the day of the assembly when you said: "If I hear the voice of the LORD my God any more, or ever again see this great fire, I will die." 17 Then the LORD replied to me: "They are right in what they have said. 18 I will raise up for them a prophet[t] like you from among their own people; I will put my words in the mouth of the prophet,[v] who shall speak to them everything that I command. 19 Anyone who does not heed the words that the prophet[w] shall speak in my name, I myself will hold accountable. 20 But any prophet who speaks in the name of other gods, or who presumes to speak in my name a word that I have not commanded the prophet to speak—that prophet shall die." 21 You may say to yourself, "How can we recognize a word that the LORD has not spoken?" 22 If a prophet speaks in the name of the LORD but the thing does not take place or prove true, it is a word that the LORD has not spoken. The prophet has spoken it presumptuously; do not be frightened by it.

Laws concerning the Cities of Refuge
(Num 35.9–28; Josh 20.1–9)

When the LORD your God has cut off the nations whose land the LORD your God is giving you, and you have dispossessed them and settled in their towns and in their houses, 2 you shall set apart three cities in the land that the LORD your God is giving you to possess. 3 You shall calculate the distances[x] and divide into three regions the land that the LORD your God gives you as a possession, so that any homicide can flee to one of them.

4 Now this is the case of a homicide who might flee there and live, that is, someone who has killed another person unintentionally when the two had not been at enmity before: 5 Suppose someone goes into the forest with another to cut

---

r Meaning of Heb uncertain   s Heb *him*   t Or *prophets*
u Or *such prophets*   v Or *mouths of the prophets*   w Heb *he*
x Or *prepare roads to them*

wood, and when one of them swings the ax to cut down a tree, the head slips from the handle and strikes the other person who then dies; the killer may flee to one of these cities and live. 6 But if the distance is too great, the avenger of blood in hot anger might pursue and overtake and put the killer to death, although a death sentence was not deserved, since the two had not been at enmity before. 7 Therefore I command you: You shall set apart three cities.

8 If the LORD your God enlarges your territory, as he swore to your ancestors—and he will give you all the land that he promised your ancestors to give you, 9 provided you diligently observe this entire commandment that I command you today, by loving the LORD your God and walking always in his ways—then you shall add three more cities to these three, 10 so that the blood of an innocent person may not be shed in the land that the LORD your God is giving you as an inheritance, thereby bringing bloodguilt upon you.

11 But if someone at enmity with another lies in wait and attacks and takes the life of that person, and flees into one of these cities, 12 then the elders of the killer's city shall send to have the culprit taken from there and handed over to the avenger of blood to be put to death. 13 Show no pity; you shall purge the guilt of innocent blood from Israel, so that it may go well with you.

Property Boundaries

14 You must not move your neighbor's boundary marker, set up by former generations, on the property that will be allotted to you in the land that the LORD your God is giving you to possess.

Law concerning Witnesses

15 A single witness shall not suffice to convict a person of any crime or wrongdoing in connection with any offense that may be committed. Only on the evidence of two or three witnesses shall a charge be sustained. 16 If a malicious witness comes forward to accuse someone of wrongdoing, 17 then both parties to the dispute shall appear before the LORD, before the priests and the judges who are in office in those days, 18 and the judges shall make a thorough inquiry. If the witness is a false witness, having testified falsely against another, 19 then you shall do to the false witness just as the false witness had meant to do to the other. So you shall purge the evil from your midst. 20 The rest shall hear and be afraid, and a crime such as this shall never again be committed among you. 21 Show no pity: life for life, eye for eye, tooth for tooth, hand for hand, foot for foot.

Rules of Warfare

When you go out to war against your enemies, and see horses and chariots, an army larger than your own, you shall not be afraid of them; for the LORD your God is with you, who brought you up from the land of Egypt. 2 Before you engage in battle, the priest shall come forward and speak to the troops, 3 and shall say to them: "Hear, O Israel! Today you are drawing near to do battle against your enemies. Do not lose heart, or be afraid, or panic, or be in dread of them; 4 for it is the LORD your God who goes with you, to fight for you against your enemies, to give you victory." 5 Then the officials shall address the troops, saying, "Has anyone built a new house but not dedicated it? He should go back to his house, or he might die in

DEUT

Facing Life's Battles

LIVE IT!

What are the wars in your life? Where do you experience conflict and lack of peace? We all hope that we will not face war in armed conflict. But in a sense, war is around us in the conflicts of everyday life.

We have fights with family and friends. We battle the pressures of society and our peers. We are at odds with the future. Deuteronomy 20.1 tells us that we are not to fear times of war because our God is with us and will be our strength.

When we face conflict, our faith will be tested, but we must hold strong and true to what God tells us. If we let our heart be filled with God, the wars that we face will become opportunities for God's love to triumph.

What conflicts do you encounter these days? Do you sense God is with you in these conflicts? If so, how? Pray for peace-filled ways to resolve conflict.

▶ Deut 20.1

the battle and another dedicate it. 6 Has anyone planted a vineyard but not yet enjoyed its fruit? He should go back to his house, or he might die in the battle and another be first to enjoy its fruit. 7 Has anyone become engaged to a woman but not yet married her? He should go back to his house, or he might die in the battle and another marry her." 8 The officials shall continue to address the troops, saying, "Is anyone afraid or disheartened? He should go back to his house, or he might cause the heart of his comrades to melt like his own." 9 When the officials have finished addressing the troops, then the commanders shall take charge of them.

10 When you draw near to a town to fight against it, offer it terms of peace. 11 If it accepts your terms of peace and surrenders to you, then all the people in it shall serve you at forced labor. 12 If it does not submit to you peacefully, but makes war against you, then you shall besiege it; 13 and when the LORD your God gives it into your hand, you shall put all its males to the sword. 14 You may, however, take as your booty the women, the children, livestock, and everything else in the town, all its spoil. You may enjoy the spoil of your enemies, which the LORD your God has given you. 15 Thus you shall treat all the towns that are very far from you, which are not towns of the nations here. 16 But as for the towns of these peoples that the LORD your God is giving you as an inheritance, you must not let anything that breathes remain alive. 17 You shall annihilate them—the Hit′tites and the Am′o·rites, the Ca′naan·ites and the Per′iz·zites, the Hi′vites and the Jeb′u·sites—just as the LORD your God has commanded, 18 so that they may not teach you to do all the abhorrent things that they do for their gods, and you thus sin against the LORD your God.

19 If you besiege a town for a long time, making war against it in order to take it, you must not destroy its trees by wielding an ax against them. Although you may take food from them, you must not cut them down. Are trees in the field human beings that they should come under siege from you? 20 You may destroy only the trees that you know do not produce food; you may cut them down for use in building siegeworks against the town that makes war with you, until it falls.

Law concerning Murder by Persons Unknown

If, in the land that the LORD your God is giving you to possess, a body is found lying in open country, and it is not known who struck the person down, 2 then your elders and your judges shall come out to measure the distances to the towns that are near the body. 3 The elders of the town nearest the body shall take a heifer that has never been worked, one that has not pulled in the yoke; 4 the elders of that town shall bring the heifer down to a wadi with running water, which is neither plowed nor sown, and shall break the heifer's neck there in the wadi. 5 Then the priests, the sons of Levi, shall come forward, for the LORD your God has chosen them to minister to him and to pronounce blessings in the name of the LORD, and by their decision all cases of dispute and assault shall be settled. 6 All the elders of that town nearest the body shall wash their hands over the heifer whose neck was broken in the wadi, 7 and they shall declare: "Our hands did not shed this blood, nor were we witnesses to it. 8 Absolve, O LORD, your people Israel, whom you redeemed; do not let the guilt of innocent blood remain in the midst of your people Israel." Then they will be absolved of bloodguilt. 9 So you shall purge the guilt of innocent blood from your midst, because you must do what is right in the sight of the LORD.

Female Captives

10 When you go out to war against your enemies, and the LORD your God hands them over to you and you take them captive, 11 suppose you see among the captives a beautiful woman whom you desire and want to marry, 12 and so you bring her home to your house: she shall shave her head, pare her nails, 13 discard her captive's garb, and shall remain in your house a full month, mourning for her father and mother; after that you may go in to her and be her husband, and she shall be your wife. 14 But if you are not satisfied with her, you shall let her go free and not sell her for money. You must not treat her as a slave, since you have dishonored her.

The Right of the Firstborn

15 If a man has two wives, one of them loved and the other disliked, and if both the loved and the disliked have borne him sons, the firstborn being the son of the one who is disliked, 16 then on the day when he wills his possessions to his sons, he is not permitted to treat the son of the loved as the firstborn in preference to the son of the disliked, who is the firstborn. 17 He must acknowledge as firstborn the son of the one who is disliked, giving him a double portion𝑦 of all that he has; since he is the first issue of his virility, the right of the firstborn is his.

𝑦 Heb *two-thirds*

Rebellious Children

18 If someone has a stubborn and rebellious son who will not obey his father and mother, who does not heed them when they discipline him, ¹⁹ then his father and his mother shall take hold of him and bring him out to the elders of his town at the gate of that place. ²⁰ They shall say to the elders of his town, "This son of ours is stubborn and rebellious. He will not obey us. He is a glutton and a drunkard." ²¹ Then all the men of the town shall stone him to death. So you shall purge the evil from your midst; and all Israel will hear, and be afraid.

Miscellaneous Laws

22 When someone is convicted of a crime punishable by death and is executed, and you hang him on a tree, ²³ his corpse must not remain all night upon the tree; you shall bury him that same day, for anyone hung on a tree is under God's curse. You must not defile the land that the LORD your God is giving you for possession. You shall not watch your neighbor's ox or sheep straying away and ignore them; you shall take them back to their owner. ² If the owner does not reside near you or you do not know who the owner is, you shall bring it to your own house, and it shall remain with you until the owner claims it; then you shall return it. ³ You shall do the same with a neighbor's donkey; you shall do the same with a neighbor's garment; and you shall do the same with anything else that your neighbor loses and you find. You may not withhold your help.

4 You shall not see your neighbor's donkey or ox fallen on the road and ignore it; you shall help to lift it up.

5 A woman shall not wear a man's apparel, nor shall a man put on a woman's garment; for whoever does such things is abhorrent to the LORD your God.

6 If you come on a bird's nest, in any tree or on the ground, with fledglings or eggs, with the mother sitting on the fledglings or on the eggs, you shall not take the mother with the young. ⁷ Let the mother go, taking only the young for yourself, in order that it may go well with you and you may live long.

8 When you build a new house, you shall make a parapet for your roof; otherwise you might have bloodguilt on your house, if anyone should fall from it.

9 You shall not sow your vineyard with a second kind of seed, or the whole yield will have to be forfeited, both the crop that you have sown and the yield of the vineyard itself.

10 You shall not plow with an ox and a donkey yoked together.

11 You shall not wear clothes made of wool and linen woven together.

12 You shall make tassels on the four corners of the cloak with which you cover yourself.

Laws concerning Sexual Relations

13 Suppose a man marries a woman, but after going in to her, he dislikes her ¹⁴ and makes up charges against her, slandering her by saying, "I married this woman; but when I lay with her, I did not find evidence of her virginity." ¹⁵ The father of the young woman and her mother shall then submit the evidence of the young woman's virginity to the elders of the city at the gate. ¹⁶ The father of the young woman shall say to the elders: "I gave my daughter in marriage to this man but he dislikes her; ¹⁷ now he has made up charges against her, saying, 'I did not find evidence of your daughter's virginity.' But here is the evidence of my daughter's virginity." Then they shall spread out the cloth before the elders of the town. ¹⁸ The elders of that town shall take the man and punish him; ¹⁹ they shall fine him one hundred shekels of silver (which they shall give to the young woman's father) because he has slandered a virgin of Israel. She shall remain his wife; he shall not be permitted to divorce her as long as he lives.

20 If, however, this charge is true, that evidence of the young woman's virginity was not found, ²¹ then they shall bring the young woman out to the entrance of her father's house and the men of her town shall stone her to death, because she committed a disgraceful act in Israel by prostituting herself in her father's house. So you shall purge the evil from your midst.

22 If a man is caught lying with the wife of another man, both of them shall die, the man who lay with the woman as well as the woman. So you shall purge the evil from Israel.

23 If there is a young woman, a virgin already engaged to be married, and a man meets her in the town and lies with her, ²⁴ you shall bring both of them to the gate of that town and stone them to death, the young woman because she did not cry for help in the town and the man because he violated his neighbor's wife. So you shall purge the evil from your midst.

25 But if the man meets the engaged woman in the open country, and the man seizes her and lies with her, then only the man who lay with her shall die. ²⁶ You shall do nothing to the young woman; the young woman has not committed an

offense punishable by death, because this case is like that of someone who attacks and murders a neighbor. 27 Since he found her in the open country, the engaged woman may have cried for help, but there was no one to rescue her.

28 If a man meets a virgin who is not engaged, and seizes her and lies with her, and they are caught in the act, 29 the man who lay with her shall give fifty shekels of silver to the young woman's father, and she shall become his wife. Because he violated her he shall not be permitted to divorce her as long as he lives.

30ᶻ A man shall not marry his father's wife, thereby violating his father's rights.ᵃ

Those Excluded from the Assembly

No one whose testicles are crushed or whose penis is cut off shall be admitted to the assembly of the LORD.

2 Those born of an illicit union shall not be admitted to the assembly of the LORD. Even to the tenth generation, none of their descendants shall be admitted to the assembly of the LORD.

3 No Am'mon·ite or Mō'ab·ite shall be admitted to the assembly of the LORD. Even to the tenth generation, none of their descendants shall be admitted to the assembly of the LORD, 4 because they did not meet you with food and water on your journey out of Egypt, and because they hired against you Bā'laam son of Bē'or, from Pē'thor of Mes·o·po·tā'mi·a, to curse you. 5 (Yet the LORD your God refused to heed Bā'laam; the LORD your God turned the curse into a blessing for you, because the LORD your God loved you.) 6 You shall never promote their welfare or their prosperity as long as you live.

7 You shall not abhor any of the Ē'dom·ītes, for they are your kin. You shall not abhor any of the Egyptians, because you were an alien residing in their land. 8 The children of the third generation that are born to them may be admitted to the assembly of the LORD.

Sanitary, Ritual, and Humanitarian Precepts

9 When you are encamped against your enemies you shall guard against any impropriety.

10 If one of you becomes unclean because of a nocturnal emission, then he shall go outside the camp; he must not come within the camp. 11 When evening comes, he shall wash himself with water, and when the sun has set, he may come back into the camp.

12 You shall have a designated area outside the camp to which you shall go. 13 With your utensils you shall have a trowel; when you relieve yourself outside, you shall dig a hole with it and then cover up your excrement. 14 Because the LORD your God travels along with your camp, to save you and to hand over your enemies to you, therefore your camp must be holy, so that he may not see anything indecent among you and turn away from you.

15 Slaves who have escaped to you from their owners shall not be given back to them. 16 They shall reside with you, in your midst, in any place they choose in any one of your towns, wherever they please; you shall not oppress them.

17 None of the daughters of Israel shall be a temple prostitute; none of the sons of Israel shall be a temple prostitute. 18 You shall not bring the fee of a prostitute or the wages of a male prostituteᵇ into the house of the LORD your God in payment for any vow, for both of these are abhorrent to the LORD your God.

19 You shall not charge interest on loans to another Israelite, interest on money, interest on provisions, interest on anything that is lent. 20 On loans to a foreigner you may charge interest, but on loans to another Israelite you may not charge interest, so that the LORD your God may bless you in all your undertakings in the land that you are about to enter and possess.

21 If you make a vow to the LORD your God, do not postpone fulfilling it; for the LORD your God will surely require it of you, and you would incur guilt. 22 But if you refrain from vowing, you will not incur guilt. 23 Whatever your lips utter you must diligently perform, just as you have freely vowed to the LORD your God with your own mouth.

24 If you go into your neighbor's vineyard, you may eat your fill of grapes, as many as you wish, but you shall not put any in a container.

25 If you go into your neighbor's standing grain, you may pluck the ears with your hand, but you shall not put a sickle to your neighbor's standing grain.

Laws concerning Marriage and Divorce

Suppose a man enters into marriage with a woman, but she does not please him because he finds something objectionable about her, and so he writes her a certificate of divorce, puts it in her hand, and sends her out of his house; she then leaves his house 2 and goes off to become another man's wife. 3 Then suppose the second man dislikes her, writes her a bill of divorce, puts it in her hand, and sends her out of his house (or the second man who married her dies); 4 her first hus-

---

ᶻ Ch 23.1 in Heb   ᵃ Heb *uncovering his father's skirt*
ᵇ Heb *a dog*

band, who sent her away, is not permitted to take her again to be his wife after she has been defiled; for that would be abhorrent to the LORD, and you shall not bring guilt on the land that the LORD your God is giving you as a possession.

Miscellaneous Laws

5 When a man is newly married, he shall not go out with the army or be charged with any related duty. He shall be free at home one year, to be happy with the wife whom he has married.

6 No one shall take a mill or an upper millstone in pledge, for that would be taking a life in pledge.

7 If someone is caught kidnaping another Israelite, enslaving or selling the Israelite, then that kidnaper shall die. So you shall purge the evil from your midst.

8 Guard against an outbreak of a leprous*c* skin disease by being very careful; you shall carefully observe whatever the levitical priests instruct you, just as I have commanded them. 9 Remember what the LORD your God did to Miriam on your journey out of Egypt.

10 When you make your neighbor a loan of any kind, you shall not go into the house to take the pledge. 11 You shall wait outside, while the person to whom you are making the loan brings the pledge out to you. 12 If the person is poor, you shall not sleep in the garment given you as*d* pledge. 13 You shall give the pledge back by sunset, so that your neighbor may sleep in the cloak and bless you; and it will be to your credit before the LORD your God.

14 You shall not withhold the wages of poor and needy laborers, whether other Israelites or aliens who reside in your land in one of your towns. 15 You shall pay them their wages daily before sunset, because they are poor and their livelihood depends on them; otherwise they might cry to the LORD against you, and you would incur guilt.

16 Parents shall not be put to death for their children, nor shall children be put to death for their parents; only for their own crimes may persons be put to death.

17 You shall not deprive a resident alien or an orphan of justice; you shall not take a widow's garment in pledge. 18 Remember that you were a slave in Egypt and the LORD your God redeemed you from there; therefore I command you to do this.

19 When you reap your harvest in your field and forget a sheaf in the field, you shall not go back to get it; it shall be left for the alien, the or-

The Poor, the Strangers, the Widows, and the Orphans

One remarkable aspect of Israel's Covenant was the command to care for the poor, the strangers, the widows, and the orphans. These four groups were the outsiders in ancient Israel because they fell outside Israel's socioeconomic system. The poor often had no means to sustain themselves. Strangers were not part of Israel's tribal organization. Widows depended on the charity of others. Orphans were destitute because they had no family to help them survive.

God provides a reason why Israel must care for the poor and oppressed. Just as the Israelites were enslaved in Egypt—when they were poor, oppressed, orphans in a foreign land—and God responded to their cry for help, so they must care for the poor, oppressed, forgotten, and marginalized in their midst. Can this be any less true for us today?

▶ Deut 24.10–21

phan, and the widow, so that the LORD your God may bless you in all your undertakings. 20 When you beat your olive trees, do not strip what is left; it shall be for the alien, the orphan, and the widow.

21 When you gather the grapes of your vineyard, do not glean what is left; it shall be for the alien, the orphan, and the widow. 22 Remember that you were a slave in the land of Egypt; therefore I am commanding you to do this.

Suppose two persons have a dispute and enter into litigation, and the judges decide between them, declaring one to be in the right and the other to be in the wrong. 2 If the one in the wrong deserves to be flogged, the judge shall make that person lie down and be beaten in his presence with the number of lashes proportionate to the offense. 3 Forty lashes may be given but not more; if more lashes

c A term for several skin diseases; precise meaning uncertain   *d* Heb lacks *the garment given you as*

than these are given, your neighbor will be degraded in your sight.

4 You shall not muzzle an ox while it is treading out the grain.

Levirate Marriage

5 When brothers reside together, and one of them dies and has no son, the wife of the deceased shall not be married outside the family to a stranger. Her husband's brother shall go in to her, taking her in marriage, and performing the duty of a husband's brother to her, 6 and the firstborn whom she bears shall succeed to the name of the deceased brother, so that his name may not be blotted out of Israel. 7 But if the man has no desire to marry his brother's widow, then his brother's widow shall go up to the elders at the gate and say, "My husband's brother refuses to perpetuate his brother's name in Israel; he will not perform the duty of a husband's brother to me." 8 Then the elders of his town shall summon him and speak to him. If he persists, saying, "I have no desire to marry her," 9 then his brother's wife shall go up to him in the presence of the elders, pull his sandal off his foot, spit in his face, and declare, "This is what is done to the man who does not build up his brother's house." 10 Throughout Israel his family shall be known as "the house of him whose sandal was pulled off."

Various Commands

11 If men get into a fight with one another, and the wife of one intervenes to rescue her husband from the grip of his opponent by reaching out and seizing his genitals, 12 you shall cut off her hand; show no pity.

13 You shall not have in your bag two kinds of weights, large and small. 14 You shall not have in your house two kinds of measures, large and small. 15 You shall have only a full and honest weight; you shall have only a full and honest measure, so that your days may be long in the land that the LORD your God is giving you. 16 For all who do such things, all who act dishonestly, are abhorrent to the LORD your God.

17 Remember what Am'a•lek did to you on your journey out of Egypt, 18 how he attacked you on the way, when you were faint and weary, and struck down all who lagged behind you; he did not fear God. 19 Therefore when the LORD your God has given you rest from all your enemies on every hand, in the land that the LORD your God is giving you as an inheritance to possess, you shall blot out the remembrance of Am'a•lek from under heaven; do not forget.

First Fruits and Tithes

When you have come into the land that the LORD your God is giving you as an inheritance to possess, and you possess it, and settle in it, 2 you shall take some of the first of all the fruit of the ground, which you harvest from the land that the LORD your God is giving you, and you shall put it in a basket and go to the place that the LORD your God will choose as a dwelling for his name. 3 You shall go to the priest who is in office at that time, and say to him, "Today I declare to the LORD your God that I have come into the land that the LORD swore to our ancestors to give us." 4 When the priest takes the basket from your hand and sets it down before the altar of the LORD your God, 5 you shall make this response before the LORD your God: "A wandering Ar•a•mē'an was my ancestor; he went down into Egypt and lived there as an alien, few in number, and there he became a great nation, mighty and populous. 6 When the Egyptians treated us harshly and afflicted us, by imposing hard labor on us, 7 we cried to the LORD, the God of our ancestors; the LORD heard our voice and saw our affliction, our toil, and our oppression. 8 The LORD brought us out of Egypt with a mighty hand and an outstretched arm, with a terrifying display of power, and with signs and wonders; 9 and he brought us into this place and gave us this land, a land flowing with milk and honey. 10 So now I bring the first of the fruit of the ground that you, O LORD, have given me." You shall set it down before the LORD your God and bow down before the LORD your God. 11 Then you, together with the Lē'vītes and the aliens who reside among you, shall celebrate with all the bounty that the LORD your God has given to you and to your house.

12 When you have finished paying all the tithe of your produce in the third year (which is the year of the tithe), giving it to the Lē'vītes, the aliens, the orphans, and the widows, so that they may eat their fill within your towns, 13 then you shall say before the LORD your God: "I have removed the sacred portion from the house, and I have given it to the Lē'vītes, the resident aliens, the orphans, and the widows, in accordance with your entire commandment that you commanded me; I have neither transgressed nor forgotten any of your commandments: 14 I have not eaten of it while in mourning; I have not removed any of it while I was unclean; and I have not offered any of it to the dead. I have obeyed the LORD my God, doing just as you commanded me. 15 Look down from your holy habitation, from heaven, and bless your people Israel and the ground that you have

given us, as you swore to our ancestors—a land flowing with milk and honey."

Concluding Exhortation

16 This very day the LORD your God is commanding you to observe these statutes and ordinances; so observe them diligently with all your heart and with all your soul. [17] Today you have obtained the LORD's agreement: to be your God; and for you to walk in his ways, to keep his statutes, his commandments, and his ordinances, and to obey him. [18] Today the LORD has obtained your agreement: to be his treasured people, as he promised you, and to keep his commandments; [19] for him to set you high above all nations that he has made, in praise and in fame and in honor; and for you to be a people holy to the LORD your God, as he promised.

The Inscribed Stones and Altar on Mount Ebal

Then Moses and the elders of Israel charged all the people as follows: Keep the entire commandment that I am commanding you today. [2] On the day that you cross over the Jordan into the land that the LORD your God is giving you, you shall set up large stones and cover them with plaster. [3] You shall write on them all the words of this law when you have crossed over, to enter the land that the LORD your God is giving you, a land flowing with milk and honey, as the LORD, the God of your ancestors, promised you. [4] So when you have crossed over the Jordan, you shall set up these stones, about which I am commanding you today, on Mount Ê'bal, and you shall cover them with plaster. [5] And you shall build an altar there to the LORD your God, an altar of stones on which you have not used an iron tool. [6] You must build the altar of the LORD your God of unhewn[e] stones. Then offer up burnt offerings on it to the LORD your God, [7] make sacrifices of well-being, and eat them there, rejoicing before the LORD your God. [8] You shall write on the stones all the words of this law very clearly.

9 Then Moses and the levitical priests spoke to all Israel, saying: Keep silence and hear, O Israel! This very day you have become the people of the LORD your God. [10] Therefore obey the LORD your God, observing his commandments and his statutes that I am commanding you today.

Twelve Curses

11 The same day Moses charged the people as follows: [12] When you have crossed over the Jordan, these shall stand on Mount Ger'i•zim for the blessing of the people: Sim'ê•on, Levi, Judah, Is'sa•char, Joseph, and Benjamin. [13] And these shall stand on

Mount Ê'bal for the curse: Reuben, Gad, Ash'er, Zeb'û•lun, Dan, and Naph'ta•lī. [14] Then the Lē'vītes shall declare in a loud voice to all the Israelites:

15 "Cursed be anyone who makes an idol or casts an image, anything abhorrent to the LORD, the work of an artisan, and sets it up in secret." All the people shall respond, saying, "Amen!"

16 "Cursed be anyone who dishonors father or mother." All the people shall say, "Amen!"

17 "Cursed be anyone who moves a neighbor's boundary marker." All the people shall say, "Amen!"

18 "Cursed be anyone who misleads a blind person on the road." All the people shall say, "Amen!"

19 "Cursed be anyone who deprives the alien, the orphan, and the widow of justice." All the people shall say, "Amen!"

20 "Cursed be anyone who lies with his father's wife, because he has violated his father's rights."[f] All the people shall say, "Amen!"

21 "Cursed be anyone who lies with any animal." All the people shall say, "Amen!"

22 "Cursed be anyone who lies with his sister, whether the daughter of his father or the daughter of his mother." All the people shall say, "Amen!"

23 "Cursed be anyone who lies with his mother-in-law." All the people shall say, "Amen!"

24 "Cursed be anyone who strikes down a neighbor in secret." All the people shall say, "Amen!"

25 "Cursed be anyone who takes a bribe to shed innocent blood." All the people shall say, "Amen!"

26 "Cursed be anyone who does not uphold the words of this law by observing them." All the people shall say, "Amen!"

Blessings for Obedience
(Lev 26.1–13; Deut 7.12–24)

If you will only obey the LORD your God, by diligently observing all his commandments that I am commanding you today, the LORD your God will set you high above all the nations of the earth; [2] all these blessings shall come upon you and overtake you, if you obey the LORD your God:

3 Blessed shall you be in the city, and blessed shall you be in the field.

4 Blessed shall be the fruit of your womb, the fruit of your ground, and the fruit of your livestock, both the increase of your cattle and the issue of your flock.

5 Blessed shall be your basket and your kneading bowl.

---

e Heb *whole*   f Heb *uncovered his father's skirt*

6 Blessed shall you be when you come in, and blessed shall you be when you go out.

7 The LORD will cause your enemies who rise against you to be defeated before you; they shall come out against you one way, and flee before you seven ways. 8 The LORD will command the blessing upon you in your barns, and in all that you undertake; he will bless you in the land that the LORD your God is giving you. 9 The LORD will establish you as his holy people, as he has sworn to you, if you keep the commandments of the LORD your God and walk in his ways. 10 All the peoples of the earth shall see that you are called by the name of the LORD, and they shall be afraid of you. 11 The LORD will make you abound in prosperity, in the fruit of your womb, in the fruit of your livestock, and in the fruit of your ground in the land that the LORD swore to your ancestors to give you. 12 The LORD will open for you his rich storehouse, the heavens, to give the rain of your land in its season and to bless all your undertakings. You will lend to many nations, but you will not borrow. 13 The LORD will make you the head, and not the tail; you shall be only at the top, and not at the bottom—if you obey the commandments of the LORD your God, which I am commanding you today, by diligently observing them, 14 and if you do not turn aside from any of the words that I am commanding you today, either to the right or to the left, following other gods to serve them.

Warnings against Disobedience
(Ex 9.8–12; Lev 26.14–46)

15 But if you will not obey the LORD your God by diligently observing all his commandments and decrees, which I am commanding you today, then all these curses shall come upon you and overtake you:

16 Cursed shall you be in the city, and cursed shall you be in the field.

17 Cursed shall be your basket and your kneading bowl.

18 Cursed shall be the fruit of your womb, the fruit of your ground, the increase of your cattle and the issue of your flock.

19 Cursed shall you be when you come in, and cursed shall you be when you go out.

20 The LORD will send upon you disaster, panic, and frustration in everything you attempt to do, until you are destroyed and perish quickly, on account of the evil of your deeds, because you have forsaken me. 21 The LORD will make the pestilence cling to you until it has consumed you off the land that you are entering to possess. 22 The LORD will afflict you with consumption, fever, inflammation, with fiery heat and drought, and with

Catholic Connections

HAIL MARY

Deuteronomy 28.4 might sound familiar to you. These words, also found in Lk 1.42, are part of a prayer called the Hail Mary. In this passage, Moses reminds the Israelites that they shall be blessed because of their obedience, and Mary is the ultimate example of the blessings that come from obedience to God's will.

▶ Deut 28.1–6

blight and mildew; they shall pursue you until you perish. 23 The sky over your head shall be bronze, and the earth under you iron. 24 The LORD will change the rain of your land into powder, and only dust shall come down upon you from the sky until you are destroyed.

25 The LORD will cause you to be defeated before your enemies; you shall go out against them one way and flee before them seven ways. You shall become an object of horror to all the kingdoms of the earth. 26 Your corpses shall be food for every bird of the air and animal of the earth, and there shall be no one to frighten them away. 27 The LORD will afflict you with the boils of Egypt, with ulcers, scurvy, and itch, of which you cannot be healed. 28 The LORD will afflict you with madness, blindness, and confusion of mind; 29 you shall grope about at noon as blind people grope in darkness, but you shall be unable to find your way; and you shall be continually abused and robbed, without anyone to help. 30 You shall become engaged to a woman, but another man shall lie with her. You shall build a house, but not live in it. You shall plant a vineyard, but not enjoy its fruit. 31 Your ox shall be butchered before your eyes, but you shall not eat of it. Your donkey shall be stolen in front of you, and shall not be restored to you. Your sheep shall be given to your enemies, without anyone to help you. 32 Your sons and daughters shall be given to another people, while

D
E
U
T

you look on; you will strain your eyes looking for them all day but be powerless to do anything. 33 A people whom you do not know shall eat up the fruit of your ground and of all your labors; you shall be continually abused and crushed, 34 and driven mad by the sight that your eyes shall see. 35 The LORD will strike you on the knees and on the legs with grievous boils of which you cannot be healed, from the sole of your foot to the crown of your head. 36 The LORD will bring you, and the king whom you set over you, to a nation that neither you nor your ancestors have known, where you shall serve other gods, of wood and stone. 37 You shall become an object of horror, a proverb, and a byword among all the peoples where the LORD will lead you.

38 You shall carry much seed into the field but shall gather little in, for the locust shall consume it. 39 You shall plant vineyards and dress them, but you shall neither drink the wine nor gather the grapes, for the worm shall eat them. 40 You shall have olive trees throughout all your territory, but you shall not anoint yourself with the oil, for your olives shall drop off. 41 You shall have sons and daughters, but they shall not remain yours, for they shall go into captivity. 42 All your trees and the fruit of your ground the cicada shall take over. 43 Aliens residing among you shall ascend above you higher and higher, while you shall descend lower and lower. 44 They shall lend to you but you shall not lend to them; they shall be the head and you shall be the tail.

45 All these curses shall come upon you, pursuing and overtaking you until you are destroyed, because you did not obey the LORD your God, by observing the commandments and the decrees that he commanded you. 46 They shall be among you and your descendants as a sign and a portent forever.

47 Because you did not serve the LORD your God joyfully and with gladness of heart for the abundance of everything, 48 therefore you shall serve your enemies whom the LORD will send against you, in hunger and thirst, in nakedness and lack of everything. He will put an iron yoke on your neck until he has destroyed you. 49 The LORD will bring a nation from far away, from the end of the earth, to swoop down on you like an eagle, a nation whose language you do not understand, 50 a grim-faced nation showing no respect to the old or favor to the young. 51 It shall consume the fruit of your livestock and the fruit of your ground until you are destroyed, leaving you neither grain, wine, and oil, nor the increase of your cattle and the issue of your flock, until it has made you perish. 52 It shall besiege you in all your towns until your high and fortified walls, in which you trusted, come down throughout your land; it shall besiege you in all your towns throughout the land that the LORD your God has given you. 53 In the desperate straits to which the enemy siege reduces you, you will eat the fruit of your womb, the flesh of your own sons and daughters whom the LORD your God has given you. 54 Even the most refined and gentle of men among you will begrudge food to his own brother, to the wife whom he embraces, and to the last of his remaining children, 55 giving to none of them any of the flesh of his children whom he is eating, because nothing else remains to him, in the desperate straits to which the enemy siege will reduce you in all your towns. 56 She who is the most refined and gentle among you, so gentle and refined that she does not venture to set the sole of her foot on the ground, will begrudge food to the husband whom she embraces, to her own son, and to her own daughter, 57 begrudging even the afterbirth that comes out from between her thighs, and the children that she bears, because she is eating them in secret for lack of anything else, in the desperate straits to which the enemy siege will reduce you in your towns.

58 If you do not diligently observe all the words of this law that are written in this book, fearing this glorious and awesome name, the LORD your God, 59 then the LORD will overwhelm both you and your offspring with severe and lasting afflictions and grievous and lasting maladies. 60 He will bring back upon you all the diseases of Egypt, of which you were in dread, and they shall cling to you. 61 Every other malady and affliction, even though not recorded in the book of this law, the LORD will inflict on you until you are destroyed. 62 Although once you were as numerous as the stars in heaven, you shall be left few in number, because you did not obey the LORD your God. 63 And just as the LORD took delight in making you prosperous and numerous, so the LORD will take delight in bringing you to ruin and destruction; you shall be plucked off the land that you are entering to possess. 64 The LORD will scatter you among all peoples, from one end of the earth to the other; and there you shall serve other gods, of wood and stone, which neither you nor your ancestors have known. 65 Among those nations you shall find no ease, no resting place for the sole of your foot. There the LORD will give you a trembling heart, failing eyes, and a languishing spirit. 66 Your life shall hang in doubt before you; night and day you shall be in dread, with no assurance of your life. 67 In the morning you shall say, "If only it were evening!" and at evening you shall say, "If only it were morning!"—because of the dread that

your heart shall feel and the sights that your eyes shall see. 68 The LORD will bring you back in ships to Egypt, by a route that I promised you would never see again; and there you shall offer yourselves for sale to your enemies as male and female slaves, but there will be no buyer.

g These are the words of the covenant that the LORD commanded Moses to make with the Israelites in the land of Mō′ab, in addition to the covenant that he had made with them at Hō′reb.

The Covenant Renewed in Moab

2 h Moses summoned all Israel and said to them: You have seen all that the LORD did before your eyes in the land of Egypt, to Pharaoh and to all his servants and to all his land, 3 the great trials that your eyes saw, the signs, and those great wonders. 4 But to this day the LORD has not given you a mind to understand, or eyes to see, or ears to hear. 5 I have led you forty years in the wilderness. The clothes on your back have not worn out, and the sandals on your feet have not worn out; 6 you have not eaten bread, and you have not drunk wine or strong drink—so that you may know that I am the LORD your God. 7 When you came to this place, King Sī′hon of Hesh′bon and King Og of Bā′shan came out against us for battle, but we defeated them. 8 We took their land and gave it as an inheritance to the Reü′ben•ites, the Gad′ites, and the half-tribe of Ma•nas′seh. 9 Therefore diligently observe the words of this covenant, in order that you may succeed i in everything that you do.

10 You stand assembled today, all of you, before the LORD your God—the leaders of your tribes, j your elders, and your officials, all the men of Israel, 11 your children, your women, and the aliens who are in your camp, both those who cut your wood and those who draw your water— 12 to enter into the covenant of the LORD your God, sworn by an oath, which the LORD your God is making with you today; 13 in order that he may establish you today as his people, and that he may be your God, as he promised you and as he swore to your ancestors, to Abraham, to Isaac, and to Jacob. 14 I am making this covenant, sworn by an oath, not only with you who stand here with us today before the LORD our God, 15 but also with those who are not here with us today. 16 You know how we lived in the land of Egypt, and how we came through the midst of the nations through which you passed. 17 You have seen their detestable things, the filthy idols of wood and stone, of silver and gold, that were among them. 18 It may be that there is among you a man or woman, or a family or tribe, whose heart is already turning away from the LORD our God to serve the gods of those nations. It may be that there is among you a root sprouting poisonous and bitter growth. 19 All who hear the words of this oath and bless themselves, thinking in their hearts, "We are safe even though we go our own stubborn ways" (thus bringing disaster on moist and dry alike) k — 20 the LORD will be unwilling to pardon them, for the LORD's anger and passion will smoke against them. All the curses written in this book will descend on them, and the LORD will blot out their names from under heaven. 21 The LORD will single them out from all the tribes of Israel for calamity, in accordance with all the curses of the covenant written in this book of the law. 22 The next generation, your children who rise up after you, as well as the foreigner who comes from a distant country, will see the devastation of that land and the afflictions with which the LORD has afflicted it— 23 all its soil burned out by sulfur and salt, nothing planted, nothing sprouting, unable to support any vegetation, like the destruction of Sod′om and Go•mor′rah, Ad′mah and Ze•boi′im, which the LORD destroyed in his fierce anger— 24 they and indeed all the nations will wonder, "Why has the LORD done thus to this land? What caused this great display of anger?" 25 They will conclude, "It is because they abandoned the covenant of the LORD, the God of their ancestors, which he made with them when he brought them out of the land of Egypt. 26 They turned and served other gods, worshiping them, gods whom they had not known and whom he had not allotted to them; 27 so the anger of the LORD was kindled against that land, bringing on it every curse written in this book. 28 The LORD uprooted them from their land in anger, fury, and great wrath, and cast them into another land, as is now the case." 29 The secret things belong to the LORD our God, but the revealed things belong to us and to our children forever, to observe all the words of this law.

God's Fidelity Assured

When all these things have happened to you, the blessings and the curses that I have set before you, if you call them to mind among all the nations where the LORD your God has driven you, 2 and return to the LORD your God, and you and your children obey him with all your heart and with all your soul, just as I am commanding you today, 3 then the LORD your God will restore your fortunes and have compassion on you, gathering you again from all the peoples among whom the LORD your God has scattered you. 4 Even if you are exiled to

---

g Ch 28.69 in Heb   h Ch 29.1 in Heb   i Or *deal wisely*
j Gk Syr: Heb *your leaders, your tribes*   k Meaning of Heb uncertain

the ends of the world,[l] from there the LORD your God will gather you, and from there he will bring you back. 5 The LORD your God will bring you into the land that your ancestors possessed, and you will possess it; he will make you more prosperous and numerous than your ancestors.

6 Moreover, the LORD your God will circumcise your heart and the heart of your descendants, so that you will love the LORD your God with all your heart and with all your soul, in order that you may live. 7 The LORD your God will put all these curses on your enemies and on the adversaries who took advantage of you. 8 Then you shall again obey the LORD, observing all his commandments that I am commanding you today, 9 and the LORD your God will make you abundantly prosperous in all your undertakings, in the fruit of your body, in the fruit of your livestock, and in the fruit of your soil. For the LORD will again take delight in prospering you, just as he delighted in prospering your ancestors, 10 when you obey the LORD your God by observing his commandments and decrees that are written in this book of the law, because you turn to the LORD your God with all your heart and with all your soul.

Exhortation to Choose Life

11 Surely, this commandment that I am commanding you today is not too hard for you, nor is it too far away. 12 It is not in heaven, that you should say, "Who will go up to heaven for us, and get it for us so that we may hear it and observe it?" 13 Neither is it beyond the sea, that you should say, "Who will cross to the other side of the sea for us, and get it for us so that we may hear it and observe it?" 14 No, the word is very near to you; it is in your mouth and in your heart for you to observe.

15 See, I have set before you today life and prosperity, death and adversity. 16 If you obey the commandments of the LORD your God[m] that I am commanding you today, by loving the LORD your God, walking in his ways, and observing his commandments, decrees, and ordinances, then you shall live and become numerous, and the LORD your God will bless you in the land that you are entering to possess. 17 But if your heart turns away and you do not hear, but are led astray to bow down to other gods and serve them, 18 I declare to you today that you shall perish; you shall not live long in the land that you are crossing the Jordan to enter and possess. 19 I call heaven and earth to witness against you today that I have set before you life and death, blessings and curses. Choose life so that you and your descendants may live, 20 loving the LORD your God, obeying him, and holding fast

Choose Life so that you and your descendants may LIVE

30.19

to him; for that means life to you and length of days, so that you may live in the land that the LORD swore to give to your ancestors, to Abraham, to Isaac, and to Jacob.

Joshua Becomes Moses' Successor
(Num 27.12–23)

When Moses had finished speaking all[n] these words to all Israel, 2 he said to them: "I am now one hundred twenty years old. I am no longer able to get about, and the LORD has told me, 'You shall not cross over this Jordan.' 3 The LORD your God himself will cross over before you. He will destroy these nations before you, and you shall dispossess them. Joshua also will cross over before you, as the LORD promised. 4 The LORD will do to them as he did to Si'hon and Og, the kings of the Am'o·rites, and to their land, when he destroyed them. 5 The LORD will give them over to you and you shall deal with them in full accord with the command that I have given to you. 6 Be strong and bold; have no fear or dread of them, because it is the LORD your God who goes with you; he will not fail you or forsake you."

7 Then Moses summoned Joshua and said to him in the sight of all Israel: "Be strong and bold, for you are the one who will go with this people into the land that the LORD has sworn to their ancestors to give them; and you will put them in possession of it. 8 It is the LORD who goes before you. He will be with you; he will not fail you or forsake you. Do not fear or be dismayed."

---

[l] Heb of heaven   [m] Gk: Heb lacks *If you obey the commandments of the LORD your God*   [n] Q Ms Gk: MT *Moses went and spoke*

DEUT

The Law to Be Read Every Seventh Year

9 Then Moses wrote down this law, and gave it to the priests, the sons of Levi, who carried the ark of the covenant of the LORD, and to all the elders of Israel. ¹⁰Moses commanded them: "Every seventh year, in the scheduled year of remission, during the festival of booths,ᵒ ¹¹when all Israel comes to appear before the LORD your God at the place that

and learn to fear the LORD your God, as long as you live in the land that you are crossing over the Jordan to possess."

Moses and Joshua Receive God's Charge

14 The LORD said to Moses, "Your time to die is near; call Joshua and present yourselves in the tent of meeting, so that I may commission him." So

HISPANICS LIVE THE HISTORY OF SALVATION!

HISPANIC ¡Los hispanos viven la historia de salvación!

As Moses did, Hispanics express their faith in the Lord of history:

Lord, you who are the Lord of all,
we, the Hispanic people of the United States,
conscious of being a people with its own identity,
born of common roots,
cultural traditions, language, and faith,
and in diversity united,
direct this prayer to you.

Lord and master of history,
we, a people, as we experience the same hungers and hurts,
make a preferential option for the poor,
and we stand in solidarity with this suffering humanity.

From your creative womb, we have been born;
we are your family, your believing people.
In this moment of grace, we feel ourselves called
to a "prophetic mission";
working together and participating in community,
we speak in your name to church and society.

Raised up as a people, intent on being authors
of our own history,
we walk with hope and in a progressive process.
Together we contribute to the coming of
the Kingdom of God here and now,
struggling to establish the new society, with an economy, relationships, and values
*   based on the love and the justice of your Son, Jesus Christ.*

We ask this in company with Mary,
the mother of all believers.
Amen.

(Secretariat for Hispanic Affairs, Prophetic Voices, p. 23)

he will choose, you shall read this law before all Israel in their hearing. ¹²Assemble the people— men, women, and children, as well as the aliens residing in your towns—so that they may hear and learn to fear the LORD your God and to observe diligently all the words of this law, ¹³and so that their children, who have not known it, may hear

Moses and Joshua went and presented themselves in the tent of meeting, ¹⁵and the LORD appeared at the tent in a pillar of cloud; the pillar of cloud stood at the entrance to the tent.

ᵒ Or *tabernacles*; Heb *succoth*

16 The LORD said to Moses, "Soon you will lie down with your ancestors. Then this people will begin to prostitute themselves to the foreign gods in their midst, the gods of the land into which they are going; they will forsake me, breaking my covenant that I have made with them. 17 My anger will be kindled against them in that day. I will forsake them and hide my face from them; they will become easy prey, and many terrible troubles will come upon them. In that day they will say, 'Have not these troubles come upon us because our God is not in our midst?' 18 On that day I will surely hide my face on account of all the evil they have done by turning to other gods. 19 Now therefore write this song, and teach it to the Israelites; put it in their mouths, in order that this song may be a witness for me against the Israelites. 20 For when I have brought them into the land flowing with milk and honey, which I promised on oath to their ancestors, and they have eaten their fill and grown fat, they will turn to other gods and serve them, despising me and breaking my covenant. 21 And when many terrible troubles come upon them, this song will confront them as a witness, because it will not be lost from the mouths of their descendants. For I know what they are inclined to do even now, before I have brought them into the land that I promised them on oath." 22 That very day Moses wrote this song and taught it to the Israelites.

23 Then the LORD commissioned Joshua son of Nun and said, "Be strong and bold, for you shall bring the Israelites into the land that I promised them; I will be with you."

24 When Moses had finished writing down in a book the words of this law to the very end, 25 Moses commanded the Lē′vītes who carried the ark of the covenant of the LORD, saying, 26 "Take this book of the law and put it beside the ark of the covenant of the LORD your God; let it remain there as a witness against you. 27 For I know well how rebellious and stubborn you are. If you already have been so rebellious toward the LORD while I am still alive among you, how much more after my death! 28 Assemble to me all the elders of your tribes and your officials, so that I may recite these words in their hearing and call heaven and earth to witness against them. 29 For I know that after my death you will surely act corruptly, turning aside from the way that I have commanded you. In time to come trouble will befall you, because you will do what is evil in the sight of the LORD, provoking him to anger through the work of your hands."

The Song of Moses

30 Then Moses recited the words of this song, to the very end, in the hearing of the whole assembly of Israel:

Give ear, O heavens, and I will speak;
    let the earth hear the words of my
      mouth.
2 May my teaching drop like the rain,
    my speech condense like the dew;
like gentle rain on grass,
    like showers on new growth.
3 For I will proclaim the name of the LORD;
    ascribe greatness to our God!

4 The Rock, his work is perfect,
    and all his ways are just.
A faithful God, without deceit,
    just and upright is he;
5 yet his degenerate children have dealt falsely
      with him, p
    a perverse and crooked generation.
6 Do you thus repay the LORD,
    O foolish and senseless people?
Is not he your father, who created you,
    who made you and established you?
7 Remember the days of old,
    consider the years long past;
ask your father, and he will inform you;
    your elders, and they will tell you.
8 When the Most High q apportioned the
      nations,
    when he divided humankind,
he fixed the boundaries of the peoples
    according to the number of the gods; r
9 the LORD's own portion was his people,
    Jacob his allotted share.

10 He sustained s him in a desert land,
    in a howling wilderness waste;
he shielded him, cared for him,
    guarded him as the apple of his eye.
11 As an eagle stirs up its nest,
    and hovers over its young;
as it spreads its wings, takes them up,
    and bears them aloft on its pinions,
12 the LORD alone guided him;
    no foreign god was with him.
13 He set him atop the heights of the land,
    and fed him with t produce of the field;
he nursed him with honey from the crags,
    with oil from flinty rock;

p Meaning of Heb uncertain   q Traditional rendering of Heb *Elyon*   r Q Ms Compare Gk Tg: MT *the Israelites*   s Sam Gk Compare Tg: MT *found*   t Sam Gk Syr Tg: MT *he ate*

14 curds from the herd, and milk from the
        flock,
    with fat of lambs and rams;
    Ba'shan bulls and goats,
        together with the choicest wheat—
    you drank fine wine from the blood of
        grapes.
15 Jacob ate his fill;*u*
    Jesh'ū•run grew fat, and kicked.
    You grew fat, bloated, and gorged!
    He abandoned God who made him,
        and scoffed at the Rock of his salvation.
16 They made him jealous with strange gods,
        with abhorrent things they provoked him.
17 They sacrificed to demons, not God,
        to deities they had never known,
    to new ones recently arrived,
        whom your ancestors had not feared.
18 You were unmindful of the Rock that bore
        you;*v*
    you forgot the God who gave you birth.

19 The LORD saw it, and was jealous;*w*
        he spurned*x* his sons and daughters.
20 He said: I will hide my face from them,
        I will see what their end will be;
    for they are a perverse generation,
        children in whom there is no
        faithfulness.
21 They made me jealous with what is no god,
        provoked me with their idols.
    So I will make them jealous with what is no
        people,
        provoke them with a foolish nation.
22 For a fire is kindled by my anger,
        and burns to the depths of Shē'ōl;
    it devours the earth and its increase,
        and sets on fire the foundations of the
        mountains.
23 I will heap disasters upon them,
        spend my arrows against them:
24 wasting hunger,
        burning consumption,
        bitter pestilence.
    The teeth of beasts I will send against them,
        with venom of things crawling in the
        dust.
25 In the street the sword shall bereave,
        and in the chambers terror,
    for young man and woman alike,
        nursing child and old gray head.
26 I thought to scatter them*y*
        and blot out the memory of them from
        humankind;
27 but I feared provocation by the enemy,
        for their adversaries might misunderstand

    and say, "Our hand is triumphant;
        it was not the LORD who did all this."

28 They are a nation void of sense;
        there is no understanding in them.
29 If they were wise, they would understand
        this;
    they would discern what the end would
        be.
30 How could one have routed a thousand,
        and two put a myriad to flight,
    unless their Rock had sold them,
        the LORD had given them up?
31 Indeed their rock is not like our Rock;
        our enemies are fools.*y*
32 Their vine comes from the vinestock of
        Sod'om,
        from the vineyards of Go•mor'rah;
    their grapes are grapes of poison,
        their clusters are bitter;
33 their wine is the poison of serpents,
        the cruel venom of asps.

34 Is not this laid up in store with me,
        sealed up in my treasuries?
35 Vengeance is mine, and recompense,
        for the time when their foot shall slip;
    because the day of their calamity is at hand,
        their doom comes swiftly.

36 Indeed the LORD will vindicate his people,
        have compassion on his servants,
    when he sees that their power is gone,
        neither bond nor free remaining.
37 Then he will say: Where are their gods,
        the rock in which they took refuge,
38 who ate the fat of their sacrifices,
        and drank the wine of their libations?
    Let them rise up and help you,
        let them be your protection!

39 See now that I, even I, am he;
        there is no god besides me.
    I kill and I make alive;
        I wound and I heal;
    and no one can deliver from my hand.
40 For I lift up my hand to heaven,
        and swear: As I live forever,
41 when I whet my flashing sword,
        and my hand takes hold on judgment;
    I will take vengeance on my adversaries,
        and will repay those who hate me.
42 I will make my arrows drunk with blood,
        and my sword shall devour flesh—

---

u Q Mss Sam Gk: MT lacks *Jacob ate his fill*   *v* Or *that
begot you*   *w* Q Mss Gk: MT lacks *was jealous*
x Cn: Heb *he spurned because of provocation*
y Gk: Meaning of Heb uncertain

with the blood of the slain and the captives,
from the long-haired enemy.

43 Praise, O heavens,^{z} his people,
worship him, all you gods!^{a}
For he will avenge the blood of his
children,^{b}
and take vengeance on his adversaries;
he will repay those who hate him,^{a}
and cleanse the land for his people.^{c}

44 Moses came and recited all the words of
this song in the hearing of the people, he and
Joshua^d son of Nun. 45 When Moses had finished
reciting all these words to all Israel, 46 he said to
them: "Take to heart all the words that I am giving
in witness against you today; give them as a command to your children, so that they may diligently
observe all the words of this law. 47 This is no tri-
fling matter for you, but rather your very life;
through it you may live long in the land that you
are crossing over the Jordan to possess."

Moses' Death Foretold

48 On that very day the LORD addressed Moses
as follows: 49 "Ascend this mountain of the Ab'a-
rim, Mount Ne'bo, which is in the land of Mo'ab,
across from Jericho, and view the land of Ca'naan,
which I am giving to the Israelites for a possession;
50 you shall die there on the mountain that you
ascend and shall be gathered to your kin, as your
brother Aaron died on Mount Hor and was gathered to his kin; 51 because both of you broke faith
with me among the Israelites at the waters of Mer'-
i•bath-ka'desh in the wilderness of Zin, by failing
to maintain my holiness among the Israelites.
52 Although you may view the land from a distance, you shall not enter it—the land that I am
giving to the Israelites."

Moses' Final Blessing on Israel

This is the blessing with which Moses, the man of
God, blessed the Israelites before his death. 2 He
said:
The LORD came from Sinai,
and dawned from Se'ir upon us;^{e}
he shone forth from Mount Par'an.
With him were myriads of holy ones;^{f}
at his right, a host of his own.^{g}
3 Indeed, O favorite among^h peoples,
all his holy ones were in your charge;
they marched at your heels,
accepted direction from you.
4 Moses charged us with the law,
as a possession for the assembly of Jacob.

5 There arose a king in Jesh'u•run,
when the leaders of the people
assembled—
the united tribes of Israel.

6 May Reuben live, and not die out,
even though his numbers are few.

7 And this he said of Judah:
O LORD, give heed to Judah,
and bring him to his people;
strengthen his hands for him,^{i}
and be a help against his adversaries.

8 And of Levi he said:
Give to Levi^j your Thum'mim,
and your U'rim to your loyal one,
whom you tested at Mas'sah,
with whom you contended at the waters
of Mer'i•bah;
9 who said of his father and mother,
"I regard them not";
he ignored his kin,
and did not acknowledge his children.
For they observed your word,
and kept your covenant.
10 They teach Jacob your ordinances,
and Israel your law;
they place incense before you,
and whole burnt offerings on your altar.
11 Bless, O LORD, his substance,
and accept the work of his hands;
crush the loins of his adversaries,
of those that hate him, so that they do
not rise again.

12 Of Benjamin he said:
The beloved of the LORD rests in safety—
the High God^k surrounds him all day long—
the beloved^l rests between his shoulders.

13 And of Joseph he said:
Blessed by the LORD be his land,
with the choice gifts of heaven above,
and of the deep that lies beneath;
14 with the choice fruits of the sun,
and the rich yield of the months;
15 with the finest produce of the ancient
mountains,
and the abundance of the everlasting hills;

---

^{z} Q Ms Gk: MT *nations* ^{a} Q Ms Gk: MT lacks this line
^{b} Q Ms Gk: MT *his servants* ^{c} Q Ms Sam Gk Vg: MT *his
land his people* ^{d} Sam Gk Syr Vg: MT *Hoshea* ^{e} Gk Syr
Vg Compare Tg: Heb *upon them* ^{f} Cn Compare Gk Sam
Syr Vg: MT *He came from Ribeboth-kodesh,* ^{g} Cn Compare
Gk: meaning of Heb uncertain ^{h} Or *O lover of the*
^{i} Cn: Heb *with his hands he contended* ^{j} Q Ms Gk: MT
lacks *Give to Levi* ^{k} Heb *above him* ^{l} Heb *he*

16 with the choice gifts of the earth and its
    fullness,
and the favor of the one who dwells on
    Sinai.[m]
Let these come on the head of Joseph,
    on the brow of the prince among his
    brothers.
17 A firstborn[n] bull—majesty is his!
    His horns are the horns of a wild ox;
with them he gores the peoples,
    driving them to[o] the ends of the
    earth;
such are the myriads of Ē′phra·im,
    such the thousands of Ma·nas′seh.

18 And of Zeb′u·lun he said:
Rejoice, Zeb′u·lun, in your going out;
    and Is′sa·char, in your tents.
19 They call peoples to the mountain;
    there they offer the right sacrifices;
for they suck the affluence of the seas
    and the hidden treasures of the sand.

20 And of Gad he said:
Blessed be the enlargement of Gad!
    Gad lives like a lion;
    he tears at arm and scalp.
21 He chose the best for himself,
    for there a commander's allotment was
    reserved;
he came at the head of the people,
    he executed the justice of the LORD,
    and his ordinances for Israel.

22 And of Dan he said:
Dan is a lion's whelp
    that leaps forth from Bā′shan.

23 And of Naph′ta·li he said:
O Naph′ta·li, sated with favor,
    full of the blessing of the LORD,
    possess the west and the south.

24 And of Ash′er he said:
Most blessed of sons be Ash′er;
    may he be the favorite of his brothers,
    and may he dip his foot in oil.
25 Your bars are iron and bronze;
    and as your days, so is your strength.

26 There is none like God, O Jesh′u·run,
    who rides through the heavens to your
    help,
    majestic through the skies.
27 He subdues the ancient gods,[p]
    shatters[q] the forces of old;[r]
he drove out the enemy before you,
    and said, "Destroy!"

28 So Israel lives in safety,
    untroubled is Jacob's abode[s]
in a land of grain and wine,
    where the heavens drop down dew.
29 Happy are you, O Israel! Who is like you,
    a people saved by the LORD,
the shield of your help,
    and the sword of your triumph!
Your enemies shall come fawning to you,
    and you shall tread on their backs.

Moses Dies and Is Buried in the Land of Moab

34 Then Moses went up from the plains of Mō′ab to Mount Nē′bō, to the top of Pis′gah, which is opposite Jericho, and the LORD showed him the whole land: Gil′e·ad as far as Dan, 2 all Naph′ta·li, the land of Ē′phra·im and Ma·nas′seh, all the land of Judah as far as the Western Sea, 3 the Neg′eb, and the Plain—that is, the valley of Jericho, the city of palm trees—as far as Zō′ar. 4 The LORD said to him, "This is the land of which I swore to Abra-

---

[m] Cn: Heb *in the bush*   [n] Q Ms Gk Syr Vg: MT *His firstborn*   [o] Cn: Heb *the peoples, together*   [p] Or *The eternal God is a dwelling place*   [q] Cn: Heb *from underneath*   [r] Or *the everlasting arms*   [s] Or *fountain*

MOSES' DEATH

Why did Moses die on the brink of entering the Promised Land? This question has disturbed many generations of believers. The one who received God's call to lead the Israelites out of slavery; who amazed Pharaoh with wonders and called down plagues on Egypt; who opened the Red Sea and received the tablets of the Law on Mount Sinai—this great leader did not get to enjoy the success of his work (Num 20.12)! Deuteronomy 34.1–6 simply tells us that Moses died on Mount Nebo and that his burial place was forgotten.

But consider this: By the time Deuteronomy was written, Moses had become a legendary figure. Many of the details of his life had been forgotten. Perhaps it is fitting that Moses' story ends as it began: shrouded in mystery, tragedy, and hope. What hope? The hope for another prophet like Moses (18.15) that remained alive and strong in the Israelites' hearts.

▶ Deuteronomy, chapter 34

ham, to Isaac, and to Jacob, saying, 'I will give it to your descendants'; I have let you see it with your eyes, but you shall not cross over there." 5 Then Moses, the servant of the LORD, died there in the land of Mō'ab, at the LORD's command. 6 He was buried in a valley in the land of Mō'ab, opposite Beth-pĕ'or, but no one knows his burial place to this day. 7 Moses was one hundred twenty years old when he died; his sight was unimpaired and his vigor had not abated. 8 The Israelites wept for Moses in the plains of Mō'ab thirty days; then the period of mourning for Moses was ended.

9 Joshua son of Nun was full of the spirit of wisdom, because Moses had laid his hands on him; and the Israelites obeyed him, doing as the LORD had commanded Moses.

10 Never since has there arisen a prophet in Israel like Moses, whom the LORD knew face to face. 11 He was unequaled for all the signs and wonders that the LORD sent him to perform in the land of Egypt, against Pharaoh and all his servants and his entire land, 12 and for all the mighty deeds and all the terrifying displays of power that Moses performed in the sight of all Israel.

DEUT

Introduction to the

Historical
Books

Have you ever noticed that many older people enjoy telling stories about the past? Sometimes, it seems that their past experiences are more real to them than present-day events. Those of us who are younger may get tired of hearing about the "good old days." Still, a lot is to be gained from listening carefully to the memories of our elders. The sixteen historical books of the Old Testament, like the voices of respected elders, tell the stories of God at work in ancient Israel. In reading these stories, we can see more clearly how God works in today's world.

In-depth

THE HISTORICAL BOOKS RECOUNT THE PERIOD of Israelite history from 1250 to 100 B.C. In those books, we read about the following events:

- the Israelites' settlement in the Promised Land and their struggle to protect themselves from their enemies (the Books of Joshua and Judges)
- the rise of a united kingdom under David (1 and 2 Samuel, 1 Kings)
- the division of the kingdom into northern and southern kingdoms, and the various kings and prophets of each, until the fall of Jerusalem in 587 B.C. (1 and 2 Kings, 1 and 2 Chronicles)
- the return from Exile and the rebuilding of the nation (Ezra and Nehemiah)
- the Jewish resistance to Greek domination in the second century before Christ (1 and 2 Maccabees)

In addition, the books contain three "novels" about the human challenge to trust God in difficult times (Tobit, Judith, and Esther).

The historical books of the Old Testament are not like the history books that we read in school. Those who write history books today generally try to report the facts with little interpretation. "Let the events speak for themselves," they say. However, those who wrote the historical books of the Old Testament had a different purpose: "Let us tell you what the events *mean in the light of our faith in God."* Thus, the history contained in these books is often called sacred history because it reveals God's message and God's purpose in history.

Scripture scholars find evidence of two general groups shaping the final form of the historical books. The first group is called the Deuteronomic school of writers because it was responsible for the highly influential Book of Deuteronomy. This group also wrote Joshua, Judges, 1 and 2 Samuel, and 1 and 2 Kings. The Deuteronomists were convinced that God rewarded the good and punished the wicked in this world. Thus, you will find in these books a repeated pattern of (1) God's offer of love, (2) the people's faithlessness and sin, (3) God's just punishment, (4) the people's repentance and cry for help, (5) God's forgiveness and mercy, and (6) the people's repeated sin.

The second group (or person), sometimes called the Chronicler, is responsible for 1 and 2 Chronicles, and probably Ezra and Nehemiah. The Chronicler still emphasized that God rewards the faithful and punishes the unfaithful, but the measurement for what is faithful had changed. Instead of emphasizing faithfulness to the Sinai Covenant, the Chronicler emphasized faithfulness to proper worship, particularly worship at the Temple in Jerusalem. The Chronicler wrote after the destruction of the northern and southern kingdoms, to nurture the faith of a small community trying to rebuild itself.

Some of the religious truths you will learn from reading these books are as follows:

- God is not removed from the affairs of this world, but cares deeply about what is happening in human history.
- People are happier when they follow the law of God than when they turn away from the Law.
- All human beings, from the beginning of history, are joined in a common struggle to find sense and meaning in the ups and downs of life.

As you read these books, remember that the authors' understanding of God is not the same as Jesus' understanding. Although not denying the truths about God taught by these books, Christians have a larger context for understanding God's unconditional love and unlimited mercy: Jesus' teaching in the New Testament.

Other Background

- **The Book of Ruth was not originally one of the historical books. It was written later than the books it is now sandwiched between.**

- **The Books of 1 and 2 Chronicles review the same historical period as 1 and 2 Samuel and 1 and 2 Kings.**

- **Tobit, Judith, and Esther are fictional works that use history only as a backdrop. Their purpose is to encourage fidelity to God's law in hard times.**

- **Tobit, Judith, 1 and 2 Maccabees, and parts of Esther are not found in every translation of the Old Testament and are not contained in many Protestant Bibles. See "The Case of the Missing Books," near Tob 1.16.**

When you were young, did you ask to hear your favorite book over and over again? Do you remember feeling secure because you knew how the story would turn out? Often, familiar stories appeal to us because of their simple justice: evil is punished, and good is rewarded. The author of the Book of Joshua applies this simple justice to the conquest of the Promised Land: those who follow God are rewarded, and those who do not are destroyed.

At a Glance

- **Chapters 1–12.** the conquest of the land of Canaan
- **Chapters 13–22.** the division of the land among the twelve tribes
- **Chapters 23–24.** Joshua's last words and death

In-depth

The Book of Joshua is named after the Israelite hero who succeeds Moses and leads the people in their takeover of the Promised Land. At the beginning of the book, Joshua promises the Israelites that they will conquer the land of Canaan and make it their own if they are faithful to the Covenant of Moses. They respond with enthusiasm, "Just as we obeyed Moses in all things, so we will obey you" (1.17). The author describes how by remaining true to the Commandments of God, the various Israelite tribes, under Joshua's leadership, take over the land and settle in it with their families and livestock (see map 2, "The Exodus from Egypt").

Today, biblical scholars doubt that the conquest of the Promised Land by the twelve tribes of Israel was as complete and easy as it is written in Joshua. Archaeologists have found evidence that Canaanites continued to live in the area after the "conquest." The historical memories preserved in the book were reshaped by the author to emphasize an important lesson of faith: God would preserve the Israelites on their land as long as they obeyed the Commandments.

The belief in the triumph of good and the punishment of evil is at the heart of the Book of Joshua. Like Judges, 1 and 2 Samuel, and 1 and 2 Kings, the Book of Joshua is inspired by the Book of Deuteronomy, which insists that God rewards the just and punishes the wicked in this world (see Deut 30.15–20). The Book of Joshua challenges us to remember that God is our surest hope in all the ups and downs of history.

Quick Facts

Period Covered
after the desert wandering, from about 1250 to 1200 B.C.

Author
unknown, from the Deuteronomic tradition, writing in the seventh or sixth century B.C.

Themes
Israel's conquest of the Promised Land, the triumph of good and the punishment of evil

Of Note
The name Jesus is the Greek form of Joshua, which means "God saves."

The Book of Joshua

Joshua

3.14

God's Commission to Joshua

After the death of Moses the servant of the LORD, the LORD spoke to Joshua son of Nun, Moses' assistant, saying, 2 "My servant Moses is dead. Now proceed to cross the Jordan, you and all this people, into the land that I am giving to them, to the Israelites. 3 Every place that the sole of your foot will tread upon I have given to you, as I promised to Moses. 4 From the wilderness and the Lebanon as far as the great river, the river Euphrates, all the land of the Hit'tites, to the Great Sea in the west shall be your territory. 5 No one shall be able to stand against you all the days of your life. As I was with Moses, so I will be with you; I will not fail you or forsake you. 6 Be strong and courageous; for you shall put this people in possession of the land that I swore to their ancestors to give them. 7 Only be strong and very courageous, being careful to act in accordance with all the law that my servant Moses commanded you; do not turn from it to the right hand or to the left, so that you may be successful wherever you go. 8 This book of the law shall not depart out of your mouth; you shall meditate on it day and night, so that you may be careful to act in accordance with all that is written in it. For then you shall make your way prosperous, and then you shall be successful. 9 I hereby command you: Be strong and courageous; do not be frightened or dismayed, for the LORD your God is with you wherever you go."

Preparations for the Invasion

10 Then Joshua commanded the officers of the people, 11 "Pass through the camp, and command the people: 'Prepare your provisions; for in three days you are to cross over the Jordan, to go in to take possession of the land that the LORD your God gives you to possess.' "

12 To the Reu'ben·ites, the Gad'ites, and the half-tribe of Ma·nas'seh Joshua said, 13 "Remember the word that Moses the servant of the LORD commanded you, saying, 'The LORD your God is providing you a place of rest, and will give you this land.' 14 Your wives, your little ones, and your livestock shall remain in the land that Moses gave you beyond the Jordan. But all the warriors among you shall cross over armed before your kindred and shall help them, 15 until the LORD gives rest to your kindred as well as to you, and they too take possession of the land that the LORD your God is giving them. Then you shall return to your own land and take possession of it, the land that Moses the servant of the LORD gave you beyond the Jordan to the east."

16 They answered Joshua: "All that you have commanded us we will do, and wherever you send us we will go. 17 Just as we obeyed Moses in all things, so we will obey you. Only may the LORD your God be with you, as he was with Moses! 18 Whoever rebels against your orders and disobeys your words, whatever you command, shall be put to death. Only be strong and courageous."

Be Not Afraid

"Be strong and courageous; do not be frightened or dismayed, for the LORD your God is with you wherever you go" (Josh 1.9).

Living proof:

Saint Joan of Arc was a humble, uneducated peasant maiden from fifteenth-century France. Inspired by saintly voices, she overcame numerous obstacles to lead the French troops into battle against British invaders.

Saint Thomas More, a distinguished scholar and lawyer, refused to approve King Henry VIII's divorce and remarriage and establishment of the Church of England.

Dorothy Day, twentieth-century American cofounder of the Catholic Worker Movement, challenged all Christians to serve poor and homeless people and dedicated her life to nonviolence.

Archbishop Oscar Romero of El Salvador was shot while saying Mass in 1980 because he dared to speak against the military groups that were terrorizing and killing the poor people of his diocese.

These four people, along with many others, have taken to heart God's words to Joshua. If you are not familiar with their stories, take time to learn more about these Catholic heroes.

▶ Josh 1.5–9

Spies Sent to Jericho
(Heb 11.31)

Then Joshua son of Nun sent two men secretly from Shit'tim as spies, saying, "Go, view the land, especially Jericho." So they went, and entered the house of a prostitute whose name was Rā'hab, and spent the night there. 2 The king of Jericho was told, "Some Israelites have come here tonight to search out the land." 3 Then the king of Jericho sent orders to Rā'hab, "Bring out the men who have come to you, who entered your house, for they have come only to search out the whole land." 4 But the woman took the two men and hid them. Then she said, "True, the men came to me, but I did not know where they came from. 5 And when it was time to close the gate at dark, the men went out. Where the men went I do not know. Pursue them quickly, for you can overtake them." 6 She had, however, brought them up to the roof and hidden them with the stalks of flax that she had laid out on the roof. 7 So the men pursued them on the way to the Jordan as far as the fords. As soon as the pursuers had gone out, the gate was shut.

8 Before they went to sleep, she came up to them on the roof 9 and said to the men: "I know that the LORD has given you the land, and that dread of you has fallen on us, and that all the inhabitants of the land melt in fear before you. 10 For we have heard how the LORD dried up the water of the Red Sea[a] before you when you came out of Egypt, and what you did to the two kings of the Am'o•rītes that were beyond the Jordan, to Sī'hon and Og, whom you utterly destroyed. 11 As soon as we heard it, our hearts melted, and there was no courage left in any of us because of you. The LORD your God is indeed God in heaven above and on earth below. 12 Now then, since I have dealt kindly with you, swear to me by the LORD that you in turn will deal kindly with my family. Give me a sign of good faith 13 that you will spare my father and mother, my brothers and sisters, and all who belong to them, and deliver our lives from death." 14 The men said to her, "Our life for yours! If you do not tell this business of ours, then we will deal kindly and faithfully with you when the LORD gives us the land."

15 Then she let them down by a rope through the window, for her house was on the outer side of the city wall and she resided within the wall itself. 16 She said to them, "Go toward the hill country, so that the pursuers may not come upon you. Hide yourselves there three days, until the pursuers have returned; then afterward you may go your way." 17 The men said to her, "We will be released from this oath that you have made us swear to you 18 if we invade the land and you do not tie this crimson cord in the window through which you let us down, and you do not gather into your house your father and mother, your brothers, and all your family. 19 If any of you go out of the doors of your house into the street, they shall be respon-

a Or Sea of Reeds

sible for their own death, and we shall be innocent; but if a hand is laid upon any who are with
you in the house, we shall bear the responsibility
for their death. 20 But if you tell this business of
ours, then we shall be released from this oath that
you made us swear to you." 21 She said, "According
to your words, so be it." She sent them away and
they departed. Then she tied the crimson cord in
the window.

22 They departed and went into the hill country and stayed there three days, until the pursuers
returned. The pursuers had searched all along the
way and found nothing. 23 Then the two men
came down again from the hill country. They
crossed over, came to Joshua son of Nun, and told
him all that had happened to them. 24 They said to
Joshua, "Truly the LORD has given all the land into
our hands; moreover all the inhabitants of the
land melt in fear before us."

PRAY IT!

A Prayer Against Prejudice

Creator of diverse people, the Israelites united themselves with Rahab, someone outside their group, and trusted her. Lead me to be open to befriending those who are different from me so that I may learn to trust them as well.

Forgive my friends and me for every time we have looked at someone different and considered them to be of lesser quality. Forgive us for each time we have talked about certain people as if we were superior. Forgive our cliques that look down on others and won't associate with them. And help us forgive those who have looked down on us. Amen.

▸ Joshua, chapter 2

Israel Crosses the Jordan

Early in the morning Joshua rose and set out from
Shit′tim with all the Israelites, and they came to
the Jordan. They camped there before crossing
over. 2 At the end of three days the officers went
through the camp 3 and commanded the people,
"When you see the ark of the covenant of the LORD
your God being carried by the levitical priests,
then you shall set out from your place. Follow it,
4 so that you may know the way you should go, for
you have not passed this way before. Yet there
shall be a space between you and it, a distance
of about two thousand cubits; do not come any
nearer to it." 5 Then Joshua said to the people,
"Sanctify yourselves; for tomorrow the LORD will
do wonders among you." 6 To the priests Joshua
said, "Take up the ark of the covenant, and pass
on in front of the people." So they took up the
ark of the covenant and went in front of the
people.

7 The LORD said to Joshua, "This day I will begin to exalt you in the sight of all Israel, so that
they may know that I will be with you as I was
with Moses. 8 You are the one who shall command
the priests who bear the ark of the covenant,
'When you come to the edge of the waters of the
Jordan, you shall stand still in the Jordan.' "
9 Joshua then said to the Israelites, "Draw near and
hear the words of the LORD your God." 10 Joshua
said, "By this you shall know that among you is
the living God who without fail will drive out
from before you the Cā′naan•ites, Hit′tites,
Hī′vites, Per′iz•zites, Gir′ga•shites, Am′o•rites, and
Jeb′ū•sites: 11 the ark of the covenant of the Lord of
all the earth is going to pass before you into the
Jordan. 12 So now select twelve men from the
tribes of Israel, one from each tribe. 13 When
the soles of the feet of the priests who bear the ark
of the LORD, the Lord of all the earth, rest in the
waters of the Jordan, the waters of the Jordan flowing from above shall be cut off; they shall stand in
a single heap."

14 When the people set out from their tents to
cross over the Jordan, the priests bearing the ark of
the covenant were in front of the people. 15 Now
the Jordan overflows all its banks throughout the
time of harvest. So when those who bore the ark
had come to the Jordan, and the feet of the priests
bearing the ark were dipped in the edge of the water, 16 the waters flowing from above stood still,
rising up in a single heap far off at Adam, the city
that is beside Zar′e•than, while those flowing toward the sea of the Ar′a•bah, the Dead Sea,*b* were
wholly cut off. Then the people crossed over opposite Jericho. 17 While all Israel were crossing over
on dry ground, the priests who bore the ark of the
covenant of the LORD stood on dry ground in the
middle of the Jordan, until the entire nation finished crossing over the Jordan.

---

b Heb *Salt Sea*

JOSH

Twelve Stones Set Up at Gilgal

When the entire nation had finished crossing over the Jordan, the LORD said to Joshua: 2 "Select twelve men from the people, one from each tribe, 3 and command them, 'Take twelve stones from here out of the middle of the Jordan, from the place where the priests' feet stood, carry them over with you, and lay them down in the place where you camp tonight.' " 4 Then Joshua summoned the twelve men from the Israelites, whom he had appointed, one from each tribe. 5 Joshua said to them, "Pass on before the ark of the LORD your God into the middle of the Jordan, and each of you take up a stone on his shoulder, one for each of the tribes of the Israelites, 6 so that this may be a sign among you. When your children ask in time to come, 'What do those stones mean to you?' 7 then you shall tell them that the waters of the Jordan were cut off in front of the ark of the covenant of the LORD. When it crossed over the Jordan, the waters of the Jordan were cut off. So these stones shall be to the Israelites a memorial forever."

8 The Israelites did as Joshua commanded. They took up twelve stones out of the middle of the Jordan, according to the number of the tribes of the Israelites, as the LORD told Joshua, carried them over with them to the place where they camped, and laid them down there. 9 (Joshua set up twelve stones in the middle of the Jordan, in the place where the feet of the priests bearing the ark of the covenant had stood; and they are there to this day.)

10 The priests who bore the ark remained standing in the middle of the Jordan, until everything was finished that the LORD commanded Joshua to tell the people, according to all that Moses had commanded Joshua. The people crossed over in haste. 11 As soon as all the people had finished crossing over, the ark of the LORD, and the priests, crossed over in front of the people. 12 The Reü'ben·ites, the Gad'ites, and the half-tribe of Manas'seh crossed over armed before the Israelites, as Moses had ordered them. 13 About forty thousand armed for war crossed over before the LORD to the plains of Jericho for battle.

14 On that day the LORD exalted Joshua in the sight of all Israel; and they stood in awe of him, as they had stood in awe of Moses, all the days of his life.

15 The LORD said to Joshua, 16 "Command the priests who bear the ark of the covenant,c to come up out of the Jordan." 17 Joshua therefore commanded the priests, "Come up out of the Jordan." 18 When the priests bearing the ark of the covenant of the LORD came up from the middle of the Jor-

dan, and the soles of the priests' feet touched dry ground, the waters of the Jordan returned to their place and overflowed all its banks, as before.

19 The people came up out of the Jordan on the tenth day of the first month, and they camped in Gil'gal on the east border of Jericho. 20 Those twelve stones, which they had taken out of the Jordan, Joshua set up in Gil'gal, 21 saying to the Israelites, "When your children ask their parents in time to come, 'What do these stones mean?' 22 then you shall let your children know, 'Israel crossed over the Jordan here on dry ground.' 23 For the LORD your God dried up the waters of the Jordan for you until you crossed over, as the LORD your God did to the Red Sea,d which he dried up for us until we crossed over, 24 so that all the peoples of the earth may know that the hand of the LORD is mighty, and so that you may fear the LORD your God forever."

The New Generation Circumcised

When all the kings of the Am'o·rītes beyond the Jordan to the west, and all the kings of the Cā'-naan·ites by the sea, heard that the LORD had dried up the waters of the Jordan for the Israelites until they had crossed over, their hearts melted, and there was no longer any spirit in them, because of the Israelites.

2 At that time the LORD said to Joshua, "Make flint knives and circumcise the Israelites a second time." 3 So Joshua made flint knives, and circumcised the Israelites at Gib'e·ath-ha·ar'a·loth.e 4 This is the reason why Joshua circumcised them: all the males of the people who came out of Egypt, all the warriors, had died during the journey through the wilderness after they had come out of Egypt. 5 Although all the people who came out had been circumcised, yet all the people born on the journey through the wilderness after they had come out of Egypt had not been circumcised. 6 For the Israelites traveled forty years in the wilderness, until all the nation, the warriors who came out of Egypt, perished, not having listened to the voice of the LORD. To them the LORD swore that he would not let them see the land that he had sworn to their ancestors to give us, a land flowing with milk and honey. 7 So it was their children, whom he raised up in their place, that Joshua circumcised; for they were uncircumcised, because they had not been circumcised on the way.

8 When the circumcising of all the nation was done, they remained in their places in the camp until they were healed. 9 The LORD said to Joshua,

c Or treaty, or testimony; Heb eduth   d Or Sea of Reeds
e That is the Hill of the Foreskins

"Today I have rolled away from you the disgrace of Egypt." And so that place is called Gil'gal *f* to this day.

The Passover at Gilgal

10 While the Israelites were camped in Gil'gal they kept the passover in the evening on the fourteenth day of the month in the plains of Jericho. 11 On the day after the passover, on that very day, they ate the produce of the land, unleavened cakes and parched grain. 12 The manna ceased on the day they ate the produce of the land, and the Israelites no longer had manna; they ate the crops of the land of Cā'naan that year.

Joshua's Vision

13 Once when Joshua was by Jericho, he looked up and saw a man standing before him with a drawn sword in his hand. Joshua went to him and said to him, "Are you one of us, or one of our adversaries?" 14 He replied, "Neither; but as commander of the army of the LORD I have now come." And Joshua fell on his face to the earth and worshiped, and he said to him, "What do you command your servant, my lord?" 15 The commander of the army of the LORD said to Joshua, "Remove the sandals from your feet, for the place where you stand is holy." And Joshua did so.

Jericho Taken and Destroyed

Now Jericho was shut up inside and out because of the Israelites; no one came out and no one went in. 2 The LORD said to Joshua, "See, I have handed Jericho over to you, along with its king and soldiers. 3 You shall march around the city, all the warriors circling the city once. Thus you shall do for six days, 4 with seven priests bearing seven trumpets of rams' horns before the ark. On the seventh day you shall march around the city seven times, the priests blowing the trumpets. 5 When they make a long blast with the ram's horn, as soon as you hear the sound of the trumpet, then all the people shall shout with a great shout; and the wall of the city will fall down flat, and all the people shall charge straight ahead." 6 So Joshua son of Nun summoned the priests and said to them, "Take up the ark of the covenant, and have seven priests carry seven trumpets of rams' horns in front of the ark of the LORD." 7 To the people he said, "Go forward and march around the city; have the armed men pass on before the ark of the LORD."

8 As Joshua had commanded the people, the seven priests carrying the seven trumpets of rams' horns before the LORD went forward, blowing the trumpets, with the ark of the covenant of the LORD following them. 9 And the armed men went before the priests who blew the trumpets; the rear guard came after the ark, while the trumpets blew continually. 10 To the people Joshua gave this command: "You shall not shout or let your voice be heard, nor shall you utter a word, until the day I tell you to shout. Then you shall shout." 11 So the ark of the LORD went around the city, circling it once; and they came into the camp, and spent the night in the camp.

12 Then Joshua rose early in the morning, and the priests took up the ark of the LORD. 13 The seven priests carrying the seven trumpets of rams' horns before the ark of the LORD passed on, blowing the trumpets continually. The armed men went before them, and the rear guard came after the ark of the LORD, while the trumpets blew continually. 14 On the second day they marched around the city once and then returned to the camp. They did this for six days.

15 On the seventh day they rose early, at dawn, and marched around the city in the same manner seven times. It was only on that day that they marched around the city seven times. 16 And at the seventh time, when the priests had blown the trumpets, Joshua said to the people, "Shout! For the LORD has given you the city. 17 The city and all that is in it shall be devoted to the LORD for destruction. Only Rā'hab the prostitute and all who are with her in her house shall live because she hid the messengers we sent. 18 As for you, keep away from the things devoted to destruction, so as not to covet *g* and take any of the devoted things and make the camp of Israel an object for destruction, bringing trouble upon it. 19 But all silver and gold, and vessels of bronze and iron, are sacred to the LORD; they shall go into the treasury of the LORD." 20 So the people shouted, and the trumpets were blown. As soon as the people heard the sound of the trumpets, they raised a great shout, and the wall fell down flat; so the people charged straight ahead into the city and captured it. 21 Then they devoted to destruction by the edge of the sword all in the city, both men and women, young and old, oxen, sheep, and donkeys.

22 Joshua said to the two men who had spied out the land, "Go into the prostitute's house, and bring the woman out of it and all who belong to her, as you swore to her." 23 So the young men who had been spies went in and brought Rā'hab out, along with her father, her mother, her brothers, and all who belonged to her—they brought all her kindred out—and set them outside the camp of

---

f Related to Heb *galal* to roll   *g* Gk: Heb *devote to destruction* Compare 7.21

Israel. 24 They burned down the city, and everything in it; only the silver and gold, and the vessels of bronze and iron, they put into the treasury of the house of the LORD. 25 But Rāʾhab the prostitute, with her family and all who belonged to her, Joshua spared. Her family[h] has lived in Israel ever since. For she hid the messengers whom Joshua sent to spy out Jericho.

26 Joshua then pronounced this oath, saying,
"Cursed before the LORD be anyone who
       tries
   to build this city—this Jericho!
At the cost of his firstborn he shall lay its
       foundation,
   and at the cost of his youngest he shall
       set up its gates!"

27 So the LORD was with Joshua; and his fame was in all the land.

The Sin of Achan and Its Punishment

But the Israelites broke faith in regard to the devoted things: Āʾchan son of Carʾmī son of Zabʾdī son of Zēʾrah, of the tribe of Judah, took some of the devoted things; and the anger of the LORD burned against the Israelites.

2 Joshua sent men from Jericho to Aī, which is near Beth-āʾven, east of Bethʾel, and said to them, "Go up and spy out the land." And the men went up and spied out Aī. 3 Then they returned to Joshua and said to him, "Not all the people need go up; about two or three thousand men should go up and attack Aī. Since they are so few, do not make the whole people toil up there." 4 So about three thousand of the people went up there; and they fled before the men of Aī. 5 The men of Aī killed about thirty-six of them, chasing them from outside the gate as far as Shebʾaʹrim and killing them on the slope. The hearts of the people melted and turned to water.

6 Then Joshua tore his clothes, and fell to the ground on his face before the ark of the LORD until the evening, he and the elders of Israel; and they put dust on their heads. 7 Joshua said, "Ah, Lord GOD! Why have you brought this people across the Jordan at all, to hand us over to the Amʾoʹrites so as to destroy us? Would that we had been content to settle beyond the Jordan! 8 O Lord, what can I say, now that Israel has turned their backs to their enemies! 9 The Cāʾnaanʹites and all the inhabitants of the land will hear of it, and surround us, and cut off our name from the earth. Then what will you do for your great name?"

10 The LORD said to Joshua, "Stand up! Why have you fallen upon your face? 11 Israel has sinned; they have transgressed my covenant that I imposed on them. They have taken some of the devoted things; they have stolen, they have acted deceitfully, and they have put them among their own belongings. 12 Therefore the Israelites are unable to stand before their enemies; they turn their backs to their enemies, because they have become a thing devoted for destruction themselves. I will be with you no more, unless you destroy the devoted things from among you. 13 Proceed to sanctify the people, and say, 'Sanctify yourselves for tomorrow; for thus says the LORD, the God of Israel, "There are devoted things among you, O Israel; you will be unable to stand before your enemies until you take away the devoted things from among you." 14 In the morning therefore you shall come forward tribe by tribe. The tribe that the LORD takes shall come near by clans, the clan that the LORD takes shall come near by households, and the household that the LORD takes shall come near one by one. 15 And the one who is taken as having the devoted things shall be burned with fire, together with all that he has, for having transgressed the covenant of the LORD, and for having done an outrageous thing in Israel.' "

16 So Joshua rose early in the morning, and brought Israel near tribe by tribe, and the tribe of Judah was taken. 17 He brought near the clans of Judah, and the clan of the Zēʾraʹhites was taken; and he brought near the clan of the Zēʾraʹhites, family by family,[i] and Zabʾdī was taken. 18 And he brought near his household one by one, and Āʾchan son of Carʾmī son of Zabʾdī son of Zēʾrah, of the tribe of Judah, was taken. 19 Then Joshua said to Āʾchan, "My son, give glory to the LORD God of Israel and make confession to him. Tell me now what you have done; do not hide it from me." 20 And Āʾchan answered Joshua, "It is true; I am the one who sinned against the LORD God of Israel. This is what I did: 21 when I saw among the spoil a beautiful mantle from Shiʾnar, and two hundred shekels of silver, and a bar of gold weighing fifty shekels, then I coveted them and took them. They now lie hidden in the ground inside my tent, with the silver underneath."

22 So Joshua sent messengers, and they ran to the tent; and there it was, hidden in his tent with the silver underneath. 23 They took them out of the tent and brought them to Joshua and all the Israelites; and they spread them out before the LORD. 24 Then Joshua and all Israel with him took Āʾchan son of Zēʾrah, with the silver, the mantle, and the bar of gold, with his sons and daughters, with his oxen, donkeys, and sheep, and his tent and all that he had; and they brought them up to the Valley of Āʾchor. 25 Joshua said, "Why did you bring trouble

---

h Heb *She*   i Mss Syr: MT *man by man*

on us? The LORD is bringing trouble on you today." And all Israel stoned him to death; they burned them with fire, cast stones on them, 26 and raised over him a great heap of stones that remains to this day. Then the LORD turned from his burning anger. Therefore that place to this day is called the Valley of Ā′chor.*j*

Ai Captured by a Stratagem and Destroyed

Then the LORD said to Joshua, "Do not fear or be dismayed; take all the fighting men with you, and go up now to Aī. See, I have handed over to you the king of Aī with his people, his city, and his land. 2 You shall do to Aī and its king as you did to Jericho and its king; only its spoil and its livestock you may take as booty for yourselves. Set an ambush against the city, behind it."

3 So Joshua and all the fighting men set out to go up against Aī. Joshua chose thirty thousand warriors and sent them out by night 4 with the command, "You shall lie in ambush against the city, behind it; do not go very far from the city, but all of you stay alert. 5 I and all the people who are with me will approach the city. When they come out against us, as before, we shall flee from them. 6 They will come out after us until we have drawn them away from the city; for they will say, 'They are fleeing from us, as before.' While we flee from them, 7 you shall rise up from the ambush and seize the city; for the LORD your God will give it into your hand. 8 And when you have taken the city, you shall set the city on fire, doing as the LORD has ordered; see, I have commanded you." 9 So Joshua sent them out; and they went to the place of ambush, and lay between Beth′el and Aī, to the west of Aī; but Joshua spent that night in the camp.*k*

10 In the morning Joshua rose early and mustered the people, and went up, with the elders of Israel, before the people to Aī. 11 All the fighting men who were with him went up, and drew near before the city, and camped on the north side of Aī, with a ravine between them and Aī. 12 Taking about five thousand men, he set them in ambush between Beth′el and Aī, to the west of the city. 13 So they stationed the forces, the main encampment that was north of the city and its rear guard west of the city. But Joshua spent that night in the valley. 14 When the king of Aī saw this, he and all his people, the inhabitants of the city, hurried out early in the morning to the meeting place facing the Ar′a•bah to meet Israel in battle; but he did not know that there was an ambush against him behind the city. 15 And Joshua and all Israel made a pretense of being beaten before them, and fled in the direction of the wilderness. 16 So all the people

who were in the city were called together to pursue them, and as they pursued Joshua they were drawn away from the city. 17 There was not a man left in Aī or Beth′el who did not go out after Israel; they left the city open, and pursued Israel.

18 Then the LORD said to Joshua, "Stretch out the sword that is in your hand toward Aī; for I will give it into your hand." And Joshua stretched out the sword that was in his hand toward the city. 19 As soon as he stretched out his hand, the troops in ambush rose quickly out of their place and rushed forward. They entered the city, took it, and at once set the city on fire. 20 So when the men of Aī looked back, the smoke of the city was rising to the sky. They had no power to flee this way or that, for the people who fled to the wilderness turned back against the pursuers. 21 When Joshua and all Israel saw that the ambush had taken the city and that the smoke of the city was rising, then they turned back and struck down the men of Aī. 22 And the others came out from the city against them; so they were surrounded by Israelites, some on one side, and some on the other; and Israel struck them down until no one was left who survived or escaped. 23 But the king of Aī was taken alive and brought to Joshua.

24 When Israel had finished slaughtering all the inhabitants of Aī in the open wilderness where they pursued them, and when all of them to the very last had fallen by the edge of the sword, all Israel returned to Aī, and attacked it with the edge of the sword. 25 The total of those who fell that day, both men and women, was twelve thousand— all the people of Aī. 26 For Joshua did not draw back his hand, with which he stretched out the sword, until he had utterly destroyed all the inhabitants of Aī. 27 Only the livestock and the spoil of that city Israel took as their booty, according to the word of the LORD that he had issued to Joshua. 28 So Joshua burned Aī, and made it forever a heap of ruins, as it is to this day. 29 And he hanged the king of Aī on a tree until evening; and at sunset Joshua commanded, and they took his body down from the tree, threw it down at the entrance of the gate of the city, and raised over it a great heap of stones, which stands there to this day.

Joshua Renews the Covenant
(*Cp Deut 27.4–5*)

30 Then Joshua built on Mount Ē′bal an altar to the LORD, the God of Israel, 31 just as Moses the servant of the LORD had commanded the Israelites, as it is written in the book of the law of Moses, "an altar of unhewn*l* stones, on which no iron

---

j That is *Trouble*   *k* Heb *among the people*   *l* Heb *whole* tool has been used"; and they offered on it burnt offerings to the LORD, and sacrificed offerings of well-being. 32 And there, in the presence of the Israelites, Joshua[m] wrote on the stones a copy of the law of Moses, which he had written. 33 All Israel, alien as well as citizen, with their elders and officers and their judges, stood on opposite sides of the ark in front of the levitical priests who carried the ark of the covenant of the LORD, half of them in front of Mount Ger′i·zim and half of them in front of Mount E′bal, as Moses the servant of the LORD had commanded at the first, that they should bless the people of Israel. 34 And afterward he read all the words of the law, blessings and curses, according to all that is written in the book of the law. 35 There was not a word of all that Moses commanded that Joshua did not read before all the assembly of Israel, and the women, and the little ones, and the aliens who resided among them.

The Gibeonites Save Themselves by Trickery

Now when all the kings who were beyond the Jordan in the hill country and in the lowland all along the coast of the Great Sea toward Lebanon—the Hit′tites, the Am′o·rites, the Ca′naan·ites, the Per′iz·zites, the Hi′vites, and the Jeb′u·sites—heard of this, 2 they gathered together with one accord to fight Joshua and Israel.

3 But when the inhabitants of Gib′e·on heard what Joshua had done to Jericho and to Ai, 4 they on their part acted with cunning: they went and prepared provisions,[n] and took worn-out sacks for their donkeys, and wineskins, worn-out and torn and mended, 5 with worn-out, patched sandals on their feet, and worn-out clothes; and all their provisions were dry and moldy. 6 They went to Joshua in the camp at Gil′gal, and said to him and to the Israelites, "We have come from a far country; so now make a treaty with us." 7 But the Israelites said to the Hi′vites, "Perhaps you live among us; then how can we make a treaty with you?" 8 They said to Joshua, "We are your servants." And Joshua said to them, "Who are you? And where do you come from?" 9 They said to him, "Your servants have come from a very far country, because of the name of the LORD your God; for we have heard a report of him, of all that he did in Egypt, 10 and of all that he did to the two kings of the Am′o·rites who were beyond the Jordan, King Si′hon of Hesh′bon, and King Og of Ba′shan who lived in Ash′ta·roth. 11 So our elders and all the inhabitants of our country said to us, 'Take provisions in your hand for the journey; go to meet them, and say to them, "We are your servants; come now, make a treaty with us." ' 12 Here is our bread; it was still warm when we took it from our houses as our food for the

Catholic Connections

THE IMPORTANCE OF ALTARS

As soon as the Israelites were able, they built an altar in the Promised Land and renewed their Covenant with God. The altar was a visible sign of the constant need for rededication and renewal.

The altar is an important symbol for Catholics. Catholics gather around the altar to remember and celebrate Jesus' sacrificial death, his Resurrection, and our new Covenant with God. And we gather around the altar to share a meal. We remember the story of our faith, and we are joined together as a community of faith.

The next time you are in church, look at the altar and think about all the other altars in Catholic churches around the world. Think about all the other people who are celebrating the Mass even as you sit there. Think about all the people, beginning with Jesus and the Apostles, who have celebrated their Christian faith around an altar. You are united with them just as surely as the Israelite people were united with one another at Mount Ebal.

▶ Josh 8.30–35

journey, on the day we set out to come to you, but now, see, it is dry and moldy; 13 these wineskins were new when we filled them, and see, they are burst; and these garments and sandals of ours are worn out from the very long journey." 14 So the leaders[o] partook of their provisions, and did not ask direction from the LORD. 15 And Joshua made peace with them, guaranteeing their lives by a treaty; and the leaders of the congregation swore an oath to them.

---

[m] Heb *he*   [n] Cn: Meaning of Heb uncertain   [o] Gk: Heb *men*

16 But when three days had passed after they had made a treaty with them, they heard that they were their neighbors and were living among them. 17 So the Israelites set out and reached their cities on the third day. Now their cities were Gib′e•on, Che•phi′rah, Be•er′oth, and Kir′i•ath-je′a•rim. 18 But the Israelites did not attack them, because the leaders of the congregation had sworn to them by the LORD, the God of Israel. Then all the congregation murmured against the leaders. 19 But all the leaders said to all the congregation, "We have sworn to them by the LORD, the God of Israel, and now we must not touch them. 20 This is what we will do to them: We will let them live, so that wrath may not come upon us, because of the oath that we swore to them." 21 The leaders said to them, "Let them live." So they became hewers of wood and drawers of water for all the congregation, as the leaders had decided concerning them.

22 Joshua summoned them, and said to them, "Why did you deceive us, saying, 'We are very far from you,' while in fact you are living among us? 23 Now therefore you are cursed, and some of you shall always be slaves, hewers of wood and drawers of water for the house of my God." 24 They answered Joshua, "Because it was told to your servants for a certainty that the LORD your God had commanded his servant Moses to give you all the land, and to destroy all the inhabitants of the land before you; so we were in great fear for our lives because of you, and did this thing. 25 And now we are in your hand: do as it seems good and right in your sight to do to us." 26 This is what he did for them: he saved them from the Israelites; and they did not kill them. 27 But on that day Joshua made them hewers of wood and drawers of water for the congregation and for the altar of the LORD, to continue to this day, in the place that he should choose.

The Sun Stands Still

When King A•do′ni-ze′dek of Jerusalem heard how Joshua had taken Aī, and had utterly destroyed it, doing to Aī and its king as he had done to Jericho and its king, and how the inhabitants of Gib′e•on had made peace with Israel and were among them, 2 he*p* became greatly frightened, because Gib′e•on was a large city, like one of the royal cities, and was larger than Aī, and all its men were warriors. 3 So King A•do′ni-ze′dek of Jerusalem sent a message to King Ho′ham of He′bron, to King Pi′ram of Jar′muth, to King Ja•phi′a of La′chish, and to King De′bir of Eg′lon, saying, 4 "Come up and help me, and let us attack Gib′e•on; for it has made peace with Joshua and with the Israelites." 5 Then the five kings of the Am′o•rites—the king of Jerusa-lem, the king of He′bron, the king of Jar′muth, the king of La′chish, and the king of Eg′lon—gathered their forces, and went up with all their armies and camped against Gib′e•on, and made war against it.

6 And the Gib′e•on•ites sent to Joshua at the camp in Gil′gal, saying, "Do not abandon your servants; come up to us quickly, and save us, and help us; for all the kings of the Am′o•rites who live in the hill country are gathered against us." 7 So Joshua went up from Gil′gal, he and all the fighting force with him, all the mighty warriors. 8 The LORD said to Joshua, "Do not fear them, for I have handed them over to you; not one of them shall stand before you." 9 So Joshua came upon them suddenly, having marched up all night from Gil′gal. 10 And the LORD threw them into a panic before Israel, who inflicted a great slaughter on them at Gib′e•on, chased them by the way of the ascent of Beth-ho′ron, and struck them down as far as A•ze′kah and Mak•ke′dah. 11 As they fled before Israel, while they were going down the slope of Beth-ho′ron, the LORD threw down huge stones from heaven on them as far as A•ze′kah, and they died; there were more who died because of the hailstones than the Israelites killed with the sword.

12 On the day when the LORD gave the Am′o•rites over to the Israelites, Joshua spoke to the LORD; and he said in the sight of Israel,

"Sun, stand still at Gib′e•on,
and Moon, in the valley of Aī′ja•lon."
13 And the sun stood still, and the moon
      stopped,
   until the nation took vengeance on their
      enemies.

Is this not written in the Book of Jash′ar? The sun stopped in midheaven, and did not hurry to set for about a whole day. 14 There has been no day like it before or since, when the LORD heeded a human voice; for the LORD fought for Israel.

15 Then Joshua returned, and all Israel with him, to the camp at Gil′gal.

Five Kings Defeated

16 Meanwhile, these five kings fled and hid themselves in the cave at Mak•ke′dah. 17 And it was told Joshua, "The five kings have been found, hidden in the cave at Mak•ke′dah." 18 Joshua said, "Roll large stones against the mouth of the cave, and set men by it to guard them; 19 but do not stay there yourselves; pursue your enemies, and attack them from the rear. Do not let them enter their towns, for the LORD your God has given them into your hand." 20 When Joshua and the Israelites had finished inflicting a very great slaughter on them,

---

p Heb *they*

until they were wiped out, and when the survivors had entered into the fortified towns, 21 all the people returned safe to Joshua in the camp at Mak•kē′-dah; no one dared to speak*q* against any of the Israelites.

22 Then Joshua said, "Open the mouth of the cave, and bring those five kings out to me from the cave." 23 They did so, and brought the five kings out to him from the cave, the king of Jerusalem, the king of Hē′bron, the king of Jar′muth, the king of Lā′chish, and the king of Eg′lon. 24 When they brought the kings out to Joshua, Joshua summoned all the Israelites, and said to the chiefs of the warriors who had gone with him, "Come near, put your feet on the necks of these kings." Then they came near and put their feet on their necks. 25 And Joshua said to them, "Do not be afraid or dismayed; be strong and courageous; for thus the LORD will do to all the enemies against whom you fight." 26 Afterward Joshua struck them down and put them to death, and he hung them on five trees. And they hung on the trees until evening. 27 At sunset Joshua commanded, and they took them down from the trees and threw them into the cave where they had hidden themselves; they set large stones against the mouth of the cave, which remain to this very day.

28 Joshua took Mak•kē′dah on that day, and struck it and its king with the edge of the sword; he utterly destroyed every person in it; he left no one remaining. And he did to the king of Mak•kē′-dah as he had done to the king of Jericho.

29 Then Joshua passed on from Mak•kē′dah, and all Israel with him, to Lib′nah, and fought against Lib′nah. 30 The LORD gave it also and its king into the hand of Israel; and he struck it with the edge of the sword, and every person in it; he left no one remaining in it; and he did to its king as he had done to the king of Jericho.

31 Next Joshua passed on from Lib′nah, and all Israel with him, to Lā′chish, and laid siege to it, and assaulted it. 32 The LORD gave Lā′chish into the hand of Israel, and he took it on the second day, and struck it with the edge of the sword, and every person in it, as he had done to Lib′nah.

33 Then King Hō′ram of Gē′zer came up to help Lā′chish; and Joshua struck him and his people, leaving him no survivors.

34 From Lā′chish Joshua passed on with all Israel to Eg′lon; and they laid siege to it, and assaulted it; 35 and they took it that day, and struck it with the edge of the sword; and every person in it he utterly destroyed that day, as he had done to Lā′chish.

36 Then Joshua went up with all Israel from Eg′lon to Hē′bron; they assaulted it, 37 and took it,

and struck it with the edge of the sword, and its king and its towns, and every person in it; he left no one remaining, just as he had done to Eg′lon, and utterly destroyed it with every person in it.

38 Then Joshua, with all Israel, turned back to Dē′bir and assaulted it, 39 and he took it with its king and all its towns; they struck them with the edge of the sword, and utterly destroyed every person in it; he left no one remaining; just as he had done to Hē′bron, and, as he had done to Lib′nah and its king, so he did to Dē′bir and its king.

40 So Joshua defeated the whole land, the hill country and the Neg′eb and the lowland and the slopes, and all their kings; he left no one remaining, but utterly destroyed all that breathed, as the LORD God of Israel commanded. 41 And Joshua defeated them from Kā′desh-bar′nē•a to Gā′za, and all the country of Gō′shen, as far as Gib′e•on. 42 Joshua took all these kings and their land at one time, because the LORD God of Israel fought for Israel. 43 Then Joshua returned, and all Israel with him, to the camp at Gil′gal.

The United Kings of Northern Canaan Defeated

11 When King Jā′bin of Hā′zor heard of this, he sent to King Jō′bab of Mā′don, to the king of Shim′-ron, to the king of Ach′shaph, 2 and to the kings who were in the northern hill country, and in the Ar′a•bah south of Chin′ne•roth, and in the lowland, and in Nā′photh-dor on the west, 3 to the Cā′-naan•ites in the east and the west, the Am′o•rītes, the Hit′tītes, the Per′iz•zītes, and the Jeb′u•sītes in the hill country, and the Hī′vītes under Hermon in the land of Miz′pah. 4 They came out, with all their troops, a great army, in number like the sand on the seashore, with very many horses and chariots. 5 All these kings joined their forces, and came and camped together at the waters of Mē′rom, to fight with Israel.

6 And the LORD said to Joshua, "Do not be afraid of them, for tomorrow at this time I will hand over all of them, slain, to Israel; you shall hamstring their horses, and burn their chariots with fire." 7 So Joshua came suddenly upon them with all his fighting force, by the waters of Mē′-rom, and fell upon them. 8 And the LORD handed them over to Israel, who attacked them and chased them as far as Great Sī′don and Mis′rē•photh-mā′im, and eastward as far as the valley of Miz′-peh. They struck them down, until they had left no

---

q Heb *moved his tongue*

one remaining. ⁹ And Joshua did to them as the
LORD commanded him; he hamstrung their horses,
and burned their chariots with fire.

10 Joshua turned back at that time, and took
Hā′zor, and struck its king down with the sword.
Before that time Hā′zor was the head of all those
kingdoms. ¹¹ And they put to the sword all who
were in it, utterly destroying them; there was no
one left who breathed, and he burned Hā′zor with
fire. ¹² And all the towns of those kings, and all
their kings, Joshua took, and struck them with the
edge of the sword, utterly destroying them, as Moses the servant of the LORD had commanded. ¹³ But
Israel burned none of the towns that stood on
mounds except Hā′zor, which Joshua did burn.
¹⁴ All the spoil of these towns, and the livestock,
the Israelites took for their booty; but all the people they struck down with the edge of the sword,
until they had destroyed them, and they did not
leave any who breathed. ¹⁵ As the LORD had commanded his servant Moses, so Moses commanded Joshua, and so Joshua did; he left nothing
undone of all that the LORD had commanded
Moses.

Summary of Joshua's Conquests

16 So Joshua took all that land: the hill country and all the Neg′eb and all the land of Gō′shen
and the lowland and the Ar′a•bah and the hill
country of Israel and its lowland, ¹⁷ from Mount
Hā′lak, which rises toward Sē′ir, as far as Bā′al-gad
in the valley of Lebanon below Mount Hermon.
He took all their kings, struck them down, and put
them to death. ¹⁸ Joshua made war a long time
with all those kings. ¹⁹ There was not a town that
made peace with the Israelites, except the Hī′vites,
the inhabitants of Gib′e•on; all were taken in battle. ²⁰ For it was the LORD's doing to harden their
hearts so that they would come against Israel in
battle, in order that they might be utterly destroyed, and might receive no mercy, but be
exterminated, just as the LORD had commanded
Moses.

21 At that time Joshua came and wiped out the
An′a•kim from the hill country, from Hē′bron,
from Dē′bir, from Ā′nab, and from all the hill
country of Judah, and from all the hill country of
Israel; Joshua utterly destroyed them with their
towns. ²² None of the An′a•kim was left in the land
of the Israelites; some remained only in Gā′za, in
Gath, and in Ash′dod. ²³ So Joshua took the whole
land, according to all that the LORD had spoken to
Moses; and Joshua gave it for an inheritance to
Israel according to their tribal allotments. And the
land had rest from war.

The Kings Conquered by Moses
(Cp Num 21.21–35)

Now these are the kings of the land, whom the
Israelites defeated, whose land they occupied beyond the Jordan toward the east, from the Wadi
Ar′non to Mount Hermon, with all the Ar′a•bah
eastward: ² King Sī′hon of the Am′o•rītes who lived
at Hesh′bon, and ruled from A•rō′er, which is on
the edge of the Wadi Ar′non, and from the middle
of the valley as far as the river Jab′bok, the boundary of the Am′mon•ites, that is, half of Gil′e•ad,
³ and the Ar′a•bah to the Sea of Chin′ne•roth eastward, and in the direction of Beth-jesh′i•moth, to
the sea of the Ar′a•bah, the Dead Sea,ʳ southward
to the foot of the slopes of Pis′gah; ⁴ and King Ogˢ
of Bā′shan, one of the last of the Reph′a•im, who
lived at Ash′ta•roth and at Ed′rē•ī ⁵ and ruled over
Mount Hermon and Sal′e•cah and all Bā′shan to
the boundary of the Gesh′ū•rītes and the Mā′a•ca-
thītes, and over half of Gil′e•ad to the boundary of
King Sī′hon of Hesh′bon. ⁶ Moses, the servant of
the LORD, and the Israelites defeated them; and
Moses the servant of the LORD gave their land for a
possession to the Reū′ben•ītes and the Gad′ītes and
the half-tribe of Ma•nas′seh.

The Kings Conquered by Joshua

7 The following are the kings of the land
whom Joshua and the Israelites defeated on the
west side of the Jordan, from Bā′al-gad in the valley of Lebanon to Mount Hā′lak, that rises toward
Sē′ir (and Joshua gave their land to the tribes of
Israel as a possession according to their allotments, ⁸ in the hill country, in the lowland, in the
Ar′a•bah, in the slopes, in the wilderness, and in
the Neg′eb, the land of the Hit′tites, Am′o•rītes,
Cā′naan•ītes, Per′iz•zītes, Hī′vites, and Jeb′ū•sītes):

⁹ the king of Jericho	one
the king of Aī, which is next to Beth′el	one
¹⁰ the king of Jerusalem	one
the king of Hē′bron	one
¹¹ the king of Jar′muth	one
the king of Lā′chish	one
¹² the king of Eg′lon	one
the king of Gē′zer	one
¹³ the king of Dē′bir	one
the king of Gē′der	one
¹⁴ the king of Hor′mah	one
the king of Ar′ad	one
¹⁵ the king of Lib′nah	one
the king of A•dul′lam	one
¹⁶ the king of Mak•kē′dah	one
the king of Beth′el	one
¹⁷ the king of Tap′pū•ah	one

ʳ Heb *Salt Sea*   ˢ Gk: Heb *the boundary of King Og*

?did you KNOW?

The Conquest of Canaan

A strong parallel connects the beginning of the story of Joshua—the crossing of the Jordan River, God's direction and protection of the Israelites (symbolized by the ark), and the renewal of the Covenant at Mount Ebal—and the events of the Exodus from Egypt. The parallel reinforces how the conquest of Canaan was part of God's continued liberation of the Chosen People and a key moment in the history of Israel.

As the Israelites moved in on the Promised Land, the Canaanites were one of several groups of people that the Israelites had to deal with. Joshua 12.8 also mentions Hittites, Amorites, Perizzites, Hivites, and Jebusites. But the Canaanites seemed to be the dominant inhabitants. They were primarily an agricultural society and believed that their gods, called baals, controlled the rains, the seasons, and the fertility of the soil. For the Israelites, God was revealed as the only God over all creation and history.

The conquest of the Canaanites through violence might make you wonder what the Israelites believed about God. Basically, they believed the Canaanite baals were an offense against God. Because the Canaanites would not change, the Israelites felt justified in killing them and taking their land. (See "Holy War," near Num 2.1.) Later, Christians would not be able to justify such actions because of Jesus' teaching that everyone is loved by God and that we must love even our enemies. But at the time Joshua was written, God and God's plan for humanity had not yet been fully revealed.

▶ Joshua, chapter 12

	the king of He′pher	one
18	the king of A′phek	one
	the king of La·shar′on	one
19	the king of Ma′don	one
	the king of Ha′zor	one
20	the king of Shim′ron-me′ron	one
	the king of Ach′shaph	one

21	the king of Ta′a·nach	one
	the king of Me·gid′do	one
22	the king of Ke′desh	one
	the king of Jok′ne·am in Car′mel	one
23	the king of Dor in Na′phath-dor	one
	the king of Goi′im in Galilee,ᵗ	one
24	the king of Tir′zah	one

thirty-one kings in all.

The Parts of Canaan Still Unconquered

Now Joshua was old and advanced in years; and the LORD said to him, "You are old and advanced in years, and very much of the land still remains to be possessed. ²This is the land that still remains: all the regions of the Phi·lis′tines, and all those of the Gesh′u·rites ³(from the Shi′hor, which is east of Egypt, northward to the boundary of Ek′ron, it is reckoned as Ca′naan·ite; there are five rulers of the Phi·lis′tines, those of Ga′za, Ash′dod, Ash′ke-lon, Gath, and Ek′ron), and those of the Av′vim ⁴in the south; all the land of the Ca′naan·ites, and Me·ar′ah that belongs to the Si·do′ni·ans, to A′phek, to the boundary of the Am′o·rites, ⁵and the land of the Ge′bal·ites, and all Lebanon, toward the east, from Ba′al-gad below Mount Hermon to Le′bo-ha′math, ⁶all the inhabitants of the hill country from Lebanon to Mis′re·photh-ma′im, even all the Si·do′ni·ans. I will myself drive them out from before the Israelites; only allot the land to Israel for an inheritance, as I have commanded you. ⁷Now therefore divide this land for an inheritance to the nine tribes and the half-tribe of Ma·nas′seh."

The Territory East of the Jordan

8 With the other half-tribe of Ma·nas′sehᵘ the Reu′ben·ites and the Gad′ites received their inheritance, which Moses gave them, beyond the Jordan eastward, as Moses the servant of the LORD gave them: ⁹from A·ro′er, which is on the edge of the Wadi Ar′non, and the town that is in the middle of the valley, and all the tableland fromᵛ Med′e·ba as far as Di′bon; ¹⁰and all the cities of King Si′hon of the Am′o·rites, who reigned in Hesh′bon, as far as the boundary of the Am′mon·ites; ¹¹and Gil′e·ad, and the region of the Gesh′u·rites and Ma′a·ca-thites, and all Mount Hermon, and all Ba′shan to Sal′e·cah; ¹²all the kingdom of Og in Ba′shan, who reigned in Ash′ta·roth and in Ed′re·i (he alone was left of the survivors of the Reph′a·im); these Moses had defeated and driven out. ¹³Yet the Israelites did not drive out the Gesh′u·rites or the Ma′a·ca-thites; but Ge′shur and Ma′a·cath live within Israel to this day.

ᵗ Gk: Heb Gilgal   ᵘ Cn: Heb With it   ᵛ Compare Gk: Heb lacks from

14 To the tribe of Levi alone Moses gave no inheritance; the offerings by fire to the LORD God of Israel are their inheritance, as he said to them.

The Territory of Reuben

15 Moses gave an inheritance to the tribe of the Reũ′ben·ites according to their clans. ¹⁶ Their territory was from A·rō′er, which is on the edge of the Wadi Ar′non, and the town that is in the middle of the valley, and all the tableland by Med′e·ba; ¹⁷ with Hesh′bon, and all its towns in the tableland; Dī′bon, and Bā′moth-bā′al, and Beth-bā′al-mē′on, ¹⁸ and Jā′haz, and Ked′e·moth, and Meph′a·ath, ¹⁹ and Kir·i·a·thā′im, and Sib′mah, and Zē′reth-shā′har on the hill of the valley, ²⁰ and Beth-pē′or, and the slopes of Pis′gah, and Beth-jesh′i·moth, ²¹ that is, all the towns of the tableland, and all the kingdom of King Sī′hon of the Am′o·rītes, who reigned in Hesh′bon, whom Moses defeated with the leaders of Mid′i·an, E′vi and Rē′kem and Zur and Hur and Rē′ba, as princes of Sī′hon, who lived in the land. ²² Along with the rest of those they put to death, the Israelites also put to the sword Bā′laam son of Bē′or, who practiced divination. ²³ And the border of the Reũ′ben-ites was the Jordan and its banks. This was the inheritance of the Reũ′ben·ites according to their families, with their towns and villages.

The Territory of Gad

24 Moses gave an inheritance also to the tribe of the Gad′ites, according to their families. ²⁵ Their territory was Jā′zer, and all the towns of Gil′e·ad, and half the land of the Am′mon·ites, to A·rō′er, which is east of Rab′bah, ²⁶ and from Hesh′bon to Rā′math-miz′peh and Bet′o·nim, and from Mā·ha-nā′im to the territory of De′bir,ʷ ²⁷ and in the valley Beth-hā′ram, Beth-nim′rah, Suc′coth, and Zā′phon, the rest of the kingdom of King Sī′hon of Hesh′bon, the Jordan and its banks, as far as the lower end of the Sea of Chin′ne·reth, eastward beyond the Jordan. ²⁸ This is the inheritance of the Gad′ites according to their clans, with their towns and villages.

The Territory of the Half-Tribe of Manasseh (East)

29 Moses gave an inheritance to the half-tribe of Ma·nas′seh; it was allotted to the half-tribe of the Ma·nas′sītes according to their families. ³⁰ Their territory extended from Mā·ha·nā′im, through all Bā′shan, the whole kingdom of King Og of Bā′-shan, and all the settlements of Jā′ir, which are in Bā′shan, sixty towns, ³¹ and half of Gil′e·ad, and Ash′ta·roth, and Ed′re·ī, the towns of the kingdom of Og in Bā′shan; these were allotted to the people of Mā′chir son of Ma·nas′seh according to their clans—for half the Mā′chir·ites.

32 These are the inheritances that Moses distributed in the plains of Mō′ab, beyond the Jordan east of Jericho. ³³ But to the tribe of Levi Moses gave no inheritance; the LORD God of Israel is their inheritance, as he said to them.

The Distribution of Territory West of the Jordan

These are the inheritances that the Israelites received in the land of Cā′naan, which the priest El·e·ā′zar, and Joshua son of Nun, and the heads of the families of the tribes of the Israelites distributed to them. ² Their inheritance was by lot, as the LORD had commanded Moses for the nine and one-half tribes. ³ For Moses had given an inheritance to the two and one-half tribes beyond the Jordan; but to the Lē′vites he gave no inheritance among them. ⁴ For the people of Joseph were two tribes, Ma·nas′seh and E′phra·im; and no portion was given to the Lē′vites in the land, but only towns to live in, with their pasture lands for their flocks and herds. ⁵ The Israelites did as the LORD commanded Moses; they allotted the land.

Hebron Allotted to Caleb

6 Then the people of Judah came to Joshua at Gil′gal; and Caleb son of Je·phũn′neh the Ken′iz-zīte said to him, "You know what the LORD said to Moses the man of God in Kā′desh-bar′ne·a concerning you and me. ⁷ I was forty years old when Moses the servant of the LORD sent me from Kā′-desh-bar′ne·a to spy out the land; and I brought him an honest report. ⁸ But my companions who went up with me made the heart of the people melt; yet I wholeheartedly followed the LORD my God. ⁹ And Moses swore on that day, saying, 'Surely the land on which your foot has trodden shall be an inheritance for you and your children forever, because you have wholeheartedly followed the LORD my God.' ¹⁰ And now, as you see, the LORD has kept me alive, as he said, these forty-five years since the time that the LORD spoke this word to Moses, while Israel was journeying through the wilderness; and here I am today, eighty-five years old. ¹¹ I am still as strong today as I was on the day that Moses sent me; my strength now is as my strength was then, for war, and for going and coming. ¹² So now give me this hill country of which the LORD spoke on that day; for you heard on that day how the An′a·kim were there, with great fortified cities; it may be that the LORD will be with me, and I shall drive them out, as the LORD said."

ʷ Gk Syr Vg: Heb *Lidebir*

13 Then Joshua blessed him, and gave Hē′-bron to Caleb son of Je·phŭn′neh for an inheritance. 14 So Hē′bron became the inheritance of Caleb son of Je·phŭn′neh the Ken′iz·zīte to this day, because he wholeheartedly followed the LORD, the God of Israel. 15 Now the name of Hē′bron formerly was Kir′i·ath-ar′ba;ˣ this Ar′ba wasʸ the greatest man among the An′a·kim. And the land had rest from war.

The Territory of Judah

The lot for the tribe of the people of Judah according to their families reached southward to the boundary of Ē′dom, to the wilderness of Zin at the farthest south. 2 And their south boundary ran from the end of the Dead Sea,ᶻ from the bay that faces southward; 3 it goes out southward of the ascent of Ak·rab′bim, passes along to Zin, and goes up south of Kā′desh-bar′nē·a, along by Hez′ron, up to Ad′dar, makes a turn to Kar′ka, 4 passes along to Az′mon, goes out by the Wadi of Egypt, and comes to its end at the sea. This shall be your south boundary. 5 And the east boundary is the Dead Sea,ᶻ to the mouth of the Jordan. And the boundary on the north side runs from the bay of the sea at the mouth of the Jordan; 6 and the boundary goes up to Beth-hog′lah, and passes along north of Beth-ar′a·bah; and the boundary goes up to the Stone of Bō′han, Reuben′s son; 7 and the boundary goes up to Dē′bir from the Valley of Ā′chor, and so northward, turning toward Gil′gal, which is opposite the ascent of A·dum′-mim, which is on the south side of the valley; and the boundary passes along to the waters of En-shē′mesh, and ends at En-ro′gel; 8 then the boundary goes up by the valley of the son of Hin′nom at the southern slope of the Jeb′u·sites (that is, Jerusalem); and the boundary goes up to the top of the mountain that lies over against the valley of Hin′-nom, on the west, at the northern end of the valley of Reph′a·im; 9 then the boundary extends from the top of the mountain to the spring of the Waters of Neph·tō′ah, and from there to the towns of Mount Ē′phron; then the boundary bends around to Bā′a·lah (that is, Kir′i·ath-jē′a·rim); 10 and the boundary circles west of Bā′a·lah to Mount Sē′ir, passes along to the northern slope of Mount Jē′a·rim (that is, Ches′a·lon), and goes down to Beth-shē′mesh, and passes along by Tim′nah; 11 the boundary goes out to the slope of the hill north of Ek′ron, then the boundary bends around to Shik′ke·ron, and passes along to Mount Bā′a·lah, and goes out to Jab′nē·el; then the boundary comes to an end at the sea. 12 And the west boundary was the Mediterranean with its coast. This is the boundary surrounding the people of Judah according to their families.

Caleb Occupies His Portion
(Judg 1.11–15)

13 According to the commandment of the LORD to Joshua, he gave to Caleb son of Je·phŭn′-neh a portion among the people of Judah, Kir′i-ath-ar′ba,ˣ that is, Hē′bron (Ar′ba was the father of Ā′nak). 14 And Caleb drove out from there the three sons of Ā′nak: Shē′shai, A·hī′man, and Tal′mai, the descendants of Ā′nak. 15 From there he went up against the inhabitants of Dē′bir; now the name of Dē′bir formerly was Kir′i·ath-sē′pher. 16 And Caleb said, "Whoever attacks Kir′i·ath-sē′-pher and takes it, to him I will give my daughter Ach′sah as wife." 17 Oth′ni·el son of Kē′naz, the brother of Caleb, took it; and he gave him his daughter Ach′sah as wife. 18 When she came to him, she urged him to ask her father for a field. As she dismounted from her donkey, Caleb said to her, "What do you wish?" 19 She said to him, "Give me a present; since you have set me in the land of the Neg′eb, give me springs of water as well." So Caleb gave her the upper springs and the lower springs.

The Towns of Judah

20 This is the inheritance of the tribe of the people of Judah according to their families. 21 The towns belonging to the tribe of the people of Judah in the extreme south, toward the boundary of Ē′dom, were Kab′zē·el, Ē′der, Jā′gur, 22 Kī′nah, Di·mō′nah, A·dā′dah, 23 Kē′desh, Hā′zor, Ith′nan, 24 Ziph, Tē′lem, Be·ā′loth, 25 Hā′zor-ha·dat′tah, Ker′-i·oth-hezron (that is, Hā′zor), 26 Ā′mam, Shē′ma, Mō′la·dah, 27 Hā′zar-gad′dah, Hesh′mon, Beth-pel′et, 28 Hā′zar-shū′al, Bē′er-shē′ba, Biz·i·o·thī′ah, 29 Bā′a·lah, Ī′im, Ē′zem, 30 El·tō′lad, Chē′sil, Hor′-mah, 31 Zik′lag, Mad·man′nah, San·san′nah, 32 Le-bā′oth, Shil′him, Ā′in, and Rim′mon: in all, twenty-nine towns, with their villages.

33 And in the lowland, Esh′tā·ol, Zō′rah, Ash′-nah, 34 Za·nō′ah, En-gan′nim, Tap′pū·ah, Ē′nam, 35 Jar′muth, A·dul′lam, Sō′cōh, A·zē′kah, 36 Shā·a-rā′im, Ad·i·thā′im, Ge·dē′rah, Ged·e·rō·thā′im: fourteen towns with their villages.

37 Zē′nan, Ha·dash′ah, Mig′dal-gad, 38 Dil′an, Miz′peh, Jok′thē-el, 39 Lā′chish, Boz′kath, Eg′lon, 40 Cab′bon, Lah′mam, Chit′lish, 41 Ge·dē′roth, Beth-dā′gon, Nā′a·mah, and Mak·kē′dah: sixteen towns with their villages.

42 Lib′nah, Ē′ther, Ā′shan, 43 Iph′tah, Ash′-nah, Nē′zib, 44 Kē·ī′lah, Ach′zib, and Ma·rē′shah: nine towns with their villages.

ˣ That is *the city of Arba*   ʸ Heb lacks *this Arba was*
ᶻ Heb *Salt Sea*

45 Ek'ron, with its dependencies and its villages; 46 from Ek'ron to the sea, all that were near Ash'dod, with their villages.

47 Ash'dod, its towns and its villages; Ga'za, its towns and its villages; to the Wadi of Egypt, and the Great Sea with its coast.

48 And in the hill country, Sha'mir, Jat'tir, So'coh, 49 Dan'nah, Kir'i•ath-san'nah (that is, De'bir), 50 A'nab, Esh'te•moh, A'nim, 51 Go'shen, Ho'lon, and Gi'loh: eleven towns with their villages.

52 A'rab, Du'mah, E'shan, 53 Ja'nim, Beth-tap'pu•ah, A•phe'kah, 54 Hum'tah, Kir'i•ath-ar'ba (that is, He'bron), and Zi'or: nine towns with their villages.

55 Ma'on, Car'mel, Ziph, Jut'tah, 56 Jez're•el, Jok'de•am, Za•no'ah, 57 Ka'in, Gib'e•ah, and Tim'nah: ten towns with their villages.

58 Hal'hul, Beth-zur, Ge'dor, 59 Ma'a•rath, Beth-a'noth, and El'te•kon: six towns with their villages.

60 Kir'i•ath-ba'al (that is, Kir'i•ath-je'a•rim) and Rab'bah: two towns with their villages.

61 In the wilderness, Beth-ar'a•bah, Mid'din, Se•ca'cah, 62 Nib'shan, the City of Salt, and En-ge'di: six towns with their villages.

63 But the people of Judah could not drive out the Jeb'u•sites, the inhabitants of Jerusalem; so the Jeb'u•sites live with the people of Judah in Jerusalem to this day.

The Territory of Ephraim

The allotment of the Jo'seph•ites went from the Jordan by Jericho, east of the waters of Jericho, into the wilderness, going up from Jericho into the hill country to Beth'el; 2 then going from Beth'el to Luz, it passes along to At'a•roth, the territory of the Ar'chites; 3 then it goes down westward to the territory of the Japh'let•ites, as far as the territory of Lower Beth-ho'ron, then to Ge'zer, and it ends at the sea.

4 The Jo'seph•ites—Ma•nas'seh and E'phra•im—received their inheritance.

5 The territory of the E'phra•im•ites by their families was as follows: the boundary of their inheritance on the east was At'a•roth-ad'dar as far as Upper Beth-ho'ron, 6 and the boundary goes from there to the sea; on the north is Mich•me'thath; then on the east the boundary makes a turn toward Taanath-shiloh, and passes along beyond it on the east to Ja•no'ah, 7 then it goes down from Ja•no'ah to At'a•roth and to Na'a•rah, and touches Jericho, ending at the Jordan. 8 From Tap'pu•ah the boundary goes westward to the Wadi Ka'nah, and ends at the sea. Such is the inheritance of the tribe of the E'phra•im•ites by their families, 9 together with the towns that were set apart for the E'phra-

im•ites within the inheritance of the Ma•nas'sites, all those towns with their villages. 10 They did not, however, drive out the Ca'naan•ites who lived in Ge'zer: so the Ca'naan•ites have lived within E'phra•im to this day but have been made to do forced labor.

The Other Half-Tribe of Manasseh (West)

Then allotment was made to the tribe of Ma•nas'seh, for he was the firstborn of Joseph. To Ma'chir the firstborn of Ma•nas'seh, the father of Gil'e•ad, were allotted Gil'e•ad and Ba'shan, because he was a warrior. 2 And allotments were made to the rest of the tribe of Ma•nas'seh, by their families, A•bi•e'zer, He'lek, As'ri•el, She'chem, He'pher, and She•mi'da; these were the male descendants of Ma•nas'seh son of Joseph, by their families.

3 Now Ze•loph'e•had son of He'pher son of Gil'e•ad son of Ma'chir son of Ma•nas'seh had no sons, but only daughters; and these are the names of his daughters: Mah'lah, Noah, Hog'lah, Mil'cah, and Tir'zah. 4 They came before the priest El•e•a'zar and Joshua son of Nun and the leaders, and said, "The LORD commanded Moses to give us an inheritance along with our male kin." So according to the commandment of the LORD he gave them an inheritance among the kinsmen of their father. 5 Thus there fell to Ma•nas'seh ten portions, besides the land of Gil'e•ad and Ba'shan, which is on the other side of the Jordan, 6 because the daughters of Ma•nas'seh received an inheritance along with his sons. The land of Gil'e•ad was allotted to the rest of the Ma•nas'sites.

7 The territory of Ma•nas'seh reached from Ash'er to Mich•me'thath, which is east of She'chem; then the boundary goes along southward to the inhabitants of En-tap'pu•ah. 8 The land of Tap'pu•ah belonged to Ma•nas'seh, but the town of Tap'pu•ah on the boundary of Ma•nas'seh belonged to the E'phra•im•ites. 9 Then the boundary went down to the Wadi Ka'nah. The towns here, to the south of the wadi, among the towns of Ma•nas'seh, belong to E'phra•im. Then the boundary of Ma•nas'seh goes along the north side of the wadi and ends at the sea. 10 The land to the south is E'phra•im's and that to the north is Ma•nas'seh's, with the sea forming its boundary; on the north Ash'er is reached, and on the east Is'sa•char. 11 Within Is'sa•char and Ash'er, Ma•nas'seh had Beth-she'an and its villages, Ib'le•am and its villages, the inhabitants of Dor and its villages, the inhabitants of En-dor and its villages, the inhabitants of Ta'a•nach and its villages, and the inhabitants of Me•gid'do and its villages (the third is Na'phath).ᵃ 12 Yet the

---

ᵃ Meaning of Heb uncertain

JOSH

Ma•nas'sītes could not take possession of those towns; but the Cā'naan•ītes continued to live in that land. 13 But when the Israelites grew strong, they put the Cā'naan•ītes to forced labor, but did not utterly drive them out.

The Tribe of Joseph Protests

14 The tribe of Joseph spoke to Joshua, saying, "Why have you given me but one lot and one portion as an inheritance, since we are a numerous people, whom all along the LORD has blessed?" 15 And Joshua said to them, "If you are a numerous people, go up to the forest, and clear ground there for yourselves in the land of the Per'iz•zites and the Reph'a•im, since the hill country of E'phra•im is too narrow for you." 16 The tribe of Joseph said, "The hill country is not enough for us; yet all the Cā'naan•ītes who live in the plain have chariots of iron, both those in Beth-shē'an and its villages and those in the Valley of Jez'rē•el." 17 Then Joshua said to the house of Joseph, to E'phra•im and Ma•nas'seh, "You are indeed a numerous people, and have great power; you shall not have one lot only, 18 but the hill country shall be yours, for though it is a forest, you shall clear it and possess it to its farthest borders; for you shall drive out the Cā'naan•ītes, though they have chariots of iron, and though they are strong."

The Territories of the Remaining Tribes

Then the whole congregation of the Israelites assembled at Shī'lōh, and set up the tent of meeting there. The land lay subdued before them.

2 There remained among the Israelites seven tribes whose inheritance had not yet been apportioned. 3 So Joshua said to the Israelites, "How long will you be slack about going in and taking possession of the land that the LORD, the God of your ancestors, has given you? 4 Provide three men from each tribe, and I will send them out that they may begin to go throughout the land, writing a description of it with a view to their inheritances. Then come back to me. 5 They shall divide it into seven portions, Judah continuing in its territory on the south, and the house of Joseph in their territory on the north. 6 You shall describe the land in seven divisions and bring the description here to me; and I will cast lots for you here before the LORD our God. 7 The Lē'vītes have no portion among you, for the priesthood of the LORD is their heritage; and Gad and Reuben and the half-tribe of Ma•nas'seh have received their inheritance beyond the Jordan eastward, which Moses the servant of the LORD gave them."

8 So the men started on their way; and Joshua charged those who went to write the description of the land, saying, "Go throughout the land and write a description of it, and come back to me; and I will cast lots for you here before the LORD in Shī'lōh." 9 So the men went and traversed the land and set down in a book a description of it by towns in seven divisions; then they came back to Joshua in the camp at Shī'lōh, 10 and Joshua cast lots for them in Shī'lōh before the LORD; and there Joshua apportioned the land to the Israelites, to each a portion.

The Territory of Benjamin

11 The lot of the tribe of Benjamin according to its families came up, and the territory allotted to it fell between the tribe of Judah and the tribe of Joseph. 12 On the north side their boundary began at the Jordan; then the boundary goes up to the slope of Jericho on the north, then up through the hill country westward; and it ends at the wilderness of Beth-ā'ven. 13 From there the boundary passes along southward in the direction of Luz, to the slope of Luz (that is, Beth'el), then the boundary goes down to At'a•roth-ad'dar, on the mountain that lies south of Lower Beth-hō'ron. 14 Then the boundary goes in another direction, turning on the western side southward from the mountain that lies to the south, opposite Beth-hō'ron, and it ends at Kir'i•ath-bā'al (that is, Kir'i•ath-jē'a•rim), a town belonging to the tribe of Judah. This forms the western side. 15 The southern side begins at the outskirts of Kir'i•ath-jē'a•rim; and the boundary goes from there to E'phron,[b] to the spring of the Waters of Neph•tō'ah; 16 then the boundary goes down to the border of the mountain that overlooks the valley of the son of Hin'nom, which is at the north end of the valley of Reph'a•im; and it then goes down the valley of Hin'nom, south of the slope of the Jeb'ū•sites, and downward to En-rō'gel; 17 then it bends in a northerly direction going on to En-shē'mesh, and from there goes to Ge•li'loth, which is opposite the ascent of A•dum'-mim; then it goes down to the Stone of Bō'han, Reuben's son; 18 and passing on to the north of the slope of Beth-ar'a•bah[c] it goes down to the Ar'a-bah; 19 then the boundary passes on to the north of the slope of Beth-hog'lah; and the boundary ends at the northern bay of the Dead Sea,[d] at the south end of the Jordan: this is the southern border. 20 The Jordan forms its boundary on the eastern side. This is the inheritance of the tribe of Benjamin, according to its families, boundary by boundary all around.

---

b Cn See 15.9. Heb *westward*   c Gk: Heb *to the slope over against the Arabah*   d Heb *Salt Sea*

21 Now the towns of the tribe of Benjamin according to their families were Jericho, Beth-hog′lah, Ē′mek-kē′ziz, 22 Beth-ar′a•bah, Zem•a•rā′im, Beth′el, 23 Av′vim, Par′ah, Oph′rah, 24 Chē′phar-am′mo•nī, Oph′nī, and Gē′ba—twelve towns with their villages: 25 Gib′ē•on, Rā′mah, Be•er′oth, 26 Miz′peh, Chē•phī′rah, Mō′zah, 27 Rē′kem, Ir′pē•el, Tar′a•lah, 28 Zē′la, Ha•ē′leph, Jē′bus*e* (that is, Jerusalem), Gib′ē•ah*f* and Kir′i•ath-jē′a•rim*g*—fourteen towns with their villages. This is the inheritance of the tribe of Benjamin according to its families.

The Territory of Simeon

The second lot came out for Sim′ē•on, for the tribe of Sim′ē•on, according to its families; its inheritance lay within the inheritance of the tribe of Judah. 2 It had for its inheritance Bē′er-shē′ba, Shē′ba, Mō′la•dah, 3 Hā′zar-shū′al, Bā′lah, Ē′zem, 4 El•tō′lad, Bē′thul, Hor′mah, 5 Zik′lag, Beth-mar′ca•both, Hā′zar-sū′sah, 6 Beth-le•bā′oth, and Sha•rū′hen—thirteen towns with their villages; 7 Ā′in, Rim′mon, Ē′ther, and Ā′shan—four towns with their villages; 8 together with all the villages all around these towns as far as Bā′a•lath-bē′er, Rā′mah of the Neg′eb. This was the inheritance of the tribe of Sim′ē•on according to its families. 9 The inheritance of the tribe of Sim′ē•on formed part of the territory of Judah; because the portion of the tribe of Judah was too large for them, the tribe of Sim′ē•on obtained an inheritance within their inheritance.

The Territory of Zebulun

10 The third lot came up for the tribe of Zeb′u•lun, according to its families. The boundary of its inheritance reached as far as Sā′rid; 11 then its boundary goes up westward, and on to Mar′a•lah, and touches Dab′be•sheth, then the wadi that is east of Jok′nē•am; 12 from Sā′rid it goes in the other direction eastward toward the sunrise to the boundary of Chis′loth-tā′bor; from there it goes to Dab′e•rath, then up to Ja•phī′a; 13 from there it passes along on the east toward the sunrise to Gath-hē′pher, to Eth-kā′zin, and going on to Rim′mon it bends toward Nē′ah; 14 then on the north the boundary makes a turn to Han•na′thon, and it ends at the valley of Iph′tah-el; 15 and Kat′tath, Na•hal′al, Shim′ron, I′da•lah, and Bethlehem—twelve towns with their villages. 16 This is the inheritance of the tribe of Zeb′u•lun, according to its families—these towns with their villages.

The Territory of Issachar

17 The fourth lot came out for Is′sa•char, for the tribe of Is′sa•char, according to its families. 18 Its territory included Jez′rē•el, Che•sul′loth, Shū′nem, 19 Haph•a•rā′im, Shi′on, A•nā′ha•rath, 20 Rab′bith, Kish′i•on, Ē′bez, 21 Rē′meth, En-gan′nim, En-had′dah, Beth-paz′zez; 22 the boundary also touches Tā′bor, Sha•ha•zū′mah, and Beth-shē′mesh, and its boundary ends at the Jordan—sixteen towns with their villages. 23 This is the inheritance of the tribe of Is′sa•char, according to its families—the towns with their villages.

The Territory of Asher

24 The fifth lot came out for the tribe of Ash′er according to its families. 25 Its boundary included Hel′kath, Hā′lī, Bē′ten, Ach′shaph, 26 Al•lam′me-lech, Ā′mad, and Mī′shal; on the west it touches Car′mel and Shī•hor-lib′nath, 27 then it turns eastward, goes to Beth-dā′gon, and touches Zeb′u•lun and the valley of Iph′tah-el northward to Beth-ē′mek and Nē•ī′el; then it continues in the north to Cā′bul, 28 Ē′bron, Rē′hob, Ham′mon, Kā′nah, as far as Great Sī′don; 29 then the boundary turns to Rā′mah, reaching to the fortified city of Tȳre; then the boundary turns to Hō′sah, and it ends at the sea; Ma•hā′lab,*h* Ach′zib, 30 Um′mah, Ā′phek, and Rē′hob—twenty-two towns with their villages. 31 This is the inheritance of the tribe of Ash′er according to its families—these towns with their villages.

The Territory of Naphtali

32 The sixth lot came out for the tribe of Naph′ta•lī, for the tribe of Naph′ta•lī, according to its families. 33 And its boundary ran from Hē′leph, from the oak in Zā•a•nan′nim, and Ad′a•mī-nek′eb, and Jab′nē•el, as far as Lak′kum; and it ended at the Jordan; 34 then the boundary turns westward to Az′noth-tā′bor, and goes from there to Huk′kok, touching Zeb′u•lun at the south, and Ash′er on the west, and Judah on the east at the Jordan. 35 The fortified towns are Zid′dim, Zer, Ham′math, Rak′kath, Chin′ne•reth, 36 Ad′a•mah, Rā′mah, Hā′zor, 37 Kē′desh, Ed′rē•ī, En-hā′zor, 38 I′ron, Mig′dal-el, Hō′rem, Beth-ā′nath, and Beth-shē′mesh—nineteen towns with their villages. 39 This is the inheritance of the tribe of Naph′ta•lī according to its families—the towns with their villages.

---

e Gk Syr Vg: Heb *the Jebusite* *f* Heb *Gibeath* *g* Gk: Heb *Kiriath* *h* Cn Compare Gk: Heb *Mehebel*

JOSH

The Territory of Dan

40 The seventh lot came out for the tribe of Dan, according to its families. 41 The territory of its inheritance included Zō′rah, Esh′ta·ol, Ir-she′mesh, 42 Shā·a·lab′bin, Aī′ja·lon, Ith′lah, 43 Ē′lon, Tim′nah, Ek′ron, 44 El′te·keh, Gib′be·thon, Bā′a·lath, 45 Je′hud, Ben′e-be′rak, Gath-rim′mon, 46 Me·jar′kon, and Rak′kon at the border opposite Jop′pa. 47 When the territory of the Dan′ites was lost to them, the Dan′ites went up and fought against Le′shem, and after capturing it and putting it to the sword, they took possession of it and settled in it, calling Le′shem, Dan, after their ancestor Dan. 48 This is the inheritance of the tribe of Dan, according to their families—these towns with their villages.

Joshua's Inheritance

49 When they had finished distributing the several territories of the land as inheritances, the Israelites gave an inheritance among them to Joshua son of Nun. 50 By command of the LORD they gave him the town that he asked for, Tim′-nath-se′rah in the hill country of Ē′phra·im; he rebuilt the town, and settled in it.

51 These are the inheritances that the priest El-e·a′zar and Joshua son of Nun and the heads of the families of the tribes of the Israelites distributed by lot at Shi′loh before the LORD, at the entrance of the tent of meeting. So they finished dividing the land.

The Cities of Refuge
(Num 35.9–28; Deut 19.1–13)

Then the LORD spoke to Joshua, saying, 2 "Say to the Israelites, 'Appoint the cities of refuge, of which I spoke to you through Moses, 3 so that anyone who kills a person without intent or by mistake may flee there; they shall be for you a refuge from the avenger of blood. 4 The slayer shall flee to one of these cities and shall stand at the entrance of the gate of the city, and explain the case to the elders of that city; then the fugitive shall be taken into the city, and given a place, and shall remain with them. 5 And if the avenger of blood is in pursuit, they shall not give up the slayer, because the neighbor was killed by mistake, there having been no enmity between them before. 6 The slayer shall remain in that city until there is a trial before the congregation, until the death of the one who is high priest at the time: then the slayer may return home, to the town in which the deed was done.' "

7 So they set apart Ke′desh in Galilee in the hill country of Naph′ta·li, and She′chem in the hill country of Ē′phra·im, and Kir′i·ath-ar′ba (that is,

He′bron) in the hill country of Judah. 8 And beyond the Jordan east of Jericho, they appointed Be′zer in the wilderness on the tableland, from the tribe of Reuben, and Rā′moth in Gil′e·ad, from the tribe of Gad, and Gō′lan in Bā′shan, from the tribe of Ma·nas′seh. 9 These were the cities designated for all the Israelites, and for the aliens residing among them, that anyone who killed a person without intent could flee there, so as not to die by the hand of the avenger of blood, until there was a trial before the congregation.

Cities Allotted to the Levites
(1 Chr 6.54–81)

Then the heads of the families of the Le′vites came to the priest El·e·a′zar and to Joshua son of Nun and to the heads of the families of the tribes of the Israelites; 2 they said to them at Shi′loh in the land of Ca′naan, "The LORD commanded through Moses that we be given towns to live in, along with their pasture lands for our livestock." 3 So by command of the LORD the Israelites gave to the Le′vites the following towns and pasture lands out of their inheritance.

4 The lot came out for the families of the Kō′hath·ites. So those Le′vites who were descendants of Aaron the priest received by lot thirteen towns from the tribes of Judah, Sim′e·on, and Benjamin.

5 The rest of the Kō′hath·ites received by lot ten towns from the families of the tribe of Ē′phra·im, from the tribe of Dan, and the half-tribe of Ma·nas′seh.

6 The Ger′shon·ites received by lot thirteen towns from the families of the tribe of Is′sa·char, from the tribe of Ash′er, from the tribe of Naph′ta·li, and from the half-tribe of Ma·nas′seh in Bā′shan.

7 The Me·rar′ites according to their families received twelve towns from the tribe of Reuben, the tribe of Gad, and the tribe of Zeb′u·lun.

8 These towns and their pasture lands the Israelites gave by lot to the Le′vites, as the LORD had commanded through Moses.

9 Out of the tribe of Judah and the tribe of Sim′e·on they gave the following towns mentioned by name, 10 which went to the descendants of Aaron, one of the families of the Kō′hath·ites who belonged to the Le′vites, since the lot fell to them first. 11 They gave them Kir′i·ath-ar′ba (Ar′ba being the father of Ā′nak), that is He′bron, in the hill country of Judah, along with the pasture lands around it. 12 But the fields of the town and its villages had been given to Caleb son of Je·phun′neh as his holding.

13 To the descendants of Aaron the priest they gave He′bron, the city of refuge for the slayer, with

its pasture lands, Lib'nah with its pasture lands, [14] Jat'tir with its pasture lands, Esh•te•mō'a with its pasture lands, [15] Hō'lon with its pasture lands, Dē'bir with its pasture lands, [16] Ā'in with its pasture lands, Jut'tah with its pasture lands, and Beth-shē'mesh with its pasture lands—nine towns out of these two tribes. [17] Out of the tribe of Benjamin: Gib'e•on with its pasture lands, Gē'ba with its pasture lands, [18] An'a•thoth with its pasture lands, and Al'mon with its pasture lands—four towns. [19] The towns of the descendants of Aaron—the priests—were thirteen in all, with their pasture lands.

20 As to the rest of the Kō'hath•ites belonging to the Kō'hath•ite families of the Lē'vites, the towns allotted to them were out of the tribe of Ē'phra•im. [21] To them were given Shē'chem, the city of refuge for the slayer, with its pasture lands in the hill country of Ē'phra•im, Gē'zer with its pasture lands, [22] Kib'zā•im with its pasture lands, and Beth-hō'ron with its pasture lands—four towns. [23] Out of the tribe of Dan: El'te•ke with its pasture lands, Gib'be•thon with its pasture lands, [24] Aī'ja•lon with its pasture lands, Gath-rim'mon with its pasture lands—four towns. [25] Out of the half-tribe of Ma•nas'seh: Tā'a•nach with its pasture lands, and Gath-rim'mon with its pasture lands—two towns. [26] The towns of the families of the rest of the Kō'hath•ites were ten in all, with their pasture lands.

27 To the Ger'shon•ites, one of the families of the Lē'vites, were given out of the half-tribe of Ma-nas'seh, Gō'lan in Bā'shan with its pasture lands, the city of refuge for the slayer, and Be•esh•te'rah with its pasture lands—two towns. [28] Out of the tribe of Is'sa•char: Kish'i•on with its pasture lands, Dab'e•rath with its pasture lands, [29] Jar'muth with its pasture lands, En-gan'nim with its pasture lands—four towns. [30] Out of the tribe of Ash'er: Mī'shal with its pasture lands, Ab'don with its pasture lands, [31] Hel'kath with its pasture lands, and Rē'hob with its pasture lands—four towns. [32] Out of the tribe of Naph'ta•lī: Kē'desh in Galilee with its pasture lands, the city of refuge for the slayer, Ham'moth-dor with its pasture lands, and Kar'tan with its pasture lands—three towns. [33] The towns of the several families of the Ger'shon•ites were in all thirteen, with their pasture lands.

34 To the rest of the Lē'vites—the Me•rar'īte families—were given out of the tribe of Zeb'ū•lun: Jok'ne•am with its pasture lands, Kar'tah with its pasture lands, [35] Dim'nah with its pasture lands, Na•hal'al with its pasture lands—four towns. [36] Out of the tribe of Reuben: Bē'zer with its pasture lands, Jah'zah with its pasture lands, [37] Ked'e•moth with its pasture lands, and Meph'a•ath with its pasture lands—four towns. [38] Out of the tribe of Gad:

Rā'moth in Gil'e•ad with its pasture lands, the city of refuge for the slayer, Mā•ha•nā'im with its pasture lands, [39] Hesh'bon with its pasture lands, Jā'zer with its pasture lands—four towns in all. [40] As for the towns of the several Me•rar'īte families, that is, the remainder of the families of the Lē'vites, those allotted to them were twelve in all.

41 The towns of the Lē'vites within the holdings of the Israelites were in all forty-eight towns with their pasture lands. [42] Each of these towns had its pasture lands around it; so it was with all these towns.

43 Thus the LORD gave to Israel all the land that he swore to their ancestors that he would give them; and having taken possession of it, they settled there. [44] And the LORD gave them rest on every side just as he had sworn to their ancestors; not one of all their enemies had withstood them, for the LORD had given all their enemies into their hands. [45] Not one of all the good promises that the LORD had made to the house of Israel had failed; all came to pass.

The Eastern Tribes Return to Their Territory

Then Joshua summoned the Reū'ben•ites, the Gad'ites, and the half-tribe of Ma•nas'seh, [2] and said to them, "You have observed all that Moses the servant of the LORD commanded you, and have obeyed me in all that I have commanded you; [3] you have not forsaken your kindred these many days, down to this day, but have been careful to keep the charge of the LORD your God. [4] And now the LORD your God has given rest to your kindred, as he promised them; therefore turn and go to your tents in the land where your possession lies, which Moses the servant of the LORD gave you on the other side of the Jordan. [5] Take good care to observe the commandment and instruction that Moses the servant of the LORD commanded you, to love the LORD your God, to walk in all his ways, to keep his commandments, and to hold fast to him, and to serve him with all your heart and with all your soul." [6] So Joshua blessed them and sent them away, and they went to their tents.

7 Now to the one half of the tribe of Ma•nas'-seh Moses had given a possession in Bā'shan; but to the other half Joshua had given a possession beside their fellow Israelites in the land west of the Jordan. And when Joshua sent them away to their tents and blessed them, [8] he said to them, "Go back to your tents with much wealth, and with very much livestock, with silver, gold, bronze, and iron, and with a great quantity of clothing; divide the spoil of your enemies with your kindred." [9] So the Reū'ben•ites and the Gad'ites and the half-tribe of Ma•nas'seh returned home, parting from the

Israelites at Shi'lōh, which is in the land of Cā'naan, to go to the land of Gil'e·ad, their own land of which they had taken possession by command of the LORD through Moses.

A Memorial Altar East of the Jordan

10 When they came to the region[i] near the Jordan that lies in the land of Cā'naan, the Reū'-ben·ites and the Gad'ites and the half-tribe of Ma-nas'seh built there an altar by the Jordan, an altar of great size. 11 The Israelites heard that the Reū'-ben·ites and the Gad'ites and the half-tribe of Ma-nas'seh had built an altar at the frontier of the land of Cā'naan, in the region[j] near the Jordan, on the side that belongs to the Israelites. 12 And when the people of Israel heard of it, the whole assembly of the Israelites gathered at Shi'lōh, to make war against them.

13 Then the Israelites sent the priest Phin'e·has son of El·ē·ā'zar to the Reū'ben·ites and the Gad'ites and the half-tribe of Ma·nas'seh, in the land of Gil'e·ad, 14 and with him ten chiefs, one from each of the tribal families of Israel, every one of them the head of a family among the clans of Israel. 15 They came to the Reū'ben·ites, the Gad'ites, and the half-tribe of Ma·nas'seh, in the land of Gil'e·ad, and they said to them, 16 "Thus says the whole congregation of the LORD, 'What is this treachery that you have committed against the God of Israel in turning away today from following the LORD, by building yourselves an altar today in rebellion against the LORD? 17 Have we not had enough of the sin at Pē'or from which even yet we have not cleansed ourselves, and for which a plague came upon the congregation of the LORD, 18 that you must turn away today from following the LORD! If you rebel against the LORD today, he will be angry with the whole congregation of Israel tomorrow. 19 But now, if your land is unclean, cross over into the LORD's land where the LORD's tabernacle now stands, and take for yourselves a possession among us; only do not rebel against the LORD, or rebel against us[k] by building yourselves an altar other than the altar of the LORD our God. 20 Did not Ā'chan son of Zē'rah break faith in the matter of the devoted things, and wrath fell upon all the congregation of Israel? And he did not perish alone for his iniquity!' "

21 Then the Reū'ben·ites, the Gad'ites, and the half-tribe of Ma·nas'seh said in answer to the heads of the families of Israel, 22 "The LORD, God of gods! The LORD, God of gods! He knows; and let Israel itself know! If it was in rebellion or in breach of faith toward the LORD, do not spare us today 23 for building an altar to turn away from following the LORD; or if we did so to offer burnt offerings or

grain offerings or offerings of well-being on it, may the LORD himself take vengeance. 24 No! We did it from fear that in time to come your children might say to our children, 'What have you to do

PRAY IT!
A Prayer for Understanding

When the Israelite tribes located east of the Jordan build a large altar to worship God, the Israelite tribes who settled west of the Jordan become concerned. They think that by building more altars, the tribes to the east are compromising their belief in one God. Some are ready to go to war over this issue. But maintaining unity among the tribes is also important. So, the western tribes wisely send Phinehas and others to insist on the importance of one place of worship. Listening to the eastern tribes, Phinehas understands their good intentions, and war is avoided.

Think about times when you have jumped to conclusions about other people's actions. Then say the following prayer:

God of love and wisdom, a misunderstanding almost led to war among the Israelites. Help me to avoid jumping to conclusions about the actions of others. Help me to listen and understand their intentions, as Phinehas did. And let me be gracious in recognizing when I am wrong. Amen.

▶ Josh 22.13–20

with the LORD, the God of Israel? 25 For the LORD has made the Jordan a boundary between us and you, you Reū'ben·ites and Gad'ites; you have no portion in the LORD.' So your children might make our children cease to worship the LORD. 26 Therefore we said, 'Let us now build an altar, not for burnt offering, nor for sacrifice, 27 but to be a witness between us and you, and between the generations after us, that we do perform the service of the LORD in his presence with our burnt offerings and sacrifices and offerings of well-being; so that your

---

i Or to Geliloth   j Or at Geliloth   k Or make rebels of us

children may never say to our children in time to come, "You have no portion in the LORD." ' ²⁸And we thought, If this should be said to us or to our descendants in time to come, we could say, 'Look at this copy of the altar of the LORD, which our ancestors made, not for burnt offerings, nor for sacrifice, but to be a witness between us and you.' ²⁹Far be it from us that we should rebel against the LORD, and turn away this day from following the LORD by building an altar for burnt offering, grain offering, or sacrifice, other than the altar of the LORD our God that stands before his tabernacle!"

30 When the priest Phin'e•has and the chiefs of the congregation, the heads of the families of Israel who were with him, heard the words that the Reū'ben•ites and the Gad'ites and the Ma•nas'sites spoke, they were satisfied. ³¹The priest Phin'e•has son of El•ē•ā'zar said to the Reū'ben•ites and the Gad'ites and the Ma•nas'sites, "Today we know that the LORD is among us, because you have not committed this treachery against the LORD; now you have saved the Israelites from the hand of the LORD."

32 Then the priest Phin'e•has son of El•ē•ā'zar and the chiefs returned from the Reū'ben•ites and the Gad'ites in the land of Gil'e•ad to the land of Cā'naan, to the Israelites, and brought back word to them. ³³The report pleased the Israelites; and the Israelites blessed God and spoke no more of making war against them, to destroy the land where the Reū'ben•ites and the Gad'ites were settled. ³⁴The Reū'ben•ites and the Gad'ites called the altar Witness;ᶦ "For," said they, "it is a witness between us that the LORD is God."

Joshua Exhorts the People

A long time afterward, when the LORD had given rest to Israel from all their enemies all around, and Joshua was old and well advanced in years, ²Joshua summoned all Israel, their elders and heads, their judges and officers, and said to them, "I am now old and well advanced in years; ³and you have seen all that the LORD your God has done to all these nations for your sake, for it is the LORD your God who has fought for you. ⁴I have allotted to you as an inheritance for your tribes those nations that remain, along with all the nations that I have already cut off, from the Jordan to the Great Sea in the west. ⁵The LORD your God will push them back before you, and drive them out of your sight; and you shall possess their land, as the LORD your God promised you. ⁶Therefore be very steadfast to observe and do all that is written in the book of the law of Moses, turning aside from it neither to the right nor to the left, ⁷so that you

may not be mixed with these nations left here among you, or make mention of the names of their gods, or swear by them, or serve them, or bow yourselves down to them, ⁸but hold fast to the LORD your God, as you have done to this day. ⁹For the LORD has driven out before you great and strong nations; and as for you, no one has been able to withstand you to this day. ¹⁰One of you puts to flight a thousand, since it is the LORD your God who fights for you, as he promised you. ¹¹Be very careful, therefore, to love the LORD your God. ¹²For if you turn back, and join the survivors of these nations left here among you, and intermarry with them, so that you marry their women and they yours, ¹³know assuredly that the LORD your God will not continue to drive out these nations before you; but they shall be a snare and a trap for you, a scourge on your sides, and thorns in your eyes, until you perish from this good land that the LORD your God has given you.

14 "And now I am about to go the way of all the earth, and you know in your hearts and souls, all of you, that not one thing has failed of all the good things that the LORD your God promised concerning you; all have come to pass for you, not one of them has failed. ¹⁵But just as all the good things that the LORD your God promised concerning you have been fulfilled for you, so the LORD will bring upon you all the bad things, until he has destroyed you from this good land that the LORD your God has given you. ¹⁶If you transgress the covenant of the LORD your God, which he enjoined on you, and go and serve other gods and bow down to them, then the anger of the LORD will be kindled against you, and you shall perish quickly from the good land that he has given to you."

The Tribes Renew the Covenant
(Cp Ex 24.9–18)

Then Joshua gathered all the tribes of Israel to Shē'chem, and summoned the elders, the heads, the judges, and the officers of Israel; and they presented themselves before God. ²And Joshua said to all the people, "Thus says the LORD, the God of Israel: Long ago your ancestors—Tē'rah and his sons Abraham and Nā'hor—lived beyond the Euphrates and served other gods. ³Then I took your father Abraham from beyond the River and led him through all the land of Cā'naan and made his offspring many. I gave him Isaac; ⁴and to Isaac I gave Jacob and Esau. I gave Esau the hill country of Sē'ir to possess, but Jacob and his children went down to Egypt. ⁵Then I sent Moses and Aaron,

---

ᶦ Cn Compare Syr: Heb lacks *Witness*

J
O
S
H

and I plagued Egypt with what I did in its midst; and afterwards I brought you out. ⁶When I brought your ancestors out of Egypt, you came to the sea; and the Egyptians pursued your ancestors with chariots and horsemen to the Red Sea.*m* ⁷When they cried out to the LORD, he put darkness between you and the Egyptians, and made the sea come upon them and cover them; and your eyes saw what I did to Egypt. Afterwards you lived in the wilderness a long time. ⁸Then I brought you to the land of the Am′o•rītes, who lived on the other side of the Jordan; they fought with you, and I handed them over to you, and you took possession of their land, and I destroyed them before you. ⁹Then King Bā′lak son of Zip′por of Mō′ab, set out to fight against Israel. He sent and invited Bā′laam son of Bē′or to curse you, ¹⁰but I would not listen to Bā′laam; therefore he blessed you; so I rescued you out of his hand. ¹¹When you went over the Jordan and came to Jericho, the citizens of Jericho fought against you, and also the Am′o•rītes, the Per′iz•zītes, the Cā′naan•ītes, the Hit′tītes, the Gir′ga•shītes, the Hī′vītes, and the Jeb′ū•sītes; and I handed them over to you. ¹²I sent the hornet*n* ahead of you, which drove out before you the two kings of the Am′o•rītes; it was not by your sword or by your bow. ¹³I gave you a land on which you had not labored, and towns that you had not

built, and you live in them; you eat the fruit of vineyards and oliveyards that you did not plant.

14 "Now therefore revere the LORD, and serve him in sincerity and in faithfulness; put away the gods that your ancestors served beyond the River and in Egypt, and serve the LORD. ¹⁵Now if you are unwilling to serve the LORD, choose this day whom you will serve, whether the gods your ancestors served in the region beyond the River or the gods of the Am′o•rītes in whose land you are living; but as for me and my household, we will serve the LORD."

16 Then the people answered, "Far be it from us that we should forsake the LORD to serve other gods; ¹⁷for it is the LORD our God who brought us and our ancestors up from the land of Egypt, out of the house of slavery, and who did those great signs in our sight. He protected us along all the way that we went, and among all the peoples through whom we passed; ¹⁸and the LORD drove out before us all the peoples, the Am′o•rītes who lived in the land. Therefore we also will serve the LORD, for he is our God."

19 But Joshua said to the people, "You cannot serve the LORD, for he is a holy God. He is a jealous God; he will not forgive your transgressions or

---

m Or *Sea of Reeds*   *n* Meaning of Heb uncertain

LIVING **THE COVENANT** TODAY!

Some people think the Israelites were completely unified and without differences, but nothing could be further from the truth. Joshua 24.1 tells how Joshua summoned the leaders of the twelve tribes to present themselves before God. In this gathering, they embraced their common faith in God and renewed the Covenant of Sinai, setting aside their differences and political struggles.

The twelve tribes were not unlike schools and neighborhoods in many parts of this country where young people gather in clubs, cliques, and even gangs, oftentimes dividing themselves by ethnic group or social class. Such division frequently leads to turf issues, conflict, and even violence.

Imagine if all the people in your school and neighborhood could come together, as the tribes did in Joshua's time, and embrace a common identity before God. Imagine the unity and strength you would have to help one another face life's challenges!

■ What can you do to foster this type of vision in your school and neighborhood? With whom can you start to share this vision so that it becomes a reality?

■ Pray for the courage and ability you need to be God's instrument of unity, love, and peace.

▶ Josh 24.1–28

Revere the LORD, and serve him in sincerity and in faithfulness

24.14

these words in the book of the law of God; and he took a large stone, and set it up there under the oak in the sanctuary of the LORD. ²⁷ Joshua said to all the people, "See, this stone shall be a witness against us; for it has heard all the words of the LORD that he spoke to us; therefore it shall be a witness against you, if you deal falsely with your God." ²⁸ So Joshua sent the people away to their inheritances.

Death of Joshua and Eleazar

29 After these things Joshua son of Nun, the servant of the LORD, died, being one hundred ten years old. ³⁰ They buried him in his own inheritance at Tim′nath-se̅′rah, which is in the hill country of E̅′phra·im, north of Mount Ga̅′ash.

31 Israel served the LORD all the days of Joshua, and all the days of the elders who outlived Joshua and had known all the work that the LORD did for Israel.

32 The bones of Joseph, which the Israelites had brought up from Egypt, were buried at She̅′chem, in the portion of ground that Jacob had bought from the children of Ha̅′mor, the father of She̅′chem, for one hundred pieces of money;ᵒ it became an inheritance of the descendants of Joseph.

33 El·e·a̅′zar son of Aaron died; and they buried him at Gib′e̅·ah, the town of his son Phin′e·has, which had been given him in the hill country of E̅′phra·im.

your sins. ²⁰ If you forsake the LORD and serve foreign gods, then he will turn and do you harm, and consume you, after having done you good." ²¹ And the people said to Joshua, "No, we will serve the LORD!" ²² Then Joshua said to the people, "You are witnesses against yourselves that you have chosen the LORD, to serve him." And they said, "We are witnesses." ²³ He said, "Then put away the foreign gods that are among you, and incline your hearts to the LORD, the God of Israel." ²⁴ The people said to Joshua, "The LORD our God we will serve, and him we will obey." ²⁵ So Joshua made a covenant with the people that day, and made statutes and ordinances for them at She̅′chem. ²⁶ Joshua wrote

---

o Heb *one hundred qesitah*

Mom and Dad treat me like such a child." "I can't get a job without experience, but how can I get experience if I can't get a job?" The teenage years often feel like an in-between time, when young people pass from being children to becoming adults who must take responsibility for their own life. This time of transition holds many challenges. In some ways, the Book of Judges is about Israel's "teenage years." It tells about the difficulties faced by God's people in an in-between time: the two hundred years between the conquest of Canaan under Joshua and the establishment of the kingdom of Israel under Saul.

At a Glance

- **1.1—3.6.** historical introduction
- **3.7—16.31.** the stories of individual judges
- **Chapters 17–21.** two appendices

In-depth

In the Book of Judges, the twelve tribes of Israel face two especially difficult challenges: how to live peacefully with one another and how to withstand the attacks of foreign armies. God answers the Israelites' prayers for help by raising up extraordinary men and women to lead the tribes. These famous leaders—Gideon, Deborah, Samson, and nine others—are called judges, but they aren't judges in courtrooms wearing black robes. They are local elders and military heroes who are chosen by God's spirit to lead the Israelites in times of crisis.

The pattern that we observed in the Book of Joshua also appears in the Book of Judges: when the people obey God's laws, they thrive; when they are disobedient, they suffer and need to be rescued by a leader raised up by God's spirit. The stories in Judges probably began as regional tales about local heroes. As they were collected and edited by the author of Judges, they became national stories influenced by the message of Deuteronomy: faithfulness to God is the only road to personal and tribal security.

Judges reminds us that the challenges of life, especially in the in-between times, are best handled through prayer and reliance on God. God can be trusted to lead us through all difficulties, both great and small.

Quick Facts

Period Covered
from 1220 to 1000 B.C.

Author
The book was put into final form by an unknown person from the Deuteronomic school, after the fall of Jerusalem (587 B.C.).

Themes
God raises up mighty heroes to protect the people. God works even through flawed heroes.

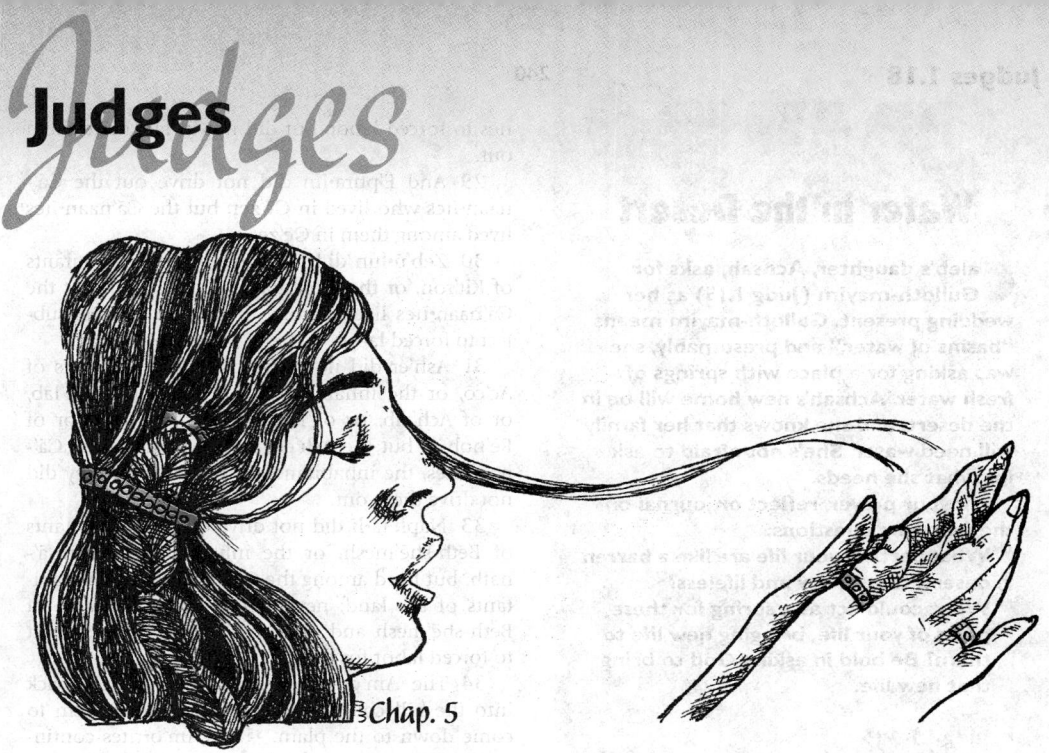

Judges

Chap. 5

Israel's Failure to Complete the
Conquest of Canaan
(Josh 15.13–19)

After the death of Joshua, the Israelites inquired of the LORD, "Who shall go up first for us against the Cā'naan·ītes, to fight against them?" ² The LORD said, "Judah shall go up. I hereby give the land into his hand." ³ Judah said to his brother Sim'ē·on, "Come up with me into the territory allotted to me, that we may fight against the Cā'naan·ītes; then I too will go with you into the territory allotted to you." So Sim'ē·on went with him. ⁴ Then Judah went up and the LORD gave the Cā'naan·ītes and the Per'iz-zītes into their hand; and they defeated ten thousand of them at Bē'zek. ⁵ They came upon A·dō'-ni-bē'zek at Bē'zek, and fought against him, and defeated the Cā'naan·ītes and the Per'iz·zītes. ⁶ A·dō'ni-bē'zek fled; but they pursued him, and caught him, and cut off his thumbs and big toes. ⁷ A·dō'ni-bē'zek said, "Seventy kings with their thumbs and big toes cut off used to pick up scraps under my table; as I have done, so God has paid me back." They brought him to Jerusalem, and he died there.

8 Then the people of Judah fought against Jerusalem and took it. They put it to the sword and set the city on fire. ⁹ Afterward the people of Judah went down to fight against the Cā'naan·ītes who lived in the hill country, in the Neg'eb, and in the lowland. ¹⁰ Judah went against the Cā'naan·ītes who lived in Hē'bron (the name of Hē'bron was formerly Kir'i·ath-ar'ba); and they defeated Shē'-shaī and A·hī'man and Tal'maī.

11 From there they went against the inhabitants of Dē'bir (the name of Dē'bir was formerly Kir'i·ath-sē'pher). ¹² Then Caleb said, "Whoever attacks Kir'i·ath-sē'pher and takes it, I will give him my daughter Ach'sah as wife." ¹³ And Oth'ni·el son of Kē'naz, Caleb's younger brother, took it; and he gave him his daughter Ach'sah as wife. ¹⁴ When she came to him, she urged him to ask her father for a field. As she dismounted from her donkey, Caleb said to her, "What do you wish?" ¹⁵ She said to him, "Give me a present; since you have set me in the land of the Neg'eb, give me also Gul'loth-māy'im."ᵃ So Caleb gave her Upper Gul'loth and Lower Gul'loth.

16 The descendants of Hō'babᵇ the Ken'īte, Moses' father-in-law, went up with the people of Judah from the city of palms into the wilderness of Judah, which lies in the Neg'eb near Ar'ad. Then they went and settled with the A·mal'e·kītes.ᶜ ¹⁷ Judah went with his brother Sim'ē·on, and they defeated the Cā'naan·ītes who inhabited Zē'phath,

ᵃ That is *Basins of Water*   ᵇ Gk: Heb lacks *Hobab*
ᶜ See 1 Sam 15.6: Heb *people*

239

PRAY IT

Water in the Desert

Caleb's daughter, Achsah, asks for Gulloth-mayim (Judg 1.15) as her wedding present. Gulloth-mayim means "basins of water," and presumably, she was asking for a place with springs of fresh water. Achsah's new home will be in the desert, and she knows that her family will need water. She's not afraid to ask for what she needs.

In your prayer, reflect or journal on the following questions:

- What parts of your life are like a barren desert, that is, dry and lifeless?
- What could act as a spring for these parts of your life, bringing new life to them? Be bold in asking God to bring that new life.

▶ Judg 1.14–15

and devoted it to destruction. So the city was called Hor'mah. 18 Judah took Gā'za with its territory, Ash'ke·lon with its territory, and Ek'ron with its territory. 19 The LORD was with Judah, and he took possession of the hill country, but could not drive out the inhabitants of the plain, because they had chariots of iron. 20 Hē'bron was given to Caleb, as Moses had said; and he drove out from it the three sons of Ā'nak. 21 But the Ben'ja·min·ites did not drive out the Jeb'ū·sītes who lived in Jerusalem; so the Jeb'ū·sītes have lived in Jerusalem among the Ben'ja·min·ites to this day.

22 The house of Joseph also went up against Beth'el; and the LORD was with them. 23 The house of Joseph sent out spies to Beth'el (the name of the city was formerly Luz). 24 When the spies saw a man coming out of the city, they said to him, "Show us the way into the city, and we will deal kindly with you." 25 So he showed them the way into the city; and they put the city to the sword, but they let the man and all his family go. 26 So the man went to the land of the Hit'tītes and built a city, and named it Luz; that is its name to this day.

27 Ma·nas'seh did not drive out the inhabitants of Beth-shē'an and its villages, or Tā'a·nach and its villages, or the inhabitants of Dor and its villages, or the inhabitants of Ib'lē·am and its villages, or the inhabitants of Me·gid'dō and its villages; but the Cā'naan·ītes continued to live in that land. 28 When Israel grew strong, they put the Cā'naan-

ītes to forced labor, but did not in fact drive them out.

29 And Ē'phra·im did not drive out the Cā'-naan·ītes who lived in Gē'zer; but the Cā'naan·ītes lived among them in Gē'zer.

30 Zeb'ū·lun did not drive out the inhabitants of Kit'ron, or the inhabitants of Na·hal'ol; but the Cā'naan·ītes lived among them, and became subject to forced labor.

31 Ash'er did not drive out the inhabitants of Ac'cō, or the inhabitants of Sī'don, or of Ah'lab, or of Ach'zib, or of Hel'bah, or of Ā'phik, or of Rē'hob; 32 but the Ash'er·ītes lived among the Cā'-naan·ītes, the inhabitants of the land; for they did not drive them out.

33 Naph'ta·li did not drive out the inhabitants of Beth-shē'mesh, or the inhabitants of Beth-ā'-nath, but lived among the Cā'naan·ītes, the inhabitants of the land; nevertheless the inhabitants of Beth-shē'mesh and of Beth-ā'nath became subject to forced labor for them.

34 The Am'o·rītes pressed the Dan'ītes back into the hill country; they did not allow them to come down to the plain. 35 The Am'o·rītes continued to live in Har-hē'rēs, in Aī'ja·lon, and in Shā-al'bim, but the hand of the house of Joseph rested heavily on them, and they became subject to forced labor. 36 The border of the Am'o·rītes ran from the ascent of Ak·rab'bim, from Sē'la and upward.

Israel's Disobedience

Now the angel of the LORD went up from Gil'gal to Bō'chim, and said, "I brought you up from Egypt, and brought you into the land that I had promised to your ancestors. I said, 'I will never break my covenant with you. 2 For your part, do not make a covenant with the inhabitants of this land; tear down their altars.' But you have not obeyed my command. See what you have done! 3 So now I say, I will not drive them out before you; but they shall become adversaries^d to you, and their gods shall be a snare to you." 4 When the angel of the LORD spoke these words to all the Israelites, the people lifted up their voices and wept. 5 So they named that place Bō'chim,^{e} and there they sacrificed to the LORD.

Death of Joshua
(Josh 24.29–31)

6 When Joshua dismissed the people, the Israelites all went to their own inheritances to take possession of the land. 7 The people worshiped the LORD all the days of Joshua, and all the days of the

---

^{d} OL Vg Compare Gk: Heb sides ^{e} That is *Weepers*

Obeying Authority

Have you ever decided to disobey your parents, your teachers, or maybe a boss at work? What were the consequences? Disobedience to legitimate authority tends to bring about bad consequences. Just read Judg 2.11–15. The people turned from God, and their separation from God led to defeat at the hands of their enemies.

God places parents, teachers, and other authority figures in our life to protect and support us. Their love and caring are an extension of God's love and caring. From their vantage point, they often see a bigger picture than we do. When we disobey their reasonable requests, we build walls between them and us, preventing God's love from reaching us. On the other hand, obedience leads to more trust, responsibility, and freedom. Of course, as Jesus himself showed us, no one is obligated to obey requests or directions that are abusive, demeaning, or immoral.

So, the next time you are having a problem with a person in authority, ask yourself, Might obedience in this situation somehow bring me closer to God?

▶ Judg 2.11–15

---

elders who outlived Joshua, who had seen all the great work that the LORD had done for Israel. 8 Joshua son of Nun, the servant of the LORD, died at the age of one hundred ten years. 9 So they buried him within the bounds of his inheritance in Tim′nath-hē′rēs, in the hill country of Ē′phra•im, north of Mount Gā′ash. 10 Moreover, that whole generation was gathered to their ancestors, and another generation grew up after them, who did not know the LORD or the work that he had done for Israel.

Israel's Unfaithfulness

11 Then the Israelites did what was evil in the sight of the LORD and worshiped the Bā′als; 12 and they abandoned the LORD, the God of their ancestors, who had brought them out of the land of Egypt; they followed other gods, from among the gods of the peoples who were all around them, and bowed down to them; and they provoked the LORD to anger. 13 They abandoned the LORD, and worshiped Bā′al and the As•tar′tēs. 14 So the anger of the LORD was kindled against Israel, and he gave them over to plunderers who plundered them, and he sold them into the power of their enemies all around, so that they could no longer withstand their enemies. 15 Whenever they marched out, the hand of the LORD was against them to bring misfortune, as the LORD had warned them and sworn to them; and they were in great distress.

16 Then the LORD raised up judges, who delivered them out of the power of those who plundered them. 17 Yet they did not listen even to their judges; for they lusted after other gods and bowed down to them. They soon turned aside from the

way in which their ancestors had walked, who had obeyed the commandments of the LORD; they did not follow their example. 18 Whenever the LORD raised up judges for them, the LORD was with the judge, and he delivered them from the hand of their enemies all the days of the judge; for the LORD would be moved to pity by their groaning because of those who persecuted and oppressed them. 19 But whenever the judge died, they would relapse and behave worse than their ancestors, following other gods, worshiping them and bowing down to them. They would not drop any of their practices or their stubborn ways. 20 So the anger of the LORD was kindled against Israel; and he said, "Because this people have transgressed my covenant that I commanded their ancestors, and have not obeyed my voice, 21 I will no longer drive out before them any of the nations that Joshua left when he died." 22 In order to test Israel, whether or not they would take care to walk in the way of the LORD as their ancestors did, 23 the LORD had left those nations, not driving them out at once, and had not handed them over to Joshua.

Nations Remaining in the Land

Now these are the nations that the LORD left to test all those in Israel who had no experience of any war in Cā′naan 2 (it was only that successive generations of Israelites might know war, to teach those who had no experience of it before): 3 the five lords of the Phi•lis′tines, and all the Cā′naan•ites, and the Sī•dō′ni•ans, and the Hī′vītes who lived on Mount Lebanon, from Mount Bā′al-her′mon as far as Lē′bō-hā′math. 4 They were for the testing of Israel, to know whether Israel would obey the

JUDG

commandments of the LORD, which he commanded their ancestors by Moses. 5 So the Israelites lived among the Cā'naan·ites, the Hit'tītes, the Am'o·rītes, the Per'iz·zītes, the Hī'vītes, and the Jeb'ū·sītes; 6 and they took their daughters as wives for themselves, and their own daughters they gave to their sons; and they worshiped their gods.

Othniel

7 The Israelites did what was evil in the sight of the LORD, forgetting the LORD their God, and worshiping the Bā'als and the A·shē'rahs. 8 Therefore the anger of the LORD was kindled against Israel, and he sold them into the hand of King Cū'shan-rish·a·thā'im of Ar'am-nā·ha·rā'im; and the Israelites served Cū'shan-rish·a·thā'im eight years. 9 But when the Israelites cried out to the LORD, the LORD raised up a deliverer for the Israelites, who delivered them, Oth'ni·el son of Kē'naz, Caleb's younger brother. 10 The spirit of the LORD came upon him, and he judged Israel; he went out to war, and the LORD gave King Cū'shan-rish·a·thā'im of Ar'am into his hand; and his hand prevailed over Cū'shan-rish·a·thā'im. 11 So the land had rest forty years. Then Oth'ni·el son of Kē'naz died.

Ehud

12 The Israelites again did what was evil in the sight of the LORD; and the LORD strengthened King Eg'lon of Mō'ab against Israel, because they had done what was evil in the sight of the LORD. 13 In alliance with the Am'mon·ites and the A·mal'e·kites, he went and defeated Israel; and they took possession of the city of palms. 14 So the Israelites served King Eg'lon of Mō'ab eighteen years.

15 But when the Israelites cried out to the LORD, the LORD raised up for them a deliverer, Ē'hud son of Gē'ra, the Ben'ja·min·ite, a left-handed man. The Israelites sent tribute by him to King Eg'lon of Mō'ab. 16 Ē'hud made for himself a sword with two edges, a cubit in length; and he fastened it on his right thigh under his clothes. 17 Then he presented the tribute to King Eg'lon of Mō'ab. Now Eg'lon was a very fat man. 18 When Ē'hud had finished presenting the tribute, he sent the people who carried the tribute on their way. 19 But he himself turned back at the sculptured stones near Gil'gal, and said, "I have a secret message for you, O king." So the king said,*f* "Silence!" and all his attendants went out from his presence. 20 Ē'hud came to him, while he was sitting alone in his cool roof chamber, and said, "I have a message from God for you." So he rose from his seat. 21 Then Ē'hud reached with his left hand, took the sword from his right thigh, and thrust it into Eg'-

lon's*g* belly; 22 the hilt also went in after the blade, and the fat closed over the blade, for he did not draw the sword out of his belly; and the dirt came out.*h* 23 Then Ē'hud went out into the vestibule,*i* and closed the doors of the roof chamber on him, and locked them.

24 After he had gone, the servants came. When they saw that the doors of the roof chamber were locked, they thought, "He must be relieving himself*j* in the cool chamber." 25 So they waited until they were embarrassed. When he still did not open the doors of the roof chamber, they took the key and opened them. There was their lord lying dead on the floor.

26 Ē'hud escaped while they delayed, and passed beyond the sculptured stones, and escaped to Sē·ī'rah. 27 When he arrived, he sounded the trumpet in the hill country of Ē'phra·im; and the Israelites went down with him from the hill country, having him at their head. 28 He said to them, "Follow after me; for the LORD has given your enemies the Mō'ab·ites into your hand." So they went down after him, and seized the fords of the Jordan against the Mō'ab·ites, and allowed no one to cross over. 29 At that time they killed about ten thousand of the Mō'ab·ites, all strong, able-bodied men; no one escaped. 30 So Mō'ab was subdued that day under the hand of Israel. And the land had rest eighty years.

Shamgar

31 After him came Sham'gar son of Ā'nath, who killed six hundred of the Phi·lis'tines with an oxgoad. He too delivered Israel.

Deborah and Barak

The Israelites again did what was evil in the sight of the LORD, after Ē'hud died. 2 So the LORD sold them into the hand of King Jā'bin of Cā'naan, who reigned in Hā'zor; the commander of his army was Sis'e·ra, who lived in Ha·rō'sheth-ha-goi'im. 3 Then the Israelites cried out to the LORD for help; for he had nine hundred chariots of iron, and had oppressed the Israelites cruelly twenty years.

4 At that time Deb'or·ah, a prophetess, wife of Lap'pi·doth, was judging Israel. 5 She used to sit under the palm of Deb'or·ah between Rā'mah and Beth'el in the hill country of Ē'phra·im; and the Israelites came up to her for judgment. 6 She sent

---

f Heb *he said*   *g* Heb *his*   *h* With Tg Vg: Meaning of Heb uncertain   *i* Meaning of Heb uncertain
j Heb *covering his feet*

and summoned Bar′ak son of A•bin′ō•am from Kē′-desh in Naph′ta•lī, and said to him, "The LORD, the God of Israel, commands you, 'Go, take position at Mount Tā′bor, bringing ten thousand from the tribe of Naph′ta•lī and the tribe of Zeb′ū•lun. ⁷I will draw out Sis′e•ra, the general of Jā′bin's army, to meet you by the Wadi Kī′shon with his chariots and his troops; and I will give him into your hand.' " ⁸Bar′ak said to her, "If you will go with me, I will go; but if you will not go with me, I will not go." ⁹And she said, "I will surely go with you; nevertheless, the road on which you are going will not lead to your glory, for the LORD will sell Sis′e•ra into the hand of a woman." Then Deb′or•ah got up and went with Bar′ak to Kē′desh. ¹⁰Bar′ak summoned Zeb′ū•lun and Naph′ta•lī to Kē′desh; and

PRAY IT!
Wartime Women

In Judges, chapter 4, Deborah, a judge and prophet, rallies Barak and the Israelites to war, and Jael, another woman (who is not an Israelite), delivers the final blow to the enemy's commander, Sisera. In chapter 5, Deborah leads the victory celebration with an elaborate prayer-song that is probably one of the oldest texts in the Bible (see also Exodus, chapter 15).

In the Bible, women are often innocent victims of war. Usually, they do not do the fighting but are raped, killed, or widowed. Is Jael's violence the answer to this abuse? Is Jael a hero? Or is she still a victim of war, forced to make a violent choice in order to survive in a violent world? The writer of the Book of Judges gives no judgment on her actions.

When we are no longer victims, but have become people who abuse others, has the situation really improved? Or are we just doing to others what we would never want done to ourselves? In light of Jesus' teachings, these are important questions to ask. Let us pray:

God of love, please deliver us from being both victims of violence and agents of violence. Amen.

▸ Judges, chapter 4

ten thousand warriors went up behind him; and Deb′or•ah went up with him.

11 Now Hē′ber the Ken′īte had separated from the other Ken′ītes,ᵏ that is, the descendants of Hō′bab the father-in-law of Moses, and had encamped as far away as Ē′lon-be•zā-a•nan′nim, which is near Kē′desh.

12 When Sis′e•ra was told that Bar′ak son of A•bin′ō•am had gone up to Mount Tā′bor, ¹³Sis′e•ra called out all his chariots, nine hundred chariots of iron, and all the troops who were with him, from Ha•rō′sheth-ha-goi′im to the Wadi Kī′shon. ¹⁴Then Deb′or•ah said to Bar′ak, "Up! For this is the day on which the LORD has given Sis′e•ra into your hand. The LORD is indeed going out before you." So Bar′ak went down from Mount Tā′bor with ten thousand warriors following him. ¹⁵And the LORD threw Sis′e•ra and all his chariots and all his army into a panicˡ before Bar′ak; Sis′e•ra got down from his chariot and fled away on foot, ¹⁶while Bar′ak pursued the chariots and the army to Ha•rō′sheth-ha-goi′im. All the army of Sis′e•ra fell by the sword; no one was left.

17 Now Sis′e•ra had fled away on foot to the tent of Jā′el wife of Hē′ber the Ken′īte; for there was peace between King Jā′bin of Hā′zor and the clan of Hē′ber the Ken′īte. ¹⁸Jā′el came out to meet Sis′e•ra, and said to him, "Turn aside, my lord, turn aside to me; have no fear." So he turned aside to her into the tent, and she covered him with a rug. ¹⁹Then he said to her, "Please give me a little water to drink; for I am thirsty." So she opened a skin of milk and gave him a drink and covered him. ²⁰He said to her, "Stand at the entrance of the tent, and if anybody comes and asks you, 'Is anyone here?' say, 'No.' " ²¹But Jā′el wife of Hē′ber took a tent peg, and took a hammer in her hand, and went softly to him and drove the peg into his temple, until it went down into the ground—he was lying fast asleep from weariness—and he died. ²²Then, as Bar′ak came in pursuit of Sis′e•ra, Jā′el went out to meet him, and said to him, "Come, and I will show you the man whom you are seeking." So he went into her tent; and there was Sis′e•ra lying dead, with the tent peg in his temple.

23 So on that day God subdued King Jā′bin of Cā′naan before the Israelites. ²⁴Then the hand of the Israelites bore harder and harder on King Jā′bin of Cā′naan, until they destroyed King Jā′bin of Cā′naan.

ᵏ Heb *from the Kain*   ˡ Heb adds *to the sword*; compare verse 16

The Battle Within

Although the story of Deborah is inspiring, partly because so few women leaders are portrayed in the Bible, it is also a story of war and violence. The Book of Judges records one battle after another. It is wearying to read of so much fighting, and of rejoicing over someone's having a tent peg pounded into their head.

We need to keep our perspective here and understand that the way the Israelites viewed life at that time was simple: If they were victorious, God was with them. If they were defeated, God had been offended and had turned away from them.

What can we learn from this story? It teaches that God never turns away from us. The real victories to celebrate are the personal battles we win each day as we strive to become more faithful to God. Jesus calls us to make peace rather than war. Our greatest enemy is often within, as we strive to be the person God wants us to be, whether our name is Deborah or Joshua, Jennifer or Carlos.

What battle is going on inside you today? What choice in this battle leads to greater faithfulness to God?

▶ Judges, chapter 4

The Song of Deborah

Then Deb'or•ah and Bar'ak son of A•bin'ō•am sang on that day, saying:

2 "When locks are long in Israel,
      when the people offer themselves
            willingly—
      bless ^{m} the LORD!

3 "Hear, O kings; give ear, O princes;
      to the LORD I will sing,
      I will make melody to the LORD, the God
            of Israel.

4 "LORD, when you went out from Sē'ir,
      when you marched from the region of
            Ē'dom,
      the earth trembled,
      and the heavens poured,
      the clouds indeed poured water.

5 The mountains quaked before the LORD, the
            One of Sinai,
      before the LORD, the God of Israel.

6 "In the days of Sham'gar son of Ā'nath,
      in the days of Jā'el, caravans ceased
      and travelers kept to the byways.

7 The peasantry prospered in Israel,
      they grew fat on plunder,
      because you arose, Deb'or•ah,
      arose as a mother in Israel.

8 When new gods were chosen,
      then war was in the gates.
      Was shield or spear to be seen
      among forty thousand in Israel?

9 My heart goes out to the commanders of
            Israel
      who offered themselves willingly among
            the people.
      Bless the LORD.

10 "Tell of it, you who ride on white donkeys,
      you who sit on rich carpets ^{n}
      and you who walk by the way.

11 To the sound of musicians ^{n} at the watering
            places,
      there they repeat the triumphs of the LORD,
      the triumphs of his peasantry in Israel.

"Then down to the gates marched the
            people of the LORD.

12 "Awake, awake, Deb'or•ah!
      Awake, awake, utter a song!
      Arise, Bar'ak, lead away your captives,
      O son of A•bin'ō•am.

13 Then down marched the remnant of the
            noble;
      the people of the LORD marched down for
            him ^{o} against the mighty.

14 From Ē'phra•im they set out ^{p} into the
            valley, ^{q}
      following you, Benjamin, with your kin;
      from Mā'chir marched down the commanders,
      and from Zeb'ū•lun those who bear the
            marshal's staff;

---

^{m} Or *You who offer yourselves willingly among the people, bless* ^{n} Meaning of Heb uncertain ^{o} Gk: Heb *me* ^{p} Cn: Heb *From Ephraim their root* ^{q} Gk: Heb *in Amalek*

15 the chiefs of Is'sa•char came with
    Deb'or•ah,
  and Is'sa•char faithful to Bar'ak;
    into the valley they rushed out at his
      heels.
  Among the clans of Reuben
    there were great searchings of heart.
16 Why did you tarry among the sheepfolds,
    to hear the piping for the flocks?
  Among the clans of Reuben
    there were great searchings of heart.
17 Gil'e•ad stayed beyond the Jordan;
    and Dan, why did he abide with the
      ships?
  Ash'er sat still at the coast of the sea,
    settling down by his landings.
18 Zeb'ū•lun is a people that scorned death;
    Naph'ta•lī too, on the heights of the field.

19 "The kings came, they fought;
    then fought the kings of Cā'naan,
  at Tā'a•nach, by the waters of Me•gid'dō;
    they got no spoils of silver.
20 The stars fought from heaven,
    from their courses they fought against
      Sis'e•ra.
21 The torrent Kī'shon swept them away,
    the onrushing torrent, the torrent
      Kī'shon.
  March on, my soul, with might!

22 "Then loud beat the horses' hoofs
    with the galloping, galloping of his
      steeds.

23 "Curse Me'roz, says the angel of the LORD,
    curse bitterly its inhabitants,
  because they did not come to the help of
    the LORD,
    to the help of the LORD against the
      mighty.

24 "Most blessed of women be Jā'el,
    the wife of Hē'ber the Ken'īte,
  of tent-dwelling women most blessed.
25 He asked water and she gave him milk,
    she brought him curds in a lordly
      bowl.
26 She put her hand to the tent peg
    and her right hand to the workmen's
      mallet;
  she struck Sis'e•ra a blow,
    she crushed his head,
    she shattered and pierced his temple.
27 He sank, he fell,
    he lay still at her feet;
  at her feet he sank, he fell;
    where he sank, there he fell dead.

28 "Out of the window she peered,
    the mother of Sis'e•ra gazed^r through the
      lattice:
  'Why is his chariot so long in coming?
    Why tarry the hoofbeats of his chariots?'
29 Her wisest ladies make answer,
    indeed, she answers the question herself:
30 'Are they not finding and dividing the
      spoil?—
    A girl or two for every man;
  spoil of dyed stuffs for Sis'e•ra,
    spoil of dyed stuffs embroidered,
    two pieces of dyed work embroidered for
      my neck as spoil?'

31 "So perish all your enemies, O LORD!
    But may your friends be like the sun as it
      rises in its might."

And the land had rest forty years.

The Midianite Oppression

The Israelites did what was evil in the sight of the LORD, and the LORD gave them into the hand of Mid'i•an seven years. 2 The hand of Mid'i•an prevailed over Israel; and because of Mid'i•an the Israelites provided for themselves hiding places in the mountains, caves and strongholds. 3 For whenever the Israelites put in seed, the Mid'i•an•ītes and the A•mal'e•kītes and the people of the east would come up against them. 4 They would encamp against them and destroy the produce of the land, as far as the neighborhood of Gā'za, and leave no sustenance in Israel, and no sheep or ox or donkey. 5 For they and their livestock would come up, and they would even bring their tents, as thick as locusts; neither they nor their camels could be counted; so they wasted the land as they came in. 6 Thus Israel was greatly impoverished because of Mid'i•an; and the Israelites cried out to the LORD for help.

7 When the Israelites cried to the LORD on account of the Mid'i•an•ītes, 8 the LORD sent a prophet to the Israelites; and he said to them, "Thus says the LORD, the God of Israel: I led you up from Egypt, and brought you out of the house of slavery; 9 and I delivered you from the hand of the Egyptians, and from the hand of all who oppressed you, and drove them out before you, and gave you their land; 10 and I said to you, 'I am the LORD your God; you shall not pay reverence to the gods of the Am'o•rītes, in whose land you live.' But you have not given heed to my voice."

---

r Gk Compare Tg: Heb *exclaimed*

The Call of Gideon

11 Now the angel of the LORD came and sat under the oak at Oph'rah, which belonged to Jŏ'ash the Ā·bi·ez'rīte, as his son Gideon was beating out wheat in the wine press, to hide it from the Mid'i·an·ītes. 12 The angel of the LORD appeared to him and said to him, "The LORD is with you, you mighty warrior." 13 Gideon answered him, "But sir, if the LORD is with us, why then has all this happened to us? And where are all his wonderful deeds that our ancestors recounted to us, saying, 'Did not the LORD bring us up from Egypt?' But now the LORD has cast us off, and given us into the hand of Mid'i·an." 14 Then the LORD turned to him and said, "Go in this might of yours and deliver Israel from the hand of Mid'i·an; I hereby commission you." 15 He responded, "But sir, how can I deliver Israel? My clan is the weakest in Ma·nas'seh, and I am the least in my family." 16 The LORD said to him, "But I will be with you, and you shall strike down the Mid'i·an·ītes, every one of them." 17 Then he said to him, "If now I have found favor with you, then show me a sign that it is you who speak with me. 18 Do not depart from here until I come to you, and bring out my present, and set it before you." And he said, "I will stay until you return."

19 So Gideon went into his house and prepared a kid, and unleavened cakes from an ephah of flour; the meat he put in a basket, and the broth he put in a pot, and brought them to him under the oak and presented them. 20 The angel of God said to him, "Take the meat and the unleavened cakes, and put them on this rock, and pour out the broth." And he did so. 21 Then the angel of the LORD reached out the tip of the staff that was in his hand, and touched the meat and the unleavened cakes; and fire sprang up from the rock and consumed the meat and the unleavened cakes; and the angel of the LORD vanished from his sight. 22 Then Gideon perceived that it was the angel of the LORD; and Gideon said, "Help me, Lord GOD! For I have seen the angel of the LORD face to face." 23 But the LORD said to him, "Peace be to you; do not fear, you shall not die." 24 Then Gideon built an altar there to the LORD, and called it, The LORD is peace. To this day it still stands at Oph'rah, which belongs to the Ā·bi·ez'rītes.

25 That night the LORD said to him, "Take your father's bull, the second bull seven years old, and pull down the altar of Bā'al that belongs to your father, and cut down the sacred poleˢ that is beside it; 26 and build an altar to the LORD your God on the top of the stronghold here, in proper order; then take the second bull, and offer it as a burnt offering with the wood of the sacred poleˢ that

you shall cut down." 27 So Gideon took ten of his servants, and did as the LORD had told him; but because he was too afraid of his family and the townspeople to do it by day, he did it by night.

Gideon Destroys the Altar of Baal

28 When the townspeople rose early in the morning, the altar of Bā'al was broken down, and the sacred poleˢ beside it was cut down, and the second bull was offered on the altar that had been built. 29 So they said to one another, "Who has done this?" After searching and inquiring, they were told, "Gideon son of Jŏ'ash did it." 30 Then the townspeople said to Jŏ'ash, "Bring out your son, so that he may die, for he has pulled down the altar of Bā'al and cut down the sacred poleˢ beside it." 31 But Jŏ'ash said to all who were arrayed against him, "Will you contend for Bā'al? Or will you defend his cause? Whoever contends for him shall be put to death by morning. If he is a god, let him contend for himself, because his altar has been pulled down." 32 Therefore on that day Gideonᵗ was called Jer·ub·bā'al, that is to say, "Let Bā'al contend against him," because he pulled down his altar.

33 Then all the Mid'i·an·ītes and the A·mal'e-kītes and the people of the east came together, and crossing the Jordan they encamped in the Valley of Jez're·el. 34 But the spirit of the LORD took possession of Gideon; and he sounded the trumpet, and the Ā·bi·ez'rītes were called out to follow him. 35 He sent messengers throughout all Ma·nas'seh, and they too were called out to follow him. He also sent messengers to Ash'er, Zeb'ŭ·lun, and Naph'-ta·lī, and they went up to meet them.

The Sign of the Fleece

36 Then Gideon said to God, "In order to see whether you will deliver Israel by my hand, as you have said, 37 I am going to lay a fleece of wool on the threshing floor; if there is dew on the fleece alone, and it is dry on all the ground, then I shall know that you will deliver Israel by my hand, as you have said." 38 And it was so. When he rose early next morning and squeezed the fleece, he wrung enough dew from the fleece to fill a bowl with water. 39 Then Gideon said to God, "Do not let your anger burn against me, let me speak one more time; let me, please, make trial with the fleece just once more; let it be dry only on the fleece, and on all the ground let there be dew." 40 And God did so that night. It was dry on the fleece only, and on all the ground there was dew.

ˢ Heb *Asherah*   ᵗ Heb *he*

Gideon Surprises and Routs the Midianites

Then Jer·ub·bā′al (that is, Gideon) and all the troops that were with him rose early and encamped beside the spring of Har′od; and the camp of Mid′i·an was north of them, below*u* the hill of Mō′reh, in the valley.

2 The LORD said to Gideon, "The troops with you are too many for me to give the Mid′i·an·ītes into their hand. Israel would only take the credit away from me, saying, 'My own hand has delivered me.' 3 Now therefore proclaim this in the hearing of the troops, 'Whoever is fearful and trembling, let him return home.' " Thus Gideon sifted them out;*v* twenty-two thousand returned, and ten thousand remained.

Trusting God

The true test of love is loving without testing.

Gideon keeps testing God; he cannot bring himself to believe God's promises. Judges, chapters 6–8, gives a full picture of this hero who never quite understands what loving God is all about. Even after his victory, and his words of devotion to God, he makes a gold idol (8.22–28).

Most people are tempted to test God in some way: "God, I'll know you are there for me if I get this job." Fortunately, God is big enough to accept our testing. Just do not expect God to answer every request—at least not exactly the way you would like God to answer it.

How do you test God? Is your prayer more trusting than Gideon's prayer? The next time you feel anxious or afraid, use one of these Scripture passages for your prayer: Psalm 25; Psalm 27; John, chapter 14; 1 Jn 4.7–21. Challenge yourself to trust God without testing.

▸ Judg 6.36–40

4 Then the LORD said to Gideon, "The troops are still too many; take them down to the water and I will sift them out for you there. When I say, 'This one shall go with you,' he shall go with you; and when I say, 'This one shall not go with you,' he shall not go." 5 So he brought the troops down to the water; and the LORD said to Gideon, "All those who lap the water with their tongues, as a dog laps, you shall put to one side; all those who kneel down to drink, putting their hands to their mouths,*w* you shall put to the other side." 6 The number of those that lapped was three hundred; but all the rest of the troops knelt down to drink water. 7 Then the LORD said to Gideon, "With the three hundred that lapped I will deliver you, and give the Mid′i·an·ītes into your hand. Let all the others go to their homes." 8 So he took the jars of the troops from their hands,*x* and their trumpets; and he sent all the rest of Israel back to their own tents, but retained the three hundred. The camp of Mid′i·an was below him in the valley.

9 That same night the LORD said to him, "Get up, attack the camp; for I have given it into your hand. 10 But if you fear to attack, go down to the camp with your servant Pŭ′rah; 11 and you shall hear what they say, and afterward your hands shall be strengthened to attack the camp." Then he went down with his servant Pŭ′rah to the outposts of the armed men that were in the camp. 12 The Mid′i·an·ītes and the A·mal′e·kītes and all the people of the east lay along the valley as thick as locusts; and their camels were without number, countless as the sand on the seashore. 13 When Gideon arrived, there was a man telling a dream to his comrade; and he said, "I had a dream, and in it a cake of barley bread tumbled into the camp of Mid′i·an, and came to the tent, and struck it so that it fell; it turned upside down, and the tent collapsed." 14 And his comrade answered, "This is no other than the sword of Gideon son of Jō′ash, a man of Israel; into his hand God has given Mid′i·an and all the army."

15 When Gideon heard the telling of the dream and its interpretation, he worshiped; and he returned to the camp of Israel, and said, "Get up; for the LORD has given the army of Mid′i·an into your hand." 16 After he divided the three hundred men into three companies, and put trumpets into the hands of all of them, and empty jars, with torches inside the jars, 17 he said to them, "Look at me, and do the same; when I come to the outskirts of the camp, do as I do. 18 When I blow the trumpet, I and all who are with me, then you also blow the trumpets around the whole camp, and shout, 'For the LORD and for Gideon!' "

19 So Gideon and the hundred who were with him came to the outskirts of the camp at the beginning of the middle watch, when they had just

---

u Heb *from*   *v* Cn: Heb *home, and depart from Mount Gilead'* "   *w* Heb places the words *putting their hands to their mouths* after the word *lapped* in verse 6   *x* Cn: Heb *So the people took provisions in their hands*

J
U
D
G

set the watch; and they blew the trumpets and smashed the jars that were in their hands. 20 So the three companies blew the trumpets and broke the jars, holding in their left hands the torches, and in their right hands the trumpets to blow; and they cried, "A sword for the LORD and for Gideon!" 21 Every man stood in his place all around the camp, and all the men in camp ran; they cried out and fled. 22 When they blew the three hundred trumpets, the LORD set every man's sword against his fellow and against all the army; and the army fled as far as Beth-shit'tah toward Zer'e•rah,ʸ as far as the border of Ā'bel-me•hō'lah, by Tab'bath. 23 And the men of Israel were called out from Naph'ta•lī and from Ash'er and from all Ma•nas'seh, and they pursued after the Mid'i•an•ītes.

24 Then Gideon sent messengers throughout all the hill country of Ē'phra•im, saying, "Come down against the Mid'i•an•ītes and seize the waters against them, as far as Beth-bar'ah, and also the Jordan." So all the men of Ē'phra•im were called out, and they seized the waters as far as Beth-bar'ah, and also the Jordan. 25 They captured the two captains of Mid'i•an, Or'eb and Zē'eb; they killed Or'eb at the rock of Or'eb, and Zē'eb they killed at the wine press of Zē'eb, as they pursued the Mid'i•an•ītes. They brought the heads of Or'eb and Zē'eb to Gideon beyond the Jordan.

Gideon's Triumph and Vengeance

Then the Ē'phra•im•ītes said to him, "What have you done to us, not to call us when you went to fight against the Mid'i•an•ītes?" And they upbraided him violently. 2 So he said to them, "What have I done now in comparison with you? Is not the gleaning of the grapes of Ē'phra•im better than the vintage of Ā•bi•ē'zer? 3 God has given into your hands the captains of Mid'i•an, Or'eb and Zē'eb; what have I been able to do in comparison with you?" When he said this, their anger against him subsided.

4 Then Gideon came to the Jordan and crossed over, he and the three hundred who were with him, exhausted and famished.ᶻ 5 So he said to the people of Suc'coth, "Please give some loaves of bread to my followers, for they are exhausted, and I am pursuing Zē'bah and Zal•mun'na, the kings of Mid'i•an." 6 But the officials of Suc'coth said, "Do you already have in your possession the hands of Zē'bah and Zal•mun'na, that we should give bread to your army?" 7 Gideon replied, "Well then, when the LORD has given Zē'bah and Zal•mun'na into my hand, I will trample your flesh on the thorns of the wilderness and on briers." 8 From there he went up to Pe•nū'el, and made the same request of them; and the people of Pe•nū'el answered him as

the people of Suc'coth had answered. 9 So he said to the people of Pe•nū'el, "When I come back victorious, I will break down this tower."

10 Now Zē'bah and Zal•mun'na were in Kar'kor with their army, about fifteen thousand men, all who were left of all the army of the people of the east; for one hundred twenty thousand men bearing arms had fallen. 11 So Gideon went up by the caravan route east of Nō'bah and Jog'be•hah, and attacked the army; for the army was off its guard. 12 Zē'bah and Zal•mun'na fled; and he pursued them and took the two kings of Mid'i•an, Zē'bah and Zal•mun'na, and threw all the army into a panic.

13 When Gideon son of Jō'ash returned from the battle by the ascent of Heres, 14 he caught a young man, one of the people of Suc'coth, and questioned him; and he listed for him the officials and elders of Suc'coth, seventy-seven people. 15 Then he came to the people of Suc'coth, and said, "Here are Zē'bah and Zal•mun'na, about whom you taunted me, saying, 'Do you already have in your possession the hands of Zē'bah and Zal•mun'na, that we should give bread to your troops who are exhausted?' " 16 So he took the elders of the city and he took thorns of the wilderness and briers and with them he trampledᵃ the people of Suc'coth. 17 He also broke down the tower of Pe•nū'el, and killed the men of the city.

18 Then he said to Zē'bah and Zal•mun'na, "What about the men whom you killed at Tā'bor?" They answered, "As you are, so were they, every one of them; they resembled the sons of a king." 19 And he replied, "They were my brothers, the sons of my mother; as the LORD lives, if you had saved them alive, I would not kill you." 20 So he said to Jē'ther his firstborn, "Go kill them!" But the boy did not draw his sword, for he was afraid, because he was still a boy. 21 Then Zē'bah and Zal•mun'na said, "You come and kill us; for as the man is, so is his strength." So Gideon proceeded to kill Zē'bah and Zal•mun'na; and he took the crescents that were on the necks of their camels.

Gideon's Idolatry

22 Then the Israelites said to Gideon, "Rule over us, you and your son and your grandson also; for you have delivered us out of the hand of Mid'i•an." 23 Gideon said to them, "I will not rule over you, and my son will not rule over you; the LORD will rule over you." 24 Then Gideon said to them, "Let me make a request of you; each of you give me an earring he has taken as booty." (For the en-

---

ʸ Another reading is *Zeredah*   ᶻ Gk: Heb *pursuing*
ᵃ With verse 7, Compare Gk: Heb *he taught*

emy[b] had golden earrings, because they were Ish'·ma·el·ites.) 25 "We will willingly give them," they answered. So they spread a garment, and each threw into it an earring he had taken as booty. 26 The weight of the golden earrings that he requested was one thousand seven hundred shekels of gold (apart from the crescents and the pendants and the purple garments worn by the kings of Mid'i·an, and the collars that were on the necks of their camels). 27 Gideon made an ephod of it and put it in his town, in Oph'rah; and all Israel prostituted themselves to it there, and it became a snare to Gideon and to his family. 28 So Mid'i·an was subdued before the Israelites, and they lifted up their heads no more. So the land had rest forty years in the days of Gideon.

Death of Gideon

29 Jer·ub·ba'al son of Jo'ash went to live in his own house. 30 Now Gideon had seventy sons, his own offspring, for he had many wives. 31 His concubine who was in She'chem also bore him a son, and he named him A·bim'e·lech. 32 Then Gideon son of Jo'ash died at a good old age, and was buried in the tomb of his father Jo'ash at Oph'rah of the Ā·bi·ez'rītes.

33 As soon as Gideon died, the Israelites relapsed and prostituted themselves with the Bā'als, making Bā'al-be'rith their god. 34 The Israelites did not remember the LORD their God, who had rescued them from the hand of all their enemies on every side; 35 and they did not exhibit loyalty to the house of Jer·ub·ba'al (that is, Gideon) in return for all the good that he had done to Israel.

Abimelech Attempts to Establish a Monarchy

Now A·bim'e·lech son of Jer·ub·ba'al went to She'chem to his mother's kinsfolk and said to them and to the whole clan of his mother's family, 2 "Say in the hearing of all the lords of She'chem, 'Which is better for you, that all seventy of the sons of Jer·ub·ba'al rule over you, or that one rule over you?' Remember also that I am your bone and your flesh." 3 So his mother's kinsfolk spoke all these words on his behalf in the hearing of all the lords of She'chem; and their hearts inclined to follow A·bim'e·lech, for they said, "He is our brother." 4 They gave him seventy pieces of silver out of the temple of Bā'al-be'rith with which A·bim'e·lech hired worthless and reckless fellows, who followed him. 5 He went to his father's house at Oph'rah, and killed his brothers the sons of Jer·ub·ba'al, seventy men, on one stone; but Jo'tham, the youngest son of Jer·ub·ba'al, survived, for he hid himself. 6 Then all the lords of She'chem and all Beth-mil'lo came together, and they went and made A·bim'e·lech king, by the oak of the pillar[c] at She'chem.

The Parable of the Trees

7 When it was told to Jo'tham, he went and stood on the top of Mount Ger'i·zim, and cried aloud and said to them, "Listen to me, you lords of She'chem, so that God may listen to you.

PRAY IT!
The Fable of the Trees

Such stupid violence. The would-be king Abimelech kills his seventy brothers and assumes the role of king. But his youngest brother, Jotham, survives and prophesies against him using a fable about trees. Jotham tries to tell the Israelites that replacing God's leadership with a king will only bring them trouble. Like the bramble in the fable, an abusive leader will have nothing to offer but trouble and pain.

What qualities do good leaders demonstrate? What qualities bring trouble and pain? How do leaders show humility and trust in God?

God, send your spirit to the hearts of the world's leaders so that they are inspired to make wise choices. Help them to be sources of love and justice and not sources of trouble and pain. Amen.

▸ **Judg 9.7–15**

8   The trees once went out
        to anoint a king over themselves.
    So they said to the olive tree,
        'Reign over us.'
9   The olive tree answered them,
        'Shall I stop producing my rich oil
            by which gods and mortals are
                honored,
            and go to sway over the trees?'
10 Then the trees said to the fig tree,
        'You come and reign over us.'
11 But the fig tree answered them,
        'Shall I stop producing my sweetness
            and my delicious fruit,
            and go to sway over the trees?'

---

[b] Heb *they*   [c] Cn: Meaning of Heb uncertain

JUDG

12 Then the trees said to the vine,
   'You come and reign over us.'
13 But the vine said to them,
   'Shall I stop producing my wine
     that cheers gods and mortals,
     and go to sway over the trees?'
14 So all the trees said to the bramble,
   'You come and reign over us.'
15 And the bramble said to the trees,
   'If in good faith you are anointing me
     king over you,
   then come and take refuge in my
     shade;
   but if not, let fire come out of the
     bramble
   and devour the cedars of Lebanon.'

16 "Now therefore, if you acted in good faith and honor when you made A•bim′e•lech king, and if you have dealt well with Jer•ub•ba′al and his house, and have done to him as his actions deserved— 17 for my father fought for you, and risked his life, and rescued you from the hand of Mid′i•an; 18 but you have risen up against my father's house this day, and have killed his sons, seventy men on one stone, and have made A•bim′e•lech, the son of his slave woman, king over the lords of She′chem, because he is your kinsman— 19 if, I say, you have acted in good faith and honor with Jer•ub•ba′al and with his house this day, then rejoice in A•bim′e•lech, and let him also rejoice in you; 20 but if not, let fire come out from A•bim′e•lech, and devour the lords of She′chem, and Beth-mil′lo; and let fire come out from the lords of She′chem, and from Beth-mil′lo, and devour A•bim′e•lech." 21 Then Jo′tham ran away and fled, going to Be′er, where he remained for fear of his brother A•bim′e•lech.

The Downfall of Abimelech

22 A•bim′e•lech ruled over Israel three years. 23 But God sent an evil spirit between A•bim′e•lech and the lords of She′chem; and the lords of She′chem dealt treacherously with A•bim′e•lech. 24 This happened so that the violence done to the seventy sons of Jer•ub•ba′al might be avenged[d] and their blood be laid on their brother A•bim′e•lech, who killed them, and on the lords of She′chem, who strengthened his hands to kill his brothers. 25 So, out of hostility to him, the lords of She′chem set ambushes on the mountain tops. They robbed all who passed by them along that way; and it was reported to A•bim′e•lech.

26 When Ga′al son of E′bed moved into She′chem with his kinsfolk, the lords of She′chem put confidence in him. 27 They went out into the field and gathered the grapes from their vineyards, trod them, and celebrated. Then they went into the temple of their god, ate and drank, and ridiculed A•bim′e•lech. 28 Ga′al son of E′bed said, "Who is A•bim′e•lech, and who are we of She′chem, that we should serve him? Did not the son of Jer•ub•ba′al and Ze′bul his officer serve the men of Ha′mor father of She′chem? Why then should we serve him? 29 If only this people were under my command! Then I would remove A•bim′e•lech; I would say[e] to him, 'Increase your army, and come out.' "

30 When Ze′bul the ruler of the city heard the words of Ga′al son of E′bed, his anger was kindled. 31 He sent messengers to A•bim′e•lech at A•ru′mah,[f] saying, "Look, Ga′al son of E′bed and his kinsfolk have come to She′chem, and they are stirring up[g] the city against you. 32 Now therefore, go by night, you and the troops that are with you, and lie in wait in the fields. 33 Then early in the morning, as soon as the sun rises, get up and rush on the city; and when he and the troops that are with him come out against you, you may deal with them as best you can."

34 So A•bim′e•lech and all the troops with him got up by night and lay in wait against She′chem in four companies. 35 When Ga′al son of E′bed went out and stood in the entrance of the gate of the city, A•bim′e•lech and the troops with him rose from the ambush. 36 And when Ga′al saw them, he said to Ze′bul, "Look, people are coming down from the mountain tops!" And Ze′bul said to him, "The shadows on the mountains look like people to you." 37 Ga′al spoke again and said, "Look, people are coming down from Tab•bur′-e′rez, and one company is coming from the direction of E′lon-me•on′e•nim."[h] 38 Then Ze′bul said to him, "Where is your boast[i] now, you who said, 'Who is A•bim′-e•lech, that we should serve him?' Are not these the troops you made light of? Go out now and fight with them." 39 So Ga′al went out at the head of the lords of She′chem, and fought with A•bim′e•lech. 40 A•bim′e•lech chased him, and he fled before him. Many fell wounded, up to the entrance of the gate. 41 So A•bim′e•lech resided at A•ru′mah; and Ze′bul drove out Ga′al and his kinsfolk, so that they could not live on at She′chem.

42 On the following day the people went out into the fields. When A•bim′e•lech was told, 43 he took his troops and divided them into three companies, and lay in wait in the fields. When he looked and saw the people coming out of the city, he rose against them and killed them. 44 A•bim′e•lech and the company that was[j] with him rushed

---

d Heb might come   e Gk: Heb and he said   f Cn See 9.41. Heb Tormah   g Cn: Heb are besieging   h That is Diviners' Oak   i Heb mouth   j Vg and some Gk Mss: Heb companies that were

forward and stood at the entrance of the gate of the city, while the two companies rushed on all who were in the fields and killed them. 45 A·bim′e·lech fought against the city all that day; he took the city, and killed the people that were in it; and he razed the city and sowed it with salt.

46 When all the lords of the Tower of Shĕ′-chem heard of it, they entered the stronghold of the temple of El-bĕ′rith. 47 A·bim′e·lech was told that all the lords of the Tower of Shĕ′chem were gathered together. 48 So A·bim′e·lech went up to Mount Zal′mon, he and all the troops that were with him. A·bim′e·lech took an ax in his hand, cut down a bundle of brushwood, and took it up and laid it on his shoulder. Then he said to the troops with him, "What you have seen me do, do quickly, as I have done." 49 So every one of the troops cut down a bundle and following A·bim′e-lech put it against the stronghold, and they set the stronghold on fire over them, so that all the people of the Tower of Shĕ′chem also died, about a thousand men and women.

50 Then A·bim′e·lech went to Thĕ′bez, and encamped against Thĕ′bez, and took it. 51 But there was a strong tower within the city, and all the men and women and all the lords of the city fled to it and shut themselves in; and they went to the roof of the tower. 52 A·bim′e·lech came to the tower, and fought against it, and came near to the entrance of the tower to burn it with fire. 53 But a certain woman threw an upper millstone on A·bim′e·lech's head, and crushed his skull. 54 Immediately he called to the young man who carried his armor and said to him, "Draw your sword and kill me, so people will not say about me, 'A woman killed him.' " So the young man thrust him through, and he died. 55 When the Israelites saw that A·bim′e·lech was dead, they all went home. 56 Thus God repaid A·bim′e·lech for the crime he committed against his father in killing his seventy brothers; 57 and God also made all the wickedness of the people of Shĕ′chem fall back on their heads, and on them came the curse of Jŏ′tham son of Jer·ub·bā′al.

Tola and Jair

After A·bim′e·lech, Tō′la son of Pū′ah son of Dō′dō, a man of Is′sa·char, who lived at Shā′mir in the hill country of Ē′phra·im, rose to deliver Israel. 2 He judged Israel twenty-three years. Then he died, and was buried at Shā′mir.

3 After him came Jā′ir the Gil′e·ad·īte, who judged Israel twenty-two years. 4 He had thirty sons who rode on thirty donkeys; and they had thirty towns, which are in the land of Gil′e·ad, and

are called Hav′voth-jā′ir to this day. 5 Jā′ir died, and was buried in Kā′mon.

Oppression by the Ammonites

6 The Israelites again did what was evil in the sight of the LORD, worshiping the Bā′als and the As·tar′tēs, the gods of Ar′am, the gods of Sī′don, the gods of Mō′ab, the gods of the Am′mon·ītes, and the gods of the Phi·lis′tines. Thus they abandoned the LORD, and did not worship him. 7 So the anger of the LORD was kindled against Israel, and he sold them into the hand of the Phi·lis′tines and into the hand of the Am′mon·ītes, 8 and they crushed and oppressed the Israelites that year. For eighteen years they oppressed all the Israelites that were beyond the Jordan in the land of the Am′orītes, which is in Gil′e·ad. 9 The Am′mon·ītes also crossed the Jordan to fight against Judah and

PRAY IT!
The Effects of Sin

Once again, the Israelites lapse into sin and worship other gods (Judg 10.6). Once again, they cry out to God to save them (verse 10). Did they think their sins would have no effect on their lives?

Listen to these words from Pope John Paul II:

There is no sin, not even the most intimate and secret one, the most strictly individual one, that exclusively concerns the person committing it. With greater or lesser violence, with greater or lesser harm, every sin has repercussions on the . . . whole human family.

Have you done anything today that brought harm to you or others? Have you used your gifts and talents as God intended them to be used? Have you neglected an opportunity to share God's love with another person?

Lord, you know all things. Look on me with love and hear my prayer. Forgive my sins and give me strength to turn away from the lure of sin. Help me to be more generous in serving you and my neighbor. Help me to be a true follower of your Son, Jesus. Amen.

▶ Judg 10.10–16

against Benjamin and against the house of É'phra·im; so that Israel was greatly distressed.

10 So the Israelites cried to the LORD, saying, "We have sinned against you, because we have abandoned our God and have worshiped the Bā'-als." 11 And the LORD said to the Israelites, "Did I not deliver you[k] from the Egyptians and from the Am'o·rītes, from the Am'mon·ītes and from the Phi·lis'tines? 12 The Sī·dō'ni·ans also, and the A·mal'-e·kītes, and the Mā'on·ītes, oppressed you; and you cried to me, and I delivered you out of their hand. 13 Yet you have abandoned me and worshiped other gods; therefore I will deliver you no more. 14 Go and cry to the gods whom you have chosen; let them deliver you in the time of your distress." 15 And the Israelites said to the LORD, "We have sinned; do to us whatever seems good to you; but deliver us this day!" 16 So they put away the foreign gods from among them and worshiped the LORD; and he could no longer bear to see Israel suffer.

17 Then the Am'mon·ītes were called to arms, and they encamped in Gil'e·ad; and the Israelites came together, and they encamped at Miz'pah. 18 The commanders of the people of Gil'e·ad said to one another, "Who will begin the fight against the Am'mon·ītes? He shall be head over all the inhabitants of Gil'e·ad."

Jephthah

Now Jeph'thah the Gil'e·ad·ite, the son of a prostitute, was a mighty warrior. Gil'e·ad was the father of Jeph'thah. 2 Gil'e·ad's wife also bore him sons; and when his wife's sons grew up, they drove Jeph'thah away, saying to him, "You shall not inherit anything in our father's house; for you are the son of another woman." 3 Then Jeph'thah fled from his brothers and lived in the land of Tob. Outlaws collected around Jeph'thah and went raiding with him.

4 After a time the Am'mon·ītes made war against Israel. 5 And when the Am'mon·ītes made war against Israel, the elders of Gil'e·ad went to bring Jeph'thah from the land of Tob. 6 They said to Jeph'thah, "Come and be our commander, so that we may fight with the Am'mon·ītes." 7 But Jeph'thah said to the elders of Gil'e·ad, "Are you not the very ones who rejected me and drove me out of my father's house? So why do you come to me now when you are in trouble?" 8 The elders of Gil'e·ad said to Jeph'thah, "Nevertheless, we have now turned back to you, so that you may go with us and fight with the Am'mon·ītes, and become head over us, over all the inhabitants of Gil'e·ad." 9 Jeph'thah said to the elders of Gil'e·ad, "If you bring me home again to fight with the Am'mon-̄tes, and the LORD gives them over to me, I will be

your head." 10 And the elders of Gil'e·ad said to Jeph'thah, "The LORD will be witness between us; we will surely do as you say." 11 So Jeph'thah went with the elders of Gil'e·ad, and the people made him head and commander over them; and Jeph'thah spoke all his words before the LORD at Miz'-pah.

12 Then Jeph'thah sent messengers to the king of the Am'mon·ītes and said, "What is there between you and me, that you have come to me to fight against my land?" 13 The king of the Am'mon-ītes answered the messengers of Jeph'thah, "Because Israel, on coming from Egypt, took away my land from the Ar'non to the Jab'bok and to the Jordan; now therefore restore it peaceably." 14 Once again Jeph'thah sent messengers to the king of the Am'mon·ītes 15 and said to him: "Thus says Jeph'-thah: Israel did not take away the land of Mō'ab or the land of the Am'mon·ītes, 16 but when they came up from Egypt, Israel went through the wilderness to the Red Sea[l] and came to Kā'desh. 17 Israel then sent messengers to the king of É'dom, saying, 'Let us pass through your land'; but the king of É'dom would not listen. They also sent to the king of Mō'ab, but he would not consent. So Israel remained at Kā'desh. 18 Then they journeyed through the wilderness, went around the land of É'dom and the land of Mō'ab, arrived on the east side of the land of Mō'ab, and camped on the other side of the Ar'non. They did not enter the territory of Mō'ab, for the Ar'non was the boundary of Mō'ab. 19 Israel then sent messengers to King Sī'hon of the Am'o·rītes, king of Hesh'bon; and Israel said to him, 'Let us pass through your land to our country.' 20 But Sī'hon did not trust Israel to pass through his territory; so Sī'hon gathered all his people together, and encamped at Jā'-haz, and fought with Israel. 21 Then the LORD, the God of Israel, gave Sī'hon and all his people into the hand of Israel, and they defeated them; so Israel occupied all the land of the Am'o·rītes, who inhabited that country. 22 They occupied all the territory of the Am'o·rītes from the Ar'non to the Jab'bok and from the wilderness to the Jordan. 23 So now the LORD, the God of Israel, has conquered the Am'o·rītes for the benefit of his people Israel. Do you intend to take their place? 24 Should you not possess what your god Chē'mosh gives you to possess? And should we not be the ones to possess everything that the LORD our God has conquered for our benefit? 25 Now are you any better than King Bā'lak son of Zip'por of Mō'ab? Did he ever enter into conflict with Israel, or did he ever go to war with them? 26 While Israel lived in

---

[k] Heb lacks *Did I not deliver you*   [l] Or *Sea of Reeds*

Hesh'bon and its villages, and in A•rō'er and its villages, and in all the towns that are along the Ar'non, three hundred years, why did you not recover them within that time? [27] It is not I who have sinned against you, but you are the one who does me wrong by making war on me. Let the LORD, who is judge, decide today for the Israelites or for the Am'mon•ites." [28] But the king of the Am'mon•ites did not heed the message that Jeph'thah sent him.

Jephthah's Vow

29 Then the spirit of the LORD came upon Jeph'thah, and he passed through Gil'e•ad and Ma•nas'seh. He passed on to Miz'pah of Gil'e•ad, and from Miz'pah of Gil'e•ad he passed on to the Am'mon•ites. [30] And Jeph'thah made a vow to the LORD, and said, "If you will give the Am'mon•ites into my hand, [31] then whoever comes out of the doors of my house to meet me, when I return victorious from the Am'mon•ites, shall be the LORD's, to be offered up by me as a burnt offering." [32] So Jeph'thah crossed over to the Am'mon•ites to fight against them; and the LORD gave them into his hand. [33] He inflicted a massive defeat on them from A•rō'er to the neighborhood of Min'nith, twenty towns, and as far as Ā'bel-ker'a•mim. So the Am'mon•ites were subdued before the people of Israel.

Jephthah's Daughter

34 Then Jeph'thah came to his home at Miz'pah; and there was his daughter coming out to meet him with timbrels and with dancing. She was his only child; he had no son or daughter except her. [35] When he saw her, he tore his clothes, and said, "Alas, my daughter! You have brought me very low; you have become the cause of great trouble to me. For I have opened my mouth to the LORD, and I cannot take back my vow." [36] She said to him, "My father, if you have opened your mouth to the LORD, do to me according to what has gone out of your mouth, now that the LORD has given you vengeance against your enemies, the Am'mon•ites." [37] And she said to her father, "Let this thing be done for me: Grant me two months, so that I may go and wander[m] on the mountains, and bewail my virginity, my companions and I." [38] "Go," he said and sent her away for two months. So she departed, she and her companions, and bewailed her virginity on the mountains. [39] At the end of two months, she returned to her father, who did with her according to the vow he had made. She had never slept with a man. So there arose an Israelite custom that [40] for four days every year the daughters of Israel would go out to lament the daughter of Jeph'thah the Gil'e•ad•ite.

Intertribal Dissension

The men of Ē'phra•im were called to arms, and they crossed to Zā'phon and said to Jeph'thah, "Why did you cross over to fight against the Am'mon•ites, and did not call us to go with you? We will burn your house down over you!" [2] Jeph'thah said to them, "My people and I were engaged in conflict with the Am'mon•ites who oppressed us[n] severely. But when I called you, you did not deliver me from their hand. [3] When I saw that you would not deliver me, I took my life in my hand, and crossed over against the Am'mon•ites, and the LORD gave them into my hand. Why then have you come up to me this day, to fight against me?" [4] Then Jeph'thah gathered all the men of Gil'e•ad and fought with Ē'phra•im; and the men of Gil'e•ad defeated Ē'phra•im, because they said, "You are fugitives from Ē'phra•im, you Gil'e•ad•ites—in the heart of Ē'phra•im and Ma•nas'seh.[o] [5] Then the Gil'e•ad•ites took the fords of the Jordan against the Ē'phra•im•ites. Whenever one of the fugitives of Ē'phra•im said, "Let me go over," the men of Gil'e•ad would say to him, "Are you an Ē'phra•im•ite?" When he said, "No," [6] they said to him, "Then say Shib'bo•leth," and he said, "Sib'bo•leth," for he could not pronounce it right. Then they seized him and killed him at the fords of the Jordan. Forty-two thousand of the Ē'phra•im•ites fell at that time.

7 Jeph'thah judged Israel six years. Then Jeph'thah the Gil'e•ad•ite died, and was buried in his town in Gil'e•ad.[p]

Ibzan, Elon, and Abdon

8 After him Ib'zan of Bethlehem judged Israel. [9] He had thirty sons. He gave his thirty daughters in marriage outside his clan and brought in thirty young women from outside for his sons. He judged Israel seven years. [10] Then Ib'zan died, and was buried at Bethlehem.

11 After him Ē'lon the Zeb'ū•lun•ite judged Israel; and he judged Israel ten years. [12] Then Ē'lon the Zeb'ū•lun•ite died, and was buried at Aī'ja•lon in the land of Zeb'ū•lun.

13 After him Ab'don son of Hil'lel the Pir'a•thon•īte judged Israel. [14] He had forty sons and thirty grandsons, who rode on seventy donkeys; he judged Israel eight years. [15] Then Ab'don son of Hil'lel the Pir'a•thon•īte died, and was buried at

---

m Cn: Heb go down   n Gk OL, Syr H: Heb l⁻ oppressed us   o Meaning of Heb uncertain: (because . . . Manasseh   p Gk: Heb in the town.

Pir'a•thon in the land of Ē'phra•im, in the hill country of the A•mal'e•kītes.

The Birth of Samson
(Cp Num 6.1–21)

The Israelites again did what was evil in the sight of the LORD, and the LORD gave them into the hand of the Phi•lis'tines forty years. 2 There was a certain man of Zō'rah, of the tribe of the Dan'ītes, whose name was Ma•nō'ah. His wife was barren, having borne no children. 3 And the angel of the LORD appeared to the woman and said to her, "Although you are barren, having borne no children, you shall conceive and bear a son. 4 Now be careful not to drink wine or strong drink, or to eat anything unclean, 5 for you shall conceive and bear a son. No razor is to come on his head, for the boy shall be a nazirite^q to God

again to the woman as she sat in the field; but her husband Ma•nō'ah was not with her. 10 So the woman ran quickly and told her husband, "The man who came to me the other day has appeared to me." 11 Ma•nō'ah got up and followed his wife, and came to the man and said to him, "Are you the man who spoke to this woman?" And he said, "I am." 12 Then Ma•nō'ah said, "Now when your words come true, what is to be the boy's rule of life; what is he to do?" 13 The angel of the LORD said to Ma•nō'ah, "Let the woman give heed to all that I said to her. 14 She may not eat of anything that comes from the vine. She is not to drink wine or strong drink, or eat any unclean thing. She is to observe everything that I commanded her."

15 Ma•nō'ah said to the angel of the LORD, "Allow us to detain you, and prepare a kid for you." 16 The angel of the LORD said to Ma•nō'ah, "If you

Introducing ▶ SAMSON

The story of Samson in Judges, chapters 13–16, is one of the most well known in the Bible. Most of us know Samson for his great feats of strength, such as killing a lion bare-handed and slaying a thousand men with the jawbone of a donkey. But did you also know that Samson's birth was announced by an angel and that the Book of Judges says "the spirit of the LORD rushed on him" more often for Samson than for any other judge? Samson was a nazirite as well as a judge. Nazirites took vows to abstain from alcohol, avoid contact with dead bodies, and refrain from cutting their hair.

Like many of the other judges, Samson was a flawed hero. He broke all his nazirite vows, was controlled by lust, and used his great strength for personal revenge. Despite these flaws, God chose to use Samson. Samson paid for his sins, but ultimately, his tragic death brought victory over the Philistines. Once again, God's purposes were accomplished, even through a flawed and sinful human being.

from birth. It is he who shall begin to deliver Israel from the hand of the Phi•lis'tines." 6 Then the woman came and told her husband, "A man of God came to me, and his appearance was like that of an angel^r of God, most awe-inspiring; I did not ask him where he came from, and he did not tell me his name; 7 but he said to me, 'You shall conceive and bear a son. So then drink no wine or strong drink, and eat nothing unclean, for the boy shall be a nazirite^q to God from birth to the day of his death.'" 8 Then Ma•nō'ah entreated the LORD, and said, "O LORD, I pray, let the man of God whom you sent come to us again and teach us what we are to do concerning the boy who will be born." 9 God 'istened to Ma•nō'ah, and the angel of God came

detain me, I will not eat your food; but if you want to prepare a burnt offering, then offer it to the LORD." (For Ma•nō'ah did not know that he was the angel of the LORD.) 17 Then Ma•nō'ah said to the angel of the LORD, "What is your name, so that we may honor you when your words come true?" 18 But the angel of the LORD said to him, "Why do you ask my name? It is too wonderful." 19 So Ma•nō'ah took the kid with the grain offering, and offered it on the rock to the LORD, to him who works^s wonders.^{t} 20 When the flame went up toward heaven from the altar, the angel of the LORD ascended in the flame of the altar while

---

^{q} That is *one separated* or *one consecrated* ^{r} Or *the angel*
^{s} Gk Vg: Heb *and working* ^{t} Heb *wonders, while Manoah and his wife looked on*

Ma•nō′ah and his wife looked on; and they fell on their faces to the ground. 21 The angel of the Lord did not appear again to Ma•nō′ah and his wife. Then Ma•nō′ah realized that it was the angel of the Lord. 22 And Ma•nō′ah said to his wife, "We shall surely die, for we have seen God." 23 But his wife said to him, "If the Lord had meant to kill us, he would not have accepted a burnt offering and a grain offering at our hands, or shown us all these things, or now announced to us such things as these."

24 The woman bore a son, and named him Samson. The boy grew, and the Lord blessed him. 25 The spirit of the Lord began to stir him in Mā′-ha•neh-dan, between Zō′rah and Esh′tā•ol.

Samson's Marriage

Once Samson went down to Tim′nah, and at Tim′nah he saw a Phi•lis′tine woman. 2 Then he came up, and told his father and mother, "I saw a Phi•lis′tine woman at Tim′nah; now get her for me as my wife." 3 But his father and mother said to him, "Is there not a woman among your kin, or among all our^u people, that you must go to take a wife from the uncircumcised Phi•lis′tines?" But Samson said to his father, "Get her for me, because she pleases me." 4 His father and mother did not know that this was from the Lord; for he was seeking a pretext to act against the Phi•lis′tines. At that time the Phi•lis′tines had dominion over Israel.

5 Then Samson went down with his father and mother to Tim′nah. When he came to the vineyards of Tim′nah, suddenly a young lion roared at him. 6 The spirit of the Lord rushed on him, and he tore the lion apart barehanded as one might tear apart a kid. But he did not tell his father or his mother what he had done. 7 Then he went down and talked with the woman, and she pleased Samson. 8 After a while he returned to marry her, and he turned aside to see the carcass of the lion, and there was a swarm of bees in the body of the lion, and honey. 9 He scraped it out into his hands, and went on, eating as he went. When he came to his father and mother, he gave some to them, and they ate it. But he did not tell them that he had taken the honey from the carcass of the lion.

10 His father went down to the woman, and Samson made a feast there as the young men were accustomed to do. 11 When the people saw him, they brought thirty companions to be with him. 12 Samson said to them, "Let me now put a riddle to you. If you can explain it to me within the seven days of the feast, and find it out, then I will give you thirty linen garments and thirty festal gar-

ments. 13 But if you cannot explain it to me, then you shall give me thirty linen garments and thirty festal garments." So they said to him, "Ask your riddle; let us hear it." 14 He said to them,

"Out of the eater came something to eat.

Out of the strong came something sweet."

But for three days they could not explain the riddle.

15 On the fourth^v day they said to Samson's wife, "Coax your husband to explain the riddle to us, or we will burn you and your father's house with fire. Have you invited us here to impoverish us?" 16 So Samson's wife wept before him, saying, "You hate me; you do not really love me. You have asked a riddle of my people, but you have not explained it to me." He said to her, "Look, I have not told my father or my mother. Why should I tell you?" 17 She wept before him the seven days that their feast lasted; and because she nagged him, on the seventh day he told her. Then she explained the riddle to her people. 18 The men of the town said to him on the seventh day before the sun went down,

"What is sweeter than honey?

What is stronger than a lion?"

And he said to them,

"If you had not plowed with my heifer,

you would not have found out my riddle."

19 Then the spirit of the Lord rushed on him, and he went down to Ash′ke•lon. He killed thirty men of the town, took their spoil, and gave the festal garments to those who had explained the riddle. In hot anger he went back to his father's house. 20 And Samson's wife was given to his companion, who had been his best man.

Samson Defeats the Philistines

After a while, at the time of the wheat harvest, Samson went to visit his wife, bringing along a kid. He said, "I want to go into my wife's room." But her father would not allow him to go in. 2 Her father said, "I was sure that you had rejected her; so I gave her to your companion. Is not her younger sister prettier than she? Why not take her instead?" 3 Samson said to them, "This time, when I do mischief to the Phi•lis′tines, I will be without blame." 4 So Samson went and caught three hundred foxes, and took some torches; and he turned the foxes^w tail to tail, and put a torch between each pair of tails. 5 When he had set fire to the torches, he let the foxes go into the standing grain of the

---

^{u} Cn: Heb *my* ^{v} Gk Syr: Heb *seventh* ^{w} He

Phi·lis'tines, and burned up the shocks and the standing grain, as well as the vineyards and[x] olive groves. 6 Then the Phi·lis'tines asked, "Who has done this?" And they said, "Samson, the son-in-law of the Tim'nīte, because he has taken Samson's wife and given her to his companion." So the Phi·lis'tines came up, and burned her and her father. 7 Samson said to them, "If this is what you do, I swear I will not stop until I have taken revenge on you." 8 He struck them down hip and thigh with great slaughter; and he went down and stayed in the cleft of the rock of Ē'tam.

9 Then the Phi·lis'tines came up and encamped in Judah, and made a raid on Lē'hī. 10 The men of Judah said, "Why have you come up against us?" They said, "We have come up to bind Samson, to do to him as he did to us." 11 Then three thousand men of Judah went down to the cleft of the rock of Ē'tam, and they said to Samson, "Do you not know that the Phi·lis'tines are rulers over us? What then have you done to us?" He replied, "As they did to me, so I have done to them." 12 They said to him, "We have come down to bind you, so that we may give you into the hands of the Phi·lis'tines." Samson answered them, "Swear to me that you yourselves will not attack me." 13 They said to him, "No, we will only bind you and give you into their hands; we will not kill you." So they bound him with two new ropes, and brought him up from the rock.

14 When he came to Lē'hī, the Phi·lis'tines came shouting to meet him; and the spirit of the LORD rushed on him, and the ropes that were on his arms became like flax that has caught fire, and his bonds melted off his hands. 15 Then he found a fresh jawbone of a donkey, reached down and took it, and with it he killed a thousand men. 16 And Samson said,

"With the jawbone of a donkey,
    heaps upon heaps,
 with the jawbone of a donkey
    I have slain a thousand men."

17 When he had finished speaking, he threw away the jawbone; and that place was called Rā'math-lē'hī.[y]

18 By then he was very thirsty, and he called on the LORD, saying, "You have granted this great victory by the hand of your servant. Am I now to die of thirst, and fall into the hands of the uncircumcised?" 19 So God split open the hollow place that is at Lē'hī, and water came from it. When he drank, his spirit returned, and he revived. Therefore it was named En-hak·kor'ē,[z] which is at Lē'hī to this day. 20 And he judged Israel in the days of the Phi·lis'tines twenty years.

Samson and Delilah

16 Once Samson went to Gā'za, where he saw a prostitute and went in to her. 2 The Gā'zītes were told,[a] "Samson has come here." So they circled around and lay in wait for him all night at the city gate. They kept quiet all night, thinking, "Let us wait until the light of the morning; then we will kill him." 3 But Samson lay only until midnight. Then at midnight he rose up, took hold of the doors of the city gate and the two posts, pulled them up, bar and all, put them on his shoulders, and carried them to the top of the hill that is in front of Hē'bron.

4 After this he fell in love with a woman in the valley of Sō'rek, whose name was Dē·lī'lah. 5 The lords of the Phi·lis'tines came to her and said to her, "Coax him, and find out what makes his strength so great, and how we may overpower him, so that we may bind him in order to subdue him; and we will each give you eleven hundred pieces of silver." 6 So Dē·lī'lah said to Samson, "Please tell me what makes your strength so great, and how you could be bound, so that one could subdue you." 7 Samson said to her, "If they bind me with seven fresh bowstrings that are not dried out, then I shall become weak, and be like anyone else." 8 Then the lords of the Phi·lis'tines brought her seven fresh bowstrings that had not dried out, and she bound him with them. 9 While men were lying in wait in an inner chamber, she said to him, "The Phi·lis'tines are upon you, Samson!" But he snapped the bowstrings, as a strand of fiber snaps when it touches the fire. So the secret of his strength was not known.

10 Then Dē·lī'lah said to Samson, "You have mocked me and told me lies; please tell me how you could be bound." 11 He said to her, "If they bind me with new ropes that have not been used, then I shall become weak, and be like anyone else." 12 So Dē·lī'lah took new ropes and bound him with them, and said to him, "The Phi·lis'tines are upon you, Samson!" (The men lying in wait were in an inner chamber.) But he snapped the ropes off his arms like a thread.

13 Then Dē·lī'lah said to Samson, "Until now you have mocked me and told me lies; tell me how you could be bound." He said to her, "If you weave the seven locks of my head with the web and make it tight with the pin, then I shall become weak, and be like anyone else." 14 So while he slept, Dē·lī'lah took the seven locks of his head and wove

---

x Gk Tg Vg: Heb lacks *and*   y That is *The Hill of the Jawbone*
z That is *The Spring of the One who Called*
a Gk: Heb lacks *were told*

them into the web,[b] and made them tight with the pin. Then she said to him, "The Phi·lis'tines are upon you, Samson!" But he awoke from his sleep, and pulled away the pin, the loom, and the web.

15 Then she said to him, "How can you say, 'I love you,' when your heart is not with me? You have mocked me three times now and have not told me what makes your strength so great." 16 Finally, after she had nagged him with her words day after day, and pestered him, he was tired to death. 17 So he told her his whole secret, and said to her, "A razor has never come upon my head; for I have been a nazirite[c] to God from my mother's womb. If my head were shaved, then my strength would leave me; I would become weak, and be like anyone else."

18 When De·li'lah realized that he had told her his whole secret, she sent and called the lords of the Phi·lis'tines, saying, "This time come up, for he has told his whole secret to me." Then the lords of the Phi·lis'tines came up to her, and brought the money in their hands. 19 She let him fall asleep on her lap; and she called a man, and had him shave off the seven locks of his head. He began to weaken,[d] and his strength left him. 20 Then she said, "The Phi·lis'tines are upon you, Samson!" When he awoke from his sleep, he thought, "I will go out as at other times, and shake myself free." But he did not know that the LORD had left him. 21 So the Phi·lis'tines seized him and gouged out his eyes. They brought him down to Ga'za and bound him with bronze shackles; and he ground at the mill in the prison. 22 But the hair of his head began to grow again after it had been shaved.

Samson's Death

23 Now the lords of the Phi·lis'tines gathered to offer a great sacrifice to their god Da'gon, and to rejoice; for they said, "Our god has given Samson our enemy into our hand." 24 When the people saw him, they praised their god; for they said, "Our god has given our enemy into our hand, the ravager of our country, who has killed many of us." 25 And when their hearts were merry, they said, "Call Samson, and let him entertain us." So they called Samson out of the prison, and he performed for them. They made him stand between the pillars; 26 and Samson said to the attendant who held him by the hand, "Let me feel the pillars on which the house rests, so that I may lean against them." 27 Now the house was full of men and women; all the lords of the Phi·lis'tines were there, and on the roof there were about three thousand men and women, who looked on while Samson performed.

28 Then Samson called to the LORD and said, "Lord GOD, remember me and strengthen me only this once, O God, so that with this one act of revenge I may pay back the Phi·lis'tines for my two eyes."[e] 29 And Samson grasped the two middle pillars on which the house rested, and he leaned his weight against them, his right hand on the one and his left hand on the other. 30 Then Samson said, "Let me die with the Phi·lis'tines." He strained with all his might; and the house fell on the lords

---

[b] Compare Gk: in verses 13-14, Heb lacks *and make it tight . . . into the web*   [c] That is *one separated* or *one consecrated*   [d] Gk: Heb *She began to torment him*   [e] Or *so that I may be avenged upon the Philistines for one of my two eyes*

Manipulation   LIVE IT!

You'd think that Samson would catch on, wouldn't you? Delilah tries to coax from Samson the secret of his strength. By the third attempt, it seems rather obvious that she wants to betray him to the Philistines. Nonetheless, Samson finally is pestered into revealing his secret, and Delilah uses the information to betray him.

Have you ever had a confidence betrayed? Have you ever trusted someone with a secret only to discover later that your secret is out? It makes it that much harder to trust again, to be open and to share yourself with another. When the person who betrays your confidence is someone you love, the betrayal is even more painful.

We need to do some soul-searching here. Ask yourself: Am I the kind of person who can be trusted with someone's secret? Have I ever betrayed a confidence?

It is easier than we like to think to be like Delilah—abusing the trust built up in a relationship and manipulating another person, even someone we care deeply about. We need to resolve to be people of integrity, who would never betray a confidence for personal gain.

▸ Judg 16.4–22

16.28–31

and all the people who were in it. So those he killed at his death were more than those he had killed during his life. ³¹ Then his brothers and all his family came down and took him and brought him up and buried him between Zō′rah and Esh′-tā•ol in the tomb of his father Ma•nō′ah. He had judged Israel twenty years.

Micah and the Levite

There was a man in the hill country of Ē′phra•im whose name was Mī′cah. ² He said to his mother, "The eleven hundred pieces of silver that were taken from you, about which you uttered a curse, and even spoke it in my hearing,—that silver is in my possession; I took it; but now I will return it to you."ᶠ And his mother said, "May my son be blessed by the LORD!" ³ Then he returned the eleven hundred pieces of silver to his mother; and his mother said, "I consecrate the silver to the LORD from my hand for my son, to make an idol of cast metal." ⁴ So when he returned the money to his mother, his mother took two hundred pieces of silver, and gave it to the silversmith, who made it into an idol of cast metal; and it was in the house of Mī′cah. ⁵ This man Mī′cah had a shrine, and he made an ephod and teraphim, and installed one of his sons, who became his priest. ⁶ In those days there was no king in Israel; all the people did what was right in their own eyes.

7 Now there was a young man of Bethlehem in Judah, of the clan of Judah. He was a Lē′vīte residing there. ⁸ This man left the town of Bethlehem in Judah, to live wherever he could find a place. He came to the house of Mī′cah in the hill country of Ē′phra•im to carry on his work.ᵍ ⁹ Mī′cah said to

him, "From where do you come?" He replied, "I am a Lē′vīte of Bethlehem in Judah, and I am going to live wherever I can find a place." ¹⁰ Then Mī′cah said to him, "Stay with me, and be to me a father and a priest, and I will give you ten pieces of silver a year, a set of clothes, and your living."ʰ ¹¹ The Lē′vīte agreed to stay with the man; and the young man became to him like one of his sons. ¹² So Mī′cah installed the Lē′vīte, and the young man became his priest, and was in the house of Mī′cah. ¹³ Then Mī′cah said, "Now I know that the LORD will prosper me, because the Lē′vīte has become my priest."

The Migration of Dan

In those days there was no king in Israel. And in those days the tribe of the Dan′ītes was seeking for itself a territory to live in; for until then no territory among the tribes of Israel had been allotted to them. ² So the Dan′ītes sent five valiant men from the whole number of their clan, from Zō′rah and from Esh′tā•ol, to spy out the land and to explore it; and they said to them, "Go, explore the land." When they came to the hill country of Ē′phra•im, to the house of Mī′cah, they stayed there. ³ While they were at Mī′cah's house, they recognized the voice of the young Lē′vīte; so they went over and asked him, "Who brought you here? What are you doing in this place? What is your business here?" ⁴ He said to them, "Mī′cah did such and such for me, and he hired me, and I have become his priest." ⁵ Then they said to him, "Inquire of God that we may know whether the mission we are undertaking will succeed." ⁶ The priest replied, "Go in peace. The mission you are on is under the eye of the LORD."

7 The five men went on, and when they came to Lā′ish, they observed the people who were there living securely, after the manner of the Sī•dō′ni•ans, quiet and unsuspecting, lackingⁱ nothing on earth, and possessing wealth.ʲ Furthermore, they were far from the Sī•dō′ni•ans and had no dealings with Ar′am.ᵏ ⁸ When they came to their kinsfolk at Zō′-rah and Esh′tā•ol, they said to them, "What do you report?" ⁹ They said, "Come, let us go up against them; for we have seen the land, and it is very good. Will you do nothing? Do not be slow to go, but enter in and possess the land. ¹⁰ When you go,

---

ᶠ The words *but now I will return it to you* are transposed from the end of verse 3 in Heb   ᵍ Or *Ephraim, continuing his journey*   ʰ Heb *living, and the Levite went* ⁱ Cn Compare 18.10: Meaning of Heb uncertain ʲ Meaning of Heb uncertain   ᵏ Symmachus: Heb *with anyone*

you will come to an unsuspecting people. The land is broad—God has indeed given it into your hands—a place where there is no lack of anything on earth."

11 Six hundred men of the Dan′īte clan, armed with weapons of war, set out from Zō′rah and Esh′tā·ol, 12 and went up and encamped at Kir′i·ath-jē′a·rim in Judah. On this account that place is called Mā′ha·neh-dan[l] to this day; it is west of Kir′i·ath-jē′a·rim. 13 From there they passed on to the hill country of Ē′phra·im, and came to the house of Mī′cah.

14 Then the five men who had gone to spy out the land (that is, Lā′ish) said to their comrades, "Do you know that in these buildings there are an ephod, teraphim, and an idol of cast metal? Now therefore consider what you will do." 15 So they turned in that direction and came to the house of the young Lē′vīte, at the home of Mī′cah, and greeted him. 16 While the six hundred men of the Dan′ītes, armed with their weapons of war, stood by the entrance of the gate, 17 the five men who had gone to spy out the land proceeded to enter and take the idol of cast metal, the ephod, and the teraphim.[m] The priest was standing by the entrance of the gate with the six hundred men armed with weapons of war. 18 When the men went into Mī′cah's house and took the idol of cast metal, the ephod, and the teraphim, the priest said to them, "What are you doing?" 19 They said to him, "Keep quiet! Put your hand over your mouth, and come with us, and be to us a father and a priest. Is it better for you to be priest to the house of one person, or to be priest to a tribe and clan in Israel?" 20 Then the priest accepted the offer. He took the ephod, the teraphim, and the idol, and went along with the people.

21 So they resumed their journey, putting the little ones, the livestock, and the goods in front of them. 22 When they were some distance from the home of Mī′cah, the men who were in the houses near Mī′cah's house were called out, and they overtook the Dan′ītes. 23 They shouted to the Dan′ītes, who turned around and said to Mī′cah, "What is the matter that you come with such a company?" 24 He replied, "You take my gods that I made, and the priest, and go away, and what have I left? How then can you ask me, 'What is the matter?' " 25 And the Dan′ītes said to him, "You had better not let your voice be heard among us or else hot-tempered fellows will attack you, and you will lose your life and the lives of your household." 26 Then the Dan′ītes went their way. When Mī′cah saw that they were too strong for him, he turned and went back to his home.

The Danites Settle in Laish

27 The Dan′ītes, having taken what Mī′cah had made, and the priest who belonged to him, came to Lā′ish, to a people quiet and unsuspecting, put them to the sword, and burned down the city. 28 There was no deliverer, because it was far from Sī′don and they had no dealings with Ar′am.[n] It was in the valley that belongs to Beth-rē′hob. They rebuilt the city, and lived in it. 29 They named the city Dan, after their ancestor Dan, who was born to Israel; but the name of the city was formerly Lā′ish. 30 Then the Dan′ītes set up the idol for themselves. Jonathan son of Ger′shom, son of Moses,[o] and his sons were priests to the tribe of the Dan′ītes until the time the land went into captivity. 31 So they maintained as their own Mī′cah's idol that he had made, as long as the house of God was at Shī′lōh.

The Levite's Concubine

In those days, when there was no king in Israel, a certain Lē′vīte, residing in the remote parts of the hill country of Ē′phra·im, took to himself a concubine from Bethlehem in Judah. 2 But his concubine became angry with[p] him, and she went away from him to her father's house at Bethlehem in Judah, and was there some four months. 3 Then her husband set out after her, to speak tenderly to her and bring her back. He had with him his servant and a couple of donkeys. When he reached[q] her father's house, the girl's father saw him and came with joy to meet him. 4 His father-in-law, the girl's father, made him stay, and he remained with him three days; so they ate and drank, and he[r] stayed there. 5 On the fourth day they got up early in the morning, and he prepared to go; but the girl's father said to his son-in-law, "Fortify yourself with a bit of food, and after that you may go." 6 So the two men sat and ate and drank together; and the girl's father said to the man, "Why not spend the night and enjoy yourself?" 7 When the man got up to go, his father-in-law kept urging him until he spent the night there again. 8 On the fifth day he got up early in the morning to leave; and the girl's father said, "Fortify yourself." So they lingered[s] until the day declined, and the two of them ate and drank.[t] 9 When the man with his concubine and his servant got up to leave, his father-in-law, the girl's father, said to him, "Look, the day has worn on until it is almost evening. Spend the night. See, the

---

[l] That is Camp of Dan   [m] Compare 17.4, 5; 18.14: Heb teraphim and the cast metal   [n] Cn Compare verse 7: Heb with anyone   [o] Another reading is son of Manasseh   [p] Gk OL: Heb prostituted herself against   [q] Gk: Lᴛ ⁱ brought him to   [r] Compare verse 7 and Gk: ʜ   [s] Cn: Heb Linger   [t] Gk: Heb lacks and drank

day has drawn to a close. Spend the night here and enjoy yourself. Tomorrow you can get up early in the morning for your journey, and go home."

10 But the man would not spend the night; he got up and departed, and arrived opposite Jĕ′bus (that is, Jerusalem). He had with him a couple of saddled donkeys, and his concubine was with him. [11] When they were near Jĕ′bus, the day was far spent, and the servant said to his master, "Come now, let us turn aside to this city of the Jeb′u•sītes, and spend the night in it." [12] But his master said to him, "We will not turn aside into a city of foreigners, who do not belong to the people of Israel; but we will continue on to Gib′ē•ah." [13] Then he said to his servant, "Come, let us try to reach one of these places, and spend the night at Gib′ē•ah or at Rā′mah." [14] So they passed on and went their way; and the sun went down on them near Gib′ē•ah, which belongs to Benjamin. [15] They turned aside there, to go in and spend the night at Gib′ē•ah. He went in and sat down in the open square of the city, but no one took them in to spend the night.

16 Then at evening there was an old man coming from his work in the field. The man was from the hill country of Ē′phra•im, and he was residing in Gib′ē•ah. (The people of the place were Ben′ja•min•ītes.) [17] When the old man looked up and saw the wayfarer in the open square of the city, he said, "Where are you going and where do you come from?" [18] He answered him, "We are passing from Bethlehem in Judah to the remote parts of the hill country of Ē′phra•im, from which I come. I went to Bethlehem in Judah; and I am going to my home.[u] Nobody has offered to take me in. [19] We your servants have straw and fodder for our donkeys, with bread and wine for me and the woman and the young man along with us. We need nothing more." [20] The old man said, "Peace be to you. I will care for all your wants; only do not spend the night in the square." [21] So he brought him into his house, and fed the donkeys; they washed their feet, and ate and drank.

Gibeah's Crime

22 While they were enjoying themselves, the men of the city, a perverse lot, surrounded the house, and started pounding on the door. They said to the old man, the master of the house, "Bring out the man who came into your house, so that we may have intercourse with him." [23] And the man, the master of the house, went out to them and said to them, "No, my brothers, do not act so wickedly. Since this man is my guest, do not do this vile thing. [24] Here are my virgin daughter and his concubine; let me bring them out now. Ravish

them and do whatever you want to them; but against this man do not do such a vile thing." [25] But the men would not listen to him. So the man seized his concubine, and put her out to them. They wantonly raped her, and abused her all through the night until the morning. And as the dawn began to break, they let her go. [26] As morning appeared, the woman came and fell down at the door of the man's house where her master was, until it was light.

27 In the morning her master got up, opened the doors of the house, and when he went out to go on his way, there was his concubine lying at the door of the house, with her hands on the threshold. [28] "Get up," he said to her, "we are going." But there was no answer. Then he put her on the donkey; and the man set out for his home. [29] When he had entered his house, he took a knife, and grasping his concubine he cut her into twelve pieces, limb by limb, and sent her throughout all the territory of Israel. [30] Then he commanded the men whom he sent, saying, "Thus shall you say to all the Israelites, 'Has such a thing ever happened[v] since the day that the Israelites came up from the land of Egypt until this day? Consider it, take counsel, and speak out.' "

The Other Tribes Attack Benjamin

Then all the Israelites came out, from Dan to Bĕ′-er-shĕ′ba, including the land of Gil′e•ad, and the congregation assembled in one body before the LORD at Miz′pah. [2] The chiefs of all the people, of all the tribes of Israel, presented themselves in the assembly of the people of God, four hundred thousand foot-soldiers bearing arms. [3] (Now the Ben′ja•min•ītes heard that the people of Israel had gone up to Miz′pah.) And the Israelites said, "Tell us, how did this criminal act come about?" [4] The Lē′vīte, the husband of the woman who was murdered, answered, "I came to Gib′ē•ah that belongs to Benjamin, I and my concubine, to spend the night. [5] The lords of Gib′ē•ah rose up against me, and surrounded the house at night. They intended to kill me, and they raped my concubine until she died. [6] Then I took my concubine and cut her into pieces, and sent her throughout the whole extent of Israel's territory; for they have committed a vile outrage in Israel. [7] So now, you Israelites, all of you, give your advice and counsel here."

8 All the people got up as one, saying, "We will not any of us go to our tents, nor will any of us return to our houses. [9] But now this is what we

---

u Gk Compare 19.29. Heb *to the house of the LORD*
v Compare Gk: Heb [30] *And all who saw it said, "Such a thing has not happened or been seen*

will do to Gib′ē·ah: we will go up[w] against it by lot. [10]We will take ten men of a hundred throughout all the tribes of Israel, and a hundred of a thousand, and a thousand of ten thousand, to bring provisions for the troops, who are going to repay[x] Gib′ē·ah of Benjamin for all the disgrace that they have done in Israel." [11]So all the men of Israel gathered against the city, united as one.

12 The tribes of Israel sent men through all the tribe of Benjamin, saying, "What crime is this that has been committed among you? [13]Now then, hand over those scoundrels in Gib′ē·ah, so that we may put them to death, and purge the evil from Israel." But the Ben′ja·min·ītes would not listen to their kinsfolk, the Israelites. [14]The Ben′ja·min·ītes came together out of the towns to Gib′ē·ah, to go out to battle against the Israelites. [15]On that day the Ben′ja·min·ītes mustered twenty-six thousand armed men from their towns, besides the inhabitants of Gib′ē·ah. [16]Of all this force, there were seven hundred picked men who were left-handed; every one could sling a stone at a hair, and not miss. [17]And the Israelites, apart from Benjamin, mustered four hundred thousand armed men, all of them warriors.

18 The Israelites proceeded to go up to Beth′el, where they inquired of God, "Which of us shall go up first to battle against the Ben′ja·min·ītes?" And the LORD answered, "Judah shall go up first."

19 Then the Israelites got up in the morning, and encamped against Gib′ē·ah. [20]The Israelites went out to battle against Benjamin; and the Israelites drew up the battle line against them at Gib′ē·ah. [21]The Ben′ja·min·ītes came out of Gib′ē·ah, and struck down on that day twenty-two thousand of the Israelites. [23][y]The Israelites went up and wept before the LORD until the evening; and they inquired of the LORD, "Shall we again draw near to battle against our kinsfolk the Ben′ja·min·ītes?" And the LORD said, "Go up against them." [22]The Israelites took courage, and again formed the battle line in the same place where they had formed it on the first day.

24 So the Israelites advanced against the Ben′ja·min·ītes the second day. [25]Benjamin moved out against them from Gib′ē·ah the second day, and struck down eighteen thousand of the Israelites, all of them armed men. [26]Then all the Israelites, the whole army, went back to Beth′el and wept, sitting there before the LORD; they fasted that day until evening. Then they offered burnt offerings and sacrifices of well-being before the LORD. [27]And the Israelites inquired of the LORD (for the ark of the covenant of God was there in those days, [28]and Phin′e·has son of El·e·ā′zar, son of Aaron, ministered before it in those days), saying, "Shall we go

out once more to battle against our kinsfolk the Ben′ja·min·ītes, or shall we desist?" The LORD answered, "Go up, for tomorrow I will give them into your hand."

29 So Israel stationed men in ambush around Gib′ē·ah. [30]Then the Israelites went up against the Ben′ja·min·ītes on the third day, and set themselves in array against Gib′ē·ah, as before. [31]When the Ben′ja·min·ītes went out against the army, they were drawn away from the city. As before they began to inflict casualties on the troops, along the main roads, one of which goes up to Beth′el and the other to Gib′ē·ah, as well as in the open country, killing about thirty men of Israel. [32]The Ben′ja·min·ītes thought, "They are being routed before us, as previously." But the Israelites said, "Let us retreat and draw them away from the city toward the roads." [33]The main body of the Israelites drew back its battle line to Bā′al-tā′mar, while those Israelites who were in ambush rushed out of their place west[z] of Gē′ba. [34]There came against Gib′ē·ah ten thousand picked men out of all Israel, and the battle was fierce. But the Ben′ja·min·ītes did not realize that disaster was close upon them.

35 The LORD defeated Benjamin before Israel; and the Israelites destroyed twenty-five thousand one hundred men of Benjamin that day, all of them armed.

36 Then the Ben′ja·min·ītes saw that they were defeated.[a]

The Israelites gave ground to Benjamin, because they trusted to the troops in ambush that they had stationed against Gib′ē·ah. [37]The troops in ambush rushed quickly upon Gib′ē·ah. Then they put the whole city to the sword. [38]Now the agreement between the main body of Israel and the men in ambush was that when they sent up a cloud of smoke out of the city [39]the main body of Israel should turn in battle. But Benjamin had begun to inflict casualties on the Israelites, killing about thirty of them; so they thought, "Surely they are defeated before us, as in the first battle." [40]But when the cloud, a column of smoke, began to rise out of the city, the Ben′ja·min·ītes looked behind them—and there was the whole city going up in smoke toward the sky! [41]Then the main body of Israel turned, and the Ben′ja·min·ītes were dismayed, for they saw that disaster was close upon them. [42]Therefore they turned away from the Israelites in the direction of the wilderness; but the battle overtook them, and those who came out of the city[b] were

---

[w] Gk: Heb lacks *we will go up*   [x] Compare Gk: Meaning of Heb uncertain   [y] Verses 22 and 23 are transposed   [z] Gk Vg: Heb *in the plain*   [a] This sentence is ⌐ by verse 45.   [b] Compare Vg and some Gk M⟨ *cities*

slaughtering them in between.*c* ⁴³ Cutting down*d* the Ben′ja•min•ites, they pursued them from Nō′-hah*e* and trod them down as far as a place east of Gib′ē•ah. ⁴⁴ Eighteen thousand Ben′ja•min•ites fell, all of them courageous fighters. ⁴⁵ When they turned and fled toward the wilderness to the rock of Rim′mon, five thousand of them were cut down on the main roads, and they were pursued as far as Gī′dom, and two thousand of them were slain. ⁴⁶ So all who fell that day of Benjamin were twenty-five thousand arms-bearing men, all of them courageous fighters. ⁴⁷ But six hundred turned and fled toward the wilderness to the rock of Rim′mon, and remained at the rock of Rim′-mon for four months. ⁴⁸ Meanwhile, the Israelites turned back against the Ben′ja•min•ites, and put them to the sword—the city, the people, the animals, and all that remained. Also the remaining towns they set on fire.

The Benjaminites Saved from Extinction

Now the Israelites had sworn at Miz′pah, "No one of us shall give his daughter in marriage to Benjamin." ² And the people came to Beth′el, and sat there until evening before God, and they lifted up their voices and wept bitterly. ³ They said, "O LORD, the God of Israel, why has it come to pass that today there should be one tribe lacking in Israel?" ⁴ On the next day, the people got up early, and built an altar there, and offered burnt offerings and sacrifices of well-being. ⁵ Then the Israelites said, "Which of all the tribes of Israel did not come up in the assembly to the LORD?" For a solemn oath had been taken concerning whoever did not come up to the LORD to Miz′pah, saying, "That one shall be put to death." ⁶ But the Israelites had compassion for Benjamin their kin, and said, "One tribe is cut off from Israel this day. ⁷ What shall we do for wives for those who are left, since we have sworn by the LORD that we will not give them any of our daughters as wives?"

8 Then they said, "Is there anyone from the tribes of Israel who did not come up to the LORD to Miz′pah?" It turned out that no one from Jā′besh-gil′ē•ad had come to the camp, to the assembly. ⁹ For when the roll was called among the people, not one of the inhabitants of Jā′besh-gil′ē•ad was there. ¹⁰ So the congregation sent twelve thousand soldiers there and commanded them, "Go, put the inhabitants of Jā′besh-gil′ē•ad to the sword, including the women and the little ones. ¹¹ This is what

you shall do; every male and every woman that has lain with a male you shall devote to destruction." ¹² And they found among the inhabitants of Jā′besh-gil′ē•ad four hundred young virgins who had never slept with a man and brought them to the camp at Shī′lōh, which is in the land of Cā′-naan.

13 Then the whole congregation sent word to the Ben′ja•min•ites who were at the rock of Rim′-mon, and proclaimed peace to them. ¹⁴ Benjamin returned at that time; and they gave them the women whom they had saved alive of the women of Jā′besh-gil′ē•ad; but they did not suffice for them.

15 The people had compassion on Benjamin because the LORD had made a breach in the tribes of Israel. ¹⁶ So the elders of the congregation said, "What shall we do for wives for those who are left, since there are no women left in Benjamin?" ¹⁷ And they said, "There must be heirs for the survivors of Benjamin, in order that a tribe may not be blotted out from Israel. ¹⁸ Yet we cannot give any of our daughters to them as wives." For the Israelites had sworn, "Cursed be anyone who gives a wife to Benjamin." ¹⁹ So they said, "Look, the yearly festival of the LORD is taking place at Shī′lōh, which is north of Beth′el, on the east of the highway that goes up from Beth′el to Shē′chem, and south of Le•bō′nah." ²⁰ And they instructed the Ben′ja•min-ites, saying, "Go and lie in wait in the vineyards, ²¹ and watch; when the young women of Shī′lōh come out to dance in the dances, then come out of the vineyards and each of you carry off a wife for himself from the young women of Shī′lōh, and go to the land of Benjamin. ²² Then if their fathers or their brothers come to complain to us, we will say to them, 'Be generous and allow us to have them; because we did not capture in battle a wife for each man. But neither did you incur guilt by giving your daughters to them.' " ²³ The Ben′ja•min•ites did so; they took wives for each of them from the dancers whom they abducted. Then they went and returned to their territory, and rebuilt the towns, and lived in them. ²⁴ So the Israelites departed from there at that time by tribes and families, and they went out from there to their own territories.

25 In those days there was no king in Israel; all the people did what was right in their own eyes.

---

c Compare Syr: Meaning of Heb uncertain   *d* Gk: Heb Surrounding   *e* Gk: Heb *pursued them at their resting place*

Tracing one's family tree has become a popular pastime. People comb through courthouse files, study old tombstones in search of names and dates, and write to churches in foreign countries looking for baptismal and marriage records. In learning about our ancestors, we gain a better sense of our place in history and who we should be in light of that history. Ruth is a beautiful story of love and loyalty about one of Israel's ancestors. The story helps God's people understand who they are and how they should live.

At a Glance

- **Chapter 1.** Ruth goes with her mother-in-law to Bethlehem.

- **Chapters 2–3.** Ruth encounters Boaz.

- **Chapter 4.** the marriage of Ruth and Boaz, Ruth's descendants

In-depth

The Book of Ruth offers a surprising revelation about the family tree of King David: Ruth, King David's great-grandmother, was a foreigner, born and reared in the land of Moab. The Book of Ruth was written long after the death of her famous great-grandson, but it seems to preserve an accurate memory: King David was of mixed ancestry. Israelites who insisted on racial purity were probably shocked that God worked through a member of an enemy tribe to advance the divine plan.

The Book of Ruth is sandwiched between Judges and 1 Samuel because its events take place during the time of the judges. It teaches some extremely important lessons:

- Ruth was faithful to Naomi, her mother-in-law, even though she was of a different race and different faith. Ruth challenged the ancient Israelites, who tended to view foreigners with suspicion and to see nothing good in their enemies.

- If God's plan included a Moabite woman among David's ancestors, then God's love and favor must extend beyond the boundaries of Israel. After the Exile, when Jewish marriages to foreigners were outlawed, the little Book of Ruth presented a huge challenge!

- God works through the faithfulness of ordinary people living ordinary lives. No kings, wars, or dramatic miracles appear in the Book of Ruth.

The Book of Ruth is action packed and full of dialog; it is a dramatic story like the Books of Judith and Tobit. Some of the traditions of ancient Israel may seem strange to us today, but we can still gain a deeper understanding of ourselves and our faith by reading the story of King David's great-grandmother.

Quick Facts

Period Covered
sometime from 1200 to 1000 B.C.

Author
unknown, probably writing sometime during the monarchy (1000–800 B.C.)

Themes
God's plan includes non-Israelites. God works through ordinary people.

The Book of **Ruth**

Ruth

Elimelech's Family Goes to Moab

In the days when the judges ruled, there was a famine in the land, and a certain man of Bethlehem in Judah went to live in the country of Mō'ab, he and his wife and two sons. 2 The name of the man was Ē•lim'e•lech and the name of his wife Nā'o•mī, and the names of his two sons were Mah'lon and Chil'i•on; they were Eph'ra•thītes from Bethlehem in Judah. They went into the country of Mō'ab and remained there. 3 But Ē•lim'-e•lech, the husband of Nā'o•mī, died, and she was left with her two sons. 4 These took Mō'ab•īte wives; the name of the one was Or'pah and the name of the other Ruth. When they had lived there about ten years, 5 both Mah'lon and Chil'i•on also died, so that the woman was left without her two sons and her husband.

Naomi and Her Moabite Daughters-in-Law

6 Then she started to return with her daughters-in-law from the country of Mō'ab, for she had heard in the country of Mō'ab that the LORD had considered his people and given them food. 7 So she set out from the place where she had been living, she and her two daughters-in-law, and they went on their way to go back to the land of Judah. 8 But Nā'o•mī said to her two daughters-in-law, "Go back each of you to your mother's house. May the LORD deal kindly with you, as you have dealt with the dead and with me. 9 The LORD grant that you may find security, each of you in the house of your husband." Then she kissed them, and they wept aloud. 10 They said to her, "No, we will return with you to your people." 11 But Nā'o•mī said, "Turn back, my daughters, why will you go with me? Do I still have sons in my womb that they may become your husbands? 12 Turn back, my daughters, go your way, for I am too old to have a husband. Even if I thought there was hope for me, even if I should have a husband tonight and bear sons, 13 would you then wait until they were grown? Would you then refrain from marrying? No, my daughters, it has been far more bitter for me than for you, because the hand of the LORD has turned against me." 14 Then they wept aloud again. Or'pah kissed her mother-in-law, but Ruth clung to her.

15 So she said, "See, your sister-in-law has gone back to her people and to her gods; return after your sister-in-law." 16 But Ruth said,

"Do not press me to leave you
    or to turn back from following you!
Where you go, I will go;
    where you lodge, I will lodge;
your people shall be my people,
    and your God my God.
17   Where you die, I will die—
    there will I be buried.

May the LORD do thus and so to me,
>and more as well,
>if even death parts me from you!"

18 When Nā'o•mī saw that she was determined to go with her, she said no more to her.

19 So the two of them went on until they came to Bethlehem. When they came to Bethlehem, the whole town was stirred because of them; and the women said, "Is this Nā'o•mī?" 20 She said to them,

"Call me no longer Nā'o•mī,ᵃ
>call me Mar'a,ᵇ
>for the Almightyᶜ has dealt bitterly with
>>me.
21 I went away full,
>but the LORD has brought me back empty;
>why call me Nā'o•mī
>when the LORD has dealt harshly withᵈ
>>me,
>and the Almightyᶜ has brought calamity
>>upon me?"

22 So Nā'o•mī returned together with Ruth the Mō'ab•īte, her daughter-in-law, who came back with her from the country of Mō'ab. They came to Bethlehem at the beginning of the barley harvest.

LORD bless you." 5 Then Bō'az said to his servant who was in charge of the reapers, "To whom does this young woman belong?" 6 The servant who was in charge of the reapers answered, "She is the Mō'-ab•īte who came back with Nā'o•mī from the country of Mō'ab. 7 She said, 'Please, let me glean and gather among the sheaves behind the reapers.' So she came, and she has been on her feet from early this morning until now, without resting even for a moment."ᵉ

8 Then Bō'az said to Ruth, "Now listen, my daughter, do not go to glean in another field or leave this one, but keep close to my young women. 9 Keep your eyes on the field that is being reaped, and follow behind them. I have ordered the young men not to bother you. If you get thirsty, go to the vessels and drink from what the young men have drawn." 10 Then she fell prostrate, with her face to the ground, and said to him, "Why have I found favor in your sight, that you should take notice of me, when I am a foreigner?" 11 But Bō'az answered her, "All that you have done for your mother-in-law since the death of your husband has been fully told me, and how you left

Bill

Bill is a special person. He is different looking. Most people walk by Bill and ignore him. But the people who have looked beyond Bill's appearance have discovered one of the most beautiful people they will ever come to know.

Many people who have gotten to know Bill feel that they have found someone who is close to God. They have discovered a person who brings out the best in themselves.

In the same way, Ruth easily could have been overlooked by Boaz as just another poor person scavenging in his fields. Boaz took the opportunity to get to know her and found someone with inspiring faith and loyalty. God can be found in the ones who are forgotten. Reach out to them, and you might find God too.

▶ **Ruth 2.1–16**

Ruth Meets Boaz

Now Nā'o•mī had a kinsman on her husband's side, a prominent rich man, of the family of Ē•lim'-e•lech, whose name was Bō'az. 2 And Ruth the Mō'-ab•īte said to Nā'o•mī, "Let me go to the field and glean among the ears of grain, behind someone in whose sight I may find favor." She said to her, "Go, my daughter." 3 So she went. She came and gleaned in the field behind the reapers. As it happened, she came to the part of the field belonging to Bō'az, who was of the family of Ē•lim'e•lech. 4 Just then Bō'az came from Bethlehem. He said to the reapers, "The LORD be with you." They answered, "The

your father and mother and your native land and came to a people that you did not know before. 12 May the LORD reward you for your deeds, and may you have a full reward from the LORD, the God of Israel, under whose wings you have come for refuge!" 13 Then she said, "May I continue to find favor in your sight, my lord, for you have comforted me and spoken kindly to your servant, even though I am not one of your servants."

ᵃ That is *Pleasant*   ᵇ That is *Bitter*   ᶜ Traditional rendering of Heb *Shaddai*   ᵈ Or *has testified ag*
ᵉ Compare Gk Vg: Meaning of Heb uncertain

14 At mealtime Bō'az said to her, "Come here, and eat some of this bread, and dip your morsel in the sour wine." So she sat beside the reapers, and he heaped up for her some parched grain. She ate until she was satisfied, and she had some left over. 15 When she got up to glean, Bō'az instructed his young men, "Let her glean even among the standing sheaves, and do not reproach her. 16 You must also pull out some handfuls for her from the bundles, and leave them for her to glean, and do not rebuke her."

17 So she gleaned in the field until evening. Then she beat out what she had gleaned, and it was about an ephah of barley. 18 She picked it up and came into the town, and her mother-in-law saw how much she had gleaned. Then she took out and gave her what was left over after she herself had been satisfied. 19 Her mother-in-law said to her, "Where did you glean today? And where have you worked? Blessed be the man who took notice of you." So she told her mother-in-law with whom she had worked, and said, "The name of the man with whom I worked today is Bō'az." 20 Then Nā'o•mī said to her daughter-in-law, "Blessed be he by the LORD, whose kindness has not forsaken the living or the dead!" Nā'o•mī also said to her, "The man is a relative of ours, one of our nearest kin." *f* 21 Then Ruth the Mō'ab•īte said, "He even said to me, 'Stay close by my servants, until they have finished all my harvest.' " 22 Nā'o•mī said to Ruth, her daughter-in-law, "It is better, my daughter, that you go out with his young women, otherwise you might be bothered in another field."

23 So she stayed close to the young women of Bō'az, gleaning until the end of the barley and wheat harvests; and she lived with her mother-in-law.

Ruth and Boaz at the Threshing Floor

Nā'o•mī her mother-in-law said to her, "My daughter, I need to seek some security for you, so that it may be well with you. 2 Now here is our kinsman Bō'az, with whose young women you have been working. See, he is winnowing barley tonight at the threshing floor. 3 Now wash and anoint yourself, and put on your best clothes and go down to the threshing floor; but do not make yourself known to the man until he has finished eating and drinking. 4 When he lies down, observe the place where he lies; then, go and uncover his feet and lie down; and he will tell you what to do." 5 She said to her, "All that you tell me I will do."

6 So she went down to the threshing floor and did just as her mother-in-law had instructed her. 7 When Bō'az had eaten and drunk, and he was in a contented mood, he went to lie down at the end of the heap of grain. Then she came stealthily and uncovered his feet, and lay down. 8 At midnight the man was startled, and turned over, and there, lying at his feet, was a woman! 9 He said, "Who are you?" And she answered, "I am Ruth, your servant; spread your cloak over your servant, for you are next-of-kin." *f* 10 He said, "May you be blessed by the LORD, my daughter; this last instance of your loyalty is better than the first; you have not gone

f Or one with the right to redeem

SERVICE TO THE POOR AND THE COMMUNITY!

The story of Ruth was a challenge to Israel's laws of racial purity. It is also an example of how service to the poor was an integral part of Israel's society. For in the story, Boaz, a wealthy and respected person, both provides for the poor and looks beyond the differences of race and faith to marry Ruth. Boaz's goal is to do God's will. His marriage to Ruth ensures that Naomi's land is redeemed and that she will have descendants to claim the land. Ruth's faithfulness and Boaz's integrity serve to gradually restore Naomi's hope in God's care.

In the New Testament, it becomes even clearer that God makes no distinctions between people of different races and cultures. And Jesus teaches that caring for the poor is one of the requirements for being God's people.

■ How do you treat people of different races, and how much is service to poor people a part of your life?

■ Pray that you can follow Ruth and Boaz's example and be an instrument of faith, hope, and justice for people in need.

after young men, whether poor or rich. ¹¹And now, my daughter, do not be afraid, I will do for you all that you ask, for all the assembly of my people know that you are a worthy woman. ¹²But now, though it is true that I am a near kinsman, there is another kinsman more closely related than I. ¹³Remain this night, and in the morning, if he will act as next-of-kin⁸ for you, good; let him do it. If he is not willing to act as next-of-kin⁸ for you, then, as the LORD lives, I will act as next-of-kin⁸ for you. Lie down until the morning."

14 So she lay at his feet until morning, but got up before one person could recognize another; for he said, "It must not be known that the woman came to the threshing floor." ¹⁵Then he said, "Bring the cloak you are wearing and hold it out." So she held it, and he measured out six measures of barley, and put it on her back; then he went into the city. ¹⁶She came to her mother-in-law, who said, "How did things go with you,ʰ my daughter?" Then she told her all that the man had done for her, ¹⁷saying, "He gave me these six measures of barley, for he said, 'Do not go back to your mother-in-law empty-handed.' " ¹⁸She replied, "Wait, my daughter, until you learn how the matter turns out, for the man will not rest, but will settle the matter today."

The Marriage of Boaz and Ruth

No sooner had Bō′az gone up to the gate and sat down there than the next-of-kin,⁸ of whom Bō′az had spoken, came passing by. So Bō′az said, "Come over, friend; sit down here." And he went over and sat down. ²Then Bō′az took ten men of the elders of the city, and said, "Sit down here"; so they sat down. ³He then said to the next-of-kin,⁸ "Nā′o•mī, who has come back from the country of Mō′ab, is selling the parcel of land that belonged to our kinsman Ē•lim′e•lech. ⁴So I thought I would tell you of it, and say: Buy it in the presence of those sitting here, and in the presence of the elders of my people. If you will redeem it, redeem it; but if you will not, tell me, so that I may know; for there is no one prior to you to redeem it, and I come after you." So he said, "I will redeem it." ⁵Then Bō′az said, "The day you acquire the field from the hand of Nā′o•mī, you are also acquiring Ruthⁱ the Mō′ab•īte, the widow of the dead man, to maintain the dead man's name on his inheritance." ⁶At this, the next-of-kin⁸ said, "I cannot redeem it for myself without damaging my own inheritance. Take my right of redemption yourself, for I cannot redeem it."

7 Now this was the custom in former times in Israel concerning redeeming and exchanging: to confirm a transaction, the one took off a sandal

and gave it to the other; this was the manner of attesting in Israel. ⁸So when the next-of-kin⁸ said to Bō′az, "Acquire it for yourself," he took off his sandal. ⁹Then Bō′az said to the elders and all the people, "Today you are witnesses that I have acquired from the hand of Nā′o•mī all that belonged to Ē•lim′e•lech and all that belonged to Chil′i•on and Mah′lon. ¹⁰I have also acquired Ruth the Mō′ab•īte, the wife of Mah′lon, to be my wife, to maintain the dead man's name on his inheritance, in order that the name of the dead may not be cut off from his kindred and from the gate of his native place; today you are witnesses." ¹¹Then all the people who were at the gate, along with the elders, said, "We are witnesses. May the LORD make the woman who is coming into your house like Rachel and Leah, who together built up the house of Israel. May you produce children in Eph′ra•thah and bestow a name in Bethlehem; ¹²and, through the children that the LORD will give you by this young woman, may your house be like the house of Per′ez, whom Tā′mar bore to Judah."

---

⁸ Or *one with the right to redeem*   ʰ Or *"Who are you,*
ⁱ OL Vg: Heb *from the hand of Naomi and from Ruth*

PRAY IT!
Wherever You Go

Ruth is under no obligation to leave her homeland and go to Israel with her mother-in-law, very likely facing a life of poverty. But her loyalty is rewarded, and she finds new life among God's people.

After reading Ruth's story, reflect on these questions:

- What do you find inspiring in Ruth's story?
- Who are you faithful to?
- What would have to be present in a relationship for you to have the kind of loyalty Ruth showed to Naomi?
- Can you make Ruth's words to Naomi your prayer to God?

Where you lead, I will follow; where you direct me, I will live; your people shall be my family; and you shall always be my God. (Adapted from Ruth 1.16)

An ongoing national debate these days involves, on the one side, those who want more laws to protect workers, poor people, and the environment, and on the other side, those who want fewer laws and less government. The First Book of Samuel reflects a similar tension in Israel as the days of the judges come to an end and the first kings make their appearance. This period of Israelite history is filled with mighty struggles and colorful personalities, including a king who gradually loses his sanity and the shining hero who replaces him.

At a Glance

- **Chapters 1–7.** stories of Eli and Samuel
- **Chapters 8–15.** the beginning of Saul's kingship
- **Chapters 16–31.** stories of King Saul and the young David

In-depth

This book is named after Samuel, the last of the judges and a reluctant king-maker. Samuel, a prophet anointed to speak God's word to the nation, represents one way of governing. God works through the prophet's words to remind the people of Israel to be faithful to the terms of the Covenant. A second way of governing is represented by Saul, the first king anointed by Samuel to rule over the whole nation. God works through the king's laws and regulations to ensure that the people of Israel are faithful to the terms of the Covenant. In 1 Samuel, the former way of governing the Israelite nation gradually gives way to the latter, with an obvious gain and an obvious loss for the people.

When kings begin to rule Israel in place of judges and prophets, the people gain a more structured way of life and develop a greater national identity. These changes also make them stronger in facing threats from other nations. But at the same time, the people lose a great deal of personal freedom and independence. They are taxed and even forced into labor to support the king's government and building plans. Echoes of this debate on governing styles can be found throughout 1 Samuel (see "Doublets," near 9.1).

Israel's kings were understood as being chosen by God and as being responsible for God's interests. First Samuel clearly emphasizes that the success of kings depends on their obedience to God's law. First Samuel reminds us that final authority in human affairs rests in no human being, but in God alone. Human systems are never perfect, but must constantly be reviewed and renewed.

Quick Facts

Period Covered
approximately 1080 to 1040 B.C.

Author
unknown, from the Deuteronomic tradition, probably using ancient court records and hero stories

Theme
tension between the need for a king and the people's reliance on God

Of Note
First and Second Samuel, originally one book, were made into two books when they were translated from Hebrew into Greek.

The First Book of *Samuel*

1 Samuel

Samuel's Birth and Dedication

There was a certain man of Rā·ma·thā'im, a Zuph'īte*a* from the hill country of Ē'phra·im, whose name was El·kā'nah son of Je·rō'ham son of E·lī'hū son of Tō'hū son of Zuph, an Ē'phra·im·īte. ²He had two wives; the name of the one was Hannah, and the name of the other Pe·nin'nah. Pe·nin'nah had children, but Hannah had no children.

3 Now this man used to go up year by year from his town to worship and to sacrifice to the LORD of hosts at Shī'lōh, where the two sons of Ē'lī, Hoph'nī and Phin'e·has, were priests of the LORD. ⁴On the day when El·kā'nah sacrificed, he would give portions to his wife Pe·nin'nah and to all her sons and daughters; ⁵but to Hannah he gave a double portion,*b* because he loved her, though the LORD had closed her womb. ⁶Her rival used to provoke her severely, to irritate her, because the LORD had closed her womb. ⁷So it went on year by year; as often as she went up to the house of the LORD, she used to provoke her. Therefore Hannah wept and would not eat. ⁸Her husband El·kā'nah said to her, "Hannah, why do you weep? Why do you not eat? Why is your heart sad? Am I not more to you than ten sons?"

9 After they had eaten and drunk at Shī'lōh, Hannah rose and presented herself before the LORD.*c* Now Ē'lī the priest was sitting on the seat beside the doorpost of the temple of the LORD. ¹⁰She was deeply distressed and prayed to the LORD, and wept bitterly. ¹¹She made this vow: "O LORD of hosts, if only you will look on the misery of your servant, and remember me, and not forget your servant, but will give to your servant a male child, then I will set him before you as a nazirite*d* until the day of his death. He shall drink neither wine nor intoxicants,*e* and no razor shall touch his head."

12 As she continued praying before the LORD, Ē'lī observed her mouth. ¹³Hannah was praying silently; only her lips moved, but her voice was not heard; therefore Ē'lī thought she was drunk. ¹⁴So Ē'lī said to her, "How long will you make a drunken spectacle of yourself? Put away your wine." ¹⁵But Hannah answered, "No, my lord, I am a woman deeply troubled; I have drunk neither wine nor strong drink, but I have been pouring out my soul before the LORD. ¹⁶Do not regard your servant as a worthless woman, for I have been speaking out of my great anxiety and vexation all this time." ¹⁷Then Ē'lī answered, "Go in peace; the God of Israel grant the petition you have made to him." ¹⁸And she said, "Let your servant find favor in your sight." Then the woman went to her quar-

a Compare Gk and 1 Chr 6.35-36: Heb *Ramathaim-zophim*
b Syr: Meaning of Heb uncertain   *c* Gk: Heb lacks *and presented herself before the* LORD   *d* That is *one separated* or *one consecrated*   *e* Cn Compare Gk Q Ms 1.22: MT *then I will give him to the* LORD *all the days of his life*

ters,*f* ate and drank with her husband,*g* and her countenance was sad no longer.*h*

19 They rose early in the morning and worshiped before the LORD; then they went back to their house at Rā′mah. El·kā′nah knew his wife Hannah, and the LORD remembered her. 20 In due time Hannah conceived and bore a son. She named him Samuel, for she said, "I have asked him of the LORD."

Prayers of Strong and Holy Women

Compare Hannah's prayer in 1 Sam 2.1–10 to Mary's prayer in Lk 1.46–55. Notice the joy, the confident faith in God's way, and the understanding that God will raise up those who are hungry, poor, and in need. Notice also how God will deal with the proud, the powerful, and the rich, especially in Mary's prayer. These holy women identify in their lives and in their prayers the bigger picture of what God is all about.

What strong and holy women in your life keep you in their prayers?

▸ 1 Sam 2.1–10

21 The man El·kā′nah and all his household went up to offer to the LORD the yearly sacrifice, and to pay his vow. 22 But Hannah did not go up, for she said to her husband, "As soon as the child is weaned, I will bring him, that he may appear in the presence of the LORD, and remain there forever; I will offer him as a nazirite*i* for all time."*j* 23 Her husband El·kā′nah said to her, "Do what seems best to you, wait until you have weaned him; only—may the LORD establish his word."*k* So the woman remained and nursed her son, until she weaned him. 24 When she had weaned him, she took him up with her, along with a three-year-old bull,*l* an ephah of flour, and a skin of wine. She brought him to the house of the LORD at Shī′lōh; and the child was young. 25 Then they slaughtered the bull, and they brought the child to Ē′lī. 26 And she said, "Oh, my lord! As you live, my lord, I am the woman who was standing here in your presence, praying to the LORD. 27 For this child I prayed; and the LORD has granted me the petition that I

made to him. 28 Therefore I have lent him to the LORD; as long as he lives, he is given to the LORD." She left him there for*m* the LORD.

Hannah's Prayer
(Cp Lk 1.46–55)

Hannah prayed and said,
  "My heart exults in the LORD;
    my strength is exalted in my God.*n*
  My mouth derides my enemies,
    because I rejoice in my*o* victory.

2 "There is no Holy One like the LORD,
    no one besides you;
  there is no Rock like our God.
3 Talk no more so very proudly,
    let not arrogance come from your mouth;
  for the LORD is a God of knowledge,
    and by him actions are weighed.
4 The bows of the mighty are broken,
    but the feeble gird on strength.
5 Those who were full have hired themselves
      out for bread,
  but those who were hungry are fat with
      spoil.
  The barren has borne seven,
    but she who has many children is
      forlorn.
6 The LORD kills and brings to life;
    he brings down to Shē′ōl and raises up.
7 The LORD makes poor and makes rich;
    he brings low, he also exalts.
8 He raises up the poor from the dust;
    he lifts the needy from the ash heap,
  to make them sit with princes
    and inherit a seat of honor.*p*
  For the pillars of the earth are the LORD's,
    and on them he has set the world.

9 "He will guard the feet of his faithful ones,
    but the wicked shall be cut off in
      darkness;
  for not by might does one prevail.
10 The LORD! His adversaries shall be shattered;
    the Most High*q* will thunder in heaven.

---

f Gk: Heb *went her way*   *g* Gk: Heb lacks *and drank with her husband*   *h* Gk: Meaning of Heb uncertain   *i* That is *one separated* or *one consecrated*   *j* Cn Compare Q Ms: MT lacks *I will offer him as a nazirite for all time*   *k* MT: Q Ms Gk Compare Syr *that which goes out of your mouth*   *l* Q Ms Gk Syr: MT *three bulls*   *m* Gk (Compare Q Ms) and Gk at 2.11: MT *And he* (that is, Elkanah) *worshiped there before*   *n* Gk: Heb *the LORD*   *o* Ms: MT *your*   *p* Gk (Compare Q Ms) adds *He grants the vow of the one who vows, and blesses the years of the just*   *q* Cn Heb *against him he*

The LORD will judge the ends of the earth;
he will give strength to his king,
and exalt the power of his anointed."

Eli's Wicked Sons

11 Then El•kā′nah went home to Rā′mah, while the boy remained to minister to the LORD, in the presence of the priest Ē′lī.

12 Now the sons of Ē′lī were scoundrels; they had no regard for the LORD 13 or for the duties of the priests to the people. When anyone offered sacrifice, the priest's servant would come, while the meat was boiling, with a three-pronged fork in his hand, 14 and he would thrust it into the pan, or kettle, or caldron, or pot; all that the fork brought up the priest would take for himself.r This is what they did at Shi′lōh to all the Israelites who came there. 15 Moreover, before the fat was burned, the priest's servant would come and say to the one who was sacrificing, "Give meat for the priest to roast; for he will not accept boiled meat from you, but only raw." 16 And if the man said to him, "Let them burn the fat first, and then take whatever you wish," he would say, "No, you must give it now; if not, I will take it by force." 17 Thus the sin of the young men was very great in the sight of the LORD; for they treated the offerings of the LORD with contempt.

The Child Samuel at Shiloh

18 Samuel was ministering before the LORD, a boy wearing a linen ephod. 19 His mother used to make for him a little robe and take it to him each year, when she went up with her husband to offer the yearly sacrifice. 20 Then Ē′lī would bless El•kā′-nah and his wife, and say, "May the LORD repays you with children by this woman for the gift that she made tot the LORD"; and then they would return to their home.

21 Andu the LORD took note of Hannah; she conceived and bore three sons and two daughters. And the boy Samuel grew up in the presence of the LORD.

Prophecy against Eli's Household

22 Now Ē′lī was very old. He heard all that his sons were doing to all Israel, and how they lay with the women who served at the entrance to the tent of meeting. 23 He said to them, "Why do you do such things? For I hear of your evil dealings from all these people. 24 No, my sons; it is not a good report that I hear the people of the LORD spreading abroad. 25 If one person sins against another, someone can intercede for the sinner with the LORD;v but if someone sins against the LORD, who can make intercession?" But they would not listen to the voice of their father; for it was the will of the LORD to kill them.

26 Now the boy Samuel continued to grow both in stature and in favor with the LORD and with the people.

27 A man of God came to Ē′lī and said to him, "Thus the LORD has said, 'I revealedw myself to the family of your ancestor in Egypt when they were slavesx to the house of Pharaoh. 28 I chose him out of all the tribes of Israel to be my priest, to go up to my altar, to offer incense, to wear an ephod before me; and I gave to the family of your ancestor all my offerings by fire from the people of Israel. 29 Why then look with greedy eyey at my sacrifices and my offerings that I commanded, and honor your sons more than me by fattening yourselves on the choicest parts of every offering of my people Israel?' 30 Therefore the LORD the God of Israel declares: 'I promised that your family and the family of your ancestor should go in and out before me forever'; but now the LORD declares: 'Far be it from me; for those who honor me I will honor, and those who despise me shall be treated with contempt. 31 See, a time is coming when I will cut off your strength and the strength of your ancestor's family, so that no one in your family will live to old age. 32 Then in distress you will look with greedy eyez on all the prosperity that shall be bestowed upon Israel; and no one in your family shall ever live to old age. 33 The only one of you whom I shall not cut off from my altar shall be spared to weep out hisa eyes and grieve hisb heart; all the members of your household shall die by the sword.c 34 The fate of your two sons, Hoph′nī and Phin′e•has, shall be the sign to you—both of them shall die on the same day. 35 I will raise up for myself a faithful priest, who shall do according to what is in my heart and in my mind. I will build him a sure house, and he shall go in and out before my anointed one forever. 36 Everyone who is left in your family shall come to implore him for a piece of silver or a loaf of bread, and shall say, Please put me in one of the priest's places, that I may eat a morsel of bread.' "

---

r Gk Syr Vg: Heb *with it*   s Q Ms Gk: MT *give*   t Q Ms Gk: MT *for the petition that she asked of*   u Q Ms Gk: MT *When*   v Gk Compare Q Ms: MT *another, God will mediate for him*   w Gk Tg Syr: Heb *Did I reveal*   x Q Ms Gk: MT lacks *slaves*   y Q Ms Gk: MT *then kick*   z Q Ms Gk: MT *will kick*   a Q Ms Gk: MT *your*   b Q Ms Gk: Heb *your*   c Q Ms See Gk: MT *die like mortals*

Samuel's Calling and Prophetic Activity

Now the boy Samuel was ministering to the LORD under Ē'lī. The word of the LORD was rare in those days; visions were not widespread.

2 At that time Ē'lī, whose eyesight had begun to grow dim so that he could not see, was lying down in his room; 3 the lamp of God had not yet gone out, and Samuel was lying down in the temple of the LORD, where the ark of God was. 4 Then the LORD called, "Samuel! Samuel!"*d* and he said, "Here I am!" 5 and ran to Ē'lī, and said, "Here I am, for you called me." But he said, "I did not call;

PRAY IT

Eli Teaches Samuel How to Pray

Eli taught Samuel to listen to God's voice with a simple sentence: "Speak, LORD, for your servant is listening" (1 Sam 3.9). Let's look at that sentence as a prayer:

"Speak, LORD . . ." This is an invitation. It shows openness and readiness. It shows your recognition of God: "You are the Almighty, and I am ready to hear what you have to say."

". . . for your servant . . ." This shows humility. It is a recognition of yourself: "I am your servant. It is my desire to do what you want. My life's purpose is to serve you."

". . . is listening." This demonstrates your response: "I am not going to ignore you. I am not going to daydream or just pretend to pay attention. I will take in your message, and it will become part of me."

▶ 1 Sam 3.1–19

lie down again." So he went and lay down. 6 The LORD called again, "Samuel!" Samuel got up and went to Ē'lī, and said, "Here I am, for you called me." But he said, "I did not call, my son; lie down again." 7 Now Samuel did not yet know the LORD, and the word of the LORD had not yet been revealed to him. 8 The LORD called Samuel again, a third time. And he got up and went to Ē'lī, and said, "Here I am, for you called me." Then Ē'lī perceived that the LORD was calling the boy. 9 Therefore Ē'lī said to Samuel, "Go, lie down; and if he calls you, you shall say, 'Speak, LORD, for your servant is listening.'" So Samuel went and lay down in his place.

10 Now the LORD came and stood there, calling as before, "Samuel! Samuel!" And Samuel said, "Speak, for your servant is listening." 11 Then the LORD said to Samuel, "See, I am about to do something in Israel that will make both ears of anyone who hears of it tingle. 12 On that day I will fulfill against Ē'lī all that I have spoken concerning his house, from beginning to end. 13 For I have told him that I am about to punish his house forever, for the iniquity that he knew, because his sons were blaspheming God,*e* and he did not restrain them. 14 Therefore I swear to the house of Ē'lī that the iniquity of Ē'lī's house shall not be expiated by sacrifice or offering forever."

15 Samuel lay there until morning; then he opened the doors of the house of the LORD. Samuel was afraid to tell the vision to Ē'lī. 16 But Ē'lī called Samuel and said, "Samuel, my son." He said, "Here I am." 17 Ē'lī said, "What was it that he told you? Do not hide it from me. May God do so to you and more also, if you hide anything from me of all that he told you." 18 So Samuel told him everything and hid nothing from him. Then he said, "It is the LORD; let him do what seems good to him."

19 As Samuel grew up, the LORD was with him and let none of his words fall to the ground. 20 And all Israel from Dan to Bē'er-shē'ba knew that Samuel was a trustworthy prophet of the LORD. 21 The LORD continued to appear at Shī'lōh, for the LORD revealed himself to Samuel at Shī'lōh by the word of the LORD. 1 And the word of Samuel came to all Israel.

The Ark of God Captured

In those days the Phi•lis'tines mustered for war against Israel,*f* and Israel went out to battle against them;*g* they encamped at Eb•e•nē'zer, and the Phi•lis'tines encamped at Ā'phek. 2 The Phi•lis'tines drew up in line against Israel, and when the battle was joined,*h* Israel was defeated by the Phi•lis'tines, who killed about four thousand men on the field of battle. 3 When the troops came to the camp, the elders of Israel said, "Why has the LORD

---

d Q Ms Gk See 3.10: MT *the LORD called Samuel*
e Another reading is *for themselves*   *f* Gk: Heb lacks *In those days the Philistines mustered for war against Israel*
g Gk: Heb *against the Philistines*   *h* Meaning of Heb uncertain

put us to rout today before the Phi·lis′tines? Let us bring the ark of the covenant of the LORD here from Shī′lōh, so that he may come among us and save us from the power of our enemies." ⁴So the people sent to Shī′lōh, and brought from there the ark of the covenant of the LORD of hosts, who is enthroned on the cherubim. The two sons of Ē′lī, Hoph′nī and Phin′e·has, were there with the ark of the covenant of God.

5 When the ark of the covenant of the LORD came into the camp, all Israel gave a mighty shout, so that the earth resounded. ⁶When the Phi·lis′tines heard the noise of the shouting, they said, "What does this great shouting in the camp of the Hebrews mean?" When they learned that the ark of the LORD had come to the camp, ⁷the Phi·lis′tines were afraid; for they said, "Gods have[i] come into the camp." They also said, "Woe to us! For nothing like this has happened before. ⁸Woe to us! Who can deliver us from the power of these mighty gods? These are the gods who struck the Egyptians with every sort of plague in the wilderness. ⁹Take courage, and be men, O Phi·lis′tines, in order not to become slaves to the Hebrews as they have been to you; be men and fight."

10 So the Phi·lis′tines fought; Israel was defeated, and they fled, everyone to his home. There was a very great slaughter, for there fell of Israel thirty thousand foot soldiers. ¹¹The ark of God was captured; and the two sons of Ē′lī, Hoph′nī and Phin′e·has, died.

Death of Eli

12 A man of Benjamin ran from the battle line, and came to Shī′lōh the same day, with his clothes torn and with earth upon his head. ¹³When he arrived, Ē′lī was sitting upon his seat by the road watching, for his heart trembled for the ark of God. When the man came into the city and told the news, all the city cried out. ¹⁴When Ē′lī heard the sound of the outcry, he said, "What is this uproar?" Then the man came quickly and told Ē′lī. ¹⁵Now Ē′lī was ninety-eight years old and his eyes were set, so that he could not see. ¹⁶The man said to Ē′lī, "I have just come from the battle; I fled from the battle today." He said, "How did it go, my son?" ¹⁷The messenger replied, "Israel has fled before the Phi·lis′tines, and there has also been a great slaughter among the troops; your two sons also, Hoph′nī and Phin′e·has, are dead, and the ark of God has been captured." ¹⁸When he mentioned the ark of God, Ē′lī fell over backward from his seat by the side of the gate; and his neck was broken and he died, for he was an old man, and heavy. He had judged Israel forty years.

19 Now his daughter-in-law, the wife of Phin′e·has, was pregnant, about to give birth. When she heard the news that the ark of God was captured, and that her father-in-law and her husband were dead, she bowed and gave birth; for her labor pains overwhelmed her. ²⁰As she was about to die, the women attending her said to her, "Do not be afraid, for you have borne a son." But she did not answer or give heed. ²¹She named the child Ich′a-bod, meaning, "The glory has departed from Israel," because the ark of God had been captured and because of her father-in-law and her husband. ²²She said, "The glory has departed from Israel, for the ark of God has been captured."

The Philistines and the Ark

When the Phi·lis′tines captured the ark of God, they brought it from Eb·e·nē′zer to Ash′dod; ²then the Phi·lis′tines took the ark of God and brought it into the house of Dā′gon and placed it beside Dā′-gon. ³When the people of Ash′dod rose early the next day, there was Dā′gon, fallen on his face to the ground before the ark of the LORD. So they took Dā′gon and put him back in his place. ⁴But when they rose early on the next morning, Dā′gon had fallen on his face to the ground before the ark of the LORD, and the head of Dā′gon and both his hands were lying cut off upon the threshold; only the trunk of[k] Dā′gon was left to him. ⁵This is why the priests of Dā′gon and all who enter the house of Dā′gon do not step on the threshold of Dā′gon in Ash′dod to this day.

6 The hand of the LORD was heavy upon the people of Ash′dod, and he terrified and struck them with tumors, both in Ash′dod and in its territory. ⁷And when the inhabitants of Ash′dod saw how things were, they said, "The ark of the God of Israel must not remain with us; for his hand is heavy on us and on our god Dā′gon." ⁸So they sent and gathered together all the lords of the Phi·lis′tines, and said, "What shall we do with the ark of the God of Israel?" The inhabitants of Gath replied, "Let the ark of God be moved on to us."[l] So they moved the ark of the God of Israel to Gath.[m] ⁹But after they had brought it to Gath,[n] the hand of the LORD was against the city, causing a very great panic; he struck the inhabitants of the city, both young and old, so that tumors broke out on them. ¹⁰So they sent the ark of the God of Israel[o] to Ek′ron. But when the ark of God came to Ek′ron, the people of Ek′ron cried out, "Why[p] have they

---

[i] Or A god has   [j] Heb he   [k] Heb lacks the trunk of
[l] Gk Compare Q Ms: MT They answered, "Let the ark of the God of Israel be brought around to Gath."   [m] Gk: Heb lacks to Gath   [n] Q Ms: MT lacks to Gath   [o] Q Ms Gk: MT lacks of Israel   [p] Q Ms Gk: MT lacks Why

brought around to us^q the ark of the God of Israel to kill us^q and our^r people?" 11 They sent therefore and gathered together all the lords of the Phi·lis′-tines, and said, "Send away the ark of the God of Israel, and let it return to its own place, that it may not kill us and our people." For there was a deathly panic^s throughout the whole city. The hand of God was very heavy there; 12 those who did not die were stricken with tumors, and the cry of the city went up to heaven.

The Ark Returned to Israel

The ark of the LORD was in the country of the Phi·lis′tines seven months. 2 Then the Phi·lis′tines called for the priests and the diviners and said, "What shall we do with the ark of the LORD? Tell us what we should send with it to its place." 3 They said, "If you send away the ark of the God of Israel, do not send it empty, but by all means return him a guilt offering. Then you will be healed and will be ransomed;^{t} will not his hand then turn from you?" 4 And they said, "What is the guilt offering that we shall return to him?" They answered, "Five gold tumors and five gold mice, according to the number of the lords of the Phi·lis′tines; for the same plague was upon all of you and upon your lords. 5 So you must make images of your tumors and images of your mice that ravage the land, and give glory to the God of Israel; perhaps he will lighten his hand on you and your gods and your land. 6 Why should you harden your hearts as the Egyptians and Pharaoh hardened their hearts? After he had made fools of them, did they not let the people go, and they departed? 7 Now then, get ready a new cart and two milch cows that have never borne a yoke, and yoke the cows to the cart, but take their calves home, away from them. 8 Take the ark of the LORD and place it on the cart, and put in a box at its side the figures of gold, which you are returning to him as a guilt offering. Then send it off, and let it go its way. 9 And watch; if it goes up on the way to its own land, to Beth-shē′-mesh, then it is he who has done us this great harm; but if not, then we shall know that it is not his hand that struck us; it happened to us by chance."

10 The men did so; they took two milch cows and yoked them to the cart, and shut up their calves at home. 11 They put the ark of the LORD on the cart, and the box with the gold mice and the images of their tumors. 12 The cows went straight in the direction of Beth-shē′mesh along one highway, lowing as they went; they turned neither to the right nor to the left, and the lords of the Phi·lis′tines went after them as far as the border of Beth-shē′mesh.

13 Now the people of Beth-shē′mesh were reaping their wheat harvest in the valley. When they looked up and saw the ark, they went with rejoicing to meet it.^{u} 14 The cart came into the field of Joshua of Beth-shē′mesh, and stopped there. A large stone was there; so they split up the wood of the cart and offered the cows as a burnt offering to the LORD. 15 The Lē′vītes took down the ark of the LORD and the box that was beside it, in which were the gold objects, and set them upon the large stone. Then the people of Beth-shē′mesh offered burnt offerings and presented sacrifices on that day to the LORD. 16 When the five lords of the Phi·lis′tines saw it, they returned that day to Ek′ron.

17 These are the gold tumors, which the Phi·lis′tines returned as a guilt offering to the LORD: one for Ash′dod, one for Gā′za, one for Ash′ke·lon, one for Gath, one for Ek′ron; 18 also the gold mice, according to the number of all the cities of the Phi·lis′tines belonging to the five lords, both fortified cities and unwalled villages. The great stone, beside which they set down the ark of the LORD, is a witness to this day in the field of Joshua of Beth-shē′mesh.

The Ark at Kiriath-jearim

19 The descendants of Jec·o·nī′ah did not rejoice with the people of Beth-shē′mesh when they greeted^v the ark of the LORD; and he killed seventy men of them.^{w} The people mourned because the LORD had made a great slaughter among the people. 20 Then the people of Beth-shē′mesh said, "Who is able to stand before the LORD, this holy God? To whom shall he go so that we may be rid of him?" 21 So they sent messengers to the inhabitants of Kir′i·ath-jē′a·rim, saying, "The Phi·lis′tines have returned the ark of the LORD. Come down and take it up to you." 1 And the people of Kir′i·ath-jē′a·rim came and took up the ark of the LORD, and brought it to the house of A·bin′a·dab on the hill. They consecrated his son, El·ē·ā′zar, to have charge of the ark of the LORD.

2 From the day that the ark was lodged at Kir′i·ath-jē′a·rim, a long time passed, some twenty years, and all the house of Israel lamented^x after the LORD.

---

^{q} Heb me ^{r} Heb my ^{s} Q Ms reads *a panic from the LORD* ^{t} Q Ms Gk: MT *and it will be known to you* ^{u} Gk: Heb *rejoiced to see it* ^{v} Gk: Heb *And he killed some of the people of Beth-shemesh, because they looked into* ^{w} Heb *killed seventy men, fifty thousand men* ^{x} Meani- Heb uncertain

Samuel as Judge

3 Then Samuel said to all the house of Israel, "If you are returning to the LORD with all your heart, then put away the foreign gods and the Astar′tēs from among you. Direct your heart to the LORD, and serve him only, and he will deliver you out of the hand of the Phi·lis′tines." 4 So Israel put away the Bā′als and the As·tar′tēs, and they served the LORD only.

5 Then Samuel said, "Gather all Israel at Miz′pah, and I will pray to the LORD for you." 6 So they gathered at Miz′pah, and drew water and poured it out before the LORD. They fasted that day, and said, "We have sinned against the LORD." And Samuel judged the people of Israel at Miz′pah.

7 When the Phi·lis′tines heard that the people of Israel had gathered at Miz′pah, the lords of the Phi·lis′tines went up against Israel. And when the people of Israel heard of it they were afraid of the Phi·lis′tines. 8 The people of Israel said to Samuel, "Do not cease to cry out to the LORD our God for us, and pray that he may save us from the hand of the Phi·lis′tines." 9 So Samuel took a sucking lamb and offered it as a whole burnt offering to the LORD; Samuel cried out to the LORD for Israel, and the LORD answered him. 10 As Samuel was offering up the burnt offering, the Phi·lis′tines drew near to attack Israel; but the LORD thundered with a mighty voice that day against the Phi·lis′tines and threw them into confusion; and they were routed before Israel. 11 And the men of Israel went out of Miz′pah and pursued the Phi·lis′tines, and struck them down as far as beyond Beth-car.

12 Then Samuel took a stone and set it up between Miz′pah and Je·shā′nah,ʸ and named it Eb·e·nē′zer;ᶻ for he said, "Thus far the LORD has helped us." 13 So the Phi·lis′tines were subdued and did not again enter the territory of Israel; the hand of the LORD was against the Phi·lis′tines all the days of Samuel. 14 The towns that the Phi·lis′tines had taken from Israel were restored to Israel, from Ek′ron to Gath; and Israel recovered their territory from the hand of the Phi·lis′tines. There was peace also between Israel and the Am′o·rītes.

15 Samuel judged Israel all the days of his life. 16 He went on a circuit year by year to Beth′el, Gil′gal, and Miz′pah; and he judged Israel in all these places. 17 Then he would come back to Rā′mah, for his home was there; he administered justice there to Israel, and built there an altar to the LORD.

Israel Demands a King

When Samuel became old, he made his sons judges over Israel. 2 The name of his firstborn son was Jō′el, and the name of his second, A·bī′jah; they were judges in Bē′er-shē′ba. 3 Yet his sons did not follow in his ways, but turned aside after gain; they took bribes and perverted justice.

4 Then all the elders of Israel gathered together and came to Samuel at Rā′mah, 5 and said to him, "You are old and your sons do not follow in your ways; appoint for us, then, a king to govern us, like other nations." 6 But the thing displeased Samuel when they said, "Give us a king to govern us." Samuel prayed to the LORD, 7 and the LORD said to Samuel, "Listen to the voice of the people in all that they say to you; for they have not rejected you, but they have rejected me from being king over them. 8 Just as they have done to me,ᵃ from the day I brought them up out of Egypt to this day, forsaking me and serving other gods, so also they are doing to you. 9 Now then, listen to their voice; only—you shall solemnly warn them, and show them the ways of the king who shall reign over them."

10 So Samuel reported all the words of the LORD to the people who were asking him for a king. 11 He said, "These will be the ways of the king who will reign over you: he will take your sons and appoint them to his chariots and to be his horsemen, and to run before his chariots; 12 and he will appoint for himself commanders of thousands and commanders of fifties, and some to plow his ground and to reap his harvest, and to make his implements of war and the equipment of his chariots. 13 He will take your daughters to be perfumers and cooks and bakers. 14 He will take the best of your fields and vineyards and olive orchards and give them to his courtiers. 15 He will take one-tenth of your grain and of your vineyards and give it to his officers and his courtiers. 16 He will take your male and female slaves, and the best of your cattleᵇ and donkeys, and put them to his work. 17 He will take one-tenth of your flocks, and you shall be his slaves. 18 And in that day you will cry out because of your king, whom you have chosen for yourselves; but the LORD will not answer you in that day."

Israel's Request for a King Granted

19 But the people refused to listen to the voice of Samuel; they said, "No! but we are determined to have a king over us, 20 so that we also may be like other nations, and that our king may govern

---

y Gk Syr: Heb *Shen*   z That is *Stone of Help*   a Gk: Heb lacks *to me*   b Gk: Heb *young men*

us and go out before us and fight our battles." ²¹When Samuel had heard all the words of the people, he repeated them in the ears of the LORD. ²²The LORD said to Samuel, "Listen to their voice and set a king over them." Samuel then said to the people of Israel, "Each of you return home."

?did you KNOW?

Doublets

Often, more than one version of a story is recorded in the Bible. Genesis has two stories of the Creation (1.1—2.4; 2.4—25). The First Book of Samuel has two different attitudes toward the request to have a king in Israel. Compare the anti-king passages of 8.10–22 and 10.17–19 with the pro-king passages of 9.15–16 and chapter 11. Most likely, the difference of opinion comes from different parts of Israel. The Bible often combines two versions of a story, called doublets, to allow consideration of both sides of an issue.

Saul Chosen to Be King

There was a man of Benjamin whose name was Kish son of A•bī′el son of Zē′ror son of Be•cō′rath son of A•phī′ah, a Ben′ja•min•ite, a man of wealth. ²He had a son whose name was Saul, a handsome young man. There was not a man among the people of Israel more handsome than he; he stood head and shoulders above everyone else.

3 Now the donkeys of Kish, Saul's father, had strayed. So Kish said to his son Saul, "Take one of the boys with you; go and look for the donkeys." ⁴He passed through the hill country of Ē′phra•im and passed through the land of Shal′i•shah, but they did not find them. And they passed through the land of Shā′a•lim, but they were not there. Then he passed through the land of Benjamin, but they did not find them.

5 When they came to the land of Zuph, Saul said to the boy who was with him, "Let us turn back, or my father will stop worrying about the donkeys and worry about us." ⁶But he said to him, "There is a man of God in this town; he is a man held in honor. Whatever he says always comes true. Let us go there now; perhaps he will tell us about the journey on which we have set out." ⁷Then Saul replied to the boy, "But if we go, what

can we bring the man? For the bread in our sacks is gone, and there is no present to bring to the man of God. What have we?" ⁸The boy answered Saul again, "Here, I have with me a quarter shekel of silver; I will give it to the man of God, to tell us our way." ⁹(Formerly in Israel, anyone who went to inquire of God would say, "Come, let us go to the seer"; for the one who is now called a prophet was formerly called a seer.) ¹⁰Saul said to the boy, "Good; come, let us go." So they went to the town where the man of God was.

11 As they went up the hill to the town, they met some girls coming out to draw water, and said to them, "Is the seer here?" ¹²They answered, "Yes, there he is just ahead of you. Hurry; he has come just now to the town, because the people have a sacrifice today at the shrine. ¹³As soon as you enter the town, you will find him, before he goes up to the shrine to eat. For the people will not eat until he comes, since he must bless the sacrifice; afterward those eat who are invited. Now go up, for you will meet him immediately." ¹⁴So they went up to the town. As they were entering the town, they saw Samuel coming out toward them on his way up to the shrine.

15 Now the day before Saul came, the LORD had revealed to Samuel: ¹⁶"Tomorrow about this time I will send to you a man from the land of Benjamin, and you shall anoint him to be ruler over my people Israel. He shall save my people from the hand of the Phi•lis′tines; for I have seen the suffering of ᶜ my people, because their outcry has come to me." ¹⁷When Samuel saw Saul, the LORD told him, "Here is the man of whom I spoke to you. He it is who shall rule over my people." ¹⁸Then Saul approached Samuel inside the gate, and said, "Tell me, please, where is the house of the seer?" ¹⁹Samuel answered Saul, "I am the seer; go up before me to the shrine, for today you shall eat with me, and in the morning I will let you go and will tell you all that is on your mind. ²⁰As for your donkeys that were lost three days ago, give no further thought to them, for they have been found. And on whom is all Israel's desire fixed, if not on you and on all your ancestral house?" ²¹Saul answered, "I am only a Ben′ja•min•ite, from the least of the tribes of Israel, and my family is the humblest of all the families of the tribe of Benjamin. Why then have you spoken to me in this way?"

22 Then Samuel took Saul and his servant-boy and brought them into the hall, and gave them a place at the head of those who had been invited, of whom there were about thirty. ²³And Samuel said to the cook, "Bring the portion I gave you, the

---

ᶜ Gk: Heb lacks *the suffering of*

one I asked you to put aside." 24 The cook took up the thigh and what went with it*d* and set them before Saul. Samuel said, "See, what was kept is set before you. Eat; for it is set*e* before you at the appointed time, so that you might eat with the guests."*f*

So Saul ate with Samuel that day. 25 When they came down from the shrine into the town, a bed was spread for Saul*g* on the roof, and he lay down to sleep.*h* 26 Then at the break of dawn*i* Samuel called to Saul upon the roof, "Get up, so that I may send you on your way." Saul got up, and both he and Samuel went out into the street.

Samuel Anoints Saul

27 As they were going down to the outskirts of the town, Samuel said to Saul, "Tell the boy to go on before us, and when he has passed on, stop here yourself for a while, that I may make known to you the word of God." 1 Samuel took a vial of oil and poured it on his head, and kissed him; he said, "The LORD has anointed you ruler over his people Israel. You shall reign over the people of the LORD and you will save them from the hand of their enemies all around. Now this shall be the sign to you that the LORD has anointed you ruler*j* over his heritage: 2 When you depart from me today you will meet two men by Rachel's tomb in the territory of Benjamin at Zel'zah; they will say to you, 'The donkeys that you went to seek are found, and now your father has stopped worrying about them and is worrying about you, saying: What shall I do about my son?' 3 Then you shall go on from there further and come to the oak of Tā'-bor; three men going up to God at Beth'el will meet you there, one carrying three kids, another carrying three loaves of bread, and another carrying a skin of wine. 4 They will greet you and give you two loaves of bread, which you shall accept from them. 5 After that you shall come to Gib'ē-ath-e•lō'him,*k* at the place where the Phi•lis'tine garrison is; there, as you come to the town, you will meet a band of prophets coming down from the shrine with harp, tambourine, flute, and lyre playing in front of them; they will be in a prophetic frenzy. 6 Then the spirit of the LORD will possess you, and you will be in a prophetic frenzy along with them and be turned into a different person. 7 Now when these signs meet you, do whatever you see fit to do, for God is with you. 8 And you shall go down to Gil'gal ahead of me; then I will come down to you to present burnt offerings and offer sacrifices of well-being. Seven days you shall wait, until I come to you and show you what you shall do."

Saul Prophesies

9 As he turned away to leave Samuel, God gave him another heart; and all these signs were fulfilled that day. 10 When they were going from there*l* to Gib'ē•ah,*m* a band of prophets met him; and the spirit of God possessed him, and he fell into a prophetic frenzy along with them. 11 When all who knew him before saw how he prophesied with the prophets, the people said to one another, "What has come over the son of Kish? Is Saul also among the prophets?" 12 A man of the place answered, "And who is their father?" Therefore it became a proverb, "Is Saul also among the prophets?" 13 When his prophetic frenzy had ended, he went home.*n*

14 Saul's uncle said to him and to the boy, "Where did you go?" And he replied, "To seek the donkeys; and when we saw they were not to be found, we went to Samuel." 15 Saul's uncle said, "Tell me what Samuel said to you." 16 Saul said to his uncle, "He told us that the donkeys had been found." But about the matter of the kingship, of which Samuel had spoken, he did not tell him anything.

Saul Proclaimed King

17 Samuel summoned the people to the LORD at Miz'pah 18 and said to them,*o* "Thus says the LORD, the God of Israel, 'I brought up Israel out of Egypt, and I rescued you from the hand of the Egyptians and from the hand of all the kingdoms that were oppressing you.' 19 But today you have rejected your God, who saves you from all your calamities and your distresses; and you have said, 'No! but set a king over us.' Now therefore present yourselves before the LORD by your tribes and by your clans."

20 Then Samuel brought all the tribes of Israel near, and the tribe of Benjamin was taken by lot. 21 He brought the tribe of Benjamin near by its families, and the family of the Mā'trites was taken by lot. Finally he brought the family of the Mā'trites near man by man,*p* and Saul the son of Kish was taken by lot. But when they sought him, he could not be found. 22 So they inquired again of the LORD, "Did the man come here?"*q* and the LORD

d Meaning of Heb uncertain   *e* Q Ms Gk: MT *it was kept*
f Cn: Heb *it was kept for you, saying, I have invited the people*
g Gk: Heb *and he spoke with Saul*   *h* Gk: Heb lacks *and he lay down to sleep*   *i* Gk: Heb *and they arose early and at break of dawn*   *j* Gk: Heb *over his people Israel. You shall . . . anointed you ruler*   *k* Or *the Hill of God*
l Gk: Heb *they came there*   *m* Or *the hill*   *n* Cn: Heb *he came to the shrine*   *o* Heb *to the people of Israel*
p Gk: Heb lacks *Finally . . . man by man*   *q* Gk: Heb *Is there yet a man to come here?*

said, "See, he has hidden himself among the baggage." 23 Then they ran and brought him from there. When he took his stand among the people, he was head and shoulders taller than any of them. 24 Samuel said to all the people, "Do you see the one whom the LORD has chosen? There is no one like him among all the people." And all the people shouted, "Long live the king!"

25 Samuel told the people the rights and duties of the kingship; and he wrote them in a book and laid it up before the LORD. Then Samuel sent all the people back to their homes. 26 Saul also went to his home at Gib′e·ah, and with him went warriors whose hearts God had touched. 27 But some worthless fellows said, "How can this man save us?" They despised him and brought him no present. But he held his peace.

Now Nā′hash, king of the Am′mon·ites, had been grievously oppressing the Gad′ītes and the Reū′ben·ites. He would gouge out the right eye of each of them and would not grant Israel a deliverer. No one was left of the Israelites across the Jordan whose right eye Nā′hash, king of the Am′mon·ites, had not gouged out. But there were seven thousand men who had escaped from the Am′mon·ites and had entered Jā′besh-gil′ē·ad.[r]

Saul Defeats the Ammonites

11 About a month later,[s] Nā′hash the Am′mon·ite went up and besieged Jā′besh-gil′ē·ad; and all the men of Jā′besh said to Nā′hash, "Make a treaty with us, and we will serve you." 2 But Nā′hash the Am′mon·ite said to them, "On this condition I will make a treaty with you, namely that I gouge out everyone's right eye, and thus put disgrace upon all Israel." 3 The elders of Jā′besh said to him, "Give us seven days' respite that we may send messengers through all the territory of Israel. Then, if there is no one to save us, we will give ourselves up to you." 4 When the messengers came to Gib′ē·ah of Saul, they reported the matter in the hearing of the people; and all the people wept aloud.

5 Now Saul was coming from the field behind the oxen; and Saul said, "What is the matter with the people, that they are weeping?" So they told him the message from the inhabitants of Jā′besh. 6 And the spirit of God came upon Saul in power when he heard these words, and his anger was greatly kindled. 7 He took a yoke of oxen, and cut them in pieces and sent them throughout all the territory of Israel by messengers, saying, "Whoever does not come out after Saul and Samuel, so shall it be done to his oxen!" Then the dread of the LORD fell upon the people, and they came out as one. 8 When he mustered them at Bē′zek, those from Israel were three hundred thousand, and those

from Judah seventy[t] thousand. 9 They said to the messengers who had come, "Thus shall you say to the inhabitants of Jā′besh-gil′ē·ad: 'Tomorrow, by the time the sun is hot, you shall have deliverance.' " When the messengers came and told the inhabitants of Jā′besh, they rejoiced. 10 So the inhabitants of Jā′besh said, "Tomorrow we will give ourselves up to you, and you may do to us whatever seems good to you." 11 The next day Saul put the people in three companies. At the morning watch they came into the camp and cut down the Am′mon·ites until the heat of the day; and those who survived were scattered, so that no two of them were left together.

12 The people said to Samuel, "Who is it that said, 'Shall Saul reign over us?' Give them to us so that we may put them to death." 13 But Saul said, "No one shall be put to death this day, for today the LORD has brought deliverance to Israel."

14 Samuel said to the people, "Come, let us go to Gil′gal and there renew the kingship." 15 So all the people went to Gil′gal, and there they made Saul king before the LORD in Gil′gal. There they sacrificed offerings of well-being before the LORD, and there Saul and all the Israelites rejoiced greatly.

Samuel's Farewell Address

12 Samuel said to all Israel, "I have listened to you in all that you have said to me, and have set a king over you. 2 See, it is the king who leads you now; I am old and gray, but my sons are with you. I have led you from my youth until this day. 3 Here I am; testify against me before the LORD and before his anointed. Whose ox have I taken? Or whose donkey have I taken? Or whom have I defrauded? Whom have I oppressed? Or from whose hand have I taken a bribe to blind my eyes with it? Testify against me[u] and I will restore it to you." 4 They said, "You have not defrauded us or oppressed us or taken anything from the hand of anyone." 5 He said to them, "The LORD is witness against you, and his anointed is witness this day, that you have not found anything in my hand." And they said, "He is witness."

6 Samuel said to the people, "The LORD is witness, who[v] appointed Moses and Aaron and brought your ancestors up out of the land of Egypt. 7 Now therefore take your stand, so that I may enter into judgment with you before the LORD, and I will declare to you[w] all the saving deeds of

---

r Q Ms Compare Josephus, *Antiquities* VI.v.1 (68-71): MT lacks *Now Nahash . . . entered Jabesh-gilead.*   s Q Ms Gk: MT lacks *About a month later*   t Q Ms Gk: MT *thirty*   u Gk: Heb lacks *Testify against me*   v Gk: Heb lacks *is witness, who*   w Gk: Heb lacks *and I will declare to you*

the LORD that he performed for you and for your ancestors. [8] When Jacob went into Egypt and the Egyptians oppressed them,[x] then your ancestors cried to the LORD and the LORD sent Moses and Aaron, who brought forth your ancestors out of Egypt, and settled them in this place. [9] But they forgot the LORD their God; and he sold them into the hand of Sis'e·ra, commander of the army of King Ja'bin of[y] Ha'zor, and into the hand of the Phi·lis'tines, and into the hand of the king of Mo'ab; and they fought against them. [10] Then they cried to the LORD, and said, 'We have sinned, because we have forsaken the LORD, and have served the Ba'als and the As·tar'tes; but now rescue us out of the hand of our enemies, and we will serve you.' [11] And the LORD sent Jer·ub·ba'al and Bar'ak,[z] and Jeph'thah, and Samson,[a] and rescued you out of the hand of your enemies on every side; and you lived in safety. [12] But when you saw that King Na'hash of the Am'mon·ites came against you, you said to me, 'No, but a king shall reign over us,' though the LORD your God was your king. [13] See, here is the king whom you have chosen, for whom you have asked; see, the LORD has set a king over you. [14] If you will fear the LORD and serve him and heed his voice and not rebel against the commandment of the LORD, and if both you and the king who reigns over you will follow the LORD your God, it will be well; [15] but if you will not heed the voice of the LORD, but rebel against the commandment of the LORD, then the hand of the LORD will be against you and your king.[b] [16] Now therefore take your stand and see this great thing that the LORD will do before your eyes. [17] Is it not the wheat harvest today? I will call upon the LORD, that he may send thunder and rain; and you shall know and see that the wickedness that you have done in the sight of the LORD is great in demanding a king for yourselves." [18] So Samuel called upon the LORD, and the LORD sent thunder and rain that day; and all the people greatly feared the LORD and Samuel.

19 All the people said to Samuel, "Pray to the LORD your God for your servants, so that we may not die; for we have added to all our sins the evil of demanding a king for ourselves." [20] And Samuel said to the people, "Do not be afraid; you have done all this evil, yet do not turn aside from following the LORD, but serve the LORD with all your heart; [21] and do not turn aside after useless things that cannot profit or save, for they are useless. [22] For the LORD will not cast away his people, for his great name's sake, because it has pleased the LORD to make you a people for himself. [23] Moreover as for me, far be it from me that I should sin against the LORD by ceasing to pray for you; and I will instruct you in the good and the right way.

[24] Only fear the LORD, and serve him faithfully with all your heart; for consider what great things he has done for you. [25] But if you still do wickedly, you shall be swept away, both you and your king."

Saul's Unlawful Sacrifice

Saul was . . .[c] years old when he began to reign; and he reigned . . . and two[d] years over Israel.

2 Saul chose three thousand out of Israel; two thousand were with Saul in Mich'mash and the hill country of Beth'el, and a thousand were with Jonathan in Gib'e·ah of Benjamin; the rest of the people he sent home to their tents. [3] Jonathan defeated the garrison of the Phi·lis'tines that was at Ge'ba; and the Phi·lis'tines heard of it. And Saul blew the trumpet throughout all the land, saying, "Let the Hebrews hear!" [4] When all Israel heard that Saul had defeated the garrison of the Phi·lis'tines, and also that Israel had become odious to the Phi·lis'tines, the people were called out to join Saul at Gil'gal.

5 The Phi·lis'tines mustered to fight with Israel, thirty thousand chariots, and six thousand horsemen, and troops like the sand on the seashore in multitude; they came up and encamped at Mich'mash, to the east of Beth-a'ven. [6] When the Israelites saw that they were in distress (for the troops were hard pressed), the people hid themselves in caves and in holes and in rocks and in tombs and in cisterns. [7] Some Hebrews crossed the Jordan to the land of Gad and Gil'e·ad. Saul was still at Gil'gal, and all the people followed him trembling.

8 He waited seven days, the time appointed by Samuel; but Samuel did not come to Gil'gal, and the people began to slip away from Saul.[e] [9] So Saul said, "Bring the burnt offering here to me, and the offerings of well-being." And he offered the burnt offering. [10] As soon as he had finished offering the burnt offering, Samuel arrived; and Saul went out to meet him and salute him. [11] Samuel said, "What have you done?" Saul replied, "When I saw that the people were slipping away from me, and that you did not come within the days appointed, and that the Phi·lis'tines were mustering at Mich'mash, [12] I said, 'Now the Phi·lis'tines will come down upon me at Gil'gal, and I have not entreated the favor of the LORD'; so I forced myself, and offered the burnt offering." [13] Samuel said to Saul, "You have done foolishly; you have not kept the commandment of the LORD your God, which he

---

[x] Gk: Heb lacks *and the Egyptians oppressed them*
[y] Gk: Heb lacks *King Jabin of*   [z] Gk Syr: Heb *Bedan*
[a] Gk: Heb *Samuel*   [b] Gk: Heb *and your ancestors*
[c] The number is lacking in the Heb text (the verse is lacking in the Septuagint).   [d] *Two* is not the entire number; something has dropped out.   [e] Heb *him*

commanded you. The LORD would have established your kingdom over Israel forever, 14 but now your kingdom will not continue; the LORD has sought out a man after his own heart; and the LORD has appointed him to be ruler over his people, because you have not kept what the LORD commanded you." 15 And Samuel left and went on his way from Gil'gal.*f* The rest of the people followed Saul to join the army; they went up from Gil'gal toward Gib'e·ah of Benjamin.*g*

Preparations for Battle

Saul counted the people who were present with him, about six hundred men. 16 Saul, his son Jonathan, and the people who were present with them stayed in Ge'ba of Benjamin; but the Phi·lis'tines encamped at Mich'mash. 17 And raiders came out of the camp of the Phi·lis'tines in three companies; one company turned toward Oph'rah, to the land of Shu'al, 18 another company turned toward Beth-ho'ron, and another company turned toward the mountain*h* that looks down upon the valley of Ze-bo'im toward the wilderness.

19 Now there was no smith to be found throughout all the land of Israel; for the Phi·lis'-tines said, "The Hebrews must not make swords or spears for themselves"; 20 so all the Israelites went down to the Phi·lis'tines to sharpen their plowshares, mattocks, axes, or sickles;*i* 21 The charge was two-thirds of a shekel*j* for the plowshares and for the mattocks, and one-third of a shekel for sharpening the axes and for setting the goads.*k* 22 So on the day of the battle neither sword nor spear was to be found in the possession of any of the people with Saul and Jonathan; but Saul and his son Jonathan had them.

Jonathan Surprises and Routs the Philistines

23 Now a garrison of the Phi·lis'tines had gone out to the pass of Mich'mash. 1 One day Jonathan son of Saul said to the young man who carried his armor, "Come, let us go over to the Phi·lis'tine garrison on the other side." But he did not tell his father. 2 Saul was staying in the outskirts of Gib'-e·ah under the pomegranate tree that is at Mig'ron; the troops that were with him were about six hundred men, 3 along with A·hi'jah son of A·hi'tub, Ich'a·bod's brother, son of Phin'e·has son of E'li, the priest of the LORD in Shi'loh, carrying an ephod. Now the people did not know that Jonathan had gone. 4 In the pass,*l* by which Jonathan tried to go over to the Phi·lis'tine garrison, there was a rocky crag on one side and a rocky crag on the other; the name of the one was Bo'zez, and the name of the other Se'neh. 5 One crag rose on the

north in front of Mich'mash, and the other on the south in front of Ge'ba.

6 Jonathan said to the young man who carried his armor, "Come, let us go over to the garrison of these uncircumcised; it may be that the LORD will act for us; for nothing can hinder the LORD from saving by many or by few." 7 His armor-bearer said to him, "Do all that your mind inclines to.*m* I am with you; as your mind is, so is mine."*n* 8 Then Jonathan said, "Now we will cross over to those men and will show ourselves to them. 9 If they say to us, 'Wait until we come to you,' then we will stand still in our place, and we will not go up to them. 10 But if they say, 'Come up to us,' then we will go up; for the LORD has given them into our hand. That will be the sign for us." 11 So both of them showed themselves to the garrison of the Phi·lis'-tines; and the Phi·lis'tines said, "Look, Hebrews are coming out of the holes where they have hidden themselves." 12 The men of the garrison hailed Jonathan and his armor-bearer, saying, "Come up to us, and we will show you something." Jonathan said to his armor-bearer, "Come up after me; for the LORD has given them into the hand of Israel." 13 Then Jonathan climbed up on his hands and feet, with his armor-bearer following after him. The Phi·lis'tines*o* fell before Jonathan, and his armor-bearer, coming after him, killed them. 14 In that first slaughter Jonathan and his armor-bearer killed about twenty men within an area about half a furrow long in an acre*p* of land. 15 There was a panic in the camp, in the field, and among all the people; the garrison and even the raiders trembled; the earth quaked; and it became a very great panic.

16 Saul's lookouts in Gib'e·ah of Benjamin were watching as the multitude was surging back and forth.*q* 17 Then Saul said to the troops that were with him, "Call the roll and see who has gone from us." When they had called the roll, Jonathan and his armor-bearer were not there. 18 Saul said to A·hi'jah, "Bring the ark*r* of God here." For at that time the ark*r* of God went with the Israelites. 19 While Saul was talking to the priest, the tumult in the camp of the Phi·lis'tines increased more and more; and Saul said to the priest, "Withdraw your hand." 20 Then Saul and all the people who were with him rallied and went into the battle; and every sword was against the other, so that there was

---

f Gk: Heb *went up from Gilgal to Gibeah of Benjamin*
g Gk: Heb lacks *The rest . . . of Benjamin*   *h* Cn Compare
Gk: Heb *toward the border*   *i* Gk: Heb *plowshare*
j Heb *was a pim*   *k* Cn: Meaning of Heb uncertain
l Heb *Between the passes*   *m* Gk: Heb *Do all that is in your
mind. Turn*   *n* Gk: Heb lacks *so is mine*   *o* Heb *They*
p Heb *yoke*   *q* Gk: Heb *they went and there*   *r* Gk *the
ephod*

very great confusion. 21 Now the Hebrews who previously had been with the Phi·lis′tines and had gone up with them into the camp turned and joined the Israelites who were with Saul and Jonathan. 22 Likewise, when all the Israelites who had gone into hiding in the hill country of E′phra·im heard that the Phi·lis′tines were fleeing, they too followed closely after them in the battle. 23 So the LORD gave Israel the victory that day.

The battle passed beyond Beth-a′ven, and the troops with Saul numbered altogether about ten thousand men. The battle spread out over the hill country of E′phra·im.

Saul's Rash Oath

24 Now Saul committed a very rash act on that day.[s] He had laid an oath on the troops, saying, "Cursed be anyone who eats food before it is evening and I have been avenged on my enemies." So none of the troops tasted food. 25 All the troops[t] came upon a honeycomb; and there was honey on the ground. 26 When the troops came upon the honeycomb, the honey was dripping out; but they did not put their hands to their mouths, for they feared the oath. 27 But Jonathan had not heard his father charge the troops with the oath; so he extended the staff that was in his hand, and dipped the tip of it in the honeycomb, and put his hand to his mouth; and his eyes brightened. 28 Then one of the soldiers said, "Your father strictly charged the troops with an oath, saying, 'Cursed be anyone who eats food this day.' And so the troops are faint." 29 Then Jonathan said, "My father has troubled the land; see how my eyes have brightened because I tasted a little of this honey. 30 How much better if today the troops had eaten freely of the spoil taken from their enemies; for now the slaughter among the Phi·lis′tines has not been great."

31 After they had struck down the Phi·lis′tines that day from Mich′mash to Ai′ja·lon, the troops were very faint; 32 so the troops flew upon the spoil, and took sheep and oxen and calves, and slaughtered them on the ground; and the troops ate them with the blood. 33 Then it was reported to Saul, "Look, the troops are sinning against the LORD by eating with the blood." And he said, "You have dealt treacherously; roll a large stone before me here."[u] 34 Saul said, "Disperse yourselves among the troops, and say to them, 'Let all bring their oxen or their sheep, and slaughter them here, and eat; and do not sin against the LORD by eating with the blood.' " So all of the troops brought their oxen with them that night, and slaughtered them there. 35 And Saul built an altar to the LORD; it was the first altar that he built to the LORD.

Jonathan in Danger of Death

36 Then Saul said, "Let us go down after the Phi·lis′tines by night and despoil them until the morning light; let us not leave one of them." They said, "Do whatever seems good to you." But the priest said, "Let us draw near to God here." 37 So Saul inquired of God, "Shall I go down after the Phi·lis′tines? Will you give them into the hand of Israel?" But he did not answer him that day. 38 Saul said, "Come here, all you leaders of the people; and let us find out how this sin has arisen today. 39 For as the LORD lives who saves Israel, even if it is in my son Jonathan, he shall surely die!" But there was no one among all the people who answered him. 40 He said to all Israel, "You shall be on one side, and I and my son Jonathan will be on the other side." The people said to Saul, "Do what seems good to you." 41 Then Saul said, "O LORD God of Israel, why have you not answered your servant today? If this guilt is in me or in my son Jonathan, O LORD God of Israel, give U′rim; but if this guilt is in your people Israel,[v] give Thum′mim." And Jonathan and Saul were indicated by the lot, but the people were cleared. 42 Then Saul said, "Cast the lot between me and my son Jonathan." And Jonathan was taken.

43 Then Saul said to Jonathan, "Tell me what you have done." Jonathan told him, "I tasted a little honey with the tip of the staff that was in my hand; here I am, I will die." 44 Saul said, "God do so to me and more also; you shall surely die, Jonathan!" 45 Then the people said to Saul, "Shall Jonathan die, who has accomplished this great victory in Israel? Far from it! As the LORD lives, not one hair of his head shall fall to the ground; for he has worked with God today." So the people ransomed Jonathan, and he did not die. 46 Then Saul withdrew from pursuing the Phi·lis′tines; and the Phi·lis′tines went to their own place.

Saul's Continuing Wars

47 When Saul had taken the kingship over Israel, he fought against all his enemies on every side—against Mo′ab, against the Am′mon·ites, against E′dom, against the kings of Zo′bah, and against the Phi·lis′tines; wherever he turned he routed them. 48 He did valiantly, and struck down the A·mal′e·kites, and rescued Israel out of the hands of those who plundered them.

49 Now the sons of Saul were Jonathan, Ish′vi, and Mal·chi·shu′a; and the names of his two daughters were these: the name of the firstborn was Me′-

---

s Gk: Heb *The Israelites were distressed that day*   t Heb *land*
u Gk: Heb *me this day*   v Vg Compare Gk: Heb *41 Saul said to the LORD, the God of Israel*

1
S
A
M

rab, and the name of the younger, Mi′chal. 50 The name of Saul's wife was A·hin′ō·am daughter of A·him′a·az. And the name of the commander of his army was Abner son of Ner, Saul's uncle; 51 Kish was the father of Saul, and Ner the father of Abner was the son of A·bi′el.

52 There was hard fighting against the Phi·lis′-tines all the days of Saul; and when Saul saw any strong or valiant warrior, he took him into his service.

Saul Defeats the Amalekites but Spares Their King

Samuel said to Saul, "The LORD sent me to anoint you king over his people Israel; now therefore listen to the words of the LORD. 2 Thus says the LORD of hosts, 'I will punish the A·mal′e·kites for what they did in opposing the Israelites when they came up out of Egypt. 3 Now go and attack Am′a·lek, and utterly destroy all that they have; do not spare them, but kill both man and woman, child and infant, ox and sheep, camel and donkey.' "

4 So Saul summoned the people, and numbered them in Te·la′im, two hundred thousand foot soldiers, and ten thousand soldiers of Judah. 5 Saul came to the city of the A·mal′e·kites and lay in wait in the valley. 6 Saul said to the Ken′ites, "Go! Leave! Withdraw from among the A·mal′e-kites, or I will destroy you with them; for you showed kindness to all the people of Israel when they came up out of Egypt." So the Ken′ites withdrew from the A·mal′e·kites. 7 Saul defeated the A·mal′e·kites, from Hav′i·lah as far as Shur, which is east of Egypt. 8 He took King Ā′gag of the A·mal′e-kites alive, but utterly destroyed all the people with the edge of the sword. 9 Saul and the people spared Ā′gag, and the best of the sheep and of the cattle and of the fatlings, and the lambs, and all that was valuable, and would not utterly destroy

them; all that was despised and worthless they utterly destroyed.

Saul Rejected as King

10 The word of the LORD came to Samuel: 11 "I regret that I made Saul king, for he has turned back from following me, and has not carried out my commands." Samuel was angry; and he cried out to the LORD all night. 12 Samuel rose early in the morning to meet Saul, and Samuel was told, "Saul went to Car′mel, where he set up a monument for himself, and on returning he passed on down to Gil′gal." 13 When Samuel came to Saul, Saul said to him, "May you be blessed by the LORD; I have carried out the command of the LORD." 14 But Samuel said, "What then is this bleating of sheep in my ears, and the lowing of cattle that I hear?" 15 Saul said, "They have brought them from the A·mal′e·kites; for the people spared the best of the sheep and the cattle, to sacrifice to the LORD your God; but the rest we have utterly destroyed." 16 Then Samuel said to Saul, "Stop! I will tell you what the LORD said to me last night." He replied, "Speak."

17 Samuel said, "Though you are little in your own eyes, are you not the head of the tribes of Israel? The LORD anointed you king over Israel. 18 And the LORD sent you on a mission, and said, 'Go, utterly destroy the sinners, the A·mal′e·kites, and fight against them until they are consumed.' 19 Why then did you not obey the voice of the LORD? Why did you swoop down on the spoil, and do what was evil in the sight of the LORD?" 20 Saul said to Samuel, "I have obeyed the voice of the LORD, I have gone on the mission on which the LORD sent me, I have brought Ā′gag the king of Am′a·lek, and I have utterly destroyed the A·mal′e-kites. 21 But from the spoil the people took sheep and cattle, the best of the things devoted to

Power and Corruption

Power corrupts. We have often heard that phrase. And in 1 Sam 15.22–23, we have a vivid example. King Saul once again has decided to take matters in his own hands and goes against the word of the Lord. He seems to assume that his role as king exempts him from obedience to God. But Samuel reminds Saul that he has assumed way too much. No king, no president, no prime minster is above the law. Especially when that Law comes from God.

Have you ever been in a position of leadership and been tempted to abuse your privileges?

▶ I Sam 15.22–23

destruction, to sacrifice to the LORD your God in Gil'gal." 22 And Samuel said,

"Has the LORD as great delight in burnt
offerings and sacrifices,
as in obedience to the voice of the LORD?
Surely, to obey is better than sacrifice,
and to heed than the fat of rams.
23 For rebellion is no less a sin than
divination,
and stubbornness is like iniquity and
idolatry.
Because you have rejected the word of the
LORD,
he has also rejected you from being king."

24 Saul said to Samuel, "I have sinned; for I have transgressed the commandment of the LORD and your words, because I feared the people and obeyed their voice. 25 Now therefore, I pray, pardon my sin, and return with me, so that I may worship the LORD." 26 Samuel said to Saul, "I will not return with you; for you have rejected the word of the LORD, and the LORD has rejected you from being king over Israel." 27 As Samuel turned to go away, Saul caught hold of the hem of his robe, and it tore. 28 And Samuel said to him, "The LORD has torn the kingdom of Israel from you this very day, and has given it to a neighbor of yours, who is better than you. 29 Moreover the Glory of Israel will not recant[w] or change his mind; for he is not a mortal, that he should change his mind." 30 Then Saul[x] said, "I have sinned; yet honor me now before the elders of my people and before Israel, and return with me, so that I may worship the LORD your God." 31 So Samuel turned back after Saul; and Saul worshiped the LORD.

32 Then Samuel said, "Bring Ā'gag king of the A•mal'e•kītes here to me." And Ā'gag came to him haltingly.[y] Ā'gag said, "Surely this is the bitterness of death."[z] 33 But Samuel said,

"As your sword has made women childless,
so your mother shall be childless among
women."

And Samuel hewed Ā'gag in pieces before the LORD in Gil'gal.

34 Then Samuel went to Rā'mah; and Saul went up to his house in Gib'ē•ah of Saul. 35 Samuel did not see Saul again until the day of his death, but Samuel grieved over Saul. And the LORD was sorry that he had made Saul king over Israel.

David Anointed as King

The LORD said to Samuel, "How long will you grieve over Saul? I have rejected him from being king over Israel. Fill your horn with oil and set out; I will send you to Jesse the Beth'le•hem•īte, for I have provided for myself a king among his sons."

2 Samuel said, "How can I go? If Saul hears of it, he will kill me." And the LORD said, "Take a heifer with you, and say, 'I have come to sacrifice to the LORD.' 3 Invite Jesse to the sacrifice, and I will show you what you shall do; and you shall anoint for me the one whom I name to you." 4 Samuel did what the LORD commanded, and came to Bethlehem. The elders of the city came to meet him trembling, and said, "Do you come peaceably?" 5 He said, "Peaceably; I have come to sacrifice to the LORD; sanctify yourselves and come with me to the sacrifice." And he sanctified Jesse and his sons and invited them to the sacrifice.

6 When they came, he looked on E•li'ab and thought, "Surely the LORD's anointed is now before the LORD."[a] 7 But the LORD said to Samuel, "Do not look on his appearance or on the height of his stature, because I have rejected him; for the LORD does not see as mortals see; they look on the out-

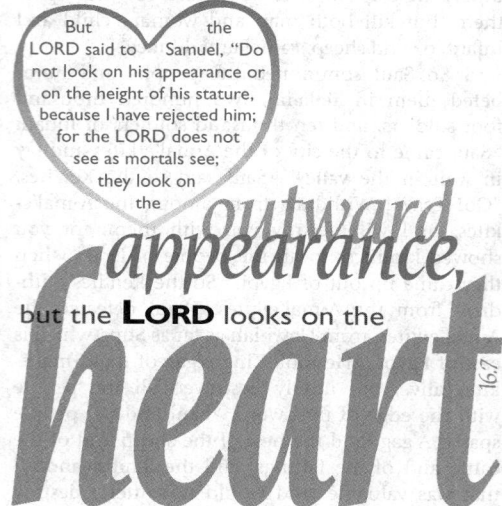

But the LORD said to Samuel, "Do not look on his appearance or on the height of his stature, because I have rejected him; for the LORD does not see as mortals see; they look on the outward appearance, but the LORD looks on the heart.
16.7

ward appearance, but the LORD looks on the heart." 8 Then Jesse called A•bin'a•dab, and made him pass before Samuel. He said, "Neither has the LORD chosen this one." 9 Then Jesse made Sham'mah pass by. And he said, "Neither has the LORD chosen this one." 10 Jesse made seven of his sons pass before Samuel, and Samuel said to Jesse, "The LORD has not chosen any of these." 11 Samuel said to Jesse, "Are all your sons here?" And he said, "There remains yet the youngest, but he is keeping the sheep." And Samuel said to Jesse, "Send and bring him; for we will not sit down until he comes here." 12 He sent and brought him in. Now he was ruddy,

w Q Ms Gk: MT deceive   x Heb he   y Cn Compare Gk: Meaning of Heb uncertain   z Q Ms Gk: MT Surely the bitterness of death is past   a Heb him

David Plays the Lyre for Saul

14 Now the spirit of the LORD departed from Saul, and an evil spirit from the LORD tormented him. 15 And Saul's servants said to him, "See now, an evil spirit from God is tormenting you. 16 Let our lord now command the servants who attend you to look for someone who is skillful in playing the lyre; and when the evil spirit from God is upon you, he will play it, and you will feel better." 17 So Saul said to his servants, "Provide for me someone who can play well, and bring him to me." 18 One of the young men answered, "I have seen a son of Jesse the Beth'le•hem•ite who is skillful in playing, a man of valor, a warrior, prudent in speech, and a man of good presence; and the LORD is with him." 19 So Saul sent messengers to Jesse, and said, "Send me your son David who is with the sheep." 20 Jesse took a donkey loaded with bread, a skin of wine, and a kid, and sent them by his son David to Saul. 21 And David came to Saul, and entered his service. Saul loved him greatly, and he became his armor-bearer. 22 Saul sent to Jesse, saying, "Let David remain in my service, for he has found favor in my sight." 23 And whenever the evil spirit from God came upon Saul, David took the lyre and played it with his hand, and Saul would be relieved and feel better, and the evil spirit would depart from him.

and had beautiful eyes, and was handsome. The LORD said, "Rise and anoint him; for this is the one." 13 Then Samuel took the horn of oil, and anointed him in the presence of his brothers; and the spirit of the LORD came mightily upon David from that day forward. Samuel then set out and went to Rā'mah.

Introducing ►DAVID

Who cannot love David? This shepherd-turned-king is one of the great tragic heroes of the Old Testament. David, whose name means "beloved," was the successor to Saul and the second king (1000–961 B.C.) of the new nation formed out of the twelve tribes of Israel. The youngest son of Jesse of the tribe of Judah, David was a member of Saul's court as a young man. Later, when Saul disappointed God, Samuel the prophet anointed David as Saul's successor. After Saul was killed, David established the neutral city of Jerusalem as his capital (see map 3, "The Kingdom Years"). He moved the ark of the Covenant there, making this city the new religious center of Israel. Jerusalem is also known as the City of David.

David was a successful warrior, a capable king, and a gifted poet, having himself written some of the Psalms. He was also capable of great sin. His affair with Bathsheba seemed to lead to a string of violence and betrayal affecting his whole family. One of his sons, Absalom, even inspired a revolt against David. But through it all, David was passionately in love with God. God recognized this and promised David that someone from his house would sit upon the throne in Israel.

When Israel was destroyed and its kings taken prisoners, the people developed a hope that another anointed one, a messiah from the house of David, would rise up and lead Israel in God's ways once again. It is this hope for the Davidic messiah that is associated with Jesus in the New Testament.

David and Goliath

Now the Phi•lis'tines gathered their armies for battle; they were gathered at Sō'cōh, which belongs to Judah, and encamped between Sō'cōh and A•zē'-kah, in E'phes-dam'mim. 2 Saul and the Israelites gathered and encamped in the valley of Ē'lah, and formed ranks against the Phi•lis'tines. 3 The Phi•lis'-tines stood on the mountain on the one side, and Israel stood on the mountain on the other side, with a valley between them. 4 And there came out from the camp of the Phi•lis'tines a champion named Goliath, of Gath, whose height was six[b] cubits and a span. 5 He had a helmet of bronze on his head, and he was armed with a coat of mail; the weight of the coat was five thousand shekels of bronze. 6 He had greaves of bronze on his legs and a javelin of bronze slung between his shoulders. 7 The shaft of his spear was like a weaver's beam, and his spear's head weighed six hundred shekels of iron; and his shield-bearer went before him. 8 He stood and shouted to the ranks of Israel, "Why have you come out to draw up for battle? Am I not a Phi•lis'tine, and are you not servants of Saul? Choose a man for yourselves, and let him come down to me. 9 If he is able to fight with me and kill me, then we will be your servants; but if I prevail against him and kill him, then you shall be our servants and serve us." 10 And the Phi•lis'tine said, "Today I defy the ranks of Israel! Give me a man, that we may fight together." 11 When Saul and all Israel heard these words of the Phi•lis'tine, they were dismayed and greatly afraid.

12 Now David was the son of an Eph'ra•thīte of Bethlehem in Judah, named Jesse, who had eight sons. In the days of Saul the man was already old and advanced in years.[c] 13 The three eldest sons of Jesse had followed Saul to the battle; the names of his three sons who went to the battle were E•lī'ab the firstborn, and next to him A•bin'a-dab, and the third Sham'mah. 14 David was the youngest; the three eldest followed Saul, 15 but David went back and forth from Saul to feed his father's sheep at Bethlehem. 16 For forty days the Phi•lis'tine came forward and took his stand, morning and evening.

17 Jesse said to his son David, "Take for your brothers an ephah of this parched grain and these ten loaves, and carry them quickly to the camp to your brothers; 18 also take these ten cheeses to the commander of their thousand. See how your brothers fare, and bring some token from them."

19 Now Saul, and they, and all the men of Israel, were in the valley of Ē'lah, fighting with the Phi•lis'tines. 20 David rose early in the morning, left the sheep with a keeper, took the provisions, and went as Jesse had commanded him. He came to the encampment as the army was going forth to the battle line, shouting the war cry. 21 Israel and the Phi•lis'tines drew up for battle, army against army. 22 David left the things in charge of the keeper of the baggage, ran to the ranks, and went and greeted his brothers. 23 As he talked with them, the champion, the Phi•lis'tine of Gath, Goliath by name, came up out of the ranks of the Phi•lis'tines, and spoke the same words as before. And David heard him.

24 All the Israelites, when they saw the man, fled from him and were very much afraid. 25 The Israelites said, "Have you seen this man who has come up? Surely he has come up to defy Israel. The king will greatly enrich the man who kills him, and will give him his daughter and make his family free in Israel." 26 David said to the men who stood by him, "What shall be done for the man who kills this Phi•lis'tine, and takes away the reproach from Israel? For who is this uncircumcised Phi•lis'tine that he should defy the armies of the living God?" 27 The people answered him in the same way, "So shall it be done for the man who kills him."

28 His eldest brother E•lī'ab heard him talking to the men; and E•lī'ab's anger was kindled against David. He said, "Why have you come down? With whom have you left those few sheep in the wilderness? I know your presumption and the evil of your heart; for you have come down just to see the battle." 29 David said, "What have I done now? It was only a question." 30 He turned away from him toward another and spoke in the same way; and the people answered him again as before.

31 When the words that David spoke were heard, they repeated them before Saul; and he sent for him. 32 David said to Saul, "Let no one's heart fail because of him; your servant will go and fight with this Phi•lis'tine." 33 Saul said to David, "You are not able to go against this Phi•lis'tine to fight with him; for you are just a boy, and he has been a warrior from his youth." 34 But David said to Saul, "Your servant used to keep sheep for his father; and whenever a lion or a bear came, and took a lamb from the flock, 35 I went after it and struck it down, rescuing the lamb from its mouth; and if it turned against me, I would catch it by the jaw, strike it down, and kill it. 36 Your servant has killed both lions and bears; and this uncircumcised Phi•lis'tine shall be like one of them, since he has defied the armies of the living God." 37 David said, "The LORD, who saved me from the paw of the lion and from the paw of the bear, will save me from

---

b MT: Q Ms Gk *four*   c Gk Syr: Heb *among men*

the hand of this Phi·lis'tine." So Saul said to David, "Go, and may the LORD be with you!"

38 Saul clothed David with his armor; he put a bronze helmet on his head and clothed him with a coat of mail. 39 David strapped Saul's sword over the armor, and he tried in vain to walk, for he was not used to them. Then David said to Saul, "I cannot walk with these; for I am not used to them." So David removed them. 40 Then he took his staff in his hand, and chose five smooth stones from the wadi, and put them in his shepherd's bag, in the pouch; his sling was in his hand, and he drew near to the Phi·lis'tine.

41 The Phi·lis'tine came on and drew near to David, with his shield-bearer in front of him.

save by sword and spear; for the battle is the LORD's and he will give you into our hand."

48 When the Phi·lis'tine drew nearer to meet David, David ran quickly toward the battle line to meet the Phi·lis'tine. 49 David put his hand in his bag, took out a stone, slung it, and struck the Phi·lis'tine on his forehead; the stone sank into his forehead, and he fell face down on the ground.

50 So David prevailed over the Phi·lis'tine with a sling and a stone, striking down the Phi·lis'tine and killing him; there was no sword in David's hand. 51 Then David ran and stood over the Phi·lis'tine; he grasped his sword, drew it out of its sheath, and killed him; then he cut off his head with it.

Taking On Goliath

LIVE IT!

David makes it look so easy. A slingshot, a stone, a skillful aim, and it is all over. Goliath is dead, and the Israelites win the day. It is a story that gives hope to anyone who has ever been bullied or harassed.

A David lives in each of us, and plenty of Goliaths are out there ready to defeat us. The Goliaths we encounter can include peer pressure, an addiction, an abusive situation, or simply self-doubt. We may feel overpowered by these Goliaths, sure that they are too big for us to handle. But they are not! Those of us who believe in God, as David did, know that we are not alone. As followers of Jesus, we rely not on violence but on love and the support of the Christian community to defeat the Goliaths in our life. We can make David's story our own.

Identify a Goliath in your life right now and journal about it. What stepping-stone can you take in defeating it?

▶ I Samuel, chapter 17

42 When the Phi·lis'tine looked and saw David, he disdained him, for he was only a youth, ruddy and handsome in appearance. 43 The Phi·lis'tine said to David, "Am I a dog, that you come to me with sticks?" And the Phi·lis'tine cursed David by his gods. 44 The Phi·lis'tine said to David, "Come to me, and I will give your flesh to the birds of the air and to the wild animals of the field." 45 But David said to the Phi·lis'tine, "You come to me with sword and spear and javelin; but I come to you in the name of the LORD of hosts, the God of the armies of Israel, whom you have defied. 46 This very day the LORD will deliver you into my hand, and I will strike you down and cut off your head; and I will give the dead bodies of the Phi·lis'tine army this very day to the birds of the air and to the wild animals of the earth, so that all the earth may know that there is a God in Israel, 47 and that all this assembly may know that the LORD does not

When the Phi·lis'tines saw that their champion was dead, they fled. 52 The troops of Israel and Judah rose up with a shout and pursued the Phi·lis'-tines as far as Gath[d] and the gates of Ek'ron, so that the wounded Phi·lis'tines fell on the way from Shã·a·rã'im as far as Gath and Ek'ron. 53 The Israelites came back from chasing the Phi·lis'tines, and they plundered their camp. 54 David took the head of the Phi·lis'tine and brought it to Jerusalem; but he put his armor in his tent.

55 When Saul saw David go out against the Phi·lis'tine, he said to Abner, the commander of the army, "Abner, whose son is this young man?" Abner said, "As your soul lives, O king, I do not know." 56 The king said, "Inquire whose son the stripling is." 57 On David's return from killing the Phi·lis'tine, Abner took him and brought him before Saul, with the head of the Phi·lis'tine in his

d Gk Syr: Heb Gai

hand. 58 Saul said to him, "Whose son are you, young man?" And David answered, "I am the son of your servant Jesse the Beth'le·hem·ite."

Jonathan's Covenant with David

When David[e] had finished speaking to Saul, the soul of Jonathan was bound to the soul of David, and Jonathan loved him as his own soul. 2 Saul took him that day and would not let him return to his father's house. 3 Then Jonathan made a covenant with David, because he loved him as his own soul. 4 Jonathan stripped himself of the robe that he was wearing, and gave it to David, and his armor, and even his sword and his bow and his belt. 5 David went out and was successful wherever Saul sent him; as a result, Saul set him over the army. And all the people, even the servants of Saul, approved.

6 As they were coming home, when David returned from killing the Phi·lis'tine, the women came out of all the towns of Israel, singing and dancing, to meet King Saul, with tambourines, with songs of joy, and with musical instruments.[f] 7 And the women sang to one another as they made merry,

"Saul has killed his thousands,
and David his ten thousands."

8 Saul was very angry, for this saying displeased him. He said, "They have ascribed to David ten thousands, and to me they have ascribed thousands; what more can he have but the kingdom?" 9 So Saul eyed David from that day on.

Saul Tries to Kill David

10 The next day an evil spirit from God rushed upon Saul, and he raved within his house, while David was playing the lyre, as he did day by day. Saul had his spear in his hand; 11 and Saul threw the spear, for he thought, "I will pin David to the wall." But David eluded him twice.

12 Saul was afraid of David, because the LORD was with him but had departed from Saul. 13 So Saul removed him from his presence, and made him a commander of a thousand; and David marched out and came in, leading the army. 14 David had success in all his undertakings; for the LORD was with him. 15 When Saul saw that he had great success, he stood in awe of him. 16 But all Israel and Judah loved David; for it was he who marched out and came in leading them.

David Marries Michal

17 Then Saul said to David, "Here is my elder daughter Mē'rab; I will give her to you as a wife; only be valiant for me and fight the LORD's battles." For Saul thought, "I will not raise a hand against him; let the Phi·lis'tines deal with him." 18 David said to Saul, "Who am I and who are my kinsfolk, my father's family in Israel, that I should be son-in-law to the king?" 19 But at the time when Saul's daughter Mē'rab should have been given to David, she was given to A'dri·el the Me·hō'la·thīte as a wife.

20 Now Saul's daughter Mi'chal loved David. Saul was told, and the thing pleased him. 21 Saul thought, "Let me give her to him that she may be a snare for him and that the hand of the Phi·lis'-tines may be against him." Therefore Saul said to David a second time,[g] "You shall now be my son-in-law." 22 Saul commanded his servants, "Speak to David in private and say, 'See, the king is delighted with you, and all his servants love you; now then, become the king's son-in-law.' " 23 So Saul's servants reported these words to David in private. And David said, "Does it seem to you a little thing to become the king's son-in-law, seeing that I am a poor man and of no repute?" 24 The servants of Saul told him, "This is what David said." 25 Then Saul said, "Thus shall you say to David, 'The king desires no marriage present except a hundred foreskins of the Phi·lis'tines, that he may be avenged on the king's enemies.' " Now Saul planned to make David fall by the hand of the Phi·lis'tines. 26 When his servants told David these words, David was well pleased to be the king's son-in-law. Before the time had expired, 27 David rose and went, along with his men, and killed one hundred[h] of the Phi·lis'tines; and David brought their foreskins, which were given in full number to the king, that he might become the king's son-in-law. Saul gave him his daughter Mi'chal as a wife. 28 But when Saul realized that the LORD was with David, and that Saul's daughter Mi'chal loved him, 29 Saul was still more afraid of David. So Saul was David's enemy from that time forward.

30 Then the commanders of the Phi·lis'tines came out to battle; and as often as they came out, David had more success than all the servants of Saul, so that his fame became very great.

Jonathan Intercedes for David

Saul spoke with his son Jonathan and with all his servants about killing David. But Saul's son Jonathan took great delight in David. 2 Jonathan told David, "My father Saul is trying to kill you; therefore be on guard tomorrow morning; stay in a secret place and hide yourself. 3 I will go out and stand beside my father in the field where you are, and I will speak to my father about you; if I learn

---

e Heb he   f Or triangles, or three-stringed instruments
g Heb by two   h Gk Compare 2 Sam 3.14: Heb two hundred

anything I will tell you." ⁴ Jonathan spoke well of David to his father Saul, saying to him, "The king should not sin against his servant David, because he has not sinned against you, and because his deeds have been of good service to you; ⁵ for he took his life in his hand when he attacked the Philis'tine, and the LORD brought about a great victory for all Israel. You saw it, and rejoiced; why then will you sin against an innocent person by killing David without cause?" ⁶ Saul heeded the voice of Jonathan; Saul swore, "As the LORD lives, he shall not be put to death." ⁷ So Jonathan called David and related all these things to him. Jonathan then brought David to Saul, and he was in his presence as before.

Michal Helps David Escape from Saul

8 Again there was war, and David went out to fight the Phi·lis'tines. He launched a heavy attack on them, so that they fled before him. ⁹ Then an evil spirit from the LORD came upon Saul, as he sat in his house with his spear in his hand, while David was playing music. ¹⁰ Saul sought to pin David to the wall with the spear; but he eluded Saul, so that he struck the spear into the wall. David fled and escaped that night.

11 Saul sent messengers to David's house to keep watch over him, planning to kill him in the morning. David's wife Mi'chal told him, "If you do not save your life tonight, tomorrow you will be killed." ¹² So Mi'chal let David down through the window; he fled away and escaped. ¹³ Mi'chal took an idol[i] and laid it on the bed; she put a net[j] of goats' hair on its head, and covered it with the clothes. ¹⁴ When Saul sent messengers to take David, she said, "He is sick." ¹⁵ Then Saul sent the messengers to see David for themselves. He said, "Bring him up to me in the bed, that I may kill him." ¹⁶ When the messengers came in, the idol[k] was in the bed, with the covering[j] of goats' hair on its head. ¹⁷ Saul said to Mi'chal, "Why have you deceived me like this, and let my enemy go, so that he has escaped?" Mi'chal answered Saul, "He said to me, 'Let me go; why should I kill you?' "

David Joins Samuel in Ramah

18 Now David fled and escaped; he came to Samuel at Rā'mah, and told him all that Saul had done to him. He and Samuel went and settled at Nai'ōth. ¹⁹ Saul was told, "David is at Nai'ōth in Rā'mah." ²⁰ Then Saul sent messengers to take David. When they saw the company of the prophets in a frenzy, with Samuel standing in charge of[j] them, the spirit of God came upon the messengers of Saul, and they also fell into a prophetic frenzy. ²¹ When Saul was told, he sent other messengers,

and they also fell into a frenzy. Saul sent messengers again the third time, and they also fell into a frenzy. ²² Then he himself went to Rā'mah. He came to the great well that is in Sē'cū;[l] he asked, "Where are Samuel and David?" And someone said, "They are at Nai'ōth in Rā'mah." ²³ He went there, toward Nai'ōth in Rā'mah; and the spirit of God came upon him. As he was going, he fell into a prophetic frenzy, until he came to Nai'ōth in Rā'mah. ²⁴ He too stripped off his clothes, and he too fell into a frenzy before Samuel. He lay naked all that day and all that night. Therefore it is said, "Is Saul also among the prophets?"

The Friendship of David and Jonathan

David fled from Nai'ōth in Rā'mah. He came before Jonathan and said, "What have I done? What is my guilt? And what is my sin against your father that he is trying to take my life?" ² He said to him, "Far from it! You shall not die. My father does nothing either great or small without disclosing it to me; and why should my father hide this from me? Never!" ³ But David also swore, "Your father knows well that you like me; and he thinks, 'Do not let Jonathan know this, or he will be grieved.' But truly, as the LORD lives and as you yourself live, there is but a step between me and death." ⁴ Then Jonathan said to David, "Whatever you say, I will do for you." ⁵ David said to Jonathan, "Tomorrow is the new moon, and I should not fail to sit with the king at the meal; but let me go, so that I may hide in the field until the third evening. ⁶ If your father misses me at all, then say, 'David earnestly asked leave of me to run to Bethlehem his city; for there is a yearly sacrifice there for all the family.' ⁷ If he says, 'Good!' it will be well with your servant; but if he is angry, then know that evil has been determined by him. ⁸ Therefore deal kindly with your servant, for you have brought your servant into a sacred covenant[m] with you. But if there is guilt in me, kill me yourself; why should you bring me to your father?" ⁹ Jonathan said, "Far be it from you! If I knew that it was decided by my father that evil should come upon you, would I not tell you?" ¹⁰ Then David said to Jonathan, "Who will tell me if your father answers you harshly?" ¹¹ Jonathan replied to David, "Come, let us go out into the field." So they both went out into the field.

12 Jonathan said to David, "By the LORD, the God of Israel! When I have sounded out my father, about this time tomorrow, or on the third

---

[i] Heb *took the teraphim*   [j] Meaning of Heb uncertain   [k] Heb *the teraphim*   [l] Gk reads *to the well of the threshing floor on the bare height*   [m] Heb *a covenant of the* LORD

day, if he is well disposed toward David, shall I not then send and disclose it to you? 13 But if my father intends to do you harm, the LORD do so to Jonathan, and more also, if I do not disclose it to you, and send you away, so that you may go in safety. May the LORD be with you, as he has been with my father. 14 If I am still alive, show me the faithful love of the LORD; but if I die,*n* 15 never cut off your faithful love from my house, even if the LORD were to cut off every one of the enemies of David from the face of the earth." 16 Thus Jonathan made a covenant with the house of David, saying, "May the LORD seek out the enemies of David." 17 Jonathan made David swear again by his love for him; for he loved him as he loved his own life.

18 Jonathan said to him, "Tomorrow is the new moon; you will be missed, because your place will be empty. 19 On the day after tomorrow, you shall go a long way down; go to the place where you hid yourself earlier, and remain beside the stone there.*n* 20 I will shoot three arrows to the side of it, as though I shot at a mark. 21 Then I will send the boy, saying, 'Go, find the arrows.' If I say to the boy, 'Look, the arrows are on this side of you, collect them,' then you are to come, for, as the LORD lives, it is safe for you and there is no danger. 22 But if I say to the young man, 'Look, the arrows are beyond you,' then go; for the LORD has sent you away. 23 As for the matter about which you and I have spoken, the LORD is witness*o* between you and me forever."

24 So David hid himself in the field. When the new moon came, the king sat at the feast to eat. 25 The king sat upon his seat, as at other times, upon the seat by the wall. Jonathan stood, while Abner sat by Saul's side; but David's place was empty.

26 Saul did not say anything that day; for he thought, "Something has befallen him; he is not clean, surely he is not clean." 27 But on the second day, the day after the new moon, David's place was empty. And Saul said to his son Jonathan, "Why has the son of Jesse not come to the feast, either yesterday or today?" 28 Jonathan answered Saul, "David earnestly asked leave of me to go to Bethlehem; 29 he said, 'Let me go; for our family is holding a sacrifice in the city, and my brother has commanded me to be there. So now, if I have found favor in your sight, let me get away, and see my brothers.' For this reason he has not come to the king's table."

30 Then Saul's anger was kindled against Jonathan. He said to him, "You son of a perverse, rebellious woman! Do I not know that you have chosen the son of Jesse to your own shame, and to the shame of your mother's nakedness? 31 For as long as the son of Jesse lives upon the earth, neither you nor your kingdom shall be established. Now send and bring him to me, for he shall surely die." 32 Then Jonathan answered his father Saul, "Why should he be put to death? What has he done?" 33 But Saul threw his spear at him to strike him; so Jonathan knew that it was the decision of his father to put David to death. 34 Jonathan rose from the table in fierce anger and ate no food on the second day of the month, for he was grieved for David, and because his father had disgraced him.

Friends Forever

David and Jonathan have one of the most touching stories of friendship in the Bible. In 1 Sam 18.1–4, Jonathan makes a special covenant with David. In chapter 20, their deep love leads them to risk their lives for each other. Saul, the king and Jonathan's father, is acting like a madman. He is insanely jealous of David and wants him dead.

Yet, Jonathan and David bring God into their relationship. This gives them the wisdom to see what is right and do it. When they have to part (see 20.41–42), they weep and kiss and remind each other of their vows.

Not many teenagers deal with situations as drastic as this, but tension with parents over your choice of friends can be common. Parents may not understand why you like a person whom they dislike. It can leave you with a sense of being stuck in the middle.

Your response should be like David and Jonathan's, keeping God part of all your relationships. Each friendship then becomes a living prayer, and God will guide you through conflicts and help you make good decisions.

▶ I Samuel, chapter 20

35 In the morning Jonathan went out into the field to the appointment with David, and with him was a little boy. 36 He said to the boy, "Run and find the arrows that I shoot." As the boy ran, he shot an arrow beyond him. 37 When the boy came to the place where Jonathan's arrow had fallen, Jonathan called after the boy and said, "Is the ar-

n Meaning of Heb uncertain   *o* Gk: Heb lacks *witness*

row not beyond you?" ³⁸ Jonathan called after the boy, "Hurry, be quick, do not linger." So Jonathan's boy gathered up the arrows and came to his master. ³⁹ But the boy knew nothing; only Jonathan and David knew the arrangement. ⁴⁰ Jonathan gave his weapons to the boy and said to him, "Go and carry them to the city." ⁴¹ As soon as the boy had gone, David rose from beside the stone heap*p* and prostrated himself with his face to the ground. He bowed three times, and they kissed each other, and wept with each other; David wept the more.*q* ⁴² Then Jonathan said to David, "Go in peace, since both of us have sworn in the name of the LORD, saying, 'The LORD shall be between me and you, and between my descendants and your descendants, forever.' " He got up and left; and Jonathan went into the city.*r*

David and the Holy Bread

s David came to Nob to the priest A·him′e·lech. A·him′e·lech came trembling to meet David, and said to him, "Why are you alone, and no one with you?" ² David said to the priest A·him′e·lech, "The king has charged me with a matter, and said to me, 'No one must know anything of the matter about which I send you, and with which I have charged you.' I have made an appointment*t* with the young men for such and such a place. ³ Now then, what have you at hand? Give me five loaves of bread, or whatever is here." ⁴ The priest answered David, "I have no ordinary bread at hand, only holy bread—provided that the young men have kept themselves from women." ⁵ David answered the priest, "Indeed women have been kept from us as always when I go on an expedition; the vessels of the young men are holy even when it is a common journey; how much more today will their vessels be holy?" ⁶ So the priest gave him the holy bread; for there was no bread there except the bread of the Presence, which is removed from before the LORD, to be replaced by hot bread on the day it is taken away.

⁷ Now a certain man of the servants of Saul was there that day, detained before the LORD; his name was Dō′eg the Ē′dom·ite, the chief of Saul's shepherds.

⁸ David said to A·him′e·lech, "Is there no spear or sword here with you? I did not bring my sword or my weapons with me, because the king's business required haste." ⁹ The priest said, "The sword of Goliath the Phi·lis′tine, whom you killed in the valley of Ē′lah, is here wrapped in a cloth behind the ephod; if you will take that, take it, for there is none here except that one." David said, "There is none like it; give it to me."

David Flees to Gath

¹⁰ David rose and fled that day from Saul; he went to King Ā′chish of Gath. ¹¹ The servants of Ā′chish said to him, "Is this not David the king of the land? Did they not sing to one another of him in dances,

'Saul has killed his thousands,
    and David his ten thousands'?"

¹² David took these words to heart and was very much afraid of King Ā′chish of Gath. ¹³ So he changed his behavior before them; he pretended to be mad when in their presence.*u* He scratched marks on the doors of the gate, and let his spittle run down his beard. ¹⁴ Ā′chish said to his servants, "Look, you see the man is mad; why then have you brought him to me? ¹⁵ Do I lack madmen, that you have brought this fellow to play the madman in my presence? Shall this fellow come into my house?"

David and His Followers at Adullam

David left there and escaped to the cave of A·dul′-lam; when his brothers and all his father's house heard of it, they went down there to him. ² Everyone who was in distress, and everyone who was in debt, and everyone who was discontented gathered to him; and he became captain over them. Those who were with him numbered about four hundred.

³ David went from there to Miz′peh of Mō′ab. He said to the king of Mō′ab, "Please let my father and mother come*v* to you, until I know what God will do for me." ⁴ He left them with the king of Mō′ab, and they stayed with him all the time that David was in the stronghold. ⁵ Then the prophet Gad said to David, "Do not remain in the stronghold; leave, and go into the land of Judah." So David left, and went into the forest of Hē′reth.

Saul Slaughters the Priests at Nob

⁶ Saul heard that David and those who were with him had been located. Saul was sitting at Gib′e·ah, under the tamarisk tree on the height, with his spear in his hand, and all his servants were standing around him. ⁷ Saul said to his servants who stood around him, "Hear now, you Ben′ja·min·ites; will the son of Jesse give every one of you fields and vineyards, will he make you all commanders of thousands and commanders of

---

p Gk: Heb *from beside the south*   *q* Vg: Meaning of Heb uncertain   *r* This sentence is 21.1 in Heb   *s* Ch 21.2 in Heb   *t* Q Ms Vg Compare Gk: Meaning of MT uncertain   *u* Heb *in their hands*   *v* Syr Vg: Heb *come out*

hundreds? [8] Is that why all of you have conspired against me? No one discloses to me when my son makes a league with the son of Jesse, none of you is sorry for me or discloses to me that my son has stirred up my servant against me, to lie in wait, as he is doing today." [9] Dō′eg the Ē′dom·ite, who was in charge of Saul's servants, answered, "I saw the son of Jesse coming to Nob, to A·him′e·lech son of A·hī′tub; [10] he inquired of the LORD for him, gave him provisions, and gave him the sword of Goliath the Phi·lis′tine."

11 The king sent for the priest A·him′e·lech son of A·hī′tub and for all his father's house, the priests who were at Nob; and all of them came to the king. [12] Saul said, "Listen now, son of A·hī′tub." He answered, "Here I am, my lord." [13] Saul said to him, "Why have you conspired against me, you and the son of Jesse, by giving him bread and a sword, and by inquiring of God for him, so that he has risen against me, to lie in wait, as he is doing today?"

14 Then A·him′e·lech answered the king, "Who among all your servants is so faithful as David? He is the king's son-in-law, and is quick[w] to do your bidding, and is honored in your house. [15] Is today the first time that I have inquired of God for him? By no means! Do not let the king impute anything to his servant or to any member of his father's house; for your servant has known nothing of all this, much or little." [16] The king said, "You shall surely die, A·him′e·lech, you and all your father's house." [17] The king said to the guard who stood around him, "Turn and kill the priests of the LORD, because their hand also is with David; they knew that he fled, and did not disclose it to me." But the servants of the king would not raise their hand to attack the priests of the LORD. [18] Then the king said to Dō′eg, "You, Dō′eg, turn and attack the priests." Dō′eg the Ē′dom·ite turned and attacked the priests; on that day he killed eighty-five who wore the linen ephod. [19] Nob, the city of the priests, he put to the sword; men and women, children and infants, oxen, donkeys, and sheep, he put to the sword.

20 But one of the sons of A·him′e·lech son of A·hī′tub, named A·bī′a·thar, escaped and fled after David. [21] A·bī′a·thar told David that Saul had killed the priests of the LORD. [22] David said to A·bī′a·thar, "I knew on that day, when Dō′eg the Ē′dom·ite was there, that he would surely tell Saul. I am responsible[x] for the lives of all your father's house. [23] Stay with me, and do not be afraid; for the one who seeks my life seeks your life; you will be safe with me."

David Saves the City of Keilah

Now they told David, "The Phi·lis′tines are fighting against Kē·ī′lah, and are robbing the threshing floors." [2] David inquired of the LORD, "Shall I go and attack these Phi·lis′tines?" The LORD said to David, "Go and attack the Phi·lis′tines and save Kē·ī′lah." [3] But David's men said to him, "Look, we are afraid here in Judah; how much more then if we go to Kē·ī′lah against the armies of the Phi·lis′tines?" [4] Then David inquired of the LORD again. The LORD answered him, "Yes, go down to Kē·ī′lah; for I will give the Phi·lis′tines into your hand." [5] So David and his men went to Kē·ī′lah, fought with the Phi·lis′tines, brought away their livestock, and dealt them a heavy defeat. Thus David rescued the inhabitants of Kē·ī′lah.

6 When A·bī′a·thar son of A·him′e·lech fled to David at Kē·ī′lah, he came down with an ephod in his hand. [7] Now it was told Saul that David had come to Kē·ī′lah. And Saul said, "God has given[y] him into my hand; for he has shut himself in by entering a town that has gates and bars." [8] Saul summoned all the people to war, to go down to Kē·ī′lah, to besiege David and his men. [9] When David learned that Saul was plotting evil against him, he said to the priest A·bī′a·thar, "Bring the ephod here." [10] David said, "O LORD, the God of Israel, your servant has heard that Saul seeks to come to Kē·ī′lah, to destroy the city on my account. [11] And now, will[z] Saul come down as your servant has heard? O LORD, the God of Israel, I beseech you, tell your servant." The LORD said, "He will come down." [12] Then David said, "Will the men of Kē·ī′lah surrender me and my men into the hand of Saul?" The LORD said, "They will surrender you." [13] Then David and his men, who were about six hundred, set out and left Kē·ī′lah; they wandered wherever they could go. When Saul was told that David had escaped from Kē·ī′lah, he gave up the expedition. [14] David remained in the strongholds in the wilderness, in the hill country of the Wilderness of Ziph. Saul sought him every day, but the LORD[a] did not give him into his hand.

David Eludes Saul in the Wilderness

15 David was in the Wilderness of Ziph at Hō′resh when he learned that[b] Saul had come out to seek his life. [16] Saul's son Jonathan set out and came to David at Hō′resh; there he strengthened his hand through the LORD.[c] [17] He said to him,

---

[w] Heb *and turns aside*   [x] Gk Vg: Meaning of Heb uncertain   [y] Gk Tg: Heb *made a stranger of*   [z] Q Ms Compare Gk: MT *Will the men of Keilah surrender me into his hand? Will*   [a] Q Ms Gk: MT *God*   [b] Or *saw that* [c] Compare Q Ms Gk: MT *God*

"Do not be afraid; for the hand of my father Saul shall not find you; you shall be king over Israel, and I shall be second to you; my father Saul also knows that this is so." 18 Then the two of them made a covenant before the LORD; David remained at Hō'resh, and Jonathan went home.

19 Then some Ziph'ites went up to Saul at Gib'ē•ah and said, "David is hiding among us in the strongholds of Hō'resh, on the hill of Ha•chī'-lah, which is south of Jĕ•shī'mon. 20 Now, O king, whenever you wish to come down, do so; and our part will be to surrender him into the king's hand." 21 Saul said, "May you be blessed by the LORD for showing me compassion! 22 Go and make sure once more; find out exactly where he is, and who has seen him there; for I am told that he is very cunning. 23 Look around and learn all the hiding places where he lurks, and come back to me with sure information. Then I will go with you; and if he is in the land, I will search him out among all the thousands of Judah." 24 So they set out and went to Ziph ahead of Saul.

David and his men were in the wilderness of Mā'on, in the Ar'a•bah to the south of Jĕ•shī'mon. 25 Saul and his men went to search for him. When David was told, he went down to the rock and stayed in the wilderness of Mā'on. When Saul heard that, he pursued David into the wilderness of Mā'on. 26 Saul went on one side of the mountain, and David and his men on the other side of the mountain. David was hurrying to get away from Saul, while Saul and his men were closing in on David and his men to capture them. 27 Then a messenger came to Saul, saying, "Hurry and come; for the Phi•lis'tines have made a raid on the land." 28 So Saul stopped pursuing David, and went against the Phi•lis'tines; therefore that place was called the Rock of Escape.d 29 eDavid then went up from there, and lived in the strongholds of En-ge'di.

David Spares Saul's Life

When Saul returned from following the Phi•lis'-tines, he was told, "David is in the wilderness of En-ge'di." 2 Then Saul took three thousand chosen men out of all Israel, and went to look for David and his men in the direction of the Rocks of the Wild Goats. 3 He came to the sheepfolds beside the road, where there was a cave; and Saul went in to relieve himself.f Now David and his men were sitting in the innermost parts of the cave. 4 The men of David said to him, "Here is the day of which the LORD said to you, 'I will give your enemy into your hand, and you shall do to him as it seems good to you.' " Then David went and stealthily cut off a corner of Saul's cloak. 5 Afterward David was stricken to the heart because he had cut off a corner of Saul's cloak. 6 He said to his men, "The LORD forbid that I should do this thing to my lord, the LORD's anointed, to raise my hand against him; for he is the LORD's anointed." 7 So David scolded his men severely and did not permit them to attack Saul. Then Saul got up and left the cave, and went on his way.

did you KNOW?
The Lord's Anointed

Israelite kings and prophets were anointed with oil to symbolize the powerful spirit of God that was present to them as they fulfilled their important role. The Hebrew word *mashiah*, translated in 1 Sam 24.6 as "anointed [one]," is the root of the English word *messiah*. Often applied to kings in the Old Testament, this title was attached in the second century B.C. to the one "like David" who was expected to come (see Dan 9.25). *Mashiah* translated into Greek is *christos*, which became the title given to Jesus by his followers: Jesus, the Christ; Jesus, the anointed one; Jesus, the Messiah.

8 Afterwards David also rose up and went out of the cave and called after Saul, "My lord the king!" When Saul looked behind him, David bowed with his face to the ground, and did obeisance. 9 David said to Saul, "Why do you listen to the words of those who say, 'David seeks to do you harm'? 10 This very day your eyes have seen how the LORD gave you into my hand in the cave; and some urged me to kill you, but I sparedg you. I said, 'I will not raise my hand against my lord; for he is the LORD's anointed.' 11 See, my father, see the corner of your cloak in my hand; for by the fact that I cut off the corner of your cloak, and did not kill you, you may know for certain that there is no wrong or treason in my hands. I have not sinned against you, though you are hunting me to take my life. 12 May the LORD judge between me and you! May the LORD avenge me on you; but my hand shall not be against you. 13 As the ancient

---

d Or *Rock of Division*; meaning of Heb uncertain
e Ch 24.1 in Heb   f Heb *to cover his feet*   g Gk Syr Tg Vg: Heb *it* (my eye) *spared*

proverb says, 'Out of the wicked comes forth wickedness'; but my hand shall not be against you. [14]Against whom has the king of Israel come out? Whom do you pursue? A dead dog? A single flea? [15]May the LORD therefore be judge, and give sentence between me and you. May he see to it, and plead my cause, and vindicate me against you."

16 When David had finished speaking these words to Saul, Saul said, "Is this your voice, my son David?" Saul lifted up his voice and wept. [17]He said to David, "You are more righteous than I; for you have repaid me good, whereas I have repaid you evil. [18]Today you have explained how you have dealt well with me, in that you did not kill me when the LORD put me into your hands. [19]For who has ever found an enemy, and sent the enemy safely away? So may the LORD reward you with good for what you have done to me this day. [20]Now I know that you shall surely be king, and that the kingdom of Israel shall be established in your hand. [21]Swear to me therefore by the LORD that you will not cut off my descendants after me, and that you will not wipe out my name from my father's house." [22]So David swore this to Saul. Then Saul went home; but David and his men went up to the stronghold.

Death of Samuel

Now Samuel died; and all Israel assembled and mourned for him. They buried him at his home in Rā′mah.

Then David got up and went down to the wilderness of Par′an.

David and the Wife of Nabal

2 There was a man in Mā′on, whose property was in Car′mel. The man was very rich; he had three thousand sheep and a thousand goats. He was shearing his sheep in Car′mel. [3]Now the name of the man was Nā′bal, and the name of his wife Ab′i•gāil. The woman was clever and beautiful, but the man was surly and mean; he was a Cā′-leb•ite. [4]David heard in the wilderness that Nā′bal was shearing his sheep. [5]So David sent ten young men; and David said to the young men, "Go up to Car′mel, and go to Nā′bal, and greet him in my name. [6]Thus you shall salute him: 'Peace be to you, and peace be to your house, and peace be to all that you have. [7]I hear that you have shearers; now your shepherds have been with us, and we did them no harm, and they missed nothing, all the time they were in Car′mel. [8]Ask your young men, and they will tell you. Therefore let my young men find favor in your sight; for we have come on a feast day. Please give whatever you have at hand to your servants and to your son David.' "

9 When David's young men came, they said all this to Nā′bal in the name of David; and then they waited. [10]But Nā′bal answered David's servants, "Who is David? Who is the son of Jesse? There are many servants today who are breaking away from their masters. [11]Shall I take my bread and my water and the meat that I have butchered for my shearers, and give it to men who come from I do not know where?" [12]So David's young men turned away, and came back and told him all this. [13]David said to his men, "Every man strap on his sword!" And every one of them strapped on his sword; David also strapped on his sword; and about four hundred men went up after David, while two hundred remained with the baggage.

14 But one of the young men told Ab′i•gāil, Nā′bal's wife, "David sent messengers out of the wilderness to salute our master; and he shouted insults at them. [15]Yet the men were very good to us, and we suffered no harm, and we never missed anything when we were in the fields, as long as we were with them; [16]they were a wall to us both by night and by day, all the while we were with them keeping the sheep. [17]Now therefore know this and consider what you should do; for evil has been decided against our master and against all his house; he is so ill-natured that no one can speak to him."

18 Then Ab′i•gāil hurried and took two hundred loaves, two skins of wine, five sheep ready dressed, five measures of parched grain, one hundred clusters of raisins, and two hundred cakes of figs. She loaded them on donkeys [19]and said to her young men, "Go on ahead of me; I am coming after you." But she did not tell her husband Nā′bal. [20]As she rode on the donkey and came down under cover of the mountain, David and his men came down toward her; and she met them. [21]Now David had said, "Surely it was in vain that I protected all that this fellow has in the wilderness, so that nothing was missed of all that belonged to him; but he has returned me evil for good. [22]God do so to David[h] and more also, if by morning I leave so much as one male of all who belong to him."

23 When Ab′i•gāil saw David, she hurried and alighted from the donkey, and fell before David on her face, bowing to the ground. [24]She fell at his feet and said, "Upon me alone, my lord, be the guilt; please let your servant speak in your ears, and hear the words of your servant. [25]My lord, do not take seriously this ill-natured fellow, Nā′bal; for as his name is, so is he; Nā′bal[i] is his name,

---

h Gk Compare Syr: Heb the enemies of David
i That is Fool

and folly is with him; but I, your servant, did not see the young men of my lord, whom you sent. 26 "Now then, my lord, as the LORD lives, and as you yourself live, since the LORD has restrained you from bloodguilt and from taking vengeance with your own hand, now let your enemies and those who seek to do evil to my lord be like Nā'-bal. 27 And now let this present that your servant has brought to my lord be given to the young men who follow my lord. 28 Please forgive the trespass of your servant; for the LORD will certainly make my lord a sure house, because my lord is fighting the battles of the LORD; and evil shall not be found in you so long as you live. 29 If anyone should rise up to pursue you and to seek your life, the life of my lord shall be bound in the bundle of the living under the care of the LORD your God; but the lives of your enemies he shall sling out as from the hollow of a sling. 30 When the LORD has done to my lord according to all the good that he has spoken concerning you, and has appointed you prince over Israel, 31 my lord shall have no cause of grief, or pangs of conscience, for having shed blood without cause or for having saved himself. And when the LORD has dealt well with my lord, then remember your servant."

32 David said to Ab'i·gāil, "Blessed be the LORD, the God of Israel, who sent you to meet me today! 33 Blessed be your good sense, and blessed be you, who have kept me today from bloodguilt and from avenging myself by my own hand! 34 For as surely as the LORD the God of Israel lives, who has restrained me from hurting you, unless you had hurried and come to meet me, truly by morning there would not have been left to Nā'bal so much as one male." 35 Then David received from her hand what she had brought him; he said to her, "Go up to your house in peace; see, I have heeded your voice, and I have granted your petition."

36 Ab'i·gāil came to Nā'bal; he was holding a feast in his house, like the feast of a king. Nā'bal's heart was merry within him, for he was very drunk; so she told him nothing at all until the morning light. 37 In the morning, when the wine had gone out of Nā'bal, his wife told him these things, and his heart died within him; he became like a stone. 38 About ten days later the LORD struck Nā'bal, and he died.

39 When David heard that Nā'bal was dead, he said, "Blessed be the LORD who has judged the case of Nā'bal's insult to me, and has kept back his servant from evil; the LORD has returned the evildoing of Nā'bal upon his own head." Then David sent and wooed Ab'i·gāil, to make her his wife. 40 When David's servants came to Ab'i·gāil at Car'mel, they said to her, "David has sent us to you to take you to him as his wife." 41 She rose and bowed down, with her face to the ground, and said, "Your servant is a slave to wash the feet of the servants of my lord." 42 Ab'i·gāil got up hurriedly and rode away on a donkey; her five maids attended her. She went after the messengers of David and became his wife.

43 David also married A·hin'o·am of Jez'rē·el; both of them became his wives. 44 Saul had given his daughter Mī'chal, David's wife, to Pal'tī son of Lā'ish, who was from Gal'lim.

David Spares Saul's Life a Second Time

Then the Ziph'ites came to Saul at Gib'ē·ah, saying, "David is in hiding on the hill of Ha·chī'lah, which is opposite Jē·shī'mon."[j] 2 So Saul rose and went down to the Wilderness of Ziph, with three thousand chosen men of Israel, to seek David in the Wilderness of Ziph. 3 Saul encamped on the hill of Ha·chī'lah, which is opposite Jē·shī'mon[j] beside the road. But David remained in the wilderness. When he learned that Saul had come after him into the wilderness, 4 David sent out spies, and learned that Saul had indeed arrived. 5 Then David set out and came to the place where Saul had encamped; and David saw the place where Saul lay, with Abner son of Ner, the commander of his army. Saul was lying within the encampment, while the army was encamped around him.

6 Then David said to A·him'e·lech the Hit'tīte, and to Jō'ab's brother A·bi'shaī son of Ze·rū'i·ah, "Who will go down with me into the camp to Saul?" A·bi'shaī said, "I will go down with you." 7 So David and A·bi'shaī went to the army by night; there Saul lay sleeping within the encampment, with his spear stuck in the ground at his head; and Abner and the army lay around him. 8 A·bi'shaī said to David, "God has given your enemy into your hand today; now therefore let me pin him to the ground with one stroke of the spear; I will not strike him twice." 9 But David said to A·bi'shaī, "Do not destroy him; for who can raise his hand against the LORD's anointed, and be guiltless?" 10 David said, "As the LORD lives, the LORD will strike him down; or his day will come to die; or he will go down into battle and perish. 11 The LORD forbid that I should raise my hand against the LORD's anointed; but now take the spear that is at his head, and the water jar, and let us go." 12 So David took the spear that was at Saul's head and the water jar, and they went away. No one saw it, or knew it, nor did anyone awake; for they were all

---

j Or opposite the wasteland

asleep, because a deep sleep from the Lord had fallen upon them.

13 Then David went over to the other side, and stood on top of a hill far away, with a great distance between them. 14 David called to the army and to Abner son of Ner, saying, "Abner! Will you not answer?" Then Abner replied, "Who are you that calls to the king?" 15 David said to Abner, "Are you not a man? Who is like you in Israel? Why then have you not kept watch over your lord the king? For one of the people came in to destroy your lord the king. 16 This thing that you have done is not good. As the Lord lives, you deserve to die, because you have not kept watch over your lord, the Lord's anointed. See now, where is the king's spear, or the water jar that was at his head?"

17 Saul recognized David's voice, and said, "Is this your voice, my son David?" David said, "It is my voice, my lord, O king." 18 And he added, "Why does my lord pursue his servant? For what have I done? What guilt is on my hands? 19 Now therefore let my lord the king hear the words of his servant. If it is the Lord who has stirred you up against me, may he accept an offering; but if it is mortals, may they be cursed before the Lord, for they have driven me out today from my share in the heritage of the Lord, saying, 'Go, serve other gods.' 20 Now therefore, do not let my blood fall to the ground, away from the presence of the Lord; for the king of Israel has come out to seek a single flea, like one who hunts a partridge in the mountains."

21 Then Saul said, "I have done wrong; come back, my son David, for I will never harm you again, because my life was precious in your sight today; I have been a fool, and have made a great mistake." 22 David replied, "Here is the spear, O king! Let one of the young men come over and get it. 23 The Lord rewards everyone for his righteousness and his faithfulness; for the Lord gave you into my hand today, but I would not raise my hand against the Lord's anointed. 24 As your life was precious today in my sight, so may my life be precious in the sight of the Lord, and may he rescue me from all tribulation." 25 Then Saul said to David, "Blessed be you, my son David! You will do many things and will succeed in them." So David went his way, and Saul returned to his place.

David Serves King Achish of Gath

David said in his heart, "I shall now perish one day by the hand of Saul; there is nothing better for me than to escape to the land of the Phi·lis'tines; then Saul will despair of seeking me any longer within the borders of Israel, and I shall escape out of his hand." 2 So David set out and went over, he and the six hundred men who were with him, to King Ā'chish son of Mā'och of Gath. 3 David stayed with Ā'chish at Gath, he and his troops, every man with his household, and David with his two wives, A·hin'o·am of Jez're·el, and Ab'i·gail of Car'mel, Nā'bal's widow. 4 When Saul was told that David had fled to Gath, he no longer sought for him.

5 Then David said to Ā'chish, "If I have found favor in your sight, let a place be given me in one of the country towns, so that I may live there; for why should your servant live in the royal city with you?" 6 So that day Ā'chish gave him Zik'lag; therefore Zik'lag has belonged to the kings of Judah to this day. 7 The length of time that David lived in the country of the Phi·lis'tines was one year and four months.

8 Now David and his men went up and made raids on the Gesh'u·rites, the Gir'zites, and the A·mal'e·kites; for these were the landed settlements from Tē'lam[k] on the way to Shur and on to the land of Egypt. 9 David struck the land, leaving neither man nor woman alive, but took away the sheep, the oxen, the donkeys, the camels, and the clothing, and came back to Ā'chish. 10 When Ā'chish asked, "Against whom[l] have you made a raid today?" David would say, "Against the Neg'eb of Judah," or "Against the Neg'eb of the Je·rah'me·el·ites," or, "Against the Neg'eb of the Ken'ites." 11 David left neither man nor woman alive to be brought back to Gath, thinking, "They might tell about us, and say, 'David has done so and so.' " Such was his practice all the time he lived in the country of the Phi·lis'tines. 12 Ā'chish trusted David, thinking, "He has made himself utterly abhorrent to his people Israel; therefore he shall always be my servant."

In those days the Phi·lis'tines gathered their forces for war, to fight against Israel. Ā'chish said to David, "You know, of course, that you and your men are to go out with me in the army." 2 David said to Ā'chish, "Very well, then you shall know what your servant can do." Ā'chish said to David, "Very well, I will make you my bodyguard for life."

Saul Consults a Medium
(Cp Deut 18.9–14)

3 Now Samuel had died, and all Israel had mourned for him and buried him in Rā'mah, his own city. Saul had expelled the mediums and the wizards from the land. 4 The Phi·lis'tines assembled, and came and encamped at Shū'nem. Saul gathered all Israel, and they encamped at Gil·bō'a.

k Compare Gk 15.4: Heb *from of old*   l Q Ms Gk Vg: MT lacks *whom*

5 When Saul saw the army of the Phi•lis'tines, he was afraid, and his heart trembled greatly. 6 When Saul inquired of the LORD, the LORD did not answer him, not by dreams, or by Ū'rim, or by prophets. 7 Then Saul said to his servants, "Seek out for me a woman who is a medium, so that I may go to her and inquire of her." His servants said to him, "There is a medium at En'dor."

8 So Saul disguised himself and put on other clothes and went there, he and two men with him. They came to the woman by night. And he said, "Consult a spirit for me, and bring up for me the one whom I name to you." 9 The woman said to him, "Surely you know what Saul has done, how he has cut off the mediums and the wizards from the land. Why then are you laying a snare for my life to bring about my death?" 10 But Saul swore to her by the LORD, "As the LORD lives, no punishment shall come upon you for this thing." 11 Then the woman said, "Whom shall I bring up for you?" He answered, "Bring up Samuel for me." 12 When the woman saw Samuel, she cried out with a loud voice; and the woman said to Saul, "Why have you deceived me? You are Saul!" 13 The king said to her, "Have no fear; what do you see?" The woman said to Saul, "I see a divine being^m coming up out of the ground." 14 He said to her, "What is his appearance?" She said, "An old man is coming up; he is wrapped in a robe." So Saul knew that it was Samuel, and he bowed with his face to the ground, and did obeisance.

15 Then Samuel said to Saul, "Why have you disturbed me by bringing me up?" Saul answered, "I am in great distress, for the Phi•lis'tines are warring against me, and God has turned away from me and answers me no more, either by prophets or by dreams; so I have summoned you to tell me what I should do." 16 Samuel said, "Why then do you ask me, since the LORD has turned from you and become your enemy? 17 The LORD has done to you just as he spoke by me; for the LORD has torn the kingdom out of your hand, and given it to your neighbor, David. 18 Because you did not obey the voice of the LORD, and did not carry out his fierce wrath against Am'a•lek, therefore the LORD has done this thing to you today. 19 Moreover the LORD will give Israel along with you into the hands of the Phi•lis'tines; and tomorrow you and your sons shall be with me; the LORD will also give the army of Israel into the hands of the Phi•lis'tines."

20 Immediately Saul fell full length on the ground, filled with fear because of the words of Samuel; and there was no strength in him, for he had eaten nothing all day and all night. 21 The woman came to Saul, and when she saw that he was terrified, she said to him, "Your servant has listened to you; I have taken my life in my hand, and have listened to what you have said to me. 22 Now therefore, you also listen to your servant; let me set a morsel of bread before you. Eat, that you may have strength when you go on your way." 23 He refused, and said, "I will not eat." But his servants, together with the woman, urged him; and he listened to their words. So he got up from the ground and sat on the bed. 24 Now the woman had a fatted calf in the house. She quickly slaughtered it, and she took flour, kneaded it, and baked unleavened cakes. 25 She put them before Saul and his servants, and they ate. Then they rose and went away that night.

The Philistines Reject David

Now the Phi•lis'tines gathered all their forces at Ā'phek, while the Israelites were encamped by the fountain that is in Jez're•el. 2 As the lords of the Phi•lis'tines were passing on by hundreds and by thousands, and David and his men were passing on in the rear with Ā'chish, 3 the commanders of the Phi•lis'tines said, "What are these Hebrews doing here?" Ā'chish said to the commanders of the Phi•lis'tines, "Is this not David, the servant of King Saul of Israel, who has been with me now for days and years? Since he deserted to me I have found no fault in him to this day." 4 But the commanders of the Phi•lis'tines were angry with him; and the commanders of the Phi•lis'tines said to him, "Send the man back, so that he may return to the place that you have assigned to him; he shall not go down with us to battle, or else he may become an adversary to us in the battle. For how could this fellow reconcile himself to his lord? Would it not be with the heads of the men here? 5 Is this not David, of whom they sing to one another in dances,

'Saul has killed his thousands,
    and David his ten thousands'?"

6 Then Ā'chish called David and said to him, "As the LORD lives, you have been honest, and to me it seems right that you should march out and in with me in the campaign; for I have found nothing wrong in you from the day of your coming to me until today. Nevertheless the lords do not approve of you. 7 So go back now; and go peaceably; do nothing to displease the lords of the Phi•lis'tines." 8 David said to Ā'chish, "But what have I done? What have you found in your servant from the day I entered your service until now, that I should not go and fight against the enemies of my lord the king?" 9 Ā'chish replied to David, "I know that you are as blameless in my sight as an

---

^m Or *a god*; or *gods*

angel of God; nevertheless, the commanders of the Phi•lis'tines have said, 'He shall not go up with us to the battle.' [10] Now then rise early in the morning, you and the servants of your lord who came with you, and go to the place that I appointed for you. As for the evil report, do not take it to heart, for you have done well before me.[n] Start early in the morning, and leave as soon as you have light." [11] So David set out with his men early in the morning, to return to the land of the Phi•lis'tines. But the Phi•lis'tines went up to Jez're•el.

David Avenges the Destruction of Ziklag

Now when David and his men came to Zik'lag on the third day, the A•mal'e•kites had made a raid on the Neg'eb and on Zik'lag. They had attacked Zik'lag, burned it down, [2] and taken captive the women and all[o] who were in it, both small and great; they killed none of them, but carried them off, and went their way. [3] When David and his men came to the city, they found it burned down, and their wives and sons and daughters taken captive. [4] Then David and the people who were with him raised their voices and wept, until they had no more strength to weep. [5] David's two wives also had been taken captive, A•hin'o•am of Jez're•el, and Ab'i•gail the widow of Nā'bal of Car'mel. [6] David was in great danger; for the people spoke of stoning him, because all the people were bitter in spirit for their sons and daughters. But David strengthened himself in the LORD his God.

[7] David said to the priest A•bi'a•thar son of A•him'e•lech, "Bring me the ephod." So A•bi'a•thar brought the ephod to David. [8] David inquired of the LORD, "Shall I pursue this band? Shall I overtake them?" He answered him, "Pursue; for you shall surely overtake and shall surely rescue." [9] So David set out, he and the six hundred men who were with him. They came to the Wadi Bē'sor, where those stayed who were left behind. [10] But David went on with the pursuit, he and four hundred men; two hundred stayed behind, too exhausted to cross the Wadi Bē'sor.

[11] In the open country they found an Egyptian, and brought him to David. They gave him bread and he ate; they gave him water to drink; [12] they also gave him a piece of fig cake and two clusters of raisins. When he had eaten, his spirit revived; for he had not eaten bread or drunk water for three days and three nights. [13] Then David said to him, "To whom do you belong? Where are you from?" He said, "I am a young man of Egypt, servant to an A•mal'e•kite. My master left me behind because I fell sick three days ago. [14] We had made a raid on the Neg'eb of the Cher'e•thites and on that which belongs to Judah and on the Neg'eb of Caleb; and we burned Zik'lag down." [15] David said to him, "Will you take me down to this raiding party?" He said, "Swear to me by God that you will not kill me, or hand me over to my master, and I will take you down to them."

[16] When he had taken him down, they were spread out all over the ground, eating and drinking and dancing, because of the great amount of spoil they had taken from the land of the Phi•lis'tines and from the land of Judah. [17] David attacked them from twilight until the evening of the next day. Not one of them escaped, except four hundred young men, who mounted camels and fled. [18] David recovered all that the A•mal'e•kites had taken; and David rescued his two wives. [19] Nothing was missing, whether small or great, sons or daughters, spoil or anything that had been taken; David brought back everything. [20] David also captured all the flocks and herds, which were driven ahead of the other cattle; people said, "This is David's spoil."

[21] Then David came to the two hundred men who had been too exhausted to follow David, and who had been left at the Wadi Bē'sor. They went out to meet David and to meet the people who were with him. When David drew near to the people he saluted them. [22] Then all the corrupt and worthless fellows among the men who had gone with David said, "Because they did not go with us, we will not give them any of the spoil that we have recovered, except that each man may take his wife and children, and leave." [23] But David said, "You shall not do so, my brothers, with what the LORD has given us; he has preserved us and handed over to us the raiding party that attacked us. [24] Who would listen to you in this matter? For the share of the one who goes down into the battle shall be the same as the share of the one who stays by the baggage; they shall share alike." [25] From that day forward he made it a statute and an ordinance for Israel; it continues to the present day.

[26] When David came to Zik'lag, he sent part of the spoil to his friends, the elders of Judah, saying, "Here is a present for you from the spoil of the enemies of the LORD"; [27] it was for those in Beth'el, in Rā'moth of the Neg'eb, in Jat'tir, [28] in A•rō'er, in Siph'moth, in Esh•te•mō'a, [29] in Rā'cal, in the towns of the Je•rah'me•el•ites, in the towns of the Ken'ites, [30] in Hor'mah, in Bor-ash'an, in Ā'thach, [31] in Hē'bron, all the places where David and his men had roamed.

---

n Gk: Heb lacks *and go to the place . . . done well before me*
o Gk: Heb lacks *and all*

Suicide Is Not an Answer

In 1 Sam 31.4, Saul commits suicide out of fear of what his enemies would do to him. His death leaves a gap for the Israelites, and David, Saul's enemy, deeply mourns his death in 2 Samuel, chapter 1.

A popular newspaper advice columnist printed a letter from someone who was writing to share a thought on suicide. He had decided that his life was not worth living anymore and planned to kill himself. The moment before he was about to do it, he thought about who would find him, and then he stopped. He realized that he couldn't put someone through the pain and suffering of finding him dead from suicide. Because he thought of another, he no longer looked at his life as hopeless.

No life is worthless! No pain is invincible! No matter how overwhelming your struggles and challenges seem, there are people who can help you, and people who could not bear to lose you. Seek God for help, seek others for help—suicide is never a solution!

For more on suicide, see "Judas's Suicide," Mt 27.3–10.

▸ 1 Sam 31.1–7

The Death of Saul and His Sons
(1 Chr 10.1–14)

Now the Phi·lis'tines fought against Israel; and the men of Israel fled before the Phi·lis'tines, and many fell*p* on Mount Gil·bō'a. ²The Phi·lis'tines overtook Saul and his sons; and the Phi·lis'tines killed Jonathan and A·bin'a·dab and Mal·chi·shū'a, the sons of Saul. ³The battle pressed hard upon Saul; the archers found him, and he was badly wounded by them. ⁴Then Saul said to his armor-bearer, "Draw your sword and thrust me through with it, so that these uncircumcised may not come and thrust me through, and make sport of me." But his armor-bearer was unwilling; for he was terrified. So Saul took his own sword and fell upon it. ⁵When his armor-bearer saw that Saul was dead, he also fell upon his sword and died with him. ⁶So Saul and his three sons and his armor-bearer and all his men died together on the same day. ⁷When the men of Israel who were on the other side of the valley and those beyond the Jordan saw

that the men of Israel had fled and that Saul and his sons were dead, they forsook their towns and fled; and the Phi·lis'tines came and occupied them.

8 The next day, when the Phi·lis'tines came to strip the dead, they found Saul and his three sons fallen on Mount Gil·bō'a. ⁹They cut off his head, stripped off his armor, and sent messengers throughout the land of the Phi·lis'tines to carry the good news to the houses of their idols and to the people. ¹⁰They put his armor in the temple of As·tar'te;*q* and they fastened his body to the wall of Beth-shan. ¹¹But when the inhabitants of Jā'besh-gil'ē·ad heard what the Phi·lis'tines had done to Saul, ¹²all the valiant men set out, traveled all night long, and took the body of Saul and the bodies of his sons from the wall of Beth-shan. They came to Jā'besh and burned them there. ¹³Then they took their bones and buried them under the tamarisk tree in Jā'besh, and fasted seven days.

p Heb *and they fell slain*   *q* Heb plural

Samuel

Politician Guilty of Taking Foreign Bribes!" "Minister Accused of Sexual Misconduct!" "Athlete Arrested on Drug Charges!" Sometimes it seems as if the news is filled with one scandal after another. "What's happening in the world today?" we may ask in despair. "Are there no honest, decent people left?" After reading 2 Samuel, you will realize that scandals among the rich and powerful are nothing new. But somehow, God's will is accomplished despite human sin.

At a Glance

- **Chapter 1.** David mourns Saul's death.

- **Chapters 2–20.** the reign of David

- **Chapters 21–24.** miscellaneous texts, including David's last words

In-depth

The main character in 2 Samuel is King David, whom we already met in 1 Samuel. The youngest of Jesse's sons, David is secretly anointed to succeed King Saul; he kills Goliath, plays music in Saul's court, and is befriended by the king's son Jonathan. At the beginning of 2 Samuel, when David takes the throne and quickly extends Israel's boundaries in every direction, everything looks hopeful for the nation.

As 2 Samuel continues, however, we discover that this hero is far from perfect: he sleeps with Bathsheba, the wife of one of his soldiers, and then tries to deceive the man when Bathsheba reports that she is pregnant. Later, he has the soldier killed and takes Bathsheba as his own. Soon, several tragedies befall his family and further bad decisions hurt his reign, leaving us with a mixed picture of the second king of Israel. Was David a great saint or a great sinner?

It was through David that God established a new Covenant with the people of Israel (7.1–17). This fact is underlined in a memorable way when David, after completing his own magnificent palace, declares that he will build a house for God. But God does not want a temple; God wishes to maintain a covenantal relationship with the people of Israel through all history: "Your throne shall be established forever" (verse 16).

Although a talented military leader and a powerful ruler, King David shared our broken human nature. The author of 2 Samuel reminds us that even the great and the mighty stand in need of God's help and mercy; even they must keep God's Covenant. Because of David's reliance on God, he became a symbol of the ideal king and of the future messiah. David's greatness—and our own—comes from a willing reliance on God.

Quick Facts

Period Covered
from 1040 to 1000 B.C.

Author
same as for 1 Samuel

Theme
David's rise to power and his fall into sin

Of Note
Samuel does not appear in this book, although it carries his name.

2 Samuel

David Mourns for Saul and Jonathan

After the death of Saul, when David had returned from defeating the A•mal′e•kites, David remained two days in Zik′lag. 2 On the third day, a man came from Saul's camp, with his clothes torn and dirt on his head. When he came to David, he fell to the ground and did obeisance. 3 David said to him, "Where have you come from?" He said to him, "I have escaped from the camp of Israel." 4 David said to him, "How did things go? Tell me!" He answered, "The army fled from the battle, but also many of the army fell and died; and Saul and his son Jonathan also died." 5 Then David asked the young man who was reporting to him, "How do you know that Saul and his son Jonathan died?" 6 The young man reporting to him said, "I happened to be on Mount Gil•bō′a; and there was Saul leaning on his spear, while the chariots and the horsemen drew close to him. 7 When he looked behind him, he saw me, and called to me. I answered, 'Here sir.' 8 And he said to me, 'Who are you?' I answered him, 'I am an A•mal′e•kīte.' 9 He said to me, 'Come, stand over me and kill me; for convulsions have seized me, and yet my life still lingers.' 10 So I stood over him, and killed him, for I knew that he could not live after he had fallen. I took the crown that was on his head and the arm-

let that was on his arm, and I have brought them here to my lord."

11 Then David took hold of his clothes and tore them; and all the men who were with him did the same. 12 They mourned and wept, and fasted until evening for Saul and for his son Jonathan, and for the army of the LORD and for the house of Israel, because they had fallen by the sword. 13 David said to the young man who had reported to him, "Where do you come from?" He answered, "I am the son of a resident alien, an A•mal′e•kīte." 14 David said to him, "Were you not afraid to lift your hand to destroy the LORD's anointed?" 15 Then David called one of the young men and said, "Come here and strike him down." So he struck him down and he died. 16 David said to him, "Your blood be on your head; for your own mouth has testified against you, saying, 'I have killed the LORD's anointed.' "

17 David intoned this lamentation over Saul and his son Jonathan. 18 (He ordered that The Song of the Bow[a] be taught to the people of Judah; it is written in the Book of Jash′ar.) He said:
19   Your glory, O Israel, lies slain upon your
        high places!
  How the mighty have fallen!

---

a Heb *that The Bow*

20 Tell it not in Gath,
> proclaim it not in the streets of
> > Ash′ke•lon;
> or the daughters of the Phi•lis′tines will
> > rejoice,
> > the daughters of the uncircumcised will
> > > exult.

21 You mountains of Gil•bō′a,
> > let there be no dew or rain upon you,
> > nor bounteous fields!^b
> For there the shield of the mighty was
> > defiled,
> > the shield of Saul, anointed with oil no
> > > more.

David the Musician

?did you KNOW?

David's song of mourning for Saul and Jonathan is another example of David's many talents. The Bible speaks in several places about David's ability as a musician and songwriter. One tradition says that he wrote all the Psalms, but no proof of this exists. His legendary reputation probably became exaggerated over the years to include many things only remotely related to his life.

▶ **2 Sam 1.19–27**

22 From the blood of the slain,
> > from the fat of the mighty,
> > the bow of Jonathan did not turn back,
> > > nor the sword of Saul return empty.

23 Saul and Jonathan, beloved and lovely!
> > In life and in death they were not
> > > divided;
> they were swifter than eagles,
> > they were stronger than lions.

24 O daughters of Israel, weep over Saul,
> > who clothed you with crimson, in luxury,
> > who put ornaments of gold on your
> > > apparel.

25 How the mighty have fallen
> > in the midst of the battle!

Jonathan lies slain upon your high places.
26 I am distressed for you, my brother
> > Jonathan;
> greatly beloved were you to me;
> > your love to me was wonderful,
> > passing the love of women.

27 How the mighty have fallen,
> > and the weapons of war perished!

David Anointed King of Judah

After this David inquired of the LORD, "Shall I go up into any of the cities of Judah?" The LORD said to him, "Go up." David said, "To which shall I go up?" He said, "To Hē′bron." ²So David went up there, along with his two wives, A•hin′ō•am of Jez′rē•el, and Ab′i•gail the widow of Nā′bal of Car′mel. ³David brought up the men who were with him, every one with his household; and they settled in the towns of Hē′bron. ⁴Then the people of Judah came, and there they anointed David king over the house of Judah.

When they told David, "It was the people of Jā′besh-gil′ē•ad who buried Saul," ⁵David sent messengers to the people of Jā′besh-gil′ē•ad, and said to them, "May you be blessed by the LORD, because you showed this loyalty to Saul your lord, and buried him! ⁶Now may the LORD show steadfast love and faithfulness to you! And I too will reward you because you have done this thing. ⁷Therefore let your hands be strong, and be valiant; for Saul your lord is dead, and the house of Judah has anointed me king over them."

Ishbaal King of Israel

8 But Abner son of Ner, commander of Saul's army, had taken Ish′bā•al^c son of Saul, and brought him over to Mā•ha•nā′im. ⁹He made him king over Gil′e•ad, the Ash′ur•ites, Jez′rē•el, Ē′phra•im, Benjamin, and over all Israel. ¹⁰Ish′-bā•al,^c Saul's son, was forty years old when he began to reign over Israel, and he reigned two years. But the house of Judah followed David. ¹¹The time that David was king in Hē′bron over the house of Judah was seven years and six months.

The Battle of Gibeon

12 Abner son of Ner, and the servants of Ish′-bā•al^c son of Saul, went out from Mā•ha•nā′im to Gib′ē•on. ¹³Jō′ab son of Ze•rū′i•ah, and the servants of David, went out and met them at the pool of Gib′ē•on. One group sat on one side of the pool, while the other sat on the other side of the pool. ¹⁴Abner said to Jō′ab, "Let the young men come

---

^b Meaning of Heb uncertain   ^c Gk Compare 1 Chr 8.33; 9.39: Heb *Ish-bosheth*, "man of shame"

forward and have a contest before us." Jō'ab said, "Let them come forward." 15 So they came forward and were counted as they passed by, twelve for Benjamin and Ish'bā·al*d* son of Saul, and twelve of the servants of David. 16 Each grasped his opponent by the head, and thrust his sword in his opponent's side; so they fell down together. Therefore that place was called Hel'kath-haz·zū'rim,*e* which is at Gib'ē·on. 17 The battle was very fierce that day; and Abner and the men of Israel were beaten by the servants of David.

18 The three sons of Ze·rū'i·ah were there, Jō'ab, A·bi'shaī, and As'a·hel. Now As'a·hel was as swift of foot as a wild gazelle. 19 As'a·hel pursued Abner, turning neither to the right nor to the left as he followed him. 20 Then Abner looked back and said, "Is it you, As'a·hel?" He answered, "Yes, it is." 21 Abner said to him, "Turn to your right or to your left, and seize one of the young men, and take his spoil." But As'a·hel would not turn away from following him. 22 Abner said again to As'a·hel, "Turn away from following me; why should I strike you to the ground? How then could I show my face to your brother Jō'ab?" 23 But he refused to turn away. So Abner struck him in the stomach with the butt of his spear, so that the spear came out at his back. He fell there, and died where he lay. And all those who came to the place where As'a·hel had fallen and died, stood still.

24 But Jō'ab and A·bi'shaī pursued Abner. As the sun was going down they came to the hill of Am'mah, which lies before Gī'ah on the way to the wilderness of Gib'ē·on. 25 The Ben'ja·min·ītes rallied around Abner and formed a single band; they took their stand on the top of a hill. 26 Then Abner called to Jō'ab, "Is the sword to keep devouring forever? Do you not know that the end will be bitter? How long will it be before you order your people to turn from the pursuit of their kinsmen?" 27 Jō'ab said, "As God lives, if you had not spoken, the people would have continued to pursue their kinsmen, not stopping until morning." 28 Jō'ab sounded the trumpet and all the people stopped; they no longer pursued Israel or engaged in battle any further.

29 Abner and his men traveled all that night through the Ar'a·bah; they crossed the Jordan, and, marching the whole forenoon,*f* they came to Mā·ha·nā'im. 30 Jō'ab returned from the pursuit of Abner; and when he had gathered all the people together, there were missing of David's servants nineteen men besides As'a·hel. 31 But the servants of David had killed of Benjamin three hundred sixty of Abner's men. 32 They took up As'a·hel and buried him in the tomb of his father, which was at

Bethlehem. Jō'ab and his men marched all night, and the day broke upon them at Hē'bron.

Abner Defects to David

There was a long war between the house of Saul and the house of David; David grew stronger and stronger, while the house of Saul became weaker and weaker.

2 Sons were born to David at Hē'bron: his firstborn was Am'non, of A·hin'ō·am of Jez'rē·el; 3 his second, Chil'ē·ab, of Ab'i·gāil the widow of Nā'bal of Car'mel; the third, Ab'sa·lom son of Mā'a·cah, daughter of King Tal'maī of Gē'shur; 4 the fourth, Ad·o·nī'jah son of Hag'gith; the fifth, Sheph·a·tī'ah son of A·bī'tal; 5 and the sixth, Ith'rē·am, of David's wife Eg'lah. These were born to David in Hē'bron.

6 While there was war between the house of Saul and the house of David, Abner was making himself strong in the house of Saul. 7 Now Saul had a concubine whose name was Riz'pah daughter of Āi'ah. And Ish'bā·al*g* said to Abner, "Why have you gone in to my father's concubine?" 8 The words of Ish'bā·al*d* made Abner very angry; he said, "Am I a dog's head for Judah? Today I keep showing loyalty to the house of your father Saul, to his brothers, and to his friends, and have not given you into the hand of David; and yet you charge me now with a crime concerning this woman. 9 So may God do to Abner and so may he add to it! For just what the LORD has sworn to David, that will I accomplish for him, 10 to transfer the kingdom from the house of Saul, and set up the throne of David over Israel and over Judah, from Dan to Bē'er-shē'ba." 11 And Ish'bā·al*g* could not answer Abner another word, because he feared him.

12 Abner sent messengers to David at Hē'bron,*h* saying, "To whom does the land belong? Make your covenant with me, and I will give you my support to bring all Israel over to you." 13 He said, "Good; I will make a covenant with you. But one thing I require of you: you shall never appear in my presence unless you bring Saul's daughter Mī'chal when you come to see me." 14 Then David sent messengers to Saul's son Ish'bā·al,*i* saying, "Give me my wife Mī'chal, to whom I became engaged at the price of one hundred foreskins of the Phi·lis'tines." 15 Ish'bā·al*i* sent and took her from her husband Pal'ti·el the son of Lā'ish. 16 But her husband went with her, weeping as he walked

---

d Gk Compare 1 Chr 8.33; 9.39: Heb *Ish-bosheth*, "man of shame"   *e* That is *Field of Sword-edges*   *f* Meaning of Heb uncertain   *g* Heb *And he*   *h* Gk: Heb *where he was*   *i* Heb *Ish-bosheth*

behind her all the way to Ba•hū'rim. Then Abner said to him, "Go back home!" So he went back.

17 Abner sent word to the elders of Israel, saying, "For some time past you have been seeking David as king over you. 18 Now then bring it about; for the LORD has promised David: Through my servant David I will save my people Israel from the hand of the Phi•lis'tines, and from all their enemies." 19 Abner also spoke directly to the Ben'ja-min•ītes; then Abner went to tell David at Hē'bron all that Israel and the whole house of Benjamin were ready to do.

20 When Abner came with twenty men to David at Hē'bron, David made a feast for Abner and the men who were with him. 21 Abner said to David, "Let me go and rally all Israel to my lord the king, in order that they may make a covenant with you, and that you may reign over all that your heart desires." So David dismissed Abner, and he went away in peace.

Abner Is Killed by Joab

22 Just then the servants of David arrived with Jō'ab from a raid, bringing much spoil with them. But Abner was not with David at Hē'bron, for David[j] had dismissed him, and he had gone away in peace. 23 When Jō'ab and all the army that was with him came, it was told Jō'ab, "Abner son of Ner came to the king, and he has dismissed him, and he has gone away in peace." 24 Then Jō'ab went to the king and said, "What have you done? Abner came to you; why did you dismiss him, so that he got away? 25 You know that Abner son of Ner came to deceive you, and to learn your comings and goings and to learn all that you are doing."

26 When Jō'ab came out from David's presence, he sent messengers after Abner, and they brought him back from the cistern of Sī'rah; but David did not know about it. 27 When Abner returned to Hē'bron, Jō'ab took him aside in the gateway to speak with him privately, and there he stabbed him in the stomach. So he died for shedding[k] the blood of As'a•hel, Jō'ab's[l] brother. 28 Afterward, when David heard of it, he said, "I and my kingdom are forever guiltless before the LORD for the blood of Abner son of Ner. 29 May the guilt[m] fall on the head of Jō'ab, and on all his father's house; and may the house of Jō'ab never be without one who has a discharge, or who is leprous,[n] or who holds a spindle, or who falls by the sword, or who lacks food!" 30 So Jō'ab and his brother A•bi'shai murdered Abner because he had killed their brother As'a•hel in the battle at Gib'-ē•on.

31 Then David said to Jō'ab and to all the people who were with him, "Tear your clothes, and put on sackcloth, and mourn over Abner." And King David followed the bier. 32 They buried Abner at Hē'bron. The king lifted up his voice and wept at the grave of Abner, and all the people wept. 33 The king lamented for Abner, saying,

"Should Abner die as a fool dies?
34 Your hands were not bound,
    your feet were not fettered;
as one falls before the wicked
    you have fallen."

And all the people wept over him again. 35 Then all the people came to persuade David to eat something while it was still day; but David swore, saying, "So may God do to me, and more, if I taste bread or anything else before the sun goes down!" 36 All the people took notice of it, and it pleased them; just as everything the king did pleased all the people. 37 So all the people and all Israel understood that day that the king had no part in the killing of Abner son of Ner. 38 And the king said to his servants, "Do you not know that a prince and a great man has fallen this day in Israel? 39 Today I am powerless, even though anointed king; these men, the sons of Ze•rū'i•ah, are too violent for me. The LORD pay back the one who does wickedly in accordance with his wickedness!"

Ishbaal Assassinated

When Saul's son Ish'bā•al[o] heard that Abner had died at Hē'bron, his courage failed, and all Israel was dismayed. 2 Saul's son had two captains of raiding bands; the name of the one was Bā'a•nah, and the name of the other Rē'chab. They were sons of Rim'mon a Ben'ja•min•īte from Be•er'oth—for Be•er'oth is considered to belong to Benjamin. 3 (Now the people of Be•er'oth had fled to Git'ta•im and are there as resident aliens to this day).

4 Saul's son Jonathan had a son who was crippled in his feet. He was five years old when the news about Saul and Jonathan came from Jez'rē•el. His nurse picked him up and fled; and, in her haste to flee, it happened that he fell and became lame. His name was Me•phib'o•sheth.[p]

5 Now the sons of Rim'mon the Be•er'oth•īte, Rē'chab and Bā'a•nah, set out, and about the heat of the day they came to the house of Ish'bā•al,[q] while he was taking his noonday rest. 6 They came inside the house as though to take wheat, and they struck him in the stomach; then Rē'chab and his brother Bā'a•nah escaped.[r] 7 Now they had come into the house while he was lying on his couch in

---

[j] Heb he   [k] Heb lacks *shedding*   [l] Heb *his*   [m] Heb *May it*   [n] A term for several skin diseases; precise meaning uncertain   [o] Heb lacks *Ishbaal*   [p] In 1 Chr 8.34 and 9.40, *Merib-baal*   [q] Heb *Ish-bosheth*   [r] Meaning of Heb of verse 6 uncertain

his bedchamber; they attacked him, killed him, and beheaded him. Then they took his head and traveled by way of the Ar′a‑bah all night long. [8] They brought the head of Ish′bā‑al[s] to David at Hē′bron and said to the king, "Here is the head of Ish′bā‑al,[s] son of Saul, your enemy, who sought your life; the LORD has avenged my lord the king this day on Saul and on his offspring."

9 David answered Rē′chab and his brother Bā′‑a‑nah, the sons of Rim′mon the Be‑er′oth‑īte, "As the LORD lives, who has redeemed my life out of every adversity, [10] when the one who told me, 'See, Saul is dead,' thought he was bringing good news, I seized him and killed him at Zik′lag—this was the reward I gave him for his news. [11] How much more then, when wicked men have killed a righteous man on his bed in his own house! And now shall I not require his blood at your hand, and destroy you from the earth?" [12] So David commanded the young men, and they killed them; they cut off their hands and feet, and hung their bodies beside the pool at Hē′bron. But the head of Ish′bā‑al[s] they took and buried in the tomb of Abner at Hē′bron.

David Anointed King of All Israel
(1 Chr 11.1–3)

Then all the tribes of Israel came to David at Hē′bron, and said, "Look, we are your bone and flesh. [2] For some time, while Saul was king over us, it was you who led out Israel and brought it in. The LORD said to you: It is you who shall be shepherd of my people Israel, you who shall be ruler over Israel." [3] So all the elders of Israel came to the king at Hē′bron; and King David made a covenant with them at Hē′bron before the LORD, and they anointed David king over Israel. [4] David was thirty years old when he began to reign, and he reigned forty years. [5] At Hē′bron he reigned over Judah seven years and six months; and at Jerusalem he reigned over all Israel and Judah thirty-three years.

Jerusalem Made Capital of
the United Kingdom
(1 Chr 11.4–9; 14.1–7)

6 The king and his men marched to Jerusalem against the Jeb′u‑sītes, the inhabitants of the land, who said to David, "You will not come in here, even the blind and the lame will turn you back"—thinking, "David cannot come in here." [7] Nevertheless David took the stronghold of Zion, which is now the city of David. [8] David had said on that day, "Whoever would strike down the Jeb′u‑sītes,

let him get up the water shaft to attack the lame and the blind, those whom David hates."[t] Therefore it is said, "The blind and the lame shall not come into the house." [9] David occupied the stronghold, and named it the city of David. David built the city all around from the Mil′lō inward. [10] And David became greater and greater, for the LORD, the God of hosts, was with him.

11 King Hiram of Tȳre sent messengers to David, along with cedar trees, and carpenters and masons who built David a house. [12] David then perceived that the LORD had established him king over Israel, and that he had exalted his kingdom for the sake of his people Israel.

13 In Jerusalem, after he came from Hē′bron, David took more concubines and wives; and more sons and daughters were born to David. [14] These are the names of those who were born to him in Jerusalem: Sham′mū‑a, Shō′bab, Nathan, Solomon, [15] Ib′har, E‑lish′ū‑a, Nē′pheg, Ja‑phi′a, [16] E‑lish′‑a‑ma, E‑lī′a‑da, and E‑liph′e‑let.

Philistine Attack Repulsed
(1 Chr 14.8–17)

17 When the Phi‑lis′tines heard that David had been anointed king over Israel, all the Phi‑lis′tines went up in search of David; but David heard about it and went down to the stronghold. [18] Now the Phi‑lis′tines had come and spread out in the valley of Reph′a‑im. [19] David inquired of the LORD, "Shall I go up against the Phi‑lis′tines? Will you give them into my hand?" The LORD said to David, "Go up; for I will certainly give the Phi‑lis′tines into your hand." [20] So David came to Bā′al‑pe‑rā′zim, and David defeated them there. He said, "The LORD has burst forth against[u] my enemies before me, like a bursting flood." Therefore that place is called Bā′al‑pe‑rā′zim.[v] [21] The Phi‑lis′tines abandoned their idols there, and David and his men carried them away.

22 Once again the Phi‑lis′tines came up, and were spread out in the valley of Reph′a‑im. [23] When David inquired of the LORD, he said, "You shall not go up; go around to their rear, and come upon them opposite the balsam trees. [24] When you hear the sound of marching in the tops of the balsam trees, then be on the alert; for then the LORD has gone out before you to strike down the army of the Phi‑lis′tines." [25] David did just as the LORD had commanded him; and he struck down the Phi‑lis′tines from Gē′ba all the way to Gē′zer.

---

[s] Heb *Ish-bosheth*   [t] Another reading is *those who hate David*   [u] Heb *paraz*   [v] That is *Lord of Bursting Forth*

2
S
A
M

The Dance of Life

It's a party! How else could we describe the festivities surrounding the triumphant bringing of the ark of the Covenant into Jerusalem? And King David is leading the way, dancing before the Lord "with all his might" (2 Sam 6.14). What a scene that must have been! What a wonderfully uninhibited way for David to express his great joy at escorting the ark into the city he has made his own.

So often we attend religious rituals as mere observers, much like Michal, David's wife, being critical and uninvolved. David shows us the true way to celebrate—with singing and dancing and eating. We need to celebrate together the presence of the Lord in our life! Here, David is our role model. Let us sing the song in our heart, and dance to the music God has planted within us.

How can we do a better job of celebrating the Lord in our life? Are we observers or participants in the dance of life?

▶ 2 Sam 6.12–19

David Brings the Ark to Jerusalem
(1 Chr 13.1–14; 15.25—16.3)

David again gathered all the chosen men of Israel, thirty thousand. ²David and all the people with him set out and went from Bā′a·lē·jū′dah, to bring up from there the ark of God, which is called by the name of the LORD of hosts who is enthroned on the cherubim. ³They carried the ark of God on a new cart, and brought it out of the house of A·bin′a·dab, which was on the hill. Uz′zah and A·hi′ō,ʷ the sons of A·bin′a·dab, were driving the new cart ⁴with the ark of God;ˣ and A·hi′ōʷ went in front of the ark. ⁵David and all the house of Israel were dancing before the LORD with all their might, with songsʸ and lyres and harps and tambourines and castanets and cymbals.

6 When they came to the threshing floor of Na′con, Uz′zah reached out his hand to the ark of God and took hold of it, for the oxen shook it. ⁷The anger of the LORD was kindled against Uz′zah; and God struck him there because he reached out his hand to the ark;ᶻ and he died there beside the ark of God. ⁸David was angry because the LORD had burst forth with an outburst upon Uz′zah; so that place is called Per′ez-uz′zah,ᵃ to this day. ⁹David was afraid of the LORD that day; he said, "How can the ark of the LORD come into my care?" ¹⁰So David was unwilling to take the ark of the LORD into his care in the city of David; instead David took it to the house of Ō′bed-ē′dom the Git′tīte. ¹¹The ark of the LORD remained in the house of Ō′bed-ē′dom the Git′tīte three months; and the LORD blessed Ō′bed-ē′dom and all his household.

12 It was told King David, "The LORD has blessed the household of Ō′bed-ē′dom and all that belongs to him, because of the ark of God." So

David went and brought up the ark of God from the house of Ō′bed-ē′dom to the city of David with rejoicing; ¹³and when those who bore the ark of the LORD had gone six paces, he sacrificed an ox and a fatling. ¹⁴David danced before the LORD with all his might; David was girded with a linen ephod. ¹⁵So David and all the house of Israel brought up the ark of the LORD with shouting, and with the sound of the trumpet.

16 As the ark of the LORD came into the city of David, Mi′chal daughter of Saul looked out of the window, and saw King David leaping and dancing before the LORD; and she despised him in her heart.

17 They brought in the ark of the LORD, and set it in its place, inside the tent that David had pitched for it; and David offered burnt offerings and offerings of well-being before the LORD. ¹⁸When David had finished offering the burnt offerings and the offerings of well-being, he blessed the people in the name of the LORD of hosts, ¹⁹and distributed food among all the people, the whole multitude of Israel, both men and women, to each a cake of bread, a portion of meat,ᵇ and a cake of raisins. Then all the people went back to their homes.

20 David returned to bless his household. But Mi′chal the daughter of Saul came out to meet David, and said, "How the king of Israel honored himself today, uncovering himself today before the eyes of his servants' maids, as any vulgar fellow

---

ʷ Or *and his brother*　　ˣ Compare Gk: Heb *and brought it out of the house of Abinadab, which was on the hill with the ark of God*　　ʸ Q Ms Gk 1 Chr 13.8: Heb *fir trees*　　ᶻ 1 Chr 13.10 Compare Q Ms: Meaning of Heb uncertain　　ᵃ That is *Bursting Out Against Uzzah*　　ᵇ Vg: Meaning of Heb uncertain

might shamelessly uncover himself!" 21 David said to Mi'chal, "It was before the LORD, who chose me in place of your father and all his household, to appoint me as prince over Israel, the people of the LORD, that I have danced before the LORD. 22 I will make myself yet more contemptible than this, and I will be abased in my own eyes; but by the maids of whom you have spoken, by them I shall be held in honor." 23 And Mi'chal the daughter of Saul had no child to the day of her death.

God's Covenant with David
(1 Chr 17.1–15)

Now when the king was settled in his house, and the LORD had given him rest from all his enemies around him, 2 the king said to the prophet Nathan, "See now, I am living in a house of cedar, but the ark of God stays in a tent." 3 Nathan said to the king, "Go, do all that you have in mind; for the LORD is with you."

4 But that same night the word of the LORD came to Nathan: 5 Go and tell my servant David: Thus says the LORD: Are you the one to build me a house to live in? 6 I have not lived in a house since the day I brought up the people of Israel from Egypt to this day, but I have been moving about in a tent and a tabernacle. 7 Wherever I have moved about among all the people of Israel, did I ever speak a word with any of the tribal leaders*c* of Israel, whom I commanded to shepherd my people Israel, saying, "Why have you not built me a house of cedar?" 8 Now therefore thus you shall say to my servant David: Thus says the LORD of hosts: I took you from the pasture, from following the sheep to be prince over my people Israel; 9 and I have been with you wherever you went, and have cut off all your enemies from before you; and I will make for you a great name, like the name of the great ones of the earth. 10 And I will appoint a place for my people Israel and will plant them, so that they may live in their own place, and be disturbed no more; and evildoers shall afflict them no more, as formerly, 11 from the time that I appointed judges over my people Israel; and I will give you rest from all your enemies. Moreover the LORD declares to you that the LORD will make you a house. 12 When your days are fulfilled and you lie down with your ancestors, I will raise up your offspring after you, who shall come forth from your body, and I will establish his kingdom. 13 He shall build a house for my name, and I will establish the throne of his kingdom forever. 14 I will be a father to him, and he shall be a son to me. When he commits iniquity, I will punish him with a rod such as mortals use, with blows inflicted by human beings. 15 But I will not take*d* my steadfast

love from him, as I took it from Saul, whom I put away from before you. 16 Your house and your kingdom shall be made sure forever before me;*e* your throne shall be established forever. 17 In accordance with all these words and with all this vision, Nathan spoke to David.

David's Prayer
(1 Chr 17.16–27)

18 Then King David went in and sat before the LORD, and said, "Who am I, O Lord GOD, and what is my house, that you have brought me thus far?

PRAY IT
David Praises God

Then King David went in and sat before the LORD, and said, 'Who am I, O LORD GOD, and what is my house, that you have brought me thus far?'" (2 Sam 7.18). When was the last time you brought yourself before God, like King David, simply to offer praise for all God has done for you?

It is easy for us to feel too busy to take time for God. Then, we complain and get frustrated because God does not seem to be around, giving our life direction. Taking quiet moments to place ourselves in humility before our God and to praise God for the good we experience is important.

Find a quiet place, take just fifteen minutes. No radio, no television, no book. Think of all the positive and happy things in your life, and in your own words, say, "Thank you, God, for caring for me and the people I love!"

▶ 2 Sam 7.18–29

19 And yet this was a small thing in your eyes, O Lord GOD; you have spoken also of your servant's house for a great while to come. May this be instruction for the people,*f* O Lord GOD! 20 And what more can David say to you? For you know your servant, O Lord GOD! 21 Because of your promise, and according to your own heart, you

c Or *any of the tribes*   *d* Gk Syr Vg 1 Chr 17.13: Heb *shall not depart*   *e* Gk Heb Mss: MT *before you*; Compare 2 Sam 7.26, 29   *f* Meaning of Heb uncertain

have wrought all this greatness, so that your servant may know it. 22 Therefore you are great, O LORD God; for there is no one like you, and there is no God besides you, according to all that we have heard with our ears. 23 Who is like your people, like Israel? Is there another*g* nation on earth whose God went to redeem it as a people, and to make a name for himself, doing great and awesome things for them,*h* by driving out*i* before his people nations and their gods?*j* 24 And you established your people Israel for yourself to be your people forever; and you, O LORD, became their God. 25 And now, O LORD God, as for the word that you have spoken concerning your servant and concerning his house, confirm it forever; do as you have promised. 26 Thus your name will be magnified forever in the saying, 'The LORD of hosts is God over Israel'; and the house of your servant David will be established before you. 27 For you, O LORD of hosts, the God of Israel, have made this revelation to your servant, saying, 'I will build you a house'; therefore your servant has found courage to pray this prayer to you. 28 And now, O Lord GOD, you are God, and your words are true, and you have promised this good thing to your servant; 29 now therefore may it please you to bless the house of your servant, so that it may continue forever before you; for you, O Lord GOD, have spoken, and with your blessing shall the house of your servant be blessed forever."

David's Wars
(1 Chr 18.1–13)

Some time afterward, David attacked the Phi·lis'·tines and subdued them; David took Meth'eg-am'·mah out of the hand of the Phi·lis'tines.

2 He also defeated the Mo'ab·ites and, making them lie down on the ground, measured them off with a cord; he measured two lengths of cord for those who were to be put to death, and one length*k* for those who were to be spared. And the Mo'ab·ites became servants to David and brought tribute.

3 David also struck down King Had·a·de'zer son of Re'hob of Zo'bah, as he went to restore his monument*l* at the river Euphrates. 4 David took from him one thousand seven hundred horsemen, and twenty thousand foot soldiers. David hamstrung all the chariot horses, but left enough for a hundred chariots. 5 When the Ar·a·me'ans of Damascus came to help King Had·a·de'zer of Zo'bah, David killed twenty-two thousand men of the Ar·a·me'ans. 6 Then David put garrisons among the Ar·a·me'ans of Damascus; and the Ar·a·me'ans became servants to David and brought tribute. The LORD

gave victory to David wherever he went. 7 David took the gold shields that were carried by the servants of Had·a·de'zer, and brought them to Jerusalem. 8 From Be'tah and from Be·ro'thai, towns of Had·a·de'zer, King David took a great amount of bronze.

9 When King To'i of Ha'math heard that David had defeated the whole army of Had·a·de'zer, 10 To'i sent his son Jo'ram to King David, to greet him and to congratulate him because he had fought against Had·a·de'zer and defeated him. Now Had·a·de'zer had often been at war with To'i. Jo'ram brought with him articles of silver, gold, and bronze; 11 these also King David dedicated to the LORD, together with the silver and gold that he dedicated from all the nations he subdued, 12 from E'dom, Mo'ab, the Am'mon·ites, the Phi·lis'tines, Am'a·lek, and from the spoil of King Had·a·de'zer son of Re'hob of Zo'bah.

13 David won a name for himself. When he returned, he killed eighteen thousand E'dom·ites*m* in the Valley of Salt. 14 He put garrisons in E'dom; throughout all E'dom he put garrisons, and all the E'dom·ites became David's servants. And the LORD gave victory to David wherever he went.

David's Officers
(1 Chr 18.14–17)

15 So David reigned over all Israel; and David administered justice and equity to all his people. 16 Jo'ab son of Ze·ru'i·ah was over the army; Je·hosh'a·phat son of A·hi'lud was recorder; 17 Za'dok son of A·hi'tub and A·him'e·lech son of A·bi'a·thar were priests; Se·rai'ah was secretary; 18 Be·na'i·ah son of Je·hoi'a·da was over*n* the Cher'e·thites and the Pel'eth·ites; and David's sons were priests.

David's Kindness to Mephibosheth

David asked, "Is there still anyone left of the house of Saul to whom I may show kindness for Jonathan's sake?" 2 Now there was a servant of the house of Saul whose name was Zi'ba, and he was summoned to David. The king said to him, "Are you Zi'ba?" And he said, "At your service!" 3 The king said, "Is there anyone remaining of the house of Saul to whom I may show the kindness of God?" Zi'ba said to the king, "There remains a son of Jonathan; he is crippled in his feet." 4 The king said

g Gk: Heb *one*   *h* Heb *you*   *i* Gk 1 Chr 17.21: Heb *for your land*   *j* Cn: Heb *before your people, whom you redeemed for yourself from Egypt, nations and its gods*   *k* Heb *one full length*   *l* Compare 1 Sam 15.12 and 2 Sam 18.18   *m* Gk: Heb *returned from striking down eighteen thousand Arameans*   *n* Syr Tg Vg 20.23; 1 Chr 18.17: Heb lacks *was over*

to him, "Where is he?" Zī'ba said to the king, "He
is in the house of Mā'chir son of Am'mi•el, at Lō-
dē'bar." 5 Then King David sent and brought him
from the house of Mā'chir son of Am'mi•el, at Lō-
dē'bar. 6 Me•phib'o•sheth[o] son of Jonathan son of
Saul came to David, and fell on his face and did
obeisance. David said, "Me•phib'o•sheth!"[o] He answered, "I am your servant." 7 David said to him,
"Do not be afraid, for I will show you kindness for
the sake of your father Jonathan; I will restore to
you all the land of your grandfather Saul, and you
yourself shall eat at my table always." 8 He did obeisance and said, "What is your servant, that you
should look upon a dead dog such as I?"

9 Then the king summoned Saul's servant
Zī'ba, and said to him, "All that belonged to Saul
and to all his house I have given to your master's
grandson. 10 You and your sons and your servants
shall till the land for him, and shall bring in the
produce, so that your master's grandson may have
food to eat; but your master's grandson Me•phib'o-
sheth[o] shall always eat at my table." Now Zī'ba had
fifteen sons and twenty servants. 11 Then Zī'ba said
to the king, "According to all that my lord the
king commands his servant, so your servant will
do." Me•phib'o•sheth[o] ate at David's[p] table, like one
of the king's sons. 12 Me•phib'o•sheth[o] had a young
son whose name was Mī'ca. And all who lived in
Zī'ba's house became Me•phib'o•sheth's[q] servants.
13 Me•phib'o•sheth[o] lived in Jerusalem, for he always ate at the king's table. Now he was lame in
both his feet.

The Ammonites and Arameans Are Defeated

(1 Chr 19.1–19)

10 Some time afterward, the king of the Am'mon•ītes
died, and his son Hā'nun succeeded him. 2 David
said, "I will deal loyally with Hā'nun son of Nā'-
hash, just as his father dealt loyally with me." So
David sent envoys to console him concerning his
father. When David's envoys came into the land of
the Am'mon•ītes, 3 the princes of the Am'mon•ītes
said to their lord Hā'nun, "Do you really think
that David is honoring your father just because he
has sent messengers with condolences to you? Has
not David sent his envoys to you to search the city,
to spy it out, and to overthrow it?" 4 So Hā'nun
seized David's envoys, shaved off half the beard of
each, cut off their garments in the middle at their
hips, and sent them away. 5 When David was told,
he sent to meet them, for the men were greatly
ashamed. The king said, "Remain at Jericho until
your beards have grown, and then return."

6 When the Am'mon•ītes saw that they had become odious to David, the Am'mon•ītes sent and
hired the Ar•a•mē'ans of Beth-rē'hob and the Ar•a-
mē'ans of Zō'bah, twenty thousand foot soldiers,
as well as the king of Mā'a•cah, one thousand men,
and the men of Tob, twelve thousand men. 7 When
David heard of it, he sent Jō'ab and all the army
with the warriors. 8 The Am'mon•ītes came out and
drew up in battle array at the entrance of the gate;
but the Ar•a•mē'ans of Zō'bah and of Rē'hob, and
the men of Tob and Mā'a•cah, were by themselves
in the open country.

9 When Jō'ab saw that the battle was set
against him both in front and in the rear, he chose
some of the picked men of Israel, and arrayed
them against the Ar•a•mē'ans; 10 the rest of his men
he put in the charge of his brother A•bi'shaī, and
he arrayed them against the Am'mon•ītes. 11 He
said, "If the Ar•a•mē'ans are too strong for me, then
you shall help me; but if the Am'mon•ites are too
strong for you, then I will come and help you.
12 Be strong, and let us be courageous for the sake
of our people, and for the cities of our God; and
may the LORD do what seems good to him." 13 So
Jō'ab and the people who were with him moved
forward into battle against the Ar•a•mē'ans; and
they fled before him. 14 When the Am'mon•ītes saw
that the Ar•a•mē'ans fled, they likewise fled before
A•bi'shaī, and entered the city. Then Jō'ab returned
from fighting against the Am'mon•ītes, and came
to Jerusalem.

15 But when the Ar•a•mē'ans saw that they had
been defeated by Israel, they gathered themselves
together. 16 Had•a•dē'zer sent and brought out the
Ar•a•mē'ans who were beyond the Euphrates; and
they came to Hē'lam, with Shō'bach the commander of the army of Had•a•dē'zer at their head.
17 When it was told David, he gathered all Israel
together, and crossed the Jordan, and came to Hē'-
lam. The Ar•a•mē'ans arrayed themselves against
David and fought with him. 18 The Ar•a•mē'ans fled
before Israel; and David killed of the Ar•a•mē'ans
seven hundred chariot teams, and forty thousand
horsemen,[r] and wounded Shō'bach the commander of their army, so that he died there.
19 When all the kings who were servants of Had•a-
dē'zer saw that they had been defeated by Israel,
they made peace with Israel, and became subject
to them. So the Ar•a•mē'ans were afraid to help the
Am'mon•ītes any more.

---

[o] Or *Merib-baal*: See 4.4 note [p] Gk: Heb *my*
[q] Or *Merib-baal's*: See 4.4 note [r] 1 Chr 19.18 and some Gk Mss read *foot soldiers*

David Commits Adultery with Bathsheba

In the spring of the year, the time when kings go out to battle, David sent Jōʹab with his officers and all Israel with him; they ravaged the Amʹmonītes, and besieged Rabʹbah. But David remained at Jerusalem.

2 It happened, late one afternoon, when David rose from his couch and was walking about on the roof of the king's house, that he saw from the roof a woman bathing; the woman was very beautiful. ³David sent someone to inquire about the woman. It was reported, "This is Bath·sheʹba daughter of E·liʹam, the wife of U·riʹah the Hitʹtīte." ⁴So David sent messengers to get her, and she came to him, and he lay with her. (Now she was purifying herself after her period.) Then she returned to her house. ⁵The woman conceived; and she sent and told David, "I am pregnant."

6 So David sent word to Jōʹab, "Send me U·riʹah the Hitʹtīte." And Jōʹab sent U·riʹah to David. ⁷When U·riʹah came to him, David asked how Jōʹab and the people fared, and how the war was going. ⁸Then David said to U·riʹah, "Go down to your house, and wash your feet." U·riʹah went out of the king's house, and there followed him a present from the king. ⁹But U·riʹah slept at the entrance of the king's house with all the servants of his lord, and did not go down to his house. ¹⁰When they told David, "U·riʹah did not go down to his house," David said to U·riʹah, "You have just come from a journey. Why did you not go down to your house?" ¹¹U·riʹah said to David, "The ark and Israel and Judah remain in booths;⁵ and my lord Jōʹab and the servants of my lord are camping in the open field; shall I then go to my house, to eat and to drink, and to lie with my wife? As you live, and as your soul lives, I will not do such a thing." ¹²Then David said to U·riʹah, "Remain here today also, and tomorrow I will send you back." So U·riʹah remained in Jerusalem that day. On the next day, ¹³David invited him to eat and drink in his presence and made him drunk; and in the evening he went out to lie on his couch with the servants of his lord, but he did not go down to his house.

David Has Uriah Killed

14 In the morning David wrote a letter to Jōʹab, and sent it by the hand of U·riʹah. ¹⁵In the letter he wrote, "Set U·riʹah in the forefront of the hardest fighting, and then draw back from him, so that he may be struck down and die." ¹⁶As Jōʹab was besieging the city, he assigned U·riʹah to the place where he knew there were valiant warriors. ¹⁷The men of the city came out and fought with Jōʹab; and some of the servants of David among the people fell. U·riʹah the Hitʹtīte was killed as well. ¹⁸Then Jōʹab sent and told David all the news about the fighting; ¹⁹and he instructed the messenger, "When you have finished telling the king all the news about the fighting, ²⁰then, if the king's anger rises, and if he says to you, 'Why did you go so near the city to fight? Did you not

⁵ Or *at Succoth*

LIVE IT!

Lust and Its Consequences

What the king wants, the king gets.
    That seems to be the message of 2 Sam 11.1–5. We are spared many of the details about the encounter between David and Bathsheba, but we do know this: Bathsheba is married to Uriah, so David has coveted another man's wife and committed adultery. When Bathsheba becomes pregnant, David attempts to deceive Uriah into thinking the baby is Uriah's, by bringing him home to have sex with Bathsheba. But Uriah refuses to do so because he and his comrades are in the midst of a war. Finally, David arranges for Uriah to be murdered in battle.
    In one brief episode, David has broken four commandments. He has given in to lust, and it has led him into a situation that will affect his family, his kingship, and the whole nation of Israel.
    It is so easy to give in to temptation, especially lust, because it can be so alluring, and because we generally fail to think beyond the moment. A dangerous thing.
    Take a few moments to reflect on how you deal with your own sexual desires and temptations.

▶ **2 Sam 11.1–5**

The Power of a Good Story

LIVE IT!

A story can be a powerful thing. Jesus knew the power of stories, so he often responded to questions by telling a story.

The prophet Nathan also knew the power of stories. His challenge was to force David to come to grips with what he had done with Bathsheba and Uriah. In 2 Samuel, Nathan cleverly creates a story in which David is to assume his familiar role as judge. David hears the case and is furious at the actions of the rich man in it, declaring that he should die for what he has done. Then, with four words, Nathan turns David's world upside down:

"You are the man!" (12.7).

What can David say? He just condemned himself, and he knows it. Nathan has cleverly forced him into a moment of truth. You may want to read Psalm 51, which poetically records David's confession.

Yes, a story can be a powerful thing. Just ask Nathan. Or David. Or Jesus.

▶ 2 Sam 12.1–12

---

know that they would shoot from the wall? 21 Who killed A·bim′e·lech son of Jer·ub·ba′al?[t] Did not a woman throw an upper millstone on him from the wall, so that he died at The′bez? Why did you go so near the wall?' then you shall say, 'Your servant Ū·rī′ah the Hit′tīte is dead too.' "

22 So the messenger went, and came and told David all that Jō′ab had sent him to tell. 23 The messenger said to David, "The men gained an advantage over us, and came out against us in the field; but we drove them back to the entrance of the gate. 24 Then the archers shot at your servants from the wall; some of the king's servants are dead; and your servant Ū·rī′ah the Hit′tīte is dead also." 25 David said to the messenger, "Thus you shall say to Jō′ab, 'Do not let this matter trouble you, for the sword devours now one and now another; press your attack on the city, and overthrow it.' And encourage him."

26 When the wife of Ū·rī′ah heard that her husband was dead, she made lamentation for him. 27 When the mourning was over, David sent and brought her to his house, and she became his wife, and bore him a son.

Nathan Condemns David

But the thing that David had done displeased the LORD, 1 and the LORD sent Nathan to David. He came to him, and said to him, "There were two men in a certain city, the one rich and the other poor. 2 The rich man had very many flocks and herds; 3 but the poor man had nothing but one little ewe lamb, which he had bought. He brought it up, and it grew up with him and with his children; it used to eat of his meager fare, and drink

from his cup, and lie in his bosom, and it was like a daughter to him. 4 Now there came a traveler to the rich man, and he was loath to take one of his own flock or herd to prepare for the wayfarer who had come to him, but he took the poor man's lamb, and prepared that for the guest who had come to him." 5 Then David's anger was greatly kindled against the man. He said to Nathan, "As the LORD lives, the man who has done this deserves to die; 6 he shall restore the lamb fourfold, because he did this thing, and because he had no pity."

7 Nathan said to David, "You are the man! Thus says the LORD, the God of Israel: I anointed you king over Israel, and I rescued you from the hand of Saul; 8 I gave you your master's house, and your master's wives into your bosom, and gave you the house of Israel and of Judah; and if that had been too little, I would have added as much more. 9 Why have you despised the word of the LORD, to do what is evil in his sight? You have struck down Ū·rī′ah the Hit′tīte with the sword, and have taken his wife to be your wife, and have killed him with the sword of the Am′mon·ites. 10 Now therefore the sword shall never depart from your house, for you have despised me, and have taken the wife of Ū·rī′ah the Hit′tīte to be your wife. 11 Thus says the LORD: I will raise up trouble against you from within your own house; and I will take your wives before your eyes, and give them to your neighbor, and he shall lie with your wives in the sight of this very sun. 12 For you did it secretly; but I will do this thing before all Israel, and before the sun." 13 David said to Nathan, "I have sinned against the LORD." Nathan said to

---

[t] Gk Syr Judg 7.1: Heb *Jerubbesheth*

David, "Now the LORD has put away your sin; you shall not die. ¹⁴ Nevertheless, because by this deed you have utterly scorned the LORD,ᵘ the child that is born to you shall die." ¹⁵ Then Nathan went to his house.

Bathsheba's Child Dies

The LORD struck the child that Ū•rī'ah's wife bore to David, and it became very ill. ¹⁶ David therefore pleaded with God for the child; David fasted, and went in and lay all night on the ground. ¹⁷ The elders of his house stood beside him, urging him to rise from the ground; but he would not, nor did he eat food with them. ¹⁸ On the seventh day the child died. And the servants of David were afraid to tell him that the child was dead; for they said, "While the child was still alive, we spoke to him, and he did not listen to us; how then can we tell him the child is dead? He may do himself some harm." ¹⁹ But when David saw that his servants were whispering together, he perceived that the child was dead; and David said to his servants, "Is the child dead?" They said, "He is dead."

20 Then David rose from the ground, washed, anointed himself, and changed his clothes. He went into the house of the LORD, and worshiped; he then went to his own house; and when he asked, they set food before him and he ate. ²¹ Then his servants said to him, "What is this thing that you have done? You fasted and wept for the child while it was alive; but when the child died, you rose and ate food." ²² He said, "While the child was still alive, I fasted and wept; for I said, 'Who knows? The LORD may be gracious to me, and the child may live.' ²³ But now he is dead; why should I fast? Can I bring him back again? I shall go to him, but he will not return to me."

Solomon Is Born

24 Then David consoled his wife Bath•she'ba, and went to her, and lay with her; and she bore a son, and he named him Solomon. The LORD loved him, ²⁵ and sent a message by the prophet Nathan; so he named him Jed•i•di'ah,ᵛ because of the LORD.

The Ammonites Crushed
(1 Chr 20.1–3)

26 Now Jō'ab fought against Rab'bah of the Am'mon•ites, and took the royal city. ²⁷ Jō'ab sent messengers to David, and said, "I have fought against Rab'bah; moreover, I have taken the water city. ²⁸ Now, then, gather the rest of the people together, and encamp against the city, and take it; or I myself will take the city, and it will be called by my name." ²⁹ So David gathered all the people together and went to Rab'bah, and fought against

it and took it. ³⁰ He took the crown of Mil'com ᵂ from his head; the weight of it was a talent of gold, and in it was a precious stone; and it was placed on David's head. He also brought forth the spoil of the city, a very great amount. ³¹ He brought out the people who were in it, and set them to work with saws and iron picks and iron axes, or sent them to the brickworks. Thus he did to all the cities of the Am'mon•ites. Then David and all the people returned to Jerusalem.

Amnon and Tamar

Some time passed. David's son Ab'sa•lom had a beautiful sister whose name was Tā'mar; and David's son Am'non fell in love with her. ² Am'non was so tormented that he made himself ill because of his sister Tā'mar, for she was a virgin and it seemed impossible to Am'non to do anything to her. ³ But Am'non had a friend whose name was Jon'a•dab, the son of David's brother Shim'ē•ah; and Jon'a•dab was a very crafty man. ⁴ He said to him, "O son of the king, why are you so haggard morning after morning? Will you not tell me?" Am'non said to him, "I love Tā'mar, my brother Ab'sa•lom's sister." ⁵ Jon'a•dab said to him, "Lie down on your bed, and pretend to be ill; and when your father comes to see you, say to him, 'Let my sister Tā'mar come and give me something to eat, and prepare the food in my sight, so that I may see it and eat it from her hand.' " ⁶ So Am'non lay down, and pretended to be ill; and when the king came to see him, Am'non said to the king, "Please let my sister Tā'mar come and make a couple of cakes in my sight, so that I may eat from her hand."

7 Then David sent home to Tā'mar, saying, "Go to your brother Am'non's house, and prepare food for him." ⁸ So Tā'mar went to her brother Am'non's house, where he was lying down. She took dough, kneaded it, made cakes in his sight, and baked the cakes. ⁹ Then she took the pan and set themˣ out before him, but he refused to eat. Am'non said, "Send out everyone from me." So everyone went out from him. ¹⁰ Then Am'non said to Tā'mar, "Bring the food into the chamber, so that I may eat from your hand." So Tā'mar took the cakes she had made, and brought them into the chamber to Am'non her brother. ¹¹ But when she brought them near him to eat, he took hold of her, and said to her, "Come, lie with me, my sister." ¹² She answered him, "No, my brother, do not force me; for such a thing is not done in Israel; do

---

ᵘ Ancient scribal tradition: Compare 1 Sam 25.22 note: Heb *scorned the enemies of the LORD* ᵛ That is *Beloved of the LORD* ᵂ Gk See 1 Kings 11.5, 33: Heb *their kings* ˣ Heb *and poured*

not do anything so vile! 13 As for me, where could I carry my shame? And as for you, you would be as one of the scoundrels in Israel. Now therefore, I beg you, speak to the king; for he will not withhold me from you." 14 But he would not listen to her; and being stronger than she, he forced her and lay with her.

15 Then Am'non was seized with a very great loathing for her; indeed, his loathing was even greater than the lust he had felt for her. Am'non said to her, "Get out!" 16 But she said to him, "No, my brother;ʸ for this wrong in sending me away is greater than the other that you did to me." But he would not listen to her. 17 He called the young man who served him and said, "Put this woman out of my presence, and bolt the door after her." 18 (Now she was wearing a long robe with sleeves; for this is how the virgin daughters of the king were clothed in earlier times.ᶻ) So his servant put her out, and bolted the door after her. 19 But Tā'mar put ashes on her head, and tore the long robe that she was wearing; she put her hand on her head, and went away, crying aloud as she went.

20 Her brother Ab'sa•lom said to her, "Has Am'non your brother been with you? Be quiet for now, my sister; he is your brother; do not take this to heart." So Tā'mar remained, a desolate woman, in her brother Ab'sa•lom's house. 21 When King David heard of all these things, he became very angry, but he would not punish his son Am'non, because he loved him, for he was his firstborn.ᵃ 22 But Ab'sa•lom spoke to Am'non neither good nor bad; for Ab'sa•lom hated Am'non, because he had raped his sister Tā'mar.

Absalom Avenges the Violation of His Sister

23 After two full years Ab'sa•lom had sheepshearers at Bā'al-hā'zor, which is near Ē'phra•im, and Ab'sa•lom invited all the king's sons. 24 Ab'salom came to the king, and said, "Your servant has sheepshearers; will the king and his servants please go with your servant?" 25 But the king said to Ab'salom, "No, my son, let us not all go, or else we will be burdensome to you." He pressed him, but he would not go but gave him his blessing. 26 Then Ab'sa•lom said, "If not, please let my brother Am'non go with us." The king said to him, "Why should he go with you?" 27 But Ab'sa•lom pressed him until he let Am'non and all the king's sons go with him. Ab'sa•lom made a feast like a king's feast.ᵇ 28 Then Ab'sa•lom commanded his servants, "Watch when Am'non's heart is merry with wine, and when I say to you, 'Strike Am'non,' then kill him. Do not be afraid; have I not myself commanded you? Be courageous and valiant." 29 So the

servants of Ab'sa•lom did to Am'non as Ab'sa•lom had commanded. Then all the king's sons rose, and each mounted his mule and fled.

30 While they were on the way, the report came to David that Ab'sa•lom had killed all the king's sons, and not one of them was left. 31 The king rose, tore his garments, and lay on the ground; and all his servants who were standing by tore their garments. 32 But Jon'a•dab, the son of David's brother Shim'ē•ah, said, "Let not my lord suppose that they have killed all the young men the king's sons; Am'non alone is dead. This has been determined by Ab'sa•lom from the day Am'nonᶜ raped his sister Tā'mar. 33 Now therefore, do not let my lord the king take it to heart, as if all the king's sons were dead; for Am'non alone is dead."

34 But Ab'sa•lom fled. When the young man who kept watch looked up, he saw many people coming from the Hor•ō•nā'im roadᵈ by the side of the mountain. 35 Jon'a•dab said to the king, "See, the king's sons have come; as your servant said, so it has come about." 36 As soon as he had finished speaking, the king's sons arrived, and raised their voices and wept; and the king and all his servants also wept very bitterly.

37 But Ab'sa•lom fled, and went to Tal'maī son of Am•mī'hud, king of Gē'shur. David mourned for his son day after day. 38 Ab'sa•lom, having fled to Gē'shur, stayed there three years. 39 And the heart ofᵉ the king went out, yearning for Ab'salom; for he was now consoled over the death of Am'non.

Absalom Returns to Jerusalem

Now Jō'ab son of Ze•rū'i•ah perceived that the king's mind was on Ab'sa•lom. 2 Jō'ab sent to Te•kō'a and brought from there a wise woman. He said to her, "Pretend to be a mourner; put on mourning garments, do not anoint yourself with oil, but behave like a woman who has been mourning many days for the dead. 3 Go to the king and speak to him as follows." And Jō'ab put the words into her mouth.

4 When the woman of Te•kō'a came to the king, she fell on her face to the ground and did obeisance, and said, "Help, O king!" 5 The king asked her, "What is your trouble?" She answered, "Alas, I am a widow; my husband is dead. 6 Your servant had two sons, and they fought with one another in the field; there was no one to part

ʸ Cn Compare Gk Vg: Meaning of Heb uncertain
ᶻ Cn: Heb *were clothed in robes*   ᵃ Q Ms Gk: MT lacks *but he would not punish . . . firstborn*   ᵇ Gk Compare Q Ms: MT lacks *Absalom made a feast like a king's feast*   ᶜ Heb *he*   ᵈ Cn Compare Gk: Heb *the road behind him*   ᵉ Q Ms Gk: MT *And David*

them, and one struck the other and killed him. 7 Now the whole family has risen against your servant. They say, 'Give up the man who struck his brother, so that we may kill him for the life of his brother whom he murdered, even if we destroy the heir as well.' Thus they would quench my one remaining ember, and leave to my husband neither name nor remnant on the face of the earth."

8 Then the king said to the woman, "Go to your house, and I will give orders concerning you." 9 The woman of Te·kō'a said to the king, "On me be the guilt, my lord the king, and on my father's house; let the king and his throne be guiltless." 10 The king said, "If anyone says anything to you, bring him to me, and he shall never touch you again." 11 Then she said, "Please, may the king keep the LORD your God in mind, so that the avenger of blood may kill no more, and my son not be destroyed." He said, "As the LORD lives, not one hair of your son shall fall to the ground."

12 Then the woman said, "Please let your servant speak a word to my lord the king." He said, "Speak." 13 The woman said, "Why then have you planned such a thing against the people of God? For in giving this decision the king convicts himself, inasmuch as the king does not bring his banished one home again. 14 We must all die; we are like water spilled on the ground, which cannot be gathered up. But God will not take away a life; he will devise plans so as not to keep an outcast banished forever from his presence.ƒ 15 Now I have come to say this to my lord the king because the people have made me afraid; your servant thought, 'I will speak to the king; it may be that the king will perform the request of his servant. 16 For the king will hear, and deliver his servant from the hand of the man who would cut both me and my son off from the heritage of God.' 17 Your servant thought, 'The word of my lord the king will set me at rest'; for my lord the king is like the angel of God, discerning good and evil. The LORD your God be with you!"

18 Then the king answered the woman, "Do not withhold from me anything I ask you." The woman said, "Let my lord the king speak." 19 The king said, "Is the hand of Jō'ab with you in all this?" The woman answered and said, "As surely as you live, my lord the king, one cannot turn right or left from anything that my lord the king has said. For it was your servant Jō'ab who commanded me; it was he who put all these words into the mouth of your servant. 20 In order to change the course of affairs your servant Jō'ab did this. But my lord has wisdom like the wisdom of the angel of God to know all things that are on the earth."

21 Then the king said to Jō'ab, "Very well, I grant this; go, bring back the young man Ab'sa·lom." 22 Jō'ab prostrated himself with his face to the ground and did obeisance, and blessed the king; and Jō'ab said, "Today your servant knows that I have found favor in your sight, my lord the king, in that the king has granted the request of his servant." 23 So Jō'ab set off, went to Gē'shur, and brought Ab'sa·lom to Jerusalem. 24 The king said, "Let him go to his own house; he is not to come into my presence." So Ab'sa·lom went to his own house, and did not come into the king's presence.

David Forgives Absalom

25 Now in all Israel there was no one to be praised so much for his beauty as Ab'sa·lom; from the sole of his foot to the crown of his head there was no blemish in him. 26 When he cut the hair of his head (for at the end of every year he used to cut it; when it was heavy on him, he cut it), he weighed the hair of his head, two hundred shekels by the king's weight. 27 There were born to Ab'sa·lom three sons, and one daughter whose name was Tā'mar; she was a beautiful woman.

28 So Ab'sa·lom lived two full years in Jerusalem, without coming into the king's presence. 29 Then Ab'sa·lom sent for Jō'ab to send him to the king; but Jō'ab would not come to him. He sent a second time, but Jō'ab would not come. 30 Then he said to his servants, "Look, Jō'ab's field is next to mine, and he has barley there; go and set it on fire." So Ab'sa·lom's servants set the field on fire. 31 Then Jō'ab rose and went to Ab'sa·lom at his house, and said to him, "Why have your servants set my field on fire?" 32 Ab'sa·lom answered Jō'ab, "Look, I sent word to you: Come here, that I may send you to the king with the question, 'Why have I come from Gē'shur? It would be better for me to be there still.' Now let me go into the king's presence; if there is guilt in me, let him kill me!" 33 Then Jō'ab went to the king and told him; and he summoned Ab'sa·lom. So he came to the king and prostrated himself with his face to the ground before the king; and the king kissed Ab'sa·lom.

Absalom Usurps the Throne

After this Ab'sa·lom got himself a chariot and horses, and fifty men to run ahead of him. 2 Ab'sa·lom used to rise early and stand beside the road into the gate; and when anyone brought a suit before the king for judgment, Ab'sa·lom would call out and say, "From what city are you?" When the person said, "Your servant is of such and such a tribe in Israel," 3 Ab'sa·lom would say, "See, your

ƒ Meaning of Heb uncertain

claims are good and right; but there is no one deputed by the king to hear you." 4 Ab'sa·lom said moreover, "If only I were judge in the land! Then all who had a suit or cause might come to me, and I would give them justice." 5 Whenever people came near to do obeisance to him, he would put out his hand and take hold of them, and kiss them. 6 Thus Ab'sa·lom did to every Israelite who came to the king for judgment; so Ab'sa·lom stole the hearts of the people of Israel.

7 At the end of four*g* years Ab'sa·lom said to the king, "Please let me go to He'bron and pay the vow that I have made to the LORD. 8 For your servant made a vow while I lived at Ge'shur in Ar'am: If the LORD will indeed bring me back to Jerusalem, then I will worship the LORD in He'-bron."*h* 9 The king said to him, "Go in peace." So he got up, and went to He'bron. 10 But Ab'sa·lom sent secret messengers throughout all the tribes of Israel, saying, "As soon as you hear the sound of the trumpet, then shout: Ab'sa·lom has become king at He'bron!" 11 Two hundred men from Jerusalem went with Ab'sa·lom; they were invited guests, and they went in their innocence, knowing nothing of the matter. 12 While Ab'sa·lom was offering the sacrifices, he sent for*i* A·hith'o·phel the Gi'lo·nite, David's counselor, from his city Gi'loh. The conspiracy grew in strength, and the people with Ab'sa·lom kept increasing.

David Flees from Jerusalem

13 A messenger came to David, saying, "The hearts of the Israelites have gone after Ab'sa·lom." 14 Then David said to all his officials who were with him at Jerusalem, "Get up! Let us flee, or there will be no escape for us from Ab'sa·lom. Hurry, or he will soon overtake us, and bring disaster down upon us, and attack the city with the edge of the sword." 15 The king's officials said to the king, "Your servants are ready to do whatever our lord the king decides." 16 So the king left, followed by all his household, except ten concubines whom he left behind to look after the house. 17 The king left, followed by all the people; and they stopped at the last house. 18 All his officials passed by him; and all the Cher'e·thites, and all the Pel'eth·ites, and all the six hundred Git'tites who had followed him from Gath, passed on before the king.

19 Then the king said to It'tai the Git'tite, "Why are you also coming with us? Go back, and stay with the king; for you are a foreigner, and also an exile from your home. 20 You came only yesterday, and shall I today make you wander about with us, while I go wherever I can? Go back, and take your kinsfolk with you; and may the LORD show*j* steadfast love and faithfulness to you." 21 But

It'tai answered the king, "As the LORD lives, and as my lord the king lives, wherever my lord the king may be, whether for death or for life, there also your servant will be." 22 David said to It'tai, "Go then, march on." So It'tai the Git'tite marched on, with all his men and all the little ones who were with him. 23 The whole country wept aloud as all the people passed by; the king crossed the Wadi Kid'ron, and all the people moved on toward the wilderness.

24 A·bi'a·thar came up, and Za'dok also, with all the Le'vites, carrying the ark of the covenant of God. They set down the ark of God, until the people had all passed out of the city. 25 Then the king said to Za'dok, "Carry the ark of God back into the city. If I find favor in the eyes of the LORD, he will bring me back and let me see both it and the place where it stays. 26 But if he says, 'I take no pleasure in you,' here I am, let him do to me what seems good to him." 27 The king also said to the priest Za'dok, "Look,*k* go back to the city in peace, you and A·bi'a·thar,*l* with your two sons, A·him'a·az your son, and Jonathan son of A·bi'a·thar. 28 See, I will wait at the fords of the wilderness until word comes from you to inform me." 29 So Za'dok and A·bi'a·thar carried the ark of God back to Jerusalem, and they remained there.

30 But David went up the ascent of the Mount of Olives, weeping as he went, with his head covered and walking barefoot; and all the people who were with him covered their heads and went up, weeping as they went. 31 David was told that A·hith'o·phel was among the conspirators with Ab'sa·lom. And David said, "O LORD, I pray you, turn the counsel of A·hith'o·phel into foolishness."

Hushai Becomes David's Spy

32 When David came to the summit, where God was worshiped, Hu'shai the Ar'chite came to meet him with his coat torn and earth on his head. 33 David said to him, "If you go on with me, you will be a burden to me. 34 But if you return to the city and say to Ab'sa·lom, 'I will be your servant, O king; as I have been your father's servant in time past, so now I will be your servant,' then you will defeat for me the counsel of A·hith'o·phel. 35 The priests Za'dok and A·bi'a·thar will be with you there. So whatever you hear from the king's house, tell it to the priests Za'dok and A·bi'a·thar. 36 Their two sons are with them there, Za'dok's son A·him'-a·az and A·bi'a·thar's son Jonathan; and by them you shall report to me everything you hear." 37 So

g Gk Syr: Heb *forty*   *h* Gk Mss: Heb lacks *in Hebron*
i Or *he sent*   *j* Gk Compare 2.6: Heb lacks *may the LORD show*   *k* Gk: Heb *Are you a seer* or *Do you see?*
l Cn: Heb lacks *and Abiathar*

Hū'shaī, David's friend, came into the city, just as
Ab'sa·lom was entering Jerusalem.

David's Adversaries

When David had passed a little beyond the summit, Zī'ba the servant of Me·phib'o·sheth[m] met
him, with a couple of donkeys saddled, carrying
two hundred loaves of bread, one hundred
bunches of raisins, one hundred of summer fruits,
and one skin of wine. 2 The king said to Zī'ba,
"Why have you brought these?" Zī'ba answered,
"The donkeys are for the king's household to ride,
the bread and summer fruit for the young men to
eat, and the wine is for those to drink who faint in
the wilderness." 3 The king said, "And where is your
master's son?" Zī'ba said to the king, "He remains
in Jerusalem; for he said, 'Today the house of Israel will give me back my grandfather's kingdom.' "
4 Then the king said to Zī'ba, "All that belonged to
Me·phib'o·sheth[m] is now yours." Zī'ba said, "I do
obeisance; let me find favor in your sight, my lord
the king."

Shimei Curses David

5 When King David came to Ba·hū'rim, a man
of the family of the house of Saul came out whose
name was Shim'ē·ī son of Gē'ra; he came out cursing. 6 He threw stones at David and at all the servants of King David; now all the people and all the
warriors were on his right and on his left. 7 Shim'ē·ī
shouted while he cursed, "Out! Out! Murderer!
Scoundrel! 8 The LORD has avenged on all of you
the blood of the house of Saul, in whose place you
have reigned; and the LORD has given the kingdom
into the hand of your son Ab'sa·lom. See, disaster
has overtaken you; for you are a man of blood."

9 Then A·bi'shaī son of Ze·rū'i·ah said to the
king, "Why should this dead dog curse my lord
the king? Let me go over and take off his head."
10 But the king said, "What have I to do with you,
you sons of Ze·rū'i·ah? If he is cursing because the
LORD has said to him, 'Curse David,' who then
shall say, 'Why have you done so?' " 11 David said
to A·bi'shaī and to all his servants, "My own son
seeks my life; how much more now may this Ben'-
ja·min·ite! Let him alone, and let him curse; for the
LORD has bidden him. 12 It may be that the LORD
will look on my distress,[n] and the LORD will repay
me with good for this cursing of me today." 13 So
David and his men went on the road, while
Shim'ē·ī went along on the hillside opposite him
and cursed as he went, throwing stones and fling-
ing dust at him. 14 The king and all the people who
were with him arrived weary at the Jordan;[o] and
there he refreshed himself.

The Counsel of Ahithophel

15 Now Ab'sa·lom and all the Israelites[p] came
to Jerusalem; A·hith'o·phel was with him. 16 When
Hū'shaī the Ar'chīte, David's friend, came to Ab'-
sa·lom, Hū'shaī said to Ab'sa·lom, "Long live the
king! Long live the king!" 17 Ab'sa·lom said to Hū'-
shaī, "Is this your loyalty to your friend? Why did
you not go with your friend?" 18 Hū'shaī said to
Ab'sa·lom, "No; but the one whom the LORD and
this people and all the Israelites have chosen, his I
will be, and with him I will remain. 19 Moreover,
whom should I serve? Should it not be his son?
Just as I have served your father, so I will serve
you."

20 Then Ab'sa·lom said to A·hith'o·phel, "Give
us your counsel; what shall we do?" 21 A·hith'o·phel
said to Ab'sa·lom, "Go in to your father's concubines, the ones he has left to look after the house;
and all Israel will hear that you have made yourself odious to your father, and the hands of all
who are with you will be strengthened." 22 So they
pitched a tent for Ab'sa·lom upon the roof; and
Ab'sa·lom went in to his father's concubines in the
sight of all Israel. 23 Now in those days the counsel
that A·hith'o·phel gave was as if one consulted the
oracle[q] of God; so all the counsel of A·hith'o·phel
was esteemed, both by David and by Ab'sa·lom.
Moreover A·hith'o·phel said to Ab'sa·lom, "Let me
choose twelve thousand men, and I will set out
and pursue David tonight. 2 I will come upon him
while he is weary and discouraged, and throw him
into a panic; and all the people who are with
him will flee. I will strike down only the king,
3 and I will bring all the people back to you as a
bride comes home to her husband. You seek the
life of only one man,[r] and all the people will be at
peace." 4 The advice pleased Ab'sa·lom and all the
elders of Israel.

The Counsel of Hushai

5 Then Ab'sa·lom said, "Call Hū'shaī the Ar'-
chīte also, and let us hear too what he has to say."
6 When Hū'shaī came to Ab'sa·lom, Ab'sa·lom said
to him, "This is what A·hith'o·phel has said; shall
we do as he advises? If not, you tell us." 7 Then
Hū'shaī said to Ab'sa·lom, "This time the counsel
that A·hith'o·phel has given is not good." 8 Hū'shaī
continued, "You know that your father and his
men are warriors, and that they are enraged, like a
bear robbed of her cubs in the field. Besides, your
father is expert in war; he will not spend the night

---

m Or *Merib-baal:* See 4.4 note   n Gk Vg: Heb *iniquity*
o Gk: Heb lacks *at the Jordan*   p Gk: Heb *all the people, the
men of Israel*   q Heb *word*   r Gk: Heb *like the return of
the whole (is) the man whom you seek*

with the troops. ⁹Even now he has hidden himself in one of the pits, or in some other place. And when some of our troopsˢ fall at the first attack, whoever hears it will say, 'There has been a slaughter among the troops who follow Ab'sa•lom.' ¹⁰Then even the valiant warrior, whose heart is like the heart of a lion, will utterly melt with fear; for all Israel knows that your father is a warrior, and that those who are with him are valiant warriors. ¹¹But my counsel is that all Israel be gathered to you, from Dan to Bē'er-shē'ba, like the sand by the sea for multitude, and that you go to battle in person. ¹²So we shall come upon him in whatever place he may be found, and we shall light on him as the dew falls on the ground; and he will not survive, nor will any of those with him. ¹³If he withdraws into a city, then all Israel will bring ropes to that city, and we shall drag it into the valley, until not even a pebble is to be found there." ¹⁴Ab'sa•lom and all the men of Israel said, "The counsel of Hū'shaī the Ar'chīte is better than the counsel of A•hith'o•phel." For the LORD had ordained to defeat the good counsel of A•hith'o•phel, so that the LORD might bring ruin on Ab'sa•lom.

Hushai Warns David to Escape

15 Then Hū'shaī said to the priests Zā'dok and A•bī'a•thar, "Thus and so did A•hith'o•phel counsel Ab'sa•lom and the elders of Israel; and thus and so I have counseled. ¹⁶Therefore send quickly and tell David, 'Do not lodge tonight at the fords of the wilderness, but by all means cross over; otherwise the king and all the people who are with him will be swallowed up.' " ¹⁷Jonathan and A•him'a•az were waiting at En-rō'gel; a servant-girl used to go and tell them, and they would go and tell King David; for they could not risk being seen entering the city. ¹⁸But a boy saw them, and told Ab'sa•lom; so both of them went away quickly, and came to the house of a man at Ba•hū'rim, who had a well in his courtyard; and they went down into it. ¹⁹The man's wife took a covering, stretched it over the well's mouth, and spread out grain on it; and nothing was known of it. ²⁰When Ab'sa•lom's servants came to the woman at the house, they said, "Where are A•him'a•az and Jonathan?" The woman said to them, "They have crossed over the brookᵗ of water." And when they had searched and could not find them, they returned to Jerusalem.

21 After they had gone, the men came up out of the well, and went and told King David. They said to David, "Go and cross the water quickly; for thus and so has A•hith'o•phel counseled against you." ²²So David and all the people who were with him set out and crossed the Jordan; by daybreak not one was left who had not crossed the Jordan.

23 When A•hith'o•phel saw that his counsel was not followed, he saddled his donkey and went off home to his own city. He set his house in order, and hanged himself; he died and was buried in the tomb of his father.

24 Then David came to Mā•ha•nā'im, while Ab'sa•lom crossed the Jordan with all the men of Israel. ²⁵Now Ab'sa•lom had set A•mā'sa over the army in the place of Jō'ab. A•mā'sa was the son of a man named Ith'ra the Ish'ma•el•īte,ᵘ who had married Ab'i•gāl daughter of Nā'hash, sister of Ze•rū'i•ah, Jō'ab's mother. ²⁶The Israelites and Ab'sa•lom encamped in the land of Gil'e•ad.

27 When David came to Mā•ha•nā'im, Shō'bī son of Nā'hash from Rab'bah of the Am'mon•ites, and Mā'chir son of Am'mi•el from Lō-dē'bar, and Bar•zil'laī the Gil'e•ad•īte from Rō'ge•lim, ²⁸brought beds, basins, and earthen vessels, wheat, barley, meal, parched grain, beans and lentils,ᵛ ²⁹honey and curds, sheep, and cheese from the herd, for David and the people with him to eat; for they said, "The troops are hungry and weary and thirsty in the wilderness."

The Defeat and Death of Absalom

Then David mustered the men who were with him, and set over them commanders of thousands and commanders of hundreds. ²And David divided the army into three groups:ᵂ one third under the command of Jō'ab, one third under the command of A•bi'shaī son of Ze•rū'i•ah, Jō'ab's brother, and one third under the command of It'taī the Git'tīte. The king said to the men, "I myself will also go out with you." ³But the men said, "You shall not go out. For if we flee, they will not care about us. If half of us die, they will not care about us. But you are worth ten thousand of us;ˣ therefore it is better that you send us help from the city." ⁴The king said to them, "Whatever seems best to you I will do." So the king stood at the side of the gate, while all the army marched out by hundreds and by thousands. ⁵The king ordered Jō'ab and A•bi'shaī and It'taī, saying, "Deal gently for my sake with the young man Ab'sa•lom." And all the people heard when the king gave orders to all the commanders concerning Ab'sa•lom.

6 So the army went out into the field against Israel; and the battle was fought in the forest of Ē'phra•im. ⁷The men of Israel were defeated there by the servants of David, and the slaughter there was great on that day, twenty thousand men. ⁸The battle spread over the face of all the country; and

---

ˢ Gk Mss: Heb *some of them*   ᵗ Meaning of Heb uncertain
ᵘ 1 Chr 2.17: Heb *Israelite*   ᵛ Heb *and lentils and parched grain*   ᵂ Gk: Heb *sent forth the army*   ˣ Gk Vg
Symmachus: Heb *for now there are ten thousand such as we*

the forest claimed more victims that day than the sword.

9 Ab'sa•lom happened to meet the servants of David. Ab'sa•lom was riding on his mule, and the mule went under the thick branches of a great oak. His head caught fast in the oak, and he was left hanging^y between heaven and earth, while the mule that was under him went on. 10 A man saw it, and told Jō'ab, "I saw Ab'sa•lom hanging in an oak." 11 Jō'ab said to the man who told him, "What, you saw him! Why then did you not strike him there to the ground? I would have been glad to give you ten pieces of silver and a belt." 12 But the man said to Jō'ab, "Even if I felt in my hand the weight of a thousand pieces of silver, I would not raise my hand against the king's son; for in our hearing the king commanded you and A•bi'shaī and It'taī, saying: For my sake protect the young man Ab'sa•lom! 13 On the other hand, if I had dealt treacherously against his life^z (and there is nothing hidden from the king), then you yourself would have stood aloof." 14 Jō'ab said, "I will not waste time like this with you." He took three spears in his hand, and thrust them into the heart of Ab'-sa•lom, while he was still alive in the oak. 15 And ten young men, Jō'ab's armor-bearers, surrounded Ab'sa•lom and struck him, and killed him.

16 Then Jō'ab sounded the trumpet, and the troops came back from pursuing Israel, for Jō'ab restrained the troops. 17 They took Ab'sa•lom, threw him into a great pit in the forest, and raised over him a very great heap of stones. Meanwhile all the Israelites fled to their homes. 18 Now Ab'sa-lom in his lifetime had taken and set up for him-self a pillar that is in the King's Valley, for he said, "I have no son to keep my name in remembrance"; he called the pillar by his own name. It is called Ab'sa•lom's Monument to this day.

David Hears of Absalom's Death

19 Then A•him'a•az son of Zā'dok said, "Let me run, and carry tidings to the king that the LORD has delivered him from the power of his enemies." 20 Jō'ab said to him, "You are not to carry tidings today; you may carry tidings another day, but to-day you shall not do so, because the king's son is dead." 21 Then Jō'ab said to a Cū'shīte, "Go, tell the king what you have seen." The Cū'shīte bowed be-fore Jō'ab, and ran. 22 Then A•him'a•az son of Zā'-dok said again to Jō'ab, "Come what may, let me also run after the Cū'shīte." And Jō'ab said, "Why will you run, my son, seeing that you have no reward^a for the tidings?" 23 "Come what may," he said, "I will run." So he said to him, "Run." Then A•him'a•az ran by the way of the Plain, and outran the Cū'shīte.

24 Now David was sitting between the two gates. The sentinel went up to the roof of the gate by the wall, and when he looked up, he saw a man running alone. 25 The sentinel shouted and told the king. The king said, "If he is alone, there are tidings in his mouth." He kept coming, and drew near. 26 Then the sentinel saw another man running; and the sentinel called to the gatekeeper and said, "See, another man running alone!" The king said, "He also is bringing tidings." 27 The sentinel said, "I think the running of the first one is like the running of A•him'a•az son of Zā'dok." The king said, "He is a good man, and comes with good tidings."

28 Then A•him'a•az cried out to the king, "All is well!" He prostrated himself before the king with his face to the ground, and said, "Blessed be the LORD your God, who has delivered up the men who raised their hand against my lord the king." 29 The king said, "Is it well with the young man Ab'sa•lom?" A•him'a•az answered, "When Jō'ab sent your servant,^b I saw a great tumult, but I do not know what it was." 30 The king said, "Turn aside, and stand here." So he turned aside, and stood still.

31 Then the Cū'shīte came; and the Cū'shīte said, "Good tidings for my lord the king! For the LORD has vindicated you this day, delivering you from the power of all who rose up against you." 32 The king said to the Cū'shīte, "Is it well with the young man Ab'sa•lom?" The Cū'shīte answered, "May the enemies of my lord the king, and all who rise up to do you harm, be like that young man."

David Mourns for Absalom

33^c The king was deeply moved, and went up to the chamber over the gate, and wept; and as he went, he said, "O my son Ab'sa•lom, my son, my son Ab'sa•lom! Would I had died instead of you, O Ab'sa•lom, my son, my son!"

It was told Jō'ab, "The king is weeping and mourning for Ab'sa•lom." 2 So the victory that day was turned into mourning for all the troops; for the troops heard that day, "The king is grieving for his son." 3 The troops stole into the city that day as soldiers steal in who are ashamed when they flee in battle. 4 The king covered his face, and the king cried with a loud voice, "O my son Ab'sa•lom, O Ab'sa•lom, my son, my son!" 5 Then Jō'ab came into the house to the king, and said, "Today you have covered with shame the faces of all your offi-cers who have saved your life today, and the lives

---

y Gk Syr Tg: Heb *was put*   z Another reading is *at the risk of my life*   a Meaning of Heb uncertain   b Heb *the king's servant, your servant*   c Ch 19.1 in Heb

David Recalled to Jerusalem

Meanwhile, all the Israelites had fled to their homes. 9 All the people were disputing throughout all the tribes of Israel, saying, "The king delivered us from the hand of our enemies, and saved us from the hand of the Phi·lis′tines; and now he has fled out of the land because of Ab′sa·lom. 10 But Ab′sa·lom, whom we anointed over us, is dead in battle. Now therefore why do you say nothing about bringing the king back?"

11 King David sent this message to the priests Zā′dok and A·bī′a·thar, "Say to the elders of Judah, 'Why should you be the last to bring the king back to his house? The talk of all Israel has come to the king.ᵈ 12 You are my kin, you are my bone and my flesh; why then should you be the last to bring back the king?' 13 And say to A·mā′sa, 'Are you not my bone and my flesh? So may God do to me, and more, if you are not the commander of my army from now on, in place of Jō′ab.'" 14 A·mā′saᵉ swayed the hearts of all the people of Judah as one, and they sent word to the king, "Return, both you and all your servants." 15 So the king came back to the Jordan; and Judah came to Gil′gal to meet the king and to bring him over the Jordan.

16 Shim′ē·ī son of Gē′ra, the Ben′ja·min·īte, from Ba·hū′rim, hurried to come down with the people of Judah to meet King David; 17 with him were a thousand people from Benjamin. And Zī′ba, the servant of the house of Saul, with his fifteen sons and his twenty servants, rushed down to the Jordan ahead of the king, 18 while the

---

ᵈ Gk: Heb *to the king, to his house*   ᵉ Heb *He*

of your sons and your daughters, and the lives of your wives and your concubines, 6 for love of those who hate you and for hatred of those who love you. You have made it clear today that commanders and officers are nothing to you; for I perceive that if Ab′sa·lom were alive and all of us were dead today, then you would be pleased. 7 So go out at once and speak kindly to your servants; for I swear by the LORD, if you do not go, not a man will stay with you this night; and this will be worse for you than any disaster that has come upon you from your youth until now." 8 Then the king got up and took his seat in the gate. The troops were all told, "See, the king is sitting in the gate"; and all the troops came before the king.

2 S A M

Surviving Grief

LIVE IT!

It is a cold winter day when the state trooper comes to the door with the news that James Washington has just lost his son in an automobile accident. James falls to the ground in utter pain. Michael was just sixteen years old. James weeps as the trooper helps him up; the young officer begins to cry as he thinks of his own son, just three years of age.

There is no greater loss for parents than the death of a child. In 2 Sam 19.1, King David is devastated by the death of his son Absalom, despite Absalom's betrayal. There is no easy answer or explanation when someone we love dies. How could God allow this? It is too hard to understand. What helps is to allow ourselves to mourn like David and to place ourselves into God's healing hands.

Life continues. Joab challenges David not to forget the people who have served him faithfully and count on his leadership (verses 5–7). In our grief, we must not forget the family and friends who grieve with us. We need them, and they need us to heal the pain of loss.

▶ 2 Sam 18.33—19.8

crossing was taking place,*f* to bring over the king's household, and to do his pleasure.

David's Mercy to Shimei

Shim′ē•ī son of Gē′ra fell down before the king, as he was about to cross the Jordan, 19 and said to the king, "May my lord not hold me guilty or remember how your servant did wrong on the day my lord the king left Jerusalem; may the king not bear it in mind. 20 For your servant knows that I have sinned; therefore, see, I have come this day, the first of all the house of Joseph to come down to meet my lord the king." 21 A•bi′shaī son of Ze•rū′i•ah answered, "Shall not Shim′ē•ī be put to death for this, because he cursed the LORD's anointed?" 22 But David said, "What have I to do with you, you sons of Ze•rū′i•ah, that you should today become an adversary to me? Shall anyone be put to death in Israel this day? For do I not know that I am this day king over Israel?" 23 The king said to Shim′ē•ī, "You shall not die." And the king gave him his oath.

David and Mephibosheth Meet

24 Me•phib′o•sheth*g* grandson of Saul came down to meet the king; he had not taken care of his feet, or trimmed his beard, or washed his clothes, from the day the king left until the day he came back in safety. 25 When he came from Jerusalem to meet the king, the king said to him, "Why did you not go with me, Me•phib′o•sheth?"*g* 26 He answered, "My lord, O king, my servant deceived me; for your servant said to him, 'Saddle a donkey for me,*h* so that I may ride on it and go with the king.' For your servant is lame. 27 He has slandered your servant to my lord the king. But my lord the king is like the angel of God; do therefore what seems good to you. 28 For all my father's house were doomed to death before my lord the king; but you set your servant among those who eat at your table. What further right have I, then, to appeal to the king?" 29 The king said to him, "Why speak any more of your affairs? I have decided: you and Zī′ba shall divide the land." 30 Me•phib′o•sheth*g* said to the king, "Let him take it all, since my lord the king has arrived home safely."

David's Kindness to Barzillai

31 Now Bar•zil′laī the Gil′e•ad•īte had come down from Rō′ge•lim; he went on with the king to the Jordan, to escort him over the Jordan. 32 Bar•zil′laī was a very aged man, eighty years old. He had provided the king with food while he stayed at Mā•ha•nā′im, for he was a very wealthy man. 33 The king said to Bar•zil′laī, "Come over with me, and I will provide for you in Jerusalem at my side."

34 But Bar•zil′laī said to the king, "How many years have I still to live, that I should go up with the king to Jerusalem? 35 Today I am eighty years old; can I discern what is pleasant and what is not? Can your servant taste what he eats or what he drinks? Can I still listen to the voice of singing men and singing women? Why then should your servant be an added burden to my lord the king? 36 Your servant will go a little way over the Jordan with the king. Why should the king recompense me with such a reward? 37 Please let your servant return, so that I may die in my own town, near the graves of my father and my mother. But here is your servant Chim′ham; let him go over with my lord the king; and do for him whatever seems good to you." 38 The king answered, "Chim′ham shall go over with me, and I will do for him whatever seems good to you; and all that you desire of me I will do for you." 39 Then all the people crossed over the Jordan, and the king crossed over; the king kissed Bar•zil′laī and blessed him, and he returned to his own home. 40 The king went on to Gil′gal, and Chim′ham went on with him; all the people of Judah, and also half the people of Israel, brought the king on his way.

41 Then all the people of Israel came to the king, and said to him, "Why have our kindred the people of Judah stolen you away, and brought the king and his household over the Jordan, and all David's men with him?" 42 All the people of Judah answered the people of Israel, "Because the king is near of kin to us. Why then are you angry over this matter? Have we eaten at all at the king's expense? Or has he given us any gift?" 43 But the people of Israel answered the people of Judah, "We have ten shares in the king, and in David also we have more than you. Why then did you despise us? Were we not the first to speak of bringing back our king?" But the words of the people of Judah were fiercer than the words of the people of Israel.

The Rebellion of Sheba

Now a scoundrel named Shē′ba son of Bich′rī, a Ben′ja•min•ite, happened to be there. He sounded the trumpet and cried out,

"We have no portion in David,
  no share in the son of Jesse!
Everyone to your tents, O Israel!"

2 So all the people of Israel withdrew from David and followed Shē′ba son of Bich′rī; but the people of Judah followed their king steadfastly from the Jordan to Jerusalem.

---

f Cn: Heb *the ford crossed*   *g* Or *Merib-baal*: See 4.4 note
h Gk Syr Vg: Heb *said, 'I will saddle a donkey for myself*

3 David came to his house at Jerusalem; and the king took the ten concubines whom he had left to look after the house, and put them in a house under guard, and provided for them, but did not go in to them. So they were shut up until the day of their death, living as if in widowhood.

4 Then the king said to A•ma′sa, "Call the men of Judah together to me within three days, and be here yourself." 5 So A•ma′sa went to summon Judah; but he delayed beyond the set time that had been appointed him. 6 David said to A•bi′shaī, "Now She′ba son of Bich′rī will do us more harm than Ab′sa•lom; take your lord's servants and pursue him, or he will find fortified cities for himself, and escape from us." 7 Jō′ab's men went out after him, along with the Cher′e•thītes, the Pel′eth•ītes, and all the warriors; they went out from Jerusalem to pursue She′ba son of Bich′rī. 8 When they were at the large stone that is in Gib′e•on, A•ma′sa came to meet them. Now Jō′ab was wearing a soldier's garment and over it was a belt with a sword in its sheath fastened at his waist; as he went forward it fell out. 9 Jō′ab said to A•ma′sa, "Is it well with you, my brother?" And Jō′ab took A•ma′sa by the beard with his right hand to kiss him. 10 But A•ma′sa did not notice the sword in Jō′ab's hand; Jō′ab struck him in the belly so that his entrails poured out on the ground, and he died. He did not strike a second blow.

Then Jō′ab and his brother A•bi′shaī pursued She′ba son of Bich′rī. 11 And one of Jō′ab's men took his stand by A•ma′sa, and said, "Whoever favors Jō′ab, and whoever is for David, let him follow Jō′ab." 12 A•ma′sa lay wallowing in his blood on the highway, and the man saw that all the people were stopping. Since he saw that all who came by him were stopping, he carried A•ma′sa from the highway into a field, and threw a garment over him. 13 Once he was removed from the highway, all the people went on after Jō′ab to pursue She′ba son of Bich′rī.

14 She′ba[i] passed through all the tribes of Israel to Abel of Beth-ma′a•cah;[j] and all the Bich′-rītes[k] assembled, and followed him inside. 15 Jō′ab's forces[l] came and besieged him in Abel of Beth-ma′a•cah; they threw up a siege ramp against the city, and it stood against the rampart. Jō′ab's forces were battering the wall to break it down. 16 Then a wise woman called from the city, "Listen! Listen! Tell Jō′ab, 'Come here, I want to speak to you.' " 17 He came near her; and the woman said, "Are you Jō′ab?" He answered, "I am." Then she said to him, "Listen to the words of your servant." He answered, "I am listening." 18 Then she said, "They used to say in the old days, 'Let them inquire at Abel'; and so they would settle a matter.

19 I am one of those who are peaceable and faithful in Israel; you seek to destroy a city that is a mother in Israel; why will you swallow up the heritage of the LORD?" 20 Jō′ab answered, "Far be it from me, far be it, that I should swallow up or destroy! 21 That is not the case! But a man of the hill country of E′phra•im, called She′ba son of Bich′rī, has lifted up his hand against King David; give him up alone, and I will withdraw from the city." The woman said to Jō′ab, "His head shall be thrown over the wall to you." 22 Then the woman went to all the people with her wise plan. And they cut off the head of She′ba son of Bich′rī, and threw it out to Jō′ab. So he blew the trumpet, and they dispersed from the city, and all went to their homes, while Jō′ab returned to Jerusalem to the king.

23 Now Jō′ab was in command of all the army of Israel;[m] Be•na′i•ah son of Je•hoi′a•da was in command of the Cher′e•thītes and the Pel′eth•ītes; 24 A•dor′am was in charge of the forced labor; Je-hosh′a•phat son of A•hi′lud was the recorder; 25 She′va was secretary; Za′dok and A•bi′a•thar were priests; 26 and Ira the Ja′i•rīte was also David's priest.

David Avenges the Gibeonites

Now there was a famine in the days of David for three years, year after year; and David inquired of the LORD. The LORD said, "There is bloodguilt on Saul and on his house, because he put the Gib′e•on•ites to death." 2 So the king called the Gib′e•on•ites and spoke to them. (Now the Gib′e•on•ites were not of the people of Israel, but of the remnant of the Am′o•rītes; although the people of Israel had sworn to spare them, Saul had tried to wipe them out in his zeal for the people of Israel and Judah.) 3 David said to the Gib′e•on•ites, "What shall I do for you? How shall I make expiation, that you may bless the heritage of the LORD?" 4 The Gib′e•on•ites said to him, "It is not a matter of silver or gold between us and Saul or his house; neither is it for us to put anyone to death in Israel." He said, "What do you say that I should do for you?" 5 They said to the king, "The man who consumed us and planned to destroy us, so that we should have no place in all the territory of Israel— 6 let seven of his sons be handed over to us, and we will impale them before the LORD at Gib′e•on on the mountain of the LORD."[n] The king said, "I will hand them over."

---

i Heb *He*   j Compare 20.15: Heb *and Beth-maacah*
k Compare Gk Vg: Heb *Berites*   l Heb *They*   m Cn: Heb
Joab to all the army, Israel   n Cn Compare Gk and 21.9:
Heb *at Gibeah of Saul, the chosen of the LORD*

7 But the king spared Me·phib'o·sheth,⁰ the son of Saul's son Jonathan, because of the oath of the LORD that was between them, between David and Jonathan son of Saul. ⁸The king took the two sons of Riz'pah daughter of Ā'i·ah, whom she bore to Saul, Ar·mō'ni and Me·phib'o·sheth;⁰ and the five sons of Mē'rab ᵖ daughter of Saul, whom she bore to Ā'dri·el son of Bar·zil'lai the Me·hō'la·thite; ⁹he gave them into the hands of the Gib'e·on·ites, and they impaled them on the mountain before the LORD. The seven of them perished together. They were put to death in the first days of harvest, at the beginning of barley harvest.

10 Then Riz'pah the daughter of Ā'i·ah took sackcloth, and spread it on a rock for herself, from the beginning of harvest until rain fell on them from the heavens; she did not allow the birds of the air to come on the bodies ᑫ by day, or the wild animals by night. ¹¹When David was told what Riz'pah daughter of Ā'i·ah, the concubine of Saul, had done, ¹²David went and took the bones of Saul and the bones of his son Jonathan from the people of Jā'besh-gil'e·ad, who had stolen them from the public square of Beth-shan, where the Phi·lis'tines had hung them up, on the day the Phi·lis'tines killed Saul on Gil·bō'a. ¹³He brought up from there the bones of Saul and the bones of his son Jonathan; and they gathered the bones of those who had been impaled. ¹⁴They buried the bones of Saul and of his son Jonathan in the land of Benjamin in Zē'la, in the tomb of his father Kish; they did all that the king commanded. After that, God heeded supplications for the land.

Exploits of David's Men
(1 Chr 20.4–8)

15 The Phi·lis'tines went to war again with Israel, and David went down together with his servants. They fought against the Phi·lis'tines, and David grew weary. ¹⁶Ish'bi-bē'nob, one of the descendants of the giants, whose spear weighed three hundred shekels of bronze, and who was fitted out with new weapons,ʳ said he would kill David. ¹⁷But A·bi'shai son of Ze·rū'i·ah came to his aid, and attacked the Phi·lis'tine and killed him. Then David's men swore to him, "You shall not go out with us to battle any longer, so that you do not quench the lamp of Israel."

18 After this a battle took place with the Phi·lis'tines, at Gob; then Sib'be·cai the Hū'sha·thite killed Saph, who was one of the descendants of the giants. ¹⁹Then there was another battle with the Phi·lis'tines at Gob; and El·hā'nan son of Jā'a·rē·or'e·gim, the Beth'le·hem·ite, killed Goliath the Git'tite, the shaft of whose spear was like a weaver's beam. ²⁰There was again war at Gath, where there

was a man of great size, who had six fingers on each hand, and six toes on each foot, twenty-four in number; he too was descended from the giants. ²¹When he taunted Israel, Jonathan son of David's brother Shim'e·i, killed him. ²²These four were descended from the giants in Gath; they fell by the hands of David and his servants.

David's Song of Thanksgiving
(Ps 18.1–50)

David spoke to the LORD the words of this song on the day when the LORD delivered him from the hand of all his enemies, and from the hand of Saul. ²He said:

The LORD is my rock, my fortress, and my
    deliverer,
3   my God, my rock, in whom I take refuge,
my shield and the horn of my salvation,
    my stronghold and my refuge,
    my savior; you save me from violence.
4 I call upon the LORD, who is worthy to be
    praised,
    and I am saved from my enemies.

5 For the waves of death encompassed me,
    the torrents of perdition assailed me;
6 the cords of Shē'ōl entangled me,
    the snares of death confronted me.

7 In my distress I called upon the LORD;
    to my God I called.
From his temple he heard my voice,
    and my cry came to his ears.

8 Then the earth reeled and rocked;
    the foundations of the heavens trembled
    and quaked, because he was angry.
9 Smoke went up from his nostrils,
    and devouring fire from his mouth;
    glowing coals flamed forth from him.
10 He bowed the heavens, and came down;
    thick darkness was under his feet.
11 He rode on a cherub, and flew;
    he was seen upon the wings of the wind.
12 He made darkness around him a canopy,
    thick clouds, a gathering of water.
13 Out of the brightness before him
    coals of fire flamed forth.
14 The LORD thundered from heaven;
    the Most High uttered his voice.
15 He sent out arrows, and scattered them
    —lightning, and routed them.

⁰ Or *Merib-baal:* See 4.4 note   ᵖ Two Heb Mss Syr Compare Gk: MT *Michal*   ᑫ Heb *them*   ʳ Heb *was belted anew*

16 Then the channels of the sea were seen,
    the foundations of the world were laid bare
  at the rebuke of the LORD,
    at the blast of the breath of his nostrils.

17 He reached from on high, he took me,
    he drew me out of mighty waters.

18 He delivered me from my strong enemy,
    from those who hated me;
  for they were too mighty for me.

19 They came upon me in the day of my calamity,
    but the LORD was my stay.

20 He brought me out into a broad place;
    he delivered me, because he delighted in me.

27 with the pure you show yourself pure,
    and with the crooked you show yourself
      perverse.

28 You deliver a humble people,
    but your eyes are upon the haughty to
      bring them down.

29 Indeed, you are my lamp, O LORD,
    the LORD lightens my darkness.

30 By you I can crush a troop,
    and by my God I can leap over a wall.

31 This God—his way is perfect;
    the promise of the LORD proves true;
  he is a shield for all who take refuge in
      him.

The Lord Is My Rock

Build on the rock! What exactly does that mean? Have you ever watched a house being built? One of the first things that a contractor does is level the ground and put in a foundation. Upon the foundation, the structure begins to grow. A solid foundation will enable that house to stand for many years.

The same goes for our life, both personally and communally. What is your foundation—the rock—that your life is built on? In 2 Sam 22.1–2, King David says to the Lord, "[You are] my rock, my fortress, and my deliverer." David built his life on the rock and foundation of the Lord. As a result, he found refuge in times of fear. It was this rock that saved David and the people of Israel from the hands of their enemies. Because of David's reliance on God, his kingdom is seen by later generations of Jews as the ideal kingdom for Israel.

You too can find this same refuge, this same saving grace. Starting today, build your life with the Lord as your foundation (see Mt 7.24–27). The next time you face a battle, be it drugs or envy or anger or lust, *stand on the rock!*

▶ 2 Sam 22.1–4

21 The LORD rewarded me according to my
      righteousness;
    according to the cleanness of my hands
      he recompensed me.

22 For I have kept the ways of the LORD,
    and have not wickedly departed from my
      God.

23 For all his ordinances were before me,
    and from his statutes I did not
      turn aside.

24 I was blameless before him,
    and I kept myself from guilt.

25 Therefore the LORD has recompensed me
      according to my righteousness,
    according to my cleanness in his sight.

26 With the loyal you show yourself loyal;
    with the blameless you show yourself
      blameless;

32 For who is God, but the LORD?
    And who is a rock, except our God?

33 The God who has girded me with strength[s]
    has opened wide my path.[t]

34 He made my[u] feet like the feet of deer,
    and set me secure on the heights.

35 He trains my hands for war,
    so that my arms can bend a bow of
      bronze.

36 You have given me the shield of your
      salvation,
    and your help[v] has made me great.

37 You have made me stride freely,
    and my feet do not slip;

[s] Q Ms Gk Syr Vg Compare Ps 18.32: MT *God is my strong refuge*   [t] Meaning of Heb uncertain   [u] Another reading is *his*   [v] Q Ms: MT *your answering*

2
S
A
M

38 I pursued my enemies and destroyed them,
    and did not turn back until they were
      consumed.
39 I consumed them; I struck them down, so
    that they did not rise;
    they fell under my feet.
40 For you girded me with strength for the
      battle;
    you made my assailants sink under me.
41 You made my enemies turn their backs to me,
    those who hated me, and I destroyed
      them.
42 They looked, but there was no one to save
    them;
    they cried to the LORD, but he did not
      answer them.
43 I beat them fine like the dust of the earth,
    I crushed them and stamped them down
      like the mire of the streets.

44 You delivered me from strife with the
      peoples;*w*
    you kept me as the head of the nations;
    people whom I had not known served
      me.
45 Foreigners came cringing to me;
    as soon as they heard of me, they obeyed
      me.
46 Foreigners lost heart,
    and came trembling out of their
      strongholds.

47 The LORD lives! Blessed be my rock,
    and exalted be my God, the rock of my
      salvation,
48 the God who gave me vengeance
    and brought down peoples under me,
49 who brought me out from my enemies;
    you exalted me above my adversaries,
    you delivered me from the violent.

50 For this I will extol you, O LORD, among the
      nations,
    and sing praises to your name.
51 He is a tower of salvation for his king,
    and shows steadfast love to his anointed,
    to David and his descendants forever.

The Last Words of David

Now these are the last words of David:
    The oracle of David, son of Jesse,
    the oracle of the man whom God
      exalted,*x*
    the anointed of the God of Jacob,
    the favorite of the Strong One of Israel:

2 The spirit of the LORD speaks through me,
    his word is upon my tongue.

3 The God of Israel has spoken,
    the Rock of Israel has said to me:
    One who rules over people justly,
    ruling in the fear of God,
4 is like the light of morning,
    like the sun rising on a cloudless
      morning,
    gleaming from the rain on the grassy
      land.

5 Is not my house like this with God?
    For he has made with me an everlasting
      covenant,
    ordered in all things and secure.
    Will he not cause to prosper
    all my help and my desire?
6 But the godless are*y* all like thorns that are
      thrown away;
    for they cannot be picked up with the
      hand;
7 to touch them one uses an iron bar
    or the shaft of a spear.
    And they are entirely consumed in fire on
      the spot.*z*

David's Mighty Men
(1 Chr 11.10–47)

8 These are the names of the warriors whom David had: Jŏ′sheb-bas•shĕ′beth a Tah•chĕ′mo•nīte; he was chief of the Three;*a* he wielded his spear*b* against eight hundred whom he killed at one time. 9 Next to him among the three warriors was El•ē•ā′zar son of Dō′dō son of A•hō′hī. He was with David when they defied the Phi•lis′tines who were gathered there for battle. The Israelites withdrew, 10 but he stood his ground. He struck down the Phi•lis′tines until his arm grew weary, though his hand clung to the sword. The LORD brought about a great victory that day. Then the people came back to him—but only to strip the dead.

11 Next to him was Sham′mah son of Ā′gee, the Har′a•rīte. The Phi•lis′tines gathered together at Lē′hī, where there was a plot of ground full of lentils; and the army fled from the Phi•lis′tines. 12 But he took his stand in the middle of the plot, defended it, and killed the Phi•lis′tines; and the LORD brought about a great victory.

13 Towards the beginning of harvest three of the thirty*c* chiefs went down to join David at the cave of A•dul′lam, while a band of Phi•lis′tines was encamped in the valley of Reph′a•im. 14 David was

---

w Gk: Heb *from strife with my people*   *x* Q Ms: MT *who was raised on high*   *y* Heb *But worthlessness*   *z* Heb *in sitting*
a Gk Vg Compare 1 Chr 11.11: Meaning of Heb uncertain
b 1 Chr 11.11: Meaning of Heb uncertain   *c* Heb adds *head*

then in the stronghold; and the garrison of the Phi•lis'tines was then at Bethlehem. [15] David said longingly, "O that someone would give me water to drink from the well of Bethlehem that is by the gate!" [16] Then the three warriors broke through the camp of the Phi•lis'tines, drew water from the well of Bethlehem that was by the gate, and brought it to David. But he would not drink of it; he poured it out to the LORD, [17] for he said, "The LORD forbid that I should do this. Can I drink the blood of the men who went at the risk of their lives?" Therefore he would not drink it. The three warriors did these things.

18 Now A•bi'shaī son of Ze•rū'i•ah, the brother of Jō'ab, was chief of the Thirty.[d] With his spear he fought against three hundred men and killed them, and won a name beside the Three. [19] He was the most renowned of the Thirty,[e] and became their commander; but he did not attain to the Three.

20 Be•nā'i•ah son of Je•hoi'a•da was a valiant warrior[f] from Kab'zē•el, a doer of great deeds; he struck down two sons of Ar'i•el[g] of Mō'ab. He also went down and killed a lion in a pit on a day when snow had fallen. [21] And he killed an Egyptian, a handsome man. The Egyptian had a spear in his hand; but Be•nā'i•ah went against him with a staff, snatched the spear out of the Egyptian's hand, and killed him with his own spear. [22] Such were the things Be•nā'i•ah son of Je•hoi'a•da did, and won a name beside the three warriors. [23] He was renowned among the Thirty, but he did not attain to the Three. And David put him in charge of his bodyguard.

24 Among the Thirty were As'a•hel brother of Jō'ab; El•hā'nan son of Dō'dō of Bethlehem; [25] Sham'mah of Har'od; E•lī'ka of Har'od; [26] Hē'lez the Pal'tīte; Ira son of Ik'kesh of Te•kō'a; [27] A•bi•ē'-zer of An'a•thoth; Me•bun'naī the Hū'sha•thīte; [28] Zal'mon the A•hō'hīte; Mā'ha•raī of Ne•toph'ah; [29] Hē'leb son of Bā'a•nah of Ne•toph'ah; It'taī son of Rī'baī of Gib'ē•ah of the Ben'ja•min•ītes; [30] Be•nā'-i•ah of Pir'a•thon; Hid'daī of the torrents of Gā'ash; [31] Ā'bi-al'bon the Ar'ba•thīte; Az'ma•veth of Ba•hū'-rim; [32] Ē•lī'ah•ba of Shā•al'bon; the sons of Jā'shen; Jonathan [33] son of[h] Sham'mah the Har'a•rīte; A•hī'am son of Shar'ar the Har'a•rīte; [34] E•liph'e•let son of A•has'baī of Mā'a•cah; E•lī'am son of A•hith'-o•phel the Gi'lo•nīte; [35] Hez'rō[i] of Car'mel; Pā'a•raī the Ar'bīte; [36] I'gal son of Nathan of Zō'bah; Bā'nī the Gad'īte; [37] Zē'lek the Am'mon•īte; Nā'ha•raī of Be•er'oth, the armor-bearer of Jō'ab son of Ze•rū'-i•ah; [38] Ira the Ith'rīte; Gā'reb the Ith'rīte; [39] Ū•rī'ah the Hit'tīte—thirty-seven in all.

David's Census of Israel and Judah
(1 Chr 21.1–6)

Again the anger of the LORD was kindled against Israel, and he incited David against them, saying, "Go, count the people of Israel and Judah." [2] So the king said to Jō'ab and the commanders of the army,[j] who were with him, "Go through all the tribes of Israel, from Dan to Bē'er-shē'ba, and take a census of the people, so that I may know how many there are." [3] But Jō'ab said to the king, "May the LORD your God increase the number of the people a hundredfold, while the eyes of my lord the king can still see it! But why does my lord the king want to do this?" [4] But the king's word prevailed against Jō'ab and the commanders of the army. So Jō'ab and the commanders of the army went out from the presence of the king to take a census of the people of Israel. [5] They crossed the Jordan, and began from[k] A•rō'er and from the city that is in the middle of the valley, toward Gad and on to Jā'zer. [6] Then they came to Gil'e•ad, and to Kā'desh in the land of the Hit'tītes;[l] and they came to Dan, and from Dan[m] they went around to Sī'don, [7] and came to the fortress of Tyre and to all the cities of the Hī'vītes and Cā'naan•ītes; and they went out to the Neg'eb of Judah at Bē'er-shē'ba. [8] So when they had gone through all the land, they came back to Jerusalem at the end of nine months and twenty days. [9] Jō'ab reported to the king the number of those who had been recorded: in Israel there were eight hundred thousand soldiers able to draw the sword, and those of Judah were five hundred thousand.

Judgment on David's Sin
(1 Chr 21.7–17)

10 But afterward, David was stricken to the heart because he had numbered the people. David said to the LORD, "I have sinned greatly in what I have done. But now, O LORD, I pray you, take away the guilt of your servant; for I have done very foolishly." [11] When David rose in the morning, the word of the LORD came to the prophet Gad, David's seer, saying, [12] "Go and say to David: Thus says the LORD: Three things I offer[n] you; choose one of them, and I will do it to you." [13] So Gad came to David and told him; he asked him, "Shall

d Two Heb Mss Syr: MT *Three*   e Syr Compare
1 Chr 11.25: Heb *Was he the most renowned of the Three?*
f Another reading is *the son of Ish-hai*   g Gk: Heb lacks *sons of*   h Gk: Heb lacks *son of*   i Another reading is *Hezrai*   j 1 Chr 21.2 Gk: Heb *to Joab the commander of the army*   k Gk Mss: Heb *encamped in Aroer south of*   l Gk: Heb *to the land of Tahtim-hodshi*   m Cn Compare Gk: Heb *they came to Dan-jaan and*   n Or *hold over*

three° years of famine come to you on your land? Or will you flee three months before your foes while they pursue you? Or shall there be three days' pestilence in your land? Now consider, and decide what answer I shall return to the one who sent me." 14 Then David said to Gad, "I am in great distress; let us fall into the hand of the LORD, for his mercy is great; but let me not fall into human hands."

15 So the LORD sent a pestilence on Israel from that morning until the appointed time; and seventy thousand of the people died, from Dan to Be'er-she'ba. 16 But when the angel stretched out his hand toward Jerusalem to destroy it, the LORD relented concerning the evil, and said to the angel who was bringing destruction among the people, "It is enough; now stay your hand." The angel of the LORD was then by the threshing floor of A·rau'nah the Jeb'u·site. 17 When David saw the angel who was destroying the people, he said to the LORD, "I alone have sinned, and I alone have done wickedly; but these sheep, what have they done? Let your hand, I pray, be against me and against my father's house."

David's Altar on the Threshing Floor
(1 Chr 21.18–27)

18 That day Gad came to David and said to him, "Go up and erect an altar to the LORD on the threshing floor of A·rau'nah the Jeb'u·site." 19 Following Gad's instructions, David went up, as the LORD had commanded. 20 When A·rau'nah looked down, he saw the king and his servants coming toward him; and A·rau'nah went out and prostrated himself before the king with his face to the ground. 21 A·rau'nah said, "Why has my lord the king come to his servant?" David said, "To buy the threshing floor from you in order to build an altar to the LORD, so that the plague may be averted from the people." 22 Then A·rau'nah said to David, "Let my lord the king take and offer up what seems good to him; here are the oxen for the burnt offering, and the threshing sledges and the yokes of the oxen for the wood. 23 All this, O king, A·rau'nah gives to the king." And A·rau'nah said to the king, "May the LORD your God respond favorably to you."

24 But the king said to A·rau'nah, "No, but I will buy them from you for a price; I will not offer burnt offerings to the LORD my God that cost me nothing." So David bought the threshing floor and the oxen for fifty shekels of silver. 25 David built there an altar to the LORD, and offered burnt offerings and offerings of well-being. So the LORD answered his supplication for the land, and the plague was averted from Israel.

° 1 Chr 21.12 Gk: Heb *seven*

The ancient Egyptians had an advanced civilization, yet today, the remains of their handiwork lie buried under centuries of sand. The great Roman Empire spanned the Western world at the time of Jesus, yet today, only scattered ruins testify to its existence. The same is true of the glorious but short-lived Israelite kingdom. The Books of 1 and 2 Kings trace its tragic collapse from the glories of Solomon's Temple to the Babylonian Exile.

At a Glance

- **1 Kings, chapters 1–11.** the reign of King Solomon

- **1 Kings, chapter 12, to 2 Kings, chapter 17.** the various kings of Israel and Judah

- **2 Kings, chapters 18–30.** the kingdom of Judah until its fall in 587 B.C.

In-depth

If the kingships of Saul and David could be described as the spring and summer of the Israelite kingdom, the Books of 1 and 2 Kings describe its fall and winter. The beginning of 1 Kings covers the glorious late summer under King Solomon. Solomon accumulated great riches, constructed a beautiful Temple, and built Jerusalem into a city rivaling any other center of power. But the summer was quickly over at Solomon's death, when the kingdom was split in two (see map 3, "The Kingdom Years"). The northern kingdom, called Israel, and the southern kingdom, called Judah, were ruled by a succession of kings, most of whom proved to be weak and sinful leaders. Their incompetence had disastrous consequences: the two kingdoms fell to foreign powers. Israel fell to the Assyrians in 722 B.C., and Judah to the Babylonians in 587 B.C.

The sorrow that we hear in 1 and 2 Kings is accompanied by a clear explanation: the people have fallen because of their wickedness and the wickedness of their leaders. Not surprisingly, the author of 1 and 2 Kings fashioned the history of God's people into a kind of morality tale, emphasizing the importance of faithfulness to the Covenant and the Law.

Of special interest in these books is the appearance of the classical prophet. Unlike the prophets of other lands, who were mere tools in the ruler's hand, the great prophets of Israel and Judah, like Elijah and Elisha, often directly opposed royal decisions and actions. Their job was not to pamper the ruler's pride, but to speak God's word clearly and boldly.

As we read about the terrible crises that the kingdoms of Judah and Israel faced, we can reflect on one of the basic truths of human history: Apart from God there is no hope. Only one thing remains as history passes: God's promise.

Quick Facts

Period Covered
from 961 to 587 B.C.

Author
unknown, from the Deuteronomic tradition, writing after the fall of Jerusalem

Theme
the history of Israel's and Judah's kings from Solomon until the fall of Jerusalem

Of Note
The two books of Kings were originally one book.

Kings

1 Kings

10.23

The Struggle for the Succession

King David was old and advanced in years; and although they covered him with clothes, he could not get warm. ²So his servants said to him, "Let a young virgin be sought for my lord the king, and let her wait on the king, and be his attendant; let her lie in your bosom, so that my lord the king may be warm." ³So they searched for a beautiful girl throughout all the territory of Israel, and found Ab'i•shag the Shū'nam•mīte, and brought her to the king. ⁴The girl was very beautiful. She became the king's attendant and served him, but the king did not know her sexually.

5 Now Ad•o•nī'jah son of Hag'gith exalted himself, saying, "I will be king"; he prepared for himself chariots and horsemen, and fifty men to run before him. ⁶His father had never at any time displeased him by asking, "Why have you done thus and so?" He was also a very handsome man, and he was born next after Ab'sa•lom. ⁷He conferred with Jō'ab son of Ze•rū'i•ah and with the priest A•bī'a•thar, and they supported Ad•o•nī'jah. ⁸But the priest Zā'dok, and Be•nā'i•ah son of Je•hoi'a•da, and the prophet Nathan, and Shim'e•ī, and Rē'ī, and David's own warriors did not side with Ad•o•nī'jah.

9 Ad•o•nī'jah sacrificed sheep, oxen, and fatted cattle by the stone Zō'he•leth, which is beside En-rō'gel, and he invited all his brothers, the king's sons, and all the royal officials of Judah, ¹⁰but he did not invite the prophet Nathan or Be•nā'i•ah or the warriors or his brother Solomon.

11 Then Nathan said to Bath•shē'ba, Solomon's mother, "Have you not heard that Ad•o•nī'jah son of Hag'gith has become king and our lord David does not know it? ¹²Now therefore come, let me give you advice, so that you may save your own life and the life of your son Solomon. ¹³Go in at once to King David, and say to him, 'Did you not, my lord the king, swear to your servant, saying: Your son Solomon shall succeed me as king, and he shall sit on my throne? Why then is Ad•o•nī'jah king?' ¹⁴Then while you are still there speaking with the king, I will come in after you and confirm your words."

15 So Bath•shē'ba went to the king in his room. The king was very old; Ab'i•shag the Shū'-nam•mīte was attending the king. ¹⁶Bath•shē'ba bowed and did obeisance to the king, and the king said, "What do you wish?" ¹⁷She said to him, "My lord, you swore to your servant by the LORD your God, saying: Your son Solomon shall succeed me as king, and he shall sit on my throne. ¹⁸But now suddenly Ad•o•nī'jah has become king, though you, my lord the king, do not know it. ¹⁹He has sacrificed oxen, fatted cattle, and sheep in abundance, and has invited all the children of the king, the priest A•bī'a•thar, and Jō'ab the commander of the army; but your servant Solomon he has not in-

vited. 20 But you, my lord the king—the eyes of all Israel are on you to tell them who shall sit on the throne of my lord the king after him. 21 Otherwise it will come to pass, when my lord the king sleeps with his ancestors, that my son Solomon and I will be counted offenders."

22 While she was still speaking with the king, the prophet Nathan came in. 23 The king was told, "Here is the prophet Nathan." When he came in before the king, he did obeisance to the king, with his face to the ground. 24 Nathan said, "My lord

from every adversity, 30 as I swore to you by the LORD, the God of Israel, 'Your son Solomon shall succeed me as king, and he shall sit on my throne in my place,' so will I do this day." 31 Then Bath-she′ba bowed with her face to the ground, and did obeisance to the king, and said, "May my lord King David live forever!"

32 King David said, "Summon to me the priest Za′dok, the prophet Nathan, and Be•nā′i•ah son of Je•hoi′a•da." When they came before the king, 33 the king said to them, "Take with you the ser-

Introducing ▶ SOLOMON

Solomon was one of the sons of David and Bathsheba. He ruled for forty years after King David died, and he was the third and last king to rule over the united kingdom of Israel.

There is an old saying that often, our personal strengths are our greatest weaknesses. This is true of Solomon. He was a tremendous organizer, an able ruler, a clever politician, and a great builder—it was during his reign that the first Temple was built in Jerusalem. To fulfill these great accomplishments, however, Solomon taxed his people heavily, married foreign women to seal political alliances with other nations, and used forced labor to complete his building projects. These things offended God and made Solomon unpopular with the people of Israel.

When Solomon died, ten of the original twelve tribes from the northern part of Israel left the kingdom owing to these harsh practices and set up their own kingdom. Israel never again existed as a united kingdom ruled by an Israelite king. The author of Kings attributes this more to Solomon's acceptance of other gods near the end of his life than to his political mistakes.

the king, have you said, 'Ad•o•ni′jah shall succeed me as king, and he shall sit on my throne'? 25 For today he has gone down and has sacrificed oxen, fatted cattle, and sheep in abundance, and has invited all the king's children, Jō′ab the commander*a* of the army, and the priest A•bi′a•thar, who are now eating and drinking before him, and saying, 'Long live King Ad•o•ni′jah!' 26 But he did not invite me, your servant, and the priest Za′dok, and Be•nā′i•ah son of Je•hoi′a•da, and your servant Solomon. 27 Has this thing been brought about by my lord the king and you have not let your servants know who should sit on the throne of my lord the king after him?"

The Accession of Solomon
(1 Chr 29.22b–25)

28 King David answered, "Summon Bath-she′ba to me." So she came into the king's presence, and stood before the king. 29 The king swore, saying, "As the LORD lives, who has saved my life

vants of your lord, and have my son Solomon ride on my own mule, and bring him down to Gī′hon. 34 There let the priest Za′dok and the prophet Nathan anoint him king over Israel; then blow the trumpet, and say, 'Long live King Solomon!' 35 You shall go up following him. Let him enter and sit on my throne; he shall be king in my place; for I have appointed him to be ruler over Israel and over Judah." 36 Be•nā′i•ah son of Je•hoi′a•da answered the king, "Amen! May the LORD, the God of my lord the king, so ordain. 37 As the LORD has been with my lord the king, so may he be with Solomon, and make his throne greater than the throne of my lord King David."

38 So the priest Za′dok, the prophet Nathan, and Be•nā′i•ah son of Je•hoi′a•da, and the Cher′e-thītes and the Pel′eth•ītes, went down and had Solomon ride on King David's mule, and led him to Gī′hon. 39 There the priest Za′dok took the horn of oil from the tent and anointed Solomon. Then

a Gk: Heb *the commanders*

they blew the trumpet, and all the people said, "Long live King Solomon!" 40And all the people went up following him, playing on pipes and rejoicing with great joy, so that the earth quaked at their noise.

41 Ad·o·ni′jah and all the guests who were with him heard it as they finished feasting. When Jo′ab heard the sound of the trumpet, he said, "Why is the city in an uproar?" 42While he was still speaking, Jonathan son of the priest A·bi′a·thar arrived. Ad·o·ni′jah said, "Come in, for you are a worthy man and surely you bring good news." 43Jonathan answered Ad·o·ni′jah, "No, for our lord King David has made Solomon king; 44the king has sent with him the priest Za′dok, the prophet Nathan, and Be·nai′ah son of Je·hoi′a·da, and the Cher′e·thites and the Pel′eth·ites; and they had him ride on the king's mule; 45the priest Za′dok and the prophet Nathan have anointed him king at Gi′hon; and they have gone up from there rejoicing, so that the city is in an uproar. This is the noise that you heard. 46Solomon now sits on the royal throne. 47Moreover the king's servants came to congratulate our lord King David, saying, 'May God make the name of Solomon more famous than yours, and make his throne greater than your throne.' The king bowed in worship on the bed 48and went on to pray thus, 'Blessed be the LORD, the God of Israel, who today has granted one of my offspring[b] to sit on my throne and permitted me to witness it.' "

49 Then all the guests of Ad·o·ni′jah got up trembling and went their own ways. 50Ad·o·ni′jah, fearing Solomon, got up and went to grasp the horns of the altar. 51Solomon was informed, "Ad·o·ni′jah is afraid of King Solomon; see, he has laid hold of the horns of the altar, saying, 'Let King Solomon swear to me first that he will not kill his servant with the sword.' " 52So Solomon responded, "If he proves to be a worthy man, not one of his hairs shall fall to the ground; but if wickedness is found in him, he shall die." 53Then King Solomon sent to have him brought down from the altar. He came to do obeisance to King Solomon; and Solomon said to him, "Go home."

David's Instruction to Solomon

When David's time to die drew near, he charged his son Solomon, saying: 2"I am about to go the way of all the earth. Be strong, be courageous, 3and keep the charge of the LORD your God, walking in his ways and keeping his statutes, his commandments, his ordinances, and his testimonies, as it is written in the law of Moses, so that you may prosper in all that you do and wherever you turn. 4Then the LORD will establish his word that

he spoke concerning me: 'If your heirs take heed to their way, to walk before me in faithfulness with all their heart and with all their soul, there shall not fail you a successor on the throne of Israel.'

5 "Moreover you know also what Jo′ab son of Ze·ru′i·ah did to me, how he dealt with the two commanders of the armies of Israel, Abner son of Ner, and A·ma′sa son of Je′ther, whom he murdered, retaliating in time of peace for blood that had been shed in war, and putting the blood of war on the belt around his waist, and on the sandals on his feet. 6Act therefore according to your wisdom, but do not let his gray head go down to She′ol in peace. 7Deal loyally, however, with the sons of Bar·zil′lai the Gil′e·ad·ite, and let them be among those who eat at your table; for with such loyalty they met me when I fled from your brother Ab′sa·lom. 8There is also with you Shim′e·i son of Ge′ra, the Ben′ja·min·ite from Ba·hu′rim, who cursed me with a terrible curse on the day when I went to Ma·ha·na′im; but when he came down to meet me at the Jordan, I swore to him by the LORD, 'I will not put you to death with the sword.' 9Therefore do not hold him guiltless, for you are a wise man; you will know what you ought to do to him, and you must bring his gray head down with blood to She′ol."

Death of David
(1 Chr 3.4; 29.26–28)

10 Then David slept with his ancestors, and was buried in the city of David. 11The time that David reigned over Israel was forty years; he reigned seven years in He′bron, and thirty-three years in Jerusalem. 12So Solomon sat on the throne of his father David; and his kingdom was firmly established.

Solomon Consolidates His Reign

13 Then Ad·o·ni′jah son of Hag′gith came to Bath·she′ba, Solomon's mother. She asked, "Do you come peaceably?" He said, "Peaceably." 14Then he said, "May I have a word with you?" She said, "Go on." 15He said, "You know that the kingdom was mine, and that all Israel expected me to reign; however, the kingdom has turned about and become my brother's, for it was his from the LORD. 16And now I have one request to make of you; do not refuse me." She said to him, "Go on." 17He said, "Please ask King Solomon—he will not refuse you—to give me Ab′i·shag the Shu′nam·mite as my wife." 18Bath·she′ba said, "Very well; I will speak to the king on your behalf."

b Gk: Heb one

19 So Bath•she′ba went to King Solomon, to speak to him on behalf of Ad•o•ni′jah. The king rose to meet her, and bowed down to her; then he sat on his throne, and had a throne brought for the king's mother, and she sat on his right. ²⁰Then she said, "I have one small request to make of you; do not refuse me." And the king said to her, "Make your request, my mother; for I will not refuse you." ²¹She said, "Let Ab′i•shag the Shū′nam•mīte be given to your brother Ad•o•ni′jah as his wife." ²²King Solomon answered his mother, "And why do you ask Ab′i•shag the Shū′nam•mīte for Ad•o•ni′jah? Ask for him the kingdom as well! For he is my elder brother; ask not only for him but also for the priest A•bi′a•thar and for Jō′ab son of Ze•rū′i•ah!" ²³Then King Solomon swore by the LORD, "So may God do to me, and more also, for Ad•o•ni′jah has devised this scheme at the risk of his life! ²⁴Now therefore as the LORD lives, who has established me and placed me on the throne of my father David, and who has made me a house as he promised, today Ad•o•ni′jah shall be put to death." ²⁵So King Solomon sent Be•na′i•ah son of Je•hoi′a•da; he struck him down, and he died.

26 The king said to the priest A•bi′a•thar, "Go to An′a•thoth, to your estate; for you deserve death. But I will not at this time put you to death, because you carried the ark of the Lord GOD before my father David, and because you shared in all the hardships my father endured." ²⁷So Solomon banished A•bi′a•thar from being priest to the LORD, thus fulfilling the word of the LORD that he had spoken concerning the house of E′li in Shi′loh.

28 When the news came to Jō′ab—for Jō′ab had supported Ad•o•ni′jah though he had not supported Ab′sa•lom—Jō′ab fled to the tent of the LORD and grasped the horns of the altar. ²⁹When it was told King Solomon, "Jō′ab has fled to the tent of the LORD and now is beside the altar," Solomon sent Be•na′i•ah son of Je•hoi′a•da, saying, "Go, strike him down." ³⁰So Be•na′i•ah came to the tent of the LORD and said to him, "The king commands, 'Come out.'" But he said, "No, I will die here." Then Be•na′i•ah brought the king word again, saying, "Thus said Jō′ab, and thus he answered me." ³¹The king replied to him, "Do as he has said, strike him down and bury him; and thus take away from me and from my father's house the guilt for the blood that Jō′ab shed without cause. ³²The LORD will bring back his bloody deeds on his own head, because, without the knowledge of my father David, he attacked and killed with the sword two men more righteous and better than himself, Abner son of Ner, commander of the army of Israel, and A•ma′sa son of Je′ther, commander of the army of Judah. ³³So shall their blood come back on the

head of Jō′ab and on the head of his descendants forever; but to David, and to his descendants, and to his house, and to his throne, there shall be peace from the LORD forevermore." ³⁴Then Be•na′i•ah son of Je•hoi′a•da went up and struck him down and killed him; and he was buried at his own house near the wilderness. ³⁵The king put Be•na′i•ah son of Je•hoi′a•da over the army in his place, and the king put the priest Zā′dok in the place of A•bi′a•thar.

36 Then the king sent and summoned Shim′e•ī, and said to him, "Build yourself a house in Jerusalem, and live there, and do not go out from there to any place whatever. ³⁷For on the day you go out, and cross the Wadi Kid′ron, know for certain that you shall die; your blood shall be on your own head." ³⁸And Shim′e•ī said to the king, "The sentence is fair; as my lord the king has said, so will your servant do." So Shim′e•ī lived in Jerusalem many days.

39 But it happened at the end of three years that two of Shim′e•ī's slaves ran away to King Ā′chish son of Mā′a•cah of Gath. When it was told Shim′e•ī, "Your slaves are in Gath," ⁴⁰Shim′e•ī arose and saddled a donkey, and went to Ā′chish in Gath, to search for his slaves; Shim′e•ī went and brought his slaves from Gath. ⁴¹When Solomon was told that Shim′e•ī had gone from Jerusalem to Gath and returned, ⁴²the king sent and summoned Shim′e•ī, and said to him, "Did I not make you swear by the LORD, and solemnly adjure you, saying, 'Know for certain that on the day you go out and go to any place whatever, you shall die'? And you said to me, 'The sentence is fair; I accept.' ⁴³Why then have you not kept your oath to the LORD and the commandment with which I charged you?" ⁴⁴The king also said to Shim′e•ī, "You know in your own heart all the evil that you did to my father David; so the LORD will bring back your evil on your own head. ⁴⁵But King Solomon shall be blessed, and the throne of David shall be established before the LORD forever." ⁴⁶Then the king commanded Be•na′i•ah son of Je•hoi′a•da; and he went out and struck him down, and he died.

So the kingdom was established in the hand of Solomon.

Solomon's Prayer for Wisdom
(2 Chr 1.2–13)

Solomon made a marriage alliance with Pharaoh king of Egypt; he took Pharaoh's daughter and brought her into the city of David, until he had finished building his own house and the house of the LORD and the wall around Jerusalem. ²The people were sacrificing at the high places, however, because no house had yet been built for the name of the LORD.

3 Solomon loved the LORD, walking in the statutes of his father David; only, he sacrificed and offered incense at the high places. 4 The king went to Gib′e·on to sacrifice there, for that was the principal high place; Solomon used to offer a thousand burnt offerings on that altar. 5 At Gib′e·on the LORD appeared to Solomon in a dream by night; and God said, "Ask what I should give you." 6 And Solomon said, "You have shown great and steadfast love to your servant my father David, because he walked before you in faithfulness, in righteousness, and in uprightness of heart toward you; and you have kept for him this great and steadfast love, and have given him a son to sit on his throne today. 7 And now, O LORD my God, you have made your servant king in place of my father David, although I am only a little child; I do not know how to go out or come in. 8 And your servant is in the midst of the people whom you have chosen, a great people, so numerous they cannot be numbered or counted. 9 Give your servant therefore an understanding mind to govern your people, able to discern between good and evil; for who can govern this your great people?"

PRAY IT!
A Wise Heart

A famous prayer, often called the Peace Prayer, by Saint Francis of Assisi (A.D. 1181–1226), contains the line "Lord, grant that I may not so much seek to be . . . understood, as to understand."

It is almost as if Saint Francis is echoing the prayer of King Solomon, who lived two thousand years before him. The request is the same. Both men ask God to give them the gift of a wise heart—the ability to see things as God sees them.

What a difference wisdom can make in our life. What a wonderful thing to pray for. What a blessing to increase the amount of wisdom in our world. What inspiring examples we have in the prayers of Solomon a millennium before Jesus, and of Francis a millennium after.

Let us ask God daily for a wise heart.

▶ 1 Kings 3.9

GOD, GIVE ME WISDOM!

At the beginning of his reign, Solomon asked God for wisdom to govern his people. Under the advice of the prophet Nathan, Solomon became a great king. His failure came later because he betrayed God by accepting other gods and exploiting his people with work and taxes to build his magnificent royal city of Jerusalem.

Whenever you are in a leadership position, remember that you must use the power or authority you have in service to God and God's people; never use it to exploit others or for your own selfishness.

- Ask God for the wisdom necessary to discern how to respond to the needs of people you lead.
- Examine your leadership style frequently to see if you remain faithful to God's call to be a servant of those in need.

▶ 1 Kings 3.4–15

¡Dios mío, dame Sabiduría Para discernir! HISPANIC

1 KINGS

10 It pleased the Lord that Solomon had asked this. 11 God said to him, "Because you have asked this, and have not asked for yourself long life or riches, or for the life of your enemies, but have asked for yourself understanding to discern what is right, 12 I now do according to your word. Indeed I give you a wise and discerning mind; no one like you has been before you and no one like you shall arise after you. 13 I give you also what you have not asked, both riches and honor all your life; no other king shall compare with you. 14 If you will walk in my ways, keeping my statutes and my commandments, as your father David walked, then I will lengthen your life."

15 Then Solomon awoke; it had been a dream. He came to Jerusalem where he stood before the ark of the covenant of the LORD. He offered up burnt offerings and offerings of well-being, and provided a feast for all his servants.

Solomon's Wisdom in Judgment

16 Later, two women who were prostitutes came to the king and stood before him. 17 The one woman said, "Please, my lord, this woman and I live in the same house; and I gave birth while she was in the house. 18 Then on the third day after I gave birth, this woman also gave birth. We were together; there was no one else with us in the house, only the two of us were in the house. 19 Then this woman's son died in the night, because she lay on him. 20 She got up in the middle of the night and took my son from beside me while your servant slept. She laid him at her breast, and laid her dead son at my breast. 21 When I rose in the morning to nurse my son, I saw that he was dead; but when I looked at him closely in the morning, clearly it was not the son I had borne." 22 But the other woman said, "No, the living son is mine, and the dead son is yours." The first said, "No, the dead son is yours, and the living son is mine." So they argued before the king.

23 Then the king said, "The one says, 'This is my son that is alive, and your son is dead'; while the other says, 'Not so! Your son is dead, and my son is the living one.'" 24 So the king said, "Bring me a sword," and they brought a sword before the king. 25 The king said, "Divide the living boy in two; then give half to the one, and half to the other." 26 But the woman whose son was alive said to the king—because compassion for her son burned within her—"Please, my lord, give her the living boy; certainly do not kill him!" The other said, "It shall be neither mine nor yours; divide it." 27 Then the king responded: "Give the first woman the living boy; do not kill him. She is his mother." 28 All Israel heard of the judgment that the king had rendered; and they stood in awe of the king, because they perceived that the wisdom of God was in him, to execute justice.

Solomon's Administrative Officers

King Solomon was king over all Israel, 2 and these were his high officials: Az·a·rī'ah son of Zā'dok was the priest; 3 El·i·hōr'eph and A·hī'jah sons of Shī'sha were secretaries; Je·hosh'a·phat son of A·hī'lud was recorder; 4 Be·nā'i·ah son of Je·hoi'a·da was in command of the army; Zā'dok and A·bī'a·thar were priests; 5 Az·a·rī'ah son of Nathan was over the officials; Zā'bud son of Nathan was priest and king's friend; 6 A·hī'shar was in charge of the palace; and Ad·o·nī'ram son of Ab'da was in charge of the forced labor.

7 Solomon had twelve officials over all Israel, who provided food for the king and his household; each one had to make provision for one month in the year. 8 These were their names: Benhur, in the hill country of Ē'phra·im; 9 Ben-de'ker, in Mā'kaz, Shā·al'bim, Beth-shē'mesh, and Ē'lonbeth-hā'nan; 10 Ben-hē'sed, in A·rūb'both (to him belonged Sō'cōh and all the land of Hē'pher); 11 Ben-a·bin'a·dab, in all Nā'phath-dor (he had Tā'phath, Solomon's daughter, as his wife); 12 Bā'a·na son of A·hī'lud, in Tā'a·nach, Me·gid'dō, and all Beth-shē'an, which is beside Zar'e·than below Jez'rē·el, and from Beth-shē'an to A'bel-me·hō'lah, as far as the other side of Jok'mē·am; 13 Ben-ge'ber, in Rā'moth-gil'ē·ad (he had the villages of Jā'ir son of Ma·nas'seh, which are in Gil'e·ad, and he had the region of Ar'gob, which is in Bā'shan, sixty great cities with walls and bronze bars); 14 A·hin'a·dab son of Id'dō, in Mā·ha·nā'im; 15 A·him'a·az, in Naph'ta·lī (he had taken Bas'e·math, Solomon's daughter, as his wife); 16 Bā'a·na son of Hū'shaī, in Ash'er and Be·ā'loth; 17 Je·hosh'a·phat son of Pa·rū'ah, in Is'sa·char; 18 Shim'e·ī son of Ē'la, in Benjamin; 19 Ge'ber son of Ū'rī, in the land of Gil'e·ad, the country of King Sī'hon of the Am'o·rītes and of King Og of Bā'shan. And there was one official in the land of Judah.

Magnificence of Solomon's Rule

20 Judah and Israel were as numerous as the sand by the sea; they ate and drank and were happy. 21c Solomon was sovereign over all the kingdoms from the Euphrates to the land of the Phi·lis'tines, even to the border of Egypt; they brought tribute and served Solomon all the days of his life.

22 Solomon's provision for one day was thirty cors of choice flour, and sixty cors of meal, 23 ten fat oxen, and twenty pasture-fed cattle, one hundred sheep, besides deer, gazelles, roebucks, and fatted fowl. 24 For he had dominion over all the region west of the Euphrates from Tiph'sah to Gā'za, over all the kings west of the Euphrates; and he had peace on all sides. 25 During Solomon's lifetime Judah and Israel lived in safety, from Dan even to Bē'er-shē'ba, all of them under their vines and fig trees. 26 Solomon also had forty thousand stalls of horses for his chariots, and twelve thousand horsemen. 27 Those officials supplied provisions for King Solomon and for all who came to King Solomon's table, each one in his month; they let nothing be lacking. 28 They also brought to the required place barley and straw for the horses and swift steeds, each according to his charge.

c Ch 5.1 in Heb

Fame of Solomon's Wisdom

29 God gave Solomon very great wisdom, discernment, and breadth of understanding as vast as the sand on the seashore, 30 so that Solomon's wisdom surpassed the wisdom of all the people of the

AFRICAN AMERICAN

How Excellent

The First Book of Kings says, "Solomon's wisdom surpassed the wisdom of all the people of the east, and all the wisdom of Egypt" (4.30).

This should be a source of pride for young African Americans. The people of Egypt and of the East are dark-skinned people. Ancient southern Egypt actually included the country of modern Ethiopia. The people in these countries must have been well known for their wisdom in order for the biblical author to use them in a comparison with Solomon. African Americans can praise God for their African ancestors: the wise, black people from Egypt and the East.

▶ I Kings 4.30

east, and all the wisdom of Egypt. 31 He was wiser than anyone else, wiser than E'than the Ez'ra•hīte, and Hē'man, Cal'col, and Dar'da, children of Mā'-hol; his fame spread throughout all the surrounding nations. 32 He composed three thousand proverbs, and his songs numbered a thousand and five. 33 He would speak of trees, from the cedar that is in the Lebanon to the hyssop that grows in the wall; he would speak of animals, and birds, and reptiles, and fish. 34 People came from all the nations to hear the wisdom of Solomon; they came from all the kings of the earth who had heard of his wisdom.

Preparations and Materials
for the Temple
(2 Chr 2.1–18)

dNow King Hiram of Tyre sent his servants to Solomon, when he heard that they had anointed him king in place of his father; for Hiram had always been a friend to David. 2 Solomon sent word to Hiram, saying, 3 "You know that my father David

could not build a house for the name of the LORD his God because of the warfare with which his enemies surrounded him, until the LORD put them under the soles of his feet.e 4 But now the LORD my God has given me rest on every side; there is neither adversary nor misfortune. 5 So I intend to build a house for the name of the LORD my God, as the LORD said to my father David, 'Your son, whom I will set on your throne in your place, shall build the house for my name.' 6 Therefore command that cedars from the Lebanon be cut for me. My servants will join your servants, and I will give you whatever wages you set for your servants; for you know that there is no one among us who knows how to cut timber like the Sī•dō'ni•ans."

7 When Hiram heard the words of Solomon, he rejoiced greatly, and said, "Blessed be the LORD today, who has given to David a wise son to be over this great people." 8 Hiram sent word to Solomon, "I have heard the message that you have sent to me; I will fulfill all your needs in the matter of cedar and cypress timber. 9 My servants shall bring it down to the sea from the Lebanon; I will make it into rafts to go by sea to the place you indicate. I will have them broken up there for you to take away. And you shall meet my needs by providing food for my household." 10 So Hiram supplied Solomon's every need for timber of cedar and cypress. 11 Solomon in turn gave Hiram twenty thousand cors of wheat as food for his household, and twenty cors of fine oil. Solomon gave this to Hiram year by year. 12 So the LORD gave Solomon wisdom, as he promised him. There was peace between Hiram and Solomon; and the two of them made a treaty.

13 King Solomon conscripted forced labor out of all Israel; the levy numbered thirty thousand men. 14 He sent them to the Lebanon, ten thousand a month in shifts; they would be a month in the Lebanon and two months at home; Ad•o•ni'ram was in charge of the forced labor. 15 Solomon also had seventy thousand laborers and eighty thousand stonecutters in the hill country, 16 besides Solomon's three thousand three hundred supervisors who were over the work, having charge of the people who did the work. 17 At the king's command, they quarried out great, costly stones in order to lay the foundation of the house with dressed stones. 18 So Solomon's builders and Hiram's builders and the Gē'bal•ītes did the stonecutting and prepared the timber and the stone to build the house.

d Ch 5.15 in Heb   e Gk Tg Vg: Heb *my feet* or *his feet*

Solomon Builds the Temple
(2 Chr 3.1–14)

In the four hundred eightieth year after the Israelites came out of the land of Egypt, in the fourth year of Solomon's reign over Israel, in the month of Ziv, which is the second month, he began to build the house of the LORD. 2 The house that King Solomon built for the LORD was sixty cubits long, twenty cubits wide, and thirty cubits high. 3 The vestibule in front of the nave of the house was twenty cubits wide, across the width of the house. Its depth was ten cubits in front of the house. 4 For the house he made windows with recessed frames.*f* 5 He also built a structure against the wall of the house, running around the walls of the house, both the nave and the inner sanctuary; and he made side chambers all around. 6 The lowest story*g* was five cubits wide, the middle one was six cubits wide, and the third was seven cubits wide; for around the outside of the house he made offsets on the wall in order that the supporting beams should not be inserted into the walls of the house.

7 The house was built with stone finished at the quarry, so that neither hammer nor ax nor any tool of iron was heard in the temple while it was being built.

8 The entrance for the middle story was on the south side of the house: one went up by winding stairs to the middle story, and from the middle story to the third. 9 So he built the house, and finished it; he roofed the house with beams and planks of cedar. 10 He built the structure against the whole house, each story*h* five cubits high, and it was joined to the house with timbers of cedar.

11 Now the word of the LORD came to Solomon, 12 "Concerning this house that you are building, if you will walk in my statutes, obey my ordinances, and keep all my commandments by walking in them, then I will establish my promise with you, which I made to your father David. 13 I will dwell among the children of Israel, and will not forsake my people Israel."

14 So Solomon built the house, and finished it. 15 He lined the walls of the house on the inside with boards of cedar; from the floor of the house to the rafters of the ceiling, he covered them on the inside with wood; and he covered the floor of the house with boards of cypress. 16 He built twenty cubits of the rear of the house with boards of cedar from the floor to the rafters, and he built this within as an inner sanctuary, as the most holy place. 17 The house, that is, the nave in front of the inner sanctuary, was forty cubits long. 18 The cedar within the house had carvings of gourds and open flowers; all was cedar, no stone was seen. 19 The

inner sanctuary he prepared in the innermost part of the house, to set there the ark of the covenant of the LORD. 20 The interior of the inner sanctuary was twenty cubits long, twenty cubits wide, and twenty cubits high; he overlaid it with pure gold. He also overlaid the altar with cedar.*i* 21 Solomon overlaid the inside of the house with pure gold, then he drew chains of gold across, in front of the inner sanctuary, and overlaid it with gold. 22 Next he overlaid the whole house with gold, in order that the whole house might be perfect; even the whole altar that belonged to the inner sanctuary he overlaid with gold.

---

f Gk: Meaning of Heb uncertain   *g* Gk: Heb *structure*
h Heb lacks *each story*   *i* Meaning of Heb uncertain

The Temple of Solomon

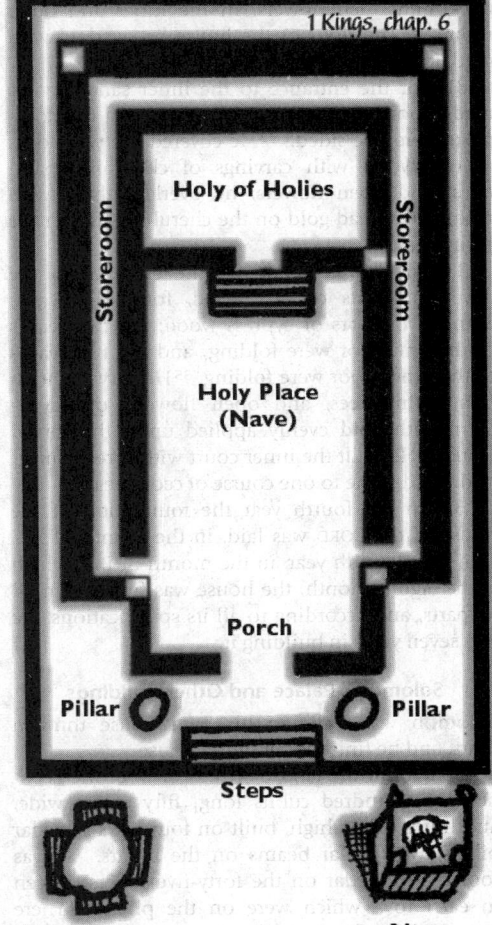

1 Kings, chap. 6

Holy of Holies

Storeroom

Storeroom

Holy Place (Nave)

Porch

Pillar

Pillar

Steps

Sea of Bronze

Altar

The Furnishings of the Temple
(2 Chr 4.1–10, 19–22; 5.1)

23 In the inner sanctuary he made two cherubim of olivewood, each ten cubits high. 24 Five cubits was the length of one wing of the cherub, and five cubits the length of the other wing of the cherub; it was ten cubits from the tip of one wing to the tip of the other. 25 The other cherub also measured ten cubits; both cherubim had the same measure and the same form. 26 The height of one cherub was ten cubits, and so was that of the other cherub. 27 He put the cherubim in the innermost part of the house; the wings of the cherubim were spread out so that a wing of one was touching the one wall, and a wing of the other cherub was touching the other wall; their other wings toward the center of the house were touching wing to wing. 28 He also overlaid the cherubim with gold.

29 He carved the walls of the house all around about with carved engravings of cherubim, palm trees, and open flowers, in the inner and outer rooms. 30 The floor of the house he overlaid with gold, in the inner and outer rooms.

31 For the entrance to the inner sanctuary he made doors of olivewood; the lintel and the doorposts were five-sided.*i* 32 He covered the two doors of olivewood with carvings of cherubim, palm trees, and open flowers; he overlaid them with gold, and spread gold on the cherubim and on the palm trees.

33 So also he made for the entrance to the nave doorposts of olivewood, four-sided each, 34 and two doors of cypress wood; the two leaves of the one door were folding, and the two leaves of the other door were folding. 35 He carved cherubim, palm trees, and open flowers, overlaying them with gold evenly applied upon the carved work. 36 He built the inner court with three courses of dressed stone to one course of cedar beams.

37 In the fourth year the foundation of the house of the LORD was laid, in the month of Ziv. 38 In the eleventh year, in the month of Bul, which is the eighth month, the house was finished in all its parts, and according to all its specifications. He was seven years in building it.

Solomon's Palace and Other Buildings

Solomon was building his own house thirteen years, and he finished his entire house.

2 He built the House of the Forest of the Lebanon one hundred cubits long, fifty cubits wide, and thirty cubits high, built on four rows of cedar pillars, with cedar beams on the pillars. 3 It was roofed with cedar on the forty-five rafters, fifteen in each row, which were on the pillars. 4 There were window frames in the three rows, facing each other in the three rows. 5 All the doorways and doorposts had four-sided frames, opposite, facing each other in the three rows.

6 He made the Hall of Pillars fifty cubits long and thirty cubits wide. There was a porch in front with pillars, and a canopy in front of them.

7 He made the Hall of the Throne where he was to pronounce judgment, the Hall of Justice, covered with cedar from floor to floor.

8 His own house where he would reside, in the other court back of the hall, was of the same construction. Solomon also made a house like this hall for Pharaoh's daughter, whom he had taken in marriage.

9 All these were made of costly stones, cut according to measure, sawed with saws, back and front, from the foundation to the coping, and from outside to the great court. 10 The foundation was of costly stones, huge stones, stones of eight and ten cubits. 11 There were costly stones above, cut to measure, and cedarwood. 12 The great court had three courses of dressed stone to one layer of cedar beams all around; so had the inner court of the house of the LORD, and the vestibule of the house.

Products of Hiram the Bronzeworker
(2 Chr 3.15–17; 4.11–18)

13 Now King Solomon invited and received Hiram from Tyre. 14 He was the son of a widow of the tribe of Naph′ta•li, whose father, a man of Tyre, had been an artisan in bronze; he was full of skill, intelligence, and knowledge in working bronze. He came to King Solomon, and did all his work.

15 He cast two pillars of bronze. Eighteen cubits was the height of the one, and a cord of twelve cubits would encircle it; the second pillar was the same.*j* 16 He also made two capitals of molten bronze, to set on the tops of the pillars; the height of the one capital was five cubits, and the height of the other capital was five cubits. 17 There were nets of checker work with wreaths of chain work for the capitals on the tops of the pillars; seven*k* for the one capital, and seven*k* for the other capital. 18 He made the columns with two rows around each latticework to cover the capitals that were above the pomegranates; he did the same with the other capital. 19 Now the capitals that were on the tops of the pillars in the vestibule were of lily-work, four cubits high. 20 The capitals were on the two pillars and also above the rounded projection that was beside the latticework; there were two hundred

---

i Meaning of Heb uncertain   *j* Cn: Heb *and a cord of twelve cubits encircled the second pillar*; Compare Jer 52.21   *k* Heb: Gk *a net*

pomegranates in rows all around; and so with the other capital. 21 He set up the pillars at the vestibule of the temple; he set up the pillar on the south and called it Jā′chin; and he set up the pillar on the north and called it Bō′az. 22 On the tops of the pillars was lily-work. Thus the work of the pillars was finished.

23 Then he made the molten sea; it was round, ten cubits from brim to brim, and five cubits high. A line of thirty cubits would encircle it completely. 24 Under its brim were panels all around it, each of ten cubits, surrounding the sea; there were two rows of panels, cast when it was cast. 25 It stood on twelve oxen, three facing north, three facing west, three facing south, and three facing east; the sea was set on them. The hindquarters of each were toward the inside. 26 Its thickness was a handbreadth; its brim was made like the brim of a cup, like the flower of a lily; it held two thousand baths.*l*

27 He also made the ten stands of bronze; each stand was four cubits long, four cubits wide, and three cubits high. 28 This was the construction of the stands: they had borders; the borders were within the frames; 29 on the borders that were set in the frames were lions, oxen, and cherubim. On the frames, both above and below the lions and oxen, there were wreaths of beveled work. 30 Each stand had four bronze wheels and axles of bronze; at the four corners were supports for a basin. The supports were cast with wreaths at the side of each. 31 Its opening was within the crown whose height was one cubit; its opening was round, as a pedestal is made; it was a cubit and a half wide. At its opening there were carvings; its borders were four-sided, not round. 32 The four wheels were underneath the borders; the axles of the wheels were in the stands; and the height of a wheel was a cubit and a half. 33 The wheels were made like a chariot wheel; their axles, their rims, their spokes, and their hubs were all cast. 34 There were four supports at the four corners of each stand; the supports were of one piece with the stands. 35 On the top of the stand there was a round band half a cubit high; on the top of the stand, its stays and its borders were of one piece with it. 36 On the surfaces of its stays and on its borders he carved cherubim, lions, and palm trees, where each had space, with wreaths all around. 37 In this way he made the ten stands; all of them were cast alike, with the same size and the same form.

38 He made ten basins of bronze; each basin held forty baths,*l* each basin measured four cubits; there was a basin for each of the ten stands. 39 He set five of the stands on the south side of the house, and five on the north side of the house; he set the sea on the southeast corner of the house.

40 Hiram also made the pots, the shovels, and the basins. So Hiram finished all the work that he did for King Solomon on the house of the LORD: 41 the two pillars, the two bowls of the capitals that were on the tops of the pillars, the two latticeworks to cover the two bowls of the capitals that were on the tops of the pillars; 42 the four hundred pomegranates for the two latticeworks, two rows of pomegranates for each latticework, to cover the two bowls of the capitals that were on the pillars; 43 the ten stands, the ten basins on the stands; 44 the one sea, and the twelve oxen underneath the sea.

45 The pots, the shovels, and the basins, all these vessels that Hiram made for King Solomon for the house of the LORD were of burnished bronze. 46 In the plain of the Jordan the king cast them, in the clay ground between Suc′coth and Zar′e•than. 47 Solomon left all the vessels unweighed, because there were so many of them; the weight of the bronze was not determined.

48 So Solomon made all the vessels that were in the house of the LORD: the golden altar, the golden table for the bread of the Presence, 49 the lampstands of pure gold, five on the south side and five on the north, in front of the inner sanctuary; the flowers, the lamps, and the tongs, of gold; 50 the cups, snuffers, basins, dishes for incense, and firepans, of pure gold; the sockets for the doors of the innermost part of the house, the most holy place, and for the doors of the nave of the temple, of gold.

51 Thus all the work that King Solomon did on the house of the LORD was finished. Solomon brought in the things that his father David had dedicated, the silver, the gold, and the vessels, and stored them in the treasuries of the house of the LORD.

Dedication of the Temple
(2 Chr 5.2—6.2)

Then Solomon assembled the elders of Israel and all the heads of the tribes, the leaders of the ancestral houses of the Israelites, before King Solomon in Jerusalem, to bring up the ark of the covenant of the LORD out of the city of David, which is Zion. 2 All the people of Israel assembled to King Solomon at the festival in the month Eth′a•nim, which is the seventh month. 3 And all the elders of Israel came, and the priests carried the ark. 4 So they brought up the ark of the LORD, the tent of meeting, and all the holy vessels that were in the tent; the priests and the Lē′vītes brought them up.

1

K
I
N
G
S

---

l A Heb measure of volume

5 King Solomon and all the congregation of Israel, who had assembled before him, were with him before the ark, sacrificing so many sheep and oxen that they could not be counted or numbered. 6 Then the priests brought the ark of the covenant of the LORD to its place, in the inner sanctuary of the house, in the most holy place, underneath the wings of the cherubim. 7 For the cherubim spread out their wings over the place of the ark, so that the cherubim made a covering above the ark and its poles. 8 The poles were so long that the ends of the poles were seen from the holy place in front of the inner sanctuary; but they could not be seen from outside; they are there to this day. 9 There was nothing in the ark except the two tablets of stone that Moses had placed there at Hō'reb, where the LORD made a covenant with the Israelites, when they came out of the land of Egypt. 10 And when the priests came out of the holy place, a cloud filled the house of the LORD, 11 so that the priests could not stand to minister because of the cloud; for the glory of the LORD filled the house of the LORD.

12 Then Solomon said,

"The LORD has said that he would dwell in
     thick darkness.
13   I have built you an exalted house,
     a place for you to dwell in forever."

Solomon's Speech
(2 Chr 6.3–11)

14 Then the king turned around and blessed all the assembly of Israel, while all the assembly of Israel stood. 15 He said, "Blessed be the LORD, the God of Israel, who with his hand has fulfilled what he promised with his mouth to my father David, saying, 16 'Since the day that I brought my people Israel out of Egypt, I have not chosen a city from any of the tribes of Israel in which to build a house, that my name might be there; but I chose David to be over my people Israel.' 17 My father David had it in mind to build a house for the name of the LORD, the God of Israel. 18 But the LORD said to my father David, 'You did well to consider building a house for my name; 19 nevertheless you shall not build the house, but your son who shall be born to you shall build the house for my name.' 20 Now the LORD has upheld the promise that he made; for I have risen in the place of my father David; I sit on the throne of Israel, as the LORD promised, and have built the house for the name of the LORD, the God of Israel. 21 There I have provided a place for the ark, in which is the covenant of the LORD that he made with our ancestors when he brought them out of the land of Egypt."

Solomon's Prayer of Dedication
(2 Chr 6.12–39)

22 Then Solomon stood before the altar of the LORD in the presence of all the assembly of Israel, and spread out his hands to heaven. 23 He said, "O LORD, God of Israel, there is no God like you in heaven above or on earth beneath, keeping covenant and steadfast love for your servants who walk before you with all their heart, 24 the covenant that you kept for your servant my father David as you declared to him; you promised with your mouth and have this day fulfilled with your hand. 25 Therefore, O LORD, God of Israel, keep for your servant my father David that which you promised him, saying, 'There shall never fail you a successor before me to sit on the throne of Israel, if only your children look to their way, to walk before me as you have walked before me.' 26 Therefore, O God of Israel, let your word be confirmed, which you promised to your servant my father David.

PRAY IT?
Holy Places

Solomon knows that the Temple will not hold God. Holy places are not cages to keep God contained. People need holy places more than God does. We gather together in public holy places to experience God's presence as a community. But we can also meet God one-on-one in private holy places, special to us alone.

Try creating a holy space in your bedroom. Clear out a corner and put in it a small table, and a chair or rug to sit on. On the table, put your Bible and an object or two to help you focus on God. You might use a candle, a special picture or statue, or something from a retreat or a special place. Try to spend a little time each day in your holy space with God.

▸ 1 Kings 8.27–30

27 "But will God indeed dwell on the earth? Even heaven and the highest heaven cannot contain you, much less this house that I have built! 28 Regard your servant's prayer and his plea,

O LORD my God, heeding the cry and the prayer that your servant prays to you today; 29 that your eyes may be open night and day toward this house, the place of which you said, 'My name shall be there,' that you may heed the prayer that your servant prays toward this place. 30 Hear the plea of your servant and of your people Israel when they pray toward this place; O hear in heaven your dwelling place; heed and forgive.

31 "If someone sins against a neighbor and is given an oath to swear, and comes and swears before your altar in this house, 32 then hear in heaven, and act, and judge your servants, condemning the guilty by bringing their conduct on their own head, and vindicating the righteous by rewarding them according to their righteousness.

33 "When your people Israel, having sinned against you, are defeated before an enemy but turn again to you, confess your name, pray and plead with you in this house, 34 then hear in heaven, forgive the sin of your people Israel, and bring them again to the land that you gave to their ancestors.

35 "When heaven is shut up and there is no rain because they have sinned against you, and then they pray toward this place, confess your name, and turn from their sin, because you punish*m* them, 36 then hear in heaven, and forgive the sin of your servants, your people Israel, when you teach them the good way in which they should walk; and grant rain on your land, which you have given to your people as an inheritance.

37 "If there is famine in the land, if there is plague, blight, mildew, locust, or caterpillar; if their enemy besieges them in any*n* of their cities; whatever plague, whatever sickness there is; 38 whatever prayer, whatever plea there is from any individual or from all your people Israel, all knowing the afflictions of their own hearts so that they stretch out their hands toward this house; 39 then hear in heaven your dwelling place, forgive, act, and render to all whose hearts you know—according to all their ways, for only you know what is in every human heart— 40 so that they may fear you all the days that they live in the land that you gave to our ancestors.

41 "Likewise when a foreigner, who is not of your people Israel, comes from a distant land because of your name 42 —for they shall hear of your great name, your mighty hand, and your outstretched arm—when a foreigner comes and prays toward this house, 43 then hear in heaven your dwelling place, and do according to all that the foreigner calls to you, so that all the peoples of the earth may know your name and fear you, as do your people Israel, and so that they may know that

your name has been invoked on this house that I have built.

44 "If your people go out to battle against their enemy, by whatever way you shall send them, and they pray to the LORD toward the city that you have chosen and the house that I have built for your name, 45 then hear in heaven their prayer and their plea, and maintain their cause.

46 "If they sin against you—for there is no one who does not sin—and you are angry with them and give them to an enemy, so that they are carried away captive to the land of the enemy, far off or near; 47 yet if they come to their senses in the land to which they have been taken captive, and repent, and plead with you in the land of their captors, saying, 'We have sinned, and have done wrong; we have acted wickedly'; 48 if they repent with all their heart and soul in the land of their enemies, who took them captive, and pray to you toward their land, which you gave to their ancestors, the city that you have chosen, and the house that I have built for your name; 49 then hear in heaven your dwelling place their prayer and their plea, maintain their cause 50 and forgive your people who have sinned against you, and all their transgressions that they have committed against you; and grant them compassion in the sight of their captors, so that they may have compassion on them 51 (for they are your people and heritage, which you brought out of Egypt, from the midst of the iron-smelter). 52 Let your eyes be open to the plea of your servant, and to the plea of your people Israel, listening to them whenever they call to you. 53 For you have separated them from among all the peoples of the earth, to be your heritage, just as you promised through Moses, your servant, when you brought our ancestors out of Egypt, O Lord GOD."

Solomon Blesses the Assembly
(2 Chr 6.40–42)

54 Now when Solomon finished offering all this prayer and this plea to the LORD, he arose from facing the altar of the LORD, where he had knelt with hands outstretched toward heaven; 55 he stood and blessed all the assembly of Israel with a loud voice:

56 "Blessed be the LORD, who has given rest to his people Israel according to all that he promised; not one word has failed of all his good promise, which he spoke through his servant Moses. 57 The LORD our God be with us, as he was with our ancestors; may he not leave us or abandon us, 58 but incline our hearts to him, to walk in all his ways,

---

m Or *when you answer*   *n* Gk Syr: Heb *in the land*

and to keep his commandments, his statutes, and his ordinances, which he commanded our ancestors. ⁵⁹ Let these words of mine, with which I pleaded before the LORD, be near to the LORD our God day and night, and may he maintain the cause of his servant and the cause of his people Israel, as each day requires; ⁶⁰ so that all the peoples of the earth may know that the LORD is God; there is no other. ⁶¹ Therefore devote yourselves completely to the LORD our God, walking in his statutes and keeping his commandments, as at this day."

Solomon Offers Sacrifices
(2 Chr 7.4–11)

62 Then the king, and all Israel with him, offered sacrifice before the LORD. ⁶³ Solomon offered as sacrifices of well-being to the LORD twenty-two thousand oxen and one hundred twenty thousand sheep. So the king and all the people of Israel dedicated the house of the LORD. ⁶⁴ The same day the king consecrated the middle of the court that was in front of the house of the LORD; for there he offered the burnt offerings and the grain offerings and the fat pieces of the sacrifices of well-being, because the bronze altar that was before the LORD was too small to receive the burnt offerings and the grain offerings and the fat pieces of the sacrifices of well-being.

65 So Solomon held the festival at that time, and all Israel with him—a great assembly, people from Lēʹboʹ-hāʹmath to the Wadi of Egypt—before the LORD our God, seven days.ᵒ ⁶⁶ On the eighth day he sent the people away; and they blessed the king, and went to their tents, joyful and in good spirits because of all the goodness that the LORD had shown to his servant David and to his people Israel.

God Appears Again to Solomon
(2 Chr 7.11–22)

When Solomon had finished building the house of the LORD and the king's house and all that Solomon desired to build, ² the LORD appeared to Solomon a second time, as he had appeared to him at Gibʹeʹ·on. ³ The LORD said to him, "I have heard your prayer and your plea, which you made before me; I have consecrated this house that you have built, and put my name there forever; my eyes and my heart will be there for all time. ⁴ As for you, if you will walk before me, as David your father walked, with integrity of heart and uprightness, doing according to all that I have commanded you, and keeping my statutes and my ordinances, ⁵ then I will establish your royal throne over Israel forever, as I promised your father David, saying,

'There shall not fail you a successor on the throne of Israel.'

6 "If you turn aside from following me, you or your children, and do not keep my commandments and my statutes that I have set before you, but go and serve other gods and worship them,

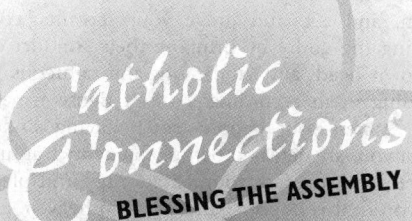

Catholic Connections

BLESSING THE ASSEMBLY

The *assembly* is a phrase used to describe people gathered to pray together. Think of how the assembly is blessed at the end of Mass. With raised hands, the priest speaks with words similar to Solomon's in 1 Kings 8.56–61. The people are sent forth to know God's love and to do what God wants.

Let us praise God who loves us, and let us go in peace to love and serve God and one another.

▶ 1 Kings 8.56–61

⁷ then I will cut Israel off from the land that I have given them; and the house that I have consecrated for my name I will cast out of my sight; and Israel will become a proverb and a taunt among all peoples. ⁸ This house will become a heap of ruins;ᵖ everyone passing by it will be astonished, and will hiss; and they will say, 'Why has the LORD done such a thing to this land and to this house?' ⁹ Then they will say, 'Because they have forsaken the LORD their God, who brought their ancestors out of the land of Egypt, and embraced other gods, worshiping them and serving them; therefore the LORD has brought this disaster upon them.' "

10 At the end of twenty years, in which Solomon had built the two houses, the house of the LORD and the king's house, ¹¹ King Hiram of Tȳre having supplied Solomon with cedar and cypress timber and gold, as much as he desired, King Solomon gave to Hiram twenty cities in the land of

---

ᵒ Compare Gk: Heb *seven days and seven days, fourteen days*
ᵖ Syr Old Latin: Heb *will become high*

Galilee. [12] But when Hiram came from Tyre to see the cities that Solomon had given him, they did not please him. [13] Therefore he said, "What kind of cities are these that you have given me, my brother?" So they are called the land of Ca'bul[q] to this day. [14] But Hiram had sent to the king one hundred twenty talents of gold.

Other Acts of Solomon
(2 Chr 8.3–16)

15 This is the account of the forced labor that King Solomon conscripted to build the house of the LORD and his own house, the Mil'lo and the wall of Jerusalem, Ha'zor, Me•gid'do, Ge'zer [16] (Pharaoh king of Egypt had gone up and captured Ge'zer and burned it down, had killed the Ca'naan•ites who lived in the city, and had given it as dowry to his daughter, Solomon's wife; [17] so Solomon rebuilt Ge'zer), Lower Beth-ho'ron, [18] Ba'a•lath, Ta'mar in the wilderness, within the land, [19] as well as all of Solomon's storage cities, the cities for his chariots, the cities for his cavalry, and whatever Solomon desired to build, in Jerusalem, in Lebanon, and in all the land of his dominion. [20] All the people who were left of the Am'o•rites, the Hit'tites, the Per'iz•zites, the Hi'vites, and the Jeb'u•sites, who were not of the people of Israel— [21] their descendants who were still left in the land, whom the Israelites were unable to destroy completely—these Solomon conscripted for slave labor, and so they are to this day. [22] But of the Israelites Solomon made no slaves; they were the soldiers, they were his officials, his commanders, his captains, and the commanders of his chariotry and cavalry.

23 These were the chief officers who were over Solomon's work: five hundred fifty, who had charge of the people who carried on the work.

24 But Pharaoh's daughter went up from the city of David to her own house that Solomon had built for her; then he built the Mil'lo.

25 Three times a year Solomon used to offer up burnt offerings and sacrifices of well-being on the altar that he built for the LORD, offering incense[r] before the LORD. So he completed the house.

Solomon's Commercial Activity
(2 Chr 8.17–18)

26 King Solomon built a fleet of ships at E'zi-on-ge'ber, which is near E'loth on the shore of the Red Sea,[s] in the land of E'dom. [27] Hiram sent his servants with the fleet, sailors who were familiar with the sea, together with the servants of Solomon. [28] They went to O'phir, and imported from

there four hundred twenty talents of gold, which they delivered to King Solomon.

Visit of the Queen of Sheba
(2 Chr 9.1–28)

10 When the queen of She'ba heard of the fame of Solomon (fame due to[t] the name of the LORD), she came to test him with hard questions. [2] She came to Jerusalem with a very great retinue, with camels bearing spices, and very much gold, and precious stones; and when she came to Solomon, she told him all that was on her mind. [3] Solomon answered all her questions; there was nothing hidden from the king that he could not explain to her. [4] When the queen of She'ba had observed all the wisdom of Solomon, the house that he had built, [5] the food of his table, the seating of his officials, and the attendance of his servants, their clothing, his valets, and his burnt offerings that he offered at the house of the LORD, there was no more spirit in her.

6 So she said to the king, "The report was true that I heard in my own land of your accomplishments and of your wisdom, [7] but I did not believe the reports until I came and my own eyes had seen it. Not even half had been told me; your wisdom and prosperity far surpass the report that I had heard. [8] Happy are your wives![u] Happy are these your servants, who continually attend you and hear your wisdom! [9] Blessed be the LORD your God, who has delighted in you and set you on the throne of Israel! Because the LORD loved Israel forever, he has made you king to execute justice and righteousness." [10] Then she gave the king one hundred twenty talents of gold, a great quantity of spices, and precious stones; never again did spices come in such quantity as that which the queen of She'ba gave to King Solomon.

11 Moreover, the fleet of Hiram, which carried gold from O'phir, brought from O'phir a great quantity of almug wood and precious stones. [12] From the almug wood the king made supports for the house of the LORD, and for the king's house, lyres also and harps for the singers; no such almug wood has come or been seen to this day.

13 Meanwhile King Solomon gave to the queen of She'ba every desire that she expressed, as well as what he gave her out of Solomon's royal bounty. Then she returned to her own land, with her servants.

14 The weight of gold that came to Solomon in one year was six hundred sixty-six talents of

---

q Perhaps meaning *a land good for nothing*   *r* Gk: Heb *offering incense with it that was*   *s* Or *Sea of Reeds*   *t* Meaning of Heb uncertain   *u* Gk Syr: Heb *men* gold, 15 besides that which came from the traders and from the business of the merchants, and from all the kings of Arabia and the governors of the land. 16 King Solomon made two hundred large shields of beaten gold; six hundred shekels of gold went into each large shield. 17 He made three hundred shields of beaten gold; three minas of gold went into each shield; and the king put them in the House of the Forest of Lebanon. 18 The king also made a great ivory throne, and overlaid it with the finest gold. 19 The throne had six steps. The top of the throne was rounded in the back, and on each side of the seat were arm rests and two lions standing beside the arm rests, 20 while twelve lions were standing, one on each end of a step on the six steps. Nothing like it was ever made in any kingdom. 21 All King Solomon's drinking vessels were of gold, and all the vessels of the House of the Forest of Lebanon were of pure gold; none were of silver—it was not considered as anything in the days of Solomon. 22 For the king had a fleet of ships of Tar'shish at sea with the fleet of Hiram. Once every three years the fleet of ships of Tar'shish used to come bringing gold, silver, ivory, apes, and peacocks.^v

23 Thus King Solomon excelled all the kings of the earth in riches and in wisdom. 24 The whole earth sought the presence of Solomon to hear his wisdom, which God had put into his mind. 25 Every one of them brought a present, objects of silver and gold, garments, weaponry, spices, horses, and mules, so much year by year.

26 Solomon gathered together chariots and horses; he had fourteen hundred chariots and twelve thousand horses, which he stationed in the chariot cities and with the king in Jerusalem. 27 The king made silver as common in Jerusalem as stones, and he made cedars as numerous as the sycamores of the She·phē'lah. 28 Solomon's import of horses was from Egypt and Kū'e, and the king's traders received them from Kū'e at a price. 29 A chariot could be imported from Egypt for six hundred shekels of silver, and a horse for one hundred fifty; so through the king's traders they were exported to all the kings of the Hit'tītes and the kings of Ar'am.

Solomon's Errors

King Solomon loved many foreign women along with the daughter of Pharaoh: Mō'ab·īte, Am'mon·īte, E'dom·īte, Sī·dō'ni·an, and Hit'tīte women, 2 from the nations concerning which the LORD had said to the Israelites, "You shall not enter into marriage with them, neither shall they with you; for they will surely incline your heart to follow their gods"; Solomon clung to these in love.

3 Among his wives were seven hundred princesses and three hundred concubines; and his wives turned away his heart. 4 For when Solomon was old, his wives turned away his heart after other gods; and his heart was not true to the LORD his God, as was the heart of his father David. 5 For Solomon followed As·tar'tē the goddess of the Sī·dō'ni·ans, and Mil'com the abomination of the Am'mon·ites. 6 So Solomon did what was evil in the sight of the LORD, and did not completely follow the LORD, as his father David had done. 7 Then Solomon built a high place for Chē'mosh the abomination of Mō'ab, and for Mō'lech the abomination of the Am'mon·ites, on the mountain

PRAY IT!
Solomon's Sin

Sometimes, when we think we are strongest, we are actually weakest. Solomon replaces his poverty of spirit with pride (see 1 Kings 3.4–14). He seems to believe that he is strong enough to go against God's command not to take foreign wives and that he can withstand the influence of their foreign gods. But Solomon falls into the sin of idolatry (worshiping other gods), breaking the Covenant.

Have you ever considered doing something that you knew was wrong? Did you tell yourself, "It won't hurt to do it just this once"? Maybe that is what Solomon said when he took his first foreign wife.

In your prayer time, reflect or journal on the following questions:
- What takes your attention away from God?
- Have you ever used the excuse, "I'm strong enough to handle this," to lead you in doing something wrong?
- Pray Ps 86.11 to end your prayer.

▶ 1 Kings 11.1–8

east of Jerusalem. 8 He did the same for all his foreign wives, who offered incense and sacrificed to their gods.

9 Then the LORD was angry with Solomon, because his heart had turned away from the LORD, the God of Israel, who had appeared to him twice,

^v Or baboons

¹⁰ and had commanded him concerning this matter, that he should not follow other gods; but he did not observe what the LORD commanded. ¹¹ Therefore the LORD said to Solomon, "Since this has been your mind and you have not kept my covenant and my statutes that I have commanded you, I will surely tear the kingdom from you and give it to your servant. ¹² Yet for the sake of your father David I will not do it in your lifetime; I will tear it out of the hand of your son. ¹³ I will not, however, tear away the entire kingdom; I will give one tribe to your son, for the sake of my servant David and for the sake of Jerusalem, which I have chosen."

Adversaries of Solomon

14 Then the LORD raised up an adversary against Solomon, Hă′dad the Ē′dom•īte; he was of the royal house in Ē′dom. ¹⁵ For when David was in Ē′dom, and Jō′ab the commander of the army went up to bury the dead, he killed every male in Ē′dom ¹⁶ (for Jō′ab and all Israel remained there six months, until he had eliminated every male in Ē′dom); ¹⁷ but Hă′dad fled to Egypt with some Ē′dom•ītes who were servants of his father. He was a young boy at that time. ¹⁸ They set out from Mĭd′i•an and came to Par′an; they took people with them from Par′an and came to Egypt, to Pharaoh king of Egypt, who gave him a house, assigned him an allowance of food, and gave him land. ¹⁹ Hă′dad found great favor in the sight of Pharaoh, so that he gave him his sister-in-law for a wife, the sister of Queen Tah′pe•nēs. ²⁰ The sister of Tah′pe•nēs gave birth by him to his son Gĕ•nū′bath, whom Tah′pe•nēs weaned in Pharaoh's house; Gĕ-nū′bath was in Pharaoh's house among the children of Pharaoh. ²¹ When Hă′dad heard in Egypt that David slept with his ancestors and that Jō′ab the commander of the army was dead, Hă′dad said to Pharaoh, "Let me depart, that I may go to my own country." ²² But Pharaoh said to him, "What do you lack with me that you now seek to go to your own country?" And he said, "No, do let me go."

23 God raised up another adversary against Solomon,^w Rē′zon son of Ĕ•lī′a•da, who had fled from his master, King Hăd•a•dē′zer of Zō′bah. ²⁴ He gathered followers around him and became leader of a marauding band, after the slaughter by David; they went to Damascus, settled there, and made him king in Damascus. ²⁵ He was an adversary of Israel all the days of Solomon, making trouble as Hă′dad did; he despised Israel and reigned over Ar′am.

Jeroboam's Rebellion

26 Jer•o•bō′am son of Nē′bat, an Ē′phra•im•īte of Zer′e•dah, a servant of Solomon, whose mother's name was Ze•rū′ah, a widow, rebelled against the king. ²⁷ The following was the reason he rebelled against the king. Solomon built the Mil′lō, and closed up the gap in the wall^x of the city of his father David. ²⁸ The man Jer•o•bō′am was very able, and when Solomon saw that the young man was industrious he gave him charge over all the forced labor of the house of Joseph. ²⁹ About that time, when Jer•o•bō′am was leaving Jerusalem, the prophet A•hī′jah the Shī′lo•nīte found him on the road. A•hī′jah had clothed himself with a new garment. The two of them were alone in the open country ³⁰ when A•hī′jah laid hold of the new garment he was wearing and tore it into twelve pieces. ³¹ He then said to Jer•o•bō′am: Take for yourself ten pieces; for thus says the LORD, the God of Israel, "See, I am about to tear the kingdom from the hand of Solomon, and will give you ten tribes. ³² One tribe will remain his, for the sake of my servant David and for the sake of Jerusalem, the city that I have chosen out of all the tribes of Israel. ³³ This is because he has^y forsaken me, worshiped As•tar′tē the goddess of the Sī•dō′ni•ans, Chĕ′mosh the god of Mō′ab, and Mil′com the god of the Am′mon•ītes, and has^y not walked in my ways, doing what is right in my sight and keeping my statutes and my ordinances, as his father David did. ³⁴ Nevertheless I will not take the whole kingdom away from him but will make him ruler all the days of his life, for the sake of my servant David whom I chose and who did keep my commandments and my statutes; ³⁵ but I will take the kingdom away from his son and give it to you—that is, the ten tribes. ³⁶ Yet to his son I will give one tribe, so that my servant David may always have a lamp before me in Jerusalem, the city where I have chosen to put my name. ³⁷ I will take you, and you shall reign over all that your soul desires; you shall be king over Israel. ³⁸ If you will listen to all that I command you, walk in my ways, and do what is right in my sight by keeping my statutes and my commandments, as David my servant did, I will be with you, and will build you an enduring house, as I built for David, and I will give Israel to you. ³⁹ For this reason I will punish the descendants of David, but not forever." ⁴⁰ Solomon sought therefore to kill Jer•o•bō′am; but Jer•o•bō′am promptly fled to Egypt, to King Shī′shak of Egypt, and remained in Egypt until the death of Solomon.

---

w Heb *him*   x Heb lacks *in the wall*   y Gk Syr Vg: Heb *they have*

Death of Solomon
(2 Chr 9.29–31)

41 Now the rest of the acts of Solomon, all that he did as well as his wisdom, are they not written in the Book of the Acts of Solomon? 42 The time that Solomon reigned in Jerusalem over all Israel was forty years. 43 Solomon slept with his ancestors and was buried in the city of his father David; and his son Rĕ·ho·bō′am succeeded him.

The Northern Tribes Secede
(2 Chr 10.1–19)

Rĕ·ho·bō′am went to Shĕ′chem, for all Israel had come to Shĕ′chem to make him king. 2 When Jer·o·bō′am son of Nĕ′bat heard of it (for he was still in Egypt, where he had fled from King Solomon), then Jer·o·bō′am returned from z Egypt. 3 And they sent and called him; and Jer·o·bō′am and all the assembly of Israel came and said to Rĕ·ho·bō′am, 4 "Your father made our yoke heavy. Now therefore lighten the hard service of your father and his heavy yoke that he placed on us, and we will serve you." 5 He said to them, "Go away for three days, then come again to me." So the people went away.

6 Then King Rĕ·ho·bō′am took counsel with the older men who had attended his father Solomon while he was still alive, saying, "How do you advise me to answer this people?" 7 They answered him, "If you will be a servant to this people today and serve them, and speak good words to them when you answer them, then they will be your servants forever." 8 But he disregarded the advice that the older men gave him, and consulted with the young men who had grown up with him and now attended him. 9 He said to them, "What do you advise that we answer this people who have said to me, 'Lighten the yoke that your father put on us'?" 10 The young men who had grown up with him said to him, "Thus you should say to this people who spoke to you, 'Your father made our yoke heavy, but you must lighten it for us'; thus you should say to them, 'My little finger is thicker than my father's loins. 11 Now, whereas my father laid on you a heavy yoke, I will add to your yoke. My father disciplined you with whips, but I will discipline you with scorpions.' "

12 So Jer·o·bō′am and all the people came to Rĕ·ho·bō′am the third day, as the king had said, "Come to me again the third day." 13 The king answered the people harshly. He disregarded the advice that the older men had given him 14 and spoke to them according to the advice of the young men, "My father made your yoke heavy, but I will add to your yoke; my father disciplined

z Gk Vg Compare 2 Chr 10.2: Heb *lived in*

?did you KNOW?

The Kingdom of Israel Splits

When the people of Israel first came to settle in Canaan, they organized into twelve tribes, ruled by chieftains, that supported and protected one another. As Israel grew in size, it was necessary to have one central ruler who would unite the tribes into one nation. Saul was the first king of this united Israel. David followed Saul and expanded the kingdom's territory. David's son Solomon continued ruling over the expanded kingdom, and engaged in expensive building projects.

At Solomon's death, many Israelites wanted a less demanding king. They had suffered under the burden of heavy taxes and forced labor. When Solomon's son Rehoboam refused to make any changes (1 Kings 12.11), ten of the northern tribes pulled away and placed their own king, Jeroboam, on the throne. The northern kingdom was called Israel. The southern kingdom, composed of two tribes, was called Judah (see map 3, "The Kingdom Years"). The kingdom was now split in two, and it was never again reunited.

Saul (1020 B.C.)
|
David (1000 B.C.)
|
Solomon (961 B.C.)
|
Kingdom splits
(931 B.C.)

JUDAH (south)	ISRAEL (north)
Capital: Jerusalem	Capital: Samaria
Twenty kings	Twenty kings
Falls to Babylonians (587 B.C.)	Falls to Assyrians (721 B.C.)
Exile to Babylon	Exile to Assyria

▶ 1 Kings 12.1–19

you with whips, but I will discipline you with scorpions." ¹⁵ So the king did not listen to the people, because it was a turn of affairs brought about by the LORD that he might fulfill his word, which the LORD had spoken by A•hiʹjah the Shiʹlo•nīte to Jer•o•boʹam son of Neʹbat.

16 When all Israel saw that the king would not listen to them, the people answered the king,

"What share do we have in David?
   We have no inheritance in the son of
      Jesse.
To your tents, O Israel!
   Look now to your own house, O David."

So Israel went away to their tents. ¹⁷ But Re•ho•boʹam reigned over the Israelites who were living in the towns of Judah. ¹⁸ When King Re•ho•boʹam sent A•dorʹam, who was taskmaster over the forced labor, all Israel stoned him to death. King Re•ho•boʹam then hurriedly mounted his chariot to flee to Jerusalem. ¹⁹ So Israel has been in rebellion against the house of David to this day.

First Dynasty: Jeroboam Reigns over Israel
(2 Chr 11.1–4)

20 When all Israel heard that Jer•o•boʹam had returned, they sent and called him to the assembly and made him king over all Israel. There was no one who followed the house of David, except the tribe of Judah alone.

21 When Re•ho•boʹam came to Jerusalem, he assembled all the house of Judah and the tribe of Benjamin, one hundred eighty thousand chosen troops to fight against the house of Israel, to restore the kingdom to Re•ho•boʹam son of Solomon. ²² But the word of God came to She•maiʹah the man of God: ²³ Say to King Re•ho•boʹam of Judah, son of Solomon, and to all the house of Judah and Benjamin, and to the rest of the people, ²⁴ "Thus says the LORD, You shall not go up or fight against your kindred the people of Israel. Let everyone go home, for this thing is from me." So they heeded the word of the LORD and went home again, according to the word of the LORD.

Jeroboam's Golden Calves

25 Then Jer•o•boʹam built Sheʹchem in the hill country of Eʹphra•im, and resided there; he went out from there and built Pe•nuʹel. ²⁶ Then Jer•o•boʹam said to himself, "Now the kingdom may well revert to the house of David. ²⁷ If this people continues to go up to offer sacrifices in the house of the LORD at Jerusalem, the heart of this people will turn again to their master, King Re•ho•boʹam of Judah; they will kill me and return to King Re•ho-

boʹam of Judah." ²⁸ So the king took counsel, and made two calves of gold. He said to the people,ᵃ "You have gone up to Jerusalem long enough. Here are your gods, O Israel, who brought you up out of the land of Egypt." ²⁹ He set one in Bethʹel, and the other he put in Dan. ³⁰ And this thing became a sin, for the people went to worship before the one at Bethʹel and before the other as far as Dan.ᵇ ³¹ He also made housesᶜ on high places, and appointed priests from among all the people, who were not Leʹvītes. ³² Jer•o•boʹam appointed a festival on the fifteenth day of the eighth month like the festival that was in Judah, and he offered sacrifices on the altar; so he did in Bethʹel, sacrificing to the calves that he had made. And he placed in Bethʹel the priests of the high places that he had made. ³³ He went up to the altar that he had made in Bethʹel on the fifteenth day in the eighth month, in the month that he alone had devised; he appointed a festival for the people of Israel, and he went up to the altar to offer incense.

A Man of God from Judah

While Jer•o•boʹam was standing by the altar to offer incense, a man of God came out of Judah by the word of the LORD to Bethʹel ² and proclaimed against the altar by the word of the LORD, and said, "O altar, altar, thus says the LORD: 'A son shall be born to the house of David, Jō•sīʹah by name; and he shall sacrifice on you the priests of the high places who offer incense on you, and human bones shall be burned on you.' " ³ He gave a sign the same day, saying, "This is the sign that the LORD has spoken: 'The altar shall be torn down, and the ashes that are on it shall be poured out.' " ⁴ When the king heard what the man of God cried out against the altar at Bethʹel, Jer•o•boʹam stretched out his hand from the altar, saying, "Seize him!" But the hand that he stretched out against him withered so that he could not draw it back to himself. ⁵ The altar also was torn down, and the ashes poured out from the altar, according to the sign that the man of God had given by the word of the LORD. ⁶ The king said to the man of God, "Entreat now the favor of the LORD your God, and pray for me, so that my hand may be restored to me." So the man of God entreated the LORD; and the king's hand was restored to him, and became as it was before. ⁷ Then the king said to the man of God, "Come home with me and dine, and I will give you a gift." ⁸ But the man of God said to the king, "If you give me half your kingdom, I will not go in with you; nor will I eat food or drink water

---

ᵃ Gk: Heb *to them*   ᵇ Compare Gk: Heb *went to the one as far as Dan*   ᶜ Gk Vg Compare 13.32: Heb *a house*

in this place. ⁹For thus I was commanded by the word of the LORD: You shall not eat food, or drink water, or return by the way that you came." ¹⁰So he went another way, and did not return by the way that he had come to Beth'el.

11 Now there lived an old prophet in Beth'el. One of his sons came and told him all that the man of God had done that day in Beth'el; the words also that he had spoken to the king, they told to their father. ¹²Their father said to them, "Which way did he go?" And his sons showed him the way that the man of God who came from Judah had gone. ¹³Then he said to his sons, "Saddle a donkey for me." So they saddled a donkey for him, and he mounted it. ¹⁴He went after the man of God, and found him sitting under an oak tree. He said to him, "Are you the man of God who came from Judah?" He answered, "I am." ¹⁵Then he said to him, "Come home with me and eat some food." ¹⁶But he said, "I cannot return with you, or go in with you; nor will I eat food or drink water with you in this place; ¹⁷for it was said to me by the word of the LORD: You shall not eat food or drink water there, or return by the way that you came." ¹⁸Then the other*d* said to him, "I also am a prophet as you are, and an angel spoke to me by the word of the LORD: Bring him back with you into your house so that he may eat food and drink water." But he was deceiving him. ¹⁹Then the man of God*d* went back with him, and ate food and drank water in his house.

20 As they were sitting at the table, the word of the LORD came to the prophet who had brought him back; ²¹and he proclaimed to the man of God who came from Judah, "Thus says the LORD: Because you have disobeyed the word of the LORD, and have not kept the commandment that the LORD your God commanded you, ²²but have come back and have eaten food and drunk water in the place of which he said to you, 'Eat no food, and drink no water,' your body shall not come to your ancestral tomb." ²³After the man of God*d* had eaten food and had drunk, they saddled for him a donkey belonging to the prophet who had brought him back. ²⁴Then as he went away, a lion met him on the road and killed him. His body was thrown in the road, and the donkey stood beside it; the lion also stood beside the body. ²⁵People passed by and saw the body thrown in the road, with the lion standing by the body. And they came and told it in the town where the old prophet lived.

26 When the prophet who had brought him back from the way heard of it, he said, "It is the man of God who disobeyed the word of the LORD; therefore the LORD has given him to the lion, which has torn him and killed him according to

the word that the LORD spoke to him." ²⁷Then he said to his sons, "Saddle a donkey for me." So they saddled one, ²⁸and he went and found the body thrown in the road, with the donkey and the lion standing beside the body. The lion had not eaten the body or attacked the donkey. ²⁹The prophet took up the body of the man of God, laid it on the donkey, and brought it back to the city,*e* to mourn and to bury him. ³⁰He laid the body in his own grave; and they mourned over him, saying, "Alas, my brother!" ³¹After he had buried him, he said to his sons, "When I die, bury me in the grave in which the man of God is buried; lay my bones beside his bones. ³²For the saying that he proclaimed by the word of the LORD against the altar in Beth'el, and against all the houses of the high places that are in the cities of Sa·mar'i·a, shall surely come to pass."

33 Even after this event Jer·o·bo'am did not turn from his evil way, but made priests for the high places again from among all the people; any who wanted to be priests he consecrated for the high places. ³⁴This matter became sin to the house of Jer·o·bo'am, so as to cut it off and to destroy it from the face of the earth.

Judgment on the House of Jeroboam

At that time A·bi'jah son of Jer·o·bo'am fell sick. ²Jer·o·bo'am said to his wife, "Go, disguise yourself, so that it will not be known that you are the wife of Jer·o·bo'am, and go to Shi'loh; for the prophet A·hi'jah is there, who said of me that I should be king over this people. ³Take with you ten loaves, some cakes, and a jar of honey, and go to him; he will tell you what shall happen to the child."

4 Jer·o·bo'am's wife did so; she set out and went to Shi'loh, and came to the house of A·hi'jah. Now A·hi'jah could not see, for his eyes were dim because of his age. ⁵But the LORD said to A·hi'jah, "The wife of Jer·o·bo'am is coming to inquire of you concerning her son; for he is sick. Thus and thus you shall say to her."

When she came, she pretended to be another woman. ⁶But when A·hi'jah heard the sound of her feet, as she came in at the door, he said, "Come in, wife of Jer·o·bo'am; why do you pretend to be another? For I am charged with heavy tidings for you. ⁷Go, tell Jer·o·bo'am, 'Thus says the LORD, the God of Israel: Because I exalted you from among the people, made you leader over my people Israel, ⁸and tore the kingdom away from the house of David to give it to you; yet you have not been like my servant David, who kept my command-

d Heb *he*   *e* Gk: Heb *he came to the town of the old prophet*

ments and followed me with all his heart, doing only that which was right in my sight, [9]but you have done evil above all those who were before you and have gone and made for yourself other gods, and cast images, provoking me to anger, and have thrust me behind your back; [10]therefore, I will bring evil upon the house of Jer·o·bo′am. I will cut off from Jer·o·bo′am every male, both bond and free in Israel, and will consume the house of Jer·o·bo′am, just as one burns up dung until it is all gone. [11]Anyone belonging to Jer·o·bo′am who dies in the city, the dogs shall eat; and anyone who dies in the open country, the birds of the air shall eat; for the LORD has spoken.' [12]Therefore set out, go to your house. When your feet enter the city, the child shall die. [13]All Israel shall mourn for him and bury him; for he alone of Jer·o·bo′am's family shall come to the grave, because in him there is found something pleasing to the LORD, the God of Israel, in the house of Jer·o·bo′am. [14]Moreover the LORD will raise up for himself a king over Israel, who shall cut off the house of Jer·o·bo′am today, even right now! [f]

[15] "The LORD will strike Israel, as a reed is shaken in the water; he will root up Israel out of this good land that he gave to their ancestors, and scatter them beyond the Euphrates, because they have made their sacred poles, [g] provoking the LORD to anger. [16]He will give Israel up because of the sins of Jer·o·bo′am, which he sinned and which he caused Israel to commit."

[17] Then Jer·o·bo′am's wife got up and went away, and she came to Tir′zah. As she came to the threshold of the house, the child died. [18]All Israel buried him and mourned for him, according to the word of the LORD, which he spoke by his servant the prophet A·hi′jah.

Death of Jeroboam

[19] Now the rest of the acts of Jer·o·bo′am, how he warred and how he reigned, are written in the Book of the Annals of the Kings of Israel. [20]The time that Jer·o·bo′am reigned was twenty-two years; then he slept with his ancestors, and his son Na′dab succeeded him.

Rehoboam Reigns over Judah:
(2 Chr 11.5—12.16)

[21] Now Re·ho·bo′am son of Solomon reigned in Judah. Re·ho·bo′am was forty-one years old when he began to reign, and he reigned seventeen years in Jerusalem, the city that the LORD had chosen out of all the tribes of Israel, to put his name there. His mother's name was Na′a·mah the Am′mon·ite. [22]Judah did what was evil in the sight of the LORD; they provoked him to jealousy with their sins that they committed, more than all that their ancestors had done. [23]For they also built for themselves high places, pillars, and sacred poles [g] on every high hill and under every green tree; [24]there were also male temple prostitutes in the land. They committed all the abominations of the nations that the LORD drove out before the people of Israel.

[25] In the fifth year of King Re·ho·bo′am, King Shi′shak of Egypt came up against Jerusalem; [26]he took away the treasures of the house of the LORD and the treasures of the king's house; he took everything. He also took away all the shields of gold that Solomon had made; [27]so King Re·ho·bo′am made shields of bronze instead, and committed them to the hands of the officers of the guard, who kept the door of the king's house. [28]As often as the king went into the house of the LORD, the guard carried them and brought them back to the guardroom.

[29] Now the rest of the acts of Re·ho·bo′am, and all that he did, are they not written in the Book of the Annals of the Kings of Judah? [30]There was war between Re·ho·bo′am and Jer·o·bo′am continually. [31]Re·ho·bo′am slept with his ancestors and was buried with his ancestors in the city of David. His mother's name was Na′a·mah the Am′mon·ite. His son A·bi′jam succeeded him.

Abijam Reigns over Judah:
Idolatry and War
(2 Chr 13.1—14.1)

Now in the eighteenth year of King Jer·o·bo′am son of Ne′bat, A·bi′jam began to reign over Judah. [2]He reigned for three years in Jerusalem. His mother's name was Ma′a·cah daughter of A·bish′a·lom. [3]He committed all the sins that his father did before him; his heart was not true to the LORD his God, like the heart of his father David. [4]Nevertheless for David's sake the LORD his God gave him a lamp in Jerusalem, setting up his son after him, and establishing Jerusalem; [5]because David did what was right in the sight of the LORD, and did not turn aside from anything that he commanded him all the days of his life, except in the matter of U·ri′ah the Hit′tite. [6]The war begun between Re·ho·bo′am and Jer·o·bo′am continued all the days of his life. [7]The rest of the acts of A·bi′jam, and all that he did, are they not written in the Book of the Annals of the Kings of Judah? There was war between A·bi′jam and Jer·o·bo′am. [8]A·bi′jam slept with his ancestors, and they buried him in the city of David. Then his son Asa succeeded him.

---

f Meaning of Heb uncertain　　*g* Heb *Asherim*

Asa Reigns over Judah
(2 Chr 14.1—15.19)

9 In the twentieth year of King Jer•o•bō′am of Israel, Asa began to reign over Judah; 10 he reigned forty-one years in Jerusalem. His mother's name was Mā′a•cah daughter of A•bish′a•lom. 11 Asa did what was right in the sight of the LORD, as his father David had done. 12 He put away the male temple prostitutes out of the land, and removed all the idols that his ancestors had made. 13 He also removed his mother Mā′a•cah from being queen mother, because she had made an abominable image for A•shē′rah; Asa cut down her image and burned it at the Wadi Kid′ron. 14 But the high places were not taken away. Nevertheless the heart of Asa was true to the LORD all his days. 15 He brought into the house of the LORD the votive gifts of his father and his own votive gifts—silver, gold, and utensils.

Alliance with Aram against Israel
(2 Chr 16.1—17.1)

16 There was war between Asa and King Bā′a•sha of Israel all their days. 17 King Bā′a•sha of Israel went up against Judah, and built Rā′mah, to prevent anyone from going out or coming in to King Asa of Judah. 18 Then Asa took all the silver and the gold that were left in the treasures of the house of the LORD and the treasures of the king's house, and gave them into the hands of his servants. King Asa sent them to King Ben-hā′dad son of Tab•rim′-mon son of Hē′zi•on of Ar′am, who resided in Damascus, saying, 19 "Let there be an alliance between me and you, like that between my father and your father: I am sending you a present of silver and gold; go, break your alliance with King Bā′a•sha of Israel, so that he may withdraw from me." 20 Ben-hā′dad listened to King Asa, and sent the commanders of his armies against the cities of Israel. He conquered Ī′jon, Dan, Ā′bel-beth-mā′a•cah, and all Chin′ne•roth, with all the land of Naph′ta•lī. 21 When Bā′a•sha heard of it, he stopped building Rā′mah and lived in Tir′zah. 22 Then King Asa made a proclamation to all Judah, none was exempt: they carried away the stones of Rā′mah and its timber, with which Bā′a•sha had been building; with them King Asa built Gē′ba of Benjamin and Miz′pah. 23 Now the rest of all the acts of Asa, all his power, all that he did, and the cities that he built, are they not written in the Book of the Annals of the Kings of Judah? But in his old age he was diseased in his feet. 24 Then Asa slept with his ancestors, and was buried with his ancestors in the city of his father David; his son Je•hosh′-a•phat succeeded him.

Nadab Reigns over Israel

25 Nā′dab son of Jer•o•bō′am began to reign over Israel in the second year of King Asa of Judah; he reigned over Israel two years. 26 He did what was evil in the sight of the LORD, walking in the way of his ancestor and in the sin that he caused Israel to commit.

27 Bā′a•sha son of A•hī′jah, of the house of Is′-sa•char, conspired against him; and Bā′a•sha struck him down at Gib′be•thon, which belonged to the Phi•lis′tines; for Nā′dab and all Israel were laying siege to Gib′be•thon. 28 So Bā′a•sha killed Nā′dab[h] in the third year of King Asa of Judah, and succeeded him. 29 As soon as he was king, he killed all the house of Jer•o•bō′am; he left to the house of Jer•o•bō′am not one that breathed, until he had destroyed it, according to the word of the LORD that he spoke by his servant A•hī′jah the Shī′lo•nīte— 30 because of the sins of Jer•o•bō′am that he committed and that he caused Israel to commit, and because of the anger to which he provoked the LORD, the God of Israel.

31 Now the rest of the acts of Nā′dab, and all that he did, are they not written in the Book of the Annals of the Kings of Israel? 32 There was war between Asa and King Bā′a•sha of Israel all their days.

Second Dynasty: Baasha
Reigns over Israel

33 In the third year of King Asa of Judah, Bā′a•sha son of A•hī′jah began to reign over all Israel at Tir′zah; he reigned twenty-four years. 34 He did what was evil in the sight of the LORD, walking in the way of Jer•o•bō′am and in the sin that he caused Israel to commit.

16 The word of the LORD came to Jē′hū son of Ha•nā′nī against Bā′a•sha, saying, 2 "Since I exalted you out of the dust and made you leader over my people Israel, and you have walked in the way of Jer•o•bō′am, and have caused my people Israel to sin, provoking me to anger with their sins, 3 therefore, I will consume Bā′a•sha and his house, and I will make your house like the house of Jer•o•bō′am son of Ne′bat. 4 Anyone belonging to Bā′a•sha who dies in the city the dogs shall eat; and anyone of his who dies in the field the birds of the air shall eat."

5 Now the rest of the acts of Bā′a•sha, what he did, and his power, are they not written in the Book of the Annals of the Kings of Israel? 6 Bā′a•sha slept with his ancestors, and was buried at Tir′zah; and his son Ē′lah succeeded him. 7 Moreover the

---

h Heb *him*

word of the LORD came by the prophet Jĕ′hū son of Ha·nā′nī against Bā′a·sha and his house, both because of all the evil that he did in the sight of the LORD, provoking him to anger with the work of his hands, in being like the house of Jer·o·bō′am, and also because he destroyed it.

Elah Reigns over Israel

8 In the twenty-sixth year of King Asa of Judah, Ē′lah son of Bā′a·sha began to reign over Israel in Tir′zah; he reigned two years. 9 But his servant Zim′rī, commander of half his chariots, conspired against him. When he was at Tir′zah, drinking himself drunk in the house of Ar′za, who was in charge of the palace at Tir′zah, 10 Zim′rī came in and struck him down and killed him, in the twenty-seventh year of King Asa of Judah, and succeeded him.

11 When he began to reign, as soon as he had seated himself on his throne, he killed all the house of Bā′a·sha; he did not leave him a single male of his kindred or his friends. 12 Thus Zim′rī destroyed all the house of Bā′a·sha, according to the word of the LORD, which he spoke against Bā′a·sha by the prophet Jĕ′hū— 13 because of all the sins of Bā′a·sha and the sins of his son Ē′lah that they committed, and that they caused Israel to commit, provoking the LORD God of Israel to anger with their idols. 14 Now the rest of the acts of Ē′lah, and all that he did, are they not written in the Book of the Annals of the Kings of Israel?

Third Dynasty: Zimri Reigns over Israel

15 In the twenty-seventh year of King Asa of Judah, Zim′rī reigned seven days in Tir′zah. Now the troops were encamped against Gib′be·thon, which belonged to the Phi·lis′tines, 16 and the troops who were encamped heard it said, "Zim′rī has conspired, and he has killed the king"; therefore all Israel made Om′rī, the commander of the army, king over Israel that day in the camp. 17 So Om′rī went up from Gib′be·thon, and all Israel with him, and they besieged Tir′zah. 18 When Zim′rī saw that the city was taken, he went into the citadel of the king's house; he burned down the king's house over himself with fire, and died— 19 because of the sins that he committed, doing evil in the sight of the LORD, walking in the way of Jer·o·bō′am, and for the sin that he committed, causing Israel to sin. 20 Now the rest of the acts of Zim′rī, and the conspiracy that he made, are they not written in the Book of the Annals of the Kings of Israel?

Fourth Dynasty: Omri Reigns over Israel

21 Then the people of Israel were divided into two parts; half of the people followed Tib′nī son of Gī′nath, to make him king, and half followed Om′rī. 22 But the people who followed Om′rī overcame the people who followed Tib′nī son of Gī′nath; so Tib′nī died, and Om′rī became king. 23 In the thirty-first year of King Asa of Judah, Om′rī began to reign over Israel; he reigned for twelve years, six of them in Tir′zah.

Samaria the New Capital

24 He bought the hill of Sa·mār′i·a from Shĕ′-mer for two talents of silver; he fortified the hill, and called the city that he built, Sa·mār′i·a, after the name of Shĕ′mer, the owner of the hill.

25 Om′rī did what was evil in the sight of the LORD; he did more evil than all who were before him. 26 For he walked in all the way of Jer·o·bō′am son of Nĕ′bat, and in the sins that he caused Israel to commit, provoking the LORD, the God of Israel, to anger by their idols. 27 Now the rest of the acts of Om′rī that he did, and the power that he showed, are they not written in the Book of the Annals of the Kings of Israel? 28 Om′rī slept with his ancestors, and was buried in Sa·mār′i·a; his son Ā′hab succeeded him.

Ahab Reigns over Israel

29 In the thirty-eighth year of King Asa of Judah, Ā′hab son of Om′rī began to reign over Israel; Ā′hab son of Om′rī reigned over Israel in Sa·mār′i·a twenty-two years. 30 Ā′hab son of Om′rī did evil in the sight of the LORD more than all who were before him.

Ahab Marries Jezebel and Worships Baal

31 And as if it had been a light thing for him to walk in the sins of Jer·o·bō′am son of Nĕ′bat, he took as his wife Jez′e·bel daughter of King Eth·bā′al of the Sī·dō′ni·ans, and went and served Bā′al, and worshiped him. 32 He erected an altar for Bā′al in the house of Bā′al, which he built in Sa·mār′i·a. 33 Ā′hab also made a sacred pole.*i* Ā′hab did more to provoke the anger of the LORD, the God of Israel, than had all the kings of Israel who were before him. 34 In his days Hī′el of Beth′el built Jericho; he laid its foundation at the cost of A·bī′ram his first-born, and set up its gates at the cost of his youngest son Sĕ′gub, according to the word of the LORD, which he spoke by Joshua son of Nun.

---

i Heb *Asherah*

Elijah Predicts a Drought

Now E•li′jah the Tish′bite, of Tish′bei in Gil′e•ad, said to A′hab, "As the LORD the God of Israel lives, before whom I stand, there shall be neither dew nor rain these years, except by my word." 2 The word of the LORD came to him, saying, 3 "Go from here and turn eastward, and hide yourself by the Wadi Chē′rith, which is east of the Jordan. 4 You shall drink from the wadi, and I have commanded the ravens to feed you there." 5 So he went and did according to the word of the LORD; he went and lived by the Wadi Chē′rith, which is east of the Jordan. 6 The ravens brought him bread and meat in the morning, and bread and meat in the evening; and he drank from the wadi. 7 But after a while the wadi dried up, because there was no rain in the land.

The Widow of Zarephath

8 Then the word of the LORD came to him, saying, 9 "Go now to Zar′e•phath, which belongs to Si′don, and live there; for I have commanded a widow there to feed you." 10 So he set out and went to Zar′e•phath. When he came to the gate of the town, a widow was there gathering sticks; he called to her and said, "Bring me a little water in a vessel, so that I may drink." 11 As she was going to bring it, he called to her and said, "Bring me a morsel of bread in your hand." 12 But she said, "As the LORD your God lives, I have nothing baked, only a handful of meal in a jar, and a little oil in a jug; I am now gathering a couple of sticks, so that I may go home and prepare it for myself and my son, that we may eat it, and die." 13 E•li′jah said to her, "Do not be afraid; go and do as you have said; but first make me a little cake of it and bring it to me, and afterwards make something for yourself and your son. 14 For thus says the LORD the God of Israel: The jar of meal will not be emptied and the jug of oil will not fail until the day that the LORD sends rain on the earth." 15 She went and did as E•li′jah said, so that she as well as he and her household ate for many days. 16 The jar of meal was not emptied, neither did the jug of oil fail, according to the word of the LORD that he spoke by E•li′jah.

Elijah Revives the Widow's Son

17 After this the son of the woman, the mistress of the house, became ill; his illness was so severe that there was no breath left in him. 18 She then said to E•li′jah, "What have you against me,

_j_ Gk: Heb _of the settlers_

Introducing
►ELIJAH AND ELISHA

You didn't want to mess with Elijah and Elisha. They were take-no-prisoners kinds of prophets. According to 1 Kings, Elijah has 450 prophets of Baal killed after publicly humiliating them (18.40). And when a bunch of boys call Elisha "baldy," they are attacked by bears (2 Kings 2.23–24).

Elijah, whose name means "Yahweh is my God," shows up in the second half of 1 Kings reminding the Israelites that God is their God alone, and that keeping God's Covenant means not worshiping the Canaanite baals (gods). In a dramatic story, he shows the idol-worshiping King Ahab and Queen Jezebel that God is superior to their false gods (1 Kings 18.20–40).

Elijah was recorded as being carried to heaven in a fiery chariot (2 Kings 2.11) as a sign of his greatness, and he was expected to reappear before the "day of the LORD" arrived (Mal 4.5). By New Testament times, Elijah had come to represent the prophets as Moses had come to represent the Law. Referring to Moses and Elijah was a way of summarizing everything that God had revealed before Christ.

Elisha was Elijah's disciple and successor. He plays an important role in the first half of 2 Kings. Elisha's name means "God is salvation." He was a man of wisdom and a miracle worker.

These "tough guys" also had tender hearts. Both miraculously multiplied food for widows (1 Kings 17.16; 2 Kings 4.5), and both brought a dead child back to life (1 Kings 17.22; 2 Kings 4.34). Elijah and Elisha are revered both for their uncompromising faith and their compassion for the "little ones."

1
K
I
N
G
S

O man of God? You have come to me to bring my sin to remembrance, and to cause the death of my son!" ¹⁹ But he said to her, "Give me your son." He took him from her bosom, carried him up into the upper chamber where he was lodging, and laid him on his own bed. ²⁰ He cried out to the LORD, "O LORD my God, have you brought calamity even upon the widow with whom I am staying, by killing her son?" ²¹ Then he stretched himself upon the child three times, and cried out to the LORD, "O LORD my God, let this child's life come into him again." ²² The LORD listened to the voice of E·li′jah; the life of the child came into him again, and he revived. ²³ E·li′jah took the child, brought him down from the upper chamber into the house, and gave him to his mother; then E·li′jah said, "See, your son is alive." ²⁴ So the woman said to E·li′jah, "Now I know that you are a man of God, and that the word of the LORD in your mouth is truth."

Elijah's Message to Ahab

After many days the word of the LORD came to E·li′jah, in the third year of the drought,ᵏ saying, "Go, present yourself to Ā′hab; I will send rain on the earth." ² So E·li′jah went to present himself to Ā′hab. The famine was severe in Sa·mār′i·a. ³ Ā′hab summoned Ō·ba·dī′ah, who was in charge of the palace. (Now Ō·ba·dī′ah revered the LORD greatly; ⁴ when Jez′e·bel was killing off the prophets of the LORD, Ō·ba·dī′ah took a hundred prophets, hid them fifty to a cave, and provided them with bread and water.) ⁵ Then Ā′hab said to Ō·ba·dī′ah, "Go through the land to all the springs of water and to all the wadis; perhaps we may find grass to keep the horses and mules alive, and not lose some of the animals." ⁶ So they divided the land between them to pass through it; Ā′hab went in one direction by himself, and Ō·ba·dī′ah went in another direction by himself.

⁷ As Ō·ba·dī′ah was on the way, E·li′jah met him; Ō·ba·dī′ah recognized him, fell on his face, and said, "Is it you, my lord E·li′jah?" ⁸ He answered him, "It is I. Go, tell your lord that E·li′jah is here." ⁹ And he said, "How have I sinned, that you would hand your servant over to Ā′hab, to kill me? ¹⁰ As the LORD your God lives, there is no nation or kingdom to which my lord has not sent to seek you; and when they would say, 'He is not here,' he would require an oath of the kingdom or nation, that they had not found you. ¹¹ But now you say, 'Go, tell your lord that E·li′jah is here.' ¹² As soon as I have gone from you, the spirit of the LORD will carry you I know not where; so, when I come and tell Ā′hab and he cannot find you, he will kill me, although I your servant have revered the LORD from my youth. ¹³ Has it not been told

my lord what I did when Jez′e·bel killed the prophets of the LORD, how I hid a hundred of the LORD's prophets fifty to a cave, and provided them with bread and water? ¹⁴ Yet now you say, 'Go, tell your lord that E·li′jah is here'; he will surely kill me." ¹⁵ E·li′jah said, "As the LORD of hosts lives, before whom I stand, I will surely show myself to him today." ¹⁶ So Ō·ba·dī′ah went to meet Ā′hab, and told him; and Ā′hab went to meet E·li′jah.

17 When Ā′hab saw E·li′jah, Ā′hab said to him, "Is it you, you troubler of Israel?" ¹⁸ He answered, "I have not troubled Israel; but you have, and your father's house, because you have forsaken the commandments of the LORD and followed the Bā′als. ¹⁹ Now therefore have all Israel assemble for me at Mount Car′mel, with the four hundred fifty prophets of Bā′al and the four hundred prophets of A·shē′rah, who eat at Jez′e·bel's table."

Elijah's Triumph over the Priests of Baal

20 So Ā′hab sent to all the Israelites, and assembled the prophets at Mount Car′mel. ²¹ E·li′jah then came near to all the people, and said, "How long will you go limping with two different opinions? If the LORD is God, follow him; but if Bā′al, then follow him." The people did not answer him a word. ²² Then E·li′jah said to the people, "I, even I only, am left a prophet of the LORD; but Bā′al's prophets number four hundred fifty. ²³ Let two bulls be given to us; let them choose one bull for themselves, cut it in pieces, and lay it on the wood, but put no fire to it; I will prepare the other bull and lay it on the wood, but put no fire to it. ²⁴ Then you call on the name of your god and I will call on the name of the LORD; the god who answers by fire is indeed God." All the people answered, "Well spoken!" ²⁵ Then E·li′jah said to the prophets of Bā′al, "Choose for yourselves one bull and prepare it first, for you are many; then call on the name of your god, but put no fire to it." ²⁶ So they took the bull that was given them, prepared it, and called on the name of Bā′al from morning until noon, crying, "O Bā′al, answer us!" But there was no voice, and no answer. They limped about the altar that they had made. ²⁷ At noon E·li′jah mocked them, saying, "Cry aloud! Surely he is a god; either he is meditating, or he has wandered away, or he is on a journey, or perhaps he is asleep and must be awakened." ²⁸ Then they cried aloud and, as was their custom, they cut themselves with swords and lances until the blood gushed out over them. ²⁹ As midday passed, they raved on until the time of the offering of the oblation, but there was no voice, no answer, and no response.

ᵏ Heb lacks *of the drought*

30 Then E•lī′jah said to all the people, "Come closer to me"; and all the people came closer to him. First he repaired the altar of the LORD that had been thrown down; 31 E•lī′jah took twelve stones, according to the number of the tribes of the sons of Jacob, to whom the word of the LORD came, saying, "Israel shall be your name"; 32 with the stones he built an altar in the name of the LORD. Then he made a trench around the altar, large enough to contain two measures of seed. 33 Next he put the wood in order, cut the bull in pieces, and laid it on the wood. He said, "Fill four jars with water and pour it on the burnt offering and on the wood." 34 Then he said, "Do it a second time"; and they did it a second time. Again he said, "Do it a third time"; and they did it a third time, 35 so that the water ran all around the altar, and filled the trench also with water.

36 At the time of the offering of the oblation, the prophet E•lī′jah came near and said, "O LORD, God of Abraham, Isaac, and Israel, let it be known this day that you are God in Israel, that I am your servant, and that I have done all these things at your bidding. 37 Answer me, O LORD, answer me, so that this people may know that you, O LORD, are God, and that you have turned their hearts back." 38 Then the fire of the LORD fell and consumed the burnt offering, the wood, the stones, and the dust, and even licked up the water that was in the trench. 39 When all the people saw it, they fell on their faces and said, "The LORD indeed is God; the LORD indeed is God." 40 E•lī′jah said to them, "Seize the prophets of Bā′al; do not let one of them escape." Then they seized them; and E•lī′jah brought them down to the Wadi Kī′shon, and killed them there.

The Drought Ends

41 E•lī′jah said to Ā′hab, "Go up, eat and drink; for there is a sound of rushing rain." 42 So Ā′hab went up to eat and to drink. E•lī′jah went up to the top of Car′mel; there he bowed himself down upon the earth and put his face between his knees. 43 He said to his servant, "Go up now, look toward the sea." He went up and looked, and said, "There is nothing." Then he said, "Go again seven times." 44 At the seventh time he said, "Look, a little cloud no bigger than a person's hand is rising out of the sea." Then he said, "Go say to Ā′hab, 'Harness your chariot and go down before the rain stops you.' " 45 In a little while the heavens grew black with clouds and wind; there was a heavy rain. Ā′hab rode off and went to Jez′rē•el. 46 But the hand of the LORD was on E•lī′jah; he girded up his loins and ran in front of Ā′hab to the entrance of Jez′rē•el.

Elijah Flees from Jezebel

Ā′hab told Jez′e•bel all that E•lī′jah had done, and how he had killed all the prophets with the sword. 2 Then Jez′e•bel sent a messenger to E•lī′jah, saying, "So may the gods do to me, and more also, if I do not make your life like the life of one of them by this time tomorrow." 3 Then he was afraid; he got up and fled for his life, and came to Bē′er-shē′ba, which belongs to Judah; he left his servant there.

4 But he himself went a day's journey into the wilderness, and came and sat down under a solitary broom tree. He asked that he might die: "It is enough; now, O LORD, take away my life, for I am no better than my ancestors." 5 Then he lay down under the broom tree and fell asleep. Suddenly an angel touched him and said to him, "Get up and eat." 6 He looked, and there at his head was a cake baked on hot stones, and a jar of water. He ate and drank, and lay down again. 7 The angel of the LORD came a second time, touched him, and said, "Get up and eat, otherwise the journey will be too much for you." 8 He got up, and ate and drank; then he went in the strength of that food forty days and forty nights to Hō′reb the mount of God. 9 At that place he came to a cave, and spent the night there.

Then the word of the LORD came to him, saying, "What are you doing here, E•lī′jah?" 10 He answered, "I have been very zealous for the LORD, the God of hosts; for the Israelites have forsaken your covenant, thrown down your altars, and killed your prophets with the sword. I alone am left, and they are seeking my life, to take it away."

Elijah Meets God at Horeb

11 He said, "Go out and stand on the mountain before the LORD, for the LORD is about to pass by." Now there was a great wind, so strong that it was splitting mountains and breaking rocks in pieces before the LORD, but the LORD was not in the wind; and after the wind an earthquake, but the LORD was not in the earthquake; 12 and after the earthquake a fire, but the LORD was not in the fire; and after the fire a sound of sheer silence. 13 When E•lī′jah heard it, he wrapped his face in his mantle and went out and stood at the entrance of the cave. Then there came a voice to him that said, "What are you doing here, E•lī′jah?" 14 He answered, "I have been very zealous for the LORD, the God of hosts; for the Israelites have forsaken your covenant, thrown down your altars, and killed your prophets with the sword. I alone am left, and they are seeking my life, to take it away." 15 Then the LORD said to him, "Go, return on your way to the wilderness of Damascus; when you arrive, you

shall anoint Haz′a•el as king over Ar′am. ¹⁶Also you shall anoint Jē′hū son of Nim′shī as king over Israel; and you shall anoint E•lī′sha son of Shā′-phat of Ā′bel-me•hō′lah as prophet in your place. ¹⁷Whoever escapes from the sword of Haz′a•el, Jē′hū shall kill; and whoever escapes from the sword of Jē′hū, E•lī′sha shall kill. ¹⁸Yet I will leave seven thousand in Israel, all the knees that have not bowed to Bā′al, and every mouth that has not kissed him."

PRAY IT!
Looking for God

E lijah was told to meet God on the mountain. God's presence could have been in fire, an earthquake, a great wind, but God was in none of these. God was in the stillness of sheer silence.

All of us have a need for God. We might not know it, but it is there: a God-shaped hole in our soul that no one and nothing else can fill. Without God, we will always feel empty.

Sometimes, we look for loud and spectacular things to fill that empty space. We buy expensive clothing or toys. Or we smoke cigarettes, drink alcohol, use other illegal drugs, or have sex without commitment. And we still feel empty.

The irony is that through all this, God is there, in the quiet depths of our heart. We need to be like Elijah—tuning out things that are not God and tuning in to God's presence. Taking quiet time to think and pray is a great start.

▸ 1 Kings 19.9–13

Elisha Becomes Elijah's Disciple

19 So he set out from there, and found E•lī′sha son of Shā′phat, who was plowing. There were twelve yoke of oxen ahead of him, and he was with the twelfth. E•lī′jah passed by him and threw his mantle over him. ²⁰He left the oxen, ran after E•lī′jah, and said, "Let me kiss my father and my mother, and then I will follow you." Then E•lī′jah*l* said to him, "Go back again; for what have I done to you?" ²¹He returned from following him, took the yoke of oxen, and slaughtered them; using the equipment from the oxen, he boiled their flesh,

and gave it to the people, and they ate. Then he set out and followed E•lī′jah, and became his servant.

Ahab's Wars with the Arameans

King Ben-hā′dad of Ar′am gathered all his army together; thirty-two kings were with him, along with horses and chariots. He marched against Sa-mār′i•a, laid siege to it, and attacked it. ²Then he sent messengers into the city to King Ā′hab of Is-rael, and said to him: "Thus says Ben-hā′dad: ³Your silver and gold are mine; your fairest wives and children also are mine." ⁴The king of Israel an-swered, "As you say, my lord, O king, I am yours, and all that I have." ⁵The messengers came again and said: "Thus says Ben-hā′dad: I sent to you, saying, 'Deliver to me your silver and gold, your wives and children'; ⁶nevertheless I will send my servants to you tomorrow about this time, and they shall search your house and the houses of your servants, and lay hands on whatever pleases them,*m* and take it away."

7 Then the king of Israel called all the elders of the land, and said, "Look now! See how this man is seeking trouble; for he sent to me for my wives, my children, my silver, and my gold; and I did not refuse him." ⁸Then all the elders and all the people said to him, "Do not listen or consent." ⁹So he said to the messengers of Ben-hā′dad, "Tell my lord the king: All that you first demanded of your ser-vant I will do; but this thing I cannot do." The messengers left and brought him word again. ¹⁰Ben-hā′dad sent to him and said, "The gods do so to me, and more also, if the dust of Sa•mār′i•a will provide a handful for each of the people who follow me." ¹¹The king of Israel answered, "Tell him: One who puts on armor should not brag like one who takes it off." ¹²When Ben-hā′dad heard this message—now he had been drinking with the kings in the booths—he said to his men, "Take your positions!" And they took their positions against the city.

Prophetic Opposition to Ahab

13 Then a certain prophet came up to King Ā′hab of Israel and said, "Thus says the LORD, Have you seen all this great multitude? Look, I will give it into your hand today; and you shall know that I am the LORD." ¹⁴Ā′hab said, "By whom?" He said, "Thus says the LORD, By the young men who serve the district governors." Then he said, "Who shall begin the battle?" He answered, "You." ¹⁵Then he mustered the young men who served the dis-trict governors, two hundred thirty-two; after them

l Heb *he*   *m* Gk Syr Vg: Heb *you*

he mustered all the people of Israel, seven thousand.

16 They went out at noon, while Ben-hā′dad was drinking himself drunk in the booths, he and the thirty-two kings allied with him. 17 The young men who served the district governors went out first. Ben-hā′dad had sent out scouts,*n* and they reported to him, "Men have come out from Sa-mār′i•a." 18 He said, "If they have come out for peace, take them alive; if they have come out for war, take them alive."

19 But these had already come out of the city: the young men who served the district governors, and the army that followed them. 20 Each killed his man; the Ar•a•mē′ans fled and Israel pursued them, but King Ben-hā′dad of Ar′am escaped on a horse with the cavalry. 21 The king of Israel went out, attacked the horses and chariots, and defeated the Ar•a•mē′ans with a great slaughter.

22 Then the prophet approached the king of Israel and said to him, "Come, strengthen yourself, and consider well what you have to do; for in the spring the king of Ar′am will come up against you."

The Arameans Are Defeated

23 The servants of the king of Ar′am said to him, "Their gods are gods of the hills, and so they were stronger than we; but let us fight against them in the plain, and surely we shall be stronger than they. 24 Also do this: remove the kings, each from his post, and put commanders in place of them; 25 and muster an army like the army that you have lost, horse for horse, and chariot for chariot; then we will fight against them in the plain, and surely we shall be stronger than they." He heeded their voice, and did so.

26 In the spring Ben-hā′dad mustered the Ar•a-mē′ans and went up to Ā′phek to fight against Israel. 27 After the Israelites had been mustered and provisioned, they went out to engage them; the people of Israel encamped opposite them like two little flocks of goats, while the Ar•a•mē′ans filled the country. 28 A man of God approached and said to the king of Israel, "Thus says the LORD: Because the Ar•a•mē′ans have said, 'The LORD is a god of the hills but he is not a god of the valleys,' therefore I will give all this great multitude into your hand, and you shall know that I am the LORD." 29 They encamped opposite one another seven days. Then on the seventh day the battle began; the Israelites killed one hundred thousand Ar•a•mē′an foot soldiers in one day. 30 The rest fled into the city of Ā′phek; and the wall fell on twenty-seven thousand men that were left.

Ben-hā′dad also fled, and entered the city to hide. 31 His servants said to him, "Look, we have heard that the kings of the house of Israel are merciful kings; let us put sackcloth around our waists and ropes on our heads, and go out to the king of Israel; perhaps he will spare your life." 32 So they tied sackcloth around their waists, put ropes on their heads, went to the king of Israel, and said, "Your servant Ben-hā′dad says, 'Please let me live.' " And he said, "Is he still alive? He is my brother." 33 Now the men were watching for an omen; they quickly took it up from him and said, "Yes, Ben-hā′dad is your brother." Then he said, "Go and bring him." So Ben-hā′dad came out to him; and he had him come up into the chariot. 34 Ben-hā′dad*o* said to him, "I will restore the towns that my father took from your father; and you may establish bazaars for yourself in Damascus, as my father did in Sa•mār′i•a." The king of Israel responded,*p* "I will let you go on those terms." So he made a treaty with him and let him go.

A Prophet Condemns Ahab

35 At the command of the LORD a certain member of a company of prophets*q* said to another, "Strike me!" But the man refused to strike him. 36 Then he said to him, "Because you have not obeyed the voice of the LORD, as soon as you have left me, a lion will kill you." And when he had left him, a lion met him and killed him. 37 Then he found another man and said, "Strike me!" So the man hit him, striking and wounding him. 38 Then the prophet departed, and waited for the king along the road, disguising himself with a bandage over his eyes. 39 As the king passed by, he cried to the king and said, "Your servant went out into the thick of the battle; then a soldier turned and brought a man to me, and said, 'Guard this man; if he is missing, your life shall be given for his life, or else you shall pay a talent of silver.' 40 While your servant was busy here and there, he was gone." The king of Israel said to him, "So shall your judgment be; you yourself have decided it." 41 Then he quickly took the bandage away from his eyes. The king of Israel recognized him as one of the prophets. 42 Then he said to him, "Thus says the LORD, 'Because you have let the man go whom I had devoted to destruction, therefore your life shall be for his life, and your people for his people.' " 43 The king of Israel set out toward home, resentful and sullen, and came to Sa•mār′i•a.

---

n Heb lacks *scouts*   *o* Heb *He*   *p* Heb lacks *The king of Israel responded,*   *q* Heb *of the sons of the prophets*

Naboth's Vineyard

Later the following events took place: Nā'both the Jez're·el·īte had a vineyard in Jez're'el, beside the palace of King Ā'hab of Sa·mār'i·a. ² And Ā'hab said to Nā'both, "Give me your vineyard, so that I may have it for a vegetable garden, because it is near my house; I will give you a better vineyard for it; or, if it seems good to you, I will give you its value in money." ³ But Nā'both said to Ā'hab, "The LORD forbid that I should give you my ancestral inheritance." ⁴ Ā'hab went home resentful and sullen because of what Nā'both the Jez're·el·īte had said to him; for he had said, "I will not give you my ancestral inheritance." He lay down on his bed, turned away his face, and would not eat.

5 His wife Jez'e·bel came to him and said, "Why are you so depressed that you will not eat?" ⁶ He said to her, "Because I spoke to Nā'both the Jez're·el·īte and said to him, 'Give me your vineyard for money; or else, if you prefer, I will give you another vineyard for it'; but he answered, 'I will not give you my vineyard.'" ⁷ His wife Jez'e·bel said to him, "Do you now govern Israel? Get up, eat some food, and be cheerful; I will give you the vineyard of Nā'both the Jez're·el·īte."

8 So she wrote letters in Ā'hab's name and sealed them with his seal; she sent the letters to the elders and the nobles who lived with Nā'both in his city. ⁹ She wrote in the letters, "Proclaim a fast, and seat Nā'both at the head of the assembly; ¹⁰ seat two scoundrels opposite him, and have them bring a charge against him, saying, 'You have cursed God and the king.' Then take him out, and stone him to death." ¹¹ The men of his city, the elders and the nobles who lived in his city, did as Jez'e·bel had sent word to them. Just as it was written in the letters that she had sent to them, ¹² they proclaimed a fast and seated Nā'both at the head of the assembly. ¹³ The two scoundrels came in and sat opposite him; and the scoundrels brought a charge against Nā'both, in the presence of the people, saying, "Nā'both cursed God and the king." So they took him outside the city, and stoned him to death. ¹⁴ Then they sent to Jez'e·bel, saying, "Nā'both has been stoned; he is dead."

15 As soon as Jez'e·bel heard that Nā'both had been stoned and was dead, Jez'e·bel said to Ā'hab, "Go, take possession of the vineyard of Nā'both the Jez're·el·īte, which he refused to give you for money; for Nā'both is not alive, but dead." ¹⁶ As soon as Ā'hab heard that Nā'both was dead, Ā'hab set out to go down to the vineyard of Nā'both the Jez're·el·īte, to take possession of it.

Elijah Pronounces God's Sentence

17 Then the word of the LORD came to E·li'jah the Tish'bīte, saying: ¹⁸ Go down to meet King Ā'hab of Israel, who rules^r in Sa·mār'i·a; he is now in the vineyard of Nā'both, where he has gone to take possession. ¹⁹ You shall say to him, "Thus says the LORD: Have you killed, and also taken possession?" You shall say to him, "Thus says the LORD: In the place where dogs licked up the blood of Nā'both, dogs will also lick up your blood."

20 Ā'hab said to E·li'jah, "Have you found me, O my enemy?" He answered, "I have found you. Because you have sold yourself to do what is evil in the sight of the LORD, ²¹ I will bring disaster on you; I will consume you, and will cut off from Ā'hab every male, bond or free, in Israel; ²² and I will make your house like the house of Jer·o·bō'am son of Ne'bat, and like the house of Bā'a·sha son of A·hī'jah, because you have provoked me to anger and have caused Israel to sin. ²³ Also concerning Jez'e·bel the LORD said, 'The dogs shall eat Jez'e·bel within the bounds of Jez're'el.' ²⁴ Anyone belonging to Ā'hab who dies in the city the dogs shall eat; and anyone of his who dies in the open country the birds of the air shall eat."

25 (Indeed, there was no one like Ā'hab, who sold himself to do what was evil in the sight of the LORD, urged on by his wife Jez'e·bel. ²⁶ He acted most abominably in going after idols, as the Am'o·rītes had done, whom the LORD drove out before the Israelites.)

27 When Ā'hab heard those words, he tore his clothes and put sackcloth over his bare flesh; he fasted, lay in the sackcloth, and went about dejectedly. ²⁸ Then the word of the LORD came to E·li'jah the Tish'bīte: ²⁹ "Have you seen how Ā'hab has humbled himself before me? Because he has humbled himself before me, I will not bring the disaster in his days; but in his son's days I will bring the disaster on his house."

Joint Campaign with Judah
against Aram
(2 Chr 18.1–11)

For three years Ar'am and Israel continued without war. ² But in the third year King Je·hosh'a·phat of Judah came down to the king of Israel. ³ The king of Israel said to his servants, "Do you know that Rā'moth-gil'e·ad belongs to us, yet we are doing nothing to take it out of the hand of the king of Ar'am?" ⁴ He said to Je·hosh'a·phat, "Will you go with me to battle at Rā'moth-gil'e·ad?" Je·hosh'a·phat replied to the king of Israel, "I am as you are;

---

r Heb *who is*

my people are your people, my horses are your horses."

5 But Je•hosh´a•phat also said to the king of Israel, "Inquire first for the word of the LORD." 6 Then the king of Israel gathered the prophets together, about four hundred of them, and said to them, "Shall I go to battle against Rā´moth-gil´e•ad, or shall I refrain?" They said, "Go up; for the LORD will give it into the hand of the king." 7 But Je•hosh´a•phat said, "Is there no other prophet of the LORD here of whom we may inquire?" 8 The king of Israel said to Je•hosh´a•phat, "There is still one other by whom we may inquire of the LORD, Mī•cāi´ah son of Im´lah; but I hate him, for he never prophesies anything favorable about me, but only disaster." Je•hosh´a•phat said, "Let the king not say such a thing." 9 Then the king of Israel summoned an officer and said, "Bring quickly Mī•cāi´ah son of Im´lah." 10 Now the king of Israel and King Je•hosh´a•phat of Judah were sitting on their thrones, arrayed in their robes, at the threshing floor at the entrance of the gate of Sa•mār´i•a; and all the prophets were prophesying before them. 11 Zed•e•kī´ah son of Che•nā´a•nah made for himself horns of iron, and he said, "Thus says the LORD: With these you shall gore the Ar•a•mē´ans until they are destroyed." 12 All the prophets were prophesying the same and saying, "Go up to Rā´moth-gil´e•ad and triumph; the LORD will give it into the hand of the king."

Micaiah Predicts Failure
(2 Chr 18.12–27)

13 The messenger who had gone to summon Mī•cāi´ah said to him, "Look, the words of the prophets with one accord are favorable to the king; let your word be like the word of one of them, and speak favorably." 14 But Mī•cāi´ah said, "As the LORD lives, whatever the LORD says to me, that I will speak."

15 When he had come to the king, the king said to him, "Mī•cāi´ah, shall we go to Rā´moth-gil´e•ad to battle, or shall we refrain?" He answered him, "Go up and triumph; the LORD will give it into the hand of the king." 16 But the king said to him, "How many times must I make you swear to tell me nothing but the truth in the name of the LORD?" 17 Then Mī•cāi´ah[s] said, "I saw all Israel scattered on the mountains, like sheep that have no shepherd; and the LORD said, 'These have no master; let each one go home in peace.' " 18 The king of Israel said to Je•hosh´a•phat, "Did I not tell you that he would not prophesy anything favorable about me, but only disaster?"

19 Then Mī•cāi´ah[s] said, "Therefore hear the word of the LORD: I saw the LORD sitting on his throne, with all the host of heaven standing beside him to the right and to the left of him. 20 And the LORD said, 'Who will entice Ā´hab, so that he may go up and fall at Rā´moth-gil´e•ad?' Then one said one thing, and another said another, 21 until a spirit came forward and stood before the LORD, saying, 'I will entice him.' 22 'How?' the LORD asked him. He replied, 'I will go out and be a lying spirit in the mouth of all his prophets.' Then the LORD[s] said, 'You are to entice him, and you shall succeed; go out and do it.' 23 So you see, the LORD has put a lying spirit in the mouth of all these your prophets; the LORD has decreed disaster for you."

24 Then Zed•e•kī´ah son of Che•nā´a•nah came up to Mī•cāi´ah, slapped him on the cheek, and said, "Which way did the spirit of the LORD pass from me to speak to you?" 25 Mī•cāi´ah replied, "You will find out on that day when you go in to hide in an inner chamber." 26 The king of Israel then ordered, "Take Mī•cāi´ah, and return him to Ā´mon the governor of the city and to Jō´ash the king's son, 27 and say, 'Thus says the king: Put this fellow in prison, and feed him on reduced rations of bread and water until I come in peace.' " 28 Mī•cāi´ah said, "If you return in peace, the LORD has not spoken by me." And he said, "Hear, you peoples, all of you!"

Defeat and Death of Ahab
(2 Chr 18.28–34)

29 So the king of Israel and King Je•hosh´a•phat of Judah went up to Rā´moth-gil´e•ad. 30 The king of Israel said to Je•hosh´a•phat, "I will disguise myself and go into battle, but you wear your robes." So the king of Israel disguised himself and went into battle. 31 Now the king of Ar´am had commanded the thirty-two captains of his chariots, "Fight with no one small or great, but only with the king of Israel." 32 When the captains of the chariots saw Je•hosh´a•phat, they said, "It is surely the king of Israel." So they turned to fight against him; and Je•hosh´a•phat cried out. 33 When the captains of the chariots saw that it was not the king of Israel, they turned back from pursuing him. 34 But a certain man drew his bow and unknowingly struck the king of Israel between the scale armor and the breastplate; so he said to the driver of his chariot, "Turn around, and carry me out of the battle, for I am wounded." 35 The battle grew hot that day, and the king was propped up in his chariot facing the Ar•a•mē´ans, until at evening he died; the blood from the wound had flowed into the bottom of the chariot. 36 Then about sunset a shout went

---

[s] Heb *he*

through the army, "Every man to his city, and every man to his country!"

37 So the king died, and was brought to Sa·mār'i·a; they buried the king in Sa·mār'i·a. 38 They washed the chariot by the pool of Sa·mār'i·a; the dogs licked up his blood, and the prostitutes washed themselves in it,[t] according to the word of the LORD that he had spoken. 39 Now the rest of the acts of Ā'hab, and all that he did, and the ivory house that he built, and all the cities that he built, are they not written in the Book of the Annals of the Kings of Israel? 40 So Ā'hab slept with his ancestors; and his son A·ha·zī'ah succeeded him.

Jehoshaphat Reigns over Judah
(2 Chr 20.31—21.1)

41 Je·hosh'a·phat son of Asa began to reign over Judah in the fourth year of King Ā'hab of Israel. 42 Je·hosh'a·phat was thirty-five years old when he began to reign, and he reigned twenty-five years in Jerusalem. His mother's name was A·zū'bah daughter of Shil'hi. 43 He walked in all the way of his father Asa; he did not turn aside from it, doing what was right in the sight of the LORD; yet the high places were not taken away, and the people still sacrificed and offered incense on the high places. 44 Je·hosh'a·phat also made peace with the king of Israel.

45 Now the rest of the acts of Je·hosh'a·phat, and his power that he showed, and how he waged war, are they not written in the Book of the Annals of the Kings of Judah? 46 The remnant of the male temple prostitutes who were still in the land in the days of his father Asa, he exterminated.

47 There was no king in Ē'dom; a deputy was king. 48 Je·hosh'a·phat made ships of the Tar'shish type to go to Ō'phir for gold; but they did not go, for the ships were wrecked at Ē'zi·on-gē'ber. 49 Then A·ha·zī'ah son of Ā'hab said to Je·hosh'a·phat, "Let my servants go with your servants in the ships," but Je·hosh'a·phat was not willing. 50 Je·hosh'a·phat slept with his ancestors and was buried with his ancestors in the city of his father David; his son Je·hō'ram succeeded him.

Ahaziah Reigns over Israel

51 A·ha·zī'ah son of Ā'hab began to reign over Israel in Sa·mār'i·a in the seventeenth year of King Je·hosh'a·phat of Judah; he reigned two years over Israel. 52 He did what was evil in the sight of the LORD, and walked in the way of his father and mother, and in the way of Jer·o·bō'am son of Nē'bat, who caused Israel to sin. 53 He served Bā'al and worshiped him; he provoked the LORD, the God of Israel, to anger, just as his father had done.

---

t Heb lacks *in it*

2 Kings

Chap. 25

Elijah Denounces Ahaziah

After the death of Ā'hab, Mō'ab rebelled against Israel.

2 A·ha·zī'ah had fallen through the lattice in his upper chamber in Sa·mār'i·a, and lay injured; so he sent messengers, telling them, "Go, inquire of Bā'-al-zē'bub, the god of Ek'ron, whether I shall recover from this injury." ³ But the angel of the LORD said to E·lī'jah the Tish'bīte, "Get up, go to meet the messengers of the king of Sa·mār'i·a, and say to them, 'Is it because there is no God in Israel that you are going to inquire of Bā'al-zē'bub, the god of Ek'ron?' ⁴ Now therefore thus says the LORD, 'You shall not leave the bed to which you have gone, but you shall surely die.' " So E·lī'jah went.

5 The messengers returned to the king, who said to them, "Why have you returned?" ⁶ They answered him, "There came a man to meet us, who said to us, 'Go back to the king who sent you, and say to him: Thus says the LORD: Is it because there is no God in Israel that you are sending to inquire of Bā'al-zē'bub, the god of Ek'ron? Therefore you shall not leave the bed to which you have gone, but shall surely die.' " ⁷ He said to them, "What sort of man was he who came to meet you and told you these things?" ⁸ They answered him, "A hairy man, with a leather belt around his waist." He said, "It is E·lī'jah the Tish'bīte."

9 Then the king sent to him a captain of fifty with his fifty men. He went up to E·lī'jah, who was sitting on the top of a hill, and said to him, "O man of God, the king says, 'Come down.' " ¹⁰ But E·lī'jah answered the captain of fifty, "If I am a man of God, let fire come down from heaven and consume you and your fifty." Then fire came down from heaven, and consumed him and his fifty.

11 Again the king sent to him another captain of fifty with his fifty. He went up*a* and said to him, "O man of God, this is the king's order: Come down quickly!" ¹² But E·lī'jah answered them, "If I am a man of God, let fire come down from heaven and consume you and your fifty." Then the fire of God came down from heaven and consumed him and his fifty.

13 Again the king sent the captain of a third fifty with his fifty. So the third captain of fifty went up, and came and fell on his knees before E·lī'jah, and entreated him, "O man of God, please let my life, and the life of these fifty servants of yours, be precious in your sight. ¹⁴ Look, fire came down from heaven and consumed the two former captains of fifty men with their fifties; but now let my life be precious in your sight." ¹⁵ Then the angel of the LORD said to E·lī'jah, "Go down with him; do not be afraid of him." So he set out and went down with him to the king, ¹⁶ and said to him, "Thus says the LORD: Because you have sent messengers to inquire of Bā'al-zē'bub, the god of Ek'ron,—is it

---

a Gk Compare verses 9, 13: Heb *He answered*

because there is no God in Israel to inquire of his word?—therefore you shall not leave the bed to which you have gone, but you shall surely die."

Death of Ahaziah

17 So he died according to the word of the LORD that E·lī′jah had spoken. His brother,[b] Je·hō′-ram succeeded him as king in the second year of King Je·hō′ram son of Je·hosh′a·phat of Judah, because A·ha·zī′ah had no son. 18 Now the rest of the acts of A·ha·zī′ah that he did, are they not written in the Book of the Annals of the Kings of Israel?

Elijah Ascends to Heaven

Now when the LORD was about to take E·lī′jah up to heaven by a whirlwind, E·lī′jah and E·lī′sha were on their way from Gil′gal. 2 E·lī′jah said to E·lī′sha, "Stay here; for the LORD has sent me as far as Beth′el." But E·lī′sha said, "As the LORD lives, and as you yourself live, I will not leave you." So they went down to Beth′el. 3 The company of prophets[c] who were in Beth′el came out to E·lī′sha, and said to him, "Do you know that today the LORD will take your master away from you?" And he said, "Yes, I know; keep silent."

4 E·lī′jah said to him, "E·lī′sha, stay here; for the LORD has sent me to Jericho." But he said, "As the LORD lives, and as you yourself live, I will not leave you." So they came to Jericho. 5 The company of prophets[c] who were at Jericho drew near to E·lī′-sha, and said to him, "Do you know that today the LORD will take your master away from you?" And he answered, "Yes, I know; be silent."

6 Then E·lī′jah said to him, "Stay here; for the LORD has sent me to the Jordan." But he said, "As the LORD lives, and as you yourself live, I will not leave you." So the two of them went on. 7 Fifty men of the company of prophets[c] also went, and stood at some distance from them, as they both were standing by the Jordan. 8 Then E·lī′jah took his mantle and rolled it up, and struck the water; the water was parted to the one side and to the other, until the two of them crossed on dry ground.

9 When they had crossed, E·lī′jah said to E·lī′-sha, "Tell me what I may do for you, before I am taken from you." E·lī′sha said, "Please let me inherit a double share of your spirit." 10 He responded, "You have asked a hard thing; yet, if you see me as I am being taken from you, it will be granted you; if not, it will not." 11 As they continued walking and talking, a chariot of fire and horses of fire separated the two of them, and E·lī′jah ascended in a whirlwind into heaven. 12 E·lī′sha kept watching and crying out, "Father, father! The chariots of Israel and its horsemen!" But when he could no longer see him, he grasped his own clothes and tore them in two pieces.

---

b Gk Syr: Heb lacks *His brother*   *c* Heb *sons of the prophets*

ELIJAH, PROPHET OF GOD IN SOLIDARITY WITH THE PEOPLE!

¡Elías, profeta de Dios en/con el pueblo, solidaridad con el pueblo! HISPANIC

Elijah was a passionate prophet who read the history of the monarchy (Israel's kings) from the perspective of God. He saw division in the people of Israel. On the one hand were the kings, the noblemen, and the leaders of the army; on the other hand were the peasants, the widows, and the persecuted prophets. The Covenant had been broken. Elijah denounced the unfaithfulness of Queen Jezebel and Kings Ahab and Ahaziah. They had introduced idolatry in the form of the false god Baal, who favored the powerful and allowed injustices.

Elijah's faithfulness to the Covenant and his solidarity with the poor led him to speak against kings and queens, to fight false prophets, and to intervene in national affairs. The powerful rulers wanted to kill him and silence his voice. After his dramatic departure (2 Kings 2.11), the people never forgot him; they always expected his return.

- If you saw today's world through the prism that Elijah used to view the world of his time, what would you see? Who would you support with your words and actions? Who would you challenge?
- Through your Baptism, you are called to be a prophet. As a prophet, how can you promote justice in society?

2 KINGS

Elisha Succeeds Elijah

13 He picked up the mantle of E•lī′jah that had fallen from him, and went back and stood on the bank of the Jordan. 14 He took the mantle of E•lī′jah that had fallen from him, and struck the water, saying, "Where is the LORD, the God of E•lī′jah?" When he had struck the water, the water was parted to the one side and to the other, and E•lī′sha went over.

15 When the company of prophets*d* who were at Jericho saw him at a distance, they declared, "The spirit of E•lī′jah rests on E•lī′sha." They came to meet him and bowed to the ground before him. 16 They said to him, "See now, we have fifty strong men among your servants; please let them go and seek your master; it may be that the spirit of the LORD has caught him up and thrown him down on some mountain or into some valley." He responded, "No, do not send them." 17 But when they urged him until he was ashamed, he said, "Send them." So they sent fifty men who searched for three days but did not find him. 18 When they came back to him (he had remained at Jericho), he said to them, "Did I not say to you, Do not go?"

Elisha Performs Miracles

19 Now the people of the city said to E•lī′sha, "The location of this city is good, as my lord sees; but the water is bad, and the land is unfruitful." 20 He said, "Bring me a new bowl, and put salt in it." So they brought it to him. 21 Then he went to the spring of water and threw the salt into it, and said, "Thus says the LORD, I have made this water wholesome; from now on neither death nor miscarriage shall come from it." 22 So the water has been wholesome to this day, according to the word that E•lī′sha spoke.

23 He went up from there to Beth′el; and while he was going up on the way, some small boys came out of the city and jeered at him, saying, "Go away, baldhead! Go away, baldhead!" 24 When he turned around and saw them, he cursed them in the name of the LORD. Then two she-bears came out of the woods and mauled forty-two of the boys. 25 From there he went on to Mount Car′mel, and then returned to Sa•mār′i•a.

Jehoram Reigns over Israel

In the eighteenth year of King Je•hosh′a•phat of Judah, Je•hō′ram son of Ā′hab became king over Israel in Sa•mār′i•a; he reigned twelve years. 2 He did what was evil in the sight of the LORD, though not like his father and mother, for he removed the pillar of Bā′al that his father had made. 3 Nevertheless he clung to the sin of Jer•o•bō′am son of Ne′bat, which he caused Israel to commit; he did not depart from it.

War with Moab

4 Now King Me′sha of Mō′ab was a sheep breeder, who used to deliver to the king of Israel one hundred thousand lambs, and the wool of one hundred thousand rams. 5 But when Ā′hab died, the king of Mō′ab rebelled against the king of Israel. 6 So King Je•hō′ram marched out of Sa•mār′i•a at that time and mustered all Israel. 7 As he went he sent word to King Je•hosh′a•phat of Judah, "The king of Mō′ab has rebelled against me; will you go with me to battle against Mō′ab?" He answered, "I will; I am with you, my people are your people, my horses are your horses." 8 Then he asked, "By which way shall we march?" Je•hō′ram answered, "By the way of the wilderness of Ē′dom."

9 So the king of Israel, the king of Judah, and the king of Ē′dom set out; and when they had made a roundabout march of seven days, there was no water for the army or for the animals that were with them. 10 Then the king of Israel said, "Alas! The LORD has summoned us, three kings, only to be handed over to Mō′ab." 11 But Je•hosh′a•phat said, "Is there no prophet of the LORD here, through whom we may inquire of the LORD?" Then one of the servants of the king of Israel answered, "E•lī′sha son of Shā′phat, who used to pour water on the hands of E•lī′jah, is here." 12 Je•hosh′a•phat said, "The word of the LORD is with him." So the king of Israel and Je•hosh′a•phat and the king of Ē′dom went down to him.

13 E•lī′sha said to the king of Israel, "What have I to do with you? Go to your father's prophets or to your mother's." But the king of Israel said to him, "No; it is the LORD who has summoned us, three kings, only to be handed over to Mō′ab." 14 E•lī′sha said, "As the LORD of hosts lives, whom I serve, were it not that I have regard for King Je•hosh′a•phat of Judah, I would give you neither a look nor a glance. 15 But get me a musician." And then, while the musician was playing, the power of the LORD came on him. 16 And he said, "Thus says the LORD, 'I will make this wadi full of pools.' 17 For thus says the LORD, 'You shall see neither wind nor rain, but the wadi shall be filled with water, so that you shall drink, you, your cattle, and your animals.' 18 This is only a trifle in the sight of the LORD, for he will also hand Mō′ab over to you. 19 You shall conquer every fortified city and every choice city; every good tree you shall fell, all springs of water you shall stop up, and every good piece of land you shall ruin with stones." 20 The

---

d Heb *sons of the prophets*

next day, about the time of the morning offering, suddenly water began to flow from the direction of Ē'dom, until the country was filled with water.

21 When all the Mō'ab•ītes heard that the kings had come up to fight against them, all who were able to put on armor, from the youngest to the oldest, were called out and were drawn up at the frontier. 22 When they rose early in the morning, and the sun shone upon the water, the Mō'ab•ītes saw the water opposite them as red as blood. 23 They said, "This is blood; the kings must have fought together, and killed one another. Now then, Mō'ab, to the spoil!" 24 But when they came to the camp of Israel, the Israelites rose up and attacked the Mō'ab•ītes, who fled before them; as they entered Mō'ab they continued the attack.[e] 25 The cities they overturned, and on every good piece of land everyone threw a stone, until it was covered; every spring of water they stopped up, and every good tree they felled. Only at Kir-har'e-seth did the stone walls remain, until the slingers surrounded and attacked it. 26 When the king of Mō'ab saw that the battle was going against him, he took with him seven hundred swordsmen to break through, opposite the king of Ē'dom; but they could not. 27 Then he took his firstborn son who was to succeed him, and offered him as a burnt offering on the wall. And great wrath came upon Israel, so they withdrew from him and returned to their own land.

Elisha and the Widow's Oil
(Cp 1 Kings 17.14–16)

Now the wife of a member of the company of prophets[f] cried to E•lī'sha, "Your servant my husband is dead; and you know that your servant feared the LORD, but a creditor has come to take my two children as slaves." 2 E•lī'sha said to her, "What shall I do for you? Tell me, what do you have in the house?" She answered, "Your servant has nothing in the house, except a jar of oil." 3 He said, "Go outside, borrow vessels from all your neighbors, empty vessels and not just a few. 4 Then go in, and shut the door behind you and your children, and start pouring into all these vessels; when each is full, set it aside." 5 So she left him and shut the door behind her and her children; they kept bringing vessels to her, and she kept pouring. 6 When the vessels were full, she said to her son, "Bring me another vessel." But he said to her, "There are no more." Then the oil stopped flowing. 7 She came and told the man of God, and he said, "Go sell the oil and pay your debts, and you and your children can live on the rest."

Elisha Raises the Shunammite's Son
(Cp 1 Kings 17.17–24)

8 One day E•lī'sha was passing through Shū'nem, where a wealthy woman lived, who urged him to have a meal. So whenever he passed that way, he would stop there for a meal. 9 She said to her husband, "Look, I am sure that this man who regularly passes our way is a holy man of God. 10 Let us make a small roof chamber with walls, and put there for him a bed, a table, a chair, and a lamp, so that he can stay there whenever he comes to us."

11 One day when he came there, he went up to the chamber and lay down there. 12 He said to his servant Ge•hā'zī, "Call the Shū'nam•mīte woman." When he had called her, she stood before him. 13 He said to him, "Say to her, Since you have taken all this trouble for us, what may be done for you? Would you have a word spoken on your behalf to the king or to the commander of the army?" She answered, "I live among my own people." 14 He said, "What then may be done for her?" Ge•hā'zī answered, "Well, she has no son, and her husband is old." 15 He said, "Call her." When he had called her, she stood at the door. 16 He said, "At this season, in due time, you shall embrace a son." She replied, "No, my lord, O man of God; do not deceive your servant."

4.1–7

17 The woman conceived and bore a son at that season, in due time, as E•lī'sha had declared to her.

18 When the child was older, he went out one day to his father among the reapers. 19 He

---

e Compare Gk Syr: Meaning of Heb uncertain   *f* Heb *the sons of the prophets*

complained to his father, "Oh, my head, my head!" The father said to his servant, "Carry him to his mother." 20 He carried him and brought him to his mother; the child sat on her lap until noon, and he died. 21 She went up and laid him on the bed of the man of God, closed the door on him, and left. 22 Then she called to her husband, and said, "Send me one of the servants and one of the donkeys, so that I may quickly go to the man of God and come back again." 23 He said, "Why go to him today? It is neither new moon nor sabbath." She said, "It will be all right." 24 Then she saddled the donkey and said to her servant, "Urge the animal on; do not hold back for me unless I tell you." 25 So she set out, and came to the man of God at Mount Car'mel.

When the man of God saw her coming, he said to Ge·ha′zī his servant, "Look, there is the Shū′nam·mīte woman; 26 run at once to meet her, and say to her, Are you all right? Is your husband all right? Is the child all right?" She answered, "It is all right." 27 When she came to the man of God at the mountain, she caught hold of his feet. Ge·ha′zī approached to push her away. But the man of God said, "Let her alone, for she is in bitter distress; the LORD has hidden it from me and has not told me." 28 Then she said, "Did I ask my lord for a son? Did I not say, Do not mislead me?" 29 He said to Ge·ha′zī, "Gird up your loins, and take my staff in your hand, and go. If you meet anyone, give no greeting, and if anyone greets you, do not answer; and lay my staff on the face of the child." 30 Then the mother of the child said, "As the LORD lives, and as you yourself live, I will not leave without you." So he rose up and followed her. 31 Ge·ha′zī went on ahead and laid the staff on the face of the child, but there was no sound or sign of life. He came back to meet him and told him, "The child has not awakened."

32 When E·li′sha came into the house, he saw the child lying dead on his bed. 33 So he went in and closed the door on the two of them, and prayed to the LORD. 34 Then he got up on the bed*g* and lay upon the child, putting his mouth upon his mouth, his eyes upon his eyes, and his hands upon his hands; and while he lay bent over him, the flesh of the child became warm. 35 He got down, walked once to and fro in the room, then got up again and bent over him; the child sneezed seven times, and the child opened his eyes. 36 E·li′sha*h* summoned Ge·ha′zī and said, "Call the Shū′nam·mīte woman." So he called her. When she came to him, he said, "Take your son." 37 She came and fell at his feet, bowing to the ground; then she took her son and left.

Elisha Purifies the Pot of Stew

38 When E·li′sha returned to Gil′gal, there was a famine in the land. As the company of prophets was*i* sitting before him, he said to his servant, "Put the large pot on, and make some stew for the company of prophets."*j* 39 One of them went out into the field to gather herbs; he found a wild vine and gathered from it a lapful of wild gourds, and came and cut them up into the pot of stew, not knowing what they were. 40 They served some for the men to eat. But while they were eating the stew, they cried out, "O man of God, there is death in the pot!" They could not eat it. 41 He said, "Then bring some flour." He threw it into the pot, and said, "Serve the people and let them eat." And there was nothing harmful in the pot.

did you KNOW?

New Testament Parallels

The story in 2 Kings 4.42–44 reminds us of a famous story about Jesus feeding a crowd of people with a tiny amount of food. This story is famous because it is the only one told six times in the Gospels. Jesus feeds a crowd of five thousand in all four Gospels (Mt 14.13–21; Mk 6.30–44; Lk 9.10–17; Jn 6.1–14) and a crowd of four thousand in two Gospels (Mt 15.32–39; Mk 8.1–10).

    Several events in the Old Testament have close parallels in the New Testament. For Christians, these Old Testament parallels have even richer meaning in the light of Jesus' life and ministry.

▶ **2 Kings 4.42–44**

Elisha Feeds One Hundred Men
(Cp Mt 14.13–21; 15.32–39)

42 A man came from Ba′al-shal′i·shah, bringing food from the first fruits to the man of God: twenty loaves of barley and fresh ears of grain in his sack. E·li′sha said, "Give it to the people and let them eat." 43 But his servant said, "How can I set this before a hundred people?" So he repeated, "Give it to the people and let them eat, for thus

---

g Heb lacks *on the bed*   *h* Heb *he*   *i* Heb *sons of the prophets were*   *j* Heb *sons of the prophets*

says the LORD, 'They shall eat and have some left.' "
44 He set it before them, they ate, and had some
left, according to the word of the LORD.

The Healing of Naaman

Nā´a•man, commander of the army of the king of
Ar´am, was a great man and in high favor with his
master, because by him the LORD had given victory
to Ar´am. The man, though a mighty warrior, suffered from leprosy.[k] 2 Now the Ar•a•mē´ans on one
of their raids had taken a young girl captive from
the land of Israel, and she served Nā´a•man's wife.

seven times, and your flesh shall be restored and
you shall be clean." 11 But Nā´a•man became angry
and went away, saying, "I thought that for me he
would surely come out, and stand and call on the
name of the LORD his God, and would wave his
hand over the spot, and cure the leprosy![k] 12 Are
not A•bā´na[m] and Phar´par, the rivers of Damascus,
better than all the waters of Israel? Could I not
wash in them, and be clean?" He turned and went
away in a rage. 13 But his servants approached and
said to him, "Father, if the prophet had commanded you to do something difficult, would you

Feed Your Soul

Elisha's miracle in 2 Kings 4.44 fed the body, but it is just as important to feed the
the appetite of the soul, such as the need for hope, for affirmation, for being loved.
It's easy to go to the nearest fast-food restaurant to satisfy your physical appetite,
but when it comes to feeding your soul, where do you go?

God gives us plenty of opportunities to feed our soul. We just need to take advantage of
them. Go to church. Participate in your youth program. Start a Bible study. Go on a retreat
or to a youth conference. Talk to friends about your faith and theirs. Take a walk and pray.
You'll find feeding your faith can be fun, and it often costs less than a value meal at your
local fast-food restaurant.

▸ 2 Kings 4.42–44

3 She said to her mistress, "If only my lord were
with the prophet who is in Sa•mār´i•a! He would
cure him of his leprosy."[k] 4 So Nā´a•man[l] went in
and told his lord just what the girl from the land
of Israel had said. 5 And the king of Ar´am said,
"Go then, and I will send along a letter to the king
of Israel."

He went, taking with him ten talents of silver,
six thousand shekels of gold, and ten sets of garments. 6 He brought the letter to the king of Israel,
which read, "When this letter reaches you, know
that I have sent to you my servant Nā´a•man, that
you may cure him of his leprosy."[k] 7 When the king
of Israel read the letter, he tore his clothes and
said, "Am I God, to give death or life, that this
man sends word to me to cure a man of his leprosy?[k] Just look and see how he is trying to pick a
quarrel with me."

8 But when E•lī´sha the man of God heard that
the king of Israel had torn his clothes, he sent a
message to the king, "Why have you torn your
clothes? Let him come to me, that he may learn
that there is a prophet in Israel." 9 So Nā´a•man
came with his horses and chariots, and halted at
the entrance of E•lī´sha's house. 10 E•lī´sha sent a
messenger to him, saying, "Go, wash in the Jordan

not have done it? How much more, when all he
said to you was, 'Wash, and be clean'?" 14 So he
went down and immersed himself seven times in
the Jordan, according to the word of the man of
God; his flesh was restored like the flesh of a
young boy, and he was clean.

15 Then he returned to the man of God, he
and all his company; he came and stood before
him and said, "Now I know that there is no God
in all the earth except in Israel; please accept a
present from your servant." 16 But he said, "As the
LORD lives, whom I serve, I will accept nothing!" He
urged him to accept, but he refused. 17 Then Nā´a-
man said, "If not, please let two mule-loads of
earth be given to your servant; for your servant will
no longer offer burnt offering or sacrifice to any
god except the LORD. 18 But may the LORD pardon
your servant on one count: when my master goes
into the house of Rim´mon to worship there, leaning on my arm, and I bow down in the house of
Rim´mon, when I do bow down in the house of
Rim´mon, may the LORD pardon your servant on
this one count." 19 He said to him, "Go in peace."

---

[k] A term for several skin diseases; precise meaning
uncertain   [l] Heb *he*   [m] Another reading is *Amana*

2 KINGS

Gehazi's Greed

But when Nā′a•man had gone from him a short distance, 20 Ge•hā′zī, the servant of E•lī′sha the man of God, thought, "My master has let that Ar•a•mē′an Nā′a•man off too lightly by not accepting from him what he offered. As the LORD lives, I will run after him and get something out of him." 21 So Ge•hā′zī went after Nā′a•man. When Nā′a•man saw someone running after him, he jumped down from the chariot to meet him and said, "Is everything all right?" 22 He replied, "Yes, but my master has sent me to say, 'Two members of a company of prophets[n] have just come to me from the hill country of E′phra•im; please give them a talent of silver and two changes of clothing.' " 23 Nā′a•man said, "Please accept two talents." He urged him, and tied up two talents of silver in two bags, with two changes of clothing, and gave them to two of his servants, who carried them in front of Ge•hā′zī.[o] 24 When he came to the citadel, he took the bags[p] from them, and stored them inside; he dismissed the men, and they left.

25 He went in and stood before his master; and E•lī′sha said to him, "Where have you been, Ge•hā′zī?" He answered, "Your servant has not gone anywhere at all." 26 But he said to him, "Did I not go with you in spirit when someone left his chariot to meet you? Is this a time to accept money and to accept clothing, olive orchards and vineyards, sheep and oxen, and male and female slaves? 27 Therefore the leprosy[q] of Nā′a•man shall cling to you, and to your descendants forever." So he left his presence leprous,[q] as white as snow.

The Miracle of the Ax Head

Now the company of prophets[n] said to E•lī′sha, "As you see, the place where we live under your charge is too small for us. 2 Let us go to the Jordan, and let us collect logs there, one for each of us, and build a place there for us to live." He answered, "Do so." 3 Then one of them said, "Please come with your servants." And he answered, "I will." 4 So he went with them. When they came to the Jordan, they cut down trees. 5 But as one was felling a log, his ax head fell into the water; he cried out, "Alas, master! It was borrowed." 6 Then the man of God said, "Where did it fall?" When he showed him the place, he cut off a stick, and threw it in there, and made the iron float. 7 He said, "Pick it up." So he reached out his hand and took it.

The Aramean Attack Is Thwarted

8 Once when the king of Ar′am was at war with Israel, he took counsel with his officers. He said, "At such and such a place shall be my camp." 9 But the man of God sent word to the king of Israel, "Take care not to pass this place, because the Ar•a•mē′ans are going down there." 10 The king of Israel sent word to the place of which the man of God spoke. More than once or twice he warned such a place[r] so that it was on the alert.

11 The mind of the king of Ar′am was greatly perturbed because of this; he called his officers and said to them, "Now tell me who among us sides with the king of Israel?" 12 Then one of his officers said, "No one, my lord king. It is E•lī′sha, the prophet in Israel, who tells the king of Israel the words that you speak in your bedchamber." 13 He said, "Go and find where he is; I will send and seize him." He was told, "He is in Dō′than." 14 So he sent horses and chariots there and a great army; they came by night, and surrounded the city.

15 When an attendant of the man of God rose early in the morning and went out, an army with horses and chariots was all around the city. His servant said, "Alas, master! What shall we do?" 16 He replied, "Do not be afraid, for there are more with us than there are with them." 17 Then E•lī′sha prayed: "O LORD, please open his eyes that he may see." So the LORD opened the eyes of the servant, and he saw; the mountain was full of horses and chariots of fire all around E•lī′sha. 18 When the Ar•a•mē′ans[s] came down against him, E•lī′sha prayed to the LORD, and said, "Strike this people, please, with blindness." So he struck them with blindness as E•lī′sha had asked. 19 E•lī′sha said to them, "This is not the way, and this is not the city; follow me, and I will bring you to the man whom you seek." And he led them to Sa•mār′i•a.

20 As soon as they entered Sa•mār′i•a, E•lī′sha said, "O LORD, open the eyes of these men so that they may see." The LORD opened their eyes, and they saw that they were inside Sa•mār′i•a. 21 When the king of Israel saw them he said to E•lī′sha, "Father, shall I kill them? Shall I kill them?" 22 He answered, "No! Did you capture with your sword and your bow those whom you want to kill? Set food and water before them so that they may eat and drink; and let them go to their master." 23 So he prepared for them a great feast; after they ate and drank, he sent them on their way, and they went to their master. And the Ar•a•mē′ans no longer came raiding into the land of Israel.

---

n Heb *sons of the prophets*   *o* Heb *him*   *p* Heb lacks *the bags*   *q* A term for several skin diseases; precise meaning uncertain   *r* Heb *warned it*   *s* Heb *they*

Ben-hadad's Siege of Samaria

24 Some time later King Ben-hā′dad of Ar′am mustered his entire army; he marched against Sa-mār′i•a and laid siege to it. 25 As the siege continued, famine in Sa•mār′i•a became so great that a donkey's head was sold for eighty shekels of silver, and one-fourth of a kab of dove's dung for five shekels of silver. 26 Now as the king of Israel was walking on the city wall, a woman cried out to him, "Help, my lord king!" 27 He said, "No! Let the Lord help you. How can I help you? From the threshing floor or from the wine press?" 28 But then the king asked her, "What is your complaint?" She answered, "This woman said to me, 'Give up your son; we will eat him today, and we will eat my son tomorrow.' 29 So we cooked my son and ate him. The next day I said to her, 'Give up your son and we will eat him.' But she has hidden her son." 30 When the king heard the words of the woman he tore his clothes—now since he was walking on the city wall, the people could see that he had sackcloth on his body underneath— 31 and he said, "So may God do to me, and more, if the head of E•lī′sha son of Shā′phat stays on his shoulders today." 32 So he dispatched a man from his presence.

Now E•lī′sha was sitting in his house, and the elders were sitting with him. Before the messenger arrived, E•lī′sha said to the elders, "Are you aware that this murderer has sent someone to take off my head? When the messenger comes, see that you shut the door and hold it closed against him. Is not the sound of his master's feet behind him?" 33 While he was still speaking with them, the king[t] came down to him and said, "This trouble is from the Lord! Why should I hope in the Lord any longer?" 1 But E•lī′sha said, "Hear the word of the Lord: thus says the Lord, Tomorrow about this time a measure of choice meal shall be sold for a shekel, and two measures of barley for a shekel, at the gate of Sa•mār′i•a." 2 Then the captain on whose hand the king leaned said to the man of God, "Even if the Lord were to make windows in the sky, could such a thing happen?" But he said, "You shall see it with your own eyes, but you shall not eat from it."

The Arameans Flee

3 Now there were four leprous[u] men outside the city gate, who said to one another, "Why should we sit here until we die? 4 If we say, 'Let us enter the city,' the famine is in the city, and we shall die there; but if we sit here, we shall also die. Therefore, let us desert to the Ar•a•mē′an camp; if they spare our lives, we shall live; and if they kill us, we shall but die." 5 So they arose at twilight to go to the Ar•a•mē′an camp; but when they came to the edge of the Ar•a•mē′an camp, there was no one there at all. 6 For the Lord had caused the Ar•a•mē′an army to hear the sound of chariots, and of horses, the sound of a great army, so that they said to one another, "The king of Israel has hired the kings of the Hit′tītes and the kings of Egypt to fight against us." 7 So they fled away in the twilight and abandoned their tents, their horses, and their donkeys leaving the camp just as it was, and fled for their lives. 8 When these leprous[u] men had come to the edge of the camp, they went into a tent, ate and drank, carried off silver, gold, and clothing, and went and hid them. Then they came back, entered another tent, carried off things from it, and went and hid them.

9 Then they said to one another, "What we are doing is wrong. This is a day of good news; if we are silent and wait until the morning light, we will be found guilty; therefore let us go and tell the king's household." 10 So they came and called to the gatekeepers of the city, and told them, "We went to the Ar•a•mē′an camp, but there was no one to be seen or heard there, nothing but the horses tied, the donkeys tied, and the tents as they were." 11 Then the gatekeepers called out and proclaimed it to the king's household. 12 The king got up in the night, and said to his servants, "I will tell you what the Ar•a•mē′ans have prepared against us. They know that we are starving; so they have left the camp to hide themselves in the open country, thinking, 'When they come out of the city, we shall take them alive and get into the city.'" 13 One of his servants said, "Let some men take five of the remaining horses, since those left here will suffer the fate of the whole multitude of Israel that have perished already;[v] let us send and find out." 14 So they took two mounted men, and the king sent them after the Ar•a•mē′an army, saying, "Go and find out." 15 So they went after them as far as the Jordan; the whole way was littered with garments and equipment that the Ar•a•mē′ans had thrown away in their haste. So the messengers returned, and told the king.

16 Then the people went out, and plundered the camp of the Ar•a•mē′ans. So a measure of choice meal was sold for a shekel, and two measures of barley for a shekel, according to the word of the Lord. 17 Now the king had appointed the captain on whose hand he leaned to have charge of the gate; the people trampled him to death in the gate, just as the man of God had said when the king

---

t See 7.2: Heb *messenger*   u A term for several skin diseases; precise meaning uncertain   v Compare Gk Syr Vg: Meaning of Heb uncertain

came down to him. 18 For when the man of God had said to the king, "Two measures of barley shall be sold for a shekel, and a measure of choice meal for a shekel, about this time tomorrow in the gate of Sa•mār'i•a," 19 the captain had answered the man of God, "Even if the LORD were to make windows in the sky, could such a thing happen?" And he had answered, "You shall see it with your own eyes, but you shall not eat from it." 20 It did indeed happen to him; the people trampled him to death in the gate.

The Shunammite Woman's Land Restored

Now E•lī'sha had said to the woman whose son he had restored to life, "Get up and go with your household, and settle wherever you can; for the LORD has called for a famine, and it will come on the land for seven years." 2 So the woman got up and did according to the word of the man of God; she went with her household and settled in the land of the Phi•lis'tines seven years. 3 At the end of the seven years, when the woman returned from the land of the Phi•lis'tines, she set out to appeal to the king for her house and her land. 4 Now the king was talking with Ge•hā'zī the servant of the man of God, saying, "Tell me all the great things that E•lī'sha has done." 5 While he was telling the king how E•lī'sha had restored a dead person to life, the woman whose son he had restored to life appealed to the king for her house and her land. Ge•hā'zī said, "My lord king, here is the woman, and here is her son whom E•lī'sha restored to life." 6 When the king questioned the woman, she told him. So the king appointed an official for her, saying, "Restore all that was hers, together with all the revenue of the fields from the day that she left the land until now."

Death of Ben-hadad

7 E•lī'sha went to Damascus while King Ben-hā'dad of Ar'am was ill. When it was told him, "The man of God has come here," 8 the king said to Haz'a•el, "Take a present with you and go to meet the man of God. Inquire of the LORD through him, whether I shall recover from this illness." 9 So Haz'-a•el went to meet him, taking a present with him, all kinds of goods of Damascus, forty camel loads. When he entered and stood before him, he said, "Your son King Ben-hā'dad of Ar'am has sent me to you, saying, 'Shall I recover from this illness?' " 10 E•lī'sha said to him, "Go, say to him, 'You shall certainly recover'; but the LORD has shown me that he shall certainly die." 11 He fixed his gaze and stared at him, until he was ashamed. Then the man of God wept. 12 Haz'a•el asked, "Why does

my lord weep?" He answered, "Because I know the evil that you will do to the people of Israel; you will set their fortresses on fire, you will kill their young men with the sword, dash in pieces their little ones, and rip up their pregnant women." 13 Haz'a•el said, "What is your servant, who is a mere dog, that he should do this great thing?" E•lī'sha answered, "The LORD has shown me that you are to be king over Ar'am." 14 Then he left E•lī'sha, and went to his master Ben-hā'dad,[w] who said to him, "What did E•lī'sha say to you?" And he answered, "He told me that you would certainly recover." 15 But the next day he took the bed-cover and dipped it in water and spread it over the king's face, until he died. And Haz'a•el succeeded him.

Jehoram Reigns over Judah
(2 Chr 21.1–20)

16 In the fifth year of King Jō'ram son of Ā'hab of Israel,[x] Je•hō'ram son of King Je•hosh'a-phat of Judah began to reign. 17 He was thirty-two years old when he became king, and he reigned eight years in Jerusalem. 18 He walked in the way of the kings of Israel, as the house of Ā'hab had done, for the daughter of Ā'hab was his wife. He

did you KNOW?

Grading Kings

As you read the remaining chapters of Second Kings, notice that the author gives a kind of report card for each of the rulers of Israel and Judah. Jehoram, for example, receives an F: "He did what was evil in the sight of the LORD" (8.18). Josiah receives an A: "He did what was right in the sight of the LORD" (22.2). The author, who wrote after the fall of both kingdoms, provides a theological reason for Israel's and Judah's failure. Because most of the rulers continually violated God's law, they were largely responsible for the fall of the kingdoms.

did what was evil in the sight of the LORD. 19 Yet the LORD would not destroy Judah, for the sake of his servant David, since he had promised to give a lamp to him and to his descendants forever.

---

w Heb lacks Ben-hadad   x Gk Syr: Heb adds Jehoshaphat being king of Judah,

20 In his days Ē'dom revolted against the rule of Judah, and set up a king of their own. 21 Then Jō'ram crossed over to Zā'ir with all his chariots. He set out by night and attacked the Ē'dom·ites and their chariot commanders who had surrounded him;*y* but his army fled home. 22 So Ē'dom has been in revolt against the rule of Judah to this day. Lib'nah also revolted at the same time. 23 Now the rest of the acts of Jō'ram, and all that he did, are they not written in the Book of the Annals of the Kings of Judah? 24 So Jō'ram slept with his ancestors, and was buried with them in the city of David; his son A·ha·zī'ah succeeded him.

Ahaziah Reigns over Judah
(2 Chr 22.1–6)

25 In the twelfth year of King Jō'ram son of Ā'hab of Israel, A·ha·zī'ah son of King Je·hō'ram of Judah began to reign. 26 A·ha·zī'ah was twenty-two years old when he began to reign; he reigned one year in Jerusalem. His mother's name was Ath·a·lī'ah, a granddaughter of King Om'rī of Israel. 27 He also walked in the way of the house of Ā'hab, doing what was evil in the sight of the LORD, as the house of Ā'hab had done, for he was son-in-law to the house of Ā'hab.

28 He went with Jō'ram son of Ā'hab to wage war against King Haz'a·el of Ar'am at Rā'moth-gil'-ē·ad, where the Ar·a·mē'ans wounded Jō'ram. 29 King Jō'ram returned to be healed in Jez'rē·el of the wounds that the Ar·a·mē'ans had inflicted on him at Rā'mah, when he fought against King Haz'-a·el of Ar'am. King A·ha·zī'ah son of Je·hō'ram of Judah went down to see Jō'ram son of Ā'hab in Jez'rē·el, because he was wounded.

Anointing of Jehu

Then the prophet E·lī'sha called a member of the company of prophets*z* and said to him, "Gird up your loins; take this flask of oil in your hand, and go to Rā'moth-gil'ē·ad. 2 When you arrive, look there for Jē'hū son of Je·hosh'a·phat, son of Nim'shī; go in and get him to leave his companions, and take him into an inner chamber. 3 Then take the flask of oil, pour it on his head, and say, 'Thus says the LORD: I anoint you king over Israel.' Then open the door and flee; do not linger."

4 So the young man, the young prophet, went to Rā'moth-gil'ē·ad. 5 He arrived while the commanders of the army were in council, and he announced, "I have a message for you, commander." "For which one of us?" asked Jē'hū. "For you, commander." 6 So Jē'hū*a* got up and went inside; the young man poured the oil on his head, saying to him, "Thus says the LORD the God of Israel: I anoint you king over the people of the LORD, over

Israel. 7 You shall strike down the house of your master Ā'hab, so that I may avenge on Jez'e·bel the blood of my servants the prophets, and the blood of all the servants of the LORD. 8 For the whole house of Ā'hab shall perish; I will cut off from Ā'hab every male, bond or free, in Israel. 9 I will make the house of Ā'hab like the house of Jer·o·bō'am son of Nē'bat, and like the house of Bā'a·sha son of A·hī'jah. 10 The dogs shall eat Jez'e·bel in the territory of Jez'rē·el, and no one shall bury her." Then he opened the door and fled.

11 When Jē'hū came back to his master's officers, they said to him, "Is everything all right? Why did that madman come to you?" He answered them, "You know the sort and how they babble." 12 They said, "Liar! Come on, tell us!" So he said, "This is just what he said to me: 'Thus says the LORD, I anoint you king over Israel.' " 13 Then hurriedly they all took their cloaks and spread them for him on the bare*y* steps; and they blew the trumpet, and proclaimed, "Jē'hū is king."

Joram of Israel Killed

14 Thus Jē'hū son of Je·hosh'a·phat son of Nim'shī conspired against Jō'ram. Jō'ram with all Israel had been on guard at Rā'moth-gil'ē·ad against King Haz'a·el of Ar'am; 15 but King Jō'ram had returned to be healed in Jez'rē·el of the wounds that the Ar·a·mē'ans had inflicted on him, when he fought against King Haz'a·el of Ar'am. So Jē'hū said, "If this is your wish, then let no one slip out of the city to go and tell the news in Jez'-rē·el." 16 Then Jē'hū mounted his chariot and went to Jez'rē·el, where Jō'ram was lying ill. King A·ha·zī'ah of Judah had come down to visit Jō'ram.

17 In Jez'rē·el, the sentinel standing on the tower spied the company of Jē'hū arriving, and said, "I see a company." Jō'ram said, "Take a horseman; send him to meet them, and let him say, 'Is it peace?' " 18 So the horseman went to meet him; he said, "Thus says the king, 'Is it peace?' " Jē'hū responded, "What have you to do with peace? Fall in behind me." The sentinel reported, saying, "The messenger reached them, but he is not coming back." 19 Then he sent out a second horseman, who came to them and said, "Thus says the king, 'Is it peace?' " Jē'hū answered, "What have you to do with peace? Fall in behind me." 20 Again the sentinel reported, "He reached them, but he is not coming back. It looks like the driving of Jē'hū son of Nim'shī; for he drives like a maniac."

---

y Meaning of Heb uncertain   *z* Heb *sons of the prophets*
a Heb *he*

21 Jō′ram said, "Get ready." And they got his chariot ready. Then King Jō′ram of Israel and King A•ha•zī′ah of Judah set out, each in his chariot, and went to meet Jē′hū; they met him at the property of Nā′both the Jez′re•el•īte. 22 When Jō′ram saw Jē′hū, he said, "Is it peace, Jē′hū?" He answered, "What peace can there be, so long as the many whoredoms and sorceries of your mother Jez′e•bel continue?" 23 Then Jō′ram reined about and fled, saying to A•ha•zī′ah, "Treason, A•ha•zī′ah!" 24 Jē′hū drew his bow with all his strength, and shot Jō′-ram between the shoulders, so that the arrow pierced his heart; and he sank in his chariot. 25 Jē′hū said to his aide Bid′kar, "Lift him out, and throw him on the plot of ground belonging to Nā′both the Jez′re•el•īte; for remember, when you and I rode side by side behind his father Ā′hab how the LORD uttered this oracle against him: 26 'For the blood of Nā′both and for the blood of his children that I saw yesterday, says the LORD, I swear I will repay you on this very plot of ground.' Now therefore lift him out and throw him on the plot of ground, in accordance with the word of the LORD."

Ahaziah of Judah Killed
(2 Chr 22.7–9)

27 When King A•ha•zī′ah of Judah saw this, he fled in the direction of Beth-hag′gan. Jē′hū pursued him, saying, "Shoot him also!" And they shot him*b* in the chariot at the ascent to Gur, which is by Ib′le•am. Then he fled to Me•gid′do, and died there. 28 His officers carried him in a chariot to Jerusalem, and buried him in his tomb with his ancestors in the city of David.

29 In the eleventh year of Jō′ram son of Ā′hab, A•ha•zī′ah began to reign over Judah.

Jezebel's Violent Death

30 When Jē′hū came to Jez′re•el, Jez′e•bel heard of it; she painted her eyes, and adorned her head, and looked out of the window. 31 As Jē′hū entered the gate, she said, "Is it peace, Zim′rī, murderer of your master?" 32 He looked up to the window and said, "Who is on my side? Who?" Two or three eunuchs looked out at him. 33 He said, "Throw her down." So they threw her down; some of her blood spattered on the wall and on the horses, which trampled on her. 34 Then he went in and ate and drank; he said, "See to that cursed woman and bury her; for she is a king's daughter." 35 But when they went to bury her, they found no more of her than the skull and the feet and the palms of her hands. 36 When they came back and told him, he said, "This is the word of the LORD, which he spoke by his servant E•lī′jah the Tish′bīte, 'In the territory

of Jez′re•el the dogs shall eat the flesh of Jez′e•bel; 37 the corpse of Jez′e•bel shall be like dung on the field in the territory of Jez′re•el, so that no one can say, This is Jez′e•bel.' "

Massacre of Ahab's Descendants

Now Ā′hab had seventy sons in Sa•mār′i•a. So Jē′hū wrote letters and sent them to Sa•mār′i•a, to the rulers of Jez′re•el,*c* to the elders, and to the guardians of the sons of*d* Ā′hab, saying, 2 "Since your master's sons are with you and you have at your disposal chariots and horses, a fortified city, and weapons, 3 select the son of your master who is the best qualified, set him on his father's throne, and fight for your master's house." 4 But they were utterly terrified and said, "Look, two kings could not withstand him; how then can we stand?" 5 So the steward of the palace, and the governor of the city, along with the elders and the guardians, sent word to Jē′hū: "We are your servants; we will do anything you say. We will not make anyone king; do whatever you think right." 6 Then he wrote them a second letter, saying, "If you are on my side, and if you are ready to obey me, take the heads of your master's sons and come to me at Jez′re•el tomorrow at this time." Now the king's sons, seventy persons, were with the leaders of the city, who were charged with their upbringing. 7 When the letter reached them, they took the king's sons and killed them, seventy persons; they put their heads in baskets and sent them to him at Jez′re•el. 8 When the messenger came and told him, "They have brought the heads of the king's sons," he said, "Lay them in two heaps at the entrance of the gate until the morning." 9 Then in the morning when he went out, he stood and said to all the people, "You are innocent. It was I who conspired against my master and killed him; but who struck down all these? 10 Know then that there shall fall to the earth nothing of the word of the LORD, which the LORD spoke concerning the house of Ā′hab; for the LORD has done what he said through his servant E•lī′jah." 11 So Jē′hū killed all who were left of the house of Ā′hab in Jez′re•el, all his leaders, close friends, and priests, until he left him no survivor.

12 Then he set out and went to Sa•mār′i•a. On the way, when he was at Beth-ek′ed of the Shepherds, 13 Jē′hū met relatives of King A•ha•zī′ah of Judah and said, "Who are you?" They answered, "We are kin of A•ha•zī′ah; we have come down to visit the royal princes and the sons of the queen mother." 14 He said, "Take them alive." They took

b Syr Vg Compare Gk: Heb lacks *and they shot him*
c Or *of the city;* Vg Compare Gk   *d* Gk: Heb lacks *of the sons of*

them alive, and slaughtered them at the pit of Beth-ek′ed, forty-two in all; he spared none of them.

15 When he left there, he met Je•hon′a•dab son of Rē′chab coming to meet him; he greeted him, and said to him, "Is your heart as true to mine as mine is to yours?"*e* Je•hon′a•dab answered, "It is." Jē′hū said,*f* "If it is, give me your hand." So he gave him his hand. Jē′hū took him up with him into the chariot. 16 He said, "Come with me, and see my zeal for the LORD." So he*g* had him ride in his chariot. 17 When he came to Sa•mār′i•a, he killed all who were left to Ā′hab in Sa•mār′i•a, until he had wiped them out, according to the word of the LORD that he spoke to E•lī′jah.

Slaughter of Worshipers of Baal

18 Then Jē′hū assembled all the people and said to them, "Ā′hab offered Bā′al small service; but Jē′hū will offer much more. 19 Now therefore summon to me all the prophets of Bā′al, all his worshipers, and all his priests; let none be missing, for I have a great sacrifice to offer to Bā′al; whoever is missing shall not live." But Jē′hū was acting with cunning in order to destroy the worshipers of Bā′al. 20 Jē′hū decreed, "Sanctify a solemn assembly for Bā′al." So they proclaimed it. 21 Jē′hū sent word throughout all Israel; all the worshipers of Bā′al came, so that there was no one left who did not come. They entered the temple of Bā′al, until the temple of Bā′al was filled from wall to wall. 22 He said to the keeper of the wardrobe, "Bring out the vestments for all the worshipers of Bā′al." So he brought out the vestments for them. 23 Then Jē′hū entered the temple of Bā′al with Je•hon′a•dab son of Rē′chab; he said to the worshipers of Bā′al, "Search and see that there is no worshiper of the LORD here among you, but only worshipers of Bā′al." 24 Then they proceeded to offer sacrifices and burnt offerings.

Now Jē′hū had stationed eighty men outside, saying, "Whoever allows any of those to escape whom I deliver into your hands shall forfeit his life." 25 As soon as he had finished presenting the burnt offering, Jē′hū said to the guards and to the officers, "Come in and kill them; let no one escape." So they put them to the sword. The guards and the officers threw them out, and then went into the citadel of the temple of Bā′al. 26 They brought out the pillar*h* that was in the temple of Bā′al, and burned it. 27 Then they demolished the pillar of Bā′al, and destroyed the temple of Bā′al, and made it a latrine to this day.

28 Thus Jē′hū wiped out Bā′al from Israel. 29 But Jē′hū did not turn aside from the sins of Jer•o•bō′am son of Nē′bat, which he caused Israel

to commit—the golden calves that were in Beth′el and in Dan. 30 The LORD said to Jē′hū, "Because you have done well in carrying out what I consider right, and in accordance with all that was in my heart have dealt with the house of Ā′hab, your sons of the fourth generation shall sit on the throne of Israel." 31 But Jē′hū was not careful to follow the law of the LORD the God of Israel with all his heart; he did not turn from the sins of Jer•o•bō′am, which he caused Israel to commit.

Death of Jehu

32 In those days the LORD began to trim off parts of Israel. Haz′a•el defeated them throughout the territory of Israel: 33 from the Jordan eastward, all the land of Gil′e•ad, the Gad′ites, the Reū′ben-ites, and the Ma•nas′sītes, from A•rō′er, which is by the Wadi Ar′non, that is, Gil′e•ad and Bā′shan. 34 Now the rest of the acts of Jē′hū, all that he did, and all his power, are they not written in the Book of the Annals of the Kings of Israel? 35 So Jē′hū slept with his ancestors, and they buried him in Sa•mār′i•a. His son Je•hō′a•haz succeeded him. 36 The time that Jē′hū reigned over Israel in Sa•mār′i•a was twenty-eight years.

Athaliah Reigns over Judah
(2 Chr 22.10–12)

Now when Ath•a•lī′ah, A•ha•zī′ah's mother, saw that her son was dead, she set about to destroy all the royal family. 2 But Je•hosh′e•ba, King Jō′ram's daughter, A•ha•zī′ah's sister, took Jō′ash son of A•ha-zī′ah, and stole him away from among the king's children who were about to be killed; she put*i* him and his nurse in a bedroom. Thus she*j* hid him from Ath•a•lī′ah, so that he was not killed; 3 he remained with her six years, hidden in the house of the LORD, while Ath•a•lī′ah reigned over the land.

Jehoiada Anoints the Child Joash
(2 Chr 23.1–11)

4 But in the seventh year Je•hoi′a•da summoned the captains of the Cār′i•tes and of the guards and had them come to him in the house of the LORD. He made a covenant with them and put them under oath in the house of the LORD; then he showed them the king's son. 5 He commanded them, "This is what you are to do: one-third of you, those who go off duty on the sabbath and guard the king's house 6 (another third being at the gate Sur and a third at the gate behind the guards), shall guard

---

e Gk: Heb *Is it right with your heart, as my heart is with your heart?* *f* Gk: Heb lacks *Jehu said* *g* Gk Syr Tg: Heb *they* *h* Gk Vg Syr Tg: Heb *pillars* *i* With 2 Chr 22.11: Heb lacks *she put* *j* Gk Syr Vg Compare 2 Chr 22.11: Heb *they*

the palace; 7 and your two divisions that come on duty in force on the sabbath and guard the house of the LORD *k* 8 shall surround the king, each with weapons in hand; and whoever approaches the ranks is to be killed. Be with the king in his comings and goings."

9 The captains did according to all that the priest Je•hoi'a•da commanded; each brought his men who were to go off duty on the sabbath, with those who were to come on duty on the sabbath, and came to the priest Je•hoi'a•da. 10 The priest delivered to the captains the spears and shields that had been King David's, which were in the house of the LORD; 11 the guards stood, every man with his weapons in his hand, from the south side of the house to the north side of the house, around the altar and the house, to guard the king on every side. 12 Then he brought out the king's son, put the crown on him, and gave him the covenant;*l* they proclaimed him king, and anointed him; they clapped their hands and shouted, "Long live the king!"

Death of Athaliah
(2 Chr 23.12—24.1)

13 When Ath•a•li'ah heard the noise of the guard and of the people, she went into the house of the LORD to the people; 14 when she looked, there was the king standing by the pillar, according to custom, with the captains and the trumpeters beside the king, and all the people of the land rejoicing and blowing trumpets. Ath•a•li'ah tore her clothes and cried, "Treason! Treason!" 15 Then the priest Je•hoi'a•da commanded the captains who were set over the army, "Bring her out between the ranks, and kill with the sword anyone who follows her." For the priest said, "Let her not be killed in the house of the LORD." 16 So they laid hands on her; she went through the horses' entrance to the king's house, and there she was put to death.

17 Je•hoi'a•da made a covenant between LORD and the king and people, that they should be the LORD's people; also between the king and the people. 18 Then all the people of the land went to the house of Ba'al, and tore it down; his altars and his images they broke in pieces, and they killed Mat'tan, the priest of Ba'al, before the altars. The priest posted guards over the house of the LORD. 19 He took the captains, the Cãr'ī•tes, the guards, and all the people of the land; then they brought the king down from the house of the LORD, marching through the gate of the guards to the king's house. He took his seat on the throne of the kings. 20 So all the people of the land rejoiced; and the city was quiet after Ath•a•li'ah had been killed with the sword at the king's house.

21 *m* Je•hō'ash*n* was seven years old when he began to reign.

The Temple Repaired
(2 Chr 24.1–14)

In the seventh year of Jē'hū, Je•hō'ash began to reign; he reigned forty years in Jerusalem. His mother's name was Zib'i•ah of Bē'er-shē'ba. 2 Je•hō'ash did what was right in the sight of the LORD all his days, because the priest Je•hoi'a•da instructed him. 3 Nevertheless the high places were not taken away; the people continued to sacrifice and make offerings on the high places.

4 Je•hō'ash said to the priests, "All the money offered as sacred donations that is brought into the house of the LORD, the money for which each person is assessed—the money from the assessment of persons—and the money from the voluntary offerings brought into the house of the LORD, 5 let the priests receive from each of the donors; and let them repair the house wherever any need of repairs is discovered." 6 But by the twenty-third year of King Je•hō'ash the priests had made no repairs on the house. 7 Therefore King Je•hō'ash summoned the priest Je•hoi'a•da with the other priests and said to them, "Why are you not repairing the house? Now therefore do not accept any more money from your donors but hand it over for the repair of the house." 8 So the priests agreed that they would neither accept more money from the people nor repair the house.

9 Then the priest Je•hoi'a•da took a chest, made a hole in its lid, and set it beside the altar on the right side as one entered the house of the LORD; the priests who guarded the threshold put in it all the money that was brought into the house of the LORD. 10 Whenever they saw that there was a great deal of money in the chest, the king's secretary and the high priest went up, counted the money that was found in the house of the LORD, and tied it up in bags. 11 They would give the money that was weighed out into the hands of the workers who had the oversight of the house of the LORD; then they paid it out to the carpenters and the builders who worked on the house of the LORD, 12 to the masons and the stonecutters, as well as to buy timber and quarried stone for making repairs on the house of the LORD, as well as for any outlay for repairs of the house. 13 But for the house of the LORD no basins of silver, snuffers, bowls, trumpets, or any vessels of gold, or of silver, were made from the money that was brought into the house of the

---

k Heb *the* LORD *to the king*   *l* Or *treaty* or *testimony*; Heb *eduth*   *m* Ch 12.1 in Heb   *n* Another spelling is *Joash*; see verse 19

LORD, 14 for that was given to the workers who were repairing the house of the LORD with it. 15 They did not ask an accounting from those into whose hand they delivered the money to pay out to the workers, for they dealt honestly. 16 The money from the guilt offerings and the money from the sin offerings was not brought into the house of the LORD; it belonged to the priests.

Hazael Threatens Jerusalem

17 At that time King Haz'a•el of Ar'am went up, fought against Gath, and took it. But when Haz'a•el set his face to go up against Jerusalem, 18 King Je•hō'ash of Judah took all the votive gifts that Je•hosh'a•phat, Je•hō'ram, and A•ha•zī'ah, his ancestors, the kings of Judah, had dedicated, as well as his own votive gifts, all the gold that was found in the treasuries of the house of the LORD and of the king's house, and sent these to King Haz'a•el of Ar'am. Then Haz'a•el withdrew from Jerusalem.

Death of Joash
(2 Chr 24.23–27)

19 Now the rest of the acts of Jō'ash, and all that he did, are they not written in the Book of the Annals of the Kings of Judah? 20 His servants arose, devised a conspiracy, and killed Jō'ash in the house of Mil'lō, on the way that goes down to Sil'la. 21 It was Jō'za•car son of Shim'ē•ath and Je•hō'za•bad son of Shō'mer, his servants, who struck him down, so that he died. He was buried with his ancestors in the city of David; then his son Am•a•zī'ah succeeded him.

Jehoahaz Reigns over Israel

In the twenty-third year of King Jō'ash son of A•ha•zī'ah of Judah, Je•hō'a•haz son of Jē'hū began to reign over Israel in Sa•mār'i•a; he reigned seventeen years. 2 He did what was evil in the sight of the LORD, and followed the sins of Jer•o•bō'am son of Nē'bat, which he caused Israel to sin; he did not depart from them. 3 The anger of the LORD was kindled against Israel, so that he gave them repeatedly into the hand of King Haz'a•el of Ar'am, then into the hand of Ben-hā'dad son of Haz'a•el. 4 But Je•hō'a•haz entreated the LORD, and the LORD heeded him; for he saw the oppression of Israel, how the king of Ar'am oppressed them. 5 Therefore the LORD gave Israel a savior, so that they escaped from the hand of the Ar•a•mē'ans; and the people of Israel lived in their homes as formerly. 6 Nevertheless they did not depart from the sins of the house of Jer•o•bō'am, which he caused Israel to sin, but walked^o in them; the sacred pole^p also remained in Sa•mār'i•a. 7 So Je•hō'a•haz was left with an army of not more than fifty horsemen, ten chariots and

ten thousand footmen; for the king of Ar'am had destroyed them and made them like the dust at threshing. 8 Now the rest of the acts of Je•hō'a•haz and all that he did, including his might, are they not written in the Book of the Annals of the Kings of Israel? 9 So Je•hō'a•haz slept with his ancestors, and they buried him in Sa•mār'i•a; then his son Jō'ash succeeded him.

Jehoash Reigns over Israel

10 In the thirty-seventh year of King Jō'ash of Judah, Je•hō'ash son of Je•hō'a•haz began to reign over Israel in Sa•mār'i•a; he reigned sixteen years. 11 He also did what was evil in the sight of the LORD; he did not depart from all the sins of Jer•o•bō'am son of Nē'bat, which he caused Israel to sin, but he walked in them. 12 Now the rest of the acts of Jō'ash, and all that he did, as well as the might with which he fought against King Am•a•zī'ah of Judah, are they not written in the Book of the Annals of the Kings of Israel? 13 So Jō'ash slept with his ancestors, and Jer•o•bō'am sat upon his throne; Jō'ash was buried in Sa•mār'i•a with the kings of Israel.

Death of Elisha

14 Now when E•lī'sha had fallen sick with the illness of which he was to die, King Jō'ash of Israel went down to him, and wept before him, crying, "My father, my father! The chariots of Israel and its horsemen!" 15 E•lī'sha said to him, "Take a bow and arrows"; so he took a bow and arrows. 16 Then he said to the king of Israel, "Draw the bow"; and he drew it. E•lī'sha laid his hands on the king's hands. 17 Then he said, "Open the window eastward"; and he opened it. E•lī'sha said, "Shoot"; and he shot. Then he said, "The LORD's arrow of victory, the arrow of victory over Ar'am! For you shall fight the Ar•a•mē'ans in Ā'phek until you have made an end of them." 18 He continued, "Take the arrows"; and he took them. He said to the king of Israel, "Strike the ground with them"; he struck three times, and stopped. 19 Then the man of God was angry with him, and said, "You should have struck five or six times; then you would have struck down Ar'am until you had made an end of it, but now you will strike down Ar'am only three times."

20 So E•lī'sha died, and they buried him. Now bands of Mō'ab•ites used to invade the land in the spring of the year. 21 As a man was being buried, a marauding band was seen and the man was thrown into the grave of E•lī'sha; as soon as the

---

o Gk Syr Tg Vg: Heb *he walked*   p Heb *Asherah*

man touched the bones of E•lī'sha, he came to life and stood on his feet.

Israel Recaptures Cities from Aram

22 Now King Haz'a•el of Ar'am oppressed Israel all the days of Je•hō'a•haz. 23 But the LORD was gracious to them and had compassion on them; he turned toward them, because of his covenant with Abraham, Isaac, and Jacob, and would not destroy them; nor has he banished them from his presence until now.

24 When King Haz'a•el of Ar'am died, his son Ben-ha'dad succeeded him. 25 Then Je•hō'ash son of Je•hō'a•haz took again from Ben-ha'dad son of Haz'a•el the towns that he had taken from his father Je•hō'a•haz in war. Three times Jō'ash defeated him and recovered the towns of Israel.

Amaziah Reigns over Judah
(2 Chr 25.1—26.2)

In the second year of King Jō'ash son of Jō'a•haz of Israel, King Am•a•zī'ah son of Jō'ash of Judah, began to reign. 2 He was twenty-five years old when he began to reign, and he reigned twenty-nine years in Jerusalem. His mother's name was Jē•hō-ad'din of Jerusalem. 3 He did what was right in the sight of the LORD, yet not like his ancestor David; in all things he did as his father Jō'ash had done. 4 But the high places were not removed; the people still sacrificed and made offerings on the high places. 5 As soon as the royal power was firmly in his hand he killed his servants who had murdered his father the king. 6 But he did not put to death the children of the murderers; according to what is written in the book of the law of Moses, where the LORD commanded, "The parents shall not be put to death for the children, or the children be put to death for the parents; but all shall be put to death for their own sins."

7 He killed ten thousand Ē'dom•ites in the Valley of Salt and took Sē'la by storm; he called it Jok'thē-el, which is its name to this day.

8 Then Am•a•zī'ah sent messengers to King Je•hō'ash son of Je•hō'a•haz, son of Jē'hū, of Israel, saying, "Come, let us look one another in the face." 9 King Je•hō'ash of Israel sent word to King Am•a•zī'ah of Judah, "A thornbush on Lebanon sent to a cedar on Lebanon, saying, 'Give your daughter to my son for a wife'; but a wild animal of Lebanon passed by and trampled down the thornbush. 10 You have indeed defeated Ē'dom, and your heart has lifted you up. Be content with your glory, and stay at home; for why should you provoke trouble so that you fall, you and Judah with you?"

11 But Am•a•zī'ah would not listen. So King Je•hō'ash of Israel went up; he and King Am•a•zī'ah of Judah faced one another in battle at Beth-shē'mesh, which belongs to Judah. 12 Judah was defeated by Israel; everyone fled home. 13 King Je•hō'ash of Israel captured King Am•a•zī'ah of Judah son of Je•hō'ash, son of A•ha•zī'ah, at Beth-shē'mesh; he came to Jerusalem, and broke down the wall of Jerusalem from the Ē'phra•im Gate to the Corner Gate, a distance of four hundred cubits. 14 He seized all the gold and silver, and all the vessels that were found in the house of the LORD and in the treasuries of the king's house, as well as hostages; then he returned to Sa•mār'i•a.

15 Now the rest of the acts that Je•hō'ash did, his might, and how he fought with King Am•a•zī'ah of Judah, are they not written in the Book of the Annals of the Kings of Israel? 16 Je•hō'ash slept with his ancestors, and was buried in Sa•mār'i•a with the kings of Israel; then his son Jer•o•bō'am succeeded him.

17 King Am•a•zī'ah son of Jō'ash of Judah lived fifteen years after the death of King Je•hō'ash son of Je•hō'a•haz of Israel. 18 Now the rest of the deeds of Am•a•zī'ah, are they not written in the Book of the Annals of the Kings of Judah? 19 They made a conspiracy against him in Jerusalem, and he fled to Lā'chish. But they sent after him to Lā'chish, and killed him there. 20 They brought him on horses; he was buried in Jerusalem with his ancestors in the city of David. 21 All the people of Judah took Az•a•rī'ah, who was sixteen years old, and made him king to succeed his father Am•a•zī'ah. 22 He rebuilt Ē'lath and restored it to Judah, after King Am•a•zī'ah*q* slept with his ancestors.

Jeroboam II Reigns over Israel

23 In the fifteenth year of King Am•a•zī'ah son of Jō'ash of Judah, King Jer•o•bō'am son of Jō'ash of Israel began to reign in Sa•mār'i•a; he reigned forty-one years. 24 He did what was evil in the sight of the LORD; he did not depart from all the sins of Jer•o•bō'am son of Nē'bat, which he caused Israel to sin. 25 He restored the border of Israel from Lē'bo-ha'math as far as the Sea of the Ar'a•bah, according to the word of the LORD, the God of Israel, which he spoke by his servant Jonah son of A•mit'tai, the prophet, who was from Gath-hē'pher. 26 For the LORD saw that the distress of Israel was very bitter; there was no one left, bond or free, and no one to help Israel. 27 But the LORD had not said that he would blot out the name of Israel from under heaven, so he saved them by the hand of Jer•o•bō'am son of Jō'ash.

28 Now the rest of the acts of Jer•o•bō'am, and all that he did, and his might, how he fought, and

q Heb the king

how he recovered for Israel Damascus and Hā'-math, which had belonged to Judah, are they not written in the Book of the Annals of the Kings of Israel? 29 Jer•o•bō'am slept with his ancestors, the kings of Israel; his son Zech•a•rī'ah succeeded him.

Azariah Reigns over Judah
(2 Chr 26.3–23)

In the twenty-seventh year of King Jer•o•bō'am of Israel King Az•a•rī'ah son of Am•a•zī'ah of Judah be-gan to reign. 2 He was sixteen years old when he began to reign, and he reigned fifty-two years in Jerusalem. His mother's name was Jec•o•lī'ah of Je-rusalem. 3 He did what was right in the sight of the LORD, just as his father Am•a•zī'ah had done. 4 Nev-ertheless the high places were not taken away; the people still sacrificed and made offerings on the high places. 5 The LORD struck the king, so that he was leprous^r to the day of his death, and lived in a separate house. Jō'tham the king's son was in charge of the palace, governing the people of the land. 6 Now the rest of the acts of Az•a•rī'ah, and all that he did, are they not written in the Book of the Annals of the Kings of Judah? 7 Az•a•rī'ah slept with his ancestors; they buried him with his ancestors in the city of David; his son Jō'tham succeeded him.

Zechariah Reigns over Israel

8 In the thirty-eighth year of King Az•a•rī'ah of Judah, Zech•a•rī'ah son of Jer•o•bō'am reigned over Israel in Sa•mār'i•a six months. 9 He did what was evil in the sight of the LORD, as his ancestors had done. He did not depart from the sins of Jer•o•bō'am son of Nē'bat, which he caused Israel to sin. 10 Shal'lum son of Jā'besh conspired against him, and struck him down in public and killed him, and reigned in place of him. 11 Now the rest of the deeds of Zech•a•rī'ah are written in the Book of the Annals of the Kings of Israel. 12 This was the promise of the LORD that he gave to Jē'hū, "Your sons shall sit on the throne of Israel to the fourth generation." And so it happened.

Shallum Reigns over Israel

13 Shal'lum son of Jā'besh began to reign in the thirty-ninth year of King Uz•zī'ah of Judah; he reigned one month in Sa•mār'i•a. 14 Then Men'a•hem son of Gā'dī came up from Tir'zah and came to Sa•mār'i•a; he struck down Shal'lum son of Jā'besh in Sa•mār'i•a and killed him; he reigned in place of him. 15 Now the rest of the deeds of Shal'-lum, including the conspiracy that he made, are written in the Book of the Annals of the Kings of Israel. 16 At that time Men'a•hem sacked Tiph'sah, all who were in it and its territory from Tir'zah on;

because they did not open it to him, he sacked it. He ripped open all the pregnant women in it.

Menahem Reigns over Israel

17 In the thirty-ninth year of King Az•a•rī'ah of Judah, Men'a•hem son of Gā'dī began to reign over Israel; he reigned ten years in Sa•mār'i•a. 18 He did what was evil in the sight of the LORD; he did not depart all his days from any of the sins of Jer•o•bō'am son of Nē'bat, which he caused Israel to sin. 19 King Pūl of Assyria came against the land; Men'a•hem gave Pūl a thousand talents of silver, so that he might help him confirm his hold on the royal power. 20 Men'a•hem exacted the money from Israel, that is, from all the wealthy, fifty shekels of silver from each one, to give to the king of Assyria. So the king of Assyria turned back, and did not stay there in the land. 21 Now the rest of the deeds of Men'a•hem, and all that he did, are they not written in the Book of the Annals of the Kings of Israel? 22 Men'a•hem slept with his ancestors, and his son Pek•a•hī'ah succeeded him.

Pekahiah Reigns over Israel

23 In the fiftieth year of King Az•a•rī'ah of Ju-dah, Pek•a•hī'ah son of Men'a•hem began to reign over Israel in Sa•mār'i•a; he reigned two years. 24 He did what was evil in the sight of the LORD; he did not turn away from the sins of Jer•o•bō'am son of Nē'bat, which he caused Israel to sin. 25 Pē'kah son of Rem•a•lī'ah, his captain, conspired against him with fifty of the Gil'e•ad•ites, and attacked him in Sa•mār'i•a, in the citadel of the palace along with Ar'gob and A•rī'eh; he killed him, and reigned in place of him. 26 Now the rest of the deeds of Pek•a•hī'ah, and all that he did, are written in the Book of the Annals of the Kings of Israel.

Pekah Reigns over Israel

27 In the fifty-second year of King Az•a•rī'ah of Judah, Pē'kah son of Rem•a•lī'ah began to reign over Israel in Sa•mār'i•a; he reigned twenty years. 28 He did what was evil in the sight of the LORD; he did not depart from the sins of Jer•o•bō'am son of Nē'bat, which he caused Israel to sin.

29 In the days of King Pē'kah of Israel, King Tig'lath-pi•lē'ser of Assyria came and captured I'jon, Ā'bel-beth-mā'a•cah, Ja•nō'ah, Kē'desh, Hā'-zor, Gil'e•ad, and Galilee, all the land of Naph'ta•lī; and he carried the people captive to Assyria. 30 Then Hō•shē'a son of Ē'lah made a conspiracy against Pē'kah son of Rem•a•lī'ah, attacked him, and killed him; he reigned in place of him, in the

---

r A term for several skin diseases; precise meaning uncertain

twentieth year of Jō'tham son of Uz·zī'ah. ³¹ Now the rest of the acts of Pē'kah, and all that he did, are written in the Book of the Annals of the Kings of Israel.

Jotham Reigns over Judah
(2 Chr 27.1–9)

32 In the second year of King Pē'kah son of Rem·a·lī'ah of Israel, King Jō'tham son of Uz·zī'ah of Judah began to reign. ³³ He was twenty-five years old when he began to reign and reigned sixteen years in Jerusalem. His mother's name was Je·rū'sha daughter of Zā'dok. ³⁴ He did what was right in the sight of the LORD, just as his father Uz·zī'ah had done. ³⁵ Nevertheless the high places were not removed; the people still sacrificed and made offerings on the high places. He built the upper gate of the house of the LORD. ³⁶ Now the rest of the acts of Jō'tham, and all that he did, are they not written in the Book of the Annals of the Kings of Judah? ³⁷ In those days the LORD began to send King Rē'zin of Ar'am and Pē'kah son of Rem·a·lī'ah against Judah. ³⁸ Jō'tham slept with his ancestors, and was buried with his ancestors in the city of David, his ancestor; his son Ā'haz succeeded him.

Ahaz Reigns over Judah
(2 Chr 28.1–27)

In the seventeenth year of Pē'kah son of Rem·a·lī'ah, King Ā'haz son of Jō'tham of Judah began to reign. ² Ā'haz was twenty years old when he began to reign; he reigned sixteen years in Jerusalem. He did not do what was right in the sight of the LORD his God, as his ancestor David had done, ³ but he walked in the way of the kings of Israel. He even made his son pass through fire, according to the abominable practices of the nations whom the LORD drove out before the people of Israel. ⁴ He sacrificed and made offerings on the high places, on the hills, and under every green tree.

5 Then King Rē'zin of Ar'am and King Pē'kah son of Rem·a·lī'ah of Israel came up to wage war on Jerusalem; they besieged Ā'haz but could not conquer him. ⁶ At that time the king of Ē'dom ˢ recovered Ē'lath for Ē'dom, ᵗ and drove the Judeans from Ē'lath; and the Ē'dom·ites came to Ē'lath, where they live to this day. ⁷ Ā'haz sent messengers to King Tig'lath-pi·lē'ser of Assyria, saying, "I am your servant and your son. Come up, and rescue me from the hand of the king of Ar'am and from the hand of the king of Israel, who are attacking me." ⁸ Ā'haz also took the silver and gold found in the house of the LORD and in the treasures of the king's house, and sent a present to the king of Assyria. ⁹ The king of Assyria listened to him; the

king of Assyria marched up against Damascus, and took it, carrying its people captive to Kir; then he killed Rē'zin.

10 When King Ā'haz went to Damascus to meet King Tig'lath-pi·lē'ser of Assyria, he saw the altar that was at Damascus. King Ā'haz sent to the priest Ū·rī'ah a model of the altar, and its pattern, exact in all its details. ¹¹ The priest Ū·rī'ah built the altar; in accordance with all that King Ā'haz had sent from Damascus, just so did the priest Ū·rī'ah build it, before King Ā'haz arrived from Damascus. ¹² When the king came from Damascus, the king viewed the altar. Then the king drew near to the altar, went up on it, ¹³ and offered his burnt offering and his grain offering, poured his drink offering, and dashed the blood of his offerings of well-being against the altar. ¹⁴ The bronze altar that was before the LORD he removed from the front of the house, from the place between his altar and the house of the LORD, and put it on the north side of his altar. ¹⁵ King Ā'haz commanded the priest Ū·rī'ah, saying, "Upon the great altar offer the morning burnt offering, and the evening grain offering, and the king's burnt offering, and his grain offering, with the burnt offering of all the people of the land, their grain offering, and their drink offering; then dash against it all the blood of the burnt offering, and all the blood of the sacrifice; but the bronze altar shall be for me to inquire by." ¹⁶ The priest Ū·rī'ah did everything that King Ā'haz commanded.

17 Then King Ā'haz cut off the frames of the stands, and removed the laver from them; he removed the sea from the bronze oxen that were under it, and put it on a pediment of stone. ¹⁸ The covered portal for use on the sabbath that had been built inside the palace, and the outer entrance for the king he removed from ᵘ the house of the LORD. He did this because of the king of Assyria. ¹⁹ Now the rest of the acts of Ā'haz that he did, are they not written in the Book of the Annals of the Kings of Judah? ²⁰ Ā'haz slept with his ancestors, and was buried with his ancestors in the city of David; his son Hez·e·kī'ah succeeded him.

Hoshea Reigns over Israel

In the twelfth year of King Ā'haz of Judah, Hō·shē'a son of Ē'lah began to reign in Sa·mār'i·a over Israel; he reigned nine years. ² He did what was evil in the sight of the LORD, yet not like the kings of Israel who were before him. ³ King Shal·man·ē'ser of Assyria came up against him; Hō·shē'a became his vassal, and paid him tribute. ⁴ But the

---

ˢ Cn: Heb *King Rezin of Aram*   ᵗ Cn: Heb *Aram*
ᵘ Cn: Heb lacks *from*

king of Assyria found treachery in Hō·shē′a; for he had sent messengers to King So of Egypt, and offered no tribute to the king of Assyria, as he had done year by year; therefore the king of Assyria confined him and imprisoned him.

Israel Carried Captive to Assyria

5 Then the king of Assyria invaded all the land and came to Sa·mār′i·a; for three years he besieged it. 6 In the ninth year of Hō·shē′a the king of Assyria captured Sa·mār′i·a; he carried the Israelites away to Assyria. He placed them in Hā′lah, on the Hā′bor, the river of Gō′zan, and in the cities of the Mēdes.

did you KNOW?

The First Captivity

The Second Book of Kings describes two captivities and exiles. The first one is the Assyrian conquest of the northern kingdom, Israel, which occurred in 721 B.C. (see map 4, "The Assyrian Empire"). According to the author of 2 Kings, Israel fell first because its kings and people were even less faithful to God than the kings and people of Judah, the southern kingdom. Notice that the Assyrian conquest is described in the briefest detail (17.5–6), but the reasons for it are described in great detail (verses 7–18).

▶ **2 Kings 17.5–18**

7 This occurred because the people of Israel had sinned against the LORD their God, who had brought them up out of the land of Egypt from under the hand of Pharaoh king of Egypt. They had worshiped other gods 8 and walked in the customs of the nations whom the LORD drove out before the people of Israel, and in the customs that the kings of Israel had introduced.ᵛ 9 The people of Israel secretly did things that were not right against the LORD their God. They built for themselves high places at all their towns, from watchtower to fortified city; 10 they set up for themselves pillars and sacred polesʷ on every high hill and under every green tree; 11 there they made offerings on all the high places, as the nations did whom the LORD car-

ried away before them. They did wicked things, provoking the LORD to anger; 12 they served idols, of which the LORD had said to them, "You shall not do this." 13 Yet the LORD warned Israel and Judah by every prophet and every seer, saying, "Turn from your evil ways and keep my commandments and my statutes, in accordance with all the law that I commanded your ancestors and that I sent to you by my servants the prophets." 14 They would not listen but were stubborn, as their ancestors had been, who did not believe in the LORD their God. 15 They despised his statutes, and his covenant that he made with their ancestors, and the warnings that he gave them. They went after false idols and became false; they followed the nations that were around them, concerning whom the LORD had commanded them that they should not do as they did. 16 They rejected all the commandments of the LORD their God and made for themselves cast images of two calves; they made a sacred pole,ˣ worshiped all the host of heaven, and served Bā′al. 17 They made their sons and their daughters pass through fire; they used divination and augury; and they sold themselves to do evil in the sight of the LORD, provoking him to anger. 18 Therefore the LORD was very angry with Israel and removed them out of his sight; none was left but the tribe of Judah alone.

19 Judah also did not keep the commandments of the LORD their God but walked in the customs that Israel had introduced. 20 The LORD rejected all the descendants of Israel; he punished them and gave them into the hand of plunderers, until he had banished them from his presence.

21 When he had torn Israel from the house of David, they made Jer·o·bō′am son of Nē′bat king. Jer·o·bō′am drove Israel from following the LORD and made them commit great sin. 22 The people of Israel continued in all the sins that Jer·o·bō′am committed; they did not depart from them 23 until the LORD removed Israel out of his sight, as he had foretold through all his servants the prophets. So Israel was exiled from their own land to Assyria until this day.

Assyria Resettles Samaria

24 The king of Assyria brought people from Babylon, Cū′thah, Av′va, Hā′math, and Seph·ar·vā′im, and placed them in the cities of Sa·mār′i·a in place of the people of Israel; they took possession of Sa·mār′i·a, and settled in its cities. 25 When they first settled there, they did not worship the LORD; therefore the LORD sent lions among them, which

---

ᵛ Meaning of Heb uncertain   ʷ Heb *Asherim*
ˣ Heb *Asherah*

killed some of them. 26 So the king of Assyria was told, "The nations that you have carried away and placed in the cities of Sa•mār′i•a do not know the law of the god of the land; therefore he has sent lions among them; they are killing them, because they do not know the law of the god of the land." 27 Then the king of Assyria commanded, "Send there one of the priests whom you carried away from there; let him*y* go and live there, and teach them the law of the god of the land." 28 So one of the priests whom they had carried away from Sa•mār′i•a came and lived in Beth′el; he taught them how they should worship the LORD.

29 But every nation still made gods of its own and put them in the shrines of the high places that the people of Sa•mār′i•a had made, every nation in the cities in which they lived; 30 the people of Babylon made Suc′coth-bē′noth, the people of Cuth made Ner′gal, the people of Hā′math made A•shī′ma; 31 the Av′vites made Nib′haz and Tar′tak; the Se•phar′vites burned their children in the fire to A•dram′me•lech and A•nam′me•lech, the gods of Seph•ar•vā′im. 32 They also worshiped the LORD and appointed from among themselves all sorts of people as priests of the high places, who sacrificed for them in the shrines of the high places. 33 So they worshiped the LORD but also served their own gods, after the manner of the nations from among whom they had been carried away. 34 To this day they continue to practice their former customs.

They do not worship the LORD and they do not follow the statutes or the ordinances or the law or the commandment that the LORD commanded the children of Jacob, whom he named Israel. 35 The LORD had made a covenant with them and commanded them, "You shall not worship other gods or bow yourselves to them or serve them or sacrifice to them, 36 but you shall worship the LORD, who brought you out of the land of Egypt with great power and with an outstretched arm; you shall bow yourselves to him, and to him you shall sacrifice. 37 The statutes and the ordinances and the law and the commandment that he wrote for you, you shall always be careful to observe. You shall not worship other gods; 38 you shall not forget the covenant that I have made with you. You shall not worship other gods; 39 but you shall worship the LORD your God; he will deliver you out of the hand of all your enemies." 40 They would not listen, however, but they continued to practice their former custom.

41 So these nations worshiped the LORD, but also served their carved images; to this day their children and their children's children continue to do as their ancestors did.

Hezekiah's Reign over Judah
(2 Chr 29.1–2; 31.1)

In the third year of King Hō•shē′a son of Ē′lah of Israel, Hez•e•kī′ah son of King Ā′haz of Judah began to reign. 2 He was twenty-five years old when he began to reign; he reigned twenty-nine years in Jerusalem. His mother's name was Ā′bī daughter of Zech•a•rī′ah. 3 He did what was right in the sight of the LORD just as his ancestor David had done. 4 He removed the high places, broke down the pillars, and cut down the sacred pole.*z* He broke in pieces the bronze serpent that Moses had made, for until those days the people of Israel had made offerings to it; it was called Ne•hush′tan. 5 He trusted in the LORD the God of Israel; so that there was no one like him among all the kings of Judah after him, or among those who were before him. 6 For he held fast to the LORD; he did not depart from following him but kept the commandments that the LORD commanded Moses. 7 The LORD was with him; wherever he went, he prospered. He rebelled against the king of Assyria and would not serve him. 8 He attacked the Phi•lis′tines as far as Ga′za and its territory, from watchtower to fortified city.

9 In the fourth year of King Hez•e•kī′ah, which was the seventh year of King Hō•shē′a son of Ē′lah of Israel, King Shal•man•ē′ser of Assyria came up against Sa•mār′i•a, besieged it, 10 and at the end of three years, took it. In the sixth year of Hez•e•kī′ah, which was the ninth year of King Hō•shē′a of Israel, Sa•mār′i•a was taken. 11 The king of Assyria carried the Israelites away to Assyria, settled them in Hā′lah, on the Hā′bor, the river of Gō′zan, and in the cities of the Mēdes, 12 because they did not obey the voice of the LORD their God but transgressed his covenant—all that Moses the servant of the LORD had commanded; they neither listened nor obeyed.

Sennacherib Invades Judah
(Isa 36.1–22; 2 Chr 32.1–19)

13 In the fourteenth year of King Hez•e•kī′ah, King Sen•nach′e•rib of Assyria came up against all the fortified cities of Judah and captured them. 14 King Hez•e•kī′ah of Judah sent to the king of Assyria at Lā′chish, saying, "I have done wrong; withdraw from me; whatever you impose on me I will bear." The king of Assyria demanded of King Hez•e•kī′ah of Judah three hundred talents of silver and thirty talents of gold. 15 Hez•e•kī′ah gave him all the silver that was found in the house of the LORD and in the treasuries of the king's house. 16 At that time Hez•e•kī′ah stripped the gold from the

---

y Syr Vg: Heb *them*   *z* Heb *Asherah*

doors of the temple of the LORD, and from the doorposts that King Hez•e•kī'ah of Judah had overlaid and gave it to the king of Assyria. ¹⁷The king of Assyria sent the Tar'tan, the Rab'sar'is, and the Rab'sha•keh with a great army from Lā'chish to King Hez•e•kī'ah at Jerusalem. They went up and came to Jerusalem. When they arrived, they came and stood by the conduit of the upper pool, which is on the highway to the Fuller's Field. ¹⁸When they called for the king, there came out to them E•lī'a•kim son of Hil•kī'ah, who was in charge of the palace, and Sheb'nah the secretary, and Jō'ah son of Ā'saph, the recorder.

19 The Rab'sha•keh said to them, "Say to Hez•e•kī'ah: Thus says the great king, the king of Assyria: On what do you base this confidence of yours? ²⁰Do you think that mere words are strategy and power for war? On whom do you now rely, that you have rebelled against me? ²¹See, you are relying now on Egypt, that broken reed of a staff, which will pierce the hand of anyone who leans on it. Such is Pharaoh king of Egypt to all who rely on him. ²²But if you say to me, 'We rely on the LORD our God,' is it not he whose high places and altars Hez•e•kī'ah has removed, saying to Judah and to Jerusalem, 'You shall worship before this altar in Jerusalem'? ²³Come now, make a wager with my master the king of Assyria: I will give you two thousand horses, if you are able on your part to set riders on them. ²⁴How then can you repulse a single captain among the least of my master's servants, when you rely on Egypt for chariots and for horsemen? ²⁵Moreover, is it without the LORD that I have come up against this place to destroy it? The LORD said to me, Go up against this land, and destroy it."

26 Then E•lī'a•kim son of Hil•kī'ah, and Sheb'-nah, and Jō'ah said to the Rab'sha•keh, "Please speak to your servants in the Ar•a•mā'ic language, for we understand it; do not speak to us in the language of Judah within the hearing of the people who are on the wall." ²⁷But the Rab'sha•keh said to them, "Has my master sent me to speak these words to your master and to you, and not to the people sitting on the wall, who are doomed with you to eat their own dung and to drink their own urine?"

28 Then the Rab'sha•keh stood and called out in a loud voice in the language of Judah, "Hear the word of the great king, the king of Assyria! ²⁹Thus says the king: 'Do not let Hez•e•kī'ah deceive you, for he will not be able to deliver you out of my hand. ³⁰Do not let Hez•e•kī'ah make you rely on the LORD by saying, The LORD will surely deliver us, and this city will not be given into the hand of the king of Assyria.' ³¹Do not listen to Hez•e•kī'ah;

for thus says the king of Assyria: 'Make your peace with me and come out to me; then every one of you will eat from your own vine and your own fig tree, and drink water from your own cistern, ³²until I come and take you away to a land like your own land, a land of grain and wine, a land of bread and vineyards, a land of olive oil and honey, that you may live and not die. Do not listen to Hez•e•kī'ah when he misleads you by saying, The LORD will deliver us. ³³Has any of the gods of the nations ever delivered its land out of the hand of the king of Assyria? ³⁴Where are the gods of Hā'-math and Ar'pad? Where are the gods of Sephar•vā'im, Hē'na, and Iv'vah? Have they delivered Sa•mār'i•a out of my hand? ³⁵Who among all the gods of the countries have delivered their countries out of my hand, that the LORD should deliver Jerusalem out of my hand?' "

36 But the people were silent and answered him not a word, for the king's command was, "Do not answer him." ³⁷Then E•lī'a•kim son of Hil•kī'ah, who was in charge of the palace, and Sheb'na the secretary, and Jō'ah son of Ā'saph, the recorder, came to Hez•e•kī'ah with their clothes torn and told him the words of the Rab'sha•keh.

Hezekiah Consults Isaiah
(Isa 37.1–7)

19 When King Hez•e•kī'ah heard it, he tore his clothes, covered himself with sackcloth, and went into the house of the LORD. ²And he sent E•lī'a•kim, who was in charge of the palace, and Sheb'na the secretary, and the senior priests, covered with sackcloth, to the prophet Ī•sāi'ah son of Ā'moz. ³They said to him, "Thus says Hez•e•kī'ah, This day is a day of distress, of rebuke, and of disgrace; children have come to the birth, and there is no strength to bring them forth. ⁴It may be that the LORD your God heard all the words of the Rab'sha•keh, whom his master the king of Assyria has sent to mock the living God, and will rebuke the words that the LORD your God has heard; therefore lift up your prayer for the remnant that is left." ⁵When the servants of King Hez•e•kī'ah came to Ī•sāi'ah, ⁶Ī•sāi'ah said to them, "Say to your master, 'Thus says the LORD: Do not be afraid because of the words that you have heard, with which the servants of the king of Assyria have reviled me. ⁷I myself will put a spirit in him, so that he shall hear a rumor and return to his own land; I will cause him to fall by the sword in his own land.' "

Sennacherib's Threat
(Isa 37.8–13)

8 The Rab'sha•keh returned, and found the king of Assyria fighting against Lib'nah; for he had

heard that the king had left Lāʹchish. 9 When the kingᵃ heard concerning King Tirʹhāʹkah of Ethiopia,ᵇ "See, he has set out to fight against you," he sent messengers again to Hezʹeʹkīʹah, saying, 10 "Thus shall you speak to King Hezʹeʹkīʹah of Judah: Do not let your God on whom you rely deceive you by promising that Jerusalem will not be given into the hand of the king of Assyria. 11 See, you have heard what the kings of Assyria have done to all lands, destroying them utterly. Shall you be delivered? 12 Have the gods of the nations delivered them, the nations that my predecessors destroyed, Gōʹzan, Harʹan, Rĕʹzeph, and the people of Eden who were in Teʹlasʹsar? 13 Where is the king of Hāʹmath, the king of Arʹpad, the king of the city of Sephʹarʹvāʹim, the king of Hĕʹna, or the king of Ivʹvah?"

Hezekiah's Prayer
(Isa 37.14–35)

14 Hezʹeʹkīʹah received the letter from the hand of the messengers and read it; then Hezʹeʹkīʹah went up to the house of the LORD and spread it before the LORD. 15 And Hezʹeʹkīʹah prayed before the LORD, and said: "O LORD the God of Israel, who are enthroned above the cherubim, you are God, you alone, of all the kingdoms of the earth; you have made heaven and earth. 16 Incline your ear, O LORD, and hear; open your eyes, O LORD, and see; hear the words of Senʹnachʹeʹrib, which he has sent to mock the living God. 17 Truly, O LORD, the kings of Assyria have laid waste the nations and their lands, 18 and have hurled their gods into the fire, though they were no gods but the work of human hands—wood and stone—and so they were destroyed. 19 So now, O LORD our God, save us, I pray you, from his hand, so that all the kingdoms of the earth may know that you, O LORD, are God alone."

20 Then Īʹsāiʹah son of Āʹmoz sent to Hezʹeʹkīʹah, saying, "Thus says the LORD, the God of Israel: I have heard your prayer to me about King Senʹnachʹeʹrib of Assyria. 21 This is the word that the LORD has spoken concerning him:

She despises you, she scorns you—
  virgin daughter Zion;
she tosses her head—behind your back,
  daughter Jerusalem.

22 "Whom have you mocked and reviled?
  Against whom have you raised your
    voice
and haughtily lifted your eyes?
  Against the Holy One of Israel!

23 By your messengers you have mocked the Lord,
  and you have said, 'With my many chariots
I have gone up the heights of the
    mountains,
  to the far recesses of Lebanon;
I felled its tallest cedars,
  its choicest cypresses;
I entered its farthest retreat,
  its densest forest.
24 I dug wells
  and drank foreign waters,
I dried up with the sole of my foot
  all the streams of Egypt.'

25 "Have you not heard
  that I determined it long ago?
I planned from days of old
  what now I bring to pass,
that you should make fortified cities
  crash into heaps of ruins,
26 while their inhabitants, shorn of strength,
  are dismayed and confounded;
they have become like plants of the field
  and like tender grass,
like grass on the housetops,
  blighted before it is grown.

27 "But I know your risingᶜ and your sitting,
  your going out and coming in,
  and your raging against me.
28 Because you have raged against me
  and your arrogance has come to my ears,
I will put my hook in your nose
  and my bit in your mouth;
I will turn you back on the way
  by which you came.

29 "And this shall be the sign for you: This year you shall eat what grows of itself, and in the second year what springs from that; then in the third year sow, reap, plant vineyards, and eat their fruit. 30 The surviving remnant of the house of Judah shall again take root downward, and bear fruit upward; 31 for from Jerusalem a remnant shall go out, and from Mount Zion a band of survivors. The zeal of the LORD of hosts will do this.

32 "Therefore thus says the LORD concerning the king of Assyria: He shall not come into this city, shoot an arrow there, come before it with a shield, or cast up a siege ramp against it. 33 By the way that he came, by the same he shall return; he shall not come into this city, says the LORD. 34 For I will defend this city to save it, for my own sake and for the sake of my servant David."

ᵃ Heb *he*   ᵇ Or *Nubia*; Heb *Cush*   ᶜ Gk Compare Isa 37.27 Q Ms: MT lacks *rising*

Sennacherib's Defeat and Death
(Isa 37.36–38; 2 Chr 32.20–23)

35 That very night the angel of the LORD set out and struck down one hundred eighty-five thousand in the camp of the Assyrians; when morning dawned, they were all dead bodies. 36 Then King Sen•nach'e•rib of Assyria left, went home, and lived at Nin'e•veh. 37 As he was worshiping in the house of his god Nis'roch, his sons A•dram'me•lech and Sha•re'zer killed him with the sword, and they escaped into the land of Ar'a•rat. His son E'sar-had'don succeeded him.

Hezekiah's Illness
(2 Chr 32.24–26; Isa 38.1–8)

In those days Hez•e•kī'ah became sick and was at the point of death. The prophet Ī•sāi'ah son of Ā'moz came to him, and said to him, "Thus says the LORD: Set your house in order, for you shall die; you shall not recover." 2 Then Hez•e•kī'ah turned his face to the wall and prayed to the LORD: 3 "Remember now, O LORD, I implore you, how I have walked before you in faithfulness with a whole heart, and have done what is good in your sight." Hez•e•kī'ah wept bitterly. 4 Before Ī•sāi'ah had gone out of the middle court, the word of the LORD came to him: 5 "Turn back, and say to Hez•e•kī'ah prince of my people, Thus says the LORD, the God of your ancestor David: I have heard your prayer, I have seen your tears; indeed, I will heal you; on the third day you shall go up to the house of the LORD. 6 I will add fifteen years to your life. I will deliver you and this city out of the hand of the king of Assyria; I will defend this city for my own sake and for my servant David's sake." 7 Then Ī•sāi'ah said, "Bring a lump of figs. Let them take it and apply it to the boil, so that he may recover."

8 Hez•e•kī'ah said to Ī•sāi'ah, "What shall be the sign that the LORD will heal me, and that I shall go up to the house of the LORD on the third day?" 9 Ī•sāi'ah said, "This is the sign to you from the LORD, that the LORD will do the thing that he has promised: the shadow has now advanced ten intervals; shall it retreat ten intervals?" 10 Hez•e•kī'ah answered, "It is normal for the shadow to lengthen ten intervals; rather let the shadow retreat ten intervals." 11 The prophet Ī•sāi'ah cried to the LORD; and he brought the shadow back the ten intervals, by which the sun[d] had declined on the dial of Ā'haz.

Envoys from Babylon
(Isa 39.1–8)

12 At that time King Mer'o•dach-bal'a•dan son of Bal'a•dan of Babylon sent envoys with letters and a present to Hez•e•kī'ah, for he had heard that Hez•e•kī'ah had been sick. 13 Hez•e•kī'ah welcomed them;[e] he showed them all his treasure house, the silver, the gold, the spices, the precious oil, his armory, all that was found in his storehouses; there was nothing in his house or in all his realm that Hez•e•kī'ah did not show them. 14 Then the prophet Ī•sāi'ah came to King Hez•e•kī'ah, and said to him, "What did these men say? From where did they come to you?" Hez•e•kī'ah answered, "They have come from a far country, from Babylon." 15 He said, "What have they seen in your house?" Hez•e•kī'ah answered, "They have seen all that is in my house; there is nothing in my storehouses that I did not show them."

16 Then Ī•sāi'ah said to Hez•e•kī'ah, "Hear the word of the LORD: 17 Days are coming when all that is in your house, and that which your ancestors have stored up until this day, shall be carried to Babylon; nothing shall be left, says the LORD. 18 Some of your own sons who are born to you shall be taken away; they shall be eunuchs in the palace of the king of Babylon." 19 Then Hez•e•kī'ah said to Ī•sāi'ah, "The word of the LORD that you have spoken is good." For he thought, "Why not, if there will be peace and security in my days?"

Death of Hezekiah
(2 Chr 32.32–33)

20 The rest of the deeds of Hez•e•kī'ah, all his power, how he made the pool and the conduit and brought water into the city, are they not written in the Book of the Annals of the Kings of Judah? 21 Hez•e•kī'ah slept with his ancestors; and his son Ma•nas'seh succeeded him.

Manasseh Reigns over Judah
(2 Chr 33.1–20)

Ma•nas'seh was twelve years old when he began to reign; he reigned fifty-five years in Jerusalem. His mother's name was Heph'zi•bah. 2 He did what was evil in the sight of the LORD, following the abominable practices of the nations that the LORD drove out before the people of Israel. 3 For he rebuilt the high places that his father Hez•e•kī'ah had destroyed; he erected altars for Bā'al, made a sacred pole,[f] as King Ā'hab of Israel had done, worshiped all the host of heaven, and served them. 4 He built altars in the house of the LORD, of which the LORD had said, "In Jerusalem I will put my name." 5 He built altars for all the host of heaven in the two courts of the house of the LORD. 6 He made his son pass through fire; he practiced soothsaying

---

d Syr See Isa 38.8 and Tg: Heb *it*   e Gk Vg Syr: Heb *When Hezekiah heard about them*   f Heb *Asherah*

---

and augury, and dealt with mediums and with wizards. He did much evil in the sight of the LORD, provoking him to anger. 7 The carved image of A•shĕ'rah that he had made he set in the house of which the LORD said to David and to his son Solomon, "In this house, and in Jerusalem, which I have chosen out of all the tribes of Israel, I will put my name forever; 8 I will not cause the feet of Israel to wander any more out of the land that I gave to their ancestors, if only they will be careful to do according to all that I have commanded them, and according to all the law that my servant Moses commanded them." 9 But they did not listen; Manas'seh misled them to do more evil than the nations had done that the LORD destroyed before the people of Israel.

10 The LORD said by his servants the prophets, 11 "Because King Ma•nas'seh of Judah has committed these abominations, has done things more wicked than all that the Am'o•rītes did, who were before him, and has caused Judah also to sin with his idols; 12 therefore thus says the LORD, the God of Israel, I am bringing upon Jerusalem and Judah such evil that the ears of everyone who hears of it will tingle. 13 I will stretch over Jerusalem the measuring line for Sa•mār'i•a, and the plummet for the house of Ā'hab; I will wipe Jerusalem as one wipes a dish, wiping it and turning it upside down. 14 I will cast off the remnant of my heritage, and give them into the hand of their enemies; they shall become a prey and a spoil to all their enemies, 15 because they have done what is evil in my sight and have provoked me to anger, since the day their ancestors came out of Egypt, even to this day."

16 Moreover Ma•nas'seh shed very much innocent blood, until he had filled Jerusalem from one end to another, besides the sin that he caused Judah to sin so that they did what was evil in the sight of the LORD.

17 Now the rest of the acts of Ma•nas'seh, all that he did, and the sin that he committed, are they not written in the Book of the Annals of the Kings of Judah? 18 Ma•nas'seh slept with his ancestors, and was buried in the garden of his house, in the garden of Uz'za. His son Ā'mon succeeded him.

Amon Reigns over Judah
(2 Chr 33.21–25)

19 Ā'mon was twenty-two years old when he began to reign; he reigned two years in Jerusalem. His mother's name was Me•shul'le•meth daughter of Hā'ruz of Jot'bah. 20 He did what was evil in the sight of the LORD, as his father Ma•nas'seh had done. 21 He walked in all the way in which his father walked, served the idols that his father

served, and worshiped them; 22 he abandoned the LORD, the God of his ancestors, and did not walk in the way of the LORD. 23 The servants of Ā'mon conspired against him, and killed the king in his house. 24 But the people of the land killed all those who had conspired against King Ā'mon, and the people of the land made his son Jō•sī'ah king in place of him. 25 Now the rest of the acts of Ā'mon that he did, are they not written in the Book of the Annals of the Kings of Judah? 26 He was buried in his tomb in the garden of Uz'za; then his son Jō•sī'ah succeeded him.

Josiah Reigns over Judah
(2 Chr 34.1–2)

Jō•sī'ah was eight years old when he began to reign; he reigned thirty-one years in Jerusalem. His mother's name was Je•dī'dah daughter of A•dāi'ah of Boz'kath. 2 He did what was right in the sight of the LORD, and walked in all the way of his father David; he did not turn aside to the right or to the left.

Hilkiah Finds the Book of the Law
(2 Chr 34.8–28)

3 In the eighteenth year of King Jō•sī'ah, the king sent Shā'phan son of Az•a•lī'ah, son of Meshul'lam, the secretary, to the house of the LORD, saying, 4 "Go up to the high priest Hil•kī'ah, and have him count the entire sum of the money that has been brought into the house of the LORD, which the keepers of the threshold have collected from the people; 5 let it be given into the hand of the workers who have the oversight of the house of the LORD; let them give it to the workers who are at the house of the LORD, repairing the house, 6 that is, to the carpenters, to the builders, to the masons; and let them use it to buy timber and quarried stone to repair the house. 7 But no accounting shall be asked from them for the money that is delivered into their hand, for they deal honestly."

8 The high priest Hil•kī'ah said to Shā'phan the secretary, "I have found the book of the law in the house of the LORD." When Hil•kī'ah gave the book to Shā'phan, he read it. 9 Then Shā'phan the secretary came to the king, and reported to the king, "Your servants have emptied out the money that was found in the house, and have delivered it into the hand of the workers who have oversight of the house of the LORD." 10 Shā'phan the secretary informed the king, "The priest Hil•kī'ah has given me a book." Shā'phan then read it aloud to the king.

11 When the king heard the words of the book of the law, he tore his clothes. 12 Then the king commanded the priest Hil•kī'ah, A•hī'kam son of

PRAY IT!

Josiah Brings Back the Ways of God

What happened to the Covenant? What happened to the Israelites' true traditions and prayer rituals? After worshiping false gods for so long, it seems as if people just forgot about the Covenant! Then in 2 Kings 22.8, Hilkiah discovers an old book, King Josiah reads it, and a religious reform is started. Josiah's reform is an effort to know and obey God's law and to restore worship to the one, true God. The holy days and holy ways of God are back—at least for a while (see also 2 Chronicles, chapters 34–35).

Reading can be powerful. Christians have a tremendous tradition of spiritual writings that inspire and renew faith. Spiritual autobiographies like *The Confessions of St. Augustine; The Story of a Soul*, by Saint Thérèse of Lisieux; and *The Seven Storey Mountain*, by Thomas Merton, are classics. You might try starting with entertaining fictional books with a strong spiritual message, like the seven volumes of *The Chronicles of Narnia*, by C. S. Lewis, or the Joshua books, by Joseph F. Girzone. For other suggestions of spiritual writings you might enjoy, ask a parent, youth minister, teacher, or pastor.

▸ 2 Kings, chapters 22–23

Shā'phan, Ach'bor son of Mī•cāi'ah, Shā'phan the secretary, and the king's servant A•sāi'ah, saying, 13 "Go, inquire of the LORD for me, for the people, and for all Judah, concerning the words of this book that has been found; for great is the wrath of the LORD that is kindled against us, because our ancestors did not obey the words of this book, to do according to all that is written concerning us."

14 So the priest Hil•kī'ah, A•hī'kam, Ach'bor, Shā'phan, and A•sāi'ah went to the prophetess Hul'dah the wife of Shal'lum son of Tik'vah, son of Har'has, keeper of the wardrobe; she resided in Jerusalem in the Second Quarter, where they consulted her. 15 She declared to them, "Thus says the LORD, the God of Israel: Tell the man who sent you to me, 16 Thus says the LORD, I will indeed bring disaster on this place and on its inhabitants—all

the words of the book that the king of Judah has read. 17 Because they have abandoned me and have made offerings to other gods, so that they have provoked me to anger with all the work of their hands, therefore my wrath will be kindled against this place, and it will not be quenched. 18 But as to the king of Judah, who sent you to inquire of the LORD, thus shall you say to him, Thus says the LORD, the God of Israel: Regarding the words that you have heard, 19 because your heart was penitent, and you humbled yourself before the LORD, when you heard how I spoke against this place, and against its inhabitants, that they should become a desolation and a curse, and because you have torn your clothes and wept before me, I also have heard you, says the LORD. 20 Therefore, I will gather you to your ancestors, and you shall be gathered to your grave in peace; your eyes shall not see all the disaster that I will bring on this place." They took the message back to the king.

Josiah's Reformation
(2 Chr 34.29–33)

Then the king directed that all the elders of Judah and Jerusalem should be gathered to him. 2 The king went up to the house of the LORD, and with him went all the people of Judah, all the inhabitants of Jerusalem, the priests, the prophets, and all the people, both small and great; he read in their hearing all the words of the book of the covenant that had been found in the house of the LORD. 3 The king stood by the pillar and made a covenant before the LORD, to follow the LORD, keeping his commandments, his decrees, and his statutes, with all his heart and all his soul, to perform the words of this covenant that were written in this book. All the people joined in the covenant.

4 The king commanded the high priest Hil-kī'ah, the priests of the second order, and the guardians of the threshold, to bring out of the temple of the LORD all the vessels made for Bā'al, for A•shē'rah, and for all the host of heaven; he burned them outside Jerusalem in the fields of the Kid'ron, and carried their ashes to Beth'el. 5 He deposed the idolatrous priests whom the kings of Judah had ordained to make offerings in the high places at the cities of Judah and around Jerusalem; those also who made offerings to Bā'al, to the sun, the moon, the constellations, and all the host of the heavens. 6 He brought out the image of𝑔 A•shē'rah from the house of the LORD, outside Jerusalem, to the Wadi Kid'ron, burned it at the Wadi Kid'ron, beat it to dust and threw the dust of it upon

g Heb lacks *image of*

2

K
I
N
G
S

the graves of the common people. 7 He broke down the houses of the male temple prostitutes that were in the house of the LORD, where the women did weaving for A·she′rah. 8 He brought all the priests out of the towns of Judah, and defiled the high places where the priests had made offerings, from Ge′ba to Be′er-she′ba; he broke down the high places of the gates that were at the entrance of the gate of Joshua the governor of the city, which were on the left at the gate of the city. 9 The priests of the high places, however, did not come up to the altar of the LORD in Jerusalem, but ate unleavened bread among their kindred. 10 He defiled To′pheth, which is in the valley of Ben-hin′nom, so that no one would make a son or a daughter pass through fire as an offering to Mo′-lech. 11 He removed the horses that the kings of Judah had dedicated to the sun, at the entrance to the house of the LORD, by the chamber of the eunuch Na′than-me′lech, which was in the precincts;h then he burned the chariots of the sun with fire. 12 The altars on the roof of the upper chamber of A′haz, which the kings of Judah had made, and the altars that Ma·nas′seh had made in the two courts of the house of the LORD, he pulled down from there and broke in pieces, and threw the rubble into the Wadi Kid′ron. 13 The king defiled the high places that were east of Jerusalem, to the south of the Mount of Destruction, which King Solomon of Israel had built for As·tar′te the abomination of the Si·do′ni·ans, for Che′mosh the abomination of Mo′ab, and for Mil′com the abomination of the Am′mon·ites. 14 He broke the pillars in pieces, cut down the sacred poles,i and covered the sites with human bones.

15 Moreover, the altar at Beth′el, the high place erected by Jer·o·bo′am son of Ne′bat, who caused Israel to sin—he pulled down that altar along with the high place. He burned the high place, crushing it to dust; he also burned the sacred pole.j 16 As Jo·si′ah turned, he saw the tombs there on the mount; and he sent and took the bones out of the tombs, and burned them on the altar, and defiled it, according to the word of the LORD that the man of God proclaimed,k when Jer·o·bo′am stood by the altar at the festival; he turned and looked up at the tomb of the man of God who had predicted these things. 17 Then he said, "What is that monument that I see?" The people of the city told him, "It is the tomb of the man of God who came from Judah and predicted these things that you have done against the altar at Beth′el." 18 He said, "Let him rest; let no one move his bones." So they let his bones alone, with the bones of the prophet who came out of Sa·mar′i·a. 19 Moreover, Jo·si′ah removed all the shrines of the

high places that were in the towns of Sa·mar′i·a, which kings of Israel had made, provoking the LORD to anger; he did to them just as he had done at Beth′el. 20 He slaughtered on the altars all the priests of the high places who were there, and burned human bones on them. Then he returned to Jerusalem.

The Passover Celebrated
(2 Chr 35.1–19)

21 The king commanded all the people, "Keep the passover to the LORD your God as prescribed in this book of the covenant." 22 No such passover had been kept since the days of the judges who judged Israel, even during all the days of the kings of Israel and of the kings of Judah; 23 but in the eighteenth year of King Jo·si′ah this passover was kept to the LORD in Jerusalem.

24 Moreover Jo·si′ah put away the mediums, wizards, teraphim,l idols, and all the abominations that were seen in the land of Judah and in Jerusalem, so that he established the words of the law that were written in the book that the priest Hil·ki′ah had found in the house of the LORD. 25 Before him there was no king like him, who turned to the LORD with all his heart, with all his soul, and with all his might, according to all the law of Moses; nor did any like him arise after him.

26 Still the LORD did not turn from the fierceness of his great wrath, by which his anger was kindled against Judah, because of all the provocations with which Ma·nas′seh had provoked him. 27 The LORD said, "I will remove Judah also out of my sight, as I have removed Israel; and I will reject this city that I have chosen, Jerusalem, and the house of which I said, My name shall be there."

Josiah Dies in Battle
(2 Chr 35.20—36.1)

28 Now the rest of the acts of Jo·si′ah, and all that he did, are they not written in the Book of the Annals of the Kings of Judah? 29 In his days Pharaoh Ne′co king of Egypt went up to the king of Assyria to the river Euphrates. King Jo·si′ah went to meet him; but when Pharaoh Ne′co met him at Me·gid′do, he killed him. 30 His servants carried him dead in a chariot from Me·gid′do, brought him to Jerusalem, and buried him in his own tomb. The people of the land took Je·ho′a·haz son of Jo·si′ah, anointed him, and made him king in place of his father.

h Meaning of Heb uncertain   i Heb Asherim
j Heb Asherah   k Gk: Heb proclaimed, who had predicted these things   l Or household gods

Reign and Captivity of Jehoahaz
(2 Chr 36.1–4)

31 Je•hō'a•haz was twenty-three years old when he began to reign; he reigned three months in Jerusalem. His mother's name was Ha•mū'tal daughter of Jer•e•mī'ah of Lib'nah. 32 He did what was evil in the sight of the LORD, just as his ancestors had done. 33 Pharaoh Nē'cō confined him at Rib'lah in the land of Hā'math, so that he might not reign in Jerusalem, and imposed tribute on the land of one hundred talents of silver and a talent of gold. 34 Pharaoh Nē'cō made E•lī'a•kim son of Jō•sī'ah king in place of his father Jō•sī'ah, and changed his name to Je•hoi'a•kim. But he took Je•hō'a•haz away; he came to Egypt, and died there. 35 Je•hoi'a•kim gave the silver and the gold to Pharaoh, but he taxed the land in order to meet Pharaoh's demand for money. He exacted the silver and the gold from the people of the land, from all according to their assessment, to give it to Pharaoh Nē'cō.

Jehoiakim Reigns over Judah
(2 Chr 36.5–8)

36 Je•hoi'a•kim was twenty-five years old when he began to reign; he reigned eleven years in Jerusalem. His mother's name was Ze•bī'dah daughter of Pe•dāi'ah of Rū'mah. 37 He did what was evil in the sight of the LORD, just as all his ancestors had done.

Judah Overrun by Enemies

In his days King Ne•bū•chad•nez'zar of Babylon came up; Je•hoi'a•kim became his servant for three years; then he turned and rebelled against him. 2 The LORD sent against him bands of the Chal•dē'ans, bands of the Ar•a•mē'ans, bands of the Mō'ab-ites, and bands of the Am'mon•ites; he sent them against Judah to destroy it, according to the word of the LORD that he spoke by his servants the prophets. 3 Surely this came upon Judah at the command of the LORD, to remove them out of his sight, for the sins of Ma•nas'seh, for all that he had committed, 4 and also for the innocent blood that he had shed; for he filled Jerusalem with innocent blood, and the LORD was not willing to pardon. 5 Now the rest of the deeds of Je•hoi'a•kim, and all that he did, are they not written in the Book of the Annals of the Kings of Judah? 6 So Je•hoi'a•kim slept with his ancestors; then his son Je•hoi'a•chin succeeded him. 7 The king of Egypt did not come again out of his land, for the king of Babylon had taken over all that belonged to the king of Egypt from the Wadi of Egypt to the River Euphrates.

Reign and Captivity of Jehoiachin
(2 Chr 36.9–10)

8 Je•hoi'a•chin was eighteen years old when he began to reign; he reigned three months in Jerusalem. His mother's name was Ne•hush'ta daughter of El•nā'than of Jerusalem. 9 He did what was evil in the sight of the LORD, just as his father had done.

10 At that time the servants of King Ne•bū•chad•nez'zar of Babylon came up to Jerusalem, and the city was besieged. 11 King Ne•bū•chad•nez'zar of Babylon came to the city, while his servants were besieging it; 12 King Je•hoi'a•chin of Judah gave himself up to the king of Babylon, himself, his mother, his servants, his officers, and his palace officials. The king of Babylon took him prisoner in the eighth year of his reign.

Capture of Jerusalem

13 He carried off all the treasures of the house of the LORD, and the treasures of the king's house; he cut in pieces all the vessels of gold in the temple of the LORD, which King Solomon of Israel had made, all this as the LORD had foretold. 14 He carried away all Jerusalem, all the officials, all the warriors, ten thousand captives, all the artisans and the smiths; no one remained, except the poorest people of the land. 15 He carried away Je•hoi'a•chin to Babylon; the king's mother, the king's wives, his officials, and the elite of the land, he took into captivity from Jerusalem to Babylon. 16 The king of Babylon brought captive to Babylon all the men of valor, seven thousand, the artisans and the smiths, one thousand, all of them strong and fit for war. 17 The king of Babylon made Mat-ta•ni'ah, Je•hoi'a•chin's uncle, king in his place, and changed his name to Zed•e•kī'ah.

Zedekiah Reigns over Judah
(2 Chr 36.11–14; Jer 52.1–3a)

18 Zed•e•kī'ah was twenty-one years old when he began to reign; he reigned eleven years in Jerusalem. His mother's name was Ha•mū'tal daughter of Jer•e•mī'ah of Lib'nah. 19 He did what was evil in the sight of the LORD, just as Je•hoi'a•kim had done. 20 Indeed, Jerusalem and Judah so angered the LORD that he expelled them from his presence.

The Fall and Captivity of Judah
(2 Chr 36.15–21; Jer 52.3b–30)

Zed•e•kī'ah rebelled against the king of Babylon. 1 And in the ninth year of his reign, in the tenth month, on the tenth day of the month, King Ne•bū•chad•nez'zar of Babylon came with all his army against Jerusalem, and laid siege to it; they built siegeworks against it all around. 2 So the city was besieged until the eleventh year of King Zed•e•kī′ah. ³ On the ninth day of the fourth month the famine became so severe in the city that there was no food for the people of the land. ⁴ Then a breach was made in the city wall;ᵐ the king with all the soldiers fledⁿ by night by the way of the gate between the two walls, by the king's garden, though the Chal•dē′ans were all around the city. They went in the direction of the Ar′a•bah. ⁵ But the army of the Chal•dē′ans pursued the king, and overtook him in the plains of Jericho; all his army was scattered, deserting him. ⁶ Then they captured the king and brought him up to the king of Babylon at Rib′lah, who passed sentence on him. ⁷ They slaughtered the sons of Zed•e•kī′ah before his eyes, then put out the eyes of Zed•e•kī′ah; they bound him in fetters and took him to Babylon.

did you KNOW?

The Fall of Jerusalem

The second conquest and exile described in 2 Kings (see "The First Captivity," 17.5–18, for the first) involves the southern kingdom, Judah. Judah was conquered by the Babylonians in 587 B.C., which is why that event is often referred to as the Babylonian Exile (see map 5, "The Babylonian Empire"). The author of Kings implies that the kingdom of Judah lasted longer than the kingdom of Israel because it had faithful reformer kings like Hezekiah and Josiah. The fall of Judah was particularly devastating because both Jerusalem, David's city, and the Temple, the central place of worship, were destroyed. The whole Book of Lamentations is an expression of the sorrow and grief the people experienced as a result.

▶ **2 Kings 25.1–21**

8 In the fifth month, on the seventh day of the month—which was the nineteenth year of King Ne•bū•chad•nez′zar, king of Babylon—Ne•bū•za•rad′an, the captain of the bodyguard, a servant of the king of Babylon, came to Jerusalem. ⁹ He burned the house of the LORD, the king's house, and all the houses of Jerusalem; every great house he burned

down. ¹⁰ All the army of the Chal•dē′ans who were with the captain of the guard broke down the walls around Jerusalem. ¹¹ Ne•bū•za•rad′an the captain of the guard carried into exile the rest of the people who were left in the city and the deserters who had defected to the king of Babylon—all the rest of the population. ¹² But the captain of the guard left some of the poorest people of the land to be vinedressers and tillers of the soil.

13 The bronze pillars that were in the house of the LORD, as well as the stands and the bronze sea that were in the house of the LORD, the Chal•dē′ans broke in pieces, and carried the bronze to Babylon. ¹⁴ They took away the pots, the shovels, the snuffers, the dishes for incense, and all the bronze vessels used in the temple service, ¹⁵ as well as the firepans and the basins. What was made of gold the captain of the guard took away for the gold, and what was made of silver, for the silver. ¹⁶ As for the two pillars, the one sea, and the stands, which Solomon had made for the house of the LORD, the bronze of all these vessels was beyond weighing. ¹⁷ The height of the one pillar was eighteen cubits, and on it was a bronze capital; the height of the capital was three cubits; latticework and pomegranates, all of bronze, were on the capital all around. The second pillar had the same, with the latticework.

18 The captain of the guard took the chief priest Se•rāi′ah, the second priest Zeph•a•nī′ah, and the three guardians of the threshold; ¹⁹ from the city he took an officer who had been in command of the soldiers, and five men of the king's council who were found in the city; the secretary who was the commander of the army who mustered the people of the land; and sixty men of the people of the land who were found in the city. ²⁰ Ne•bū•za•rad′an the captain of the guard took them, and brought them to the king of Babylon at Rib′lah. ²¹ The king of Babylon struck them down and put them to death at Rib′lah in the land of Hā′math. So Judah went into exile out of its land.

Gedaliah Made Governor of Judah
(Jer 40.5—41.18)

22 He appointed Ged•a•lī′ah son of A•hī′kam son of Shā′phan as governor over the people who remained in the land of Judah, whom King Ne•bū•chad•nez′zar of Babylon had left. ²³ Now when all the captains of the forces and their men heard that the king of Babylon had appointed Ged•a•lī′ah as governor, they came with their men to Ged•a•lī′ah

---

ᵐ Heb lacks *wall*   ⁿ Gk Compare Jer 39.4; 52.7: Heb lacks *the king* and lacks *fled*

at Miz'pah, namely, Ish'ma·el son of Neth·a·ni'ah, Jō·hā'nan son of Ka·rē'ah, Se·rāi'ah son of Tan'hu·meth the Ne·toph'a·thīte, and Jā·az·a·ni'ah son of the Mā'a·ca·thīte. 24 Ged·a·lī'ah swore to them and their men, saying, "Do not be afraid because of the Chal·dē'an officials; live in the land, serve the king of Babylon, and it shall be well with you." 25 But in the seventh month, Ish'ma·el son of Neth·a·ni'ah son of E·lish'a·ma, of the royal family, came with ten men; they struck down Ged·a·lī'ah so that he died, along with the Judeans and Chal·dē'ans who were with him at Miz'pah. 26 Then all the people, high and low,ᵒ and the captains of the forces set out and went to Egypt; for they were afraid of the Chal·dē'ans.

Jehoiachin Released from Prison
(Jer 52.31–34)

27 In the thirty-seventh year of the exile of King Je·hoi'a·chin of Judah, in the twelfth month, on the twenty-seventh day of the month, King Ē'vil-me·rō'dach of Babylon, in the year that he began to reign, released King Je·hoi'a·chin of Judah from prison; 28 he spoke kindly to him, and gave him a seat above the other seats of the kings who were with him in Babylon. 29 So Je·hoi'a·chin put aside his prison clothes. Every day of his life he dined regularly in the king's presence. 30 For his allowance, a regular allowance was given him by the king, a portion every day, as long as he lived.

ᵒ Or *young and old*

Have you ever had a friendly disagreement with someone over the interpretation of a movie? Did you each emphasize different aspects of the movie to support your interpretation? The First and Second Books of Chronicles are another interpretation of the history of the people of Israel. These books downplay the Covenant and emphasize the importance of institutional ritual and worship of God.

At a Glance

- **1 Chronicles, chapters 1–9.** genealogies of Israel
- **1 Chronicles, chapters 10–29.** David's kingship
- **2 Chronicles, chapters 1–9.** Solomon's kingship
- **2 Chronicles, chapters 10–36.** the kings of Judah after Solomon's death

In-depth

The Chronicler is the name given to the unknown author (or authors) of 1 and 2 Chronicles. The Chronicler, writing after the Israelites returned from the Exile in Babylon, has a unique perspective, so unique that he almost never mentions the Sinai Covenant or Moses (central themes throughout other parts of the Old Testament). Because the Israelites cannot have their own king, the Chronicler emphasizes a new type of reign, one governed by priests instead of kings.

The Chronicler uses two types of material—genealogies and lively sermons—to summarize Israel's history from the Creation to around 525 B.C. But he primarily focuses on Kings David and Solomon. They are praised extensively because of their role in centralizing worship in Jerusalem and building the Temple. Many of the negative stories about David from 2 Samuel—such as his affair with Bathsheba—are not even mentioned. The Chronicler wants nothing to tarnish the people's memory of an ideal kingdom that might one day be restored.

Second Chronicles also focuses on the southern kingdom of Judah and ignores the northern kingdom of Israel after Solomon's death. This may well be due to a bias of the priestly class in Jerusalem against the religious practice of the northern tribes. This bias lasted into Jesus' time.

The goal of 1 and 2 Chronicles was to give the Israelites hope for the future after returning from the Exile. The Chronicler reminded them that if they maintained their religious practices and worship of God, they would continue to be God's people.

Quick Facts

Period Covered
Creation to the end of the Babylonian captivity

Author
a Levite cantor and scribe writing after the return to Jerusalem in the fourth century B.C.

Theme
Israel can secure its future by continuing its worship in the pattern established by David.

386

1 Chronicles

Chap. 15

From Adam to Abraham
(Gen 5.1–32; 10.1–32; 11.10–26;
Lk 3.34–38)

Adam, Seth, Ē′nosh; 2 Kē′nan, Ma•hal′a•lel, Jar′ed; 3 Ē′noch, Me•thū′se•lah, Lā′mech; 4 Noah, Shem, Ham, and Jā′pheth.

5 The descendants of Jā′pheth: Gō′mer, Mā′gog, Mā′daī, Jā′van, Tū′bal, Mē′shech, and Tī′ras. 6 The descendants of Gō′mer: Ash′ke•naz, Dī′phath,*a* and Tō•gar′mah. 7 The descendants of Jā′van: E•lī′shah, Tar′shish, Kit′tim, and Rod′a•nim.*b*

8 The descendants of Ham: Cush, Egypt, Put, and Cā′naan. 9 The descendants of Cush: Sē′ba, Hav′i•lah, Sab′ta, Rā′a•ma, and Sab′te•ca. The descendants of Rā′a•mah: Shē′ba and Dē′dan. 10 Cush became the father of Nim′rod; he was the first to be a mighty one on the earth.

11 Egypt became the father of Lū′dim, An′a•mim, Le•hā′bim, Naph•tū′him, 12 Path•rū′sim, Cas•lū′him, and Caph′to•rim, from whom the Phi•lis′tines come.*c*

13 Cā′naan became the father of Sī′don his firstborn, and Heth, 14 and the Jeb′ū•sītes, the Am′o•rītes, the Gir′ga•shītes, 15 the Hī′vītes, the Ar′kītes, the Sī′nītes, 16 the Ar′vad•ītes, the Zem′a•rītes, and the Hā′math•ītes.

17 The descendants of Shem: Ē′lam, As′shur, Ar•pach′shad, Lud, Ar′am, Uz, Hul, Gē′ther, and Mē′shech.*d* 18 Ar•pach′shad became the father of

Shē′lah; and Shē′lah became the father of Ē′ber. 19 To Ē′ber were born two sons: the name of the one was Pē′leg (for in his days the earth was divided), and the name of his brother Jok′tan. 20 Jok′tan became the father of Al•mō′dad, Shē′leph, Hā•zar•mā′veth, Jē′rah, 21 Ha•dor′am, Ū′zal, Dik′lah, 22 Ē′bal, A•bim′a•el, Shē′ba, 23 Ō′phir, Hav′i•lah, and Jō′bab; all these were the descendants of Jok′tan.

24 Shem, Ar•pach′shad, Shē′lah; 25 Ē′ber, Pē′leg, Rē′ū; 26 Sē′rug, Nā′hor, Tē′rah; 27 Abram, that is, Abraham.

From Abraham to Jacob
(Gen 25.1–4, 12–16; 36.1–30)

28 The sons of Abraham: Isaac and Ish′ma•el. 29 These are their genealogies: the firstborn of Ish′ma•el, Ne•bā′i•oth; and Kē′dar, Ad′bē•el, Mib′sam, 30 Mish′ma, Dū′mah, Mas′sa, Hā′dad, Tē′ma, 31 Jē′tur, Nā′phish, and Ked′e•mah. These are the sons of Ish′ma•el. 32 The sons of Ke•tū′rah, Abraham′s concubine: she bore Zim′ran, Jok′shan, Mē′dan, Mid′i•an, Ish′bak, and Shū′ah. The sons of Jok′shan: Shē′ba and Dē′dan. 33 The sons of Mid′i•an: Ē′phah, Ē′pher, Hā′noch, A•bī′da, and El•dā′ah. All these were the descendants of Ke•tū′rah.

a Gen 10.3 *Ripath;* See Gk Vg   *b* Gen 10.4 *Dodanim;* See Syr Vg   *c* Heb *Casluhim, from which the Philistines come, Caphtorim;* See Am 9.7, Jer 47.4   *d* *Mash* in Gen 10.23

34 Abraham became the father of Isaac. The sons of Isaac: Esau and Israel. 35 The sons of Esau: E·li′phaz, Reü′el, Jë′ush, Jä′lam, and Kō′rah. 36 The sons of E·li′phaz: Tē′man, Ō′mar, Zē′phi, Gā′tam, Kē′naz, Tim′na, and Am′a·lek. 37 The sons of Reü′el: Nä′hath, Zē′rah, Sham′mah, and Miz′zah.

38 The sons of Sē′ir: Lō′tan, Shō′bal, Zib′ē·on, An′ah, Dī′shon, Ē′zer, and Dī′shan. 39 The sons of Lō′tan: Hō′ri and Hō′mam; and Lō′tan′s sister was Tim′na. 40 The sons of Shō′bal: Al′i·an, Man′a·hath, Ē′bal, Shē′phi, and Ō′nam. The sons of Zib′ē·on: Ā′i·ah and An′ah. 41 The sons of An′ah: Dī′shon. The sons of Dī′shon: Ham′ran, Esh′ban, Ith′ran, and Chē′ran. 42 The sons of Ē′zer: Bil′han, Zā′a·van, and Jā′a·kan.ᵉ The sons of Dī′shan:ᶠ Uz and Ar′an.

43 These are the kings who reigned in the land of Ē′dom before any king reigned over the Israelites: Bē′la son of Bē′or, whose city was called Din′ha·bah. 44 When Bē′la died, Jō′bab son of Zē′rah of Boz′rah succeeded him. 45 When Jō′bab died, Hū′sham of the land of the Tē′man·ites succeeded him. 46 When Hū′sham died, Hā′dad son of Bē′dad, who defeated Mid′i·an in the country of Mō′ab, succeeded him; and the name of his city was Ā′vith. 47 When Hā′dad died, Sam′lah of Mas·rē′kah succeeded him. 48 When Sam′lah died, Shā′ulᵍ of Re·hō′both on the Euphrates succeeded him. 49 When Shā′ulᵍ died, Bā′al-hā′nan son of Ach′bor succeeded him. 50 When Bā′al-hā′nan died, Hā′dad succeeded him; the name of his city was Pā′i, and his wife′s name Me·het′a·bel daughter of Mā′tred, daughter of Me-za·hab′. 51 And Hā′dad died.

The clansʰ of Ē′dom were: clansʰ Tim′na, Al′i·ah,ⁱ Jē′theth, 52 Ō·hol·i·bā′mah, Ē′lah, Pī′non, 53 Kē′naz, Tē′man, Mib′zar, 54 Mag′di·el, and Ī′ram; these are the clansʰ of Ē′dom.

The Sons of Israel and the Descendants of Judah
(Gen 29.31—30.24; 35.16–18; 46.8–25; Ruth 4.18–22; Mt 1.2–6; Lk 33.1–33)

These are the sons of Israel: Reuben, Sim′ē·on, Levi, Judah, Is′sa·char, Zeb′ū·lun, 2 Dan, Joseph, Benjamin, Naph′ta·li, Gad, and Ash′er. 3 The sons of Judah: Er, Ō′nan, and Shē′lah; these three the Cä′naan·ite woman Bath-shū′a bore to him. Now Er, Judah′s firstborn, was wicked in the sight of the LORD, and he put him to death. 4 His daughter-in-law Tä′mar also bore him Per′ez and Zē′rah. Judah had five sons in all.

5 The sons of Per′ez: Hez′ron and Hā′mul. 6 The sons of Zē′rah: Zim′ri, Ē′than, Hē′man, Cal′col, and Dar′a,ʲ five in all. 7 The sons of Car′mi: Ā′char, the troubler of Israel, who transgressed in the matter of the devoted thing; 8 and Ē′than′s son was Az·a·ri′ah.

9 The sons of Hez′ron, who were born to him: Je·rah′mē·el, Ram, and Che·lū′bai. 10 Ram became the father of Am·min′a·dab, and Am·min′a·dab became the father of Nah′shon, prince of the sons of Judah. 11 Nah′shon became the father of Sal′ma, Sal′ma of Bō′az, 12 Bō′az of Ō′bed, Ō′bed of Jesse. 13 Jesse became the father of E·li′ab his firstborn, A·bin′a·dab the second, Shim′ē·a the third, 14 Nethan′el the fourth, Rad′dai the fifth, 15 Ō′zem the sixth, David the seventh; 16 and their sisters were Ze·rū′i·ah and Ab′i·gāil. The sons of Ze·rū′i·ah: A·bi′shai, Jō′ab, and As′a·hel, three. 17 Ab′i·gāil bore A·mā′sa, and the father of A·mā′sa was Jē′ther the Ish′ma·el·īte.

18 Caleb son of Hez′ron had children by his wife A·zū′bah, and by Jer′i·oth; these were her sons: Jē′sher, Shō′bab, and Ar′don. 19 When A·zū′bah died, Caleb married Eph′rath, who bore him Hur. 20 Hur became the father of Ū′ri, and Ū′ri became the father of Bez′a·lel.

21 Afterward Hez′ron went in to the daughter of Mā′chir father of Gil′e·ad, whom he married when he was sixty years old; and she bore him Sē′gub; 22 and Sē′gub became the father of Jā′ir, who had twenty-three towns in the land of Gil′e·ad. 23 But Gē′shur and Ar′am took from them Hav′voth-jā′ir, Kē′nath and its villages, sixty towns. All these were descendants of Mā′chir, father of Gil′e·ad. 24 After the death of Hez′ron, in Cā′leb-eph′ra·thah, A·bi′jah wife of Hez′ron bore him Ash′hur, father of Te·kō′a.

25 The sons of Je·rah′mē·el, the firstborn of Hez′ron: Ram his firstborn, Bū′nah, Ō′ren, Ō′zem, and A·hi′jah. 26 Je·rah′mē·el also had another wife, whose name was At′a·rah; she was the mother of Ō′nam. 27 The sons of Ram, the firstborn of Je·rah′mē·el: Mā′az, Jā′min, and Ē′ker. 28 The sons of Ō′nam: Sham′mai and Jā′da. The sons of Sham′mai: Nā′dab and A·bi′shur. 29 The name of A·bi′shur′s wife was Ab·i·hā′il, and she bore him Ah′ban and Mō′lid. 30 The sons of Nā′dab: Sē′led and Ap′pa·im; and Sē′led died childless. 31 The sonᵏ of Ap′pa·im: Ish′i. The sonᵏ of Ish′i: Shē′shan. The sonᵏ of Shē′shan: Ah′lai. 32 The sons of Jā′da, Sham′mai′s brother: Jē′ther and Jonathan; and Jē′ther died childless. 33 The sons of Jonathan: Pē′leth and Zā′za. These were the descendants of Je·rah′mē·el. 34 Now Shē′shan had no sons, only daughters; but Shē′shan had an Egyptian slave, whose name was Jar′ha. 35 So Shē′shan

---

ᵉ Or *and Akan*; See Gen 36.27   ᶠ See 1.38: Heb *Dishon*
ᵍ Or *Saul*   ʰ Or *chiefs*   ⁱ Or *Alvah*; See Gen 36.40
ʲ Or *Darda*; Compare Syr Tg some Gk Mss; See
1 Kings 4.31   ᵏ Heb *sons*

gave his daughter in marriage to his slave Jar'ha; and she bore him At'tai. ³⁶ At'tai became the father of Nathan, and Nathan of Zā'bad. ³⁷ Zā'bad became the father of Eph'lal, and Eph'lal of O'bed. ³⁸ O'bed became the father of Jē'hū, and Jē'hū of Az•a•rī'ah. ³⁹ Az•a•rī'ah became the father of Hē'lez, and Hē'lez of El•e•ā'sah. ⁴⁰ El•e•ā'sah became the father of Sis'mai, and Sis'mai of Shal'lum. ⁴¹ Shal'lum became the father of Jek•a•mī'ah, and Jek•a•mī'ah of E•lish'a•ma.

42 The sons of Caleb brother of Je•rah'mē•el: Mē'sha[l] his firstborn, who was father of Ziph. The sons of Ma•rē'shah father of Hē'bron. ⁴³ The sons of Hē'bron: Kō'rah, Tap'pū•ah, Rē'kem, and Shē'ma. ⁴⁴ Shē'ma became father of Rā'ham, father of Jor'kĕ•am; and Rē'kem became the father of Sham'mai. ⁴⁵ The son of Sham'mai: Mā'on; and Mā'on was the father of Beth-zur. ⁴⁶ Ē'phah also, Caleb's concubine, bore Har'an, Mō'za, and Gā'zez; and Har'an became the father of Gā'zez. ⁴⁷ The sons of Jah'dai: Rē'gem, Jō'tham, Gē'shan, Pĕ'let, Ē'phah, and Shā'aph. ⁴⁸ Mā'a•cah, Caleb's concubine, bore Shē'ber and Tir'ha•nah. ⁴⁹ She also bore Shā'aph father of Mad•man'nah, Shē'va father of Mach•bē'nah and father of Gib'ē•a; and the daughter of Caleb was Ach'sah. ⁵⁰ These were the descendants of Caleb.

The sons[m] of Hur the firstborn of Eph'ra•thah: Shō'bal father of Kir'i•ath-jē'a•rim, ⁵¹ Sal'ma father of Bethlehem, and Har'eph father of Beth-gā'der. ⁵² Shō'bal father of Kir'i•ath-jē'a•rim had other sons: Ha•rō'eh, half of the Me•nū'hoth. ⁵³ And the families of Kir'i•ath-jē'a•rim: the Ith'rites, the Pū'thites, the Shū'ma•thites, and the Mish'ra•ites; from these came the Zō'ra•thites and the Esh'ta•o•lites. ⁵⁴ The sons of Sal'ma: Bethlehem, the Ne•toph'a•thites, At'roth-beth-jō'ab, and half of the Man•a•hā'thites, the Zō'rites. ⁵⁵ The families also of the scribes that lived at Jā'bez: the Tī'ra•thites, the Shim'ē•a•thites, and the Sū'ca•thites. These are the Ken'ites who came from Ham'math, father of the house of Rē'chab.

Descendants of David and Solomon
(Mt 1.6–12)

These are the sons of David who were born to him in Hē'bron: the firstborn Am'non, by A•hin'ō•am the Jez'rē•el•ite; the second Daniel, by Ab'i•gāil the Car'mel•ite; ² the third Ab'sa•lom, son of Mā'a•cah, daughter of King Tal'mai of Gē'shur; the fourth Ad•o•nī'jah, son of Hag'gith; ³ the fifth Sheph•a•tī'ah, by A•bī'tal; the sixth Ith'rē•am, by his wife Eg'lah; ⁴ six were born to him in Hē'bron, where he reigned for seven years and six months. And he reigned thirty-three years in Jerusalem. ⁵ These were born to him in Jerusalem: Shim'ē•a, Shō'bab,

---

did you KNOW?

Genealogies

Look at all these names! Our present-day interest in family trees obviously has ancient roots. The first nine chapters of I Chronicles consist entirely of family trees—or genealogies—tracing the history of Israel from Adam to Saul. In a culture where not only money and identity but also the offices of priest and king passed from one generation to another, it was essential to be able to trace one's bloodline.

The many genealogies of the Old Testament answer important questions: How were the various tribes related to one another? Who were a particular tribe's ancestors? What right did a certain group or person have to the office of priest or king? The Chronicler lists the genealogies of David and Levi in considerable detail. The kingship and the priesthood were clearly of special interest to him.

▶ **I Chronicles, chapters I–9**

Nathan, and Solomon, four by Bath-shū'a, daughter of Am'mi•el; ⁶ then Ib'har, E•lish'a•ma, E•liph'e•let, ⁷ Nō'gah, Nē'pheg, Ja•phī'a, ⁸ E•lish'a•ma, E•lī'a•da, and E•liph'e•let, nine. ⁹ All these were David's sons, besides the sons of the concubines; and Tā'mar was their sister.

10 The descendants of Solomon: Rē•ho•bō'am, A•bī'jah his son, Asa his son, Je•hosh'a•phat his son, ¹¹ Jō'ram his son, A•ha•zī'ah his son, Jō'ash his son, ¹² Am•a•zī'ah his son, Az•a•rī'ah his son, Jō'tham his son, ¹³ Ā'haz his son, Hez•e•kī'ah his son, Ma•nas'seh his son, ¹⁴ Ā'mon his son, Jō•sī'ah his son. ¹⁵ The sons of Jō•sī'ah: Jō•hā'nan the firstborn, the second Je•hoi'a•kim, the third Zed•e•kī'ah, the fourth Shal'lum. ¹⁶ The descendants of Je•hoi'a•kim: Jec•o•nī'ah his son, Zed•e•kī'ah his son; ¹⁷ and the sons of Jec•o•nī'ah, the captive: She•al'ti•el his son, ¹⁸ Mal•chī'ram, Pe•dāi'ah, Shen•az'zar, Jek•a•mī'ah, Hosh'a•ma, and Ned•a•bī'ah; ¹⁹ The sons of Pe•dāi'ah: Ze•rub'ba•bel and Shim'ē•i; and the sons of Ze•rub'ba•bel: Me•shul'lam and Han•a•nī'ah, and She•lō'mith was their sister; ²⁰ and Ha•shū'bah, O'hel,

---

[l] Gk reads *Mareshah*   [m] Gk Vg: Heb *son*

Ber·e·chī'ah, Has·a·dī'ah, and Jū'shab-hē'sed, five. [21] The sons of Han·a·nī'ah: Pel·a·tī'ah and Je·shā'i·ah, his son[n] Reph·āi'ah, his son[n] Ar'nan, his son[n] Ō·ba·dī'ah, his son[n] Shec·a·nī'ah. [22] The son[o] of Shec·a·nī'ah: She·māi'ah. And the sons of She·māi'ah: Hat'tush, Ī'gal, Ba·rī'ah, Nē·a·rī'ah, and Shā'phat, six. [23] The sons of Nē·a·rī'ah: El·i·ō·ē'nai, Hiz·kī'ah, and Az·rī'kam, three. [24] The sons of El·i·ō·ē'nai: Hod·a·vī'ah, E·lī'a·shib, Pe·lāi'ah, Ak'kub, Jō·hā'nan, De·lāi'ah, and A·nā'nī, seven.

Descendants of Judah

The sons of Judah: Per'ez, Hez'ron, Car'mī, Hur, and Shō'bal. [2] Re·āi'ah son of Shō'bal became the father of Ja'hath, and Ja'hath became the father of A·hū'māi and Lā'had. These were the families of the Zō'ra·thītes. [3] These were the sons[p] of Ē'tam: Jez'rē·el, Ish'ma, and Id'bash; and the name of their sister was Haz·ze·lel·pō'nī, [4] and Pe·nū'el was the father of Ge'dor, and Ē'zer the father of Hū'shah. These were the sons of Hur, the firstborn of Eph'ra·thah, the father of Bethlehem. [5] Ash'hur father of Te·kō'a had two wives, Hē'lah and Nā'a·rah; [6] Nā'a·rah bore him A·huz'zam, Hē'pher, Tē'me·nī, and Hā·a·hash'ta·rī.[q] These were the sons of Nā'a·rah. [7] The sons of Hē'lah: Zē'reth, Iz'har,[r] and Eth'nan. [8] Koz became the father of Ā'nub, Zō·bē'bah, and the families of A·har'hel son of Har'um. [9] Jā'bez was honored more than his brothers; and his mother named him Jā'bez, saying, "Because I bore him in pain." [10] Jā'bez called on the God of Israel, saying, "Oh that you would bless me and enlarge my border, and that your hand might be with me, and that you would keep me from hurt and harm!" And God granted what he asked. [11] Chē'lub the brother of Shū'hah became the father of Mē'hir, who was the father of Esh'ton. [12] Esh'ton became the father of Beth-rā'pha, Pa·sē'ah, and Te·hin'nah the father of Ir-nā'hash. These are the men of Rē'cah. [13] The sons of Kē'naz: Oth'ni·el and Se·rāi'ah; and the sons of Oth'ni·el: Hā'thath and Me·ō'no·thai.[s] [14] Me·ō'no·thai became the father of Oph'rah; and Se·rāi'ah became the father of Jō'ab father of Ge-har'a·shim,[t] so-called because they were artisans. [15] The sons of Caleb son of Je·phūn'neh: I'rū, Ē'lah, and Nā'am; and the son[o] of Ē'lah: Kē'naz. [16] The sons of Je·hal'le·lel: Ziph, Zī'phah, Tir'i·a, and As'a·rel. [17] The sons of Ez'rah: Jē'ther, Mē'red, Ē'pher, and Jā'lon. These are the sons of Bith'i·ah, daughter of Pharaoh, whom Mē'red married;[u] and she conceived and bore[v] Miriam, Sham'māi, and Ish'bah father of Esh·te·mō'a. [18] And his Judean wife bore Jē'red father of Ge'dor, Hē'ber father of Sō'cō, and Je·kū'thi·el father of Za·nō'ah. [19] The sons of the wife of Hō·dī'ah, the sister of Nā'ham, were the fathers of

Kē·ī'lah the Gar'mīte and Esh·te·mō'a the Mā'a·ca·thīte. [20] The sons of Shī'mon: Am'non, Rin'nah, Ben-hā'nan, and Ti'lon. The sons of Ish'ī: Zō'heth and Ben-zō'heth. [21] The sons of Shē'lah son of Judah: Er father of Lē'cah, Lā'a·dah father of Ma·rē'-shah, and the families of the guild of linen workers at Beth-ash·bē'a; [22] and Jō'kim, and the men of Cō·zē'ba, and Jō'ash, and Sar'aph, who married into Mō'ab but returned to Lē'hem[w] (now the records[x] are ancient). [23] These were the potters and inhabitants of Ne·tā'im and Ge·dē'rah; they lived there with the king in his service.

Descendants of Simeon
(Gen 46.10)

24 The sons of Sim'ē·on: Nem'ū·el, Jā'min, Jā'rib, Zē'rah, Shā'ūl;[y] [25] Shal'lum was his son, Mib'sam his son, Mish'ma his son. [26] The sons of Mish'ma: Ham'mū·el his son, Zac'cur his son, Shim'ē·ī his son. [27] Shim'ē·ī had sixteen sons and six daughters; but his brothers did not have many children, nor did all their family multiply like the Judeans. [28] They lived in Bē'er-shē'ba, Mō'la·dah, Hā'zar-shū'al, [29] Bil'hah, Ē'zem, Tō'lad, [30] Be·thū'el, Hor'mah, Zik'lag, [31] Beth-mar'ca·both, Hā'zar-sū'sim, Beth-bi'rī, and Shā·a·rā'im. These were their towns until David became king. [32] And their villages were Ē'tam, Ā'in, Rim'mon, Tō'chen, and Ā'shan, five towns, [33] along with all their villages that were around these towns as far as Bā'al. These were their settlements. And they kept a genealogical record.

34 Me·shō'bab, Jam'lech, Jō'shah son of Am·a·zī'ah, [35] Jō'el, Jē'hū son of Josh·i·bī'ah son of Se·rāi'ah son of As'i·el, [36] El·i·ō·ē'nai, Jā·a·kō'bah, Jesh·ō·hāi'ah, A·sāi'ah, Ad'i·el, Je·sim'i·el, Be·nā'i·ah, [37] Zī'za son of Shī'phī son of Al'lon son of Je·dāi'ah son of Shim'rī son of She·māi'ah— [38] these mentioned by name were leaders in their families, and their clans increased greatly. [39] They journeyed to the entrance of Ge'dor, to the east side of the valley, to seek pasture for their flocks, [40] where they found rich, good pasture, and the land was very broad, quiet, and peaceful; for the former inhabitants there belonged to Ham. [41] These, registered by name, came in the days of King Hez·e·kī'ah of Judah, and attacked their tents and the Me·ū'nim who were found there, and exterminated them to this day, and settled in their place, be-

---

[n] Gk Compare Syr Vg: Heb *sons of*   [o] Heb *sons*
[p] Gk Compare Vg: Heb *the father*   [q] Or *Ahashtari*
[r] Another reading is *Zohar*   [s] Gk Vg: Heb lacks *and Meonothai*   [t] That is *Valley of artisans*   [u] The clause: *These are . . . married* is transposed from verse 18
[v] Heb lacks *and bore*   [w] Vg Compare Gk: Heb *and Jashubi-lahem*   [x] Or *matters*   [y] Or *Saul*

cause there was pasture there for their flocks. [42]And some of them, five hundred men of the Sim'e·on·ites, went to Mount Se'ir, having as their leaders Pel·a·ti'ah, Ne·a·ri'ah, Reph·ai'ah, and Uz'zi·el, sons of Ish'i; [43]they destroyed the remnant of the A·mal'e·kites that had escaped, and they have lived there to this day.

Descendants of Reuben
(Gen 46.8–9)

The sons of Reuben the firstborn of Israel. (He was the firstborn, but because he defiled his father's bed his birthright was given to the sons of Joseph son of Israel, so that he is not enrolled in the genealogy according to the birthright; [2]though Judah became prominent among his brothers and a ruler came from him, yet the birthright belonged to Joseph.) [3]The sons of Reuben, the firstborn of Israel: Ha'noch, Pal'lu, Hez'ron, and Car'mi. [4]The sons of Jo'el: She·mai'ah his son, Gog his son, Shim'e·i his son, [5]Mi'cah his son, Re·ai'ah his son, Ba'al his son, [6]Be·er'ah his son, whom King Til'gath-pil·ne'ser of Assyria carried away into exile; he was a chieftain of the Reu'ben·ites. [7]And his kindred by their families, when the genealogy of their generations was reckoned: the chief, Je·i'el, and Zech·a·ri'ah, [8]and Be'la son of A'zaz, son of She'ma, son of Jo'el, who lived in A·ro'er, as far as Ne'bo and Ba'al-me'on. [9]He also lived to the east as far as the beginning of the desert this side of the Euphrates, because their cattle had multiplied in the land of Gil'e·ad. [10]And in the days of Saul they made war on the Hag'rites, who fell by their hand; and they lived in their tents throughout all the region east of Gil'e·ad.

Descendants of Gad

[11]The sons of Gad lived beside them in the land of Ba'shan as far as Sal'e·cah: [12]Jo'el the chief, Sha'pham the second, Ja'nai, and Sha'phat in Ba'shan. [13]And their kindred according to their clans: Michael, Me·shul'lam, She'ba, Jo'rai, Ja'can, Zi'a, and E'ber, seven. [14]These were the sons of Ab·i·ha'il son of Hu'ri, son of Ja·ro'ah, son of Gil'e·ad, son of Michael, son of Je·shish'ai, son of Jah'do, son of Buz; [15]A'hi son of Ab'di·el, son of Gu'ni, was chief in their clan; [16]and they lived in Gil'e·ad, in Ba'shan and in its towns, and in all the pasture lands of Sharon to their limits. [17]All of these were enrolled by genealogies in the days of King Jo'tham of Judah, and in the days of King Jer·o·bo'am of Israel.

[18]The Reu'ben·ites, the Gad'ites, and the half-tribe of Ma·nas'seh had valiant warriors, who carried shield and sword, and drew the bow, expert in war, forty-four thousand seven hundred sixty,

ready for service. [19]They made war on the Hag'rites, Je'tur, Na'phish, and No'dab; [20]and when they received help against them, the Hag'rites and all who were with them were given into their hands, for they cried to God in the battle, and he granted their entreaty because they trusted in him. [21]They captured their livestock: fifty thousand of their camels, two hundred fifty thousand sheep, two thousand donkeys, and one hundred thousand captives. [22]Many fell slain, because the war was of God. And they lived in their territory until the exile.

The Half-Tribe of Manasseh

[23] The members of the half-tribe of Ma·nas'seh lived in the land; they were very numerous from Ba'shan to Ba'al-her'mon, Se'nir, and Mount Hermon. [24]These were the heads of their clans: E'pher,[z] Ish'i, E·li'el, Az'ri·el, Jer·e·mi'ah, Hoda·vi'ah, and Jah'di·el, mighty warriors, famous men, heads of their clans. [25]But they transgressed against the God of their ancestors, and prostituted themselves to the gods of the peoples of the land, whom God had destroyed before them. [26]So the God of Israel stirred up the spirit of King Pul of Assyria, the spirit of King Til'gath-pil·ne'ser of Assyria, and he carried them away, namely, the Reu'ben·ites, the Gad'ites, and the half-tribe of Ma·nas'seh, and brought them to Ha'lah, Ha'bor, Har'a, and the river Go'zan, to this day.

Descendants of Levi
(Gen 46.11)

[a]The sons of Levi: Ger'shom,[b] Ko'hath, and Me·rar'i. [2]The sons of Ko'hath: Am'ram, Iz'har, He'bron, and Uz'zi·el. [3]The children of Am'ram: Aaron, Moses, and Miriam. The sons of Aaron: Na'dab, A·bi'hu, El·e·a'zar, and Ith'a·mar. [4]El·e·a'zar became the father of Phin'e·has, Phin'e·has of Ab·i·shu'a, [5]Ab·i·shu'a of Buk'ki, Buk'ki of Uz'zi, [6]Uz'zi of Zer·a·hi'ah, Zer·a·hi'ah of Me·ra'i·oth, [7]Me·ra'i·oth of Am·a·ri'ah, Am·a·ri'ah of A·hi'tub, [8]A·hi'tub of Za'dok, Za'dok of A·him'a·az, [9]A·him'a·az of Az·a·ri'ah, Az·a·ri'ah of Jo·ha'nan, [10]and Jo·ha'nan of Az·a·ri'ah (it was he who served as priest in the house that Solomon built in Jerusalem). [11]Az·a·ri'ah became the father of Am·a·ri'ah, Am·a·ri'ah of A·hi'tub, [12]A·hi'tub of Za'dok, Za'dok of Shal'lum, [13]Shal'lum of Hil·ki'ah, Hil·ki'ah of Az·a·ri'ah, [14]Az·a·ri'ah of Se·rai'ah, Se·rai'ah of Je·hoz'a·dak; [15]and Je·hoz'a·dak went into exile when the LORD sent Judah and Jerusalem into exile by the hand of Ne·bu·chad·nez'zar.

---

z Gk Vg: Heb and Epher　　a Ch 5.27 in Heb
b Heb Gershon, variant of Gershom; See 6.16

16[c] The sons of Levi: Ger'shom, Kō'hath, and Me·rar'ī. 17 These are the names of the sons of Ger'shom: Lib'nī and Shim'e·ī. 18 The sons of Kō'hath: Am'ram, Iz'har, Hē'bron, and Uz'zi·el. 19 The sons of Me·rar'ī: Mah'lī and Mū'shī. These are the clans of the Lē'vītes according to their ancestry. 20 Of Ger'shom: Lib'nī his son, Jā'hath his son, Zim'mah his son, 21 Jō'ah his son, Id'dō his son, Zē'rah his son, Jē·ath'e·raī his son. 22 The sons of Kō'hath: Am·min'a·dab his son, Kō'rah his son, As'sir his son, 23 El·kā'nah his son, E·bī'a·saph his son, As'sir his son, 24 Tā'hath his son, Ū·rī'el his son, Uz·zī'ah his son, and Shā'ul his son. 25 The sons of El·kā'nah: A·mā'saī and A·hī'moth, 26 El·kā'nah his son, Zō'phaī his son, Nā'hath his son, 27 E·lī'ab his son, Je·rō'ham his son, El·kā'nah his son. 28 The sons of Samuel: Jō'el[d] his firstborn, the second A·bī'jah.[e] 29 The sons of Me·rar'ī: Mah'lī, Lib'nī his son, Shim'e·ī his son, Uz'zah his son, 30 Shim'e·a his son, Hag·gī'ah his son, and A·sāi'ah his son.

Musicians Appointed by David

31 These are the men whom David put in charge of the service of song in the house of the LORD, after the ark came to rest there. 32 They ministered with song before the tabernacle of the tent of meeting, until Solomon had built the house of the LORD in Jerusalem; and they performed their service in due order. 33 These are the men who served; and their sons were: Of the Kō'hath·ites: Hē'man, the singer, son of Jō'el, son of Samuel, 34 son of El·kā'nah, son of Je·rō'ham, son of E·lī'el, son of Tō'ah, 35 son of Zuph, son of El·kā'nah, son of Mā'hath, son of A·mā'saī, 36 son of El·kā'nah, son of Jō'el, son of Az·a·rī'ah, son of Zeph·a·nī'ah, 37 son of Tā'hath, son of As'sir, son of E·bī'a·saph, son of Kō'rah, 38 son of Iz'har, son of Kō'hath, son of Levi, son of Israel; 39 and his brother Ā'saph, who stood on his right, namely, Ā'saph son of Ber·e·chī'ah, son of Shim'e·a, 40 son of Michael, son of Bā·a·sē'i·ah, son of Mal·chī'jah, 41 son of Eth'nī, son of Zē'rah, son of A·dāi'ah, 42 son of Ē'than, son of Zim'mah, son of Shim'e·ī, 43 son of Jā'hath, son of Ger'shom, son of Levi. 44 On the left were their kindred the sons of Me·rar'ī: Ē'than son of Kish'ī, son of Ab'dī, son of Mal'luch, 45 son of Hash·a·bī'ah, son of Am·a·zī'ah, son of Hil·kī'ah, 46 son of Am'zī, son of Bā'nī, son of Shē'mer, 47 son of Mah'lī, son of Mū'shī, son of Me·rar'ī, son of Levi; 48 and their kindred the Lē'vītes were appointed for all the service of the tabernacle of the house of God.

49 But Aaron and his sons made offerings on the altar of burnt offering and on the altar of incense, doing all the work of the most holy place, to make atonement for Israel, according to all that Moses the servant of God had commanded. 50 These are the sons of Aaron: El·e·ā'zar his son, Phin'e·has his son, Ab·i·shū'a his son, 51 Buk'kī his son, Uz'zī his son, Zer·a·hī'ah his son, 52 Me·rā'i·oth his son, Am·a·rī'ah his son, A·hī'tub his son, 53 Zā'dok his son, A·him'a·az his son.

Settlements of the Levites
(Josh 21.1–42)

54 These are their dwelling places according to their settlements within their borders: to the sons of Aaron of the families of Kō'hath·ites—for the lot fell to them first— 55 to them they gave Hē'bron in the land of Judah and its surrounding pasture lands, 56 but the fields of the city and its villages they gave to Caleb son of Je·phūn'neh. 57 To the sons of Aaron they gave the cities of refuge: Hē'bron, Lib'nah with its pasture lands, Jat'tir, Esh·te·mō'a with its pasture lands, 58 Hī'len[f] with its pasture lands, Dē'bir with its pasture lands, 59 Ā'shan with its pasture lands, and Beth-shē'mesh with its pasture lands. 60 From the tribe of Benjamin, Gē'ba with its pasture lands, Al'e·meth with its pasture lands, and An'a·thoth with its pasture lands. All their towns throughout their families were thirteen.

61 To the rest of the Kō'hath·ites were given by lot out of the family of the tribe, out of the half-tribe, the half of Ma·nas'seh, ten towns. 62 To the Ger'shom·ites according to their families were allotted thirteen towns out of the tribes of Is'sa·char, Ash'er, Naph'ta·lī, and Ma·nas'seh in Bā'shan. 63 To the Me·rar'ītes according to their families were allotted twelve towns out of the tribes of Reuben, Gad, and Zeb'u·lun. 64 So the people of Israel gave the Lē'vītes the towns with their pasture lands. 65 They also gave them by lot out of the tribes of Judah, Sim'e·on, and Benjamin these towns that are mentioned by name.

66 And some of the families of the sons of Kō'hath had towns of their territory out of the tribe of Ē'phra·im. 67 They were given the cities of refuge: Shē'chem with its pasture lands in the hill country of Ē'phra·im, Gē'zer with its pasture lands, 68 Jok'mē·am with its pasture lands, Beth-hō'ron with its pasture lands, 69 Aī'ja·lon with its pasture lands, Gath-rim'mon with its pasture lands; 70 and out of the half-tribe of Ma·nas'seh, Ā'ner with its pasture lands, and Bil'e·am with its pasture lands, for the rest of the families of the Kō'hath·ites.

71 To the Ger'shom·ites: out of the half-tribe of Ma·nas'seh: Gō'lan in Bā'shan with its pasture

---

[c] Ch 6.1 in Heb   [d] Gk Syr Compare verse 33 and 1 Sam 8.2: Heb lacks *Joel*   [e] Heb reads *Vashni, and Abijah* for *the second Abijah*, taking *the second* as a proper name
[f] Other readings *Hilez, Holon*; See Josh 21.15

lands and Ash'ta•roth with its pasture lands; 72 and out of the tribe of Is'sa•char: Ke'desh with its pasture lands, Dab'e•rath*g* with its pasture lands, 73 Ra'moth with its pasture lands, and A'nem with its pasture lands; 74 out of the tribe of Ash'er: Ma'-shal with its pasture lands, Ab'don with its pasture lands, 75 Hu'kok with its pasture lands, and Re'-hob with its pasture lands; 76 and out of the tribe of Naph'ta•li: Ke'desh in Galilee with its pasture lands, Ham'mon with its pasture lands, and Kir•i•a-tha'im with its pasture lands. 77 To the rest of the Me•rar'ites out of the tribe of Zeb'u•lun: Rim'mo•nō with its pasture lands, Ta'bor with its pasture lands, 78 and across the Jordan from Jericho, on the east side of the Jordan, out of the tribe of Reuben: Be'zer in the steppe with its pasture lands, Jah'zah with its pasture lands, 79 Ked'e•moth with its pasture lands, and Meph'a•ath with its pasture lands; 80 and out of the tribe of Gad: Ra'moth in Gil'e•ad with its pasture lands, Ma•ha•na'im with its pasture lands, 81 Hesh'bon with its pasture lands, and Ja'zer with its pasture lands.

Descendants of Issachar
(Gen 46.13)

The sons*h* of Is'sa•char: Tō'la, Pū'ah, Jash'ub, and Shim'ron, four. 2 The sons of Tō'la: Uz'zī, Reph-āi'ah, Je'ri•el, Jah'maī, Ib'sam, and She•mū'el, heads of their ancestral houses, namely of Tō'la, mighty warriors of their generations, their number in the days of David being twenty-two thousand six hundred. 3 The son*i* of Uz'zī: Iz•ra•hī'ah. And the sons of Iz•ra•hī'ah: Michael, Ō•ba•dī'ah, Jō'el, and Is•shī'ah, five, all of them chiefs; 4 and along with them, by their generations, according to their ancestral houses, were units of the fighting force, thirty-six thousand, for they had many wives and sons. 5 Their kindred belonging to all the families of Is'sa•char were in all eighty-seven thousand mighty warriors, enrolled by genealogy.

Descendants of Benjamin
(Gen 46.21)

6 The sons of Benjamin: Be'la, Be'cher, and Je-dī'a•el, three. 7 The sons of Be'la: Ez'bon, Uz'zī, Uz'zi•el, Jer'i•moth, and I'rī, five, heads of ancestral houses, mighty warriors; and their enrollment by genealogies was twenty-two thousand thirty-four. 8 The sons of Be'cher: Ze•mī'rah, Jō'ash, El•i•e'zer, El•i•ō•e'naī, Om'rī, Jer'e•moth, A•bī'jah, An'a•thoth, and Al'e•meth. All these were the sons of Be'cher; 9 and their enrollment by genealogies, according to their generations, as heads of their ancestral houses, mighty warriors, was twenty thousand two hundred. 10 The sons of Je•dī'a•el: Bil'han. And the sons of Bil'han: Je'ush, Benjamin, E'hud, Che•nā'a-

nah, Ze'than, Tar'shish, and A•hish'a•har. 11 All these were the sons of Je•dī'a•el according to the heads of their ancestral houses, mighty warriors, seventeen thousand two hundred, ready for service in war. 12 And Shup'pim and Hup'pim were the sons of Ir, Hū'shim the son*i* of A'her.

Descendants of Naphtali
(Gen 46.24)

13 The descendants of Naph'ta•li: Jah'zi•el, Gū'nī, Je'zer, and Shal'lum, the descendants of Bil'hah.

Descendants of Manasseh

14 The sons of Ma•nas'seh: As'ri•el, whom his Ar•a•me'an concubine bore; she bore Ma'chir the father of Gil'e•ad. 15 And Ma'chir took a wife for Hup'pim and for Shup'pim. The name of his sister was Ma'a•cah. And the name of the second was Ze-loph'e•had; and Ze•loph'e•had had daughters. 16 Ma'a•cah the wife of Ma'chir bore a son, and she named him Pe'resh; the name of his brother was She'resh; and his sons were Ū'lam and Re'kem. 17 The son*i* of Ū'lam: Be'dan. These were the sons of Gil'e•ad son of Ma'chir, son of Ma•nas'seh. 18 And his sister Ham•mō'le•cheth bore Ish'hod, A•bi•e'zer, and Mah'lah. 19 The sons of She•mī'da were A•hī'an, She'chem, Lik'hī, and A•nī'am.

Descendants of Ephraim

20 The sons of E'phra•im: Shū•the'lah, and Be'-red his son, Ta'hath his son, El•e•a'dah his son, Ta'-hath his son, 21 Za'bad his son, Shū•the'lah his son, and E'zer and E'le•ad. Now the people of Gath, who were born in the land, killed them, because they came down to raid their cattle. 22 And their father E'phra•im mourned many days, and his brothers came to comfort him. 23 E'phra•im*j* went in to his wife, and she conceived and bore a son; and he named him Be•rī'ah, because disaster*k* had befallen his house. 24 His daughter was She'e•rah, who built both Lower and Upper Beth-hō'ron, and Uz'zen-she'e•rah. 25 Re'phah was his son, Re'-sheph his son, Te'lah his son, Ta'han his son, 26 Lā'dan his son, Am•mī'hud his son, E•lish'a•ma his son, 27 Nun*l* his son, Joshua his son. 28 Their possessions and settlements were Beth'el and its towns, and eastward Nā'a•ran, and westward Ge'-zer and its towns, She'chem and its towns, as far as Āy'yah and its towns; 29 also along the borders of the Ma•nas'sites, Beth-she'an and its towns, Ta'-a•nach and its towns, Me•gid'dō and its towns, Dor

---

g Or *Dobrath*   *h* Syr Compare Vg: Heb *And to the sons*   *i* Heb *sons*   *j* Heb *He*   *k* Heb *beraah*   *l* Here spelled *Non*; see Ex 33.11

and its towns. In these lived the sons of Joseph son of Israel.

Descendants of Asher
(Gen 46.17)

30 The sons of Ash'er: Im'nah, Ish'vah, Ish'vi, Bē·rī'ah, and their sister Sē'rah. 31 The sons of Bē·rī'ah: Hē'ber and Mal'chi·el, who was the father of Bir'zā·ith. 32 Hē'ber became the father of Japh'let, Shō'mer, Hō'tham, and their sister Shū'a. 33 The sons of Japh'let: Pā'sach, Bim'hal, and Ash'vath. These are the sons of Japh'let. 34 The sons of Shē'mer: Ā'hī, Rōh'gah, Hub'bah, and Ar'am. 35 The sons of Hē'lem[m] his brother: Zō'phah, Im'na, Shē'lesh, and Ā'mal. 36 The sons of Zō'phah: Sū'ah, Har'ne·pher, Shū'al, Bē'rī, Im'rah, 37 Bē'zer, Hod, Sham'ma, Shil'shah, Ith'ran, and Be·ē'ra. 38 The sons of Jē'ther: Je·phun'neh, Pis'pa, and Ar'a. 39 The sons of Ul'la: Ā'rah, Han'ni·el, and Rī·zī'a. 40 All of these were men of Ash'er, heads of ancestral houses, select mighty warriors, chief of the princes. Their number enrolled by genealogies, for service in war, was twenty-six thousand men.

Descendants of Benjamin
(Gen 46.21)

Benjamin became the father of Bē'la his firstborn, Ash'bel the second, A'har·ah the third, 2 Nō'hah the fourth, and Rā'pha the fifth. 3 And Bē'la had sons: Ad'dar, Gē'ra, A·bī'hud,[n] 4 Ab·i·shū'a, Nā'a·man, A·hō'ah, 5 Gē'ra, She·phū'phan, and Hū'ram. 6 These are the sons of Ē'hud (they were heads of ancestral houses of the inhabitants of Gē'ba, and they were carried into exile to Man'a·hath): 7 Nā'a·man,[o] A·hī'jah, and Gē'ra, that is, Heg'lam,[p] who became the father of Uz'za and A·hī'hud. 8 And Shā·ha·rā'im had sons in the country of Mō'ab after he had sent away his wives Hū'shim and Bā'a·ra. 9 He had sons by his wife Hō'desh: Jō'bab, Zib'i·a, Mē'sha, Mal'cam, 10 Jē'uz, Sa·chī'a, and Mir'mah. These were his sons, heads of ancestral houses. 11 He also had sons by Hū'shim: A·bī'tub and El·pā'al. 12 The sons of El·pā'al: Ē'ber, Mī'sham, and Shē'med, who built Ō'nō and Lod with its towns, 13 and Bē·rī'ah and Shē'ma (they were heads of ancestral houses of the inhabitants of Ai'ja·lon, who put to flight the inhabitants of Gath); 14 and A·hī'ō, Shā'shak, and Jer'e·moth. 15 Zeb·a·dī'ah, Ar'ad, Ē'der, 16 Michael, Ish'pah, and Jō'ha were sons of Bē·rī'ah. 17 Zeb·a·dī'ah, Me·shul'lam, Hiz'kī, Hē'ber, 18 Ish'me·raī, Iz·lī'ah, and Jō'bab were the sons of El·pā'al. 19 Jā'kim, Zich'rī, Zab'dī, 20 E·li·ē'naī, Zil'le·thaī, E·lī'el, 21 A·dāi'ah, Be·rā'i·ah, and Shim'rath were the sons of Shim'ē·ī. 22 Ish'pan, Ē'ber, E·lī'el, 23 Ab'don, Zich'rī, Hā'nan, 24 Han·a·nī'ah, Ē'lam, An·tho·thī'jah, 25 Iph·dē'i·ah, and Pe·nū'el were the

sons of Shā'shak. 26 Sham'she·raī, Shē·ha·rī'ah, Ath·a·lī'ah, 27 Jā·ar·e·shī'ah, E·lī'jah, and Zich'rī were the sons of Je·rō'ham. 28 These were the heads of ancestral houses, according to their generations, chiefs. These lived in Jerusalem.

29 Je·i'el[q] the father of Gib'e·on lived in Gib'e·on, and the name of his wife was Mā'a·cah. 30 His firstborn son: Ab'don, then Zur, Kish, Bā'al,[r] Nā'dab, 31 Gē'dor, A·hī'ō, Zē'cher, 32 and Mik'loth, who became the father of Shim'ē·ah. Now these also lived opposite their kindred in Jerusalem, with their kindred. 33 Ner became the father of Kish, Kish of Saul,[s] Saul[s] of Jonathan, Mal·chi·shū'a, A·bin'a·dab, and Esh-bā'al; 34 and the son of Jonathan was Mer'ib-bā'al; and Mer'ib-bā'al became the father of Mī'cah. 35 The sons of Mī'cah: Pī'thon, Mē'lech, Ta·rē'a, and Ā'haz. 36 Ā'haz became the father of Je·hō'ad·dah; and Je·hō'ad·dah became the father of Al'e·meth, Az'ma·veth, and Zim'rī; Zim'rī became the father of Mō'za. 37 Mō'za became the father of Bin'ē·a; Rā'phah was his son, El·e·ā'sah his son, Ā'zel his son. 38 Ā'zel had six sons, and these are their names: Az·rī'kam, Bō'che·rū, Ish'ma·el, Shē·a·rī'ah, Ō·ba·dī'ah, and Hā'nan; all these were the sons of Ā'zel. 39 The sons of his brother Ē'shek: Ū'lam his firstborn, Jē'ush the second, and E·liph'e·let the third. 40 The sons of Ū'lam were mighty warriors, archers, having many children and grandchildren, one hundred fifty. All these were Ben'ja·min·ītes.

So all Israel was enrolled by genealogies; and these are written in the Book of the Kings of Israel. And Judah was taken into exile in Babylon because of their unfaithfulness. 2 Now the first to live again in their possessions in their towns were Israelites, priests, Lē'vītes, and temple servants.

Inhabitants of Jerusalem after the Exile

3 And some of the people of Judah, Benjamin, Ē'phra·im, and Ma·nas'seh lived in Jerusalem: 4 Ū'thaī son of Am·mī'hud, son of Om'rī, son of Im'rī, son of Bā'nī, from the sons of Per'ez son of Judah. 5 And of the Shī'lo·nītes: A·sāi'ah the firstborn, and his sons. 6 Of the sons of Zē'rah: Je·ū'el and their kin, six hundred ninety. 7 Of the Ben'ja·min·ītes: Sal'lū son of Me·shul'lam, son of Hod·a·vī'ah, son of Has'se·nū'ah, 8 Ib·nē'i·ah son of Je·rō'ham, Ē'lah son of Uz'zī, son of Mich'rī, and Me·shul'lam son of Sheph·a·tī'ah, son of Reū'el, son of Ib·nī'jah; 9 and their kindred according to their generations, nine hundred fifty-six. All these were

m Or Hotham; see 7.32   n Or father of Ehud; see 8.6
o Heb and Naaman   p Or he carried them into exile
q Compare 9.35: Heb lacks Jeiel   r Gk Ms adds Ner;
Compare 8.33 and 9.36   s Or Shaul

heads of families according to their ancestral houses.

Priestly Families

10 Of the priests: Je•daī′ah, Je•hoi′a•rib, Jā′chin, ¹¹ and Az•a•rī′ah son of Hil•kī′ah, son of Me•shul′lam, son of Zā′dok, son of Me•rā′i•oth, son of A•hī′tub, the chief officer of the house of God; ¹² and A•dāi′ah son of Je•rō′ham, son of Pash′hur, son of Mal•chī′jah, and Mā′a•saī son of Ad′i•el, son of Jah′ze•rah, son of Me•shul′lam, son of Me•shil′le•mith, son of Im′mer; ¹³ besides their kindred, heads of their ancestral houses, one thousand seven hundred sixty, qualified for the work of the service of the house of God.

Levitical Families

14 Of the Lē′vites: She•māi′ah son of Has′shub, son of Az•rī′kam, son of Hash•a•bī′ah, of the sons of Me•rar′ī; ¹⁵ and Bak•bak′kar, Hē′resh, Gā′lal, and Mat•ta•nī′ah son of Mī′ca, son of Zich′rī, son of Ā′saph; ¹⁶ and Ō•ba•dī′ah son of She•māi′ah, son of Gā′lal, son of Je•dū′thun, and Ber•e•chī′ah son of Asa, son of El•kā′nah, who lived in the villages of the Ne•toph′a•thītes.

17 The gatekeepers were: Shal′lum, Ak′kub, Tal′mon, A•hī′man; and their kindred Shal′lum was the chief, ¹⁸ stationed previously in the king's gate on the east side. These were the gatekeepers of the camp of the Lē′vites. ¹⁹ Shal′lum son of Kō′re, son of E•bī′a•saph, son of Kō′rah, and his kindred of his ancestral house, the Kō′ra•hītes, were in charge of the work of the service, guardians of the thresholds of the tent, as their ancestors had been in charge of the camp of the LORD, guardians of the entrance. ²⁰ And Phin′e•has son of El•e•ā′zar was chief over them in former times; the LORD was with him. ²¹ Zech•a•rī′ah son of Me•shel•e•mī′ah was gatekeeper at the entrance of the tent of meeting. ²² All these, who were chosen as gatekeepers at the thresholds, were two hundred twelve. They were enrolled by genealogies in their villages. David and the seer Samuel established them in their office of trust. ²³ So they and their descendants were in charge of the gates of the house of the LORD, that is, the house of the tent, as guards. ²⁴ The gatekeepers were on the four sides, east, west, north, and south; ²⁵ and their kindred who were in their villages were obliged to come in every seven days, in turn, to be with them; ²⁶ for the four chief gatekeepers, who were Lē′vites, were in charge of the chambers and the treasures of the house of God. ²⁷ And they would spend the night near the house of God; for on them lay the duty of watching, and they had charge of opening it every morning.

28 Some of them had charge of the utensils of service, for they were required to count them when they were brought in and taken out. ²⁹ Others of them were appointed over the furniture, and over all the holy utensils, also over the choice flour, the wine, the oil, the incense, and the spices. ³⁰ Others, of the sons of the priests, prepared the mixing of the spices, ³¹ and Mat•ti•thī′ah, one of the Lē′vites, the firstborn of Shal′lum the Kō′ra•hīte, was in charge of making the flat cakes. ³² Also some of their kindred of the Kō′hath•ītes had charge of the rows of bread, to prepare them for each sabbath.

33 Now these are the singers, the heads of ancestral houses of the Lē′vites, living in the chambers of the temple free from other service, for they were on duty day and night. ³⁴ These were heads of ancestral houses of the Lē′vites, according to their generations; these leaders lived in Jerusalem.

The Family of King Saul

35 In Gib′e•on lived the father of Gib′e•on, Je•ī′el, and the name of his wife was Mā′a•cah. ³⁶ His firstborn son was Ab′don, then Zur, Kish, Bā′al, Ner, Nā′dab, ³⁷ Gē′dor, A•hī′ō, Zech•a•rī′ah, and Mik′loth; ³⁸ and Mik′loth became the father of Shim′e•am; and these also lived opposite their kindred in Jerusalem, with their kindred. ³⁹ Ner became the father of Kish, Kish of Saul, Saul of Jonathan, Mal•chī•shū′a, A•bin′a•dab, and Esh-bā′al; ⁴⁰ and the son of Jonathan was Mer′ib-bā′al; and Mer′ib-bā′al became the father of Mī′cah. ⁴¹ The sons of Mī′cah: Pī′thon, Mē′lech, Tah′rē•a, and Ā′haz;ᵗ ⁴² and Ā′haz became the father of Jar′ah, and Jar′ah of Al′e•meth, Az′ma•veth, and Zim′rī; and Zim′rī became the father of Mō′za. ⁴³ Mō′za became the father of Bin′e•a; and Reph•ai′ah was his son, El•e•ā′sah his son, Ā′zel his son. ⁴⁴ Ā′zel had six sons, and these are their names: Az•rī′kam, Bō′che•rū, Ish′ma•el, Shē•a•rī′ah, Ō•ba•dī′ah, and Hā′nan; these were the sons of Ā′zel.

Death of Saul and His Sons
(1 Sam 31.1–13)

Now the Phi•lis′tines fought against Israel; and the men of Israel fled before the Phi•lis′tines, and fell slain on Mount Gil•bō′a. ²The Phi•lis′tines overtook Saul and his sons; and the Phi•lis′tines killed Jonathan and A•bin′a•dab and Mal•chī•shū′a, sons of Saul. ³The battle pressed hard on Saul; and the archers found him, and he was wounded by the archers. ⁴Then Saul said to his armor-bearer, "Draw your sword, and thrust me through with it, so that these uncircumcised may not come and make sport of me." But his armor-bearer was

---

ᵗ Compare 8.35: Heb lacks *and Ahaz*

unwilling, for he was terrified. So Saul took his own sword and fell on it. ⁵When his armor-bearer saw that Saul was dead, he also fell on his sword and died. ⁶Thus Saul died; he and his three sons and all his house died together. ⁷When all the men of Israel who were in the valley saw that the armyᵘ had fled and that Saul and his sons were dead, they abandoned their towns and fled; and the Phi·lis'tines came and occupied them.

8 The next day when the Phi·lis'tines came to strip the dead, they found Saul and his sons fallen on Mount Gil·bō'a. ⁹They stripped him and took his head and his armor, and sent messengers throughout the land of the Phi·lis'tines to carry the good news to their idols and to the people. ¹⁰They put his armor in the temple of their gods, and fastened his head in the temple of Dā'gon. ¹¹But when all Jā'besh-gil'ē·ad heard everything that the Phi·lis'tines had done to Saul, ¹²all the valiant warriors got up and took away the body of Saul and the bodies of his sons, and brought them to Jā'besh. Then they buried their bones under the oak in Jā'besh, and fasted seven days.

13 So Saul died for his unfaithfulness; he was unfaithful to the LORD in that he did not keep the command of the LORD; moreover, he had consulted a medium, seeking guidance, ¹⁴and did not seek guidance from the LORD. Therefore the LORDᵛ put him to death and turned the kingdom over to David son of Jesse.

David Anointed King of All Israel
(2 Sam 5.1–3)

Then all Israel gathered together to David at Hē'bron and said, "See, we are your bone and flesh. ²For some time now, even while Saul was king, it was you who commanded the army of Israel. The LORD your God said to you: It is you who shall be shepherd of my people Israel, you who shall be ruler over my people Israel." ³So all the elders of Israel came to the king at Hē'bron, and David made a covenant with them at Hē'bron before the LORD. And they anointed David king over Israel, according to the word of the LORD by Samuel.

Jerusalem Captured
(2 Sam 5.6–10)

4 David and all Israel marched to Jerusalem, that is Jē'bus, where the Jeb'ū·sites were, the inhabitants of the land. ⁵The inhabitants of Jē'bus said to David, "You will not come in here." Nevertheless David took the stronghold of Zion, now the city of David. ⁶David had said, "Whoever attacks the Jeb'ū·sites first shall be chief and commander." And Jō'ab son of Ze·rū'i·ah went up first, and became chief. ⁷David resided in the stronghold;

therefore it was called the city of David. ⁸He built the city all around, from the Mil'lō in complete circuit; and Jō'ab repaired the rest of the city. ⁹And David became greater and greater, for the LORD of hosts was with him.

David's Mighty Men and Their Exploits
(2 Sam 23.8–39)

10 Now these are the chiefs of David's warriors, who gave him strong support in his kingdom, together with all Israel, to make him king, according to the word of the LORD concerning Israel. ¹¹This is an account of David's mighty warriors: Ja·shō'bē·am, son of Hach'mo·ni,ʷ was chief of the Three;ˣ he wielded his spear against three hundred whom he killed at one time.

12 And next to him among the three warriors was El·ē·ā'zar son of Dō'dō, the A·hō'hīte. ¹³He was with David at Pas-dam'mim when the Phi·lis'tines were gathered there for battle. There was a plot of ground full of barley. Now the people had fled from the Phi·lis'tines, ¹⁴but he and David took their stand in the middle of the plot, defended it, and killed the Phi·lis'tines; and the LORD saved them by a great victory.

15 Three of the thirty chiefs went down to the rock to David at the cave of A·dul'lam, while the army of Phi·lis'tines was encamped in the valley of Reph'a·im. ¹⁶David was then in the stronghold; and the garrison of the Phi·lis'tines was then at Bethlehem. ¹⁷David said longingly, "O that someone would give me water to drink from the well of Bethlehem that is by the gate!" ¹⁸Then the Three broke through the camp of the Phi·lis'tines, and drew water from the well of Bethlehem that was by the gate, and they brought it to David. But David would not drink of it; he poured it out to the LORD, ¹⁹and said, "My God forbid that I should do this. Can I drink the blood of these men? For at the risk of their lives they brought it." Therefore he would not drink it. The three warriors did these things.

20 Now A·bi'shaī,ʸ the brother of Jō'ab, was chief of the Thirty.ᶻ With his spear he fought against three hundred and killed them, and won a name beside the Three. ²¹He was the most renownedᵃ of the Thirty,ᶻ and became their commander; but he did not attain to the Three.

22 Be·nā'i·ah son of Je·hoi'a·da was a valiant manᵇ of Kab'ze·el, a doer of great deeds; he struck down two sons ofᶜ Ar'i·el of Mō'ab. He also went

---

ᵘ Heb they   ᵛ Heb he   ʷ Or a Hachmonite   ˣ Compare
2 Sam 23.8: Heb Thirty or captains   ʸ Gk Vg Tg Compare
2 Sam 23.18: Heb Abshai   ᶻ Syr: Heb Three
ᵃ Compare 2 Sam 23.19: Heb more renowned among the two
ᵇ Syr: Heb the son of a valiant man   ᶜ See 2 Sam 23.20:
Heb lacks sons of

down and killed a lion in a pit on a day when snow had fallen. 23 And he killed an Egyptian, a man of great stature, five cubits tall. The Egyptian had in his hand a spear like a weaver's beam; but Be·nā′i·ah went against him with a staff, snatched the spear out of the Egyptian's hand, and killed him with his own spear. 24 Such were the things Be·nā′i·ah son of Je·hoi′a·da did, and he won a name beside the three warriors. 25 He was renowned among the Thirty, but he did not attain to the Three. And David put him in charge of his bodyguard.

26 The warriors of the armies were As′a·hel brother of Jō′ab, El·hā′nan son of Dō′dō of Bethlehem, 27 Sham′moth of Har′od,*d* Hē′lez the Pel′o·nīte, 28 Ira son of Ik′kesh of Te·kō′a, A·bi·ē′zer of An′a·thoth, 29 Sib′be·cai the Hū′sha·thite, I′lai the A·hō′hīte, 30 Mā′ha·rai of Ne·toph′ah, Hē′led son of Bā′a·nah of Ne·toph′ah, 31 Ith′ai son of Rī′bai of Gib′ē·ah of the Ben′ja·min·ītes, Be·nā′i·ah of Pir′a·thon, 32 Hū′rai of the wadis of Gā′ash, A·bi′el the Ar′ba·thīte, 33 Az′ma·veth of Ba·hā′rum, Ē·li′ah·ba of Shā·al′bon, 34 Hā′sheme* the Gī′zō·nīte, Jonathan son of Shā′gee the Har′a·rīte, 35 A·hī′am son of Sā′char the Har′a·rīte, E·lī′phal son of Ūr, 36 Hē′pher the Me·chē′ra·thīte, A·hī′jah the Pel′o·nīte, 37 Hez′rō of Car′mel, Nā′a·rai son of Ez′bai, 38 Jō′el the brother of Nathan, Mib′har son of Hag′rī, 39 Zē′lek the Am′mon·īte, Nā′ha·rai of Be·er′oth, the armorbearer of Jō′ab son of Ze·rū′i·ah, 40 Ira the Ith′rīte, Gā′reb the Ith′rīte, 41 Ū·rī′ah the Hit′tīte, Zā′bad son of Ah′lai, 42 Ad′i·na son of Shī′za the Reū′ben·īte, a leader of the Reū′ben·ītes, and thirty with him, 43 Hā′nan son of Mā′a·cah, and Josh′a·phat the Mith′nīte, 44 Uz·zī′a the Ash′te·ra·thīte, Shā′ma and Je·ī′el sons of Hō′tham the A·rō′er·īte, 45 Je·dī′a·el son of Shim′rī, and his brother Jō′ha the Tī′zīte, 46 E·lī′el the Mā′ha·vīte, and Jer′i·bai and Josh·a·vī′ah sons of El′nā·am, and Ith′mah the Mō′ab·īte, 47 E·lī′el, and Ō′bed, and Jā·a·sī′el the Me·zō′ba·īte.

David's Followers in the Wilderness
(1 Sam 22.1–2)

The following are those who came to David at Zik′lag, while he could not move about freely because of Saul son of Kish; they were among the mighty warriors who helped him in war. 2 They were archers, and could shoot arrows and sling stones with either the right hand or the left; they were Ben′ja·min·ītes, Saul's kindred. 3 The chief was Ā·hī·ē′zer, then Jō′ash, both sons of She·mā′ah of Gib′ē·ah; also Jē′zi·el and Pē′let sons of Az′ma·veth; Ber′a·cah, Jē′hū of An′a·thoth, 4 Ish·mā′i·ah of Gib′ē·on, a warrior among the Thirty and a leader over the Thirty; Jer·e·mī′ah,*f* Ja·hā′zi·el, Jō·hā′nan, Joz′a·bad of Ge·dē′rah, 5 E·lū′zai,*g* Jer′i·moth, Be·a·lī′ah,

Shem·a·rī′ah, Sheph·a·tī′ah the Ha·rū′phite; 6 El·kā′nah, Is·shī′ah, Az′a·rel, Jō·ē′zer, and Ja·shō′bē·am, the Kō′ra·hītes; 7 and Jō·ē′lah and Zeb·a·dī′ah, sons of Je·rō′ham of Gē′dor.

8 From the Gad′ītes there went over to David at the stronghold in the wilderness mighty and experienced warriors, expert with shield and spear, whose faces were like the faces of lions, and who were swift as gazelles on the mountains: 9 Ē′zer the chief, Ō·ba·dī′ah second, E·lī′ab third, 10 Mish′man′nah fourth, Jer·e·mī′ah fifth, 11 At′tai sixth, E·lī′el seventh, 12 Jō·hā′nan eighth, El·zā′bad ninth, 13 Jer·e·mī′ah tenth, Mach′ban·nai eleventh. 14 These Gad′ītes were officers of the army, the least equal to a hundred and the greatest to a thousand. 15 These are the men who crossed the Jordan in the first month, when it was overflowing all its banks, and put to flight all those in the valleys, to the east and to the west.

16 Some Ben′ja·min·ītes and Jū′dah·ītes came to the stronghold to David. 17 David went out to meet them and said to them, "If you have come to me in friendship, to help me, then my heart will be knit to you; but if you have come to betray me to my adversaries, though my hands have done no wrong, then may the God of our ancestors see and give judgment." 18 Then the spirit came upon A·mā′sai, chief of the Thirty, and he said,

> "We are yours, O David;
> and with you, O son of Jesse!
> Peace, peace to you,
> and peace to the one who helps you!
> For your God is the one who helps you."

Then David received them, and made them officers of his troops.

19 Some of the Ma·nas′sītes deserted to David when he came with the Phi·lis′tines for the battle against Saul. (Yet he did not help them, for the rulers of the Phi·lis′tines took counsel and sent him away, saying, "He will desert to his master Saul at the cost of our heads.") 20 As he went to Zik′lag these Ma·nas′sītes deserted to him: Ad′nah, Joz′a·bad, Je·dī′a·el, Michael, Joz′a·bad, E·lī′hū, and Zil′le·thai, chiefs of the thousands in Ma·nas′seh. 21 They helped David against the band of raiders,*h* for they were all warriors and commanders in the army. 22 Indeed from day to day people kept coming to David to help him, until there was a great army, like an army of God.

---

d Compare 2 Sam 23.25: Heb *the Harorite*   *e* Compare Gk and 2 Sam 23.32: Heb *the sons of Hashem*   *f* Heb verse 5   *g* Heb verse 6   *h* Or *as officers of his troops*

David's Army at Hebron

23 These are the numbers of the divisions of the armed troops who came to David in Hē′bron to turn the kingdom of Saul over to him, according to the word of the LORD. 24 The people of Judah bearing shield and spear numbered six thousand eight hundred armed troops. 25 Of the Sim′e•on•ites, mighty warriors, seven thousand one hundred. 26 Of the Lē′vites four thousand six hundred. 27 Jehoi′a•da, leader of the house of Aaron, and with him three thousand seven hundred. 28 Zā′dok, a young warrior, and twenty-two commanders from his own ancestral house. 29 Of the Ben′ja•min•ites, the kindred of Saul, three thousand, of whom the majority had continued to keep their allegiance to the house of Saul. 30 Of the Ē′phra•im•ites, twenty thousand eight hundred, mighty warriors, notables in their ancestral houses. 31 Of the half-tribe of Ma•nas′seh, eighteen thousand, who were expressly named to come and make David king. 32 Of Is′sa•char, those who had understanding of the times, to know what Israel ought to do, two hundred chiefs, and all their kindred under their command. 33 Of Zeb′u•lun, fifty thousand seasoned troops, equipped for battle with all the weapons of war, to help David*i* with singleness of purpose. 34 Of Naph′ta•li, a thousand commanders, with whom there were thirty-seven thousand armed with shield and spear. 35 Of the Dan′ites, twenty-eight thousand six hundred equipped for battle. 36 Of Ash′er, forty thousand seasoned troops ready for battle. 37 Of the Reū′ben•ites and Gad′ites and the half-tribe of Ma•nas′seh from beyond the Jordan, one hundred twenty thousand armed with all the weapons of war.

38 All these, warriors arrayed in battle order, came to Hē′bron with full intent to make David king over all Israel; likewise all the rest of Israel were of a single mind to make David king. 39 They were there with David for three days, eating and drinking, for their kindred had provided for them. 40 And also their neighbors, from as far away as Is′sa•char and Zeb′u•lun and Naph′ta•li, came bringing food on donkeys, camels, mules, and oxen — abundant provisions of meal, cakes of figs, clusters of raisins, wine, oil, oxen, and sheep, for there was joy in Israel.

The Ark Brought from Kiriath-jearim
(2 Sam 6.1–11)

David consulted with the commanders of the thousands and of the hundreds, with every leader. 2 David said to the whole assembly of Israel, "If it seems good to you, and if it is the will of the LORD our God, let us send abroad to our kindred who remain in all the land of Israel, including the priests and Lē′vites in the cities that have pasture lands, that they may come together to us. 3 Then let us bring again the ark of our God to us; for we did not turn to it in the days of Saul." 4 The whole assembly agreed to do so, for the thing pleased all the people.

5 So David assembled all Israel from the Shī′hor of Egypt to Lē′bo-ha′math, to bring the ark of God from Kir′i•ath-je′a•rim. 6 And David and all Israel went up to Bā′a•lah, that is, to Kir′i•ath-je′a•rim, which belongs to Judah, to bring up from there the ark of God, the LORD, who is enthroned on the cherubim, which is called by his*j* name. 7 They carried the ark of God on a new cart, from the house of A•bin′a•dab, and Uz′zah and A•hi′ō*k* were driving the cart. 8 David and all Israel were dancing before God with all their might, with song and lyres and harps and tambourines and cymbals and trumpets.

9 When they came to the threshing floor of Chī′don, Uz′zah put out his hand to hold the ark, for the oxen shook it. 10 The anger of the LORD was kindled against Uz′zah; he struck him down because he put out his hand to the ark; and he died there before God. 11 David was angry because the LORD had burst out against Uz′zah; so that place is called Per′ez-uz′zah*l* to this day. 12 David was afraid of God that day; he said, "How can I bring the ark of God into my care?" 13 So David did not take the ark into his care into the city of David; he took it instead to the house of Ō′bed-e′dom the Git′tite. 14 The ark of God remained with the household of Ō′bed-e′dom in his house three months, and the LORD blessed the household of Ō′bed-e′dom and all that he had.

David Established at Jerusalem
(2 Sam 5.11–16)

King Hiram of Tyre sent messengers to David, along with cedar logs, and masons and carpenters to build a house for him. 2 David then perceived that the LORD had established him as king over Israel, and that his kingdom was highly exalted for the sake of his people Israel.

3 David took more wives in Jerusalem, and David became the father of more sons and daughters. 4 These are the names of the children whom he had in Jerusalem: Sham′mū•a, Shō′bab, and Nathan; Solomon, 5 Ib′har, E•lish′ū•a, and El′pe•let; 6 Nō′gah, Nē′pheg, and Ja•phi′a; 7 E•lish′a•ma, Bē•e•li′a•da, and E•liph′e•let.

i Gk: Heb lacks *David*   *j* Heb lacks *his*   *k* Or *and his brother*   *l* That is *Bursting Out Against Uzzah*

Defeat of the Philistines
(2 Sam 5.17–25)

8 When the Phi·lis'tines heard that David had been anointed king over all Israel, all the Phi·lis'tines went up in search of David; and David heard of it and went out against them. 9 Now the Phi·lis'tines had come and made a raid in the valley of Reph'a·im. 10 David inquired of God, "Shall I go up against the Phi·lis'tines? Will you give them into my hand?" The LORD said to him, "Go up, and I will give them into your hand." 11 So he went up to Bā'al-pe·rā'zim, and David defeated them there. David said, "God has burst out^m against my enemies by my hand, like a bursting flood." Therefore that place is called Bā'al-pe·rā'zim.^n 12 They abandoned their gods there, and at David's command they were burned.

13 Once again the Phi·lis'tines made a raid in the valley. 14 When David again inquired of God, God said to him, "You shall not go up after them; go around and come on them opposite the balsam trees. 15 When you hear the sound of marching in the tops of the balsam trees, then go out to battle; for God has gone out before you to strike down the army of the Phi·lis'tines." 16 David did as God had commanded him, and they struck down the Phi·lis'tine army from Gib'e·on to Gē'zer. 17 The fame of David went out into all lands, and the LORD brought the fear of him on all nations.

The Ark Brought to Jerusalem
(2 Sam 6.12–16)

David^o built houses for himself in the city of David, and he prepared a place for the ark of God and pitched a tent for it. 2 Then David commanded that no one but the Lē'vites were to carry the ark of God, for the LORD had chosen them to carry the ark of the LORD and to minister to him forever. 3 David assembled all Israel in Jerusalem to bring up the ark of the LORD to its place, which he had prepared for it. 4 Then David gathered together the descendants of Aaron and the Lē'vites: 5 of the sons of Kō'hath, Ū·rī'el the chief, with one hundred twenty of his kindred; 6 of the sons of Me·rar'ī, A·sāi'ah the chief, with two hundred twenty of his kindred; 7 of the sons of Ger'shom, Jō'el the chief, with one hundred thirty of his kindred; 8 of the sons of E·li·zā'phan, She·māi'ah the chief, with two hundred of his kindred; 9 of the sons of Hē'bron, E·lī'el the chief, with eighty of his kindred; 10 of the sons of Uz'zi·el, Am·min'a·dab the chief, with one hundred twelve of his kindred.

11 David summoned the priests Zā'dok and A·bi'a·thar, and the Lē'vites Ū·rī'el, A·sāi'ah, Jō'el, She·māi'ah, E·lī'el, and Am·min'a·dab. 12 He said to them, "You are the heads of families of the Lē'vites; sanctify yourselves, you and your kindred, so that you may bring up the ark of the LORD, the God of Israel, to the place that I have prepared for it. 13 Because you did not carry it the first time,^p the LORD our God burst out against us, because we did not give it proper care." 14 So the priests and the Lē'vites sanctified themselves to bring up the ark of the LORD, the God of Israel. 15 And the Lē'vites carried the ark of God on their shoulders with the poles, as Moses had commanded according to the word of the LORD.

16 David also commanded the chiefs of the Lē'vites to appoint their kindred as the singers to play on musical instruments, on harps and lyres and cymbals, to raise loud sounds of joy. 17 So the Lē'vites appointed Hē'man son of Jō'el; and of his kindred Ā'saph son of Ber·e·chī'ah; and of the sons of Me·rar'ī, their kindred, Ē'than son of Kū·shā'i·ah; 18 and with them their kindred of the second order, Zech·a·rī'ah, Ja·ā'zi·el, She·mir'a·moth, Je·hī'el, Un'nī, E·lī'ab, Be·nā'i·ah, Mā·a·sēi'ah, Mat·ti·thī'ah, E·liph'e·le·hū, and Mik·nē'i·ah, and the gatekeepers Ō'bed-ē'dom and Je·ī'el. 19 The singers Hē'man, Ā'saph, and Ē'than were to sound bronze cymbals; 20 Zech·a·rī'ah, Ā'zi·el, She·mir'a·moth, Je·hī'el, Un'nī, E·lī'ab, Mā·a·sēi'ah, and Be·nā'i·ah were to play harps according to Al'a·moth; 21 but Mat·ti·thī'ah, E·liph'e·le·hū, Mik·nē'i·ah, Ō'bed-ē'dom, Je·ī'el, and Az·a·zī'ah were to lead with lyres according to the Shem'i·nith. 22 Chen·a·nī'ah, leader of the Lē'vites in music, was to direct the music, for he understood it. 23 Ber·e·chī'ah and El·kā'nah were to be gatekeepers for the ark. 24 Sheb·a·nī'ah, Josh'a·phat, Ne·than'el, A·mā'sai, Zech·a·rī'ah, Be·nā'i·ah, and El·i·e'zer, the priests, were to blow the trumpets before the ark of God. Ō'bed-ē'dom and Je·hī'ah also were to be gatekeepers for the ark.

25 So David and the elders of Israel, and the commanders of the thousands, went to bring up the ark of the covenant of the LORD from the house of Ō'bed-ē'dom with rejoicing. 26 And because God helped the Lē'vites who were carrying the ark of the covenant of the LORD, they sacrificed seven bulls and seven rams. 27 David was clothed with a robe of fine linen, as also were all the Lē'vites who were carrying the ark, and the singers, and Chen·a·nī'ah the leader of the music of the singers; and David wore a linen ephod. 28 So all Israel brought up the ark of the covenant of the LORD with shouting, to the sound of the horn, trumpets, and cymbals, and made loud music on harps and lyres.

---

m Heb *paraz*   n That is *Lord of Bursting Out*   o Heb *He*
p Meaning of Heb uncertain

29 As the ark of the covenant of the LORD came to the city of David, Mi'chal daughter of Saul looked out of the window, and saw King David leaping and dancing; and she despised him in her heart.

The Ark Placed in the Tent
(2 Sam 6.17–19)

They brought in the ark of God, and set it inside the tent that David had pitched for it; and they offered burnt offerings and offerings of well-being before God. ²When David had finished offering the burnt offerings and the offerings of well-being, he blessed the people in the name of the LORD; ³and he distributed to every person in Israel—man and woman alike—to each a loaf of bread, a portion of meat,*q* and a cake of raisins.

4 He appointed certain of the Lē'vītes as ministers before the ark of the LORD, to invoke, to thank, and to praise the LORD, the God of Israel. ⁵Ā'saph was the chief, and second to him Zech•a•rī'ah, Je•ī'el, She•mir'a•moth, Je•hī'el, Mat•ti•thī'ah, E•lī'ab, Be•nā'-i•ah, Ō'bed-ē'dom, and Je•ī'el, with harps and lyres; Ā'saph was to sound the cymbals, ⁶and the priests Be•nā'i•ah and Ja•hā'zi•el were to blow trumpets regularly, before the ark of the covenant of God.

David's Psalm of Thanksgiving
(Ps 96.1–13; 105.1–15; 106.1, 47–48)

7 Then on that day David first appointed the singing of praises to the LORD by Ā'saph and his kindred.

8 O give thanks to the LORD, call on his name,
    make known his deeds among the
        peoples.
⁹ Sing to him, sing praises to him,
    tell of all his wonderful works.

¹⁰ Glory in his holy name;
    let the hearts of those who seek the LORD
        rejoice.
¹¹ Seek the LORD and his strength,
    seek his presence continually.
¹² Remember the wonderful works he has done,
    his miracles, and the judgments he
        uttered,
¹³ O offspring of his servant Israel,*r*
    children of Jacob, his chosen ones.

¹⁴ He is the LORD our God;
    his judgments are in all the earth.
¹⁵ Remember his covenant forever,
    the word that he commanded, for a
        thousand generations,
¹⁶ the covenant that he made with Abraham,
    his sworn promise to Isaac,
¹⁷ which he confirmed to Jacob as a statute,
    to Israel as an everlasting covenant,
¹⁸ saying, "To you I will give the land of
        Ca'naan
    as your portion for an inheritance."

¹⁹ When they were few in number,
    of little account, and strangers in the land,*s*
²⁰ wandering from nation to nation,
    from one kingdom to another people,
²¹ he allowed no one to oppress them;
    he rebuked kings on their account,
²² saying, "Do not touch my anointed ones;
    do my prophets no harm."

²³ Sing to the LORD, all the earth.
    Tell of his salvation from day to day.
²⁴ Declare his glory among the nations,
    his marvelous works among all the
        peoples.
²⁵ For great is the LORD, and greatly to be
        praised;
    he is to be revered above all gods.
²⁶ For all the gods of the peoples are idols,
    but the LORD made the heavens.
²⁷ Honor and majesty are before him;
    strength and joy are in his place.

²⁸ Ascribe to the LORD, O families of the peoples,
    ascribe to the LORD glory and strength.
²⁹ Ascribe to the LORD the glory due his name;
    bring an offering, and come before him.
    Worship the LORD in holy splendor;
³⁰   tremble before him, all the earth.
    The world is firmly established; it shall
        never be moved.

---

q Compare Gk Syr Vg: Meaning of Heb uncertain
r Another reading is *Abraham* (compare Ps 105.6)
s Heb *in it*

31 Let the heavens be glad, and let the earth
rejoice,
and let them say among the nations,
"The LORD is king!"
32 Let the sea roar, and all that fills it;
let the field exult, and everything in it.
33 Then shall the trees of the forest sing for joy
before the LORD, for he comes to judge
the earth.
34 O give thanks to the LORD,
for he is good;
for his steadfast love endures forever.

35 Say also:
"Save us, O God of our salvation,
and gather and rescue us from among the
nations,
that we may give thanks to your
holy name,
and glory in your praise.
36 Blessed be the LORD, the God of Israel,
from everlasting to everlasting."
Then all the people said "Amen!" and praised the
LORD.

Regular Worship Maintained

37 David left Ā'saph and his kinsfolk there before the ark of the covenant of the LORD to minister
regularly before the ark as each day required,
38 and also Ō'bed-ē'dom and his^t sixty-eight kinsfolk; while Ō'bed-ē'dom son of Je•dū'thun and
Hō'sah were to be gatekeepers. 39 And he left the
priest Zā'dok and his kindred the priests before
the tabernacle of the LORD in the high place that
was at Gib'ē•on, 40 to offer burnt offerings to the
LORD on the altar of burnt offering regularly, morning and evening, according to all that is written in
the law of the LORD that he commanded Israel.
41 With them were Hē'man and Je•dū'thun, and the
rest of those chosen and expressly named to render thanks to the LORD, for his steadfast love endures forever. 42 Hē'man and Je•dū'thun had with
them trumpets and cymbals for the music, and instruments for sacred song. The sons of Je•dū'thun
were appointed to the gate.
43 Then all the people departed to their
homes, and David went home to bless his household.

God's Covenant with David
(2 Sam 7.1–17)

Now when David settled in his house, David said
to the prophet Nathan, "I am living in a house of
cedar, but the ark of the covenant of the LORD is
under a tent." 2 Nathan said to David, "Do all that
you have in mind, for God is with you."

3 But that same night the word of the LORD
came to Nathan, saying: 4 Go and tell my servant
David: Thus says the LORD: You shall not build me
a house to live in. 5 For I have not lived in a house
since the day I brought out Israel to this very day,
but I have lived in a tent and a tabernacle.^u

Catholic Connections

RITUAL PRAYER

King David established times of regular,
ritual prayer at the ark. Regular, ritual
prayer is a practice of many of the world's
great religions and, in the eyes of the
Chronicler, is a key ingredient of true religious practice. Catholics also have ancient
traditions of regular, ritual prayer. (Regular,
in this instance, does not mean "ordinary,"
but rather "at certain, established times.")
We start the day with prayer, we end the
day with prayer, we have special blessings
for special occasions, and we gather to celebrate the Eucharist each week. Regular,
ritual prayer helps to remind us of God's
presence and of our identity as God's people.
How do you pray? Do you pray regularly? Do you have any personal rituals as part
of your prayer life?

▶ 1 Chr 16.37–43

6 Wherever I have moved about among all Israel,
did I ever speak a word with any of the judges of
Israel, whom I commanded to shepherd my people, saying, Why have you not built me a house of
cedar? 7 Now therefore thus you shall say to my
servant David: Thus says the LORD of hosts: I took
you from the pasture, from following the sheep, to
be ruler over my people Israel; 8 and I have been
with you wherever you went, and have cut off all
your enemies before you; and I will make for you

---

^t Gk Syr Vg: Heb *their*   ^u Gk 2 Sam 7.6: Heb *but I have
been from tent to tent and from tabernacle*

a name, like the name of the great ones of the earth. 9 I will appoint a place for my people Israel, and will plant them, so that they may live in their own place, and be disturbed no more; and evildoers shall wear them down no more, as they did formerly, 10 from the time that I appointed judges over my people Israel; and I will subdue all your enemies.

vant? You know your servant. 19 For your servant's sake, O LORD, and according to your own heart, you have done all these great deeds, making known all these great things. 20 There is no one like you, O LORD, and there is no God besides you, according to all that we have heard with our ears. 21 Who is like your people Israel, one nation on the earth whom God went to redeem to be his

Where Do We Place God?

How the world loves boxes and containers and compartments! Remember the old saying, A place for everything and everything in its place? There is something comforting in knowing that everything is where it should be.

Don't we often try to put God away in a special place? Isn't it more convenient to think of God as residing "up there" in the tabernacle or sanctuary? Perhaps that is why in I Chr 17.4–6, God seems less than enthusiastic about David's desire to build a temple. The danger is clear: identify God with a building, however grand and beautiful, and in people's minds, God *stays* there.

When we enter a chapel or a church, we become reverent, sensing that we are in the presence of God. And, indeed, we are. But we need to remember that we do not leave God behind when we step out of that structure. Simply put, God cannot and will not be confined, despite our best efforts.

Our God walks with us. God's place is everywhere.

How can you practice living in the constant presence of God?

▶ I Chr 17.1–15

Moreover I declare to you that the LORD will build you a house. 11 When your days are fulfilled to go to be with your ancestors, I will raise up your offspring after you, one of your own sons, and I will establish his kingdom. 12 He shall build a house for me, and I will establish his throne forever. 13 I will be a father to him, and he shall be a son to me. I will not take my steadfast love from him, as I took it from him who was before you, 14 but I will confirm him in my house and in my kingdom forever, and his throne shall be established forever. 15 In accordance with all these words and all this vision, Nathan spoke to David.

David's Prayer
(2 Sam 7.18–29)

16 Then King David went in and sat before the LORD, and said, "Who am I, O LORD God, and what is my house, that you have brought me thus far? 17 And even this was a small thing in your sight, O God; you have also spoken of your servant's house for a great while to come. You regard me as someone of high rank,ᵛ O LORD God! 18 And what more can David say to you for honoring your ser-

people, making for yourself a name for great and terrible things, in driving out nations before your people whom you redeemed from Egypt? 22 And you made your people Israel to be your people forever; and you, O LORD, became their God.

23 "And now, O LORD, as for the word that you have spoken concerning your servant and concerning his house, let it be established forever, and do as you have promised. 24 Thus your name will be established and magnified forever in the saying, 'The LORD of hosts, the God of Israel, is Israel's God'; and the house of your servant David will be established in your presence. 25 For you, my God, have revealed to your servant that you will build a house for him; therefore your servant has found it possible to pray before you. 26 And now, O LORD, you are God, and you have promised this good thing to your servant; 27 therefore may it please you to bless the house of your servant, that it may continue forever before you. For you, O LORD, have blessed and are blessedʷ forever."

ᵛ Meaning of Heb uncertain   ʷ Or *and it is blessed*

David's Kingdom Established
and Extended
(2 Sam 8.1–14)

Some time afterward, David attacked the Phi·lis′tines and subdued them; he took Gath and its villages from the Phi·lis′tines. 2 He defeated Mō′ab, and the Mō′ab·ites became subject to David and brought tribute. 3 David also struck down King Had·a·dē′zer of Zō′bah, toward Hā′math,ˣ as he went to set up a monument at the river Euphrates. 4 David took from him one thousand chariots, seven thousand cavalry, and twenty thousand foot soldiers. David hamstrung all the chariot horses, but left one hundred of them. 5 When the Ar·a·mē′ans of Damascus came to help King Had·a·dē′zer of Zō′bah, David killed twenty-two thousand Ar·a·mē′ans. 6 Then David put garrisonsʸ in Ar′am of Damascus; and the Ar·a·mē′ans became subject to David, and brought tribute. The LORD gave victory to David wherever he went. 7 David took the gold shields that were carried by the servants of Had·a·dē′zer, and brought them to Jerusalem. 8 From Tib′hath and from Cūn, cities of Had·a·dē′zer, David took a vast quantity of bronze; with it Solomon made the bronze sea and the pillars and the vessels of bronze.

9 When King Tō′ū of Hā′math heard that David had defeated the whole army of King Had·a·dē′zer of Zō′bah, 10 he sent his son Ha·dor′am to King David, to greet him and to congratulate him, because he had fought against Had·a·dē′zer and defeated him. Now Had·a·dē′zer had often been at war with Tō′ū. He sent all sorts of articles of gold, of silver, and of bronze; 11 these also King David dedicated to the LORD, together with the silver and gold that he had carried off from all the nations, from Ē′dom, Mō′ab, the Am′mon·ites, the Phi·lis′tines, and Am′a·lek.

12 A·bi′shaī son of Ze·rū′i·ah killed eighteen thousand Ē′dom·ites in the Valley of Salt. 13 He put garrisons in Ē′dom; and all the Ē′dom·ites became subject to David. And the LORD gave victory to David wherever he went.

David's Administration
(2 Sam 8.15–18)

14 So David reigned over all Israel; and he administered justice and equity to all his people. 15 Jō′ab son of Ze·rū′i·ah was over the army; Je·hosh′a·phat son of A·hī′lud was recorder; 16 Zā′dok son of A·hī′tub and A·him′e·lech son of A·bī′a·thar were priests; Shav′sha was secretary; 17 Be·nā′i·ah son of Je·hoi′a·da was over the Cher′e·thītes and the Pel′eth·ites; and David's sons were the chief officials in the service of the king.

Defeat of the Ammonites
and Arameans
(2 Sam 10.1–19)

Some time afterward, King Nā′hash of the Am′mon·ites died, and his son succeeded him. 2 David said, "I will deal loyally with Hā′nun son of Nā′hash, for his father dealt loyally with me." So David sent messengers to console him concerning his father. When David's servants came to Hā′nun in the land of the Am′mon·ites, to console him, 3 the officials of the Am′mon·ites said to Hā′nun, "Do you think, because David has sent consolers to you, that he is honoring your father? Have not his servants come to you to search and to overthrow and to spy out the land?" 4 So Hā′nun seized David's servants, shaved them, cut off their garments in the middle at their hips, and sent them away; 5 and they departed. When David was told about the men, he sent messengers to them, for they felt greatly humiliated. The king said, "Remain at Jericho until your beards have grown, and then return."

6 When the Am′mon·ites saw that they had made themselves odious to David, Hā′nun and the Am′mon·ites sent a thousand talents of silver to hire chariots and cavalry from Mes·o·po·ta′mi·a, from Ar′am-mā′a·cah and from Zō′bah. 7 They hired thirty-two thousand chariots and the king of Mā′a·cah with his army, who came and camped before Med′e·ba. And the Am′mon·ites were mustered from their cities and came to battle. 8 When David heard of it, he sent Jō′ab and all the army of the warriors. 9 The Am′mon·ites came out and drew up in battle array at the entrance of the city, and the kings who had come were by themselves in the open country.

10 When Jō′ab saw that the line of battle was set against him both in front and in the rear, he chose some of the picked men of Israel and arrayed them against the Ar·a·mē′ans; 11 the rest of his troops he put in the charge of his brother A·bi′shaī, and they were arrayed against the Am′mon·ites. 12 He said, "If the Ar·a·mē′ans are too strong for me, then you shall help me; but if the Am′mon·ites are too strong for you, then I will help you. 13 Be strong, and let us be courageous for our people and for the cities of our God; and may the LORD do what seems good to him." 14 So Jō′ab and the troops who were with him advanced toward the Ar·a·mē′ans for battle; and they fled before him. 15 When the Am′mon·ites saw that the Ar·a·mē′ans fled, they likewise fled before A·bi′shaī, Jō′ab's

---

ˣ Meaning of Heb uncertain   ʸ Gk Vg 2 Sam 8.6
Compare Syr: Heb lacks *garrisons*

brother, and entered the city. Then Jō'ab came to Jerusalem.

16 But when the Ar•a•mē'ans saw that they had been defeated by Israel, they sent messengers and brought out the Ar•a•mē'ans who were beyond the Euphrates, with Shō'phach the commander of the army of Had•a•dē'zer at their head. [17] When David was informed, he gathered all Israel together, crossed the Jordan, came to them, and drew up his forces against them. When David set the battle in array against the Ar•a•mē'ans, they fought with him. [18] The Ar•a•mē'ans fled before Israel; and David killed seven thousand Ar•a•mē'an charioteers and forty thousand foot soldiers, and also killed Shō'-phach the commander of their army. [19] When the servants of Had•a•dē'zer saw that they had been defeated by Israel, they made peace with David, and became subject to him. So the Ar•a•mē'ans were not willing to help the Am'mon•ites any more.

Siege and Capture of Rabbah
(2 Sam 11.1; 12.26–31)

In the spring of the year, the time when kings go out to battle, Jō'ab led out the army, ravaged the country of the Am'mon•ites, and came and be-sieged Rab'bah. But David remained at Jerusalem. Jō'ab attacked Rab'bah, and overthrew it. [2] David took the crown of Mil'com[z] from his head; he found that it weighed a talent of gold, and in it was a precious stone; and it was placed on David's head. He also brought out the booty of the city, a very great amount. [3] He brought out the people who were in it, and set them to work[a] with saws and iron picks and axes.[b] Thus David did to all the cities of the Am'mon•ites. Then David and all the people returned to Jerusalem.

Exploits against the Philistines
(2 Sam 21.15–22)

4 After this, war broke out with the Phi•lis'tines at Gē'zer; then Sib'be•caī the Hū'sha•thīte killed Sip'paī, who was one of the descendants of the giants; and the Phi•lis'tines were subdued. [5] Again there was war with the Phi•lis'tines; and El•hā'nan son of Jā'ir killed Lah'mī the brother of Goliath the Git'tīte, the shaft of whose spear was like a weaver's beam. [6] Again there was war at Gath, where there was a man of great size, who had six fingers on each hand, and six toes on each foot, twenty-four in number; he also was descended from the giants. [7] When he taunted Israel, Jona-than son of Shim'ē•a, David's brother, killed him. [8] These were descended from the giants in Gath; they fell by the hand of David and his servants.

The Census and Plague
(2 Sam 24.1–17)

Satan stood up against Israel, and incited David to count the people of Israel. [2] So David said to Jō'ab and the commanders of the army, "Go, number Israel, from Be'er-shē'ba to Dan, and bring me a report, so that I may know their number." [3] But Jō'ab said, "May the LORD increase the number of his people a hundredfold! Are they not, my lord the king, all of them my lord's servants? Why then should my lord require this? Why should he bring

PRAY IT!
True Repentance

Think of a time when you said, "I'm sorry," just because you had to. Now, think of a time when you were truly sorry. What is the difference between these two experiences? There is a big difference between going through the motions of repentance and being truly repentant. For example, David sinned—although it is not clear to us why—by ordering a census to count his people (1 Chr 21.2). He accepted a consequence that he hoped would be the easiest (verse 13). But when he saw the harm he had caused his people, he became truly repentant and accepted complete responsibility for his sin (verse 17).

Repentance requires true sorrow and a change of heart. It leads to an active response to make amends to those who are affected by our sin. Such repentance is called reconciliation, and Catholics celebrate it in the sacrament of Recon-ciliation.

▶ 1 Chr 21.1–17

guilt on Israel?" [4] But the king's word prevailed against Jō'ab. So Jō'ab departed and went throughout all Israel, and came back to Jerusalem. [5] Jō'ab gave the total count of the people to David. In all Israel there were one million one hundred thousand men who drew the sword, and in Judah four hundred seventy thousand who drew the

---

z Gk Vg See 1 Kings 11.5, 33: MT *of their king*
a Compare 2 Sam 12.31: Heb *and he sawed*   b Compare 2 Sam 12.31: Heb *saws*

sword. ⁶ But he did not include Levi and Benjamin in the numbering, for the king's command was abhorrent to Jo'ab.

7 But God was displeased with this thing, and he struck Israel. ⁸ David said to God, "I have sinned greatly in that I have done this thing. But now, I pray you, take away the guilt of your servant; for I have done very foolishly." ⁹ The LORD spoke to Gad, David's seer, saying, ¹⁰ "Go and say to David, 'Thus says the LORD: Three things I offer you; choose one of them, so that I may do it to you.' " ¹¹ So Gad came to David and said to him, "Thus says the LORD, 'Take your choice: ¹² either three years of famine; or three months of devastation by your foes, while the sword of your enemies overtakes you; or three days of the sword of the LORD, pestilence on the land, and the angel of the LORD destroying throughout all the territory of Israel.' Now decide what answer I shall return to the one who sent me." ¹³ Then David said to Gad, "I am in great distress; let me fall into the hand of the LORD, for his mercy is very great; but let me not fall into human hands."

14 So the LORD sent a pestilence on Israel; and seventy thousand persons fell in Israel. ¹⁵ And God sent an angel to Jerusalem to destroy it; but when he was about to destroy it, the LORD took note and relented concerning the calamity; he said to the destroying angel, "Enough! Stay your hand." The angel of the LORD was then standing by the threshing floor of Or'nan the Jeb'u·site. ¹⁶ David looked up and saw the angel of the LORD standing between earth and heaven, and in his hand a drawn sword stretched out over Jerusalem. Then David and the elders, clothed in sackcloth, fell on their faces. ¹⁷ And David said to God, "Was it not I who gave the command to count the people? It is I who have sinned and done very wickedly. But these sheep, what have they done? Let your hand, I pray, O LORD my God, be against me and against my father's house; but do not let your people be plagued!"

David's Altar and Sacrifice
(2 Sam 24.18–25)

18 Then the angel of the LORD commanded Gad to tell David that he should go up and erect an altar to the LORD on the threshing floor of Or'nan the Jeb'u·site. ¹⁹ So David went up following Gad's instructions, which he had spoken in the name of the LORD. ²⁰ Or'nan turned and saw the angel; and while his four sons who were with him hid themselves, Or'nan continued to thresh wheat. ²¹ As David came to Or'nan, Or'nan looked and saw David; he went out from the threshing floor, and did obeisance to David with his face to the

ground. ²² David said to Or'nan, "Give me the site of the threshing floor that I may build on it an altar to the LORD—give it to me at its full price—so that the plague may be averted from the people." ²³ Then Or'nan said to David, "Take it; and let my lord the king do what seems good to him; see, I present the oxen for burnt offerings, and the threshing sledges for the wood, and the wheat for a grain offering. I give it all." ²⁴ But King David said to Or'nan, "No; I will buy them for the full price. I will not take for the LORD what is yours, nor offer burnt offerings that cost me nothing." ²⁵ So David paid Or'nan six hundred shekels of gold by weight for the site. ²⁶ David built there an altar to the LORD and presented burnt offerings and offerings of well-being. He called upon the LORD, and he answered him with fire from heaven on the altar of burnt offering. ²⁷ Then the LORD commanded the angel, and he put his sword back into its sheath.

The Place Chosen for the Temple

28 At that time, when David saw that the LORD had answered him at the threshing floor of Or'nan the Jeb'u·site, he made his sacrifices there. ²⁹ For the tabernacle of the LORD, which Moses had made in the wilderness, and the altar of burnt offering were at that time in the high place at Gib'e·on; ³⁰ but David could not go before it to inquire of God, for he was afraid of the sword of the angel of the LORD. ¹ Then David said, "Here shall be the house of the LORD God and here the altar of burnt offering for Israel."

David Prepares to Build the Temple

2 David gave orders to gather together the aliens who were residing in the land of Israel, and he set stonecutters to prepare dressed stones for building the house of God. ³ David also provided great stores of iron for nails for the doors of the gates and for clamps, as well as bronze in quantities beyond weighing, ⁴ and cedar logs without number—for the Si·do'ni·ans and Ty'ri·ans brought great quantities of cedar to David. ⁵ For David said, "My son Solomon is young and inexperienced, and the house that is to be built for the LORD must be exceedingly magnificent, famous and glorified throughout all lands; I will therefore make preparation for it." So David provided materials in great quantity before his death.

David's Charge to Solomon and the Leaders

6 Then he called for his son Solomon and charged him to build a house for the LORD, the God of Israel. ⁷ David said to Solomon, "My son, I had planned to build a house to the name of the

LORD my God. 8 But the word of the LORD came to me, saying, 'You have shed much blood and have waged great wars; you shall not build a house to my name, because you have shed so much blood in my sight on the earth. 9 See, a son shall be born to you; he shall be a man of peace. I will give him peace from all his enemies on every side; for his name shall be Solomon,c and I will give peaced and quiet to Israel in his days. 10 He shall build a house for my name. He shall be a son to me, and I will be a father to him, and I will establish his royal throne in Israel forever.' 11 Now, my son, the LORD be with you, so that you may succeed in building the house of the LORD your God, as he has spoken concerning you. 12 Only, may the LORD grant you discretion and understanding, so that when he gives you charge over Israel you may keep the law of the LORD your God. 13 Then you will prosper if you are careful to observe the statutes and the ordinances that the LORD commanded Moses for Israel. Be strong and of good courage. Do not be afraid or dismayed. 14 With great pains I have provided for the house of the LORD one hundred thousand talents of gold, one million talents of silver, and bronze and iron beyond weighing, for there is so much of it; timber and stone too I have provided. To these you must add more. 15 You have an abundance of workers: stonecutters, masons, carpenters, and all kinds of artisans without number, skilled in working 16 gold, silver, bronze, and iron. Now begin the work, and the LORD be with you."

17 David also commanded all the leaders of Israel to help his son Solomon, saying, 18 "Is not the LORD your God with you? Has he not given you peace on every side? For he has delivered the inhabitants of the land into my hand; and the land is subdued before the LORD and his people. 19 Now set your mind and heart to seek the LORD your God. Go and build the sanctuary of the LORD God so that the ark of the covenant of the LORD and the holy vessels of God may be brought into a house built for the name of the LORD."

Families of the Levites and Their Functions

When David was old and full of days, he made his son Solomon king over Israel.

2 David assembled all the leaders of Israel and the priests and the Le'vites. 3 The Le'vites, thirty years old and upward, were counted, and the total was thirty-eight thousand. 4 "Twenty-four thousand of these," David said, "shall have charge of the work in the house of the LORD, six thousand shall be officers and judges, 5 four thousand gatekeepers, and four thousand shall offer praises to

the LORD with the instruments that I have made for praise." 6 And David organized them in divisions corresponding to the sons of Levi: Ger'shon,e Ko'hath, and Me·rar'i.

7 The sons of Ger'shonf were La'dan and Shim'e·i. 8 The sons of La'dan: Je·hi'el the chief, Ze'tham, and Jo'el, three. 9 The sons of Shim'e·i: She·lo'moth, Ha'zi·el, and Har'an, three. These were the heads of families of La'dan. 10 And the sons of Shim'e·i: Ja'hath, Zi'na, Je'ush, and Be·ri'ah. These four were the sons of Shim'e·i. 11 Ja'hath was the chief, and Zi'zah the second; but Je'ush and Be·ri'ah did not have many sons, so they were enrolled as a single family.

12 The sons of Ko'hath: Am'ram, Iz'har, He'bron, and Uz'zi·el, four. 13 The sons of Am'ram: Aaron and Moses. Aaron was set apart to consecrate the most holy things, so that he and his sons forever should make offerings before the LORD, and minister to him and pronounce blessings in his name forever; 14 but as for Moses the man of God, his sons were to be reckoned among the tribe of Levi. 15 The sons of Moses: Ger'shom and El·i·e'zer. 16 The sons of Ger'shom: She·bu'el the chief. 17 The sons of El·i·e'zer: Re·ha·bi'ah the chief; El·i·e'zer had no other sons, but the sons of Re·ha·bi'ah were very numerous. 18 The sons of Iz'har: She·lo'mith the chief. 19 The sons of He'bron: Je·ri'ah the chief, Am·a·ri'ah the second, Ja·ha'zi·el the third, and Jek·a·me'am the fourth. 20 The sons of Uz'zi·el: Mi'cah the chief and Is·shi'ah the second.

21 The sons of Me·rar'i: Mah'li and Mu'shi. The sons of Mah'li: El·e·a'zar and Kish. 22 El·e·a'zar died having no sons, but only daughters; their kindred, the sons of Kish, married them. 23 The sons of Mu'shi: Mah'li, E'der, and Jer'e·moth, three.

24 These were the sons of Levi by their ancestral houses, the heads of families as they were enrolled according to the number of the names of the individuals from twenty years old and upward who were to do the work for the service of the house of the LORD. 25 For David said, "The LORD, the God of Israel, has given rest to his people; and he resides in Jerusalem forever. 26 And so the Le'vites no longer need to carry the tabernacle or any of the things for its service" — 27 for according to the last words of David these were the number of the Le'vites from twenty years old and upward— 28 "but their duty shall be to assist the descendants of Aaron for the service of the house of the LORD, having the care of the courts and the chambers, the cleansing of all that is holy, and any work for

c Heb Shelomoh   d Heb shalom   e Or Gershom; See 1 Chr 6.1, note, and 23.15   f Vg Compare Gk Syr: Heb to the Gershonite

the service of the house of God; ²⁹ to assist also with the rows of bread, the choice flour for the grain offering, the wafers of unleavened bread, the baked offering, the offering mixed with oil, and all measures of quantity or size. ³⁰ And they shall stand every morning, thanking and praising the LORD, and likewise at evening, ³¹ and whenever burnt offerings are offered to the LORD on sabbaths, new moons, and appointed festivals, according to the number required of them, regularly before the LORD. ³² Thus they shall keep charge of the tent of meeting and the sanctuary, and shall attend the descendants of Aaron, their kindred, for the service of the house of the LORD."

Divisions of the Priests

The divisions of the descendants of Aaron were these. The sons of Aaron: Nā′dab, A·bī′hū, El·ē·ā′-zar, and Ith′a·mar. ² But Nā′dab and A·bī′hū died before their father, and had no sons; so El·ē·ā′zar and Ith′a·mar became the priests. ³ Along with Zā′-dok of the sons of El·ē·ā′zar, and A·him′e·lech of the sons of Ith′a·mar, David organized them according to the appointed duties in their service. ⁴ Since more chief men were found among the sons of El·ē·ā′zar than among the sons of Ith′a·mar, they organized them under sixteen heads of ancestral houses of the sons of El·ē·ā′zar, and eight of the sons of Ith′a·mar. ⁵ They organized them by lot, all alike, for there were officers of the sanctuary and officers of God among both the sons of El·ē·ā′zar and the sons of Ith′a·mar. ⁶ The scribe She·māi′ah son of Ne·than′el, a Lē′vīte, recorded them in the presence of the king, and the officers, and Zā′dok the priest, and A·him′e·lech son of A·bī′a·thar, and the heads of ancestral houses of the priests and of the Lē′vītes; one ancestral house being chosen for El·ē·ā′zar and one chosen for Ith′a·mar.

7 The first lot fell to Je·hoi′a·rib, the second to Je·daī′ah, ⁸ the third to Hā′rim, the fourth to Se·ō′-rim, ⁹ the fifth to Mal·chī′jah, the sixth to Mij′a·min, ¹⁰ the seventh to Hak′koz, the eighth to A·bī′jah, ¹¹ the ninth to Jesh′ū·a, the tenth to Shec·a·nī′-ah, ¹² the eleventh to E·lī′a·shib, the twelfth to Jā′-kim, ¹³ the thirteenth to Hup′pah, the fourteenth to Je·sheb′e·ab, ¹⁴ the fifteenth to Bil′gah, the sixteenth to Im′mer, ¹⁵ the seventeenth to Hē′zir, the eighteenth to Hap′piz·zez, ¹⁶ the nineteenth to Peth·a·hī′ah, the twentieth to Je·hez′kel, ¹⁷ the twenty-first to Jā′chin, the twenty-second to Gā′mul, ¹⁸ the twenty-third to De·laī′ah, the twenty-fourth to Mā·a·zī′ah. ¹⁹ These had as their appointed duty in their service to enter the house of the LORD according to the procedure established for them by their ancestor Aaron, as the LORD God of Israel had commanded him.

Other Levites

20 And of the rest of the sons of Levi: of the sons of Am′ram, Shū′ba·el; of the sons of Shū′ba·el, Jeh·dē′i·ah. ²¹ Of Rē·ha·bī′ah: of the sons of Rē·ha-bī′ah, Is·shī′ah the chief. ²² Of the Iz′har·ītes, She-lō′moth; of the sons of She·lō′moth, Jā′hath. ²³ The sons of Hē′bron:ᵍ Je·rī′ah the chief,ʰ Am·a·rī′ah the second, Ja·hā′zi·el the third, Jek·a·mē′am the fourth. ²⁴ The sons of Uz′zi·el, Mī′cah; of the sons of Mī′cah, Shā′mir. ²⁵ The brother of Mī′cah, Is-shī′ah; of the sons of Is·shī′ah, Zech·a·rī′ah. ²⁶ The sons of Me·rar′ī: Mah′li and Mū′shi. The sons of Jā·a·zī′ah: Bē′no.ⁱ ²⁷ The sons of Me·rar′ī: of Jā·a-zī′ah, Bē′no,ⁱ Shō′ham, Zac′cur, and Ib′rī. ²⁸ Of Mah′li: El·e·ā′zar, who had no sons. ²⁹ Of Kish, the sons of Kish: Je·rah′mē·el. ³⁰ The sons of Mū′shi: Mah′li, Ē′der, and Jer′i·moth. These were the sons of the Lē′vītes according to their ancestral houses. ³¹ These also cast lots corresponding to their kindred, the descendants of Aaron, in the presence of King David, Zā′dok, A·him′e·lech, and the heads of ancestral houses of the priests and of the Lē′vītes, the chief as well as the youngest brother.

The Temple Musicians

David and the officers of the army also set apart for the service the sons of Ā′saph, and of Hē′man, and of Je·dū′thun, who should prophesy with lyres, harps, and cymbals. The list of those who did the work and of their duties was: ² Of the sons of Ā′saph: Zac′cur, Joseph, Neth·a·nī′ah, and As·a·rē′-lah, sons of Ā′saph, under the direction of Ā′saph, who prophesied under the direction of the king. ³ Of Je·dū′thun, the sons of Je·dū′thun: Ged·a·lī′ah, Zē′rī, Je·shā′i·ah, Shim′ē·i,ʲ Hash·a·bī′ah, and Mat·ti-thī′ah, six, under the direction of their father Je-dū′thun, who prophesied with the lyre in thanksgiving and praise to the LORD. ⁴ Of Hē′man, the sons of Hē′man: Buk·kī′ah, Mat·ta·nī′ah, Uz′-zi·el, She·bū′el, and Jer′i·moth, Han·a·nī′ah, Ha·nā′nī, E·lī′a·thah, Gid·dal′tī, and Rō·mam′ti-ē′zer, Josh·be-kash′ah, Mal·lō′thī, Hō′thir, Ma·hā′zi·oth. ⁵ All these were the sons of Hē′man the king's seer, according to the promise of God to exalt him; for God had given Hē′man fourteen sons and three daughters. ⁶ They were all under the direction of their father for the music in the house of the LORD with cymbals, harps, and lyres for the service of the house of God. Ā′saph, Je·dū′thun, and Hē′man were under the order of the king. ⁷ They and their kindred, who were trained in singing to the LORD, all of whom were skillful, numbered two hundred

---

g See 23.19: Heb lacks *Hebron*　　*h* See 23.19: Heb lacks *the chief*　　*i* Or *his son*: Meaning of Heb uncertain
j One Ms: Gk: MT lacks *Shimei*

eighty-eight. ⁸ And they cast lots for their duties, small and great, teacher and pupil alike.

9 The first lot fell for Ā'saph to Joseph; the second to Ged·a·lī'ah, to him and his brothers and his sons, twelve; ¹⁰ the third to Zac'cur, his sons and his brothers, twelve; ¹¹ the fourth to Iz'rī, his sons and his brothers, twelve; ¹² the fifth to Neth·a·nī'ah, his sons and his brothers, twelve; ¹³ the sixth to Buk·kī'ah, his sons and his brothers, twelve; ¹⁴ the seventh to Jes·a·rē'lah,ᵏ his sons and his brothers, twelve; ¹⁵ the eighth to Je·shā'i·ah, his sons and his brothers, twelve; ¹⁶ the ninth to Mat·ta·nī'ah, his sons and his brothers, twelve; ¹⁷ the tenth to Shim'ē·ī, his sons and his brothers, twelve; ¹⁸ the eleventh to Az'a·rel, his sons and his brothers, twelve; ¹⁹ the twelfth to Hash·a·bī'ah, his sons and his brothers, twelve; ²⁰ to the thirteenth, Shū'ba·el, his sons and his brothers, twelve; ²¹ to the fourteenth, Mat·ti·thī'ah, his sons and his brothers, twelve; ²² to the fifteenth, to Jer'e·moth, his sons and his brothers, twelve; ²³ to the sixteenth, to Han·a·nī'ah, his sons and his brothers, twelve; ²⁴ to the seventeenth, to Josh·be·kash'ah, his sons and his brothers, twelve; ²⁵ to the eighteenth, to Ha·nā'nī, his sons and his brothers, twelve; ²⁶ to the nineteenth, to Mal·lō'thī, his sons and his brothers, twelve; ²⁷ to the twentieth, to E·lī'a·thah, his sons and his brothers, twelve; ²⁸ to the twenty-first, to Hō'thir, his sons and his brothers, twelve; ²⁹ to the twenty-second, to Gid·dal'tī, his sons and his brothers, twelve; ³⁰ to the twenty-third, to Ma·hā'zi·oth, his sons and his brothers, twelve; ³¹ to the twenty-fourth, to Rō·mam'ti-e'zer, his sons and his brothers, twelve.

The Gatekeepers

As for the divisions of the gatekeepers: of the Kō'ra·hītes, Me·shel·e·mī'ah son of Kō're, of the sons of Ā'saph. ² Me·shel·e·mī'ah had sons: Zech·a·rī'ah the firstborn, Je·dī'a·el the second, Zeb·a·dī'ah the third, Jath'ni·el the fourth, ³ Ē'lam the fifth, Jē·hō·hā'nan the sixth, El·i·e·hō·ē'nai the seventh. ⁴ Ō'bed-ē'dom had sons: She·māi'ah the firstborn, Je·hō'za·bad the second, Jō'ah the third, Sā'char the fourth, Ne·than'el the fifth, ⁵ Am'mi·el the sixth, Is'sa·char the seventh, Pe·ul'le·thai the eighth; for God blessed him. ⁶ Also to his son She·māi'ah were born who exercised authority in their ancestral houses, for they were men of great ability. ⁷ The sons of She·māi'ah: Oth'nī, Reph'a·el, Ō'bed, and El·zā'bad, whose brothers were able men, E·lī'hū and Sem·a·chī'ah. ⁸ All these, sons of Ō'bed-ē'dom with their sons and brothers, were able men qualified for the service; sixty-two of Ō'bed-ē'dom. ⁹ Me·shel·e·mī'ah had sons and brothers, able men, eighteen. ¹⁰ Hō'sah, of the sons of Me·rar'ī, had sons:

Shim'rī the chief (for though he was not the firstborn, his father made him chief), ¹¹ Hil·kī'ah the second, Teb·a·lī'ah the third, Zech·a·rī'ah the fourth: all the sons and brothers of Hō'sah totaled thirteen.

12 These divisions of the gatekeepers, corresponding to their leaders, had duties, just as their kindred did, ministering in the house of the LORD; ¹³ and they cast lots by ancestral houses, small and great alike, for their gates. ¹⁴ The lot for the east fell to Shel·e·mī'ah. They cast lots also for his son Zech·a·rī'ah, a prudent counselor, and his lot came out for the north. ¹⁵ Ō'bed-ē'dom's came out for the south, and to his sons was allotted the storehouse. ¹⁶ For Shup'pim and Hō'sah it came out for the west, at the gate of Shal'le·cheth on the ascending road. Guard corresponded to guard. ¹⁷ On the east there were six Lē'vītes each day,ˡ on the north four each day, on the south four each day, as well as two and two at the storehouse; ¹⁸ and for the colonnadeᵐ on the west there were four at the road and two at the colonnade.ᵐ ¹⁹ These were the divisions of the gatekeepers among the Kō'ra·hītes and the sons of Me·rar'ī.

The Treasurers, Officers, and Judges

20 And of the Lē'vītes, A·hī'jah had charge of the treasuries of the house of God and the treasuries of the dedicated gifts. ²¹ The sons of Lā'dan, the sons of the Ger'shon·ites belonging to Lā'dan, the heads of families belonging to Lā'dan the Ger'shon·ite: Je·hī'e·lī.ⁿ ²² The sons of Je·hī'e·lī, Zē'tham and his brother Jō'el, were in charge of the treasuries of the house of the LORD. ²³ Of the Am'ram·ites, the Iz'har·ites, the Hē'bron·ites, and the Uz'zi·el·ites: ²⁴ She·bū'el son of Ger'shom, son of Moses, was chief officer in charge of the treasuries. ²⁵ His brothers: from El·i·e'zer were his son Rē·ha·bī'ah, his son Je·shā'i·ah, his son Jō'ram, his son Zich'rī, and his son She·lō'moth. ²⁶ This She·lō'moth and his brothers were in charge of all the treasuries of the dedicated gifts that King David, and the heads of families, and the officers of the thousands and the hundreds, and the commanders of the army, had dedicated. ²⁷ From booty won in battles they dedicated gifts for the maintenance of the house of the LORD. ²⁸ Also all that Samuel the seer, and Saul son of Kish, and Abner son of Ner, and Jō'ab son of Ze·rū'i·ah had dedicated — all dedicated gifts were in the care of She·lō'mothᵒ and his brothers.

ᵏ Or *Asarelah*; see 25.2   ˡ Gk: Heb lacks *each day*
ᵐ Heb *parbar*: meaning uncertain   ⁿ The Hebrew text of verse 21 is confused   ᵒ Gk Compare 26.28: Heb *Shelomith*

29 Of the Iz′har·ites, Chen·a·ni′ah and his sons were appointed to outside duties for Israel, as officers and judges. 30 Of the Hē′bron·ites, Hash·a·bi′ah and his brothers, one thousand seven hundred men of ability, had the oversight of Israel west of the Jordan for all the work of the LORD and for the service of the king. 31 Of the Hē′bron·ites, Je·rī′jah was chief of the Hē′bron·ites. (In the fortieth year of David's reign search was made, of whatever genealogy or family, and men of great ability among them were found at Jā′zer in Gil′e·ad.) 32 King David appointed him and his brothers, two thousand seven hundred men of ability, heads of families, to have the oversight of the Reū′ben·ites, the Gad′ites, and the half-tribe of the Ma·nas′sites for everything pertaining to God and for the affairs of the king.

The Military Divisions

This is the list of the people of Israel, the heads of families, the commanders of the thousands and the hundreds, and their officers who served the king in all matters concerning the divisions that came and went, month after month throughout the year, each division numbering twenty-four thousand:

2 Ja·shō′bē·am son of Zab′di·el was in charge of the first division in the first month; in his division were twenty-four thousand. 3 He was a descendant of Per′ez, and was chief of all the commanders of the army for the first month. 4 Dō′daī the A·hō′hīte was in charge of the division of the second month; Mik′loth was the chief officer of his division. In his division were twenty-four thousand. 5 The third commander, for the third month, was Be·nā′i·ah son of the priest Je·hoi′a·da, as chief; in his division were twenty-four thousand. 6 This is the Be·nā′i·ah who was a mighty man of the Thirty and in command of the Thirty; his son Am·miz′a·bad was in charge of his division.ᵖ 7 As′a·hel brother of Jō′ab was fourth, for the fourth month, and his son Zeb·a·di′ah after him; in his division were twenty-four thousand. 8 The fifth commander, for the fifth month, was Sham′huth, the Iz′ra·hīte; in his division were twenty-four thousand. 9 Sixth, for the sixth month, was Ira son of Ik′kesh the Te·kō′ite; in his division were twenty-four thousand. 10 Seventh, for the seventh month, was Hē′lez the Pel′o·nīte, of the Ē′phra·im·ites; in his division were twenty-four thousand. 11 Eighth, for the eighth month, was Sib′be·caī the Hū′sha·thīte, of the Zē′ra·hītes; in his division were twenty-four thousand. 12 Ninth, for the ninth month, was Ā·bi·e′zer of An′a·thoth, a Ben′ja·min·ite; in his division were twenty-four thousand. 13 Tenth, for the tenth month, was Mā′ha·raī of Ne·toph′ah, of the Zē′ra·hītes; in his division were twenty-four thousand.

14 Eleventh, for the eleventh month, was Be·nā′i·ah of Pir′a·thon, of the Ē′phra·im·ites; in his division were twenty-four thousand. 15 Twelfth, for the twelfth month, was Hel′daī the Ne·toph′a·thīte, of Oth′ni·el; in his division were twenty-four thousand.

Leaders of Tribes

16 Over the tribes of Israel, for the Reū′ben·ites, El·i·e′zer son of Zich′rī was chief officer; for the Sim′e·on·ites, Sheph·a·tī′ah son of Mā′a·cah; 17 for Levi, Hash·a·bi′ah son of Ke·mū′el; for Aaron, Zā′dok; 18 for Judah, E·lī′hū, one of David's brothers; for Is′sa·char, Om′rī son of Michael; 19 for Zeb′u·lun, Ish·mā′i·ah son of Ō·ba·di′ah; for Naph′ta·lī, Jer′i·moth son of Az′ri·el; 20 for the Ē′phra·im·ites, Hō·shē′a son of Az·a·zī′ah; for the half-tribe of Manas′seh, Jō′el son of Pe·dāi′ah; 21 for the half-tribe of Ma·nas′seh in Gil′e·ad, Id′dō son of Zech·a·rī′ah; for Benjamin, Jā·a·sī′el son of Abner; 22 for Dan, Az′a·rel son of Je·rō′ham. These were the leaders of the tribes of Israel. 23 David did not count those below twenty years of age, for the LORD had promised to make Israel as numerous as the stars of heaven. 24 Jō′ab son of Ze·rū′i·ah began to count them, but did not finish; yet wrath came upon Israel for this, and the number was not entered into the account of the Annals of King David.

Other Civic Officials

25 Over the king's treasuries was Az′ma·veth son of Ad′i·el. Over the treasuries in the country, in the cities, in the villages and in the towers, was Jonathan son of Uz·zī′ah. 26 Over those who did the work of the field, tilling the soil, was Ez′rī son of Chē′lub. 27 Over the vineyards was Shim′e·ī the Rā′ma·thīte. Over the produce of the vineyards for the wine cellars was Zab′dī the Shiph′mīte. 28 Over the olive and sycamore trees in the She·phē′lah was Bā′al-hā′nan the Ge·dē′rīte. Over the stores of oil was Jō′ash. 29 Over the herds that pastured in Sharon was Shit′raī the Shār′on·īte. Over the herds in the valleys was Shā′phat son of Ad′lā·ī. 30 Over the camels was Ō′bil the Ish′ma·el·ite. Over the donkeys was Jeh·dē′i·ah the Me·ron′o·thīte. Over the flocks was Jā′ziz the Hag′rīte. 31 All these were stewards of King David's property.

32 Jonathan, David's uncle, was a counselor, being a man of understanding and a scribe; Je·hī′el son of Hach′mo·nī attended the king's sons. 33 A·hith′o·phel was the king's counselor, and Hū′shaī the Ar′chīte was the king's friend. 34 After A·hith′o·phel came Je·hoi′a·da son of Be·nā′i·ah, and

---

ᵖ Gk Vg: Heb *Ammizabad was his division*

A•bī'a•thar. Jō'ab was commander of the king's
army.

Solomon Instructed to Build the Temple

28 David assembled at Jerusalem all the officials of
Israel, the officials of the tribes, the officers of the
divisions that served the king, the commanders of
the thousands, the commanders of the hundreds,
the stewards of all the property and cattle of the
king and his sons, together with the palace officials, the mighty warriors, and all the warriors.
2 Then King David rose to his feet and said: "Hear
me, my brothers and my people. I had planned to
build a house of rest for the ark of the covenant of
the LORD, for the footstool of our God; and I made
preparations for building. 3 But God said to me,
'You shall not build a house for my name, for you
are a warrior and have shed blood.' 4 Yet the LORD
God of Israel chose me from all my ancestral
house to be king over Israel forever; for he chose
Judah as leader, and in the house of Judah my
father's house, and among my father's sons he
took delight in making me king over all Israel.
5 And of all my sons, for the LORD has given me
many, he has chosen my son Solomon to sit upon
the throne of the kingdom of the LORD over Israel.
6 He said to me, 'It is your son Solomon who shall
build my house and my courts, for I have chosen
him to be a son to me, and I will be a father to
him. 7 I will establish his kingdom forever if he
continues resolute in keeping my commandments
and my ordinances, as he is today.' 8 Now therefore in the sight of all Israel, the assembly of the
LORD, and in the hearing of our God, observe and
search out all the commandments of the LORD your
God; that you may possess this good land, and
leave it for an inheritance to your children after
you forever.

9 "And you, my son Solomon, know the God
of your father, and serve him with single mind and
willing heart; for the LORD searches every mind,
and understands every plan and thought. If you
seek him, he will be found by you; but if you forsake him, he will abandon you forever. 10 Take
heed now, for the LORD has chosen you to build a
house as the sanctuary; be strong, and act."

11 Then David gave his son Solomon the plan
of the vestibule of the temple, and of its houses, its
treasuries, its upper rooms, and its inner chambers, and of the room for the mercy seat;[q] 12 and
the plan of all that he had in mind: for the courts
of the house of the LORD, all the surrounding
chambers, the treasuries of the house of God, and
the treasuries for dedicated gifts; 13 for the divisions of the priests and of the Lē'vītes, and all the
work of the service in the house of the LORD; for all
the vessels for the service in the house of the LORD,
14 the weight of gold for all golden vessels for each
service, the weight of silver vessels for each service,
15 the weight of the golden lampstands and their
lamps, the weight of gold for each lampstand and
its lamps, the weight of silver for a lampstand and
its lamps, according to the use of each in the service, 16 the weight of gold for each table for the
rows of bread, the silver for the silver tables, 17 and
pure gold for the forks, the basins, and the cups;
for the golden bowls and the weight of each; for
the silver bowls and the weight of each; 18 for the
altar of incense made of refined gold, and its
weight; also his plan for the golden chariot of the
cherubim that spread their wings and covered the
ark of the covenant of the LORD.

19 "All this, in writing at the LORD's direction,
he made clear to me—the plan of all the works."

20 David said further to his son Solomon, "Be
strong and of good courage, and act. Do not be
afraid or dismayed; for the LORD God, my God, is
with you. He will not fail you or forsake you, until
all the work for the service of the house of the
LORD is finished. 21 Here are the divisions of the
priests and the Lē'vītes for all the service of
the house of God; and with you in all the work
will be every volunteer who has skill for any kind
of service; also the officers and all the people will
be wholly at your command."

Offerings for Building the Temple

29 King David said to the whole assembly, "My son
Solomon, whom alone God has chosen, is young
and inexperienced, and the work is great; for the
temple[r] will not be for mortals but for the LORD
God. 2 So I have provided for the house of my
God, so far as I was able, the gold for the things of
gold, the silver for the things of silver, and the
bronze for the things of bronze, the iron for the
things of iron, and wood for the things of wood,
besides great quantities of onyx and stones for
setting, antimony, colored stones, all sorts of precious stones, and marble in abundance. 3 Moreover, in addition to all that I have provided for
the holy house, I have a treasure of my own of
gold and silver, and because of my devotion to the
house of my God I give it to the house of my God:
4 three thousand talents of gold, of the gold of
Ō'phir, and seven thousand talents of refined silver, for overlaying the walls of the house, 5 and for
all the work to be done by artisans, gold for the
things of gold and silver for the things of silver.

[q] Or *the cover*   [r] Heb *fortress*

American

Asian

God's Name

As David neared the end of his life and reign, he blessed God's name in the midst of the people. The Israelites, who believed in one God, were surrounded by other cultures who believed in many different gods, both good and evil. The name of the Israelites' one God was sacred and precious to them, and they often associated God's name with power, glory, majesty, and victory over all creation.

In Hmong, the name of God is Huab Tais Ntuj, which can be translated as Highest One or Emperor Spirit or Overriding Spirit. The Hmong culture developed as a subculture within the Central Highlands of China. The Hmong believed in different spirits, both good and evil, angelic and demonic. So, in naming God Highest Emperor, overriding all other spirits, they clearly also developed a belief in one God with power over all creation.

▶ **I Chr 29.10–22**

Who then will offer willingly, consecrating themselves today to the LORD?"

6 Then the leaders of ancestral houses made their freewill offerings, as did also the leaders of the tribes, the commanders of the thousands and of the hundreds, and the officers over the king's work. 7 They gave for the service of the house of God five thousand talents and ten thousand darics of gold, ten thousand talents of silver, eighteen thousand talents of bronze, and one hundred thousand talents of iron. 8 Whoever had precious stones gave them to the treasury of the house of the LORD, into the care of Je·hi′el the Ger′shon·ite. 9 Then the people rejoiced because these had given willingly, for with single mind they had offered freely to the LORD; King David also rejoiced greatly.

David's Praise to God

10 Then David blessed the LORD in the presence of all the assembly; David said: "Blessed are you, O LORD, the God of our ancestor Israel, forever and ever. 11 Yours, O LORD, are the greatness,

the power, the glory, the victory, and the majesty; for all that is in the heavens and on the earth is yours; yours is the kingdom, O LORD, and you are exalted as head above all. 12 Riches and honor come from you, and you rule over all. In your hand are power and might; and it is in your hand to make great and to give strength to all. 13 And now, our God, we give thanks to you and praise your glorious name.

14 "But who am I, and what is my people, that we should be able to make this freewill offering? For all things come from you, and of your own have we given you. 15 For we are aliens and transients before you, as were all our ancestors; our days on the earth are like a shadow, and there is no hope. 16 O LORD our God, all this abundance that we have provided for building you a house for your holy name comes from your hand and is all your own. 17 I know, my God, that you search the heart, and take pleasure in uprightness; in the uprightness of my heart I have freely offered all these things, and now I have seen your people, who are present here, offering freely and joyously to you. 18 O LORD, the God of Abraham, Isaac, and Israel, our ancestors, keep forever such purposes and thoughts in the hearts of your people, and direct their hearts toward you. 19 Grant to my son Solomon that with single mind he may keep your commandments, your decrees, and your statutes, performing all of them, and that he may build the temple*s* for which I have made provision."

20 Then David said to the whole assembly, "Bless the LORD your God." And all the assembly blessed the LORD, the God of their ancestors, and bowed their heads and prostrated themselves before the LORD and the king. 21 On the next day they offered sacrifices and burnt offerings to the LORD, a thousand bulls, a thousand rams, and a thousand lambs, with their libations, and sacrifices in abundance for all Israel; 22 and they ate and drank before the LORD on that day with great joy.

Solomon Anointed King
(1 Kings 1.38–40; 2.12)

They made David's son Solomon king a second time; they anointed him as the LORD's prince, and Za′dok as priest. 23 Then Solomon sat on the throne of the LORD, succeeding his father David as king; he prospered, and all Israel obeyed him. 24 All the leaders and the mighty warriors, and also all the sons of King David, pledged their allegiance to King Solomon. 25 The LORD highly exalted Solomon in the sight of all Israel, and bestowed upon

s Heb *fortress*

1

C H R

him such royal majesty as had not been on any king before him in Israel.

Summary of David's Reign

26 Thus David son of Jesse reigned over all Israel. 27 The period that he reigned over Israel was forty years; he reigned seven years in Hĕ′bron, and thirty-three years in Jerusalem. 28 He died in a good old age, full of days, riches, and honor; and his son Solomon succeeded him. 29 Now the acts of King David, from first to last, are written in the records of the seer Samuel, and in the records of the prophet Nathan, and in the records of the seer Gad, 30 with accounts of all his rule and his might and of the events that befell him and Israel and all the kingdoms of the earth.

2 Chronicles

For background on this book, see the introduction to 1 and 2 Chronicles, before 1 Chronicles.

Chap. 3

Solomon Requests Wisdom
(1 Kings 3.1–15)

Solomon son of David established himself in his kingdom; the LORD his God was with him and made him exceedingly great.

2 Solomon summoned all Israel, the commanders of the thousands and of the hundreds, the judges, and all the leaders of all Israel, the heads of families. ³Then Solomon, and the whole assembly with him, went to the high place that was at Gib′e•on; for God's tent of meeting, which Moses the servant of the LORD had made in the wilderness, was there. ⁴(But David had brought the ark of God up from Kir′i•ath-je′a•rim to the place that David had prepared for it; for he had pitched a tent for it in Jerusalem.) ⁵Moreover the bronze altar that Bez′a•lel son of U′ri, son of Hur, had made, was there in front of the tabernacle of the LORD. And Solomon and the assembly inquired at it. ⁶Solomon went up there to the bronze altar before the LORD, which was at the tent of meeting, and offered a thousand burnt offerings on it.

7 That night God appeared to Solomon, and said to him, "Ask what I should give you." ⁸Solomon said to God, "You have shown great and steadfast love to my father David, and have made me succeed him as king. ⁹O LORD God, let your promise to my father David now be fulfilled, for you have made me king over a people as numerous as the dust of the earth. ¹⁰Give me now wisdom and knowledge to go out and come in before this people, for who can rule this great people of yours?" ¹¹God answered Solomon, "Because this was in your heart, and you have not asked for possessions, wealth, honor, or the life of those who hate you, and have not even asked for long life, but have asked for wisdom and knowledge for yourself that you may rule my people over whom I have made you king, ¹²wisdom and knowledge are granted to you. I will also give you riches, possessions, and honor, such as none of the kings had who were before you, and none after you shall have the like." ¹³So Solomon came from*ᵃ* the high place at Gib′e•on, from the tent of meeting, to Jerusalem. And he reigned over Israel.

Solomon's Military and Commercial Activity
(1 Kings 10.26–29; 2 Chr 9.25–28)

14 Solomon gathered together chariots and horses; he had fourteen hundred chariots and twelve thousand horses, which he stationed in the chariot cities and with the king in Jerusalem. ¹⁵The king made silver and gold as common in Jerusalem as stone, and he made cedar as plentiful as the sycamore of the She•phe′lah. ¹⁶Solomon's horses were imported from Egypt and Ku′e; the king's traders received them from Ku′e at the prevailing price. ¹⁷They imported from Egypt, and then

---

ᵃ Gk Vg: Heb *to*

exported, a chariot for six hundred shekels of silver, and a horse for one hundred fifty; so through them these were exported to all the kings of the Hit'tites and the kings of Ar'am.

Preparations for Building the Temple

*b*Solomon decided to build a temple for the name of the LORD, and a royal palace for himself. 2 *c* Solomon conscripted seventy thousand laborers and eighty thousand stonecutters in the hill country, with three thousand six hundred to oversee them.

Alliance with Huram of Tyre
(1 Kings 5.1–18)

3 Solomon sent word to King Hū'ram of Tyre: "Once you dealt with my father David and sent him cedar to build himself a house to live in. 4 I am now about to build a house for the name of the LORD my God and dedicate it to him for offering fragrant incense before him, and for the regular offering of the rows of bread, and for burnt offerings morning and evening, on the sabbaths and the new moons and the appointed festivals of the LORD our God, as ordained forever for Israel.

5 The house that I am about to build will be great, for our God is greater than other gods. 6 But who is able to build him a house, since heaven, even highest heaven, cannot contain him? Who am I to build a house for him, except as a place to make offerings before him? 7 So now send me an artisan skilled to work in gold, silver, bronze, and iron, and in purple, crimson, and blue fabrics, trained also in engraving, to join the skilled workers who are with me in Judah and Jerusalem, whom my father David provided. 8 Send me also cedar, cypress, and algum timber from Lebanon, for I know that your servants are skilled in cutting Lebanon timber. My servants will work with your servants 9 to prepare timber for me in abundance, for the house I am about to build will be great and wonderful. 10 I will provide for your servants, those who cut the timber, twenty thousand cors of crushed wheat, twenty thousand cors of barley, twenty thousand baths*d* of wine, and twenty thousand baths of oil."

11 Then King Hū'ram of Tyre answered in a letter that he sent to Solomon, "Because the LORD loves his people he has made you king over them." 12 Hū'ram also said, "Blessed be the LORD God of Israel, who made heaven and earth, who has given King David a wise son, endowed with discretion and understanding, who will build a temple for the LORD, and a royal palace for himself.

13 "I have dispatched Hū'ram-a'bī, a skilled artisan, endowed with understanding, 14 the son of one of the Dan'īte women, his father a Ty'ri•an. He is trained to work in gold, silver, bronze, iron, stone, and wood, and in purple, blue, and crimson fabrics and fine linen, and to do all sorts of engraving and execute any design that may be assigned him, with your artisans, the artisans of my lord, your father David. 15 Now, as for the wheat, barley, oil, and wine, of which my lord has spoken, let him send them to his servants. 16 We will cut whatever timber you need from Lebanon, and bring it to you as rafts by sea to Jop'pa; you will take it up to Jerusalem."

17 Then Solomon took a census of all the aliens who were residing in the land of Israel, after the census that his father David had taken; and there were found to be one hundred fifty-three thousand six hundred. 18 Seventy thousand of them he assigned as laborers, eighty thousand as stonecutters in the hill country, and three thousand six hundred as overseers to make the people work.

---

b Ch 1.18 in Heb　　*c* Ch 2.1 in Heb　　*d* A Hebrew measure of volume

Solomon Builds the Temple
(1 Kings 6.1–22)

Solomon began to build the house of the LORD in Jerusalem on Mount Mō·rī'ah, where the LORD had appeared to his father David, at the place that David had designated, on the threshing floor of Or'nan the Jeb'ū·sīte. 2 He began to build on the second day of the second month of the fourth year of his reign. 3 These are Solomon's measurements[e] for building the house of God: the length, in cubits of the old standard, was sixty cubits, and the width twenty cubits. 4 The vestibule in front of the nave of the house was twenty cubits long, across the width of the house;[f] and its height was one hundred twenty cubits. He overlaid it on the inside with pure gold. 5 The nave he lined with cypress, covered it with fine gold, and made palms and chains on it. 6 He adorned the house with settings of precious stones. The gold was gold from Par·vā'im. 7 So he lined the house with gold—its beams, its thresholds, its walls, and its doors; and he carved cherubim on the walls.

8 He made the most holy place; its length, corresponding to the width of the house, was twenty cubits, and its width was twenty cubits; he overlaid it with six hundred talents of fine gold. 9 The weight of the nails was fifty shekels of gold. He overlaid the upper chambers with gold.

10 In the most holy place he made two carved cherubim and overlaid[g] them with gold. 11 The wings of the cherubim together extended twenty cubits: one wing of the one, five cubits long, touched the wall of the house, and its other wing, five cubits long, touched the wing of the other cherub; 12 and of this cherub, one wing, five cubits long, touched the wall of the house, and the other wing, also five cubits long, was joined to the wing of the first cherub. 13 The wings of these cherubim extended twenty cubits; the cherubim[h] stood on their feet, facing the nave. 14 And Solomon[i] made the curtain of blue and purple and crimson fabrics and fine linen, and worked cherubim into it.

15 In front of the house he made two pillars thirty-five cubits high, with a capital of five cubits on the top of each. 16 He made encircling[j] chains and put them on the tops of the pillars; and he made one hundred pomegranates, and put them on the chains. 17 He set up the pillars in front of the temple, one on the right, the other on the left; the one on the right he called Jā'chin, and the one on the left, Bō'az.

Furnishings of the Temple
(1 Kings 6.23–38; 7.13–51)

He made an altar of bronze, twenty cubits long, twenty cubits wide, and ten cubits high. 2 Then he made the molten sea; it was round, ten cubits from rim to rim, and five cubits high. A line of thirty cubits would encircle it completely. 3 Under it were panels all around, each of ten cubits, surrounding the sea; there were two rows of panels, cast when it was cast. 4 It stood on twelve oxen, three facing north, three facing west, three facing south, and three facing east; the sea was set on them. The hindquarters of each were toward the inside. 5 Its thickness was a handbreadth; its rim was made like the rim of a cup, like the flower of a lily; it held three thousand baths.[k] 6 He also made ten basins in which to wash, and set five on the right side, and five on the left. In these they were to rinse what was used for the burnt offering. The sea was for the priests to wash in.

7 He made ten golden lampstands as prescribed, and set them in the temple, five on the south side and five on the north. 8 He also made ten tables and placed them in the temple, five on the right side and five on the left. And he made one hundred basins of gold. 9 He made the court of the priests, and the great court, and doors for the court; he overlaid their doors with bronze. 10 He set the sea at the southeast corner of the house.

11 And Hū'ram made the pots, the shovels, and the basins. Thus Hū'ram finished the work that he did for King Solomon on the house of God: 12 the two pillars, the bowls, and the two capitals on the top of the pillars; and the two latticeworks to cover the two bowls of the capitals that were on the top of the pillars; 13 the four hundred pomegranates for the two latticeworks, two rows of pomegranates for each latticework, to cover the two bowls of the capitals that were on the pillars. 14 He made the stands, the basins on the stands, 15 the one sea, and the twelve oxen underneath it. 16 The pots, the shovels, the forks, and all the equipment for these Hū'ram-ā'bī made of burnished bronze for King Solomon for the house of the LORD. 17 In the plain of the Jordan the king cast them, in the clay ground between Suc'coth and Zer'e·dah. 18 Solomon made all these things in great quantities, so that the weight of the bronze was not determined.

---

e Syr: Heb *foundations*   f Compare 1 Kings 6.3: Meaning of Heb uncertain   g Heb *they overlaid*   h Heb *they*
i Heb *he*   j Cn: Heb *in the inner sanctuary*   k A Hebrew measure of volume

19 So Solomon made all the things that were in the house of God: the golden altar, the tables for the bread of the Presence, 20 the lampstands and their lamps of pure gold to burn before the inner sanctuary, as prescribed; 21 the flowers, the lamps, and the tongs, of purest gold; 22 the snuffers, basins, ladles, and firepans, of pure gold. As for the entrance to the temple: the inner doors to the most holy place and the doors of the nave of the temple were of gold.

Thus all the work that Solomon did for the house of the LORD was finished. Solomon brought in the things that his father David had dedicated, and stored the silver, the gold, and all the vessels in the treasuries of the house of God.

The Ark Brought into the Temple
(1 Kings 8.1–11)

2 Then Solomon assembled the elders of Israel and all the heads of the tribes, the leaders of the ancestral houses of the people of Israel, in Jerusalem, to bring up the ark of the covenant of the LORD out of the city of David, which is Zion. 3 And all the Israelites assembled before the king at the festival that is in the seventh month. 4 And all the elders of Israel came, and the Lě'vites carried the ark. 5 So they brought up the ark, the tent of meeting, and all the holy vessels that were in the tent; the priests and the Lě'vites brought them up. 6 King Solomon and all the congregation of Israel, who had assembled before him, were before the ark, sacrificing so many sheep and oxen that they could not be numbered or counted. 7 Then the priests brought the ark of the covenant of the LORD to its place, in the inner sanctuary of the house, in the most holy place, underneath the wings of the cherubim. 8 For the cherubim spread out their wings over the place of the ark, so that the cherubim made a covering above the ark and its poles. 9 The poles were so long that the ends of the poles were seen from the holy place in front of the inner sanctuary; but they could not be seen from outside; they are there to this day. 10 There was nothing in the ark except the two tablets that Moses put there at Hŏ'reb, where the LORD made a covenant*l* with the people of Israel after they came out of Egypt.

11 Now when the priests came out of the holy place (for all the priests who were present had sanctified themselves, without regard to their divisions), 12 all the levitical singers, Ā'saph, Hē'man, and Je•dū'thun, their sons and kindred, arrayed in fine linen, with cymbals, harps, and lyres, stood east of the altar with one hundred twenty priests who were trumpeters. 13 It was the duty of the trumpeters and singers to make themselves heard in unison in praise and thanksgiving to the LORD, and when the song was raised, with trumpets and cymbals and other musical instruments, in praise to the LORD,

"For he is good,
   for his steadfast love endures forever,"

the house, the house of the LORD, was filled with a cloud, 14 so that the priests could not stand to minister because of the cloud; for the glory of the LORD filled the house of God.

Dedication of the Temple
(1 Kings 8.12–21)

Then Solomon said, "The LORD has said that he would reside in thick darkness. 2 I have built you an exalted house, a place for you to reside in forever."

3 Then the king turned around and blessed all the assembly of Israel, while all the assembly of Israel stood. 4 And he said, "Blessed be the LORD, the God of Israel, who with his hand has fulfilled what he promised with his mouth to my father David, saying, 5 'Since the day that I brought my people out of the land of Egypt, I have not chosen a city from any of the tribes of Israel in which to build a house, so that my name might be there, and I chose no one as ruler over my people Israel; 6 but I have chosen Jerusalem in order that my name may be there, and I have chosen David to be over my people Israel.' 7 My father David had it in mind to build a house for the name of the LORD, the God of Israel. 8 But the LORD said to my father David, 'You did well to consider building a house for my name; 9 nevertheless you shall not build the house, but your son who shall be born to you shall build the house for my name.' 10 Now the LORD has fulfilled his promise that he made; for I have succeeded my father David, and sit on the throne of Israel, as the LORD promised, and have built the house for the name of the LORD, the God of Israel. 11 There I have set the ark, in which is the covenant of the LORD that he made with the people of Israel."

Solomon's Prayer of Dedication
(1 Kings 8.22–53)

12 Then Solomon*m* stood before the altar of the LORD in the presence of the whole assembly of Israel, and spread out his hands. 13 Solomon had made a bronze platform five cubits long, five cubits wide, and three cubits high, and had set it in the court; and he stood on it. Then he knelt on his knees in the presence of the whole assembly of Israel, and spread out his hands toward heaven.

---

l Heb lacks *a covenant*   *m* Heb *he*

14 He said, "O LORD, God of Israel, there is no God like you, in heaven or on earth, keeping covenant in steadfast love with your servants who walk before you with all their heart— 15 you who have kept for your servant, my father David, what you promised to him. Indeed, you promised with your mouth and this day have fulfilled with your hand. 16 Therefore, O LORD, God of Israel, keep for your servant, my father David, that which you promised him, saying, 'There shall never fail you a successor before me to sit on the throne of Israel, if only your children keep to their way, to walk in my law as you have walked before me.' 17 Therefore, O LORD, God of Israel, let your word be confirmed, which you promised to your servant David.

18 "But will God indeed reside with mortals on earth? Even heaven and the highest heaven cannot contain you, how much less this house that I have built! 19 Regard your servant's prayer and his plea, O LORD my God, heeding the cry and the prayer that your servant prays to you. 20 May your eyes be open day and night toward this house, the place where you promised to set your name, and may you heed the prayer that your servant prays toward this place. 21 And hear the plea of your servant and of your people Israel, when they pray toward this place; may you hear from heaven your dwelling place; hear and forgive.

22 "If someone sins against another and is required to take an oath and comes and swears before your altar in this house, 23 may you hear from heaven, and act, and judge your servants, repaying the guilty by bringing their conduct on their own head, and vindicating those who are in the right by rewarding them in accordance with their righteousness.

24 "When your people Israel, having sinned against you, are defeated before an enemy but turn again to you, confess your name, pray and plead with you in this house, 25 may you hear from heaven, and forgive the sin of your people Israel, and bring them again to the land that you gave to them and to their ancestors.

26 "When heaven is shut up and there is no rain because they have sinned against you, and then they pray toward this place, confess your name, and turn from their sin, because you punish them, 27 may you hear in heaven, forgive the sin of your servants, your people Israel, when you teach them the good way in which they should walk; and send down rain upon your land, which you have given to your people as an inheritance. 28 "If there is famine in the land, if there is plague, blight, mildew, locust, or caterpillar; if their enemies besiege them in any of the settlements of the lands; whatever suffering, whatever

sickness there is; 29 whatever prayer, whatever plea from any individual or from all your people Israel, all knowing their own suffering and their own sorrows so that they stretch out their hands toward this house; 30 may you hear from heaven, your dwelling place, forgive, and render to all whose heart you know, according to all their ways, for only you know the human heart. 31 Thus may they fear you and walk in your ways all the days that they live in the land that you gave to our ancestors.

32 "Likewise when foreigners, who are not of your people Israel, come from a distant land because of your great name, and your mighty hand, and your outstretched arm, when they come and pray toward this house, 33 may you hear from heaven your dwelling place, and do whatever the foreigners ask of you, in order that all the peoples of the earth may know your name and fear you, as do your people Israel, and that they may know that your name has been invoked on this house that I have built.

34 "If your people go out to battle against their enemies, by whatever way you shall send them, and they pray to you toward this city that you have chosen and the house that I have built for your name, 35 then hear from heaven their prayer and their plea, and maintain their cause.

36 "If they sin against you—for there is no one who does not sin—and you are angry with them and give them to an enemy, so that they are carried away captive to a land far or near; 37 then if they come to their senses in the land to which they have been taken captive, and repent, and plead with you in the land of their captivity, saying, 'We have sinned, and have done wrong; we have acted wickedly'; 38 if they repent with all their heart and soul in the land of their captivity, to which they were taken captive, and pray toward their land, which you gave to their ancestors, the city that you have chosen, and the house that I have built for your name, 39 then hear from heaven your dwelling place their prayer and their pleas, maintain their cause and forgive your people who have sinned against you. 40 Now, O my God, let your eyes be open and your ears attentive to prayer from this place.

41 "Now rise up, O LORD God, and go to your
resting place,
you and the ark of your might.
Let your priests, O LORD God, be clothed
with salvation,
and let your faithful rejoice in your goodness.
42 O LORD God, do not reject your anointed one.
Remember your steadfast love for your
servant David."

Solomon Dedicates the Temple
(1 Kings 8.62–66)

When Solomon had ended his prayer, fire came down from heaven and consumed the burnt offering and the sacrifices; and the glory of the LORD filled the temple. 2 The priests could not enter the house of the LORD, because the glory of the LORD filled the LORD's house. 3 When all the people of Israel saw the fire come down and the glory of the LORD on the temple, they bowed down on the pavement with their faces to the ground, and worshiped and gave thanks to the LORD, saying,

"For he is good,
for his steadfast love endures
forever."

4 Then the king and all the people offered sacrifice before the LORD. 5 King Solomon offered as a sacrifice twenty-two thousand oxen and one hundred twenty thousand sheep. So the king and all the people dedicated the house of God. 6 The priests stood at their posts; the Le'vītes also, with the instruments for music to the LORD that King David had made for giving thanks to the LORD—for his steadfast love endures forever—whenever David offered praises by their ministry. Opposite them the priests sounded trumpets; and all Israel stood.

7 Solomon consecrated the middle of the court that was in front of the house of the LORD; for there he offered the burnt offerings and the fat of the offerings of well-being because the bronze altar Solomon had made could not hold the burnt offering and the grain offering and the fat parts.

8 At that time Solomon held the festival for seven days, and all Israel with him, a very great congregation, from Le'bō-ha'math to the Wadi of Egypt. 9 On the eighth day they held a solemn assembly; for they had observed the dedication of the altar seven days and the festival seven days. 10 On the twenty-third day of the seventh month he sent the people away to their homes, joyful and in good spirits because of the goodness that the LORD had shown to David and to Solomon and to his people Israel.

11 Thus Solomon finished the house of the LORD and the king's house; all that Solomon had planned to do in the house of the LORD and in his own house he successfully accomplished.

God's Second Appearance to Solomon
(1 Kings 9.1–9)

12 Then the LORD appeared to Solomon in the night and said to him: "I have heard your prayer, and have chosen this place for myself as a house of sacrifice. 13 When I shut up the heavens so that there is no rain, or command the locust to devour the land, or send pestilence among my people, 14 if my people who are called by my name humble themselves, pray, seek my face, and turn from their wicked ways, then I will hear from heaven, and will forgive their sin and heal their land. 15 Now my eyes will be open and my ears attentive to the prayer that is made in this place. 16 For now I have chosen and consecrated this house so that my name may be there forever; my eyes and my heart will be there for all time. 17 As for you, if you walk before me, as your father David walked, doing according to all that I have commanded you and keeping my statutes and my ordinances, 18 then I will establish your royal throne, as I made covenant with your father David saying, 'You shall never lack a successor to rule over Israel.'

19 "But if you[n] turn aside and forsake my statutes and my commandments that I have set before you, and go and serve other gods and worship them, 20 then I will pluck you[o] up from the land that I have given you;[o] and this house, which I have consecrated for my name, I will cast out of my sight, and will make it a proverb and a byword among all peoples. 21 And regarding this house, now exalted, everyone passing by will be astonished, and say, 'Why has the LORD done such a thing to this land and to this house?' 22 Then they will say, 'Because they abandoned the LORD the God of their ancestors who brought them out of the land of Egypt, and they adopted other gods, and worshiped them and served them; therefore he has brought all this calamity upon them.' "

Various Activities of Solomon
(1 Kings 9.10–28)

At the end of twenty years, during which Solomon had built the house of the LORD and his own house, 2 Solomon rebuilt the cities that Hū'ram had given to him, and settled the people of Israel in them.

3 Solomon went to Hā'math-zō'bah, and captured it. 4 He built Tad'mor in the wilderness and all the storage towns that he built in Hā'math. 5 He also built Upper Beth-hō'ron and Lower Beth-hō'ron, fortified cities, with walls, gates, and bars, 6 and Bā'a•lath, as well as all Solomon's storage towns, and all the towns for his chariots, the towns for his cavalry, and whatever Solomon desired to build, in Jerusalem, in Lebanon, and in all the land of his dominion. 7 All the people who were left of the Hit'tītes, the Am'o•rītes, the Per'iz-zītes, the Hī'vītes, and the Jeb'u•sītes, who were not of Israel, 8 from their descendants who were

---

n The word you in this verse is plural   o Heb them

still left in the land, whom the people of Israel had
not destroyed—these Solomon conscripted for
forced labor, as is still the case today. 9 But of the
people of Israel Solomon made no slaves for his
work; they were soldiers, and his officers, the commanders of his chariotry and cavalry. 10 These were
the chief officers of King Solomon, two hundred
fifty of them, who exercised authority over the
people.

11 Solomon brought Pharaoh's daughter from
the city of David to the house that he had built for
her, for he said, "My wife shall not live in the
house of King David of Israel, for the places to
which the ark of the LORD has come are holy."

Chap. 9

12 Then Solomon offered up burnt offerings to
the LORD on the altar of the LORD that he had built
in front of the vestibule, 13 as the duty of each day
required, offering according to the commandment
of Moses for the sabbaths, the new moons, and
the three annual festivals—the festival of unleavened bread, the festival of weeks, and the festival
of booths. 14 According to the ordinance of his
father David, he appointed the divisions of the
priests for their service, and the Lē′vītes for their
offices of praise and ministry alongside the priests
as the duty of each day required, and the gatekeepers in their divisions for the several gates; for so
David the man of God had commanded. 15 They
did not turn away from what the king had commanded the priests and Lē′vītes regarding anything at all, or regarding the treasuries.

16 Thus all the work of Solomon was accomplished from[p] the day the foundation of the house
of the LORD was laid until the house of the LORD
was finished completely.

17 Then Solomon went to Ē′zi•on-gē′ber and
Ē′loth on the shore of the sea, in the land of
Ē′dom. 18 Hū′ram sent him, in the care of his ser-
vants, ships and servants familiar with the sea.
They went to Ō′phir, together with the servants of
Solomon, and imported from there four hundred
fifty talents of gold and brought it to King Sol-
omon.

Visit of the Queen of Sheba
(1 Kings 10.1–13)

9 When the queen of Shē′ba heard of the fame of
Solomon, she came to Jerusalem to test him with
hard questions, having a very great retinue and
camels bearing spices and very much gold and precious stones. When she came to Solomon, she
discussed with him all that was on her mind.
2 Solomon answered all her questions; there was
nothing hidden from Solomon that he could not
explain to her. 3 When the queen of Shē′ba had
observed the wisdom of Solomon, the house that
he had built, 4 the food of his table, the seating of
his officials, and the attendance of his servants,
and their clothing, his valets, and their clothing,
and his burnt offerings[q] that he offered at the
house of the LORD, there was no more spirit left in
her.

5 So she said to the king, "The report was true
that I heard in my own land of your accomplishments and of your wisdom, 6 but I did not believe
the[r] reports until I came and my own eyes saw it.
Not even half of the greatness of your wisdom had
been told to me; you far surpass the report that I
had heard. 7 Happy are your people! Happy are
these your servants, who continually attend you
and hear your wisdom! 8 Blessed be the LORD your
God, who has delighted in you and set you on his
throne as king for the LORD your God. Because
your God loved Israel and would establish them
forever, he has made you king over them, that you
may execute justice and righteousness." 9 Then she
gave the king one hundred twenty talents of gold,
a very great quantity of spices, and precious stones:
there were no spices such as those that the queen
of Shē′ba gave to King Solomon.

10 Moreover the servants of Hū′ram and the
servants of Solomon who brought gold from
Ō′phir brought algum wood and precious stones.
11 From the algum wood, the king made steps[s] for
the house of the LORD and for the king's house,
lyres also and harps for the singers; there never

[p] Gk Syr Vg: Heb *to ascent* [q] Gk Syr Vg 1 Kings 10.5: Heb [r] Heb *their* [s] Gk Vg: Meaning of Heb uncertain

was seen the like of them before in the land of Judah.

12 Meanwhile King Solomon granted the queen of Shĕ′ba every desire that she expressed, well beyond what she had brought to the king. Then she returned to her own land, with her servants.

Solomon's Great Wealth
(1 Kings 10.14–29; 2 Chr 1.14–17)

13 The weight of gold that came to Solomon in one year was six hundred sixty-six talents of gold, 14 besides that which the traders and merchants brought; and all the kings of Arabia and the governors of the land brought gold and silver to

Hŭ′ram; once every three years the ships of Tar′shish used to come bringing gold, silver, ivory, apes, and peacocks.*t*

22 Thus King Solomon excelled all the kings of the earth in riches and in wisdom. 23 All the kings of the earth sought the presence of Solomon to hear his wisdom, which God had put into his mind. 24 Every one of them brought a present, objects of silver and gold, garments, weaponry, spices, horses, and mules, so much year by year. 25 Solomon had four thousand stalls for horses and chariots, and twelve thousand horses, which he stationed in the chariot cities and with the king in Jerusalem. 26 He ruled over all the kings from the Euphrates to the land of the Phi·lis′tines, and

Money Talks

LIVE IT!

You can't take it with you.
How often have we heard this statement? We know it's true. Yet we are so easily impressed with wealth and riches. King Solomon, whose wealth is described in 2 Chr 9.13–28, would be right at home in our world, which seems so taken with the rich and the famous.

The Chronicler seems to suggest that Solomon's wealth is a sign of his being blessed by God (see 1.12). And some Jews and Christians still see wealth as a sign of God's blessing. But we need to remember Jesus' words, "Where your treasure is, there your heart will be also" (Mt 6.21), and "Blessed are you who are poor, / for yours is the kingdom of God" (Lk 6.20). Jesus saw that the accumulation of wealth was usually the result of injustice (see "The Greed Trap," Lk 12.13–21). Simply put, Jesus probably would not have approved of Solomon's wealth. How do you view wealth? What is your attitude toward poor people?

▶ 2 Chr 9.13–28

Solomon. 15 King Solomon made two hundred large shields of beaten gold; six hundred shekels of beaten gold went into each large shield. 16 He made three hundred shields of beaten gold; three hundred shekels of gold went into each shield; and the king put them in the House of the Forest of Lebanon. 17 The king also made a great ivory throne, and overlaid it with pure gold. 18 The throne had six steps and a footstool of gold, which were attached to the throne, and on each side of the seat were arm rests and two lions standing beside the arm rests, 19 while twelve lions were standing, one on each end of a step on the six steps. The like of it was never made in any kingdom. 20 All King Solomon's drinking vessels were of gold, and all the vessels of the House of the Forest of Lebanon were of pure gold; silver was not considered as anything in the days of Solomon. 21 For the king's ships went to Tar′shish with the servants of

to the border of Egypt. 27 The king made silver as common in Jerusalem as stone, and cedar as plentiful as the sycamore of the She·phē′lah. 28 Horses were imported for Solomon from Egypt and from all lands.

Death of Solomon
(1 Kings 11.41–43)

29 Now the rest of the acts of Solomon, from first to last, are they not written in the history of the prophet Nathan, and in the prophecy of A·hi′jah the Shi′lo·nite, and in the visions of the seer Id′dō concerning Jer·o·bō′am son of Nĕ′bat? 30 Solomon reigned in Jerusalem over all Israel forty years. 31 Solomon slept with his ancestors and was buried in the city of his father David; and his son Rĕ·ho·bō′am succeeded him.

t Or baboons

The Revolt against Rehoboam
(1 Kings 12.1–19)

Rē·ho·bō'am went to Shĕ'chem, for all Israel had come to Shĕ'chem to make him king. ² When Jer·o·bō'am son of Nĕ'bat heard of it (for he was in Egypt, where he had fled from King Solomon), then Jer·o·bō'am returned from Egypt. ³ They sent and called him; and Jer·o·bō'am and all Israel came and said to Rē·ho·bō'am, ⁴ "Your father made our yoke heavy. Now therefore lighten the hard service of your father and his heavy yoke that he placed on us, and we will serve you." ⁵ He said to them, "Come to me again in three days." So the people went away.

6 Then King Rē·ho·bō'am took counsel with the older men who had attended his father Solomon while he was still alive, saying, "How do you advise me to answer this people?" ⁷ They answered him, "If you will be kind to this people and please them, and speak good words to them, then they will be your servants forever." ⁸ But he rejected the advice that the older men gave him, and consulted the young men who had grown up with him and now attended him. ⁹ He said to them, "What do you advise that we answer this people who have said to me, 'Lighten the yoke that your father put on us'?" ¹⁰ The young men who had grown up with him said to him, "Thus should you speak to the people who said to you, 'Your father made our yoke heavy, but you must lighten it for us'; tell them, 'My little finger is thicker than my father's loins. ¹¹ Now, whereas my father laid on you a heavy yoke, I will add to your yoke. My father disciplined you with whips, but I will discipline you with scorpions.' "

12 So Jer·o·bō'am and all the people came to Rē·ho·bō'am the third day, as the king had said, "Come to me again the third day." ¹³ The king answered them harshly. King Rē·ho·bō'am rejected the advice of the older men; ¹⁴ he spoke to them in accordance with the advice of the young men, "My father made your yoke heavy, but I will add to it; my father disciplined you with whips, but I will discipline you with scorpions." ¹⁵ So the king did not listen to the people, because it was a turn of affairs brought about by God so that the LORD might fulfill his word, which he had spoken by A·hi'jah the Shi'lo·nīte to Jer·o·bō'am son of Nĕ'bat.

16 When all Israel saw that the king would not listen to them, the people answered the king,

"What share do we have in David?
    We have no inheritance in the son of
    Jesse.
Each of you to your tents, O Israel!
    Look now to your own house, O David."

So all Israel departed to their tents. ¹⁷ But Rē·ho·bō'am reigned over the people of Israel who were living in the cities of Judah. ¹⁸ When King Rē·ho·bō'am sent Ha·dor'am, who was taskmaster over the forced labor, the people of Israel stoned him to death. King Rē·ho·bō'am hurriedly mounted his chariot to flee to Jerusalem. ¹⁹ So Israel has been in rebellion against the house of David to this day.

Judah and Benjamin Fortified
(1 Kings 12.20–24)

When Rē·ho·bō'am came to Jerusalem, he assembled one hundred eighty thousand chosen troops of the house of Judah and Benjamin to fight against Israel, to restore the kingdom to Rē·ho·bō'am. ² But the word of the LORD came to She·māi'ah the man of God: ³ Say to King Rē·ho·bō'am of Judah, son of Solomon, and to all Israel in Judah and Benjamin, ⁴ "Thus says the LORD: You shall not go up or fight against your kindred. Let everyone return home, for this thing is from me." So they heeded the word of the LORD and turned back from the expedition against Jer·o·bō'am.

5 Rē·ho·bō'am resided in Jerusalem, and he built cities for defense in Judah. ⁶ He built up Bethlehem, E'tam, Te·kō'a, ⁷ Beth-zur, Sō'cō, A·dul'lam, ⁸ Gath, Ma·rē'shah, Ziph, ⁹ Ad·o·rā'im, Lā'chish, A·zē'kah, ¹⁰ Zō'rah, Ai'ja·lon, and Hē'bron, fortified cities that are in Judah and in Benjamin. ¹¹ He made the fortresses strong, and put commanders in them, and stores of food, oil, and wine. ¹² He also put large shields and spears in all the cities, and made them very strong. So he held Judah and Benjamin.

Priests and Levites Support Rehoboam
(1 Kings 14.21–24)

13 The priests and the Lē'vītes who were in all Israel presented themselves to him from all their territories. ¹⁴ The Lē'vītes had left their common lands and their holdings and had come to Judah and Jerusalem, because Jer·o·bō'am and his sons had prevented them from serving as priests of the LORD, ¹⁵ and had appointed his own priests for the high places, and for the goat-demons, and for the calves that he had made. ¹⁶ Those who had set their hearts to seek the LORD God of Israel came after them from all the tribes of Israel to Jerusalem to sacrifice to the LORD, the God of their ancestors. ¹⁷ They strengthened the kingdom of Judah, and for three years they made Rē·ho·bō'am son of Solomon secure, for they walked for three years in the way of David and Solomon.

Rehoboam's Marriages

18 Rĕ•ho•bō′am took as his wife Mā′ha•lath daughter of Jer′i•moth son of David, and of Ab•i•hā′il daughter of E•lī′ab son of Jesse. 19 She bore him sons: Jĕ′ush, Shem•a•rī′ah, and Zā′ham. 20 After her he took Mā′a•cah daughter of Ab′sa•lom, who bore him A•bī′jah, At′tai, Zī′za, and She•lō′mith. 21 Rĕ•ho•bō′am loved Mā′a•cah daughter of Ab′sa•lom more than all his other wives and concubines (he took eighteen wives and sixty concubines, and became the father of twenty-eight sons and sixty daughters). 22 Rĕ•ho•bō′am appointed A•bī′jah son of Mā′a•cah as chief prince among his brothers, for he intended to make him king. 23 He dealt wisely, and distributed some of his sons through all the districts of Judah and Benjamin, in all the fortified cities; he gave them abundant provisions, and found many wives for them.

Egypt Attacks Judah
(1 Kings 14.25–28)

When the rule of Rĕ•ho•bō′am was established and he grew strong, he abandoned the law of the LORD, he and all Israel with him. 2 In the fifth year of King Rĕ•ho•bō′am, because they had been unfaithful to the LORD, King Shī′shak of Egypt came up against Jerusalem 3 with twelve hundred chariots and sixty thousand cavalry. A countless army came with him from Egypt—Libyans, Suk′ki•im, and Ethiopians.ᵘ 4 He took the fortified cities of Judah and came as far as Jerusalem. 5 Then the prophet She•mai′ah came to Rĕ•ho•bō′am and to the officers of Judah, who had gathered at Jerusalem because of Shī′shak, and said to them, "Thus says the LORD: You abandoned me, so I have abandoned you to the hand of Shī′shak." 6 Then the officers of Israel and the king humbled themselves and said, "The LORD is in the right." 7 When the LORD saw that they

humbled themselves, the word of the LORD came to She•mai′ah, saying: "They have humbled themselves; I will not destroy them, but I will grant them some deliverance, and my wrath shall not be poured out on Jerusalem by the hand of Shī′shak. 8 Nevertheless they shall be his servants, so that they may know the difference between serving me and serving the kingdoms of other lands."

9 So King Shī′shak of Egypt came up against Jerusalem; he took away the treasures of the house of the LORD and the treasures of the king's house; he took everything. He also took away the shields of gold that Solomon had made; 10 but King Rĕ•ho•bō′am made in place of them shields of bronze, and committed them to the hands of the officers of the guard, who kept the door of the king's house. 11 Whenever the king went into the house of the LORD, the guard would come along bearing them, and would then bring them back to the guardroom. 12 Because he humbled himself the wrath of the LORD turned from him, so as not to destroy them completely; moreover, conditions were good in Judah.

Death of Rehoboam
(1 Kings 14.21–22, 29–31)

13 So King Rĕ•ho•bō′am established himself in Jerusalem and reigned. Rĕ•ho•bō′am was forty-one years old when he began to reign; he reigned seventeen years in Jerusalem, the city that the LORD had chosen out of all the tribes of Israel to put his name there. His mother's name was Nā′a•mah the Am′mon•īte. 14 He did evil, for he did not set his heart to seek the LORD.

15 Now the acts of Rĕ•ho•bō′am, from first to last, are they not written in the records of the

ᵘ Or Nubians; Heb Cushites

Selling Out

LIVE IT!

King Rehoboam, son of Solomon, sold out and abandoned the law of the Lord after he thought his rule was secure (2 Chr 12.1). The Chronicler tells us that the Lord abandoned Rehoboam to the Egyptians because of this. Fortunately, Rehoboam and his officers repented, and the Lord showed mercy on them.

It is tempting to compromise our values in order to succeed and become popular, even though doing this ends up hurting the people around us. Maybe you have experienced some success like Rehoboam and figure you can have even more if you just bend the rules a bit. Maybe you feel life has given you a rotten deal and the only way to get ahead is to forget your principles. But before you sell out, think again. Ultimately, abandoning your good and holy principles won't get you ahead; it will only lead to your downfall.

▶ 2 Chr 12.1–12

prophet She•māi′ah and of the seer Id′dō, recorded by genealogy? There were continual wars between Rē•ho•bō′am and Jer•o•bō′am. [16] Rē•ho•bō′am slept with his ancestors and was buried in the city of David; and his son A•bī′jah succeeded him.

Abijah Reigns over Judah
(1 Kings 15.1–8)

In the eighteenth year of King Jer•o•bō′am, A•bī′jah began to reign over Judah. [2] He reigned for three years in Jerusalem. His mother's name was Mi•cāi′ah daughter of Ū•rī′el of Gib′ē•ah.

Now there was war between A•bī′jah and Jer•o•bō′am. [3] A•bī′jah engaged in battle, having an army of valiant warriors, four hundred thousand picked men; and Jer•o•bō′am drew up his line of battle against him with eight hundred thousand picked mighty warriors. [4] Then A•bī′jah stood on the slope of Mount Zem•a•rā′im that is in the hill country of Ē′phra•im, and said, "Listen to me, Jer•o•bō′am and all Israel! [5] Do you not know that the LORD God of Israel gave the kingship over Israel forever to David and his sons by a covenant of salt? [6] Yet Jer•o•bō′am son of Nē′bat, a servant of Solomon son of David, rose up and rebelled against his lord; [7] and certain worthless scoundrels gathered around him and defied Rē•ho•bō′am son of Solomon, when Rē•ho•bō′am was young and irresolute and could not withstand them.

[8] "And now you think that you can withstand the kingdom of the LORD in the hand of the sons of David, because you are a great multitude and have with you the golden calves that Jer•o•bō′am made as gods for you. [9] Have you not driven out the priests of the LORD, the descendants of Aaron, and the Lē′vītes, and made priests for yourselves like the peoples of other lands? Whoever comes to be consecrated with a young bull or seven rams becomes a priest of what are no gods. [10] But as for us, the LORD is our God, and we have not abandoned him. We have priests ministering to the LORD who are descendants of Aaron, and Lē′vītes for their service. [11] They offer to the LORD every morning and every evening burnt offerings and fragrant incense, set out the rows of bread on the table of pure gold, and care for the golden lampstand so that its lamps may burn every evening; for we keep the charge of the LORD our God, but you have abandoned him. [12] See, God is with us at our head, and his priests have their battle trumpets to sound the call to battle against you. O Israelites, do not fight against the LORD, the God of your ancestors; for you cannot succeed."

[13] Jer•o•bō′am had sent an ambush around to come on them from behind; thus his troops[v] were in front of Judah, and the ambush was behind them. [14] When Judah turned, the battle was in front of them and behind them. They cried out to the LORD, and the priests blew the trumpets. [15] Then the people of Judah raised the battle shout. And when the people of Judah shouted, God defeated Jer•o•bō′am and all Israel before A•bī′jah and Judah. [16] The Israelites fled before Judah, and God gave them into their hands. [17] A•bī′jah and his army defeated them with great slaughter; five hundred thousand picked men of Israel fell slain. [18] Thus the Israelites were subdued at that time, and the people of Judah prevailed, because they relied on the LORD, the God of their ancestors. [19] A•bī′jah pursued Jer•o•bō′am, and took cities from him: Beth′el with its villages and Je•shā′nah with its villages and Ē′phron[w] with its villages. [20] Jer•o•bō′am did not recover his power in the days of A•bī′jah; the LORD struck him down, and he died. [21] But A•bī′jah grew strong. He took fourteen wives, and became the father of twenty-two sons and sixteen daughters. [22] The rest of the acts of A•bī′jah, his behavior and his deeds, are written in the story of the prophet Id′dō.

Asa Reigns
(1 Kings 15.9–15)

[x] So A•bī′jah slept with his ancestors, and they buried him in the city of David. His son Asa succeeded him. In his days the land had rest for ten years. [2][y] Asa did what was good and right in the sight of the LORD his God. [3] He took away the foreign altars and the high places, broke down the pillars, hewed down the sacred poles,[z] [4] and commanded Judah to seek the LORD, the God of their ancestors, and to keep the law and the commandment. [5] He also removed from all the cities of Judah the high places and the incense altars. And the kingdom had rest under him. [6] He built fortified cities in Judah while the land had rest. He had no war in those years, for the LORD gave him peace. [7] He said to Judah, "Let us build these cities, and surround them with walls and towers, gates and bars; the land is still ours because we have sought the LORD our God; we have sought him, and he has given us peace on every side." So they built and prospered. [8] Asa had an army of three hundred thousand from Judah, armed with large shields and spears, and two hundred eighty thousand troops from Benjamin who carried shields and drew bows; all these were mighty warriors.

---

v Heb *they*   w Another reading is *Ephraim* in Heb   y Ch 14.1 in Heb   x Ch 13.23   z Heb *Asherim*

2
CHR

Ethiopian Invasion Repulsed

9 Zĕ′rah the Ethiopian[a] came out against them with an army of a million men and three hundred chariots, and came as far as Ma•rē′shah. [10] Asa went out to meet him, and they drew up their lines of battle in the valley of Zeph′a•thah at Ma•rē′shah. [11] Asa cried to the LORD his God, "O LORD, there is no difference for you between helping the mighty and the weak. Help us, O LORD our God, for we rely on you, and in your name we have come against this multitude. O LORD, you are our God; let no mortal prevail against you." [12] So the LORD defeated the Ethiopians[b] before Asa and before Judah, and the Ethiopians[b] fled. [13] Asa and the army with him pursued them as far as Gĕ′rar, and the Ethiopians[b] fell until no one remained alive; for they were broken before the LORD and his army. The people of Judah[c] carried away a great quantity of booty. [14] They defeated all the cities around Gĕ′rar, for the fear of the LORD was on them. They plundered all the cities; for there was much plunder in them. [15] They also attacked the tents of those who had livestock,[d] and carried away sheep and goats in abundance, and camels. Then they returned to Jerusalem.

The spirit of God came upon Az•a•rī′ah son of O′ded. [2] He went out to meet Asa and said to him, "Hear me, Asa, and all Judah and Benjamin: The LORD is with you, while you are with him. If you seek him, he will be found by you, but if you abandon him, he will abandon you. [3] For a long time Israel was without the true God, and without a teaching priest, and without law; [4] but when in their distress they turned to the LORD, the God of Israel, and sought him, he was found by them. [5] In those times it was not safe for anyone to go or come, for great disturbances afflicted all the inhabitants of the lands. [6] They were broken in pieces, nation against nation and city against city, for God troubled them with every sort of distress. [7] But you, take courage! Do not let your hands be weak, for your work shall be rewarded."

8 When Asa heard these words, the prophecy of Az•a•rī′ah son of O′ded,[e] he took courage, and put away the abominable idols from all the land of Judah and Benjamin and from the towns that he had taken in the hill country of E′phra•im. He repaired the altar of the LORD that was in front of the vestibule of the house of the LORD.[f] [9] He gathered all Judah and Benjamin, and those from E′phra•im, Ma•nas′seh, and Sim′ē•on who were residing as aliens with them, for great numbers had deserted to him from Israel when they saw that the LORD his God was with him. [10] They were gathered at Jerusalem in the third month of the fifteenth year of the reign of Asa. [11] They sacrificed to the LORD on that day, from the booty that they had brought, seven hundred oxen and seven thousand sheep. [12] They entered into a covenant to seek the LORD, the God of their ancestors, with all their heart and with all their soul. [13] Whoever would not seek the LORD, the God of Israel, should be put to death, whether young or old, man or woman. [14] They took an oath to the LORD with a loud voice,

---

a Or *Nubian*; Heb *Cushite*   *b* Or *Nubians*; Heb *Cushites*
c Heb *They*   *d* Meaning of Heb uncertain   *e* Compare Syr Vg: Heb *the prophecy, the prophet Obed*   *f* Heb *the vestibule of the LORD*

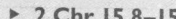

Keep On Turning   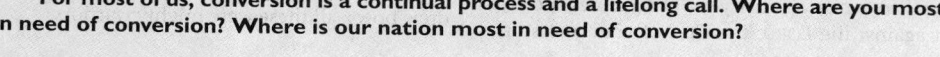 LIVE IT!

Conversion.
A very important word for Christians. Its Latin root means "to turn around." That pretty much sums up what conversion is all about. We turn from sin and toward God, as individuals and as a people. In 2 Chr 15.8–15, we read about King Asa and his people hearing the words of the prophet Azariah and then turning away from idols and turning back to God.

Conversion is usually not a onetime event. For most of us, conversion is something we need to do again and again. We are reminded of that especially during the season of Lent. On Ash Wednesday, as individuals and as a community, we hear the words, "Turn away from sin and be faithful to the gospel" (*The Sacramentary*, p. 77). The Israelites went through the same thing. Again and again, they were called to turn back to God.

For most of us, conversion is a continual process and a lifelong call. Where are you most in need of conversion? Where is our nation most in need of conversion?

▶ 2 Chr 15.8–15

and with shouting, and with trumpets, and with horns. ¹⁵ All Judah rejoiced over the oath; for they had sworn with all their heart, and had sought him with their whole desire, and he was found by them, and the LORD gave them rest all around.

16 King Asa even removed his mother Mā′a•cah from being queen mother because she had made an abominable image for A•shē′rah. Asa cut down her image, crushed it, and burned it at the Wadi Kid′ron. ¹⁷ But the high places were not taken out of Israel. Nevertheless the heart of Asa was true all his days. ¹⁸ He brought into the house of God the votive gifts of his father and his own votive gifts— silver, gold, and utensils. ¹⁹ And there was no more war until the thirty-fifth year of the reign of Asa.

Alliance with Aram Condemned
(1 Kings 15.16–22)

In the thirty-sixth year of the reign of Asa, King Bā′a•sha of Israel went up against Judah, and built Rā′mah, to prevent anyone from going out or coming into the territory of*g* King Asa of Judah. ² Then Asa took silver and gold from the treasures of the house of the LORD and the king's house, and sent them to King Ben-hā′dad of Ar′am, who re-sided in Damascus, saying, ³ "Let there be an alli-ance between me and you, like that between my father and your father; I am sending to you silver and gold; go, break your alliance with King Bā′a-sha of Israel, so that he may withdraw from me." ⁴ Ben-hā′dad listened to King Asa, and sent the commanders of his armies against the cities of Is-rael. They conquered Ī′jon, Dan, Ā′bel-mā′im, and all the store-cities of Naph′ta•lī. ⁵ When Bā′a•sha heard of it, he stopped building Rā′mah, and let his work cease. ⁶ Then King Asa brought all Judah, and they carried away the stones of Rā′mah and its timber, with which Bā′a•sha had been building, and with them he built up Gē′ba and Miz′pah.

7 At that time the seer Ha•nā′nī came to King Asa of Judah, and said to him, "Because you relied on the king of Ar′am, and did not rely on the LORD your God, the army of the king of Ar′am has es-caped you. ⁸ Were not the Ethiopians*h* and the Lib-yans a huge army with exceedingly many chariots and cavalry? Yet because you relied on the LORD, he gave them into your hand. ⁹ For the eyes of the LORD range throughout the entire earth, to strengthen those whose heart is true to him. You have done foolishly in this; for from now on you will have wars." ¹⁰ Then Asa was angry with the seer, and put him in the stocks, in prison, for he was in a rage with him because of this. And Asa inflicted cruelties on some of the people at the same time.

Asa's Disease and Death
(1 Kings 15.23–24)

11 The acts of Asa, from first to last, are written in the Book of the Kings of Judah and Israel. ¹² In the thirty-ninth year of his reign Asa was diseased in his feet, and his disease became severe; yet even in his disease he did not seek the LORD, but sought help from physicians. ¹³ Then Asa slept with his ancestors, dying in the forty-first year of his reign. ¹⁴ They buried him in the tomb that he had hewn out for himself in the city of David. They laid him on a bier that had been filled with various kinds of spices prepared by the perfumer's art; and they made a very great fire in his honor.

Jehoshaphat's Reign

His son Je•hosh′a•phat succeeded him, and strengthened himself against Israel. ² He placed forces in all the fortified cities of Judah, and set garrisons in the land of Judah, and in the cities of E′phra•im that his father Asa had taken. ³ The LORD was with Je•hosh′a•phat, because he walked in the earlier ways of his father;*i* he did not seek the Bā′-als, ⁴ but sought the God of his father and walked in his commandments, and not according to the ways of Israel. ⁵ Therefore the LORD established the kingdom in his hand. All Judah brought tribute to Je•hosh′a•phat, and he had great riches and honor. ⁶ His heart was courageous in the ways of the LORD; and furthermore he removed the high places and the sacred poles*j* from Judah.

7 In the third year of his reign he sent his offi-cials, Ben-hā′il, Ō•ba•dī′ah, Zech•a•rī′ah, Ne•than′el, and Mī•cāi′ah, to teach in the cities of Judah. ⁸ With them were the Lē′vites, She•māi′ah, Neth•a•nī′ah, Zeb•a•dī′ah, As′a•hel, She•mir′a•moth, Je•hon′a•than, Ad•o•nī′jah, Tō•bī′jah, and Tob-ad•o•nī′jah; and with these Lē′vites, the priests E•lish′a•ma and Je•hō′ram. ⁹ They taught in Judah, having the book of the law of the LORD with them; they went around through all the cities of Judah and taught among the people.

10 The fear of the LORD fell on all the king-doms of the lands around Judah, and they did not make war against Je•hosh′a•phat. ¹¹ Some of the Phi•lis′tines brought Je•hosh′a•phat presents, and sil-ver for tribute; and the Arabs also brought him seven thousand seven hundred rams and seven thousand seven hundred male goats. ¹² Je•hosh′a-phat grew steadily greater. He built fortresses and storage cities in Judah. ¹³ He carried out great works in the cities of Judah. He had soldiers, mighty warriors, in Jerusalem. ¹⁴ This was the

---

g Heb lacks *the territory of*   *h* Or *Nubians;* Heb *Cushites*
i Another reading is *his father David*   *j* Heb *Asherim*

muster of them by ancestral houses: Of Judah, the commanders of the thousands: Ad'nah the commander, with three hundred thousand mighty warriors, 15 and next to him Jĕ·hŏ·hă'nan the commander, with two hundred eighty thousand, 16 and next to him Am·a·si'ah son of Zich'rī, a volunteer for the service of the LORD, with two hundred thousand mighty warriors. 17 Of Benjamin: E·li'a·da, a mighty warrior, with two hundred thousand armed with bow and shield, 18 and next to him Je·hŏ'za·bad with one hundred eighty thousand armed for war. 19 These were in the service of the king, besides those whom the king had placed in the fortified cities throughout all Judah.

Micaiah Predicts Failure
(1 Kings 22.1–28)

Now Je·hosh'a·phat had great riches and honor; and he made a marriage alliance with A'hab. 2 After some years he went down to A'hab in Sa·mār'i·a. A'hab slaughtered an abundance of sheep and oxen for him and for the people who were with him, and induced him to go up against Ra'moth-gil'ē·ad. 3 King A'hab of Israel said to King Je·hosh'a·phat of Judah, "Will you go with me to Ra'moth-gil'ē·ad?" He answered him, "I am with you, my people are your people. We will be with you in the war."

4 But Je·hosh'a·phat also said to the king of Israel, "Inquire first for the word of the LORD." 5 Then the king of Israel gathered the prophets together, four hundred of them, and said to them, "Shall we go to battle against Ra'moth-gil'ē·ad, or shall I refrain?" They said, "Go up; for God will give it into the hand of the king." 6 But Je·hosh'a·phat said, "Is there no other prophet of the LORD here of whom we may inquire?" 7 The king of Israel said to Je·hosh'a·phat, "There is still one other by whom we may inquire of the LORD, Mī·cāi'ah son of Im'lah; but I hate him, for he never prophesies anything favorable about me, but only disaster." Je·hosh'a·phat said, "Let the king not say such a thing." 8 Then the king of Israel summoned an officer and said, "Bring quickly Mī·cāi'ah son of Im'lah." 9 Now the king of Israel and King Je·hosh'a·phat of Judah were sitting on their thrones, arrayed in their robes; and they were sitting at the threshing floor at the entrance of the gate of Sa·mār'i·a; and all the prophets were prophesying before them. 10 Zed·e·kī'ah son of Che·nā'a·nah made for himself horns of iron, and he said, "Thus says the LORD: With these you shall gore the Ar·a·mē'ans until they are destroyed." 11 All the prophets were prophesying the same and saying, "Go up to Ra'moth-gil'ē·ad and triumph; the LORD will give it into the hand of the king."

12 The messenger who had gone to summon Mī·cāi'ah said to him, "Look, the words of the prophets with one accord are favorable to the king; let your word be like the word of one of them, and speak favorably." 13 But Mī·cāi'ah said, "As the LORD lives, whatever my God says, that I will speak."

14 When he had come to the king, the king said to him, "Mī·cāi'ah, shall we go to Ra'moth-gil'ē·ad to battle, or shall I refrain?" He answered, "Go up and triumph; they will be given into your hand." 15 But the king said to him, "How many times must I make you swear to tell me nothing but the truth in the name of the LORD?" 16 Then Mī·cāi'ah*k* said, "I saw all Israel scattered on the mountains, like sheep without a shepherd; and the LORD said, 'These have no master; let each one go home in peace.'" 17 The king of Israel said to Je·hosh'a·phat, "Did I not tell you that he would not prophesy anything favorable about me, but only disaster?"

18 Then Mī·cāi'ah*k* said, "Therefore hear the word of the LORD: I saw the LORD sitting on his throne, with all the host of heaven standing to the right and to the left of him. 19 And the LORD said, 'Who will entice King A'hab of Israel, so that he may go up and fall at Ra'moth-gil'ē·ad?' Then one said one thing, and another said another, 20 until a spirit came forward and stood before the LORD, saying, 'I will entice him.' The LORD asked him, 'How?' 21 He replied, 'I will go out and be a lying spirit in the mouth of all his prophets.' Then the LORD*k* said, 'You are to entice him, and you shall succeed; go out and do it.' 22 So you see, the LORD has put a lying spirit in the mouth of these your prophets; the LORD has decreed disaster for you."

23 Then Zed·e·kī'ah son of Che·nā'a·nah came up to Mī·cāi'ah, slapped him on the cheek, and said, "Which way did the spirit of the LORD pass from me to speak to you?" 24 Mī·cāi'ah replied, "You will find out on that day when you go in to hide in an inner chamber." 25 The king of Israel then ordered, "Take Mī·cāi'ah, and return him to A'mon the governor of the city and to Jō'ash the king's son; 26 and say, 'Thus says the king: Put this fellow in prison, and feed him on reduced rations of bread and water until I return in peace.'" 27 Mī·cāi'ah said, "If you return in peace, the LORD has not spoken by me." And he said, "Hear, you peoples, all of you!"

Defeat and Death of Ahab
(1 Kings 22.29–40)

28 So the king of Israel and King Je·hosh'a·phat of Judah went up to Ra'moth-gil'ē·ad. 29 The king

k Heb he

of Israel said to Je•hosh′a•phat, "I will disguise my-self and go into battle, but you wear your robes." So the king of Israel disguised himself, and they went into battle. 30 Now the king of Ar′am had com-manded the captains of his chariots, "Fight with no one small or great, but only with the king of Israel." 31 When the captains of the chariots saw Je-hosh′a•phat, they said, "It is the king of Israel." So they turned to fight against him; and Je•hosh′a•phat cried out, and the LORD helped him. God drew them away from him, 32 for when the captains of the chariots saw that it was not the king of Israel, they turned back from pursuing him. 33 But a cer-tain man drew his bow and unknowingly struck the king of Israel between the scale armor and the breastplate; so he said to the driver of his chariot, "Turn around, and carry me out of the battle, for I am wounded." 34 The battle grew hot that day, and the king of Israel propped himself up in his char-iot facing the Ar•a•mē′ans until evening; then at sunset he died.

King Je•hosh′a•phat of Judah returned in safety to his house in Jerusalem. 2 Jē′hū son of Ha•nā′nī the seer went out to meet him and said to King Je-hosh′a•phat, "Should you help the wicked and love those who hate the LORD? Because of this, wrath has gone out against you from the LORD. 3 Nevertheless, some good is found in you, for you destroyed the sacred poles*ˡ* out of the land, and have set your heart to seek God."

The Reforms of Jehoshaphat

4 Je•hosh′a•phat resided at Jerusalem; then he went out again among the people, from Bē′er-shē′ba to the hill country of É′phra•im, and brought them back to the LORD, the God of their ancestors. 5 He appointed judges in the land in all the fortified cities of Judah, city by city, 6 and said to the judges, "Consider what you are doing, for you judge not on behalf of human beings but on the LORD's behalf; he is with you in giving judg-ment. 7 Now, let the fear of the LORD be upon you; take care what you do, for there is no perversion of justice with the LORD our God, or partiality, or tak-ing of bribes."

8 Moreover in Jerusalem Je•hosh′a•phat ap-pointed certain Lē′vītes and priests and heads of families of Israel, to give judgment for the LORD and to decide disputed cases. They had their seat at Jerusalem. 9 He charged them: "This is how you shall act: in the fear of the LORD, in faithfulness, and with your whole heart; 10 whenever a case comes to you from your kindred who live in their cities, concerning bloodshed, law or command-ment, statutes or ordinances, then you shall in-struct them, so that they may not incur guilt before

the LORD and wrath may not come on you and your kindred. Do so, and you will not incur guilt. 11 See, Am•a•rī′ah the chief priest is over you in all matters of the LORD; and Zeb•a•dī′ah son of Ish′-ma•el, the governor of the house of Judah, in all the king's matters; and the Lē′vītes will serve you as officers. Deal courageously, and may the LORD be with the good!"

Invasion from the East

After this the Mō′ab•ītes and Am′mon•ites, and with them some of the Me•ū′nītes,*ᵐ* came against Je•hosh′a•phat for battle. 2 Messengers*ⁿ* came and told Je•hosh′a•phat, "A great multitude is coming against you from É′dom,*ᵒ* from beyond the sea; already they are at Haz′a•zon-tā′mar" (that is, En-ge′di). 3 Je•hosh′a•phat was afraid; he set himself to seek the LORD, and proclaimed a fast throughout all Judah. 4 Judah assembled to seek help from the LORD; from all the towns of Judah they came to seek the LORD.

Jehoshaphat's Prayer and Victory

5 Je•hosh′a•phat stood in the assembly of Judah and Jerusalem, in the house of the LORD, before the new court, 6 and said, "O LORD, God of our ances-tors, are you not God in heaven? Do you not rule over all the kingdoms of the nations? In your hand are power and might, so that no one is able to withstand you. 7 Did you not, O our God, drive out the inhabitants of this land before your people Israel, and give it forever to the descendants of your friend Abraham? 8 They have lived in it, and in it have built you a sanctuary for your name, saying, 9 'If disaster comes upon us, the sword, judgment,*ᵖ* or pestilence, or famine, we will stand before this house, and before you, for your name is in this house, and cry to you in our distress, and you will hear and save.' 10 See now, the people of Am′mon, Mō′ab, and Mount Sē′ir, whom you would not let Israel invade when they came from the land of Egypt, and whom they avoided and did not destroy— 11 they reward us by coming to drive us out of your possession that you have given us to inherit. 12 O our God, will you not execute judg-ment upon them? For we are powerless against this great multitude that is coming against us. We do not know what to do, but our eyes are on you."

13 Meanwhile all Judah stood before the LORD, with their little ones, their wives, and their chil-dren. 14 Then the spirit of the LORD came upon Ja-hā′zi•el son of Zech•a•rī′ah, son of Be•nā′i•ah, son of

---

ˡ Heb *Asheroth*   *ᵐ* Compare 26.7: Heb *Ammonites*
ⁿ Heb *They*   *ᵒ* One Ms: MT *Aram*   *ᵖ* Or *the sword of judgment*

Je·ī′el, son of Mat·ta·nī′ah, a Lē′vīte of the sons of Ā′saph, in the middle of the assembly. ¹⁵ He said, "Listen, all Judah and inhabitants of Jerusalem, and King Je·hosh′a·phat: Thus says the LORD to you: 'Do not fear or be dismayed at this great multitude; for the battle is not yours but God's. ¹⁶ Tomorrow go down against them; they will come up by the ascent of Ziz; you will find them at the end of the valley, before the wilderness of Je·rū′el. ¹⁷ This battle is not for you to fight; take your position, stand still, and see the victory of the LORD on your behalf, O Judah and Jerusalem.' Do not fear or be dismayed; tomorrow go out against them, and the LORD will be with you."

18 Then Je·hosh′a·phat bowed down with his face to the ground, and all Judah and the inhabitants of Jerusalem fell down before the LORD, worshiping the LORD. ¹⁹ And the Lē′vītes, of the Kō′hath·ites and the Kō′ra·hites, stood up to praise the LORD, the God of Israel, with a very loud voice.

20 They rose early in the morning and went out into the wilderness of Te·kō′a; and as they went out, Je·hosh′a·phat stood and said, "Listen to me, O Judah and inhabitants of Jerusalem! Believe in the LORD your God and you will be established; believe his prophets." ²¹ When he had taken counsel with the people, he appointed those who were to sing to the LORD and praise him in holy splendor, as they went before the army, saying,

"Give thanks to the LORD,
    for his steadfast love endures forever."

²² As they began to sing and praise, the LORD set an ambush against the Am′mon·ites, Mō′ab, and Mount Sē′ir, who had come against Judah, so that they were routed. ²³ For the Am′mon·ites and Mō′ab attacked the inhabitants of Mount Sē′ir, destroying them utterly; and when they had made an end of the inhabitants of Sē′ir, they all helped to destroy one another.

24 When Judah came to the watchtower of the wilderness, they looked toward the multitude; they were corpses lying on the ground; no one had escaped. ²⁵ When Je·hosh′a·phat and his people came to take the booty from them, they found livestock⁹ in great numbers, goods, clothing, and precious things, which they took for themselves until they could carry no more. They spent three days taking the booty, because of its abundance. ²⁶ On the fourth day they assembled in the Valley of Ber′a·cah, for there they blessed the LORD; therefore that place has been called the Valley of Ber′a·cahʳ to this day. ²⁷ Then all the people of Judah and Jerusalem, with Je·hosh′a·phat at their head, returned to Jerusalem with joy, for the LORD had enabled them to rejoice over their enemies. ²⁸ They came to Jerusalem, with harps and lyres and trumpets, to the house of the LORD. ²⁹ The fear of God came on all the kingdoms of the countries when they heard that the LORD had fought against the enemies of Israel. ³⁰ And the realm of Je·hosh′a·phat was quiet, for his God gave him rest all around.

The End of Jehoshaphat's Reign
(1 Kings 22.41–50)

31 So Je·hosh′a·phat reigned over Judah. He was thirty-five years old when he began to reign; he reigned twenty-five years in Jerusalem. His mother's name was A·zū′bah daughter of Shil′hī. ³² He walked in the way of his father Asa and did not turn aside from it, doing what was right in the sight of the LORD. ³³ Yet the high places were not removed; the people had not yet set their hearts upon the God of their ancestors.

34 Now the rest of the acts of Je·hosh′a·phat, from first to last, are written in the Annals of Jē′hū son of Ha·nā′nī, which are recorded in the Book of the Kings of Israel.

35 After this King Je·hosh′a·phat of Judah joined with King A·ha·zī′ah of Israel, who did wickedly. ³⁶ He joined him in building ships to go to Tar′shish; they built the ships in Ē′zi·on·gē′ber. ³⁷ Then El·i·ē′zer son of Dō·dav′a·hū of Ma·rē′shah prophesied against Je·hosh′a·phat, saying, "Because you have joined with A·ha·zī′ah, the LORD will destroy what you have made." And the ships were wrecked and were not able to go to Tar′shish.

Jehoram's Reign
(1 Kings 22.50; 2 Kings 8.16–19)

Je·hosh′a·phat slept with his ancestors and was buried with his ancestors in the city of David; his son Je·hō′ram succeeded him. ²He had brothers, the sons of Je·hosh′a·phat: Az·a·rī′ah, Je·hī′el, Zech·a·rī′ah, Az·a·rī′ah, Michael, and Sheph·a·tī′ah; all these were the sons of King Je·hosh′a·phat of Judah.ˢ ³Their father gave them many gifts, of silver, gold, and valuable possessions, together with fortified cities in Judah; but he gave the kingdom to Je·hō′ram, because he was the firstborn. ⁴When Je·hō′ram had ascended the throne of his father and was established, he put all his brothers to the sword, and also some of the officials of Israel. ⁵Je·hō′ram was thirty-two years old when he began to reign; he reigned eight years in Jerusalem. ⁶He walked in the way of the kings of Israel, as the house of Ā′hab had done; for the daughter of Ā′hab was his wife. He did what was evil in the sight of the LORD. ⁷Yet the LORD would not destroy the house of David because of the covenant that he had made with

---

⁹ Gk: Heb *among them*   ʳ That is *Blessing*   ˢ Gk Syr: Heb *Israel*

David, and since he had promised to give a lamp to him and to his descendants forever.

Revolt of Edom
(2 Kings 8.20–22)

8 In his days E'dom revolted against the rule of Judah and set up a king of their own. 9 Then Je·hō'-ram crossed over with his commanders and all his chariots. He set out by night and attacked the E'dom·ites, who had surrounded him and his chariot commanders. 10 So E'dom has been in revolt against the rule of Judah to this day. At that time Lib'nah also revolted against his rule, because he had forsaken the LORD, the God of his ancestors.

Elijah's Letter

11 Moreover he made high places in the hill country of Judah, and led the inhabitants of Jerusalem into unfaithfulness, and made Judah go astray. 12 A letter came to him from the prophet E·li'jah, saying: "Thus says the LORD, the God of your father David: Because you have not walked in the ways of your father Je·hosh'a·phat or in the

The Role of the Prophet

The letter from Elijah to King Jehoram discussed in 2 Chr 21.12–15 underscores the principal role of the Hebrew prophet: to be God's voice, the one who speaks for God. Although many early figures are called prophets, including Moses and Deborah, the classical prophet—*nabi'* in Hebrew—appeared later in Israelite history. The primary function of the prophet was not to foretell the future, but to announce God's judgment, to confront those who violated God's law, and to console those who suffered. In short, the prophets were the conscience of the Israelite nation.

▶ **2 Chr 21.12–15**

ways of King Asa of Judah, 13 but have walked in the way of the kings of Israel, and have led Judah and the inhabitants of Jerusalem into unfaithfulness, as the house of A'hab led Israel into unfaithfulness, and because you also have killed your

brothers, members of your father's house, who were better than yourself, 14 see, the LORD will bring a great plague on your people, your children, your wives, and all your possessions, 15 and you yourself will have a severe sickness with a disease of your bowels, until your bowels come out, day after day, because of the disease."

16 The LORD aroused against Je·hō'ram the anger of the Phi·lis'tines and of the Arabs who are near the Ethiopians.[t] 17 They came up against Judah, invaded it, and carried away all the possessions they found that belonged to the king's house, along with his sons and his wives, so that no son was left to him except Je·hō'a·haz, his youngest son.

Disease and Death of Jehoram
(2 Kings 8.23–24)

18 After all this the LORD struck him in his bowels with an incurable disease. 19 In course of time, at the end of two years, his bowels came out because of the disease, and he died in great agony. His people made no fire in his honor, like the fires made for his ancestors. 20 He was thirty-two years old when he began to reign; he reigned eight years in Jerusalem. He departed with no one's regret. They buried him in the city of David, but not in the tombs of the kings.

Ahaziah's Reign
(2 Kings 8.25–29; 9.14–16, 27–29)

The inhabitants of Jerusalem made his youngest son A·ha·zi'ah king as his successor; for the troops who came with the Arabs to the camp had killed all the older sons. So A·ha·zi'ah son of Je·hō'ram reigned as king of Judah. 2 A·ha·zi'ah was forty-two years old when he began to reign; he reigned one year in Jerusalem. His mother's name was Ath·a·li'ah, a granddaughter of Om'ri. 3 He also walked in the ways of the house of A'hab, for his mother was his counselor in doing wickedly. 4 He did what was evil in the sight of the LORD, as the house of A'hab had done; for after the death of his father they were his counselors, to his ruin. 5 He even followed their advice, and went with Je·hō'ram son of King A'hab of Israel to make war against King Haz'a·el of Ar'am at Rā'moth-gil'e·ad. The Ar·a·mē'ans wounded Jō'ram, 6 and he returned to be healed in Jez're·el of the wounds that he had received at Rā'mah, when he fought King Haz'a·el of Ar'am. And A·ha·zi'ah son of King Je·hō'ram of Judah went down to see Jō'ram son of A'hab in Jez're·el, because he was sick.

---

t Or *Nubians*; Heb *Cushites*

7 But it was ordained by God that the downfall of A•ha•zī'ah should come about through his going to visit Jō'ram. For when he came there he went out with Je•hō'ram to meet Jē'hū son of Nim'shī, whom the LORD had anointed to destroy the house of Ā'hab. 8 When Jē'hū was executing judgment on the house of Ā'hab, he met the officials of Judah and the sons of A•ha•zī'ah's brothers, who attended A•ha•zī'ah, and he killed them. 9 He searched for A•ha•zī'ah, who was captured while hiding in Sa•mār'i•a and was brought to Jē'hū, and put to death. They buried him, for they said, "He is the grandson of Je•hosh'a•phat, who sought the LORD with all his heart." And the house of A•ha•zī'ah had no one able to rule the kingdom.

Athaliah Seizes the Throne
(2 Kings 11.1–8)

10 Now when Ath•a•lī'ah, A•ha•zī'ah's mother, saw that her son was dead, she set about to destroy all the royal family of the house of Judah. 11 But Jē•hō•shab'e•ath, the king's daughter, took Jō'ash son of A•ha•zī'ah, and stole him away from among the king's children who were about to be killed; she put him and his nurse in a bedroom. Thus Jē•hō•shab'e•ath, daughter of King Je•hō'ram and wife of the priest Je•hoi'a•da—because she was a sister of A•ha•zī'ah—hid him from Ath•a•lī'ah, so that she did not kill him; 12 he remained with them six years, hidden in the house of God, while Ath•a•lī'ah reigned over the land.

But in the seventh year Je•hoi'a•da took courage, and entered into a compact with the commanders of the hundreds, Az•a•rī'ah son of Je•rō'ham, Ish'-ma•el son of Jē•hō•hā'nan, Az•a•rī'ah son of Ō'bed, Mā•a•sēi'ah son of A•dāi'ah, and El•i•shā'phat son of Zich'rī. 2 They went around through Judah and gathered the Lē'vītes from all the towns of Judah, and the heads of families of Israel, and they came to Jerusalem. 3 Then the whole assembly made a covenant with the king in the house of God. Je•hoi'a•da*u* said to them, "Here is the king's son! Let him reign, as the LORD promised concerning the sons of David. 4 This is what you are to do: one-third of you, priests and Lē'vītes, who come on duty on the sabbath, shall be gatekeepers, 5 one-third shall be at the king's house, and one-third at the Gate of the Foundation; and all the people shall be in the courts of the house of the LORD. 6 Do not let anyone enter the house of the LORD except the priests and ministering Lē'vītes; they may enter, for they are holy, but all the other*v* people shall observe the instructions of the LORD. 7 The Lē'vītes shall surround the king, each with his weapons in his hand; and whoever enters the house shall be killed. Stay with the king in his comings and goings."

Joash Crowned King
(2 Kings 11.9–12)

8 The Lē'vītes and all Judah did according to all that the priest Je•hoi'a•da commanded; each brought his men, who were to come on duty on the sabbath, with those who were to go off duty on the sabbath; for the priest Je•hoi'a•da did not dismiss the divisions. 9 The priest Je•hoi'a•da delivered to the captains the spears and the large and small shields that had been King David's, which were in the house of God; 10 and he set all the people as a guard for the king, everyone with weapon in hand, from the south side of the house to the north side of the house, around the altar and the house. 11 Then he brought out the king's son, put the crown on him, and gave him the covenant;*w* they proclaimed him king, and Je•hoi'a•da and his sons anointed him; and they shouted, "Long live the king!"

Athaliah Murdered
(2 Kings 11.13–20)

12 When Ath•a•lī'ah heard the noise of the people running and praising the king, she went into the house of the LORD to the people; 13 and when she looked, there was the king standing by his pillar at the entrance, and the captains and the trumpeters beside the king, and all the people of the land rejoicing and blowing trumpets, and the singers with their musical instruments leading in the celebration. Ath•a•lī'ah tore her clothes, and cried, "Treason! Treason!" 14 Then the priest Je•hoi'a•da brought out the captains who were set over the army, saying to them, "Bring her out between the ranks; anyone who follows her is to be put to the sword." For the priest said, "Do not put her to death in the house of the LORD." 15 So they laid hands on her; she went into the entrance of the Horse Gate of the king's house, and there they put her to death.

16 Je•hoi'a•da made a covenant between himself and all the people and the king that they should be the LORD's people. 17 Then all the people went to the house of Bā'al, and tore it down; his altars and his images they broke in pieces, and they killed Mat'tan, the priest of Bā'al, in front of the altars. 18 Je•hoi'a•da assigned the care of the house of the LORD to the levitical priests whom David had organized to be in charge of the house of the LORD, to offer burnt offerings to the LORD, as it

---

u Heb *He*   *v* Heb lacks *other*   *w* Or *treaty*, or *testimony*; Heb *eduth*

is written in the law of Moses, with rejoicing and with singing, according to the order of David. ¹⁹He stationed the gatekeepers at the gates of the house of the LORD so that no one should enter who was in any way unclean. ²⁰And he took the captains, the nobles, the governors of the people, and all the people of the land, and they brought the king down from the house of the LORD, marching through the upper gate to the king's house. They set the king on the royal throne. ²¹So all the people of the land rejoiced, and the city was quiet after Ath·a·lī'ah had been killed with the sword.

Joash Repairs the Temple
(2 Kings 11.21 — 12.16)

Jō'ash was seven years old when he began to reign; he reigned forty years in Jerusalem; his mother's name was Zib'i·ah of Bē'er-shē'ba. ²Jō'ash did what was right in the sight of the LORD all the days of the priest Je·hoi'a·da. ³Je·hoi'a·da got two wives for him, and he became the father of sons and daughters.

4 Some time afterward Jō'ash decided to restore the house of the LORD. ⁵He assembled the priests and the Lē'vītes and said to them, "Go out to the cities of Judah and gather money from all Israel to repair the house of your God, year by year; and see that you act quickly." But the Lē'vītes did not act quickly. ⁶So the king summoned Je·hoi'a·da the chief, and said to him, "Why have you not required the Lē'vītes to bring in from Judah and Jerusalem the tax levied by Moses, the servant of the LORD, on^x the congregation of Israel for the tent of the covenant?"^y ⁷For the children of Ath·a·lī'ah, that wicked woman, had broken into the house of God, and had even used all the dedicated things of the house of the LORD for the Bā'als.

8 So the king gave command, and they made a chest, and set it outside the gate of the house of the LORD. ⁹A proclamation was made throughout Judah and Jerusalem to bring in for the LORD the tax that Moses the servant of God laid on Israel in the wilderness. ¹⁰All the leaders and all the people rejoiced and brought their tax and dropped it into the chest until it was full. ¹¹Whenever the chest was brought to the king's officers by the Lē'vītes, when they saw that there was a large amount of money in it, the king's secretary and the officer of the chief priest would come and empty the chest and take it and return it to its place. So they did day after day, and collected money in abundance. ¹²The king and Je·hoi'a·da gave it to those who had charge of the work of the house of the LORD, and they hired masons and carpenters to restore the house of the LORD, and also workers in iron and bronze to repair the house of the LORD. ¹³So those

who were engaged in the work labored, and the repairing went forward at their hands, and they restored the house of God to its proper condition and strengthened it. ¹⁴When they had finished, they brought the rest of the money to the king and Je·hoi'a·da, and with it were made utensils for the house of the LORD, utensils for the service and for the burnt offerings, and ladles, and vessels of gold and silver. They offered burnt offerings in the house of the LORD regularly all the days of Je·hoi'a·da.

Apostasy of Joash

15 But Je·hoi'a·da grew old and full of days, and died; he was one hundred thirty years old at his death. ¹⁶And they buried him in the city of David among the kings, because he had done good in Israel, and for God and his house.

17 Now after the death of Je·hoi'a·da the officials of Judah came and did obeisance to the king; then the king listened to them. ¹⁸They abandoned the house of the LORD, the God of their ancestors, and served the sacred poles^z and the idols. And wrath came upon Judah and Jerusalem for this guilt of theirs. ¹⁹Yet he sent prophets among them to bring them back to the LORD; they testified against them, but they would not listen.

20 Then the spirit of God took possession of^a Zech·a·rī'ah son of the priest Je·hoi'a·da; he stood above the people and said to them, "Thus says God: Why do you transgress the commandments of the LORD, so that you cannot prosper? Because you have forsaken the LORD, he has also forsaken you." ²¹But they conspired against him, and by command of the king they stoned him to death in the court of the house of the LORD. ²²King Jō'ash did not remember the kindness that Je·hoi'a·da, Zech·a·rī'ah's father, had shown him, but killed his son. As he was dying, he said, "May the LORD see and avenge!"

Death of Joash
(2 Kings 12.19–21)

23 At the end of the year the army of Ar'am came up against Jō'ash. They came to Judah and Jerusalem, and destroyed all the officials of the people from among them, and sent all the booty they took to the king of Damascus. ²⁴Although the army of Ar'am had come with few men, the LORD delivered into their hand a very great army, because they had abandoned the LORD, the God of their ancestors. Thus they executed judgment on Jō'ash.

x Compare Vg: Heb *and eduth*   y Or *treaty*, or *testimony*; Heb   z Heb *Asherim*   a Heb *clothed itself with*

2
CHR

25 When they had withdrawn, leaving him severely wounded, his servants conspired against him because of the blood of the son[b] of the priest Je·hoi′a·da, and they killed him on his bed. So he died; and they buried him in the city of David, but they did not bury him in the tombs of the kings. 26 Those who conspired against him were Zā′bad son of Shim′ē·ath the Am′mon·ite, and Je·hō′za·bad son of Shim′rith the Mō′ab·īte. 27 Accounts of his sons, and of the many oracles against him, and of the rebuilding[c] of the house of God are written in the Commentary on the Book of the Kings. And his son Am·a·zī′ah succeeded him.

Reign of Amaziah
(2 Kings 14.1–6)

Am·a·zī′ah was twenty-five years old when he began to reign, and he reigned twenty-nine years in Jerusalem. His mother's name was Jē·hō·ad′dan of Jerusalem. 2 He did what was right in the sight of the LORD, yet not with a true heart. 3 As soon as the royal power was firmly in his hand he killed his servants who had murdered his father the king. 4 But he did not put their children to death, according to what is written in the law, in the book of Moses, where the LORD commanded, "The parents shall not be put to death for the children, or the children be put to death for the parents; but all shall be put to death for their own sins."

Slaughter of the Edomites
(2 Kings 14.7)

5 Am·a·zī′ah assembled the people of Judah, and set them by ancestral houses under commanders of the thousands and of the hundreds for all Judah and Benjamin. He mustered those twenty years old and upward, and found that they were three hundred thousand picked troops fit for war, able to handle spear and shield. 6 He also hired one hundred thousand mighty warriors from Israel for one hundred talents of silver. 7 But a man of God came to him and said, "O king, do not let the army of Israel go with you, for the LORD is not with Israel—all these Ē′phra·im·ītes. 8 Rather, go by yourself and act; be strong in battle, or God will fling you down before the enemy; for God has power to help or to overthrow." 9 Am·a·zī′ah said to the man of God, "But what shall we do about the hundred talents that I have given to the army of Israel?" The man of God answered, "The LORD is able to give you much more than this." 10 Then Am·a·zī′ah discharged the army that had come to him from Ē′phra·im, letting them go home again. But they became very angry with Judah, and returned home in fierce anger.

11 Am·a·zī′ah took courage, and led out his people; he went to the Valley of Salt, and struck down ten thousand men of Sē′ir. 12 The people of Judah captured another ten thousand alive, took them to the top of Sē′la, and threw them down from the top of Sē′la, so that all of them were dashed to pieces. 13 But the men of the army whom Am·a·zī′ah sent back, not letting them go with him to battle, fell on the cities of Judah from Sa·mār′i·a to Beth-hō′ron; they killed three thousand people in them, and took much booty.

14 Now after Am·a·zī′ah came from the slaughter of the Ē′dom·ītes, he brought the gods of the people of Sē′ir, set them up as his gods, and worshiped them, making offerings to them. 15 The LORD was angry with Am·a·zī′ah and sent to him a prophet, who said to him, "Why have you resorted to a people's gods who could not deliver their own people from your hand?" 16 But as he was speaking the king[d] said to him, "Have we made you a royal counselor? Stop! Why should you be put to death?" So the prophet stopped, but said, "I know that God has determined to destroy you, because you have done this and have not listened to my advice."

Israel Defeats Judah
(2 Kings 14.8–14)

17 Then King Am·a·zī′ah of Judah took counsel and sent to King Jō′ash son of Je·hō′a·haz son of Jē′hū of Israel, saying, "Come, let us look one another in the face." 18 King Jō′ash of Israel sent word to King Am·a·zī′ah of Judah, "A thornbush on Lebanon sent to a cedar on Lebanon, saying, 'Give your daughter to my son for a wife'; but a wild animal of Lebanon passed by and trampled down the thornbush. 19 You say, 'See, I have defeated Ē′dom,' and your heart has lifted you up in boastfulness. Now stay at home; why should you provoke trouble so that you fall, you and Judah with you?"

20 But Am·a·zī′ah would not listen—it was God's doing, in order to hand them over, because they had sought the gods of Ē′dom. 21 So King Jō′ash of Israel went up; he and King Am·a·zī′ah of Judah faced one another in battle at Beth-shē′mesh, which belongs to Judah. 22 Judah was defeated by Israel; everyone fled home. 23 King Jō′ash of Israel captured King Am·a·zī′ah of Judah, son of Jō′ash, son of A·ha·zī′ah, at Beth-shē′mesh; he brought him to Jerusalem, and broke down the wall of Jerusalem from the Ē′phra·im Gate to the Corner Gate, a distance of four hundred cubits. 24 He seized all the gold and silver, and all the ves-

---

b Gk Vg: Heb sons   c Heb founding   d Heb he

sels that were found in the house of God, and Oʹbed-eʹdom with them; he seized also the treasuries of the king's house, also hostages; then he returned to Sa•marʹi•a.

Death of Amaziah
(2 Kings 14.17–20)

25 King Am•a•ziʹah son of Joʹash of Judah, lived fifteen years after the death of King Joʹash son of Je•hoʹa•haz of Israel. 26 Now the rest of the deeds of Am•a•ziʹah, from first to last, are they not written in the Book of the Kings of Judah and Israel? 27 From the time that Am•a•ziʹah turned away from the LORD they made a conspiracy against him in Jerusalem, and he fled to Laʹchish. But they sent after him to Laʹchish, and killed him there. 28 They brought him back on horses; he was buried with his ancestors in the city of David.

Reign of Uzziah
(2 Kings 14.21–22; 15.1–3)

Then all the people of Judah took Uz•ziʹah, who was sixteen years old, and made him king to succeed his father Am•a•ziʹah. 2 He rebuilt Eʹloth and restored it to Judah, after the king slept with his ancestors. 3 Uz•ziʹah was sixteen years old when he began to reign, and he reigned fifty-two years in Jerusalem. His mother's name was Jec•o•liʹah of Jerusalem. 4 He did what was right in the sight of the LORD, just as his father Am•a•ziʹah had done. 5 He set himself to seek God in the days of Zech•a•riʹah, who instructed him in the fear of God; and as long as he sought the LORD, God made him prosper.

6 He went out and made war against the Phi•lisʹtines, and broke down the wall of Gath and the wall of Jabʹneh and the wall of Ashʹdod; he built cities in the territory of Ashʹdod and elsewhere among the Phi•lisʹtines. 7 God helped him against the Phi•lisʹtines, against the Arabs who lived in Gur-baʹal, and against the Me•uʹnites. 8 The Amʹmon•ites paid tribute to Uz•ziʹah, and his fame spread even to the border of Egypt, for he became very strong. 9 Moreover Uz•ziʹah built towers in Jerusalem at the Corner Gate, at the Valley Gate, and at the Angle, and fortified them. 10 He built towers in the wilderness and hewed out many cisterns, for he had large herds, both in the She•pheʹlah and in the plain, and he had farmers and vinedressers in the hills and in the fertile lands, for he loved the soil. 11 Moreover Uz•ziʹah had an army of soldiers, fit for war, in divisions according to the numbers in the muster made by the secretary Je•iʹel and the officer Ma•a•seiʹah, under the direction of Han•a•niʹah, one of the king's commanders. 12 The whole number of the heads of ancestral houses of mighty warriors was two thousand six hundred. 13 Under

their command was an army of three hundred seven thousand five hundred, who could make war with mighty power, to help the king against the enemy. 14 Uz•ziʹah provided for all the army the shields, spears, helmets, coats of mail, bows, and stones for slinging. 15 In Jerusalem he set up machines, invented by skilled workers, on the towers and the corners for shooting arrows and large stones. And his fame spread far, for he was marvelously helped until he became strong.

Pride and Apostasy
(2 Kings 15.4–7)

16 But when he had become strong he grew proud, to his destruction. For he was false to the LORD his God, and entered the temple of the LORD to make offering on the altar of incense. 17 But the priest Az•a•riʹah went in after him, with eighty priests of the LORD who were men of valor; 18 they withstood King Uz•ziʹah, and said to him, "It is not for you, Uz•ziʹah, to make offering to the LORD, but for the priests the descendants of Aaron, who are consecrated to make offering. Go out of the sanctuary; for you have done wrong, and it will bring you no honor from the LORD God." 19 Then Uz•ziʹah was angry. Now he had a censer in his hand to make offering, and when he became angry with the priests a leprous*e* disease broke out on his forehead, in the presence of the priests in the house of the LORD, by the altar of incense. 20 When the chief priest Az•a•riʹah, and all the priests, looked at him, he was leprous*e* in his forehead. They hurried him out, and he himself hurried to get out, because the LORD had struck him. 21 King Uz•ziʹah was leprous*e* to the day of his death, and being leprous*e* lived in a separate house, for he was excluded from the house of the LORD. His son Joʹtham was in charge of the palace of the king, governing the people of the land.

22 Now the rest of the acts of Uz•ziʹah, from first to last, the prophet I•saiʹah son of Aʹmoz wrote. 23 Uz•ziʹah slept with his ancestors; they buried him near his ancestors in the burial field that belonged to the kings, for they said, "He is leprous."*e* His son Joʹtham succeeded him.

Reign of Jotham
(2 Kings 15.32–38)

Joʹtham was twenty-five years old when he began to reign; he reigned sixteen years in Jerusalem. His mother's name was Je•ruʹshah daughter of Zaʹdok. 2 He did what was right in the sight of the LORD just as his father Uz•ziʹah had done—only he did not

---

e A term for several skin diseases; precise meaning uncertain

invade the temple of the LORD. But the people still followed corrupt practices. 3 He built the upper gate of the house of the LORD, and did extensive building on the wall of O'phel. 4 Moreover he built cities in the hill country of Judah, and forts and towers on the wooded hills. 5 He fought with the king of the Am'mon·ites and prevailed against them. The Am'mon·ites gave him that year one hundred talents of silver, ten thousand cors of wheat and ten thousand of barley. The Am'mon-ites paid him the same amount in the second and the third years. 6 So Jō'tham became strong because he ordered his ways before the LORD his God. 7 Now the rest of the acts of Jō'tham, and all his wars and his ways, are written in the Book of the Kings of Israel and Judah. 8 He was twenty-five years old when he began to reign; he reigned sixteen years in Jerusalem. 9 Jō'tham slept with his ancestors, and they buried him in the city of David; and his son Ā'haz succeeded him.

Reign of Ahaz
(2 Kings 16.1–4)

Ā'haz was twenty years old when he began to reign; he reigned sixteen years in Jerusalem. He did not do what was right in the sight of the LORD, as his ancestor David had done, 2 but he walked in the ways of the kings of Israel. He even made cast images for the Bā'als; 3 and he made offerings in the valley of the son of Hin'nom, and made his sons pass through fire, according to the abominable practices of the nations whom the LORD drove out before the people of Israel. 4 He sacrificed and made offerings on the high places, on the hills, and under every green tree.

Aram and Israel Defeat Judah
(2 Kings 16.5–6; Isa 7.1)

5 Therefore the LORD his God gave him into the hand of the king of Ar'am, who defeated him and took captive a great number of his people and brought them to Damascus. He was also given into the hand of the king of Israel, who defeated him with great slaughter. 6 Pē'kah son of Rem·a-lī'ah killed one hundred twenty thousand in Judah in one day, all of them valiant warriors, because they had abandoned the LORD, the God of their ancestors. 7 And Zich'rī, a mighty warrior of Ē'phra·im, killed the king's son Mā·a·sēi'ah, Az·rī'-kam the commander of the palace, and El·kā'nah the next in authority to the king.

Intervention of Oded

8 The people of Israel took captive two hundred thousand of their kin, women, sons, and daughters; they also took much booty from them and brought the booty to Sa·mār'i·a. 9 But a prophet of the LORD was there, whose name was Ō'ded; he went out to meet the army that came to Sa·mār'i·a, and said to them, "Because the LORD, the God of your ancestors, was angry with Judah, he gave them into your hand, but you have killed them in a rage that has reached up to heaven. 10 Now you intend to subjugate the people of Judah and Jerusalem, male and female, as your slaves. But what have you except sins against the LORD your God? 11 Now hear me, and send back the captives whom you have taken from your kindred, for the fierce wrath of the LORD is upon you." 12 Moreover, certain chiefs of the Ē'phra·im·ites, Az·a·rī'ah son of Jō·hā'-nan, Ber·e·chī'ah son of Me·shil'le·moth, Jē·hiz·kī'ah son of Shal'lum, and A·mā'sa son of Had'laī, stood up against those who were coming from the war, 13 and said to them, "You shall not bring the captives in here, for you propose to bring on us guilt against the LORD in addition to our present sins and guilt. For our guilt is already great, and there is fierce wrath against Israel." 14 So the warriors left the captives and the booty before the officials and all the assembly. 15 Then those who were mentioned by name got up and took the captives, and with the booty they clothed all that were naked among them; they clothed them, gave them sandals, provided them with food and drink, and anointed them; and carrying all the feeble among them on donkeys, they brought them to their kindred at Jericho, the city of palm trees. Then they returned to Sa·mār'i·a.

Assyria Refuses to Help Judah
(2 Kings 16.7–9)

16 At that time King Ā'haz sent to the king*f* of Assyria for help. 17 For the Ē'dom·ites had again invaded and defeated Judah, and carried away captives. 18 And the Phi·lis'tines had made raids on the cities in the She·phē'lah and the Neg'eb of Judah, and had taken Beth-shē'mesh, Ai'ja·lon, Ge·dē'roth, Sō'cō with its villages, Tim'nah with its villages, and Gim'zō with its villages; and they settled there. 19 For the LORD brought Judah low because of King Ā'haz of Israel, for he had behaved without restraint in Judah and had been faithless to the LORD. 20 So King Til'gath-pil·nē'ser of Assyria came against him, and oppressed him instead of strengthening him. 21 For Ā'haz plundered the house of the LORD and the houses of the king and of the officials, and gave tribute to the king of Assyria; but it did not help him.

f Gk Syr Vg Compare 2 Kings 16.7: Heb *kings*

Apostasy and Death of Ahaz
(2 Kings 16.12–20)

22 In the time of his distress he became yet more faithless to the LORD—this same King Ā'haz. 23 For he sacrificed to the gods of Damascus, which had defeated him, and said, "Because the gods of the kings of Ar'am helped them, I will sacrifice to them so that they may help me." But they were the ruin of him, and of all Israel. 24 Ā'haz gathered together the utensils of the house of God, and cut in pieces the utensils of the house of God. He shut up the doors of the house of the LORD and made himself altars in every corner of Jerusalem. 25 In every city of Judah he made high places to make offerings to other gods, provoking to anger the LORD, the God of his ancestors. 26 Now the rest of his acts and all his ways, from first to last, are written in the Book of the Kings of Judah and Israel. 27 Ā'haz slept with his ancestors, and they buried him in the city, in Jerusalem; but they did not bring him into the tombs of the kings of Israel. His son Hez•e•kī'ah succeeded him.

Reign of Hezekiah
(2 Kings 18.1–3)

Hez•e•kī'ah began to reign when he was twenty-five years old; he reigned twenty-nine years in Jerusalem. His mother's name was A•bī'jah daughter of Zech•a•rī'ah. 2 He did what was right in the sight of the LORD, just as his ancestor David had done.

The Temple Cleansed

3 In the first year of his reign, in the first month, he opened the doors of the house of the LORD and repaired them. 4 He brought in the priests and the Lē'vites and assembled them in the square on the east. 5 He said to them, "Listen to me, Lē'vites! Sanctify yourselves, and sanctify the house of the LORD, the God of your ancestors, and carry out the filth from the holy place. 6 For our ancestors have been unfaithful and have done what was evil in the sight of the LORD our God; they have forsaken him, and have turned away their faces from the dwelling of the LORD, and turned their backs. 7 They also shut the doors of the vestibule and put out the lamps, and have not offered incense or made burnt offerings in the holy place to the God of Israel. 8 Therefore the wrath of the LORD came upon Judah and Jerusalem, and he has made them an object of horror, of astonishment, and of hissing, as you see with your own eyes. 9 Our fathers have fallen by the sword and our sons and our daughters and our wives are in captivity for this. 10 Now it is in my heart to make a covenant with the LORD, the God of Israel, so that his fierce anger may turn away from us. 11 My sons, do not now be negligent, for the LORD has chosen you to stand in his presence to minister to him, and to be his ministers and make offerings to him."

PRAY IT!
Renewing Your Prayer Life

Hezekiah was one of Judah's reformer kings. Before he became king, the people had neglected the Temple in Jerusalem for a long time. At the beginning of Hezekiah's reign, the Temple needed some intense effort to get it back in order.

Sometimes, our prayer life suffers from neglect too. We get busy and do not take enough time to pray, or forget to pray altogether. When we decide to commit ourselves to regular prayer, it may take some intense effort to get rid of our bad habits.

Imagine your prayer life as being like the Temple. How does it look? Is it in need of a little dusting? full of cobwebs? ready for major renovation? What steps can you take to make sure you do not neglect your prayer life?

▸ 2 Chr 29.3–11

12 Then the Lē'vites arose, Mā'hath son of A•mā'saī, and Jō'el son of Az•a•rī'ah, of the sons of the Kō'hath•ites; and of the sons of Me•rar'ī, Kish son of Ab'dī, and Az•a•rī'ah son of Je•hal'le•lel; and of the Ger'shon•ites, Jō'ah son of Zim'mah, and Eden son of Jō'ah; 13 and of the sons of E•li•zā'phan, Shim'rī and Je•u'el; and of the sons of Ā'saph, Zech•a•rī'ah and Mat•ta•nī'ah; 14 and of the sons of Hē'man, Jē•hū'el and Shim'ē•ī; and of the sons of Je•dū'thun, She•mā'iah and Uz'zi•el. 15 They gathered their brothers, sanctified themselves, and went in as the king had commanded, by the words of the LORD, to cleanse the house of the LORD. 16 The priests went into the inner part of the house of the LORD to cleanse it, and they brought out all the unclean things that they found in the temple of the LORD into the court of the house of the LORD; and the Lē'vites took them and carried them out

to the Wadi Kid'ron. 17 They began to sanctify on the first day of the first month, and on the eighth day of the month they came to the vestibule of the LORD; then for eight days they sanctified the house of the LORD, and on the sixteenth day of the first month they finished. 18 Then they went inside to King Hez•e•ki′ah and said, "We have cleansed all the house of the LORD, the altar of burnt offering and all its utensils, and the table for the rows of bread and all its utensils. 19 All the utensils that King Ā′haz repudiated during his reign when he was faithless, we have made ready and sanctified; see, they are in front of the altar of the LORD."

Temple Worship Restored

20 Then King Hez•e•ki′ah rose early, assembled the officials of the city, and went up to the house of the LORD. 21 They brought seven bulls, seven rams, seven lambs, and seven male goats for a sin offering for the kingdom and for the sanctuary and for Judah. He commanded the priests the descendants of Aaron to offer them on the altar of the LORD. 22 So they slaughtered the bulls, and the priests received the blood and dashed it against the altar; they slaughtered the rams and their blood was dashed against the altar; they also slaughtered the lambs and their blood was dashed against the altar. 23 Then the male goats for the sin offering were brought to the king and the assembly; they laid their hands on them, 24 and the priests slaughtered them and made a sin offering with their blood at the altar, to make atonement for all Israel. For the king commanded that the burnt offering and the sin offering should be made for all Israel.

25 He stationed the Lē′vītes in the house of the LORD with cymbals, harps, and lyres, according to the commandment of David and of Gad the king's seer and of the prophet Nathan, for the commandment was from the LORD through his prophets. 26 The Lē′vītes stood with the instruments of David, and the priests with the trumpets. 27 Then Hez•e•ki′ah commanded that the burnt offering be offered on the altar. When the burnt offering began, the song to the LORD began also, and the trumpets, accompanied by the instruments of King David of Israel. 28 The whole assembly worshiped, the singers sang, and the trumpeters sounded; all this continued until the burnt offering was finished. 29 When the offering was finished, the king and all who were present with him bowed down and worshiped. 30 King Hez•e•ki′ah and the officials commanded the Lē′vītes to sing praises to the LORD with the words of David and of the seer Ā′saph. They sang praises

with gladness, and they bowed down and worshiped.

31 Then Hez•e•ki′ah said, "You have now consecrated yourselves to the LORD; come near, bring sacrifices and thank offerings to the house of the LORD." The assembly brought sacrifices and thank offerings; and all who were of a willing heart brought burnt offerings. 32 The number of the burnt offerings that the assembly brought was seventy bulls, one hundred rams, and two hundred lambs; all these were for a burnt offering to the LORD. 33 The consecrated offerings were six hundred bulls and three thousand sheep. 34 But the priests were too few and could not skin all the burnt offerings, so, until other priests had sanctified themselves, their kindred, the Lē′vītes, helped them until the work was finished—for the Lē′vītes were more conscientious⁸ than the priests in sanctifying themselves. 35 Besides the great number of burnt offerings there was the fat of the offerings of well-being, and there were the drink offerings for the burnt offerings. Thus the service of the house of the LORD was restored. 36 And Hez•e•ki′ah and all the people rejoiced because of what God had done for the people; for the thing had come about suddenly.

The Great Passover

Hez•e•ki′ah sent word to all Israel and Judah, and wrote letters also to Ē′phra•im and Ma•nas′seh, that they should come to the house of the LORD at Jerusalem, to keep the passover to the LORD the God of Israel. 2 For the king and his officials and all the assembly in Jerusalem had taken counsel to keep the passover in the second month 3 (for they could not keep it at its proper time because the priests had not sanctified themselves in sufficient number, nor had the people assembled in Jerusalem). 4 The plan seemed right to the king and all the assembly. 5 So they decreed to make a proclamation throughout all Israel, from Bē′er-shē′ba to Dan, that the people should come and keep the passover to the LORD the God of Israel, at Jerusalem; for they had not kept it in great numbers as prescribed. 6 So couriers went throughout all Israel and Judah with letters from the king and his officials, as the king had commanded, saying, "O people of Israel, return to the LORD, the God of Abraham, Isaac, and Israel, so that he may turn again to the remnant of you who have escaped from the hand of the kings of Assyria. 7 Do not be like your ancestors and your kindred, who were faithless to the LORD God of their ancestors, so that he made them a desolation, as you see. 8 Do not

---

⁸ Heb *upright in heart*

now be stiff-necked as your ancestors were, but yield yourselves to the LORD and come to his sanctuary, which he has sanctified forever, and serve the LORD your God, so that his fierce anger may turn away from you. 9 For as you return to the LORD, your kindred and your children will find compassion with their captors, and return to this land. For the LORD your God is gracious and merciful, and will not turn away his face from you, if you return to him."

10 So the couriers went from city to city through the country of E′phra·im and Ma·nas′seh, and as far as Zeb′u·lun; but they laughed them to scorn, and mocked them. 11 Only a few from Ash′er, Ma·nas′seh, and Zeb′u·lun humbled themselves and came to Jerusalem. 12 The hand of God was also on Judah to give them one heart to do what the king and the officials commanded by the word of the LORD.

13 Many people came together in Jerusalem to keep the festival of unleavened bread in the second month, a very large assembly. 14 They set to work and removed the altars that were in Jerusalem, and all the altars for offering incense they took away and threw into the Wadi Kid′ron. 15 They slaughtered the passover lamb on the fourteenth day of the second month. The priests and the Le′vites were ashamed, and they sanctified themselves and brought burnt offerings into the house of the LORD. 16 They took their accustomed posts according to the law of Moses the man of God; the priests dashed the blood that they received[h] from the hands of the Le′vites. 17 For there were many in the assembly who had not sanctified themselves; therefore the Le′vites had to slaughter the passover lamb for everyone who was not clean, to make it holy to the LORD. 18 For a multitude of the people, many of them from E′phra·im, Ma·nas′seh, Is′sa·char, and Zeb′u·lun, had not cleansed themselves, yet they ate the passover otherwise than as prescribed. But Hez·e·ki′ah prayed for them, saying, "The good LORD pardon all 19 who set their hearts to seek God, the LORD the God of their ancestors, even though not in accordance with the sanctuary's rules of cleanness." 20 The LORD heard Hez·e·ki′ah, and healed the people. 21 The people of Israel who were present at Jerusalem kept the festival of unleavened bread seven days with great gladness; and the Le′vites and the priests praised the LORD day by day, accompanied by loud instruments for the LORD. 22 Hez·e·ki′ah spoke encouragingly to all the Le′vites who showed good skill in the service of the LORD. So the people ate the food of the festival for seven days, sacrificing offerings of well-being and giving thanks to the LORD the God of their ancestors.

23 Then the whole assembly agreed together to keep the festival for another seven days; so they kept it for another seven days with gladness. 24 For King Hez·e·ki′ah of Judah gave the assembly a thousand bulls and seven thousand sheep for offerings, and the officials gave the assembly a thousand bulls and ten thousand sheep. The priests sanctified themselves in great numbers. 25 The whole assembly of Judah, the priests and the Le′vites, and the whole assembly that came out of Israel, and the resident aliens who came out of the land of Israel, and the resident aliens who lived in Judah, rejoiced. 26 There was great joy in Jerusalem, for since the time of Solomon son of King David of Israel there had been nothing like this in Jerusalem. 27 Then the priests and the Le′vites stood up and blessed the people, and their voice was heard; their prayer came to his holy dwelling in heaven.

Pagan Shrines Destroyed
(2 Kings 18.4)

Now when all this was finished, all Israel who were present went out to the cities of Judah and broke down the pillars, hewed down the sacred poles,[i] and pulled down the high places and the altars throughout all Judah and Benjamin, and in E′phra·im and Ma·nas′seh, until they had destroyed them all. Then all the people of Israel returned to their cities, all to their individual properties.

2 Hez·e·ki′ah appointed the divisions of the priests and of the Le′vites, division by division, everyone according to his service, the priests and the Le′vites, for burnt offerings and offerings of well-being, to minister in the gates of the camp of the LORD and to give thanks and praise. 3 The contribution of the king from his own possessions was for the burnt offerings: the burnt offerings of morning and evening, and the burnt offerings for the sabbaths, the new moons, and the appointed festivals, as it is written in the law of the LORD. 4 He commanded the people who lived in Jerusalem to give the portion due to the priests and the Le′vites, so that they might devote themselves to the law of the LORD. 5 As soon as the word spread, the people of Israel gave in abundance the first fruits of grain, wine, oil, honey, and of all the produce of the field; and they brought in abundantly the tithe of everything. 6 The people of Israel and Judah who lived in the cities of Judah also brought in the tithe of cattle and sheep, and the tithe of the dedicated things that had been consecrated to the LORD their God, and laid them in heaps. 7 In the third month they began to pile up the heaps, and finished them in the seventh month. 8 When Hez·e·ki′ah and the

---

h Heb lacks *that they received*   i Heb *Asherim*

Giving the Best of the Best

In 2 Chr 31.5, we read about how the people "gave in abundance the first fruits of grain, wine, oil, honey, and of all the produce of the field." They gave the best of the best, in gratitude for the gifts from God. That is what being generous is all about. True generosity springs from the heart and motivates us to give the best of what we have, not just what we do not want or need anymore.

The word *tithe* appears in this verse. For the Israelites, to tithe meant to give 10 percent of one's earnings as a tax for the upkeep of the Temple. Some Christians continue the spirit of tithing by giving 10 percent of all they earn to the church and other charities. They are offering God their best, the firstfruits of their labor.

We all need to search our heart and continue this tradition of offering our best back to God—not because it makes us look good and gives us "extra points" with God, but because it comes from our gratitude for the gifts we have received.

▶ 2 Chr 31.2–10

officials came and saw the heaps, they blessed the LORD and his people Israel. 9 Hez·e·kī′ah questioned the priests and the Lē′vītes about the heaps. 10 The chief priest Az·a·rī′ah, who was of the house of Zā′-dok, answered him, "Since they began to bring the contributions into the house of the LORD, we have had enough to eat and have plenty to spare; for the LORD has blessed his people, so that we have this great supply left over."

Reorganization of Priests and Levites

11 Then Hez·e·kī′ah commanded them to prepare store-chambers in the house of the LORD; and they prepared them. 12 Faithfully they brought in the contributions, the tithes and the dedicated things. The chief officer in charge of them was Con·a·nī′ah the Lē′vīte, with his brother Shim′e·ī as second; 13 while Je·hī′el, Az·a·zī′ah, Nā′hath, As′a-hel, Jer′i·moth, Joz′a·bad, E·lī′el, Is·ma·chī′ah, Mā′-hath, and Be·nā′i·ah were overseers assisting Con·a·nī′ah and his brother Shim′e·ī, by the appointment of King Hez·e·kī′ah and of Az·a·rī′ah the chief officer of the house of God. 14 Kō′re son of Im′nah the Lē′vīte, keeper of the east gate, was in charge of the freewill offerings to God, to apportion the contribution reserved for the LORD and the most holy offerings. 15 Eden, Mi·nī′a·min, Jesh′ū·a, She·māi′ah, Am·a·rī′ah, and Shec·a·nī′ah were faithfully assisting him in the cities of the priests, to distribute the portions to their kindred, old and young alike, by divisions, 16 except those enrolled by genealogy, males from three years old and upwards, all who entered the house of the LORD as the duty of each day required, for their service according to their offices, by their divisions. 17 The enroll-

ment of the priests was according to their ancestral houses; that of the Lē′vītes from twenty years old and upwards was according to their offices, by their divisions. 18 The priests were enrolled with all their little children, their wives, their sons, and their daughters, the whole multitude; for they were faithful in keeping themselves holy. 19 And for the descendants of Aaron, the priests, who were in the fields of common land belonging to their towns, town by town, the people designated by name were to distribute portions to every male among the priests and to everyone among the Lē′vītes who was enrolled.

20 Hez·e·kī′ah did this throughout all Judah; he did what was good and right and faithful before the LORD his God. 21 And every work that he undertook in the service of the house of God, and in accordance with the law and the commandments, to seek his God, he did with all his heart; and he prospered.

Sennacherib's Invasion
(2 Kings 18.13 — 19.34; Isa 36.2–22)

After these things and these acts of faithfulness, King Sen·nach′e·rib of Assyria came and invaded Judah and encamped against the fortified cities, thinking to win them for himself. 2 When Hez·e·kī′ah saw that Sen·nach′e·rib had come and intended to fight against Jerusalem, 3 he planned with his officers and his warriors to stop the flow of the springs that were outside the city; and they helped him. 4 A great many people were gathered, and they stopped all the springs and the wadi that flowed through the land, saying, "Why should the Assyrian kings come and find water in abundance?"

5 Hez•e•kī′ah[j] set to work resolutely and built up the entire wall that was broken down, and raised towers on it,[k] and outside it he built another wall; he also strengthened the Mil′lō in the city of David, and made weapons and shields in abundance. 6 He appointed combat commanders over the people, and gathered them together to him in the square at the gate of the city and spoke encouragingly to them, saying, 7 "Be strong and of good courage. Do not be afraid or dismayed before the king of Assyria and all the horde that is with him; for there is one greater with us than with him. 8 With him is an arm of flesh; but with us is the LORD our God, to help us and to fight our battles." The people were encouraged by the words of King Hez•e•kī′ah of Judah.

9 After this, while King Sen•nach′e•rib of Assyria was at Lā′chish with all his forces, he sent his servants to Jerusalem to King Hez•e•kī′ah of Judah and to all the people of Judah that were in Jerusalem, saying, 10 "Thus says King Sen•nach′e•rib of Assyria: On what are you relying, that you undergo the siege of Jerusalem? 11 Is not Hez•e•kī′ah misleading you, handing you over to die by famine and by thirst, when he tells you, 'The LORD our God will save us from the hand of the king of Assyria'? 12 Was it not this same Hez•e•kī′ah who took away his high places and his altars and commanded Judah and Jerusalem, saying, 'Before one altar you shall worship, and upon it you shall make your offerings'? 13 Do you not know what I and my ancestors have done to all the peoples of other lands? Were the gods of the nations of those lands at all able to save their lands out of my hand? 14 Who among all the gods of those nations that my ancestors utterly destroyed was able to save his people from my hand, that your God should be able to save you from my hand? 15 Now therefore do not let Hez•e•kī′ah deceive you or mislead you in this fashion, and do not believe him, for no god of any nation or kingdom has been able to save his people from my hand or from the hand of my ancestors. How much less will your God save you out of my hand!"

16 His servants said still more against the Lord GOD and against his servant Hez•e•kī′ah. 17 He also wrote letters to throw contempt on the LORD the God of Israel and to speak against him, saying, "Just as the gods of the nations in other lands did not rescue their people from my hands, so the God of Hez•e•kī′ah will not rescue his people from my hand." 18 They shouted it with a loud voice in the language of Judah to the people of Jerusalem who were on the wall, to frighten and terrify them, in order that they might take the city. 19 They spoke of the God of Jerusalem as if he were like the gods of the peoples of the earth, which are the work of human hands.

Sennacherib's Defeat and Death
(2 Kings 19.35–37)

20 Then King Hez•e•kī′ah and the prophet I•sāi′ah son of Ā′moz prayed because of this and cried to heaven. 21 And the LORD sent an angel who cut off all the mighty warriors and commanders and officers in the camp of the king of Assyria. So he returned in disgrace to his own land. When he came into the house of his god, some of his own sons struck him down there with the sword. 22 So the LORD saved Hez•e•kī′ah and the inhabitants of Jerusalem from the hand of King Sen•nach′e•rib of Assyria and from the hand of all his enemies; he gave them rest[l] on every side. 23 Many brought gifts to the LORD in Jerusalem and precious things to King Hez•e•kī′ah of Judah, so that he was exalted in the sight of all nations from that time onward.

Hezekiah's Sickness
(2 Kings 20.1–11; Isa 38.1–8)

24 In those days Hez•e•kī′ah became sick and was at the point of death. He prayed to the LORD, and he answered him and gave him a sign. 25 But Hez•e•kī′ah did not respond according to the benefit done to him, for his heart was proud. Therefore wrath came upon him and upon Judah and Jerusalem. 26 Then Hez•e•kī′ah humbled himself for the pride of his heart, both he and the inhabitants of Jerusalem, so that the wrath of the LORD did not come upon them in the days of Hez•e•kī′ah.

Hezekiah's Prosperity and Achievements
(2 Kings 20.12–21; Isa 39.1–8)

27 Hez•e•kī′ah had very great riches and honor; and he made for himself treasuries for silver, for gold, for precious stones, for spices, for shields, and for all kinds of costly objects; 28 storehouses also for the yield of grain, wine, and oil; and stalls for all kinds of cattle, and sheepfolds.[m] 29 He likewise provided cities for himself, and flocks and herds in abundance; for God had given him very great possessions. 30 This same Hez•e•kī′ah closed the upper outlet of the waters of Gī′hon and directed them down to the west side of the city of David. Hez•e•kī′ah prospered in all his works. 31 So also in the matter of the envoys of the officials of Babylon, who had been sent to him to inquire about the sign that had been done in the land, God left him to himself, in order to test him and to know all that was in his heart.

---

j Heb *He*   *k* Vg: Heb *and raised on the towers*   *l* Gk Vg: Heb *guided them*   *m* Gk Vg: Heb *flocks for folds*

Perseverance in Leadership

King Hezekiah persevered and prospered. He had many riches and provided for the people in his kingdom. One great accomplishment was a tunnel he had dug under the City of David (2 Chr 32.30). The tunnel allowed the springs of Gihon to flow into the city so that the people had easier access to the water.

That tunnel, more than seventeen hundred feet long, was carved through the stone. Today, it would not take much to complete such a task, but in Hezekiah's time, it was done little by little with simple tools.

A great leader needs perseverance. People can get discouraged and lose heart when faced with difficult tasks. A good leader provides the encouragement and vision to get the job done. Who is an encouraging leader in your life? How do you encourage other people you work or go to school or live with?

▶ 2 Chr 32.27–33

32 Now the rest of the acts of Hez•e•kī′ah, and his good deeds, are written in the vision of the prophet Ī•sāi′ah son of Ā′moz in the Book of the Kings of Judah and Israel. 33 Hez•e•kī′ah slept with his ancestors, and they buried him on the ascent to the tombs of the descendants of David; and all Judah and the inhabitants of Jerusalem did him honor at his death. His son Ma•nas′seh succeeded him.

Reign of Manasseh
(2 Kings 21.1–9)

Ma•nas′seh was twelve years old when he began to reign; he reigned fifty-five years in Jerusalem. 2 He did what was evil in the sight of the LORD, according to the abominable practices of the nations whom the LORD drove out before the people of Israel. 3 For he rebuilt the high places that his father Hez•e•kī′ah had pulled down, and erected altars to the Bā′als, made sacred poles,ⁿ worshiped all the host of heaven, and served them. 4 He built altars in the house of the LORD, of which the LORD had said, "In Jerusalem shall my name be forever." 5 He built altars for all the host of heaven in the two courts of the house of the LORD. 6 He made his son pass through fire in the valley of the son of Hin′nom, practiced soothsaying and augury and sorcery, and dealt with mediums and with wizards. He did much evil in the sight of the LORD, provoking him to anger. 7 The carved image of the idol that he had made he set in the house of God, of which God said to David and to his son Solomon, "In this house, and in Jerusalem, which I have chosen out of all the tribes of Israel, I will put my name forever; 8 I will never again remove the feet of Israel from the land that I appointed for your ancestors, if only they will be careful to do all that

I have commanded them, all the law, the statutes, and the ordinances given through Moses." 9 Ma•nas′seh misled Judah and the inhabitants of Jerusalem, so that they did more evil than the nations whom the LORD had destroyed before the people of Israel.

Manasseh Restored after Repentance

10 The LORD spoke to Ma•nas′seh and to his people, but they gave no heed. 11 Therefore the LORD brought against them the commanders of the army of the king of Assyria, who took Ma•nas′seh captive in manacles, bound him with fetters, and brought him to Babylon. 12 While he was in distress he entreated the favor of the LORD his God and humbled himself greatly before the God of his ancestors. 13 He prayed to him, and God received his entreaty, heard his plea, and restored him again to Jerusalem and to his kingdom. Then Ma•nas′seh knew that the LORD indeed was God.

14 Afterward he built an outer wall for the city of David west of Gī′hon, in the valley, reaching the entrance at the Fish Gate; he carried it around Ō′phel, and raised it to a very great height. He also put commanders of the army in all the fortified cities in Judah. 15 He took away the foreign gods and the idol from the house of the LORD, and all the altars that he had built on the mountain of the house of the LORD and in Jerusalem, and he threw them out of the city. 16 He also restored the altar of the LORD and offered on it sacrifices of well-being and of thanksgiving; and he commanded Judah to serve the LORD the God of Israel. 17 The people, however, still sacrificed at the high places, but only to the LORD their God.

ⁿ Heb Asheroth

Death of Manasseh
(2 Kings 21.17–18)

18 Now the rest of the acts of Ma•nas′seh, his prayer to his God, and the words of the seers who spoke to him in the name of the LORD God of Israel, these are in the Annals of the Kings of Israel. 19 His prayer, and how God received his entreaty, all his sin and his faithlessness, the sites on which he built high places and set up the sacred poles*o* and the images, before he humbled himself, these are written in the records of the seers.*p* 20 So Manas′seh slept with his ancestors, and they buried him in his house. His son Ā′mon succeeded him.

Amon's Reign and Death
(2 Kings 21.19–26)

21 Ā′mon was twenty-two years old when he began to reign; he reigned two years in Jerusalem. 22 He did what was evil in the sight of the LORD, as his father Ma•nas′seh had done. Ā′mon sacrificed to all the images that his father Ma•nas′seh had made, and served them. 23 He did not humble himself before the LORD, as his father Ma•nas′seh had humbled himself, but this Ā′mon incurred more and more guilt. 24 His servants conspired against him and killed him in his house. 25 But the people of the land killed all those who had conspired against King Ā′mon; and the people of the land made his son Jō•sī′ah king to succeed him.

Reign of Josiah
(2 Kings 22.1–2)

Jō•sī′ah was eight years old when he began to reign; he reigned thirty-one years in Jerusalem. 2 He did what was right in the sight of the LORD, and walked in the ways of his ancestor David; he did not turn aside to the right or to the left. 3 For in the eighth year of his reign, while he was still a boy, he began to seek the God of his ancestor David, and in the twelfth year he began to purge Judah and Jerusalem of the high places, the sacred poles,*o* and the carved and the cast images. 4 In his presence they pulled down the altars of the Bā′als; he demolished the incense altars that stood above them. He broke down the sacred poles*o* and the carved and the cast images; he made dust of them and scattered it over the graves of those who had sacrificed to them. 5 He also burned the bones of the priests on their altars, and purged Judah and Jerusalem. 6 In the towns of Ma•nas′seh, Ē′phra•im, and Sim′ē•on, and as far as Naph′ta•lī, in their ruins*q* all around, 7 he broke down the altars, beat the sacred poles*o* and the images into powder, and demolished all the incense altars throughout all the land of Israel. Then he returned to Jerusalem.

Discovery of the Book of the Law
(2 Kings 22.3–20)

8 In the eighteenth year of his reign, when he had purged the land and the house, he sent Shā′phan son of Az•a•lī′ah, Mā•a•sēi′ah the governor of the city, and Jō′ah son of Jō′a•haz, the recorder, to repair the house of the LORD his God. 9 They came to the high priest Hil•kī′ah and delivered the money that had been brought into the house of God, which the Lē′vites, the keepers of the threshold, had collected from Ma•nas′seh and Ē′phra•im and from all the remnant of Israel and from all Judah and Benjamin and from the inhabitants of Jerusalem. 10 They delivered it to the workers who had the oversight of the house of the LORD, and the workers who were working in the house of the LORD gave it for repairing and restoring the house. 11 They gave it to the carpenters and the builders to buy quarried stone, and timber for binders, and beams for the buildings that the kings of Judah had let go to ruin. 12 The people did the work faithfully. Over them were appointed the Lē′vites Jā′hath and Ō•ba•dī′ah, of the sons of Me•rar′ī, along with Zech•a•rī′ah and Me•shul′lam, of the sons of the Kō′hath•ites, to have oversight. Other Lē′vites, all skillful with instruments of music, 13 were over the burden bearers and directed all who did work in every kind of service; and some of the Lē′vites were scribes, and officials, and gatekeepers.

14 While they were bringing out the money that had been brought into the house of the LORD, the priest Hil•kī′ah found the book of the law of the LORD given through Moses. 15 Hil•kī′ah said to the secretary Shā′phan, "I have found the book of the law in the house of the LORD"; and Hil•kī′ah gave the book to Shā′phan. 16 Shā′phan brought the book to the king, and further reported to the king, "All that was committed to your servants they are doing. 17 They have emptied out the money that was found in the house of the LORD and have delivered it into the hand of the overseers and the workers." 18 The secretary Shā′phan informed the king, "The priest Hil•kī′ah has given me a book." Shā′phan then read it aloud to the king.

19 When the king heard the words of the law he tore his clothes. 20 Then the king commanded Hil•kī′ah, A•hī′kam son of Shā′phan, Ab′don son of Mī′cah, the secretary Shā′phan, and the king's servant A•sāi′ah: 21 "Go, inquire of the LORD for me and for those who are left in Israel and in Judah, concerning the words of the book that has been found; for the wrath of the LORD that is poured out

---

o Heb *Asherim*   *p* One Ms Gk: MT *of Hozai*   *q* Meaning of Heb uncertain

2
C
H
R

on us is great, because our ancestors did not keep the word of the LORD, to act in accordance with all that is written in this book."

The Prophet Huldah Consulted

22 So Hil•ki'ah and those whom the king had sent went to the prophet Hul'dah, the wife of Shal'lum son of Tok'hath son of Has'rah, keeper of the wardrobe (who lived in Jerusalem in the Second Quarter) and spoke to her to that effect. 23 She declared to them, "Thus says the LORD, the God of Israel: Tell the man who sent you to me, 24 Thus says the LORD: I will indeed bring disaster upon this place and upon its inhabitants, all the curses that are written in the book that was read before the king of Judah. 25 Because they have forsaken me and have made offerings to other gods, so that they have provoked me to anger with all the works of their hands, my wrath will be poured out on this place and will not be quenched. 26 But as to the king of Judah, who sent you to inquire of the LORD, thus shall you say to him: Thus says the LORD, the God of Israel: Regarding the words that you have heard, 27 because your heart was penitent and you humbled yourself before God when you heard his words against this place and its inhabitants, and you have humbled yourself before me, and have torn your clothes and wept before me, I also have heard you, says the LORD. 28 I will gather you to your ancestors and you shall be gathered to your grave in peace; your eyes shall not see all the disaster that I will bring on this place and its inhabitants." They took the message back to the king.

The Covenant Renewed
(2 Kings 23.1–20)

29 Then the king sent word and gathered together all the elders of Judah and Jerusalem. 30 The king went up to the house of the LORD, with all the people of Judah, the inhabitants of Jerusalem, the priests and the Le'vites, all the people both great and small; he read in their hearing all the words of the book of the covenant that had been found in the house of the LORD. 31 The king stood in his place and made a covenant before the LORD, to follow the LORD, keeping his commandments, his decrees, and his statutes, with all his heart and all his soul, to perform the words of the covenant that were written in this book. 32 Then he made all who were present in Jerusalem and in Benjamin pledge themselves to it. And the inhabitants of Jerusalem acted according to the covenant of God, the God of their ancestors. 33 Jō•si'ah took away all the abominations from all the territory that belonged to the people of Israel, and made all who were in Israel worship the LORD their God. All his days they

did not turn away from following the LORD the God of their ancestors,

Celebration of the Passover
(2 Kings 23.21–23)

Jō•si'ah kept a passover to the LORD in Jerusalem; they slaughtered the passover lamb on the fourteenth day of the first month. 2 He appointed the priests to their offices and encouraged them in the service of the house of the LORD. 3 He said to the Le'vites who taught all Israel and who were holy to the LORD, "Put the holy ark in the house that Solomon son of David, king of Israel, built; you need no longer carry it on your shoulders. Now serve the LORD your God and his people Israel. 4 Make preparations by your ancestral houses by your divisions, following the written directions of King David of Israel and the written directions of his son Solomon. 5 Take position in the holy place according to the groupings of the ancestral houses of your kindred the people, and let there be Le'vites for each division of an ancestral house.[r] 6 Slaughter the passover lamb, sanctify yourselves, and on behalf of your kindred make preparations, acting according to the word of the LORD by Moses."

7 Then Jō•si'ah contributed to the people, as passover offerings for all that were present, lambs and kids from the flock to the number of thirty thousand, and three thousand bulls; these were from the king's possessions. 8 His officials contributed willingly to the people, to the priests, and to the Le'vites. Hil•ki'ah, Zech•a•ri'ah, and Je•hi'el, the chief officers of the house of God, gave to the priests for the passover offerings two thousand six hundred lambs and kids and three hundred bulls. 9 Con•a•ni'ah also, and his brothers She•mai'ah and Ne•than'el, and Hash•a•bi'ah and Je•i'el and Joz'a-bad, the chiefs of the Le'vites, gave to the Le'vites for the passover offerings five thousand lambs and kids and five hundred bulls.

10 When the service had been prepared for, the priests stood in their place, and the Le'vites in their divisions according to the king's command. 11 They slaughtered the passover lamb, and the priests dashed the blood that they received[s] from them, while the Le'vites did the skinning. 12 They set aside the burnt offerings so that they might distribute them according to the groupings of the ancestral houses of the people, to offer to the LORD, as it is written in the book of Moses. And they did the same with the bulls. 13 They roasted the passover lamb with fire according to the ordinance; and

---

r Meaning of Heb uncertain   s Heb lacks *that they received*

they boiled the holy offerings in pots, in caldrons, and in pans, and carried them quickly to all the people. ¹⁴ Afterward they made preparations for themselves and for the priests, because the priests the descendants of Aaron were occupied in offering the burnt offerings and the fat parts until night; so the Lĕ′vītes made preparations for themselves and for the priests, the descendants of Aaron. ¹⁵ The singers, the descendants of Ā′saph, were in their place according to the command of David, and Ā′saph, and Hĕ′man, and the king's seer Je•dū′thun. The gatekeepers were at each gate; they did not need to interrupt their service, for their kindred the Lĕ′vītes made preparations for them.

16 So all the service of the LORD was prepared that day, to keep the passover and to offer burnt offerings on the altar of the LORD, according to the command of King Jō•sī′ah. ¹⁷ The people of Israel who were present kept the passover at that time, and the festival of unleavened bread seven days. ¹⁸ No passover like it had been kept in Israel since the days of the prophet Samuel; none of the kings of Israel had kept such a passover as was kept by Jō•sī′ah, by the priests and the Lĕ′vītes, by all Judah and Israel who were present, and by the inhabitants of Jerusalem. ¹⁹ In the eighteenth year of the reign of Jō•sī′ah this passover was kept.

Defeat by Pharaoh Neco and
Death of Josiah
(2 Kings 23.28–30)

20 After all this, when Jō•sī′ah had set the temple in order, King Nĕ′cō of Egypt went up to fight at Car′chem•ish on the Euphrates, and Jō•sī′ah went out against him. ²¹ But Nĕ′cōᵗ sent envoys to him, saying, "What have I to do with you, king of Judah? I am not coming against you today, but against the house with which I am at war; and God has commanded me to hurry. Cease opposing God, who is with me, so that he will not destroy you." ²² But Jō•sī′ah would not turn away from him, but disguised himself in order to fight with him. He did not listen to the words of Nĕ′cō from the mouth of God, but joined battle in the plain of Me•gid′dō. ²³ The archers shot King Jō•sī′ah; and the king said to his servants, "Take me away, for I am badly wounded." ²⁴ So his servants took him out of the chariot and carried him in his second chariotᵘ and brought him to Jerusalem. There he died, and was buried in the tombs of his ancestors. All Judah and Jerusalem mourned for Jō•sī′ah. ²⁵ Jer•e•mī′ah also uttered a lament for Jō•sī′ah, and all the singing men and singing women have spoken of Jō•sī′ah in their laments to this day. They made these a custom in Israel; they are recorded in the La-

ments. ²⁶ Now the rest of the acts of Jō•sī′ah and his faithful deeds in accordance with what is written in the law of the LORD, ²⁷ and his acts, first and last, are written in the Book of the Kings of Israel and Judah.

Reign of Jehoahaz
(2 Kings 23.31–33)

The people of the land took Je•hō′a•haz son of Jō•sī′ah and made him king to succeed his father in Jerusalem. ² Je•hō′a•haz was twenty-three years old when he began to reign; he reigned three months in Jerusalem. ³ Then the king of Egypt deposed him in Jerusalem and laid on the land a tribute of one hundred talents of silver and one talent of gold. ⁴ The king of Egypt made his brother E•lī′a•kim king over Judah and Jerusalem, and changed his name to Je•hoi′a•kim; but Nĕ′cō took his brother Je•hō′a•haz and carried him to Egypt.

Reign and Captivity of Jehoiakim
(2 Kings 23.34—24.7)

5 Je•hoi′a•kim was twenty-five years old when he began to reign; he reigned eleven years in Jerusalem. He did what was evil in the sight of the LORD his God. ⁶ Against him King Ne•bū•chad•nez′zar of Babylon came up, and bound him with fetters to take him to Babylon. ⁷ Ne•bū•chad•nez′zar also carried some of the vessels of the house of the LORD to Babylon and put them in his palace in Babylon. ⁸ Now the rest of the acts of Je•hoi′a•kim, and the abominations that he did, and what was found against him, are written in the Book of the Kings of Israel and Judah; and his son Je•hoi′a•chin succeeded him.

Reign and Captivity of Jehoiachin
(2 Kings 24.8–17)

9 Je•hoi′a•chin was eight years old when he began to reign; he reigned three months and ten days in Jerusalem. He did what was evil in the sight of the LORD. ¹⁰ In the spring of the year King Ne•bū•chad•nez′zar sent and brought him to Babylon, along with the precious vessels of the house of the LORD, and made his brother Zed•e•kī′ah king over Judah and Jerusalem.

Reign of Zedekiah
(2 Kings 24.18–20; Jer 52.1–3a)

11 Zed•e•kī′ah was twenty-one years old when he began to reign; he reigned eleven years in Jerusalem. ¹² He did what was evil in the sight of the LORD his God. He did not humble himself before the prophet Jer•e•mī′ah who spoke from the mouth

---

ᵗ Heb *he*   ᵘ Or *the chariot of his deputy*

Stiff Necks

It happened so quickly. I was waiting at a stoplight when the car behind me slammed into my car and my neck snapped back. Whiplash! It hurt, but it didn't seem very serious. I was much more upset at the damage that had been done to my car. But by the next morning, I was in agony. I could barely move my head, and my neck was stiff and sore. By the end of the day, my neck was in a brace, and I was taking pain medication.

Now I understand a little better why the Bible so often uses the metaphor of stiff-necked people (2 Chr 36.13). To be unable or unwilling to turn their heads deprives people of the ability to look toward God. They just keep looking straight ahead as if it were not possible to look in any other direction. You miss out on a lot if you don't or can't look from side to side, believe me!

How often have you refused to turn toward God, or to gain a new perspective on life?

▶ 2 Chr 36.11–14

of the LORD. 13 He also rebelled against King Ne·bū-chad·nez′zar, who had made him swear by God; he stiffened his neck and hardened his heart against turning to the LORD, the God of Israel. 14 All the leading priests and the people also were exceedingly unfaithful, following all the abominations of the nations; and they polluted the house of the LORD that he had consecrated in Jerusalem.

The Fall of Jerusalem
(2 Kings 25.1–21; Jer 52.3b–30)

15 The LORD, the God of their ancestors, sent persistently to them by his messengers, because he had compassion on his people and on his dwelling place; 16 but they kept mocking the messengers of God, despising his words, and scoffing at his prophets, until the wrath of the LORD against his people became so great that there was no remedy. 17 Therefore he brought up against them the king of the Chal·dē′ans, who killed their youths with the sword in the house of their sanctuary, and had no compassion on young man or young woman, the aged or the feeble; he gave them all into his hand. 18 All the vessels of the house of God, large and small, and the treasures of the house of the LORD, and the treasures of the king

and of his officials, all these he brought to Babylon. 19 They burned the house of God, broke down the wall of Jerusalem, burned all its palaces with fire, and destroyed all its precious vessels. 20 He took into exile in Babylon those who had escaped from the sword, and they became servants to him and to his sons until the establishment of the kingdom of Persia, 21 to fulfill the word of the LORD by the mouth of Jer·e·mī′ah, until the land had made up for its sabbaths. All the days that it lay desolate it kept sabbath, to fulfill seventy years.

Cyrus Proclaims Liberty for the Exiles
(Ezra 1.1–4)

22 In the first year of King Cyrus of Persia, in fulfillment of the word of the LORD spoken by Jer·e·mī′ah, the LORD stirred up the spirit of King Cyrus of Persia so that he sent a herald throughout all his kingdom and also declared in a written edict: 23 "Thus says King Cyrus of Persia: The LORD, the God of heaven, has given me all the kingdoms of the earth, and he has charged me to build him a house at Jerusalem, which is in Judah. Whoever is among you of all his people, may the LORD his God be with him! Let him go up."

I magine the worst vacation ever. The car breaks down twice, you are sick almost the whole time, and the weather is awful. You can't wait to get home—but when you walk in the front door, the house is trashed. Now, imagine how the Israelites felt. They didn't just have a bad vacation; they spent fifty years as captives in a foreign land. When they finally returned home, they faced the overwhelming task of rebuilding Jerusalem and starting their new life. Fortunately, they had Ezra and Nehemiah to help lead and encourage them.

In-depth

In 587 B.C., the land of Judah and the city of Jerusalem were conquered by the Babylonians, and many Israelites were exiled to Babylon. The Books of Ezra and Nehemiah pick up the story with the return of some Israelites from Babylon to Judah in 538 B.C. The two books were originally a single work, perhaps written in their final form by the same person (or persons) who wrote 1 and 2 Chronicles.

Ezra, a descendant of Israelite priests, was born in Babylonian captivity and became a priest. Because priests couldn't exercise their religious functions during the Exile, they dedicated themselves to studying the Scriptures. Eventually, Ezra was sent to Judah by the Persian emperor Artaxerxes to restore Israel's faithfulness to God. Ezra appointed scribes and judges to establish civil and moral order in the new community returned from Exile.

Nehemiah was a Jewish cupbearer for Emperor Artaxerxes (a cupbearer tastes the contents of whatever the emperor drinks to assure it is not poisoned). When Nehemiah heard reports of Jerusalem's poverty and ruin, he persuaded the emperor to appoint him governor of Judah to help rebuild the city. Nehemiah turned out to be a gifted governor. Under Nehemiah's direction, Jerusalem's walls were rebuilt, and economic and social reforms helped restore order and hope to the community.

Ezra and Nehemiah's leadership was extremely important to Israel as the people returned and began the difficult task of rebuilding Jerusalem. The need to save the faith and customs of the Israelites led to a strict observance of the Law and the beginnings of modern Judaism.

At a Glance

- **Ezra, chapters 1–6.** Israel's return to Judah

- **Ezra, chapters 7–10.** Ezra's coming and works

- **Neh 1.1–7.72.** Nehemiah's appointment as governor

- **Neh 7.73–9.38.** Ezra's proclaiming of the Torah

- **Nehemiah, chapters 10–13.** the various reforms of Nehemiah

Quick Facts

Period Covered
from the Exiles' return to Jerusalem through Nehemiah's tenure as governor of Judah, from 538 to about 400 B.C.

Author
a scribe (the Chronicler?) drawing on Ezra's and Nehemiah's memoirs

Themes
the return of the Israelites from captivity, the rebuilding of Jerusalem and the Temple

The Books of Ezra and Nehemiah

Ezra

6.3

End of the Babylonian Captivity
(2 Chr 36.22–23)

In the first year of King Cyrus of Persia, in order that the word of the LORD by the mouth of Jer·e·mī′ah might be accomplished, the LORD stirred up the spirit of King Cyrus of Persia so that he sent a herald throughout all his kingdom, and also in a written edict declared:

2 "Thus says King Cyrus of Persia: The LORD, the God of heaven, has given me all the kingdoms of the earth, and he has charged me to build him a house at Jerusalem in Judah. ³ Any of those among you who are of his people—may their God be with them!—are now permitted to go up to Jerusalem in Judah, and rebuild the house of the LORD, the God of Israel—he is the God who is in Jerusalem; ⁴ and let all survivors, in whatever place they reside, be assisted by the people of their place with silver and gold, with goods and with animals, besides freewill offerings for the house of God in Jerusalem."

5 The heads of the families of Judah and Benjamin, and the priests and the Lē′vītes—everyone whose spirit God had stirred—got ready to go up and rebuild the house of the LORD in Jerusalem. ⁶ All their neighbors aided them with silver vessels, with gold, with goods, with animals, and with valuable gifts, besides all that was freely offered. ⁷ King Cyrus himself brought out the vessels of the house of the LORD that Ne·bū·chad·nez′zar had carried away from Jerusalem and placed in the house

of his gods. ⁸ King Cyrus of Persia had them released into the charge of Mith′re·dath the treasurer, who counted them out to Shesh·baz′zar the prince of Judah. ⁹ And this was the inventory: gold basins, thirty; silver basins, one thousand; knives,ᵃ twenty-nine; ¹⁰ gold bowls, thirty; other silver bowls, four hundred ten; other vessels, one thousand; ¹¹ the total of the gold and silver vessels was five thousand four hundred. All these Shesh·baz′zar brought up, when the exiles were brought up from Babylonia to Jerusalem.

List of the Returned Exiles
(Neh 7.6–73)

Now these were the people of the province who came from those captive exiles whom King Ne·bū·chad·nez′zar of Babylon had carried captive to Babylonia; they returned to Jerusalem and Judah, all to their own towns. ² They came with Ze·rub′ba·bel, Jesh′ū·a, Nē·he·mī′ah, Se·rāi′ah, Rē·el·āi′ah, Mor′de·cai, Bil′shan, Mis′par, Big′vaī, Rē′hum, and Bā′a·nah.

The number of the Israelite people: ³ the descendants of Pā′rosh, two thousand one hundred seventy-two. ⁴ Of Sheph·a·tī′ah, three hundred seventy-two. ⁵ Of Ā′rah, seven hundred seventy-five. ⁶ Of Pā′hath-mō′ab, namely the descendants of Jesh′ū·a and Jō′ab, two thousand eight hundred twelve. ⁷ Of Ē′lam, one thousand two hundred fifty-four. ⁸ Of Zat′tū, nine hundred forty-five. ⁹ Of

---

ᵃ Vg: Meaning of Heb uncertain

Zac'caī, seven hundred sixty. ¹⁰ Of Bā'nī, six hundred forty-two. ¹¹ Of Bē'baī, six hundred twenty-three. ¹² Of Az'gad, one thousand two hundred twenty-two. ¹³ Of Ad•o•nī'kam, six hundred sixty-six. ¹⁴ Of Big'vaī, two thousand fifty-six. ¹⁵ Of Ā'din, four hundred fifty-four. ¹⁶ Of Ā'ter, namely of Hez•e•kī'ah, ninety-eight. ¹⁷ Of Bē'zaī, three hundred twenty-three. ¹⁸ Of Jō'rah, one hundred twelve. ¹⁹ Of Hā'shum, two hundred twenty-three. ²⁰ Of Gib'bar, ninety-five. ²¹ Of Bethlehem, one hundred twenty-three. ²² The people of Ne•toph'ah, fifty-six. ²³ Of An'a•thoth, one hundred twenty-eight. ²⁴ The descendants of Az'ma•veth, forty-two. ²⁵ Of Kir•i•ath•ar'im, Chē•phī'rah, and Be•er'oth, seven hundred forty-three. ²⁶ Of Rā'mah and Gē'ba, six hundred twenty-one. ²⁷ The people of Mich'mas, one hundred twenty-two. ²⁸ Of Beth'el and Aī, two hundred twenty-three. ²⁹ The descendants of Nē'bō, fifty-two. ³⁰ Of Mag'bish, one hundred fifty-six. ³¹ Of the other Ē'lam, one thousand two hundred fifty-four. ³² Of Hā'rim, three hundred twenty. ³³ Of Lod, Hā'did, and Ō'nō, seven hundred twenty-five. ³⁴ Of Jericho, three hundred forty-five. ³⁵ Of Se•nā'ah, three thousand six hundred thirty.

36 The priests: the descendants of Je•daī'ah, of the house of Jesh'ū•a, nine hundred seventy-three. ³⁷ Of Im'mer, one thousand fifty-two. ³⁸ Of Pash'-hur, one thousand two hundred forty-seven. ³⁹ Of Hā'rim, one thousand seventeen.

40 The Lē'vītes: the descendants of Jesh'ū•a and Kad'mi•el, of the descendants of Hod•a•vī'ah, seventy-four. ⁴¹ The singers: the descendants of Ā'saph, one hundred twenty-eight. ⁴² The descen-

dants of the gatekeepers: of Shal'lum, of Ā'ter, of Tal'mon, of Ak'kub, of Ha•tī'ta, and of Shō'baī, in all one hundred thirty-nine.

43 The temple servants: the descendants of Zī'ha, Ha•sū'pha, Tab•bā'oth, ⁴⁴ Kē'ros, Sī'a•ha, Pā'-don, ⁴⁵ Le•bā'nah, Hag'a•bah, Ak'kub, ⁴⁶ Hā'gab, Sham'laī, Hā'nan, ⁴⁷ Gid'del, Gā'har, Rē•ai'ah, ⁴⁸ Rē'zin, Ne•kō'da, Gaz'zam, ⁴⁹ Uz'za, Pa•sē'ah, Bē'saī, ⁵⁰ As'nah, Me•ū'nim, Ne•phī'sim, ⁵¹ Bak'buk, Ha•kū'pha, Har'hur, ⁵² Baz'luth, Me•hī'da, Har'sha, ⁵³ Bar'kos, Sis'e•ra, Tē'mah, ⁵⁴ Ne•zī'ah, and Ha•tī'-pha.

55 The descendants of Solomon's servants: Sō'taī, Has•sō'phe•reth, Pe•rū'da, ⁵⁶ Jā'a•lah, Dar'kon, Gid'del, ⁵⁷ Sheph•a•tī'ah, Hat'til, Pō'che•reth-haz•ze-bā'im, and Ā'mī.

58 All the temple servants and the descendants of Solomon's servants were three hundred ninety-two.

59 The following were those who came up from Tel-mē'lah, Tel-har'sha, Chē'rub, Ad'dan, and Im'mer, though they could not prove their families or their descent, whether they belonged to Israel: ⁶⁰ the descendants of De•laī'ah, Tō•bī'ah, and Ne•kō'da, six hundred fifty-two. ⁶¹ Also, of the descendants of the priests: the descendants of Ha-baī'ah, Hak'koz, and Bar•zil'laī (who had married one of the daughters of Bar•zil'laī the Gil'e•ad•īte, and was called by their name). ⁶² These looked for their entries in the genealogical records, but they were not found there, and so they were excluded from the priesthood as unclean; ⁶³ the governor told them that they were not to partake of the

The Spirit of Giving

LIVE IT!

It was Christmas Eve, and Sally was depressed because she had little to give her three children for Christmas. The father of Sally's children had left suddenly one day, and each day since had been a struggle. The children each had a gift that they wanted from Santa, and Sally could not afford what they were hoping for. Friends and family had offered to help, but she was too proud to accept their charity.

As Sally and the children headed home after church, Sally's heart was heavy because she knew her children would be disappointed. But when they arrived home, they found a pile of presents in the middle of the living room. The children had each received their special gift. Sally never found out who was responsible for this special Christmas.

For the Jews returning to Jerusalem, the task of rebuilding Jerusalem must have seemed overwhelming. King Cyrus understood this and asked that family, friends, and neighbors help by giving whatever they could. Who has been there to help you when you have felt completely overwhelmed? How do you offer help to others?

▶ Ezra 1.6–11

most holy food, until there should be a priest to consult U'rim and Thum'mim.

64 The whole assembly together was forty-two thousand three hundred sixty, [65] besides their male and female servants, of whom there were seven thousand three hundred thirty-seven; and they had two hundred male and female singers. [66] They had seven hundred thirty-six horses, two hundred forty-five mules, [67] four hundred thirty-five camels, and six thousand seven hundred twenty donkeys.

68 As soon as they came to the house of the LORD in Jerusalem, some of the heads of families made freewill offerings for the house of God, to erect it on its site. [69] According to their resources they gave to the building fund sixty-one thousand darics of gold, five thousand minas of silver, and one hundred priestly robes.

70 The priests, the Lē'vītes, and some of the people lived in Jerusalem and its vicinity;[b] and the singers, the gatekeepers, and the temple servants lived in their towns, and all Israel in their towns.

Worship Restored at Jerusalem

When the seventh month came, and the Israelites were in the towns, the people gathered together in Jerusalem. [2] Then Jesh'ū·a son of Jō'za·dak, with his fellow priests, and Ze·rub'ba·bel son of She·al'ti·el with his kin set out to build the altar of the God of Israel, to offer burnt offerings on it, as prescribed in the law of Moses the man of God. [3] They set up the altar on its foundation, because they were in dread of the neighboring peoples, and they offered burnt offerings upon it to the LORD, morning and evening. [4] And they kept the festival of booths,[c] as prescribed, and offered the daily burnt offerings by number according to the ordinance, as required for each day, [5] and after that the regular burnt offerings, the offerings at the new moon and at all the sacred festivals of the LORD, and the offerings of everyone who made a freewill offering to the LORD. [6] From the first day of the seventh month they began to offer burnt offerings to the LORD. But the foundation of the temple of the LORD was not yet laid. [7] So they gave money to the masons and the carpenters, and food, drink, and oil to the Sī·dō'ni·ans and the Tȳ'ri·ans to bring cedar trees from Lebanon to the sea, to Jop'pa, according to the grant that they had from King Cyrus of Persia.

Foundation Laid for the Temple

8 In the second year after their arrival at the house of God at Jerusalem, in the second month, Ze·rub'ba·bel son of She·al'ti·el and Jesh'ū·a son of Jō'za·dak made a beginning, together with the rest of their people, the priests and the Lē'vītes and all who had come to Jerusalem from the captivity.

They appointed the Lē'vītes, from twenty years old and upward, to have the oversight of the work on the house of the LORD. [9] And Jesh'ū·a with his sons and his kin, and Kad'mi·el and his sons, Bin'nū·ī and Hod·a·vī'ah[d] along with the sons of Hen'a·dad, the Lē'vītes, their sons and kin, together took charge of the workers in the house of God.

PRAY IT!
Holy Tears

Ezra 3.12 tells us that many of the older Israelites who remembered the first Temple wept at the grand celebration that marked its rebirth. Were they shedding tears of joy that the Temple was being built again? Or were they shedding tears of sorrow over what they had lost and never regained? Most likely, they were doing both.

Weeping can be a holy and healing part of life. Unfortunately, some people believe that strong men and women never cry. But tears are appropriate on many occasions: the loss of a dear friend or family member, a reconciliation with someone after a long separation, and the moment we recognize we have sinned and hurt someone deeply, to name a few. We should bring our tears to God in prayer. They will turn into holy tears as God's healing love enters our life.

▶ Ezra 3.10–13

10 When the builders laid the foundation of the temple of the LORD, the priests in their vestments were stationed to praise the LORD with trumpets, and the Lē'vītes, the sons of Ā'saph, with cymbals, according to the directions of King David of Israel; [11] and they sang responsively, praising and giving thanks to the LORD,

"For he is good,
for his steadfast love endures forever toward Israel."

And all the people responded with a great shout when they praised the LORD, because the foundation of the house of the LORD was laid. [12] But many

---

b 1 Esdras 5.46: Heb lacks *lived in Jerusalem and its vicinity*
c Or *tabernacles*; Heb *succoth*   d Compare 2.40; Neh 7.43;
1 Esdras 5.58: Heb *sons of Judah*

of the priests and Lĕ′vītes and heads of families, old people who had seen the first house on its foundations, wept with a loud voice when they saw this house, though many shouted aloud for joy, [13] so that the people could not distinguish the sound of the joyful shout from the sound of the people's weeping, for the people shouted so loudly that the sound was heard far away.

Resistance to Rebuilding the Temple

When the adversaries of Judah and Benjamin heard that the returned exiles were building a temple to the LORD, the God of Israel, [2] they approached Ze·rub′ba·bel and the heads of families and said to them, "Let us build with you, for we worship your God as you do, and we have been sacrificing to him ever since the days of King Ē′sar-had′don of Assyria who brought us here." [3] But Ze·rub′ba·bel, Jesh′ū·a, and the rest of the heads of families in Israel said to them, "You shall have no part with us in building a house to our God; but we alone will build to the LORD, the God of Israel, as King Cyrus of Persia has commanded us."

[4] Then the people of the land discouraged the people of Judah, and made them afraid to build, [5] and they bribed officials to frustrate their plan throughout the reign of King Cyrus of Persia and until the reign of King Da·rī′us of Persia.

Rebuilding of Jerusalem Opposed

[6] In the reign of A·has·ū·ē′rus, in his accession year, they wrote an accusation against the inhabitants of Judah and Jerusalem.

[7] And in the days of Ar·ta·xerx′ēs, Bish′lam and Mith′re·dath and Tā′bē·el and the rest of their associates wrote to King Ar·ta·xerx′ēs of Persia; the letter was written in Ar·a·mā′ic and translated.[e] [8] Rĕ′hum the royal deputy and Shim′shaī the scribe wrote a letter against Jerusalem to King Ar·ta·xerx′ēs as follows [9] (then Rĕ′hum the royal deputy, Shim′shaī the scribe, and the rest of their associates, the judges, the envoys, the officials, the Persians, the people of Ē′rech, the Babylonians, the people of Su′sa, that is, the Ē′lam·ītes, [10] and the rest of the nations whom the great and noble Os·nap′par deported and settled in the cities of Sa·mār′i·a and in the rest of the province Beyond the River wrote— and now [11] this is a copy of the letter that they sent):

"To King Ar·ta·xerx′ēs: Your servants, the people of the province Beyond the River, send greeting. And now [12] may it be known to the king that the Jews who came up from you to us have gone to Jerusalem. They are rebuilding that rebellious and wicked city; they are finishing the walls and repairing the foundations. [13] Now may it be known to

the king that, if this city is rebuilt and the walls finished, they will not pay tribute, custom, or toll, and the royal revenue will be reduced. [14] Now because we share the salt of the palace and it is not fitting for us to witness the king's dishonor, therefore we send and inform the king, [15] so that a search may be made in the annals of your ancestors. You will discover in the annals that this is a rebellious city, hurtful to kings and provinces, and that sedition was stirred up in it from long ago. On that account this city was laid waste. [16] We make known to the king that, if this city is rebuilt and its walls finished, you will then have no possession in the province Beyond the River."

[17] The king sent an answer: "To Rĕ′hum the royal deputy and Shim′shaī the scribe and the rest of their associates who live in Sa·mār′i·a and in the rest of the province Beyond the River, greeting. And now [18] the letter that you sent to us has been read in translation before me. [19] So I made a decree, and someone searched and discovered that this city has risen against kings from long ago, and that rebellion and sedition have been made in it. [20] Jerusalem has had mighty kings who ruled over the whole province Beyond the River, to whom tribute, custom, and toll were paid. [21] Therefore issue an order that these people be made to cease, and that this city not be rebuilt, until I make a decree. [22] Moreover, take care not to be slack in this matter; why should damage grow to the hurt of the king?"

[23] Then when the copy of King Ar·ta·xerx′ēs′ letter was read before Rĕ′hum and the scribe Shim′-shaī and their associates, they hurried to the Jews in Jerusalem and by force and power made them cease. [24] At that time the work on the house of God in Jerusalem stopped and was discontinued until the second year of the reign of King Da·rī′us of Persia.

Restoration of the Temple Resumed
(Hag 1.1; Zech 1.1)

Now the prophets, Hag′gaī[f] and Zech·a·rī′ah son of Id′dō, prophesied to the Jews who were in Judah and Jerusalem, in the name of the God of Israel who was over them. [2] Then Ze·rub′ba·bel son of She·al′ti·el and Jesh′ū·a son of Jō′za·dak set out to rebuild the house of God in Jerusalem; and with them were the prophets of God, helping them.

[3] At the same time Tat′te·naī the governor of the province Beyond the River and Shĕ′thar-boz′-e·naī and their associates came to them and spoke

---

e Heb adds *in Aramaic*, indicating that 4.8–6.18 is in Aramaic. Another interpretation is *The letter was written in the Aramaic script and set forth in the Aramaic language*
f Aram adds *the prophet*

to them thus, "Who gave you a decree to build this house and to finish this structure?" [4] They[g] also asked them this, "What are the names of the men who are building this building?" [5] But the eye of their God was upon the elders of the Jews, and they did not stop them until a report reached Da·rī'us and then answer was returned by letter in reply to it.

[6] The copy of the letter that Tat'te·nai the governor of the province Beyond the River and Shē'thar-boz'e·nai and his associates the envoys who were in the province Beyond the River sent to King Da·rī'us; [7] they sent him a report, in which was written as follows: "To Da·rī'us the king, all peace! [8] May it be known to the king that we went to the province of Judah, to the house of the great God. It is being built of hewn stone, and timber is laid in the walls; this work is being done diligently and prospers in their hands. [9] Then we spoke to those elders and asked them, 'Who gave you a decree to

did you KNOW?

The Second Temple

The first Temple, built during Solomon's reign, was destroyed in 587 B.C. when the southern kingdom of Judah was conquered by the Babylonians. The Persian king, Cyrus II, conquered Babylon in 539 B.C. and a year later liberated the Jewish exiles in Babylon. He also decreed that the Temple in Jerusalem be rebuilt (Ezra 6.3). Between the years 520 and 515 the second Temple was rebuilt in Jerusalem. The second Temple was an essential aspect of the Israelites' rebuilding of their life, culture, and religion after the Babylonian Exile. This Temple, rather than a king, became the central focus of Jewish identity, until its destruction in A.D. 70.

build this house and to finish this structure?' [10] We also asked them their names, for your information, so that we might write down the names of the men at their head. [11] This was their reply to us: 'We are the servants of the God of heaven and earth, and we are rebuilding the house that was built many years ago, which a great king of Israel built and finished. [12] But because our ancestors had angered the God of heaven, he gave them into the hand of King Ne·bū·chad·nez'zar of Babylon, the Chal·dē'an, who destroyed this house and carried away the people to Babylonia. [13] However, King Cyrus of Babylon, in the first year of his reign, made a decree that this house of God should be rebuilt. [14] Moreover, the gold and silver vessels of the house of God, which Ne·bū·chad·nez'zar had taken out of the temple in Jerusalem and had brought into the temple of Babylon, these King Cyrus took out of the temple of Babylon, and they were delivered to a man named Shesh·baz'zar, whom he had made governor. [15] He said to him, "Take these vessels; go and put them in the temple in Jerusalem, and let the house of God be rebuilt on its site." [16] Then this Shesh·baz'zar came and laid the foundations of the house of God in Jerusalem; and from that time until now it has been under construction, and it is not yet finished.' [17] And now, if it seems good to the king, have a search made in the royal archives there in Babylon, to see whether a decree was issued by King Cyrus for the rebuilding of this house of God in Jerusalem. Let the king send us his pleasure in this matter."

The Decree of Darius

Then King Da·rī'us made a decree, and they searched the archives where the documents were stored in Babylon. [2] But it was in Ec·bat'a·na, the capital in the province of Mēd'i·a, that a scroll was found on which this was written: "A record. [3] In the first year of his reign, King Cyrus issued a decree: Concerning the house of God at Jerusalem, let the house be rebuilt, the place where sacrifices are offered and burnt offerings are brought;[h] its height shall be sixty cubits and its width sixty cubits, [4] with three courses of hewn stones and one course of timber; let the cost be paid from the royal treasury. [5] Moreover, let the gold and silver vessels of the house of God, which Ne·bū·chad·nez'zar took out of the temple in Jerusalem and brought to Babylon, be restored and brought back to the temple in Jerusalem, each to its place; you shall put them in the house of God."

[6] "Now you, Tat'te·nai, governor of the province Beyond the River, Shē'thar-boz'e·nai, and you, their associates, the envoys in the province Beyond the River, keep away; [7] let the work on this house of God alone; let the governor of the Jews and the elders of the Jews rebuild this house of God on its site. [8] Moreover I make a decree regarding what you shall do for these elders of the Jews for the rebuilding of this house of God: the cost is to be

---

g Gk Syr: Aram *We*   h Meaning of Aram uncertain

paid to these people, in full and without delay, from the royal revenue, the tribute of the province Beyond the River. 9 Whatever is needed—young bulls, rams, or sheep for burnt offerings to the God of heaven, wheat, salt, wine, or oil, as the priests in Jerusalem require—let that be given to them day by day without fail, 10 so that they may offer pleasing sacrifices to the God of heaven, and pray for the life of the king and his children. 11 Furthermore I decree that if anyone alters this edict, a beam shall be pulled out of the house of the perpetrator, who then shall be impaled on it. The house shall be made a dunghill. 12 May the God who has established his name there overthrow any king or people that shall put forth a hand to alter this, or to destroy this house of God in Jerusalem. I, Da•rī′us, make a decree; let it be done with all diligence."

Completion and Dedication of the Temple

13 Then, according to the word sent by King Da•rī′us, Tat′te•naī, the governor of the province Beyond the River, Shĕ′thar-boz′e•naī, and their associates did with all diligence what King Da•rī′us had ordered. 14 So the elders of the Jews built and prospered, through the prophesying of the prophet Hag′gaī and Zech•a•rī′ah son of Id′dō. They finished their building by command of the God of Israel and by decree of Cyrus, Da•rī′us, and King Ar•ta•xerx′ēs of Persia; 15 and this house was finished on the third day of the month of Ā′dar, in the sixth year of the reign of King Da•rī′us.

16 The people of Israel, the priests and the Lē′-vītes, and the rest of the returned exiles, celebrated the dedication of this house of God with joy. 17 They offered at the dedication of this house of God one hundred bulls, two hundred rams, four hundred lambs, and as a sin offering for all Israel, twelve male goats, according to the number of the tribes of Israel. 18 Then they set the priests in their divisions and the Lē′vītes in their courses for the service of God at Jerusalem, as it is written in the book of Moses.

The Passover Celebrated
(Cp Deut 16.1–8)

19 On the fourteenth day of the first month the returned exiles kept the passover. 20 For both the priests and the Lē′vītes had purified themselves; all of them were clean. So they killed the passover lamb for all the returned exiles, for their fellow priests, and for themselves. 21 It was eaten by the people of Israel who had returned from exile, and also by all who had joined them and separated themselves from the pollutions of the

nations of the land to worship the LORD, the God of Israel. 22 With joy they celebrated the festival of unleavened bread seven days; for the LORD had made them joyful, and had turned the heart of the king of Assyria to them, so that he aided them in the work on the house of God, the God of Israel.

The Coming and Work of Ezra

7 After this, in the reign of King Ar•ta•xerx′ēs of Persia, Ezra son of Se•rāi′ah, son of Az•a•rī′ah, son of Hil-kī′ah, 2 son of Shal′lum, son of Zā′dok, son of A•hī′tub, 3 son of Am•a•rī′ah, son of Az•a•rī′ah, son of Me•rā′i•oth, 4 son of Zer•a•hī′ah, son of Uz′zī, son of Buk′kī, 5 son of Ab•i•shū′a, son of Phin′e•has, son of El•ē•ā′zar, son of the chief priest Aaron— 6 this Ezra went up from Babylonia. He was a scribe skilled in the law of Moses that the LORD the God of Israel had given; and the king granted him all that he asked, for the hand of the LORD his God was upon him.

7 Some of the people of Israel, and some of the priests and Lē′vītes, the singers and gatekeepers, and the temple servants also went up to Jerusalem, in the seventh year of King Ar•ta•xerx′ēs. 8 They came to Jerusalem in the fifth month, which was in the seventh year of the king. 9 On the first day of the first month the journey up from Babylon was begun, and on the first day of the fifth month he came to Jerusalem, for the gracious hand of his God was upon him. 10 For Ezra had set his heart to study the law of the LORD, and to do it, and to teach the statutes and ordinances in Israel.

The Letter of Artaxerxes to Ezra

11 This is a copy of the letter that King Ar•ta-xerx′ēs gave to the priest Ezra, the scribe, a scholar of the text of the commandments of the LORD and his statutes for Israel: 12 "Ar•ta•xerx′ēs, king of kings, to the priest Ezra, the scribe of the law of the God of heaven: Peace.[i] And now 13 I decree that any of the people of Israel or their priests or Lē′vītes in my kingdom who freely offers to go to Jerusalem may go with you. 14 For you are sent by the king and his seven counselors to make inquiries about Judah and Jerusalem according to the law of your God, which is in your hand, 15 and also to convey the silver and gold that the king and his counselors have freely offered to the God of Israel, whose dwelling is in Jerusalem, 16 with all the silver and gold that you shall find in the whole province of Babylonia, and with the freewill offerings of the people and the priests, given willingly for the house of their God in Jerusalem. 17 With this money, then, you shall with all diligence buy

---

i Syr Vg 1 Esdras 8.9: Aram *Perfect*

bulls, rams, and lambs, and their grain offerings and their drink offerings, and you shall offer them on the altar of the house of your God in Jerusalem. [18]Whatever seems good to you and your colleagues to do with the rest of the silver and gold, you may do, according to the will of your God. [19]The vessels that have been given you for the service of the house of your God, you shall deliver before the God of Jerusalem. [20]And whatever else is required for the house of your God, which you are responsible for providing, you may provide out of the king's treasury.

[21] "I, King Ar·ta·xerx'ēs, decree to all the treasurers in the province Beyond the River: Whatever the priest Ezra, the scribe of the law of the God of heaven, requires of you, let it be done with all diligence, [22]up to one hundred talents of silver, one hundred cors of wheat, one hundred baths[j] of wine, one hundred baths[j] of oil, and unlimited salt. [23]Whatever is commanded by the God of heaven, let it be done with zeal for the house of the God of heaven, or wrath will come upon the realm of the king and his heirs. [24]We also notify you that it shall not be lawful to impose tribute, custom, or toll on any of the priests, the Lē'vītes, the singers, the doorkeepers, the temple servants, or other servants of this house of God.

[25] "And you, Ezra, according to the God-given wisdom you possess, appoint magistrates and judges who may judge all the people in the province Beyond the River who know the laws of your God; and you shall teach those who do not know them. [26]All who will not obey the law of your God and the law of the king, let judgment be strictly executed on them, whether for death or for banishment or for confiscation of their goods or for imprisonment."

[27] Blessed be the LORD, the God of our ancestors, who put such a thing as this into the heart of the king to glorify the house of the LORD in Jerusalem, [28]and who extended to me steadfast love before the king and his counselors, and before all the king's mighty officers. I took courage, for the hand of the LORD my God was upon me, and I gathered leaders from Israel to go up with me.

Heads of Families Who Returned with Ezra

These are their family heads, and this is the genealogy of those who went up with me from Babylonia, in the reign of King Ar·ta·xerx'ēs: [2]Of the descendants of Phin'e·has, Ger'shom. Of Ith'a·mar, Daniel. Of David, Hat'tush, [3]of the descendants of Shec·a·nī'ah. Of Pā'rosh, Zech·a·rī'ah, with whom were registered one hundred fifty males. [4]Of the descendants of Pā'hath-mō'ab, El·i·e·hō·ē'naī son of

Zer·a·hī'ah, and with him two hundred males. [5]Of the descendants of Zat'tū,[k] Shec·a·nī'ah son of Ja·hā'zi·el, and with him three hundred males. [6]Of the descendants of Ā'din, Ē'bed son of Jonathan, and with him fifty males. [7]Of the descendants of Ē'lam, Je·shā'i·ah son of Ath·a·lī'ah, and with him seventy males. [8]Of the descendants of Sheph·a·tī'ah, Zeb·a·dī'ah son of Michael, and with him eighty males. [9]Of the descendants of Jō'ab, Ō·ba·dī'ah son of Je·hī'el, and with him two hundred eighteen males. [10]Of the descendants of Bā'nī,[l] She·lō'mith son of Jos·i·phī'ah, and with him one hundred sixty males. [11]Of the descendants of Bē'baī, Zech·a·rī'ah son of Bē'baī, and with him twenty-eight males. [12]Of the descendants of Az'gad, Jō·hā'nan son of Hak'ka·tan, and with him one hundred ten males. [13]Of the descendants of Ad·o·nī'kam, those who came later, their names being E·liph'e·let, Je·ū'el, and She·mā'i·ah, and with them sixty males. [14]Of the descendants of Big'vaī, Ū'thaī and Zac'cur, and with them seventy males.

Servants for the Temple

[15] I gathered them by the river that runs to A·hā'va, and there we camped three days. As I reviewed the people and the priests, I found there none of the descendants of Levi. [16]Then I sent for El·i·e·ē'zer, Ar'i·el, She·mā'i·ah, El·nā'than, Jā'rib, El·nā'than, Nathan, Zech·a·rī'ah, and Me·shul'lam, who were leaders, and for Joi'a·rib and El·nā'than, who were wise, [17]and sent them to Id'dō, the leader at the place called Cas·i·phī'a, telling them what to say to Id'dō and his colleagues the temple servants at Cas·i·phī'a, namely, to send us ministers for the house of our God. [18]Since the gracious hand of our God was upon us, they brought us a man of discretion, of the descendants of Mah'lī son of Levi son of Israel, namely Sher·e·bī'ah, with his sons and kin, eighteen; [19]also Hash·a·bī'ah and with him Je·shā'i·ah of the descendants of Me·rar'ī, with his kin and their sons, twenty; [20]besides two hundred twenty of the temple servants, whom David and his officials had set apart to attend the Lē'vītes. These were all mentioned by name.

Fasting and Prayer for Protection

[21] Then I proclaimed a fast there, at the river A·hā'va, that we might deny ourselves[m] before our God, to seek from him a safe journey for ourselves, our children, and all our possessions. [22]For I was ashamed to ask the king for a band of soldiers and cavalry to protect us against the enemy on our

---

[j] A Heb measure of volume   [k] Gk 1 Esdras 8.32: Heb lacks *of Zattu*   [l] Gk 1 Esdras 8.36: Heb lacks *Bani*   [m] Or *might fast*

way, since we had told the king that the hand of our God is gracious to all who seek him, but his power and his wrath are against all who forsake him. 23 So we fasted and petitioned our God for this, and he listened to our entreaty.

Gifts for the Temple

24 Then I set apart twelve of the leading priests: Sher•e•bī′ah, Hash•a•bī′ah, and ten of their kin with them. 25 And I weighed out to them the silver and the gold and the vessels, the offering for the house of our God that the king, his counselors, his lords, and all Israel there present had offered; 26 I weighed out into their hand six hundred fifty talents of silver, and one hundred silver vessels worth . . . talents,[n] and one hundred talents of gold, 27 twenty gold bowls worth a thousand darics, and two vessels of fine polished bronze as precious as gold. 28 And I said to them, "You are holy to the LORD, and the vessels are holy; and the silver and the gold are a freewill offering to the LORD, the God of your ancestors. 29 Guard them and keep them until you weigh them before the chief priests and the Lē′vītes and the heads of families in Israel at Jerusalem, within the chambers of the house of the LORD." 30 So the priests and the Lē′vītes took over the silver, the gold, and the vessels as they were weighed out, to bring them to Jerusalem, to the house of our God.

The Return to Jerusalem

31 Then we left the river A•hā′va on the twelfth day of the first month, to go to Jerusalem; the hand of our God was upon us, and he delivered us from the hand of the enemy and from ambushes along the way. 32 We came to Jerusalem and remained there three days. 33 On the fourth day, within the house of our God, the silver, the gold, and the vessels were weighed into the hands of the priest Mer′e•moth son of U•rī′ah, and with him was El•ē•ā′zar son of Phin′e•has, and with them were the Lē′vītes, Joz′a•bad son of Jesh′ū•a and Nō•a•dī′ah son of Bin′nū•i. 34 The total was counted and weighed, and the weight of everything was recorded.

35 At that time those who had come from captivity, the returned exiles, offered burnt offerings to the God of Israel, twelve bulls for all Israel, ninety-six rams, seventy-seven lambs, and as a sin offering twelve male goats; all this was a burnt offering to the LORD. 36 They also delivered the king's commissions to the king's satraps and to the governors of the province Beyond the River; and they supported the people and the house of God.

Denunciation of Mixed Marriages

After these things had been done, the officials approached me and said, "The people of Israel, the priests, and the Lē′vītes have not separated themselves from the peoples of the lands with their abominations, from the Cā′naan•ites, the Hit′tītes, the Per′iz•zītes, the Jeb′ū•sītes, the Am′mon•ites, the Mō′ab•ites, the Egyptians, and the Am′o•rītes. 2 For they have taken some of their daughters as wives for themselves and for their sons. Thus the holy seed has mixed itself with the peoples of the lands, and in this faithlessness the officials and leaders have led the way." 3 When I heard this, I tore my garment and my mantle, and pulled hair from my

---

[n] The number of talents is lacking

Who Belongs, and Who Does Not?

In Ezra, chapters 9–10, Ezra tells the people to reject their foreign wives and children. Nehemiah does the same in Neh 13.23–27. This probably strikes us as harsh, but we can try to understand the Israelites' situation. Only a remnant of the Israelites was left to re-establish Israel's identity. History had taught the Israelites that intermarriage led to a watering down of their faith and of the people's loyalty to their religious practices. The only way to survive as a people was to separate themselves from outsiders.

This separation led to an even greater animosity between the Jews from Judah and their cousins in faith, the Samaritans. We see some of this prejudice in the Gospels (see Jn 4.1–42 and "Discrimination in Jesus' Time," Lk 10.25–37). Christians have had similar separations throughout our history. Today, the church teaches us to be faithful to our beliefs but also to be open to others who believe differently and discover together what we have in common.

▶ Ezra, chapters 9–10

head and beard, and sat appalled. 4 Then all who trembled at the words of the God of Israel, because of the faithlessness of the returned exiles, gathered around me while I sat appalled until the evening sacrifice.

Ezra's Prayer

5 At the evening sacrifice I got up from my fasting, with my garments and my mantle torn, and fell on my knees, spread out my hands to the LORD my God, 6 and said,

"O my God, I am too ashamed and embarrassed to lift my face to you, my God, for our iniquities have risen higher than our heads, and our guilt has mounted up to the heavens. 7 From the days of our ancestors to this day we have been deep in guilt, and for our iniquities we, our kings, and our priests have been handed over to the kings of the lands, to the sword, to captivity, to plundering, and to utter shame, as is now the case. 8 But now for a brief moment favor has been shown by the LORD our God, who has left us a remnant, and given us a stake in his holy place, in order that heo may brighten our eyes and grant us a little sustenance in our slavery. 9 For we are slaves; yet our God has not forsaken us in our slavery, but has extended to us his steadfast love before the kings of Persia, to give us new life to set up the house of our God, to repair its ruins, and to give us a wall in Judea and Jerusalem.

10 "And now, our God, what shall we say after this? For we have forsaken your commandments, 11 which you commanded by your servants the prophets, saying, 'The land that you are entering to possess is a land unclean with the pollutions of the peoples of the lands, with their abominations. They have filled it from end to end with their uncleanness. 12 Therefore do not give your daughters to their sons, neither take their daughters for your sons, and never seek their peace or prosperity, so that you may be strong and eat the good of the land and leave it for an inheritance to your children forever.' 13 After all that has come upon us for our evil deeds and for our great guilt, seeing that you, our God, have punished us less than our iniquities deserved and have given us such a remnant as this, 14 shall we break your commandments again and intermarry with the peoples who practice these abominations? Would you not be angry with us until you destroy us without remnant or survivor? 15 O LORD, God of Israel, you are just, but we have escaped as a remnant, as is now the case. Here we are before you in our guilt, though no one can face you because of this."

The People's Response

While Ezra prayed and made confession, weeping and throwing himself down before the house of God, a very great assembly of men, women, and children gathered to him out of Israel; the people also wept bitterly. 2 Shec·a·ni'ah son of Je·hi'el, of the descendants of E'lam, addressed Ezra, saying, "We have broken faith with our God and have married foreign women from the peoples of the land, but even now there is hope for Israel in spite of this. 3 So now let us make a covenant with our God to send away all these wives and their children, according to the counsel of my lord and of those who tremble at the commandment of our God; and let it be done according to the law. 4 Take action, for it is your duty, and we are with you; be strong, and do it." 5 Then Ezra stood up and made the leading priests, the Le'vites, and all Israel swear that they would do as had been said. So they swore.

Foreign Wives and Their Children Rejected

6 Then Ezra withdrew from before the house of God, and went to the chamber of Je·hō·hā'nan son of E·li'a·shib, where he spent the night.p He did not eat bread or drink water, for he was mourning over the faithlessness of the exiles. 7 They made a proclamation throughout Judah and Jerusalem to all the returned exiles that they should assemble at Jerusalem, 8 and that if any did not come within three days, by order of the officials and the elders all their property should be forfeited, and they themselves banned from the congregation of the exiles.

9 Then all the people of Judah and Benjamin assembled at Jerusalem within the three days; it was the ninth month, on the twentieth day of the month. All the people sat in the open square before the house of God, trembling because of this matter and because of the heavy rain. 10 Then Ezra the priest stood up and said to them, "You have trespassed and married foreign women, and so increased the guilt of Israel. 11 Now make confession to the LORD the God of your ancestors, and do his will; separate yourselves from the peoples of the land and from the foreign wives." 12 Then all the assembly answered with a loud voice, "It is so; we must do as you have said. 13 But the people are many, and it is a time of heavy rain; we cannot stand in the open. Nor is this a task for one day or for two, for many of us have transgressed in this matter. 14 Let our officials represent the whole assembly, and let all in our towns who have taken

---

o Heb *our God*   p 1 Esdras 9.2: Heb *where he went*

foreign wives come at appointed times, and with them the elders and judges of every town, until the fierce wrath of our God on this account is averted from us." 15 Only Jonathan son of As′a•hel and Jah-zēi′ah son of Tik′vah opposed this, and Me•shul′-lam and Shab′be•thaī the Lē′vītes supported them.

16 Then the returned exiles did so. Ezra the priest selected men,q heads of families, according to their families, each of them designated by name. On the first day of the tenth month they sat down to examine the matter. 17 By the first day of the first month they had come to the end of all the men who had married foreign women.

18 There were found of the descendants of the priests who had married foreign women, of the descendants of Jesh′u•a son of Jō′za•dak and his brothers: Mā•a•sēi′ah, El•i•ē′zer, Jā′rib, and Ged•a-lī′ah. 19 They pledged themselves to send away their wives, and their guilt offering was a ram of the flock for their guilt. 20 Of the descendants of Im′mer: Ha•nā′nī and Zeb•a•dī′ah. 21 Of the descendants of Hā′rim: Mā•a•sēi′ah, E•lī′jah, She•māi′ah, Je-hī′el, and Uz•zī′ah. 22 Of the descendants of Pash′hur: El•i•ō•ē′nai, Mā•a•sēi′ah, Ish′ma•el, Ne-than′el, Joz′a•bad, and El•ā′sah.

23 Of the Lē′vītes: Joz′a•bad, Shim′ē•i, Ke•lāi′ah (that is, Ke•lī′ta), Peth•a•hī′ah, Judah, and El•i•ē′zer. 24 Of the singers: E•lī′a•shib. Of the gatekeepers: Shal′lum, Tē′lem, and Ū′rī.

25 And of Israel: of the descendants of Pā′-rosh: Ra•mī′ah, Iz•zī′ah, Mal•chī′jah, Mij′a•min, El•ē-

ā′zar, Hash•a•bī′ah,r and Be•nā′i•ah. 26 Of the descendants of Ē′lam: Mat•ta•nī′ah, Zech•a•rī′ah, Je-hī′el, Ab′dī, Jer′e•moth, and E•lī′jah. 27 Of the de-scendants of Zat′tū: El•i•ō•ē′nai, E•lī′a•shib, Mat•ta•nī′ah, Jer′e•moth, Zā′bad, and A•zī′za. 28 Of the descendants of Bē′baī: Jē•hō•hā′nan, Han•a•nī′ah, Zab′baī, and Ath′laī. 29 Of the descendants of Bā′nī: Me•shul′lam, Mal′luch, A•dāi′ah, Jash′ub, Shē′al, and Jer′e•moth. 30 Of the descendants of Pā′hath-mō′ab: Ad′na, Chē′lal, Be•nā′i•ah, Mā•a-sēi′ah, Mat•ta•nī′ah, Bez′a•lel, Bin•nū•ī, and Ma•nas′-seh. 31 Of the descendants of Hā′rim: El•i•ē′zer, Is•shī′jah, Mal•chī′jah, She•māi′ah, Shim′ē•on, 32 Benjamin, Mal′luch, and Shem•a•rī′ah. 33 Of the descendants of Hā′shum: Mat•tē′naī, Mat•tat′tah, Zā′bad, E•liph′e•let, Jer′e•maī, Ma•nas′seh, and Shim′ē•ī. 34 Of the descendants of Bā′nī: Mā•a•dā′ī, Am′ram, Ū′el, 35 Be•nā′i•ah, Bē•dēi′ah, Chel′ū•hī, 36 Va•nī′ah, Mer′e•moth, E•lī′a•shib, 37 Mat•ta•nī′ah, Mat•tē′naī, and Jā•a′sū. 38 Of the descendants of Bin•nū•ī:s Shim′ē•ī, 39 Shel•e•mī′ah, Nathan, A•dāi′ah, 40 Mach•nad′e•baī, Shā′shaī, Shā′raī, 41 Az′a•rel, Shel-e•mī′ah, Shem•a•rī′ah, 42 Shal′lum, Am•a•rī′ah, and Joseph. 43 Of the descendants of Nē′bō: Je•ī′el, Mat-ti•thī′ah, Zā′bad, Ze•bī′na, Jad′daī, Jō′el, and Be•nā′-i•ah. 44 All these had married foreign women, and they sent them away with their children.t

---

q 1 Esdras 9.16: Syr: Heb *And there were selected Ezra,*
r 1 Esdras 9.26 Gk: Heb *Malchijah*   s Gk: Heb *Bani,*
Binnui   t 1 Esdras 9.36; meaning of Heb uncertain

Nehemiah

For background on this book, see the introduction to Ezra and Nehemiah, before Ezra.

Nehemiah Prays for His People

The words of Nē•he•mī′ah son of Hac•a•lī′ah. In the month of Chis′lev, in the twentieth year, while I was in Su′sa the capital, ²one of my brothers, Ha•nā′nī, came with certain men from Judah; and I asked them about the Jews that survived, those who had escaped the captivity, and about Jerusalem. ³They replied, "The survivors there in the province who escaped captivity are in great trouble and shame; the wall of Jerusalem is broken down, and its gates have been destroyed by fire."

4 When I heard these words I sat down and wept, and mourned for days, fasting and praying before the God of heaven. ⁵I said, "O LORD God of heaven, the great and awesome God who keeps covenant and steadfast love with those who love him and keep his commandments; ⁶let your ear be attentive and your eyes open to hear the prayer of your servant that I now pray before you day and night for your servants, the people of Israel, confessing the sins of the people of Israel, which we have sinned against you. Both I and my family have sinned. ⁷We have offended you deeply, failing to keep the commandments, the statutes, and the ordinances that you commanded your servant Moses. ⁸Remember the word that you commanded your servant Moses, 'If you are unfaithful, I will scatter you among the peoples; ⁹but if you return to me and keep my commandments and do them, though your outcasts are under the farthest skies, I will gather them from there and bring

them to the place at which I have chosen to establish my name.' ¹⁰They are your servants and your people, whom you redeemed by your great power and your strong hand. ¹¹O Lord, let your ear be attentive to the prayer of your servant, and to the prayer of your servants who delight in revering your name. Give success to your servant today, and grant him mercy in the sight of this man!"

At the time, I was cupbearer to the king.

Nehemiah Sent to Judah

In the month of Nī′san, in the twentieth year of King Ar•ta•xerx′ēs, when wine was served him, I carried the wine and gave it to the king. Now, I had never been sad in his presence before. ²So the king said to me, "Why is your face sad, since you are not sick? This can only be sadness of the heart." Then I was very much afraid. ³I said to the king, "May the king live forever! Why should my face not be sad, when the city, the place of my ancestors' graves, lies waste, and its gates have been destroyed by fire?" ⁴Then the king said to me, "What do you request?" So I prayed to the God of heaven. ⁵Then I said to the king, "If it pleases the king, and if your servant has found favor with you, I ask that you send me to Judah, to the city of my ancestors' graves, so that I may rebuild it." ⁶The king said to me (the queen also was sitting beside him), "How long will you be gone, and when will you return?" So it pleased the king to send me, and I set him a date. ⁷Then I said to the king, "If it pleases

PRAY IT!

Nehemiah Prepares for Action

Do you ever watch the news and think, Why bother trying to make the world a better place? Christians are called to social action—action for justice, action to make the world a better place. But social sin can scare Christians away from social action. Social sin—such as poverty, racism, violence, materialism, and indifference—seems too big for any individual to do much about. In the overwhelming face of social sin, it is easy to say, "I give up."

But then we have Nehemiah's example. When Nehemiah heard of the results of Israel's collective sin, he could have said, "I give up." Instead, he turned to God in fasting and prayer. Fasting and prayer help us focus on what is important. Fasting and prayer help us remember that God calls us only to be faithful in taking action. Let God worry about the results.

In your prayer, reflect or journal on the following questions:

- **What social issue are you concerned about?**
- **What can you fast from to help yourself gain a new perspective on that issue? (You can fast from many things: food, television, a particular activity, a particular place.)**
- **What group can you get involved with to address this concern?**
- **What do you need to bring to God in prayer?**

▶ Nehemiah, chapter 1

the king, let letters be given me to the governors of the province Beyond the River, that they may grant me passage until I arrive in Judah; 8 and a letter to Ā'saph, the keeper of the king's forest, directing him to give me timber to make beams for the gates of the temple fortress, and for the wall of the city, and for the house that I shall occupy." And the king granted me what I asked, for the gracious hand of my God was upon me.

9 Then I came to the governors of the province Beyond the River, and gave them the king's letters. Now the king had sent officers of the army and cavalry with me. 10 When San·bal'lat the Hor'o·nīte and Tō·bī'ah the Am'mon·ite official heard this, it displeased them greatly that someone had come to seek the welfare of the people of Israel.

Nehemiah's Inspection of the Walls

11 So I came to Jerusalem and was there for three days. 12 Then I got up during the night, I and a few men with me; I told no one what my God had put into my heart to do for Jerusalem. The only animal I took was the animal I rode. 13 I went out by night by the Valley Gate past the Dragon's Spring and to the Dung Gate, and I inspected the walls of Jerusalem that had been broken down and its gates that had been destroyed by fire. 14 Then I went on to the Fountain Gate and to the King's Pool; but there was no place for the animal I was riding to continue. 15 So I went up by way of the valley by night and inspected the wall. Then I turned back and entered by the Valley Gate, and so returned. 16 The officials did not know where I had gone or what I was doing; I had not yet told the Jews, the priests, the nobles, the officials, and the rest that were to do the work.

Decision to Restore the Walls

17 Then I said to them, "You see the trouble we are in, how Jerusalem lies in ruins with its gates burned. Come, let us rebuild the wall of Jerusalem, so that we may no longer suffer disgrace." 18 I told them that the hand of my God had been gracious upon me, and also the words that the king had spoken to me. Then they said, "Let us start building!" So they committed themselves to the common good. 19 But when San·bal'lat the Hor'o·nīte and Tō·bī'ah the Am'mon·ite official, and Gē'shem the A'rab heard of it, they mocked and ridiculed us, saying, "What is this that you are doing? Are you rebelling against the king?" 20 Then I replied to them, "The God of heaven is the one who will give us success, and we his servants are going to start building; but you have no share or claim or historic right in Jerusalem."

Organization of the Work

Then the high priest E·lī'a·shib set to work with his fellow priests and rebuilt the Sheep Gate. They consecrated it and set up its doors; they consecrated it as far as the Tower of the Hundred and as far as the Tower of Ha·nan'el. 2 And the men of

Jericho built next to him. And next to them*a* Zac'-cur son of Im'ri built.

3 The sons of Has·se·nā'ah built the Fish Gate; they laid its beams and set up its doors, its bolts, and its bars. 4 Next to them Mer'e·moth son of Ū·rī'ah son of Hak'koz made repairs. Next to them Me·shul'lam son of Ber·e·chī'ah son of Me·shez'a·bel made repairs. Next to them Zā'dok son of Bā'a·na made repairs. 5 Next to them the Te·kō'ites made repairs; but their nobles would not put their shoulders to the work of their Lord.*b*

6 Joi'a·da son of Pa·sē'ah and Me·shul'lam son of Bes·o·dēi'ah repaired the Old Gate; they laid its beams and set up its doors, its bolts, and its bars. 7 Next to them repairs were made by Me·la·tī'ah the Gib'ē·on·ite and Jā'don the Me·ron'o·thīte—the men of Gib'ē·on and of Miz'pah—who were under the jurisdiction of*c* the governor of the province Beyond the River. 8 Next to them Uz'zi·el son of Har·haī'ah, one of the goldsmiths, made repairs. Next to him Han·a·nī'ah, one of the perfumers, made repairs; and they restored Jerusalem as far as the Broad Wall. 9 Next to them Reph·aī'ah son of Hur, ruler of half the district of*d* Jerusalem, made repairs. 10 Next to them Je·dai'ah son of Har·ū'maph made repairs opposite his house; and next to him Hat'tush son of Hash·ab·neī'ah made repairs. 11 Mal·chī'jah son of Hā'rim and Has'shub son of Pā'hath-mō'ab repaired another section and the Tower of the Ovens. 12 Next to him Shal'lum son of Hal·lō'hesh, ruler of half the district of*d* Jerusalem, made repairs, he and his daughters.

13 Hā'nun and the inhabitants of Za·nō'ah repaired the Valley Gate; they rebuilt it and set up its doors, its bolts, and its bars, and repaired a thousand cubits of the wall, as far as the Dung Gate.

14 Mal·chī'jah son of Rē'chab, ruler of the district of*e* Beth-hac·chē'rem, repaired the Dung Gate; he rebuilt it and set up its doors, its bolts, and its bars.

15 And Shal'lum son of Col-hō'zeh, ruler of the district of*e* Miz'pah, repaired the Fountain Gate; he rebuilt it and covered it and set up its doors, its bolts, and its bars; and he built the wall of the Pool of Shē'lah of the king's garden, as far as the stairs that go down from the City of David. 16 After him Nē·he·mī'ah son of Az'buk, ruler of half the district of*d* Beth-zur, repaired from a point opposite the graves of David, as far as the artificial pool and the house of the warriors. 17 After him the Lē'vites made repairs: Rē'hum son of Bā'ni; next to him Hash·a·bī'ah, ruler of half the district of*d* Kē·i'lah, made repairs for his district. 18 After him their kin made repairs: Bin'nū·i,*f* son of Hen'a·dad, ruler of half the district of*d* Kē·i'lah; 19 next to him E'zer son of Jesh'ū·a, ruler*g* of Miz'pah, re-

paired another section opposite the ascent to the armory at the Angle. 20 After him Bar'uch son of Zab'bai repaired another section from the Angle to the door of the house of the high priest E·lī'a·shib. 21 After him Mer'e·moth son of Ū·rī'ah son of Hak'koz repaired another section from the door of the house of E·lī'a·shib to the end of the house of E·lī'a·shib. 22 After him the priests, the men of the surrounding area, made repairs. 23 After them Benjamin and Has'shub made repairs opposite their house. After them Az·a·rī'ah son of Mā·a·sēi'ah son of An·a·nī'ah made repairs beside his own house. 24 After him Bin'nū·i son of Hen'a·dad repaired another section, from the house of Az·a·rī'ah to the Angle and to the corner. 25 Pā'lal son of Ū'zai repaired opposite the Angle and the tower projecting from the upper house of the king at the court of the guard. After him Pe·dāi'ah son of Pā'rosh 26 and the temple servants living*h* on Ō'phel made repairs up to a point opposite the Water Gate on the east and the projecting tower. 27 After him the Te·kō'ites repaired another section opposite the great projecting tower as far as the wall of Ō'phel.

28 Above the Horse Gate the priests made repairs, each one opposite his own house. 29 After them Zā'dok son of Im'mer made repairs opposite his own house. After him She·māi'ah son of Shec·a·nī'ah, the keeper of the East Gate, made repairs. 30 After him Han·a·nī'ah son of Shel·e·mī'ah and Hā'nun sixth son of Zā'laph repaired another section. After him Me·shul'lam son of Ber·e·chī'ah made repairs opposite his living quarters. 31 After him Mal·chī'jah, one of the goldsmiths, made repairs as far as the house of the temple servants and of the merchants, opposite the Muster Gate,*i* and to the upper room of the corner. 32 And between the upper room of the corner and the Sheep Gate the goldsmiths and the merchants made repairs.

Hostile Plots Thwarted

4 *j*Now when San·bal'lat heard that we were building the wall, he was angry and greatly enraged, and he mocked the Jews. 2 He said in the presence of his associates and of the army of Sa·mār'i·a, "What are these feeble Jews doing? Will they restore things? Will they sacrifice? Will they finish it in a day? Will they revive the stones out of the heaps of rubbish—and burned ones at that?" 3 Tō·bī'ah the Am'mon·īte was beside him, and he said, "That stone wall they are building—any fox going

---

a Heb *him*   *b* Or *lords*   *c* Meaning of Heb uncertain
d Or *supervisor of half the portion assigned to*   *e* Or *supervisor of the portion assigned to*   *f* Gk Syr Compare verse 24, 10.9: Heb *Bavvai*   *g* Or *supervisor*   *h* Cn: Heb *were living*
i Or *Hammiphkad Gate*   *j* Ch 3.33 in Heb

up on it would break it down!" [4] Hear, O our God, for we are despised; turn their taunt back on their own heads, and give them over as plunder in a land of captivity. [5] Do not cover their guilt, and do not let their sin be blotted out from your sight; for they have hurled insults in the face of the builders.

6 So we rebuilt the wall, and all the wall was joined together to half its height; for the people had a mind to work.

and awesome, and fight for your kin, your sons, your daughters, your wives, and your homes."

15 When our enemies heard that their plot was known to us, and that God had frustrated it, we all returned to the wall, each to his work. [16] From that day on, half of my servants worked on construction, and half held the spears, shields, bows, and body-armor; and the leaders posted themselves behind the whole house of Judah, [17] who were build-

Nehemiah's Strength

Many young people have traumatic experiences, such as the divorce of their parents, domestic and community violence, the death of a parent or sibling, prejudice, and poverty. Some young people come through these experiences as victims, unable to take any control of their life. Others take the attitude If you can't beat them, join them, and become cynical, violent, or antisocial. But some rise above their hurt to live a happy and healthy life. What can account for the difference in people's reactions?

Perhaps Nehemiah provides a clue. He was confronted by cynical people (Neh 4.2–3) and violent people (verses 7–9). But he trusted in something bigger than himself. "The God of heaven is the one who will give us success" (2.20), he proclaimed to those with negative attitudes.

Prayer and faith in God gave Nehemiah strength to take action in difficult times. They can work for us too. Don't let life's traumas make you powerless. Don't let them make you cynical and part of the problem. Pray and have faith, and you too will have the strength to meet your problems with action.

▶ Nehemiah, chapter 4

7[k] But when San·bal'lat and Tō·bī'ah and the Arabs and the Am'mon·ites and the Ash'dod·ites heard that the repairing of the walls of Jerusalem was going forward and the gaps were beginning to be closed, they were very angry, [8] and all plotted together to come and fight against Jerusalem and to cause confusion in it. [9] So we prayed to our God, and set a guard as a protection against them day and night.

10 But Judah said, "The strength of the burden bearers is failing, and there is too much rubbish so that we are unable to work on the wall." [11] And our enemies said, "They will not know or see anything before we come upon them and kill them and stop the work." [12] When the Jews who lived near them came, they said to us ten times, "From all the places where they live[l] they will come up against us."[m] [13] So in the lowest parts of the space behind the wall, in open places, I stationed the people according to their families,[n] with their swords, their spears, and their bows. [14] After I looked these things over, I stood up and said to the nobles and the officials and the rest of the people, "Do not be afraid of them. Remember the LORD, who is great

ing the wall. The burden bearers carried their loads in such a way that each labored on the work with one hand and with the other held a weapon. [18] And each of the builders had his sword strapped at his side while he built. The man who sounded the trumpet was beside me. [19] And I said to the nobles, the officials, and the rest of the people, "The work is great and widely spread out, and we are separated far from one another on the wall. [20] Rally to us wherever you hear the sound of the trumpet. Our God will fight for us."

21 So we labored at the work, and half of them held the spears from break of dawn until the stars came out. [22] I also said to the people at that time, "Let every man and his servant pass the night inside Jerusalem, so that they may be a guard for us by night and may labor by day." [23] So neither I nor my brothers nor my servants nor the men of the guard who followed me ever took off our clothes; each kept his weapon in his right hand.[o]

---

[k] Ch 4.1 in Heb   [l] Cn: Heb *you return*   [m] Compare Gk Syr: Meaning of Heb uncertain   [n] Meaning of Heb uncertain   [o] Cn: Heb *each his weapon the water*

Nehemiah Deals with Oppression

Now there was a great outcry of the people and of their wives against their Jewish kin. 2 For there were those who said, "With our sons and our daughters, we are many; we must get grain, so that we may eat and stay alive." 3 There were also those who said, "We are having to pledge our fields, our vineyards, and our houses in order to get grain during the famine." 4 And there were those who said, "We are having to borrow money on our fields and vineyards to pay the king's tax. 5 Now our flesh is the same as that of our kindred; our children are the same as their children; and yet we are forcing our sons and daughters to be slaves, and some of our daughters have been ravished; we are powerless, and our fields and vineyards now belong to others."

6 I was very angry when I heard their outcry and these complaints. 7 After thinking it over, I brought charges against the nobles and the officials; I said to them, "You are all taking interest from your own people." And I called a great assembly to deal with them, 8 and said to them, "As far as we were able, we have bought back our Jewish kindred who had been sold to other nations; but now you are selling your own kin, who must then be bought back by us!" They were silent, and could not find a word to say. 9 So I said, "The thing that you are doing is not good. Should you not walk in the fear of our God, to prevent the taunts of the nations our enemies? 10 Moreover I and my brothers and my servants are lending them money and grain. Let us stop this taking of interest. 11 Restore to them, this very day, their fields, their vineyards, their olive orchards, and their houses, and the interest on money, grain, wine, and oil that you have been exacting from them." 12 Then they said, "We will restore everything and demand nothing more from them. We will do as you say." And I called the priests, and made them take an oath to do as they had promised. 13 I also shook out the fold of my garment and said, "So may God shake out everyone from house and from property who does not perform this promise. Thus may they be shaken out and emptied." And all the assembly said, "Amen," and praised the LORD. And the people did as they had promised.

The Generosity of Nehemiah

14 Moreover from the time that I was appointed to be their governor in the land of Judah, from the twentieth year to the thirty-second year of King Ar·ta·xerx′es, twelve years, neither I nor my brothers ate the food allowance of the governor.

LIVE IT!

Hunger Pains

"I'm hungry."

"Yeah, I'm starved. Let's go get something to eat."

How many times have we uttered those words or heard them said? It's so easy. If we're hungry, we eat. If we're thirsty, we grab something to drink. If we're not feeling well, we get something to make us feel better. We forget sometimes that our way of doing things is the exception in the world, not the rule. Right now, people in this country and in the rest of the world are starving and have no idea where their next meal is coming from.

When Nehemiah's people were hungry, he saw the problem right away. The problem was not a lack of food. It was that some people were using their wealth and influence to control who got the food (Neh 5.7–8). Nehemiah took the radical step of demanding that the powerful and wealthy stop taking advantage of those less well off. He suggested that the wealthy redistribute their property to the poor so that they could feed themselves (verses 10–11).

Experts tell us that much the same is true today. People are starving not because food is scarce but because political and economic conditions prevent them from getting the food. If only we could be like Nehemiah and demand that the powerful and wealthy reform. Well, you know what? We can! We can educate ourselves and speak out through letters and phone calls to elected officials. And while we are calling for society to change, let's volunteer at a neighborhood pantry or soup kitchen to help feed the poor people in our own backyard.

▸ Nehemiah, chapter 5

15 The former governors who were before me laid heavy burdens on the people, and took food and wine from them, besides forty shekels of silver. Even their servants lorded it over the people. But I did not do so, because of the fear of God. 16 Indeed, I devoted myself to the work on this wall, and acquired no land; and all my servants were gathered there for the work. 17 Moreover there were at my table one hundred fifty people, Jews and officials, besides those who came to us from the nations around us. 18 Now that which was prepared for one day was one ox and six choice sheep; also fowls were prepared for me, and every ten days skins of wine in abundance; yet with all this I did not demand the food allowance of the governor, because of the heavy burden of labor on the people. 19 Remember for my good, O my God, all that I have done for this people.

Intrigues of Enemies Foiled

Now when it was reported to San·bal'lat and Tō·bi'ah and to Gē'shem the A'rab and to the rest of our enemies that I had built the wall and that there was no gap left in it (though up to that time I had not set up the doors in the gates), 2 San·bal'-lat and Gē'shem sent to me, saying, "Come and let us meet together in one of the villages in the plain of O'nō." But they intended to do me harm. 3 So I sent messengers to them, saying, "I am doing a great work and I cannot come down. Why should the work stop while I leave it to come down to you?" 4 They sent to me four times in this way, and I answered them in the same manner. 5 In the same way San·bal'lat for the fifth time sent his servant to me with an open letter in his hand. 6 In it was written, "It is reported among the nations—and Gē'shem p also says it—that you and the Jews intend to rebel; that is why you are building the wall; and according to this report you wish to become their king. 7 You have also set up prophets to proclaim in Jerusalem concerning you, 'There is a king in Judah!' And now it will be reported to the king according to these words. So come, therefore, and let us confer together." 8 Then I sent to him, saying, "No such things as you say have been done; you are inventing them out of your own mind" 9 —for they all wanted to frighten us, thinking, "Their hands will drop from the work, and it will not be done." But now, O God, strengthen my hands.

10 One day when I went into the house of She·māi'ah son of De·lai'ah son of Me·het'a·bel, who was confined to his house, he said, "Let us meet together in the house of God, within the temple, and let us close the doors of the temple, for they are coming to kill you; indeed, tonight they are coming to kill you." 11 But I said, "Should a man like me run away? Would a man like me go into the temple to save his life? I will not go in!" 12 Then I perceived and saw that God had not sent him at all, but he had pronounced the prophecy against me because Tō·bi'ah and San·bal'lat had hired him. 13 He was hired for this purpose, to intimidate me and make me sin by acting in this way, and so they could give me a bad name, in order to taunt me. 14 Remember Tō·bi'ah and San-bal'lat, O my God, according to these things that they did, and also the prophetess Nō·a·di'ah and the rest of the prophets who wanted to make me afraid.

The Wall Completed

15 So the wall was finished on the twenty-fifth day of the month Ē'lul, in fifty-two days. 16 And when all our enemies heard of it, all the nations around us were afraid q and fell greatly in their own esteem; for they perceived that this work had been accomplished with the help of our God. 17 Moreover in those days the nobles of Judah sent many letters to Tō·bi'ah, and Tō·bi'ah's letters came to them. 18 For many in Judah were bound by oath to him, because he was the son-in-law of Shec·a·ni'ah son of A'rah: and his son Jē·hō·hā'nan had married the daughter of Me·shul'lam son of Ber·e·chi'ah. 19 Also they spoke of his good deeds in my presence, and reported my words to him. And Tō·bi'ah sent letters to intimidate me.

Now when the wall had been built and I had set up the doors, and the gatekeepers, the singers, and the Lē'vites had been appointed, 2 I gave my brother Ha·na'ni charge over Jerusalem, along with Han·a·ni'ah the commander of the citadel—for he was a faithful man and feared God more than many. 3 And I said to them, "The gates of Jerusalem are not to be opened until the sun is hot; while the gatekeepers r are still standing guard, let them shut and bar the doors. Appoint guards from among the inhabitants of Jerusalem, some at their watch posts, and others before their own houses." 4 The city was wide and large, but the people within it were few and no houses had been built.

Lists of the Returned Exiles
(Ezra 2.1–70)

5 Then my God put it into my mind to assemble the nobles and the officials and the people to be enrolled by genealogy. And I found the book of the genealogy of those who were the first to come back, and I found the following written in it:

---

p Heb *Gashmu*   q Another reading is *saw*   r Heb *while they*

6 These are the people of the province who came up out of the captivity of those exiles whom King Ne•bu•chad•nez′zar of Babylon had carried into exile; they returned to Jerusalem and Judah, each to his town. 7 They came with Ze•rub′ba•bel, Jesh′u•a, Ne•he•mi′ah, Az•a•ri′ah, Ra•a•mi′ah, Na•ham′a•ni, Mor′de•cai, Bil′shan, Mis′pe•reth, Big′vai, Ne′hum, Ba′a•nah.

The number of the Israelite people: 8 the descendants of Pa′rosh, two thousand one hundred seventy-two. 9 Of Sheph•a•ti′ah, three hundred seventy-two. 10 Of A′rah, six hundred fifty-two. 11 Of Pa′hath-mo′ab, namely the descendants of Jesh′u•a and Jo′ab, two thousand eight hundred eighteen. 12 Of E′lam, one thousand two hundred fifty-four. 13 Of Zat′tu, eight hundred forty-five. 14 Of Zac′cai, seven hundred sixty. 15 Of Bin′nu•i, six hundred forty-eight. 16 Of Be′bai, six hundred twenty-eight. 17 Of Az′gad, two thousand three hundred twenty-two. 18 Of Ad•o•ni′kam, six hundred sixty-seven. 19 Of Big′vai, two thousand sixty-seven. 20 Of A′din, six hundred fifty-five. 21 Of A′ter, namely of Hez•e•ki′ah, ninety-eight. 22 Of Ha′shum, three hundred twenty-eight. 23 Of Be′zai, three hundred twenty-four. 24 Of Ha′riph, one hundred twelve. 25 Of Gib′e•on, ninety-five. 26 The people of Bethlehem and Ne•toph′ah, one hundred eighty-eight. 27 Of An′a•thoth, one hundred twenty-eight. 28 Of Beth-az′ma•veth, forty-two. 29 Of Kir′i•ath-je′a•rim, Che•phi′rah, and Be•er′oth, seven hundred forty-three. 30 Of Ra′mah and Ge′ba, six hundred twenty-one. 31 Of Mich′mas, one hundred twenty-two. 32 Of Beth′el and Ai, one hundred twenty-three. 33 Of the other Ne′bo, fifty-two. 34 The descendants of the other E′lam, one thousand two hundred fifty-four. 35 Of Ha′rim, three hundred twenty. 36 Of Jericho, three hundred forty-five. 37 Of Lod, Ha′did, and O′no, seven hundred twenty-one. 38 Of Se•na′ah, three thousand nine hundred thirty.

39 The priests: the descendants of Je•dai′ah, namely the house of Jesh′u•a, nine hundred seventy-three. 40 Of Im′mer, one thousand fifty-two. 41 Of Pash′hur, one thousand two hundred forty-seven. 42 Of Ha′rim, one thousand seventeen.

43 The Le′vites: the descendants of Jesh′u•a, namely of Kad′mi•el of the descendants of Ho′de•vah, seventy-four. 44 The singers: the descendants of A′saph, one hundred forty-eight. 45 The gatekeepers: the descendants of Shal′lum, of A′ter, of Tal′mon, of Ak′kub, of Ha•ti′ta, of Sho′bai, one hundred thirty-eight.

46 The temple servants: the descendants of Zi′ha, of Ha•su′pha, of Tab•ba′oth, 47 of Ke′ros, of Si′a, of Pa′don, 48 of Le•ba′na, of Hag′a•ba, of Shal′-mai, 49 of Ha′nan, of Gid′del, of Ga′har, 50 of Re•ai′ah, of Re′zin, of Ne•ko′da, 51 of Gaz′zam, of Uz′za, of Pa•se′ah, 52 of Be′sai, of Me•u′nim, of Ne•phush′e•sim, 53 of Bak′buk, of Ha•ku′pha, of Har′-hur, 54 of Baz′lith, of Me•hi′da, of Har′sha, 55 of Bar′kos, of Sis′e•ra, of Te′mah, 56 of Ne•zi′ah, of Ha•ti′pha.

57 The descendants of Solomon's servants: of So′tai, of So′phe•reth, of Pe•ri′da, 58 of Ja′a•la, of Dar′kon, of Gid′del, 59 of Sheph•a•ti′ah, of Hat′til, of Po′che•reth-haz•ze•ba′im, of A′mon.

60 All the temple servants and the descendants of Solomon's servants were three hundred ninety-two.

61 The following were those who came up from Tel-me′lah, Tel-har′sha, Che′rub, Ad′don, and Im′mer, but they could not prove their ancestral houses or their descent, whether they belonged to Israel: 62 the descendants of De•lai′ah, of To•bi′ah, of Ne•ko′da, six hundred forty-two. 63 Also, of the priests: the descendants of Ho•bai′ah, of Hak′koz, of Bar•zil′lai (who had married one of the daughters of Bar•zil′lai the Gil′e•ad•ite and was called by their name). 64 These sought their registration among those enrolled in the genealogies, but it was not found there, so they were excluded from the priesthood as unclean; 65 the governor told them that they were not to partake of the most holy food, until a priest with U′rim and Thum′mim should come.

66 The whole assembly together was forty-two thousand three hundred sixty, 67 besides their male and female slaves, of whom there were seven thousand three hundred thirty-seven; and they had two hundred forty-five singers, male and female. 68 They had seven hundred thirty-six horses, two hundred forty-five mules,ˢ 69 four hundred thirty-five camels, and six thousand seven hundred twenty donkeys.

70 Now some of the heads of ancestral houses contributed to the work. The governor gave to the treasury one thousand darics of gold, fifty basins, and five hundred thirty priestly robes. 71 And some of the heads of ancestral houses gave into the building fund twenty thousand darics of gold and two thousand two hundred minas of silver. 72 And what the rest of the people gave was twenty thousand darics of gold, two thousand minas of silver, and sixty-seven priestly robes.

73 So the priests, the Le′vites, the gatekeepers, the singers, some of the people, the temple servants, and all Israel settled in their towns.

ˢ Ezra 2.66 and the margins of some Hebrew Mss: MT lacks *They had . . . forty-five mules*

Ezra Summons the People to Obey the Law

When the seventh month came—the people of Israel being settled in their towns— [1] all the people gathered together into the square before the Water Gate. They told the scribe Ezra to bring the book of the law of Moses, which the LORD had given to Israel. [2] Accordingly, the priest Ezra brought the law before the assembly, both men and women and all who could hear with understanding. This was on the first day of the seventh month. [3] He read from it facing the square before the Water Gate from early morning until midday, in the presence of the men and the women and those who could understand; and the ears of all the people were attentive to the book of the law. [4] The scribe Ezra stood on a wooden platform that had been made for the purpose; and beside him stood Mat·ti·thi'ah, She'ma, A·nai'ah, U·ri'ah, Hil·ki'ah, and Ma·a·sei'ah on his right hand; and Pe·dai'ah, Mish'a·el, Mal·chi'jah, Ha'shum, Hash·bad'da·nah, Zech·a·ri'ah, and Me·shul'lam on his left hand. [5] And Ezra opened the book in the sight of all the people, for he was standing above all the people; and when he opened it, all the people stood up. [6] Then Ezra blessed the LORD, the great God, and all the people answered, "Amen, Amen," lifting up their hands. Then they bowed their heads and worshiped the LORD with their faces to the ground. [7] Also Jesh'u·a, Ba'ni, Sher·e·bi'ah, Ja'min, Ak'kub, Shab'be·thai, Ho·di'ah, Ma·a·sei'ah, Ke·li'ta, Az·a·ri'ah, Joz'a·bad, Ha'nan, Pe·lai'ah, the Le'vites,[t] helped the people to understand the law, while the people remained in their places. [8] So they read from the book, from the law of God, with interpretation. They gave the sense, so that the people understood the reading.

[9] And Ne·he·mi'ah, who was the governor, and Ezra the priest and scribe, and the Le'vites who taught the people said to all the people, "This day is holy to the LORD your God; do not mourn or weep." For all the people wept when they heard the words of the law. [10] Then he said to them, "Go your way, eat the fat and drink sweet wine and send portions of them to those for whom nothing is prepared, for this day is holy to our LORD; and do not be grieved, for the joy of the LORD is your strength." [11] So the Le'vites stilled all the people, saying, "Be quiet, for this day is holy; do not be grieved." [12] And all the people went their way to eat and drink and to send portions and to make great rejoicing, because they had understood the words that were declared to them.

The Festival of Booths Celebrated
(Cp Lev 23.33–43)

[13] On the second day the heads of ancestral houses of all the people, with the priests and the Le'vites, came together to the scribe Ezra in order to study the words of the law. [14] And they found it written in the law, which the LORD had commanded by Moses, that the people of Israel should live in booths[u] during the festival of the seventh month, [15] and that they should publish and proclaim in all their towns and in Jerusalem as follows, "Go out to the hills and bring branches of olive, wild olive, myrtle, palm, and other leafy

Catholic Connections

GATHERING TO PRAY

It is good for us to gather as church and worship God.

Notice how the event described in Neh 8.1–12 sounds similar to some parts of the Mass. The people gather, read and reflect, renew a covenant with God, and offer a great "Amen, Amen!" Finally, they are blessed to go forth and share what they have with one another.

Several times, the people at this event heard, "This day is holy." We set aside Sunday as a holy day, a Sabbath day. What do you do to make this day holy? Can you do something to make it even more special?

▸ Neh 8.1–12

trees to make booths,[u] as it is written." [16] So the people went out and brought them, and made booths[u] for themselves, each on the roofs of their houses, and in their courts and in the courts of the house of God, and in the square at the Water Gate and in the square at the Gate of E'phra·im. [17] And all the assembly of those who had returned from

t 1 Esdras 9.48 Vg: Heb and the Levites   u Or tabernacles; Heb succoth

the captivity made booths[v] and lived in them; for from the days of Jesh'ū•a son of Nun to that day the people of Israel had not done so. And there was very great rejoicing. 18 And day by day, from the first day to the last day, he read from the book of the law of God. They kept the festival seven days; and on the eighth day there was a solemn assembly, according to the ordinance.

National Confession

Now on the twenty-fourth day of this month the people of Israel were assembled with fasting and in sackcloth, and with earth on their heads.[w] 2 Then those of Israelite descent separated themselves from all foreigners, and stood and confessed their sins and the iniquities of their ancestors. 3 They stood up in their place and read from the book of the law of the LORD their God for a fourth part of the day, and for another fourth they made confession and worshiped the LORD their God. 4 Then Jesh'ū•a, Bā'nī, Kad'mi•el, Sheb•a•nī'ah, Bun'nī, Sher•e•bī'ah, Bā'nī, and Che•nā'nī stood on the stairs of the Lē'vītes and cried out with a loud voice to the LORD their God. 5 Then the Lē'vītes, Jesh'ū•a, Kad'mi•el, Bā'nī, Hash•ab•neī'ah, Sher•e•bī'ah, Hō•dī'ah, Sheb•a•nī'ah, and Peth•a•hī'ah, said, "Stand up and bless the LORD your God from everlasting to everlasting. Blessed be your glorious name, which is exalted above all blessing and praise."

and

bless the LORD your God

STAND UP

from everlasting to everlasting

9.5

6 And Ezra said:[x] "You are the LORD, you alone; you have made heaven, the heaven of heavens, with all their host, the earth and all that is on it, the seas and all that is in them. To all of them you give life, and the host of heaven worships you. 7 You are the LORD, the God who chose Abram and brought him out of Ūr of the Chal•dē'ans and gave him the name Abraham; 8 and you found his heart

faithful before you, and made with him a covenant to give to his descendants the land of the Cā'naan•īte, the Hit'tīte, the Am'o•rīte, the Per'iz•zīte, the Jeb'ū•sīte, and the Gir'ga•shīte; and you have fulfilled your promise, for you are righteous.

9 "And you saw the distress of our ancestors in Egypt and heard their cry at the Red Sea.[y] 10 You performed signs and wonders against Pharaoh and all his servants and all the people of his land, for you knew that they acted insolently against our ancestors. You made a name for yourself, which remains to this day. 11 And you divided the sea before them, so that they passed through the sea on dry land, but you threw their pursuers into the depths, like a stone into mighty waters. 12 Moreover, you led them by day with a pillar of cloud, and by night with a pillar of fire, to give them light on the way in which they should go. 13 You came down also upon Mount Sinai, and spoke with them from heaven, and gave them right ordinances and true laws, good statutes and commandments, 14 and you made known your holy sabbath to them and gave them commandments and statutes and a law through your servant Moses. 15 For their hunger you gave them bread from heaven, and for their thirst you brought water for them out of the rock, and you told them to go in to possess the land that you swore to give them.

16 "But they and our ancestors acted presumptuously and stiffened their necks and did not obey your commandments; 17 they refused to obey, and were not mindful of the wonders that you performed among them; but they stiffened their necks and determined to return to their slavery in Egypt. But you are a God ready to forgive, gracious and merciful, slow to anger and abounding in steadfast love, and you did not forsake them. 18 Even when they had cast an image of a calf for themselves and said, 'This is your God who brought you up out of Egypt,' and had committed great blasphemies, 19 you in your great mercies did not forsake them in the wilderness; the pillar of cloud that led them in the way did not leave them by day, nor the pillar of fire by night that gave them light on the way by which they should go. 20 You gave your good spirit to instruct them, and did not withhold your manna from their mouths, and gave them water for their thirst. 21 Forty years you sustained them in the wilderness so that they lacked nothing; their clothes did not wear out and their feet did not swell. 22 And you gave them kingdoms and peoples, and allotted to them every corner,[z] so they took possession of the land of King Sī'hon of

---

v Or *tabernacles;* Heb *succoth*　　*w* Heb *on them*　　*x* Gk: Heb lacks *And Ezra said*　　*y* Or *Sea of Reeds*　　*z* Meaning of Heb uncertain

Hesh'bon and the land of King Og of Bā'shan. 23 You multiplied their descendants like the stars of heaven, and brought them into the land that you had told their ancestors to enter and possess. 24 So the descendants went in and possessed the land, and you subdued before them the inhabitants of the land, the Cā'naan·ites, and gave them into their hands, with their kings and the peoples of the land, to do with them as they pleased. 25 And they captured fortress cities and a rich land, and took possession of houses filled with all sorts of goods, hewn cisterns, vineyards, olive orchards, and fruit trees in abundance; so they ate, and were filled and became fat, and delighted themselves in your great goodness.

26 "Nevertheless they were disobedient and rebelled against you and cast your law behind their backs and killed your prophets, who had warned them in order to turn them back to you, and they committed great blasphemies. 27 Therefore you gave them into the hands of their enemies, who made them suffer. Then in the time of their suffering they cried out to you and you heard them from heaven, and according to your great mercies you gave them saviors who saved them from the hands of their enemies. 28 But after they had rest, they again did evil before you, and you abandoned them to the hands of their enemies, so that they had dominion over them; yet when they turned and cried to you, you heard from heaven, and many times you rescued them according to your mercies. 29 And you warned them in order to turn them back to your law. Yet they acted presumptuously and did not obey your commandments, but sinned against your ordinances, by the observance of which a person shall live. They turned a stubborn shoulder and stiffened their neck and would not obey. 30 Many years you were patient with them, and warned them by your spirit through your prophets; yet they would not listen. Therefore you handed them over to the peoples of the lands. 31 Nevertheless, in your great mercies you did not make an end of them or forsake them, for you are a gracious and merciful God.

32 "Now therefore, our God—the great and mighty and awesome God, keeping covenant and steadfast love—do not treat lightly all the hardship that has come upon us, upon our kings, our officials, our priests, our prophets, our ancestors, and all your people, since the time of the kings of Assyria until today. 33 You have been just in all that has come upon us, for you have dealt faithfully and we have acted wickedly; 34 our kings, our officials, our priests, and our ancestors have not kept your law or heeded the commandments and the warnings that you gave them. 35 Even in their own

kingdom, and in the great goodness you bestowed on them, and in the large and rich land that you set before them, they did not serve you and did not turn from their wicked works. 36 Here we are, slaves to this day—slaves in the land that you gave to our ancestors to enjoy its fruit and its good gifts. 37 Its rich yield goes to the kings whom you have set over us because of our sins; they have power also over our bodies and over our livestock at their pleasure, and we are in great distress."

Those Who Signed the Covenant

38 a Because of all this we make a firm agreement in writing, and on that sealed document are inscribed the names of our officials, our Lē'vites, and our priests.

b Upon the sealed document are the names of Nēhe·mī'ah the governor, son of Hac·a·lī'ah, and Zed·e·kī'ah; 2 Se·rāi'ah, Az·a·rī'ah, Jer·e·mī'ah, 3 Pash'hur, Am·a·rī'ah, Mal·chī'jah, 4 Hat'tush, Sheb·a·nī'ah, Mal'luch, 5 Hā'rim, Mer'e·moth, Ō·ba·dī'ah, 6 Daniel, Gin'ne·thon, Bar'uch, 7 Me·shul'lam, A·bī'jah, Mij'a·min, 8 Mā·a·zī'ah, Bil'gai, She·māi'ah; these are the priests. 9 And the Lē'vites: Jesh'ū·a son of Az·a·nī'ah, Bin'nū·ī of the sons of Hen'a·dad, Kad'mi·el; 10 and their associates, Sheb·a·nī'ah, Hō·dī'ah, Ke·lī'ta, Pe·lāi'ah, Hā'nan, 11 Mī'ca, Rē'hob, Hasha·bī'ah, 12 Zac'cur, Sher·e·bī'ah, Sheb·a·nī'ah, 13 Hō·dī'ah, Bā'ni, Be·nī'nū. 14 The leaders of the people: Pā'rosh, Pā'hath-mō'ab, Ē'lam, Zat'tū, Bā'ni, 15 Bun'ni, Az'gad, Bē'bai, 16 Ad·o·nī'jah, Big'vai, Ā'din, 17 Ā'ter, Hez·e·kī'ah, Az'zur, 18 Hō·dī'ah, Hā'shum, Bē'zai, 19 Hā'riph, An'a·thoth, Nē'bai, 20 Mag'pi·ash, Me·shul'lam, Hē'zir, 21 Meshez'a·bel, Zā'dok, Jad'dū·a, 22 Pel·a·tī'ah, Hā'nan, A·nai'ah, 23 Hō·shē'a, Han·a·nī'ah, Has'shub, 24 Hallō'hesh, Pil'ha, Shō'bek, 25 Rē'hum, Ha·shab'nah, Mā·a·sēi'ah, 26 A·hī'ah, Hā'nan, Ā'nan, 27 Mal'luch, Hā'rim, and Bā'a·nah.

Summary of the Covenant

28 The rest of the people, the priests, the Lē'vites, the gatekeepers, the singers, the temple servants, and all who have separated themselves from the peoples of the lands to adhere to the law of God, their wives, their sons, their daughters, all who have knowledge and understanding, 29 join with their kin, their nobles, and enter into a curse and an oath to walk in God's law, which was given by Moses the servant of God, and to observe and do all the commandments of the LORD our Lord and his ordinances and his statutes. 30 We will not give our daughters to the peoples of the land or take their daughters for our sons; 31 and if the

a Ch 10.1 in Heb   b Ch 10.2 in Heb

peoples of the land bring in merchandise or any grain on the sabbath day to sell, we will not buy it from them on the sabbath or on a holy day; and we will forego the crops of the seventh year and the exaction of every debt.

32 We also lay on ourselves the obligation to charge ourselves yearly one-third of a shekel for the service of the house of our God: 33 for the rows of bread, the regular grain offering, the regular burnt offering, the sabbaths, the new moons, the appointed festivals, the sacred donations, and the sin offerings to make atonement for Israel, and for all the work of the house of our God. 34 We have also cast lots among the priests, the Le′vītes, and the people, for the wood offering, to bring it into the house of our God, by ancestral houses, at appointed times, year by year, to burn on the altar of the LORD our God, as it is written in the law. 35 We obligate ourselves to bring the first fruits of our soil and the first fruits of all fruit of every tree, year by year, to the house of the LORD; 36 also to bring to the house of our God, to the priests who minister in the house of our God, the firstborn of our sons and of our livestock, as it is written in the law, and the firstlings of our herds and of our flocks; 37 and to bring the first of our dough, and our contributions, the fruit of every tree, the wine and the oil, to the priests, to the chambers of the house of our God; and to bring to the Le′vītes the tithes from our soil, for it is the Le′vītes who collect the tithes in all our rural towns. 38 And the priest, the descendant of Aaron, shall be with the Le′vītes when the Le′vītes receive the tithes; and the Le′vītes shall bring up a tithe of the tithes to the house of our God, to the chambers of the storehouse. 39 For the people of Israel and the sons of Levi shall bring the contribution of grain, wine, and oil to the storerooms where the vessels of the sanctuary are, and where the priests that minister, and the gatekeepers and the singers are. We will not neglect the house of our God.

Population of the City Increased

Now the leaders of the people lived in Jerusalem; and the rest of the people cast lots to bring one out of ten to live in the holy city Jerusalem, while nine-tenths remained in the other towns. 2 And the people blessed all those who willingly offered to live in Jerusalem.

3 These are the leaders of the province who lived in Jerusalem; but in the towns of Judah all lived on their property in their towns: Israel, the priests, the Le′vītes, the temple servants, and the descendants of Solomon's servants. 4 And in Jerusalem lived some of the Ju′dah·ītes and of the Ben′ja·min·ītes. Of the Ju′dah·ītes: A·thai′ah son of

Uz·zī′ah son of Zech·a·rī′ah son of Am·a·rī′ah son of Sheph·a·tī′ah son of Ma·hal′a·lel, of the descendants of Per′ez; 5 and Mā·a·sēi′ah son of Bar′uch son of Col-hō′zeh son of Ha·zai′ah son of A·dāi′ah son of Joi′a·rib son of Zech·a·rī′ah son of the Shī′lo·nīte. 6 All the descendants of Per′ez who lived in Jerusalem were four hundred sixty-eight valiant warriors.

7 And these are the Ben′ja·min·ītes: Sal′lū son of Me·shul′lam son of Jō′ed son of Pe·dāi′ah son of Kō′lai′ah son of Mā·a·sēi′ah son of Ith′i·el son of Je·shā′i·ah. 8 And his brothers[c] Gab·bā′ī, Sal′lai: nine hundred twenty-eight. 9 Jō′el son of Zich′rī was their overseer; and Judah son of Has·se·nū′ah was second in charge of the city.

10 Of the priests: Je·dai′ah son of Joi′a·rib, Jā′chin, 11 Se·rāi′ah son of Hil·kī′ah son of Me·shul′lam son of Zā′dok son of Me·rā′i·oth son of A·hī′tub, officer of the house of God, 12 and their associates who did the work of the house, eight hundred twenty-two; and A·dāi′ah son of Je·rō′ham son of Pel·a·lī′ah son of Am′zī son of Zech·a·rī′ah son of Pash′hur son of Mal·chī′jah, 13 and his associates, heads of ancestral houses, two hundred forty-two; and A·mash′sai son of Az′a·rel son of Ah′zaī son of Me·shil′le·moth son of Im′mer, 14 and their associates, valiant warriors, one hundred twenty-eight; their overseer was Zab′di·el son of Hag·ge·dō′lim.

15 And of the Le′vītes: She·māi′ah son of Has′shub son of Az·rī′kam son of Hash·a·bī′ah son of Bun′ni; 16 and Shab′be·thai and Joz′a·bad, of the leaders of the Le′vītes, who were over the outside work of the house of God; 17 and Mat·ta·nī′ah son of Mī′ca son of Zab′dī son of Ā′saph, who was the leader to begin the thanksgiving in prayer, and Bak·bū·kī′ah, the second among his associates; and Ab′da son of Sham·mū′a son of Gā′lal son of Je·dū′thun. 18 All the Le′vītes in the holy city were two hundred eighty-four.

19 The gatekeepers, Ak′kub, Tal′mon and their associates, who kept watch at the gates, were one hundred seventy-two. 20 And the rest of Israel, and of the priests and the Le′vītes, were in all the towns of Judah, all of them in their inheritance. 21 But the temple servants lived on Ō′phel; and Zī′ha and Gish′pa were over the temple servants.

22 The overseer of the Le′vītes in Jerusalem was Uz′zī son of Bā′ni son of Hash·a·bī′ah son of Mat·ta·nī′ah son of Mī′ca, of the descendants of Ā′saph, the singers, in charge of the work of the house of God. 23 For there was a command from the king concerning them, and a settled provision for the singers, as was required every day. 24 And Peth·a·hī′ah son of Me·shez′a·bel, of the descendants

---

c Gk Mss: Heb *And after him*

of Ze′rah son of Judah, was at the king's hand in all matters concerning the people.

Villages outside Jerusalem

25 And as for the villages, with their fields, some of the people of Judah lived in Kir′i·ath-ar′ba and its villages, and in Di′bon and its villages, and in Je·kab′ze·el and its villages, 26 and in Jesh′u·a and in Mo′la·dah and Beth-pel′et, 27 in Ha′zar-shu′al, in Be′er-she′ba and its villages, 28 in Zik′lag, in Me·co′nah and its villages, 29 in En-rim′mon, in Zo′rah, in Jar′muth, 30 Za·no′ah, A·dul′lam, and their villages, La′chish and its fields, and A·ze′kah and its villages. So they camped from Be′er-she′ba to the valley of Hin′nom. 31 The people of Benjamin also lived from Ge′ba onward, at Mich′mash, Ai′ja, Beth′el and its villages, 32 An′a·thoth, Nob, An·a·ni′ah, 33 Ha′zor, Ra′mah, Git′ta·im, 34 Ha′did, Ze·bo′im, Ne·bal′lat, 35 Lod, and O′no, the valley of artisans. 36 And certain divisions of the Le′vites in Judah were joined to Benjamin.

A List of Priests and Levites
(Cp Ezra 2.36–40)

These are the priests and the Le′vites who came up with Ze·rub′ba·bel son of She·al′ti·el, and Jesh′u·a: Se·rai′ah, Jer·e·mi′ah, Ezra, 2 Am·a·ri′ah, Mal′luch, Hat′tush, 3 Shec·a·ni′ah, Re′hum, Mer′e·moth, 4 Id′do, Gin′ne·thoi, A·bi′jah, 5 Mij′a·min, Ma·a·di′ah, Bil′gah, 6 She·mai′ah, Joi′a·rib, Je·dai′ah, 7 Sal′lu, A′mok, Hil·ki′ah, Je·dai′ah. These were the leaders of the priests and of their associates in the days of Jesh′u·a.

8 And the Le′vites: Jesh′u·a, Bin′nu·i, Kad′mi·el, Sher·e·bi′ah, Judah, and Mat·ta·ni′ah, who with his associates was in charge of the songs of thanksgiving. 9 And Bak·bu·ki′ah and Un′no their associates stood opposite them in the service. 10 Jesh′u·a was the father of Joi′a·kim, Joi′a·kim the father of E·li′a·shib, E·li′a·shib the father of Joi′a·da, 11 Joi′a·da the father of Jonathan, and Jonathan the father of Jad′du·a.

12 In the days of Joi′a·kim the priests, heads of ancestral houses, were: of Se·rai′ah, Me·rai′ah; of Jer·e·mi′ah, Han·a·ni′ah; 13 of Ezra, Me·shul′lam; of Am·a·ri′ah, Je·ho·ha′nan; 14 of Mal′lu·chi, Jonathan; of Sheb·a·ni′ah, Joseph; 15 of Ha′rim, Ad′na; of Me·rai′oth, Hel′kai; 16 of Id′do, Zech·a·ri′ah; of Gin′ne·thon, Me·shul′lam; 17 of A·bi′jah, Zich′ri; of Mi·ni′a·min, of Mo·a·di′ah, Pil′tai; 18 of Bil′gah, Sham′mu·a; of She·mai′ah, Je·hon′a·than; 19 of Joi′a·rib, Mat·te′nai; of Je·dai′ah, Uz′zi; 20 of Sal′lai, Kal′lai; of A′mok, E′ber; 21 of Hil·ki′ah, Hash·a·bi′ah; of Je·dai′ah, Ne·than′el.

22 As for the Le′vites, in the days of E·li′a·shib, Joi′a·da, Jo·ha′nan, and Jad′du·a, there were recorded the heads of ancestral houses; also the priests until the reign of Da·ri′us the Persian. 23 The Le′vites, heads of ancestral houses, were recorded in the Book of the Annals until the days of Jo·ha′nan son of E·li′a·shib. 24 And the leaders of the Le′vites: Hash·a·bi′ah, Sher·e·bi′ah, and Jesh′u·a son of Kad′mi·el, with their associates over against them, to praise and to give thanks, according to the commandment of David the man of God, section opposite to section. 25 Mat·ta·ni′ah, Bak·bu·ki′ah, O·ba·di′ah, Me·shul′lam, Tal′mon, and Ak′kub were gatekeepers standing guard at the storehouses of the gates. 26 These were in the days of Joi′a·kim son of Jesh′u·a son of Jo′za·dak, and in the days of the governor Ne·he·mi′ah and of the priest Ezra, the scribe.

Dedication of the City Wall

27 Now at the dedication of the wall of Jerusalem they sought out the Le′vites in all their places, to bring them to Jerusalem to celebrate the dedication with rejoicing, with thanksgivings and with singing, with cymbals, harps, and lyres. 28 The companies of the singers gathered together from the circuit around Jerusalem and from the villages of the Ne·toph′a·thites; 29 also from Beth-gil′gal and from the region of Ge′ba and Az′ma·veth; for the singers had built for themselves villages around Jerusalem. 30 And the priests and the Le′vites purified themselves; and they purified the people and the gates and the wall.

31 Then I brought the leaders of Judah up onto the wall, and appointed two great companies that gave thanks and went in procession. One went to the right on the wall to the Dung Gate; 32 and after them went Ho·shai′ah and half the officials of Judah, 33 and Az·a·ri′ah, Ezra, Me·shul′lam, 34 Judah, Benjamin, She·mai′ah, and Jer·e·mi′ah, 35 and some of the young priests with trumpets: Zech·a·ri′ah son of Jonathan son of She·mai′ah son of Mat·ta·ni′ah son of Mi·cai′ah son of Zac′cur son of A′saph; 36 and his kindred, She·mai′ah, Az′a·rel, Mil′a·lai, Gil′a·lai, Ma′ai, Ne·than′el, Judah, and Ha·na′ni, with the musical instruments of David the man of God; and the scribe Ezra went in front of them. 37 At the Fountain Gate, in front of them, they went straight up by the stairs of the city of David, at the ascent of the wall, above the house of David, to the Water Gate on the east.

38 The other company of those who gave thanks went to the left,*d* and I followed them with half of the people on the wall, above the Tower of the Ovens, to the Broad Wall, 39 and above the Gate of E′phra·im, and by the Old Gate, and by

---

d Cn: Heb *opposite*

the Fish Gate and the Tower of Ha·nan'el and the Tower of the Hundred, to the Sheep Gate; and they came to a halt at the Gate of the Guard. ⁴⁰ So both companies of those who gave thanks stood in the house of God, and I and half of the officials with me; ⁴¹ and the priests E·li'a·kim, Mā·a·sēi'ah, Mi·ni'a·min, Mī·cāi'ah, El·i·ō·ē'naī, Zech·a·rī'ah, and Han·a·ni'ah, with trumpets; ⁴² and Mā·a·sēi'ah, She·mai'ah, El·e·ā'zar, Uz'zī, Jē·hō·hā'nan, Mal·chī'jah, Ē'lam, and Ē'zer. And the singers sang with Jez·ra·hī'ah as their leader. ⁴³ They offered great sacrifices that day and rejoiced, for God had made them rejoice with great joy; the women and children also rejoiced. The joy of Jerusalem was heard far away.

Temple Responsibilities

44 On that day men were appointed over the chambers for the stores, the contributions, the first fruits, and the tithes, to gather into them the portions required by the law for the priests and for the Lē'vītes from the fields belonging to the towns; for Judah rejoiced over the priests and the Lē'vītes who ministered. ⁴⁵ They performed the service of their God and the service of purification, as did the singers and the gatekeepers, according to the command of David and his son Solomon. ⁴⁶ For in the days of David and Ā'saph long ago there was a leader of the singers, and there were songs of praise and thanksgiving to God. ⁴⁷ In the days of Ze·rub'ba·bel and in the days of Nē·he·mī'ah all Israel gave the daily portions for the singers and the gatekeepers. They set apart that which was for the Lē'vītes; and the Lē'vītes set apart that which was for the descendants of Aaron.

Foreigners Separated from Israel
(Num 22.1 — 24.25)

On that day they read from the book of Moses in the hearing of the people; and in it was found written that no Am'mon·īte or Mō'ab·īte should ever enter the assembly of God, ² because they did not meet the Israelites with bread and water, but hired Bā'laam against them to curse them — yet our God turned the curse into a blessing. ³ When the people heard the law, they separated from Israel all those of foreign descent.

The Reforms of Nehemiah

4 Now before this, the priest E·li'a·shib, who was appointed over the chambers of the house of our God, and who was related to Tō·bī'ah, ⁵ prepared for Tō·bī'ah a large room where they had previously put the grain offering, the frankincense, the vessels, and the tithes of grain, wine, and oil, which were given by commandment to the Lē'vītes, singers, and gatekeepers, and the contribu-

tions for the priests. ⁶ While this was taking place I was not in Jerusalem, for in the thirty-second year of King Ar·ta·xerx'ēs of Babylon I went to the king. After some time I asked leave of the king ⁷ and returned to Jerusalem. I then discovered the wrong that E·li'a·shib had done on behalf of Tō·bī'ah, preparing a room for him in the courts of the house of God. ⁸ And I was very angry, and I threw all the household furniture of Tō·bī'ah out of the room. ⁹ Then I gave orders and they cleansed the chambers, and I brought back the vessels of the house of God, with the grain offering and the frankincense.

10 I also found out that the portions of the Lē'vītes had not been given to them; so that the Lē'vītes and the singers, who had conducted the service, had gone back to their fields. ¹¹ So I remonstrated with the officials and said, "Why is the house of God forsaken?" And I gathered them together and set them in their stations. ¹² Then all Judah brought the tithe of the grain, wine, and oil into the storehouses. ¹³ And I appointed as treasurers over the storehouses the priest Shel·e·mī'ah, the scribe Zā'dok, and Pe·dāi'ah of the Lē'vītes, and as their assistant Hā'nan son of Zac'cur son of Mat·ta·ni'ah, for they were considered faithful; and their duty was to distribute to their associates. ¹⁴ Remember me, O my God, concerning this, and do not wipe out my good deeds that I have done for the house of my God and for his service.

Sabbath Reforms Begun

15 In those days I saw in Judah people treading wine presses on the sabbath, and bringing in heaps of grain and loading them on donkeys; and also wine, grapes, figs, and all kinds of burdens, which they brought into Jerusalem on the sabbath day; and I warned them at that time against selling food. ¹⁶ Tÿ'ri·ans also, who lived in the city, brought in fish and all kinds of merchandise and sold them on the sabbath to the people of Judah, and in Jerusalem. ¹⁷ Then I remonstrated with the nobles of Judah and said to them, "What is this evil thing that you are doing, profaning the sabbath day? ¹⁸ Did not your ancestors act in this way, and did not our God bring all this disaster on us and on this city? Yet you bring more wrath on Israel by profaning the sabbath."

19 When it began to be dark at the gates of Jerusalem before the sabbath, I commanded that the doors should be shut and gave orders that they should not be opened until after the sabbath. And I set some of my servants over the gates, to prevent any burden from being brought in on the sabbath day. ²⁰ Then the merchants and sellers of all kinds of merchandise spent the night outside Jerusalem

once or twice. 21 But I warned them and said to them, "Why do you spend the night in front of the wall? If you do so again, I will lay hands on you." From that time on they did not come on the sabbath. 22 And I commanded the Lēʹvītes that they should purify themselves and come and guard the gates, to keep the sabbath day holy. Remember this also in my favor, O my God, and spare me according to the greatness of your steadfast love.

Mixed Marriages Condemned
(Cp Ezra 9.1–4)

23 In those days also I saw Jews who had married women of Ashʹdod, Amʹmon, and Mōʹab; 24 and half of their children spoke the language of Ashʹdod, and they could not speak the language of Judah, but spoke the language of various peoples. 25 And I contended with them and cursed them and beat some of them and pulled out their hair; and I made them take an oath in the name of God, saying, "You shall not give your daughters to their sons, or take their daughters for your sons or for yourselves. 26 Did not King Solomon of Israel sin on account of such women? Among the many nations there was no king like him, and he was beloved by his God, and God made him king over all Israel; nevertheless, foreign women made even him to sin. 27 Shall we then listen to you and do all this great evil and act treacherously against our God by marrying foreign women?"

28 And one of the sons of Je•hoiʹa•da, son of the high priest E•liʹa•shib, was the son-in-law of San•balʹlat the Horʹo•nite; I chased him away from me. 29 Remember them, O my God, because they have defiled the priesthood, the covenant of the priests and the Lēʹvītes.

30 Thus I cleansed them from everything foreign, and I established the duties of the priests and Lēʹvītes, each in his work; 31 and I provided for the wood offering, at appointed times, and for the first fruits. Remember me, O my God, for good.

Good people suffering, love that must overcome a frightening obstacle, an undercover angel—the Book of Tobit has it all. Part fairy tale, part love story, this book will bring a smile to your face and perhaps a tear to your eye. Enjoy!

In-depth

For the author of the Book of Tobit, understanding God's will was not difficult. The conviction that God rewards good people, especially those who have experienced great suffering, is evident on every page. In the story, the faithful Tobit, who is blinded after doing a good deed, and the virtuous Sarah, who is ridiculed because she has had seven husbands die on their wedding night, pray for death because of their suffering and humiliation. In answer to their prayers, God sends the angel Raphael to lead Tobit's son Tobias on a journey to Sarah's town. The story ends happily—but you will have to read it yourself to find out exactly how.

The Book of Tobit is a novel, that is, a fiction book. The author was writing at a time when the Jews were governed by oppressive Greek rulers, and the people needed the reassurance of this happy tale. They had not forgotten the fall of Jerusalem or the Exile in Babylon, and Israel's suffering weighed heavily on them. What was the advantage of following God's law if all they had to look forward to was more suffering? (Belief in an afterlife had not yet developed among the Jewish people.) The book assured the faithful that God would eventually reward them: it was just a matter of time.

Although the book's miraculous answers may seem too simple to modern-day readers, its insistence on God's presence in human life and God's concern for those who suffer remains as important as ever. All people—even Christians who believe in life after death—need encouragement to face the challenges of this world with faith and hope.

At a Glance

- **Chapters 1–3.** the sufferings of Tobit and Sarah
- **Chapters 4–10.** the journey of Tobias and his marriage to Sarah
- **Chapters 11–12.** Tobias's homecoming and Tobit's cure
- **Chapters 13–14.** Tobit's prayer of thanksgiving, and death

Quick Facts

Setting
although fictional, the book reflects the historical situation of the Jews who were dispersed after the fall of Jerusalem in 587 B.C.

Author
unknown, writing sometime in the second century B.C.

Theme
In time, God will aid the faithful who suffer.

Of Note
Raphael is one of only three angels named in the Bible; the others are Michael and Gabriel.

The Book of Tobit

Tobit

This book tells the story of Tō′bit son of Tō′bi•el son of Ha•nan′i•el son of A•du′el son of Gab′a•el son of Raph′a•el son of Rag′u•el of the descendants*a* of As′i•el, of the tribe of Naph′ta•lī, ² who in the days of King Shal•man•e′ser*b* of the Assyrians was taken into captivity from This′bē, which is to the south of Kē′desh Naph′ta•lī in Upper Galilee, above Ash′er toward the west, and north of Phō′gor.

Tobit's Youth and Virtuous Life
(Cp Deut 12.11–14; 16.16; 1 Kings 12.28–29)

3 I, Tō′bit, walked in the ways of truth and righteousness all the days of my life. I performed many acts of charity for my kindred and my people who had gone with me in exile to Nin′e•veh in the land of the Assyrians. ⁴ When I was in my own country, in the land of Israel, while I was still a young man, the whole tribe of my ancestor Naph′-ta•lī deserted the house of David and Jerusalem. This city had been chosen from among all the tribes of Israel, where all the tribes of Israel should offer sacrifice and where the temple, the dwelling of God, had been consecrated and established for all generations forever.

5 All my kindred and our ancestral house of Naph′ta•lī sacrificed to the calf*c* that King Jer•o-bō′am of Israel had erected in Dan and on all the mountains of Galilee. ⁶ But I alone went often to Jerusalem for the festivals, as it is prescribed for all Israel by an everlasting decree. I would hurry off to Jerusalem with the first fruits of the crops and the firstlings of the flock, the tithes of the cattle, and the first shearings of the sheep. ⁷ I would give these to the priests, the sons of Aaron, at the altar; likewise the tenth of the grain, wine, olive oil, pomegranates, figs, and the rest of the fruits to the sons of Levi who ministered at Jerusalem. Also for six years I would save up a second tenth in money and go and distribute it in Jerusalem. ⁸ A third tenth*d* I would give to the orphans and widows and to the converts who had attached themselves to Israel. I would bring it and give it to them in the third year, and we would eat it according to the ordinance decreed concerning it in the law of Moses and according to the instructions of Deb′or•ah, the mother of my father Tō′bi•el,*e* for my father had died and left me an orphan. ⁹ When I became a man I married a woman,*f* a member of our own family, and by her I became the father of a son whom I named Tō′bi•as.

Taken Captive to Nineveh

10 After I was carried away captive to Assyria and came as a captive to Nin′e•veh, everyone of my kindred and my people ate the food of the

---

a Other ancient authorities lack *of Raphael son of Raguel of the descendants* *b* Gk *Enemessaros* *c* Other ancient authorities read *heifer* *d* A third tenth added from other ancient authorities *e* Lat: Gk *Hananiel* *f* Other ancient authorities add *Anna*

471

Gentiles, [11] but I kept myself from eating the food of the Gentiles. [12] Because I was mindful of God with all my heart, [13] the Most High gave me favor and good standing with Shal·man·ē′ser,[g] and I used to buy everything he needed. [14] Until his death I used to go into Mēd′i·a, and buy for him there. While in the country of Mēd′i·a I left bags of silver worth ten talents in trust with Gab′a·el, the brother of Gā′brī. [15] But when Shal·man·ē′ser[g] died, and his son Sen-nach′e·rib reigned in his place, the highways into Mēd′i·a became unsafe and I could no longer go there.

Courage in Burying the Dead
(Cp Num 19.11–13)

[16] In the days of Shal·man·ē′ser[g] I performed many acts of charity to my kindred, those of my tribe. [17] I would give my food to the hungry and my clothing to the naked; and if I saw the dead body of any of my people thrown out behind the wall of Nin′e·veh, I would bury it. [18] I also buried any whom King Sen·nach′e·rib put to death when he came fleeing from Judea in those days of judgment that the king of heaven executed upon him because of his blasphemies. For in his anger he put to death many Israelites; but I would secretly remove the bodies and bury them. So when Sen-nach′e·rib looked for them he could not find them. [19] Then one of the Ninevites went and informed the king about me, that I was burying them; so I hid myself. But when I realized that the king knew about me and that I was being searched for to be put to death, I was afraid and ran away. [20] Then all my property was confiscated; nothing was left to me that was not taken into the royal treasury except my wife Anna and my son Tō′bī·as.

[21] But not forty[h] days passed before two of Sen·nach′e·rib′s[i] sons killed him, and they fled to the mountains of Ar′a·rat, and his son Ē′sar-had′-don[j] reigned after him. He appointed A·hī′kar, the son of my brother Han′a·el[k] over all the accounts of his kingdom, and he had authority over the entire administration. [22] A·hī′kar interceded for me, and I returned to Nin′e·veh. Now A·hī′kar was chief cupbearer, keeper of the signet, and in charge of administration of the accounts under King Sen-nach′e·rib of Assyria; so Ē′sar-had′don[j] reappointed him. He was my nephew and so a close relative.
Then during the reign of Ē′sar-had′don[j] I returned home, and my wife Anna and my son Tō′bī·as were restored to me. At our festival of Pentecost, which is the sacred festival of weeks, a good dinner was prepared for me and I reclined to eat. [2] When the table was set for me and an abundance of food placed before me, I said to my son Tō′bī·as, "Go,

? did you KNOW?
The Case of the Missing Books

The Book of Tobit is treated differently in some versions of the Bible. Some put it in a section of books separated from the rest of the Old Testament. Some do not include it at all. This may seem puzzling, but we can find an explanation, if we look back many centuries.

Sometime after the second fall of Jerusalem, in A.D. 70, Jewish scholars developed an official list, or canon, of thirty-nine holy books, arranged in three groups: the Law, the Prophets, and the Writings. The scholars rejected certain books that had been included in a popular Greek translation of the Old Testament from Alexandria, Egypt. This Greek translation was adopted as the official canon by the early church, however, and the rejected books were accepted along with the Law, the Prophets, and the Writings. Thus, Tobit, Judith, 1 and 2 Maccabees, Wisdom, Sirach, Baruch, and additions to the Books of Esther and Daniel eventually became part of the Christian Bible, although they were not in the Jewish Bible.

Many centuries later, the Christian reformer Martin Luther used the Jewish canon of the Old Testament in his translation of the Bible. He placed the additional books in a separate section, entitling them the Apocrypha (from the Greek for "hidden"). Although most Christian churches today follow Luther's lead, the Catholic church continues to use the fuller Greek canon, preferring the term deuterocanonical (from the Greek for "second canon") for the disputed books.

my child, and bring whatever poor person you may find of our people among the exiles in Nin′e·veh, who is wholeheartedly mindful of God,[l] and he shall eat together with me. I will wait for you, until you come back." [3] So Tō′bī·as went to look for

---

[g] Gk *Enemessaros*   [h] Other ancient authorities read either *forty-five* or *fifty*   [i] Gk *his*   [j] Gk *Sacherdonos*   [k] Other authorities read *Hananael*   [l] Lat: Gk *wholeheartedly mindful*

some poor person of our people. When he had returned he said, "Father!" And I replied, "Here I am, my child." Then he went on to say, "Look, father, one of our own people has been murdered and thrown into the market place, and now he lies there strangled." 4 Then I sprang up, left the dinner before even tasting it, and removed the body[m] from the square[n] and laid it[m] in one of the rooms until sunset when I might bury it.[m] 5 When I returned, I washed myself and ate my food in sorrow. 6 Then I remembered the prophecy of Ā´mos, how he said against Beth´el,[o]

> "Your festivals shall be turned into
>   mourning,
>   and all your songs into lamentation."

And I wept.

Tobit Becomes Blind

7 When the sun had set, I went and dug a grave and buried him. 8 And my neighbors laughed and said, "Is he still not afraid? He has already been hunted down to be put to death for doing this, and he ran away; yet here he is again burying the dead!" 9 That same night I washed myself and went into my courtyard and slept by the wall of the courtyard; and my face was uncovered because of the heat. 10 I did not know that there were sparrows on the wall; their fresh droppings fell into my eyes and produced white films. I went to physicians to be healed, but the more they treated me with ointments the more my vision was obscured by the white films, until I became completely blind. For four years I remained unable to see. All my kindred were sorry for me, and A•hī´kar took care of me for two years before he went to El•y-mā´is.

Tobit's Wife Earns Their Livelihood

11 At that time, also, my wife Anna earned money at women's work. 12 She used to send what she made to the owners and they would pay wages to her. One day, the seventh of Dys´trus, when she cut off a piece she had woven and sent it to the owners, they paid her full wages and also gave her a young goat for a meal. 13 When she returned to me, the goat began to bleat. So I called her and said, "Where did you get this goat? It is surely not stolen, is it? Return it to the owners; for we have no right to eat anything stolen." 14 But she said to me, "It was given to me as a gift in addition to my wages." But I did not believe her, and told her to return it to the owners. I became flushed with anger against her over this. Then she replied to me, "Where are your acts of charity? Where are your righteous deeds? These things are known about you!"[p]

Tobit's Prayer

3 Then with much grief and anguish of heart I wept, and with groaning began to pray:
2 "You are righteous, O Lord,
    and all your deeds are just;
  all your ways are mercy and truth;
    you judge the world.[q]
3 And now, O Lord, remember me
    and look favorably upon me.
  Do not punish me for my sins
    and for my unwitting offenses
    and those that my ancestors committed
      before you.
  They sinned against you,
4   and disobeyed your commandments.
  So you gave us over to plunder, exile, and
      death,
    to become the talk, the byword, and an
      object of reproach
    among all the nations among whom you
      have dispersed us.
5 And now your many judgments are true
    in exacting penalty from me for my sins.
  For we have not kept your commandments
    and have not walked in accordance with
      truth before you.
6 So now deal with me as you will;
    command my spirit to be taken from me,
    so that I may be released from the face of
      the earth and become dust.
  For it is better for me to die than to live,
    because I have had to listen to
      undeserved insults,
    and great is the sorrow within me.
  Command, O Lord, that I be released from
      this distress;
    release me to go to the eternal home,
    and do not, O Lord, turn your face away
      from me.
  For it is better for me to die
    than to see so much distress in my life
    and to listen to insults."

Sarah Falsely Accused

7 On the same day, at Ec•bat´a•na in Mēd´i•a, it also happened that Sarah, the daughter of Rag´u•el, was reproached by one of her father's maids. 8 For she had been married to seven husbands, and the wicked demon As•mō•dē´us had killed each of them before they had been with her as is customary for wives. So the maid said to her, "You are the one

---

m Gk *him*   n Other ancient authorities lack *from the square*   o Other ancient authorities read *against Bethlehem*   p Or *to you*; Gk *with you*   q Other ancient authorities read *you render true and righteous judgment forever*

who kills[r] your husbands! See, you have already been married to seven husbands and have not borne the name of[s] a single one of them. 9 Why do you beat us? Because your husbands are dead? Go with them! May we never see a son or daughter of yours!"

PRAY IT!

Praying for Death?

Tobit and Sarah are at the end of their rope. They have experienced such suffering and disgrace that life no longer has any meaning for them. They know suicide is wrong, so they each pray that God will send death to end their suffering and humiliation (Tob 3.6,10).

It is not uncommon for people who are very sick or in great pain or very old to pray for death, like Tobit. Unfortunately, young people who have experienced great loss or trauma often wish for death too, like Sarah. No one can completely explain the mystery of why we—both young and old—suffer. But through our loving actions and prayers, we can support one another in our suffering.

What people do you know who are suffering to the point of despair? Take a few moments every day to remember those people in prayer, and call or write to let them know you are thinking of them.

▸ Tobit, chapter 3

Sarah's Prayer for Death

10 On that day she was grieved in spirit and wept. When she had gone up to her father's upper room, she intended to hang herself. But she thought it over and said, "Never shall they reproach my father, saying to him, 'You had only one beloved daughter but she hanged herself because of her distress.' And I shall bring my father in his old age down in sorrow to Hades. It is better for me not to hang myself, but to pray the Lord that I may die and not listen to these reproaches anymore." 11 At that same time, with hands outstretched toward the window, she prayed and said,

"Blessed are you, merciful God!
 Blessed is your name forever;
 let all your works praise you forever.
12 And now, Lord,[t] I turn my face to you,
 and raise my eyes toward you.
13 Command that I be released from the earth
 and not listen to such reproaches any
 more.
14 You know, O Master, that I am innocent
 of any defilement with a man,
15 and that I have not disgraced my name
 or the name of my father in the land of
 my exile.
I am my father's only child;
 he has no other child to be his heir;
and he has no close relative or other
 kindred
 for whom I should keep myself as wife.
Already seven husbands of mine have died.
 Why should I still live?
But if it is not pleasing to you, O Lord, to
 take my life,
 hear me in my disgrace."

An Answer to Prayer
(Num 36.6–9)

16 At that very moment, the prayers of both of them were heard in the glorious presence of God. 17 So Raph′a•el was sent to heal both of them: Tō′bit, by removing the white films from his eyes, so that he might see God's light with his eyes; and Sarah, daughter of Rag′ū•el, by giving her in marriage to Tō•bī′as son of Tō′bit, and by setting her free from the wicked demon As•mō•dě′us. For Tō•bī′as was entitled to have her before all others who had desired to marry her. At the same time that Tō′bit returned from the courtyard into his house, Sarah daughter of Rag′ū•el came down from her upper room.

Tobit Gives Instructions to His Son
(Deut 15.7–8; Mt 6.2–4)

That same day Tō′bit remembered the money that he had left in trust with Gab′a•el at Rā′gēs in Mēd′i•a, 2 and he said to himself, "Now I have asked for death. Why do I not call my son Tō•bī′as and explain to him about the money before I die?" 3 Then he called his son Tō•bī′as, and when he came to him he said, "My son, when I die,[u] give me a proper burial. Honor your mother and do

---

r Other ancient authorities read *strangles* s Other ancient authorities read *have had no benefit from* t Other ancient authorities lack *Lord* u Lat

not abandon her all the days of her life. Do whatever pleases her, and do not grieve her in anything. 4 Remember her, my son, because she faced many dangers for you while you were in her womb. And when she dies, bury her beside me in the same grave.

5 "Revere the Lord all your days, my son, and refuse to sin or to transgress his commandments. Live uprightly all the days of your life, and do not walk in the ways of wrongdoing; 6 for those who act in accordance with truth will prosper in all their activities. To all those who practice righteousness*v* 7 give alms from your possessions, and do not let your eye begrudge the gift when you make it. Do not turn your face away from anyone who is poor, and the face of God will not be turned away

Asian American

Give Food to the Hungry

In China, whenever you see a friend, it is customary to ask whether he or she has eaten a meal yet. If your friend responds, "No, I haven't eaten yet," it may mean that his or her last meal was yesterday or even the day before that. Then, you invite your friend to your home and share whatever food you have. This custom goes back to the great famine of China (1958–59), when people were dying of starvation and even eating tree bark.

Tobit gives his son good advice when he instructs him to share his food with the hungry and his clothing with the poor (Tob 4.16). Read Mt 25.31–46 to hear how seriously Jesus wants us to follow this advice.

▶ **Tob 4.16**

from you. 8 If you have many possessions, make your gift from them in proportion; if few, do not be afraid to give according to the little you have. 9 So you will be laying up a good treasure for yourself against the day of necessity. 10 For almsgiving delivers from death and keeps you from going into the Darkness. 11 Indeed, almsgiving, for all who

practice it, is an excellent offering in the presence of the Most High.

12 "Beware, my son, of every kind of fornication. First of all, marry a woman from among the descendants of your ancestors; do not marry a foreign woman, who is not of your father's tribe; for we are the descendants of the prophets. Remember, my son, that Noah, Abraham, Isaac, and Jacob, our ancestors of old, all took wives from among their kindred. They were blessed in their children, and their posterity will inherit the land. 13 So now, my son, love your kindred, and in your heart do not disdain your kindred, the sons and daughters of your people, by refusing to take a wife for yourself from among them. For in pride there is ruin and great confusion. And in idleness there is loss and dire poverty, because idleness is the mother of famine.

14 "Do not keep over until the next day the wages of those who work for you, but pay them at once. If you serve God you will receive payment. Watch yourself, my son, in everything you do, and discipline yourself in all your conduct. 15 And what you hate, do not do to anyone. Do not drink wine to excess or let drunkenness go with you on your way. 16 Give some of your food to the hungry, and some of your clothing to the naked. Give all your surplus as alms, and do not let your eye begrudge your giving of alms. 17 Place your bread on the grave of the righteous, but give none to sinners. 18 Seek advice from every wise person and do not despise any useful counsel. 19 At all times bless the Lord God, and ask him that your ways may be made straight and that all your paths and plans may prosper. For none of the nations has understanding, but the Lord himself will give them good counsel; but if he chooses otherwise, he casts down to deepest Hades. So now, my child, remember these commandments, and do not let them be erased from your heart.

Money Left in Trust with Gabael

20 "And now, my son, let me explain to you that I left ten talents of silver in trust with Gab'a•el son of Ga'bri•as, at Ra'gēs in Mēd'i•a. 21 Do not be afraid, my son, because we have become poor. You have great wealth if you fear God and flee from every sin and do what is good in the sight of the Lord your God."

---

v The text of codex Sinaiticus goes directly from verse 6 to verse 19, reading *To those who practice righteousness* 19*the Lord will give good counsel.* In order to fill the lacuna verses 7 to 18 are derived from other ancient authorities

The Angel Raphael

(Heb 13.2)

Then Tŏ·bī′as answered his father Tŏ′bit, "I will do everything that you have commanded me, father; ²but how can I obtain the money[w] from him, since he does not know me and I do not know him? What evidence[x] am I to give him so that he will recognize and trust me, and give me the money? Also, I do not know the roads to Mēd′i·a, or how to get there." ³Then Tŏ′bit answered his son Tŏ·bī′as, "He gave me his bond and I gave him my bond. I[y] divided his in two; we each took one part, and I put one with the money. And now twenty years have passed since I left this money in trust. So now, my son, find yourself a trustworthy man to go with you, and we will pay him wages until you return. But get back the money from Gab′a·el."[z]

4 So Tŏ·bī′as went out to look for a man to go with him to Mēd′i·a, someone who was acquainted with the way. He went out and found the angel Raph′a·el standing in front of him; but he did not perceive that he was an angel of God. ⁵Tŏ·bī′as[a] said to him, "Where do you come from, young man?" "From your kindred, the Israelites," he replied, "and I have come here to work." Then Tŏ·bī′as[b] said to him, "Do you know the way to go to Mēd′i·a?" ⁶"Yes," he replied, "I have been there many times; I am acquainted with it and know all the roads. I have often traveled to Mēd′i·a, and would stay with our kinsman Gab′a·el who lives in Rā′gēs of Mēd′i·a. It is a journey of two days from Ec·bat′a·na to Rā′gēs; for it lies in a mountainous area, while Ec·bat′a·na is in the middle of the plain." ⁷Then Tŏ·bī′as said to him, "Wait for me, young man, until I go in and tell my father; for I do need you to travel with me, and I will pay you your wages." ⁸He replied, "All right, I will wait; but do not take too long."

9 So Tŏ·bī′as[b] went in to tell his father Tŏ′bit and said to him, "I have just found a man who is one of our own Israelite kindred!" He replied, "Call the man in, my son, so that I may learn about his family and to what tribe he belongs, and whether he is trustworthy enough to go with you."

10 Then Tŏ·bī′as went out and called him, and said, "Young man, my father is calling for you." So he went in to him, and Tŏ′bit greeted him first. He replied, "Joyous greetings to you!" But Tŏ′bit retorted, "What joy is left for me any more? I am a man without eyesight; I cannot see the light of heaven, but I lie in darkness like the dead who no longer see the light. Although still alive, I am among the dead. I hear people but I cannot see

them." But the young man[b] said, "Take courage; the time is near for God to heal you; take courage." Then Tŏ′bit said to him, "My son Tŏ·bī′as wishes to go to Mēd′i·a. Can you accompany him and guide him? I will pay your wages, brother." He answered, "I can go with him and I know all the roads, for I have often gone to Mēd′i·a and have crossed all its plains, and I am familiar with its mountains and all of its roads."

11 Then Tŏ′bit[b] said to him, "Brother, of what family are you and from what tribe? Tell me, brother." ¹²He replied, "Why do you need to know my tribe?" But Tŏ′bit[b] said, "I want to be sure, brother, whose son you are and what your name is." ¹³He replied, "I am Az·a·rī′ah, the son of the great Han·a·nī′ah, one of your relatives." ¹⁴Then Tŏ′bit said to him, "Welcome! God save you, brother. Do not feel bitter toward me, brother, because I wanted to be sure about your ancestry. It turns out that you are a kinsman, and of good and noble lineage. For I knew Han·a·nī′ah and Nathan,[c] the two sons of Shem·e·lī′ah,[d] and they used to go with me to Jerusalem and worshiped with me there, and were not led astray. Your kindred are good people; you come of good stock. Hearty welcome!"

15 Then he added, "I will pay you a drachma a day as wages, as well as expenses for yourself and my son. So go with my son, ¹⁶and[e] I will add something to your wages." Raph′a·el[a] answered, "I will go with him; so do not fear. We shall leave in good health and return to you in good health, because the way is safe." ¹⁷So Tŏ′bit[b] said to him, "Blessings be upon you, brother."

Then he called his son and said to him, "Son, prepare supplies for the journey and set out with your brother. May God in heaven bring you safely there and return you in good health to me; and may his angel, my son, accompany you both for your safety."

Before he went out to start his journey, he kissed his father and mother. Tŏ′bit then said to him, "Have a safe journey."

18 But his mother[f] began to weep, and said to Tŏ′bit, "Why is it that you have sent my child away? Is he not the staff of our hand as he goes in and out before us? ¹⁹Do not heap money upon money, but let it be a ransom for our child. ²⁰For the life that is given to us by the Lord is enough for us." ²¹Tŏ′bit[a] said to her, "Do not worry; our

---

w Gk *it* *x* Gk *sign* *y* Other authorities read *He* *z* Gk *from him* *a* Gk *He* *b* Gk *he* *c* Other ancient authorities read *Jathan* or *Nathaniah* *d* Other ancient authorities read *Shemaiah* *e* Other ancient authorities add *when you return safely* *f* Other ancient authorities add *Anna*

child will leave in good health and return to us in good health. Your eyes will see him on the day when he returns to you in good health. Say no more! Do not fear for them, my sister. 22 For a good angel will accompany him; his journey will be successful, and he will come back in good health." 1 So she stopped weeping.

6
Journey to Rages

The young man went out and the angel went with him; 2 and the dog came out with him and went along with them. So they both journeyed along, and when the first night overtook them they camped by the Tigris river. 3 Then the young man went down to wash his feet in the Tigris river. Suddenly a large fish leaped up from the water and tried to swallow the young man's foot, and he cried out. 4 But the angel said to the young man, "Catch hold of the fish and hang on to it!" So the young man grasped the fish and drew it up on the land. 5 Then the angel said to him, "Cut open the fish and take out its gall, heart, and liver. Keep them with you, but throw away the intestines. For its gall, heart, and liver are useful as medicine." 6 So after cutting open the fish the young man gathered together the gall, heart, and liver; then he roasted and ate some of the fish, and kept some to be salted.

The two continued on their way together until they were near Mēd′i•a.g 7 Then the young man questioned the angel and said to him, "Brother Az•a•rī′ah, what medicinal value is there in the fish's heart and liver, and in the gall?" 8 He replied, "As for the fish's heart and liver, you must burn them to make a smoke in the presence of a man or woman afflicted by a demon or evil spirit, and every affliction will flee away and never remain with that person any longer. 9 And as for the gall, anoint a person's eyes where white films have appeared on them; blow upon them, upon the white films, and the eyesh will be healed."

Raphael's Instructions
(Num 36.6–9)

10 When he entered Mēd′i•a and already was approaching Ec•bat′a•na,i 11 Raph′a•el said to the young man, "Brother Tō•bī′as." "Here I am," he answered. Then Raph′a•elj said to him, "We must stay this night in the home of Rag′ū•el. He is your relative, and he has a daughter named Sarah. 12 He has no male heir and no daughter except Sarah only, and you, as next of kin to her, have before all other men a hereditary claim on her. Also it is right for you to inherit her father's possessions. Moreover, the girl is sensible, brave, and very

beautiful, and her father is a good man." 13 He continued, "You have every right to take her in marriage. So listen to me, brother; tonight I will speak to her father about the girl, so that we may take her to be your bride. When we return from Rā′gēs we will celebrate her marriage. For I know that Rag′ū•el can by no means keep her from you or promise her to another man without incurring the penalty of death according to the decree of the book of Moses. Indeed he knows that you, rather than any other man, are entitled to marry his daughter. So now listen to me, brother, and tonight we shall speak concerning the girl and arrange her engagement to you. And when we return from Rā′gēs we will take her and bring her back with us to your house."

14 Then Tō•bī′as said in answer to Raph′a•el, "Brother Az•a•rī′ah, I have heard that she already has been married to seven husbands and that they died in the bridal chamber. On the night when they went in to her, they would die. I have heard people saying that it was a demon that killed them. 15 It does not harm her, but it kills anyone who desires to approach her. So now, since I am the only son my father has, I am afraid that I may die and bring my father's and mother's life down to their grave, grieving for me—and they have no other son to bury them."

16 But Raph′a•elj said to him, "Do you not remember your father's orders when he commanded you to take a wife from your father's house? Now listen to me, brother, and say no more about this demon. Take her. I know that this very night she will be given to you in marriage. 17 When you enter the bridal chamber, take some of the fish's liver and heart, and put them on the embers of the incense. An odor will be given off; 18 the demon will smell it and flee, and will never be seen near her any more. Now when you are about to go to bed with her, both of you must first stand up and pray, imploring the Lord of heaven that mercy and safety may be granted to you. Do not be afraid, for she was set apart for you before the world was made. You will save her, and she will go with you. I presume that you will have children by her, and they will be as brothers to you. Now say no more!" When Tō•bī′as heard the words of Raph′a•el and learned that she was his kinswoman,k related through his father's lineage, he loved her very much, and his heart was drawn to her.

g Other ancient authorities read *Ecbatana*　h Gk *they*
i Other ancient authorities read *Rages*　j Gk *he*
k Gk *sister*

Arrival at Home of Raguel

Now when they[l] entered Ec·bat′a·na, Tō·bī′as[m] said to him, "Brother Az·a·rī′ah, take me straight to our brother Rag′ū·el." So he took him to Rag′ū·el's house, where they found him sitting beside the courtyard door. They greeted him first, and he replied, "Joyous greetings, brothers; welcome and good health!" Then he brought them into his house. [2] He said to his wife Edna, "How much the young man resembles my kinsman Tō′bit!" [3] Then Edna questioned them, saying, "Where are you from, brothers?" They answered, "We belong to the descendants of Naph′ta·lī who are exiles in Nin′e·veh." [4] She said to them, "Do you know our kinsman Tō′bit?" And they replied, "Yes, we know him." Then she asked them, "Is he[n] in good health?" [5] They replied, "He is alive and in good health." And Tō·bī′as added, "He is my father!" [6] At that Rag′ū·el jumped up and kissed him and wept. [7] He also spoke to him as follows, "Blessings on you, my child, son of a good and noble father![o] O most miserable of calamities that such an upright and beneficent man has become blind!" He then embraced his kinsman Tō·bī′as and wept. [8] His wife Edna also wept for him, and their daughter Sarah likewise wept. [9] Then Rag′ū·el[m] slaughtered a ram from the flock and received them very warmly.

Marriage of Tobias and Sarah

When they had bathed and washed themselves and had reclined to dine, Tō·bī′as said to Raph′a·el, "Brother Az·a·rī′ah, ask Rag′ū·el to give me my kinswoman[p] Sarah." [10] But Rag′ū·el overheard it and said to the lad, "Eat and drink, and be merry tonight. For no one except you, brother, has the right to marry my daughter Sarah. Likewise I am not at liberty to give her to any other man than yourself, because you are my nearest relative. But let me explain to you the true situation more fully, my child. [11] I have given her to seven men of our kinsmen, and all died on the night when they went in to her. But now, my child, eat and drink, and the Lord will act on behalf of you both." But Tō·bī′as said, "I will neither eat nor drink anything until you settle the things that pertain to me." So Rag′ū·el said, "I will do so. She is given to you in accordance with the decree in the book of Moses, and it has been decreed from heaven that she be given to you. Take your kinswoman;[p] from now on you are her brother and she is your sister. She is given to you from today and forever. May the Lord of heaven, my child, guide and prosper you both this night and grant you mercy and peace." [12] Then Rag′ū·el summoned his daughter Sarah. When she came to him he took her by the hand and gave her to Tō·bī′as,[q] saying, "Take her to be your wife in accordance with the law and decree written in the book of Moses. Take her and bring her safely to your father. And may the God of heaven prosper your journey with his peace." [13] Then he called her mother and told her to bring writing material; and he wrote out a copy of a marriage contract, to the effect that he gave her to him as wife according to the decree of the law of Moses. [14] Then they began to eat and drink.

15 Rag′ū·el called his wife Edna and said to her, "Sister, get the other room ready, and take her there." [16] So she went and made the bed in the room as he had told her, and brought Sarah[r] there. She wept for her daughter.[r] Then, wiping away the tears,[s] she said to her, "Take courage, my daughter; the Lord of heaven grant you joy[t] in place of your sorrow. Take courage, my daughter." Then she went out.

Tobias Routs the Demon
(Cp Mt 12.43–45)

When they had finished eating and drinking they wanted to retire; so they took the young man and brought him into the bedroom. [2] Then Tō·bī′as remembered the words of Raph′a·el, and he took the fish's liver and heart out of the bag where he had them and put them on the embers of the incense. [3] The odor of the fish so repelled the demon that he fled to the remotest parts[u] of Egypt. But Raph′a·el followed him, and at once bound him there hand and foot.

4 When the parents[v] had gone out and shut the door of the room, Tō·bī′as got out of bed and said to Sarah,[r] "Sister, get up, and let us pray and implore our Lord that he grant us mercy and safety." [5] So she got up, and they began to pray and implore that they might be kept safe. Tō·bī′as[w] began by saying,

"Blessed are you, O God of our ancestors,
    and blessed is your name in all
        generations forever.
Let the heavens and the whole creation
    bless you forever.
6 You made Adam, and for him you made his
      wife Eve
    as a helper and support.

---

[l] Other ancient authorities read *he*   [m] Gk *he*   [n] Other ancient authorities add *alive and*   [o] Other ancient authorities add *When he heard that Tobit had lost his sight, he was stricken with grief and wept. Then he said,*   [p] Gk *sister*   [q] Gk *him*   [r] Gk *her*   [s] Other ancient authorities read *the tears of her daughter*   [t] Other ancient authorities read *favor*   [u] Or *fled through the air to the parts*   [v] Gk *they*   [w] Gk *He*

Angels Among Us

Many older Catholics were taught as children that they were to leave a bit of space on their chair for their guardian angel. We smile at that story, partly because it was a creative way to make angels real in the lives of children, and partly because it points to a truth about God's presence in our life.

In the fictional story of Tobit, we meet the angel Raphael. In other parts of the Bible, angels serve primarily as God's messengers. But Raphael is much more than a messenger. He disguises himself as a kindly but unknown relative who guides Tobias to the secrets he needs to know to relieve both Tobit's and Sarah's suffering.

The truth is that many angels are around us. Most of us have heard stories about kind strangers who appear seemingly out of nowhere to help and then disappear. Our seat may not have a lot of room for an angel, but our world certainly does. They remind us that God is with us, protecting us and guiding us.

Have you or someone you know been touched by an angel? In return, why don't you look for opportunities to be someone else's "angel"?

From the two of them the human race
    has sprung.
You said, 'It is not good that the man
    should be alone;
    let us make a helper for him like
      himself.'
7 I now am taking this kinswoman of mine,
    not because of lust,
    but with sincerity.
Grant that she and I may find mercy
    and that we may grow old together."
8 And they both said, "Amen, Amen." 9 Then they went to sleep for the night.

But Rag′u‧el arose and called his servants to him, and they went and dug a grave, 10 for he said, "It is possible that he will die and we will become an object of ridicule and derision." 11 When they had finished digging the grave, Rag′u‧el went into his house and called his wife, 12 saying, "Send one of the maids and have her go in to see if he is alive. But if he is dead, let us bury him without anyone knowing it." 13 So they sent the maid, lit a lamp, and opened the door; and she went in and found them sound asleep together. 14 Then the maid came out and informed them that he was alive and that nothing was wrong. 15 So they blessed the God of heaven, and Rag′u‧el[x] said,
"Blessed are you, O God, with every pure
    blessing;
    let all your chosen ones bless you.[y]
    Let them bless you forever.
16 Blessed are you because you have made me
    glad.
    It has not turned out as I expected,
    but you have dealt with us according to
      your great mercy.

17 Blessed are you because you had
      compassion
    on two only children.
Be merciful to them, O Master, and keep
    them safe;
    bring their lives to fulfillment
    in happiness and mercy."
18 Then he ordered his servants to fill in the grave before daybreak.

Wedding Feast

19 After this he asked his wife to bake many loaves of bread; and he went out to the herd and brought two steers and four rams and ordered them to be slaughtered. So they began to make preparations. 20 Then he called for Tō‧bī′as and swore on oath to him in these words:[z] "You shall not leave here for fourteen days, but shall stay here eating and drinking with me; and you shall cheer up my daughter, who has been depressed. 21 Take at once half of what I own and return in safety to your father; the other half will be yours when my wife and I die. Take courage, my child. I am your father and Edna is your mother, and we belong to you as well as to your wife[a] now and forever. Take courage, my child."

The Money Recovered

Then Tō‧bī′as called Raph′a‧el and said to him, 2 "Brother Az‧a‧rī′ah, take four servants and two camels with you and travel to Rā′gēs. Go to the home of Gab′a‧el, give him the bond, get the money, and then bring him with you to the

---

x Gk they   y Other ancient authorities lack this line
z Other ancient authorities read Tobias and said to him
a Gk sister

T
O
B

wedding celebration. [4] For you know that my father must be counting the days, and if I delay even one day I will upset him very much. [3] You are witness to the oath Rag′ū•el has sworn, and I cannot violate his oath."[b] [5] So Raph′a•el with the four servants and two camels went to Rā′gēs in Mēd′i•a and stayed with Gab′a•el. Raph′a•el[c] gave him the bond and informed him that Tō′bit's son Tō•bī′as had married and was inviting him to the wedding celebration. So Gab′a•el[d] got up and counted out to him the money bags, with their seals intact; then they loaded them on the camels.[e] [6] In the morning they both got up early and went to the wedding celebration. When they came into Rag′ū•el's house they found Tō•bī′as reclining at table. He sprang up and greeted Gab′a•el,[f] who wept and blessed him with the words, "Good and noble son of a father good and noble, upright and generous! May the Lord grant the blessing of heaven to you and your wife, and to your wife's father and mother. Blessed be God, for I see in Tō•bī′as the very image of my cousin Tō′bit."

Anxiety of the Parents

Now, day by day, Tō′bit kept counting how many days Tō•bī′as[d] would need for going and for returning. And when the days had passed and his son did not appear, [2] he said, "Is it possible that he has been detained? Or that Gab′a•el has died, and there is no one to give him the money?" [3] And he began to worry. [4] His wife Anna said, "My child has perished and is no longer among the living." And she began to weep and mourn for her son, saying, [5] "Woe to me, my child, the light of my eyes, that I let you make the journey." [6] But Tō′bit kept saying to her, "Be quiet and stop worrying, my dear;[g] he is all right. Probably something unexpected has happened there. The man who went with him is trustworthy and is one of our own kin. Do not grieve for him, my dear;[g] he will soon be here." [7] She answered him, "Be quiet yourself! Stop trying to deceive me! My child has perished." She would rush out every day and watch the road her son had taken, and would heed no one.[h] When the sun had set she would go in and mourn and weep all night long, getting no sleep at all.

Tobias and Sarah Start for Home

Now when the fourteen days of the wedding celebration had ended that Rag′ū•el had sworn to observe for his daughter, Tō•bī′as came to him and said, "Send me back, for I know that my father and mother do not believe that they will see me again. So I beg of you, father, to let me go so that I may return to my own father. I have already explained to you how I left him." [8] But Rag′ū•el said to

Tō•bī′as, "Stay, my child, stay with me; I will send messengers to your father Tō′bit and they will inform him about you." [9] But he said, "No! I beg you to send me back to my father." [10] So Rag′ū•el promptly gave Tō•bī′as his wife Sarah, as well as half of all his property: male and female slaves, oxen and sheep, donkeys and camels, clothing, money, and household goods. [11] Then he saw them safely off; he embraced Tō•bī′as[f] and said, "Farewell, my child; have a safe journey. The Lord of heaven prosper you and your wife Sarah, and may I see children of yours before I die." [12] Then he kissed his daughter Sarah and said to her, "My daughter, honor your father-in-law and your mother-in-law,[i] since from now on they are as much your parents as those who gave you birth. Go in peace, daughter, and may I hear a good report about you as long as I live." Then he bade them farewell and let them go. Then Edna said to Tō•bī′as, "My child and dear brother, the Lord of heaven bring you back safely, and may I live long enough to see children of you and of my daughter Sarah before I die. In the sight of the Lord I entrust my daughter to you; do nothing to grieve her all the days of your life. Go in peace, my child. From now on I am your mother and Sarah is your beloved wife.[g] May we all prosper together all the days of our lives." Then she kissed them both and saw them safely off. [13] Tō•bī′as parted from Rag′ū•el with happiness and joy, praising the Lord of heaven and earth, King over all, because he had made his journey a success. Finally, he blessed Rag′ū•el and his wife Edna, and said, "I have been commanded by the Lord to honor you all the days of my life."[j]

Homeward Journey

When they came near to Ka•ser′in, which is opposite Nin′e•veh, Raph′a•el said, [2] "You are aware of how we left your father. [3] Let us run ahead of your wife and prepare the house while they are still on the way." [4] As they went on together Raph′a•el[d] said to him, "Have the gall ready." And the dog[k] went along behind them.

[5] Meanwhile Anna sat looking intently down the road by which her son would come. [6] When she caught sight of him coming, she said to his father, "Look, your son is coming, and the man who went with him!"

---

[b] In other ancient authorities verse 3 precedes verse 4
[c] Gk *He*   [d] Gk *he*   [e] Other ancient authorities lack *on the camels*   [f] Gk *him*   [g] Gk *sister*   [h] Other ancient authorities read *and she would eat nothing*   [i] Other ancient authorities lack parts of *Then . . . mother-in-law*
[j] Lat: Meaning of Gk uncertain   [k] Codex Sinaiticus reads *And the Lord*

Tobit's Sight Restored
(Cp Acts 9.18)

7 Raph′a•el said to Tō•bī′as, before he had approached his father, "I know that his eyes will be opened. 8 Smear the gall of the fish on his eyes; the medicine will make the white films shrink and peel off from his eyes, and your father will regain his sight and see the light."

9 Then Anna ran up to her son and threw her arms around him, saying, "Now that I have seen you, my child, I am ready to die." And she wept. 10 Then Tō′bit got up and came stumbling out through the courtyard door. Tō•bī′as went up to him, 11 with the gall of the fish in his hand, and holding him firmly, he blew into his eyes, saying, "Take courage, father." With this he applied the medicine on his eyes, 12 and it made them smart.*l* 13 Next, with both his hands he peeled off the white films from the corners of his eyes. Then Tō′-bit*m* saw his son and*n* threw his arms around him, 14 and he wept and said to him, "I see you, my son, the light of my eyes!" Then he said,

"Blessed be God,
    and blessed be his great name,
    and blessed be all his holy angels.
May his holy name be blessed*o*
    throughout all the ages.
15 Though he afflicted me,
    he has had mercy upon me.*p*
Now I see my son Tō•bī′as!"

So Tō′bit went in rejoicing and praising God at the top of his voice. Tō•bī′as reported to his father that his journey had been successful, that he had brought the money, that he had married Rag′ū•el's daughter Sarah, and that she was, indeed, on her way there, very near to the gate of Nin′e•veh.

16 Then Tō′bit, rejoicing and praising God, went out to meet his daughter-in-law at the gate of Nin′e•veh. When the people of Nin′e•veh saw him coming, walking along in full vigor and with no one leading him, they were amazed. 17 Before them all, Tō′bit acknowledged that God had been merciful to him and had restored his sight. When Tō′bit met Sarah the wife of his son Tō•bī′as, he blessed her saying, "Come in, my daughter, and welcome. Blessed be your God who has brought you to us, my daughter. Blessed be your father and your mother, blessed be my son Tō•bī′as, and blessed be you, my daughter. Come in now to your home, and welcome, with blessing and joy. Come in, my daughter." So on that day there was rejoicing among all the Jews who were in Nin′e•veh. 18 A•hī′kar and his nephew Nā′dab were also present to share Tō′bit's joy. With merriment they celebrated Tō•bī′as's wedding feast for seven days, and many gifts were given to him.*q*

Raphael's Wages

When the wedding celebration was ended, Tō′bit called his son Tō•bī′as and said to him, "My child, see to paying the wages of the man who went with you, and give him a bonus as well." 2 He replied, "Father, how much shall I pay him? It would do no harm to give him half of the possessions brought back with me. 3 For he has led me back to you safely, he cured my wife, he brought the money back with me, and he healed you. How much extra shall I give him as a bonus?" 4 Tō′bit said, "He deserves, my child, to receive half of all that he brought back." 5 So Tō′bī′as*m* called him and said, "Take for your wages half of all that you brought back, and farewell."

Raphael's Exhortation
(Sir 29.8–13; Mt 6.1–18)

6 Then Raph′a•el*m* called the two of them privately and said to them, "Bless God and acknowledge him in the presence of all the living for the good things he has done for you. Bless and sing praise to his name. With fitting honor declare to all people the deeds*r* of God. Do not be slow to acknowledge him. 7 It is good to conceal the secret of a king, but to acknowledge and reveal the works of God, and with fitting honor to acknowledge him. Do good and evil will not overtake you. 8 Prayer with fasting*s* is good, but better than both is almsgiving with righteousness. A little with righteousness is better than wealth with wrongdoing.*t* It is better to give alms than to lay up gold. 9 For almsgiving saves from death and purges away every sin. Those who give alms will enjoy a full life, 10 but those who commit sin and do wrong are their own worst enemies.

Raphael Discloses His Identity

11 "I will now declare the whole truth to you and will conceal nothing from you. Already I have declared it to you when I said, 'It is good to conceal the secret of a king, but to reveal with due honor the works of God.' 12 So now when you and Sarah prayed, it was I who brought and read*u* the record of your prayer before the glory of the Lord,

---

l Lat: Meaning of Gk uncertain   *m* Gk *he*   *n* Other ancient authorities lack *saw his son and*   *o* Codex Sinaiticus reads *May his great name be upon us and blessed be all the angels*   *p* Lat: Gk lacks this line   *q* Other ancient authorities lack parts of this sentence
r Gk *words*; other ancient authorities read *words of the deeds*   *s* Codex Sinaiticus *with sincerity*   *t* Lat   *u* Lat: Gk lacks *and read*

and likewise whenever you would bury the dead. ¹³ And that time when you did not hesitate to get up and leave your dinner to go and bury the dead, ¹⁴ I was sent to you to test you. And at the same time God sent me to heal you and Sarah your daughter-in-law. ¹⁵ I am Raph′a·el, one of the seven angels who stand ready and enter before the glory of the Lord."

16 The two of them were shaken; they fell face down, for they were afraid. ¹⁷ But he said to them, "Do not be afraid; peace be with you. Bless God forevermore. ¹⁸ As for me, when I was with you, I was not acting on my own will, but by the will of God. Bless him each and every day; sing his praises. ¹⁹ Although you were watching me, I really did not eat or drink anything—but what you saw was a vision. ²⁰ So now get up from the ground,ᵛ and acknowledge God. See, I am ascending to him who sent me. Write down all these things that have happened to you." And he ascended. ²¹ Then they stood up, and could see him no more. ²² They kept blessing God and singing his praises, and they acknowledged God for these marvelous deeds of his, when an angel of God had appeared to them.

Tobit's Thanksgiving to God
(Rev 21.9 — 22.5)

Then To′bitʷ said:

"Blessed be God who lives forever,
    because his kingdomˣ lasts throughout
        all ages.

² For he afflicts, and he shows mercy;
        he leads down to Hades in the lowest
            regions of the earth,
        and he brings up from the great abyss,ʸ
        and there is nothing that can escape his
            hand.
³ Acknowledge him before the nations,
        O children of Israel;
    for he has scattered you among them.
⁴   He has shown you his greatness even
            there.
    Exalt him in the presence of every living
        being,
        because he is our Lord and he is our
            God;
        he is our Father and he is God forever.
⁵ He will afflictᶻ you for your iniquities,
        but he will again show mercy on all of
            you.
    He will gather you from all the nations
        among whom you have been
            scattered.
⁶ If you turn to him with all your heart and
            with all your soul,
        to do what is true before him,
    then he will turn to you
        and will no longer hide his face from
            you.

ᵛ Other ancient authorities read *now bless the Lord on earth*   ʷ Gk *he*   ˣ Other ancient authorities read *forever, and his kingdom*   ʸ Gk *from destruction*   ᶻ Other ancient authorities read *He afflicted*

HOPE FOR THE FAITHFUL!

When the Jews lived under the influence of Greek culture, there was a great need for hope. The story of Tobit and Tobias, whose names mean "goodness" and "God is good," was written to give hope to those who continue to be faithful to God, even in difficult times.

Tobit is the model of the good Israelite at all times and places. God's saving actions for him and his family symbolize God's actions toward Israel. In this spirit, before his death, Tobit sings a beautiful hymn in thanksgiving for God's goodness and with hope in the triumph of Jerusalem over its oppressors.

■ **Recognize the goodness of God in your life and the way in which you fail God.**
■ **Take a moment to pray in Tobit's style. Praise God for the blessings in your life; ask forgiveness for the times you have failed God; give thanks for the times God has answered your prayers in a wiser way than what you had asked for. Pray not only for yourself but for all people, with hope for the triumph of God's love and peace over the egoism, hatred, and violence so common today.**

▶ **Tobit, chapter 13**

So now see what he has done for you;
  acknowledge him at the top of your
    voice.
Bless the Lord of righteousness,
  and exalt the King of the ages.*a*
In the land of my exile I acknowledge him,
  and show his power and majesty to a
    nation of sinners:
'Turn back, you sinners, and do what is
    right before him;
  perhaps he may look with favor upon
    you and show you mercy.'

7 As for me, I exalt my God,
  and my soul rejoices in the King of
    heaven.
8 Let all people speak of his majesty,
  and acknowledge him in Jerusalem.
9 O Jerusalem, the holy city,
  he afflicted*b* you for the deeds of your
    hands,*c*
  but will again have mercy on the children
    of the righteous.
10 Acknowledge the Lord, for he is good,*d*
  and bless the King of the ages,
  so that his tent*e* may be rebuilt in you in
    joy.
May he cheer all those within you who are
    captives,
  and love all those within you who are
    distressed,
  to all generations forever.
11 A bright light will shine to all the ends of
    the earth;
  many nations will come to you from far
    away,
  the inhabitants of the remotest parts of the
    earth to your holy name,
  bearing gifts in their hands for the King
    of heaven.
Generation after generation will give joyful
    praise in you;
  the name of the chosen city will endure
    forever.
12 Cursed are all who speak a harsh word
    against you;
  cursed are all who conquer you
    and pull down your walls,
  all who overthrow your towers
    and set your homes on fire.
  But blessed forever will be all who revere
    you.*f*
13 Go, then, and rejoice over the children of
    the righteous,
  for they will be gathered together
    and will praise the Lord of the ages.

14 Happy are those who love you,
  and happy are those who rejoice in your
    prosperity.
Happy also are all people who grieve with you
    because of your afflictions;
  for they will rejoice with you
    and witness all your glory forever.
15 My soul blesses*g* the Lord, the great King!
16 For Jerusalem will be built*h* as his house
    for all ages.
How happy I will be if a remnant of my
    descendants should survive
  to see your glory and acknowledge the
    King of heaven.
The gates of Jerusalem will be built with
    sapphire and emerald,
  and all your walls with precious stones.
The towers of Jerusalem will be built with
    gold,
  and their battlements with pure gold.
The streets of Jerusalem will be paved
    with ruby and with stones of O'phir.
17 The gates of Jerusalem will sing hymns of
    joy,
  and all her houses will cry, 'Hallelujah!
Blessed be the God of Israel!'
  and the blessed will bless the holy name
    forever and ever."

Tobit's Final Counsel
(Nah 1.2—3.19; Zech 8.20–23)

So ended To'bit's words of praise.

2 To'bit*i* died in peace when he was one hundred twelve years old, and was buried with great honor in Nin'e·veh. He was sixty-two*j* years old when he lost his eyesight, and after regaining it he lived in prosperity, giving alms and continually blessing God and acknowledging God's majesty.

3 When he was about to die, he called his son To'bi'as and the seven sons of To'bi'as*k* and gave this command: "My son, take your children 4 and hurry off to Med'i·a, for I believe the word of God that Na'hum spoke about Nin'e·veh, that all these things will take place and overtake Assyria and Nin'e·veh. Indeed, everything that was spoken by the prophets of Israel, whom God sent, will occur. None of all their words will fail, but all will come

---

a The lacuna in codex Sinaiticus, verses 6b to 10a, is filled in from other ancient authorities   *b* Other ancient authorities read *will afflict*   *c* Other ancient authorities read *your children*   *d* Other ancient authorities read *Lord worthily*   *e* Or *tabernacle*   *f* Other ancient authorities read *who build you up*   *g* Or *O my soul, bless*   *h* Other ancient authorities add *for a city*   *i* Gk *He*   *j* Other ancient authorities read *fifty-eight*   *k* Lat: Gk lacks *and the seven sons of Tobias*

true at their appointed times. So it will be safer in Mēd′i•a than in Assyria and Babylon. For I know and believe that whatever God has said will be fulfilled and will come true; not a single word of the prophecies will fail. All of our kindred, inhabitants of the land of Israel, will be scattered and taken as captives from the good land; and the whole land of Israel will be desolate, even Sa•mār′i•a and Jerusalem will be desolate. And the temple of God in it will be burned to the ground, and it will be desolate for a while.*l*

5 "But God will again have mercy on them, and God will bring them back into the land of Israel; and they will rebuild the temple of God, but not like the first one until the period when the times of fulfillment shall come. After this they all will return from their exile and will rebuild Jerusalem in splendor; and in it the temple of God will be rebuilt, just as the prophets of Israel have said concerning it. ⁶Then the nations in the whole world will all be converted and worship God in truth. They will all abandon their idols, which deceitfully have led them into their error; ⁷and in righteousness they will praise the eternal God. All the Israelites who are saved in those days and are truly mindful of God will be gathered together; they will go to Jerusalem and live in safety forever in the land of Abraham, and it will be given over to them. Those who sincerely love God will rejoice, but those who commit sin and injustice will vanish from all the earth. ⁸,⁹So now, my children, I command you, serve God faithfully and do what is pleasing in his sight. Your children are also to be commanded to do what is right and to give alms, and to be mindful of God and to bless his name at all times with sincerity and with all their strength. So now, my son, leave Nin′e•veh; do not remain here. ¹⁰On whatever day you bury your mother beside me, do not stay overnight within the confines of the city. For I see that there is much wickedness within it, and that much deceit is practiced

within it, while the people are without shame. See, my son, what Nā′dab did to A•hī′kar who had reared him. Was he not, while still alive, brought down into the earth? For God repaid him to his face for this shameful treatment. A•hī′kar came out into the light, but Nā′dab went into the eternal darkness, because he tried to kill A•hī′kar. Because he gave alms, A•hī′kar*m* escaped the fatal trap that Nā′dab had set for him, but Nā′dab fell into it himself, and was destroyed. ¹¹So now, my children, see what almsgiving accomplishes, and what injustice does—it brings death! But now my breath fails me."

Death of Tobit and Anna

Then they laid him on his bed, and he died; and he received an honorable funeral. ¹²When Tōbī′as′s mother died, he buried her beside his father. Then he and his wife and children*n* returned to Mēd′i•a and settled in Ec•bat′a•na with Rag′ū•el his father-in-law. ¹³He treated his parents-in-law*o* with great respect in their old age, and buried them in Ec•bat′a•na of Mēd′i•a. He inherited both the property of Rag′ū•el and that of his father Tō′bit. ¹⁴He died highly respected at the age of one hundred seventeen*p* years. ¹⁵Before he died he heard*q* of the destruction of Nin′e•veh, and he saw its prisoners being led into Mēd′i•a, those whom King Cȳ•ax′a•rēs*r* of Mēd′i•a had taken captive. Tōbī′as*s* praised God for all he had done to the people of Nin′e•veh and Assyria; before he died he rejoiced over Nin′e•veh, and he blessed the Lord God forever and ever. Amen.*t*

---

l Lat: Other ancient authorities read *of God will be in distress and will be burned for a while*   *m* Gk *he*; other ancient authorities read *Manasses*   *n* Codex Sinaiticus lacks *and children*   *o* Gk *them*   *p* Other authorities read other numbers   *q* Codex Sinaiticus reads *saw and heard*   *r* Cn: Codex Sinaiticus *Ahikar*; other ancient authorities read *Nebuchadnezzar and Ahasuerus*   *s* Gk *He*   *t* Other ancient authorities lack *Amen*

Do you like to cheer for the underdog? If so, you are like most people. Whether in a law court, on a football field, or in politics, we get a thrill from seeing the high and mighty toppled by a courageous and determined underdog. This theme is evident in some of the most popular stories of the Old Testament: a group of Hebrew slaves escapes from Pharaoh's army; the teenage David topples the giant Goliath; the prophet Daniel escapes injury in the lions' den. Judith's story is another in which the little people —against all odds—somehow come out on top.

At a Glance

- **Chapters 1–7.** the Jews in danger
- **Chapters 8–16.** Judith to the rescue

In-depth

As the Book of Judith opens, the mighty Assyrian army is on the march against Jerusalem. To block the advance, the citizens of the small town of Bethulia are asked by the high priest to resist the army's movement. With little hope of success but a great deal of courage, the Bethulians accept the challenge. When they are at the point of surrender, a childless widow named Judith steps forward. Putting all her trust in "the God of the lowly, helper of the oppressed, upholder of the weak, protector of the forsaken, savior of those without hope" (Jdt 9.11), she bravely delivers her nation from certain defeat.

The story of Judith must have presented a challenge to the male-dominated world of the Israelites. As a childless widow, Judith would have had little social standing. Yet she succeeds where the king, the priests, and the leaders of the city fail. It is interesting that the name Judith is probably not even a proper name. It simply means "Jewish woman." In a sense, Judith stands for all the Jewish women of the past who have served God through their faith, courage, and decisive action.

Because of its many historical errors, the Book of Judith is clearly a fictional work. With remarkable storytelling flair, the author underlines one of the major elements of Hebrew faith: "O Lord, you are great and glorious, / wonderful in strength, invincible" (16.13). This was the kind of faith that the underdog people of God needed as they faced the growing might of the Roman Empire.

Quick Facts

Setting
a fictional book without a clear historical setting

Author
unknown, writing early in the last century B.C.

Themes
a woman of faith and courage, God's saving power

The Book of *Judith*

485

Judith

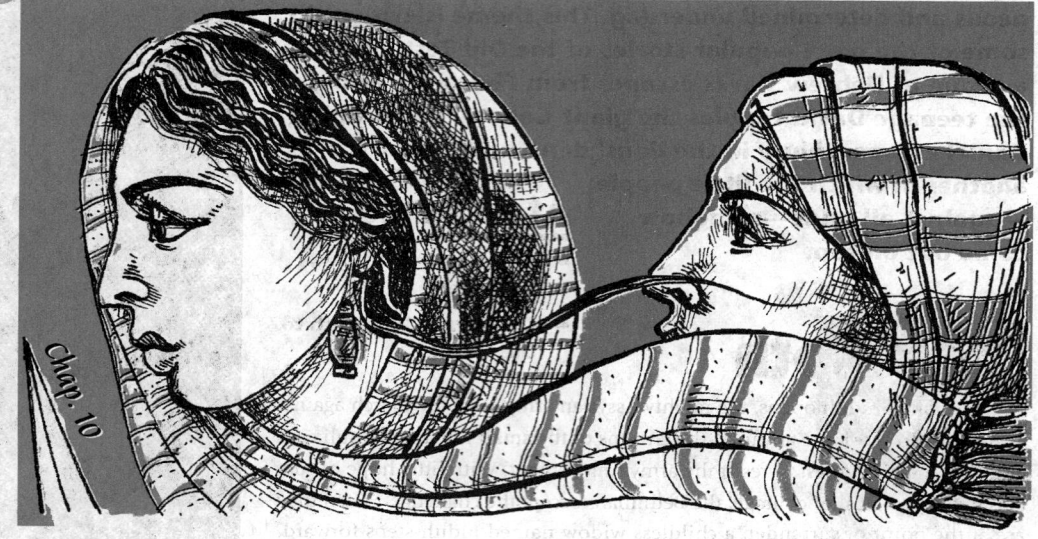

Chap. 10

Arphaxad Fortifies Ecbatana
(Cp Ezra 6.2)

It was the twelfth year of the reign of Ne·bū·chad-nez′zar, who ruled over the Assyrians in the great city of Nin′e·veh. In those days Ar·pha′xad ruled over the Mēdes in Ec·bat′a·na. ²He built walls around Ec·bat′a·na with hewn stones three cubits thick and six cubits long; he made the walls seventy cubits high and fifty cubits wide. ³At its gates he raised towers one hundred cubits high and sixty cubits wide at the foundations. ⁴He made its gates seventy cubits high and forty cubits wide to allow his armies to march out in force and his infantry to form their ranks. ⁵Then King Ne·bū·chad·nez′zar made war against King Ar·pha′xad in the great plain that is on the borders of Rā′gau. ⁶There rallied to him all the people of the hill country and all those who lived along the Euphrates, the Tigris, and the Hȳ·das′pēs, and, on the plain, Ar′i·och, king of the El·y·mē′ans. Thus, many nations joined the forces of the Chal·dē′ans.ᵃ

Nebuchadnezzar Issues Ultimatum

7 Then Ne·bū·chad·nez′zar, king of the Assyrians, sent messengers to all who lived in Persia and to all who lived in the west, those who lived in Ci·li′ci·a and Damascus, Lebanon and An·ti·leb′a-non, and all who lived along the seacoast, ⁸and those among the nations of Car′mel and Gil′e·ad, and Upper Galilee and the great plain of Es·dra·ē′-lon, ⁹and all who were in Sa·mar′i·a and its towns, and beyond the Jordan as far as Jerusalem and Beth′a·ny and Chel′ous and Kā′desh and the river of Egypt, and Tah′pan·hēs and Rā·am′sēs and the whole land of Gō′shen, ¹⁰even beyond Tā′nis and Memphis, and all who lived in Egypt as far as the borders of Ethiopia. ¹¹But all who lived in the whole region disregarded the summons of Ne·bū-chad·nez′zar, king of the Assyrians, and refused to join him in the war; for they were not afraid of him, but regarded him as only one man.ᵇ So they sent back his messengers empty-handed and in disgrace.

12 Then Ne·bū·chad·nez′zar became very angry with this whole region, and swore by his throne and kingdom that he would take revenge on the whole territory of Ci·li′ci·a and Damascus and Syria, that he would kill with his sword also all the inhabitants of the land of Mō′ab, and the people

---

ᵃ Syr: Gk *Cheleoudites*   ᵇ Or *a man*

of Am′mon, and all Judea, and every one in Egypt, as far as the coasts of the two seas.

Arphaxad Is Defeated

13 In the seventeenth year he led his forces against King Ar·phā′xad and defeated him in battle, overthrowing the whole army of Ar·phā′xad and all his cavalry and all his chariots. 14 Thus he took possession of his towns and came to Ec·bat′a·na, captured its towers, plundered its markets, and turned its glory into disgrace. 15 He captured Ar·phā′xad in the mountains of Rā′gau and struck him down with his spears, thus destroying him once and for all. 16 Then he returned to Nin′e·veh, he and all his combined forces, a vast body of troops; and there he and his forces rested and feasted for one hundred twenty days.

The Expedition against the West

In the eighteenth year, on the twenty-second day of the first month, there was talk in the palace of Ne·bū·chad·nez′zar, king of the Assyrians, about carrying out his revenge on the whole region, just as he had said. 2 He summoned all his ministers and all his nobles and set before them his secret plan and recounted fully, with his own lips, all the wickedness of the region.c 3 They decided that every one who had not obeyed his command should be destroyed.

4 When he had completed his plan, Ne·bū·chad·nez′zar, king of the Assyrians, called Hol·o·fer′nēs, the chief general of his army, second only to himself, and said to him, 5 "Thus says the Great King, the lord of the whole earth: Leave my presence and take with you men confident in their strength, one hundred twenty thousand foot soldiers and twelve thousand cavalry. 6 March out against all the land to the west, because they disobeyed my orders. 7 Tell them to prepare earth and water, for I am coming against them in my anger, and will cover the whole face of the earth with the feet of my troops, to whom I will hand them over to be plundered. 8 Their wounded shall fill their ravines and gullies, and the swelling river shall be filled with their dead. 9 I will lead them away captive to the ends of the whole earth. 10 You shall go and seize all their territory for me in advance. They must yield themselves to you, and you shall hold them for me until the day of their punishment. 11 But to those who resist show no mercy, but hand them over to slaughter and plunder throughout your whole region. 12 For as I live, and by the power of my kingdom, what I have spoken I will accomplish by my own hand. 13 And you—take

care not to transgress any of your lord's commands, but carry them out exactly as I have ordered you; do it without delay."

Campaign of Holofernes

14 So Hol·o·fer′nēs left the presence of his lord, and summoned all the commanders, generals, and officers of the Assyrian army. 15 He mustered the picked troops by divisions as his lord had ordered him to do, one hundred twenty thousand of them, together with twelve thousand archers on horseback, 16 and he organized them as a great army is marshaled for a campaign. 17 He took along a vast number of camels and donkeys and mules for transport, and innumerable sheep and oxen and goats for food; 18 also ample rations for everyone, and a huge amount of gold and silver from the royal palace.

19 Then he set out with his whole army, to go ahead of King Ne·bū·chad·nez′zar and to cover the whole face of the earth to the west with their chariots and cavalry and picked foot soldiers. 20 Along with them went a mixed crowd like a swarm of locusts, like the dustd of the earth—a multitude that could not be counted.

21 They marched for three days from Nin′e·veh to the plain of Bec′ti·leth, and camped opposite Bec′ti·leth near the mountain that is to the north of Upper Ci·li′ci·a. 22 From there Hol·o·fer′nēse took his whole army, the infantry, cavalry, and chariots, and went up into the hill country. 23 He ravaged Put and Lud, and plundered all the Ras′si·sites and the Ish′ma·el·ītes on the border of the desert, south of the country of the Chel′le·ans. 24 Then he followedf the Euphrates and passed through Mes·o·po·tā′mi·a and destroyed all the fortified towns along the brook Ab′ron, as far as the sea. 25 He also seized the territory of Ci·li′ci·a, and killed everyone who resisted him. Then he came to the southern borders of Jā′pheth, facing Arabia. 26 He surrounded all the Mid′i·an·ites, and burned their tents and plundered their sheepfolds. 27 Then he went down into the plain of Damascus during the wheat harvest, and burned all their fields and destroyed their flocks and herds and sacked their towns and ravaged their lands and put all their young men to the sword.

28 So fear and dread of him fell upon all the people who lived along the seacoast, at Sī′don and Tyre, and those who lived in Sur and Ō·cī′na and all who lived in Jam′ni·a. Those who lived in A·zō′tus and As′ca·lon feared him greatly.

---

c Meaning of Gk uncertain   d Gk sand   e Gk he
f Or crossed

Entreaties for Peace
(Cp Dan 3.1–7)

They therefore sent messengers to him to sue for peace in these words: 2 "We, the servants of Ne•bū-chad•nez′zar, the Great King, lie prostrate before you. Do with us whatever you will. 3 See, our buildings and all our land and all our wheat fields and our flocks and herds and all our encampments*g* lie before you; do with them as you please. 4 Our towns and their inhabitants are also your slaves; come and deal with them as you see fit."

5 The men came to Hol•o•fer′nēs and told him all this. 6 Then he went down to the seacoast with his army and stationed garrisons in the fortified towns and took picked men from them as auxiliaries. 7 These people and all in the countryside welcomed him with garlands and dances and tambourines. 8 Yet he demolished all their shrines*h* and cut down their sacred groves; for he had been commissioned to destroy all the gods of the land, so that all nations should worship Ne•bū•chad•nez′zar alone, and that all their dialects and tribes should call upon him as a god.

9 Then he came toward Es•dra•ē′lon, near Dō′than, facing the great ridge of Judea; 10 he camped between Gē′ba and Scyth•op′o•lis, and remained for a whole month in order to collect all the supplies for his army.

Judea on the Alert

When the Israelites living in Judea heard of everything that Hol•o•fer′nēs, the general of Ne•bū•chad•nez′zar, the king of the Assyrians, had done to the nations, and how he had plundered and destroyed all their temples, 2 they were therefore greatly terrified at his approach; they were alarmed both for Jerusalem and for the temple of the Lord their God. 3 For they had only recently returned from exile, and all the people of Judea had just now gathered together, and the sacred vessels and the altar and the temple had been consecrated after their profanation. 4 So they sent word to every district of Sa•mār′i•a, and to Kō′na, Beth-hō′ron, Bel′-māin, and Jericho, and to Chō′ba and Aē•sor′a, and the valley of Salem. 5 They immediately seized all the high hilltops and fortified the villages on them and stored up food in preparation for war—since their fields had recently been harvested.

6 The high priest, Jō′a•kim, who was in Jerusalem at the time, wrote to the people of Beth•ū′li•a and Bet•o•mes•thā′im, which faces Es•dra•ē′lon opposite the plain near Dō′than, 7 ordering them to seize the mountain passes, since by them Judea could be invaded; and it would be easy to stop any

who tried to enter, for the approach was narrow, wide enough for only two at a time to pass.

Prayer and Penance

8 So the Israelites did as they had been ordered by the high priest Jō′a•kim and the senate of the whole people of Israel, in session at Jerusalem. 9 And every man of Israel cried out to God with great fervor, and they humbled themselves with much fasting. 10 They and their wives and their children and their cattle and every resident alien and hired laborer and purchased slave—they all put sackcloth around their waists. 11 And all the Israelite men, women, and children living at Jerusalem prostrated themselves before the temple and put ashes on their heads and spread out their sackcloth before the Lord. 12 They even draped the altar with sackcloth and cried out in unison, praying fervently to the God of Israel not to allow their infants to be carried off and their wives to be taken as booty, and the towns they had inherited to be destroyed, and the sanctuary to be profaned and desecrated to the malicious joy of the Gentiles.

13 The Lord heard their prayers and had regard for their distress; for the people fasted many days throughout Judea and in Jerusalem before the sanctuary of the Lord Almighty. 14 The high priest Jō′a•kim and all the priests who stood before the Lord and ministered to the Lord, with sackcloth around their loins, offered the daily burnt offerings, the votive offerings, and freewill offerings of the people. 15 With ashes on their turbans, they cried out to the Lord with all their might to look with favor on the whole house of Israel.

Council against the Israelites

It was reported to Hol•o•fer′nēs, the general of the Assyrian army, that the people of Israel had prepared for war and had closed the mountain passes and fortified all the high hilltops and set up barricades in the plains. 2 In great anger he called together all the princes of Mō′ab and the commanders of Am′mon and all the governors of the coastland, 3 and said to them, "Tell me, you Cā′naan•ītes, what people is this that lives in the hill country? What towns do they inhabit? How large is their army, and in what does their power and strength consist? Who rules over them as king and leads their army? 4 And why have they alone, of all who live in the west, refused to come out and meet me?"

---

g Gk *all the sheepfolds of our tents*   *h* Syr: Gk *borders*

Achior's Report
(Gen 11.27 — 12.5; Ex 7.1 — 12.46; 14.21 – 22)

5 Then Ā′chi•or, the leader of all the Am′mon-
ītes, said to him, "May my lord please listen to a
report from the mouth of your servant, and I will
tell you the truth about this people that lives in
the mountain district near you. No falsehood shall
come from your servant's mouth. 6 These people
are descended from the Chal•dē′ans. 7 At one time
they lived in Mes•o•po•tā′mi•a, because they did not
wish to follow the gods of their ancestors who
were in Chal•dē′a. 8 Since they had abandoned the
ways of their ancestors, and worshiped the God of
heaven, the God they had come to know, their ancestors[i] drove them out from the presence of their
gods. So they fled to Mes•o•po•tā′mi•a, and lived
there for a long time. 9 Then their God commanded them to leave the place where they were
living and go to the land of Cā′naan. There they
settled, and grew very prosperous in gold and silver and very much livestock. 10 When a famine
spread over the land of Cā′naan they went down
to Egypt and lived there as long as they had food.
There they became so great a multitude that their
race could not be counted. 11 So the king of Egypt
became hostile to them; he exploited them and
forced them to make bricks. 12 They cried out to
their God, and he afflicted the whole land of Egypt
with incurable plagues. So the Egyptians drove
them out of their sight. 13 Then God dried up the
Red Sea before them, 14 and he led them by the
way of Sinai and Kā′desh-bar′nē•a. They drove out
all the people of the desert, 15 and took up residence in the land of the Am′o•rītes, and by their
might destroyed all the inhabitants of Hesh′bon;
and crossing over the Jordan they took possession
of all the hill country. 16 They drove out before
them the Cā′naan•ītes, the Per′iz•zītes, the Jeb′ū-
sītes, the Shē′chem•ītes, and all the Ger′ge•sītes, and
lived there a long time.

17 "As long as they did not sin against their
God they prospered, for the God who hates iniquity is with them. 18 But when they departed from
the way he had prescribed for them, they were utterly defeated in many battles and were led away
captive to a foreign land. The temple of their God
was razed to the ground, and their towns were occupied by their enemies. 19 But now they have returned to their God, and have come back from the
places where they were scattered, and have occupied Jerusalem, where their sanctuary is, and have
settled in the hill country, because it was uninhabited.

20 "So now, my master and lord, if there is
any oversight in this people and they sin against

their God and we find out their offense, then we
can go up and defeat them. 21 But if they are not a
guilty nation, then let my lord pass them by; for
their Lord and God will defend them, and we shall
become the laughingstock of the whole world."

22 When Ā′chi•or had finished saying these
things, all the people standing around the tent began to complain; Hol•o•fer′nēs' officers and all the
inhabitants of the seacoast and Mō′ab insisted that
he should be cut to pieces. 23 They said, "We are
not afraid of the Israelites; they are a people with
no strength or power for making war. 24 Therefore
let us go ahead, Lord Hol•o•fer′nēs, and your vast
army will swallow them up."

Achior Handed over to the Israelites

When the disturbance made by the people outside
the council had died down, Hol•o•fer′nēs, the commander of the Assyrian army, said to Ā′chi•or[j] in
the presence of all the foreign contingents:

2 "Who are you, Ā′chi•or and you mercenaries
of Ē′phra•im, to prophesy among us as you have
done today and tell us not to make war against the
people of Israel because their God will defend
them? What god is there except Ne•bū•chad•nez′zar?
He will send his forces and destroy them from the
face of the earth. Their God will not save them;
3 we the king's[k] servants will destroy them as one
man. They cannot resist the might of our cavalry.
4 We will overwhelm them;[l] their mountains will
be drunk with their blood, and their fields will be
full of their dead. Not even their footprints will
survive our attack; they will utterly perish. So says
King Ne•bū•chad•nez′zar, lord of the whole earth.
For he has spoken; none of his words shall be in
vain.

5 "As for you, Ā′chi•or, you Am′mon•ite mercenary, you have said these words in a moment of
perversity; you shall not see my face again from
this day until I take revenge on this race that came
out of Egypt. 6 Then at my return the sword of my
army and the spear[m] of my servants shall pierce
your sides, and you shall fall among their
wounded. 7 Now my slaves are going to take you
back into the hill country and put you in one of
the towns beside the passes. 8 You will not die until you perish along with them. 9 If you really hope
in your heart that they will not be taken, then do
not look downcast! I have spoken, and none of
my words fail to come true."

10 Then Hol•o•fer′nēs ordered his slaves, who
waited on him in his tent, to seize Ā′chi•or and

---

[i] Gk *they*   [j] Other ancient authorities add *and to all the*
Moabites   [k] Gk *his*   [l] Other ancient authorities add *with*
it   [m] Lat Syr: Gk *people*

take him away to Beth·u'li·a and hand him over to the Israelites. ¹¹ So the slaves took him and led him out of the camp into the plain, and from the plain they went up into the hill country and came to the springs below Beth·u'li·a. ¹² When the men of the town saw them,ⁿ they seized their weapons and ran out of the town to the top of the hill, and all the slingers kept them from coming up by throwing stones at them. ¹³ So having taken shelter below the hill, they bound A'chi·or and left him lying at the foot of the hill, and returned to their master.

14 Then the Israelites came down from their town and found him; they untied him and brought him into Beth·u'li·a and placed him before the magistrates of their town, ¹⁵ who in those days were Uz·zi'ah son of Mi'cah, of the tribe of Sim'e·on, and Chab'ris son of Go·thon'i·el, and Char'mis son of Mel'chi·el. ¹⁶ They called together all the elders of the town, and all their young men and women ran to the assembly. They set A'chi·or in the midst of all their people, and Uz·zi'ah questioned him about what had happened. ¹⁷ He answered and told them what had taken place at the council of Hol·o·fer'nēs, and all that he had said in the presence of the Assyrian leaders, and all that Hol·o·fer'nēs had boasted he would do against the house of Israel. ¹⁸ Then the people fell down and worshiped God, and cried out:

19 "O Lord God of heaven, see their arrogance, and have pity on our people in their humiliation, and look kindly today on the faces of those who are consecrated to you."

20 Then they reassured A'chi·or, and praised him highly. ²¹ Uz·zi'ah took him from the assembly to his own house and gave a banquet for the elders; and all that night they called on the God of Israel for help.

The Campaign against Bethulia

The next day Hol·o·fer'nēs ordered his whole army, and all the allies who had joined him, to break camp and move against Beth·u'li·a, and to seize the passes up into the hill country and make war on the Israelites. ² So all their warriors marched off that day; their fighting forces numbered one hundred seventy thousand infantry and twelve thousand cavalry, not counting the baggage and the foot soldiers handling it, a very great multitude. ³ They encamped in the valley near Beth·u'li·a, beside the spring, and they spread out in breadth over Do'than as far as Bal·ba'im and in length from Beth·u'li·a to Cy'a·mon, which faces Es·dra·e'lon.

4 When the Israelites saw their vast numbers, they were greatly terrified and said to one another,

"They will now strip clean the whole land; neither the high mountains nor the valleys nor the hills will bear their weight." ⁵ Yet they all seized their weapons, and when they had kindled fires on their towers, they remained on guard all that night.

6 On the second day Hol·o·fer'nēs led out all his cavalry in full view of the Israelites in Beth·u'li·a. ⁷ He reconnoitered the approaches to their town, and visited the springs that supplied their water; he seized them and set guards of soldiers over them, and then returned to his army.

8 Then all the chieftains of the E'dom·ites and all the leaders of the Mo'ab·ites and the commanders of the coastland came to him and said, ⁹ "Listen to what we have to say, my lord, and your army will suffer no losses. ¹⁰ This people, the Israelites, do not rely on their spears but on the height of the mountains where they live, for it is not easy to reach the tops of their mountains. ¹¹ Therefore, my lord, do not fight against them in regular formation, and not a man of your army will fall. ¹² Remain in your camp, and keep all the men in your forces with you; let your servants take possession of the spring of water that flows from the foot of the mountain, ¹³ for this is where all the people of Beth·u'li·a get their water. So thirst will destroy them, and they will surrender their town. Meanwhile, we and our people will go up to the tops of the nearby mountains and camp there to keep watch to see that no one gets out of the town. ¹⁴ They and their wives and children will waste away with famine, and before the sword reaches them they will be strewn about in the streets where they live. ¹⁵ Thus you will pay them back with evil, because they rebelled and did not receive you peaceably."

16 These words pleased Hol·o·fer'nēs and all his attendants, and he gave orders to do as they had said. ¹⁷ So the army of the Am'mon·ites moved forward, together with five thousand Assyrians, and they encamped in the valley and seized the water supply and the springs of the Israelites. ¹⁸ And the E'dom·ites and Am'mon·ites went up and encamped in the hill country opposite Do'than; and they sent some of their men toward the south and the east, toward Eg're·beh, which is near Chu'sī beside the Wadi Moch'mur. The rest of the Assyrian army encamped in the plain, and covered the whole face of the land. Their tents and supply trains spread out in great number, and they formed a vast multitude.

ⁿ Other ancient authorities add *on the top of the hill*

The Distress of the Israelites

19 The Israelites then cried out to the Lord their God, for their courage failed, because all their enemies had surrounded them, and there was no way of escape from them. 20 The whole Assyrian army, their infantry, chariots, and cavalry, surrounded them for thirty-four days, until all the water containers of every inhabitant of Beth·ū′li·a were empty; 21 their cisterns were going dry, and on no day did they have enough water to drink, for their drinking water was rationed. 22 Their children were listless, and the women and young men fainted from thirst and were collapsing in the streets of the town and in the gateways; they no longer had any strength.

23 Then all the people, the young men, the women, and the children, gathered around Uz-zi′ah and the rulers of the town and cried out with a loud voice, and said before all the elders, 24 "Let God judge between you and us! You have done us a great injury in not making peace with the Assyrians. 25 For now we have no one to help us; God has sold us into their hands, to be strewn before them in thirst and exhaustion. 26 Now summon them and surrender the whole town as booty to the army of Hol·o·fer′nēs and to all his forces. 27 For it would be better for us to be captured by them.[o] We shall indeed become slaves, but our lives will be spared, and we shall not witness our little ones dying before our eyes, and our wives and children drawing their last breath. 28 We call to witness against you heaven and earth and our God, the Lord of our ancestors, who punishes us for our sins and the sins of our ancestors; do today the things that we have described!"

29 Then great and general lamentation arose throughout the assembly, and they cried out to the Lord God with a loud voice. 30 But Uz·zī′ah said to them, "Courage, my brothers and sisters![p] Let us hold out for five days more; by that time the Lord our God will turn his mercy to us again, for he will not forsake us utterly. 31 But if these days pass by, and no help comes for us, I will do as you say."

32 Then he dismissed the people to their various posts, and they went up on the walls and towers of their town. The women and children he sent home. In the town they were in great misery.

The Character of Judith

Now in those days Judith heard about these things: she was the daughter of Me·rar′ī son of Ox son of Joseph son of Ō′zi·el son of El·kī′ah son of An·a·nī′as son of Gideon son of Raph′a·in son of A·hī′tub son of E·lī′jah son of Hil·kī′ah son of E·lī′ab son of Na·than′a·el son of Sa·lā′mi·el son of Sar·a-

sad′aī son of Israel. 2 Her husband Ma·nas′seh, who belonged to her tribe and family, had died during the barley harvest. 3 For as he stood overseeing those who were binding sheaves in the field, he was overcome by the burning heat, and took to his bed and died in his town Beth·ū′li·a. So they buried him with his ancestors in the field between Dō′than and Bal′a·mon. 4 Judith remained as a widow for three years and four months 5 at home where she set up a tent for herself on the roof of her house. She put sackcloth around her waist and dressed in widow's clothing. 6 She fasted all the days of her widowhood, except the day before the sabbath and the sabbath itself, the day before the new moon and the day of the new moon, and the festivals and days of rejoicing of the house of Israel. 7 She was beautiful in appearance, and was very lovely to behold. Her husband Ma·nas′seh had left her gold and silver, men and women slaves, livestock, and fields; and she maintained this estate. 8 No one spoke ill of her, for she feared God with great devotion.

Judith and the Elders
(Gen 22.1–18; 29.1—31.55; Deut 6.16; Rom 11.33–34)

9 When Judith heard the harsh words spoken by the people against the ruler, because they were faint for lack of water, and when she heard all that Uz·zi′ah said to them, and how he promised them under oath to surrender the town to the Assyrians after five days, 10 she sent her maid, who was in charge of all she possessed, to summon Uz·zi′ah and[q] Chab′ris and Char′mis, the elders of her town. 11 They came to her, and she said to them:

"Listen to me, rulers of the people of Beth·ū′li·a! What you have said to the people today is not right; you have even sworn and pronounced this oath between God and you, promising to surrender the town to our enemies unless the Lord turns and helps us within so many days. 12 Who are you to put God to the test today, and to set yourselves up in the place of[r] God in human affairs? 13 You are putting the Lord Almighty to the test, but you will never learn anything! 14 You cannot plumb the depths of the human heart or understand the workings of the human mind; how do you expect to search out God, who made all these things, and find out his mind or comprehend his thought? No, my brothers, do not anger the Lord our God. 15 For if he does not choose to help us within these five days, he has power to protect us within any

o Other ancient authorities add *than to die of thirst*
p Gk *Courage, brothers*   q Other ancient authorities lack *Uzziah and* (see verses 28 and 35)   r Or *above*

time he pleases, or even to destroy us in the presence of our enemies. 16 Do not try to bind the purposes of the Lord our God; for God is not like a human being, to be threatened, or like a mere mortal, to be won over by pleading. 17 Therefore, while we wait for his deliverance, let us call upon

AFRICAN AMERICAN
The Principle of *Kujichagulia*

"That man over there says that women need to be helped into carriages, and lifted over ditches, and to have the best place everywhere. Nobody ever helps me into carriages, or over mud puddles, or gives me any best place! And ain't I a woman?" (Sojourner Truth, 1851)

When people who are abused cower quietly in corners, injustice lives on. Bent heads, muffled voices, and terrified spirits invite wrongs to continue.

Judith was a biblical heroine who refused to let her role be determined by others. As a woman and a widow, she had little social standing in ancient Israel. Yet, she did not let this keep her from speaking out and challenging the community leaders to action.

Sojourner Truth was a modern hero who refused to keep quiet despite being mistreated and devalued. Her womanhood was slighted, and her personhood was trampled, yet she traveled America to tell all who would listen about the evils of slavery.

The Kwanzaa principle of *kujichagulia* (see "Kwanzaa as a Way of Life," Deut 10.12–22), or self-determination, sometimes requires us to stand up and speak out. Silence can be compliance. Thank God for the gift of boldness of speech! It gives us the power to speak the truth even in the most oppressive situations.

Dear God, give me the boldness of Judith and Sojourner Truth to address the wrongs of this world. Amen.

▶ Jdt 8.9–36

him to help us, and he will hear our voice, if it pleases him.

18 "For never in our generation, nor in these present days, has there been any tribe or family or people or town of ours that worships gods made with hands, as was done in days gone by. 19 That was why our ancestors were handed over to the sword and to pillage, and so they suffered a great catastrophe before our enemies. 20 But we know no other god but him, and so we hope that he will not disdain us or any of our nation. 21 For if we are captured, all Judea will be captured and our sanctuary will be plundered; and he will make us pay for its desecration with our blood. 22 The slaughter of our kindred and the captivity of the land and the desolation of our inheritance—all this he will bring on our heads among the Gentiles, wherever we serve as slaves; and we shall be an offense and a disgrace in the eyes of those who acquire us. 23 For our slavery will not bring us into favor, but the Lord our God will turn it to dishonor.

24 "Therefore, my brothers, let us set an example for our kindred, for their lives depend upon us, and the sanctuary—both the temple and the altar—rests upon us. 25 In spite of everything let us give thanks to the Lord our God, who is putting us to the test as he did our ancestors. 26 Remember what he did with Abraham, and how he tested Isaac, and what happened to Jacob in Syrian Mes•o•po•tā′-mi•a, while he was tending the sheep of Lā′ban, his mother's brother. 27 For he has not tried us with fire, as he did them, to search their hearts, nor has he taken vengeance on us; but the Lord scourges those who are close to him in order to admonish them."

28 Then Uz•zī′ah said to her, "All that you have said was spoken out of a true heart, and there is no one who can deny your words. 29 Today is not the first time your wisdom has been shown, but from the beginning of your life all the people have recognized your understanding, for your heart's disposition is right. 30 But the people were so thirsty that they compelled us to do for them what we have promised, and made us take an oath that we cannot break. 31 Now since you are a God-fearing woman, pray for us, so that the Lord may send us rain to fill our cisterns. Then we will no longer feel faint from thirst."

32 Then Judith said to them, "Listen to me. I am about to do something that will go down through all generations of our descendants. 33 Stand at the town gate tonight so that I may go out with my maid; and within the days after which you have promised to surrender the town to our enemies, the Lord will deliver Israel by my hand. 34 Only, do not try to find out what I am doing; for

I will not tell you until I have finished what I am about to do."

35 Uz•zi′ah and the rulers said to her, "Go in peace, and may the Lord God go before you, to take vengeance on our enemies." 36 So they returned from the tent and went to their posts.

The Prayer of Judith
(Gen 34.1–31)

Then Judith prostrated herself, put ashes on her head, and uncovered the sackcloth she was wearing. At the very time when the evening incense was being offered in the house of God in Jerusalem, Judith cried out to the Lord with a loud voice, and said,

2 "O Lord God of my ancestor Sim′e•on, to whom you gave a sword to take revenge on those strangers who had torn off a virgin's clothing[s] to defile her, and exposed her thighs to put her to shame, and polluted her womb to disgrace her; for you said, 'It shall not be done'—yet they did it; 3 so you gave up their rulers to be killed, and their bed, which was ashamed of the deceit they had practiced, was stained with blood, and you struck down slaves along with princes, and princes on their thrones. 4 You gave up their wives for booty and their daughters to captivity, and all their booty to be divided among your beloved children who burned with zeal for you and abhorred the pollution of their blood and called on you for help. O God, my God, hear me also, a widow.

5 "For you have done these things and those that went before and those that followed. You have designed the things that are now, and those that are to come. What you had in mind has happened; 6 the things you decided on presented themselves and said, 'Here we are!' For all your ways are prepared in advance, and your judgment is with foreknowledge.

7 "Here now are the Assyrians, a greatly increased force, priding themselves in their horses and riders, boasting in the strength of their foot soldiers, and trusting in shield and spear, in bow and sling. They do not know that you are the Lord who crushes wars; the Lord is your name. 8 Break their strength by your might, and bring down their power in your anger; for they intend to defile your sanctuary, and to pollute the tabernacle where your glorious name resides, and to break off the horns[t] of your altar with the sword. 9 Look at their pride, and send your wrath upon their heads. Give to me, a widow, the strong hand to do what I plan. 10 By the deceit of my lips strike down the slave with the prince and the prince with his servant; crush their arrogance by the hand of a woman.

Catholic Connections
THE BODY PRAYER

To pray, Judith prostrated herself, which means she lay facedown on the ground. This position demonstrates humility and surrender. Judith also wore ashes and sackcloth, additional symbols of repentance and sorrow.

You will see this prayer posture on Good Friday, when the priests lie down on the floor at the beginning of the service. It is a sign of reverence and humility as we remember in a special way Jesus' sacrifice on the cross. You will see priest and deacon candidates prostrate themselves during the ordination ceremony as a sign of humility and their dependence on God's strength to carry out their ministry—a sign not just for themselves but for the whole Christian community.

▶ Jdt 9.1

11 "For your strength does not depend on numbers, nor your might on the powerful. But you are the God of the lowly, helper of the oppressed, upholder of the weak, protector of the forsaken, savior of those without hope. 12 Please, please, God of my father, God of the heritage of Israel, Lord of heaven and earth, Creator of the waters, King of all your creation, hear my prayer! 13 Make my deceitful words bring wound and bruise on those who have planned cruel things against your covenant, and against your sacred house, and against Mount Zion, and against the house your children possess. 14 Let your whole nation and every tribe know and understand that you are God, the God of all power and might, and that there is no other who protects the people of Israel but you alone!"

---

s Cn: Gk *loosed her womb*   t Syr: Gk *horn*

Judith Prepares to Go to Holofernes

When Judith[u] had stopped crying out to the God of Israel, and had ended all these words, 2 she rose from where she lay prostrate. She called her maid and went down into the house where she lived on sabbaths and on her festal days. 3 She removed the sackcloth she had been wearing, took off her widow's garments, bathed her body with water, and anointed herself with precious ointment. She combed her hair, put on a tiara, and dressed herself in the festive attire that she used to wear while her husband Ma·nas′seh was living. 4 She put sandals on her feet, and put on her anklets, bracelets, rings, earrings, and all her other jewelry. Thus she made herself very beautiful, to entice the eyes of all the men who might see her. 5 She gave her maid a skin of wine and a flask of oil, and filled a bag with roasted grain, dried fig cakes, and fine bread;[v] then she wrapped up all her dishes and gave them to her to carry.

6 Then they went out to the town gate of Beth·u′li·a and found Uz·zi′ah standing there with the elders of the town, Chab′ris and Char′mis. 7 When they saw her transformed in appearance and dressed differently, they were very greatly astounded at her beauty and said to her, 8 "May the God of our ancestors grant you favor and fulfill your plans, so that the people of Israel may glory and Jerusalem may be exalted." She bowed down to God.

9 Then she said to them, "Order the gate of the town to be opened for me so that I may go out and accomplish the things you have just said to me." So they ordered the young men to open the gate for her, as she requested. 10 When they had done this, Judith went out, accompanied by her maid. The men of the town watched her until she had gone down the mountain and passed through the valley, where they lost sight of her.

Judith Is Captured

11 As the women[w] were going straight on through the valley, an Assyrian patrol met her 12 and took her into custody. They asked her, "To what people do you belong, and where are you coming from, and where are you going?" She replied, "I am a daughter of the Hebrews, but I am fleeing from them, for they are about to be handed over to you to be devoured. 13 I am on my way to see Hol·o·fer′nēs the commander of your army, to give him a true report; I will show him a way by which he can go and capture all the hill country without losing one of his men, captured or slain."

14 When the men heard her words, and observed her face—she was in their eyes marvelously beautiful—they said to her, 15 "You have saved your life by hurrying down to see our lord. Go at once to his tent; some of us will escort you and hand you over to him. 16 When you stand before him, have no fear in your heart, but tell him what you have just said, and he will treat you well."

17 They chose from their number a hundred men to accompany her and her maid, and they brought them to the tent of Hol·o·fer′nēs. 18 There was great excitement in the whole camp, for her arrival was reported from tent to tent. They came and gathered around her as she stood outside the tent of Hol·o·fer′nēs, waiting until they told him about her. 19 They marveled at her beauty and admired the Israelites, judging them by her. They said to one another, "Who can despise these people, who have women like this among them? It is not wise to leave one of their men alive, for if we let them go they will be able to beguile the whole world!"

Judith Is Brought before Holofernes

20 Then the guards of Hol·o·fer′nēs and all his servants came out and led her into the tent. 21 Hol·o·fer′nēs was resting on his bed under a canopy that was woven with purple and gold, emeralds and other precious stones. 22 When they told him of her, he came to the front of the tent, with silver lamps carried before him. 23 When Judith came into the presence of Hol·o·fer′nēs[x] and his servants, they all marveled at the beauty of her face. She prostrated herself and did obeisance to him, but his slaves raised her up.

Then Hol·o·fer′nēs said to her, "Take courage, woman, and do not be afraid in your heart, for I have never hurt anyone who chose to serve Ne·bū·chad·nez′zar, king of all the earth. 2 Even now, if your people who live in the hill country had not slighted me, I would never have lifted my spear against them. They have brought this on themselves. 3 But now tell me why you have fled from them and have come over to us. In any event, you have come to safety. Take courage! You will live tonight and ever after. 4 No one will hurt you. Rather, all will treat you well, as they do the servants of my lord King Ne·bū·chad·nez′zar."

Judith Explains Her Presence

5 Judith answered him, "Accept the words of your slave, and let your servant speak in your presence. I will say nothing false to my lord this night. 6 If you follow out the words of your servant, God will accomplish something through you, and my

---

u Gk she   v Other ancient authorities add and cheese
w Gk they   x Gk him

lord will not fail to achieve his purposes. 7 By the life of Ne•bū•chad•nez'zar, king of the whole earth, and by the power of him who has sent you to direct every living being! Not only do human beings serve him because of you, but also the animals of the field and the cattle and the birds of the air will live, because of your power, under Ne•bū•chad•nez'zar and all his house. 8 For we have heard of your wisdom and skill, and it is reported throughout the whole world that you alone are the best in the whole kingdom, the most informed and the most astounding in military strategy.

9 "Now as for Ā'chi•or's speech in your council, we have heard his words, for the people of Beth•ū'li•a spared him and he told them all he had said to you. 10 Therefore, lord and master, do not disregard what he said, but keep it in your mind, for it is true. Indeed our nation cannot be punished, nor can the sword prevail against them, unless they sin against their God.

11 "But now, in order that my lord may not be defeated and his purpose frustrated, death will fall upon them, for a sin has overtaken them by which they are about to provoke their God to anger when they do what is wrong. 12 Since their food supply is exhausted and their water has almost given out, they have planned to kill their livestock and have determined to use all that God by his laws has forbidden them to eat. 13 They have decided to consume the first fruits of the grain and the tithes of the wine and oil, which they had consecrated and set aside for the priests who minister in the presence of our God in Jerusalem—things it is not lawful for any of the people even to touch with their hands. 14 Since even the people in Jerusalem have been doing this, they have sent messengers there in order to bring back permission from the council of the elders. 15 When the response reaches them and they act upon it, on that very day they will be handed over to you to be destroyed.

16 "So when I, your slave, learned all this, I fled from them. God has sent me to accomplish with you things that will astonish the whole world wherever people shall hear about them. 17 Your servant is indeed God-fearing and serves the God of heaven night and day. So, my lord, I will remain with you; but every night your servant will go out into the valley and pray to God. He will tell me when they have committed their sins. 18 Then I will come and tell you, so that you may go out with your whole army, and not one of them will be able to withstand you. 19 Then I will lead you through Judea, until you come to Jerusalem; there I will set your throne.y You will drive them like sheep that have no shepherd, and no dog will so much as growl at you. For this was told to me to give

me foreknowledge; it was announced to me, and I was sent to tell you."

20 Her words pleased Hol•o•fer'nēs and all his servants. They marveled at her wisdom and said, 21 "No other woman from one end of the earth to the other looks so beautiful or speaks so wisely!" 22 Then Hol•o•fer'nēs said to her, "God has done well to send you ahead of the people, to strengthen our hands and bring destruction on those who have despised my lord. 23 You are not only beautiful in appearance, but wise in speech. If you do as you have said, your God shall be my God, and you shall live in the palace of King Ne•bū•chad•nez'zar and be renowned throughout the whole world."

Judith as a Guest of Holofernes
(Cp Dan 1.3–8)

Then he commanded them to bring her in where his silver dinnerware was kept, and ordered them to set a table for her with some of his own delicacies, and with some of his own wine to drink. 2 But Judith said, "I cannot partake of them, or it will be an offense; but I will have enough with the things I brought with me." 3 Hol•o•fer'nēs said to her, "If your supply runs out, where can we get you more of the same? For none of your people are here with us." 4 Judith replied, "As surely as you live, my lord, your servant will not use up the supplies I have with me before the Lord carries out by my hand what he has determined."

5 Then the servants of Hol•o•fer'nēs brought her into the tent, and she slept until midnight. Toward the morning watch she got up 6 and sent this message to Hol•o•fer'nēs: "Let my lord now give orders

y Or *chariot*

Dead Drunk!

Have you ever wondered why people get drunk? Why would anyone want to drink enough alcohol to pass out? Getting drunk has lots of negative consequences, and getting very drunk can even be fatal.

In the Book of Judith, chapter 13, Judith takes advantage of Holofernes' drunkenness to kill him. She gives the term *dead drunk* a whole new meaning. If you do not believe that getting drunk can destroy your life, then think again. It doesn't take a widow with a sword to help drunkenness destroy your life.

▸ Jdt 12.16—13.10

to allow your servant to go out and pray." 7 So Hol·o·fer'nēs commanded his guards not to hinder her. She remained in the camp three days. She went out each night to the valley of Beth·ū'li·a, and bathed at the spring in the camp.ᶻ 8 After bathing, she prayed the Lord God of Israel to direct her way for the triumph of hisᵃ people. 9 Then she returned purified and stayed in the tent until she ate her food toward evening.

Judith Attends Holofernes' Banquet

10 On the fourth day Hol·o·fer'nēs held a banquet for his personal attendants only, and did not invite any of his officers. 11 He said to Ba·gō'as, the eunuch who had charge of his personal affairs, "Go and persuade the Hebrew woman who is in your care to join us and to eat and drink with us. 12 For it would be a disgrace if we let such a woman go without having intercourse with her. If we do not seduce her, she will laugh at us."

13 So Ba·gō'as left the presence of Hol·o·fer'nēs, and approached her and said, "Let this pretty girl not hesitate to come to my lord to be honored in his presence, and to enjoy drinking wine with us, and to become today like one of the Assyrian women who serve in the palace of Ne·bū·chad·nez'-zar." 14 Judith replied, "Who am I to refuse my lord? Whatever pleases him I will do at once, and it will be a joy to me until the day of my death." 15 So she proceeded to dress herself in all her woman's finery. Her maid went ahead and spread for her on the ground before Hol·o·fer'nēs the lambskins she had received from Ba·gō'as for her daily use in reclining.

16 Then Judith came in and lay down. Hol·o·fer'nēs' heart was ravished with her and his passion was aroused, for he had been waiting for an opportunity to seduce her from the day he first saw her. 17 So Hol·o·fer'nēs said to her, "Have a drink and be merry with us!" 18 Judith said, "I will gladly drink, my lord, because today is the greatest day in my whole life." 19 Then she took what her maid had prepared and ate and drank before him. 20 Hol·o·fer'nēs was greatly pleased with her, and drank a great quantity of wine, much more than he had ever drunk in any one day since he was born.

Judith Beheads Holofernes

When evening came, his slaves quickly withdrew. Ba·gō'as closed the tent from outside and shut out the attendants from his master's presence. They went to bed, for they all were weary because the banquet had lasted so long. 2 But Judith was left alone in the tent, with Hol·o·fer'nēs stretched out on his bed, for he was dead drunk.

3 Now Judith had told her maid to stand outside the bedchamber and to wait for her to come out, as she did on the other days; for she said she would be going out for her prayers. She had said the same thing to Ba·gō'as. 4 So everyone went out, and no one, either small or great, was left in the bedchamber. Then Judith, standing beside his bed, said in her heart, "O Lord God of all might, look in this hour on the work of my hands for the exaltation of Jerusalem. 5 Now indeed is the time to help your heritage and to carry out my design to destroy the enemies who have risen up against us."

6 She went up to the bedpost near Hol·o·fer'nēs' head, and took down his sword that hung there. 7 She came close to his bed, took hold of the hair of his head, and said, "Give me strength today, O Lord God of Israel!" 8 Then she struck his neck twice with all her might, and cut off his head. 9 Next she rolled his body off the bed and pulled down the canopy from the posts. Soon afterward she went out and gave Hol·o·fer'nēs' head to her maid, 10 who placed it in her food bag.

ᶻ Other ancient authorities lack *in the camp*
ᵃ Other ancient authorities read *her*

Is God a Fan of Violence?

Is it hard to believe that God strengthened Judith to cut off Holofernes' head
(Jdt 13.7–8)? Or that God was angry
at Saul for not destroying Agag and his
possessions (1 Sam 15.18–19)? Or that
Jephthah had to sacrifice his daughter
because of a vow he had made (Judg
11.29–40)? The violence portrayed in the
Old Testament is often horrifying, especially when the Old Testament authors
view it as part of God's will.

In the ancient world, tribes and nations viewed their gods as the leaders of
their armies. The Hebrews were no exception. One of God's oldest titles is
"LORD God of hosts" (Ps 89.8; Isa 6.3);
the image is of an almighty warrior who
fought on Israel's side (see Ex 15.3; 1 Sam
14.23). The enemies of Israel were seen as
God's enemies, and their destruction
as God's will. The military victories of
Joshua, Saul, and David were understood
as proof of heaven's blessing on the nation.

Later in history, as the Israelites experienced one agonizing defeat after another and the prophets challenged them
to consider God's love for all nations, a
new understanding of God's will began to
develop in certain Jewish circles. Later
prophets spoke of beating "swords into
plowshares" (Isa 2.4), of making "a covenant of peace" (Ezek 37.26), of seeking
"to do justice, and to love kindness, / and
to walk humbly with your God" (Mic 6.8).
From their own painful history, the Chosen People started to see that war and
violence always meant unspeakable suffering for many, and they began to question whether holy war was part of God's
will.

▶ Jdt 13.1–10

Judith Returns to Bethulia

Then the two of them went out together, as they
were accustomed to do for prayer. They passed
through the camp, circled around the valley, and
went up the mountain to Beth·ū′li·a, and came to
its gates. [11] From a distance Judith called out to the
sentries at the gates, "Open, open the gate! God,
our God, is with us, still showing his power in
Israel and his strength against our enemies, as he
has done today!"

[12] When the people of her town heard her
voice, they hurried down to the town gate and
summoned the elders of the town. [13] They all ran
together, both small and great, for it seemed unbelievable that she had returned. They opened the
gate and welcomed them. Then they lit a fire to
give light, and gathered around them. [14] Then she
said to them with a loud voice, "Praise God,
O praise him! Praise God, who has not withdrawn
his mercy from the house of Israel, but has destroyed our enemies by my hand this very night!"

[15] Then she pulled the head out of the bag
and showed it to them, and said, "See here, the
head of Hol·o·fer′nes, the commander of the Assyrian army, and here is the canopy beneath which
he lay in his drunken stupor. The Lord has struck
him down by the hand of a woman. [16] As the Lord
lives, who has protected me in the way I went, I
swear that it was my face that seduced him to his
destruction, and that he committed no sin with
me, to defile and shame me."

[17] All the people were greatly astonished. They
bowed down and worshiped God, and said with
one accord, "Blessed are you our God, who have
this day humiliated the enemies of your people."

[18] Then Uz·zī′ah said to her, "O daughter, you
are blessed by the Most High God above all other
women on earth; and blessed be the Lord God,
who created the heavens and the earth, who has
guided you to cut off the head of the leader of our
enemies. [19] Your praise[b] will never depart from the
hearts of those who remember the power of God.
[20] May God grant this to be a perpetual honor to
you, and may he reward you with blessings, because you risked your own life when our nation
was brought low, and you averted our ruin, walking in the straight path before our God." And all the
people said, "Amen. Amen."

Judith's Counsel

Then Judith said to them, "Listen to me, my
friends. Take this head and hang it upon the parapet of your wall. [2] As soon as day breaks and the
sun rises on the earth, each of you take up your
weapons, and let every able-bodied man go out of
the town; set a captain over them, as if you were
going down to the plain against the Assyrian outpost; only do not go down. [3] Then they will seize
their arms and go into the camp and rouse the

---

b Other ancient authorities read *hope*

officers of the Assyrian army. They will rush into the tent of Hol•o•fer'nēs and will not find him. Then panic will come over them, and they will flee before you. ⁴Then you and all who live within the borders of Israel will pursue them and cut them down in their tracks. ⁵But before you do all this, bring Ā'chi•or the Am'mon•ite to me so that he may see and recognize the man who despised the house of Israel and sent him to us as if to his death."

6 So they summoned Ā'chi•or from the house of Uz•zī'ah. When he came and saw the head of Hol•o•fer'nēs in the hand of one of the men in the assembly of the people, he fell down on his face in a faint. ⁷When they raised him up he threw himself at Judith's feet, and did obeisance to her, and said, "Blessed are you in every tent of Judah! In every nation those who hear your name will be alarmed. ⁸Now tell me what you have done during these days."

So Judith told him in the presence of the people all that she had done, from the day she left until the moment she began speaking to them. ⁹When she had finished, the people raised a great shout and made a joyful noise in their town. ¹⁰When Ā'chi•or saw all that the God of Israel had done, he believed firmly in God. So he was circumcised, and joined the house of Israel, remaining so to this day.

Holofernes' Death Is Discovered

11 As soon as it was dawn they hung the head of Hol•o•fer'nēs on the wall. Then they all took their weapons, and they went out in companies to the mountain passes. ¹²When the Assyrians saw them they sent word to their commanders, who then went to the generals and the captains and to all their other officers. ¹³They came to Hol•o•fer'-nēs' tent and said to the steward in charge of all his personal affairs, "Wake up our lord, for the slaves have been so bold as to come down against us to give battle, to their utter destruction."

14 So Ba•gō'as went in and knocked at the entry of the tent, for he supposed that he was sleeping with Judith. ¹⁵But when no one answered, he opened it and went into the bedchamber and found him sprawled on the floor dead, with his head missing. ¹⁶He cried out with a loud voice and wept and groaned and shouted, and tore his clothes. ¹⁷Then he went to the tent where Judith had stayed, and when he did not find her, he rushed out to the people and shouted, ¹⁸"The slaves have tricked us! One Hebrew woman has brought disgrace on the house of King Ne•bū•chad-

nez'zar. Look, Hol•o•fer'nēs is lying on the ground, and his head is missing!"

19 When the leaders of the Assyrian army heard this, they tore their tunics and were greatly dismayed, and their loud cries and shouts rose up throughout the camp.

The Assyrians Flee in Panic

When the men in the tents heard it, they were amazed at what had happened. ²Overcome with fear and trembling, they did not wait for one another, but with one impulse all rushed out and fled by every path across the plain and through the hill country. ³Those who had camped in the hills around Beth•ū'li•a also took to flight. Then the Israelites, everyone that was a soldier, rushed out upon them. ⁴Uz•zī'ah sent men to Bet•o•mas•thā'imᶜ and Chō'ba and Kō'la, and to all the frontiers of Israel, to tell what had taken place and to urge all to rush out upon the enemy to destroy them. ⁵When the Israelites heard it, with one accord they fell upon the enemy,ᵈ and cut them down as far as Chō'ba. Those in Jerusalem and all the hill country also came, for they were told what had happened in the camp of the enemy. The men in Gil'e•ad and in Galilee outflanked them with great slaughter, even beyond Damascus and its borders. ⁶The rest of the people of Beth•ū'li•a fell upon the Assyrian camp and plundered it, acquiring great riches. ⁷And the Israelites, when they returned from the slaughter, took possession of what remained. Even the villages and towns in the hill country and in the plain got a great amount of booty, since there was a vast quantity of it.

The Israelites Celebrate Their Victory
(Cp 1 Sam 18.6)

8 Then the high priest Jō'a•kim and the elders of the Israelites who lived in Jerusalem came to witness the good things that the Lord had done for Israel, and to see Judith and to wish her well. ⁹When they met her, they all blessed her with one accord and said to her, "You are the glory of Jerusalem, you are the great boast of Israel, you are the great pride of our nation! ¹⁰You have done all this with your own hand; you have done great good to Israel, and God is well pleased with it. May the Almighty Lord bless you forever!" And all the people said, "Amen."

11 All the people plundered the camp for thirty days. They gave Judith the tent of Hol•o•fer'-nēs and all his silver dinnerware, his beds, his bowls, and all his furniture. She took them and

ᶜ Other ancient authorities add *and Bebai*   ᵈ Gk *them*

loaded her mules and hitched up her carts and piled the things on them.

12 All the women of Israel gathered to see her, and blessed her, and some of them performed a dance in her honor. She took ivy-wreathed wands in her hands and distributed them to the women who were with her; 13 and she and those who were with her crowned themselves with olive wreaths. She went before all the people in the dance, leading all the women, while all the men of Israel followed, bearing their arms and wearing garlands and singing hymns.

PRAY IT!

Judith Leads the Prayer-Song

In the Book of Judith, chapter 16, Judith sings praises to God and leads the people in a holy celebration after victory over the enemy.

Notice the similarity to Miriam's song (Exodus, chapter 15), Deborah's song (Judges, chapter 5), and even Tobit's song (Tobit, chapter 13).

Singing, dancing, and retelling special stories go hand in hand with praising God.

▶ Jdt 16.1–20

Judith Offers Her Hymn of Praise
(Cp Ex 15.20–21; Judg 5.1–31; Tob 13.1–17)

14 Judith began this thanksgiving before all Israel, and all the people loudly sang this song of praise. 1 And Judith said,

Begin a song to my God with tambourines,
　　sing to my Lord with cymbals.
Raise to him a new psalm;*e*
　　exalt him, and call upon his name.
2 For the Lord is a God who crushes wars;
　　he sets up his camp among his people;
　　he delivered me from the hands of my
　　　　pursuers.
3 The Assyrian came down from the
　　　　mountains of the north;
　　he came with myriads of his warriors;
　　their numbers blocked up the wadis,
　　　　and their cavalry covered the hills.
4 He boasted that he would burn up my
　　　　territory,
　　and kill my young men with the sword,

and dash my infants to the ground,
　　and seize my children as booty,
　　and take my virgins as spoil.
5 But the Lord Almighty has foiled them
　　by the hand of a woman.*f*
6 For their mighty one did not fall by the
　　　　hands of the young men,
　　nor did the sons of the Titans strike him down,
　　nor did tall giants set upon him;
but Judith daughter of Me•rar′i
　　with the beauty of her countenance
　　　　undid him.

7 For she put away her widow's clothing
　　to exalt the oppressed in Israel.
She anointed her face with perfume;
8 　　she fastened her hair with a tiara
　　and put on a linen gown to beguile him.
9 Her sandal ravished his eyes,
　　her beauty captivated his mind,
　　and the sword severed his neck!
10 The Persians trembled at her boldness,
　　the Mēdes were daunted at her daring.

11 Then my oppressed people shouted;
　　my weak people cried out,*g* and the
　　　　enemy*h* trembled;
　　they lifted up their voices, and the
　　　　enemy*h* were turned back.
12 Sons of slave-girls pierced them through
　　and wounded them like the children of
　　　　fugitives;
　　they perished before the army of my Lord.

13 I will sing to my God a new song:
　　O Lord, you are great and glorious,
　　　　wonderful in strength, invincible.
14 Let all your creatures serve you,
　　for you spoke, and they were made.
You sent forth your spirit,*i* and it formed them;*j*
　　there is none that can resist your voice.
15 For the mountains shall be shaken to their
　　　　foundations with the waters;
　　before your glance the rocks shall melt
　　　　like wax.
But to those who fear you
　　you show mercy.
16 For every sacrifice as a fragrant offering is a
　　　　small thing,
　　and the fat of all whole burnt offerings to
　　　　you is a very little thing;
　　but whoever fears the Lord is great forever.

---

e Other ancient authorities read *a psalm and praise*
f Other ancient authorities add *he has confounded them*
g Other ancient authorities read *feared*　　*h* Gk *they*
i Or *breath*　　*j* Other ancient authorities read *they were created*

17 Woe to the nations that rise up against my
    people!
  The Lord Almighty will take vengeance
    on them in the day of judgment;
he will send fire and worms into their
    flesh;
  they shall weep in pain forever.

18 When they arrived at Jerusalem, they worshiped God. As soon as the people were purified, they offered their burnt offerings, their freewill offerings, and their gifts. 19 Judith also dedicated to God all the possessions of Hol•o•fer'nēs, which the people had given her; and the canopy that she had taken for herself from his bedchamber she gave as a votive offering. 20 For three months the people continued feasting in Jerusalem before the sanctuary, and Judith remained with them.

The Renown and Death of Judith

21 After this they all returned home to their own inheritances. Judith went to Beth•ū'li•a, and remained on her estate. For the rest of her life she was honored throughout the whole country. 22 Many desired to marry her, but she gave herself to no man all the days of her life after her husband Ma•nas'seh died and was gathered to his people. 23 She became more and more famous, and grew old in her husband's house, reaching the age of one hundred five. She set her maid free. She died in Beth•ū'li•a, and they buried her in the cave of her husband Ma•nas'seh; 24 and the house of Israel mourned her for seven days. Before she died she distributed her property to all those who were next of kin to her husband Ma•nas'seh, and to her own nearest kindred. 25 No one ever again spread terror among the Israelites during the lifetime of Judith, or for a long time after her death.

Most of us cannot understand what would possess a group of people to plot the complete destruction of another group of people. Yet, in our own time, ethnic groups have been targeted for extinction through wars, concentration camps, and death squads. The Book of Esther is the story of a genocidal plot against a Jewish population and how that plot was prevented by Mordecai and his courageous cousin Esther.

In-depth

In the five centuries before Jesus, many of the Jewish people who were uprooted from their homeland had to be on the lookout for their safety. Several of the late Old Testament books—Sirach, Tobit, and Daniel—reflect the challenges that these emigrant Jews had to face. The fictional story of Queen Esther belongs to this group. Like Joseph in Egypt, Esther rose to a position of power in a foreign government. When a plot was hatched to destroy the Jews, she used her influence with the king of Persia to save her people. Each year, Esther's victory is celebrated in the Jewish feast of Purim (Esth 9.18–32)—the feast of little people who have triumphed over larger forces.

Like Daniel, the Book of Esther has come down to us in two versions: the Hebrew and the Greek. The difference in style between these two versions is obvious:

■ The shorter Hebrew text is clearly fictional and does not even mention God's name. The Greek text, a later reworking of the Hebrew, adds sections to bring out the religious dimension of the story and to make the book appear more historical.

■ The Hebrew version emphasizes the human actors; the Greek version, the divine Actor. The two versions stress different aspects of the same truth: God is the savior of the Chosen People (Greek), but works through human beings to achieve that goal (Hebrew).

Despite the confusing numbering, the book reads as a unified story; it's full of action and has a happy ending. What is more, it challenges us to recognize in our hatred of others the seeds of unthinkable destruction.

At a Glance

■ **Addition A.** prologue
■ **Chapters 1–2.** the choice of Esther as queen
■ **Chapters 3–5,13–15.** the plot against the Jews
■ **6.1—10.3; chapter 16.** the rescue of the Jews
■ **10.4–13.** epilogue

Quick Facts

Setting
Persia after the Babylonian Exile

Authors
Hebrew version. unknown, probably writing in the late fourth century B.C.
Greek version. unknown, writing about two centuries later

Themes
God's love for the little ones, the origin of the feast of Purim

Of Note
Catholic Bibles include the Greek version of Esther, inserted as additions A to F.

The Book of Esther

Esther

Chap. 15

NOTE. The deuterocanonical portions of the Book of Esther are several additional passages found in the Greek translation of the Hebrew Book of Esther, a translation that differs also in other respects from the Hebrew text (the latter is translated in the NRSV Old Testament). The disordered chapter numbers come from the displacement of the additions to the end of the canonical Book of Esther by Jerome in his Latin translation and from the subsequent division of the Bible into chapters by Stephen Langton, who numbered the additions consecutively as though they formed a direct continuation of the Hebrew text. So that the additions may be read in their proper context, the whole of the Greek version is here translated, though certain familiar names are given according to their Hebrew rather than their Greek form; for example, Mordecai and Vashti instead of Mardocheus and Astin. The order followed is that of the Greek text, but the chapter and verse numbers conform to those of the King James or Authorized Version. The additions, conveniently indicated by the letters A — F, are located as follows: A, before 1.1; B, after 3.13; C and D, after 4.17; E, after 8.12; F, after 10.3.

ADDITION A

Mordecai's Dream

a 2 In the second year of the reign of A•has•u•e′rus the Great, on the first day of Ni′san, Mor′de•cai son of Ja′ir son of Shim′e•i *b* son of Kish, of the tribe of Benjamin, had a dream. 3 He was a Jew living in the city of Su′sa, a great man, serving in the court of the king. 4 He was one of the captives whom King Ne•bu•chad•nez′zar of Babylon had brought from Jerusalem with King Jec•o•ni′ah of Judah. And this was his dream: 5 Noises *c* and confusion, thunders and earthquake, tumult on the earth! 6 Then two great dragons came forward, both ready to fight, and they roared terribly. 7 At their roaring every nation prepared for war, to fight against the righteous nation. 8 It was a day of darkness and gloom, of tribulation and distress, affliction and great tumult on the earth! 9 And the whole righteous nation was troubled; they feared the evils that threatened them, *d* and were ready to perish. 10 Then they cried out to God; and at their outcry, as though from a tiny spring, there came a great river, with abundant water; 11 light came, and the sun rose, and the lowly were exalted and devoured those held in honor.

---

a Chapters 11.2—12.6 correspond to chapter A 1-17 in some translations. *b* Gk *Semeios* *c* Or *Voices* *d* Gk *their own evils*

12 Mor′de·caī saw in this dream what God had determined to do, and after he awoke he had it on his mind, seeking all day to understand it in every detail.

A Plot against the King

Now Mor′de·caī took his rest in the courtyard with Big′than and Tē′resh, the two eunuchs of the king who kept watch in the courtyard. 2 He overheard their conversation and inquired into their purposes, and learned that they were preparing to lay hands on King A·has·ū·ē′rus; and he informed the king concerning them. 3 Then the king examined the two eunuchs, and after they had confessed it, they were led away to execution. 4 The king made a permanent record of these things, and Mor′de·caī wrote an account of them. 5 And the king ordered Mor′de·caī to serve in the court, and rewarded him for these things. 6 But Hā′man son of Ham·me·dā′-tha the Ag′ag·ite, who was in great honor with the king, determined to injure Mor′de·caī and his people because of the two eunuchs of the king.

END OF ADDITION A

King Ahasuerus Deposes Queen Vashti

This happened in the days of A·has·ū·ē′rus, the same A·has·ū·ē′rus who ruled over one hundred twenty-seven provinces from India to Ethiopia.*e* 2 In those days when King A·has·ū·ē′rus sat on his royal throne in the citadel of Su′sa, 3 in the third year of his reign, he gave a banquet for all his officials and ministers. The army of Persia and Mēd′i·a and the nobles and governors of the provinces were present, 4 while he displayed the great wealth of his kingdom and the splendor and pomp of his majesty for many days, one hundred eighty days in all.

5 When these days were completed, the king gave for all the people present in the citadel of Su′sa, both great and small, a banquet lasting for seven days, in the court of the garden of the king's palace. 6 There were white cotton curtains and blue hangings tied with cords of fine linen and purple to silver rings*f* and marble pillars. There were couches of gold and silver on a mosaic pavement of porphyry, marble, mother-of-pearl, and colored stones. 7 Drinks were served in golden goblets, goblets of different kinds, and the royal wine was lavished according to the bounty of the king. 8 Drinking was by flagons, without restraint; for the king had given orders to all the officials of his palace to do as each one desired. 9 Furthermore, Queen Vash′tī gave a banquet for the women in the palace of King A·has·ū·ē′rus.

10 On the seventh day, when the king was merry with wine, he commanded Me·hū′man, Biz′-tha, Har·bō′na, Big′tha and A·bag′tha, Zē′thar and Car′kas, the seven eunuchs who attended him, 11 to bring Queen Vash′tī before the king, wearing the royal crown, in order to show the peoples and the officials her beauty; for she was fair to behold. 12 But Queen Vash′tī refused to come at the king's command conveyed by the eunuchs. At this the king was enraged, and his anger burned within him.

13 Then the king consulted the sages who knew the laws*g* (for this was the king's procedure toward all who were versed in law and custom, 14 and those next to him were Car·shē′na, Shē′thar, Ad·mā′tha, Tar′shish, Mē′rēs, Mar·sē′na, and Mē·mū′can, the seven officials of Persia and Mēd′i·a, who had access to the king, and sat first in the kingdom): 15 "According to the law, what is to be done to Queen Vash′tī because she has not performed the command of King A·has·ū·ē′rus conveyed by the eunuchs?" 16 Then Mē·mū′can said in the presence of the king and the officials, "Not only has Queen Vash′tī done wrong to the king, but also to all the officials and all the peoples who are in all the provinces of King A·has·ū·ē′rus. 17 For this deed of the queen will be made known to all women, causing them to look with contempt on their husbands, since they will say, 'King A·has·ū·ē′-rus commanded Queen Vash′tī to be brought before him, and she did not come.' 18 This very day the noble ladies of Persia and Mēd′i·a who have heard of the queen's behavior will rebel against*h* the king's officials, and there will be no end of contempt and wrath! 19 If it pleases the king, let a royal order go out from him, and let it be written among the laws of the Persians and the Mēdes so that it may not be altered, that Vash′tī is never again to come before King A·has·ū·ē′rus; and let the king give her royal position to another who is better than she. 20 So when the decree made by the king is proclaimed throughout all his kingdom, vast as it is, all women will give honor to their husbands, high and low alike."

21 This advice pleased the king and the officials, and the king did as Mē·mū′can proposed; 22 he sent letters to all the royal provinces, to every province in its own script and to every people in its own language, declaring that every man should be master in his own house.*i*

---

e Or *Nubia;* Heb *Cush*   *f* Or *rods*   *g* Cn: Heb *times*
h Cn: Heb *will tell*   *i* Heb adds *and speak according to the language of his people*

ESTH

Esther Becomes Queen

After these things, when the anger of King A·has·ū·ē′rus had abated, he remembered Vash′tī and what she had done and what had been decreed against her. 2 Then the king's servants who attended him said, "Let beautiful young virgins be sought out for the king. 3 And let the king appoint commissioners in all the provinces of his kingdom to gather all the beautiful young virgins to the harem in the citadel of Su′sa under custody of Heg′aī, the king's eunuch, who is in charge of the women; let their cosmetic treatments be given them. 4 And let the girl who pleases the king be queen instead of Vash′tī." This pleased the king, and he did so.

did you KNOW?

Diaspora Jews

The fictional story of Esther implies that Mordecai and Esther were members of the Diaspora. The Greek word *diaspora* means "scattered abroad." It refers to the Jews who lived outside of Palestine. When the Babylonians destroyed Jerusalem (587 B.C.), many of the Jews who were forced to leave the land of Israel decided to settle in various Greco-Roman cities and not return home. They maintained their Jewish identity by adapting the language and customs of their new home into their Jewish traditions. The Diaspora Jews were responsible for the translation of the Hebrew Bible into Greek, a translation called the Septuagint.

5 Now there was a Jew in the citadel of Su′sa whose name was Mor′de·caī son of Jā′ir son of Shim′ē·ī son of Kish, a Ben′ja·min·īte. 6 Kish[j] had been carried away from Jerusalem among the captives carried away with King Jec·o·nī′ah of Judah, whom King Ne·bū·chad·nez′zar of Babylon had carried away. 7 Mor′de·caī[k] had brought up Ha·das′sah, that is Esther, his cousin, for she had neither father nor mother; the girl was fair and beautiful, and when her father and her mother died, Mor′de·caī adopted her as his own daughter. 8 So when the king's order and his edict were proclaimed, and when many young women were gathered in the citadel of Su′sa in custody of Heg′aī, Esther

also was taken into the king's palace and put in custody of Heg′aī, who had charge of the women. 9 The girl pleased him and won his favor, and he quickly provided her with her cosmetic treatments and her portion of food, and with seven chosen maids from the king's palace, and advanced her and her maids to the best place in the harem. 10 Esther did not reveal her people or kindred, for Mor′de·caī had charged her not to tell. 11 Every day Mor′de·caī would walk around in front of the court of the harem, to learn how Esther was and how she fared.

12 The turn came for each girl to go in to King A·has·ū·ē′rus, after being twelve months under the regulations for the women, since this was the regular period of their cosmetic treatment, six months with oil of myrrh and six months with perfumes and cosmetics for women. 13 When the girl went in to the king she was given whatever she asked for to take with her from the harem to the king's palace. 14 In the evening she went in; then in the morning she came back to the second harem in custody of Sha·ash′gaz, the king's eunuch, who was in charge of the concubines; she did not go in to the king again, unless the king delighted in her and she was summoned by name.

15 When the turn came for Esther daughter of Ab·i·hā′il the uncle of Mor′de·caī, who had adopted her as his own daughter, to go in to the king, she asked for nothing except what Heg′aī the king's eunuch, who had charge of the women, advised. Now Esther was admired by all who saw her. 16 When Esther was taken to King A·has·ū·ē′rus in his royal palace in the tenth month, which is the month of Tē′beth, in the seventh year of his reign, 17 the king loved Esther more than all the other women; of all the virgins she won his favor and devotion, so that he set the royal crown on her head and made her queen instead of Vash′tī. 18 Then the king gave a great banquet to all his officials and ministers—"Esther's banquet." He also granted a holiday[l] to the provinces, and gave gifts with royal liberality.

Mordecai Discovers a Plot

19 When the virgins were being gathered together,[m] Mor′de·caī was sitting at the king's gate. 20 Now Esther had not revealed her kindred or her people, as Mor′de·caī had charged her; for Esther obeyed Mor′de·caī just as when she was brought up by him. 21 In those days, while Mor′de·caī was sitting at the king's gate, Big′than and Tē′resh, two of the king's eunuchs, who guarded the threshold,

---

j Heb *a Benjaminite* 6 *who*   *k* Heb *He*   *l* Or *an amnesty*
m Heb adds *a second time*

LIVE IT!

Body Count

Genocide. Such a frightening word. The complete destruction of a people. This is what King Ahasuerus plots in the Book of Esther: to destroy all the Jews in his kingdom. Fortunately, he does not succeed.

In our time, we know only too well that the past two centuries have been marked by many attempts to exterminate whole groups of people. The most systematic and ambitious of these attempts was that of Adolf Hitler and the Third Reich. Six million Jews were put to death in Nazi concentration camps, along with four million other "undesirables." Yet, we in the Americas need to look no farther than our own shores. Many Native American peoples were slaughtered simply because they were defending their homes and way of life. Others were wiped out by diseases brought by European settlers in the name of progress, civilization, and Christianity.

Such atrocities begin with a them-and-us attitude. The first step is to set apart a group of people and blame them for whatever is going wrong. The second is to give them a label, like "savages" or "communists," to make them seem less human and easier to destroy. The ghosts of too many victims of genocide remind us that the only accurate pronoun to describe our human family is *we*.

▶ Esth 3.1–7

became angry and conspired to assassinate[n] King A·has·u·e′rus. 22 But the matter came to the knowledge of Mor′de·cai, and he told it to Queen Esther, and Esther told the king in the name of Mor′de·cai. 23 When the affair was investigated and found to be so, both the men were hanged on the gallows. It was recorded in the book of the annals in the presence of the king.

Haman Undertakes to Destroy the Jews

After these things King A·has·u·e′rus promoted Hā′man son of Ham·me·dā′tha the Ag′ag·ite, and advanced him and set his seat above all the officials who were with him. 2 And all the king's servants who were at the king's gate bowed down and did obeisance to Hā′man; for the king had so commanded concerning him. But Mor′de·cai did not bow down or do obeisance. 3 Then the king's servants who were at the king's gate said to Mor′de·cai, "Why do you disobey the king's command?" 4 When they spoke to him day after day and he would not listen to them, they told Hā′man, in order to see whether Mor′de·cai's words would avail; for he had told them that he was a Jew. 5 When Hā′man saw that Mor′de·cai did not bow down or do obeisance to him, Hā′man was infuriated. 6 But he thought it beneath him to lay hands on Mor′de·cai alone. So, having been told who Mor′de·cai's people were, Hā′man plotted to destroy all the Jews, the people of Mor′de·cai, throughout the whole kingdom of A·has·u·e′rus.

7 In the first month, which is the month of Ni′san, in the twelfth year of King A·has·u·e′rus, they cast Pūr—which means "the lot"—before Hā′man for the day and for the month, and the lot fell on the thirteenth day[o] of the twelfth month, which is the month of Ā′dar. 8 Then Hā′man said to King A·has·u·e′rus, "There is a certain people scattered and separated among the peoples in all the provinces of your kingdom; their laws are different from those of every other people, and they do not keep the king's laws, so that it is not appropriate for the king to tolerate them. 9 If it pleases the king, let a decree be issued for their destruction, and I will pay ten thousand talents of silver into the hands of those who have charge of the king's business, so that they may put it into the king's treasuries." 10 So the king took his signet ring from his hand and gave it to Hā′man son of Ham·me·dā′tha the Ag′ag·ite, the enemy of the Jews. 11 The king said to Hā′man, "The money is given to you, and the people as well, to do with them as it seems good to you."

12 Then the king's secretaries were summoned on the thirteenth day of the first month, and an edict, according to all that Hā′man commanded, was written to the king's satraps and to the governors over all the provinces and to the officials of all the peoples, to every province in its own script and every people in its own language; it was written in the name of King A·has·u·e′rus and sealed

n Heb *to lay hands on*   o Cn Compare Gk and verse 13 below: Heb *the twelfth month*

E
S
T
H

with the king's ring. [13] Letters were sent by couriers to all the king's provinces, giving orders to destroy, to kill, and to annihilate all Jews, young and old, women and children, in one day, the thirteenth day of the twelfth month, which is the month of Ā'dar, and to plunder their goods.

ADDITION B

The King's Letter

p This is a copy of the letter: "The Great King, A·has·ū·ē'rus, writes the following to the governors of the hundred twenty-seven provinces from India to Ethiopia and to the officials under them:

2 "Having become ruler of many nations and master of the whole world (not elated with presumption of authority but always acting reasonably and with kindness), I have determined to settle the lives of my subjects in lasting tranquility and, in order to make my kingdom peaceable and open to travel throughout all its extent, to restore the peace desired by all people.

3 "When I asked my counselors how this might be accomplished, Hā'man—who excels among us in sound judgment, and is distinguished for his unchanging goodwill and steadfast fidelity, and has attained the second place in the kingdom— [4] pointed out to us that among all the nations in the world there is scattered a certain hostile people, who have laws contrary to those of every nation and continually disregard the ordinances of kings, so that the unifying of the kingdom that we honorably intend cannot be brought about. [5] We understand that this people, and it alone, stands constantly in opposition to every nation, perversely following a strange manner of life and laws, and is ill-disposed to our government, doing all the harm they can so that our kingdom may not attain stability.

6 "Therefore we have decreed that those indicated to you in the letters written by Hā'man, who is in charge of affairs and is our second father, shall all—wives and children included—be utterly destroyed by the swords of their enemies, without pity or restraint, on the fourteenth day of the twelfth month, Ā'dar, of this present year, [7] so that those who have long been hostile and remain so may in a single day go down in violence to Hades, and leave our government completely secure and untroubled hereafter."

END OF ADDITION B

---

[14] A copy of the document was to be issued as a decree in every province by proclamation, calling on all the peoples to be ready for that day. [15] The couriers went quickly by order of the king, and the decree was issued in the citadel of Su'sa. The king and Hā'man sat down to drink; but the city of Su'sa was thrown into confusion.

Esther Agrees to Help the Jews

When Mor'de·cai learned all that had been done, Mor'de·cai tore his clothes and put on sackcloth and ashes, and went through the city, wailing with a loud and bitter cry; [2] he went up to the entrance of the king's gate, for no one might enter the king's gate clothed with sackcloth. [3] In every province, wherever the king's command and his decree came, there was great mourning among the Jews, with fasting and weeping and lamenting, and most of them lay in sackcloth and ashes.

4 When Esther's maids and her eunuchs came and told her, the queen was deeply distressed; she sent garments to clothe Mor'de·cai, so that he might take off his sackcloth; but he would not accept them. [5] Then Esther called for Hā'thach, one of the king's eunuchs, who had been appointed to attend her, and ordered him to go to Mor'de·cai to learn what was happening and why. [6] Hā'thach went out to Mor'de·cai in the open square of the city in front of the king's gate, [7] and Mor'de·cai told him all that had happened to him, and the exact sum of money that Hā'man had promised to pay into the king's treasuries for the destruction of the Jews. [8] Mor'de·cai also gave him a copy of the written decree issued in Su'sa for their destruction, that he might show it to Esther, explain it to her, and charge her to go to the king to make supplication to him and entreat him for her people.

9 Hā'thach went and told Esther what Mor'-de·cai had said. [10] Then Esther spoke to Hā'thach and gave him a message for Mor'de·cai, saying, [11] "All the king's servants and the people of the king's provinces know that if any man or woman goes to the king inside the inner court without being called, there is but one law—all alike are to be put to death. Only if the king holds out the golden scepter to someone, may that person live. I myself have not been called to come in to the king for thirty days." [12] When they told Mor'de·cai what Esther had said, [13] Mor'de·cai told them to reply to Esther, "Do not think that in the king's palace you will escape any more than all the other Jews. [14] For

---

?did you KNOW?

The Silent Women of the Bible

"Mordecai then went away and did everything as Esther had ordered him" (Esth 4.17). What a surprise: to hear of a man in the ancient world taking orders from a woman! Esther, like Judith, has an exceptional role in the Old Testament. Many other important women are not even named: Jephthah's daughter, Samson's mother, and Job's wife, for instance. Even the Hebrew women whose names have become famous—Sarah, Rebekah, Rachel, Miriam, Bathsheba—played second fiddle to their more famous husbands. They depended on indirect influence or trickery to get what they wanted.

In the biblical world, a woman was defined by her relationships with men. Before marriage, she belonged to her father's household and had no status outside of it. Once married, a woman left her father's family and joined the family of her husband. If her husband died, she remained in the new family, rearing children for her deceased spouse or, if childless, marrying a brother-in-law. Although many women undoubtedly lived happily under this system, many others just as surely suffered abuse or felt oppressed. The stories of Lot's daughters (Gen 19.8) and the woman of Gibeah (Judg 19.24–30) testify to this horrifying truth.

A system of scriptural interpretation that was developed during recent decades attempts to give voice to the many silent, forgotten, abused women of the Bible. More and more biblical scholars reread the familiar stories, searching for quiet messages that have long been overlooked. All of us—males and females alike—can benefit from this effort to listen to the voices of these women who have been silenced for so many centuries.

▶ Esth 4.15–17

if you keep silence at such a time as this, relief and deliverance will rise for the Jews from another quarter, but you and your father's family will perish. Who knows? Perhaps you have come to royal dignity for just such a time as this." 15 Then Esther said in reply to Mor·de·caī, 16 "Go, gather all the Jews to be found in Su'sa, and hold a fast on my behalf, and neither eat nor drink for three days, night or day. I and my maids will also fast as you do. After that I will go to the king, though it is against the law; and if I perish, I perish." 17 Mor'-de·caī then went away and did everything as Esther had ordered him.

ADDITION C
Mordecai's Prayer

8 *q* Then Mor·de·caī[r] prayed to the Lord, calling to remembrance all the works of the Lord.

9 He said, "O Lord, Lord, you rule as King over all things, for the universe is in your power and there is no one who can oppose you when it is your will to save Israel, 10 for you have made heaven and earth and every wonderful thing under heaven. 11 You are Lord of all, and there is no one who can resist you, the Lord. 12 You know all things; you know, O Lord, that it was not in insolence or pride or for any love of glory that I did this, and refused to bow down to this proud Hā'-man; 13 for I would have been willing to kiss the soles of his feet to save Israel! 14 But I did this so that I might not set human glory above the glory of God, and I will not bow down to anyone but you, who are my Lord; and I will not do these things in pride. 15 And now, O Lord God and King, God of Abraham, spare your people; for the eyes of our foes are upon us[s] to annihilate us, and they desire to destroy the inheritance that has been yours from the beginning. 16 Do not neglect your portion, which you redeemed for yourself out of the land of Egypt. 17 Hear my prayer, and have mercy upon your inheritance; turn our mourning into feasting that we may live and sing praise to your name, O Lord; do not destroy the lips[t] of those who praise you."

18 And all Israel cried out mightily, for their death was before their eyes.

Esther's Prayer

Then Queen Esther, seized with deadly anxiety, fled to the Lord. 2 She took off her splendid apparel and put on the garments of distress and mourning, and instead of costly perfumes she

q Chapters 13.8—15.16 correspond to chapters C 1-30 and D 1-16 in some translations.　*r* Gk he　*s* Gk for they are eying us　*t* Gk mouth

covered her head with ashes and dung, and she utterly humbled her body; every part that she loved to adorn she covered with her tangled hair. ³ She prayed to the Lord God of Israel, and said: "O my Lord, you only are our king; help me, who am alone and have no helper but you, ⁴ for my danger is in my hand. ⁵ Ever since I was born I have heard in the tribe of my family that you, O Lord, took Israel out of all the nations, and our ancestors from among all their forebears, for an everlasting inheritance, and that you did for them all that you promised. ⁶ And now we have sinned before you, and you have handed us over to our enemies ⁷ because we glorified their gods. You are righteous, O Lord! ⁸ And now they are not satisfied that we are in bitter slavery, but they have covenanted with their idols ⁹ to abolish what your mouth has ordained, and to destroy your inheritance, to stop the mouths of those who praise you and to quench your altar and the glory of your house, ¹⁰ to open the mouths of the nations for the praise of vain idols, and to magnify forever a mortal king.

11 "O Lord, do not surrender your scepter to what has no being; and do not let them laugh at our downfall; but turn their plan against them, and make an example of him who began this against us. ¹² Remember, O Lord; make yourself known in this time of our affliction, and give me courage, O King of the gods and Master of all dominion! ¹³ Put eloquent speech in my mouth before the lion, and turn his heart to hate the man who is fighting against us, so that there may be an end of him and those who agree with him. ¹⁴ But save us by your hand, and help me, who am alone and have no helper but you, O Lord. ¹⁵ You have knowledge of all things, and you know that I hate the splendor of the wicked and abhor the bed of the uncircumcised and of any alien. ¹⁶ You know my necessity—that I abhor the sign of my proud position, which is upon my head on days when I appear in public. I abhor it like a filthy rag, and I do not wear it on the days when I am at leisure. ¹⁷ And your servant has not eaten at Hā′man's table, and I have not honored the king's feast or drunk the wine of libations. ¹⁸ Your servant has had no joy since the day that I was brought here until now, except in you, O Lord God of Abraham. ¹⁹ O God, whose might is over all, hear the voice of the despairing, and save us from the hands of evildoers. And save me from my fear!"

END OF ADDITION C

ADDITION D
Esther Is Received by the King
(Esth 5.1–2)

On the third day, when she ended her prayer, she took off the garments in which she had worshiped, and arrayed herself in splendid attire. ² Then, majestically adorned, after invoking the aid of the all-seeing God and Savior, she took two maids with her; ³ on one she leaned gently for support, ⁴ while the other followed, carrying her train. ⁵ She was radiant with perfect beauty, and she looked happy, as if beloved, but her heart was frozen with fear. ⁶ When she had gone through all the doors, she stood before the king. He was seated on his royal throne, clothed in the full array of his majesty, all covered with gold and precious stones. He was most terrifying.

7 Lifting his face, flushed with splendor, he looked at her in fierce anger. The queen faltered, and turned pale and faint, and collapsed on the head of the maid who went in front of her. ⁸ Then God changed the spirit of the king to gentleness, and in alarm he sprang from his throne and took her in his arms until she came to herself. He comforted her with soothing words, and said to her, ⁹ "What is it, Esther? I am your husband.ᵘ Take courage; ¹⁰ You shall not die, for our law applies only to our subjects.ᵛ Come near."

11 Then he raised the golden scepter and touched her neck with it; ¹² he embraced her, and said, "Speak to me." ¹³ She said to him, "I saw you, my lord, like an angel of God, and my heart was shaken with fear at your glory. ¹⁴ For you are wonderful, my lord, and your countenance is full of grace." ¹⁵ And while she was speaking, she fainted and fell. ¹⁶ Then the king was agitated, and all his servants tried to comfort her.

END OF ADDITION D

Esther's Banquet

ʷ ³ The king said to her, "What is it, Queen Esther? What is your request? It shall be given you, even to the half of my kingdom." ⁴ Then Esther said, "If it pleases the king, let the king and Hā′man come today to a banquet that I have prepared for the king." ⁵ Then the king said, "Bring Hā′man quickly, so that we may do as Esther desires." So the king and Hā′man came to the banquet that Esther had prepared. ⁶ While they were drinking wine, the king said to Esther, "What is your petition? It shall be granted you. And what is your request? Even to the half of my kingdom, it shall be fulfilled." ⁷ Then

ᵘ Gk *brother*   ᵛ Meaning of Gk uncertain   ʷ In Greek, Chapter D replaces verses 1 and 2 in Hebrew.

Esther said, "This is my petition and request: 8 If I have won the king's favor, and if it pleases the king to grant my petition and fulfill my request, let the king and Hā′man come tomorrow to the banquet that I will prepare for them, and then I will do as the king has said."

Haman Plans to Have Mordecai Hanged

9 Hā′man went out that day happy and in good spirits. But when Hā′man saw Mor′de•caī in the king's gate, and observed that he neither rose nor trembled before him, he was infuriated with Mor′de•caī; 10 nevertheless Hā′man restrained himself and went home. Then he sent and called for his friends and his wife Zē′resh, 11 and Hā′man recounted to them the splendor of his riches, the number of his sons, all the promotions with which the king had honored him, and how he had advanced him above the officials and the ministers of the king. 12 Hā′man added, "Even Queen Esther let no one but myself come with the king to the banquet that she prepared. Tomorrow also I am invited by her, together with the king. 13 Yet all this does me no good so long as I see the Jew Mor′-de•caī sitting at the king's gate." 14 Then his wife Zē′-resh and all his friends said to him, "Let a gallows fifty cubits high be made, and in the morning tell the king to have Mor′de•caī hanged on it; then go with the king to the banquet in good spirits." This advice pleased Hā′man, and he had the gallows made.

The King Honors Mordecai

On that night the king could not sleep, and he gave orders to bring the book of records, the annals, and they were read to the king. 2 It was found written how Mor′de•caī had told about Big•thā′na and Tē′resh, two of the king's eunuchs, who guarded the threshold, and who had conspired to assassinate[x] King A•has•ū•ē′rus. 3 Then the king said, "What honor or distinction has been bestowed on Mor′de•caī for this?" The king's servants who attended him said, "Nothing has been done for him." 4 The king said, "Who is in the court?" Now Hā′man had just entered the outer court of the king's palace to speak to the king about having Mor′de•caī hanged on the gallows that he had prepared for him. 5 So the king's servants told him, "Hā′man is there, standing in the court." The king said, "Let him come in." 6 So Hā′man came in, and the king said to him, "What shall be done for the man whom the king wishes to honor?" Hā′man said to himself, "Whom would the king wish to honor more than me?" 7 So Hā′man said to the king, "For the man whom the king wishes to honor, 8 let royal robes be brought, which the king

has worn, and a horse that the king has ridden, with a royal crown on its head. 9 Let the robes and the horse be handed over to one of the king's most noble officials; let him[y] robe the man whom the king wishes to honor, and let him[y] conduct the man on horseback through the open square of the city, proclaiming before him: 'Thus shall it be done for the man whom the king wishes to honor.' " 10 Then the king said to Hā′man, "Quickly, take the robes and the horse, as you have said, and do so to the Jew Mor′de•caī who sits at the king's gate. Leave out nothing that you have mentioned." 11 So Hā′man took the robes and the horse and robed Mor′de•caī and led him riding through the open square of the city, proclaiming, "Thus shall it be done for the man whom the king wishes to honor."

12 Then Mor′de•caī returned to the king's gate, but Hā′man hurried to his house, mourning and with his head covered. 13 When Hā′man told his wife Zē′resh and all his friends everything that had happened to him, his advisers and his wife Zē′resh said to him, "If Mor′de•caī, before whom your downfall has begun, is of the Jewish people, you will not prevail against him, but will surely fall before him."

Haman's Downfall and Mordecai's Advancement

14 While they were still talking with him, the king's eunuchs arrived and hurried Hā′man off to the banquet that Esther had prepared. 1 So the king and Hā′man went in to feast with Queen Esther. 2 On the second day, as they were drinking wine, the king again said to Esther, "What is your petition, Queen Esther? It shall be granted you. And what is your request? Even to the half of my kingdom, it shall be fulfilled." 3 Then Queen Esther answered, "If I have won your favor, O king, and if it pleases the king, let my life be given me—that is my petition—and the lives of my people—that is my request. 4 For we have been sold, I and my people, to be destroyed, to be killed, and to be annihilated. If we had been sold merely as slaves, men and women, I would have held my peace; but no enemy can compensate for this damage to the king."[z] 5 Then King A•has•ū•ē′rus said to Queen Esther, "Who is he, and where is he, who has presumed to do this?" 6 Esther said, "A foe and enemy, this wicked Hā′man!" Then Hā′man was terrified before the king and the queen. 7 The king rose from the feast in wrath and went into the palace garden, but Hā′man stayed to beg his life from

---

x Heb *to lay hands on*   y Heb *them*   z Meaning of Heb uncertain

Queen Esther, for he saw that the king had determined to destroy him. [8] When the king returned from the palace garden to the banquet hall, Hā′man had thrown himself on the couch where Esther was reclining; and the king said, "Will he even assault the queen in my presence, in my own house?" As the words left the mouth of the king, they covered Hā′man's face. [9] Then Har·bō′na, one of the eunuchs in attendance on the king, said, "Look, the very gallows that Hā′man has prepared for Mor′de·caī, whose word saved the king, stands at Hā′man's house, fifty cubits high." And the king said, "Hang him on that." [10] So they hanged Hā′man on the gallows that he had prepared for Mor′de·caī. Then the anger of the king abated. [1] On that day King A·has·ū·ē′rus gave to Queen Esther the house of Hā′man, the enemy of the Jews; and Mor′de·caī came before the king, for Esther had told what he was to her. [2] Then the king took off his signet ring, which he had taken from Hā′man, and gave it to Mor′de·caī. So Esther set Mor′de·caī over the house of Hā′man.

Esther Saves the Jews

[3] Then Esther spoke again to the king; she fell at his feet, weeping and pleading with him to avert the evil design of Hā′man the Ag′ag·īte and the plot that he had devised against the Jews. [4] The king held out the golden scepter to Esther, [5] and Esther rose and stood before the king. She said, "If it pleases the king, and if I have won his favor, and if the thing seems right before the king, and I have his approval, let an order be written to revoke the letters devised by Hā′man son of Ham·me·dā′tha the Ag′ag·īte, which he wrote giving orders to destroy the Jews who are in all the provinces of the king. [6] For how can I bear to see the calamity that is coming on my people? Or how can I bear to see the destruction of my kindred?" [7] Then King A·has·ū·ē′rus said to Queen Esther and to the Jew Mor′de·caī, "See, I have given Esther the house of Hā′man, and they have hanged him on the gallows, because he plotted to lay hands on the Jews. [8] You may write as you please with regard to the Jews, in the name of the king, and seal it with the king's ring; for an edict written in the name of the king and sealed with the king's ring cannot be revoked."

[9] The king's secretaries were summoned at that time, in the third month, which is the month of Sī′van, on the twenty-third day; and an edict was written, according to all that Mor′de·caī commanded, to the Jews and to the satraps and the governors and the officials of the provinces from India to Ethiopia,[a] one hundred twenty-seven provinces, to every province in its own script and

to every people in its own language, and also to the Jews in their script and their language. [10] He wrote letters in the name of King A·has·ū·ē′rus, sealed them with the king's ring, and sent them by mounted couriers riding on fast steeds bred from the royal herd.[b] [11] By these letters the king allowed the Jews who were in every city to assemble and defend their lives, to destroy, to kill, and to annihilate any armed force of any people or province that might attack them, with their children and women, and to plunder their goods [12] on a single day throughout all the provinces of King A·has·ū·ē′rus, on the thirteenth day of the twelfth month, which is the month of Ā′dar.

ADDITION E

The Decree of Ahasuerus

[c] The following is a copy of this letter:

"The Great King, A·has·ū·ē′rus, to the governors of the provinces from India to Ethiopia, one hundred twenty-seven provinces, and to those who are loyal to our government, greetings.

[2] "Many people, the more they are honored with the most generous kindness of their benefactors, the more proud do they become, [3] and not only seek to injure our subjects, but in their inability to stand prosperity, they even undertake to scheme against their own benefactors. [4] They not only take away thankfulness from others, but, carried away by the boasts of those who know nothing of goodness, they even assume that they will escape the evil-hating justice of God, who always sees everything. [5] And often many of those who are set in places of authority have been made in part responsible for the shedding of innocent blood, and have been involved in irremediable calamities, by the persuasion of friends who have been entrusted with the administration of public affairs, [6] when these persons by the false trickery of their evil natures beguile the sincere goodwill of their sovereigns.

[7] "What has been wickedly accomplished through the pestilent behavior of those who exercise authority unworthily can be seen, not so much from the more ancient records that we hand on, as from investigation of matters close at hand.[d] [8] In the future we will take care to render our kingdom quiet and peaceable for all, [9] by changing our methods and always judging what

---

a Or *Nubia*; Heb *Cush*   *b* Meaning of Heb uncertain   *c* Chapter 16.1-24 corresponds to chapter E 1-24 in some translations.   *d* Gk *matters beside* (your) *feet*

comes before our eyes with more equitable consideration. [10] For Hā′man son of Ham·me·dā′tha, a Mac·e·dō′ni·an (really an alien to the Persian blood, and quite devoid of our kindliness), having become our guest, [11] enjoyed so fully the goodwill that we have for every nation that he was called our father and was continually bowed down to by all as the person second to the royal throne. [12] But, unable to restrain his arrogance, he undertook to deprive us of our kingdom and our life,[e] [13] and with intricate craft and deceit asked for the destruction of Mor′de·caī, our savior and perpetual benefactor, and of Esther, the blameless partner of our kingdom, together with their whole nation. [14] He thought that by these methods he would catch us undefended and would transfer the kingdom of the Persians to the Mac·e·dō′ni·ans.

[15] "But we find that the Jews, who were consigned to annihilation by this thrice-accursed man, are not evildoers, but are governed by most righteous laws [16] and are children of the living God, most high, most mighty,[f] who has directed the kingdom both for us and for our ancestors in the most excellent order.

[17] "You will therefore do well not to put in execution the letters sent by Hā′man son of Hamme·dā′tha, [18] since he, the one who did these things, has been hanged at the gate of Su′sa with all his household—for God, who rules over all things, has speedily inflicted on him the punishment that he deserved.

[19] "Therefore post a copy of this letter publicly in every place, and permit the Jews to live under their own laws. [20] And give them reinforcements, so that on the thirteenth day of the twelfth month, Ā′dar, on that very day, they may defend themselves against those who attack them at the time of oppression. [21] For God, who rules over all things, has made this day to be a joy for his chosen people instead of a day of destruction for them.

[22] "Therefore you shall observe this with all good cheer as a notable day among your commemorative festivals, [23] so that both now and hereafter it may represent deliverance for you[g] and the loyal Persians, but that it may be a reminder of destruction for those who plot against us.

[24] "Every city and country, without exception, that does not act accordingly shall be destroyed in wrath with spear and fire. It shall be made not only impassable for human beings, but also most hateful to wild animals and birds for all time."

END OF ADDITION E

[13] A copy of the writ was to be issued as a decree in every province and published to all peoples, and the Jews were to be ready on that day to take revenge on their enemies. [14] So the couriers, mounted on their swift royal steeds, hurried out, urged by the king's command. The decree was issued in the citadel of Su′sa.

[15] Then Mor′de·caī went out from the presence of the king, wearing royal robes of blue and white, with a great golden crown and a mantle of fine linen and purple, while the city of Su′sa shouted and rejoiced. [16] For the Jews there was light and gladness, joy and honor. [17] In every province and in every city, wherever the king's command and his edict came, there was gladness and joy among the Jews, a festival and a holiday. Furthermore, many of the peoples of the country professed to be Jews, because the fear of the Jews had fallen upon them.

Destruction of the Enemies of the Jews
(Cp. 1 Macc 7.49)

Now in the twelfth month, which is the month of Ā′dar, on the thirteenth day, when the king's command and edict were about to be executed, on the very day when the enemies of the Jews hoped to gain power over them, but which had been changed to a day when the Jews would gain power over their foes, [2] the Jews gathered in their cities throughout all the provinces of King A·has·u·ē′rus to lay hands on those who had sought their ruin; and no one could withstand them, because the fear of them had fallen upon all peoples. [3] All the officials of the provinces, the satraps and the governors, and the royal officials were supporting the Jews, because the fear of Mor′de·caī had fallen upon them. [4] For Mor′de·caī was powerful in the king's house, and his fame spread throughout all the provinces as the man Mor′de·caī grew more and more powerful. [5] So the Jews struck down all their enemies with the sword, slaughtering, and destroying them, and did as they pleased to those who hated them. [6] In the citadel of Su′sa the Jews killed and destroyed five hundred people. [7] They killed Par·shan·dā′tha, Dal′phon, As·pā′tha, [8] Pō·rā′tha, A·dā′li·a, Ar·i·dā′tha, [9] Par·mash′ta, Ar′i·saī, Ar′i·daī, Vaī·zā′tha, [10] the ten sons of Hā′man son of Hamme·dā′tha, the enemy of the Jews; but they did not touch the plunder.

[11] That very day the number of those killed in the citadel of Su′sa was reported to the king. [12] The king said to Queen Esther, "In the citadel of Su′sa the Jews have killed five hundred people and also

---

e Gk *our spirit*   f Gk *greatest*   g Other ancient authorities read *for us*

the ten sons of Hā′man. What have they done in the rest of the king's provinces? Now what is your petition? It shall be granted you. And what further is your request? It shall be fulfilled." 13 Esther said, "If it pleases the king, let the Jews who are in Su′sa be allowed tomorrow also to do according to this day's edict, and let the ten sons of Hā′man be hanged on the gallows." 14 So the king commanded this to be done; a decree was issued in Su′sa, and the ten sons of Hā′man were hanged. 15 The Jews who were in Su′sa gathered also on the fourteenth day of the month of Ā′dar and they killed three hundred persons in Su′sa; but they did not touch the plunder.

16 Now the other Jews who were in the king's provinces also gathered to defend their lives, and gained relief from their enemies, and killed seventy-five thousand of those who hated them; but they laid no hands on the plunder. 17 This was on the thirteenth day of the month of Ā′dar, and on the fourteenth day they rested and made that a day of feasting and gladness.

The Feast of Purim Inaugurated
(Esth 3.7)

18 But the Jews who were in Su′sa gathered on the thirteenth day and on the fourteenth, and rested on the fifteenth day, making that a day of feasting and gladness. 19 Therefore the Jews of the villages, who live in the open towns, hold the fourteenth day of the month of Ā′dar as a day for gladness and feasting, a holiday on which they send gifts of food to one another.

20 Mor′de·caī recorded these things, and sent letters to all the Jews who were in all the provinces of King A·has·u·ē′rus, both near and far, 21 enjoining them that they should keep the fourteenth day of the month Ā′dar and also the fifteenth day of the same month, year by year, 22 as the days on which the Jews gained relief from their enemies, and as the month that had been turned for them from sorrow into gladness and from mourning into a holiday; that they should make them days of feasting and gladness, days for sending gifts of food to one another and presents to the poor. 23 So the Jews adopted as a custom what they had begun to do, as Mor′de·caī had written to them.

24 Hā′man son of Ham·me·dā′tha the Ag′ag·īte, the enemy of all the Jews, had plotted against the Jews to destroy them, and had cast Pūr—that is "the lot"—to crush and destroy them; 25 but when Esther came before the king, he gave orders in writing that the wicked plot that he had devised against the Jews should come upon his own head, and that he and his sons should be hanged on the gallows. 26 Therefore these days are called Pūr′im,

from the word Pūr. Thus because of all that was written in this letter, and of what they had faced in this matter, and of what had happened to them, 27 the Jews established and accepted as a custom for themselves and their descendants and all who joined them, that without fail they would continue to observe these two days every year, as it was written and at the time appointed. 28 These days should be remembered and kept throughout every generation, in every family, province, and city; and these days of Pūr′im should never fall into disuse among the Jews, nor should the commemoration of these days cease among their descendants.

did you KNOW?

Purim

The feast of Purim ("lots" in Hebrew) commemorates the legendary victory of Queen Esther and Mordecai. A minor festival in the Jewish calendar, Purim is celebrated in late winter and is marked by the exchange of gifts and the sharing of meals.

▶ Esth 9.24–32

29 Queen Esther daughter of Ab·i·hā′il, along with the Jew Mor′de·caī, gave full written authority, confirming this second letter about Pūr′im. 30 Letters were sent wishing peace and security to all the Jews, to the one hundred twenty-seven provinces of the kingdom of A·has·u·ē′rus, 31 and giving orders that these days of Pūr′im should be observed at their appointed seasons, as the Jew Mor′de·caī and Queen Esther enjoined on the Jews, just as they had laid down for themselves and for their descendants regulations concerning their fasts and their lamentations. 32 The command of Queen Esther fixed these practices of Pūr′im, and it was recorded in writing.

10 King A·has·u·ē′rus laid tribute on the land and on the islands of the sea. 2 All the acts of his power and might, and the full account of the high honor of Mor′de·caī, to which the king advanced him, are they not written in the annals of the kings of Mēd′i·a and Persia? 3 For Mor′de·caī the Jew was next in rank to King A·has·u·ē′rus, and he was powerful among the Jews and popular with his many kindred, for he sought the good of his people and interceded for the welfare of all his descendants.

Mordecai's Dream Fulfilled

4 *h* And Mor·de·caī said, "These things have come from God; 5 for I remember the dream that I had concerning these matters, and none of them has failed to be fulfilled. 6 There was the little spring that became a river, and there was light and sun and abundant water—the river is Esther, whom the king married and made queen. 7 The two dragons are Hā′man and myself. 8 The nations are those that gathered to destroy the name of the Jews. 9 And my nation, this is Israel, who cried out to God and was saved. The Lord has saved his people; the Lord has rescued us from all these evils; God has done great signs and wonders, wonders that have never happened among the nations. 10 For this purpose he made two lots, one for the people of God and one for all the nations, 11 and these two lots came to the hour and moment and day of decision before God and among all the na-

tions. 12 And God remembered his people and vindicated his inheritance. 13 So they will observe these days in the month of Ā′dar, on the fourteenth and fifteenth*i* of that month, with an assembly and joy and gladness before God, from generation to generation forever among his people Israel."

Postscript

1 In the fourth year of the reign of Ptol′e·my and Cleopatra, Dō·sith′e·us, who said that he was a priest and a Lē′vīte,*j* and his son Ptol′e·my brought to Egypt*k* the preceding Letter about Pūr′im, which they said was authentic and had been translated by Lȳ·sim′a·chus son of Ptol′e·my, one of the residents of Jerusalem.

---

h Chapter 10.4-13 and 11.1 correspond to chapter F 1-11 in some translations.   *i* Other ancient authorities lack *and fifteenth*   *j* Or *priest, and Levitas*   *k* Cn: Gk *brought in*

Have you ever listened as two fighting siblings tell their parents about a conflict? Usually, each child blames the other one and protests his or her complete innocence. Sometimes you have to wonder if they are even talking about the same fight. In a similar way, the author of 1 Maccabees, reporting on the Jewish resistance to the persecution of the Seleucid (Greek) rulers, tells one version of the story. The book defends the violent resistance of the family of Mattathias. Second Maccabees, on the other hand, has a broader perspective in telling of other forms of Jewish resistance.

At a Glance

- **Chapters 1–2.** the revolt of the Jews
- **3.1—9.22.** the leadership of Judas Maccabeus
- **9.23—16.24.** the leadership of Judas's brothers Jonathan and Simon

In-depth

The writer of 1 Maccabees has a clear purpose in mind: to defend the family of Mattathias, whose sons—the Maccabees—held positions of authority in the Jewish community. The most famous of them, Judas Maccabeus, led the Jews in a successful revolt (167–164 B.C.) against the Greek persecution—an incredible feat given the military might of the Greeks. After Judas's death, his brothers and nephews held positions of power, and Israel remained free from foreign domination for the next hundred years.

For traditional Jews, the power of the Maccabees posed a problem: because Mattathias's bloodline could be traced to neither King David nor Aaron the priest, by what right had his descendants assumed kingly and priestly authority? Against such criticism, the author of 1 Maccabees tries to prove that God's plan was accomplished through Mattathias's family.

Quick Facts

Period Covered
from 175 to 134 B.C.
Author
unknown, writing shortly after 100 B.C.
Theme
God brings Israel to freedom through the family of Mattathias.
Of Note
First Maccabees is not found in every translation of the Old Testament (see "The Case of the Missing Books," near Tob 1.16).

The interpretation of Jewish history contained in 1 Maccabees invites us to believe in God's choice of Mattathias's sons as saviors of the nation. Even more important, it invites us to believe in the utter reliability of God: "And so observe, from generation to generation, that none of those who put their trust in [God] will lack strength" (2.61).

1 Maccabees

1.56

Alexander the Great

After Alexander son of Philip, the Mac•e•dō′ni•an, who came from the land of Kit′tim, had defeated^a King Da•rī′us of the Persians and the Mēdes, he succeeded him as king. (He had previously become king of Greece.) ²He fought many battles, conquered strongholds, and put to death the kings of the earth. ³He advanced to the ends of the earth, and plundered many nations. When the earth became quiet before him, he was exalted, and his heart was lifted up. ⁴He gathered a very strong army and ruled over countries, nations, and princes, and they became tributary to him.

5 After this he fell sick and perceived that he was dying. ⁶So he summoned his most honored officers, who had been brought up with him from youth, and divided his kingdom among them while he was still alive. ⁷And after Alexander had reigned twelve years, he died.

8 Then his officers began to rule, each in his own place. ⁹They all put on crowns after his death, and so did their descendants after them for many years; and they caused many evils on the earth.

Antiochus Epiphanes and Renegade Jews
(2 Macc 4.7–17)

10 From them came forth a sinful root, An•tī′o•chus E•piph′a•nēs, son of King An•tī′o•chus; he had been a hostage in Rome. He began to reign in the one hundred thirty-seventh year of the kingdom of the Greeks.^b

11 In those days certain renegades came out from Israel and misled many, saying, "Let us go and make a covenant with the Gentiles around us, for since we separated from them many disasters have come upon us." ¹²This proposal pleased them, ¹³and some of the people eagerly went to the king, who authorized them to observe the ordinances of the Gentiles. ¹⁴So they built a gymnasium in Jerusalem, according to Gentile custom, ¹⁵and removed the marks of circumcision, and abandoned the holy covenant. They joined with the Gentiles and sold themselves to do evil.

Antiochus in Egypt
(2 Macc 5.1, 11–26)

16 When An•tī′o•chus saw that his kingdom was established, he determined to become king of the land of Egypt, in order that he might reign over both kingdoms. ¹⁷So he invaded Egypt with a strong force, with chariots and elephants and cavalry and with a large fleet. ¹⁸He engaged King Ptol′e•my of Egypt in battle, and Ptol′e•my turned and fled before him, and many were wounded and fell. ¹⁹They captured the fortified cities in the land of Egypt, and he plundered the land of Egypt.

---

^a Gk adds *and he defeated*   ^b 175 B.C.

Persecution of the Jews

20 After subduing Egypt, An•ti′o•chus returned in the one hundred forty-third year.[c] He went up against Israel and came to Jerusalem with a strong force. 21 He arrogantly entered the sanctuary and took the golden altar, the lampstand for the light, and all its utensils. 22 He took also the table for the bread of the Presence, the cups for drink offerings, the bowls, the golden censers, the curtain, the crowns, and the gold decoration on the front of the temple; he stripped it all off. 23 He took the silver and the gold, and the costly vessels; he took also the hidden treasures that he found. 24 Taking them all, he went into his own land.

He shed much blood,
and spoke with great arrogance.
25 Israel mourned deeply in every community,
26 rulers and elders groaned,
young women and young men became faint,
the beauty of the women faded.
27 Every bridegroom took up the lament;
she who sat in the bridal chamber was mourning.
28 Even the land trembled for its inhabitants,
and all the house of Jacob was clothed with shame.

The Occupation of Jerusalem

29 Two years later the king sent to the cities of Judah a chief collector of tribute, and he came to Jerusalem with a large force. 30 Deceitfully he spoke peaceable words to them, and they believed him; but he suddenly fell upon the city, dealt it a severe blow, and destroyed many people of Israel. 31 He plundered the city, burned it with fire, and tore down its houses and its surrounding walls. 32 They took captive the women and children, and seized the livestock. 33 Then they fortified the city of David with a great strong wall and strong towers, and it became their citadel. 34 They stationed there a sinful people, men who were renegades. These strengthened their position; 35 they stored up arms and food, and collecting the spoils of Jerusalem they stored them there, and became a great menace,
36 for the citadel[d] became an ambush against the sanctuary,
an evil adversary of Israel at all times.
37 On every side of the sanctuary they shed innocent blood;
they even defiled the sanctuary.
38 Because of them the residents of Jerusalem fled;
she became a dwelling of strangers;

she became strange to her offspring,
and her children forsook her.
39 Her sanctuary became desolate like a desert;
her feasts were turned into mourning,
her sabbaths into a reproach,
her honor into contempt.
40 Her dishonor now grew as great as her glory;
her exaltation was turned into mourning.

Installation of Gentile Cults
(Cp 2 Macc 6.1–17; Mt 24.15; Mk 13.14)

41 Then the king wrote to his whole kingdom that all should be one people, 42 and that all should give up their particular customs. 43 All the Gentiles accepted the command of the king. Many even from Israel gladly adopted his religion; they sacrificed to idols and profaned the sabbath. 44 And the king sent letters by messengers to Jerusalem and the towns of Judah; he directed them to follow customs strange to the land, 45 to forbid burnt offerings and sacrifices and drink offerings in the sanctuary, to profane sabbaths and festivals, 46 to defile the sanctuary and the priests, 47 to build altars and sacred precincts and shrines for idols, to sacrifice swine and other unclean animals, 48 and to leave their sons uncircumcised. They were to make themselves abominable by everything unclean and profane, 49 so that they would forget the law and change all the ordinances. 50 He added,[e] "And whoever does not obey the command of the king shall die."

51 In such words he wrote to his whole kingdom. He appointed inspectors over all the people and commanded the towns of Judah to offer sacrifice, town by town. 52 Many of the people, everyone who forsook the law, joined them, and they did evil in the land; 53 they drove Israel into hiding in every place of refuge they had.

54 Now on the fifteenth day of Chis′lev, in the one hundred forty-fifth year,[f] they erected a desolating sacrilege on the altar of burnt offering. They also built altars in the surrounding towns of Judah, 55 and offered incense at the doors of the houses and in the streets. 56 The books of the law that they found they tore to pieces and burned with fire. 57 Anyone found possessing the book of the covenant, or anyone who adhered to the law, was condemned to death by decree of the king. 58 They kept using violence against Israel, against those who were found month after month in the towns. 59 On the twenty-fifth day of the month they offered sacrifice on the altar that was on top of the altar of burnt offering. 60 According to the

decree, they put to death the women who had their children circumcised, 61 and their families and those who circumcised them; and they hung the infants from their mothers' necks.

62 But many in Israel stood firm and were resolved in their hearts not to eat unclean food. 63 They chose to die rather than to be defiled by food or to profane the holy covenant; and they did die. 64 Very great wrath came upon Israel.

Mattathias and His Sons

In those days Mat·ta·thi′as son of John son of Sim′-ē·on, a priest of the family of Jō′a·rib, moved from Jerusalem and settled in Mō′dēin. 2 He had five sons, John surnamed Gad′dī, 3 Simon called Thas′sī, 4 Judas called Mac·ca·bē′us, 5 El·ē·ā′zar called Av′a·ran, and Jonathan called Ap′phus. 6 He saw the blasphemies being committed in Judah and Jerusalem, 7 and said,

"Alas! Why was I born to see this,
    the ruin of my people, the ruin of the
        holy city,
and to live there when it was given over to
        the enemy,
    the sanctuary given over to aliens?
8   Her temple has become like a person
            without honor; 8
9   her glorious vessels have been carried
            into exile.
    Her infants have been killed in her streets,
        her youths by the sword of the foe.
10   What nation has not inherited her palaces[h]
        and has not seized her spoils?
11   All her adornment has been taken away;
        no longer free, she has become a slave.
12   And see, our holy place, our beauty,
        and our glory have been laid waste;
    the Gentiles have profaned them.
13   Why should we live any longer?"

14 Then Mat·ta·thi′as and his sons tore their clothes, put on sackcloth, and mourned greatly.

Pagan Worship Refused

15 The king's officers who were enforcing the apostasy came to the town of Mō′dēin to make them offer sacrifice. 16 Many from Israel came to them; and Mat·ta·thi′as and his sons were assembled. 17 Then the king's officers spoke to Mat·ta·thi′as as follows: "You are a leader, honored and great in this town, and supported by sons and brothers. 18 Now be the first to come and do what the king commands, as all the Gentiles and the people of Judah and those that are left in Jerusalem have done. Then you and your sons will be numbered among the Friends of the king, and you and your sons will be honored with silver and gold and many gifts."

19 But Mat·ta·thi′as answered and said in a loud voice: "Even if all the nations that live under the rule of the king obey him, and have chosen to obey his commandments, everyone of them abandoning the religion of their ancestors, 20 I and my sons and my brothers will continue to live by the covenant of our ancestors. 21 Far be it from us to desert the law and the ordinances. 22 We will not obey the king's words by turning aside from our religion to the right hand or to the left."

23 When he had finished speaking these words, a Jew came forward in the sight of all to offer sacrifice on the altar in Mō′dēin, according to the king's command. 24 When Mat·ta·thi′as saw it, he burned with zeal and his heart was stirred. He gave vent to righteous anger; he ran and killed him on the altar. 25 At the same time he killed the king's officer who was forcing them to sacrifice, and he tore down the altar. 26 Thus he burned with zeal for the law, just as Phin′e·has did against Zim′rī son of Sa′lū.

27 Then Mat·ta·thi′as cried out in the town with a loud voice, saying: "Let every one who is zealous for the law and supports the covenant come out

---

g Meaning of Gk uncertain   h Other ancient authorities read *has not had a part in her kingdom*

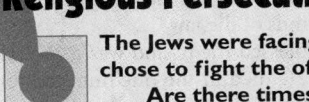

Religious Persecution

The Jews were facing a societal attack on their faith. But Mattathias and his sons chose to fight the official and cultural pressure to turn away from their faith.
    Are there times when you feel persecuted because of your belief in God? In what subtle ways does contemporary society ridicule people with religious beliefs? If you were to be persecuted because of your religion, how would you respond?

▶ 1 Macc 2.19–22

with me!" 28 Then he and his sons fled to the hills and left all that they had in the town.

29 At that time many who were seeking righteousness and justice went down to the wilderness to live there, 30 they, their sons, their wives, and their livestock, because troubles pressed heavily upon them. 31 And it was reported to the king's officers, and to the troops in Jerusalem the city of David, that those who had rejected the king's command had gone down to the hiding places in the wilderness. 32 Many pursued them, and overtook them; they encamped opposite them and prepared for battle against them on the sabbath day. 33 They said to them, "Enough of this! Come out and do what the king commands, and you will live." 34 But they said, "We will not come out, nor will we do what the king commands and so profane the sabbath day." 35 Then the enemy*i* quickly attacked them. 36 But they did not answer them or hurl a stone at them or block up their hiding places, 37 for they said, "Let us all die in our innocence; heaven and earth testify for us that you are killing us unjustly." 38 So they attacked them on the sabbath, and they died, with their wives and children and livestock, to the number of a thousand persons.

39 When Mat·ta·thi′as and his friends learned of it, they mourned for them deeply. 40 And all said to their neighbors: "If we all do as our kindred have done and refuse to fight with the Gentiles for our lives and for our ordinances, they will quickly destroy us from the earth." 41 So they made this decision that day: "Let us fight against anyone who comes to attack us on the sabbath day; let us not all die as our kindred died in their hiding places."

Counter-Attack

42 Then there united with them a company of Has·i·dē′ans, mighty warriors of Israel, all who offered themselves willingly for the law. 43 And all who became fugitives to escape their troubles joined them and reinforced them. 44 They organized an army, and struck down sinners in their anger and renegades in their wrath; the survivors fled to the Gentiles for safety. 45 And Mat·ta·thi′as and his friends went around and tore down the altars; 46 they forcibly circumcised all the uncircumcised boys that they found within the borders of Israel. 47 They hunted down the arrogant, and the work prospered in their hands. 48 They rescued the law out of the hands of the Gentiles and kings, and they never let the sinner gain the upper hand.

The Last Words of Mattathias

(Gen 22.1–18; 39.1—45.28; Num 13.1—14.10; Josh 1.1–9)

49 Now the days drew near for Mat·ta·thi′as to die, and he said to his sons: "Arrogance and scorn have now become strong; it is a time of ruin and furious anger. 50 Now, my children, show zeal for the law, and give your lives for the covenant of our ancestors.

51 "Remember the deeds of the ancestors, which they did in their generations; and you will receive great honor and an everlasting name. 52 Was not Abraham found faithful when tested, and it was reckoned to him as righteousness? 53 Joseph in the time of his distress kept the commandment, and became lord of Egypt. 54 Phin′e·has our ancestor, because he was deeply zealous, received the covenant of everlasting priesthood. 55 Joshua, because he fulfilled the command, became a judge in Israel. 56 Caleb, because he testified in the assembly, received an inheritance in the land. 57 David, because he was merciful, inherited the throne of the kingdom forever. 58 E·li′jah, because of great zeal for the law, was taken up into heaven. 59 Han·a·ni′ah, Az·a·ri′ah, and Mish′a·el believed and were saved from the flame. 60 Daniel, because of his innocence, was delivered from the mouth of the lions.

61 "And so observe, from generation to generation, that none of those who put their trust in him will lack strength. 62 Do not fear the words of sinners, for their splendor will turn into dung and worms. 63 Today they will be exalted, but tomorrow they will not be found, because they will have returned to the dust, and their plans will have perished. 64 My children, be courageous and grow strong in the law, for by it you will gain honor.

65 "Here is your brother Sim′e·on who, I know, is wise in counsel; always listen to him; he shall be your father. 66 Judas Mac·ca·bē′us has been a mighty warrior from his youth; he shall command the army for you and fight the battle against the peoples.*j* 67 You shall rally around you all who observe the law, and avenge the wrong done to your people. 68 Pay back the Gentiles in full, and obey the commands of the law."

69 Then he blessed them, and was gathered to his ancestors. 70 He died in the one hundred forty-sixth year*k* and was buried in the tomb of his ancestors at Mō′dein. And all Israel mourned for him with great lamentation.

---

i Gk *they*   *j* Or *of the people*   *k* 166 B.C.

The Early Victories of Judas
(2 Macc 8.1–7)

Then his son Judas, who was called Mac•ca•bēʹus, took command in his place. ²All his brothers and all who had joined his father helped him; they gladly fought for Israel.

³ He extended the glory of his people.
   Like a giant he put on his breastplate;
   he bound on his armor of war and waged battles,
     protecting the camp by his sword.
⁴ He was like a lion in his deeds,
   like a lion's cub roaring for prey.
⁵ He searched out and pursued those who broke the law;
   he burned those who troubled his people.
⁶ Lawbreakers shrank back for fear of him;
   all the evildoers were confounded;
   and deliverance prospered by his hand.
⁷ He embittered many kings,
   but he made Jacob glad by his deeds,
   and his memory is blessed forever.
⁸ He went through the cities of Judah;
   he destroyed the ungodly out of the land;ˡ
     thus he turned away wrath from Israel.
⁹ He was renowned to the ends of the earth;
   he gathered in those who were perishing.

10 Ap•ol•lōʹni•us now gathered together Gentiles and a large force from Sa•mārʹi•a to fight against Israel. ¹¹When Judas learned of it, he went out to meet him, and he defeated and killed him. Many were wounded and fell, and the rest fled. ¹²Then they seized their spoils; and Judas took the sword of Ap•ol•lōʹni•us, and used it in battle the rest of his life.

13 When Sērʹon, the commander of the Syrian army, heard that Judas had gathered a large company, including a body of faithful soldiers who stayed with him and went out to battle, ¹⁴he said, "I will make a name for myself and win honor in the kingdom. I will make war on Judas and his companions, who scorn the king's command." ¹⁵Once again a strong army of godless men went up with him to help him, to take vengeance on the Israelites.

16 When he approached the ascent of Beth-hōʹron, Judas went out to meet him with a small company. ¹⁷But when they saw the army coming to meet them, they said to Judas, "How can we, few as we are, fight against so great and so strong a multitude? And we are faint, for we have eaten nothing today." ¹⁸Judas replied, "It is easy for many to be hemmed in by few, for in the sight of Heaven there is no difference between saving by many or by few. ¹⁹It is not on the size of the army that victory in battle depends, but strength comes from Heaven. ²⁰They come against us in great insolence and lawlessness to destroy us and our wives and our children, and to despoil us; ²¹but we fight for our lives and our laws. ²²He himself will crush them before us; as for you, do not be afraid of them."

23 When he finished speaking, he rushed suddenly against Sērʹon and his army, and they were crushed before him. ²⁴They pursued themᵐ down the descent of Beth-hōʹron to the plain; eight hundred of them fell, and the rest fled into the land of the Phi•lisʹtines. ²⁵Then Judas and his brothers began to be feared, and terror fell on the Gentiles all around them. ²⁶His fame reached the king, and the Gentiles talked of the battles of Judas.

The Policy of Antiochus

27 When King An•tiʹo•chus heard these reports, he was greatly angered; and he sent and gathered all the forces of his kingdom, a very strong army. ²⁸He opened his coffers and gave a year's pay to his forces, and ordered them to be ready for any need. ²⁹Then he saw that the money in the treasury was exhausted, and that the revenues from the country were small because of the dissension and disaster that he had caused in the land by abolishing the laws that had existed from the earliest days. ³⁰He feared that he might not have such funds as he had before for his expenses and for the gifts that he used to give more lavishly than preceding kings. ³¹He was greatly perplexed in mind; then he determined to go to Persia and collect the revenues from those regions and raise a large fund.

32 He left Lysʹi•as, a distinguished man of royal lineage, in charge of the king's affairs from the river Euphrates to the borders of Egypt. ³³Lysʹi•as was also to take care of his son An•tiʹo•chus until he returned. ³⁴And he turned over to Lysʹi•asⁿ half of his forces and the elephants, and gave him orders about all that he wanted done. As for the residents of Judea and Jerusalem, ³⁵Lysʹi•as was to send a force against them to wipe out and destroy the strength of Israel and the remnant of Jerusalem; he was to banish the memory of them from the place, ³⁶settle aliens in all their territory, and distribute their land by lot. ³⁷Then the king took the remaining half of his forces and left Anʹti•och his capital in the one hundred and forty-seventh year.ᵒ He crossed the Euphrates river and went through the upper provinces.

ˡ Gk it   ᵐ Other ancient authorities read *him*   ⁿ Gk *him*
ᵒ 165 B.C.

Preparations for Battle

(2 Macc 8.8–20)

38 Lys'i•as chose Ptol'e•my son of Dor•ym'e•nēs,
and Nī•cā'nor and Gor'gi•as, able men among the
Friends of the king, 39 and sent with them forty
thousand infantry and seven thousand cavalry to
go into the land of Judah and destroy it, as the
king had commanded. 40 So they set out with their
entire force, and when they arrived they encamped
near Em•mā'us in the plain. 41 When the traders of
the region heard what was said to them, they took
silver and gold in immense amounts, and fetters,[p]
and went to the camp to get the Israelites for
slaves. And forces from Syria and the land of the
Phi•lis'tines joined with them.

42 Now Judas and his brothers saw that misfortunes had increased and that the forces were encamped in their territory. They also learned what
the king had commanded to do to the people to
cause their final destruction. 43 But they said to
one another, "Let us restore the ruins of our people, and fight for our people and the sanctuary."
44 So the congregation assembled to be ready for
battle, and to pray and ask for mercy and compassion.

45 Jerusalem was uninhabited like a wilderness;
not one of her children went in or out.
The sanctuary was trampled down,
and aliens held the citadel;
it was a lodging place for the Gentiles.
Joy was taken from Jacob;
the flute and the harp ceased to play.

46 Then they gathered together and went to
Miz'pah, opposite Jerusalem, because Israel formerly had a place of prayer in Miz'pah. 47 They
fasted that day, put on sackcloth and sprinkled
ashes on their heads, and tore their clothes. 48 And
they opened the book of the law to inquire into
those matters about which the Gentiles consulted
the likenesses of their gods. 49 They also brought
the vestments of the priesthood and the first fruits
and the tithes, and they stirred up the nazirites[q]
who had completed their days; 50 and they cried
aloud to Heaven, saying,

"What shall we do with these?
Where shall we take them?
51 Your sanctuary is trampled down and
profaned,
and your priests mourn in humiliation.
52 Here the Gentiles are assembled against us
to destroy us;
you know what they plot against us.
53 How will we be able to withstand them,
if you do not help us?"

54 Then they sounded the trumpets and gave a
loud shout. 55 After this Judas appointed leaders of
the people, in charge of thousands and hundreds
and fifties and tens. 56 Those who were building
houses, or were about to be married, or were
planting a vineyard, or were fainthearted, he told
to go home again, according to the law. 57 Then
the army marched out and encamped to the south
of Em•mā'us.

58 And Judas said, "Arm yourselves and be
courageous. Be ready early in the morning to fight
with these Gentiles who have assembled against us
to destroy us and our sanctuary. 59 It is better for us
to die in battle than to see the misfortunes of our
nation and of the sanctuary. 60 But as his will in
heaven may be, so shall he do."

The Battle at Emmaus

(2 Macc 8.21–29, 34–36)

4 Now Gor'gi•as took five thousand infantry and one
thousand picked cavalry, and this division moved
out by night 2 to fall upon the camp of the Jews
and attack them suddenly. Men from the citadel
were his guides. 3 But Judas heard of it, and he and
his warriors moved out to attack the king's force in
Em•mā'us 4 while the division was still absent from
the camp. 5 When Gor'gi•as entered the camp of
Judas by night, he found no one there, so he
looked for them in the hills, because he said,
"These men are running away from us."

6 At daybreak Judas appeared in the plain with
three thousand men, but they did not have armor
and swords such as they desired. 7 And they saw
the camp of the Gentiles, strong and fortified, with
cavalry all around it; and these men were trained
in war. 8 But Judas said to those who were with
him, "Do not fear their numbers or be afraid
when they charge. 9 Remember how our ancestors
were saved at the Red Sea, when Pharaoh with his
forces pursued them. 10 And now, let us cry to
Heaven, to see whether he will favor us and remember his covenant with our ancestors and
crush this army before us today. 11 Then all the
Gentiles will know that there is one who redeems
and saves Israel."

12 When the foreigners looked up and saw
them coming against them, 13 they went out from
their camp to battle. Then the men with Judas
blew their trumpets 14 and engaged in battle. The
Gentiles were crushed, and fled into the plain,
15 and all those in the rear fell by the sword. They
pursued them to Ga•zā'ra, and to the plains of Id•ū-
mē'a, and to A•zō'tus and Jam'ni•a; and three thou-

---

[p] Syr: Gk Mss, Vg *slaves* [q] That is *those separated* or *those consecrated*

sand of them fell. 16 Then Judas and his force turned back from pursuing them, 17 and he said to the people, "Do not be greedy for plunder, for there is a battle before us; 18 Gor·gi·as and his force are near us in the hills. But stand now against our enemies and fight them, and afterward seize the plunder boldly."

19 Just as Judas was finishing this speech, a detachment appeared, coming out of the hills. 20 They saw that their army^r had been put to flight, and that the Jews^r were burning the camp, for the smoke that was seen showed what had happened. 21 When they perceived this, they were greatly frightened, and when they also saw the army of Judas drawn up in the plain for battle, 22 they all fled into the land of the Phi·lis'tines. 23 Then Judas returned to plunder the camp, and they seized a great amount of gold and silver, and cloth dyed blue and sea purple, and great riches. 24 On their return they sang hymns and praises to Heaven— "For he is good, for his mercy endures forever." 25 Thus Israel had a great deliverance that day.

First Campaign of Lysias
(2 Macc 11.1–12)

26 Those of the foreigners who escaped went and reported to Lys'i·as all that had happened. 27 When he heard it, he was perplexed and discouraged, for things had not happened to Israel as he had intended, nor had they turned out as the king had ordered. 28 But the next year he mustered sixty thousand picked infantry and five thousand cavalry to subdue them. 29 They came into Id·u·me'a and encamped at Beth-zur, and Judas met them with ten thousand men.

30 When he saw that their army was strong, he prayed, saying, "Blessed are you, O Savior of Israel, who crushed the attack of the mighty warrior by the hand of your servant David, and gave the camp of the Phi·lis'tines into the hands of Jonathan son of Saul, and of the man who carried his armor. 31 Hem in this army by the hand of your people Israel, and let them be ashamed of their troops and their cavalry. 32 Fill them with cowardice; melt the boldness of their strength; let them tremble in their destruction. 33 Strike them down with the sword of those who love you, and let all who know your name praise you with hymns."

34 Then both sides attacked, and there fell of the army of Lys'i·as five thousand men; they fell in action.^{s} 35 When Lys'i·as saw the rout of his troops and observed the boldness that inspired those of Judas, and how ready they were either to live or to die nobly, he withdrew to An'ti·och and enlisted mercenaries in order to invade Judea again with an even larger army.

Cleansing and Dedication of the Temple
(2 Macc 10.1–9)

36 Then Judas and his brothers said, "See, our enemies are crushed; let us go up to cleanse the sanctuary and dedicate it." 37 So all the army assembled and went up to Mount Zion. 38 There they saw the sanctuary desolate, the altar profaned, and the gates burned. In the courts they saw bushes sprung up as in a thicket, or as on one of the mountains. They saw also the chambers of the priests in ruins. 39 Then they tore their clothes and mourned with great lamentation; they sprinkled themselves with ashes 40 and fell face down on the ground. And when the signal was given with the trumpets, they cried out to Heaven.

41 Then Judas detailed men to fight against those in the citadel until he had cleansed the sanctuary. 42 He chose blameless priests devoted to the law, 43 and they cleansed the sanctuary and removed the defiled stones to an unclean place. 44 They deliberated what to do about the altar of burnt offering, which had been profaned. 45 And they thought it best to tear it down, so that it would not be a lasting shame to them that the Gentiles had defiled it. So they tore down the altar, 46 and stored the stones in a convenient place on the temple hill until a prophet should come to tell what to do with them. 47 Then they took unhewn^t stones, as the law directs, and built a new altar like the former one. 48 They also rebuilt the sanctuary and the interior of the temple, and consecrated the courts. 49 They made new holy vessels, and brought the lampstand, the altar of incense, and the table into the temple. 50 Then they offered incense on the altar and lit the lamps on the lampstand, and these gave light in the temple. 51 They placed the bread on the table and hung up the curtains. Thus they finished all the work they had undertaken.

52 Early in the morning on the twenty-fifth day of the ninth month, which is the month of Chis'lev, in the one hundred forty-eighth year,^{u} 53 they rose and offered sacrifice, as the law directs, on the new altar of burnt offering that they had built. 54 At the very season and on the very day that the Gentiles had profaned it, it was dedicated with songs and harps and lutes and cymbals. 55 All the people fell on their faces and worshiped and blessed Heaven, who had prospered them. 56 So they celebrated the dedication of the altar for eight days, and joyfully offered burnt offerings; they offered a sacrifice of well-being and a thanksgiving offering. 57 They decorated the front of the temple

---

^{r} Gk they ^{s} Or and some fell on the opposite side
^{t} Gk whole ^{u} 164 B.C.

with golden crowns and small shields; they re-stored the gates and the chambers for the priests, and fitted them with doors. 58 There was very great joy among the people, and the disgrace brought by the Gentiles was removed.

?did you KNOW?

Hanukkah

Hanukkah, or the feast of dedication, is a joyful eight-day celebration in the month of Chislev (December). On each night of the festival, a candle is lit in joyful re-membrance of the Maccabees' rededica-tion of the Temple in Jerusalem after it was robbed and desecrated by Antiochus IV Epiphanes (1 Macc 4.56). Even more deeply, the candlelight symbolizes the gratitude of the Jewish people for the survival, often against great odds, of their age-old faith.

▸ **1 Macc 4.52–59**

59 Then Judas and his brothers and all the as-sembly of Israel determined that every year at that season the days of dedication of the altar should be observed with joy and gladness for eight days, beginning with the twenty-fifth day of the month of Chis'lev.

60 At that time they fortified Mount Zion with high walls and strong towers all around, to keep the Gentiles from coming and trampling them down as they had done before. 61 Judas[v] stationed a garrison there to guard it; he also fortified Beth-zur to guard it, so that the people might have a stronghold that faced Id·u·mē'a.

Wars with Neighboring Peoples
(2 Macc 10.14–33)

When the Gentiles all around heard that the altar had been rebuilt and the sanctuary dedicated as it was before, they became very angry, 2 and they de-termined to destroy the descendants of Jacob who lived among them. So they began to kill and de-stroy among the people. 3 But Judas made war on the descendants of Esau in Id·u·mē'a, at Ak·ra·bat'-te·nē, because they kept lying in wait for Israel. He dealt them a heavy blow and humbled them and despoiled them. 4 He also remembered the wicked-

ness of the sons of Bae'an, who were a trap and a snare to the people and ambushed them on the highways. 5 They were shut up by him in their[w] towers; and he encamped against them, vowed their complete destruction, and burned with fire their towers and all who were in them. 6 Then he crossed over to attack the Am'mon·ites, where he found a strong band and many people, with Timo-thy as their leader. 7 He engaged in many battles with them, and they were crushed before him; he struck them down. 8 He also took Jā'zer and its villages; then he returned to Judea.

Liberation of Galilean Jews
(2 Macc 12.10–25)

9 Now the Gentiles in Gil'e·ad gathered to-gether against the Israelites who lived in their terri-tory, and planned to destroy them. But they fled to the stronghold of Dath'e·ma, 10 and sent to Judas and his brothers a letter that said, "The Gentiles around us have gathered together to destroy us. 11 They are preparing to come and capture the stronghold to which we have fled, and Timothy is leading their forces. 12 Now then, come and rescue us from their hands, for many of us have fallen, 13 and all our kindred who were in the land of Tob have been killed; the enemy[x] have captured their wives and children and goods, and have destroyed about a thousand persons there."

14 While the letter was still being read, other messengers, with their garments torn, came from Galilee and made a similar report; 15 they said that the people of Ptol·e·mā'is and Tÿre and Sï'don, and all Galilee of the Gentiles,[y] had gathered together against them "to annihilate us." 16 When Judas and the people heard these messages, a great assembly was called to determine what they should do for their kindred who were in distress and were being attacked by enemies.[z] 17 Then Judas said to his brother Simon, "Choose your men and go and rescue your kindred in Galilee; Jonathan my brother and I will go to Gil'e·ad." 18 But he left Jo-seph, son of Zech·a·rī'ah, and Az·a·rī'ah, a leader of the people, with the rest of the forces, in Judea to guard it; 19 and he gave them this command, "Take charge of this people, but do not engage in battle with the Gentiles until we return." 20 Then three thousand men were assigned to Simon to go to Galilee, and eight thousand to Judas for Gil'-e·ad.

21 So Simon went to Galilee and fought many battles against the Gentiles, and the Gentiles were crushed before him. 22 He pursued them to the

---

v Gk He   *w* Gk her   *x* Gk they   *y* Gk aliens
z Gk them

gate of Ptol•e•mā'is; as many as three thousand of the Gentiles fell, and he despoiled them. 23 Then he took the Jews[a] of Galilee and Ar•bat'ta, with their wives and children, and all they possessed, and led them to Judea with great rejoicing.

Judas and Jonathan in Gilead

24 Judas Mac•ca•bē'us and his brother Jonathan crossed the Jordan and made three days' journey into the wilderness. 25 They encountered the Na•ba•tē'ans, who met them peaceably and told them all that had happened to their kindred in Gil'e•ad: 26 "Many of them have been shut up in Boz'rah and Bō'sor, in Al'e•ma and Chas'phō, Mā'ked and Car'na•im"—all these towns were strong and large— 27 "and some have been shut up in the other towns of Gil'e•ad; the enemy[b] are getting ready to attack the strongholds tomorrow and capture and destroy all these people in a single day."

28 Then Judas and his army quickly turned back by the wilderness road to Boz'rah; and he took the town, and killed every male by the edge of the sword; then he seized all its spoils and burned it with fire. 29 He left the place at night, and they went all the way to the stronghold of Dath'e•ma.[c] 30 At dawn they looked out and saw a large company, which could not be counted, carrying ladders and engines of war to capture the stronghold, and attacking the Jews within.[d] 31 So Judas saw that the battle had begun and that the cry of the town went up to Heaven, with trumpets and loud shouts, 32 and he said to the men of his forces, "Fight today for your kindred!" 33 Then he came up behind them in three companies, who sounded their trumpets and cried aloud in prayer. 34 And when the army of Timothy realized that it was Mac•ca•bē'us, they fled before him, and he dealt them a heavy blow. As many as eight thousand of them fell that day.

35 Next he turned aside to Mā'a•pha,[e] and fought against it and took it; and he killed every male in it, plundered it, and burned it with fire. 36 From there he marched on and took Chas'phō, Mā'ked, and Bō'sor, and the other towns of Gil'e•ad.

37 After these things Timothy gathered another army and encamped opposite Rā'phon, on the other side of the stream. 38 Judas sent men to spy out the camp, and they reported to him, "All the Gentiles around us have gathered to him; it is a very large force. 39 They also have hired Arabs to help them, and they are encamped across the stream, ready to come and fight against you." And Judas went to meet them.

40 Now as Judas and his army drew near to the stream of water, Timothy said to the officers of his forces, "If he crosses over to us first, we will not be able to resist him, for he will surely defeat us. 41 But if he shows fear and camps on the other side of the river, we will cross over to him and defeat him." 42 When Judas approached the stream of water, he stationed the officers[f] of the army at the stream and gave them this command, "Permit no one to encamp, but make them all enter the battle." 43 Then he crossed over against them first, and the whole army followed him. All the Gentiles were defeated before him, and they threw away their arms and fled into the sacred precincts at Car'na•im. 44 But he took the town and burned the sacred precincts with fire, together with all who were in them. Thus Car'na•im was conquered; they could stand before Judas no longer.

The Return to Jerusalem
(2 Macc 12.26–31)

45 Then Judas gathered together all the Israelites in Gil'e•ad, the small and the great, with their wives and children and goods, a very large company, to go to the land of Judah. 46 So they came to E'phron. This was a large and very strong town on the road, and they could not go around it to the right or to the left; they had to go through it. 47 But the people of the town shut them out and blocked up the gates with stones.

48 Judas sent them this friendly message, "Let us pass through your land to get to our land. No one will do you harm; we will simply pass by on foot." But they refused to open to him. 49 Then Judas ordered proclamation to be made to the army that all should encamp where they were. 50 So the men of the forces encamped, and he fought against the town all that day and all the night, and the town was delivered into his hands. 51 He destroyed every male by the edge of the sword, and razed and plundered the town. Then he passed through the town over the bodies of the dead.

52 Then they crossed the Jordan into the large plain before Beth-shan. 53 Judas kept rallying the laggards and encouraging the people all the way until he came to the land of Judah. 54 So they went up to Mount Zion with joy and gladness, and offered burnt offerings, because they had returned in safety; not one of them had fallen.

Joseph and Azariah Defeated

55 Now while Judas and Jonathan were in Gil'e•ad and their[g] brother Simon was in Galilee before Ptol•e•mā'is, 56 Joseph son of Zech•a•rī'ah, and

---

a Gk *those*   b Gk *they*   c Gk lacks *of Dathema.* See verse 9   d Gk *and they were attacking them*   e Other ancient authorities read *Alema*   f Or *scribes*   g Gk *his*

Az·a·ri'ah, the commanders of the forces, heard of their brave deeds and of the heroic war they had fought. [57] So they said, "Let us also make a name for ourselves; let us go and make war on the Gentiles around us." [58] So they issued orders to the men of the forces that were with them and marched against Jam'ni·a. [59] Gor'gi·as and his men came out of the town to meet them in battle. [60] Then Joseph and Az·a·ri'ah were routed, and were pursued to the borders of Judea; as many as two thousand of the people of Israel fell that day. [61] Thus the people suffered a great rout because, thinking to do a brave deed, they did not listen to Judas and his brothers. [62] But they did not belong to the family of those men through whom deliverance was given to Israel.

63 The man Judas and his brothers were greatly honored in all Israel and among all the Gentiles, wherever their name was heard. [64] People gathered to them and praised them.

Success at Hebron and Philistia

65 Then Judas and his brothers went out and fought the descendants of Esau in the land to the south. He struck He'bron and its villages and tore down its strongholds and burned its towers on all sides. [66] Then he marched off to go into the land of the Phi·lis'tines, and passed through Mar'i·sa.[h] [67] On that day some priests, who wished to do a brave deed, fell in battle, for they went out to battle unwisely. [68] But Judas turned aside to A·zo'tus in the land of the Phi·lis'tines; he tore down their altars, and the carved images of their gods he burned with fire; he plundered the towns and returned to the land of Judah.

The Last Days of Antiochus Epiphanes
(2 Macc 1.11–17; 9.1–29; 10.9–13)

King An·ti'o·chus was going through the upper provinces when he heard that El·y·ma'is in Persia was a city famed for its wealth in silver and gold. [2] Its temple was very rich, containing golden shields, breastplates, and weapons left there by Alexander son of Philip, the Mac·e·do'ni·an king who first reigned over the Greeks. [3] So he came and tried to take the city and plunder it, but he could not because his plan had become known to the citizens [4] and they withstood him in battle. So he fled and in great disappointment left there to return to Babylon.

5 Then someone came to him in Persia and reported that the armies that had gone into the land of Judah had been routed; [6] that Lys'i·as had gone first with a strong force, but had turned and fled before the Jews;[i] that the Jews[j] had grown strong from the arms, supplies, and abundant

spoils that they had taken from the armies they had cut down; [7] that they had torn down the abomination that he had erected on the altar in Jerusalem; and that they had surrounded the sanctuary with high walls as before, and also Beth-zur, his town.

8 When the king heard this news, he was astounded and badly shaken. He took to his bed and became sick from disappointment, because things had not turned out for him as he had planned. [9] He lay there for many days, because deep disappointment continually gripped him, and he realized that he was dying. [10] So he called all his Friends and said to them, "Sleep has departed from my eyes and I am downhearted with worry. [11] I said to myself, 'To what distress I have come! And into what a great flood I now am plunged! For I was kind and beloved in my power.' [12] But now I remember the wrong I did in Jerusalem. I seized all its vessels of silver and gold, and I sent to destroy the inhabitants of Judah without good reason. [13] I know that it is because of this that these misfortunes have come upon me; here I am, perishing of bitter disappointment in a strange land."

14 Then he called for Philip, one of his Friends, and made him ruler over all his kingdom. [15] He gave him the crown and his robe and the signet, so that he might guide his son An·ti'o·chus and bring him up to be king. [16] Thus King An·ti'o·chus died there in the one hundred forty-ninth year.[k] [17] When Lys'i·as learned that the king was dead, he set up An·ti'o·chus the king's[l] son to reign. Lys'i·as[m] had brought him up from boyhood; he named him Eu'pa·tor.

Renewed Attacks from Syria
(2 Macc 11.22–26; 13.1–26)

18 Meanwhile the garrison in the citadel kept hemming Israel in around the sanctuary. They were trying in every way to harm them and strengthen the Gentiles. [19] Judas therefore resolved to destroy them, and assembled all the people to besiege them. [20] They gathered together and besieged the citadel[n] in the one hundred fiftieth year;[o] and he built siege towers and other engines of war. [21] But some of the garrison escaped from the siege and some of the ungodly Israelites joined them. [22] They went to the king and said, "How long will you fail to do justice and to avenge our kindred? [23] We were happy to serve your father, to live by what he said, and to follow his commands.

---

h Other ancient authorities read *Samaria*   i Gk *them*
j Gk *they*   k 163 B.C.   l Gk *his*   m Gk *He*   n Gk *it*
o 162 B.C.

²⁴ For this reason the sons of our people besieged the citadel*ᵖ* and became hostile to us; moreover, they have put to death as many of us as they have caught, and they have seized our inheritances. ²⁵ It

they have fortified both the sanctuary and Beth-zur; ²⁷ unless you quickly prevent them, they will do still greater things, and you will not be able to stop them."

28 The king was enraged when he heard this. He assembled all his Friends, the commanders of his forces and those in authority.*q* ²⁹ Mercenary forces also came to him from other kingdoms and from islands of the seas. ³⁰ The number of his forces was one hundred thousand foot soldiers, twenty thousand horsemen, and thirty-two elephants accustomed to war. ³¹ They came through Id·ū·mē′a and encamped against Beth-zur, and for many days they fought and built engines of war; but the Jews*ʳ* sallied out and burned these with fire, and fought courageously.

The Battle at Beth-zechariah

32 Then Judas marched away from the citadel and encamped at Beth-zech·a·rī′ah, opposite the camp of the king. ³³ Early in the morning the king set out and took his army by a forced march along the road to Beth-zech·a·rī′ah, and his troops made ready for battle and sounded their trumpets. ³⁴ They offered the elephants the juice of grapes and mulberries, to arouse them for battle. ³⁵ They distributed the animals among the phalanxes; with each elephant they stationed a thousand men armed with coats of mail, and with brass helmets on their heads; and five hundred picked horsemen were assigned to each beast. ³⁶ These took their position beforehand wherever the animal was; wherever it went, they went with it, and they never left it. ³⁷ On the elephants*ˢ* were wooden towers, strong and covered; they were fastened on each animal by special harness, and on each were four*ᵗ* armed men who fought from there, and also its Indian driver. ³⁸ The rest of the cavalry were stationed on either side, on the two flanks of the army, to harass the enemy while being themselves protected by the phalanxes. ³⁹ When the sun shone on the shields of gold and brass, the hills were ablaze with them and gleamed like flaming torches.

40 Now a part of the king's army was spread out on the high hills, and some troops were on the plain, and they advanced steadily and in good order. ⁴¹ All who heard the noise made by their multitude, by the marching of the multitude and the clanking of their arms, trembled, for the army was very large and strong. ⁴² But Judas and his army advanced to the battle, and six hundred of the

did you KNOW?

A Just War

Have you ever believed in something so strongly that you could justify a war to protect it? The Maccabees did, and they led a violent resistance against terrible religious persecution.

The Catholic church teaches that "all citizens and all governments are obliged to work for the avoidance of war" (*Catechism*, no. 2308). But it also teaches that there can be occasions for legitimate defense by military force (no. 2309), or what is sometimes called a just war. The criteria for a just war are as follows:

- All other means to avoid war must be exhausted.
- The damage done by the aggressor must be grave and certain.
- There must be serious prospects of success.
- The use of arms must not produce evils that are greater than the evil to be eliminated.

No Catholic Christian can participate in good conscience in any war that does not meet all these criteria. And many people say that no war today can meet these criteria because of our modern weapons of mass destruction.

War is not the answer; peace is. But at times in history, some Christians have felt that the only response to a grave injustice was violent resistance. However, no Christian is obligated to fight in a war, and nonviolent resistance is always an option (see "Nonviolent Resistance," near 2 Macc 7.42).

is not against us alone that they have stretched out their hands; they have also attacked all the lands on their borders. ²⁶ And see, today they have encamped against the citadel in Jerusalem to take it;

---

p Meaning of Gk uncertain   *q* Gk *those over the reins*   *r* Gk *they*   *s* Gk *them*   *t* Cn: Some authorities read *thirty*; others *thirty-two*

king's army fell. 43 Now El•ē•ā′zar, called Av′a•ran, saw that one of the animals was equipped with royal armor. It was taller than all the others, and he supposed that the king was on it. 44 So he gave his life to save his people and to win for himself an everlasting name. 45 He courageously ran into the midst of the phalanx to reach it; he killed men right and left, and they parted before him on both sides. 46 He got under the elephant, stabbed it from beneath, and killed it; but it fell to the ground upon him and he died. 47 When the Jews*u* saw the royal might and the fierce attack of the forces, they turned away in flight.

The Siege of the Temple

48 The soldiers of the king's army went up to Jerusalem against them, and the king encamped in Judea and at Mount Zion. 49 He made peace with the people of Beth-zur, and they evacuated the town because they had no provisions there to withstand a siege, since it was a sabbatical year for the land. 50 So the king took Beth-zur and stationed a guard there to hold it. 51 Then he encamped before the sanctuary for many days. He set up siege towers, engines of war to throw fire and stones, machines to shoot arrows, and catapults. 52 The Jews*u* also made engines of war to match theirs, and fought for many days. 53 But they had no food in storage,*v* because it was the seventh year; those who had found safety in Judea from the Gentiles had consumed the last of the stores. 54 Only a few men were left in the sanctuary; the rest scattered to their own homes, for the famine proved too much for them.

Syria Offers Terms

55 Then Lys′i•as heard that Philip, whom King An•tī′o•chus while still living had appointed to bring up his son An•tī′o•chus to be king, 56 had returned from Persia and Mēd′i•a with the forces that had gone with the king, and that he was trying to seize control of the government. 57 So he quickly gave orders to withdraw, and said to the king, to the commanders of the forces, and to the troops, "Daily we grow weaker, our food supply is scant, the place against which we are fighting is strong, and the affairs of the kingdom press urgently on us. 58 Now then let us come to terms with these people, and make peace with them and with all their nation. 59 Let us agree to let them live by their laws as they did before; for it was on account of their laws that we abolished that they became angry and did all these things."

60 The speech pleased the king and the commanders, and he sent to the Jews*w* an offer of peace, and they accepted it. 61 So the king and the commanders gave them their oath. On these conditions the Jews*u* evacuated the stronghold. 62 But when the king entered Mount Zion and saw what a strong fortress the place was, he broke the oath he had sworn and gave orders to tear down the wall all around. 63 Then he set off in haste and returned to An′ti•och. He found Philip in control of the city, but he fought against him, and took the city by force.

Expedition of Bacchides and Alcimus
(2 Macc 14.1–14)

In the one hundred fifty-first year*x* De•mē′tri•us son of Se•leū′cus set out from Rome, sailed with a few men to a town by the sea, and there began to reign. 2 As he was entering the royal palace of his ancestors, the army seized An•tī′o•chus and Lys′i•as to bring them to him. 3 But when this act became known to him, he said, "Do not let me see their faces!" 4 So the army killed them, and De•mē′tri•us took his seat on the throne of his kingdom.

5 Then there came to him all the renegade and godless men of Israel; they were led by Al′ci•mus, who wanted to be high priest. 6 They brought to the king this accusation against the people: "Judas and his brothers have destroyed all your Friends, and have driven us out of our land. 7 Now then send a man whom you trust; let him go and see all the ruin that Judas*y* has brought on us and on the land of the king, and let him punish them and all who help them."

8 So the king chose Bac′chi•dēs, one of the king's Friends, governor of the province Beyond the River; he was a great man in the kingdom and was faithful to the king. 9 He sent him, and with him he sent the ungodly Al′ci•mus, whom he made high priest; and he commanded him to take vengeance on the Israelites. 10 So they marched away and came with a large force into the land of Judah; and he sent messengers to Judas and his brothers with peaceable but treacherous words. 11 But they paid no attention to their words, for they saw that they had come with a large force.

12 Then a group of scribes appeared in a body before Al′ci•mus and Bac′chi•dēs to ask for just terms. 13 The Has•i•dē′ans were first among the Israelites to seek peace from them, 14 for they said, "A priest of the line of Aaron has come with the army, and he will not harm us." 15 Al′ci•mus*z* spoke peaceable words to them and swore this oath to them, "We will not seek to injure you or your friends." 16 So they trusted him; but he seized sixty of them

u Gk *they*   *v* Other ancient authorities read *in the sanctuary*   *w* Gk *them*   *x* 161 B.C.   *y* Gk *he*   *z* Gk *He*

and killed them in one day, in accordance with the word that was written,

17 "The flesh of your faithful ones and their
> blood
> they poured out all around Jerusalem,
> and there was no one to bury them."

18 Then the fear and dread of them fell on all the people, for they said, "There is no truth or justice in them, for they have violated the agreement and the oath that they swore."

19 Then Bac'chi•dēs withdrew from Jerusalem and encamped in Beth-zā'ith. And he sent and seized many of the men who had deserted to him,[a] and some of the people, and killed them and threw them into a great pit. 20 He placed Al'ci•mus in charge of the country and left with him a force to help him; then Bac'chi•dēs went back to the king.

21 Al'ci•mus struggled to maintain his high priesthood, 22 and all who were troubling their people joined him. They gained control of the land of Judah and did great damage in Israel. 23 And Judas saw all the wrongs that Al'ci•mus and those with him had done among the Israelites; it was more than the Gentiles had done. 24 So Judas[b] went out into all the surrounding parts of Judea, taking vengeance on those who had deserted and preventing those in the city[c] from going out into the country. 25 When Al'ci•mus saw that Judas and those with him had grown strong, and realized that he could not withstand them, he returned to the king and brought malicious charges against them.

Nicanor in Judea
(2 Macc 14.15—15.19)

26 Then the king sent Nī•cā'nor, one of his honored princes, who hated and detested Israel, and he commanded him to destroy the people. 27 So Nī•cā'nor came to Jerusalem with a large force, and treacherously sent to Judas and his brothers this peaceable message, 28 "Let there be no fighting between you and me; I shall come with a few men to see you face to face in peace." 29 So he came to Judas, and they greeted one another peaceably; but the enemy were preparing to kidnap Judas. 30 It became known to Judas that Nī•cā'nor[b] had come to him with treacherous intent, and he was afraid of him and would not meet him again. 31 When Nī•cā'nor learned that his plan had been disclosed, he went out to meet Judas in battle near Caph'ar-sal'a•ma. 32 About five hundred of the army of Nī•cā'nor fell, and the rest[d] fled into the city of David.

Nicanor Threatens the Temple

33 After these events Nī•cā'nor went up to Mount Zion. Some of the priests from the sanctuary and some of the elders of the people came out to greet him peaceably and to show him the burnt offering that was being offered for the king. 34 But he mocked them and derided them and defiled them and spoke arrogantly, 35 and in anger he swore this oath, "Unless Judas and his army are delivered into my hands this time, then if I return safely I will burn up this house." And he went out in great anger. 36 At this the priests went in and stood before the altar and the temple; they wept and said,

37 "You chose this house to be called by your
> name,
> and to be for your people a house of
> prayer and supplication.
38 Take vengeance on this man and on his
> army,
> and let them fall by the sword;
> remember their blasphemies,
> and let them live no longer."

The Death of Nicanor
(2 Macc 15.20–37)

39 Now Nī•cā'nor went out from Jerusalem and encamped in Beth-hō'ron, and the Syrian army joined him. 40 Judas encamped in Ad'a•sa with three thousand men. Then Judas prayed and said, 41 "When the messengers from the king spoke blasphemy, your angel went out and struck down one hundred eighty-five thousand of the Assyrians.[e] 42 So also crush this army before us today; let the rest learn that Nī•cā'nor[b] has spoken wickedly against the sanctuary, and judge him according to this wickedness."

43 So the armies met in battle on the thirteenth day of the month of Ā'dar. The army of Nī•cā'nor was crushed, and he himself was the first to fall in the battle. 44 When his army saw that Nī•cā'nor had fallen, they threw down their arms and fled. 45 The Jews[d] pursued them a day's journey, from Ad'a•sa as far as Ga•zā'ra, and as they followed they kept sounding the battle call on the trumpets. 46 People came out of all the surrounding villages of Judea, and they outflanked the enemy[f] and drove them back to their pursuers,[g] so that they all fell by the sword; not even one of them was left. 47 Then the Jews[d] seized the spoils and the plunder; they cut off Nī•cā'nor's head and the right hand that he had so arrogantly stretched

---

a Or many of his men who had deserted   b Gk he
c Gk and they were prevented   d Gk they   e Gk of them
f Gk them   g Gk these

out, and brought them and displayed them just outside Jerusalem. [48] The people rejoiced greatly and celebrated that day as a day of great gladness. [49] They decreed that this day should be celebrated each year on the thirteenth day of A'dar. [50] So the land of Judah had rest for a few days.

A Eulogy of the Romans

Now Judas heard of the fame of the Romans, that they were very strong and were well-disposed toward all who made an alliance with them, that they pledged friendship to those who came to them, [2] and that they were very strong. He had been told of their wars and of the brave deeds that they were doing among the Gauls, how they had defeated them and forced them to pay tribute, [3] and what they had done in the land of Spain to get control of the silver and gold mines there, [4] and how they had gained control of the whole region by their planning and patience, even though the place was far distant from them. They also subdued the kings who came against them from the ends of the earth, until they crushed them and inflicted great disaster on them; the rest paid them tribute every year. [5] They had crushed in battle and conquered Philip, and King Per'se·us of the Mac·e·do'ni·ans,[h] and the others who rose up against them. [6] They also had defeated An·ti'o·chus the Great, king of Asia, who went to fight against them with one hundred twenty elephants and with cavalry and chariots and a very large army. He was crushed by them; [7] they took him alive and decreed that he and those who would reign after him should pay a heavy tribute and give hostages and surrender some of their best provinces, [8] the countries of India, Med'i·a, and Lyd'i·a. These they took from him and gave to King Eu'me·nes. [9] The Greeks planned to come and destroy them, [10] but this became known to them, and they sent a general against the Greeks[i] and attacked them. Many of them were wounded and fell, and the Romans[j] took captive their wives and children; they plundered them, conquered the land, tore down their strongholds, and enslaved them to this day. [11] The remaining kingdoms and islands, as many as ever opposed them, they destroyed and enslaved; [12] but with their friends and those who rely on them they have kept friendship. They have subdued kings far and near, and as many as have heard of their fame have feared them. [13] Those whom they wish to help and to make kings, they make kings, and those whom they wish they depose; and they have been greatly exalted. [14] Yet for all this not one of them has put on a crown or worn purple as a mark of pride, [15] but they have built for themselves a senate chamber, and every day three hundred twenty senators constantly deliberate concerning the people, to govern them well. [16] They trust one man each year to rule over them and to control all their land; they all heed the one man, and there is no envy or jealousy among them.

An Alliance with Rome

17 So Judas chose Eu·pol'e·mus son of John son of Ac'cos, and Jason son of El·e·a'zar, and sent them to Rome to establish friendship and alliance, [18] and to free themselves from the yoke; for they saw that the kingdom of the Greeks was enslaving Israel completely. [19] They went to Rome, a very long journey; and they entered the senate chamber and spoke as follows: [20] "Judas, who is also called Mac·ca·be'us, and his brothers and the people of the Jews have sent us to you to establish alliance and peace with you, so that we may be enrolled as your allies and friends." [21] The proposal pleased them, [22] and this is a copy of the letter that they wrote in reply, on bronze tablets, and sent to Jerusalem to remain with them there as a memorial of peace and alliance:

23 "May all go well with the Romans and with the nation of the Jews at sea and on land forever, and may sword and enemy be far from them. [24] If war comes first to Rome or to any of their allies in all their dominion, [25] the nation of the Jews shall act as their allies wholeheartedly, as the occasion may indicate to them. [26] To the enemy that makes war they shall not give or supply grain, arms, money, or ships, just as Rome has decided; and they shall keep their obligations without receiving any return. [27] In the same way, if war comes first to the nation of the Jews, the Romans shall willingly act as their allies, as the occasion may indicate to them. [28] And to their enemies there shall not be given grain, arms, money, or ships, just as Rome has decided; and they shall keep these obligations and do so without deceit. [29] Thus on these terms the Romans make a treaty with the Jewish people. [30] If after these terms are in effect both parties shall determine to add or delete anything, they shall do so at their discretion, and any addition or deletion that they may make shall be valid.

31 "Concerning the wrongs that King De·me'tri·us is doing to them, we have written to him as follows, 'Why have you made your yoke heavy on our friends and allies the Jews? [32] If now they appeal again for help against you, we will defend their rights and fight you on sea and on land.' "

---

h Or Kittim   i Gk them   j Gk they

What Makes a Hero?

History is full of heroes, those bigger-than-life men and women like Judas Maccabeus who have made a difference because of their courageous acts and their willingness to take risks that frighten other people. What makes someone a hero? Is each of us capable of heroism?

Someone we have grown up with, who now seems ordinary, could one day be a hero. None of us knows when we could be called on to do something heroic. We need an openness to God's call and a willingness to take a risk—to let go of our fears and to reach deep within ourselves for courage and strength. You may amaze yourself at what you can accomplish in extraordinary situations. The stuff of heroes, of great and brave persons such as Judas Maccabeus, is already within us. We need only to believe in ourselves and believe that God is with us.

You may not end up in a history book or be memorialized in a statue, but you can make a difference in the life of one or perhaps many people. What really counts is to be a hero in the eyes of God.

▶ 1 Macc 9.19–22

Bacchides Returns to Judea

When De·mē′tri·us heard that Nī·cā′nor and his army had fallen in battle, he sent Bac′chi·dēs and Al′ci·mus into the land of Judah a second time, and with them the right wing of the army. ²They went by the road that leads to Gil′gal and encamped against Mes′a·loth in Ar·bē′la, and they took it and killed many people. ³In the first month of the one hundred fifty-second year*ᵏ* they encamped against Jerusalem; ⁴then they marched off and went to Be·rē′a with twenty thousand foot soldiers and two thousand cavalry.

5 Now Judas was encamped in El′a·sa, and with him were three thousand picked men. ⁶When they saw the huge number of the enemy forces, they were greatly frightened, and many slipped away from the camp, until no more than eight hundred of them were left.

7 When Judas saw that his army had slipped away and the battle was imminent, he was crushed in spirit, for he had no time to assemble them. ⁸He became faint, but he said to those who were left, "Let us get up and go against our enemies. We may have the strength to fight them." ⁹But they tried to dissuade him, saying, "We do not have the strength. Let us rather save our own lives now, and let us come back with our kindred and fight them; we are too few." ¹⁰But Judas said, "Far be it from us to do such a thing as to flee from them. If our time has come, let us die bravely for our kindred, and leave no cause to question our honor."

The Last Battle of Judas

11 Then the army of Bac′chi·dēs*ˡ* marched out from the camp and took its stand for the encounter. The cavalry was divided into two companies, and the slingers and the archers went ahead of the army, as did all the chief warriors. ¹²Bac′chi·dēs was on the right wing. Flanked by the two companies, the phalanx advanced to the sound of the trumpets; and the men with Judas also blew their trumpets. ¹³The earth was shaken by the noise of the armies, and the battle raged from morning until evening.

14 Judas saw that Bac′chi·dēs and the strength of his army were on the right; then all the stouthearted men went with him, ¹⁵and they crushed the right wing, and he pursued them as far as Mount A·zō′tus. ¹⁶When those on the left wing saw that the right wing was crushed, they turned and followed close behind Judas and his men. ¹⁷The battle became desperate, and many on both sides were wounded and fell. ¹⁸Judas also fell, and the rest fled.

19 Then Jonathan and Simon took their brother Judas and buried him in the tomb of their ancestors at Mō′dein, ²⁰and wept for him. All Israel made great lamentation for him; they mourned many days and said,

21 "How is the mighty fallen,
    the savior of Israel!"

²²Now the rest of the acts of Judas, and his wars and the brave deeds that he did, and his greatness, have not been recorded, but they were very many.

---

k 160 B.C.   *l* Gk lacks *of Bacchides*

1
M
A
C
C

Jonathan Succeeds Judas

23 After the death of Judas, the renegades emerged in all parts of Israel; all the wrongdoers reappeared. 24 In those days a very great famine occurred, and the country went over to their side. 25 Bac'chi•dēs chose the godless and put them in charge of the country. 26 They made inquiry and searched for the friends of Judas, and brought them to Bac'chi•dēs, who took vengeance on them and made sport of them. 27 So there was great distress in Israel, such as had not been since the time that prophets ceased to appear among them.

28 Then all the friends of Judas assembled and said to Jonathan, 29 "Since the death of your brother Judas there has been no one like him to go against our enemies and Bac'chi•dēs, and to deal with those of our nation who hate us. 30 Now therefore we have chosen you today to take his place as our ruler and leader, to fight our battle." 31 So Jonathan accepted the leadership at that time in place of his brother Judas.

The Campaigns of Jonathan

32 When Bac'chi•dēs learned of this, he tried to kill him. 33 But Jonathan and his brother Simon and all who were with him heard of it, and they fled into the wilderness of Te•kō'a and camped by the water of the pool of As'phar. 34 Bac'chi•dēs found this out on the sabbath day, and he with all his army crossed the Jordan.

35 So Jonathan[m] sent his brother as leader of the multitude and begged the Na•ba•tē'ans, who were his friends, for permission to store with them the great amount of baggage that they had. 36 But the family of Jam'brī from Med'e•ba came out and seized John and all that he had, and left with it.

37 After these things it was reported to Jonathan and his brother Simon, "The family of Jam'brī are celebrating a great wedding, and are conducting the bride, a daughter of one of the great nobles of Cā'naan, from Nad'a•bath with a large escort." 38 Remembering how their brother John had been killed, they went up and hid under cover of the mountain. 39 They looked out and saw a tumultuous procession with a great amount of baggage; and the bridegroom came out with his friends and his brothers to meet them with tambourines and musicians and many weapons. 40 Then they rushed on them from the ambush and began killing them. Many were wounded and fell, and the rest fled to the mountain; and the Jews[n] took all their goods. 41 So the wedding was turned into mourning and the voice of their musicians into a funeral dirge. 42 After they had fully avenged the blood of their brother, they returned to the marshes of the Jordan.

43 When Bac'chi•dēs heard of this, he came with a large force on the sabbath day to the banks of the Jordan. 44 And Jonathan said to those with him, "Let us get up now and fight for our lives, for today things are not as they were before. 45 For look! the battle is in front of us and behind us; the water of the Jordan is on this side and on that, with marsh and thicket; there is no place to turn. 46 Cry out now to Heaven that you may be delivered from the hands of our enemies." 47 So the battle began, and Jonathan stretched out his hand to strike Bac'chi•dēs, but he eluded him and went to the rear. 48 Then Jonathan and the men with him leaped into the Jordan and swam across to the other side, and the enemy[n] did not cross the Jordan to attack them. 49 And about one thousand of Bac'chi•dēs' men fell that day.

Bacchides Builds Fortifications

50 Then Bac'chi•dēs[m] returned to Jerusalem and built strong cities in Judea: the fortress in Jericho, and Em•mā'us, and Beth-hō'ron, and Beth'el, and Tim'nath, and[o] Phar'a•thon, and Tē'phon, with high walls and gates and bars. 51 And he placed garrisons in them to harass Israel. 52 He also fortified the town of Beth-zur, and Ga•zā'ra, and the citadel, and in them he put troops and stores of food. 53 And he took the sons of the leading men of the land as hostages and put them under guard in the citadel at Jerusalem.

54 In the one hundred and fifty-third year,[p] in the second month, Al'ci•mus gave orders to tear down the wall of the inner court of the sanctuary. He tore down the work of the prophets! 55 But he only began to tear it down, for at that time Al'ci•mus was stricken and his work was hindered; his mouth was stopped and he was paralyzed, so that he could no longer say a word or give commands concerning his house. 56 And Al'ci•mus died at that time in great agony. 57 When Bac'chi•dēs saw that Al'ci•mus was dead, he returned to the king, and the land of Judah had rest for two years.

The End of the War

58 Then all the lawless plotted and said, "See! Jonathan and his men are living in quiet and confidence. So now let us bring Bac'chi•dēs back, and he will capture them all in one night." 59 And they went and consulted with him. 60 He started to come with a large force, and secretly sent letters to all his allies in Judea, telling them to seize Jona-

---

m Gk he   n Gk they   o Some authorities omit and
p 159 B.C.

than and his men; but they were unable to do it, because their plan became known. 61 And Jonathan's men[q] seized about fifty of the men of the country who were leaders in this treachery, and killed them.

62 Then Jonathan with his men, and Simon, withdrew to Beth•bā'sī in the wilderness; he rebuilt the parts of it that had been demolished, and they fortified it. 63 When Bac'chi•dēs learned of this, he assembled all his forces, and sent orders to the men of Judea. 64 Then he came and encamped against Beth•bā'sī; he fought against it for many days and made machines of war.

65 But Jonathan left his brother Simon in the town, while he went out into the country; and he went with only a few men. 66 He struck down Od-o•mē'ra and his kindred and the people of Phas'i-ron in their tents. 67 Then he[r] began to attack and went into battle with his forces; and Simon and his men sallied out from the town and set fire to the machines of war. 68 They fought with Bac'chi-dēs, and he was crushed by them. They pressed him very hard, for his plan and his expedition had been in vain. 69 So he was very angry at the renegades who had counseled him to come into the country, and he killed many of them. Then he decided to go back to his own land.

70 When Jonathan learned of this, he sent ambassadors to him to make peace with him and obtain release of the captives. 71 He agreed, and did as he said; and he swore to Jonathan[s] that he would not try to harm him as long as he lived. 72 He restored to him the captives whom he had taken previously from the land of Judah; then he turned and went back to his own land, and did not come again into their territory. 73 Thus the sword ceased from Israel. Jonathan settled in Mich'mash and began to judge the people; and he destroyed the godless out of Israel.

Revolt of Alexander Epiphanes

10 In the one hundred sixtieth year[t] Alexander E•piph'a•nēs, son of An•tī'o•chus, landed and occupied Ptol•e•mā'is. They welcomed him, and there he began to reign. 2 When King De•mē'tri•us heard of it, he assembled a very large army and marched out to meet him in battle. 3 De•mē'tri•us sent Jonathan a letter in peaceable words to honor him; 4 for he said to himself, "Let us act first to make peace with him[u] before he makes peace with Alexander against us, 5 for he will remember all the wrongs that we did to him and to his brothers and his nation." 6 So De•mē'tri•us[v] gave him authority to recruit troops, to equip them with arms, and to become his ally; and he commanded that the hostages in the citadel should be released to him.

7 Then Jonathan came to Jerusalem and read the letter in the hearing of all the people and of those in the citadel. 8 They were greatly alarmed when they heard that the king had given him authority to recruit troops. 9 But those in the citadel released the hostages to Jonathan, and he returned them to their parents.

10 And Jonathan took up residence in Jerusalem and began to rebuild and restore the city. 11 He directed those who were doing the work to build the walls and encircle Mount Zion with squared stones, for better fortification; and they did so.

12 Then the foreigners who were in the strongholds that Bac'chi•dēs had built fled; 13 all of them left their places and went back to their own lands. 14 Only in Beth-zur did some remain who had forsaken the law and the commandments, for it served as a place of refuge.

15 Now King Alexander heard of all the promises that De•mē'tri•us had sent to Jonathan, and he heard of the battles that Jonathan[v] and his brothers had fought, of the brave deeds that they had done, and of the troubles that they had endured. 16 So he said, "Shall we find another such man? Come now, we will make him our friend and ally." 17 And he wrote a letter and sent it to him, in the following words:

Jonathan Becomes High Priest

18 "King Alexander to his brother Jonathan, greetings. 19 We have heard about you, that you are a mighty warrior and worthy to be our friend. 20 And so we have appointed you today to be the high priest of your nation; you are to be called the king's Friend and you are to take our side and keep friendship with us." He also sent him a purple robe and a golden crown.

21 So Jonathan put on the sacred vestments in the seventh month of the one hundred sixtieth year,[t] at the festival of booths,[w] and he recruited troops and equipped them with arms in abundance. 22 When De•mē'tri•us heard of these things he was distressed and said, 23 "What is this that we have done? Alexander has gotten ahead of us in forming a friendship with the Jews to strengthen himself. 24 I also will write them words of encouragement and promise them honor and gifts, so that I may have their help." 25 So he sent a message to them in the following words:

---

q Gk *they* r Other ancient authorities read *they*
s Gk *him* t 152 B.C. u Gk *them* v Gk *he*
w Or *tabernacles*

A Letter from Demetrius to Jonathan

"King De•mē'tri•us to the nation of the Jews, greetings. 26 Since you have kept your agreement with us and have continued your friendship with us, and have not sided with our enemies, we have heard of it and rejoiced. 27 Now continue still to keep faith with us, and we will repay you with good for what you do for us. 28 We will grant you many immunities and give you gifts.

29 "I now free you and exempt all the Jews from payment of tribute and salt tax and crown levies, 30 and instead of collecting the third of the grain and the half of the fruit of the trees that I should receive, I release them from this day and henceforth. I will not collect them from the land of Judah or from the three districts added to it from Sa•mār'i•a and Galilee, from this day and for all time. 31 Jerusalem and its environs, its tithes and its revenues, shall be holy and free from tax. 32 I release also my control of the citadel in Jerusalem and give it to the high priest, so that he may station in it men of his own choice to guard it. 33 And everyone of the Jews taken as a captive from the land of Judah into any part of my kingdom, I set free without payment; and let all officials cancel also the taxes on their livestock.

34 "All the festivals and sabbaths and new moons and appointed days, and the three days before a festival and the three after a festival—let them all be days of immunity and release for all the Jews who are in my kingdom. 35 No one shall have authority to exact anything from them or annoy any of them about any matter.

36 "Let Jews be enrolled in the king's forces to the number of thirty thousand men, and let the maintenance be given them that is due to all the forces of the king. 37 Let some of them be stationed in the great strongholds of the king, and let some of them be put in positions of trust in the kingdom. Let their officers and leaders be of their own number, and let them live by their own laws, just as the king has commanded in the land of Judah.

38 "As for the three districts that have been added to Judea from the country of Sa•mār'i•a, let them be annexed to Judea so that they may be considered to be under one ruler and obey no other authority than the high priest. 39 Ptol•e•mā'is and the land adjoining it I have given as a gift to the sanctuary in Jerusalem, to meet the necessary expenses of the sanctuary. 40 I also grant fifteen thousand shekels of silver yearly out of the king's revenues from appropriate places. 41 And all the additional funds that the government officials have not paid as they did in the first years,ˣ they shall give from now on for the service of the tem-

ple.ʸ 42 Moreover, the five thousand shekels of silver that my officialsᶻ have received every year from the income of the services of the temple, this too is canceled, because it belongs to the priests who minister there. 43 And all who take refuge at the temple in Jerusalem, or in any of its precincts, because they owe money to the king or are in debt, let them be released and receive back all their property in my kingdom.

44 "Let the cost of rebuilding and restoring the structures of the sanctuary be paid from the revenues of the king. 45 And let the cost of rebuilding the walls of Jerusalem and fortifying it all around, and the cost of rebuilding the walls in Judea, also be paid from the revenues of the king."

Death of Demetrius

46 When Jonathan and the people heard these words, they did not believe or accept them, because they remembered the great wrongs that De•mē'tri•usᵃ had done in Israel and how much he had oppressed them. 47 They favored Alexander, because he had been the first to speak peaceable words to them, and they remained his allies all his days.

48 Now King Alexander assembled large forces and encamped opposite De•mē'tri•us. 49 The two kings met in battle, and the army of De•mē'tri•us fled, and Alexanderᵇ pursued him and defeated them. 50 He pressed the battle strongly until the sun set, and on that day De•mē'tri•us fell.

Treaty of Ptolemy and Alexander

51 Then Alexander sent ambassadors to Ptol'e•my king of Egypt with the following message: 52 "Since I have returned to my kingdom and have taken my seat on the throne of my ancestors, and established my rule—for I crushed De•mē'tri•us and gained control of our country; 53 I met him in battle, and he and his army were crushed by us, and we have taken our seat on the throne of his kingdom— 54 now therefore let us establish friendship with one another; give me now your daughter as my wife, and I will become your son-in-law, and will make gifts to you and to her in keeping with your position."

55 Ptol'e•my the king replied and said, "Happy was the day on which you returned to the land of your ancestors and took your seat on the throne of their kingdom. 56 And now I will do for you as you wrote, but meet me at Ptol•e•mā'is, so that we may

---

x Meaning of Gk uncertain   y Gk house   z Gk they
a Gk he   b Other ancient authorities read Alexander fled, and Demetrius

see one another, and I will become your father-in-law, as you have said."

57 So Ptol·e·my set out from Egypt, he and his daughter Cleopatra, and came to Ptol·e·mā'is in the one hundred sixty-second year.[c] 58 King Alexander met him, and Ptol·e·my[d] gave him his daughter Cleopatra in marriage, and celebrated her wedding at Ptol·e·mā'is with great pomp, as kings do.

59 Then King Alexander wrote to Jonathan to come and meet him. 60 So he went with pomp to Ptol·e·mā'is and met the two kings; he gave them and their Friends silver and gold and many gifts, and found favor with them. 61 A group of malcontents from Israel, renegades, gathered together against him to accuse him; but the king paid no attention to them. 62 The king gave orders to take off Jonathan's garments and to clothe him in purple, and they did so. 63 The king also seated him at his side; and he said to his officers, "Go out with him into the middle of the city and proclaim that no one is to bring charges against him about any matter, and let no one annoy him for any reason." 64 When his accusers saw the honor that was paid him, in accord with the proclamation, and saw him clothed in purple, they all fled. 65 Thus the king honored him and enrolled him among his chief[e] Friends, and made him general and governor of the province. 66 And Jonathan returned to Jerusalem in peace and gladness.

Apollonius Is Defeated by Jonathan

67 In the one hundred sixty-fifth year[f] De·mē'tri·us son of De·mē'tri·us came from Crete to the land of his ancestors. 68 When King Alexander heard of it, he was greatly distressed and returned to An'ti·och. 69 And De·mē'tri·us appointed Ap·ol·lō'ni·us the governor of Coe·le·syr'i·a, and he assembled a large force and encamped against Jam'ni·a. Then he sent the following message to the high priest Jonathan:

70 "You are the only one to rise up against us, and I have fallen into ridicule and disgrace because of you. Why do you assume authority against us in the hill country? 71 If you now have confidence in your forces, come down to the plain to meet us, and let us match strength with each other there, for I have with me the power of the cities. 72 Ask and learn who I am and who the others are that are helping us. People will tell you that you cannot stand before us, for your ancestors were twice put to flight in their own land. 73 And now you will not be able to withstand my cavalry and such an army in the plain, where there is no stone or pebble, or place to flee."

74 When Jonathan heard the words of Ap·ol·lō'ni·us, his spirit was aroused. He chose ten thousand men and set out from Jerusalem, and his brother Simon met him to help him. 75 He encamped before Jop'pa, but the people of the city closed its gates, for Ap·ol·lō'ni·us had a garrison in Jop'pa. 76 So they fought against it, and the people of the city became afraid and opened the gates, and Jonathan gained possession of Jop'pa.

77 When Ap·ol·lō'ni·us heard of it, he mustered three thousand cavalry and a large army, and went to A·zō'tus as though he were going farther. At the same time he advanced into the plain, for he had a large troop of cavalry and put confidence in it. 78 Jonathan[d] pursued him to A·zō'tus, and the armies engaged in battle. 79 Now Ap·ol·lō'ni·us had secretly left a thousand cavalry behind them. 80 Jonathan learned that there was an ambush behind him, for they surrounded his army and shot arrows at his men from early morning until late afternoon. 81 But his men stood fast, as Jonathan had commanded, and the enemy's[g] horses grew tired.

82 Then Simon brought forward his force and engaged the phalanx in battle (for the cavalry was exhausted); they were overwhelmed by him and fled, 83 and the cavalry was dispersed in the plain. They fled to A·zō'tus and entered Beth-dā'gon, the temple of their idol, for safety. 84 But Jonathan burned A·zō'tus and the surrounding towns and plundered them; and the temple of Dā'gon, and those who had taken refuge in it, he burned with fire. 85 The number of those who fell by the sword, with those burned alive, came to eight thousand.

86 Then Jonathan left there and encamped against As'ka·lon, and the people of the city came out to meet him with great pomp.

87 He and those with him then returned to Jerusalem with a large amount of booty. 88 When King Alexander heard of these things, he honored Jonathan still more; 89 and he sent to him a golden buckle, such as it is the custom to give to the King's Kinsmen. He also gave him Ek'ron and all its environs as his possession.

Ptolemy Invades Syria

Then the king of Egypt gathered great forces, like the sand by the seashore, and many ships; and he tried to get possession of Alexander's kingdom by trickery and add it to his own kingdom. 2 He set out for Syria with peaceable words, and the people of the towns opened their gates to him and went to meet him, for King Alexander had commanded them to meet him, since he was Alexander's[h] father-in-law. 3 But when Ptol·e·my entered the

c 150 B.C. *d* Gk *he* *e* Gk *first* *f* 147 B.C. *g* Gk *their* *h* Gk *his*

towns he stationed forces as a garrison in each town.

4 When he[i] approached A·zō′tus, they showed him the burnt-out temple of Dā′gon, and A·zō′tus and its suburbs destroyed, and the corpses lying about, and the charred bodies of those whom Jonathan[j] had burned in the war, for they had piled them in heaps along his route. 5 They also told the king what Jonathan had done, to throw blame on him; but the king kept silent. 6 Jonathan met the king at Jop′pa with pomp, and they greeted one another and spent the night there. 7 And Jonathan went with the king as far as the river called E·leū′ther·us; then he returned to Jerusalem.

8 So King Ptol′e·my gained control of the coastal cities as far as Se·leū′ci·a by the sea, and he kept devising wicked designs against Alexander. 9 He sent envoys to King De·mē′tri·us, saying, "Come, let us make a covenant with each other, and I will give you in marriage my daughter who was Alexander's wife, and you shall reign over your father's kingdom. 10 I now regret that I gave him my daughter, for he has tried to kill me." 11 He threw blame on Alexander[k] because he coveted his kingdom. 12 So he took his daughter away from him and gave her to De·mē′tri·us. He was estranged from Alexander, and their enmity became manifest.

13 Then Ptol′e·my entered An′ti·och and put on the crown of Asia. Thus he put two crowns on his head, the crown of Egypt and that of Asia. 14 Now King Alexander was in Ci·li′ci·a at that time, because the people of that region were in revolt. 15 When Alexander heard of it, he came against him in battle. Ptol′e·my marched out and met him with a strong force, and put him to flight. 16 So Alexander fled into Arabia to find protection there, and King Ptol′e·my was triumphant. 17 Zab′di·el the A′rab cut off the head of Alexander and sent it to Ptol′e·my. 18 But King Ptol′e·my died three days later, and his troops in the strongholds were killed by the inhabitants of the strongholds. 19 So De·mē′tri·us became king in the one hundred sixty-seventh year.[l]

Jonathan's Diplomacy

20 In those days Jonathan assembled the Judeans to attack the citadel in Jerusalem, and he built many engines of war to use against it. 21 But certain renegades who hated their nation went to the king and reported to him that Jonathan was besieging the citadel. 22 When he heard this he was angry, and as soon as he heard it he set out and came to Ptol·e·mā′is; and he wrote Jonathan not to continue the siege, but to meet him for a conference at Ptol·e·mā′is as quickly as possible.

23 When Jonathan heard this, he gave orders to continue the siege. He chose some of the elders of Israel and some of the priests, and put himself in danger, 24 for he went to the king at Ptol·e·mā′is, taking silver and gold and clothing and numerous other gifts. And he won his favor. 25 Although certain renegades of his nation kept making complaints against him, 26 the king treated him as his predecessors had treated him; he exalted him in the presence of all his Friends. 27 He confirmed him in the high priesthood and in as many other honors as he had formerly had, and caused him to be reckoned among his chief[m] Friends. 28 Then Jonathan asked the king to free Judea and the three districts of Sa·mār′i·a[n] from tribute, and promised him three hundred talents. 29 The king consented, and wrote a letter to Jonathan about all these things; its contents were as follows:

30 "King De·mē′tri·us to his brother Jonathan and to the nation of the Jews, greetings. 31 This copy of the letter that we wrote concerning you to our kinsman Las′the·nēs we have written to you also, so that you may know what it says. 32 'King De·mē′tri·us to his father Las′the·nēs, greetings. 33 We have determined to do good to the nation of the Jews, who are our friends and fulfill their obligations to us, because of the goodwill they show toward us. 34 We have confirmed as their possession both the territory of Judea and the three districts of A·phāir′e·ma and Lyd′da and Rath′a·min; the latter, with all the region bordering them, were added to Judea from Sa·mār′i·a. To all those who offer sacrifice in Jerusalem we have granted release from[o] the royal taxes that the king formerly received from them each year, from the crops of the land and the fruit of the trees. 35 And the other payments henceforth due to us of the tithes, and the taxes due to us, and the salt pits and the crown taxes due to us—from all these we shall grant them release. 36 And not one of these grants shall be canceled from this time on forever. 37 Now therefore take care to make a copy of this, and let it be given to Jonathan and put up in a conspicuous place on the holy mountain.' "

The Intrigue of Trypho

38 When King De·mē′tri·us saw that the land was quiet before him and that there was no opposition to him, he dismissed all his troops, all of them to their own homes, except the foreign troops that he had recruited from the islands of the nations. So all the troops who had served un-

---
i Other ancient authorities read *they*   j Gk *he*   k Gk *him*
l 145 B.C.   m Gk *first*   n Cn: Gk *the three districts and Samaria*   o Or *Samaria, for all those who offer sacrifice in Jerusalem, in place of*

der his predecessors hated him. 39 A certain Trÿ′-phō had formerly been one of Alexander's supporters; he saw that all the troops were grumbling against De•mē′tri•us. So he went to I•mal′kū•ē the A′rab, who was bringing up An•tī′o•chus, the young son of Alexander, 40 and insistently urged him to hand An•tī′o•chus*p* over to him, to become king in place of his father. He also reported to I•mal′kū•ē*p* what De•mē′tri•us had done and told of the hatred that the troops of De•mē′tri•us*q* had for him; and he stayed there many days.

41 Now Jonathan sent to King De•mē′tri•us the request that he remove the troops of the citadel from Jerusalem, and the troops in the strongholds; for they kept fighting against Israel. 42 And De•mē′-tri•us sent this message back to Jonathan: "Not only will I do these things for you and your nation, but I will confer great honor on you and your nation, if I find an opportunity. 43 Now then you will do well to send me men who will help me, for all my troops have revolted." 44 So Jonathan sent three thousand stalwart men to him at An′ti•och, and when they came to the king, the king rejoiced at their arrival.

45 Then the people of the city assembled within the city, to the number of a hundred and twenty thousand, and they wanted to kill the king. 46 But the king fled into the palace. Then the people of the city seized the main streets of the city and began to fight. 47 So the king called the Jews to his aid, and they all rallied around him and then spread out through the city; and they killed on that day about one hundred thousand. 48 They set fire to the city and seized a large amount of spoil on that day, and saved the king. 49 When the people of the city saw that the Jews had gained control of the city as they pleased, their courage failed and they cried out to the king with this entreaty: 50 "Grant us peace, and make the Jews stop fighting against us and our city." 51 And they threw down their arms and made peace. So the Jews gained glory in the sight of the king and of all the people in his kingdom, and they returned to Jerusalem with a large amount of spoil.

52 So King De•mē′tri•us sat on the throne of his kingdom, and the land was quiet before him. 53 But he broke his word about all that he had promised; he became estranged from Jonathan and did not repay the favors that Jonathan*r* had done him, but treated him very harshly.

Trypho Seizes Power

54 After this Trÿ′phō returned, and with him the young boy An•tī′o•chus who began to reign and put on the crown. 55 All the troops that De•mē′tri•us had discharged gathered around him; they fought against De•mē′tri•us,*p* and he fled and was routed. 56 Trÿ′phō captured the elephants*s* and gained control of An′ti•och. 57 Then the young An•tī′o•chus wrote to Jonathan, saying, "I confirm you in the high priesthood and set you over the four districts and make you one of the king's Friends." 58 He also sent him gold plates and a table service, and granted him the right to drink from gold cups and dress in purple and wear a gold buckle. 59 He appointed Jonathan's*t* brother Simon governor from the Ladder of Tÿre to the borders of Egypt.

Campaigns of Jonathan and Simon

60 Then Jonathan set out and traveled beyond the river and among the towns, and all the army of Syria gathered to him as allies. When he came to As′ka•lon, the people of the city met him and paid him honor. 61 From there he went to Gā′za, but the people of Gā′za shut him out. So he besieged it and burned its suburbs with fire and plundered them. 62 Then the people of Gā′za pleaded with Jonathan, and he made peace with them, and took the sons of their rulers as hostages and sent them to Jerusalem. And he passed through the country as far as Damascus.

63 Then Jonathan heard that the officers of De•mē′tri•us had come to Kā′desh in Galilee with a large army, intending to remove him from office. 64 He went to meet them, but left his brother Simon in the country. 65 Simon encamped before Beth-zur and fought against it for many days and hemmed it in. 66 Then they asked him to grant them terms of peace, and he did so. He removed them from there, took possession of the town, and set a garrison over it.

67 Jonathan and his army encamped by the waters of Gen•nes′a•ret. Early in the morning they marched to the plain of Hā′zor, 68 and there in the plain the army of the foreigners met him; they had set an ambush against him in the mountains, but they themselves met him face to face. 69 Then the men in ambush emerged from their places and joined battle. 70 All the men with Jonathan fled; not one of them was left except Mat•ta•thī′as son of Ab′sa•lom and Judas son of Chal′phī, commanders of the forces of the army. 71 Jonathan tore his clothes, put dust on his head, and prayed. 72 Then he turned back to the battle against the enemy*u* and routed them, and they fled. 73 When his men who were fleeing saw this, they returned to him and joined him in the pursuit as far as Kā′desh, to their camp, and there they encamped. 74 As many

---

p Gk him   *q* Gk his troops   *r* Gk he   *s* Gk animals
t Gk his   *u* Gk them

as three thousand of the foreigners fell that day. And Jonathan returned to Jerusalem.

Alliances with Rome and Sparta

Now when Jonathan saw that the time was favorable for him, he chose men and sent them to Rome to confirm and renew the friendship with them. ² He also sent letters to the same effect to the Spartans and to other places. ³ So they went to Rome and entered the senate chamber and said, "The high priest Jonathan and the Jewish nation have sent us to renew the former friendship and alliance with them." ⁴ And the Romans° gave them letters to the people in every place, asking them to provide for the envoysᵂ safe conduct to the land of Judah.

5 This is a copy of the letter that Jonathan wrote to the Spartans: ⁶ "The high priest Jonathan, the senate of the nation, the priests, and the rest of the Jewish people to their brothers the Spartans, greetings. ⁷ Already in time past a letter was sent to the high priest Ō·nī'as from Ar'i·us,ˣ who was king among you, stating that you are our brothers, as the appended copy shows. ⁸ Ō·nī'as welcomed the envoy with honor, and received the letter, which contained a clear declaration of alliance and friendship. ⁹ Therefore, though we have no need of these things, since we have as encouragement the holy books that are in our hands, ¹⁰ we have undertaken to send to renew our family ties and friendship with you, so that we may not become estranged from you, for considerable time has passed since you sent your letter to us. ¹¹ We therefore remember you constantly on every occasion, both at our festivals and on other appropriate days, at the sacrifices that we offer and in our prayers, as it is right and proper to remember brothers. ¹² And we rejoice in your glory. ¹³ But as for ourselves, many trials and many wars have encircled us; the kings around us have waged war against us. ¹⁴ We were unwilling to annoy you and our other allies and friends with these wars, ¹⁵ for we have the help that comes from Heaven for our aid, and so we were delivered from our enemies, and our enemies were humbled. ¹⁶ We therefore have chosen Nū·mē'ni·us son of An·ti'o·chus and An·tip'a·ter son of Jason, and have sent them to Rome to renew our former friendship and alliance with them. ¹⁷ We have commanded them to go also to you and greet you and deliver to you this letter from us concerning the renewal of our family ties. ¹⁸ And now please send us a reply to this."

19 This is a copy of the letter that they sent to Ō·nī'as: ²⁰ "King Ar'i·us of the Spartans, to the high priest Ō·nī'as, greetings. ²¹ It has been found in writing concerning the Spartans and the Jews that they are brothers and are of the family of Abraham. ²² And now that we have learned this, please write us concerning your welfare; ²³ we on our part write to you that your livestock and your property belong to us, and ours belong to you. We therefore command that our envoys° report to you accordingly."

Further Campaigns of Jonathan and Simon

24 Now Jonathan heard that the commanders of De·mē'tri·us had returned, with a larger force than before, to wage war against him. ²⁵ So he marched away from Jerusalem and met them in the region of Hā'math, for he gave them no opportunity to invade his own country. ²⁶ He sent spies to their camp, and they returned and reported to him that the enemy° were being drawn up in formation to attack the Jewsᵂ by night. ²⁷ So when the sun had set, Jonathan commanded his troops to be alert and to keep their arms at hand so as to be ready all night for battle, and he stationed outposts around the camp. ²⁸ When the enemy heard that Jonathan and his troops were prepared for battle, they were afraid and were terrified at heart; so they kindled fires in their camp and withdrew.ʸ ²⁹ But Jonathan and his troops did not know it until morning, for they saw the fires burning. ³⁰ Then Jonathan pursued them, but he did not overtake them, for they had crossed the E·leū'ther·us river. ³¹ So Jonathan turned aside against the Arabs who are called Zab·a·dē'ans, and he crushed them and plundered them. ³² Then he broke camp and went to Damascus, and marched through all that region.

33 Simon also went out and marched through the country as far as As'ka·lon and the neighboring strongholds. He turned aside to Jop'pa and took it by surprise, ³⁴ for he had heard that they were ready to hand over the stronghold to those whom De·mē'tri·us had sent. And he stationed a garrison there to guard it.

35 When Jonathan returned he convened the elders of the people and planned with them to build strongholds in Judea, ³⁶ to build the walls of Jerusalem still higher, and to erect a high barrier between the citadel and the city to separate it from the city, in order to isolate it so that its garrison° could neither buy nor sell. ³⁷ So they gathered together to rebuild the city; part of the wall on the valley to the east had fallen, and he repaired the section called Cha·phen'a·tha. ³⁸ Simon also built Ad'i·da in the She·phē'lah; he fortified it and installed gates with bolts.

Trypho Captures Jonathan

39 Then Trý′phō attempted to become king in Asia and put on the crown, and to raise his hand against King An•ti′o•chus. 40 He feared that Jonathan might not permit him to do so, but might make war on him, so he kept seeking to seize and kill him, and he marched out and came to Bethshan. 41 Jonathan went out to meet him with forty

thousand picked warriors, and he came to Bethshan. 42 When Trý′phō saw that he had come with a large army, he was afraid to raise his hand against him. 43 So he received him with honor and commended him to all his Friends, and he gave him gifts and commanded his Friends and his troops to obey him as they would himself. 44 Then he said to Jonathan, "Why have you put all these people to so much trouble when we are not at war? 45 Dismiss them now to their homes and choose for yourself a few men to stay with you, and come with me to Ptol•e•mā′is. I will hand it over to you as well as the other strongholds and the remaining troops and all the officials, and will turn around and go home. For that is why I am here."

46 Jonathanᶻ trusted him and did as he said; he sent away the troops, and they returned to the land of Judah. 47 He kept with himself three thousand men, two thousand of whom he left in Galilee, while one thousand accompanied him. 48 But when Jonathan entered Ptol•e•mā′is, the people of Ptol•e•mā′is closed the gates and seized him, and they killed with the sword all who had entered with him.

49 Then Trý′phō sent troops and cavalry into Galilee and the Great Plain to destroy all Jonathan's soldiers. 50 But they realized that Jonathan had been seized and had perished along with his men, and they encouraged one another and kept marching in close formation, ready for battle. 51 When their pursuers saw that they would fight for their lives, they turned back. 52 So they all reached the land of Judah safely, and they mourned for Jonathan and his companions and were in great fear; and all Israel mourned deeply. 53 All the nations around them tried to destroy them, for they said, "They have no leader or helper. Now therefore let us make war on them and blot out the memory of them from humankind."

Simon Takes Command

Simon heard that Trý′phō had assembled a large army to invade the land of Judah and destroy it, 2 and he saw that the people were trembling with fear. So he went up to Jerusalem, and gathering the people together 3 he encouraged them, saying to them, "You yourselves know what great things my brothers and I and the house of my father have done for the laws and the sanctuary; you know also the wars and the difficulties that my brothers and I have seen. 4 By reason of this all my brothers have perished for the sake of Israel, and I alone am left. 5 And now, far be it from me to spare my life in any time of distress, for I am not better than my brothers. 6 But I will avenge my nation and the sanctuary and your wives and children, for all the nations have gathered together out of hatred to destroy us."

7 The spirit of the people was rekindled when they heard these words, 8 and they answered in a loud voice, "You are our leader in place of Judas and your brother Jonathan. 9 Fight our battles, and all that you say to us we will do." 10 So he assembled all the warriors and hurried to complete the walls of Jerusalem, and he fortified it on every side. 11 He sent Jonathan son of Ab′sa•lom to Jop′pa, and with him a considerable army; he drove out its occupants and remained there.

Deceit and Treachery of Trypho

12 Then Trý′phō left Ptol•e•mā′is with a large army to invade the land of Judah, and Jonathan was with him under guard. 13 Simon encamped in Ad′i•da, facing the plain. 14 Trý′phō learned that Simon had risen up in place of his brother Jonathan, and that he was about to join battle with him, so he sent envoys to him and said, 15 "It is for the money that your brother Jonathan owed the royal treasury, in connection with the offices he held,

z Gk he

that we are detaining him. ¹⁶ Send now one hundred talents of silver and two of his sons as hostages, so that when released he will not revolt against us, and we will release him."

17 Simon knew that they were speaking deceitfully to him, but he sent to get the money and the sons, so that he would not arouse great hostility among the people, who might say, ¹⁸ "It was because Simon^a did not send him the money and the sons, that Jonathan^b perished." ¹⁹ So he sent the sons and the hundred talents, but Trýphō^b broke his word and did not release Jonathan.

20 After this Trýphō came to invade the country and destroy it, and he circled around by the way to A·dor'a. But Simon and his army kept marching along opposite him to every place he went. ²¹ Now the men in the citadel kept sending envoys to Trýphō urging him to come to them by way of the wilderness and to send them food. ²² So Trýphō got all his cavalry ready to go, but that night a very heavy snow fell, and he did not go because of the snow. He marched off and went into the land of Gil'e·ad. ²³ When he approached Bas'ka·ma, he killed Jonathan, and he was buried there. ²⁴ Then Trýphō turned and went back to his own land.

Jonathan's Tomb

25 Simon sent and took the bones of his brother Jonathan, and buried him in Mō'dein, the city of his ancestors. ²⁶ All Israel bewailed him with great lamentation, and mourned for him many days. ²⁷ And Simon built a monument over the tomb of his father and his brothers; he made it high so that it might be seen, with polished stone at the front and back. ²⁸ He also erected seven pyramids, opposite one another, for his father and mother and four brothers. ²⁹ For the pyramids^c he devised an elaborate setting, erecting about them great columns, and on the columns he put suits of armor for a permanent memorial, and beside the suits of armor he carved ships, so that they could be seen by all who sail the sea. ³⁰ This is the tomb that he built in Mō'dein; it remains to this day.

Judea Gains Independence

31 Trýphō dealt treacherously with the young King An·ti'o·chus; he killed him ³² and became king in his place, putting on the crown of Asia; and he brought great calamity on the land. ³³ But Simon built up the strongholds of Judea and walled them all around, with high towers and great walls and gates and bolts, and he stored food in the strongholds. ³⁴ Simon also chose emissaries and sent them to King De·mē'tri·us with a request to grant relief to the country, for all that Trýphō did was to

plunder. ³⁵ King De·mē'tri·us sent him a favorable reply to this request, and wrote him a letter as follows, ³⁶ "King De·mē'tri·us to Simon, the high priest and friend of kings, and to the elders and nation of the Jews, greetings. ³⁷ We have received the gold crown and the palm branch that you^d sent, and we are ready to make a general peace with you and to write to our officials to grant you release from tribute. ³⁸ All the grants that we have made to you remain valid, and let the strongholds that you have built be your possession. ³⁹ We pardon any errors and offenses committed to this day, and cancel the crown tax that you owe; and whatever other tax has been collected in Jerusalem shall be collected no longer. ⁴⁰ And if any of you are qualified to be enrolled in our bodyguard,^{e} let them be enrolled, and let there be peace between us."

41 In the one hundred seventieth year^f the yoke of the Gentiles was removed from Israel, ⁴² and the people began to write in their documents and contracts, "In the first year of Simon the great high priest and commander and leader of the Jews."

The Capture of Gazara by Simon

43 In those days Simon^b encamped against Ga·zā'ra^g and surrounded it with troops. He made a siege engine, brought it up to the city, and battered and captured one tower. ⁴⁴ The men in the siege engine leaped out into the city, and a great tumult arose in the city. ⁴⁵ The men in the city, with their wives and children, went up on the wall with their clothes torn, and they cried out with a loud voice, asking Simon to make peace with them; ⁴⁶ they said, "Do not treat us according to our wicked acts but according to your mercy." ⁴⁷ So Simon reached an agreement with them and stopped fighting against them. But he expelled them from the city and cleansed the houses in which the idols were located, and then entered it with hymns and praise. ⁴⁸ He removed all uncleanness from it, and settled in it those who observed the law. He also strengthened its fortifications and built in it a house for himself.

Simon Regains the Citadel at Jerusalem

49 Those who were in the citadel at Jerusalem were prevented from going in and out to buy and sell in the country. So they were very hungry, and many of them perished from famine. ⁵⁰ Then they cried to Simon to make peace with them, and he

---

^{a} Gk I ^{b} Gk he ^{c} Gk For these ^{d} The word *you* in verses 37-40 is plural ^{e} Or *court* ^{f} 142 B.C. ^{g} Cn: Gk *Gaza*

did so. But he expelled them from there and cleansed the citadel from its pollutions. 51 On the twenty-third day of the second month, in the one hundred seventy-first year,[h] the Jews[i] entered it with praise and palm branches, and with harps and cymbals and stringed instruments, and with hymns and songs, because a great enemy had been crushed and removed from Israel. 52 Simon[j] decreed that every year they should celebrate this day with rejoicing. He strengthened the fortifications of the temple hill alongside the citadel, and he and his men lived there. 53 Simon saw that his son John had reached manhood, and so he made him commander of all the forces; and he lived at Gazʹra.

Capture of Demetrius

In the one hundred seventy-second year[k] King Deméʹtriʹus assembled his forces and marched into Mēdʹiʹa to obtain help, so that he could make war against Tryʹphō. 2 When King Arʹsaʹcēs of Persia and Mēdʹiʹa heard that Deʹméʹtriʹus had invaded his territory, he sent one of his generals to take him alive. 3 The general[j] went and defeated the army of Deʹméʹtriʹus, and seized him and took him to Arʹsaʹcēs, who put him under guard.

Eulogy of Simon

4 The land[l] had rest all the days of Simon.
　　He sought the good of his nation;
　　his rule was pleasing to them,
　　　as was the honor shown him, all his days.
5 To crown all his honors he took Jopʹpa for
　　　a harbor,
　　and opened a way to the isles of the sea.
6 He extended the borders of his nation,
　　and gained full control of the country.
7 He gathered a host of captives;
　　he ruled over Gaʹzāʹra and Beth-zur and
　　　the citadel,
　　and he removed its uncleanness from it;
　　and there was none to oppose him.
8 They tilled their land in peace;
　　the ground gave its increase,
　　and the trees of the plains their fruit.
9 Old men sat in the streets;
　　they all talked together of good things,
　　and the youths put on splendid military
　　　attire.
10 He supplied the towns with food,
　　and furnished them with the means of
　　　defense,
　　until his renown spread to the ends of
　　　the earth.
11 He established peace in the land,
　　and Israel rejoiced with great joy.

12 All the people sat under their own vines
　　and fig trees,
　　and there was none to make them afraid.
13 No one was left in the land to fight them,
　　and the kings were crushed in those days.
14 He gave help to all the humble among his
　　　people;
　　he sought out the law,
　　and did away with all the renegades and
　　　outlaws.
15 He made the sanctuary glorious,
　　and added to the vessels of the sanctuary.

Diplomacy with Rome and Sparta

16 It was heard in Rome, and as far away as Sparta, that Jonathan had died, and they were deeply grieved. 17 When they heard that his brother Simon had become high priest in his stead, and that he was ruling over the country and the towns in it, 18 they wrote to him on bronze tablets to renew with him the friendship and alliance that they had established with his brothers Judas and Jonathan. 19 And these were read before the assembly in Jerusalem.

20 This is a copy of the letter that the Spartans sent:

"The rulers and the city of the Spartans to the high priest Simon and to the elders and the priests and the rest of the Jewish people, our brothers, greetings. 21 The envoys who were sent to our people have told us about your glory and honor, and we rejoiced at their coming. 22 We have recorded what they said in our public decrees, as follows, 'Nūʹméʹniʹus son of Anʹtīʹoʹchus and Anʹtipʹaʹter son of Jason, envoys of the Jews, have come to us to renew their friendship with us. 23 It has pleased our people to receive these men with honor and to put a copy of their words in the public archives, so that the people of the Spartans may have a record of them. And they have sent a copy of this to the high priest Simon.' "

24 After this Simon sent Nūʹméʹniʹus to Rome with a large gold shield weighing one thousand minas, to confirm the alliance with the Romans.[m]

Official Honors for Simon

25 When the people heard these things they said, "How shall we thank Simon and his sons? 26 For he and his brothers and the house of his father have stood firm; they have fought and repulsed Israel's enemies and established its

---

[h] 141 B.C.　[i] Gk they　[j] Gk He　[k] 140 B.C.　[l] Other ancient authorities add of Judah　[m] Gk them

freedom." [27] So they made a record on bronze tablets and put it on pillars on Mount Zion.

This is a copy of what they wrote: "On the eighteenth day of Ĕ′lul, in the one hundred seventy-second year,[n] which is the third year of the great high priest Simon, [28] in A·sar′a·mel,[o] in the great assembly of the priests and the people and the rulers of the nation and the elders of the country, the following was proclaimed to us:

[29] "Since wars often occurred in the country, Simon son of Mat·ta·thī′as, a priest of the sons[p] of Jō′a·rib, and his brothers, exposed themselves to danger and resisted the enemies of their nation, in order that their sanctuary and the law might be preserved; and they brought great glory to their nation. [30] Jonathan rallied the[q] nation, became their high priest, and was gathered to his people. [31] When their enemies decided to invade their country and lay hands on their sanctuary, [32] then Simon rose up and fought for his nation. He spent great sums of his own money; he armed the soldiers of his nation and paid them wages. [33] He fortified the towns of Judea, and Beth-zur on the borders of Judea, where formerly the arms of the enemy had been stored, and he placed there a garrison of Jews. [34] He also fortified Jop′pa, which is by the sea, and Ga·zā′ra, which is on the borders of A·zō′tus, where the enemy formerly lived. He settled Jews there, and provided in those towns[r] whatever was necessary for their restoration.

[35] "The people saw Simon's faithfulness[s] and the glory that he had resolved to win for his nation, and they made him their leader and high priest, because he had done all these things and because of the justice and loyalty that he had maintained toward his nation. He sought in every way to exalt his people. [36] In his days things prospered in his hands, so that the Gentiles were put out of the[q] country, as were also those in the city of David in Jerusalem, who had built themselves a citadel from which they used to sally forth and defile the environs of the sanctuary, doing great damage to its purity. [37] He settled Jews in it and fortified it for the safety of the country and of the city, and built the walls of Jerusalem higher.

[38] "In view of these things King De·mē′tri·us confirmed him in the high priesthood, [39] made him one of his Friends, and paid him high honors. [40] For he had heard that the Jews were addressed by the Romans as friends and allies and brothers, and that the Romans[t] had received the envoys of Simon with honor.

[41] "The Jews and their priests have resolved that Simon should be their leader and high priest forever, until a trustworthy prophet should arise, [42] and that he should be governor over them and

that he should take charge of the sanctuary and appoint officials over its tasks and over the country and the weapons and the strongholds, and that he should take charge of the sanctuary, [43] and that he should be obeyed by all, and that all contracts in the country should be written in his name, and that he should be clothed in purple and wear gold.

[44] "None of the people or priests shall be permitted to nullify any of these decisions or to oppose what he says, or to convene an assembly in the country without his permission, or to be clothed in purple or put on a gold buckle. [45] Whoever acts contrary to these decisions or rejects any of them shall be liable to punishment."

[46] All the people agreed to grant Simon the right to act in accordance with these decisions. [47] So Simon accepted and agreed to be high priest, to be commander and ethnarch of the Jews and priests, and to be protector of them all.[u] [48] And they gave orders to inscribe this decree on bronze tablets, to put them up in a conspicuous place in the precincts of the sanctuary, [49] and to deposit copies of them in the treasury, so that Simon and his sons might have them.

Letter of Antiochus VII

An·tī′o·chus, son of King De·mē′tri·us, sent a letter from the islands of the sea to Simon, the priest and ethnarch of the Jews, and to all the nation; [2] its contents were as follows: "King An·tī′o·chus to Simon the high priest and ethnarch and to the nation of the Jews, greetings. [3] Whereas certain scoundrels have gained control of the kingdom of our ancestors, and I intend to lay claim to the kingdom so that I may restore it as it formerly was, and have recruited a host of mercenary troops and have equipped warships, [4] and intend to make a landing in the country so that I may proceed against those who have destroyed our country and those who have devastated many cities in my kingdom, [5] now therefore I confirm to you all the tax remissions that the kings before me have granted you, and a release from all the other payments from which they have released you. [6] I permit you to mint your own coinage as money for your country, [7] and I grant freedom to Jerusalem and the sanctuary. All the weapons that you have prepared and the strongholds that you have built and now hold shall remain yours. [8] Every debt you owe to the royal treasury and any such future debts shall be canceled for you from henceforth and for

---

[n] 140 B.C.   [o] This word resembles the Hebrew words for *the court of the people of God* or *the prince of the people of God*   [p] Meaning of Gk uncertain   [q] Gk *their*   [r] Gk *them*   [s] Other ancient authorities read *conduct*   [t] Gk *they*   [u] Or *to preside over them all*

all time. 9 When we gain control of our kingdom, we will bestow great honor on you and your nation and the temple, so that your glory will become manifest in all the earth."

10 In the one hundred seventy-fourth year[v] An•tī′o•chus set out and invaded the land of his ancestors. All the troops rallied to him, so that there were only a few with Trȳ′phō. 11 An•tī′o•chus pursued him, and Trȳ′phō[w] came in his flight to Dor, which is by the sea; 12 for he knew that troubles had converged on him, and his troops had deserted him. 13 So An•tī′o•chus encamped against Dor, and with him were one hundred twenty thousand warriors and eight thousand cavalry. 14 He surrounded the town, and the ships joined battle from the sea; he pressed the town hard from land and sea, and permitted no one to leave or enter it.

Rome Supports the Jews

15 Then Nū•mē′ni•us and his companions arrived from Rome, with letters to the kings and countries, in which the following was written: 16 "Lucius, consul of the Romans, to King Ptol′e•my, greetings. 17 The envoys of the Jews have come to us as our friends and allies to renew our ancient friendship and alliance. They had been sent by the high priest Simon and by the Jewish people 18 and have brought a gold shield weighing one thousand minas. 19 We therefore have decided to write to the kings and countries that they should not seek their harm or make war against them and their cities and their country, or make alliance with those who war against them. 20 And it has seemed good to us to accept the shield from them. 21 Therefore if any scoundrels have fled to you from their country, hand them over to the high priest Simon, so that he may punish them according to their law."

22 The consul[x] wrote the same thing to King De•mē′tri•us and to At′ta•lus and Ar•i•a•rā′thēs and Ar′sa•cēs, 23 and to all the countries, and to Samp′sa•mēs,[y] and to the Spartans, and to Dē′los, and to Myn′dos, and to Si′cy•on, and to Cār′i•a, and to Sā′mos, and to Pam•phyl′i•a, and to Ly′ci•a, and to Hal•i•car•nas′sus, and to Rhōdes, and to Pha•sē′lis, and to Cōs, and to Si′de, and to Ar′a•dus and Gor•tȳ′na and Cnī′dus and Cyprus and Cȳ•rē′nē. 24 They also sent a copy of these things to the high priest Simon.

Antiochus VII Threatens Simon

25 King An•tī′o•chus besieged Dor for the second time, continually throwing his forces against it and making engines of war; and he shut Trȳ′phō up and kept him from going out or in. 26 And Si-

mon sent to An•tī′o•chus[z] two thousand picked troops, to fight for him, and silver and gold and a large amount of military equipment. 27 But he refused to receive them, and broke all the agreements he formerly had made with Simon, and became estranged from him. 28 He sent to him Ath•e•nō′bi•us, one of his Friends, to confer with him, saying, "You hold control of Jop′pa and Ga•zā′ra and the citadel in Jerusalem; they are cities of my kingdom. 29 You have devastated their territory, you have done great damage in the land, and you have taken possession of many places in my kingdom. 30 Now then, hand over the cities that you have seized and the tribute money of the places that you have conquered outside the borders of Judea; 31 or else pay me five hundred talents of silver for the destruction that you have caused and five hundred talents more for the tribute money of the cities. Otherwise we will come and make war on you."

32 So Ath•e•nō′bi•us, the king's Friend, came to Jerusalem, and when he saw the splendor of Simon, and the sideboard with its gold and silver plate, and his great magnificence, he was amazed. When he reported to him the king's message, 33 Simon said to him in reply: "We have neither taken foreign land nor seized foreign property, but only the inheritance of our ancestors, which at one time had been unjustly taken by our enemies. 34 Now that we have the opportunity, we are firmly holding the inheritance of our ancestors. 35 As for Jop′pa and Ga•zā′ra, which you demand, they were causing great damage among the people and to our land; for them we will give you one hundred talents."

Ath•e•nō′bi•us[x] did not answer him a word, 36 but returned in wrath to the king and reported to him these words, and also the splendor of Simon and all that he had seen. And the king was very angry.

Victory over Cendebeus

37 Meanwhile Trȳ′phō embarked on a ship and escaped to Or•thō′si•a. 38 Then the king made Cen•de•bē′us commander-in-chief of the coastal country, and gave him troops of infantry and cavalry. 39 He commanded him to encamp against Judea, to build up Kēd′ron and fortify its gates, and to make war on the people; but the king pursued Trȳ′phō. 40 So Cen•de•bē′us came to Jam′ni•a and began to provoke the people and invade Judea and take the people captive and kill them. 41 He built up Kēd′ron and stationed horsemen and troops there, so that they might go out and make raids

v 138 B.C.　　*w* Gk *he*　　*x* Gk *He*　　*y* The name is uncertain　　*z* Gk *him*

along the highways of Judea, as the king had ordered him.

John went up from Ga·zā'ra and reported to his father Simon what Cen·de·bē'us had done. 2 And Simon called in his two eldest sons Judas and John, and said to them: "My brothers and I and my father's house have fought the wars of Israel from our youth until this day, and things have prospered in our hands so that we have delivered Israel many times. 3 But now I have grown old, and you by Heaven's*a* mercy are mature in years. Take my place and my brother's, and go out and fight for our nation, and may the help that comes from Heaven be with you."

4 So John*b* chose out of the country twenty thousand warriors and cavalry, and they marched against Cen·de·bē'us and camped for the night in Mō'dēin. 5 Early in the morning they started out and marched into the plain, where a large force of infantry and cavalry was coming to meet them; and a stream lay between them. 6 Then he and his army lined up against them. He saw that the soldiers were afraid to cross the stream, so he crossed over first; and when his troops saw him, they crossed over after him. 7 Then he divided the army and placed the cavalry in the center of the infantry, for the cavalry of the enemy were very numerous. 8 They sounded the trumpets, and Cen·de·bē'us and his army were put to flight; many of them fell wounded and the rest fled into the stronghold. 9 At that time Judas the brother of John was wounded, but John pursued them until Cen·de·bē'us*c* reached Kēd'ron, which he had built. 10 They also fled into the towers that were in the fields of A·zō'tus, and John*c* burned it with fire, and about two thousand of them fell. He then returned to Judea safely.

Murder of Simon and His Sons

11 Now Ptol'e·my son of A·bū'bus had been appointed governor over the plain of Jericho; he had a large store of silver and gold, 12 for he was son-in-law of the high priest. 13 His heart was lifted up; he determined to get control of the country, and made treacherous plans against Simon and his sons, to do away with them. 14 Now Simon was visiting the towns of the country and attending to their needs, and he went down to Jericho with his sons Mat·ta·thī'as and Judas, in the one hundred seventy-seventh year,*d* in the eleventh month, which is the month of She·bat'. 15 The son of A·bū'-bus received them treacherously in the little stronghold called Dok, which he had built; he gave them a great banquet, and hid men there. 16 When Simon and his sons were drunk, Ptol'e·my and his men rose up, took their weapons, rushed in against Simon in the banquet hall and killed him and his two sons, as well as some of his servants. 17 So he committed an act of great treachery and returned evil for good.

John Succeeds Simon

18 Then Ptol'e·my wrote a report about these things and sent it to the king, asking him to send troops to aid him and to turn over to him the towns and the country. 19 He sent other troops to Ga·zā'ra to do away with John; he sent letters to the captains asking them to come to him so that he might give them silver and gold and gifts; 20 and he sent other troops to take possession of Jerusalem and the temple hill. 21 But someone ran ahead and reported to John at Ga·zā'ra that his father and brothers had perished, and that "he has sent men to kill you also." 22 When he heard this, he was greatly shocked; he seized the men who came to destroy him and killed them, for he had found out that they were seeking to destroy him.

23 The rest of the acts of John and his wars and the brave deeds that he did, and the building of the walls that he completed, and his achievements, 24 are written in the annals of his high priesthood, from the time that he became high priest after his father.

a Gk *his*   *b* Other ancient authorities read *he*   *c* Gk *he*
d 134 B.C.

When you are suffering, what is your first response? to escape? to look for relief? to cry out in pain? These are normal and healthy responses: no well-adjusted person chooses to suffer willingly. Sometimes, though, people inflict unspeakable suffering on one another, especially through violence such as rape and torture. What meaning could there be in such suffering? In response, 2 Maccabees insists that God will vindicate all those who suffer innocently at the hands of the unjust.

At a Glance

- **Chapters 1–2.** two letters to the Jews in Egypt, the author's preface

- **Chapters 3–7.** the persecution of the Jews

- **8.1—10.9.** the victory of Judas

- **10.10—15.39.** the renewal of persecution

In-depth

In 167 B.C., the Jewish people faced a new persecution under the Seleucid (Greek) king Antiochus IV Epiphanes. In an effort to unify the many different peoples under his rule, Antiochus imposed his own language, customs, and religion on all of them, including the Jews. Second Maccabees covers some of the same history as First Maccabees but with different purposes: to show the variety of ways the Jews resisted persecution and to give hope to persecuted Jews in the author's time.

The Book of Job had already struggled with the mystery of human suffering and concluded that only God could understand it. Not content with this answer, the author of 2 Maccabees presses forward with new insights:

- In the famous story of the martyrdom of a Jewish mother and her seven sons (7.1–42), 2 Maccabees talks about the resurrection of the dead.
- In chapter 12, the value of praying for the dead is commended.
- In chapter 15, the book speaks confidently of the prayers of the saints in heaven for those on earth.

Second Maccabees is less concerned with the facts of history than with the meaning of history. It insists that whenever God's faithful people suffer, they can be assured of receiving justice—if not in this life, then in the resurrection. The book shows how the Jewish faith continued to develop as it faced the sometimes painful events of history.

Quick Facts

Period Covered
from 180 to 160 B.C.

Author
someone around 100 B.C., summarizing a lost work by Jason of Cyrene

Themes
differing responses to persecution, the just and suffering

Of Note
Second Maccabees is not found in every translation of the Old Translation (see "The Case of the Missing Books," near Tob 1.16).

Second Maccabees is not found in every translation of the Old Testament (see "The Case of the Missing Books," near Tob 1.16).

Maccabees

The Second Book of

543

2 Maccabees

A Letter to the Jews in Egypt

The Jews in Jerusalem and those in the land of Judea,

To their Jewish kindred in Egypt,

Greetings and true peace.

2 May God do good to you, and may he remember his covenant with Abraham and Isaac and Jacob, his faithful servants. ³ May he give you all a heart to worship him and to do his will with a strong heart and a willing spirit. ⁴ May he open your heart to his law and his commandments, and may he bring peace. ⁵ May he hear your prayers and be reconciled to you, and may he not forsake you in time of evil. ⁶ We are now praying for you here.

7 In the reign of De•mē′tri•us, in the one hundred sixty-ninth year,*a* we Jews wrote to you, in the critical distress that came upon us in those years after Jason and his company revolted from the holy land and the kingdom ⁸ and burned the gate and shed innocent blood. We prayed to the Lord and were heard, and we offered sacrifice and grain offering, and we lit the lamps and set out the loaves. ⁹ And now see that you keep the festival of booths in the month of Chis′lev, in the one hundred eighty-eighth year.*b*

A Letter to Aristobulus

(Cp 1 Macc 6.1–4)

10 The people of Jerusalem and of Judea and the senate and Judas,

To Ar•is•tob′ū•lus, who is of the family of the anointed priests, teacher of King Ptol′e•my, and to the Jews in Egypt,

Greetings and good health.

11 Having been saved by God out of grave dangers we thank him greatly for taking our side against the king,*c* ¹² for he drove out those who fought against the holy city. ¹³ When the leader reached Persia with a force that seemed irresistible, they were cut to pieces in the temple of Na•nē′a by a deception employed by the priests of the goddess*d* Na•nē′a. ¹⁴ On the pretext of intending to marry her, An•ti′o•chus came to the place together with his Friends, to secure most of its treasures as a dowry. ¹⁵ When the priests of the temple of Na-nē′a had set out the treasures and An•ti′o•chus had come with a few men inside the wall of the sacred precinct, they closed the temple as soon as he entered it. ¹⁶ Opening a secret door in the ceiling, they threw stones and struck down the leader and

---

a 143 B.C.   *b* 124 B.C.   *c* Cn: Gk *as those who array themselves against a king*   *d* Gk lacks *the goddess*

544

his men; they dismembered them and cut off their heads and threw them to the people outside. [17] Blessed in every way be our God, who has brought judgment on those who have behaved impiously.

Fire Consumes Nehemiah's Sacrifice

18 Since on the twenty-fifth day of Chis'lev we shall celebrate the purification of the temple, we thought it necessary to notify you, in order that you also may celebrate the festival of booths and the festival of the fire given when Nē•he•mī'ah, who built the temple and the altar, offered sacrifices.

19 For when our ancestors were being led captive to Persia, the pious priests of that time took some of the fire of the altar and secretly hid it in the hollow of a dry cistern, where they took such precautions that the place was unknown to anyone. [20] But after many years had passed, when it pleased God, Nē•he•mī'ah, having been commissioned by the king of Persia, sent the descendants of the priests who had hidden the fire to get it. And when they reported to us that they had not found fire but only a thick liquid, he ordered them to dip it out and bring it. [21] When the materials for the sacrifices were presented, Nē•he•mī'ah ordered the priests to sprinkle the liquid on the wood and on the things laid upon it. [22] When this had been done and some time had passed, and when the sun, which had been clouded over, shone out, a great fire blazed up, so that all marveled. [23] And while the sacrifice was being consumed, the priests offered prayer—the priests and everyone. Jonathan led, and the rest responded, as did Nē•he•mī'ah. [24] The prayer was to this effect:

"O Lord, Lord God, Creator of all things, you are awe-inspiring and strong and just and merciful, you alone are king and are kind, [25] you alone are bountiful, you alone are just and almighty and eternal. You rescue Israel from every evil; you chose the ancestors and consecrated them. [26] Accept this sacrifice on behalf of all your people Israel and preserve your portion and make it holy. [27] Gather together our scattered people, set free those who are slaves among the Gentiles, look on those who are rejected and despised, and let the Gentiles know that you are our God. [28] Punish those who oppress and are insolent with pride. [29] Plant your people in your holy place, as Moses promised."

30 Then the priests sang the hymns. [31] After the materials of the sacrifice had been consumed, Nē•he•mī'ah ordered that the liquid that was left should be poured on large stones. [32] When this was done, a flame blazed up; but when the light from the altar shone back, it went out. [33] When this matter became known, and it was reported to the king of the Persians that, in the place where the exiled priests had hidden the fire, the liquid had appeared with which Nē•he•mī'ah and his associates had burned the materials of the sacrifice, [34] the king investigated the matter, and enclosed the place and made it sacred. [35] And with those persons whom the king favored he exchanged many excellent gifts. [36] Nē•he•mī'ah and his associates called this "nephthar," which means purification, but by most people it is called naphtha.[e]

Jeremiah Hides the Tent, Ark, and Altar

One finds in the records that the prophet Jer•e•mī'ah ordered those who were being deported to take some of the fire, as has been mentioned, [2] and that the prophet, after giving them the law, instructed those who were being deported not to forget the commandments of the Lord, or to be led astray in their thoughts on seeing the gold and silver statues and their adornment. [3] And with other similar words he exhorted them that the law should not depart from their hearts.

4 It was also in the same document that the prophet, having received an oracle, ordered that the tent and the ark should follow with him, and that he went out to the mountain where Moses had gone up and had seen the inheritance of God. [5] Jer•e•mī'ah came and found a cave-dwelling, and he brought there the tent and the ark and the altar of incense; then he sealed up the entrance. [6] Some of those who followed him came up intending to mark the way, but could not find it. [7] When Jer•e•mī'ah learned of it, he rebuked them and declared: "The place shall remain unknown until God gathers his people together again and shows his mercy. [8] Then the Lord will disclose these things, and the glory of the Lord and the cloud will appear, as they were shown in the case of Moses, and as Solomon asked that the place should be specially consecrated."

9 It was also made clear that being possessed of wisdom Solomon[f] offered sacrifice for the dedication and completion of the temple. [10] Just as Moses prayed to the Lord, and fire came down from heaven and consumed the sacrifices, so also Solomon prayed, and the fire came down and consumed the whole burnt offerings. [11] And Moses said, "They were consumed because the sin offering had not been eaten." [12] Likewise Solomon also kept the eight days.

13 The same things are reported in the records and in the memoirs of Nē•he•mī'ah, and also that he founded a library and collected the books

e Gk *nephthai*   f Gk *he*

about the kings and prophets, and the writings of David, and letters of kings about votive offerings. 14 In the same way Judas also collected all the books that had been lost on account of the war that had come upon us, and they are in our possession. 15 So if you have need of them, send people to get them for you.

16 Since, therefore, we are about to celebrate the purification, we write to you. Will you therefore please keep the days? 17 It is God who has saved all his people, and has returned the inheritance to all, and the kingship and the priesthood and the consecration, 18 as he promised through the law. We have hope in God that he will soon have mercy on us and will gather us from everywhere under heaven into his holy place, for he has rescued us from great evils and has purified the place.

The Compiler's Preface

19 The story of Judas Mac·ca·bē′us and his brothers, and the purification of the great temple, and the dedication of the altar, 20 and further the wars against An·ti′o·chus E·piph′a·nēs and his son Eū′pa·tor, 21 and the appearances that came from heaven to those who fought bravely for Jū′da·ism, so that though few in number they seized the whole land and pursued the barbarian hordes, 22 and regained possession of the temple famous throughout the world, and liberated the city, and re-established the laws that were about to be abolished, while the Lord with great kindness became gracious to them— 23 all this, which has been set forth by Jason of Cȳ·rē′nē in five volumes, we shall attempt to condense into a single book. 24 For considering the flood of statistics involved and the difficulty there is for those who wish to enter upon the narratives of history because of the mass of material, 25 we have aimed to please those who wish to read, to make it easy for those who are inclined to memorize, and to profit all readers. 26 For us who have undertaken the toil of abbreviating, it is no light matter but calls for sweat and loss of sleep, 27 just as it is not easy for one who prepares a banquet and seeks the benefit of others. Nevertheless, to secure the gratitude of many we will gladly endure the uncomfortable toil, 28 leaving the responsibility for exact details to the compiler, while devoting our effort to arriving at the outlines of the condensation. 29 For as the master builder of a new house must be concerned with the whole construction, while the one who undertakes its painting and decoration has to consider only what is suitable for its adornment, such in my judgment is the case with us. 30 It is the duty of the original historian to occupy the ground, to discuss matters from every side, and to take trouble with details, 31 but the one who recasts the narrative should be allowed to strive for brevity of expression and to forego exhaustive treatment. 32 At this point therefore let us begin our narrative, without adding any more to what has already been said; for it would be foolish to lengthen the preface while cutting short the history itself.

Arrival of Heliodorus in Jerusalem

While the holy city was inhabited in unbroken peace and the laws were strictly observed because of the piety of the high priest Ō·nī′as and his hatred of wickedness, 2 it came about that the kings themselves honored the place and glorified the temple with the finest presents, 3 even to the extent that King Se·leū′cus of Asia defrayed from his own revenues all the expenses connected with the service of the sacrifices.

4 But a man named Simon, of the tribe of Benjamin, who had been made captain of the temple, had a disagreement with the high priest about the administration of the city market. 5 Since he could not prevail over O·ni′as, he went to Ap·ol·lō′ni·us of Tar′sus,*g* who at that time was governor of Coē·le·syr′i·a and Phoe·ni′ci·a, 6 and reported to him that the treasury in Jerusalem was full of untold sums of money, so that the amount of the funds could not be reckoned, and that they did not belong to the account of the sacrifices, but that it was possible for them to fall under the control of the king. 7 When Ap·ol·lō′ni·us met the king, he told him of the money about which he had been informed. The king*h* chose Hē·li·o·dor′us, who was in charge of his affairs, and sent him with commands to effect the removal of the reported wealth. 8 Hē·li·o·dor′us at once set out on his journey, ostensibly to make a tour of inspection of the cities of Coē·le·syr′i·a and Phoe·ni′ci·a, but in fact to carry out the king's purpose.

9 When he had arrived at Jerusalem and had been kindly welcomed by the high priest of*i* the city, he told about the disclosure that had been made and stated why he had come, and he inquired whether this really was the situation. 10 The high priest explained that there were some deposits belonging to widows and orphans, 11 and also some money of Hyr·cā′nus son of Tō·bi′as, a man of very prominent position, and that it totaled in all four hundred talents of silver and two hundred of gold. To such an extent the impious Simon had

---

g Gk *Apollonius son of Tharseas*   *h* Gk *He*   *i* Other ancient authorities read *and*

misrepresented the facts. 12 And he said that it was utterly impossible that wrong should be done to those people who had trusted in the holiness of the place and in the sanctity and inviolability of the temple that is honored throughout the whole world.

Heliodorus Plans to Rob the Temple

13 But Hē·li·o·dor′us, because of the orders he had from the king, said that this money must in any case be confiscated for the king's treasury. 14 So he set a day and went in to direct the inspection of these funds.

There was no little distress throughout the whole city. 15 The priests prostrated themselves before the altar in their priestly vestments and called toward heaven upon him who had given the law about deposits, that he should keep them safe for those who had deposited them. 16 To see the appearance of the high priest was to be wounded at heart, for his face and the change in his color disclosed the anguish of his soul. 17 For terror and bodily trembling had come over the man, which plainly showed to those who looked at him the pain lodged in his heart. 18 People also hurried out of their houses in crowds to make a general supplication because the holy place was about to be brought into dishonor. 19 Women, girded with sackcloth under their breasts, thronged the streets. Some of the young women who were kept indoors ran together to the gates, and some to the walls, while others peered out of the windows. 20 And holding up their hands to heaven, they all made supplication. 21 There was something pitiable in the prostration of the whole populace and the anxiety of the high priest in his great anguish.

The Lord Protects His Temple

22 While they were calling upon the Almighty Lord that he would keep what had been entrusted safe and secure for those who had entrusted it, 23 Hē·li·o·dor′us went on with what had been decided. 24 But when he arrived at the treasury with his bodyguard, then and there the Sovereign of spirits and of all authority caused so great a manifestation that all who had been so bold as to accompany him were astounded by the power of God, and became faint with terror. 25 For there appeared to them a magnificently caparisoned horse, with a rider of frightening mien; it rushed furiously at Hē·li·o·dor′us and struck at him with its front hoofs. Its rider was seen to have armor and weapons of gold. 26 Two young men also appeared to him, remarkably strong, gloriously beautiful and splendidly dressed, who stood on either side

of him and flogged him continuously, inflicting many blows on him. 27 When he suddenly fell to the ground and deep darkness came over him, his men took him up, put him on a stretcher, 28 and carried him away—this man who had just entered the aforesaid treasury with a great retinue and all his bodyguard but was now unable to help himself. They recognized clearly the sovereign power of God.

Onias Prays for Heliodorus

29 While he lay prostrate, speechless because of the divine intervention and deprived of any hope of recovery, 30 they praised the Lord who had acted marvelously for his own place. And the temple, which a little while before was full of fear and disturbance, was filled with joy and gladness, now that the Almighty Lord had appeared.

31 Some of Hē·li·o·dor′us's friends quickly begged Ō·ni′as to call upon the Most High to grant life to one who was lying quite at his last breath. 32 So the high priest, fearing that the king might get the notion that some foul play had been perpetrated by the Jews with regard to Hē·li·o·dor′us, offered sacrifice for the man's recovery. 33 While the high priest was making an atonement, the same young men appeared again to Hē·li·o·dor′us dressed in the same clothing, and they stood and said, "Be very grateful to the high priest Ō·ni′as, since for his sake the Lord has granted you your life. 34 And see that you, who have been flogged by heaven, report to all people the majestic power of God." Having said this they vanished.

The Conversion of Heliodorus

35 Then Hē·li·o·dor′us offered sacrifice to the Lord and made very great vows to the Savior of his life, and having bidden Ō·ni′as farewell, he marched off with his forces to the king. 36 He bore testimony to all concerning the deeds of the supreme God, which he had seen with his own eyes. 37 When the king asked Hē·li·o·dor′us what sort of person would be suitable to send on another mission to Jerusalem, he replied, 38 "If you have any enemy or plotter against your government, send him there, for you will get him back thoroughly flogged, if he survives at all; for there is certainly some power of God about the place. 39 For he who has his dwelling in heaven watches over that place himself and brings it aid, and he strikes and destroys those who come to do it injury." 40 This was the outcome of the episode of Hē·li·o·dor′us and the protection of the treasury.

Simon Accuses Onias

The previously mentioned Simon, who had informed about the money against[j] his own country, slandered Ō·nī′as, saying that it was he who had incited Hē·li·o·dor′us and had been the real cause of the misfortune. [2] He dared to designate as a plotter against the government the man who was the benefactor of the city, the protector of his compatriots, and a zealot for the laws. [3] When his hatred progressed to such a degree that even murders were committed by one of Simon's approved agents, [4] Ō·nī′as recognized that the rivalry was serious and that Ap·ol·lō′ni·us son of Me·nes′thē·us,[k] and governor of Coē·le·syr′i·a and Phoe·ni′ci·a, was intensifying the malice of Simon. [5] So he appealed to the king, not accusing his compatriots but having in view the welfare, both public and private, of all the people. [6] For he saw that without the king's attention public affairs could not again reach a peaceful settlement, and that Simon would not stop his folly.

Jason's Reforms
(Cp 1 Macc 1.10–19)

7 When Se·leū′cus died and An·tī′o·chus, who was called E·piph′a·nēs, succeeded to the kingdom, Jason the brother of Ō·nī′as obtained the high priesthood by corruption, [8] promising the king at an interview[l] three hundred sixty talents of silver, and from another source of revenue eighty talents. [9] In addition to this he promised to pay one hundred fifty more if permission were given to establish by his authority a gymnasium and a body of youth for it, and to enroll the people of Jerusalem as citizens of An′ti·och. [10] When the king assented and Jason[m] came to office, he at once shifted his compatriots over to the Greek way of life.

11 He set aside the existing royal concessions to the Jews, secured through John the father of Eū·pol′e·mus, who went on the mission to establish friendship and alliance with the Romans; and he destroyed the lawful ways of living and introduced new customs contrary to the law. [12] He took delight in establishing a gymnasium right under the citadel, and he induced the noblest of the young men to wear the Greek hat. [13] There was such an extreme of Hellenization and increase in the adoption of foreign ways because of the surpassing wickedness of Jason, who was ungodly and no true[n] high priest, [14] that the priests were no longer intent upon their service at the altar. Despising the sanctuary and neglecting the sacrifices, they hurried to take part in the unlawful proceedings in the wrestling arena after the signal for the discus-throwing, [15] disdaining the honors prized by their ancestors and putting the highest value upon Greek forms of prestige. [16] For this reason heavy disaster overtook them, and those whose ways of living they admired and wished to imitate completely became their enemies and punished them. [17] It is no light thing to show irreverence to the divine laws—a fact that later events will make clear.

Jason Introduces Greek Customs

18 When the quadrennial games were being held at Tyre and the king was present, [19] the vile Jason sent envoys, chosen as being An·ti·och′i·an cit-

PRAY IT!

Arrogance

Arrogance seems to run in the family of Simon. First, Simon seeks to embarrass the high priest, Onias, because of a minor disagreement (2 Macc 3.4–12). When that fails, he falsely accuses Onias of a crime (4.1–5). Several years later, Simon's brother bribes his way into power (verses 23–29).

We have all encountered arrogant people who think that they can do no wrong, and when they do err, cover it up by attacking others. Many of us are intimidated by such people and resent that we felt talked down to or easily dismissed as unimportant. So, how should we respond to arrogant people? The most obvious solution is to ignore them. If that is not possible, then we need to react to them calmly and confidently. Finally, we should keep them in our prayers. Their arrogance can be masking an insecurity or a hurt that needs God's healing touch.

In your prayer, reflect or journal on the following questions:

- Who intimidates you by her or his arrogant behavior?
- How could you respond in a loving and just way?
- What do you need to bring to God in prayer?

▶ 2 Macc 3.4—4.29

---

j Gk *and*
uncertain   *l* Or *by a petition*   *m* Gk *he*   *n* Gk lacks *true*
k Vg Compare verse 21: Meaning of Gk

izens from Jerusalem, to carry three hundred silver drachmas for the sacrifice to Hercules. Those who carried the money, however, thought best not to use it for sacrifice, because that was inappropriate, but to expend it for another purpose. 20 So this money was intended by the sender for the sacrifice to Hercules, but by the decision of its carriers it was applied to the construction of triremes.

21 When Ap·ol·lō′ni·us son of Me·nes′thē·us was sent to Egypt for the coronation*o* of Phil·o·mē′-tor as king, An·tī′o·chus learned that Phil·o·mē′tor*p* had become hostile to his government, and he took measures for his own security. Therefore upon arriving at Jop′pa he proceeded to Jerusalem. 22 He was welcomed magnificently by Jason and the city, and ushered in with a blaze of torches and with shouts. Then he marched his army into Phoe·nī′-ci·a.

Menelaus Becomes High Priest

23 After a period of three years Jason sent Men·e·lā′us, the brother of the previously mentioned Simon, to carry the money to the king and to complete the records of essential business. 24 But he, when presented to the king, extolled him with an air of authority, and secured the high priesthood for himself, outbidding Jason by three hundred talents of silver. 25 After receiving the king's orders he returned, possessing no qualification for the high priesthood, but having the hot temper of a cruel tyrant and the rage of a savage wild beast. 26 So Jason, who after supplanting his own brother was supplanted by another man, was driven as a fugitive into the land of Am′mon. 27 Although Men·e·lā′us continued to hold the office, he did not pay regularly any of the money promised to the king. 28 When Sos′tra·tus the captain of the citadel kept requesting payment—for the collection of the revenue was his responsibility—the two of them were summoned by the king on account of this issue. 29 Men·e·lā′us left his own brother Lȳ-sim′a·chus as deputy in the high priesthood, while Sos′tra·tus left Crā′tēs, the commander of the Cyp′-ri·an troops.

The Murder of Onias

30 While such was the state of affairs, it happened that the people of Tar′sus and of Mal′lus revolted because their cities had been given as a present to An·tī′o·chis, the king's concubine. 31 So the king went hurriedly to settle the trouble, leaving An·dron′i·cus, a man of high rank, to act as his deputy. 32 But Men·e·lā′us, thinking he had obtained a suitable opportunity, stole some of the gold vessels of the temple and gave them to An·dron′i·cus; other vessels, as it happened, he had

sold to Tȳre and the neighboring cities. 33 When Ō·nī′as became fully aware of these acts, he publicly exposed them, having first withdrawn to a place of sanctuary at Daphne near An′ti·och. 34 Therefore Men·e·lā′us, taking An·dron′i·cus aside, urged him to kill Ō·nī′as. An·dron′i·cus*q* came to Ō·nī′as, and resorting to treachery, offered him sworn pledges and gave him his right hand; he persuaded him, though still suspicious, to come out from the place of sanctuary; then, with no regard for justice, he immediately put him out of the way.

Andronicus Is Punished

35 For this reason not only Jews, but many also of other nations, were grieved and displeased at the unjust murder of the man. 36 When the king returned from the region of Ci·li′ci·a, the Jews in the city*r* appealed to him with regard to the unreasonable murder of Ō·nī′as, and the Greeks shared their hatred of the crime. 37 Therefore An·tī′o·chus was grieved at heart and filled with pity, and wept because of the moderation and good conduct of the deceased. 38 Inflamed with anger, he immediately stripped off the purple robe from An·dron′i-cus, tore off his clothes, and led him around the whole city to that very place where he had committed the outrage against Ō·nī′as, and there he dispatched the bloodthirsty fellow. The Lord thus repaid him with the punishment he deserved.

Unpopularity of Lysimachus and Menelaus

39 When many acts of sacrilege had been committed in the city by Lȳ·sim′a·chus with the connivance of Men·e·lā′us, and when report of them had spread abroad, the populace gathered against Lȳ-sim′a·chus, because many of the gold vessels had already been stolen. 40 Since the crowds were becoming aroused and filled with anger, Lȳ·sim′a-chus armed about three thousand men and launched an unjust attack, under the leadership of a certain Au·rā′nus, a man advanced in years and no less advanced in folly. 41 But when the Jews*s* became aware that Lȳ·sim′a·chus was attacking them, some picked up stones, some blocks of wood, and others took handfuls of the ashes that were lying around, and threw them in wild confusion at Lȳ·sim′a·chus and his men. 42 As a result, they wounded many of them, and killed some, and put all the rest to flight; the temple robber himself they killed close by the treasury.

43 Charges were brought against Men·e·lā′us about this incident. 44 When the king came to Tȳre,

---

o Meaning of Gk uncertain   *p* Gk *he*   *q* Gk *He*
r Or *in each city*   *s* Gk *they*

three men sent by the senate presented the case before him. 45 But Men•e•lā′us, already as good as beaten, promised a substantial bribe to Ptol′e•my son of Dor•ym′e•nēs to win over the king. 46 Therefore Ptol′e•my, taking the king aside into a colonnade as if for refreshment, induced the king to change his mind. 47 Men•e•lā′us, the cause of all the trouble, he acquitted of the charges against him, while he sentenced to death those unfortunate men, who would have been freed uncondemned if they had pleaded even before Scyth′i•ans. 48 And so those who had spoken for the city and the villages[t] and the holy vessels quickly suffered the unjust penalty. 49 Therefore even the Tȳ′ri•ans, showing their hatred of the crime, provided magnificently for their funeral. 50 But Men•e•lā′us, because of the greed of those in power, remained in office, growing in wickedness, having become the chief plotter against his compatriots.

Jason Tries to Regain Control

About this time An•tī′o•chus made his second invasion of Egypt. 2 And it happened that, for almost forty days, there appeared over all the city golden-clad cavalry charging through the air, in companies fully armed with lances and drawn swords—3 troops of cavalry drawn up, attacks and counterattacks made on this side and on that, brandishing of shields, massing of spears, hurling of missiles, the flash of golden trappings, and armor of all kinds. 4 Therefore everyone prayed that the apparition might prove to have been a good omen.

5 When a false rumor arose that An•tī′o•chus was dead, Jason took no fewer than a thousand men and suddenly made an assault on the city. When the troops on the wall had been forced back and at last the city was being taken, Men•e•lā′us took refuge in the citadel. 6 But Jason kept relentlessly slaughtering his compatriots, not realizing that success at the cost of one's kindred is the greatest misfortune, but imagining that he was setting up trophies of victory over enemies and not over compatriots. 7 He did not, however, gain control of the government; in the end he got only disgrace from his conspiracy, and fled again into the country of the Am′mon•ites. 8 Finally he met a miserable end. Accused[u] before Ar′e•tas the ruler of the Arabs, fleeing from city to city, pursued by everyone, hated as a rebel against the laws, and abhorred as the executioner of his country and his compatriots, he was cast ashore in Egypt. 9 There he who had driven many from their own country into exile died in exile, having embarked to go to the Lac•e•dae•mō′ni•ans in hope of finding protection because of their kinship. 10 He who had cast out many to lie unburied had no one to mourn for

him; he had no funeral of any sort and no place in the tomb of his ancestors.

11 When news of what had happened reached the king, he took it to mean that Judea was in revolt. So, raging inwardly, he left Egypt and took the city by storm. 12 He commanded his soldiers to cut down relentlessly everyone they met and to kill those who went into their houses. 13 Then there was massacre of young and old, destruction of boys, women, and children, and slaughter of young girls and infants. 14 Within the total of three days eighty thousand were destroyed, forty thousand in hand-to-hand fighting, and as many were sold into slavery as were killed.

Pillage of the Temple
(1 Macc 1.20–40)

15 Not content with this, An•tī′o•chus[v] dared to enter the most holy temple in all the world, guided by Men•e•lā′us, who had become a traitor both to the laws and to his country. 16 He took the holy vessels with his polluted hands, and swept away with profane hands the votive offerings that other kings had made to enhance the glory and honor of the place. 17 An•tī′o•chus was elated in spirit, and did not perceive that the Lord was angered for a little while because of the sins of those who lived in the city, and that this was the reason he was disregarding the holy place. 18 But if it had not happened that they were involved in many sins, this man would have been flogged and turned back from his rash act as soon as he came forward, just as Hē•li•o•dor′us had been, whom King Se•leu′cus sent to inspect the treasury. 19 But the Lord did not choose the nation for the sake of the holy place, but the place for the sake of the nation. 20 Therefore the place itself shared in the misfortunes that befell the nation and afterward participated in its benefits; and what was forsaken in the wrath of the Almighty was restored again in all its glory when the great Lord became reconciled.

21 So An•tī′o•chus carried off eighteen hundred talents from the temple, and hurried away to An′ti•och, thinking in his arrogance that he could sail on the land and walk on the sea, because his mind was elated. 22 He left governors to oppress the people: at Jerusalem, Philip, by birth a Phryg′i•an and in character more barbarous than the man who appointed him; 23 and at Ger′i•zim, An•dron′i•cus; and besides these Men•e•lā′us, who lorded it over his compatriots worse than the others did. In his malice toward the Jewish citizens,[w] 24 An•tī′o•chus[v]

---

[t] Other ancient authorities read *the people* [u] Cn: Gk *Imprisoned* [v] Gk *he* [w] Or *worse than the others did in his malice toward the Jewish citizens*

sent Ap·ol·lō′ni·us, the captain of the My′si·ans, with an army of twenty-two thousand, and commanded him to kill all the grown men and to sell the women and boys as slaves. 25 When this man arrived in Jerusalem, he pretended to be peaceably disposed and waited until the holy sabbath day; then, finding the Jews not at work, he ordered his troops to parade under arms. 26 He put to the sword all those who came out to see them, then rushed into the city with his armed warriors and killed great numbers of people.

27 But Judas Mac·ca·bē′us, with about nine others, got away to the wilderness, and kept himself and his companions alive in the mountains as wild animals do; they continued to live on what grew wild, so that they might not share in the defilement.

The Suppression of Judaism
(1 Macc 1.41–64)

Not long after this, the king sent an Athenian[x] senator[y] to compel the Jews to forsake the laws of their ancestors and no longer to live by the laws of God; 2 also to pollute the temple in Jerusalem and to call it the temple of Olympian Zeūs, and to call the one in Ger′i·zim the temple of Zeūs-the-Friend-of-Strangers, as did the people who lived in that place.

3 Harsh and utterly grievous was the onslaught of evil. 4 For the temple was filled with debauchery and reveling by the Gentiles, who dallied with prostitutes and had intercourse with women within the sacred precincts, and besides brought in things for sacrifice that were unfit. 5 The altar was covered with abominable offerings that were forbidden by the laws. 6 People could neither keep the sabbath, nor observe the festivals of their ancestors, nor so much as confess themselves to be Jews.

7 On the monthly celebration of the king's birthday, the Jews[z] were taken, under bitter constraint, to partake of the sacrifices; and when a festival of Dī·o·nȳ′sus was celebrated, they were compelled to wear wreaths of ivy and to walk in the procession in honor of Dī·o·nȳ′sus. 8 At the suggestion of the people of Ptol·e·mā′is[a] a decree was issued to the neighboring Greek cities that they should adopt the same policy toward the Jews and make them partake of the sacrifices, 9 and should kill those who did not choose to change over to Greek customs. One could see, therefore, the misery that had come upon them. 10 For example, two women were brought in for having circumcised their children. They publicly paraded

them around the city, with their babies hanging at their breasts, and then hurled them down headlong from the wall. 11 Others who had assembled in the caves nearby, in order to observe the seventh day secretly, were betrayed to Philip and were all burned together, because their piety kept them from defending themselves, in view of their regard for that most holy day.

Providential Significance of the Persecution

12 Now I urge those who read this book not to be depressed by such calamities, but to recognize that these punishments were designed not to destroy but to discipline our people. 13 In fact, it is a sign of great kindness not to let the impious alone for long, but to punish them immediately. 14 For in the case of the other nations the Lord waits patiently to punish them until they have reached the full measure of their sins; but he does not deal in this way with us, 15 in order that he may not take vengeance on us afterward when our sins have reached their height. 16 Therefore he never withdraws his mercy from us. Although he disciplines us with calamities, he does not forsake his own people. 17 Let what we have said serve as a reminder; we must go on briefly with the story.

The Martyrdom of Eleazar
(Lev 11.7–8; 4 Macc 5–7)

18 El·e·ā′zar, one of the scribes in high position, a man now advanced in age and of noble presence, was being forced to open his mouth to eat swine's flesh. 19 But he, welcoming death with honor rather than life with pollution, went up to the rack of his own accord, spitting out the flesh, 20 as all ought to go who have the courage to refuse things that it is not right to taste, even for the natural love of life.

21 Those who were in charge of that unlawful sacrifice took the man aside because of their long acquaintance with him, and privately urged him to bring meat of his own providing, proper for him to use, and to pretend that he was eating the flesh of the sacrificial meal that had been commanded by the king, 22 so that by doing this he might be saved from death, and be treated kindly on account of his old friendship with them. 23 But making a high resolve, worthy of his years

---

x Other ancient authorities read *Antiochian*   y Or *Geron an Athenian*   z Gk *they*   a Cn: Gk *suggestion of the Ptolemies* (or *of Ptolemy*)

Teaching by Example

Second Maccabees tells the story of Eleazar, a dignified, elderly scribe who has followed God his whole life. Rather than compromise his principles, Eleazar courageously accepts death by torture. He knows that his example will influence younger people (6.28). His example gives others courage (verse 31).

Young people watch and learn. An old television commercial showed a father and son driving along in a car. The son had a toy steering wheel in front of him and imitated his father's driving. When the father turned the wheel, so did the son. When the father switched the turn signal, so did the son.

Then the father pulled a cigarette from a pack. He lit it and began smoking. The next scene showed the son going for the pack of cigarettes.

The next time you find yourself struggling to make the right choice, think about the example you might be giving to someone younger than you.

▶ 2 Macc 6.18–31

---

and the dignity of his old age and the gray hairs that he had reached with distinction and his excellent life even from childhood, and moreover according to the holy God-given law, he declared himself quickly, telling them to send him to Hades.

24 "Such pretense is not worthy of our time of life," he said, "for many of the young might suppose that El·e·a′zar in his ninetieth year had gone over to an alien religion, 25 and through my pretense, for the sake of living a brief moment longer, they would be led astray because of me, while I defile and disgrace my old age. 26 Even if for the present I would avoid the punishment of mortals, yet whether I live or die I will not escape the hands of the Almighty. 27 Therefore, by bravely giving up my life now, I will show myself worthy of my old age 28 and leave to the young a noble example of how to die a good death willingly and nobly for the revered and holy laws."

When he had said this, he went[b] at once to the rack. 29 Those who a little before had acted toward him with goodwill now changed to ill will, because the words he had uttered were in their opinion sheer madness.[c] 30 When he was about to die under the blows, he groaned aloud and said: "It is clear to the Lord in his holy knowledge that, though I might have been saved from death, I am enduring terrible sufferings in my body under this beating, but in my soul I am glad to suffer these things because I fear him."

31 So in this way he died, leaving in his death an example of nobility and a memorial of courage, not only to the young but to the great body of his nation.

The Martyrdom of Seven Brothers
(4 Macc 8—18)

It happened also that seven brothers and their mother were arrested and were being compelled by the king, under torture with whips and thongs, to partake of unlawful swine's flesh. 2 One of them, acting as their spokesman, said, "What do you intend to ask and learn from us? For we are ready to die rather than transgress the laws of our ancestors."

3 The king fell into a rage, and gave orders to have pans and caldrons heated. 4 These were heated immediately, and he commanded that the tongue of their spokesman be cut out and that they scalp him and cut off his hands and feet, while the rest of the brothers and the mother looked on. 5 When he was utterly helpless, the king[d] ordered them to take him to the fire, still breathing, and to fry him in a pan. The smoke from the pan spread widely, but the brothers[e] and their mother encouraged one another to die nobly, saying, 6 "The Lord God is watching over us and in truth has compassion on us, as Moses declared in his song that bore witness against the people to their faces, when he said, 'And he will have compassion on his servants.' "[f]

7 After the first brother had died in this way, they brought forward the second for their sport. They tore off the skin of his head with the hair, and asked him, "Will you eat rather than have your body punished limb by limb?" 8 He replied in the language of his ancestors and said to them, "No." Therefore he in turn underwent tortures as

---

b Other ancient authorities read *was dragged*   *c* Meaning of Gk uncertain   *d* Gk *he*   *e* Gk *they*   *f* Gk *slaves*

the first brother had done. 9 And when he was at his last breath, he said, "You accursed wretch, you dismiss us from this present life, but the King of the universe will raise us up to an everlasting renewal of life, because we have died for his laws."

Asian *American*

I Will Sacrifice Myself

If I were a bird
and able to fly afar,
I would like to be a white dove
to guide the people to freedom.
If I were the cloud in the sky,
I would shelter and bring rains
to the rice field.
If I were a grain of sand
I would throw myself down
to make a path for the people.
I will sacrifice my life
for the suffering people.
I would sacrifice myself
no matter how many times
I would have to die.

(From Maren C. Tirabassi and
Kathy Wonson Eddy, editors,
Gifts of Many Cultures, p. 208)

This song was written by a twenty-two-year-old Thai student. He was later shot and killed by police officers at a demonstration against the return of a corrupt leader. His love for Thailand echoes the love of the mother and her seven sons for God and their Jewish faith in chapter 7 of 2 Maccabees.

▶ **2 Maccabees, chapter 7**

10 After him, the third was the victim of their sport. When it was demanded, he quickly put out his tongue and courageously stretched forth his hands, 11 and said nobly, "I got these from Heaven, and because of his laws I disdain them, and from him I hope to get them back again." 12 As a result the king himself and those with him were astonished at the young man's spirit, for he regarded his sufferings as nothing.

13 After he too had died, they maltreated and tortured the fourth in the same way. 14 When he was near death, he said, "One cannot but choose to die at the hands of mortals and to cherish the hope God gives of being raised again by him. But for you there will be no resurrection to life!"

15 Next they brought forward the fifth and maltreated him. 16 But he looked at the king, *g* and said, "Because you have authority among mortals, though you also are mortal, you do what you please. But do not think that God has forsaken our people. 17 Keep on, and see how his mighty power will torture you and your descendants!"

18 After him they brought forward the sixth. And when he was about to die, he said, "Do not deceive yourself in vain. For we are suffering these things on our own account, because of our sins against our own God. Therefore*h* astounding things have happened. 19 But do not think that you will go unpunished for having tried to fight against God!"

20 The mother was especially admirable and worthy of honorable memory. Although she saw her seven sons perish within a single day, she bore it with good courage because of her hope in the Lord. 21 She encouraged each of them in the language of their ancestors. Filled with a noble spirit, she reinforced her woman's reasoning with a man's courage, and said to them, 22 "I do not know how you came into being in my womb. It was not I who gave you life and breath, nor I who set in order the elements within each of you. 23 Therefore the Creator of the world, who shaped the beginning of humankind and devised the origin of all things, will in his mercy give life and breath back to you again, since you now forget yourselves for the sake of his laws."

24 An•ti′o•chus felt that he was being treated with contempt, and he was suspicious of her reproachful tone. The youngest brother being still alive, An•ti′o•chus*i* not only appealed to him in words, but promised with oaths that he would make him rich and enviable if he would turn from the ways of his ancestors, and that he would take him for his Friend and entrust him with public affairs. 25 Since the young man would not listen to him at all, the king called the mother to him and urged her to advise the youth to save himself. 26 After much urging on his part, she undertook to persuade her son. 27 But, leaning close to him, she spoke in their native language as follows, deriding the cruel tyrant: "My son, have pity on me. I carried you nine months in my womb, and nursed you for three years, and have reared you and brought you up to this point in your life, and have

g Gk *at him*   *h* Lat: Other ancient authorities lack *Therefore*   *i* Gk *he* taken care of you.^{j} ^{28}I beg you, my child, to look at the heaven and the earth and see everything that is in them, and recognize that God did not make them out of things that existed.^{k} And in the same way the human race came into being. ^{29}Do not fear this butcher, but prove worthy of your brothers. Accept death, so that in God's mercy I may get you back again along with your brothers."

30 While she was still speaking, the young man said, "What are you^l waiting for? I will not obey the king's command, but I obey the command of the law that was given to our ancestors through Moses. ^{31}But you,^{m} who have contrived all sorts of evil against the Hebrews, will certainly not escape the hands of God. ^{32}For we are suffering because of our own sins. ^{33}And if our living Lord is angry for a little while, to rebuke and discipline us, he will again be reconciled with his own servants.^{n} ^{34}But you, unholy wretch, you most defiled of all mortals, do not be elated in vain and puffed up by uncertain hopes, when you raise your hand against the children of heaven. ^{35}You have not yet escaped the judgment of the almighty, all-seeing God. ^{36}For our brothers after enduring a brief suffering have drunk^o of ever-flowing life, under God's covenant; but you, by the judgment of God, will receive just punishment for your arrogance. ^{37}I, like my brothers, give up body and life for the laws of our ancestors, appealing to God to show mercy soon to our nation and by trials and plagues to make you confess that he alone is God, ^{38}and through me and my brothers to bring to an end the wrath of the Almighty that has justly fallen on our whole nation."

39 The king fell into a rage, and handled him worse than the others, being exasperated at his scorn. ^{40}So he died in his integrity, putting his whole trust in the Lord.

41 Last of all, the mother died, after her sons.

42 Let this be enough, then, about the eating of sacrifices and the extreme tortures.

The Revolt of Judas Maccabeus
(1 Macc 3.1–26)

Meanwhile Judas, who was also called Mac·cabe'us, and his companions secretly entered the villages and summoned their kindred and enlisted those who had continued in the Jewish faith, and so they gathered about six thousand. ^{2}They implored the Lord to look upon the people who were oppressed by all; and to have pity on the temple that had been profaned by the godless; ^{3}to have mercy on the city that was being destroyed and about to be leveled to the ground; to hearken to the blood that cried out to him; ^{4}to remember

did you KNOW?

Nonviolent Resistance

The article "A Just War," near 1 Macc 6.32, discusses just war as a response to the Seleucid persecution of the Jews. Second Maccabees, chapters 6–7, hints at another response—nonviolent resistance. Despite being ordered to forsake their faith and to adopt Greek customs, Jews resisted. We read of women continuing to have their baby boys circumcised (6.10), of secret gatherings to celebrate the Sabbath (6.11), and of martyrs refusing to eat unlawful meat (6.19; 7.1). Although the stories focus on the violent responses and tortures inflicted by the Greeks, they indicate that at least part of the population neither gave up their religious practices nor took up arms in violent conflict.

Christians have continued to develop the concept of nonviolent resistance—sometimes called pacifism. Nonviolent resistance is rooted in Jesus' teachings to turn the other cheek (Mt 5.39) and "love your enemies" (5.44). Nonviolent resistance is not passive. It confronts evil and refuses to cooperate with it without resorting to violence. Those who practice nonviolent resistance accept the suffering that results because they know God can bring good out of the suffering of the just. The Catholic church teaches that nonviolent resistance gives witness to God's redeeming love and that no person who objects to committing violence should be forced into military service.

Christian nonviolence is a challenge for everyone. How do you practice it in your relationships with others? In what situations, if any, do you think it is necessary to respond with violence? In what situations would you refuse to participate in military service?

also the lawless destruction of the innocent babies and the blasphemies committed against his name; and to show his hatred of evil.

---

^{j} Or *have borne the burden of your education* ^{k} Or *God made them out of things that did not exist* ^{l} The Gk here for *you* is plural ^{m} The Gk here for *you* is singular ^{n} Gk *slaves* ^{o} Cn: Gk *fallen*

5 As soon as Mac·ca·bē′us got his army organized, the Gentiles could not withstand him, for the wrath of the Lord had turned to mercy. 6 Coming without warning, he would set fire to towns and villages. He captured strategic positions and put to flight not a few of the enemy. 7 He found the nights most advantageous for such attacks. And talk of his valor spread everywhere.

8 When Philip saw that the man was gaining ground little by little, and that he was pushing ahead with more frequent successes, he wrote to Ptol′e·my, the governor of Coē·le·syr′i·a and Phoeni′ci·a, to come to the aid of the king's government. 9 Then Ptol′e·my*p* promptly appointed Nī·cā′nor son of Pa·trō′clus, one of the king's chief*q* Friends, and sent him, in command of no fewer than twenty thousand Gentiles of all nations, to wipe out the whole race of Judea. He associated with him Gor′gi·as, a general and a man of experience in military service. 10 Nī·cā′nor determined to make up for the king the tribute due to the Romans, two thousand talents, by selling the captured Jews into slavery. 11 So he immediately sent to the towns on the seacoast, inviting them to buy Jewish slaves and promising to hand over ninety slaves for a talent, not expecting the judgment from the Almighty that was about to overtake him.

Preparation for Battle
(1 Macc 3.38–53)

12 Word came to Judas concerning Nī·cā′nor's invasion; and when he told his companions of the arrival of the army, 13 those who were cowardly and distrustful of God's justice ran off and got away. 14 Others sold all their remaining property, and at the same time implored the Lord to rescue those who had been sold by the ungodly Nī·cā′nor before he ever met them, 15 if not for their own sake, then for the sake of the covenants made with their ancestors, and because he had called them by his holy and glorious name. 16 But Mac·ca·bē′us gathered his forces together, to the number six thousand, and exhorted them not to be frightened by the enemy and not to fear the great multitude of Gentiles who were wickedly coming against them, but to fight nobly, 17 keeping before their eyes the lawless outrage that the Gentiles*r* had committed against the holy place, and the torture of the derided city, and besides, the overthrow of their ancestral way of life. 18 "For they trust to arms and acts of daring," he said, "but we trust in the Almighty God, who is able with a single nod to strike down those who are coming against us, and even, if necessary, the whole world."

19 Moreover, he told them of the occasions when help came to their ancestors; how, in the time of Sen·nach′e·rib, when one hundred eighty-five thousand perished, 20 and the time of the battle against the Galatians that took place in Babylonia, when eight thousand Jews*s* fought along with four thousand Mac·e·dō′ni·ans; yet when the Mac·e·dō′ni·ans were hard pressed, the eight thousand, by the help that came to them from heaven, destroyed one hundred twenty thousand Galatians*t* and took a great amount of booty.

Judas Defeats Nicanor
(1 Macc 3.54—4.25)

21 With these words he filled them with courage and made them ready to die for their laws and their country; then he divided his army into four parts. 22 He appointed his brothers also, Simon and Joseph and Jonathan, each to command a division, putting fifteen hundred men under each. 23 Besides, he appointed El·ē·ā′zar to read aloud*u* from the holy book, and gave the watchword, "The help of God"; then, leading the first division himself, he joined battle with Nī·cā′nor.

24 With the Almighty as their ally, they killed more than nine thousand of the enemy, and wounded and disabled most of Nī·cā′nor's army, and forced them all to flee. 25 They captured the money of those who had come to buy them as slaves. After pursuing them for some distance, they were obliged to return because the hour was late. 26 It was the day before the sabbath, and for that reason they did not continue their pursuit. 27 When they had collected the arms of the enemy and stripped them of their spoils, they kept the sabbath, giving great praise and thanks to the Lord, who had preserved them for that day and allotted it to them as the beginning of mercy. 28 After the sabbath they gave some of the spoils to those who had been tortured and to the widows and orphans, and distributed the rest among themselves and their children. 29 When they had done this, they made common supplication and implored the merciful Lord to be wholly reconciled with his servants.*v*

Judas Defeats Timothy and Bacchides

30 In encounters with the forces of Timothy and Bac′chi·dēs they killed more than twenty thousand of them and got possession of some exceedingly high strongholds, and they divided a very large amount of plunder, giving to those who had

p Gk he   *q* Gk one of the first   *r* Gk they   *s* Gk lacks Jews   *t* Gk lacks Galatians   *u* Meaning of Gk uncertain   *v* Gk slaves

been tortured and to the orphans and widows, and also to the aged, shares equal to their own. ³¹They collected the arms of the enemy,ʷ and carefully stored all of them in strategic places; the rest of the spoils they carried to Jerusalem. ³²They killed the commander of Timothy's forces, a most wicked man, and one who had greatly troubled the Jews. ³³While they were celebrating the victory in the city of their ancestors, they burned those who had set fire to the sacred gates, Cal·lis'the·nēs and some others, who had fled into one little house; so these received the proper reward for their impiety.ˣ

34 The thrice-accursed Nī·cā'nor, who had brought the thousand merchants to buy the Jews, ³⁵having been humbled with the help of the Lord by opponents whom he regarded as of the least account, took off his splendid uniform and made his way alone like a runaway slave across the country until he reached An'ti·och, having succeeded chiefly in the destruction of his own army! ³⁶So he who had undertaken to secure tribute for the Romans by the capture of the people of Jerusalem proclaimed that the Jews had a Defender, and that therefore the Jews were invulnerable, because they followed the laws ordained by him.

The Last Campaign of Antiochus Epiphanes
(1 Macc 6.1–7; 2 Macc 1.11–17)

About that time, as it happened, An·ti'o·chus had retreated in disorder from the region of Persia. ²He had entered the city called Per·sep'o·lis and attempted to rob the temples and control the city. Therefore the people rushed to the rescue with arms, and An·ti'o·chus and his army were defeated,ʸ with the result that An·ti'o·chus was put to flight by the inhabitants and beat a shameful retreat. ³While he was in Ec·bat'a·na, news came to him of what had happened to Nī·cā'nor and the forces of Timothy. ⁴Transported with rage, he conceived the idea of turning upon the Jews the injury done by those who had put him to flight; so he ordered his charioteer to drive without stopping until he completed the journey. But the judgment of heaven rode with him! For in his arrogance he said, "When I get there I will make Jerusalem a cemetery of Jews."

5 But the all-seeing Lord, the God of Israel, struck him with an incurable and invisible blow. As soon as he stopped speaking he was seized with a pain in his bowels, for which there was no relief, and with sharp internal tortures— ⁶and that very justly, for he had tortured the bowels of others with many and strange inflictions. ⁷Yet he did not in any way stop his insolence, but was even more filled with arrogance, breathing fire in his rage

against the Jews, and giving orders to drive even faster. And so it came about that he fell out of his chariot as it was rushing along, and the fall was so hard as to torture every limb of his body. ⁸Thus he who only a little while before had thought in his superhuman arrogance that he could command the waves of the sea, and had imagined that he could weigh the high mountains in a balance, was brought down to earth and carried in a litter, making the power of God manifest to all. ⁹And so the ungodly man's body swarmed with worms, and while he was still living in anguish and pain, his flesh rotted away, and because of the stench the whole army felt revulsion at his decay. ¹⁰Because of his intolerable stench no one was able to carry the man who a little while before had thought that he could touch the stars of heaven. ¹¹Then it was that, broken in spirit, he began to lose much of his arrogance and to come to his senses under the scourge of God, for he was tortured with pain every moment. ¹²And when he could not endure his own stench, he uttered these words, "It is right to be subject to God; mortals should not think that they are equal to God."ᶻ

Antiochus Makes a Promise to God
(1 Macc 6.8–17)

13 Then the abominable fellow made a vow to the Lord, who would no longer have mercy on him, stating ¹⁴that the holy city, which he was hurrying to level to the ground and to make a cemetery, he was now declaring to be free; ¹⁵and the Jews, whom he had not considered worth burying but had planned to throw out with their children for the wild animals and for the birds to eat, he would make, all of them, equal to citizens of Athens; ¹⁶and the holy sanctuary, which he had formerly plundered, he would adorn with the finest offerings; and all the holy vessels he would give back, many times over; and the expenses incurred for the sacrifices he would provide from his own revenues; ¹⁷and in addition to all this he also would become a Jew and would visit every inhabited place to proclaim the power of God. ¹⁸But when his sufferings did not in any way abate, for the judgment of God had justly come upon him, he gave up all hope for himself and wrote to the Jews the following letter, in the form of a supplication. This was its content:

Antiochus's Letter and Death

19 "To his worthy Jewish citizens, An·ti'o·chus their king and general sends hearty greetings and

---

ʷ Gk *their arms*   ˣ Meaning of Gk uncertain   ʸ Gk *they were defeated*   ᶻ Or *not think thoughts proper only to God* good wishes for their health and prosperity. 20 If you and your children are well and your affairs are as you wish, I am glad. As my hope is in heaven, 21 I remember with affection your esteem and goodwill. On my way back from the region of Persia I suffered an annoying illness, and I have deemed it necessary to take thought for the general security of all. 22 I do not despair of my condition, for I have good hope of recovering from my illness, 23 but I observed that my father, on the occasions when he made expeditions into the upper country, appointed his successor, 24 so that, if anything unexpected happened or any unwelcome news came, the people throughout the realm would not be troubled, for they would know to whom the government was left. 25 Moreover, I understand how the princes along the borders and the neighbors of my kingdom keep watching for opportunities and waiting to see what will happen. So I have appointed my son An·ti′o·chus to be king, whom I have often entrusted and commended to most of you when I hurried off to the upper provinces; and I have written to him what is written here. 26 I therefore urge and beg you to remember the public and private services rendered to you and to maintain your present goodwill, each of you, toward me and my son. 27 For I am sure that he will follow my policy and will treat you with moderation and kindness."

28 So the murderer and blasphemer, having endured the more intense suffering, such as he had inflicted on others, came to the end of his life by a most pitiable fate, among the mountains in a strange land. 29 And Philip, one of his courtiers, took his body home; then, fearing the son of An·ti′o·chus, he withdrew to Ptol′e·my Phil·o·me′tor in Egypt.

Purification of the Temple
(1 Macc 4.36–61)

Now Mac·ca·be′us and his followers, the Lord leading them on, recovered the temple and the city; 2 they tore down the altars that had been built in the public square by the foreigners, and also destroyed the sacred precincts. 3 They purified the sanctuary, and made another altar of sacrifice; then, striking fire out of flint, they offered sacrifices, after a lapse of two years, and they offered incense and lighted lamps and set out the bread of the Presence. 4 When they had done this, they fell prostrate and implored the Lord that they might never again fall into such misfortunes, but that, if they should ever sin, they might be disciplined by him with forbearance and not be handed over to blasphemous and barbarous nations. 5 It happened that on the same day on which the sanctu-

10.6

ary had been profaned by the foreigners, the purification of the sanctuary took place, that is, on the twenty-fifth day of the same month, which was Chis′lev. 6 They celebrated it for eight days with rejoicing, in the manner of the festival of booths, remembering how not long before, during the festival of booths, they had been wandering in the mountains and caves like wild animals. 7 Therefore, carrying ivy-wreathed wands and beautiful branches and also fronds of palm, they offered hymns of thanksgiving to him who had given success to the purifying of his own holy place. 8 They decreed by public edict, ratified by vote, that the whole nation of the Jews should observe these days every year.

9 Such then was the end of An·ti′o·chus, who was called E·piph′a·nes.

Accession of Antiochus Eupator
(1 Macc 6.17)

10 Now we will tell what took place under An·ti′o·chus Eu′pa·tor, who was the son of that ungodly man, and will give a brief summary of the principal calamities of the wars. 11 This man, when he succeeded to the kingdom, appointed one Lys′i·as to have charge of the government and to be chief governor of Coe·le·syr′i·a and Phoe·ni′ci·a. 12 Ptol′e·my, who was called Ma′cron, took the lead in showing justice to the Jews because of the wrong that had been done to them, and attempted to maintain peaceful relations with them. 13 As a result he was accused before Eu′pa·tor by the king's Friends. He heard himself called a traitor at every turn, because he had abandoned Cyprus, which Phil·o·me′tor had entrusted to him, and had gone over to An·ti′o·chus E·piph′a·nes. Unable to

command the respect due his office,[a] he took poison and ended his life.

Campaign in Idumea
(1 Macc 5.1–8)

14 When Gor'gi•as became governor of the region, he maintained a force of mercenaries, and at every turn kept attacking the Jews. 15 Besides this, the Id•ū•mē'ans, who had control of important strongholds, were harassing the Jews; they received those who were banished from Jerusalem, and endeavored to keep up the war. 16 But Mac•ca•bē'us and his forces, after making solemn supplication and imploring God to fight on their side, rushed to the strongholds of the Id•ū•mē'ans. 17 Attacking them vigorously, they gained possession of the places, and beat off all who fought upon the wall, and slaughtered those whom they encountered, killing no fewer than twenty thousand.

18 When at least nine thousand took refuge in two very strong towers well equipped to withstand a siege, 19 Mac•ca•bē'us left Simon and Joseph, and also Zac•chaē'us and his troops, a force sufficient to besiege them; and he himself set off for places where he was more urgently needed. 20 But those with Simon, who were money-hungry, were bribed by some of those who were in the towers, and on receiving seventy thousand drachmas let some of them slip away. 21 When word of what had happened came to Mac•ca•bē'us, he gathered the leaders of the people, and accused these men of having sold their kindred for money by setting their enemies free to fight against them. 22 Then he killed these men who had turned traitor, and immediately captured the two towers. 23 Having success at arms in everything he undertook, he destroyed more than twenty thousand in the two strongholds.

Judas Defeats Timothy

24 Now Timothy, who had been defeated by the Jews before, gathered a tremendous force of mercenaries and collected the cavalry from Asia in no small number. He came on, intending to take Judea by storm. 25 As he drew near, Mac•ca•bē'us and his men sprinkled dust on their heads and girded their loins with sackcloth, in supplication to God. 26 Falling upon the steps before the altar, they implored him to be gracious to them and to be an enemy to their enemies and an adversary to their adversaries, as the law declares. 27 And rising from their prayer they took up their arms and advanced a considerable distance from the city; and when they came near the enemy they halted. 28 Just as dawn was breaking, the two armies joined battle, the one having as pledge of success

and victory not only their valor but also their reliance on the Lord, while the other made rage their leader in the fight.

29 When the battle became fierce, there appeared to the enemy from heaven five resplendent men on horses with golden bridles, and they were leading the Jews. 30 Two of them took Mac•ca•bē'us between them, and shielding him with their own armor and weapons, they kept him from being wounded. They showered arrows and thunderbolts on the enemy, so that, confused and blinded, they were thrown into disorder and cut to pieces. 31 Twenty thousand five hundred were slaughtered, besides six hundred cavalry.

32 Timothy himself fled to a stronghold called Ga•zā'ra, especially well garrisoned, where Chaēr'e•as was commander. 33 Then Mac•ca•bē'us and his men were glad, and they besieged the fort for four days. 34 The men within, relying on the strength of the place, kept blaspheming terribly and uttering wicked words. 35 But at dawn of the fifth day, twenty young men in the army of Mac•ca•bē'us, fired with anger because of the blasphemies, bravely stormed the wall and with savage fury cut down everyone they met. 36 Others who came up in the same way wheeled around against the defenders and set fire to the towers; they kindled fires and burned the blasphemers alive. Others broke open the gates and let in the rest of the force, and they occupied the city. 37 They killed Timothy, who was hiding in a cistern, and his brother Chaēr'e•as, and Ap•ol•loph'a•nēs. 38 When they had accomplished these things, with hymns and thanksgivings they blessed the Lord who shows great kindness to Israel and gives them the victory.

Lysias Besieges Beth-zur
(1 Macc 4.26–35)

Very soon after this, Lys'i•as, the king's guardian and kinsman, who was in charge of the government, being vexed at what had happened, 2 gathered about eighty thousand infantry and all his cavalry and came against the Jews. He intended to make the city a home for Greeks, 3 and to levy tribute on the temple as he did on the sacred places of the other nations, and to put up the high priesthood for sale every year. 4 He took no account whatever of the power of God, but was elated with his ten thousands of infantry, and his thousands of cavalry, and his eighty elephants. 5 Invading Judea, he approached Beth-zur, which was a fortified

---

[a] Cn: Meaning of Gk uncertain

place about five stadia*b* from Jerusalem, and pressed it hard.

6 When Mac•ca•bē'us and his men got word that Lys'i•as*c* was besieging the strongholds, they and all the people, with lamentations and tears, prayed the Lord to send a good angel to save Israel. 7 Mac•ca•bē'us himself was the first to take up arms, and he urged the others to risk their lives with him to aid their kindred. Then they eagerly rushed off together. 8 And there, while they were still near Jerusalem, a horseman appeared at their head, clothed in white and brandishing weapons of gold. 9 And together they all praised the merciful God, and were strengthened in heart, ready to assail not only humans but the wildest animals or walls of iron. 10 They advanced in battle order, having their heavenly ally, for the Lord had mercy on them. 11 They hurled themselves like lions against the enemy, and laid low eleven thousand of them and sixteen hundred cavalry, and forced all the rest to flee. 12 Most of them got away stripped and wounded, and Lys'i•as himself escaped by disgraceful flight.

Lysias Makes Peace with the Jews
(1 Macc 6.55–63)

13 As he was not without intelligence, he pondered over the defeat that had befallen him, and realized that the Hebrews were invincible because the mighty God fought on their side. So he sent to them 14 and persuaded them to settle everything on just terms, promising that he would persuade the king, constraining him to be their friend.*b* 15 Mac•ca•bē'us, having regard for the common good, agreed to all that Lys'i•as urged. For the king granted every request in behalf of the Jews which Mac•ca•bē'us delivered to Lys'i•as in writing.

16 The letter written to the Jews by Lys'i•as was to this effect:

"Lys'i•as to the people of the Jews, greetings. 17 John and Ab'sa•lom, who were sent by you, have delivered your signed communication and have asked about the matters indicated in it. 18 I have informed the king of everything that needed to be brought before him, and he has agreed to what was possible. 19 If you will maintain your goodwill toward the government, I will endeavor in the future to help promote your welfare. 20 And concerning such matters and their details, I have ordered these men and my representatives to confer with you. 21 Farewell. The one hundred forty-eighth year,*d* Di•os•co•rin'thi•us twenty-fourth."

22 The king's letter ran thus:

"King An•ti'o•chus to his brother Lys'i•as, greetings. 23 Now that our father has gone on to the gods, we desire that the subjects of the kingdom be undisturbed in caring for their own affairs. 24 We have heard that the Jews do not consent to our father's change to Greek customs, but prefer their own way of living and ask that their own customs be allowed them. 25 Accordingly, since we choose that this nation also should be free from disturbance, our decision is that their temple be restored to them and that they shall live according to the customs of their ancestors. 26 You will do well, therefore, to send word to them and give them pledges of friendship, so that they may know our policy and be of good cheer and go on happily in the conduct of their own affairs."

27 To the nation the king's letter was as follows:

"King An•ti'o•chus to the senate of the Jews and to the other Jews, greetings. 28 If you are well, it is as we desire. We also are in good health. 29 Men•e•lā'us has informed us that you wish to return home and look after your own affairs. 30 Therefore those who go home by the thirtieth of Xan'thi•cus will have our pledge of friendship and full permission 31 for the Jews to enjoy their own food and laws, just as formerly, and none of them shall be molested in any way for what may have been done in ignorance. 32 And I have also sent Men•e•lā'us to encourage you. 33 Farewell. The one hundred forty-eighth year,*d* Xan'thi•cus fifteenth."

34 The Romans also sent them a letter, which read thus:

"Quin'tus Mem'mi•us and Titus Mā'ni•us, envoys of the Romans, to the people of the Jews, greetings. 35 With regard to what Lys'i•as the kinsman of the king has granted you, we also give consent. 36 But as to the matters that he decided are to be referred to the king, as soon as you have considered them, send some one promptly so that we may make proposals appropriate for you. For we are on our way to An'ti•och. 37 Therefore make haste and send messengers so that we may have your judgment. 38 Farewell. The one hundred forty-eighth year,*d* Xan'thi•cus fifteenth."

Incidents at Joppa and Jamnia

When this agreement had been reached, Lys'i•as returned to the king, and the Jews went about their farming.

2 But some of the governors in various places, Timothy and Ap•ol•lō'ni•us son of Gen•nae'us, as well as Hi•e•ron'y•mus and Dem'o•phon, and in addition to these Ni•cā'nor the governor of Cyprus,

would not let them live quietly and in peace. ³And the people of Jop′pa did so ungodly a deed as this: they invited the Jews who lived among them to embark, with their wives and children, on boats that they had provided, as though there were no ill will to the Jews;*e* ⁴and this was done by public vote of the city. When they accepted, because they wished to live peaceably and suspected nothing, the people of Jop′pa*f* took them out to sea and drowned them, at least two hundred. ⁵When Judas heard of the cruelty visited on his compatriots, he gave orders to his men ⁶and, calling upon God, the righteous judge, attacked the murderers of his kindred. He set fire to the harbor by night, burned the boats, and massacred those who had taken refuge there. ⁷Then, because the city's gates were closed, he withdrew, intending to come again and root out the whole community of Jop′pa. ⁸But learning that the people in Jam′ni·a meant in the same way to wipe out the Jews who were living among them, ⁹he attacked the Jam′nites by night and set fire to the harbor and the fleet, so that the glow of the light was seen in Jerusalem, thirty miles*g* distant.

The Campaign in Gilead
(1 Macc 5.9–36)

10 When they had gone more than a mile*h* from there, on their march against Timothy, at least five thousand Arabs with five hundred cavalry attacked them. ¹¹After a hard fight, Judas and his companions, with God's help, were victorious. The defeated nomads begged Judas to grant them pledges of friendship, promising to give him livestock and to help his people*i* in all other ways. ¹²Judas, realizing that they might indeed be useful in many ways, agreed to make peace with them; and after receiving his pledges they went back to their tents.

13 He also attacked a certain town that was strongly fortified with earthworks*j* and walls, and inhabited by all sorts of Gentiles. Its name was Cas′pin. ¹⁴Those who were within, relying on the strength of the walls and on their supply of provisions, behaved most insolently toward Judas and his men, railing at them and even blaspheming and saying unholy things. ¹⁵But Judas and his men, calling upon the great Sovereign of the world, who without battering rams or engines of war overthrew Jericho in the days of Joshua, rushed furiously upon the walls. ¹⁶They took the town by the will of God, and slaughtered untold numbers, so that the adjoining lake, a quarter of a mile*k* wide, appeared to be running over with blood.

Judas Defeats Timothy's Army
(1 Macc 5.37–44)

17 When they had gone ninety-five miles*l* from there, they came to Chār′ax, to the Jews who are called Toū·bi·ā′nī. ¹⁸They did not find Timothy in that region, for he had by then left there without accomplishing anything, though in one place he had left a very strong garrison. ¹⁹Dō·sith′e·us and Sō·sip′a·ter, who were captains under Mac·ca·bē′us, marched out and destroyed those whom Timothy had left in the stronghold, more than ten thousand men. ²⁰But Mac·ca·bē′us arranged his army in divisions, set men*i* in command of the divisions, and hurried after Timothy, who had with him one hundred twenty thousand infantry and two thousand five hundred cavalry. ²¹When Timothy learned of the approach of Judas, he sent off the women and the children and also the baggage to a place called Car′na·im; for that place was hard to besiege and difficult of access because of the narrowness of all the approaches. ²²But when Judas's first division appeared, terror and fear came over the enemy at the manifestation to them of him who sees all things. In their flight they rushed headlong in every direction, so that often they were injured by their own men and pierced by the points of their own swords. ²³Judas pressed the pursuit with the utmost vigor, putting the sinners to the sword, and destroyed as many as thirty thousand.

24 Timothy himself fell into the hands of Dō·sith′e·us and Sō·sip′a·ter and their men. With great guile he begged them to let him go in safety, because he held the parents of most of them, and the brothers of some, to whom no consideration would be shown. ²⁵And when with many words he had confirmed his solemn promise to restore them unharmed, they let him go, for the sake of saving their kindred.

Judas Wins Other Victories
(1 Macc 5.45–54)

26 Then Judas*m* marched against Car′na·im and the temple of A·tar′ga·tis, and slaughtered twenty-five thousand people. ²⁷After the rout and destruction of these, he marched also against Ē′phron, a fortified town where Lys′i·as lived with multitudes of people of all nationalities.*j* Stalwart young men took their stand before the walls and made a vigorous defense; and great stores of war engines and missiles were there. ²⁸But the Jews*f* called upon

---

e Gk to them   f Gk they   g Gk two hundred forty stadia
h Gk nine stadia   i Gk them   j Meaning of Gk uncertain
k Gk two stadia   l Gk seven hundred fifty stadia   m Gk he

the Sovereign who with power shatters the might of his enemies, and they got the town into their hands, and killed as many as twenty-five thousand of those who were in it.

29 Setting out from there, they hastened to Scyth•op'o•lis, which is seventy-five miles[n] from Jerusalem. 30 But when the Jews who lived there bore witness to the goodwill that the people of Scyth-op'o•lis had shown them and their kind treatment of them in times of misfortune, 31 they thanked them and exhorted them to be well disposed to their race in the future also. Then they went up to Jerusalem, as the festival of weeks was close at hand.

Judas Defeats Gorgias

32 After the festival called Pentecost, they hurried against Gor'gi•as, the governor of Id•u•mē'a, 33 who came out with three thousand infantry and four hundred cavalry. 34 When they joined battle, it happened that a few of the Jews fell. 35 But a certain Do•sith'e•us, one of Ba•cē'nor's men, who was on horseback and was a strong man, caught hold of Gor'gi•as, and grasping his cloak was dragging him off by main strength, wishing to take the accursed man alive, when one of the Thrā'ci•an cavalry bore down on him and cut off his arm; so Gor'gi•as escaped and reached Mar'i•sa.

36 As Es'dris and his men had been fighting for a long time and were weary, Judas called upon the Lord to show himself their ally and leader in the battle. 37 In the language of their ancestors he raised the battle cry, with hymns; then he charged against Gor'gi•as's troops when they were not expecting it, and put them to flight.

Prayers for Those Killed in Battle

38 Then Judas assembled his army and went to the city of A•dul'lam. As the seventh day was coming on, they purified themselves according to the custom, and kept the sabbath there.

39 On the next day, as had now become necessary, Judas and his men went to take up the bodies of the fallen and to bring them back to lie with their kindred in the sepulchres of their ancestors. 40 Then under the tunic of each one of the dead they found sacred tokens of the idols of Jam'ni•a, which the law forbids the Jews to wear. And it became clear to all that this was the reason these men had fallen. 41 So they all blessed the ways of the Lord, the righteous judge, who reveals the things that are hidden; 42 and they turned to supplication, praying that the sin that had been committed might be wholly blotted out. The noble Judas exhorted the people to keep themselves free

from sin, for they had seen with their own eyes what had happened as the result of the sin of those who had fallen. 43 He also took up a collection, man by man, to the amount of two thousand drachmas of silver, and sent it to Jerusalem to provide for a sin offering. In doing this he acted very well and honorably, taking account of the resurrection. 44 For if he were not expecting that those who had fallen would rise again, it would have been superfluous and foolish to pray for the dead. 45 But if he was looking to the splendid reward that is laid up for those who fall asleep in godliness, it was a holy and pious thought. Therefore he made atonement for the dead, so that they might be delivered from their sin.

Menelaus Is Put to Death

In the one hundred forty-ninth year[o] word came to Judas and his men that An•ti'o•chus Eū'pa•tor was coming with a great army against Judea, 2 and with him Lys'i•as, his guardian, who had charge of the government. Each of them had a Greek force of one hundred ten thousand infantry, five thousand three hundred cavalry, twenty-two elephants, and three hundred chariots armed with scythes.

3 Men•e•lā'us also joined them and with utter hypocrisy urged An•ti'o•chus on, not for the sake of his country's welfare, but because he thought that he would be established in office. 4 But the King of kings aroused the anger of An•ti'o•chus against the scoundrel; and when Lys'i•as informed him that this man was to blame for all the trouble, he ordered them to take him to Be•roē'a and to put him to death by the method that is customary in that place. 5 For there is a tower there, fifty cubits high, full of ashes, and it has a rim running around it that on all sides inclines precipitously into the ashes. 6 There they all push to destruction anyone guilty of sacrilege or notorious for other crimes. 7 By such a fate it came about that Men•e•lā'us the lawbreaker died, without even burial in the earth. 8 And this was eminently just; because he had committed many sins against the altar whose fire and ashes were holy, he met his death in ashes.

A Battle Near the City of Modein
(1 Macc 6.43–46)

9 The king with barbarous arrogance was coming to show the Jews things far worse than those that had been done[p] in his father's time. 10 But when Judas heard of this, he ordered the people to call upon the Lord day and night, now if ever to

---

n Gk six hundred stadia   o 163 B.C.   p Or the worst of the things that had been done

help those who were on the point of being deprived of the law and their country and the holy temple, [11] and not to let the people who had just begun to revive fall into the hands of the blasphemous Gentiles. [12] When they had all joined in the same petition and had implored the merciful Lord with weeping and fasting and lying prostrate for three days without ceasing, Judas exhorted them and ordered them to stand ready.

[13] After consulting privately with the elders, he determined to march out and decide the matter by the help of God before the king's army could enter Judea and get possession of the city. [14] So, committing the decision to the Creator of the world and exhorting his troops to fight bravely to the death for the laws, temple, city, country, and commonwealth, he pitched his camp near Mŏ′dein. [15] He gave his troops the watchword, "God's victory," and with a picked force of the bravest young men, he attacked the king's pavilion at night and killed as many as two thousand men in the camp. He stabbed[q] the leading elephant and its rider. [16] In the end they filled the camp with terror and confusion and withdrew in triumph. [17] This happened, just as day was dawning, because the Lord's help protected him.

Antiochus Makes a Treaty with the Jews
(1 Macc 6.48–63)

[18] The king, having had a taste of the daring of the Jews, tried strategy in attacking their positions. [19] He advanced against Beth-zur, a strong fortress of the Jews, was turned back, attacked again,[r] and was defeated. [20] Judas sent in to the garrison whatever was necessary. [21] But Rhod′o•cus, a man from the ranks of the Jews, gave secret information to the enemy; he was sought for, caught, and put in prison. [22] The king negotiated a second time with the people in Beth-zur, gave pledges, received theirs, withdrew, attacked Judas and his men, was defeated; [23] he got word that Philip, who had been left in charge of the government, had revolted in An′ti•och; he was dismayed, called in the Jews, yielded and swore to observe all their rights, settled with them and offered sacrifice, honored the sanctuary and showed generosity to the holy place. [24] He received Mac•ca•bē′us, left Heg•e•mō′ni•dēs as governor from Ptol•e•mā′is to Gē′rar, [25] and went to Ptol•e•mā′is. The people of Ptol•e•mā′is were indignant over the treaty; in fact they were so angry that they wanted to annul its terms.[q] [26] Lys′i•as took the public platform, made the best possible defense, convinced them, appeased them, gained their goodwill, and set out for An′ti•och. This is how the king's attack and withdrawal turned out.

Alcimus Speaks against Judas
(1 Macc 7.1–25)

Three years later, word came to Judas and his men that De•mē′tri•us son of Se•leu′cus had sailed into the harbor of Trip′o•lis with a strong army and a fleet, [2] and had taken possession of the country, having made away with An•ti′o•chus and his guardian Lys′i•as.

[3] Now a certain Al′ci•mus, who had formerly been high priest but had willfully defiled himself in the times of separation,[s] realized that there was no way for him to be safe or to have access again to the holy altar, [4] and went to King De•mē′tri•us in about the one hundred fifty-first year,[t] presenting to him a crown of gold and a palm, and besides these some of the customary olive branches from the temple. During that day he kept quiet. [5] But he found an opportunity that furthered his mad purpose when he was invited by De•mē′tri•us to a meeting of the council and was asked about the attitude and intentions of the Jews. He answered:

[6] "Those of the Jews who are called Has•i•dē′ans, whose leader is Judas Mac•ca•bē′us, are keeping up war and stirring up sedition, and will not let the kingdom attain tranquility. [7] Therefore I have laid aside my ancestral glory—I mean the high priesthood—and have now come here, [8] first because I am genuinely concerned for the interests of the king, and second because I have regard also for my compatriots. For through the folly of those whom I have mentioned our whole nation is now in no small misfortune. [9] Since you are acquainted, O king, with the details of this matter, may it please you to take thought for our country and our hard-pressed nation with the gracious kindness that you show to all. [10] For as long as Judas lives, it is impossible for the government to find peace." [11] When he had said this, the rest of the king's Friends,[u] who were hostile to Judas, quickly inflamed De•mē′tri•us still more. [12] He immediately chose Nī•cā′nor, who had been in command of the elephants, appointed him governor of Judea, and sent him off [13] with orders to kill Judas and scatter his troops, and to install Al′ci•mus as high priest of the great[v] temple. [14] And the Gentiles throughout Judea, who had fled before[q] Judas, flocked to join Nī•cā′nor, thinking that the misfortunes and calamities of the Jews would mean prosperity for themselves.

---

[q] Meaning of Gk uncertain   [r] Or faltered   [s] Other ancient authorities read of mixing   [t] 161 B.C.   [u] Gk of the Friends   [v] Gk greatest

Nicanor Makes Friends with Judas
(1 Macc 7.26–28)

15 When the Jews[w] heard of Nĭ·cā'nor's coming and the gathering of the Gentiles, they sprinkled dust on their heads and prayed to him who established his own people forever and always upholds his own heritage by manifesting himself. 16 At the command of the leader, they[x] set out from there immediately and engaged them in battle at a village called Des'sau.[y] 17 Simon, the brother of Judas, had encountered Nĭ·cā'nor, but had been temporarily[z] checked because of the sudden consternation created by the enemy.

18 Nevertheless Nĭ·cā'nor, hearing of the valor of Judas and his troops and their courage in battle for their country, shrank from deciding the issue by bloodshed. 19 Therefore he sent Pos·i·dō'ni·us, Thē·od'o·tus, and Mat·ta·thī'as to give and receive pledges of friendship. 20 When the terms had been fully considered, and the leader had informed the people, and it had appeared that they were of one mind, they agreed to the covenant. 21 The leaders[a] set a day on which to meet by themselves. A chariot came forward from each army; seats of honor were set in place; 22 Judas posted armed men in readiness at key places to prevent sudden treachery on the part of the enemy; so they duly held the consultation.

23 Nĭ·cā'nor stayed on in Jerusalem and did nothing out of the way, but dismissed the flocks of people that had gathered. 24 And he kept Judas always in his presence; he was warmly attached to the man. 25 He urged him to marry and have children; so Judas[x] married, settled down, and shared the common life.

Nicanor Turns against Judas
(1 Macc 7.29–30)

26 But when Al'ci·mus noticed their goodwill for one another, he took the covenant that had been made and went to De·mē'tri·us. He told him that Nĭ·cā'nor was disloyal to the government, since he had appointed that conspirator against the kingdom, Judas, to be his successor. 27 The king became excited and, provoked by the false accusations of that depraved man, wrote to Nĭ·cā'nor, stating that he was displeased with the covenant and commanding him to send Mac·ca·bē'us to An'ti·och as a prisoner without delay.

28 When this message came to Nĭ·cā'nor, he was troubled and grieved that he had to annul their agreement when the man had done no wrong. 29 Since it was not possible to oppose the king, he watched for an opportunity to accomplish this by a stratagem. 30 But Mac·ca·bē'us, noticing that Nĭ·cā'nor was more austere in his dealings with him and was meeting him more rudely than had been his custom, concluded that this austerity did not spring from the best motives. So he gathered not a few of his men, and went into hiding from Nĭ·cā'nor. 31 When the latter became aware that he had been cleverly outwitted by the man, he went to the great[b] and holy temple while the priests were offering the customary sacrifices, and commanded them to hand the man over. 32 When they declared on oath that they did not know where the man was whom he wanted, 33 he stretched out his right hand toward the sanctuary, and swore this oath: "If you do not hand Judas over to me as a prisoner, I will level this shrine of God to the ground and tear down the altar, and build here a splendid temple to Dĭ·o·nў'sus."

34 Having said this, he went away. Then the priests stretched out their hands toward heaven and called upon the constant Defender of our nation, in these words: 35 "O Lord of all, though you have need of nothing, you were pleased that there should be a temple for your habitation among us; 36 so now, O holy One, Lord of all holiness, keep undefiled forever this house that has been so recently purified."

Razis Dies for His Country

37 A certain Rā'zis, one of the elders of Jerusalem, was denounced to Nĭ·cā'nor as a man who loved his compatriots and was very well thought of and for his goodwill was called father of the Jews. 38 In former times, when there was no mingling with the Gentiles, he had been accused of Jū'da·ism, and he had most zealously risked body and life for Jū'da·ism. 39 Nĭ·cā'nor, wishing to exhibit the enmity that he had for the Jews, sent more than five hundred soldiers to arrest him; 40 for he thought that by arresting[y] him he would do them an injury. 41 When the troops were about to capture the tower and were forcing the door of the courtyard, they ordered that fire be brought and the doors burned. Being surrounded, Rā'zis[x] fell upon his own sword, 42 preferring to die nobly rather than to fall into the hands of sinners and suffer outrages unworthy of his noble birth. 43 But in the heat of the struggle he did not hit exactly, and the crowd was now rushing in through the doors. He courageously ran up on the wall, and bravely threw himself down into the crowd. 44 But as they quickly drew back, a space opened and he fell in the middle of the empty space. 45 Still alive

---

w Gk *they*   *x* Gk *he*   *y* Meaning of Gk uncertain
z Other ancient authorities read *slowly*   *a* Gk *They*
b Gk *greatest*

and aflame with anger, he rose, and though his blood gushed forth and his wounds were severe he ran through the crowd; and standing upon a steep rock, ⁴⁶with his blood now completely drained from him, he tore out his entrails, took them in both hands and hurled them at the crowd, calling upon the Lord of life and spirit to give them back to him again. This was the manner of his death.

Nicanor's Arrogance

When Nĭ•cā'nor heard that Judas and his troops were in the region of Sa•mār'i•a, he made plans to attack them with complete safety on the day of rest. ²When the Jews who were compelled to follow him said, "Do not destroy so savagely and barbarously, but show respect for the day that he who sees all things has honored and hallowed above other days," ³the thrice-accursed wretch asked if there were a sovereign in heaven who had commanded the keeping of the sabbath day. ⁴When they declared, "It is the living Lord himself, the Sovereign in heaven, who ordered us to observe the seventh day," ⁵he replied, "But I am a sovereign also, on earth, and I command you to take up arms and finish the king's business." Nevertheless, he did not succeed in carrying out his abominable design.

Judas Prepares the Jews for Battle

6 This Nĭ•cā'nor in his utter boastfulness and arrogance had determined to erect a public monument of victory over Judas and his forces. ⁷But Mac•ca•bē'us did not cease to trust with all confidence that he would get help from the Lord. ⁸He exhorted his troops not to fear the attack of the Gentiles, but to keep in mind the former times when help had come to them from heaven, and so to look for the victory that the Almighty would give them. ⁹Encouraging them from the law and the prophets, and reminding them also of the struggles they had won, he made them the more eager. ¹⁰When he had aroused their courage, he issued his orders, at the same time pointing out the perfidy of the Gentiles and their violation of oaths. ¹¹He armed each of them not so much with confidence in shields and spears as with the inspiration of brave words, and he cheered them all by relating a dream, a sort of vision,ᶜ which was worthy of belief.

12 What he saw was this: Ō•nī'as, who had been high priest, a noble and good man, of modest bearing and gentle manner, one who spoke fittingly and had been trained from childhood in all that belongs to excellence, was praying with outstretched hands for the whole body of the Jews. ¹³Then in the same fashion another appeared, distinguished by his gray hair and dignity, and of marvelous majesty and authority. ¹⁴And Ō•nī'as spoke, saying, "This is a man who loves the family of Israel and prays much for the people and the holy city—Jer•e•mī'ah, the prophet of God." ¹⁵Jer•e•mī'ah stretched out his right hand and gave to Judas a golden sword, and as he gave it he addressed him thus: ¹⁶"Take this holy sword, a gift from God, with which you will strike down your adversaries."

17 Encouraged by the words of Judas, so noble and so effective in arousing valor and awaking courage in the souls of the young, they determined not to carry on a campaignᵈ but to attack bravely, and to decide the matter by fighting hand to hand with all courage, because the city and the sanctuary and the temple were in danger. ¹⁸Their concern for wives and children, and also for brothers and sistersᵉ and relatives, lay upon them less heavily; their greatest and first fear was for the consecrated sanctuary. ¹⁹And those who had to remain in the city were in no little distress, being anxious over the encounter in the open country.

The Defeat and Death of Nicanor
(1 Macc 7.39–50)

20 When all were now looking forward to the coming issue, and the enemy was already close at hand with their army drawn up for battle, the elephantsᶠ strategically stationed and the cavalry deployed on the flanks, ²¹Mac•ca•bē'us, observing the masses that were in front of him and the varied supply of arms and the savagery of the elephants, stretched out his hands toward heaven and called upon the Lord who works wonders; for he knew that it is not by arms, but as the Lordᵍ decides, that he gains the victory for those who deserve it. ²²He called upon him in these words: "O Lord, you sent your angel in the time of King Hez•e•kī'ah of Judea, and he killed fully one hundred eighty-five thousand in the camp of Sen•nach'e•rib. ²³So now, O Sovereign of the heavens, send a good angel to spread terror and trembling before us. ²⁴By the might of your arm may these blasphemers who come against your holy people be struck down." With these words he ended his prayer.

25 Nĭ•cā'nor and his troops advanced with trumpets and battle songs, ²⁶but Judas and his troops met the enemy in battle with invocations to God and prayers. ²⁷So, fighting with their hands and praying to God in their hearts, they laid low at least thirty-five thousand, and were greatly gladdened by God's manifestation.

ᶜ Meaning of Gk uncertain   ᵈ Or *to remain in camp*
ᵉ Gk *for brothers*   ᶠ Gk *animals*   ᵍ Gk *he*

28 When the action was over and they were returning with joy, they recognized Nĭ•cā′nor, lying dead, in full armor. ²⁹Then there was shouting and tumult, and they blessed the Sovereign Lord in the language of their ancestors. ³⁰Then the man who was ever in body and soul the defender of his people, the man who maintained his youthful goodwill toward his compatriots, ordered them to cut off Nĭ•cā′nor's head and arm and carry them to Jerusalem. ³¹When he arrived there and had called his compatriots together and stationed the priests before the altar, he sent for those who were in the citadel. ³²He showed them the vile Nĭ•cā′nor's head and that profane man's arm, which had been boastfully stretched out against the holy house of the Almighty. ³³He cut out the tongue of the ungodly Nĭ•cā′nor and said that he would feed it piecemeal to the birds and would hang up these rewards of his folly opposite the sanctuary. ³⁴And they all, looking to heaven, blessed the Lord who had manifested himself, saying, "Blessed is he who has kept his own place undefiled!" ³⁵Judas[h]

hung Nĭ•cā′nor's head from the citadel, a clear and conspicuous sign to everyone of the help of the Lord. ³⁶And they all decreed by public vote never to let this day go unobserved, but to celebrate the thirteenth day of the twelfth month—which is called Ā′dar in the Ar•a•mā′ic language—the day before Mor′de•caī's day.

37 This, then, is how matters turned out with Nĭ•cā′nor, and from that time the city has been in the possession of the Hebrews. So I will here end my story.

The Compiler's Epilogue

38 If it is well told and to the point, that is what I myself desired; if it is poorly done and mediocre, that was the best I could do. ³⁹For just as it is harmful to drink wine alone, or, again, to drink water alone, while wine mixed with water is sweet and delicious and enhances one's enjoyment, so also the style of the story delights the ears of those who read the work. And here will be the end.

h Gk *He*

Introducing

► JEWISH SECTS

In the last two centuries before Christ, a diversity of ways of being Jewish emerged. Different groups arose emphasizing different ways of remaining faithful to their Jewish heritage. These groups, or factions, within a religion are sometimes called sects. Primarily three sects emerged within Judaism.

Pharisees. The Pharisees were descendants of the Hasidim, Jews devoted to a strict observance of the Law who opposed King Antiochus IV Epiphanes' attempts to destroy the Jewish religion. Pharisee means "separated" and probably reflects the Pharisees' rigorous observance of the Law. They were often greatly respected. In the New Testament, Jesus argues with some Pharisees but is also a guest of others. Saint Paul was a Pharisee. Not surprisingly, some of the Pharisees' teachings were similar to those of the early Christians.

Sadducees. The Sadducees were a conservative Jewish sect that emerged in the first century B.C. and lasted only to around A.D. 70. The Sadducees were wealthy and politically influential landowners, and some of them had important roles in the Temple. They emphasized the necessity of worshiping at the Temple in Jerusalem. Unlike the Pharisees, they did not believe in the resurrection of the body.

Essenes. The Essenes, like the Pharisees, seem to have descended from the Hasidim. They existed in the first century B.C. and disappeared after A.D. 70. The name Essene can mean "healer" or "pious." The Essenes did not believe in the necessity of Temple sacrifice and often lived together in isolated communities where they practiced a simple lifestyle. Some of them were connected with the desert monastery at Qumran, and were responsible for writing the Dead Sea Scrolls. John the Baptist's preaching and some of Jesus' teaching in the Gospels closely reflected the writings and teachings of the Essenes.

2
M
A
C
C

Introduction to the
Wisdom
and Poetry Books

The LORD is my shepherd, I shall not want. (Ps 23.1)

A soft answer turns away wrath,
but a harsh word stirs up anger.
(Prov 15.1)

For everything there is a season, and a time for every matter
under heaven. (Eccl 3.1)

The books these words are taken from, the wisdom and poetry books of the Old Testament, are among the most quoted books of the Bible. The distilled wisdom they contain and the beauty of the language they use have universal appeal. Across cultures and across time, these books touch thoughtful minds and inquiring hearts.

In-depth

THIS SECTION OF THE BIBLE CONTAINS A VARIETY of books. The Book of Psalms consists of religious hymns, many written for use in Jewish worship. The Song of Solomon is a love poem. The Book of Job is a debate on why innocent people suffer. The Wisdom of Solomon, Proverbs, and Sirach give advice on moral and virtuous living. And Ecclesiastes is a sort of journal on the purpose of human life. The most obvious common element among these books is the use of poetic language to convey their message. Not that these are the only books of the Old Testament that use poetry. But they make such extensive application of it that a little background on the nature of Hebrew poetry is helpful for reading them.

The most important feature of Hebrew poetry is parallelism. Parallelism involves the repetition of words or ideas in successive lines of a verse. Sometimes, the second line contrasts with the first:

For the LORD watches over the way of the
righteous,
but the way of the wicked will perish.

(Ps 1.6)

Other times, the second line completes the thought of the first:

> The LORD looks down from heaven on
> humankind
> to see if there are any who are wise.
> (14.2)

Still other times, the second line seems to restate the first line more forcefully:

> For I know my transgressions,
> and my sin is ever before me.
> (51.3)

In its many forms, parallelism—not a rhythmic pattern or rhyming words—is the organizing principle of Hebrew poetry.

Hebrew poetry also uses symbolic language that is characteristic of poetry in any language. This includes metaphors ("The LORD is my rock" [18.2]) and similes ("As a deer longs for flowing streams, / so my soul longs for you, O God" [42.1]). To appreciate the beauty of Old Testament poetry and feel its impact, one must be willing to wrestle with symbolic ways of interpreting words and phrases.

Whereas the other books of the Old Testament emphasize ancient Israel's distinctive religious values, the wisdom and poetry books focus on its unique view of wisdom. Wisdom literature is something the ancient Israelites shared with neighboring cultures. The Egyptians, Sumerians, and Babylonians all had literature that offered practical, time-tested advice for people seeking trustworthy guidance. For the Israelites, however, true wisdom was more than mere common sense: it was a gift from God given to those who sought it. Some passages of the wisdom literature even describe wisdom as a divine person, a feminine form of the one God (see Wis 7.22—8.8 and Sirach, chapter 1).

In general, the wisdom writings have these characteristics:

- few references to the Law or the Covenant
- a minimal interest in Israel's history
- a search for harmony and the meaning of life
- a willingness to explore the difficult mysteries of life, such as suffering and death
- a commitment to discovering the moral lessons of everyday experiences
- a fundamental belief that good and wise living is rewarded whereas evil and foolish ways lead to ruin

The poetry and wisdom books of the Old Testament had an enormous influence on the writers of the New Testament and continue to be popular. Their poetic structure, which often makes them difficult to comprehend, also gives them a richness and depth that centuries of reading and rereading have not exhausted. Each time you read from these books, you will discover new treasures to enrich your life.

Other Background

- **The Book of Psalms is quoted more often in the New Testament than is any other Old Testament book. Also, it is used extensively in the church's liturgy.**

- **Job and Ecclesiastes posed serious challenges to the traditional understanding of Israelite faith. For help in understanding why, see the introductions to these books.**

- **Solomon's reputation for wisdom was so great that he was indicated as the author of four books actually written by others: Proverbs and Ecclesiastes, and two books that carry his name, the Song of Solomon and the Wisdom of Solomon.**

- **The Wisdom of Solomon and Sirach are not found in all translations of the Old Testament (see "The Case of the Missing Books," near Tob 1.16).**

You've seen the picture—a mother holding her poor, dead child, against the background of a country ravaged by drought. Or perhaps you have watched someone you love suffer from a devastating illness. And you found yourself wondering, Why, God? This is the basic question struggled with in the Book of Job. How can God allow innocent people to suffer?

At a Glance

- **Chapters 1–2.** God and an adversary (Satan) agree to test Job.

- **Chapters 3–37.** Job and his friends debate the cause of his suffering.

- **38.1—42.6.** God responds to Job.

- **42.7–17.** The story has a happy ending.

In-depth

At the time Job was written, most Israelites believed that if they obeyed God's commandments, God would bless them and protect them. The Israelites also believed that if people were suffering or poor, God was punishing them for some sin they or their parents had committed, even if they did not know what that sin was. The Israelites' thinking was extremely logical—because God is all-powerful and completely just, God will not allow people or communities to suffer unless they have sinned in some way.

The Book of Job challenges that way of thinking. Job is a good man, who has received great wealth and a wonderful family from God. In fact, Job's final defense in chapter 31 is one of the finest summaries of the Old Testament vision of a righteous person. The Book of Job begins with God allowing Job's wealth and children and health to be taken from him. Three friends come to mourn with Job. In a series of lengthy debates, they point out that his misfortunes must be the result of some sin or wrong he has committed. Job maintains his innocence, sometimes forcefully, and demands another explanation from God. Finally, God appears to Job and overwhelms him with questions about the nature of the universe. Job realizes that God is beyond human knowledge and that some mysteries—including suffering—can never be completely understood, they can only be accepted.

The Book of Job does not give the final answer about why bad things happen to good people. But it does make it clear that good people do suffer and their suffering is not a punishment sent by God. And Job is a reminder to the Israelites and to us that God's purposes are too far beyond human understanding for anyone to claim to know everything there is to know about God.

Quick Facts

Author
unknown, writing at an unknown date

Theme
Why do good people suffer?

Of Note
Job is a story within a story: chapters 1–2 and 42.7–17 constitute a folktale; set within that tale, in 3.1—42.6, is a poetic debate about the cause of suffering.

The Book of Job

568

Job

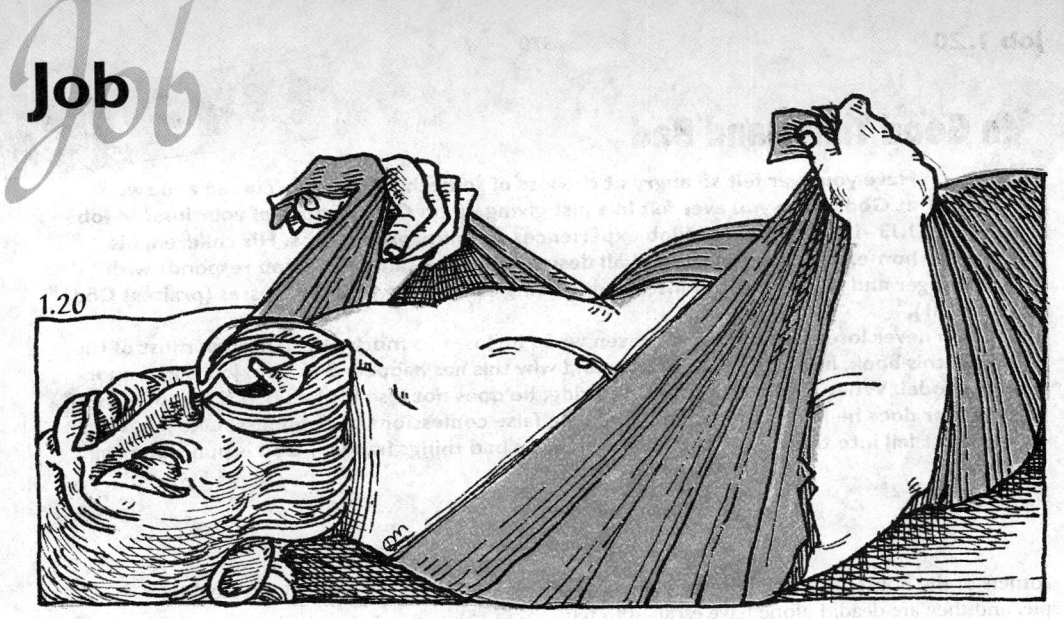

1.20

Job and His Family

There was once a man in the land of Uz whose name was Jōb. That man was blameless and upright, one who feared God and turned away from evil. ² There were born to him seven sons and three daughters. ³ He had seven thousand sheep, three thousand camels, five hundred yoke of oxen, five hundred donkeys, and very many servants; so that this man was the greatest of all the people of the east. ⁴ His sons used to go and hold feasts in one another's houses in turn; and they would send and invite their three sisters to eat and drink with them. ⁵ And when the feast days had run their course, Jōb would send and sanctify them, and he would rise early in the morning and offer burnt offerings according to the number of them all; for Jōb said, "It may be that my children have sinned, and cursed God in their hearts." This is what Jōb always did.

Attack on Job's Character

6 One day the heavenly beings[a] came to present themselves before the LORD, and Satan[b] also came among them. ⁷ The LORD said to Satan,[b] "Where have you come from?" Satan[b] answered the LORD, "From going to and fro on the earth, and from walking up and down on it." ⁸ The LORD said to Satan,[b] "Have you considered my servant Jōb? There is no one like him on the earth, a blameless and upright man who fears God and turns away from evil." ⁹ Then Satan[b] answered the LORD, "Does Jōb fear God for nothing? ¹⁰ Have you not put a fence around him and his house and all that he has, on every side? You have blessed the work of his hands, and his possessions have increased in the land. ¹¹ But stretch out your hand now, and touch all that he has, and he will curse you to your face." ¹² The LORD said to Satan,[b] "Very well, all that he has is in your power; only do not stretch out your hand against him!" So Satan[b] went out from the presence of the LORD.

Job Loses Property and Children

13 One day when his sons and daughters were eating and drinking wine in the eldest brother's house, ¹⁴ a messenger came to Jōb and said, "The oxen were plowing and the donkeys were feeding beside them, ¹⁵ and the Sa·bē'ans fell on them and carried them off, and killed the servants with the edge of the sword; I alone have escaped to tell you." ¹⁶ While he was still speaking, another came and said, "The fire of God fell from heaven and burned up the sheep and the servants, and consumed them; I alone have escaped to tell you." ¹⁷ While he was still speaking, another came and said, "The Chal·dē'ans formed three columns, made a raid on the camels and carried them off, and killed the servants with the edge of the sword; I alone have escaped to tell you." ¹⁸ While he was still speaking, another came and said, "Your sons and daughters were eating and drinking wine in their eldest brother's house, ¹⁹ and suddenly a great wind came across the desert, struck the four

a Heb *sons of God*   b Or *the Accuser*; Heb *ha-satan*

569

In Good Times and Bad

Have you ever felt so angry at the loss of something that you cursed and swore at God? Have you ever felt like just giving up on God because of your loss? In Job 1.13–19, a man named Job experiences an unimaginable loss. His children, his home, and his property are all destroyed at the same time. Job responds with great anger and great pain, but instead of cursing or blaming God, he blesses (praises) God (verse 21).

Job never loses his faith in God, even when he loses so much else. Through most of the rest of this book, he struggles to understand why this has happened to him. Job is an important model. When faced with great suffering, he does not lose his belief in the goodness of God, nor does he let his friends talk him into false confessions of sinfulness. Like Job, we must not fall into the trap of thinking that when bad things happen, God is punishing us.

▶ Job 1.13–21

corners of the house, and it fell on the young people, and they are dead; I alone have escaped to tell you."

20 Then Jōb arose, tore his robe, shaved his head, and fell on the ground and worshiped. 21 He said, "Naked I came from my mother's womb, and naked shall I return there; the LORD gave, and the LORD has taken away; blessed be the name of the LORD."

22 In all this Jōb did not sin or charge God with wrongdoing.

Attack on Job's Health

One day the heavenly beings*c* came to present themselves before the LORD, and Satan*d* also came among them to present himself before the LORD. 2 The LORD said to Satan,*d* "Where have you come from?" Satan*d* answered the LORD, "From going to and fro on the earth, and from walking up and down on it." 3 The LORD said to Satan,*d* "Have you considered my servant Jōb? There is no one like

---

c Heb *sons of God*   *d* Or *the Accuser;* Heb *ha-satan*

Introducing ▶ SATAN

Does the word Satan conjure for you an image of a demon with horns and a tail, torturing people in the fires of hell? or perhaps an evil presence wandering the world looking for souls to corrupt? Does it surprise you that Job 6.1 and Zech 3.1 present Satan as actually working for God? In fact, the word Satan is more of a job description than a name; it means "adversary." In the Old Testament, Satan is depicted as a member of God's court whose responsibility it was to accuse or test humans before God. (Although, contrary to popular belief, the snake in the Garden of Eden is never identified as Satan in the Bible!)

It is only much later that Satan is seen as the enemy of God and the controller of the forces of evil. The notion of Satan as an evildoer seems to have been borrowed from a similar figure in Persian religion and developed in Israel as time passed. By the New Testament period, Satan is identified as a powerful agent of evil fighting against God (1 Thess 2.18), is instrumental in Jesus' death (Lk 22.3), tempts people to sin (1 Cor 7.5), and is called the devil (Rev 12.9). The good news is that in the death and Resurrection of Jesus, God overcomes the evil associated with Satan, both now and forever.

▶ Job 1.6—2.10

him on the earth, a blameless and upright man who fears God and turns away from evil. He still persists in his integrity, although you incited me against him, to destroy him for no reason." 4 Then Satan*e* answered the LORD, "Skin for skin! All that people have they will give to save their lives.*f* 5 But stretch out your hand now and touch his bone and his flesh, and he will curse you to your face." 6 The LORD said to Satan,*e* "Very well, he is in your power; only spare his life."

7 So Satan*e* went out from the presence of the LORD, and inflicted loathsome sores on Jōb from the sole of his foot to the crown of his head. 8 Jōb*g* took a potsherd with which to scrape himself, and sat among the ashes.

9 Then his wife said to him, "Do you still persist in your integrity? Curse*h* God, and die." 10 But he said to her, "You speak as any foolish woman would speak. Shall we receive the good at the hand of God, and not receive the bad?" In all this Jōb did not sin with his lips.

Job's Three Friends

11 Now when Jōb's three friends heard of all these troubles that had come upon him, each of them set out from his home—E•li′phaz the Tē′-man•ite, Bil′dad the Shū′hīte, and Zō′phar the Nā′-a•ma•thīte. They met together to go and console and comfort him. 12 When they saw him from a distance, they did not recognize him, and they raised their voices and wept aloud; they tore their robes and threw dust in the air upon their heads. 13 They sat with him on the ground seven days and seven nights, and no one spoke a word to him, for they saw that his suffering was very great.

Job Curses the Day He Was Born

After this Jōb opened his mouth and cursed the day of his birth. 2 Jōb said:
3 "Let the day perish in which I was born,
   and the night that said,
   'A man-child is conceived.'
4 Let that day be darkness!
   May God above not seek it,
   or light shine on it.
5 Let gloom and deep darkness claim it.
   Let clouds settle upon it;
   let the blackness of the day terrify it.
6 That night—let thick darkness seize it!
   let it not rejoice among the days of the year;
   let it not come into the number of the months.
7 Yes, let that night be barren;
   let no joyful cry be heard*i* in it.
8 Let those curse it who curse the Sea,*j*
   those who are skilled to rouse up Le•vī′a•than.
9 Let the stars of its dawn be dark;
   let it hope for light, but have none;
   may it not see the eyelids of the morning—
10 because it did not shut the doors of my mother's womb,
   and hide trouble from my eyes.

e Or *the Accuser;* Heb *ha-satan*   *f* Or *All that the man has he will give for his life*   *g* Heb *He*   *h* Heb *Bless*   *i* Heb *come*   *j* Cn: Heb *day*

Being There · LIVE IT!

What is the best way to respond to the suffering of another? Many of us shy away from funerals and hospitals because we just don't know what to say or how to act. In Job 2.11–13, Job was visited by three friends. They did not recognize him at first because of his great suffering; then they cried. And then something remarkable happened: "They sat with him on the ground seven days and seven nights, and no one spoke a word to him, for they saw that his suffering was very great."

We must give Job's friends credit for being there, for spending time with him, and for letting him know they cared, especially when they first arrived. That is all we have to do for a friend who is hurting—offer a hug and a simple "I'm sorry," and then just stay around. Though this sounds easy, it can be very hard; we can feel so helpless. We need to keep in mind that what matters most is that we are there. That is what will be remembered.

If you know people are suffering or grieving, don't avoid them. Go up to them, let them know how you feel, and just be there for them. That is all. And that is a lot.

▸ Job 2.11–13

11 "Why did I not die at birth,
  come forth from the womb and expire?
12 Why were there knees to receive me,
  or breasts for me to suck?
13 Now I would be lying down and quiet;
  I would be asleep; then I would be at rest
14 with kings and counselors of the earth
  who rebuild ruins for themselves,
15 or with princes who have gold,
  who fill their houses with silver.
16 Or why was I not buried like a stillborn
    child,
  like an infant that never sees the light?
17 There the wicked cease from troubling,
  and there the weary are at rest.
18 There the prisoners are at ease together;
  they do not hear the voice of the
    taskmaster.
19 The small and the great are there,
  and the slaves are free from their masters.

20 "Why is light given to one in misery,
  and life to the bitter in soul,
21 who long for death, but it does not come,
  and dig for it more than for hidden
    treasures;
22 who rejoice exceedingly,
  and are glad when they find the grave?
23 Why is light given to one who cannot see
    the way,
  whom God has fenced in?
24 For my sighing comes like^k my bread,
  and my groanings are poured out like
    water.
25 Truly the thing that I fear comes
    upon me,
  and what I dread befalls me.
26 I am not at ease, nor am I quiet;
  I have no rest; but trouble comes."

Eliphaz Speaks: Job Has Sinned

Then E·li′phaz the Te′man·ite answered:
2 "If one ventures a word with you, will you
    be offended?
  But who can keep from speaking?
3 See, you have instructed many;
  you have strengthened the weak hands.
4 Your words have supported those who were
    stumbling,
  and you have made firm the feeble knees.
5 But now it has come to you, and you are
    impatient;
  it touches you, and you are dismayed.
6 Is not your fear of God your confidence,
  and the integrity of your ways your hope?

7 "Think now, who that was innocent ever
    perished?
  Or where were the upright cut off?
8 As I have seen, those who plow iniquity
  and sow trouble reap the same.
9 By the breath of God they perish,
  and by the blast of his anger they are
    consumed.
10 The roar of the lion, the voice of the fierce
    lion,
  and the teeth of the young lions are
    broken.
11 The strong lion perishes for lack of prey,
  and the whelps of the lioness are
    scattered.

12 "Now a word came stealing to me,
  my ear received the whisper of it.
13 Amid thoughts from visions of the night,
  when deep sleep falls on mortals,
14 dread came upon me, and trembling,
  which made all my bones shake.
15 A spirit glided past my face;
  the hair of my flesh bristled.
16 It stood still,
  but I could not discern its appearance.
  A form was before my eyes;
  there was silence, then I heard a voice:
17 'Can mortals be righteous before^l God?
  Can human beings be pure before^l their
    Maker?
18 Even in his servants he puts no trust,
  and his angels he charges with error;
19 how much more those who live in houses
    of clay,
  whose foundation is in the dust,
  who are crushed like a moth.
20 Between morning and evening they are
    destroyed;
  they perish forever without any
    regarding it.
21 Their tent-cord is plucked up within them,
  and they die devoid of wisdom.'

Job Is Corrected by God

"Call now; is there anyone who will
    answer you?
To which of the holy ones will you turn?
2 Surely vexation kills the fool,
  and jealousy slays the simple.
3 I have seen fools taking root,
  but suddenly I cursed their dwelling.

---

^k Heb *before*   ^l Or *more than*

4 Their children are far from safety,
  they are crushed in the gate,
  and there is no one to deliver them.
5 The hungry eat their harvest,
  and they take it even out of the thorns;[m]
  and the thirsty[n] pant after their wealth.
6 For misery does not come from the earth,
  nor does trouble sprout from the ground;
7 but human beings are born to trouble
  just as sparks[o] fly upward.

8 "As for me, I would seek God,
  and to God I would commit my cause.
9 He does great things and unsearchable,
  marvelous things without number.
10 He gives rain on the earth
  and sends waters on the fields;
11 he sets on high those who are lowly,
  and those who mourn are lifted to safety.
12 He frustrates the devices of the crafty,
  so that their hands achieve no success.
13 He takes the wise in their own craftiness;
  and the schemes of the wily are brought
  to a quick end.
14 They meet with darkness in the daytime,
  and grope at noonday as in the night.
15 But he saves the needy from the sword of
  their mouth,
  from the hand of the mighty.
16 So the poor have hope,
  and injustice shuts its mouth.

17 "How happy is the one whom God
  reproves;
  therefore do not despise the discipline of
  the Almighty.[p]
18 For he wounds, but he binds up;
  he strikes, but his hands heal.
19 He will deliver you from six troubles;
  in seven no harm shall touch you.
20 In famine he will redeem you from death,
  and in war from the power of the sword.
21 You shall be hidden from the scourge of the
  tongue,
  and shall not fear destruction when it
  comes.
22 At destruction and famine you shall laugh,
  and shall not fear the wild animals of the
  earth.
23 For you shall be in league with the stones
  of the field,
  and the wild animals shall be at peace
  with you.
24 You shall know that your tent is safe,
  you shall inspect your fold and miss
  nothing.

25 You shall know that your descendants will
  be many,
  and your offspring like the grass of the
  earth.
26 You shall come to your grave in ripe old age,
  as a shock of grain comes up to the
  threshing floor in its season.
27 See, we have searched this out; it is true.
  Hear, and know it for yourself."

Job Replies: My Complaint Is Just

Then Job answered:
2 "O that my vexation were weighed,
  and all my calamity laid in the balances!
3 For then it would be heavier than the sand
  of the sea;
  therefore my words have been rash.
4 For the arrows of the Almighty[p] are in me;
  my spirit drinks their poison;
  the terrors of God are arrayed against me.
5 Does the wild ass bray over its grass,
  or the ox low over its fodder?
6 Can that which is tasteless be eaten without
  salt,
  or is there any flavor in the juice of
  mallows?[m]
7 My appetite refuses to touch them;
  they are like food that is loathsome
  to me.[m]

8 "O that I might have my request,
  and that God would grant my desire;
9 that it would please God to crush me,
  that he would let loose his hand and cut
  me off!
10 This would be my consolation;
  I would even exult[m] in unrelenting pain;
  for I have not denied the words of the
  Holy One.
11 What is my strength, that I should wait?
  And what is my end, that I should be
  patient?
12 Is my strength the strength of stones,
  or is my flesh bronze?
13 In truth I have no help in me,
  and any resource is driven from me.

14 "Those who withhold[q] kindness from a
  friend
  forsake the fear of the Almighty.[p]
15 My companions are treacherous like a
  torrent-bed,
  like freshets that pass away,

---

m Meaning of Heb uncertain   n Aquila Symmachus Syr
Vg: Heb *snare*   o Or *birds*; Heb *sons of Resheph*
p Traditional rendering of Heb *Shaddai*   q Syr Vg
Compare Tg: Meaning of Heb uncertain

JOB

16   that run dark with ice,
        turbid with melting snow.
17   In time of heat they disappear;
        when it is hot, they vanish from their
            place.
18   The caravans turn aside from their course;
        they go up into the waste, and perish.
19   The caravans of Tē′ma look,
        the travelers of Shē′ba hope.
20   They are disappointed because they were
            confident;
        they come there and are confounded.

PRAY IT!

Suffering

Job's words in Job, chapter 7, are almost
a prayer describing his suffering and
asking, Why me? Job isn't worried about
being polite; he says it like it is. What can
you learn from Job about prayer during
suffering?

   First, you need to be honest with God
and yourself. If you are hurt or in pain,
don't play games with God. Tell God what
you are feeling in your own words. Write
it down in a journal if you want to. And be
honest. Because if you aren't honest with
God, you probably aren't being honest
with yourself.

   Second, let all your feelings out, just
like Job did—including your anger. God is
big enough to handle it. When you suppress your negative feelings, they may
come out in unhealthy ways. So, let God
help you deal with them.

   Finally, let your prayer lead you to
take some action. Job debated with his
friends. That's probably how people did
counseling back then! Your prayer to God
for help might lead you to a counselor, a
minister, or a support group. God works
in many ways.

▶ Job 7.1–21

21   Such you have now become to me;[r]
        you see my calamity, and are afraid.
22   Have I said, 'Make me a gift'?
        Or, 'From your wealth offer a bribe
            for me'?

23   Or, 'Save me from an opponent's hand'?
        Or, 'Ransom me from the hand of
            oppressors'?
24   "Teach me, and I will be silent;
        make me understand how I have gone
            wrong.
25   How forceful are honest words!
        But your reproof, what does it reprove?
26   Do you think that you can reprove words,
        as if the speech of the desperate were
            wind?
27   You would even cast lots over the orphan,
        and bargain over your friend.

28   "But now, be pleased to look at me;
        for I will not lie to your face.
29   Turn, I pray, let no wrong be done.
        Turn now, my vindication is at stake.
30   Is there any wrong on my tongue?
        Cannot my taste discern calamity?

Job: My Suffering Is without End

"Do not human beings have a hard service
        on earth,
    and are not their days like the days of a
            laborer?
2   Like a slave who longs for the shadow,
        and like laborers who look for their
            wages,
3   so I am allotted months of emptiness,
        and nights of misery are apportioned
            to me.
4   When I lie down I say, 'When shall I rise?'
        But the night is long,
    and I am full of tossing until dawn.
5   My flesh is clothed with worms and dirt;
        my skin hardens, then breaks out again.
6   My days are swifter than a weaver's shuttle,
        and come to their end without hope.[s]

7   "Remember that my life is a breath;
        my eye will never again see good.
8   The eye that beholds me will see me no
            more;
        while your eyes are upon me, I shall be
            gone.
9   As the cloud fades and vanishes,
        so those who go down to Shē′ol do not
            come up;
10   they return no more to their houses,
        nor do their places know them any more.

11   "Therefore I will not restrain my mouth;
        I will speak in the anguish of my spirit;

---

r Cn Compare Gk Syr: Meaning of Heb uncertain
s Or *as the thread runs out*

I will complain in the bitterness of my
soul.

12 Am I the Sea, or the Dragon,
that you set a guard over me?

13 When I say, 'My bed will comfort me,
my couch will ease my complaint,'

14 then you scare me with dreams
and terrify me with visions,

15 so that I would choose strangling
and death rather than this body.

16 I loathe my life; I would not live forever.
Let me alone, for my days are a breath.

17 What are human beings, that you make so
much of them,
that you set your mind on them,

18 visit them every morning,
test them every moment?

19 Will you not look away from me for a
while,
let me alone until I swallow my spittle?

20 If I sin, what do I do to you, you watcher of
humanity?
Why have you made me your target?
Why have I become a burden to you?

21 Why do you not pardon my transgression
and take away my iniquity?
For now I shall lie in the earth;
you will seek me, but I shall not be."

Bildad Speaks: Job Should Repent

Then Bil'dad the Shū'hite answered:

2 "How long will you say these things,
and the words of your mouth be a great
wind?

3 Does God pervert justice?
Or does the Almighty*t* pervert the right?

4 If your children sinned against him,
he delivered them into the power of their
transgression.

5 If you will seek God
and make supplication to the Almighty,*t*

6 if you are pure and upright,
surely then he will rouse himself for you
and restore to you your rightful place.

7 Though your beginning was small,
your latter days will be very great.

8 "For inquire now of bygone generations,
and consider what their ancestors have
found;

9 for we are but of yesterday, and we know
nothing,
for our days on earth are but a shadow.

10 Will they not teach you and tell you
and utter words out of their
understanding?

11 "Can papyrus grow where there is no
marsh?
Can reeds flourish where there is no
water?

12 While yet in flower and not cut down,
they wither before any other plant.

13 Such are the paths of all who forget God;
the hope of the godless shall perish.

14 Their confidence is gossamer,
a spider's house their trust.

15 If one leans against its house, it will not
stand;
if one lays hold of it, it will not endure.

16 The wicked thrive*u* before the sun,
and their shoots spread over the garden.

17 Their roots twine around the stoneheap;
they live among the rocks.*v*

18 If they are destroyed from their place,
then it will deny them, saying, 'I have
never seen you.'

19 See, these are their happy ways,*w*
and out of the earth still others will
spring.

20 "See, God will not reject a blameless
person,
nor take the hand of evildoers.

21 He will yet fill your mouth with laughter,
and your lips with shouts of joy.

22 Those who hate you will be clothed with
shame,
and the tent of the wicked will be no
more."

Job Replies: There Is No Mediator

Then Job answered:

2 "Indeed I know that this is so;
but how can a mortal be just
before God?

3 If one wished to contend with him,
one could not answer him once in a
thousand.

4 He is wise in heart, and mighty in strength
—who has resisted him, and succeeded?—

5 he who removes mountains, and they do
not know it,
when he overturns them in his anger;

6 who shakes the earth out of its place,
and its pillars tremble;

7 who commands the sun, and it does not
rise;
who seals up the stars;

8 who alone stretched out the heavens

---

t Traditional rendering of Heb *Shaddai*   *u* Heb *He thrives*
v Gk Vg: Meaning of Heb uncertain   *w* Meaning of Heb
uncertain

and trampled the waves of the Sea;*

9 who made the Bear and Ō·rī'on,
the Plēi'a·dēs and the chambers of the
south;
10 who does great things beyond
understanding,
and marvelous things without number.
11 Look, he passes by me, and I do not
see him;
he moves on, but I do not perceive him.
12 He snatches away; who can stop him?
Who will say to him, 'What are you
doing?'
13 "God will not turn back his anger;
the helpers of Rā'hab bowed
beneath him.
14 How then can I answer him,
choosing my words with him?
15 Though I am innocent, I cannot
answer him;
I must appeal for mercy to my accuser.*
16 If I summoned him and he answered me,
I do not believe that he would listen to
my voice.
17 For he crushes me with a tempest,
and multiplies my wounds without cause;
18 he will not let me get my breath,
but fills me with bitterness.
19 If it is a contest of strength, he is the
strong one!
If it is a matter of justice, who can
summon him?*
20 Though I am innocent, my own mouth
would condemn me;
though I am blameless, he would prove
me perverse.
21 I am blameless; I do not know myself;
I loathe my life.
22 It is all one; therefore I say,
he destroys both the blameless and the
wicked.
23 When disaster brings sudden death,
he mocks at the calamity* of the
innocent.
24 The earth is given into the hand of the
wicked;
he covers the eyes of its judges—
if it is not he, who then is it?
25 "My days are swifter than a runner;
they flee away, they see no good.
26 They go by like skiffs of reed,
like an eagle swooping on the prey.
27 If I say, 'I will forget my complaint;
I will put off my sad countenance and be
of good cheer,'

28 I become afraid of all my suffering,
for I know you will not hold me
innocent.
29 I shall be condemned;
why then do I labor in vain?
30 If I wash myself with soap
and cleanse my hands with lye,
31 yet you will plunge me into filth,
and my own clothes will abhor me.
32 For he is not a mortal, as I am, that I might
answer him,
that we should come to trial together.
33 There is no umpire* between us,
who might lay his hand on us both.
34 If he would take his rod away from me,
and not let dread of him terrify me,
35 then I would speak without fear of him,
for I know I am not what I am thought
to be.*

Job: I Loathe My Life

10 "I loathe my life;
I will give free utterance to my
complaint;
I will speak in the bitterness of my soul.
2 I will say to God, Do not condemn me;
let me know why you contend
against me.
3 Does it seem good to you to oppress,
to despise the work of your hands
and favor the schemes of the wicked?
4 Do you have eyes of flesh?
Do you see as humans see?
5 Are your days like the days of mortals,
or your years like human years,
6 that you seek out my iniquity
and search for my sin,
7 although you know that I am not guilty,
and there is no one to deliver out of your
hand?
8 Your hands fashioned and made me;
and now you turn and destroy me.*
9 Remember that you fashioned me like clay;
and will you turn me to dust again?
10 Did you not pour me out like milk
and curdle me like cheese?
11 You clothed me with skin and flesh,
and knit me together with bones and
sinews.
12 You have granted me life and steadfast love,
and your care has preserved my spirit.

---

x Or *trampled the back of the sea dragon*   *y* Or *for my right*
z Compare Gk: Heb *me*   *a* Meaning of Heb uncertain
b Another reading is *Would that there were an umpire*
c Cn: Heb *for I am not so in myself*   *d* Cn Compare Gk
Syr: Heb *made me together all around, and you destroy me*

13 Yet these things you hid in your heart;
    I know that this was your purpose.
14 If I sin, you watch me,
    and do not acquit me of my iniquity.
15 If I am wicked, woe to me!
    If I am righteous, I cannot lift up my
        head,
    for I am filled with disgrace
    and look upon my affliction.
16 Bold as a lion you hunt me;
    you repeat your exploits against me.
17 You renew your witnesses against me,
    and increase your vexation toward me;
    you bring fresh troops against me.[e]
18 "Why did you bring me forth from the
        womb?
    Would that I had died before any eye
        had seen me,
19 and were as though I had not been,
    carried from the womb to the grave.
20 Are not the days of my life few?[f]
    Let me alone, that I may find a little
        comfort[g]
21 before I go, never to return,
    to the land of gloom and deep darkness,
22 the land of gloom[h] and chaos,
    where light is like darkness."

Zophar Speaks: Job's Guilt Deserves Punishment

Then Zō′phar the Nā′a·ma·thīte answered:
2 "Should a multitude of words go
        unanswered,
    and should one full of talk be vindicated?
3 Should your babble put others to silence,
    and when you mock, shall no one
        shame you?
4 For you say, 'My conduct[i] is pure,
    and I am clean in God's[j] sight.'
5 But O that God would speak,
    and open his lips to you,
6 and that he would tell you the secrets of
        wisdom!
    For wisdom is many-sided.[k]
    Know then that God exacts of you less than
        your guilt deserves.

7 "Can you find out the deep things of God?
    Can you find out the limit of the
        Almighty?[l]
8 It is higher than heaven[m]—what can you do?
    Deeper than Shē′ōl—what can you know?
9 Its measure is longer than the earth,
    and broader than the sea.
10 If he passes through, and imprisons,

and assembles for judgment, who can
        hinder him?
11 For he knows those who are worthless;
    when he sees iniquity, will he not
        consider it?
12 But a stupid person will get understanding,
    when a wild ass is born human.[k]

13 "If you direct your heart rightly,
    you will stretch out your hands
        toward him.
14 If iniquity is in your hand, put it far away,
    and do not let wickedness reside in your
        tents.
15 Surely then you will lift up your face
        without blemish;
    you will be secure, and will not fear.
16 You will forget your misery;
    you will remember it as waters that have
        passed away.
17 And your life will be brighter than the
        noonday;
    its darkness will be like the morning.
18 And you will have confidence, because there
        is hope;
    you will be protected[n] and take your rest
        in safety.
19 You will lie down, and no one will make
        you afraid;
    many will entreat your favor.
20 But the eyes of the wicked will fail;
    all way of escape will be lost to them,
    and their hope is to breathe their last."

Job Replies: I Am a Laughingstock

Then Job answered:
2 "No doubt you are the people,
    and wisdom will die with you.
3 But I have understanding as well as you;
    I am not inferior to you.
    Who does not know such things as these?
4 I am a laughingstock to my friends;
    I, who called upon God and he
        answered me,
    a just and blameless man, I am a
        laughingstock.
5 Those at ease have contempt for
        misfortune,[k]

---

[e] Cn Compare Gk: Heb *toward me; changes and a troop are with me*   [f] Cn Compare Gk Syr: Heb *Are not my days few? Let him cease!*   [g] Heb *that I may brighten up a little*   [h] Heb *gloom as darkness, deep darkness*   [i] Gk: Heb *teaching*   [j] Heb *your*   [k] Meaning of Heb uncertain   [l] Traditional rendering of Heb *Shaddai*   [m] Heb *The heights of heaven*   [n] Or *you will look around*

but it is ready for those whose feet are
   unstable.
6 The tents of robbers are at peace,
   and those who provoke God are secure,
   who bring their god in their hands.*o*

7 "But ask the animals, and they will
      teach you;
   the birds of the air, and they will
      tell you;
8 ask the plants of the earth,*p* and they will
      teach you;
   and the fish of the sea will declare
      to you.
9 Who among all these does not know
   that the hand of the LORD has done this?
10 In his hand is the life of every living thing
   and the breath of every human being.
11 Does not the ear test words
   as the palate tastes food?
12 Is wisdom with the aged,
   and understanding in length of days?

13 "With God*q* are wisdom and strength;
   he has counsel and understanding.
14 If he tears down, no one can rebuild;
   if he shuts someone in, no one can
      open up.
15 If he withholds the waters, they dry up;
   if he sends them out, they overwhelm the
      land.
16 With him are strength and wisdom;
   the deceived and the deceiver are his.
17 He leads counselors away stripped,
   and makes fools of judges.
18 He looses the sash of kings,
   and binds a waistcloth on their loins.
19 He leads priests away stripped,
   and overthrows the mighty.
20 He deprives of speech those who are
      trusted,
   and takes away the discernment of the
      elders.
21 He pours contempt on princes,
   and looses the belt of the strong.
22 He uncovers the deeps out of darkness,
   and brings deep darkness to light.
23 He makes nations great, then destroys them;
   he enlarges nations, then leads them
      away.
24 He strips understanding from the leaders*r* of
      the earth,
   and makes them wander in a pathless
      waste.
25 They grope in the dark without light;
   he makes them stagger like a drunkard.

"Look, my eye has seen all this,
   my ear has heard and understood it.
2 What you know, I also know;
   I am not inferior to you.
3 But I would speak to the Almighty,*s*
   and I desire to argue my case with God.
4 As for you, you whitewash with lies;
   all of you are worthless physicians.
5 If you would only keep silent,
   that would be your wisdom!
6 Hear now my reasoning,
   and listen to the pleadings of my lips.
7 Will you speak falsely for God,
   and speak deceitfully for him?
8 Will you show partiality toward him,
   will you plead the case for God?
9 Will it be well with you when he searches
      you out?
   Or can you deceive him, as one person
      deceives another?
10 He will surely rebuke you
   if in secret you show partiality.
11 Will not his majesty terrify you,
   and the dread of him fall upon you?
12 Your maxims are proverbs of ashes,
   your defenses are defenses of clay.

13 "Let me have silence, and I will speak,
   and let come on me what may.
14 I will take my flesh in my teeth,
   and put my life in my hand.*t*
15 See, he will kill me; I have no hope;*u*
   but I will defend my ways to his face.
16 This will be my salvation,
   that the godless shall not come
      before him.
17 Listen carefully to my words,
   and let my declaration be in your ears.
18 I have indeed prepared my case;
   I know that I shall be vindicated.
19 Who is there that will contend with me?
   For then I would be silent and die.

Job's Despondent Prayer

20 Only grant two things to me,
   then I will not hide myself from your
      face:
21 withdraw your hand far from me,
   and do not let dread of you terrify me.
22 Then call, and I will answer;
   or let me speak, and you reply to me.

---

o Or *whom God brought forth by his hand;* Meaning of Heb
uncertain   *p* Or *speak to the earth*   *q* Heb *him*
r Heb adds *of the people*   *s* Traditional rendering of Heb
Shaddai   *t* Gk: Heb *Why should I take . . . in my hand?*
u Or *Though he kill me, yet I will trust in him*

23 How many are my iniquities and my sins?
　　Make me know my transgression and
　　　my sin.
24 Why do you hide your face,
　　and count me as your enemy?
25 Will you frighten a windblown leaf
　　and pursue dry chaff?
26 For you write bitter things against me,
　　and make me reap^v the iniquities of my
　　　youth.
27 You put my feet in the stocks,
　　and watch all my paths;
　　you set a bound to the soles of my feet.
28 One wastes away like a rotten thing,
　　like a garment that is moth-eaten.

14 "A mortal, born of woman, few of days and
　　full of trouble,
2 　comes up like a flower and withers,
　　flees like a shadow and does not last.
3 Do you fix your eyes on such a one?
　　Do you bring me into judgment
　　　with you?
4 Who can bring a clean thing out of an
　　unclean?
　　No one can.
5 Since their days are determined,
　　and the number of their months is
　　　known to you,
　　and you have appointed the bounds that
　　　they cannot pass,
6 look away from them, and desist,^w
　　that they may enjoy, like laborers, their
　　　days.

7 "For there is hope for a tree,
　　if it is cut down, that it will sprout again,
　　and that its shoots will not cease.
8 Though its root grows old in the earth,
　　and its stump dies in the ground,
9 yet at the scent of water it will bud
　　and put forth branches like a young
　　　plant.
10 But mortals die, and are laid low;
　　humans expire, and where are they?
11 As waters fail from a lake,
　　and a river wastes away and dries up,
12 so mortals lie down and do not rise again;
　　until the heavens are no more, they will
　　　not awake
　　or be roused out of their sleep.
13 O that you would hide me in Shĕ′ōl,
　　that you would conceal me until your
　　　wrath is past,
　　that you would appoint me a set time,
　　and remember me!
14 If mortals die, will they live again?

All the days of my service I would wait
　　until my release should come.
15 You would call, and I would answer you;
　　you would long for the work of your
　　　hands.
16 For then you would not^x number my steps,
　　you would not keep watch over my sin;
17 my transgression would be sealed up in
　　a bag,
　　and you would cover over my iniquity.

18 "But the mountain falls and crumbles away,
　　and the rock is removed from its place;
19 the waters wear away the stones;
　　the torrents wash away the soil of the
　　　earth;
　　so you destroy the hope of mortals.
20 You prevail forever against them, and they
　　pass away;
　　you change their countenance, and send
　　　them away.
21 Their children come to honor, and they do
　　not know it;
　　they are brought low, and it goes
　　　unnoticed.
22 They feel only the pain of their own bodies,
　　and mourn only for themselves."

Eliphaz Speaks: Job Undermines Religion

Then E•li′phaz the Te′man•ite answered:
2 "Should the wise answer with windy
　　knowledge,
　　and fill themselves with the east wind?
3 Should they argue in unprofitable talk,
　　or in words with which they can do no
　　　good?
4 But you are doing away with the fear
　　of God,
　　and hindering meditation before God.
5 For your iniquity teaches your mouth,
　　and you choose the tongue of the crafty.
6 Your own mouth condemns you, and not I;
　　your own lips testify against you.

7 "Are you the firstborn of the human race?
　　Were you brought forth before the hills?
8 Have you listened in the council of God?
　　And do you limit wisdom to yourself?
9 What do you know that we do not know?
　　What do you understand that is not clear
　　　to us?
10 The gray-haired and the aged are on our
　　side,

---

v Heb *inherit*　　*w* Cn: Heb *that they may desist*
x Syr: Heb lacks *not*

those older than your father.

11 Are the consolations of God too small
for you,
or the word that deals gently with you?
12 Why does your heart carry you away,
and why do your eyes flash,*y*
13 so that you turn your spirit against God,
and let such words go out of your
mouth?
14 What are mortals, that they can be clean?
Or those born of woman, that they can
be righteous?
15 God puts no trust even in his holy ones,
and the heavens are not clean in his
sight;
16 how much less one who is abominable and
corrupt,
one who drinks iniquity like water!

17 "I will show you; listen to me;
what I have seen I will declare—
18 what sages have told,
and their ancestors have not hidden,
19 to whom alone the land was given,
and no stranger passed among them.
20 The wicked writhe in pain all their days,
through all the years that are laid up for
the ruthless.
21 Terrifying sounds are in their ears;
in prosperity the destroyer will come
upon them.
22 They despair of returning from darkness,
and they are destined for the sword.
23 They wander abroad for bread, saying,
'Where is it?'
They know that a day of darkness is
ready at hand;
24 distress and anguish terrify them;
they prevail against them, like a king
prepared for battle.
25 Because they stretched out their hands
against God,
and bid defiance to the Almighty,*z*
26 running stubbornly against him
with a thick-bossed shield;
27 because they have covered their faces with
their fat,
and gathered fat upon their loins,
28 they will live in desolate cities,
in houses that no one should inhabit,
houses destined to become heaps of
ruins;
29 they will not be rich, and their wealth will
not endure,
nor will they strike root in the earth;*a*
30 they will not escape from darkness;

the flame will dry up their shoots,
and their blossom*b* will be swept away*c*
by the wind.
31 Let them not trust in emptiness, deceiving
themselves;
for emptiness will be their recompense.
32 It will be paid in full before their time,
and their branch will not be green.
33 They will shake off their unripe grape, like
the vine,
and cast off their blossoms, like the olive
tree.
34 For the company of the godless is barren,
and fire consumes the tents of bribery.
35 They conceive mischief and bring forth evil
and their heart prepares deceit."

Job Reaffirms His Innocence

Then Job answered:
2 "I have heard many such things;
miserable comforters are you all.
3 Have windy words no limit?
Or what provokes you that you keep on
talking?
4 I also could talk as you do,
if you were in my place;
I could join words together against you,
and shake my head at you.
5 I could encourage you with my mouth,
and the solace of my lips would assuage
your pain.

6 "If I speak, my pain is not assuaged,
and if I forbear, how much of it
leaves me?
7 Surely now God has worn me out;
he has*d* made desolate all my company.
8 And he has*d* shriveled me up,
which is a witness against me;
my leanness has risen up against me,
and it testifies to my face.
9 He has torn me in his wrath, and hated me;
he has gnashed his teeth at me;
my adversary sharpens his eyes
against me.
10 They have gaped at me with their mouths;
they have struck me insolently on the
cheek;
they mass themselves together
against me.
11 God gives me up to the ungodly,
and casts me into the hands of the
wicked.

---

y Meaning of Heb uncertain   *z* Traditional rendering of
Heb *Shaddai*   *a* Vg: Meaning of Heb uncertain
b Gk: Heb *mouth*   *c* Cn: Heb *will depart*   *d* Heb *you have*

12 I was at ease, and he broke me in two;
　　he seized me by the neck and dashed me
　　　　to pieces;
　　he set me up as his target;
13　　his archers surround me.
　　He slashes open my kidneys, and shows no
　　　　mercy;
　　he pours out my gall on the ground.
14 He bursts upon me again and again;
　　he rushes at me like a warrior.
15 I have sewed sackcloth upon my skin,
　　and have laid my strength in the dust.
16 My face is red with weeping,
　　and deep darkness is on my eyelids,
17 though there is no violence in my hands,
　　and my prayer is pure.

18 "O earth, do not cover my blood;
　　let my outcry find no resting place.
19 Even now, in fact, my witness is in heaven,
　　and he that vouches for me is on high.
20 My friends scorn me;
　　my eye pours out tears to God,
21 that he would maintain the right of a
　　　　mortal with God,
　　as*e* one does for a neighbor.
22 For when a few years have come,
　　I shall go the way from which I shall not
　　　　return.

Job Prays for Relief

My spirit is broken, my days are extinct,
　　the grave is ready for me.
2 Surely there are mockers around me,
　　and my eye dwells on their provocation.

3 "Lay down a pledge for me with yourself;
　　who is there that will give surety for me?
4 Since you have closed their minds to
　　　　understanding,
　　therefore you will not let them triumph.
5 Those who denounce friends for reward—
　　the eyes of their children will fail.

6 "He has made me a byword of the peoples,
　　and I am one before whom people spit.
7 My eye has grown dim from grief,
　　and all my members are like a shadow.
8 The upright are appalled at this,
　　and the innocent stir themselves up
　　　　against the godless.
9 Yet the righteous hold to their way,
　　and they that have clean hands grow
　　　　stronger and stronger.

10 But you, come back now, all of you,
　　and I shall not find a sensible person
　　　　among you.

11 My days are past, my plans are broken off,
　　the desires of my heart.
12 They make night into day;
　　'The light,' they say, 'is near to the
　　　　darkness.'*f*
13 If I look for She′ol as my house,
　　if I spread my couch in darkness,
14 if I say to the Pit, 'You are my father,'
　　and to the worm, 'My mother,' or 'My
　　　　sister,'
15 where then is my hope?
　　Who will see my hope?
16 Will it go down to the bars of She′ol?
　　Shall we descend together into the dust?"

Bildad Speaks: God Punishes
the Wicked

Then Bil′dad the Shu′hite answered:
2 "How long will you hunt for words?
　　Consider, and then we shall speak.
3 Why are we counted as cattle?
　　Why are we stupid in your sight?
4 You who tear yourself in your anger—
　　shall the earth be forsaken because
　　　　of you,
　　or the rock be removed out of its place?

5 "Surely the light of the wicked is put out,
　　and the flame of their fire does not
　　　　shine.
6 The light is dark in their tent,
　　and the lamp above them is put out.
7 Their strong steps are shortened,
　　and their own schemes throw them
　　　　down.
8 For they are thrust into a net by their own
　　　　feet,
　　and they walk into a pitfall.
9 A trap seizes them by the heel;
　　a snare lays hold of them.
10 A rope is hid for them in the ground,
　　a trap for them in the path.
11 Terrors frighten them on every side,
　　and chase them at their heels.
12 Their strength is consumed by hunger,*g*
　　and calamity is ready for their stumbling.
13 By disease their skin is consumed,*h*
　　the firstborn of Death consumes their
　　　　limbs.
14 They are torn from the tent in which they
　　　　trusted,
　　and are brought to the king of terrors.
15 In their tents nothing remains;

---

e Syr Vg Tg: Heb *and*　　*f* Meaning of Heb uncertain
g Or *Disaster is hungry for them*　　*h* Cn: Heb *It consumes the
limbs of his skin*

sulfur is scattered upon their habitations.

16 Their roots dry up beneath,
and their branches wither above.

17 Their memory perishes from the earth,
and they have no name in the street.

18 They are thrust from light into darkness,
and driven out of the world.

19 They have no offspring or descendant
among their people,
and no survivor where they used to live.

20 They of the west are appalled at their fate,
and horror seizes those of the east.

21 Surely such are the dwellings of the
ungodly,
such is the place of those who do not
know God."

Job Replies: I Know That My Redeemer Lives

Then Job answered:

2 "How long will you torment me,
and break me in pieces with words?

3 These ten times you have cast reproach
upon me;
are you not ashamed to wrong me?

4 And even if it is true that I have erred,
my error remains with me.

5 If indeed you magnify yourselves
against me,
and make my humiliation an argument
against me,

6 know then that God has put me in the
wrong,
and closed his net around me.

7 Even when I cry out, 'Violence!' I am not
answered;
I call aloud, but there is no justice.

8 He has walled up my way so that I cannot
pass,
and he has set darkness upon my paths.

9 He has stripped my glory from me,
and taken the crown from my head.

10 He breaks me down on every side, and I am
gone,
he has uprooted my hope like a tree.

11 He has kindled his wrath against me,
and counts me as his adversary.

12 His troops come on together;
they have thrown up siegeworks[i]
against me,
and encamp around my tent.

13 "He has put my family far from me,
and my acquaintances are wholly
estranged from me.

14 My relatives and my close friends have
failed me;

15 the guests in my house have
forgotten me;
my serving girls count me as a stranger;
I have become an alien in their eyes.

16 I call to my servant, but he gives me no
answer;
I must myself plead with him.

17 My breath is repulsive to my wife;
I am loathsome to my own family.

18 Even young children despise me;
when I rise, they talk against me.

19 All my intimate friends abhor me,
and those whom I loved have turned
against me.

20 My bones cling to my skin and to my flesh,
and I have escaped by the skin of my
teeth.

21 Have pity on me, have pity on me, O you
my friends,
for the hand of God has touched me!

22 Why do you, like God, pursue me,
never satisfied with my flesh?

23 "O that my words were written down!
O that they were inscribed in a book!

24 O that with an iron pen and with lead
they were engraved on a rock forever!

25 For I know that my Redeemer[j] lives,
and that at the last he[k] will stand upon
the earth;[l]

26 and after my skin has been thus destroyed,
then in[m] my flesh I shall see God,[n]

27 whom I shall see on my side,[o]
and my eyes shall behold, and not
another.
My heart faints within me!

28 If you say, 'How we will persecute him!'
and, 'The root of the matter is found
in him';

29 be afraid of the sword,
for wrath brings the punishment of the
sword,
so that you may know there is a
judgment."

Zophar Speaks: Wickedness Receives Just Retribution

Then Zō′phar the Nā′a•ma•thīte answered:

2 "Pay attention! My thoughts urge me to
answer,
because of the agitation within me.

3 I hear censure that insults me,

---

i Cn: Heb *their way*   *j* Or *Vindicator*   *k* Or *that he the*
Last   *l* Heb *dust*   *m* Or *without*   *n* Meaning of Heb of
this verse uncertain   *o* Or *for myself*

and a spirit beyond my understanding
answers me.

4 Do you not know this from of old,
ever since mortals were placed on earth,

5 that the exulting of the wicked is short,
and the joy of the godless is but for a
moment?

6 Even though they mount up high as the
heavens,
and their head reaches to the clouds,

7 they will perish forever like their own dung;
those who have seen them will say,
'Where are they?'

8 They will fly away like a dream, and not be
found;
they will be chased away like a vision of
the night.

9 The eye that saw them will see them no
more,
nor will their place behold them any
longer.

10 Their children will seek the favor of the
poor,
and their hands will give back their
wealth.

11 Their bodies, once full of youth,
will lie down in the dust with them.

12 "Though wickedness is sweet in their
mouth,
though they hide it under their tongues,

13 though they are loath to let it go,
and hold it in their mouths,

14 yet their food is turned in their stomachs;
it is the venom of asps within them.

15 They swallow down riches and vomit them
up again;
God casts them out of their bellies.

16 They will suck the poison of asps;
the tongue of a viper will kill them.

17 They will not look on the rivers,
the streams flowing with honey and
curds.

18 They will give back the fruit of their toil,
and will not swallow it down;
from the profit of their trading
they will get no enjoyment.

19 For they have crushed and abandoned the
poor,
they have seized a house that they did
not build.

20 "They knew no quiet in their bellies;
in their greed they let nothing escape.

21 There was nothing left after they had eaten;
therefore their prosperity will not endure.

22 In full sufficiency they will be in distress;

all the force of misery will come upon
them.

23 To fill their belly to the full
God*p* will send his fierce anger into
them,
and rain it upon them as their food.*q*

24 They will flee from an iron weapon;
a bronze arrow will strike them through.

25 It is drawn forth and comes out of their
body,
and the glittering point comes out of
their gall;
terrors come upon them.

26 Utter darkness is laid up for their treasures;
a fire fanned by no one will devour
them;
what is left in their tent will be
consumed.

27 The heavens will reveal their iniquity,
and the earth will rise up against them.

28 The possessions of their house will be
carried away,
dragged off in the day of God's*r* wrath.

29 This is the portion of the wicked from God,
the heritage decreed for them by God."

Job Replies: The Wicked Often Go Unpunished

Then Jōb answered:

2 "Listen carefully to my words,
and let this be your consolation.

3 Bear with me, and I will speak;
then after I have spoken, mock on.

4 As for me, is my complaint addressed to
mortals?
Why should I not be impatient?

5 Look at me, and be appalled,
and lay your hand upon your mouth.

6 When I think of it I am dismayed,
and shuddering seizes my flesh.

7 Why do the wicked live on,
reach old age, and grow mighty in
power?

8 Their children are established in their
presence,
and their offspring before their eyes.

9 Their houses are safe from fear,
and no rod of God is upon them.

10 Their bull breeds without fail;
their cow calves and never miscarries.

11 They send out their little ones like a flock,
and their children dance around.

12 They sing to the tambourine and the lyre,
and rejoice to the sound of the pipe.

---

p Heb *he*   *q* Cn: Meaning of Heb uncertain   *r* Heb *his*

JOB

13 They spend their days in prosperity,
and in peace they go down to Shĕ'ōl.
14 They say to God, 'Leave us alone!
We do not desire to know your ways.
15 What is the Almighty,[s] that we should
serve him?
And what profit do we get if we pray
to him?'
16 Is not their prosperity indeed their own
achievement?[t]
The plans of the wicked are repugnant
to me.

17 "How often is the lamp of the wicked
put out?
How often does calamity come upon
them?
How often does God[u] distribute pains in
his anger?
18 How often are they like straw before the
wind,
and like chaff that the storm carries
away?
19 You say, 'God stores up their iniquity for
their children.'
Let it be paid back to them, so that they
may know it.
20 Let their own eyes see their destruction,
and let them drink of the wrath of the
Almighty.[s]
21 For what do they care for their household
after them,
when the number of their months is
cut off?
22 Will any teach God knowledge,
seeing that he judges those that are on
high?
23 One dies in full prosperity,
being wholly at ease and secure,
24 his loins full of milk
and the marrow of his bones moist.
25 Another dies in bitterness of soul,
never having tasted of good.
26 They lie down alike in the dust,
and the worms cover them.

27 "Oh, I know your thoughts,
and your schemes to wrong me.
28 For you say, 'Where is the house of the
prince?
Where is the tent in which the wicked
lived?'
29 Have you not asked those who travel the
roads,
and do you not accept their testimony,
30 that the wicked are spared in the day of
calamity,

and are rescued in the day of wrath?
31 Who declares their way to their face,
and who repays them for what they have
done?
32 When they are carried to the grave,
a watch is kept over their tomb.
33 The clods of the valley are sweet to them;
everyone will follow after,
and those who went before are
innumerable.
34 How then will you comfort me with empty
nothings?
There is nothing left of your answers but
falsehood."

Eliphaz Speaks: Job's Wickedness Is Great

Then E·li′phaz the Te′man·īte answered:
2 "Can a mortal be of use to God?
Can even the wisest be of service to him?
3 Is it any pleasure to the Almighty[s] if you
are righteous,
or is it gain to him if you make your
ways blameless?
4 Is it for your piety that he reproves you,
and enters into judgment with you?
5 Is not your wickedness great?
There is no end to your iniquities.
6 For you have exacted pledges from your
family for no reason,
and stripped the naked of their clothing.
7 You have given no water to the weary to
drink,
and you have withheld bread from the
hungry.
8 The powerful possess the land,
and the favored live in it.
9 You have sent widows away empty-handed,
and the arms of the orphans you have
crushed.[v]
10 Therefore snares are around you,
and sudden terror overwhelms you,
11 or darkness so that you cannot see;
a flood of water covers you.

12 "Is not God high in the heavens?
See the highest stars, how lofty they are!
13 Therefore you say, 'What does God know?
Can he judge through the deep darkness?
14 Thick clouds enwrap him, so that he does
not see,
and he walks on the dome of heaven.'
15 Will you keep to the old way
that the wicked have trod?

---

s Traditional rendering of Heb *Shaddai*   t Heb *in their*
hand   u Heb *he*   v Gk Syr Tg Vg: Heb *were crushed*

16 They were snatched away before their time;
    their foundation was washed away by a
        flood.
17 They said to God, 'Leave us alone,'
    and 'What can the Almighty[w] do to us?'[x]
18 Yet he filled their houses with good things—
    but the plans of the wicked are repugnant
        to me.
19 The righteous see it and are glad;
    the innocent laugh them to scorn,
20 saying, 'Surely our adversaries are cut off,
    and what they left, the fire has
        consumed.'

21 "Agree with God,[y] and be at peace;
    in this way good will come to you.
22 Receive instruction from his mouth,
    and lay up his words in your heart.
23 If you return to the Almighty,[w] you will be
        restored,
    if you remove unrighteousness from your
        tents,
24 if you treat gold like dust,
    and gold of O'phir like the stones of the
        torrent-bed,
25 and if the Almighty[w] is your gold
    and your precious silver,
26 then you will delight yourself in the
        Almighty,[w]
    and lift up your face to God.
27 You will pray to him, and he will hear you,
    and you will pay your vows.
28 You will decide on a matter, and it will be
        established for you,
    and light will shine on your ways.
29 When others are humiliated, you say it is
        pride;
    for he saves the humble.
30 He will deliver even those who are guilty;
    they will escape because of the cleanness
        of your hands."[z]

Job Replies: My Complaint Is Bitter

Then Job answered:
2 "Today also my complaint is bitter;[a]
    his[b] hand is heavy despite my groaning.
3 Oh, that I knew where I might find him,
    that I might come even to his dwelling!
4 I would lay my case before him,
    and fill my mouth with arguments.
5 I would learn what he would answer me,
    and understand what he would say
        to me.
6 Would he contend with me in the greatness
        of his power?
    No; but he would give heed to me.

7 There an upright person could reason
        with him,
    and I should be acquitted forever by my
        judge.
8 "If I go forward, he is not there;
    or backward, I cannot perceive him;
9 on the left he hides, and I cannot
        behold him;
    I turn[c] to the right, but I cannot see him.
10 But he knows the way that I take;
    when he has tested me, I shall come out
        like gold.
11 My foot has held fast to his steps;
    I have kept his way and have not turned
        aside.
12 I have not departed from the
        commandment of his lips;
    I have treasured in[d] my bosom the words
        of his mouth.
13 But he stands alone and who can
        dissuade him?
    What he desires, that he does.
14 For he will complete what he appoints
        for me;
    and many such things are in his mind.
15 Therefore I am terrified at his presence;
    when I consider, I am in dread of him.
16 God has made my heart faint;
    the Almighty[w] has terrified me;
17 If only I could vanish in darkness,
    and thick darkness would cover my face![e]

Job Complains of Violence on the Earth

"Why are times not kept by the Almighty,[w]
    and why do those who know him never
        see his days?
2 The wicked[f] remove landmarks;
    they seize flocks and pasture them.
3 They drive away the donkey of the orphan;
    they take the widow's ox for a pledge.
4 They thrust the needy off the road;
    the poor of the earth all hide themselves.
5 Like wild asses in the desert
    they go out to their toil,
scavenging in the wasteland
    food for their young.

---

w Traditional rendering of Heb *Shaddai*   x Gk Syr: Heb
them   y Heb *him*   z Meaning of Heb uncertain
a Syr Vg Tg: Heb *rebellious*   b Gk Syr: Heb *my*   c Syr Vg:
Heb *he turns*   d Gk Vg: Heb *from*   e Or *But I am not
destroyed by the darkness; he has concealed the thick darkness
from me*   f Gk: Heb *they*

6 They reap in a field not their own
    and they glean in the vineyard of the
        wicked.
7 They lie all night naked, without clothing,
    and have no covering in the cold.
8 They are wet with the rain of the mountains,
    and cling to the rock for want of shelter.

9 "There are those who snatch the orphan
        child from the breast,
    and take as a pledge the infant of the
        poor.

did you KNOW?

A Long Debate

Why are Job's friends so insistent that sin and suffering are connected? Why do they go on, chapter after chapter, telling Job that his suffering is a punishment for his sins? The author of the Book of Job uses the debate of Job and his friends to contrast two positions. The position of Job's friends is that God rewards people who are good and punishes those who are wicked: if Job is suffering terribly, then Job must have sinned terribly. Job's repeated denial of sin reveals the second position, which is that sometimes innocent people suffer. This second position is harder to argue because it leaves a huge question: Why?

Because Job has too much integrity to repent for sins he never committed (Job 27.1–6), he keeps searching for another answer. Finally, Job makes an oath of innocence. Such an oath has God as its witness, and if it is false, it requires God to strike down the person who made it. But God appears to Job in an awesome show of power (chapters 38–41) and reminds Job that human intelligence is too limited to comprehend the deeper mysteries of creation. God alone knows why innocent people suffer; Job must trust God's plan.

Read chapters 20–24 to get a sense of the long debate in Job about human suffering. This debate reflects the long history of the Israelites wrestling with this complex question.

10 They go about naked, without clothing;
    though hungry, they carry the sheaves;
11 between their terraces*g* they press out oil;
    they tread the wine presses, but suffer
        thirst.
12 From the city the dying groan,
    and the throat of the wounded cries for
        help;
    yet God pays no attention to their prayer.

13 "There are those who rebel against the light,
    who are not acquainted with its ways,
    and do not stay in its paths.
14 The murderer rises at dusk
    to kill the poor and needy,
    and in the night is like a thief.
15 The eye of the adulterer also waits for the
        twilight,
    saying, 'No eye will see me';
    and he disguises his face.
16 In the dark they dig through houses;
    by day they shut themselves up;
    they do not know the light.
17 For deep darkness is morning to all of them;
    for they are friends with the terrors of
        deep darkness.

18 "Swift are they on the face of the waters;
    their portion in the land is cursed;
    no treader turns toward their vineyards.
19 Drought and heat snatch away the snow
        waters;
    so does She'ōl those who have sinned.
20 The womb forgets them;
    the worm finds them sweet;
    they are no longer remembered;
    so wickedness is broken like a tree.

21 "They harm*h* the childless woman,
    and do no good to the widow.
22 Yet God*i* prolongs the life of the mighty by
        his power;
    they rise up when they despair of life.
23 He gives them security, and they are
        supported;
    his eyes are upon their ways.
24 They are exalted a little while, and then are
        gone;
    they wither and fade like the mallow;*j*
    they are cut off like the heads of grain.
25 If it is not so, who will prove me a liar,
    and show that there is nothing in what
        I say?"

---

g Meaning of Heb uncertain   *h* Gk Tg: Heb *feed on* or
associate with   *i* Heb *he*   *j* Gk: Heb *like all others*

Bildad Speaks: How Can a Mortal Be Righteous Before God?

Then Bil'dad the Shū'hīte answered:

2 "Dominion and fear are with God;[k]
  he makes peace in his high heaven.
3 Is there any number to his armies?
  Upon whom does his light not arise?
4 How then can a mortal be righteous
    before God?
  How can one born of woman be pure?
5 If even the moon is not bright
  and the stars are not pure in his sight,
6 how much less a mortal, who is a maggot,
  and a human being, who is a worm!"

Job Replies: God's Majesty Is Unsearchable

Then Jōb answered:

2 "How you have helped one who has no
    power!
  How you have assisted the arm that has
    no strength!
3 How you have counseled one who has no
    wisdom,
  and given much good advice!
4 With whose help have you uttered words,
  and whose spirit has come forth
    from you?
5 The shades below tremble,
  the waters and their inhabitants.
6 Shē'ōl is naked before God,
  and A•bad'don has no covering.
7 He stretches out Zā'phon[l] over the void,
  and hangs the earth upon nothing.
8 He binds up the waters in his thick clouds,
  and the cloud is not torn open by them.
9 He covers the face of the full moon,
  and spreads over it his cloud.
10 He has described a circle on the face of the
    waters,
  at the boundary between light and
    darkness.
11 The pillars of heaven tremble,
  and are astounded at his rebuke.
12 By his power he stilled the Sea;
  by his understanding he struck down
    Rā'hab.
13 By his wind the heavens were made fair;
  his hand pierced the fleeing serpent.
14 These are indeed but the outskirts of his
    ways;
  and how small a whisper do we hear
    of him!
  But the thunder of his power who can
    understand?"

Job Maintains His Integrity

Jōb again took up his discourse and said:

2 "As God lives, who has taken away my right,
  and the Almighty,[m] who has made my
    soul bitter,
3 as long as my breath is in me
  and the spirit of God is in my nostrils,
4 my lips will not speak falsehood,
  and my tongue will not utter deceit.
5 Far be it from me to say that you are right;
  until I die I will not put away my
    integrity from me.
6 I hold fast my righteousness, and will not
    let it go;
  my heart does not reproach me for any
    of my days.

7 "May my enemy be like the wicked,
  and may my opponent be like the
    unrighteous.
8 For what is the hope of the godless when
    God cuts them off,
  when God takes away their lives?
9 Will God hear their cry
  when trouble comes upon them?
10 Will they take delight in the Almighty?[m]
  Will they call upon God at all times?
11 I will teach you concerning the hand
    of God;
  that which is with the Almighty[m] I will
    not conceal.
12 All of you have seen it yourselves;
  why then have you become altogether
    vain?

13 "This is the portion of the wicked
    with God,
  and the heritage that oppressors receive
    from the Almighty:[m]
14 If their children are multiplied, it is for the
    sword;
  and their offspring have not enough
    to eat.
15 Those who survive them the pestilence
    buries,
  and their widows make no lamentation.
16 Though they heap up silver like dust,
  and pile up clothing like clay—
17 they may pile it up, but the just will wear it,
  and the innocent will divide the silver.
18 They build their houses like nests,
  like booths made by sentinels of the
    vineyard.

---

k Heb *him*   *l* Or *the North*   *m* Traditional rendering of
Heb *Shaddai*

19 They go to bed with wealth, but will do so
　　no more;
　　they open their eyes, and it is gone.
20 Terrors overtake them like a flood;
　　in the night a whirlwind carries them off.
21 The east wind lifts them up and they are
　　gone;
　　it sweeps them out of their place.
22 It[n] hurls at them without pity;
　　they flee from its[o] power in headlong
　　flight.
23 It[n] claps its[o] hands at them,
　　and hisses at them from its[o] place.

Interlude: Where Wisdom Is Found

28 "Surely there is a mine for silver,
　　and a place for gold to be refined.
2 Iron is taken out of the earth,
　　and copper is smelted from ore.
3 Miners put[p] an end to darkness,
　　and search out to the farthest bound
　　the ore in gloom and deep darkness.
4 They open shafts in a valley away from
　　human habitation;
　　they are forgotten by travelers,
　　they sway suspended, remote from
　　people.
5 As for the earth, out of it comes bread;
　　but underneath it is turned up as by fire.
6 Its stones are the place of sapphires,[q]
　　and its dust contains gold.

7 "That path no bird of prey knows,
　　and the falcon's eye has not seen it.
8 The proud wild animals have not trodden it;
　　the lion has not passed over it.

9 "They put their hand to the flinty rock,
　　and overturn mountains by the roots.
10 They cut out channels in the rocks,
　　and their eyes see every precious thing.
11 The sources of the rivers they probe;[r]
　　hidden things they bring to light.

12 "But where shall wisdom be found?
　　And where is the place of understanding?
13 Mortals do not know the way to it,[s]
　　and it is not found in the land of the
　　living.
14 The deep says, 'It is not in me,'
　　and the sea says, 'It is not with me.'
15 It cannot be gotten for gold,
　　and silver cannot be weighed out as its
　　price.
16 It cannot be valued in the gold of O'phir,
　　in precious onyx or sapphire.[q]
17 Gold and glass cannot equal it,

nor can it be exchanged for jewels of fine
　　gold.
18 No mention shall be made of coral or of
　　crystal;
　　the price of wisdom is above pearls.
19 The chrysolite of Ethiopia[t] cannot compare
　　with it,
　　nor can it be valued in pure gold.

20 "Where then does wisdom come from?
　　And where is the place of understanding?
21 It is hidden from the eyes of all living,
　　and concealed from the birds of the air.
22 A•bad'don and Death say,
　　'We have heard a rumor of it with our
　　ears.'

23 "God understands the way to it,
　　and he knows its place.
24 For he looks to the ends of the earth,
　　and sees everything under the heavens.
25 When he gave to the wind its weight,
　　and apportioned out the waters by
　　measure;
26 when he made a decree for the rain,
　　and a way for the thunderbolt;
27 then he saw it and declared it;
　　he established it, and searched it out.
28 And he said to humankind,
　　'Truly, the fear of the Lord, that is wisdom;
　　and to depart from evil is
　　understanding.' "

Job Finishes His Defense

29 Job again took up his discourse and said:
2 "O that I were as in the months of old,
　　as in the days when God watched
　　over me;
3 when his lamp shone over my head,
　　and by his light I walked through
　　darkness;
4 when I was in my prime,
　　when the friendship of God was upon
　　my tent;
5 when the Almighty[u] was still with me,
　　when my children were around me;
6 when my steps were washed with milk,
　　and the rock poured out for me streams
　　of oil!
7 When I went out to the gate of the city,
　　when I took my seat in the square,
8 the young men saw me and withdrew,
　　and the aged rose up and stood;

---

n Or *He* (that is God)　o Or *his*　p Heb *He puts*
q Or *lapis lazuli*　r Gk Vg: Heb *bind*　s Gk: Heb *its price*
t Or *Nubia*; Heb *Cush*　u Traditional rendering of Heb
Shaddai

J O B

9 the nobles refrained from talking,
and laid their hands on their mouths;
10 the voices of princes were hushed,
and their tongues stuck to the roof of
their mouths.
11 When the ear heard, it commended me,
and when the eye saw, it approved;
12 because I delivered the poor who cried,
and the orphan who had no helper.
13 The blessing of the wretched came
upon me,
and I caused the widow's heart to sing
for joy.
14 I put on righteousness, and it clothed me;
my justice was like a robe and a turban.
15 I was eyes to the blind,
and feet to the lame.
16 I was a father to the needy,
and I championed the cause of the
stranger.
17 I broke the fangs of the unrighteous,
and made them drop their prey from
their teeth.
18 Then I thought, 'I shall die in my nest,
and I shall multiply my days like the
phoenix;*v*
19 my roots spread out to the waters,
with the dew all night on my branches;
20 my glory was fresh with me,
and my bow ever new in my hand.'
21 "They listened to me, and waited,
and kept silence for my counsel.
22 After I spoke they did not speak again,
and my word dropped upon them
like dew.*w*
23 They waited for me as for the rain;
they opened their mouths as for the
spring rain.
24 I smiled on them when they had no
confidence;
and the light of my countenance they did
not extinguish.*x*
25 I chose their way, and sat as chief,
and I lived like a king among his troops,
like one who comforts mourners.

30 "But now they make sport of me,
those who are younger than I,
whose fathers I would have disdained
to set with the dogs of my flock.
2 What could I gain from the strength of their
hands?
All their vigor is gone.
3 Through want and hard hunger
they gnaw the dry and desolate ground,
4 they pick mallow and the leaves of bushes,

and to warm themselves the roots of
broom.
5 They are driven out from society;
people shout after them as after a thief.
6 In the gullies of wadis they must live,
in holes in the ground, and in the rocks.
7 Among the bushes they bray;
under the nettles they huddle together.
8 A senseless, disreputable brood,
they have been whipped out of the land.

9 "And now they mock me in song;
I am a byword to them.
10 They abhor me, they keep aloof from me;
they do not hesitate to spit at the sight
of me.
11 Because God has loosed my bowstring and
humbled me,
they have cast off restraint in my
presence.
12 On my right hand the rabble rise up;
they send me sprawling,
and build roads for my ruin.
13 They break up my path,
they promote my calamity;
no one restrains*y* them.
14 As through a wide breach they come;
amid the crash they roll on.
15 Terrors are turned upon me;
my honor is pursued as by the wind,
and my prosperity has passed away like a
cloud.

16 "And now my soul is poured out
within me;
days of affliction have taken hold of me.
17 The night racks my bones,
and the pain that gnaws me takes no rest.
18 With violence he seizes my garment;*z*
he grasps me by*a* the collar of my tunic.
19 He has cast me into the mire,
and I have become like dust and ashes.
20 I cry to you and you do not answer me;
I stand, and you merely look at me.
21 You have turned cruel to me;
with the might of your hand you
persecute me.
22 You lift me up on the wind, you make me
ride on it,
and you toss me about in the roar of the
storm.
23 I know that you will bring me to death,
and to the house appointed for all living.

v Or *like sand*   *w* Heb lacks *like dew*   *x* Meaning of Heb
uncertain   *y* Cn: Heb *helps*   *z* Gk: Heb *my garment is
disfigured*   *a* Heb *like*

24 "Surely one does not turn against the
       needy,*b*
   when in disaster they cry for help.*c*
25 Did I not weep for those whose day was
       hard?
   Was not my soul grieved for the poor?
26 But when I looked for good, evil came;
   and when I waited for light, darkness
       came.
27 My inward parts are in turmoil, and are
       never still;
   days of affliction come to meet me.
28 I go about in sunless gloom;
   I stand up in the assembly and cry for
       help.
29 I am a brother of jackals,
   and a companion of ostriches.
30 My skin turns black and falls from me,
   and my bones burn with heat.
31 My lyre is turned to mourning,
   and my pipe to the voice of those who
       weep.

"I have made a covenant with my eyes;
   how then could I look upon a virgin?
2 What would be my portion from God
       above,
   and my heritage from the Almighty*d* on
       high?
3 Does not calamity befall the unrighteous,
   and disaster the workers of iniquity?
4 Does he not see my ways,
   and number all my steps?

5 "If I have walked with falsehood,
   and my foot has hurried to deceit—
6 let me be weighed in a just balance,
   and let God know my integrity!—
7 if my step has turned aside from the way,
   and my heart has followed my eyes,
   and if any spot has clung to my hands;
8 then let me sow, and another eat;
   and let what grows for me be rooted out.

9 "If my heart has been enticed by a woman,
   and I have lain in wait at my neighbor's
       door;
10 then let my wife grind for another,
   and let other men kneel over her.
11 For that would be a heinous crime;
   that would be a criminal offense;
12 for that would be a fire consuming down to
       A·bad′don,
   and it would burn to the root all my
       harvest.

13 "If I have rejected the cause of my male or
       female slaves,

   when they brought a complaint
       against me;
14 what then shall I do when God rises up?
   When he makes inquiry, what shall I
       answer him?
15 Did not he who made me in the womb
       make them?
   And did not one fashion us in the
       womb?

16 "If I have withheld anything that the poor
       desired,
   or have caused the eyes of the widow to
       fail,
17 or have eaten my morsel alone,
   and the orphan has not eaten from it—
18 for from my youth I reared the orphan*e* like
       a father,
   and from my mother's womb I guided
       the widow*f*—
19 if I have seen anyone perish for lack of
       clothing,
   or a poor person without covering,
20 whose loins have not blessed me,
   and who was not warmed with the fleece
       of my sheep;
21 if I have raised my hand against the orphan,
   because I saw I had supporters at the
       gate;
22 then let my shoulder blade fall from my
       shoulder,
   and let my arm be broken from its
       socket.
23 For I was in terror of calamity from God,
   and I could not have faced his majesty.

24 "If I have made gold my trust,
   or called fine gold my confidence;
25 if I have rejoiced because my wealth was
       great,
   or because my hand had gotten much;
26 if I have looked at the sun*g* when it shone,
   or the moon moving in splendor,
27 and my heart has been secretly enticed,
   and my mouth has kissed my hand;
28 this also would be an iniquity to be
       punished by the judges,
   for I should have been false to God
       above.

29 "If I have rejoiced at the ruin of those who
       hated me,
   or exulted when evil overtook them—
30 I have not let my mouth sin

---

b Heb *ruin*   *c* Cn: Meaning of Heb uncertain
d Traditional rendering of Heb *Shaddai*   *e* Heb *him*
f Heb *her*   *g* Heb *the light*

by asking for their lives with a curse—
31 if those of my tent ever said,
     'O that we might be sated with his
          flesh!'*h*—
32 the stranger has not lodged in the street;
     I have opened my doors to the traveler—
33 if I have concealed my transgressions as
          others do,*i*
     by hiding my iniquity in my bosom,
34 because I stood in great fear of the
          multitude,
     and the contempt of families terrified me,
     so that I kept silence, and did not go out
          of doors—
35 O that I had one to hear me!
     (Here is my signature! Let the Almighty*j*
          answer me!)
     O that I had the indictment written by
          my adversary!
36 Surely I would carry it on my shoulder;
     I would bind it on me like a crown;
37 I would give him an account of all my
          steps;
     like a prince I would approach him.

38 "If my land has cried out against me,
     and its furrows have wept together;
39 if I have eaten its yield without payment,
     and caused the death of its owners;
40 let thorns grow instead of wheat,
     and foul weeds instead of barley."

The words of Jōb are ended.

Elihu Rebukes Job's Friends

So these three men ceased to answer Jōb, because
he was righteous in his own eyes. 2 Then E•lī′hū
son of Bar′a•chel the Būz′īte, of the family of Ram,
became angry. He was angry at Jōb because he justified himself rather than God; 3 he was angry also
at Jōb's three friends because they had found no
answer, though they had declared Jōb to be in the
wrong.*k* 4 Now E•lī′hū had waited to speak to Jōb,
because they were older than he. 5 But when E•lī′hū
saw that there was no answer in the mouths of
these three men, he became angry.

6 E•lī′hū son of Bar′a•chel the Būz′īte answered:
     "I am young in years,
          and you are aged;
     therefore I was timid and afraid
          to declare my opinion to you.
7 I said, 'Let days speak,
     and many years teach wisdom.'
8 But truly it is the spirit in a mortal,
     the breath of the Almighty,*j* that makes
          for understanding.
9 It is not the old*l* that are wise,

nor the aged that understand what is
     right.
10 Therefore I say, 'Listen to me;
     let me also declare my opinion.'

11 "See, I waited for your words,
     I listened for your wise sayings,
     while you searched out what to say.
12 I gave you my attention,
     but there was in fact no one that
          confuted Jōb,
     no one among you that answered his
          words.
13 Yet do not say, 'We have found wisdom;
     God may vanquish him, not a human.'
14 He has not directed his words against me,
     and I will not answer him with your
          speeches.

15 "They are dismayed, they answer no more;
     they have not a word to say.
16 And am I to wait, because they do not speak,
     because they stand there, and answer no
          more?

But truly it is the *spirit* in a mortal, the *breath* of the Almighty; that makes for understanding
32.8

17 I also will give my answer;
     I also will declare my opinion.
18 For I am full of words;
     the spirit within me constrains me.
19 My heart is indeed like wine that has no vent;
     like new wineskins, it is ready to burst.
20 I must speak, so that I may find relief;
     I must open my lips and answer.

---

h Meaning of Heb uncertain   *i* Or *as Adam did*
j Traditional rendering of Heb *Shaddai*   *k* Another
ancient tradition reads *answer, and had put God in the*
wrong   *l* Gk Syr Vg: Heb *many*

J
O
B

21 I will not show partiality to any person
   or use flattery toward anyone.
22 For I do not know how to flatter—
   or my Maker would soon put an end
      to me!

Elihu Rebukes Job

"But now, hear my speech, O Job,
   and listen to all my words.
2 See, I open my mouth;
   the tongue in my mouth speaks.
3 My words declare the uprightness of my
      heart,
   and what my lips know they speak
      sincerely.
4 The spirit of God has made me,
   and the breath of the Almighty[m] gives me
      life.
5 Answer me, if you can;
   set your words in order before me; take
      your stand.
6 See, before God I am as you are;
   I too was formed from a piece of clay.
7 No fear of me need terrify you;
   my pressure will not be heavy on you.

8 "Surely, you have spoken in my hearing,
   and I have heard the sound of your
      words.
9 You say, 'I am clean, without transgression;
   I am pure, and there is no iniquity
      in me.
10 Look, he finds occasions against me,
   he counts me as his enemy;
11 he puts my feet in the stocks,
   and watches all my paths.'

12 "But in this you are not right. I will
      answer you:
   God is greater than any mortal.
13 Why do you contend against him,
   saying, 'He will answer none of my[n]
      words'?
14 For God speaks in one way,
   and in two, though people do not
      perceive it.
15 In a dream, in a vision of the night,
   when deep sleep falls on mortals,
   while they slumber on their beds,
16 then he opens their ears,
   and terrifies them with warnings,
17 that he may turn them aside from their
      deeds,
   and keep them from pride,
18 to spare their souls from the Pit,
   their lives from traversing the River.

19 They are also chastened with pain upon
      their beds,
   and with continual strife in their bones,
20 so that their lives loathe bread,
   and their appetites dainty food.
21 Their flesh is so wasted away that it cannot
      be seen;
   and their bones, once invisible, now
      stick out.
22 Their souls draw near the Pit,
   and their lives to those who bring death.
23 Then, if there should be for one of them an
      angel,
   a mediator, one of a thousand,
   one who declares a person upright,
24 and he is gracious to that person, and says,
   'Deliver him from going down into
      the Pit;
   I have found a ransom;
25 let his flesh become fresh with youth;
   let him return to the days of his youthful
      vigor';
26 then he prays to God, and is accepted
      by him,
   he comes into his presence with joy,
and God[o] repays him for his righteousness.
27   That person sings to others and says,
   'I sinned, and perverted what was right,
   and it was not paid back to me.
28 He has redeemed my soul from going down
      to the Pit,
   and my life shall see the light.'

29 "God indeed does all these things,
   twice, three times, with mortals,
30 to bring back their souls from the Pit,
   so that they may see the light of life.[p]
31 Pay heed, Job, listen to me;
   be silent, and I will speak.
32 If you have anything to say, answer me;
   speak, for I desire to justify you.
33 If not, listen to me;
   be silent, and I will teach you wisdom."

Elihu Proclaims God's Justice

Then E·li´hu continued and said:
2 "Hear my words, you wise men,
   and give ear to me, you who know;
3 for the ear tests words
   as the palate tastes food.
4 Let us choose what is right;
   let us determine among ourselves what is
      good.

---

[m] Traditional rendering of Heb *Shaddai*   [n] Compare Gk:
Heb *his*   [o] Heb *he*   [p] Syr: Heb *to be lighted with the light
of life*

5 For Jōb has said, 'I am innocent,
and God has taken away my right;

6 in spite of being right I am counted a liar;
my wound is incurable, though I am
without transgression.'

7 Who is there like Jōb,
who drinks up scoffing like water,

8 who goes in company with evildoers
and walks with the wicked?

9 For he has said, 'It profits one nothing
to take delight in God.'

10 "Therefore, hear me, you who have sense,
far be it from God that he should do
wickedness,
and from the Almighty*q* that he should
do wrong.

11 For according to their deeds he will repay
them,
and according to their ways he will make
it befall them.

12 Of a truth, God will not do wickedly,
and the Almighty*q* will not pervert
justice.

13 Who gave him charge over the earth
and who laid on him*r* the whole world?

14 If he should take back his spirit*s* to himself,
and gather to himself his breath,

15 all flesh would perish together,
and all mortals return to dust.

16 "If you have understanding, hear this;
listen to what I say.

17 Shall one who hates justice govern?
Will you condemn one who is righteous
and mighty,

18 who says to a king, 'You scoundrel!'
and to princes, 'You wicked men!';

19 who shows no partiality to nobles,
nor regards the rich more than the poor,
for they are all the work of his hands?

20 In a moment they die;
at midnight the people are shaken and
pass away,
and the mighty are taken away by no
human hand.

21 "For his eyes are upon the ways of mortals,
and he sees all their steps.

22 There is no gloom or deep darkness
where evildoers may hide themselves.

23 For he has not appointed a time*t* for
anyone
to go before God in judgment.

24 He shatters the mighty without
investigation,
and sets others in their place.

25 Thus, knowing their works,
he overturns them in the night, and they
are crushed.

26 He strikes them for their wickedness
while others look on,

27 because they turned aside from
following him,
and had no regard for any of his ways,

28 so that they caused the cry of the poor to
come to him,
and he heard the cry of the afflicted—

29 When he is quiet, who can condemn?
When he hides his face, who can
behold him,
whether it be a nation or an individual?—

30 so that the godless should not reign,
or those who ensnare the people.

31 "For has anyone said to God,
'I have endured punishment; I will not
offend any more;

32 teach me what I do not see;
if I have done iniquity, I will do it no
more'?

33 Will he then pay back to suit you,
because you reject it?
For you must choose, and not I;
therefore declare what you know.*u*

34 Those who have sense will say to me,
and the wise who hear me will say,

35 'Jōb speaks without knowledge,
his words are without insight.'

36 Would that Jōb were tried to the limit,
because his answers are those of the
wicked.

37 For he adds rebellion to his sin;
he claps his hands among us,
and multiplies his words against God."

Elihu Condemns Self-Righteousness

E•lī′hū continued and said:

2 "Do you think this to be just?
You say, 'I am in the right before God.'

3 If you ask, 'What advantage have I?
How am I better off than if I had
sinned?'

4 I will answer you
and your friends with you.

5 Look at the heavens and see;
observe the clouds, which are higher
than you.

6 If you have sinned, what do you accomplish
against him?

---

q Traditional rendering of Heb *Shaddai*   *r* Heb lacks *on
him*   *s* Heb *his heart his spirit*   *t* Cn: Heb *yet*
u Meaning of Heb of verses 29-33 uncertain

And if your transgressions are multiplied,
what do you do to him?

7 If you are righteous, what do you give
to him;
or what does he receive from your hand?

8 Your wickedness affects others like you,
and your righteousness, other human
beings.

9 "Because of the multitude of oppressions
people cry out;
they call for help because of the arm of
the mighty.

10 But no one says, 'Where is God my Maker,
who gives strength in the night,

11 who teaches us more than the animals of
the earth,
and makes us wiser than the birds of
the air?'

12 There they cry out, but he does not answer,
because of the pride of evildoers.

13 Surely God does not hear an empty cry,
nor does the Almighty[v] regard it.

14 How much less when you say that you do
not see him,
that the case is before him, and you are
waiting for him!

15 And now, because his anger does not
punish,
and he does not greatly heed
transgression,[w]

16 Jōb opens his mouth in empty talk,
he multiplies words without knowledge."

Elihu Exalts God's Goodness

E•lī′hū continued and said:
2 "Bear with me a little, and I will show you,
for I have yet something to say on God's
behalf.

3 I will bring my knowledge from far away,
and ascribe righteousness to my Maker.

4 For truly my words are not false;
one who is perfect in knowledge is
with you.

5 "Surely God is mighty and does not
despise any;
he is mighty in strength of
understanding.

6 He does not keep the wicked alive,
but gives the afflicted their right.

7 He does not withdraw his eyes from the
righteous,
but with kings on the throne
he sets them forever, and they are
exalted.

8 And if they are bound in fetters

and caught in the cords of affliction,

9 then he declares to them their work
and their transgressions, that they are
behaving arrogantly.

10 He opens their ears to instruction,
and commands that they return from
iniquity.

11 If they listen, and serve him,
they complete their days in prosperity,
and their years in pleasantness.

12 But if they do not listen, they shall perish
by the sword,
and die without knowledge.

13 "The godless in heart cherish anger;
they do not cry for help when he binds
them.

14 They die in their youth,
and their life ends in shame.[x]

15 He delivers the afflicted by their affliction,
and opens their ear by adversity.

16 He also allured you out of distress
into a broad place where there was no
constraint,
and what was set on your table was full
of fatness.

17 "But you are obsessed with the case of the
wicked;
judgment and justice seize you.

18 Beware that wrath does not entice you into
scoffing,
and do not let the greatness of the
ransom turn you aside.

19 Will your cry avail to keep you from
distress,
or will all the force of your strength?

20 Do not long for the night,
when peoples are cut off in their place.

21 Beware! Do not turn to iniquity;
because of that you have been tried by
affliction.

22 See, God is exalted in his power;
who is a teacher like him?

23 Who has prescribed for him his way,
or who can say, 'You have done wrong'?

Elihu Proclaims God's Majesty

24 "Remember to extol his work,
of which mortals have sung.

25 All people have looked on it;
everyone watches it from far away.

---

v Traditional rendering of Heb *Shaddai*   *w* Theodotion
Symmachus Compare Vg: Meaning of Heb uncertain
x Heb *ends among the temple prostitutes*

26 Surely God is great, and we do not
     know him;
   the number of his years is unsearchable.
27 For he draws up the drops of water;
   he distills[y] his mist in rain,
28 which the skies pour down
   and drop upon mortals abundantly.
29 Can anyone understand the spreading of the
     clouds,
   the thunderings of his pavilion?
30 See, he scatters his lightning around him
   and covers the roots of the sea.
31 For by these he governs peoples;
   he gives food in abundance.
32 He covers his hands with the lightning,
   and commands it to strike the mark.
33 Its crashing[z] tells about him;
   he is jealous[z] with anger against iniquity.

"At this also my heart trembles,
   and leaps out of its place.
2 Listen, listen to the thunder of his voice
   and the rumbling that comes from his
     mouth.
3 Under the whole heaven he lets it loose,
   and his lightning to the corners of the
     earth.
4 After it his voice roars;
   he thunders with his majestic voice
   and he does not restrain the lightnings[a]
     when his voice is heard.
5 God thunders wondrously with his voice;
   he does great things that we cannot
     comprehend.
6 For to the snow he says, 'Fall on the earth';
   and the shower of rain, his heavy shower
     of rain,
7 serves as a sign on everyone's hand,
   so that all whom he has made may
     know it.[b]
8 Then the animals go into their lairs
   and remain in their dens.
9 From its chamber comes the whirlwind,
   and cold from the scattering winds.
10 By the breath of God ice is given,
   and the broad waters are frozen fast.
11 He loads the thick cloud with moisture;
   the clouds scatter his lightning.
12 They turn round and round by his guidance,
   to accomplish all that he commands
     them
   on the face of the habitable world.
13 Whether for correction, or for his land,
   or for love, he causes it to happen.

14 "Hear this, O Jōb;
   stop and consider the wondrous works
     of God.
15 Do you know how God lays his command
     upon them,
   and causes the lightning of his cloud to
     shine?
16 Do you know the balancings of the clouds,
   the wondrous works of the one whose
     knowledge is perfect,
17 you whose garments are hot
   when the earth is still because of the
     south wind?
18 Can you, like him, spread out the skies,
   hard as a molten mirror?
19 Teach us what we shall say to him;
   we cannot draw up our case because of
     darkness.
20 Should he be told that I want to speak?
   Did anyone ever wish to be
     swallowed up?
21 Now, no one can look on the light
   when it is bright in the skies,
   when the wind has passed and cleared
     them.
22 Out of the north comes golden splendor;
   around God is awesome majesty.
23 The Almighty[c]—we cannot find him;
   he is great in power and justice,
   and abundant righteousness he will not
     violate.
24 Therefore mortals fear him;
   he does not regard any who are wise in
     their own conceit."

The LORD Answers Job
(Cp Gen 1.1–10)

Then the LORD answered Jōb out of the whirlwind:
2 "Who is this that darkens counsel by words
     without knowledge?
3 Gird up your loins like a man,
   I will question you, and you shall declare
     to me.

4 "Where were you when I laid the
     foundation of the earth?
   Tell me, if you have understanding.
5 Who determined its measurements—surely
     you know!
   Or who stretched the line upon it?
6 On what were its bases sunk,
   or who laid its cornerstone
7 when the morning stars sang together

---

[y] Cn: Heb *they distill*   [z] Meaning of Heb uncertain
[a] Heb *them*   [b] Meaning of Heb of verse 7 uncertain
[c] Traditional rendering of Heb *Shaddai*

J
O
B

and all the heavenly beings[d] shouted
for joy?

8 "Or who shut in the sea with doors
when it burst out from the womb?—
9 when I made the clouds its garment,
and thick darkness its swaddling band,
10 and prescribed bounds for it,
and set bars and doors,
11 and said, 'Thus far shall you come, and no
farther,
and here shall your proud waves be
stopped'?

did you KNOW?

Heaven and Earth

The questions God asks Job about the
formation of the cosmos (Job 38.4–38)
give us a clue about how the ancient Israelites thought the universe was put
together. They believed that God had
created it in three levels: the heavens,
which were contained in a giant vault
above the earth; the earth itself, which
was a disk that rested on the waters of
the abyss; and the abyss, which was the
underworld. Over time, the heavens and
the earth developed symbolic meanings.
The heavens became known as the place
where God dwells and the earth as the
place that humans inhabit. Even later,
the abyss became known as the place of
the dead.

▶ Job 38.4–38

12 "Have you commanded the morning since
your days began,
and caused the dawn to know its place,
13 so that it might take hold of the skirts of
the earth,
and the wicked be shaken out of it?
14 It is changed like clay under the seal,
and it is dyed[e] like a garment.
15 Light is withheld from the wicked,
and their uplifted arm is broken.

16 "Have you entered into the springs of
the sea,
or walked in the recesses of the deep?

17 Have the gates of death been revealed
to you,
or have you seen the gates of deep
darkness?
18 Have you comprehended the expanse of the
earth?
Declare, if you know all this.

19 "Where is the way to the dwelling of light,
and where is the place of darkness,
20 that you may take it to its territory
and that you may discern the paths to its
home?
21 Surely you know, for you were born then,
and the number of your days is great!

22 "Have you entered the storehouses of the
snow,
or have you seen the storehouses of the
hail,
23 which I have reserved for the time of
trouble,
for the day of battle and war?
24 What is the way to the place where the light
is distributed,
or where the east wind is scattered upon
the earth?

25 "Who has cut a channel for the torrents of
rain,
and a way for the thunderbolt,
26 to bring rain on a land where no one lives,
on the desert, which is empty of human
life,
27 to satisfy the waste and desolate land,
and to make the ground put forth grass?

28 "Has the rain a father,
or who has begotten the drops of dew?
29 From whose womb did the ice come forth,
and who has given birth to the hoarfrost
of heaven?
30 The waters become hard like stone,
and the face of the deep is frozen.

31 "Can you bind the chains of the Plēi′a•dēs,
or loose the cords of O•ri′on?
32 Can you lead forth the Maz′za•roth in their
season,
or can you guide the Bear with its
children?
33 Do you know the ordinances of the
heavens?
Can you establish their rule on the earth?

34 "Can you lift up your voice to the clouds,
so that a flood of waters may cover you?

d Heb sons of God   e Cn: Heb and they stand forth

35 Can you send forth lightnings, so that they
        may go
    and say to you, 'Here we are'?
36 Who has put wisdom in the inward parts,*f*
    or given understanding to the mind?*f*
37 Who has the wisdom to number the clouds?
    Or who can tilt the waterskins of the
        heavens,
38 when the dust runs into a mass
    and the clods cling together?

39 "Can you hunt the prey for the lion,
    or satisfy the appetite of the young lions,
40 when they crouch in their dens,
    or lie in wait in their covert?
41 Who provides for the raven its prey,
    when its young ones cry to God,
    and wander about for lack of food?

"Do you know when the mountain goats
        give birth?
    Do you observe the calving of the deer?
2 Can you number the months that they
        fulfill,
    and do you know the time when they
        give birth,
3 when they crouch to give birth to their
        offspring,
    and are delivered of their young?
4 Their young ones become strong, they grow
        up in the open;
    they go forth, and do not return to them.

5 "Who has let the wild ass go free?
    Who has loosed the bonds of the
        swift ass,
6 to which I have given the steppe for its
        home,
    the salt land for its dwelling place?
7 It scorns the tumult of the city;
    it does not hear the shouts of the driver.
8 It ranges the mountains as its pasture,
    and it searches after every green thing.

9 "Is the wild ox willing to serve you?
    Will it spend the night at your crib?
10 Can you tie it in the furrow with ropes,
    or will it harrow the valleys after you?
11 Will you depend on it because its strength is
        great,
    and will you hand over your labor to it?
12 Do you have faith in it that it will return,
    and bring your grain to your threshing
        floor?*g*

13 "The ostrich's wings flap wildly,
    though its pinions lack plumage.*f*
14 For it leaves its eggs to the earth,

and lets them be warmed on the ground,
15 forgetting that a foot may crush them,
    and that a wild animal may trample
        them.
16 It deals cruelly with its young, as if they
        were not its own;
    though its labor should be in vain, yet it
        has no fear;
17 because God has made it forget wisdom,
    and given it no share in understanding.
18 When it spreads its plumes aloft,*f*
    it laughs at the horse and its rider.

19 "Do you give the horse its might?
    Do you clothe its neck with mane?
20 Do you make it leap like the locust?
    Its majestic snorting is terrible.
21 It paws*h* violently, exults mightily;
    it goes out to meet the weapons.
22 It laughs at fear, and is not dismayed;
    it does not turn back from the sword.
23 Upon it rattle the quiver,
    the flashing spear, and the javelin.
24 With fierceness and rage it swallows the
        ground;
    it cannot stand still at the sound of the
        trumpet.
25 When the trumpet sounds, it says 'Aha!'
    From a distance it smells the battle,
    the thunder of the captains, and the
        shouting.

26 "Is it by your wisdom that the hawk soars,
    and spreads its wings toward the south?
27 Is it at your command that the eagle
        mounts up
    and makes its nest on high?
28 It lives on the rock and makes its home
    in the fastness of the rocky crag.
29 From there it spies the prey;
    its eyes see it from far away.
30 Its young ones suck up blood;
    and where the slain are, there it is."

And the LORD said to Jōb:
2 "Shall a faultfinder contend with the
        Almighty?*i*
    Anyone who argues with God must
        respond."

Job's Response to God

3 Then Jōb answered the LORD:
4 "See, I am of small account; what shall I
        answer you?

f Meaning of Heb uncertain   g Heb *your grain and your*
threshing floor   h Gk Syr Vg: Heb *they dig*   i Traditional
rendering of Heb *Shaddai*

I lay my hand on my mouth.

5 I have spoken once, and I will not answer;
twice, but will proceed no further."

PRAY IT?

Too Big to Understand

All the questions God asks Job about
creation and good and evil in Job,
chapters 38–41, are intended to make
one simple point: "You can never understand me. I am too big. You are too
small."

The author of Job seems to be saying to readers, "If you think you've got
God all figured out—like Job's friends
thought they had or like even Job wanted
to have—you're wrong." The author is
reminding readers that God is a mystery
—powerful and awesome beyond our
imagination and control.

In your prayer, reflect or journal on
the following questions:

■ Do you expect God to provide you
with happiness? peace? friends?

■ What happens if God doesn't meet
your expectations in the way you want
them to be met? Can you let go of
your expectations and trust in God's
love? Why or why not?

▶ Job, chapters 38–41

God's Challenge to Job

6 Then the LORD answered Jōb out of the whirlwind:

7 "Gird up your loins like a man;
I will question you, and you declare
to me.

8 Will you even put me in the wrong?
Will you condemn me that you may be
justified?

9 Have you an arm like God,
and can you thunder with a voice
like his?

10 "Deck yourself with majesty and dignity;
clothe yourself with glory and splendor.

11 Pour out the overflowings of your anger,
and look on all who are proud, and
abase them.

12 Look on all who are proud, and bring
them low;
tread down the wicked where they stand.

13 Hide them all in the dust together;
bind their faces in the world below.j

14 Then I will also acknowledge to you
that your own right hand can give you
victory.

15 "Look at Bēʹheʹmoth,
which I made just as I made you;
it eats grass like an ox.

16 Its strength is in its loins,
and its power in the muscles of its belly.

17 It makes its tail stiff like a cedar;
the sinews of its thighs are knit together.

18 Its bones are tubes of bronze,
its limbs like bars of iron.

19 "It is the first of the great acts of God—
only its Maker can approach it with the
sword.

20 For the mountains yield food for it
where all the wild animals play.

21 Under the lotus plants it lies,
in the covert of the reeds and in the
marsh.

22 The lotus trees cover it for shade;
the willows of the wadi surround it.

23 Even if the river is turbulent, it is not
frightened;
it is confident though Jordan rushes
against its mouth.

24 Can one take it with hooksk
or pierce its nose with a snare?

l"Can you draw out Leʹviʹaʹthanm with a
fishhook,
or press down its tongue with a cord?

2 Can you put a rope in its nose,
or pierce its jaw with a hook?

3 Will it make many supplications to you?
Will it speak soft words to you?

4 Will it make a covenant with you
to be taken as your servant forever?

5 Will you play with it as with a bird,
or will you put it on leash for your girls?

6 Will traders bargain over it?
Will they divide it up among the
merchants?

7 Can you fill its skin with harpoons,
or its head with fishing spears?

8 Lay hands on it;
think of the battle; you will not do it
again!

---

j Heb *the hidden place* k Cn: Heb *in his eyes*
l Ch 40.25 in Heb m Or *the crocodile*

^9n Any hope of capturing it^o will be
　　disappointed;
　　were not even the gods^p overwhelmed at
　　　the sight of it?
10 No one is so fierce as to dare to stir it up.
　　Who can stand before it?^{q}
11 Who can confront it^q and be safe?^{r}
　　—under the whole heaven, who?^{s}

12 "I will not keep silence concerning its
　　　limbs,
　　or its mighty strength, or its splendid
　　　frame.
13 Who can strip off its outer garment?
　　Who can penetrate its double coat of
　　　mail?^{t}
14 Who can open the doors of its face?
　　There is terror all around its teeth.
15 Its back^u is made of shields in rows,
　　shut up closely as with a seal.
16 One is so near to another
　　that no air can come between them.
17 They are joined one to another;
　　they clasp each other and cannot be
　　　separated.
18 Its sneezes flash forth light,
　　and its eyes are like the eyelids of the
　　　dawn.
19 From its mouth go flaming torches;
　　sparks of fire leap out.
20 Out of its nostrils comes smoke,
　　as from a boiling pot and burning rushes.
21 Its breath kindles coals,
　　and a flame comes out of its mouth.
22 In its neck abides strength,
　　and terror dances before it.
23 The folds of its flesh cling together;
　　it is firmly cast and immovable.
24 Its heart is as hard as stone,
　　as hard as the lower millstone.
25 When it raises itself up the gods are afraid;
　　at the crashing they are beside
　　　themselves.
26 Though the sword reaches it, it does not
　　　avail,
　　nor does the spear, the dart, or the
　　　javelin.
27 It counts iron as straw,
　　and bronze as rotten wood.
28 The arrow cannot make it flee;
　　slingstones, for it, are turned to chaff.
29 Clubs are counted as chaff;
　　it laughs at the rattle of javelins.
30 Its underparts are like sharp potsherds;
　　it spreads itself like a threshing sledge on
　　　the mire.

31 It makes the deep boil like a pot;
　　it makes the sea like a pot of ointment.
32 It leaves a shining wake behind it;
　　one would think the deep to be
　　　white-haired.
33 On earth it has no equal,
　　a creature without fear.
34 It surveys everything that is lofty;
　　it is king over all that are proud."

Job Is Humbled and Satisfied

Then Jōb answered the LORD:
2 "I know that you can do all things,
　　and that no purpose of yours can be
　　　thwarted.
3 'Who is this that hides counsel without
　　　knowledge?'
　　Therefore I have uttered what I did not
　　　understand,
　　things too wonderful for me, which I did
　　　not know.
4 'Hear, and I will speak;
　　I will question you, and you declare
　　　to me.'
5 I had heard of you by the hearing of
　　　the ear,
　　but now my eye sees you;
6 therefore I despise myself,
　　and repent in dust and ashes."

Job's Friends Are Humiliated

7 After the LORD had spoken these words to
Jōb, the LORD said to E·lī'phaz the Tē'man·ite: "My
wrath is kindled against you and against your two
friends; for you have not spoken of me what is
right, as my servant Jōb has. 8 Now therefore take
seven bulls and seven rams, and go to my servant
Jōb, and offer up for yourselves a burnt offering;
and my servant Jōb shall pray for you, for I will
accept his prayer not to deal with you according to
your folly; for you have not spoken of me what is
right, as my servant Jōb has done." 9 So E·lī'phaz the
Tē'man·ite and Bil'dad the Shū'hīte and Zō'phar
the Nā'a·ma·thīte went and did what the LORD had
told them; and the LORD accepted Jōb's prayer.

Job's Fortunes Are Restored Twofold

10 And the LORD restored the fortunes of Jōb
when he had prayed for his friends; and the LORD
gave Jōb twice as much as he had before. 11 Then
there came to him all his brothers and sisters and
all who had known him before, and they ate bread

---

^{n} Ch 41.1 in Heb　^{o} Heb *of it*　^{p} Cn Compare
Symmachus Syr: Heb *one is*　^{q} Heb *me*　^{r} Gk: Heb *that
I shall repay*　^{s} Heb *to me*　^{t} Gk: Heb *bridle*
^{u} Cn Compare Gk Vg: Heb *pride*

Why?

So, that's it? God just shows up, overwhelms Job with a bunch of questions he can't answer, and then gives Job back double everything he lost? God doesn't even answer Job's question about why he had to suffer!

And what about *our* questions? Why do innocent children die? Why is someone we love taken from us? Why do people die from hunger in a world that has so much? Why did that plane crash? Why did our friend die?

Why was Job satisfied with God's response? Perhaps Job's mind and his heart struggled with God's answer, and his heart won. Maybe his heart told him to trust in God's love even when his mind couldn't understand the mystery of his suffering.

With Job, the Israelite people began to see the suffering of innocent people as mystery and not as punishment. In the New Testament, this suffering would continue to be seen as mystery but also as something more. The death of Jesus—the ultimate innocent suffering person—and his Resurrection led to the understanding that God ultimately brings good out of the suffering of faithful people (see Jn 12.24–25 and the introduction to 1 Peter).

▶ Job 38.1—42.6

with him in his house; they showed him sympathy and comforted him for all the evil that the LORD had brought upon him; and each of them gave him a piece of money*v* and a gold ring. ¹²The LORD blessed the latter days of Jōb more than his beginning; and he had fourteen thousand sheep, six thousand camels, a thousand yoke of oxen, and a thousand donkeys. ¹³He also had seven sons and three daughters. ¹⁴He named the first Je•mī′mah,

the second Ke•zī′ah, and the third Ker′en-hap′-puch. ¹⁵In all the land there were no women so beautiful as Jōb's daughters; and their father gave them an inheritance along with their brothers. ¹⁶After this Jōb lived one hundred and forty years, and saw his children, and his children's children, four generations. ¹⁷And Jōb died, old and full of days.

---

v Heb *a qesitah*

Rock! Pop! Salsa! Rhythm and blues! Hip-hop! Rap! Jazz! Country! Alternative! We each have our own favorite music that somehow resonates with our being, and maybe even expresses our attitude and philosophy toward life. So much so that we often refer to it as *our* music, even though it was written by someone else. In the same way, we can say that the Psalms are Israel's music. They are the hymns or songs that Israel used in its Temple worship. They give voice to the souls of the Israelites and tell about the ups and downs of the Israelites' relationship with God.

At a Glance

Psalms is divided into five books without any particular organizing theme:

- **Psalms 1–41.** Book I
- **Psalms 42–72.** Book II
- **Psalms 73–89.** Book III
- **Psalms 90–106.** Book IV
- **Psalms 107–150.** Book V

In-depth

The Hebrew version of Psalms is titled Tehillim, or Praises, because its hymns praise God. The Greek translation calls them Psalmoi, or Psalms, which means "religious songs performed to music." The 150 Psalms can be grouped into one or more of five general categories:

- The *hymns of praise and thanksgiving* sing of God's majesty, power, and wisdom (for example, Psalms 8, 24, 47, 93, 95–99, 113–118, 136, and 150).
- The *hymns of lament or petition* include both individual and communal cries to God for help in some need (for example, Psalms 38, 51, 55, 58, 59, 74, 78, 105, and 106).
- The *hymns of wisdom* sing of Israel's insights into how to live according to God's law and what brings true happiness (for example, Psalms 1, 34, 37, 49, 73, 112, and 128).
- The *liturgical or worship psalms* are used for entrance hymns at liturgies or during worship services at the Temple (for example, Psalms 15, 24, and 134).
- The *historical psalms* sing of the great wonders God has worked throughout the history of Israel (for example, Psalms 78, 105, 106, 135, and 136).

Quick Facts

Authors
many, sometimes called psalmists

Themes
a variety

Of Note
The psalms are used by Catholic Christians regularly at Mass and in the church's official prayer, the liturgy of the hours.

Because of King David's reputation for writing and performing music, he is named as the author of many of the Psalms. Actually, though, many of them were written long after his death. It is more accurate to understand the Psalms as a collection of songs that reflect different times and experiences throughout Israel's existence. Just as your favorite music might tell others what you value as a person, the Psalms tell us about Israel and its wondrous relationship with God.

The Book of Psalms

Psalms

BOOK I
(Psalms 1–41)

Psalm 1
The Two Ways

1 Happy are those
    who do not follow the advice of the
        wicked,
    or take the path that sinners tread,
        or sit in the seat of scoffers;
2 but their delight is in the law of
        the LORD,
    and on his law they meditate day and
        night.
3 They are like trees
    planted by streams of water,
    which yield their fruit in its season,
        and their leaves do not wither.
    In all that they do, they prosper.

4 The wicked are not so,
    but are like chaff that the wind drives
        away.
5 Therefore the wicked will not stand in the
        judgment,
    nor sinners in the congregation of the
        righteous;
6 for the LORD watches over the way of the
        righteous,
    but the way of the wicked will perish.

Psalm 2
God's Promise to His Anointed
(Acts 4.23–31)

1 Why do the nations conspire,
    and the peoples plot in vain?
2 The kings of the earth set themselves,
    and the rulers take counsel together,
    against the LORD and his anointed, saying,
3 "Let us burst their bonds asunder,
    and cast their cords from us."

4 He who sits in the heavens laughs;
    the LORD has them in derision.
5 Then he will speak to them in his wrath,
    and terrify them in his fury, saying,
6 "I have set my king on Zion, my holy hill."
7 I will tell of the decree of the LORD:
    He said to me, "You are my son;
        today I have begotten you.
8 Ask of me, and I will make the nations your
        heritage,
    and the ends of the earth your
        possession.
9 You shall break them with a rod of iron,
    and dash them in pieces like a potter's
        vessel."

10 Now therefore, O kings, be wise;
    be warned, O rulers of the earth.
11 Serve the LORD with fear,

with trembling [12] kiss his feet,[a]
or he will be angry, and you will perish in
the way;
for his wrath is quickly kindled.

Happy are all who take refuge in him.

did you KNOW?

Understanding the Psalms

**"Praise God!" "Why am I suffering?"
"Save us from oppression and injustice."
"God, give me rest." These phrases illustrate types of prayer: praise, lament, and
petition. The Book of Psalms includes
these and many other kinds of prayer,
made by individuals, small groups, or the
whole Jewish nation. Yet, throughout the
Psalms, there is one constant: human
experience is viewed through the eyes of
faith. For example, Psalm 3 reflects the
human experience of being attacked by
others (verses 1–2). The writer of this
psalm, rather than losing all hope, calls
God to the rescue (verse 7). In a similar
way, all the Psalms teach us that every
human experience can also be a faith
experience.**

Psalm 3

Trust in God under Adversity

A Psalm of David, when he fled from his son Ab'sa·lom.

[1] O LORD, how many are my foes!
Many are rising against me;
[2] many are saying to me,
"There is no help for you[b] in God."   *Sĕ'lah*

[3] But you, O LORD, are a shield around me,
my glory, and the one who lifts up my
head.
[4] I cry aloud to the LORD,
and he answers me from his holy hill.
Sĕ'lah

[5] I lie down and sleep;
I wake again, for the LORD sustains me.
[6] I am not afraid of ten thousands of people
who have set themselves against me all
around.

[7] Rise up, O LORD!
Deliver me, O my God!
For you strike all my enemies on the cheek;
you break the teeth of the wicked.

[8] Deliverance belongs to the LORD;
may your blessing be on your people!
Sĕ'lah

Psalm 4

Confident Plea for Deliverance
from Enemies

*To the leader: with stringed instruments. A Psalm
of David.*

[1] Answer me when I call, O God of my right!
You gave me room when I was in
distress.
Be gracious to me, and hear my prayer.

[2] How long, you people, shall my honor
suffer shame?
How long will you love vain words, and
seek after lies?   *Sĕ'lah*
[3] But know that the LORD has set apart the
faithful for himself;
the LORD hears when I call to him.

[4] When you are disturbed,[c] do not sin;
ponder it on your beds, and be silent.
Sĕ'lah

[5] Offer right sacrifices,
and put your trust in the LORD.
[6] There are many who say, "O that we might
see some good!
Let the light of your face shine on us,
O LORD!"
[7] You have put gladness in my heart
more than when their grain and wine
abound.

[8] I will both lie down and sleep in peace;
for you alone, O LORD, make me lie down
in safety.

Psalm 5

Trust in God for Deliverance
from Enemies

To the leader: for the flutes. A Psalm of David.

[1] Give ear to my words, O LORD;
give heed to my sighing.
[2] Listen to the sound of my cry,
my King and my God,
for to you I pray.
[3] O LORD, in the morning you hear my voice;

---

a Cn: Meaning of Heb of verses 11b and 12a is uncertain
b Syr: Heb *him*   *c* Or *are angry*

in the morning I plead my case to you,
and watch.

4 For you are not a God who delights in
wickedness;
evil will not sojourn with you.
5 The boastful will not stand before your eyes;
you hate all evildoers.
6 You destroy those who speak lies;
the LORD abhors the bloodthirsty and
deceitful.

7 But I, through the abundance of your
steadfast love,
will enter your house,
I will bow down toward your holy temple
in awe of you.
8 Lead me, O LORD, in your righteousness
because of my enemies;
make your way straight before me.

9 For there is no truth in their mouths;
their hearts are destruction;
their throats are open graves;
they flatter with their tongues.
10 Make them bear their guilt, O God;
let them fall by their own counsels;
because of their many transgressions cast
them out,
for they have rebelled against you.

11 But let all who take refuge in you rejoice;
let them ever sing for joy.
Spread your protection over them,
so that those who love your name may
exult in you.
12 For you bless the righteous, O LORD;
you cover them with favor as with a
shield.

Psalm 6
Prayer for Recovery

*To the leader: with stringed instruments; according to
The Shem'i·nith. A Psalm of David.*

1 O LORD, do not rebuke me in your
anger,
or discipline me in your wrath.
2 Be gracious to me, O LORD, for I am
languishing;
O LORD, heal me, for my bones are
shaking with terror.
3 My soul also is struck with terror,
while you, O LORD—how long?

4 Turn, O LORD, save my life;
deliver me for the sake of your steadfast
love.
5 For in death there is no remembrance
of you;
in She'ōl who can give you praise?

6 I am weary with my moaning;
every night I flood my bed with tears;
I drench my couch with my weeping.
7 My eyes waste away because of grief;
they grow weak because of all my foes.

8 Depart from me, all you workers of evil,
for the LORD has heard the sound of my
weeping.
9 The LORD has heard my supplication;
the LORD accepts my prayer.
10 All my enemies shall be ashamed and struck
with terror;
they shall turn back, and in a moment be
put to shame.

Our Cross to Bear

In Psalm 6, the psalmist is praying for deliverance from physical and mental suffering. Christians often refer to the suffering or sacrifice that comes as part of life as their cross to bear, because they see it as connected to Jesus' own suffering on the cross. Indeed, we all have crosses to bear. Some crosses are heavier than others, and like the psalmist, we ask God to deliver us from them. But unlike the psalmist, Christians also pray that God will transform their suffering and use it in some way for the good of others.

What are some of the crosses that you have had to bear? How were you saved from your suffering? How has someone else's suffering or sacrifice helped or inspired you?

▶ Psalm 6

Psalm 7

Plea for Help against Persecutors

A Shig·gāi'on of David, which he sang to the LORD concerning Cush, a Ben'ja·min·ite.

1 O LORD my God, in you I take refuge;
  save me from all my pursuers, and
    deliver me,
2 or like a lion they will tear me apart;
  they will drag me away, with no one to
    rescue.

3 O LORD my God, if I have done this,
  if there is wrong in my hands,
4 if I have repaid my ally with harm
  or plundered my foe without cause,
5 then let the enemy pursue and overtake me,
  trample my life to the ground,
  and lay my soul in the dust.   *Sē'lah*

6 Rise up, O LORD, in your anger;
  lift yourself up against the fury of my
    enemies;
  awake, O my God;*d* you have appointed
    a judgment.
7 Let the assembly of the peoples be gathered
    around you,
  and over it take your seat*e* on high.
8 The LORD judges the peoples;
  judge me, O LORD, according to my
    righteousness
  and according to the integrity that is
    in me.

9 O let the evil of the wicked come to an end,
  but establish the righteous,
you who test the minds and hearts,
  O righteous God.
10 God is my shield,
  who saves the upright in heart.
11 God is a righteous judge,
  and a God who has indignation
    every day.

12 If one does not repent, God*f* will whet his
    sword;
  he has bent and strung his bow;
13 he has prepared his deadly weapons,
  making his arrows fiery shafts.
14 See how they conceive evil,
  and are pregnant with mischief,
  and bring forth lies.
15 They make a pit, digging it out,
  and fall into the hole that they have
    made.
16 Their mischief returns upon their own
    heads,

and on their own heads their violence
  descends.

17 I will give to the LORD the thanks due to his
    righteousness,
  and sing praise to the name of the LORD,
    the Most High.

Psalm 8

Divine Majesty and Human Dignity

*To the leader: according to The Git'tith. A Psalm
of David.*

1 O LORD, our Sovereign,
  how majestic is your name in all the
    earth!

You have set your glory above the heavens.
2   Out of the mouths of babes and infants
you have founded a bulwark because of
    your foes,
  to silence the enemy and the avenger.

3 When I look at your heavens, the work of
    your fingers,
  the moon and the stars that you have
    established;
4 what are human beings that you are
    mindful of them,
  mortals*g* that you care for them?

5 Yet you have made them a little lower
    than God,*h*
  and crowned them with glory and honor.
6 You have given them dominion over the
    works of your hands;
  you have put all things under their feet,
7 all sheep and oxen,
  and also the beasts of the field,
8 the birds of the air, and the fish of the sea,
  whatever passes along the paths of the
    seas.

9 O LORD, our Sovereign,
  how majestic is your name in all the
    earth!

Psalm 9

God's Power and Justice

*To the leader: according to Muth-lab'ben.
A Psalm of David.*

1 I will give thanks to the LORD with my
    whole heart;
  I will tell of all your wonderful deeds.

---

d Or *awake for me*   *e* Cn: Heb *return*   *f* Heb *he*
g Heb *ben adam*, lit. *son of man*   *h* Or *than the divine
beings* or *angels*: Heb *elohim*

2 I will be glad and exult in you;
   I will sing praise to your name, O Most
     High.

3 When my enemies turned back,
   they stumbled and perished before you.
4 For you have maintained my just cause;
   you have sat on the throne giving
     righteous judgment.

5 You have rebuked the nations, you have
     destroyed the wicked;
   you have blotted out their name forever
     and ever.
6 The enemies have vanished in everlasting
     ruins;
   their cities you have rooted out;
   the very memory of them has perished.

7 But the LORD sits enthroned forever,
   he has established his throne for
     judgment.
8 He judges the world with righteousness;
   he judges the peoples with equity.

9 The LORD is a stronghold for the oppressed,
   a stronghold in times of trouble.
10 And those who know your name put their
     trust in you,
   for you, O LORD, have not forsaken those
     who seek you.

11 Sing praises to the LORD, who dwells in
     Zion.
   Declare his deeds among the peoples.
12 For he who avenges blood is mindful of
     them;
   he does not forget the cry of the afflicted.

13 Be gracious to me, O LORD.
   See what I suffer from those who
     hate me;
   you are the one who lifts me up from the
     gates of death,
14 so that I may recount all your praises,
   and, in the gates of daughter Zion,
   rejoice in your deliverance.

15 The nations have sunk in the pit that they
     made;
   in the net that they hid has their own
     foot been caught.
16 The LORD has made himself known, he has
     executed judgment;
   the wicked are snared in the work of
     their own hands.   *Hig·gāi'on. Sě'lah*

17 The wicked shall depart to Shě'ōl,
   all the nations that forget God.
18 For the needy shall not always be forgotten,
   nor the hope of the poor perish forever.

19 Rise up, O LORD! Do not let mortals prevail;
   let the nations be judged before you.
20 Put them in fear, O LORD;
   let the nations know that they are only
     human.   *Sě'lah*

Psalm 10
Prayer for Deliverance from Enemies

1 Why, O LORD, do you stand far off?
   Why do you hide yourself in times of
     trouble?
2 In arrogance the wicked persecute the poor—
   let them be caught in the schemes they
     have devised.

3 For the wicked boast of the desires of their
     heart,
   those greedy for gain curse and renounce
     the LORD.
4 In the pride of their countenance the wicked
   say, "God will not seek it out";
   all their thoughts are, "There is no God."

5 Their ways prosper at all times;
   your judgments are on high, out of their
     sight;
   as for their foes, they scoff at them.
6 They think in their heart, "We shall not be
     moved;
   throughout all generations we shall not
     meet adversity."

7 Their mouths are filled with cursing and
     deceit and oppression;
   under their tongues are mischief and
     iniquity.
8 They sit in ambush in the villages;
   in hiding places they murder the
     innocent.

   Their eyes stealthily watch for the helpless;
9   they lurk in secret like a lion in its covert;
   they lurk that they may seize the poor;
   they seize the poor and drag them off in
     their net.

10 They stoop, they crouch,
   and the helpless fall by their might.
11 They think in their heart, "God has
     forgotten,
   he has hidden his face, he will never
     see it."

12 Rise up, O LORD; O God, lift up your hand;
    do not forget the oppressed.
13 Why do the wicked renounce God,
    and say in their hearts, "You will not call
        us to account"?

14 But you do see! Indeed you note trouble
        and grief,
    that you may take it into your hands;
    the helpless commit themselves to you;
    you have been the helper of the
        orphan.

15 Break the arm of the wicked and
        evildoers;
    seek out their wickedness until you find
        none.
16 The LORD is king forever and ever;
    the nations shall perish from his
        land.

17 O LORD, you will hear the desire of the
        meek;
    you will strengthen their heart, you will
        incline your ear
18 to do justice for the orphan and the
        oppressed,
    so that those from earth may strike terror
        no more.[i]

Psalm 11
Song of Trust in God

To the leader. Of David.

1 In the LORD I take refuge; how can you say
    to me,
    "Flee like a bird to the mountains;[j]
2 for look, the wicked bend the bow,
    they have fitted their arrow to the string,
    to shoot in the dark at the upright in
        heart.
3 If the foundations are destroyed,
    what can the righteous do?"

4 The LORD is in his holy temple;
    the LORD's throne is in heaven.
    His eyes behold, his gaze examines
        humankind.
5 The LORD tests the righteous and the wicked,
    and his soul hates the lover of violence.
6 On the wicked he will rain coals of fire and
        sulfur;
    a scorching wind shall be the portion of
        their cup.
7 For the LORD is righteous;
    he loves righteous deeds;
    the upright shall behold his face.

Psalm 12
Plea for Help in Evil Times

*To the leader: according to The Shem'i•nith.
A Psalm of David.*

1 Help, O LORD, for there is no longer anyone
    who is godly;
    the faithful have disappeared from
        humankind.
2 They utter lies to each other;
    with flattering lips and a double heart
        they speak.

3 May the LORD cut off all flattering lips,
    the tongue that makes great boasts,
4 those who say, "With our tongues we will
        prevail;
    our lips are our own—who is our master?"

5 "Because the poor are despoiled, because
    the needy groan,
    I will now rise up," says the LORD;
    "I will place them in the safety for which
        they long."
6 The promises of the LORD are promises that
    are pure,
    silver refined in a furnace on the ground,
    purified seven times.

7 You, O LORD, will protect us;
    you will guard us from this generation
        forever.
8 On every side the wicked prowl,
    as vileness is exalted among humankind.

Psalm 13
Prayer for Deliverance from Enemies

To the leader. A Psalm of David.

1 How long, O LORD? Will you forget me
    forever?
    How long will you hide your face
        from me?
2 How long must I bear pain[k] in my soul,
    and have sorrow in my heart all day
        long?
    How long shall my enemy be exalted
        over me?

3 Consider and answer me, O LORD my God!
    Give light to my eyes, or I will sleep the
        sleep of death,
4 and my enemy will say, "I have prevailed";
    my foes will rejoice because I am shaken.

5 But I trusted in your steadfast love;
    my heart shall rejoice in your salvation.

---

i Meaning of Heb uncertain   *j* Gk Syr Jerome Tg: Heb
flee to your mountain, O bird   *k* Syr: Heb *hold counsels*

Believing

> **Angel.** My Lord, the earth is filled with those who say, "There is no God!"
>
> **God.** So, my messenger, what do we do with these people?
>
> **Angel.** My Lord, they are fools.
>
> **God.** Perhaps, but they are free. I force no one to believe in me.

Angel. Yet, the wise always seem to find you.

God. That is because they seek me. Those who seek—

Angel. Yes, I know, Lord, they shall find. But how do we get through to those others, the godless ones?

God. You must trust. My signs and wonders surround them. There is the witness of those who believe. And there are a few angels.

Angel. But they keep explaining all that away.

God. So they do. They are free, after all. Their destiny is in their hands, in the choices they make.

Angel. Including the most basic choice of all.

God. Yes. Especially that. True love is not forced. It gives and awaits a response. We must trust in love.

Angel. And hope?

God. Yes, always hope.

▸ Psalm 14

---

6 I will sing to the LORD,
> because he has dealt bountifully with me.

Psalm 14

Denunciation of Godlessness

(Ps 53.1–6)

To the leader. Of David.

1 Fools say in their hearts, "There is no God."
> They are corrupt, they do abominable
> deeds;
> there is no one who does good.

2 The LORD looks down from heaven on
> humankind
> to see if there are any who are wise,
> who seek after God.

3 They have all gone astray, they are all alike
> perverse;
> there is no one who does good,
> no, not one.

4 Have they no knowledge, all the evildoers
> who eat up my people as they eat bread,
> and do not call upon the LORD?

5 There they shall be in great terror,
> for God is with the company of the
> righteous.

6 You would confound the plans of the poor,
> but the LORD is their refuge.

7 O that deliverance for Israel would come
> from Zion!
> When the LORD restores the fortunes of
> his people,
> Jacob will rejoice; Israel will be glad.

Psalm 15

Who Shall Abide in God's Sanctuary?

A Psalm of David.

1 O LORD, who may abide in your tent?
> Who may dwell on your holy hill?

2 Those who walk blamelessly, and do what is
> right,
> and speak the truth from their heart;

3 who do not slander with their tongue,
> and do no evil to their friends,
> nor take up a reproach against their
> neighbors;

4 in whose eyes the wicked are despised,
> but who honor those who fear the LORD;
> who stand by their oath even to their hurt;

5 who do not lend money at interest,
> and do not take a bribe against the
> innocent.

Those who do these things shall never be
> moved.

Psalm 16

Song of Trust and Security in God

A Mik'tam of David.

1 Protect me, O God, for in you I take
   refuge.
2 I say to the Lord, "You are my Lord;
   I have no good apart from you."[l]

3 As for the holy ones in the land, they are
   the noble,
   in whom is all my delight.
4 Those who choose another god multiply
   their sorrows;[m]
   their drink offerings of blood I will not
   pour out
   or take their names upon my lips.

5 The Lord is my chosen portion and my cup;
   you hold my lot.

NATIVE AMERICAN

Living in Your Tent, on Your Holy Hill

Native Americans can appreciate the imagery of Psalm 15. Both tents and hills have a sacred meaning for them. The Lakota have the phrase *mit-a-ku-ye O-ya-sin*, which means "all my relatives." This phrase is often used at the end of a prayer, much like *amen*. It expresses the deep belief that all human beings are our brothers and sisters, and we all belong in the Holy Tent of the Great Spirit. All creatures—the two legged and the four legged, those that crawl and those that fly—are our relatives. In fact, we are related to all of creation—the sea, the rocks, the caves, the sky, the trees, the holy hills. Native Americans understand human beings as connected to all creation, and believe that any harm we do to creation we do to ourselves.

▶ Psalm 15

6 The boundary lines have fallen for me in
   pleasant places;
   I have a goodly heritage.

7 I bless the Lord who gives me counsel;
   in the night also my heart instructs me.
8 I keep the Lord always before me;
   because he is at my right hand, I shall
   not be moved.

9 Therefore my heart is glad, and my soul
   rejoices;
   my body also rests secure.
10 For you do not give me up to Shē'ōl,
   or let your faithful one see the Pit.

11 You show me the path of life.
   In your presence there is fullness of joy;
   in your right hand are pleasures
   forevermore.

Psalm 17

Prayer for Deliverance from Persecutors

A Prayer of David.

1 Hear a just cause, O Lord; attend to my cry;
   give ear to my prayer from lips free of
   deceit.
2 From you let my vindication come;
   let your eyes see the right.

3 If you try my heart, if you visit me by night,
   if you test me, you will find no
   wickedness in me;
   my mouth does not transgress.
4 As for what others do, by the word of your
   lips
   I have avoided the ways of the violent.
5 My steps have held fast to your paths;
   my feet have not slipped.

6 I call upon you, for you will answer me,
   O God;
   incline your ear to me, hear my words.
7 Wondrously show your steadfast love,
   O savior of those who seek refuge
   from their adversaries at your right hand.

8 Guard me as the apple of the eye;
   hide me in the shadow of your wings,
9 from the wicked who despoil me,
   my deadly enemies who surround me.
10 They close their hearts to pity;
   with their mouths they speak arrogantly.
11 They track me down;[n] now they
   surround me;

---

[l] Jerome Tg: Meaning of Heb uncertain   [m] Cn: Meaning of Heb uncertain   [n] One Ms Compare Syr: MT *Our steps*

they set their eyes to cast me to the
ground.

12 They are like a lion eager to tear,
like a young lion lurking in ambush.

13 Rise up, O LORD, confront them, overthrow
them!
By your sword deliver my life from the
wicked,

14 from mortals—by your hand, O LORD—
from mortals whose portion in life is in
this world.
May their bellies be filled with what you
have stored up for them;
may their children have more than
enough;
may they leave something over to their
little ones.

15 As for me, I shall behold your face in
righteousness;
when I awake I shall be satisfied,
beholding your likeness.

Psalm 18

Royal Thanksgiving for Victory
(2 Sam 22.1–51)

To the leader. A Psalm of David the servant of the
LORD, who addressed the words of this song to the LORD
on the day when the LORD delivered him from the hand
of all his enemies, and from the hand of Saul. He said:

1 I love you, O LORD, my strength.

2 The LORD is my rock, my fortress, and my
deliverer,
my God, my rock in whom I take refuge,
my shield, and the horn of my salvation,
my stronghold.

3 I call upon the LORD, who is worthy to be
praised,
so I shall be saved from my enemies.

4 The cords of death encompassed me;
the torrents of perdition assailed me;

5 the cords of She'ōl entangled me;
the snares of death confronted me.

6 In my distress I called upon the LORD;
to my God I cried for help.
From his temple he heard my voice,
and my cry to him reached his ears.

7 Then the earth reeled and rocked;
the foundations also of the mountains
trembled
and quaked, because he was angry.

8 Smoke went up from his nostrils,
and devouring fire from his mouth;
glowing coals flamed forth from him.

9 He bowed the heavens, and came down;
thick darkness was under his feet.

10 He rode on a cherub, and flew;
he came swiftly upon the wings of the
wind.

11 He made darkness his covering around him,
his canopy thick clouds dark with water.

12 Out of the brightness before him
there broke through his clouds
hailstones and coals of fire.

13 The LORD also thundered in the heavens,
and the Most High uttered his voice.*o*

14 And he sent out his arrows, and scattered
them;
he flashed forth lightnings, and routed
them.

15 Then the channels of the sea were seen,
and the foundations of the world were
laid bare
at your rebuke, O LORD,
at the blast of the breath of your nostrils.

16 He reached down from on high, he
took me;
he drew me out of mighty waters.

17 He delivered me from my strong enemy,
and from those who hated me;
for they were too mighty for me.

18 They confronted me in the day of my
calamity;
but the LORD was my support.

19 He brought me out into a broad place;
he delivered me, because he delighted
in me.

20 The LORD rewarded me according to my
righteousness;
according to the cleanness of my hands
he recompensed me.

21 For I have kept the ways of the LORD,
and have not wickedly departed from
my God.

22 For all his ordinances were before me,
and his statutes I did not put away
from me.

23 I was blameless before him,
and I kept myself from guilt.

24 Therefore the LORD has recompensed me
according to my righteousness,
according to the cleanness of my hands
in his sight.

25 With the loyal you show yourself loyal;
with the blameless you show yourself
blameless;

26 with the pure you show yourself pure;

---

o Gk See 2 Sam 22.14: Heb adds *hailstones and coals of fire*

and with the crooked you show yourself
　　perverse.

27 For you deliver a humble people,
　　but the haughty eyes you bring down.

28 It is you who light my lamp;
　　the LORD, my God, lights up my darkness.

29 By you I can crush a troop,
　　and by my God I can leap over a wall.

30 This God—his way is perfect;
　　the promise of the LORD proves true;
　　he is a shield for all who take refuge
　　　　in him.

31 For who is God except the LORD?
　　And who is a rock besides our God?—

32 the God who girded me with strength,
　　and made my way safe.

33 He made my feet like the feet of a deer,
　　and set me secure on the heights.

34 He trains my hands for war,
　　so that my arms can bend a bow of
　　　　bronze.

35 You have given me the shield of your
　　　　salvation,
　　and your right hand has supported me;
　　your help*p* has made me great.

36 You gave me a wide place for my steps
　　　　under me,
　　and my feet did not slip.

37 I pursued my enemies and overtook them;
　　and did not turn back until they were
　　　　consumed.

38 I struck them down, so that they were not
　　　　able to rise;
　　they fell under my feet.

39 For you girded me with strength for the
　　　　battle;
　　you made my assailants sink under me.

40 You made my enemies turn their backs
　　　　to me,
　　and those who hated me I destroyed.

41 They cried for help, but there was no one to
　　　　save them;
　　they cried to the LORD, but he did not
　　　　answer them.

42 I beat them fine, like dust before the wind;
　　I cast them out like the mire of the
　　　　streets.

43 You delivered me from strife with the
　　　　peoples;*q*
　　you made me head of the nations;
　　people whom I had not known
　　　　served me.

44 As soon as they heard of me they
　　　　obeyed me;
　　foreigners came cringing to me.

45 Foreigners lost heart,
　　and came trembling out of their
　　　　strongholds.

46 The LORD lives! Blessed be my rock,
　　and exalted be the God of my salvation,

47 the God who gave me vengeance
　　and subdued peoples under me;

48 who delivered me from my enemies;
　　indeed, you exalted me above my
　　　　adversaries;
　　you delivered me from the violent.

49 For this I will extol you, O LORD, among the
　　　　nations,
　　and sing praises to your name.

50 Great triumphs he gives to his king,
　　and shows steadfast love to his anointed,
　　to David and his descendants forever.

Psalm 19

God's Glory in Creation and the Law

To the leader. A Psalm of David.

1 The heavens are telling the glory of God;
　　and the firmament*r* proclaims his
　　　　handiwork.

2 Day to day pours forth speech,
　　and night to night declares knowledge.

3 There is no speech, nor are there words;
　　their voice is not heard;

4 yet their voice*s* goes out through all the
　　　　earth,
　　and their words to the end of the world.

In the heavens*t* he has set a tent for
　　the sun,

5 which comes out like a bridegroom from
　　　　his wedding canopy,
　　and like a strong man runs its course
　　　　with joy.

6 Its rising is from the end of the heavens,
　　and its circuit to the end of them;
　　and nothing is hid from its heat.

7 The law of the LORD is perfect,
　　reviving the soul;
　　the decrees of the LORD are sure,
　　making wise the simple;

8 the precepts of the LORD are right,
　　rejoicing the heart;
　　the commandment of the LORD is clear,
　　enlightening the eyes;

9 the fear of the LORD is pure,
　　enduring forever;

---

p Or *gentleness*　　*q* Gk Tg: Heb *people*　　*r* Or *dome*
s Gk Jerome Compare Syr: Heb *line*　　*t* Heb *In them*

the ordinances of the LORD are true
and righteous altogether.
10 More to be desired are they than gold,
even much fine gold;
sweeter also than honey,
and drippings of the honeycomb.

11 Moreover by them is your servant
warned;
in keeping them there is great reward.
12 But who can detect their errors?
Clear me from hidden faults.
13 Keep back your servant also from the
insolent;[u]
do not let them have dominion over me.
Then I shall be blameless,
and innocent of great transgression.

14 Let the words of my mouth and the
meditation of my heart
be acceptable to you,
O LORD, my rock and my redeemer.

PRAY IT

"The Heavens Are Telling the Glory of God"

Does that opening line of Psalm 19 sound familiar? Perhaps you've seen it on a poster or sung it at Mass. The sky constantly tells us how glorious and magnificent God is!

Have you ever watched the awesome show of a thunder and lightning storm? been delighted by a rainbow? marveled at the power behind a tornado or a hurricane? been tickled by a gentle spring breeze? caught snowflakes on your tongue? had leaves dance around you in a brisk autumn wind? lost yourself looking up into a star-filled night? felt breathless watching a magnificent sunset?

As amazing as the sky is, it only hints at how amazing God is! And in the second half of Psalm 19, the psalmist reminds us that God's law is equally wonderful. Read Psalm 19 as your own prayer of praise to God for the many ways God communicates to us.

▶ Psalm 19

Psalm 20
Prayer for Victory

To the leader. A Psalm of David.

1 The LORD answer you in the day of trouble!
The name of the God of Jacob
protect you!
2 May he send you help from the sanctuary,
and give you support from Zion.
3 May he remember all your offerings,
and regard with favor your burnt
sacrifices.   *Se'lah*

4 May he grant you your heart's desire,
and fulfill all your plans.
5 May we shout for joy over your victory,
and in the name of our God set up our
banners.
May the LORD fulfill all your petitions.

6 Now I know that the LORD will help his
anointed;
he will answer him from his holy heaven
with mighty victories by his right hand.
7 Some take pride in chariots, and some in
horses,
but our pride is in the name of the LORD
our God.
8 They will collapse and fall,
but we shall rise and stand upright.

9 Give victory to the king, O LORD;
answer us when we call.[v]

Psalm 21
Thanksgiving for Victory

To the leader. A Psalm of David.

1 In your strength the king rejoices, O LORD,
and in your help how greatly he exults!
2 You have given him his heart's desire,
and have not withheld the request of his
lips.   *Se'lah*
3 For you meet him with rich blessings;
you set a crown of fine gold on his head.
4 He asked you for life; you gave it to him—
length of days forever and ever.
5 His glory is great through your help;
splendor and majesty you bestow
on him.
6 You bestow on him blessings forever;
you make him glad with the joy of your
presence.
7 For the king trusts in the LORD,
and through the steadfast love of the
Most High he shall not be moved.

---

u Or *from proud thoughts*   v Gk: Heb *give victory, O LORD;
let the King answer us when we call*

8 Your hand will find out all your enemies;
   your right hand will find out those who
       hate you.
9 You will make them like a fiery furnace
   when you appear.
   The LORD will swallow them up in his wrath,
   and fire will consume them.
10 You will destroy their offspring from the
       earth,
   and their children from among
       humankind.
11 If they plan evil against you,
   if they devise mischief, they will not
       succeed.
12 For you will put them to flight;
   you will aim at their faces with your
       bows.

13 Be exalted, O LORD, in your strength!
   We will sing and praise your power.

Psalm 22

Plea for Deliverance from Suffering
and Hostility

*To the leader: according to The Deer of the Dawn.
A Psalm of David.*

1 My God, my God, why have you
       forsaken me?
   Why are you so far from helping me,
       from the words of my groaning?
2 O my God, I cry by day, but you do not
       answer;
   and by night, but find no rest.

3 Yet you are holy,
   enthroned on the praises of Israel.
4 In you our ancestors trusted;
   they trusted, and you delivered them.
5 To you they cried, and were saved;
   in you they trusted, and were not put to
       shame.

6 But I am a worm, and not human;
   scorned by others, and despised by the
       people.
7 All who see me mock at me;
   they make mouths at me, they shake
       their heads;
8 "Commit your cause to the LORD; let him
       deliver—
   let him rescue the one in whom he
       delights!"

9 Yet it was you who took me from the
       womb;
   you kept me safe on my mother's breast.
10 On you I was cast from my birth,

and since my mother bore me you have
       been my God.
11 Do not be far from me,
   for trouble is near
   and there is no one to help.

12 Many bulls encircle me,
   strong bulls of Ba'shan surround me;
13 they open wide their mouths at me,
   like a ravening and roaring lion.

14 I am poured out like water,
   and all my bones are out of joint;
   my heart is like wax;
   it is melted within my breast;
15 my mouth^w is dried up like a potsherd,
   and my tongue sticks to my jaws;
   you lay me in the dust of death.

Catholic Connections

HOPE IN DESPAIR

The Gospel writers make many references to Psalm 22 in telling the story of Jesus' suffering and death. During the long Gospel readings on Palm Sunday and Good Friday, you will hear them. Try reading Mt 27.45–50 and then reading Psalm 22. What sound like words of despair in Matthew are actually words of promise for those familiar with the psalm. This is because Psalm 22 is a hymn of hope, which ends by praising God for hearing and rescuing those who cry out. So, even in the horrible suffering of Jesus' death, there was already the promise of God's saving action.

▶ Psalm 22

16 For dogs are all around me;
   a company of evildoers encircles me.
   My hands and feet have shriveled;^{x}
17 I can count all my bones.
   They stare and gloat over me;

---

w Cn: Heb *strength* x Meaning of Heb uncertain

THE GOOD SHEPHERD LOOKS AFTER US!

The famous Psalm 23 offers two images of God: the Good Shepherd and a generous host. Both images speak of God's nearness and gentle care for us. In the New Testament, Jesus appears as the Good Shepherd who gives his life for the life of his sheep (Jn 10.1–29). He also appears several times as a host, particularly in the stories about the multiplication of the loaves and the Last Supper.

Similar images repeat time and again in Hispanic homes. The following traditional sayings are just some examples of the caring and generous attitudes among Hispanic families: "My home is your home" (*Mi casa es su casa*); "God help you! What can I do for you?" (*¡Dios te ampare! ¿Cómo puedo ayudarte?*); "Where two eat, three eat; where six eat, seven eat" (*Donde comen dos comen tres; donde comen seis comen siete*); "Welcome! We just add water to the beans" (*¡Bienvenidos! Le echamos más agua a los frijoles*); and "Stay with us! From wall to wall, all is mattress" (*¡Quédense con nosotros! De pared a pared todo es colchón!*).

As a Christian, you should pray Psalm 23 feeling the nearness of Jesus, the Good Shepherd, and asking his help to be a good shepherd for people in need:

- Pray the psalm slowly, letting God fill you with peace and security.
- Pray the psalm again, this time thinking of friends who might be feeling like sheep without a shepherd. How can you lead them to Jesus? How can you care more for them?

▶ Psalm 23

18 they divide my clothes among themselves,
　　and for my clothing they cast lots.

19 But you, O LORD, do not be far away!
　　O my help, come quickly to my aid!
20 Deliver my soul from the sword,
　　my life*y* from the power of the dog!
21 Save me from the mouth of the lion!

From the horns of the wild oxen you have
　　rescued*z* me.
22 I will tell of your name to my brothers and
　　sisters;*a*
　　in the midst of the congregation I will
　　praise you:
23 You who fear the LORD, praise him!
　　All you offspring of Jacob, glorify him;
　　stand in awe of him, all you offspring of
　　Israel!
24 For he did not despise or abhor
　　the affliction of the afflicted;
　　he did not hide his face from me,*b*
　　but heard when I*c* cried to him.

25 From you comes my praise in the great
　　congregation;
　　my vows I will pay before those who
　　fear him.

26 The poor*d* shall eat and be satisfied;
　　those who seek him shall praise the LORD.
　　May your hearts live forever!
27 All the ends of the earth shall remember
　　and turn to the LORD;
　　and all the families of the nations
　　shall worship before him.*e*
28 For dominion belongs to the LORD,
　　and he rules over the nations.
29 To him,*f* indeed, shall all who sleep in*g* the
　　earth bow down;
　　before him shall bow all who go down
　　to the dust,
　　and I shall live for him.*h*
30 Posterity will serve him;
　　future generations will be told about the
　　Lord,
31 and*i* proclaim his deliverance to a people
　　yet unborn,
　　saying that he has done it.

---

y Heb *my only one*　*z* Heb *answered*　*a* Or *kindred*
b Heb *him*　*c* Heb *he*　*d* Or *afflicted*　*e* Gk Syr Jerome:
Heb *you*　*f* Cn: Heb *They have eaten and*　*g* Cn: Heb *all
the fat ones*　*h* Compare Gk Syr Vg: Heb *and he who
cannot keep himself alive*　*i* Compare Gk: Heb *it will be
told about the Lord to the generation,* 31*they will come and*

Psalm 23
The Divine Shepherd
A Psalm of David.

1 The LORD is my shepherd, I shall not want.
2   He makes me lie down in green pastures;
he leads me beside still waters;*j*
3   he restores my soul.*k*
He leads me in right paths*l*
   for his name's sake.

4 Even though I walk through the darkest
            valley,*m*
      I fear no evil;
for you are with me;
      your rod and your staff—
      they comfort me.

5 You prepare a table before me
      in the presence of my enemies;
you anoint my head with oil;
      my cup overflows.
6 Surely*n* goodness and mercy*o* shall
            follow me
      all the days of my life,
and I shall dwell in the house of the LORD
      my whole life long.*p*

Psalm 24
Entrance into the Temple
Of David. A Psalm.

1 The earth is the LORD's and all that is in it,
      the world, and those who live in it;
2 for he has founded it on the seas,
      and established it on the rivers.

3 Who shall ascend the hill of the LORD?
      And who shall stand in his holy place?
4 Those who have clean hands and pure
            hearts,
      who do not lift up their souls to what is
            false,
      and do not swear deceitfully.
5 They will receive blessing from the LORD,
      and vindication from the God of their
            salvation.
6 Such is the company of those who
            seek him,
      who seek the face of the God of Jacob.*q*
                                            Sĕ'lah

7 Lift up your heads, O gates!
      and be lifted up, O ancient doors!
      that the King of glory may come in.
8 Who is the King of glory?
      The LORD, strong and mighty,
      the LORD, mighty in battle.

9 Lift up your heads, O gates!
      and be lifted up, O ancient doors!
      that the King of glory may come in.
10 Who is this King of glory?
      The LORD of hosts,
      he is the King of glory.   *Sĕ'lah*

---

j Heb *waters of rest*   *k* Or *life*   *l* Or *paths of righteousness*
m Or *the valley of the shadow of death*   *n* Or *Only*
o Or *kindness*   *p* Heb *for length of days*   *q* Gk Syr: Heb
your face, O Jacob

did you KNOW?

Temple Worship

When Israel was ruled by kings (1000–587 B.C.), worship in the Temple at Jerusalem was an important part of the people's religious life. Many of the psalms, like Psalm 24, refer to going up to the Temple (the "holy place" in verse 3). Although the first Temple was destroyed in 587 B.C., it was later rebuilt. Temple worship started again and continued into Jesus' time. This is what the priests did during some of the Temple ceremonies:

Daily Temple worship
- every morning, presented a burnt offering (a year-old male lamb), grain, drink, and an incense offering
- every evening, presented a second burnt offering and a cereal offering

Sabbath (weekly) Temple worship
- gave two additional burnt offerings
- replaced the twelve loaves of bread, called the Bread of Presence, recalling the manna with which God fed Israel in the desert
- made an incense offering

Monthly and festival Temple worship
- blew the trumpet
- presented additional burnt offerings and a sin offering (a male goat)
- on the Day of Atonement, laid their hands on a living goat while confessing the people's sins and then sent the goat away into the wilderness

P
S
A
L
M
S

PSALMS

Psalm 25

Prayer for Guidance and for Deliverance

Of David.

1 To you, O LORD, I lift up my soul.
2 O my God, in you I trust;
    do not let me be put to shame;
    do not let my enemies exult over me.
3 Do not let those who wait for you be put to shame;
    let them be ashamed who are wantonly treacherous.

4 Make me to know your ways, O LORD;
    teach me your paths.
5 Lead me in your truth, and teach me,
    for you are the God of my salvation;
    for you I wait all day long.

6 Be mindful of your mercy, O LORD, and of your steadfast love,
    for they have been from of old.
7 Do not remember the sins of my youth or my transgressions;
    according to your steadfast love remember me,
    for your goodness' sake, O LORD!

8 Good and upright is the LORD;
    therefore he instructs sinners in the way.
9 He leads the humble in what is right,
    and teaches the humble his way.
10 All the paths of the LORD are steadfast love and faithfulness,
    for those who keep his covenant and his decrees.

11 For your name's sake, O LORD,
    pardon my guilt, for it is great.
12 Who are they that fear the LORD?
    He will teach them the way that they should choose.

13 They will abide in prosperity,
    and their children shall possess the land.
14 The friendship of the LORD is for those who fear him,
    and he makes his covenant known to them.
15 My eyes are ever toward the LORD,
    for he will pluck my feet out of the net.

16 Turn to me and be gracious to me,
    for I am lonely and afflicted.
17 Relieve the troubles of my heart,
    and bring me[r] out of my distress.
18 Consider my affliction and my trouble,
    and forgive all my sins.

19 Consider how many are my foes,
    and with what violent hatred they hate me.
20 O guard my life, and deliver me;
    do not let me be put to shame, for I take refuge in you.
21 May integrity and uprightness preserve me,
    for I wait for you.

22 Redeem Israel, O God,
    out of all its troubles.

Psalm 26

Plea for Justice and Declaration of Righteousness

Of David.

1 Vindicate me, O LORD,
    for I have walked in my integrity,
    and I have trusted in the LORD without wavering.
2 Prove me, O LORD, and try me;
    test my heart and mind.
3 For your steadfast love is before my eyes,
    and I walk in faithfulness to you.[s]

4 I do not sit with the worthless,
    nor do I consort with hypocrites;
5 I hate the company of evildoers,
    and will not sit with the wicked.

6 I wash my hands in innocence,
    and go around your altar, O LORD,
7 singing aloud a song of thanksgiving,
    and telling all your wondrous deeds.

8 O LORD, I love the house in which you dwell,
    and the place where your glory abides.
9 Do not sweep me away with sinners,
    nor my life with the bloodthirsty,
10 those in whose hands are evil devices,
    and whose right hands are full of bribes.

11 But as for me, I walk in my integrity;
    redeem me, and be gracious to me.
12 My foot stands on level ground;
    in the great congregation I will bless the LORD.

Psalm 27

Triumphant Song of Confidence

Of David.

1 The LORD is my light and my salvation;
    whom shall I fear?

---

r Or *The troubles of my heart are enlarged; bring me* s Or *in your faithfulness*

The LORD is the stronghold[t] of my life;
  of whom shall I be afraid?

2 When evildoers assail me
  to devour my flesh—
my adversaries and foes—
  they shall stumble and fall.

3 Though an army encamp against me,
  my heart shall not fear;
though war rise up against me,
  yet I will be confident.

PRAY IT!

Integrity and Values

People with integrity know what they value and have a commitment to being consistent in what they believe and what they do. It is impossible for us to have integrity if we follow one set of values in one situation and another set of values in a different situation. The integrity of the writer of Psalm 26 comes from following God in everything (Ps 26.1). The psalmist even wants to be tested by God (verse 2) to be sure of complete faithfulness! To have the kind of integrity that the psalmist writes about, we have to let God be the only ruler of our life. Being able to do that takes a lifetime of growth and conversion.

What values are you committed to consistently? Can you think of times when your actions did not reflect your values or beliefs? Pray that God will give you strength to do what is right, even when it is most difficult.

▶ Psalm 26

4 One thing I asked of the LORD,
  that will I seek after:
to live in the house of the LORD
  all the days of my life,
to behold the beauty of the LORD,
  and to inquire in his temple.

5 For he will hide me in his shelter
  in the day of trouble;
he will conceal me under the cover of his
    tent;
  he will set me high on a rock.

6 Now my head is lifted up
  above my enemies all around me,
and I will offer in his tent
  sacrifices with shouts of joy;
I will sing and make melody to the LORD.

7 Hear, O LORD, when I cry aloud,
  be gracious to me and answer me!
8 "Come," my heart says, "seek his face!"
  Your face, LORD, do I seek.
9   Do not hide your face from me.

Do not turn your servant away in anger,
  you who have been my help.
Do not cast me off, do not forsake me,
  O God of my salvation!
10 If my father and mother forsake me,
  the LORD will take me up.

11 Teach me your way, O LORD,
  and lead me on a level path
  because of my enemies.
12 Do not give me up to the will of
  my adversaries,
  for false witnesses have risen against me,
  and they are breathing out violence.

13 I believe that I shall see the goodness of the
  LORD
  in the land of the living.
14 Wait for the LORD;
  be strong, and let your heart take
    courage;
  wait for the LORD!

Psalm 28
Prayer for Help and Thanksgiving for It
Of David.

1 To you, O LORD, I call;
  my rock, do not refuse to hear me,
for if you are silent to me,
  I shall be like those who go down to
    the Pit.
2 Hear the voice of my supplication,
  as I cry to you for help,
as I lift up my hands
  toward your most holy sanctuary.[u]

3 Do not drag me away with the wicked,
  with those who are workers of evil,
who speak peace with their neighbors,
  while mischief is in their hearts.
4 Repay them according to their work,
  and according to the evil of their deeds;
repay them according to the work of their
    hands;

---

t Or *refuge*   *u* Heb *your innermost sanctuary*

P
S
A
L
M
S

render them their due reward.

5 Because they do not regard the works of the
    LORD,
    or the work of his hands,
  he will break them down and build them
    up no more.

6 Blessed be the LORD,
    for he has heard the sound of my
      pleadings.
7 The LORD is my strength and my shield;
    in him my heart trusts;
  so I am helped, and my heart exults,
    and with my song I give thanks to him.

8 The LORD is the strength of his people;
    he is the saving refuge of his anointed.
9 O save your people, and bless your heritage;
    be their shepherd, and carry them
      forever.

Psalm 29

The Voice of God in a Great Storm

A Psalm of David.

1 Ascribe to the LORD, O heavenly beings,[v]
    ascribe to the LORD glory and strength.
2 Ascribe to the LORD the glory of his name;
    worship the LORD in holy splendor.

3 The voice of the LORD is over the waters;
    the God of glory thunders,
    the LORD, over mighty waters.
4 The voice of the LORD is powerful;
    the voice of the LORD is full of majesty.

5 The voice of the LORD breaks the cedars;
    the LORD breaks the cedars of Lebanon.
6 He makes Lebanon skip like a calf,
    and Sir'i•on like a young wild ox.

7 The voice of the LORD flashes forth flames of
    fire.
8 The voice of the LORD shakes the wilderness;
    the LORD shakes the wilderness of
      Kā'desh.

9 The voice of the LORD causes the oaks to
    whirl,[w]
  and strips the forest bare;
    and in his temple all say, "Glory!"

10 The LORD sits enthroned over the flood;
     the LORD sits enthroned as king forever.
11 May the LORD give strength to his people!
     May the LORD bless his people with
       peace!

Psalm 30

Thanksgiving for Recovery from Grave Illness

*A Psalm. A Song at the dedication of the temple.
Of David.*

1 I will extol you, O LORD, for you have drawn
    me up,
  and did not let my foes rejoice over me.
2 O LORD my God, I cried to you for help,
    and you have healed me.
3 O LORD, you brought up my soul from
    Shē'ōl,
  restored me to life from among those
    gone down to the Pit.[x]

4 Sing praises to the LORD, O you his faithful
    ones,
  and give thanks to his holy name.
5 For his anger is but for a moment;
    his favor is for a lifetime.
  Weeping may linger for the night,
    but joy comes with the morning.

The Eye of the Storm

Thunderstorms can be frightening. They often
come up quickly and without warning. The
winds and lightning that accompany them can
be destructive. Children and animals (okay,
lots of adults too) are often afraid at the sheer
force of it all.

It would be difficult to read Psalm 29
aloud and not be expressive. Phrases such as
"the God of glory thunders" (verse 3), and
"the voice of the LORD breaks the cedars"
(verse 5) and "flashes forth flames of fire"
(verse 7) evoke a divine splendor that we do
not often hear about. The psalmist speaks with
admiration about the power and majesty of
God.

When have you experienced the awesome
power of God?

▸ **Psalm 29**

6 As for me, I said in my prosperity,
    "I shall never be moved."
7 By your favor, O LORD,

---
v Heb *sons of gods*   *w* Or *causes the deer to calve*
x Or *that I should not go down to the Pit*

you had established me as a strong
  mountain;
you hid your face;
  I was dismayed.

8 To you, O LORD, I cried,
  and to the LORD I made supplication:
9 "What profit is there in my death,
  if I go down to the Pit?
  Will the dust praise you?
  Will it tell of your faithfulness?
10 Hear, O LORD, and be gracious to me!
  O LORD, be my helper!"

11 You have turned my mourning into
  dancing;
  you have taken off my sackcloth
  and clothed me with joy,
12 so that my soul*y* may praise you and not be
  silent.
  O LORD my God, I will give thanks to you
  forever.

Psalm 31

Prayer and Praise for Deliverance
from Enemies

To the leader. A Psalm of David.

1 In you, O LORD, I seek refuge;
  do not let me ever be put to shame;
  in your righteousness deliver me.
2 Incline your ear to me;
  rescue me speedily.
  Be a rock of refuge for me,
  a strong fortress to save me.

3 You are indeed my rock and my fortress;
  for your name's sake lead me and
  guide me,
4 take me out of the net that is hidden
  for me,
  for you are my refuge.
5 Into your hand I commit my spirit;
  you have redeemed me, O LORD,
  faithful God.

6 You hate*z* those who pay regard to
  worthless idols,
  but I trust in the LORD.
7 I will exult and rejoice in your steadfast
  love,
  because you have seen my affliction;
  you have taken heed of my adversities,
8 and have not delivered me into the hand of
  the enemy;
  you have set my feet in a broad place.

9 Be gracious to me, O LORD, for I am in
  distress;
  my eye wastes away from grief,
  my soul and body also.
10 For my life is spent with sorrow,
  and my years with sighing;
  my strength fails because of my misery,*a*
  and my bones waste away.

11 I am the scorn of all my adversaries,
  a horror*b* to my neighbors,
  an object of dread to my acquaintances;
  those who see me in the street flee
  from me.
12 I have passed out of mind like one who is
  dead;
  I have become like a broken vessel.
13 For I hear the whispering of many—
  terror all around!—
  as they scheme together against me,
  as they plot to take my life.

14 But I trust in you, O LORD;
  I say, "You are my God."
15 My times are in your hand;
  deliver me from the hand of my enemies
  and persecutors.
16 Let your face shine upon your servant;
  save me in your steadfast love.
17 Do not let me be put to shame, O LORD,
  for I call on you;
  let the wicked be put to shame;
  let them go dumbfounded to She'ol.
18 Let the lying lips be stilled
  that speak insolently against the righteous
  with pride and contempt.

19 O how abundant is your goodness
  that you have laid up for those who
  fear you,
  and accomplished for those who take refuge
  in you,
  in the sight of everyone!
20 In the shelter of your presence you hide
  them
  from human plots;
  you hold them safe under your shelter
  from contentious tongues.

21 Blessed be the LORD,
  for he has wondrously shown his
  steadfast love to me
  when I was beset as a city under siege.
22 I had said in my alarm,

---

y Heb *that glory*   *z* One Heb Ms Gk Syr Jerome: MT *I hate*
a Gk Syr: Heb *my iniquity*   *b* Cn: Heb *exceedingly*

"I am driven far^c from your sight."
But you heard my supplications
    when I cried out to you for help.

23 Love the LORD, all you his saints.
    The LORD preserves the faithful,
    but abundantly repays the one who acts
        haughtily.
24 Be strong, and let your heart take courage,
    all you who wait for the LORD.

NATIVE AMERICAN

Courage

Psalm 31 ends "Be strong, and let your heart take courage, / all you who wait for the LORD" (verse 24). Courage is an important value for many Native American peoples. For the Lakota tribe, it is one of four primary values. The Lakota word for courage is *woo-hit-i-ka.*

Leaders particularly have to be brave. It takes courage to make unpopular decisions, and to go against peer pressure. It takes courage to do the right thing when the wrong thing might be easier or more enjoyable. It takes courage to protect others and care for their needs. Because these kinds of actions take courage, practicing them will earn you honor.

What is the most courageous thing you have done for the sake of someone else?

To explore the other primary Lakota virtues, see the Native American articles for Psalms 73, 89, and 112.

▸ Psalm 31

Psalm 32
The Joy of Forgiveness

Of David. A Mas'kil.

1 Happy are those whose transgression is
        forgiven,
    whose sin is covered.

2 Happy are those to whom the LORD imputes
        no iniquity,
    and in whose spirit there is no deceit.

3 While I kept silence, my body wasted away
    through my groaning all day long.
4 For day and night your hand was heavy
        upon me;
    my strength was dried up^d as by the heat
        of summer.   *Se'lah*

5 Then I acknowledged my sin to you,
    and I did not hide my iniquity;
I said, "I will confess my transgressions to
        the LORD,"
    and you forgave the guilt of my sin.
             Se'lah

6 Therefore let all who are faithful
      offer prayer to you;
at a time of distress,^e the rush of mighty
        waters
    shall not reach them.
7 You are a hiding place for me;
    you preserve me from trouble;
    you surround me with glad cries of
        deliverance.   *Se'lah*

8 I will instruct you and teach you the way
        you should go;
    I will counsel you with my eye upon you.
9 Do not be like a horse or a mule, without
        understanding,
    whose temper must be curbed with bit
        and bridle,
    else it will not stay near you.

10 Many are the torments of the wicked,
    but steadfast love surrounds those who
        trust in the LORD.
11 Be glad in the LORD and rejoice, O righteous,
    and shout for joy, all you upright in
        heart.

Psalm 33
The Greatness and Goodness of God

1 Rejoice in the LORD, O you righteous.
    Praise befits the upright.
2 Praise the LORD with the lyre;
    make melody to him with the harp of
        ten strings.
3 Sing to him a new song;
    play skillfully on the strings, with loud
        shouts.

---

c Another reading is *cut off*   *d* Meaning of Heb uncertain
e Cn: Heb *at a time of finding only*

4 For the word of the LORD is upright,
  and all his work is done in faithfulness.
5 He loves righteousness and justice;
  the earth is full of the steadfast love of
    the LORD.

6 By the word of the LORD the heavens were
    made,
  and all their host by the breath of his
    mouth.
7 He gathered the waters of the sea as in a
    bottle;
  he put the deeps in storehouses.

8 Let all the earth fear the LORD;
  let all the inhabitants of the world stand
    in awe of him.
9 For he spoke, and it came to be;
  he commanded, and it stood firm.

10 The LORD brings the counsel of the nations
     to nothing;
   he frustrates the plans of the peoples.
11 The counsel of the LORD stands forever,
   the thoughts of his heart to all
     generations.
12 Happy is the nation whose God is the LORD,
   the people whom he has chosen as his
     heritage.

13 The LORD looks down from heaven;
   he sees all humankind.
14 From where he sits enthroned he watches
   all the inhabitants of the earth—
15 he who fashions the hearts of them all,
   and observes all their deeds.
16 A king is not saved by his great army;
   a warrior is not delivered by his great
     strength.
17 The war horse is a vain hope for victory,
   and by its great might it cannot save.

18 Truly the eye of the LORD is on those who
     fear him,
   on those who hope in his steadfast love,
19 to deliver their soul from death,
   and to keep them alive in famine.

20 Our soul waits for the LORD;
   he is our help and shield.
21 Our heart is glad in him,
   because we trust in his holy name.
22 Let your steadfast love, O LORD, be upon us,
   even as we hope in you.

Psalm 34

Praise for Deliverance from Trouble

*Of David, when he feigned madness before A·bim′e·lech,
so that he drove him out, and he went away.*

1 I will bless the LORD at all times;
  his praise shall continually be in my
    mouth.
2 My soul makes its boast in the LORD;
  let the humble hear and be glad.
3 O magnify the LORD with me,
  and let us exalt his name together.

4 I sought the LORD, and he answered me,
  and delivered me from all my fears.
5 Look to him, and be radiant;
  so your*f* faces shall never be ashamed.
6 This poor soul cried, and was heard by the
    LORD,
  and was saved from every trouble.
7 The angel of the LORD encamps
  around those who fear him, and delivers
    them.
8 O taste and see that the LORD is good;
  happy are those who take refuge in him.
9 O fear the LORD, you his holy ones,
  for those who fear him have no want.
10 The young lions suffer want and hunger,
   but those who seek the LORD lack no
     good thing.

11 Come, O children, listen to me;
   I will teach you the fear of the LORD.
12 Which of you desires life,
   and covets many days to enjoy good?
13 Keep your tongue from evil,
   and your lips from speaking deceit.
14 Depart from evil, and do good;
   seek peace, and pursue it.

15 The eyes of the LORD are on the righteous,
   and his ears are open to their cry.
16 The face of the LORD is against evildoers,
   to cut off the remembrance of them from
     the earth.
17 When the righteous cry for help, the LORD
     hears,
   and rescues them from all their troubles.
18 The LORD is near to the brokenhearted,
   and saves the crushed in spirit.

19 Many are the afflictions of the righteous,
   but the LORD rescues them from them all.
20 He keeps all their bones;
   not one of them will be broken.
21 Evil brings death to the wicked,

f Gk Syr Jerome: Heb *their*

and those who hate the righteous will be
    condemned.
22 The LORD redeems the life of his servants;
    none of those who take refuge in him
        will be condemned.

Psalm 35
Prayer for Deliverance from Enemies
Of David.

1 Contend, O LORD, with those who contend
        with me;
    fight against those who fight against me!
2 Take hold of shield and buckler,
    and rise up to help me!
3 Draw the spear and javelin
    against my pursuers;
    say to my soul,
        "I am your salvation."

4 Let them be put to shame and dishonor
    who seek after my life.
    Let them be turned back and confounded
    who devise evil against me.
5 Let them be like chaff before the wind,
    with the angel of the LORD driving
        them on.
6 Let their way be dark and slippery,
    with the angel of the LORD pursuing
        them.

7 For without cause they hid their net*g*
        for me;
    without cause they dug a pit*h* for my life.
8 Let ruin come on them unawares.
    And let the net that they hid ensnare them;
        let them fall in it—to their ruin.

9 Then my soul shall rejoice in the LORD,
    exulting in his deliverance.
10 All my bones shall say,
    "O LORD, who is like you?
    You deliver the weak
        from those too strong for them,
        the weak and needy from those who
            despoil them."

11 Malicious witnesses rise up;
    they ask me about things I do not know.
12 They repay me evil for good;
    my soul is forlorn.
13 But as for me, when they were sick,
    I wore sackcloth;
    I afflicted myself with fasting.
    I prayed with head bowed*i* on my bosom,
14   as though I grieved for a friend or a
        brother;

I went about as one who laments for a
        mother,
    bowed down and in mourning.

15 But at my stumbling they gathered in glee,
    they gathered together against me;
    ruffians whom I did not know
        tore at me without ceasing;
16 they impiously mocked more and more,*j*
        gnashing at me with their teeth.

17 How long, O LORD, will you look on?
    Rescue me from their ravages,
    my life from the lions!
18 Then I will thank you in the great
        congregation;
    in the mighty throng I will praise you.

19 Do not let my treacherous enemies rejoice
        over me,
    or those who hate me without cause
        wink the eye.
20 For they do not speak peace,
    but they conceive deceitful words
        against those who are quiet in the land.
21 They open wide their mouths against me;
    they say, "Aha, Aha,
        our eyes have seen it."

22 You have seen, O LORD; do not be silent!
    O Lord, do not be far from me!
23 Wake up! Bestir yourself for my defense,
    for my cause, my God and my Lord!
24 Vindicate me, O LORD, my God,
    according to your righteousness,
    and do not let them rejoice over me.
25 Do not let them say to themselves,
    "Aha, we have our heart's desire."
    Do not let them say, "We have swallowed
        you*k* up."

26 Let all those who rejoice at my calamity
        be put to shame and confusion;
    let those who exalt themselves against me
        be clothed with shame and dishonor.

27 Let those who desire my vindication
        shout for joy and be glad,
    and say evermore,
    "Great is the LORD,
        who delights in the welfare of his servant."
28 Then my tongue shall tell of your
        righteousness
    and of your praise all day long.

---

g Heb *a pit, their net*   *h* The word *pit* is transposed from
the preceding line   *i* Or *My prayer turned back*
j Cn Compare Gk: Heb *like the profanest of mockers of a
cake*   *k* Heb *him*

Psalm 36

Human Wickedness and Divine Goodness

To the leader. Of David, the servant of the LORD.

1 Transgression speaks to the wicked
deep in their hearts;
there is no fear of God
before their eyes.
2 For they flatter themselves in their own eyes
that their iniquity cannot be found out
and hated.
3 The words of their mouths are mischief and
deceit;
they have ceased to act wisely and do
good.
4 They plot mischief while on their beds;
they are set on a way that is not good;
they do not reject evil.

5 Your steadfast love, O LORD, extends to the
heavens,
your faithfulness to the clouds.
6 Your righteousness is like the mighty
mountains,
your judgments are like the great deep;
you save humans and animals alike,
O LORD.

7 How precious is your steadfast love, O God!
All people may take refuge in the shadow
of your wings.
8 They feast on the abundance of your house,
and you give them drink from the river
of your delights.
9 For with you is the fountain of life;
in your light we see light.

10 O continue your steadfast love to those who
know you,
and your salvation to the upright of
heart!
11 Do not let the foot of the arrogant tread
on me,
or the hand of the wicked drive me away.
12 There the evildoers lie prostrate;
they are thrust down, unable to rise.

Psalm 37

Exhortation to Patience and Trust

Of David.

1 Do not fret because of the wicked;
do not be envious of wrongdoers,
2 for they will soon fade like the grass,
and wither like the green herb.

3 Trust in the LORD, and do good;
so you will live in the land, and enjoy
security.
4 Take delight in the LORD,
and he will give you the desires of your
heart.
5 Commit your way to the LORD;
trust in him, and he will act.
6 He will make your vindication shine like
the light,
and the justice of your cause like the
noonday.

7 Be still before the LORD, and wait patiently
for him;
do not fret over those who prosper in
their way,
over those who carry out evil devices.
8 Refrain from anger, and forsake wrath.
Do not fret—it leads only to evil.
9 For the wicked shall be cut off,
but those who wait for the LORD shall
inherit the land.

10 Yet a little while, and the wicked will be no
more;
though you look diligently for their
place, they will not be there.
11 But the meek shall inherit the land,
and delight themselves in abundant
prosperity.

12 The wicked plot against the righteous,
and gnash their teeth at them;
13 but the LORD laughs at the wicked,
for he sees that their day is coming.

14 The wicked draw the sword and bend their
bows
to bring down the poor and needy,
to kill those who walk uprightly;
15 their sword shall enter their own heart,
and their bows shall be broken.

16 Better is a little that the righteous
person has
than the abundance of many wicked.
17 For the arms of the wicked shall be broken,
but the LORD upholds the righteous.

18 The LORD knows the days of the blameless,
and their heritage will abide forever;
19 they are not put to shame in evil times,
in the days of famine they have
abundance.

20 But the wicked perish,
  and the enemies of the LORD are like the
    glory of the pastures;
  they vanish—like smoke they vanish away.

21 The wicked borrow, and do not pay back,
  but the righteous are generous and keep
    giving;
22 for those blessed by the LORD shall inherit
    the land,
  but those cursed by him shall be cut off.

23 Our steps*l* are made firm by the LORD,
  when he delights in our*m* way;
24 though we stumble,*n* we*o* shall not fall
    headlong,
  for the LORD holds us*p* by the hand.

25 I have been young, and now am old,
  yet I have not seen the righteous forsaken
  or their children begging bread.
26 They are ever giving liberally and lending,
  and their children become a blessing.

27 Depart from evil, and do good;
  so you shall abide forever.
28 For the LORD loves justice;
  he will not forsake his faithful ones.

  The righteous shall be kept safe forever,
  but the children of the wicked shall be
    cut off.
29 The righteous shall inherit the land,
  and live in it forever.

30 The mouths of the righteous utter wisdom,
  and their tongues speak justice.
31 The law of their God is in their hearts;
  their steps do not slip.

32 The wicked watch for the righteous,
  and seek to kill them.
33 The LORD will not abandon them to their
    power,
  or let them be condemned when they are
    brought to trial.

34 Wait for the LORD, and keep to his way,
  and he will exalt you to inherit the land;
  you will look on the destruction of the
    wicked.

35 I have seen the wicked oppressing,
  and towering like a cedar of Lebanon.*q*
36 Again I*r* passed by, and they were no more;
  though I sought them, they could not be
    found.

37 Mark the blameless, and behold the upright,
  for there is posterity for the peaceable.

38 But transgressors shall be altogether
    destroyed;
  the posterity of the wicked shall be
    cut off.

39 The salvation of the righteous is from the
    LORD;
  he is their refuge in the time of trouble.
40 The LORD helps them and rescues them;
  he rescues them from the wicked, and
    saves them,
  because they take refuge in him.

Psalm 38

A Penitent Sufferer's Plea for Healing

A Psalm of David, for the memorial offering.

1 O LORD, do not rebuke me in your anger,
  or discipline me in your wrath.
2 For your arrows have sunk into me,
  and your hand has come down on me.

3 There is no soundness in my flesh
  because of your indignation;
  there is no health in my bones
  because of my sin.
4 For my iniquities have gone over my head;
  they weigh like a burden too heavy
    for me.

5 My wounds grow foul and fester
  because of my foolishness;
6 I am utterly bowed down and prostrate;
  all day long I go around mourning.
7 For my loins are filled with burning,
  and there is no soundness in my flesh.
8 I am utterly spent and crushed;
  I groan because of the tumult of my
    heart.

9 O Lord, all my longing is known to you;
  my sighing is not hidden from you.
10 My heart throbs, my strength fails me;
  as for the light of my eyes—it also has
    gone from me.
11 My friends and companions stand aloof
    from my affliction,
  and my neighbors stand far off.

12 Those who seek my life lay their snares;
  those who seek to hurt me speak of ruin,
  and meditate treachery all day long.

13 But I am like the deaf, I do not hear;
  like the mute, who cannot speak.

---

l Heb *A man's steps*   *m* Heb *his*   *n* Heb *he stumbles*
o Heb *he*   *p* Heb *him*   *q* Gk: Meaning of Heb uncertain
r Gk Syr Jerome: Heb *he*

14 Truly, I am like one who does not hear,
    and in whose mouth is no retort.

15 But it is for you, O LORD, that I wait;
    it is you, O Lord my God, who will
        answer.
16 For I pray, "Only do not let them rejoice
        over me,
    those who boast against me when my
        foot slips."

17 For I am ready to fall,
    and my pain is ever with me.
18 I confess my iniquity;
    I am sorry for my sin.
19 Those who are my foes without cause[s] are
        mighty,
    and many are those who hate me
        wrongfully.
20 Those who render me evil for good
    are my adversaries because I follow after
        good.

21 Do not forsake me, O LORD;
    O my God, do not be far from me;
22 make haste to help me,
    O Lord, my salvation.

Psalm 39

Prayer for Wisdom and Forgiveness

To the leader: to Je·dŭ'thun. A Psalm of David.

1 I said, "I will guard my ways
    that I may not sin with my tongue;
  I will keep a muzzle on my mouth
    as long as the wicked are in my presence."
2 I was silent and still;
    I held my peace to no avail;
  my distress grew worse,
3   my heart became hot within me.
  While I mused, the fire burned;
    then I spoke with my tongue:

4 "LORD, let me know my end,
    and what is the measure of my days;
  let me know how fleeting my life is.
5 You have made my days a few
        handbreadths,
    and my lifetime is as nothing in your
        sight.
  Surely everyone stands as a mere breath.
                                    Sĕ'lah

6   Surely everyone goes about like a
        shadow.
  Surely for nothing they are in turmoil;
    they heap up, and do not know who will
        gather.

7 "And now, O Lord, what do I wait for?
    My hope is in you.
8 Deliver me from all my transgressions.
    Do not make me the scorn of the fool.
9 I am silent; I do not open my mouth,
    for it is you who have done it.
10 Remove your stroke from me;
    I am worn down by the blows[t] of your
        hand.

11 "You chastise mortals
    in punishment for sin,
  consuming like a moth what is dear to
        them;
  surely everyone is a mere breath.   *Sĕ'lah*

12 "Hear my prayer, O LORD,
    and give ear to my cry;
  do not hold your peace at my tears.
  For I am your passing guest,
    an alien, like all my forebears.
13 Turn your gaze away from me, that I may
        smile again,
    before I depart and am no more."

Psalm 40

Thanksgiving for Deliverance and Prayer for Help

(Ps 70.1–5)

To the leader. Of David. A Psalm.

1 I waited patiently for the LORD;
    he inclined to me and heard my cry.
2 He drew me up from the desolate pit,[u]
    out of the miry bog,
  and set my feet upon a rock,
    making my steps secure.
3 He put a new song in my mouth,
    a song of praise to our God.
  Many will see and fear,
    and put their trust in the LORD.

4 Happy are those who make
    the LORD their trust,
  who do not turn to the proud,
    to those who go astray after false gods.
5 You have multiplied, O LORD my God,
    your wondrous deeds and your thoughts
        toward us;
  none can compare with you.
  Were I to proclaim and tell of them,
    they would be more than can be
        counted.

---

[s] Q Ms: MT *my living foes*   [t] Heb *hostility*   [u] Cn: Heb *pit
of tumult*

6 Sacrifice and offering you do
    not desire,
  but you have given me an
    open ear.*v*
  Burnt offering and sin offering
    you have not required.
7 Then I said, "Here I am;
  in the scroll of the book it is written
    of me.*w*
8 I delight to do your will, O my God;
  your law is within my heart."

9 I have told the glad news of deliverance
    in the great congregation;
  see, I have not restrained my lips,
    as you know, O LORD.
10 I have not hidden your saving help within
    my heart,
  I have spoken of your faithfulness and
    your salvation;
  I have not concealed your steadfast love and
    your faithfulness
  from the great congregation.

11 Do not, O LORD, withhold
    your mercy from me;
  let your steadfast love and your
    faithfulness
  keep me safe forever.
12 For evils have encompassed me
    without number;
  my iniquities have overtaken me,
    until I cannot see;
  they are more than the hairs of my head,
    and my heart fails me.

13 Be pleased, O LORD, to deliver me;
  O LORD, make haste to help me.
14 Let all those be put to shame and
    confusion
  who seek to snatch away my life;
  let those be turned back and brought to
    dishonor
  who desire my hurt.
15 Let those be appalled because of their
    shame
  who say to me, "Aha, Aha!"

16 But may all who seek you
    rejoice and be glad in you;
  may those who love your salvation
    say continually, "Great is the LORD!"
17 As for me, I am poor and needy,
  but the Lord takes thought for me.
  You are my help and my deliverer;
    do not delay, O my God.

Psalm 41

Assurance of God's Help and
a Plea for Healing

To the leader. A Psalm of David.

1 Happy are those who consider the poor;*x*
  the LORD delivers them in the day of
    trouble.
2 The LORD protects them and keeps them
    alive;
  they are called happy in the land.
  You do not give them up to the will of
    their enemies.
3 The LORD sustains them on their sickbed;
  in their illness you heal all their
    infirmities.*y*

4 As for me, I said, "O LORD, be gracious
    to me;
  heal me, for I have sinned against you."
5 My enemies wonder in malice
  when I will die, and my name perish.
6 And when they come to see me, they utter
    empty words,
  while their hearts gather mischief;
  when they go out, they tell it abroad.
7 All who hate me whisper together
    about me;
  they imagine the worst for me.

8 They think that a deadly thing has fastened
    on me,

---

v Heb *ears you have dug for me*   *w* Meaning of Heb uncertain
x Or *weak*   *y* Heb *you change all his bed*

42.1/b

that I will not rise again from where
 I lie.
9 Even my bosom friend in whom I trusted,
 who ate of my bread, has lifted the heel
  against me.
10 But you, O LORD, be gracious to me,
 and raise me up, that I may repay them.

11 By this I know that you are pleased
  with me;
 because my enemy has not triumphed
  over me.
12 But you have upheld me because of my
  integrity,
 and set me in your presence forever.

13 Blessed be the LORD, the God of Israel,
 from everlasting to everlasting.
   Amen and Amen.

BOOK II
(Psalms 42–72)
Psalm 42
Longing for God and His
Help in Distress

To the leader. A Mas'kil of the Ko'ra·hites.

1 As a deer longs for flowing streams,
 so my soul longs for you, O God.
2 My soul thirsts for God,
 for the living God.
When shall I come and behold
 the face of God?
3 My tears have been my food
 day and night,
while people say to me continually,
 "Where is your God?"

4 These things I remember,
 as I pour out my soul:
how I went with the throng,z
 and led them in procession to the house
  of God,
with glad shouts and songs of thanksgiving,
 a multitude keeping festival.
5 Why are you cast down, O my soul,
 and why are you disquieted within me?
Hope in God; for I shall again praise him,
 my help 6 and my God.

My soul is cast down within me;
 therefore I remember you
from the land of Jordan and of Hermon,
 from Mount Mi'zar.
7 Deep calls to deep
 at the thunder of your cataracts;

all your waves and your billows
 have gone over me.
8 By day the LORD commands his steadfast
  love,
 and at night his song is with me,
 a prayer to the God of my life.

PRAY IT!
Randy's First Day of School

Randy and his family have just moved to a new town. Randy is hopeful about this move because he didn't like his old neighborhood and school. There, he was often made fun of for his size. So, he figures this will be a new start for him, and just maybe the kids here will give him a chance.

The first day of school is exciting. Randy is nervous, but can't wait to meet some new people. As the principal walks him down to his new homeroom, he has hopeful visions of how great it will be. When they walk into the classroom, all that changes. As the principal introduces him, someone yells from the back of the room, "Hey, hey, hey, it's Fat Albert!" Everyone laughs. Randy smiles, only to hide the pain and anger he feels inside.

Have you ever experienced painful moments like the one Randy went through? Psalm 42 is a good prayer to turn to during moments like these. Verse 5 says, "Hope in God; for I shall again praise him, / my help and my God." If you follow this advice, the situation may not change, but your heart may find peace rather than anger.

▶ **Psalm 42**

9 I say to God, my rock,
 "Why have you forgotten me?
Why must I walk about mournfully
 because the enemy oppresses me?"
10 As with a deadly wound in my body,
 my adversaries taunt me,
while they say to me continually,
 "Where is your God?"

z Meaning of Heb uncertain

11 Why are you cast down, O my soul,
and why are you disquieted within me?
Hope in God; for I shall again praise him,
my help and my God.

Psalm 43
Prayer to God in Time of Trouble

1 Vindicate me, O God, and defend my cause
against an ungodly people;
from those who are deceitful and unjust
deliver me!
2 For you are the God in whom I take refuge;
why have you cast me off?
Why must I walk about mournfully
because of the oppression of the enemy?

3 O send out your light and your truth;
let them lead me;
let them bring me to your holy hill
and to your dwelling.
4 Then I will go to the altar of God,
to God my exceeding joy;
and I will praise you with the harp,
O God, my God.

5 Why are you cast down, O my soul,
and why are you disquieted within me?
Hope in God; for I shall again praise him,
my help and my God.

Psalm 44
National Lament and Prayer for Help

To the leader. Of the Kō'ra·hites. A Mas'kil.

1 We have heard with our ears, O God,
our ancestors have told us,
what deeds you performed in their days,
in the days of old:
2 you with your own hand drove out the
nations,
but them you planted;
you afflicted the peoples,
but them you set free;
3 for not by their own sword did they win the
land,
nor did their own arm give them victory;
but your right hand, and your arm,
and the light of your countenance,
for you delighted in them.

4 You are my King and my God;
you command*a* victories for Jacob.
5 Through you we push down our foes;
through your name we tread down our
assailants.
6 For not in my bow do I trust,
nor can my sword save me.

7 But you have saved us from our foes,
and have put to confusion those who
hate us.
8 In God we have boasted continually,
and we will give thanks to your name
forever. *Se'lah*

9 Yet you have rejected us and abased us,
and have not gone out with our armies.
10 You made us turn back from the foe,
and our enemies have gotten spoil.
11 You have made us like sheep for slaughter,
and have scattered us among the nations.
12 You have sold your people for a trifle,
demanding no high price for them.

13 You have made us the taunt of our
neighbors,
the derision and scorn of those
around us.
14 You have made us a byword among the
nations,
a laughingstock*b* among the peoples.
15 All day long my disgrace is before me,
and shame has covered my face
16 at the words of the taunters and revilers,
at the sight of the enemy and the
avenger.

17 All this has come upon us,
yet we have not forgotten you,
or been false to your covenant.
18 Our heart has not turned back,
nor have our steps departed from
your way,
19 yet you have broken us in the haunt of
jackals,
and covered us with deep darkness.

20 If we had forgotten the name of our God,
or spread out our hands to a strange god,
21 would not God discover this?
For he knows the secrets of the heart.
22 Because of you we are being killed all day
long,
and accounted as sheep for the slaughter.

23 Rouse yourself! Why do you sleep, O Lord?
Awake, do not cast us off forever!
24 Why do you hide your face?
Why do you forget our affliction and
oppression?
25 For we sink down to the dust;
our bodies cling to the ground.
26 Rise up, come to our help.

---

a Gk Syr: Heb *You are my King, O God; command*
b Heb *a shaking of the head*

Redeem us for the sake of your steadfast
love.

Psalm 45
Ode for a Royal Wedding

*To the leader: according to Lilies. Of the Kō'ra•hītes.
A Mas'kil. A love song.*

1 My heart overflows with a goodly theme;
　　I address my verses to the king;
　　my tongue is like the pen of a ready
　　　　scribe.

2 You are the most handsome of men;
　　grace is poured upon your lips;
　　therefore God has blessed you forever.

3 Gird your sword on your thigh,
　　　　O mighty one,
　　in your glory and majesty.

4 In your majesty ride on victoriously
　　for the cause of truth and to defend[c] the
　　　　right;
　　let your right hand teach you dread
　　　　deeds.

5 Your arrows are sharp
　　in the heart of the king's enemies;
　　the peoples fall under you.

6 Your throne, O God,[d] endures forever and
　　　　ever.
　　Your royal scepter is a scepter of equity;

7 　you love righteousness and hate
　　　　wickedness.
　　Therefore God, your God, has anointed you
　　　　with the oil of gladness beyond your
　　　　companions;

8 　your robes are all fragrant with myrrh
　　　　and aloes and cassia.
　　From ivory palaces stringed instruments
　　　　make you glad;

9 　daughters of kings are among your ladies
　　　　of honor;
　　at your right hand stands the queen in
　　　　gold of Ō'phir.

10 Hear, O daughter, consider and incline
　　　　your ear;
　　forget your people and your father's
　　　　house,

11 　and the king will desire your beauty.
　　Since he is your lord, bow to him;

12 　the people[e] of Tÿre will seek your favor
　　　　with gifts,
　　the richest of the people 13 with all kinds
　　　　of wealth.

The princess is decked in her chamber with
　　gold-woven robes;[f]

14 　in many-colored robes she is led to the
　　　　king;
　　behind her the virgins, her companions,
　　　　follow.

15 With joy and gladness they are led along
　　as they enter the palace of the king.

16 In the place of ancestors you, O king,[g] shall
　　　　have sons;
　　you will make them princes in all the
　　　　earth.

17 I will cause your name to be celebrated in
　　　　all generations;
　　therefore the peoples will praise you
　　　　forever and ever.

Psalm 46
God's Defense of His City and People

*To the leader. Of the Kō'ra•hītes.
According to Al'a•moth. A Song.*

1 God is our refuge and strength,
　　a very present[h] help in trouble.

2 Therefore we will not fear, though the earth
　　　　should change,
　　though the mountains shake in the heart
　　　　of the sea;

3 though its waters roar and foam,
　　though the mountains tremble with its
　　　　tumult.　　　　　　　　　　*Sē'lah*

4 There is a river whose streams make glad
　　　　the city of God,
　　the holy habitation of the Most High.

5 God is in the midst of the city;[i] it shall not
　　　　be moved;
　　God will help it when the morning
　　　　dawns.

6 The nations are in an uproar, the kingdoms
　　　　totter;
　　he utters his voice, the earth melts.

7 The LORD of hosts is with us;
　　the God of Jacob is our refuge.[j]　　*Sē'lah*

8 Come, behold the works of the LORD;
　　see what desolations he has brought on
　　　　the earth.

9 He makes wars cease to the end of the
　　　　earth;
　　he breaks the bow, and shatters the spear;
　　he burns the shields with fire.

10 "Be still, and know that I am God!
　　I am exalted among the nations,

---

c Cn: Heb *and the meekness of*　　*d* Or *Your throne is a
throne of God, it*　　*e* Heb *daughter*　　*f* Or *people.* 13 *All
glorious is the princess within, gold embroidery is her clothing*
g Heb lacks *O king*　　*h* Or *well proved*　　*i* Heb *of it*
j Or *fortress*

I am exalted in the earth."
11 The LORD of hosts is with us;
    the God of Jacob is our refuge.*k*   *Sē'lah*

Psalm 47
God's Rule over the Nations

To the leader. Of the Kō'ra·hites. A Psalm.

1 Clap your hands, all you peoples;
    shout to God with loud songs of joy.
2 For the LORD, the Most High, is awesome,
    a great king over all the earth.
3 He subdued peoples under us,
    and nations under our feet.
4 He chose our heritage for us,
    the pride of Jacob whom he loves.   *Sē'lah*

5 God has gone up with a shout,
    the LORD with the sound of a trumpet.
6 Sing praises to God, sing praises;
    sing praises to our King, sing praises.
7 For God is the king of all the earth;
    sing praises with a psalm.*l*

8 God is king over the nations;
    God sits on his holy throne.
9 The princes of the peoples gather
    as the people of the God of Abraham.
For the shields of the earth belong to God;
    he is highly exalted.

Psalm 48
The Glory and Strength of Zion

A Song. A Psalm of the Kō'ra·hites.

1 Great is the LORD and greatly to be praised
    in the city of our God.
His holy mountain, 2 beautiful in elevation,
    is the joy of all the earth,
Mount Zion, in the far north,
    the city of the great King.
3 Within its citadels God
    has shown himself a sure defense.

4 Then the kings assembled,
    they came on together.
5 As soon as they saw it, they were astounded;
    they were in panic, they took to flight;
6 trembling took hold of them there,
    pains as of a woman in labor,
7 as when an east wind shatters
    the ships of Tar'shish.
8 As we have heard, so have we seen
    in the city of the LORD of hosts,
in the city of our God,
    which God establishes forever.   *Sē'lah*

9 We ponder your steadfast love, O God,
    in the midst of your temple.
10 Your name, O God, like your praise,
    reaches to the ends of the earth.
Your right hand is filled with victory.
11   Let Mount Zion be glad,
let the towns*m* of Judah rejoice
    because of your judgments.

12 Walk about Zion, go all around it,
    count its towers,
13 consider well its ramparts;
    go through its citadels,
that you may tell the next generation
14   that this is God,
our God forever and ever.
    He will be our guide forever.

Psalm 49
The Folly of Trust in Riches

To the leader. Of the Kō'ra·hites. A Psalm.

1 Hear this, all you peoples;
    give ear, all inhabitants of the world,
2 both low and high,
    rich and poor together.
3 My mouth shall speak wisdom;
    the meditation of my heart shall be
        understanding.
4 I will incline my ear to a proverb;
    I will solve my riddle to the music of the
        harp.

5 Why should I fear in times of trouble,
    when the iniquity of my persecutors
        surrounds me,
6 those who trust in their wealth
    and boast of the abundance of their
        riches?
7 Truly, no ransom avails for one's life,*n*
    there is no price one can give to God
        for it.
8 For the ransom of life is costly,
    and can never suffice,
9 that one should live on forever
    and never see the grave.*o*

10 When we look at the wise, they die;
    fool and dolt perish together
    and leave their wealth to others.
11 Their graves*p* are their homes forever,
    their dwelling places to all generations,
        though they named lands their own.

---

k Or *fortress*   *l* Heb *Maskil*   *m* Heb *daughters*
n Another reading is *no one can ransom a brother*
o Heb *the pit*   *p* Gk Syr Compare Tg: Heb *their inward*
(thought)

12 Mortals cannot abide in their pomp;
    they are like the animals that perish.

13 Such is the fate of the foolhardy,
    the end of those*q* who are pleased with
        their lot.   *Se′lah*
14 Like sheep they are appointed for She′ōl;
    Death shall be their shepherd;
straight to the grave they descend,*r*
    and their form shall waste away;
    She′ōl shall be their home.*s*
15 But God will ransom my soul from the
        power of She′ōl,
    for he will receive me.   *Se′lah*

16 Do not be afraid when some become rich,
    when the wealth of their houses
        increases.
17 For when they die they will carry nothing
        away;
    their wealth will not go down after them.
18 Though in their lifetime they count
        themselves happy
    —for you are praised when you do well
        for yourself—
19 they*t* will go to the company of their
        ancestors,
    who will never again see the light.
20 Mortals cannot abide in their pomp;
    they are like the animals that perish.

Psalm 50

The Acceptable Sacrifice

A Psalm of Ā′saph.

1 The mighty one, God the LORD,
    speaks and summons the earth
    from the rising of the sun to its setting.
2 Out of Zion, the perfection of beauty,
    God shines forth.

3 Our God comes and does not keep silence,
    before him is a devouring fire,
    and a mighty tempest all around him.
4 He calls to the heavens above
    and to the earth, that he may judge his
        people:
5 "Gather to me my faithful ones,
    who made a covenant with me by
        sacrifice!"
6 The heavens declare his righteousness,
    for God himself is judge.   *Se′lah*

7 "Hear, O my people, and I will speak,
    O Israel, I will testify against you.
    I am God, your God.

8 Not for your sacrifices do I rebuke you;
    your burnt offerings are continually
        before me.
9 I will not accept a bull from your house,
    or goats from your folds.
10 For every wild animal of the forest is mine,
    the cattle on a thousand hills.
11 I know all the birds of the air,*u*
    and all that moves in the field is mine.

12 "If I were hungry, I would not tell you,
    for the world and all that is in it is mine.
13 Do I eat the flesh of bulls,
    or drink the blood of goats?
14 Offer to God a sacrifice of thanksgiving,*v*
    and pay your vows to the Most High.
15 Call on me in the day of trouble;
    I will deliver you, and you shall
        glorify me."

16 But to the wicked God says:
    "What right have you to recite my
        statutes,
    or take my covenant on your lips?
17 For you hate discipline,
    and you cast my words behind you.
18 You make friends with a thief when you
        see one,
    and you keep company with adulterers.

19 "You give your mouth free rein for evil,
    and your tongue frames deceit.
20 You sit and speak against your kin;
    you slander your own mother's child.
21 These things you have done and I have been
        silent;
    you thought that I was one just like
        yourself.
    But now I rebuke you, and lay the charge
        before you.

22 "Mark this, then, you who forget God,
    or I will tear you apart, and there will be
        no one to deliver.
23 Those who bring thanksgiving as their
        sacrifice honor me;
    to those who go the right way*w*
    I will show the salvation of God."

---

q Tg: Heb *after them*   *r* Cn: Heb *the upright shall have
dominion over them in the morning*   *s* Meaning of Heb
uncertain   *t* Cn: Heb *you*   *u* Gk Syr Tg: Heb *mountains*
v Or *make thanksgiving your sacrifice to God*   *w* Heb *who set
a way*

A Fresh Start

Psalm 51 is a beautiful prayer of sorrow and remorse. It is attributed to King David, who would have written it seeking forgiveness and a fresh start after committing adultery with Bathsheba. Take a few minutes to read this psalm prayerfully and reflect on the marvelous way it asks for God's help in starting over.

In our time too, people can fall into a sinful pattern of having sex outside of marriage. Many people experience a deep regret and sadness in losing their virginity in a short-term and uncommitted relationship. Thinking they can never regain their moral virtue, they then pursue one loveless relationship after another. The promise of Psalm 51 is that they can start fresh at any point in this cycle! Some people call this new beginning a secondary virginity—not, of course, a physical virginity, but a virginity of the heart and soul. It means a commitment not to have sex again except with the person they marry.

So, whenever you are feeling the weight of sin, whether it is premarital sex or some other sin, pray Psalm 51. Let it mark your commitment to start fresh with God's help. Ask God to show you what situations to avoid and what people you need to ask to support you. Remember, God is always ready to forgive you, and all of heaven rejoices each time you make a fresh start!

▶ Psalm 51

Psalm 51

Prayer for Cleansing and Pardon

To the leader. A Psalm of David, when the prophet Nathan came to him, after he had gone in to Bath·she'ba.

1 Have mercy on me, O God,
according to your steadfast love;
according to your abundant mercy
blot out my transgressions.
2 Wash me thoroughly from my iniquity,
and cleanse me from my sin.

3 For I know my transgressions,
and my sin is ever before me.
4 Against you, you alone, have I sinned,
and done what is evil in your sight,
so that you are justified in your sentence
and blameless when you pass judgment.
5 Indeed, I was born guilty,
a sinner when my mother conceived me.

6 You desire truth in the inward being;[x]
therefore teach me wisdom in my secret heart.
7 Purge me with hyssop, and I shall be clean;
wash me, and I shall be whiter than snow.
8 Let me hear joy and gladness;
let the bones that you have crushed rejoice.
9 Hide your face from my sins,
and blot out all my iniquities.

10 Create in me a clean heart, O God,
and put a new and right[y] spirit within me.
11 Do not cast me away from your presence,
and do not take your holy spirit from me.
12 Restore to me the joy of your salvation,
and sustain in me a willing[z] spirit.

13 Then I will teach transgressors your ways,
and sinners will return to you.
14 Deliver me from bloodshed, O God,
O God of my salvation,
and my tongue will sing aloud of your deliverance.

15 O Lord, open my lips,
and my mouth will declare your praise.
16 For you have no delight in sacrifice;
if I were to give a burnt offering, you would not be pleased.
17 The sacrifice acceptable to God[a] is a broken spirit;
a broken and contrite heart, O God, you will not despise.

18 Do good to Zion in your good pleasure;
rebuild the walls of Jerusalem,
19 then you will delight in right sacrifices,

---

[x] Meaning of Heb uncertain   [y] Or *steadfast*
[z] Or *generous*   [a] Or *My sacrifice, O God,*

in burnt offerings and whole burnt
offerings;
then bulls will be offered on your altar.

Psalm 52

Judgment on the Deceitful

*To the leader. A Mas'kil of David, when Dō'eg the
Ē'dom·ite came to Saul and said to him, "David has
come to the house of A·him'e·lech."*

1 Why do you boast, O mighty one,
of mischief done against the godly?[b]
All day long 2 you are plotting
destruction.
Your tongue is like a sharp razor,
you worker of treachery.
3 You love evil more than good,
and lying more than speaking the truth.
Sē'lah

4 You love all words that devour,
O deceitful tongue.

5 But God will break you down forever;
he will snatch and tear you from your
tent;
he will uproot you from the land of the
living.   *Sē'lah*
6 The righteous will see, and fear,
and will laugh at the evildoer,[c] saying,
7 "See the one who would not take
refuge in God,
but trusted in abundant riches,
and sought refuge in wealth!"[d]

8 But I am like a green olive tree
in the house of God.
I trust in the steadfast love of God
forever and ever.
9 I will thank you forever,
because of what you have done.
In the presence of the faithful
I will proclaim[e] your name, for it is
good.

Psalm 53

Denunciation of Godlessness
(Ps 14.1–7)

*To the leader: according to Mā'ha·lath. A Mas'kil
of David.*

1 Fools say in their hearts, "There is no God."
They are corrupt, they commit
abominable acts;
there is no one who does good.

2 God looks down from heaven on
humankind

to see if there are any who are wise,
who seek after God.

3 They have all fallen away, they are all alike
perverse;
there is no one who does good,
no, not one.

4 Have they no knowledge, those evildoers,
who eat up my people as they eat bread,
and do not call upon God?

5 There they shall be in great terror,
in terror such as has not been.
For God will scatter the bones of the
ungodly;[f]
they will be put to shame,[g] for God has
rejected them.

6 O that deliverance for Israel would come
from Zion!
When God restores the fortunes of his
people,
Jacob will rejoice; Israel will be glad.

Psalm 54

Prayer for Vindication

*To the leader: with stringed instruments. A Mas'kil
of David, when the Ziph'ites went and told Saul,
"David is in hiding among us."*

1 Save me, O God, by your name,
and vindicate me by your might.
2 Hear my prayer, O God;
give ear to the words of my mouth.

3 For the insolent have risen against me,
the ruthless seek my life;
they do not set God before them.   *Sē'lah*

4 But surely, God is my helper;
the Lord is the upholder of[h] my life.
5 He will repay my enemies for their evil.
In your faithfulness, put an end to them.

6 With a freewill offering I will sacrifice
to you;
I will give thanks to your name, O LORD,
for it is good.
7 For he has delivered me from every trouble,
and my eye has looked in triumph on
my enemies.

---

b Cn Compare Syr: Heb *the kindness of God*   c Heb *him*
d Syr Tg: Heb *in his destruction*   e Cn: Heb *wait for*
f Cn Compare Gk Syr: Heb *him who encamps against you*
g Gk: Heb *you have put (them) to shame*   h Gk Syr Jerome:
Heb *is of those who uphold* or *is with those who uphold*

Psalm 55

Complaint about a Friend's Treachery

To the leader: with stringed instruments. A Mas'kil of David.

1 Give ear to my prayer, O God;
  do not hide yourself from my
    supplication.
2 Attend to me, and answer me;
  I am troubled in my complaint.
I am distraught 3 by the noise of the enemy,
  because of the clamor of the wicked.
For they bring[i] trouble upon me,
  and in anger they cherish enmity
    against me.

4 My heart is in anguish within me,
  the terrors of death have fallen upon me.
5 Fear and trembling come upon me,
  and horror overwhelms me.
6 And I say, "O that I had wings like a dove!
  I would fly away and be at rest;
7 truly, I would flee far away;
  I would lodge in the wilderness;   *Sē'lah*
8 I would hurry to find a shelter for myself
  from the raging wind and tempest."

9 Confuse, O Lord, confound their speech;
  for I see violence and strife in the city.
10 Day and night they go around it
  on its walls,
and iniquity and trouble are within it;
11   ruin is in its midst;
oppression and fraud
  do not depart from its marketplace.
12 It is not enemies who taunt me—
  I could bear that;
it is not adversaries who deal insolently
    with me—
  I could hide from them.
13 But it is you, my equal,
  my companion, my familiar friend,
14 with whom I kept pleasant company;
  we walked in the house of God with the
    throng.
15 Let death come upon them;
  let them go down alive to Shē'ōl;
  for evil is in their homes and in their
    hearts.
16 But I call upon God,
  and the LORD will save me.
17 Evening and morning and at noon
  I utter my complaint and moan,
  and he will hear my voice.
18 He will redeem me unharmed
  from the battle that I wage,

for many are arrayed against me.
19 God, who is enthroned from of old,   *Sē'lah*
  will hear, and will humble them—
because they do not change,
  and do not fear God.

20 My companion laid hands on a friend
  and violated a covenant with me[j]
21 with speech smoother than butter,
  but with a heart set on war;
with words that were softer than oil,
  but in fact were drawn swords.

22 Cast your burden[k] on the LORD,
  and he will sustain you;
he will never permit
  the righteous to be moved.

23 But you, O God, will cast them down
  into the lowest pit;
the bloodthirsty and treacherous
  shall not live out half their days.
But I will trust in you.

PRAY IT!

Betrayed!

How long, O God, will I feel this miserable? How long can this go on?
My friend betrayed me. I trusted and was made a fool. Everyone is laughing at me. I feel humiliated. How can I ever recover from this?
I don't think I can take it much longer!
But I still trust you, God. I want to believe you are with me. Help me to know it's true. You're all I have now.

▸ Psalm 55

Psalm 56

Trust in God under Persecution

To the leader: according to The Dove on Far-off Terebinths. Of David. A Mik'tam, when the Phi·lis'tines seized him in Gath.

1 Be gracious to me, O God, for people
    trample on me;
  all day long foes oppress me;
2 my enemies trample on me all day long,
  for many fight against me.

---

i Cn Compare Gk: Heb *they cause to totter*   *j* Heb lacks *with me*   *k* Or *Cast what he has given you*

O Most High, [3] when I am afraid,
I put my trust in you.
[4] In God, whose word I praise,
in God I trust; I am not afraid;
what can flesh do to me?

[5] All day long they seek to injure my cause;
all their thoughts are against me for evil.
[6] They stir up strife, they lurk,
they watch my steps.
As they hoped to have my life,
[7] so repay[l] them for their crime;
in wrath cast down the peoples, O God!

[8] You have kept count of my tossings;
put my tears in your bottle.
Are they not in your record?
[9] Then my enemies will retreat
in the day when I call.
This I know, that[m] God is for me.
[10] In God, whose word I praise,
in the LORD, whose word I praise,
[11] in God I trust; I am not afraid.
What can a mere mortal do to me?

[12] My vows to you I must perform, O God;
I will render thank offerings to you.
[13] For you have delivered my soul from death,
and my feet from falling,
so that I may walk before God
in the light of life.

Psalm 57

Praise and Assurance
under Persecution
(Cp Ps 108.1–5)

To the leader: Do Not Destroy. Of David. A Mik'tam,
when he fled from Saul, in the cave.

[1] Be merciful to me, O God, be merciful
to me,
for in you my soul takes refuge;
in the shadow of your wings I will take
refuge,
until the destroying storms pass by.
[2] I cry to God Most High,
to God who fulfills his purpose for me.
[3] He will send from heaven and save me,
he will put to shame those who trample
on me. *Sẽ'lah*
God will send forth his steadfast love and
his faithfulness.

[4] I lie down among lions
that greedily devour[n] human prey;
their teeth are spears and arrows,
their tongues sharp swords.

[5] Be exalted, O God, above the heavens.
Let your glory be over all the earth.

[6] They set a net for my steps;
my soul was bowed down.
They dug a pit in my path,
but they have fallen into it themselves. *Sẽ'lah*

[7] My heart is steadfast, O God,
my heart is steadfast.
I will sing and make melody.
[8] Awake, my soul!
Awake, O harp and lyre!
I will awake the dawn.
[9] I will give thanks to you, O Lord, among
the peoples;
I will sing praises to you among the
nations.
[10] For your steadfast love is as high as the
heavens;
your faithfulness extends to the clouds.

[11] Be exalted, O God, above the heavens.
Let your glory be over all the earth.

Psalm 58

Prayer for Vengeance

To the leader: Do Not Destroy. Of David. A Mik'tam.

[1] Do you indeed decree what is right, you
gods?[o]
Do you judge people fairly?
[2] No, in your hearts you devise wrongs;
your hands deal out violence on earth.

[3] The wicked go astray from the womb;
they err from their birth, speaking lies.
[4] They have venom like the venom of a
serpent,
like the deaf adder that stops its ear,
[5] so that it does not hear the voice of
charmers
or of the cunning enchanter.

[6] O God, break the teeth in their mouths;
tear out the fangs of the young lions,
O LORD!
[7] Let them vanish like water that runs away;
like grass let them be trodden down[p] and
wither.
[8] Let them be like the snail that dissolves into
slime;
like the untimely birth that never sees
the sun.
[9] Sooner than your pots can feel the heat of
thorns,

---

[l] Cn: Heb *rescue*   [m] Or *because*   [n] Cn: Heb *are aflame*
for   [o] Or *mighty lords*   [p] Cn: Meaning of Heb uncertain

whether green or ablaze, may he sweep
them away!

10 The righteous will rejoice when they see
vengeance done;
they will bathe their feet in the blood of
the wicked.

11 People will say, "Surely there is a reward for
the righteous;
surely there is a God who judges on
earth."

Psalm 59
Prayer for Deliverance from Enemies

*To the leader: Do Not Destroy. Of David. A Mik'tam,
when Saul ordered his house to be watched in order
to kill him.*

1 Deliver me from my enemies, O my God;
protect me from those who rise up
against me.
2 Deliver me from those who work evil;
from the bloodthirsty save me.

3 Even now they lie in wait for my life;
the mighty stir up strife against me.
For no transgression or sin of mine, O LORD,
4 for no fault of mine, they run and make
ready.

Rouse yourself, come to my help and see!
5 You, LORD God of hosts, are God of
Israel.
Awake to punish all the nations;
spare none of those who treacherously
plot evil.   *Sē'lah*

6 Each evening they come back,
howling like dogs
and prowling about the city.
7 There they are, bellowing with their mouths,
with sharp words*q* on their lips—
for "Who," they think,*r* "will hear us?"

8 But you laugh at them, O LORD;
you hold all the nations in derision.
9 O my strength, I will watch for you;
for you, O God, are my fortress.
10 My God in his steadfast love will meet me;
my God will let me look in triumph on
my enemies.

11 Do not kill them, or my people may forget;
make them totter by your power, and
bring them down,
O Lord, our shield.
12 For the sin of their mouths, the words of
their lips,
let them be trapped in their pride.

For the cursing and lies that they utter,
13 consume them in wrath;
consume them until they are no more.
Then it will be known to the ends of the
earth
that God rules over Jacob.   *Sē'lah*

14 Each evening they come back,
howling like dogs
and prowling about the city.
15 They roam about for food,
and growl if they do not get their fill.

16 But I will sing of your might;
I will sing aloud of your steadfast love in
the morning.
For you have been a fortress for me
and a refuge in the day of my distress.
17 O my strength, I will sing praises to you,
for you, O God, are my fortress,
the God who shows me steadfast love.

Psalm 60
Prayer for National Victory
after Defeat
(Cp Ps 108.6–13)

*To the leader: according to the Lily of the Covenant.
A Mik'tam of David; for instruction; when he struggled
with Ar'am-nā·ha·rā'im and with Ar'am-zō'bah, and
when Jō'ab on his return killed twelve thousand
É'dom·ites in the Valley of Salt.*

1 O God, you have rejected us, broken our
defenses;
you have been angry; now restore us!
2 You have caused the land to quake; you
have torn it open;
repair the cracks in it, for it is tottering.
3 You have made your people suffer hard
things;
you have given us wine to drink that
made us reel.

4 You have set up a banner for those who
fear you,
to rally to it out of bowshot.*s*   *Sē'lah*
5 Give victory with your right hand, and
answer us,*t*
so that those whom you love may be
rescued.

6 God has promised in his sanctuary:*u*
"With exultation I will divide up
Shē'chem,
and portion out the Vale of Suc'coth.

q Heb *with swords*   *r* Heb lacks *they think*   *s* Gk Syr
Jerome: Heb *because of the truth*   *t* Another reading is *me*
u Or *by his holiness*

7 Gil'e•ad is mine, and Ma•nas'seh is mine;
  Ē'phra•im is my helmet;
  Judah is my scepter.
8 Mō'ab is my washbasin;
  on Ē'dom I hurl my shoe;
  over Phi•lis'ti•a I shout in triumph."

9 Who will bring me to the fortified city?
  Who will lead me to Ē'dom?
10 Have you not rejected us, O God?
   You do not go out, O God, with our
     armies.
11 O grant us help against the foe,
   for human help is worthless.
12 With God we shall do valiantly;
   it is he who will tread down our foes.

Psalm 61
Assurance of God's Protection
To the leader: with stringed instruments. Of David.

1 Hear my cry, O God;
  listen to my prayer.
2 From the end of the earth I call to you,
  when my heart is faint.

  Lead me to the rock
    that is higher than I;
3 for you are my refuge,
  a strong tower against the enemy.

4 Let me abide in your tent forever,
  find refuge under the shelter of your
    wings.   *Sē'lah*
5 For you, O God, have heard my vows;
  you have given me the heritage of those
    who fear your name.

6 Prolong the life of the king;
  may his years endure to all generations!
7 May he be enthroned forever before God;
  appoint steadfast love and faithfulness to
    watch over him!

8 So I will always sing praises to your name,
  as I pay my vows day after day.

Psalm 62
Song of Trust in God Alone
To the leader: according to Je•dū'thun. A Psalm of David.

1 For God alone my soul waits in silence;
  from him comes my salvation.
2 He alone is my rock and my salvation,
  my fortress; I shall never be shaken.

3 How long will you assail a person,
  will you batter your victim, all of you,

as you would a leaning wall, a tottering
  fence?
4 Their only plan is to bring down a person
  of prominence.
  They take pleasure in falsehood;
they bless with their mouths,
  but inwardly they curse.   *Sē'lah*

5 For God alone my soul waits in silence,
  for my hope is from him.
6 He alone is my rock and my salvation,
  my fortress; I shall not be shaken.
7 On God rests my deliverance and my
    honor;
  my mighty rock, my refuge is in God.

8 Trust in him at all times, O people;
  pour out your heart before him;
  God is a refuge for us.   *Sē'lah*

9 Those of low estate are but a breath,
  those of high estate are a delusion;
in the balances they go up;
  they are together lighter than a breath.
10 Put no confidence in extortion,
   and set no vain hopes on robbery;
   if riches increase, do not set your heart
     on them.

11 Once God has spoken;
   twice have I heard this:
that power belongs to God,

PRAY IT! Decide!

Who are you going to trust? Where will you find your power? in the right people? in the right clothes? in money? in the right job?
  Or can you trust God to be your rock and your salvation (Ps 62.2)? Will you let God be your refuge (61.4; 62.7) in times of hardship? Why is it so hard sometimes to let your soul wait for God in silence (62.1)?

God, I am weak. Help me every day to put my trust in you.
  Help me to believe that you and I can do anything together.

▶ Psalm 62

12 and steadfast love belongs to you,
O Lord.
For you repay to all
according to their work.

Psalm 63

Comfort and Assurance in
God's Presence

*A Psalm of David, when he was in the Wilderness
of Judah.*

1 O God, you are my God, I seek you,
my soul thirsts for you;
my flesh faints for you,
as in a dry and weary land where there is
no water.
2 So I have looked upon you in the sanctuary,
beholding your power and glory.
3 Because your steadfast love is better than
life,
my lips will praise you.
4 So I will bless you as long as I live;
I will lift up my hands and call on your
name.
5 My soul is satisfied as with a rich feast,[v]
and my mouth praises you with joyful
lips
6 when I think of you on my bed,
and meditate on you in the watches of
the night;
7 for you have been my help,
and in the shadow of your wings I sing
for joy.
8 My soul clings to you;
your right hand upholds me.

9 But those who seek to destroy my life
shall go down into the depths of the
earth;
10 they shall be given over to the power of the
sword,
they shall be prey for jackals.
11 But the king shall rejoice in God;
all who swear by him shall exult,
for the mouths of liars will be stopped.

Psalm 64

Prayer for Protection from Enemies

To the leader. A Psalm of David.

1 Hear my voice, O God, in my complaint;
preserve my life from the dread enemy.
2 Hide me from the secret plots of the
wicked,
from the scheming of evildoers,
3 who whet their tongues like swords,

who aim bitter words like arrows,
4 shooting from ambush at the blameless;
they shoot suddenly and without fear.
5 They hold fast to their evil purpose;
they talk of laying snares secretly,
thinking, "Who can see us?[w]
6 Who can search out our crimes?[x]
We have thought out a cunningly conceived
plot."
For the human heart and mind are deep.

7 But God will shoot his arrow at them;
they will be wounded suddenly.
8 Because of their tongue he will bring them
to ruin;[y]
all who see them will shake with horror.
9 Then everyone will fear;
they will tell what God has brought about,
and ponder what he has done.

10 Let the righteous rejoice in the LORD
and take refuge in him.
Let all the upright in heart glory.

Psalm 65

Thanksgiving for Earth's Bounty

To the leader. A Psalm of David. A Song.

1 Praise is due to you,
O God, in Zion;
and to you shall vows be performed,
2 O you who answer prayer!
To you all flesh shall come.
3 When deeds of iniquity overwhelm us,
you forgive our transgressions.
4 Happy are those whom you choose and
bring near
to live in your courts.
We shall be satisfied with the goodness of
your house,
your holy temple.

5 By awesome deeds you answer us with
deliverance,
O God of our salvation;
you are the hope of all the ends of the earth
and of the farthest seas.
6 By your[z] strength you established the
mountains;
you are girded with might.
7 You silence the roaring of the seas,
the roaring of their waves,
the tumult of the peoples.

---

v Heb *with fat and fatness*   *w* Syr: Heb *them*   *x* Cn: Heb
They search out crimes   *y* Cn: Heb *They will bring him to
ruin, their tongue being against them*   *z* Gk Jerome: Heb
his

8 Those who live at earth's farthest bounds are
   awed by your signs;
you make the gateways of the morning and
   the evening shout for joy.

9 You visit the earth and water it,
   you greatly enrich it;
the river of God is full of water;
   you provide the people with grain,
   for so you have prepared it.
10 You water its furrows abundantly,
   settling its ridges,
softening it with showers,
   and blessing its growth.
11 You crown the year with your bounty;
   your wagon tracks overflow with richness.
12 The pastures of the wilderness overflow,
   the hills gird themselves with joy,
13 the meadows clothe themselves with flocks,
   the valleys deck themselves with grain,
   they shout and sing together for joy.

Psalm 66

Praise for God's Goodness to Israel

To the leader. A Song. A Psalm.

1 Make a joyful noise to God, all the earth;
2 sing the glory of his name;
   give to him glorious praise.
3 Say to God, "How awesome are your deeds!
   Because of your great power, your
   enemies cringe before you.
4 All the earth worships you;
   they sing praises to you,
   sing praises to your name."   *Sĕ'lah*

5 Come and see what God has done:
   he is awesome in his deeds among
   mortals.
6 He turned the sea into dry land;
   they passed through the river on foot.
There we rejoiced in him,
7   who rules by his might forever,
whose eyes keep watch on the nations—
   let the rebellious not exalt themselves.
                                          Sĕ'lah

8 Bless our God, O peoples,
   let the sound of his praise be heard,
9 who has kept us among the living,
   and has not let our feet slip.
10 For you, O God, have tested us;
   you have tried us as silver is tried.
11 You brought us into the net;
   you laid burdens on our backs;

12 you let people ride over our heads;
   we went through fire and through water;
yet you have brought us out to a spacious
   place.*a*

13 I will come into your house with burnt
   offerings;
   I will pay you my vows,
14 those that my lips uttered
   and my mouth promised when I was in
   trouble.
15 I will offer to you burnt offerings of fatlings,
   with the smoke of the sacrifice of rams;
I will make an offering of bulls and goats.
                                          Sĕ'lah

16 Come and hear, all you who fear God,
   and I will tell what he has done for me.
17 I cried aloud to him,
   and he was extolled with my tongue.
18 If I had cherished iniquity in my heart,
   the Lord would not have listened.
19 But truly God has listened;
   he has given heed to the words of my
   prayer.

20 Blessed be God,
   because he has not rejected my prayer
   or removed his steadfast love from me.

Psalm 67

The Nations Called to Praise God

To the leader: with stringed instruments. A Psalm.
A Song.

1 May God be gracious to us and bless us
   and make his face to shine upon us,
                                          Sĕ'lah
2 that your way may be known upon earth,
   your saving power among all nations.
3 Let the peoples praise you, O God;
   let all the peoples praise you.

4 Let the nations be glad and sing for joy,
   for you judge the peoples with equity
   and guide the nations upon earth.   *Sĕ'lah*
5 Let the peoples praise you, O God;
   let all the peoples praise you.

6 The earth has yielded its increase;
   God, our God, has blessed us.
7 May God continue to bless us;
   let all the ends of the earth revere him.

a Cn Compare Gk Syr Jerome Tg: Heb *to a saturation*

Psalm 68

Praise and Thanksgiving

To the leader. Of David. A Psalm. A Song.

1 Let God rise up, let his enemies be
        scattered;
    let those who hate him flee before him.
2 As smoke is driven away, so drive them
        away;
    as wax melts before the fire,
    let the wicked perish before God.
3 But let the righteous be joyful;
    let them exult before God;
    let them be jubilant with joy.

4 Sing to God, sing praises to his name;
    lift up a song to him who rides upon the
        clouds[b]—
    his name is the LORD—
    be exultant before him.
5 Father of orphans and protector of widows
    is God in his holy habitation.
6 God gives the desolate a home to live in;
    he leads out the prisoners to prosperity,
    but the rebellious live in a parched land.

7 O God, when you went out before your
        people,
    when you marched through the
        wilderness,   *Sĕ'lah*
8 the earth quaked, the heavens poured down
        rain
    at the presence of God, the God of Sinai,
    at the presence of God, the God of Israel.
9 Rain in abundance, O God, you showered
        abroad;
    you restored your heritage when it
        languished;
10 your flock found a dwelling in it;
    in your goodness, O God, you provided
        for the needy.

11 The Lord gives the command;
    great is the company of those[c] who bore
        the tidings:
12 "The kings of the armies, they flee, they
        flee!"
    The women at home divide the spoil,
13 though they stay among the sheepfolds—
    the wings of a dove covered with silver,
    its pinions with green gold.
14 When the Almighty[d] scattered kings there,
    snow fell on Zal'mon.

15 O mighty mountain, mountain of Bā'shan;
    O many-peaked mountain, mountain of
        Bā'shan!

16 Why do you look with envy,
        O many-peaked mountain,
    at the mount that God desired for his
        abode,
    where the LORD will reside forever?
17 With mighty chariotry, twice ten thousand,
        thousands upon thousands,
    the Lord came from Sinai into the holy
        place.[e]
18 You ascended the high mount,
        leading captives in your train
    and receiving gifts from people,
    even from those who rebel against the LORD
        God's abiding there.
19 Blessed be the Lord,
    who daily bears us up;
    God is our salvation.   *Sĕ'lah*
20 Our God is a God of salvation,
    and to GOD, the Lord, belongs escape
        from death.

21 But God will shatter the heads of his
        enemies,
    the hairy crown of those who walk in
        their guilty ways.
22 The Lord said,
    "I will bring them back from Bā'shan,
    I will bring them back from the depths of
        the sea,
23 so that you may bathe[f] your feet in blood,
    so that the tongues of your dogs may
        have their share from the foe."

24 Your solemn processions are seen,[g] O God,
    the processions of my God, my King, into
        the sanctuary—
25 the singers in front, the musicians last,
    between them girls playing tambourines:
26 "Bless God in the great congregation,
    the LORD, O you who are of Israel's
        fountain!"
27 There is Benjamin, the least of them, in the
        lead,
    the princes of Judah in a body,
    the princes of Zeb'ū·lun, the princes of
        Naph'ta·lī.

28 Summon your might, O God;
    show your strength, O God, as you have
        done for us before.
29 Because of your temple at Jerusalem
    kings bear gifts to you.

---

b Or *cast up a highway for him who rides through the deserts*
c Or *company of the women*   d Traditional rendering of
Heb *Shaddai*   e Cn: Heb *The Lord among them Sinai in the
holy* (place)   f Gk Syr Tg: Heb *shatter*   g Or *have been
seen*

30 Rebuke the wild animals that live among
     the reeds,
    the herd of bulls with the calves of the
       peoples.
  Trample*h* under foot those who lust after
     tribute;
    scatter the peoples who delight in war.*i*

31 Let bronze be brought from Egypt;
    let Ethiopia*j* hasten to stretch out its
      hands to God.

32 Sing to God, O kingdoms of the earth;
    sing praises to the Lord,   *Sě'lah*

33 O rider in the heavens, the ancient heavens;
    listen, he sends out his voice, his mighty
      voice.

34 Ascribe power to God,
    whose majesty is over Israel;
    and whose power is in the skies.

35 Awesome is God in his*k* sanctuary,
    the God of Israel;
  he gives power and strength to his
      people.

Blessed be God!

Psalm 69
Prayer for Deliverance
from Persecution

To the leader: according to Lilies. Of David.

1 Save me, O God,
    for the waters have come up to my neck.
2 I sink in deep mire,
    where there is no foothold;
  I have come into deep waters,
    and the flood sweeps over me.
3 I am weary with my crying;
    my throat is parched.
  My eyes grow dim
    with waiting for my God.

4 More in number than the hairs of my head
    are those who hate me without cause;
  many are those who would destroy me,
    my enemies who accuse me falsely.
  What I did not steal
    must I now restore?
5 O God, you know my folly;
    the wrongs I have done are not hidden
      from you.

6 Do not let those who hope in you be put to
      shame because of me,
    O Lord GOD of hosts;
  do not let those who seek you be
      dishonored because of me,
    O God of Israel.

AFRICAN
AMERICAN
Black People
Praise the Lord

Psalm 68 commands us to sing praises to the Lord. We are told to praise the Lord because God is the "Father of orphans and protector of widows" (verse 5), and "gives the desolate a home to live in" and "leads out the prisoners to prosperity" (verse 6), and "daily bears us up" (verse 19), and "will shatter the heads of his enemies" (verse 21).

Near the end of all this praise, the psalmist says, "Let bronze be brought from Egypt; / let Ethiopia hasten to stretch out its hands to God" (verse 31). The psalmist's call to Egypt and Ethiopia is significant for African Americans because the Egyptians and the Ethiopians were North African black people.

Nevertheless, the message of Psalm 68 is for all people, whether they are black, brown, red, yellow, or white. All people ought to submit to the Lord, all people ought to praise the Lord, and all people ought to render their whole self and their whole substance to the Lord. It matters not who we are or where we come from; the Lord is God and worthy of all praise!

▶ Psalm 68

7 It is for your sake that I have borne
      reproach,
    that shame has covered my face.
8 I have become a stranger to my kindred,
    an alien to my mother's children.

9 It is zeal for your house that has
      consumed me;
    the insults of those who insult you have
      fallen on me.
10 When I humbled my soul with fasting,*l*
    they insulted me for doing so.
11 When I made sackcloth my clothing,
    I became a byword to them.

h Cn: Heb *Trampling*   *i* Meaning of Heb of verse 30 is uncertain   *j* Or *Nubia*; Heb *Cush*   *k* Gk: Heb *from your* *l* Gk Syr: Heb *I wept, with fasting my soul*, or *I made my soul mourn with fasting*

12 I am the subject of gossip for those who sit
      in the gate,
   and the drunkards make songs about me.

13 But as for me, my prayer is to you, O LORD.
   At an acceptable time, O God,
      in the abundance of your steadfast love,
         answer me.
   With your faithful help 14 rescue me
      from sinking in the mire;
   let me be delivered from my enemies
      and from the deep waters.
15 Do not let the flood sweep over me,
   or the deep swallow me up,
   or the Pit close its mouth over me.

16 Answer me, O LORD, for your steadfast love
      is good;
   according to your abundant mercy, turn
      to me.
17 Do not hide your face from your servant,
   for I am in distress—make haste to
      answer me.
18 Draw near to me, redeem me,
   set me free because of my enemies.

19 You know the insults I receive,
   and my shame and dishonor;
   my foes are all known to you.
20 Insults have broken my heart,
   so that I am in despair.
   I looked for pity, but there was none;
   and for comforters, but I found none.
21 They gave me poison for food,
   and for my thirst they gave me vinegar to
      drink.

22 Let their table be a trap for them,
   a snare for their allies.
23 Let their eyes be darkened so that they
      cannot see,
   and make their loins tremble continually.
24 Pour out your indignation upon them,
   and let your burning anger overtake
      them.
25 May their camp be a desolation;
   let no one live in their tents.
26 For they persecute those whom you have
      struck down,
   and those whom you have wounded,
      they attack still more.*m*
27 Add guilt to their guilt;
   may they have no acquittal from you.
28 Let them be blotted out of the book of the
      living;
   let them not be enrolled among the
      righteous.

29 But I am lowly and in pain;
   let your salvation, O God, protect me.
30 I will praise the name of God with a song;
   I will magnify him with thanksgiving.
31 This will please the LORD more than an ox
   or a bull with horns and hoofs.
32 Let the oppressed see it and be glad;
   you who seek God, let your hearts revive.
33 For the LORD hears the needy,
   and does not despise his own that are in
      bonds.

34 Let heaven and earth praise him,
   the seas and everything that moves in
      them.
35 For God will save Zion
   and rebuild the cities of Judah;
   and his servants shall live*n* there and
      possess it;
36 the children of his servants shall
      inherit it,
   and those who love his name shall live
      in it.

Psalm 70

Prayer for Deliverance from Enemies
(Ps 40.13–17)

To the leader. Of David, for the memorial offering.

1 Be pleased, O God, to deliver me.
   O LORD, make haste to help me!
2 Let those be put to shame and confusion
   who seek my life.
   Let those be turned back and brought to
      dishonor
   who desire to hurt me.
3 Let those who say, "Aha, Aha!"
   turn back because of their shame.

4 Let all who seek you
   rejoice and be glad in you.
   Let those who love your salvation
   say evermore, "God is great!"
5 But I am poor and needy;
   hasten to me, O God!
   You are my help and my deliverer;
   O LORD, do not delay!

Psalm 71

Prayer for Lifelong Protection and Help

1 In you, O LORD, I take refuge;
   let me never be put to shame.
2 In your righteousness deliver me and
   rescue me;

---

m Gk Syr: Heb *recount the pain of*   *n* Syr: Heb *and they
shall live*

incline your ear to me and save me.

3 Be to me a rock of refuge,
 　a strong fortress,*o* to save me,
 　for you are my rock and my fortress.

4 Rescue me, O my God, from the hand of
 　　the wicked,
 　from the grasp of the unjust and cruel.

5 For you, O Lord, are my hope,
 　my trust, O LORD, from my youth.

6 Upon you I have leaned from my birth;
 　it was you who took me from my
 　　mother's womb.
 My praise is continually of you.

7 I have been like a portent to many,
 　but you are my strong refuge.

8 My mouth is filled with your praise,
 　and with your glory all day long.

9 Do not cast me off in the time of old age;
 　do not forsake me when my strength is
 　　spent.

10 For my enemies speak concerning me,
 　and those who watch for my life consult
 　　together.

11 They say, "Pursue and seize that person
 　whom God has forsaken,
 　for there is no one to deliver."

12 O God, do not be far from me;
 　O my God, make haste to help me!

13 Let my accusers be put to shame and
 　　consumed;
 　let those who seek to hurt me
 　be covered with scorn and disgrace.

14 But I will hope continually,
 　and will praise you yet more and more.

15 My mouth will tell of your righteous acts,
 　of your deeds of salvation all day long,
 　though their number is past my
 　　knowledge.

16 I will come praising the mighty deeds of the
 　　Lord GOD,
 　I will praise your righteousness, yours
 　　alone.

17 O God, from my youth you have taught me,
 　and I still proclaim your wondrous deeds.

18 So even to old age and gray hairs,
 　O God, do not forsake me,
 　until I proclaim your might
 　　to all the generations to come.*p*
 Your power 19 and your righteousness,
 　　O God,
 　reach the high heavens.

You who have done great things,
 　O God, who is like you?

20 You who have made me see many troubles
 　　and calamities
 　will revive me again;
 from the depths of the earth
 　you will bring me up again.

21 You will increase my honor,
 　and comfort me once again.

22 I will also praise you with the harp
 　for your faithfulness, O my God;
 I will sing praises to you with the lyre,
 　O Holy One of Israel.

23 My lips will shout for joy
 　when I sing praises to you;
 　my soul also, which you have rescued.

24 All day long my tongue will talk of your
 　　righteous help,
 for those who tried to do me harm
 　have been put to shame, and disgraced.

Psalm 72

Prayer for Guidance and Support
for the King

Of Solomon.

1 Give the king your justice, O God,
 　and your righteousness to a king's son.

2 May he judge your people with
 　　righteousness,
 　and your poor with justice.

3 May the mountains yield prosperity for the
 　　people,
 　and the hills, in righteousness.

4 May he defend the cause of the poor of the
 　　people,
 　give deliverance to the needy,
 　and crush the oppressor.

5 May he live*q* while the sun endures,
 　and as long as the moon, throughout all
 　　generations.

6 May he be like rain that falls on the mown
 　　grass,
 　like showers that water the earth.

7 In his days may righteousness flourish
 　and peace abound, until the moon is no
 　　more.

8 May he have dominion from sea to sea,
 　and from the River to the ends of the
 　　earth.

9 May his foes*r* bow down before him,
 　and his enemies lick the dust.

---

o Gk Compare 31.3: Heb *to come continually you have
commanded*　　*p* Gk Compare Syr: Heb *to a generation, to
all that come*　　*q* Gk: Heb *may they fear you*　　*r* Cn: Heb
those who live in the wilderness

P
S
A
L
M
S

¹⁰ May the kings of Tar'shish and of the isles
    render him tribute,
may the kings of Shē'ba and Sē'ba
    bring gifts.
¹¹ May all kings fall down before him,
    all nations give him service.

¹² For he delivers the needy when they call,
    the poor and those who have no helper.
¹³ He has pity on the weak and the needy,
    and saves the lives of the needy.
¹⁴ From oppression and violence he redeems
        their life;
    and precious is their blood in his sight.

¹⁵ Long may he live!
    May gold of Shē'ba be given to him.
May prayer be made for him continually,
    and blessings invoked for him all day
        long.
¹⁶ May there be abundance of grain in the
        land;
    may it wave on the tops of the
        mountains;
    may its fruit be like Lebanon;
and may people blossom in the cities
    like the grass of the field.
¹⁷ May his name endure forever,
    his fame continue as long as the sun.
May all nations be blessed in him;^s
    may they pronounce him happy.

¹⁸ Blessed be the LORD, the God of Israel,
    who alone does wondrous things.
¹⁹ Blessed be his glorious name forever;
    may his glory fill the whole earth.
        Amen and Amen.

²⁰ The prayers of David son of Jesse are ended.

BOOK III
(Psalms 73–89)

Psalm 73

Plea for Relief from Oppressors

A Psalm of A'saph.

¹ Truly God is good to the upright,^t
    to those who are pure in heart.
² But as for me, my feet had almost stumbled;
    my steps had nearly slipped.
³ For I was envious of the arrogant;
    I saw the prosperity of the wicked.

⁴ For they have no pain;
    their bodies are sound and sleek.
⁵ They are not in trouble as others are;
    they are not plagued like other people.

AFRICAN AMERICAN
Open Up Your Treasure

If you are black, you may have thought that
you've been left out, that God doesn't need you
or your talents. African Americans and other
ethnic groups have often been relegated to the
background. But as Eccl 3.1 says, "For everything there is a season, and a time for every
matter under heaven." And from Psalm 72, we
see there is a timing for God's call to us.

Psalm 72.10 says the kings of Sheba and
Seba shall come to pay tribute to the King of
Israel. Sheba, or Seba, was an ancient kingdom,
located near Ethiopia, that included black-
skinned people.

In Matthew's story of Jesus' birth, God
sends a message in the heavens to inform the
dark-skinned wise men from the East when it
is time to come and open up their treasures to
the King.

God is sending a star to us now. God is
talking loud to us, including blacks as a people.
"Get yourself ready, and be prepared to bring
your gifts to me," God says. God has opened
the door for us to come, but we must be willing
to fall down and worship God and open up our
treasures. If we do that, we too will be wise
people who acknowledge the One who is born
King. Are you ready to acknowledge our real
King?

▸ **Psalm 72.10–11**

⁶ Therefore pride is their necklace;
    violence covers them like a garment.
⁷ Their eyes swell out with fatness;
    their hearts overflow with follies.
⁸ They scoff and speak with malice;
    loftily they threaten oppression.
⁹ They set their mouths against heaven,
    and their tongues range over the earth.

¹⁰ Therefore the people turn and praise them,^u
    and find no fault in them.^v
¹¹ And they say, "How can God know?
    Is there knowledge in the Most High?"

---

^s Or *bless themselves by him*   ^t Or *good to Israel*
^u Cn: Heb *his people return here*   ^v Cn: Heb *abundant
waters are drained by them*

12 Such are the wicked;
    always at ease, they increase in riches.
13 All in vain I have kept my heart clean
    and washed my hands in innocence.
14 For all day long I have been plagued,
    and am punished every morning.

15 If I had said, "I will talk on in this way,"
    I would have been untrue to the circle of
        your children.
16 But when I thought how to understand this,
    it seemed to me a wearisome task,
17 until I went into the sanctuary of God;
    then I perceived their end.
18 Truly you set them in slippery places;
    you make them fall to ruin.
19 How they are destroyed in a moment,
    swept away utterly by terrors!
20 They are*w* like a dream when one awakes;
    on awaking you despise their phantoms.

21 When my soul was embittered,
    when I was pricked in heart,
22 I was stupid and ignorant,
    I was like a brute beast toward you.
23 Nevertheless I am continually with you;
    you hold my right hand.
24 You guide me with your counsel,
    and afterward you will receive me with
        honor.*x*
25 Whom have I in heaven but you?
    And there is nothing on earth that I
        desire other than you.
26 My flesh and my heart may fail,
    but God is the strength*y* of my heart and
        my portion forever.

27 Indeed, those who are far from you will
        perish;
    you put an end to those who are false
        to you.
28 But for me it is good to be near God;
    I have made the Lord GOD my refuge,
    to tell of all your works.

Psalm 74
Plea for Help in Time of National Humiliation

A Mas'kil of Ā'saph.

1 O God, why do you cast us off forever?
    Why does your anger smoke against the
        sheep of your pasture?
2 Remember your congregation, which you
        acquired long ago,
    which you redeemed to be the tribe of
        your heritage.

NATIVE AMERICAN

Wisdom

Psalm 73 explores the common wisdom question of why the wicked prosper (verse 3). The psalmist finally sees clearly that the wicked eventually fall to ruin (verse 17). The gift of wisdom is also an important value for many Native American peoples. For the Lakota tribe, it is one of four primary values. The Lakota word for wisdom is *wok-sa-pe*.

Wisdom is the ability to see clearly and not be taken in by illusions or outer appearances. The wise person knows that what is inside someone is more important than what is outside. The wise person also knows that we are nothing without the power of Wakan-Tanka, the Great Spirit. Because the sun helps us see things the way they really are, many Native Americans face the rising sun each day to pray to God for wisdom.

To explore the other primary Lakota virtues, see the Native American articles for Psalms 31, 89, and 112.

▶ Psalm 73

Remember Mount Zion, where you came
        to dwell.
3 Direct your steps to the perpetual ruins;
    the enemy has destroyed everything in
        the sanctuary.

4 Your foes have roared within your holy
        place;
    they set up their emblems there.
5 At the upper entrance they hacked
    the wooden trellis with axes.*z*
6 And then, with hatchets and hammers,
    they smashed all its carved work.
7 They set your sanctuary on fire;
    they desecrated the dwelling place of
        your name,

---

w Cn: Heb *Lord*   *x* Or *to glory*   *y* Heb *rock*
z Cn Compare Gk Syr: Meaning of Heb uncertain

bringing it to the ground.

8 They said to themselves, "We will utterly
      subdue them";
    they burned all the meeting places of
      God in the land.

9 We do not see our emblems;
      there is no longer any prophet,
      and there is no one among us who
        knows how long.
10 How long, O God, is the foe to scoff?
      Is the enemy to revile your name
        forever?
11 Why do you hold back your hand;
      why do you keep your hand in[a] your
        bosom?

12 Yet God my King is from of old,
      working salvation in the earth.
13 You divided the sea by your might;
      you broke the heads of the dragons in
        the waters.
14 You crushed the heads of Le·vi′a·than;
      you gave him as food[b] for the creatures
        of the wilderness.
15 You cut openings for springs and torrents;
      you dried up ever-flowing streams.
16 Yours is the day, yours also the night;
      you established the luminaries[c] and
        the sun.
17 You have fixed all the bounds of
        the earth;
      you made summer and winter.

18 Remember this, O LORD, how the enemy
        scoffs,
      and an impious people reviles your
        name.
19 Do not deliver the soul of your dove to the
        wild animals;
      do not forget the life of your poor
        forever.

20 Have regard for your[d] covenant,
      for the dark places of the land are full of
        the haunts of violence.
21 Do not let the downtrodden be put to
        shame;
      let the poor and needy praise
        your name.
22 Rise up, O God, plead your cause;
      remember how the impious scoff at you
        all day long.
23 Do not forget the clamor of your foes,
      the uproar of your adversaries that goes
        up continually.

Psalm 75

Thanksgiving for God's Wondrous Deeds

*To the leader: Do Not Destroy. A Psalm of Ā′saph.
A Song.*

1 We give thanks to you, O God;
      we give thanks; your name is near.
    People tell of your wondrous deeds.

2 At the set time that I appoint
      I will judge with equity.
3 When the earth totters, with all its
        inhabitants,
      it is I who keep its pillars steady.   *Se′lah*
4 I say to the boastful, "Do not boast,"
      and to the wicked, "Do not lift up your
        horn;
5 do not lift up your horn on high,
      or speak with insolent neck."

6 For not from the east or from the west
      and not from the wilderness comes
        lifting up;
7 but it is God who executes judgment,
      putting down one and lifting up another.
8 For in the hand of the LORD there is a cup
      with foaming wine, well mixed;
    he will pour a draught from it,
      and all the wicked of the earth
      shall drain it down to the dregs.
9 But I will rejoice[e] forever;
      I will sing praises to the God of Jacob.

10 All the horns of the wicked I will cut off,
      but the horns of the righteous shall be
        exalted.

Psalm 76

Israel's God—Judge of All the Earth

*To the leader: with stringed instruments. A Psalm
of Ā′saph. A Song.*

1 In Judah God is known,
      his name is great in Israel.
2 His abode has been established in Salem,
      his dwelling place in Zion.
3 There he broke the flashing arrows,
      the shield, the sword, and the weapons
        of war.   *Se′lah*

4 Glorious are you, more majestic
      than the everlasting mountains.[f]
5 The stouthearted were stripped of their
        spoil;

a Cn: Heb *do you consume your right hand from*
b Heb *food for the people*   c Or *moon;* Heb *light*
d Gk Syr: Heb *the*   e Gk: Heb *declare*   f Gk: Heb *the
mountains of prey*

they sank into sleep;
none of the troops
was able to lift a hand.

6 At your rebuke, O God of Jacob,
both rider and horse lay stunned.

7 But you indeed are awesome!
Who can stand before you
when once your anger is roused?

8 From the heavens you uttered judgment;
the earth feared and was still

9 when God rose up to establish judgment,
to save all the oppressed of the earth.
Sĕ'lah

10 Human wrath serves only to praise you,
when you bind the last bit of your*g*
wrath around you.

11 Make vows to the LORD your God, and
perform them;
let all who are around him bring gifts
to the one who is awesome,

12 who cuts off the spirit of princes,
who inspires fear in the kings of the
earth.

Psalm 77
God's Mighty Deeds Recalled

To the leader: according to Je•dŭ'thun. Of Ā'saph.
A Psalm.

1 I cry aloud to God,
aloud to God, that he may hear me.

2 In the day of my trouble I seek the Lord;
in the night my hand is stretched out
without wearying;
my soul refuses to be comforted.

3 I think of God, and I moan;
I meditate, and my spirit faints.   *Sĕ'lah*

4 You keep my eyelids from closing;
I am so troubled that I cannot speak.

5 I consider the days of old,
and remember the years of long ago.

6 I commune*h* with my heart in the night;
I meditate and search my spirit:*i*

7 "Will the Lord spurn forever,
and never again be favorable?

8 Has his steadfast love ceased forever?
Are his promises at an end for all time?

9 Has God forgotten to be gracious?
Has he in anger shut up his compassion?"
Sĕ'lah

10 And I say, "It is my grief
that the right hand of the Most High has
changed."

11 I will call to mind the deeds of the LORD;
I will remember your wonders of old.

12 I will meditate on all your work,
and muse on your mighty deeds.

13 Your way, O God, is holy.
What god is so great as our God?

14 You are the God who works wonders;
you have displayed your might among
the peoples.

15 With your strong arm you redeemed your
people,
the descendants of Jacob and Joseph.
Sĕ'lah

16 When the waters saw you, O God,
when the waters saw you, they were
afraid;
the very deep trembled.

17 The clouds poured out water;
the skies thundered;
your arrows flashed on every side.

18 The crash of your thunder was in the
whirlwind;
your lightnings lit up the world;
the earth trembled and shook.

19 Your way was through the sea,
your path, through the mighty waters;
yet your footprints were unseen.

20 You led your people like a flock
by the hand of Moses and Aaron.

Psalm 78
God's Goodness and
Israel's Ingratitude

A Mas'kil of Ā'saph.

1 Give ear, O my people, to my teaching;
incline your ears to the words of my
mouth.

2 I will open my mouth in a parable;
I will utter dark sayings from of old,

3 things that we have heard and known,
that our ancestors have told us.

4 We will not hide them from their children;
we will tell to the coming generation
the glorious deeds of the LORD, and his
might,
and the wonders that he has done.

5 He established a decree in Jacob,
and appointed a law in Israel,
which he commanded our ancestors
to teach to their children;

6 that the next generation might know them,
the children yet unborn,

g Heb lacks *your*   *h* Gk Syr: Heb *My music*
i Syr Jerome: Heb *my spirit searches*

P
S
A
L
M
S

The Big Picture

Perspective is a valuable thing. It is easy for us to get caught up in the moment, overwhelmed by the urgency of school assignments, sports, and time with family and friends. As difficult as it is, we need to step back for a moment or two and try to grasp the big picture.

You've probably heard the maxim Hindsight is twenty-twenty. When we look back at our life and see where we have come from, the path often makes sense. The twists and turns that were so frustrating and confusing can now be recognized as temporary diversions on our journey. Everything we experienced—the good and the bad—contains lessons for us. The question is, How good a student are we?

The key to wisdom is reflection. Psalm 77 keeps saying this in different ways: "I meditate" (verses 3,6,12), "I consider" (verse 5), "I will call to mind" (verse 11), and "I will remember" (verse 11). How do you take the time to remember where you have been and to meditate on where you hope to go? Do you learn from the great teacher, life experience? Do you see the whole forest, or only the trees right in front of you?

If you don't already spend some time at the end of each day reflecting on the events of that day, begin doing so. Perhaps keep a journal on how you felt or what you learned. Over time, you will see the big picture emerge and even have a greater sense of God's presence in your life.

▶ Psalm 77

and rise up and tell them to their children,
7   so that they should set their hope
      in God,
and not forget the works of God,
    but keep his commandments;
8 and that they should not be like their
      ancestors,
    a stubborn and rebellious generation,
a generation whose heart was not steadfast,
    whose spirit was not faithful to God.

9 The Ē′phra•im•ites, armed with[j] the bow,
    turned back on the day of battle.
10 They did not keep God's covenant,
    but refused to walk according to his law.
11 They forgot what he had done,
    and the miracles that he had shown
      them.
12 In the sight of their ancestors he worked
      marvels
    in the land of Egypt, in the fields of
      Zō′an.
13 He divided the sea and let them pass
      through it,
    and made the waters stand like a heap.
14 In the daytime he led them with a cloud,
    and all night long with a fiery light.
15 He split rocks open in the wilderness,

and gave them drink abundantly as from
      the deep.
16 He made streams come out of the rock,
    and caused waters to flow down like
      rivers.

17 Yet they sinned still more against him,
    rebelling against the Most High in the
      desert.
18 They tested God in their heart
    by demanding the food they craved.
19 They spoke against God, saying,
    "Can God spread a table in the
      wilderness?
20 Even though he struck the rock so that
      water gushed out
    and torrents overflowed,
can he also give bread,
    or provide meat for his people?"

21 Therefore, when the LORD heard, he was full
      of rage;
    a fire was kindled against Jacob,
    his anger mounted against Israel,
22 because they had no faith in God,
    and did not trust his saving power.
23 Yet he commanded the skies above,
    and opened the doors of heaven;

_____

j Heb armed with shooting

24 he rained down on them manna to eat,
    and gave them the grain of heaven.
25 Mortals ate of the bread of angels;
    he sent them food in abundance.
26 He caused the east wind to blow in the
        heavens,
    and by his power he led out the south
        wind;
27 he rained flesh upon them like dust,
    winged birds like the sand of the seas;
28 he let them fall within their camp,
    all around their dwellings.
29 And they ate and were well filled,
    for he gave them what they craved.
30 But before they had satisfied their craving,
    while the food was still in their mouths,
31 the anger of God rose against them
    and he killed the strongest of them,
    and laid low the flower of Israel.

32 In spite of all this they still sinned;
    they did not believe in his wonders.
33 So he made their days vanish like a breath,
    and their years in terror.
34 When he killed them, they sought for him;
    they repented and sought God earnestly.
35 They remembered that God was their rock,
    the Most High God their redeemer.
36 But they flattered him with their mouths;
    they lied to him with their tongues.
37 Their heart was not steadfast toward him;
    they were not true to his covenant.
38 Yet he, being compassionate,
    forgave their iniquity,
    and did not destroy them;
often he restrained his anger,
    and did not stir up all his wrath.
39 He remembered that they were but flesh,
    a wind that passes and does not come
        again.
40 How often they rebelled against him in the
        wilderness
    and grieved him in the desert!
41 They tested God again and again,
    and provoked the Holy One of Israel.
42 They did not keep in mind his power,
    or the day when he redeemed them from
        the foe;
43 when he displayed his signs in Egypt,
    and his miracles in the fields of Zō'an.
44 He turned their rivers to blood,
    so that they could not drink of their
        streams.
45 He sent among them swarms of flies, which
        devoured them,
    and frogs, which destroyed them.

46 He gave their crops to the caterpillar,
    and the fruit of their labor to the locust.
47 He destroyed their vines with hail,
    and their sycamores with frost.
48 He gave over their cattle to the hail,
    and their flocks to thunderbolts.
49 He let loose on them his fierce anger,
    wrath, indignation, and distress,
    a company of destroying angels.
50 He made a path for his anger;
    he did not spare them from death,
    but gave their lives over to the plague.
51 He struck all the firstborn in Egypt,
    the first issue of their strength in the
        tents of Ham.
52 Then he led out his people like sheep,
    and guided them in the wilderness like a
        flock.
53 He led them in safety, so that they were not
        afraid;
    but the sea overwhelmed their enemies.
54 And he brought them to his holy hill,
    to the mountain that his right hand
        had won.
55 He drove out nations before them;
    he apportioned them for a possession
    and settled the tribes of Israel in their
        tents.

56 Yet they tested the Most High God,
    and rebelled against him.
    They did not observe his decrees,
57 but turned away and were faithless like their
        ancestors;
    they twisted like a treacherous bow.
58 For they provoked him to anger with their
        high places;
    they moved him to jealousy with their
        idols.
59 When God heard, he was full of wrath,
    and he utterly rejected Israel.
60 He abandoned his dwelling at Shī'lōh,
    the tent where he dwelt among mortals,
61 and delivered his power to captivity,
    his glory to the hand of the foe.
62 He gave his people to the sword,
    and vented his wrath on his heritage.
63 Fire devoured their young men,
    and their girls had no marriage song.
64 Their priests fell by the sword,
    and their widows made no lamentation.
65 Then the Lord awoke as from sleep,
    like a warrior shouting because of wine.
66 He put his adversaries to rout;
    he put them to everlasting disgrace.

P
S
A
L
M
S

67 He rejected the tent of Joseph,
    he did not choose the tribe of Ē′phra·im;
68 but he chose the tribe of Judah,
    Mount Zion, which he loves.
69 He built his sanctuary like the high heavens,
    like the earth, which he has founded
      forever.
70 He chose his servant David,
    and took him from the sheepfolds;
71 from tending the nursing ewes he
      brought him
    to be the shepherd of his people Jacob,
    of Israel, his inheritance.
72 With upright heart he tended them,
    and guided them with skillful hand.

Psalm 79

Plea for Mercy for Jerusalem

A Psalm of Ā′saph.

1 O God, the nations have come into your
      inheritance;
    they have defiled your holy temple;
    they have laid Jerusalem in ruins.
2 They have given the bodies of your servants
    to the birds of the air for food,
    the flesh of your faithful to the wild
      animals of the earth.
3 They have poured out their blood like water
    all around Jerusalem,
    and there was no one to bury them.
4 We have become a taunt to our neighbors,
    mocked and derided by those around us.
5 How long, O LORD? Will you be angry
      forever?
    Will your jealous wrath burn like fire?
6 Pour out your anger on the nations
    that do not know you,
  and on the kingdoms
    that do not call on your name.
7 For they have devoured Jacob
    and laid waste his habitation.

8 Do not remember against us the iniquities
      of our ancestors;
    let your compassion come speedily to
      meet us,
    for we are brought very low.
9 Help us, O God of our salvation,
    for the glory of your name;
  deliver us, and forgive our sins,
    for your name's sake.
10 Why should the nations say,
    "Where is their God?"
  Let the avenging of the outpoured blood of
      your servants

be known among the nations before our
    eyes.
11 Let the groans of the prisoners come
      before you;
    according to your great power preserve
      those doomed to die.
12 Return sevenfold into the bosom of our
      neighbors
    the taunts with which they taunted you,
      O Lord!
13 Then we your people, the flock of your
      pasture,
    will give thanks to you forever;
    from generation to generation we will
      recount your praise.

Psalm 80

Prayer for Israel's Restoration

*To the leader: on Lilies, a Covenant. Of Ā′saph.
A Psalm.*

1 Give ear, O Shepherd of Israel,
    you who lead Joseph like a flock!
  You who are enthroned upon the cherubim,
      shine forth
2   before Ē′phra·im and Benjamin and
        Ma·nas′seh.
  Stir up your might,
    and come to save us!

3 Restore us, O God;
    let your face shine, that we may be saved.

4 O LORD God of hosts,
    how long will you be angry with your
      people's prayers?
5 You have fed them with the bread of tears,
    and given them tears to drink in full
      measure.
6 You make us the scorn[k] of our neighbors;
    our enemies laugh among themselves.

7 Restore us, O God of hosts;
    let your face shine, that we may be saved.

8 You brought a vine out of Egypt;
    you drove out the nations and planted it.
9 You cleared the ground for it;
    it took deep root and filled the land.
10 The mountains were covered with its shade,
    the mighty cedars with its branches;
11 it sent out its branches to the sea,
    and its shoots to the River.
12 Why then have you broken down its walls,
    so that all who pass along the way pluck
      its fruit?

---

k Syr: Heb *strife*

13 The boar from the forest ravages it,
    and all that move in the field feed on it.

14 Turn again, O God of hosts;
    look down from heaven, and see;
have regard for this vine,
15   the stock that your right hand planted.[l]
16 They have burned it with fire, they have cut
        it down;[m]
    may they perish at the rebuke of your
        countenance.
17 But let your hand be upon the one at your
        right hand,
    the one whom you made strong for
        yourself.
18 Then we will never turn back from you;
    give us life, and we will call on your
        name.

19 Restore us, O LORD God of hosts;
    let your face shine, that we may be saved.

Psalm 81
God's Appeal to Stubborn Israel

To the leader: according to The Git'tith. Of Ā'saph.

1 Sing aloud to God our strength;
    shout for joy to the God of Jacob.
2 Raise a song, sound the tambourine,
    the sweet lyre with the harp.
3 Blow the trumpet at the new moon,
    at the full moon, on our festal day.
4 For it is a statute for Israel,
    an ordinance of the God of Jacob.
5 He made it a decree in Joseph,
    when he went out over[n] the land of
        Egypt.

I hear a voice I had not known:
6 "I relieved your[o] shoulder of the burden;
    your[o] hands were freed from the basket.
7 In distress you called, and I rescued you;
    I answered you in the secret place of
        thunder;
    I tested you at the waters of Mer'i·bah.
                                        Sē'lah
8 Hear, O my people, while I admonish you;
    O Israel, if you would but listen to me!
9 There shall be no strange god among you;
    you shall not bow down to a
        foreign god.
10 I am the LORD your God,
    who brought you up out of the land of
        Egypt.
    Open your mouth wide and I will fill it.

11 "But my people did not listen to my voice;
    Israel would not submit to me.

12 So I gave them over to their stubborn
        hearts,
    to follow their own counsels.
13 O that my people would listen to me,
    that Israel would walk in my ways!
14 Then I would quickly subdue their enemies,
    and turn my hand against their foes.
15 Those who hate the LORD would cringe
        before him,
    and their doom would last forever.
16 I would feed you[p] with the finest of the
        wheat,
    and with honey from the rock I would
        satisfy you."

Psalm 82
A Plea for Justice

A Psalm of Ā'saph.

1 God has taken his place in the divine
        council;
    in the midst of the gods he holds
        judgment:
2 "How long will you judge unjustly
    and show partiality to the wicked?   *Sē'lah*
3 Give justice to the weak and the orphan;
    maintain the right of the lowly and the
        destitute.
4 Rescue the weak and the needy;
    deliver them from the hand of the
        wicked."

5 They have neither knowledge nor
        understanding,
    they walk around in darkness;
    all the foundations of the earth are
        shaken.

6 I say, "You are gods,
    children of the Most High, all of you;
7 nevertheless, you shall die like mortals,
    and fall like any prince."[q]

8 Rise up, O God, judge the earth;
    for all the nations belong to you!

Psalm 83
Prayer for Judgment on Israel's Foes

A Song. A Psalm of Ā'saph.

1 O God, do not keep silence;
    do not hold your peace or be still,
        O God!
2 Even now your enemies are in tumult;

---

[l] Heb adds from verse 17 *and upon the one whom you
made strong for yourself*   [m] Cn: Heb *it is cut down*
[n] Or *against*   [o] Heb *his*   [p] Cn Compare verse 16b: Heb
he would feed him   [q] Or *fall as one man, O princes*

P
S
A
L
M
S

AIDS—a Matter of Justice

Jerry died of complications due to the AIDS virus. The paper carried an article about his life. The writer said: "His worst fears were not realized. His church did not reject him in the end. It surrounded him with love." What an awesome example of love and justice. Jerry's parish did not condemn him; it showed compassion for his life.

We are tempted, in our society, to blame the weakest and the poorest for their situation and to excuse ourselves from any need to help. We say that people who are poor are too lazy to work. That those who are hungry should get a job. That people dying of AIDS deserve it because of their choices. These attitudes portray a cold justice without mercy. They are not from the mind of God. For God, mercy and justice go hand in hand. Thank goodness, the people of Jerry's parish understood that.

Psalm 82 is a plea for God's justice, a cry to "maintain the right of the lowly" (verse 3). Take these words to heart, pray for those who judge without mercy, and remember the reporter's words about Jerry: "His church . . . surrounded him with love."

▶ **Psalm 82**

those who hate you have raised their
  heads.
3 They lay crafty plans against your people;
  they consult together against those you
    protect.
4 They say, "Come, let us wipe them out as a
    nation;
  let the name of Israel be remembered no
    more."
5 They conspire with one accord;
  against you they make a covenant—
6 the tents of Ē'dom and the Ish'ma·el·ites,
  Mō'ab and the Hag'rites,
7 Gē'bal and Am'mon and Am'a·lek,
  Phi·lis'ti·a with the inhabitants of Tȳre;
8 Assyria also has joined them;
  they are the strong arm of the children of
    Lot.   *Sē'lah*

9 Do to them as you did to Mid'i·an,
  as to Sis'e·ra and Jā'bin at the Wadi
    Ki'shon,
10 who were destroyed at En-dor,
  who became dung for the ground.
11 Make their nobles like Or'eb and Zē'eb,
  all their princes like Zē'bah and
    Zal·mun'na,
12 who said, "Let us take the pastures of God
  for our own possession."
13 O my God, make them like whirling dust,*r*
  like chaff before the wind.
14 As fire consumes the forest,
  as the flame sets the mountains ablaze,
15 so pursue them with your tempest

and terrify them with your hurricane.
16 Fill their faces with shame,
  so that they may seek your name,
    O LORD.
17 Let them be put to shame and dismayed
    forever;
  let them perish in disgrace.
18 Let them know that you alone,
  whose name is the LORD,
  are the Most High over all the earth.

Psalm 84
The Joy of Worship in the Temple

To the leader: according to The Git'tith.
Of the Kō'ra·hītes. A Psalm.

1 How lovely is your dwelling place,
  O LORD of hosts!
2 My soul longs, indeed it faints
  for the courts of the LORD;
  my heart and my flesh sing for joy
  to the living God.

3 Even the sparrow finds a home,
  and the swallow a nest for herself,
  where she may lay her young,
  at your altars, O LORD of hosts,
    my King and my God.
4 Happy are those who live in your house,
  ever singing your praise.   *Sē'lah*

5 Happy are those whose strength is in you,
  in whose heart are the highways to
    Zion.*s*

---

r Or *a tumbleweed*   *s* Heb lacks *to Zion*

6 As they go through the valley of Bā′ca
     they make it a place of springs;
     the early rain also covers it with pools.
7 They go from strength to strength;
     the God of gods will be seen in Zion.

8 O LORD God of hosts, hear my prayer;
     give ear, O God of Jacob!   *Sē′lah*
9 Behold our shield, O God;
     look on the face of your anointed.

10 For a day in your courts is better
     than a thousand elsewhere.
   I would rather be a doorkeeper in the house
        of my God
     than live in the tents of wickedness.
11 For the LORD God is a sun and shield;
     he bestows favor and honor.
   No good thing does the LORD withhold
     from those who walk uprightly.
12 O LORD of hosts,
     happy is everyone who trusts in you.

Psalm 85

Prayer for the Restoration
of God's Favor

To the leader. Of the Kō′ra·hītes. A Psalm.

1 LORD, you were favorable to your land;
     you restored the fortunes of Jacob.
2 You forgave the iniquity of your people;
     you pardoned all their sin.   *Sē′lah*
3 You withdrew all your wrath;
     you turned from your hot anger.

4 Restore us again, O God of our salvation,
     and put away your indignation
        toward us.
5 Will you be angry with us forever?
     Will you prolong your anger to all
        generations?
6 Will you not revive us again,
     so that your people may rejoice in you?
7 Show us your steadfast love, O LORD,
     and grant us your salvation.

8 Let me hear what God the LORD will speak,
     for he will speak peace to his people,
     to his faithful, to those who turn to him
        in their hearts.[t]
9 Surely his salvation is at hand for those who
        fear him,
     that his glory may dwell in our land.

10 Steadfast love and faithfulness will meet;
     righteousness and peace will kiss each
        other.
11 Faithfulness will spring up from the ground,

and righteousness will look down from
     the sky.
12 The LORD will give what is good,
     and our land will yield its increase.
13 Righteousness will go before him,
     and will make a path for his steps.

Psalm 86

Supplication for Help against Enemies

A Prayer of David.

1 Incline your ear, O LORD, and answer me,
     for I am poor and needy.
2 Preserve my life, for I am devoted to you;
     save your servant who trusts in you.
   You are my God; 3 be gracious to me,
        O Lord,
     for to you do I cry all day long.
4 Gladden the soul of your servant,
     for to you, O Lord, I lift up my soul.
5 For you, O Lord, are good and forgiving,
     abounding in steadfast love to all who
        call on you.
6 Give ear, O LORD, to my prayer;
     listen to my cry of supplication.
7 In the day of my trouble I call on you,
     for you will answer me.

8 There is none like you among the gods,
        O Lord,
     nor are there any works like yours.
9 All the nations you have made shall come
     and bow down before you, O Lord,
     and shall glorify your name.
10 For you are great and do wondrous things;
     you alone are God.
11 Teach me your way, O LORD,
     that I may walk in your truth;
     give me an undivided heart to revere
        your name.
12 I give thanks to you, O Lord my God, with
        my whole heart,
     and I will glorify your name forever.
13 For great is your steadfast love toward me;
     you have delivered my soul from the
        depths of She′ōl.

14 O God, the insolent rise up against me;
     a band of ruffians seeks my life,
     and they do not set you before them.
15 But you, O Lord, are a God merciful and
        gracious,
     slow to anger and abounding in steadfast
        love and faithfulness.
16 Turn to me and be gracious to me;
     give your strength to your servant;

---

t Gk: Heb *but let them not turn back to folly*

save the child of your serving girl.
17 Show me a sign of your favor,
  so that those who hate me may see it
    and be put to shame,
  because you, LORD, have helped me and
    comforted me.

Psalm 87

The Joy of Living in Zion

Of the Kōʹraˑhites. A Psalm. A Song.

1 On the holy mount stands the city he
    founded;
2   the LORD loves the gates of Zion
    more than all the dwellings of Jacob.
3 Glorious things are spoken of you,
    O city of God.   *Seʹlah*

4 Among those who know me I mention
    Rāʹhab and Babylon;
  Phiˑlisʹtiˑa too, and Tȳre, with Ethiopiaᵘ—
  "This one was born there," they say.
5 And of Zion it shall be said,
  "This one and that one were born in it";
  for the Most High himself will
    establish it.
6 The LORD records, as he registers the peoples,
  "This one was born there."   *Seʹlah*

7 Singers and dancers alike say,
  "All my springs are in you."

Psalm 88

Prayer for Help in Despondency

*A Song. A Psalm of the Kōʹraˑhites. To the leader:
according to Māʹhaˑlath Leˑanʹnoth. A Masʹkil
of Hēʹman the Ezʹraˑhite.*

1 O LORD, God of my salvation,
  when, at night, I cry out in your
    presence,
2 let my prayer come before you;
  incline your ear to my cry.

3 For my soul is full of troubles,
  and my life draws near to Shēʹōl.
4 I am counted among those who go down to
    the Pit;
  I am like those who have no help,
5 like those forsaken among the dead,
  like the slain that lie in the grave,
  like those whom you remember no more,
  for they are cut off from your hand.
6 You have put me in the depths of the Pit,
  in the regions dark and deep.
7 Your wrath lies heavy upon me,
  and you overwhelm me with all your
    waves.   *Seʹlah*

8 You have caused my companions to
    shun me;
  you have made me a thing of horror to
    them.
  I am shut in so that I cannot escape;
9   my eye grows dim through sorrow.
  Every day I call on you, O LORD;
  I spread out my hands to you.
10 Do you work wonders for the dead?
  Do the shades rise up to praise you?
                                      Seʹlah
11 Is your steadfast love declared in the grave,
  or your faithfulness in Aˑbadʹdon?
12 Are your wonders known in the darkness,
  or your saving help in the land of
    forgetfulness?
13 But I, O LORD, cry out to you;
  in the morning my prayer comes
    before you.
14 O LORD, why do you cast me off?
  Why do you hide your face from me?
15 Wretched and close to death from my
    youth up,
  I suffer your terrors; I am desperate.ᵛ
16 Your wrath has swept over me;
  your dread assaults destroy me.
17 They surround me like a flood all day long;
  from all sides they close in on me.
18 You have caused friend and neighbor to
    shun me;
  my companions are in darkness.

Psalm 89

God's Covenant with David

A Masʹkil of Ēʹthan the Ezʹraˑhite.

1 I will sing of your steadfast love, O LORD,ʷ
    forever;
  with my mouth I will proclaim your
    faithfulness to all generations.
2 I declare that your steadfast love is
    established forever;
  your faithfulness is as firm as the
    heavens.
3 You said, "I have made a covenant with my
    chosen one,
  I have sworn to my servant David:
4 'I will establish your descendants forever,
  and build your throne for all
    generations.' "   *Seʹlah*

5 Let the heavens praise your wonders,
    O LORD,

ᵘ Or *Nubia*; Heb *Cush*   ᵛ Meaning of Heb uncertain
ʷ Gk: Heb *the steadfast love of the LORD*

your faithfulness in the assembly of the
holy ones.

6 For who in the skies can be compared to
the LORD?
Who among the heavenly beings is like
the LORD,

7 a God feared in the council of the holy
ones,
great and awesome[x] above all that are
around him?

8 O LORD God of hosts,
who is as mighty as you, O LORD?
Your faithfulness surrounds you.

9 You rule the raging of the sea;
when its waves rise, you still them.

10 You crushed Ra'hab like a carcass;
you scattered your enemies with your
mighty arm.

11 The heavens are yours, the earth also is
yours;
the world and all that is in it—you have
founded them.

12 The north and the south[y]—you created
them;
Ta'bor and Hermon joyously praise your
name.

13 You have a mighty arm;
strong is your hand, high your right
hand.

14 Righteousness and justice are the foundation
of your throne;
steadfast love and faithfulness go
before you.

15 Happy are the people who know the festal
shout,
who walk, O LORD, in the light of your
countenance;

16 they exult in your name all day long,
and extol[z] your righteousness.

17 For you are the glory of their strength;
by your favor our horn is exalted.

18 For our shield belongs to the LORD,
our king to the Holy One of Israel.

19 Then you spoke in a vision to your faithful
one, and said:
"I have set the crown[a] on one who is
mighty,
I have exalted one chosen from the
people.

20 I have found my servant David;
with my holy oil I have anointed him;

21 my hand shall always remain with him;
my arm also shall strengthen him.

22 The enemy shall not outwit him,
the wicked shall not humble him.

NATIVE AMERICAN

Respect

Respect is an important value for many Native American peoples. For the Lakota tribe, it is one of four primary values. The Lakota word for respect is *wo-wac-in-tan-ka*.

    Psalm 89.6–9 speaks to the Lakota people of the power and the awesomeness of the Great Spirit. We owe reverence and respect not only to our God but also to all our God has created—the earth, the animals, and one another. The young respect the elders because the elders are people of history and experience. The old respect the young because they are the future of the world. When everyone lives in respect, the earth is at peace.

    To explore the other primary Lakota virtues, see the Native American articles for Psalms 31, 73, and 112.

▶ **Psalm 89**

23 I will crush his foes before him
and strike down those who hate him.

24 My faithfulness and steadfast love shall be
with him;
and in my name his horn shall be
exalted.

25 I will set his hand on the sea
and his right hand on the rivers.

26 He shall cry to me, 'You are my Father,
my God, and the Rock of my salvation!'

27 I will make him the firstborn,
the highest of the kings of the earth.

28 Forever I will keep my steadfast love
for him,
and my covenant with him will stand
firm.

29 I will establish his line forever,
and his throne as long as the heavens
endure.

---

x Gk Syr: Heb *greatly awesome*   y Or *Zaphon and Yamin*
z Cn: Heb *are exalted in*   a Cn: Heb *help*

30 If his children forsake my law
  and do not walk according to my
    ordinances,
31 if they violate my statutes
  and do not keep my commandments,
32 then I will punish their transgression with
    the rod
  and their iniquity with scourges;
33 but I will not remove from him my
    steadfast love,
  or be false to my faithfulness.
34 I will not violate my covenant,
  or alter the word that went forth from
    my lips.
35 Once and for all I have sworn by my
    holiness;
  I will not lie to David.
36 His line shall continue forever,
  and his throne endure before me like
    the sun.
37 It shall be established forever like the moon,
  an enduring witness in the skies."   *Sĕ'lah*

38 But now you have spurned and
    rejected him;
  you are full of wrath against your
    anointed.
39 You have renounced the covenant with your
    servant;
  you have defiled his crown in the dust.
40 You have broken through all his walls;
  you have laid his strongholds in ruins.
41 All who pass by plunder him;
  he has become the scorn of his
    neighbors.
42 You have exalted the right hand of his foes;
  you have made all his enemies rejoice.
43 Moreover, you have turned back the edge of
    his sword,
  and you have not supported him in
    battle.
44 You have removed the scepter from his
    hand,[b]
  and hurled his throne to the ground.
45 You have cut short the days of his youth;
  you have covered him with shame.   *Sĕ'lah*

46 How long, O LORD? Will you hide yourself
    forever?
  How long will your wrath burn like fire?
47 Remember how short my time is—[c]
  for what vanity you have created all
    mortals!
48 Who can live and never see death?
  Who can escape the power of Shĕ'ōl?
                                          Sĕ'lah

49 Lord, where is your steadfast love of old,
  which by your faithfulness you swore to
    David?
50 Remember, O Lord, how your servant is
    taunted;
  how I bear in my bosom the insults of
    the peoples,[d]
51 with which your enemies taunt, O LORD,
  with which they taunted the footsteps of
    your anointed.

52 Blessed be the LORD forever.
    Amen and Amen.

BOOK IV
(Psalms 90–106)
Psalm 90
God's Eternity and Human Frailty

A Prayer of Moses, the man of God.

1 Lord, you have been our dwelling place[e]
  in all generations.
2 Before the mountains were brought forth,
  or ever you had formed the earth and the
    world,
  from everlasting to everlasting you
    are God.

3 You turn us[f] back to dust,
  and say, "Turn back, you mortals."
4 For a thousand years in your sight
  are like yesterday when it is past,
  or like a watch in the night.

5 You sweep them away; they are like a
    dream,
  like grass that is renewed in the morning;
6 in the morning it flourishes and is renewed;
  in the evening it fades and withers.

7 For we are consumed by your anger;
  by your wrath we are overwhelmed.
8 You have set our iniquities before you,
  our secret sins in the light of your
    countenance.

9 For all our days pass away under your
    wrath;
  our years come to an end[g] like a sigh.
10 The days of our life are seventy years,
  or perhaps eighty, if we are strong;

---

b Cn: Heb *removed his cleanness*   c Meaning of Heb
uncertain   d Cn: Heb *bosom all of many peoples*
e Another reading is *our refuge*   f Heb *humankind*
g Syr: Heb *we bring our years to an end*

even then their span[h] is only toil and
    trouble;
    they are soon gone, and we fly away.

11 Who considers the power of your anger?
    Your wrath is as great as the fear that is
        due you.
12 So teach us to count our days
    that we may gain a wise heart.

13 Turn, O LORD! How long?
    Have compassion on your servants!
14 Satisfy us in the morning with your
        steadfast love,
    so that we may rejoice and be glad all
        our days.
15 Make us glad as many days as you have
        afflicted us,
    and as many years as we have seen evil.
16 Let your work be manifest to your servants,
    and your glorious power to their
        children.
17 Let the favor of the Lord our God be
        upon us,
    and prosper for us the work of our
        hands—
    O prosper the work of our hands!

Psalm 91

Assurance of God's Protection

1 You who live in the shelter of the Most
        High,
    who abide in the shadow of the
        Almighty,[i]
2 will say to the LORD, "My refuge and my
        fortress;
    my God, in whom I trust."
3 For he will deliver you from the snare of the
        fowler
    and from the deadly pestilence;
4 he will cover you with his pinions,
    and under his wings you will find refuge;
    his faithfulness is a shield and buckler.
5 You will not fear the terror of the night,
    or the arrow that flies by day,
6 or the pestilence that stalks in darkness,
    or the destruction that wastes at
        noonday.
7 A thousand may fall at your side,
    ten thousand at your right hand,
    but it will not come near you.
8 You will only look with your eyes
    and see the punishment of the wicked.

9 Because you have made the LORD your
    refuge,[j]

the Most High your dwelling place,
10 no evil shall befall you,
    no scourge come near your tent.

11 For he will command his angels
        concerning you
    to guard you in all your ways.
12 On their hands they will bear you up,
    so that you will not dash your foot
        against a stone.
13 You will tread on the lion and the adder,
    the young lion and the serpent you will
        trample under foot.

14 Those who love me, I will deliver;
    I will protect those who know my name.
15 When they call to me, I will answer them;
    I will be with them in trouble,
    I will rescue them and honor them.
16 With long life I will satisfy them,
    and show them my salvation.

---

h Cn Compare Gk Syr Jerome Tg: Heb *pride*
i Traditional rendering of Heb *Shaddai*   j Cn: Heb
Because you, LORD, are my refuge; you have made

PRAY IT?

Have You Sung This Before?

Psalm 91 might sound familiar! Have
you ever sung "On Eagle's Wings" or
"Blest Be the Lord"? Both are based on
this psalm. Both express confidence that
God will protect us, no matter what. This
idea was sung long before Jesus lived, and
we still sing it today.

    And He will raise you up on eagle's
      wings,
    bear you on the breath of dawn,
    make you to shine like the sun,
    and hold you in the palm of His hand.
      (Michael Joncas, "On Eagle's Wings")

    Blest be the Lord; blest be the Lord,
    the God of mercy, the God who saves.
    I shall not fear the dark of night,
    nor the arrow that flies by day.
      (Dan Schutte, "Blest Be the Lord")

▶ Psalm 91

P
S
A
L
M
S

Psalm 92
Thanksgiving for Vindication
A Psalm. A Song for the Sabbath Day.

1 It is good to give thanks to the LORD,
  to sing praises to your name, O Most
  High;
2 to declare your steadfast love in the
  morning,
  and your faithfulness by night,
3 to the music of the lute and the harp,
  to the melody of the lyre.
4 For you, O LORD, have made me glad by
  your work;
  at the works of your hands I sing for joy.

5 How great are your works, O LORD!
  Your thoughts are very deep!
6 The dullard cannot know,
  the stupid cannot understand this:
7 though the wicked sprout like grass
  and all evildoers flourish,
  they are doomed to destruction forever,
8 but you, O LORD, are on high forever.
9 For your enemies, O LORD,
  for your enemies shall perish;
  all evildoers shall be scattered.

10 But you have exalted my horn like that of
  the wild ox;
  you have poured over me[k] fresh oil.
11 My eyes have seen the downfall of my
  enemies;
  my ears have heard the doom of my evil
  assailants.

12 The righteous flourish like the palm tree,
  and grow like a cedar in Lebanon.
13 They are planted in the house of the LORD;
  they flourish in the courts of our God.
14 In old age they still produce fruit;
  they are always green and full of sap,
15 showing that the LORD is upright;
  he is my rock, and there is no
  unrighteousness in him.

Psalm 93
The Majesty of God's Rule

1 The LORD is king, he is robed in majesty;
  the LORD is robed, he is girded with
  strength.
  He has established the world; it shall never
  be moved;
2 your throne is established from of old;
  you are from everlasting.

3 The floods have lifted up, O LORD,
  the floods have lifted up their voice;

  the floods lift up their roaring.
4 More majestic than the thunders of mighty
  waters,
  more majestic than the waves[l] of the sea,
  majestic on high is the LORD!

5 Your decrees are very sure;
  holiness befits your house,
  O LORD, forevermore.

Psalm 94
God the Avenger of the Righteous

1 O LORD, you God of vengeance,
  you God of vengeance, shine forth!
2 Rise up, O judge of the earth;
  give to the proud what they deserve!
3 O LORD, how long shall the wicked,
  how long shall the wicked exult?

4 They pour out their arrogant words;
  all the evildoers boast.
5 They crush your people, O LORD,
  and afflict your heritage.
6 They kill the widow and the stranger,
  they murder the orphan,
7 and they say, "The LORD does not see;
  the God of Jacob does not perceive."

8 Understand, O dullest of the people;
  fools, when will you be wise?
9 He who planted the ear, does he not hear?
  He who formed the eye, does he not see?
10 He who disciplines the nations,
  he who teaches knowledge to humankind,
  does he not chastise?
11 The LORD knows our thoughts,[m]
  that they are but an empty breath.

12 Happy are those whom you discipline,
  O LORD,
  and whom you teach out of your law,
13 giving them respite from days of trouble,
  until a pit is dug for the wicked.
14 For the LORD will not forsake his people;
  he will not abandon his heritage;
15 for justice will return to the righteous,
  and all the upright in heart will follow it.

16 Who rises up for me against the wicked?
  Who stands up for me against evildoers?
17 If the LORD had not been my help,
  my soul would soon have lived in the
  land of silence.
18 When I thought, "My foot is slipping,"
  your steadfast love, O LORD, held me up.

---

k Syr: Meaning of Heb uncertain   *l* Cn: Heb *majestic are
the waves*   *m* Heb *the thoughts of humankind*

19 When the cares of my heart are many,
    your consolations cheer my soul.
20 Can wicked rulers be allied with you,
    those who contrive mischief by statute?
21 They band together against the life of the
    righteous,
    and condemn the innocent to death.
22 But the LORD has become my stronghold,
    and my God the rock of my refuge.
23 He will repay them for their iniquity
    and wipe them out for their wickedness;
    the LORD our God will wipe them out.

Psalm 95
A Call to Worship and Obedience

1 O come, let us sing to the LORD;
    let us make a joyful noise to the rock of
    our salvation!
2 Let us come into his presence with
    thanksgiving;
    let us make a joyful noise to him with
    songs of praise!
3 For the LORD is a great God,
    and a great King above all gods.
4 In his hand are the depths of the earth;
    the heights of the mountains are his also.
5 The sea is his, for he made it,
    and the dry land, which his hands have
    formed.

6 O come, let us worship and bow down,
    let us kneel before the LORD, our Maker!
7 For he is our God,
    and we are the people of his pasture,
    and the sheep of his hand.

    O that today you would listen to his voice!
8   Do not harden your hearts, as at
    Mer'i·bah,
    as on the day at Mas'sah in the
    wilderness,
9 when your ancestors tested me,
    and put me to the proof, though they
    had seen my work.
10 For forty years I loathed that generation
    and said, "They are a people whose
    hearts go astray,
    and they do not regard my ways."
11 Therefore in my anger I swore,
    "They shall not enter my rest."

Psalm 96
Praise to God Who Comes in Judgment
(1 Chr 16.23–33)

1 O sing to the LORD a new song;
    sing to the LORD, all the earth.

O sing to the LORD a new song; sing to the LORD, all the earth. Sing to the LORD, bless his name; tell of his salvation from day to day.

Sing to the LORD

96.1–2

2 Sing to the LORD, bless his name;
    tell of his salvation from day to day.
3 Declare his glory among the nations,
    his marvelous works among all the
    peoples.
4 For great is the LORD, and greatly to be
    praised;
    he is to be revered above all gods.
5 For all the gods of the peoples are idols,
    but the LORD made the heavens.
6 Honor and majesty are before him;
    strength and beauty are in his sanctuary.

7 Ascribe to the LORD, O families of the
    peoples,
    ascribe to the LORD glory and strength.
8 Ascribe to the LORD the glory due his name;
    bring an offering, and come into his
    courts.
9 Worship the LORD in holy splendor;
    tremble before him, all the earth.

10 Say among the nations, "The LORD is king!
    The world is firmly established; it shall
    never be moved.
    He will judge the peoples with equity."
11 Let the heavens be glad, and let the earth
    rejoice;
    let the sea roar, and all that fills it;
12   let the field exult, and everything in it.
    Then shall all the trees of the forest sing
    for joy
13   before the LORD; for he is coming,
    for he is coming to judge the earth.
    He will judge the world with righteousness,
    and the peoples with his truth.

Psalm 97

The Glory of God's Reign

1 The LORD is king! Let the earth rejoice;
  let the many coastlands be glad!
2 Clouds and thick darkness are all
    around him;
  righteousness and justice are the
    foundation of his throne.
3 Fire goes before him,
  and consumes his adversaries on every
    side.
4 His lightnings light up the world;
  the earth sees and trembles.
5 The mountains melt like wax before the
    LORD,
  before the Lord of all the earth.

6 The heavens proclaim his righteousness;
  and all the peoples behold his glory.
7 All worshipers of images are put to shame,
  those who make their boast in worthless
    idols;
  all gods bow down before him.
8 Zion hears and is glad,
  and the towns[n] of Judah rejoice,
  because of your judgments, O God.
9 For you, O LORD, are most high over all the
    earth;
  you are exalted far above all gods.

10 The LORD loves those who hate[o] evil;
  he guards the lives of his faithful;
  he rescues them from the hand of the
    wicked.
11 Light dawns[p] for the righteous,
  and joy for the upright in heart.
12 Rejoice in the LORD, O you righteous,
  and give thanks to his holy name!

Psalm 98

Praise the Judge of the World

A Psalm.

1 O sing to the LORD a new song,
  for he has done marvelous things.
His right hand and his holy arm
  have gotten him victory.
2 The LORD has made known his victory;
  he has revealed his vindication in the
    sight of the nations.
3 He has remembered his steadfast love and
    faithfulness
  to the house of Israel.
All the ends of the earth have seen
  the victory of our God.

4 Make a joyful noise to the LORD, all the
    earth;
  break forth into joyous song and sing
    praises.
5 Sing praises to the LORD with the lyre,
  with the lyre and the sound of melody.
6 With trumpets and the sound of the horn
  make a joyful noise before the King, the
    LORD.

7 Let the sea roar, and all that fills it;
  the world and those who live in it.
8 Let the floods clap their hands;
  let the hills sing together for joy
9 at the presence of the LORD, for he is coming
  to judge the earth.
He will judge the world with righteousness,
  and the peoples with equity.

Psalm 99

Praise to God for His Holiness

1 The LORD is king; let the peoples tremble!
  He sits enthroned upon the cherubim; let
    the earth quake!
2 The LORD is great in Zion;
  he is exalted over all the peoples.
3 Let them praise your great and awesome
    name.
  Holy is he!
4 Mighty King,[q] lover of justice,
  you have established equity;
you have executed justice
  and righteousness in Jacob.
5 Extol the LORD our God;
  worship at his footstool.
  Holy is he!

6 Moses and Aaron were among his priests,
  Samuel also was among those who called
    on his name.
  They cried to the LORD, and he answered
    them.
7 He spoke to them in the pillar of cloud;
  they kept his decrees,
  and the statutes that he gave them.

8 O LORD our God, you answered them;
  you were a forgiving God to them,
  but an avenger of their wrongdoings.
9 Extol the LORD our God,
  and worship at his holy mountain;
  for the LORD our God is holy.

---

n Heb *daughters*   o Cn: Heb *You who love the LORD hate*
p Gk Syr Jerome: Heb *is sown*   q Cn: Heb *And a king's
strength*

Psalm 100

All Lands Summoned to Praise God

A Psalm of thanksgiving.

1 Make a joyful noise to the LORD, all the
　 earth.
2 　Worship the LORD with gladness;
　 come into his presence with singing.

3 Know that the LORD is God.
　 It is he that made us, and we are his;[r]
　 we are his people, and the sheep of his
　 pasture.

4 Enter his gates with thanksgiving,
　 and his courts with praise.
　 Give thanks to him, bless his name.

5 For the LORD is good;
　 his steadfast love endures forever,
　 and his faithfulness to all generations.

Psalm 101

A Sovereign's Pledge of Integrity
and Justice

Of David. A Psalm.

1 I will sing of loyalty and of justice;
　 to you, O LORD, I will sing.
2 I will study the way that is blameless.
　 When shall I attain it?

　 I will walk with integrity of heart
　 within my house;
3 I will not set before my eyes
　 anything that is base.

　 I hate the work of those who fall away;
　 it shall not cling to me.
4 Perverseness of heart shall be far from me;
　 I will know nothing of evil.

5 One who secretly slanders a neighbor
　 I will destroy.
　 A haughty look and an arrogant heart
　 I will not tolerate.

6 I will look with favor on the faithful in the
　 land,
　 so that they may live with me;
　 whoever walks in the way that is blameless
　 shall minister to me.

7 No one who practices deceit
　 shall remain in my house;
　 no one who utters lies
　 shall continue in my presence.

8 Morning by morning I will destroy
　 all the wicked in the land,

cutting off all evildoers
　 from the city of the LORD.

Psalm 102

Prayer to the Eternal King for Help

*A prayer of one afflicted, when faint and pleading
before the LORD.*

1 Hear my prayer, O LORD;
　 let my cry come to you.
2 Do not hide your face from me
　 in the day of my distress.
　 Incline your ear to me;
　 answer me speedily in the day when I
　 call.

3 For my days pass away like smoke,
　 and my bones burn like a furnace.
4 My heart is stricken and withered like grass;
　 I am too wasted to eat my bread.
5 Because of my loud groaning
　 my bones cling to my skin.
6 I am like an owl of the wilderness,
　 like a little owl of the waste places.
7 I lie awake;
　 I am like a lonely bird on the housetop.
8 All day long my enemies taunt me;
　 those who deride me use my name for a
　 curse.
9 For I eat ashes like bread,
　 and mingle tears with my drink,
10 because of your indignation and anger;
　 for you have lifted me up and thrown me
　 aside.
11 My days are like an evening shadow;
　 I wither away like grass.

12 But you, O LORD, are enthroned forever;
　 your name endures to all generations.
13 You will rise up and have compassion on
　 Zion,
　 for it is time to favor it;
　 the appointed time has come.
14 For your servants hold its stones dear,
　 and have pity on its dust.
15 The nations will fear the name of the LORD,
　 and all the kings of the earth your glory.
16 For the LORD will build up Zion;
　 he will appear in his glory.
17 He will regard the prayer of the destitute,
　 and will not despise their prayer.

18 Let this be recorded for a generation to
　 come,
　 so that a people yet unborn may praise
　 the LORD:

---

r Another reading is *and not we ourselves*

P
S
A
L
M
S

P
S
A
L
M
S

19 that he looked down from his holy height,
      from heaven the LORD looked at the earth,
20 to hear the groans of the prisoners,
      to set free those who were doomed
            to die;
21 so that the name of the LORD may be
            declared in Zion,
      and his praise in Jerusalem,
22 when peoples gather together,
      and kingdoms, to worship the LORD.

23 He has broken my strength in midcourse;
      he has shortened my days.
24 "O my God," I say, "do not take me away
      at the midpoint of my life,
   you whose years endure
      throughout all generations."

25 Long ago you laid the foundation of the
            earth,
      and the heavens are the work of your
            hands.
26 They will perish, but you endure;
      they will all wear out like a garment.
   You change them like clothing, and they
            pass away;
27   but you are the same, and your years
            have no end.
28 The children of your servants shall live
            secure;
      their offspring shall be established in
            your presence.

Psalm 103

Thanksgiving for God's Goodness

Of David.

1 Bless the LORD, O my soul,
      and all that is within me,
      bless his holy name.
2 Bless the LORD, O my soul,
      and do not forget all his benefits—
3 who forgives all your iniquity,
      who heals all your diseases,
4 who redeems your life from the Pit,
      who crowns you with steadfast love and
            mercy,
5 who satisfies you with good as long as you
            lives
      so that your youth is renewed like the
            eagle's.

6 The LORD works vindication
      and justice for all who are oppressed.
7 He made known his ways to Moses,
      his acts to the people of Israel.
8 The LORD is merciful and gracious,

slow to anger and abounding in steadfast
      love.
9 He will not always accuse,
      nor will he keep his anger forever.
10 He does not deal with us according to our
            sins,
      nor repay us according to our iniquities.
11 For as the heavens are high above the earth,
      so great is his steadfast love toward those
            who fear him;
12 as far as the east is from the west,
      so far he removes our transgressions
            from us.
13 As a father has compassion for his children,
      so the LORD has compassion for those
            who fear him.
14 For he knows how we were made;
      he remembers that we are dust.

15 As for mortals, their days are like grass;
      they flourish like a flower of the field;
16 for the wind passes over it, and it is gone,
      and its place knows it no more.
17 But the steadfast love of the LORD is from
            everlasting to everlasting
      on those who fear him,
      and his righteousness to children's
            children,
18 to those who keep his covenant
      and remember to do his commandments.

19 The LORD has established his throne in the
            heavens,
      and his kingdom rules over all.
20 Bless the LORD, O you his angels,
      you mighty ones who do his bidding,
      obedient to his spoken word.
21 Bless the LORD, all his hosts,
      his ministers that do his will.
22 Bless the LORD, all his works,
      in all places of his dominion.
   Bless the LORD, O my soul.

Psalm 104

God the Creator and Provider

(Cp Gen 1.1–31)

1 Bless the LORD, O my soul.
   O LORD my God, you are very great.
   You are clothed with honor and majesty,
2   wrapped in light as with a garment.
   You stretch out the heavens like a tent,
3   you set the beams of yourt chambers on
            the waters,
   you make the clouds yourt chariot,
      you ride on the wings of the wind,

---
s Meaning of Heb uncertain   t Heb *his*

Letting Go of Anger

Psalm 103 is a beautiful prayer praising God's love and compassion. Verse 9 reminds us that God will not stay angry forever. What better lesson could we learn from our God? Anger is a natural human emotion—but in imitation of God, we should not hold on to it. When we let go of our anger, we build better relationships, because hidden anger puts other people on the defensive and destroys trust.

How do you let go of anger? Here are some suggestions:

- Express your feelings in a letter or a journal.
- Tell the person you are angry with how you feel and that you would like to reconcile.
- Go for a fast walk or run, or use another form of exercise to "vent" your anger.
- Relax with some quiet, reflective music.
- Try to identify why you feel angry—often, anger is a symptom of another feeling such as hurt, disappointment, or even tiredness.
- Express your anger in prayer to God and ask for help in forgiveness.

God's way and God's goodness can be yours if you desire them. Make an effort; God does!

▸ Psalm 103

4 you make the winds your[u] messengers,
　　fire and flame your[u] ministers.
5 You set the earth on its foundations,
　　so that it shall never be shaken.
6 You cover it with the deep as with a garment;
　　the waters stood above the mountains.
7 At your rebuke they flee;
　　at the sound of your thunder they take to flight.
8 They rose up to the mountains, ran down to the valleys
　　to the place that you appointed for them.
9 You set a boundary that they may not pass,
　　so that they might not again cover the earth.

10 You make springs gush forth in the valleys;
　　they flow between the hills,
11 giving drink to every wild animal;
　　the wild asses quench their thirst.
12 By the streams[v] the birds of the air have their habitation;
　　they sing among the branches.
13 From your lofty abode you water the mountains;
　　the earth is satisfied with the fruit of your work.
14 You cause the grass to grow for the cattle,
　　and plants for people to use,[w]
　　to bring forth food from the earth,
15 　and wine to gladden the human heart,
　　oil to make the face shine,

and bread to strengthen the human heart.
16 The trees of the LORD are watered abundantly,
　　the cedars of Lebanon that he planted.
17 In them the birds build their nests;
　　the stork has its home in the fir trees.
18 The high mountains are for the wild goats;
　　the rocks are a refuge for the coneys.
19 You have made the moon to mark the seasons;
　　the sun knows its time for setting.
20 You make darkness, and it is night,
　　when all the animals of the forest come creeping out.
21 The young lions roar for their prey,
　　seeking their food from God.
22 When the sun rises, they withdraw
　　and lie down in their dens.
23 People go out to their work
　　and to their labor until the evening.

24 O LORD, how manifold are your works!
　　In wisdom you have made them all;
　　the earth is full of your creatures.
25 Yonder is the sea, great and wide,
　　creeping things innumerable are there,
　　living things both small and great.
26 There go the ships,
　　and Le·vi′a·than that you formed to sport in it.

27 These all look to you
　　to give them their food in due season;

u Heb his　　v Heb By them　　w Or to cultivate

28 when you give to them, they gather it up;
   when you open your hand, they are filled
      with good things.
29 When you hide your face, they are
      dismayed;
   when you take away their breath,
      they die
   and return to their dust.
30 When you send forth your spirit,ˣ they are
      created;
   and you renew the face of the ground.

31 May the glory of the LORD endure forever;
   may the LORD rejoice in his works—
32 who looks on the earth and it trembles,
   who touches the mountains and they
      smoke.
33 I will sing to the LORD as long as I live;
   I will sing praise to my God while I have
      being.
34 May my meditation be pleasing to him,
   for I rejoice in the LORD.
35 Let sinners be consumed from the earth,
   and let the wicked be no more.
   Bless the LORD, O my soul.
   Praise the LORD!

Psalm 105
God's Faithfulness to Israel
(Ex 7.8 — 11.10; 1 Chr 16.8—22)

1 O give thanks to the LORD, call on his name,
   make known his deeds among the
      peoples.
2 Sing to him, sing praises to him;
   tell of all his wonderful works.
3 Glory in his holy name;
   let the hearts of those who seek the LORD
      rejoice.
4 Seek the LORD and his strength;
   seek his presence continually.
5 Remember the wonderful works he has
      done,
   his miracles, and the judgments he has
      uttered,
6 O offspring of his servant Abraham,ʸ
   children of Jacob, his chosen ones.

7 He is the LORD our God;
   his judgments are in all the earth.
8 He is mindful of his covenant forever,
   of the word that he commanded, for a
      thousand generations,
9 the covenant that he made with Abraham,
   his sworn promise to Isaac,
10 which he confirmed to Jacob as a statute,
   to Israel as an everlasting covenant,

11 saying, "To you I will give the land of
      Cā´naan
   as your portion for an inheritance."

12 When they were few in number,
   of little account, and strangers in it,
13 wandering from nation to nation,
   from one kingdom to another people,
14 he allowed no one to oppress them;
   he rebuked kings on their account,
15 saying, "Do not touch my anointed ones;
   do my prophets no harm."

16 When he summoned famine against the
      land,
   and broke every staff of bread,
17 he had sent a man ahead of them,
   Joseph, who was sold as a slave.
18 His feet were hurt with fetters,
   his neck was put in a collar of iron;
19 until what he had said came to pass,
   the word of the LORD kept testing him.
20 The king sent and released him;
   the ruler of the peoples set him free.
21 He made him lord of his house,
   and ruler of all his possessions,
22 to instructᶻ his officials at his pleasure,
   and to teach his elders wisdom.

23 Then Israel came to Egypt;
   Jacob lived as an alien in the land
      of Ham.
24 And the LORD made his people very fruitful,
   and made them stronger than their foes,
25 whose hearts he then turned to hate his
      people,
   to deal craftily with his servants.

26 He sent his servant Moses,
   and Aaron whom he had chosen.
27 They performed his signs among them,
   and miracles in the land of Ham.
28 He sent darkness, and made the land dark;
   they rebelledᵃ against his words.
29 He turned their waters into blood,
   and caused their fish to die.
30 Their land swarmed with frogs,
   even in the chambers of their kings.
31 He spoke, and there came swarms of flies,
   and gnats throughout their country.
32 He gave them hail for rain,
   and lightning that flashed through their
      land.
33 He struck their vines and fig trees,

---

x Or *your breath*   y Another reading is *Israel* (compare
1 Chr 16.13)   z Gk Syr Jerome: Heb *to bind*
a Cn Compare Gk Syr: Heb *they did not rebel*

and shattered the trees of their country.
34 He spoke, and the locusts came,
    and young locusts without number;
35 they devoured all the vegetation in their
    land,
    and ate up the fruit of their ground.
36 He struck down all the firstborn in their
    land,
    the first issue of all their strength.

37 Then he brought Israel[b] out with silver and
    gold,
    and there was no one among their tribes
    who stumbled.
38 Egypt was glad when they departed,
    for dread of them had fallen upon it.
39 He spread a cloud for a covering,
    and fire to give light by night.
40 They asked, and he brought quails,
    and gave them food from heaven in
    abundance.
41 He opened the rock, and water gushed out;
    it flowed through the desert like a river.
42 For he remembered his holy promise,
    and Abraham, his servant.

43 So he brought his people out with joy,
    his chosen ones with singing.
44 He gave them the lands of the nations,
    and they took possession of the wealth of
    the peoples,
45 that they might keep his statutes
    and observe his laws.
    Praise the LORD!

Psalm 106
A Confession of Israel's Sins

1 Praise the LORD!
    O give thanks to the LORD, for he is good;
    for his steadfast love endures forever.
2 Who can utter the mighty doings of the
    LORD,
    or declare all his praise?
3 Happy are those who observe justice,
    who do righteousness at all times.

4 Remember me, O LORD, when you show
    favor to your people;
    help me when you deliver them;
5 that I may see the prosperity of your chosen
    ones,
    that I may rejoice in the gladness of your
    nation,
    that I may glory in your heritage.

6 Both we and our ancestors have sinned;
    we have committed iniquity, have done
    wickedly.
7 Our ancestors, when they were in Egypt,
    did not consider your wonderful works;
    they did not remember the abundance of
    your steadfast love,
    but rebelled against the Most High[c] at
    the Red Sea.[d]
8 Yet he saved them for his name's sake,
    so that he might make known his mighty
    power.
9 He rebuked the Red Sea,[d] and it
    became dry;
    he led them through the deep as through
    a desert.
10 So he saved them from the hand of the foe,
    and delivered them from the hand of the
    enemy.
11 The waters covered their adversaries;
    not one of them was left.
12 Then they believed his words;
    they sang his praise.

13 But they soon forgot his works;
    they did not wait for his counsel.
14 But they had a wanton craving in the
    wilderness,
    and put God to the test in the desert;
15 he gave them what they asked,
    but sent a wasting disease among them.

16 They were jealous of Moses in the camp,
    and of Aaron, the holy one of the LORD.
17 The earth opened and swallowed
    up Dā′than,
    and covered the faction of A·bī′ram.
18 Fire also broke out in their company;
    the flame burned up the wicked.

19 They made a calf at Hō′reb
    and worshiped a cast image.
20 They exchanged the glory of God[e]
    for the image of an ox that eats grass.
21 They forgot God, their Savior,
    who had done great things in Egypt,
22 wondrous works in the land of Ham,
    and awesome deeds by the Red Sea.[d]
23 Therefore he said he would destroy them—
    had not Moses, his chosen one,
    stood in the breach before him,
    to turn away his wrath from destroying
    them.

b Heb them   c Cn Compare 78.17, 56: Heb rebelled at the
sea   d Or Sea of Reeds   e Compare Gk Mss: Heb
exchanged their glory

P
S
A
L
M
S

24 Then they despised the pleasant land,
   having no faith in his promise.
25 They grumbled in their tents,
   and did not obey the voice of the LORD.
26 Therefore he raised his hand and swore to
   them
   that he would make them fall in the
   wilderness,
27 and would disperse*f* their descendants
   among the nations,
   scattering them over the lands.

28 Then they attached themselves to the Bā′al
   of Pē′or,
   and ate sacrifices offered to the dead;
29 they provoked the LORD to anger with their
   deeds,
   and a plague broke out among them.
30 Then Phin′e•has stood up and interceded,
   and the plague was stopped.
31 And that has been reckoned to him as
   righteousness
   from generation to generation forever.

32 They angered the LORD *g* at the waters of
   Mer′i•bah,
   and it went ill with Moses on their
   account;
33 for they made his spirit bitter,
   and he spoke words that were rash.

34 They did not destroy the peoples,
   as the LORD commanded them,
35 but they mingled with the nations
   and learned to do as they did.
36 They served their idols,
   which became a snare to them.
37 They sacrificed their sons
   and their daughters to the demons;
38 they poured out innocent blood,
   the blood of their sons and daughters,
   whom they sacrificed to the idols of
   Cā′naan;
   and the land was polluted with blood.
39 Thus they became unclean by their acts,
   and prostituted themselves in their
   doings.

40 Then the anger of the LORD was kindled
   against his people,
   and he abhorred his heritage;
41 he gave them into the hand of the nations,
   so that those who hated them ruled over
   them.
42 Their enemies oppressed them,
   and they were brought into subjection
   under their power.

Asian American

Thankfulness

It's good and natural for people to express thankfulness for their blessings. Psalm 107 is an extended thanksgiving for God's love and saving power. Indonesians have a custom for offering thanks on certain special occasions, such as after a new house is built, during the seventh month of pregnancy, and thirty-five days after the birth of a child.

During a thanksgiving for a new house, the family gathers in the house and offers prayers for the people who will live, eat, work, and die there. Similar prayers are said for a mother during pregnancy and for a child after birth—in thanksgiving for their health, well-being, and happiness. After the prayers, those who are gathered share a simple traditional meal of rice, vegetables, fish or chicken, and fruit.

▶ Psalm 107

43 Many times he delivered them,
   but they were rebellious in their
   purposes,
   and were brought low through their
   iniquity.
44 Nevertheless he regarded their distress
   when he heard their cry.
45 For their sake he remembered his
   covenant,
   and showed compassion according to the
   abundance of his steadfast love.
46 He caused them to be pitied
   by all who held them captive.

47 Save us, O LORD our God,
   and gather us from among the nations,
   that we may give thanks to your holy name
   and glory in your praise.

48 Blessed be the LORD, the God of Israel,
   from everlasting to everlasting.
   And let all the people say, "Amen."
   Praise the LORD!

---

f Syr Compare Ezek 20.23: Heb *cause to fall*   *g* Heb *him*

BOOK V
(Psalms 107–150)
Psalm 107
Thanksgiving for Deliverance
from Many Troubles

1 O give thanks to the LORD, for he is good;
   for his steadfast love endures forever.
2 Let the redeemed of the LORD say so,
   those he redeemed from trouble
3 and gathered in from the lands,
   from the east and from the west,
   from the north and from the south.*h*

4 Some wandered in desert wastes,
   finding no way to an inhabited town;
5 hungry and thirsty,
   their soul fainted within them.
6 Then they cried to the LORD in their trouble,
   and he delivered them from their
   distress;
7 he led them by a straight way,
   until they reached an inhabited town.
8 Let them thank the LORD for his steadfast
   love,
   for his wonderful works to humankind.
9 For he satisfies the thirsty,
   and the hungry he fills with good things.

10 Some sat in darkness and in gloom,
   prisoners in misery and in irons,
11 for they had rebelled against the words
   of God,
   and spurned the counsel of the Most
   High.
12 Their hearts were bowed down with hard
   labor;
   they fell down, with no one to help.
13 Then they cried to the LORD in their trouble,
   and he saved them from their distress;
14 he brought them out of darkness and
   gloom,
   and broke their bonds asunder.
15 Let them thank the LORD for his steadfast
   love,
   for his wonderful works to humankind.
16 For he shatters the doors of bronze,
   and cuts in two the bars of iron.

17 Some were sick*i* through their sinful ways,
   and because of their iniquities endured
   affliction;
18 they loathed any kind of food,
   and they drew near to the gates of death.
19 Then they cried to the LORD in their trouble,
   and he saved them from their distress;
20 he sent out his word and healed them,
   and delivered them from destruction.

21 Let them thank the LORD for his steadfast
   love,
   for his wonderful works to humankind.
22 And let them offer thanksgiving sacrifices,
   and tell of his deeds with songs of joy.

23 Some went down to the sea in ships,
   doing business on the mighty waters;
24 they saw the deeds of the LORD,
   his wondrous works in the deep.
25 For he commanded and raised the stormy
   wind,
   which lifted up the waves of the sea.
26 They mounted up to heaven, they went
   down to the depths;
   their courage melted away in their
   calamity;
27 they reeled and staggered like drunkards,
   and were at their wits' end.
28 Then they cried to the LORD in their trouble,
   and he brought them out from their
   distress;
29 he made the storm be still,
   and the waves of the sea were hushed.
30 Then they were glad because they had quiet,
   and he brought them to their desired
   haven.
31 Let them thank the LORD for his steadfast
   love,
   for his wonderful works to humankind.
32 Let them extol him in the congregation of
   the people,
   and praise him in the assembly of the
   elders.

33 He turns rivers into a desert,
   springs of water into thirsty ground,
34 a fruitful land into a salty waste,
   because of the wickedness of its
   inhabitants.
35 He turns a desert into pools of water,
   a parched land into springs of water.
36 And there he lets the hungry live,
   and they establish a town to live in;
37 they sow fields, and plant vineyards,
   and get a fruitful yield.
38 By his blessing they multiply greatly,
   and he does not let their cattle decrease.

39 When they are diminished and brought low
   through oppression, trouble, and sorrow,
40 he pours contempt on princes
   and makes them wander in trackless
   wastes;
41 but he raises up the needy out of distress,
   and makes their families like flocks.

h Cn: Heb *sea*   *i* Cn: Heb *fools*

42 The upright see it and are glad;
and all wickedness stops its mouth.
43 Let those who are wise give heed to these things,
and consider the steadfast love of the LORD.

Psalm 108

Praise and Prayer for Victory

(Ps 57.7–11; 60.5–12)

A Song. A Psalm of David.

1 My heart is steadfast, O God, my heart is steadfast;[j]
I will sing and make melody.
Awake, my soul![k]
2 Awake, O harp and lyre!
I will awake the dawn.
3 I will give thanks to you, O LORD, among the peoples,
and I will sing praises to you among the nations.
4 For your steadfast love is higher than the heavens,
and your faithfulness reaches to the clouds.

5 Be exalted, O God, above the heavens,
and let your glory be over all the earth.
6 Give victory with your right hand, and answer me,
so that those whom you love may be rescued.

7 God has promised in his sanctuary:[l]
"With exultation I will divide up Shĕ′chem,
and portion out the Vale of Suc′coth.
8 Gil′e·ad is mine; Ma·nas′seh is mine;
E′phra·im is my helmet;
Judah is my scepter.
9 Mō′ab is my washbasin;
on E′dom I hurl my shoe;
over Phi·lis′ti·a I shout in triumph."

10 Who will bring me to the fortified city?
Who will lead me to E′dom?
11 Have you not rejected us, O God?
You do not go out, O God, with our armies.
12 O grant us help against the foe,
for human help is worthless.
13 With God we shall do valiantly;
it is he who will tread down our foes.

Psalm 109

Prayer for Vindication and Vengeance

To the leader. Of David. A Psalm.

1 Do not be silent, O God of my praise.
2 For wicked and deceitful mouths are opened against me,
speaking against me with lying tongues.
3 They beset me with words of hate,
and attack me without cause.
4 In return for my love they accuse me,
even while I make prayer for them.[m]
5 So they reward me evil for good,
and hatred for my love.

6 They say,[n] "Appoint a wicked man against him;
let an accuser stand on his right.
7 When he is tried, let him be found guilty;
let his prayer be counted as sin.
8 May his days be few;
may another seize his position.
9 May his children be orphans,
and his wife a widow.
10 May his children wander about and beg;
may they be driven out of[o] the ruins they inhabit.
11 May the creditor seize all that he has;
may strangers plunder the fruits of his toil.
12 May there be no one to do him a kindness,
nor anyone to pity his orphaned children.
13 May his posterity be cut off;
may his name be blotted out in the second generation.
14 May the iniquity of his father[p] be remembered before the LORD,
and do not let the sin of his mother be blotted out.
15 Let them be before the LORD continually,
and may his[q] memory be cut off from the earth.
16 For he did not remember to show kindness,
but pursued the poor and needy
and the brokenhearted to their death.
17 He loved to curse; let curses come on him.
He did not like blessing; may it be far from him.
18 He clothed himself with cursing as his coat,
may it soak into his body like water,
like oil into his bones.

---

j Heb Mss Gk Syr: MT lacks *my heart is steadfast*
k Compare 57.8: Heb *also my soul*   l Or *by his holiness*
m Syr: Heb *I prayer*   n Heb lacks *They say*   o Gk: Heb *and seek*   p Cn: Heb *fathers*   q Gk: Heb *their*

19 May it be like a garment that he wraps
    around himself,
  like a belt that he wears every day."

20 May that be the reward of my accusers from
    the LORD,
  of those who speak evil against my life.
21 But you, O LORD my Lord,
    act on my behalf for your name's sake;
  because your steadfast love is good,
    deliver me.
22 For I am poor and needy,
  and my heart is pierced within me.
23 I am gone like a shadow at evening;
  I am shaken off like a locust.
24 My knees are weak through fasting;
  my body has become gaunt.
25 I am an object of scorn to my accusers;
  when they see me, they shake their
    heads.

26 Help me, O LORD my God!
  Save me according to your steadfast love.
27 Let them know that this is your hand;
  you, O LORD, have done it.
28 Let them curse, but you will bless.
    Let my assailants be put to shame;ʳ may
      your servant be glad.
29 May my accusers be clothed with dishonor;
  may they be wrapped in their own shame
    as in a mantle.
30 With my mouth I will give great thanks to
    the LORD;
  I will praise him in the midst of the
    throng.
31 For he stands at the right hand of the
    needy,
  to save them from those who would
    condemn them to death.

Psalm 110
Assurance of Victory for God's Priest-King
(Mt 22.44; Acts 2.34–35)

Of David. A Psalm.

1 The LORD says to my lord,
  "Sit at my right hand
  until I make your enemies your footstool."

2 The LORD sends out from Zion
    your mighty scepter.
  Rule in the midst of your foes.
3 Your people will offer themselves willingly
    on the day you lead your forces
    on the holy mountains.ˢ
  From the womb of the morning,
    like dew, your youthᵗ will come to you.

4 The LORD has sworn and will not change his
    mind,
  "You are a priest forever according to the
    order of Mel•chiz′e•dek."ᵘ

5 The Lord is at your right hand;
  he will shatter kings on the day of his
    wrath.
6 He will execute judgment among the
    nations,
  filling them with corpses;
  he will shatter heads
  over the wide earth.
7 He will drink from the stream by the path;
  therefore he will lift up his head.

Psalm 111
Praise for God's Wonderful Works

1 Praise the LORD!
  I will give thanks to the LORD with my
    whole heart,
  in the company of the upright, in the
    congregation.
2 Great are the works of the LORD,
  studied by all who delight in them.
3 Full of honor and majesty is his work,
  and his righteousness endures forever.
4 He has gained renown by his wonderful
    deeds;
  the LORD is gracious and merciful.
5 He provides food for those who fear him;
  he is ever mindful of his covenant.
6 He has shown his people the power of his
    works,
  in giving them the heritage of the
    nations.
7 The works of his hands are faithful and just;
  all his precepts are trustworthy.
8 They are established forever and ever,
  to be performed with faithfulness and
    uprightness.
9 He sent redemption to his people;
  he has commanded his covenant forever.
  Holy and awesome is his name.
10 The fear of the LORD is the beginning of
    wisdom;
  all those who practice itᵛ have a good
    understanding.
  His praise endures forever.

ʳ Gk: Heb *They have risen up and have been put to shame*
ˢ Another reading is *in holy splendor*   ᵗ Cn: Heb *the dew of
your youth*   ᵘ Or *forever, a rightful king by my edict*
ᵛ Gk Syr: Heb *them*

Psalm 112
Blessings of the Righteous

1 Praise the LORD!
  Happy are those who fear the LORD,
  who greatly delight in his
  commandments.
2 Their descendants will be mighty in the
  land;
  the generation of the upright will be
  blessed.
3 Wealth and riches are in their houses,
  and their righteousness endures forever.
4 They rise in the darkness as a light for the
  upright;
  they are gracious, merciful, and righteous.
5 It is well with those who deal generously
  and lend,
  who conduct their affairs with justice.
6 For the righteous will never be moved;
  they will be remembered forever.
7 They are not afraid of evil tidings;
  their hearts are firm, secure in the LORD.
8 Their hearts are steady, they will not be
  afraid;
  in the end they will look in triumph on
  their foes.
9 They have distributed freely, they have given
  to the poor;
  their righteousness endures forever;
  their horn is exalted in honor.
10 The wicked see it and are angry;
  they gnash their teeth and melt away;
  the desire of the wicked comes
  to nothing.

Psalm 113
God the Helper of the Needy

1 Praise the LORD!
  Praise, O servants of the LORD;
  praise the name of the LORD.
2 Blessed be the name of the LORD
  from this time on and forevermore.
3 From the rising of the sun to its setting
  the name of the LORD is to be praised.
4 The LORD is high above all nations,
  and his glory above the heavens.

5 Who is like the LORD our God,
  who is seated on high,
6 who looks far down
  on the heavens and the earth?
7 He raises the poor from the dust,
  and lifts the needy from the ash heap,
8 to make them sit with princes,
  with the princes of his people.

NATIVE AMERICAN

Generosity

"It is well with those who deal generously and
lend, / who conduct their affairs with justice"
(Ps 112.5). Generosity is an important value for
many Native American peoples. For the Lakota tribe, it is one of four primary values. The
Lakota word for generosity is *wa-can-tog-na-ka*.

In this Native American culture, it is a
great insult to be called selfish, and a high
compliment to be called generous. You are not
able to raise your social status by showing off
the things that you own. You can do it only by
giving things away. In fact, there is a special
ceremony called the *otuhan*, or the "giveaway,"
in which people give away many of their possessions to honor one another. For example,
young people may have a giveaway when they
graduate from high school, as a way of honoring all who have helped them along the way.

To explore the other primary Lakota virtues, see the Native American articles for
Psalms 31, 73, and 89.

▶ Psalm 112

9 He gives the barren woman a home,
  making her the joyous mother of
  children.
  Praise the LORD!

Psalm 114
God's Wonders at the Exodus
(*Cp Ex 14.1–31*)

1 When Israel went out from Egypt,
  the house of Jacob from a people of
  strange language,
2 Judah became God's[w] sanctuary,
  Israel his dominion.

3 The sea looked and fled;
  Jordan turned back.

---

w Heb *his*

4 The mountains skipped like rams,
the hills like lambs.

5 Why is it, O sea, that you flee?
O Jordan, that you turn back?
6 O mountains, that you skip like rams?
O hills, like lambs?
7 Tremble, O earth, at the presence of the
LORD,
at the presence of the God of Jacob,
8 who turns the rock into a pool of water,
the flint into a spring of water.

Psalm 115
The Impotence of Idols and the Greatness of God

1 Not to us, O LORD, not to us, but to your
name give glory,
for the sake of your steadfast love and
your faithfulness.
2 Why should the nations say,
"Where is their God?"

3 Our God is in the heavens;
he does whatever he pleases.
4 Their idols are silver and gold,
the work of human hands.
5 They have mouths, but do not speak;
eyes, but do not see.
6 They have ears, but do not hear;
noses, but do not smell.
7 They have hands, but do not feel;
feet, but do not walk;
they make no sound in their throats.
8 Those who make them are like them;
so are all who trust in them.

9 O Israel, trust in the LORD!
He is their help and their shield.
10 O house of Aaron, trust in the LORD!
He is their help and their shield.

11 You who fear the LORD, trust in the LORD!
He is their help and their shield.
12 The LORD has been mindful of us; he will
bless us;
he will bless the house of Israel;
he will bless the house of Aaron;
13 he will bless those who fear the LORD,
both small and great.

14 May the LORD give you increase,
both you and your children.
15 May you be blessed by the LORD,
who made heaven and earth.
16 The heavens are the LORD's heavens,
but the earth he has given to human
beings.
17 The dead do not praise the LORD,
nor do any that go down into silence.
18 But we will bless the LORD
from this time on and forevermore.
Praise the LORD!

Psalm 116
Thanksgiving for Recovery from Illness

1 I love the LORD, because he has heard
my voice and my supplications.
2 Because he inclined his ear to me,
therefore I will call on him as long as I
live.
3 The snares of death encompassed me;
the pangs of Shĕ'ōl laid hold on me;
I suffered distress and anguish.
4 Then I called on the name of the LORD:
"O LORD, I pray, save my life!"

5 Gracious is the LORD, and righteous;
our God is merciful.
6 The LORD protects the simple;
when I was brought low, he saved me.
7 Return, O my soul, to your rest,

What Lasts?

LIVE IT!

Will a car last forever? a house? the sun? Does anything other than God truly have no end? No matter how much you look, you won't find such a thing. So, why do we spend much of our time with what won't last, rather than what *will* last?
Psalm 115 proclaims the greatness of God and the foolishness of idols. In the end, the things that matter most won't be how many awards you were given, how much money you made, or how many possessions you had, but rather how much you loved others, how much you served, and how much you loved God!

▶ Psalm 115

Gratitude

Roy. Thank God, I'm feeling better.

Maria. Exactly!

Roy. Exactly what?

Maria. That's exactly what Psalm 116 is all about. Feeling better, and thanking God for it.

Roy. Really? I thought the Psalms were about praising God and winning victories.

Maria. Some are. In a way, that's what Psalm 116 is about too. You can use it to praise God for your victory over illness.

Roy. I never really thought of it that way.

Maria. You prayed to get well, didn't you?

Roy. Yes, a lot.

Maria. Well, there you are. God heard your prayers. Now, how about some genuine gratitude?

Roy. You're right. Thank you, God! I'm feeling so much better!

Maria. Amen!

▸ Psalm 116

for the LORD has dealt bountifully
   with you.

8 For you have delivered my soul from death,
   my eyes from tears,
   my feet from stumbling.
9 I walk before the LORD
   in the land of the living.
10 I kept my faith, even when I said,
   "I am greatly afflicted";
11 I said in my consternation,
   "Everyone is a liar."

12 What shall I return to the LORD
   for all his bounty to me?
13 I will lift up the cup of salvation
   and call on the name of the LORD,
14 I will pay my vows to the LORD
   in the presence of all his people.
15 Precious in the sight of the LORD
   is the death of his faithful ones.
16 O LORD, I am your servant;
   I am your servant, the child of your
      serving girl.
   You have loosed my bonds.
17 I will offer to you a thanksgiving sacrifice
   and call on the name of the LORD.
18 I will pay my vows to the LORD
   in the presence of all his people,
19 in the courts of the house of the LORD,
   in your midst, O Jerusalem.
   Praise the LORD!

Psalm 117
Universal Call to Worship

1 Praise the LORD, all you nations!
   Extol him, all you peoples!
2 For great is his steadfast love toward us,
   and the faithfulness of the LORD endures
      forever.
   Praise the LORD!

Psalm 118
A Song of Victory

1 O give thanks to the LORD, for he is good;
   his steadfast love endures forever!

2 Let Israel say,
   "His steadfast love endures forever."
3 Let the house of Aaron say,
   "His steadfast love endures forever."
4 Let those who fear the LORD say,
   "His steadfast love endures forever."

5 Out of my distress I called on the LORD;
   the LORD answered me and set me in a
      broad place.
6 With the LORD on my side I do not fear.
   What can mortals do to me?
7 The LORD is on my side to help me;
   I shall look in triumph on those who
      hate me.
8 It is better to take refuge in the LORD
   than to put confidence in mortals.
9 It is better to take refuge in the LORD
   than to put confidence in princes.

10 All nations surrounded me;
       in the name of the LORD I cut them off!
11 They surrounded me, surrounded me on
          every side;
       in the name of the LORD I cut them off!
12 They surrounded me like bees;
       they blazed^x like a fire of thorns;
       in the name of the LORD I cut them off!
13 I was pushed hard,^y so that I was falling,
       but the LORD helped me.
14 The LORD is my strength and my might;
       he has become my salvation.

15 There are glad songs of victory in the tents
          of the righteous:
    "The right hand of the LORD does valiantly;
16   the right hand of the LORD is exalted;
       the right hand of the LORD does valiantly."
17 I shall not die, but I shall live,
       and recount the deeds of the LORD.
18 The LORD has punished me severely,
       but he did not give me over to death.

19 Open to me the gates of righteousness,
       that I may enter through them
       and give thanks to the LORD.

20 This is the gate of the LORD;
       the righteous shall enter through it.

21 I thank you that you have answered me
       and have become my salvation.
22 The stone that the builders rejected
       has become the chief cornerstone.
23 This is the LORD's doing;
       it is marvelous in our eyes.
24 This is the day that the LORD has made;
       let us rejoice and be glad in it.^z
25 Save us, we beseech you, O LORD!
       O LORD, we beseech you, give us success!

26 Blessed is the one who comes in the name
          of the LORD.^a
       We bless you from the house of the LORD.
27 The LORD is God,
       and he has given us light.
       Bind the festal procession with branches,
       up to the horns of the altar.^b

28 You are my God, and I will give thanks
          to you;
       you are my God, I will extol you.

29 O give thanks to the LORD, for he is good,
       for his steadfast love endures forever.

Psalm 119
The Glories of God's Law

1 Happy are those whose way is blameless,
       who walk in the law of the LORD.

The Longest Psalm

Psalm 119 is the longest psalm. Also, it has an interesting structure that you cannot appreciate in the English translation: it consists of twenty-two sections, and all the lines of a particular section begin with the same letter of the Hebrew alphabet. All the lines of the first section begin with *Aleph*, the Hebrew equivalent of the letter A. All the lines of the second section begin with *Beth*, the Hebrew equivalent of the letter B. And so on through the whole Hebrew alphabet!

This structure is called an acrostic. An acrostic is a poem in which the beginning letters of each line form a word or a phrase or a logical sequence. You may have written a poem like this in grade school using the word *mother* or *father*.

Write your own acrostic prayer, beginning the lines of the prayer with the letters of your name or of the name of someone or something you would like to pray for.

▶ Psalm 119

2 Happy are those who keep his decrees,
       who seek him with their whole heart,
3 who also do no wrong,
       but walk in his ways.
4 You have commanded your precepts
       to be kept diligently.
5 O that my ways may be steadfast
       in keeping your statutes!
6 Then I shall not be put to shame,
       having my eyes fixed on all your
          commandments.
7 I will praise you with an upright heart,
       when I learn your righteous ordinances.

x Gk: Heb *were extinguished*   y Gk Syr Jerome: Heb *You pushed me hard*   z Or *in him*   a Or *Blessed in the name of the LORD is the one who comes*   b Meaning of Heb uncertain

8 I will observe your statutes;
  do not utterly forsake me.

9 How can young people keep their way pure?
  By guarding it according to your word.

10 With my whole heart I seek you;
  do not let me stray from your
    commandments.

11 I treasure your word in my heart,
  so that I may not sin against you.

12 Blessed are you, O LORD;
  teach me your statutes.

13 With my lips I declare
  all the ordinances of your mouth.

14 I delight in the way of your decrees
  as much as in all riches.

15 I will meditate on your precepts,
  and fix my eyes on your ways.

16 I will delight in your statutes;
  I will not forget your word.

17 Deal bountifully with your servant,
  so that I may live and observe your word.

18 Open my eyes, so that I may behold
  wondrous things out of your law.

19 I live as an alien in the land;
  do not hide your commandments
    from me.

20 My soul is consumed with longing
  for your ordinances at all times.

21 You rebuke the insolent, accursed ones,
  who wander from your commandments;

22 take away from me their scorn and
    contempt,
  for I have kept your decrees.

23 Even though princes sit plotting against me,
  your servant will meditate on your
    statutes.

24 Your decrees are my delight,
  they are my counselors.

25 My soul clings to the dust;
  revive me according to your word.

26 When I told of my ways, you answered me;
  teach me your statutes.

27 Make me understand the way of your
    precepts,
  and I will meditate on your wondrous
    works.

28 My soul melts away for sorrow;
  strengthen me according to your word.

29 Put false ways far from me;
  and graciously teach me your law.

30 I have chosen the way of faithfulness;
  I set your ordinances before me.

31 I cling to your decrees, O LORD;
  let me not be put to shame.

32 I run the way of your commandments,
  for you enlarge my understanding.

33 Teach me, O LORD, the way of your statutes,
  and I will observe it to the end.

34 Give me understanding, that I may keep
    your law
  and observe it with my whole heart.

35 Lead me in the path of your
    commandments,
  for I delight in it.

36 Turn my heart to your decrees,
  and not to selfish gain.

37 Turn my eyes from looking at vanities;
  give me life in your ways.

38 Confirm to your servant your promise,
  which is for those who fear you.

39 Turn away the disgrace that I dread,
  for your ordinances are good.

40 See, I have longed for your precepts;
  in your righteousness give me life.

41 Let your steadfast love come to me, O LORD,
  your salvation according to your promise.

42 Then I shall have an answer for those who
    taunt me,
  for I trust in your word.

43 Do not take the word of truth utterly out of
    my mouth,
  for my hope is in your ordinances.

44 I will keep your law continually,
  forever and ever.

45 I shall walk at liberty,
  for I have sought your precepts.

46 I will also speak of your decrees before
    kings,
  and shall not be put to shame;

47 I find my delight in your commandments,
  because I love them.

48 I revere your commandments, which I love,
  and I will meditate on your statutes.

49 Remember your word to your servant,
  in which you have made me hope.

50 This is my comfort in my distress,
  that your promise gives me life.

51 The arrogant utterly deride me,
  but I do not turn away from your law.

52 When I think of your ordinances from
    of old,
  I take comfort, O LORD.

53 Hot indignation seizes me because of the
    wicked,
  those who forsake your law.

54 Your statutes have been my songs
  wherever I make my home.

55 I remember your name in the night, O LORD,

and keep your law.
56 This blessing has fallen to me,
for I have kept your precepts.

57 The LORD is my portion;
I promise to keep your words.
58 I implore your favor with all my heart;
be gracious to me according to your
promise.
59 When I think of your ways,
I turn my feet to your decrees;
60 I hurry and do not delay
to keep your commandments.
61 Though the cords of the wicked ensnare me,
I do not forget your law.
62 At midnight I rise to praise you,
because of your righteous ordinances.
63 I am a companion of all who fear you,
of those who keep your precepts.
64 The earth, O LORD, is full of your steadfast
love;
teach me your statutes.

65 You have dealt well with your servant,
O LORD, according to your word.
66 Teach me good judgment and knowledge,
for I believe in your commandments.
67 Before I was humbled I went astray,
but now I keep your word.
68 You are good and do good;
teach me your statutes.
69 The arrogant smear me with lies,
but with my whole heart I keep your
precepts.
70 Their hearts are fat and gross,
but I delight in your law.
71 It is good for me that I was humbled,
so that I might learn your statutes.
72 The law of your mouth is better to me
than thousands of gold and silver pieces.

73 Your hands have made and fashioned me;
give me understanding that I may learn
your commandments.
74 Those who fear you shall see me and
rejoice,
because I have hoped in your word.
75 I know, O LORD, that your judgments are
right,
and that in faithfulness you have
humbled me.
76 Let your steadfast love become my comfort
according to your promise to your
servant.
77 Let your mercy come to me, that I may live;
for your law is my delight.
78 Let the arrogant be put to shame,

because they have subverted me with
guile;
as for me, I will meditate on your
precepts.
79 Let those who fear you turn to me,
so that they may know your decrees.
80 May my heart be blameless in your statutes,
so that I may not be put to shame.

81 My soul languishes for your salvation;
I hope in your word.
82 My eyes fail with watching for your
promise;
I ask, "When will you comfort me?"
83 For I have become like a wineskin in the
smoke,
yet I have not forgotten your statutes.
84 How long must your servant endure?
When will you judge those who
persecute me?
85 The arrogant have dug pitfalls for me;
they flout your law.
86 All your commandments are enduring;
I am persecuted without cause; help me!
87 They have almost made an end of me on
earth;
but I have not forsaken your precepts.
88 In your steadfast love spare my life,
so that I may keep the decrees of your
mouth.

89 The LORD exists forever;
your word is firmly fixed in heaven.
90 Your faithfulness endures to all generations;
you have established the earth, and it
stands fast.
91 By your appointment they stand today,
for all things are your servants.
92 If your law had not been my delight,
I would have perished in my misery.
93 I will never forget your precepts,
for by them you have given me life.
94 I am yours; save me,
for I have sought your precepts.
95 The wicked lie in wait to destroy me,
but I consider your decrees.
96 I have seen a limit to all perfection,
but your commandment is exceedingly
broad.

97 Oh, how I love your law!
It is my meditation all day long.
98 Your commandment makes me wiser than
my enemies,
for it is always with me.
99 I have more understanding than all my
teachers,

for your decrees are my meditation.
100 I understand more than the aged,
for I keep your precepts.
101 I hold back my feet from every evil way,
in order to keep your word.
102 I do not turn away from your ordinances,
for you have taught me.
103 How sweet are your words to my taste,
sweeter than honey to my mouth!
104 Through your precepts I get understanding;
therefore I hate every false way.

105 Your word is a lamp to my feet
and a light to my path.
106 I have sworn an oath and confirmed it,
to observe your righteous ordinances.
107 I am severely afflicted;
give me life, O LORD, according to your
word.
108 Accept my offerings of praise, O LORD,
and teach me your ordinances.
109 I hold my life in my hand continually,
but I do not forget your law.
110 The wicked have laid a snare for me,
but I do not stray from your precepts.
111 Your decrees are my heritage forever;
they are the joy of my heart.
112 I incline my heart to perform your statutes
forever, to the end.

113 I hate the double-minded,
but I love your law.
114 You are my hiding place and my shield;
I hope in your word.
115 Go away from me, you evildoers,
that I may keep the commandments of
my God.
116 Uphold me according to your promise, that
I may live,
and let me not be put to shame in my
hope.
117 Hold me up, that I may be safe
and have regard for your statutes
continually.
118 You spurn all who go astray from your
statutes;
for their cunning is in vain.
119 All the wicked of the earth you count as
dross;
therefore I love your decrees.
120 My flesh trembles for fear of you,
and I am afraid of your judgments.

121 I have done what is just and right;
do not leave me to my oppressors.
122 Guarantee your servant's well-being;
do not let the godless oppress me.

123 My eyes fail from watching for your
salvation,
and for the fulfillment of your righteous
promise.
124 Deal with your servant according to your
steadfast love,
and teach me your statutes.
125 I am your servant; give me understanding,
so that I may know your decrees.
126 It is time for the LORD to act,
for your law has been broken.
127 Truly I love your commandments
more than gold, more than fine gold.
128 Truly I direct my steps by all your
precepts;[c]
I hate every false way.

129 Your decrees are wonderful;
therefore my soul keeps them.
130 The unfolding of your words gives light;
it imparts understanding to the simple.
131 With open mouth I pant,
because I long for your commandments.
132 Turn to me and be gracious to me,
as is your custom toward those who love
your name.
133 Keep my steps steady according to your
promise,
and never let iniquity have dominion
over me.
134 Redeem me from human oppression,
that I may keep your precepts.
135 Make your face shine upon your servant,
and teach me your statutes.
136 My eyes shed streams of tears
because your law is not kept.

137 You are righteous, O LORD,
and your judgments are right.
138 You have appointed your decrees in
righteousness
and in all faithfulness.
139 My zeal consumes me
because my foes forget your words.
140 Your promise is well tried,
and your servant loves it.
141 I am small and despised,
yet I do not forget your precepts.
142 Your righteousness is an everlasting
righteousness,
and your law is the truth.
143 Trouble and anguish have come upon me,
but your commandments are my delight.
144 Your decrees are righteous forever;
give me understanding that I may live.

---

c Gk Jerome: Meaning of Heb uncertain

145 With my whole heart I cry; answer me,
    O LORD.
  I will keep your statutes.
146 I cry to you; save me,
  that I may observe your decrees.
147 I rise before dawn and cry for help;
  I put my hope in your words.
148 My eyes are awake before each watch of the
    night,
  that I may meditate on your promise.
149 In your steadfast love hear my voice;
  O LORD, in your justice preserve my life.
150 Those who persecute me with evil purpose
    draw near;
  they are far from your law.
151 Yet you are near, O LORD,
  and all your commandments are true.
152 Long ago I learned from your decrees
  that you have established them forever.

153 Look on my misery and rescue me,
  for I do not forget your law.
154 Plead my cause and redeem me;
  give me life according to your promise.
155 Salvation is far from the wicked,
  for they do not seek your statutes.
156 Great is your mercy, O LORD;
  give me life according to your justice.
157 Many are my persecutors and my
    adversaries,
  yet I do not swerve from your decrees.
158 I look at the faithless with disgust,
  because they do not keep your
    commands.
159 Consider how I love your precepts;
  preserve my life according to your
    steadfast love.
160 The sum of your word is truth;
  and every one of your righteous
    ordinances endures forever.

161 Princes persecute me without cause,
  but my heart stands in awe of your
    words.
162 I rejoice at your word
  like one who finds great spoil.
163 I hate and abhor falsehood,
  but I love your law.
164 Seven times a day I praise you
  for your righteous ordinances.
165 Great peace have those who love your law;
  nothing can make them stumble.
166 I hope for your salvation, O LORD,
  and I fulfill your commandments.
167 My soul keeps your decrees;
  I love them exceedingly.

168 I keep your precepts and decrees,
  for all my ways are before you.

169 Let my cry come before you, O LORD;
  give me understanding according to your
    word.
170 Let my supplication come before you;
  deliver me according to your promise.
171 My lips will pour forth praise,
  because you teach me your statutes.
172 My tongue will sing of your promise,
  for all your commandments are right.
173 Let your hand be ready to help me,
  for I have chosen your precepts.
174 I long for your salvation, O LORD,
  and your law is my delight.
175 Let me live that I may praise you,
  and let your ordinances help me.
176 I have gone astray like a lost sheep; seek
    out your servant,
  for I do not forget your commandments.

Psalm 120
Prayer for Deliverance from Slanderers

A Song of Ascents.

1 In my distress I cry to the LORD,
  that he may answer me:
2 "Deliver me, O LORD,
  from lying lips,
  from a deceitful tongue."

3 What shall be given to you?
  And what more shall be done to you,
  you deceitful tongue?
4 A warrior's sharp arrows,
  with glowing coals of the broom tree!

5 Woe is me, that I am an alien in Me'shech,
  that I must live among the tents of
    Ke'dar.
6 Too long have I had my dwelling
  among those who hate peace.
7 I am for peace;
  but when I speak,
  they are for war.

Psalm 121
Assurance of God's Protection

A Song of Ascents.

1 I lift up my eyes to the hills—
  from where will my help come?
2 My help comes from the LORD,
  who made heaven and earth.

3 He will not let your foot be moved;
  he who keeps you will not slumber.

⁴ He who keeps Israel
  will neither slumber nor sleep.

⁵ The LORD is your keeper;
  the LORD is your shade at your right hand.
⁶ The sun shall not strike you by day,
  nor the moon by night.

⁷ The LORD will keep you from all evil;
  he will keep your life.
⁸ The LORD will keep
  your going out and your coming in
  from this time on and forevermore.

Psalm 122
Song of Praise and Prayer
for Jerusalem

A Song of Ascents. Of David.

¹ I was glad when they said to me,
  "Let us go to the house of the LORD!"
² Our feet are standing
  within your gates, O Jerusalem.

³ Jerusalem—built as a city
  that is bound firmly together.
⁴ To it the tribes go up,
  the tribes of the LORD,
  as was decreed for Israel,
  to give thanks to the name of the LORD.
⁵ For there the thrones for judgment were
      set up,
  the thrones of the house of David.

⁶ Pray for the peace of Jerusalem:
  "May they prosper who love you.
⁷ Peace be within your walls,
  and security within your towers."
⁸ For the sake of my relatives and friends
  I will say, "Peace be within you."

⁹ For the sake of the house of the LORD
      our God,
  I will seek your good.

Psalm 123
Supplication for Mercy

A Song of Ascents.

¹ To you I lift up my eyes,
  O you who are enthroned in the
      heavens!
² As the eyes of servants
  look to the hand of their master,
  as the eyes of a maid
    to the hand of her mistress,
  so our eyes look to the LORD our God,
    until he has mercy upon us.
³ Have mercy upon us, O LORD, have mercy
      upon us,
  for we have had more than enough of
      contempt.
⁴ Our soul has had more than its fill
  of the scorn of those who are at ease,
  of the contempt of the proud.

Psalm 124
Thanksgiving for Israel's Deliverance

A Song of Ascents. Of David.

¹ If it had not been the LORD who was on our
      side
  —let Israel now say—
² if it had not been the LORD who was on our
      side,
  when our enemies attacked us,
³ then they would have swallowed us up
      alive,
  when their anger was kindled against us;

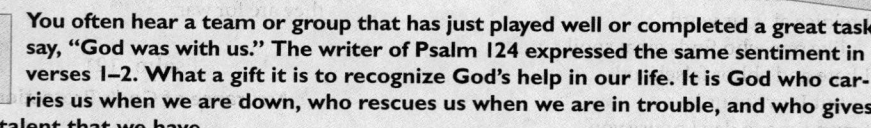

The Lord Was on Our Side

You often hear a team or group that has just played well or completed a great task
say, "God was with us." The writer of Psalm 124 expressed the same sentiment in
verses 1–2. What a gift it is to recognize God's help in our life. It is God who carries us when we are down, who rescues us when we are in trouble, and who gives
us the talent that we have.

Are you ever afraid, or do you ever feel lost? Read Psalm 124 and be assured that others have felt the same way. Whether you are unsure about school, a job, a relationship, or
your future, just remember, "Our help is in the name of the LORD, / who made heaven and
earth" (verse 8).

▸ Psalm 124

4 then the flood would have swept us away,
  the torrent would have gone over us;
5 then over us would have gone
  the raging waters.

6 Blessed be the LORD,
  who has not given us
  as prey to their teeth.
7 We have escaped like a bird
  from the snare of the fowlers;
  the snare is broken,
  and we have escaped.

8 Our help is in the name of the LORD,
  who made heaven and earth.

Psalm 125
The Security of God's People
A Song of Ascents.

1 Those who trust in the LORD are like Mount
    Zion,
  which cannot be moved, but abides
    forever.
2 As the mountains surround Jerusalem,
  so the LORD surrounds his people,
  from this time on and forevermore.
3 For the scepter of wickedness shall not rest
    on the land allotted to the righteous,
  so that the righteous might not stretch out
    their hands to do wrong.
4 Do good, O LORD, to those who are good,
  and to those who are upright in their
    hearts.
5 But those who turn aside to their own
    crooked ways
  the LORD will lead away with evildoers.
  Peace be upon Israel!

Psalm 126
A Harvest of Joy
A Song of Ascents.

1 When the LORD restored the fortunes of
    Zion,*d*
  we were like those who dream.
2 Then our mouth was filled with laughter,
  and our tongue with shouts of joy;
  then it was said among the nations,
  "The LORD has done great things for
    them."
3 The LORD has done great things for us,
  and we rejoiced.

4 Restore our fortunes, O LORD,
  like the watercourses in the Neg'eb.

5 May those who sow in tears
  reap with shouts of joy.
6 Those who go out weeping,
  bearing the seed for sowing,
shall come home with shouts of joy,
  carrying their sheaves.

Psalm 127
God's Blessings in the Home
A Song of Ascents. Of Solomon.

1 Unless the LORD builds the house,
  those who build it labor in vain.
Unless the LORD guards the city,
  the guard keeps watch in vain.
2 It is in vain that you rise up early
  and go late to rest,
eating the bread of anxious toil;
  for he gives sleep to his beloved.*e*
3 Sons are indeed a heritage from the LORD,
  the fruit of the womb a reward.
4 Like arrows in the hand of a warrior
  are the sons of one's youth.
5 Happy is the man who has
  his quiver full of them.
He shall not be put to shame
  when he speaks with his enemies in the
    gate.

Psalm 128
The Happy Home of the Faithful
A Song of Ascents.

1 Happy is everyone who fears the LORD,
  who walks in his ways.
2 You shall eat the fruit of the labor of your
    hands;
  you shall be happy, and it shall go well
    with you.

3 Your wife will be like a fruitful vine
  within your house;
  your children will be like olive shoots
    around your table.
4 Thus shall the man be blessed
  who fears the LORD.

5 The LORD bless you from Zion.
  May you see the prosperity of
    Jerusalem
  all the days of your life.
6 May you see your children's children.
  Peace be upon Israel!

---

d Or *brought back those who returned to Zion*   *e* Or *for he*
provides for his beloved during sleep

P
S
A
L
M
S

Psalm 129

Prayer for the Downfall of Israel's Enemies

A Song of Ascents.

1 "Often have they attacked me from my
  youth"
  —let Israel now say—
2 "often have they attacked me from my
  youth,
  yet they have not prevailed against me.
3 The plowers plowed on my back;
  they made their furrows long."
4 The LORD is righteous;
  he has cut the cords of the wicked.
5 May all who hate Zion
  be put to shame and turned backward.
6 Let them be like the grass on the housetops
  that withers before it grows up,
7 with which reapers do not fill their hands
  or binders of sheaves their arms,
8 while those who pass by do not say,
  "The blessing of the LORD be upon you!
  We bless you in the name of the LORD!"

PRAY IT

Hold Me, Mother God

Psalm 131 is a humble prayer of child-like trust. It gives the wonderful image of God holding us like a child in a mother's lap. Like a mother, God hugs us close, and keeps us safe and warm and protected. We don't need to solve problems or be concerned about our performance. We are loved just because we are us. God created us; God loves us and cradles us.

Do you remember sitting quietly in your mother's or grandmother's lap when you were a small child? If so, do you recall her telling you stories or singing you lullabies? If you do not have such memories, have you ever seen a mother calm her child with songs and stories? How is God's love like that? In prayer, imagine being held by God, as a child is held by a mother. You might be surprised at how safe and secure you feel!

▸ Psalm 131

Psalm 130

Waiting for Divine Redemption

A Song of Ascents.

1 Out of the depths I cry to you, O LORD.
2   Lord, hear my voice!
  Let your ears be attentive
    to the voice of my supplications!

3 If you, O LORD, should mark iniquities,
  Lord, who could stand?
4 But there is forgiveness with you,
  so that you may be revered.

5 I wait for the LORD, my soul waits,
  and in his word I hope;
6 my soul waits for the Lord
  more than those who watch for the
    morning,
  more than those who watch for the
    morning.

7 O Israel, hope in the LORD!
  For with the LORD there is steadfast love,
  and with him is great power to redeem.
8 It is he who will redeem Israel
  from all its iniquities.

Psalm 131

Song of Quiet Trust

A Song of Ascents. Of David.

1 O LORD, my heart is not lifted up,
  my eyes are not raised too high;
  I do not occupy myself with things
  too great and too marvelous for me.
2 But I have calmed and quieted my soul,
  like a weaned child with its mother;
  my soul is like the weaned child that is
    with me. *f*

3 O Israel, hope in the LORD
  from this time on and forevermore.

Psalm 132

The Eternal Dwelling of God in Zion

A Song of Ascents.

1 O LORD, remember in David's favor
  all the hardships he endured;
2 how he swore to the LORD
  and vowed to the Mighty One of Jacob,
3 "I will not enter my house
  or get into my bed;
4 I will not give sleep to my eyes
  or slumber to my eyelids,
5 until I find a place for the LORD,

f Or *my soul within me is like a weaned child*

a dwelling place for the Mighty One of
   Jacob."

6 We heard of it in Eph'ra•thah;
      we found it in the fields of Jā'ar.
7 "Let us go to his dwelling place;
      let us worship at his footstool."

8 Rise up, O LORD, and go to your resting
      place,
      you and the ark of your might.
9 Let your priests be clothed with
      righteousness,
      and let your faithful shout for joy.
10 For your servant David's sake
      do not turn away the face of your
      anointed one.

11 The LORD swore to David a sure oath
      from which he will not turn back:
   "One of the sons of your body
      I will set on your throne.
12 If your sons keep my covenant
      and my decrees that I shall teach them,
   their sons also, forevermore,
      shall sit on your throne."

13 For the LORD has chosen Zion;
      he has desired it for his habitation:
14 "This is my resting place forever;
      here I will reside, for I have desired it.
15 I will abundantly bless its provisions;
      I will satisfy its poor with bread.
16 Its priests I will clothe with salvation,
      and its faithful will shout for joy.
17 There I will cause a horn to sprout up for
      David;
   I have prepared a lamp for my
      anointed one.
18 His enemies I will clothe with disgrace,
      but on him, his crown will gleam."

Psalm 133
The Blessedness of Unity

A Song of Ascents.

1 How very good and pleasant it is
      when kindred live together in unity!
2 It is like the precious oil on the head,
      running down upon the beard,
   on the beard of Aaron,
      running down over the collar of his
      robes.
3 It is like the dew of Hermon,
      which falls on the mountains of Zion.
   For there the LORD ordained his blessing,
      life forevermore.

did you KNOW?

Jerusalem, Zion, City of David

Jerusalem, Zion, City of David—you have probably noticed that these three names keep popping up throughout the Psalms. They all refer to the heart of Israel, the city of Jerusalem. When David became king of the united tribes of Israel, he needed a neutral place between the northern and southern tribes. He conquered Jerusalem and elevated it as the political and religious center—thus, Jerusalem was also known as the City of David. Mount Zion, located within Jerusalem, was the site of the Temple—the sacred place where God dwelt. So, Zion became another way to refer to Jerusalem.

At that time, the Israelites felt that Jerusalem was invincible because it was God's dwelling place. But eventually, Jerusalem and the Temple were destroyed. Afterward, a hope arose that one day, a messiah from David's line would renew Jerusalem and true worship of God on Zion. The New Testament portrays Jesus as the fulfillment of this hope.

▶ **Psalm 132**

Psalm 134
Praise in the Night

A Song of Ascents.

1 Come, bless the LORD, all you servants of the
      LORD,
      who stand by night in the house of the
      LORD!
2 Lift up your hands to the holy place,
      and bless the LORD.

3 May the LORD, maker of heaven and earth,
      bless you from Zion.

Psalm 135
Praise for God's Goodness and Might

1 Praise the LORD!
      Praise the name of the LORD;
      give praise, O servants of the LORD,

P
S
A
L
M
S

2 you that stand in the house of the LORD,
  in the courts of the house of our God.
3 Praise the LORD, for the LORD is good;
  sing to his name, for he is gracious.
4 For the LORD has chosen Jacob for himself,
  Israel as his own possession.

5 For I know that the LORD is great;
  our Lord is above all gods.
6 Whatever the LORD pleases he does,
  in heaven and on earth,
  in the seas and all deeps.
7 He it is who makes the clouds rise at the
      end of the earth;
  he makes lightnings for the rain
  and brings out the wind from his
      storehouses.

8 He it was who struck down the firstborn of
      Egypt,
  both human beings and animals;
9 he sent signs and wonders
  into your midst, O Egypt,
  against Pharaoh and all his servants.
10 He struck down many nations
  and killed mighty kings—
11 Sī'hon, king of the Am'o•rites,
  and Og, king of Bā'shan,
  and all the kingdoms of Cā'naan—
12 and gave their land as a heritage,
  a heritage to his people Israel.

13 Your name, O LORD, endures forever,
  your renown, O LORD, throughout all
      ages.
14 For the LORD will vindicate his people,
  and have compassion on his servants.

15 The idols of the nations are silver and gold,
  the work of human hands.
16 They have mouths, but they do not speak;
  they have eyes, but they do not see;
17 they have ears, but they do not hear,
  and there is no breath in their mouths.
18 Those who make them
  and all who trust them
  shall become like them.

19 O house of Israel, bless the LORD!
  O house of Aaron, bless the LORD!
20 O house of Levi, bless the LORD!
  You that fear the LORD, bless the LORD!
21 Blessed be the LORD from Zion,
  he who resides in Jerusalem.
  Praise the LORD!

Psalm 136

God's Work in Creation and in History

1 O give thanks to the LORD, for he is good,
  for his steadfast love endures forever.
2 O give thanks to the God of gods,
  for his steadfast love endures forever.
3 O give thanks to the Lord of lords,
  for his steadfast love endures forever;

4 who alone does great wonders,
  for his steadfast love endures forever;
5 who by understanding made the heavens,
  for his steadfast love endures forever;
6 who spread out the earth on the waters,
  for his steadfast love endures forever;
7 who made the great lights,
  for his steadfast love endures forever;
8 the sun to rule over the day,
  for his steadfast love endures forever;
9 the moon and stars to rule over the night,
  for his steadfast love endures forever;
10 who struck Egypt through their firstborn,
  for his steadfast love endures forever;
11 and brought Israel out from among them,
  for his steadfast love endures forever;
12 with a strong hand and an
      outstretched arm,
  for his steadfast love endures forever;
13 who divided the Red Sea8 in two,
  for his steadfast love endures forever;
14 and made Israel pass through the midst
      of it,
  for his steadfast love endures forever;
15 but overthrew Pharaoh and his army in the
      Red Sea,8
  for his steadfast love endures forever;
16 who led his people through the wilderness,
  for his steadfast love endures forever;
17 who struck down great kings,
  for his steadfast love endures forever;
18 and killed famous kings,
  for his steadfast love endures forever;
19 Sī'hon, king of the Am'o•rītes,
  for his steadfast love endures forever;
20 and Og, king of Bā'shan,
  for his steadfast love endures forever;
21 and gave their land as a heritage,
  for his steadfast love endures forever;
22 a heritage to his servant Israel,
  for his steadfast love endures forever.

23 It is he who remembered us in our low
      estate,
  for his steadfast love endures forever;

---

8 Or Sea of Reeds

24 and rescued us from our foes,
  for his steadfast love endures forever;
25 who gives food to all flesh,
  for his steadfast love endures forever.

26 O give thanks to the God of heaven,
  for his steadfast love endures forever.

Psalm 137
Lament over the Destruction of Jerusalem

1 By the rivers of Babylon—
  there we sat down and there we wept
    when we remembered Zion.
2 On the willows[h] there
  we hung up our harps.
3 For there our captors
  asked us for songs,
  and our tormentors asked for mirth, saying,
    "Sing us one of the songs of Zion!"

4 How could we sing the LORD's song
  in a foreign land?
5 If I forget you, O Jerusalem,
  let my right hand wither!
6 Let my tongue cling to the roof of my
    mouth,
  if I do not remember you,
if I do not set Jerusalem
  above my highest joy.

7 Remember, O LORD, against the Ē′dom•ites
    the day of Jerusalem's fall,
  how they said, "Tear it down! Tear it down!
    Down to its foundations!"
8 O daughter Babylon, you devastator![i]
    Happy shall they be who pay you back
    what you have done to us!
9 Happy shall they be who take your little
      ones
    and dash them against the rock!

Psalm 138
Thanksgiving and Praise
Of David.

1 I give you thanks, O LORD, with my whole
    heart;
  before the gods I sing your praise;
2 I bow down toward your holy temple
  and give thanks to your name for your
      steadfast love and your faithfulness;
  for you have exalted your name and your
      word
  above everything.[j]

3 On the day I called, you answered me,
  you increased my strength of soul.[k]

4 All the kings of the earth shall praise you,
    O LORD,
  for they have heard the words of your
      mouth.
5 They shall sing of the ways of the LORD,
  for great is the glory of the LORD.
6 For though the LORD is high, he regards the
      lowly;
  but the haughty he perceives from far
      away.

7 Though I walk in the midst of trouble,
  you preserve me against the wrath of my
      enemies;
  you stretch out your hand,
  and your right hand delivers me.
8 The LORD will fulfill his purpose for me;
  your steadfast love, O LORD, endures
      forever.
  Do not forsake the work of your hands.

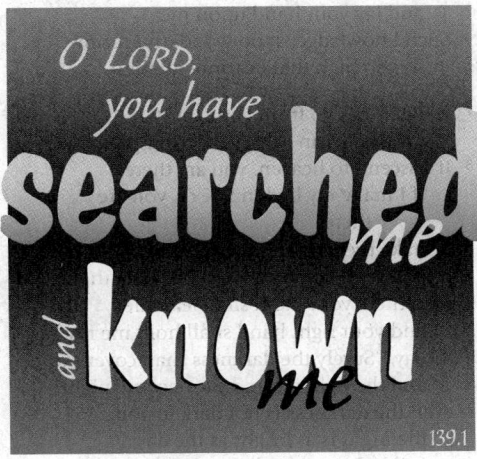

Psalm 139
The Inescapable God
To the leader. Of David. A Psalm.

1 O LORD, you have searched me and
    known me.
2 You know when I sit down and when I
    rise up;
  you discern my thoughts from far away.
3 You search out my path and my lying
    down,
  and are acquainted with all my ways.
4 Even before a word is on my tongue,
    O LORD, you know it completely.

h Or *poplars*   i Or *you who are devastated*   j Cn: Heb *you have exalted your word above all your name*   k Syr Compare Gk Tg: Heb *you made me arrogant in my soul with strength*

The Sacredness of Life

"For it was you who formed my inward parts; / you knit me together in my mother's womb" (Ps 139.13).

Psalm 139 speaks poetically of God's intimate care for each of us, long before we were even formed. It is perhaps the most powerful argument against abortion in the entire Bible. Who can deny that God gave us life long before we actually saw the light of day? How can we deny that every unborn child is fashioned by the hand of God?

It is easy to get caught up in arguments about individual rights and scientific terminology. But this is not about science or government or even when life begins. It is about poetry and love and the faith that God has knit each of us together in our mother's womb. God has great plans for each of us, whether we have been born, are in the womb, or have not yet even been thought of. God knows and loves us, and has through all eternity.

What else is there to say?

▸ Psalm 139

5 You hem me in, behind and before,
  and lay your hand upon me.
6 Such knowledge is too wonderful for me;
  it is so high that I cannot attain it.

7 Where can I go from your spirit?
  Or where can I flee from your presence?
8 If I ascend to heaven, you are there;
  if I make my bed in Shē'ōl, you are
    there.
9 If I take the wings of the morning
  and settle at the farthest limits of the sea,
10 even there your hand shall lead me,
  and your right hand shall hold me fast.
11 If I say, "Surely the darkness shall cover me,
  and the light around me become night,"
12 even the darkness is not dark to you;
  the night is as bright as the day,
  for darkness is as light to you.

13 For it was you who formed my inward
    parts;
  you knit me together in my mother's
    womb.
14 I praise you, for I am fearfully and
    wonderfully made.
  Wonderful are your works;
that I know very well.
15 My frame was not hidden from you,
  when I was being made in secret,
  intricately woven in the depths of the
    earth.
16 Your eyes beheld my unformed substance.
  In your book were written
    all the days that were formed for me,
    when none of them as yet existed.

17 How weighty to me are your thoughts,
    O God!
  How vast is the sum of them!
18 I try to count them—they are more than the
    sand;
  I come to the end[l]—I am still with you.

19 O that you would kill the wicked, O God,
  and that the bloodthirsty would depart
    from me—
20 those who speak of you maliciously,
  and lift themselves up against you for
    evil![m]
21 Do I not hate those who hate you, O LORD?
  And do I not loathe those who rise up
    against you?
22 I hate them with perfect hatred;
  I count them my enemies.
23 Search me, O God, and know my heart;
  test me and know my thoughts.
24 See if there is any wicked[n] way in me,
  and lead me in the way everlasting.[o]

Psalm 140

Prayer for Deliverance from Enemies

To the leader. A Psalm of David.

1 Deliver me, O LORD, from evildoers;
  protect me from those who are violent,
2 who plan evil things in their minds
  and stir up wars continually.
3 They make their tongue sharp as a snake's,
  and under their lips is the venom of
    vipers.   *Sē'lah*

---

[l] Or *I awake*   [m] Cn: Meaning of Heb uncertain
[n] Heb *hurtful*   [o] Or *the ancient way.* Compare Jer 6.16

4 Guard me, O LORD, from the hands of the
      wicked;
   protect me from the violent
   who have planned my downfall.
5 The arrogant have hidden a trap
      for me,
   and with cords they have spread
      a net,ᵖ
   along the road they have set snares for
      me.   Sĕ'lah

6 I say to the LORD, "You are my God;
   give ear, O LORD, to the voice of my
      supplications."
7 O LORD, my Lord, my strong deliverer,
   you have covered my head in the day
      of battle.
8 Do not grant, O LORD, the desires of the
      wicked;
   do not further their evil plot.q   Sĕ'lah

9 Those who surround me lift up their
      heads;ʳ
   let the mischief of their lips overwhelm
      them!
10 Let burning coals fall on them!
   Let them be flung into pits, no more
      to rise!
11 Do not let the slanderer be established in
      the land;
   let evil speedily hunt down the violent!

12 I know that the LORD maintains the cause of
      the needy,
   and executes justice for the poor.
13 Surely the righteous shall give thanks to
      your name;
   the upright shall live in your presence.

ᵖ Or *they have spread cords as a net*   q Heb adds *they are
exalted*   ʳ Cn Compare Gk: Heb *those who surround me
are uplifted in head*; Heb divides verses 8 and 9 differently

GOD CARES FOR THOSE WHO SUFFER PERSECUTION!

Many of us like to think that persecution rarely occurs. Unfortunately, this is not true. All too frequently, people are persecuted because of their color, their ethnic origin, their political beliefs, or even their faith. Harassment can be as subtle as a rude comment or a patronizing attitude, or as aggressive as a beating or death. Young people know the feeling of persecution. They may experience it because of their origin, the way they look or talk, or what they believe.

Psalm 140 is one of several psalms (see also Psalms 35, 86) and prayers seeking God's help in times of persecution. These typically have two parts. The first part asks for God's protection against persecutors, and the second part praises God's love, justice, and mercy. This illustrates the continual tension for all believers: feeling the need for God's action while at the same time being certain that God cares for them in the midst of their persecution.

For Christians, Jesus is the perfect model of the persecuted person. He was persecuted without reason (Lk 23.4), and he felt God's absence (Mk 15.34), but he still put his entire faith and trust in God's will (Mt 26.39). Following Jesus' example, Christians throughout history have bravely endured persecution, and even death, for their faith.

■ Have you or your family experienced some kind of persecution? If so, how and why? If you have ever participated in some kind of persecution of someone else, pray for forgiveness and if possible make amends.

■ Thank God for the blessings you have, and ask God for the strength to endure whatever persecutions come your way. Pray for those who are suffering persecution, regardless of the motive.

▸ Psalm 140

Psalm 141

Prayer for Preservation from Evil

A Psalm of David.

1 I call upon you, O LORD; come quickly
        to me;
    give ear to my voice when I call to you.
2 Let my prayer be counted as incense
        before you,
    and the lifting up of my hands as an
        evening sacrifice.

3 Set a guard over my mouth, O LORD;
    keep watch over the door of my lips.
4 Do not turn my heart to any evil,
    to busy myself with wicked deeds
in company with those who work iniquity;
    do not let me eat of their delicacies.

5 Let the righteous strike me;
    let the faithful correct me.
Never let the oil of the wicked anoint my
        head,*s*
    for my prayer is continually*t* against their
        wicked deeds.
6 When they are given over to those who
        shall condemn them,
    then they shall learn that my words were
        pleasant.
7 Like a rock that one breaks apart and
        shatters on the land,
so shall their bones be strewn at the
        mouth of She′ol.*u*

8 But my eyes are turned toward you, O GOD,
        my Lord;
    in you I seek refuge; do not leave me
        defenseless.
9 Keep me from the trap that they have laid
        for me,
    and from the snares of evildoers.
10 Let the wicked fall into their own nets,
    while I alone escape.

Psalm 142

Prayer for Deliverance from Persecutors

A Mas′kil of David. When he was in the cave.
A Prayer.

1 With my voice I cry to the LORD;
    with my voice I make supplication to the
        LORD.
2 I pour out my complaint before him;
    I tell my trouble before him.
3 When my spirit is faint,
    you know my way.

In the path where I walk
    they have hidden a trap for me.
4 Look on my right hand and see—
    there is no one who takes notice of me;
no refuge remains to me;
    no one cares for me.

5 I cry to you, O LORD;
    I say, "You are my refuge,
    my portion in the land of the living."
6 Give heed to my cry,
    for I am brought very low.

Save me from my persecutors,
    for they are too strong for me.
7 Bring me out of prison,
    so that I may give thanks to your name.
The righteous will surround me,
    for you will deal bountifully with me.

Psalm 143

Prayer for Deliverance from Enemies

A Psalm of David.

1 Hear my prayer, O LORD;
    give ear to my supplications in your
        faithfulness;
    answer me in your righteousness.
2 Do not enter into judgment with your
        servant,
    for no one living is righteous before you.
3 For the enemy has pursued me,
    crushing my life to the ground,
    making me sit in darkness like those long
        dead.
4 Therefore my spirit faints within me;
    my heart within me is appalled.

5 I remember the days of old,
    I think about all your deeds,
    I meditate on the works of your hands.
6 I stretch out my hands to you;
    my soul thirsts for you like a parched
        land.   *Se′lah*

7 Answer me quickly, O LORD;
    my spirit fails.
Do not hide your face from me,
    or I shall be like those who go down to
        the Pit.
8 Let me hear of your steadfast love in the
        morning,
    for in you I put my trust.

---

s Gk: Meaning of Heb uncertain   *t* Cn: Heb *for
continually and my prayer*   *u* Meaning of Heb of
verses 5-7 is uncertain

Teach me the way I should go,
   for to you I lift up my soul.

9 Save me, O LORD, from my enemies;
   I have fled to you for refuge.[v]
10 Teach me to do your will,
   for you are my God.
   Let your good spirit lead me
   on a level path.

11 For your name's sake, O LORD, preserve my
      life.
   In your righteousness bring me out of
      trouble.
12 In your steadfast love cut off my enemies,
   and destroy all my adversaries,
   for I am your servant.

Psalm 144

Prayer for National Deliverance and Security

Of David.

1 Blessed be the LORD, my rock,
   who trains my hands for war, and my
      fingers for battle;
2 my rock[w] and my fortress,
   my stronghold and my deliverer,
   my shield, in whom I take refuge,
   who subdues the peoples[x] under me.

3 O LORD, what are human beings that you
      regard them,
   or mortals that you think of them?
4 They are like a breath;
   their days are like a passing shadow.

5 Bow your heavens, O LORD, and come down;
   touch the mountains so that they smoke.
6 Make the lightning flash and scatter them;
   send out your arrows and rout them.
7 Stretch out your hand from on high;
   set me free and rescue me from the
      mighty waters,
   from the hand of aliens,
8 whose mouths speak lies,
   and whose right hands are false.

9 I will sing a new song to you, O God;
   upon a ten-stringed harp I will play
      to you,
10 the one who gives victory to kings,
   who rescues his servant David.
11 Rescue me from the cruel sword,
   and deliver me from the hand of aliens,
   whose mouths speak lies,
   and whose right hands are false.

12 May our sons in their youth
   be like plants full grown,
   our daughters like corner pillars,
   cut for the building of a palace.
13 May our barns be filled,
   with produce of every kind;
   may our sheep increase by thousands,
   by tens of thousands in our fields,
14 and may our cattle be heavy with young.
   May there be no breach in the walls,[y] no
      exile,
   and no cry of distress in our streets.

15 Happy are the people to whom such
      blessings fall;
   happy are the people whose God is the
      LORD.

PRAY IT!

A Prayer for the Young

We praise you, God, for all our nation's
      blessings!
We thank you for our young people, our
   sons and daughters who come forward to
   serve the people of God.
We ask you to make them strong, to call
   them into a trusting relationship with you,
   to live a faithful life, and to be leaders
   and examples for others.
Happy the people whose God is the Lord!

▸ Psalm 144

Psalm 145

The Greatness and the Goodness of God

Praise. Of David.

1 I will extol you, my God and King,
   and bless your name forever and ever.
2 Every day I will bless you,
   and praise your name forever and ever.
3 Great is the LORD, and greatly to be praised;
   his greatness is unsearchable.

4 One generation shall laud your works to
      another,
   and shall declare your mighty acts.
5 On the glorious splendor of your majesty,

---

v One Heb Ms Gk: MT *to you I have hidden*   w With 18.2
and 2 Sam 22.2: Heb *my steadfast love*   x Heb Mss Syr
Aquila Jerome: MT *my people*   y Heb lacks *in the walls*

and on your wondrous works, I will
meditate.

6 The might of your awesome deeds shall be
proclaimed,
and I will declare your greatness.

7 They shall celebrate the fame of your
abundant goodness,
and shall sing aloud of your
righteousness.

8 The LORD is gracious and merciful,
slow to anger and abounding in steadfast
love.

9 The LORD is good to all,
and his compassion is over all that he
has made.

10 All your works shall give thanks to you,
O LORD,
and all your faithful shall bless you.

11 They shall speak of the glory of your
kingdom,
and tell of your power,

12 to make known to all people your^z mighty
deeds,
and the glorious splendor of your^a
kingdom.

13 Your kingdom is an everlasting kingdom,
and your dominion endures throughout
all generations.

The LORD is faithful in all his words,
and gracious in all his deeds.^b

14 The LORD upholds all who are falling,
and raises up all who are bowed down.

15 The eyes of all look to you,
and you give them their food in due
season.

16 You open your hand,
satisfying the desire of every living thing.

17 The LORD is just in all his ways,
and kind in all his doings.

18 The LORD is near to all who call on him,
to all who call on him in truth.

19 He fulfills the desire of all who fear him;
he also hears their cry, and saves them.

20 The LORD watches over all who love him,
but all the wicked he will destroy.

21 My mouth will speak the praise of the LORD,
and all flesh will bless his holy name
forever and ever.

Psalm 146
Praise for God's Help

1 Praise the LORD!
Praise the LORD, O my soul!

2 I will praise the LORD as long as I live;
I will sing praises to my God all my life
long.

3 Do not put your trust in princes,
in mortals, in whom there is no help.

4 When their breath departs, they return to
the earth;
on that very day their plans perish.

5 Happy are those whose help is the God of
Jacob,
whose hope is in the LORD their God,

6 who made heaven and earth,
the sea, and all that is in them;
who keeps faith forever;

7 who executes justice for the
oppressed;
who gives food to the hungry.

The LORD sets the prisoners free;

8 the LORD opens the eyes of the blind.
The LORD lifts up those who are bowed
down;
the LORD loves the righteous.

9 The LORD watches over the strangers;
he upholds the orphan and the
widow,
but the way of the wicked he brings to
ruin.

10 The LORD will reign forever,
your God, O Zion, for all generations.
Praise the LORD!

Psalm 147
Praise for God's Care for Jerusalem

1 Praise the LORD!
How good it is to sing praises to our God;
for he is gracious, and a song of praise is
fitting.

2 The LORD builds up Jerusalem;
he gathers the outcasts of Israel.

3 He heals the brokenhearted,
and binds up their wounds.

4 He determines the number of the stars;
he gives to all of them their names.

5 Great is our Lord, and abundant in power;
his understanding is beyond measure.

6 The LORD lifts up the downtrodden;
he casts the wicked to the ground.

7 Sing to the LORD with thanksgiving;
make melody to our God on the lyre.

---

^z Gk Jerome Syr: Heb *his*   ^a Heb *his*   ^b These two lines
supplied by Q Ms Gk Syr

8 He covers the heavens with clouds,
         prepares rain for the earth,
         makes grass grow on the hills.
9 He gives to the animals their food,
         and to the young ravens when they cry.
10 His delight is not in the strength of the
              horse,
         nor his pleasure in the speed of
              a runner;^c
11 but the LORD takes pleasure in those who
              fear him,
         in those who hope in his steadfast
              love.

12 Praise the LORD, O Jerusalem!
         Praise your God, O Zion!
13 For he strengthens the bars of your gates;
         he blesses your children within you.
14 He grants peace^d within your borders;
         he fills you with the finest of wheat.
15 He sends out his command to the earth;
         his word runs swiftly.
16 He gives snow like wool;
         he scatters frost like ashes.
17 He hurls down hail like crumbs—
         who can stand before his cold?
18 He sends out his word, and melts them;
         he makes his wind blow, and the waters
              flow.
19 He declares his word to Jacob,
         his statutes and ordinances to Israel.
20 He has not dealt thus with any other
              nation;
         they do not know his ordinances.
    Praise the LORD!

Psalm 148
Praise for God's Universal Glory

1 Praise the LORD!
   Praise the LORD from the heavens;
         praise him in the heights!
2 Praise him, all his angels;
         praise him, all his host!

3 Praise him, sun and moon;
         praise him, all you shining stars!
4 Praise him, you highest heavens,
         and you waters above the heavens!

5 Let them praise the name of the LORD,
         for he commanded and they
              were created.
6 He established them forever and ever;
         he fixed their bounds, which cannot be
              passed.^e

7 Praise the LORD from the earth,
         you sea monsters and all deeps,
8 fire and hail, snow and frost,
         stormy wind fulfilling his command!

9 Mountains and all hills,
         fruit trees and all cedars!
10 Wild animals and all cattle,
         creeping things and flying birds!

11 Kings of the earth and all peoples,
         princes and all rulers of the earth!
12 Young men and women alike,
         old and young together!

13 Let them praise the name of the LORD,
         for his name alone is exalted;
         his glory is above earth and heaven.
14 He has raised up a horn for his people,
         praise for all his faithful,
         for the people of Israel who are close
              to him.
    Praise the LORD!

Psalm 149
Praise for God's Goodness to Israel

1 Praise the LORD!
   Sing to the LORD a new song,
         his praise in the assembly of the
              faithful.
2 Let Israel be glad in its Maker;
         let the children of Zion rejoice in their
              King.
3 Let them praise his name with dancing,
         making melody to him with tambourine
              and lyre.
4 For the LORD takes pleasure in his
              people;
         he adorns the humble with victory.
5 Let the faithful exult in glory;
         let them sing for joy on their couches.
6 Let the high praises of God be in their
              throats
         and two-edged swords in their hands,
7 to execute vengeance on the nations
         and punishment on the peoples,
8 to bind their kings with fetters
         and their nobles with chains of iron,
9 to execute on them the judgment
              decreed.
         This is glory for all his faithful ones.
    Praise the LORD!

---

c Heb *legs of a person*   d Or *prosperity*   e Or *he set a law
that cannot pass away*

Psalm 150

Praise for God's Surpassing Greatness

1 Praise the LORD!
  Praise God in his sanctuary;
    praise him in his mighty firmament!*f*
2 Praise him for his mighty deeds;
    praise him according to his surpassing
      greatness!
3 Praise him with trumpet sound;
    praise him with lute and harp!
4 Praise him with tambourine and dance;
    praise him with strings and pipe!
5 Praise him with clanging cymbals;
    praise him with loud clashing cymbals!
6 Let everything that breathes praise the LORD!
  Praise the LORD!

f Or dome

PRAY IT!

Psalm 150, Part 2

Praise God with clarinet and saxophone;
  praise God with flute and oboe!
Praise God with French horn and tuba;
  praise God with marimba and
    xylophone!
Praise God with guitar and fiddle;
  praise God with banjo and ukulele!
Praise God with bagpipe and accordion;
  praise God with piano and calliope!
Praise God with steel drum and harmonica;
  praise God with bongo and maracas!
Praise God with soaring classical music;
  praise God with mellow blues, and tango!
Praise God with reggae and rap;
  praise God with jazz and rock!
Praise God with square dancing and line
    dancing;
  praise God with polka and waltz!
Let everyone who has breath and hands
    and feet and voices—
  sopranos, altos, tenors, and basses—
    praise the Lord!

▶ Psalm 150

When we pick up the daily newspaper, many of us turn first to the advice columns. "My mom just doesn't understand me" we read. "Why won't she let me make my own decisions?" Or "I think my boyfriend is cheating on me. Should I show him the door?" Or "All my friends take drugs. How do I resist the pressure?" The Book of Proverbs is the advice column of the Old Testament. It covers everything from raising children to choosing friends.

At a Glance

- **Chapters 1–9.** introduction and instructions for young people
- **10.1—31.9.** assorted collections of proverbs
- **31.10–31.** a reflection on being a good wife

In-depth

"Hear, my child" (Prov 1.8)—this, in a nutshell, is the teaching of Proverbs. The wise person listens to the "voices" of history: experience, intelligence, and common sense. The ancient Israelites had a long tradition of reflecting on the challenges of life. Over the centuries, a whole body of writings developed to record their reflections. These writings gave advice on common problems and questions that people faced, and directions for wise living.

Proverbs is the best-known example of this type of literature in the Old Testament. It contains two basic kinds of writings: longer instructions addressed to young people and short sayings addressed to all. With advice on matters ranging from laziness (6.6–11), cheating (11.1), pride (16.18), and the training of children (22.6), to laughter (14.13), eyewinking (16.30), visiting neighbors (25.17), and being a good wife (31.10–31), Proverbs is a treasure chest of advice from the ancient world. Although some of the sayings may seem outdated or funny to us today, the overall lesson is something that Jesus insists in the Gospels: Faith is not just a matter of right believing; it is also a matter of right living.

The poetic structure of this book—a feature of most wisdom literature—reveals another basic insight of our ancestors in faith: How something is said is as important as what is said. In addition, parallelism makes the generally short sayings in this book easy to memorize. We would do well to consult Proverbs regularly for good advice, and to remember what we read. To all who care to hear, this book tells of the rewards of virtue and the dangers of vice.

Quick Facts

Author

King Solomon is introduced as the author, probably because of his legendary wisdom. However, the actual author is unknown, writing from the reign of King Solomon (970–931 B.C.) to sometime after the Babylonian Exile (587–538 B.C.).

Of Note

The book is made up of several collections of proverbs.

Proverbs

The proverbs of Solomon son of David, king of Israel:

Prologue

2 For learning about wisdom and instruction,
   for understanding words of insight,
3 for gaining instruction in wise dealing,
   righteousness, justice, and equity;
4 to teach shrewdness to the simple,
   knowledge and prudence to the young—
5 let the wise also hear and gain in learning,
   and the discerning acquire skill,
6 to understand a proverb and a figure,
   the words of the wise and their riddles.

7 The fear of the LORD is the beginning of
      knowledge;
   fools despise wisdom and instruction.

Warnings against Evil Companions

8 Hear, my child, your father's instruction,
   and do not reject your mother's teaching;
9 for they are a fair garland for your head,
   and pendants for your neck.
10 My child, if sinners entice you,
   do not consent.
11 If they say, "Come with us, let us lie in wait
      for blood;
   let us wantonly ambush the innocent;

12 like Sheʹōl let us swallow them alive
      and whole, like those who go down to
      the Pit.
13 We shall find all kinds of costly things;
   we shall fill our houses with booty.
14 Throw in your lot among us;
   we will all have one purse"—
15 my child, do not walk in their way,
   keep your foot from their paths;
16 for their feet run to evil,
   and they hurry to shed blood.
17 For in vain is the net baited
   while the bird is looking on;
18 yet they lie in wait—to kill themselves!
   and set an ambush—for their own lives!
19 Such is the end[a] of all who are greedy for
      gain;
   it takes away the life of its possessors.

The Call of Wisdom

20 Wisdom cries out in the street;
   in the squares she raises her voice.
21 At the busiest corner she cries out;
   at the entrance of the city gates she
      speaks:
22 "How long, O simple ones, will you love
      being simple?

---

[a] Gk: Heb are the ways

692

LIVE IT!

Media Literacy

Our society today has a powerful, persuasive tool. It is called the media. We are influenced in many ways by what we read, watch, and hear in the many forms of modern media.

We might buy things because something we read says it's the best. We might look the other way when someone is being robbed, because we see so much violence at the movies it doesn't seem to bother us. We might dance to the beat of a song and not even realize that the words are suggesting an immoral behavior.

Certainly not all the messages in the media are bad. But to resist the influence of the media's negative messages, we must educate ourselves to watch for them. In Prov 1.10, we read "My child, if sinners entice you, / do not consent." Take time to really think about a message in the media before you choose to follow it. Verse 7 says it best: Only a fool despises wisdom!

▸ **Prov 1.10**

How long will scoffers delight in their
    scoffing
    and fools hate knowledge?
23 Give heed to my reproof;
I will pour out my thoughts to you;
    I will make my words known to you.
24 Because I have called and you refused,
    have stretched out my hand and no one
      heeded,
25 and because you have ignored all my
    counsel
    and would have none of my reproof,
26 I also will laugh at your calamity;
    I will mock when panic strikes you,
27 when panic strikes you like a storm,
    and your calamity comes like a
      whirlwind,
    when distress and anguish come
      upon you.
28 Then they will call upon me, but I will not
    answer;
    they will seek me diligently, but will not
      find me.
29 Because they hated knowledge
    and did not choose the fear of
      the LORD,
30 would have none of my counsel,
    and despised all my reproof,
31 therefore they shall eat the fruit of their way
    and be sated with their own devices.
32 For waywardness kills the simple,
    and the complacency of fools destroys
      them;
33 but those who listen to me will be secure
    and will live at ease, without dread of
      disaster."

The Value of Wisdom

My child, if you accept my words
    and treasure up my commandments
      within you,
2 making your ear attentive to wisdom
    and inclining your heart to
      understanding;
3 if you indeed cry out for insight,
    and raise your voice for understanding;
4 if you seek it like silver,
    and search for it as for hidden treasures—
5 then you will understand the fear of the
    LORD
    and find the knowledge of God.
6 For the LORD gives wisdom;
    from his mouth come knowledge and
      understanding;
7 he stores up sound wisdom for the upright;
    he is a shield to those who walk
      blamelessly,
8 guarding the paths of justice
    and preserving the way of his faithful
      ones.
9 Then you will understand righteousness and
    justice
    and equity, every good path;
10 for wisdom will come into your heart,
    and knowledge will be pleasant to your
      soul;
11 prudence will watch over you;
    and understanding will guard you.
12 It will save you from the way of evil,
    from those who speak perversely,
13 who forsake the paths of uprightness
    to walk in the ways of darkness,
14 who rejoice in doing evil

and delight in the perverseness of evil;
15 those whose paths are crooked,
 and who are devious in their ways.

16 You will be saved from the loose[b] woman,
 from the adulteress with her smooth
 words,
17 who forsakes the partner of her youth
 and forgets her sacred covenant;
18 for her way[c] leads down to death,
 and her paths to the shades;
19 those who go to her never come back,
 nor do they regain the paths of life.

20 Therefore walk in the way of the good,
 and keep to the paths of the just.
21 For the upright will abide in the land,
 and the innocent will remain in it;
22 but the wicked will be cut off from the
 land,
 and the treacherous will be rooted out
 of it.

Admonition to Trust and Honor God

My child, do not forget my teaching,
 but let your heart keep my
 commandments;
2 for length of days and years of life
 and abundant welfare they will give you.

3 Do not let loyalty and faithfulness
 forsake you;
 bind them around your neck,
 write them on the tablet of your heart.
4 So you will find favor and good repute
 in the sight of God and of people.

5 Trust in the LORD with all your heart,
 and do not rely on your own insight.
6 In all your ways acknowledge him,
 and he will make straight your paths.
7 Do not be wise in your own eyes;
 fear the LORD, and turn away from evil.
8 It will be a healing for your flesh
 and a refreshment for your body.

9 Honor the LORD with your substance
 and with the first fruits of all your
 produce;
10 then your barns will be filled with plenty,
 and your vats will be bursting with wine.

11 My child, do not despise the LORD's
 discipline
 or be weary of his reproof,
12 for the LORD reproves the one he loves,
 as a father the son in whom he delights.

The True Wealth

13 Happy are those who find wisdom,
 and those who get understanding,
14 for her income is better than silver,
 and her revenue better than gold.
15 She is more precious than jewels,
 and nothing you desire can compare
 with her.
16 Long life is in her right hand;
 in her left hand are riches and honor.
17 Her ways are ways of pleasantness,
 and all her paths are peace.
18 She is a tree of life to those who lay hold
 of her;
 those who hold her fast are called happy.

PRAY IT!
Your Future

Read Prov 3.5–8 and think about your
plans for the future. How does God
play a part in them? Do they include
discernment of (prayerful listening to)
God's plans for you? Here are some clues
for discerning where God is calling you:

■ Pray about your future and ask for
 God's direction.
■ Look at your talents and interests.
 These are gifts from God to be used for
 the good of others as well as yourself.
■ Imagine yourself doing whatever you
 are considering. What feelings surface?
 Peace and joy are usually signs of God's
 presence. Excessive anxiety, fear, and
 shame are usually signs of God's absence.
■ Talk with a trusted adult about your
 options. If this person is wise, she or he
 will not give you a direct answer but
 will help you sort out where God is
 leading.

▶ Prov 3.5–8

God's Wisdom in Creation

19 The LORD by wisdom founded the earth;
 by understanding he established the
 heavens;
20 by his knowledge the deeps broke open,
 and the clouds drop down the dew.

b Heb strange   c Cn: Heb house

P
R
O
V

The True Security

21 My child, do not let these escape from your
    sight:
    keep sound wisdom and prudence,
22 and they will be life for your soul
    and adornment for your neck.
23 Then you will walk on your way securely
    and your foot will not stumble.
24 If you sit down,d you will not be afraid;
    when you lie down, your sleep will be
    sweet.
25 Do not be afraid of sudden panic,
    or of the storm that strikes the wicked;
26 for the LORD will be your confidence
    and will keep your foot from being
    caught.

27 Do not withhold good from those to whom
    it is due,e
    when it is in your power to do it.
28 Do not say to your neighbor, "Go, and
    come again,
    tomorrow I will give it"—when you have it
    with you.
29 Do not plan harm against your neighbor
    who lives trustingly beside you.
30 Do not quarrel with anyone without cause,
    when no harm has been done to you.
31 Do not envy the violent
    and do not choose any of their ways;
32 for the perverse are an abomination to the
    LORD,
    but the upright are in his confidence.
33 The LORD's curse is on the house of the wicked,
    but he blesses the abode of the righteous.
34 Toward the scorners he is scornful,
    but to the humble he shows favor.
35 The wise will inherit honor,
    but stubborn fools, disgrace.

Parental Advice

Listen, children, to a father's instruction,
    and be attentive, that you may gainf
    insight;
2 for I give you good precepts:
    do not forsake my teaching.
3 When I was a son with my father,
    tender, and my mother's favorite,
4 he taught me, and said to me,
    "Let your heart hold fast my words;
    keep my commandments, and live.
5 Get wisdom; get insight: do not forget, nor
    turn away
    from the words of my mouth.
6 Do not forsake her, and she will keep you;
    love her, and she will guard you.

TRUE SECURITY

We often hear: When the going gets tough, the tough get going.

But how do we know how to get going? Where do we get going to? Our faith gives us sound wisdom (Prov 3.21). Prayer keeps us close to God (verse 26). Clear thinking guides us to prudent (right) decisions (verse 21). And knowing we have made the right decision is true security.

When the going gets tough, first the tough get faithful, and prayerful, and thoughtful. Then they get going.

▶ Prov 3.21–26

7 The beginning of wisdom is this: Get
    wisdom,
    and whatever else you get, get insight.
8 Prize her highly, and she will exalt you;
    she will honor you if you embrace her.
9 She will place on your head a fair garland;
    she will bestow on you a beautiful
    crown."

Admonition to Keep to the Right Path

10 Hear, my child, and accept my words,
    that the years of your life may be many.
11 I have taught you the way of wisdom;
    I have led you in the paths of
    uprightness.
12 When you walk, your step will not be
    hampered;
    and if you run, you will not stumble.
13 Keep hold of instruction; do not let go;
    guard her, for she is your life.
14 Do not enter the path of the wicked,
    and do not walk in the way of evildoers.
15 Avoid it; do not go on it;
    turn away from it and pass on.
16 For they cannot sleep unless they have done
    wrong;
    they are robbed of sleep unless they have
    made someone stumble.
17 For they eat the bread of wickedness
    and drink the wine of violence.
18 But the path of the righteous is like the
    light of dawn,

---

d Gk: Heb lie down   e Heb from its owners   f Heb know

which shines brighter and brighter until
full day.

19 The way of the wicked is like deep darkness;
they do not know what they stumble
over.

20 My child, be attentive to my words;
incline your ear to my sayings.

21 Do not let them escape from your sight;
keep them within your heart.

22 For they are life to those who find them,
and healing to all their flesh.

23 Keep your heart with all vigilance,
for from it flow the springs of life.

24 Put away from you crooked speech,
and put devious talk far from you.

25 Let your eyes look directly forward,
and your gaze be straight before you.

26 Keep straight the path of your feet,
and all your ways will be sure.

27 Do not swerve to the right or to the left;
turn your foot away from evil.

Warning against Impurity and Infidelity

My child, be attentive to my wisdom;
incline your ear to my understanding,

2 so that you may hold on to prudence,
and your lips may guard knowledge.

3 For the lips of a loose*g* woman drip honey,
and her speech is smoother than oil;

4 but in the end she is bitter as wormwood,
sharp as a two-edged sword.

5 Her feet go down to death;
her steps follow the path to She'ōl.

6 She does not keep straight to the path of
life;

her ways wander, and she does not
know it.

7 And now, my child,*h* listen to me,
and do not depart from the words of my
mouth.

8 Keep your way far from her,
and do not go near the door of her
house;

9 or you will give your honor to others,
and your years to the merciless,

10 and strangers will take their fill of your
wealth,
and your labors will go to the house of
an alien;

11 and at the end of your life you will groan,
when your flesh and body are consumed,

12 and you say, "Oh, how I hated discipline,
and my heart despised reproof!

13 I did not listen to the voice of my teachers
or incline my ear to my instructors.

14 Now I am at the point of utter ruin
in the public assembly."

15 Drink water from your own cistern,
flowing water from your own well.

16 Should your springs be scattered abroad,
streams of water in the streets?

17 Let them be for yourself alone,
and not for sharing with strangers.

18 Let your fountain be blessed,
and rejoice in the wife of your youth,

19 a lovely deer, a graceful doe.
May her breasts satisfy you at all times;
may you be intoxicated always by her
love.

g Heb *strange*   *h* Gk Vg: Heb *children*

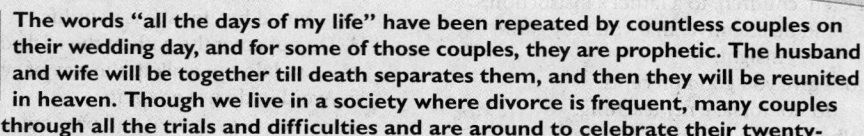

All the Days of My Life

The words "all the days of my life" have been repeated by countless couples on their wedding day, and for some of those couples, they are prophetic. The husband and wife will be together till death separates them, and then they will be reunited in heaven. Though we live in a society where divorce is frequent, many couples make it through all the trials and difficulties and are around to celebrate their twenty-fifth and fiftieth anniversaries.

The writer of Prov 5.15–23 is warning men, in particular, against adultery, which remains, even today, a primary reason marriages break up. But the author's wish in verse 19 could easily be rephrased to address both husbands and wives: "May you always be intoxicated (as in elated, not drunk) by each other's love."

What a wonderful wedding toast!

▶ Prov 5.15–23

20 Why should you be intoxicated, my son, by
    another woman
    and embrace the bosom of an adulteress?
21 For human ways are under the eyes of the
    LORD,
    and he examines all their paths.
22 The iniquities of the wicked ensnare them,
    and they are caught in the toils of
    their sin.
23 They die for lack of discipline,
    and because of their great folly they are
    lost.

Practical Admonitions

My child, if you have given your pledge to
    your neighbor,
    if you have bound yourself to another,*i*
2 you are snared by the utterance of your lips,*j*
    caught by the words of your mouth.
3 So do this, my child, and save yourself,
    for you have come into your neighbor's
    power:

a little folding of the hands to rest,
11 and poverty will come upon you like a
    robber,
    and want, like an armed warrior.

12 A scoundrel and a villain
    goes around with crooked speech,
13 winking the eyes, shuffling the feet,
    pointing the fingers,
14 with perverted mind devising evil,
    continually sowing discord;
15 on such a one calamity will descend
    suddenly;
    in a moment, damage beyond repair.

16 There are six things that the LORD hates,
    seven that are an abomination to him:
17 haughty eyes, a lying tongue,
    and hands that shed innocent blood,
18 a heart that devises wicked plans,
    feet that hurry to run to evil,
19 a lying witness who testifies falsely,
    and one who sows discord in a family.

P
R
O
V

Leaders with Character

Look at the list of the things the Lord hates in Prov 6.17–19. It looks like a popular description of a corrupt politician or businessperson! Now take the list and put it in the positive: humble eyes, a truthful tongue, hands that protect the innocent, a heart that plans good, feet that hurry to help, a truthful witness, and someone who brings harmony to families. That's the kind of leader everyone wants!

The author of Proverbs is constantly reminding us to be of good character. Especially when you are called to be a leader—and we all will be at some time in our life—keep the advice of Proverbs in mind. Be a leader of character by doing the things the Lord loves, not the things the Lord hates.

▸ **Prov 6.16–19**

    go, hurry,*k* and plead with your neighbor.
4 Give your eyes no sleep
    and your eyelids no slumber;
5 save yourself like a gazelle from the hunter,*l*
    like a bird from the hand of the fowler.

6 Go to the ant, you lazybones;
    consider its ways, and be wise.
7 Without having any chief
    or officer or ruler,
8 it prepares its food in summer,
    and gathers its sustenance in harvest.
9 How long will you lie there, O lazybones?
    When will you rise from your sleep?
10 A little sleep, a little slumber,

20 My child, keep your father's commandment,
    and do not forsake your mother's
    teaching.
21 Bind them upon your heart always;
    tie them around your neck.
22 When you walk, they*m* will lead you;
    when you lie down, they*m* will watch
    over you;
    and when you awake, they*m* will talk
    with you.
23 For the commandment is a lamp and the
    teaching a light,

---

i Or *a stranger*   *j* Cn Compare Gk Syr: Heb *the words of your mouth*   *k* Or *humble yourself*   *l* Cn: Heb *from the hand*   *m* Heb *it*

and the reproofs of discipline are the way
of life,

24 to preserve you from the wife of another,[n]
from the smooth tongue of the
adulteress.

25 Do not desire her beauty in your heart,
and do not let her capture you with her
eyelashes;

26 for a prostitute's fee is only a loaf of bread,[o]
but the wife of another stalks a man's
very life.

27 Can fire be carried in the bosom
without burning one's clothes?

28 Or can one walk on hot coals
without scorching the feet?

29 So is he who sleeps with his neighbor's
wife;
no one who touches her will go
unpunished.

30 Thieves are not despised who steal only
to satisfy their appetite when they are
hungry.

31 Yet if they are caught, they will pay
sevenfold;
they will forfeit all the goods of their
house.

32 But he who commits adultery has no sense;
he who does it destroys himself.

33 He will get wounds and dishonor,
and his disgrace will not be wiped away.

34 For jealousy arouses a husband's fury,
and he shows no restraint when he takes
revenge.

35 He will accept no compensation,
and refuses a bribe no matter how great.

The False Attractions of Adultery

My child, keep my words
and store up my commandments
with you;

2 keep my commandments and live,
keep my teachings as the apple of
your eye;

3 bind them on your fingers,
write them on the tablet of your heart.

4 Say to wisdom, "You are my sister,"
and call insight your intimate friend,

5 that they may keep you from the loose[p]
woman,
from the adulteress with her smooth
words.

6 For at the window of my house
I looked out through my lattice,

7 and I saw among the simple ones,
I observed among the youths,

a young man without sense,

8 passing along the street near her corner,
taking the road to her house

9 in the twilight, in the evening,
at the time of night and darkness.

10 Then a woman comes toward him,
decked out like a prostitute, wily of
heart.[q]

11 She is loud and wayward;
her feet do not stay at home;

12 now in the street, now in the squares,
and at every corner she lies in wait.

13 She seizes him and kisses him,
and with impudent face she says to him:

14 "I had to offer sacrifices,
and today I have paid my vows;

15 so now I have come out to meet you,
to seek you eagerly, and I have
found you!

16 I have decked my couch with coverings,
colored spreads of Egyptian linen;

17 I have perfumed my bed with myrrh,
aloes, and cinnamon.

18 Come, let us take our fill of love until
morning;
let us delight ourselves with love.

19 For my husband is not at home;
he has gone on a long journey.

20 He took a bag of money with him;
he will not come home until full moon."

21 With much seductive speech she
persuades him;
with her smooth talk she compels him.

22 Right away he follows her,
and goes like an ox to the slaughter,
or bounds like a stag toward the trap[r]

23 until an arrow pierces its entrails.
He is like a bird rushing into a snare,
not knowing that it will cost him his life.

24 And now, my children, listen to me,
and be attentive to the words of my
mouth.

25 Do not let your hearts turn aside to her
ways;
do not stray into her paths.

26 For many are those she has laid low,
and numerous are her victims.

27 Her house is the way to Shĕ'ōl,
going down to the chambers of death.

---

n Gk: MT *the evil woman*   o Cn Compare Gk Syr Vg Tg:
Heb *for because of a harlot to a piece of bread*
p Heb *strange*   q Meaning of Heb uncertain
r Cn Compare Gk: Meaning of Heb uncertain

The Gifts of Wisdom

To gain wisdom, you have to hunger for it, really want it, and actively seek it out. You will not find it by yourself: wisdom is found where other people are—"beside the gates" where people meet (Prov 8.3).

Wisdom's gifts described in Proverbs, chapter 8, include prudence or caution, insight, truth, knowledge, understanding, discretion, fear of the Lord (hatred of evil), insight, strength, and justice and righteousness. Which of these gifts do you have? Which would you like to develop? Who could help you? Write a prayer to the Holy Spirit, asking for the strength and courage to actively seek out these gifts.

▶ Prov 8.1–21

The Gifts of Wisdom

Does not wisdom call,
     and does not understanding raise her
         voice?
2 On the heights, beside the way,
     at the crossroads she takes her stand;
3 beside the gates in front of the town,
     at the entrance of the portals she
         cries out:

4 "To you, O people, I call,
     and my cry is to all that live.
5 O simple ones, learn prudence;
     acquire intelligence, you who lack it.
6 Hear, for I will speak noble things,
     and from my lips will come what is right;
7 for my mouth will utter truth;
     wickedness is an abomination to my lips.
8 All the words of my mouth are righteous;
     there is nothing twisted or crooked in
         them.
9 They are all straight to one who understands
     and right to those who find knowledge.
10 Take my instruction instead of silver,
     and knowledge rather than choice gold;
11 for wisdom is better than jewels,
     and all that you may desire cannot
         compare with her.
12 I, wisdom, live with prudence,*
     and I attain knowledge and discretion.
13 The fear of the LORD is hatred of evil.
     Pride and arrogance and the way of evil
     and perverted speech I hate.
14 I have good advice and sound wisdom;
     I have insight, I have strength.
15 By me kings reign,
     and rulers decree what is just;
16 by me rulers rule,
     and nobles, all who govern rightly.
17 I love those who love me,
     and those who seek me diligently
         find me.
18 Riches and honor are with me,
     enduring wealth and prosperity.

---

* Meaning of Heb uncertain

Introducing ▶ LADY WISDOM

As you read the description of wisdom in Prov 8.1—9.6, you might get the impression that you are reading about a goddess. But that's not the case. The wisdom writers borrowed from neighboring cultures the idea of describing wisdom as a beautiful and eternal aspect of God. They exquisitely embodied the idea of wisdom in the figure of Lady Wisdom. Lady Wisdom comes from God. She was present at the Creation of the world, and she has a special understanding of the world and its workings. For the wisdom writers, Lady Wisdom was an aspect of God that wise people would want to pursue, because she reveals the right ways to live and behave.

▶ Prov 8.1—9.6

¹⁹ My fruit is better than gold, even fine gold,
   and my yield than choice silver.
²⁰ I walk in the way of righteousness,
   along the paths of justice,
²¹ endowing with wealth those who love
   me,
   and filling their treasuries.

Wisdom's Part in Creation
(Cp Jn 1.1–3)

²² The LORD created me at the beginningˢ of
   his work,ᵗ
   the first of his acts of long ago.
²³ Ages ago I was set up,
   at the first, before the beginning of the
   earth.
²⁴ When there were no depths I was brought
   forth,
   when there were no springs abounding
   with water.
²⁵ Before the mountains had been shaped,
   before the hills, I was brought forth—
²⁶ when he had not yet made earth and
   fields,ᵘ
   or the world's first bits of soil.
²⁷ When he established the heavens, I was
   there,
   when he drew a circle on the face of the
   deep,
²⁸ when he made firm the skies above,
   when he established the fountains of the
   deep,
²⁹ when he assigned to the sea its limit,
   so that the waters might not transgress
   his command,
   when he marked out the foundations of the
   earth,
³⁰ then I was beside him, like a master
   worker;ᵛ
   and I was daily hisʷ delight,
   rejoicing before him always,
³¹ rejoicing in his inhabited world
   and delighting in the human race.

³² "And now, my children, listen to me:
   happy are those who keep my ways.
³³ Hear instruction and be wise,
   and do not neglect it.
³⁴ Happy is the one who listens to me,
   watching daily at my gates,
   waiting beside my doors.
³⁵ For whoever finds me finds life
   and obtains favor from the LORD;
³⁶ but those who miss me injure themselves;
   all who hate me love death."

Wisdom's Feast

Wisdom has built her house,
   she has hewn her seven pillars.
² She has slaughtered her animals, she has
   mixed her wine,
   she has also set her table.
³ She has sent out her servant-girls, she calls
   from the highest places in the town,
⁴ "You that are simple, turn in here!"
   To those without sense she says,
⁵ "Come, eat of my bread
   and drink of the wine I have mixed.
⁶ Lay aside immaturity,ˣ and live,
   and walk in the way of insight."

General Maxims

⁷ Whoever corrects a scoffer wins abuse;
   whoever rebukes the wicked gets hurt.
⁸ A scoffer who is rebuked will only hate you;
   the wise, when rebuked, will love you.
⁹ Give instructionʸ to the wise, and they will
   become wiser still;
   teach the righteous and they will gain in
   learning.
¹⁰ The fear of the LORD is the beginning of
   wisdom,
   and the knowledge of the Holy One is
   insight.
¹¹ For by me your days will be multiplied,
   and years will be added to your life.

ˢ Or me as the beginning   ᵗ Heb way   ᵘ Meaning of Heb
uncertain   ᵛ Another reading is little child   ʷ Gk: Heb
lacks his   ˣ Or simpleness   ʸ Heb lacks instruction

The fear of the **Lord** is the beginning of **wisdom**, and the knowledge of the **Holy One** is **insight**

9.10

12 If you are wise, you are wise for yourself;
    if you scoff, you alone will bear it.

Folly's Invitation and Promise

13 The foolish woman is loud;
    she is ignorant and knows nothing.
14 She sits at the door of her house,
    on a seat at the high places of the town,
15 calling to those who pass by,
    who are going straight on their way,
16 "You who are simple, turn in here!"
    And to those without sense she says,
17 "Stolen water is sweet,
    and bread eaten in secret is pleasant."
18 But they do not know that the dead[z] are
            there,
    that her guests are in the depths of
        She'ol.

Wise Sayings of Solomon

The proverbs of Solomon.

A wise child makes a glad father,
    but a foolish child is a mother's grief.
2 Treasures gained by wickedness do not
        profit,
    but righteousness delivers from death.
3 The LORD does not let the righteous go
        hungry,
    but he thwarts the craving of the wicked.
4 A slack hand causes poverty,
    but the hand of the diligent makes rich.
5 A child who gathers in summer is prudent,
    but a child who sleeps in harvest brings
        shame.
6 Blessings are on the head of the righteous,

but the mouth of the wicked conceals
        violence.
7 The memory of the righteous is a blessing,
    but the name of the wicked will rot.
8 The wise of heart will heed commandments,
    but a babbling fool will come to ruin.
9 Whoever walks in integrity walks securely,
    but whoever follows perverse ways will
        be found out.
10 Whoever winks the eye causes trouble,
    but the one who rebukes boldly makes
        peace.[a]
11 The mouth of the righteous is a fountain of life,
    but the mouth of the wicked conceals
        violence.
12 Hatred stirs up strife,
    but love covers all offenses.
13 On the lips of one who has understanding
        wisdom is found,
    but a rod is for the back of one who
        lacks sense.
14 The wise lay up knowledge,
    but the babbling of a fool brings ruin
        near.
15 The wealth of the rich is their fortress;
    the poverty of the poor is their ruin.
16 The wage of the righteous leads to life,
    the gain of the wicked to sin.
17 Whoever heeds instruction is on the path to
        life,
    but one who rejects a rebuke goes astray.
18 Lying lips conceal hatred,
    and whoever utters slander is a fool.

---

z Heb *shades*   a Gk: Heb *but a babbling fool will come to
ruin*

P
R
O
V

Nothing But the Truth

"Do you swear to tell the truth, the whole truth, and nothing but the truth, so help you God?"
        We have all heard these words. They are asked of every witness about to testify in a courtroom. In addition to responding positively to this crucial question, witnesses are called to place a hand on the Bible. All of this is to try to ensure that they will be honest. But despite this oath, some witnesses lie. We call that crime perjury, and it carries a severe penalty, because someone's innocence or guilt may be hanging on the sworn testimony.
        Proverbs 10.18 tells us, "Lying lips conceal hatred." Just as dishonesty is an act of hatred, so is honesty an act of love. Ultimately, our lies end up hurting others and damaging our integrity. Whether in the courtroom or in everyday life, we must always strive to tell "the truth, the whole truth, and nothing but the truth."

▶ Prov 10.18–21

P
R
O
V

19 When words are many, transgression is not
    lacking,
      but the prudent are restrained in speech.
20 The tongue of the righteous is choice silver;
      the mind of the wicked is of little worth.
21 The lips of the righteous feed many,
      but fools die for lack of sense.
22 The blessing of the LORD makes rich,
      and he adds no sorrow with it.[b]
23 Doing wrong is like sport to a fool,
      but wise conduct is pleasure to a person
      of understanding.
24 What the wicked dread will come upon
    them,
      but the desire of the righteous will be
      granted.
25 When the tempest passes, the wicked are no
    more,
      but the righteous are established forever.
26 Like vinegar to the teeth, and smoke to the
    eyes,
      so are the lazy to their employers.
27 The fear of the LORD prolongs life,
      but the years of the wicked will be short.
28 The hope of the righteous ends in gladness,
      but the expectation of the wicked comes
      to nothing.
29 The way of the LORD is a stronghold for the
    upright,
      but destruction for evildoers.
30 The righteous will never be removed,
      but the wicked will not remain in the
      land.
31 The mouth of the righteous brings forth
    wisdom,
      but the perverse tongue will be cut off.
32 The lips of the righteous know what is
    acceptable,
      but the mouth of the wicked what is
      perverse.

A false balance is an abomination to the
    LORD,
      but an accurate weight is his delight.
2 When pride comes, then comes disgrace;
      but wisdom is with the humble.
3 The integrity of the upright guides them,
      but the crookedness of the treacherous
      destroys them.
4 Riches do not profit in the day of wrath,
      but righteousness delivers from death.
5 The righteousness of the blameless keeps
    their ways straight,
      but the wicked fall by their own
      wickedness.
6 The righteousness of the upright saves them,

but the treacherous are taken captive by
      their schemes.
7 When the wicked die, their hope perishes,
      and the expectation of the godless comes
      to nothing.
8 The righteous are delivered from trouble,
      and the wicked get into it instead.
9 With their mouths the godless would
      destroy their neighbors,
      but by knowledge the righteous are
      delivered.
10 When it goes well with the righteous, the
    city rejoices;
      and when the wicked perish, there is
      jubilation.
11 By the blessing of the upright a city is
    exalted,
      but it is overthrown by the mouth of the
      wicked.
12 Whoever belittles another lacks sense,
      but an intelligent person remains silent.

PRAY IT!

Gossip

Oh, God, forgive me!
  I gossiped about someone's family
today.
I don't even know if what I said was true.
But it made me feel important to tell it to
  my friends.
Help me keep my mouth shut!
When someone tells me a secret, seal it
  into my heart,
and keep it away from my lips!
Gossip can seem like fun, but it hurts
  people.
I can't stop thinking about how the target
  of my gossip would feel
if she or he knew what I said about the
  family.
Oh, God, teach me to be trustworthy!
Amen.

▶ Prov 11.13

13 A gossip goes about telling secrets,
      but one who is trustworthy in spirit keeps
      a confidence.
14 Where there is no guidance, a nation[c] falls,

---

[b] Or *and toil adds nothing to it*   [c] Or *an army*

but in an abundance of counselors there
    is safety.

15 To guarantee loans for a stranger brings
    trouble,
    but there is safety in refusing to do so.

16 A gracious woman gets honor,
    but she who hates virtue is covered with
      shame.*d*
    The timid become destitute,*e*
    but the aggressive gain riches.

17 Those who are kind reward themselves,
    but the cruel do themselves harm.

18 The wicked earn no real gain,
    but those who sow righteousness get a
      true reward.

19 Whoever is steadfast in righteousness will
    live,
    but whoever pursues evil will die.

20 Crooked minds are an abomination to the
    LORD,
    but those of blameless ways are his
      delight.

21 Be assured, the wicked will not go
    unpunished,
    but those who are righteous will escape.

22 Like a gold ring in a pig's snout
    is a beautiful woman without good sense.

23 The desire of the righteous ends only in
    good;
    the expectation of the wicked in wrath.

24 Some give freely, yet grow all the richer;
    others withhold what is due, and only
      suffer want.

25 A generous person will be enriched,
    and one who gives water will get water.

26 The people curse those who hold back grain,
    but a blessing is on the head of those
      who sell it.

27 Whoever diligently seeks good seeks favor,
    but evil comes to the one who searches
      for it.

28 Those who trust in their riches will wither,*f*
    but the righteous will flourish like green
      leaves.

29 Those who trouble their households will
    inherit wind,
    and the fool will be servant to the wise.

30 The fruit of the righteous is a tree of life,
    but violence*g* takes lives away.

31 If the righteous are repaid on earth,
    how much more the wicked and the
      sinner!

Whoever loves discipline loves knowledge,
    but those who hate to be rebuked are
      stupid.

2 The good obtain favor from the LORD,

but those who devise evil he condemns.

3 No one finds security by wickedness,
    but the root of the righteous will never
      be moved.

4 A good wife is the crown of her husband,
    but she who brings shame is like
      rottenness in his bones.

5 The thoughts of the righteous are just;
    the advice of the wicked is treacherous.

6 The words of the wicked are a deadly
    ambush,
    but the speech of the upright delivers
      them.

7 The wicked are overthrown and are no
    more,
    but the house of the righteous will stand.

8 One is commended for good sense,
    but a perverse mind is despised.

9 Better to be despised and have a servant,
    than to be self-important and lack food.

10 The righteous know the needs of their
    animals,
    but the mercy of the wicked is cruel.

11 Those who till their land will have plenty of
    food,
    but those who follow worthless pursuits
      have no sense.

12 The wicked covet the proceeds of
    wickedness,*h*
    but the root of the righteous bears fruit.

13 The evil are ensnared by the transgression of
    their lips,
    but the righteous escape from trouble.

14 From the fruit of the mouth one is filled
    with good things,
    and manual labor has its reward.

15 Fools think their own way is right,
    but the wise listen to advice.

16 Fools show their anger at once,
    but the prudent ignore an insult.

17 Whoever speaks the truth gives honest
    evidence,
    but a false witness speaks deceitfully.

18 Rash words are like sword thrusts,
    but the tongue of the wise brings healing.

19 Truthful lips endure forever,
    but a lying tongue lasts only a moment.

20 Deceit is in the mind of those who plan
    evil,
    but those who counsel peace have joy.

21 No harm happens to the righteous,

---

d Compare Gk Syr: Heb lacks *but she . . . shame*
e Gk: Heb lacks *The timid . . . destitute*   *f* Cn: Heb *fall*
g Cn Compare Gk Syr: Heb *a wise man*   *h* Or *covet the*
catch of the wicked

but the wicked are filled with trouble.

22 Lying lips are an abomination to the LORD,
   but those who act faithfully are his
      delight.

23 One who is clever conceals knowledge,
   but the mind of a fool[i] broadcasts folly.

24 The hand of the diligent will rule,
   while the lazy will be put to forced labor.

25 Anxiety weighs down the human heart,
   but a good word cheers it up.

26 The righteous gives good advice to friends,[j]
   but the way of the wicked leads astray.

27 The lazy do not roast[k] their game,
   but the diligent obtain precious wealth.[k]

28 In the path of righteousness there is life,
   in walking its path there is no death.

13 A wise child loves discipline,[l]
   but a scoffer does not listen to rebuke.

2 From the fruit of their words good persons
      eat good things,
   but the desire of the treacherous is for
      wrongdoing.

3 Those who guard their mouths preserve
      their lives;
   those who open wide their lips come to
      ruin.

4 The appetite of the lazy craves, and gets
      nothing,
   while the appetite of the diligent is richly
      supplied.

5 The righteous hate falsehood,
   but the wicked act shamefully and
      disgracefully.

6 Righteousness guards one whose way is
      upright,

but sin overthrows the wicked.

7 Some pretend to be rich, yet have nothing;
   others pretend to be poor, yet have great
      wealth.

8 Wealth is a ransom for a person's life,
   but the poor get no threats.

9 The light of the righteous rejoices,
   but the lamp of the wicked goes out.

10 By insolence the heedless make strife,
   but wisdom is with those who take
      advice.

11 Wealth hastily gotten[m] will dwindle,
   but those who gather little by little will
      increase it.

12 Hope deferred makes the heart sick,
   but a desire fulfilled is a tree of life.

13 Those who despise the word bring
      destruction on themselves,
   but those who respect the commandment
      will be rewarded.

14 The teaching of the wise is a fountain of
      life,
   so that one may avoid the snares of
      death.

15 Good sense wins favor,
   but the way of the faithless is their
      ruin.[n]

16 The clever do all things intelligently,
   but the fool displays folly.

17 A bad messenger brings trouble,
   but a faithful envoy, healing.

---

i Heb *the heart of fools*   j Syr: Meaning of Heb uncertain
k Meaning of Heb uncertain   l Cn: Heb *A wise child the*
discipline of his father   m Gk Vg: Heb *from vanity*
n Cn Compare Gk Syr Vg Tg: Heb *is enduring*

The Company of Fools

LIVE IT!

Lucy found out the hard way. She was neglected at home, and she had few friends in her neighborhood. Her need for belonging was answered one day when she met a group who asked her to join them. She quickly felt that she had a family and that people liked her for who she was.

Lucy spent a great deal of time with her new friends. Before long, they were encouraging her to do things she didn't feel comfortable with. They fed her anger toward her family and the society that had neglected her.

Lucy is now in prison, serving time for armed robbery. And her gang is recruiting her replacement. There are a lot more vulnerable kids where Lucy came from.

Proverbs 13.11 tells us that quick wealth doesn't last. And verse 20 says that the companion of fools will suffer harm. That's wisdom that Lucy—along with most of us—needs to hear.

▶ Prov 13.11,20

18 Poverty and disgrace are for the one who
     ignores instruction,
    but one who heeds reproof is honored.
19 A desire realized is sweet to the soul,
    but to turn away from evil is an
     abomination to fools.
20 Whoever walks with the wise becomes wise,
    but the companion of fools suffers harm.
21 Misfortune pursues sinners,
    but prosperity rewards the righteous.
22 The good leave an inheritance to their
     children's children,
    but the sinner's wealth is laid up for the
     righteous.
23 The field of the poor may yield much food,
    but it is swept away through injustice.
24 Those who spare the rod hate their children,
    but those who love them are diligent to
     discipline them.
25 The righteous have enough to satisfy their
     appetite,
    but the belly of the wicked is empty.
The wise woman*o* builds her house,
    but the foolish tears it down with her
     own hands.
2 Those who walk uprightly fear the LORD,
    but one who is devious in conduct
     despises him.
3 The talk of fools is a rod for their backs,*p*
    but the lips of the wise preserve them.
4 Where there are no oxen, there is no grain;
    abundant crops come by the strength of
     the ox.
5 A faithful witness does not lie,
    but a false witness breathes out lies.
6 A scoffer seeks wisdom in vain,
    but knowledge is easy for one who
     understands.
7 Leave the presence of a fool,
    for there you do not find words of
     knowledge.
8 It is the wisdom of the clever to understand
     where they go,
    but the folly of fools misleads.
9 Fools mock at the guilt offering,*q*
    but the upright enjoy God's favor.
10 The heart knows its own bitterness,
    and no stranger shares its joy.
11 The house of the wicked is destroyed,
    but the tent of the upright flourishes.
12 There is a way that seems right to a person,
    but its end is the way to death.*r*
13 Even in laughter the heart is sad,
    and the end of joy is grief.
14 The perverse get what their ways deserve,
    and the good, what their deeds deserve.*s*

15 The simple believe everything,
    but the clever consider their steps.
16 The wise are cautious and turn away from
     evil,
    but the fool throws off restraint and is
     careless.
17 One who is quick-tempered acts foolishly,
    and the schemer is hated.
18 The simple are adorned with*t* folly,
    but the clever are crowned with
     knowledge.
19 The evil bow down before the good,
    the wicked at the gates of the righteous.
20 The poor are disliked even by their
     neighbors,
    but the rich have many friends.
21 Those who despise their neighbors are
     sinners,
    but happy are those who are kind to the
     poor.
22 Do they not err that plan evil?
    Those who plan good find loyalty and
     faithfulness.
23 In all toil there is profit,
    but mere talk leads only to poverty.
24 The crown of the wise is their wisdom,*u*
    but folly is the garland*v* of fools.
25 A truthful witness saves lives,
    but one who utters lies is a betrayer.
26 In the fear of the LORD one has strong
     confidence,
    and one's children will have a refuge.
27 The fear of the LORD is a fountain of life,
    so that one may avoid the snares of
     death.
28 The glory of a king is a multitude of people;
    without people a prince is ruined.
29 Whoever is slow to anger has great
     understanding,
    but one who has a hasty temper exalts
     folly.
30 A tranquil mind gives life to the flesh,
    but passion makes the bones rot.
31 Those who oppress the poor insult their
     Maker,
    but those who are kind to the needy
     honor him.
32 The wicked are overthrown by their
     evildoing,
    but the righteous find a refuge in their
     integrity.*w*

---

o Heb *Wisdom of women*   *p* Cn: Heb *a rod of pride*
q Meaning of Heb uncertain   *r* Heb *ways of death*
s Cn: Heb *from upon him*   *t* Or *inherit*   *u* Cn Compare
Gk: Heb *riches*   *v* Cn: Heb *is the folly*   *w* Gk Syr: Heb *in
their death*

33 Wisdom is at home in the mind of one who
     has understanding,
     but it is not[x] known in the heart of fools.
34 Righteousness exalts a nation,
     but sin is a reproach to any people.
35 A servant who deals wisely has the king's
     favor,
     but his wrath falls on one who acts
     shamefully.

A soft answer turns away wrath,
     but a harsh word stirs up anger.
2 The tongue of the wise dispenses
     knowledge,[y]
     but the mouths of fools pour out folly.
3 The eyes of the LORD are in every place,
     keeping watch on the evil and the good.
4 A gentle tongue is a tree of life,
     but perverseness in it breaks the spirit.
5 A fool despises a parent's instruction,
     but the one who heeds admonition is
     prudent.
6 In the house of the righteous there is much
     treasure,
     but trouble befalls the income of the
     wicked.
7 The lips of the wise spread knowledge;
     not so the minds of fools.
8 The sacrifice of the wicked is an
     abomination to the LORD,
     but the prayer of the upright is his
     delight.
9 The way of the wicked is an abomination to
     the LORD,
     but he loves the one who pursues
     righteousness.
10 There is severe discipline for one who
     forsakes the way,
     but one who hates a rebuke will die.
11 Shĕ′ōl and A·bad′don lie open before the
     LORD,
     how much more human hearts!
12 Scoffers do not like to be rebuked;
     they will not go to the wise.
13 A glad heart makes a cheerful countenance,
     but by sorrow of heart the spirit is
     broken.
14 The mind of one who has understanding
     seeks knowledge,
     but the mouths of fools feed on folly.
15 All the days of the poor are hard,
     but a cheerful heart has a continual feast.
16 Better is a little with the fear of the LORD
     than great treasure and trouble with it.
17 Better is a dinner of vegetables where love is
     than a fatted ox and hatred with it.
18 Those who are hot-tempered stir up strife,
     but those who are slow to anger calm
     contention.
19 The way of the lazy is overgrown with
     thorns,
     but the path of the upright is a level
     highway.
20 A wise child makes a glad father,
     but the foolish despise their mothers.
21 Folly is a joy to one who has no sense,
     but a person of understanding walks
     straight ahead.
22 Without counsel, plans go wrong,
     but with many advisers they succeed.
23 To make an apt answer is a joy to anyone,
     and a word in season, how good it is!
24 For the wise the path of life leads upward,
     in order to avoid Shĕ′ōl below.
25 The LORD tears down the house of the
     proud,
     but maintains the widow's boundaries.
26 Evil plans are an abomination to the LORD,
     but gracious words are pure.
27 Those who are greedy for unjust gain make
     trouble for their households,
     but those who hate bribes will live.
28 The mind of the righteous ponders how to
     answer,
     but the mouth of the wicked pours out
     evil.
29 The LORD is far from the wicked,
     but he hears the prayer of the righteous.
30 The light of the eyes rejoices the heart,
     and good news refreshes the body.
31 The ear that heeds wholesome admonition
     will lodge among the wise.
32 Those who ignore instruction despise
     themselves,
     but those who heed admonition gain
     understanding.
33 The fear of the LORD is instruction in
     wisdom,
     and humility goes before honor.

The plans of the mind belong to mortals,
     but the answer of the tongue is from the
     LORD.
2 All one's ways may be pure in one's own
     eyes,
     but the LORD weighs the spirit.
3 Commit your work to the LORD,
     and your plans will be established.
4 The LORD has made everything for its
     purpose,
     even the wicked for the day of trouble.

---

x Gk Syr: Heb lacks *not*   y Cn: Heb *makes knowledge good*

than to divide the spoil with the proud.
20 Those who are attentive to a matter will
      prosper,
   and happy are those who trust in the
      LORD.
21 The wise of heart is called perceptive,
   and pleasant speech increases
      persuasiveness.
22 Wisdom is a fountain of life to one who
      has it,
   but folly is the punishment of fools.
23 The mind of the wise makes their speech
      judicious,
   and adds persuasiveness to their lips.
24 Pleasant words are like a honeycomb,
   sweetness to the soul and health to the
      body.
25 Sometimes there is a way that seems to be
      right,
   but in the end it is the way to death.
26 The appetite of workers works for them;
   their hunger urges them on.
27 Scoundrels concoct evil,
   and their speech is like a scorching fire.
28 A perverse person spreads strife,
   and a whisperer separates close friends.
29 The violent entice their neighbors,
   and lead them in a way that is not good.
30 One who winks the eyes plansᶻ perverse
      things;
   one who compresses the lips brings evil
      to pass.
31 Gray hair is a crown of glory;
   it is gained in a righteous life.
32 One who is slow to anger is better than the
      mighty,
   and one whose temper is controlled than
      one who captures a city.
33 The lot is cast into the lap,
   but the decision is the LORD's alone.
   Better is a dry morsel with quiet
      than a house full of feasting with strife.
2 A slave who deals wisely will rule over a
      child who acts shamefully,
   and will share the inheritance as one of
      the family.
3 The crucible is for silver, and the furnace is
      for gold,
   but the LORD tests the heart.
4 An evildoer listens to wicked lips;
   and a liar gives heed to a mischievous
      tongue.
5 Those who mock the poor insult their
      Maker;

Offering Your Day to God

Follow the advice of Prov 16.3 and start each day with a prayer like this one:

Dearest Lord, today, I offer you all my thoughts, deeds, and words. Let everything I do reflect your love and goodness. Amen.

▸ Prov 16.3

5 All those who are arrogant are an
      abomination to the LORD;
   be assured, they will not go unpunished.
6 By loyalty and faithfulness iniquity is
      atoned for,
   and by the fear of the LORD one avoids
      evil.
7 When the ways of people please the LORD,
   he causes even their enemies to be at
      peace with them.
8 Better is a little with righteousness
   than large income with injustice.
9 The human mind plans the way,
   but the LORD directs the steps.
10 Inspired decisions are on the lips of a king;
   his mouth does not sin in judgment.
11 Honest balances and scales are the LORD's;
   all the weights in the bag are his work.
12 It is an abomination to kings to do evil,
   for the throne is established by
      righteousness.
13 Righteous lips are the delight of a king,
   and he loves those who speak what is
      right.
14 A king's wrath is a messenger of death,
   and whoever is wise will appease it.
15 In the light of a king's face there is life,
   and his favor is like the clouds that bring
      the spring rain.
16 How much better to get wisdom than gold!
   To get understanding is to be chosen
      rather than silver.
17 The highway of the upright avoids evil;
   those who guard their way preserve their
      lives.
18 Pride goes before destruction,
   and a haughty spirit before a fall.
19 It is better to be of a lowly spirit among the
      poor

z Gk Syr Vg Tg: Heb *to plan*

those who are glad at calamity will not
go unpunished.
6 Grandchildren are the crown of the aged,
and the glory of children is their parents.
7 Fine speech is not becoming to a fool;
still less is false speech to a ruler.*a*
8 A bribe is like a magic stone in the eyes of
those who give it;
wherever they turn they prosper.
9 One who forgives an affront fosters
friendship,
but one who dwells on disputes will
alienate a friend.

16 Why should fools have a price in hand
to buy wisdom, when they have no mind
to learn?
17 A friend loves at all times,
and kinsfolk are born to share adversity.
18 It is senseless to give a pledge,
to become surety for a neighbor.
19 One who loves transgression loves strife;
one who builds a high threshold invites
broken bones.
20 The crooked of mind do not prosper,
and the perverse of tongue fall into
calamity.

Count to Ten

"The beginning of strife is like letting out water; / so stop before the quarrel breaks out" (Prov 17.14).

Have you ever noticed how people quickly congregate whenever a fight breaks out, especially at school? Many of the spectators seem to be in entertainment mode, and are generally on one side or the other. Others want the fight to stop but lack the courage or confidence to break it up. So, everyone ends up waiting until someone in authority comes along to intervene, or until one of the contenders is hurt and the fight stops.

A fight can begin so quickly. A word. A taunting phrase. A sudden turn and a punch. And there is an instant fight. Some of us have a shorter fuse than others. Some of us have a temper that flares easily or an ego that won't allow us to walk away when provoked. To paraphrase the image used in Prov 17.14, once the water breaks through the dike, it is very hard to stop.

How do you react when you see a quarrel or a fight? How quickly do you get involved in fights or quarrels? If you have a quick temper, what can you do to control it?

▸ **Prov 17.14**

10 A rebuke strikes deeper into a discerning
person
than a hundred blows into a fool.
11 Evil people seek only rebellion,
but a cruel messenger will be sent against
them.
12 Better to meet a she-bear robbed of its cubs
than to confront a fool immersed in
folly.
13 Evil will not depart from the house
of one who returns evil for good.
14 The beginning of strife is like letting out
water;
so stop before the quarrel breaks out.
15 One who justifies the wicked and one who
condemns the righteous
are both alike an abomination to the
LORD.

21 The one who begets a fool gets trouble;
the parent of a fool has no joy.
22 A cheerful heart is a good medicine,
but a downcast spirit dries up the bones.
23 The wicked accept a concealed bribe
to pervert the ways of justice.
24 The discerning person looks to wisdom,
but the eyes of a fool to the ends of the
earth.
25 Foolish children are a grief to their father
and bitterness to her who bore them.
26 To impose a fine on the innocent is not right,
or to flog the noble for their integrity.
27 One who spares words is knowledgeable;
one who is cool in spirit has
understanding.
28 Even fools who keep silent are considered wise;

a Or *a noble person*

when they close their lips, they are
  deemed intelligent.
The one who lives alone is self-indulgent,
  showing contempt for all who have
    sound judgment.[b]
2 A fool takes no pleasure in understanding,
  but only in expressing personal opinion.
3 When wickedness comes, contempt comes
    also;
  and with dishonor comes disgrace.
4 The words of the mouth are deep waters;
  the fountain of wisdom is a gushing
    stream.
5 It is not right to be partial to the guilty,
  or to subvert the innocent in judgment.
6 A fool's lips bring strife,
  and a fool's mouth invites a flogging.
7 The mouths of fools are their ruin,
  and their lips a snare to themselves.
8 The words of a whisperer are like delicious
    morsels;
  they go down into the inner parts of the
    body.
9 One who is slack in work
  is close kin to a vandal.
10 The name of the LORD is a strong tower;
  the righteous run into it and are safe.
11 The wealth of the rich is their strong city;
  in their imagination it is like a high wall.
12 Before destruction one's heart is haughty,
  but humility goes before honor.
13 If one gives answer before hearing,
  it is folly and shame.
14 The human spirit will endure sickness;
  but a broken spirit—who can bear?
15 An intelligent mind acquires knowledge,
  and the ear of the wise seeks knowledge.
16 A gift opens doors;
  it gives access to the great.
17 The one who first states a case seems right,
  until the other comes and cross-examines.
18 Casting the lot puts an end to disputes
  and decides between powerful
    contenders.
19 An ally offended is stronger than a city;[c]
  such quarreling is like the bars of a
    castle.
20 From the fruit of the mouth one's stomach
    is satisfied;
  the yield of the lips brings satisfaction.
21 Death and life are in the power of the
    tongue,
  and those who love it will eat its fruits.
22 He who finds a wife finds a good thing,
  and obtains favor from the LORD.
23 The poor use entreaties,

but the rich answer roughly.
24 Some[d] friends play at friendship[e]
  but a true friend sticks closer than one's
    nearest kin.
Better the poor walking in integrity
  than one perverse of speech who is a
    fool.
2 Desire without knowledge is not good,
  and one who moves too hurriedly misses
    the way.
3 One's own folly leads to ruin,
  yet the heart rages against the LORD.
4 Wealth brings many friends,
  but the poor are left friendless.
5 A false witness will not go unpunished,
  and a liar will not escape.
6 Many seek the favor of the generous,
  and everyone is a friend to a giver of
    gifts.
7 If the poor are hated even by their kin,
  how much more are they shunned by
    their friends!
When they call after them, they are not
    there.[b]
8 To get wisdom is to love oneself;
  to keep understanding is to prosper.
9 A false witness will not go unpunished,
  and the liar will perish.
10 It is not fitting for a fool to live in luxury,
  much less for a slave to rule over princes.
11 Those with good sense are slow to anger,
  and it is their glory to overlook an
    offense.
12 A king's anger is like the growling of a lion,
  but his favor is like dew on the grass.
13 A stupid child is ruin to a father,
  and a wife's quarreling is a continual
    dripping of rain.
14 House and wealth are inherited from
    parents,
  but a prudent wife is from the LORD.
15 Laziness brings on deep sleep;
  an idle person will suffer hunger.
16 Those who keep the commandment will
    live;
  those who are heedless of their ways
    will die.
17 Whoever is kind to the poor lends to the
    LORD,
  and will be repaid in full.
18 Discipline your children while there is hope;

---

b Meaning of Heb uncertain   c Gk Syr Vg Tg: Meaning of
Heb uncertain   d Syr Tg: Heb *A man of*   e Cn Compare
Syr Vg Tg: Meaning of Heb uncertain

do not set your heart on their
destruction.

19 A violent tempered person will pay the
penalty;
if you effect a rescue, you will only have
to do it again.*f*

20 Listen to advice and accept instruction,
that you may gain wisdom for the future.

21 The human mind may devise many plans,
but it is the purpose of the LORD that will
be established.

22 What is desirable in a person is loyalty,
and it is better to be poor than a liar.

23 The fear of the LORD is life indeed;
filled with it one rests secure
and suffers no harm.

P
R
O
V

PRAY IT!

Fear of the Lord

The phrase "fear of the LORD" is used
fourteen times in Proverbs (see, for
example, 19.23). You might ask why the
author of Proverbs keeps telling us to be
afraid of God. But in the Bible, fear of the
Lord has less to do with terror and fright
than with awe, reverence, and respect.
It's a reminder that God is far from ordinary. To fear the Lord is to take God very
seriously.

Take some time to reflect or journal
on the question What does it mean to
fear the Lord? Describe a time when
you were awed by something about God.
Explain how you give God respect.

▶ Prov 19.23

24 The lazy person buries a hand in the dish,
and will not even bring it back to the
mouth.

25 Strike a scoffer, and the simple will learn
prudence;
reprove the intelligent, and they will gain
knowledge.

26 Those who do violence to their father and
chase away their mother
are children who cause shame and bring
reproach.

27 Cease straying, my child, from the words of
knowledge,
in order that you may hear instruction.

28 A worthless witness mocks at justice,
and the mouth of the wicked devours
iniquity.

29 Condemnation is ready for scoffers,
and flogging for the backs of fools.

20 Wine is a mocker, strong drink a brawler,
and whoever is led astray by it is not
wise.

2 The dread anger of a king is like the
growling of a lion;
anyone who provokes him to anger
forfeits life itself.

3 It is honorable to refrain from strife,
but every fool is quick to quarrel.

4 The lazy person does not plow in season;
harvest comes, and there is nothing to be
found.

5 The purposes in the human mind are like
deep water,
but the intelligent will draw them out.

6 Many proclaim themselves loyal,
but who can find one worthy of trust?

7 The righteous walk in integrity—
happy are the children who follow them!

8 A king who sits on the throne of judgment
winnows all evil with his eyes.

9 Who can say, "I have made my heart clean;
I am pure from my sin"?

10 Diverse weights and diverse measures
are both alike an abomination to the
LORD.

11 Even children make themselves known by
their acts,
by whether what they do is pure and
right.

12 The hearing ear and the seeing eye—
the LORD has made them both.

13 Do not love sleep, or else you will come to
poverty;
open your eyes, and you will have plenty
of bread.

14 "Bad, bad," says the buyer,
then goes away and boasts.

15 There is gold, and abundance of costly
stones;
but the lips informed by knowledge are a
precious jewel.

16 Take the garment of one who has given
surety for a stranger;
seize the pledge given as surety for
foreigners.

17 Bread gained by deceit is sweet,
but afterward the mouth will be full of
gravel.

f Meaning of Heb uncertain

18 Plans are established by taking advice;
    wage war by following wise guidance.
19 A gossip reveals secrets;
    therefore do not associate with a babbler.
20 If you curse father or mother,
    your lamp will go out in utter darkness.
21 An estate quickly acquired in the beginning
    will not be blessed in the end.
22 Do not say, "I will repay evil";
    wait for the LORD, and he will help you.
23 Differing weights are an abomination to the
    LORD,
    and false scales are not good.
24 All our steps are ordered by the LORD;
    how then can we understand our own
    ways?
25 It is a snare for one to say rashly, "It is
    holy,"
    and begin to reflect only after making
    a vow.
26 A wise king winnows the wicked,
    and drives the wheel over them.
27 The human spirit is the lamp of the LORD,
    searching every inmost part.
28 Loyalty and faithfulness preserve the king,
    and his throne is upheld by
    righteousness. g
29 The glory of youths is their strength,
    but the beauty of the aged is their gray
    hair.
30 Blows that wound cleanse away evil;
    beatings make clean the innermost parts.

The king's heart is a stream of water in the
    hand of the LORD;
    he turns it wherever he will.
2 All deeds are right in the sight of the doer,
    but the LORD weighs the heart.
3 To do righteousness and justice
    is more acceptable to the LORD than
    sacrifice.
4 Haughty eyes and a proud heart—
    the lamp of the wicked—are sin.
5 The plans of the diligent lead surely to
    abundance,
    but everyone who is hasty comes only to
    want.
6 The getting of treasures by a lying tongue
    is a fleeting vapor and a snare h of death.
7 The violence of the wicked will sweep them
    away,
    because they refuse to do what is just.
8 The way of the guilty is crooked,
    but the conduct of the pure is right.
9 It is better to live in a corner of the
    housetop

than in a house shared with a
    contentious wife.
10 The souls of the wicked desire evil;
    their neighbors find no mercy in their
    eyes.
11 When a scoffer is punished, the simple
    become wiser;
    when the wise are instructed, they
    increase in knowledge.
12 The Righteous One observes the house of
    the wicked;
    he casts the wicked down to ruin.
13 If you close your ear to the cry of the poor,
    you will cry out and not be heard.
14 A gift in secret averts anger;
    and a concealed bribe in the bosom,
    strong wrath.
15 When justice is done, it is a joy to the
    righteous,
    but dismay to evildoers.
16 Whoever wanders from the way of
    understanding
    will rest in the assembly of the dead.
17 Whoever loves pleasure will suffer want;
    whoever loves wine and oil will not be
    rich.
18 The wicked is a ransom for the righteous,
    and the faithless for the upright.
19 It is better to live in a desert land
    than with a contentious and fretful wife.
20 Precious treasure remains i in the house of
    the wise,
    but the fool devours it.
21 Whoever pursues righteousness and
    kindness
    will find life j and honor.
22 One wise person went up against a city of
    warriors
    and brought down the stronghold in
    which they trusted.
23 To watch over mouth and tongue
    is to keep out of trouble.
24 The proud, haughty person, named "Scoffer,"
    acts with arrogant pride.
25 The craving of the lazy person is fatal,
    for lazy hands refuse to labor.
26 All day long the wicked covet, k
    but the righteous give and do not hold
    back.
27 The sacrifice of the wicked is an
    abomination;

---

g Gk: Heb *loyalty*   h Gk: Heb *seekers*   i Gk: Heb *and oil*
j Gk: Heb *life and righteousness*   k Gk: Heb *all day long one
covets covetously*

how much more when brought with evil
   intent.
28 A false witness will perish,
   but a good listener will testify
      successfully.
29 The wicked put on a bold face,
   but the upright give thought to[l] their
      ways.
30 No wisdom, no understanding, no counsel,
   can avail against the LORD.
31 The horse is made ready for the day of
      battle,
   but the victory belongs to the LORD.

A good name is to be chosen rather than
      great riches,
   and favor is better than silver or gold.
2 The rich and the poor have this in common:
   the LORD is the maker of them all.
3 The clever see danger and hide;
   but the simple go on, and suffer for it.
4 The reward for humility and fear of the LORD
   is riches and honor and life.
5 Thorns and snares are in the way of the
      perverse;
   the cautious will keep far from them.
6 Train children in the right way,
   and when old, they will not stray.
7 The rich rule over the poor,
   and the borrower is the slave of the
      lender.
8 Whoever sows injustice will reap calamity,
   and the rod of anger will fail.
9 Those who are generous are blessed,
   for they share their bread with the poor.
10 Drive out a scoffer, and strife goes out;
   quarreling and abuse will cease.
11 Those who love a pure heart and are
      gracious in speech
   will have the king as a friend.
12 The eyes of the LORD keep watch over
      knowledge,
   but he overthrows the words of the
      faithless.
13 The lazy person says, "There is a lion
      outside!
   I shall be killed in the streets!"
14 The mouth of a loose[m] woman is a deep pit;
   he with whom the LORD is angry falls
      into it.
15 Folly is bound up in the heart of a boy,
   but the rod of discipline drives it far
      away.
16 Oppressing the poor in order to enrich
      oneself,
   and giving to the rich, will lead only to
      loss.

Sayings of the Wise

17 The words of the wise:

Incline your ear and hear my words,[n]
   and apply your mind to my teaching;
18 for it will be pleasant if you keep them
      within you,
   if all of them are ready on your lips.
19 So that your trust may be in the LORD,
   I have made them known to you today—
      yes, to you.
20 Have I not written for you thirty sayings
   of admonition and knowledge,
21 to show you what is right and true,
   so that you may give a true answer to
      those who sent you?

22 Do not rob the poor because they are poor,
   or crush the afflicted at the gate;
23 for the LORD pleads their cause
   and despoils of life those who despoil
      them.
24 Make no friends with those given to anger,
   and do not associate with hotheads,
25 or you may learn their ways
   and entangle yourself in a snare.

PRAY IT!

Hotheads

We need to be careful who our friends
are, who we hang out with (Prov
22.24). Their worst habits easily become
ours.

*God of patience and calm, be with us when
we get angry. Help us not to do and say
things we will surely regret. And remind us
to be forgiving when someone else's quick
temper hurts us. Amen.*

▶ **Prov 22.24–25**

26 Do not be one of those who give pledges,
   who become surety for debts.
27 If you have nothing with which to pay,
   why should your bed be taken from
      under you?
28 Do not remove the ancient landmark
   that your ancestors set up.

---

l Another reading is *establish*   m Heb *strange*
n Cn Compare Gk: Heb *Incline your ear, and hear the words
of the wise*

29 Do you see those who are skillful in their
        work?
    They will serve kings;
    they will not serve common people.

When you sit down to eat with a ruler,
    observe carefully what[o] is before you,
2 and put a knife to your throat
    if you have a big appetite.
3 Do not desire the ruler's[p] delicacies,
    for they are deceptive food.
4 Do not wear yourself out to get rich;
    be wise enough to desist.
5 When your eyes light upon it, it is gone;
    for suddenly it takes wings to itself,
    flying like an eagle toward heaven.
6 Do not eat the bread of the stingy;
    do not desire their delicacies;
7 for like a hair in the throat, so are they.[q]
    "Eat and drink!" they say to you;
    but they do not mean it.
8 You will vomit up the little you have eaten,
    and you will waste your pleasant words.
9 Do not speak in the hearing of a fool,
    who will only despise the wisdom of
        your words.
10 Do not remove an ancient landmark
    or encroach on the fields of orphans,
11 for their redeemer is strong;
    he will plead their cause against you.
12 Apply your mind to instruction
    and your ear to words of knowledge.
13 Do not withhold discipline from your
        children;
    if you beat them with a rod, they will
        not die.
14 If you beat them with the rod,
    you will save their lives from Shĕ'ōl.
15 My child, if your heart is wise,
    my heart too will be glad.
16 My soul will rejoice
    when your lips speak what is right.
17 Do not let your heart envy sinners,
    but always continue in the fear of the
        LORD.
18 Surely there is a future,
    and your hope will not be cut off.

19 Hear, my child, and be wise,
    and direct your mind in the way.
20 Do not be among winebibbers,
    or among gluttonous eaters of meat;
21 for the drunkard and the glutton will come
        to poverty,
    and drowsiness will clothe them with
        rags.

22 Listen to your father who begot you,
    and do not despise your mother when
        she is old.
23 Buy truth, and do not sell it;
    buy wisdom, instruction, and
        understanding.
24 The father of the righteous will greatly
        rejoice;
    he who begets a wise son will be glad
        in him.
25 Let your father and mother be glad;
    let her who bore you rejoice.

26 My child, give me your heart,
    and let your eyes observe[r] my ways.
27 For a prostitute is a deep pit;
    an adulteress[s] is a narrow well.
28 She lies in wait like a robber
    and increases the number of the faithless.

29 Who has woe? Who has sorrow?
    Who has strife? Who has complaining?
    Who has wounds without cause?
    Who has redness of eyes?
30 Those who linger late over wine,
    those who keep trying mixed wines.
31 Do not look at wine when it is red,
    when it sparkles in the cup
    and goes down smoothly.
32 At the last it bites like a serpent,
    and stings like an adder.
33 Your eyes will see strange things,
    and your mind utter perverse things.
34 You will be like one who lies down in the
        midst of the sea,
    like one who lies on the top of a mast.[q]
35 "They struck me," you will say,[t] "but I was
        not hurt;
    they beat me, but I did not feel it.
    When shall I awake?
    I will seek another drink."

Do not envy the wicked,
    nor desire to be with them;
2 for their minds devise violence,
    and their lips talk of mischief.

3 By wisdom a house is built,
    and by understanding it is established;
4 by knowledge the rooms are filled
    with all precious and pleasant riches.
5 Wise warriors are mightier than strong
        ones,[u]

o Or who   p Heb his   q Meaning of Heb uncertain
r Another reading is delight in   s Heb an alien woman
t Gk Syr Vg Tg: Heb lacks you will say   u Gk Compare Syr
Tg: Heb A wise man is strength

NATIVE AMERICAN

Wisdom and the Elders

"By wisdom a house is built . . . / by knowledge the rooms are filled" (Prov 24.3–4). Becoming wise is like building and furnishing a house. It doesn't happen all at once; it takes time, experience, and work. Native American cultures understand this. Wisdom is an important value for them.

In many Native American cultures, the elders have the highest place of honor because of their wisdom. Native Americans understand it takes an entire life to grow wise. The elders have lived through much, and their advice is always worth seeking. They are relied on to settle disagreements because they have learned to judge people by their heart and their integrity, not by their money or possessions. The others in the tribe know that through listening to the elders, they too, over time, will grow wise.

▶ Prov 24.3–4

and those who have knowledge than
    those who have strength;
6 for by wise guidance you can wage
    your war,
   and in abundance of counselors there is
    victory.
7 Wisdom is too high for fools;
   in the gate they do not open
    their mouths.

8 Whoever plans to do evil
   will be called a mischief-maker.
9 The devising of folly is sin,
   and the scoffer is an abomination to all.

10 If you faint in the day of adversity,
   your strength being small;
11 if you hold back from rescuing those taken
    away to death,
   those who go staggering to the slaughter;

12 if you say, "Look, we did not know this"—
   does not he who weighs the heart
    perceive it?
   Does not he who keeps watch over your
    soul know it?
   And will he not repay all according to
    their deeds?

13 My child, eat honey, for it is good,
   and the drippings of the honeycomb are
    sweet to your taste.
14 Know that wisdom is such to your soul;
   if you find it, you will find a future,
   and your hope will not be cut off.

15 Do not lie in wait like an outlaw against the
    home of the righteous;
   do no violence to the place where the
    righteous live;
16 for though they fall seven times, they will
    rise again;
   but the wicked are overthrown by
    calamity.

17 Do not rejoice when your enemies fall,
   and do not let your heart be glad when
    they stumble,
18 or else the LORD will see it and be
    displeased,
   and turn away his anger from them.

19 Do not fret because of evildoers.
   Do not envy the wicked;
20 for the evil have no future;
   the lamp of the wicked will go out.

21 My child, fear the LORD and the king,
   and do not disobey either of them;*v*
22 for disaster comes from them suddenly,
   and who knows the ruin that both can
    bring?

Further Sayings of the Wise

23   These also are sayings of the wise:

Partiality in judging is not good.
24 Whoever says to the wicked, "You are
    innocent,"
   will be cursed by peoples, abhorred by
    nations;
25 but those who rebuke the wicked will have
    delight,
   and a good blessing will come upon
    them.
26 One who gives an honest answer
   gives a kiss on the lips.

v Gk: Heb *do not associate with those who change*

27 Prepare your work outside,
   get everything ready for you in the field;
   and after that build your house.

28 Do not be a witness against your neighbor
      without cause,
   and do not deceive with your lips.

29 Do not say, "I will do to others as they
      have done to me;
   I will pay them back for what they have
      done."

30 I passed by the field of one who was lazy,
   by the vineyard of a stupid person;

31 and see, it was all overgrown with thorns;
   the ground was covered with nettles,
   and its stone wall was broken down.

32 Then I saw and considered it;
   I looked and received instruction.

33 A little sleep, a little slumber,
   a little folding of the hands to rest,

34 and poverty will come upon you like a
      robber,
   and want, like an armed warrior.

Further Wise Sayings of Solomon

These are other proverbs of Solomon that the officials of King Hez·e·ki′ah of Judah copied.

2 It is the glory of God to conceal things,
   but the glory of kings is to search
      things out.

3 Like the heavens for height, like the earth
      for depth,
   so the mind of kings is unsearchable.

4 Take away the dross from the silver,
   and the smith has material for a vessel;

5 take away the wicked from the presence of
      the king,
   and his throne will be established in
      righteousness.

6 Do not put yourself forward in the king's
      presence
   or stand in the place of the great;

7 for it is better to be told, "Come up here,"
   than to be put lower in the presence of a
      noble.

   What your eyes have seen

8   do not hastily bring into court;
   for[w] what will you do in the end,
   when your neighbor puts you to shame?

9 Argue your case with your neighbor directly,
   and do not disclose another's secret;

10 or else someone who hears you will bring
      shame upon you,
   and your ill repute will have no end.

11 A word fitly spoken
   is like apples of gold in a setting of silver.

12 Like a gold ring or an ornament of gold
   is a wise rebuke to a listening ear.

13 Like the cold of snow in the time of harvest
   are faithful messengers to those who send
      them;
   they refresh the spirit of their masters.

14 Like clouds and wind without rain
   is one who boasts of a gift never given.

15 With patience a ruler may be persuaded,
   and a soft tongue can break bones.

16 If you have found honey, eat only enough
      for you,
   or else, having too much, you will
      vomit it.

17 Let your foot be seldom in your neighbor's
      house,
   otherwise the neighbor will become
      weary of you and hate you.

18 Like a war club, a sword, or a sharp arrow
   is one who bears false witness against a
      neighbor.

19 Like a bad tooth or a lame foot
   is trust in a faithless person in time of
      trouble.

20 Like vinegar on a wound[x]
   is one who sings songs to a heavy heart.
   Like a moth in clothing or a worm in wood,
   sorrow gnaws at the human heart.[y]

21 If your enemies are hungry, give them bread
      to eat;
   and if they are thirsty, give them water to
      drink;

22 for you will heap coals of fire on their
      heads,
   and the LORD will reward you.

23 The north wind produces rain,
   and a backbiting tongue, angry looks.

24 It is better to live in a corner of the
      housetop
   than in a house shared with a
      contentious wife.

25 Like cold water to a thirsty soul,
   so is good news from a far country.

26 Like a muddied spring or a polluted
      fountain
   are the righteous who give way before the
      wicked.

27 It is not good to eat much honey,
   or to seek honor on top of honor.

28 Like a city breached, without walls,

---

w Cn: Heb *or else*   x Gk: Heb *Like one who takes off a
garment on a cold day, like vinegar on lye*   y Gk Syr Tg:
Heb lacks *Like a moth . . . human heart*

P
R
O
V

is one who lacks self-control.
Like snow in summer or rain in harvest,
  so honor is not fitting for a fool.
2 Like a sparrow in its flitting, like a swallow
    in its flying,
  an undeserved curse goes nowhere.
3 A whip for the horse, a bridle for the
    donkey,
  and a rod for the back of fools.
4 Do not answer fools according to their folly,
  or you will be a fool yourself.
5 Answer fools according to their folly,
  or they will be wise in their own eyes.
6 It is like cutting off one's foot and drinking
    down violence,
  to send a message by a fool.
7 The legs of a disabled person hang limp;
  so does a proverb in the mouth of a fool.
8 It is like binding a stone in a sling
  to give honor to a fool.
9 Like a thornbush brandished by the hand of
    a drunkard
  is a proverb in the mouth of a fool.
10 Like an archer who wounds everybody
  is one who hires a passing fool or
    drunkard.z
11 Like a dog that returns to its vomit
  is a fool who reverts to his folly.
12 Do you see persons wise in their own eyes?
  There is more hope for fools than for
    them.
13 The lazy person says, "There is a lion in the
    road!
  There is a lion in the streets!"
14 As a door turns on its hinges,
  so does a lazy person in bed.
15 The lazy person buries a hand in the dish,
  and is too tired to bring it back to the
    mouth.
16 The lazy person is wiser in self-esteem
  than seven who can answer discreetly.
17 Like somebody who takes a passing dog by
    the ears
  is one who meddles in the quarrel of
    another.
18 Like a maniac who shoots deadly firebrands
    and arrows,
19 so is one who deceives a neighbor
  and says, "I am only joking!"
20 For lack of wood the fire goes out,
  and where there is no whisperer,
    quarreling ceases.
21 As charcoal is to hot embers and wood to
    fire,
  so is a quarrelsome person for kindling
    strife.

22 The words of a whisperer are like delicious
    morsels;
  they go down into the inner parts of the
    body.
23 Like the glazea covering an earthen vessel
  are smoothb lips with an evil heart.
24 An enemy dissembles in speaking
  while harboring deceit within;
25 when an enemy speaks graciously, do not
    believe it,
  for there are seven abominations
    concealed within;
26 though hatred is covered with guile,
  the enemy's wickedness will be exposed
    in the assembly.
27 Whoever digs a pit will fall into it,
  and a stone will come back on the one
    who starts it rolling.
28 A lying tongue hates its victims,
  and a flattering mouth works ruin.

DO NOT BOAST ABOUT *Tomorrow,* FOR YOU DO NOT KNOW WHAT A DAY MAY BRING

27.1

Do not boast about tomorrow,
  for you do not know what a day may
    bring.
2 Let another praise you, and not your own
    mouth—
  a stranger, and not your own lips.
3 A stone is heavy, and sand is weighty,
  but a fool's provocation is heavier than
    both.
4 Wrath is cruel, anger is overwhelming,
  but who is able to stand before jealousy?
5 Better is open rebuke
  than hidden love.
6 Well meant are the wounds a friend inflicts,
  but profuse are the kisses of an enemy.
7 The sated appetite spurns honey,
  but to a ravenous appetite even the bitter
    is sweet.
8 Like a bird that strays from its nest

z Meaning of Heb uncertain   a Cn: Heb *silver of dross*
b Gk: Heb *burning*

is one who strays from home.

9 Perfume and incense make the heart glad,
  but the soul is torn by trouble.*c*

10 Do not forsake your friend or the friend of
   your parent;
   do not go to the house of your kindred
   in the day of your calamity.
   Better is a neighbor who is nearby
   than kindred who are far away.

11 Be wise, my child, and make my heart glad,
   so that I may answer whoever
   reproaches me.

12 The clever see danger and hide;
   but the simple go on, and suffer for it.

13 Take the garment of one who has given
   surety for a stranger;
   seize the pledge given as surety for
   foreigners.*d*

14 Whoever blesses a neighbor with a loud
   voice,
   rising early in the morning,
   will be counted as cursing.

15 A continual dripping on a rainy day
   and a contentious wife are alike;

16 to restrain her is to restrain the wind
   or to grasp oil in the right hand.*e*

17 Iron sharpens iron,
   and one person sharpens the wits*f* of
   another.

18 Anyone who tends a fig tree will eat its
   fruit,
   and anyone who takes care of a master
   will be honored.

19 Just as water reflects the face,
   so one human heart reflects another.

20 She'ōl and A·bad'don are never satisfied,
   and human eyes are never satisfied.

21 The crucible is for silver, and the furnace is
   for gold,
   so a person is tested*g* by being praised.

22 Crush a fool in a mortar with a pestle
   along with crushed grain,
   but the folly will not be driven out.

23 Know well the condition of your flocks,
   and give attention to your herds;

24 for riches do not last forever,
   nor a crown for all generations.

25 When the grass is gone, and new growth
   appears,
   and the herbage of the mountains is
   gathered,

26 the lambs will provide your clothing,
   and the goats the price of a field;

27 there will be enough goats' milk for your
   food,

for the food of your household
and nourishment for your servant-girls.

28 The wicked flee when no one pursues,
  but the righteous are as bold as a lion.

2 When a land rebels
  it has many rulers;
  but with an intelligent ruler
  there is lasting order.*e*

3 A ruler*h* who oppresses the poor
  is a beating rain that leaves no food.

4 Those who forsake the law praise the
  wicked,
  but those who keep the law struggle
  against them.

5 The evil do not understand justice,
  but those who seek the LORD understand
  it completely.

6 Better to be poor and walk in integrity
  than to be crooked in one's ways even
  though rich.

PRAY IT!

Integrity

A person with integrity does the right thing, even if it doesn't lead to fame or riches. A person with integrity won't lie, steal, or cheat; won't gossip, betray, or insult. Not even when everyone else seems to be doing it. A person with integrity is trustworthy, dependable, and reliable. Such a person admits making mistakes and apologizes. Such a person forgives freely and doesn't hold grudges.

Lord, I'm far from perfect. But, with every word I speak, every action I take, every choice I make, may I become more aware of how I am growing into a person of integrity.

▶ Prov 28.6

7 Those who keep the law are wise children,
  but companions of gluttons shame their
  parents.

8 One who augments wealth by exorbitant
  interest

---

c Gk: Heb *the sweetness of a friend is better than one's own counsel*   *d* Vg and 20.16: Heb *for a foreign woman*
e Meaning of Heb uncertain   *f* Heb *face*   *g* Heb *lacks is tested*   *h* Cn: Heb *A poor person*

gathers it for another who is kind to the
poor.

9 When one will not listen to the law,
even one's prayers are an abomination.

10 Those who mislead the upright into evil
ways
will fall into pits of their own making,
but the blameless will have a goodly
inheritance.

11 The rich is wise in self-esteem,
but an intelligent poor person sees
through the pose.

12 When the righteous triumph, there is great
glory,
but when the wicked prevail, people go
into hiding.

13 No one who conceals transgressions will
prosper,
but one who confesses and forsakes them
will obtain mercy.

14 Happy is the one who is never without fear,
but one who is hard-hearted will fall into
calamity.

15 Like a roaring lion or a charging bear
is a wicked ruler over a poor people.

16 A ruler who lacks understanding is a cruel
oppressor;
but one who hates unjust gain will enjoy
a long life.

17 If someone is burdened with the blood of
another,
let that killer be a fugitive until death;
let no one offer assistance.

18 One who walks in integrity will be safe,
but whoever follows crooked ways will
fall into the Pit.[i]

19 Anyone who tills the land will have plenty
of bread,
but one who follows worthless pursuits
will have plenty of poverty.

20 The faithful will abound with blessings,
but one who is in a hurry to be rich will
not go unpunished.

21 To show partiality is not good—
yet for a piece of bread a person may do
wrong.

22 The miser is in a hurry to get rich
and does not know that loss is sure to
come.

23 Whoever rebukes a person will afterward
find more favor
than one who flatters with the tongue.

24 Anyone who robs father or mother
and says, "That is no crime,"
is partner to a thug.

25 The greedy person stirs up strife,

but whoever trusts in the LORD will be
enriched.

26 Those who trust in their own wits are fools;
but those who walk in wisdom come
through safely.

27 Whoever gives to the poor will lack nothing,
but one who turns a blind eye will get
many a curse.

28 When the wicked prevail, people go into
hiding;
but when they perish, the righteous
increase.

One who is often reproved, yet remains
stubborn,
will suddenly be broken beyond healing.

2 When the righteous are in authority, the
people rejoice;
but when the wicked rule, the people
groan.

3 A child who loves wisdom makes a parent
glad,
but to keep company with prostitutes is
to squander one's substance.

4 By justice a king gives stability to the land,
but one who makes heavy exactions
ruins it.

5 Whoever flatters a neighbor
is spreading a net for the neighbor's feet.

6 In the transgression of the evil there is a
snare,
but the righteous sing and rejoice.

7 The righteous know the rights of the poor;
the wicked have no such understanding.

8 Scoffers set a city aflame,
but the wise turn away wrath.

9 If the wise go to law with fools,
there is ranting and ridicule without
relief.

10 The bloodthirsty hate the blameless,
and they seek the life of the upright.

11 A fool gives full vent to anger,
but the wise quietly holds it back.

12 If a ruler listens to falsehood,
all his officials will be wicked.

13 The poor and the oppressor have this in
common:
the LORD gives light to the eyes of both.

14 If a king judges the poor with equity,
his throne will be established forever.

15 The rod and reproof give wisdom,
but a mother is disgraced by a neglected
child.

16 When the wicked are in authority,
transgression increases,

_____
i Syr: Heb *fall all at once*

but the righteous will look upon their
   downfall.
17 Discipline your children, and they will give
      you rest;
   they will give delight to your heart.
18 Where there is no prophecy, the people cast
      off restraint,
   but happy are those who keep the law.
19 By mere words servants are not disciplined,
   for though they understand, they will not
      give heed.
20 Do you see someone who is hasty
      in speech?
   There is more hope for a fool than for
      anyone like that.
21 A slave pampered from childhood
   will come to a bad end. *j*
22 One given to anger stirs up strife,
   and the hothead causes much
      transgression.
23 A person's pride will bring humiliation,
   but one who is lowly in spirit will obtain
      honor.
24 To be a partner of a thief is to hate one's
      own life;
   one hears the victim's curse, but discloses
      nothing. *k*
25 The fear of others *l* lays a snare,
   but one who trusts in the LORD is secure.
26 Many seek the favor of a ruler,
   but it is from the LORD that one gets
      justice.
27 The unjust are an abomination to the
      righteous,
   but the upright are an abomination to
      the wicked.

Sayings of Agur

The words of A'gur son of Ja'keh. An oracle.

Thus says the man: I am weary, O God,
   I am weary, O God. How can I prevail? *m*
2 Surely I am too stupid to be human;
   I do not have human understanding.
3 I have not learned wisdom,
   nor have I knowledge of the holy ones. *n*
4 Who has ascended to heaven and come
      down?
   Who has gathered the wind in the hollow
      of the hand?
   Who has wrapped up the waters in a
      garment?
   Who has established all the ends of the
      earth?
   What is the person's name?

And what is the name of the person's
      child?
   Surely you know!

5 Every word of God proves true;
   he is a shield to those who take refuge
      in him.
6 Do not add to his words,
   or else he will rebuke you, and you will
      be found a liar.
7 Two things I ask of you;
   do not deny them to me before I die:
8 Remove far from me falsehood and lying;
   give me neither poverty nor riches;
   feed me with the food that I need,
9 or I shall be full, and deny you,
   and say, "Who is the LORD?"
   or I shall be poor, and steal,
   and profane the name of my God.

10 Do not slander a servant to a master,
   or the servant will curse you, and you
      will be held guilty.

11 There are those who curse their fathers
   and do not bless their mothers.
12 There are those who are pure in their own
      eyes
   yet are not cleansed of their filthiness.
13 There are those—how lofty are their eyes,
   how high their eyelids lift!—
14 there are those whose teeth are swords,
   whose teeth are knives,
   to devour the poor from off the earth,
   the needy from among mortals.

15 The leech *k* has two daughters;
   "Give, give," they cry.
   Three things are never satisfied;
   four never say, "Enough":
16 She'ol, the barren womb,
   the earth ever thirsty for water,
   and the fire that never says, "Enough." *k*

17 The eye that mocks a father
   and scorns to obey a mother
   will be pecked out by the ravens of the
      valley
   and eaten by the vultures.

18 Three things are too wonderful for me;
   four I do not understand:
19 the way of an eagle in the sky,
   the way of a snake on a rock,

---

j Vg: Meaning of Heb uncertain   *k* Meaning of Heb
uncertain   *l* Or *human fear*   *m* Or *I am spent.* Meaning
of Heb uncertain   *n* Or *Holy One*

PROV

Ravens and Vultures

> The eye that mocks a father
>   and scorns to obey a mother
> will be pecked out by the ravens of the valley
>   and eaten by the vultures.
>
> (Prov 30.17)

If this passage reflected reality, most of us would already have been eaten by those vultures hovering overhead. For who among us has not at one time mocked our parents, if not to their face, then perhaps to our friends? And is there anyone who has not disobeyed a parent?

We live in a time when families have many different forms. You might live with biological parents, stepparents, adopted parents, or foster parents. Whatever kind and number of parents you have, they need your respect, despite their weaknesses and flaws (although you must not accept verbal, physical, sexual, or other abuse).

The vast majority of us are loved by our parents. In most cases, they are trying their hardest to do what is best for us, even though it doesn't always seem that way. If we can accept this, then it might be easier to forgive them their faults and overlook some of the things they do that irritate us.

Let's keep the vultures far away!

- What can you do to let your parents know that you love them?
- What can you do today to show them more respect?

▶ Prov 30.17

the way of a ship on the high seas,
    and the way of a man with a girl.

20 This is the way of an adulteress:
    she eats, and wipes her mouth,
    and says, "I have done no wrong."

21 Under three things the earth trembles;
    under four it cannot bear up:
22 a slave when he becomes king,
    and a fool when glutted with food;
23 an unloved woman when she gets
        a husband,
    and a maid when she succeeds her
        mistress.

24 Four things on earth are small,
    yet they are exceedingly wise:
25 the ants are a people without strength,
    yet they provide their food in
        the summer;
26 the badgers are a people without power,
    yet they make their homes in the rocks;
27 the locusts have no king,
    yet all of them march in rank;
28 the lizard*o* can be grasped in the hand,
    yet it is found in kings' palaces.

29 Three things are stately in their stride;
    four are stately in their gait:
30 the lion, which is mightiest among wild
        animals
    and does not turn back before any;
31 the strutting rooster,*p* the he-goat,
    and a king striding before*q* his people.

32 If you have been foolish, exalting yourself,
    or if you have been devising evil,
    put your hand on your mouth.
33 For as pressing milk produces curds,
    and pressing the nose produces blood,
    so pressing anger produces strife.

The Teaching of King Lemuel's Mother

The words of King Lem′u·el. An oracle that his mother taught him:

2 No, my son! No, son of my womb!
    No, son of my vows!
3 Do not give your strength to women,
    your ways to those who destroy kings.
4 It is not for kings, O Lem′u·el,
    it is not for kings to drink wine,

---

o Or *spider*   *p* Gk Syr Tg Compare Vg: Meaning of Heb uncertain   *q* Meaning of Heb uncertain

or for rulers to desire[r] strong drink;
5 or else they will drink and forget what has
   been decreed,
   and will pervert the rights of all the
   afflicted.
6 Give strong drink to one who is perishing,
   and wine to those in bitter distress;
7 let them drink and forget their poverty,
   and remember their misery no more.
8 Speak out for those who cannot speak,
   for the rights of all the destitute.[s]
9 Speak out, judge righteously,
   defend the rights of the poor and needy.

Ode to a Capable Wife

10 A capable wife who can find?
   She is far more precious than jewels.
11 The heart of her husband trusts in her,
   and he will have no lack of gain.
12 She does him good, and not harm,
   all the days of her life.
13 She seeks wool and flax,
   and works with willing hands.
14 She is like the ships of the merchant,
   she brings her food from far away.
15 She rises while it is still night
   and provides food for her household
   and tasks for her servant-girls.
16 She considers a field and buys it;
   with the fruit of her hands she plants a
   vineyard.
17 She girds herself with strength,
   and makes her arms strong.
18 She perceives that her merchandise is
   profitable.
   Her lamp does not go out at night.
19 She puts her hands to the distaff,
   and her hands hold the spindle.
20 She opens her hand to the poor,
   and reaches out her hands to the needy.
21 She is not afraid for her household when it
   snows,
   for all her household are clothed in
   crimson.
22 She makes herself coverings;
   her clothing is fine linen and purple.
23 Her husband is known in the city gates,
   taking his seat among the elders of the
   land.
24 She makes linen garments and sells them;
   she supplies the merchant with sashes.
25 Strength and dignity are her clothing,
   and she laughs at the time to come.
26 She opens her mouth with wisdom,
   and the teaching of kindness is on her
   tongue.
27 She looks well to the ways of her
   household,
   and does not eat the bread of idleness.
28 Her children rise up and call her happy;
   her husband too, and he praises her:
29 "Many women have done excellently,
   but you surpass them all."
30 Charm is deceitful, and beauty is vain,
   but a woman who fears the LORD is to be
   praised.
31 Give her a share in the fruit of her hands,
   and let her works praise her in the city
   gates.

---

r Cn: Heb *where*   s Heb *all children of passing away*

PROV

T here is nothing new under the sun."
"Sorrow is better than laughter."
"No one can anticipate the time of disaster."
If you saw these comments on the Internet, what
would you think? That you had just found the web site
of the National Association of Pessimists? Would you be
surprised to learn that all these lines come from the Bible?

The author of Ecclesiastes, who
was called the Teacher (Eccl 1.1),
wrote all of them. Yet, the book
is hardly a defense of pessimism.
The Teacher was pointing out to
the Israelites the need for a new
understanding of God and life.

At a Glance

- **1.1—6.9.** thoughts on life's difficulties, along with the Teacher's advice
- **6.10—12.8.** thoughts on the future
- **12.9–14.** the final editor's addition, affirming the traditional teaching

In-depth

After a long life of careful observation, the author of Ecclesiastes was disturbed by many things:
- that wise people perished just like fools (2.12–17)
- that those who worked hard for a living had to leave their possessions behind in death (5.13–17)
- that sometimes bad people lived longer than good people (7.15–16)
- that the most deserving did not always get what they had earned (9.11–12)

Observing these puzzling things, the Teacher asked the obvious question: "Why should we work so hard to be wise and good?" For centuries, believers had struggled to be honest, law-abiding people in the hope of being rewarded by God. And what had they gotten? Sickness, suffering, and death—like everyone else! "Something's wrong!" the Teacher insisted. "Something's terribly wrong!"

After raising the question, the author of Ecclesiastes did not provide an answer—nor is a convincing one to be found in the writings of others in the Old Testament. However, later generations of Jews, pondering the possibility of life after death—a concept that developed late in Jewish religion—began to see things in a different light. Does God possibly reward the faithful in a life beyond the grave? For Christians, the New Testament answers that question with a resounding yes.

The Book of Ecclesiastes stands as a reminder to believers that all things change, even our understanding of God. The Teacher was not a pessimist, but a realist with a mission—to stretch the traditional understanding of faith in order to embrace the difficult questions of life.

Quick Facts

Author
the Teacher, writing in the fourth or third century B.C.

Themes
Life is not always fair. There are no easy answers.

Of Note
Ecclesiastes is often attributed to King Solomon, although he did not write it.

The Book of Ecclesiastes

722

Ecclesiastes

Reflections of a Royal Philosopher

The words of the Teacher,[a] the son of David, king in Jerusalem.

2 Vanity of vanities, says the Teacher,[a]
    vanity of vanities! All is vanity.
3 What do people gain from all the toil
    at which they toil under the sun?
4 A generation goes, and a generation comes,
    but the earth remains forever.
5 The sun rises and the sun goes down,
    and hurries to the place where it rises.
6 The wind blows to the south,
    and goes around to the north;
round and round goes the wind,
    and on its circuits the wind returns.
7 All streams run to the sea,
    but the sea is not full;
to the place where the streams flow,
    there they continue to flow.
8 All things[b] are wearisome;
    more than one can express;
the eye is not satisfied with seeing,
    or the ear filled with hearing.
9 What has been is what will be,
    and what has been done is what will be
        done;
    there is nothing new under the sun.
10 Is there a thing of which it is said,
    "See, this is new"?
It has already been,

in the ages before us.
11 The people of long ago are not
        remembered,
    nor will there be any remembrance
of people yet to come
    by those who come after them.

The Futility of Seeking Wisdom

12 I, the Teacher,[a] when king over Israel in Jerusalem, 13 applied my mind to seek and to search out by wisdom all that is done under heaven; it is an unhappy business that God has given to human beings to be busy with. 14 I saw all the deeds that are done under the sun; and see, all is vanity and a chasing after wind.[c]
15 What is crooked cannot be made straight,
    and what is lacking cannot be counted.

16 I said to myself, "I have acquired great wisdom, surpassing all who were over Jerusalem before me; and my mind has had great experience of wisdom and knowledge." 17 And I applied my mind to know wisdom and to know madness and folly. I perceived that this also is but a chasing after wind.[c]
18 For in much wisdom is much vexation,
    and those who increase knowledge increase
        sorrow.

a Heb Qoheleth, traditionally rendered Preacher
b Or words   c Or a feeding on wind. See Hos 12.1

723

New and Improved!

NEW! IMPROVED! These two words are basic to many ad campaigns. No matter how good a product is, sooner or later, it will be "new and improved." The reason is simple: the advertisers want us to think the product is even better.

The writer of Ecclesiastes would not be very impressed with the claims of advertisers today. The author sounds skeptical in 1.9: "There is nothing new under the sun." The Teacher is not going to be taken in by claims that something is new and improved. This person has seen it all before.

Advertising can get us thinking that our life isn't good enough, that we have to have more things and new things in order to be happy. In fact, we need to have a little bit of the attitude of the Teacher if we want to find contentment. Throughout the Book of Ecclesiastes, this writer invites us to enjoy what we have now.

Have you ever gotten something because of its advertising, only to be disappointed afterward? Are you enjoying the things you have right now?

▸ Eccl 1.1–11

The Futility of Self-Indulgence
(Cp 1 Kings 4.20–28)

I said to myself, "Come now, I will make a test of pleasure; enjoy yourself." But again, this also was vanity. 2 I said of laughter, "It is mad," and of pleasure, "What use is it?" 3 I searched with my mind how to cheer my body with wine—my mind still guiding me with wisdom—and how to lay hold on folly, until I might see what was good for mortals to do under heaven during the few days of their life. 4 I made great works; I built houses and planted vineyards for myself; 5 I made myself gardens and parks, and planted in them all kinds of fruit trees. 6 I made myself pools from which to water the forest of growing trees. 7 I bought male and female slaves, and had slaves who were born in my house; I also had great possessions of herds and flocks, more than any who had been before me in Jerusalem. 8 I also gathered for myself silver and gold and the treasure of kings and of the provinces; I got singers, both men and women, and delights of the flesh, and many concubines.[d]

9 So I became great and surpassed all who were before me in Jerusalem; also my wisdom remained with me. 10 Whatever my eyes desired I did not keep from them; I kept my heart from no pleasure, for my heart found pleasure in all my toil, and this was my reward for all my toil. 11 Then I considered all that my hands had done and the toil I had spent in doing it, and again, all was vanity and a chasing after wind,[e] and there was nothing to be gained under the sun.

Wisdom and Joy Given to One
Who Pleases God

12 So I turned to consider wisdom and madness and folly; for what can the one do who comes after the king? Only what has already been done. 13 Then I saw that wisdom excels folly as light excels darkness.

14   The wise have eyes in their head,
       but fools walk in darkness.

Yet I perceived that the same fate befalls all of them. 15 Then I said to myself, "What happens to the fool will happen to me also; why then have I been so very wise?" And I said to myself that this also is vanity. 16 For there is no enduring remembrance of the wise or of fools, seeing that in the days to come all will have been long forgotten. How can the wise die just like fools? 17 So I hated life, because what is done under the sun was grievous to me; for all is vanity and a chasing after wind.[e]

18 I hated all my toil in which I had toiled under the sun, seeing that I must leave it to those who come after me 19 —and who knows whether they will be wise or foolish? Yet they will be master of all for which I toiled and used my wisdom under the sun. This also is vanity. 20 So I turned and gave my heart up to despair concerning all the toil of my labors under the sun, 21 because sometimes one who has toiled with wisdom and knowledge and skill must leave all to be enjoyed by another who did not toil for it. This also is vanity

---

d Meaning of Heb uncertain   e Or *a feeding on wind*. See Hos 12.1

and a great evil. ²²What do mortals get from all the toil and strain with which they toil under the sun? ²³For all their days are full of pain, and their work is a vexation; even at night their minds do not rest. This also is vanity.

24 There is nothing better for mortals than to eat and drink, and find enjoyment in their toil. This also, I saw, is from the hand of God; ²⁵for apart from him*f* who can eat or who can have enjoyment? ²⁶For to the one who pleases him God gives wisdom and knowledge and joy; but to the sinner he gives the work of gathering and heaping, only to give to one who pleases God. This also is vanity and a chasing after wind.*g*

Everything Has Its Time

For everything there is a season, and a time for every matter under heaven:
2 a time to be born, and a time to die;
  a time to plant, and a time to pluck up
    what is planted;
3 a time to kill, and a time to heal;
  a time to break down, and a time to
    build up;
4 a time to weep, and a time to laugh;

a time to mourn, and a time to dance;
5 a time to throw away stones, and a time to
    gather stones together;
  a time to embrace, and a time to refrain
    from embracing;
6 a time to seek, and a time to lose;
  a time to keep, and a time to throw away;
7 a time to tear, and a time to sew;
  a time to keep silence, and a time to speak;
8 a time to love, and a time to hate;
  a time for war, and a time for peace.

Asian American
A Time for Connections

The Tao te Ching (pronounced "Dow deh JING") is the ancient Chinese Book of the Way. This piece of Chinese wisdom literature was written by Lao-tzu, who probably lived about 500 B.C., close to the time of the author of Ecclesiastes. See how similar the following passage from the Tao te Ching is to Eccl 3.1–8:

> There is a time for being ahead,
> a time for being behind;
> a time for being in motion,
> a time for being at rest;
> a time for being vigorous,
> a time for being exhausted;
> a time for being safe,
> a time for being in danger.
> (Stephen Mitchell, translator,
> *Tao te Ching*, no. 29)

▸ Eccl 3.1–8

PRAY IT
The Balance of Life

God of all seasons,
  Help me to remember the sun when it is raining.
Help me to remember the rain when the sun is shining.
Teach me to respect the seniors when I am a sophomore.
Teach me to respect the sophomores when I am a senior.
When I win on the field, let me remember the times I lost.
When I lose on the field, let me remember the times I won.
Guide me to appreciate studying when I'm taking a hard test.
Guide me to appreciate hard tests when I'm studying.
During times with friends, remind me of times alone.
During times alone, remind me of times with friends.
Help me to live all moments and remember there is a balance to life.
Amen.

▸ Eccl 3.1–8

The God-Given Task

9 What gain have the workers from their toil? ¹⁰I have seen the business that God has given to everyone to be busy with. ¹¹He has made everything suitable for its time; moreover he has put a sense of past and future into their minds, yet they cannot find out what God has done from the

f Gk Syr: Heb *apart from me*　　*g* Or *a feeding on wind.* See Hos 12.1

beginning to the end. [12] I know that there is nothing better for them than to be happy and enjoy themselves as long as they live; [13] moreover, it is God's gift that all should eat and drink and take pleasure in all their toil. [14] I know that whatever God does endures forever; nothing can be added to it, nor anything taken from it; God has done this, so that all should stand in awe before him. [15] That which is, already has been; that which is to be, already is; and God seeks out what has gone by.[h]

Judgment and the Future
Belong to God

16 Moreover I saw under the sun that in the place of justice, wickedness was there, and in the place of righteousness, wickedness was there as well. [17] I said in my heart, God will judge the righteous and the wicked, for he has appointed a time for every matter, and for every work. [18] I said in my heart with regard to human beings that God is testing them to show that they are but animals. [19] For the fate of humans and the fate of animals is the same; as one dies, so dies the other. They all have the same breath, and humans have no advantage over the animals; for all is vanity. [20] All go to one place; all are from the dust, and all turn to dust again. [21] Who knows whether the human spirit goes upward and the spirit of animals goes downward to the earth? [22] So I saw that there is nothing better than that all should enjoy their work, for that is their lot; who can bring them to see what will be after them?

Again I saw all the oppressions that are practiced under the sun. Look, the tears of the oppressed—with no one to comfort them! On the side of their oppressors there was power—with no one to comfort them. [2] And I thought the dead, who have already died, more fortunate than the living, who are still alive; [3] but better than both is the one who has not yet been, and has not seen the evil deeds that are done under the sun.

4 Then I saw that all toil and all skill in work come from one person's envy of another. This also is vanity and a chasing after wind.[i]

5 Fools fold their hands
   and consume their own flesh.
6 Better is a handful with quiet
   than two handfuls with toil,
   and a chasing after wind.[i]

7 Again, I saw vanity under the sun: [8] the case of solitary individuals, without sons or brothers; yet there is no end to all their toil, and their eyes are never satisfied with riches. "For whom am I toiling," they ask, "and depriving myself of pleasure?" This also is vanity and an unhappy business.

The Value of a Friend

9 Two are better than one, because they have a good reward for their toil. [10] For if they fall, one will lift up the other; but woe to one who is alone and falls and does not have another to help.

---

[h] Heb *what is pursued*   [i] Or *a feeding on wind*. See Hos 12.1

Eat, Drink, and Be Merry

LIVE IT!

Shirley. Do you know what the Bible says about the purpose of life?
Brian. Well, it says a lot of things. What did you find?
Shirley. Eat, drink, and be merry!
Brian. What? Where did you find that?
Shirley. Ecclesiastes 3.13.
Brian. It really says that?
Shirley. It says, "It is God's gift that all should eat and drink and take pleasure in all their toil." So, eat, drink, and be merry!
Brian. But remember the first part of the passage: "It is God's gift." To look on the simple pleasures of life as gifts from God changes the focus a bit.
Shirley. You're right. It adds a deeper purpose to the enjoyment. All those pleasures are gifts from a God who wants us to be happy and enjoy ourselves as long as we live, as it says in verse 12.
Brian. Yes, and verse 1 says, "For everything there is a season, and a time for every matter under heaven."
Shirley. I guess this is a time to be grateful for the simple gifts!

▶ Eccl 3.9–15

How Much Is Enough?

LIVE IT!

How much wealth does one need? In surveys, most young people reply they want just enough money to be happy. It's an interesting answer because they are implying they don't want to be greedy, but it takes money to be happy!

According to the Teacher, in Eccl 5.10, those who love money will always want more. What is God trying to tell us here? Maybe that real happiness is not found in material wealth. The more we want, the less satisfied we are. Money can be an evil when it is all we want and think about.

For a week, try to do things with your family and friends that do not cost anything. Play board games, go for walks or hikes, even volunteer some time at a community organization. Consider taking the money you save and donating it to a worthy cause.

▶ Eccl 5.10

11 Again, if two lie together, they keep warm; but how can one keep warm alone? 12 And though one might prevail against another, two will withstand one. A threefold cord is not quickly broken.

13 Better is a poor but wise youth than an old but foolish king, who will no longer take advice. 14 One can indeed come out of prison to reign, even though born poor in the kingdom. 15 I saw all the living who, moving about under the sun, follow that^j youth who replaced the king;^{k} 16 there was no end to all those people whom he led. Yet those who come later will not rejoice in him. Surely this also is vanity and a chasing after wind.^{l}

Reverence, Humility, and Contentment

^{m}Guard your steps when you go to the house of God; to draw near to listen is better than the sacrifice offered by fools; for they do not know how to keep from doing evil.^{n} ^{2} ^{o}Never be rash with your mouth, nor let your heart be quick to utter a word before God, for God is in heaven, and you upon earth; therefore let your words be few.

3 For dreams come with many cares, and a fool's voice with many words.

4 When you make a vow to God, do not delay fulfilling it; for he has no pleasure in fools. Fulfill what you vow. 5 It is better that you should not vow than that you should vow and not fulfill it. 6 Do not let your mouth lead you into sin, and do not say before the messenger that it was a mistake; why should God be angry at your words, and destroy the work of your hands?

7 With many dreams come vanities and a multitude of words;^{p} but fear God.

8 If you see in a province the oppression of the poor and the violation of justice and right, do not be amazed at the matter; for the high official is watched by a higher, and there are yet higher ones

over them. 9 But all things considered, this is an advantage for a land: a king for a plowed field.^{p}

10 The lover of money will not be satisfied with money; nor the lover of wealth, with gain. This also is vanity.

11 When goods increase, those who eat them increase; and what gain has their owner but to see them with his eyes?

12 Sweet is the sleep of laborers, whether they eat little or much; but the surfeit of the rich will not let them sleep.

13 There is a grievous ill that I have seen under the sun: riches were kept by their owners to their hurt, 14 and those riches were lost in a bad venture; though they are parents of children, they have nothing in their hands. 15 As they came from their mother's womb, so they shall go again, naked as they came; they shall take nothing for their toil, which they may carry away with their hands. 16 This also is a grievous ill: just as they came, so shall they go; and what gain do they have from toiling for the wind? 17 Besides, all their days they eat in darkness, in much vexation and sickness and resentment.

18 This is what I have seen to be good: it is fitting to eat and drink and find enjoyment in all the toil with which one toils under the sun the few days of the life God gives us; for this is our lot. 19 Likewise all to whom God gives wealth and possessions and whom he enables to enjoy them, and to accept their lot and find enjoyment in their toil—this is the gift of God. 20 For they will scarcely brood over the days of their lives, because God keeps them occupied with the joy of their hearts.

---

^{j} Heb *the second* ^{k} Heb *him* ^{l} Or *a feeding on wind.* See Hos 12.1 ^{m} Ch 4.17 in Heb ^{n} Cn: Heb *they do not know how to do evil* ^{o} Ch 5.1 in Heb ^{p} Meaning of Heb uncertain

The Frustration of Desires

There is an evil that I have seen under the sun, and it lies heavy upon humankind: ² those to whom God gives wealth, possessions, and honor, so that they lack nothing of all that they desire, yet God does not enable them to enjoy these things, but a stranger enjoys them. This is vanity; it is a grievous ill. ³ A man may beget a hundred children, and live many years; but however many are the days of his years, if he does not enjoy life's good things, or has no burial, I say that a stillborn child is better off than he. ⁴ For it comes into vanity and goes into darkness, and in darkness its name is covered; ⁵ moreover it has not seen the sun or known anything; yet it finds rest rather than he. ⁶ Even though he should live a thousand years twice over, yet enjoy no good—do not all go to one place?

7 All human toil is for the mouth, yet the appetite is not satisfied. ⁸ For what advantage have the wise over fools? And what do the poor have who know how to conduct themselves before the living? ⁹ Better is the sight of the eyes than the wandering of desire; this also is vanity and a chasing after wind.*q*

10 Whatever has come to be has already been named, and it is known what human beings are, and that they are not able to dispute with those who are stronger. ¹¹ The more words, the more vanity, so how is one the better? ¹² For who knows what is good for mortals while they live the few days of their vain life, which they pass like a shadow? For who can tell them what will be after them under the sun?

A Disillusioned View of Life

A good name is better than precious
    ointment,
  and the day of death, than the day of
    birth.
² It is better to go to the house of mourning
    than to go to the house of feasting;
  for this is the end of everyone,
    and the living will lay it to heart.
³ Sorrow is better than laughter,
    for by sadness of countenance the heart
      is made glad.
⁴ The heart of the wise is in the house of
      mourning;
  but the heart of fools is in the house of
      mirth.
⁵ It is better to hear the rebuke of the wise
    than to hear the song of fools.
⁶ For like the crackling of thorns under a pot,
    so is the laughter of fools;
  this also is vanity.

7 Surely oppression makes the wise foolish,
    and a bribe corrupts the heart.
⁸ Better is the end of a thing than its
      beginning;
  the patient in spirit are better than the
      proud in spirit.
⁹ Do not be quick to anger,
    for anger lodges in the bosom of fools.
¹⁰ Do not say, "Why were the former days
      better than these?"
  For it is not from wisdom that you ask
    this.
¹¹ Wisdom is as good as an inheritance,
    an advantage to those who see the sun.
¹² For the protection of wisdom is like the
      protection of money,
  and the advantage of knowledge is that
      wisdom gives life to the one who
      possesses it.
¹³ Consider the work of God;
  who can make straight what he has made
    crooked?

14 In the day of prosperity be joyful, and in the day of adversity consider; God has made the one as well as the other, so that mortals may not find out anything that will come after them.

The Riddles of Life

15 In my vain life I have seen everything; there are righteous people who perish in their righteousness, and there are wicked people who prolong their life in their evildoing. ¹⁶ Do not be too righteous, and do not act too wise; why should you destroy yourself? ¹⁷ Do not be too wicked, and do not be a fool; why should you die before your time? ¹⁸ It is good that you should take hold of the one, without letting go of the other; for the one who fears God shall succeed with both.

19 Wisdom gives strength to the wise more than ten rulers that are in a city.

20 Surely there is no one on earth so righteous as to do good without ever sinning.

21 Do not give heed to everything that people say, or you may hear your servant cursing you; ²² your heart knows that many times you have yourself cursed others.

23 All this I have tested by wisdom; I said, "I will be wise," but it was far from me. ²⁴ That which is, is far off, and deep, very deep; who can find it out? ²⁵ I turned my mind to know and to search out and to seek wisdom and the sum of things, and to know that wickedness is folly and that foolishness is madness. ²⁶ I found more bitter than death the woman who is a trap, whose heart is

---

q Or *a feeding on wind.* See Hos 12.1

snares and nets, whose hands are fetters; one who pleases God escapes her, but the sinner is taken by her. 27 See, this is what I found, says the Teacher,[r] adding one thing to another to find the sum, 28 which my mind has sought repeatedly, but I have not found. One man among a thousand I found, but a woman among all these I have not found. 29 See, this alone I found, that God made human beings straightforward, but they have devised many schemes.

Obey the King and Enjoy Yourself

Who is like the wise man?
    And who knows the interpretation of a
        thing?
Wisdom makes one's face shine,
    and the hardness of one's countenance is
        changed.

2 Keep[s] the king's command because of your sacred oath. 3 Do not be terrified; go from his presence, do not delay when the matter is unpleasant, for he does whatever he pleases. 4 For the word of the king is powerful, and who can say to him, "What are you doing?" 5 Whoever obeys a command will meet no harm, and the wise mind will know the time and way. 6 For every matter has its time and way, although the troubles of mortals lie heavy upon them. 7 Indeed, they do not know what is to be, for who can tell them how it will be? 8 No one has power over the wind[t] to restrain the wind,[t] or power over the day of death; there is no discharge from the battle, nor does wickedness deliver those who practice it. 9 All this I observed, applying my mind to all that is done under the sun, while one person exercises authority over another to the other's hurt.

God's Ways Are Inscrutable

10 Then I saw the wicked buried; they used to go in and out of the holy place, and were praised in the city where they had done such things.[u] This also is vanity. 11 Because sentence against an evil deed is not executed speedily, the human heart is fully set to do evil. 12 Though sinners do evil a hundred times and prolong their lives, yet I know that it will be well with those who fear God, because they stand in fear before him, 13 but it will not be well with the wicked, neither will they prolong their days like a shadow, because they do not stand in fear before God.

14 There is a vanity that takes place on earth, that there are righteous people who are treated according to the conduct of the wicked, and there are wicked people who are treated according to the conduct of the righteous. I said that this also is vanity. 15 So I commend enjoyment, for there is nothing better for people under the sun than to eat, and drink, and enjoy themselves, for this will go with them in their toil through the days of life that God gives them under the sun.

16 When I applied my mind to know wisdom, and to see the business that is done on earth, how one's eyes see sleep neither day nor night, 17 then I saw all the work of God, that no one can find out what is happening under the sun. However much they may toil in seeking, they will not find it out; even though those who are wise claim to know, they cannot find it out.

Take Life as It Comes

All this I laid to heart, examining it all, how the righteous and the wise and their deeds are in the hand of God; whether it is love or hate one does not know. Everything that confronts them 2 is vanity,[v] since the same fate comes to all, to the righteous and the wicked, to the good and the evil,[w] to the clean and the unclean, to those who sacrifice and those who do not sacrifice. As are the good, so are the sinners; those who swear are like those who shun an oath. 3 This is an evil in all that happens under the sun, that the same fate comes to everyone. Moreover, the hearts of all are full of

---

[r] Qoheleth, traditionally rendered *Preacher*   [s] Heb *I keep*
[t] Or *breath*   [u] Meaning of Heb uncertain
[v] Syr Compare Gk: Heb *Everything that confronts them* 2*is everything*   [w] Gk Syr Vg: Heb lacks *and the evil*

did you KNOW?

Imagine There Is No Heaven

Some people assume that the ancient Israelites believed in an afterlife as we do today. However, Ecclesiastes speaks of the end of earthly life without any hint of eternal life: "The dead know nothing; they have no more reward, and even the memory of them is lost" (9.5). The book reflects the author's belief that all life ends with death. It was not until the last two centuries before Jesus that the idea of life after death began to take root among the Jewish people.

▸ **Eccl 9.5**

evil; madness is in their hearts while they live, and after that they go to the dead. 4 But whoever is joined with all the living has hope, for a living dog is better than a dead lion. 5 The living know that they will die, but the dead know nothing; they have no more reward, and even the memory of them is lost. 6 Their love and their hate and their envy have already perished; never again will they have any share in all that happens under the sun.

7 Go, eat your bread with enjoyment, and drink your wine with a merry heart; for God has long ago approved what you do. 8 Let your garments always be white; do not let oil be lacking on your head. 9 Enjoy life with the wife whom you love, all the days of your vain life that are given you under the sun, because that is your portion in life and in your toil at which you toil under the sun. 10 Whatever your hand finds to do, do with your might; for there is no work or thought or knowledge or wisdom in She'ōl, to which you are going.

11 Again I saw that under the sun the race is not to the swift, nor the battle to the strong, nor bread to the wise, nor riches to the intelligent, nor favor to the skillful; but time and chance happen to them all. 12 For no one can anticipate the time of disaster. Like fish taken in a cruel net, and like birds caught in a snare, so mortals are snared at a time of calamity, when it suddenly falls upon them.

Wisdom Superior to Folly

13 I have also seen this example of wisdom under the sun, and it seemed great to me. 14 There was a little city with few people in it. A great king came against it and besieged it, building great siegeworks against it. 15 Now there was found in it a poor wise man, and he by his wisdom delivered the city. Yet no one remembered that poor man. 16 So I said, "Wisdom is better than might; yet the poor man's wisdom is despised, and his words are not heeded."

17 The quiet words of the wise are more to be
    heeded
    than the shouting of a ruler among fools.
18 Wisdom is better than weapons of war,
    but one bungler destroys much good.

Miscellaneous Observations

Dead flies make the perfumer's ointment give
    off a foul odor;
    so a little folly outweighs wisdom and
    honor.
2 The heart of the wise inclines to the right,
    but the heart of a fool to the left.

9.7

3 Even when fools walk on the road, they lack
    sense,
    and show to everyone that they are fools.
4 If the anger of the ruler rises against you, do
    not leave your post,
    for calmness will undo great offenses.
5 There is an evil that I have seen under the sun, as great an error as if it proceeded from the ruler: 6 folly is set in many high places, and the rich sit in a low place. 7 I have seen slaves on horseback, and princes walking on foot like slaves.
8 Whoever digs a pit will fall into it;
    and whoever breaks through a wall will
    be bitten by a snake.
9 Whoever quarries stones will be hurt by them;
    and whoever splits logs will be
    endangered by them.
10 If the iron is blunt, and one does not whet
    the edge,
    then more strength must be exerted;
    but wisdom helps one to succeed.
11 If the snake bites before it is charmed,
    there is no advantage in a charmer.
12 Words spoken by the wise bring them favor,
    but the lips of fools consume them.
13 The words of their mouths begin in
    foolishness,
    and their talk ends in wicked madness;
14 yet fools talk on and on.
    No one knows what is to happen,
    and who can tell anyone what the future
    holds?
15 The toil of fools wears them out,
    for they do not even know the way to town.

Carpe Diem—"Seize the Day"!

LIVE IT!

"Youth is wasted on the young."
Perhaps you have heard that statement uttered by not-so-young adults struggling with growing older. There is some truth in it: many young people do not reflect on life and do not pause to appreciate being young.

The Teacher says some beautiful and profound things about youthfulness. He advises young people to "follow the inclination of your heart" (Eccl 11.9) and to "banish anxiety from your mind" (verse 10). Someone like the Teacher might say today: "Follow your heart, and do not spend so much time worrying. It is a blessing to be young, to have so much energy and so many dreams. There are many pressures and stresses on young people today, but do not let them dominate your life. Enjoy this special time of growth and discovery."

It is good to be young. Seize the day!

▶ Eccl 11.7–10

16 Alas for you, O land, when your king is a
servant,*
and your princes feast in the morning!
17 Happy are you, O land, when your king is a
nobleman,
and your princes feast at the proper
time—
for strength, and not for drunkenness!
18 Through sloth the roof sinks in,
and through indolence the house leaks.
19 Feasts are made for laughter;
wine gladdens life,
and money meets every need.
20 Do not curse the king, even in your
thoughts,
or curse the rich, even in your bedroom;
for a bird of the air may carry your voice,
or some winged creature tell the matter.

The Value of Diligence

Send out your bread upon the waters,
for after many days you will get it back.
2 Divide your means seven ways, or even
eight,
for you do not know what disaster may
happen on earth.
3 When clouds are full,
they empty rain on the earth;
whether a tree falls to the south or to the
north,
in the place where the tree falls, there it
will lie.
4 Whoever observes the wind will not sow;
and whoever regards the clouds will not
reap.
5 Just as you do not know how the breath
comes to the bones in the mother's womb, so you

do not know the work of God, who makes everything.
6 In the morning sow your seed, and at evening do not let your hands be idle; for you do not know which will prosper, this or that, or whether both alike will be good.

Youth and Old Age

7 Light is sweet, and it is pleasant for the eyes to see the sun.
8 Even those who live many years should rejoice in them all; yet let them remember that the days of darkness will be many. All that comes is vanity.
9 Rejoice, young man, while you are young, and let your heart cheer you in the days of your youth. Follow the inclination of your heart and the desire of your eyes, but know that for all these things God will bring you into judgment.
10 Banish anxiety from your mind, and put away pain from your body; for youth and the dawn of life are vanity.
Remember your creator in the days of your youth, before the days of trouble come, and the years draw near when you will say, "I have no pleasure in them"; 2 before the sun and the light and the moon and the stars are darkened and the clouds return with* the rain; 3 in the day when the guards of the house tremble, and the strong men are bent, and the women who grind cease working because they are few, and those who look through the windows see dimly; 4 when the doors on the street are shut, and the sound of the grinding is low, and one rises up at the sound of a bird, and all the daughters of song are brought low; 5 when one is afraid of heights, and terrors are in the road; the

* Or a child y Or after; Heb 'ahar

Remember the Elderly

Ecclesiastes 12.1–8 is a bittersweet poem about the difficulties of the aging process. To understand it, you need to be aware of the metaphors used, like these:

- **Guards of the house = arms and hands**
- **Strong men = legs**
- **Women who grind = teeth**
- **Windows = eyes**
- **Doors = ears or lips**
- **Silver cord, golden bowl = life itself**

    Aging is a natural part of life, but it is a struggle for many people. No one enjoys its accompanying loss of mobility, loss of strength, and problems with seeing and hearing. The struggle is even greater if one is alone. If you have aging grandparents, family friends, or neighbors, keep in mind how much they need to be noticed by you. Stay in touch with them so that you can learn from their wisdom, and they can be strengthened by your youth!

▶ **Eccl 12.1–8**

almond tree blossoms, the grasshopper drags itself along[z] and desire fails; because all must go to their eternal home, and the mourners will go about the streets; [6] before the silver cord is snapped,[a] and the golden bowl is broken, and the pitcher is broken at the fountain, and the wheel broken at the cistern, [7] and the dust returns to the earth as it was, and the breath[b] returns to God who gave it. [8] Vanity of vanities, says the Teacher;[c] all is vanity.

Epilogue

9 Besides being wise, the Teacher[c] also taught the people knowledge, weighing and studying and arranging many proverbs. [10] The Teacher[c] sought to find pleasing words, and he wrote words of truth plainly.

11 The sayings of the wise are like goads, and like nails firmly fixed are the collected sayings that are given by one shepherd.[d] [12] Of anything beyond these, my child, beware. Of making many books there is no end, and much study is a weariness of the flesh.

13 The end of the matter; all has been heard. Fear God, and keep his commandments; for that is the whole duty of everyone. [14] For God will bring every deed into judgment, including[e] every secret thing, whether good or evil.

z Or *is a burden* a Syr Vg Compare Gk: Heb *is removed*
b Or *the spirit* c *Qoheleth*, traditionally rendered *Preacher*
d Meaning of Heb uncertain e Or *into the judgment on*

Sex sells. When we see an ad with a beautiful woman slipping out of a sports car or a bare-chested man grabbing an ice-cold soda, we sit up and take notice. Advertisers love to take advantage of our fascination with sex. Once they have our attention, they can sell us something we might not even be interested in! The Song of Solomon—a collection of ancient love poems— reminds us that this powerful force is ultimately a gift from God.

At a Glance

- **1.1–6.** introduction
- **1.7—2.7.** opening dialog between the lovers
- **2.8—8.4.** various reflections and other dialogs
- **8.5–14.** final thoughts

In-depth

From an advertiser's point of view, the Song of Solomon is a well-kept secret. How many people are aware of its explicit sexual images? Consider these verses:

- "Let him kiss me with the kisses of his mouth!" (1.2).
- "Your lips distill nectar, my bride; / honey and milk are under your tongue" (4.11).
- "Oh, may your breasts be like clusters of the vine, / and the scent of your breath like apples" (7.8).

Some people find these images so surprising that they wonder why the Song of Solomon is found in the Bible at all.

Scholars believe that the naming of King Solomon in the Song's first verse is the main reason that this book was preserved and eventually included with the Jewish holy books. Although written long after Solomon's death, this book—like Proverbs and Ecclesiastes—was attributed to him to give it authority.

Through the centuries, some people have not been able to accept the Song of Solomon as simply love poetry, and have hunted for a deeper meaning. Many people believe that the lover and the beloved in this book stand for Israel and God, or for Jesus and the church. Modern-day scholars, however, begin their interpretation of the Song of Solomon at the literal level, that is, as a collection of love poems. The book's inclusion among the other holy books, they insist, is an affirmation of the goodness of human sexuality: human love is holy because it is a gift from God. The passion and beauty of human sexual attraction is a reflection of the passion and beauty of God's love for us!

Quick Facts

Author
unknown, probably writing after the Jews' return from the Babylonian Exile in 538 B.C.

Theme
poetry that expresses the goodness and passion of human love

Of Note
In other translations, this book is called the Song of Songs or the Canticle of Canticles.

The Song of Solomon

Song of Solomon

The Song of Songs, which is Solomon's.

Love's Desires

2 Let him kiss me with the kisses of his
mouth!
For your love is better than wine,
3   your anointing oils are fragrant,
your name is perfume poured out;
    therefore the maidens love you.
4 Draw me after you, let us make haste.
    The king has brought me into his
    chambers.
We will exult and rejoice in you;
    we will extol your love more than wine;
    rightly do they love you.

Love's Boast

5 I am black and beautiful,
    O daughters of Jerusalem,
like the tents of Kē'dar,
    like the curtains of Solomon.
6 Do not gaze at me because I am dark,
    because the sun has gazed on me.
My mother's sons were angry with me;
    they made me keeper of the vineyards,
    but my own vineyard I have not kept!
7 Tell me, you whom my soul loves,
    where you pasture your flock,
    where you make it lie down at noon;

for why should I be like one who is veiled
    beside the flocks of your companions?
8 If you do not know,
    O fairest among women,
follow the tracks of the flock,
    and pasture your kids
    beside the shepherds' tents.

Vision of the Beloved

9 I compare you, my love,
    to a mare among Pharaoh's chariots.
10 Your cheeks are comely with ornaments,
    your neck with strings of jewels.
11 We will make you ornaments of gold,
    studded with silver.

12 While the king was on his couch,
    my nard gave forth its fragrance.
13 My beloved is to me a bag of myrrh
    that lies between my breasts.
14 My beloved is to me a cluster of henna
    blossoms
    in the vineyards of En-ge'di.

15 Ah, you are beautiful, my love;
    ah, you are beautiful;
    your eyes are doves.
16 Ah, you are beautiful, my beloved,
    truly lovely.

AFRICAN AMERICAN

Black and Beautiful

I am black and beautiful,
O daughters of Jerusalem,
like the tents of Kē′dar,
like the curtains of Solomon.
(Song 1.5)

Who is speaking to us in this Scripture text? Who is so boldly and confidently proclaiming to us that she is black and beautiful? Some traditions say this is the bride of Solomon, the son of David and the third king of Israel.

Most of the people in the Old Testament world were black Africans or Afro-Asiatics (Asians of black African heritage). They had various shades of dark skin. In Song 1.5, the bride describes herself as black as the tents of Kē′dar; in 5.10, she describes her lover as ruddy (reddish) in color.

Some African Americans are ruddy; others are darker. Together, all African Americans are a rainbow of blackness. Whatever shade they are, it is good. And if you are one of them, you are black and beautiful!

▸ Song 1.5

Our couch is green;
17   the beams of our house are cedar,
our rafters*a* are pine.

I am a rose*b* of Sharon,
a lily of the valleys.

2 As a lily among brambles,
so is my love among maidens.

3 As an apple tree among the trees of the
wood,
so is my beloved among young men.
With great delight I sat in his shadow,
and his fruit was sweet to my taste.
4 He brought me to the banqueting house,
and his intention toward me was love.
5 Sustain me with raisins,
refresh me with apples;
for I am faint with love.
6 O that his left hand were under my head,
and that his right hand embraced me!

7 I adjure you, O daughters of Jerusalem,
by the gazelles or the wild does:
do not stir up or awaken love
until it is ready!

Springtime Rhapsody

8 The voice of my beloved!
Look, he comes,
leaping upon the mountains,
bounding over the hills.
9 My beloved is like a gazelle
or a young stag.
Look, there he stands
behind our wall,
gazing in at the windows,
looking through the lattice.

---

a Meaning of Heb uncertain   *b* Heb *crocus*

NATIVE AMERICAN

Romantic Love

God loves us passionately and seeks us with the enthusiasm of a lover who memorizes every detail and cherishes every moment (Song 1.9–17). Romantic, playful love was created by God for us to enjoy. The way we express such love can bring joy and delight; it also can devastate and destroy if it is abused and not respected. Be careful with love. God gave us our sexuality as a gift, not as a weapon.

Hear the tender respect of this love poem from the Cherokee tradition:

You are part of me now
You touched me.
With your kindness and love
So enchanted.
Your soft lips are kind.
Your eyes glow with life.
I'm glad you touched me.
You're part of me now.
(Lloyd Carl Owle, "You Are Part of Me")

▸ Song 1.9–17

S
O
N
G

10 My beloved speaks and says to me:
   "Arise, my love, my fair one,
      and come away;
11 for now the winter is past,
      the rain is over and gone.
12 The flowers appear on the earth;
      the time of singing has come,
   and the voice of the turtledove
      is heard in our land.
13 The fig tree puts forth its figs,
      and the vines are in blossom;
      they give forth fragrance.
   Arise, my love, my fair one,
      and come away.
14 O my dove, in the clefts of
         the rock,
      in the covert of the cliff,
   let me see your face,
      let me hear your voice;
   for your voice is sweet,
      and your face is lovely.
15 Catch us the foxes,
      the little foxes,
   that ruin the vineyards—
      for our vineyards are in blossom."

16 My beloved is mine and I am his;
      he pastures his flock among
         the lilies.
17 Until the day breathes
      and the shadows flee,
   turn, my beloved, be like a gazelle
      or a young stag on the cleft
         mountains.^c

Love's Dream

Upon my bed at night
   I sought him whom my soul loves;
I sought him, but found him not;
   I called him, but he gave no answer.^d
2 "I will rise now and go about the city,
      in the streets and in the squares;
   I will seek him whom my soul loves."
      I sought him, but found him not.
3 The sentinels found me,
      as they went about in the city.
   "Have you seen him whom my soul loves?"
4 Scarcely had I passed them,
      when I found him whom my soul loves.
   I held him, and would not let him go
      until I brought him into my mother's
         house,
      and into the chamber of her that
         conceived me.
5 I adjure you, O daughters of Jerusalem,
      by the gazelles or the wild does:
   do not stir up or awaken love
      until it is ready!

The Groom and His Party Approach

6 What is that coming up from the
         wilderness,
   like a column of smoke,
   perfumed with myrrh and frankincense,
      with all the fragrant powders of the
         merchant?

---

c Or *on the mountains of Bether*; meaning of Heb uncertain
d Gk: Heb lacks this line

The Illusion of Pornography

LIVE IT!

"1-900-CALL IF YOU'RE LONELY!" Everywhere you look it seems, you can find ads for phone sex, pornographic magazines and videos, and Internet porn sites. People are lured into the immoral world of false love through an industry that preys on those who are weak and lost, those unfortunate souls searching for love in all the wrong places.

One interpretation proposes that the Song of Solomon is about passion and sexual longing between a bride and a bridegroom. Their love is committed: "My beloved is mine and I am his" (Song 2.16). Their love is at once both urgent ("Draw me after you, let us make haste" [1.4]) and patient ("Do not stir up or awaken love / until it is ready" [2.7]). This is not the kind of love offered to us in pornography, which has nothing at all to do with real love.

If you find yourself drawn to pornography, ask yourself: Is this God's purpose for human sexuality? Is this enriching to human love, or degrading? Pray for the strength to avoid the temptation and illusion of pornography.

▶  Song 2.1–17

7 Look, it is the litter of Solomon!
  Around it are sixty mighty men
    of the mighty men of Israel,
8 all equipped with swords
    and expert in war,
  each with his sword at his thigh
    because of alarms by night.
9 King Solomon made himself a palanquin
    from the wood of Lebanon.
10 He made its posts of silver,
    its back of gold, its seat of purple;
  its interior was inlaid with love.[e]
    Daughters of Jerusalem,
11   come out.
  Look, O daughters of Zion,
    at King Solomon,
  at the crown with which his mother
      crowned him
    on the day of his wedding,
    on the day of the gladness of his heart.

The Bride's Beauty Extolled

How beautiful you are, my love,
  how very beautiful!
Your eyes are doves
  behind your veil.
Your hair is like a flock of goats,
  moving down the slopes of Gil'e•ad.
2 Your teeth are like a flock of shorn ewes
    that have come up from the washing,
  all of which bear twins,
    and not one among them is bereaved.
3 Your lips are like a crimson thread,
    and your mouth is lovely.
  Your cheeks are like halves of a
      pomegranate
    behind your veil.
4 Your neck is like the tower of David,
    built in courses;
  on it hang a thousand bucklers,
    all of them shields of warriors.
5 Your two breasts are like two fawns,
    twins of a gazelle,
    that feed among the lilies.
6 Until the day breathes
    and the shadows flee,
  I will hasten to the mountain of myrrh
    and the hill of frankincense.
7 You are altogether beautiful, my love;
    there is no flaw in you.
8 Come with me from Lebanon, my bride;
    come with me from Lebanon.
  Depart[f] from the peak of A•ma'na,
    from the peak of Se̅'nir and Hermon,
  from the dens of lions,
    from the mountains of leopards.

9 You have ravished my heart, my sister, my
      bride,
  you have ravished my heart with a glance
      of your eyes,
    with one jewel of your necklace.

10 How sweet is your love, my sister, my bride!
    how much better is your love than wine,
    and the fragrance of your oils than any
      spice!
11 Your lips distill nectar, my bride;
    honey and milk are under your tongue;
  the scent of your garments is like the
      scent of Lebanon.
12 A garden locked is my sister, my bride,
    a garden locked, a fountain sealed.
13 Your channel[e] is an orchard of
      pomegranates
    with all choicest fruits,
    henna with nard,
14 nard and saffron, calamus and cinnamon,
    with all trees of frankincense,
  myrrh and aloes,
    with all chief spices—
15 a garden fountain, a well of living water,
    and flowing streams from Lebanon.

16 Awake, O north wind,
    and come, O south wind!
  Blow upon my garden
    that its fragrance may be wafted abroad.
  Let my beloved come to his garden,
    and eat its choicest fruits.

I come to my garden, my sister, my bride;
  I gather my myrrh with my spice,
  I eat my honeycomb with my honey,
  I drink my wine with my milk.

Eat, friends, drink,
  and be drunk with love.

_____
e Meaning of Heb uncertain   *f* Or *Look*

Another Dream

2 I slept, but my heart was awake.
  Listen! my beloved is knocking.
  "Open to me, my sister, my love,
    my dove, my perfect one;
  for my head is wet with dew,
    my locks with the drops of the night."
3 I had put off my garment;
    how could I put it on again?
  I had bathed my feet;
    how could I soil them?
4 My beloved thrust his hand into the
    opening,
    and my inmost being yearned for him.
5 I arose to open to my beloved,
    and my hands dripped with myrrh,
  my fingers with liquid myrrh,
    upon the handles of the bolt.

PRAY IT
The Song of Songs

If human love is a reflection of divine
love, then could parts of this love poem
called the Song of Solomon be understood as prayers? Could you read parts of
it as your words to God, and other parts
as God's words to you? Look at these
sections:

■ **2.2–6.** a prayer describing your passion
  for God
■ **5.6–8.** a prayer to God when God
  seems absent
■ **8.6–7.** God's words of love to you

The words may seem strange in this
context, but if we are passionate about
pursuing a human relationship, why
can't we be passionate about pursuing
our relationship with God? Some of the
greatest saints expressed their love of
God as a passionate, romantic love. You
can do the same in your prayer with God!

6 I opened to my beloved,
    but my beloved had turned and was
      gone.
  My soul failed me when he spoke.
  I sought him, but did not find him;
    I called him, but he gave no answer.
7 Making their rounds in the city
    the sentinels found me;

they beat me, they wounded me,
  they took away my mantle,
    those sentinels of the walls.
8 I adjure you, O daughters of Jerusalem,
    if you find my beloved,
  tell him this:
    I am faint with love.

Praise for the Bridegroom

9 What is your beloved more than another
      beloved,
    O fairest among women?
  What is your beloved more than another
      beloved,
    that you thus adjure us?

10 My beloved is all radiant and ruddy,
    distinguished among ten thousand.
11 His head is the finest gold;
    his locks are wavy,
    black as a raven.
12 His eyes are like doves
    beside springs of water,
  bathed in milk,
    fitly set. g
13 His cheeks are like beds of spices,
    yielding fragrance.
  His lips are lilies,
    distilling liquid myrrh.
14 His arms are rounded gold,
    set with jewels.
  His body is ivory work, g
    encrusted with sapphires.h
15 His legs are alabaster columns,
    set upon bases of gold.
  His appearance is like Lebanon,
    choice as the cedars.
16 His speech is most sweet,
    and he is altogether desirable.
  This is my beloved and this is my friend,
    O daughters of Jerusalem.

Where has your beloved gone,
  O fairest among women?
Which way has your beloved turned,
  that we may seek him with you?

2 My beloved has gone down to his garden,
    to the beds of spices,
  to pasture his flock in the gardens,
    and to gather lilies.
3 I am my beloved's and my beloved is mine;
    he pastures his flock among the lilies.

g Meaning of Heb uncertain   h Heb *lapis lazuli*

The Bride's Matchless Beauty

4 You are beautiful as Tir'zah, my love,
    comely as Jerusalem,
    terrible as an army with banners.

did you KNOW?

Sex in the Old Testament

Through its surprisingly graphic sexual content (see, for example, 7.1–9), the Song of Solomon has surprised many generations of readers. It reminds us that one of the richest images of the Old Testament is a sexual one: God as the faithful lover of Israel. In Ex 20.5, we hear of God's jealous love of the Chosen People. By the time of the early prophets, the image of God as lover was fully developed: "On that day, says the LORD, you will call me, 'My husband'" (Hos 2.16).

Because of ancient Israel's conviction that human love reflects divine love—and vice versa—there was a high regard for human sexuality. This regard was reflected in Israel's sexual morality. Free-for-all sex stood in clear contradiction of the holiness of God, whose faithful love was the model for all human love. The Ten Commandments prohibit not only having sex with someone else's spouse but also desiring someone else's spouse.

Despite these high standards, some Bible stories do not comment on the morality of behavior that would be unacceptable in Christian morality. They make no comment on the many patriarchs and kings who have more than one wife, and take for granted an inferior status of women in marriage. Because of problems like these, we must remember to read biblical passages in light of the *whole* Bible and the Christian tradition. In the Old Testament, we find the seeds of Christian sexual morality, not its full flower.

5 Turn away your eyes from me,
    for they overwhelm me!
  Your hair is like a flock of goats,
    moving down the slopes of Gil'e·ad.
6 Your teeth are like a flock of ewes,
    that have come up from the washing;

all of them bear twins,
    and not one among them is bereaved.
7 Your cheeks are like halves of a
        pomegranate
    behind your veil.
8 There are sixty queens and eighty
        concubines,
    and maidens without number.
9 My dove, my perfect one, is the only one,
    the darling of her mother,
    flawless to her that bore her.
  The maidens saw her and called her happy;
    the queens and concubines also, and they
        praised her.
10 "Who is this that looks forth like the dawn,
    fair as the moon, bright as the sun,
    terrible as an army with banners?"

11 I went down to the nut orchard,
    to look at the blossoms of the valley,
  to see whether the vines had budded,
    whether the pomegranates were in
        bloom.
12 Before I was aware, my fancy set me
    in a chariot beside my prince.*i*

13*j* Return, return, O Shū'lam·mīte!
    Return, return, that we may look
        upon you.

  Why should you look upon the
        Shū'lam·mīte,
    as upon a dance before two armies?*k*

Expressions of Praise

7 How graceful are your feet in sandals,
    O queenly maiden!
  Your rounded thighs are like jewels,
    the work of a master hand.
2 Your navel is a rounded bowl
    that never lacks mixed wine.
  Your belly is a heap of wheat,
    encircled with lilies.
3 Your two breasts are like two fawns,
    twins of a gazelle.
4 Your neck is like an ivory tower.
  Your eyes are pools in Hesh'bon,
    by the gate of Bath-rab'bim.
  Your nose is like a tower of Lebanon,
    overlooking Damascus.
5 Your head crowns you like Car'mel,
    and your flowing locks are like purple;
    a king is held captive in the tresses.*l*

---

i Cn: Meaning of Heb uncertain   *j* Ch 7.1 in Heb
k Or *dance of Mahanaim*   *l* Meaning of Heb uncertain

6 How fair and pleasant you are,
     O loved one, delectable maiden! [m]
7 You are stately [n] as a palm tree,
     and your breasts are like its clusters.
8 I say I will climb the palm tree
     and lay hold of its branches.
   O may your breasts be like clusters of the
          vine,
     and the scent of your breath like apples,
9 and your kisses [o] like the best wine
     that goes down [p] smoothly,
     gliding over lips and teeth. [q]

10 I am my beloved's,
     and his desire is for me.
11 Come, my beloved,
     let us go forth into the fields,
     and lodge in the villages;
12 let us go out early to the vineyards,
     and see whether the vines have budded,
   whether the grape blossoms have opened
     and the pomegranates are in bloom.
   There I will give you my love.
13 The mandrakes give forth fragrance,
     and over our doors are all choice fruits,
   new as well as old,
     which I have laid up for you, O my
          beloved.
   O that you were like a brother to me,
     who nursed at my mother's breast!
   If I met you outside, I would kiss you,
     and no one would despise me.
2 I would lead you and bring you
     into the house of my mother,
     and into the chamber of the one who
          bore me. [r]
   I would give you spiced wine to drink,
     the juice of my pomegranates.
3 O that his left hand were under my head,
     and that his right hand embraced me!
4 I adjure you, O daughters of Jerusalem,
     do not stir up or awaken love
     until it is ready!

Homecoming

5 Who is that coming up from the wilderness,
     leaning upon her beloved?

   Under the apple tree I awakened you.
   There your mother was in labor with you;
     there she who bore you was in labor.

6 Set me as a seal upon your heart,
     as a seal upon your arm;
   for love is strong as death,
     passion fierce as the grave.
   Its flashes are flashes of fire,
     a raging flame.
7 Many waters cannot quench love,
     neither can floods drown it.
   If one offered for love
     all the wealth of one's house,
     it would be utterly scorned.

8 We have a little sister,
     and she has no breasts.
   What shall we do for our sister,
     on the day when she is spoken for?
9 If she is a wall,
     we will build upon her a battlement of
          silver;
   but if she is a door,
     we will enclose her with boards of cedar.
10 I was a wall,
     and my breasts were like towers;
   then I was in his eyes
     as one who brings [s] peace.
11 Solomon had a vineyard at Bāʹal-haʹmon;
     he entrusted the vineyard to keepers;
     each one was to bring for its fruit a
          thousand pieces of silver.
12 My vineyard, my very own, is for myself;
     you, O Solomon, may have the
          thousand,
   and the keepers of the fruit two
          hundred!

13 O you who dwell in the gardens,
     my companions are listening for your
          voice;
     let me hear it.

14 Make haste, my beloved,
     and be like a gazelle
   or a young stag
     upon the mountains of spices!

---

m Syr: Heb *in delights*   *n* Heb *This your stature is*
o Heb *palate*   *p* Heb *down for my lover*   *q* Gk Syr Vg:
Heb *lips of sleepers*   *r* Gk Syr: Heb *my mother; she* (or *you*)
will teach me   *s* Or *finds*

Do you know what life was like for your great-grandparents? Were they, or other members of your family, immigrants to the United States? How much of their history do you know? Time and distance have a way of fading the memories that keep our roots alive. The same was true for the ancient Jewish people after they had settled in different countries. The Wisdom of Solomon was written to remind them of their roots and the wisdom of their traditions.

In-depth

The Jewish people living in Alexandria, Egypt, in the first century B.C. had long forgotten the difficult transition their ancestors had experienced in moving from Judea. In fact, they had come to feel so much at home in Alexandria that certain leaders began to fear that the Jewish faith and way of life might be lost (see "Diaspora Jews," near Esth 2.5). One of those leaders wrote the Wisdom of Solomon to encourage the "displaced" Jews to remain faithful to their heritage. Although incorporating new ideas into traditional arguments, the author insists that true wisdom is, in fact, very old. Its course can be traced "from the beginning of creation" (Wis 6.22).

The Wisdom of Solomon grapples with another problem—good versus evil—in a refreshing way. The author is convinced that there will be a final judgment, in which good people "will stand with great confidence," and evil people will shake "with dreadful fear" (5.1,2). What is more, the good will live forever (5.15), whereas the evil will disappear without a trace (4.18–19). Like Second Maccabees, the Wisdom of Solomon sees life after death as the answer to the troubling question Why do innocent people suffer when God is good and just?

The Wisdom of Solomon claims King Solomon as its honorary author, even though it was written long after his death. In this quiet way, it reminds the Jewish faithful that they must never forget their roots in their ancient faith, even though they feel at home in their new land. The book shows how people of faith take the best of their history and tradition to find new answers in new situations.

Quick Facts

Author
unknown, writing around 50 B.C., making this the latest of all Old Testament books

Theme
the reward of the righteous, the praise of wisdom, the importance of trust in God

Of Note
The book is not found in every translation of the Old Testament (see "The Case of the Missing Books," near Tob 1.16).

Wisdom

Exhortation to Uprightness
(Wis 6.1–11)

Love righteousness, you rulers of the earth,
think of the Lord in goodness
and seek him with sincerity of heart;
2 because he is found by those who do not
put him to the test,
and manifests himself to those who do not
distrust him.
3 For perverse thoughts separate people
from God,
and when his power is tested, it exposes the
foolish;
4 because wisdom will not enter a deceitful
soul,
or dwell in a body enslaved to sin.
5 For a holy and disciplined spirit will flee
from deceit,
and will leave foolish thoughts behind,
and will be ashamed at the approach of
unrighteousness.

6 For wisdom is a kindly spirit,
but will not free blasphemers from the guilt
of their words;
because God is witness of their inmost
feelings,
and a true observer of their hearts, and a
hearer of their tongues.

7 Because the spirit of the Lord has filled the
world,
and that which holds all things together
knows what is said,
8 therefore those who utter unrighteous things
will not escape notice,
and justice, when it punishes, will not pass
them by.
9 For inquiry will be made into the counsels
of the ungodly,
and a report of their words will come to the
Lord,
to convict them of their lawless deeds;
10 because a jealous ear hears all things,
and the sound of grumbling does not go
unheard.
11 Beware then of useless grumbling,
and keep your tongue from slander;
because no secret word is without result,*a*
and a lying mouth destroys the soul.
12 Do not invite death by the error of your
life,
or bring on destruction by the works of
your hands;
13 because God did not make death,
and he does not delight in the death of the
living.

---

a Or will go unpunished

14 For he created all things so that they might exist;
the generative forces[b] of the world are wholesome,
and there is no destructive poison in them,
and the dominion[c] of Hades is not on earth.
15 For righteousness is immortal.

PRAY IT!

God Knows Our Heart

God, you know my heart (Wis 1.6) even better than I do. This could scare me, or it could give me peace—the peace of knowing that despite my weakness and sin, you still love me. I choose to feel peace! And knowing that you see my heart truly and still love me, I choose to do good. Give me the courage to do the right thing. Help me never to say a word meant to injure another person. Give me too the wisdom of loving justice, so that my heart might be a reflection of your own. Amen.

▸ Wis 1.6–15

Life as the Ungodly See It

16 But the ungodly by their words and deeds summoned death;[d]
considering him a friend, they pined away and made a covenant with him,
because they are fit to belong to his company.
For they reasoned unsoundly, saying to themselves,
"Short and sorrowful is our life,
and there is no remedy when a life comes to its end,
and no one has been known to return from Hades.
2 For we were born by mere chance,
and hereafter we shall be as though we had never been,
for the breath in our nostrils is smoke,
and reason is a spark kindled by the beating of our hearts;
3 when it is extinguished, the body will turn to ashes,
and the spirit will dissolve like empty air.
4 Our name will be forgotten in time,
and no one will remember our works;
our life will pass away like the traces of a cloud,
and be scattered like mist
that is chased by the rays of the sun
and overcome by its heat.
5 For our allotted time is the passing of a shadow,
and there is no return from our death,
because it is sealed up and no one turns back.
6 "Come, therefore, let us enjoy the good things that exist,
and make use of the creation to the full as in youth.
7 Let us take our fill of costly wine and perfumes,
and let no flower of spring pass us by.
8 Let us crown ourselves with rosebuds before they wither.
9 Let none of us fail to share in our revelry;
everywhere let us leave signs of enjoyment,
because this is our portion, and this our lot.
10 Let us oppress the righteous poor man;
let us not spare the widow
or regard the gray hairs of the aged.
11 But let our might be our law of right,
for what is weak proves itself to be useless.
12 "Let us lie in wait for the righteous man,
because he is inconvenient to us and opposes our actions;
he reproaches us for sins against the law,
and accuses us of sins against our training.
13 He professes to have knowledge of God,
and calls himself a child[e] of the Lord.
14 He became to us a reproof of our thoughts;
15 the very sight of him is a burden to us,
because his manner of life is unlike that of others,
and his ways are strange.
16 We are considered by him as something base,
and he avoids our ways as unclean;
he calls the last end of the righteous happy,
and boasts that God is his father.
17 Let us see if his words are true,
and let us test what will happen at the end of his life;
18 for if the righteous man is God's child, he will help him,
and will deliver him from the hand of his adversaries.
19 Let us test him with insult and torture,

WIS

so that we may find out how gentle he is,
and make trial of his forbearance.
20 Let us condemn him to a shameful death,
for, according to what he says, he will be
protected."

Error of the Wicked
(Cp Gen 1.26–27)

21 Thus they reasoned, but they were led
astray,
for their wickedness blinded them,
22 and they did not know the secret purposes
of God,
nor hoped for the wages of holiness,
nor discerned the prize for blameless souls;
23 for God created us for incorruption,
and made us in the image of his own
eternity,*f*
24 but through the devil's envy death entered
the world,
and those who belong to his company
experience it.

The Destiny of the Righteous
(Wis 4.17)

But the souls of the righteous are in the hand
of God,
and no torment will ever touch them.
2 In the eyes of the foolish they seemed to
have died,
and their departure was thought to be a
disaster,
3 and their going from us to be their
destruction;
but they are at peace.
4 For though in the sight of others they were
punished,
their hope is full of immortality.
5 Having been disciplined a little, they will
receive great good,
because God tested them and found them
worthy of himself;
6 like gold in the furnace he tried them,
and like a sacrificial burnt offering he
accepted them.
7 In the time of their visitation they will shine
forth,
and will run like sparks through the stubble.
8 They will govern nations and rule over
peoples,
and the Lord will reign over them forever.
9 Those who trust in him will understand
truth,
and the faithful will abide with him in love,

because grace and mercy are upon his holy
ones,
and he watches over his elect.*g*

The Destiny of the Ungodly

10 But the ungodly will be punished as their
reasoning deserves,
those who disregarded the righteous*h*
and rebelled against the Lord;
11 for those who despise wisdom and
instruction are miserable.
Their hope is vain, their labors are
unprofitable,
and their works are useless.
12 Their wives are foolish, and their children
evil;
13 their offspring are accursed.

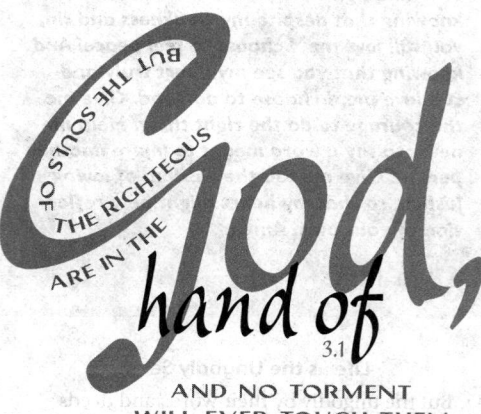

BUT THE SOULS
OF THE RIGHTEOUS
ARE IN THE
God,
hand of
3.1
AND NO TORMENT
WILL EVER TOUCH THEM

On Childlessness
(Sir 16.3)

For blessed is the barren woman who is
undefiled,
who has not entered into a sinful union;
she will have fruit when God examines
souls.
14 Blessed also is the eunuch whose hands
have done no lawless deed,
and who has not devised wicked things
against the Lord;
for special favor will be shown him for his
faithfulness,
and a place of great delight in the temple of
the Lord.
15 For the fruit of good labors is renowned,
and the root of understanding does not fail.

---

f Other ancient authorities read *nature*   *g* Text of this
line uncertain; omitted by some ancient authorities.
Compare 4.15   *h* Or *what is right*

16 But children of adulterers will not come to
maturity,
and the offspring of an unlawful union will
perish.
17 Even if they live long they will be held of
no account,
and finally their old age will be without
honor.
18 If they die young, they will have no hope
and no consolation on the day of judgment.
19 For the end of an unrighteous generation is
grievous.

Better than this is childlessness with virtue,
for in the memory of virtue[i] is immortality,
because it is known both by God and by
mortals.
2 When it is present, people imitate[j] it,
and they long for it when it has gone;
throughout all time it marches, crowned in
triumph,
victor in the contest for prizes that are
undefiled.
3 But the prolific brood of the ungodly will
be of no use,
and none of their illegitimate seedlings will
strike a deep root
or take a firm hold.
4 For even if they put forth boughs for a
while,
standing insecurely they will be shaken by
the wind,
and by the violence of the winds they will
be uprooted.
5 The branches will be broken off before they
come to maturity,
and their fruit will be useless,
not ripe enough to eat, and good for
nothing.
6 For children born of unlawful unions
are witnesses of evil against their parents
when God examines them.[k]
7 But the righteous, though they die early,
will be at rest.
8 For old age is not honored for length of
time,
or measured by number of years;
9 but understanding is gray hair for anyone,
and a blameless life is ripe old age.
10 There were some who pleased God and
were loved by him,
and while living among sinners were
taken up.
11 They were caught up so that evil might not
change their understanding
or guile deceive their souls.

12 For the fascination of wickedness obscures
what is good,
and roving desire perverts the innocent
mind.
13 Being perfected in a short time, they
fulfilled long years;
14 for their souls were pleasing to the Lord,
therefore he took them quickly from the
midst of wickedness.
15 Yet the peoples saw and did not understand,
or take such a thing to heart,
that God's grace and mercy are with his
elect,
and that he watches over his holy ones.

The Triumph of the Righteous

16 The righteous who have died will condemn
the ungodly who are living,
and youth that is quickly perfected[l] will
condemn the prolonged old age of
the unrighteous.
17 For they will see the end of the wise,
and will not understand what the Lord
purposed for them,
and for what he kept them safe.
18 The unrighteous[m] will see, and will have
contempt for them,
but the Lord will laugh them to scorn.
After this they will become dishonored
corpses,
and an outrage among the dead forever;
19 because he will dash them speechless to the
ground,
and shake them from the foundations;
they will be left utterly dry and barren,
and they will suffer anguish,
and the memory of them will perish.

The Final Judgment

20 They will come with dread when their sins
are reckoned up,
and their lawless deeds will convict them to
their face.
Then the righteous will stand with great
confidence
in the presence of those who have
oppressed them
and those who make light of their labors.
2 When the unrighteous[n] see them, they will
be shaken with dreadful fear,
and they will be amazed at the unexpected
salvation of the righteous.

---

i Gk it   j Other ancient authorities read *honor*   k Gk *at
their examination*   l Or *ended*   m Gk *They*   n Gk *they*

3 They will speak to one another in
        repentance,
    and in anguish of spirit they will groan,
        and say,
4 "These are persons whom we once held in
        derision
    and made a byword of reproach—fools that
        we were!
    We thought that their lives were madness
    and that their end was without honor.
5 Why have they been numbered among the
        children of God?
    And why is their lot among the saints?
6 So it was we who strayed from the way of
        truth,
    and the light of righteousness did not shine
        on us,
    and the sun did not rise upon us.
7 We took our fill of the paths of lawlessness
        and destruction,
    and we journeyed through trackless deserts,
    but the way of the Lord we have not
        known.
8 What has our arrogance profited us?
    And what good has our boasted wealth
        brought us?
9 "All those things have vanished like a
        shadow,
    and like a rumor that passes by;
10 like a ship that sails through the billowy
        water,
    and when it has passed no trace can be
        found,
    no track of its keel in the waves;
11 or as, when a bird flies through the air,
    no evidence of its passage is found;
    the light air, lashed by the beat of its
        pinions
    and pierced by the force of its rushing
        flight,
    is traversed by the movement of its wings,
    and afterward no sign of its coming is
        found there;
12 or as, when an arrow is shot at a target,
    the air, thus divided, comes together at
        once,
    so that no one knows its pathway.
13 So we also, as soon as we were born, ceased
        to be,
    and we had no sign of virtue to show,
    but were consumed in our wickedness."
14 Because the hope of the ungodly is like
        thistledown*o* carried by the wind,
    and like a light frost*p* driven away by a
        storm;

it is dispersed like smoke before the wind,
    and it passes like the remembrance of a
        guest who stays but a day.

The Reward of the Righteous
(Eph 6.10–20)

15 But the righteous live forever,
    and their reward is with the Lord;
    the Most High takes care of them.
16 Therefore they will receive a glorious crown
    and a beautiful diadem from the hand of
        the Lord,
    because with his right hand he will cover
        them,
    and with his arm he will shield them.
17 The Lord*q* will take his zeal as his whole
        armor,
    and will arm all creation to repel*r* his enemies;
18 he will put on righteousness as a
        breastplate,
    and wear impartial justice as a helmet;
19 he will take holiness as an invincible shield,
20 and sharpen stern wrath for a sword,
    and creation will join with him to fight
        against his frenzied foes.
21 Shafts of lightning will fly with true aim,
    and will leap from the clouds to the target,
        as from a well-drawn bow,
22 and hailstones full of wrath will be hurled
        as from a catapult;
    the water of the sea will rage against them,
    and rivers will relentlessly overwhelm them;
23 a mighty wind will rise against them,
    and like a tempest it will winnow them away.
    Lawlessness will lay waste the whole earth,
    and evildoing will overturn the thrones of
        rulers.

Kings Should Seek Wisdom
(Rom 13.1)

6 Listen therefore, O kings, and understand;
    learn, O judges of the ends of the earth.
2 Give ear, you that rule over multitudes,
    and boast of many nations.
3 For your dominion was given you from the
        Lord,
    and your sovereignty from the Most High;
    he will search out your works and inquire
        into your plans.
4 Because as servants of his kingdom you did
        not rule rightly,
    or keep the law,
    or walk according to the purpose of God,

---

o Other ancient authorities read *dust*   *p* Other ancient
authorities read *spider's web*   *q* Gk He   *r* Or *punish*

5 he will come upon you terribly and swiftly,
  because severe judgment falls on those in
      high places.
6 For the lowliest may be pardoned
      in mercy,
  but the mighty will be mightily tested.
7 For the Lord of all will not stand in awe of
      anyone,
  or show deference to greatness;
  because he himself made both small and
      great,
  and he takes thought for all alike.
8 But a strict inquiry is in store for the
      mighty.
9 To you then, O monarchs, my words are
      directed,
  so that you may learn wisdom and not
      transgress.
10 For they will be made holy who observe
      holy things in holiness,
  and those who have been taught them will
      find a defense.
11 Therefore set your desire on my words;
  long for them, and you will be
      instructed.

Description of Wisdom
(Cp Prov 8.1–36)

12 Wisdom is radiant and unfading,
  and she is easily discerned by those who
      love her,
  and is found by those who seek her.
13 She hastens to make herself known to those
      who desire her.
14 One who rises early to seek her will have no
      difficulty,

for she will be found sitting at the gate.
15 To fix one's thought on her is perfect
      understanding,
  and one who is vigilant on her account will
      soon be free from care,
16 because she goes about seeking those
      worthy of her,
  and she graciously appears to them in their
      paths,
  and meets them in every thought.
17 The beginning of wisdom[s] is the most
      sincere desire for instruction,
  and concern for instruction is love of her,
18 and love of her is the keeping of her laws,
  and giving heed to her laws is assurance of
      immortality,
19 and immortality brings one near to God;
20 so the desire for wisdom leads to a
      kingdom.

21 Therefore if you delight in thrones and
      scepters, O monarchs over the
      peoples,
  honor wisdom, so that you may reign
      forever.
22 I will tell you what wisdom is and how she
      came to be,
  and I will hide no secrets from you,
  but I will trace her course from the
      beginning of creation,
  and make knowledge of her clear,
  and I will not pass by the truth;
23 nor will I travel in the company of sickly
      envy,

---

[s] Gk *Her beginning*

Wisdom Speaks

> My name is Wisdom. In Greek, I am called Sophia. The Bible speaks of me as an aspect, or image, of God. I am sought after by many. I reveal myself to few. I appear many times in the Scriptures, yet I am elusive. What is it about me that is so attractive, so appealing? Solomon prayed for understanding, and I came to him. Indeed, wisdom is often associated with his name.

Those who seek me must desire deep in their heart to know me. That desire is the first step to finding me. The next is patience. Nothing of true and lasting importance comes quickly. I am not "fast food." In fact, you must experience a deep hunger before you can taste me. Quiet time is essential. You must be willing to simply be present, with no agenda. Imagine a "radiant and unfading" flame (Wis 6.12). Let that be your focus.

Soon, I will come to you. I will seek you out. I will meet you in your thoughts, and we will become friends. We will dance together, you and I. You will be changed, transformed. You will grow deeper, quieter, and peace will begin to fill your soul.

My name is Wisdom. I want to be your friend. I wait for you.

for envy*t* does not associate with wisdom.

24 The multitude of the wise is the salvation of
the world,
and a sensible king is the stability of any
people.

25 Therefore be instructed by my words, and
you will profit.

Solomon Like Other Mortals

I also am mortal, like everyone else,
a descendant of the first-formed child of
earth;
and in the womb of a mother I was molded
into flesh,

2 within the period of ten months, compacted
with blood,
from the seed of a man and the pleasure of
marriage.

3 And when I was born, I began to breathe
the common air,
and fell upon the kindred earth;
my first sound was a cry, as is true of all.

4 I was nursed with care in swaddling cloths.

5 For no king has had a different beginning of
existence;

6 there is for all one entrance into life, and
one way out.

Solomon's Respect for Wisdom
(1 Kings 3.3–9; Wis 9.1–18)

7 Therefore I prayed, and understanding was
given me;
I called on God, and the spirit of wisdom
came to me.

8 I preferred her to scepters and thrones,
and I accounted wealth as nothing in
comparison with her.

9 Neither did I liken to her any priceless gem,
because all gold is but a little sand in her
sight,
and silver will be accounted as clay
before her.

10 I loved her more than health and beauty,
and I chose to have her rather than light,
because her radiance never ceases.

11 All good things came to me along with her,
and in her hands uncounted wealth.

12 I rejoiced in them all, because wisdom leads
them;
but I did not know that she was their
mother.

13 I learned without guile and I impart without
grudging;
I do not hide her wealth,

NATIVE AMERICAN

The Source of Wisdom

Solomon valued wisdom above riches, authority, health, and beauty (Wis 7.7–10). Native
American spirituality values wisdom in a similar way. The elders are seen as the people's
connection to history and experience; they
are a source of wisdom and sound advice. In
fact, all of God's creation is seen as a potential
source of wisdom. Notice how this is reflected
in the following prayer from the Ojibwa (or
Anishinabe) tradition:

> *Oh Great Spirit, whose voice I hear in the*
> *winds*
> *And whose breath gives life to everyone,*
> *Hear me.*
> *I come to you as one of your many children;*
> *I am weak . . . I am small . . . I need your*
> *wisdom and your strength.*
> *Let me walk in beauty, and make my eyes ever*
> *behold the red and purple sunsets.*
> *Make my hands respect the things you have*
> *made, and make my ears sharp so I may*
> *hear your voice.*
> *Make me wise, so that I may understand what*
> *you have taught my people and*
> *The lessons you have hidden in each leaf and*
> *each rock.*
> *I ask for wisdom and strength,*
> *Not to be superior to my brothers, but to be*
> *able to fight my greatest enemy, myself.*
> *Make me ever ready to come before you with*
> *clean hands and a straight eye,*
> *So as life fades away as a fading sunset,*
> *My spirit may come to you without shame.*
> *(Author unknown, "Ojibwa Prayer")*

▶ Wis 7.7–14

14 for it is an unfailing treasure for mortals;
those who get it obtain friendship
with God,

---

t Gk *this*

commended for the gifts that come from
　　instruction.

Solomon Prays for Wisdom

15 May God grant me to speak with judgment,
　　and to have thoughts worthy of what I have
　　　　received;
　　for he is the guide even of wisdom
　　and the corrector of the wise.
16 For both we and our words are in his hand,
　　as are all understanding and skill in crafts.
17 For it is he who gave me unerring
　　　　knowledge of what exists,
　　to know the structure of the world and the
　　　　activity of the elements;
18 the beginning and end and middle of times,
　　the alternations of the solstices and the
　　　　changes of the seasons,
19 the cycles of the year and the constellations
　　　　of the stars,
20 the natures of animals and the tempers of
　　　　wild animals,
　　the powers of spirits[u] and the thoughts of
　　　　human beings,
　　the varieties of plants and the virtues of
　　　　roots;
21 I learned both what is secret and what is
　　　　manifest,
22 for wisdom, the fashioner of all things,
　　　　taught me.

The Nature of Wisdom
(Jn 1.1–14; Heb 1.1–4)

There is in her a spirit that is intelligent,
　　　　holy,
unique, manifold, subtle,
mobile, clear, unpolluted,
distinct, invulnerable, loving the good, keen,
irresistible, 23 beneficent, humane,
steadfast, sure, free from anxiety,
all-powerful, overseeing all,
and penetrating through all spirits
that are intelligent, pure, and altogether
　　　　subtle.
24 For wisdom is more mobile than any
　　　　motion;
　　because of her pureness she pervades and
　　　　penetrates all things.
25 For she is a breath of the power of God,
　　and a pure emanation of the glory of the
　　　　Almighty;
　　therefore nothing defiled gains entrance
　　　　into her.
26 For she is a reflection of eternal light,
　　a spotless mirror of the working of God,

and an image of his goodness.
27 Although she is but one, she can do all
　　　　things,
　　and while remaining in herself, she renews
　　　　all things;
　　in every generation she passes into holy
　　　　souls
　　and makes them friends of God, and
　　　　prophets;
28 for God loves nothing so much as the
　　　　person who lives with wisdom.
29 She is more beautiful than the sun,
　　and excels every constellation of the stars.
　　Compared with the light she is found to be
　　　　superior,
30 for it is succeeded by the night,
　　but against wisdom evil does not prevail.

---

u Or *winds*

How Do You Image God?

Old Testament writers sometimes
used attributes of God, such as spirit,
word, and justice, as titles for God. Wisdom is another of these titles. Each title
gives us some insight into God's nature,
although no one of them, or even all of
them together, can give us the whole
picture. The author of the Wisdom of
Solomon describes God's wisdom as a
woman, which gives us insight into God's
feminine dimension.

Read the qualities of wisdom given
in Wis 7.23—8.1. This passage summarizes the author's understanding of God's
nature. It was probably familiar to New
Testament authors. Aspects of it show up
in the Letter to the Hebrews (1.1–4) and
in the Gospel of John (1.1–14).

Explore your images of God. Choose
an attribute of God that is significant for
you. It might be love, faithfulness, truth,
or some other quality. Write a poem, like
the one in Wis 8.2–8, that describes this
quality as a person.

▶ Wis 7.23—8.8

W
I
S

She reaches mightily from one end of the
    earth to the other,
and she orders all things well.

Solomon's Love for Wisdom
(Cp Prov 8.22–31)

2 I loved her and sought her from my youth;
    I desired to take her for my bride,
    and became enamored of her beauty.
3 She glorifies her noble birth by living
        with God,
    and the Lord of all loves her.
4 For she is an initiate in the knowledge
        of God,
    and an associate in his works.
5 If riches are a desirable possession in life,
    what is richer than wisdom, the active cause
        of all things?
6 And if understanding is effective,
    who more than she is fashioner of what
        exists?
7 And if anyone loves righteousness,
    her labors are virtues;
    for she teaches self-control and prudence,
        justice and courage;
    nothing in life is more profitable for
        mortals than these.
8 And if anyone longs for wide experience,
    she knows the things of old, and infers the
        things to come;
    she understands turns of speech and the
        solutions of riddles;
    she has foreknowledge of signs and wonders
    and of the outcome of seasons and times.

Wisdom Indispensible to Rulers

9 Therefore I determined to take her to live
        with me,
    knowing that she would give me good
        counsel
    and encouragement in cares and grief.
10 Because of her I shall have glory among the
        multitudes
    and honor in the presence of the elders,
        though I am young.
11 I shall be found keen in judgment,
    and in the sight of rulers I shall be admired.
12 When I am silent they will wait for me,
    and when I speak they will give heed;
    if I speak at greater length,
    they will put their hands on their mouths.
13 Because of her I shall have immortality,
    and leave an everlasting remembrance to
        those who come after me.
14 I shall govern peoples,
    and nations will be subject to me;

15 dread monarchs will be afraid of me when
        they hear of me;
    among the people I shall show myself
        capable, and courageous in war.
16 When I enter my house, I shall find rest
        with her;
    for companionship with her has no
        bitterness,
    and life with her has no pain, but gladness
        and joy.
17 When I considered these things inwardly,
    and pondered in my heart
    that in kinship with wisdom there is
        immortality,
18 and in friendship with her, pure delight,
    and in the labors of her hands, unfailing
        wealth,
    and in the experience of her company,
        understanding,
    and renown in sharing her words,
    I went about seeking how to get her for
        myself.
19 As a child I was naturally gifted,
    and a good soul fell to my lot;
20 or rather, being good, I entered an undefiled
        body.
21 But I perceived that I would not possess
        wisdom unless God gave her
        to me—
    and it was a mark of insight to know whose
        gift she was—
    so I appealed to the Lord and
        implored him,
    and with my whole heart I said:

Solomon's Prayer for Wisdom
(1 Kings 3.3–9; Wis 7.7–22a)

"O God of my ancestors and Lord of mercy,
    who have made all things by your word,
2 and by your wisdom have formed
        humankind
    to have dominion over the creatures you
        have made,
3 and rule the world in holiness and
        righteousness,
    and pronounce judgment in uprightness of
        soul,
4 give me the wisdom that sits by your
        throne,
    and do not reject me from among your
        servants.
5 For I am your servant[v] the son of your
        serving girl,
    a man who is weak and short-lived,

---

v Gk *slave*

with little understanding of judgment and
laws;
6 for even one who is perfect among human
beings
will be regarded as nothing without the
wisdom that comes from you.
7 You have chosen me to be king of your
people
and to be judge over your sons and
daughters.
8 You have given command to build a temple
on your holy mountain,
and an altar in the city of your habitation,
a copy of the holy tent that you prepared
from the beginning.
9 With you is wisdom, she who knows your
works
and was present when you made the
world;
she understands what is pleasing in your
sight
and what is right according to your
commandments.
10 Send her forth from the holy heavens,
and from the throne of your glory
send her,
that she may labor at my side,
and that I may learn what is pleasing
to you.
11 For she knows and understands all things,
and she will guide me wisely in my
actions
and guard me with her glory.
12 Then my works will be acceptable,
and I shall judge your people justly,
and shall be worthy of the throne[w] of my
father.
13 For who can learn the counsel of God?
Or who can discern what the Lord wills?
14 For the reasoning of mortals is worthless,
and our designs are likely to fail;
15 for a perishable body weighs down
the soul,
and this earthy tent burdens the thoughtful[x]
mind.
16 We can hardly guess at what is on earth,
and what is at hand we find with labor;
but who has traced out what is in the
heavens?
17 Who has learned your counsel,
unless you have given wisdom
and sent your holy spirit from on high?
18 And thus the paths of those on earth were
set right,
and people were taught what pleases you,
and were saved by wisdom."

The Work of Wisdom
from Adam to Moses

Wisdom[y] protected the first-formed father of
the world, when he alone had been
created;
she delivered him from his transgression,
2 and gave him strength to rule all things.
3 But when an unrighteous man departed
from her in his anger,
he perished because in rage he killed his
brother.
4 When the earth was flooded because of
him, wisdom again saved it,
steering the righteous man by a paltry piece
of wood.
5 Wisdom[y] also, when the nations in wicked
agreement had been put to
confusion,
recognized the righteous man and preserved
him blameless before God,
and kept him strong in the face of his
compassion for his child.
6 Wisdom[y] rescued a righteous man when the
ungodly were perishing;
he escaped the fire that descended on the
Five Cities.[z]
7 Evidence of their wickedness still remains:
a continually smoking wasteland,
plants bearing fruit that does not ripen,
and a pillar of salt standing as a monument
to an unbelieving soul.
8 For because they passed wisdom by,
they not only were hindered from
recognizing the good,
but also left for humankind a reminder of
their folly,
so that their failures could never go
unnoticed.
9 Wisdom rescued from troubles those who
served her.
10 When a righteous man fled from his
brother's wrath,
she guided him on straight paths;
she showed him the kingdom of God,
and gave him knowledge of holy things;
she prospered him in his labors,
and increased the fruit of his toil.
11 When his oppressors were covetous,
she stood by him and made him rich.
12 She protected him from his enemies,
and kept him safe from those who lay in
wait for him;

w Gk *thrones*   x Or *anxious*   y Gk *She*   z Or *on
Pentapolis*

WORDS FROM A FATHER TO HIS SON!

The following translation of a text originally written in Nahuatl is the wisdom of a native father in sixteenth-century Mexico. This spirit of wisdom still exists in many Mexican families.

My son, . . . my precious feather, you have come to life, been born, been blessed to come into the world in the land of our Lord. The One for whom we live forged your life, gave you shape. We, your mother and father, have watched over you; your aunts and uncles, all your family, have watched over you, have cried for you, have suffered for you that you might be born. (P. 49)

Love and serve others in holiness; respect and obey your mother and father, and do their hearts' desire. Your gift of service, obedience, and respect will be the recompense they deserve. (P. 53)

Push away from you all that is not good: that which is wrong, all the things that dishonor you. . . . Do no damage to the community, or the peace. Because if you do bad things, you will not come away unscathed: you must eventually suffer for such actions. (P. 79)

With these words, I encourage and strengthen you; through them, I console you. Throw away nothing I have told you, nothing you have heard. May all this be your inspiration, helping you always to remember the Lord, our God. (P. 86)

(Miguel Léon-Portilla and Librado Silva Galeana, *Huehuehtlahtolli*, as translated by Richard Wood)

in his arduous contest she gave him the
victory,
so that he might learn that godliness is
more powerful than anything else.

13 When a righteous man was sold, wisdom[a]
did not desert him,
but delivered him from sin.
She descended with him into the dungeon,
14 and when he was in prison she did not
leave him,
until she brought him the scepter of a
kingdom
and authority over his masters.
Those who accused him she showed to be
false,
and she gave him everlasting honor.

Wisdom Led the Israelites out of Egypt
(Ex 13—15)

15 A holy people and blameless race
wisdom delivered from a nation of
oppressors.
16 She entered the soul of a servant of the
Lord,
and withstood dread kings with wonders
and signs.

17 She gave to holy people the reward of their
labors;
she guided them along a marvelous way,
and became a shelter to them by day,
and a starry flame through the night.
18 She brought them over the Red Sea,
and led them through deep waters;
19 but she drowned their enemies,
and cast them up from the depth of the sea.
20 Therefore the righteous plundered the ungodly;
they sang hymns, O Lord, to your holy name,
and praised with one accord your defending
hand;
21 for wisdom opened the mouths of those
who were mute,
and made the tongues of infants speak
clearly.

Wisdom Led the Israelites
through the Desert
(Ex 15—17)

11 Wisdom[b] prospered their works by the hand
of a holy prophet.
2 They journeyed through an uninhabited
wilderness,

---

a Gk *she*   b Gk *She*

and pitched their tents in untrodden
      places.

3 They withstood their enemies and fought off
      their foes.

4 When they were thirsty, they called
      upon you,
and water was given them out of flinty
      rock,
and from hard stone a remedy for their
      thirst.

5 For through the very things by which their
      enemies were punished,
they themselves received benefit in their
      need.

6 Instead of the fountain of an ever-flowing
      river,
stirred up and defiled with blood

7 in rebuke for the decree to kill the infants,
you gave them abundant water
      unexpectedly,

8 showing by their thirst at that time
how you punished their enemies.

9 For when they were tried, though they were
      being disciplined in mercy,
they learned how the ungodly were
      tormented when judged in wrath.

10 For you tested them as a parent*c* does in
      warning,
but you examined the ungodly*d* as a stern
      king does in condemnation.

11 Whether absent or present, they were
      equally distressed,

12 for a twofold grief possessed them,
and a groaning at the memory of what had
      occurred.

13 For when they heard that through their own
      punishments
the righteous*e* had received benefit, they
      perceived it was the Lord's doing.

14 For though they had mockingly rejected him
      who long before had been cast out
      and exposed,
at the end of the events they marveled
      at him,
when they felt thirst in a different way from
      the righteous.

Punishment of the Wicked
(Ex 7—11)

15 In return for their foolish and wicked
      thoughts,
which led them astray to worship irrational
      serpents and worthless animals,
you sent upon them a multitude of
      irrational creatures to punish them,

16 so that they might learn that one is
      punished by the very things by
      which one sins.

17 For your all-powerful hand,
which created the world out of formless
      matter,
did not lack the means to send upon them
      a multitude of bears, or bold lions,

18 or newly-created unknown beasts full of
      rage,
or such as breathe out fiery breath,
or belch forth a thick pall of smoke,
or flash terrible sparks from their eyes;

19 not only could the harm they did destroy
      people,*f*
but the mere sight of them could kill by
      fright.

20 Even apart from these, people*e* could fall at
      a single breath
when pursued by justice
and scattered by the breath of your power.
But you have arranged all things by measure
      and number and weight.

God Is Powerful and Merciful

21 For it is always in your power to show great
      strength,
and who can withstand the might of
      your arm?

22 Because the whole world before you is like
      a speck that tips the scales,
and like a drop of morning dew that falls
      on the ground.

23 But you are merciful to all, for you can do
      all things,
and you overlook people's sins, so that they
      may repent.

24 For you love all things that exist,
and detest none of the things that you have
      made,
for you would not have made anything if
      you had hated it.

25 How would anything have endured if you
      had not willed it?
Or how would anything not called forth by
      you have been preserved?

26 You spare all things, for they are yours,
      O Lord, you who love the living.
For your immortal spirit is in all things.

2 Therefore you correct little by little those
      who trespass,
and you remind and warn them of the
      things through which they sin,

---

c Gk *a father*   *d* Gk *those*   *e* Gk *they*   *f* Gk *them*

so that they may be freed from wickedness
     and put their trust in you, O Lord.

The Sins of the Canaanites
(Ex 23.20–33; Deut 18.9–14)

3 Those who lived long ago in your
          holy land
4 you hated for their detestable practices,
     their works of sorcery and unholy rites,
5 their merciless slaughter*g* of children,
     and their sacrificial feasting on human flesh
          and blood.
These initiates from the midst of a heathen
          cult,*h*

and sent wasps*j* as forerunners of your army
     to destroy them little by little,
9 though you were not unable to give the
          ungodly into the hands of the
          righteous in battle,
or to destroy them at one blow by dread
          wild animals or your stern word.
10 But judging them little by little you gave
          them an opportunity to repent,
though you were not unaware that their
          origin*k* was evil
and their wickedness inborn,
and that their way of thinking would never
          change.

WORDS FROM A MOTHER TO HER DAUGHTER!

HISPANIC

¡Palabras de una madre a su hija!

The following translation of a text originally written in Nahuatl is the wisdom of
a native mother in sixteenth-century Mexico. This spirit of wisdom still exists in
many Mexican families.

Now, my daughter, my turtledove, little woman: you have life, you are born.
You have entered the world, emerged from my womb, nourished at my breast.
Our Lord forged your life, shaped you, made you within me. . . . Our Lord
makes each of us earn our reputation, our honor, our warmth, our passion, our
sweetness, our savor. . . .

Sing well, speak well, converse deeply, respond to all, pray deeply; words are
not to be bought and sold. Never allow the world to make you stupid, or silly.
. . . In this way, you will live among the people, and you will be worthy of all
you need . . . you will please our Lord and be worthy of our Lord's kindness
and mercy. (Pp. 91–92)

Be not a friend to liars, to thieves, to evil women, to meddlers, to those
who are lazy. . . .

And if you have belongings or property, do not waste them; do not display
them when you go out to the market. . . . Then you will leave what is yours
to your children and grandchildren after you.

If you live in this way, as I have taught you, then in truth, you will live well
among your own people, favored by all. (Pp. 95–97)

(Miguel Léon-Portilla and Librado Silva Galeana,
Huehuehtlahtolli, as translated by Richard Wood)

WIS

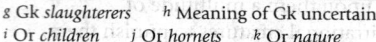

6 these parents who murder helpless lives,
     you willed to destroy by the hands of our
          ancestors,
7 so that the land most precious of all to you
     might receive a worthy colony of the
          servants*i* of God.
8 But even these you spared, since they were
          but mortals,

11 For they were an accursed race from the
          beginning,
     and it was not through fear of anyone that you
          left them unpunished for their sins.

---

g Gk *slaughterers*   *h* Meaning of Gk uncertain
i Or *children*   *j* Or *hornets*   *k* Or *nature*

God Is Sovereign

12 For who will say, "What have you done?"
or will resist your judgment?
Who will accuse you for the destruction of
nations that you made?
Or who will come before you to plead as an
advocate for the unrighteous?
13 For neither is there any god besides you,
whose care is for all people,[l]
to whom you should prove that you have
not judged unjustly;
14 nor can any king or monarch confront you
about those whom you have
punished.
15 You are righteous and you rule all things
righteously,
deeming it alien to your power
to condemn anyone who does not deserve
to be punished.
16 For your strength is the source of
righteousness,
and your sovereignty over all causes you to
spare all.
17 For you show your strength when people
doubt the completeness of your
power,
and you rebuke any insolence among those
who know it.[m]
18 Although you are sovereign in strength, you
judge with mildness,
and with great forbearance you govern us;
for you have power to act whenever you
choose.

God's Lessons for Israel

19 Through such works you have taught your
people
that the righteous must be kind,
and you have filled your children with good
hope,
because you give repentance for sins.
20 For if you punished with such great care
and indulgence[n]
the enemies of your servants[o] and those
deserving of death,
granting them time and opportunity to give
up their wickedness,
21 with what strictness you have judged your
children,
to whose ancestors you gave oaths and
covenants full of good promises!
22 So while chastening us you scourge our
enemies ten thousand times more,
so that, when we judge, we may meditate
upon your goodness,

and when we are judged, we may expect
mercy.

The Punishment of the Egyptians

23 Therefore those who lived unrighteously, in
a life of folly,
you tormented through their own
abominations.
24 For they went far astray on the paths of
error,
accepting as gods those animals that even
their enemies[p] despised;
they were deceived like foolish infants.
25 Therefore, as though to children who cannot
reason,
you sent your judgment to mock them.
26 But those who have not heeded the warning
of mild rebukes
will experience the deserved judgment
of God.
27 For when in their suffering they became
incensed
at those creatures that they had thought to
be gods, being punished by means
of them,
they saw and recognized as the true God the
one whom they had before refused
to know.
Therefore the utmost condemnation came
upon them.

The Foolishness of Nature Worship

For all people who were ignorant of God
were foolish by nature;
and they were unable from the good things
that are seen to know the one who
exists,
nor did they recognize the artisan while
paying heed to his works;
2 but they supposed that either fire or wind
or swift air,
or the circle of the stars, or turbulent water,
or the luminaries of heaven were the gods
that rule the world.
3 If through delight in the beauty of these
things people assumed them to be
gods,
let them know how much better than these
is their Lord,
for the author of beauty created them.
4 And if people[p] were amazed at their power
and working,

---

[l] Or all things   [m] Meaning of Gk uncertain   [n] Other
ancient authorities lack and indulgence; others read and
entreaty   [o] Or children   [p] Gk they

let them perceive from them
how much more powerful is the one who
formed them.
5 For from the greatness and beauty of created
things
comes a corresponding perception of their
Creator.
6 Yet these people are little to be blamed,
for perhaps they go astray
while seeking God and desiring to find him.
7 For while they live among his works, they
keep searching,
and they trust in what they see, because the
things that are seen are beautiful.
8 Yet again, not even they are to be excused;
9 for if they had the power to know so much
that they could investigate the world,
how did they fail to find sooner the Lord of
these things?

The Foolishness of Idolatry
(Isa 44.9–20; Jer 10.1–16; Let Jer 8–73)

10 But miserable, with their hopes set on dead
things, are those
who give the name "gods" to the works of
human hands,
gold and silver fashioned with skill,
and likenesses of animals,
or a useless stone, the work of an ancient
hand.
11 A skilled woodcutter may saw down a tree
easy to handle
and skillfully strip off all its bark,
and then with pleasing workmanship
make a useful vessel that serves life's needs,
12 and burn the cast-off pieces of his work
to prepare his food, and eat his fill.
13 But a cast-off piece from among them,
useful for nothing,
a stick crooked and full of knots,
he takes and carves with care in his leisure,
and shapes it with skill gained in idleness;*q*
he forms it in the likeness of a human
being,
14 or makes it like some worthless animal,
giving it a coat of red paint and coloring its
surface red
and covering every blemish in it with paint;
15 then he makes a suitable niche for it,
and sets it in the wall, and fastens it there
with iron.
16 He takes thought for it, so that it may not
fall,
because he knows that it cannot help itself,
for it is only an image and has need of
help.

17 When he prays about possessions and his
marriage and children,
he is not ashamed to address a lifeless
thing.
18 For health he appeals to a thing that is
weak;
for life he prays to a thing that is dead;
for aid he entreats a thing that is utterly
inexperienced;
for a prosperous journey, a thing that
cannot take a step;
19 for money-making and work and success
with his hands
he asks strength of a thing whose hands
have no strength.

Folly of a Navigator Praying to an Idol

Again, one preparing to sail and about to
voyage over raging waves
14 calls upon a piece of wood more fragile
than the ship that carries him.
2 For it was desire for gain that planned that
vessel,
and wisdom was the artisan who built it;
3 but it is your providence, O Father, that
steers its course,
because you have given it a path in the sea,
and a safe way through the waves,
4 showing that you can save from every
danger,
so that even a person who lacks skill may
put to sea.
5 It is your will that works of your wisdom
should not be without effect;
therefore people trust their lives even to the
smallest piece of wood,
and passing through the billows on a raft
they come safely to land.
6 For even in the beginning, when arrogant
giants were perishing,
the hope of the world took refuge on a raft,
and guided by your hand left to the world
the seed of a new generation.
7 For blessed is the wood by which
righteousness comes.

8 But the idol made with hands is accursed,
and so is the one who made it—
he for having made it, and the perishable
thing because it was named a god.
9 For equally hateful to God are the ungodly
and their ungodliness;
10 for what was done will be punished
together with the one who did it.

---

q Other ancient authorities read *with intelligent skill*

11 Therefore there will be a visitation also
upon the heathen idols,
because, though part of what God created,
they became an abomination,
snares for human souls
and a trap for the feet of the foolish.

The Origin and Evils of Idolatry

12 For the idea of making idols was the
beginning of fornication,
and the invention of them was the
corruption of life;
13 for they did not exist from the beginning,
nor will they last forever.
14 For through human vanity they entered the
world,
and therefore their speedy end has been
planned.
15 For a father, consumed with grief at an
untimely bereavement,
made an image of his child, who had been
suddenly taken from him;
he now honored as a god what was once a
dead human being,
and handed on to his dependents secret
rites and initiations.
16 Then the ungodly custom, grown strong
with time, was kept as a law,
and at the command of monarchs carved
images were worshiped.
17 When people could not honor monarchs*r*
in their presence, since they lived at
a distance,
they imagined their appearance far away,
and made a visible image of the king whom
they honored,
so that by their zeal they might flatter the
absent one as though present.

18 Then the ambition of the artisan impelled
even those who did not know the king to
intensify their worship.
19 For he, perhaps wishing to please his ruler,
skillfully forced the likeness to take more
beautiful form,
20 and the multitude, attracted by the charm of
his work,
now regarded as an object of worship the
one whom shortly before they had
honored as a human being.
21 And this became a hidden trap for
humankind,
because people, in bondage to misfortune
or to royal authority,
bestowed on objects of stone or wood the
name that ought not to be shared.

22 Then it was not enough for them to err
about the knowledge of God,
but though living in great strife due to
ignorance,
they call such great evils peace.
23 For whether they kill children in their
initiations, or celebrate secret
mysteries,
or hold frenzied revels with strange customs,
24 they no longer keep either their lives or
their marriages pure,
but they either treacherously kill one
another, or grieve one another by
adultery,
25 and all is a raging riot of blood and murder,
theft and deceit, corruption,
faithlessness, tumult, perjury,
26 confusion over what is good, forgetfulness
of favors,
defiling of souls, sexual perversion,

---

r Gk *them*

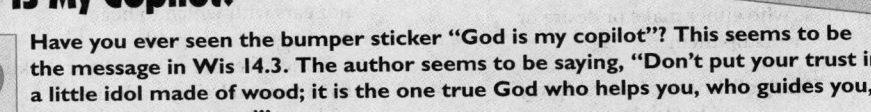

God Is My Copilot!

Have you ever seen the bumper sticker "God is my copilot"? This seems to be
the message in Wis 14.3. The author seems to be saying, "Don't put your trust in
a little idol made of wood; it is the one true God who helps you, who guides you,
who sets your course!"
  Your life has many challenges. One way to face those challenges is to take God along
on the journey. When you feel like you can't go on, call on God. When you fail and stumble,
call on God. When you succeed, call on God and celebrate. God is here to be your copilot,
to help you navigate through life, so just let go and let God!

▶ Wis 14.1–7

disorder in marriages, adultery, and
debauchery.

27 For the worship of idols not to be named
is the beginning and cause and end of every
evil.

28 For their worshipers[s] either rave in
exultation,
or prophesy lies, or live unrighteously, or
readily commit perjury;

29 for because they trust in lifeless idols
they swear wicked oaths and expect to suffer
no harm.

30 But just penalties will overtake them on two
counts:
because they thought wrongly about God in
devoting themselves to idols,
and because in deceit they swore
unrighteously through contempt for
holiness.

31 For it is not the power of the things by
which people swear,[t]
but the just penalty for those who sin,
that always pursues the transgression of the
unrighteous.

Benefits of Worshiping the True God

But you, our God, are kind and true,
patient, and ruling all things[u] in mercy.

2 For even if we sin we are yours, knowing
your power;
but we will not sin, because we know that
you acknowledge us as yours.

3 For to know you is complete righteousness,
and to know your power is the root of
immortality.

4 For neither has the evil intent of human art
misled us,
nor the fruitless toil of painters,
a figure stained with varied colors,

5 whose appearance arouses yearning in fools,
so that they desire[v] the lifeless form of a
dead image.

6 Lovers of evil things and fit for such objects
of hope[w]
are those who either make or desire or
worship them.

The Foolishness of Worshiping
Clay Idols

7 A potter kneads the soft earth
and laboriously molds each vessel for our
service,
fashioning out of the same clay
both the vessels that serve clean uses
and those for contrary uses, making all
alike;

but which shall be the use of each of them
the worker in clay decides.

8 With misspent toil, these workers form a
futile god from the same clay—
these mortals who were made of earth a
short time before
and after a little while go to the earth from
which all mortals are taken,
when the time comes to return the souls
that were borrowed.

9 But the workers are not concerned that
mortals are destined to die
or that their life is brief,
but they compete with workers in gold and
silver,
and imitate workers in copper;
and they count it a glorious thing to mold
counterfeit gods.

10 Their heart is ashes, their hope is cheaper
than dirt,
and their lives are of less worth than clay,

11 because they failed to know the one who
formed them
and inspired them with active souls
and breathed a living spirit into them.

12 But they considered our existence an idle
game,
and life a festival held for profit,
for they say one must get money however
one can, even by base means.

13 For these persons, more than all others,
know that they sin
when they make from earthy matter fragile
vessels and carved images.

14 But most foolish, and more miserable than
an infant,
are all the enemies who oppressed your
people.

15 For they thought that all their heathen idols
were gods,
though these have neither the use of their
eyes to see with,
nor nostrils with which to draw breath,
nor ears with which to hear,
nor fingers to feel with,
and their feet are of no use for walking.

16 For a human being made them,
and one whose spirit is borrowed formed
them;
for none can form gods that are like
themselves.

17 People are mortal, and what they make with
lawless hands is dead;

---

s Gk they   t Or of the oaths people swear   u Or ruling the
universe   v Gk and he desires   w Gk such hopes

for they are better than the objects they
worship,
since[x] they have life, but the idols[y]
never had.

Serpents in the Desert
(Num 11.31–35; 21.6–9)

18 Moreover, they worship even the most
hateful animals,
which are worse than all others when
judged by their lack of intelligence;

19 and even as animals they are not so
beautiful in appearance that one
would desire them,
but they have escaped both the praise of
God and his blessing.
Therefore those people[z] were deservedly
punished through such creatures,
and were tormented by a multitude of
animals.

2 Instead of this punishment you showed
kindness to your people,
and you prepared quails to eat,
a delicacy to satisfy the desire of appetite;

3 in order that those people, when they
desired food,
might lose the least remnant of appetite[a]
because of the odious creatures sent to
them,
while your people,[z] after suffering want a
short time,
might partake of delicacies.

4 For it was necessary that upon those
oppressors inescapable want should
come,
while to these others it was merely shown
how their enemies were being
tormented.

5 For when the terrible rage of wild animals
came upon your people[b]
and they were being destroyed by the bites
of writhing serpents,
your wrath did not continue to the end;

6 they were troubled for a little while as a
warning,
and received a symbol of deliverance to
remind them of your law's
command.

7 For the one who turned toward it was
saved, not by the thing that was
beheld,
but by you, the Savior of all.

8 And by this also you convinced our enemies
that it is you who deliver from every evil.

9 For they were killed by the bites of locusts
and flies,
and no healing was found for them,
because they deserved to be punished by
such things.

10 But your children were not conquered even
by the fangs of venomous serpents,
for your mercy came to their help and
healed them.

11 To remind them of your oracles they were
bitten,
and then were quickly delivered,
so that they would not fall into deep
forgetfulness
and become unresponsive[c] to your
kindness.

12 For neither herb nor poultice cured them,
but it was your word, O Lord, that heals all
people.

13 For you have power over life and death;
you lead mortals down to the gates of
Hades and back again.

14 A person in wickedness kills another,
but cannot bring back the departed spirit,
or set free the imprisoned soul.

Disastrous Storms Strike Egypt

15 To escape from your hand is impossible;

16 for the ungodly, refusing to know you,
were flogged by the strength of your arm,
pursued by unusual rains and hail and
relentless storms,
and utterly consumed by fire.

17 For—most incredible of all—in water, which
quenches all things,
the fire had still greater effect,
for the universe defends the righteous.

18 At one time the flame was restrained,
so that it might not consume the creatures
sent against the ungodly,
but that seeing this they might know
that they were being pursued by the
judgment of God;

19 and at another time even in the midst of
water it burned more intensely than
fire,
to destroy the crops of the unrighteous land.

The Israelites Receive Manna
(Ex 16.1–21)

20 Instead of these things you gave your people
food of angels,

---

x Other ancient authorities read *of which*   y Gk *but they*
z Gk *they*   a Gk *loathed the necessary appetite*   b Gk *them*
c Meaning of Gk uncertain

and without their toil you supplied them
      from heaven with bread ready
      to eat,
providing every pleasure and suited to every
      taste.

21 For your sustenance manifested your
      sweetness toward your children;
and the bread, ministering[d] to the desire of
      the one who took it,
was changed to suit everyone's liking.

22 Snow and ice withstood fire without
      melting,
so that they might know that the crops of
      their enemies
were being destroyed by the fire that blazed
      in the hail
and flashed in the showers of rain;

23 whereas the fire,[e] in order that the righteous
      might be fed,
even forgot its native power.

24 For creation, serving you who made it,
exerts itself to punish the unrighteous,
and in kindness relaxes on behalf of those
      who trust in you.

25 Therefore at that time also, changed into all
      forms,
it served your all-nourishing bounty,
according to the desire of those who had
      need,[f]

26 so that your children, whom you loved,
      O Lord, might learn
that it is not the production of crops that
      feeds humankind
but that your word sustains those who trust
      in you.

27 For what was not destroyed by fire
was melted when simply warmed by a
      fleeting ray of the sun,

28 to make it known that one must rise before
      the sun to give you thanks,
and must pray to you at the dawning of the
      light;

29 for the hope of an ungrateful person will
      melt like wintry frost,
and flow away like waste water.

Terror Strikes the Egyptians at Night
(Ex 10.21–23)

17 Great are your judgments and hard to
      describe;
therefore uninstructed souls have gone
      astray.

2 For when lawless people supposed that they
      held the holy nation in their power,

did you KNOW?
The Exodus Pattern

The **Exodus** refers to all the events surrounding God's leading the formerly enslaved Israelites out of Egypt as recorded in the Books of Exodus, Leviticus, Numbers, and Deuteronomy. Because the Exodus was an important experience in the Israelites' religious history, later biblical writers began to see in it a pattern in which God rescued the just and punished the wicked.

    The author of the Wisdom of Solomon applies the Exodus pattern to explain how the righteous will be rewarded and sinners will be punished in the author's time. Throughout chapters 11–15, the writer refers to the journey through the desert, the Egyptians, the plagues, the manna in the desert, the pillars of fire, and the Red Sea. The author even takes the liberty of adding details that were not recorded in the original books! In doing so, the writer reminds the people of that time that the pattern of the Exodus is being repeated in their life now, so they should not lose hope that God will be with them always.

▶ **Wis 11.1—19.22**

they themselves lay as captives of darkness
      and prisoners of long night,
shut in under their roofs, exiles from eternal
      providence.

3 For thinking that in their secret sins they
      were unobserved
behind a dark curtain of forgetfulness,
they were scattered, terribly[g] alarmed,
and appalled by specters.

4 For not even the inner chamber that held
      them protected them from fear,
but terrifying sounds rang out around them,
and dismal phantoms with gloomy faces
      appeared.

---

d Gk *and it, ministering*   *e* Gk *this*   *f* Or *who made
supplication*   *g* Other ancient authorities read *unobserved,
they were darkened behind a dark curtain of forgetfulness,
terribly*

5 And no power of fire was able to give light,
nor did the brilliant flames of the stars
avail to illumine that hateful night.

6 Nothing was shining through to them
except a dreadful, self-kindled fire,
and in terror they deemed the things that
they saw
to be worse than that unseen appearance.

7 The delusions of their magic art lay
humbled,
and their boasted wisdom was scornfully
rebuked.

8 For those who promised to drive off the
fears and disorders of a sick soul
were sick themselves with ridiculous fear.

9 For even if nothing disturbing frightened
them,
yet, scared by the passing of wild animals
and the hissing of snakes

10 they perished in trembling fear,
refusing to look even at the air, though it
nowhere could be avoided.

11 For wickedness is a cowardly thing,
condemned by its own testimony;[h]
distressed by conscience, it has always
exaggerated[i] the difficulties.

12 For fear is nothing but a giving up of the
helps that come from reason;

13 and hope, defeated by this inward weakness,
prefers ignorance of what causes the
torment.

14 But throughout the night, which was really
powerless
and which came upon them from the
recesses of powerless Hades,
they all slept the same sleep,

15 and now were driven by monstrous specters,
and now were paralyzed by their souls'
surrender;
for sudden and unexpected fear
overwhelmed them.

16 And whoever was there fell down,
and thus was kept shut up in a prison not
made of iron;

17 for whether they were farmers or shepherds
or workers who toiled in the wilderness,
they were seized, and endured the
inescapable fate;
for with one chain of darkness they all were
bound.

18 Whether there came a whistling wind,
or a melodious sound of birds in
wide-spreading branches,
or the rhythm of violently rushing water,

19 or the harsh crash of rocks hurled down,
or the unseen running of leaping animals,

or the sound of the most savage roaring
beasts,
or an echo thrown back from a hollow of
the mountains,
it paralyzed them with terror.

20 For the whole world was illumined with
brilliant light,
and went about its work unhindered,

21 while over those people alone heavy night
was spread,
an image of the darkness that was destined
to receive them;
but still heavier than darkness were they to
themselves.

Light Shines on the Israelites
(Ex 13.17–22)

But for your holy ones there was very great
light.
Their enemies[j] heard their voices but did
not see their forms,
and counted them happy for not having
suffered,

2 and were thankful that your holy ones,[h]
though previously wronged, were
doing them no injury;
and they begged their pardon for having
been at variance with them.[h]

3 Therefore you provided a flaming pillar of
fire
as a guide for your people's[k] unknown
journey,
and a harmless sun for their glorious
wandering.

4 For their enemies[i] deserved to be deprived
of light and imprisoned in darkness,
those who had kept your children
imprisoned,
through whom the imperishable light of the
law was to be given to the world.

The Death of the Egyptian Firstborn
(Ex 12.29–30; 14.26–31)

5 When they had resolved to kill the infants
of your holy ones,
and one child had been abandoned and
rescued,
you in punishment took away a multitude
of their children;
and you destroyed them all together by a
mighty flood.

---

h Meaning of Gk uncertain　　*i* Other ancient authorities
read *anticipated*　　*j* Gk *They*　　*k* Gk *their*　　*l* Gk *those*
persons

6 That night was made known beforehand to
our ancestors,
so that they might rejoice in sure knowledge
of the oaths in which they trusted.
7 The deliverance of the righteous and the
destruction of their enemies
were expected by your people.
8 For by the same means by which you
punished our enemies
you called us to yourself and glorified us.
9 For in secret the holy children of good
people offered sacrifices,
and with one accord agreed to the
divine law,
so that the saints would share alike the
same things,
both blessings and dangers;
and already they were singing the praises of
the ancestors.*m*
10 But the discordant cry of their enemies
echoed back,
and their piteous lament for their children
was spread abroad.
11 The slave was punished with the same
penalty as the master,
and the commoner suffered the same loss as
the king;
12 and they all together, by the one form*n* of
death,
had corpses too many to count.
For the living were not sufficient even to
bury them,
since in one instant their most valued
children had been destroyed.
13 For though they had disbelieved everything
because of their magic arts,
yet, when their firstborn were destroyed,
they acknowledged your people to
be God's child.
14 For while gentle silence enveloped all
things,
and night in its swift course was now half
gone,
15 your all-powerful word leaped from heaven,
from the royal throne,
into the midst of the land that was doomed,
a stern warrior
16 carrying the sharp sword of your authentic
command,
and stood and filled all things with death,
and touched heaven while standing on the
earth.
17 Then at once apparitions in dreadful dreams
greatly troubled them,

and unexpected fears assailed them;
18 and one here and another there, hurled
down half dead,
made known why they were dying;
19 for the dreams that disturbed them
forewarned them of this,
so that they might not perish without
knowing why they suffered.

Threat of Annihilation in the Desert
(Num 16.41–50)

20 The experience of death touched also the
righteous,
and a plague came upon the multitude in
the desert,
but the wrath did not long continue.
21 For a blameless man was quick to act as
their champion;
he brought forward the shield of his
ministry,
prayer and propitiation by incense;
he withstood the anger and put an end to
the disaster,
showing that he was your servant.
22 He conquered the wrath*o* not by strength of
body,
not by force of arms,
but by his word he subdued the avenger,
appealing to the oaths and covenants given
to our ancestors.
23 For when the dead had already fallen on
one another in heaps,
he intervened and held back the wrath,
and cut off its way to the living.
24 For on his long robe the whole world was
depicted,
and the glories of the ancestors were
engraved on the four rows of
stones,
and your majesty was on the diadem upon
his head.
25 To these the destroyer yielded, these he*p*
feared;
for merely to test the wrath was enough.

The Red Sea

But the ungodly were assailed to the end by
pitiless anger,
for God*q* knew in advance even their future
actions:

---

m Other ancient authorities read *dangers, the ancestors
already leading the songs of praise*   *n* Gk *name*   *o* Cn: Gk
multitude   *p* Other ancient authorities read *they*
q Gk *he*

2 how, though they themselves had
  permitted[r] your people to depart
and hastily sent them out,
they would change their minds and pursue
  them.
3 For while they were still engaged in
  mourning,
and were lamenting at the graves of their
  dead,
they reached another foolish decision,
and pursued as fugitives those whom they
  had begged and compelled to leave.
4 For the fate they deserved drew them on to
  this end,
and made them forget what had happened,
in order that they might fill up the
  punishment that their torments still
  lacked,
5 and that your people might experience[s] an
  incredible journey,
but they themselves might meet a strange
  death.

God Guides and Protects His People
(Num 11.1–35)

6 For the whole creation in its nature was
  fashioned anew,
complying with your commands,
so that your children[t] might be kept
  unharmed.
7 The cloud was seen overshadowing the
  camp,
and dry land emerging where water had
  stood before,
an unhindered way out of the Red Sea,
and a grassy plain out of the raging waves,
8 where those protected by your hand passed
  through as one nation,
after gazing on marvelous wonders.
9 For they ranged like horses,
and leaped like lambs,
praising you, O Lord, who delivered
  them.
10 For they still recalled the events of their
  sojourn,
how instead of producing animals the earth
  brought forth gnats,
and instead of fish the river spewed out vast
  numbers of frogs.
11 Afterward they saw also a new kind[u] of
  birds,
when desire led them to ask for luxurious
  food;
12 for, to give them relief, quails came up from
  the sea.

The Punishment of the Egyptians

13 The punishments did not come upon the
  sinners
without prior signs in the violence of
  thunder,
for they justly suffered because of their
  wicked acts;
for they practiced a more bitter hatred of
  strangers.
14 Others had refused to receive strangers when
  they came to them,
but these made slaves of guests who were
  their benefactors.
15 And not only so—but, while punishment of
  some sort will come upon the
  former
for having received strangers with
  hostility,
16 the latter, having first received them with
  festal celebrations,
afterward afflicted with terrible
  sufferings
those who had already shared the same
  rights.
17 They were stricken also with loss
  of sight—
just as were those at the door of the
  righteous man—
when, surrounded by yawning
  darkness,
all of them tried to find the way through
  their own doors.

A New Harmony in Nature

18 For the elements changed[v] places with one
  another,
as on a harp the notes vary the nature of
  the rhythm,
while each note remains the same.[w]
This may be clearly inferred from the sight
  of what took place.
19 For land animals were transformed into
  water creatures,
and creatures that swim moved over to the
  land.
20 Fire even in water retained its normal
  power,

---

r Other ancient authorities read *had changed their minds
to permit* s Other ancient authorities read *accomplish*
t Or *servants* u Or *production* v Gk *changing*
w Meaning of Gk uncertain

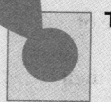

Supernatural Resources

The Wisdom of Solomon ends with an inspiring statement of faith:

> For in everything, O Lord, you have exalted and glorified your people,
> and you have not neglected to help them at all times and in all places.
>
> (19.22)

Could you say these words? Do you have the kind of faith that is able to see the hand of God at work through everything that happens?

So many times, we pray for God's help, especially if we are struggling or someone we love is suffering. Later, when that particular crisis is over, we quickly forget how God helped us through. The Bible's message is that God is at work through all the times in our life, even in ways that we do not realize at the moment. The church's word for God's help is *grace*. Unlike most of our natural resources, the supernatural resource of grace is never in danger of being used up. In fact, the more we use it, the more of it there is!

Find a way of keeping track of how God has helped you through life. Perhaps you can maintain a journal of the difficult times you've made it through and the people who have supported you. You might be surprised by this record of how God's grace has been active!

▶ Wis 19.22

---

and water forgot its fire-quenching nature.
21 Flames, on the contrary, failed to consume
  the flesh of perishable creatures that walked
      among them,
  nor did they melt*x* the crystalline,
      quick-melting kind of heavenly
      food.

Conclusion

22 For in everything, O Lord, you have exalted
      and glorified your people,
  and you have not neglected to help them at
      all times and in all places.

---

x Cn: Gk *nor could be melted*

I magine that many years ago, your grandfather—
a learned and wise man—wrote a book summarizing
all his wisdom. Recently, you read the book and discovered it has answers to many of the problems you and
your friends are struggling with. But the book is written
in your grandfather's native language, which your friends
don't understand. So, what do you do? You translate the
book! This is exactly what the
grandson of Jesus Ben Sira did.
He translated into Greek the
book his grandfather had written in Hebrew.

At a Glance

- **Chapters 1–43.** praise of wisdom and general moral teaching
- **Chapters 44–50.** praise of the heroes of Israel
- **Chapter 51.** a concluding prayer and poem

In-depth

The Book of Sirach is unique in the Old Testament because it clearly identifies its
author: Jesus Ben Sira, a wise teacher who lived early in the second century B.C.
Living in Jerusalem during a time of great change, he saw many of his people—
especially those who were rich—deserting traditional Jewish beliefs in favor of
more fashionable ideas coming from Greece. A book underlining the superiority
of Jewish wisdom was needed, Ben Sira thought. So, he collected his class notes
into a single volume and offered it to those who desired to learn the ways of living well. Though full of many different kinds of writing—sayings, hymns, prayers,
and lists—the book is unified in its overall conviction: "All wisdom is from the
Lord, / and with him it remains forever" (1.1).

The Book of Sirach holds fast to the long-standing belief that in this life,
good is rewarded and evil is punished. Unlike Second Maccabees and Daniel—
also written in the second century B.C.—Sirach never mentions the possibility of
life after death. But like other wisdom books, it celebrates the glories of wisdom
(chapter 1) and recalls the heroes of Jewish faith (chapters 44–50). Its view of
women is harsher than that of most of the Old Testament, though. In interpreting Sirach, you must take special care not to
conclude that women are the source of most of
men's troubles!

Sometimes called Ecclesiasticus or Ben Sira
(which is the short form for "son of Sirach"),
the Book of Sirach was well known among the
ancient Jews. It was popular in the early Christian church as well. Its influence can be found
in the New Testament, especially in the Letter of
James. Long after his death, Ben Sira continues
to share the wisdom of the past and offers us
trustworthy guidance for the present.

Quick Facts

Author
Jesus Ben Sira, writing
around 180 B.C.

Theme
the superiority of Jewish
wisdom over Greek wis-
dom

Of Note
Sirach is not found in
every translation of the
Old Testament (see
"The Case of the Missing
Books," near Tob 1.16).

The Book of **Sirach (Ecclesiasticus)**

Sirach

THE PROLOGUE

Many great teachings have been given to us through the Law and the Prophets and the others[a] that followed them, and for these we should praise Israel for instruction and wisdom. Now, those who read the scriptures must not only themselves understand them, but must also as lovers of learning be able through the spoken and written word to help the outsiders. So my grandfather Jesus, who had devoted himself especially to the reading of the Law and the Prophets and the other books of our ancestors, and had acquired considerable proficiency in them, was himself also led to write something pertaining to instruction and wisdom, so that by becoming familiar also with his book[b] those who love learning might make even greater progress in living according to the law.

You are invited therefore to read it with good-will and attention, and to be indulgent in cases where, despite our diligent labor in translating, we may seem to have rendered some phrases imperfectly. For what was originally expressed in Hebrew does not have exactly the same sense when translated into another language. Not only this book, but even the Law itself, the Prophecies, and the rest of the books differ not a little when read in the original.

When I came to Egypt in the thirty-eighth year of the reign of Eū·er′ge·tēs and stayed for some time, I found opportunity for no little instruc-

tion.[c] It seemed highly necessary that I should myself devote some diligence and labor to the translation of this book. During that time I have applied my skill day and night to complete and publish the book for those living abroad who wished to gain learning and are disposed to live according to the law.

In Praise of Wisdom

(Cp Prov 3.13–20; 8.22–31; Rom 11.33)

1 All wisdom is from the Lord,
   and with him it remains forever.

2 The sand of the sea, the drops of rain,
   and the days of eternity—who can count
      them?

3 The height of heaven, the breadth of the
      earth,
   the abyss, and wisdom[d]—who can search
      them out?

4 Wisdom was created before all other things,
   and prudent understanding from
      eternity.[e]

6 The root of wisdom—to whom has it been
   revealed?

---

[a] Or *other books* [b] Gk *with these things* [c] Other ancient authorities read *I found a copy affording no little instruction*
[d] Other ancient authorities read *the depth of the abyss*
[e] Other ancient authorities add as verse 5, *The source of wisdom is God's word in the highest heaven, and her ways are the eternal commandments.*

Her subtleties—who knows them?*f*

8 There is but one who is wise, greatly to be
      feared,
   seated upon his throne—the Lord.
9 It is he who created her;
   he saw her and took her measure;
   he poured her out upon all his works,
10 upon all the living according to his gift;
   he lavished her upon those who
      love him.*g*

Fear of the Lord Is True Wisdom
(Job 28.28; Prov 1.7)

11 The fear of the Lord is glory and exultation,
   and gladness and a crown of rejoicing.
12 The fear of the Lord delights the heart,
   and gives gladness and joy and long life.*h*
13 Those who fear the Lord will have a
      happy end;
   on the day of their death they will be
      blessed.
14 To fear the Lord is the beginning of
      wisdom;
   she is created with the faithful in the
      womb.
15 She made*i* among human beings an eternal
      foundation,
   and among their descendants she will
      abide faithfully.
16 To fear the Lord is fullness of wisdom;
   she inebriates mortals with her fruits;
17 she fills their*j* whole house with desirable
      goods,
   and their*j* storehouses with her produce.
18 The fear of the Lord is the crown of
      wisdom,
   making peace and perfect health to
      flourish.*k*
19 She rained down knowledge and discerning
      comprehension,
   and she heightened the glory of those
      who held her fast.
20 To fear the Lord is the root of wisdom,
   and her branches are long life.*l*

22 Unjust anger cannot be justified,
   for anger tips the scale to one's ruin.
23 Those who are patient stay calm until the
      right moment,
   and then cheerfulness comes back to
      them.
24 They hold back their words until the right
      moment;
   then the lips of many tell of their good
      sense.

25 In the treasuries of wisdom are wise sayings,
   but godliness is an abomination to a
      sinner.
26 If you desire wisdom, keep the
      commandments,
   and the Lord will lavish her upon you.
27 For the fear of the Lord is wisdom and
      discipline,
   fidelity and humility are his delight.
28 Do not disobey the fear of the Lord;
   do not approach him with a divided
      mind.
29 Do not be a hypocrite before others,
   and keep watch over your lips.
30 Do not exalt yourself, or you may fall
   and bring dishonor upon yourself.
   The Lord will reveal your secrets
   and overthrow you before the whole
      congregation,
   because you did not come in the fear of the
      Lord,
   and your heart was full of deceit.

Duties toward God
(Jas 1.2–4, 12–16; Wis 3.1–9)

My child, when you come to serve the Lord,
   prepare yourself for testing.*m*
2 Set your heart right and be steadfast,
   and do not be impetuous in time of
      calamity.
3 Cling to him and do not depart,
   so that your last days may be prosperous.
4 Accept whatever befalls you,
   and in times of humiliation be patient.
5 For gold is tested in the fire,
   and those found acceptable, in the
      furnace of humiliation.*n*
6 Trust in him, and he will help you;
   make your ways straight, and hope
      in him.

7 You who fear the Lord, wait for his mercy;
   do not stray, or else you may fall.

f Other ancient authorities add as verse 7, *The knowledge of
wisdom—to whom was it manifested? And her abundant
experience—who has understood it?* *g* Other ancient
authorities add *Love of the Lord is glorious wisdom; to those
to whom he appears he apportions her, that they may see him.*
h Other ancient authorities add *The fear of the Lord is a gift
from the Lord; also for love he makes firm paths.* *i* Gk made
as a nest *j* Other ancient authorities read *her* *k* Other
ancient authorities add *Both are gifts of God for peace; glory
opens out for those who love him. He saw her and took her
measure.* *l* Other ancient authorities add as verse 21, *The
fear of the Lord drives away sins; and where it abides, it will
turn away all anger.* *m* Or *trials* *n* Other ancient
authorities add *in sickness and poverty put your trust in him*

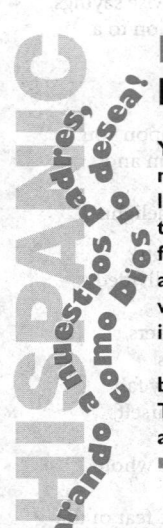

HONORING OUR PARENTS IN GOD'S WAY!

You hear Sir 3.1–7 every year on Holy Family Sunday, the weekend after Christmas. This reading calls us to honor our parents, because this is the way God established children's responsibilities toward parents. To honor our parents is to respect them (verse 6), to be kind to them (verse 14), to not dishonor them in order to feel superior (verse 10), and to take care of them and be patient with them as they age (verses 12–13). According to Ben Sira, God assures many blessings to those who honor their parents, including safety, happiness, forgiveness of sins, the hearing of their prayers, and a long life.

Hispanics have a long tradition of being parented not only by birth parents but by the extended family, including grandparents, godparents, aunts, and uncles. Today, many young people are also parented by foster parents, stepparents, and adoptive parents.

■ Take a moment to think of the adults who have parented you. In what specific ways do you honor and show your love to them? In what ways might you have failed to do so?

■ Thank God, our heavenly parent, for the love and sacrifices of all the people who have parented you. Ask God to give you love, understanding, strength, and patience to honor them in word and deed.

► Sir 3.1–16

8 You who fear the Lord, trust in him,
  and your reward will not be lost.
9 You who fear the Lord, hope for good things,
  for lasting joy and mercy.*o*
10 Consider the generations of old and see:
  has anyone trusted in the Lord and been disappointed?
  Or has anyone persevered in the fear of the Lord*p* and been forsaken?
  Or has anyone called upon him and been neglected?
11 For the Lord is compassionate and merciful;
  he forgives sins and saves in time of distress.
12 Woe to timid hearts and to slack hands,
  and to the sinner who walks a double path!
13 Woe to the fainthearted who have no trust!
  Therefore they will have no shelter.
14 Woe to you who have lost your nerve!
  What will you do when the Lord's reckoning comes?
15 Those who fear the Lord do not disobey his words,

and those who love him keep his ways.
16 Those who fear the Lord seek to please him,
  and those who love him are filled with his law.
17 Those who fear the Lord prepare their hearts,
  and humble themselves before him.
18 Let us fall into the hands of the Lord,
  but not into the hands of mortals;
  for equal to his majesty is his mercy,
  and equal to his name are his works.*q*

Duties toward Parents
(Ex 20.12; Deut 5.16; Eph 6.1–3)

Listen to me your father, O children;
  act accordingly, that you may be kept in safety.
2 For the Lord honors a father above his children,
  and he confirms a mother's right over her children.
3 Those who honor their father atone for sins,

---

o Other ancient authorities add *For his reward is an everlasting gift with joy.*   *p* Gk *of him*   *q* Syr: Gk lacks this line

4   and those who respect their mother are
          like those who lay up treasure.
5   Those who honor their father will have joy
          in their own children,
          and when they pray they will be heard.
6   Those who respect their father will have
          long life,
          and those who honor^r their mother obey
          the Lord;
7   they will serve their parents as their
          masters.^s
8   Honor your father by word and deed,
          that his blessing may come upon you.
9   For a father's blessing strengthens the
          houses of the children,
          but a mother's curse uproots their
          foundations.
10   Do not glorify yourself by dishonoring your
          father,
          for your father's dishonor is no glory
          to you.
11   The glory of one's father is one's own glory,
          and it is a disgrace for children not to
          respect their mother.

12   My child, help your father in his old age,
          and do not grieve him as long as he
          lives;
13   even if his mind fails, be patient with him;
          because you have all your faculties do
          not despise him.
14   For kindness to a father will not be
          forgotten,
          and will be credited to you against your
          sins;
15   in the day of your distress it will be
          remembered in your favor;
          like frost in fair weather, your sins will
          melt away.
16   Whoever forsakes a father is like a
          blasphemer,
          and whoever angers a mother is cursed
          by the Lord.

Humility
(Mt 20.26–28; Phil 2.3–8)

17   My child, perform your tasks with
          humility;^t
          then you will be loved by those whom
          God accepts.
18   The greater you are, the more you must
          humble yourself;
          so you will find favor in the sight of the
          Lord.^u
20   For great is the might of the Lord;
          but by the humble he is glorified.

Asian American

Celebrating Families

Ben Sira holds family relationships in high esteem. In chapter 3, he empha-sizes the importance of honor and respect between family members. Many cultures have special days honoring par-ents and children. In the United States, we celebrate Mother's Day, Father's Day, and Grandparent's Day.

Japan also has special days honoring family members. Girls' Festival (Hina-matsuri) is celebrated on 3 March with doll displays and peach blossoms. Boys' Festival (Kodomo No Hi) is celebrated on 5 May with streamers. Respect for the Aged Day (Keiro No Hi) is celebrat-ed on 15 September. On 15 January, the Coming of Age Festival (Seigin No Hi) takes place. This day celebrates all young people who have turned twenty during the previous year—the age when young adults are permitted to vote, drink, and smoke.

If you have Japanese friends or ac-quaintances, consider marking these holidays on your calendar and sending a card or note with a prayer on the ap-propriate day.

▶ Sir 3.1–16

21   Neither seek what is too difficult for you,
          nor investigate what is beyond your
          power.
22   Reflect upon what you have been
          commanded,
          for what is hidden is not your concern.
23   Do not meddle in matters that are
          beyond you,
          for more than you can understand has
          been shown you.
24   For their conceit has led many astray,
          and wrong opinion has impaired their
          judgment.

---

^r Heb: Other ancient authorities read *comfort*   ^s In other
ancient authorities this line is preceded by *Those who fear
the Lord honor their father,*   ^t Heb: Gk *meekness*
^u Other ancient authorities add as verse 19, *Many are lofty
and renowned, but to the humble he reveals his secrets.*

25 Without eyes there is no light;
   without knowledge there is no wisdom.*v*
26 A stubborn mind will fare badly at the end,
   and whoever loves danger will perish
      in it.
27 A stubborn mind will be burdened by
      troubles,
   and the sinner adds sin to sins.
28 When calamity befalls the proud, there is no
      healing,
   for an evil plant has taken root in him.
29 The mind of the intelligent appreciates
      proverbs,
   and an attentive ear is the desire of the
      wise.

Alms for the Poor
(Tob 4.7–11)

30 As water extinguishes a blazing fire,
   so almsgiving atones for sin.
31 Those who repay favors give thought to the
      future;
   when they fall they will find support.

Duties toward the Poor and the Oppressed
(Deut 15.7–11)

My child, do not cheat the poor of their
      living,
   and do not keep needy eyes waiting.
2 Do not grieve the hungry,
   or anger one in need.
3 Do not add to the troubles of the desperate,
   or delay giving to the needy.
4 Do not reject a suppliant in distress,
   or turn your face away from the poor.
5 Do not avert your eye from the needy,
   and give no one reason to curse you;
6 for if in bitterness of soul some should
      curse you,
   their Creator will hear their prayer.

7 Endear yourself to the congregation;
   bow your head low to the great.
8 Give a hearing to the poor,
   and return their greeting politely.
9 Rescue the oppressed from the oppressor;
   and do not be hesitant in giving a
      verdict.
10 Be a father to orphans,
   and be like a husband to their mother;
you will then be like a son of the Most
      High,
   and he will love you more than does
      your mother.

The Rewards of Wisdom
(Prov 3.13–18; Wis 8.17–18)

11 Wisdom teaches*w* her children
   and gives help to those who seek her.
12 Whoever loves her loves life,
   and those who seek her from early
      morning are filled with joy.
13 Whoever holds her fast inherits glory,
   and the Lord blesses the place she*x*
      enters.
14 Those who serve her minister to the
      Holy One;
   the Lord loves those who love her.
15 Those who obey her will judge the nations,
   and all who listen to her will live secure.
16 If they remain faithful, they will inherit her;
   their descendants will also obtain her.
17 For at first she will walk with them on
      tortuous paths;
   she will bring fear and dread upon them,
and will torment them by her discipline
   until she trusts them,*y*
and she will test them with her ordinances.
18 Then she will come straight back to them
      again and gladden them,
   and will reveal her secrets to them.
19 If they go astray she will forsake them,
   and hand them over to their ruin.

20 Watch for the opportune time, and beware
      of evil,
   and do not be ashamed to be yourself.
21 For there is a shame that leads to sin,
   and there is a shame that is glory and
      favor.
22 Do not show partiality, to your own harm,
   or deference, to your downfall.
23 Do not refrain from speaking at the proper
      moment,*z*
   and do not hide your wisdom.*a*
24 For wisdom becomes known through
      speech,
   and education through the words of the
      tongue.
25 Never speak against the truth,
   but be ashamed of your ignorance.
26 Do not be ashamed to confess your sins,
   and do not try to stop the current of a
      river.
27 Do not subject yourself to a fool,
   or show partiality to a ruler.

v Heb: Other ancient authorities lack verse 25 *w* Heb
Syr: Gk *exalts* *x* Or *he* *y* Or *until they remain
faithful in their heart* *z* Heb: Gk *at a time of salvation*
a So some Gk Mss and Heb Syr Lat: Other Gk Mss lack
and do not hide your wisdom

28 Fight to the death for truth,
and the Lord God will fight for you.

29 Do not be reckless in your speech,
or sluggish and remiss in your deeds.

30 Do not be like a lion in your home,
or suspicious of your servants.

31 Do not let your hand be stretched out to
receive
and closed when it is time to give.

Precepts for Everyday Living

Do not rely on your wealth,
or say, "I have enough."

2 Do not follow your inclination and strength
in pursuing the desires of your heart.

3 Do not say, "Who can have power over me?"
for the Lord will surely punish you.

4 Do not say, "I sinned, yet what has
happened to me?"
for the Lord is slow to anger.

5 Do not be so confident of forgiveness[b]
that you add sin to sin.

6 Do not say, "His mercy is great,
he will forgive[c] the multitude of my sins,"
for both mercy and wrath are with him,
and his anger will rest on sinners.

7 Do not delay to turn back to the Lord,
and do not postpone it from day to day;
for suddenly the wrath of the Lord will
come upon you,
and at the time of punishment you will
perish.

8 Do not depend on dishonest wealth,
for it will not benefit you on the day of
calamity.

9 Do not winnow in every wind,
or follow every path.[d]

10 Stand firm for what you know,
and let your speech be consistent.

11 Be quick to hear,
but deliberate in answering.

12 If you know what to say, answer your
neighbor;
but if not, put your hand over your
mouth.

13 Honor and dishonor come from speaking,
and the tongue of mortals may be their
downfall.

14 Do not be called double-tongued[e]
and do not lay traps with your tongue;
for shame comes to the thief,
and severe condemnation to the
double-tongued.

15 In great and small matters cause no harm,[f]

1 and do not become an enemy instead of
a friend;
for a bad name incurs shame and reproach;
so it is with the double-tongued sinner.

2 Do not fall into the grip of passion,[g]
or you may be torn apart as by a bull.[h]

3 Your leaves will be devoured and your fruit
destroyed,
and you will be left like a withered tree.

4 Evil passion destroys those who have it,
and makes them the laughingstock of
their enemies.

PRAY IT!

Friends

God of friendship,
Thank you for my friends, especially
for those who give me wise advice.
Thank you for my closest friends whom I
see every day, who motivate me to grow
and serve.
Thank you for all the good friends whom I
used to see more often but don't see as
much anymore.
Lord, continue to give me good friends
throughout my life, and help me be a
better friend to all. Amen.

▶ Sir 6.5–17

Friendship, False and True

5 Pleasant speech multiplies friends,
and a gracious tongue multiplies
courtesies.

6 Let those who are friendly with you be
many,
but let your advisers be one in a
thousand.

7 When you gain friends, gain them through
testing,
and do not trust them hastily.

8 For there are friends who are such when it
suits them,

---

b Heb: Gk *atonement*   c Heb: Gk *he* (or *it*) *will atone for*
d Gk adds *so it is with the double-tongued sinner* (see 6.1)
e Heb: Gk *a slanderer*   f Heb Syr: Gk *be ignorant*
g Heb: Meaning of Gk uncertain   h Meaning of Gk uncertain

but they will not stand by you in time of
trouble.

9 And there are friends who change into
enemies,
and tell of the quarrel to your disgrace.

10 And there are friends who sit at your table,
but they will not stand by you in time of
trouble.

11 When you are prosperous, they become
your second self,
and lord it over your servants;

12 but if you are brought low, they turn
against you,
and hide themselves from you.

13 Keep away from your enemies,
and be on guard with your friends.

14 Faithful friends are a sturdy shelter:
whoever finds one has found a treasure.

15 Faithful friends are beyond price;
no amount can balance their worth.

16 Faithful friends are life-saving medicine;
and those who fear the Lord will find
them.

17 Those who fear the Lord direct their
friendship aright,
for as they are, so are their neighbors
also.

Blessings of Wisdom

18 My child, from your youth choose discipline,
and when you have gray hair you will
still find wisdom.

19 Come to her like one who plows and sows,
and wait for her good harvest.
For when you cultivate her you will toil but
little,
and soon you will eat of her produce.

20 She seems very harsh to the undisciplined;
fools cannot remain with her.

21 She will be like a heavy stone to test them,
and they will not delay in casting her
aside.

22 For wisdom is like her name;
she is not readily perceived by many.

23 Listen, my child, and accept my judgment;
do not reject my counsel.

24 Put your feet into her fetters,
and your neck into her collar.

25 Bend your shoulders and carry her,
and do not fret under her bonds.

26 Come to her with all your soul,
and keep her ways with all your might.

27 Search out and seek, and she will become
known to you;

and when you get hold of her, do not let
her go.

28 For at last you will find the rest she gives,
and she will be changed into joy for you.

29 Then her fetters will become for you a
strong defense,
and her collar a glorious robe.

30 Her yoke[i] is a golden ornament,
and her bonds a purple cord.

31 You will wear her like a glorious robe,
and put her on like a splendid crown.[j]

32 If you are willing, my child, you can be
disciplined,
and if you apply yourself you will
become clever.

33 If you love to listen you will gain
knowledge,
and if you pay attention you will become
wise.

34 Stand in the company of the elders.
Who is wise? Attach yourself to such
a one.

35 Be ready to listen to every godly discourse,
and let no wise proverbs escape you.

36 If you see an intelligent person, rise early to
visit him;
let your foot wear out his doorstep.

37 Reflect on the statutes of the Lord,
and meditate at all times on his
commandments.
It is he who will give insight to[k] your mind,
and your desire for wisdom will be
granted.

Miscellaneous Advice

7 Do no evil, and evil will never overtake you.

2 Stay away from wrong, and it will turn
away from you.

3 Do[l] not sow in the furrows of injustice,
and you will not reap a sevenfold crop.

4 Do not seek from the Lord high office,
or the seat of honor from the king.

5 Do not assert your righteousness before the
Lord,
or display your wisdom before the king.

6 Do not seek to become a judge,
or you may be unable to root out
injustice;
you may be partial to the powerful,
and so mar your integrity.

7 Commit no offense against the public,

---

i Heb: Gk *Upon her*   j Heb: Gk *crown of gladness*
k Heb: Gk *will confirm*   l Gk *My child, do*

and do not disgrace yourself among the people.

8 Do not commit a sin twice;
  not even for one will you go unpunished.
9 Do not say, "He will consider the great
      number of my gifts,
    and when I make an offering to the Most
      High God, he will accept it."
10 Do not grow weary when you pray;
    do not neglect to give alms.
11 Do not ridicule a person who is embittered
      in spirit,
    for there is One who humbles and exalts.
12 Do not devise[m] a lie against your brother,
    or do the same to a friend.
13 Refuse to utter any lie,
    for it is a habit that results in no good.
14 Do not babble in the assembly of the
      elders,
    and do not repeat yourself when you
      pray.
15 Do not hate hard labor
    or farm work, which was created by the
      Most High.
16 Do not enroll in the ranks of sinners;
    remember that retribution does not delay.
17 Humble yourself to the utmost,
    for the punishment of the ungodly is fire
      and worms.[n]

Relations with Others

18 Do not exchange a friend for money,
    or a real brother for the gold of O'phir.
19 Do not dismiss[o] a wise and good wife,
    for her charm is worth more than gold.
20 Do not abuse slaves who work faithfully,
    or hired laborers who devote themselves
      to their task.
21 Let your soul love intelligent slaves;[p]
    do not withhold from them their
      freedom.
22 Do you have cattle? Look after them;
    if they are profitable to you, keep them.
23 Do you have children? Discipline them,
    and make them obedient[q] from their
      youth.
24 Do you have daughters? Be concerned for
      their chastity,[r]
    and do not show yourself too indulgent
      with them.
25 Give a daughter in marriage, and you
      complete a great task;
    but give her to a sensible man.

26 Do you have a wife who pleases you?[s] Do
      not divorce her;
    but do not trust yourself to one whom
      you detest.
27 With all your heart honor your father,
    and do not forget the birth pangs of your
      mother.
28 Remember that it was of your parents[t] you
      were born;
    how can you repay what they have given
      to you?
29 With all your soul fear the Lord,
    and revere his priests.
30 With all your might love your Maker,
    and do not neglect his ministers.
31 Fear the Lord and honor the priest,
    and give him his portion, as you have
      been commanded:
    the first fruits, the guilt offering, the gift of
      the shoulders,
    the sacrifice of sanctification, and the first
      fruits of the holy things.
32 Stretch out your hand to the poor,
    so that your blessing may be complete.
33 Give graciously to all the living;
    do not withhold kindness even from the
      dead.
34 Do not avoid those who weep,
    but mourn with those who mourn.
35 Do not hesitate to visit the sick,
    because for such deeds you will be loved.
36 In all you do, remember the end of your
      life,
    and then you will never sin.

Prudence and Common Sense

Do not contend with the powerful,
    or you may fall into their hands.
2 Do not quarrel with the rich,
    in case their resources outweigh yours;
  for gold has ruined many,
    and has perverted the minds of kings.
3 Do not argue with the loud of mouth,
    and do not heap wood on their fire.
4 Do not make fun of one who is ill-bred,
    or your ancestors may be insulted.
5 Do not reproach one who is turning away
      from sin;
    remember that we all deserve
      punishment.

---

m Heb: Gk *plow*   n Heb *for the expectation of mortals is worms*   o Heb: Gk *deprive yourself of*   p Heb *Love a wise slave as yourself*   q Gk *bend their necks*   r Gk *body*   s Heb Syr *lack who pleases you*   t Gk *them*

6 Do not disdain one who is old,
for some of us are also growing old.
7 Do not rejoice over anyone's death;
remember that we must all die.

8 Do not slight the discourse of the sages,
but busy yourself with their maxims;
because from them you will learn
discipline
and how to serve princes.
9 Do not ignore the discourse of the aged,
for they themselves learned from their
parents;^u
from them you learn how to understand
and to give an answer when the need
arises.

10 Do not kindle the coals of sinners,
or you may be burned in their flaming
fire.
11 Do not let the insolent bring you to your
feet,
or they may lie in ambush against your
words.
12 Do not lend to one who is stronger
than you;
but if you do lend anything, count it as a
loss.
13 Do not give surety beyond your means;
but if you give surety, be prepared
to pay.

14 Do not go to law against a judge,
for the decision will favor him because of
his standing.
15 Do not go traveling with the reckless,
or they will be burdensome to you;
for they will act as they please,
and through their folly you will perish
with them.
16 Do not pick a fight with the
quick-tempered,
and do not journey with them through
lonely country,
because bloodshed means nothing
to them,
and where no help is at hand, they will
strike you down.
17 Do not consult with fools,
for they cannot keep a secret.
18 In the presence of strangers do nothing that
is to be kept secret,
for you do not know what they will
divulge.^v
19 Do not reveal your thoughts to anyone,
or you may drive away your happiness.^w

Advice Concerning Women
(Cp Num 5.11–15)

Do not be jealous of the wife of your bosom,
or you will teach her an evil lesson to
your own hurt.
2 Do not give yourself to a woman
and let her trample down your strength.
3 Do not go near a loose woman,
or you will fall into her snares.
4 Do not dally with a singing girl,
or you will be caught by her tricks.
5 Do not look intently at a virgin,
or you may stumble and incur penalties
for her.
6 Do not give yourself to prostitutes,
or you may lose your inheritance.
7 Do not look around in the streets of a city,
or wander about in its deserted sections.
8 Turn away your eyes from a shapely
woman,
and do not gaze at beauty belonging to
another;
many have been seduced by a woman's
beauty,
and by it passion is kindled like a fire.
9 Never dine with another man's wife,
or revel with her at wine;
or your heart may turn aside to her,
and in blood^x you may be plunged into
destruction.

Choice of Friends

10 Do not abandon old friends,
for new ones cannot equal them.
A new friend is like new wine;
when it has aged, you can drink it with
pleasure.
11 Do not envy the success of sinners,
for you do not know what their end will
be like.
12 Do not delight in what pleases the ungodly;
remember that they will not be held
guiltless all their lives.
13 Keep far from those who have power to kill,
and you will not be haunted by the fear
of death.
But if you approach them, make no misstep,
or they may rob you of your life.
Know that you are stepping among snares,
and that you are walking on the city
battlements.

u Or ancestors   v Or it will bring forth   w Heb: Gk and let
him not return a favor to you   x Heb: Gk by your spirit

14 As much as you can, aim to know your
      neighbors,
   and consult with the wise.
15 Let your conversation be with intelligent
      people,
   and let all your discussion be about the
      law of the Most High.
16 Let the righteous be your dinner
      companions,
   and let your glory be in the fear of the
      Lord.

Concerning Rulers
(Prov 8.15–16; Wis 6.1–11)

17 A work is praised for the skill of the artisan;
   so a people's leader is proved wise by his
      words.
18 The loud of mouth are feared in their city,
   and the one who is reckless in speech is
      hated.
A wise magistrate educates his people,
   and the rule of an intelligent person is
      well ordered.
2 As the people's judge is, so are his officials;
   as the ruler of the city is, so are all its
      inhabitants.
3 An undisciplined king ruins his people,
   but a city becomes fit to live in through
      the understanding of its rulers.
4 The government of the earth is in the hand
      of the Lord,
   and over it he will raise up the right
      leader for the time.
5 Human success is in the hand of the Lord,

and it is he who confers honor upon the
   lawgiver.*y*

The Sin of Pride

6 Do not get angry with your neighbor for
      every injury,
   and do not resort to acts of insolence.
7 Arrogance is hateful to the Lord and to
      mortals,
   and injustice is outrageous to both.
8 Sovereignty passes from nation to nation
   on account of injustice and insolence and
      wealth.*z*
9 How can dust and ashes be proud?
   Even in life the human body decays.*a*
10 A long illness baffles the physician;*b*
   the king of today will die tomorrow.
11 For when one is dead
   he inherits maggots and vermin*c* and
      worms.
12 The beginning of human pride is to forsake
      the Lord;
   the heart has withdrawn from its Maker.
13 For the beginning of pride is sin,
   and the one who clings to it pours out
      abominations.
Therefore the Lord brings upon them
   unheard-of calamities,
   and destroys them completely.
14 The Lord overthrows the thrones of rulers,

---

y Heb: Gk *scribe*   *z* Other ancient authorities add here or
after verse 9a, *Nothing is more wicked than one who loves
money, for such a person puts his own soul up for sale.*
a Heb: Meaning of Gk uncertain   *b* Heb Lat: Meaning of
Gk uncertain   *c* Heb: Gk *wild animals*

Friends, Old and New

LIVE IT!

Out there, somewhere, is a special person you have not yet met. He or she will
eventually become a key person in your life, perhaps even a life partner. In fact, a
lot of such people are out there, somewhere—including future classmates, co-
workers, roommates, and friends. The challenge is in finding the particular people who will become close to you, your soul mates.

Ben Sira reminds us in Wis 9.10 that in the excitement that accompanies making new
friends, we should not forget the pleasure and comfort that an old friend brings us. A friend
we have known for a long time is someone to trust, someone who knows and accepts us,
warts and all. And when the circumstances of life cause separation from old friends, there is
value in reconnecting occasionally to share where life has taken us or even to seek direction
and support if life has become confusing or hard. We need to treasure our tried-and-true
friendships, as well as welcome new ones.

Spend some time reflecting on your friends, old and new, and their value in your life.

▶ Sir 9.10

S
I
R

and enthrones the lowly in their place.
15 The Lord plucks up the roots of the
    nations,*d*
    and plants the humble in their place.
16 The Lord lays waste the lands of the
    nations,
    and destroys them to the foundations of
        the earth.
17 He removes some of them and destroys
        them,
    and erases the memory of them from the
        earth.
18 Pride was not created for human beings,
    or violent anger for those born of
        women.

Persons Deserving Honor
(Cp Jer 9.23–24; 1 Cor 1.26–31)

19 Whose offspring are worthy of honor?
        Human offspring.
    Whose offspring are worthy of honor?
        Those who fear the Lord.
    Whose offspring are unworthy of honor?
        Human offspring.
    Whose offspring are unworthy of honor?
        Those who break the commandments.
20 Among family members their leader is
        worthy of honor,
    but those who fear the Lord are worthy
        of honor in his eyes.*e*
22 The rich, and the eminent, and the poor—
    their glory is the fear of the Lord.
23 It is not right to despise one who is
        intelligent but poor,
    and it is not proper to honor one who is
        sinful.
24 The prince and the judge and the ruler are
        honored,
    but none of them is greater than the one
        who fears the Lord.
25 Free citizens will serve a wise servant,
    and an intelligent person will not
        complain.

Concerning Humility

26 Do not make a display of your wisdom
        when you do your work,
    and do not boast when you are in need.
27 Better is the worker who has goods in
        plenty
    than the boaster who lacks bread.

28 My child, honor yourself with humility,
    and give yourself the esteem you deserve.
29 Who will acquit those who condemn*f*
        themselves?

And who will honor those who dishonor
        themselves?*g*
30 The poor are honored for their knowledge,
    while the rich are honored for their
        wealth.
31 One who is honored in poverty, how much
        more in wealth!
    And one dishonored in wealth, how
        much more in poverty!

The Deceptiveness of Appearances

The wisdom of the humble lifts their heads
        high,
    and seats them among the great.
2 Do not praise individuals for their good
        looks,
    or loathe anyone because of appearance
        alone.
3 The bee is small among flying creatures,
    but what it produces is the best of sweet
        things.
4 Do not boast about wearing fine clothes,
    and do not exalt yourself when you are
        honored;
    for the works of the Lord are wonderful,
    and his works are concealed from
        humankind.
5 Many kings have had to sit on the ground,
    but one who was never thought of has
        worn a crown.
6 Many rulers have been utterly disgraced,
    and the honored have been handed over
        to others.

Deliberation and Caution
(Prov 18.13)

7 Do not find fault before you investigate;
    examine first, and then criticize.
8 Do not answer before you listen,
    and do not interrupt when another is
        speaking.
9 Do not argue about a matter that does not
        concern you,
    and do not sit with sinners when they
        judge a case.

10 My child, do not busy yourself with many
        matters;
    if you multiply activities, you will not be
        held blameless.
    If you pursue, you will not overtake,

---

d Other ancient authorities read *proud nations*   *e* Other
ancient authorities add as verse 21, *The fear of the Lord is
the beginning of acceptance; obduracy and pride are the
beginning of rejection.*   *f* Heb: Gk *sin against*   *g* Heb Lat:
Gk *their own life*

and by fleeing you will not escape.
11 There are those who work and struggle and
        hurry,
    but are so much the more in want.
12 There are others who are slow and need
        help,
    who lack strength and abound in poverty;
    but the eyes of the Lord look kindly upon
        them;
    he lifts them out of their lowly condition
13 and raises up their heads
    to the amazement of the many.

14 Good things and bad, life and death,
    poverty and wealth, come from the
        Lord.*h*
17 The Lord's gift remains with the devout,
    and his favor brings lasting success.
18 One becomes rich through diligence and
        self-denial,
    and the reward allotted to him is this:
19 when he says, "I have found rest,
        and now I shall feast on my goods!"
    he does not know how long it will be
    until he leaves them to others and dies.

20 Stand by your agreement and attend to it,
    and grow old in your work.
21 Do not wonder at the works of a sinner,
        but trust in the Lord and keep at
        your job;
    for it is easy in the sight of the Lord
        to make the poor rich suddenly, in an
        instant.
22 The blessing of the Lord is*i* the reward of
        the pious,
    and quickly God causes his blessing to
        flourish.
23 Do not say, "What do I need,
    and what further benefit can be mine?"
24 Do not say, "I have enough,
    and what harm can come to me now?"
25 In the day of prosperity, adversity is
        forgotten,
    and in the day of adversity, prosperity is
        not remembered.
26 For it is easy for the Lord on the day of
        death
    to reward individuals according to their
        conduct.
27 An hour's misery makes one forget past
        delights,
    and at the close of one's life one's deeds
        are revealed.
28 Call no one happy before his death;
    by how he ends, a person becomes
        known.*j*

Care in Choosing Friends
(Prov 19.4, 6)

29 Do not invite everyone into your home,
    for many are the tricks of the crafty.
30 Like a decoy partridge in a cage, so is the
        mind of the proud,
    and like spies they observe your
        weakness;*k*
31 for they lie in wait, turning good into evil,
    and to worthy actions they attach blame.
32 From a spark many coals are kindled,
    and a sinner lies in wait to shed blood.
33 Beware of scoundrels, for they devise evil,
    and they may ruin your reputation
        forever.
34 Receive strangers into your home and they
        will stir up trouble for you,
    and will make you a stranger to your
        own family.

If you do good, know to whom you do it,
    and you will be thanked for your good
        deeds.
2 Do good to the devout, and you will be
        repaid—
    if not by them, certainly by the Most
        High.
3 No good comes to one who persists in evil
    or to one who does not give alms.
4 Give to the devout, but do not help the
        sinner.
5   Do good to the humble, but do not give
        to the ungodly;
    hold back their bread, and do not give it to
        them,
        for by means of it they might
        subdue you;
    then you will receive twice as much evil
        for all the good you have done to them.
6 For the Most High also hates sinners
    and will inflict punishment on the
        ungodly.*l*
7 Give to the one who is good, but do not
        help the sinner.
8 A friend is not known*m* in prosperity,
    nor is an enemy hidden in adversity.

---

h Other ancient authorities add as verses 15 and 16,
*15Wisdom, understanding, and knowledge of the law come
from the Lord; affection and the ways of good works come from
him. 16Error and darkness were created with sinners; evil grows
old with those who take pride in malice.*   *i* Heb: Gk is in
j Heb: Gk *and through his children a person becomes known*
k Heb: Gk *downfall*   *l* Other ancient authorities add *and
he is keeping them for the day of their punishment*   *m* Other
ancient authorities read *punished*

9 One's enemies are friendly[n] when one
    prospers,
  but in adversity even one's friend
    disappears.
10 Never trust your enemy,
  for like corrosion in copper, so is his
    wickedness.
11 Even if he humbles himself and walks
    bowed down,
  take care to be on your guard
    against him.
  Be to him like one who polishes a mirror,
    to be sure it does not become completely
    tarnished.
12 Do not put him next to you,
  or he may overthrow you and take your
    place.
  Do not let him sit at your right hand,
  or else he may try to take your own seat,
  and at last you will realize the truth of my
    words,
  and be stung by what I have said.
13 Who pities a snake charmer when he is
    bitten,
  or all those who go near wild animals?
14 So no one pities a person who associates
    with a sinner
  and becomes involved in the other's sins.
15 He stands by you for a while,
  but if you falter, he will not be there.
16 An enemy speaks sweetly with his lips,
  but in his heart he plans to throw you
    into a pit;
  an enemy may have tears in his eyes,
  but if he finds an opportunity he will
    never have enough of your blood.
17 If evil comes upon you, you will find him
    there ahead of you;
  pretending to help, he will trip you up.
18 Then he will shake his head, and clap his
    hands,
  and whisper much, and show his true
    face.

Caution Regarding Associates

Whoever touches pitch gets dirty,
  and whoever associates with a proud
    person becomes like him.
2 Do not lift a weight too heavy for you,
  or associate with one mightier and richer
    than you.
  How can the clay pot associate with the
    iron kettle?
  The pot will strike against it and be
    smashed.

3 A rich person does wrong, and even adds
    insults;
  a poor person suffers wrong, and must
    add apologies.
4 A rich person[o] will exploit you if you can
    be of use to him,
  but if you are in need he will
    abandon you.
5 If you own something, he will live
    with you;
  he will drain your resources without a
    qualm.
6 When he needs you he will deceive you,
  and will smile at you and encourage you;
  he will speak to you kindly and say,
    "What do you need?"
7 He will embarrass you with his delicacies,
  until he has drained you two or three
    times,
  and finally he will laugh at you.
  Should he see you afterwards, he will pass
    you by
  and shake his head at you.
8 Take care not to be led astray
  and humiliated when you are enjoying
    yourself.[p]
9 When an influential person invites you, be
    reserved,
  and he will invite you more insistently.
10 Do not be forward, or you may be rebuffed;
  do not stand aloof, or you will be
    forgotten.
11 Do not try to treat him as an equal,
  or trust his lengthy conversations;
  for he will test you by prolonged talk,
  and while he smiles he will be
    examining you.
12 Cruel are those who do not keep your
    secrets;
  they will not spare you harm or
    imprisonment.
13 Be on your guard and very careful,
  for you are walking about with your own
    downfall.[q]

15 Every creature loves its like,
  and every person the neighbor.
16 All living beings associate with their own
    kind,
  and people stick close to those like
    themselves.

---

[n] Heb: Gk *grieved*   [o] Gk *He*   [p] Other ancient
authorities read *in your folly*   [q] Other ancient authorities
add as verse 14, *When you hear these things in your sleep,
wake up! During all your life love the Lord, and call on him
for your salvation.*

17 What does a wolf have in common with a
  lamb?
  No more has a sinner with the devout.
18 What peace is there between a hyena and
  a dog?
  And what peace between the rich and the
  poor?
19 Wild asses in the wilderness are the prey of
  lions;
  likewise the poor are feeding grounds for
  the rich.
20 Humility is an abomination to the proud;
  likewise the poor are an abomination to
  the rich.

21 When the rich person totters, he is
  supported by friends,
  but when the humble[r] falls, he is pushed
  away even by friends.
22 If the rich person slips, many come to the
  rescue;
  he speaks unseemly words, but they
  justify him.
  If the humble person slips, they even
  criticize him;
  he talks sense, but is not given a hearing.
23 The rich person speaks and all are silent;
  they extol to the clouds what he says.
  The poor person speaks and they say, "Who
  is this fellow?"
  And should he stumble, they even push
  him down.
24 Riches are good if they are free from sin;
  poverty is evil only in the opinion of the
  ungodly.

25 The heart changes the countenance,
  either for good or for evil.[s]
26 The sign of a happy heart is a cheerful face,
  but to devise proverbs requires painful
  thinking.

Happy are those who do not blunder with
  their lips,
  and need not suffer remorse for sin.
2 Happy are those whose hearts do not
  condemn them,
  and who have not given up their hope.

Responsible Use of Wealth

3 Riches are inappropriate for a small-minded
  person;
  and of what use is wealth to a miser?
4 What he denies himself he collects for
  others;
  and others will live in luxury on his
  goods.

5 If one is mean to himself, to whom will he
  be generous?
  He will not enjoy his own riches.
6 No one is worse than one who is grudging
  to himself;
  this is the punishment for his meanness.
7 If ever he does good, it is by mistake;
  and in the end he reveals his meanness.
8 The miser is an evil person;
  he turns away and disregards people.
9 The eye of the greedy person is not satisfied
  with his share;
  greedy injustice withers the soul.
10 A miser begrudges bread,
  and it is lacking at his table.

11 My child, treat yourself well, according to
  your means,
  and present worthy offerings to the Lord.
12 Remember that death does not tarry,
  and the decree[t] of Hades has not been
  shown to you.
13 Do good to friends before you die,
  and reach out and give to them as much
  as you can.
14 Do not deprive yourself of a day's
  enjoyment;
  do not let your share of desired good
  pass by you.
15 Will you not leave the fruit of your labors
  to another,
  and what you acquired by toil to be
  divided by lot?
16 Give, and take, and indulge yourself,
  because in Hades one cannot look for
  luxury.
17 All living beings become old like a garment,
  for the decree[u] from of old is, "You
  must die!"
18 Like abundant leaves on a spreading tree
  that sheds some and puts forth others,
  so are the generations of flesh and blood:
  one dies and another is born.
19 Every work decays and ceases to exist,
  and the one who made it will pass away
  with it.

The Happiness of Seeking Wisdom
(Prov 8.32–36)

20 Happy is the person who meditates on[v]
  wisdom
  and reasons intelligently,

---

r Other ancient authorities read *poor*   s Other ancient
authorities add *and a glad heart makes a cheerful
countenance*   t Heb Syr: Gk *covenant*   u Heb: Gk
covenant   v Other ancient authorities read *dies in*

21 who*w* reflects in his heart on her ways
     and ponders her secrets,
22 pursuing her like a hunter,
     and lying in wait on her paths;
23 who peers through her windows
     and listens at her doors;
24 who camps near her house
     and fastens his tent peg to her walls;
25 who pitches his tent near her,
     and so occupies an excellent lodging
         place;
26 who places his children under her shelter,
     and lodges under her boughs;
27 who is sheltered by her from the heat,
     and dwells in the midst of her glory.

Whoever fears the Lord will do this,
     and whoever holds to the law will obtain
         wisdom.*x*
2 She will come to meet him like a mother,
     and like a young bride she will
         welcome him.
3 She will feed him with the bread of
         learning,
     and give him the water of wisdom to
         drink.
4 He will lean on her and not fall,
     and he will rely on her and not be put to
         shame.
5 She will exalt him above his neighbors,
     and will open his mouth in the midst of
         the assembly.
6 He will find gladness and a crown of
         rejoicing,
     and will inherit an everlasting name.
7 The foolish will not obtain her,
     and sinners will not see her.
8 She is far from arrogance,
     and liars will never think of her.
9 Praise is unseemly on the lips of a sinner,
     for it has not been sent from the Lord.
10 For in wisdom must praise be uttered,
     and the Lord will make it prosper.

Freedom of Choice
(Cp Sir 17.1–12)

11 Do not say, "It was the Lord's doing that I
         fell away";
     for he does not do*y* what he hates.
12 Do not say, "It was he who led me astray";
     for he has no need of the sinful.
13 The Lord hates all abominations;
     such things are not loved by those who
         fear him.
14 It was he who created humankind in the
         beginning,

Taking Responsibility

"It isn't my fault; she made me do it."
"He started it!" "The devil made me
do it!" We have lots of ways of blaming
others when bad things happen. Sir 15.11
tells of one way people in Ben Sira's time
tried to put the blame on someone else:
"It was the Lord's doing." Evidently, some
people blamed God when they fell into
sin. Ben Sira tells us it isn't God's will
when bad things happen as a result of
human choice (verses 14–17)—which is
why we need to stop the blame game and
take responsibility for our own actions.

   In your prayer, take some time to
reflect or journal on the following questions:
■ **Do you tend to blame others when bad
   things happen?**
■ **Have there been hurtful situations in
   which you would not accept your part
   of the responsibility? If so, describe one
   and explain how you could have owned
   up to your responsibility.**

▶ Sir 15.11–20

and he left them in the power of their
         own free choice.
15 If you choose, you can keep the
         commandments,
     and to act faithfully is a matter of your
         own choice.
16 He has placed before you fire and water;
     stretch out your hand for whichever you
         choose.
17 Before each person are life and death,
     and whichever one chooses will be given.
18 For great is the wisdom of the Lord;
     he is mighty in power and sees
         everything;
19 his eyes are on those who fear him,
     and he knows every human action.
20 He has not commanded anyone to be
         wicked,
     and he has not given anyone permission
         to sin.

---

w The structure adopted in verses 21-27 follows the Heb
x Gk *her*   *y* Heb: Gk *you ought not to do*

God's Punishment of Sinners

16 Do not desire a multitude of worthless[z]
    children,
  and do not rejoice in ungodly offspring.
2 If they multiply, do not rejoice in them,
  unless the fear of the Lord is in them.
3 Do not trust in their survival,
  or rely on their numbers;[a]
for one can be better than a thousand,
  and to die childless is better than to have
    ungodly children.
4 For through one intelligent person a city can
    be filled with people,
  but through a clan of outlaws it becomes
    desolate.

5 Many such things my eye has seen,
  and my ear has heard things more
    striking than these.
6 In an assembly of sinners a fire is kindled,
  and in a disobedient nation wrath
    blazes up.
7 He did not forgive the ancient giants
  who revolted in their might.
8 He did not spare the neighbors of Lot,
  whom he loathed on account of their
    arrogance.
9 He showed no pity on the doomed nation,
  on those dispossessed because of their
    sins;[b]
10 or on the six hundred thousand foot
    soldiers
  who assembled in their stubbornness.[c]
11 Even if there were only one stiff-necked
    person,
  it would be a wonder if he remained
    unpunished.
For mercy and wrath are with the Lord;[d]
  he is mighty to forgive—but he also pours
    out wrath.
12 Great as is his mercy, so also is his
    chastisement;
  he judges a person according to his or
    her deeds.
13 The sinner will not escape with plunder,
  and the patience of the godly will not be
    frustrated.
14 He makes room for every act of mercy;
  everyone receives in accordance with his
    or her deeds.[e]

17 Do not say, "I am hidden from the Lord,
  and who from on high has me in mind?
Among so many people I am unknown,
  for what am I in a boundless creation?
18 Lo, heaven and the highest heaven,

the abyss and the earth, tremble at his
  visitation![f]
19 The very mountains and the foundations of
    the earth
  quiver and quake when he looks upon them.
20 But no human mind can grasp this,
  and who can comprehend his ways?
21 Like a tempest that no one can see,
  so most of his works are concealed.[g]
22 Who is to announce his acts of justice?
  Or who can await them? For his decree[h]
    is far off."[i]
23 Such are the thoughts of one devoid of
    understanding;
  a senseless and misguided person thinks
    foolishly.

God's Wisdom Seen in Creation
(Gen 1.1—2.4a)

24 Listen to me, my child, and acquire
    knowledge,
  and pay close attention to my words.
25 I will impart discipline precisely[j]
  and declare knowledge accurately.

26 When the Lord created[k] his works from the
    beginning,
  and, in making them, determined their
    boundaries,
27 he arranged his works in an eternal order,
  and their dominion[l] for all generations.
They neither hunger nor grow weary,
  and they do not abandon their tasks.
28 They do not crowd one another,
  and they never disobey his word.
29 Then the Lord looked upon the earth,
  and filled it with his good things.
30 With all kinds of living beings he covered
    its surface,
  and into it they must return.

z Heb: Gk *unprofitable*   a Other ancient authorities add *For you will groan in untimely mourning, and will know of their sudden end.*   b Other ancient authorities add *All these things he did to the hard-hearted nations, and by the multitude of his holy ones he was not appeased.*   c Other ancient authorities add *Chastising, showing mercy, striking, healing, the Lord persisted in mercy and discipline.* d Gk *him*   e Other ancient authorities add [15]*The Lord hardened Pharaoh so that he did not recognize him, in order that his works might be known under heaven.* [16]*His mercy is manifest to the whole of creation, and he divided his light and darkness with a plumb line.*   f Other ancient authorities add *The whole world past and present is in his will.* g Meaning of Gk uncertain: Heb Syr *If I sin, no eye can see me, and if I am disloyal all in secret, who is to know?* h Heb *the decree*: Gk *the covenant*   i Other ancient authorities add *and a scrutiny for all comes at the end* j Gk *by weight*   k Heb: Gk *judged*   l Or *elements*

The Lord created human beings out of earth,
and makes them return to it again.
2 He gave them a fixed number of days,
but granted them authority over
everything on the earth.[m]
3 He endowed them with strength like
his own,[n]
and made them in his own image.
4 He put the fear of them[o] in all living
beings,
and gave them dominion over beasts and
birds.[p]
6 Discretion and tongue and eyes,
ears and a mind for thinking he gave
them.
7 He filled them with knowledge and
understanding,
and showed them good and evil.
8 He put the fear of him into[q] their hearts
to show them the majesty of his
works.[r]
10 And they will praise his holy name,
9 to proclaim the grandeur of his works.
11 He bestowed knowledge upon them,
and allotted to them the law of life.[s]
12 He established with them an eternal
covenant,
and revealed to them his decrees.
13 Their eyes saw his glorious majesty,
and their ears heard the glory of his
voice.
14 He said to them, "Beware of all evil."
And he gave commandment to each of
them concerning the neighbor.
15 Their ways are always known to him;
they will not be hid from his eyes.[t]
17 He appointed a ruler for every nation,
but Israel is the Lord's own portion.[u]
19 All their works are as clear as the sun
before him,
and his eyes are ever upon their ways.
20 Their iniquities are not hidden from him,
and all their sins are before the Lord.[v]
22 One's almsgiving is like a signet ring with
the Lord,[w]
and he will keep a person's kindness like
the apple of his eye.[x]
23 Afterward he will rise up and repay them,
and he will bring their recompense on
their heads.
24 Yet to those who repent he grants a
return,
and he encourages those who are losing
hope.

A Call to Repentance

25 Turn back to the Lord and forsake your sins;
pray in his presence and lessen your
offense.
26 Return to the Most High and turn away
from iniquity,[y]
and hate intensely what he abhors.
27 Who will sing praises to the Most High in
Hades
in place of the living who give thanks?
28 From the dead, as from one who does not
exist, thanksgiving has ceased;
those who are alive and well sing the
Lord's praises.
29 How great is the mercy of the Lord,
and his forgiveness for those who return
to him!
30 For not everything is within human
capability,
since human beings are not immortal.
31 What is brighter than the sun? Yet it can be
eclipsed.
So flesh and blood devise evil.
32 He marshals the host of the height of
heaven;
but all human beings are dust and ashes.

The Majesty of God

He who lives forever created the whole
universe;
2 the Lord alone is just.[z]

---

m Lat: Gk it   n Lat: Gk *proper to them*   o Syr: Gk *him*
p Other ancient authorities add as verse 5, *They obtained
the use of the five faculties of the Lord; as sixth he distributed
to them the gift of mind, and as seventh, reason, the interpreter
of one's faculties.*   q Other ancient authorities read *He set
his eye upon*   r Other ancient authorities add *and he gave
them to boast of his marvels forever*   s Other ancient
authorities add *so that they may know that they who are alive
now are mortal*   t Other ancient authorities add 16*Their
ways from youth tend toward evil, and they are unable to make
for themselves hearts of flesh in place of their stony hearts.*
17*For in the division of the nations of the whole earth, he
appointed*   u Other ancient authorities add as verse 18,
*whom, being his firstborn, he brings up with discipline, and
allotting to him the light of his love, he does not neglect him.*
v Other ancient authorities add as verse 21, *But the Lord,
who is gracious and knows how they are formed, has neither
left them nor abandoned them, but has spared them.*
w Gk *him* x Other ancient authorities add *apportioning
repentance to his sons and daughters* y Other ancient
authorities add *for he will lead you out of darkness to the
light of health.*   z Other ancient authorities add *and there
is no other beside him;* 3*he steers the world with the span of his
hand, and all things obey his will; for he is king of all things
by his power, separating among them the holy things from the
profane.*

4 To none has he given power to proclaim his
   works;
  and who can search out his mighty
   deeds?
5 Who can measure his majestic power?
  And who can fully recount his mercies?
6 It is not possible to diminish or increase
   them,
  nor is it possible to fathom the wonders
   of the Lord.
7 When human beings have finished, they are
   just beginning,
  and when they stop, they are still
   perplexed.
8 What are human beings, and of what use
   are they?
  What is good in them, and what is evil?
9 The number of days in their life is great if
   they reach one hundred years.[a]
10 Like a drop of water from the sea and a
   grain of sand,
  so are a few years among the days of
   eternity.
11 That is why the Lord is patient with them
  and pours out his mercy upon them.
12 He sees and recognizes that their end is
   miserable;
  therefore he grants them forgiveness all
   the more.
13 The compassion of human beings is for
   their neighbors,
  but the compassion of the Lord is for
   every living thing.
  He rebukes and trains and teaches them,
  and turns them back, as a shepherd his
   flock.
14 He has compassion on those who accept his
   discipline
  and who are eager for his precepts.

The Right Spirit in Giving Alms

15 My child, do not mix reproach with your
   good deeds,
  or spoil your gift by harsh words.
16 Does not the dew give relief from the
   scorching heat?
  So a word is better than a gift.
17 Indeed, does not a word surpass a good
   gift?
  Both are to be found in a gracious
   person.
18 A fool is ungracious and abusive,
  and the gift of a grudging giver makes the
   eyes dim.

The Need of Reflection and Self-control

19 Before you speak, learn;
  and before you fall ill, take care of your
   health.
20 Before judgment comes, examine yourself;
  and at the time of scrutiny you will find
   forgiveness.
21 Before falling ill, humble yourself;
  and when you have sinned, repent.
22 Let nothing hinder you from paying a vow
   promptly,
  and do not wait until death to be
   released from it.
23 Before making a vow, prepare yourself;
  do not be like one who puts the Lord to
   the test.
24 Think of his wrath on the day of death,
  and of the moment of vengeance when
   he turns away his face.
25 In the time of plenty think of the time of
   hunger;
  in days of wealth think of poverty and
   need.
26 From morning to evening conditions
   change;
  all things move swiftly before the Lord.

27 One who is wise is cautious in everything;
  when sin is all around, one guards
   against wrongdoing.
28 Every intelligent person knows wisdom,
  and praises the one who finds her.
29 Those who are skilled in words become wise
   themselves,
  and pour forth apt proverbs.[b]

SELF-CONTROL[c]

30 Do not follow your base desires,
  but restrain your appetites.
31 If you allow your soul to take pleasure in
   base desire,
  it will make you the laughingstock of
   your enemies.
32 Do not revel in great luxury,
  or you may become impoverished by its
   expense.
33 Do not become a beggar by feasting with
   borrowed money,
  when you have nothing in your purse.[d]

---

a Other ancient authorities add *but the death of each one is
beyond the calculation of all*   b Other ancient authorities
add *Better is confidence in the one Lord than clinging with a
dead heart to a dead one.*   c This heading is included in
the Gk text.   d Other ancient authorities add *for you will
be plotting against your own life*

S
I
R

Don't Get Burned

It is easy to give in to temptation. Every day, we face decisions that can hurt our relationship with God. Ben Sira soundly advises us not to give in to our base desires (Sir 18.30). These are attitudes and practices, like laziness, drunkenness, and lust, that might bring some immediate pleasure but also lead to long-term problems. Self-control is the strength to resist the base desires that lead to lifelong problems.

An old saying—If you play with matches, you might get burned—is often used by people recovering from addictions. It reminds them that risky behaviors often end up hurting them. It helps them stay focused on their long-term goal of leading a healthy and happy life. If they follow Ben Sira's advice—practice self-control—they won't end up getting burned!

What base desires tempt you the most? What do you need to do to avoid getting burned by them?

▶ Sir 18.30—19.3

The one who does this*e* will not become rich;
    one who despises small things will fail
        little by little.
2 Wine and women lead intelligent men
        astray,
    and the man who consorts with
        prostitutes is reckless.
3 Decay and worms will take possession
        of him,
    and the reckless person will be snatched
        away.

Against Loose Talk

4 One who trusts others too quickly has a
        shallow mind,
    and one who sins does wrong to himself.
5 One who rejoices in wickedness*f* will be
        condemned,*g*
6   but one who hates gossip has less evil.
7 Never repeat a conversation,
    and you will lose nothing at all.
8 With friend or foe do not report it,
    and unless it would be a sin for you, do
        not reveal it;
9 for someone may have heard you and
        watched you,
    and in time will hate you.
10 Have you heard something? Let it die
        with you.
    Be brave, it will not make you burst!
11 Having heard something, the fool suffers
        birth pangs
    like a woman in labor with a child.
12 Like an arrow stuck in a person's thigh,
    so is gossip inside a fool.

13 Question a friend; perhaps he did not do it;
    or if he did, so that he may not do it
        again.
14 Question a neighbor; perhaps he did not
        say it;
    or if he said it, so that he may not
        repeat it.
15 Question a friend, for often it is slander;
    so do not believe everything you hear.
16 A person may make a slip without
        intending it.
    Who has not sinned with his tongue?
17 Question your neighbor before you
        threaten him;
    and let the law of the Most High take its
        course.*h*

True and False Wisdom

20 The whole of wisdom is fear of the Lord,
    and in all wisdom there is the fulfillment
        of the law.*i*
22 The knowledge of wickedness is not
        wisdom,
    nor is there prudence in the counsel of
        sinners.
23 There is a cleverness that is detestable,

e Heb: Gk *A worker who is a drunkard*   *f* Other ancient authorities read *heart*   *g* Other ancient authorities add *but one who withstands pleasures crowns his life.* *6One who controls the tongue will live without strife.*   *h* Other ancient authorities add *and do not be angry.* *18The fear of the Lord is the beginning of acceptance, and wisdom obtains his love.* *19The knowledge of the Lord's commandments is life-giving discipline; and those who do what is pleasing to him enjoy the fruit of the tree of immortality.*   *i* Other ancient authorities add *and the knowledge of his omnipotence.* *21When a slave says to his master, "I will not act as you wish," even if later he does it, he angers the one who supports him.*

S
I
R

and there is a fool who merely lacks
    wisdom.

24 Better are the God-fearing who lack
    understanding
than the highly intelligent who transgress
    the law.

25 There is a cleverness that is exact but unjust,
    and there are people who abuse favors to
    gain a verdict.

26 There is the villain bowed down in
    mourning,
but inwardly he is full of deceit.

27 He hides his face and pretends not to hear,
    but when no one notices, he will take
    advantage of you.

28 Even if lack of strength keeps him from
    sinning,
he will nevertheless do evil when he
    finds the opportunity.

29 A person is known by his appearance,
    and a sensible person is known when
    first met, face to face.

30 A person's attire and hearty laughter,
    and the way he walks, show what he is.

Silence and Speech

There is a rebuke that is untimely,
    and there is the person who is wise
    enough to keep silent.

2 How much better it is to rebuke than to
    fume!

3 And the one who admits his fault will be
    kept from failure.

4 Like a eunuch lusting to violate a girl
    is the person who does right under
    compulsion.

5 Some people keep silent and are thought to
    be wise,
while others are detested for being
    talkative.

6 Some people keep silent because they have
    nothing to say,
while others keep silent because they
    know when to speak.

7 The wise remain silent until the right
    moment,
but a boasting fool misses the right
    moment.

8 Whoever talks too much is detested,
    and whoever pretends to authority is
    hated.*j*

Paradoxes

9 There may be good fortune for a person in
    adversity,
and a windfall may result in a loss.

10 There is the gift that profits you nothing,
    and the gift to be paid back double.

11 There are losses for the sake of glory,
    and there are some who have raised their
    heads from humble circumstances.

12 Some buy much for little,
    but pay for it seven times over.

13 The wise make themselves beloved by only
    few words,*k*
but the courtesies of fools are wasted.

14 A fool's gift will profit you nothing,*l*
    for he looks for recompense sevenfold.*m*

15 He gives little and upbraids much;
    he opens his mouth like a town crier.
Today he lends and tomorrow he asks it
    back;
such a one is hateful to God and
    humans.*n*

16 The fool says, "I have no friends,
    and I get no thanks for my good deeds.
Those who eat my bread are
    evil-tongued."

17 How many will ridicule him, and how
    often!*o*

Inappropriate Speech

18 A slip on the pavement is better than a slip
    of the tongue;
the downfall of the wicked will occur just
    as speedily.

19 A coarse person is like an inappropriate
    story,
continually on the lips of the ignorant.

20 A proverb from a fool's lips will be
    rejected,
for he does not tell it at the proper time.

21 One may be prevented from sinning by
    poverty;
so when he rests he feels no remorse.

22 One may lose his life through shame,
    or lose it because of human respect.*p*

23 Another out of shame makes promises to a
    friend,
and so makes an enemy for nothing.

---

j Other ancient authorities add *How good it is to show
repentance when you are reproved, for so you will escape
deliberate sin!*   *k* Heb: Gk *by words*   *l* Other ancient
authorities add *so it is with the envious who give under
compulsion*   *m* Syr: Gk *he has many eyes instead of one*
n Other ancient authorities lack *to God and humans*
o Other ancient authorities add *for he has not honestly
received what he has, and what he does not have is
unimportant to him*   *p* Other ancient authorities read *his
foolish look*

Lying

24 A lie is an ugly blot on a person;
    it is continually on the lips of the
        ignorant.
25 A thief is preferable to a habitual liar,
    but the lot of both is ruin.
26 A liar's way leads to disgrace,
    and his shame is ever with him.

PROVERBIAL SAYINGS q

27 The wise person advances himself by his
        words,
    and one who is sensible pleases the great.
28 Those who cultivate the soil heap up their
        harvest,
    and those who please the great atone for
        injustice.
29 Favors and gifts blind the eyes of the wise;
    like a muzzle on the mouth they stop
        reproofs.
30 Hidden wisdom and unseen treasure,
    of what value is either?
31 Better are those who hide their folly
    than those who hide their wisdom.r

Various Sins

Have you sinned, my child? Do so no more,
    but ask forgiveness for your past sins.
2 Flee from sin as from a snake;
    for if you approach sin, it will bite you.
Its teeth are lion's teeth,
    and can destroy human lives.
3 All lawlessness is like a two-edged sword;
    there is no healing for the wound it
        inflicts.

4 Panic and insolence will waste away riches;
    thus the house of the proud will be laid
        waste.s
5 The prayer of the poor goes from their lips
    to the ears of God,t
    and his judgment comes speedily.
6 Those who hate reproof walk in the sinner's
        steps,
    but those who fear the Lord repent in
        their heart.
7 The mighty in speech are widely known;
    when they slip, the sensible person
        knows it.
8 Whoever builds his house with other
        people's money
    is like one who gathers stones for his
        burial mound.u
9 An assembly of the wicked is like a bundle
        of tow,
    and their end is a blazing fire.

10 The way of sinners is paved with smooth
        stones,
    but at its end is the pit of Hades.

PRAY IT!

Examine Your Conscience

An examination of conscience is a moral inventory of one's life. When we examine our conscience, we can recognize those we have hurt, make amends where possible, and turn our life around before a pattern of sin becomes a major obstacle in our relationships with God and with others. We can also recognize the positive moral choices that we have made. Chapters 19–22 of Sirach list some of the sins from Ben Sira's time. Use them as a guide for making your own examination of conscience, as follows:

- Have you broken a confidence (19.5–12)?
- Do you offend others with your language (20.18–19)?
- Have you lied (20.24–26)?
- Have you stolen from others (21.8)?
- Have you been lazy in your use of time (22.1–2)?
- Have you disobeyed your parents (22.3–5)?

    When you have finished this examination, read 22.27—23.6 as your own prayer for God's help against sinning.

▶ Sir 19.4—23.6

Wisdom and Foolishness

11 Whoever keeps the law controls his
        thoughts,
    and the fulfillment of the fear of the Lord
        is wisdom.
12 The one who is not clever cannot be taught,
    but there is a cleverness that increases
        bitterness.

---

q This heading is included in the Gk text.   r Other ancient authorities add *32Unwearied endurance in seeking the Lord is better than a masterless charioteer of one's own life.* s Other ancient authorities read *uprooted*   t Gk *his ears* u Other ancient authorities read *for the winter*

13 The knowledge of the wise will increase like
a flood,
and their counsel like a life-giving spring.
14 The mind[v] of a fool is like a broken jar;
it can hold no knowledge.

15 When an intelligent person hears a wise
saying,
he praises it and adds to it;
when a fool[w] hears it, he laughs at[x] it
and throws it behind his back.
16 A fool's chatter is like a burden on a
journey,
but delight is found in the speech of the
intelligent.
17 The utterance of a sensible person is sought
in the assembly,
and they ponder his words in their
minds.
18 Like a house in ruins is wisdom to a fool,
and to the ignorant, knowledge is talk
that has no meaning.
19 To a senseless person education is fetters on
his feet,
and like manacles on his right hand.
20 A fool raises his voice when he laughs,
but the wise[y] smile quietly.
21 To the sensible person education is like a
golden ornament,
and like a bracelet on the right arm.

22 The foot of a fool rushes into a house,
but an experienced person waits
respectfully outside.
23 A boor peers into the house from the door,
but a cultivated person remains outside.
24 It is ill-mannered for a person to listen at a
door;
the discreet would be grieved by the
disgrace.

25 The lips of babblers speak of what is not
their concern,[z]
but the words of the prudent are weighed
in the balance.
26 The mind of fools is in their mouth,
but the mouth of the wise is in[a] their
mind.
27 When an ungodly person curses an
adversary,[b]
he curses himself.
28 A whisperer degrades himself
and is hated in his neighborhood.

The Idler

The idler is like a filthy stone,
and every one hisses at his disgrace.
2 The idler is like the filth of dunghills;
anyone that picks it up will shake it off
his hand.

Degenerate Children

3 It is a disgrace to be the father of an
undisciplined son,
and the birth of a daughter is a loss.
4 A sensible daughter obtains a husband of
her own,
but one who acts shamefully is a grief to
her father.
5 An impudent daughter disgraces father and
husband,
and is despised by both.
6 Like music in time of mourning is ill-timed
conversation,
but a thrashing and discipline are at all
times wisdom.[c]

Wisdom and Folly

9 Whoever teaches a fool is like one who
glues potsherds together,
or who rouses a sleeper from deep
slumber.
10 Whoever tells a story to a fool tells it to a
drowsy man;
and at the end he will say, "What is it?"
11 Weep for the dead, for he has left the light
behind;
and weep for the fool, for he has left
intelligence behind.
Weep less bitterly for the dead, for he is at
rest;
but the life of the fool is worse than
death.
12 Mourning for the dead lasts seven days,
but for the foolish or the ungodly it lasts
all the days of their lives.

13 Do not talk much with a senseless person
or visit an unintelligent person.[d]
Stay clear of him, or you may have trouble,

---

v Syr Lat: Gk *entrails*   w Syr: Gk *reveler*   x Syr: Gk *dislikes*
y Syr Lat: Gk *clever*   z Other ancient authorities read *of
strangers speak of these things*   a Other ancient authorities
omit *in*   b Or *curses Satan*   c Other ancient authorities
add 7*Children who are brought up in a good life, conceal the
lowly birth of their parents.* 8*Children who are disdainfully and
boorishly haughty stain the nobility of their kindred.*
d Other ancient authorities add *For being without sense he
will despise everything about you*

and be spattered when he shakes
  himself off.
Avoid him and you will find rest,
  and you will never be wearied by his lack
    of sense.
14 What is heavier than lead?
  And what is its name except "Fool"?
15 Sand, salt, and a piece of iron
  are easier to bear than a stupid person.

16 A wooden beam firmly bonded into a
    building
  is not loosened by an earthquake;
so the mind firmly resolved after due
    reflection
  will not be afraid in a crisis.
17 A mind settled on an intelligent thought
  is like stucco decoration that makes a
    wall smooth.
18 Fences[e] set on a high place
  will not stand firm against the wind;
so a timid mind with a fool's resolve
  will not stand firm against any fear.

The Preservation of Friendship

19 One who pricks the eye brings tears,
  and one who pricks the heart makes clear
    its feelings.
20 One who throws a stone at birds scares
    them away,
  and one who reviles a friend destroys a
    friendship.
21 Even if you draw your sword against a
    friend,
  do not despair, for there is a way back.
22 If you open your mouth against your friend,
  do not worry, for reconciliation is
    possible.
But as for reviling, arrogance, disclosure of
    secrets, or a treacherous blow—
  in these cases any friend will take to
    flight.

23 Gain the trust of your neighbor in his
    poverty,
  so that you may rejoice with him in his
    prosperity.
Stand by him in time of distress,
  so that you may share with him in his
    inheritance.[f]
24 The vapor and smoke of the furnace precede
    the fire;
  so insults precede bloodshed.
25 I am not ashamed to shelter a friend,
  and I will not hide from him.

26 But if harm should come to me because
    of him,
  whoever hears of it will beware of him.

A Prayer for Help against Sinning

27 Who will set a guard over my mouth,
  and an effective seal upon my lips,
so that I may not fall because of them,
  and my tongue may not destroy me?

O Lord, Father and Master of my life,
  do not abandon me to their designs,
  and do not let me fall because of them!
2 Who will set whips over my thoughts,
  and the discipline of wisdom over my
    mind,
so as not to spare me in my errors,
  and not overlook my[g] sins?
3 Otherwise my mistakes may be multiplied,
  and my sins may abound,
and I may fall before my adversaries,
  and my enemy may rejoice over me.[h]
4 O Lord, Father and God of my life,
  do not give me haughty eyes,
5 and remove evil desire from me.
6 Let neither gluttony nor lust overcome me,
  and do not give me over to shameless
    passion.

DISCIPLINE OF THE TONGUE[i]

7 Listen, my children, to instruction
    concerning the mouth;
  the one who observes it will never be
    caught.
8 Sinners are overtaken through their lips;
  by them the reviler and the arrogant are
    tripped up.
9 Do not accustom your mouth to oaths,
  nor habitually utter the name of the
    Holy One;
10 for as a servant who is constantly under
    scrutiny
  will not lack bruises,
so also the person who always swears and
    utters the Name
  will never be cleansed[j] from sin.
11 The one who swears many oaths is full of
    iniquity,
  and the scourge will not leave his house.
If he swears in error, his sin remains
    on him,

---

e Other ancient authorities read *Pebbles* f Other ancient
authorities add *For one should not always despise restricted
circumstances, or admire a rich person who is stupid.*
g Gk *their* h Other ancient authorities add *From them the
hope of your mercy is remote* i This heading is included in
the Gk text. j Syr *be free*

and if he disregards it, he sins doubly;
　if he swears a false oath, he will not be
　　　justified,
　for his house will be filled with
　　　calamities.

will not be quenched until it burns itself out;
one who commits fornication with his near
　of kin
will never cease until the fire burns
　him up.

Four-Letter Words

Four-letter words. You've heard them plenty. You have undoubtedly used them yourself. They roll off the tongue so easily. They get attention. They help you fit in with some groups of people.

You might wonder, So, what's the problem with foul language? Why does Ben Sira call it "sinful speech" (Sir 23.13)? Well, part of the problem is that using it easily becomes a habit. You become less aware of when you are using it. You can get yourself into trouble. Ben Sira warns that you may "behave like a fool through bad habit" (verse 14).

Maybe the worst part of the problem is that frequent use of foul language shows a lack of respect and reverence for others and certainly for God's name. Ben Sira reminds us, "Such conduct will be far from the godly" (verse 12).

Certainly, in a language with over six hundred thousand words, there are more creative ways to express emotion or frustration than relying on those all-too-familiar four-letter words. If you've developed the habit of using them, ask God and your friends to help you stop.

▶ Sir 23.12–15

Foul Language

12 There is a manner of speaking comparable
　　　to death;[k]
　may it never be found in the inheritance
　　　of Jacob!
　Such conduct will be far from the godly,
　　　and they will not wallow in sins.
13 Do not accustom your mouth to coarse,
　　　foul language,
　　for it involves sinful speech.
14 Remember your father and mother
　　　when you sit among the great,
　or you may forget yourself in their presence,
　　　and behave like a fool through bad habit;
　then you will wish that you had never been
　　　born,
　　and you will curse the day of your birth.
15 Those who are accustomed to using abusive
　　　language
　　will never become disciplined as long as
　　　they live.

Concerning Sexual Sins

16 Two kinds of individuals multiply sins,
　　and a third incurs wrath.
　Hot passion that blazes like a fire

17 To a fornicator all bread is sweet;
　　he will never weary until he dies.
18 The one who sins against his marriage bed
　　says to himself, "Who can see me?
　Darkness surrounds me, the walls hide me,
　　and no one sees me. Why should I worry?
　The Most High will not remember sins."
19 His fear is confined to human eyes
　　and he does not realize that the eyes of
　　　the Lord
　are ten thousand times brighter than
　　　the sun;
　they look upon every aspect of human
　　　behavior
　　and see into hidden corners.
20 Before the universe was created, it was
　　　known to him,
　　and so it is since its completion.
21 This man will be punished in the streets of
　　　the city,
　　and where he least suspects it, he will be
　　　seized.

22 So it is with a woman who leaves her
　　　husband

_____
k Other ancient authorities read _clothed about with death_

S
I
R

and presents him with an heir by
another man.

23 For first of all, she has disobeyed the law of
the Most High;
second, she has committed an offense
against her husband;
and third, through her fornication she has
committed adultery
and brought forth children by
another man.

24 She herself will be brought before the
assembly,
and her punishment will extend to her
children.

25 Her children will not take root,
and her branches will not bear fruit.

26 She will leave behind an accursed memory
and her disgrace will never be
blotted out.

27 Those who survive her will recognize
that nothing is better than the fear of the
Lord,
and nothing sweeter than to heed the
commandments of the Lord.[l]

THE PRAISE OF WISDOM [m]

24 Wisdom praises herself,
and tells of her glory in the midst of her
people.

2 In the assembly of the Most High she opens
her mouth,
and in the presence of his hosts she tells
of her glory:

3 "I came forth from the mouth of the Most
High,
and covered the earth like a mist.

4 I dwelt in the highest heavens,
and my throne was in a pillar of cloud.

5 Alone I compassed the vault of heaven
and traversed the depths of the abyss.

6 Over waves of the sea, over all the earth,
and over every people and nation I have
held sway.[n]

7 Among all these I sought a resting place;
in whose territory should I abide?

8 "Then the Creator of all things gave me a
command,
and my Creator chose the place for my
tent.
He said, 'Make your dwelling in Jacob,
and in Israel receive your inheritance.'

9 Before the ages, in the beginning, he
created me,
and for all the ages I shall not cease
to be.

10 In the holy tent I ministered before him,
and so I was established in Zion.

11 Thus in the beloved city he gave me a
resting place,
and in Jerusalem was my domain.

12 I took root in an honored people,
in the portion of the Lord, his heritage.

13 "I grew tall like a cedar in Lebanon,
and like a cypress on the heights of
Hermon.

14 I grew tall like a palm tree in En-ge'di,[o]
and like rosebushes in Jericho;
like a fair olive tree in the field,
and like a plane tree beside water[p] I grew
tall.

15 Like cassia and camel's thorn I gave forth
perfume,
and like choice myrrh I spread my
fragrance,
like galbanum, onycha, and stacte,
and like the odor of incense in the tent.

16 Like a terebinth I spread out my branches,
and my branches are glorious and
graceful.

17 Like the vine I bud forth delights,
and my blossoms become glorious and
abundant fruit.[q]

19 "Come to me, you who desire me,
and eat your fill of my fruits.

20 For the memory of me is sweeter than
honey,
and the possession of me sweeter than
the honeycomb.

21 Those who eat of me will hunger for more,
and those who drink of me will thirst for
more.

22 Whoever obeys me will not be put to
shame,
and those who work with me will
not sin."

Wisdom and the Law

23 All this is the book of the covenant of the
Most High God,
the law that Moses commanded us

---

[l] Other ancient authorities add as verse 28, *It is a great
honor to follow God, and to be received by him is long life.*
[m] This heading is included in the Gk text.   [n] Other
ancient authorities read *I have acquired a possession*
[o] Other ancient authorities read *on the beaches*   [p] Other
ancient authorities omit *beside water*   [q] Other ancient
authorities add as verse 18, *I am the mother of beautiful
love, of fear, of knowledge, and of holy hope; being eternal, I
am given to all my children, to those who are named by him.*

as an inheritance for the congregations of
   Jacob.*r*

25 It overflows, like the Pi'shon, with wisdom,
   and like the Tigris at the time of the first
      fruits.
26 It runs over, like the Euphrates, with
      understanding,
   and like the Jordan at harvest time.
27 It pours forth instruction like the Nile,*s*
   like the Gi'hon at the time of vintage.
28 The first man did not know wisdom*t* fully,
   nor will the last one fathom her.
29 For her thoughts are more abundant than
      the sea,
   and her counsel deeper than the great
      abyss.
30 As for me, I was like a canal from a river,
   like a water channel into a garden.
31 I said, "I will water my garden
   and drench my flower-beds."
   And lo, my canal became a river,
   and my river a sea.
32 I will again make instruction shine forth
      like the dawn,
   and I will make it clear from far away.
33 I will again pour out teaching like prophecy,
   and leave it to all future generations.
34 Observe that I have not labored for myself
      alone,
   but for all who seek wisdom.*t*

Those Who Are Worthy of Praise

I take pleasure in three things,
   and they are beautiful in the sight of God
      and of mortals:*u*
agreement among brothers and sisters,
      friendship among neighbors,
   and a wife and a husband who live in
      harmony.
2 I hate three kinds of people,
   and I loathe their manner of life:
a pauper who boasts, a rich person who
      lies,
   and an old fool who commits adultery.
3 If you gathered nothing in your youth,
   how can you find anything in your
      old age?
4 How attractive is sound judgment in the
      gray-haired,
   and for the aged to possess good counsel!
5 How attractive is wisdom in the aged,
   and understanding and counsel in the
      venerable!
6 Rich experience is the crown of the aged,
   and their boast is the fear of the Lord.

7 I can think of nine whom I would call
      blessed,
   and a tenth my tongue proclaims:
a man who can rejoice in his children;
   a man who lives to see the downfall of
      his foes.
8 Happy the man who lives with a sensible
      wife,
   and the one who does not plow with ox
      and ass together.*v*
Happy is the one who does not sin with the
      tongue,
   and the one who has not served an
      inferior.
9 Happy is the one who finds a friend,*w*
   and the one who speaks to attentive
      listeners.
10 How great is the one who finds wisdom!
   But none is superior to the one who fears
      the Lord.
11 Fear of the Lord surpasses everything;
   to whom can we compare the one who
      has it?*x*

Some Extreme Forms of Evil

13 Any wound, but not a wound of the heart!
   Any wickedness, but not the wickedness
      of a woman!
14 Any suffering, but not suffering from those
      who hate!
   And any vengeance, but not the
      vengeance of enemies!
15 There is no venom*y* worse than a snake's
      venom,*y*
   and no anger worse than a woman's*z*
      wrath.

The Evil of a Wicked Woman

16 I would rather live with a lion and a dragon
   than live with an evil woman.
17 A woman's wickedness changes her
      appearance,
   and darkens her face like that of a bear.
18 Her husband sits*a* among the neighbors,

---

r Other ancient authorities add as verse 24, *"Do not cease
to be strong in the Lord, cling to him so that he may
strengthen you; the Lord Almighty alone is God, and besides
him there is no savior."* *s* Syr: Gk *It makes instruction shine
forth like light* *t* Gk *her* *u* Syr Lat: Gk *In three things I
was beautiful and I stood in beauty before the Lord and
mortals.* *v* Heb Syr: Gk lacks *and the one who does not
plow with ox and ass together* *w* Lat Syr: Gk *good sense*
x Other ancient authorities add as verse 12, *The fear of the
Lord is the beginning of love for him, and faith is the
beginning of clinging to him.* *y* Syr: Gk *head* *z* Other
ancient authorities read *an enemy's* *a* Heb Syr: Gk *loses
heart*

and he cannot help sighing*b* bitterly.

19 Any iniquity is small compared to a
woman's iniquity;
may a sinner's lot befall her!

20 A sandy ascent for the feet of the aged—
such is a garrulous wife to a quiet
husband.

21 Do not be ensnared by a woman's beauty,
and do not desire a woman for her
possessions.*c*

22 There is wrath and impudence and great
disgrace
when a wife supports her husband.

23 Dejected mind, gloomy face,
and wounded heart come from an evil
wife.
Drooping hands and weak knees
come from the wife who does not make
her husband happy.

24 From a woman sin had its beginning,
and because of her we all die.

25 Allow no outlet to water,
and no boldness of speech to an evil
wife.

26 If she does not go as you direct,
separate her from yourself.

The Joy of a Good Wife

Happy is the husband of a good wife;
the number of his days will be doubled.

2 A loyal wife brings joy to her husband,
and he will complete his years in peace.

3 A good wife is a great blessing;
she will be granted among the blessings
of the man who fears the Lord.

4 Whether rich or poor, his heart is content,
and at all times his face is cheerful.

The Worst of Evils: A Wicked Wife

5 Of three things my heart is frightened,
and of a fourth I am in great fear:*d*
Slander in the city, the gathering of a mob,
and false accusation—all these are worse
than death.

6 But it is heartache and sorrow when a wife
is jealous of a rival,
and a tongue-lashing makes it known
to all.

7 A bad wife is a chafing yoke;
taking hold of her is like grasping a
scorpion.

8 A drunken wife arouses great anger;
she cannot hide her shame.

9 The haughty stare betrays an unchaste wife;
her eyelids give her away.

10 Keep strict watch over a headstrong
daughter,
or else, when she finds liberty, she will
make use of it.

11 Be on guard against her impudent eye,
and do not be surprised if she sins
against you.

12 As a thirsty traveler opens his mouth
and drinks from any water near him,
so she will sit in front of every tent peg
and open her quiver to the arrow.

The Blessing of a Good Wife

13 A wife's charm delights her husband,
and her skill puts flesh on his bones.

14 A silent wife is a gift from the Lord,
and nothing is so precious as her
self-discipline.

15 A modest wife adds charm to charm,
and no scales can weigh the value of her
chastity.

16 Like the sun rising in the heights of the
Lord,
so is the beauty of a good wife in her
well-ordered home.

17 Like the shining lamp on the holy
lampstand,
so is a beautiful face on a stately figure.

18 Like golden pillars on silver bases,
so are shapely legs and steadfast feet.

Other ancient authorities add verses 19–27:

19 *My child, keep sound the bloom of your youth,
and do not give your strength to strangers.*

20 *Seek a fertile field within the whole plain,
and sow it with your own seed, trusting in
your fine stock.*

21 *So your offspring will prosper,
and, having confidence in their good descent,
will grow great.*

22 *A prostitute is regarded as spittle,
and a married woman as a tower of death to
her lovers.*

23 *A godless wife is given as a portion to a
lawless man,
but a pious wife is given to the man who
fears the Lord.*

24 *A shameless woman constantly acts disgracefully,
but a modest daughter will even be
embarrassed before her husband.*

25 *A headstrong wife is regarded as a dog,*

b Other ancient authorities read *and listening he sighs*
c Heb Syr: Other Gk authorities read *for her beauty*
d Syr: Meaning of Gk uncertain

*but one who has a sense of shame will fear
the Lord.*
26 *A wife honoring her husband will seem wise
to all,
but if she dishonors him in her pride she will
be known to all as ungodly.
Happy is the husband of a good wife;
for the number of his years will be doubled.*
27 *A loud-voiced and garrulous wife is like a
trumpet sounding the charge,
and every person like this lives in the anarchy
of war.*

Three Depressing Things

28 At two things my heart is grieved,
and because of a third anger comes
over me:
a warrior in want through poverty,
intelligent men who are treated
contemptuously,
and a man who turns back from
righteousness to sin—
the Lord will prepare him for the sword!

The Temptations of Commerce

29 A merchant can hardly keep from
wrongdoing,
nor is a tradesman innocent of sin.
Many have committed sin for gain,*e*
and those who seek to get rich will avert
their eyes.
2 As a stake is driven firmly into a fissure
between stones,
so sin is wedged in between selling and
buying.
3 If a person is not steadfast in the fear of the
Lord,
his house will be quickly overthrown.

Tests in Life

4 When a sieve is shaken, the refuse appears;
so do a person's faults when he speaks.
5 The kiln tests the potter's vessels;
so the test of a person is in his
conversation.
6 Its fruit discloses the cultivation of a tree;
so a person's speech discloses the
cultivation of his mind.
7 Do not praise anyone before he speaks,
for this is the way people are tested.

Reward and Retribution

8 If you pursue justice, you will attain it
and wear it like a glorious robe.
9 Birds roost with their own kind,
so honesty comes home to those who
practice it.
10 A lion lies in wait for prey;
so does sin for evildoers.

Varieties of Speech

11 The conversation of the godly is always
wise,
but the fool changes like the moon.
12 Among stupid people limit your time,
but among thoughtful people linger on.
13 The talk of fools is offensive,
and their laughter is wantonly sinful.
14 Their cursing and swearing make one's hair
stand on end,
and their quarrels make others stop their
ears.
15 The strife of the proud leads to bloodshed,
and their abuse is grievous to hear.

Betraying Secrets
(Prov 20.19; 25.9)

16 Whoever betrays secrets destroys confidence,
and will never find a congenial friend.
17 Love your friend and keep faith with him;
but if you betray his secrets, do not
follow after him.
18 For as a person destroys his enemy,
so you have destroyed the friendship of
your neighbor.
19 And as you allow a bird to escape from
your hand,
so you have let your neighbor go, and
will not catch him again.
20 Do not go after him, for he is too far off,
and has escaped like a gazelle from a
snare.
21 For a wound may be bandaged,
and there is reconciliation after abuse,
but whoever has betrayed secrets is
without hope.

Hypocrisy and Retribution

22 Whoever winks the eye plots mischief,
and those who know him will keep their
distance.
23 In your presence his mouth is all sweetness,
and he admires your words;
but later he will twist his speech

---

e Other ancient authorities read *a trifle*

and with your own words he will trip
you up.

24 I have hated many things, but him
above all;
even the Lord hates him.

25 Whoever throws a stone straight up throws
it on his own head,
and a treacherous blow opens up many
wounds.

26 Whoever digs a pit will fall into it,
and whoever sets a snare will be caught
in it.

27 If a person does evil, it will roll back
upon him,
and he will not know where it came
from.

28 Mockery and abuse issue from the proud,
but vengeance lies in wait for them like a
lion.

29 Those who rejoice in the fall of the godly
will be caught in a snare,
and pain will consume them before their
death.

Anger and Vengeance

30 Anger and wrath, these also are
abominations,
yet a sinner holds on to them.

28 The vengeful will face the Lord's vengeance,
for he keeps a strict account of*f* their
sins.

2 Forgive your neighbor the wrong he has
done,
and then your sins will be pardoned
when you pray.

3 Does anyone harbor anger against another,
and expect healing from the Lord?

4 If one has no mercy toward another like
himself,
can he then seek pardon for his own
sins?

5 If a mere mortal harbors wrath,
who will make an atoning sacrifice for
his sins?

6 Remember the end of your life, and set
enmity aside;
remember corruption and death, and be
true to the commandments.

7 Remember the commandments, and do not
be angry with your neighbor;
remember the covenant of the Most
High, and overlook faults.

8 Refrain from strife, and your sins will be
fewer;
for the hot-tempered kindle strife,

9 and the sinner disrupts friendships
and sows discord among those who are
at peace.

10 In proportion to the fuel, so will the fire
burn,
and in proportion to the obstinacy, so
will strife increase;*g*
in proportion to a person's strength will be
his anger,
and in proportion to his wealth he will
increase his wrath.

11 A hasty quarrel kindles a fire,
and a hasty dispute sheds blood.

The Evil Tongue
(Jas 3.1–12)

12 If you blow on a spark, it will glow;
if you spit on it, it will be put out;
yet both come out of your mouth.

13 Curse the gossips and the double-tongued,
for they destroy the peace of many.

14 Slander*h* has shaken many,
and scattered them from nation to
nation;
it has destroyed strong cities,
and overturned the houses of the great.

15 Slander*h* has driven virtuous women from
their homes,
and deprived them of the fruit of their
toil.

16 Those who pay heed to slander*i* will not
find rest,
nor will they settle down in peace.

17 The blow of a whip raises a welt,
but a blow of the tongue crushes the
bones.

18 Many have fallen by the edge of the sword,
but not as many as have fallen because of
the tongue.

19 Happy is the one who is protected from it,
who has not been exposed to its anger,
who has not borne its yoke,
and has not been bound with its fetters.

20 For its yoke is a yoke of iron,
and its fetters are fetters of bronze;

21 its death is an evil death,
and Hades is preferable to it.

22 It has no power over the godly;
they will not be burned in its flame.

23 Those who forsake the Lord will fall into its
power;

---

f Other ancient authorities read *for he firmly establishes*
g Other ancient authorities read *burn*   *h* Gk A *third tongue*
i Gk *it*

it will burn among them and will not be
  put out.
It will be sent out against them like a lion;
  like a leopard it will mangle them.
24a As you fence in your property with thorns,
25b   so make a door and a bolt for your
          mouth.
24b As you lock up your silver and gold,
25a   so make balances and scales for your
          words.
26 Take care not to err with your tongue,*j*
      and fall victim to one lying in wait.

j Gk *with it*

On Lending and Borrowing
(Cp Ex 22.25; Lev 25.35–38)

The merciful lend to their neighbors;
  by holding out a helping hand they keep
    the commandments.
2 Lend to your neighbor in his time of need;
  repay your neighbor when a loan
    falls due.
3 Keep your promise and be honest
    with him,

Just Walk Away

"Hey, did you hear the latest about Valerie?"
"No, what?"
"Well, last Friday night, she and Maria were at Jason's party, and—"
"Wait a minute, here comes Maria. Tell me later."

Curse the gossips and the double-tongued,
  for they destroy the peace of many.
                              (Sir 28.13)

"Guess what I heard!"
"What?"
"Well, Teresa, who is usually so stuck-up—"
"I know. I can't stand her. She thinks she's so cool."
"Well, anyway, she went to this party and . . ."

Those who pay heed to slander will not find rest,
    nor will they settle down in peace.
                              (Verse 16)

"I can't believe what I just heard!"
"What? Tell me!"
"I heard that Juan and Sunyub went out last night, got totally trashed, and spent the night together."
"Are you kidding? Sunyub, little miss honor student? And Juan, athlete of the year? Are you sure?"
"I know. I can't believe it either, but I heard it from two different people . . ."

Many have fallen by the edge of the sword,
    but not as many as have fallen because of the tongue.
                              (Verse 18)

If you blow on a spark, it will glow;
    if you spit on it, it will be put out;
    yet both come out of your mouth.
                              (Verse 12)

The next time you hear a piece of gossip or a rumor, don't blow on it—spit on it and walk away. Someone's reputation is at stake. One of these times, it could be yours. Check out the third chapter of James in the New Testament for another version of the hazards of gossip and slander.

▶ Sir 28.12–18

S
I
R

and on every occasion you will find what
you need.
4 Many regard a loan as a windfall,
and cause trouble to those who help
them.
5 One kisses another's hands until he gets a
loan,
and is deferential in speaking of his
neighbor's money;
but at the time for repayment he delays,
and pays back with empty promises,
and finds fault with the time.
6 If he can pay, his creditor[k] will hardly get
back half,
and will regard that as a windfall.
If he cannot pay, the borrower[k] has robbed
the other of his money,
and he has needlessly made him an
enemy;
he will repay him with curses and
reproaches,
and instead of glory will repay him with
dishonor.
7 Many refuse to lend, not because of
meanness,
but from fear[l] of being defrauded
needlessly.

8 Nevertheless, be patient with someone in
humble circumstances,
and do not keep him waiting for your
alms.
9 Help the poor for the commandment's sake,
and in their need do not send them away
empty-handed.
10 Lose your silver for the sake of a brother or
a friend,
and do not let it rust under a stone and
be lost.
11 Lay up your treasure according to the
commandments of the Most High,
and it will profit you more than gold.
12 Store up almsgiving in your treasury,
and it will rescue you from every disaster;
13 better than a stout shield and a sturdy spear,
it will fight for you against the enemy.

On Guaranteeing Debts

14 A good person will be surety for his
neighbor,
but the one who has lost all sense of
shame will fail him.
15 Do not forget the kindness of your
guarantor,
for he has given his life for you.

16 A sinner wastes the property of his
guarantor,
17 and the ungrateful person abandons his
rescuer.
18 Being surety has ruined many who were
prosperous,
and has tossed them about like waves of
the sea;
it has driven the influential into exile,
and they have wandered among foreign
nations.
19 The sinner comes to grief through surety;
his pursuit of gain involves him in
lawsuits.
20 Assist your neighbor to the best of your
ability,
but be careful not to fall yourself.

Home and Hospitality

21 The necessities of life are water, bread, and
clothing,
and also a house to assure privacy.
22 Better is the life of the poor under their
own crude roof
than sumptuous food in the house of
others.
23 Be content with little or much,
and you will hear no reproach for being
a guest.[m]
24 It is a miserable life to go from house to
house;
as a guest you should not open your
mouth;
25 you will play the host and provide drink
without being thanked,
and besides this you will hear rude words
like these:
26 "Come here, stranger, prepare the table;
let me eat what you have there."
27 "Be off, stranger, for an honored guest is here;
my brother has come for a visit, and I
need the guest-room."
28 It is hard for a sensible person to bear
scolding about lodging[n] and the insults
of the moneylender.

CONCERNING CHILDREN [o]

30 He who loves his son will whip him
often,
so that he may rejoice at the way he
turns out.

---

[k] Gk *he*   [l] Other ancient authorities read *many refuse to
lend, therefore, because of such meanness; they are afraid*
[m] Lat: Gk *reproach from your family;* other ancient
authorities lack this line   [n] Or *scolding from the household*
[o] This heading is included in the Gk text.

2 He who disciplines his son will profit
by him,
and will boast of him among
acquaintances.
3 He who teaches his son will make his
enemies envious,
and will glory in him among his friends.
4 When the father dies he will not seem to be
dead,
for he has left behind him one like
himself,
5 whom in his life he looked upon with joy
and at death, without grief.
6 He has left behind him an avenger against
his enemies,
and one to repay the kindness of his
friends.

7 Whoever spoils his son will bind up his
wounds,
and will suffer heartache at every cry.
8 An unbroken horse turns out stubborn,
and an unchecked son turns out
headstrong.
9 Pamper a child, and he will terrorize you;
play with him, and he will grieve you.
10 Do not laugh with him, or you will have
sorrow with him,
and in the end you will gnash your teeth.
11 Give him no freedom in his youth,
and do not ignore his errors.
12 Bow down his neck in his youth,*p*
and beat his sides while he is young,
or else he will become stubborn and
disobey you,
and you will have sorrow of soul
from him.*q*
13 Discipline your son and make his yoke
heavy,*r*
so that you may not be offended by his
shamelessness.

14 Better off poor, healthy, and fit
than rich and afflicted in body.
15 Health and fitness are better than any gold,
and a robust body than countless riches.
16 There is no wealth better than health of
body,
and no gladness above joy of heart.
17 Death is better than a life of misery,
and eternal sleep*s* than chronic sickness.

CONCERNING FOODS *t*

18 Good things poured out upon a mouth that
is closed
are like offerings of food placed upon a
grave.

19 Of what use to an idol is a sacrifice?
For it can neither eat nor smell.
So is the one punished by the Lord;
20 he sees with his eyes and groans
as a eunuch groans when embracing a
girl.*u*
21 Do not give yourself over to sorrow,
and do not distress yourself deliberately.
22 A joyful heart is life itself,
and rejoicing lengthens one's life span.
23 Indulge yourself*v* and take comfort,
and remove sorrow far from you,
for sorrow has destroyed many,
and no advantage ever comes from it.
24 Jealousy and anger shorten life,
and anxiety brings on premature old age.
25 Those who are cheerful and merry at table
will benefit from their food.

Right Attitude toward Riches

Wakefulness over wealth wastes away one's
flesh,
and anxiety about it drives away sleep.
2 Wakeful anxiety prevents slumber,
and a severe illness carries off sleep.*w*
3 The rich person toils to amass a fortune,
and when he rests he fills himself with
his dainties.
4 The poor person toils to make a meager
living,
and if ever he rests he becomes needy.

5 One who loves gold will not be justified;
one who pursues money will be led
astray*x* by it.
6 Many have come to ruin because of gold,
and their destruction has met them face
to face.
7 It is a stumbling block to those who are
avid for it,
and every fool will be taken captive by it.
8 Blessed is the rich person who is found
blameless,
and who does not go after gold.
9 Who is he, that we may praise him?

---

p Other ancient authorities lack this line and the
preceding line   *q* Other ancient authorities lack this line
r Heb: Gk *take pains with him*   *s* Other ancient authorities
lack *eternal sleep*   *t* This heading is included in the Gk
text; other ancient authorities place the heading before
verse 16   *u* Other ancient authorities add *So is the person
who does right under compulsion*   *v* Other ancient
authorities read *Beguile yourself*   *w* Other ancient
authorities read *sleep carries off a severe illness*   *x* Heb Syr:
Gk *pursues destruction will be filled*

For he has done wonders among his
people.
10 Who has been tested by it and been found
perfect?
Let it be for him a ground for boasting.
Who has had the power to transgress and
did not transgress,
and to do evil and did not do it?
11 His prosperity will be established,*y*
and the assembly will proclaim his acts
of charity.

Table Etiquette

12 Are you seated at the table of the great?*z*
Do not be greedy at it,
and do not say, "How much food there
is here!"
13 Remember that a greedy eye is a bad thing.
What has been created more greedy than
the eye?
Therefore it sheds tears for any reason.
14 Do not reach out your hand for everything
you see,
and do not crowd your neighbor*a* at the
dish.
15 Judge your neighbor's feelings by your own,
and in every matter be thoughtful.
16 Eat what is set before you like a well
brought-up person,*b*
and do not chew greedily, or you will
give offense.
17 Be the first to stop, as befits good manners,
and do not be insatiable, or you will give
offense.
18 If you are seated among many persons,
do not help yourself*c* before they do.

19 How ample a little is for a well-disciplined
person!
He does not breathe heavily when
in bed.
20 Healthy sleep depends on moderate eating;
he rises early, and feels fit.
The distress of sleeplessness and of nausea
and colic are with the glutton.
21 If you are overstuffed with food,
get up to vomit, and you will have relief.
22 Listen to me, my child, and do not
disregard me,
and in the end you will appreciate my
words.
In everything you do be moderate,*d*
and no sickness will overtake you.
23 People bless the one who is liberal with
food,

and their testimony to his generosity is
trustworthy.
24 The city complains of the one who is stingy
with food,
and their testimony to his stinginess is
accurate.

Temperance in Drinking Wine

25 Do not try to prove your strength by
wine-drinking,
for wine has destroyed many.
26 As the furnace tests the work of the smith,*e*
so wine tests hearts when the insolent
quarrel.
27 Wine is very life to human beings
if taken in moderation.
What is life to one who is without wine?
It has been created to make people
happy.
28 Wine drunk at the proper time and in
moderation
is rejoicing of heart and gladness of soul.
29 Wine drunk to excess leads to bitterness of
spirit,
to quarrels and stumbling.
30 Drunkenness increases the anger of a fool to
his own hurt,
reducing his strength and adding wounds.
31 Do not reprove your neighbor at a banquet
of wine,
and do not despise him in his
merrymaking;
speak no word of reproach to him,
and do not distress him by making
demands of him.

Etiquette at a Banquet

If they make you master of the feast, do not
exalt yourself;
be among them as one of their number.
Take care of them first and then sit down;
2   when you have fulfilled all your duties,
take your place,
so that you may be merry along with them
and receive a wreath for your excellent
leadership.

3 Speak, you who are older, for it is your
right,
but with accurate knowledge, and do not
interrupt the music.

---
y Other ancient authorities add *because of this*   *z* Heb Syr:
Gk *at a great table*   *a* Gk *him*   *b* Heb: Gk *like a human
being*   *c* Gk *reach out your hand*   *d* Heb Syr: Gk
industrious   *e* Heb: Gk *tests the hardening of steel by dipping*

A Tragic Tale

LIVE IT!

Drunkenness increases the anger of a fool to his own hurt. (Sir 31.30)

This is the true story of a young man we'll call Kevin. Kevin had a drinking problem. It all began when he had his first beer at age thirteen. It tasted horrible, but all his friends told him to keep drinking, and he would grow to love the feeling it gave him. He did keep drinking, and the alcohol made him feel more outgoing and more funny. This didn't seem all that bad.

Unfortunately, Kevin became an alcoholic. Weekend drinking turned into weekday drinking, and before long, he was drinking on his way to school. Kevin drank so much that he blacked out almost every other day.

One day, Kevin had drunk nearly a fifth of vodka. He was at home and was supposed to be watching his six-year-old sister, Veronica. Kevin got angry at her and slammed her across the side of the head. She fell to the ground and laid there without moving. Kevin tried calling 911 but couldn't see the numbers well enough to dial.

Veronica died as a result of Kevin's blow. Now Kevin has to live with the horror of killing his own sister. He wishes he could tell every thirteen-year-old in the world not to try that first beer.

▶ Sir 31.25–31

4 Where there is entertainment, do not pour
    out talk;
  do not display your cleverness at the
    wrong time.
5 A ruby seal in a setting of gold
  is a concert of music at a banquet of
    wine.
6 A seal of emerald in a rich setting of gold
  is the melody of music with good wine.
7 Speak, you who are young, if you are
    obliged to,
  but no more than twice, and only if
    asked.
8 Be brief; say much in few words;
  be as one who knows and can still hold
    his tongue.
9 Among the great do not act as their equal;
  and when another is speaking, do not
    babble.
10 Lightning travels ahead of the thunder,
  and approval goes before one who is
    modest.
11 Leave in good time and do not be the last;
  go home quickly and do not linger.
12 Amuse yourself there to your heart's
    content,
  but do not sin through proud speech.
13 But above all bless your Maker,
  who fills you with his good gifts.

The Providence of God

14 The one who seeks God*f* will accept his
    discipline,
  and those who rise early to seek him*g*
    will find favor.
15 The one who seeks the law will be filled
    with it,
  but the hypocrite will stumble at it.
16 Those who fear the Lord will form true
    judgments,
  and they will kindle righteous deeds like
    a light.
17 The sinner will shun reproof,
  and will find a decision according to his
    liking.
18 A sensible person will not overlook a
    thoughtful suggestion;
  an insolent*h* and proud person will not
    be deterred by fear.*i*
19 Do nothing without deliberation,
  but when you have acted, do not
    regret it.
20 Do not go on a path full of hazards,
  and do not stumble at an obstacle twice.*j*
21 Do not be overconfident on a smooth*k*
    road,

---

f Heb: Gk *who fears the Lord*   *g* Other ancient authorities lack *to seek him*   *h* Heb: Gk *alien*   *i* Meaning of Gk uncertain. Other ancient authorities add *and after acting, with him, without deliberation*   *j* Heb: Gk *stumble on stony ground*   *k* Or *an unexplored*

S
I
R

22 and give good heed to your paths.[l]
23 Guard[m] yourself in every act,
    for this is the keeping of the
        commandments.

24 The one who keeps the law preserves
        himself,[n]
    and the one who trusts the Lord will not
        suffer loss.

No evil will befall the one who fears the
        Lord,
    but in trials such a one will be rescued
        again and again.
2 The wise will not hate the law,
    but the one who is hypocritical about it
        is like a boat in a storm.
3 The sensible person will trust in the law;
    for such a one the law is as dependable
        as a divine oracle.

4 Prepare what to say, and then you will be
        listened to;
    draw upon your training, and give your
        answer.
5 The heart of a fool is like a cart wheel,
    and his thoughts like a turning axle.
6 A mocking friend is like a stallion
    that neighs no matter who the rider is.

Differences in Nature and in Humankind

7 Why is one day more important than
        another,
    when all the daylight in the year is from
        the sun?
8 By the Lord's wisdom they were
        distinguished,
    and he appointed the different seasons
        and festivals.
9 Some days he exalted and hallowed,
    and some he made ordinary days.
10 All human beings come from the ground,
    and humankind[o] was created out of the
        dust.
11 In the fullness of his knowledge the Lord
        distinguished them
    and appointed their different ways.
12 Some he blessed and exalted,
    and some he made holy and brought
        near to himself;
    but some he cursed and brought low,
        and turned them out of their place.
13 Like clay in the hand of the potter,
    to be molded as he pleases,
    so all are in the hand of their Maker,
        to be given whatever he decides.

14 Good is the opposite of evil,
    and life the opposite of death;
    so the sinner is the opposite of the godly.
15 Look at all the works of the Most High;
    they come in pairs, one the opposite of
        the other.

16 Now I was the last to keep vigil;
    I was like a gleaner following the
        grape-pickers;
17 by the blessing of the Lord I arrived first,
    and like a grape-picker I filled my wine
        press.
18 Consider that I have not labored for myself
        alone,
    but for all who seek instruction.
19 Hear me, you who are great among the
        people,
    and you leaders of the congregation, pay
        heed!

The Advantage of Independence

20 To son or wife, to brother or friend,
    do not give power over yourself, as long
        as you live;
    and do not give your property to another,
        in case you change your mind and must
            ask for it.
21 While you are still alive and have breath
        in you,
    do not let anyone take your place.
22 For it is better that your children should ask
        from you
    than that you should look to the hand of
        your children.
23 Excel in all that you do;
    bring no stain upon your honor.
24 At the time when you end the days of your
        life,
    in the hour of death, distribute your
        inheritance.

The Treatment of Slaves

25 Fodder and a stick and burdens for a
        donkey;
    bread and discipline and work for a
        slave.
26 Set your slave to work, and you will find
        rest;
    leave his hands idle, and he will seek
        liberty.
27 Yoke and thong will bow the neck,

---

[l] Heb Syr: Gk *and beware of your children*   [m] Heb Syr: Gk
Trust   [n] Heb: Gk *who believes the law heeds the
commandments*   [o] Heb: Gk *Adam*

and for a wicked slave there are racks and
  tortures.

28 Put him to work, in order that he may not
  be idle,

29   for idleness teaches much evil.

30 Set him to work, as is fitting for him,
  and if he does not obey, make his fetters
   heavy.

Do not be overbearing toward anyone,
  and do nothing unjust.

31 If you have but one slave, treat him like
  yourself,

  because you have bought him with
   blood.

If you have but one slave, treat him like a
  brother,

  for you will need him as you need your
   life.

32 If you ill-treat him, and he leaves you and
  runs away,

33   which way will you go to seek him?

Dreams Mean Nothing
(Deut 13.1–5; 18.9–14)

34 The senseless have vain and false hopes,
  and dreams give wings to fools.

2 As one who catches at a shadow and
  pursues the wind,

  so is anyone who believes in *p* dreams.

3 What is seen in dreams is but a reflection,
  the likeness of a face looking at itself.

4 From an unclean thing what can be clean?
  And from something false what can be
   true?

5 Divinations and omens and dreams are
  unreal,

  and like a woman in labor, the mind has
   fantasies.

6 Unless they are sent by intervention from
  the Most High,

  pay no attention to them.

7 For dreams have deceived many,
  and those who put their hope in them
   have perished.

8 Without such deceptions the law will be
  fulfilled,

  and wisdom is complete in the mouth of
   the faithful.

Experience as a Teacher

9 An educated*q* person knows many things,
  and one with much experience knows
   what he is talking about.

10 An inexperienced person knows few things,

11   but he that has traveled acquires much
   cleverness.

12 I have seen many things in my travels,
  and I understand more than I can
   express.

13 I have often been in danger of death,
  but have escaped because of these
   experiences.

Fear the Lord

14 The spirit of those who fear the Lord will
  live,

15   for their hope is in him who saves them.

16 Those who fear the Lord will not be timid,
  or play the coward, for he is their hope.

17 Happy is the soul that fears the Lord!

18   To whom does he look? And who is his
   support?

19 The eyes of the Lord are on those who
  love him,

  a mighty shield and strong support,

a shelter from scorching wind and a shade
  from noonday sun,

a guard against stumbling and a help
  against falling.

20 He lifts up the soul and makes the eyes
  sparkle;

  he gives health and life and blessing.

Offering Sacrifices

21 If one sacrifices ill-gotten goods, the offering
  is blemished;*r*

22   the gifts*s* of the lawless are not
   acceptable.

23 The Most High is not pleased with the
  offerings of the ungodly,

  nor for a multitude of sacrifices does he
   forgive sins.

24 Like one who kills a son before his father's
  eyes

  is the person who offers a sacrifice from
   the property of the poor.

25 The bread of the needy is the life of the
  poor;

  whoever deprives them of it is a
   murderer.

26 To take away a neighbor's living is to
  commit murder;

27   to deprive an employee of wages is to
   shed blood.

28 When one builds and another tears down,
  what do they gain but hard work?

---

p Syr: Gk *pays heed to* *q* Other ancient authorities read *A
traveled* *r* Other ancient authorities read *is made in
mockery* *s* Other ancient authorities read *mockeries*

29 When one prays and another curses,
   to whose voice will the Lord listen?
30 If one washes after touching a corpse, and
      touches it again,
   what has been gained by washing?
31 So if one fasts for his sins,
      and goes again and does the same things,
   who will listen to his prayer?
   And what has he gained by humbling
      himself?

The Law and Sacrifices
(Cp 2 Cor 9.7)

The one who keeps the law makes many
   offerings;
2   one who heeds the commandments
   makes an offering of well-being.
3 The one who returns a kindness offers
   choice flour,
4   and one who gives alms sacrifices a thank
   offering.
5 To keep from wickedness is pleasing to the
   Lord,
   and to forsake unrighteousness is an
      atonement.
6 Do not appear before the Lord
   empty-handed,
7   for all that you offer is in fulfillment of
   the commandment.
8 The offering of the righteous enriches the
   altar,
   and its pleasing odor rises before the
      Most High.
9 The sacrifice of the righteous is acceptable,
   and it will never be forgotten.
10 Be generous when you worship the Lord,
   and do not stint the first fruits of your
      hands.
11 With every gift show a cheerful face,
   and dedicate your tithe with gladness.
12 Give to the Most High as he has given
   to you,
   and as generously as you can afford.
13 For the Lord is the one who repays,
   and he will repay you sevenfold.

Divine Justice
14 Do not offer him a bribe, for he will not
   accept it;
15   and do not rely on a dishonest sacrifice;
   for the Lord is the judge,
   and with him there is no partiality.
16 He will not show partiality to the poor;
   but he will listen to the prayer of one
      who is wronged.

GIVE to the **Most High** as he has **GIVEN**

35.12 to you, and as **generously** as you can afford

17 He will not ignore the supplication of the
   orphan,
   or the widow when she pours out her
      complaint.
18 Do not the tears of the widow run down
   her cheek
19   as she cries out against the one who
   causes them to fall?
20 The one whose service is pleasing to the
   Lord will be accepted,
   and his prayer will reach to the clouds.
21 The prayer of the humble pierces the
   clouds,
   and it will not rest until it reaches its
      goal;
   it will not desist until the Most High
      responds
22   and does justice for the righteous, and
   executes judgment.
   Indeed, the Lord will not delay,
   and like a warrior*t* will not be patient
until he crushes the loins of the unmerciful
23   and repays vengeance on the nations;
   until he destroys the multitude of the
      insolent,
   and breaks the scepters of the
      unrighteous;
24 until he repays mortals according to their
   deeds,
   and the works of all according to their
      thoughts;
25 until he judges the case of his people
   and makes them rejoice in his mercy.
26 His mercy is as welcome in time of distress
   as clouds of rain in time of drought.

---

t Heb: Gk *and with them*

A Prayer for God's People

Have mercy upon us, O God[u] of all,
2 and put all the nations in fear of you.
3 Lift up your hand against foreign nations
  and let them see your might.
4 As you have used us to show your holiness
    to them,
  so use them to show your glory to us.
5 Then they will know,[v] as we have known,
  that there is no God but you, O Lord.
6 Give new signs, and work other wonders;
7 make your hand and right arm glorious.
8 Rouse your anger and pour out your wrath;
9 destroy the adversary and wipe out the
    enemy.
10 Hasten the day, and remember the
    appointed time,[w]
  and let people recount your mighty
    deeds.
11 Let survivors be consumed in the fiery
    wrath,
  and may those who harm your people
    meet destruction.
12 Crush the heads of hostile rulers
  who say, "There is no one but ourselves."
13 Gather all the tribes of Jacob,[x]
16 and give them their inheritance, as at the
    beginning.
17 Have mercy, O Lord, on the people called
    by your name,
  on Israel, whom you have named[y] your
    firstborn,
18 Have pity on the city of your sanctuary,[z]
  Jerusalem, the place of your dwelling.[a]
19 Fill Zion with your majesty,[b]
  and your temple[c] with your glory.
20 Bear witness to those whom you created in
    the beginning,
  and fulfill the prophecies spoken in your
    name.
21 Reward those who wait for you
  and let your prophets be found
    trustworthy.
22 Hear, O Lord, the prayer of your servants,
  according to your goodwill toward[d]
    your people,
  and all who are on the earth will know
    that you are the Lord, the God of the
    ages.

Concerning Discrimination

23 The stomach will take any food,
  yet one food is better than another.
24 As the palate tastes the kinds of game,
  so an intelligent mind detects false
    words.
25 A perverse mind will cause grief,
  but a person with experience will pay
    him back.
26 A woman will accept any man as a
    husband,
  but one girl is preferable to another.
27 A woman's beauty lights up a man's face,
  and there is nothing he desires more.
28 If kindness and humility mark her speech,
  her husband is more fortunate than
    other men.
29 He who acquires a wife gets his best
    possession,[e]
  a helper fit for him and a pillar of
    support.[f]
30 Where there is no fence, the property will
    be plundered;
  and where there is no wife, a man will
    become a fugitive and a wanderer.[g]
31 For who will trust a nimble robber
  that skips from city to city?
  So who will trust a man that has no nest,
  but lodges wherever night overtakes him?

False Friends

Every friend says, "I too am a friend";
  but some friends are friends only in
    name.
2 Is it not a sorrow like that for death itself
  when a dear friend turns into an enemy?
3 O inclination to evil, why were you formed
  to cover the land with deceit?
4 Some companions rejoice in the happiness
    of a friend,
  but in time of trouble they are
    against him.
5 Some companions help a friend for their
    stomachs' sake,
  yet in battle they will carry his shield.
6 Do not forget a friend during the battle,[h]
  and do not be unmindful of him when
    you distribute your spoils.[i]

u Heb: Gk O Master, the God   v Heb: Gk And let them
know you   w Other ancient authorities read remember
your oath   x Owing to a dislocation in the Greek Mss of
Sirach, the verse numbers 14 and 15 are not used in
chapter 36, though no text is missing.   y Other ancient
authorities read you have likened to   z Or on your holy city
a Heb: Gk your rest   b Heb Syr: Gk the celebration of your
wondrous deeds   c Heb Syr: Gk Lat people   d Heb and
two Gk witnesses: Lat and most Gk witnesses read
according to the blessing of Aaron for   e Heb: Gk enters
upon a possession   f Heb: Gk rest   g Heb: Gk wander
about and sigh   h Heb: Gk in your heart   i Heb: Gk him
in your wealth

Caution in Taking Advice

7 All counselors praise the counsel they give,
but some give counsel in their own
interest.
8 Be wary of a counselor,
and learn first what is his interest,
for he will take thought for himself.
He may cast the lot against you
9 and tell you, "Your way is good,"
and then stand aside to see what happens
to you.
10 Do not consult the one who regards you
with suspicion;
hide your intentions from those who are
jealous of you.
11 Do not consult with a woman about her
rival
or with a coward about war,
with a merchant about business
or with a buyer about selling,
with a miser about generosity[j]
or with the merciless about kindness,
with an idler about any work
or with a seasonal laborer about
completing his work,
with a lazy servant about a big task—
pay no attention to any advice they give.
12 But associate with a godly person
whom you know to be a keeper of the
commandments,
who is like-minded with yourself,
and who will grieve with you if you fail.
13 And heed[k] the counsel of your own heart,
for no one is more faithful to you than
it is.
14 For our own mind sometimes keeps us
better informed
than seven sentinels sitting high on a
watchtower.
15 But above all pray to the Most High
that he may direct your way in truth.

True and False Wisdom

16 Discussion is the beginning of every work,
and counsel precedes every undertaking.
17 The mind is the root of all conduct;
18 it sprouts four branches,[l]
good and evil, life and death;
and it is the tongue that continually rules
them.
19 Some people may be clever enough to teach
many,
and yet be useless to themselves.
20 A skillful speaker may be hated;
he will be destitute of all food,

21 for the Lord has withheld the gift of charm,
since he is lacking in all wisdom.
22 If a person is wise to his own advantage,
the fruits of his good sense will be
praiseworthy.[m]
23 A wise person instructs his own people,
and the fruits of his good sense will
endure.
24 A wise person will have praise heaped
upon him,
and all who see him will call him happy.
25 The days of a person's life are numbered,
but the days of Israel are without
number.
26 One who is wise among his people will
inherit honor,[n]
and his name will live forever.

Concerning Moderation

27 My child, test yourself while you live;
see what is bad for you and do not give
in to it.
28 For not everything is good for everyone,
and no one enjoys everything.
29 Do not be greedy for every delicacy,
and do not eat without restraint;
30 for overeating brings sickness,
and gluttony leads to nausea.
31 Many have died of gluttony,
but the one who guards against it
prolongs his life.

Concerning Physicians and Health

38 Honor physicians for their services,
for the Lord created them;
2 for their gift of healing comes from the
Most High,
and they are rewarded by the king.
3 The skill of physicians makes them
distinguished,
and in the presence of the great they are
admired.
4 The Lord created medicines out of the earth,
and the sensible will not despise them.
5 Was not water made sweet with a tree
in order that its[o] power might be known?
6 And he gave skill to human beings
that he[p] might be glorified in his
marvelous works.
7 By them the physician[q] heals and takes
away pain;

---

j Heb: Gk gratitude   k Heb: Gk establish   l Heb: Gk As a
clue to changes of heart four kinds of destiny appear
m Other ancient witnesses read trustworthy   n Other
ancient authorities read confidence   o Or his   p Or they
q Heb: Gk he

8   the pharmacist makes a mixture from
       them.
     God's^r works will never be finished;
       and from him health^s spreads over all
         the earth.

9   My child, when you are ill, do not delay,
       but pray to the Lord, and he will
         heal you.
10   Give up your faults and direct your hands
       rightly,
     and cleanse your heart from all sin.
11   Offer a sweet-smelling sacrifice, and a
       memorial portion of choice flour,
     and pour oil on your offering, as much
       as you can afford.^t
12   Then give the physician his place, for the
       Lord created him;
     do not let him leave you, for you
       need him.
13   There may come a time when recovery lies
       in the hands of physicians,^u
14   for they too pray to the Lord
     that he grant them success in diagnosis^v
       and in healing, for the sake of preserving
         life.
15   He who sins against his Maker,
       will be defiant toward the physician.^w

PRAY IT!
Health-Care Providers

When was the last time you went to
the doctor? How often do you take
medicine? Did you ever spend a night in a
hospital? It's humbling to realize that the
basic health care we take for granted is
not available to millions of people in this
country and throughout the world.

God gives the skill to heal to doctors,
nurses, dentists, pharmacists, therapists,
and medical technicians of every kind
(Sir 38.2). Their jobs often demand huge
amounts of time and energy. Take a moment to remember in prayer the health-
care providers you know personally, and
ask yourself if you have a vocation in the
medical profession.

▶ Sir 38.1–15

On Mourning for the Dead
(Cp Sir 22.11–12)

16   My child, let your tears fall for the dead,
       and as one in great pain begin the
         lament.
     Lay out the body with due ceremony,
       and do not neglect the burial.
17   Let your weeping be bitter and your wailing
         fervent;
       make your mourning worthy of the
         departed,
     for one day, or two, to avoid criticism;
       then be comforted for your grief.
18   For grief may result in death,
       and a sorrowful heart saps one's strength.
19   When a person is taken away, sorrow is
         over;
       but the life of the poor weighs down the
         heart.
20   Do not give your heart to grief;
       drive it away, and remember your
         own end.
21   Do not forget, there is no coming back;
       you do the dead^x no good, and you
         injure yourself.
22   Remember his^y fate, for yours is like it;
       yesterday it was his,^z and today it is
         yours.
23   When the dead is at rest, let his
         remembrance rest too,
       and be comforted for him when his spirit
         has departed.

Trades and Crafts

24   The wisdom of the scribe depends on the
       opportunity of leisure;
     only the one who has little business can
       become wise.
25   How can one become wise who handles the
       plow,
     and who glories in the shaft of a goad,
     who drives oxen and is occupied with their
       work,
       and whose talk is about bulls?
26   He sets his heart on plowing furrows,
       and he is careful about fodder for the
         heifers.
27   So it is with every artisan and master artisan
       who labors by night as well as by day;
     those who cut the signets of seals,
       each is diligent in making a great variety;

---

^r Gk *His*   ^s Or *peace*   ^t Heb: Lat lacks *as much as you
can afford*; Meaning of Gk uncertain   ^u Gk *in their hands*
^v Heb: Gk *rest*   ^w Heb: Gk *may he fall into the hands of the
physician*   ^x Gk *him*   ^y Heb: Gk *my*   ^z Heb: Gk *mine*

S
I
R

they set their heart on painting a lifelike
image,
and they are careful to finish their work.
28 So it is with the smith, sitting by the anvil,
intent on his iron-work;
the breath of the fire melts his flesh,
and he struggles with the heat of the
furnace;
the sound of the hammer deafens his ears,[a]
and his eyes are on the pattern of the
object.
He sets his heart on finishing his
handiwork,
and he is careful to complete its
decoration.
29 So it is with the potter sitting at his work
and turning the wheel with his feet;
he is always deeply concerned over his
products,
and he produces them in quantity.
30 He molds the clay with his arm
and makes it pliable with his feet;
he sets his heart to finish the glazing,
and he takes care in firing[b] the kiln.
31 All these rely on their hands,
and all are skillful in their own work.
32 Without them no city can be inhabited,
and wherever they live, they will not go
hungry.[c]
Yet they are not sought out for the council
of the people,[d]
33 nor do they attain eminence in the public
assembly.
They do not sit in the judge's seat,
nor do they understand the decisions of
the courts;
they cannot expound discipline or
judgment,
and they are not found among the
rulers.[e]
34 But they maintain the fabric of the world,
and their concern is for[f] the exercise of
their trade.

The Activity of the Scribe

How different the one who devotes himself
to the study of the law of the Most High!
He seeks out the wisdom of all the ancients,
and is concerned with prophecies;
2 he preserves the sayings of the famous
and penetrates the subtleties of parables;
3 he seeks out the hidden meanings of
proverbs
and is at home with the obscurities of
parables.

4 He serves among the great
and appears before rulers;
he travels in foreign lands
and learns what is good and evil in the
human lot.
5 He sets his heart to rise early
to seek the Lord who made him,
and to petition the Most High;
he opens his mouth in prayer
and asks pardon for his sins.

6 If the great Lord is willing,
he will be filled with the spirit of
understanding;
he will pour forth words of wisdom of
his own
and give thanks to the Lord in prayer.
7 The Lord[g] will direct his counsel and
knowledge,
as he meditates on his mysteries.
8 He will show the wisdom of what he has
learned,
and will glory in the law of the Lord's
covenant.
9 Many will praise his understanding;
it will never be blotted out.
His memory will not disappear,
and his name will live through all
generations.
10 Nations will speak of his wisdom,
and the congregation will proclaim his
praise.
11 If he lives long, he will leave a name greater
than a thousand,
and if he goes to rest, it is enough[h]
for him.

A Hymn of Praise to God

12 I have more on my mind to express;
I am full like the full moon.
13 Listen to me, my faithful children, and
blossom
like a rose growing by a stream of water.
14 Send out fragrance like incense,
and put forth blossoms like a lily.
Scatter the fragrance, and sing a hymn of
praise;
bless the Lord for all his works.
15 Ascribe majesty to his name
and give thanks to him with praise,

---

[a] Cn: Gk *renews his ear*   [b] Cn: Gk *cleaning*   [c] Syr: Gk
and people can neither live nor walk there   [d] Most ancient
authorities lack this line   [e] Cn: Gk *among parables*
[f] Syr: Gk *prayer is in*   [g] Gk *He himself*   [h] Cn: Meaning
of Gk uncertain

with songs on your lips, and with harps;
  this is what you shall say in thanksgiving:

16 "All the works of the Lord are very good,
  and whatever he commands will be done
    at the appointed time.
17 No one can say, 'What is this?' or 'Why is
    that?'—
  for at the appointed time all such
    questions will be answered.
At his word the waters stood in a heap,
  and the reservoirs of water at the word of
    his mouth.
18 When he commands, his every purpose is
    fulfilled,
  and none can limit his saving power.
19 The works of all are before him,
  and nothing can be hidden from his eyes.
20 From the beginning to the end of time he
    can see everything,
  and nothing is too marvelous for him.
21 No one can say, 'What is this?' or 'Why is
    that?'—
  for everything has been created for its
    own purpose.

22 "His blessing covers the dry land like a
    river,
  and drenches it like a flood.
23 But his wrath drives out the nations,
  as when he turned a watered land into
    salt.
24 To the faithful his ways are straight,
  but full of pitfalls for the wicked.
25 From the beginning good things were
    created for the good,
  but for sinners good things and bad.i
26 The basic necessities of human life
  are water and fire and iron and salt
and wheat flour and milk and honey,
  the blood of the grape and oil and
    clothing.
27 All these are good for the godly,
  but for sinners they turn into evils.

28 "There are winds created for vengeance,
  and in their anger they can dislodge
    mountains;j
on the day of reckoning they will pour out
    their strength
  and calm the anger of their Maker.
29 Fire and hail and famine and pestilence,
  all these have been created for vengeance;
30 the fangs of wild animals and scorpions and
    vipers,
  and the sword that punishes the ungodly
    with destruction.

31 They take delight in doing his bidding,
  always ready for his service on earth;
  and when their time comes they never
    disobey his command."

32 So from the beginning I have been
    convinced of all this
  and have thought it out and left it in
    writing:
33 All the works of the Lord are good,
  and he will supply every need in its time.
34 No one can say, "This is not as good as
    that,"
  for everything proves good in its
    appointed time.
35 So now sing praise with all your heart and
    voice,
  and bless the name of the Lord.

Human Wretchedness

Hard work was created for everyone,
  and a heavy yoke is laid on the children
    of Adam,
from the day they come forth from their
    mother's womb
  until the day they return tok the mother
    of all the living.l
2 Perplexities and fear of heart are theirs,
  and anxious thought of the day of their
    death.
3 From the one who sits on a splendid throne
  to the one who grovels in dust and ashes,
4 from the one who wears purple and a
    crown
  to the one who is clothed in burlap,
5 there is anger and envy and trouble and
    unrest,
  and fear of death, and fury and strife.
And when one rests upon his bed,
  his sleep at night confuses his mind.
6 He gets little or no rest;
  he struggles in his sleep as he did
    by day.m
He is troubled by the visions of his mind
  like one who has escaped from the
    battlefield.
7 At the moment he reaches safety he
    wakes up,
  astonished that his fears were groundless.
8 To all creatures, human and animal,
  but to sinners seven times more,
9 come death and bloodshed and strife and
    sword,

---

i Heb Lat: Gk *sinners bad things*   j Heb Syr: Gk *can scourge
mightily*   k Other Gk and Lat authorities read *are buried
in*   l Heb: Gk *of all*   m Arm: Meaning of Gk uncertain

calamities and famine and ruin and
plague.

10 All these were created for the wicked,
and on their account the flood came.

11 All that is of earth returns to earth,
and what is from above returns above.[n]

Injustice Will Not Prosper

12 All bribery and injustice will be blotted out,
but good faith will last forever.

13 The wealth of the unjust will dry up like a
river,
and crash like a loud clap of thunder in a
storm.

14 As a generous person has cause to rejoice,
so lawbreakers will utterly fail.

15 The children of the ungodly put out few
branches;
they are unhealthy roots on sheer rock.

16 The reeds by any water or river bank
are plucked up before any grass;

17 but kindness is like a garden of blessings,
and almsgiving endures forever.

The Joys of Life

18 Wealth and wages make life sweet,[o]
but better than either is finding a
treasure.

19 Children and the building of a city establish
one's name,
but better than either is the one who
finds wisdom.
Cattle and orchards make one prosperous;[p]
but a blameless wife is accounted better
than either.

20 Wine and music gladden the heart,
but the love of friends[q] is better than
either.

21 The flute and the harp make sweet melody,
but a pleasant voice is better than either.

22 The eye desires grace and beauty,
but the green shoots of grain more than
either.

23 A friend or companion is always welcome,
but a sensible wife[r] is better than either.

24 Kindred and helpers are for a time of
trouble,
but almsgiving rescues better than either.

25 Gold and silver make one stand firm,
but good counsel is esteemed more than
either.

26 Riches and strength build up confidence,
but the fear of the Lord is better than
either.
There is no want in the fear of the Lord,

and with it there is no need to seek for
help.

27 The fear of the Lord is like a garden of
blessing,
and covers a person better than any
glory.

The Disgrace of Begging

28 My child, do not lead the life of a beggar;
it is better to die than to beg.

29 When one looks to the table of another,
one's way of life cannot be considered a
life.
One loses self-respect with another person's
food,
but one who is intelligent and well
instructed guards against that.

30 In the mouth of the shameless begging is
sweet,
but it kindles a fire inside him.

Concerning Death

O death, how bitter is the thought of you
to the one at peace among possessions,
who has nothing to worry about and is
prosperous in everything,
and still is vigorous enough to enjoy
food!

2 O death, how welcome is your sentence
to one who is needy and failing in
strength,
worn down by age and anxious about
everything;
to one who is contrary, and has lost all
patience!

3 Do not fear death's decree for you;
remember those who went before you
and those who will come after.

4 This is the Lord's decree for all flesh;
why then should you reject the will of
the Most High?
Whether life lasts for ten years or a hundred
or a thousand,
there are no questions asked in Hades.

The Fate of the Wicked

5 The children of sinners are abominable
children,
and they frequent the haunts of the
ungodly.

6 The inheritance of the children of sinners
will perish,

---

n Heb Syr: Gk Lat *from the waters returns to the sea*
o Heb: Gk *Life is sweet for the self-reliant worker*
p Heb Syr: Gk lacks *but better . . . prosperous*   q Heb: Gk
wisdom   r Heb Compare Syr: Gk *wife with her husband*

and on their offspring will be a perpetual
    disgrace.
7 Children will blame an ungodly father,
    for they suffer disgrace because of him.
8 Woe to you, the ungodly,
    who have forsaken the law of the Most
        High God!
9 If you have children, calamity will be theirs;
    you will beget them only for groaning.
When you stumble, there is lasting joy;^{s}
    and when you die, a curse is your lot.
10 Whatever comes from earth returns to earth;
    so the ungodly go from curse to
        destruction.

11 The human body is a fleeting thing,
    but a virtuous name will never be
        blotted out.^{t}
12 Have regard for your name, since it will
        outlive you
    longer than a thousand hoards of gold.
13 The days of a good life are numbered,
    but a good name lasts forever.

14 My children, be true to your training and be
        at peace;
    hidden wisdom and unseen treasure—
        of what value is either?

A Series of Contrasts

15 Better are those who hide their folly
    than those who hide their wisdom.
16 Therefore show respect for my words;
    for it is not good to feel shame in every
        circumstance,
    nor is every kind of abashment to be
        approved.^{u}

17 Be ashamed of sexual immorality, before
        your father or mother;
    and of a lie, before a prince or a ruler;
18 of a crime, before a judge or magistrate;
    and of a breach of the law, before the
        congregation and the people;
    of unjust dealing, before your partner or
        your friend;
19 and of theft, in the place where you live.
Be ashamed of breaking an oath or
        agreement,^{v}
    and of leaning on your elbow at meals;
    of surliness in receiving or giving,
20 and of silence, before those who
            greet you;
    of looking at a prostitute,
21 and of rejecting the appeal of a relative;
    of taking away someone's portion or gift,
    and of gazing at another man's wife;

22 of meddling with his servant-girl—
    and do not approach her bed;
of abusive words, before friends—
    and do not be insulting after making a
            gift.
Be ashamed of repeating what you hear,
    and of betraying secrets.
Then you will show proper shame,
    and will find favor with everyone.

Of the following things do not be ashamed,
    and do not sin to save face:
2 Do not be ashamed of the law of the Most
        High and his covenant,
    and of rendering judgment to acquit the
        ungodly;
3 of keeping accounts with a partner or with
        traveling companions,
    and of dividing the inheritance of friends;
4 of accuracy with scales and weights,
    and of acquiring much or little;
5 of profit from dealing with merchants,
    and of frequent disciplining of children,
    and of drawing blood from the back of a
        wicked slave.
6 Where there is an untrustworthy wife, a seal
        is a good thing;
    and where there are many hands, lock
        things up.
7 When you make a deposit, be sure it is
        counted and weighed,
    and when you give or receive, put it all
        in writing.
8 Do not be ashamed to correct the stupid or
        foolish
    or the aged who are guilty of sexual
        immorality.
Then you will show your sound training,
    and will be approved by all.

Daughters and Fathers
(Sir 7.24–25; 26.10–12)

9 A daughter is a secret anxiety to her father,
    and worry over her robs him of sleep;
when she is young, for fear she may not
        marry,
    or if married, for fear she may be
        disliked;
10 while a virgin, for fear she may be seduced
    and become pregnant in her father's
        house;

---

^{s} Heb: Meaning of Gk uncertain ^{t} Heb: Gk *People grieve
over the death of the body, but the bad name of sinners will be
blotted out* ^{u} Heb: Gk *and not everything is confidently
esteemed by everyone* ^{v} Heb: Gk *before the truth of God
and the covenant*

The Sexism of Sirach

Let's just get this right out in the open: Ben Sira was extremely sexist by today's standards. He didn't have a very high opinion of women. As you read Sir 42.9–14, you probably think it's a curse to have a daughter! Verse 14 says, "Better is the wickedness of a man than a woman who does good; / it is woman who brings shame and disgrace." Wow, with an attitude like that, Ben Sira wouldn't be welcomed by many modern people.

Once again, we have to remember that the Bible was written by human beings and reflects their cultural standards. Ben Sira's attitude was commonly accepted in his culture. But the cultural standards in the Bible don't always reflect God's truth. That's why we need the help of the larger church community to properly interpret the Bible. Today, the church teaches that women and men are to be treated with equal dignity and respect. Let's work together to continue making that vision a reality.

▸ Sir 42.9–14

or having a husband, for fear she may go
    astray,
or, though married, for fear she may be
    barren.

11 Keep strict watch over a headstrong
        daughter,
    or she may make you a laughingstock to
        your enemies,
a byword in the city and the assembly of[w]
        the people,
    and put you to shame in public
        gatherings.[x]
See that there is no lattice in her room,
    no spot that overlooks the approaches to
        the house.[y]

12 Do not let her parade her beauty before
        any man,
    or spend her time among married
        women;[w]

13 for from garments comes the moth,
    and from a woman comes woman's
        wickedness.

14 Better is the wickedness of a man than a
        woman who does good;
    it is woman who brings shame and
        disgrace.

The Works of God in Nature

15 I will now call to mind the works of the
        Lord,
    and will declare what I have seen.
By the word of the Lord his works are
        made,
    and all his creatures do his will.[z]

16 The sun looks down on everything with its
        light,

and the work of the Lord is full of his
        glory.

17 The Lord has not empowered even his holy
        ones
    to recount all his marvelous works,
which the Lord the Almighty has
        established
    so that the universe may stand firm in
        his glory.

18 He searches out the abyss and the human
        heart;
    he understands their innermost secrets.
For the Most High knows all that may be
        known;
    he sees from of old the things that are to
        come.[a]

19 He discloses what has been and what is
        to be,
    and he reveals the traces of hidden
        things.

20 No thought escapes him,
    and nothing is hidden from him.

21 He has set in order the splendors of his
        wisdom;
    he is from all eternity one and the same.
Nothing can be added or taken away,
    and he needs no one to be his counselor.

22 How desirable are all his works,
    and how sparkling they are to see![b]

23 All these things live and remain forever;

---

w Heb: Meaning of Gk uncertain   x Heb: Gk to shame
before the great multitude   y Heb: Gk lacks See . . . house
z Syr Compare Heb: most Gk witnesses lack and all . . .
will   a Heb: Gk he sees the sign(s) of the age   b Meaning
of Gk uncertain

each creature is preserved to meet a
    particular need.[c]

24 All things come in pairs, one opposite the
    other,
    and he has made nothing incomplete.
25 Each supplements the virtues of the other.
    Who could ever tire of seeing his glory?

The Splendor of the Sun

The pride of the higher realms is the clear
    vault of the sky,
    as glorious to behold as the sight of the
    heavens.
2 The sun, when it appears, proclaims as it
    rises
    what a marvelous instrument it is, the
    work of the Most High.
3 At noon it parches the land,
    and who can withstand its burning heat?
4 A man tending[d] a furnace works in burning
    heat,
    but three times as hot is the sun
    scorching the mountains;
    it breathes out fiery vapors,
    and its bright rays blind the eyes.
5 Great is the Lord who made it;
    at his orders it hurries on its course.

The Splendor of the Moon

6 It is the moon that marks the changing
    seasons,[e]
    governing the times, their everlasting
    sign.
7 From the moon comes the sign for festal
    days,
    a light that wanes when it completes its
    course.
8 The new moon, as its name suggests, renews
    itself;[f]
    how marvelous it is in this change,
    a beacon to the hosts on high,
    shining in the vault of the heavens!

The Glory of the Stars and the Rainbow

9 The glory of the stars is the beauty of
    heaven,
    a glittering array in the heights of the
    Lord.
10 On the orders of the Holy One they stand
    in their appointed places;
    they never relax in their watches.
11 Look at the rainbow, and praise him who
    made it;
    it is exceedingly beautiful in its
    brightness.
12 It encircles the sky with its glorious arc;

the hands of the Most High have
    stretched it out.

The Marvels of Nature

13 By his command he sends the driving snow
    and speeds the lightnings of his
    judgment.
14 Therefore the storehouses are opened,
    and the clouds fly out like birds.
15 In his majesty he gives the clouds their
    strength,
    and the hailstones are broken in pieces.
17a The voice of his thunder rebukes the earth;
16   when he appears, the mountains shake.
At his will the south wind blows;
17b   so do the storm from the north and the
    whirlwind.
He scatters the snow like birds flying down,
    and its descent is like locusts alighting.
18 The eye is dazzled by the beauty of its
    whiteness,
    and the mind is amazed as it falls.
19 He pours frost over the earth like salt,
    and icicles form like pointed thorns.
20 The cold north wind blows,
    and ice freezes on the water;
    it settles on every pool of water,
    and the water puts it on like a
    breastplate.
21 He consumes the mountains and burns up
    the wilderness,
    and withers the tender grass like fire.
22 A mist quickly heals all things;
    the falling dew gives refreshment from
    the heat.
23 By his plan he stilled the deep
    and planted islands in it.
24 Those who sail the sea tell of its dangers,
    and we marvel at what we hear.
25 In it are strange and marvelous creatures,
    all kinds of living things, and huge
    sea-monsters.
26 Because of him each of his messengers
    succeeds,
    and by his word all things hold together.
27 We could say more but could never say
    enough;
    let the final word be: "He is the all."
28 Where can we find the strength to
    praise him?
    For he is greater than all his works.

---

c Heb: Gk *forever for every need, and all are obedient*
d Other ancient authorities read *blowing upon*
e Heb: Meaning of Gk uncertain   f Heb: Gk *The month is
named after the moon*

29 Awesome is the Lord and very great,
and marvelous is his power.
30 Glorify the Lord and exalt him as much as
you can,
for he surpasses even that.
When you exalt him, summon all your
strength,
and do not grow weary, for you cannot
praise him enough.
31 Who has seen him and can describe him?
Or who can extol him as he is?
32 Many things greater than these lie hidden,
for I*g* have seen but few of his works.
33 For the Lord has made all things,
and to the godly he has given wisdom.

HYMN IN HONOR OF OUR ANCESTORS*h*

Let us now sing the praises of famous men,
our ancestors in their generations.
2 The Lord apportioned to them*i* great glory,
his majesty from the beginning.
3 There were those who ruled in their
kingdoms,
and made a name for themselves by their
valor;
those who gave counsel because they were
intelligent;
those who spoke in prophetic oracles;
4 those who led the people by their counsels
and by their knowledge of the people's
lore;
they were wise in their words of
instruction;
5 those who composed musical tunes,
or put verses in writing;
6 rich men endowed with resources,
living peacefully in their homes—
7 all these were honored in their generations,
and were the pride of their times.
8 Some of them have left behind a name,
so that others declare their praise.
9 But of others there is no memory;
they have perished as though they had
never existed;
they have become as though they had never
been born,
they and their children after them.
10 But these also were godly men,
whose righteous deeds have not been
forgotten;
11 their wealth will remain with their
descendants,
and their inheritance with their children's
children.*j*
12 Their descendants stand by the covenants;
their children also, for their sake.

13 Their offspring will continue forever,
and their glory will never be blotted out.
14 Their bodies are buried in peace,
but their name lives on generation after
generation.
15 The assembly declares*k* their wisdom,
and the congregation proclaims their
praise.

Enoch
(Gen 5.24; Heb 11.5)

16 E'noch pleased the Lord and was taken up,
an example of repentance to all
generations.

Noah
(Gen 6.9—9.17)

17 Noah was found perfect and righteous;
in the time of wrath he kept the race
alive;*l*
therefore a remnant was left on the earth
when the flood came.
18 Everlasting covenants were made with him
that all flesh should never again be
blotted out by a flood.

Abraham
(Gen 15.1—17.27; 22.1–18)

19 Abraham was the great father of a multitude
of nations,
and no one has been found like him in
glory.
20 He kept the law of the Most High,
and entered into a covenant with him;
he certified the covenant in his flesh,
and when he was tested he proved
faithful.
21 Therefore the Lord*m* assured him with an
oath
that the nations would be blessed
through his offspring;
that he would make him as numerous as
the dust of the earth,
and exalt his offspring like the stars,
and give them an inheritance from sea
to sea
and from the Euphrates*n* to the ends of
the earth.

---

g Heb: Gk *we*   *h* This title is included in the Gk text.
i Heb: Gk *created*   *j* Heb Compare Lat Syr: Meaning of
Gk uncertain   *k* Heb: Gk *Peoples declare*   *l* Heb: Gk *was
taken in exchange*   *m* Gk *he*   *n* Syr: Heb Gk *River*

Isaac and Jacob

(Gen 26.1–5; 27.1–29)

22 To Isaac also he gave the same assurance
    for the sake of his father Abraham.
The blessing of all people and the covenant
23   he made to rest on the head of Jacob;
he acknowledged him with his blessings,
    and gave him his inheritance;
he divided his portions,
    and distributed them among twelve
        tribes.

Moses

(Ex 6.28 — 11.10; 20.1–21)

From his descendants the Lord[o] brought
    forth a godly man,
who found favor in the sight of all
1 and was beloved by God and people,
    Moses, whose memory is blessed.
2 He made him equal in glory to the holy
        ones,
    and made him great, to the terror of his
        enemies.
3 By his words he performed swift miracles;[p]
    the Lord[o] glorified him in the presence of
        kings.
He gave him commandments for his people,
    and revealed to him his glory.
4 For his faithfulness and meekness he
        consecrated him,
    choosing him out of all humankind.
5 He allowed him to hear his voice,
    and led him into the dark cloud,
and gave him the commandments face to
        face,
    the law of life and knowledge,
so that he might teach Jacob the covenant,
    and Israel his decrees.

Aaron

(Ex 28.1–43; Lev 8.1–36; Num 16.1–35)

6 He exalted Aaron, a holy man like Moses[q]
    who was his brother, of the tribe of Levi.
7 He made an everlasting covenant with him,
    and gave him the priesthood of the
        people.
He blessed him with stateliness,
    and put a glorious robe on him.
8 He clothed him in perfect splendor,
    and strengthened him with the symbols
        of authority,
    the linen undergarments, the long robe,
        and the ephod.
9 And he encircled him with pomegranates,
    with many golden bells all around,

to send forth a sound as he walked,
    to make their ringing heard in the temple
    as a reminder to his people;
10 with the sacred vestment, of gold and violet
        and purple, the work of an embroiderer;
with the oracle of judgment, U'rim and
        Thum'mim;
11   with twisted crimson, the work of an
        artisan;
with precious stones engraved like seals,
    in a setting of gold, the work of a
        jeweler,
to commemorate in engraved letters
    each of the tribes of Israel;
12 with a gold crown upon his turban,
    inscribed like a seal with "Holiness,"
a distinction to be prized, the work of an
        expert,
    a delight to the eyes, richly adorned.
13 Before him such beautiful things did not
        exist.
    No outsider ever put them on,
but only his sons
    and his descendants in perpetuity.
14 His sacrifices shall be wholly burned
    twice every day continually.
15 Moses ordained him,
    and anointed him with holy oil;
it was an everlasting covenant for him
    and for his descendants as long as the
        heavens endure,
to minister to the Lord[q] and serve as priest
    and bless his people in his name.
16 He chose him out of all the living
    to offer sacrifice to the Lord,
incense and a pleasing odor as a memorial
        portion,
    to make atonement for the[r] people.
17 In his commandments he gave him
    authority and statutes and[s] judgments,
to teach Jacob the testimonies,
    and to enlighten Israel with his law.
18 Outsiders conspired against him,
    and envied him in the wilderness,
Dā'than and A·bī'ram and their followers
    and the company of Kō'rah, in wrath and
        anger.
19 The Lord saw it and was not pleased,
    and in the heat of his anger they were
        destroyed;
he performed wonders against them
    to consume them in flaming fire.

---

o Gk he   p Heb: Gk *caused signs to cease*   q Gk *him*
r Other ancient authorities read *his* or *your*   s Heb: Gk
authority in covenants of

20 He added glory to Aaron
  and gave him a heritage;
he allotted to him the best of the first fruits,
  and prepared bread of first fruits in
    abundance;
21 for they eat the sacrifices of the Lord,
  which he gave to him and his
    descendants.
22 But in the land of the people he has no
    inheritance,
  and he has no portion among the people;
for the Lord[t] himself is his[u] portion and
    inheritance.

Phinehas
(Num 25.7–13)

23 Phin'e•has son of El•ē•ā'zar ranks third in
    glory
  for being zealous in the fear of the Lord,
and standing firm, when the people turned
    away,
  in the noble courage of his soul;
  and he made atonement for Israel.
24 Therefore a covenant of friendship was
    established with him,
  that he should be leader of the sanctuary
    and of his people,
that he and his descendants should have
  the dignity of the priesthood forever.
25 Just as a covenant was established with
    David
  son of Jesse of the tribe of Judah,
that the king's heritage passes only from son
    to son,
  so the heritage of Aaron is for his
    descendants alone.

26 And now bless the Lord
  who has crowned you with glory.[v]
May the Lord[t] grant you wisdom of mind
  to judge his people with justice,
so that their prosperity may not vanish,
  and that their glory may endure through
    all their generations.

Joshua and Caleb
(Josh 6 — 11)

Joshua son of Nun was mighty in war,
  and was the successor of Moses in the
    prophetic office.
He became, as his name implies,
  a great savior of God's[w] elect,
to take vengeance on the enemies that rose
    against them,
  so that he might give Israel its
    inheritance.

2 How glorious he was when he lifted his
    hands
  and brandished his sword against the
    cities!
3 Who before him ever stood so firm?
  For he waged the wars of the Lord.
4 Was it not through him that the sun stood
    still
  and one day became as long as two?
5 He called upon the Most High, the
    Mighty One,
  when enemies pressed him on every side,
and the great Lord answered him
  with hailstones of mighty power.
6 He overwhelmed that nation in battle,
  and on the slope he destroyed his
    opponents,
so that the nations might know his
    armament,
  that he was fighting in the sight of the
    Lord;
for he was a devoted follower of the
    Mighty One.
7 And in the days of Moses he proved his
    loyalty,
  he and Caleb son of Je•phūn'neh:
they opposed the congregation,[x]
  restrained the people from sin,
  and stilled their wicked grumbling.
8 And these two alone were spared
  out of six hundred thousand infantry,
to lead the people[y] into their inheritance,
  the land flowing with milk and honey.
9 The Lord gave Caleb strength,
  which remained with him in his old age,
so that he went up to the hill country,
  and his children obtained it for an
    inheritance,
10 so that all the Israelites might see
  how good it is to follow the Lord.

The Judges
(Judg 1 — 16; 1 Sam 3.19–20)

11 The judges also, with their respective names,
  whose hearts did not fall into idolatry
and who did not turn away from the Lord—
  may their memory be blessed!
12 May their bones send forth new life from
    where they lie,
  and may the names of those who have
    been honored
  live again in their children!

---

[t] Gk he   [u] Other ancient authorities read *your*
[v] Heb: Gk lacks *And . . . glory*   [w] Gk *his*   [x] Other
ancient authorities read *the enemy*   [y] Gk *them*

Heroes

Who are your heroes? Maybe they include a teacher, a coach, a friend, or a parent. What sets them apart and makes them people you look up to? Their accomplishments? A cause they represent? Or a personal trait that only someone who knows them personally would be aware of?

Who we look to as heroes says a lot about us. If our heroes are kind and generous, then maybe we value kindness and generosity. If our heroes are wealthy, perhaps we desire wealth.

Read the last section of Sirach, starting with chapter 44, which honors many Old Testament heroes. Ben Sira considered them heroes because their hearts were fixed on the Lord (49.3). What an awesome way to describe heroes!

Who do you know who has his or her heart fixed on the Lord? What does your choice of heroes say about your dreams and values?

▶ Sirach, chapters 44–49

13 Samuel was beloved by his Lord;
     a prophet of the Lord, he established the
          kingdom
     and anointed rulers over his people.
14 By the law of the Lord he judged the
          congregation,
     and the Lord watched over Jacob.
15 By his faithfulness he was proved to be a
          prophet,
     and by his words he became known as a
          trustworthy seer.
16 He called upon the Lord, the Mighty One,
     when his enemies pressed him on every
          side,
     and he offered in sacrifice a suckling
          lamb.
17 Then the Lord thundered from heaven,
     and made his voice heard with a mighty
          sound;
18 he subdued the leaders of the enemy[z]
     and all the rulers of the Phi·lis'tines.
19 Before the time of his eternal sleep,
     Samuel[a] bore witness before the Lord
          and his anointed:
"No property, not so much as a pair of
          shoes,
     have I taken from anyone!"
And no one accused him.
20 Even after he had fallen asleep, he
          prophesied
     and made known to the king his
          death,
     and lifted up his voice from the ground
          in prophecy, to blot out the wickedness
               of the people.

Nathan
(2 Sam 7.1–3; 12.1–14)

After him Nathan rose up
     to prophesy in the days of David.

David
(1 Sam 17.12—18.7)

2 As the fat is set apart from the offering of
          well-being,
     so David was set apart from the Israelites.
3 He played with lions as though they were
          young goats,
     and with bears as though they were
          lambs of the flock.
4 In his youth did he not kill a giant,
     and take away the people's disgrace,
when he whirled the stone in the sling
     and struck down the boasting Goliath?
5 For he called on the Lord, the Most High,
     and he gave strength to his right arm
to strike down a mighty warrior,
     and to exalt the power[b] of his people.
6 So they glorified him for the tens of
          thousands he conquered,
     and praised him for the blessings
          bestowed by the Lord,
     when the glorious diadem was given
          to him.
7 For he wiped out his enemies on every side,
     and annihilated his adversaries the
          Phi·lis'tines;
     he crushed their power[b] to our own day.
8 In all that he did he gave thanks

---

z Heb: Gk *leaders of the people of Tyre*   a Gk *he*
b Gk *horn*

S
I
R

to the Holy One, the Most High,
proclaiming his glory;
he sang praise with all his heart,
and he loved his Maker.

9 He placed singers before the altar,
to make sweet melody with their voices.^c

10 He gave beauty to the festivals,
and arranged their times throughout the
year,^d
while they praised God's^e holy name,
and the sanctuary resounded from early
morning.

11 The Lord took away his sins,
and exalted his power^f forever;
he gave him a covenant of kingship
and a glorious throne in Israel.

Solomon
(1 Kings 4.20–34)

12 After him a wise son rose up
who because of him lived in security:^g

13 Solomon reigned in an age of peace,
because God made all his borders
tranquil,
so that he might build a house in his name
and provide a sanctuary to stand forever.

14 How wise you were when you were young!
You overflowed like the Nile^h with
understanding.

15 Your influence spread throughout the earth,
and you filled it with proverbs having
deep meaning.

16 Your fame reached to far-off islands,
and you were loved for your peaceful
reign.

17 Your songs, proverbs, and parables,
and the answers you gave astounded the
nations.

18 In the name of the Lord God,
who is called the God of Israel,
you gathered gold like tin
and amassed silver like lead.

19 But you brought in women to lie at your
side,
and through your body you were brought
into subjection.

20 You stained your honor,
and defiled your family line,
so that you brought wrath upon your
children,
and they were grievedⁱ at your folly,

21 because the sovereignty was divided
and a rebel kingdom arose out of
E′phra•im.

22 But the Lord will never give up his mercy,
or cause any of his works to perish;

he will never blot out the descendants of his
chosen one,
or destroy the family line of him who
loved him.
So he gave a remnant to Jacob,
and to David a root from his own family.

Rehoboam and Jeroboam
(1 Kings 12.6–33)

23 Solomon rested with his ancestors,
and left behind him one of his sons,
broad in^j folly and lacking in sense,
Rē•ho•bō′am, whose policy drove the
people to revolt.
Then Jer•o•bō′am son of Nē′bat led Israel
into sin
and started Ē′phra•im on its sinful ways.

24 Their sins increased more and more,
until they were exiled from their land.

25 For they sought out every kind of
wickedness,
until vengeance came upon them.

Elijah
(1 Kings 17.1—19.18)

Then Elijah arose, a prophet like fire,
and his word burned like a torch.

2 He brought a famine upon them,
and by his zeal he made them few in
number.

3 By the word of the Lord he shut up the
heavens,
and also three times brought down fire.

4 How glorious you were, E•lī′jah, in your
wondrous deeds!
Whose glory is equal to yours?

5 You raised a corpse from death
and from Hades, by the word of the Most
High.

6 You sent kings down to destruction,
and famous men, from their sickbeds.

7 You heard rebuke at Sinai
and judgments of vengeance at Hō′reb.

8 You anointed kings to inflict retribution,
and prophets to succeed you.^k

9 You were taken up by a whirlwind of fire,
in a chariot with horses of fire.

10 At the appointed time, it is written, you are
destined^l

---

^c Other ancient authorities add *and daily they sing his
praises* ^d Gk *to completion* ^e Gk *his* ^f Gk *horn*
^g Heb: Gk *in a broad place* ^h Heb: Gk *a river* ⁱ Other
ancient authorities read *I was grieved* ^j Heb (with a play
on the name Rehoboam) Syr: Gk *the people's* ^k Heb: Gk
him ^l Heb: Gk *are for reproofs*

to calm the wrath of God before it breaks
　　out in fury,
to turn the hearts of parents to their
　　children,
and to restore the tribes of Jacob.
11 Happy are those who saw you
　　and were adorned[m] with your love!
　For we also shall surely live.[n]

Elisha
(2 Kings 2.9–13)

12 When E·li′jah was enveloped in the
　　whirlwind,
　E·li′sha was filled with his spirit.
He performed twice as many signs,
　　and marvels with every utterance of his
　　mouth.[o]
Never in his lifetime did he tremble before
　　any ruler,
　　nor could anyone intimidate him at all.
13 Nothing was too hard for him,
　　and when he was dead, his body
　　prophesied.
14 In his life he did wonders,
　　and in death his deeds were marvelous.

15 Despite all this the people did not repent,
　　nor did they forsake their sins,
until they were carried off as plunder from
　　their land,
　and were scattered over all the earth.
The people were left very few in number,
　　but with a ruler from the house of David.
16 Some of them did what was right,
　　but others sinned more and more.

Hezekiah
(2 Kings 18.1—20.21)

17 Hez·e·ki′ah fortified his city,
　　and brought water into its midst;
he tunneled the rock with iron tools,
　　and built cisterns for the water.
18 In his days Sen·nach′e·rib invaded the
　　country;
　he sent his commander[p] and departed;
he shook his fist against Zion,
　　and made great boasts in his arrogance.
19 Then their hearts were shaken and their
　　hands trembled,
　and they were in anguish, like women in
　　labor.
20 But they called upon the Lord who is
　　merciful,
　spreading out their hands toward him.
The Holy One quickly heard them from
　　heaven,

and delivered them through I·sāi′ah.
21 The Lord[q] struck down the camp of the
　　Assyrians,
　and his angel wiped them out.
22 For Hez·e·ki′ah did what was pleasing to the
　　Lord,
　and he kept firmly to the ways of his
　　ancestor David,
as he was commanded by the prophet
　　I·sāi′ah,
　who was great and trustworthy in his
　　visions.

Isaiah
(2 Kings 20.10–11)

23 In I·sāi′ah's[r] days the sun went backward,
　　and he prolonged the life of the king.
24 By his dauntless spirit he saw the future,
　　and comforted the mourners in Zion.
25 He revealed what was to occur to the end of
　　time,
　and the hidden things before they
　　happened.

Josiah and Other Worthies

The name[s] of Jō·sī′ah is like blended incense
　　prepared by the skill of the perfumer;
his memory[t] is as sweet as honey to every
　　mouth,
　and like music at a banquet of wine.
2 He did what was right by reforming the
　　people,
　and removing the wicked abominations.
3 He kept his heart fixed on the Lord;
　　in lawless times he made godliness
　　prevail.

4 Except for David and Hez·e·ki′ah and Jō·sī′ah,
　　all of them were great sinners,
for they abandoned the law of the Most
　　High;
　the kings of Judah came to an end.
5 They[u] gave their power to others,
　　and their glory to a foreign nation,
6 who set fire to the chosen city of the
　　sanctuary,
　and made its streets desolate,
as Jer·e·mi′ah had foretold.[v]
7 For they had mistreated him,
　　who even in the womb had been
　　consecrated a prophet,

---

m Other ancient authorities read *and have died*　　n Text
and meaning of Gk uncertain　　o Heb: Gk lacks *He
performed . . . mouth*　　p Other ancient authorities add
from Lachish　　q Gk *He*　　r Gk *his*　　s Heb: Gk *memory*
t Heb: Gk *it*　　u Heb *He*　　v Gk *by the hand of Jeremiah*

S
I
R

to pluck up and ruin and destroy,
and likewise to build and to plant.

8 It was E•zēk′i•el who saw the vision of glory,
which God[w] showed him above the
chariot of the cherubim.
9 For God[x] also mentioned Jōb
who held fast to all the ways of justice.[y]
10 May the bones of the Twelve Prophets
send forth new life from where they lie,
for they comforted the people of Jacob
and delivered them with confident hope.

11 How shall we magnify Ze•rub′ba•bel?
He was like a signet ring on the right
hand,
12 and so was Jesh′ū•a son of Jō′za•dak;
in their days they built the house
and raised a temple[z] holy to the Lord,
destined for everlasting glory.
13 The memory of Nē•he•mī′ah also is lasting;
he raised our fallen walls,
and set up gates and bars,
and rebuilt our ruined houses.

Retrospect

14 Few have[a] ever been created on earth like
Ē′noch,
for he was taken up from the earth.
15 Nor was anyone ever born like Joseph;[b]
even his bones were cared for.
16 Shem and Seth and Ē′nosh were honored,[c]
but above every other created living being
was Adam.

Simon Son of Onias

The leader of his brothers and the pride of
his people[d]
was the high priest, Simon son of Ō•nī′as,
who in his life repaired the house,
and in his time fortified the temple.
2 He laid the foundations for the high double
walls,
the high retaining walls for the temple
enclosure.
3 In his days a water cistern was dug,[e]
a reservoir like the sea in circumference.
4 He considered how to save his people from
ruin,
and fortified the city against siege.
5 How glorious he was, surrounded by the
people,
as he came out of the house of the
curtain.
6 Like the morning star among the clouds,
like the full moon at the festal season;[e]

7 like the sun shining on the temple of the
Most High,
like the rainbow gleaming in splendid
clouds;
8 like roses in the days of first fruits,
like lilies by a spring of water,
like a green shoot on Lebanon on a
summer day;
9 like fire and incense in the censer,
like a vessel of hammered gold
studded with all kinds of precious stones;
10 like an olive tree laden with fruit,
and like a cypress towering in the clouds.
11 When he put on his glorious robe
and clothed himself in perfect splendor,
when he went up to the holy altar,
he made the court of the sanctuary
glorious.
12 When he received the portions from the
hands of the priests,
as he stood by the hearth of the altar
with a garland of brothers around him,
he was like a young cedar on Lebanon
surrounded by the trunks of palm trees.
13 All the sons of Aaron in their splendor
held the Lord's offering in their hands
before the whole congregation of Israel.
14 Finishing the service at the altars,[f]
and arranging the offering to the Most
High, the Almighty,
15 he held out his hand for the cup
and poured a drink offering of the blood
of the grape;
he poured it out at the foot of the altar,
a pleasing odor to the Most High, the
king of all.
16 Then the sons of Aaron shouted;
they blew their trumpets of hammered
metal;
they sounded a mighty fanfare
as a reminder before the Most High.
17 Then all the people together quickly
fell to the ground on their faces
to worship their Lord,
the Almighty, God Most High.

18 Then the singers praised him with their
voices

w Gk He   x Gk he   y Heb Compare Syr: Meaning of Gk
uncertain   z Other ancient authorities read *people*
a Heb Syr: Gk *No one has*   b Heb Syr: Gk adds *the leader
of his brothers, the support of the people*   c Heb: Gk *Shem
and Seth were honored by people*   d Heb Syr: Gk lacks this
line. Compare 49.15   e Heb: Meaning of Gk uncertain
f Other ancient authorities read *altar*

in sweet and full-toned melody.g

19 And the people of the Lord Most High
offered
their prayers before the Merciful One,
until the order of worship of the Lord was
ended,
and they completed his ritual.

20 Then Simonh came down and raised his
hands
over the whole congregation of Israelites,
to pronounce the blessing of the Lord with
his lips,
and to glory in his name;

21 and they bowed down in worship a second
time,
to receive the blessing from the Most
High.

A Benediction

22 And now bless the God of all,
who everywhere works great wonders,
who fosters our growth from birth,
and deals with us according to his mercy.

23 May he give usi gladness of heart,
and may there be peace in ourj days
in Israel, as in the days of old.

24 May he entrust to us his mercy,
and may he deliver us in ourk days!

Epilogue

25 Two nations my soul detests,
and the third is not even a people:

26 Those who live in Sē′ir,l and the
Phi•lis′tines,
and the foolish people that live in
Shē′chem.

27 Instruction in understanding and knowledge
I have written in this book,
Jesus son of El•ē•ā′zar son of Sī′rachm of
Jerusalem,
whose mind poured forth wisdom.

28 Happy are those who concern themselves
with these things,
and those who lay them to heart will
become wise.

29 For if they put them into practice, they will
be equal to anything,
for the fearn of the Lord is their path.

PRAYER OF JESUS SON OF SIRACHo

I give you thanks, O Lord and King,
and praise you, O God my Savior.
I give thanks to your name,
2 for you have been my protector and
helper

and have delivered me from destruction
and from the trap laid by a slanderous
tongue,
from lips that fabricate lies.
In the face of my adversaries
you have been my helper 3 and
delivered me,
in the greatness of your mercy and of
your name,
from grinding teeth about to devour me,
from the hand of those seeking my life,
from the many troubles I endured,

4 from choking fire on every side,
and from the midst of fire that I had not
kindled,

5 from the deep belly of Hades,
from an unclean tongue and lying
words—

6 the slander of an unrighteous tongue to
the king.
My soul drew near to death,
and my life was on the brink of Hades
below.

7 They surrounded me on every side,
and there was no one to help me;
I looked for human assistance,
and there was none.

8 Then I remembered your mercy, O Lord,
and your kindnessp from of old,
for you rescue those who wait for you
and save them from the hand of their
enemies.

9 And I sent up my prayer from the earth,
and begged for rescue from death.

10 I cried out, "Lord, you are my Father;q
do not forsake me in the days of
trouble,
when there is no help against the
proud.

11 I will praise your name continually,
and will sing hymns of thanksgiving."
My prayer was heard,

12 for you saved me from destruction
and rescued me in time of trouble.
For this reason I thank you and praise you,
and I bless the name of the Lord.

g Other ancient authorities read *in sweet melody throughout
the house*   h Gk *he*   i Other ancient authorities read *you*
j Other ancient authorities read *your*   k Other ancient
authorities read *his*   l Heb Compare Lat: Gk *on the
mountain of Samaria*   m Heb: Meaning of Gk uncertain
n Heb: Other ancient authorities read *light*   o This title is
included in the Gk text.   p Other ancient authorities
read *work*   q Heb: Gk *the Father of my lord*

Heb adds:

Give thanks to the LORD, for he is good,
for his mercy endures forever;

Give thanks to the God of praises,
for his mercy endures forever;

Give thanks to the guardian of Israel,
for his mercy endures forever;

Give thanks to him who formed all things,
for his mercy endures forever;

Give thanks to the redeemer of Israel,
for his mercy endures forever;

Give thanks to him who gathers the dispersed of
Israel,
for his mercy endures forever;

Give thanks to him who rebuilt his city and his
sanctuary,
for his mercy endures forever;

Give thanks to him who makes a horn to sprout
for the house of David,
for his mercy endures forever;

Give thanks to him who has chosen the sons of
Za'dok to be priests,
for his mercy endures forever;

Give thanks to the shield of Abraham,
for his mercy endures forever;

Give thanks to the rock of Isaac,
for his mercy endures forever;

Give thanks to the mighty one of Jacob,
for his mercy endures forever;

Give thanks to him who has chosen Zion,
for his mercy endures forever;

Give thanks to the King of the kings of kings,
for his mercy endures forever;

He has raised up a horn for his people,
praise for all his loyal ones.

For the children of Israel, the people close
to him.
Praise the LORD!

Autobiographical Poem on Wisdom

13 While I was still young, before I went on
my travels,
I sought wisdom openly in my prayer.

14 Before the temple I asked for her,
and I will search for her until the end.
15 From the first blossom to the ripening
grape
my heart delighted in her;
my foot walked on the straight path;
from my youth I followed her steps.
16 I inclined my ear a little and received her,
and I found for myself much instruction.
17 I made progress in her;
to him who gives wisdom I will give
glory.
18 For I resolved to live according to
wisdom,[r]
and I was zealous for the good,
and I shall never be disappointed.
19 My soul grappled with wisdom,[r]
and in my conduct I was strict;[s]

I spread out my hands to the heavens,
and lamented my ignorance of her.
20 I directed my soul to her,
and in purity I found her.

With her I gained understanding from the
first;
therefore I will never be forsaken.
21 My heart was stirred to seek her;
therefore I have gained a prize
possession.
22 The Lord gave me my tongue as a reward,
and I will praise him with it.

23 Draw near to me, you who are uneducated,
and lodge in the house of instruction.
24 Why do you say you are lacking in these
things,[t]
and why do you endure such great
thirst?
25 I opened my mouth and said,
Acquire wisdom[u] for yourselves without
money.

26 Put your neck under her[v] yoke,
and let your souls receive instruction;
it is to be found close by.

27 See with your own eyes that I have labored
but little

---

r Gk *her*   *s* Meaning of Gk uncertain   *t* Cn Compare
Heb Syr: Meaning of Gk uncertain   *u* Heb: Gk lacks
wisdom   *v* Heb: other ancient authorities read *the*

and found for myself much
    serenity.

28 Hear but a little of my instruction,
    and through me you will acquire
      silver and gold.*w*

29 May your soul rejoice in God's*x*
    mercy,

and may you never be ashamed to
    praise him.

30 Do your work in good time,
    and in his own time God*y* will give you
      your reward.

---

w Syr Compare Heb: Gk *Get instruction with a large sum of silver, and you will gain by it much gold.*   *x* Gk *his*   *y* Gk *he*

Introduction to the
Prophets

Have you ever heard a speaker who seemed to be talking right to you? someone who could see past external appearances and into the hearts of people and events? someone committed to total honesty even if it hurt? someone who inspired you to make some needed changes and gave you hope for the future? If so, you've encountered a modern-day prophet—a person who names what God wants to say to us. In this section of books, you will meet the prophets of the Bible —unique and courageous people who did these things for ancient Israel.

In-depth

WHAT IS A PROPHET? FIRST AND FOREMOST, A prophet is a person—or sometimes a group—who speaks for God. The prophet's words spoken in God's name—usually called prophecies or oracles—are God's words. Some people think that prophets can predict the future, but this is not their role in the Bible. The biblical prophets were called by God during times of crisis to offer God's people challenge or comfort, depending on their circumstances. So, to properly understand biblical prophecies, we must try to understand the historical situation God was addressing through the prophets.

Through the prophets' inspired messages, God reminded the Israelites of the Covenant God had made with them (see "Introduction to the Pentateuch"). If the people or their leaders were not keeping their side of the Covenant, the prophets challenged them to do so. If the people were in despair that God was not keeping God's side of the Covenant, the prophets promised that God would. Here are some common Covenant themes the prophets emphasized:

■ *Warnings against idolatry.* The Israelites were constantly tempted to worship the gods of other nations and cultures. The prophets had to keep reminding the kings and people of the first law of the Ten Commandments: "I am the LORD your God, who brought you out of the land of Egypt, out of the house of slavery; you shall have no other gods before me" (Ex 20.2–3).

- *Warnings to act justly and to treat the poor fairly.* In their greed and struggle for power, the wealthy and the ruling class often cheated and oppressed other people. Operating as Israel's conscience, the prophets were unanimous in challenging Israel to act justly and to care for the poor and marginalized. This did not always make the prophets popular with the kings and the ruling class—they were often ridiculed and even threatened with violence.

- *Attempts to deepen the understanding of God's love and mercy.* Some Israelites felt God would not forgive them after Israel (the northern kingdom) and Judah (the southern kingdom) were conquered by foreign nations. The prophets assured them that they would receive God's forgiveness if they turned to God and kept the Covenant. In addition, some of the prophets began to teach that God was Lord over—and cared for—all nations, not just Israel.

- *Promises of hope for the future.* During these troubled and often violent times, it must have seemed to many Israelites that their world was coming to an end. The prophets responded to the people's despair with hope-filled promises that ultimately God's love and justice would prevail. These hopeful prophecies took different forms: the coming of the Ideal Ruler, the restoration of Jerusalem and the Temple, a time of judgment when good is rewarded and evil punished, and so on.

The stories of the earliest prophets—Samuel, Nathan, Elijah, and Elisha—are in the Bible's historical Books of 1 and 2 Samuel and 1 and 2 Kings. God's revelation through the later prophets is recorded in the books of this section of the Bible. The introduction to each book in this section gives background about the historical situation the prophet faced. The timeline in the back of this Bible identifies the time period for each prophet.

As you read these books, keep this in mind: the role of prophets has not died, only changed. In every age, there are people who challenge us to be faithful to God, and remind us about God's faithful love for us. In fact, Christians believe that through their Baptism, God calls them to be priest, prophet, and king. You can fulfill your prophetic calling by challenging others to live justly and reminding them of God's love. It's exciting and humbling to be called into such a proud tradition.

Other Background

- Isaiah, Jeremiah, and Ezekiel are sometimes called the major prophets because their books are long.

- Hosea, Amos, Jeremiah, First Isaiah, Obadiah, Micah, Nahum, Habakkuk, and Zephaniah prophesied before the Babylonian Exile.

- Ezekiel, Second Isaiah, and Lamentations wrote during the Exile.

- Joel, Haggai, Zechariah, Malachi, Third Isaiah, and Baruch wrote after the Exile.

- Jonah isn't a real prophet, but a fictional, reluctant prophet.

- Seven of the prophets talk about "the day of the Lord"—a final time of God's judgment when evil will be punished.

Once in a while, Hollywood releases a new movie that is actually a remake of an older film. The new movie has a new director and new actors and actresses. It keeps the same basic plot as the original but is adapted to appeal to a modern audience. This is what happened with the prophet Isaiah. The original Isaiah was such a hit that years after he died, a second and even a third person or group adapted his ideas to their situation. The stories of the original Isaiah and his two "remakes" were collected into the single Book of Isaiah that we have today.

At a Glance

- **Chapters 1–39.** First Isaiah (before the Babylonian Exile)

- **Chapters 40–55.** Second Isaiah (during the Exile)

- **Chapters 56–66.** Third Isaiah (after the Exile)

In-depth

Prophets from three different periods in Israel's history contributed to the Book of Isaiah. Chapters 1–39 reflect the prophecies of the original Isaiah, called First Isaiah. His career began with his call in the Temple during the reign of Uzziah around 740 B.C. (see the timeline at the back of this Bible). First Isaiah advised the kings of Judah about the dangers of alliances with foreign nations and cautioned them to trust only in God. He cried out against the social injustices of the rich ruling class against the poor, and taught that God had a plan in which all, rich and poor, powerful and oppressed, would have a part. First Isaiah is responsible for the messianic prophecies, which tell of the coming of a perfect king.

Years later, when Israel was exiled in Babylon (587–538 B.C.), another prophet, Second Isaiah, reworked First Isaiah's prophecies to address his own people (chapters 40–55). Second Isaiah's people were struggling to understand why God allowed them to be captives in a strange land. The prophet comforted them with a hopeful message: They had been taken captive so that they would turn away from their sinful practices; now that they had learned their lesson, God would return them to rebuild Israel. Contained in this prophet's writings are the famous servant songs (see "The Servant Songs," 42.1–7).

Quick Facts

Period Covered
742–500 B.C.

Authors
the three Isaiahs or their followers

Themes
faithfulness to God, justice for the poor, hope for the future, messianic prophecies, God as lord over all nations

After the Israelites returned from exile and resettled in Judah (537–500 B.C.), they once again fell into patterns of social injustice and religious apathy. Third Isaiah responded by demanding that they practice justice toward one another, and even toward the Gentiles, non-Jews (chapters 56–66). Realizing that Israel would never be a perfect community, he spoke of "new heavens / and a new earth" (65.17), where people would live according to God's plan.

The Book of Isaiah

Isaiah

The vision of Ī•sāi'ah son of Ā'moz, which he saw concerning Judah and Jerusalem in the days of Uz-zī'ah, Jō'tham, Ā'haz, and Hez•e•kī'ah, kings of Judah.

The Wickedness of Judah

2 Hear, O heavens, and listen, O earth;
  for the LORD has spoken:
I reared children and brought them up,
  but they have rebelled against me.
3 The ox knows its owner,
  and the donkey its master's crib;
but Israel does not know,
  my people do not understand.

4 Ah, sinful nation,
  people laden with iniquity,
offspring who do evil,
  children who deal corruptly,
who have forsaken the LORD,
  who have despised the Holy One of
    Israel,
  who are utterly estranged!

5 Why do you seek further beatings?
  Why do you continue to rebel?
The whole head is sick,
  and the whole heart faint.
6 From the sole of the foot even to the head,
  there is no soundness in it,
but bruises and sores
  and bleeding wounds;
they have not been drained, or bound up,
  or softened with oil.

7 Your country lies desolate,
  your cities are burned with fire;
in your very presence
  aliens devour your land;
  it is desolate, as overthrown by
    foreigners.
8 And daughter Zion is left
  like a booth in a vineyard,
like a shelter in a cucumber field,
  like a besieged city.
9 If the LORD of hosts
  had not left us a few survivors,
we would have been like Sod'om,
  and become like Go•mor'rah.

10 Hear the word of the LORD,
  you rulers of Sod'om!
Listen to the teaching of our God,
  you people of Go•mor'rah!
11 What to me is the multitude of your
    sacrifices?
  says the LORD;
I have had enough of burnt offerings of
    rams
  and the fat of fed beasts;
I do not delight in the blood of bulls,
  or of lambs, or of goats.

I
S
A

12 When you come to appear before me,*a*
  who asked this from your hand?
  Trample my courts no more;
13 bringing offerings is futile;
  incense is an abomination to me.
  New moon and sabbath and calling of
    convocation—
  I cannot endure solemn assemblies with
    iniquity.
14 Your new moons and your appointed
    festivals
  my soul hates;
  they have become a burden to me,
  I am weary of bearing them.
15 When you stretch out your hands,
  I will hide my eyes from you;
  even though you make many prayers,
  I will not listen;
  your hands are full of blood.
16 Wash yourselves; make yourselves clean;
  remove the evil of your doings
  from before my eyes;
  cease to do evil,
17 learn to do good;
  seek justice,
  rescue the oppressed,
  defend the orphan,
  plead for the widow.

18 Come now, let us argue it out,
  says the LORD:
  though your sins are like scarlet,
  they shall be like snow;
  though they are red like crimson,
  they shall become like wool.
19 If you are willing and obedient,
  you shall eat the good of the land;
20 but if you refuse and rebel,
  you shall be devoured by the sword;
  for the mouth of the LORD has spoken.

The Degenerate City

21 How the faithful city
  has become a whore!
  She that was full of justice,
  righteousness lodged in her—
  but now murderers!
22 Your silver has become dross,
  your wine is mixed with water.
23 Your princes are rebels
  and companions of thieves.
  Everyone loves a bribe
  and runs after gifts.
  They do not defend the orphan,
  and the widow's cause does not come
    before them.

¡Dios quiere justicia, no ritos vacíos;

EL HISPANIC

GOD WANTS JUSTICE, NOT EMPTY RITES!

First Isaiah denounces the hypocrisy of practicing empty religious rituals that are not grounded in justice, sincerity, and good deeds. Speaking for God, he calls the people to do good, seek justice, rescue the oppressed, and defend the orphans and the widows.

- **How do you actively seek justice and take care of people in need?**
- **In your prayer, ask God's forgiveness for when you have not responded to God's call to practice justice or help people in need.**

▶ Isa 1.10–20

24 Therefore says the Sovereign, the LORD of
    hosts, the Mighty One of Israel:
  Ah, I will pour out my wrath on my
    enemies,
  and avenge myself on my foes!
25 I will turn my hand against you;
  I will smelt away your dross as with lye
  and remove all your alloy.
26 And I will restore your judges as at the first,
  and your counselors as at the beginning.
  Afterward you shall be called the city of
    righteousness,
  the faithful city.

27 Zion shall be redeemed by justice,
  and those in her who repent, by
    righteousness.
28 But rebels and sinners shall be destroyed
    together,
  and those who forsake the LORD shall be
    consumed.
29 For you shall be ashamed of the oaks
  in which you delighted;
  and you shall blush for the gardens

a Or *see my face*

that you have chosen.
30 For you shall be like an oak
    whose leaf withers,
    and like a garden without water.
31 The strong shall become like tinder,
    and their work[b] like a spark;
they and their work shall burn together,
    with no one to quench them.

The Future House of God
(Mic 4.1–5)

The word that I·sāi′ah son of Ā′moz saw concerning Judah and Jerusalem.

2 In days to come
    the mountain of the LORD's house
shall be established as the highest of the
        mountains,
    and shall be raised above the hills;
all the nations shall stream to it.
3   Many peoples shall come and say,
"Come, let us go up to the mountain of the
        LORD,
    to the house of the God of Jacob;
that he may teach us his ways

Swords into Plowshares

We hear Isa 2.1–5 every three years, on the first Sunday of Advent. Its swords-into-plowshares theme is all about moving from violence to nonviolence in our responses to conflict. (See also Joel 3.10 and Mic 4.3.)

Today, an organization called Swords to Plowshares sells small lapel pins that are made from parts of a U.S. Air Force Thunderjet fighter plane and shaped like a plowshare. They are actually a modern sword (tool of violence) beaten and bent into a modern plowshare (tool of life).

In your prayer, reflect or journal on the following questions:
■ Why does our culture glorify violence?
■ How do you feel about nonviolence?
■ How far are you willing to go in responding to hate and violence with love and nonviolence?

▶ Isa 2.1–5

and that we may walk in his paths."
For out of Zion shall go forth instruction,
    and the word of the LORD from Jerusalem.
4 He shall judge between the nations,
    and shall arbitrate for many peoples;
they shall beat their swords into plowshares,
    and their spears into pruning hooks;
nation shall not lift up sword against
        nation,
    neither shall they learn war any more.

Judgment Pronounced on Arrogance

5 O house of Jacob,
    come, let us walk
    in the light of the LORD!
6 For you have forsaken the ways of[c] your
        people,
    O house of Jacob.
Indeed they are full of diviners[d] from the
        east
    and of soothsayers like the Phi·lis′tines,
    and they clasp hands with foreigners.
7 Their land is filled with silver and gold,
    and there is no end to their treasures;
their land is filled with horses,
    and there is no end to their chariots.
8 Their land is filled with idols;
    they bow down to the work of their
        hands,
    to what their own fingers have made.
9 And so people are humbled,
    and everyone is brought low—
    do not forgive them!
10 Enter into the rock,
    and hide in the dust
from the terror of the LORD,
    and from the glory of his majesty.
11 The haughty eyes of people shall be
        brought low,
    and the pride of everyone shall be
        humbled;
and the LORD alone will be exalted on
        that day.
12 For the LORD of hosts has a day
    against all that is proud and lofty,
    against all that is lifted up and high;[e]
13 against all the cedars of Lebanon,
    lofty and lifted up;
    and against all the oaks of Bā′shan;
14 against all the high mountains,
    and against all the lofty hills;
15 against every high tower,
    and against every fortified wall;

---

b Or *its makers*   *c* Heb lacks *the ways of*   *d* Cn: Heb
lacks *of diviners*   *e* Cn Compare Gk: Heb *low*

16 against all the ships of Tar'shish,
  and against all the beautiful craft.*f*
17 The haughtiness of people shall be
    humbled,
  and the pride of everyone shall be
    brought low;
  and the LORD alone will be exalted on
    that day.
18 The idols shall utterly pass away.
19 Enter the caves of the rocks
  and the holes of the ground,
from the terror of the LORD,
  and from the glory of his majesty,
  when he rises to terrify the earth.
20 On that day people will throw away
  to the moles and to the bats
their idols of silver and their idols of gold,
  which they made for themselves to
    worship,
21 to enter the caverns of the rocks
  and the clefts in the crags,
from the terror of the LORD,
  and from the glory of his majesty,
  when he rises to terrify the earth.
22 Turn away from mortals,
  who have only breath in their nostrils,
  for of what account are they?

3 For now the Sovereign, the LORD of hosts,
  is taking away from Jerusalem and from
    Judah
support and staff—
  all support of bread,
  and all support of water—
2 warrior and soldier,
    judge and prophet,
    diviner and elder,
3 captain of fifty
    and dignitary,
  counselor and skillful magician
    and expert enchanter.
4 And I will make boys their princes,
  and babes shall rule over them.
5 The people will be oppressed,
    everyone by another
  and everyone by a neighbor;
the youth will be insolent to the elder,
  and the base to the honorable.

6 Someone will even seize a relative,
  a member of the clan, saying,
"You have a cloak;
  you shall be our leader,
and this heap of ruins
  shall be under your rule."
7 But the other will cry out on that day,
    saying,

"I will not be a healer;
  in my house there is neither bread nor
    cloak;
you shall not make me
  leader of the people."
8 For Jerusalem has stumbled
  and Judah has fallen,
because their speech and their deeds are
    against the LORD,
  defying his glorious presence.

9 The look on their faces bears witness against
    them;
  they proclaim their sin like Sod'om,
  they do not hide it.
Woe to them!
  For they have brought evil on themselves.
10 Tell the innocent how fortunate they are,
  for they shall eat the fruit of their labors.
11 Woe to the guilty! How unfortunate
    they are,
  for what their hands have done shall be
    done to them.
12 My people—children are their oppressors,
  and women rule over them.
O my people, your leaders mislead you,
  and confuse the course of your paths.

13 The LORD rises to argue his case;
  he stands to judge the peoples.
14 The LORD enters into judgment
  with the elders and princes of his people:
It is you who have devoured the vineyard;
  the spoil of the poor is in your houses.
15 What do you mean by crushing my people,
  by grinding the face of the poor? says the
    Lord GOD of hosts.

16 The LORD said:
Because the daughters of Zion are haughty
  and walk with outstretched necks,
    glancing wantonly with their eyes,
mincing along as they go,
  tinkling with their feet;
17 the Lord will afflict with scabs
  the heads of the daughters of Zion,
  and the LORD will lay bare their secret
    parts.

18 In that day the Lord will take away the finery of the anklets, the headbands, and the crescents; 19 the pendants, the bracelets, and the scarfs;
20 the headdresses, the armlets, the sashes, the perfume boxes, and the amulets; 21 the signet rings
and nose rings; 22 the festal robes, the mantles,
the cloaks, and the handbags; 23 the garments of

---

f Compare Gk: Meaning of Heb uncertain

gauze, the linen garments, the turbans, and the veils.

24 Instead of perfume there will be a stench;
     and instead of a sash, a rope;
and instead of well-set hair, baldness;
     and instead of a rich robe, a binding of
         sackcloth;
instead of beauty, shame. *g*

25 Your men shall fall by the sword
     and your warriors in battle.

26 And her gates shall lament and mourn;
     ravaged, she shall sit upon the ground.

Seven women shall take hold of one man in that day, saying,
     "We will eat our own bread and wear our
         own clothes;
just let us be called by your name;
     take away our disgrace."

The Future Glory of the Survivors in Zion

2 On that day the branch of the LORD shall be beautiful and glorious, and the fruit of the land shall be the pride and glory of the survivors of Israel. 3 Whoever is left in Zion and remains in Jerusalem will be called holy, everyone who has been recorded for life in Jerusalem, 4 once the Lord has washed away the filth of the daughters of Zion and cleansed the bloodstains of Jerusalem from its midst by a spirit of judgment and by a spirit of burning. 5 Then the LORD will create over the whole site of Mount Zion and over its places of assembly a cloud by day and smoke and the shining of a flaming fire by night. Indeed over all the glory there will be a canopy. 6 It will serve as a pavilion, a shade by day from the heat, and a refuge and a shelter from the storm and rain.

The Song of the Unfruitful Vineyard

Let me sing for my beloved
     my love-song concerning his vineyard:
My beloved had a vineyard
     on a very fertile hill.

2 He dug it and cleared it of stones,
     and planted it with choice vines;
he built a watchtower in the midst of it,
     and hewed out a wine vat in it;
he expected it to yield grapes,
     but it yielded wild grapes.

3 And now, inhabitants of Jerusalem
     and people of Judah,
judge between me
     and my vineyard.

4 What more was there to do for my vineyard
     that I have not done in it?

When I expected it to yield grapes,
     why did it yield wild grapes?

5 And now I will tell you
     what I will do to my vineyard.
I will remove its hedge,
     and it shall be devoured;
I will break down its wall,
     and it shall be trampled down.

6 I will make it a waste;
     it shall not be pruned or hoed,
     and it shall be overgrown with briers and
         thorns;
I will also command the clouds
     that they rain no rain upon it.

7 For the vineyard of the LORD of hosts
     is the house of Israel,
and the people of Judah
     are his pleasant planting;
he expected justice,
     but saw bloodshed;
righteousness,
     but heard a cry!

Social Injustice Denounced

8 Ah, you who join house to house,
     who add field to field,
until there is room for no one but you,
     and you are left to live alone
     in the midst of the land!

9 The LORD of hosts has sworn in my hearing:
Surely many houses shall be desolate,
     large and beautiful houses, without
         inhabitant.

10 For ten acres of vineyard shall yield but one
     bath,
     and a homer of seed shall yield a mere
         ephah. *h*

11 Ah, you who rise early in the morning
     in pursuit of strong drink,
who linger in the evening
     to be inflamed by wine,

12 whose feasts consist of lyre and harp,
     tambourine and flute and wine,
but who do not regard the deeds of the
     LORD,
     or see the work of his hands!

13 Therefore my people go into exile without
         knowledge;
their nobles are dying of hunger,
     and their multitude is parched with
         thirst.

---

g Q Ms: MT lacks *shame*   *h* The Heb *bath, homer,* and *ephah* are measures of quantity

ISA

14 Therefore Shĕ′ōl has enlarged its appetite
    and opened its mouth beyond measure;
the nobility of Jerusalem[i] and her multitude
        go down,
    her throng and all who exult in her.
15 People are bowed down, everyone is
        brought low,
    and the eyes of the haughty are humbled.
16 But the LORD of hosts is exalted by justice,
    and the Holy God shows himself holy by
        righteousness.
17 Then the lambs shall graze as in their
        pasture,
    fatlings and kids[j] shall feed among the
        ruins.

18 Ah, you who drag iniquity along with cords
        of falsehood,
    who drag sin along as with cart ropes,
19 who say, "Let him make haste,
    let him speed his work
        that we may see it;
    let the plan of the Holy One of Israel hasten
        to fulfillment,
        that we may know it!"
20 Ah, you who call evil good
        and good evil,
    who put darkness for light
        and light for darkness,
    who put bitter for sweet
        and sweet for bitter!
21 Ah, you who are wise in your own eyes,
    and shrewd in your own sight!
22 Ah, you who are heroes in drinking wine
    and valiant at mixing drink,

23 who acquit the guilty for a bribe,
    and deprive the innocent of their rights!

Foreign Invasion Predicted

24 Therefore, as the tongue of fire devours the
        stubble,
    and as dry grass sinks down in the flame,
so their root will become rotten,
    and their blossom go up like dust;
for they have rejected the instruction of the
        LORD of hosts,
    and have despised the word of the Holy
        One of Israel.

25 Therefore the anger of the LORD was kindled
        against his people,
    and he stretched out his hand against
        them and struck them;
    the mountains quaked,
and their corpses were like refuse
    in the streets.
For all this his anger has not turned away,
    and his hand is stretched out still.

26 He will raise a signal for a nation far away,
    and whistle for a people at the ends of
        the earth;
Here they come, swiftly, speedily!
27 None of them is weary, none stumbles,
    none slumbers or sleeps,
    not a loincloth is loose,
    not a sandal-thong broken;
28 their arrows are sharp,
    all their bows bent,

---

i Heb *her nobility*   *j* Cn Compare Gk: Heb *aliens*

Introducing

▶ FIRST ISAIAH

The name Isaiah means "God is salvation" in Hebrew, and First Isaiah's preaching certainly reflects that message. Born in Jerusalem, he prophesied there during the reigns of Kings Uzziah, Jotham, Ahaz, and Hezekiah, between 740 and 710 B.C. (see 2 Kings, chapters 15–20, and 2 Chronicles, chapters 26–32). He was married to a prophet, and they had two sons whose names played a symbolic role in his prophecy: Shear-jashub, meaning "a remnant shall remain," and Maher-shalal-hash-baz, meaning "the spoil speeds, the prey hastes." In his preaching, he emphasized the role of Jerusalem (Zion) as God's dwelling place and home to King David's dynasty. For this reason, he is also called Isaiah of Jerusalem.

First Isaiah had ready access to Judah's kings and was probably a member of an aristocratic family. His education shows in his use of language—he is responsible for some of the loftiest and most beautiful poetry in the Old Testament.

Here I Am, Lord!

Phrases from the sixth chapter of Isaiah may be familiar from the song "Here I Am, Lord." This chapter tells of First Isaiah's call, which follows a biblical pattern:
1. *The person has some experience of God.* **Isaiah has a dramatic vision of God in the Temple.**
2. *God gives the person a mission.* **God sends Isaiah to speak to the people.**
3. *The person may deny being worthy.* **Isaiah knows he has unclean (or sinful) lips.**
4. *God addresses the denial and reassures the person.* **God purifies Isaiah with fire and words of forgiveness.**

You can see the same pattern for Moses' call in Ex 3.1–12, Samuel's call in 1 Sam 3.1–14, Jeremiah's call in Jer 1.4–10, and Mary's call in Lk 1.26–38.

   Christians are called by God to participate in Jesus' saving mission. They believe everyone needs to discover the way God wants them to live out that call. Do you believe that God has a mission for your life? How can you use your talents to create a more loving and just world?

▶ **Isa 6.1–13**

---

their horses' hoofs seem like flint,
   and their wheels like the whirlwind.
29 Their roaring is like a lion,
   like young lions they roar;
they growl and seize their prey,
   they carry it off, and no one can rescue.
30 They will roar over it on that day,
   like the roaring of the sea.
And if one look to the land—
   only darkness and distress;
and the light grows dark with clouds.

A Vision of God in the Temple
(Cp Ezek 1.4–28)

In the year that King Uz•zī'ah died, I saw the Lord sitting on a throne, high and lofty; and the hem of his robe filled the temple. 2 Seraphs were in attendance above him; each had six wings: with two they covered their faces, and with two they covered their feet, and with two they flew. 3 And one called to another and said:
   "Holy, holy, holy is the LORD of hosts;
   the whole earth is full of his glory."
4 The pivots[k] on the thresholds shook at the voices of those who called, and the house filled with smoke. 5 And I said: "Woe is me! I am lost, for I am a man of unclean lips, and I live among a people of unclean lips; yet my eyes have seen the King, the LORD of hosts!"

6 Then one of the seraphs flew to me, holding a live coal that had been taken from the altar with a pair of tongs. 7 The seraph[l] touched my mouth with it and said: "Now that this has touched your lips, your guilt has departed and your sin is blotted out." 8 Then I heard the voice of the Lord saying, "Whom shall I send, and who will go for us?" And I said, "Here am I; send me!" 9 And he said, "Go and say to this people:
   'Keep listening, but do not comprehend;
   keep looking, but do not understand.'
10 Make the mind of this people dull,
   and stop their ears,
   and shut their eyes,
so that they may not look with their
      eyes,
   and listen with their ears,
and comprehend with their minds,
   and turn and be healed."
11 Then I said, "How long, O Lord?" And he said:
"Until cities lie waste
   without inhabitant,
and houses without people,
   and the land is utterly desolate;
12 until the LORD sends everyone far away,
   and vast is the emptiness in the midst of
      the land.
13 Even if a tenth part remain in it,
   it will be burned again,
like a terebinth or an oak
   whose stump remains standing
   when it is felled."[k]
The holy seed is its stump.

---

k Meaning of Heb uncertain   l Heb He

Isaiah Reassures King Ahaz
(2 Kings 16.5; 2 Chr 28.5–15)

In the days of Ā'haz son of Jō'tham son of Uz-zī'ah, king of Judah, King Rē'zin of Ar'am and King Pē'kah son of Rem•a•lī'ah of Israel went up to attack Jerusalem, but could not mount an attack against it. ²When the house of David heard that Ar'am had allied itself with Ē'phra•im, the heart of Ā'haz[m] and the heart of his people shook as the trees of the forest shake before the wind.

3 Then the LORD said to Ī•sāi'ah, Go out to meet Ā'haz, you and your son Shē'ar-jash'ub,[n] at the end of the conduit of the upper pool on the high-way to the Fuller's Field, ⁴and say to him, Take heed, be quiet, do not fear, and do not let your heart be faint because of these two smoldering stumps of firebrands, because of the fierce anger of Rē'zin and Ar'am and the son of Rem•a•lī'ah. ⁵Be-cause Ar'am—with Ē'phra•im and the son of Rem•a•lī'ah—has plotted evil against you, saying, ⁶Let us go up against Judah and cut off Jerusalem[o] and conquer it for ourselves and make the son of Tā'-

bē•el king in it; ⁷therefore thus says the Lord GOD:

It shall not stand,
  and it shall not come to pass.
⁸ For the head of Ar'am is Damascus,
  and the head of Damascus is Rē'zin.
(Within sixty-five years Ē'phra•im will be shat-tered, no longer a people.)
⁹ The head of Ē'phra•im is Sa•mār'i•a,
  and the head of Sa•mār'i•a is the son of
    Rem•a•lī'ah.
If you do not stand firm in faith,
  you shall not stand at all.

Isaiah Gives Ahaz the Sign of Immanuel

10 Again the LORD spoke to Ā'haz, saying, ¹¹Ask a sign of the LORD your God; let it be deep as Shē'ōl or high as heaven. ¹²But Ā'haz said, I will not ask, and I will not put the LORD to the test. ¹³Then Ī•sāi'ah[p] said: "Hear then, O house of Da-

---

m Heb *his heart*   n That is *A remnant shall return*
o Heb *cut it off*   p Heb *he*

GOD-WITH-US!

Many Bibles refer to Isaiah, chapters 7–12, as the Book of Immanuel. In these chapters, First Isaiah announces that Israel's salvation will come from a child from the family of Jesse, the father of King David. This child will be named Immanuel (also spelled Emmanuel), which means "God-with-us." With this message, Isaiah emphasizes that God is with the little ones who trust in God's saving power.

Biblical scholars agree that the child Isaiah is referring to is the son of King Ahaz—the future king Hezekiah. But the Gospel writers later see in this passage a reference to Jesus (Mt 1.23), the Son of God, who is truly Immanuel, God-with-Us.

For Hispanic people, Immanuel is a constant reality. Hispanics give witness of the nearness of God in daily affairs through the following expressions, which you may hear more than a dozen times a day in their communities: "God help you" (*Dios te ayude*), "Go with God" (*Ve con Dios*), "If God wants it" (*Si Dios quiere*), "With God's permission" (*Si Dios lo permite*), "Through the power of God" (*Dios mediante*), "Thanks to God" (*Gracias a Dios*), "For the love of God" (*Por el amor de Dios*), "God give you a good day" (*Buen día te dé Dios*), and "God bless you" (*Dios te bendiga*).

- **If you come from a family or community tradition where these faith expressions are common, feel the presence of God each time they are voiced and use them boldly yourself.**
- **Think about what happened to you today. How many of these expressions could you have applied to different situations and felt God-with-You? Choose the ex-pression that best fits the yearnings of your heart at this time, and pray with it, repeating it several times.**

▶ **Isaiah, chapters 7–12**

vid! Is it too little for you to weary mortals, that you weary my God also? 14 Therefore the Lord himself will give you a sign. Look, the young woman*q* is with child and shall bear a son, and shall name him Im•man′ū•el.*r* 15 He shall eat curds and honey by the time he knows how to refuse the evil and choose the good. 16 For before the child knows how to refuse the evil and choose the good, the land before whose two kings you are in dread will be deserted. 17 The LORD will bring on you and on your people and on your ancestral house such days as have not come since the day that Ē′phra•im departed from Judah—the king of Assyria."

18 On that day the LORD will whistle for the fly that is at the sources of the streams of Egypt, and for the bee that is in the land of Assyria. 19 And they will all come and settle in the steep ravines, and in the clefts of the rocks, and on all the thornbushes, and on all the pastures.

20 On that day the Lord will shave with a razor hired beyond the River—with the king of Assyria—the head and the hair of the feet, and it will take off the beard as well.

21 On that day one will keep alive a young cow and two sheep, 22 and will eat curds because of the abundance of milk that they give; for everyone that is left in the land shall eat curds and honey.

23 On that day every place where there used to be a thousand vines, worth a thousand shekels of silver, will become briers and thorns. 24 With bow and arrows one will go there, for all the land will be briers and thorns; 25 and as for all the hills that used to be hoed with a hoe, you will not go there for fear of briers and thorns; but they will become a place where cattle are let loose and where sheep tread.

Isaiah's Son a Sign of the Assyrian Invasion

Then the LORD said to me, Take a large tablet and write on it in common characters, "Belonging to Ma′her-shal′al-hash-baz,"*s* 2 and have it attested*t* for me by reliable witnesses, the priest Ū•rī′ah and Zech•a•rī′ah son of Je•ber•e•chī′ah. 3 And I went to the prophetess, and she conceived and bore a son. Then the LORD said to me, Name him Ma′her-shal′al-hash-baz; 4 for before the child knows how to call "My father" or "My mother," the wealth of Damascus and the spoil of Sa•mār′i•a will be carried away by the king of Assyria.

5 The LORD spoke to me again: 6 Because this people has refused the waters of Shī•lō′ah that flow gently, and melt in fear before*u* Rē′zin and the son of Rem•a•lī′ah; 7 therefore, the Lord is bringing up against it the mighty flood waters of the River, the

king of Assyria and all his glory; it will rise above all its channels and overflow all its banks; 8 it will sweep on into Judah as a flood, and, pouring over, it will reach up to the neck; and its outspread wings will fill the breadth of your land, O Im-man′ū•el.

9   Band together, you peoples, and be
       dismayed;
     listen, all you far countries;
   gird yourselves and be dismayed;
     gird yourselves and be dismayed!
10 Take counsel together, but it shall be
       brought to naught;
     speak a word, but it will not stand,
     for God is with us.*v*

11 For the LORD spoke thus to me while his hand was strong upon me, and warned me not to walk in the way of this people, saying: 12 Do not call conspiracy all that this people calls conspiracy, and do not fear what it fears, or be in dread. 13 But the LORD of hosts, him you shall regard as holy; let him be your fear, and let him be your dread. 14 He will become a sanctuary, a stone one strikes against; for both houses of Israel he will become a rock one stumbles over—a trap and a snare for the inhabitants of Jerusalem. 15 And many among them shall stumble; they shall fall and be broken; they shall be snared and taken.

Disciples of Isaiah

16 Bind up the testimony, seal the teaching among my disciples. 17 I will wait for the LORD, who is hiding his face from the house of Jacob, and I will hope in him. 18 See, I and the children whom the LORD has given me are signs and portents in Israel from the LORD of hosts, who dwells on Mount Zion. 19 Now if people say to you, "Consult the ghosts and the familiar spirits that chirp and mutter; should not a people consult their gods, the dead on behalf of the living, 20 for teaching and for instruction?" surely, those who speak like this will have no dawn! 21 They will pass through the land,*w* greatly distressed and hungry; when they are hungry, they will be enraged and will curse*x* their king and their gods. They will turn their faces upward, 22 or they will look to the earth, but will see only distress and darkness, the gloom of anguish; and they will be thrust into thick darkness.*y*

---

q Gk *the virgin*   *r* That is *God is with us*   *s* That is *The spoil speeds, the prey hastens*   *t* Q Ms Gk Syr: MT *and I caused to be attested*   *u* Cn: Meaning of Heb uncertain
v Heb *immanu el*   *w* Heb *it*   *x* Or *curse by*   *y* Meaning of Heb uncertain

The Righteous Reign
of the Coming King
(Isa 11.1–9)

z But there will be no gloom for those who were in anguish. In the former time he brought into contempt the land of Zeb'u·lun and the land of Naph'ta·li, but in the latter time he will make glorious the way of the sea, the land beyond the Jordan, Galilee of the nations.

2a The people who walked in darkness
   have seen a great light;
those who lived in a land of deep darkness—
   on them light has shined.
3 You have multiplied the nation,
   you have increased its joy;
they rejoice before you
   as with joy at the harvest,
   as people exult when dividing plunder.
4 For the yoke of their burden,
   and the bar across their shoulders,
   the rod of their oppressor,
   you have broken as on the day of
      Mid'i·an.
5 For all the boots of the tramping warriors
   and all the garments rolled in blood
   shall be burned as fuel for the fire.
6 For a child has been born for us,
   a son given to us;
authority rests upon his shoulders;
   and he is named
Wonderful Counselor, Mighty God,
   Everlasting Father, Prince of Peace.
7 His authority shall grow continually,
   and there shall be endless peace
for the throne of David and his kingdom.
   He will establish and uphold it
with justice and with righteousness
   from this time onward and forevermore.
The zeal of the LORD of hosts will do this.

Judgment on Arrogance
and Oppression

8 The Lord sent a word against Jacob,
   and it fell on Israel;
9 and all the people knew it—
   E'phra·im and the inhabitants of
      Sa·mar'i·a—
   but in pride and arrogance of heart they
      said:
10 "The bricks have fallen,
   but we will build with dressed stones;
the sycamores have been cut down,
   but we will put cedars in their place."
11 So the LORD raised adversaries[b] against them,
   and stirred up their enemies,

PRAY IT!
Christmas Light

Isaiah 9.2–7 describes Immanuel as a wise, brave, courageous, virtuous, and righteous king. Here, First Isaiah may be referring to King Hezekiah, the reformer king of Judah (see 2 Chronicles, chapters 29–33). However, after Hezekiah's death, the passage came to be understood as predicting the coming of an ideal future savior or messiah. That's why the passage is called a messianic prophecy.

Christians see in these words a perfect description of Jesus. In fact, Catholics read these verses at Christmas during midnight Mass. On one of the longest nights of the year, they imagine Jesus' presence in the world as a light dispelling the darkness of sin.

This is the opening prayer for the Christmas Mass at midnight:

Father,
You make this holy night radiant
with the splendor of Jesus Christ our
   light.
We welcome him as Lord, the true light
   of the world.
Bring us to eternal joy in the kingdom of
   heaven,
where he lives and reigns with you and
   the Holy Spirit,
one God, for ever and ever.
            (The Sacramentary, p. 40)

▶ Isa 9.2–7

12 the Ar·a·me'ans on the east and the
      Phi·lis'tines on the west,
and they devoured Israel with open
   mouth.
For all this his anger has not turned away;
   his hand is stretched out still.

13 The people did not turn to him who struck
      them,
   or seek the LORD of hosts.
14 So the LORD cut off from Israel head and
      tail,

---

z Ch 8.23 in Heb   a Ch 9.1 in Heb   b Cn: Heb *the adversaries of Rezin* palm branch and reed in one day—

15 elders and dignitaries are the head,
    and prophets who teach lies are the tail;

16 for those who led this people led them
        astray,
    and those who were led by them were
        left in confusion.

17 That is why the Lord did not have pity on[c]
        their young people,
    or compassion on their orphans and
        widows;
for everyone was godless and an evildoer,
    and every mouth spoke folly.
For all this his anger has not turned away;
    his hand is stretched out still.

18 For wickedness burned like a fire,
    consuming briers and thorns;
it kindled the thickets of the forest,
    and they swirled upward in a column of
        smoke.

19 Through the wrath of the LORD of hosts
    the land was burned,
and the people became like fuel for the fire;
    no one spared another.

20 They gorged on the right, but still were
        hungry,
    and they devoured on the left, but were
        not satisfied;
they devoured the flesh of their own
        kindred;[d]

21 Ma•nas'seh devoured Ē'phra•im, and
        Ē'phra•im Ma•nas'seh,
and together they were against Judah.
For all this his anger has not turned away;
    his hand is stretched out still.

Ah, you who make iniquitous decrees,
    who write oppressive statutes,

2 to turn aside the needy from justice
    and to rob the poor of my people of
        their right,
that widows may be your spoil,
    and that you may make the orphans your
        prey!

3 What will you do on the day of
        punishment,
    in the calamity that will come from far
        away?
To whom will you flee for help,
    and where will you leave your wealth,

4 so as not to crouch among the prisoners
    or fall among the slain?
For all this his anger has not turned away;
    his hand is stretched out still.

Arrogant Assyria Also Judged

5 Ah, Assyria, the rod of my anger—
    the club in their hands is my fury!

6 Against a godless nation I send him,
    and against the people of my wrath I
        command him,
to take spoil and seize plunder,
    and to tread them down like the mire of
        the streets.

7 But this is not what he intends,
    nor does he have this in mind;
but it is in his heart to destroy,
    and to cut off nations not a few.

8 For he says:
"Are not my commanders all kings?

9 Is not Cal'nō like Car'chem•ish?
    Is not Hā'math like Ar'pad?
    Is not Sa•mār'i•a like Damascus?

10 As my hand has reached to the kingdoms of
        the idols
    whose images were greater than those of
        Jerusalem and Sa•mār'i•a,

11 shall I not do to Jerusalem and her idols
    what I have done to Sa•mār'i•a and her
        images?"

12 When the Lord has finished all his work on Mount Zion and on Jerusalem, he[e] will punish the arrogant boasting of the king of Assyria and his haughty pride. 13 For he says:
"By the strength of my hand I have done it,
    and by my wisdom, for I have
        understanding;
I have removed the boundaries of peoples,
    and have plundered their treasures;
    like a bull I have brought down those
        who sat on thrones.

14 My hand has found, like a nest,
    the wealth of the peoples;
and as one gathers eggs that have been
        forsaken,
    so I have gathered all the earth;
and there was none that moved a wing,
    or opened its mouth, or chirped."

15 Shall the ax vaunt itself over the one who
        wields it,
    or the saw magnify itself against the one
        who handles it?
As if a rod should raise the one who lifts
        it up,
    or as if a staff should lift the one who is
        not wood!

16 Therefore the Sovereign, the LORD of hosts,

---

[c] Q Ms: MT *rejoice over*   [d] Or *arm*   [e] Heb *I*

will send wasting sickness among his
stout warriors,
and under his glory a burning will be
kindled,
like the burning of fire.
17 The light of Israel will become a fire,
and his Holy One a flame;
and it will burn and devour
his thorns and briers in one day.
18 The glory of his forest and his fruitful land
the LORD will destroy, both soul and
body,
and it will be as when an invalid wastes
away.
19 The remnant of the trees of his forest will
be so few
that a child can write them down.

The Repentant Remnant of Israel

20 On that day the remnant of Israel and the
survivors of the house of Jacob will no more lean
on the one who struck them, but will lean on the
LORD, the Holy One of Israel, in truth. 21 A remnant
will return, the remnant of Jacob, to the mighty
God. 22 For though your people Israel were like the
sand of the sea, only a remnant of them will return. Destruction is decreed, overflowing with
righteousness. 23 For the Lord GOD of hosts will
make a full end, as decreed, in all the earth.ƒ

24 Therefore thus says the Lord GOD of hosts:
O my people, who live in Zion, do not be afraid of
the Assyrians when they beat you with a rod and
lift up their staff against you as the Egyptians did.
25 For in a very little while my indignation will
come to an end, and my anger will be directed to
their destruction. 26 The LORD of hosts will wield a
whip against them, as when he struck Mid′i•an at
the rock of Or′eb; his staff will be over the sea, and
he will lift it as he did in Egypt. 27 On that day his
burden will be removed from your shoulder, and
his yoke will be destroyed from your neck.

He has gone up from Rim′mon,ℊ
28 he has come to Ai′ath;
he has passed through Mig′ron,
at Mich′mash he stores his baggage;
29 they have crossed over the pass,
at Ge′ba they lodge for the night;
Ra′mah trembles,
Gib′e•ah of Saul has fled.
30 Cry aloud, O daughter Gal′lim!
Listen, O La′i•shah!
Answer her, O An′a•thoth!
31 Mad•me′nah is in flight,
the inhabitants of Ge′bim flee for safety.
32 This very day he will halt at Nob,

he will shake his fist
at the mount of daughter Zion,
the hill of Jerusalem.

33 Look, the Sovereign, the LORD of hosts,
will lop the boughs with terrifying power;
the tallest trees will be cut down,
and the lofty will be brought low.
34 He will hack down the thickets of the forest
with an ax,
and Lebanon with its majestic treesʰ will
fall.

The Peaceful Kingdom
(Isa 9.1–7)

11 A shoot shall come out from the stump of
Jesse,
and a branch shall grow out of his roots.
2 The spirit of the LORD shall rest on him,
the spirit of wisdom and understanding,
the spirit of counsel and might,
the spirit of knowledge and the fear of
the LORD.
3 His delight shall be in the fear of the LORD.

He shall not judge by what his eyes see,
or decide by what his ears hear;
4 but with righteousness he shall judge the
poor,
and decide with equity for the meek of
the earth;
he shall strike the earth with the rod of his
mouth,

ƒ Or land　ℊ Cn: Heb and his yoke from your neck, and a
yoke will be destroyed because of fatness　ʰ Cn Compare Gk
Vg: Heb with a majestic one

and with the breath of his lips he shall
    kill the wicked.
5 Righteousness shall be the belt around his
        waist,
    and faithfulness the belt around his loins.

6 The wolf shall live with the lamb,
    the leopard shall lie down with the kid,
  the calf and the lion and the fatling
        together,
    and a little child shall lead them.
7 The cow and the bear shall graze,
    their young shall lie down together;
    and the lion shall eat straw like the ox.
8 The nursing child shall play over the hole of
        the asp,
    and the weaned child shall put its hand
        on the adder's den.
9 They will not hurt or destroy
    on all my holy mountain;
  for the earth will be full of the knowledge
        of the LORD
    as the waters cover the sea.

Return of the Remnant of
Israel and Judah

10 On that day the root of Jesse shall stand as
a signal to the peoples; the nations shall inquire of
him, and his dwelling shall be glorious.

11 On that day the Lord will extend his hand
yet a second time to recover the remnant that is
left of his people, from Assyria, from Egypt, from
Path'ros, from Ethiopia,[i] from É'lam, from Shī'-
nar, from Hā'math, and from the coastlands of the
sea.
12 He will raise a signal for the nations,

and will assemble the outcasts of Israel,
and gather the dispersed of Judah
    from the four corners of the earth.
13 The jealousy of É'phra·im shall depart,
    the hostility of Judah shall be cut off;
  É'phra·im shall not be jealous of Judah,
    and Judah shall not be hostile towards
        É'phra·im.
14 But they shall swoop down on the backs of
        the Phi·lis'tines in the west,
    together they shall plunder the people of
        the east.
  They shall put forth their hand against
        É'dom and Mō'ab,
    and the Am'mon·ites shall obey them.
15 And the LORD will utterly destroy
    the tongue of the sea of Egypt;
  and will wave his hand over the River
    with his scorching wind;
  and will split it into seven channels,
    and make a way to cross on foot;
16 so there shall be a highway from Assyria
    for the remnant that is left of his people,
  as there was for Israel
    when they came up from the land of
        Egypt.

Thanksgiving and Praise

You will say in that day:
I will give thanks to you, O LORD,
    for though you were angry with me,
your anger turned away,
    and you comforted me.

---

i Or *Nubia*; Heb *Cush*

Lions and Lambs

There are so many troubled spots in the world. It seems that almost every week, violence and ethnic clashes occur somewhere. How easily we forget that we are all members of the human family.

Yet, we are drawn to the image of the peaceable kingdom in Isa 11.6–9. To imagine natural predators such as wolves and lions living together in harmony with lambs and calves, their natural prey, gives us an insight into the Reign of God. Harmony. Peace. Gentleness. No wonder this scene has been the inspiration for numerous artists.

It is a vision we must all aim for, while we do our best to resist all the things that pull us apart as a human family. We are all in this together. We need to work to make the peaceable Reign of God a reality. It is God's work we do.

It is inspiring that First Isaiah also uses the image of youth to express his vision of peace. What can you as a young person do to help bring about the peaceable kingdom?

▶ Isa 11.6–9

In God We Trust

In God we trust. Every piece of U.S. currency bears this statement, yet many of us never notice it. First Isaiah proclaims this same message:

> Surely God is my salvation;
>   I will trust, and will not be afraid,
>   for the LORD GOD is my strength and my might.
>   (Isa 12.2)

How often does fear keep us from trusting? How often does it keep us from being and doing what God is calling us to be and do? We need to reach out to God and to others in our life and trust that God is with us. Jesus came to tell us that love is more powerful than fear, and his life and death testified to his deep trust in his Father. Many times, he told his disciples, "Do not be afraid."

Let us truly live the words In God we trust.

▶ Isa 12.1–6

2 Surely God is my salvation;
    I will trust, and will not be afraid,
for the LORD GOD[k] is my strength and my
            might;
    he has become my salvation.

3 With joy you will draw water from the wells of salvation. 4 And you will say in that day:
Give thanks to the LORD,
    call on his name;
make known his deeds among the nations;
    proclaim that his name is exalted.

5 Sing praises to the LORD, for he has done
            gloriously;
    let this be known[l] in all the earth.
6 Shout aloud and sing for joy, O royal[m]
            Zion,
    for great in your midst is the Holy One
            of Israel.

Proclamation against Babylon

The oracle concerning Babylon that I·sāi'ah son of Ā'moz saw.

2 On a bare hill raise a signal,
    cry aloud to them;
wave the hand for them to enter
    the gates of the nobles.
3 I myself have commanded my consecrated
            ones,
    have summoned my warriors, my
            proudly exulting ones,
    to execute my anger.

4 Listen, a tumult on the mountains
    as of a great multitude!

Listen, an uproar of kingdoms,
    of nations gathering together!
The LORD of hosts is mustering
    an army for battle.
5 They come from a distant land,
    from the end of the heavens,
the LORD and the weapons of his
            indignation,
    to destroy the whole earth.

6 Wail, for the day of the LORD is near;
    it will come like destruction from the
            Almighty![n]
7 Therefore all hands will be feeble,
    and every human heart will melt,
8   and they will be dismayed.
Pangs and agony will seize them;
    they will be in anguish like a woman in
            labor.
They will look aghast at one another;
    their faces will be aflame.
9 See, the day of the LORD comes,
    cruel, with wrath and fierce anger,
to make the earth a desolation,
    and to destroy its sinners from it.
10 For the stars of the heavens and their
            constellations
    will not give their light;
the sun will be dark at its rising,
    and the moon will not shed its light.
11 I will punish the world for its evil,
    and the wicked for their iniquity;

---

k Heb for Yah, the LORD   l Or this is made known
m Or O inhabitant of   n Traditional rendering of Heb
Shaddai

I will put an end to the pride of
the arrogant,
and lay low the insolence of tyrants.
12 I will make mortals more rare than fine
gold,
and humans than the gold of Ō′phir.
13 Therefore I will make the heavens tremble,
and the earth will be shaken out of its
place,
at the wrath of the LORD of hosts
in the day of his fierce anger.
14 Like a hunted gazelle,
or like sheep with no one to gather them,
all will turn to their own people,
and all will flee to their own lands.
15 Whoever is found will be thrust through,
and whoever is caught will fall by the
sword.
16 Their infants will be dashed to pieces
before their eyes;
their houses will be plundered,
and their wives ravished.
17 See, I am stirring up the Mēdes against
them,
who have no regard for silver
and do not delight in gold.
18 Their bows will slaughter the young men;
they will have no mercy on the fruit of
the womb;
their eyes will not pity children.
19 And Babylon, the glory of kingdoms,
the splendor and pride of the Chal•dē′ans,
will be like Sod′om and Go•mor′rah
when God overthrew them.
20 It will never be inhabited
or lived in for all generations;
Arabs will not pitch their tents there,
shepherds will not make their flocks lie
down there.
21 But wild animals will lie down there,
and its houses will be full of howling
creatures;
there ostriches will live,
and there goat-demons will dance.
22 Hyenas will cry in its towers,
and jackals in the pleasant palaces;
its time is close at hand,
and its days will not be prolonged.

Restoration of Judah

14 But the LORD will have compassion on Jacob and
will again choose Israel, and will set them in their
own land; and aliens will join them and attach
themselves to the house of Jacob. 2 And the nations will take them and bring them to their place,
and the house of Israel will possess the nations[o] as
male and female slaves in the LORD's land; they
will take captive those who were their captors, and
rule over those who oppressed them.

Downfall of the King of Babylon

3 When the LORD has given you rest from your
pain and turmoil and the hard service with which
you were made to serve, 4 you will take up this
taunt against the king of Babylon:
How the oppressor has ceased!
How his insolence[p] has ceased!
5 The LORD has broken the staff of the
wicked,
the scepter of rulers,
6 that struck down the peoples in wrath
with unceasing blows,
that ruled the nations in anger
with unrelenting persecution.
7 The whole earth is at rest and quiet;
they break forth into singing.
8 The cypresses exult over you,
the cedars of Lebanon, saying,
"Since you were laid low,
no one comes to cut us down."
9 Shē′ōl beneath is stirred up
to meet you when you come;
it rouses the shades to greet you,
all who were leaders of the earth;
it raises from their thrones
all who were kings of the nations.
10 All of them will speak
and say to you:
"You too have become as weak as we!
You have become like us!"
11 Your pomp is brought down to Shē′ōl,
and the sound of your harps;
maggots are the bed beneath you,
and worms are your covering.
12 How you are fallen from heaven,
O Day Star, son of Dawn!
How you are cut down to the ground,
you who laid the nations low!
13 You said in your heart,
"I will ascend to heaven;
I will raise my throne
above the stars of God;
I will sit on the mount of assembly
on the heights of Zā′phon;[q]
14 I will ascend to the tops of the clouds,
I will make myself like the Most High."
15 But you are brought down to Shē′ōl,
to the depths of the Pit.

---

[o] Heb *them* [p] Q Ms Compare Gk Syr Vg: Meaning of MT uncertain [q] Or *assembly in the far north*

16 Those who see you will stare at you,
and ponder over you:
"Is this the man who made the earth
tremble,
who shook kingdoms,
17 who made the world like a desert
and overthrew its cities,
who would not let his prisoners go
home?"
18 All the kings of the nations lie in glory,
each in his own tomb;
19 but you are cast out, away from your
grave,
like loathsome carrion,r
clothed with the dead, those pierced by the
sword,
who go down to the stones of the Pit,
like a corpse trampled underfoot.
20 You will not be joined with them in
burial,
because you have destroyed your land,
you have killed your people.

May the descendants of evildoers
nevermore be named!
21 Prepare slaughter for his sons
because of the guilt of their father.s
Let them never rise to possess the earth
or cover the face of the world with cities.

22 I will rise up against them, says the LORD of
hosts, and will cut off from Babylon name and
remnant, offspring and posterity, says the LORD.
23 And I will make it a possession of the hedgehog,
and pools of water, and I will sweep it with the
broom of destruction, says the LORD of hosts.

An Oracle concerning Assyria

24 The LORD of hosts has sworn:
As I have designed,
so shall it be;
and as I have planned,
so shall it come to pass:
25 I will break the Assyrian in my land,
and on my mountains trample him
under foot;
his yoke shall be removed from them,
and his burden from their shoulders.
26 This is the plan that is planned
concerning the whole earth;
and this is the hand that is stretched out
over all the nations.
27 For the LORD of hosts has planned,
and who will annul it?
His hand is stretched out,
and who will turn it back?

An Oracle concerning Philistia

28 In the year that King Ā′haz died this oracle
came:

29 Do not rejoice, all you Phi·lis′tines,
that the rod that struck you is broken,
for from the root of the snake will come
forth an adder,
and its fruit will be a flying fiery serpent.
30 The firstborn of the poor will graze,
and the needy lie down in safety;
but I will make your root die of famine,
and your remnant It will kill.
31 Wail, O gate; cry, O city;
melt in fear, O Phi·lis′ti·a, all of you!
For smoke comes out of the north,
and there is no straggler in its ranks.

32 What will one answer the messengers of the
nation?
"The LORD has founded Zion,
and the needy among his people
will find refuge in her."

An Oracle concerning Moab

An oracle concerning Mō′ab.

Because Ar is laid waste in a night,
Mō′ab is undone;
because Kir is laid waste in a night,
Mō′ab is undone.
2 Dī′bonu has gone up to the temple,
to the high places to weep;
over Nē′bō and over Med′e·ba
Mō′ab wails.
On every head is baldness,
every beard is shorn;
3 in the streets they bind on sackcloth;
on the housetops and in the squares
everyone wails and melts in tears.
4 Hesh′bon and Ê·le·ā′leh cry out,
their voices are heard as far as Jā′haz;
therefore the loins of Mō′ab quiver;v
his soul trembles.
5 My heart cries out for Mō′ab;
his fugitives flee to Zō′ar,
to Eg′lath-she·lish′i·yah.
For at the ascent of Lū′hith
they go up weeping;
on the road to Hor·ō·nā′im
they raise a cry of destruction;
6 the waters of Nim′rim
are a desolation;

---

r Cn Compare Gk: Heb *like a loathed branch*
s Syr Compare Gk: Heb *fathers*   t Q Ms Vg: MT *he*
u Cn: Heb *the house and Dibon*   v Cn Compare Gk Syr:
Heb *the armed men of Moab cry aloud*

did you KNOW?

Oracles

In the ancient world, an oracle was understood as a communication of the gods. By means of oracles, First Isaiah presents God's judgment on Israel's enemies, including Egypt, Babylon, Assyria, Philistia, Moab, and Edom (Isaiah, chapters 13–23). When we read these oracles today, we can understand their angry and vengeful spirit if we recall the terrible suffering that these nations inflicted on Israel. Still, we should also keep in mind the New Testament commandment to avoid revenge in all its forms (Mt 5.38–48). Jesus calls us to be peacemakers in spite of our suffering.

▶ Isaiah, chapters 13–23

the grass is withered, the new growth fails,
 the verdure is no more.
7 Therefore the abundance they have gained
 and what they have laid up
they carry away
 over the Wadi of the Willows.
8 For a cry has gone
 around the land of Mōʹab;
the wailing reaches to Eg·lāʹim,
 the wailing reaches to Bēʹer-ēʹlim.
9 For the waters of Dīʹbonʷ are full of
 blood;
 yet I will bring upon Dīʹbonʷ even
 more—
a lion for those of Mōʹab who escape,
 for the remnant of the land.
Send lambs
 to the ruler of the land,
from Sēʹla, by way of the desert,
 to the mount of daughter Zion.
2 Like fluttering birds,
 like scattered nestlings,
so are the daughters of Mōʹab
 at the fords of the Arʹnon.
3 "Give counsel,
 grant justice;
make your shade like night
 at the height of noon;
hide the outcasts,
 do not betray the fugitive;

4 let the outcasts of Mōʹab
 settle among you;
be a refuge to them
 from the destroyer."

When the oppressor is no more,
 and destruction has ceased,
and marauders have vanished from the
 land,
5 then a throne shall be established in
 steadfast love
 in the tent of David,
 and on it shall sit in faithfulness
a ruler who seeks justice
 and is swift to do what is right.

6 We have heard of the pride of Mōʹab
 —how proud he is!—
of his arrogance, his pride, and his
 insolence;
 his boasts are false.
7 Therefore let Mōʹab wail,
 let everyone wail for Mōʹab.
Mourn, utterly stricken,
 for the raisin cakes of Kir-harʹe·seth.

8 For the fields of Heshʹbon languish,
 and the vines of Sibʹmah,
whose clusters once made drunk
 the lords of the nations,
reached to Jāʹzer
 and strayed to the desert;
their shoots once spread abroad
 and crossed over the sea.
9 Therefore I weep with the weeping of Jāʹzer
 for the vines of Sibʹmah;
I drench you with my tears,
 O Heshʹbon and Ēʹle·āʹleh;
for the shout over your fruit harvest
 and your grain harvest has ceased.
10 Joy and gladness are taken away
 from the fruitful field;
and in the vineyards no songs are sung,
 no shouts are raised;
no treader treads out wine in the presses;
 the vintage-shout is hushed.ˣ
11 Therefore my heart throbs like a harp for Mōʹab,
 and my very soul for Kir-hēʹres.

12 When Mōʹab presents himself, when he wearies himself upon the high place, when he comes to his sanctuary to pray, he will not prevail.

13 This was the word that the LORD spoke concerning Mōʹab in the past. 14 But now the LORD says, In three years, like the years of a hired worker, the glory of Mōʹab will be brought into

ʷ Q Ms Vg Compare Syr: MT *Dimon*   ˣ Gk: Heb *I have hushed*

contempt, in spite of all its great multitude; and those who survive will be very few and feeble.

An Oracle concerning Damascus

An oracle concerning Damascus.

See, Damascus will cease to be a city,
    and will become a heap of ruins.
2 Her towns will be deserted forever;[y]
    they will be places for flocks,
    which will lie down, and no one will
        make them afraid.
3 The fortress will disappear from E′phra·im,
    and the kingdom from Damascus;
and the remnant of Ar′am will be
    like the glory of the children of Israel,
                    says the LORD of hosts.

4 On that day
    the glory of Jacob will be brought low,
    and the fat of his flesh will grow lean.
5 And it shall be as when reapers gather
        standing grain
    and their arms harvest the ears,
and as when one gleans the ears of grain
    in the Valley of Reph′a·im.
6 Gleanings will be left in it,
    as when an olive tree is beaten—
two or three berries
    in the top of the highest bough,
four or five
    on the branches of a fruit tree,
                    says the LORD God of Israel.

7 On that day people will regard their Maker, and their eyes will look to the Holy One of Israel; 8 they will not have regard for the altars, the work of their hands, and they will not look to what their own fingers have made, either the sacred poles[z] or the altars of incense.

9 On that day their strong cities will be like the deserted places of the Hi′vites and the Am′o·rites,[a] which they deserted because of the children of Israel, and there will be desolation.

10 For you have forgotten the God of your
        salvation,
    and have not remembered the Rock of
        your refuge;
    therefore, though you plant pleasant plants
    and set out slips of an alien god,
11 though you make them grow on the day
        that you plant them,
    and make them blossom in the morning
        that you sow;
yet the harvest will flee away
    in a day of grief and incurable pain.

12 Ah, the thunder of many peoples,
    they thunder like the thundering of
        the sea!
Ah, the roar of nations,
    they roar like the roaring of mighty
        waters!
13 The nations roar like the roaring of many
        waters,
    but he will rebuke them, and they will
        flee far away,
chased like chaff on the mountains before
        the wind
    and whirling dust before the storm.
14 At evening time, lo, terror!
    Before morning, they are no more.
This is the fate of those who despoil us,
    and the lot of those who plunder us.

An Oracle concerning Ethiopia

Ah, land of whirring wings
    beyond the rivers of Ethiopia,[b]
2 sending ambassadors by the Nile
    in vessels of papyrus on the waters!
Go, you swift messengers,
    to a nation tall and smooth,
to a people feared near and far,
    a nation mighty and conquering,
    whose land the rivers divide.

3 All you inhabitants of the world,
    you who live on the earth,
when a signal is raised on the mountains,
        look!
    When a trumpet is blown, listen!
4 For thus the LORD said to me:
I will quietly look from my dwelling
    like clear heat in sunshine,
    like a cloud of dew in the heat of harvest.
5 For before the harvest, when the blossom is
        over
    and the flower becomes a ripening grape,
he will cut off the shoots with pruning
        hooks,
    and the spreading branches he will hew
        away.
6 They shall all be left
    to the birds of prey of the mountains
    and to the animals of the earth.
And the birds of prey will summer on them,
    and all the animals of the earth will
        winter on them.

---

y Cn Compare Gk: Heb *the cities of Aroer are deserted*
z Heb *Asherim*   a Cn Compare Gk: Heb *places of the wood
and the highest bough*   b Or *Nubia*; Heb *Cush*

7 At that time gifts will be brought to the LORD of hosts from[c] a people tall and smooth, from a people feared near and far, a nation mighty and conquering, whose land the rivers divide, to Mount Zion, the place of the name of the LORD of hosts.

An Oracle concerning Egypt

An oracle concerning Egypt.

See, the LORD is riding on a swift cloud
   and comes to Egypt;
the idols of Egypt will tremble at his
     presence,
   and the heart of the Egyptians will melt
     within them.
2 I will stir up Egyptians against Egyptians,
   and they will fight, one against the other,
   neighbor against neighbor,
   city against city, kingdom against
     kingdom;
3 the spirit of the Egyptians within them will
     be emptied out,
   and I will confound their plans;
they will consult the idols and the spirits of
     the dead
   and the ghosts and the familiar spirits;
4 I will deliver the Egyptians
   into the hand of a hard master;
a fierce king will rule over them,
   says the Sovereign, the LORD of hosts.

5 The waters of the Nile will be dried up,
   and the river will be parched and dry;
6 its canals will become foul,
   and the branches of Egypt's Nile will
     diminish and dry up;
   reeds and rushes will rot away.
7 There will be bare places by the Nile,
   on the brink of the Nile;
and all that is sown by the Nile will dry up,
   be driven away, and be no more.
8 Those who fish will mourn;
   all who cast hooks in the Nile will
     lament,
   and those who spread nets on the water
     will languish.
9 The workers in flax will be in despair,
   and the carders and those at the loom
     will grow pale.
10 Its weavers will be dismayed,
   and all who work for wages will be
     grieved.

11 The princes of Zō′an are utterly foolish;
   the wise counselors of Pharaoh give
     stupid counsel.

How can you say to Pharaoh,
   "I am one of the sages,
   a descendant of ancient kings"?
12 Where now are your sages?
   Let them tell you and make known
     what the LORD of hosts has planned
     against Egypt.
13 The princes of Zō′an have become fools,
   and the princes of Memphis are deluded;
those who are the cornerstones of its tribes
   have led Egypt astray.
14 The LORD has poured into them[d]
   a spirit of confusion;
and they have made Egypt stagger in all its
     doings
   as a drunkard staggers around in vomit.
15 Neither head nor tail, palm branch or reed,
   will be able to do anything for Egypt.

16 On that day the Egyptians will be like women, and tremble with fear before the hand that the LORD of hosts raises against them. 17 And the land of Judah will become a terror to the Egyptians; everyone to whom it is mentioned will fear because of the plan that the LORD of hosts is planning against them.

Egypt, Assyria, and Israel Blessed

18 On that day there will be five cities in the land of Egypt that speak the language of Cā′naan and swear allegiance to the LORD of hosts. One of these will be called the City of the Sun.

19 On that day there will be an altar to the LORD in the center of the land of Egypt, and a pillar to the LORD at its border. 20 It will be a sign and a witness to the LORD of hosts in the land of Egypt; when they cry to the LORD because of oppressors, he will send them a savior, and will defend and deliver them. 21 The LORD will make himself known to the Egyptians; and the Egyptians will know the LORD on that day, and will worship with sacrifice and burnt offering, and they will make vows to the LORD and perform them. 22 The LORD will strike Egypt, striking and healing; they will return to the LORD, and he will listen to their supplications and heal them.

23 On that day there will be a highway from Egypt to Assyria, and the Assyrian will come into Egypt, and the Egyptian into Assyria, and the Egyptians will worship with the Assyrians.

24 On that day Israel will be the third with Egypt and Assyria, a blessing in the midst of the earth, 25 whom the LORD of hosts has blessed, saying, "Blessed be Egypt my people, and Assyria the work of my hands, and Israel my heritage."

---

c Q Ms Gk Vg: MT of   d Gk Compare Tg: Heb it

Isaiah Dramatizes the Conquest of Egypt and Ethiopia

In the year that the commander-in-chief, who was sent by King Sar′gon of Assyria, came to Ash′dod and fought against it and took it— ²at that time the LORD had spoken to Ī•sāi′ah son of Ā′moz, saying, "Go, and loose the sackcloth from your loins and take your sandals off your feet," and he had done so, walking naked and barefoot. ³Then the LORD said, "Just as my servant Ī•sāi′ah has walked naked and barefoot for three years as a sign and a portent against Egypt and Ethiopia,ᵉ ⁴so shall the king of Assyria lead away the Egyptians as captives and the Ethiopiansᶠ as exiles, both the young and the old, naked and barefoot, with buttocks uncovered, to the shame of Egypt. ⁵And they shall be dismayed and confounded because of Ethiopiaᵉ their hope and of Egypt their boast. ⁶In that day the inhabitants of this coastland will say, 'See, this is what has happened to those in whom we hoped and to whom we fled for help and deliverance from the king of Assyria! And we, how shall we escape?' "

Oracles concerning Babylon, Edom, and Arabia

The oracle concerning the wilderness of the sea.

As whirlwinds in the Neg′eb sweep on,
 it comes from the desert,
  from a terrible land.
² A stern vision is told to me;
 the betrayer betrays,
 and the destroyer destroys.
Go up, O Ē′lam,
 lay siege, O Mēd′i•a;
all the sighing she has caused
 I bring to an end.
³ Therefore my loins are filled with anguish;
 pangs have seized me,
 like the pangs of a woman in labor;
I am bowed down so that I cannot hear,
 I am dismayed so that I cannot see.
⁴ My mind reels, horror has appalled me;
 the twilight I longed for
 has been turned for me into trembling.
⁵ They prepare the table,
 they spread the rugs,
 they eat, they drink.
Rise up, commanders,
 oil the shield!
⁶ For thus the Lord said to me:
 "Go, post a lookout,
 let him announce what he sees.
⁷ When he sees riders, horsemen in pairs,
 riders on donkeys, riders on camels,
let him listen diligently,
 very diligently."

⁸ Then the watcherᵍ called out:
 "Upon a watchtower I stand, O Lord,
  continually by day,
 and at my post I am stationed
  throughout the night.
⁹ Look, there they come, riders,
 horsemen in pairs!"
Then he responded,
 "Fallen, fallen is Babylon;
 and all the images of her gods
 lie shattered on the ground."
¹⁰ O my threshed and winnowed one,
 what I have heard from the LORD of hosts,
 the God of Israel, I announce to you.

11 The oracle concerning Dū′mah.

One is calling to me from Sē′ir,
 "Sentinel, what of the night?
 Sentinel, what of the night?"
¹² The sentinel says:
 "Morning comes, and also the night.
 If you will inquire, inquire;
 come back again."

13 The oracle concerning the desert plain.

In the scrub of the desert plain you will
  lodge,
 O caravans of Ded′an•ītes.
¹⁴ Bring water to the thirsty,
 meet the fugitive with bread,
 O inhabitants of the land of Tē′ma.
¹⁵ For they have fled from the swords,
 from the drawn sword,
from the bent bow,
 and from the stress of battle.

16 For thus the Lord said to me: Within a year, according to the years of a hired worker, all the glory of Kē′dar will come to an end; ¹⁷and the remaining bows of Kē′dar's warriors will be few; for the LORD, the God of Israel, has spoken.

A Warning of Destruction of Jerusalem

The oracle concerning the valley of vision.

What do you mean that you have gone up,
 all of you, to the housetops,
² you that are full of shoutings,
 tumultuous city, exultant town?
Your slain are not slain by the sword,
 nor are they dead in battle.
³ Your rulers have all fled together;
 they were captured without the use of
  a bow.ʰ
All of you who were found were captured,

ᵉ Or *Nubia*; Heb *Cush* ᶠ Or *Nubians*; Heb *Cushites*
ᵍ Q Ms: MT *a lion* ʰ Or *without their bows*

though they had fled far away.*i*

4 Therefore I said:
Look away from me,
    let me weep bitter tears;
do not try to comfort me
    for the destruction of my beloved
        people.

"Let us eat and drink,
    for tomorrow we die."
14 The LORD of hosts has revealed himself in
        my ears:
Surely this iniquity will not be forgiven you
        until you die,
    says the Lord GOD of hosts.

Faith and Politics

Every group that we belong to has a leader. And every leader might be corrupt. Like First Isaiah, we should demand integrity from our leaders as well as practicing it ourselves.

In Isa 22.15–25, the prophet denounces the steward Shebna for his self-seeking ways. Evidently, Shebna is using his position of leadership to prepare an expensive tomb for himself (verse 16) and to acquire ornate chariots (verse 18). Isaiah prefers Eliakim to take over his position. The prophet's interest in local politics points out a biblical truth: Our faith applies to our daily life, including our political choices.

We need to search out and endorse good leaders for school, community, state, and federal governments and for organizations like school clubs, sports teams, youth groups, and Scouts. Challenge your leaders to be people of integrity by avoiding corruption and seeking the best for the people they serve.

▸ Isa 22.15–25

5 For the Lord GOD of hosts has a day
    of tumult and trampling and confusion
    in the valley of vision,
a battering down of walls
    and a cry for help to the mountains.
6 Ē'lam bore the quiver
    with chariots and cavalry,*j*
    and Kir uncovered the shield.
7 Your choicest valleys were full of chariots,
    and the cavalry took their stand at the gates.
8 He has taken away the covering of Judah.

On that day you looked to the weapons of the House of the Forest, 9 and you saw that there were many breaches in the city of David, and you collected the waters of the lower pool. 10 You counted the houses of Jerusalem, and you broke down the houses to fortify the wall. 11 You made a reservoir between the two walls for the water of the old pool. But you did not look to him who did it, or have regard for him who planned it long ago.

12 In that day the Lord GOD of hosts
    called to weeping and mourning,
    to baldness and putting on sackcloth;
13 but instead there was joy and festivity,
    killing oxen and slaughtering sheep,
    eating meat and drinking wine.

Denunciation of Self-Seeking Officials

15 Thus says the Lord GOD of hosts: Come, go to this steward, to Sheb'na, who is master of the household, and say to him: 16 What right do you have here? Who are your relatives here, that you have cut out a tomb here for yourself, cutting a tomb on the height, and carving a habitation for yourself in the rock? 17 The LORD is about to hurl you away violently, my fellow. He will seize firm hold on you, 18 whirl you round and round, and throw you like a ball into a wide land; there you shall die, and there your splendid chariots shall lie, O you disgrace to your master's house! 19 I will thrust you from your office, and you will be pulled down from your post.

20 On that day I will call my servant E•li'a•kim son of Hil•ki'ah, 21 and will clothe him with your robe and bind your sash on him. I will commit your authority to his hand, and he shall be a father to the inhabitants of Jerusalem and to the house of Judah. 22 I will place on his shoulder the key of the house of David; he shall open, and no one shall shut; he shall shut, and no one shall open. 23 I will fasten him like a peg in a secure place, and he will

i Gk Syr Vg: Heb *fled from far away*   *j* Meaning of Heb uncertain

become a throne of honor to his ancestral house. [24] And they will hang on him the whole weight of his ancestral house, the offspring and issue, every small vessel, from the cups to all the flagons. [25] On that day, says the LORD of hosts, the peg that was fastened in a secure place will give way; it will be cut down and fall, and the load that was on it will perish, for the LORD has spoken.

An Oracle concerning Tyre

The oracle concerning Tyre.

> Wail, O ships of Tar'shish,
> for your fortress is destroyed.[k]
> When they came in from Cyprus
> they learned of it.
> [2] Be still, O inhabitants of the coast,
> O merchants of Si'don,
> your messengers crossed over the sea[l]
> [3] and were on the mighty waters;
> your revenue was the grain of Shi'hor,
> the harvest of the Nile;
> you were the merchant of the nations.
> [4] Be ashamed, O Si'don, for the sea has
> spoken,
> the fortress of the sea, saying:
> "I have neither labored nor given birth,
> I have neither reared young men
> nor brought up young women."
> [5] When the report comes to Egypt,
> they will be in anguish over the report
> about Tyre.
> [6] Cross over to Tar'shish—
> wail, O inhabitants of the coast!
> [7] Is this your exultant city
> whose origin is from days of old,
> whose feet carried her
> to settle far away?
> [8] Who has planned this
> against Tyre, the bestower of crowns,
> whose merchants were princes,
> whose traders were the honored of
> the earth?
> [9] The LORD of hosts has planned it—
> to defile the pride of all glory,
> to shame all the honored of the earth.
> [10] Cross over to your own land,
> O ships of[m] Tar'shish;
> this is a harbor[n] no more.
> [11] He has stretched out his hand over the sea,
> he has shaken the kingdoms;
> the LORD has given command concerning
> Ca'naan
> to destroy its fortresses.
> [12] He said:
> You will exult no longer,

> O oppressed virgin daughter Si'don;
> rise, cross over to Cyprus—
> even there you will have no rest.

13 Look at the land of the Chal·de'ans! This is the people; it was not Assyria. They destined Tyre for wild animals. They erected their siege towers, they tore down her palaces, they made her a ruin.[o]
> [14] Wail, O ships of Tar'shish,
> for your fortress is destroyed.
[15] From that day Tyre will be forgotten for seventy years, the lifetime of one king. At the end of seventy years, it will happen to Tyre as in the song about the prostitute:
> [16] Take a harp,
> go about the city,
> you forgotten prostitute!
> Make sweet melody,
> sing many songs,
> that you may be remembered.
[17] At the end of seventy years, the LORD will visit Tyre, and she will return to her trade, and will prostitute herself with all the kingdoms of the world on the face of the earth. [18] Her merchandise and her wages will be dedicated to the LORD; her profits[p] will not be stored or hoarded, but her merchandise will supply abundant food and fine clothing for those who live in the presence of the LORD.

Impending Judgment on the Earth

> Now the LORD is about to lay waste the
> earth and make it desolate,
> and he will twist its surface and scatter its
> inhabitants.
> [2] And it shall be, as with the people, so with
> the priest;
> as with the slave, so with his master;
> as with the maid, so with her mistress;
> as with the buyer, so with the seller;
> as with the lender, so with the borrower;
> as with the creditor, so with the debtor.
> [3] The earth shall be utterly laid waste and
> utterly despoiled;
> for the LORD has spoken this word.
> [4] The earth dries up and withers,
> the world languishes and withers;
> the heavens languish together with the
> earth.
> [5] The earth lies polluted
> under its inhabitants;

---

k Cn Compare verse 14: Heb *for it is destroyed, without houses*   l Q Ms: MT *crossing over the sea, they replenished you*   m Cn Compare Gk: Heb *like the Nile, daughter*   n Cn: Heb *restraint*   o Meaning of Heb uncertain   p Heb *it*

for they have transgressed laws,
    violated the statutes,
    broken the everlasting covenant.
6 Therefore a curse devours the earth,
    and its inhabitants suffer for their guilt;
therefore the inhabitants of the earth
        dwindled,
    and few people are left.
7 The wine dries up,
    the vine languishes,
    all the merry-hearted sigh.
8 The mirth of the timbrels is stilled,
    the noise of the jubilant has ceased,
    the mirth of the lyre is stilled.
9 No longer do they drink wine with singing;
    strong drink is bitter to those who
        drink it.
10 The city of chaos is broken down,
    every house is shut up so that no one can
        enter.
11 There is an outcry in the streets for lack of
        wine;
    all joy has reached its eventide;
    the gladness of the earth is banished.
12 Desolation is left in the city,
    the gates are battered into ruins.
13 For thus it shall be on the earth
    and among the nations,
as when an olive tree is beaten,
    as at the gleaning when the grape harvest
        is ended.

14 They lift up their voices, they sing for joy;
    they shout from the west over the
        majesty of the LORD.
15 Therefore in the east give glory to the LORD;
    in the coastlands of the sea glorify the
        name of the LORD, the God of Israel.
16 From the ends of the earth we hear songs of
        praise,
    of glory to the Righteous One.
But I say, I pine away,
    I pine away. Woe is me!
For the treacherous deal treacherously,
    the treacherous deal very treacherously.
17 Terror, and the pit, and the snare
    are upon you, O inhabitant of the earth!
18 Whoever flees at the sound of the terror
    shall fall into the pit;
and whoever climbs out of the pit
    shall be caught in the snare.
For the windows of heaven are opened,
    and the foundations of the earth tremble.
19 The earth is utterly broken,
    the earth is torn asunder,
    the earth is violently shaken.

20 The earth staggers like a drunkard,
    it sways like a hut;
its transgression lies heavy upon it,
    and it falls, and will not rise again.

21 On that day the LORD will punish
    the host of heaven in heaven,
    and on earth the kings of the earth.
22 They will be gathered together
    like prisoners in a pit;
they will be shut up in a prison,
    and after many days they will be
        punished.
23 Then the moon will be abashed,
    and the sun ashamed;
for the LORD of hosts will reign
    on Mount Zion and in Jerusalem,
and before his elders he will manifest his
        glory.

Praise for Deliverance from Oppression

25 O LORD, you are my God;
    I will exalt you, I will praise your name;
for you have done wonderful things,
    plans formed of old, faithful and sure.
2 For you have made the city a heap,
    the fortified city a ruin;
the palace of aliens is a city no more,
    it will never be rebuilt.
3 Therefore strong peoples will glorify you;
    cities of ruthless nations will fear you.
4 For you have been a refuge to the poor,
    a refuge to the needy in their distress,
    a shelter from the rainstorm and a shade
        from the heat.
When the blast of the ruthless was like a
        winter rainstorm,
5   the noise of aliens like heat in a dry
        place,
you subdued the heat with the shade of
        clouds;
    the song of the ruthless was stilled.

6 On this mountain the LORD of hosts will
        make for all peoples
    a feast of rich food, a feast of well-aged
        wines,
    of rich food filled with marrow, of
        well-aged wines strained clear.
7 And he will destroy on this mountain
    the shroud that is cast over all peoples,
    the sheet that is spread over all nations;
8   he will swallow up death forever.
Then the Lord GOD will wipe away the tears
        from all faces,
    and the disgrace of his people he will
        take away from all the earth,

for the LORD has spoken.

9 It will be said on that day,
Lo, this is our God; we have waited for
him, so that he might save us.
This is the LORD for whom we have
waited;
let us be glad and rejoice in his salvation.

10 For the hand of the LORD will rest on this
mountain.

The Mōʻab·ites shall be trodden down in
their place
as straw is trodden down in a dung-pit.

11 Though they spread out their hands in the
midst of it,
as swimmers spread out their hands to
swim,
their pride will be laid low despite the
struggle*q* of their hands.

12 The high fortifications of his walls will be
brought down,
laid low, cast to the ground, even to the
dust.

Judah's Song of Victory

On that day this song will be sung in the land of
Judah:
We have a strong city;
he sets up victory
like walls and bulwarks.

2 Open the gates,
so that the righteous nation that keeps
faith
may enter in.

3 Those of steadfast mind you keep in peace—
in peace because they trust in you.

4 Trust in the LORD forever,
for in the LORD GOD*r*
you have an everlasting rock.

5 For he has brought low
the inhabitants of the height;
the lofty city he lays low.
He lays it low to the ground,
casts it to the dust.

6 The foot tramples it,
the feet of the poor,
the steps of the needy.

7 The way of the righteous is level;
O Just One, you make smooth the path
of the righteous.

8 In the path of your judgments,
O LORD, we wait for you;
your name and your renown
are the soul's desire.

9 My soul yearns for you in the night,
my spirit within me earnestly seeks you.

For when your judgments are in the earth,
the inhabitants of the world learn
righteousness.

10 If favor is shown to the wicked,
they do not learn righteousness;
in the land of uprightness they deal
perversely
and do not see the majesty of the LORD.

11 O LORD, your hand is lifted up,
but they do not see it.
Let them see your zeal for your people, and
be ashamed.
Let the fire for your adversaries consume
them.

12 O LORD, you will ordain peace for us,
for indeed, all that we have done, you
have done for us.

13 O LORD our God,
other lords besides you have ruled
over us,
but we acknowledge your name alone.

14 The dead do not live;
shades do not rise—
because you have punished and destroyed
them,
and wiped out all memory of them.

15 But you have increased the nation, O LORD,
you have increased the nation; you are
glorified;
you have enlarged all the borders of the
land.

16 O LORD, in distress they sought you,
they poured out a prayer*q*
when your chastening was on them.

17 Like a woman with child,
who writhes and cries out in her pangs
when she is near her time,
so were we because of you, O LORD;

18 we were with child, we writhed,
but we gave birth only to wind.
We have won no victories on earth,
and no one is born to inhabit the world.

19 Your dead shall live, their corpses*s* shall rise.
O dwellers in the dust, awake and sing
for joy!
For your dew is a radiant dew,
and the earth will give birth to those
long dead.*t*

20 Come, my people, enter your chambers,
and shut your doors behind you;
hide yourselves for a little while
until the wrath is past.

---

q Meaning of Heb uncertain   *r* Heb *in Yah, the* LORD
s Cn Compare Syr Tg: Heb *my corpse*   *t* Heb *to the shades*

21 For the LORD comes out from his place
  to punish the inhabitants of the earth for
    their iniquity;
the earth will disclose the blood shed on it,
  and will no longer cover its slain.

Israel's Redemption

On that day the LORD with his cruel and great and
strong sword will punish Le·vi′a·than the fleeing
serpent, Le·vi′a·than the twisting serpent, and he
will kill the dragon that is in the sea.

2 On that day:
  A pleasant vineyard, sing about it!
3   I, the LORD, am its keeper;
    every moment I water it.
  I guard it night and day
    so that no one can harm it;
4   I have no wrath.
  If it gives me thorns and briers,
    I will march to battle against it.
    I will burn it up.
5 Or else let it cling to me for protection,
    let it make peace with me,
    let it make peace with me.

6 In days to come[u] Jacob shall take root,
    Israel shall blossom and put forth shoots,
    and fill the whole world with fruit.

7 Has he struck them down as he struck down
      those who struck them?
  Or have they been killed as their killers
      were killed?
8 By expulsion,[v] by exile you struggled against
      them;
  with his fierce blast he removed them in
      the day of the east wind.
9 Therefore by this the guilt of Jacob will be
      expiated,
  and this will be the full fruit of the
      removal of his sin:
  when he makes all the stones of the altars
    like chalkstones crushed to pieces,
  no sacred poles[w] or incense altars will
      remain standing.
10 For the fortified city is solitary,
    a habitation deserted and forsaken, like
      the wilderness;
  the calves graze there,
    there they lie down, and strip its
      branches.
11 When its boughs are dry, they are broken;
    women come and make a fire
      of them.
  For this is a people without understanding;

therefore he that made them will not
    have compassion on them,
  he that formed them will show them no
    favor.

12 On that day the LORD will thresh from the
channel of the Euphrates to the Wadi of Egypt,
and you will be gathered one by one, O people of
Israel. 13 And on that day a great trumpet will be
blown, and those who were lost in the land of
Assyria and those who were driven out to the land
of Egypt will come and worship the LORD on the
holy mountain at Jerusalem.

Judgment on Corrupt Rulers,
Priests, and Prophets

Ah, the proud garland of the drunkards of
      Ē′phra·im,
  and the fading flower of its glorious
      beauty,
    which is on the head of those bloated
      with rich food, of those overcome
      with wine!
2 See, the Lord has one who is mighty and
      strong;
    like a storm of hail, a destroying tempest,
  like a storm of mighty, overflowing waters;
    with his hand he will hurl them down to
      the earth.
3 Trampled under foot will be
    the proud garland of the drunkards of
      Ē′phra·im.
4 And the fading flower of its glorious beauty,
    which is on the head of those bloated
      with rich food,
  will be like a first-ripe fig before the
      summer;
    whoever sees it, eats it up
    as soon as it comes to hand.

5 In that day the LORD of hosts will be a
      garland of glory,
    and a diadem of beauty, to the remnant
      of his people;
6 and a spirit of justice to the one who sits in
      judgment,
    and strength to those who turn back the
      battle at the gate.

7 These also reel with wine
    and stagger with strong drink;
  the priest and the prophet reel with strong
      drink,
    they are confused with wine,
    they stagger with strong drink;

---

u Heb *Those to come*   v Meaning of Heb uncertain
w Heb *Asherim*

ISA

they err in vision,
  they stumble in giving judgment.
8 All tables are covered with filthy vomit;
  no place is clean.

9 "Whom will he teach knowledge,
    and to whom will he explain
      the message?
Those who are weaned from milk,
    those taken from the breast?
10 For it is precept upon precept, precept upon
      precept,
    line upon line, line upon line,
    here a little, there a little."ˣ

11 Truly, with stammering lip
    and with alien tongue
  he will speak to this people,
12 to whom he has said,
  "This is rest;
    give rest to the weary;
  and this is repose";
    yet they would not hear.
13 Therefore the word of the LORD will be to
      them,
  "Precept upon precept, precept upon
      precept,
    line upon line, line upon line,
    here a little, there a little;"ˣ
  in order that they may go, and fall
      backward,
    and be broken, and snared, and taken.

14 Therefore hear the word of the LORD, you
      scoffers
  who rule this people in Jerusalem.
15 Because you have said, "We have made a
      covenant with death,
    and with Shē′ōl we have an agreement;
  when the overwhelming scourge passes
      through
    it will not come to us;
  for we have made lies our refuge,
    and in falsehood we have taken shelter";
16 therefore thus says the Lord GOD,
  See, I am laying in Zion a foundation stone,
    a tested stone,
  a precious cornerstone, a sure foundation:
    "One who trusts will not panic."
17 And I will make justice the line,
    and righteousness the plummet;
  hail will sweep away the refuge of lies,
    and waters will overwhelm the shelter.
18 Then your covenant with death will be
      annulled,
    and your agreement with Shē′ōl will not
      stand;

when the overwhelming scourge passes
      through
    you will be beaten down by it.
19 As often as it passes through, it will
      take you;
  for morning by morning it will pass
      through,
    by day and by night;
  and it will be sheer terror to understand the
      message.
20 For the bed is too short to stretch oneself
      on it,
    and the covering too narrow to wrap
      oneself in it.
21 For the LORD will rise up as on Mount
      Pe·rā′zim,
    he will rage as in the valley of Gib′ē·on
  to do his deed—strange is his deed!—
    and to work his work—alien is his work!
22 Now therefore do not scoff,
    or your bonds will be made stronger;
  for I have heard a decree of destruction
    from the Lord GOD of hosts upon the
      whole land.

23 Listen, and hear my voice;
    Pay attention, and hear my speech.
24 Do those who plow for sowing plow
      continually?
    Do they continually open and harrow
      their ground?
25 When they have leveled its surface,
    do they not scatter dill, sow cummin,
  and plant wheat in rows
    and barley in its proper place,
    and spelt as the border?
26 For they are well instructed;
    their God teaches them.

27 Dill is not threshed with a threshing sledge,
    nor is a cart wheel rolled over cummin;
  but dill is beaten out with a stick,
    and cummin with a rod.
28 Grain is crushed for bread,
    but one does not thresh it forever;
  one drives the cart wheel and horses over it,
    but does not pulverize it.
29 This also comes from the LORD of hosts;
    he is wonderful in counsel,
    and excellent in wisdom.

The Siege of Jerusalem.

29 Ah, Ariel, Ariel,
    the city where David encamped!
  Add year to year;

ˣ Meaning of Heb of this verse uncertain

let the festivals run their round.

2 Yet I will distress Ar′i•el,
  and there shall be moaning and
    lamentation,
  and Jerusalem*y* shall be to me like an
    Ar′i•el.*z*
3 And like David*a* I will encamp against you;
  I will besiege you with towers
  and raise siegeworks against you.
4 Then deep from the earth you shall speak,
  from low in the dust your words shall
    come;
  your voice shall come from the ground like
    the voice of a ghost,
  and your speech shall whisper out of the
    dust.

5 But the multitude of your foes*b* shall be like
    small dust,
  and the multitude of tyrants like flying
    chaff.
And in an instant, suddenly,
6   you will be visited by the LORD of hosts
  with thunder and earthquake and great
    noise,
    with whirlwind and tempest, and the
      flame of a devouring fire.
7 And the multitude of all the nations that
    fight against Ar′i•el,
  all that fight against her and her
    stronghold, and who distress her,
  shall be like a dream, a vision
    of the night.
8 Just as when a hungry person dreams of
    eating
  and wakes up still hungry,
or a thirsty person dreams of drinking
  and wakes up faint, still thirsty,
so shall the multitude of all the nations be
  that fight against Mount Zion.

9 Stupefy yourselves and be in a stupor,
  blind yourselves and be blind!
Be drunk, but not from wine;
  stagger, but not from strong drink!
10 For the LORD has poured out upon you
    a spirit of deep sleep;
  he has closed your eyes, you prophets,
    and covered your heads, you seers.

11 The vision of all this has become for you
like the words of a sealed document. If it is given
to those who can read, with the command, "Read
this," they say, "We cannot, for it is sealed." 12 And if
it is given to those who cannot read, saying, "Read
this," they say, "We cannot read."

13 The Lord said:
Because these people draw near with their
    mouths
  and honor me with their lips,
  while their hearts are far from me,
and their worship of me is a human
    commandment learned by rote;
14 so I will again do
  amazing things with this people,
  shocking and amazing.
The wisdom of their wise shall perish,
  and the discernment of the discerning
    shall be hidden.

15 Ha! You who hide a plan too deep for the
    LORD,
  whose deeds are in the dark,
  and who say, "Who sees us? Who
    knows us?"
16 You turn things upside down!
  Shall the potter be regarded as the clay?
Shall the thing made say of its maker,
  "He did not make me";
or the thing formed say of the one who
    formed it,
  "He has no understanding"?

Hope for the Future

17 Shall not Lebanon in a very little while
    become a fruitful field,
  and the fruitful field be regarded as a
    forest?
18 On that day the deaf shall hear
    the words of a scroll,
  and out of their gloom and darkness
    the eyes of the blind shall see.
19 The meek shall obtain fresh joy in the LORD,
  and the neediest people shall exult in the
    Holy One of Israel.
20 For the tyrant shall be no more,
  and the scoffer shall cease to be;
  all those alert to do evil shall be cut off—
21 those who cause a person to lose a lawsuit,
  who set a trap for the arbiter in the gate,
  and without grounds deny justice to the
    one in the right.

22 Therefore thus says the LORD, who redeemed Abraham, concerning the house of Jacob:
No longer shall Jacob be ashamed,
  no longer shall his face grow pale.
23 For when he sees his children,
  the work of my hands, in his midst,

y Heb *she*   *z* Probable meaning, *altar hearth;* compare
Ezek 43.15   *a* Gk: Meaning of Heb uncertain
b Cn: Heb *strangers*

Preference for the Poor

Isaiah 29.17–21 proclaims that God's power will transform society: the deaf will hear, the blind will see, the meek will know joy, and the neediest will exult! First Isaiah's words are reflected in Jesus' words in the Beatitudes (see Lk 6.20–26). Both Jesus and Isaiah say that in God's Reign, the rights and needs of the lowliest and the weakest come first (see Isaiah, chapters 58, 61).

The Catholic church refers to this principle as the preferential option for the poor. People who are poor and helpless have a right to a just society where they get what they need to live with dignity and where they have a voice in the structures that govern their life. One can tell how near a society is to the Reign of God by seeing how it treats the most vulnerable members of the human family. Those who are poor should never be ignored when others have the resources to share.

Write your own prayer describing God's vision for those who are poor. Use Isaiah's words and the Beatitudes for ideas. Share your prayer with your family or youth group.

▶ Isa 29.17–21

they will sanctify my name;
they will sanctify the Holy One of Jacob,
    and will stand in awe of the God of
        Israel.
24 And those who err in spirit will come to
        understanding,
    and those who grumble will accept
        instruction.

The Futility of Reliance on Egypt

Oh, rebellious children, says the LORD,
who carry out a plan, but not mine;
who make an alliance, but against my will,
    adding sin to sin;
2 who set out to go down to Egypt
    without asking for my counsel,
to take refuge in the protection of Pharaoh,
    and to seek shelter in the shadow of
        Egypt;

3 Therefore the protection of Pharaoh shall
        become your shame,
    and the shelter in the shadow of Egypt
        your humiliation.
4 For though his officials are at Zō'an
    and his envoys reach Hā'nēs,
5 everyone comes to shame
    through a people that cannot profit them,
that brings neither help nor profit,
    but shame and disgrace.

6 An oracle concerning the animals of the Neg'eb.
Through a land of trouble and distress,
    of lioness and roaring[c] lion,
    of viper and flying serpent,
they carry their riches on the backs of
        donkeys,
    and their treasures on the humps of
        camels,
    to a people that cannot profit them.
7 For Egypt's help is worthless and empty,
    therefore I have called her,
    "Rā'hab who sits still."[d]

A Rebellious People

8 Go now, write it before them on a tablet,
    and inscribe it in a book,
so that it may be for the time to come
    as a witness forever.
9 For they are a rebellious people,
    faithless children,
children who will not hear
    the instruction of the LORD;
10 who say to the seers, "Do not see";
    and to the prophets, "Do not prophesy
        to us what is right;
speak to us smooth things,
    prophesy illusions,
11 leave the way, turn aside from the path,
    let us hear no more about the Holy One
        of Israel."
12 Therefore thus says the Holy One of Israel:
Because you reject this word,
    and put your trust in oppression and
        deceit,
    and rely on them;
13 therefore this iniquity shall become for you
    like a break in a high wall, bulging out,
        and about to collapse,
    whose crash comes suddenly, in an
        instant;
14 its breaking is like that of a potter's vessel
    that is smashed so ruthlessly

---

c Cn: Heb *from them*   d Meaning of Heb uncertain

that among its fragments not a sherd is
found
for taking fire from the hearth,
or dipping water out of the cistern.

15 For thus said the Lord GOD, the Holy One
of Israel:
In returning and rest you shall be saved;
in quietness and in trust shall be your
strength.
But you refused 16 and said,
"No! We will flee upon horses"—
therefore you shall flee!
and, "We will ride upon swift steeds"—
therefore your pursuers shall be swift!
17 A thousand shall flee at the threat of one,
at the threat of five you shall flee,
until you are left
like a flagstaff on the top of a mountain,
like a signal on a hill.

God's Promise to Zion

18 Therefore the LORD waits to be gracious
to you;
therefore he will rise up to show mercy
to you.
For the LORD is a God of justice;
blessed are all those who wait for him.
19 Truly, O people in Zion, inhabitants of Jerusalem, you shall weep no more. He will surely
be gracious to you at the sound of your cry; when
he hears it, he will answer you. 20 Though the Lord
may give you the bread of adversity and the water
of affliction, yet your Teacher will not hide himself
any more, but your eyes shall see your Teacher.
21 And when you turn to the right or when you
turn to the left, your ears shall hear a word behind
you, saying, "This is the way; walk in it." 22 Then
you will defile your silver-covered idols and your
gold-plated images. You will scatter them like
filthy rags; you will say to them, "Away with you!"

23 He will give rain for the seed with which
you sow the ground, and grain, the produce of the
ground, which will be rich and plenteous. On that
day your cattle will graze in broad pastures; 24 and
the oxen and donkeys that till the ground will eat
silage, which has been winnowed with shovel and
fork. 25 On every lofty mountain and every high
hill there will be brooks running with water—on a
day of the great slaughter, when the towers fall.
26 Moreover the light of the moon will be like the
light of the sun, and the light of the sun will be
sevenfold, like the light of seven days, on the day
when the LORD binds up the injuries of his people,
and heals the wounds inflicted by his blow.

Judgment on Assyria

27 See, the name of the LORD comes from far
away,
burning with his anger, and in thick
rising smoke;[e]
his lips are full of indignation,
and his tongue is like a devouring fire;
28 his breath is like an overflowing stream
that reaches up to the neck—
to sift the nations with the sieve of
destruction,
and to place on the jaws of the peoples a
bridle that leads them astray.

29 You shall have a song as in the night when
a holy festival is kept; and gladness of heart, as
when one sets out to the sound of the flute to go
to the mountain of the LORD, to the Rock of Israel.
30 And the LORD will cause his majestic voice to be
heard and the descending blow of his arm to be
seen, in furious anger and a flame of devouring
fire, with a cloudburst and tempest and hailstones.
31 The Assyrian will be terror-stricken at the voice
of the LORD, when he strikes with his rod. 32 And
every stroke of the staff of punishment that the
LORD lays upon him will be to the sound of timbrels and lyres; battling with brandished arm he
will fight with him. 33 For his burning place[f] has
long been prepared; truly it is made ready for the
king,[g] its pyre made deep and wide, with fire and
wood in abundance; the breath of the LORD, like a
stream of sulfur, kindles it.

Alliance with Egypt Is Futile

31 Alas for those who go down to Egypt for help
and who rely on horses,
who trust in chariots because they are many
and in horsemen because they are very
strong,
but do not look to the Holy One of Israel
or consult the LORD!
2 Yet he too is wise and brings disaster;
he does not call back his words,
but will rise against the house of the
evildoers,
and against the helpers of those who
work iniquity.
3 The Egyptians are human, and not God;
their horses are flesh, and not spirit.
When the LORD stretches out his hand,
the helper will stumble, and the one
helped will fall,
and they will all perish together.

e Meaning of Heb uncertain   f Or Topheth   g Or Molech

4 For thus the LORD said to me,
As a lion or a young lion growls over its
prey,
and—when a band of shepherds is called
out against it—
is not terrified by their shouting
or daunted at their noise,
so the LORD of hosts will come down
to fight upon Mount Zion and upon its
hill.
5 Like birds hovering overhead, so the LORD of
hosts
will protect Jerusalem;
he will protect and deliver it,
he will spare and rescue it.

6 Turn back to him whom you[h] have deeply
betrayed, O people of Israel. 7 For on that day all
of you shall throw away your idols of silver and
idols of gold, which your hands have sinfully
made for you.

8 "Then the Assyrian shall fall by a sword,
not of mortals;
and a sword, not of humans, shall
devour him;
he shall flee from the sword,
and his young men shall be put to forced
labor.
9 His rock shall pass away in terror,
and his officers desert the standard in
panic,"
says the LORD, whose fire is in Zion,
and whose furnace is in Jerusalem.

Government with Justice Predicted

See, a king will reign in righteousness,
and princes will rule with justice.
2 Each will be like a hiding place from the
wind,
a covert from the tempest,
like streams of water in a dry place,
like the shade of a great rock in a weary
land.
3 Then the eyes of those who have sight will
not be closed,
and the ears of those who have hearing
will listen.
4 The minds of the rash will have good
judgment,
and the tongues of stammerers will speak
readily and distinctly.
5 A fool will no longer be called noble,
nor a villain said to be honorable.
6 For fools speak folly,
and their minds plot iniquity:
to practice ungodliness,

to utter error concerning the LORD,
to leave the craving of the hungry
unsatisfied,
and to deprive the thirsty of drink.
7 The villainies of villains are evil;
they devise wicked devices
to ruin the poor with lying words,
even when the plea of the needy is right.
8 But those who are noble plan noble things,
and by noble things they stand.

Complacent Women Warned of Disaster

9 Rise up, you women who are at ease, hear
my voice;
you complacent daughters, listen to my
speech.
10 In little more than a year
you will shudder, you complacent ones;
for the vintage will fail,
the fruit harvest will not come.
11 Tremble, you women who are at ease,
shudder, you complacent ones;
strip, and make yourselves bare,
and put sackcloth on your loins.
12 Beat your breasts for the pleasant fields,
for the fruitful vine,
13 for the soil of my people
growing up in thorns and briers;
yes, for all the joyous houses
in the jubilant city.
14 For the palace will be forsaken,
the populous city deserted;
the hill and the watchtower
will become dens forever,
the joy of wild asses,
a pasture for flocks;
15 until a spirit from on high is poured out
on us,
and the wilderness becomes a fruitful
field,
and the fruitful field is deemed a forest.

The Peace of God's Reign

16 Then justice will dwell in the wilderness,
and righteousness abide in the fruitful
field.
17 The effect of righteousness will be peace,
and the result of righteousness, quietness
and trust forever.
18 My people will abide in a peaceful
habitation,
in secure dwellings, and in quiet resting
places.

h Heb they

19 The forest will disappear completely,*i*
   and the city will be utterly laid low.
20 Happy will you be who sow beside every
      stream,
   who let the ox and the donkey range
      freely.

The treaty is broken,
   its oaths*l* are despised,
   its obligation*m* is disregarded.
9 The land mourns and languishes;
   Lebanon is confounded and withers
      away;

Shalom

In Israel, people greet one another by saying "Shalom." In the Bible, *shalom* means "peace" in its fullest sense (see Isa 32.16–20). Shalom is not just the absence of war and violence but also the presence of justice, righteousness, happiness, and fullness of life. What better way to greet your neighbors or friends than to wish them shalom.

In your own life, seek peace. Begin each day by praying for peace of mind and heart, and to act with justice in all that you do. The very prayer that you speak will become the way that you live. Peace can become a reality only when we become a shalom people. It begins with us. If we wait, it may never come.

▶ Isa 32.16–20

A Prophecy of Deliverance from Foes

33 Ah, you destroyer,
   who yourself have not been destroyed;
you treacherous one,
   with whom no one has dealt
      treacherously!
When you have ceased to destroy,
   you will be destroyed;
and when you have stopped dealing
      treacherously,
you will be dealt with treacherously.
2 O LORD, be gracious to us; we wait for you.
   Be our arm every morning,
   our salvation in the time of trouble.
3 At the sound of tumult, peoples fled;
   before your majesty, nations
      scattered.
4 Spoil was gathered as the caterpillar gathers;
   as locusts leap, they leaped*j* upon it.
5 The LORD is exalted, he dwells on high;
   he filled Zion with justice and
      righteousness;
6 he will be the stability of your times,
   abundance of salvation, wisdom, and
      knowledge;
   the fear of the LORD is Zion's treasure.*k*

7 Listen! the valiant*j* cry in the streets;
   the envoys of peace weep bitterly.
8 The highways are deserted,
   travelers have quit the road.

Sharon is like a desert;
   and Ba'shan and Car'mel shake off their
      leaves.
10 "Now I will arise," says the LORD,
   "now I will lift myself up;
   now I will be exalted.
11 You conceive chaff, you bring forth stubble;
   your breath is a fire that will
      consume you.
12 And the peoples will be as if burned to lime,
   like thorns cut down, that are burned in
      the fire."

13 Hear, you who are far away, what I have
      done;
   and you who are near, acknowledge my
      might.
14 The sinners in Zion are afraid;
   trembling has seized the godless:
"Who among us can live with the
      devouring fire?
   Who among us can live with everlasting
      flames?"
15 Those who walk righteously and speak
      uprightly,
   who despise the gain of oppression,
who wave away a bribe instead of
      accepting it,

---

i Cn: Heb *And it will hail when the forest comes down*
j Meaning of Heb uncertain   *k* Heb *his treasure*; meaning of Heb uncertain   *l* Q Ms: MT *cities*   *m* Or *everyone*

who stop their ears from hearing of
bloodshed
and shut their eyes from looking on evil,
16 they will live on the heights;
their refuge will be the fortresses of rocks;
their food will be supplied, their water
assured.

The Land of the Majestic King

17 Your eyes will see the king in his beauty;
they will behold a land that stretches far
away.
18 Your mind will muse on the terror:
"Where is the one who counted?
Where is the one who weighed the
tribute?
Where is the one who counted the
towers?"
19 No longer will you see the insolent people,
the people of an obscure speech that you
cannot comprehend,
stammering in a language that you
cannot understand.
20 Look on Zion, the city of our appointed
festivals!
Your eyes will see Jerusalem,
a quiet habitation, an immovable tent,
whose stakes will never be pulled up,
and none of whose ropes will be broken.
21 But there the LORD in majesty will be for us
a place of broad rivers and streams,
where no galley with oars can go,
nor stately ship can pass.
22 For the LORD is our judge, the LORD is our
ruler,
the LORD is our king; he will save us.

23 Your rigging hangs loose;
it cannot hold the mast firm in its place,
or keep the sail spread out.

Then prey and spoil in abundance will be
divided;
even the lame will fall to plundering.
24 And no inhabitant will say, "I am sick";
the people who live there will be forgiven
their iniquity.

Judgment on the Nations

Draw near, O nations, to hear;
O peoples, give heed!
Let the earth hear, and all that fills it;
the world, and all that comes from it.
2 For the LORD is enraged against all the
nations,
and furious against all their hordes;

he has doomed them, has given them
over for slaughter.
3 Their slain shall be cast out,
and the stench of their corpses shall rise;
the mountains shall flow with their
blood.
4 All the host of heaven shall rot away,
and the skies roll up like a scroll.
All their host shall wither
like a leaf withering on a vine,
or fruit withering on a fig tree.

5 When my sword has drunk its fill in the
heavens,
lo, it will descend upon E'dom,
upon the people I have doomed to
judgment.
6 The LORD has a sword; it is sated with
blood,
it is gorged with fat,
with the blood of lambs and goats,
with the fat of the kidneys of rams.
For the LORD has a sacrifice in Boz'rah,
a great slaughter in the land of E'dom.
7 Wild oxen shall fall with them,
and young steers with the mighty bulls.
Their land shall be soaked with blood,
and their soil made rich with fat.

8 For the LORD has a day of vengeance,
a year of vindication by Zion's cause.[n]
9 And the streams of E'dom[o] shall be turned
into pitch,
and her soil into sulfur;
her land shall become burning pitch.
10 Night and day it shall not be quenched;
its smoke shall go up forever.
From generation to generation it shall lie
waste;
no one shall pass through it forever and
ever.
11 But the hawk[p] and the hedgehog[p] shall
possess it;
the owl[p] and the raven shall live in it.
He shall stretch the line of confusion
over it,
and the plummet of chaos over[q] its
nobles.
12 They shall name it No Kingdom There,
and all its princes shall be nothing.
13 Thorns shall grow over its strongholds,
nettles and thistles in its fortresses.
It shall be the haunt of jackals,
an abode for ostriches.

---

n Or of recompense by Zion's defender   o Heb her streams
p Identification uncertain   q Heb lacks over

14 Wildcats shall meet with hyenas,
    goat-demons shall call to each other;
there too Lil'ith shall repose,
    and find a place to rest.
15 There shall the owl nest
    and lay and hatch and brood in its
        shadow;
there too the buzzards shall gather,
    each one with its mate.
16 Seek and read from the book of the LORD:
    Not one of these shall be missing;
    none shall be without its mate.
For the mouth of the LORD has commanded,
    and his spirit has gathered them.
17 He has cast the lot for them,
    his hand has portioned it out to them
        with the line;
they shall possess it forever,
    from generation to generation they shall
        live in it.

The Return of the Redeemed to Zion

The wilderness and the dry land shall be
        glad,
    the desert shall rejoice and blossom;
like the crocus 2 it shall blossom
        abundantly,
    and rejoice with joy and singing.
The glory of Lebanon shall be given to it,
    the majesty of Car'mel and Sharon.
They shall see the glory of the LORD,
    the majesty of our God.

3 Strengthen the weak hands,
    and make firm the feeble knees.
4 Say to those who are of a fearful heart,
    "Be strong, do not fear!
Here is your God.
    He will come with vengeance,
    with terrible recompense.
    He will come and save you."

5 Then the eyes of the blind shall be opened,
    and the ears of the deaf unstopped;
6 then the lame shall leap like a deer,
    and the tongue of the speechless sing
        for joy.
For waters shall break forth in the
        wilderness,
    and streams in the desert;
7 the burning sand shall become a pool,
    and the thirsty ground springs of water;
the haunt of jackals shall become
        a swamp,r
    the grass shall become reeds and rushes.

8 A highway shall be there,
    and it shall be called the Holy Way;
the unclean shall not travel on it,s
    but it shall be for God's people;t
    no traveler, not even fools, shall go
        astray.
9 No lion shall be there,
    nor shall any ravenous beast come up
        on it;
they shall not be found there,
    but the redeemed shall walk there.
10 And the ransomed of the LORD shall return,
    and come to Zion with singing;
everlasting joy shall be upon their heads;
    they shall obtain joy and gladness,
    and sorrow and sighing shall flee away.

Catholic Connections

ADVENT REJOICING

Isaiah 35.1–7,10 is read at Mass on the third
Sunday of Advent. The third candle of the
Advent wreath and the vestments that
priests wear on this Sunday are often the
color rose, which is a symbol for rejoicing.
Together, this passage from Isaiah and this
color remind us that the coming of the
Messiah is a joyful event.

▶ Isa 35.1–10

Sennacherib Threatens Jerusalem
(2 Kings 18.13–37; 2 Chr 32.1–19)

In the fourteenth year of King Hez•e•ki'ah, King
Sen•nach'e•rib of Assyria came up against all the
fortified cities of Judah and captured them. 2 The
king of Assyria sent the Rab'sha•keh from La'chish
to King Hez•e•ki'ah at Jerusalem, with a great army.
He stood by the conduit of the upper pool on the
highway to the Fuller's Field. 3 And there came
out to him E•li'a•kim son of Hil•ki'ah, who was in

---

r Cn: Heb *in the haunt of jackals is her resting place*
s Or *pass it by*   t Cn: Heb *for them*

charge of the palace, and Sheb'na the secretary, and Jō'ah son of Ā'saph, the recorder.

4 The Rab'sha•keh said to them, "Say to Hez•e•kī'ah: Thus says the great king, the king of Assyria: On what do you base this confidence of yours? [5] Do you think that mere words are strategy and power for war? On whom do you now rely, that you have rebelled against me? [6] See, you are relying on Egypt, that broken reed of a staff, which will pierce the hand of anyone who leans on it. Such is Pharaoh king of Egypt to all who rely on him. [7] But if you say to me, 'We rely on the LORD our God,' is it not he whose high places and altars Hez•e•kī'ah has removed, saying to Judah and to Jerusalem, 'You shall worship before this altar'? [8] Come now, make a wager with my master the king of Assyria: I will give you two thousand horses, if you are able on your part to set riders on them. [9] How then can you repulse a single captain among the least of my master's servants, when you rely on Egypt for chariots and for horsemen? [10] Moreover, is it without the LORD that I have come up against this land to destroy it? The LORD said to me, Go up against this land, and destroy it."

11 Then E•lī'a•kim, Sheb'na, and Jō'ah said to the Rab'sha•keh, "Please speak to your servants in Ar•a•mā'ic, for we understand it; do not speak to us in the language of Judah within the hearing of the people who are on the wall." [12] But the Rab'sha•keh said, "Has my master sent me to speak these words to your master and to you, and not to the people sitting on the wall, who are doomed with you to eat their own dung and drink their own urine?"

13 Then the Rab'sha•keh stood and called out in a loud voice in the language of Judah, "Hear the words of the great king, the king of Assyria! [14] Thus says the king: 'Do not let Hez•e•kī'ah deceive you, for he will not be able to deliver you. [15] Do not let Hez•e•kī'ah make you rely on the LORD by saying, The LORD will surely deliver us; this city will not be given into the hand of the king of Assyria.' [16] Do not listen to Hez•e•kī'ah; for thus says the king of Assyria: 'Make your peace with me and come out to me; then everyone of you will eat from your own vine and your own fig tree and drink water from your own cistern, [17] until I come and take you away to a land like your own land, a land of grain and wine, a land of bread and vineyards. [18] Do not let Hez•e•kī'ah mislead you by saying, The LORD will save us. Has any of the gods of the nations saved their land out of the hand of the king of Assyria? [19] Where are the gods of Hā'math and Ar'pad? Where are the gods of Seph•ar•vā'im? Have they delivered Sa•mār'i•a out of my hand? [20] Who among all the gods of these countries have saved their countries out of my hand, that the LORD should save Jerusalem out of my hand?'"

21 But they were silent and answered him not a word, for the king's command was, "Do not answer him." [22] Then E•lī'a•kim son of Hil•kī'ah, who was in charge of the palace, and Sheb'na the secretary, and Jō'ah son of Ā'saph, the recorder, came to Hez•e•kī'ah with their clothes torn, and told him the words of the Rab'sha•keh.

Hezekiah Consults Isaiah
(2 Kings 19.1–13)

When King Hez•e•kī'ah heard it, he tore his clothes, covered himself with sackcloth, and went into the house of the LORD. [2] And he sent E•lī'a•kim, who was in charge of the palace, and Sheb'na the secretary, and the senior priests, covered with sackcloth, to the prophet Ī•sāi'ah son of Ā'moz. [3] They said to him, "Thus says Hez•e•kī'ah, This day is a day of distress, of rebuke, and of disgrace; children have come to the birth, and there is no strength to bring them forth. [4] It may be that the LORD your God heard the words of the Rab'sha•keh, whom his master the king of Assyria has sent to mock the living God, and will rebuke the words that the LORD your God has heard; therefore lift up your prayer for the remnant that is left."

5 When the servants of King Hez•e•kī'ah came to Ī•sāi'ah, [6] Ī•sāi'ah said to them, "Say to your master, 'Thus says the LORD: Do not be afraid because of the words that you have heard, with which the servants of the king of Assyria have reviled me. [7] I myself will put a spirit in him, so that he shall hear a rumor, and return to his own land; I will cause him to fall by the sword in his own land.'"

8 The Rab'sha•keh returned, and found the king of Assyria fighting against Lib'nah; for he had heard that the king had left Lā'chish. [9] Now the king[u] heard concerning King Tir•hā'kah of Ethiopia,[v] "He has set out to fight against you." When he heard it, he sent messengers to Hez•e•kī'ah, saying, [10] "Thus shall you speak to King Hez•e•kī'ah of Judah: Do not let your God on whom you rely deceive you by promising that Jerusalem will not be given into the hand of the king of Assyria. [11] See, you have heard what the kings of Assyria have done to all lands, destroying them utterly. Shall you be delivered? [12] Have the gods of the nations delivered them, the nations that my predecessors destroyed, Gō'zan, Har'an, Rē'zeph, and the people of Eden who were in Te•las'sar? [13] Where is the king of Hā'math, the king of Ar'pad, the king of the city of Seph•ar•vā'im, the king of Hē'na, or the king of Iv'vah?"

---

u Heb *he*   *v* Or *Nubia*; Heb *Cush*

Hezekiah's Prayer
(2 Kings 19.14–34)

14 Hez•e•kī′ah received the letter from the hand of the messengers and read it; then Hez•e•kī′ah went up to the house of the LORD and spread it before the LORD. 15 And Hez•e•kī′ah prayed to the LORD, saying: 16 "O LORD of hosts, God of Israel, who are enthroned above the cherubim, you are God, you alone, of all the kingdoms of the earth; you have made heaven and earth. 17 Incline your ear, O LORD, and hear; open your eyes, O LORD, and see; hear all the words of Sen•nach′e•rib, which he has sent to mock the living God. 18 Truly, O LORD, the kings of Assyria have laid waste all the nations and their lands, 19 and have hurled their gods into the fire, though they were no gods, but the work of human hands—wood and stone—and so they were destroyed. 20 So now, O LORD our God, save us from his hand, so that all the kingdoms of the earth may know that you alone are the LORD."

21 Then Ī•sāi′ah son of Ā′moz sent to Hez•e•kī′ah, saying: "Thus says the LORD, the God of Israel: Because you have prayed to me concerning King Sen•nach′e•rib of Assyria, 22 this is the word that the LORD has spoken concerning him:

She despises you, she scorns you—
　　virgin daughter Zion;
she tosses her head—behind your back,
　　daughter Jerusalem.

23 "Whom have you mocked and reviled?
　　Against whom have you raised your voice
and haughtily lifted your eyes?
　　Against the Holy One of Israel!
24 By your servants you have mocked the Lord,
　　and you have said, 'With my many
　　　　chariots
I have gone up the heights of the
　　　　mountains,
　　to the far recesses of Lebanon;
I felled its tallest cedars,
　　its choicest cypresses;
I came to its remotest height,
　　its densest forest.
25 I dug wells
　　and drank waters,
I dried up with the sole of my foot
　　all the streams of Egypt.'

26 "Have you not heard
　　that I determined it long ago?
I planned from days of old
　　what now I bring to pass,
that you should make fortified cities
　　crash into heaps of ruins,

27 while their inhabitants, shorn of
　　strength,
　　are dismayed and confounded;
they have become like plants of the field
　　and like tender grass,
like grass on the housetops,
　　blighted[w] before it is grown.

28 "I know your rising up[x] and your sitting
　　down,
　　your going out and coming in,
　　and your raging against me.
29 Because you have raged against me
　　and your arrogance has come to
　　　　my ears,
I will put my hook in your nose
　　and my bit in your mouth;
I will turn you back on the way
　　by which you came.

30 "And this shall be the sign for you: This year eat what grows of itself, and in the second year what springs from that; then in the third year sow, reap, plant vineyards, and eat their fruit. 31 The surviving remnant of the house of Judah shall again take root downward, and bear fruit upward; 32 for from Jerusalem a remnant shall go out, and from Mount Zion a band of survivors. The zeal of the LORD of hosts will do this.

33 "Therefore thus says the LORD concerning the king of Assyria: He shall not come into this city, shoot an arrow there, come before it with a shield, or cast up a siege ramp against it. 34 By the way that he came, by the same he shall return; he shall not come into this city, says the LORD. 35 For I will defend this city to save it, for my own sake and for the sake of my servant David."

Sennacherib's Defeat and Death
(2 Kings 19.35–37)

36 Then the angel of the LORD set out and struck down one hundred eighty-five thousand in the camp of the Assyrians; when morning dawned, they were all dead bodies. 37 Then King Sen•nach′e•rib of Assyria left, went home, and lived at Nin′e•veh. 38 As he was worshiping in the house of his god Nis′roch, his sons A•dram′me•lech and Sha•rē′zer killed him with the sword, and they escaped into the land of Ar′a•rat. His son Ē′sar-had′don succeeded him.

---

w With 2 Kings 19.26: Heb *field*　　x Q Ms Gk: MT lacks *your rising up*

Hezekiah's Illness
(2 Kings 20.1–11; 2 Chr 32.24–26)

In those days Hez·e·kī′ah became sick and was at the point of death. The prophet Ī·sāi′ah son of Ā′moz came to him, and said to him, "Thus says the LORD: Set your house in order, for you shall die; you shall not recover." 2 Then Hez·e·kī′ah turned his face to the wall, and prayed to the LORD: 3 "Remember now, O LORD, I implore you, how I have walked before you in faithfulness with a whole heart, and have done what is good in your sight." And Hez·e·kī′ah wept bitterly.

4 Then the word of the LORD came to Ī·sāi′ah: 5 "Go and say to Hez·e·kī′ah, Thus says the LORD, the God of your ancestor David: I have heard your prayer, I have seen your tears; I will add fifteen years to your life. 6 I will deliver you and this city out of the hand of the king of Assyria, and defend this city.

7 "This is the sign to you from the LORD, that the LORD will do this thing that he has promised: 8 See, I will make the shadow cast by the declining sun on the dial of Ā′haz turn back ten steps." So the sun turned back on the dial the ten steps by which it had declined. *y*

9 A writing of King Hez·e·kī′ah of Judah, after he had been sick and had recovered from his sickness:

10 I said: In the noontide of my days
    I must depart;
I am consigned to the gates of Shē′ōl
    for the rest of my years.
11 I said, I shall not see the LORD
    in the land of the living;
I shall look upon mortals no more
    among the inhabitants of the world.
12 My dwelling is plucked up and removed
        from me
    like a shepherd's tent;
like a weaver I have rolled up my life;
    he cuts me off from the loom;
from day to night you bring me to an end; *y*
13   I cry for help *z* until morning;
like a lion he breaks all my bones;
    from day to night you bring me to
        an end. *y*

14 Like a swallow or a crane *y* I clamor,
    I moan like a dove.
My eyes are weary with looking upward.
    O Lord, I am oppressed; be my security!
15 But what can I say? For he has spoken
        to me,
    and he himself has done it.

All my sleep has fled *a*
    because of the bitterness of my soul.
16 O Lord, by these things people live,
    and in all these is the life of my spirit. *y*
Oh, restore me to health and make me
        live!
17 Surely it was for my welfare
    that I had great bitterness;
but you have held back *b* my life
    from the pit of destruction,
for you have cast all my sins
    behind your back.
18 For Shē′ōl cannot thank you,
    death cannot praise you;
those who go down to the Pit cannot hope
    for your faithfulness.
19 The living, the living, they thank you,
    as I do this day;
fathers make known to children
    your faithfulness.

20 The LORD will save me,
    and we will sing to stringed instruments *c*
all the days of our lives,
    at the house of the LORD.

21 Now Ī·sāi′ah had said, "Let them take a lump of figs, and apply it to the boil, so that he may recover." 22 Hez·e·kī′ah also had said, "What is the sign that I shall go up to the house of the LORD?"

---

y Meaning of Heb uncertain   *z* Cn: Meaning of Heb uncertain   *a* Cn Compare Syr: Heb *I will walk slowly all my years*   *b* Cn Compare Gk Vg: Heb *loved*   *c* Heb *my stringed instruments*

PREPARE THE WAY OF THE LORD, MAKE STRAIGHT IN THE DESERT A HIGHWAY FOR OUR GOD

40.3

Envoys from Babylon Welcomed
(2 Kings 20.12–19)

39 At that time King Mer'o•dach-bal'a•dan son of Bal'a•dan of Babylon sent envoys with letters and a present to Hez•e•kī'ah, for he heard that he had been sick and had recovered. 2 Hez•e•kī'ah welcomed them; he showed them his treasure house, the silver, the gold, the spices, the precious oil, his whole armory, all that was found in his storehouses. There was nothing in his house or in all his realm that Hez•e•kī'ah did not show them. 3 Then the prophet Ī•sāi'ah came to King Hez•e•kī'ah and said to him, "What did these men say? From where did they come to you?" Hez•e•kī'ah answered, "They have come to me from a far country, from Babylon." 4 He said, "What have they seen in your house?" Hez•e•kī'ah answered, "They have seen all that is in my house; there is nothing in my storehouses that I did not show them."

5 Then Ī•sāi'ah said to Hez•e•kī'ah, "Hear the word of the LORD of hosts: 6 Days are coming when all that is in your house, and that which your ancestors have stored up until this day, shall be carried to Babylon; nothing shall be left, says the LORD. 7 Some of your own sons who are born to you shall be taken away; they shall be eunuchs in the palace of the king of Babylon." 8 Then Hez•e•kī'ah said to Ī•sāi'ah, "The word of the LORD that you have spoken is good." For he thought, "There will be peace and security in my days."

God's People Are Comforted
(Cp Lk 3.4–6)

40 Comfort, O comfort my people,
   says your God.
2 Speak tenderly to Jerusalem,
   and cry to her
that she has served her term,
   that her penalty is paid,
that she has received from the LORD's hand
   double for all her sins.

3 A voice cries out:
"In the wilderness prepare the way of the
      LORD,
   make straight in the desert a highway for
      our God.
4 Every valley shall be lifted up,
   and every mountain and hill be
      made low;
the uneven ground shall become level,
   and the rough places a plain.
5 Then the glory of the LORD shall be revealed,
   and all people shall see it together,
for the mouth of the LORD has spoken."

6 A voice says, "Cry out!"
   And I said, "What shall I cry?"
All people are grass,
   their constancy is like the flower of the
      field.
7 The grass withers, the flower fades,
   when the breath of the LORD blows
      upon it;
   surely the people are grass.

PRAY IT?
The Hope of Second Isaiah

Second Isaiah prophesies to the Israelites living in exile in Babylon with words full of love and hope: "Comfort, O comfort my people, / says your God" (Isa 40.1). Isaiah promises these Israelites a new liberation and the eventual restoration of Jerusalem and the Temple (44.26–28).

   The author of the Gospel of Luke uses Isa 40.3–5 to describe the ministry of John the Baptist in announcing Jesus' arrival (Lk 3.4–6). This writer wants to make it clear that Isaiah's promises are answered by the coming of Jesus.

   In your prayer, reflect or journal on the following questions:
■ Is there hope for our society?
■ What are some things that you are hopeful for?
■ Imagine God is speaking words of hope to you. What is God saying?

▶ Isa 40.1–5

8 The grass withers, the flower fades;
   but the word of our God will stand forever.
9 Get you up to a high mountain,
   O Zion, herald of good tidings;*d*
lift up your voice with strength,
   O Jerusalem, herald of good tidings,*e*
   lift it up, do not fear;
say to the cities of Judah,
   "Here is your God!"

---

d Or O herald of good tidings to Zion   *e* Or O herald of good tidings to Jerusalem

Between a Rock and a Soft Place

Joe. Is God a rock or a pillow?

Valerie. A rock, I guess. God is strong and reliable. When I think of a rock, I think of something I can brace myself against when things are changing all around me.

Joe. For me, God is a pillow. God is someone I can come home to and be comfortable with. I can sit back and relax, leaning against God and feeling at ease.

Valerie. But a pillow is so ordinary and doesn't have any character. A rock is distinctive and doesn't change.

Joe. But a rock is so hard and unyielding. What kind of compassion can you get from a rock?

Valerie. What kind of strength can you draw from a pillow?

Joe. The strength that comes from relaxing and resting and being comforted. The strength that comes from being energized to go forward again.

Valerie. I'm sorry, but a pillow seems too soft to be like God.

Joe. And a rock seems much too hard.

Valerie. Isn't God both a pillow and a rock? In chapter 40 of Isaiah, it seems that the pillow image wins out. The picture of a comforting God gathering the lambs conveys a softness that is sometimes hard to find in the Old Testament.

Joe. That's true. There are times when we need a pillow to get comfortable. It is good to know that God is there waiting for us, helping us to feel at home.

Valerie. And it is also good to know that God the rock is there for the times when we need something to hold on to (see Ps 18.2).

▸ Isa 40.1–11

10 See, the Lord GOD comes with might,
  and his arm rules for him;
his reward is with him,
  and his recompense before him.
11 He will feed his flock like a shepherd;
  he will gather the lambs in his arms,
and carry them in his bosom,
  and gently lead the mother sheep.

12 Who has measured the waters in the hollow
    of his hand
  and marked off the heavens with a span,
enclosed the dust of the earth in a measure,
  and weighed the mountains in scales
    and the hills in a balance?
13 Who has directed the spirit of the LORD,
  or as his counselor has instructed him?
14 Whom did he consult for his
    enlightenment,
  and who taught him the path of justice?
Who taught him knowledge,
  and showed him the way of
    understanding?
15 Even the nations are like a drop from a
    bucket,
  and are accounted as dust on the
    scales;

see, he takes up the isles like fine dust.
16 Lebanon would not provide fuel enough,
  nor are its animals enough for a burnt
    offering.
17 All the nations are as nothing before
    him;
  they are accounted by him as less than
    nothing and emptiness.

18 To whom then will you liken God,
  or what likeness compare with him?
19 An idol? —A workman casts it,
  and a goldsmith overlays it with gold,
  and casts for it silver chains.
20 As a gift one chooses mulberry wood f
  —wood that will not rot—
then seeks out a skilled artisan
  to set up an image that will not
    topple.

21 Have you not known? Have you not heard?
  Has it not been told you from the
    beginning?
  Have you not understood from the
    foundations of the earth?

f Meaning of Heb uncertain

22 It is he who sits above the circle of the
       earth,
   and its inhabitants are like grasshoppers;
who stretches out the heavens like a curtain,
   and spreads them like a tent to live in;
23 who brings princes to naught,
   and makes the rulers of the earth as
       nothing.

▶ ➤ ➤ ➤ ➤ ➤ ➤ ➤ ➤ ➤ ➤

NATIVE AMERICAN

The Tent and the Circle

Isaiah 40.22–23 has significance in Native American spirituality for several reasons. First, the circle (verse 22) is a symbol of unity and healing. In silhouette, the sun, the moon, and the earth are all circles. The poles of a teepee are arranged in a circle, and the tee-pees of a village are placed in a circle. The people of a nation are called the hoop or the circle, and sit in a circle for the sweat lodge ceremony (see "You Will Be Cleansed," Ezek 36.25–26) and to smoke from the sacred pipe.

Second, the tent (verse 22) is a symbol of home and family for a people that traditionally dwelled in tents.

Third, the Great Spirit is well described as the one "who sits above the circle" (verse 22).

Last, the insight that God, the Great Spirit, cares very little about the status of princes and rulers (verse 23) is powerful to a people that is oppressed, treated violently, scattered, and despised in its homeland. Native Americans have been subjected to such treatment by the explorers, then the colonists, then the pioneers, and now many citizens of the United States.

Pray for the circle of humanity—that we learn to celebrate the diversity of our cultures and cease oppression of any form.

▶ Isa 40.22–23

24 Scarcely are they planted, scarcely sown,
       scarcely has their stem taken root in the
           earth,
   when he blows upon them, and they wither,
       and the tempest carries them off like
           stubble.

25 To whom then will you compare me,
       or who is my equal? says the Holy One.
26 Lift up your eyes on high and see:
       Who created these?
   He who brings out their host and numbers
           them,
       calling them all by name;
   because he is great in strength,
       mighty in power,
       not one is missing.

27 Why do you say, O Jacob,
       and speak, O Israel,
   "My way is hidden from the LORD,
       and my right is disregarded by my God"?
28 Have you not known? Have you not heard?
   The LORD is the everlasting God,
       the Creator of the ends of the earth.
   He does not faint or grow weary;
       his understanding is unsearchable.
29 He gives power to the faint,
       and strengthens the powerless.
30 Even youths will faint and be weary,
       and the young will fall exhausted;
31 but those who wait for the LORD shall renew
           their strength,
       they shall mount up with wings like
           eagles,
   they shall run and not be weary,
       they shall walk and not faint.

Israel Assured of God's Help

Listen to me in silence, O coastlands;
   let the peoples renew their strength;
let them approach, then let them speak;
   let us together draw near for judgment.

2 Who has roused a victor from the east,
       summoned him to his service?
   He delivers up nations to him,
       and tramples kings under foot;
   he makes them like dust with his sword,
       like driven stubble with his bow.
3 He pursues them and passes on safely,
       scarcely touching the path with his feet.
4 Who has performed and done this,
       calling the generations from the
           beginning?
   I, the LORD, am first,
       and will be with the last.

⁵ The coastlands have seen and are afraid,
the ends of the earth tremble;
they have drawn near and come.
⁶ Each one helps the other,
saying to one another, "Take courage!"
⁷ The artisan encourages the goldsmith,
and the one who smooths with the
hammer encourages the one who
strikes the anvil,
saying of the soldering, "It is good";
and they fasten it with nails so that it
cannot be moved.
⁸ But you, Israel, my servant,
Jacob, whom I have chosen,
the offspring of Abraham, my friend;
⁹ you whom I took from the ends of the
earth,
and called from its farthest corners,
saying to you, "You are my servant,
I have chosen you and not cast you off";
¹⁰ do not fear, for I am with you,
do not be afraid, for I am your God;
I will strengthen you, I will help you,
I will uphold you with my victorious
right hand.

¹¹ Yes, all who are incensed against you
shall be ashamed and disgraced;
those who strive against you
shall be as nothing and shall perish.
¹² You shall seek those who contend with you,
but you shall not find them;
those who war against you
shall be as nothing at all.
¹³ For I, the LORD your God,
hold your right hand;
it is I who say to you, "Do not fear,
I will help you."

¹⁴ Do not fear, you worm Jacob,
you insect[g] Israel!
I will help you, says the LORD;
your Redeemer is the Holy One of Israel.
¹⁵ Now, I will make of you a threshing sledge,
sharp, new, and having teeth;
you shall thresh the mountains and crush
them,
and you shall make the hills like chaff.
¹⁶ You shall winnow them and the wind shall
carry them away,
and the tempest shall scatter them.
Then you shall rejoice in the LORD;
in the Holy One of Israel you shall glory.

¹⁷ When the poor and needy seek water,
and there is none,
and their tongue is parched with thirst,

I the LORD will answer them,
I the God of Israel will not forsake them.
¹⁸ I will open rivers on the bare heights,[h]
and fountains in the midst of the valleys;
I will make the wilderness a pool of water,
and the dry land springs of water.
¹⁹ I will put in the wilderness the cedar,
the acacia, the myrtle, and the olive;
I will set in the desert the cypress,
the plane and the pine together,
²⁰ so that all may see and know,
all may consider and understand,
that the hand of the LORD has done this,
the Holy One of Israel has created it.

The Futility of Idols

²¹ Set forth your case, says the LORD;
bring your proofs, says the King of Jacob.
²² Let them bring them, and tell us
what is to happen.
Tell us the former things, what they are,
so that we may consider them,
and that we may know their outcome;
or declare to us the things to come.
²³ Tell us what is to come hereafter,
that we may know that you are gods;
do good, or do harm,
that we may be afraid and terrified.
²⁴ You, indeed, are nothing
and your work is nothing at all;
whoever chooses you is an abomination.

²⁵ I stirred up one from the north, and he has
come,
from the rising of the sun he was
summoned by name.[i]
He shall trample[j] on rulers as on mortar,
as the potter treads clay.
²⁶ Who declared it from the beginning, so that
we might know,
and beforehand, so that we might say,
"He is right"?
There was no one who declared it, none
who proclaimed,
none who heard your words.
²⁷ I first have declared it to Zion,[k]
and I give to Jerusalem a herald of good
tidings.
²⁸ But when I look there is no one;
among these there is no counselor
who, when I ask, gives an answer.

---

g Syr: Heb *men of*   h Or *trails*   i Cn Compare Q Ms Gk:
MT *and he shall call on my name*   j Cn: Heb *come*
k Cn: Heb *First to Zion—Behold, behold them*

29 No, they are all a delusion;
>> their works are nothing;
>> their images are empty wind.

The Servant, a Light to the Nations

Here is my servant, whom I uphold,
>> my chosen, in whom my soul delights;
I have put my spirit upon him;
>> he will bring forth justice to the nations.
2 He will not cry or lift up his voice,
>> or make it heard in the street;

5 Thus says God, the LORD,
>> who created the heavens and stretched
>>> them out,
>> who spread out the earth and what
>>> comes from it,
who gives breath to the people upon it
>> and spirit to those who walk in it:
6 I am the LORD, I have called you in
>>> righteousness,
>> I have taken you by the hand and
>>> kept you;
I have given you as a covenant to the
>>> people,*l*
>> a light to the nations,
7 to open the eyes that are blind,
to bring out the prisoners from the
>>> dungeon,
>> from the prison those who sit in
>>> darkness.

did you KNOW?

The Servant Songs

Second Isaiah's four songs of the servant (Isa 42.1–7; 49.1–6; 50.4–9; 52.13—53.12) have had an important place in Christian theology and worship. They portray the qualities of the ideal servant leader. Through these songs, the prophet speaks of hope: the faithful Israelites, though in exile, are still God's servants (42.1), chosen from the womb (49.1). Through their courageous suffering (50.7–8), Israel will be restored to bring salvation to all nations (53.5).

It is not surprising that the early Christians saw in the servant songs a remarkable similarity to Jesus' words and actions. The fourth song in particular—which talks of a suffering servant—helped the followers of Jesus understand his suffering and humiliating death on the cross. Because of this, these passages have become part of the Catholic church's formal worship during Holy Week (the week before Easter): Isaiah 42.1–7 on Monday, 49.1–6 on Tuesday, 50.4–9 on Wednesday, and 52.13—53.12 on Friday.

▶ Isa 42.1–7

PRAY IT?

The Servant's Mission

Read Isa 42.1–7 and then reflect or journal on the following questions:
- What is the servant's mission from God?
- How does Jesus fulfill this mission (compare Isa 42.6–7 with Lk 4.18)?
- How do you participate in this mission?

▶ Isa 42.1–7

8 I am the LORD, that is my name;
>> my glory I give to no other,
>> nor my praise to idols.
9 See, the former things have come to pass,
>> and new things I now declare;
before they spring forth,
>> I tell you of them.

A Hymn of Praise

10 Sing to the LORD a new song,
>> his praise from the end of the earth!
Let the sea roar*m* and all that fills it,
>> the coastlands and their inhabitants.
11 Let the desert and its towns lift up their
>>> voice,
>> the villages that Kē′dar inhabits;

3 a bruised reed he will not break,
>> and a dimly burning wick he will not
>>> quench;
>> he will faithfully bring forth justice.
4 He will not grow faint or be crushed
>> until he has established justice in the earth;
>> and the coastlands wait for his teaching.

---

l Meaning of Heb uncertain   *m* Cn Compare Ps 96.11; 98.7: Heb *Those who go down to the sea*

ISA

let the inhabitants of Sē'la sing for joy,
    let them shout from the tops of the
        mountains.
12 Let them give glory to the LORD,
    and declare his praise in the coastlands.
13 The LORD goes forth like a soldier,
    like a warrior he stirs up his fury;
he cries out, he shouts aloud,
    he shows himself mighty against his foes.

14 For a long time I have held my peace,
    I have kept still and restrained myself;
now I will cry out like a woman in labor,
    I will gasp and pant.
15 I will lay waste mountains and hills,
    and dry up all their herbage;
I will turn the rivers into islands,
    and dry up the pools.
16 I will lead the blind
    by a road they do not know,
by paths they have not known
    I will guide them.
I will turn the darkness before them into
        light,
    the rough places into level ground.
These are the things I will do,
    and I will not forsake them.
17 They shall be turned back and utterly put to
        shame—
    those who trust in carved images,
who say to cast images,
    "You are our gods."

18 Listen, you that are deaf;
    and you that are blind, look up and see!
19 Who is blind but my servant,
    or deaf like my messenger whom I send?
Who is blind like my dedicated one,
    or blind like the servant of the LORD?
20 He sees many things, but does[n] not observe
        them;
    his ears are open, but he does not hear.

Israel's Disobedience

21 The LORD was pleased, for the sake of his
        righteousness,
    to magnify his teaching and make it
        glorious.
22 But this is a people robbed and plundered,
    all of them are trapped in holes
    and hidden in prisons;
they have become a prey with no one to
        rescue,
    a spoil with no one to say, "Restore!"
23 Who among you will give heed to this,
    who will attend and listen for the time to
        come?

24 Who gave up Jacob to the spoiler,
    and Israel to the robbers?
Was it not the LORD, against whom we have
        sinned,
    in whose ways they would not walk,
    and whose law they would not obey?
25 So he poured upon him the heat of his
        anger
    and the fury of war;
it set him on fire all around, but he did not
        understand;
    it burned him, but he did not take it to
        heart.

Restoration and Protection Promised

But now thus says the LORD,
    he who created you, O Jacob,
    he who formed you, O Israel:
Do not fear, for I have redeemed you;
    I have called you by name, you are mine.

PRAY IT!
Be Not Afraid

The words of Isa 43.1–5 might sound
familiar to you. Most of the song "Be
Not Afraid" is based on these verses.
    God calls us to be disciples and lead-
ers. God calls us from within our faith
community, to serve others. How easy is
it for you to go forth and do God's work?
How easy is it to be not afraid?

Be not afraid.
I go before you always.
Come follow Me,
and I will give you rest.
    (From Bob Dufford, "Be Not Afraid")

▶ Isa 43.1–5

2 When you pass through the waters, I will be
        with you;
    and through the rivers, they shall not
        overwhelm you;
when you walk through fire you shall not
        be burned,
    and the flame shall not consume you.
3 For I am the LORD your God,
    the Holy One of Israel, your Savior.
I give Egypt as your ransom,

_____

n Heb *You see many things but do*

Ethiopia[o] and Sē'ba in exchange for you.
4 Because you are precious in my sight,
    and honored, and I love you,
I give people in return for you,
    nations in exchange for your life.
5 Do not fear, for I am with you;
    I will bring your offspring from the east,
    and from the west I will gather you;
6 I will say to the north, "Give them up,"
    and to the south, "Do not withhold;
bring my sons from far away
    and my daughters from the end of the
        earth—
7 everyone who is called by my name,
    whom I created for my glory,
    whom I formed and made."

8 Bring forth the people who are blind, yet
        have eyes,
    who are deaf, yet have ears!
9 Let all the nations gather together,
    and let the peoples assemble.
Who among them declared this,
    and foretold to us the former things?
Let them bring their witnesses to justify
        them,
    and let them hear and say, "It is true."
10 You are my witnesses, says the LORD,
    and my servant whom I have chosen,
so that you may know and believe me
    and understand that I am he.
Before me no god was formed,
    nor shall there be any after me.
11 I, I am the LORD,
    and besides me there is no savior.
12 I declared and saved and proclaimed,
    when there was no strange god
        among you;
    and you are my witnesses, says the LORD.
13 I am God, and also henceforth I am He;
    there is no one who can deliver from my
        hand;
    I work and who can hinder it?

14 Thus says the LORD,
    your Redeemer, the Holy One of Israel:
For your sake I will send to Babylon
    and break down all the bars,
    and the shouting of the Chal·dē'ans will
        be turned to lamentation. [p]
15 I am the LORD, your Holy One,
    the Creator of Israel, your King.
16 Thus says the LORD,
    who makes a way in the sea,
    a path in the mighty waters,
17 who brings out chariot and horse,
    army and warrior;

they lie down, they cannot rise,
    they are extinguished, quenched like a
        wick:
18 Do not remember the former things,
    or consider the things of old.
19 I am about to do a new thing;
    now it springs forth, do you not
        perceive it?
I will make a way in the wilderness
    and rivers in the desert.
20 The wild animals will honor me,
    the jackals and the ostriches;
for I give water in the wilderness,
    rivers in the desert,
to give drink to my chosen people,
21   the people whom I formed for myself
so that they might declare my praise.

22 Yet you did not call upon me, O Jacob;
    but you have been weary of me, O Israel!
23 You have not brought me your sheep for
        burnt offerings,
    or honored me with your sacrifices.
I have not burdened you with offerings,
    or wearied you with frankincense.
24 You have not bought me sweet cane with
        money,
    or satisfied me with the fat of your
        sacrifices.
But you have burdened me with your sins;
    you have wearied me with your
        iniquities.

25 I, I am He
    who blots out your transgressions for my
        own sake,
    and I will not remember your sins.
26 Accuse me, let us go to trial;
    set forth your case, so that you may be
        proved right.
27 Your first ancestor sinned,
    and your interpreters transgressed
        against me.
28 Therefore I profaned the princes of the
        sanctuary,
    I delivered Jacob to utter destruction,
    and Israel to reviling.

God's Blessing on Israel

But now hear, O Jacob my servant,
    Israel whom I have chosen!
2 Thus says the LORD who made you,
    who formed you in the womb and will
        help you:
Do not fear, O Jacob my servant,

---

o Or *Nubia;* Heb *Cush*   *p* Meaning of Heb uncertain

Jesh'ū•run whom I have chosen.
3 For I will pour water on the thirsty land,
and streams on the dry ground;
I will pour my spirit upon your
descendants,
and my blessing on your offspring.
4 They shall spring up like a green tamarisk,
like willows by flowing streams.
5 This one will say, "I am the LORD's,"
another will be called by the name of
Jacob,
yet another will write on the hand, "The
LORD's,"
and adopt the name of Israel.

6 Thus says the LORD, the King of Israel,
and his Redeemer, the LORD of hosts:
I am the first and I am the last;
besides me there is no god.
7 Who is like me? Let them proclaim it,
let them declare and set it forth
before me.
Who has announced from of old the things
to come?[q]
Let them tell us[r] what is yet to be.
8 Do not fear, or be afraid;
have I not told you from of old and
declared it?
You are my witnesses!
Is there any god besides me?
There is no other rock; I know not one.

The Absurdity of Idol Worship

9 All who make idols are nothing, and the
things they delight in do not profit; their witnesses
neither see nor know. And so they will be put to
shame. 10 Who would fashion a god or cast an image that can do no good? 11 Look, all its devotees
shall be put to shame; the artisans too are merely
human. Let them all assemble, let them stand up;
they shall be terrified, they shall all be put to
shame.

12 The ironsmith fashions it[s] and works it
over the coals, shaping it with hammers, and forging it with his strong arm; he becomes hungry and
his strength fails, he drinks no water and is faint.
13 The carpenter stretches a line, marks it out with
a stylus, fashions it with planes, and marks it with
a compass; he makes it in human form, with human beauty, to be set up in a shrine. 14 He cuts
down cedars or chooses a holm tree or an oak and
lets it grow strong among the trees of the forest.
He plants a cedar and the rain nourishes it. 15 Then
it can be used as fuel. Part of it he takes and warms
himself; he kindles a fire and bakes bread. Then he
makes a god and worships it, makes it a carved
image and bows down before it. 16 Half of it he
burns in the fire; over this half he roasts meat, eats
it and is satisfied. He also warms himself and says,
"Ah, I am warm, I can feel the fire!" 17 The rest of it
he makes into a god, his idol, bows down to it and
worships it; he prays to it and says, "Save me, for
you are my god!"

18 They do not know, nor do they comprehend; for their eyes are shut, so that they cannot
see, and their minds as well, so that they cannot
understand. 19 No one considers, nor is there
knowledge or discernment to say, "Half of it I
burned in the fire; I also baked bread on its coals,
I roasted meat and have eaten. Now shall I make
the rest of it an abomination? Shall I fall down
before a block of wood?" 20 He feeds on ashes; a
deluded mind has led him astray, and he cannot
save himself or say, "Is not this thing in my right
hand a fraud?"

Israel Is Not Forgotten

21 Remember these things, O Jacob,
and Israel, for you are my servant;
I formed you, you are my servant;
O Israel, you will not be forgotten by me.
22 I have swept away your transgressions like a
cloud,
and your sins like mist;
return to me, for I have redeemed you.

23 Sing, O heavens, for the LORD has done it;
shout, O depths of the earth;
break forth into singing, O mountains,
O forest, and every tree in it!
For the LORD has redeemed Jacob,
and will be glorified in Israel.

24 Thus says the LORD, your Redeemer,
who formed you in the womb:
I am the LORD, who made all things,
who alone stretched out the heavens,
who by myself spread out the earth;
25 who frustrates the omens of liars,
and makes fools of diviners;
who turns back the wise,
and makes their knowledge foolish;
26 who confirms the word of his servant,
and fulfills the prediction of his
messengers;
who says of Jerusalem, "It shall be
inhabited,"
and of the cities of Judah, "They shall be
rebuilt,
and I will raise up their ruins";

---

[q] Cn: Heb *from my placing an eternal people and things to come* [r] Tg: Heb *them* [s] Cn: Heb *an ax*

27 who says to the deep, "Be dry—
  I will dry up your rivers";
28 who says of Cyrus, "He is my shepherd,
  and he shall carry out all my purpose";
and who says of Jerusalem, "It shall be
    rebuilt,"
  and of the temple, "Your foundation
    shall be laid."

Cyrus, God's Instrument

Thus says the LORD to his anointed, to
    Cyrus,
  whose right hand I have grasped
to subdue nations before him
  and strip kings of their robes,
to open doors before him—
  and the gates shall not be closed:
2 I will go before you
  and level the mountains,[t]
I will break in pieces the doors of bronze
  and cut through the bars of iron,
3 I will give you the treasures of darkness
  and riches hidden in secret places,
so that you may know that it is I, the LORD,
  the God of Israel, who call you by your
    name.
4 For the sake of my servant Jacob,
  and Israel my chosen,
I call you by your name,
  I surname you, though you do not
    know me.
5 I am the LORD, and there is no other;
  besides me there is no god.
I arm you, though you do not know me,
6 so that they may know, from the rising of
    the sun
  and from the west, that there is no one
    besides me;
I am the LORD, and there is no other.
7 I form light and create darkness,
  I make weal and create woe;
I the LORD do all these things.

8 Shower, O heavens, from above,
  and let the skies rain down righteousness;
let the earth open, that salvation may
    spring up,[u]
  and let it cause righteousness to sprout
    up also;
I the LORD have created it.

9 Woe to you who strive with your Maker,
  earthen vessels with the potter![v]
Does the clay say to the one who fashions
  it, "What are you making"?
  or "Your work has no handles"?

10 Woe to anyone who says to a father, "What
    are you begetting?"
  or to a woman, "With what are you in
    labor?"
11 Thus says the LORD,
  the Holy One of Israel, and its Maker:
Will you question me[w] about my children,
  or command me concerning the work of
    my hands?
12 I made the earth,
  and created humankind upon it;
it was my hands that stretched out the
    heavens,
  and I commanded all their host.
13 I have aroused Cyrus[x] in righteousness,
  and I will make all his paths straight;
he shall build my city
  and set my exiles free,
not for price or reward,
  says the LORD of hosts.
14 Thus says the LORD:
The wealth of Egypt and the merchandise of
    Ethiopia,[y]
  and the Sa·bē′ans, tall of stature,
shall come over to you and be yours,
  they shall follow you;
  they shall come over in chains and bow
    down to you.
They will make supplication to you, saying,
  "God is with you alone, and there is no
    other;
  there is no god besides him."
15 Truly, you are a God who hides himself,
  O God of Israel, the Savior.
16 All of them are put to shame and
    confounded,
  the makers of idols go in confusion
    together.
17 But Israel is saved by the LORD
  with everlasting salvation;
you shall not be put to shame or
    confounded
  to all eternity.

18 For thus says the LORD,
  who created the heavens
    (he is God!),
  who formed the earth and made it
    (he established it;
  he did not create it a chaos,
    he formed it to be inhabited!):
I am the LORD, and there is no other.

---

t Q Ms Gk: MT *the swellings*   u Q Ms: MT *that they may
bring forth salvation*   v Cn: Heb *with the potsherds,* or *with
the potters*   w Cn: Heb *Ask me of things to come*
x Heb *him*   y Or *Nubia;* Heb *Cush*

19 I did not speak in secret,
  in a land of darkness;
I did not say to the offspring of Jacob,
  "Seek me in chaos."
I the LORD speak the truth,
  I declare what is right.

Idols Cannot Save Babylon

20 Assemble yourselves and come together,
  draw near, you survivors of the nations!
They have no knowledge—
  those who carry about their wooden
    idols,
and keep on praying to a god
  that cannot save.
21 Declare and present your case;
  let them take counsel together!
Who told this long ago?
  Who declared it of old?
Was it not I, the LORD?
  There is no other god besides me,
a righteous God and a Savior;
  there is no one besides me.

22 Turn to me and be saved,
  all the ends of the earth!
For I am God, and there is no other.
23 By myself I have sworn,
  from my mouth has gone forth in
    righteousness
  a word that shall not return:
"To me every knee shall bow,
  every tongue shall swear."

24 Only in the LORD, it shall be said of me,
  are righteousness and strength;
all who were incensed against him
  shall come to him and be ashamed.
25 In the LORD all the offspring of Israel
  shall triumph and glory.

Bel bows down, Nebo stoops,
  their idols are on beasts and cattle;
these things you carry are loaded
  as burdens on weary animals.
2 They stoop, they bow down together;
  they cannot save the burden,
  but themselves go into captivity.

3 Listen to me, O house of Jacob,
  all the remnant of the house of Israel,
who have been borne by me from your
    birth,
  carried from the womb;
4 even to your old age I am he,
  even when you turn gray I will carry you.
I have made, and I will bear;
  I will carry and will save.

5 To whom will you liken me and make me
    equal,
  and compare me, as though we were
    alike?
6 Those who lavish gold from the purse,
  and weigh out silver in the scales—
they hire a goldsmith, who makes it into
    a god;
  then they fall down and worship!
7 They lift it to their shoulders, they carry it,
  they set it in its place, and it stands there;
  it cannot move from its place.
If one cries out to it, it does not answer
  or save anyone from trouble.

8 Remember this and consider,z
  recall it to mind, you transgressors,
9   remember the former things of old;
for I am God, and there is no other;
  I am God, and there is no one like me,
10 declaring the end from the beginning
  and from ancient times things not yet
    done,
saying, "My purpose shall stand,
  and I will fulfill my intention,"
11 calling a bird of prey from the east,
  the man for my purpose from a far
    country.
I have spoken, and I will bring it to pass;
  I have planned, and I will do it.

12 Listen to me, you stubborn of heart,
  you who are far from deliverance:
13 I bring near my deliverance, it is not far off,
  and my salvation will not tarry;
I will put salvation in Zion,
  for Israel my glory.

The Humiliation of Babylon

Come down and sit in the dust,
  virgin daughter Babylon!
Sit on the ground without a throne,
  daughter Chal·de′a!
For you shall no more be called
  tender and delicate.
2 Take the millstones and grind meal,
  remove your veil,
strip off your robe, uncover your legs,
  pass through the rivers.
3 Your nakedness shall be uncovered,
  and your shame shall be seen.
I will take vengeance,
  and I will spare no one.

---

z Meaning of Heb uncertain

4 Our Redeemer—the LORD of hosts is his
        name—
     is the Holy One of Israel.

5 Sit in silence, and go into darkness,
        daughter Chal·dě'a!
   For you shall no more be called
        the mistress of kingdoms.
6 I was angry with my people,
        I profaned my heritage;
   I gave them into your hand,
        you showed them no mercy;
   on the aged you made your yoke
        exceedingly heavy.
7 You said, "I shall be mistress forever,"
        so that you did not lay these things to
            heart
        or remember their end.

8 Now therefore hear this, you lover of
            pleasures,
        who sit securely,
   who say in your heart,
        "I am, and there is no one besides me;
   I shall not sit as a widow
        or know the loss of children"—
9 both these things shall come upon you
        in a moment, in one day:
   the loss of children and widowhood
        shall come upon you in full measure,
   in spite of your many sorceries
        and the great power of your
            enchantments.

10 You felt secure in your wickedness;
        you said, "No one sees me."
   Your wisdom and your knowledge
        led you astray,
   and you said in your heart,
        "I am, and there is no one besides me."
11 But evil shall come upon you,
        which you cannot charm away;
   disaster shall fall upon you,
        which you will not be able to ward off;
   and ruin shall come on you suddenly,
        of which you know nothing.

12 Stand fast in your enchantments
        and your many sorceries,
        with which you have labored from your
            youth;
   perhaps you may be able to succeed,
        perhaps you may inspire terror.
13 You are wearied with your many
            consultations;
        let those who study[a] the heavens
   stand up and save you,
        those who gaze at the stars,

and at each new moon predict
        what[b] shall befall you.

14 See, they are like stubble,
        the fire consumes them;
   they cannot deliver themselves
        from the power of the flame.
   No coal for warming oneself is this,
        no fire to sit before!
15 Such to you are those with whom you have
            labored,
        who have trafficked with you from your
            youth;
   they all wander about in their own paths;
        there is no one to save you.

God the Creator and Redeemer

   Hear this, O house of Jacob,
        who are called by the name of Israel,
        and who came forth from the loins[c] of
            Judah;
   who swear by the name of the LORD,
        and invoke the God of Israel,
        but not in truth or right.
2 For they call themselves after the holy city,
        and lean on the God of Israel;
        the LORD of hosts is his name.

3 The former things I declared long ago,
        they went out from my mouth and I
            made them known;
        then suddenly I did them and they came
            to pass.
4 Because I know that you are obstinate,
        and your neck is an iron sinew
        and your forehead brass,
5 I declared them to you from long ago,
        before they came to pass I announced
            them to you,
   so that you would not say, "My idol did
            them,
        my carved image and my cast image
            commanded them."

6 You have heard; now see all this;
        and will you not declare it?
   From this time forward I make you hear
            new things,
        hidden things that you have not known.
7 They are created now, not long ago;
        before today you have never heard of
            them,
        so that you could not say, "I already
            knew them."

---

a Meaning of Heb uncertain   *b* Gk Syr Compare Vg: Heb
from what   *c* Cn: Heb *waters*

ISA

8 You have never heard, you have never
    known,
        from of old your ear has not been
            opened.
    For I knew that you would deal very
        treacherously,
        and that from birth you were called a
            rebel.

9 For my name's sake I defer my anger,
    for the sake of my praise I restrain it
        for you,
    so that I may not cut you off.
10 See, I have refined you, but not like[d] silver;
    I have tested you in the furnace of
        adversity.
11 For my own sake, for my own sake, I do it,
    for why should my name[e] be profaned?
    My glory I will not give to another.

12 Listen to me, O Jacob,
    and Israel, whom I called:
    I am He; I am the first,
    and I am the last.
13 My hand laid the foundation of the earth,
    and my right hand spread out
        the heavens;
    when I summon them,
        they stand at attention.

14 Assemble, all of you, and hear!
    Who among them has declared these
        things?
    The LORD loves him;
        he shall perform his purpose on Babylon,
        and his arm shall be against the
            Chal·de'ans.
15 I, even I, have spoken and called him,
    I have brought him, and he will prosper
        in his way.
16 Draw near to me, hear this!
    From the beginning I have not spoken in
        secret,
    from the time it came to be I have been
        there.
    And now the Lord GOD has sent me and his
        spirit.

17 Thus says the LORD,
    your Redeemer, the Holy One of Israel:
    I am the LORD your God,
        who teaches you for your own good,
        who leads you in the way you should go.
18 O that you had paid attention to my
        commandments!
    Then your prosperity would have been
        like a river,

    and your success like the waves of
        the sea;
19 your offspring would have been like the
        sand,
        and your descendants like its grains;
    their name would never be cut off
        or destroyed from before me.

20 Go out from Babylon, flee from Chal·de'a,
    declare this with a shout of joy,
        proclaim it,
    send it forth to the end of the earth;
    say, "The LORD has redeemed his servant
        Jacob!"
21 They did not thirst when he led them
        through the deserts;
    he made water flow for them from the
        rock;
    he split open the rock and the water
        gushed out.

22 "There is no peace," says the LORD, "for the
        wicked."

PRAY IT!

The Servant's Success

Isaiah 49.1–6 is the second of the four servant songs (see "The Servant Songs," Isa 42.1–7). In this passage, the servant expresses a feeling of failure (49.4). But God responds that the servant will be a success, a "light to the nations" (verse 6). In your prayer, reflect or journal on a time when you felt you failed but something good happened anyway. How do you now see God's hand at work in the situation?

▶ Isa 49.1–6

The Servant's Mission
Listen to me, O coastlands,
    pay attention, you peoples from far away!
The LORD called me before I was born,
    while I was in my mother's womb he
        named me.
2 He made my mouth like a sharp sword,
    in the shadow of his hand he hid me;
    he made me a polished arrow,
    in his quiver he hid me away.

d Cn: Heb *with*   e Gk Old Latin: Heb *for why should it*

3 And he said to me, "You are my servant,
   Israel, in whom I will be glorified."
4 But I said, "I have labored in vain,
   I have spent my strength for nothing and
      vanity;
yet surely my cause is with the LORD,
   and my reward with my God."

5 And now the LORD says,
   who formed me in the womb to be his
      servant,
to bring Jacob back to him,
   and that Israel might be gathered to him,
for I am honored in the sight of the LORD,
   and my God has become my strength—
6 he says,
"It is too light a thing that you should be
      my servant
   to raise up the tribes of Jacob
   and to restore the survivors of Israel;
I will give you as a light to the nations,

to apportion the desolate heritages;
9 saying to the prisoners, "Come out,"
   to those who are in darkness, "Show
      yourselves."
They shall feed along the ways,
   on all the bare heights ^{g} shall be their
      pasture;
10 they shall not hunger or thirst,
   neither scorching wind nor sun shall
      strike them down,
for he who has pity on them will lead
      them,
   and by springs of water will guide them.
11 And I will turn all my mountains into a
      road,
   and my highways shall be raised up.
12 Lo, these shall come from far away,
   and lo, these from the north and from
      the west,
   and these from the land of Sȳ•ē'nē. ^{h}

I Will Never Forget You, My People

God is like a loving mother: forgiving, embracing, nurturing, tender, and gentle. The Hebrew root of the word *compassion* means "womb." A God of compassion and love is by definition a God of the womb, a God of motherly tenderness.
   Picture your mother figure: perhaps your birth mother, grandmother, adoptive mother, stepmother, or godmother. How do you see God's love reflected in her love?

▶ Isa 49.13–16

that my salvation may reach to the end
      of the earth."

7 Thus says the LORD,
   the Redeemer of Israel and his Holy One,
to one deeply despised, abhorred by the
      nations,
   the slave of rulers,
"Kings shall see and stand up,
   princes, and they shall prostrate themselves,
because of the LORD, who is faithful,
   the Holy One of Israel, who has
      chosen you."

Zion's Children to Be Brought Home

8 Thus says the LORD:
In a time of favor I have answered you,
   on a day of salvation I have helped you;
I have kept you and given you
   as a covenant to the people, ^{f}
to establish the land,

13 Sing for joy, O heavens, and exult, O earth;
   break forth, O mountains, into singing!
For the LORD has comforted his people,
   and will have compassion on his
      suffering ones.

14 But Zion said, "The LORD has forsaken me,
   my Lord has forgotten me."
15 Can a woman forget her nursing child,
   or show no compassion for the child of
      her womb?
Even these may forget,
   yet I will not forget you.
16 See, I have inscribed you on the palms of
      my hands;
   your walls are continually before me.
17 Your builders outdo your destroyers, ^{i}
   and those who laid you waste go away
      from you.

---

f Meaning of Heb uncertain g Or *the trails* h Q Ms:
MT *Sinim* i Or *Your children come swiftly; your destroyers*

ISA

18 Lift up your eyes all around and see;
  they all gather, they come to you.
As I live, says the LORD,
  you shall put all of them on like an
    ornament,
  and like a bride you shall bind them on.

19 Surely your waste and your desolate places
    and your devastated land—
  surely now you will be too crowded for
    your inhabitants,
  and those who swallowed you up will be
    far away.

20 The children born in the time of your
    bereavement
  will yet say in your hearing:
  "The place is too crowded for me;
  make room for me to settle."

21 Then you will say in your heart,
  "Who has borne me these?
  I was bereaved and barren,
    exiled and put away—
  so who has reared these?
  I was left all alone—
    where then have these come from?"

22 Thus says the Lord GOD:
  I will soon lift up my hand to the nations,
    and raise my signal to the peoples;
  and they shall bring your sons in their
    bosom,
    and your daughters shall be carried on
    their shoulders.

23 Kings shall be your foster fathers,
    and their queens your nursing mothers.
  With their faces to the ground they shall
    bow down to you,
    and lick the dust of your feet.
  Then you will know that I am the LORD;
    those who wait for me shall not be put
    to shame.

24 Can the prey be taken from the mighty,
  or the captives of a tyrant*j* be rescued?

25 But thus says the LORD:
  Even the captives of the mighty shall be
    taken,
    and the prey of the tyrant be rescued;
  for I will contend with those who contend
    with you,
    and I will save your children.

26 I will make your oppressors eat their own
    flesh,
    and they shall be drunk with their own
    blood as with wine.
  Then all flesh shall know
    that I am the LORD your Savior,

and your Redeemer, the Mighty One of
    Jacob.

Thus says the LORD:
Where is your mother's bill of divorce
  with which I put her away?
Or which of my creditors is it
  to whom I have sold you?
No, because of your sins you were sold,
  and for your transgressions your mother
    was put away.

2 Why was no one there when I came?
  Why did no one answer when I called?
Is my hand shortened, that it cannot
    redeem?
  Or have I no power to deliver?
By my rebuke I dry up the sea,
  I make the rivers a desert;
their fish stink for lack of water,
  and die of thirst.*k*

3 I clothe the heavens with blackness,
  and make sackcloth their covering.

PRAY IT?

The Servant's Strength

Isaiah 50.4–9 is the third of the four servant songs (see "The Servant Songs," Isa 42.1–7). Read the song twice. The first time, think of how it reflects Jesus' relationship with his heavenly Father. The second time, meditate on the verses that inspire you and give you strength to be a prophet to other young people.

▶ Isa 50.4–9

The Servant's Humiliation and Vindication

4 The Lord GOD has given me
    the tongue of a teacher,*l*
  that I may know how to sustain
    the weary with a word.
Morning by morning he wakens—
    wakens my ear
  to listen as those who are taught.

5 The Lord GOD has opened my ear,
    and I was not rebellious,
    I did not turn backward.

6 I gave my back to those who struck me,

---

j Q Ms Syr Vg: MT *of a righteous person*   *k* Or *die on the thirsty ground*   *l* Cn: Heb *of those who are taught*

and my cheeks to those who pulled out
the beard;
I did not hide my face
from insult and spitting.

7 The Lord GOD helps me;
therefore I have not been disgraced;
therefore I have set my face like flint,
and I know that I shall not be put to
shame;
8 he who vindicates me is near.
Who will contend with me?
Let us stand up together.
Who are my adversaries?
Let them confront me.
9 It is the Lord GOD who helps me;
who will declare me guilty?
All of them will wear out like a garment;
the moth will eat them up.

10 Who among you fears the LORD
and obeys the voice of his servant,
who walks in darkness
and has no light,
yet trusts in the name of the LORD
and relies upon his God?
11 But all of you are kindlers of fire,
lighters of firebrands.[m]
Walk in the flame of your fire,
and among the brands that you have
kindled!
This is what you shall have from my hand:
you shall lie down in torment.

Blessings in Store for God's People
(Cp Gen 12.1–3)

Listen to me, you that pursue righteousness,
you that seek the LORD.
Look to the rock from which you were
hewn,
and to the quarry from which
you were dug.
2 Look to Abraham your father
and to Sarah who bore you;
for he was but one when I called him,
but I blessed him and made him many.
3 For the LORD will comfort Zion;
he will comfort all her waste places,
and will make her wilderness like Eden,
her desert like the garden of the LORD;
joy and gladness will be found in her,
thanksgiving and the voice of song.

4 Listen to me, my people,
and give heed to me, my nation;
for a teaching will go out from me,
and my justice for a light to the peoples.

5 I will bring near my deliverance swiftly,
my salvation has gone out
and my arms will rule the peoples;
the coastlands wait for me,
and for my arm they hope.
6 Lift up your eyes to the heavens,
and look at the earth beneath;
for the heavens will vanish like smoke,
the earth will wear out like a garment,
and those who live on it will die like
gnats;[n]
but my salvation will be forever,
and my deliverance will never be ended.

7 Listen to me, you who know righteousness,
you people who have my teaching in
your hearts;
do not fear the reproach of others,
and do not be dismayed when they
revile you.
8 For the moth will eat them up like a
garment,
and the worm will eat them like wool;
but my deliverance will be forever,
and my salvation to all generations.

9 Awake, awake, put on strength,
O arm of the LORD!
Awake, as in days of old,
the generations of long ago!
Was it not you who cut Rahab in pieces,
who pierced the dragon?
10 Was it not you who dried up the sea,
the waters of the great deep;
who made the depths of the sea a way
for the redeemed to cross over?
11 So the ransomed of the LORD shall return,
and come to Zion with singing;
everlasting joy shall be upon their heads;
they shall obtain joy and gladness,
and sorrow and sighing shall flee away.

12 I, I am he who comforts you;
why then are you afraid of a mere mortal
who must die,
a human being who fades like grass?
13 You have forgotten the LORD, your Maker,
who stretched out the heavens
and laid the foundations of the earth.
You fear continually all day long
because of the fury of the oppressor,
who is bent on destruction.
But where is the fury of the oppressor?

---

m Syr: Heb *you gird yourselves with firebrands* n Or *in like manner*

ISA

14 The oppressed shall speedily be released;
  they shall not die and go down to
   the Pit,
  nor shall they lack bread.
15 For I am the LORD your God,
  who stirs up the sea so that its waves
   roar—
  the LORD of hosts is his name.
16 I have put my words in your mouth,
  and hidden you in the shadow of my
   hand,
 stretching out*o* the heavens
  and laying the foundations of the earth,
  and saying to Zion, "You are my people."

17 Rouse yourself, rouse yourself!
  Stand up, O Jerusalem,
 you who have drunk at the hand of the
   LORD
  the cup of his wrath,
 who have drunk to the dregs
  the bowl of staggering.
18 There is no one to guide her
  among all the children she has borne;
 there is no one to take her by the hand
  among all the children she has
   brought up.
19 These two things have befallen you
  —who will grieve with you?—
 devastation and destruction, famine and
   sword—
  who will comfort you?*p*
20 Your children have fainted,
  they lie at the head of every street
  like an antelope in a net;
 they are full of the wrath of the LORD,
  the rebuke of your God.

21 Therefore hear this, you who are
   wounded,*q*
  who are drunk, but not with wine:
22 Thus says your Sovereign, the LORD,
  your God who pleads the cause of his
   people:
 See, I have taken from your hand the cup of
   staggering;
 you shall drink no more
  from the bowl of my wrath.
23 And I will put it into the hand of your
   tormentors,
  who have said to you,
 "Bow down, that we may walk on you";
 and you have made your back like the
   ground
  and like the street for them to walk on.

Let Zion Rejoice

Awake, awake,
  put on your strength, O Zion!
Put on your beautiful garments,
  O Jerusalem, the holy city;
for the uncircumcised and the unclean
  shall enter you no more.
2 Shake yourself from the dust, rise up,
  O captive*r* Jerusalem;
loose the bonds from your neck,
  O captive daughter Zion!

3 For thus says the LORD: You were sold for nothing, and you shall be redeemed without money. 4 For thus says the Lord GOD: Long ago, my people went down into Egypt to reside there as aliens; the Assyrian, too, has oppressed them without cause. 5 Now therefore what am I doing here, says the LORD, seeing that my people are taken away without cause? Their rulers howl, says the LORD, and continually, all day long, my name is despised. 6 Therefore my people shall know my name; therefore in that day they shall know that it is I who speak; here am I.

7 How beautiful upon the mountains
  are the feet of the messenger who
   announces peace,
 who brings good news,
  who announces salvation,
  who says to Zion, "Your God reigns."
8 Listen! Your sentinels lift up their voices,
  together they sing for joy;
 for in plain sight they see
  the return of the LORD to Zion.
9 Break forth together into singing,
  you ruins of Jerusalem;
 for the LORD has comforted his people,
  he has redeemed Jerusalem.
10 The LORD has bared his holy arm
  before the eyes of all the nations;
 and all the ends of the earth shall see
  the salvation of our God.

11 Depart, depart, go out from there!
  Touch no unclean thing;
 go out from the midst of it, purify
   yourselves,
  you who carry the vessels of the LORD.
12 For you shall not go out in haste,
  and you shall not go in flight;
 for the LORD will go before you,
  and the God of Israel will be your rear
   guard.

---

o Syr: Heb *planting* *p* Q Ms Gk Syr Vg: MT *how may I comfort you?* *q* Or *humbled* *r* Cn: Heb *rise up, sit*

ISA

The Suffering Servant

13 See, my servant shall prosper;
     he shall be exalted and lifted up,
     and shall be very high.
14 Just as there were many who were
           astonished at him[s]
     —so marred was his appearance, beyond
           human semblance,
     and his form beyond that of mortals—
15 so he shall startle[t] many nations;
     kings shall shut their mouths because
           of him;
   for that which had not been told them they
           shall see,
     and that which they had not heard they
           shall contemplate.

Who has believed what we have heard?
     And to whom has the arm of the LORD
           been revealed?
2 For he grew up before him like a young
           plant,
   and like a root out of dry ground;
   he had no form or majesty that we should
           look at him,
     nothing in his appearance that we should
           desire him.
3 He was despised and rejected by others;
     a man of suffering[u] and acquainted with
           infirmity;
   and as one from whom others hide their
           faces[v]
     he was despised, and we held him of no
           account.

4 Surely he has borne our infirmities
     and carried our diseases;
   yet we accounted him stricken,
     struck down by God, and afflicted.
5 But he was wounded for our transgressions,
     crushed for our iniquities;
   upon him was the punishment that made
           us whole,
     and by his bruises we are healed.
6 All we like sheep have gone astray;
     we have all turned to our own way,
   and the LORD has laid on him
     the iniquity of us all.

7 He was oppressed, and he was afflicted,
     yet he did not open his mouth;
   like a lamb that is led to the slaughter,
     and like a sheep that before its shearers is
           silent,
     so he did not open his mouth.
8 By a perversion of justice he was taken
           away.

Who could have imagined his future?
     For he was cut off from the land of the
           living,
     stricken for the transgression of my
           people.
9 They made his grave with the wicked
     and his tomb[w] with the rich,[x]
   although he had done no violence,
     and there was no deceit in his mouth.

10 Yet it was the will of the LORD to crush him
           with pain.[y]
   When you make his life an offering for sin,[t]
     he shall see his offspring, and shall
           prolong his days;
   through him the will of the LORD shall
           prosper.

Catholic Connections

THE SUFFERING SERVANT

Isaiah 52.13—53.12 is the fourth of the four servant songs (see "The Servant Songs," Isa 42.1–7). In it, the servant suffers for the salvation of others. Can you see how this description fits Jesus? Take a moment to say your own prayer of thanksgiving to Jesus for saving us from sin and death.

▸ Isa 52.13—53.12

11   Out of his anguish he shall see light;[z]
     he shall find satisfaction through his
           knowledge.
     The righteous one,[a] my servant, shall
           make many righteous,
     and he shall bear their iniquities.

---

s Syr Tg: Heb *you*   t Meaning of Heb uncertain   u Or *a man of sorrows*   v Or *as one who hides his face from us*   w Q Ms: MT *and in his death*   x Cn: Heb *with a rich person*   y Or *by disease*; meaning of Heb uncertain   z Q Mss: MT lacks *light*   a Or *and he shall find satisfaction. Through his knowledge, the righteous one*

ISA

12 Therefore I will allot him a portion with the
        great,
    and he shall divide the spoil with the
        strong;
  because he poured out himself to death,
    and was numbered with the transgressors;
  yet he bore the sin of many,
    and made intercession for the
        transgressors.

The Eternal Covenant of Peace

Sing, O barren one who did not bear;
    burst into song and shout,
    you who have not been in labor!
For the children of the desolate woman will
        be more
    than the children of her that is married,
        says the LORD.
2 Enlarge the site of your tent,
    and let the curtains of your habitations
        be stretched out;
  do not hold back; lengthen your cords
    and strengthen your stakes.
3 For you will spread out to the right and to
        the left,
    and your descendants will possess the
        nations
    and will settle the desolate towns.

4 Do not fear, for you will not be ashamed;
    do not be discouraged, for you will not
        suffer disgrace;
  for you will forget the shame of your youth,
    and the disgrace of your widowhood you
        will remember no more.
5 For your Maker is your husband,
    the LORD of hosts is his name;
  the Holy One of Israel is your Redeemer,
    the God of the whole earth he is called.
6 For the LORD has called you
    like a wife forsaken and grieved in spirit,
  like the wife of a man's youth when she is
        cast off,
    says your God.
7 For a brief moment I abandoned you,
    but with great compassion I will
        gather you.
8 In overflowing wrath for a moment
    I hid my face from you,
  but with everlasting love I will have
        compassion on you,
    says the LORD, your Redeemer.

9 This is like the days of Noah to me:
    Just as I swore that the waters of Noah
        would never again go over the earth,

so I have sworn that I will not be angry
        with you
    and will not rebuke you.
10 For the mountains may depart
    and the hills be removed,
  but my steadfast love shall not depart
        from you,
    and my covenant of peace shall not be
        removed,
  says the LORD, who has compassion
        on you.

11 O afflicted one, storm-tossed, and not
        comforted,
    I am about to set your stones in
        antimony,
    and lay your foundations with
        sapphires.b
12 I will make your pinnacles of rubies,
    your gates of jewels,
    and all your wall of precious stones.
13 All your children shall be taught by the
        LORD,
    and great shall be the prosperity of your
        children.
14 In righteousness you shall be established;
    you shall be far from oppression, for you
        shall not fear;
    and from terror, for it shall not come
        near you.
15 If anyone stirs up strife,
    it is not from me;
  whoever stirs up strife with you
    shall fall because of you.
16 See it is I who have created the smith
    who blows the fire of coals,
    and produces a weapon fit for
        its purpose;
  I have also created the ravager to destroy.
17   No weapon that is fashioned against you
        shall prosper,
    and you shall confute every tongue that
        rises against you in judgment.
  This is the heritage of the servants of the
        LORD
    and their vindication from me, says the
        LORD.

An Invitation to Abundant Life

Ho, everyone who thirsts,
    come to the waters;
  and you that have no money,
    come, buy and eat!
  Come, buy wine and milk
    without money and without price.

---

b Or *lapis lazuli*

2 Why do you spend your money for that
        which is not bread,
    and your labor for that which does not
        satisfy?
Listen carefully to me, and eat what is good,
    and delight yourselves in rich food.
3 Incline your ear, and come to me;
    listen, so that you may live.
I will make with you an everlasting
        covenant,
    my steadfast, sure love for David.
4 See, I made him a witness to the peoples,
    a leader and commander for the peoples.
5 See, you shall call nations that you do not
        know,
    and nations that do not know you shall
        run to you,
because of the LORD your God, the Holy
        One of Israel,
    for he has glorified you.

6 Seek the LORD while he may be found,
    call upon him while he is near;
7 let the wicked forsake their way,
    and the unrighteous their thoughts;
let them return to the LORD, that he may
        have mercy on them,
    and to our God, for he will abundantly
        pardon.
8 For my thoughts are not your thoughts,
    nor are your ways my ways, says the
        LORD.
9 For as the heavens are higher than the earth,
    so are my ways higher than your ways
    and my thoughts than your thoughts.

10 For as the rain and the snow come down
        from heaven,
    and do not return there until they have
        watered the earth,

making it bring forth and sprout,
    giving seed to the sower and bread to the
        eater,
11 so shall my word be that goes out from my
        mouth;
    it shall not return to me empty,
but it shall accomplish that which I
        purpose,
    and succeed in the thing for which I
        sent it.

12 For you shall go out in joy,
    and be led back in peace;
the mountains and the hills before you
    shall burst into song,
    and all the trees of the field shall clap
        their hands.
13 Instead of the thorn shall come up the
        cypress;
    instead of the brier shall come up the
        myrtle;
and it shall be to the LORD for a memorial,
    for an everlasting sign that shall not be
        cut off.

The Covenant Extended to All Who Obey

Thus says the LORD:
    Maintain justice, and do what is right,
for soon my salvation will come,
    and my deliverance be revealed.

2 Happy is the mortal who does this,
    the one who holds it fast,
who keeps the sabbath, not profaning it,
    and refrains from doing any evil.

3 Do not let the foreigner joined to the LORD say,
    "The LORD will surely separate me from
        his people";

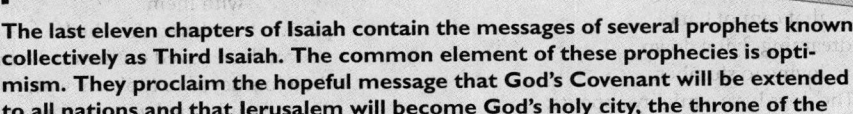

The Optimism of Third Isaiah

**The last eleven chapters of Isaiah contain the messages of several prophets known
collectively as Third Isaiah. The common element of these prophecies is opti-
mism. They proclaim the hopeful message that God's Covenant will be extended
to all nations and that Jerusalem will become God's holy city, the throne of the
Eternal King.**

**Third Isaiah, in contrast to many of the other biblical prophets, proclaims joy as a sign
of God's presence. Joy is absent in the life of many people today, as it was in the time of
Isaiah. Let us remember all the wonderful things God has done for us, and we too will find
cause for rejoicing!**

▸ **Isa 56.1—66.24**

and do not let the eunuch say,
"I am just a dry tree."
4 For thus says the LORD:
To the eunuchs who keep my sabbaths,
who choose the things that please me
and hold fast my covenant,
5 I will give, in my house and within my
walls,
a monument and a name
better than sons and daughters;
I will give them an everlasting name
that shall not be cut off.

6 And the foreigners who join themselves to
the LORD,
to minister to him, to love the name of
the LORD,
and to be his servants,
all who keep the sabbath, and do not
profane it,
and hold fast my covenant—
7 these I will bring to my holy mountain,
and make them joyful in my house of
prayer;
their burnt offerings and their sacrifices
will be accepted on my altar;
for my house shall be called a house of
prayer
for all peoples.
8 Thus says the Lord GOD,
who gathers the outcasts of Israel,
I will gather others to them
besides those already gathered.c

The Corruption of Israel's Rulers

9 All you wild animals,
all you wild animals in the forest, come
to devour!
10 Israel'sd sentinels are blind,
they are all without knowledge;
they are all silent dogs
that cannot bark;
dreaming, lying down,
loving to slumber.
11 The dogs have a mighty appetite;
they never have enough.
The shepherds also have no understanding;
they have all turned to their own way,
to their own gain, one and all.
12 "Come," they say, "let use get wine;
let us fill ourselves with strong drink.
And tomorrow will be like today,
great beyond measure."

Israel's Futile Idolatry

The righteous perish,
and no one takes it to heart;
the devout are taken away,
while no one understands.
For the righteous are taken away from
calamity,
2   and they enter into peace;
those who walk uprightly
will rest on their couches.
3 But as for you, come here,
you children of a sorceress,
you offspring of an adulterer and a
whore.f
4 Whom are you mocking?
Against whom do you open your mouth
wide
and stick out your tongue?
Are you not children of transgression,
the offspring of deceit—
5 you that burn with lust among the oaks,
under every green tree;
you that slaughter your children in the
valleys,
under the clefts of the rocks?
6 Among the smooth stones of the valley is
your portion;
they, they, are your lot;
to them you have poured out a drink
offering,
you have brought a grain offering.
Shall I be appeased for these things?
7 Upon a high and lofty mountain
you have set your bed,
and there you went up to offer sacrifice.
8 Behind the door and the doorpost
you have set up your symbol;
for, in deserting me,g you have uncovered
your bed,
you have gone up to it,
you have made it wide;
and you have made a bargain for yourself
with them,
you have loved their bed,
you have gazed on their nakedness.h
9 You journeyed to Mō'lechi with oil,
and multiplied your perfumes;
you sent your envoys far away,
and sent down even to Shē'ol.
10 You grew weary from your many
wanderings,

---

c Heb besides his gathered ones   d Heb His   e Q Ms Syr
Vg Tg: MT me   f Heb an adulterer and she plays the whore
g Meaning of Heb uncertain   h Or their phallus; Heb the
hand   i Or the king

but you did not say, "It is useless."
You found your desire rekindled,
    and so you did not weaken.

11 Whom did you dread and fear
    so that you lied,
and did not remember me
    or give me a thought?
Have I not kept silent and closed my eyes,*j*
    and so you do not fear me?
12 I will concede your righteousness and your
    works,
    but they will not help you.
13 When you cry out, let your collection of
    idols deliver you!
    The wind will carry them off,
    a breath will take them away.
But whoever takes refuge in me shall
    possess the land
    and inherit my holy mountain.

A Promise of Help and Healing

14 It shall be said,
"Build up, build up, prepare the way,
    remove every obstruction from my
    people's way."
15 For thus says the high and lofty one
    who inhabits eternity, whose name is
    Holy:
I dwell in the high and holy place,
    and also with those who are contrite and
    humble in spirit,
to revive the spirit of the humble,
    and to revive the heart of the contrite.
16 For I will not continually accuse,
    nor will I always be angry;
for then the spirits would grow faint
    before me,
    even the souls that I have made.
17 Because of their wicked covetousness I
    was angry;
    I struck them, I hid and was angry;
but they kept turning back to their own
    ways.
18 I have seen their ways, but I will heal them;
    I will lead them and repay them with
    comfort,
    creating for their mourners the fruit of
    the lips.*k*
19 Peace, peace, to the far and the near, says
    the LORD;
    and I will heal them.
20 But the wicked are like the tossing sea
    that cannot keep still;
    its waters toss up mire and mud.

21 There is no peace, says my God, for the
    wicked.

False and True Worship

Shout out, do not hold back!
    Lift up your voice like a trumpet!
Announce to my people their rebellion,
    to the house of Jacob their sins.
2 Yet day after day they seek me
    and delight to know my ways,
as if they were a nation that practiced
    righteousness
    and did not forsake the ordinance of
    their God;
they ask of me righteous judgments,
    they delight to draw near to God.
3 "Why do we fast, but you do not see?
    Why humble ourselves, but you do not
    notice?"
Look, you serve your own interest on your
    fast day,
    and oppress all your workers.
4 Look, you fast only to quarrel and to fight
    and to strike with a wicked fist.
Such fasting as you do today
    will not make your voice heard on high.
5 Is such the fast that I choose,
    a day to humble oneself?
Is it to bow down the head like a bulrush,
    and to lie in sackcloth and ashes?
Will you call this a fast,
    a day acceptable to the LORD?

---

j Gk Vg: Heb *silent even for a long time*   *k* Meaning of Heb
uncertain

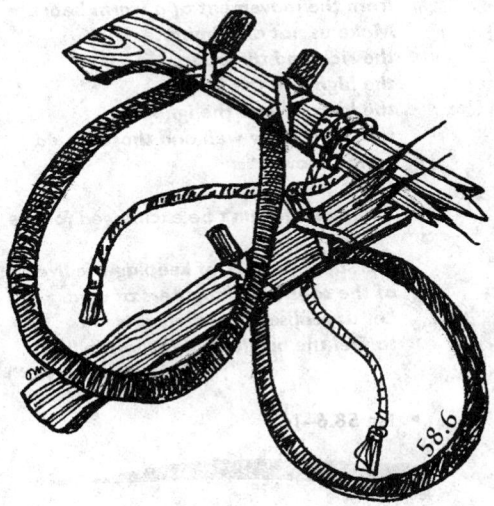

6 Is not this the fast that I choose:
　to loose the bonds of injustice,
　to undo the thongs of the yoke,
to let the oppressed go free,
　and to break every yoke?

Asian American

"If You Want Peace, Work for Justice"

**"If you want peace, work for justice"
is a famous quote of Pope Paul VI.
We hear a similar message in Isa 56.1,
and 58.6–14 gives us clear examples of
works that create justice and peace.**

　　**At the core of justice is the under-
standing that life—all life—is precious.
All people are to be honored, protected, and celebrated. Ensuring that this
happens is our responsibility, even when
it seems to be a burden. The following
prayer by a worker of Peace Market in
Korea reflects this passion:**

*Make us keep the sputtering lantern
　burning
and not to break a wounded reed.
Make us understand
the secret of eternal life
from the pulse of blood in our veins
and realise the worth of a life
from the movement of a warm heart.
Make us not discriminate
the rich and the poor,
the high and the low,
the learned and the ignorant
those we know well and those we do
　not know.
Oh!
A human life can't be exchanged for the
　whole world
this supreme task of keeping the lives
of the sons and daughters of God.
Let us realise how lovely it is
to feel the burdens of responsibility.*
　　　　　　　　　　("Our Prayer")

▶ Isa 58.6–14

7 Is it not to share your bread with the
　　hungry,
　and bring the homeless poor into your
　　house;
when you see the naked, to cover them,
　and not to hide yourself from your
　　own kin?
8 Then your light shall break forth like the
　　dawn,
　and your healing shall spring up
　　quickly;
your vindicator[l] shall go before you,
　the glory of the LORD shall be your rear
　　guard.
9 Then you shall call, and the LORD will
　　answer;
　you shall cry for help, and he will say,
　　Here I am.

If you remove the yoke from among you,
　the pointing of the finger, the speaking of
　　evil,
10 if you offer your food to the hungry
　and satisfy the needs of the afflicted,
then your light shall rise in the darkness
　and your gloom be like the noonday.
11 The LORD will guide you continually,
　and satisfy your needs in parched places,
　and make your bones strong;
and you shall be like a watered garden,
　like a spring of water,
　whose waters never fail.
12 Your ancient ruins shall be rebuilt;
　you shall raise up the foundations of
　　many generations;
you shall be called the repairer of the
　　breach,
　the restorer of streets to live in.

13 If you refrain from trampling the sabbath,
　from pursuing your own interests on my
　　holy day;
if you call the sabbath a delight
　and the holy day of the LORD honorable;
if you honor it, not going your own ways,
　serving your own interests, or pursuing
　　your own affairs;[m]
14 then you shall take delight in the LORD,
　and I will make you ride upon the
　　heights of the earth;
I will feed you with the heritage of your
　　ancestor Jacob,
　for the mouth of the LORD has spoken.

---

[l] Or *vindication*　　[m] Heb *or speaking words*

Injustice and Oppression to Be Punished

See, the LORD's hand is not too short to save,
  nor his ear too dull to hear.
2 Rather, your iniquities have been barriers
    between you and your God,
  and your sins have hidden his face
      from you
    so that he does not hear.
3 For your hands are defiled with blood,
    and your fingers with iniquity;
  your lips have spoken lies,
    your tongue mutters wickedness.
4 No one brings suit justly,
    no one goes to law honestly;
  they rely on empty pleas, they speak lies,
    conceiving mischief and begetting
      iniquity.
5 They hatch adders' eggs,
    and weave the spider's web;
  whoever eats their eggs dies,
    and the crushed egg hatches out a viper.
6 Their webs cannot serve as clothing;
    they cannot cover themselves with what
      they make.
  Their works are works of iniquity,
    and deeds of violence are in their hands.
7 Their feet run to evil,
    and they rush to shed innocent blood;
  their thoughts are thoughts of iniquity,
    desolation and destruction are in
      their highways.
8 The way of peace they do not know,
    and there is no justice in their paths.
  Their roads they have made crooked;
    no one who walks in them knows peace.

9 Therefore justice is far from us,
    and righteousness does not reach us;
  we wait for light, and lo! there is darkness;
    and for brightness, but we walk in
      gloom.
10 We grope like the blind along a wall,
    groping like those who have no eyes;
  we stumble at noon as in the twilight,
    among the vigorous*n* as though we were
      dead.
11 We all growl like bears;
    like doves we moan mournfully.
  We wait for justice, but there is none;
    for salvation, but it is far from us.
12 For our transgressions before you are many,
    and our sins testify against us.
  Our transgressions indeed are with us,
    and we know our iniquities:
13 transgressing, and denying the LORD,

  and turning away from following
      our God,
  talking oppression and revolt,
    conceiving lying words and uttering them
      from the heart.
14 Justice is turned back,
    and righteousness stands at a distance;
  for truth stumbles in the public square,
    and uprightness cannot enter.
15 Truth is lacking,
    and whoever turns from evil is despoiled.

  The LORD saw it, and it displeased him
    that there was no justice.
16 He saw that there was no one,
    and was appalled that there was no one
      to intervene;
  so his own arm brought him victory,
    and his righteousness upheld him.
17 He put on righteousness like a breastplate,
    and a helmet of salvation on his head;
  he put on garments of vengeance for
      clothing,
    and wrapped himself in fury as in a
      mantle.
18 According to their deeds, so will he repay;
    wrath to his adversaries, requital to his
      enemies;
  to the coastlands he will render requital.
19 So those in the west shall fear the name of
      the LORD,
    and those in the east, his glory;
  for he will come like a pent-up stream
    that the wind of the LORD drives on.

20 And he will come to Zion as Redeemer,
    to those in Jacob who turn from
      transgression, says the LORD.
21 And as for me, this is my covenant with them,
says the LORD: my spirit that is upon you, and my
words that I have put in your mouth, shall not
depart out of your mouth, or out of the mouths of
your children, or out of the mouths of your children's children, says the LORD, from now on and
forever.

The Ingathering of the Dispersed

Arise, shine; for your light has come,
    and the glory of the LORD has risen
      upon you.
2 For darkness shall cover the earth,
    and thick darkness the peoples;
  but the LORD will arise upon you,
    and his glory will appear over you.

---

n Meaning of Heb uncertain

3 Nations shall come to your light,
  and kings to the brightness of your dawn.

4 Lift up your eyes and look around;
  they all gather together, they come
    to you;
  your sons shall come from far away,
  and your daughters shall be carried on
    their nurses' arms.

5 Then you shall see and be radiant;
  your heart shall thrill and rejoice,*o*
  because the abundance of the sea shall be
    brought to you,
  the wealth of the nations shall come
    to you.

6 A multitude of camels shall cover you,
  the young camels of Mid'i·an and E'phah;
  all those from She'ba shall come.
  They shall bring gold and frankincense,
  and shall proclaim the praise of the LORD.

7 All the flocks of Ke'dar shall be gathered
    to you,
  the rams of Ne·ba'i·oth shall minister
    to you;
  they shall be acceptable on my altar,
  and I will glorify my glorious house.

8 Who are these that fly like a cloud,
  and like doves to their windows?

9 For the coastlands shall wait for me,
  the ships of Tar'shish first,
  to bring your children from far away,
  their silver and gold with them,
  for the name of the LORD your God,
  and for the Holy One of Israel,
  because he has glorified you.

10 Foreigners shall build up your walls,
  and their kings shall minister to you;
  for in my wrath I struck you down,
  but in my favor I have had mercy
    on you.

11 Your gates shall always be open;
  day and night they shall not be shut,
  so that nations shall bring you their wealth,
  with their kings led in procession.

12 For the nation and kingdom
  that will not serve you shall perish;
  those nations shall be utterly laid waste.

13 The glory of Lebanon shall come to you,
  the cypress, the plane, and the pine,
  to beautify the place of my sanctuary;
  and I will glorify where my feet rest.

14 The descendants of those who
    oppressed you
  shall come bending low to you,
  and all who despised you
  shall bow down at your feet;

they shall call you the City of the LORD,
  the Zion of the Holy One of Israel.

15 Whereas you have been forsaken and hated,
  with no one passing through,
  I will make you majestic forever,
  a joy from age to age.

16 You shall suck the milk of nations,
  you shall suck the breasts of kings;
  and you shall know that I, the LORD, am
    your Savior
  and your Redeemer, the Mighty One of
    Jacob.

17 Instead of bronze I will bring gold,
  instead of iron I will bring silver;
  instead of wood, bronze,
  instead of stones, iron.
  I will appoint Peace as your overseer
  and Righteousness as your taskmaster.

18 Violence shall no more be heard in your
    land,
  devastation or destruction within your
    borders;
  you shall call your walls Salvation,
  and your gates Praise.

God the Glory of Zion

19 The sun shall no longer be
    your light by day,
  nor for brightness shall the moon
    give light to you by night;*p*
  but the LORD will be your everlasting light,
  and your God will be your glory.

20 Your sun shall no more go down,
  or your moon withdraw itself;
  for the LORD will be your everlasting light,
  and your days of mourning shall be
    ended.

21 Your people shall all be righteous;
  they shall possess the land forever.
  They are the shoot that I planted, the work
    of my hands,
  so that I might be glorified.

22 The least of them shall become a clan,
  and the smallest one a mighty nation;
  I am the LORD;
  in its time I will accomplish it quickly.

The Good News of Deliverance

61 The spirit of the Lord GOD is upon me,
  because the LORD has anointed me;
  he has sent me to bring good news to the
    oppressed,
  to bind up the brokenhearted,

---

o Heb *be enlarged*   *p* Q Ms Gk Old Latin Tg: MT lacks *by night*

to proclaim liberty to the captives,
   and release to the prisoners;
2 to proclaim the year of the LORD's favor,
   and the day of vengeance of our God;
   to comfort all who mourn;
3 to provide for those who mourn in Zion—
   to give them a garland instead of ashes,
the oil of gladness instead of mourning,
   the mantle of praise instead of a faint
      spirit.
They will be called oaks of righteousness,
   the planting of the LORD, to display his
      glory.
4 They shall build up the ancient ruins,
   they shall raise up the former
      devastations;
they shall repair the ruined cities,
   the devastations of many generations.

5 Strangers shall stand and feed your flocks,
   foreigners shall till your land and dress
      your vines;
6 but you shall be called priests of the LORD,
   you shall be named ministers of
      our God;
you shall enjoy the wealth of the nations,
   and in their riches you shall glory.
7 Because their*q* shame was double,
   and dishonor was proclaimed as their lot,
therefore they shall possess a double
      portion;
   everlasting joy shall be theirs.

8 For I the LORD love justice,
   I hate robbery and wrongdoing;*r*
I will faithfully give them their recompense,
   and I will make an everlasting covenant
      with them.
9 Their descendants shall be known among
      the nations,
   and their offspring among the peoples;
all who see them shall acknowledge
   that they are a people whom the LORD
      has blessed.
10 I will greatly rejoice in the LORD,
   my whole being shall exult in my God;
for he has clothed me with the garments of
      salvation,
   he has covered me with the robe of
      righteousness,
as a bridegroom decks himself with a
      garland,
   and as a bride adorns herself with her
      jewels.
11 For as the earth brings forth its shoots,
   and as a garden causes what is sown in it
      to spring up,

so the Lord GOD will cause righteousness
      and praise
   to spring up before all the nations.

The Vindication and Salvation of Zion

For Zion's sake I will not keep silent,
   and for Jerusalem's sake I will not rest,
until her vindication shines out like the
      dawn,
   and her salvation like a burning torch.
2 The nations shall see your vindication,
   and all the kings your glory;
and you shall be called by a new name
   that the mouth of the LORD will give.
3 You shall be a crown of beauty in the hand
      of the LORD,
   and a royal diadem in the hand of
      your God.
4 You shall no more be termed Forsaken,*s*
   and your land shall no more be termed
      Desolate;*t*

---

q Heb *your*   *r* Or *robbery with a burnt offering*
s Heb *Azubah*   *t* Heb *Shemamah*

did you KNOW?
Bride and Bridegroom

In ancient Israel, the bride and bridegroom gradually became a metaphor, or symbol, for the relationship between Israel and God as pictured in Isa 61.10 and 62.5. In these passages, Israel is the bride, and God is the faithful bridegroom, who loves her, lavishes her with blessings, and continues to be faithful to her. When Israel strays from the Covenant or goes after foreign gods, she is compared to an unfaithful lover, even a prostitute who pursues other partners (for a graphic example, see Ezek 16.1–43). The prophet Hosea even marries a prostitute as a living example of God's faithfulness (Hos 1.2)! The wonder of God's love is that through all of Israel's infidelity (and ours), God always remains willing to take it (and us) back.

▶ Isa 61.10

but you shall be called My Delight Is
in Her,[u]
and your land Married;[v]
for the LORD delights in you,
and your land shall be married.
5 For as a young man marries a young
woman,
so shall your builder[w] marry you,
and as the bridegroom rejoices over the
bride,
so shall your God rejoice over you.
6 Upon your walls, O Jerusalem,
I have posted sentinels;
all day and all night
they shall never be silent.
You who remind the LORD,
take no rest,
7 and give him no rest
until he establishes Jerusalem
and makes it renowned throughout the
earth.
8 The LORD has sworn by his right hand
and by his mighty arm:
I will not again give your grain
to be food for your enemies,
and foreigners shall not drink the wine
for which you have labored;
9 but those who garner it shall eat it
and praise the LORD,
and those who gather it shall drink it
in my holy courts.
10 Go through, go through the gates,
prepare the way for the people;
build up, build up the highway,
clear it of stones,
lift up an ensign over the peoples.
11 The LORD has proclaimed
to the end of the earth:
Say to daughter Zion,
"See, your salvation comes;
his reward is with him,
and his recompense before him."
12 They shall be called, "The Holy People,
The Redeemed of the LORD";
and you shall be called, "Sought Out,
A City Not Forsaken."

Vengeance on Edom

"Who is this that comes from Edom,
from Boz'rah in garments stained
crimson?
Who is this so splendidly robed,
marching in his great might?"

"It is I, announcing vindication,
mighty to save."

2 "Why are your robes red,
and your garments like theirs who tread
the wine press?"
3 "I have trodden the wine press alone,
and from the peoples no one was
with me;
I trod them in my anger
and trampled them in my wrath;
their juice spattered on my garments,
and stained all my robes.
4 For the day of vengeance was in my heart,
and the year for my redeeming work had
come.
5 I looked, but there was no helper;
I stared, but there was no one to
sustain me;
so my own arm brought me victory,
and my wrath sustained me.
6 I trampled down peoples in my anger,
I crushed them in my wrath,
and I poured out their lifeblood on the
earth."

God's Mercy Remembered

7 I will recount the gracious deeds of the LORD,
the praiseworthy acts of the LORD,
because of all that the LORD has done for us,
and the great favor to the house of Israel
that he has shown them according to his
mercy,
according to the abundance of his
steadfast love.
8 For he said, "Surely they are my people,
children who will not deal falsely";
and he became their savior
9 in all their distress.
It was no messenger[x] or angel
but his presence that saved them;[y]
in his love and in his pity he redeemed
them;
he lifted them up and carried them all
the days of old.
10 But they rebelled
and grieved his holy spirit;
therefore he became their enemy;
he himself fought against them.
11 Then they[z] remembered the days of old,
of Moses his servant.[a]
Where is the one who brought them up out
of the sea

---

[u] Heb *Hephzibah*   [v] Heb *Beulah*   [w] Cn: Heb *your sons*
[x] Gk: Heb *anguish*   [y] Or *savior.* 9 *In all their distress he was
distressed; the angel of his presence saved them;*   [z] Heb *he*
[a] Cn: Heb *his people*

with the shepherds of his flock?
  Where is the one who put within them
    his holy spirit,
12 who caused his glorious arm
    to march at the right hand of Moses,
  who divided the waters before them
    to make for himself an everlasting name,
13   who led them through the depths?
  Like a horse in the desert,
    they did not stumble.
14 Like cattle that go down into the valley,
    the spirit of the LORD gave them rest.
  Thus you led your people,
    to make for yourself a glorious name.

A Prayer of Penitence

15 Look down from heaven and see,
    from your holy and glorious habitation.
  Where are your zeal and your might?
    The yearning of your heart and your
      compassion?
  They are withheld from me.
16 For you are our father,
    though Abraham does not know us
  and Israel does not acknowledge us;
  you, O LORD, are our father;
    our Redeemer from of old is your name.
17 Why, O LORD, do you make us stray from
      your ways
    and harden our heart, so that we do not
      fear you?
  Turn back for the sake of your servants,
    for the sake of the tribes that are your
      heritage.
18 Your holy people took possession for a little
      while;
  but now our adversaries have trampled
    down your sanctuary.
19 We have long been like those whom you do
      not rule,
  like those not called by your name.

64 O that you would tear open the heavens and
      come down,
  so that the mountains would quake at
    your presence—
2b as when fire kindles brushwood
    and the fire causes water to boil—
  to make your name known to your
      adversaries,
    so that the nations might tremble at your
      presence!
3 When you did awesome deeds that we did
      not expect,
  you came down, the mountains quaked
    at your presence.

4 From ages past no one has heard,
    no ear has perceived,
  no eye has seen any God besides you,
    who works for those who wait for him.
5 You meet those who gladly do right,
    those who remember you in your ways.
  But you were angry, and we sinned;
    because you hid yourself we
      transgressed.c
6 We have all become like one who is
      unclean,
    and all our righteous deeds are like a
      filthy cloth.
  We all fade like a leaf,
    and our iniquities, like the wind, take us
      away.
7 There is no one who calls on your name,
    or attempts to take hold of you;
  for you have hidden your face from us,
    and have deliveredd us into the hand of
      our iniquity.
8 Yet, O LORD, you are our Father;
    we are the clay, and you are our potter;
    we are all the work of your hand.
9 Do not be exceedingly angry, O LORD,
    and do not remember iniquity forever.
    Now consider, we are all your people.
10 Your holy cities have become a wilderness,
    Zion has become a wilderness,
    Jerusalem a desolation.
11 Our holy and beautiful house,
    where our ancestors praised you,
  has been burned by fire,
    and all our pleasant places have become
      ruins.
12 After all this, will you restrain yourself,
    O LORD?
    Will you keep silent, and punish us so
      severely?

The Righteousness of God's Judgment

65 I was ready to be sought out by those who
      did not ask,
    to be found by those who did not
      seek me.
  I said, "Here I am, here I am,"
    to a nation that did not call on my
      name.
2 I held out my hands all day long
    to a rebellious people,
  who walk in a way that is not good,
    following their own devices;

---

b Ch 64.1 in Heb   c Meaning of Heb uncertain
d Gk Syr Old Latin Tg: Heb *melted*

PRAY IT!

The Master Potter

Have you ever seen a potter at work? Perhaps you have even made a pot yourself. Pot making is still practiced today much as it was at the time of Third Isaiah: The potter takes a lump of moist clay and begins to shape it by hand, with an image in mind of what the finished product will look like. The artisan then puts the piece of clay on a potter's wheel and spins the wheel, continuing to form the pot with his or her hands. Because it is designed by hand, rather than mass-produced by machine, each work of the potter is original; there is no other just like it.

The image of God as a potter and each of us as a clay pot reminds us of the second Creation story, where God scoops up clay from the earth and forms the first human being and breathes life into the being (Gen 2.7). It also reminds us of Psalm 139's description of our being knit together in our mother's womb.

The idea of God's hands shaping us like clay is intimate and comforting. No one but the potter knows how much time and love went into the fashioning of a particular pot. The potter gives each pot its own special design and markings. The potter also knows its flaws. The potter and the pot share a bond that seems much like the one between each of us and God. Isaiah 64.8 indeed gives us a vivid and beautiful image for God's relationship with each of us (see also Jer 18.1–6).

In your prayer, reflect or journal on the following questions:

■ How has God molded you as a unique person?
■ What are your special features and markings (gifts), and what are your flaws (weaknesses)?
■ How is God still molding you?

▶ Isa 64.8

3 a people who provoke me
    to my face continually,
sacrificing in gardens
    and offering incense on bricks;

4 who sit inside tombs,
    and spend the night in secret places;
who eat swine's flesh,
    with broth of abominable things in their
        vessels;
5 who say, "Keep to yourself,
    do not come near me, for I am too holy
        for you."
These are a smoke in my nostrils,
    a fire that burns all day long.
6 See, it is written before me:
    I will not keep silent, but I will repay;
I will indeed repay into their laps
7   their*e* iniquities and their*e* ancestors'
        iniquities together,
                                    says the LORD;
because they offered incense on the
        mountains
    and reviled me on the hills,
I will measure into their laps
    full payment for their actions.
8 Thus says the LORD:
As the wine is found in the cluster,
    and they say, "Do not destroy it,
    for there is a blessing in it,"
so I will do for my servants' sake,
    and not destroy them all.
9 I will bring forth descendants*f* from Jacob,
    and from Judah inheritors*g* of my
        mountains;
my chosen shall inherit it,
    and my servants shall settle there.
10 Sharon shall become a pasture for flocks,
    and the Valley of A'chor a place for herds
        to lie down,
    for my people who have sought me.
11 But you who forsake the LORD,
    who forget my holy mountain,
who set a table for Fortune
    and fill cups of mixed wine for Destiny;
12 I will destine you to the sword,
    and all of you shall bow down to the
        slaughter;
because, when I called, you did not answer,
    when I spoke, you did not listen,
but you did what was evil in my sight,
    and chose what I did not delight in.
13 Therefore thus says the Lord GOD:
My servants shall eat,
    but you shall be hungry;
my servants shall drink,
    but you shall be thirsty;
my servants shall rejoice,
    but you shall be put to shame;

e Gk Syr: Heb *your*   *f* Or *a descendant*   *g* Or *an inheritor*

14 my servants shall sing for gladness of heart,
        but you shall cry out for pain of heart,
        and shall wail for anguish of spirit.
15 You shall leave your name to my chosen to
            use as a curse,
        and the Lord GOD will put you to death;
        but to his servants he will give a different
            name.
16 Then whoever invokes a blessing in the land
        shall bless by the God of faithfulness,
    and whoever takes an oath in the land
        shall swear by the God of faithfulness;
    because the former troubles are forgotten
        and are hidden from my sight.

The Glorious New Creation

17 For I am about to create new heavens
        and a new earth;
    the former things shall not be remembered
        or come to mind.
18 But be glad and rejoice forever
        in what I am creating;
    for I am about to create Jerusalem as a joy,
        and its people as a delight.
19 I will rejoice in Jerusalem,
        and delight in my people;
    no more shall the sound of weeping be
            heard in it,
        or the cry of distress.
20 No more shall there be in it
        an infant that lives but a few days,
        or an old person who does not live out a
            lifetime;
    for one who dies at a hundred years will be
            considered a youth,
        and one who falls short of a hundred
            will be considered accursed.
21 They shall build houses and inhabit them;
        they shall plant vineyards and eat their
            fruit.
22 They shall not build and another inhabit;
        they shall not plant and another eat;
    for like the days of a tree shall the days of
            my people be,
        and my chosen shall long enjoy the work
            of their hands.
23 They shall not labor in vain,
        or bear children for calamity;[h]
    for they shall be offspring blessed by the
            LORD—
        and their descendants as well.
24 Before they call I will answer,
        while they are yet speaking I will hear.
25 The wolf and the lamb shall feed together,
        the lion shall eat straw like the ox;
        but the serpent—its food shall be dust!

They shall not hurt or destroy
        on all my holy mountain,
                    says the LORD.

The Worship God Demands

Thus says the LORD:
Heaven is my throne
        and the earth is my footstool;
what is the house that you would build
            for me,
        and what is my resting place?
2 All these things my hand has made,
        and so all these things are mine,[i]
                    says the LORD.
But this is the one to whom I will look,
        to the humble and contrite in spirit,
        who trembles at my word.

3 Whoever slaughters an ox is like one who
            kills a human being;
    whoever sacrifices a lamb, like one who
            breaks a dog's neck;
    whoever presents a grain offering, like one
            who offers swine's blood;[j]
    whoever makes a memorial offering of
            frankincense, like one who blesses
            an idol.
These have chosen their own ways,
        and in their abominations they take
            delight;
4 I also will choose to mock[k] them,
        and bring upon them what they fear;
    because, when I called, no one answered,
        when I spoke, they did not listen;
    but they did what was evil in my sight,
        and chose what did not please me.

The LORD Vindicates Zion

5 Hear the word of the LORD,
        you who tremble at his word:
Your own people who hate you
        and reject you for my name's sake
have said, "Let the LORD be glorified,
        so that we may see your joy";
        but it is they who shall be put to shame.

6 Listen, an uproar from the city!
        A voice from the temple!
The voice of the LORD,
        dealing retribution to his enemies!

7 Before she was in labor
        she gave birth;
    before her pain came upon her
        she delivered a son.

---

h Or sudden terror   i Gk Syr: Heb these things came to be
j Meaning of Heb uncertain   k Or to punish

8 Who has heard of such a thing?
   Who has seen such things?
Shall a land be born in one day?
   Shall a nation be delivered in one
      moment?
Yet as soon as Zion was in labor
   she delivered her children.
9 Shall I open the womb and not deliver?
   says the LORD;
shall I, the one who delivers, shut the
      womb?
   says your God.

10 Rejoice with Jerusalem, and be glad for her,
   all you who love her;
rejoice with her in joy,
   all you who mourn over her—
11 that you may nurse and be satisfied
   from her consoling breast;
that you may drink deeply with delight
   from her glorious bosom.

12 For thus says the LORD:
I will extend prosperity to her like a river,
   and the wealth of the nations like an
      overflowing stream;
and you shall nurse and be carried on
      her arm,
   and dandled on her knees.
13 As a mother comforts her child,
   so I will comfort you;
   you shall be comforted in Jerusalem.

The Reign and Indignation of God

14 You shall see, and your heart shall rejoice;
   your bodies[l] shall flourish like the grass;
and it shall be known that the hand of the
      LORD is with his servants,
   and his indignation is against
      his enemies.
15 For the LORD will come in fire,
   and his chariots like the whirlwind,
to pay back his anger in fury,
   and his rebuke in flames of fire.
16 For by fire will the LORD execute judgment,

and by his sword, on all flesh;
   and those slain by the LORD shall be
      many.

17 Those who sanctify and purify themselves to go into the gardens, following the one in the center, eating the flesh of pigs, vermin, and rodents, shall come to an end together, says the LORD.

18 For I know[m] their works and their thoughts, and I am[n] coming to gather all nations and tongues; and they shall come and shall see my glory, 19 and I will set a sign among them. From them I will send survivors to the nations, to Tar'shish, Put,[o] and Lud—which draw the bow—to Tū'bal and Jā'van, to the coastlands far away that have not heard of my fame or seen my glory; and they shall declare my glory among the nations. 20 They shall bring all your kindred from all the nations as an offering to the LORD, on horses, and in chariots, and in litters, and on mules, and on dromedaries, to my holy mountain Jerusalem, says the LORD, just as the Israelites bring a grain offering in a clean vessel to the house of the LORD. 21 And I will also take some of them as priests and as Lē'vītes, says the LORD.

22 For as the new heavens and the new earth,
   which I will make,
shall remain before me, says the LORD;
   so shall your descendants and your name
      remain.
23 From new moon to new moon,
   and from sabbath to sabbath,
all flesh shall come to worship before me,
   says the LORD.

24 And they shall go out and look at the dead bodies of the people who have rebelled against me; for their worm shall not die, their fire shall not be quenched, and they shall be an abhorrence to all flesh.

---

l Heb bones   m Gk Syr: Heb lacks know   n Gk Syr Vg Tg: Heb it is   o Gk: Heb Pul

I magine you're watching a movie. One of the leading characters imposes severe hardships on others and then goes off to dine in luxury. Immediately, you know the character is a villain. Another leading character calls for others to endure sacrifice and lives under the same conditions as they do. You know this is a hero, because heroes practice what they preach. Jeremiah the prophet was such a hero; he not only preached a hard message but accepted the trials that came with it.

At a Glance

- **Chapter 1.** Jeremiah's call
- **Chapters 2–25.** prophecies against Judah and Jerusalem
- **Chapters 26–45.** biographical material and a discussion of the restoration of Israel
- **Chapters 46–52.** prophecies against other nations

In-depth

At the beginning of Jeremiah's prophetic ministry, King Josiah ruled the southern kingdom of Judah (2 Chronicles, chapters 34–35). He was a good king who expanded Judah's territory and started a religious reform. Jeremiah approved of Josiah and Josiah's reforms, but he was afraid they were too little, too late. Chapters 2–5 of his book contain his prophecies during Josiah's rule. In them, he speaks out against Israel's sin and corruption but hopes that things will improve if the people turn to God (4.1–2). Unfortunately, King Josiah was suddenly killed in battle, and things went from bad to worse.

Kings Jehoiakim and Zedekiah were the main rulers who followed Josiah, and they were Josiah's complete opposite (2 Chr 36.1–14). Both were ruthless, power hungry, and corrupt. During Jehoiakim's reign, Jeremiah had to go into hiding out of fear for his life. Chapters 7–20 of Jeremiah's book contain his prophecies during this time, when his preaching against the sins of Israel became stronger. Chapters 21–29 and 34–45 record his life and preaching during Zedekiah's reign—the last few years before the Babylonian Exile. While Zedekiah ruled, Jeremiah was imprisoned, beaten, and thrown into a well to die.

Jeremiah survived his experience in the well to see Jerusalem and the Temple destroyed by the Babylonians. To give the people hope that God was still on their side, he prophesied the destruction of all Israel's enemies, especially Babylon (see chapters 46–51).

Ultimately, Jeremiah realized that even a new king like David would not be enough to correct what was wrong. The people were unable to fulfill God's commandments because they had hearts of stone. In chapters 30–33, the Book of Consolation, Jeremiah said that the Lord would make a new Covenant with Israel in the future, and this time, the Law would be written on the people's hearts (31.33–34).

Quick Facts

Period Covered
626–583 B.C.

Authors
Jeremiah and his disciples, including Baruch

Themes
Israel's need for repentance, Jeremiah's struggles, the New Covenant

The Book of *Jeremiah*

Jeremiah

Before I formed you in the womb I knew you.

The words of Jer•e•mī′ah son of Hil•kī′ah, of the priests who were in An′a•thoth in the land of Benjamin, ²to whom the word of the LORD came in the days of King Jō•sī′ah son of Ā′mon of Judah, in the thirteenth year of his reign. ³It came also in the days of King Je•hoi′a•kim son of Jō•sī′ah of Judah, and until the end of the eleventh year of King Zed•e•kī′ah son of Jō•sī′ah of Judah, until the captivity of Jerusalem in the fifth month.

Jeremiah's Call and Commission

4 Now the word of the LORD came to me saying,
5 "Before I formed you in the womb I
        knew you,
    and before you were born I consecrated you;
    I appointed you a prophet to the nations."
⁶Then I said, "Ah, Lord GOD! Truly I do not know how to speak, for I am only a boy." ⁷But the LORD said to me,
    "Do not say, 'I am only a boy';
    for you shall go to all to whom I send you,
    and you shall speak whatever I
        command you.
8   Do not be afraid of them,
    for I am with you to deliver you,
                            says the LORD."
⁹Then the LORD put out his hand and touched my mouth; and the LORD said to me,

"Now I have put my words in your mouth.
10 See, today I appoint you over nations and
        over kingdoms,
    to pluck up and to pull down,
    to destroy and to overthrow,
    to build and to plant."

11 The word of the LORD came to me, saying, "Jer•e•mī′ah, what do you see?" And I said, "I see a branch of an almond tree."ᵃ ¹²Then the LORD said to me, "You have seen well, for I am watchingᵇ over my word to perform it." ¹³The word of the LORD came to me a second time, saying, "What do you see?" And I said, "I see a boiling pot, tilted away from the north."

14 Then the LORD said to me: Out of the north disaster shall break out on all the inhabitants of the land. ¹⁵For now I am calling all the tribes of the kingdoms of the north, says the LORD; and they shall come and all of them shall set their thrones at the entrance of the gates of Jerusalem, against all its surrounding walls and against all the cities of Judah. ¹⁶And I will utter my judgments against them, for all their wickedness in forsaking me; they have made offerings to other gods, and worshiped the works of their own hands. ¹⁷But you, gird up your loins; stand up and tell them everything that I command you. Do not break down before them, or I will break you before them.

ᵃ Heb *shaqed*   ᵇ Heb *shoqed*

JER

18 And I for my part have made you today a forti-fied city, an iron pillar, and a bronze wall, against the whole land—against the kings of Judah, its princes, its priests, and the people of the land. 19 They will fight against you; but they shall not prevail against you, for I am with you, says the LORD, to deliver you.

God Pleads with Israel to Repent

The word of the LORD came to me, saying: 2 Go and proclaim in the hearing of Jerusalem, Thus says the LORD:
> I remember the devotion of your youth,
>   your love as a bride,
> how you followed me in the wilderness,
>   in a land not sown.
3 Israel was holy to the LORD,
>   the first fruits of his harvest.
> All who ate of it were held guilty;
>   disaster came upon them,
>
>   says the LORD.

4 Hear the word of the LORD, O house of Jacob, and all the families of the house of Israel. 5 Thus says the LORD:
> What wrong did your ancestors find in me
>   that they went far from me,
> and went after worthless things, and became
>   worthless themselves?
6 They did not say, "Where is the LORD

> who brought us up from the land of
>   Egypt,
> who led us in the wilderness,
>   in a land of deserts and pits,
> in a land of drought and deep darkness,
>   in a land that no one passes through,
>   where no one lives?"
7 I brought you into a plentiful land
>   to eat its fruits and its good things.
> But when you entered you defiled my land,
>   and made my heritage an abomination.
8 The priests did not say, "Where is the LORD?"
>   Those who handle the law did not
>   know me;
> the rulers[c] transgressed against me;
>   the prophets prophesied by Bā'al,
>   and went after things that do not profit.

9 Therefore once more I accuse you,
>   says the LORD,
>   and I accuse your children's children.
10 Cross to the coasts of Cyprus and look,
>   send to Kē'dar and examine with care;
>   see if there has ever been such a thing.
11 Has a nation changed its gods,
>   even though they are no gods?
> But my people have changed their glory
>   for something that does not profit.
12 Be appalled, O heavens, at this,

---

c Heb shepherds

Who, Me?

LIVE IT!

"Who, me?"
How many times have we said those two words? or heard others say them? Usually, some type of excuse follows: "No, I didn't do it!" or "I wasn't there" or "I'm too busy right now." Why are we so eager to get out of a challenging situation or avoid taking on some responsibility?

Jeremiah is no exception. The story of his calling follows a classic pattern (see "Here I Am, Lord!" Isa 6.1–13). God gives him a clear summons and a definite direction for his life: "I appointed you a prophet to the nations" (Jer 1.5). Jeremiah tries to claim that he is too young and to get out of what he is being called to do. The Lord reassures him: "Do not be afraid . . . / for I am with you to deliver you" (verse 8).

How can Jeremiah—indeed, any of us—turn down a call like this? God has known each of us from the beginning of time. Each of us has a call to be prophetic. And God has a dream for us, a challenge, no matter what our age or situation. Can you be open to that challenge?

"Who, me?"

Yes, you!

What is God calling you to? What excuses do you use to avoid deepening your relationship with God?

▶ Jer 1.4–10

be shocked, be utterly desolate,
says the LORD,

13 for my people have committed two evils:
    they have forsaken me,
the fountain of living water,
    and dug out cisterns for themselves,
cracked cisterns
    that can hold no water.

14 Is Israel a slave? Is he a homeborn servant?
    Why then has he become plunder?

15 The lions have roared against him,
    they have roared loudly.
They have made his land a waste;
    his cities are in ruins, without inhabitant.

16 Moreover, the people of Memphis and
    Tah'pan•hēs

19 Your wickedness will punish you,
    and your apostasies will convict you.
Know and see that it is evil and bitter
    for you to forsake the LORD your God;
    the fear of me is not in you,
        says the Lord GOD of hosts.

20 For long ago you broke your yoke
    and burst your bonds,
    and you said, "I will not serve!"
On every high hill
    and under every green tree
    you sprawled and played the whore.

21 Yet I planted you as a choice vine,
    from the purest stock.
How then did you turn degenerate
    and become a wild vine?

Introducing ▶ JEREMIAH

Have you ever felt ridiculed for defending your values or doing a good deed? If so, then you can probably relate to Jeremiah, who once told God:

O LORD, you have enticed me,
    and I was enticed;

I have become a laughingstock all day long;
    everyone mocks me.
(Jer 20.7)

Jeremiah knew what it was like to be rejected for delivering God's message.

Jeremiah was born in 645 B.C. of a priestly family from a northern Israelite tribe. He was very young when he began his prophetic career. Like Isaiah, Jeremiah was a prophet for all seasons. He was both optimistic (chapter 31) and condemning (22.18–23). He was courageous (chapter 37), enduring beatings, imprisonment, and even being thrown into a well to die (38.1–6) for the sake of delivering God's message. He loved his people so much that he was sometimes called the weeping prophet because of his bitter tears for them and their fast approaching doom (9.1; 13.7).

The Book of Jeremiah gives us a fascinating inside look at the prophet's relationship with God. Several passages, called the Confessions of Jeremiah, are personal accounts of his struggles with God (12.1–6; 15.10–21; 17.12–18; 18.18–23; 20.7–18). If you take the time to read these passages, you may find that your own doubts and struggles aren't all that different.

have broken the crown of your head.

17 Have you not brought this upon yourself
    by forsaking the LORD your God,
    while he led you in the way?

18 What then do you gain by going to Egypt,
    to drink the waters of the Nile?
Or what do you gain by going to Assyria,
    to drink the waters of the Euphrates?

22 Though you wash yourself with lye
    and use much soap,
    the stain of your guilt is still before me,
        says the Lord GOD.

23 How can you say, "I am not defiled,
    I have not gone after the Ba'als"?
Look at your way in the valley;
    know what you have done—

HISPANICS ASSUME THEIR MISSION AS PROPHETS!

Jeremiah, and many of the other Old Testament prophets, calls for solidarity with the poor and oppressed. During the Third Encuentro Nacional Hispano de Pastoral, in 1985, Hispanics assumed their mission as prophets in contemporary society. They expressed their solidarity with the social groups in need of liberation and their desire to live and promote justice. The following statements are from the Encuentro:

- We, as Hispanic people, make a preferential option for and in solidarity with the poor and marginalized.
- We, as Hispanic people, make a preferential option for Hispanic youth so that they will participate at all levels of pastoral ministry.
- We, as Hispanic people, want to follow the line of a Church that promotes and exemplifies justice.
- We, as Hispanic people, wish to follow an approach of valuing and promoting women, recognizing their equality and dignity and their role in the Church, the family, and society.

(Secretariat for Hispanic Affairs, *Prophetic Voices*, p. 6)

a restive young camel interlacing her tracks,
24 　　a wild ass at home in the wilderness,
in her heat sniffing the wind!
　　Who can restrain her lust?
None who seek her need weary themselves;
　　in her month they will find her.
25 Keep your feet from going unshod
　　and your throat from thirst.
But you said, "It is hopeless,
for I have loved strangers,
　　and after them I will go."

26 As a thief is shamed when caught,
　　so the house of Israel shall be shamed—
they, their kings, their officials,
　　their priests, and their prophets,
27 who say to a tree, "You are my father,"
　　and to a stone, "You gave me birth."
For they have turned their backs to me,
　　and not their faces.
But in the time of their trouble they say,
　　"Come and save us!"
28 But where are your gods
　　that you made for yourself?
Let them come, if they can save you,
　　in your time of trouble;
for you have as many gods
　　as you have towns, O Judah.

29 Why do you complain against me?
　　You have all rebelled against me,
　　　　　　　　　　　　　　says the LORD.

30 In vain I have struck down your children;
　　they accepted no correction.
Your own sword devoured your prophets
　　like a ravening lion.
31 And you, O generation, behold the word of
　　　　the LORD!d
Have I been a wilderness to Israel,
　　or a land of thick darkness?
Why then do my people say, "We are free,
　　we will come to you no more"?
32 Can a girl forget her ornaments,
　　or a bride her attire?
Yet my people have forgotten me,
　　days without number.

33 How well you direct your course
　　to seek lovers!
So that even to wicked women
　　you have taught your ways.
34 Also on your skirts is found
　　the lifeblood of the innocent poor,
though you did not catch them breaking in.
　　Yet in spite of all these thingsd
35 you say, "I am innocent;
　　surely his anger has turned from me."
Now I am bringing you to judgment
　　for saying, "I have not sinned."
36 How lightly you gad about,
　　changing your ways!
You shall be put to shame by Egypt

---

d Meaning of Heb uncertain

JER

as you were put to shame by Assyria.
37 From there also you will come away
  with your hands on your head;
  for the LORD has rejected those in whom you
    trust,
  and you will not prosper through them.

Unfaithful Israel

If[e] a man divorces his wife
  and she goes from him
and becomes another man's wife,
  will he return to her?
Would not such a land be greatly polluted?
You have played the whore with many
    lovers;
  and would you return to me?
                                says the LORD.
2 Look up to the bare heights,[f] and see!
  Where have you not been lain with?
By the waysides you have sat waiting for
    lovers,
  like a nomad in the wilderness.
You have polluted the land
  with your whoring and wickedness.
3 Therefore the showers have been withheld,
  and the spring rain has not come;
yet you have the forehead of a whore,
  you refuse to be ashamed.
4 Have you not just now called to me,
  "My Father, you are the friend of my
    youth—
5 will he be angry forever,
  will he be indignant to the end?"
This is how you have spoken,
  but you have done all the evil that you
    could.

A Call to Repentance

6 The LORD said to me in the days of King Jō-sī'ah: Have you seen what she did, that faithless one, Israel, how she went up on every high hill and under every green tree, and played the whore there? 7 And I thought, "After she has done all this she will return to me"; but she did not return, and her false sister Judah saw it. 8 She[g] saw that for all the adulteries of that faithless one, Israel, I had sent her away with a decree of divorce; yet her false sister Judah did not fear, but she too went and played the whore. 9 Because she took her whoredom so lightly, she polluted the land, committing adultery with stone and tree. 10 Yet for all this her false sister Judah did not return to me with her whole heart, but only in pretense, says the LORD.

11 Then the LORD said to me: Faithless Israel has shown herself less guilty than false Judah.

12 Go, and proclaim these words toward the north, and say:
  Return, faithless Israel,
                                says the LORD.
I will not look on you in anger,
  for I am merciful,
                                says the LORD;
I will not be angry forever.

Catholic Connections

CONTRITION

Jeremiah calls the people to acknowledge their sin and return to God. In Catholic Tradition, the word *contrition* describes sorrow for sins and the commitment not to sin again. Jeremiah is calling the people to contrition with the promise that God wants their return and is eager to welcome them back.

An act of contrition is a prayer in which you express your sorrow and hate for your sin and your resolve not to sin again. You may have learned an act of contrition to prepare to celebrate the sacrament of Reconciliation (or Penance). You can use this prayer form any time you need to acknowledge a sin and ask God's forgiveness.

Try writing your own act of contrition. Use it whenever sin has separated you from God—knowing that God is merciful and wants nothing to separate you from God's love.

▸ Jer 3.12–14

13 Only acknowledge your guilt,
  that you have rebelled against the LORD
    your God,
and scattered your favors among strangers
  under every green tree,

---

[e] Q Ms Gk Syr: MT *Saying, If*   [f] Or *the trails*   [g] Q Ms Gk Mss Syr: MT *I*

and have not obeyed my voice,
>
> says the LORD.

14 Return, O faithless children,
>
> says the LORD,

for I am your master;
I will take you, one from a city and two
> from a family,
and I will bring you to Zion.

15 I will give you shepherds after my own heart, who will feed you with knowledge and understanding. 16 And when you have multiplied and increased in the land, in those days, says the LORD, they shall no longer say, "The ark of the covenant of the LORD." It shall not come to mind, or be remembered, or missed; nor shall another one be made. 17 At that time Jerusalem shall be called the throne of the LORD, and all nations shall gather to it, to the presence of the LORD in Jerusalem, and they shall no longer stubbornly follow their own evil will. 18 In those days the house of Judah shall join the house of Israel, and together they shall come from the land of the north to the land that I gave your ancestors for a heritage.

19 I thought
> how I would set you among my children,
and give you a pleasant land,
> the most beautiful heritage of all the
> nations.
And I thought you would call me, My
> Father,
and would not turn from following me.
20 Instead, as a faithless wife leaves her
> husband,
> so you have been faithless to me,
> O house of Israel,
>
> says the LORD.

21 A voice on the bare heights[h] is heard,
> the plaintive weeping of Israel's children,
because they have perverted their way,
> they have forgotten the LORD their God:
22 Return, O faithless children,
> I will heal your faithlessness.

"Here we come to you;
> for you are the LORD our God.
23 Truly the hills are[i] a delusion,
> the orgies on the mountains.
Truly in the LORD our God
> is the salvation of Israel.

24 "But from our youth the shameful thing has devoured all for which our ancestors had labored, their flocks and their herds, their sons and their daughters. 25 Let us lie down in our shame, and let our dishonor cover us; for we have sinned against the LORD our God, we and our ancestors,

from our youth even to this day; and we have not obeyed the voice of the LORD our God."

If you return, O Israel,
>
> says the LORD,

> if you return to me,
if you remove your abominations from my
> presence,
> and do not waver,
2 and if you swear, "As the LORD lives!"
> in truth, in justice, and in uprightness,
then nations shall be blessed[j] by him,
> and by him they shall boast.

3 For thus says the LORD to the people of Judah and to the inhabitants of Jerusalem:
Break up your fallow ground,
> and do not sow among thorns.
4 Circumcise yourselves to the LORD,
> remove the foreskin of your hearts,
> O people of Judah and inhabitants of
> Jerusalem,
or else my wrath will go forth like fire,
> and burn with no one to quench it,
> because of the evil of your doings.

Invasion and Desolation of
Judah Threatened

5 Declare in Judah, and proclaim in Jerusalem, and say:
Blow the trumpet through the land;
> shout aloud[k] and say,
"Gather together, and let us go
> into the fortified cities!"
6 Raise a standard toward Zion,
> flee for safety, do not delay,
for I am bringing evil from the north,
> and a great destruction.
7 A lion has gone up from its thicket,
> a destroyer of nations has set out;
> he has gone out from his place
to make your land a waste;
> your cities will be ruins
> without inhabitant.
8 Because of this put on sackcloth,
> lament and wail:
"The fierce anger of the LORD
> has not turned away from us."

9 On that day, says the LORD, courage shall fail the king and the officials; the priests shall be appalled and the prophets astounded. 10 Then I said, "Ah, Lord GOD, how utterly you have deceived this

---

h Or *the trails*   i Gk Syr Vg: Heb *Truly from the hills is*
j Or *shall bless themselves*   k Or *shout, take your weapons:*
Heb *shout, fill* (your hand)

JER

people and Jerusalem, saying, 'It shall be well with you,' even while the sword is at the throat!"

11 At that time it will be said to this people and to Jerusalem: A hot wind comes from me out of the bare heights[l] in the desert toward my poor people, not to winnow or cleanse— 12 a wind too strong for that. Now it is I who speak in judgment against them.

13 Look! He comes up like clouds,
 his chariots like the whirlwind;
his horses are swifter than eagles—
 woe to us, for we are ruined!
14 O Jerusalem, wash your heart clean of
 wickedness
 so that you may be saved.
How long shall your evil schemes
 lodge within you?
15 For a voice declares from Dan
 and proclaims disaster from Mount
 Ē′phra•im.
16 Tell the nations, "Here they are!"
 Proclaim against Jerusalem,
"Besiegers come from a distant land;
 they shout against the cities of Judah.
17 They have closed in around her like
 watchers of a field,
because she has rebelled against me,
 says the LORD.
18 Your ways and your doings
 have brought this upon you.
This is your doom; how bitter it is!
 It has reached your very heart."

Sorrow for a Doomed Nation

19 My anguish, my anguish! I writhe in pain!
 Oh, the walls of my heart!
My heart is beating wildly;
 I cannot keep silent;
for I[m] hear the sound of the trumpet,
 the alarm of war.
20 Disaster overtakes disaster,
 the whole land is laid waste.
Suddenly my tents are destroyed,
 my curtains in a moment.
21 How long must I see the standard,
 and hear the sound of the trumpet?
22 "For my people are foolish,
 they do not know me;
they are stupid children,
 they have no understanding.
They are skilled in doing evil,
 but do not know how to do good."

23 I looked on the earth, and lo, it was waste
 and void;

and to the heavens, and they had no
 light.
24 I looked on the mountains, and lo, they
 were quaking,
 and all the hills moved to and fro.
25 I looked, and lo, there was no one at all,
 and all the birds of the air had fled.
26 I looked, and lo, the fruitful land was a
 desert,
 and all its cities were laid in ruins
 before the LORD, before his fierce anger.
27 For thus says the LORD: The whole land shall be a desolation; yet I will not make a full end.
28 Because of this the earth shall mourn,
 and the heavens above grow black;
for I have spoken, I have purposed;
 I have not relented nor will I turn back.

29 At the noise of horseman and archer
 every town takes to flight;
they enter thickets; they climb among rocks;
 all the towns are forsaken,
 and no one lives in them.
30 And you, O desolate one,
what do you mean that you dress in
 crimson,
 that you deck yourself with ornaments of
 gold,
 that you enlarge your eyes with paint?
In vain you beautify yourself.
 Your lovers despise you;
 they seek your life.
31 For I heard a cry as of a woman in labor,
 anguish as of one bringing forth her first
 child,
the cry of daughter Zion gasping for breath,
 stretching out her hands,
"Woe is me! I am fainting before killers!"

The Utter Corruption of God's People

Run to and fro through the streets of
 Jerusalem,
 look around and take note!
Search its squares and see
 if you can find one person
who acts justly
 and seeks truth—
so that I may pardon Jerusalem.[n]
2 Although they say, "As the LORD lives,"
 yet they swear falsely.
3 O LORD, do your eyes not look for truth?
You have struck them,
 but they felt no anguish;
you have consumed them,

---

l Or *the trails*   m Another reading is *for you, O my soul,*
n Heb *it*

but they refused to take correction.
They have made their faces harder than
  rock;
  they have refused to turn back.

4 Then I said, "These are only the poor,
  they have no sense;
for they do not know the way of the LORD,
  the law of their God.
5 Let me go to the rich⁰
  and speak to them;
surely they know the way of the LORD,
  the law of their God."
But they all alike had broken the yoke,
  they had burst the bonds.

6 Therefore a lion from the forest shall kill
      them,
  a wolf from the desert shall destroy them.
A leopard is watching against their cities;
  everyone who goes out of them shall be
      torn in pieces—
because their transgressions are many,
  their apostasies are great.

7 How can I pardon you?
  Your children have forsaken me,
  and have sworn by those who are no
      gods.
When I fed them to the full,
  they committed adultery
and trooped to the houses of prostitutes.
8 They were well-fed lusty stallions,
  each neighing for his neighbor's wife.
9 Shall I not punish them for these things?
                              says the LORD;
  and shall I not bring retribution
  on a nation such as this?

10 Go up through her vine-rows and destroy,
  but do not make a full end;
strip away her branches,
  for they are not the LORD's.
11 For the house of Israel and the house of
      Judah
  have been utterly faithless to me,
                              says the LORD.
12 They have spoken falsely of the LORD,
  and have said, "He will do nothing.
No evil will come upon us,
  and we shall not see sword or famine."
13 The prophets are nothing but wind,
  for the word is not in them.
Thus shall it be done to them!

14 Therefore thus says the LORD, the God of
      hosts:
Because theyᵖ have spoken this word,

I am now making my words in your mouth
      a fire,
  and this people wood, and the fire shall
      devour them.
15 I am going to bring upon you
  a nation from far away, O house of
      Israel,
                              says the LORD.
It is an enduring nation,
  it is an ancient nation,
a nation whose language you do not know,
  nor can you understand what they say.
16 Their quiver is like an open tomb;
  all of them are mighty warriors.
17 They shall eat up your harvest and your
      food;
  they shall eat up your sons and your
      daughters;
  they shall eat up your flocks and your
      herds;
  they shall eat up your vines and your fig
      trees;
  they shall destroy with the sword
  your fortified cities in which you trust.

18 But even in those days, says the LORD, I will
not make a full end of you. 19 And when your people say, "Why has the LORD our God done all these
things to us?" you shall say to them, "As you have
forsaken me and served foreign gods in your land,
so you shall serve strangers in a land that is not
yours."

20 Declare this in the house of Jacob,
  proclaim it in Judah:
21 Hear this, O foolish and senseless people,
  who have eyes, but do not see,
  who have ears, but do not hear.
22 Do you not fear me? says the LORD;
  Do you not tremble before me?
I placed the sand as a boundary for the sea,
  a perpetual barrier that it cannot pass;
though the waves toss, they cannot prevail,
  though they roar, they cannot pass
      over it.
23 But this people has a stubborn and
      rebellious heart;
  they have turned aside and gone away.
24 They do not say in their hearts,
  "Let us fear the LORD our God,
who gives the rain in its season,
  the autumn rain and the spring rain,
and keeps for us
  the weeks appointed for the harvest."
25 Your iniquities have turned these away,

---

o Or *the great*   p Heb *you*

and your sins have deprived you of good.

26 For scoundrels are found among my people;
  they take over the goods of others.
Like fowlers they set a trap;*q*
  they catch human beings.

27 Like a cage full of birds,
  their houses are full of treachery;
therefore they have become great and rich,

28   they have grown fat and sleek.
They know no limits in deeds of
    wickedness;
  they do not judge with justice
the cause of the orphan, to make it prosper,
  and they do not defend the rights of the
    needy.

29 Shall I not punish them for these things?
                    says the LORD,
  and shall I not bring retribution
  on a nation such as this?

30 An appalling and horrible thing
  has happened in the land:

31 the prophets prophesy falsely,
  and the priests rule as the prophets
    direct;*r*
my people love to have it so,
  but what will you do when the end
    comes?

The Imminence and Horror
of the Invasion

Flee for safety, O children of Benjamin,
  from the midst of Jerusalem!
Blow the trumpet in Te·kō′a,
  and raise a signal on Beth-hac·che′rem;
for evil looms out of the north,
  and great destruction.

2 I have likened daughter Zion
  to the loveliest pasture.*s*

3 Shepherds with their flocks shall come
    against her.
They shall pitch their tents around her;
  they shall pasture, all in their places.

4 "Prepare war against her;
  up, and let us attack at noon!"
"Woe to us, for the day declines,
  the shadows of evening lengthen!"

5 "Up, and let us attack by night,
  and destroy her palaces!"

6 For thus says the LORD of hosts:
Cut down her trees;
  cast up a siege ramp against Jerusalem.
This is the city that must be punished;*t*
  there is nothing but oppression
    within her.

7 As a well keeps its water fresh,
  so she keeps fresh her wickedness;
violence and destruction are heard
    within her;
  sickness and wounds are ever before me.

8 Take warning, O Jerusalem,
  or I shall turn from you in disgust,
and make you a desolation,
  an uninhabited land.

9 Thus says the LORD of hosts:
Glean*u* thoroughly as a vine
  the remnant of Israel;
like a grape-gatherer, pass your hand again
  over its branches.

10 To whom shall I speak and give warning,
  that they may hear?
See, their ears are closed,*v*
  they cannot listen.
The word of the LORD is to them an object
    of scorn;
  they take no pleasure in it.

11 But I am full of the wrath of the LORD;
  I am weary of holding it in.

Pour it out on the children in the street,
  and on the gatherings of young men as
    well;
both husband and wife shall be taken,
  the old folk and the very aged.

12 Their houses shall be turned over to others,
  their fields and wives together;
for I will stretch out my hand
  against the inhabitants of the land,
                    says the LORD.

13 For from the least to the greatest of them,
  everyone is greedy for unjust gain;
and from prophet to priest,
  everyone deals falsely.

14 They have treated the wound of my people
    carelessly,
  saying, "Peace, peace,"
  when there is no peace.

15 They acted shamefully, they committed
    abomination;
  yet they were not ashamed,
  they did not know how to blush.
Therefore they shall fall among those who
    fall;
  at the time that I punish them, they shall
    be overthrown,
                    says the LORD.

---

q Meaning of Heb uncertain   *r* Or *rule by their own*
authority   *s* Or *I will destroy daughter Zion, the loveliest*
pasture   *t* Or *the city of license*   *u* Cn: Heb *They shall*
glean   *v* Heb *are uncircumcised*

16 Thus says the LORD:
 Stand at the crossroads, and look,
  and ask for the ancient paths,
 where the good way lies; and walk in it,
  and find rest for your souls.
 But they said, "We will not walk in it."
17 Also I raised up sentinels for you:
  "Give heed to the sound of the trumpet!"
 But they said, "We will not give heed."
18 Therefore hear, O nations,
  and know, O congregation, what will
   happen to them.
19 Hear, O earth; I am going to bring disaster
   on this people,
  the fruit of their schemes,
 because they have not given heed to my words;
  and as for my teaching, they have
   rejected it.
20 Of what use to me is frankincense that
   comes from She'ba,
  or sweet cane from a distant land?
 Your burnt offerings are not acceptable,
  nor are your sacrifices pleasing to me.
21 Therefore thus says the LORD:
 See, I am laying before this people
  stumbling blocks against which they shall
   stumble;
 parents and children together,
  neighbor and friend shall perish.

22 Thus says the LORD:
 See, a people is coming from the land of
   the north,
  a great nation is stirring from the farthest
   parts of the earth.
23 They grasp the bow and the javelin,
  they are cruel and have no mercy,
  their sound is like the roaring sea;
 they ride on horses,
  equipped like a warrior for battle,
  against you, O daughter Zion!
24 "We have heard news of them,
  our hands fall helpless;
 anguish has taken hold of us,
  pain as of a woman in labor.
25 Do not go out into the field,
  or walk on the road;
 for the enemy has a sword,
  terror is on every side."

26 O my poor people, put on sackcloth,
  and roll in ashes;
 make mourning as for an only child,
  most bitter lamentation:
 for suddenly the destroyer
  will come upon us.

27 I have made you a tester and a refiner[w]
   among my people
  so that you may know and test their
   ways.
28 They are all stubbornly rebellious,
  going about with slanders;
 they are bronze and iron,
  all of them act corruptly.
29 The bellows blow fiercely,
  the lead is consumed by the fire;
 in vain the refining goes on,
  for the wicked are not removed.
30 They are called "rejected silver,"
  for the LORD has rejected them.

Jeremiah Proclaims God's Judgment on the Nation
(Cp Jer 26.4–6)

The word that came to Jer•e•mi'ah from the LORD: 2 Stand in the gate of the LORD's house, and proclaim there this word, and say, Hear the word of the LORD, all you people of Judah, you that enter these gates to worship the LORD. 3 Thus says the LORD of hosts, the God of Israel: Amend your ways and your doings, and let me dwell with you[x] in this place. 4 Do not trust in these deceptive words: "This is[y] the temple of the LORD, the temple of the LORD, the temple of the LORD."

5 For if you truly amend your ways and your doings, if you truly act justly one with another, 6 if you do not oppress the alien, the orphan, and the widow, or shed innocent blood in this place, and if you do not go after other gods to your own hurt, 7 then I will dwell with you in this place, in the land that I gave of old to your ancestors forever and ever.

8 Here you are, trusting in deceptive words to no avail. 9 Will you steal, murder, commit adultery, swear falsely, make offerings to Ba'al, and go after other gods that you have not known, 10 and then come and stand before me in this house, which is called by my name, and say, "We are safe!"—only to go on doing all these abominations? 11 Has this house, which is called by my name, become a den of robbers in your sight? You know, I too am watching, says the LORD. 12 Go now to my place that was in Shi'loh, where I made my name dwell at first, and see what I did to it for the wickedness of my people Israel. 13 And now, because you have done all these things, says the LORD, and when I spoke to you persistently, you did not listen, and when I called you, you did not answer, 14 therefore I will do to the house that is called by

---

w Or a fortress   x Or and I will let you dwell   y Heb They are

my name, in which you trust, and to the place that I gave to you and to your ancestors, just what I did to Shi'lōh. 15 And I will cast you out of my sight, just as I cast out all your kinsfolk, all the offspring of Ē'phra‧im.

did you KNOW?

The Prophet and the Temple

In ancient Israel, the Temple was considered the dwelling place of God. Most Israelites felt that as long as the Temple stood, God was keeping the Covenant promise to stay with Israel. They believed this because Jerusalem and Judea had been spared when the northern kingdom fell to Assyria (721 B.C.). The Israelites failed to remember that God's Covenant with them was a mutual one—that they in turn had to keep their commitment to worship God alone.

Speaking for God at the gates of the Temple, Jeremiah told the people the Temple would be destroyed if Israel continued to disobey the commandments of the Covenant (see how the sins he accused them of in Jer 7.8–9 reflect the Ten Commandments). The destruction of the Temple would be a visible sign that the Covenant had been broken—not by God, but by the people.

The Temple was destroyed, and then rebuilt. Centuries later, Jesus preached to a new generation who thought that the Temple was a guarantee of God's presence and favor. He predicted the Temple would be destroyed again (Mt 24.1–2).

▶ Jer 7.1–14

The People's Disobedience

16 As for you, do not pray for this people, do not raise a cry or prayer on their behalf, and do not intercede with me, for I will not hear you. 17 Do you not see what they are doing in the towns of Judah and in the streets of Jerusalem? 18 The children gather wood, the fathers kindle fire, and the women knead dough, to make cakes for the queen of heaven; and they pour out drink offerings to other gods, to provoke me to anger. 19 Is it I whom they provoke? says the LORD. Is it not themselves, to their own hurt? 20 Therefore thus says the Lord GOD: My anger and my wrath shall be poured out on this place, on human beings and animals, on the trees of the field and the fruit of the ground; it will burn and not be quenched.

21 Thus says the LORD of hosts, the God of Israel: Add your burnt offerings to your sacrifices, and eat the flesh. 22 For in the day that I brought your ancestors out of the land of Egypt, I did not speak to them or command them concerning burnt offerings and sacrifices. 23 But this command I gave them, "Obey my voice, and I will be your God, and you shall be my people; and walk only in the way that I command you, so that it may be well with you." 24 Yet they did not obey or incline their ear, but, in the stubbornness of their evil will, they walked in their own counsels, and looked backward rather than forward. 25 From the day that your ancestors came out of the land of Egypt until this day, I have persistently sent all my servants the prophets to them, day after day; 26 yet they did not listen to me, or pay attention, but they stiffened their necks. They did worse than their ancestors did.

27 So you shall speak all these words to them, but they will not listen to you. You shall call to them, but they will not answer you. 28 You shall say to them: This is the nation that did not obey the voice of the LORD their God, and did not accept discipline; truth has perished; it is cut off from their lips.

29 Cut off your hair and throw it away;
    raise a lamentation on the bare heights,z
  for the LORD has rejected and forsaken
    the generation that provoked his wrath.

30 For the people of Judah have done evil in my sight, says the LORD; they have set their abominations in the house that is called by my name, defiling it. 31 And they go on building the high placea of Tō'pheth, which is in the valley of the son of Hin'nom, to burn their sons and their daughters in the fire—which I did not command, nor did it come into my mind. 32 Therefore, the days are surely coming, says the LORD, when it will no more be called Tō'pheth, or the valley of the son of Hin'nom, but the valley of Slaughter: for they will bury in Tō'pheth until there is no more room. 33 The corpses of this people will be food for the birds of the air, and for the animals of the earth; and no one will frighten them away. 34 And I will bring to an end the sound of mirth and glad-

z Or the trails   a Gk Tg: Heb high places

ness, the voice of the bride and bridegroom in the cities of Judah and in the streets of Jerusalem; for the land shall become a waste.

At that time, says the LORD, the bones of the kings of Judah, the bones of its officials, the bones of the priests, the bones of the prophets, and the bones of the inhabitants of Jerusalem shall be brought out of their tombs; 2 and they shall be spread before the sun and the moon and all the host of heaven, which they have loved and served, which they have followed, and which they have inquired of and worshiped; and they shall not be gathered or buried; they shall be like dung on the surface of the ground. 3 Death shall be preferred to life by all the remnant that remains of this evil family in all the places where I have driven them, says the LORD of hosts.

The Blind Perversity of the Whole Nation

4 You shall say to them, Thus says the LORD:
When people fall, do they not get up again?
If they go astray, do they not turn back?
5 Why then has this people[b] turned away
in perpetual backsliding?
They have held fast to deceit,
they have refused to return.
6 I have given heed and listened,
but they do not speak honestly;
no one repents of wickedness,
saying, "What have I done!"
All of them turn to their own course,
like a horse plunging headlong into
battle.
7 Even the stork in the heavens
knows its times;
and the turtledove, swallow, and crane[c]
observe the time of their coming;
but my people do not know
the ordinance of the LORD.

8 How can you say, "We are wise,
and the law of the LORD is with us,"
when, in fact, the false pen of the scribes
has made it into a lie?
9 The wise shall be put to shame,
they shall be dismayed and taken;
since they have rejected the word of the
LORD,
what wisdom is in them?
10 Therefore I will give their wives to others
and their fields to conquerors,
because from the least to the greatest
everyone is greedy for unjust gain;
from prophet to priest
everyone deals falsely.

11 They have treated the wound of my people
carelessly,
saying, "Peace, peace,"
when there is no peace.
12 They acted shamefully, they committed
abomination;
yet they were not at all ashamed,
they did not know how to blush.
Therefore they shall fall among those who
fall;
at the time when I punish them, they
shall be overthrown,
says the LORD.
13 When I wanted to gather them, says the
LORD,
there are[d] no grapes on the vine,
nor figs on the fig tree;
even the leaves are withered,
and what I gave them has passed away
from them.[c]

14 Why do we sit still?
Gather together, let us go into the fortified
cities
and perish there;
for the LORD our God has doomed us to
perish,
and has given us poisoned water to
drink,
because we have sinned against the LORD.
15 We look for peace, but find no good,
for a time of healing, but there is terror
instead.

16 The snorting of their horses is heard
from Dan;
at the sound of the neighing of their
stallions
the whole land quakes.
They come and devour the land and all that
fills it,
the city and those who live in it.
17 See, I am letting snakes loose among you,
adders that cannot be charmed,
and they shall bite you,
says the LORD.

The Prophet Mourns for the People

18 My joy is gone, grief is upon me,
my heart is sick.
19 Hark, the cry of my poor people
from far and wide in the land:
"Is the LORD not in Zion?

b One Ms Gk: MT *this people, Jerusalem,*   c Meaning of Heb uncertain   d Or *I will make an end of them, says the* LORD. *There are*

Is her King not in her?"
("Why have they provoked me to anger
    with their images,
    with their foreign idols?")
20 "The harvest is past, the summer is ended,
    and we are not saved."
21 For the hurt of my poor people I am hurt,
    I mourn, and dismay has taken hold
    of me.
22 Is there no balm in Gil'e·ad?
    Is there no physician there?
Why then has the health of my poor people
    not been restored?
e O that my head were a spring of water,
    and my eyes a fountain of tears,
so that I might weep day and night
    for the slain of my poor people!
2f O that I had in the desert
    a traveler's lodging place,
that I might leave my people
    and go away from them!
For they are all adulterers,
    a band of traitors.
3 They bend their tongues like bows;
    they have grown strong in the land for
      falsehood, and not for truth;
for they proceed from evil to evil,
    and they do not know me,
      says the LORD.

4 Beware of your neighbors,
    and put no trust in any of your kin;g
for all your kinh are supplanters,
    and every neighbor goes around like a
      slanderer.
5 They all deceive their neighbors,
    and no one speaks the truth;
they have taught their tongues to speak lies;
    they commit iniquity and are too weary
      to repent.i
6 Oppression upon oppression, deceitj upon
    deceit!
They refuse to know me, says the LORD.

7 Therefore thus says the LORD of hosts:
I will now refine and test them,
    for what else can I do with my sinful
      people?k
8 Their tongue is a deadly arrow;
    it speaks deceit through the mouth.
They all speak friendly words to their
    neighbors,
    but inwardly are planning to lay an
      ambush.
9 Shall I not punish them for these things?
    says the LORD;

and shall I not bring retribution
    on a nation such as this?

10 Take upl weeping and wailing for the mountains,
    and a lamentation for the pastures of the
      wilderness,
because they are laid waste so that no one
      passes through,
    and the lowing of cattle is not heard;
both the birds of the air and the animals
    have fled and are gone.
11 I will make Jerusalem a heap of ruins,
    a lair of jackals;
and I will make the towns of Judah a
      desolation,
    without inhabitant.

12 Who is wise enough to understand this? To whom has the mouth of the LORD spoken, so that they may declare it? Why is the land ruined and laid waste like a wilderness, so that no one passes through? 13 And the LORD says: Because they have forsaken my law that I set before them, and have not obeyed my voice, or walked in accordance with it, 14 but have stubbornly followed their own hearts and have gone after the Ba'als, as their ancestors taught them. 15 Therefore thus says the LORD of hosts, the God of Israel: I am feeding this people with wormwood, and giving them poisonous water to drink. 16 I will scatter them among nations that neither they nor their ancestors have known; and I will send the sword after them, until I have consumed them.

The People Mourn in Judgment

17 Thus says the LORD of hosts:
Consider, and call for the mourning women
    to come;
    send for the skilled women to come;
18 let them quickly raise a dirge over us,
    so that our eyes may run down with
      tears,
    and our eyelids flow with water.
19 For a sound of wailing is heard from Zion:
    "How we are ruined!
We are utterly shamed,
because we have left the land,
    because they have cast down our
      dwellings."

---

e Ch 8.23 in Heb   f Ch 9.1 in Heb   g Heb *in a brother*
h Heb *for every brother*   i Cn Compare Gk: Heb *they weary
themselves with iniquity.* 6*Your dwelling*   j Cn: Heb *Your
dwelling in the midst of deceit*   k Or *my poor people*
l Gk Syr: Heb *I will take up*

20 Hear, O women, the word of the LORD,
   and let your ears receive the word of his
      mouth;
teach to your daughters a dirge,
   and each to her neighbor a lament.
21 "Death has come up into our windows,
   it has entered our palaces,
to cut off the children from the streets
   and the young men from the squares."
22 Speak! Thus says the LORD:
   "Human corpses shall fall
      like dung upon the open field,
   like sheaves behind the reaper,
      and no one shall gather them."

23 Thus says the LORD: Do not let the wise boast in their wisdom, do not let the mighty boast in their might, do not let the wealthy boast in their wealth; 24 but let those who boast boast in this, that they understand and know me, that I am the LORD; I act with steadfast love, justice, and righteousness in the earth, for in these things I delight, says the LORD.

25 The days are surely coming, says the LORD, when I will attend to all those who are circumcised only in the foreskin: 26 Egypt, Judah, E′dom, the Am′mon•ites, Mō′ab, and all those with shaven temples who live in the desert. For all these nations are uncircumcised, and all the house of Israel is uncircumcised in heart.

Idolatry Has Brought Ruin on Israel

Hear the word that the LORD speaks to you, O house of Israel. 2 Thus says the LORD:
   Do not learn the way of the nations,
      or be dismayed at the signs of the
         heavens;
   for the nations are dismayed at them.
3 For the customs of the peoples are false:
   a tree from the forest is cut down,
      and worked with an ax by the hands of
         an artisan;
4 people deck it with silver and gold;
   they fasten it with hammer and nails
      so that it cannot move.
5 Their idols*m* are like scarecrows in a
      cucumber field,
   and they cannot speak;
they have to be carried,
   for they cannot walk.
Do not be afraid of them,
   for they cannot do evil,
      nor is it in them to do good.

6 There is none like you, O LORD;
   you are great, and your name is great in
      might.

7 Who would not fear you, O King of the
      nations?
   For that is your due;
among all the wise ones of the nations
   and in all their kingdoms
      there is no one like you.
8 They are both stupid and foolish;
   the instruction given by idols
      is no better than wood!*n*
9 Beaten silver is brought from Tar′shish,
   and gold from U′phaz.
They are the work of the artisan and of the
      hands of the goldsmith;
   their clothing is blue and purple;
      they are all the product of skilled
         workers.
10 But the LORD is the true God;
   he is the living God and the everlasting
      King.
At his wrath the earth quakes,
   and the nations cannot endure his
      indignation.

11 Thus shall you say to them: The gods who did not make the heavens and the earth shall perish from the earth and from under the heavens.*o*

12 It is he who made the earth by his power,
   who established the world by
      his wisdom,
   and by his understanding stretched out
      the heavens.
13 When he utters his voice, there is a tumult
      of waters in the heavens,
   and he makes the mist rise from the ends
      of the earth.
He makes lightnings for the rain,
   and he brings out the wind from his
      storehouses.
14 Everyone is stupid and without knowledge;
   goldsmiths are all put to shame by their
      idols;
for their images are false,
   and there is no breath in them.
15 They are worthless, a work of delusion;
   at the time of their punishment they
      shall perish.
16 Not like these is the LORD,*p* the portion of
      Jacob,
   for he is the one who formed all things,
      and Israel is the tribe of his inheritance;
   the LORD of hosts is his name.

---

m Heb *They*   *n* Meaning of Heb uncertain   *o* This verse
is in Aramaic   *p* Heb lacks *the LORD*

The Coming Exile

17 Gather up your bundle from the
ground,
O you who live under siege!

18 For thus says the LORD:
I am going to sling out the inhabitants of
the land
at this time,
and I will bring distress on them,
so that they shall feel it.

19 Woe is me because of my hurt!
My wound is severe.
But I said, "Truly this is my punishment,
and I must bear it."

20 My tent is destroyed,
and all my cords are broken;
my children have gone from me,
and they are no more;
there is no one to spread my tent again,
and to set up my curtains.

21 For the shepherds are stupid,
and do not inquire of the LORD;
therefore they have not prospered,
and all their flock is scattered.

22 Hear, a noise! Listen, it is coming—
a great commotion from the land of the
north
to make the cities of Judah a desolation,
a lair of jackals.

23 I know, O LORD, that the way of human
beings is not in their control,
that mortals as they walk cannot direct
their steps.

24 Correct me, O LORD, but in just measure;
not in your anger, or you will bring me
to nothing.

25 Pour out your wrath on the nations that do
not know you,
and on the peoples that do not call on
your name;
for they have devoured Jacob;
they have devoured him and
consumed him,
and have laid waste his habitation.

Israel and Judah Have Broken
the Covenant

The word that came to Jer•e•mi'ah from the LORD:
2 Hear the words of this covenant, and speak to the
people of Judah and the inhabitants of Jerusalem.
3 You shall say to them, Thus says the LORD, the
God of Israel: Cursed be anyone who does not

heed the words of this covenant, 4 which I commanded your ancestors when I brought them out
of the land of Egypt, from the iron-smelter, saying,
Listen to my voice, and do all that I command
you. So shall you be my people, and I will be your
God, 5 that I may perform the oath that I swore to
your ancestors, to give them a land flowing with
milk and honey, as at this day. Then I answered,
"So be it, LORD."

6 And the LORD said to me: Proclaim all these
words in the cities of Judah, and in the streets of
Jerusalem: Hear the words of this covenant and
do them. 7 For I solemnly warned your ancestors
when I brought them up out of the land of Egypt,
warning them persistently, even to this day, saying, Obey my voice. 8 Yet they did not obey or
incline their ear, but everyone walked in the
stubbornness of an evil will. So I brought upon
them all the words of this covenant, which I commanded them to do, but they did not.

9 And the LORD said to me: Conspiracy exists
among the people of Judah and the inhabitants of
Jerusalem. 10 They have turned back to the iniquities of their ancestors of old, who refused to heed
my words; they have gone after other gods to serve
them; the house of Israel and the house of Judah
have broken the covenant that I made with their
ancestors. 11 Therefore, thus says the LORD, assuredly I am going to bring disaster upon them
that they cannot escape; though they cry out to
me, I will not listen to them. 12 Then the cities of
Judah and the inhabitants of Jerusalem will go and
cry out to the gods to whom they make offerings,
but they will never save them in the time of their
trouble. 13 For your gods have become as many as
your towns, O Judah; and as many as the streets of
Jerusalem are the altars to shame you have set up,
altars to make offerings to Ba'al.

14 As for you, do not pray for this people, or
lift up a cry or prayer on their behalf, for I will not
listen when they call to me in the time of their
trouble. 15 What right has my beloved in my
house, when she has done vile deeds? Can vows*q*
and sacrificial flesh avert your doom? Can you
then exult? 16 The LORD once called you, "A green
olive tree, fair with goodly fruit"; but with the roar
of a great tempest he will set fire to it, and its
branches will be consumed. 17 The LORD of hosts,
who planted you, has pronounced evil against
you, because of the evil that the house of Israel
and the house of Judah have done, provoking me
to anger by making offerings to Ba'al.

---

q Gk: Heb *Can many*

Jeremiah's Life Threatened

18 It was the LORD who made it known to me,
and I knew;
then you showed me their evil deeds.

19 But I was like a gentle lamb
led to the slaughter.
And I did not know it was against me
that they devised schemes, saying,
"Let us destroy the tree with its fruit,
let us cut him off from the land of the
living,
so that his name will no longer be
remembered!"

20 But you, O LORD of hosts, who judge
righteously,
who try the heart and the mind,
let me see your retribution upon them,
for to you I have committed my cause.

21 Therefore thus says the LORD concerning the
people of An'a•thoth, who seek your life, and say,
"You shall not prophesy in the name of the LORD,
or you will die by our hand" — 22 therefore thus says
the LORD of hosts: I am going to punish them; the
young men shall die by the sword; their sons and
their daughters shall die by famine; 23 and not
even a remnant shall be left of them. For I will
bring disaster upon the people of An'a•thoth, the
year of their punishment.

Jeremiah's First Confession

You will be in the right, O LORD,
when I lay charges against you;
but let me put my case to you.
Why does the way of the guilty prosper?
Why do all who are treacherous thrive?

2 You plant them, and they take root;
they grow and bring forth fruit;
you are near in their mouths
yet far from their hearts.

3 But you, O LORD, know me;
You see me and test me — my heart is
with you.
Pull them out like sheep for the slaughter,
and set them apart for the day
of slaughter.

4 How long will the land mourn,
and the grass of every field wither?
For the wickedness of those who live in it
the animals and the birds are swept
away,
and because people said, "He is blind to
our ways."ʳ

5 If you have raced with foot-runners and
they have wearied you,
how will you compete with horses?

And if in a safe land you fall down,
how will you fare in the thickets of the
Jordan?

6 For even your kinsfolk and your own
family,
even they have dealt treacherously
with you;
they are in full cry after you;
do not believe them,
though they speak friendly words to you.

ʳ Gk: Heb *to our future*

?did youKNOW?

The Confessions of Jeremiah

Jeremiah 12.1–6 is the first of five passages that are sometimes called the Confessions of Jeremiah (12.1–6; 15.10–21; 17.12–18; 18.18–23; 20.7–18). In the confessions, Jeremiah speaks to God in a very personal, very direct way. He complains to God about the people's stubbornness, he complains about his treatment, and he accuses God of deceiving him. Some scholars believe the confessions are a private journal kept by Jeremiah that he never intended to be made public.

In 12.1–4, Jeremiah asks God why God lets evil people prosper—why doesn't God just slaughter them like sheep? God's reply in verses 5–6 is that things are going to get worse before they get better and that even Jeremiah's own family will turn against him. God never answers Jeremiah directly in any of the confessions—although in 15.19–21, God does promise to support Jeremiah.

If this famous prophet shared his anger, doubts, and fears with God honestly, so can we. Jeremiah's confessions are a good reminder that God wants to share everything with us—not just our happy thoughts.

▶ Jer 12.1–6

God Replies to Jeremiah

7 I have forsaken my house,
     I have abandoned my heritage;
     I have given the beloved of my heart
        into the hands of her enemies.
8 My heritage has become to me
     like a lion in the forest;
     she has lifted up her voice against
        me—
        therefore I hate her.
9 Is the hyena greedy*s* for my heritage at my
        command?
     Are the birds of prey all around her?
     Go, assemble all the wild animals;
        bring them to devour her.
10 Many shepherds have destroyed
        my vineyard,
     they have trampled down my
        portion,
     they have made my pleasant portion
        a desolate wilderness.
11 They have made it a desolation;
     desolate, it mourns to me.
     The whole land is made desolate,
        but no one lays it to heart.
12 Upon all the bare heights*t* in the
        desert
     spoilers have come;
     for the sword of the LORD devours
        from one end of the land to the
        other;
        no one shall be safe.
13 They have sown wheat and have reaped
        thorns,
     they have tired themselves out but profit
        nothing.
     They shall be ashamed of their*u*
        harvests
     because of the fierce anger of
        the LORD.

14 Thus says the LORD concerning all my evil neighbors who touch the heritage that I have given my people Israel to inherit: I am about to pluck them up from their land, and I will pluck up the house of Judah from among them. 15 And after I have plucked them up, I will again have compassion on them, and I will bring them again to their heritage and to their land, everyone of them. 16 And then, if they will diligently learn the ways of my people, to swear by my name, "As the LORD lives," as they taught my people to swear by Ba′al, then they shall be built up in the midst of my people. 17 But if any nation will not listen, then I will completely uproot it and destroy it, says the LORD.

The Linen Loincloth

Thus said the LORD to me, "Go and buy yourself a linen loincloth, and put it on your loins, but do not dip it in water." 2 So I bought a loincloth according to the word of the LORD, and put it on my loins. 3 And the word of the LORD came to me a second time, saying, 4 "Take the loincloth that you bought and are wearing, and go now to the Euphrates,*v* and hide it there in a cleft of the rock." 5 So I went, and hid it by the Euphrates,*w* as the LORD commanded me. 6 And after many days the LORD said to me, "Go now to the Euphrates,*v* and take from there the loincloth that I commanded you to hide there." 7 Then I went to the Euphrates,*v* and dug, and I took the loincloth from the place where I had hidden it. But now the loincloth was ruined; it was good for nothing.

8 Then the word of the LORD came to me: 9 Thus says the LORD: Just so I will ruin the pride of Judah and the great pride of Jerusalem. 10 This evil people, who refuse to hear my words, who stubbornly follow their own will and have gone after other gods to serve them and worship them, shall be like this loincloth, which is good for nothing. 11 For as the loincloth clings to one's loins, so I made the whole house of Israel and the whole house of Judah cling to me, says the LORD, in order that they might be for me a people, a name, a praise, and a glory. But they would not listen.

Symbol of the Wine-Jars

12 You shall speak to them this word: Thus says the LORD, the God of Israel: Every wine-jar should be filled with wine. And they will say to you, "Do you think we do not know that every wine-jar should be filled with wine?" 13 Then you shall say to them: Thus says the LORD: I am about to fill all the inhabitants of this land—the kings who sit on David's throne, the priests, the prophets, and all the inhabitants of Jerusalem—with drunkenness. 14 And I will dash them one against another, parents and children together, says the LORD. I will not pity or spare or have compassion when I destroy them.

Exile Threatened

15 Hear and give ear; do not be haughty,
     for the LORD has spoken.
16 Give glory to the LORD your God
     before he brings darkness,
     and before your feet stumble
     on the mountains at twilight;

---

s Cn: Heb *Is the hyena, the bird of prey*   *t* Or *the trails*
u Heb *your*   *v* Or *to Parah;* Heb *perath*   *w* Or *by Parah;*
Heb *perath*

while you look for light,
    he turns it into gloom
    and makes it deep darkness.
17 But if you will not listen,
    my soul will weep in secret for your
        pride;
my eyes will weep bitterly and run down
    with tears,
    because the LORD's flock has been taken
    captive.

18 Say to the king and the queen mother:
    "Take a lowly seat,
for your beautiful crown
    has come down from your head."*x*
19 The towns of the Neg'eb are shut up
    with no one to open them;
all Judah is taken into exile,
    wholly taken into exile.

20 Lift up your eyes and see
    those who come from the north.
Where is the flock that was given you,
    your beautiful flock?
21 What will you say when they set as head
        over you
    those whom you have trained
    to be your allies?
Will not pangs take hold of you,
    like those of a woman in labor?
22 And if you say in your heart,
    "Why have these things come upon me?"
it is for the greatness of your iniquity
    that your skirts are lifted up,
    and you are violated.
23 Can Ethiopians*y* change their skin
    or leopards their spots?
Then also you can do good
    who are accustomed to do evil.
24 I will scatter you*z* like chaff
    driven by the wind from the desert.
25 This is your lot,
    the portion I have measured out to you,
        says the LORD,
because you have forgotten me
    and trusted in lies.
26 I myself will lift up your skirts over your
    face,
    and your shame will be seen.
27 I have seen your abominations,
    your adulteries and neighings, your
        shameless prostitutions
    on the hills of the countryside.
Woe to you, O Jerusalem!
    How long will it be
    before you are made clean?

The Great Drought

The word of the LORD that came to Jer•e•mi'ah concerning the drought:
2 Judah mourns
    and her gates languish;
they lie in gloom on the ground,
    and the cry of Jerusalem goes up.
3 Her nobles send their servants for water;
    they come to the cisterns,
they find no water,
    they return with their vessels empty.
They are ashamed and dismayed
    and cover their heads,
4 because the ground is cracked.
    Because there has been no rain on the
        land
the farmers are dismayed;
    they cover their heads.
5 Even the doe in the field forsakes her
        newborn fawn
    because there is no grass.
6 The wild asses stand on the bare heights,*a*
    they pant for air like jackals;
their eyes fail
    because there is no herbage.

7 Although our iniquities testify against us,
    act, O LORD, for your name's sake;
our apostasies indeed are many,
    and we have sinned against you.
8 O hope of Israel,
    its savior in time of trouble,
why should you be like a stranger in the
        land,
    like a traveler turning aside for the night?
9 Why should you be like someone confused,
    like a mighty warrior who cannot give
        help?
Yet you, O LORD, are in the midst of us,
    and we are called by your name;
    do not forsake us!

10 Thus says the LORD concerning this people:
Truly they have loved to wander,
    they have not restrained their feet;
therefore the LORD does not accept them,
    now he will remember their iniquity
    and punish their sins.

11 The LORD said to me: Do not pray for the
welfare of this people. 12 Although they fast, I do
not hear their cry, and although they offer burnt
offering and grain offering, I do not accept them;
but by the sword, by famine, and by pestilence I
consume them.

x Gk Syr Vg: Meaning of Heb uncertain   *y* Or *Nubians;*
Heb *Cushites*   *z* Heb *them*   *a* Or *the trails*

Denunciation of Lying Prophets

13 Then I said: "Ah, Lord GOD! Here are the prophets saying to them, 'You shall not see the sword, nor shall you have famine, but I will give you true peace in this place.' " 14And the LORD said to me: The prophets are prophesying lies in my name; I did not send them, nor did I command them or speak to them. They are prophesying to you a lying vision, worthless divination, and the deceit of their own minds. 15Therefore thus says the LORD concerning the prophets who prophesy in my name though I did not send them, and who say, "Sword and famine shall not come on this land": By sword and famine those prophets shall be consumed. 16And the people to whom they prophesy shall be thrown out into the streets of Jerusalem, victims of famine and sword. There shall be no one to bury them—themselves, their wives, their sons, and their daughters. For I will pour out their wickedness upon them.

PRAY IT?

The Empty Promises of False Prophets

In Jer 14.13–16, Jeremiah attacks prophets who preach what the people want to hear. The people want peace and plenty, so that is what the false prophets preach. They offer false and dangerous security.

People deceive themselves when they listen only to what they want to hear. Sometimes, God tells us things that are hard to hear or asks us to do things that are hard to do.

In your prayer, reflect or journal on the following questions:

- When have you tried to ignore God's message for you?
- When have you heard and responded to God even if God's message was difficult?
- What are the hardest things for you to hear or do?

▸ Jer 14.13–16

17 You shall say to them this word:
Let my eyes run down with tears night
and day,
and let them not cease,

for the virgin daughter—my people—is struck
down with a crushing blow,
with a very grievous wound.
18 If I go out into the field,
look—those killed by the sword!
And if I enter the city,
look—those sick with[b] famine!
For both prophet and priest ply their trade
throughout the land,
and have no knowledge.

The People Plead for Mercy

19 Have you completely rejected Judah?
Does your heart loathe Zion?
Why have you struck us down
so that there is no healing for us?
We look for peace, but find no good;
for a time of healing, but there is terror
instead.
20 We acknowledge our wickedness, O LORD,
the iniquity of our ancestors,
for we have sinned against you.
21 Do not spurn us, for your name's sake;
do not dishonor your glorious throne;
remember and do not break your
covenant with us.
22 Can any idols of the nations bring rain?
Or can the heavens give showers?
Is it not you, O LORD our God?
We set our hope on you,
for it is you who do all this.

Punishment Is Inevitable

Then the LORD said to me: Though Moses and Samuel stood before me, yet my heart would not turn toward this people. Send them out of my sight, and let them go! 2And when they say to you, "Where shall we go?" you shall say to them: Thus says the LORD:
Those destined for pestilence, to pestilence,
and those destined for the sword, to the
sword;
those destined for famine, to famine,
and those destined for captivity, to
captivity.
3And I will appoint over them four kinds of destroyers, says the LORD: the sword to kill, the dogs to drag away, and the birds of the air and the wild animals of the earth to devour and destroy. 4I will make them a horror to all the kingdoms of the earth because of what King Ma•nas'seh son of Hez-e•ki'ah of Judah did in Jerusalem.

5 Who will have pity on you, O Jerusalem,
or who will bemoan you?

b Heb look—the sicknesses of

Who will turn aside
    to ask about your welfare?
6 You have rejected me, says the LORD,
    you are going backward;
so I have stretched out my hand against you
      and destroyed you—
    I am weary of relenting.
7 I have winnowed them with a winnowing
      fork
    in the gates of the land;
I have bereaved them, I have destroyed my
      people;
    they did not turn from their ways.
8 Their widows became more numerous
    than the sand of the seas;
I have brought against the mothers of
      youths
    a destroyer at noonday;
I have made anguish and terror
    fall upon her suddenly.
9 She who bore seven has languished;
    she has swooned away;
her sun went down while it was yet day;
    she has been shamed and disgraced.
And the rest of them I will give to the sword
    before their enemies,
                says the LORD.

Jeremiah's Second Confession

10 Woe is me, my mother, that you ever bore
me, a man of strife and contention to the whole
land! I have not lent, nor have I borrowed, yet all
of them curse me. 11 The LORD said: Surely I have
intervened in your life[c] for good, surely I have imposed enemies on you in a time of trouble and in
a time of distress.[d] 12 Can iron and bronze break
iron from the north?

13 Your wealth and your treasures I will give as
plunder, without price, for all your sins, throughout all your territory. 14 I will make you serve your
enemies in a land that you do not know, for in my
anger a fire is kindled that shall burn forever.
15 O LORD, you know;
    remember me and visit me,
    and bring down retribution for me on
        my persecutors.
In your forbearance do not take me away;
    know that on your account I suffer insult.
16 Your words were found, and I ate them,
    and your words became to me a joy
    and the delight of my heart;
for I am called by your name,
    O LORD, God of hosts.
17 I did not sit in the company of
      merrymakers,
    nor did I rejoice;

under the weight of your hand I sat alone,
    for you had filled me with indignation.
18 Why is my pain unceasing,
    my wound incurable,
    refusing to be healed?
Truly, you are to me like a deceitful brook,
    like waters that fail.
19 Therefore thus says the LORD:
If you turn back, I will take you back,
    and you shall stand before me.
If you utter what is precious, and not what
      is worthless,
    you shall serve as my mouth.
It is they who will turn to you,
    not you who will turn to them.
20 And I will make you to this people
    a fortified wall of bronze;
they will fight against you,
    but they shall not prevail over you,
for I am with you
    to save you and deliver you,
                says the LORD.
21 I will deliver you out of the hand of the
      wicked,
    and redeem you from the grasp of the
      ruthless.

Jeremiah's Celibacy and Message

The word of the LORD came to me: 2 You shall not
take a wife, nor shall you have sons or daughters
in this place. 3 For thus says the LORD concerning
the sons and daughters who are born in this place,
and concerning the mothers who bear them and
the fathers who beget them in this land: 4 They
shall die of deadly diseases. They shall not be lamented, nor shall they be buried; they shall become like dung on the surface of the ground. They
shall perish by the sword and by famine, and their
dead bodies shall become food for the birds of the
air and for the wild animals of the earth.

5 For thus says the LORD: Do not enter the
house of mourning, or go to lament, or bemoan
them; for I have taken away my peace from this
people, says the LORD, my steadfast love and
mercy. 6 Both great and small shall die in this land;
they shall not be buried, and no one shall lament
for them; there shall be no gashing, no shaving of
the head for them. 7 No one shall break bread[e] for
the mourner, to offer comfort for the dead; nor
shall anyone give them the cup of consolation to
drink for their fathers or their mothers. 8 You shall
not go into the house of feasting to sit with them,

---

c Heb *intervened with you*   d Meaning of Heb uncertain
e Two Mss Gk: MT *break for them*

to eat and drink. ⁹ For thus says the LORD of hosts, the God of Israel: I am going to banish from this place, in your days and before your eyes, the voice of mirth and the voice of gladness, the voice of the bridegroom and the voice of the bride.

10 And when you tell this people all these words, and they say to you, "Why has the LORD pronounced all this great evil against us? What is our iniquity? What is the sin that we have committed against the LORD our God?" ¹¹ then you shall say to them: It is because your ancestors have forsaken me, says the LORD, and have gone after other gods and have served and worshiped them, and have forsaken me and have not kept my law; ¹² and because you have behaved worse than your ancestors, for here you are, every one of you, following your stubborn evil will, refusing to listen to me. ¹³ Therefore I will hurl you out of this land into a land that neither you nor your ancestors have known, and there you shall serve other gods day and night, for I will show you no favor.

God Will Restore Israel
(Cp Jer 23.7–8)

14 Therefore, the days are surely coming, says the LORD, when it shall no longer be said, "As the LORD lives who brought the people of Israel up out of the land of Egypt," ¹⁵ but "As the LORD lives who brought the people of Israel up out of the land of the north and out of all the lands where he had driven them." For I will bring them back to their own land that I gave to their ancestors.

16 I am now sending for many fishermen, says the LORD, and they shall catch them; and afterward I will send for many hunters, and they shall hunt them from every mountain and every hill, and out of the clefts of the rocks. ¹⁷ For my eyes are on all their ways; they are not hidden from my presence, nor is their iniquity concealed from my sight. ¹⁸ And*f* I will doubly repay their iniquity and their sin, because they have polluted my land with the carcasses of their detestable idols, and have filled my inheritance with their abominations.

19 O LORD, my strength and my stronghold,
  my refuge in the day of trouble,
to you shall the nations come
  from the ends of the earth and say:
Our ancestors have inherited nothing but
    lies,
  worthless things in which there is no
    profit.
20 Can mortals make for themselves gods?
  Such are no gods!

21 "Therefore I am surely going to teach them, this time I am going to teach them my power and

my might, and they shall know that my name is the LORD."

Judah's Sin and Punishment

The sin of Judah is written with an iron pen; with a diamond point it is engraved on the tablet of their hearts, and on the horns of their altars, ² while their children remember their altars and their sacred poles, *g* beside every green tree, and on the high hills, ³ on the mountains in the open country. Your wealth and all your treasures I will give for spoil as the price of your sin*h* throughout all your territory. ⁴ By your own act you shall lose the heritage that I gave you, and I will make you serve your enemies in a land that you do not know, for in my anger a fire is kindled*i* that shall burn forever.

5 Thus says the LORD:
  Cursed are those who trust in mere mortals
    and make mere flesh their strength,
    whose hearts turn away from the LORD.
6 They shall be like a shrub in the desert,
    and shall not see when relief comes.
  They shall live in the parched places of the
      wilderness,
    in an uninhabited salt land.

7 Blessed are those who trust in the LORD,
    whose trust is the LORD.
8 They shall be like a tree planted by water,
    sending out its roots by the stream.
  It shall not fear when heat comes,
    and its leaves shall stay green;
  in the year of drought it is not anxious,
    and it does not cease to bear fruit.

9 The heart is devious above all else;
    it is perverse—
    who can understand it?
10 I the LORD test the mind
    and search the heart,
  to give to all according to their ways,
    according to the fruit of their doings.

11 Like the partridge hatching what it did
      not lay,
    so are all who amass wealth unjustly;
  in mid-life it will leave them,
    and at their end they will prove to be
      fools.

12 O glorious throne, exalted from the
      beginning,
    shrine of our sanctuary!

---

f Gk: Heb *And first* *g* Heb *Asherim* *h* Cn: Heb *spoil your high places for sin* *i* Two Mss Theodotion: *you kindled*

▶▶▶▶▶▶▶▶

NATIVE AMERICAN

Children and Green Trees

The land is very important in Native American spirituality; trees, grass, and flowers are given reverence similar to that afforded people, because all are connected. It is the greatest wish of the elders that the children learn this lesson and carry it on to their own children. Native Americans would view the loss and destruction of the land described in Jer 17.1–3 as a horrible punishment. See how their value for the land is reflected in this prayer from the Mohawk tradition:

> *Oh Great Spirit, Creator of all things;*
> *Human Beings, trees, grass, berries.*
> *Help us, be kind to us.*
> *Let us be happy on earth.*
> *Let us lead our children*
> *To a good life and old age.*
> *These our people; give them good minds*
> *To love one another.*
> *Oh Great Spirit,*
> *Be kind to us.*
> *Give these people the favour*
> *To see green trees,*
> *Green grass, flowers, and berries*
> *This next spring;*
> *So we all meet again.*
> *Oh Great Spirit,*
> *We ask of you.*
> *(Author unknown, "Mohawk Indian Prayer")*

▶ Jer 17.1–3

▶▶▶▶▶▶▶▶

13 O hope of Israel! O LORD!
   All who forsake you shall be put to
      shame;
   those who turn away from you*j* shall be
      recorded in the underworld,*k*
   for they have forsaken the fountain of
      living water, the LORD.

Jeremiah's Third Confession

14 Heal me, O LORD, and I shall be healed;
   save me, and I shall be saved;
   for you are my praise.
15 See how they say to me,
   "Where is the word of the LORD?
   Let it come!"
16 But I have not run away from being a
         shepherd*l* in your service,
      nor have I desired the fatal day.
   You know what came from my lips;
      it was before your face.
17 Do not become a terror to me;
   you are my refuge in the day of disaster;
18 Let my persecutors be shamed,
      but do not let me be shamed;
   let them be dismayed,
      but do not let me be dismayed;
   bring on them the day of disaster;
      destroy them with double destruction!

Hallow the Sabbath Day

19 Thus said the LORD to me: Go and stand in the People's Gate, by which the kings of Judah enter and by which they go out, and in all the gates of Jerusalem, 20 and say to them: Hear the word of the LORD, you kings of Judah, and all Judah, and all the inhabitants of Jerusalem, who enter by these gates. 21 Thus says the LORD: For the sake of your lives, take care that you do not bear a burden on the sabbath day or bring it in by the gates of Jerusalem. 22 And do not carry a burden out of your houses on the sabbath or do any work, but keep the sabbath day holy, as I commanded your ancestors. 23 Yet they did not listen or incline their ear; they stiffened their necks and would not hear or receive instruction.

24 But if you listen to me, says the LORD, and bring in no burden by the gates of this city on the sabbath day, but keep the sabbath day holy and do no work on it, 25 then there shall enter by the gates of this city kings*m* who sit on the throne of David, riding in chariots and on horses, they and their officials, the people of Judah and the inhabitants of Jerusalem; and this city shall be inhabited forever. 26 And people shall come from the towns of Judah and the places around Jerusalem, from the land of Benjamin, from the She•phē'lah, from the hill country, and from the Neg'eb, bringing burnt offerings and sacrifices, grain offerings and frankincense, and bringing thank offerings to the house of the LORD. 27 But if you do not listen to me, to keep the sabbath day holy, and to carry in

j Heb *me*   *k* Or *in the earth*   *l* Meaning of Heb
uncertain   *m* Cn: Heb *kings and officials*

no burden through the gates of Jerusalem on the sabbath day, then I will kindle a fire in its gates; it shall devour the palaces of Jerusalem and shall not be quenched.

The Potter and the Clay

The word that came to Jer•e•mi′ah from the LORD: 2 "Come, go down to the potter's house, and there I will let you hear my words." 3 So I went down to the potter's house, and there he was working at his wheel. 4 The vessel he was making of clay was spoiled in the potter's hand, and he reworked it into another vessel, as seemed good to him.

5 Then the word of the LORD came to me: 6 Can I not do with you, O house of Israel, just as this potter has done? says the LORD. Just like the clay in the potter's hand, so are you in my hand, O house of Israel. 7 At one moment I may declare concerning a nation or a kingdom, that I will pluck up and break down and destroy it, 8 but if that nation, concerning which I have spoken, turns from its evil, I will change my mind about the disaster that I intended to bring on it. 9 And at another moment I may declare concerning a nation or a kingdom that I will build and plant it, 10 but if it does evil in my sight, not listening to my voice, then I will change my mind about the good that I had intended to do to it. 11 Now, therefore, say to the people of Judah and the inhabitants of Jerusalem: Thus says the LORD: Look, I am a potter shaping evil against you and devising a plan against you. Turn now, all of you from your evil way, and amend your ways and your doings.

Israel's Stubborn Idolatry

12 But they say, "It is no use! We will follow our own plans, and each of us will act according to the stubbornness of our evil will."

13 Therefore thus says the LORD:
Ask among the nations:
    Who has heard the like of this?
The virgin Israel has done
    a most horrible thing.
14 Does the snow of Lebanon leave
    the crags of Sir′i•on?[n]
Do the mountain[o] waters run dry,[p]
    the cold flowing streams?
15 But my people have forgotten me,
    they burn offerings to a delusion;
they have stumbled[q] in their ways,
    in the ancient roads,
and have gone into bypaths,
    not the highway,
16 making their land a horror,
    a thing to be hissed at forever.

All who pass by it are horrified
    and shake their heads.
17 Like the wind from the east,
    I will scatter them before the enemy.
I will show them my back, not my face,
    in the day of their calamity.

Jeremiah's Fourth Confession

18 Then they said, "Come, let us make plots against Jer•e•mi′ah—for instruction shall not perish from the priest, nor counsel from the wise, nor the word from the prophet. Come, let us bring charges against him,[r] and let us not heed any of his words."

19 Give heed to me, O LORD,
    and listen to what my adversaries say!
20 Is evil a recompense for good?
    Yet they have dug a pit for my life.
Remember how I stood before you
    to speak good for them,
    to turn away your wrath from them.
21 Therefore give their children over to famine;
    hurl them out to the power of the sword,
let their wives become childless and
        widowed.
    May their men meet death by pestilence,
    their youths be slain by the sword in
        battle.
22 May a cry be heard from their houses,
    when you bring the marauder suddenly
        upon them!
For they have dug a pit to catch me,
    and laid snares for my feet.
23 Yet you, O LORD, know
    all their plotting to kill me.
Do not forgive their iniquity,
    do not blot out their sin from your sight.
Let them be tripped up before you;
    deal with them while you are angry.

The Broken Earthenware Jug

Thus said the LORD: Go and buy a potter's earthenware jug. Take with you[s] some of the elders of the people and some of the senior priests, 2 and go out to the valley of the son of Hin′nom at the entry of the Potsherd Gate, and proclaim there the words that I tell you. 3 You shall say: Hear the word of the LORD, O kings of Judah and inhabitants of Jerusalem. Thus says the LORD of hosts, the God of Israel: I am going to bring such disaster upon this place that the ears of everyone who hears of it will tingle. 4 Because the people have forsaken me, and

---

n Cn: Heb *of the field*   o Cn: Heb *foreign*   p Cn: Heb *Are
. . . plucked up?*   q Gk Syr Vg: Heb *they made them stumble*
r Heb *strike him with the tongue*   s Syr Tg Compare Gk:
Heb lacks *take with you*

have profaned this place by making offerings in it to other gods whom neither they nor their ancestors nor the kings of Judah have known, and because they have filled this place with the blood of the innocent, 5 and gone on building the high places of Bā′al to burn their children in the fire as burnt offerings to Bā′al, which I did not command or decree, nor did it enter my mind; 6 therefore the days are surely coming, says the LORD, when this place shall no more be called Tō′pheth, or the valley of the son of Hin′nom, but the valley of Slaughter. 7 And in this place I will make void the plans of Judah and Jerusalem, and will make them fall by the sword before their enemies, and by the hand of those who seek their life. I will give their dead bodies for food to the birds of the air and to the wild animals of the earth. 8 And I will make this city a horror, a thing to be hissed at; everyone who passes by it will be horrified and will hiss because of all its disasters. 9 And I will make them eat the flesh of their sons and the flesh of their daughters, and all shall eat the flesh of their neighbors in the siege, and in the distress with which their enemies and those who seek their life afflict them.

10 Then you shall break the jug in the sight of those who go with you, 11 and shall say to them: Thus says the LORD of hosts: So will I break this people and this city, as one breaks a potter's vessel, so that it can never be mended. In Tō′pheth they shall bury until there is no more room to bury. 12 Thus will I do to this place, says the LORD, and to its inhabitants, making this city like Tō′pheth. 13 And the houses of Jerusalem and the houses of the kings of Judah shall be defiled like the place of Tō′pheth—all the houses upon whose roofs offerings have been made to the whole host of heaven, and libations have been poured out to other gods.

14 When Jer•e•mi′ah came from Tō′pheth, where the LORD had sent him to prophesy, he stood in the court of the LORD's house and said to all the people: 15 Thus says the LORD of hosts, the God of Israel: I am now bringing upon this city and upon all its towns all the disaster that I have pronounced against it, because they have stiffened their necks, refusing to hear my words.

Jeremiah Persecuted by Pashhur

Now the priest Pash′hur son of Im′mer, who was chief officer in the house of the LORD, heard Jer•e•mi′ah prophesying these things. 2 Then Pash′hur struck the prophet Jer•e•mi′ah, and put him in the stocks that were in the upper Benjamin Gate of the house of the LORD. 3 The next morning when Pash′hur released Jer•e•mi′ah from the stocks, Jer•e•mi′ah said to him, The LORD has named you not Pash′hur

but "Terror-all-around." 4 For thus says the LORD: I am making you a terror to yourself and to all your friends; and they shall fall by the sword of their enemies while you look on. And I will give all Judah into the hand of the king of Babylon; he shall carry them captive to Babylon, and shall kill them with the sword. 5 I will give all the wealth of this city, all its gains, all its prized belongings, and all the treasures of the kings of Judah into the hand of their enemies, who shall plunder them, and seize them, and carry them to Babylon. 6 And you, Pash′hur, and all who live in your house, shall go into captivity, and to Babylon you shall go; there you shall die, and there you shall be buried, you and all your friends, to whom you have prophesied falsely.

Jeremiah's Fifth Confession

7 O LORD, you have enticed me,
  and I was enticed;
you have overpowered me,
  and you have prevailed.
I have become a laughingstock all day long;
  everyone mocks me.
8 For whenever I speak, I must cry out,
  I must shout, "Violence and destruction!"
For the word of the LORD has become
    for me
  a reproach and derision all day long.
9 If I say, "I will not mention him,
  or speak any more in his name,"
then within me there is something like a
    burning fire
  shut up in my bones;
I am weary with holding it in,
  and I cannot.
10 For I hear many whispering:
  "Terror is all around!
Denounce him! Let us denounce him!"
  All my close friends
  are watching for me to stumble.
"Perhaps he can be enticed,
  and we can prevail against him,
  and take our revenge on him."
11 But the LORD is with me like a dread
    warrior;
  therefore my persecutors will stumble;
  and they will not prevail.
They will be greatly shamed,
  for they will not succeed.
Their eternal dishonor
  will never be forgotten.
12 O LORD of hosts, you test the righteous,
  you see the heart and the mind;
let me see your retribution upon them,
  for to you I have committed my cause.

13 Sing to the LORD;
　　praise the LORD!
For he has delivered the life of the needy
　　from the hands of evildoers.

14 Cursed be the day
　　on which I was born!
The day when my mother bore me,
　　let it not be blessed!
15 Cursed be the man
　　who brought the news to my father,
　　　　saying,
"A child is born to you, a son,"
　　making him very glad.
16 Let that man be like the cities
　　that the LORD overthrew without pity;
let him hear a cry in the morning
　　and an alarm at noon,
17 because he did not kill me in the womb;
　　so my mother would have been my
　　　　grave,
　　and her womb forever great.
18 Why did I come forth from the womb
　　to see toil and sorrow,
　　and spend my days in shame?

Jerusalem Will Fall to Nebuchadrezzar

This is the word that came to Jer·e·mi′ah from the
LORD, when King Zed·e·ki′ah sent to him Pash′hur
son of Mal·chi′ah and the priest Zeph·a·ni′ah son of
Mā·a·sēi′ah, saying, 2 "Please inquire of the LORD on
our behalf, for King Ne·bū·chad·rez′zar of Babylon
is making war against us; perhaps the LORD will
perform a wonderful deed for us, as he has often
done, and will make him withdraw from us."

3 Then Jer·e·mi′ah said to them: 4 Thus you shall
say to Zed·e·ki′ah: Thus says the LORD, the God of
Israel: I am going to turn back the weapons of war
that are in your hands and with which you are
fighting against the king of Babylon and against
the Chal·dē′ans who are besieging you outside the
walls; and I will bring them together into the center of this city. 5 I myself will fight against you with
outstretched hand and mighty arm, in anger, in
fury, and in great wrath. 6 And I will strike down
the inhabitants of this city, both human beings
and animals; they shall die of a great pestilence.
7 Afterward, says the LORD, I will give King Zed·e·
ki′ah of Judah, and his servants, and the people
in this city—those who survive the pestilence,
sword, and famine—into the hands of King
Ne·bū·chad·rez′zar of Babylon, into the hands of
their enemies, into the hands of those who seek
their lives. He shall strike them down with the edge
of the sword; he shall not pity them, or spare them,
or have compassion.

8 And to this people you shall say: Thus says
the LORD: See, I am setting before you the way of
life and the way of death. 9 Those who stay in this
city shall die by the sword, by famine, and by pestilence; but those who go out and surrender to the
Chal·dē′ans who are besieging you shall live and
shall have their lives as a prize of war. 10 For I have
set my face against this city for evil and not for
good, says the LORD: it shall be given into the
hands of the king of Babylon, and he shall burn it
with fire.

Message to the House of David

11 To the house of the king of Judah say: Hear
the word of the LORD, 12 O house of David! Thus
says the LORD:
　　Execute justice in the morning,
　　　　and deliver from the hand of the
　　　　　　oppressor
　　　　anyone who has been robbed,
　　or else my wrath will go forth like fire,
　　　　and burn, with no one to quench it,
　　　　because of your evil doings.

13 See, I am against you, O inhabitant of the
　　　　valley,
　　O rock of the plain,
　　　　　　　　　　　　says the LORD;
　　you who say, "Who can come down
　　　　against us,
　　or who can enter our places of refuge?"
14 I will punish you according to the fruit of
　　　　your doings,
　　　　　　　　　　　　says the LORD;
　　I will kindle a fire in its forest,
　　and it shall devour all that is around it.

Exhortation to Repent

Thus says the LORD: Go down to the house of the
king of Judah, and speak there this word, 2 and
say: Hear the word of the LORD, O King of Judah
sitting on the throne of David—you, and your servants, and your people who enter these gates.
3 Thus says the LORD: Act with justice and righteousness, and deliver from the hand of the oppressor anyone who has been robbed. And do no
wrong or violence to the alien, the orphan, and
the widow, or shed innocent blood in this place.
4 For if you will indeed obey this word, then
through the gates of this house shall enter kings
who sit on the throne of David, riding in chariots
and on horses, they, and their servants, and their
people. 5 But if you will not heed these words, I
swear by myself, says the LORD, that this house
shall become a desolation. 6 For thus says the LORD
concerning the house of the king of Judah:

You are like Gil'e•ad to me,
    like the summit of Lebanon;
but I swear that I will make you a desert,
    an uninhabited city.[t]
7 I will prepare destroyers against you,
    all with their weapons;
they shall cut down your choicest cedars
    and cast them into the fire.

8 And many nations will pass by this city, and all of them will say one to another, "Why has the LORD dealt in this way with that great city?" 9 And they will answer, "Because they abandoned the covenant of the LORD their God, and worshiped other gods and served them."

10 Do not weep for him who is dead,
    nor bemoan him;
weep rather for him who goes away,
    for he shall return no more
    to see his native land.

Message to the Sons of Josiah

11 For thus says the LORD concerning Shal'lum son of King Jō•sī'ah of Judah, who succeeded his father Jō•sī'ah, and who went away from this place: He shall return here no more, 12 but in the place where they have carried him captive he shall die, and he shall never see this land again.

13 Woe to him who builds his house by
    unrighteousness,
    and his upper rooms by injustice;
who makes his neighbors work for nothing,
    and does not give them their wages;
14 who says, "I will build myself a spacious
    house
    with large upper rooms,"
and who cuts out windows for it,
    paneling it with cedar,
    and painting it with vermilion.
15 Are you a king
    because you compete in cedar?
Did not your father eat and drink
    and do justice and righteousness?
    Then it was well with him.
16 He judged the cause of the poor and needy;
    then it was well.
Is not this to know me?
    says the LORD.
17 But your eyes and heart
    are only on your dishonest gain,
for shedding innocent blood,
    and for practicing oppression and
    violence.

18 Therefore thus says the LORD concerning King Je•hoi'a•kim son of Jō•sī'ah of Judah:
They shall not lament for him, saying,

"Alas, my brother!" or "Alas, sister!"
They shall not lament for him, saying,
    "Alas, lord!" or "Alas, his majesty!"
19 With the burial of a donkey he shall be
    buried—
    dragged off and thrown out beyond the
    gates of Jerusalem.

PRAY IT!
Admit It!

Jeremiah's words against King Jehoiakim in Jer 22.21–23 are harsh. Jehoiakim is guilty of some serious sin and is leading the nation to destruction. But he doesn't want to hear about it. In fact, when Jehoiakim is presented with a scroll of Jeremiah's prophecies, he burns it (36.23)!

Forgiving God,
Help us to hear the prophets in today's
    world who call us to own our sin.
The prophets who call us to end
    discrimination,
    who call us to care for the needy,
    who call us to care for the earth,
    who call us to end violence,
    who call us to healthy relationships,
    who call us to be people of integrity,
    avoiding sin in all its forms.
May we be humble enough to admit our
    faults
and courageous enough to do something
    about them.

▶ Jer 22.18–23

20 Go up to Lebanon, and cry out,
    and lift up your voice in Bā'shan;
cry out from Ab'a•rim,
    for all your lovers are crushed.
21 I spoke to you in your prosperity,
    but you said, "I will not listen."
This has been your way from your youth,
    for you have not obeyed my voice.
22 The wind shall shepherd all your shepherds,
    and your lovers shall go into captivity;
then you will be ashamed and dismayed
    because of all your wickedness.
23 O inhabitant of Lebanon,
    nested among the cedars,

---

t Cn: Heb *uninhabited cities*

how you will groan[u] when pangs come
      upon you,
  pain as of a woman in labor!

Judgment on Coniah (Jehoiachin)

24 As I live, says the LORD, even if King Cō·nī′ah son of Je·hoi′a·kim of Judah were the signet ring on my right hand, even from there I would tear you off 25 and give you into the hands of those who seek your life, into the hands of those of whom you are afraid, even into the hands of King Ne·būchad·rez′zar of Babylon and into the hands of the Chal·dē′ans. 26 I will hurl you and the mother who bore you into another country, where you were not born, and there you shall die. 27 But they shall not return to the land to which they long to return.

28 Is this man Cō·nī′ah a despised broken pot,
    a vessel no one wants?
Why are he and his offspring hurled out
    and cast away in a land that they do not
        know?
29 O land, land, land,
    hear the word of the LORD!
30 Thus says the LORD:
Record this man as childless,
    a man who shall not succeed in his days;
for none of his offspring shall succeed
    in sitting on the throne of David,
    and ruling again in Judah.

Restoration after Exile

Woe to the shepherds who destroy and scatter the sheep of my pasture! says the LORD. 2 Therefore thus says the LORD, the God of Israel, concerning the shepherds who shepherd my people: It is you who have scattered my flock, and have driven them away, and you have not attended to them. So I will attend to you for your evil doings, says the LORD. 3 Then I myself will gather the remnant of my flock out of all the lands where I have driven them, and I will bring them back to their fold, and they shall be fruitful and multiply. 4 I will raise up shepherds over them who will shepherd them, and they shall not fear any longer, or be dismayed, nor shall any be missing, says the LORD.

The Righteous Branch of David
(Cp Jer 16.14–15)

5 The days are surely coming, says the LORD, when I will raise up for David a righteous Branch, and he shall reign as king and deal wisely, and shall execute justice and righteousness in the land. 6 In his days Judah will be saved and Israel will live in safety. And this is the name by which he will be called: "The LORD is our righteousness."

7 Therefore, the days are surely coming, says the LORD, when it shall no longer be said, "As the LORD lives who brought the people of Israel up out of the land of Egypt," 8 but "As the LORD lives who brought out and led the offspring of the house of Israel out of the land of the north and out of all the lands where he[v] had driven them." Then they shall live in their own land.

False Prophets of Hope Denounced

9 Concerning the prophets:
My heart is crushed within me,
    all my bones shake;
I have become like a drunkard,
    like one overcome by wine,
because of the LORD
    and because of his holy words.
10 For the land is full of adulterers;
    because of the curse the land mourns,
    and the pastures of the wilderness are
        dried up.
Their course has been evil,
    and their might is not right.
11 Both prophet and priest are ungodly;
    even in my house I have found their
        wickedness,
                says the LORD.
12 Therefore their way shall be to them
    like slippery paths in the darkness,
    into which they shall be driven and fall;
for I will bring disaster upon them
    in the year of their punishment,
                says the LORD.
13 In the prophets of Sa·mār′i·a
    I saw a disgusting thing:
they prophesied by Bā′al
    and led my people Israel astray.
14 But in the prophets of Jerusalem
    I have seen a more shocking thing:
they commit adultery and walk in lies;
    they strengthen the hands of evildoers,
    so that no one turns from wickedness;
all of them have become like Sod′om
    to me,
    and its inhabitants like Go·mor′rah.
15 Therefore thus says the LORD of hosts
    concerning the prophets:
"I am going to make them eat wormwood,
    and give them poisoned water to drink;
for from the prophets of Jerusalem
    ungodliness has spread throughout the
        land."

---

u Gk Vg Syr: Heb *will be pitied*   v Gk: Heb *I*

16 Thus says the LORD of hosts: Do not listen to the words of the prophets who prophesy to you; they are deluding you. They speak visions of their own minds, not from the mouth of the LORD. 17 They keep saying to those who despise the word of the LORD, "It shall be well with you"; and to all who stubbornly follow their own stubborn hearts, they say, "No calamity shall come upon you."

18 For who has stood in the council of the LORD
　　so as to see and to hear his word?
　　Who has given heed to his word so as to
　　　　proclaim it?
19 Look, the storm of the LORD!
　　Wrath has gone forth,
　　a whirling tempest;
　　it will burst upon the head of the wicked.
20 The anger of the LORD will not turn back
　　until he has executed and accomplished
　　　　the intents of his mind.
　　In the latter days you will understand it
　　　　clearly.
21 I did not send the prophets,
　　yet they ran;
　　I did not speak to them,
　　yet they prophesied.
22 But if they had stood in my council,
　　then they would have proclaimed my
　　　　words to my people,
　　and they would have turned them from
　　　　their evil way,
　　and from the evil of their doings.

23 Am I a God near by, says the LORD, and not a God far off? 24 Who can hide in secret places so that I cannot see them? says the LORD. Do I not fill heaven and earth? says the LORD. 25 I have heard what the prophets have said who prophesy lies in my name, saying, "I have dreamed, I have dreamed!" 26 How long? Will the hearts of the prophets ever turn back—those who prophesy lies, and who prophesy the deceit of their own heart? 27 They plan to make my people forget my name by their dreams that they tell one another, just as their ancestors forgot my name for Bāʾal. 28 Let the prophet who has a dream tell the dream, but let the one who has my word speak my word faithfully. What has straw in common with wheat? says the LORD. 29 Is not my word like fire, says the LORD, and like a hammer that breaks a rock in pieces? 30 See, therefore, I am against the prophets, says the LORD, who steal my words from one another. 31 I am against the prophets, says the LORD, who use their own tongues and say, "Says the LORD." 32 See, I am against those who prophesy ly-

ing dreams, says the LORD, and who tell them, and who lead my people astray by their lies and their recklessness, when I did not send them or appoint them; so they do not profit this people at all, says the LORD.

33 When this people, or a prophet, or a priest asks you, "What is the burden of the LORD?" you shall say to them, "You are the burden,w and I will cast you off, says the LORD." 34 And as for the prophet, priest, or the people who say, "The burden of the LORD," I will punish them and their households. 35 Thus shall you say to one another, among yourselves, "What has the LORD answered?" or "What has the LORD spoken?" 36 But "the burden of the LORD" you shall mention no more, for the burden is everyone's own word, and so you pervert the words of the living God, the LORD of hosts, our God. 37 Thus you shall ask the prophet, "What has the LORD answered you?" or "What has the LORD spoken?" 38 But if you say, "the burden of the LORD," thus says the LORD: Because you have said these words, "the burden of the LORD," when I sent to you, saying, You shall not say, "the burden of the LORD," 39 therefore, I will surely lift you upx and cast you away from my presence, you and the city that I gave to you and your ancestors. 40 And I will bring upon you everlasting disgrace and perpetual shame, which shall not be forgotten.

The Good and the Bad Figs

The LORD showed me two baskets of figs placed before the temple of the LORD. This was after King Ne•bū•chad•rez′zar of Babylon had taken into exile from Jerusalem King Jec•o•ni′ah son of Je•hoi′a•kim of Judah, together with the officials of Judah, the artisans, and the smiths, and had brought them to Babylon. 2 One basket had very good figs, like first-ripe figs, but the other basket had very bad figs, so bad that they could not be eaten. 3 And the LORD said to me, "What do you see, Jer•e•mi′ah?" I said, "Figs, the good figs very good, and the bad figs very bad, so bad that they cannot be eaten."

4 Then the word of the LORD came to me: 5 Thus says the LORD, the God of Israel: Like these good figs, so I will regard as good the exiles from Judah, whom I have sent away from this place to the land of the Chal•dē′ans. 6 I will set my eyes upon them for good, and I will bring them back to this land. I will build them up, and not tear them down; I will plant them, and not pluck them up. 7 I will give them a heart to know that I am the LORD; and they shall be my people and I will be

---

w Gk Vg: Heb *What burden*　x Heb Mss Gk Vg: MT *forget you*

their God, for they shall return to me with their whole heart.

8 But thus says the LORD: Like the bad figs that are so bad they cannot be eaten, so will I treat King Zed•e•ki′ah of Judah, his officials, the remnant of Jerusalem who remain in this land, and those who live in the land of Egypt. 9 I will make them a horror, an evil thing, to all the kingdoms of the earth—a disgrace, a byword, a taunt, and a curse in all the places where I shall drive them. 10 And I will send sword, famine, and pestilence upon them, until they are utterly destroyed from the land that I gave to them and their ancestors.

did you KNOW?

Fig Trees

The fig tree was widely cultivated in the ancient Near East. Its sweet fruit was a delight to taste, and its broad leaves offered welcome shade from the scorching summer sun. In Jer 24.5–7, ripe figs are presented as an image of the faithful exiles in Babylon. In I Kings 4.25, fig leaves symbolize protection and safety. Jesus tells a parable about a fig tree in Lk 13.6–9. Think about it the next time you eat a Fig Newton!

▶ Jer 24.1–10

The Babylonian Captivity Foretold

The word that came to Jer•e•mi′ah concerning all the people of Judah, in the fourth year of King Je•hoi′a•kim son of Jo̅•si′ah of Judah (that was the first year of King Ne•bu̅•chad•rez′zar of Babylon), 2 which the prophet Jer•e•mi′ah spoke to all the people of Judah and all the inhabitants of Jerusalem: 3 For twenty-three years, from the thirteenth year of King Jo̅•si′ah son of A̅′mon of Judah, to this day, the word of the LORD has come to me, and I have spoken persistently to you, but you have not listened. 4 And though the LORD persistently sent you all his servants the prophets, you have neither listened nor inclined your ears to hear 5 when they said, "Turn now, everyone of you, from your evil way and wicked doings, and you will remain upon the land that the LORD has given to you and your ancestors from of old and forever; 6 do not go after other gods to serve and worship them, and do not

provoke me to anger with the work of your hands. Then I will do you no harm." 7 Yet you did not listen to me, says the LORD, and so you have provoked me to anger with the work of your hands to your own harm.

8 Therefore thus says the LORD of hosts: Because you have not obeyed my words, 9 I am going to send for all the tribes of the north, says the LORD, even for King Ne•bu̅•chad•rez′zar of Babylon, my servant, and I will bring them against this land and its inhabitants, and against all these nations around; I will utterly destroy them, and make them an object of horror and of hissing, and an everlasting disgrace.y 10 And I will banish from them the sound of mirth and the sound of gladness, the voice of the bridegroom and the voice of the bride, the sound of the millstones and the light of the lamp. 11 This whole land shall become a ruin and a waste, and these nations shall serve the king of Babylon seventy years. 12 Then after seventy years are completed, I will punish the king of Babylon and that nation, the land of the Chal•de′ans, for their iniquity, says the LORD, making the land an everlasting waste. 13 I will bring upon that land all the words that I have uttered against it, everything written in this book, which Jer•e•mi′ah prophesied against all the nations. 14 For many nations and great kings shall make slaves of them also; and I will repay them according to their deeds and the work of their hands.

The Cup of God's Wrath

15 For thus the LORD, the God of Israel, said to me: Take from my hand this cup of the wine of wrath, and make all the nations to whom I send you drink it. 16 They shall drink and stagger and go out of their minds because of the sword that I am sending among them.

17 So I took the cup from the LORD's hand, and made all the nations to whom the LORD sent me drink it: 18 Jerusalem and the towns of Judah, its kings and officials, to make them a desolation and a waste, an object of hissing and of cursing, as they are today; 19 Pharaoh king of Egypt, his servants, his officials, and all his people; 20 all the mixed people;z all the kings of the land of Uz; all the kings of the land of the Phi•lis′tines—Ash′ke•lon, Ga̅′za, Ek′ron, and the remnant of Ash′dod; 21 E̅′dom, Mo̅′ab, and the Am′mon•ites; 22 all the kings of Ty̅re, all the kings of Si′don, and the kings of the coastland across the sea; 23 De̅′dan, Te̅′ma, Buz, and all who have shaven temples; 24 all the kings of Arabia and all the kings of the mixed peo-

y Gk Compare Syr: Heb *and everlasting desolations*
z Meaning of Heb uncertain

ples*a* that live in the desert; 25 all the kings of Zim'rī, all the kings of Ē'lam, and all the kings of Mēd'i•a; 26 all the kings of the north, far and near, one after another, and all the kingdoms of the world that are on the face of the earth. And after them the king of Shē'shach*b* shall drink.

27 Then you shall say to them, Thus says the LORD of hosts, the God of Israel: Drink, get drunk and vomit, fall and rise no more, because of the sword that I am sending among you.

28 And if they refuse to accept the cup from your hand to drink, then you shall say to them: Thus says the LORD of hosts: You must drink! 29 See, I am beginning to bring disaster on the city that is called by my name, and how can you possibly avoid punishment? You shall not go unpunished, for I am summoning a sword against all the inhabitants of the earth, says the LORD of hosts.

30 You, therefore, shall prophesy against them all these words, and say to them:

The LORD will roar from on high,
and from his holy habitation utter his
voice;
he will roar mightily against his fold,
and shout, like those who tread grapes,
against all the inhabitants of the earth.
31 The clamor will resound to the ends of the
earth,
for the LORD has an indictment against
the nations;
he is entering into judgment with all flesh,
and the guilty he will put to the sword,
says the LORD.

32 Thus says the LORD of hosts:
See, disaster is spreading
from nation to nation,
and a great tempest is stirring
from the farthest parts of the earth!

33 Those slain by the LORD on that day shall extend from one end of the earth to the other. They shall not be lamented, or gathered, or buried; they shall become dung on the surface of the ground.

34 Wail, you shepherds, and cry out;
roll in ashes, you lords of the flock,
for the days of your slaughter have come—
and your dispersions,*a*
and you shall fall like a choice vessel.
35 Flight shall fail the shepherds,
and there shall be no escape for the lords
of the flock.
36 Hark! the cry of the shepherds,
and the wail of the lords of the flock!
For the LORD is despoiling their pasture,
37 and the peaceful folds are devastated,

because of the fierce anger of the LORD.
38 Like a lion he has left his covert;
for their land has become a waste
because of the cruel sword,
and because of his fierce anger.

Jeremiah's Prophecies in the Temple
(Cp Jer 7.1–15)

At the beginning of the reign of King Je•hoi'a•kim son of Jō•si'ah of Judah, this word came from the LORD: 2 Thus says the LORD: Stand in the court of the LORD's house, and speak to all the cities of Judah that come to worship in the house of the LORD; speak to them all the words that I command you; do not hold back a word. 3 It may be that they will listen, all of them, and will turn from their evil way, that I may change my mind about the disaster that I intend to bring on them because of their evil doings. 4 You shall say to them: Thus says the LORD: If you will not listen to me, to walk in my law that I have set before you, 5 and to heed the words of my servants the prophets whom I send to you urgently—though you have not heeded— 6 then I will make this house like Shi'lōh, and I will make this city a curse for all the nations of the earth.

7 The priests and the prophets and all the people heard Jer•e•mi'ah speaking these words in the house of the LORD. 8 And when Jer•e•mi'ah had finished speaking all that the LORD had commanded him to speak to all the people, then the priests and the prophets and all the people laid hold of him, saying, "You shall die! 9 Why have you prophesied in the name of the LORD, saying, 'This house shall be like Shi'lōh, and this city shall be desolate, without inhabitant'?" And all the people gathered around Jer•e•mi'ah in the house of the LORD.

10 When the officials of Judah heard these things, they came up from the king's house to the house of the LORD and took their seat in the entry of the New Gate of the house of the LORD. 11 Then the priests and the prophets said to the officials and to all the people, "This man deserves the sentence of death because he has prophesied against this city, as you have heard with your own ears."

12 Then Jer•e•mi'ah spoke to all the officials and all the people, saying, "It is the LORD who sent me to prophesy against this house and this city all the words you have heard. 13 Now therefore amend your ways and your doings, and obey the voice of the LORD your God, and the LORD will change his mind about the disaster that he has pronounced against you. 14 But as for me, here I

---

a Meaning of Heb uncertain   *b* Sheshach is a cryptogram for *Babel*, Babylon

am in your hands. Do with me as seems good and right to you. ¹⁵ Only know for certain that if you put me to death, you will be bringing innocent blood upon yourselves and upon this city and its inhabitants, for in truth the LORD sent me to you to speak all these words in your ears."

27.2

16 Then the officials and all the people said to the priests and the prophets, "This man does not deserve the sentence of death, for he has spoken to us in the name of the LORD our God." ¹⁷ And some of the elders of the land arose and said to all the assembled people, ¹⁸ "Mi′cah of Mō′re·sheth, who prophesied during the days of King Hez·e·ki′ah of Judah, said to all the people of Judah: 'Thus says the LORD of hosts,

Zion shall be plowed as a field;
    Jerusalem shall become a heap of ruins,
    and the mountain of the house a wooded
        height.'
¹⁹ Did King Hez·e·ki′ah of Judah and all Judah actually put him to death? Did he not fear the LORD and entreat the favor of the LORD, and did not the LORD change his mind about the disaster that he had pronounced against them? But we are about to bring great disaster on ourselves!"

20 There was another man prophesying in the name of the LORD, Ū·ri′ah son of She·mai′ah from Kir′i·ath-jē′a·rim. He prophesied against this city and against this land in words exactly like those of Jer·e·mi′ah. ²¹ And when King Je·hoi′a·kim, with all his warriors and all the officials, heard his words, the king sought to put him to death; but when Ū·ri′ah heard of it, he was afraid and fled and escaped to Egypt. ²² Then King Je·hoi′a·kim sentᶜ El-

na′than son of Ach′bor and men with him to Egypt, ²³ and they took Ū·ri′ah from Egypt and brought him to King Je·hoi′a·kim, who struck him down with the sword and threw his dead body into the burial place of the common people.

24 But the hand of A·hi′kam son of Shā′phan was with Jer·e·mi′ah so that he was not given over into the hands of the people to be put to death.

The Sign of the Yoke

In the beginning of the reign of King Zed·e·ki′ahᵈ son of Jō·si′ah of Judah, this word came to Jer·e·mi′ah from the LORD. ² Thus the LORD said to me: Make yourself a yoke of straps and bars, and put them on your neck. ³ Send wordᵉ to the king of Ē′dom, the king of Mō′ab, the king of the Am′mon·ites, the king of Tyre, and the king of Si′don by the hand of the envoys who have come to Jerusalem to King Zed·e·ki′ah of Judah. ⁴ Give them this charge for their masters: Thus says the LORD of hosts, the God of Israel: This is what you shall say to your masters: ⁵ It is I who by my great power and my outstretched arm have made the earth, with the people and animals that are on the earth, and I give it to whomever I please. ⁶ Now I have given all these lands into the hand of King Ne·bū·chad·nez′zar of Babylon, my servant, and I have given him even the wild animals of the field to serve him. ⁷ All the nations shall serve him and his son and his grandson, until the time of his own land comes; then many nations and great kings shall make him their slave.

8 But if any nation or kingdom will not serve this king, Ne·bū·chad·nez′zar of Babylon, and put its neck under the yoke of the king of Babylon, then I will punish that nation with the sword, with famine, and with pestilence, says the LORD, until I have completed itsᶠ destruction by his hand. ⁹ You, therefore, must not listen to your prophets, your diviners, your dreamers,ᵍ your soothsayers, or your sorcerers, who are saying to you, "You shall not serve the king of Babylon." ¹⁰ For they are prophesying a lie to you, with the result that you will be removed far from your land; I will drive you out, and you will perish. ¹¹ But any nation that will bring its neck under the yoke of the king of Babylon and serve him, I will leave on its own land, says the LORD, to till it and live there.

12 I spoke to King Zed·e·ki′ah of Judah in the same way: Bring your necks under the yoke of the king of Babylon, and serve him and his people, and live. ¹³ Why should you and your people die

ᶜ Heb adds *men to Egypt*   ᵈ Another reading is *Jehoiakim*
ᵉ Cn: Heb *send them*   ᶠ Heb *their*   ᵍ Gk Syr Vg: Heb *dreams*

by the sword, by famine, and by pestilence, as the LORD has spoken concerning any nation that will not serve the king of Babylon? 14 Do not listen to the words of the prophets who are telling you not to serve the king of Babylon, for they are prophesying a lie to you. 15 I have not sent them, says the LORD, but they are prophesying falsely in my name, with the result that I will drive you out and you will perish, you and the prophets who are prophesying to you.

16 Then I spoke to the priests and to all this people, saying, Thus says the LORD: Do not listen to the words of your prophets who are prophesying to you, saying, "The vessels of the LORD's house will soon be brought back from Babylon," for they are prophesying a lie to you. 17 Do not listen to them; serve the king of Babylon and live. Why should this city become a desolation? 18 If indeed they are prophets, and if the word of the LORD is with them, then let them intercede with the LORD of hosts, that the vessels left in the house of the LORD, in the house of the king of Judah, and in Jerusalem may not go to Babylon. 19 For thus says the LORD of hosts concerning the pillars, the sea, the stands, and the rest of the vessels that are left in this city, 20 which King Ne·bū·chad·nez'zar of Babylon did not take away when he took into exile from Jerusalem to Babylon King Jec·o·nī'ah son of Je·hoi'a·kim of Judah, and all the nobles of Judah and Jerusalem— 21 thus says the LORD of hosts, the God of Israel, concerning the vessels left in the house of the LORD, in the house of the king of Judah, and in Jerusalem: 22 They shall be carried to Babylon, and there they shall stay, until the day when I give attention to them, says the LORD. Then I will bring them up and restore them to this place.

Hananiah Opposes Jeremiah and Dies

In that same year, at the beginning of the reign of King Zed·e·kī'ah of Judah, in the fifth month of the fourth year, the prophet Han·a·nī'ah son of Az'zur, from Gib'e·on, spoke to me in the house of the LORD, in the presence of the priests and all the people, saying, 2 "Thus says the LORD of hosts, the God of Israel: I have broken the yoke of the king of Babylon. 3 Within two years I will bring back to this place all the vessels of the LORD's house, which King Ne·bū·chad·nez'zar of Babylon took away from this place and carried to Babylon. 4 I will also bring back to this place King Jec·o·nī'ah son of Je·hoi'a·kim of Judah, and all the exiles from Judah who went to Babylon, says the LORD, for I will break the yoke of the king of Babylon."

5 Then the prophet Jer·e·mī'ah spoke to the prophet Han·a·nī'ah in the presence of the priests

and all the people who were standing in the house of the LORD; 6 and the prophet Jer·e·mī'ah said, "Amen! May the LORD do so; may the LORD fulfill the words that you have prophesied, and bring back to this place from Babylon the vessels of the house of the LORD, and all the exiles. 7 But listen now to this word that I speak in your hearing and in the hearing of all the people. 8 The prophets who preceded you and me from ancient times prophesied war, famine, and pestilence against many countries and great kingdoms. 9 As for the prophet who prophesies peace, when the word of that prophet comes true, then it will be known that the LORD has truly sent the prophet."

10 Then the prophet Han·a·nī'ah took the yoke from the neck of the prophet Jer·e·mī'ah, and broke it. 11 And Han·a·nī'ah spoke in the presence of all the people, saying, "Thus says the LORD: This is how I will break the yoke of King Ne·bū·chad·nez'zar of Babylon from the neck of all the nations within two years." At this, the prophet Jer·e·mī'ah went his way.

12 Sometime after the prophet Han·a·nī'ah had broken the yoke from the neck of the prophet Jer·e·mī'ah, the word of the LORD came to Jer·e·mī'ah: 13 Go, tell Han·a·nī'ah, Thus says the LORD: You have broken wooden bars only to forge iron bars in place of them! 14 For thus says the LORD of hosts, the God of Israel: I have put an iron yoke on the neck of all these nations so that they may serve King Ne·bū·chad·nez'zar of Babylon, and they shall indeed serve him; I have even given him the wild animals. 15 And the prophet Jer·e·mī'ah said to the prophet Han·a·nī'ah, "Listen, Han·a·nī'ah, the LORD has not sent you, and you made this people trust in a lie. 16 Therefore thus says the LORD: I am going to send you off the face of the earth. Within this year you will be dead, because you have spoken rebellion against the LORD."

17 In that same year, in the seventh month, the prophet Han·a·nī'ah died.

Jeremiah's Letter to the Exiles in Babylon

These are the words of the letter that the prophet Jer·e·mī'ah sent from Jerusalem to the remaining elders among the exiles, and to the priests, the prophets, and all the people, whom Ne·bū·chad·nez'zar had taken into exile from Jerusalem to Babylon. 2 This was after King Jec·o·nī'ah, and the queen mother, the court officials, the leaders of Judah and Jerusalem, the artisans, and the smiths had departed from Jerusalem. 3 The letter was sent by the hand of El·ā'sah son of Shā'phan and Gem·a·rī'ah son of Hil·kī'ah, whom King Zed·e·kī'ah of Judah sent to Babylon to King Ne·bū·chad·nez'zar of

Babylon. It said: 4 Thus says the LORD of hosts, the God of Israel, to all the exiles whom I have sent into exile from Jerusalem to Babylon: 5 Build houses and live in them; plant gardens and eat what they produce. 6 Take wives and have sons and daughters; take wives for your sons, and give your daughters in marriage, that they may bear sons and daughters; multiply there, and do not decrease. 7 But seek the welfare of the city where I have sent you into exile, and pray to the LORD on its behalf, for in its welfare you will find your welfare. 8 For thus says the LORD of hosts, the God of Israel: Do not let the prophets and the diviners who are among you deceive you, and do not listen to the dreams that they dream,*h* 9 for it is a lie that they are prophesying to you in my name; I did not send them, says the LORD.

10 For thus says the LORD: Only when Babylon's seventy years are completed will I visit you, and I will fulfill to you my promise and bring you back to this place. 11 For surely I know the plans I have for you, says the LORD, plans for your welfare and not for harm, to give you a future with hope. 12 Then when you call upon me and come and pray to me, I will hear you. 13 When you search for me, you will find me; if you seek me with all your heart, 14 I will let you find me, says the LORD, and I will restore your fortunes and gather you from all the nations and all the places where I have driven you, says the LORD, and I will bring you back to the place from which I sent you into exile.

15 Because you have said, "The LORD has raised up prophets for us in Babylon,"— 16 Thus says the LORD concerning the king who sits on the throne of David, and concerning all the people who live in this city, your kinsfolk who did not go out with you into exile: 17 Thus says the LORD of hosts, I am going to let loose on them sword, famine, and pestilence, and I will make them like rotten figs that are so bad they cannot be eaten. 18 I will pursue them with the sword, with famine, and with pestilence, and will make them a horror to all the kingdoms of the earth, to be an object of cursing, and horror, and hissing, and a derision among all the nations where I have driven them, 19 because they did not heed my words, says the LORD, when I persistently sent to you my servants the prophets, but they*i* would not listen, says the LORD. 20 But now, all you exiles whom I sent away from Jerusalem to Babylon, hear the word of the LORD: 21 Thus says the LORD of hosts, the God of Israel, concerning Āʹhab son of Kōʹlaiʹah and Zedeʹkīʹah son of Māʹaʹseiʹah, who are prophesying a lie to you in my name: I am going to deliver them into the hand of King Neʹbūʹchadʹrezʹzar of Babylon, and he shall kill them before your eyes.

22 And on account of them this curse shall be used by all the exiles from Judah in Babylon: "The LORD make you like Zedʹeʹkīʹah and Āʹhab, whom the king of Babylon roasted in the fire," 23 because they have perpetrated outrage in Israel and have committed adultery with their neighbors' wives, and have spoken in my name lying words that I did not command them; I am the one who knows and bears witness, says the LORD.

The Letter of Shemaiah

24 To Sheʹmaiʹah of Neʹhelʹam you shall say: 25 Thus says the LORD of hosts, the God of Israel: In your own name you sent a letter to all the people who are in Jerusalem, and to the priest Zephʹaʹniʹah son of Māʹaʹseiʹah, and to all the priests, saying, 26 The LORD himself has made you priest instead of the priest Jeʹhoiʹaʹda, so that there may be officers in the house of the LORD to control any madman who plays the prophet, to put him in the stocks and the collar. 27 So now why have you not rebuked Jerʹeʹmiʹah of Anʹaʹthoth who plays the prophet for you? 28 For he has actually sent to us in Babylon, saying, "It will be a long time; build houses and live in them, and plant gardens and eat what they produce."

29 The priest Zephʹaʹniʹah read this letter in the hearing of the prophet Jerʹeʹmiʹah. 30 Then the word of the LORD came to Jerʹeʹmiʹah: 31 Send to all the exiles, saying, Thus says the LORD concerning Sheʹmaiʹah of Neʹhelʹam: Because Sheʹmaiʹah has prophesied to you, though I did not send him, and has led you to trust in a lie, 32 therefore thus says the LORD: I am going to punish Sheʹmaiʹah of Neʹhelʹam and his descendants; he shall not have anyone living among this people to see*j* the good that I am going to do to my people, says the LORD, for he has spoken rebellion against the LORD.

Restoration Promised for Israel and Judah

The word that came to Jerʹeʹmiʹah from the LORD: 2 Thus says the LORD, the God of Israel: Write in a book all the words that I have spoken to you. 3 For the days are surely coming, says the LORD, when I will restore the fortunes of my people, Israel and Judah, says the LORD, and I will bring them back to the land that I gave to their ancestors and they shall take possession of it.

4 These are the words that the LORD spoke concerning Israel and Judah:

5 Thus says the LORD:
    We have heard a cry of panic,

---

h Cn: Heb *your dreams that you cause to dream*   *i* Syr: Heb *you*   *j* Gk: Heb *and he shall not see*

of terror, and no peace.
6 Ask now, and see,
    can a man bear a child?
Why then do I see every man
    with his hands on his loins like a woman
        in labor?
Why has every face turned pale?
7 Alas! that day is so great
    there is none like it;
it is a time of distress for Jacob;
    yet he shall be rescued from it.

8 On that day, says the LORD of hosts, I will break the yoke from off his[k] neck, and I will burst his[k] bonds, and strangers shall no more make a servant of him. 9 But they shall serve the LORD their God and David their king, whom I will raise up for them.

10 But as for you, have no fear, my servant
        Jacob, says the LORD,
    and do not be dismayed, O Israel;
for I am going to save you from far away,
    and your offspring from the land of their
        captivity.
Jacob shall return and have quiet and ease,
    and no one shall make him afraid.
11 For I am with you, says the LORD, to
        save you;
I will make an end of all the nations
    among which I scattered you,
    but of you I will not make an end.
I will chastise you in just measure,
    and I will by no means leave you
        unpunished.

12 For thus says the LORD:
Your hurt is incurable,
    your wound is grievous.
13 There is no one to uphold your cause,
    no medicine for your wound,
    no healing for you.
14 All your lovers have forgotten you;
    they care nothing for you;
for I have dealt you the blow of an enemy,
    the punishment of a merciless foe,
because your guilt is great,
    because your sins are so numerous.
15 Why do you cry out over your hurt?
    Your pain is incurable.
Because your guilt is great,
    because your sins are so numerous,
    I have done these things to you.
16 Therefore all who devour you shall be
        devoured,
    and all your foes, everyone of them, shall
        go into captivity;
those who plunder you shall be plundered,

and all who prey on you I will make a
        prey.
17 For I will restore health to you,
    and your wounds I will heal,
                                    says the LORD,
because they have called you an outcast:
    "It is Zion; no one cares for her!"

18 Thus says the LORD:
I am going to restore the fortunes of the
        tents of Jacob,
    and have compassion on his dwellings;
the city shall be rebuilt upon its mound,
    and the citadel set on its rightful site.
19 Out of them shall come thanksgiving,
    and the sound of merrymakers.
I will make them many, and they shall not
        be few;
    I will make them honored, and they shall
        not be disdained.
20 Their children shall be as of old,
    their congregation shall be established
        before me;
    and I will punish all who oppress them.
21 Their prince shall be one of their own,
    their ruler shall come from their midst;
I will bring him near, and he shall
        approach me,
    for who would otherwise dare to
        approach me?
                                    says the LORD.
22 And you shall be my people,
    and I will be your God.

23 Look, the storm of the LORD!
    Wrath has gone forth,
a whirling[l] tempest;
    it will burst upon the head of the wicked.
24 The fierce anger of the LORD will not turn
        back
    until he has executed and accomplished
    the intents of his mind.
In the latter days you will understand this.

The Joyful Return of the Exiles

At that time, says the LORD, I will be the God of all the families of Israel, and they shall be my people.
2 Thus says the LORD:
The people who survived the sword
    found grace in the wilderness;
when Israel sought for rest,
3   the LORD appeared to him[m] from far
        away.[n]
I have loved you with an everlasting love;

---

k Cn: Heb your   l One Ms: Meaning of MT uncertain
m Gk: Heb me   n Or to him long ago

therefore I have continued my
faithfulness to you.

4 Again I will build you, and you shall be
built,
O virgin Israel!
Again you shall take° your tambourines,
and go forth in the dance of the
merrymakers.

5 Again you shall plant vineyards
on the mountains of Sa•mar′i•a;
the planters shall plant,
and shall enjoy the fruit.

6 For there shall be a day when sentinels will
call
in the hill country of E′phra•im:
"Come, let us go up to Zion,
to the LORD our God."

7 For thus says the LORD:
Sing aloud with gladness for Jacob,
and raise shouts for the chief of the
nations;
proclaim, give praise, and say,
"Save, O LORD, your people,
the remnant of Israel."

8 See, I am going to bring them from the land
of the north,
and gather them from the farthest parts
of the earth,
among them the blind and the lame,
those with child and those in labor,
together;
a great company, they shall return here.

9 With weeping they shall come,
and with consolations ᵖ I will lead them
back,
I will let them walk by brooks of water,
in a straight path in which they shall not
stumble;
for I have become a father to Israel,
and E′phra•im is my firstborn.

10 Hear the word of the LORD, O nations,
and declare it in the coastlands far away;
say, "He who scattered Israel will
gather him,
and will keep him as a shepherd a flock."

11 For the LORD has ransomed Jacob,
and has redeemed him from hands too
strong for him.

12 They shall come and sing aloud on the
height of Zion,
and they shall be radiant over the
goodness of the LORD,
over the grain, the wine, and the oil,
and over the young of the flock and the
herd;

their life shall become like a watered
garden,
and they shall never languish again.

13 Then shall the young women rejoice in the
dance,
and the young men and the old shall be
merry.
I will turn their mourning into joy,
I will comfort them, and give them
gladness for sorrow.

14 I will give the priests their fill of fatness,
and my people shall be satisfied with my
bounty,
says the LORD.

PRAY IT!
Rachel Weeps

Rachel was the "mother of Israel," the
favored wife of Jacob (Gen 29.28–30)
whose twelve sons formed the twelve
tribes of Israel. In Jer 31.15–17, she is
symbolically weeping over the death and
captivity of her children—the Israelites—
after the Babylonian invasion.

Rachel weeping has become an image of trauma and unrelenting grief over
violence, death, and slaughter, especially
when children are involved. For example,
Mt 2.16–18 quotes Jer 31.15–17 in a story
about the massacre of infants in Bethlehem. Project Rachel is an organized ministry for women who have had abortions.
And Rachel Weeps is a holocaust exhibition recalling the murder of millions of
Jewish men, women, and children.

Jeremiah goes on in verses 16–17 with
words of hope. God promises that the
scattered children will be brought back.
We can trust that God is with the victims of senseless violence and those who
grieve for them. Let us pray for Rachel's
grief to end.

▸ Jer 31.15–17

15 Thus says the LORD:
A voice is heard in Rā′mah,
lamentation and bitter weeping.

° Or *adorn yourself with*   ᵖ Gk Compare Vg Tg: Heb
supplications

Rachel is weeping for her children;
  she refuses to be comforted for her
    children,
  because they are no more.
16 Thus says the LORD:
  Keep your voice from weeping,
    and your eyes from tears;
  for there is a reward for your work,
                                    says the LORD:
  they shall come back from the land of
    the enemy;
17 there is hope for your future,
                                    says the LORD:
  your children shall come back to their
    own country.

18 Indeed I heard E´phra·im pleading:
  "You disciplined me, and I took the
    discipline;
  I was like a calf untrained.
  Bring me back, let me come back,
    for you are the LORD my God.
19 For after I had turned away I repented;
    and after I was discovered, I struck my
      thigh;
  I was ashamed, and I was dismayed
    because I bore the disgrace of my youth."
20 Is E´phra·im my dear son?
  Is he the child I delight in?
  As often as I speak against him,
    I still remember him.
  Therefore I am deeply moved for him;
    I will surely have mercy on him,
                                    says the LORD.

21 Set up road markers for yourself,
    make yourself signposts;
  consider well the highway,
    the road by which you went.
  Return, O virgin Israel,
    return to these your cities.
22 How long will you waver,
    O faithless daughter?
  For the LORD has created a new thing on the
    earth:
  a woman encompasses*q* a man.

23 Thus says the LORD of hosts, the God of Israel: Once more they shall use these words in the
land of Judah and in its towns when I restore their
fortunes:
  "The LORD bless you, O abode of
    righteousness,
  O holy hill!"
24 And Judah and all its towns shall live there together, and the farmers and those who wander*r*
with their flocks.

25 I will satisfy the weary,
    and all who are faint I will replenish.
26 Thereupon I awoke and looked, and my
sleep was pleasant to me.

Individual Retribution

27 The days are surely coming, says the LORD,
when I will sow the house of Israel and the house
of Judah with the seed of humans and the seed of
animals. 28 And just as I have watched over them
to pluck up and break down, to overthrow, destroy, and bring evil, so I will watch over them to
build and to plant, says the LORD. 29 In those days
they shall no longer say:
  "The parents have eaten sour grapes,
    and the children's teeth are set on edge."
30 But all shall die for their own sins; the teeth of
everyone who eats sour grapes shall be set on
edge.

A New Covenant

31 The days are surely coming, says the LORD,
when I will make a new covenant with the house
of Israel and the house of Judah. 32 It will not be
like the covenant that I made with their ancestors
when I took them by the hand to bring them out
of the land of Egypt—a covenant that they broke,
though I was their husband,*s* says the LORD. 33 But
this is the covenant that I will make with the
house of Israel after those days, says the LORD: I
will put my law within them, and I will write it on
their hearts; and I will be their God, and they shall
be my people. 34 No longer shall they teach one
another, or say to each other, "Know the LORD," for
they shall all know me, from the least of them to
the greatest, says the LORD; for I will forgive their
iniquity, and remember their sin no more.

35 Thus says the LORD,
    who gives the sun for light by day
      and the fixed order of the moon and the
        stars for light by night,
    who stirs up the sea so that its waves roar—
      the LORD of hosts is his name:
36 If this fixed order were ever to cease
    from my presence, says the LORD,
  then also the offspring of Israel would cease
    to be a nation before me forever.

37 Thus says the LORD:
    If the heavens above can be measured,
      and the foundations of the earth below
        can be explored,
    then I will reject all the offspring of Israel

---

q Meaning of Heb uncertain   *r* Cn Compare Syr Vg Tg:
Heb *and they shall wander*   *s* Or *master*

The Heart of the Matter

The Ten Commandments. The stone tablets on which they were written are the most famous stone tablets in the world, and yet no one knows where they are. The ark of the Covenant, in which they were once kept, was taken during a raid on the Temple (Jer 52.17–23). What a find they would be today! Imagine all the people flocking to see the original Ten Commandments.

But perhaps their absence makes Jeremiah's beautiful words about the new Covenant in Jer 31.31–34 even more fitting. What was etched in stone on those tablets needs to be etched in our heart. We keep in our heart what is most valuable to us. If we keep God's law there, we have no need for it written in stone.

When you look into your heart, what do you find written there?

▶ Jer 31.31–34

because of all they have done,

says the LORD.

Jerusalem to Be Enlarged

38 The days are surely coming, says the LORD, when the city shall be rebuilt for the LORD from the tower of Ha·nan′el to the Corner Gate. 39 And the measuring line shall go out farther, straight to the hill Gā′reb, and shall then turn to Gō′ah. 40 The whole valley of the dead bodies and the ashes, and all the fields as far as the Wadi Kid′ron, to the corner of the Horse Gate toward the east, shall be sacred to the LORD. It shall never again be uprooted or overthrown.

Jeremiah Buys a Field During the Siege

The word that came to Jer·e·mi′ah from the LORD in the tenth year of King Zed·e·kī′ah of Judah, which was the eighteenth year of Ne·bū·chad·rez′zar. 2 At that time the army of the king of Babylon was besieging Jerusalem, and the prophet Jer·e·mi′ah was confined in the court of the guard that was in the palace of the king of Judah, 3 where King Zed·e·kī′ah of Judah had confined him. Zed·e·kī′ah had said, "Why do you prophesy and say: Thus says the LORD: I am going to give this city into the hand of the king of Babylon, and he shall take it; 4 King Zed·e·kī′ah of Judah shall not escape out of the hands of the Chal·dē′ans, but shall surely be given into the hands of the king of Babylon, and shall speak with him face to face and see him eye to eye; 5 and he shall take Zed·e·kī′ah to Babylon, and there he shall remain until I attend to him, says the LORD; though you fight against the Chal·dē′ans, you shall not succeed?"

6 Jer·e·mi′ah said, The word of the LORD came to me: 7 Han′a·mel son of your uncle Shal′lum is going to come to you and say, "Buy my field that is at An′a·thoth, for the right of redemption by purchase is yours." 8 Then my cousin Han′a·mel came to me in the court of the guard, in accordance with the word of the LORD, and said to me, "Buy my field that is at An′a·thoth in the land of Benjamin, for the right of possession and redemption is yours; buy it for yourself." Then I knew that this was the word of the LORD.

9 And I bought the field at An′a·thoth from my cousin Han′a·mel, and weighed out the money to him, seventeen shekels of silver. 10 I signed the deed, sealed it, got witnesses, and weighed the money on scales. 11 Then I took the sealed deed of purchase, containing the terms and conditions, and the open copy; 12 and I gave the deed of purchase to Bar′uch son of Ne·rī′ah son of Mah′sēi·ah, in the presence of my cousin Han′a·mel, in the presence of the witnesses who signed the deed of purchase, and in the presence of all the Judeans who were sitting in the court of the guard. 13 In their presence I charged Bar′uch, saying, 14 Thus says the LORD of hosts, the God of Israel: Take these deeds, both this sealed deed of purchase and this open deed, and put them in an earthenware jar, in order that they may last for a long time. 15 For thus says the LORD of hosts, the God of Israel: Houses and fields and vineyards shall again be bought in this land.

Jeremiah Prays for Understanding

16 After I had given the deed of purchase to Bar′uch son of Ne·rī′ah, I prayed to the LORD, saying: 17 Ah Lord GOD! It is you who made the heavens and the earth by your great power and by your outstretched arm! Nothing is too hard for you. 18 You show steadfast love to the thousandth gen-

eration,[t] but repay the guilt of parents into the laps of their children after them, O great and mighty God whose name is the LORD of hosts, [19] great in counsel and mighty in deed; whose eyes are open to all the ways of mortals, rewarding all according to their ways and according to the fruit of their doings. [20] You showed signs and wonders in the land of Egypt, and to this day in Israel and among all humankind, and have made yourself a name that continues to this very day. [21] You brought your people Israel out of the land of Egypt with signs and wonders, with a strong hand and outstretched arm, and with great terror; [22] and you gave them this land, which you swore to their ancestors to give them, a land flowing with milk and honey; [23] and they entered and took possession of it. But they did not obey your voice or follow your law; of all you commanded them to do, they did nothing. Therefore you have made all these disasters come upon them. [24] See, the siege ramps have been cast up against the city to take it, and the city, faced with sword, famine, and pestilence, has been given into the hands of the Chal·dē′ans who are fighting against it. What you spoke has happened, as you yourself can see. [25] Yet you, O Lord GOD, have said to me, "Buy the field for money and get witnesses"—though the city has been given into the hands of the Chal·dē′ans.

God's Assurance of the People's Return

26 The word of the LORD came to Jer·e·mi′ah: [27] See, I am the LORD, the God of all flesh; is anything too hard for me? [28] Therefore, thus says the LORD: I am going to give this city into the hands of the Chal·dē′ans and into the hand of King Ne·bu·chad·rez′zar of Babylon, and he shall take it. [29] The Chal·dē′ans who are fighting against this city shall come, set it on fire, and burn it, with the houses on whose roofs offerings have been made to Bā′al and libations have been poured out to other gods, to provoke me to anger. [30] For the people of Israel and the people of Judah have done nothing but evil in my sight from their youth; the people of Israel have done nothing but provoke me to anger by the work of their hands, says the LORD. [31] This city has aroused my anger and wrath, from the day it was built until this day, so that I will remove it from my sight [32] because of all the evil of the people of Israel and the people of Judah that they did to provoke me to anger—they, their kings and their officials, their priests and their prophets, the citizens of Judah and the inhabitants of Jerusalem. [33] They have turned their backs to me, not their faces; though I have taught them persistently, they would not listen and accept correction. [34] They set up their abominations in the house that bears my name, and defiled it. [35] They built the high places of Bā′al in the valley of the son of Hin′nom, to offer up their sons and daughters to Mō′lech, though I did not command them, nor did it enter my mind that they should do this abomination, causing Judah to sin.

36 Now therefore thus says the LORD, the God of Israel, concerning this city of which you say, "It is being given into the hand of the king of Babylon by the sword, by famine, and by pestilence": [37] See, I am going to gather them from all the lands to which I drove them in my anger and my wrath and in great indignation; I will bring them back to this place, and I will settle them in safety. [38] They shall be my people, and I will be their God. [39] I will give them one heart and one way, that they may fear me for all time, for their own good and the good of their children after them. [40] I will make an everlasting covenant with them, never to draw back from doing good to them; and I will put the fear of me in their hearts, so that they may not turn from me. [41] I will rejoice in doing good to them, and I will plant them in this land in faithfulness, with all my heart and all my soul.

42 For thus says the LORD: Just as I have brought all this great disaster upon this people, so I will bring upon them all the good fortune that I now promise them. [43] Fields shall be bought in this land of which you are saying, It is a desolation, without human beings or animals; it has been given into the hands of the Chal·dē′ans. [44] Fields shall be bought for money, and deeds shall be signed and sealed and witnessed, in the land of Benjamin, in the places around Jerusalem, and in the cities of Judah, of the hill country, of the She·phē′lah, and of the Neg′eb; for I will restore their fortunes, says the LORD.

Healing after Punishment

The word of the LORD came to Jer·e·mi′ah a second time, while he was still confined in the court of the guard: [2] Thus says the LORD who made the earth,[u] the LORD who formed it to establish it—the LORD is his name: [3] Call to me and I will answer you, and will tell you great and hidden things that you have not known. [4] For thus says the LORD, the God of Israel, concerning the houses of this city and the houses of the kings of Judah that were torn down to make a defense against the siege ramps and before the sword:[v] [5] The Chal·dē′ans are coming in to fight[w] and to fill them with the dead bodies of those whom I shall strike down in my

---

[t] Or *to thousands*   [u] Gk: Heb *it*   [v] Meaning of Heb uncertain   [w] Cn: Heb *They are coming in to fight against the Chaldeans*

anger and my wrath, for I have hidden my face from this city because of all their wickedness. 6 I am going to bring it recovery and healing; I will heal them and reveal to them abundance[x] of prosperity and security. 7 I will restore the fortunes of Judah and the fortunes of Israel, and rebuild them as they were at first. 8 I will cleanse them from all the guilt of their sin against me, and I will forgive all the guilt of their sin and rebellion against me. 9 And this city[y] shall be to me a name of joy, a praise and a glory before all the nations of the earth who shall hear of all the good that I do for them; they shall fear and tremble because of all the good and all the prosperity I provide for it.

10 Thus says the LORD: In this place of which you say, "It is a waste without human beings or animals," in the towns of Judah and the streets of Jerusalem that are desolate, without inhabitants, human or animal, there shall once more be heard 11 the voice of mirth and the voice of gladness, the voice of the bridegroom and the voice of the bride, the voices of those who sing, as they bring thank offerings to the house of the LORD:

"Give thanks to the LORD of hosts,
    for the LORD is good,
    for his steadfast love endures forever!"

For I will restore the fortunes of the land as at first, says the LORD.

12 Thus says the LORD of hosts: In this place that is waste, without human beings or animals, and in all its towns there shall again be pasture for shepherds resting their flocks. 13 In the towns of the hill country, of the She·phe′lah, and of the Neg′eb, in the land of Benjamin, the places around Jerusalem, and in the towns of Judah, flocks shall again pass under the hands of the one who counts them, says the LORD.

The Righteous Branch and the Covenant with David

14 The days are surely coming, says the LORD, when I will fulfill the promise I made to the house of Israel and the house of Judah. 15 In those days and at that time I will cause a righteous Branch to spring up for David; and he shall execute justice and righteousness in the land. 16 In those days Judah will be saved and Jerusalem will live in safety. And this is the name by which it will be called: "The LORD is our righteousness."

17 For thus says the LORD: David shall never lack a man to sit on the throne of the house of Israel, 18 and the levitical priests shall never lack a man in my presence to offer burnt offerings, to make grain offerings, and to make sacrifices for all time.

19 The word of the LORD came to Jer·e·mi′ah: 20 Thus says the LORD: If any of you could break my covenant with the day and my covenant with the night, so that day and night would not come at their appointed time, 21 only then could my covenant with my servant David be broken, so that he would not have a son to reign on his throne, and my covenant with my ministers the Le′vites. 22 Just as the host of heaven cannot be numbered and the sands of the sea cannot be measured, so I will increase the offspring of my servant David, and the Le′vites who minister to me.

23 The word of the LORD came to Jer·e·mi′ah: 24 Have you not observed how these people say, "The two families that the LORD chose have been rejected by him," and how they hold my people in such contempt that they no longer regard them as a nation? 25 Thus says the LORD: Only if I had not established my covenant with day and night and the ordinances of heaven and earth, 26 would I reject the offspring of Jacob and of my servant David and not choose any of his descendants as rulers over the offspring of Abraham, Isaac, and Jacob. For I will restore their fortunes, and will have mercy upon them.

Death in Captivity Predicted for Zedekiah

The word that came to Jer·e·mi′ah from the LORD, when King Ne·bu·chad·rez′zar of Babylon and all his army and all the kingdoms of the earth and all the peoples under his dominion were fighting against Jerusalem and all its cities: 2 Thus says the LORD, the God of Israel: Go and speak to King Zed·e·ki′ah of Judah and say to him: Thus says the LORD: I am going to give this city into the hand of the king of Babylon, and he shall burn it with fire. 3 And you yourself shall not escape from his hand, but shall surely be captured and handed over to him; you shall see the king of Babylon eye to eye and speak with him face to face; and you shall go to Babylon. 4 Yet hear the word of the LORD, O King Zed·e·ki′ah of Judah! Thus says the LORD concerning you: You shall not die by the sword; 5 you shall die in peace. And as spices were burned[z] for your ancestors, the earlier kings who preceded you, so they shall burn spices[a] for you and lament for you, saying, "Alas, lord!" For I have spoken the word, says the LORD.

6 Then the prophet Jer·e·mi′ah spoke all these words to Zed·e·ki′ah king of Judah, in Jerusalem, 7 when the army of the king of Babylon was fighting against Jerusalem and against all the cities of Judah that were left, La′chish and A·ze′kah; for

---

[x] Meaning of Heb uncertain   [y] Heb *And it*   [z] Heb *as there was burning*   [a] Heb *shall burn*

these were the only fortified cities of Judah that remained.

Treacherous Treatment of Slaves

8 The word that came to Jer•e•mi′ah from the LORD, after King Zed•e•ki′ah had made a covenant with all the people in Jerusalem to make a proclamation of liberty to them— 9 that all should set free their Hebrew slaves, male and female, so that no one should hold another Judean in slavery. 10 And they obeyed, all the officials and all the people who had entered into the covenant that all would set free their slaves, male or female, so that they would not be enslaved again; they obeyed and set them free. 11 But afterward they turned around and took back the male and female slaves they had set free, and brought them again into subjection as slaves. 12 The word of the LORD came to Jer•e•mi′ah from the LORD: 13 Thus says the LORD, the God of Israel: I myself made a covenant with your ancestors when I brought them out of the land of Egypt, out of the house of slavery, saying, 14 "Every seventh year each of you must set free any Hebrews who have been sold to you and have served you six years; you must set them free from your service." But your ancestors did not listen to me or incline their ears to me. 15 You yourselves recently repented and did what was right in my sight by proclaiming liberty to one another, and you made a covenant before me in the house that is called by my name; 16 but then you turned around and profaned my name when each of you took back your male and female slaves, whom you had set free according to their desire, and you brought them again into subjection to be your slaves. 17 Therefore, thus says the LORD: You have not obeyed me by granting a release to your neighbors and friends; I am going to grant a release to you, says the LORD—a release to the sword, to pestilence, and to famine. I will make you a horror to all the kingdoms of the earth. 18 And those who transgressed my covenant and did not keep the terms of the covenant that they made before me, I will make like[b] the calf when they cut it in two and passed between its parts: 19 the officials of Judah, the officials of Jerusalem, the eunuchs, the priests, and all the people of the land who passed between the parts of the calf 20 shall be handed over to their enemies and to those who seek their lives. Their corpses shall become food for the birds of the air and the wild animals of the earth. 21 And as for King Zed•e•ki′ah of Judah and his officials, I will hand them over to their enemies and to those who seek their lives, to the army of the king of Babylon, which has withdrawn from you. 22 I am going to command, says the LORD, and will bring them back

to this city; and they will fight against it, and take it, and burn it with fire. The towns of Judah I will make a desolation without inhabitant.

The Rechabites Commended

The word that came to Jer•e•mi′ah from the LORD in the days of King Je•hoi′a•kim son of Jō•si′ah of Judah: 2 Go to the house of the Rē′chab•ites, and speak with them, and bring them to the house of the LORD, into one of the chambers; then offer them wine to drink. 3 So I took Jā•az•a•ni′ah son of Jer•e•mi′ah son of Ha•baz•zi•ni′ah, and his brothers, and all his sons, and the whole house of the Rē′chab•ites. 4 I brought them to the house of the LORD into the chamber of the sons of Hā′nan son of Ig•da•li′ah, the man of God, which was near the chamber of the officials, above the chamber of Mā•a•sēi′ah son of Shal′lum, keeper of the threshold. 5 Then I set before the Rē′chab•ites pitchers full of wine, and cups; and I said to them, "Have some wine." 6 But they answered, "We will drink no wine, for our ancestor Jon′a•dab son of Rē′chab commanded us, 'You shall never drink wine, neither you nor your children; 7 nor shall you ever build a house, or sow seed; nor shall you plant a vineyard, or even own one; but you shall live in tents all your days, that you may live many days in the land where you reside.' 8 We have obeyed the charge of our ancestor Jon′a•dab son of Rē′chab in all that he commanded us, to drink no wine all our days, ourselves, our wives, our sons, or our daughters, 9 and not to build houses to live in. We have no vineyard or field or seed; 10 but we have lived in tents, and have obeyed and done all that our ancestor Jon′a•dab commanded us. 11 But when King Ne•bū•chad•rez′zar of Babylon came up against the land, we said, 'Come, and let us go to Jerusalem for fear of the army of the Chal•dē′ans and the army of the Ar•a•mē′ans.' That is why we are living in Jerusalem."

12 Then the word of the LORD came to Jer•emi′ah: 13 Thus says the LORD of hosts, the God of Israel: Go and say to the people of Judah and the inhabitants of Jerusalem, Can you not learn a lesson and obey my words? says the LORD. 14 The command has been carried out that Jon′a•dab son of Rē′chab gave to his descendants to drink no wine; and they drink none to this day, for they have obeyed their ancestor's command. But I myself have spoken to you persistently, and you have not obeyed me. 15 I have sent to you all my servants the prophets, sending them persistently, saying, "Turn now everyone of you from your evil way, and amend your doings, and do not go after

---

b Cn: Heb lacks like

other gods to serve them, and then you shall live in the land that I gave to you and your ancestors." But you did not incline your ear or obey me. 16 The descendants of Jon′a·dab son of Rē′chab have carried out the command that their ancestor gave them, but this people has not obeyed me. 17 Therefore, thus says the LORD, the God of hosts, the God of Israel: I am going to bring on Judah and on all the inhabitants of Jerusalem every disaster that I have pronounced against them; because I have spoken to them and they have not listened, I have called to them and they have not answered.

18 But to the house of the Rē′chab·ites Jer·e·mī′ah said: Thus says the LORD of hosts, the God of Israel: Because you have obeyed the command of your ancestor Jon′a·dab, and kept all his precepts, and done all that he commanded you, 19 therefore thus says the LORD of hosts, the God of Israel: Jon′a·dab son of Rē′chab shall not lack a descendant to stand before me for all time.

The Scroll Read in the Temple

In the fourth year of King Je·hoi′a·kim son of Jō·sī′ah of Judah, this word came to Jer·e·mī′ah from the LORD: 2 Take a scroll and write on it all the words that I have spoken to you against Israel and Judah and all the nations, from the day I spoke to you, from the days of Jō·sī′ah until today. 3 It may be that when the house of Judah hears of all the disasters that I intend to do to them, all of them may turn from their evil ways, so that I may forgive their iniquity and their sin.

4 Then Jer·e·mī′ah called Bar′uch son of Ne·rī′ah, and Bar′uch wrote on a scroll at Jer·e·mī′ah's dictation all the words of the LORD that he had spoken to him. 5 And Jer·e·mī′ah ordered Bar′uch, saying, "I am prevented from entering the house of the LORD; 6 so you go yourself, and on a fast day in the hearing of the people in the LORD's house you shall read the words of the LORD from the scroll that you have written at my dictation. You shall read them also in the hearing of all the people of Judah who come up from their towns. 7 It may be that their plea will come before the LORD, and that all of them will turn from their evil ways, for great is the anger and wrath that the LORD has pronounced against this people." 8 And Bar′uch son of Ne·rī′ah did all that the prophet Jer·e·mī′ah ordered him about reading from the scroll the words of the LORD in the LORD's house.

9 In the fifth year of King Je·hoi′a·kim son of Jō·sī′ah of Judah, in the ninth month, all the people in Jerusalem and all the people who came from the towns of Judah to Jerusalem proclaimed a fast before the LORD. 10 Then, in the hearing of all the people, Bar′uch read the words of Jer·e·mī′ah

from the scroll, in the house of the LORD, in the chamber of Gem·a·rī′ah son of Shā′phan the secretary, which was in the upper court, at the entry of the New Gate of the LORD's house.

The Scroll Read in the Palace

11 When Mī·cāi′ah son of Gem·a·rī′ah son of Shā′phan heard all the words of the LORD from the scroll, 12 he went down to the king's house, into the secretary's chamber; and all the officials were sitting there: E·lish′a·ma the secretary, De·laī′ah son of She·māi′ah, El·nā′than son of Ach′bor, Gem·a·rī′ah son of Shā′phan, Zed·e·kī′ah son of Han·a·nī′ah, and all the officials. 13 And Mī·cāi′ah told them all the words that he had heard, when Bar′uch read the scroll in the hearing of the people. 14 Then all the officials sent Je·hū′dī son of Neth·a·nī′ah son of Shel·e·mī′ah son of Cū′shi to say to Bar′uch, "Bring the scroll that you read in the hearing of the people, and come." So Bar′uch son of Ne·rī′ah took the scroll in his hand and came to them. 15 And they said to him, "Sit down and read it to us." So Bar′uch read it to them. 16 When they heard all the words, they turned to one another in alarm, and said to Bar′uch, "We certainly must report all these words to the king." 17 Then they questioned Bar′uch, "Tell us now, how did you write all these words? Was it at his dictation?" 18 Bar′uch answered them, "He dictated all these words to me, and I wrote them with ink on the scroll." 19 Then the officials said to Bar′uch, "Go and hide, you and Jer·e·mī′ah, and let no one know where you are."

Jehoiakim Burns the Scroll

20 Leaving the scroll in the chamber of E·lish′a·ma the secretary, they went to the court of the king; and they reported all the words to the king. 21 Then the king sent Je·hū′dī to get the scroll, and he took it from the chamber of E·lish′a·ma the secretary; and Je·hū′dī read it to the king and all the officials who stood beside the king. 22 Now the king was sitting in his winter apartment (it was the ninth month), and there was a fire burning in the brazier before him. 23 As Je·hū′dī read three or four columns, the king^c would cut them off with a penknife and throw them into the fire in the brazier, until the entire scroll was consumed in the fire that was in the brazier. 24 Yet neither the king, nor any of his servants who heard all these words, was alarmed, nor did they tear their garments. 25 Even when El·nā′than and De·laī′ah and Gem·a·rī′ah urged the king not to burn the scroll, he would not listen to them. 26 And the king com-

---

c Heb *he*

manded Je·rah′mē·el the king's son and Se·rai′ah son of Az′ri·el and Shel·e·mi′ah son of Ab·dē′el to arrest the secretary Bar′uch and the prophet Jer·e·mi′ah. But the LORD hid them.

Jeremiah Dictates Another

27 Now, after the king had burned the scroll with the words that Bar′uch wrote at Jer·e·mi′ah's dictation, the word of the LORD came to Jer·e·mi′ah: 28 Take another scroll and write on it all the former words that were in the first scroll, which King Je·hoi′a·kim of Judah has burned. 29 And concerning King Je·hoi′a·kim of Judah you shall say: Thus says the LORD, You have dared to burn this scroll, saying, Why have you written in it that the king of Babylon will certainly come and destroy this land, and will cut off from it human beings and animals? 30 Therefore thus says the LORD concerning King Je·hoi′a·kim of Judah: He shall have no one to sit upon the throne of David, and his dead body shall be cast out to the heat by day and the frost by night. 31 And I will punish him and his offspring and his servants for their iniquity; I will bring on them, and on the inhabitants of Jerusalem, and on the people of Judah, all the disasters with which I have threatened them—but they would not listen.

32 Then Jer·e·mi′ah took another scroll and gave it to the secretary Bar′uch son of Ne·ri′ah, who wrote on it at Jer·e·mi′ah's dictation all the words of the scroll that King Je·hoi′a·kim of Judah had burned in the fire; and many similar words were added to them.

Zedekiah's Vain Hope
(2 Kings 24.17; 2 Chr 36.10)

Zed·e·ki′ah son of Jō·si′ah, whom King Ne·bū·chad·rez′zar of Babylon made king in the land of Judah, succeeded Cō·ni′ah son of Je·hoi′a·kim. 2 But neither he nor his servants nor the people of the land listened to the words of the LORD that he spoke through the prophet Jer·e·mi′ah.

3 King Zed·e·ki′ah sent Je·hū′cal son of Shel·e·mi′ah and the priest Zeph·a·ni′ah son of Mā·a·sēi′ah to the prophet Jer·e·mi′ah saying, "Please pray for us to the LORD our God." 4 Now Jer·e·mi′ah was still going in and out among the people, for he had not yet been put in prison. 5 Meanwhile, the army of Pharaoh had come out of Egypt; and when the Chal·dē′ans who were besieging Jerusalem heard news of them, they withdrew from Jerusalem.

6 Then the word of the LORD came to the prophet Jer·e·mi′ah: 7 Thus says the LORD, God of Israel: This is what the two of you shall say to the king of Judah, who sent you to me to inquire of me: Pharaoh's army, which set out to help you, is going to return to its own land, to Egypt. 8 And the

Chal·dē′ans shall return and fight against this city; they shall take it and burn it with fire. 9 Thus says the LORD: Do not deceive yourselves, saying, "The Chal·dē′ans will surely go away from us," for they will not go away. 10 Even if you defeated the whole army of Chal·dē′ans who are fighting against you, and there remained of them only wounded men in their tents, they would rise up and burn this city with fire.

PRAY IT!
Facing Fear

You can bet Jeremiah felt fear at times. For example, in Jer 37.17, King Zedekiah asks the prophet if he has had any word from God. Jeremiah has just been beaten and imprisoned (verse 15). Surely, he has some fear for what will happen to him if he delivers a message that angers the king. But Jeremiah courageously tells Zedekiah that he, Zedekiah, will be handed over to the king of Babylon (verse 17).

Throughout our life, when trying to do God's will, we will face situations that cause us to fear for our safety, for our reputation, or even that our friends will abandon us. This isn't the same fear we feel when watching a horror film or riding a roller coaster. It is an anxiety that can cause us to shut down and quit trying. We need to offer up that fear to God and ask the Lord to calm our heart.

Quiet your mind and pray:

Lord, give me the courage I need to be faithful to you. Let my love for you and for other people be so great that my fears will never be able to keep me from doing what is right. Amen!

▶ Jer 37.11–21

Jeremiah Is Imprisoned

11 Now when the Chal·dē′an army had withdrawn from Jerusalem at the approach of Pharaoh's army, 12 Jer·e·mi′ah set out from Jerusalem to go to the land of Benjamin to receive his share of property[d] among the people there. 13 When he reached the Benjamin Gate, a sentinel there named I·rī′jah son of Shel·e·mi′ah son of Han·a·ni′ah

---

d Meaning of Heb uncertain

arrested the prophet Jer•e•mi′ah saying, "You are deserting to the Chal•dē′ans." 14 And Jer•e•mi′ah said, "That is a lie; I am not deserting to the Chal•dē′-ans." But I•ri′jah would not listen to him, and arrested Jer•e•mi′ah and brought him to the officials. 15 The officials were enraged at Jer•e•mi′ah, and they beat him and imprisoned him in the house of the secretary Jonathan, for it had been made a prison. 16 Thus Jer•e•mi′ah was put in the cistern house, in the cells, and remained there many days.

17 Then King Zed•e•ki′ah sent for him, and received him. The king questioned him secretly in his house, and said, "Is there any word from the LORD?" Jer•e•mi′ah said, "There is!" Then he said, "You shall be handed over to the king of Babylon." 18 Jer•e•mi′ah also said to King Zed•e•ki′ah, "What wrong have I done to you or your servants or this people, that you have put me in prison? 19 Where are your prophets who prophesied to you, saying, 'The king of Babylon will not come against you and against this land'? 20 Now please hear me, my lord king: be good enough to listen to my plea, and do not send me back to the house of the secretary Jonathan to die there." 21 So King Zed•e•ki′ah gave orders, and they committed Jer•e•mi′ah to the court of the guard; and a loaf of bread was given him daily from the bakers' street, until all the bread of the city was gone. So Jer•e•mi′ah remained in the court of the guard.

Jeremiah in the Well

Now Sheph•a•ti′ah son of Mat′tan, Ged•a•li′ah son of Pash′hur, Jū′cal son of Shel•e•mi′ah, and Pash′hur son of Mal•chi′ah heard the words that Jer•e•mi′ah was saying to all the people, 2 Thus says the LORD, Those who stay in this city shall die by the sword, by famine, and by pestilence; but those who go out to the Chal•dē′ans shall live; they shall have their lives as a prize of war, and live. 3 Thus says the LORD, This city shall surely be handed over to the army of the king of Babylon and be taken. 4 Then the officials said to the king, "This man ought to be put to death, because he is discouraging the soldiers who are left in this city, and all the people, by speaking such words to them. For this man is not seeking the welfare of this people, but their harm." 5 King Zed•e•ki′ah said, "Here he is; he is in your hands; for the king is powerless against you." 6 So they took Jer•e•mi′ah and threw him into the cistern of Mal•chi′ah, the king's son, which was in the court of the guard, letting Jer•e•mi′ah down by ropes. Now there was no water in the cistern, but only mud, and Jer•e•mi′ah sank in the mud.

Jeremiah Is Rescued by Ebed-melech

7 Ē′bed-mē′lech the Ethiopian,*e* a eunuch in the king's house, heard that they had put Jer•e•mi′ah into the cistern. The king happened to be sitting at the Benjamin Gate, 8 So Ē′bed-mē′lech left the king's house and spoke to the king, 9 "My lord king, these men have acted wickedly in all they did to the prophet Jer•e•mi′ah by throwing him into the cistern to die there of hunger, for there is no bread left in the city." 10 Then the king commanded Ē′bed-mē′lech the Ethiopian,*e* "Take three men with you from here, and pull the prophet Jer•e•mi′ah up from the cistern before he dies." 11 So Ē′bed-mē′lech took the men with him and went to the house of the king, to a wardrobe off the storehouse, and took from there old rags and worn-out clothes, which he let down to Jer•e•mi′ah in the cistern by ropes. 12 Then Ē′bed-mē′-lech the Ethiopian*e* said to Jer•e•mi′ah, "Just put the rags and clothes between your armpits and the ropes." Jer•e•mi′ah did so. 13 Then they drew Jer•e•mi′ah up by the ropes and pulled him out of the cistern. And Jer•e•mi′ah remained in the court of the guard.

PRAY IT!

Prayer from the Well

Almighty Creator of ups and downs, like Jeremiah, I often find myself at the bottom. Sometimes, I just fall there; other times, I am thrown there. It's cold, dark, and lonely there.

Bless me with friends like Ebed-melech to care for me and pull me out. And make me an Ebed-melech for others—a friend who is loyal enough to get the rope and tug until they are up again, who is considerate enough to get rags for their armpits so that the process won't be so painful. Amen.

▶ Jer 38.1–13

Zedekiah Consults Jeremiah Again

14 King Zed•e•ki′ah sent for the prophet Jer•e•mi′ah and received him at the third entrance of the temple of the LORD. The king said to Jer•e•mi′ah,

---

e Or Nubian; Heb Cushite   *f* Cn: Heb to under

"I have something to ask you; do not hide anything from me." 15 Jer·e·mi'ah said to Zed·e·kī'ah, "If I tell you, you will put me to death, will you not? And if I give you advice, you will not listen to me." 16 So King Zed·e·kī'ah swore an oath in secret to Jer·e·mī'ah, "As the LORD lives, who gave us our lives, I will not put you to death or hand you over to these men who seek your life."

17 Then Jer·e·mī'ah said to Zed·e·kī'ah, "Thus says the LORD, the God of hosts, the God of Israel, If you will only surrender to the officials of the king of Babylon, then your life shall be spared, and this city shall not be burned with fire, and you and your house shall live. 18 But if you do not surrender to the officials of the king of Babylon, then this city shall be handed over to the Chal·dē'ans, and they shall burn it with fire, and you yourself shall not escape from their hand." 19 King Zed·e·kī'ah said to Jer·e·mī'ah, "I am afraid of the Judeans who have deserted to the Chal·dē'ans, for I might be handed over to them and they would abuse me." 20 Jer·e·mī'ah said, "That will not happen. Just obey the voice of the LORD in what I say to you, and it shall go well with you, and your life shall be spared. 21 But if you are determined not to surrender, this is what the LORD has shown me— 22 a vision of all the women remaining in the house of the king of Judah being led out to the officials of the king of Babylon and saying,

'Your trusted friends have seduced you
    and have overcome you;
Now that your feet are stuck in the mud,
    they desert you.'

23 All your wives and your children shall be led out to the Chal·dē'ans, and you yourself shall not escape from their hand, but shall be seized by the king of Babylon; and this city shall be burned with fire."

24 Then Zed·e·kī'ah said to Jer·e·mī'ah, "Do not let anyone else know of this conversation, or you will die. 25 If the officials should hear that I have spoken with you, and they should come and say to you, 'Just tell us what you said to the king; do not conceal it from us, or we will put you to death. What did the king say to you?' 26 then you shall say to them, 'I was presenting my plea to the king not to send me back to the house of Jonathan to die there.' " 27 All the officials did come to Jer·e·mī'ah and questioned him; and he answered them in the very words the king had commanded. So they stopped questioning him, for the conversation had not been overheard. 28 And Jer·e·mī'ah remained in the court of the guard until the day that Jerusalem was taken.

The Fall of Jerusalem
(2 Kings 25.1–12; Jer 52.4–16)

In the ninth year of King Zed·e·kī'ah of Judah, in the tenth month, King Ne·bū·chad·rez'zar of Babylon and all his army came against Jerusalem and besieged it; 2 in the eleventh year of Zed·e·kī'ah, in the fourth month, on the ninth day of the month, a breach was made in the city. 3 When Jerusalem was taken,g all the officials of the king of Babylon came and sat in the middle gate: Ner'gal-sha·rē'zer, Sam'gar-nē'bō, Sar'se·chim the Rab·sar'is, Ner'gal-sha·rē'zer the Rab'mag, with all the rest of the officials of the king of Babylon. 4 When King Zed·e·kī'ah of Judah and all the soldiers saw them, they fled, going out of the city at night by way of the king's garden through the gate between the two walls; and they went toward the Ar'a·bah. 5 But the army of the Chal·dē'ans pursued them, and overtook Zed·e·kī'ah in the plains of Jericho; and when they had taken him, they brought him up to King Ne·bū·chad·rez'zar of Babylon, at Rib'lah, in the land of Hā'math; and he passed sentence on him. 6 The king of Babylon slaughtered the sons of Zed·e·kī'ah at Rib'lah before his eyes; also the king of Babylon slaughtered all the nobles of Judah. 7 He put out the eyes of Zed·e·kī'ah, and bound him in fetters to take him to Babylon. 8 The Chal·dē'ans burned the king's house and the houses of the people, and broke down the walls of Jerusalem. 9 Then Ne·bū·za·rad'an the captain of the guard exiled to Babylon the rest of the people who were left in the city, those who had deserted to him, and the people who remained. 10 Ne·bū·za·rad'an the captain of the guard left in the land of Judah some of the poor people who owned nothing, and gave them vineyards and fields at the same time.

Jeremiah, Set Free, Remembers Ebed-melech

11 King Ne·bū·chad·rez'zar of Babylon gave command concerning Jer·e·mī'ah through Ne·bū·za·rad'an, the captain of the guard, saying, 12 "Take him, look after him well and do him no harm, but deal with him as he may ask you." 13 So Ne·bū·za·rad'an the captain of the guard, Ne·bū·shaz'ban the Rab·sar'is, Ner'gal-sha·rē'zer the Rab'mag, and all the chief officers of the king of Babylon sent 14 and took Jer·e·mī'ah from the court of the guard. They entrusted him to Ged·a·lī'ah son of A·hī'kam son of Shā'phan to be brought home. So he stayed with his own people.

15 The word of the LORD came to Jer·e·mī'ah while he was confined in the court of the guard:

g This clause has been transposed from 38.28

16 Go and say to Ê'bed-mē'lech the Ethiopian:*h* Thus says the LORD of hosts, the God of Israel: I am going to fulfill my words against this city for evil and not for good, and they shall be accomplished in your presence on that day. 17 But I will save you on that day, says the LORD, and you shall not be handed over to those whom you dread. 18 For I will surely save you, and you shall not fall by the sword; but you shall have your life as a prize of war, because you have trusted in me, says the LORD.

AFRICAN AMERICAN

Risky Business

Ebed-melech is a biblical character we do not hear too much about. But he played a significant role in Jeremiah's life, and he has special meaning for African Americans because he was black. The Bible refers to him as the Ethiopian.

Ebed-melech is important because he was available to God and he was willing to risk his neck. Although Ebed-melech had the king's permission to rescue Jeremiah, he would have lost his life if his plan to do so had been discovered by the king's generals and counselors (Jer 38.7–13). Ebed-melech shows us that being a servant of God is risky business. We cannot do God's will without taking risks. There is just no such thing as playing it safe and doing what God wants us to do.

Ebed-melech is also important because he was willing to help his "brother." Jeremiah was a Jew and Ebed-melech was an Ethiopian, but still they were brothers in the Lord. Ebed-melech knew that he had to act when he saw his brother in trouble. When destruction finally came upon Jerusalem, God rewarded Ebed-melech by keeping him safe (39.18), because he had trusted in God enough to help his brother Jeremiah.

Lord, grant me a large portion of trust in you, that I might step out at your bidding and not be afraid of the outcome. Amen.

▶ Jer 39.15–18

Jeremiah with Gedaliah the Governor
(2 Kings 25.22–26)

The word that came to Jer•e•mi'ah from the LORD after Ne•bū•za•rad'an the captain of the guard had let him go from Rā'mah, when he took him bound in fetters along with all the captives of Jerusalem and Judah who were being exiled to Babylon. 2 The captain of the guard took Jer•e•mi'ah and said to him, "The LORD your God threatened this place with this disaster; 3 and now the LORD has brought it about, and has done as he said, because all of you sinned against the LORD and did not obey his voice. Therefore this thing has come upon you. 4 Now look, I have just released you today from the fetters on your hands. If you wish to come with me to Babylon, come, and I will take good care of you; but if you do not wish to come with me to Babylon, you need not come. See, the whole land is before you; go wherever you think it good and right to go. 5 If you remain,*i* then return to Ged•a•li'ah son of A•hi'kam son of Shā'phan, whom the king of Babylon appointed governor of the towns of Judah, and stay with him among the people; or go wherever you think it right to go." So the captain of the guard gave him an allowance of food and a present, and let him go. 6 Then Jer•e•mi'ah went to Ged•a•li'ah son of A•hi'kam at Miz'pah, and stayed with him among the people who were left in the land.

7 When all the leaders of the forces in the open country and their troops heard that the king of Babylon had appointed Ged•a•li'ah son of A•hi'kam governor in the land, and had committed to him men, women, and children, those of the poorest of the land who had not been taken into exile to Babylon, 8 they went to Ged•a•li'ah at Miz'pah—Ish'ma•el son of Neth•a•ni'ah, Jō•hā'nan son of Ka•rē'ah, Se•rāi'ah son of Tan'hu•meth, the sons of Ê'phai the Ne•toph'a•thite, Jez•a•ni'ah son of the Mā'a•ca•thite, they and their troops. 9 Ged•a•li'ah son of A•hi'kam son of Shā'phan swore to them and their troops, saying, "Do not be afraid to serve the Chal•dē'ans. Stay in the land and serve the king of Babylon, and it shall go well with you. 10 As for me, I am staying at Miz'pah to represent you before the Chal•dē'ans who come to us; but as for you, gather wine and summer fruits and oil, and store them in your vessels, and live in the towns that you have taken over." 11 Likewise, when all the Judeans who were in Mō'ab and among the Am'mon•ītes and in Ê'dom and in other lands heard that the king of Babylon had left a remnant in Judah and had appointed Ged•a•li'ah son of A•hi'kam

---

h Or *Nubian*; Heb *Cushite*   *i* Syr: Meaning of Heb uncertain

son of Sha′phan as governor over them, ¹²then all the Judeans returned from all the places to which they had been scattered and came to the land of Judah, to Ged·a·li′ah at Miz′pah; and they gathered wine and summer fruits in great abundance.

13 Now Jō·hā′nan son of Ka·rē′ah and all the leaders of the forces in the open country came to Ged·a·li′ah at Miz′pah ¹⁴and said to him, "Are you at all aware that Bā′a·lis king of the Am′mon·ites has sent Ish′ma·el son of Neth·a·ni′ah to take your life?" But Ged·a·li′ah son of A·hi′kam would not believe them. ¹⁵Then Jō·hā′nan son of Ka·rē′ah spoke secretly to Ged·a·li′ah at Miz′pah, "Please let me go and kill Ish′ma·el son of Neth·a·ni′ah, and no one else will know. Why should he take your life, so that all the Judeans who are gathered around you would be scattered, and the remnant of Judah would perish?" ¹⁶But Ged·a·li′ah son of A·hi′kam said to Jō·hā′nan son of Ka·rē′ah, "Do not do such a thing, for you are telling a lie about Ish′ma·el."

Insurrection against Gedaliah

In the seventh month, Ish′ma·el son of Neth·a·ni′ah son of E·lish′a·ma, of the royal family, one of the chief officers of the king, came with ten men to Ged·a·li′ah son of A·hi′kam, at Miz′pah. As they ate bread together there at Miz′pah, ²Ish′ma·el son of Neth·a·ni′ah and the ten men with him got up and struck down Ged·a·li′ah son of A·hi′kam son of Sha′phan with the sword and killed him, because the king of Babylon had appointed him governor in the land. ³Ish′ma·el also killed all the Judeans who were with Ged·a·li′ah at Miz′pah, and the Chal·dē′an soldiers who happened to be there.

4 On the day after the murder of Ged·a·li′ah, before anyone knew of it, ⁵eighty men arrived from She′chem and Shi′lōh and Sa·mār′i·a, with their beards shaved and their clothes torn, and their bodies gashed, bringing grain offerings and incense to present at the temple of the LORD. ⁶And Ish′ma·el son of Neth·a·ni′ah came out from Miz′pah to meet them, weeping as he came. As he met them, he said to them, "Come to Ged·a·li′ah son of A·hi′kam." ⁷When they reached the middle of the city, Ish′ma·el son of Neth·a·ni′ah and the men with him slaughtered them, and threw them[j] into a cistern. ⁸But there were ten men among them who said to Ish′ma·el, "Do not kill us, for we have stores of wheat, barley, oil, and honey hidden in the fields." So he refrained, and did not kill them along with their companions.

9 Now the cistern into which Ish′ma·el had thrown all the bodies of the men whom he had struck down was the large cistern[k] that King Asa had made for defense against King Bā′a·sha of Israel; Ish′ma·el son of Neth·a·ni′ah filled that cistern

with those whom he had killed. ¹⁰Then Ish′ma·el took captive all the rest of the people who were in Miz′pah, the king's daughters and all the people who were left at Miz′pah, whom Ne·bū·za·rad′an, the captain of the guard, had committed to Ged·a·li′ah son of A·hi′kam. Ish′ma·el son of Neth·a·ni′ah took them captive and set out to cross over to the Am′mon·ites.

11 But when Jō·hā′nan son of Ka·rē′ah and all the leaders of the forces with him heard of all the crimes that Ish′ma·el son of Neth·a·ni′ah had done, ¹²they took all their men and went to fight against Ish′ma·el son of Neth·a·ni′ah. They came upon him at the great pool that is in Gib′ē·on. ¹³And when all the people who were with Ish′ma·el saw Jō·hā′nan son of Ka·rē′ah and all the leaders of the forces with him, they were glad. ¹⁴So all the people whom Ish′ma·el had carried away captive from Miz′pah turned around and came back, and went to Jō·hā′nan son of Ka·rē′ah. ¹⁵But Ish′ma·el son of Neth·a·ni′ah escaped from Jō·hā′nan with eight men, and went to the Am′mon·ites. ¹⁶Then Jō·hā′nan son of Ka·rē′ah and all the leaders of the forces with him took all the rest of the people whom Ish′ma·el son of Neth·a·ni′ah had carried away captive[l] from Miz′pah after he had slain Ged·a·li′ah son of A·hi′kam—soldiers, women, children, and eunuchs, whom Jō·hā′nan brought back from Gib′ē·on.[m] ¹⁷And they set out, and stopped at Gē′rūth Chim′ham near Bethlehem, intending to go to Egypt ¹⁸because of the Chal·dē′ans; for they were afraid of them, because Ish′ma·el son of Neth·a·ni′ah had killed Ged·a·li′ah son of A·hi′kam, whom the king of Babylon had made governor over the land.

Jeremiah Advises Survivors Not to Migrate

Then all the commanders of the forces, and Jō·hā′nan son of Ka·rē′ah and Az·a·ri′ah[n] son of Hō·shai′ah, and all the people from the least to the greatest, approached ²the prophet Jer·e·mi′ah and said, "Be good enough to listen to our plea, and pray to the LORD your God for us—for all this remnant. For there are only a few of us left out of many, as your eyes can see. ³Let the LORD your God show us where we should go and what we should do." ⁴The prophet Jer·e·mi′ah said to them, "Very well: I am going to pray to the LORD your God as you request, and whatever the LORD answers you I will tell you; I will keep nothing back from you." ⁵They in their turn said to Jer·e·mi′ah, "May the LORD be a true and faithful witness

j Syr: Heb lacks *and threw them*; compare verse 9
k Gk: Heb *whom he had killed by the hand of Gedaliah*
l Cn: Heb *whom he recovered from Ishmael son of Nethaniah*
m Meaning of Heb uncertain　　n Gk: Heb *Jezaniah*

against us if we do not act according to everything
that the LORD your God sends us through you.
6 Whether it is good or bad, we will obey the voice
of the LORD our God to whom we are sending you,
in order that it may go well with us when we obey
the voice of the LORD our God."

7 At the end of ten days the word of the LORD
came to Jer•e•mī'ah. 8 Then he summoned Jō•hā'nan
son of Ka•rē'ah and all the commanders of the
forces who were with him, and all the people from
the least to the greatest, 9 and said to them, "Thus
says the LORD, the God of Israel, to whom you sent
me to present your plea before him: 10 If you will
only remain in this land, then I will build you up
and not pull you down; I will plant you, and not
pluck you up; for I am sorry for the disaster that I
have brought upon you. 11 Do not be afraid of the
king of Babylon, as you have been; do not be
afraid of him, says the LORD, for I am with you, to
save you and to rescue you from his hand. 12 I will
grant you mercy, and he will have mercy on you
and restore you to your native soil. 13 But if you
continue to say, 'We will not stay in this land,'
thus disobeying the voice of the LORD your God
14 and saying, 'No, we will go to the land of Egypt,
where we shall not see war, or hear the sound of
the trumpet, or be hungry for bread, and there
we will stay,' 15 then hear the word of the LORD,
O remnant of Judah. Thus says the LORD of hosts,
the God of Israel: If you are determined to enter
Egypt and go to settle there, 16 then the sword that
you fear shall overtake you there, in the land of
Egypt; and the famine that you dread shall follow
close after you into Egypt; and there you shall die.
17 All the people who have determined to go to
Egypt to settle there shall die by the sword, by
famine, and by pestilence; they shall have no remnant or survivor from the disaster that I am bringing upon them.

18 "For thus says the LORD of hosts, the God of
Israel: Just as my anger and my wrath were poured
out on the inhabitants of Jerusalem, so my wrath
will be poured out on you when you go to Egypt.
You shall become an object of execration and horror, of cursing and ridicule. You shall see this place
no more. 19 The LORD has said to you, O remnant
of Judah, Do not go to Egypt. Be well aware that I
have warned you today 20 that you have made a
fatal mistake. For you yourselves sent me to the
LORD your God, saying, 'Pray for us to the LORD our
God, and whatever the LORD our God says, tell us
and we will do it.' 21 So I have told you today, but
you have not obeyed the voice of the LORD your
God in anything that he sent me to tell you. 22 Be
well aware, then, that you shall die by the sword,
by famine, and by pestilence in the place where
you desire to go and settle."

Taken to Egypt, Jeremiah Warns of Judgment

43 When Jer•e•mī'ah finished speaking to all the people all these words of the LORD their God, with
which the LORD their God had sent him to them,
2 Az•a•rī'ah son of Hō•shaī'ah and Jō•hā'nan son of
Ka•rē'ah and all the other insolent men said to Jer-
e•mī'ah, "You are telling a lie. The LORD our God
did not send you to say, 'Do not go to Egypt to
settle there'; 3 but Bar'uch son of Ne•rī'ah is inciting
you against us, to hand us over to the Chal•dē'ans,
in order that they may kill us or take us into exile
in Babylon." 4 So Jō•hā'nan son of Ka•rē'ah and all
the commanders of the forces and all the people
did not obey the voice of the LORD, to stay in the
land of Judah. 5 But Jō•hā'nan son of Ka•rē'ah and
all the commanders of the forces took all the remnant of Judah who had returned to settle in the
land of Judah from all the nations to which they
had been driven— 6 the men, the women, the children, the princesses, and everyone whom Ne•bū•za-
rad'an the captain of the guard had left with
Ged•a•lī'ah son of A•hī'kam son of Shā'phan; also
the prophet Jer•e•mī'ah and Bar'uch son of Ne•rī'ah.
7 And they came into the land of Egypt, for they
did not obey the voice of the LORD. And they arrived at Tah'pan•hēs.

8 Then the word of the LORD came to Jer•e•mī'ah
in Tah'pan•hēs: 9 Take some large stones in your
hands, and bury them in the clay pavement[o] that
is at the entrance to Pharaoh's palace in Tah'pan-
hēs. Let the Judeans see you do it, 10 and say to
them, Thus says the LORD of hosts, the God of Israel: I am going to send and take my servant King
Ne•bū•chad•rez'zar of Babylon, and he[p] will set his
throne above these stones that I have buried, and
he will spread his royal canopy over them. 11 He
shall come and ravage the land of Egypt, giving

those who are destined for pestilence, to
pestilence,
and those who are destined for captivity,
to captivity,
and those who are destined for the
sword, to the sword.

12 He[q] shall kindle a fire in the temples of the gods
of Egypt; and he shall burn them and carry them
away captive; and he shall pick clean the land of
Egypt, as a shepherd picks his cloak clean of vermin; and he shall depart from there safely. 13 He
shall break the obelisks of Hē•li•op'o•lis, which is in

---

[o] Meaning of Heb uncertain [p] Gk Syr: Heb *I* [q] Gk Syr Vg: Heb *I*

the land of Egypt; and the temples of the gods of Egypt he shall burn with fire.

Denunciation of Persistent Idolatry

The word that came to Jer•e•mī'ah for all the Judeans living in the land of Egypt, at Mig'dōl, at Tah'pan•hēs, at Memphis, and in the land of Path'ros, ² Thus says the LORD of hosts, the God of Israel: You yourselves have seen all the disaster that I have brought on Jerusalem and on all the towns of Judah. Look at them; today they are a desolation, without an inhabitant in them, ³ because of the wickedness that they committed, provoking me to anger, in that they went to make offerings and serve other gods that they had not known, neither they, nor you, nor your ancestors. ⁴ Yet I persistently sent to you all my servants the prophets, saying, "I beg you not to do this abominable thing that I hate!" ⁵ But they did not listen or incline their ear, to turn from their wickedness and make no offerings to other gods. ⁶ So my wrath and my anger were poured out and kindled in the towns of Judah and in the streets of Jerusalem; and they became a waste and a desolation, as they still are today. ⁷ And now thus says the LORD God of hosts, the God of Israel: Why are you doing such great harm to yourselves, to cut off man and woman, child and infant, from the midst of Judah, leaving yourselves without a remnant? ⁸ Why do you provoke me to anger with the works of your hands, making offerings to other gods in the land of Egypt where you have come to settle? Will you be cut off and become an object of cursing and ridicule among all the nations of the earth? ⁹ Have you forgotten the crimes of your ancestors, of the kings of Judah, of their^r wives, your own crimes and those of your wives, which they committed in the land of Judah and in the streets of Jerusalem? ¹⁰ They have shown no contrition or fear to this day, nor have they walked in my law and my statutes that I set before you and before your ancestors.

11 Therefore thus says the LORD of hosts, the God of Israel: I am determined to bring disaster on you, to bring all Judah to an end. ¹² I will take the remnant of Judah who are determined to come to the land of Egypt to settle, and they shall perish, everyone; in the land of Egypt they shall fall; by the sword and by famine they shall perish; from the least to the greatest, they shall die by the sword and by famine; and they shall become an object of execration and horror, of cursing and ridicule. ¹³ I will punish those who live in the land of Egypt, as I have punished Jerusalem, with the sword, with famine, and with pestilence, ¹⁴ so that none of the remnant of Judah who have come to settle in the

land of Egypt shall escape or survive or return to the land of Judah. Although they long to go back to live there, they shall not go back, except some fugitives.

15 Then all the men who were aware that their wives had been making offerings to other gods, and all the women who stood by, a great assembly, all the people who lived in Path'ros in the land of Egypt, answered Jer•e•mī'ah: ¹⁶ "As for the word that you have spoken to us in the name of the LORD, we are not going to listen to you. ¹⁷ Instead, we will do everything that we have vowed, make offerings to the queen of heaven and pour out libations to her, just as we and our ancestors, our kings and our officials, used to do in the towns of Judah and in the streets of Jerusalem. We used to have plenty of food, and prospered, and saw no misfortune. ¹⁸ But from the time we stopped making offerings to the queen of heaven and pouring out libations to her, we have lacked everything and have perished by the sword and by famine." ¹⁹ And the women said,^s "Indeed we will go on making offerings to the queen of heaven and pouring out libations to her; do you think that we made cakes for her, marked with her image, and poured out libations to her without our husbands' being involved?"

20 Then Jer•e•mī'ah said to all the people, men and women, all the people who were giving him this answer: ²¹ "As for the offerings that you made in the towns of Judah and in the streets of Jerusalem, you and your ancestors, your kings and your officials, and the people of the land, did not the LORD remember them? Did it not come into his mind? ²² The LORD could no longer bear the sight of your evil doings, the abominations that you committed; therefore your land became a desolation and a waste and a curse, without inhabitant, as it is to this day. ²³ It is because you burned offerings, and because you sinned against the LORD and did not obey the voice of the LORD or walk in his law and in his statutes and in his decrees, that this disaster has befallen you, as is still evident today."

24 Jer•e•mī'ah said to all the people and all the women, "Hear the word of the LORD, all you Judeans who are in the land of Egypt, ²⁵ Thus says the LORD of hosts, the God of Israel: You and your wives have accomplished in deeds what you declared in words, saying, 'We are determined to perform the vows that we have made, to make offerings to the queen of heaven and to pour out libations to her.' By all means, keep your vows and make your libations! ²⁶ Therefore hear the word of the LORD, all you Judeans who live in the land of

r Heb *his*   *s* Compare Syr: Heb lacks *And the women said*

Egypt: Lo, I swear by my great name, says the LORD, that my name shall no longer be pronounced on the lips of any of the people of Judah in all the land of Egypt, saying, 'As the Lord GOD lives.' ²⁷I am going to watch over them for harm and not for good; all the people of Judah who are in the land of Egypt shall perish by the sword and by famine, until not one is left. ²⁸And those who escape the sword shall return from the land of Egypt to the land of Judah, few in number; and all the remnant of Judah, who have come to the land of Egypt to settle, shall know whose words will stand, mine or theirs! ²⁹This shall be the sign to you, says the LORD, that I am going to punish you in this place, in order that you may know that my words against you will surely be carried out: ³⁰Thus says the LORD, I am going to give Pharaoh Hoph'ra, king of Egypt, into the hands of his enemies, those who seek his life, just as I gave King Zed•e•ki'ah of Judah into the hand of King Ne•bu•chad•rez'zar of Babylon, his enemy who sought his life."

A Word of Comfort to Baruch

The word that the prophet Jer•e•mi'ah spoke to Bar'uch son of Ne•ri'ah, when he wrote these words in a scroll at the dictation of Jer•e•mi'ah, in the fourth year of King Je•hoi'a•kim son of Jo•si'ah of Judah: ²Thus says the LORD, the God of Israel, to you, O Bar'uch: ³You said, "Woe is me! The LORD has added sorrow to my pain; I am weary with my groaning, and I find no rest." ⁴Thus you shall say to him, "Thus says the LORD: I am going to break down what I have built, and pluck up what I have planted—that is, the whole land. ⁵And you, do you seek great things for yourself? Do not seek them; for I am going to bring disaster upon all flesh, says the LORD; but I will give you your life as a prize of war in every place to which you may go."

Judgment on Egypt

The word of the LORD that came to the prophet Jer•e•mi'ah concerning the nations.

2 Concerning Egypt, about the army of Phar-aoh Ne'co, king of Egypt, which was by the river Euphrates at Car'chem•ish and which King Ne•bu-chad•rez'zar of Babylon defeated in the fourth year of King Je•hoi'a•kim son of Jo•si'ah of Judah:

³　Prepare buckler and shield,
　　　and advance for battle!
⁴　Harness the horses;
　　　mount the steeds!
　Take your stations with your helmets,
　　　whet your lances,
　　　put on your coats of mail!
⁵　Why do I see them terrified?
　　　They have fallen back;

did you KNOW?

Oracles Against the Nations

The Oracles Against the Nations, in Jeremiah, chapters 46–51, resemble the oracles in chapters 13–23 of Isaiah. In both, God's threats to destroy the enemies of Israel, as proclaimed by a prophet, reflect the bitterness that has welled up in the nation's heart during its long history of suffering.

Is God really as vengeful as the prophecies from Jeremiah suggest? We must balance our understanding of God's vengeance with Jesus' teachings—for example, Jesus' claim that God makes the "sun rise on the evil and on the good" (Mt 5.45). The God whom Jesus called Abba is the parent of all nations, who wants enemies to be reconciled with one another. The Oracles Against the Nations challenge Christians to be the first to offer the handshake of forgiveness and break the cycle of violence.

▶ **Jeremiah, chapters 46–51**

　　their warriors are beaten down,
　　　and have fled in haste.
　They do not look back—
　　　terror is all around!
　　　　　　　　　　says the LORD.
⁶　The swift cannot flee away,
　　　nor can the warrior escape;
　in the north by the river Euphrates
　　　they have stumbled and fallen.

⁷　Who is this, rising like the Nile,
　　　like rivers whose waters surge?
⁸　Egypt rises like the Nile,
　　　like rivers whose waters surge.
　It said, Let me rise, let me cover the earth,
　　　let me destroy cities and their
　　　　　　inhabitants.
⁹　Advance, O horses,
　　　and dash madly, O chariots!
　Let the warriors go forth:
　　　Ethiopia^t and Put who carry the shield,

^t Or *Nubia*; Heb *Cush*

the Lŭ′dim, who draw[u] the bow.
10 That day is the day of the Lord GOD of
hosts,
   a day of retribution,
      to gain vindication from his foes.
The sword shall devour and be sated,
   and drink its fill of their blood.
For the Lord GOD of hosts holds a
sacrifice
   in the land of the north by the river
Euphrates.
11 Go up to Gil′e•ad, and take balm,
   O virgin daughter Egypt!
In vain you have used many medicines;
   there is no healing for you.
12 The nations have heard of your shame,
   and the earth is full of your cry;
for warrior has stumbled against warrior;
   both have fallen together.

Babylonia Will Strike Egypt

13 The word that the LORD spoke to the
prophet Jer•e•mī′ah about the coming of King Ne-
bū•chad•rez′zar of Babylon to attack the land of
Egypt:
14 Declare in Egypt, and proclaim in Mig′dōl;
      proclaim in Memphis and Tah′pan•hēs;
Say, "Take your stations and be ready,
   for the sword shall devour those
      around you."
15 Why has Ā′pis fled?[v]
   Why did your bull not stand?
   —because the LORD thrust him
      down.
16 Your multitude stumbled[w] and fell,
   and one said to another,[x]
"Come, let us go back to our own people
   and to the land of our birth,
   because of the destroying sword."
17 Give Pharaoh, king of Egypt, the name
   "Braggart who missed his chance."

18 As I live, says the King,
   whose name is the LORD of hosts,
one is coming
   like Tā′bor among the mountains,
   and like Car′mel by the sea.
19 Pack your bags for exile,
   sheltered daughter Egypt!
For Memphis shall become a waste,
   a ruin, without inhabitant.

20 A beautiful heifer is Egypt—
   a gadfly from the north lights upon her.

21 Even her mercenaries in her midst
   are like fatted calves;
they too have turned and fled together,
   they did not stand;
for the day of their calamity has come upon
      them,
   the time of their punishment.

22 She makes a sound like a snake gliding
away;
   for her enemies march in force,
and come against her with axes,
   like those who fell trees.
23 They shall cut down her forest,
                                 says the LORD,
   though it is impenetrable,
because they are more numerous
   than locusts;
   they are without number.
24 Daughter Egypt shall be put to shame;
   she shall be handed over to a people
      from the north.

25 The LORD of hosts, the God of Israel, said:
See, I am bringing punishment upon Ā′mon of
Thēbes, and Pharaoh, and Egypt and her gods and
her kings, upon Pharaoh and those who trust in
him. 26 I will hand them over to those who seek
their life, to King Ne•bū•chad•rez′zar of Babylon and
his officers. Afterward Egypt shall be inhabited as
in the days of old, says the LORD.

God Will Save Israel
(Cp Jer 30.10–11)

27 But as for you, have no fear, my servant
Jacob,
   and do not be dismayed, O Israel;
for I am going to save you from far away,
   and your offspring from the land of their
      captivity.
Jacob shall return and have quiet and ease,
   and no one shall make him afraid.
28 As for you, have no fear, my servant Jacob,
                                 says the LORD,
   for I am with you.
I will make an end of all the nations
   among which I have banished you,
   but I will not make an end of you!
I will chastise you in just measure,
   and I will by no means leave you
      unpunished.

---

u Cn: Heb *who grasp, who draw*   v Gk: Heb *Why was it
swept away*   w Gk: Meaning of Heb uncertain
x Gk: Heb *and fell one to another and they said*

Judgment on the Philistines

The word of the LORD that came to the prophet Jer·e·mi'ah concerning the Phi·lis'tines, before Pharaoh attacked Ga'za:

2 Thus says the LORD:
See, waters are rising out of the north
and shall become an overflowing torrent;
they shall overflow the land and all that
fills it,
the city and those who live in it.
People shall cry out,
and all the inhabitants of the land shall
wail.
3 At the noise of the stamping of the hoofs of
his stallions,
at the clatter of his chariots, at the
rumbling of their wheels,
parents do not turn back for children,
so feeble are their hands,
4 because of the day that is coming
to destroy all the Phi·lis'tines,
to cut off from Tyre and Si'don
every helper that remains.
For the LORD is destroying the Phi·lis'tines,
the remnant of the coastland of Caph'tor.
5 Baldness has come upon Ga'za,
Ash'ke·lon is silenced.
O remnant of their power!y
How long will you gash yourselves?
6 Ah, sword of the LORD!
How long until you are quiet?
Put yourself into your scabbard,
rest and be still!
7 How can itz be quiet,
when the LORD has given it an order?
Against Ash'ke·lon and against the seashore—
there he has appointed it.

Judgment on Moab

Concerning Mo'ab.

Thus says the LORD of hosts, the God of Israel:
Alas for Ne'bo, it is laid waste!
Kir·i·a·tha'im is put to shame, it is taken;
the fortress is put to shame and broken
down;
2 the renown of Mo'ab is no more.
In Hesh'bon they planned evil against her:
"Come, let us cut her off from being a
nation!"
You also, O Madmen, shall be brought to
silence;a
the sword shall pursue you.

3 Hark! a cry from Hor·o·na'im,
"Desolation and great destruction!"

4 "Mo'ab is destroyed!"
her little ones cry out.
5 For at the ascent of Lu'hith
they gob up weeping bitterly;
for at the descent of Hor·o·na'im
they have heard the distressing cry of
anguish.
6 Flee! Save yourselves!
Be like a wild assc in the desert!

7 Surely, because you trusted in your
strongholdsd and your treasures,
you also shall be taken;
Che'mosh shall go out into exile,
with his priests and his attendants.
8 The destroyer shall come upon every town,
and no town shall escape;
the valley shall perish,
and the plain shall be destroyed,
as the LORD has spoken.

9 Set aside salt for Mo'ab,
for she will surely fall;
her towns shall become a desolation,
with no inhabitant in them.

10 Accursed is the one who is slack in doing the work of the LORD; and accursed is the one who keeps back the sword from bloodshed.

11 Mo'ab has been at ease from his youth,
settled like winee on its dregs;
he has not been emptied from vessel to
vessel,
nor has he gone into exile;
therefore his flavor has remained
and his aroma is unspoiled.
12 Therefore, the time is surely coming, says the LORD, when I shall send to him decanters to decant him, and empty his vessels, and break hisf jars in pieces. 13 Then Mo'ab shall be ashamed of Che'mosh, as the house of Israel was ashamed of Beth'el, their confidence.

14 How can you say, "We are heroes
and mighty warriors"?
15 The destroyer of Mo'ab and his towns have
come up,
and the choicest of his young men have
gone down to slaughter,
says the King, whose name is the LORD of
hosts.
16 The calamity of Mo'ab is near at hand

---

y Gk: Heb *their valley*   z Gk Vg: Heb *you*
a The place-name *Madmen* sounds like the Hebrew verb *to be silent*   b Cn: Heb *he goes*   c Gk Aquila: Heb *like Aroer*
d Gk: Heb *works*   e Heb lacks *like wine*   f Gk Aquila: Heb *their*

and his doom approaches swiftly.

17 Mourn over him, all you his neighbors,
    and all who know his name;
  say, "How the mighty scepter is broken,
    the glorious staff!"

18 Come down from glory,
    and sit on the parched ground,
    enthroned daughter Dī′bon!
  For the destroyer of Mō′ab has come up
    against you;
  he has destroyed your strongholds.
19 Stand by the road and watch,
    you inhabitant of A•rō′er!
  Ask the man fleeing and the woman
    escaping;
  say, "What has happened?"
20 Mō′ab is put to shame, for it is broken down;
    wail and cry!
  Tell it by the Ar′non,
    that Mō′ab is laid waste.

21 Judgment has come upon the tableland,
upon Hō′lon, and Jah′zah, and Meph′a•ath, 22 and
Dī′bon, and Nĕ′bō, and Beth-dib•la•thā′im, 23 and
Kir•i•a•thā′im, and Beth-gā′mul, and Beth-mĕ′on,
24 and Ker′i•oth, and Boz′rah, and all the towns of
the land of Mō′ab, far and near. 25 The horn of
Mō′ab is cut off, and his arm is broken, says the
LORD.
26 Make him drunk, because he magnified
himself against the LORD; let Mō′ab wallow in his
vomit; he too shall become a laughingstock. 27 Israel was a laughingstock for you, though he was
not caught among thieves; but whenever you
spoke of him you shook your head!

28 Leave the towns, and live on the rock,
    O inhabitants of Mō′ab!
  Be like the dove that nests
    on the sides of the mouth of a gorge.
29 We have heard of the pride of Mō′ab—
    he is very proud—
  of his loftiness, his pride, and his arrogance,
    and the haughtiness of his heart.
30 I myself know his insolence, says the LORD;
    his boasts are false,
    his deeds are false.
31 Therefore I wail for Mō′ab;
    I cry out for all Mō′ab;
    for the people of Kir-hē′res I mourn.
32 More than for Jā′zer I weep for you,
    O vine of Sib′mah!
  Your branches crossed over the sea,
    reached as far as Jā′zer;g
  upon your summer fruits and your vintage
    the destroyer has fallen.

33 Gladness and joy have been taken away
    from the fruitful land of Mō′ab;
  I have stopped the wine from the wine
    presses;
  no one treads them with shouts
    of joy;
  the shouting is not the shout of joy.

34 Hesh′bon and Ē•le•ā′leh cry out;h as far as
Jā′haz they utter their voice, from Zō′ar to Hor•ō-
nā′im and Eg′lath-she•lish′i•yah. For even the waters of Nim′rim have become desolate. 35 And I
will bring to an end in Mō′ab, says the LORD, those
who offer sacrifice at a high place and make offerings to their gods. 36 Therefore my heart moans for
Mō′ab like a flute, and my heart moans like a flute
for the people of Kir-hē′res; for the riches they
gained have perished.
37 For every head is shaved and every beard
cut off; on all the hands there are gashes, and on
the loins sackcloth. 38 On all the housetops of
Mō′ab and in the squares there is nothing but
lamentation; for I have broken Mō′ab like a vessel
that no one wants, says the LORD. 39 How it is broken! How they wail! How Mō′ab has turned his
back in shame! So Mō′ab has become a derision
and a horror to all his neighbors.
40 For thus says the LORD:
  Look, he shall swoop down like an eagle,
    and spread his wings against Mō′ab;
41 the townsi shall be taken
    and the strongholds seized.
  The hearts of the warriors of Mō′ab, on
    that day,
  shall be like the heart of a woman in
    labor.
42 Mō′ab shall be destroyed as a people,
    because he magnified himself against the
      LORD.
43 Terror, pit, and trap
    are before you, O inhabitants of Mō′ab!
                      says the LORD.
44 Everyone who flees from the terror
    shall fall into the pit,
  and everyone who climbs out of the pit
    shall be caught in the trap.
  For I will bring these thingsj upon Mō′ab
    in the year of their punishment,
                      says the LORD.

45 In the shadow of Hesh′bon
    fugitives stop exhausted;

---

g Two Mss and Isa 16.8: MT *the sea of Jazer*   h Cn: Heb
From the cry of Heshbon to Elealeh   i Or *Kerioth*
j Gk Syr: Heb *bring upon it*

➤➤➤➤➤➤➤➤➤➤➤

NATIVE AMERICAN

The Eagle

Jeremiah 48.40 portrays the punisher of Moab as an eagle. In the Bible, that is not an unusual description for this majestic bird (see also Job 39.27; Isa 40.31; Ezek 17.3; Dan 7.4). Native American cultures admire the eagle as the strongest and bravest of all birds, and therefore view eagle feathers as a symbol of what is high and holy.

So, in some Native American tribes, when someone is honored for being brave, strong, and holy, an eagle feather is given to her or him. Native Americans also use eagle feathers for blessings. They hold or wave the feathers over a person's head as a prayer for peace and happiness. (Note: Native Americans are able to acquire feathers for use in their rituals. But keep in mind that it is generally illegal to hunt eagles or even to take a feather you find!)

The next time you see an eagle or a picture of an eagle, remember what its feathers symbolize, and pray about those ideals of honor, peace, protection, strength, courage, and holiness.

▶ Jer 48.40

for a fire has gone out from Hesh'bon,
  a flame from the house of Sī'hon;
it has destroyed the forehead of
    Mō'ab,
  the scalp of the people of tumult.*k*
46 Woe to you, O Mō'ab!
  The people of Chē'mosh have
    perished,
for your sons have been taken
    captive,
  and your daughters into captivity.
47 Yet I will restore the fortunes of
    Mō'ab
  in the latter days, says the LORD.
Thus far is the judgment on Mō'ab.

Judgment on the Ammonites

Concerning the Am'mon·ites.

Thus says the LORD:
  Has Israel no sons?
    Has he no heir?
  Why then has Mil'com dispossessed Gad,
    and his people settled in its towns?
2 Therefore, the time is surely coming,
    says the LORD,
  when I will sound the battle alarm
    against Rab'bah of the Am'mon·ites;
  it shall become a desolate mound,
    and its villages shall be burned with fire;
  then Israel shall dispossess those who
        dispossessed him,
    says the LORD.

3 Wail, O Hesh'bon, for Aī is laid waste!
    Cry out, O daughters*l* of Rab'bah!
  Put on sackcloth,
    lament, and slash yourselves with
        whips!*m*
  For Mil'com shall go into exile,
    with his priests and his attendants.
4 Why do you boast in your strength?
    Your strength is ebbing,
  O faithless daughter.
    You trusted in your treasures, saying,
    "Who will attack me?"
5 I am going to bring terror upon you,
    says the Lord GOD of hosts,
    from all your neighbors,
  and you will be scattered, each headlong,
    with no one to gather the fugitives.
6 But afterward I will restore the fortunes of the Am'mon·ites, says the LORD.

Judgment on Edom

7 Concerning Ē'dom.

Thus says the LORD of hosts:
  Is there no longer wisdom in Tē'man?
    Has counsel perished from the prudent?
    Has their wisdom vanished?
8 Flee, turn back, get down low,
    inhabitants of Dē'dan!
  For I will bring the calamity of Esau
        upon him,
    the time when I punish him.
9 If grape-gatherers came to you,
    would they not leave gleanings?
  If thieves came by night,
    even they would pillage only what they
        wanted.

---

k Or *of Shaon*   *l* Or *villages*   *m* Cn: Meaning of Heb uncertain

10 But as for me, I have stripped Esau bare,
I have uncovered his hiding places,
and he is not able to conceal himself.
His offspring are destroyed, his kinsfolk
and his neighbors; and he is no more.
11 Leave your orphans, I will keep them alive;
and let your widows trust in me.
12 For thus says the LORD: If those who do not
deserve to drink the cup still have to drink it, shall
you be the one to go unpunished? You shall not
go unpunished; you must drink it. 13 For by myself
I have sworn, says the LORD, that Boz'rah shall become an object of horror and ridicule, a waste, and
an object of cursing; and all her towns shall be
perpetual wastes.
14 I have heard tidings from the LORD,
and a messenger has been sent among
the nations:
"Gather yourselves together and come
against her,
and rise up for battle!"
15 For I will make you least among the
nations,
despised by humankind.
16 The terror you inspire
and the pride of your heart have
deceived you,
you who live in the clefts of the rock,[n]
who hold the height of the hill.
Although you make your nest as high as the
eagle's,
from there I will bring you down,
says the LORD.
17 Ē'dom shall become an object of horror;
everyone who passes by it will be horrified and
will hiss because of all its disasters. 18 As when
Sod'om and Go•mor'rah and their neighbors were
overthrown, says the LORD, no one shall live there,
nor shall anyone settle in it. 19 Like a lion coming
up from the thickets of the Jordan against a perennial pasture, I will suddenly chase Ē'dom[o] away
from it; and I will appoint over it whomever I
choose.[p] For who is like me? Who can summon
me? Who is the shepherd who can stand before
me? 20 Therefore hear the plan that the LORD has
made against Ē'dom and the purposes that he has
formed against the inhabitants of Tē'man: Surely
the little ones of the flock shall be dragged away;
surely their fold shall be appalled at their fate. 21 At
the sound of their fall the earth shall tremble; the
sound of their cry shall be heard at the Red Sea.[q]
22 Look, he shall mount up and swoop down like
an eagle, and spread his wings against Boz'rah,
and the heart of the warriors of Ē'dom in that day
shall be like the heart of a woman in labor.

Judgment on Damascus

23 Concerning Damascus.
Hā'math and Ar'pad are confounded,
for they have heard bad news;
they melt in fear, they are troubled like the
sea[r]
that cannot be quiet.
24 Damascus has become feeble, she turned to
flee,
and panic seized her;
anguish and sorrows have taken hold of her,
as of a woman in labor.
25 How the famous city is forsaken,[s]
the joyful town![t]
26 Therefore her young men shall fall in her
squares,
and all her soldiers shall be destroyed in
that day,
says the LORD of hosts.
27 And I will kindle a fire at the wall of
Damascus,
and it shall devour the strongholds of
Ben-hā'dad.

Judgment on Kedar and Hazor

28 Concerning Kē'dar and the kingdoms of
Hā'zor that King Ne•bū•chad•rez'zar of Babylon defeated.

Thus says the LORD:
Rise up, advance against Kē'dar!
Destroy the people of the east!
29 Take their tents and their flocks,
their curtains and all their goods;
carry off their camels for yourselves,
and a cry shall go up: "Terror is all
around!"
30 Flee, wander far away, hide in deep places,
O inhabitants of Hā'zor!
says the LORD.
For King Ne•bū•chad•rez'zar of Babylon
has made a plan against you
and formed a purpose against you.

31 Rise up, advance against a nation at ease,
that lives secure,
says the LORD,
that has no gates or bars,
that lives alone.
32 Their camels shall become booty,
their herds of cattle a spoil.
I will scatter to every wind

[n] Or *of Sela* [o] Heb *him* [p] Or *and I will single out the choicest of his rams*: Meaning of Heb uncertain [q] Or *Sea of Reeds* [r] Cn: Heb *there is trouble in the sea* [s] Vg: Heb *is not forsaken* [t] Syr Vg Tg: Heb *the town of my joy*

those who have shaven temples,
and I will bring calamity
    against them from every side,
                          says the LORD.
33 Hā′zor shall become a lair of jackals,
    an everlasting waste;
no one shall live there,
    nor shall anyone settle in it.

Judgment on Elam

34 The word of the LORD that came to the prophet Jer•e•mi′ah concerning Ē′lam, at the beginning of the reign of King Zed•e•ki′ah of Judah. 35 Thus says the LORD of hosts: I am going to break the bow of Ē′lam, the mainstay of their might; 36 and I will bring upon Ē′lam the four winds from the four quarters of heaven; and I will scatter them to all these winds, and there shall be no nation to which the exiles from Ē′lam shall not come. 37 I will terrify Ē′lam before their enemies, and before those who seek their life; I will bring disaster upon them, my fierce anger, says the LORD. I will send the sword after them, until I have consumed them; 38 and I will set my throne in Ē′lam, and destroy their king and officials, says the LORD.

39 But in the latter days I will restore the fortunes of Ē′lam, says the LORD.

Judgment on Babylon

The word that the LORD spoke concerning Babylon, concerning the land of the Chal•dē′ans, by the prophet Jer•e•mi′ah:
2 Declare among the nations and proclaim,
    set up a banner and proclaim,
    do not conceal it, say:
Babylon is taken,
    Bel is put to shame,
    Mer′o•dach is dismayed.
Her images are put to shame,
    her idols are dismayed.

3 For out of the north a nation has come up against her; it shall make her land a desolation, and no one shall live in it; both human beings and animals shall flee away.

4 In those days and in that time, says the LORD, the people of Israel shall come, they and the people of Judah together; they shall come weeping as they seek the LORD their God. 5 They shall ask the way to Zion, with faces turned toward it, and they shall come and join[u] themselves to the LORD by an everlasting covenant that will never be forgotten.

6 My people have been lost sheep; their shepherds have led them astray, turning them away on the mountains; from mountain to hill they have gone, they have forgotten their fold. 7 All who found them have devoured them, and their enemies have said, "We are not guilty, because they have sinned against the LORD, the true pasture, the LORD, the hope of their ancestors."

8 Flee from Babylon, and go out of the land of the Chal•dē′ans, and be like male goats leading the flock. 9 For I am going to stir up and bring against Babylon a company of great nations from the land of the north; and they shall array themselves against her; from there she shall be taken. Their arrows are like the arrows of a skilled warrior who does not return empty-handed. 10 Chal•dē′a shall be plundered; all who plunder her shall be sated, says the LORD.

11 Though you rejoice, though you exult,
    O plunderers of my heritage,
though you frisk about like a heifer on the
        grass,
    and neigh like stallions,
12 your mother shall be utterly shamed,
    and she who bore you shall be disgraced.
Lo, she shall be the last of the nations,
    a wilderness, dry land, and a desert.
13 Because of the wrath of the LORD she shall
        not be inhabited,
    but shall be an utter desolation;
everyone who passes by Babylon shall be
        appalled
    and hiss because of all her wounds.
14 Take up your positions around Babylon,
    all you that bend the bow;
shoot at her, spare no arrows,
    for she has sinned against the LORD.
15 Raise a shout against her from all sides,
    "She has surrendered;
her bulwarks have fallen,
    her walls are thrown down."
For this is the vengeance of the LORD:
    take vengeance on her,
    do to her as she has done.
16 Cut off from Babylon the sower,
    and the wielder of the sickle in time of
        harvest;
because of the destroying sword
    all of them shall return to their own
        people,
    and all of them shall flee to their own
        land.

17 Israel is a hunted sheep driven away by lions. First the king of Assyria devoured it, and now at the end King Ne•bu•chad•rez′zar of Babylon has gnawed its bones. 18 Therefore, thus says the LORD of hosts, the God of Israel: I am going to punish

_____
u Gk: Heb toward it. Come! They shall join

the king of Babylon and his land, as I punished the king of Assyria. ¹⁹ I will restore Israel to its pasture, and it shall feed on Car′mel and in Ba′shan, and on the hills of E′phra•im and in Gil′e•ad its hunger shall be satisfied. ²⁰ In those days and at that time, says the LORD, the iniquity of Israel shall be sought, and there shall be none; and the sins of Judah, and none shall be found; for I will pardon the remnant that I have spared.

²¹ Go up to the land of Mer•a•tha′im;^v
    go up against her,
and attack the inhabitants of Pe′kod^w
    and utterly destroy the last of them,^x
                   says the LORD;
    do all that I have commanded you.
²² The noise of battle is in the land,
    and great destruction!
²³ How the hammer of the whole earth
    is cut down and broken!
How Babylon has become
    a horror among the nations!
²⁴ You set a snare for yourself and you were
           caught, O Babylon,
    but you did not know it;
you were discovered and seized,
    because you challenged the LORD.
²⁵ The LORD has opened his armory,
    and brought out the weapons of his
           wrath,
for the Lord GOD of hosts has a task to do
    in the land of the Chal•de′ans.
²⁶ Come against her from every quarter;
    open her granaries;
pile her up like heaps of grain, and destroy
           her utterly;
    let nothing be left of her.
²⁷ Kill all her bulls,
    let them go down to the slaughter.
Alas for them, their day has come,
    the time of their punishment!

²⁸ Listen! Fugitives and refugees from the land of Babylon are coming to declare in Zion the vengeance of the LORD our God, vengeance for his temple.

²⁹ Summon archers against Babylon, all who bend the bow. Encamp all around her; let no one escape. Repay her according to her deeds; just as she has done, do to her—for she has arrogantly defied the LORD, the Holy One of Israel. ³⁰ Therefore her young men shall fall in her squares, and all her soldiers shall be destroyed on that day, says the LORD.

³¹ I am against you, O arrogant one,
    says the Lord GOD of hosts;

for your day has come,
    the time when I will punish you.
³² The arrogant one shall stumble and fall,
    with no one to raise him up,
and I will kindle a fire in his cities,
    and it will devour everything
           around him.

³³ Thus says the LORD of hosts: The people of Israel are oppressed, and so too are the people of Judah; all their captors have held them fast and refuse to let them go. ³⁴ Their Redeemer is strong; the LORD of hosts is his name. He will surely plead their cause, that he may give rest to the earth, but unrest to the inhabitants of Babylon.

³⁵ A sword against the Chal•de′ans, says the
           LORD,
    and against the inhabitants of Babylon,
    and against her officials and her sages!
³⁶ A sword against the diviners,
    so that they may become fools!
A sword against her warriors,
    so that they may be destroyed!
³⁷ A sword against her^y horses and against
           her^y chariots,
    and against all the foreign troops in her
           midst,
    so that they may become women!
A sword against all her treasures,
    that they may be plundered!
³⁸ A drought^z against her waters,
    that they may be dried up!
For it is a land of images,
    and they go mad over idols.

³⁹ Therefore wild animals shall live with hyenas in Babylon,^a and ostriches shall inhabit her; she shall never again be peopled, or inhabited for all generations. ⁴⁰ As when God overthrew Sod′om and Go•mor′rah and their neighbors, says the LORD, so no one shall live there, nor shall anyone settle in her.

⁴¹ Look, a people is coming from the north;
    a mighty nation and many kings
    are stirring from the farthest parts of the
           earth.
⁴² They wield bow and spear,
    they are cruel and have no mercy.
The sound of them is like the roaring sea;
    they ride upon horses,
set in array as a warrior for battle,
    against you, O daughter Babylon!

---

^v Or *of Double Rebellion*   ^w Or *of Punishment*   ^x Tg: Heb *destroy after them*   ^y Cn: Heb *his*   ^z Another reading is *A sword*   ^a Heb lacks *in Babylon*

43 The king of Babylon heard news of them,
  and his hands fell helpless;
anguish seized him,
  pain like that of a woman in labor.

44 Like a lion coming up from the thickets of the Jordan against a perennial pasture, I will suddenly chase them away from her; and I will appoint over her whomever I choose.[b] For who is like me? Who can summon me? Who is the shepherd who can stand before me? 45 Therefore hear the plan that the LORD has made against Babylon, and the purposes that he has formed against the land of the Chal·dē'ans: Surely the little ones of the flock shall be dragged away; surely their[c] fold shall be appalled at their fate. 46 At the sound of the capture of Babylon the earth shall tremble, and her cry shall be heard among the nations.

Thus says the LORD:
  I am going to stir up a destructive wind[d]
  against Babylon
  and against the inhabitants of
    Leb-qā'maī;[e]
2 and I will send winnowers to Babylon,
  and they shall winnow her.
They shall empty her land
  when they come against her from every
    side
  on the day of trouble.
3 Let not the archer bend his bow,
  and let him not array himself in his coat
    of mail.
Do not spare her young men;
  utterly destroy her entire army.
4 They shall fall down slain in the land of the
    Chal·dē'ans,
  and wounded in her streets.
5 Israel and Judah have not been forsaken
  by their God, the LORD of hosts,
though their land is full of guilt
  before the Holy One of Israel.

6 Flee from the midst of Babylon,
  save your lives, each of you!
Do not perish because of her guilt,
  for this is the time of the LORD's
    vengeance;
  he is repaying her what is due.
7 Babylon was a golden cup in the LORD's
    hand,
  making all the earth drunken;
the nations drank of her wine,
  and so the nations went mad.
8 Suddenly Babylon has fallen and
    is shattered;
  wail for her!

Bring balm for her wound;
  perhaps she may be healed.
9 We tried to heal Babylon,
  but she could not be healed.
Forsake her, and let each of us go
  to our own country;
for her judgment has reached up to heaven
  and has been lifted up even to the skies.
10 The LORD has brought forth our vindication;
  come, let us declare in Zion
    the work of the LORD our God.

11 Sharpen the arrows!
  Fill the quivers!
The LORD has stirred up the spirit of the kings of the Mēdes, because his purpose concerning Babylon is to destroy it, for that is the vengeance of the LORD, vengeance for his temple.
12 Raise a standard against the walls of
    Babylon;
  make the watch strong;
post sentinels;
  prepare the ambushes;
for the LORD has both planned and done
  what he spoke concerning the inhabitants
    of Babylon.
13 You who live by mighty waters,
  rich in treasures,
your end has come,
  the thread of your life is cut.
14 The LORD of hosts has sworn by himself:
Surely I will fill you with troops like a
    swarm of locusts,
  and they shall raise a shout of victory
    over you.

15 It is he who made the earth by his power,
  who established the world by
    his wisdom,
and by his understanding stretched out the
    heavens.
16 When he utters his voice there is a tumult
    of waters in the heavens,
  and he makes the mist rise from the ends
    of the earth.
He makes lightnings for the rain,
  and he brings out the wind from his
    storehouses.
17 Everyone is stupid and without knowledge;
  goldsmiths are all put to shame by their
    idols;
for their images are false,
  and there is no breath in them.

---

b Or and I will single out the choicest of her rams: Meaning of Heb uncertain   c Syr Gk Tg Compare 49.20: Heb lacks their   d Or stir up the spirit of a destroyer   e Leb-qamai is a cryptogram for Kasdim, Chaldea

18 They are worthless, a work of delusion;
 at the time of their punishment they
  shall perish.
19 Not like these is the LORD,ƒ the portion of
 Jacob,
 for he is the one who formed all things,
and Israel is the tribe of his inheritance;
 the LORD of hosts is his name.

Israel the Creator's Instrument

20 You are my war club, my weapon of battle:
with you I smash nations;
 with you I destroy kingdoms;
21 with you I smash the horse and its rider;
 with you I smash the chariot and the
  charioteer;
22 with you I smash man and woman;
 with you I smash the old man and
  the boy;
 with you I smash the young man and the
  girl;
23 with you I smash shepherds and their
  flocks;
 with you I smash farmers and their teams;
 with you I smash governors and deputies.

The Doom of Babylon

24 I will repay Babylon and all the inhabitants
of Chal•dē′a before your very eyes for all the wrong
that they have done in Zion, says the LORD.

25 I am against you, O destroying mountain,
      says the LORD,
 that destroys the whole earth;
I will stretch out my hand against you,
 and roll you down from the crags,
 and make you a burned-out mountain.
26 No stone shall be taken from you for a
  corner
 and no stone for a foundation,
but you shall be a perpetual waste,
 says the LORD.

27 Raise a standard in the land,
 blow the trumpet among the nations;
prepare the nations for war against her,
 summon against her the kingdoms,
 Ar′a•rat, Min′nī, and Ash′ke•naz;
appoint a marshal against her,
 bring up horses like bristling locusts.
28 Prepare the nations for war against her,
 the kings of the Mēdes, with their
  governors and deputies,
 and every land under their dominion.
29 The land trembles and writhes,
 for the LORD's purposes against Babylon
  stand,

to make the land of Babylon a desolation,
 without inhabitant.
30 The warriors of Babylon have given up fighting,
 they remain in their strongholds;
their strength has failed,
 they have become women;
her buildings are set on fire,
 her bars are broken.
31 One runner runs to meet another,
 and one messenger to meet another,
to tell the king of Babylon
 that his city is taken from end to end:
32 the fords have been seized,
 the marshes have been burned with fire,
 and the soldiers are in panic.
33 For thus says the LORD of hosts, the God of
 Israel:
Daughter Babylon is like a threshing floor
 at the time when it is trodden;
yet a little while
 and the time of her harvest will come.

34 "King Ne•bū•chad•rez′zar of Babylon has
  devoured me,
 he has crushed me;
he has made me an empty vessel,
 he has swallowed me like a monster;
he has filled his belly with my delicacies,
 he has spewed me out.
35 May my torn flesh be avenged on Babylon,"
 the inhabitants of Zion shall say.
"May my blood be avenged on the
  inhabitants of Chal•dē′a,"
 Jerusalem shall say.
36 Therefore thus says the LORD:
I am going to defend your cause
 and take vengeance for you.
I will dry up her sea
 and make her fountain dry;
37 and Babylon shall become a heap of ruins,
 a den of jackals,
an object of horror and of hissing,
 without inhabitant.

38 Like lions they shall roar together;
 they shall growl like lions' whelps.
39 When they are inflamed, I will set out their
  drink
 and make them drunk, until they become
  merry
 and then sleep a perpetual sleep
 and never wake, says the LORD.
40 I will bring them down like lambs to the
  slaughter,
 like rams and goats.

ƒ Heb lacks *the LORD*

41 How Shĕ'shach*g* is taken,
    the pride of the whole earth seized!
How Babylon has become
    an object of horror among the nations!
42 The sea has risen over Babylon;
    she has been covered by its tumultuous
        waves.
43 Her cities have become an object of horror,
    a land of drought and a desert,
a land in which no one lives,
    and through which no mortal passes.
44 I will punish Bel in Babylon,
    and make him disgorge what he has
        swallowed.
The nations shall no longer stream to him;
    the wall of Babylon has fallen.

45 Come out of her, my people!
    Save your lives, each of you,
    from the fierce anger of the LORD!
46 Do not be fainthearted or fearful
    at the rumors heard in the land—
one year one rumor comes,
    the next year another,
rumors of violence in the land
    and of ruler against ruler.
47 Assuredly, the days are coming
    when I will punish the images
        of Babylon;
her whole land shall be put to shame,
    and all her slain shall fall in her midst.
48 Then the heavens and the earth,
    and all that is in them,
shall shout for joy over Babylon;
    for the destroyers shall come against
        them out of the north,
                    says the LORD.
49 Babylon must fall for the slain of Israel,
    as the slain of all the earth have fallen
        because of Babylon.

50 You survivors of the sword,
    go, do not linger!
Remember the LORD in a distant land,
    and let Jerusalem come into your mind:
51 We are put to shame, for we have heard
        insults;
    dishonor has covered our face,
for aliens have come
    into the holy places of the LORD's house.

52 Therefore the time is surely coming, says the
        LORD,
    when I will punish her idols,
and through all her land
    the wounded shall groan.

53 Though Babylon should mount up to
        heaven,
    and though she should fortify her strong
        height,
from me destroyers would come upon her,
    says the LORD.
54 Listen!—a cry from Babylon!
    A great crashing from the land of the
        Chal·dē'ans!
55 For the LORD is laying Babylon waste,
    and stilling her loud clamor.
Their waves roar like mighty waters,
    the sound of their clamor resounds;
56 for a destroyer has come against her,
        against Babylon;
her warriors are taken,
    their bows are broken;
for the LORD is a God of recompense,
    he will repay in full.
57 I will make her officials and her sages
        drunk,
    also her governors, her deputies, and her
        warriors;
they shall sleep a perpetual sleep and never
        wake,
    says the King, whose name is the LORD of
        hosts.

58 Thus says the LORD of hosts:
The broad wall of Babylon
    shall be leveled to the ground,
and her high gates
    shall be burned with fire.
The peoples exhaust themselves for nothing,
    and the nations weary themselves only
        for fire.*h*

Jeremiah's Command to Seraiah

59 The word that the prophet Jer·e·mī'ah commanded Se·rāi'ah son of Ne·rī'ah son of Mah'sēi·ah, when he went with King Zed·e·kī'ah of Judah to Babylon, in the fourth year of his reign. Se·rāi'ah was the quartermaster. 60 Jer·e·mī'ah wrote in a*i* scroll all the disasters that would come on Babylon, all these words that are written concerning Babylon. 61 And Jer·e·mī'ah said to Se·rāi'ah: "When you come to Babylon, see that you read all these words, 62 and say, 'O LORD, you yourself threatened to destroy this place so that neither human beings nor animals shall live in it, and it shall be desolate forever.' 63 When you finish reading this scroll, tie

---

g Sheshach is a cryptogram for *Babel*, Babylon   *h* Gk Syr
Compare Hab 2.13: Heb *and the nations for fire, and they
are weary   i* Or *one*

a stone to it, and throw it into the middle of the Euphrates, 64 and say, 'Thus shall Babylon sink, to rise no more, because of the disasters that I am bringing on her.' "*j*

Thus far are the words of Jer•e•mī′ah.

did you **KNOW?**

Whatever Happened to Babylon?

In his time, Jeremiah prophesied about the destruction of Babylon, the powerful empire with the most glamorous and glittering capital in the Middle East (see Jeremiah, chapters 50–51). Not long afterward, in 587 B.C., King Nebuchadrezzar (also called Nebuchadnezzar) of Babylon destroyed Jerusalem, blinded the king of Judah, and led the leaders of Judah off to exile. This seemed to be the end of Jerusalem and perhaps even the Israelites. However, the captives were eventually released when Persia defeated Babylon. Today, Jerusalem is a thriving city, and Judaism—the religion that emerged after the Exile—is a great religion. Babylon is long gone, and no one worships its chief god, Marduk.

Jeremiah saw past the immediate destruction of Jerusalem to the eventual doom of Babylon. He had a much broader vision of the future. Great cities come and go, but God is forever, and the people of God live on through all the ebbs and flows of history.

▶ Jeremiah, chapter 51

The Destruction of Jerusalem Reviewed
(2 Kings 24.18 — 25.26; 2 Chr 36.11–20; Jer 39.1–10)

Zed•e•kī′ah was twenty-one years old when he began to reign; he reigned eleven years in Jerusalem. His mother's name was Ha•mū′tal daughter of Jer•e•mī′ah of Lib′nah. 2 He did what was evil in the sight of the LORD, just as Je•hoi′a•kim had done. 3 Indeed, Jerusalem and Judah so angered the LORD that he expelled them from his presence.

Zed•e•kī′ah rebelled against the king of Babylon. 4 And in the ninth year of his reign, in the tenth month, on the tenth day of the month, King Ne•bū•chad•rez′zar of Babylon came with all his army against Jerusalem, and they laid siege to it; they built siegeworks against it all around. 5 So the city was besieged until the eleventh year of King Zed•e•kī′ah. 6 On the ninth day of the fourth month the famine became so severe in the city that there was no food for the people of the land. 7 Then a breach was made in the city wall;*k* and all the soldiers fled and went out from the city by night by the way of the gate between the two walls, by the king's garden, though the Chal•dē′ans were all around the city. They went in the direction of the Ar′a•bah. 8 But the army of the Chal•dē′ans pursued the king, and overtook Zed•e•kī′ah in the plains of Jericho; and all his army was scattered, deserting him. 9 Then they captured the king, and brought him up to the king of Babylon at Rib′lah in the land of Hā′math, and he passed sentence on him. 10 The king of Babylon killed the sons of Zed•e•kī′ah before his eyes, and also killed all the officers of Judah at Rib′lah. 11 He put out the eyes of Zed•e•kī′ah, and bound him in fetters, and the king of Babylon took him to Babylon, and put him in prison until the day of his death.

12 In the fifth month, on the tenth day of the month—which was the nineteenth year of King Ne•bū•chad•rez′zar, king of Babylon—Ne•bū•za•rad′an the captain of the bodyguard who served the king of Babylon, entered Jerusalem. 13 He burned the house of the LORD, the king's house, and all the houses of Jerusalem; every great house he burned down. 14 All the army of the Chal•dē′ans, who were with the captain of the guard, broke down all the walls around Jerusalem. 15 Ne•bū•za•rad′an the captain of the guard carried into exile some of the poorest of the people and the rest of the people who were left in the city and the deserters who had defected to the king of Babylon, together with the rest of the artisans. 16 But Ne•bū•za•rad′an the captain of the guard left some of the poorest people of the land to be vinedressers and tillers of the soil.

17 The pillars of bronze that were in the house of the LORD, and the stands and the bronze sea that were in the house of the LORD, the Chal•dē′ans broke in pieces, and carried all the bronze to Babylon. 18 They took away the pots, the shovels, the snuffers, the basins, the ladles, and all the vessels of bronze used in the temple service. 19 The captain of the guard took away the small bowls also, the firepans, the basins, the pots, the lampstands,

_____

j Gk: Heb *on her. And they shall weary themselves*
k Heb lacks *wall*

the ladles, and the bowls for libation, both those of gold and those of silver. 20 As for the two pillars, the one sea, the twelve bronze bulls that were under the sea, and the stands,[l] which King Solomon had made for the house of the LORD, the bronze of all these vessels was beyond weighing. 21 As for the pillars, the height of the one pillar was eighteen cubits, its circumference was twelve cubits; it was hollow and its thickness was four fingers. 22 Upon it was a capital of bronze; the height of the capital was five cubits; latticework and pomegranates, all of bronze, encircled the top of the capital. And the second pillar had the same, with pomegranates. 23 There were ninety-six pomegranates on the sides; all the pomegranates encircling the latticework numbered one hundred.

24 The captain of the guard took the chief priest Se·rāi′ah, the second priest Zeph·a·nī′ah, and the three guardians of the threshold; 25 and from the city he took an officer who had been in command of the soldiers, and seven men of the king's council who were found in the city; the secretary of the commander of the army who mustered the people of the land; and sixty men of the people of the land who were found inside the city. 26 Then Ne·bū·za·rad′an the captain of the guard took them, and brought them to the king of Babylon at Rib′lah. 27 And the king of Babylon struck them down, and put them to death at Rib′lah in the land of Hā′math. So Judah went into exile out of its land.

28 This is the number of the people whom Ne·bū·chad·rez′zar took into exile: in the seventh year, three thousand twenty-three Judeans; 29 in the eighteenth year of Ne·bū·chad·rez′zar he took into exile from Jerusalem eight hundred thirty-two persons; 30 in the twenty-third year of Ne·bū·chad·rez′zar, Ne·bū·za·rad′an the captain of the guard took into exile of the Judeans seven hundred forty-five persons; all the persons were four thousand six hundred.

Jehoiachin Favored in Captivity
(2 Kings 25.27–30)

31 In the thirty-seventh year of the exile of King Je·hoi′a·chin of Judah, in the twelfth month, on the twenty-fifth day of the month, King Ē′vilme·rō′dach of Babylon, in the year he began to reign, showed favor to King Je·hoi′a·chin of Judah and brought him out of prison; 32 he spoke kindly to him, and gave him a seat above the seats of the other kings who were with him in Babylon. 33 So Je·hoi′a·chin put aside his prison clothes, and every day of his life he dined regularly at the king's table. 34 For his allowance, a regular daily allowance was given him by the king of Babylon, as long as he lived, up to the day of his death.

---

l Cn: Heb *that were under the stands*

I f someone close to you has died, you know that the grief and sadness can be almost too much for words. At such times of deep emotion, many people resort to poetry or song to try to express their feelings. Written during the Babylonian Exile, the Book of Lamentations poetically expresses the overwhelming grief the Israelites felt over the loss of their homes, their freedom, their capital, and their Temple. Through its passages, we get an insight into how devastating and destructive those days actually were.

At a Glance

- **Chapter 1.** a description of the desolation of Mount Zion and Jerusalem
- **Chapter 2.** a discussion of God's wrath upon Jerusalem
- **Chapter 3.** an account moving from grief to memory to hope
- **Chapter 4.** a revisitation of Jerusalem
- **Chapter 5.** a prayer of the people

In-depth

The Book of Lamentations is a collection of five poem songs, each a separate chapter in the book. If you take a quick look, you will notice that each poem has twenty-two verses, except the third, which has sixty-six. This is not an accident. In the original Hebrew language, each verse of the first, second, fourth, and fifth poems begins with a different letter of the Hebrew alphabet, which has twenty-two letters. In the third poem, every set of three verses begins with a different letter of the alphabet. This poetic structure, called acrostic, cannot be successfully translated into English. It is found in several poetic sections of the Old Testament, including Psalm 119.

We are not sure why the Lamentation poems were written in this fashion. It may be because the structure made them easier to memorize. Some scholars believe that it may have been a mystical sign of order and completeness. Another possibility is that the poem's structure helped to give form to the people's grief, which is important because uncontrollable grief can keep people from moving on in life. Knowing that the poem had a definite end may have reminded them that their sorrow would also come to an end.

Through these beautiful poems, Israelites were able to grieve and acknowledge the sin that led to their destruction. By recalling their experience of the goodness of God in the past, they were also able to hope for the day when God would lead them back to their land to rebuild their lives in faithfulness to the Covenant.

Quick Facts

Period Covered
the Babylonian Exile, 587–538 B.C.

Authors
unknown

Theme
poems of grief over the destruction of Jerusalem and the hardships of the Exile

The Book of **Lamentations**

Lamentations

The Deserted City

How lonely sits the city
    that once was full of people!
How like a widow she has become,
    she that was great among the nations!
She that was a princess among the provinces
    has become a vassal.

2 She weeps bitterly in the night,
    with tears on her cheeks;
among all her lovers
    she has no one to comfort her;
all her friends have dealt treacherously
        with her,
    they have become her enemies.

3 Judah has gone into exile with suffering
    and hard servitude;
she lives now among the nations,
    and finds no resting place;
her pursuers have all overtaken her
    in the midst of her distress.

4 The roads to Zion mourn,
    for no one comes to the festivals;
all her gates are desolate,
    her priests groan;
her young girls grieve,*a*
    and her lot is bitter.

5 Her foes have become the masters,
    her enemies prosper,
because the LORD has made her suffer
    for the multitude of her transgressions;
her children have gone away,
    captives before the foe.

6 From daughter Zion has departed
    all her majesty.
Her princes have become like stags
    that find no pasture;
they fled without strength
    before the pursuer.

7 Jerusalem remembers,
    in the days of her affliction and
        wandering,
all the precious things
    that were hers in days of old.
When her people fell into the hand of
        the foe,
    and there was no one to help her,
the foe looked on mocking
    over her downfall.

8 Jerusalem sinned grievously,
    so she has become a mockery;
all who honored her despise her,
    for they have seen her nakedness;
she herself groans,
    and turns her face away.

---

a Meaning of Heb uncertain

9 Her uncleanness was in her skirts;
  she took no thought of her future;
her downfall was appalling,
  with none to comfort her.
"O LORD, look at my affliction,
  for the enemy has triumphed!"

10 Enemies have stretched out their hands
  over all her precious things;
she has even seen the nations
  invade her sanctuary,
those whom you forbade
  to enter your congregation.

11 All her people groan
  as they search for bread;
they trade their treasures for food
  to revive their strength.
Look, O LORD, and see
  how worthless I have become.

12 Is it nothing to you,[b] all you who pass by?
  Look and see
if there is any sorrow like my sorrow,
  which was brought upon me,
which the LORD inflicted
  on the day of his fierce anger.

13 From on high he sent fire;
  it went deep into my bones;
he spread a net for my feet;
  he turned me back;
he has left me stunned,
  faint all day long.

14 My transgressions were bound[b] into a yoke;
  by his hand they were fastened together;
they weigh on my neck,
  sapping my strength;
the Lord handed me over
  to those whom I cannot withstand.

15 The LORD has rejected
  all my warriors in the midst of me;
he proclaimed a time against me
  to crush my young men;
the Lord has trodden as in a wine press
  the virgin daughter Judah.

16 For these things I weep;
  my eyes flow with tears;
for a comforter is far from me,
  one to revive my courage;
my children are desolate,
  for the enemy has prevailed.

17 Zion stretches out her hands,
  but there is no one to comfort her;
the LORD has commanded against Jacob
that his neighbors should become his
  foes;
Jerusalem has become
  a filthy thing among them.

18 The LORD is in the right,
  for I have rebelled against his word;
but hear, all you peoples,
  and behold my suffering;
my young women and young men
  have gone into captivity.

19 I called to my lovers
  but they deceived me;
my priests and elders
  perished in the city
while seeking food
  to revive their strength.

20 See, O LORD, how distressed I am;
  my stomach churns,
my heart is wrung within me,
  because I have been very rebellious.
In the street the sword bereaves;
  in the house it is like death.

21 They heard how I was groaning,
  with no one to comfort me.
All my enemies heard of my trouble;
  they are glad that you have done it.
Bring on the day you have announced,
  and let them be as I am.

22 Let all their evil doing come before you;
  and deal with them
as you have dealt with me
  because of all my transgressions;
for my groans are many
  and my heart is faint.

God's Warnings Fulfilled

2 How the Lord in his anger
  has humiliated[b] daughter Zion!
He has thrown down from heaven to earth
  the splendor of Israel;
he has not remembered his footstool
  in the day of his anger.

2 The Lord has destroyed without mercy
  all the dwellings of Jacob;
in his wrath he has broken down
  the strongholds of daughter Judah;
he has brought down to the ground in
  dishonor
  the kingdom and its rulers.

3 He has cut down in fierce anger
  all the might of Israel;

---

b Meaning of Heb uncertain

he has withdrawn his right hand from them
    in the face of the enemy;
he has burned like a flaming fire in Jacob,
    consuming all around.

4 He has bent his bow like an enemy,
    with his right hand set like a foe;
he has killed all in whom we took pride
    in the tent of daughter Zion;
he has poured out his fury like fire.

5 The Lord has become like an enemy;
    he has destroyed Israel.
He has destroyed all its palaces,
    laid in ruins its strongholds,
and multiplied in daughter Judah
    mourning and lamentation.

6 He has broken down his booth like a
      garden,
    he has destroyed his tabernacle;
the LORD has abolished in Zion
    festival and sabbath,
and in his fierce indignation has spurned
    king and priest.

7 The Lord has scorned his altar,
    disowned his sanctuary;
he has delivered into the hand of the enemy
    the walls of her palaces;
a clamor was raised in the house of the
    LORD
    as on a day of festival.

8 The LORD determined to lay in ruins
    the wall of daughter Zion;
he stretched the line;
    he did not withhold his hand from
      destroying;
he caused rampart and wall to lament;
    they languish together.

9 Her gates have sunk into the ground;
    he has ruined and broken her bars;
her king and princes are among the nations;
    guidance is no more,
and her prophets obtain
    no vision from the LORD.

10 The elders of daughter Zion
    sit on the ground in silence;
they have thrown dust on their heads
    and put on sackcloth;
the young girls of Jerusalem
    have bowed their heads to the ground.

11 My eyes are spent with weeping;
    my stomach churns;
my bile is poured out on the ground
    because of the destruction of my people,

because infants and babes faint
    in the streets of the city.

12 They cry to their mothers,
    "Where is bread and wine?"
as they faint like the wounded
    in the streets of the city,
as their life is poured out
    on their mothers' bosom.

13 What can I say for you, to what
      compare you,
    O daughter Jerusalem?
To what can I liken you, that I may
      comfort you,
    O virgin daughter Zion?
For vast as the sea is your ruin;
    who can heal you?

14 Your prophets have seen for you
    false and deceptive visions;
they have not exposed your iniquity
    to restore your fortunes,
but have seen oracles for you
    that are false and misleading.

15 All who pass along the way
    clap their hands at you;
they hiss and wag their heads
    at daughter Jerusalem;
"Is this the city that was called
    the perfection of beauty,
    the joy of all the earth?"

16 All your enemies
    open their mouths against you;
they hiss, they gnash their teeth,
    they cry: "We have devoured her!
Ah, this is the day we longed for;
    at last we have seen it!"

17 The LORD has done what he purposed,
    he has carried out his threat;
as he ordained long ago,
    he has demolished without pity;
he has made the enemy rejoice over you,
    and exalted the might of your foes.

18 Cry aloudc to the Lord!
    O wall of daughter Zion!
Let tears stream down like a torrent
    day and night!
Give yourself no rest,
    your eyes no respite!

19 Arise, cry out in the night,
    at the beginning of the watches!
Pour out your heart like water

---

c Cn: Heb *Their heart cried*

L
A
M

PRAY IT!

Violence in Our City Streets

Verses 12, 19, and 21 of the poem in chapter 2 of Lamentations all mention hunger and violence in the streets. Are things much different in our streets? In our own time, children are hungry, young and old people are being killed, and women and men are being violated. Our voice echoes the voice of this ancient prayer, calling out for God's mercy.

When will the violence stop, Lord?
How many today will die because of drugs and domestic abuse?
How many children will go hungry while society looks on?
Have mercy on your people, Lord!

▸ **Lamentations, chapter 2**

before the presence of the Lord!
Lift your hands to him
      for the lives of your children,
who faint for hunger
      at the head of every street.

20 Look, O LORD, and consider!
      To whom have you done this?
Should women eat their offspring,
      the children they have borne?
Should priest and prophet be killed
      in the sanctuary of the Lord?

21 The young and the old are lying
      on the ground in the streets;
my young women and my young men
      have fallen by the sword;
in the day of your anger you have killed
      them,
      slaughtering without mercy.

22 You invited my enemies from all
      around
      as if for a day of festival;
and on the day of the anger of the LORD
      no one escaped or survived;
those whom I bore and reared
      my enemy has destroyed.

God's Steadfast Love Endures

I am one who has seen affliction
      under the rod of God's *d* wrath;
2 he has driven and brought me
      into darkness without any light;
3 against me alone he turns his hand,
      again and again, all day long.

4 He has made my flesh and my skin waste
      away,
      and broken my bones;
5 he has besieged and enveloped me
      with bitterness and tribulation;
6 he has made me sit in darkness
      like the dead of long ago.

7 He has walled me about so that I cannot
      escape;
      he has put heavy chains on me;
8 though I call and cry for help,
      he shuts out my prayer;
9 he has blocked my ways with hewn stones,
      he has made my paths crooked.

10 He is a bear lying in wait for me,
      a lion in hiding;
11 he led me off my way and tore me to
      pieces;
      he has made me desolate;
12 he bent his bow and set me
      as a mark for his arrow.

13 He shot into my vitals
      the arrows of his quiver;
14 I have become the laughingstock of all my
      people,
      the object of their taunt-songs all day
      long.
15 He has filled me with bitterness,
      he has sated me with wormwood.

16 He has made my teeth grind on gravel,
      and made me cower in ashes;
17 my soul is bereft of peace;
      I have forgotten what happiness is;
18 so I say, "Gone is my glory,
      and all that I had hoped for from the
      LORD."

19 The thought of my affliction and my
      homelessness
      is wormwood and gall!
20 My soul continually thinks of it
      and is bowed down within me.
21 But this I call to mind,
      and therefore I have hope:

---

d Heb *his*

²² The steadfast love of the LORD never ceases,^e
　　　　his mercies never come to an end;
²³ they are new every morning;
　　　　great is your faithfulness.
²⁴ "The LORD is my portion," says my soul,
　　　　"therefore I will hope in him."

²⁵ The LORD is good to those who wait for him,
　　　　to the soul that seeks him.
²⁶ It is good that one should wait quietly
　　　　for the salvation of the LORD.

³⁹ Why should any who draw breath
　　　　complain
　　　　about the punishment of their sins?

⁴⁰ Let us test and examine our ways,
　　　　and return to the LORD.
⁴¹ Let us lift up our hearts as well as our
　　　　hands
　　　　to God in heaven.
⁴² We have transgressed and rebelled,
　　　　and you have not forgiven.

Each New Day

The poems in Lamentations also have their hopeful side. They acknowledge that God's love never ceases (3.22) and that the Israelites will not experience God's rejection forever (verse 31). Verse 23 reminds the people that God's love is there each new day.

Imagine that at the beginning of each day, you are given $86,400. You have the whole day to spend every last penny any way you want. Does that sound exciting? Well, God gives you 86,400 seconds every day to use however you like. Try making a one-day budget of the best ways to spend your 86,400 seconds. Remember, each day is a new gift filled with God's love. Make the most of it, and do so for God!

▶ Lam 3.22–26

²⁷ It is good for one to bear
　　　　the yoke in youth,
²⁸ to sit alone in silence
　　　　when the Lord has imposed it,
²⁹ to put one's mouth to the dust
　　　　(there may yet be hope),
³⁰ to give one's cheek to the smiter,
　　　　and be filled with insults.

³¹ For the Lord will not
　　　　reject forever.
³² Although he causes grief, he will have
　　　　compassion
　　　　according to the abundance of his
　　　　steadfast love;
³³ for he does not willingly afflict
　　　　or grieve anyone.

³⁴ When all the prisoners of the land
　　　　are crushed under foot,
³⁵ when human rights are perverted
　　　　in the presence of the Most High,
³⁶ when one's case is subverted
　　　　—does the Lord not see it?

³⁷ Who can command and have it done,
　　　　if the Lord has not ordained it?
³⁸ Is it not from the mouth of the Most High
　　　　that good and bad come?

⁴³ You have wrapped yourself with anger and
　　　　pursued us,
　　　　killing without pity;
⁴⁴ you have wrapped yourself with a cloud
　　　　so that no prayer can pass through.
⁴⁵ You have made us filth and rubbish
　　　　among the peoples.

⁴⁶ All our enemies
　　　　have opened their mouths against us;
⁴⁷ panic and pitfall have come upon us,
　　　　devastation and destruction.
⁴⁸ My eyes flow with rivers of tears
　　　　because of the destruction of my people.

⁴⁹ My eyes will flow without ceasing,
　　　　without respite,
⁵⁰ until the LORD from heaven
　　　　looks down and sees.
⁵¹ My eyes cause me grief
　　　　at the fate of all the young women in my
　　　　city.

⁵² Those who were my enemies without cause
　　　　have hunted me like a bird;
⁵³ they flung me alive into a pit
　　　　and hurled stones on me;

^e Syr Tg: Heb LORD, we are not cut off

54 water closed over my head;
    I said, "I am lost."

55 I called on your name, O LORD,
    from the depths of the pit;
56 you heard my plea, "Do not close your ear
    to my cry for help, but give me relief!"
57 You came near when I called on you;
    you said, "Do not fear!"

58 You have taken up my cause, O Lord,
    you have redeemed my life.
59 You have seen the wrong done to me,
        O LORD;
    judge my cause.
60 You have seen all their malice,
    all their plots against me.

61 You have heard their taunts, O LORD,
    all their plots against me.
62 The whispers and murmurs of my assailants
    are against me all day long.
63 Whether they sit or rise—see,
    I am the object of their taunt-songs.

64 Pay them back for their deeds, O LORD,
    according to the work of their hands!
65 Give them anguish of heart;
    your curse be on them!
66 Pursue them in anger and destroy them
    from under the LORD's heavens.

The Punishment of Zion

How the gold has grown dim,
    how the pure gold is changed!
The sacred stones lie scattered
    at the head of every street.

2 The precious children of Zion,
    worth their weight in fine gold—
how they are reckoned as earthen pots,
    the work of a potter's hands!

3 Even the jackals offer the breast
    and nurse their young,
but my people has become cruel,
    like the ostriches in the wilderness.

4 The tongue of the infant sticks
    to the roof of its mouth for thirst;
the children beg for food,
    but no one gives them anything.

5 Those who feasted on delicacies
    perish in the streets;
those who were brought up in purple
    cling to ash heaps.

6 For the chastisement[f] of my people has
    been greater

than the punishment[g] of Sod'om,
    which was overthrown in a moment,
    though no hand was laid on it.[h]

7 Her princes were purer than snow,
    whiter than milk;
their bodies were more ruddy than coral,
    their hair[h] like sapphire.[i]

8 Now their visage is blacker than soot;
    they are not recognized in the streets.
Their skin has shriveled on their bones;
    it has become as dry as wood.

9 Happier were those pierced by the sword
    than those pierced by hunger,
whose life drains away, deprived
    of the produce of the field.

10 The hands of compassionate women
    have boiled their own children;
they became their food
    in the destruction of my people.

11 The LORD gave full vent to his wrath;
    he poured out his hot anger,
and kindled a fire in Zion
    that consumed its foundations.

12 The kings of the earth did not believe,
    nor did any of the inhabitants of the
        world,
that foe or enemy could enter
    the gates of Jerusalem.

13 It was for the sins of her prophets
    and the iniquities of her priests,
who shed the blood of the righteous
    in the midst of her.

14 Blindly they wandered through the streets,
    so defiled with blood
that no one was able
    to touch their garments.

15 "Away! Unclean!" people shouted at them;
    "Away! Away! Do not touch!"
So they became fugitives and wanderers;
    it was said among the nations,
    "They shall stay here no longer."

16 The LORD himself has scattered them,
    he will regard them no more;
no honor was shown to the priests,
    no favor to the elders.

17 Our eyes failed, ever watching
    vainly for help;

---

f Or *iniquity*   g Or *sin*   h Meaning of Heb uncertain
i Or *lapis lazuli*

L
A
M

we were watching eagerly
    for a nation that could not save.

18 They dogged our steps
    so that we could not walk in our streets;
our end drew near; our days were
      numbered;
    for our end had come.

19 Our pursuers were swifter
    than the eagles in the heavens;
they chased us on the mountains,
    they lay in wait for us in the wilderness.

20 The LORD's anointed, the breath of our life,
    was taken in their pits—
the one of whom we said, "Under his
      shadow
    we shall live among the nations."

21 Rejoice and be glad, O daughter Ē'dom,
    you that live in the land of Uz;
but to you also the cup shall pass;
    you shall become drunk and strip
      yourself bare.

22 The punishment of your iniquity,
    O daughter Zion, is accomplished,
he will keep you in exile no longer;
    but your iniquity, O daughter Ē'dom, he
      will punish,
he will uncover your sins.

A Plea for Mercy

Remember, O LORD, what has befallen us;
    look, and see our disgrace!
2 Our inheritance has been turned over to
      strangers,
    our homes to aliens.

3 We have become orphans, fatherless;
    our mothers are like widows.
4 We must pay for the water we drink;
    the wood we get must be bought.
5 With a yoke ^{j} on our necks we are hard
      driven;
    we are weary, we are given no rest.
6 We have made a pact with ^{k} Egypt and
      Assyria,
    to get enough bread.
7 Our ancestors sinned; they are no more,
    and we bear their iniquities.
8 Slaves rule over us;
    there is no one to deliver us from their
      hand.
9 We get our bread at the peril of our lives,
    because of the sword in the wilderness.
10 Our skin is black as an oven
    from the scorching heat of famine.
11 Women are raped in Zion,
    virgins in the towns of Judah.
12 Princes are hung up by their hands;
    no respect is shown to the elders.
13 Young men are compelled to grind,
    and boys stagger under loads of wood.
14 The old men have left the city gate,
    the young men their music.
15 The joy of our hearts has ceased;
    our dancing has been turned
      to mourning.
16 The crown has fallen from our head;
    woe to us, for we have sinned!
17 Because of this our hearts are sick,

---

j Symmachus: Heb lacks *With a yoke*   *k* Heb *have given
the hand to*

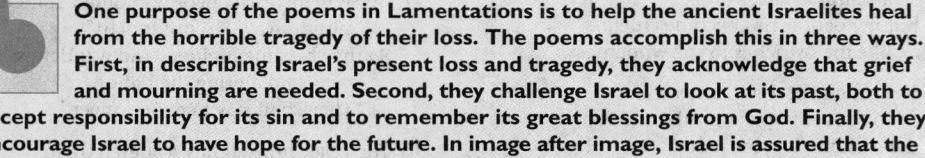

Growing Through Loss

One purpose of the poems in Lamentations is to help the ancient Israelites heal from the horrible tragedy of their loss. The poems accomplish this in three ways. First, in describing Israel's present loss and tragedy, they acknowledge that grief and mourning are needed. Second, they challenge Israel to look at its past, both to accept responsibility for its sin and to remember its great blessings from God. Finally, they encourage Israel to have hope for the future. In image after image, Israel is assured that the door to God's mercy is still open, in spite of great pain and loss.

So too must we allow ourselves to grieve when we have experienced the loss of someone we love. If we wall up our grief—and perhaps our guilt, because guilt often accompanies such a loss—we may at the same time shut out those who can help us heal. We must also reclaim our memories of the person we lost, celebrating those of good times and healing those of hurtful times. Finally, as difficult as it may seem, we must open ourselves to the future, for God's love continues to be there for us, calling us to new life.

because of these things our eyes have
grown dim:

18 because of Mount Zion, which lies desolate;
jackals prowl over it.

19 But you, O LORD, reign forever;
your throne endures to all generations.

20 Why have you forgotten us completely?

Why have you forsaken us these many
days?

21 Restore us to yourself, O LORD, that we may
be restored;
renew our days as of old—

22 unless you have utterly rejected us,
and are angry with us beyond
measure.

L
A
M

Perhaps you've seen them on the television news—long lines of refugees leaving war-torn countries. Or the camps where they set up temporary homes, waiting to return to their homeland. The sad truth is many of them can never return home. They are faced with the difficult task of building new homes in a foreign land. The Book of Baruch was written in such a situation—after many Israelites were forced to relocate following the Babylonian invasion in 587 B.C.

At a Glance

- **1.1—3.8.** an introduction and a penitential prayer
- **3.9—4.4.** a poem on wisdom
- **4.5—5.9.** words of comfort for believers
- **Chapter 6.** a letter from Jeremiah against idolatry

In-depth

In the ancient world, it was not uncommon for people to write books and letters in the name of famous ancestors or historical figures. Several Old and New Testament books, including Baruch, were written in this manner. An anonymous person collected a variety of independent writings and named them for Baruch, the famous secretary of the prophet Jeremiah, in order to emphasize their link with Jeremiah's tradition of prophecy.

The short Book of Baruch recalls the Babylonian conquest of Jerusalem in the sixth century B.C. In doing so, it points out these lessons to be learned from the painful past:

- We do not gain anything when we sin. Instead, we invite suffering into our life.
- No matter how difficult life gets, we can always rely on God's goodness.
- Believers can always approach God in prayer, even when their situation seems impossibly painful.
- The traditions we have inherited from our ancestors are a reliable guide in facing life's challenges.
- We should resist all cultural pressures to act in violation of God's will.

The core truth Baruch addresses is that no matter where they are, God's people can lead a happy and holy life by admitting their sinfulness and committing themselves to the Lord. This is an important lesson for all believers to learn. Unless we learn from history, we will repeat its mistakes.

Quick Facts

Period Covered
after the Babylonian Exile, probably 500–300 B.C.

Author
an unknown compiler who attributed the book to Baruch, Jeremiah's secretary

Theme
Even in foreign lands, God's people can live a faithful life and find hope in God's promises.

Of Note
Baruch is not found in every translation of the Old Testament (see "The Case of the Missing Books" near Tob 1.16).

The Book of Baruch

Baruch

Chap. 6

Baruch and the Jews in Babylon
(Cp 2 Kings 24.8–17; Ezra 1.7–11; Jer 36.4)

These are the words of the book that Bar′uch son of Ne·rī′ah son of Mah′sēi·ah son of Zed·e·kī′ah son of Has·a·dī′ah son of Hil·kī′ah wrote in Babylon, 2 in the fifth year, on the seventh day of the month, at the time when the Chal·dē′ans took Jerusalem and burned it with fire.

3 Bar′uch read the words of this book to Jec·o·nī′ah son of Je·hoi′a·kim, king of Judah, and to all the people who came to hear the book, 4 and to the nobles and the princes, and to the elders, and to all the people, small and great, all who lived in Babylon by the river Sud.

5 Then they wept, and fasted, and prayed before the Lord; 6 they collected as much money as each could give, 7 and sent it to Jerusalem to the high priest[a] Je·hoi′a·kim son of Hil·kī′ah son of Shal′lum, and to the priests, and to all the people who were present with him in Jerusalem. 8 At the same time, on the tenth day of Sī′van, Bar′uch[b] took the vessels of the house of the Lord, which had been carried away from the temple, to return them to the land of Judah—the silver vessels that Zed·e·kī′ah son of Jō·sī′ah, king of Judah, had made, 9 after King Ne·bū·chad·nez′zar of Babylon had carried away from Jerusalem Jec·o·nī′ah and the princes and the prisoners and the nobles and the people of the land, and brought them to Babylon.

A Letter to Jerusalem

10 They said: Here we send you money; so buy with the money burnt offerings and sin offerings and incense, and prepare a grain offering, and offer them on the altar of the Lord our God; 11 and pray for the life of King Ne·bū·chad·nez′zar of Babylon, and for the life of his son Bel·shaz′zar, so that their days on earth may be like the days of heaven. 12 The Lord will give us strength, and light to our eyes; we shall live under the protection[c] of King Ne·bū·chad·nez′zar of Babylon, and under the protection of his son Bel·shaz′zar, and we shall serve them many days and find favor in their sight. 13 Pray also for us to the Lord our God, for we have sinned against the Lord our God, and to this day the anger of the Lord and his wrath have not turned away from us. 14 And you shall read aloud this scroll that we are sending you, to make your confession in the house of the Lord on the days of the festivals and at appointed seasons.

Confession of Sins
(Cp Deut 28.15–68; Jer 11.3–5)

15 And you shall say: The Lord our God is in the right, but there is open shame on us today, on the people of Judah, on the inhabitants of Jerusalem, 16 and on our kings, our rulers, our priests, our prophets, and our ancestors, 17 because we

---

a Gk *the priest*　　*b* Gk *he*　　*c* Gk *in the shadow*

have sinned before the Lord. 18 We have disobeyed him, and have not heeded the voice of the Lord our God, to walk in the statutes of the Lord that he set before us. 19 From the time when the Lord brought our ancestors out of the land of Egypt until today, we have been disobedient to the Lord our God, and we have been negligent, in not heeding his voice. 20 So to this day there have clung to us the calamities and the curse that the Lord declared through his servant Moses at the time when he brought our ancestors out of the land of Egypt to give to us a land flowing with milk and honey. 21 We did not listen to the voice of the Lord our God in all the words of the prophets whom he sent to us, 22 but all of us followed the intent of our own wicked hearts by serving other gods and doing what is evil in the sight of the Lord our God.

So the Lord carried out the threat he spoke against us: against our judges who ruled Israel, and against our kings and our rulers and the people of Israel and Judah. 2 Under the whole heaven there has not been done the like of what he has done in Jerusalem, in accordance with the threats that were*d* written in the law of Moses. 3 Some of us ate the flesh of their sons and others the flesh of their daughters. 4 He made them subject to all the kingdoms around us, to be an object of scorn and a desolation among all the surrounding peoples, where the Lord has scattered them. 5 They were brought down and not raised up, because our nation*e* sinned against the Lord our God, in not heeding his voice.

6 The Lord our God is in the right, but there is open shame on us and our ancestors this very day. 7 All those calamities with which the Lord threatened us have come upon us. 8 Yet we have not entreated the favor of the Lord by turning away, each of us, from the thoughts of our wicked hearts. 9 And the Lord has kept the calamities ready, and the Lord has brought them upon us, for the Lord is just in all the works that he has commanded us to do. 10 Yet we have not obeyed his voice, to walk in the statutes of the Lord that he set before us.

Prayer for Deliverance
(Cp Dan 9.15–17)

11 And now, O Lord God of Israel, who brought your people out of the land of Egypt with a mighty hand and with signs and wonders and with great power and outstretched arm, and made yourself a name that continues to this day, 12 we have sinned, we have been ungodly, we have done wrong, O Lord our God, against all your ordinances. 13 Let your anger turn away from us, for we are left, few in number, among the nations where

you have scattered us. 14 Hear, O Lord, our prayer and our supplication, and for your own sake deliver us, and grant us favor in the sight of those who have carried us into exile; 15 so that all the earth may know that you are the Lord our God, for Israel and his descendants are called by your name.

16 O Lord, look down from your holy dwelling, and consider us. Incline your ear, O Lord, and hear; 17 open your eyes, O Lord, and see, for the dead who are in Hades, whose spirit has been taken from their bodies, will not ascribe glory or justice to the Lord; 18 but the person who is deeply grieved, who walks bowed and feeble, with failing eyes and famished soul, will declare your glory and righteousness, O Lord.

19 For it is not because of any righteous deeds of our ancestors or our kings that we bring before you our prayer for mercy, O Lord our God. 20 For you have sent your anger and your wrath upon us, as you declared by your servants the prophets, saying: 21 Thus says the Lord: Bend your shoulders and serve the king of Babylon, and you will remain in the land that I gave to your ancestors. 22 But if you will not obey the voice of the Lord and will not serve the king of Babylon, 23 I will make to cease from the towns of Judah and from the region around Jerusalem the voice of mirth and the voice of gladness, the voice of the bridegroom and the voice of the bride, and the whole land will be a desolation without inhabitants.

24 But we did not obey your voice, to serve the king of Babylon; and you have carried out your threats, which you spoke by your servants the prophets, that the bones of our kings and the bones of our ancestors would be brought out of their resting place; 25 and indeed they have been thrown out to the heat of day and the frost of night. They perished in great misery, by famine and sword and pestilence. 26 And the house that is called by your name you have made as it is today, because of the wickedness of the house of Israel and the house of Judah.

God's Promise Recalled
(Deut 28.58–62; Cp Jer 32.38–40)

27 Yet you have dealt with us, O Lord our God, in all your kindness and in all your great compassion, 28 as you spoke by your servant Moses on the day when you commanded him to write your law in the presence of the people of Israel, saying, 29 "If you will not obey my voice, this very great multitude will surely turn into a small number among the nations, where I will scatter them.

---

d Gk *in accordance with what is*   *e* Gk *because we*

30 For I know that they will not obey me, for they are a stiff-necked people. But in the land of their exile they will come to themselves 31 and know that I am the Lord their God. I will give them a heart that obeys and ears that hear; 32 they will praise me in the land of their exile, and will remember my name 33 and turn from their stubbornness and their wicked deeds; for they will remember the ways of their ancestors, who sinned before the Lord. 34 I will bring them again into the land that I swore to give to their ancestors, to Abraham, Isaac, and Jacob, and they will rule over it; and I will increase them, and they will not be diminished. 35 I will make an everlasting covenant with them to be their God and they shall be my people; and I will never again remove my people Israel from the land that I have given them."

O Lord Almighty, God of Israel, the soul in anguish and the wearied spirit cry out to you. 2 Hear, O Lord, and have mercy, for we have sinned before you. 3 For you are enthroned forever, and we are perishing forever. 4 O Lord Almighty, God of Israel, hear now the prayer of the people*f* of Israel, the children of those who sinned before you, who did not heed the voice of the Lord their God, so that calamities have clung to us. 5 Do not remember the iniquities of our ancestors, but in this crisis remember your power and your name. 6 For you are the Lord our God, and it is you, O Lord, whom we will praise. 7 For you have put the fear of you in our hearts so that we would call upon your name; and we will praise you in our exile, for we have put away from our hearts all the iniquity of our ancestors who sinned against you. 8 See, we are today in our exile where you have scattered us, to be reproached and cursed and punished for all the iniquities of our ancestors, who forsook the Lord our God.

In Praise of Wisdom
(Cp Job 28.23–28; Prov 8.22–31; Sir 24.1–22)

9 Hear the commandments of life, O Israel;
      give ear, and learn wisdom!
10 Why is it, O Israel, why is it that you are in
         the land of your enemies,
      that you are growing old in a foreign
         country,
      that you are defiled with the dead,
11   that you are counted among those in
         Hades?
12 You have forsaken the fountain of wisdom.
13 If you had walked in the way of God,
      you would be living in peace forever.
14 Learn where there is wisdom,
      where there is strength,
      where there is understanding,

so that you may at the same time discern
      where there is length of days, and life,
      where there is light for the eyes, and
         peace.

15 Who has found her place?
      And who has entered her storehouses?
16 Where are the rulers of the nations,
      and those who lorded it over the animals
         on earth;
17 those who made sport of the birds of
         the air,
      and who hoarded up silver and gold
in which people trust,
      and there is no end to their getting;
18 those who schemed to get silver, and were
         anxious,
      but there is no trace of their works?
19 They have vanished and gone down to
         Hades,
      and others have arisen in their place.

20 Later generations have seen the light of day,
      and have lived upon the earth;
but they have not learned the way to
         knowledge,
      nor understood her paths,
      nor laid hold of her.
21 Their descendants have strayed far from
         her*g* way.
22 She has not been heard of in Cā'naan,
      or seen in Tē'man;
23 the descendants of Hā'gar, who seek for
         understanding on the earth,
      the merchants of Mer'ran and Tē'man,
      the story-tellers and the seekers for
         understanding,
have not learned the way to wisdom,
      or given thought to her paths.

24 O Israel, how great is the house of God,
      how vast the territory that he possesses!
25 It is great and has no bounds;
      it is high and immeasurable.
26 The giants were born there, who were
         famous of old,
      great in stature, expert in war.
27 God did not choose them,
      or give them the way to knowledge;
28 so they perished because they had no
         wisdom,
      they perished through their folly.

29 Who has gone up into heaven, and
         taken her,
      and brought her down from the clouds?

---

f Gk *dead*   *g* Other ancient authorities read *their*

The House of God

It is a warm, clear summer night. You and a good friend are sitting outside talking about the struggles both of you have been having with parents. Suddenly, you see a shooting star. Both of you spend a few moments gazing at the sky and marveling at how many stars there are and how clear the night is. The problems you were just discussing seem to pale in significance next to the vastness of the universe. And you realize that the two of you are seeing only one corner of the universe, "the house of God" (Bar 3.24). You both feel a connection with the stars and the sky and with the God who created it all.

The author of Bar 3.24–34 seems to be having a similar moment. This writer describes God's wisdom as immense (verse 25) and beyond any person's grasp (verse 29), but given to Israel for salvation (verse 36). The author is saying: "Be at ease. God is bigger than your problems and in control."

When struggling with life's problems, recall the beauty of the night sky in order to put them in perspective. Spend a few moments gazing at the stars and remember who's really in control.

▶ Bar 3.24–34

---

30 Who has gone over the sea, and found her,
 and will buy her for pure gold?
31 No one knows the way to her,
 or is concerned about the path to her.
32 But the one who knows all things
  knows her,
 he found her by his understanding.
The one who prepared the earth for all time
 filled it with four-footed creatures;
33 the one who sends forth the light, and it
  goes;
 he called it, and it obeyed him,
  trembling;
34 the stars shone in their watches, and were
  glad;
 he called them, and they said, "Here
  we are!"
They shone with gladness for him who
  made them.
35 This is our God;
 no other can be compared to him.
36 He found the whole way to knowledge,
 and gave her to his servant Jacob
 and to Israel, whom he loved.
37 Afterward she appeared on earth
 and lived with humankind.

She is the book of the commandments
 of God,
 the law that endures forever.
All who hold her fast will live,
 and those who forsake her will die.
2 Turn, O Jacob, and take her;

walk toward the shining of her light.
3 Do not give your glory to another,
 or your advantages to an alien people.
4 Happy are we, O Israel,
 for we know what is pleasing to God.

Encouragement for Israel

5 Take courage, my people,
 who perpetuate Israel's name!
6 It was not for destruction
 that you were sold to the nations,
but you were handed over to your enemies
 because you angered God.
7 For you provoked the one who made you
 by sacrificing to demons and not to God.
8 You forgot the everlasting God, who
  brought you up,
 and you grieved Jerusalem, who
  reared you.
9 For she saw the wrath that came upon you
  from God,
 and she said:
Listen, you neighbors of Zion,
 God has brought great sorrow upon me;
10 for I have seen the exile of my sons and
  daughters,
 which the Everlasting brought upon
  them.
11 With joy I nurtured them,
 but I sent them away with weeping and
  sorrow.
12 Let no one rejoice over me, a widow
 and bereaved of many;

BAR

I was left desolate because of the sins of my
children,
    because they turned away from the law
    of God.
13 They had no regard for his statutes;
    they did not walk in the ways of God's
    commandments,
    or tread the paths his righteousness
    showed them.
14 Let the neighbors of Zion come;
    remember the capture of my sons and
    daughters,
    which the Everlasting brought upon
    them.
15 For he brought a distant nation against
    them,
    a nation ruthless and of a strange
    language,
    which had no respect for the aged
    and no pity for a child.
16 They led away the widow's beloved sons,
    and bereaved the lonely woman of her
    daughters.

22 For I have put my hope in the Everlasting to
    save you,
    and joy has come to me from the Holy One,
    because of the mercy that will soon come
    to you
    from your everlasting savior.*h*
23 For I sent you out with sorrow and weeping,
    but God will give you back to me with
    joy and gladness forever.
24 For as the neighbors of Zion have now seen
    your capture,
    so they soon will see your salvation by God,
    which will come to you with great glory
    and with the splendor of the Everlasting.
25 My children, endure with patience the wrath
    that has come upon you from God.
Your enemy has overtaken you,
    but you will soon see their destruction
    and will tread upon their necks.
26 My pampered children have traveled rough
    roads;
    they were taken away like a flock carried
    off by the enemy.

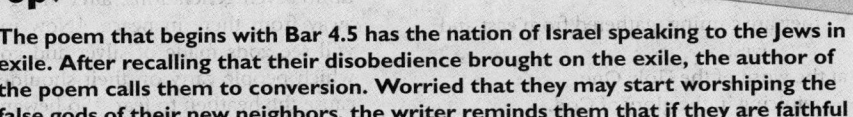

Stand Up!

LIVE IT!

The poem that begins with Bar 4.5 has the nation of Israel speaking to the Jews in
exile. After recalling that their disobedience brought on the exile, the author of
the poem calls them to conversion. Worried that they may start worshiping the
false gods of their new neighbors, the writer reminds them that if they are faithful
to God, God will not abandon them.
    It can be said that as Christians, we too live in a culture that is in some ways foreign
to our values and beliefs. How easy is it to stand up against the pressures of peers, media
values, and social standards that go against Christian values and beliefs? Are you confident
enough to do what's right if others do not?

▸ Bar 4.17–19

17 But I, how can I help you?
18 For he who brought these calamities
    upon you
    will deliver you from the hand of your
    enemies.
19 Go, my children, go;
    for I have been left desolate.
20 I have taken off the robe of peace
    and put on sackcloth for my supplication;
    I will cry to the Everlasting all my days.

21 Take courage, my children, cry to God,
    and he will deliver you from the power
    and hand of the enemy.

27 Take courage, my children,
    and cry to God,
    for you will be remembered by the one
    who brought this upon you.
28 For just as you were disposed to go astray
    from God,
    return with tenfold zeal to seek him.
29 For the one who brought these calamities
    upon you
    will bring you everlasting joy with your
    salvation.

---

h Or *from the Everlasting, your savior*

Jerusalem Is Assured of Help
(Cp Isa 52.1–10)

30 Take courage, O Jerusalem,
   for the one who named you will
     comfort you.
31 Wretched will be those who mistreated you
   and who rejoiced at your fall.
32 Wretched will be the cities that your
     children served as slaves;
   wretched will be the city that received
     your offspring.
33 For just as she rejoiced at your fall
   and was glad for your ruin,
   so she will be grieved at her own
     desolation.
34 I will take away her pride in her great
     population,
   and her insolence will be turned to grief.
35 For fire will come upon her from the
     Everlasting for many days,
   and for a long time she will be inhabited
     by demons.

36 Look toward the east, O Jerusalem,
   and see the joy that is coming to you
     from God.
37 Look, your children are coming, whom you
     sent away;
   they are coming, gathered from east and
     west,
   at the word of the Holy One,
   rejoicing in the glory of God.

5 Take off the garment of your sorrow and
     affliction, O Jerusalem,
   and put on forever the beauty of the
     glory from God.
2 Put on the robe of the righteousness that
     comes from God;
   put on your head the diadem of the glory
     of the Everlasting;
3 for God will show your splendor everywhere
     under heaven.
4 For God will give you evermore the name,
     "Righteous Peace, Godly Glory."

5 Arise, O Jerusalem, stand upon the height;
   look toward the east,
   and see your children gathered from west
     and east
   at the word of the Holy One,
   rejoicing that God has remembered them.
6 For they went out from you on foot,
   led away by their enemies;
   but God will bring them back to you,
   carried in glory, as on a royal throne.

7 For God has ordered that every high
     mountain and the everlasting hills
     be made low
   and the valleys filled up, to make level
     ground,
   so that Israel may walk safely in the glory
     of God.
8 The woods and every fragrant tree
   have shaded Israel at God's command.
9 For God will lead Israel with joy,
   in the light of his glory,
   with the mercy and righteousness that
     come from him.

The Letter of Jeremiah

[i] A copy of a letter that Jer·e·mi'ah sent to those
6 who were to be taken to Babylon as exiles by the
king of the Babylonians, to give them the message
that God had commanded him.

The People Face a Long Captivity
(Cp Jer 29.1–23)

2 Because of the sins that you have committed
before God, you will be taken to Babylon as exiles
by Ne·bu·chad·nez'zar, king of the Babylonians.
3 Therefore when you have come to Babylon you
will remain there for many years, for a long time,
up to seven generations; after that I will bring you
away from there in peace. 4 Now in Babylon you
will see gods made of silver and gold and wood,
which people carry on their shoulders, and which
cause the heathen to fear. 5 So beware of becoming
at all like the foreigners or of letting fear for these
gods[j] possess you 6 when you see the multitude
before and behind them worshiping them. But say
in your heart, "It is you, O Lord, whom we must
worship." 7 For my angel is with you, and he is
watching over your lives.

The Helplessness of Idols

8 Their tongues are smoothed by the carpenter,
and they themselves are overlaid with gold and
silver; but they are false and cannot speak. 9 People[k] take gold and make crowns for the heads of
their gods, as they might for a girl who loves ornaments. 10 Sometimes the priests secretly take gold
and silver from their gods and spend it on themselves, 11 or even give some of it to the prostitutes
on the terrace. They deck their gods[l] out with garments like human beings—these gods of silver and

---

[i] The King James Version (like the Latin Vulgate) prints
The Letter of Jeremiah as Chapter 6 of the Book of
Baruch, and the chapter and verse numbers are here
retained. In the Greek Septuagint, the Letter is separated
from Baruch by the Book of Lamentations.
[j] Gk *for them*   [k] Gk *They*   [l] Gk *them*

PRAY IT!

Lucky Charms?

The whole sixth chapter of Baruch points out the foolishness of people who worship statues of gods and goddesses. Some ancient peoples felt these images gave them luck or fertility or health. The author of this chapter is warning, "Just because you are in a foreign land, don't take up silly superstitions!"

Sometimes, modern people like to carry a special lucky charm in the belief that it will protect them or bring them good luck. Do you carry a rabbit's foot, wear a special piece of clothing for big events, or use some other good luck charm? If so, why?

Dear Lord, sometimes, when I feel like I can use every bit of luck I can get, a "lucky" object can be a comfort. Help me to remember, though, the true power over my life that comes from you.

▸ Baruch, chapter 6

gold and wood [12] that cannot save themselves from rust and corrosion. When they have been dressed in purple robes, [13] their faces are wiped because of the dust from the temple, which is thick upon them. [14] One of them holds a scepter, like a district judge, but is unable to destroy anyone who offends it. [15] Another has a dagger in its right hand, and an ax, but cannot defend itself from war and robbers. [16] From this it is evident that they are not gods; so do not fear them.

17 For just as someone's dish is useless when it is broken, [18] so are their gods when they have been set up in the temples. Their eyes are full of the dust raised by the feet of those who enter. And just as the gates are shut on every side against anyone who has offended a king, as though under sentence of death, so the priests make their temples secure with doors and locks and bars, in order that they may not be plundered by robbers. [19] They light more lamps for them than they light for themselves, though their gods[m] can see none of them. [20] They are[n] just like a beam of the temple, but their hearts, it is said, are eaten away when crawling creatures from the earth devour them and their robes. They do not notice [21] when their faces have been blackened by the smoke of the temple.

[22] Bats, swallows, and birds alight on their bodies and heads; and so do cats. [23] From this you will know that they are not gods; so do not fear them.

24 As for the gold that they wear for beauty— it[o] will not shine unless someone wipes off the tarnish; for even when they were being cast, they did not feel it. [25] They are bought without regard to cost, but there is no breath in them. [26] Having no feet, they are carried on the shoulders of others, revealing to humankind their worthlessness. And those who serve them are put to shame [27] because, if any of these gods falls[p] to the ground, they themselves must pick it up. If anyone sets it upright, it cannot move itself; and if it is tipped over, it cannot straighten itself. Gifts are placed before them just as before the dead. [28] The priests sell the sacrifices that are offered to these gods[q] and use the money themselves. Likewise their wives preserve some of the meat[r] with salt, but give none to the poor or helpless. [29] Sacrifices to them may even be touched by women in their periods or at childbirth. Since you know by these things that they are not gods, do not fear them.

30 For how can they be called gods? Women serve meals for gods of silver and gold and wood; [31] and in their temples the priests sit with their clothes torn, their heads and beards shaved, and their heads uncovered. [32] They howl and shout before their gods as some do at a funeral banquet. [33] The priests take some of the clothing of their gods[s] to clothe their wives and children. [34] Whether one does evil to them or good, they will not be able to repay it. They cannot set up a king or depose one. [35] Likewise they are not able to give either wealth or money; if one makes a vow to them and does not keep it, they will not require it. [36] They cannot save anyone from death or rescue the weak from the strong. [37] They cannot restore sight to the blind; they cannot rescue one who is in distress. [38] They cannot take pity on a widow or do good to an orphan. [39] These things that are made of wood and overlaid with gold and silver are like stones from the mountain, and those who serve them will be put to shame. [40] Why then must anyone think that they are gods, or call them gods?

The Foolishness of Worshiping Idols
(Cp Isa 46.1–13)

Besides, even the Chal·dē′ans themselves dishonor them; for when they see someone who cannot speak, they bring Bel and pray that the mute

---

[m] Gk *they*   [n] Gk *It is*   [o] Lat Syr: Gk *they*   [p] Gk *if they fall*   [q] Gk *to them*   [r] Gk *of them*   [s] Gk *some of their clothing*

may speak, as though Bel[t] were able to under-stand! [41] Yet they themselves cannot perceive this and abandon them, for they have no sense. [42] And the women, with cords around them, sit along the passageways, burning bran for incense. [43] When one of them is led off by one of the passers-by and is taken to bed by him, she derides the woman next to her, because she was not as attractive as herself and her cord was not broken. [44] Whatever is done for these idols[u] is false. Why then must any-one think that they are gods, or call them gods?

[45] They are made by carpenters and gold-smiths; they can be nothing but what the artisans wish them to be. [46] Those who make them will certainly not live very long themselves; [47] how then can the things that are made by them be gods? They have left only lies and reproach for those who come after. [48] For when war or calamity comes upon them, the priests consult together as to where they can hide themselves and their gods.[u] [49] How then can one fail to see that these are not gods, for they cannot save themselves from war or calamity? [50] Since they are made of wood and overlaid with gold and silver, it will afterward be known that they are false. [51] It will be manifest to all the nations and kings that they are not gods but the work of human hands, and that there is no work of God in them. [52] Who then can fail to know that they are not gods?[v]

[53] For they cannot set up a king over a country or give rain to people. [54] They cannot judge their own cause or deliver one who is wronged, for they have no power; [55] they are like crows between heaven and earth. When fire breaks out in a tem-ple of wooden gods overlaid with gold or silver, their priests will flee and escape, but the gods[w] will be burned up like timbers. [56] Besides, they can of-fer no resistance to king or enemy. Why then must anyone admit or think that they are gods?

[57] Gods made of wood and overlaid with sil-ver and gold are unable to save themselves from thieves or robbers. [58] Anyone who can will strip them of their gold and silver and of the robes they wear, and go off with this booty, and they will not

be able to help themselves. [59] So it is better to be a king who shows his courage, or a household uten-sil that serves its owner's need, than to be these false gods; better even the door of a house that protects its contents, than these false gods; better also a wooden pillar in a palace, than these false gods.

[60] For sun and moon and stars are bright, and when sent to do a service, they are obedient. [61] So also the lightning, when it flashes, is widely seen; and the wind likewise blows in every land. [62] When God commands the clouds to go over the whole world, they carry out his command. [63] And the fire sent from above to consume mountains and woods does what it is ordered. But these idols[x] are not to be compared with them in ap-pearance or power. [64] Therefore one must not think that they are gods, nor call them gods, for they are not able either to decide a case or to do good to anyone. [65] Since you know then that they are not gods, do not fear them.

[66] They can neither curse nor bless kings; [67] they cannot show signs in the heavens for the nations, or shine like the sun or give light like the moon. [68] The wild animals are better than they are, for they can flee to shelter and help themselves. [69] So we have no evidence whatever that they are gods; therefore do not fear them.

[70] Like a scarecrow in a cucumber bed, which guards nothing, so are their gods of wood, over-laid with gold and silver. [71] In the same way, their gods of wood, overlaid with gold and silver, are like a thornbush in a garden on which every bird perches; or like a corpse thrown out in the dark-ness. [72] From the purple and linen[y] that rot upon them you will know that they are not gods; and they will finally be consumed themselves, and be a reproach in the land. [73] Better, therefore, is some-one upright who has no idols; such a person will be far above reproach.

---

t Gk he   u Gk them   v Meaning of Gk uncertain
w Gk they   x Gk these things   y Cn: Gk marble, Syr silk

Four-headed creatures, a strange craft made up of wheels within wheels, a being of light that appears out of the sky—the first chapter of the Book of Ezekiel sounds like a preview for a science fiction movie. Ezekiel, more than any other prophet, proclaims astonishing visions that are filled with bizarre images, symbols, and creatures.

In-depth

Ezekiel lived during the last days of Judah, just before it was destroyed by the Babylonians. He was probably among an early group of captives sent into exile in Babylon before Judah and the city of Jerusalem were demolished in 587 B.C. (see the timeline at the back of this Bible). He began his prophetic ministry in 593 B.C., when he received a fantastic vision and call, described in chapters 1–3 of his book. We know that Ezekiel came from a priestly family (1.3) and that he was married (24.16–18).

Ezekiel preached many of the traditional themes of the other prophets but in a unique way. Note these examples:

- *The Lord's presence in the Temple.* Possibly because of Ezekiel's priestly heritage, he gave God's presence—or lack of presence—in the Temple a more central role than did the other prophets. In his vision, the Temple will be the center of the new Israel, and a great priest will rule instead of a king.

- *The awesomeness of God.* For Ezekiel, the Lord did not appear as a parent or someone to be argued with. Rather, God was awesome and overpowering, beyond human explanations. Ezekiel often spoke of God's glory and holiness.

- *Personal responsibility.* Ezekiel did not condemn the previous generation for the destruction of Judah, but preached that every generation is responsible for its own acts. Each individual can direct his or her life according to God's will.

- *Apocalyptic prophecy.* Some of Ezekiel's prophecies take the form of symbolic images. The images are so mysterious they require special explanation by heavenly beings. The Books of Daniel and Revelation continue this type of writing, which is called apocalyptic literature.

At a Glance

- **Chapters 1–3.** Ezekiel's call
- **Chapters 4–24.** visions and prophecies about Jerusalem
- **Chapters 25–32.** oracles against foreign nations
- **Chapters 33–39.** oracles of the restoration of Judah and Jerusalem
- **Chapters 40–48.** visions of a new Temple and a new worship

Quick Facts

Period Covered
593–573 B.C.

Authors
Ezekiel, and the scribes who recorded his words and actions

Themes
Jerusalem is being punished for its sin. God's glory will be known to all the nations. God will restore the Temple.

Ezekiel

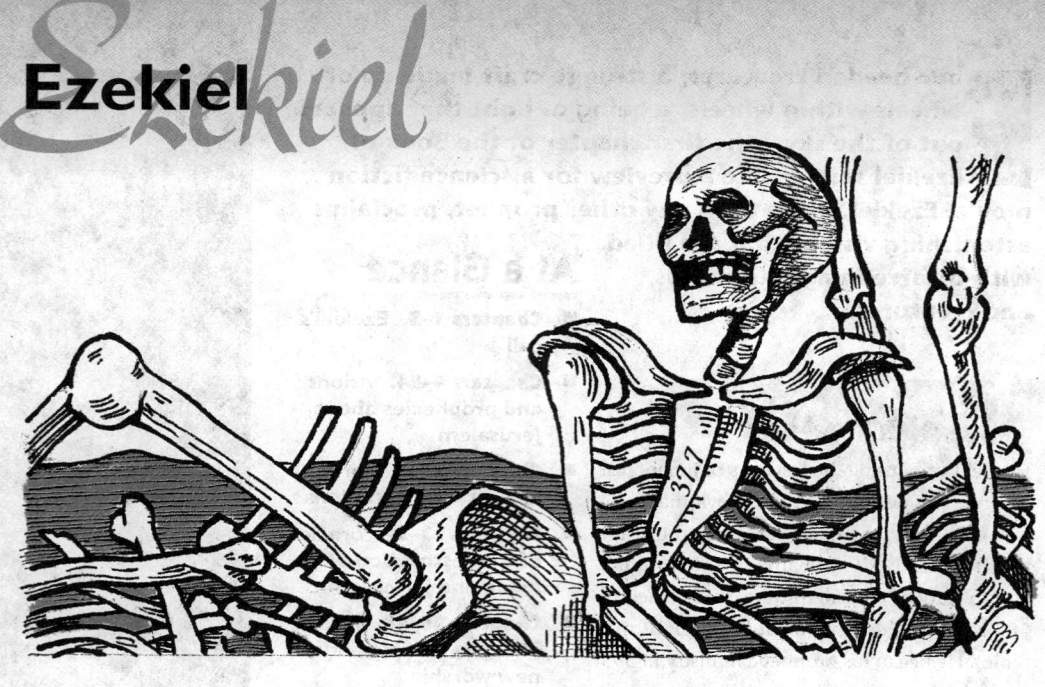

The Vision of the Chariot

In the thirtieth year, in the fourth month, on the fifth day of the month, as I was among the exiles by the river Che'bar, the heavens were opened, and I saw visions of God. ² On the fifth day of the month (it was the fifth year of the exile of King Je·hoi'a·chin), ³ the word of the LORD came to the priest E·zek'i·el son of Bu'zi, in the land of the Chal·de'ans by the river Che'bar; and the hand of the LORD was on him there.

4 As I looked, a stormy wind came out of the north: a great cloud with brightness around it and fire flashing forth continually, and in the middle of the fire, something like gleaming amber. ⁵ In the middle of it was something like four living creatures. This was their appearance: they were of human form. ⁶ Each had four faces, and each of them had four wings. ⁷ Their legs were straight, and the soles of their feet were like the sole of a calf's foot; and they sparkled like burnished bronze. ⁸ Under their wings on their four sides they had human hands. And the four had their faces and their wings thus: ⁹ their wings touched one another; each of them moved straight ahead, without turning as they moved. ¹⁰ As for the appearance of their faces: the four had the face of a human being, the face of a lion on the right side, the face of an ox on the left side, and the face of an eagle; ¹¹ such were their faces. Their wings were spread out above; each creature had two wings, each of which touched the wing of another, while two covered their bodies. ¹² Each moved straight ahead; wherever the spirit would go, they went, without turning as they went. ¹³ In the middle of *a* the living creatures there was something that looked like burning coals of fire, like torches moving to and fro among the living creatures; the fire was bright, and lightning issued from the fire. ¹⁴ The living creatures darted to and fro, like a flash of lightning.

15 As I looked at the living creatures, I saw a wheel on the earth beside the living creatures, one for each of the four of them.*b* ¹⁶ As for the appearance of the wheels and their construction: their appearance was like the gleaming of beryl; and the four had the same form, their construction being something like a wheel within a wheel. ¹⁷ When they moved, they moved in any of the four directions without veering as they moved. ¹⁸ Their rims were tall and awesome, for the rims of all four were full of eyes all around. ¹⁹ When the living creatures moved, the wheels moved beside them; and when the living creatures rose from the earth, the wheels rose. ²⁰ Wherever the spirit would go, they went, and the wheels rose along with them; for the spirit of the living creatures was in the wheels. ²¹ When they moved, the others moved;

---

a Gk OL: Heb *And the appearance of*   *b* Heb *of their faces*

972

when they stopped, the others stopped; and when they rose from the earth, the wheels rose along with them; for the spirit of the living creatures was in the wheels.

22 Over the heads of the living creatures there was something like a dome, shining like crystal,^{c} spread out above their heads. 23 Under the dome their wings were stretched out straight, one toward another; and each of the creatures had two wings covering its body. 24 When they moved, I heard the sound of their wings like the sound of mighty waters, like the thunder of the Almighty,^{d} a sound of tumult like the sound of an army; when they stopped, they let down their wings. 25 And there came a voice from above the dome over their heads; when they stopped, they let down their wings.

The Vision of the Scroll

He said to me: O mortal,^{f} stand up on your feet, and I will speak with you. 2 And when he spoke to me, a spirit entered into me and set me on my feet; and I heard him speaking to me. 3 He said to me, Mortal, I am sending you to the people of Israel, to a nation^g of rebels who have rebelled against me; they and their ancestors have transgressed against me to this very day. 4 The descendants are impudent and stubborn. I am sending you to them, and you shall say to them, "Thus says the Lord GOD." 5 Whether they hear or refuse to hear (for they are a rebellious house), they shall know that there has been a prophet among them. 6 And you, O mortal, do not be afraid of them, and do not be afraid of their words, though briers and thorns surround you and you live among scorpions; do not be

Introducing ▶ EZEKIEL

Ezekiel's name means "God strengthens." He was a complex person: priest and prophet, poet and teacher, tender and angry. He experienced God in mysterious ways, often through visions that greatly influenced his life and prophetic ministry.

Ezekiel's vision of creatures from heaven in chapters 1–3 of his book was the basis for his call and prophetic ministry. His vision of the defilement of the Temple in chapters 8–11 was a major conversion experience. He, along with most of Israel, believed that God's glory resided in the Temple and that nothing could ever change that. The vision revealed corruption in Jerusalem and that the glory of God had left the Temple and had come to Babylon. His vision of dry bones coming to life in chapter 37 helped him understand that God would breathe new life into Israel. His final visions of a new Temple in chapters 40, 43, and 47 told him that God would restore Jerusalem and the Temple.

Besides having symbolic visions, Ezekiel also performed many dramatic, symbolic actions (see "Street Theater," Ezek 4.1—5.4). These were designed to catch people's attention and transmit God's message.

26 And above the dome over their heads there was something like a throne, in appearance like sapphire;^{e} and seated above the likeness of a throne was something that seemed like a human form. 27 Upward from what appeared like the loins I saw something like gleaming amber, something that looked like fire enclosed all around; and downward from what looked like the loins I saw something that looked like fire, and there was a splendor all around. 28 Like the bow in a cloud on a rainy day, such was the appearance of the splendor all around. This was the appearance of the likeness of the glory of the LORD.

When I saw it, I fell on my face, and I heard the voice of someone speaking.

afraid of their words, and do not be dismayed at their looks, for they are a rebellious house. 7 You shall speak my words to them, whether they hear or refuse to hear; for they are a rebellious house.

8 But you, mortal, hear what I say to you; do not be rebellious like that rebellious house; open your mouth and eat what I give you. 9 I looked, and a hand was stretched out to me, and a written scroll was in it. 10 He spread it before me; it had writing on the front and on the back, and written

---

^{c} Gk: Heb *like the awesome crystal* ^{d} Traditional rendering of Heb *Shaddai* ^{e} Or *lapis lazuli* ^{f} Or *son of man*; Heb *ben adam* (and so throughout the book when Ezekiel is addressed) ^{g} Syr: Heb *to nations*

EZEK

The Word Is Sweet

God called Ezekiel to speak God's word to the people. It was a tough job; those people were rebellious. But Ezekiel opened his mouth to receive the scroll containing God's word, and the scroll was sweet (Ezek 3.3).

God gave Ezekiel words to eat. God nourished Ezekiel to carry out his calling. God gives us the Word, God's Son, Jesus Christ, to eat. God nourishes us to carry out our calling to share the Good News with others. How will you respond?

▸ **Ezek 2.1—3.11**

on it were words of lamentation and mourning and woe.
He said to me, O mortal, eat what is offered to you; eat this scroll, and go, speak to the house of Israel. 2 So I opened my mouth, and he gave me the scroll to eat. 3 He said to me, Mortal, eat this scroll that I give you and fill your stomach with it. Then I ate it; and in my mouth it was as sweet as honey.

4 He said to me: Mortal, go to the house of Israel and speak my very words to them. 5 For you are not sent to a people of obscure speech and difficult language, but to the house of Israel— 6 not to many peoples of obscure speech and difficult language, whose words you cannot understand. Surely, if I sent you to them, they would listen to you. 7 But the house of Israel will not listen to you, for they are not willing to listen to me; because all the house of Israel have a hard forehead and a stubborn heart. 8 See, I have made your face hard against their faces, and your forehead hard against their foreheads. 9 Like the hardest stone, harder than flint, I have made your forehead; do not fear them or be dismayed at their looks, for they are a rebellious house. 10 He said to me: Mortal, all my words that I shall speak to you receive in your heart and hear with your ears; 11 then go to the exiles, to your people, and speak to them. Say to them, "Thus says the Lord GOD"; whether they hear or refuse to hear.

Ezekiel at the River Chebar

12 Then the spirit lifted me up, and as the glory of the LORD rose[h] from its place, I heard behind me the sound of loud rumbling; 13 it was the sound of the wings of the living creatures brushing against one another, and the sound of the wheels beside them, that sounded like a loud rumbling. 14 The spirit lifted me up and bore me away; I went in bitterness in the heat of my spirit, the hand of the LORD being strong upon me. 15 I came to the

exiles at Tel-a·bib', who lived by the river Che'bar.[i] And I sat there among them, stunned, for seven days.

16 At the end of seven days, the word of the LORD came to me: 17 Mortal, I have made you a sentinel for the house of Israel; whenever you hear a word from my mouth, you shall give them warning from me. 18 If I say to the wicked, "You shall surely die," and you give them no warning, or speak to warn the wicked from their wicked way, in order to save their life, those wicked persons shall die for their iniquity; but their blood I will require at your hand. 19 But if you warn the wicked, and they do not turn from their wickedness, or from their wicked way, they shall die for their iniquity; but you will have saved your life. 20 Again, if the righteous turn from their righteousness and commit iniquity, and I lay a stumbling block before them, they shall die; because you have not warned them, they shall die for their sin, and their righteous deeds that they have done shall not be remembered; but their blood I will require at your hand. 21 If, however, you warn the righteous not to sin, and they do not sin, they shall surely live, because they took warning; and you will have saved your life.

Ezekiel Isolated and Silenced

22 Then the hand of the LORD was upon me there; and he said to me, Rise up, go out into the valley, and there I will speak with you. 23 So I rose up and went out into the valley; and the glory of the LORD stood there, like the glory that I had seen by the river Che'bar; and I fell on my face. 24 The spirit entered into me, and set me on my feet; and he spoke with me and said to me: Go, shut yourself inside your house. 25 As for you, mortal, cords shall be placed on you, and you shall be bound

h Cn: Heb and blessed be the glory of the LORD   i Two Mss Syr: Heb Chebar, and to where they lived. Another reading is Chebar, and I sat where they sat with them, so that you cannot go out among the people; 26 and I will make your tongue cling to the roof of your mouth, so that you shall be speechless and unable to reprove them; for they are a rebellious house. 27 But when I speak with you, I will open your mouth, and you shall say to them, "Thus says the Lord GOD"; let those who will hear, hear; and let those who refuse to hear, refuse; for they are a rebellious house.

The Siege of Jerusalem Portrayed

And you, O mortal, take a brick and set it before you. On it portray a city, Jerusalem; 2 and put siegeworks against it, and build a siege wall against it, and cast up a ramp against it; set camps also against it, and plant battering rams against it all around. 3 Then take an iron plate and place it as an iron wall between you and the city; set your face toward it, and let it be in a state of siege, and press the siege against it. This is a sign for the house of Israel.

4 Then lie on your left side, and place the punishment of the house of Israel upon it; you shall bear their punishment for the number of the days that you lie there. 5 For I assign to you a number of days, three hundred ninety days, equal to the number of the years of their punishment; and so you shall bear the punishment of the house of Israel. 6 When you have completed these, you shall lie down a second time, but on your right side, and bear the punishment of the house of Judah; forty days I assign you, one day for each year. 7 You shall set your face toward the siege of Jerusalem, and with your arm bared you shall prophesy against it. 8 See, I am putting cords on you so that you cannot turn from one side to the other until you have completed the days of your siege.

9 And you, take wheat and barley, beans and lentils, millet and spelt; put them into one vessel, and make bread for yourself. During the number of days that you lie on your side, three hundred ninety days, you shall eat it. 10 The food that you eat shall be twenty shekels a day by weight; at fixed times you shall eat it. 11 And you shall drink water by measure, one-sixth of a hin; at fixed times you shall drink. 12 You shall eat it as a barley-cake, baking it in their sight on human dung. 13 The LORD said, "Thus shall the people of Israel eat their bread, unclean, among the nations to which I will drive them." 14 Then I said, "Ah Lord GOD! I have never defiled myself; from my youth up until now I have never eaten what died of itself or was torn by animals, nor has carrion flesh come into my mouth." 15 Then he said to me, "See, I will let you have cow's dung instead of human dung, on which you may prepare your bread."

16 Then he said to me, Mortal, I am going to break the staff of bread in Jerusalem; they shall eat bread by weight and with fearfulness; and they shall drink water by measure and in dismay. 17 Lacking bread and water, they will look at one another in dismay, and waste away under their punishment.

A Sword against Jerusalem

And you, O mortal, take a sharp sword; use it as a barber's razor and run it over your head and your beard; then take balances for weighing, and divide the hair. 2 One third of the hair you shall burn in the fire inside the city, when the days of the siege are completed; one third you shall take and strike with the sword all around the city; j and one third you shall scatter to the wind, and I will unsheathe

---

j Heb *it*

Street Theater

Look over what the prophet does in Ezekiel, chapters 3–5, to get people's attention before the fall of Jerusalem in 587 B.C. He is speechless (3.22–27) as a sign that the people are rebellious and unwilling to hear God's word. He lies on his left side for days, and then his right (4.4–5), as a sign of the number of years the two kingdoms Israel and Judah will be in exile. He eats small amounts of food cooked on dung (verses 10–16) as a sign of the shortage of food during the siege of the city. Ezekiel's "street theater" is a good way of making a point that everyone can understand.

Christians today need to use creative means to raise consciousness about the ways society violates human life and harms our world. Radio and television, public prayer services, and rallies all help people get the message out. What does your church do to raise consciousness and move people to change their ways? What can you do?

▶ **Ezek 4.1—5.4**

the sword after them. 3 Then you shall take from these a small number, and bind them in the skirts of your robe. 4 From these, again, you shall take some, throw them into the fire and burn them up; from there a fire will come out against all the house of Israel.

5 Thus says the Lord GOD: This is Jerusalem; I have set her in the center of the nations, with countries all around her. 6 But she has rebelled against my ordinances and my statutes, becoming more wicked than the nations and the countries all around her, rejecting my ordinances and not following my statutes. 7 Therefore thus says the Lord GOD: Because you are more turbulent than the nations that are all around you, and have not followed my statutes or kept my ordinances, but have acted according to the ordinances of the nations that are all around you; 8 therefore thus says the Lord GOD: I, I myself, am coming against you; I will execute judgments among you in the sight of the nations. 9 And because of all your abominations, I will do to you what I have never yet done, and the like of which I will never do again. 10 Surely, parents shall eat their children in your midst, and children shall eat their parents; I will execute judgments on you, and any of you who survive I will scatter to every wind. 11 Therefore, as I live, says the Lord GOD, surely, because you have defiled my sanctuary with all your detestable things and with all your abominations—therefore I will cut you down;*k* my eye will not spare, and I will have no pity. 12 One third of you shall die of pestilence or be consumed by famine among you; one third shall fall by the sword around you; and one third I will scatter to every wind and will unsheathe the sword after them.

13 My anger shall spend itself, and I will vent my fury on them and satisfy myself; and they shall know that I, the LORD, have spoken in my jealousy, when I spend my fury on them. 14 Moreover I will make you a desolation and an object of mocking among the nations around you, in the sight of all that pass by. 15 You shall be*l* a mockery and a taunt, a warning and a horror, to the nations around you, when I execute judgments on you in anger and fury, and with furious punishments—I, the LORD, have spoken— 16 when I loose against you*m* my deadly arrows of famine, arrows for destruction, which I will let loose to destroy you, and when I bring more and more famine upon you, and break your staff of bread. 17 I will send famine and wild animals against you, and they will rob you of your children; pestilence and bloodshed shall pass through you; and I will bring the sword upon you. I, the LORD, have spoken.

Judgment on Idolatrous Israel

The word of the LORD came to me: 2 O mortal, set your face toward the mountains of Israel, and prophesy against them, 3 and say, You mountains of Israel, hear the word of the Lord GOD! Thus says the Lord GOD to the mountains and the hills, to the ravines and the valleys: I, I myself will bring a sword upon you, and I will destroy your high places. 4 Your altars shall become desolate, and your incense stands shall be broken; and I will throw down your slain in front of your idols. 5 I will lay the corpses of the people of Israel in front of their idols; and I will scatter your bones around your altars. 6 Wherever you live, your towns shall be waste and your high places ruined, so that your altars will be waste and ruined,*n* your idols broken and destroyed, your incense stands cut down, and your works wiped out. 7 The slain shall fall in your midst; then you shall know that I am the LORD.

8 But I will spare some. Some of you shall escape the sword among the nations and be scattered through the countries. 9 Those of you who escape shall remember me among the nations where they are carried captive, how I was crushed by their wanton heart that turned away from me, and their wanton eyes that turned after their idols. Then they will be loathsome in their own sight for the evils that they have committed, for all their abominations. 10 And they shall know that I am the LORD; I did not threaten in vain to bring this disaster upon them.

11 Thus says the Lord GOD: Clap your hands and stamp your foot, and say, Alas for all the vile abominations of the house of Israel! For they shall fall by the sword, by famine, and by pestilence. 12 Those far off shall die of pestilence; those nearby shall fall by the sword; and any who are left and are spared shall die of famine. Thus I will spend my fury upon them. 13 And you shall know that I am the LORD, when their slain lie among their idols around their altars, on every high hill, on all the mountain tops, under every green tree, and under every leafy oak, wherever they offered pleasing odor to all their idols. 14 I will stretch out my hand against them, and make the land desolate and waste, throughout all their settlements, from the wilderness to Rib'lah.*o* Then they shall know that I am the LORD.

---

k Another reading is *I will withdraw*   *l* Gk Syr Vg Tg: Heb *It shall be*   *m* Heb *them*   *n* Syr Vg Tg: Heb *and be made guilty*   *o* Another reading is *Diblah*

Impending Disaster

The word of the LORD came to me: 2 You, O mortal, thus says the Lord GOD to the land of Israel:
An end! The end has come
upon the four corners of the land.
3 Now the end is upon you,
I will let loose my anger upon you;
I will judge you according to your ways,
I will punish you for all your
abominations.
4 My eye will not spare you, I will have no
pity.
I will punish you for your ways,
while your abominations are among you.
Then you shall know that I am the LORD.
5 Thus says the Lord GOD:
Disaster after disaster! See, it comes.
6 An end has come, the end has come.
It has awakened against you; see, it comes!
7 Your doom*p* has come to you,
O inhabitant of the land.
The time has come, the day is near—
of tumult, not of reveling on the
mountains.
8 Soon now I will pour out my wrath
upon you;
I will spend my anger against you.
I will judge you according to your ways,
and punish you for all your
abominations.
9 My eye will not spare; I will have no pity.
I will punish you according to your ways,
while your abominations are among you.
Then you shall know that it is I the LORD who strike.
10 See, the day! See, it comes!
Your doom*p* has gone out.
The rod has blossomed, pride has budded.
11 Violence has grown into a rod
of wickedness.
None of them shall remain,
not their abundance, not their wealth;
no pre-eminence among them.*p*
12 The time has come, the day draws near;
let not the buyer rejoice, nor the seller
mourn,
for wrath is upon all their multitude.
13 For the sellers shall not return to what has been sold as long as they remain alive. For the vision concerns all their multitude; it shall not be revoked. Because of their iniquity, they cannot maintain their lives.*p*
14 They have blown the horn and made
everything ready;
but no one goes to battle,
for my wrath is upon all their multitude.
15 The sword is outside, pestilence and famine
are inside;
those in the field die by the sword;
those in the city—famine and pestilence
devour them.
16 If any survivors escape,
they shall be found on the mountains
like doves of the valleys,
all of them moaning over their iniquity.
17 All hands shall grow feeble,
all knees turn to water.
18 They shall put on sackcloth,
horror shall cover them.
Shame shall be on all faces,
baldness on all their heads.
19 They shall fling their silver into the streets,
their gold shall be treated as unclean.
Their silver and gold cannot save them on the day of the wrath of the LORD. They shall not satisfy their hunger or fill their stomachs with it. For it was the stumbling block of their iniquity. 20 From their*q* beautiful ornament, in which they took pride, they made their abominable images, their detestable things; therefore I will make of it an unclean thing to them.
21 I will hand it over to strangers as booty,
to the wicked of the earth as plunder;
they shall profane it.
22 I will avert my face from them,
so that they may profane my treasured*r*
place;
the violent shall enter it,
they shall profane it.
23 Make a chain!*p*
For the land is full of bloody crimes;
the city is full of violence.
24 I will bring the worst of the nations
to take possession of their houses.
I will put an end to the arrogance of the
strong,
and their holy places shall be profaned.
25 When anguish comes, they will seek peace,
but there shall be none.
26 Disaster comes upon disaster,
rumor follows rumor;
they shall keep seeking a vision from the
prophet;
instruction shall perish from the priest,
and counsel from the elders.
27 The king shall mourn,
the prince shall be wrapped in despair,

p Meaning of Heb uncertain   *q* Syr Symmachus: Heb *its*
r Or *secret*

and the hands of the people of the land
shall tremble.
According to their way I will deal with
them;
according to their own judgments I will
judge them.
And they shall know that I am the LORD.

Abominations in the Temple

In the sixth year, in the sixth month, on the fifth day of the month, as I sat in my house, with the elders of Judah sitting before me, the hand of the Lord GOD fell upon me there. ²I looked, and there was a figure that looked like a human being;ˢ below what appeared to be its loins it was fire, and above the loins it was like the appearance of brightness, like gleaming amber. ³It stretched out the form of a hand, and took me by a lock of my head; and the spirit lifted me up between earth and heaven, and brought me in visions of God to Jerusalem, to the entrance of the gateway of the inner court that faces north, to the seat of the image of jealousy, which provokes to jealousy. ⁴And the glory of the God of Israel was there, like the vision that I had seen in the valley.

5 Then Godᵗ said to me, "O mortal, lift up your eyes now in the direction of the north." So I lifted up my eyes toward the north, and there, north of the altar gate, in the entrance, was this image of jealousy. ⁶He said to me, "Mortal, do you see what they are doing, the great abominations that the house of Israel are committing here, to drive me far from my sanctuary? Yet you will see still greater abominations."

7 And he brought me to the entrance of the court; I looked, and there was a hole in the wall. ⁸Then he said to me, "Mortal, dig through the wall"; and when I dug through the wall, there was an entrance. ⁹He said to me, "Go in, and see the vile abominations that they are committing here." ¹⁰So I went in and looked; there, portrayed on the wall all around, were all kinds of creeping things, and loathsome animals, and all the idols of the house of Israel. ¹¹Before them stood seventy of the elders of the house of Israel, with Jā•az•a•niʹah son of Shaʹphan standing among them. Each had his censer in his hand, and the fragrant cloud of incense was ascending. ¹²Then he said to me, "Mortal, have you seen what the elders of the house of Israel are doing in the dark, each in his room of images? For they say, 'The LORD does not see us, the LORD has forsaken the land.' " ¹³He said also to me, "You will see still greater abominations that they are committing."

14 Then he brought me to the entrance of the north gate of the house of the LORD; women were sitting there weeping for Tamʹmūz. ¹⁵Then he said to me, "Have you seen this, O mortal? You will see still greater abominations than these."

16 And he brought me into the inner court of the house of the LORD; there, at the entrance of the temple of the LORD, between the porch and the altar, were about twenty-five men, with their backs to the temple of the LORD, and their faces toward the east, prostrating themselves to the sun toward the east. ¹⁷Then he said to me, "Have you seen this, O mortal? Is it not bad enough that the house of Judah commits the abominations done here? Must they fill the land with violence, and provoke my anger still further? See, they are putting the branch to their nose! ¹⁸Therefore I will act in wrath; my eye will not spare, nor will I have pity; and though they cry in my hearing with a loud voice, I will not listen to them."

The Slaughter of the Idolaters

Then he cried in my hearing with a loud voice, saying, "Draw near, you executioners of the city, each with his destroying weapon in his hand." ²And six men came from the direction of the upper gate, which faces north, each with his weapon for slaughter in his hand; among them was a man clothed in linen, with a writing case at his side. They went in and stood beside the bronze altar.

3 Now the glory of the God of Israel had gone up from the cherub on which it rested to the threshold of the house. The LORD called to the man clothed in linen, who had the writing case at his side; ⁴and said to him, "Go through the city, through Jerusalem, and put a mark on the foreheads of those who sigh and groan over all the abominations that are committed in it." ⁵To the others he said in my hearing, "Pass through the city after him, and kill; your eye shall not spare, and you shall show no pity. ⁶Cut down old men, young men and young women, little children and women, but touch no one who has the mark. And begin at my sanctuary." So they began with the elders who were in front of the house. ⁷Then he said to them, "Defile the house, and fill the courts with the slain. Go!" So they went out and killed in the city. ⁸While they were killing, and I was left alone, I fell prostrate on my face and cried out, "Ah Lord GOD! will you destroy all who remain of Israel as you pour out your wrath upon Jerusalem?" ⁹He said to me, "The guilt of the house of Israel and Judah is exceedingly great; the land is full of bloodshed and the city full of perversity; for they say, 'The LORD has forsaken the land, and the LORD does not see.' ¹⁰As for me, my eye will not

---

ˢ Gk: Heb *like fire*   ᵗ Heb *he*

spare, nor will I have pity, but I will bring down their deeds upon their heads."

11 Then the man clothed in linen, with the writing case at his side, brought back word, saying, "I have done as you commanded me."

God's Glory Leaves Jerusalem

Then I looked, and above the dome that was over the heads of the cherubim there appeared above them something like a sapphire,u in form resembling a throne. 2 He said to the man clothed in linen, "Go within the wheelwork underneath the cherubim; fill your hands with burning coals from among the cherubim, and scatter them over the city." He went in as I looked on. 3 Now the cherubim were standing on the south side of the house when the man went in; and a cloud filled the inner court. 4 Then the glory of the LORD rose up from the cherub to the threshold of the house; the house was filled with the cloud, and the court was full of the brightness of the glory of the LORD. 5 The sound of the wings of the cherubim was heard as far as the outer court, like the voice of God Almightyv when he speaks.

6 When he commanded the man clothed in linen, "Take fire from within the wheelwork, from among the cherubim," he went in and stood beside a wheel. 7 And a cherub stretched out his hand from among the cherubim to the fire that was among the cherubim, took some of it and put it into the hands of the man clothed in linen, who took it and went out. 8 The cherubim appeared to have the form of a human hand under their wings.

9 I looked, and there were four wheels beside the cherubim, one beside each cherub; and the appearance of the wheels was like gleaming beryl. 10 And as for their appearance, the four looked alike, something like a wheel within a wheel. 11 When they moved, they moved in any of the four directions without veering as they moved; but in whatever direction the front wheel faced, the others followed without veering as they moved. 12 Their entire body, their rims, their spokes, their wings, and the wheels—the wheels of the four of them—were full of eyes all around. 13 As for the wheels, they were called in my hearing "the wheelwork." 14 Each one had four faces: the first face was that of the cherub, the second face was that of a human being, the third that of a lion, and the fourth that of an eagle.

15 The cherubim rose up. These were the living creatures that I saw by the river Che'bar. 16 When the cherubim moved, the wheels moved beside them; and when the cherubim lifted up their wings to rise up from the earth, the wheels at their side did not veer. 17 When they stopped, the others stopped, and when they rose up, the others rose up with them; for the spirit of the living creatures was in them.

18 Then the glory of the LORD went out from the threshold of the house and stopped above the cherubim. 19 The cherubim lifted up their wings and rose up from the earth in my sight as they went out with the wheels beside them. They stopped at the entrance of the east gate of the house of the LORD; and the glory of the God of Israel was above them.

20 These were the living creatures that I saw underneath the God of Israel by the river Che'bar; and I knew that they were cherubim. 21 Each had four faces, each four wings, and underneath their wings something like human hands. 22 As for what their faces were like, they were the same faces whose appearance I had seen by the river Che'bar. Each one moved straight ahead.

Judgment on Wicked Counselors

The spirit lifted me up and brought me to the east gate of the house of the LORD, which faces east. There, at the entrance of the gateway, were twenty-five men; among them I saw Jā•az•a•nī'ah son of Az'-zur, and Pel•a•tī'ah son of Be•nā'i•ah, officials of the people. 2 He said to me, "Mortal, these are the men who devise iniquity and who give wicked counsel in this city; 3 they say, 'The time is not near to build houses; this city is the pot, and we are the meat.' 4 Therefore prophesy against them; prophesy, O mortal."

5 Then the spirit of the LORD fell upon me, and he said to me, "Say, Thus says the LORD: This is what you think, O house of Israel; I know the things that come into your mind. 6 You have killed many in this city, and have filled its streets with the slain. 7 Therefore thus says the Lord GOD: The slain whom you have placed within it are the meat, and this city is the pot; but you shall be taken out of it. 8 You have feared the sword; and I will bring the sword upon you, says the Lord GOD. 9 I will take you out of it and give you over to the hands of foreigners, and execute judgments upon you. 10 You shall fall by the sword; I will judge you at the border of Israel. And you shall know that I am the LORD. 11 This city shall not be your pot, and you shall not be the meat inside it; I will judge you at the border of Israel. 12 Then you shall know that I am the LORD, whose statutes you have not followed, and whose ordinances you have not kept, but you have acted according to the ordinances of the nations that are around you."

u Or *lapis lazuli*   v Traditional rendering of Heb *El Shaddai*

13 Now, while I was prophesying, Pel•a•tī'ah son of Be•nā'i•ah died. Then I fell down on my face, cried with a loud voice, and said, "Ah Lord GOD! will you make a full end of the remnant of Israel?"

God Will Restore Israel

14 Then the word of the LORD came to me: 15 Mortal, your kinsfolk, your own kin, your fellow exiles,*w* the whole house of Israel, all of them, are those of whom the inhabitants of Jerusalem have said, "They have gone far from the LORD; to us this land is given for a possession." 16 Therefore say: Thus says the Lord GOD: Though I removed them far away among the nations, and though I scattered them among the countries, yet I have been a sanctuary to them for a little while*x* in the countries where they have gone. 17 Therefore say: Thus says the Lord GOD: I will gather you from the peoples, and assemble you out of the countries where you have been scattered, and I will give you the land of Israel. 18 When they come there, they will remove from it all its detestable things and all its

they shall be my people, and I will be their God. 21 But as for those whose heart goes after their detestable things and their abominations,*z* I will bring their deeds upon their own heads, says the Lord GOD.

22 Then the cherubim lifted up their wings, with the wheels beside them; and the glory of the God of Israel was above them. 23 And the glory of the LORD ascended from the middle of the city, and stopped on the mountain east of the city. 24 The spirit lifted me up and brought me in a vision by the spirit of God into Chal•dē'a, to the exiles. Then the vision that I had seen left me. 25 And I told the exiles all the things that the LORD had shown me.

Judah's Captivity Portrayed

The word of the LORD came to me: 2 Mortal, you are living in the midst of a rebellious house, who have eyes to see but do not see, who have ears to hear but do not hear; 3 for they are a rebellious house. Therefore, mortal, prepare for yourself an exile's baggage, and go into exile by day in their sight; you shall go like an exile from your place to another place in their sight. Perhaps they will understand, though they are a rebellious house. 4 You shall bring out your baggage by day in their sight, as baggage for exile; and you shall go out yourself at evening in their sight, as those do who go into exile. 5 Dig through the wall in their sight, and carry the baggage through it. 6 In their sight you shall lift the baggage on your shoulder, and carry it out in the dark; you shall cover your face, so that you may not see the land; for I have made you a sign for the house of Israel.

7 I did just as I was commanded. I brought out my baggage by day, as baggage for exile, and in the evening I dug through the wall with my own hands; I brought it out in the dark, carrying it on my shoulder in their sight.

8 In the morning the word of the LORD came to me: 9 Mortal, has not the house of Israel, the rebellious house, said to you, "What are you doing?" 10 Say to them, "Thus says the Lord GOD: This oracle concerns the prince in Jerusalem and all the house of Israel in it." 11 Say, "I am a sign for you: as I have done, so shall it be done to them; they shall go into exile, into captivity." 12 And the prince who is among them shall lift his baggage on his shoulder in the dark, and shall go out; he*a* shall dig through the wall and carry it through; he shall cover his face, so that he may not see the land with his eyes. 13 I will spread my net over him, and he

---

PRAY IT!
Have a Heart!

The Old Testament prophets are concerned about people's hearts. The ancient Israelites understood the heart as the center of intelligence, feelings, and human will. Jeremiah says the new Covenant will be written on people's hearts (Jer 31.33), and Ezekiel says God will take away their hearts of stone and give them hearts of flesh (Ezek 11.19).

In your prayer, reflect or journal on the following questions:

■ What's the difference between having a warm heart of flesh and a cold, stony heart?

■ Why would a heart of flesh lead to obeying God (verse 20)?

■ When does your heart feel like flesh? When does it feel like stone?

▶ Ezek 11.19–20

---

abominations. 19 I will give them one*y* heart, and put a new spirit within them; I will remove the heart of stone from their flesh and give them a heart of flesh, 20 so that they may follow my statutes and keep my ordinances and obey them. Then

---

w Gk Syr: Heb *people of your kindred*   *x* Or *to some extent*   *y* Another reading is *a new*   *z* Cn: Heb *And to the heart of their detestable things and their abominations their heart goes*   *a* Gk Syr: Heb *they*

shall be caught in my snare; and I will bring him to Babylon, the land of the Chal•dē'ans, yet he shall not see it; and he shall die there. ¹⁴I will scatter to every wind all who are around him, his helpers and all his troops; and I will unsheathe the sword behind them. ¹⁵And they shall know that I am the LORD, when I disperse them among the nations and scatter them through the countries. ¹⁶But I will let a few of them escape from the sword, from famine and pestilence, so that they may tell of all their abominations among the nations where they go; then they shall know that I am the LORD.

Judgment Not Postponed

17 The word of the LORD came to me: ¹⁸Mortal, eat your bread with quaking, and drink your water with trembling and with fearfulness; ¹⁹and say to the people of the land, Thus says the Lord GOD concerning the inhabitants of Jerusalem in the land of Israel: They shall eat their bread with fearfulness, and drink their water in dismay, because their land shall be stripped of all it contains, on account of the violence of all those who live in it. ²⁰The inhabited cities shall be laid waste, and the land shall become a desolation; and you shall know that I am the LORD.

21 The word of the LORD came to me: ²²Mortal, what is this proverb of yours about the land of Israel, which says, "The days are prolonged, and every vision comes to nothing"? ²³Tell them therefore, "Thus says the Lord GOD: I will put an end to this proverb, and they shall use it no more as a proverb in Israel." But say to them, The days are near, and the fulfillment of every vision. ²⁴For there shall no longer be any false vision or flattering divination within the house of Israel. ²⁵But I the LORD will speak the word that I speak, and it will be fulfilled. It will no longer be delayed; but in your days, O rebellious house, I will speak the word and fulfill it, says the Lord GOD.

26 The word of the LORD came to me: ²⁷Mortal, the house of Israel is saying, "The vision that he sees is for many years ahead; he prophesies for distant times." ²⁸Therefore say to them, Thus says the Lord GOD: None of my words will be delayed any longer, but the word that I speak will be fulfilled, says the Lord GOD.

False Prophets Condemned

The word of the LORD came to me: ²Mortal, prophesy against the prophets of Israel who are prophesying; say to those who prophesy out of their own imagination: "Hear the word of the LORD!" ³Thus says the Lord GOD, Alas for the senseless prophets who follow their own spirit, and have

seen nothing! ⁴Your prophets have been like jackals among ruins, O Israel. ⁵You have not gone up into the breaches, or repaired a wall for the house of Israel, so that it might stand in battle on the day of the LORD. ⁶They have envisioned falsehood and lying divination; they say, "Says the LORD," when the LORD has not sent them, and yet they wait for the fulfillment of their word! ⁷Have you not seen a false vision or uttered a lying divination, when you have said, "Says the LORD," even though I did not speak?

8 Therefore thus says the Lord GOD: Because you have uttered falsehood and envisioned lies, I am against you, says the Lord GOD. ⁹My hand will be against the prophets who see false visions and utter lying divinations; they shall not be in the council of my people, nor be enrolled in the register of the house of Israel, nor shall they enter the land of Israel; and you shall know that I am the Lord GOD. ¹⁰Because, in truth, because they have misled my people, saying, "Peace," when there is no peace; and because, when the people build a wall, these prophets*b* smear whitewash on it. ¹¹Say to those who smear whitewash on it that it shall fall. There will be a deluge of rain,*c* great hailstones will fall, and a stormy wind will break out. ¹²When the wall falls, will it not be said to you, "Where is the whitewash you smeared on it?" ¹³Therefore thus says the Lord GOD: In my wrath I will make a stormy wind break out, and in my anger there shall be a deluge of rain, and hailstones in wrath to destroy it. ¹⁴I will break down the wall that you have smeared with whitewash, and bring it to the ground, so that its foundation will be laid bare; when it falls, you shall perish within it; and you shall know that I am the LORD. ¹⁵Thus I will spend my wrath upon the wall, and upon those who have smeared it with whitewash; and I will say to you, The wall is no more, nor those who smeared it— ¹⁶the prophets of Israel who prophesied concerning Jerusalem and saw visions of peace for it, when there was no peace, says the Lord GOD.

17 As for you, mortal, set your face against the daughters of your people, who prophesy out of their own imagination; prophesy against them ¹⁸and say, Thus says the Lord GOD: Woe to the women who sew bands on all wrists, and make veils for the heads of persons of every height, in the hunt for human lives! Will you hunt down lives among my people, and maintain your own lives? ¹⁹You have profaned me among my people for handfuls of barley and for pieces of bread, putting to death persons who should not die and

---

b Heb *they*   *c* Heb *rain and you*

keeping alive persons who should not live, by your lies to my people, who listen to lies.

20 Therefore thus says the Lord GOD: I am against your bands with which you hunt lives;[d] I will tear them from your arms, and let the lives go free, the lives that you hunt down like birds. 21 I will tear off your veils, and save my people from your hands; they shall no longer be prey in your hands; and you shall know that I am the LORD. 22 Because you have disheartened the righteous falsely, although I have not disheartened them, and you have encouraged the wicked not to turn from their wicked way and save their lives; 23 therefore you shall no longer see false visions or practice divination; I will save my people from your hand. Then you will know that I am the LORD.

God's Judgments Justified

Certain elders of Israel came to me and sat down before me. 2 And the word of the LORD came to me: 3 Mortal, these men have taken their idols into their hearts, and placed their iniquity as a stumbling block before them; shall I let myself be consulted by them? 4 Therefore speak to them, and say to them, Thus says the Lord GOD: Any of those of the house of Israel who take their idols into their hearts and place their iniquity as a stumbling block before them, and yet come to the prophet—I the LORD will answer those who come with the multitude of their idols, 5 in order that I may take hold of the hearts of the house of Israel, all of whom are estranged from me through their idols.

6 Therefore say to the house of Israel, Thus says the Lord GOD: Repent and turn away from your idols; and turn away your faces from all your abominations. 7 For any of those of the house of Israel, or of the aliens who reside in Israel, who separate themselves from me, taking their idols into their hearts and placing their iniquity as a stumbling block before them, and yet come to a prophet to inquire of me by him, I the LORD will answer them myself. 8 I will set my face against them; I will make them a sign and a byword and cut them off from the midst of my people; and you shall know that I am the LORD.

9 If a prophet is deceived and speaks a word, I, the LORD, have deceived that prophet, and I will stretch out my hand against him, and will destroy him from the midst of my people Israel. 10 And they shall bear their punishment—the punishment of the inquirer and the punishment of the prophet shall be the same— 11 so that the house of Israel may no longer go astray from me, nor defile themselves any more with all their transgressions. Then they shall be my people, and I will be their God, says the Lord GOD.

12 The word of the LORD came to me: 13 Mortal, when a land sins against me by acting faithlessly, and I stretch out my hand against it, and break its staff of bread and send famine upon it, and cut off from it human beings and animals, 14 even if Noah, Daniel,[e] and Job, these three, were in it, they would save only their own lives by their righteousness, says the Lord GOD. 15 If I send wild animals through the land to ravage it, so that it is made desolate, and no one may pass through because of the animals; 16 even if these three men were in it, as I live, says the Lord GOD, they would save neither sons nor daughters; they alone would be saved, but the land would be desolate. 17 Or if I bring a sword upon that land and say, "Let a sword pass through the land," and I cut off human beings and animals from it; 18 though these three men were in it, as I live, says the Lord GOD, they would save neither sons nor daughters, but they alone would be saved. 19 Or if I send a pestilence into that land, and pour out my wrath upon it with blood, to cut off humans and animals from it; 20 even if Noah, Daniel,[e] and Job were in it, as I live, says the Lord GOD, they would save neither son nor daughter; they would save only their own lives by their righteousness.

21 For thus says the Lord GOD: How much more when I send upon Jerusalem my four deadly acts of judgment, sword, famine, wild animals, and pestilence, to cut off humans and animals from it! 22 Yet, survivors shall be left in it, sons and daughters who will be brought out; they will come out to you. When you see their ways and their deeds, you will be consoled for the evil that I have brought upon Jerusalem, for all that I have brought upon it. 23 They shall console you, when you see their ways and their deeds; and you shall know that it was not without cause that I did all that I have done in it, says the Lord GOD.

The Useless Vine

The word of the LORD came to me:
2 O mortal, how does the wood of the vine
        surpass all other wood—
    the vine branch that is among the trees
        of the forest?
3 Is wood taken from it to make anything?
    Does one take a peg from it on which to
        hang any object?
4 It is put in the fire for fuel;
    when the fire has consumed both ends
        of it

---

d Gk Syr: Heb *lives for birds*   e Or, as otherwise read, *Danel*

and the middle of it is charred,
 is it useful for anything?
5 When it was whole it was used for nothing;
 how much less—when the fire has
 consumed it,
 and it is charred—
 can it ever be used for anything!

6 Therefore thus says the Lord GOD: Like the wood of the vine among the trees of the forest, which I have given to the fire for fuel, so I will give up the inhabitants of Jerusalem. 7 I will set my face against them; although they escape from the fire, the fire shall still consume them; and you shall know that I am the LORD, when I set my face against them. 8 And I will make the land desolate, because they have acted faithlessly, says the Lord GOD.

God's Faithless Bride

The word of the LORD came to me: 2 Mortal, make known to Jerusalem her abominations, 3 and say, Thus says the Lord GOD to Jerusalem: Your origin and your birth were in the land of the Cā′naan•ites; your father was an Am′o•rīte, and your mother a Hit′tīte. 4 As for your birth, on the day you were born your navel cord was not cut, nor were you washed with water to cleanse you, nor rubbed with salt, nor wrapped in cloths. 5 No eye pitied you, to do any of these things for you out of compassion for you; but you were thrown out in the open field, for you were abhorred on the day you were born.

6 I passed by you, and saw you flailing about in your blood. As you lay in your blood, I said to you, "Live! 7 and grow up f like a plant of the field." You grew up and became tall and arrived at full womanhood; g your breasts were formed, and your hair had grown; yet you were naked and bare.

8 I passed by you again and looked on you; you were at the age for love. I spread the edge of my cloak over you, and covered your nakedness: I pledged myself to you and entered into a covenant with you, says the Lord GOD, and you became mine. 9 Then I bathed you with water and washed off the blood from you, and anointed you with oil. 10 I clothed you with embroidered cloth and with sandals of fine leather; I bound you in fine linen and covered you with rich fabric.h 11 I adorned you with ornaments: I put bracelets on your arms, a chain on your neck, 12 a ring on your nose, earrings in your ears, and a beautiful crown upon your head. 13 You were adorned with gold and silver, while your clothing was of fine linen, rich fabric,h and embroidered cloth. You had choice flour and honey and oil for food. You grew exceedingly beautiful, fit to be a queen. 14 Your

fame spread among the nations on account of your beauty, for it was perfect because of my splendor that I had bestowed on you, says the Lord GOD.

15 But you trusted in your beauty, and played the whore because of your fame, and lavished your whorings on any passer-by.i 16 You took some of your garments, and made for yourself colorful shrines, and on them played the whore; nothing like this has ever been or ever shall be.h 17 You also took your beautiful jewels of my gold and my silver that I had given you, and made for yourself male images, and with them played the whore; 18 and you took your embroidered garments to cover them, and set my oil and my incense before them. 19 Also my bread that I gave you—I fed you with choice flour and oil and honey—you set it before them as a pleasing odor; and so it was, says the Lord GOD. 20 You took your sons and your daughters, whom you had borne to me, and these you sacrificed to them to be devoured. As if your whorings were not enough! 21 You slaughtered my children and delivered them up as an offering to them. 22 And in all your abominations and your whorings you did not remember the days of your youth, when you were naked and bare, flailing about in your blood.

23 After all your wickedness (woe, woe to you! says the Lord GOD), 24 you built yourself a platform and made yourself a lofty place in every square; 25 at the head of every street you built your lofty place and prostituted your beauty, offering yourself to every passer-by, and multiplying your whoring. 26 You played the whore with the Egyptians, your lustful neighbors, multiplying your whoring, to provoke me to anger. 27 Therefore I stretched out my hand against you, reduced your rations, and gave you up to the will of your enemies, the daughters of the Phi•lis′tines, who were ashamed of your lewd behavior. 28 You played the whore with the Assyrians, because you were insatiable; you played the whore with them, and still you were not satisfied. 29 You multiplied your whoring with Chal•dē′a, the land of merchants; and even with this you were not satisfied.

30 How sick is your heart, says the Lord GOD, that you did all these things, the deeds of a brazen whore; 31 building your platform at the head of every street, and making your lofty place in every square! Yet you were not like a whore, because you scorned payment. 32 Adulterous wife, who receives strangers instead of her husband! 33 Gifts are

---

f Gk Syr: Heb *Live! I made you a myriad*   g Cn: Heb *ornament of ornaments*   h Meaning of Heb uncertain   i Heb adds *let it be his*

given to all whores; but you gave your gifts to all your lovers, bribing them to come to you from all around for your whorings. 34 So you were different from other women in your whorings: no one solicited you to play the whore; and you gave payment, while no payment was given to you; you were different.

35 Therefore, O whore, hear the word of the LORD: 36 Thus says the Lord GOD, Because your lust was poured out and your nakedness uncovered in your whoring with your lovers, and because of all your abominable idols, and because of the blood of your children that you gave to them, 37 therefore, I will gather all your lovers, with whom you took pleasure, all those you loved and all those you hated; I will gather them against you from all around, and will uncover your nakedness to them, so that they may see all your nakedness. 38 I will judge you as women who commit adultery and shed blood are judged, and bring blood upon you in wrath and jealousy. 39 I will deliver you into their hands, and they shall throw down your platform and break down your lofty places; they shall strip you of your clothes and take your beautiful objects and leave you naked and bare. 40 They shall bring up a mob against you, and they shall stone you and cut you to pieces with their swords. 41 They shall burn your houses and execute judgments on you in the sight of many women; I will stop you from playing the whore, and you shall also make no more payments. 42 So I will satisfy my fury on you, and my jealousy shall turn away from you; I will be calm, and will be angry no longer. 43 Because you have not remembered the days of your youth, but have enraged me with all these things; therefore, I have returned your deeds upon your head, says the Lord GOD.

Have you not committed lewdness beyond all your abominations? 44 See, everyone who uses proverbs will use this proverb about you, "Like mother, like daughter." 45 You are the daughter of your mother, who loathed her husband and her children; and you are the sister of your sisters, who loathed their husbands and their children. Your mother was a Hit′tite and your father an Am′o•rite. 46 Your elder sister is Sa•mār′i•a, who lived with her daughters to the north of you; and your younger sister, who lived to the south of you, is Sod′om with her daughters. 47 You not only followed their ways, and acted according to their abominations; within a very little time you were more corrupt than they in all your ways. 48 As I live, says the Lord GOD, your sister Sod′om and her daughters have not done as you and your daughters have done. 49 This was the guilt of your sister Sod′om:

she and her daughters had pride, excess of food, and prosperous ease, but did not aid the poor and needy. 50 They were haughty, and did abominable things before me; therefore I removed them when I saw it. 51 Sa•mār′i•a has not committed half your sins; you have committed more abominations than they, and have made your sisters appear righteous by all the abominations that you have committed. 52 Bear your disgrace, you also, for you have brought about for your sisters a more favorable judgment; because of your sins in which you acted more abominably than they, they are more in the right than you. So be ashamed, you also, and bear your disgrace, for you have made your sisters appear righteous.

53 I will restore their fortunes, the fortunes of Sod′om and her daughters and the fortunes of Sa•mār′i•a and her daughters, and I will restore your own fortunes along with theirs, 54 in order that you may bear your disgrace and be ashamed of all that you have done, becoming a consolation to them. 55 As for your sisters, Sod′om and her daughters shall return to their former state, Sa•mār′i•a and her daughters shall return to their former state, and you and your daughters shall return to your former state. 56 Was not your sister Sod′om a byword in your mouth in the day of your pride, 57 before your wickedness was uncovered? Now you are a mockery to the daughters of Ar′am*j* and all her neighbors, and to the daughters of the Philis′tines, those all around who despise you. 58 You must bear the penalty of your lewdness and your abominations, says the LORD.

An Everlasting Covenant

59 Yes, thus says the Lord GOD: I will deal with you as you have done, you who have despised the oath, breaking the covenant; 60 yet I will remember my covenant with you in the days of your youth, and I will establish with you an everlasting covenant. 61 Then you will remember your ways, and be ashamed when I*k* take your sisters, both your elder and your younger, and give them to you as daughters, but not on account of my*l* covenant with you. 62 I will establish my covenant with you, and you shall know that I am the LORD, 63 in order that you may remember and be confounded, and never open your mouth again because of your shame, when I forgive you all that you have done, says the Lord GOD.

---

j Another reading is *Edom*   *k* Syr: Heb *you*   *l* Heb lacks *my*

The Two Eagles and the Vine

The word of the LORD came to me: [2] O mortal, propound a riddle, and speak an allegory to the house of Israel. [3] Say: Thus says the Lord GOD:

A great eagle, with great wings and long
         pinions,
    rich in plumage of many colors,
    came to the Lebanon.
He took the top of the cedar,
[4]   broke off its topmost shoot;
he carried it to a land of trade,
    set it in a city of merchants.
[5] Then he took a seed from the land,
    placed it in fertile soil;
a plant[m] by abundant waters,
    he set it like a willow twig.
[6] It sprouted and became a vine
    spreading out, but low;
its branches turned toward him,
    its roots remained where it stood.
So it became a vine;
    it brought forth branches,
    put forth foliage.

[7] There was another great eagle,
    with great wings and much plumage.
And see! This vine stretched out
    its roots toward him;
it shot out its branches toward him,
    so that he might water it.
From the bed where it was planted
[8]   it was transplanted
to good soil by abundant waters,
    so that it might produce branches
    and bear fruit
    and become a noble vine.

[9] Say: Thus says the Lord GOD:
    Will it prosper?
Will he not pull up its roots,
    cause its fruit to rot[m] and wither,
    its fresh sprouting leaves to fade?
No strong arm or mighty army will be
         needed
    to pull it from its roots.
[10] When it is transplanted, will it thrive?
When the east wind strikes it,
    will it not utterly wither,
    wither on the bed where it grew?

[11] Then the word of the LORD came to me: [12] Say now to the rebellious house: Do you not know what these things mean? Tell them: The king of Babylon came to Jerusalem, took its king and its officials, and brought them back with him to Babylon. [13] He took one of the royal offspring and made a covenant with him, putting him under oath (he had taken away the chief men of the land), [14] so that the kingdom might be humble and not lift itself up, and that by keeping his covenant it might stand. [15] But he rebelled against him by sending ambassadors to Egypt, in order that they might give him horses and a large army. Will he succeed? Can one escape who does such things? Can he break the covenant and yet escape? [16] As I live, says the Lord GOD, surely in the place where the king resides who made him king, whose oath he despised, and whose covenant with him he broke—in Babylon he shall die. [17] Pharaoh with his mighty army and great company will not help him in war, when ramps are cast up and siege walls built to cut off many lives. [18] Because he despised the oath and broke the covenant, because he gave his hand and yet did all these things, he shall not escape. [19] Therefore thus says the Lord GOD: As I live, I will surely return upon his head my oath that he despised, and my covenant that he broke. [20] I will spread my net over him, and he shall be caught in my snare; I will bring him to Babylon and enter into judgment with him there for the treason he has committed against me. [21] All the pick[n] of his troops shall fall by the sword, and the survivors shall be scattered to every wind; and you shall know that I, the LORD, have spoken.

Israel Exalted at Last
(Cp Ezek 31.1–9)

[22] Thus says the Lord GOD:
I myself will take a sprig
    from the lofty top of a cedar;
    I will set it out.
I will break off a tender one
    from the topmost of its young twigs;
I myself will plant it
    on a high and lofty mountain.
[23] On the mountain height of Israel
    I will plant it,
in order that it may produce boughs and
         bear fruit,
    and become a noble cedar.
Under it every kind of bird will live;
    in the shade of its branches will nest
    winged creatures of every kind.
[24] All the trees of the field shall know
    that I am the LORD.
I bring low the high tree,
    I make high the low tree;
I dry up the green tree
    and make the dry tree flourish.
I the LORD have spoken;
    I will accomplish it.

---

[m] Meaning of Heb uncertain   [n] Another reading is *fugitives*

E
Z
E
K

Individual Retribution

The word of the LORD came to me: 2 What do you mean by repeating this proverb concerning the land of Israel, "The parents have eaten sour grapes, and the children's teeth are set on edge"? 3 As I live, says the Lord GOD, this proverb shall no more be used by you in Israel. 4 Know that all lives are mine; the life of the parent as well as the life of the child is mine: it is only the person who sins that shall die.

5 If a man is righteous and does what is lawful and right— 6 if he does not eat upon the mountains or lift up his eyes to the idols of the house of Israel, does not defile his neighbor's wife or approach a woman during her menstrual period, 7 does not oppress anyone, but restores to the debtor his pledge, commits no robbery, gives his bread to the hungry and covers the naked with a garment, 8 does not take advance or accrued interest, withholds his hand from iniquity, executes true justice between contending parties, 9 follows my statutes, and is careful to observe my ordinances, acting faithfully—such a one is righteous; he shall surely live, says the Lord GOD.

10 If he has a son who is violent, a shedder of blood, 11 who does any of these things (though his father[o] does none of them), who eats upon the mountains, defiles his neighbor's wife, 12 oppresses the poor and needy, commits robbery, does not restore the pledge, lifts up his eyes to the idols, commits abomination, 13 takes advance or accrued interest; shall he then live? He shall not. He has done all these abominable things; he shall surely die; his blood shall be upon himself.

14 But if this man has a son who sees all the sins that his father has done, considers, and does not do likewise, 15 who does not eat upon the mountains or lift up his eyes to the idols of the house of Israel, does not defile his neighbor's wife, 16 does not wrong anyone, exacts no pledge, commits no robbery, but gives his bread to the hungry and covers the naked with a garment, 17 withholds his hand from iniquity,[p] takes no advance or accrued interest, observes my ordinances, and follows my statutes; he shall not die for his father's iniquity; he shall surely live. 18 As for his father, because he practiced extortion, robbed his brother, and did what is not good among his people, he dies for his iniquity.

19 Yet you say, "Why should not the son suffer for the iniquity of the father?" When the son has done what is lawful and right, and has been careful to observe all my statutes, he shall surely live. 20 The person who sins shall die. A child shall not suffer for the iniquity of a parent, nor a parent suffer for the iniquity of a child; the righteousness of the righteous shall be his own, and the wickedness of the wicked shall be his own.

21 But if the wicked turn away from all their sins that they have committed and keep all my statutes and do what is lawful and right, they shall surely live; they shall not die. 22 None of the transgressions that they have committed shall be remembered against them; for the righteousness that they have done they shall live. 23 Have I any pleasure in the death of the wicked, says the Lord GOD,

---

o Heb *he*   p Gk: Heb *the poor*

INDIVIDUALS ARE RESPONSIBLE FOR THEIR BEHAVIOR!

Ezekiel, chapter 18, begins with a popular proverb from Ezekiel's time that implies that children are destined to bear the burden of their parents' actions. Ezekiel goes on to explain how this is not so. He emphasizes individual responsibility for our actions. He discourages fatalistic beliefs that we will somehow suffer for the sins of our ancestors (verse 20) and that parents are responsible for the sins of their children. Ezekiel calls the people of his time—and us—to overcome immature attitudes that blame God or others for our personal faults and sins.

■ In what areas do you need to assume responsibility for your actions?
■ Pray for God's help in abandoning immature attitudes that blame others and prevent you from assuming personal responsibility for your actions.

▶ Ezek 18.1–32

and not rather that they should turn from their ways and live? 24 But when the righteous turn away from their righteousness and commit iniquity and do the same abominable things that the wicked do, shall they live? None of the righteous deeds that they have done shall be remembered; for the treachery of which they are guilty and the sin they have committed, they shall die.

25 Yet you say, "The way of the Lord is unfair." Hear now, O house of Israel: Is my way unfair? Is it not your ways that are unfair? 26 When the righteous turn away from their righteousness and commit iniquity, they shall die for it; for the iniquity that they have committed they shall die. 27 Again, when the wicked turn away from the wickedness they have committed and do what is lawful and right, they shall save their life. 28 Because they considered and turned away from all the transgressions that they had committed, they shall surely live; they shall not die. 29 Yet the house of Israel says, "The way of the Lord is unfair." O house of Israel, are my ways unfair? Is it not your ways that are unfair?

30 Therefore I will judge you, O house of Israel, all of you according to your ways, says the Lord GOD. Repent and turn from all your transgressions; otherwise iniquity will be your ruin.*q* 31 Cast away from you all the transgressions that you have committed against me, and get yourselves a new heart and a new spirit! Why will you die, O house of Israel? 32 For I have no pleasure in the death of anyone, says the Lord GOD. Turn, then, and live.

Israel Degraded

As for you, raise up a lamentation for the princes of Israel, 2 and say:
    What a lioness was your mother
        among lions!
    She lay down among young lions,
        rearing her cubs.
3   She raised up one of her cubs;
        he became a young lion,
    and he learned to catch prey;
        he devoured humans.
4   The nations sounded an alarm against him;
        he was caught in their pit;
    and they brought him with hooks
        to the land of Egypt.
5   When she saw that she was thwarted,
        that her hope was lost,
    she took another of her cubs
        and made him a young lion.
6   He prowled among the lions;
        he became a young lion,
    and he learned to catch prey;
        he devoured people.

7   And he ravaged their strongholds,*r*
        and laid waste their towns;
    the land was appalled, and all in it,
        at the sound of his roaring.
8   The nations set upon him
        from the provinces all around;
    they spread their net over him;
        he was caught in their pit.
9   With hooks they put him in a cage,
        and brought him to the king of Babylon;
        they brought him into custody,
    so that his voice should be heard no more
        on the mountains of Israel.
10 Your mother was like a vine in a vineyard*s*
        transplanted by the water,
    fruitful and full of branches
        from abundant water.
11 Its strongest stem became
        a ruler's scepter;*t*
    it towered aloft
        among the thick boughs;
    it stood out in its height
        with its mass of branches.
12 But it was plucked up in fury,
        cast down to the ground;
    the east wind dried it up;
        its fruit was stripped off,
    its strong stem was withered;
        the fire consumed it.
13 Now it is transplanted into the wilderness,
        into a dry and thirsty land.
14 And fire has gone out from its stem,
        has consumed its branches and fruit,
    so that there remains in it no strong stem,
        no scepter for ruling.

This is a lamentation, and it is used as a lamentation.

Israel's Continuing Rebellion

In the seventh year, in the fifth month, on the tenth day of the month, certain elders of Israel came to consult the LORD, and sat down before me. 2 And the word of the LORD came to me: 3 Mortal, speak to the elders of Israel, and say to them: Thus says the Lord GOD: Why are you coming? To consult me? As I live, says the Lord GOD, I will not be consulted by you. 4 Will you judge them, mortal, will you judge them? Then let them know the abominations of their ancestors, 5 and say to them: Thus says the Lord GOD: On the day when I chose Israel, I swore to the offspring of the house of Jacob—making myself known to them in the land of

---

q Or so that they shall not be a stumbling block of iniquity to you   r Heb his widows   s Cn: Heb in your blood
t Heb Its strongest stems became rulers' scepters

Egypt—I swore to them, saying, I am the LORD your God. 6 On that day I swore to them that I would bring them out of the land of Egypt into a land that I had searched out for them, a land flowing with milk and honey, the most glorious of all lands. 7 And I said to them, Cast away the detestable things your eyes feast on, every one of you, and do not defile yourselves with the idols of Egypt; I am the LORD your God. 8 But they rebelled against me and would not listen to me; not one of them cast away the detestable things their eyes feasted on, nor did they forsake the idols of Egypt.

Then I thought I would pour out my wrath upon them and spend my anger against them in the midst of the land of Egypt. 9 But I acted for the sake of my name, that it should not be profaned in the sight of the nations among whom they lived, in whose sight I made myself known to them in bringing them out of the land of Egypt. 10 So I led them out of the land of Egypt and brought them into the wilderness. 11 I gave them my statutes and showed them my ordinances, by whose observance everyone shall live. 12 Moreover I gave them my sabbaths, as a sign between me and them, so that they might know that I the LORD sanctify them. 13 But the house of Israel rebelled against me in the wilderness; they did not observe my statutes but rejected my ordinances, by whose observance everyone shall live; and my sabbaths they greatly profaned.

Then I thought I would pour out my wrath upon them in the wilderness, to make an end of them. 14 But I acted for the sake of my name, so that it should not be profaned in the sight of the nations, in whose sight I had brought them out. 15 Moreover I swore to them in the wilderness that I would not bring them into the land that I had given them, a land flowing with milk and honey, the most glorious of all lands, 16 because they rejected my ordinances and did not observe my statutes, and profaned my sabbaths; for their heart went after their idols. 17 Nevertheless my eye spared them, and I did not destroy them or make an end of them in the wilderness.

18 I said to their children in the wilderness, Do not follow the statutes of your parents, nor observe their ordinances, nor defile yourselves with their idols. 19 I the LORD am your God; follow my statutes, and be careful to observe my ordinances, 20 and hallow my sabbaths that they may be a sign between me and you, so that you may know that I the LORD am your God. 21 But the children rebelled against me; they did not follow my statutes, and were not careful to observe my ordinances, by whose observance everyone shall live; they profaned my sabbaths.

Then I thought I would pour out my wrath upon them and spend my anger against them in the wilderness. 22 But I withheld my hand, and acted for the sake of my name, so that it should not be profaned in the sight of the nations, in whose sight I had brought them out. 23 Moreover I swore to them in the wilderness that I would scatter them among the nations and disperse them through the countries, 24 because they had not executed my ordinances, but had rejected my statutes and profaned my sabbaths, and their eyes were set on their ancestors' idols. 25 Moreover I gave them statutes that were not good and ordinances by which they could not live. 26 I defiled them through their very gifts, in their offering up all their firstborn, in order that I might horrify them, so that they might know that I am the LORD.

27 Therefore, mortal, speak to the house of Israel and say to them, Thus says the Lord GOD: In this again your ancestors blasphemed me, by dealing treacherously with me. 28 For when I had brought them into the land that I swore to give them, then wherever they saw any high hill or any leafy tree, there they offered their sacrifices and presented the provocation of their offering; there they sent up their pleasing odors, and there they poured out their drink offerings. 29 (I said to them, What is the high place to which you go? So it is called Bā'mah[u] to this day.) 30 Therefore say to the house of Israel, Thus says the Lord GOD: Will you defile yourselves after the manner of your ancestors and go astray after their detestable things? 31 When you offer your gifts and make your children pass through the fire, you defile yourselves with all your idols to this day. And shall I be consulted by you, O house of Israel? As I live, says the Lord GOD, I will not be consulted by you.

32 What is in your mind shall never happen—the thought, "Let us be like the nations, like the tribes of the countries, and worship wood and stone."

God Will Restore Israel

33 As I live, says the Lord GOD, surely with a mighty hand and an outstretched arm, and with wrath poured out, I will be king over you. 34 I will bring you out from the peoples and gather you out of the countries where you are scattered, with a mighty hand and an outstretched arm, and with wrath poured out; 35 and I will bring you into the wilderness of the peoples, and there I will enter into judgment with you face to face. 36 As I entered into judgment with your ancestors in the wilderness of the land of Egypt, so I will enter into judg-

---

u That is High Place

ment with you, says the Lord GOD. 37 I will make you pass under the staff, and will bring you within the bond of the covenant. 38 I will purge out the rebels among you, and those who transgress against me; I will bring them out of the land where they reside as aliens, but they shall not enter the land of Israel. Then you shall know that I am the LORD.

39 As for you, O house of Israel, thus says the Lord GOD: Go serve your idols, everyone of you now and hereafter, if you will not listen to me; but my holy name you shall no more profane with your gifts and your idols.

40 For on my holy mountain, the mountain height of Israel, says the Lord GOD, there all the house of Israel, all of them, shall serve me in the land; there I will accept them, and there I will require your contributions and the choicest of your gifts, with all your sacred things. 41 As a pleasing odor I will accept you, when I bring you out from the peoples, and gather you out of the countries where you have been scattered; and I will manifest my holiness among you in the sight of the nations. 42 You shall know that I am the LORD, when I bring you into the land of Israel, the country that I swore to give to your ancestors. 43 There you shall remember your ways and all the deeds by which you have polluted yourselves; and you shall loathe yourselves for all the evils that you have committed. 44 And you shall know that I am the LORD, when I deal with you for my name's sake, not according to your evil ways, or corrupt deeds, O house of Israel, says the Lord GOD.

A Prophecy against the Negeb

45 v The word of the LORD came to me: 46 Mortal, set your face toward the south, preach against the south, and prophesy against the forest land in the Neg'eb; 47 say to the forest of the Neg'eb, Hear the word of the LORD: Thus says the Lord GOD, I will kindle a fire in you, and it shall devour every green tree in you and every dry tree; the blazing flame shall not be quenched, and all faces from south to north shall be scorched by it. 48 All flesh shall see that I the LORD have kindled it; it shall not be quenched. 49 Then I said, "Ah Lord GOD! they are saying of me, 'Is he not a maker of allegories?' "

The Drawn Sword of God

w The word of the LORD came to me: 2 Mortal, set your face toward Jerusalem and preach against the sanctuaries; prophesy against the land of Israel 3 and say to the land of Israel, Thus says the LORD: I am coming against you, and will draw my sword out of its sheath, and will cut off from you both righteous and wicked. 4 Because I will cut off from

you both righteous and wicked, therefore my sword shall go out of its sheath against all flesh from south to north; 5 and all flesh shall know that I the LORD have drawn my sword out of its sheath; it shall not be sheathed again. 6 Moan therefore, mortal; moan with breaking heart and bitter grief before their eyes. 7 And when they say to you, "Why do you moan?" you shall say, "Because of the news that has come. Every heart will melt and all hands will be feeble, every spirit will faint and all knees will turn to water. See, it comes and it will be fulfilled," says the Lord GOD.

8 And the word of the LORD came to me: 9 Mortal, prophesy and say: Thus says the Lord; Say:

A sword, a sword is sharpened,
   it is also polished;
10 it is sharpened for slaughter,
   honed to flash like lightning!
How can we make merry?
   You have despised the rod,
   and all discipline.x
11 The sword y is given to be polished,
   to be grasped in the hand;
it is sharpened, the sword is polished,
   to be placed in the slayer's hand.
12 Cry and wail, O mortal,
   for it is against my people;
it is against all Israel's princes;
   they are thrown to the sword,
   together with my people.
   Ah! Strike the thigh!
13 For consider: What! If you despise the rod, will it not happen?x says the Lord GOD.
14 And you, mortal, prophesy;
   strike hand to hand.
Let the sword fall twice, thrice;
   it is a sword for killing.
A sword for great slaughter—
   it surrounds them;
15 therefore hearts melt
   and many stumble.
At all their gates I have set
   the pointx of the sword.
Ah! It is made for flashing,
   it is polished z for slaughter.
16 Attack to the right!
   Engage to the left!
   —wherever your edge is directed.
17 I too will strike hand to hand,
   I will satisfy my fury;
   I the LORD have spoken.
18 The word of the LORD came to me: 19 Mortal, mark out two roads for the sword of the king of

---

v Ch 21.1 in Heb   w Ch 21.6 in Heb   x Meaning of Heb uncertain   y Heb It   z Tg: Heb wrapped up

EZEK

Babylon to come; both of them shall issue from the same land. And make a signpost, make it for a fork in the road leading to a city; 20 mark out the road for the sword to come to Rab'bah of the Am'-mon•ites or to Judah and to*a* Jerusalem the fortified. 21 For the king of Babylon stands at the parting of the way, at the fork in the two roads, to use divination; he shakes the arrows, he consults the teraphim,*b* he inspects the liver. 22 Into his right hand comes the lot for Jerusalem, to set battering rams, to call out for slaughter, for raising the battle cry, to set battering rams against the gates, to cast up ramps, to build siege towers. 23 But to them it will seem like a false divination; they have sworn solemn oaths; but he brings their guilt to remembrance, bringing about their capture.

24 Therefore thus says the Lord GOD: Because you have brought your guilt to remembrance, in that your transgressions are uncovered, so that in all your deeds your sins appear—because you have come to remembrance, you shall be taken in hand.*c*

25 As for you, vile, wicked prince of Israel,
 you whose day has come,
 the time of final punishment,
26 thus says the Lord GOD:
Remove the turban, take off the crown;
 things shall not remain as they are.
Exalt that which is low,
 abase that which is high.
27 A ruin, a ruin, a ruin—
 I will make it!
 (Such has never occurred.)
Until he comes whose right it is;
 to him I will give it.

28 As for you, mortal, prophesy, and say, Thus says the Lord GOD concerning the Am'mon•ites, and concerning their reproach; say:
A sword, a sword! Drawn for slaughter,
 polished to consume,*d* to flash like
 lightning.
29 Offering false visions for you,
 divining lies for you,
they place you over the necks
 of the vile, wicked ones—
those whose day has come,
 the time of final punishment.
30 Return it to its sheath!
In the place where you were created,
 in the land of your origin,
 I will judge you.
31 I will pour out my indignation upon you,
 with the fire of my wrath
 I will blow upon you.
I will deliver you into brutish hands,
 those skillful to destroy.

32 You shall be fuel for the fire,
 your blood shall enter the earth;
 you shall be remembered no more,
 for I the LORD have spoken.

The Bloody City

The word of the LORD came to me: 2 You, mortal, will you judge, will you judge the bloody city? Then declare to it all its abominable deeds. 3 You shall say, Thus says the Lord GOD: A city! Shedding blood within itself; its time has come; making its idols, defiling itself. 4 You have become guilty by the blood that you have shed, and defiled by the idols that you have made; you have brought your day near, the appointed time of your years has come. Therefore I have made you a disgrace before the nations, and a mockery to all the countries. 5 Those who are near and those who are far from you will mock you, you infamous one, full of tumult.

6 The princes of Israel in you, everyone according to his power, have been bent on shedding blood. 7 Father and mother are treated with contempt in you; the alien residing within you suffers extortion; the orphan and the widow are wronged in you. 8 You have despised my holy things, and profaned my sabbaths. 9 In you are those who slander to shed blood, those in you who eat upon the mountains, who commit lewdness in your midst. 10 In you they uncover their fathers' nakedness; in you they violate women in their menstrual periods. 11 One commits abomination with his neighbor's wife; another lewdly defiles his daughter-in-law; another in you defiles his sister, his father's daughter. 12 In you, they take bribes to shed blood; you take both advance interest and accrued interest, and make gain of your neighbors by extortion; and you have forgotten me, says the Lord GOD.

13 See, I strike my hands together at the dishonest gain you have made, and at the blood that has been shed within you. 14 Can your courage endure, or can your hands remain strong in the days when I shall deal with you? I the LORD have spoken, and I will do it. 15 I will scatter you among the nations and disperse you through the countries, and I will purge your filthiness out of you. 16 And I*e* shall be profaned through you in the sight of the nations; and you shall know that I am the LORD.

17 The word of the LORD came to me: 18 Mortal, the house of Israel has become dross to me; all of

---

a Gk Syr: Heb *Judah in*   *b* Or *the household gods*   *c* Or *be taken captive*   *d* Cn: Heb *to contain*   *e* Gk Syr Vg: Heb *you*

them, silver,*f* bronze, tin, iron, and lead. In the smelter they have become dross. ¹⁹Therefore thus says the Lord GOD: Because you have all become dross, I will gather you into the midst of Jerusalem. ²⁰As one gathers silver, bronze, iron, lead, and tin into a smelter, to blow the fire upon them in order to melt them; so I will gather you in my anger and in my wrath, and I will put you in and melt you. ²¹I will gather you and blow upon you with the fire of my wrath, and you shall be melted within it. ²²As silver is melted in a smelter, so you shall be melted in it; and you shall know that I the LORD have poured out my wrath upon you.

23 The word of the LORD came to me: ²⁴Mortal, say to it: You are a land that is not cleansed, not rained upon in the day of indignation. ²⁵Its princes*g* within it are like a roaring lion tearing the prey; they have devoured human lives; they have taken treasure and precious things; they have made many widows within it. ²⁶Its priests have done violence to my teaching and have profaned my holy things; they have made no distinction between the holy and the common, neither have they taught the difference between the unclean and the clean, and they have disregarded my sabbaths, so that I am profaned among them. ²⁷Its officials within it are like wolves tearing the prey, shedding blood, destroying lives to get dishonest gain. ²⁸Its prophets have smeared whitewash on their behalf, seeing false visions and divining lies for them, saying, "Thus says the Lord GOD," when the LORD has not spoken. ²⁹The people of the land have practiced extortion and committed robbery;

they have oppressed the poor and needy, and have extorted from the alien without redress. ³⁰And I sought for anyone among them who would repair the wall and stand in the breach before me on behalf of the land, so that I would not destroy it; but I found no one. ³¹Therefore I have poured out my indignation upon them; I have consumed them with the fire of my wrath; I have returned their conduct upon their heads, says the Lord GOD.

Oholah and Oholibah

The word of the LORD came to me: ²Mortal, there were two women, the daughters of one mother; ³they played the whore in Egypt; they played the whore in their youth; their breasts were caressed there, and their virgin bosoms were fondled. ⁴O•hō'lah was the name of the elder and O•hol'i•bah the name of her sister. They became mine, and they bore sons and daughters. As for their names, O•hō'lah is Sa•mār'i•a, and O•hol'i•bah is Jerusalem.

5 O•hō'lah played the whore while she was mine; she lusted after her lovers the Assyrians, warriors*h* ⁶clothed in blue, governors and commanders, all of them handsome young men, mounted horsemen. ⁷She bestowed her favors upon them, the choicest men of Assyria all of them; and she defiled herself with all the idols of everyone for whom she lusted. ⁸She did not give up her whorings that she had practiced since Egypt; for in her

f Transposed from the end of the verse; compare verse 20
g Gk: Heb *indignation.* *25A conspiracy of its prophets*
h Meaning of Heb uncertain

Irresponsible Children

LIVE IT!

Raising children is a demanding job. In teaching their children about life, parents try to help them be responsible—to accept the consequences for their actions. For example, a parent might say: "You threw the ball and broke the window. The wind had nothing to do with it! Now, what are you going to do about it?"

Chapters 13–24 of Ezekiel contain prophecies, allegories, fables, and symbolic actions, all intended to encourage the people of Judah to take responsibility for their sinful actions. In a graphic allegory in chapter 23, the northern and southern kingdoms are compared to promiscuous daughters who will sleep with almost anyone who comes their way. God is using just about every possible means to say, "Take responsibility for your actions, my children, and live with the consequences!"

We are all like little children in that we are often tempted to ignore the consequences of our actions. For instance, we may think of cheating on homework as just a little wrong. But that wrong will catch up with us. It will lead to more cheating, in bigger things. By then, our "little" wrong could mean losing a job or destroying a relationship. If you want to please God, be honest in looking at the consequences of your actions and choose responsibly!

▶ Ezek 23.1–21

youth men had lain with her and fondled her virgin bosom and poured out their lust upon her. [9]Therefore I delivered her into the hands of her lovers, into the hands of the Assyrians, for whom she lusted. [10]These uncovered her nakedness; they seized her sons and her daughters; and they killed her with the sword. Judgment was executed upon her, and she became a byword among women.

[11] Her sister Ō·hol'i·bah saw this, yet she was more corrupt than she in her lusting and in her whorings, which were worse than those of her sister. [12]She lusted after the Assyrians, governors and commanders, warriors[i] clothed in full armor, mounted horsemen, all of them handsome young men. [13]And I saw that she was defiled; they both took the same way. [14]But she carried her whorings further; she saw male figures carved on the wall, images of the Chal·dē'ans portrayed in vermilion, [15]with belts around their waists, with flowing turbans on their heads, all of them looking like officers—a picture of Babylonians whose native land was Chal·dē'a. [16]When she saw them she lusted after them, and sent messengers to them in Chal·dē'a. [17]And the Babylonians came to her into the bed of love, and they defiled her with their lust; and after she defiled herself with them, she turned from them in disgust. [18]When she carried on her whorings so openly and flaunted her nakedness, I turned in disgust from her, as I had turned from her sister. [19]Yet she increased her whorings, remembering the days of her youth, when she played the whore in the land of Egypt [20]and lusted after her paramours there, whose members were like those of donkeys, and whose emission was like that of stallions. [21]Thus you longed for the lewdness of your youth, when the Egyptians[j] fondled your bosom and caressed[k] your young breasts.

[22] Therefore, O Ō·hol'i·bah, thus says the Lord GOD: I will rouse against you your lovers from whom you turned in disgust, and I will bring them against you from every side: [23]the Babylonians and all the Chal·dē'ans, Pē'kod and Shō'a and Kō'a, and all the Assyrians with them, handsome young men, governors and commanders all of them, officers and warriors,[l] all of them riding on horses. [24]They shall come against you from the north[m] with chariots and wagons and a host of peoples; they shall set themselves against you on every side with buckler, shield, and helmet, and I will commit the judgment to them, and they shall judge you according to their ordinances. [25]I will direct my indignation against you, in order that they may deal with you in fury. They shall cut off your nose and your ears, and your survivors shall fall by the sword. They shall seize your sons and

your daughters, and your survivors shall be devoured by fire. [26]They shall also strip you of your clothes and take away your fine jewels. [27]So I will put an end to your lewdness and your whoring brought from the land of Egypt; you shall not long for them, or remember Egypt any more. [28]For thus says the Lord GOD: I will deliver you into the hands of those whom you hate, into the hands of those from whom you turned in disgust; [29]and they shall deal with you in hatred, and take away all the fruit of your labor, and leave you naked and bare, and the nakedness of your whorings shall be exposed. Your lewdness and your whorings [30]have brought this upon you, because you played the whore with the nations, and polluted yourself with their idols. [31]You have gone the way of your sister; therefore I will give her cup into your hand. [32]Thus says the Lord GOD:

You shall drink your sister's cup,
    deep and wide;
you shall be scorned and derided,
    it holds so much.
[33] You shall be filled with drunkenness and
        sorrow.
    A cup of horror and desolation
        is the cup of your sister Sa·mār'i·a;
[34] you shall drink it and drain it out,
    and gnaw its sherds,
    and tear out your breasts;

for I have spoken, says the Lord GOD. [35]Therefore thus says the Lord GOD: Because you have forgotten me and cast me behind your back, therefore bear the consequences of your lewdness and whorings.

[36] The LORD said to me: Mortal, will you judge Ō·hō'lah and Ō·hol'i·bah? Then declare to them their abominable deeds. [37]For they have committed adultery, and blood is on their hands; with their idols they have committed adultery; and they have even offered up to them for food the children whom they had borne to me. [38]Moreover this they have done to me: they have defiled my sanctuary on the same day and profaned my sabbaths. [39]For when they had slaughtered their children for their idols, on the same day they came into my sanctuary to profane it. This is what they did in my house.

[40] They even sent for men to come from far away, to whom a messenger was sent, and they came. For them you bathed yourself, painted your eyes, and decked yourself with ornaments; [41]you sat on a stately couch, with a table spread before it

---

[i] Meaning of Heb uncertain   [j] Two Mss: MT *from Egypt*
[k] Cn: Heb *for the sake of*   [l] Compare verses 6 and 12:
Heb *officers and called ones*   [m] Gk: Meaning of Heb uncertain

on which you had placed my incense and my oil. 42 The sound of a raucous multitude was around her, with many of the rabble brought in drunken from the wilderness; and they put bracelets on the arms[n] of the women, and beautiful crowns upon their heads.

43 Then I said, Ah, she is worn out with adulteries, but they carry on their sexual acts with her. 44 For they have gone in to her, as one goes in to a whore. Thus they went in to Ō·hŏʹlah and to Ō·holʹi·bah, wanton women. 45 But righteous judges shall declare them guilty of adultery and of bloodshed; because they are adulteresses and blood is on their hands.

46 For thus says the Lord GOD: Bring up an assembly against them, and make them an object of terror and of plunder. 47 The assembly shall stone them and with their swords they shall cut them down; they shall kill their sons and their daughters, and burn up their houses. 48 Thus will I put an end to lewdness in the land, so that all women may take warning and not commit lewdness as you have done. 49 They shall repay you for your lewdness, and you shall bear the penalty for your sinful idolatry; and you shall know that I am the Lord GOD.

The Boiling Pot
(Cp Jer 1.13–19)

In the ninth year, in the tenth month, on the tenth day of the month, the word of the LORD came to me: 2 Mortal, write down the name of this day, this very day. The king of Babylon has laid siege to Jerusalem this very day. 3 And utter an allegory to the rebellious house and say to them, Thus says the Lord GOD:

Set on the pot, set it on,
  pour in water also;
4 put in it the pieces,
    all the good pieces, the thigh and the
      shoulder;
    fill it with choice bones.
5 Take the choicest one of the flock,
    pile the logs[o] under it;
  boil its pieces,[p]
    seethe[q] also its bones in it.

6 Therefore thus says the Lord GOD:
Woe to the bloody city,
    the pot whose rust is in it,
    whose rust has not gone out of it!
  Empty it piece by piece,
    making no choice at all.[r]
7 For the blood she shed is inside it;
    she placed it on a bare rock;

she did not pour it out on the ground,
    to cover it with earth.
8 To rouse my wrath, to take vengeance,
    I have placed the blood she shed
    on a bare rock,
    so that it may not be covered.
9 Therefore thus says the Lord GOD:
  Woe to the bloody city!
    I will even make the pile great.
10 Heap up the logs, kindle the fire;
    boil the meat well, mix in the spices,
    let the bones be burned.
11 Stand it empty upon the coals,
    so that it may become hot, its copper
      glow,
    its filth melt in it, its rust be consumed.
12 In vain I have wearied myself;[s]
    its thick rust does not depart.
    To the fire with its rust![t]
13 Yet, when I cleansed you in your filthy
      lewdness,
    you did not become clean from your filth;
  you shall not again be cleansed
    until I have satisfied my fury upon you.
14 I the LORD have spoken; the time is coming, I will act. I will not refrain, I will not spare, I will not relent. According to your ways and your doings I will judge you, says the Lord GOD.

Ezekiel's Bereavement

15 The word of the LORD came to me: 16 Mortal, with one blow I am about to take away from you the delight of your eyes; yet you shall not mourn or weep, nor shall your tears run down. 17 Sigh, but not aloud; make no mourning for the dead. Bind on your turban, and put your sandals on your feet; do not cover your upper lip or eat the bread of mourners.[u] 18 So I spoke to the people in the morning, and at evening my wife died. And on the next morning I did as I was commanded.

19 Then the people said to me, "Will you not tell us what these things mean for us, that you are acting this way?" 20 Then I said to them: The word of the LORD came to me: 21 Say to the house of Israel, Thus says the Lord GOD: I will profane my sanctuary, the pride of your power, the delight of your eyes, and your heart's desire; and your sons and your daughters whom you left behind shall fall by the sword. 22 And you shall do as I have done; you shall not cover your upper lip or eat the bread of mourners.[u] 23 Your turbans shall be on

---

n Heb hands   o Compare verse 10: Heb the bones
p Two Mss: Heb its boilings   q Cn: Heb its bones seethe
r Heb piece, no lot has fallen on it   s Cn: Meaning of Heb
uncertain   t Meaning of Heb uncertain   u Vg Tg: Heb
of men

your heads and your sandals on your feet; you shall not mourn or weep, but you shall pine away in your iniquities and groan to one another. [24] Thus E·zēk′i·el shall be a sign to you; you shall do just as he has done. When this comes, then you shall know that I am the Lord GOD.

25 And you, mortal, on the day when I take from them their stronghold, their joy and glory, the delight of their eyes and their heart's affection, and also[v] their sons and their daughters, [26] on that day, one who has escaped will come to you to report to you the news. [27] On that day your mouth shall be opened to the one who has escaped, and you shall speak and no longer be silent. So you shall be a sign to them; and they shall know that I am the LORD.

Proclamation against Ammon

The word of the LORD came to me: [2] Mortal, set your face toward the Am′mon·ites and prophesy against them. [3] Say to the Am′mon·ites, Hear the word of the Lord GOD: Thus says the Lord GOD, Because you said, "Aha!" over my sanctuary when it was profaned, and over the land of Israel when it was made desolate, and over the house of Judah when it went into exile; [4] therefore I am handing you over to the people of the east for a possession. They shall set their encampments among you and pitch their tents in your midst; they shall eat your fruit, and they shall drink your milk. [5] I will make Rab′bah a pasture for camels and Am′mon a fold for flocks. Then you shall know that I am the LORD. [6] For thus says the Lord GOD: Because you have clapped your hands and stamped your feet and rejoiced with all the malice within you against the land of Israel, [7] therefore I have stretched out my hand against you, and will hand you over as plunder to the nations. I will cut you off from the peoples and will make you perish out of the countries; I will destroy you. Then you shall know that I am the LORD.

Proclamation against Moab

8 Thus says the Lord GOD: Because Mō′ab[w] said, The house of Judah is like all the other nations, [9] therefore I will lay open the flank of Mō′ab from the towns[x] on its frontier, the glory of the country, Beth-jesh′i·moth, Bā′al-mē′on, and Kir·i·a-thā′im. [10] I will give it along with Am′mon to the people of the east as a possession. Thus Am′mon shall be remembered no more among the nations, [11] and I will execute judgments upon Mō′ab. Then they shall know that I am the LORD.

Proclamation against Edom

12 Thus says the Lord GOD: Because Ē′dom acted revengefully against the house of Judah and has grievously offended in taking vengeance upon them, [13] therefore thus says the Lord GOD, I will stretch out my hand against Ē′dom, and cut off from it humans and animals, and I will make it desolate; from Tē′man even to Dē′dan they shall fall by the sword. [14] I will lay my vengeance upon Ē′dom by the hand of my people Israel; and they shall act in Ē′dom according to my anger and according to my wrath; and they shall know my vengeance, says the Lord GOD.

Proclamation against Philistia

15 Thus says the Lord GOD: Because with unending hostilities the Phi·lis′tines acted in vengeance, and with malice of heart took revenge in destruction; [16] therefore thus says the Lord GOD, I will stretch out my hand against the Phi·lis′tines, cut off the Cher′e·thites, and destroy the rest of the seacoast. [17] I will execute great vengeance on them with wrathful punishments. Then they shall know that I am the LORD, when I lay my vengeance on them.

Proclamation against Tyre

In the eleventh year, on the first day of the month, the word of the LORD came to me: [2] Mortal, because Tyre said concerning Jerusalem,
"Aha, broken is the gateway of the peoples;
    it has swung open to me;
I shall be replenished,
    now that it is wasted,"
[3] therefore, thus says the Lord GOD:
    See, I am against you, O Tyre!
    I will hurl many nations against you,
        as the sea hurls its waves.
4   They shall destroy the walls of Tyre
        and break down its towers.
    I will scrape its soil from it
        and make it a bare rock.
5   It shall become, in the midst of the sea,
        a place for spreading nets.
I have spoken, says the Lord GOD.
    It shall become plunder for the nations,
6   and its daughter-towns in the country
        shall be killed by the sword.
Then they shall know that I am the LORD.

7 For thus says the Lord GOD: I will bring against Tyre from the north King Ne·bu·chad·rez′zar of Babylon, king of kings, together with horses, chariots, cavalry, and a great and powerful army.

---

v Heb lacks *and also*   w Gk Old Latin: Heb *Moab and Seir*
x Heb *towns from its towns*

8 Your daughter-towns in the country
    he shall put to the sword.
He shall set up a siege wall against you,
    cast up a ramp against you,
    and raise a roof of shields against you.
9 He shall direct the shock of his battering
       rams against your walls
    and break down your towers with his
       axes.
10 His horses shall be so many
    that their dust shall cover you.
At the noise of cavalry, wheels, and chariots
    your very walls shall shake,
when he enters your gates
    like those entering a breached city.
11 With the hoofs of his horses
    he shall trample all your streets.
He shall put your people to the sword,
    and your strong pillars shall fall to the
       ground.
12 They will plunder your riches
    and loot your merchandise;
they shall break down your walls
    and destroy your fine houses.
Your stones and timber and soil
    they shall cast into the water.
13 I will silence the music of your songs;
    the sound of your lyres shall be heard no
       more.
14 I will make you a bare rock;
    you shall be a place for spreading nets.
You shall never again be rebuilt,
    for I the LORD have spoken,
    says the Lord GOD.

15 Thus says the Lord GOD to Tyre: Shall not the coastlands shake at the sound of your fall, when the wounded groan, when slaughter goes on within you? 16 Then all the princes of the sea shall step down from their thrones; they shall remove their robes and strip off their embroidered garments. They shall clothe themselves with trembling, and shall sit on the ground; they shall tremble every moment, and be appalled at you. 17 And they shall raise a lamentation over you, and say to you:

How you have vanished^y from the seas,
    O city renowned,
once mighty on the sea,
    you and your inhabitants,^z
who imposed your^a terror
    on all the mainland!^b
18 Now the coastlands tremble
    on the day of your fall;
the coastlands by the sea
    are dismayed at your passing.

19 For thus says the Lord GOD: When I make you a city laid waste, like cities that are not inhabited, when I bring up the deep over you, and the great waters cover you, 20 then I will thrust you down with those who descend into the Pit, to the people of long ago, and I will make you live in the world below, among primeval ruins, with those who go down to the Pit, so that you will not be inhabited or have a place^c in the land of the living. 21 I will bring you to a dreadful end, and you shall be no more; though sought for, you will never be found again, says the Lord GOD.

Lamentation over Tyre

The word of the LORD came to me: 2 Now you, mortal, raise a lamentation over Tyre, 3 and say to Tyre, which sits at the entrance to the sea, merchant of the peoples on many coastlands, Thus says the Lord GOD:

O Tyre, you have said,
    "I am perfect in beauty."
4 Your borders are in the heart of the seas;
    your builders made perfect your beauty.
5 They made all your planks
    of fir trees from Senir;
they took a cedar from Lebanon
    to make a mast for you.
6 From oaks of Bashan
    they made your oars;
they made your deck of pines^d
    from the coasts of Cyprus,
    inlaid with ivory.
7 Of fine embroidered linen from Egypt
    was your sail,
    serving as your ensign;
blue and purple from the coasts of E•li'shah
    was your awning.
8 The inhabitants of Sidon and Arvad
    were your rowers;
skilled men of Zemer^e were within you,
    they were your pilots.
9 The elders of Gebal and its artisans were
       within you,
    caulking your seams;
all the ships of the sea with their mariners
       were within you,
    to barter for your wares.
10 Par'as^f and Lud and Put
    were in your army,
    your mighty warriors;

---

y Gk OL Aquila: Heb *have vanished, O inhabited one,*
z Heb *it and its inhabitants*   a Heb *their*   b Cn: Heb *its inhabitants*   c Gk: Heb *I will give beauty*   d Or *boxwood*
e Cn Compare Gen 10.18: Heb *your skilled men, O Tyre*
f Or *Persia*

E
Z
E
K

they hung shield and helmet in you;
    they gave you splendor.
11 Men of Ar'vad and Hē'lech*g*
    were on your walls all around;
    men of Gā'mad were at your towers.
They hung their quivers all around your
      walls;
    they made perfect your beauty.

12 Tar'shish did business with you out of the abundance of your great wealth; silver, iron, tin, and lead they exchanged for your wares. 13 Jā'van, Tū'bal, and Mē'shech traded with you; they exchanged human beings and vessels of bronze for your merchandise. 14 Beth-tō•gar'mah exchanged for your wares horses, war horses, and mules. 15 The Rhō'di•ans*h* traded with you; many coastlands were your own special markets; they brought you in payment ivory tusks and ebony. 16 Ē'dom*i* did business with you because of your abundant goods; they exchanged for your wares turquoise, purple, embroidered work, fine linen, coral, and rubies. 17 Judah and the land of Israel traded with you; they exchanged for your merchandise wheat from Min'nith, millet,*j* honey, oil, and balm. 18 Damascus traded with you for your abundant goods—because of your great wealth of every kind—wine of Hel'bon, and white wool. 19 Vē'dan and Jā'van from Ū'zal*j* entered into trade for your wares; wrought iron, cassia, and sweet cane were bartered for your merchandise. 20 Dē'dan traded with you in saddlecloths for riding. 21 Arabia and all the princes of Kē'dar were your favored dealers in lambs, rams, and goats; in these they did business with you. 22 The merchants of Shē'ba and Rā'a•mah traded with you; they exchanged for your wares the best of all kinds of spices, and all precious stones, and gold. 23 Har'an, Can'neh, Eden, the merchants of Shē'ba, As'shur, and Chil'mad traded with you. 24 These traded with you in choice garments, in clothes of blue and embroidered work, and in carpets of colored material, bound with cords and made secure; in these they traded with you.*k* 25 The ships of Tar'shish traveled for you in your trade.

So you were filled and heavily laden
    in the heart of the seas.
26 Your rowers have brought you
    into the high seas.
The east wind has wrecked you
    in the heart of the seas.
27 Your riches, your wares, your merchandise,
    your mariners and your pilots,
    your caulkers, your dealers in merchandise,
    and all your warriors within you,
    with all the company
      that is with you,

    sink into the heart of the seas
    on the day of your ruin.
28 At the sound of the cry of your pilots
    the countryside shakes,
29 and down from their ships
    come all that handle the oar.
The mariners and all the pilots of the sea
    stand on the shore
30 and wail aloud over you,
    and cry bitterly.
They throw dust on their heads
    and wallow in ashes;
31 they make themselves bald for you,
    and put on sackcloth,
and they weep over you in bitterness of soul,
    with bitter mourning.
32 In their wailing they raise a lamentation
      for you,
    and lament over you:
"Who was ever destroyed*l* like Tȳre
    in the midst of the sea?
33 When your wares came from the seas,
    you satisfied many peoples;
with your abundant wealth and
      merchandise
    you enriched the kings of the earth.

27.34

34 Now you are wrecked by the seas,
    in the depths of the waters;
your merchandise and all your crew
    have sunk with you.
35 All the inhabitants of the coastlands
    are appalled at you;

---

g Or *and your army*   *h* Gk: Heb *The Dedanites*   *i* Another reading is *Aram*   *j* Meaning of Heb uncertain   *k* Cn: Heb *in your market*   *l* Tg Vg: Heb *like silence*

EZEK

and their kings are horribly afraid,
   their faces are convulsed.
36 The merchants among the peoples hiss
       at you;
   you have come to a dreadful end
   and shall be no more forever."

Proclamation against the King of Tyre

28 The word of the LORD came to me: 2 Mortal, say to the prince of Tyre, Thus says the Lord GOD:
   Because your heart is proud
       and you have said, "I am a god;
   I sit in the seat of the gods,
       in the heart of the seas,"
   yet you are but a mortal, and no god,
       though you compare your mind
       with the mind of a god.
3 You are indeed wiser than Daniel;[m]
       no secret is hidden from you;
4 by your wisdom and your understanding
       you have amassed wealth for yourself,
   and have gathered gold and silver
       into your treasuries.
5 By your great wisdom in trade
       you have increased your wealth,
   and your heart has become proud in your
       wealth.
6 Therefore thus says the Lord GOD:
   Because you compare your mind
       with the mind of a god,
7 therefore, I will bring strangers against you,
       the most terrible of the nations;
   they shall draw their swords against the
           beauty of your wisdom
       and defile your splendor.
8 They shall thrust you down to the Pit,
       and you shall die a violent death
       in the heart of the seas.
9 Will you still say, "I am a god,"
       in the presence of those who kill you,
   though you are but a mortal, and no god,
       in the hands of those who wound you?
10 You shall die the death of the
           uncircumcised
       by the hand of foreigners;
   for I have spoken, says the Lord GOD.

Lamentation over the King of Tyre

11 Moreover the word of the LORD came to me:
12 Mortal, raise a lamentation over the king of Tyre,
and say to him, Thus says the Lord GOD:
   You were the signet of perfection,[n]
       full of wisdom and perfect in beauty.
13 You were in Eden, the garden of God;
       every precious stone was your covering,

carnelian, chrysolite, and moonstone,
   beryl, onyx, and jasper,
sapphire,[o] turquoise, and emerald;
   and worked in gold were your settings
   and your engravings.[n]
On the day that you were created
   they were prepared.
14 With an anointed cherub as guardian I
       placed you;[n]
   you were on the holy mountain of God;
   you walked among the stones of fire.
15 You were blameless in your ways
       from the day that you were created,
       until iniquity was found in you.
16 In the abundance of your trade
       you were filled with violence, and you
           sinned;
   so I cast you as a profane thing from the
           mountain of God,
   and the guardian cherub drove you out
       from among the stones of fire.
17 Your heart was proud because of your
       beauty;
   you corrupted your wisdom for the sake
       of your splendor.
   I cast you to the ground;
       I exposed you before kings,
       to feast their eyes on you.
18 By the multitude of your iniquities,
       in the unrighteousness of your trade,
       you profaned your sanctuaries.
   So I brought out fire from within you;
       it consumed you,
   and I turned you to ashes on the earth
       in the sight of all who saw you.
19 All who know you among the peoples
       are appalled at you;
   you have come to a dreadful end
       and shall be no more forever.

Proclamation against Sidon

20 The word of the LORD came to me: 21 Mortal, set your face toward Si'don, and prophesy against it, 22 and say, Thus says the Lord GOD:
   I am against you, O Si'don,
       and I will gain glory in your midst.
   They shall know that I am the LORD
       when I execute judgments in it,
       and manifest my holiness in it;
23 for I will send pestilence into it,
       and bloodshed into its streets;
   and the dead shall fall in its midst,

---

m Or, as otherwise read, *Danel*   n Meaning of Heb
uncertain   o Or *lapis lazuli*

by the sword that is against it on every
side.
And they shall know that I am the LORD.

24 The house of Israel shall no longer find a
pricking brier or a piercing thorn among all their
neighbors who have treated them with contempt.
And they shall know that I am the Lord GOD.

Future Blessing for Israel

25 Thus says the Lord GOD: When I gather the
house of Israel from the peoples among whom
they are scattered, and manifest my holiness in
them in the sight of the nations, then they shall
settle on their own soil that I gave to my servant
Jacob. 26 They shall live in safety in it, and shall
build houses and plant vineyards. They shall live
in safety, when I execute judgments upon all their
neighbors who have treated them with contempt.
And they shall know that I am the LORD their God.

Proclamation against Egypt

In the tenth year, in the tenth month, on the
twelfth day of the month, the word of the LORD
came to me: 2 Mortal, set your face against Pharaoh
king of Egypt, and prophesy against him and
against all Egypt; 3 speak, and say, Thus says the
Lord GOD:

I am against you,
　　Pharaoh king of Egypt,
the great dragon sprawling
　　in the midst of its channels,
saying, "My Nile is my own;
　　I made it for myself."
4 I will put hooks in your jaws,
　　and make the fish of your channels stick
　　　　to your scales.
I will draw you up from your channels,
　　with all the fish of your channels
　　sticking to your scales.
5 I will fling you into the wilderness,
　　you and all the fish of your channels;
you shall fall in the open field,
　　and not be gathered and buried.
To the animals of the earth and to the birds
　　　　of the air
　　I have given you as food.
6 Then all the inhabitants of Egypt shall know
　　that I am the LORD
because you[p] were a staff of reed
　　to the house of Israel;
7 when they grasped you with the hand, you
　　broke,
　　and tore all their shoulders;
and when they leaned on you, you broke,
　　and made all their legs unsteady.[q]

8 Therefore, thus says the Lord GOD: I will
bring a sword upon you, and will cut off from you
human being and animal; 9 and the land of Egypt
shall be a desolation and a waste. Then they shall
know that I am the LORD.

Because you[r] said, "The Nile is mine, and I
made it," 10 therefore, I am against you, and against
your channels, and I will make the land of Egypt
an utter waste and desolation, from Mig′dŏl to Sȳ-
ē′nē, as far as the border of Ethiopia.[s] 11 No human foot shall pass through it, and no animal foot
shall pass through it; it shall be uninhabited forty
years. 12 I will make the land of Egypt a desolation
among desolated countries; and her cities shall be
a desolation forty years among cities that are laid
waste. I will scatter the Egyptians among the nations, and disperse them among the countries.

13 Further, thus says the Lord GOD: At the end
of forty years I will gather the Egyptians from the
peoples among whom they were scattered; 14 and I
will restore the fortunes of Egypt, and bring them
back to the land of Path′ros, the land of their origin; and there they shall be a lowly kingdom. 15 It
shall be the most lowly of the kingdoms, and
never again exalt itself above the nations; and I
will make them so small that they will never again
rule over the nations. 16 The Egyptians[t] shall never
again be the reliance of the house of Israel; they
will recall their iniquity, when they turned to them
for aid. Then they shall know that I am the Lord
GOD.

Babylonia Will Plunder Egypt

17 In the twenty-seventh year, in the first
month, on the first day of the month, the word of
the LORD came to me: 18 Mortal, King Ne•bū•chad-
rez′zar of Babylon made his army labor hard
against Tȳre; every head was made bald and every
shoulder was rubbed bare; yet neither he nor his
army got anything from Tȳre to pay for the labor
that he had expended against it. 19 Therefore thus
says the Lord GOD: I will give the land of Egypt to
King Ne•bū•chad•rez′zar of Babylon; and he shall
carry off its wealth and despoil it and plunder it;
and it shall be the wages for his army. 20 I have
given him the land of Egypt as his payment for
which he labored, because they worked for me,
says the Lord GOD.

21 On that day I will cause a horn to sprout up
for the house of Israel, and I will open your lips
among them. Then they shall know that I am the
LORD.

---

p Gk Syr Vg: Heb *they*　*q* Syr: Heb *stand*　*r* Gk Syr Vg:
Heb *he*　*s* Or Nubia; Heb *Cush*　*t* Heb *It*

Lamentation for Egypt

The word of the LORD came to me: 2 Mortal, prophesy, and say, Thus says the Lord GOD:

Wail, "Alas for the day!"
3   For a day is near,
      the day of the LORD is near;
   it will be a day of clouds,
      a time of doom*u* for the nations.
4   A sword shall come upon Egypt,
      and anguish shall be in Ethiopia,*v*
   when the slain fall in Egypt,
      and its wealth is carried away,
      and its foundations are torn down.
5 Ethiopia,*v* and Put, and Lud, and all Arabia, and Lib'ya,*w* and the people of the allied land*x* shall fall with them by the sword.

6   Thus says the LORD:
   Those who support Egypt shall fall,
      and its proud might shall come down;
   from Mig'dol to Sy·ē'nē
      they shall fall within it by the sword,
   says the Lord GOD.
7   They shall be desolated among other
      desolated countries,
      and their cities shall lie among cities laid
      waste.
8   Then they shall know that I am the LORD,
      when I have set fire to Egypt,
      and all who help it are broken.

9 On that day, messengers shall go out from me in ships to terrify the unsuspecting Ethiopians;*y* and anguish shall come upon them on the day of Egypt's doom;*z* for it is coming!

10   Thus says the Lord GOD:
   I will put an end to the hordes of Egypt,
      by the hand of King Ne·bū·chad·rez'zar of
      Babylon.
11   He and his people with him, the most
      terrible of the nations,
      shall be brought in to destroy the land;
   and they shall draw their swords against
      Egypt,
      and fill the land with the slain.
12   I will dry up the channels,
      and will sell the land into the hand of
      evildoers;
   I will bring desolation upon the land and
      everything in it
      by the hand of foreigners;
   I the LORD have spoken.

13   Thus says the Lord GOD:
   I will destroy the idols
      and put an end to the images
      in Memphis;

   there shall no longer be a prince in the land
      of Egypt;
      so I will put fear in the land of Egypt.
14   I will make Path'ros a desolation,
      and will set fire to Zō'an,
      and will execute acts of judgment on
      Thēbes.
15   I will pour my wrath upon Pe·lū'si·um,
      the stronghold of Egypt,
      and cut off the hordes of Thēbes.
16   I will set fire to Egypt;
      Pe·lū'si·um shall be in great agony;
   Thēbes shall be breached,
      and Memphis face adversaries by day.
17   The young men of On and of Pī-bē'seth
      shall fall by the sword;
      and the cities themselves*a* shall go into
      captivity.
18   At Te·haph'ne·hēs the day shall be dark,
      when I break there the dominion of
      Egypt,
      and its proud might shall come to an end;
      the city*b* shall be covered by a cloud,
      and its daughter-towns shall go into
      captivity.
19   Thus I will execute acts of judgment on
      Egypt.
      Then they shall know that I am the LORD.

Proclamation against Pharaoh

20 In the eleventh year, in the first month, on the seventh day of the month, the word of the LORD came to me: 21 Mortal, I have broken the arm of Pharaoh king of Egypt; it has not been bound up for healing or wrapped with a bandage, so that it may become strong to wield the sword. 22 Therefore thus says the Lord GOD: I am against Pharaoh king of Egypt, and will break his arms, both the strong arm and the one that was broken; and I will make the sword fall from his hand. 23 I will scatter the Egyptians among the nations, and disperse them throughout the lands. 24 I will strengthen the arms of the king of Babylon, and put my sword in his hand; but I will break the arms of Pharaoh, and he will groan before him with the groans of one mortally wounded. 25 I will strengthen the arms of the king of Babylon, but the arms of Pharaoh shall fall. And they shall know that I am the LORD, when I put my sword into the hand of the king of Babylon. He shall stretch it out against the land of Egypt, 26 and I will scatter the Egyptians among the nations and disperse them throughout

u Heb lacks *of doom*   *v* Or *Nubia;* Heb *Cush*
w Compare Gk Syr Vg: Heb *Cub*   *x* Meaning of Heb
uncertain   *y* Or *Nubians;* Heb *Cush*   *z* Heb *the day of
Egypt*   *a* Heb *and they*   *b* Heb *she*

the countries. Then they shall know that I am the LORD.

The Lofty Cedar
(Cp Ezek 17.22–24)

In the eleventh year, in the third month, on the first day of the month, the word of the LORD came to me: 2 Mortal, say to Pharaoh king of Egypt and to his hordes:

Whom are you like in your greatness?
3   Consider Assyria, a cedar of Lebanon,
with fair branches and forest shade,
    and of great height,
    its top among the clouds.*c*
4 The waters nourished it,
    the deep made it grow tall,
making its rivers flow*d*
    around the place it was planted,
sending forth its streams
    to all the trees of the field.
5 So it towered high
    above all the trees of the field;
its boughs grew large
    and its branches long,
    from abundant water in its shoots.
6 All the birds of the air
    made their nests in its boughs;
under its branches all the animals of the
        field
    gave birth to their young;
and in its shade
    all great nations lived.
7 It was beautiful in its greatness,
    in the length of its branches;
for its roots went down
    to abundant water.
8 The cedars in the garden of God could not
        rival it,
    nor the fir trees equal its boughs;
the plane trees were as nothing
    compared with its branches;
no tree in the garden of God
    was like it in beauty.
9 I made it beautiful
    with its mass of branches,
the envy of all the trees of Eden
    that were in the garden of God.

10 Therefore thus says the Lord GOD: Because it*e* towered high and set its top among the clouds,*c* and its heart was proud of its height, 11 I gave it into the hand of the prince of the nations; he has dealt with it as its wickedness deserves. I have cast it out. 12 Foreigners from the most terrible of the nations have cut it down and left it. On the mountains and in all the valleys its branches have fallen, and its boughs lie broken in all the

watercourses of the land; and all the peoples of the earth went away from its shade and left it.
13   On its fallen trunk settle
    all the birds of the air,
and among its boughs lodge
    all the wild animals.
14 All this is in order that no trees by the waters may grow to lofty height or set their tops among the clouds,*c* and that no trees that drink water may reach up to them in height.

For all of them are handed over to death,
    to the world below;
along with all mortals,
    with those who go down to the Pit.

15 Thus says the Lord GOD: On the day it went down to She'ol I closed the deep over it and covered it; I restrained its rivers, and its mighty waters were checked. I clothed Lebanon in gloom for it, and all the trees of the field fainted because of it. 16 I made the nations quake at the sound of its fall, when I cast it down to She'ol with those who go down to the Pit; and all the trees of Eden, the choice and best of Lebanon, all that were well watered, were consoled in the world below. 17 They also went down to She'ol with it, to those killed by the sword, along with its allies,*f* those who lived in its shade among the nations.

18 Which among the trees of Eden was like you in glory and in greatness? Now you shall be brought down with the trees of Eden to the world below; you shall lie among the uncircumcised, with those who are killed by the sword. This is Pharaoh and all his horde, says the Lord GOD.

Lamentation over Pharaoh and Egypt

In the twelfth year, in the twelfth month, on the first day of the month, the word of the LORD came to me: 2 Mortal, raise a lamentation over Pharaoh king of Egypt, and say to him:

You consider yourself a lion among the
        nations,
    but you are like a dragon in the seas;
you thrash about in your streams,
    trouble the water with your feet,
    and foul your*g* streams.
3 Thus says the Lord GOD:
    In an assembly of many peoples
    I will throw my net over you;
    and I*h* will haul you up in my dragnet.
4 I will throw you on the ground,
    on the open field I will fling you,

---

c Gk: Heb *thick boughs*   *d* Gk: Heb *rivers going*   *e* Syr Vg: Heb *you*   *f* Heb *its arms*   *g* Heb *their*   *h* Gk Vg: Heb *they*

and will cause all the birds of the air to
  settle on you,
  and I will let the wild animals of the
  whole earth gorge themselves
  with you.
5 I will strew your flesh on the mountains,
  and fill the valleys with your carcass.*i*
6 I will drench the land with your flowing
  blood
  up to the mountains,
  and the watercourses will be filled
  with you.
7 When I blot you out, I will cover the
  heavens,
  and make their stars dark;
I will cover the sun with a cloud,
  and the moon shall not give its light.
8 All the shining lights of the heavens
  I will darken above you,
  and put darkness on your land,
             says the Lord GOD.
9 I will trouble the hearts of many peoples,
  as I carry you captive*j* among the
  nations,
  into countries you have not known.
10 I will make many peoples appalled at you;
  their kings shall shudder because of you.
When I brandish my sword before them,
  they shall tremble every moment
for their lives, each one of them,
  on the day of your downfall.
11 For thus says the Lord GOD:
The sword of the king of Babylon shall
  come against you.
12 I will cause your hordes to fall
  by the swords of mighty ones,
  all of them most terrible among the
  nations.
They shall bring to ruin the pride of Egypt,
  and all its hordes shall perish.
13 I will destroy all its livestock
  from beside abundant waters;
and no human foot shall trouble them any
  more,
  nor shall the hoofs of cattle trouble
  them.
14 Then I will make their waters clear,
  and cause their streams to run like oil,
         says the Lord GOD.
15 When I make the land of Egypt desolate
  and when the land is stripped of all that
  fills it,
when I strike down all who live in it,
  then they shall know that I am the LORD.
16 This is a lamentation; it shall be chanted.
  The women of the nations shall chant it.

Over Egypt and all its hordes they shall
  chant it,
  says the Lord GOD.

Dirge over Egypt

17 In the twelfth year, in the first month,*k* on
the fifteenth day of the month, the word of the
LORD came to me:
18 Mortal, wail over the hordes of Egypt,
  and send them down,
with Egypt*l* and the daughters of majestic
  nations,
  to the world below,
  with those who go down to the Pit.
19 "Whom do you surpass in beauty?
  Go down! Be laid to rest with the
  uncircumcised!"
20 They shall fall among those who are killed by
the sword. Egypt*m* has been handed over to the
sword; carry away both it and its hordes. 21 The
mighty chiefs shall speak of them, with their helpers, out of the midst of Shĕ′ōl: "They have come
down, they lie still, the uncircumcised, killed by
the sword."

22 Assyria is there, and all its company, their
graves all around it, all of them killed, fallen by
the sword. 23 Their graves are set in the uttermost
parts of the Pit. Its company is all around its grave,
all of them killed, fallen by the sword, who spread
terror in the land of the living.

24 Ē′lam is there, and all its hordes around its
grave; all of them killed, fallen by the sword, who
went down uncircumcised into the world below,
who spread terror in the land of the living. They
bear their shame with those who go down to the
Pit. 25 They have made Ē′lam*l* a bed among the
slain with all its hordes, their graves all around it,
all of them uncircumcised, killed by the sword; for
terror of them was spread in the land of the living,
and they bear their shame with those who go
down to the Pit; they are placed among the slain.

26 Mĕ′shech and Tū′bal are there, and all their
multitude, their graves all around them, all of
them uncircumcised, killed by the sword; for they
spread terror in the land of the living. 27 And they
do not lie with the fallen warriors of long ago*n*
who went down to Shĕ′ōl with their weapons of
war, whose swords were laid under their heads,
and whose shields*o* are upon their bones; for the
terror of the warriors was in the land of the living.
28 So you shall be broken and lie among the uncircumcised, with those who are killed by the sword.

---

i Symmachus Syr Vg: Heb *your height*   *j* Gk: Heb *bring
your destruction*   *k* Gk: Heb lacks *in the first month*
l Heb *it*   *m* Heb *It*   *n* Gk Old Latin: Heb *of the
uncircumcised*   *o* Cn: Heb *iniquities*

E
Z
E
K

29 E'dom is there, its kings and all its princes, who for all their might are laid with those who are killed by the sword; they lie with the uncircumcised, with those who go down to the Pit.

30 The princes of the north are there, all of them, and all the Si·do'ni·ans, who have gone down in shame with the slain, for all the terror that they caused by their might; they lie uncircumcised with those who are killed by the sword, and bear their shame with those who go down to the Pit.

31 When Pharaoh sees them, he will be consoled for all his hordes—Pharaoh and all his army, killed by the sword, says the Lord GOD. 32 For he*p* spread terror in the land of the living; therefore he shall be laid to rest among the uncircumcised, with those who are slain by the sword—Pharaoh and all his multitude, says the Lord GOD.

Ezekiel Israel's Sentry

The word of the LORD came to me: 2 O Mortal, speak to your people and say to them, If I bring the sword upon a land, and the people of the land take one of their number as their sentinel; 3 and if the sentinel sees the sword coming upon the land and blows the trumpet and warns the people; 4 then if any who hear the sound of the trumpet do not take warning, and the sword comes and takes them away, their blood shall be upon their own heads. 5 They heard the sound of the trumpet and did not take warning; their blood shall be upon themselves. But if they had taken warning, they would have saved their lives. 6 But if the sentinel sees the sword coming and does not blow the trumpet, so that the people are not warned, and the sword comes and takes any of them, they are taken away in their iniquity, but their blood I will require at the sentinel's hand.

7 So you, mortal, I have made a sentinel for the house of Israel; whenever you hear a word from my mouth, you shall give them warning from me. 8 If I say to the wicked, "O wicked ones, you shall surely die," and you do not speak to warn the wicked to turn from their ways, the wicked shall die in their iniquity, but their blood I will require at your hand. 9 But if you warn the wicked to turn from their ways, and they do not turn from their ways, the wicked shall die in their iniquity, but you will have saved your life.

God's Justice and Mercy

10 Now you, mortal, say to the house of Israel, Thus you have said: "Our transgressions and our sins weigh upon us, and we waste away because of them; how then can we live?" 11 Say to them, As I live, says the Lord GOD, I have no pleasure in the death of the wicked, but that the wicked turn from their ways and live; turn back, turn back from your evil ways; for why will you die, O house of Israel? 12 And you, mortal, say to your people, The righteousness of the righteous shall not save them when they transgress; and as for the wickedness of the wicked, it shall not make them stumble when they turn from their wickedness; and the righteous shall not be able to live by their righteousness*q* when they sin. 13 Though I say to the righteous that they shall surely live, yet if they trust in their righteousness and commit iniquity, none of their righteous deeds shall be remembered; but in the iniquity that they have committed they shall die. 14 Again, though I say to the wicked, "You shall surely die," yet if they turn from their sin and do what is lawful and right— 15 if the wicked restore the pledge, give back what they have taken by robbery, and walk in the statutes of life, committing no iniquity—they shall surely live, they shall not die. 16 None of the sins that they have committed shall be remembered against them; they have done what is lawful and right, they shall surely live.

17 Yet your people say, "The way of the Lord is not just," when it is their own way that is not just. 18 When the righteous turn from their righteousness, and commit iniquity, they shall die for it.*r* 19 And when the wicked turn from their wickedness, and do what is lawful and right, they shall live by it.*r* 20 Yet you say, "The way of the Lord is not just." O house of Israel, I will judge all of you according to your ways!

The Fall of Jerusalem

21 In the twelfth year of our exile, in the tenth month, on the fifth day of the month, someone who had escaped from Jerusalem came to me and said, "The city has fallen." 22 Now the hand of the LORD had been upon me the evening before the fugitive came; but he had opened my mouth by the time the fugitive came to me in the morning; so my mouth was opened, and I was no longer unable to speak.

The Survivors in Judah

23 The word of the LORD came to me: 24 Mortal, the inhabitants of these waste places in the land of Israel keep saying, "Abraham was only one man, yet he got possession of the land; but we are many; the land is surely given us to possess." 25 Therefore say to them, Thus says the Lord GOD: You eat flesh with the blood, and lift up your eyes to your idols, and shed blood; shall you then possess the land? 26 You depend on your swords, you commit abom-

---

p Cn: Heb I   *q* Heb *by it*   *r* Heb *them*

inations, and each of you defiles his neighbor's wife; shall you then possess the land? 27 Say this to them, Thus says the Lord GOD: As I live, surely those who are in the waste places shall fall by the sword; and those who are in the open field I will give to the wild animals to be devoured; and those who are in strongholds and in caves shall die by pestilence. 28 I will make the land a desolation and a waste, and its proud might shall come to an end; and the mountains of Israel shall be so desolate that no one will pass through. 29 Then they shall know that I am the LORD, when I have made the land a desolation and a waste because of all their abominations that they have committed.

30 As for you, mortal, your people who talk together about you by the walls, and at the doors of the houses, say to one another, each to a neighbor, "Come and hear what the word is that comes from the LORD." 31 They come to you as people come, and they sit before you as my people, and they hear your words, but they will not obey them. For flattery is on their lips, but their heart is set on their gain. 32 To them you are like a singer of love songs,[s] one who has a beautiful voice and plays well on an instrument; they hear what you say, but they will not do it. 33 When this comes—and come it will!—then they shall know that a prophet has been among them.

Israel's False Shepherds

The word of the LORD came to me: 2 Mortal, prophesy against the shepherds of Israel: prophesy, and say to them—to the shepherds: Thus says the Lord GOD: Ah, you shepherds of Israel who have been feeding yourselves! Should not shepherds feed the sheep? 3 You eat the fat, you clothe yourselves with the wool, you slaughter the fatlings; but you do not feed the sheep. 4 You have not strengthened the weak, you have not healed the sick, you have not bound up the injured, you have not brought back the strayed, you have not sought the lost, but with force and harshness you have ruled them. 5 So they were scattered, because there was no shepherd; and scattered, they became food for all the wild animals. 6 My sheep were scattered, they wandered over all the mountains and on every high hill; my sheep were scattered over all the face of the earth, with no one to search or seek for them.

7 Therefore, you shepherds, hear the word of the LORD: 8 As I live, says the Lord GOD, because my sheep have become a prey, and my sheep have become food for all the wild animals, since there was no shepherd; and because my shepherds have not searched for my sheep, but the shepherds have fed themselves, and have not fed my sheep; 9 there-

fore, you shepherds, hear the word of the LORD: 10 Thus says the Lord GOD, I am against the shepherds; and I will demand my sheep at their hand, and put a stop to their feeding the sheep; no longer shall the shepherds feed themselves. I will rescue my sheep from their mouths, so that they may not be food for them.

PRAY IT?
The Good Shepherd

The theme of the good shepherd is common in the Bible. Psalm 23 compares God to a protective shepherd. Ezekiel, chapter 34, describes bad shepherds and contrasts them with God, the true shepherd, who feeds the flock with justice. In Jn 10.1–18, Jesus compares himself to a good shepherd.

God, the true shepherd, thank you for your care and protection. Today, I will do what I can to help your work. Make me aware of the people in my life who are weak, injured, straying, or lost. With your help, I will do what I can to strengthen them, heal them, and bring them back to you. Maybe I too can be more like a shepherd than like a sheep that merely follows!

▶ Ezekiel, chapter 34

God, the True Shepherd

11 For thus says the Lord GOD: I myself will search for my sheep, and will seek them out. 12 As shepherds seek out their flocks when they are among their scattered sheep, so I will seek out my sheep. I will rescue them from all the places to which they have been scattered on a day of clouds and thick darkness. 13 I will bring them out from the peoples and gather them from the countries, and will bring them into their own land; and I will feed them on the mountains of Israel, by the watercourses, and in all the inhabited parts of the land. 14 I will feed them with good pasture, and the mountain heights of Israel shall be their pasture; there they shall lie down in good grazing land, and they shall feed on rich pasture on the mountains of Israel. 15 I myself will be the shepherd of my sheep, and I will make them lie down, says the Lord GOD. 16 I will seek the lost, and I will

---

s Cn: Heb *like a love song*

bring back the strayed, and I will bind up the injured, and I will strengthen the weak, but the fat and the strong I will destroy. I will feed them with justice.

17 As for you, my flock, thus says the Lord GOD: I shall judge between sheep and sheep, between rams and goats: 18 Is it not enough for you to feed on the good pasture, but you must tread down with your feet the rest of your pasture? When you drink of clear water, must you foul the rest with your feet? 19 And must my sheep eat what you have trodden with your feet, and drink what you have fouled with your feet?

20 Therefore, thus says the Lord GOD to them: I myself will judge between the fat sheep and the lean sheep. 21 Because you pushed with flank and shoulder, and butted at all the weak animals with your horns until you scattered them far and wide, 22 I will save my flock, and they shall no longer be ravaged; and I will judge between sheep and sheep.

23 I will set up over them one shepherd, my servant David, and he shall feed them: he shall feed them and be their shepherd. 24 And I, the LORD, will be their God, and my servant David shall be prince among them; I, the LORD, have spoken.

25 I will make with them a covenant of peace and banish wild animals from the land, so that they may live in the wild and sleep in the woods securely. 26 I will make them and the region around my hill a blessing; and I will send down the showers in their season; they shall be showers of blessing. 27 The trees of the field shall yield their fruit, and the earth shall yield its increase. They shall be secure on their soil; and they shall know that I am the LORD, when I break the bars of their yoke, and save them from the hands of those who enslaved them. 28 They shall no more be plunder for the nations, nor shall the animals of the land devour them; they shall live in safety, and no one shall make them afraid. 29 I will provide for them a splendid vegetation so that they shall no more be consumed with hunger in the land, and no longer suffer the insults of the nations. 30 They shall know that I, the LORD their God, am with them, and that they, the house of Israel, are my people, says the Lord GOD. 31 You are my sheep, the sheep of my pasture[t] and I am your God, says the Lord GOD.

Judgment on Mount Seir

The word of the LORD came to me: 2 Mortal, set your face against Mount Sē'ir, and prophesy against it, 3 and say to it, Thus says the Lord GOD:
I am against you, Mount Sē'ir;
I stretch out my hand against you

to make you a desolation and a waste.
4 I lay your towns in ruins;
you shall become a desolation,
and you shall know that I am the LORD.
5 Because you cherished an ancient enmity, and gave over the people of Israel to the power of the sword at the time of their calamity, at the time of their final punishment; 6 therefore, as I live, says the Lord GOD, I will prepare you for blood, and blood shall pursue you; since you did not hate bloodshed, bloodshed shall pursue you. 7 I will make Mount Sē'ir a waste and a desolation; and I will cut off from it all who come and go. 8 I will fill its mountains with the slain; on your hills and in your valleys and in all your watercourses those killed with the sword shall fall. 9 I will make you a perpetual desolation, and your cities shall never be inhabited. Then you shall know that I am the LORD.

10 Because you said, "These two nations and these two countries shall be mine, and we will take possession of them,"—although the LORD was there—11 therefore, as I live, says the Lord GOD, I will deal with you according to the anger and envy that you showed because of your hatred against them; and I will make myself known among you,[u] when I judge you. 12 You shall know that I, the LORD, have heard all the abusive speech that you uttered against the mountains of Israel, saying, "They are laid desolate, they are given us to devour." 13 And you magnified yourselves against me with your mouth, and multiplied your words against me; I heard it. 14 Thus says the Lord GOD: As the whole earth rejoices, I will make you desolate. 15 As you rejoiced over the inheritance of the house of Israel, because it was desolate, so I will deal with you; you shall be desolate, Mount Sē'ir, and all E'dom, all of it. Then they shall know that I am the LORD.

Blessing on Israel

And you, mortal, prophesy to the mountains of Israel, and say: O mountains of Israel, hear the word of the LORD. 2 Thus says the Lord GOD: Because the enemy said of you, "Aha!" and, "The ancient heights have become our possession," 3 therefore prophesy, and say: Thus says the Lord GOD: Because they made you desolate indeed, and crushed you from all sides, so that you became the possession of the rest of the nations, and you became an object of gossip and slander among the people; 4 therefore, O mountains of Israel, hear the word of the Lord GOD: Thus says the Lord GOD to the mountains and the hills, the watercourses and the valleys, the desolate wastes and the deserted

---

[t] Gk OL: Heb *pasture, you are people*   [u] Gk: Heb *them*

towns, which have become a source of plunder and an object of derision to the rest of the nations all around; 5 therefore thus says the Lord GOD: I am speaking in my hot jealousy against the rest of the nations, and against all Ḗ'dom, who, with whole-hearted joy and utter contempt, took my land as their possession, because of its pasture, to plunder it. 6 Therefore prophesy concerning the land of Israel, and say to the mountains and hills, to the watercourses and valleys, Thus says the Lord GOD: I am speaking in my jealous wrath, because you have suffered the insults of the nations; 7 therefore thus says the Lord GOD: I swear that the nations that are all around you shall themselves suffer insults.

8 But you, O mountains of Israel, shall shoot out your branches, and yield your fruit to my people Israel; for they shall soon come home. 9 See now, I am for you; I will turn to you, and you shall be tilled and sown; 10 and I will multiply your population, the whole house of Israel, all of it; the towns shall be inhabited and the waste places rebuilt; 11 and I will multiply human beings and animals upon you. They shall increase and be fruitful; and I will cause you to be inhabited as in your former times, and will do more good to you than ever before. Then you shall know that I am the LORD. 12 I will lead people upon you—my people Israel—and they shall possess you, and you shall be their inheritance. No longer shall you bereave them of children.

13 Thus says the Lord GOD: Because they say to you, "You devour people, and you bereave your nation of children," 14 therefore you shall no longer devour people and no longer bereave your nation of children, says the Lord GOD; 15 and no longer will I let you hear the insults of the nations, no longer shall you bear the disgrace of the peoples; and no longer shall you cause your nation to stumble, says the Lord GOD.

The Renewal of Israel

16 The word of the LORD came to me: 17 Mortal, when the house of Israel lived on their own soil, they defiled it with their ways and their deeds; their conduct in my sight was like the uncleanness of a woman in her menstrual period. 18 So I poured out my wrath upon them for the blood that they had shed upon the land, and for the idols with which they had defiled it. 19 I scattered them among the nations, and they were dispersed through the countries; in accordance with their conduct and their deeds I judged them. 20 But when they came to the nations, wherever they came, they profaned my holy name, in that it was said of them, "These are the people of the LORD,

and yet they had to go out of his land." 21 But I had concern for my holy name, which the house of Israel had profaned among the nations to which they came.

22 Therefore say to the house of Israel, Thus says the Lord GOD: It is not for your sake, O house of Israel, that I am about to act, but for the sake of my holy name, which you have profaned among the nations to which you came. 23 I will sanctify my great name, which has been profaned among the nations, and which you have profaned among them; and the nations shall know that I am the LORD, says the Lord GOD, when through you I display my holiness before their eyes. 24 I will take you from the nations, and gather you from all countries, and bring you into your own land. 25 I will sprinkle clean water upon you, and you shall be clean from all your uncleannesses, and from all

NATIVE AMERICAN

You Will Be Cleansed

The sweat lodge ceremony is a Native American tradition that is still used today. It is performed whenever there is a need to be purified in order to prepare for God's blessings or ask for God's help.

   This ceremony is held in a shelter of poles and blankets that is made over a pit, with the door flap facing west, the direction the rains come from. Heated rocks fill the pit, and steam is formed when water is poured on the rocks. The ceremony consists of entering the shelter and sitting in a circle, passing a pipe, making steam, and praying toward the four directions for guidance and blessings and for maintaining an attitude of thankfulness.

   This tradition ritualizes the cleansing and conversion Ezekiel proclaims in Ezek 36.25–26. It reflects a faith that the Great Spirit, or God, will cleanse us with waters and give us a new heart and spirit.

▸ **Ezek 36.25–26**

your idols I will cleanse you. 26 A new heart I will give you, and a new spirit I will put within you; and I will remove from your body the heart of stone and give you a heart of flesh. 27 I will put my spirit within you, and make you follow my statutes and be careful to observe my ordinances. 28 Then you shall live in the land that I gave to your ancestors; and you shall be my people, and I will be your God. 29 I will save you from all your uncleannesses, and I will summon the grain and make it abundant and lay no famine upon you. 30 I will make the fruit of the tree and the produce of the field abundant, so that you may never again suffer the disgrace of famine among the nations. 31 Then you shall remember your evil ways, and your dealings that were not good; and you shall loathe yourselves for your iniquities and your abominable deeds. 32 It is not for your sake that I will act, says the Lord GOD; let that be known to you. Be ashamed and dismayed for your ways, O house of Israel.

33 Thus says the Lord GOD: On the day that I cleanse you from all your iniquities, I will cause the towns to be inhabited, and the waste places shall be rebuilt. 34 The land that was desolate shall be tilled, instead of being the desolation that it was in the sight of all who passed by. 35 And they will say, "This land that was desolate has become like the garden of Eden; and the waste and desolate and ruined towns are now inhabited and fortified." 36 Then the nations that are left all around you shall know that I, the LORD, have rebuilt the ruined places, and replanted that which was desolate; I, the LORD, have spoken, and I will do it.

37 Thus says the Lord GOD: I will also let the house of Israel ask me to do this for them: to increase their population like a flock. 38 Like the flock for sacrifices,[v] like the flock at Jerusalem during her appointed festivals, so shall the ruined towns be filled with flocks of people. Then they shall know that I am the LORD.

The Valley of Dry Bones

The hand of the LORD came upon me, and he brought me out by the spirit of the LORD and set me down in the middle of a valley; it was full of bones. 2 He led me all around them; there were very many lying in the valley, and they were very dry. 3 He said to me, "Mortal, can these bones live?" I answered, "O Lord GOD, you know." 4 Then he said to me, "Prophesy to these bones, and say to them: O dry bones, hear the word of the LORD. 5 Thus says the Lord GOD to these bones: I will cause breath[w] to enter you, and you shall live. 6 I will lay sinews on you, and will cause flesh to

come upon you, and cover you with skin, and put breath[w] in you, and you shall live; and you shall know that I am the LORD."

7 So I prophesied as I had been commanded; and as I prophesied, suddenly there was a noise, a rattling, and the bones came together, bone to its bone. 8 I looked, and there were sinews on them, and flesh had come upon them, and skin had covered them; but there was no breath in them. 9 Then he said to me, "Prophesy to the breath, prophesy, mortal, and say to the breath:[x] Thus says the Lord GOD: Come from the four winds, O breath,[x] and breathe upon these slain, that they may live." 10 I prophesied as he commanded me, and the breath came into them, and they lived, and stood on their feet, a vast multitude.

---

v Heb *flock of holy things* w Or *spirit* x Or *wind* or *spirit*

did you KNOW?

Wind, Breath, and Spirit

English has the words *wind*, *breath*, and *spirit*, with three different meanings. Hebrew has only one word for all three meanings: *ruah*. The "wind from God [that] swept over the face of the waters" at Creation (Gen 1.2) is *ruah*. The "breath of life" that God blows into the lifeless clay of the first human (Gen 2.7) is *ruah*. And the "spirit of the LORD [that] came mightily upon David" at his anointing (1 Sam 16.13) is *ruah*.

In Ezek 37.1–14, all three meanings of the word *ruah* come into play. Ezekiel cries out, "Thus says the Lord GOD: Come from the four winds, O breath [or spirit], and breathe upon these slain, that they may live" (verse 9). In the prophet's vision, the bones scattered across the battlefield are the exiled people of God, who have experienced the "death" of defeat and humiliation. God promises that the spirit (*ruah*) of God (verse 14) will bring the people of Israel back from the Exile and restore them to their land.

▶ **Ezek 37.1–14**

11 Then he said to me, "Mortal, these bones are the whole house of Israel. They say, 'Our bones are dried up, and our hope is lost; we are cut off completely.' 12 Therefore prophesy, and say to them, Thus says the Lord GOD: I am going to open your graves, and bring you up from your graves, O my people; and I will bring you back to the land of Israel. 13 And you shall know that I am the LORD, when I open your graves, and bring you up from your graves, O my people. 14 I will put my spirit within you, and you shall live, and I will place you on your own soil; then you shall know that I, the LORD, have spoken and will act, says the LORD."

from the nations among which they have gone, and will gather them from every quarter, and bring them to their own land. 22 I will make them one nation in the land, on the mountains of Israel; and one king shall be king over them all. Never again shall they be two nations, and never again shall they be divided into two kingdoms. 23 They shall never again defile themselves with their idols and their detestable things, or with any of their transgressions. I will save them from all the apostasies into which they have fallen,^z and will cleanse them. Then they shall be my people, and I will be their God.

24 My servant David shall be king over them;

Bone Dry

When have you felt dry and lifeless, like the collection of dry bones Ezekiel sees in his vision in Ezek 37.1–2? What helps you to re-energize, to put muscle and flesh back on your tired bones? What winds blow life through you to give you breath again, to make you new again?

Bones are our body's support structure, and prayer is our soul's support structure. In verse 14, God's spirit brings life. We need to pray for God's spirit—the Holy Spirit—to fill us in order to avoid shriveling up and becoming parched and lifeless. And we need to share God's spirit with others, to breathe life into the dry bones around us—the people who seem to have no energy or hope.

What are the dry bones in your life? What can you do to be re-energized by God when you feel like dry bones? How can you help to energize others who seem dry and lifeless?

▸ **Ezekiel, chapter 37**

E Z E K

The Two Sticks

15 The word of the LORD came to me: 16 Mortal, take a stick and write on it, "For Judah, and the Israelites associated with it"; then take another stick and write on it, "For Joseph (the stick of E′phra•im) and all the house of Israel associated with it"; 17 and join them together into one stick, so that they may become one in your hand. 18 And when your people say to you, "Will you not show us what you mean by these?" 19 say to them, Thus says the Lord GOD: I am about to take the stick of Joseph (which is in the hand of E′phra•im) and the tribes of Israel associated with it; and I will put the stick of Judah upon it,^y and make them one stick, in order that they may be one in my hand. 20 When the sticks on which you write are in your hand before their eyes, 21 then say to them, Thus says the Lord GOD: I will take the people of Israel

and they shall all have one shepherd. They shall follow my ordinances and be careful to observe my statutes. 25 They shall live in the land that I gave to my servant Jacob, in which your ancestors lived; they and their children and their children's children shall live there forever; and my servant David shall be their prince forever. 26 I will make a covenant of peace with them; it shall be an everlasting covenant with them; and I will bless^a them and multiply them, and will set my sanctuary among them forevermore. 27 My dwelling place shall be with them; and I will be their God, and they shall be my people. 28 Then the nations shall know that I the LORD sanctify Israel, when my sanctuary is among them forevermore.

---

y Heb *I will put them upon it*   z Another reading is *from all the settlements in which they have sinned*   a Tg: Heb *give*

Invasion by Gog

The word of the LORD came to me: 2 Mortal, set your face toward Gog, of the land of Mā'gog, the chief prince of Mē'shech and Tū'bal. Prophesy against him 3 and say: Thus says the Lord GOD: I am against you, O Gog, chief prince of Mē'shech and Tū'bal; 4 I will turn you around and put hooks into your jaws, and I will lead you out with all your army, horses and horsemen, all of them clothed in full armor, a great company, all of them with shield and buckler, wielding swords. 5 Persia, Ethiopia,*b* and Put are with them, all of them with buckler and helmet; 6 Gō'mer and all its troops; Beth-tō•gar'mah from the remotest parts of the north with all its troops—many peoples are with you.

7 Be ready and keep ready, you and all the companies that are assembled around you, and hold yourselves in reserve for them. 8 After many days you shall be mustered; in the latter years you shall go against a land restored from war, a land where people were gathered from many nations on the mountains of Israel, which had long lain waste; its people were brought out from the nations and now are living in safety, all of them. 9 You shall advance, coming on like a storm; you shall be like a cloud covering the land, you and all your troops, and many peoples with you.

10 Thus says the Lord GOD: On that day thoughts will come into your mind, and you will devise an evil scheme. 11 You will say, "I will go up against the land of unwalled villages; I will fall upon the quiet people who live in safety, all of them living without walls, and having no bars or gates"; 12 to seize spoil and carry off plunder; to assail the waste places that are now inhabited, and the people who were gathered from the nations, who are acquiring cattle and goods, who live at the center*c* of the earth. 13 Shē'ba and Dē'dan and the merchants of Tar'shish and all its young warriors*d* will say to you, "Have you come to seize spoil? Have you assembled your horde to carry off plunder, to carry away silver and gold, to take away cattle and goods, to seize a great amount of booty?"

14 Therefore, mortal, prophesy, and say to Gog: Thus says the Lord GOD: On that day when my people Israel are living securely, you will rouse yourself*e* 15 and come from your place out of the remotest parts of the north, you and many peoples with you, all of them riding on horses, a great horde, a mighty army; 16 you will come up against my people Israel, like a cloud covering the earth. In the latter days I will bring you against my land, so that the nations may know me, when through

you, O Gog, I display my holiness before their eyes.

Judgment on Gog

17 Thus says the Lord GOD: Are you he of whom I spoke in former days by my servants the prophets of Israel, who in those days prophesied for years that I would bring you against them? 18 On that day, when Gog comes against the land of Israel, says the Lord GOD, my wrath shall be aroused. 19 For in my jealousy and in my blazing wrath I declare: On that day there shall be a great shaking in the land of Israel; 20 the fish of the sea, and the birds of the air, and the animals of the field, and all creeping things that creep on the ground, and all human beings that are on the face of the earth, shall quake at my presence, and the mountains shall be thrown down, and the cliffs shall fall, and every wall shall tumble to the ground. 21 I will summon the sword against Gog*f* ing*g* all my mountains, says the Lord GOD; the swords of all will be against their comrades. 22 With pestilence and bloodshed I will enter into judgment with him; and I will pour down torrential rains and hailstones, fire and sulfur, upon him and his troops and the many peoples that are with him. 23 So I will display my greatness and my holiness and make myself known in the eyes of many nations. Then they shall know that I am the LORD.

Gog's Armies Destroyed

And you, mortal, prophesy against Gog, and say: Thus says the Lord GOD: I am against you, O Gog, chief prince of Mē'shech and Tū'bal! 2 I will turn you around and drive you forward, and bring you up from the remotest parts of the north, and lead you against the mountains of Israel. 3 I will strike your bow from your left hand, and will make your arrows drop out of your right hand. 4 You shall fall upon the mountains of Israel, you and all your troops and the peoples that are with you; I will give you to birds of prey of every kind and to the wild animals to be devoured. 5 You shall fall in the open field; for I have spoken, says the Lord GOD. 6 I will send fire on Mā'gog and on those who live securely in the coastlands; and they shall know that I am the LORD.

7 My holy name I will make known among my people Israel; and I will not let my holy name be profaned any more; and the nations shall know that I am the LORD, the Holy One in Israel. 8 It has

---

b Or *Nubia*; Heb *Cush*   *c* Heb *navel*   *d* Heb *young lions*
e Gk: Heb *will you not know?*   *f* Heb *him*   *g* Heb *to* or *for*

come! It has happened, says the Lord GOD. This is the day of which I have spoken.

9 Then those who live in the towns of Israel will go out and make fires of the weapons and burn them—bucklers and shields, bows and arrows, handpikes and spears—and they will make fires of them for seven years. 10 They will not need to take wood out of the field or cut down any trees in the forests, for they will make their fires of the weapons; they will despoil those who despoiled them, and plunder those who plundered them, says the Lord GOD.

The Burial of Gog

11 On that day I will give to Gog a place for burial in Israel, the Valley of the Travelers[h] east of the sea; it shall block the path of the travelers, for there Gog and all his horde will be buried; it shall be called the Valley of Hā′mon-gog.[i] 12 Seven months the house of Israel shall spend burying them, in order to cleanse the land. 13 All the people of the land shall bury them; and it will bring them honor on the day that I show my glory, says the Lord GOD. 14 They will set apart men to pass through the land regularly and bury any invaders[j] who remain on the face of the land, so as to cleanse it; for seven months they shall make their search. 15 As the searchers[j] pass through the land, anyone who sees a human bone shall set up a sign by it, until the buriers have buried it in the Valley of Hā′mon-gog.[i] 16 (A city Ha•mō′nah[k] is there also.) Thus they shall cleanse the land.

17 As for you, mortal, thus says the Lord GOD: Speak to the birds of every kind and to all the wild animals: Assemble and come, gather from all around to the sacrificial feast that I am preparing for you, a great sacrificial feast on the mountains of Israel, and you shall eat flesh and drink blood. 18 You shall eat the flesh of the mighty, and drink the blood of the princes of the earth—of rams, of lambs, and of goats, of bulls, all of them fatlings of Bā′shan. 19 You shall eat fat until you are filled, and drink blood until you are drunk, at the sacrificial feast that I am preparing for you. 20 And you shall be filled at my table with horses and charioteers,[l] with warriors and all kinds of soldiers, says the Lord GOD.

Israel Restored to the Land

21 I will display my glory among the nations; and all the nations shall see my judgment that I have executed, and my hand that I have laid on them. 22 The house of Israel shall know that I am the LORD their God, from that day forward. 23 And the nations shall know that the house of Israel went into captivity for their iniquity, because they

dealt treacherously with me. So I hid my face from them and gave them into the hand of their adversaries, and they all fell by the sword. 24 I dealt with them according to their uncleanness and their transgressions, and hid my face from them.

25 Therefore thus says the Lord GOD: Now I will restore the fortunes of Jacob, and have mercy on the whole house of Israel; and I will be jealous for my holy name. 26 They shall forget[m] their shame, and all the treachery they have practiced against me, when they live securely in their land with no one to make them afraid, 27 when I have brought them back from the peoples and gathered them from their enemies' lands, and through them have displayed my holiness in the sight of many nations. 28 Then they shall know that I am the LORD their God because I sent them into exile among the nations, and then gathered them into their own land. I will leave none of them behind; 29 and I will never again hide my face from them, when I pour out my spirit upon the house of Israel, says the Lord GOD.

The Vision of the New Temple

In the twenty-fifth year of our exile, at the beginning of the year, on the tenth day of the month, in the fourteenth year after the city was struck down, on that very day, the hand of the LORD was upon me, and he brought me there. 2 He brought me, in visions of God, to the land of Israel, and set me down upon a very high mountain, on which was a structure like a city to the south. 3 When he brought me there, a man was there, whose appearance shone like bronze, with a linen cord and a measuring reed in his hand; and he was standing in the gateway. 4 The man said to me, "Mortal, look closely and listen attentively, and set your mind upon all that I shall show you, for you were brought here in order that I might show it to you; declare all that you see to the house of Israel."

5 Now there was a wall all around the outside of the temple area. The length of the measuring reed in the man's hand was six long cubits, each being a cubit and a handbreadth in length; so he measured the thickness of the wall, one reed; and the height, one reed. 6 Then he went into the gateway facing east, going up its steps, and measured the threshold of the gate, one reed deep.[n] There were 7 recesses, and each recess was one reed wide and one reed deep; and the space between the recesses, five cubits; and the threshold of the gate by the vestibule of the gate at the inner end was one

---

h Or of the Abarim   i That is, *the Horde of Gog*
j Heb *travelers*   k That is *The Horde*   l Heb *chariots*
m Another reading is *They shall bear*   n Heb *deep, and one threshold, one reed deep*

reed deep. 8Then he measured the inner vestibule of the gateway, one cubit. 9Then he measured the vestibule of the gateway, eight cubits; and its pilasters, two cubits; and the vestibule of the gate was at the inner end. 10There were three recesses on either side of the east gate; the three were of the same size; and the pilasters on either side were of the same size. 11Then he measured the width of the opening of the gateway, ten cubits; and the width of the gateway, thirteen cubits. 12There was a barrier before the recesses, one cubit on either side; and the recesses were six cubits on either side. 13Then he measured the gate from the back*o* of the one recess to the back*o* of the other, a width of twenty-five cubits, from wall to wall.*p* 14He measured*q* also the vestibule, twenty cubits; and the gate next to the pilaster on every side of the court.*r* 15From the front of the gate at the entrance to the end of the inner vestibule of the gate was fifty cubits. 16The recesses and their pilasters had windows, with shutters*r* on the inside of the gateway all around, and the vestibules also had windows on the inside all around; and on the pilasters were palm trees.

17 Then he brought me into the outer court; there were chambers there, and a pavement, all around the court; thirty chambers fronted on the pavement. 18The pavement ran along the side of the gates, corresponding to the length of the gates; this was the lower pavement. 19Then he measured the distance from the inner front of*s* the lower gate to the outer front of the inner court, one hundred cubits.*t*

20 Then he measured the gate of the outer court that faced north—its depth and width. 21Its recesses, three on either side, and its pilasters and its vestibule were of the same size as those of the first gate; its depth was fifty cubits, and its width twenty-five cubits. 22Its windows, its vestibule, and its palm trees were of the same size as those of the gate that faced toward the east. Seven steps led up to it; and its vestibule was on the inside.*u* 23Opposite the gate on the north, as on the east, was a gate to the inner court; he measured from gate to gate, one hundred cubits.

24 Then he led me toward the south, and there was a gate on the south; and he measured its pilasters and its vestibule; they had the same dimensions as the others. 25There were windows all around in it and in its vestibule, like the windows of the others; its depth was fifty cubits, and its width twenty-five cubits. 26There were seven steps leading up to it; its vestibule was on the inside.*u* It had palm trees on its pilasters, one on either side. 27There was a gate on the south of the inner court;

and he measured from gate to gate toward the south, one hundred cubits.

28 Then he brought me to the inner court by the south gate, and he measured the south gate; it was of the same dimensions as the others. 29Its recesses, its pilasters, and its vestibule were of the same size as the others; and there were windows all around in it and in its vestibule; its depth was fifty cubits, and its width twenty-five cubits. 30There were vestibules all around, twenty-five cubits deep and five cubits wide. 31Its vestibule faced the outer court, and palm trees were on its pilasters, and its stairway had eight steps.

32 Then he brought me to the inner court on the east side, and he measured the gate; it was of the same size as the others. 33Its recesses, its pilasters, and its vestibule were of the same dimensions as the others; and there were windows all around in it and in its vestibule; its depth was fifty cubits, and its width twenty-five cubits. 34Its vestibule faced the outer court, and it had palm trees on its pilasters, on either side; and its stairway had eight steps.

35 Then he brought me to the north gate, and he measured it; it had the same dimensions as the others. 36Its recesses, its pilasters, and its vestibule were of the same size as the others;*v* and it had windows all around. Its depth was fifty cubits, and its width twenty-five cubits. 37Its vestibule*w* faced the outer court, and it had palm trees on its pilasters, on either side; and its stairway had eight steps.

38 There was a chamber with its door in the vestibule of the gate,*x* where the burnt offering was to be washed. 39And in the vestibule of the gate were two tables on either side, on which the burnt offering and the sin offering and the guilt offering were to be slaughtered. 40On the outside of the vestibule*y* at the entrance of the north gate were two tables; and on the other side of the vestibule of the gate were two tables. 41Four tables were on the inside, and four tables on the outside of the side of the gate, eight tables, on which the sacrifices were to be slaughtered. 42There were also four tables of hewn stone for the burnt offering, a cubit and a half long, and one cubit and a half wide, and one cubit high, on which the instruments were to be laid with which the burnt offer-

o Gk: Heb *roof*   *p* Heb *opening facing opening*
q Heb *made*   *r* Meaning of Heb uncertain   *s* Compare
Gk: Heb *from before*   *t* Heb adds *the east and the north*
u Gk: Heb *before them*   *v* One Ms: Compare verses 29
and 33: MT lacks *were of the same size as the others*
w Gk Vg Compare verses 26, 31, 34: Heb *pilasters*
x Cn: Heb *at the pilasters of the gates*   *y* Cn: Heb *to him who goes up*

ings and the sacrifices were slaughtered. ⁴³There were pegs, one handbreadth long, fastened all around the inside. And on the tables the flesh of the offering was to be laid.

44 On the outside of the inner gateway there were chambers for the singers in the inner court, one[z] at the side of the north gate facing south, the other at the side of the east gate facing north. ⁴⁵He said to me, "This chamber that faces south is for the priests who have charge of the temple, ⁴⁶and the chamber that faces north is for the priests who have charge of the altar; these are the descendants of Zā'dok, who alone among the descendants of Levi may come near to the LORD to minister to him." ⁴⁷He measured the court, one hundred cubits deep, and one hundred cubits wide, a square; and the altar was in front of the temple.

The Temple
(Cp 1 Kings 7.14–22)

48 Then he brought me to the vestibule of the temple and measured the pilasters of the vestibule, five cubits on either side; and the width of the gate was fourteen cubits; and the sidewalls of the gate were three cubits[a] on either side. ⁴⁹The depth of the vestibule was twenty cubits, and the width twelve[b] cubits; ten steps led up[c] to it; and there were pillars beside the pilasters on either side. Then he brought me to the nave, and measured the pilasters; on each side six cubits was the width of the pilasters.[d] 2The width of the entrance was ten cubits; and the sidewalls of the entrance were five cubits on either side. He measured the length of the nave, forty cubits, and its width, twenty cubits. ³Then he went into the inner room and measured the pilasters of the entrance, two cubits; and the width of the entrance, six cubits; and the sidewalls[e] of the entrance, seven cubits. ⁴He measured the depth of the room, twenty cubits, and its width, twenty cubits, beyond the nave. And he said to me, This is the most holy place.

5 Then he measured the wall of the temple, six cubits thick; and the width of the side chambers, four cubits, all around the temple. ⁶The side chambers were in three stories, one over another, thirty in each story. There were offsets[f] all around the wall of the temple to serve as supports for the side chambers, so that they should not be supported by the wall of the temple. ⁷The passageway[g] of the side chambers widened from story to story; for the structure was supplied with a stairway all around the temple. For this reason the structure became wider from story to story. One ascended from the bottom story to the uppermost story by way of the middle one. ⁸I saw also that the temple had a raised platform all around; the

foundations of the side chambers measured a full reed of six long cubits. ⁹The thickness of the outer wall of the side chambers was five cubits; and the free space between the side chambers of the temple ¹⁰and the chambers of the court was a width of twenty cubits all around the temple on every side. ¹¹The side chambers opened onto the area left free, one door toward the north, and another door toward the south; and the width of the part that was left free was five cubits all around.

12 The building that was facing the temple yard on the west side was seventy cubits wide; and the wall of the building was five cubits thick all around, and its depth ninety cubits.

13 Then he measured the temple, one hundred cubits deep; and the yard and the building with its walls, one hundred cubits deep; ¹⁴also the width of the east front of the temple and the yard, one hundred cubits.

15 Then he measured the depth of the building facing the yard at the west, together with its galleries[h] on either side, one hundred cubits.

The nave of the temple and the inner room and the outer[i] vestibule ¹⁶were paneled,[j] and, all around, all three had windows with recessed[k] frames. Facing the threshold the temple was paneled with wood all around, from the floor up to the windows (now the windows were covered), ¹⁷to the space above the door, even to the inner room, and on the outside. And on all the walls all around in the inner room and the nave there was a pattern.[l] ¹⁸It was formed of cherubim and palm trees, a palm tree between cherub and cherub. Each cherub had two faces: ¹⁹a human face turned toward the palm tree on the one side, and the face of a young lion turned toward the palm tree on the other side. They were carved on the whole temple all around; ²⁰from the floor to the area above the door, cherubim and palm trees were carved on the wall.[m]

21 The doorposts of the nave were square. In front of the holy place was something resembling ²²an altar of wood, three cubits high, two cubits long, and two cubits wide;[n] its corners, its base,[o] and its walls were of wood. He said to me, "This is the table that stands before the LORD." ²³The nave

z Heb lacks *one*   a Gk: Heb *and the width of the gate was three cubits*   b Gk: Heb *eleven*   c Gk: Heb *and by steps that went up*   d Compare Gk: Heb *tent*   e Gk: Heb *width*   f Gk Compare 1 Kings 6.6: Heb *they entered*   g Cn: Heb *it was surrounded*   h Cn: Meaning of Heb uncertain   i Gk: Heb *of the court*   j Gk: Heb *the thresholds*   k Cn Compare Gk 1 Kings 6.4: Meaning of Heb uncertain   l Gk: Heb *measures*   m Cn Compare verse 25: Heb *and the wall*   n Gk: Heb lacks *two cubits wide*   o Gk: Heb *length*

and the holy place had each a double door. 24 The doors had two leaves apiece, two swinging leaves for each door. 25 On the doors of the nave were carved cherubim and palm trees, such as were carved on the walls; and there was a canopy of wood in front of the vestibule outside. 26 And there were recessed windows and palm trees on either side, on the sidewalls of the vestibule. *p*

41.18–21

The Holy Chambers and the Outer Wall

Then he led me out into the outer court, toward the north, and he brought me to the chambers that were opposite the temple yard and opposite the building on the north. 2 The length of the building that was on the north side*q* was*r* one hundred cubits, and the width fifty cubits. 3 Across the twenty cubits that belonged to the inner court, and facing the pavement that belonged to the outer court, the chambers rose*s* gallery*t* by gallery*t* in three stories. 4 In front of the chambers was a passage on the inner side, ten cubits wide and one hundred cubits deep,*u* and its*v* entrances were on the north. 5 Now the upper chambers were narrower, for the galleries*t* took more away from them than from the lower and middle chambers in the building. 6 For they were in three stories, and they had no pillars like the pillars of the outer*w* court; for this reason the upper chambers were set back from the ground more than the lower and the middle ones. 7 There was a wall outside parallel to the chambers, toward the outer court, opposite the chambers, fifty cubits long. 8 For the chambers on the outer court were fifty cubits long, while those opposite the temple were one hundred

cubits long. 9 At the foot of these chambers ran a passage that one entered from the east in order to enter them from the outer court. 10 The width of the passage*x* was fixed by the wall of the court.

On the south*y* also, opposite the vacant area and opposite the building, there were chambers 11 with a passage in front of them; they were similar to the chambers on the north, of the same length and width, with the same exits*z* and arrangements and doors. 12 So the entrances of the chambers to the south were entered through the entrance at the head of the corresponding passage, from the east, along the matching wall.*t*

13 Then he said to me, "The north chambers and the south chambers opposite the vacant area are the holy chambers, where the priests who approach the LORD shall eat the most holy offerings; there they shall deposit the most holy offerings— the grain offering, the sin offering, and the guilt offering—for the place is holy. 14 When the priests enter the holy place, they shall not go out of it into the outer court without laying there the vestments in which they minister, for these are holy; they shall put on other garments before they go near to the area open to the people."

15 When he had finished measuring the interior of the temple area, he led me out by the gate that faces east, and measured the temple area all around. 16 He measured the east side with the measuring reed, five hundred cubits by the measuring reed. 17 Then he turned and measured*a* the north side, five hundred cubits by the measuring reed. 18 Then he turned and measured*a* the south side, five hundred cubits by the measuring reed. 19 Then he turned to the west side and measured, five hundred cubits by the measuring reed. 20 He measured it on the four sides. It had a wall around it, five hundred cubits long and five hundred cubits wide, to make a separation between the holy and the common.

The Divine Glory Returns to the Temple

Then he brought me to the gate, the gate facing east. 2 And there, the glory of the God of Israel was coming from the east; the sound was like the sound of mighty waters; and the earth shone with his glory. 3 The*b* vision I saw was like the vision

p Cn: Heb *vestibule. And the side chambers of the temple and the canopies*   *q* Gk: Heb *door*   *r* Gk: Heb *before the length*   *s* Heb lacks *the chambers rose*   *t* Meaning of Heb uncertain   *u* Gk Syr: Heb *a way of one cubit*   *v* Heb *their*   *w* Gk lacks *outer*   *x* Heb lacks *of the passage*   *y* Gk: Heb *east*   *z* Heb *and all their exits*   *a* Gk: Heb *measuring reed all around. He measured*   *b* Gk: Heb *Like the vision*

God's Dwelling Place

LIVE IT!

Ezekiel's vision of God returning to the Temple in Ezek 43.1–5 completes the circle of his prophecy. Earlier, as described in chapter 10, he had a unique vision of God's glory leaving the Temple and coming to rest in Babylon. For Ezekiel, the Temple represents the heart of Israel's relationship with God, and it is important that God's presence will return to it. This probably explains why Ezekiel carefully records the specifics of the new Temple in the remaining chapters of his book—to help make it more real.

The early Christians learned from Jesus that God's presence isn't limited to the Temple. The good news is that God is present in every person! First Corinthians 3.16 says, "Do you not know that you are God's temple and that God's Spirit dwells in you?" The basis for our self-worth should be knowing that God's spirit dwells within us. If that doesn't make us special, what will?

▶ Ezek 43.1–5

that I had seen when he came to destroy the city, and^c like the vision that I had seen by the river Che'bar; and I fell upon my face. ⁴As the glory of the LORD entered the temple by the gate facing east, ⁵the spirit lifted me up, and brought me into the inner court; and the glory of the LORD filled the temple.

6 While the man was standing beside me, I heard someone speaking to me out of the temple. ⁷He said to me: Mortal, this is the place of my throne and the place for the soles of my feet, where I will reside among the people of Israel forever. The house of Israel shall no more defile my holy name, neither they nor their kings, by their whoring, and by the corpses of their kings at their death.^d ⁸When they placed their threshold by my threshold and their doorposts beside my doorposts, with only a wall between me and them, they were defiling my holy name by their abominations that they committed; therefore I have consumed them in my anger. ⁹Now let them put away their idolatry and the corpses of their kings far from me, and I will reside among them forever.

10 As for you, mortal, describe the temple to the house of Israel, and let them measure the pattern; and let them be ashamed of their iniquities. ¹¹When they are ashamed of all that they have done, make known to them the plan of the temple, its arrangement, its exits and its entrances, and its whole form—all its ordinances and its entire plan and all its laws; and write it down in their sight, so that they may observe and follow the entire plan and all its ordinances. ¹²This is the law of the temple: the whole territory on the top of the mountain all around shall be most holy. This is the law of the temple.

The Altar

13 These are the dimensions of the altar by cubits (the cubit being one cubit and a handbreadth): its base shall be one cubit high,^e and one cubit wide, with a rim of one span around its edge. This shall be the height of the altar: ¹⁴From the base on the ground to the lower ledge, two cubits, with a width of one cubit; and from the smaller ledge to the larger ledge, four cubits, with a width of one cubit; ¹⁵and the altar hearth, four cubits; and from the altar hearth projecting upward, four horns. ¹⁶The altar hearth shall be square, twelve cubits long by twelve wide. ¹⁷The ledge also shall be square, fourteen cubits long by fourteen wide, with a rim around it half a cubit wide, and its surrounding base, one cubit. Its steps shall face east.

18 Then he said to me: Mortal, thus says the Lord GOD: These are the ordinances for the altar: On the day when it is erected for offering burnt offerings upon it and for dashing blood against it, ¹⁹you shall give to the levitical priests of the family of Za'dok, who draw near to me to minister to me, says the Lord GOD, a bull for a sin offering. ²⁰And you shall take some of its blood, and put it on the four horns of the altar, and on the four corners of the ledge, and upon the rim all around; thus you shall purify it and make atonement for it. ²¹You shall also take the bull of the sin offering, and it shall be burnt in the appointed place belonging to the temple, outside the sacred area.

22 On the second day you shall offer a male goat without blemish for a sin offering; and the

_c Syr: Heb *and the visions*   _d Or *on their high places*   _e Gk: Heb lacks *high*

altar shall be purified, as it was purified with the bull. 23 When you have finished purifying it, you shall offer a bull without blemish and a ram from the flock without blemish. 24 You shall present them before the LORD, and the priests shall throw salt on them and offer them up as a burnt offering to the LORD. 25 For seven days you shall provide daily a goat for a sin offering; also a bull and a ram from the flock, without blemish, shall be provided. 26 Seven days shall they make atonement for the altar and cleanse it, and so consecrate it. 27 When these days are over, then from the eighth day onward the priests shall offer upon the altar your burnt offerings and your offerings of well-being; and I will accept you, says the Lord GOD.

The Closed Gate

Then he brought me back to the outer gate of the sanctuary, which faces east; and it was shut. 2 The LORD said to me: This gate shall remain shut; it shall not be opened, and no one shall enter by it; for the LORD, the God of Israel, has entered by it; therefore it shall remain shut. 3 Only the prince, because he is a prince, may sit in it to eat food before the LORD; he shall enter by way of the vestibule of the gate, and shall go out by the same way.

Admission to the Temple

4 Then he brought me by way of the north gate to the front of the temple; and I looked, and lo! the glory of the LORD filled the temple of the LORD; and I fell upon my face. 5 The LORD said to me: Mortal, mark well, look closely, and listen attentively to all that I shall tell you concerning all the ordinances of the temple of the LORD and all its laws; and mark well those who may be admitted to*f* the temple and all those who are to be excluded from the sanctuary. 6 Say to the rebellious house,*g* to the house of Israel, Thus says the Lord GOD: O house of Israel, let there be an end to all your abominations 7 in admitting foreigners, uncircumcised in heart and flesh, to be in my sanctuary, profaning my temple when you offer to me my food, the fat and the blood. You*h* have broken my covenant with all your abominations. 8 And you have not kept charge of my sacred offerings; but you have appointed foreigners*i* to act for you in keeping my charge in my sanctuary.

9 Thus says the Lord GOD: No foreigner, uncircumcised in heart and flesh, of all the foreigners who are among the people of Israel, shall enter my sanctuary. 10 But the Lēʹvites who went far from me, going astray from me after their idols when Israel went astray, shall bear their punishment. 11 They shall be ministers in my sanctuary, having oversight at the gates of the temple, and serving in the temple; they shall slaughter the burnt offering and the sacrifice for the people, and they shall attend on them and serve them. 12 Because they ministered to them before their idols and made the house of Israel stumble into iniquity, therefore I have sworn concerning them, says the Lord GOD, that they shall bear their punishment. 13 They shall not come near to me, to serve me as priest, nor come near any of my sacred offerings, the things that are most sacred; but they shall bear their shame, and the consequences of the abominations that they have committed. 14 Yet I will appoint them to keep charge of the temple, to do all its chores, all that is to be done in it.

The Levitical Priests

15 But the levitical priests, the descendants of Zāʹdok, who kept the charge of my sanctuary when the people of Israel went astray from me, shall come near to me to minister to me; and they shall attend me to offer me the fat and the blood, says the Lord GOD. 16 It is they who shall enter my sanctuary, it is they who shall approach my table, to minister to me, and they shall keep my charge. 17 When they enter the gates of the inner court, they shall wear linen vestments; they shall have nothing of wool on them, while they minister at the gates of the inner court, and within. 18 They shall have linen turbans on their heads, and linen undergarments on their loins; they shall not bind themselves with anything that causes sweat. 19 When they go out into the outer court to the people, they shall remove the vestments in which they have been ministering, and lay them in the holy chambers; and they shall put on other garments, so that they may not communicate holiness to the people with their vestments. 20 They shall not shave their heads or let their locks grow long; they shall only trim the hair of their heads. 21 No priest shall drink wine when he enters the inner court. 22 They shall not marry a widow, or a divorced woman, but only a virgin of the stock of the house of Israel, or a widow who is the widow of a priest. 23 They shall teach my people the difference between the holy and the common, and show them how to distinguish between the unclean and the clean. 24 In a controversy they shall act as judges, and they shall decide it according to my judgments. They shall keep my laws and my statutes regarding all my appointed festivals, and they shall keep my sabbaths holy. 25 They shall not defile themselves by going near to a dead person; for father or mother, however, and for son or

---

f Cn: Heb *the entrance of*   *g* Gk: Heb lacks *house*
h Gk Syr Vg: Heb *They*   *i* Heb lacks *foreigners*

daughter, and for brother or unmarried sister they may defile themselves. 26 After he has become clean, they shall count seven days for him. 27 On the day that he goes into the holy place, into the inner court, to minister in the holy place, he shall offer his sin offering, says the Lord GOD.

28 This shall be their inheritance: I am their inheritance; and you shall give them no holding in Israel; I am their holding. 29 They shall eat the grain offering, the sin offering, and the guilt offering; and every devoted thing in Israel shall be theirs. 30 The first of all the first fruits of all kinds, and every offering of all kinds from all your offerings, shall belong to the priests; you shall also give to the priests the first of your dough, in order that a blessing may rest on your house. 31 The priests shall not eat of anything, whether bird or animal, that died of itself or was torn by animals.

The Holy District

When you allot the land as an inheritance, you shall set aside for the LORD a portion of the land as a holy district, twenty-five thousand cubits long and twenty*j* thousand cubits wide; it shall be holy throughout its entire extent. 2 Of this, a square plot of five hundred by five hundred cubits shall be for the sanctuary, with fifty cubits for an open space around it. 3 In the holy district you shall measure off a section twenty-five thousand cubits long and ten thousand wide, in which shall be the sanctuary, the most holy place. 4 It shall be a holy portion of the land; it shall be for the priests, who minister in the sanctuary and approach the LORD to minister to him; and it shall be both a place for their houses and a holy place for the sanctuary. 5 Another section, twenty-five thousand cubits long and ten thousand cubits wide, shall be for the Le'vites who minister at the temple, as their holding for cities to live in.*k*

6 Alongside the portion set apart as the holy district you shall assign as a holding for the city an area five thousand cubits wide, and twenty-five thousand cubits long; it shall belong to the whole house of Israel.

7 And to the prince shall belong the land on both sides of the holy district and the holding of the city, alongside the holy district and the holding of the city, on the west and on the east, corresponding in length to one of the tribal portions, and extending from the western to the eastern boundary 8 of the land. It is to be his property in Israel. And my princes shall no longer oppress my people; but they shall let the house of Israel have the land according to their tribes.

9 Thus says the Lord GOD: Enough, O princes of Israel! Put away violence and oppression, and do what is just and right. Cease your evictions of my people, says the Lord GOD.

Weights and Measures

10 You shall have honest balances, an honest ephah, and an honest bath.*l* 11 The ephah and the bath shall be of the same measure, the bath containing one-tenth of a homer, and the ephah one-tenth of a homer; the homer shall be the standard measure. 12 The shekel shall be twenty gerahs. Twenty shekels, twenty-five shekels, and fifteen shekels shall make a mina for you.

Offerings

13 This is the offering that you shall make: one-sixth of an ephah from each homer of wheat, and one-sixth of an ephah from each homer of barley, 14 and as the fixed portion of oil,*m* one-tenth of a bath from each cor (the cor,*n* like the homer, contains ten baths); 15 and one sheep from every flock of two hundred, from the pastures of Israel. This is the offering for grain offerings, burnt offerings, and offerings of well-being, to make atonement for them, says the Lord GOD. 16 All the people of the land shall join with the prince in Israel in making this offering. 17 But this shall be the obligation of the prince regarding the burnt offerings, grain offerings, and drink offerings, at the festivals, the new moons, and the sabbaths, all the appointed festivals of the house of Israel: he shall provide the sin offerings, grain offerings, the burnt offerings, and the offerings of well-being, to make atonement for the house of Israel.

Festivals
(Ex 12.1–20; Lev 23.33–43)

18 Thus says the Lord GOD: In the first month, on the first day of the month, you shall take a young bull without blemish, and purify the sanctuary. 19 The priest shall take some of the blood of the sin offering and put it on the doorposts of the temple, the four corners of the ledge of the altar, and the posts of the gate of the inner court. 20 You shall do the same on the seventh day of the month for anyone who has sinned through error or ignorance; so you shall make atonement for the temple.

21 In the first month, on the fourteenth day of the month, you shall celebrate the festival of the passover, and for seven days unleavened bread

---

j Gk: Heb *ten*   *k* Gk: Heb *as their holding, twenty chambers*
l A Heb measure of volume   *m* Cn: Heb *oil, the bath the oil*   *n* Vg: Heb *homer*

shall be eaten. 22 On that day the prince shall provide for himself and all the people of the land a young bull for a sin offering. 23 And during the seven days of the festival he shall provide as a burnt offering to the LORD seven young bulls and seven rams without blemish, on each of the seven days; and a male goat daily for a sin offering. 24 He shall provide as a grain offering an ephah for each bull, an ephah for each ram, and a hin of oil to each ephah. 25 In the seventh month, on the fifteenth day of the month and for the seven days of the festival, he shall make the same provision for sin offerings, burnt offerings, and grain offerings, and for the oil.

Miscellaneous Regulations

Thus says the Lord GOD: The gate of the inner court that faces east shall remain closed on the six working days; but on the sabbath day it shall be opened and on the day of the new moon it shall be opened. 2 The prince shall enter by the vestibule of the gate from outside, and shall take his stand by the post of the gate. The priests shall offer his burnt offering and his offerings of well-being, and he shall bow down at the threshold of the gate. Then he shall go out, but the gate shall not be closed until evening. 3 The people of the land shall bow down at the entrance of that gate before the LORD on the sabbaths and on the new moons. 4 The burnt offering that the prince offers to the LORD on the sabbath day shall be six lambs without blemish and a ram without blemish; 5 and the grain offering with the ram shall be an ephah, and the grain offering with the lambs shall be as much as he wishes to give, together with a hin of oil to each ephah. 6 On the day of the new moon he shall offer a young bull without blemish, and six lambs and a ram, which shall be without blemish; 7 as a grain offering he shall provide an ephah with the bull and an ephah with the ram, and with the lambs as much as he wishes, together with a hin of oil to each ephah. 8 When the prince enters, he shall come in by the vestibule of the gate, and shall go out by the same way.

9 When the people of the land come before the LORD at the appointed festivals, whoever enters by the north gate to worship shall go out by the south gate; and whoever enters by the south gate shall go out by the north gate: they shall not return by way of the gate by which they entered, but shall go out straight ahead. 10 When they come in, the prince shall come in with them; and when they go out, he shall go out.

11 At the festivals and the appointed seasons the grain offering with a young bull shall be an ephah, and with a ram an ephah, and with the lambs as much as one wishes to give, together with a hin of oil to an ephah. 12 When the prince provides a freewill offering, either a burnt offering or offerings of well-being as a freewill offering to the LORD, the gate facing east shall be opened for him; and he shall offer his burnt offering or his offerings of well-being as he does on the sabbath day. Then he shall go out, and after he has gone out the gate shall be closed.

13 He shall provide a lamb, a yearling, without blemish, for a burnt offering to the LORD daily; morning by morning he shall provide it. 14 And he shall provide a grain offering with it morning by morning regularly, one-sixth of an ephah, and one-third of a hin of oil to moisten the choice flour, as a grain offering to the LORD; this is the ordinance for all time. 15 Thus the lamb and the grain offering and the oil shall be provided, morning by morning, as a regular burnt offering.

16 Thus says the Lord GOD: If the prince makes a gift to any of his sons out of his inheritance,*o* it shall belong to his sons, it is their holding by inheritance. 17 But if he makes a gift out of his inheritance to one of his servants, it shall be his to the year of liberty; then it shall revert to the prince; only his sons may keep a gift from his inheritance. 18 The prince shall not take any of the inheritance of the people, thrusting them out of their holding; he shall give his sons their inheritance out of his own holding, so that none of my people shall be dispossessed of their holding.

19 Then he brought me through the entrance, which was at the side of the gate, to the north row of the holy chambers for the priests; and there I saw a place at the extreme western end of them. 20 He said to me, "This is the place where the priests shall boil the guilt offering and the sin offering, and where they shall bake the grain offering, in order not to bring them out into the outer court and so communicate holiness to the people."

21 Then he brought me out to the outer court, and led me past the four corners of the court; and in each corner of the court there was a court— 22 in the four corners of the court were small*p* courts, forty cubits long and thirty wide; the four were of the same size. 23 On the inside, around each of the four courts*q* was a row of masonry, with hearths made at the bottom of the rows all around. 24 Then he said to me, "These are the kitchens where those who serve at the temple shall boil the sacrifices of the people."

---

o Gk: Heb *it is his inheritance*   *p* Gk Syr Vg: Meaning of Heb uncertain   *q* Heb *the four of them*

Water Flowing from the Temple

Then he brought me back to the entrance of the temple; there, water was flowing from below the threshold of the temple toward the east (for the temple faced east); and the water was flowing down from below the south end of the threshold of the temple, south of the altar. 2 Then he brought me out by way of the north gate, and led me around on the outside to the outer gate that faces toward the east;*r* and the water was coming out on the south side.

3 Going on eastward with a cord in his hand, the man measured one thousand cubits, and then led me through the water; and it was ankle-deep. 4 Again he measured one thousand, and led me through the water; and it was knee-deep. Again he measured one thousand, and led me through the water; and it was up to the waist. 5 Again he measured one thousand, and it was a river that I could not cross, for the water had risen; it was deep enough to swim in, a river that could not be crossed. 6 He said to me, "Mortal, have you seen this?"

Then he led me back along the bank of the river. 7 As I came back, I saw on the bank of the river a great many trees on the one side and on the other. 8 He said to me, "This water flows toward the eastern region and goes down into the Ar'a-bah; and when it enters the sea, the sea of stagnant waters, the water will become fresh. 9 Wherever the river goes,*s* every living creature that swarms will live, and there will be very many fish, once these waters reach there. It will become fresh; and everything will live where the river goes. 10 People will stand fishing beside the sea*t* from En-ge'di to En-eg'la•im; it will be a place for the spreading of nets; its fish will be of a great many kinds, like the fish of the Great Sea. 11 But its swamps and marshes will not become fresh; they are to be left for salt. 12 On the banks, on both sides of the river, there will grow all kinds of trees for food. Their leaves will not wither nor their fruit fail, but they will bear fresh fruit every month, because the water for them flows from the sanctuary. Their fruit will be for food, and their leaves for healing."

The New Boundaries of the Land
(Cp Num 34.1–12)

13 Thus says the Lord GOD: These are the boundaries by which you shall divide the land for inheritance among the twelve tribes of Israel. Joseph shall have two portions. 14 You shall divide it equally; I swore to give it to your ancestors, and this land shall fall to you as your inheritance.

15 This shall be the boundary of the land: On the north side, from the Great Sea by way of Heth'lon to Lē'bō-hā'math, and on to Zē'dad,*u* 16 Be•rō'thah, Sib'rā•im (which lies between the border of Damascus and the border of Hā'math), as far as Hā'zer-hat'ti•con, which is on the border of Hau'ran. 17 So the boundary shall run from the sea to Hā'zar-ē'non, which is north of the border of Damascus, with the border of Hā'math to the north.*r* This shall be the north side.

18 On the east side, between Hau'ran and Damascus; along the Jordan between Gil'e•ad and the land of Israel; to the eastern sea and as far as Tā'-mar.*v* This shall be the east side.

19 On the south side, it shall run from Tā'mar as far as the waters of Mer'i•bath-kā'desh, from there along the Wadi of Egypt*w* to the Great Sea. This shall be the south side.

20 On the west side, the Great Sea shall be the boundary to a point opposite Lē'bō-hā'math. This shall be the west side.

21 So you shall divide this land among you according to the tribes of Israel. 22 You shall allot it as an inheritance for yourselves and for the aliens who reside among you and have begotten children among you. They shall be to you as citizens of Israel; with you they shall be allotted an inheritance among the tribes of Israel. 23 In whatever tribe aliens reside, there you shall assign them their inheritance, says the Lord GOD.

The Tribal Portions

These are the names of the tribes: Beginning at the northern border, on the Heth'lon road,*x* from Lē'-bō-hā'math, as far as Hā'zar-ē'non (which is on the border of Damascus, with Hā'math to the north), and*y* extending from the east side to the west,*z* Dan, one portion. 2 Adjoining the territory of Dan, from the east side to the west, Ash'er, one portion. 3 Adjoining the territory of Ash'er, from the east side to the west, Naph'ta•lī, one portion. 4 Adjoining the territory of Naph'ta•lī, from the east side to the west, Ma•nas'seh, one portion. 5 Adjoining the territory of Ma•nas'seh, from the east side to the west, Ē'phra•im, one portion. 6 Adjoining the territory of Ē'phra•im, from the east side to the west, Reuben, one portion. 7 Adjoining the territory of Reuben, from the east side to the west, Judah, one portion.

---

r Meaning of Heb uncertain　*s* Gk Syr Vg Tg: Heb *the two rivers go*　*t* Heb *it*　*u* Gk: Heb *Lebo-zedad,* 16*Hamath*　*v* Compare Syr: Heb *you shall measure*　*w* Heb lacks of Egypt　*x* Compare 47.15: Heb *by the side of the way*　*y* Cn: Heb *and they shall be his*　*z* Gk Compare verses 2-8: Heb *the east side the west*

EZEK

8 Adjoining the territory of Judah, from the east side to the west, shall be the portion that you shall set apart, twenty-five thousand cubits in width, and in length equal to one of the tribal portions, from the east side to the west, with the sanctuary in the middle of it. 9 The portion that you shall set apart for the LORD shall be twenty-five thousand cubits in length, and twenty*a* thousand in width. 10 These shall be the allotments of the holy portion: the priests shall have an allotment measuring twenty-five thousand cubits on the northern side, ten thousand cubits in width on the western side, ten thousand in width on the eastern side, and twenty-five thousand in length on the southern side, with the sanctuary of the LORD in the middle of it. 11 This shall be for the consecrated priests, the descendants*b* of Zā′dok, who kept my charge, who did not go astray when the people of Israel went astray, as the Lē′vītes did. 12 It shall belong to them as a special portion from the holy portion of the land, a most holy place, adjoining the territory of the Lē′vītes. 13 Alongside the territory of the priests, the Lē′vītes shall have an allotment twenty-five thousand cubits in length and ten thousand in width. The whole length shall be twenty-five thousand cubits and the width twenty*c* thousand. 14 They shall not sell or exchange any of it; they shall not transfer this choice portion of the land, for it is holy to the LORD.

15 The remainder, five thousand cubits in width and twenty-five thousand in length, shall be for ordinary use for the city, for dwellings and for open country. In the middle of it shall be the city; 16 and these shall be its dimensions: the north side four thousand five hundred cubits, the south side four thousand five hundred, the east side four thousand five hundred, and the west side four thousand five hundred. 17 The city shall have open land: on the north two hundred fifty cubits, on the south two hundred fifty, on the east two hundred fifty, on the west two hundred fifty. 18 The remainder of the length alongside the holy portion shall be ten thousand cubits to the east, and ten thousand to the west, and it shall be alongside the holy portion. Its produce shall be food for the workers of the city. 19 The workers of the city, from all the tribes of Israel, shall cultivate it. 20 The whole portion that you shall set apart shall be twenty-five thousand cubits square, that is, the holy portion together with the property of the city.

21 What remains on both sides of the holy portion and of the property of the city shall belong to the prince. Extending from the twenty-five thousand cubits of the holy portion to the east border, and westward from the twenty-five thousand cubits to the west border, parallel to the tribal portions, it shall belong to the prince. The holy portion with the sanctuary of the temple in the middle of it, 22 and the property of the Lē′vītes and of the city, shall be in the middle of that which belongs to the prince. The portion of the prince shall lie between the territory of Judah and the territory of Benjamin.

23 As for the rest of the tribes: from the east side to the west, Benjamin, one portion. 24 Adjoining the territory of Benjamin, from the east side to the west, Sim′ē·on, one portion. 25 Adjoining the territory of Sim′ē·on, from the east side to the west, Is′sa·char, one portion. 26 Adjoining the territory of Is′sa·char, from the east side to the west, Zeb′ū·lun, one portion. 27 Adjoining the territory of Zeb′ū·lun, from the east side to the west, Gad, one portion. 28 And adjoining the territory of Gad to the south, the boundary shall run from Tā′mar to the waters of Mer′i·bath-kā′desh, from there along the Wadi of Egypt*d* to the Great Sea. 29 This is the land that you shall allot as an inheritance among the tribes of Israel, and these are their portions, says the Lord GOD.

30 These shall be the exits of the city: On the north side, which is to be four thousand five hundred cubits by measure, 31 three gates, the gate of Reuben, the gate of Judah, and the gate of Levi, the gates of the city being named after the tribes of Israel. 32 On the east side, which is to be four thousand five hundred cubits, three gates, the gate of Joseph, the gate of Benjamin, and the gate of Dan. 33 On the south side, which is to be four thousand five hundred cubits by measure, three gates, the gate of Sim′ē·on, the gate of Is′sa·char, and the gate of Zeb′ū·lun. 34 On the west side, which is to be four thousand five hundred cubits, three gates,*e* the gate of Gad, the gate of Ash′er, and the gate of Naph′ta·lī. 35 The circumference of the city shall be eighteen thousand cubits. And the name of the city from that time on shall be, The LORD is There.

---

a Compare 45.1: Heb *ten*   *b* One Ms Gk: Heb *of the descendants*   *c* Gk: Heb *ten*   *d* Heb lacks *of Egypt*
e One Ms Gk Syr: MT *their gates three*

Do you have a favorite superhero from television or comic books? One characteristic of these larger-than-life heroes is their commitment to their own values and to saving victims of injustice. The Book of Daniel portrays just such a hero. Daniel's powers are his courage to remain faithful to God despite the threat of punishment, and his special visions, which foresee how things will turn out good even though the present situation seems far from hopeful. These powers enable him to lead his people on the right path in a foreign land filled with persecution and idolatry.

At a Glance

- **Chapters 1–6.** stories of Daniel at the Babylonian court
- **Chapters 7–12.** apocalyptic visions of Daniel
- **Chapters 13–14.** stories about Daniel that were added later

In-depth

Daniel represents the ideal leader with the spiritual and prophetic insight to lead people through troubled times. Scholars question whether he was an actual person. If he was, he lived in the sixth century B.C.—but the Book of Daniel was written four hundred years later, during the reign of an evil Greek-Syrian king, Antiochus IV Epiphanes. This was also the time of the Maccabean revolt told about in 1 and 2 Maccabees (see the timeline at the back of this Bible). King Antiochus desecrated the Temple and attempted to erase many of Israel's religious practices. To many in Israel, this seemed like the end of the world.

The author of the Book of Daniel writes about the great hero Daniel to give the people hope during this persecution. Chapters 1–6 present six stories of Daniel and three friends living their faith during the Babylonian Exile. Chapters 7–12 tell of Daniel's four visions about the empires that dominated Israel after the Exile: Media, Persia, and Greece. The visions are full of strange symbols meant to be understood by the Israelites but not the Greek rulers of the author's time.

Quick Facts

Period Covered
before the Babylonian Exile, the sixth century B.C.

Author
unknown, writing around 164 B.C., during the persecution of Israel by Antiochus IV Epiphanes

Theme
to give hope to those experiencing oppression and persecution

As you read the Book of Daniel, you will find themes familiar from other biblical books. Like Baruch, it describes living faithfully in a strange land. Like 1 and 2 Maccabees, the book shows the courage of Israelites willing to die for their beliefs. And it declares even more clearly than 2 Maccabees and the Wisdom of Solomon the belief in life after death. Daniel is shown as the ideal Jew—the embodiment of all the best of the people in exile. In the face of unjust persecution and oppression, he leads his people in faithfulness to God, even through death itself.

The Book of **Daniel**

Daniel

Chap. 6

Four Young Israelites at the Babylonian Court
(Cp. 2 Kings 24.10–17)

In the third year of the reign of King Je•hoi′a•kim of Judah, King Ne•bū•chad•nez′zar of Babylon came to Jerusalem and besieged it. ²The Lord let King Je•hoi′a•kim of Judah fall into his power, as well as some of the vessels of the house of God. These he brought to the land of Shi′nar,ᵃ and placed the vessels in the treasury of his gods.

3 Then the king commanded his palace master Ash′pe•naz to bring some of the Israelites of the royal family and of the nobility, ⁴young men without physical defect and handsome, versed in every branch of wisdom, endowed with knowledge and insight, and competent to serve in the king's palace; they were to be taught the literature and language of the Chal•dē′ans. ⁵The king assigned them a daily portion of the royal rations of food and wine. They were to be educated for three years, so that at the end of that time they could be stationed in the king's court. ⁶Among them were Daniel, Han•a•nī′ah, Mish′a•el, and Az•a•rī′ah, from the tribe of Judah. ⁷The palace master gave them other names: Daniel he called Bel•te•shaz′zar, Han•a•nī′ah he called Shad′rach, Mish′a•el he called Mē′shach, and Az•a•rī′ah he called A•bed′ne•gō.

8 But Daniel resolved that he would not defile himself with the royal rations of food and wine; so he asked the palace master to allow him not to defile himself. ⁹Now God allowed Daniel to re-ceive favor and compassion from the palace master. ¹⁰The palace master said to Daniel, "I am afraid of my lord the king; he has appointed your food and your drink. If he should see you in poorer condition than the other young men of your own age, you would endanger my head with the king." ¹¹Then Daniel asked the guard whom the palace master had appointed over Daniel, Han•a•nī′ah, Mish′a•el, and Az•a•rī′ah: ¹² "Please test your servants for ten days. Let us be given vegetables to eat and water to drink. ¹³You can then compare our appearance with the appearance of the young men who eat the royal rations, and deal with your servants according to what you observe." ¹⁴So he agreed to this proposal and tested them for ten days. ¹⁵At the end of ten days it was observed that they appeared better and fatter than all the young men who had been eating the royal rations. ¹⁶So the guard continued to withdraw their royal rations and the wine they were to drink, and gave them vegetables. ¹⁷To these four young men God gave knowledge and skill in every aspect of literature and wisdom; Daniel also had insight into all visions and dreams.

18 At the end of the time that the king had set for them to be brought in, the palace master brought them into the presence of Ne•bū•chad•nez′-zar, ¹⁹and the king spoke with them. And among them all, no one was found to compare with Dan-

---

ᵃ Gk Theodotion: Heb adds *to the house of his own gods*

iel, Han·a·nī'ah, Mish'a·el, and Az·a·rī'ah; therefore they were stationed in the king's court. 20 In every matter of wisdom and understanding concerning which the king inquired of them, he found them ten times better than all the magicians and enchanters in his whole kingdom. 21 And Daniel continued there until the first year of King Cyrus.

Nebuchadnezzar's Dream

In the second year of Ne·bū·chad·nez'zar's reign, Ne·bū·chad·nez'zar dreamed such dreams that his spirit was troubled and his sleep left him. 2 So the king commanded that the magicians, the enchanters, the sorcerers, and the Chal·dē'ans be summoned to tell the king his dreams. When they came in and stood before the king, 3 he said to them, "I have had such a dream that my spirit is troubled by the desire to understand it." 4 The Chal·dē'ans said to the king (in Ar·a·mā'ic),*b* "O king, live forever! Tell your servants the dream, and we will reveal the interpretation." 5 The king answered the Chal·dē'ans, "This is a public decree: if you do not tell me both the dream and its interpretation, you shall be torn limb from limb, and your houses shall be laid in ruins. 6 But if you do tell me the dream and its interpretation, you shall receive from me gifts and rewards and great honor. Therefore tell me the dream and its interpretation." 7 They answered a second time, "Let the king first tell his servants the dream, then we can give its interpretation." 8 The king answered, "I know with certainty that you are trying to gain time, because you see I have firmly decreed: 9 if you do not tell me the dream, there is but one verdict for you. You have agreed to speak lying and misleading words to me until things take a turn. Therefore, tell me the dream, and I shall know that you can give me its interpretation." 10 The Chal·dē'ans answered the king, "There is no one on earth who can reveal what the king demands! In fact no king, however great and powerful, has ever asked such a thing of any magician or enchanter or Chal·dē'an. 11 The thing that the king is asking is too difficult, and no one can reveal it to the king except the gods, whose dwelling is not with mortals."

12 Because of this the king flew into a violent rage and commanded that all the wise men of Babylon be destroyed. 13 The decree was issued, and the wise men were about to be executed; and they looked for Daniel and his companions, to execute them. 14 Then Daniel responded with prudence and discretion to Ar'i·och, the king's chief executioner, who had gone out to execute the wise men of Babylon; 15 he asked Ar'i·och, the royal official, "Why is the decree of the king so urgent?" Ar'i·och then explained the matter to Daniel. 16 So

Daniel went in and requested that the king give him time and he would tell the king the interpretation.

God Reveals Nebuchadnezzar's Dream

17 Then Daniel went to his home and informed his companions, Han·a·nī'ah, Mish'a·el, and Az·a·rī'ah, 18 and told them to seek mercy from the God of heaven concerning this mystery, so that Daniel and his companions with the rest of the wise men of Babylon might not perish. 19 Then the mystery was revealed to Daniel in a vision of the night, and Daniel blessed the God of heaven. 20 Daniel said:

"Blessed be the name of God from age
         to age,
      for wisdom and power are his.
21 He changes times and seasons,
      deposes kings and sets up kings;
   he gives wisdom to the wise
      and knowledge to those who have
         understanding.
22 He reveals deep and hidden things;
      he knows what is in the darkness,
      and light dwells with him.
23 To you, O God of my ancestors,
      I give thanks and praise,
   for you have given me wisdom and power,
      and have now revealed to me what we
         asked of you,
      for you have revealed to us what the king
         ordered."

Daniel Interprets the Dream

24 Therefore Daniel went to Ar'i·och, whom the king had appointed to destroy the wise men of Babylon, and said to him, "Do not destroy the wise men of Babylon; bring me in before the king, and I will give the king the interpretation." 25 Then Ar'i·och quickly brought Daniel before the king and said to him: "I have found among the exiles from Judah a man who can tell the king the interpretation." 26 The king said to Daniel, whose name was Bel·te·shaz'zar, "Are you able to tell me the dream that I have seen and its interpretation?" 27 Daniel answered the king, "No wise men, enchanters, magicians, or diviners can show to the king the mystery that the king is asking, 28 but there is a God in heaven who reveals mysteries, and he has disclosed to King Ne·bū·chad·nez'zar what will happen at the end of days. Your dream and the visions of your head as you lay in bed were these: 29 To you, O king, as you lay in bed,

b The text from this point to the end of chapter 7 is in Aramaic, except for 3.24-91a, the text of which is in Greek

came thoughts of what would be hereafter, and the revealer of mysteries disclosed to you what is to be. 30 But as for me, this mystery has not been revealed to me because of any wisdom that I have more than any other living being, but in order that the interpretation may be known to the king and that you may understand the thoughts of your mind.

31 "You were looking, O king, and lo! there was a great statue. This statue was huge, its brilliance extraordinary; it was standing before you, and its appearance was frightening. 32 The head of that statue was of fine gold, its chest and arms of silver, its middle and thighs of bronze, 33 its legs of iron, its feet partly of iron and partly of clay. 34 As you looked on, a stone was cut out, not by human hands, and it struck the statue on its feet of iron and clay and broke them in pieces. 35 Then the iron, the clay, the bronze, the silver, and the gold, were all broken in pieces and became like the chaff of the summer threshing floors; and the wind carried them away, so that not a trace of them could be found. But the stone that struck the statue became a great mountain and filled the whole earth.

36 "This was the dream; now we will tell the king its interpretation. 37 You, O king, the king of kings—to whom the God of heaven has given the kingdom, the power, the might, and the glory, 38 into whose hand he has given human beings, wherever they live, the wild animals of the field, and the birds of the air, and whom he has established as ruler over them all—you are the head of gold. 39 After you shall arise another kingdom inferior to yours, and yet a third kingdom of bronze, which shall rule over the whole earth. 40 And there shall be a fourth kingdom, strong as iron; just as iron crushes and smashes everything,^{c} it shall crush and shatter all these. 41 As you saw the feet and toes partly of potter's clay and partly of iron, it shall be a divided kingdom; but some of the strength of iron shall be in it, as you saw the iron mixed with the clay. 42 As the toes of the feet were part iron and part clay, so the kingdom shall be partly strong and partly brittle. 43 As you saw the iron mixed with clay, so will they mix with one another in marriage,^{d} but they will not hold together, just as iron does not mix with clay. 44 And in the days of those kings the God of heaven will set up a kingdom that shall never be destroyed, nor shall this kingdom be left to another people. It shall crush all these kingdoms and bring them to an end, and it shall stand forever; 45 just as you saw that a stone was cut from the mountain not by hands, and that it crushed the iron, the bronze, the clay, the silver, and the gold. The great God has

informed the king what shall be hereafter. The dream is certain, and its interpretation trustworthy."

Daniel and His Friends Promoted

46 Then King Ne·bu·chad·nez'zar fell on his face, worshiped Daniel, and commanded that a grain offering and incense be offered to him. 47 The king said to Daniel, "Truly, your God is God of gods and Lord of kings and a revealer of mysteries, for you have been able to reveal this mystery!" 48 Then the king promoted Daniel, gave him many great gifts, and made him ruler over the whole province of Babylon and chief prefect over all the wise men of Babylon. 49 Daniel made a request of the king, and he appointed Shad'rach, Me'shach, and A·bed'ne·go over the affairs of the province of Babylon. But Daniel remained at the king's court.

The Golden Image

King Ne·bu·chad·nez'zar made a golden statue whose height was sixty cubits and whose width was six cubits; he set it up on the plain of Du'ra in the province of Babylon. 2 Then King Ne·bu·chad·nez'zar sent for the satraps, the prefects, and the governors, the counselors, the treasurers, the justices, the magistrates, and all the officials of the provinces, to assemble and come to the dedication of the statue that King Ne·bu·chad·nez'zar had set up. 3 So the satraps, the prefects, and the governors, the counselors, the treasurers, the justices, the magistrates, and all the officials of the provinces, assembled for the dedication of the statue that King Ne·bu·chad·nez'zar had set up. When they were standing before the statue that Ne·bu·chad·nez'zar had set up, 4 the herald proclaimed aloud, "You are commanded, O peoples, nations, and languages, 5 that when you hear the sound of the horn, pipe, lyre, trigon, harp, drum, and entire musical ensemble, you are to fall down and worship the golden statue that King Ne·bu·chad·nez'zar has set up. 6 Whoever does not fall down and worship shall immediately be thrown into a furnace of blazing fire." 7 Therefore, as soon as all the peoples heard the sound of the horn, pipe, lyre, trigon, harp, drum, and entire musical ensemble, all the peoples, nations, and languages fell down and worshiped the golden statue that King Ne·bu·chad·nez'zar had set up.

8 Accordingly, at this time certain Chal·de'ans came forward and denounced the Jews. 9 They said to King Ne·bu·chad·nez'zar, "O king, live forever!

---

^{c} Gk Theodotion Syr Vg: Aram adds *and like iron that crushes* ^{d} Aram *by human seed*

¹⁰ You, O king, have made a decree, that everyone who hears the sound of the horn, pipe, lyre, trigon, harp, drum, and entire musical ensemble, shall fall down and worship the golden statue, ¹¹ and whoever does not fall down and worship shall be thrown into a furnace of blazing fire. ¹² There are certain Jews whom you have appointed over the affairs of the province of Babylon: Shad'rach, Mě'shach, and A·bed'ne·gō. These pay no heed to you, O king. They do not serve your gods and they do not worship the golden statue that you have set up."

13 Then Ne·bū·chad·nez'zar in furious rage commanded that Shad'rach, Mě'shach, and A·bed'ne·gō be brought in; so they brought those men before the king. ¹⁴ Ne·bū·chad·nez'zar said to them, "Is it true, O Shad'rach, Mě'shach, and A·bed'-

The Fiery Furnace

19 Then Ne·bū·chad·nez'zar was so filled with rage against Shad'rach, Mě'shach, and A·bed'ne·gō that his face was distorted. He ordered the furnace heated up seven times more than was customary, ²⁰ and ordered some of the strongest guards in his army to bind Shad'rach, Mě'shach, and A·bed'ne·gō and to throw them into the furnace of blazing fire. ²¹ So the men were bound, still wearing their tunics, g their trousers, g their hats, and their other garments, and they were thrown into the furnace of blazing fire. ²² Because the king's command was urgent and the furnace was so overheated, the raging flames killed the men who lifted Shad'rach, Mě'shach, and A·bed'ne·gō. ²³ But the three men, Shad'rach, Mě'shach, and A·bed'ne·gō, fell down, bound, into the furnace of blazing fire.

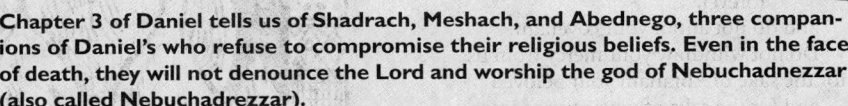

Doing the Right Thing

Chapter 3 of Daniel tells us of Shadrach, Meshach, and Abednego, three companions of Daniel's who refuse to compromise their religious beliefs. Even in the face of death, they will not denounce the Lord and worship the god of Nebuchadnezzar (also called Nebuchadrezzar).

The pressure to do what we know is wrong takes many forms. Caving in to that pressure leads many people to suffering, because by definition, sin leads to unhappy and unhealthy consequences. It may offer some short-term satisfaction, but denying what we know is right is ultimately denying God and the fullness of life God has planned for us.

Follow Shadrach, Meshach, and Abednego's example and stand up for what is right, stand up for God!

▶ Dan 3.1–24

ne·gō, that you do not serve my gods and you do not worship the golden statue that I have set up? ¹⁵ Now if you are ready when you hear the sound of the horn, pipe, lyre, trigon, harp, drum, and entire musical ensemble to fall down and worship the statue that I have made, well and good.ᵉ But if you do not worship, you shall immediately be thrown into a furnace of blazing fire, and who is the god that will deliver you out of my hands?"

16 Shad'rach, Mě'shach, and A·bed'ne·gō answered the king, "O Ne·bū·chad·nez'zar, we have no need to present a defense to you in this matter. ¹⁷ If our God whom we serve is able to deliver us from the furnace of blazing fire and out of your hand, O king, let him deliver us.ᶠ ¹⁸ But if not, be it known to you, O king, that we will not serve your gods and we will not worship the golden statue that you have set up."

The Prayer of Azariah in the Furnace

24 They walked around in the midst of the flames, singing hymns to God and blessing the Lord. ²⁵ Then Az·a·rī'ah stood still in the fire and prayed aloud:
²⁶ "Blessed are you, O Lord, God of our
         ancestors, and worthy of praise;
         and glorious is your name forever!
²⁷ For you are just in all you have done;
         all your works are true and your ways
             right,
         and all your judgments are true.
²⁸ You have executed true judgments in all you
             have brought upon us

ᵉ Aram lacks *well and good*   ᶠ Or *If our God whom we serve is able to deliver us, he will deliver us from the furnace of blazing fire and out of your hand, O king.*   ᵍ Meaning of Aram word uncertain

DAN

and upon Jerusalem, the holy city of our
ancestors;

by a true judgment you have brought all
this upon us because of our sins.

29 For we have sinned and broken your law in
turning away from you;

in all matters we have sinned grievously.

30 We have not obeyed your commandments,
we have not kept them or done what you
have commanded us for our own
good.

31 So all that you have brought upon us,
and all that you have done to us,
you have done by a true judgment.

32 You have handed us over to our enemies,
lawless and hateful rebels,
and to an unjust king, the most wicked
in all the world.

33 And now we cannot open our mouths;
we, your servants who worship you, have
become a shame and a reproach.

34 For your name's sake do not give us up
forever,
and do not annul your covenant.

35 Do not withdraw your mercy from us,
for the sake of Abraham your beloved
and for the sake of your servant Isaac
and Israel your holy one,

36 to whom you promised
to multiply their descendants like the
stars of heaven
and like the sand on the shore of the sea.

37 For we, O Lord, have become fewer than
any other nation,
and are brought low this day in all the
world because of our sins.

38 In our day we have no ruler, or prophet, or
leader,
no burnt offering, or sacrifice, or
oblation, or incense,
no place to make an offering before you
and to find mercy.

39 Yet with a contrite heart and a humble spirit
may we be accepted,

40 as though it were with burnt offerings of
rams and bulls,
or with tens of thousands of fat lambs;
such may our sacrifice be in your sight
today,
and may we unreservedly follow you,*h*
for no shame will come to those who
trust in you.

41 And now with all our heart we follow you;
we fear you and seek your presence.

42 Do not put us to shame,
but deal with us in your patience

and in your abundant mercy.

43 Deliver us in accordance with your
marvelous works,
and bring glory to your name, O Lord.

44 Let all who do harm to your servants be put
to shame;
let them be disgraced and deprived of all
power,
and let their strength be broken.

45 Let them know that you alone are the
Lord God,
glorious over the whole world."

The Song of the Three Jews

46 Now the king's servants who threw them in
kept stoking the furnace with naphtha, pitch, tow,
and brushwood. 47 And the flames poured out
above the furnace forty-nine cubits, 48 and spread
out and burned those Chal·de'ans who were
caught near the furnace. 49 But the angel of the
Lord came down into the furnace to be with Az·a-
rī'ah and his companions, and drove the fiery
flame out of the furnace, 50 and made the inside of
the furnace as though a moist wind were whistling
through it. The fire did not touch them at all and
caused them no pain or distress.

51 Then the three with one voice praised and
glorified and blessed God in the furnace:

52 "Blessed are you, O Lord, God of our
ancestors,
and to be praised and highly exalted
forever;
And blessed is your glorious, holy name,

h Meaning of Gk uncertain

DAN

and to be highly praised and highly
exalted forever.
53 Blessed are you in the temple of your holy
glory,
and to be extolled and highly glorified
forever.
54 Blessed are you who look into the depths
from your throne on the cherubim,
and to be praised and highly exalted
forever.
55 Blessed are you on the throne of your
kingdom,
and to be extolled and highly exalted
forever.
56 Blessed are you in the firmament of heaven,
and to be sung and glorified forever.

57 "Bless the Lord, all you works of the Lord;
sing praise to him and highly exalt him
forever.
58 Bless the Lord, you heavens;
sing praise to him and highly exalt him
forever.
59 Bless the Lord, you angels of the Lord;
sing praise to him and highly exalt him
forever.
60 Bless the Lord, all you waters above the
heavens;
sing praise to him and highly exalt him
forever.
61 Bless the Lord, all you powers of the Lord;
sing praise to him and highly exalt him
forever.
62 Bless the Lord, sun and moon;
sing praise to him and highly exalt him
forever.
63 Bless the Lord, stars of heaven;
sing praise to him and highly exalt him
forever.
64 "Bless the Lord, all rain and dew;
sing praise to him and highly exalt him
forever.
65 Bless the Lord, all you winds;
sing praise to him and highly exalt him
forever.
66 Bless the Lord, fire and heat;
sing praise to him and highly exalt him
forever.
67 Bless the Lord, winter cold and summer
heat;
sing praise to him and highly exalt him
forever.
68 Bless the Lord, dews and falling snow;
sing praise to him and highly exalt him
forever.
69 Bless the Lord, ice and cold;

sing praise to him and highly exalt him
forever.
70 Bless the Lord, frosts and snows;
sing praise to him and highly exalt him
forever.
71 Bless the Lord, nights and days;
sing praise to him and highly exalt him
forever.
72 Bless the Lord, light and darkness;
sing praise to him and highly exalt him
forever.
73 Bless the Lord, lightnings and clouds;
sing praise to him and highly exalt him
forever.

74 "Let the earth bless the Lord;
let it sing praise to him and highly exalt
him forever.
75 Bless the Lord, mountains and hills;
sing praise to him and highly exalt him
forever.
76 Bless the Lord, all that grows in the ground;
sing praise to him and highly exalt him
forever.
77 Bless the Lord, you springs;
sing praise to him and highly exalt him
forever.
78 Bless the Lord, seas and rivers;
sing praise to him and highly exalt him
forever.
79 Bless the Lord, you whales and all that
swim in the waters;
sing praise to him and highly exalt him
forever.
80 Bless the Lord, all birds of the air;
sing praise to him and highly exalt him
forever.
81 Bless the Lord, all wild animals and cattle;
sing praise to him and highly exalt him
forever.

82 "Bless the Lord, all people on earth;
sing praise to him and highly exalt him
forever.
83 Bless the Lord, O Israel;
sing praise to him and highly exalt him
forever.
84 Bless the Lord, you priests of the Lord;
sing praise to him and highly exalt him
forever.
85 Bless the Lord, you servants of the Lord;
sing praise to him and highly exalt him
forever.
86 Bless the Lord, spirits and souls of the
righteous;
sing praise to him and highly exalt him
forever.

DAN

87 Bless the Lord, you who are holy and
  humble in heart;
    sing praise to him and highly exalt him
      forever.

88 "Bless the Lord, Han•a•ni'ah, Az•a•ri'ah, and
  Mish'a•el;
    sing praise to him and highly exalt him
      forever.
  For he has rescued us from Hades and saved
    us from the power[i] of death,
  and delivered us from the midst of the
    burning fiery furnace;
  from the midst of the fire he has
    delivered us.

89 Give thanks to the Lord, for he is good,
  for his mercy endures forever.

90 All who worship the Lord, bless the God of
  gods,
    sing praise to him and give thanks
      to him,
  for his mercy endures forever."

91 Hearing them sing, and amazed at seeing them alive, King Ne•bu•chad•nez'zar rose up quickly. He said to his counselors, "Was it not three men that we threw bound into the fire?" They answered the king, "True, O king." 92 He replied, "But I see four men unbound, walking in the middle of the fire, and they are not hurt; and the fourth has the appearance of a god."[j] 93 Ne•bu•chad•nez'zar then approached the door of the furnace of blazing fire and said, "Shad'rach, Me'shach, and A•bed'ne•go, servants of the Most High God, come out! Come here!" So Shad'rach, Me'shach, and A•bed'ne•go came out from the fire. 94 And the satraps, the prefects, the governors, and the king's counselors gathered together and saw that the fire had not had any power over the bodies of those men; the hair of their heads was not singed, their tunics[k] were not harmed, and not even the smell of fire came from them. 95 Ne•bu•chad•nez'zar said, "Blessed be the God of Shad'rach, Me'shach, and A•bed'ne•go, who has sent his angel and delivered his servants who trusted in him. They disobeyed the king's command and yielded up their bodies rather than serve and worship any god except their own God. 96 Therefore I make a decree: Any people, nation, or language that utters blasphemy against the God of Shad'rach, Me'shach, and A•bed'ne•go shall be torn limb from limb, and their houses laid in ruins; for there is no other god who is able to deliver in this way." 97 Then the king promoted Shad'rach, Me'shach, and A•bed'ne•go in the province of Babylon.

Nebuchadnezzar's Second Dream

1 King Ne•bu•chad•nez'zar to all peoples, nations, and languages that live throughout the earth: May you have abundant prosperity! 2 The signs and wonders that the Most High God has worked for me I am pleased to recount.

3 How great are his signs,
  how mighty his wonders!
His kingdom is an everlasting kingdom,
  and his sovereignty is from generation to
    generation.

4[m] I, Ne•bu•chad•nez'zar, was living at ease in my home and prospering in my palace. 5 I saw a dream that frightened me; my fantasies in bed and the visions of my head terrified me. 6 So I made a decree that all the wise men of Babylon should be brought before me, in order that they might tell me the interpretation of the dream. 7 Then the magicians, the enchanters, the Chal•de'ans, and the diviners came in, and I told them the dream, but they could not tell me its interpretation. 8 At last Daniel came in before me—he who was named Bel•te•shaz'zar after the name of my god, and who is endowed with a spirit of the holy gods[n]—and I told him the dream: 9 "O Bel•te•shaz'zar, chief of the magicians, I know that you are endowed with a spirit of the holy gods[n] and that no mystery is too difficult for you. Hear[o] the dream that I saw; tell me its interpretation.

10[p] Upon my bed this is what I saw;
  there was a tree at the center of the earth,
    and its height was great.

11 The tree grew great and strong,
  its top reached to heaven,
    and it was visible to the ends of the
      whole earth.

12 Its foliage was beautiful,
  its fruit abundant,
    and it provided food for all.
The animals of the field found shade
    under it,
  the birds of the air nested in its branches,
    and from it all living beings were fed.

13 "I continued looking, in the visions of my head as I lay in bed, and there was a holy watcher, coming down from heaven. 14 He cried aloud and said:
  'Cut down the tree and chop off
    its branches,
  strip off its foliage and scatter its fruit.

---

i Gk hand j Aram *a son of the gods* k Meaning of Aram word uncertain l Ch 3.31 in Aram m Ch 4.1 in Aram n Or *a holy, divine spirit* o Theodotion: Aram *The visions of* p Theodotion Syr Compare Gk: Aram adds *The visions of my head*

DAN

Let the animals flee from beneath it
   and the birds from its branches.
15 But leave its stump and roots in the ground,
      with a band of iron and bronze,
      in the tender grass of the field.
   Let him be bathed with the dew of heaven,
      and let his lot be with the animals of the
         field
      in the grass of the earth.

PRAY IT!

King Nebuchadnezzar's Conversion

Sometimes, it seems God has to go to extremes to get our attention. In Daniel, chapter 4 (written like a letter from the king to his subjects), King Nebuchadnezzar tells how he had to go through some pretty intense humiliation—acting like a wild animal (verses 32–33)—before God got his attention. Even Daniel's prior warning didn't rein in his ego and bring him to his senses (see verses 26–27). After Nebuchadnezzar's reason returned, he realized the power of God and turned to praise and honor God.

Many people go through a conversion —a turning toward God—after they have suffered the consequences of their sinful actions. For others, the catalyst might be an illness or the death of a close friend or family member. Why does it take a crisis for us to realize our need for God? Maybe because during such a time, we realize that we cannot control life and that we need God's loving presence.

In your prayer, reflect or journal on the following questions:
- **Where do you recognize your need for God?**
- **Is a conversion toward God in a crisis only a temporary thing, or can it lead to a lifelong commitment? Why?**

▶ **Daniel, chapter 4**

16 Let his mind be changed from that of a
      human,
   and let the mind of an animal be given
      to him.

And let seven times pass over him.
17 The sentence is rendered by decree of the
      watchers,
   the decision is given by order of the holy
      ones,
   in order that all who live may know
      that the Most High is sovereign over the
         kingdom of mortals;
   he gives it to whom he will
      and sets over it the lowliest of human
         beings.'

18 "This is the dream that I, King Ne·bu·chad-nez'zar, saw. Now you, Bel·te·shaz'zar, declare the interpretation, since all the wise men of my kingdom are unable to tell me the interpretation. You are able, however, for you are endowed with a spirit of the holy gods."*q*

Daniel Interprets the Second Dream

19 Then Daniel, who was called Bel·te·shaz'zar, was severely distressed for a while. His thoughts terrified him. The king said, "Bel·te·shaz'zar, do not let the dream or the interpretation terrify you." Bel·te·shaz'zar answered, "My lord, may the dream be for those who hate you, and its interpretation for your enemies! 20 The tree that you saw, which grew great and strong, so that its top reached to heaven and was visible to the end of the whole earth, 21 whose foliage was beautiful and its fruit abundant, and which provided food for all, under which animals of the field lived, and in whose branches the birds of the air had nests— 22 it is you, O king! You have grown great and strong. Your greatness has increased and reaches to heaven, and your sovereignty to the ends of the earth. 23 And whereas the king saw a holy watcher coming down from heaven and saying, 'Cut down the tree and destroy it, but leave its stump and roots in the ground, with a band of iron and bronze, in the grass of the field; and let him be bathed with the dew of heaven, and let his lot be with the animals of the field, until seven times pass over him'— 24 this is the interpretation, O king, and it is a decree of the Most High that has come upon my lord the king: 25 You shall be driven away from human society, and your dwelling shall be with the wild animals. You shall be made to eat grass like oxen, you shall be bathed with the dew of heaven, and seven times shall pass over you, until you have learned that the Most High has sovereignty over the kingdom of mortals, and gives it to whom he will. 26 As it was commanded to leave the stump and roots of the tree, your kingdom shall be reestablished for you from the time that you learn

---

q Or *a holy, divine spirit*

that Heaven is sovereign. ²⁷Therefore, O king, may my counsel be acceptable to you: atone forʳ your sins with righteousness, and your iniquities with mercy to the oppressed, so that your prosperity may be prolonged."

Nebuchadnezzar's Humiliation

28 All this came upon King Ne·bū·chad·nez′zar. ²⁹At the end of twelve months he was walking on the roof of the royal palace of Babylon, ³⁰and the king said, "Is this not magnificent Babylon, which I have built as a royal capital by my mighty power and for my glorious majesty?" ³¹While the words were still in the king's mouth, a voice came from heaven: "O King Ne·bū·chad·nez′zar, to you it is declared: The kingdom has departed from you! ³²You shall be driven away from human society, and your dwelling shall be with the animals of the field. You shall be made to eat grass like oxen, and seven times shall pass over you, until you have learned that the Most High has sovereignty over the kingdom of mortals and gives it to whom he will." ³³Immediately the sentence was fulfilled against Ne·bū·chad·nez′zar. He was driven away from human society, ate grass like oxen, and his body was bathed with the dew of heaven, until his hair grew as long as eagles' feathers and his nails became like birds' claws.

Nebuchadnezzar Praises God

34 When that period was over, I, Ne·bū·chad·nez′zar, lifted my eyes to heaven, and my reason returned to me.

I blessed the Most High,
    and praised and honored the one who
        lives forever.
For his sovereignty is an everlasting
        sovereignty,
    and his kingdom endures from
        generation to generation.
³⁵ All the inhabitants of the earth are
        accounted as nothing,
    and he does what he wills with the host
        of heaven
    and the inhabitants of the earth.
There is no one who can stay his hand
    or say to him, "What are you doing?"

³⁶At that time my reason returned to me; and my majesty and splendor were restored to me for the glory of my kingdom. My counselors and my lords sought me out, I was re-established over my kingdom, and still more greatness was added to me. ³⁷Now I, Ne·bū·chad·nez′zar, praise and extol and honor the King of heaven,

for all his works are truth,
    and his ways are justice;

and he is able to bring low
    those who walk in pride.

Belshazzar's Feast

King Bel·shaz′zar made a great festival for a thousand of his lords, and he was drinking wine in the presence of the thousand.

2 Under the influence of the wine, Bel·shaz′zar commanded that they bring in the vessels of gold and silver that his father Ne·bū·chad·nez′zar had taken out of the temple in Jerusalem, so that the king and his lords, his wives, and his concubines might drink from them. ³So they brought in the vessels of gold and silverˢ that had been taken out of the temple, the house of God in Jerusalem, and the king and his lords, his wives, and his concubines drank from them. ⁴They drank the wine and praised the gods of gold and silver, bronze, iron, wood, and stone.

The Writing on the Wall

5 Immediately the fingers of a human hand appeared and began writing on the plaster of the wall of the royal palace, next to the lampstand. The king was watching the hand as it wrote. ⁶Then the king's face turned pale, and his thoughts terrified him. His limbs gave way, and his knees knocked together. ⁷The king cried aloud to bring in the enchanters, the Chal·dē′ans, and the diviners; and the king said to the wise men of Babylon, "Whoever can read this writing and tell me its interpretation shall be clothed in purple, have a chain of gold around his neck, and rank third in the kingdom." ⁸Then all the king's wise men came in, but they could not read the writing or tell the king the interpretation. ⁹Then King Bel·shaz′zar became greatly terrified and his face turned pale, and his lords were perplexed.

10 The queen, when she heard the discussion of the king and his lords, came into the banqueting hall. The queen said, "O king, live forever! Do not let your thoughts terrify you or your face grow pale. ¹¹There is a man in your kingdom who is endowed with a spirit of the holy gods.ᵗ In the days of your father he was found to have enlightenment, understanding, and wisdom like the wisdom of the gods. Your father, King Ne·bū·chad·nez′zar, made him chief of the magicians, enchanters, Chal·dē′ans, and diviners,ᵘ ¹²because an excellent spirit, knowledge, and understanding to interpret dreams, explain riddles, and solve problems were found in this Daniel, whom the king named Bel·te·shaz′zar. Now let

---

ʳ Aram *break off*   ˢ Theodotion Vg: Aram lacks *and silver*
ᵗ Or *a holy, divine spirit*   ᵘ Aram adds *the king your father*

Daniel be called, and he will give the interpretation."

The Writing on the Wall Interpreted

13 Then Daniel was brought in before the king. The king said to Daniel, "So you are Daniel, one of the exiles of Judah, whom my father the king brought from Judah? 14 I have heard of you that a spirit of the gods[v] is in you, and that enlightenment, understanding, and excellent wisdom are found in you. 15 Now the wise men, the enchanters, have been brought in before me to read this writing and tell me its interpretation, but they were not able to give the interpretation of the matter. 16 But I have heard that you can give interpretations and solve problems. Now if you are able to read the writing and tell me its interpretation, you shall be clothed in purple, have a chain of gold around your neck, and rank third in the kingdom."

17 Then Daniel answered in the presence of the king, "Let your gifts be for yourself, or give your rewards to someone else! Nevertheless I will read the writing to the king and let him know the interpretation. 18 O king, the Most High God gave your father Ne•bū•chad•nez′zar kingship, greatness, glory, and majesty. 19 And because of the greatness that he gave him, all peoples, nations, and languages trembled and feared before him. He killed those he wanted to kill, kept alive those he wanted to keep alive, honored those he wanted to honor, and degraded those he wanted to degrade. 20 But when his heart was lifted up and his spirit was hardened so that he acted proudly, he was deposed from his kingly throne, and his glory was stripped from him. 21 He was driven from human society, and his mind was made like that of an animal. His dwelling was with the wild asses, he was fed grass like oxen, and his body was bathed with the dew of heaven, until he learned that the Most High God has sovereignty over the kingdom of mortals, and sets over it whomever he will. 22 And you, Bel•shaz′zar his son, have not humbled your heart, even though you knew all this! 23 You have exalted yourself against the Lord of heaven! The vessels of his temple have been brought in before you, and you and your lords, your wives and your concubines have been drinking wine from them. You have praised the gods of silver and gold, of bronze, iron, wood, and stone, which do not see or hear or know; but the God in whose power is your very breath, and to whom belong all your ways, you have not honored.

24 "So from his presence the hand was sent and this writing was inscribed. 25 And this is the writing that was inscribed: MENE, MENE, TEKEL, and PARSIN. 26 This is the interpretation of the matter:

MENE, God has numbered the days of[w] your kingdom and brought it to an end; 27 TEKEL, you have been weighed on the scales and found wanting; 28 PERES,[x] your kingdom is divided and given to the Mēdes and Persians."

29 Then Bel•shaz′zar gave the command, and Daniel was clothed in purple, a chain of gold was put around his neck, and a proclamation was made concerning him that he should rank third in the kingdom.

30 That very night Bel•shaz′zar, the Chal•dē′an king, was killed. 31[y] And Da•rī′us the Mēde received the kingdom, being about sixty-two years old.

The Plot against Daniel

It pleased Da•rī′us to set over the kingdom one hundred twenty satraps, stationed throughout the whole kingdom, 2 and over them three presidents, including Daniel; to these the satraps gave account, so that the king might suffer no loss. 3 Soon Daniel distinguished himself above all the other presidents and satraps because an excellent spirit was in him, and the king planned to appoint him over the whole kingdom. 4 So the presidents and the satraps tried to find grounds for complaint against Daniel in connection with the kingdom. But they could find no grounds for complaint or any corruption, because he was faithful, and no negligence or corruption could be found in him. 5 The men said, "We shall not find any ground for complaint against this Daniel unless we find it in connection with the law of his God."

6 So the presidents and satraps conspired and came to the king and said to him, "O King Da•rī′us, live forever! 7 All the presidents of the kingdom, the prefects and the satraps, the counselors and the governors are agreed that the king should establish an ordinance and enforce an interdict, that whoever prays to anyone, divine or human, for thirty days, except to you, O king, shall be thrown into a den of lions. 8 Now, O king, establish the interdict and sign the document, so that it cannot be changed, according to the law of the Mēdes and the Persians, which cannot be revoked." 9 Therefore King Da•rī′us signed the document and interdict.

Daniel in the Lions' Den

10 Although Daniel knew that the document had been signed, he continued to go to his house, which had windows in its upper room open toward Jerusalem, and to get down on his knees three times a day to pray to his God and praise

---

v Or *a divine spirit*   *w* Aram lacks *the days of*
x The singular of *Parsin*   *y* Ch 6.1 in Aram

him, just as he had done previously. ¹¹ The conspirators came and found Daniel praying and seeking mercy before his God. ¹² Then they approached the king and said concerning the interdict, "O king! Did you not sign an interdict, that anyone who prays to anyone, divine or human, within thirty days except to you, O king, shall be thrown into a den of lions?" The king answered, "The thing stands fast, according to the law of the Mēdes and Persians, which cannot be revoked." ¹³ Then they responded to the king, "Daniel, one of the exiles from Judah, pays no attention to you, O king, or to the interdict you have signed, but he is saying his prayers three times a day."

14 When the king heard the charge, he was very much distressed. He was determined to save Daniel, and until the sun went down he made every effort to rescue him. ¹⁵ Then the conspirators came to the king and said to him, "Know, O king, that it is a law of the Mēdes and Persians that no interdict or ordinance that the king establishes can be changed."

16 Then the king gave the command, and Daniel was brought and thrown into the den of lions. The king said to Daniel, "May your God, whom you faithfully serve, deliver you!" ¹⁷ A stone was brought and laid on the mouth of the den, and the king sealed it with his own signet and with the signet of his lords, so that nothing might be changed concerning Daniel. ¹⁸ Then the king went to his palace and spent the night fasting; no food was brought to him, and sleep fled from him.

Daniel Saved from the Lions

19 Then, at break of day, the king got up and hurried to the den of lions. ²⁰ When he came near the den where Daniel was, he cried out anxiously to Daniel, "O Daniel, servant of the living God, has your God whom you faithfully serve been able to deliver you from the lions?" ²¹ Daniel then said to the king, "O king, live forever! ²² My God sent his angel and shut the lions' mouths so that they would not hurt me, because I was found blameless before him; and also before you, O king, I have done no wrong." ²³ Then the king was exceedingly glad and commanded that Daniel be taken up out of the den. So Daniel was taken up out of the den, and no kind of harm was found on him, because he had trusted in his God. ²⁴ The king gave a command, and those who had accused Daniel were brought and thrown into the den of lions—they, their children, and their wives. Before they reached the bottom of the den the lions overpowered them and broke all their bones in pieces.

25 Then King Da•rī′us wrote to all peoples and nations of every language throughout the whole world: "May you have abundant prosperity! ²⁶ I make a decree, that in all my royal dominion people should tremble and fear before the God of Daniel:

For he is the living God,
enduring forever.
His kingdom shall never be destroyed,
and his dominion has no end.
27 He delivers and rescues,
he works signs and wonders in heaven
and on earth;
for he has saved Daniel
from the power of the lions."

²⁸ So this Daniel prospered during the reign of Da•rī′us and the reign of Cyrus the Persian.

Visions of the Four Beasts

In the first year of King Bel•shaz′zar of Babylon, Daniel had a dream and visions of his head as he lay in bed. Then he wrote down the dream:ᶻ ²¹,ᵃ Daniel, saw in my vision by night the four winds of heaven stirring up the great sea, ³ and four great beasts came up out of the sea, different from one another. ⁴ The first was like a lion and had eagles' wings. Then, as I watched, its wings were plucked off, and it was lifted up from the ground and made to stand on two feet like a human being; and a human mind was given to it. ⁵ Another beast appeared, a second one, that looked like a bear. It was raised up on one side, had three tusksᵇ in its mouth among its teeth and was told, "Arise, devour many bodies!" ⁶ After this, as I watched, another appeared, like a leopard. The beast had four wings of a bird on its back and four heads; and dominion was given to it. ⁷ After this I saw in the visions by night a fourth beast, terrifying and dreadful and exceedingly strong. It had great iron teeth and was devouring, breaking in pieces, and stamping what was left with its feet. It was different from all the beasts that preceded it, and it had ten horns. ⁸ I was considering the horns, when another horn appeared, a little one coming up among them; to make room for it, three of the earlier horns were plucked up by the roots. There were eyes like human eyes in this horn, and a mouth speaking arrogantly.

Judgment before the Ancient One

9 As I watched,
thrones were set in place,
and an Ancient Oneᶜ took his throne,
his clothing was white as snow,

ᶻ Q Ms Theodotion: MT adds *the beginning of the words; he said*   ᵃ Theodotion: Aram *Daniel answered and said, I*
ᵇ Or *ribs*   ᶜ Aram *an Ancient of Days*

did you KNOW?

Apocalyptic Literature

As you read chapters 7–10 of Daniel, you might ask, What's with the four beasts in chapter 7, and the goat with the horn in chapter 8, and the man with a face like lightning in chapter 10? These are all examples of apocalyptic literature. *Apocalypse* is a Greek word meaning "to uncover or reveal." Apocalyptic literature is written to sound like an attempt to foretell the future by using symbols and vi-sions. But the symbols are often codes for people and events in the present. This type of literature frequently is produced during a time of persecution, when using real names could get a person into trouble or even killed. Apocalyptic literature developed in Israel around 200 B.C. when the country was enduring great persecution and suffering. The Book of Revelation in the New Testament is another example of apocalyptic literature.

The Book of Daniel contains some explanation of the visions it describes. But sometimes, you will have to consult a good Bible commentary (a book that gives additional background on Bible passages) to completely understand the symbols. For instance, you might need help recognizing that the third beast in chapter 7, which has four heads, is a symbol for Babylon, Media, Persia, and Greece—the four nations that ruled over Israel but would pass away. Or that the arrogant eleventh horn on the fourth beast's head is a symbol for Antiochus IV Epiphanes, the king who persecuted the Jews during the time Daniel was written.

Apocalyptic literature assured the people of Israel that God would triumph and the present evil would eventually pass away. It was one more way to reinforce the belief that evil would be punished and good rewarded, even when it didn't look that way at the moment.

▶ **Daniel, chapters 7–10**

and the hair of his head like pure wool;
  his throne was fiery flames,
    and its wheels were burning fire.
10 A stream of fire issued
    and flowed out from his presence.
A thousand thousands served him,
    and ten thousand times ten thousand
        stood attending him.
The court sat in judgment,
    and the books were opened.

11 I watched then because of the noise of the arrogant words that the horn was speaking. And as I watched, the beast was put to death, and its body destroyed and given over to be burned with fire. 12 As for the rest of the beasts, their dominion was taken away, but their lives were prolonged for a season and a time. 13 As I watched in the night visions,

I saw one like a human being[d]
  coming with the clouds of heaven.
And he came to the Ancient One[e]
  and was presented before him.
14 To him was given dominion
    and glory and kingship,
that all peoples, nations, and languages
    should serve him.
His dominion is an everlasting dominion
    that shall not pass away,
and his kingship is one
    that shall never be destroyed.

Daniel's Visions Interpreted

15 As for me, Daniel, my spirit was troubled within me,[f] and the visions of my head terrified me. 16 I approached one of the attendants to ask him the truth concerning all this. So he said that he would disclose to me the interpretation of the matter: 17 "As for these four great beasts, four kings shall arise out of the earth. 18 But the holy ones of the Most High shall receive the kingdom and possess the kingdom forever—forever and ever."

19 Then I desired to know the truth concerning the fourth beast, which was different from all the rest, exceedingly terrifying, with its teeth of iron and claws of bronze, and which devoured and broke in pieces, and stamped what was left with its feet; 20 and concerning the ten horns that were on its head, and concerning the other horn, which came up and to make room for which three of them fell out—the horn that had eyes and a mouth that spoke arrogantly, and that seemed greater than the others. 21 As I looked, this horn made war with the holy ones and was prevailing over them,

---

d Aram *one like a son of man*   e Aram *the Ancient of Days*
f Aram *troubled in its sheath*

D
A
N

22 until the Ancient One[g] came; then judgment was given for the holy ones of the Most High, and the time arrived when the holy ones gained possession of the kingdom.

23 This is what he said: "As for the fourth beast,

> there shall be a fourth kingdom on earth
>> that shall be different from all the other
>> kingdoms;
> it shall devour the whole earth,
>> and trample it down, and break it to
>> pieces.

24 As for the ten horns,
> out of this kingdom ten kings shall arise,
>> and another shall arise after them.
> This one shall be different from the former
>> ones,
>> and shall put down three kings.

25 He shall speak words against the Most High,
>> shall wear out the holy ones of the Most
>> High,
> and shall attempt to change the sacred
>> seasons and the law;
> and they shall be given into his power
>> for a time, two times,[h] and half a time.

26 Then the court shall sit in judgment,
>> and his dominion shall be taken away,
>> to be consumed and totally destroyed.

27 The kingship and dominion
>> and the greatness of the kingdoms under
>> the whole heaven
> shall be given to the people of the holy
>> ones of the Most High;
> their kingdom shall be an everlasting
>> kingdom,
> and all dominions shall serve and obey
>> them."

28 Here the account ends. As for me, Daniel, my thoughts greatly terrified me, and my face turned pale; but I kept the matter in my mind.

Vision of a Ram and a Goat

In the third year of the reign of King Bel·shaz'zar a vision appeared to me, Daniel, after the one that had appeared to me at first. 2 In the vision I was looking and saw myself in Su'sa the capital, in the province of E'lam,[i] and I was by the river U'lai.[j] 3 I looked up and saw a ram standing beside the river.[k] It had two horns. Both horns were long, but one was longer than the other, and the longer one came up second. 4 I saw the ram charging westward and northward and southward. All beasts were powerless to withstand it, and no one could rescue from its power; it did as it pleased and became strong.

5 As I was watching, a male goat appeared from the west, coming across the face of the whole earth without touching the ground. The goat had a horn[l] between its eyes. 6 It came toward the ram with the two horns that I had seen standing beside the river,[k] and it ran at it with savage force. 7 I saw it approaching the ram. It was enraged against it and struck the ram, breaking its two horns. The ram did not have power to withstand it; it threw the ram down to the ground and trampled upon it, and there was no one who could rescue the ram from its power. 8 Then the male goat grew exceedingly great; but at the height of its power, the great horn was broken, and in its place there came up four prominent horns toward the four winds of heaven.

9 Out of one of them came another[m] horn, a little one, which grew exceedingly great toward the south, toward the east, and toward the beautiful land. 10 It grew as high as the host of heaven. It threw down to the earth some of the host and some of the stars, and trampled on them. 11 Even against the prince of the host it acted arrogantly; it took the regular burnt offering away from him and overthrew the place of his sanctuary. 12 Because of wickedness, the host was given over to it together with the regular burnt offering;[n] it cast truth to the ground, and kept prospering in what it did. 13 Then I heard a holy one speaking, and another holy one said to the one that spoke, "For how long is this vision concerning the regular burnt offering, the transgression that makes desolate, and the giving over of the sanctuary and host to be trampled?"[n] 14 And he answered him,[o] "For two thousand three hundred evenings and mornings; then the sanctuary shall be restored to its rightful state."

Gabriel Interprets the Vision

15 When I, Daniel, had seen the vision, I tried to understand it. Then someone appeared standing before me, having the appearance of a man, 16 and I heard a human voice by the U'lai, calling, "Gabriel, help this man understand the vision." 17 So he came near where I stood; and when he came, I became frightened and fell prostrate. But he said to me, "Understand, O mortal,[p] that the vision is for the time of the end."

18 As he was speaking to me, I fell into a trance, face to the ground; then he touched me

---

g Aram *the Ancient of Days*   h Aram *a time, times*
i Gk Theodotion: MT Q Ms repeat *in the vision I was looking*
j Or *the Ulai Gate*   k Or *gate*   l Theodotion: Gk *one horn*; Heb *a horn of vision*   m Cn Compare 7.8: Heb *one*
n Meaning of Heb uncertain   o Gk Theodotion Syr Vg: Heb *me*   p Heb *son of man*

and set me on my feet. ¹⁹He said, "Listen, and I will tell you what will take place later in the period of wrath; for it refers to the appointed time of the end. ²⁰As for the ram that you saw with the two horns, these are the kings of Mēd′i•a and Persia. ²¹The male goat*q* is the king of Greece, and the great horn between its eyes is the first king. ²²As for the horn that was broken, in place of which four others arose, four kingdoms shall arise from his*r* nation, but not with his power.

²³ At the end of their rule,
   when the transgressions have reached
      their full measure,
   a king of bold countenance shall arise,
      skilled in intrigue.
²⁴ He shall grow strong in power,*s*
      shall cause fearful destruction,
      and shall succeed in what he does.
   He shall destroy the powerful
      and the people of the holy ones.
²⁵ By his cunning
      he shall make deceit prosper under his
         hand,
      and in his own mind he shall be great.
   Without warning he shall destroy many
      and shall even rise up against the Prince
         of princes.
   But he shall be broken, and not by human
      hands.
²⁶The vision of the evenings and the mornings that has been told is true. As for you, seal up the vision, for it refers to many days from now."

²⁷ So I, Daniel, was overcome and lay sick for some days; then I arose and went about the king's business. But I was dismayed by the vision and did not understand it.

Daniel's Prayer for the People

In the first year of Da•rī′us son of A•has•ū•ē′rus, by birth a Mēde, who became king over the realm of the Chal•dē′ans— ²in the first year of his reign, I, Daniel, perceived in the books the number of years that, according to the word of the LORD to the prophet Jer•e•mī′ah, must be fulfilled for the devastation of Jerusalem, namely, seventy years.

³ Then I turned to the Lord God, to seek an answer by prayer and supplication with fasting and sackcloth and ashes. ⁴I prayed to the LORD my God and made confession, saying,

"Ah, Lord, great and awesome God, keeping covenant and steadfast love with those who love you and keep your commandments, ⁵we have sinned and done wrong, acted wickedly and rebelled, turning aside from your commandments and ordinances. ⁶We have not listened to your servants the prophets, who spoke in your name to our kings, our princes, and our ancestors, and to all the people of the land.

7 "Righteousness is on your side, O Lord, but open shame, as at this day, falls on us, the people of Judah, the inhabitants of Jerusalem, and all Israel, those who are near and those who are far away, in all the lands to which you have driven them, because of the treachery that they have committed against you. ⁸Open shame, O LORD, falls on us, our kings, our officials, and our ancestors, because we have sinned against you. ⁹To the Lord our God belong mercy and forgiveness, for we have rebelled against him, ¹⁰and have not obeyed the voice of the LORD our God by following his laws, which he set before us by his servants the prophets.

11 "All Israel has transgressed your law and turned aside, refusing to obey your voice. So the curse and the oath written in the law of Moses, the servant of God, have been poured out upon us, because we have sinned against you. ¹²He has confirmed his words, which he spoke against us and against our rulers, by bringing upon us a calamity so great that what has been done against Jerusalem has never before been done under the whole heaven. ¹³Just as it is written in the law of Moses, all this calamity has come upon us. We did

---

q Or *shaggy male goat*   *r* Gk Theodotion Vg: Heb *the*
s Theodotion and one Gk Ms: Heb repeats (from 8.22) *but not with his power*

A Closer Look

Let's look closely at the prayer in chapter 9 of Daniel. Here, the prophet uses four types of prayer:

- *intercession*, because he prays on behalf of the people
- *praise*, because he proclaims God to be awesome and great
- *sorrow*, because he expresses sadness for past sinfulness and asks for forgiveness
- *petition*, because he asks God for help

   Try creating a personal prayer that includes three or all four of these types of prayer.

▸ **Daniel, chapter 9**

D
A
N

not entreat the favor of the LORD our God, turning from our iniquities and reflecting on his^t fidelity. ^{14}So the LORD kept watch over this calamity until he brought it upon us. Indeed, the LORD our God is right in all that he has done; for we have disobeyed his voice.

15 "And now, O Lord our God, who brought your people out of the land of Egypt with a mighty hand and made your name renowned even to this day—we have sinned, we have done wickedly. ^{16}O Lord, in view of all your righteous acts, let your anger and wrath, we pray, turn away from your city Jerusalem, your holy mountain; because of our sins and the iniquities of our ancestors, Jerusalem and your people have become a disgrace among all our neighbors. ^{17}Now therefore, O our God, listen to the prayer of your servant and to his supplication, and for your own sake, Lord,^{u} let your face shine upon your desolated sanctuary. ^{18}Incline your ear, O my God, and hear. Open your eyes and look at our desolation and the city that bears your name. We do not present our supplication before you on the ground of our righteousness, but on the ground of your great mercies. ^{19}O Lord, hear; O Lord, forgive; O Lord, listen and act and do not delay! For your own sake, O my God, because your city and your people bear your name!"

The Seventy Weeks

20 While I was speaking, and was praying and confessing my sin and the sin of my people Israel, and presenting my supplication before the LORD my God on behalf of the holy mountain of my God— ^{21}while I was speaking in prayer, the man Gabriel, whom I had seen before in a vision, came to me in swift flight at the time of the evening sacrifice. ^{22}He came^v and said to me, "Daniel, I have now come out to give you wisdom and understanding. ^{23}At the beginning of your supplications a word went out, and I have come to declare it, for you are greatly beloved. So consider the word and understand the vision:

24 "Seventy weeks are decreed for your people and your holy city: to finish the transgression, to put an end to sin, and to atone for iniquity, to bring in everlasting righteousness, to seal both vision and prophet, and to anoint a most holy place.^{w} ^{25}Know therefore and understand: from the time that the word went out to restore and rebuild Jerusalem until the time of an anointed prince, there shall be seven weeks; and for sixty-two weeks it shall be built again with streets and moat, but in a troubled time. ^{26}After the sixty-two weeks, an anointed one shall be cut off and shall

have nothing, and the troops of the prince who is to come shall destroy the city and the sanctuary. Its^x end shall come with a flood, and to the end there shall be war. Desolations are decreed. ^{27}He shall make a strong covenant with many for one week, and for half of the week he shall make sacrifice and offering cease; and in their place^y shall be an abomination that desolates, until the decreed end is poured out upon the desolator."

Conflict of Nations and Heavenly Powers

In the third year of King Cyrus of Persia a word was revealed to Daniel, who was named Bel·te·shaz'zar. The word was true, and it concerned a great conflict. He understood the word, having received understanding in the vision.

2 At that time I, Daniel, had been mourning for three weeks. ^{3}I had eaten no rich food, no meat or wine had entered my mouth, and I had not anointed myself at all, for the full three weeks. ^{4}On the twenty-fourth day of the first month, as I was standing on the bank of the great river (that is, the Tigris), ^{5}I looked up and saw a man clothed in linen, with a belt of gold from U'phaz around his waist. ^{6}His body was like beryl, his face like lightning, his eyes like flaming torches, his arms and legs like the gleam of burnished bronze, and the sound of his words like the roar of a multitude. ^{7}I, Daniel, alone saw the vision; the people who were with me did not see the vision, though a great trembling fell upon them, and they fled and hid themselves. ^{8}So I was left alone to see this great vision. My strength left me, and my complexion grew deathly pale, and I retained no strength. ^{9}Then I heard the sound of his words; and when I heard the sound of his words, I fell into a trance, face to the ground.

10 But then a hand touched me and roused me to my hands and knees. ^{11}He said to me, "Daniel, greatly beloved, pay attention to the words that I am going to speak to you. Stand on your feet, for I have now been sent to you." So while he was speaking this word to me, I stood up trembling. ^{12}He said to me, "Do not fear, Daniel, for from the first day that you set your mind to gain understanding and to humble yourself before your God, your words have been heard, and I have come because of your words. ^{13}But the prince of the kingdom of Persia opposed me twenty-one days. So Michael, one of the chief princes, came to help me, and I left him there with the prince of the kingdom of Persia,^{z} ^{14}and have come to help you

---

^{t} Heb your ^{u} Theodotion Vg Compare Syr: Heb *for the Lord's sake* ^{v} Gk Syr: Heb *He made to understand* ^{w} Or *thing* or *one* ^{x} Or *His* ^{y} Cn: Meaning of Heb uncertain ^{z} Gk Theodotion: Heb *I was left there with the kings of Persia*

understand what is to happen to your people at the end of days. For there is a further vision for those days."

15 While he was speaking these words to me, I turned my face toward the ground and was speechless. 16 Then one in human form touched my lips, and I opened my mouth to speak, and said to the one who stood before me, "My lord, because of the vision such pains have come upon me that I retain no strength. 17 How can my lord's servant talk with my lord? For I am shaking,*a* no strength remains in me, and no breath is left in me."

18 Again one in human form touched me and strengthened me. 19 He said, "Do not fear, greatly beloved, you are safe. Be strong and courageous!" When he spoke to me, I was strengthened and said, "Let my lord speak, for you have strengthened me." 20 Then he said, "Do you know why I have come to you? Now I must return to fight against the prince of Persia, and when I am through with him, the prince of Greece will come. 21 But I am to tell you what is inscribed in the book of truth. There is no one with me who contends against these princes except Michael, your prince. 1 As for me, in the first year of Da·rī′us the Mede, I stood up to support and strengthen him.

2 "Now I will announce the truth to you. Three more kings shall arise in Persia. The fourth shall be far richer than all of them, and when he has become strong through his riches, he shall stir up all against the kingdom of Greece. 3 Then a warrior king shall arise, who shall rule with great dominion and take action as he pleases. 4 And while still rising in power, his kingdom shall be broken and divided toward the four winds of heaven, but not to his posterity, nor according to the dominion with which he ruled; for his kingdom shall be uprooted and go to others besides these.

5 "Then the king of the south shall grow strong, but one of his officers shall grow stronger than he and shall rule a realm greater than his own realm. 6 After some years they shall make an alliance, and the daughter of the king of the south shall come to the king of the north to ratify the agreement. But she shall not retain her power, and his offspring shall not endure. She shall be given up, she and her attendants and her child and the one who supported her.

"In those times 7 a branch from her roots shall rise up in his place. He shall come against the army and enter the fortress of the king of the north, and he shall take action against them and prevail. 8 Even their gods, with their idols and with their precious vessels of silver and gold, he shall carry off to Egypt as spoils of war. For some years he shall refrain from attacking the king of the

north; 9 then the latter shall invade the realm of the king of the south, but will return to his own land.

10 "His sons shall wage war and assemble a multitude of great forces, which shall advance like a flood and pass through, and again shall carry the war as far as his fortress. 11 Moved with rage, the king of the south shall go out and do battle against the king of the north, who shall muster a great multitude, which shall, however, be defeated by his enemy. 12 When the multitude has been carried off, his heart shall be exalted, and he shall overthrow tens of thousands, but he shall not prevail. 13 For the king of the north shall again raise a multitude, larger than the former, and after some years*b* he shall advance with a great army and abundant supplies.

14 "In those times many shall rise against the king of the south. The lawless among your own people shall lift themselves up in order to fulfill the vision, but they shall fail. 15 Then the king of the north shall come and throw up siegeworks, and take a well-fortified city. And the forces of the south shall not stand, not even his picked troops, for there shall be no strength to resist. 16 But he who comes against him shall take the actions he pleases, and no one shall withstand him. He shall take a position in the beautiful land, and all of it shall be in his power. 17 He shall set his mind to come with the strength of his whole kingdom, and he shall bring terms of peace*c* and perform them. In order to destroy the kingdom,*d* he shall give him a woman in marriage; but it shall not succeed or be to his advantage. 18 Afterward he shall turn to the coastlands, and shall capture many. But a commander shall put an end to his insolence; indeed,*e* he shall turn his insolence back upon him. 19 Then he shall turn back toward the fortresses of his own land, but he shall stumble and fall, and shall not be found.

20 "Then shall arise in his place one who shall send an official for the glory of the kingdom; but within a few days he shall be broken, though not in anger or in battle. 21 In his place shall arise a contemptible person on whom royal majesty had not been conferred; he shall come in without warning and obtain the kingdom through intrigue. 22 Armies shall be utterly swept away and broken before him, and the prince of the covenant as well. 23 And after an alliance is made with him, he shall act deceitfully and become strong with a small party. 24 Without warning he shall come into the

---

a Gk: Heb *from now*   *b* Heb *and at the end of the times years*   *c* Gk: Heb *kingdom, and upright ones with him*
d Heb *it*   *e* Meaning of Heb uncertain

richest parts*f* of the province and do what none of his predecessors had ever done, lavishing plunder, spoil, and wealth on them. He shall devise plans against strongholds, but only for a time. 25 He shall stir up his power and determination against the king of the south with a great army, and the king of the south shall wage war with a much greater and stronger army. But he shall not succeed, for plots shall be devised against him 26 by those who eat of the royal rations. They shall break him, his army shall be swept away, and many shall fall slain. 27 The two kings, their minds bent on evil, shall sit at one table and exchange lies. But it shall not succeed, for there remains an end at the time appointed. 28 He shall return to his land with great wealth, but his heart shall be set against the holy covenant. He shall work his will, and return to his own land.

29 "At the time appointed he shall return and come into the south, but this time it shall not be as it was before. 30 For ships of Kit'tim shall come against him, and he shall lose heart and withdraw. He shall be enraged and take action against the holy covenant. He shall turn back and pay heed to those who forsake the holy covenant. 31 Forces sent by him shall occupy and profane the temple and fortress. They shall abolish the regular burnt offering and set up the abomination that makes desolate. 32 He shall seduce with intrigue those who violate the covenant; but the people who are loyal to their God shall stand firm and take action. 33 The wise among the people shall give understanding to many; for some days, however, they shall fall by sword and flame, and suffer captivity and plunder. 34 When they fall victim, they shall receive a little help, and many shall join them insincerely. 35 Some of the wise shall fall, so that they may be refined, purified, and cleansed,*g* until the time of the end, for there is still an interval until the time appointed.

36 "The king shall act as he pleases. He shall exalt himself and consider himself greater than any god, and shall speak horrendous things against the God of gods. He shall prosper until the period of wrath is completed, for what is determined shall be done. 37 He shall pay no respect to the gods of his ancestors, or to the one beloved by women; he shall pay no respect to any other god, for he shall consider himself greater than all. 38 He shall honor the god of fortresses instead of these; a god whom his ancestors did not know he shall honor with gold and silver, with precious stones and costly gifts. 39 He shall deal with the strongest fortresses by the help of a foreign god. Those who acknowledge him he shall make more wealthy,

and shall appoint them as rulers over many, and shall distribute the land for a price.

The Time of the End

40 "At the time of the end the king of the south shall attack him. But the king of the north shall rush upon him like a whirlwind, with chariots and horsemen, and with many ships. He shall advance against countries and pass through like a flood. 41 He shall come into the beautiful land, and tens of thousands shall fall victim, but E'dom and Mō'ab and the main part of the Am'mon•ites shall escape from his power. 42 He shall stretch out his hand against the countries, and the land of Egypt shall not escape. 43 He shall become ruler of the treasures of gold and of silver, and all the riches of Egypt; and the Libyans and the Ethiopians*h* shall follow in his train. 44 But reports from the east and the north shall alarm him, and he shall go out with great fury to bring ruin and complete destruction to many. 45 He shall pitch his palatial tents between the sea and the beautiful holy mountain. Yet he shall come to his end, with no one to help him.

The Resurrection of the Dead

"At that time Michael, the great prince, the protector of your people, shall arise. There shall be a time of anguish, such as has never occurred since nations first came into existence. But at that time your people shall be delivered, everyone who is found written in the book. 2 Many of those who sleep in the dust of the earth*i* shall awake, some to everlasting life, and some to shame and everlasting contempt. 3 Those who are wise shall shine like the brightness of the sky,*j* and those who lead many to righteousness, like the stars forever and ever. 4 But you, Daniel, keep the words secret and the book sealed until the time of the end. Many shall be running back and forth, and evil*k* shall increase."

5 Then I, Daniel, looked, and two others appeared, one standing on this bank of the stream and one on the other. 6 One of them said to the man clothed in linen, who was upstream, "How long shall it be until the end of these wonders?" 7 The man clothed in linen, who was upstream, raised his right hand and his left hand toward heaven. And I heard him swear by the one who lives forever that it would be for a time, two times, and half a time,*l* and that when the shattering of the power of the holy people comes to an end, all

---

f Or *among the richest men*   *g* Heb *made them white*   *h* Or *Nubians;* Heb *Cushites*   *i* Or *the land of dust*   *j* Or *dome*   *k* Cn Compare Gk: Heb *knowledge*   *l* Heb *a time, times, and a half*

these things would be accomplished. 8 I heard but could not understand; so I said, "My lord, what shall be the outcome of these things?" 9 He said, "Go your way, Daniel, for the words are to remain secret and sealed until the time of the end. 10 Many shall be purified, cleansed, and refined, but the wicked shall continue to act wickedly. None of the wicked shall understand, but those who are wise shall understand. 11 From the time that the regular burnt offering is taken away and the abomination that desolates is set up, there shall be one thousand two hundred ninety days. 12 Happy are those who persevere and attain the thousand three hundred thirty-five days. 13 But you, go your way,*m* and rest; you shall rise for your reward at the end of the days."

? did you KNOW?
Resurrection

Most of the Old Testament contains no indication of a belief in life after death. Daniel, however, speaks of individual resurrection, or rising to life from death. This goes beyond the less specific belief in life after death expressed in Wis 5.15 and is similar to the belief expressed in 2 Macc 7.23. The understanding of personal resurrection developed quite late in Israel's existence. It is described as the complete transformation of the human being, body and soul, after death. Daniel 12.3 says the resurrected will shine like stars.

▸ **Dan 12.1–3**

Susanna's Beauty Attracts Two Elders

There was a man living in Babylon whose name was Jō'a•kim. 2 He married the daughter of Hil-ki'ah, named Susanna, a very beautiful woman and one who feared the Lord. 3 Her parents were righteous, and had trained their daughter according to the law of Moses. 4 Jō'a•kim was very rich, and had a fine garden adjoining his house; the Jews used to come to him because he was the most honored of them all.

5 That year two elders from the people were appointed as judges. Concerning them the Lord had said: "Wickedness came forth from Babylon, from elders who were judges, who were supposed

to govern the people." 6 These men were frequently at Jō'a•kim's house, and all who had a case to be tried came to them there.

7 When the people left at noon, Susanna would go into her husband's garden to walk. 8 Every day the two elders used to see her, going in and walking about, and they began to lust for her. 9 They suppressed their consciences and turned away their eyes from looking to Heaven or remembering their duty to administer justice. 10 Both were overwhelmed with passion for her, but they did not tell each other of their distress, 11 for they were ashamed to disclose their lustful desire to seduce her. 12 Day after day they watched eagerly to see her.

13 One day they said to each other, "Let us go home, for it is time for lunch." So they both left and parted from each other. 14 But turning back, they met again; and when each pressed the other for the reason, they confessed their lust. Then together they arranged for a time when they could find her alone.

PRAY IT?
Susanna

Daniel is called the hero of chapter 13 of his book. But don't forget Susanna. A real hero, Susanna chooses to risk death rather than submitting to sin. Her prayer demanding God's justice causes the Holy Spirit to stir Daniel into action.
Prayer can challenge and inspire us. What injustices might you pray about? Whose attention do you need to get?

▸ **Daniel, chapter 13**

The Elders Attempt to Seduce Susanna

15 Once, while they were watching for an opportune day, she went in as before with only two maids, and wished to bathe in the garden, for it was a hot day. 16 No one was there except the two elders, who had hidden themselves and were watching her. 17 She said to her maids, "Bring me olive oil and ointments, and shut the garden doors so that I can bathe." 18 They did as she told them: they shut the doors of the garden and went out by the side doors to bring what they had been

m Gk Theodotion: Heb adds *to the end*

commanded; they did not see the elders, because they were hiding.

19 When the maids had gone out, the two elders got up and ran to her. 20 They said, "Look, the garden doors are shut, and no one can see us. We are burning with desire for you; so give your consent, and lie with us. 21 If you refuse, we will testify against you that a young man was with you, and this was why you sent your maids away."

22 Susanna groaned and said, "I am completely trapped. For if I do this, it will mean death for me; if I do not, I cannot escape your hands. 23 I choose not to do it; I will fall into your hands, rather than sin in the sight of the Lord."

24 Then Susanna cried out with a loud voice, and the two elders shouted against her. 25 And one of them ran and opened the garden doors. 26 When the people in the house heard the shouting in the garden, they rushed in at the side door to see what had happened to her. 27 And when the elders told their story, the servants felt very much ashamed, for nothing like this had ever been said about Susanna.

The Elders Testify against Susanna

28 The next day, when the people gathered at the house of her husband Jō'a·kim, the two elders came, full of their wicked plot to have Susanna put to death. In the presence of the people they said, 29 "Send for Susanna daughter of Hil·ki'ah, the wife of Jō'a·kim." So they sent for her. 30 And she came with her parents, her children, and all her relatives.

31 Now Susanna was a woman of great refinement and beautiful in appearance. 32 As she was veiled, the scoundrels ordered her to be unveiled, so that they might feast their eyes on her beauty. 33 Those who were with her and all who saw her were weeping.

34 Then the two elders stood up before the people and laid their hands on her head. 35 Through her tears she looked up toward Heaven, for her heart trusted in the Lord. 36 The elders said, "While we were walking in the garden alone, this woman came in with two maids, shut the garden doors, and dismissed the maids. 37 Then a young man, who was hiding there, came to her and lay with her. 38 We were in a corner of the garden, and when we saw this wickedness we ran to them. 39 Although we saw them embracing, we could not hold the man, because he was stronger than we, and he opened the doors and got away. 40 We did, however, seize this woman and asked who the young man was, 41 but she would not tell us. These things we testify."

Because they were elders of the people and judges, the assembly believed them and condemned her to death.

42 Then Susanna cried out with a loud voice, and said, "O eternal God, you know what is secret and are aware of all things before they come to be; 43 you know that these men have given false evidence against me. And now I am to die, though I have done none of the wicked things that they have charged against me!"

44 The Lord heard her cry. 45 Just as she was being led off to execution, God stirred up the holy spirit of a young lad named Daniel, 46 and he shouted with a loud voice, "I want no part in shedding this woman's blood!"

Daniel Rescues Susanna

47 All the people turned to him and asked, "What is this you are saying?" 48 Taking his stand among them he said, "Are you such fools, O Israelites, as to condemn a daughter of Israel without examination and without learning the facts? 49 Return to court, for these men have given false evidence against her."

50 So all the people hurried back. And the rest of the[n] elders said to him, "Come, sit among us and inform us, for God has given you the standing of an elder." 51 Daniel said to them, "Separate them far from each other, and I will examine them."

52 When they were separated from each other, he summoned one of them and said to him, "You old relic of wicked days, your sins have now come home, which you have committed in the past, 53 pronouncing unjust judgments, condemning the innocent and acquitting the guilty, though the Lord said, 'You shall not put an innocent and righteous person to death.' 54 Now then, if you really saw this woman, tell me this: Under what tree did you see them being intimate with each other?" He answered, "Under a mastic tree."[o] 55 And Daniel said, "Very well! This lie has cost you your head, for the angel of God has received the sentence from God and will immediately cut[o] you in two."

56 Then, putting him to one side, he ordered them to bring the other. And he said to him, "You offspring of Cā'naan and not of Judah, beauty has beguiled you and lust has perverted your heart. 57 This is how you have been treating the daughters of Israel, and they were intimate with you through fear; but a daughter of Judah would not tolerate your wickedness. 58 Now then, tell me: Under what tree did you catch them being intimate with each

n Gk lacks rest of the   o The Greek words for mastic tree and cut are similar, thus forming an ironic wordplay

other?" He answered, "Under an evergreen oak."ᵖ ⁵⁹ Daniel said to him, "Very well! This lie has cost you also your head, for the angel of God is waiting with his sword to splitᵖ you in two, so as to destroy you both."

60 Then the whole assembly raised a great shout and blessed God, who saves those who hope in him. ⁶¹ And they took action against the two elders, because out of their own mouths Daniel had convicted them of bearing false witness; they did to them as they had wickedly planned to do to their neighbor. ⁶² Acting in accordance with the law of Moses, they put them to death. Thus innocent blood was spared that day.

63 Hil·ki′ah and his wife praised God for their daughter Susanna, and so did her husband Jō′a-kim and all her relatives, because she was found innocent of a shameful deed. ⁶⁴ And from that day onward Daniel had a great reputation among the people.

Daniel and the Priests of Bel

When King As·ty′a·gēs was laid to rest with his ancestors, Cyrus the Persian succeeded to his kingdom. ² Daniel was a companion of the king, and was the most honored of all his Friends.

3 Now the Babylonians had an idol called Bel, and every day they provided for it twelve bushels of choice flour and forty sheep and six measuresᵠ of wine. ⁴ The king revered it and went every day to worship it. But Daniel worshiped his own God.

So the king said to him, "Why do you not worship Bel?" ⁵ He answered, "Because I do not revere idols made with hands, but the living God, who created heaven and earth and has dominion over all living creatures."

6 The king said to him, "Do you not think that Bel is a living god? Do you not see how much he eats and drinks every day?" ⁷ And Daniel laughed, and said, "Do not be deceived, O king, for this thing is only clay inside and bronze outside, and it never ate or drank anything."

8 Then the king was angry and called the priests of Belʳ and said to them, "If you do not tell me who is eating these provisions, you shall die. ⁹ But if you prove that Bel is eating them, Daniel shall die, because he has spoken blasphemy against Bel." Daniel said to the king, "Let it be done as you have said."

10 Now there were seventy priests of Bel, besides their wives and children. So the king went with Daniel into the temple of Bel. ¹¹ The priests of Bel said, "See, we are now going outside; you yourself, O king, set out the food and prepare the wine, and shut the door and seal it with your signet. ¹² When you return in the morning, if you do not find that Bel has eaten it all, we will die; otherwise Daniel will, who is telling lies about us." ¹³ They were unconcerned, for beneath the table they had made a hidden entrance, through which they used to go in regularly and consume the provisions. ¹⁴ After they had gone out, the king set out the food for Bel. Then Daniel ordered his servants to bring ashes, and they scattered them throughout the whole temple in the presence of the king alone. Then they went out, shut the door and sealed it with the king's signet, and departed. ¹⁵ During the night the priests came as usual, with their wives and children, and they ate and drank everything.

16 Early in the morning the king rose and came, and Daniel with him. ¹⁷ The king said, "Are the seals unbroken, Daniel?" He answered, "They are unbroken, O king." ¹⁸ As soon as the doors were opened, the king looked at the table, and shouted in a loud voice, "You are great, O Bel, and in you there is no deceit at all!"

19 But Daniel laughed and restrained the king from going in. "Look at the floor," he said, "and notice whose footprints these are." ²⁰ The king said, "I see the footprints of men and women and children."

21 Then the king was enraged, and he arrested the priests and their wives and children. They showed him the secret doors through which they used to enter to consume what was on the table. ²² Therefore the king put them to death, and gave Bel over to Daniel, who destroyed it and its temple.

Daniel Kills the Dragon

23 Now in that placeˢ there was a great dragon, which the Babylonians revered. ²⁴ The king said to Daniel, "You cannot deny that this is a living god; so worship him." ²⁵ Daniel said, "I worship the Lord my God, for he is the living God. ²⁶ But give me permission, O king, and I will kill the dragon without sword or club." The king said, "I give you permission."

27 Then Daniel took pitch, fat, and hair, and boiled them together and made cakes, which he fed to the dragon. The dragon ate them, and burst open. Then Daniel said, "See what you have been worshiping!"

28 When the Babylonians heard about it, they were very indignant and conspired against the king, saying, "The king has become a Jew; he has destroyed Bel, and killed the dragon, and

---

ᵖ The Greek words for *evergreen oak* and *split* are similar, thus forming an ironic wordplay   ᵠ A little more than fifty gallons   ʳ Gk *his priests*   ˢ Other ancient authorities lack *in that place*

CALLED TO BE PROPHETS!

HISPANIC
¡Llamados a ser Profetas!

The following excerpt from *Prophetic Voices* reveals how Hispanic young people express their prophetic mission:

As Hispanic young people, as members of the Catholic Church, we wish to raise our prophetic voice in order to announce the values of the Gospel, to denounce sin, to invite all youth to struggle for the Kingdom of God.

First of all, we announce the option for peace as against violence (Mt 26.51; 2 Cor 5.18); for love as against injustice (Jn 15.17); for good as against evil (Deut 30.15); for the family as a fundamental value through which faith is transmitted (Eph 6.4); and for maintaining one's own culture.

Likewise, we denounce materialism, which leads us to believe that the important thing in life is to have more and more in contrast to the teachings of the Gospel (Mt 6.25–30; *Populorum Progressio* 19).

We denounce the injustice and oppression that Latin America suffers as a result of the cultural, economic, military, and political intervention of wealthy nations. . . .

We denounce the Melting Pot theory and make an option for learning the culture of this country without forgetting our own (*Evangelii Nuntiandi* 20). We denounce abortion, the abuse of drugs and alcohol, and the negative and manipulative influence of commercial propaganda that creates false needs.

We do not just denounce these injustices, we also feel ourselves called to struggle for peace in the world, to live a more simple life-style in solidarity with our poor brothers and sisters. . . .

Let us be aware that we can change the world with our way of life today.

(Secretariat for Hispanic Affairs, page 12)

slaughtered the priests." 29 Going to the king, they said, "Hand Daniel over to us, or else we will kill you and your household." 30 The king saw that they were pressing him hard, and under compulsion he handed Daniel over to them.

Daniel in the Lions' Den

31 They threw Daniel into the lions' den, and he was there for six days. 32 There were seven lions in the den, and every day they had been given two human bodies and two sheep; but now they were given nothing, so that they would devour Daniel.

33 Now the prophet Ha·bak′kuk was in Judea; he had made a stew and had broken bread into a bowl, and was going into the field to take it to the reapers. 34 But the angel of the Lord said to Ha·bak′kuk, "Take the food that you have to Babylon, to Daniel, in the lions' den." 35 Ha·bak′kuk said, "Sir, I have never seen Babylon, and I know noth-

ing about the den." 36 Then the angel of the Lord took him by the crown of his head and carried him by his hair; with the speed of the wind[t] he set him down in Babylon, right over the den.

37 Then Ha·bak′kuk shouted, "Daniel, Daniel! Take the food that God has sent you." 38 Daniel said, "You have remembered me, O God, and have not forsaken those who love you." 39 So Daniel got up and ate. And the angel of God immediately returned Ha·bak′kuk to his own place.

40 On the seventh day the king came to mourn for Daniel. When he came to the den he looked in, and there sat Daniel! 41 The king shouted with a loud voice, "You are great, O Lord, the God of Daniel, and there is no other besides you!" 42 Then he pulled Daniel[u] out, and threw into the den those who had attempted his destruction, and they were instantly eaten before his eyes.

[t] Or *by the power of his spirit*   [u] Gk *him*

DAN

Go marry a prostitute." Say what, God? A picture is worth a thousand words, and Hosea's family life was a living picture of Israel's infidelity and God's continuing faithfulness. The Book of Hosea captures this faithful prophet's commitment to God and his loving faithfulness to his straying wife.

In-depth

Hosea preached to the northern kingdom of Israel before it was conquered by the Assyrians in 721 B.C. As we learn from Hosea's speeches, the situation in the northern kingdom was not good. Over twenty-five years, Hosea saw seven kings come and go, most of them corrupt (see the timeline at the back of this Bible, and 2 Kings 14.23—17.23). Pursuing their own greedy ends, and trying to play power politics, the ruling class overlooked the poor and the needy in their midst and led the people into idolatry. Through Hosea, God proclaimed, "I have been the LORD your God / ever since the land of Egypt" (Hos 13.4).

Even more powerful than Hosea's words was the living symbol of his marriage. Early in Hosea's preaching, God commanded him to marry a prostitute and have children by her. Hosea remained faithful to her, loving her even when she wandered to other men. Hosea used the image of his own marriage to preach his message to Israel. As Hosea's wife was unfaithful to him, so too was Israel unfaithful to God, wandering off in worship of other gods. However, just as Hosea was faithful to his wife and awaited her return, so too God was faithful to Israel and awaited its return from the distractions of power, wealth, and other gods.

Hosea and Amos were prophets in the northern kingdom at about the same time. But Amos had come from the southern kingdom and was more distant and cynical in describing the sins of the ruling class (see his description of well-off women in Am 4.1-3). Hosea was from the northern kingdom—these people were his people! He took their sins personally and passionately. Initially, he had hopes that the people would repent and return to God (see Hos 2.14-23). But after a succession of selfish and violent rulers, he prophesied against his people with all the passion of a scorned lover (see 13.7-11). Still, at the end, he hoped for Israel's return to God (14.1-2).

At a Glance

- **Chapters 1–3.** descriptions of Hosea's marriage and family
- **Chapters 4–14.** Hosea's speeches

Quick Facts

Period Covered
755–730 B.C.

Authors
Hosea and later scribes

Themes
God's faithful love for Israel, the image of God as a loving parent

The Book of *Hosea*

Hosea

The word of the LORD that came to Hō•sē′a son of Be•ē′rī, in the days of Kings Uz•zī′ah, Jō′tham, Ā′haz, and Hez•e•kī′ah of Judah, and in the days of King Jer•o•bō′am son of Jō′ash of Israel.

The Family of Hosea
(Cp 2 Kings 24.10–17)

2 When the LORD first spoke through Hō•sē′a, the LORD said to Hō•sē′a, "Go, take for yourself a wife of whoredom and have children of whoredom, for the land commits great whoredom by forsaking the LORD." 3 So he went and took Gō′mer daughter of Dib•lā′im, and she conceived and bore him a son.

4 And the LORD said to him, "Name him Jez′re•el;[a] for in a little while I will punish the house of Jē′hū for the blood of Jez′re•el, and I will put an end to the kingdom of the house of Israel. 5 On that day I will break the bow of Israel in the valley of Jez′re•el."

6 She conceived again and bore a daughter. Then the LORD said to him, "Name her Lō-rū•ha′mah,[b] for I will no longer have pity on the house of Israel or forgive them. 7 But I will have pity on the house of Judah, and I will save them by the LORD their God; I will not save them by bow, or by sword, or by war, or by horses, or by horsemen."

8 When she had weaned Lō-rū•ha′mah, she conceived and bore a son. 9 Then the LORD said,

"Name him Lō-am′mī,[c] for you are not my people and I am not your God."[d]

The Restoration of Israel

10[e] Yet the number of the people of Israel shall be like the sand of the sea, which can be neither measured nor numbered; and in the place where it was said to them, "You are not my people," it shall be said to them, "Children of the living God." 11 The people of Judah and the people of Israel shall be gathered together, and they shall appoint for themselves one head; and they shall take possession of[f] the land, for great shall be the day of Jez′re•el.

2 Say to your brother,[h] Am′mī,[i] and to your sister,[j] Rū•ha′mah.[k]

Israel's Infidelity, Punishment, and Redemption

2 Plead with your mother, plead—
    for she is not my wife,
    and I am not her husband—
  that she put away her whoring from her
      face,
    and her adultery from between her
      breasts,

---

a That is *God sows*   b That is *Not pitied*   c That is *Not my people*   d Heb *I am not yours*   e Ch 2.1 in Heb   f Heb *rise up from*   g Ch 2.3 in Heb   h Gk: Heb *brothers*   i That is *My people*   j Gk Vg: Heb *sisters*   k That is *Pitied*

3 or I will strip her naked
   and expose her as in the day she was
      born,
   and make her like a wilderness,
   and turn her into a parched land,
   and kill her with thirst.
4 Upon her children also I will have no pity,
   because they are children of whoredom.
5 For their mother has played the whore;
   she who conceived them has acted
      shamefully.
For she said, "I will go after my lovers;
   they give me my bread and my water,
   my wool and my flax, my oil and my
      drink."
6 Therefore I will hedge up her[l] way with
      thorns;
   and I will build a wall against her,
   so that she cannot find her paths.
7 She shall pursue her lovers,
   but not overtake them;
and she shall seek them,
   but shall not find them.
Then she shall say, "I will go
   and return to my first husband,
   for it was better with me then than now."
8 She did not know
   that it was I who gave her
   the grain, the wine, and the oil,
and who lavished upon her silver
   and gold that they used for Ba'al.
9 Therefore I will take back
   my grain in its time,
   and my wine in its season;
and I will take away my wool and my flax,
   which were to cover her nakedness.
10 Now I will uncover her shame
   in the sight of her lovers,
   and no one shall rescue her out of my
      hand.
11 I will put an end to all her mirth,
   her festivals, her new moons, her
      sabbaths,
   and all her appointed festivals.
12 I will lay waste her vines and her fig trees,
   of which she said,
   "These are my pay,
   which my lovers have given me."
I will make them a forest,
   and the wild animals shall devour them.
13 I will punish her for the festival days of the
      Ba'als,
   when she offered incense to them
   and decked herself with her ring and
      jewelry,

and went after her lovers,
   and forgot me, says the LORD.
14 Therefore, I will now allure her,
   and bring her into the wilderness,
   and speak tenderly to her.
15 From there I will give her her vineyards,
   and make the Valley of A'chor a door of
      hope.
There she shall respond as in the days of
      her youth,
   as at the time when she came out of the
      land of Egypt.
16 On that day, says the LORD, you will call me,
"My husband," and no longer will you call me,
"My Ba'al."[m] 17 For I will remove the names of the
Ba'als from her mouth, and they shall be mentioned by name no more. 18 I will make for you[n] a
covenant on that day with the wild animals, the
birds of the air, and the creeping things of the
ground; and I will abolish[o] the bow, the sword,
and war from the land; and I will make you lie
down in safety. 19 And I will take you for my wife
forever; I will take you for my wife in righteousness and in justice, in steadfast love, and in mercy.
20 I will take you for my wife in faithfulness; and
you shall know the LORD.
21 On that day I will answer, says the LORD,
   I will answer the heavens
   and they shall answer the earth;
22 and the earth shall answer the grain, the
      wine, and the oil,
   and they shall answer Jez're·el;[p]
23 and I will sow him[q] for myself in the
      land.
And I will have pity on Lo-ru·ha'mah,[r]
   and I will say to Lo-am'mi,[s] "You are
      my people";
   and he shall say, "You are my God."

Further Assurances of God's Redeeming Love

The LORD said to me again, "Go, love a woman
who has a lover and is an adulteress, just as the
LORD loves the people of Israel, though they turn to
other gods and love raisin cakes." 2 So I bought her
for fifteen shekels of silver and a homer of barley
and a measure of wine.[t] 3 And I said to her, "You
must remain as mine for many days; you shall not
play the whore, you shall not have intercourse
with a man, nor I with you." 4 For the Israelites
shall remain many days without king or prince,
without sacrifice or pillar, without ephod or

---

l Gk Syr: Heb *your*   m That is, *"My master"*   n Heb *them*
o Heb *break*   p That is *God sows*   q Cn: Heb *her*
r That is *Not pitied*   s That is *Not my people*   t Gk: Heb
a homer of barley and a lethech of barley

HOS

Unconditional Faithfulness

We don't know all the details of Hosea's relationship with his wife, Gomer. But most people understand Hos 3.1–3 to mean that Hosea accepted her back after she was unfaithful to him. We can only hope that Gomer was so touched by Hosea's unconditional forgiveness that she turned her life around and was faithful to him in return.

It is hard to be faithful to someone when they are unfaithful to you. The other person doesn't have to be an adulterous spouse. She or he can be a friend who starts spending time with someone else instead of you, or a family member who keeps breaking promises to be with you. A natural reaction is to return the hurt in some way. How much harder—and more Christlike—it is to keep being faithful and friendly.

Have you ever been hurt by someone's unfaithful behavior? If so, how did you react? How can you address a friend's or family member's unfaithful behavior and still remain faithful and loving yourself?

▸ Hos 3.1–3

---

teraphim. ⁵Afterward the Israelites shall return and seek the LORD their God, and David their king; they shall come in awe to the LORD and to his goodness in the latter days.

God Accuses Israel

Hear the word of the LORD, O people of
　　Israel;
　　for the LORD has an indictment against
　　　　the inhabitants of the land.
There is no faithfulness or loyalty,
　　and no knowledge of God in the land.
² Swearing, lying, and murder,
　　and stealing and adultery break out;
　　bloodshed follows bloodshed.
³ Therefore the land mourns,
　　and all who live in it languish;
together with the wild animals
　　and the birds of the air,
　　even the fish of the sea are perishing.

⁴ Yet let no one contend,
　　and let none accuse,
　　for with you is my contention, O priest.ᵘ
⁵ You shall stumble by day;
　　the prophet also shall stumble with you
　　　　by night,
　　and I will destroy your mother.
⁶ My people are destroyed for lack of
　　　　knowledge;
　　because you have rejected knowledge,
　　I reject you from being a priest to me.
And since you have forgotten the law of
　　　　your God,
　　I also will forget your children.

⁷ The more they increased,
　　the more they sinned against me;
　　they changedᵛ their glory into shame.
⁸ They feed on the sin of my people;
　　they are greedy for their iniquity.
⁹ And it shall be like people, like priest;
　　I will punish them for their ways,
　　and repay them for their deeds.
¹⁰ They shall eat, but not be satisfied;
　　they shall play the whore, but not
　　　　multiply;
　　because they have forsaken the LORD
　　　　to devote themselves to ¹¹whoredom.

The Idolatry of Israel

Wine and new wine
　　take away the understanding.
¹² My people consult a piece of wood,
　　and their divining rod gives them oracles.
For a spirit of whoredom has led them
　　　　astray,
　　and they have played the whore,
　　　　forsaking their God.
¹³ They sacrifice on the tops of the mountains,
　　and make offerings upon the hills,
under oak, poplar, and terebinth,
　　because their shade is good.

Therefore your daughters play the whore,
　　and your daughters-in-law commit
　　　　adultery.
¹⁴ I will not punish your daughters when they
　　　　play the whore,

ᵘ Cn: Meaning of Heb uncertain　　ᵛ Ancient Heb tradition: MT *I will change*

HOS

nor your daughters-in-law when they
   commit adultery;
for the men themselves go aside with
   whores,
   and sacrifice with temple prostitutes;
thus a people without understanding comes
   to ruin.

15 Though you play the whore, O Israel,
   do not let Judah become guilty.
Do not enter into Gil'gal,
   or go up to Beth-ā'ven,
   and do not swear, "As the LORD lives."
16 Like a stubborn heifer,
   Israel is stubborn;
can the LORD now feed them
   like a lamb in a broad pasture?

17 Ē'phra•im is joined to idols—
   let him alone.
18 When their drinking is ended, they indulge
   in sexual orgies;
   they love lewdness more than their
     glory.*w*
19 A wind has wrapped them*x* in its wings,
   and they shall be ashamed because of
     their altars.*y*

Impending Judgment on Israel and Judah

Hear this, O priests!
   Give heed, O house of Israel!
Listen, O house of the king!
   For the judgment pertains to you;
for you have been a snare at Miz'pah,
   and a net spread upon Tā'bor,
2 and a pit dug deep in Shit'tim;*z*
   but I will punish all of them.

3 I know Ē'phra•im,
   and Israel is not hidden from me;
for now, O Ē'phra•im, you have played the
     whore;
   Israel is defiled.
4 Their deeds do not permit them
   to return to their God.
For the spirit of whoredom is within them,
   and they do not know the LORD.

5 Israel's pride testifies against him;
   Ē'phra•im*a* stumbles in his guilt;
   Judah also stumbles with them.
6 With their flocks and herds they shall go
   to seek the LORD,
but they will not find him;
   he has withdrawn from them.
7 They have dealt faithlessly with the LORD;
   for they have borne illegitimate children.

Now the new moon shall devour them
   along with their fields.

8 Blow the horn in Gib'ē•ah,
   the trumpet in Rā'mah.
Sound the alarm at Beth-ā'ven;
   look behind you, Benjamin!
9 Ē'phra•im shall become a desolation
   in the day of punishment;
among the tribes of Israel
   I declare what is sure.
10 The princes of Judah have become
   like those who remove the landmark;
on them I will pour out
   my wrath like water.
11 Ē'phra•im is oppressed, crushed in judgment,
   because he was determined to go after
     vanity.*b*
12 Therefore I am like maggots to Ē'phra•im,
   and like rottenness to the house of Judah.
13 When Ē'phra•im saw his sickness,
   and Judah his wound,
then Ē'phra•im went to Assyria,
   and sent to the great king.*c*
But he is not able to cure you
   or heal your wound.
14 For I will be like a lion to Ē'phra•im,
   and like a young lion to the house of
     Judah.
I myself will tear and go away;
   I will carry off, and no one shall rescue.
15 I will return again to my place
   until they acknowledge their guilt and
     seek my face.
   In their distress they will beg my favor:

A Call to Repentance

"Come, let us return to the LORD;
   for it is he who has torn, and he will
     heal us;
he has struck down, and he will bind
     us up.
2 After two days he will revive us;
   on the third day he will raise us up,
   that we may live before him.
3 Let us know, let us press on to know the
     LORD;
   his appearing is as sure as the dawn;
he will come to us like the showers,
   like the spring rains that water the earth."

---

w Cn Compare Gk: Meaning of Heb uncertain   *x* Heb *her*
y Gk Syr: Heb *sacrifices*   *z* Cn: Meaning of Heb uncertain
a Heb *Israel and Ephraim*   *b* Gk: Meaning of Heb
uncertain   *c* Cn: Heb *to a king who will contend*

Impenitence of Israel and Judah

4 What shall I do with you, O Ē′phra•im?
    What shall I do with you, O Judah?
Your love is like a morning cloud,
    like the dew that goes away early.
5 Therefore I have hewn them by the
        prophets,
    I have killed them by the words of my
        mouth,
    and my[d] judgment goes forth as the light.
6 For I desire steadfast love and not sacrifice,
    the knowledge of God rather than burnt
        offerings.

7 But at[e] Adam they transgressed the
        covenant;
    there they dealt faithlessly with me.
8 Gil′e•ad is a city of evildoers,
    tracked with blood.
9 As robbers lie in wait[f] for someone,
    so the priests are banded together;[g]
they murder on the road to Shē′chem,
    they commit a monstrous crime.
10 In the house of Israel I have seen a horrible
        thing;
    Ē′phra•im's whoredom is there, Israel is
        defiled.

11 For you also, O Judah, a harvest
        is appointed.

When I would restore the fortunes of my
        people,
    when I would heal Israel,
    the corruption of Ē′phra•im is revealed,
    and the wicked deeds of Sa•mār′i•a;
for they deal falsely,
    the thief breaks in,
    and the bandits raid outside.
2 But they do not consider
    that I remember all their wickedness.
Now their deeds surround them,
    they are before my face.
3 By their wickedness they make the king
        glad,
    and the officials by their treachery.
4 They are all adulterers;
    they are like a heated oven,
whose baker does not need to stir the fire,
    from the kneading of the dough until it
        is leavened.
5 On the day of our king the officials
    became sick with the heat of wine;
    he stretched out his hand with mockers.
6 For they are kindled[h] like an oven, their
        heart burns within them;
    all night their anger smolders;

in the morning it blazes like a flaming
        fire.
7 All of them are hot as an oven,
    and they devour their rulers.
All their kings have fallen;
    none of them calls upon me.

8 Ē′phra•im mixes himself with the peoples;
    Ē′phra•im is a cake not turned.
9 Foreigners devour his strength,
    but he does not know it;
gray hairs are sprinkled upon him,
    but he does not know it.
10 Israel's pride testifies against[i] him;
    yet they do not return to the LORD
        their God,
    or seek him, for all this.

Futile Reliance on the Nations

11 Ē′phra•im has become like a dove,
    silly and without sense;
    they call upon Egypt, they go to Assyria.
12 As they go, I will cast my net over them;
    I will bring them down like birds of
        the air;
    I will discipline them according to the
        report made to their assembly.[j]
13 Woe to them, for they have strayed
        from me!
    Destruction to them, for they have
        rebelled against me!
I would redeem them,
    but they speak lies against me.

14 They do not cry to me from the heart,
    but they wail upon their beds;
they gash themselves for grain and wine;
    they rebel against me.
15 It was I who trained and strengthened their
        arms,
    yet they plot evil against me.
16 They turn to that which does not profit;[f]
    they have become like a defective bow;
their officials shall fall by the sword
    because of the rage of their tongue.
So much for their babbling in the land of
        Egypt.

Israel's Apostasy

Set the trumpet to your lips!
    One like a vulture[j] is over the house of
        the LORD,
because they have broken my covenant,

---

d Gk Syr: Heb *your*   e Cn: Heb *like*   f Cn: Meaning of
Heb uncertain   g Syr: Heb *are a company*   h Gk Syr:
Heb *brought near*   i Or *humbles*   j Meaning of Heb
uncertain

and transgressed my law.

2 Israel cries to me,
  "My God, we—Israel—know you!"

3 Israel has spurned the good;
  the enemy shall pursue him.

4 They made kings, but not through me;
    they set up princes, but without my
      knowledge.
  With their silver and gold they made idols
    for their own destruction.

5 Your calf is rejected, O Sa•mār′i•a.
  My anger burns against them.
  How long will they be incapable of
      innocence?

6   For it is from Israel,
  an artisan made it;
    it is not God.
  The calf of Sa•mār′i•a
    shall be broken to pieces.k

PRAY IT!

Reaping the Whirlwind

Hosea uses lots of metaphors, or symbols, in describing Israel's relationship with God. Hosea 8.7 gives one of those metaphors, saying the Israelites have sowed the wind and will reap the whirlwind. The wind is their political scheming, injustice, and idolatry; the whirlwind is violence and injustice that will destroy the whole country.

Like Israel, we are free to reject or accept God, but will have to reap the consequences of our choices.

In your prayer, reflect or journal on the following questions:

- What significant decisions have you made recently?
- What consequences are likely to follow as a result of each decision?
- Were your choices the ones that God wanted you to make?

▸ Hos 8.7

7 For they sow the wind,
    and they shall reap the whirlwind.
  The standing grain has no heads,
    it shall yield no meal;
  if it were to yield,

foreigners would devour it.

8 Israel is swallowed up;
  now they are among the nations
    as a useless vessel.

9 For they have gone up to Assyria,
    a wild ass wandering alone;
  Ē′phra•im has bargained for lovers.

10 Though they bargain with the nations,
    I will now gather them up.
  They shall soon writhe
    under the burden of kings and princes.

11 When Ē′phra•im multiplied altars
        to expiate sin,
    they became to him altars for sinning.

12 Though I write for him the multitude of my
        instructions,
    they are regarded as a strange thing.

13 Though they offer choice sacrifices,l
    though they eat flesh,
      the LORD does not accept them.
  Now he will remember their iniquity,
    and punish their sins;
    they shall return to Egypt.

14 Israel has forgotten his Maker,
    and built palaces;
  and Judah has multiplied fortified cities;
    but I will send a fire upon his cities,
    and it shall devour his strongholds.

Punishment for Israel's Sin

9 Do not rejoice, O Israel!
  Do not exultm as other nations do;
for you have played the whore, departing
        from your God.
    You have loved a prostitute's pay
    on all threshing floors.

2 Threshing floor and wine vat shall not feed
        them,
    and the new wine shall fail them.

3 They shall not remain in the land of the
        LORD;
  but Ē′phra•im shall return to Egypt,
    and in Assyria they shall eat unclean
        food.

4 They shall not pour drink offerings of wine
        to the LORD,
    and their sacrifices shall not please him.
  Such sacrifices shall be like mourners' bread;
    all who eat of it shall be defiled;
  for their bread shall be for their hunger
        only;

---

k Or shall go up in flames   l Cn: Meaning of Heb
uncertain   m Gk: Heb To exultation

it shall not come to the house of the
LORD.

5 What will you do on the day of appointed
festival,
and on the day of the festival of the
LORD?
6 For even if they escape destruction,
Egypt shall gather them,
Memphis shall bury them.
Nettles shall possess their precious things of
silver;[n]
thorns shall be in their tents.

7 The days of punishment have come,
the days of recompense have come;
Israel cries,[o]
"The prophet is a fool,
the man of the spirit is mad!"
Because of your great iniquity,
your hostility is great.
8 The prophet is a sentinel for my God over
Ē'phra·im,
yet a fowler's snare is on all his ways,
and hostility in the house of his God.
9 They have deeply corrupted themselves
as in the days of Gib'ē·ah;
he will remember their iniquity,
he will punish their sins.

10 Like grapes in the wilderness,
I found Israel.
Like the first fruit on the fig tree,
in its first season,
I saw your ancestors.
But they came to Bā'al-pē'or,
and consecrated themselves to a thing of
shame,
and became detestable like the thing they
loved.
11 Ē'phra·im's glory shall fly away like a bird—
no birth, no pregnancy, no conception!
12 Even if they bring up children,
I will bereave them until no one is left.
Woe to them indeed
when I depart from them!
13 Once I saw Ē'phra·im as a young palm
planted in a lovely meadow,[n]
but now Ē'phra·im must lead out his
children for slaughter.
14 Give them, O LORD—
what will you give?
Give them a miscarrying womb
and dry breasts.

15 Every evil of theirs began at Gil'gal;
there I came to hate them.
Because of the wickedness of their deeds

I will drive them out of my house.
I will love them no more;
all their officials are rebels.
16 Ē'phra·im is stricken,
their root is dried up,
they shall bear no fruit.
Even though they give birth,
I will kill the cherished offspring of their
womb.
17 Because they have not listened to him,
my God will reject them;
they shall become wanderers among the
nations.

Israel's Sin and Captivity

10 Israel is a luxuriant vine
that yields its fruit.
The more his fruit increased
the more altars he built;
as his country improved,
he improved his pillars.
2 Their heart is false;
now they must bear their guilt.
The LORD[p] will break down their altars,
and destroy their pillars.

3 For now they will say:
"We have no king,
for we do not fear the LORD,
and a king—what could he do for us?"
4 They utter mere words;
with empty oaths they make covenants;
so litigation springs up like poisonous
weeds
in the furrows of the field.
5 The inhabitants of Sa·mār'i·a tremble
for the calf[q] of Beth-ā'ven.
Its people shall mourn for it,
and its idolatrous priests shall wail[r]
over it,
over its glory that has departed from it.
6 The thing itself shall be carried to Assyria
as tribute to the great king.[s]
Ē'phra·im shall be put to shame,
and Israel shall be ashamed of his idol.[t]

7 Sa·mār'i·a's king shall perish
like a chip on the face of the waters.
8 The high places of Ā'ven, the sin of Israel,
shall be destroyed.
Thorn and thistle shall grow up
on their altars.

---

[n] Meaning of Heb uncertain   [o] Cn Compare Gk: Heb
shall know   [p] Heb he   [q] Gk Syr: Heb calves   [r] Cn: Heb
exult   [s] Cn: Heb to a king who will contend   [t] Cn: Heb
counsel

They shall say to the mountains, Cover us,
    and to the hills, Fall on us.

9 Since the days of Gib′ē•ah you have sinned,
    O Israel;
   there they have continued.
   Shall not war overtake them in Gib′ē•ah?
10 I will come[u] against the wayward people to
    punish them;
   and nations shall be gathered against
    them
   when they are punished[v] for their double
    iniquity.

11 Ē′phra•im was a trained heifer
   that loved to thresh,
   and I spared her fair neck;
  but I will make Ē′phra•im break the ground;
   Judah must plow;
   Jacob must harrow for himself.
12 Sow for yourselves righteousness;
   reap steadfast love;
   break up your fallow ground;
  for it is time to seek the LORD,
   that he may come and rain righteousness
    upon you.

13 You have plowed wickedness,
   you have reaped injustice,
   you have eaten the fruit of lies.
  Because you have trusted in your power
   and in the multitude of your warriors,
14 therefore the tumult of war shall rise against
   your people,
   and all your fortresses shall be destroyed,
  as Shal′man destroyed Beth-ar′bel on the
    day of battle
   when mothers were dashed in pieces with
    their children.
15 Thus it shall be done to you, O Beth′el,
   because of your great wickedness.
  At dawn the king of Israel
   shall be utterly cut off.

God's Compassion Despite
Israel's Ingratitude

11 When Israel was a child, I loved him,
   and out of Egypt I called my son.
2 The more I[w] called them,
   the more they went from me;[x]
  they kept sacrificing to the Bā′als,
   and offering incense to idols.

3 Yet it was I who taught Ē′phra•im to walk,
   I took them up in my[y] arms;
   but they did not know that I healed
    them.

4 I led them with cords of human kindness,
   with bands of love.
  I was to them like those
   who lift infants to their cheeks.[z]
  I bent down to them and fed them.

5 They shall return to the land of Egypt,
   and Assyria shall be their king,
   because they have refused to return to me.
6 The sword rages in their cities,
   it consumes their oracle-priests,
   and devours because of their schemes.
7 My people are bent on turning away
    from me.
  To the Most High they call,
   but he does not raise them up at all.[a]

A Parent's Love

Hosea, chapter 11, describes God as a loving parent. This is one of the most touching passages of the Old Testament. Despite God's tenderness and care, Israel behaves as a rebellious child. God is heartbroken by Israel's rejection, but is compassionate in calling for its return.

God, loving father and mother, thank you for your generous and unconditional love. Let me remember that you always love me even when I have done something wrong. Help me to return your love by living in a way that is pleasing to you. Amen.

▸ Hos 11.1–7

8 How can I give you up, Ē′phra•im?
   How can I hand you over, O Israel?
  How can I make you like Ad′mah?
   How can I treat you like Ze•boi′im?
  My heart recoils within me;
   my compassion grows warm and tender.
9 I will not execute my fierce anger;
   I will not again destroy Ē′phra•im;
  for I am God and no mortal,
   the Holy One in your midst,
   and I will not come in wrath.[a]

---

u Cn Compare Gk: Heb *In my desire*   v Gk: Heb *bound*
w Gk: Heb *they*   x Gk: Heb *them*   y Gk Syr Vg:
Heb *his*   z Or *who ease the yoke on their jaws*   a Meaning
of Heb uncertain

10 They shall go after the LORD,
  who roars like a lion;
when he roars,
  his children shall come trembling from
    the west.
11 They shall come trembling like birds from
    Egypt,
  and like doves from the land of Assyria;
  and I will return them to their homes,
    says the LORD.

12b Ē'phra·im has surrounded me with lies,
  and the house of Israel with deceit;
but Judah still walks[c] with God,
  and is faithful to the Holy One.
Ephraim herds the wind,
  and pursues the east wind all day long;
they multiply falsehood and violence;
  they make a treaty with Assyria,
  and oil is carried to Egypt.

The Long History of Rebellion
(Cp Gen 25—32)

2 The LORD has an indictment against Judah,
  and will punish Jacob according to his
    ways,
  and repay him according to his deeds.
3 In the womb he tried to supplant his
    brother,
  and in his manhood he strove with God.
4 He strove with the angel and prevailed,
  he wept and sought his favor;
he met him at Beth'el,
  and there he spoke with him.[d]
5 The LORD the God of hosts,
  the LORD is his name!
6 But as for you, return to your God,
  hold fast to love and justice,
  and wait continually for your God.

7 A trader, in whose hands are false balances,
  he loves to oppress.
8 Ē'phra·im has said, "Ah, I am rich,
  I have gained wealth for myself;
in all of my gain
  no offense has been found in me
  that would be sin."[e]
9 I am the LORD your God
  from the land of Egypt;
I will make you live in tents again,
  as in the days of the appointed festival.

10 I spoke to the prophets;
  it was I who multiplied visions,
  and through the prophets I will bring
    destruction.
11 In Gil'e·ad[f] there is iniquity,

they shall surely come to nothing.
In Gil'gal they sacrifice bulls,
  so their altars shall be like stone heaps
  on the furrows of the field.
12 Jacob fled to the land of Ar'am,
  there Israel served for a wife,
  and for a wife he guarded sheep.[g]

Asian American

I Therefore Commit

This prayer from Elizabeth S. Tapia of the Philippines could have been written in response to Hosea's call to live justly, to live the spirit of being a holy people of God:

*We should not oppress children,
  indigenous people,
women, the homeless, refugees and
  victims of war.
We need to live in the sense of people
  and creation.
For I believe in the interwovenness of
  life.
Creator and Creatures. Cosmic and
  Individual.
West, North, East, South. Rest and
  Prayer.
Food and Freedom. Theology and
  Ecology.
I therefore commit myself, together with
  you,
to take care for mother earth.
To advocate for peace and justice.
To choose and celebrate life.
These things I believe. Amen.*
    *(From Maren C. Tirabassi
    and Kathy Wonson Eddy,
    Gifts of Many Cultures, p. 115)*

▸ Hos 12.2–6

13 By a prophet the LORD brought Israel up
    from Egypt,
  and by a prophet he was guarded.
14 Ē'phra·im has given bitter offense,

---

b Ch 12.1 in Heb   c Heb *roams or rules*   d Gk Syr: Heb
us   e Meaning of Heb uncertain   f Compare Syr: Heb
Gilead   g Heb lacks *sheep*

so his Lord will bring his crimes down
on him
and pay him back for his insults.

Relentless Judgment on Israel

13 When Ephraim spoke, there was trembling;
he was exalted in Israel;
but he incurred guilt through Bāʹal and
died.

2 And now they keep on sinning
and make a cast image for themselves,
idols of silver made according to their
understanding,
all of them the work of artisans.
"Sacrifice to these," they say.[h]
People are kissing calves!

3 Therefore they shall be like the morning
mist
or like the dew that goes away early,
like chaff that swirls from the threshing
floor
or like smoke from a window.

4 Yet I have been the LORD your God
ever since the land of Egypt;
you know no God but me,
and besides me there is no savior.

5 It was I who fed[i] you in the wilderness,
in the land of drought.

6 When I fed[j] them, they were satisfied;
they were satisfied, and their heart was
proud;
therefore they forgot me.

7 So I will become like a lion to them,
like a leopard I will lurk beside the way.

8 I will fall upon them like a bear robbed of
her cubs,
and will tear open the covering
of their heart;
there I will devour them like a lion,
as a wild animal would mangle them.

9 I will destroy you, O Israel;
who can help you?[k]

10 Where now is[l] your king, that he may
save you?
Where in all your cities are your rulers,
of whom you said,
"Give me a king and rulers"?

11 I gave you a king in my anger,
and I took him away in my wrath.

12 Ēʹphra·im's iniquity is bound up;
his sin is kept in store.

13 The pangs of childbirth come for him,
but he is an unwise son;

for at the proper time he does not present
himself
at the mouth of the womb.

14 Shall I ransom them from the power of
Shēʹōl?
Shall I redeem them from Death?
O Death, where are[m] your plagues?
O Shēʹōl, where is[m] your destruction?
Compassion is hidden from my eyes.

15 Although he may flourish among rushes,[n]
the east wind shall come, a blast from
the LORD,
rising from the wilderness;
and his fountain shall dry up,
his spring shall be parched.
It shall strip his treasury
of every precious thing.

16o Sa·mārʹi·a shall bear her guilt,
because she has rebelled against her God;
they shall fall by the sword,
their little ones shall be dashed in pieces,
and their pregnant women ripped open.

A Plea for Repentance

14 Return, O Israel, to the LORD your God,
for you have stumbled because of your
iniquity.

2 Take words with you
and return to the LORD;
say to him,
"Take away all guilt;
accept that which is good,
and we will offer

---

h Cn Compare Gk: Heb *To these they say sacrifices of people*
i Gk Syr: Heb *knew*　　j Cn: Heb *according to their pasture*
k Gk Syr: Heb *for in me is your help*　　l Gk Syr Vg: Heb *I will be*　　m Gk Syr: Heb *I will be*　　n Or *among brothers*
o Ch 14.1 in Heb

Return, O Israel, to the LORD your God, 14.1

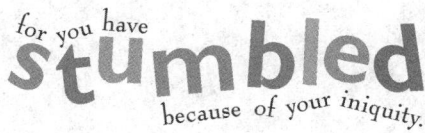

for you have stumbled because of your iniquity.

HOS

the fruit[p] of our lips.

3 Assyria shall not save us;
we will not ride upon horses;
we will say no more, 'Our God,'
to the work of our hands.
In you the orphan finds mercy."

Assurance of Forgiveness

4 I will heal their disloyalty;
I will love them freely,
for my anger has turned from them.

5 I will be like the dew to Israel;
he shall blossom like the lily,
he shall strike root like the forests of
Lebanon.[q]

6 His shoots shall spread out;
his beauty shall be like the olive tree,
and his fragrance like that of Lebanon.

7 They shall again live beneath my[r] shadow,
they shall flourish as a garden;[s]
they shall blossom like the vine,
their fragrance shall be like the wine of
Lebanon.

8 O E′phra·im, what have I[t] to do with idols?
It is I who answer and look after you.[u]
I am like an evergreen cypress;
your faithfulness[v] comes from me.

9 Those who are wise understand these things;
those who are discerning know them.
For the ways of the LORD are right,
and the upright walk in them,
but transgressors stumble in them.

---

p Gk Syr: Heb *bulls*   q Cn: Heb *like Lebanon*   r Heb *his*
s Cn: Heb *they shall grow grain*   t Or *What more has*
Ephraim   u Heb *him*   v Heb *your fruit*

You're just cruising along, in the groove, and everything is going your way. Then, it happens. You hit a major bump in the road, and everything starts falling apart. This appears to have been the situation in Joel's time, when a major plague of locusts was causing widespread destruction. Joel took it as a wake-up sign, calling Israel to rely totally on God no matter what happened.

At a Glance

- **1.1—2.17.** a discussion of a plague of locusts and the day of the Lord

- **2.18—3.21.** several prophecies promising God's salvation for Israel

In-depth

The Book of Joel does not state clearly when it was written, but it gives several clues that lead biblical scholars to believe it was written after the Babylonian Exile. During this time, Israel was ruled by the Greeks and did not have a king. The Temple and Jerusalem had been rebuilt, and Israel enjoyed relative peace, along with a growing expectancy for the coming of a messiah, a savior.

In this period, a natural disaster, perhaps a plague of locusts, occurred. In the first part of the book, Joel uses this tragedy to call Israel's attention toward God and renew its faith. He compares the plague of locusts to an invading army that brings devastation to a city. Eventually, prayer and penance end the plague and bring rain for new crops. More important, the gift of the Spirit renews the people of God (Joel 2.28–29).

A major element of this book is a warrior-type song in which Joel speaks of the coming of the day of the Lord (2.1–17). He describes this as the day when judgment will be delivered against the nations that have destroyed Israel. The day of the Lord is a theme that runs throughout the Bible. It is sometimes described as a joyful time of celebration (Isa 9.3), and other times as a day of punishment and destruction (Am 5.19–25). Initially, writers of the Scriptures applied the term *day of the Lord* only to Israel; Joel applied it to all nations. Gradually, it became connected to the final judgment (Mt 25.31–46).

The Book of Joel ends by affirming that the Lord dwells in Zion (Jerusalem) and the land will be fruitful once more. This is Joel's central message: Despite plagues and even war, God is present in Judah, and there is reason for hope.

Quick Facts

Period Covered
after the rebuilding of the Temple (515 B.C.) and before the destruction of Sidon (343 B.C.)

Authors
Joel and scribes

Theme
a plague of locusts as an occasion to call for Israel to repent and turn to the Lord

The Book of Joel

Joel

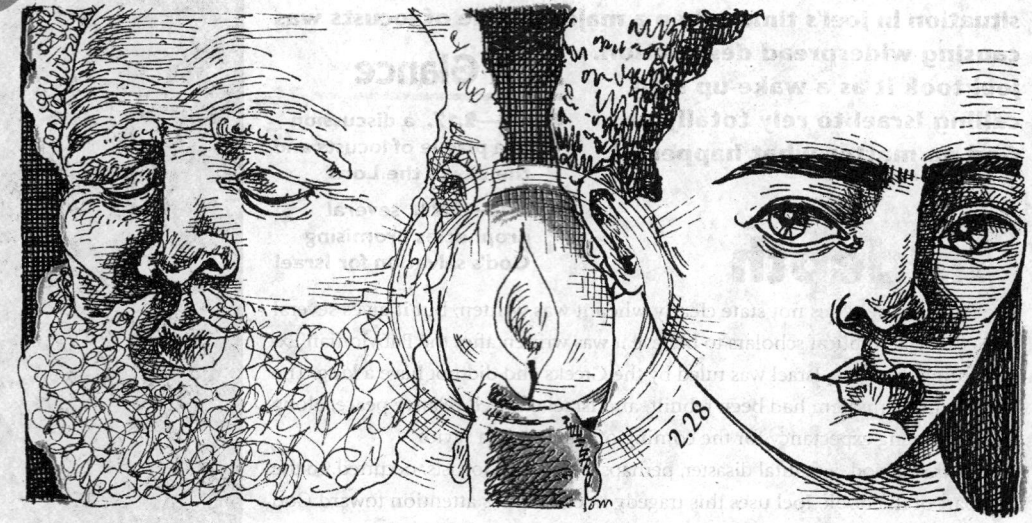

The word of the LORD that came to Jo′el son of Pe·thu′el:

Lament over the Ruin of the Country
(Ex 10.1–20)

2 Hear this, O elders,
  give ear, all inhabitants of the land!
Has such a thing happened in your days,
  or in the days of your ancestors?
3 Tell your children of it,
  and let your children tell their children,
  and their children another generation.

4 What the cutting locust left,
  the swarming locust has eaten.
What the swarming locust left,
  the hopping locust has eaten,
and what the hopping locust left,
  the destroying locust has eaten.

5 Wake up, you drunkards, and weep;
  and wail, all you wine-drinkers,
over the sweet wine,
  for it is cut off from your mouth.
6 For a nation has invaded my land,
  powerful and innumerable;
its teeth are lions' teeth,
  and it has the fangs of a lioness.
7 It has laid waste my vines,
  and splintered my fig trees;

it has stripped off their bark and thrown it
    down;
  their branches have turned white.
8 Lament like a virgin dressed in sackcloth
  for the husband of her youth.
9 The grain offering and the drink offering are
    cut off
  from the house of the LORD.
The priests mourn,
  the ministers of the LORD.
10 The fields are devastated,
  the ground mourns;
for the grain is destroyed,
  the wine dries up,
  the oil fails.

11 Be dismayed, you farmers,
  wail, you vinedressers,
over the wheat and the barley;
  for the crops of the field are
    ruined.
12 The vine withers,
  the fig tree droops.
Pomegranate, palm, and apple—
  all the trees of the field are
    dried up;
surely, joy withers away
  among the people.

A Call to Repentance and Prayer

13 Put on sackcloth and lament, you priests;
    wail, you ministers of the altar.
Come, pass the night in sackcloth,
    you ministers of my God!
Grain offering and drink offering
    are withheld from the house of
        your God.

14 Sanctify a fast,
    call a solemn assembly.
Gather the elders
    and all the inhabitants of the land
to the house of the LORD your God,
    and cry out to the LORD.

15 Alas for the day!
For the day of the LORD is near,
    and as destruction from the Almighty[a] it
        comes.

16 Is not the food cut off
    before our eyes,
joy and gladness
    from the house of our God?

17 The seed shrivels under the clods,[b]
    the storehouses are desolate;
the granaries are ruined
    because the grain has failed.

18 How the animals groan!
    The herds of cattle wander about
because there is no pasture for them;
    even the flocks of sheep are dazed.[c]

19 To you, O LORD, I cry.
For fire has devoured
    the pastures of the wilderness,
and flames have burned
    all the trees of the field.

20 Even the wild animals cry to you
    because the watercourses are dried up,
and fire has devoured
    the pastures of the wilderness.

2 Blow the trumpet in Zion;
    sound the alarm on my holy mountain!
Let all the inhabitants of the land tremble,
    for the day of the LORD is coming, it is
        near—

2 a day of darkness and gloom,
    a day of clouds and thick darkness!
Like blackness spread upon the mountains
    a great and powerful army comes;
their like has never been from of old,
    nor will be again after them
        in ages to come.

3 Fire devours in front of them,
    and behind them a flame burns.
Before them the land is like the garden of
        Eden,
    but after them a desolate wilderness,
    and nothing escapes them.

4 They have the appearance of horses,
    and like war-horses they charge.
5 As with the rumbling of chariots,
    they leap on the tops of the mountains,
like the crackling of a flame of fire
    devouring the stubble,
like a powerful army
    drawn up for battle.

6 Before them peoples are in anguish,
    all faces grow pale.[b]
7 Like warriors they charge,
    like soldiers they scale the wall.
Each keeps to its own course,
    they do not swerve from[d] their paths.
8 They do not jostle one another,
    each keeps to its own track;
they burst through the weapons
    and are not halted.
9 They leap upon the city,
    they run upon the walls;
they climb up into the houses,
    they enter through the windows like a
        thief.

10 The earth quakes before them,
    the heavens tremble.
The sun and the moon are darkened,
    and the stars withdraw their shining.
11 The LORD utters his voice
    at the head of his army;
how vast is his host!
    Numberless are those who obey his
        command.
Truly the day of the LORD is great;
    terrible indeed—who can endure it?

12 Yet even now, says the LORD,
    return to me with all your heart,
with fasting, with weeping, and with
        mourning;
13 rend your hearts and not your clothing.
Return to the LORD, your God,
    for he is gracious and merciful,
    slow to anger, and abounding in steadfast
        love,
    and relents from punishing.

---

a Traditional rendering of Heb *Shaddai*   *b* Meaning of
Heb uncertain   *c* Compare Gk Syr Vg: Meaning of Heb
uncertain   *d* Gk Syr Vg: Heb *they do not take a pledge
along*

14 Who knows whether he will not turn and
        relent,
    and leave a blessing behind him,
    a grain offering and a drink offering
        for the LORD, your God?

15 Blow the trumpet in Zion;
        sanctify a fast;
    call a solemn assembly;
16   gather the people.
    Sanctify the congregation;
        assemble the aged;
    gather the children,
        even infants at the breast.
    Let the bridegroom leave his room,
        and the bride her canopy.

17 Between the vestibule and the altar
        let the priests, the ministers of the LORD,
        weep.
    Let them say, "Spare your people, O LORD,
        and do not make your heritage a
        mockery,
    a byword among the nations.
    Why should it be said among the peoples,
    'Where is their God?'"

God's Response and Promise
(Acts 2.17)

18 Then the LORD became jealous for his land,
        and had pity on his people.
19 In response to his people the LORD said:
    I am sending you
        grain, wine, and oil,
        and you will be satisfied;
    and I will no more make you
        a mockery among the nations.

20 I will remove the northern army far
        from you,
        and drive it into a parched and desolate
        land,
    its front into the eastern sea,
        and its rear into the western sea;
    its stench and foul smell will rise up.
        Surely he has done great things!

21 Do not fear, O soil;
        be glad and rejoice,
    for the LORD has done great things!
22 Do not fear, you animals of the field,
        for the pastures of the wilderness are
        green;
    the tree bears its fruit,
        the fig tree and vine give their full yield.

23 O children of Zion, be glad
        and rejoice in the LORD your God;

for he has given the early rain*e* for your
        vindication,
    he has poured down for you abundant
        rain,
    the early and the later rain, as before.
24 The threshing floors shall be full of grain,
        the vats shall overflow with wine and oil.

Catholic Connections
ASH WEDNESDAY

Joel 2.12–18 is the first reading Catholics
hear every year on Ash Wednesday. On that
day, Catholics gather to receive ashes, and to
be reminded at the beginning of the Lenten
season of the importance of prayer, fasting,
and almsgiving. Why?
    We pray to renew our connection to
God.
    We fast to remind ourselves of how it
feels to be hungry, and to empty ourselves
so that God can fill us up spiritually.
    We give alms (money for those who are
less fortunate) to prevent ourselves from
accumulating wealth while needy people
suffer and struggle.

▸ Joel 2.12–18

25 I will repay you for the years
        that the swarming locust has eaten,
    the hopper, the destroyer, and the cutter,
        my great army, which I sent against you.

26 You shall eat in plenty and be satisfied,
        and praise the name of the LORD
        your God,
    who has dealt wondrously with you.
    And my people shall never again be put
        to shame.
27 You shall know that I am in the midst of
        Israel,

e Meaning of Heb uncertain

and that I, the LORD, am your God and
there is no other.
And my people shall never again be put to
shame.

NATIVE AMERICAN

Vision Quest

Joel 2.28 mentions young men having visions. Vision quests are a Native American tradition. A young man with only a blanket is led by a holy person to a hill to be on his own for several days. During that time, he refrains from eating and drinking and tries to focus on being very still, believing that he will receive a personal vision. That vision will give shape to his life and help him know his place in the world. The key is in the waiting. When the young man returns from his vision quest, he is considered a man and can become the person he is destined to become. He now has a vision to live out.

Jesus did his own vision quest before he began his public ministry. He went into the wilderness, fasted, and wrestled with his demons.

Joel 2.28–29 is read at Pentecost—the church feast day that celebrates the coming of the Holy Spirit. You can let the Holy Spirit help you discern the path for your life through a personal retreat, guided by a spiritual director in the Christian tradition.

▶ **Joel 2.28–29**

God's Spirit Poured Out

28 *f* Then afterward
    I will pour out my spirit on all flesh;
your sons and your daughters shall
        prophesy,
    your old men shall dream dreams,
    and your young men shall see visions.
29 Even on the male and female slaves,
    in those days, I will pour out my spirit.

30 I will show portents in the heavens and on the earth, blood and fire and columns of smoke. 31 The sun shall be turned to darkness, and the moon to blood, before the great and terrible day of the LORD comes. 32 Then everyone who calls on the name of the LORD shall be saved; for in Mount Zion and in Jerusalem there shall be those who escape, as the LORD has said, and among the survivors shall be those whom the LORD calls.

g For then, in those days and at that time, when I restore the fortunes of Judah and Jerusalem, 2 I will gather all the nations and bring them down to the valley of Je•hosh′a•phat, and I will enter into judgment with them there, on account of my people and my heritage Israel, because they have scattered them among the nations. They have divided my land, 3 and cast lots for my people, and traded boys for prostitutes, and sold girls for wine, and drunk it down.

4 What are you to me, O Tyre and Si′don, and all the regions of Phi•lis′ti•a? Are you paying me back for something? If you are paying me back, I will turn your deeds back upon your own heads swiftly and speedily. 5 For you have taken my silver and my gold, and have carried my rich treasures into your temples.*h* 6 You have sold the people of Judah and Jerusalem to the Greeks, removing them far from their own border. 7 But now I will rouse them to leave the places to which you have sold them, and I will turn your deeds back upon your own heads. 8 I will sell your sons and your daughters into the hand of the people of Judah, and they will sell them to the Sa•bē′ans, to a nation far away; for the LORD has spoken.

Judgment in the Valley of Jehoshaphat
(Cp Isa 2.4; Mic 4.3)

9   Proclaim this among the nations:
    Prepare war,*i*
        stir up the warriors.
    Let all the soldiers draw near,
        let them come up.
10 Beat your plowshares into swords,
        and your pruning hooks into spears;
        let the weakling say, "I am a warrior."

11 Come quickly,*j*
        all you nations all around,
        gather yourselves there.
    Bring down your warriors, O LORD.
12 Let the nations rouse themselves,
        and come up to the valley of
            Je•hosh′a•phat;

---

f Ch 3.1 in Heb   *g* Ch 4.1 in Heb   *h* Or *palaces*
i Heb *sanctify war*   *j* Meaning of Heb uncertain

J O E L

for there I will sit to judge
    all the neighboring nations.

13 Put in the sickle,
    for the harvest is ripe.
Go in, tread,
    for the wine press is full.
The vats overflow,
    for their wickedness is great.

14 Multitudes, multitudes,
    in the valley of decision!
For the day of the LORD is near
    in the valley of decision.
15 The sun and the moon are darkened,
    and the stars withdraw their shining.

16 The LORD roars from Zion,
    and utters his voice from Jerusalem,
    and the heavens and the earth shake.
But the LORD is a refuge for his people,
    a stronghold for the people of Israel.

The Glorious Future of Judah

17 So you shall know that I, the LORD
    your God,
    dwell in Zion, my holy mountain.

And Jerusalem shall be holy,
    and strangers shall never again pass
        through it.

18 In that day
the mountains shall drip sweet wine,
    the hills shall flow with milk,
and all the stream beds of Judah
    shall flow with water;
a fountain shall come forth from the house
    of the LORD
    and water the Wadi Shit'tim.

19 Egypt shall become a desolation
    and E'dom a desolate wilderness,
because of the violence done to the people
    of Judah,
    in whose land they have shed innocent
        blood.
20 But Judah shall be inhabited forever,
    and Jerusalem to all generations.
21 I will avenge their blood, and I will not
        clear the guilty,[k]
    for the LORD dwells in Zion.

---

[k] Gk Syr: Heb I will hold innocent their blood that I have not held innocent

You've probably run across people who bluntly state what they see going on. They don't seem to care too much about what other people think. They say, "I just tell it like it is." The prophet Amos was like that. He didn't pull any punches in describing the wealthy class's sins or the destruction that God had planned for it. He was a powerful voice calling for justice in God's plan of salvation.

In-depth

Amos lived when there were two separate kingdoms of Israelites: a northern kingdom, named Israel, and a southern kingdom, named Judah. He was born in the southern kingdom and worked as a shepherd and tree trimmer (Am 7.14). But God called him to preach to the northern kingdom. Amos was not an official prophet of the king's court, so he was free to speak against the king and the court and to be brutally honest in delivering God's message.

Among the Old Testament prophecies, Amos's are the least hopeful. Amos stresses that Israel's destruction, complete and total, is certain. He condemns Israel for its failure to be faithful to the Covenant, but he has a special anger toward the king, the priests, and the wealthy class. He accuses them of being hypocrites who lead the people of Israel astray while pretending to be faithful themselves.

What was Amos's evidence? First, the Covenant demanded special care for the poor, the outcast, and the marginalized. The king, the wealthy, and some of the priests were ignoring this demand. Instead of caring for the poor and the lowly, the wealthy were cheating them and treating them unjustly (2.6–8).

Second, with the monies they cheated out of the poor, the ruling class and the wealthy staged lavish ceremonies to God that were modeled on ceremonies honoring foreign gods. They went through the motions of worshiping God, but they ignored the demand to care for their neighbor (5.21–24). For Amos, this was the heart of Israel's hypocrisy—its sinful habit of separating its religious rituals from concern for its citizens. This phoniness was repulsive to God, and because of Israel's sin, God would bring it to destruction. Amos is rightly called the prophet of the Lord's justice.

At a Glance

- **1.1—2.3.** a condemnation of Israel's neighbors

- **2.4—9.8.** a proclamation of the destruction of the northern kingdom, Israel

- **9.9–15.** a word of hope, probably added by a later editor

Quick Facts

Period Covered
783–746 B.C.
Authors
Amos and later scribes
Theme
God's destruction of Israel because of the injustice and hypocrisy of the wealthy and the ruling class

The Book of Amos

Amos

5.24

The words of Ā'mos, who was among the shepherds of Te·kō'a, which he saw concerning Israel in the days of King Uz·zī'ah of Judah and in the days of King Jer·o·bō'am son of Jō'ash of Israel, two years[a] before the earthquake.

Judgment on Israel's Neighbors

2 And he said:

The LORD roars from Zion,
    and utters his voice from Jerusalem;
the pastures of the shepherds wither,
    and the top of Car'mel dries up.

3 Thus says the LORD:

For three transgressions of Damascus,
    and for four, I will not revoke the
      punishment;[b]
because they have threshed Gil'e·ad
    with threshing sledges of iron.
4 So I will send a fire on the house of Haz'a·el,
    and it shall devour the strongholds of
      Ben-hā'dad.
5 I will break the gate bars of Damascus,
    and cut off the inhabitants from the
      Valley of Ā'ven,
and the one who holds the scepter from
      Beth-ē'den;
and the people of Ar'am shall go into
    exile to Kir,

             says the LORD.

6 Thus says the LORD:

For three transgressions of Gā'za,
    and for four, I will not revoke the
      punishment;[b]
because they carried into exile entire
      communities,
    to hand them over to Ē'dom.
7 So I will send a fire on the wall of Gā'za,
    fire that shall devour its strongholds.
8 I will cut off the inhabitants from Ash'dod,
    and the one who holds the scepter from
      Ash'ke·lon;
I will turn my hand against Ek'ron,
    and the remnant of the Phi·lis'tines shall
      perish,

             says the Lord GOD.

9 Thus says the LORD:

For three transgressions of Tȳre,
    and for four, I will not revoke the
      punishment;[b]
because they delivered entire communities
      over to Ē'dom,
    and did not remember the covenant of
      kinship.
10 So I will send a fire on the wall of Tȳre,
    fire that shall devour its strongholds.

---

a Or *during two years*   b Heb *cause it to return*

11 Thus says the LORD:
For three transgressions of Ē′dom,
    and for four, I will not revoke the
        punishment;*c*
because he pursued his brother with the
    sword
    and cast off all pity;
he maintained his anger perpetually,*d*
    and kept his wrath*e* forever.
12 So I will send a fire on Tē′man,
    and it shall devour the strongholds of
        Boz′rah.

13 Thus says the LORD:
For three transgressions of the Am′mon•ītes,
    and for four, I will not revoke the
        punishment;*c*
because they have ripped open pregnant
    women in Gil′e•ad
    in order to enlarge their territory.
14 So I will kindle a fire against the wall of
    Rab′bah,
    fire that shall devour its strongholds,
with shouting on the day of battle,
    with a storm on the day of the
        whirlwind;
15 then their king shall go into exile,
    he and his officials together,
                                    says the LORD.

2 Thus says the LORD:
For three transgressions of Mō′ab,
    and for four, I will not revoke the
        punishment;*c*
because he burned to lime
    the bones of the king of Ē′dom.
2 So I will send a fire on Mō′ab,
    and it shall devour the strongholds of
        Ker′i•oth,
and Mō′ab shall die amid uproar,
    amid shouting and the sound of the
        trumpet;
3 I will cut off the ruler from its midst,
    and will kill all its officials with him,
                                    says the LORD.

Judgment on Judah

4 Thus says the LORD:
For three transgressions of Judah,
    and for four, I will not revoke the
        punishment;*c*
because they have rejected the law of the
    LORD,
    and have not kept his statutes,
but they have been led astray by the same
    lies
    after which their ancestors walked.

5 So I will send a fire on Judah,
    and it shall devour the strongholds of
        Jerusalem.

Judgment on Israel

6 Thus says the LORD:
For three transgressions of Israel,
    and for four, I will not revoke the
        punishment;*c*
because they sell the righteous for silver,
    and the needy for a pair of sandals—
7 they who trample the head of the poor into
    the dust of the earth,
    and push the afflicted out of the way;
father and son go in to the same girl,
    so that my holy name is profaned;
8 they lay themselves down beside every altar
    on garments taken in pledge;
and in the house of their God they drink
    wine bought with fines they imposed.

9 Yet I destroyed the Am′o•rīte before them,
    whose height was like the height of
        cedars,
    and who was as strong as oaks;
I destroyed his fruit above,
    and his roots beneath.
10 Also I brought you up out of the land of
    Egypt,
    and led you forty years in the wilderness,
    to possess the land of the Am′o•rīte.
11 And I raised up some of your children to be
    prophets
    and some of your youths to be nazirites.*f*
    Is it not indeed so, O people of Israel?
                                    says the LORD.

12 But you made the nazirites*f* drink wine,
    and commanded the prophets,
    saying, "You shall not prophesy."

13 So, I will press you down in your place,
    just as a cart presses down
    when it is full of sheaves.*g*
14 Flight shall perish from the swift,
    and the strong shall not retain their
        strength,
    nor shall the mighty save their lives;
15 those who handle the bow shall not stand,
    and those who are swift of foot shall not
        save themselves,
    nor shall those who ride horses save their
        lives;

c Heb *cause it to return*   *d* Syr Vg: Heb *and his anger tore*
perpetually   *e* Gk Syr Vg: Heb *and his wrath kept*   *f* That
is, *those separated* or *those consecrated*   *g* Meaning of Heb
uncertain

16 and those who are stout of heart among the
    mighty
    shall flee away naked in that day,
              says the LORD.

Israel's Guilt and Punishment

Hear this word that the LORD has spoken against
you, O people of Israel, against the whole family
that I brought up out of the land of Egypt:

2 You only have I known
    of all the families of the earth;
  therefore I will punish you
    for all your iniquities.

3 Do two walk together
    unless they have made an appointment?
4 Does a lion roar in the forest,
    when it has no prey?
  Does a young lion cry out from its den,
    if it has caught nothing?
5 Does a bird fall into a snare on the earth,
    when there is no trap for it?
  Does a snare spring up from the ground,
    when it has taken nothing?
6 Is a trumpet blown in a city,
    and the people are not afraid?
  Does disaster befall a city,
    unless the LORD has done it?
7 Surely the Lord GOD does nothing,
    without revealing his secret
    to his servants the prophets.
8 The lion has roared;
    who will not fear?
  The Lord GOD has spoken;
    who can but prophesy?

9 Proclaim to the strongholds in Ash′dod,
    and to the strongholds in the land of
      Egypt,
  and say, "Assemble yourselves on Mount^h
    Sa·mār′i·a,
  and see what great tumults are within it,
  and what oppressions are in its midst."
10 They do not know how to do right, says the
    LORD,
  those who store up violence and robbery
    in their strongholds.
11 Therefore thus says the Lord GOD:
  An adversary shall surround the land,
    and strip you of your defense;
    and your strongholds shall be plundered.

12 Thus says the LORD: As the shepherd rescues
from the mouth of the lion two legs, or a piece of
an ear, so shall the people of Israel who live in
Sa·mār′i·a be rescued, with the corner of a couch
and partⁱ of a bed.

13 Hear, and testify against the house of Jacob,
    says the Lord GOD, the God of hosts:
14 On the day I punish Israel for its
    transgressions,
  I will punish the altars of Beth′el,
  and the horns of the altar shall be cut off
    and fall to the ground.
15 I will tear down the winter house as well as
    the summer house;
  and the houses of ivory shall perish,
  and the great houses^j shall come to an end,
            says the LORD.

? did you KNOW?

The Remnant

**Does Amos feel that Israel is so corrupt
that God will destroy it entirely? Apparently not, because he refers in several places to a tiny portion that will be
saved (Am 3.12; 5.13). The idea that God
will save a remnant—a small part—of
the Jewish people gets picked up by others who prophesy after Amos (see Isa
10.20–22; Jer 23.3; Mic 5.7–8; Zeph 3.13).**

**The remnant that will be saved be-
comes an important biblical symbol of
God's plan not to let Israel be completely
destroyed. It will be known as a holy group
because of its faith, repentance, purification, and willingness to be God's servant.**

▸ **Am 3.12**

Hear this word, you cows of Bashan
    who are on Mount Sa·mār′i·a,
who oppress the poor, who crush the needy,
  who say to their husbands, "Bring
      something to drink!"
2 The Lord GOD has sworn by his holiness:
  The time is surely coming upon you,
  when they shall take you away with hooks,
    even the last of you with fishhooks.
3 Through breaches in the wall you shall
    leave,
  each one straight ahead;

---

^h Gk Syr: Heb *the mountains of*   ⁱ Meaning of Heb
uncertain   ^j Or *many houses*

and you shall be flung out into
    Har'mon,[k]
                     says the LORD.

4 Come to Beth'el—and transgress;
    to Gil'gal—and multiply transgression;
bring your sacrifices every morning,
    your tithes every three days;
5 bring a thank offering of leavened bread,
    and proclaim freewill offerings, publish
        them;
    for so you love to do, O people of Israel!
                 says the Lord GOD.

Israel Rejects Correction

6 I gave you cleanness of teeth in all your
        cities,
    and lack of bread in all your places,
yet you did not return to me,
                 says the LORD.

7 And I also withheld the rain from you
    when there were still three months to the
        harvest;
I would send rain on one city,
    and send no rain on another city;
one field would be rained upon,
    and the field on which it did not rain
        withered;
8 so two or three towns wandered to one
        town
    to drink water, and were not satisfied;
yet you did not return to me,
                 says the LORD.

9 I struck you with blight and mildew;
    I laid waste[l] your gardens and your
        vineyards;
    the locust devoured your fig trees and
        your olive trees;
yet you did not return to me,
                 says the LORD.

10 I sent among you a pestilence after the
        manner of Egypt;
I killed your young men with the sword;
I carried away your horses;[m]
    and I made the stench of your camp go
        up into your nostrils;
yet you did not return to me,
                 says the LORD.

11 I overthrew some of you,
    as when God overthrew Sod'om and
        Go•mor'rah,
    and you were like a brand snatched from
        the fire;
yet you did not return to me,
                 says the LORD.

12 Therefore thus I will do to you, O Israel;
    because I will do this to you,
    prepare to meet your God, O Israel!

13 For lo, the one who forms the mountains,
        creates the wind,
    reveals his thoughts to mortals,
makes the morning darkness,
    and treads on the heights of the earth—
    the LORD, the God of hosts, is his name!

A Lament for Israel's Sin

Hear this word that I take up over you in lamentation, O house of Israel:
2 Fallen, no more to rise,
    is maiden Israel;
forsaken on her land,
    with no one to raise her up.

3 For thus says the Lord GOD:
The city that marched out a thousand
    shall have a hundred left,
and that which marched out a hundred
    shall have ten left.[n]

4 For thus says the LORD to the house of Israel:
Seek me and live;
5   but do not seek Beth'el,
and do not enter into Gil'gal
    or cross over to Be'er-she'ba;
for Gil'gal shall surely go into exile,
    and Beth'el shall come to nothing.

6 Seek the LORD and live,
    or he will break out against the house of
        Joseph like fire,
    and it will devour Beth'el, with no one to
        quench it.
7 Ah, you that turn justice to wormwood,
    and bring righteousness to the ground!

8 The one who made the Plei'a•des
        and O•ri'on,
    and turns deep darkness into
        the morning,
    and darkens the day into night,
who calls for the waters of the sea,
    and pours them out on the surface of the
        earth,
    the LORD is his name,
9 who makes destruction flash out against the
        strong,
    so that destruction comes upon the
        fortress.

---

k Meaning of Heb uncertain   l Cn: Heb *the multitude of*
m Heb *with the captivity of your horses*   n Heb adds *to the
house of Israel*

10 They hate the one who reproves in the gate,
     and they abhor the one who speaks the
        truth.
11 Therefore because you trample on the poor
     and take from them levies of grain,
   you have built houses of hewn stone,
     but you shall not live in them;
   you have planted pleasant vineyards,
     but you shall not drink their wine.
12 For I know how many are your
        transgressions,
     and how great are your sins—
   you who afflict the righteous, who take a
        bribe,
   and push aside the needy in the gate.
13 Therefore the prudent will keep silent in
        such a time;
     for it is an evil time.

Prayer That Does Justice

In 5.21–24, Amos again has harsh words,
this time for the people who attend
lavish religious ceremonies but don't
practice justice in their life. Amos says
that their worship is meaningless noise to
God—just so many empty words.
    Amos's harsh words challenge us too.
The next time you attend Mass or pray,
think about the words you say and hear.
How are they challenging you to act more
justly? How would trying to act more justly change the way you pray?

▸ Am 5.21–24

14 Seek good and not evil,
     that you may live;
   and so the LORD, the God of hosts, will be
        with you,
     just as you have said.
15 Hate evil and love good,
     and establish justice in the gate;
   it may be that the LORD, the God of hosts,
     will be gracious to the remnant of Joseph.

16 Therefore thus says the LORD, the God of
        hosts, the Lord:
   In all the squares there shall be wailing;
     and in all the streets they shall say,
        "Alas! alas!"

They shall call the farmers to mourning,
     and those skilled in lamentation, to
        wailing;
17 in all the vineyards there shall be wailing,
     for I will pass through the midst of you,
        says the LORD.

The Day of the LORD a Dark Day

18 Alas for you who desire the day of the LORD!
     Why do you want the day of the LORD?
   It is darkness, not light;
19   as if someone fled from a lion,
     and was met by a bear;
   or went into the house and rested a hand
        against the wall,
     and was bitten by a snake.
20 Is not the day of the LORD darkness, not
        light,
     and gloom with no brightness in it?

21 I hate, I despise your festivals,
     and I take no delight in your solemn
        assemblies.
22 Even though you offer me your burnt
        offerings and grain offerings,
     I will not accept them;
   and the offerings of well-being of your
        fatted animals
     I will not look upon.
23 Take away from me the noise of your songs;
     I will not listen to the melody of your
        harps.
24 But let justice roll down like waters,
     and righteousness like an ever-flowing
        stream.

25 Did you bring to me sacrifices and offerings
the forty years in the wilderness, O house of Israel? 26 You shall take up Sak'kuth your king, and
Kaī'wan your star-god, your images,*o* which you
made for yourselves; 27 therefore I will take you
into exile beyond Damascus, says the LORD, whose
name is the God of hosts.

Complacent Self-Indulgence Will Be Punished

Alas for those who are at ease in Zion,
   and for those who feel secure on Mount
        Sa•mār'i•a,
the notables of the first of the nations,
   to whom the house of Israel resorts!
2 Cross over to Cal'neh, and see;
     from there go to Hā'math the great;
     then go down to Gath of the Phi•lis'tines.
   Are you better*p* than these kingdoms?

---

o Heb *your images, your star-god*   *p* Or *Are they better*

Or is your^q territory greater than their^r
　　territory,
3 O you that put far away the evil day,
　　and bring near a reign of violence?

4 Alas for those who lie on beds of ivory,
　　and lounge on their couches,
and eat lambs from the flock,
　　and calves from the stall;
5 who sing idle songs to the sound
　　of the harp,
　　and like David improvise on instruments
　　of music;
6 who drink wine from bowls,
　　and anoint themselves with the finest oils,
　　but are not grieved over the ruin of
　　Joseph!
7 Therefore they shall now be the first to go
　　into exile,
　　and the revelry of the loungers shall pass
　　away.

8 The Lord GOD has sworn by himself
　　(says the LORD, the God of hosts):
　I abhor the pride of Jacob
　　and hate his strongholds;
　and I will deliver up the city and all that
　　is in it.

9 If ten people remain in one house, they shall
die. 10 And if a relative, one who burns the dead,^s
shall take up the body to bring it out of the house,
and shall say to someone in the innermost parts of
the house, "Is anyone else with you?" the answer
will come, "No." Then the relative^t shall say,
"Hush! We must not mention the name of the
LORD."

Let **Justice**
roll down like waters,
and
righteousness
like an ever-flowing stream
5.24

11 See, the LORD commands,
　　and the great house shall be shattered to
　　bits,
　　and the little house to pieces.
12 Do horses run on rocks?
　　Does one plow the sea with oxen?^u
But you have turned justice into poison
　　and the fruit of righteousness into
　　wormwood—
13 you who rejoice in Lō-dĕ'bar,^v
　　who say, "Have we not by our own
　　strength
　　taken Kar•nā'im^w for ourselves?"
14 Indeed, I am raising up against you a
　　nation,
　　O house of Israel, says the LORD, the God
　　of hosts,
　and they shall oppress you from
　　Lē'bō-hā'math
　　to the Wadi Ar'a•bah.

Locusts, Fire, and a Plumb Line

7 This is what the Lord GOD showed me: he was
forming locusts at the time the latter growth began
to sprout (it was the latter growth after the king's
mowings). 2 When they had finished eating the
grass of the land, I said,
　"O Lord GOD, forgive, I beg you!
　　How can Jacob stand?
　　He is so small!"
3 The LORD relented concerning this;
　　"It shall not be," said the LORD.

4 This is what the Lord GOD showed me: the
Lord GOD was calling for a shower of fire,^x and it
devoured the great deep and was eating up the
land. 5 Then I said,
　"O Lord GOD, cease, I beg you!
　　How can Jacob stand?
　　He is so small!"
6 The LORD relented concerning this;
　　"This also shall not be," said the
　　Lord GOD.

7 This is what he showed me: the Lord was
standing beside a wall built with a plumb line,
with a plumb line in his hand. 8 And the LORD said
to me, "Ā'mos, what do you see?" And I said, "A
plumb line." Then the Lord said,
　"See, I am setting a plumb line
　　in the midst of my people Israel;
　I will never again pass them by;

---

^q Heb *their*　　^r Heb *your*　　^s Or *who makes a burning for
him*　　^t Heb *he*　　^u Or *Does one plow them with oxen*
^v Or *in a thing of nothingness*　　^w Or *horns*　　^x Or *for a
judgment by fire*

9 the high places of Isaac shall be made
desolate,
and the sanctuaries of Israel shall be laid
waste,
and I will rise against the house of
Jer•o•bō'am with the sword."

Amaziah Complains to the King

10 Then Am•a•zī'ah, the priest of Beth'el, sent
to King Jer•o•bō'am of Israel, saying, "Ā'mos has
conspired against you in the very center of the
house of Israel; the land is not able to bear all his
words. 11 For thus Ā'mos has said,

'Jer•o•bō'am shall die by the sword,
and Israel must go into exile
away from his land.' "

12 And Am•a•zī'ah said to Ā'mos, "O seer, go, flee
away to the land of Judah, earn your bread there,
and prophesy there; 13 but never again prophesy at
Beth'el, for it is the king's sanctuary, and it is a
temple of the kingdom."

14 Then Ā'mos answered Am•a•zī'ah, "I am*y* no
prophet, nor a prophet's son; but I am*y* a herds-
man, and a dresser of sycamore trees, 15 and the
LORD took me from following the flock, and the
LORD said to me, 'Go, prophesy to my people Israel.'
16 "Now therefore hear the word of the LORD.
You say, 'Do not prophesy against Israel,
and do not preach against the house of
Isaac.'
17 Therefore thus says the LORD:
'Your wife shall become a prostitute in the
city,

and your sons and your daughters shall
fall by the sword,
and your land shall be parceled out by
line;
you yourself shall die in an unclean land,
and Israel shall surely go into exile away
from its land.' "

The Basket of Fruit

This is what the Lord GOD showed me—a basket of
summer fruit.*z* 2 He said, "Ā'mos, what do you
see?" And I said, "A basket of summer fruit."*z* Then
the LORD said to me,

"The end*a* has come upon my people Israel;
I will never again pass them by.
3 The songs of the temple*b* shall become
wailings in that day,"
says the Lord GOD;
"the dead bodies shall be many,
cast out in every place. Be silent!"

4 Hear this, you that trample on the needy,
and bring to ruin the poor of the land,
5 saying, "When will the new moon be over
so that we may sell grain;
and the sabbath,
so that we may offer wheat for sale?
We will make the ephah small and the
shekel great,
and practice deceit with false balances,
6 buying the poor for silver
and the needy for a pair of sandals,
and selling the sweepings of the wheat."

---

y Or *was*   *z* Heb *qayits*   *a* Heb *qets*   *b* Or *palace*

Stand Up and Be Counted!

LIVE IT!

In a small-town newspaper's opinion page, a reader complains about a low-income
housing development. The reader writes: "Our town does not need more white
trash. The citizens of this town have worked hard for their homes and do not
deserve to have their home values brought down by a low-income development.
Stand up and be counted and do not let this happen!"

Amos would have had a harsh reply for the author of that letter. Read 8.4–10 for his
words condemning the people of his time who had no care or thought for the poor. Amos
says that the more we choose to think of ourselves, rather than those who are needy, the
closer we come to our own destruction. Jesus later echoes Amos in teaching that God's
reign of peace and justice will come through our efforts to support the weaker and less
fortunate people in our world (see "Jesus' Preference for the Poor!" Lk 6.17–49).

Let's be examples of God's care for those who are poor, until all opinion-page letters
read, "Stand up and be counted—let's work to end poverty and until then welcome the
people who are poor among us!"

▸ Am 8.4–8

7 The LORD has sworn by the pride of Jacob:
Surely I will never forget any of their deeds.
8 Shall not the land tremble on this account,
and everyone mourn who lives in it,
and all of it rise like the Nile,
and be tossed about and sink again, like
the Nile of Egypt?
9 On that day, says the Lord GOD,
I will make the sun go down at noon,
and darken the earth in broad daylight.
10 I will turn your feasts into mourning,
and all your songs into lamentation;
I will bring sackcloth on all loins,
and baldness on every head;
I will make it like the mourning for an
only son,
and the end of it like a bitter day.

11 The time is surely coming, says the
Lord GOD,
when I will send a famine on the land;
not a famine of bread, or a thirst for water,
but of hearing the words of the LORD.
12 They shall wander from sea to sea,
and from north to east;
they shall run to and fro, seeking the word
of the LORD,
but they shall not find it.

13 In that day the beautiful young women and
the young men
shall faint for thirst.
14 Those who swear by Ash'i•mah of Sa•mar'i•a,
and say, "As your god lives, O Dan,"
and, "As the way of Be'er-she'ba lives"—
they shall fall, and never rise again.

The Destruction of Israel

I saw the LORD standing beside*c* the altar, and he
said:
Strike the capitals until the thresholds shake,
and shatter them on the heads of all the
people;*d*
and those who are left I will kill with the
sword;
not one of them shall flee away,
not one of them shall escape.

2 Though they dig into She'ol,
from there shall my hand take them;
though they climb up to heaven,
from there I will bring them down.
3 Though they hide themselves on the top of
Car'mel,
from there I will search out and take
them;

and though they hide from my sight at the
bottom of the sea,
there I will command the sea-serpent,
and it shall bite them.
4 And though they go into captivity in front
of their enemies,
there I will command the sword, and it
shall kill them;
and I will fix my eyes on them
for harm and not for good.

5 The Lord, GOD of hosts,
he who touches the earth and it melts,
and all who live in it mourn,
and all of it rises like the Nile,
and sinks again, like the Nile of Egypt;
6 who builds his upper chambers in the
heavens,
and founds his vault upon the earth;
who calls for the waters of the sea,
and pours them out upon the surface of
the earth—
the LORD is his name.

7 Are you not like the Ethiopians*e* to me,
O people of Israel? says the LORD.
Did I not bring Israel up from the land of
Egypt,
and the Phi•lis'tines from Caph'tor and
the Ar•a•me'ans from Kir?
8 The eyes of the Lord GOD are upon the
sinful kingdom,
and I will destroy it from the face of the
earth
—except that I will not utterly destroy the
house of Jacob,
                              says the LORD.

9 For lo, I will command,
and shake the house of Israel among all
the nations
as one shakes with a sieve,
but no pebble shall fall to the ground.
10 All the sinners of my people shall die by the
sword,
who say, "Evil shall not overtake or
meet us."

The Restoration of
David's Kingdom
(Cp Acts 15.16–17)

11 On that day I will raise up
the booth of David that is fallen,
and repair its*f* breaches,
and raise up its*g* ruins,

---

c Or *on*   *d* Heb *all of them*   *e* Or *Nubians*; Heb *Cushites*
f Gk: Heb *their*   *g* Gk: Heb *his*

A
M

and rebuild it as in the days of old;

12 in order that they may possess the remnant
of E'dom
and all the nations who are called by my
name,
says the LORD who does this.

13 The time is surely coming, says the LORD,
when the one who plows shall overtake
the one who reaps,
and the treader of grapes the one who
sows the seed;
the mountains shall drip sweet wine,

and all the hills shall flow with it.

14 I will restore the fortunes of my people
Israel,
and they shall rebuild the ruined cities
and inhabit them;
they shall plant vineyards and drink their
wine,
and they shall make gardens and eat their
fruit.

15 I will plant them upon their land,
and they shall never again be plucked up
out of the land that I have given them,
says the LORD your God.

A betrayal is always difficult, and a betrayal by someone who is related to you is a particularly hard pill to swallow. We can only imagine the anger during the Civil War in the United States when family members found themselves fighting on opposite sides. It has taken the country a long time to heal from that division. Similarly, the Book of Obadiah has angry words against the nation of Edom, whose people were related to the Israelites. It should remind us that when the people we expect to care for us actually take advantage of us, the wound is especially painful.

At a Glance

- **Verses 1–9.** prophecies of Edom's destruction

- **Verses 10–14.** a discussion of Edom's cruelty to the Israelites

- **Verses 15–21.** a message about the day of the Lord

In-depth

The Book of Genesis records a conflict between Jacob (the father of the nation of Israel) and his brother Esau (the father of the nation of Edom, later called Idumea). Hundreds of years later, the Israelites still fought with the Edomites (see map 3, "The Kingdom Years"). In the Book of Obadiah, the bitterness deepens.

In 587 B.C., Jerusalem was destroyed by the Babylonians. Apparently, the Edomites not only did not aid their "brother" (Obadiah, verse 10), but took advantage of Israel's situation by gloating (verse 12), looting (verse 13), and raiding its territory (verse 14). Because of the Edomites' cruelty, the prophet Obadiah foretold the destruction of Edom by another country (verse 15).

Like many of the Old Testament prophets, Obadiah ultimately saw a hopeful future for Israel. All Israel's enemies would whither before the strong arm of the Lord. And there would come a day—"the day of the LORD" (verse 15)—when all Jews would unite and return to Mount Zion (the place where the Temple stood in Jerusalem). Mount Zion would "rule Mount Esau" and that new "kingdom shall be the LORD's" (verse 21).

We are given no clues about the identity or life of the prophet Obadiah. We know only that he wrote the shortest book in the Old Testament—just one chapter long.

Quick Facts

Period Covered
after the Babylonian Exile, the sixth or early fifth century B.C.

Author
Obadiah

Theme
God will punish Edom for its abuse of Judah.

Of Note
Obadiah means "servant" or "worshiper of the Lord."

The Book of Obadiah

Obadiah

Proud Edom Will Be Brought Low

1 The vision of O·ba·dī'ah.

Thus says the Lord GOD concerning Ē'dom:
We have heard a report from the LORD,
    and a messenger has been sent among
        the nations:
"Rise up! Let us rise against it for battle!"
2 I will surely make you least among the
        nations;
    you shall be utterly despised.
3 Your proud heart has deceived you,
    you that live in the clefts of the rock,[a]
    whose dwelling is in the heights.
You say in your heart,
    "Who will bring me down to
        the ground?"
4 Though you soar aloft like the eagle,
    though your nest is set among the stars,
    from there I will bring you down,
                    says the LORD.

Pillage and Slaughter Will Repay Edom's Cruelty

5 If thieves came to you,
    if plunderers by night
    —how you have been destroyed!—
    would they not steal only what they
        wanted?
If grape-gatherers came to you,
    would they not leave gleanings?

6 How Esau has been pillaged,
    his treasures searched out!
7 All your allies have deceived you,
    they have driven you to the border;
your confederates have prevailed
        against you;
    those who ate[b] your bread have set a trap
        for you—
    there is no understanding of it.
8 On that day, says the LORD,
    I will destroy the wise out of Ē'dom,
    and understanding out of Mount Esau.
9 Your warriors shall be shattered, O Tē'man,
    so that everyone from Mount Esau will
        be cut off.

Edom Mistreated His Brother

10 For the slaughter and violence done to your
        brother Jacob,
    shame shall cover you,
    and you shall be cut off forever.
11 On the day that you stood aside,
    on the day that strangers carried off his
        wealth,
    and foreigners entered his gates
    and cast lots for Jerusalem,
    you too were like one of them.

---

[a] Or *clefts of Sela*   [b] Cn: Heb lacks *those who ate*

What Goes Around

What goes around comes around. Have you ever heard that saying? Isn't that exactly what Obadiah is saying in verse 15?

Whatever you do comes back to affect you eventually. If you are honest, people will trust you and tell you the truth. If you lie, cheat, and steal, people will deceive you. If you respect the earth, it will take care of you. If you litter, pollute, and destroy, you ruin your home, your country, and your world.

Pray that all people take this lesson to heart. Pray that we learn to respect all living things. The results of our actions will come back to us eventually—if not to us personally, to other people and future generations.

▶ Obadiah, verse 15

12 But you should not have gloated[c] over[d]
       your brother
   on the day of his misfortune;
   you should not have rejoiced over the
       people of Judah
   on the day of their ruin;
   you should not have boasted
       on the day of distress.
13 You should not have entered the gate of my
       people
   on the day of their calamity;
   you should not have joined in the gloating
       over Judah's[e] disaster
   on the day of his calamity;
   you should not have looted his goods
       on the day of his calamity.
14 You should not have stood at the crossings
       to cut off his fugitives;
   you should not have handed over his
       survivors
   on the day of distress.

15 For the day of the LORD is near against all
       the nations.
   As you have done, it shall be done to you;
   your deeds shall return on your own
       head.
16 For as you have drunk on my
       holy mountain,
   all the nations around you shall drink;
   they shall drink and gulp down,[f]
   and shall be as though they had never
       been.

Israel's Final Triumph

17 But on Mount Zion there shall be those that
       escape,
   and it shall be holy;
   and the house of Jacob shall take possession
       of those who dispossessed them.
18 The house of Jacob shall be a fire,
   the house of Joseph a flame,
   and the house of Esau stubble;
   they shall burn them and consume them,
   and there shall be no survivor of the
       house of Esau;
               for the LORD has spoken.
19 Those of the Neg'eb shall possess Mount
       Esau,
   and those of the She•phe'lah the land of
       the Phi•lis'tines;
   they shall possess the land of E'phra•im and
       the land of Sa•mar'i•a,
   and Benjamin shall possess Gil'e•ad.
20 The exiles of the Israelites who are in
       Ha'lah[g]
   shall possess[h] Phoe•ni'ci•a as far
       as Zar'e•phath;
   and the exiles of Jerusalem who are in
       Se•phar'ad
   shall possess the towns of the Neg'eb.
21 Those who have been saved[i] shall go up to
       Mount Zion
   to rule Mount Esau;
   and the kingdom shall be the LORD's.

c Heb But do not gloat (and similarly through verse 14)
d Heb on the day of   e Heb his   f Meaning of Heb
uncertain   g Cn: Heb in this army   h Cn: Meaning of
Heb uncertain   i Or Saviors

O
B

You're watching a comedy show where someone dressed like a doctor starts making outrageous comments about a person's health. You laugh, not because sickness is funny, but because doctors are supposed to be sensitive and caring. That's the basis of satire—that someone or something that is supposed to act one way acts another way. You're about to read a biblical satire about Jonah the prophet.

The Book of Jonah uses humor to make an important point—God is the God of all people, even those we consider our enemies.

At a Glance

- **1.1–16.** Jonah being sent by God to Nineveh
- **1.17—2.10.** Jonah in the belly of a large fish
- **Chapter 3.** the Ninevites' conversion
- **Chapter 4.** Jonah's anger outside of Nineveh

In-depth

This story was written after the Jews returned from their exile in Babylon. Jewish leaders encouraged Jewish people to stay away from non-Jewish people (see Ezra, chapter 9) in order to avoid falling into idolatry again. A result was a religious bigotry against other nations—a belief that God was against every nation that opposed Israel. The Book of Jonah was written to correct that narrow attitude. Through satire, this fictional short story gently pokes fun at Israel's religious self-righteousness.

How is the book funny? Well, right off the bat, Jonah is called by God and immediately takes off in the opposite direction (1.1–3). What kind of prophet is this? When God tries to get his attention with a storm, it's the non-Jewish sailors who get the point (verse 14). Just as the reader is probably wondering how God is going to get Jonah to Nineveh, along comes a taxi in the form of a large fish's stomach (verse 17).

There's more. Readers from the author's time would have expected Jonah to be ignored at best, more likely beaten or killed by the people of Nineveh. After all, these were Israel's mortal enemies. Instead, the Ninevites immediately respond to Jonah's message and repent, even the animals (3.8)! At this point, the reader is giggling at the goofiness of pigs and sheep in sackcloth, but getting the message about God's salvation being for all nations.

Jonah's angry and upset. He didn't expect the Ninevites to convert—he wanted them punished. He goes outside the city to mope, and his favorite tree dies. The book ends with God chiding Jonah for his bigoted anger. If Jonah is so concerned for his little tree (4.6–8), shouldn't God be concerned for the great city of Nineveh with its thousands of people (verse 11)? The point is driven home, and the humor has helped to make a challenging message easier to accept.

Quick Facts

Period Covered
the eighth century B.C.
Author
unknown, probably writing in the fifth century B.C.
Theme
a fictional short story showing that God cares for all people, including Israel's enemies

The Book of Jonah

Jonah

Jonah

Jonah Tries to Run Away from God

Now the word of the LORD came to Jonah son of A•mit'tai, saying, 2 "Go at once to Nin'e•veh, that great city, and cry out against it; for their wickedness has come up before me." 3 But Jonah set out to flee to Tar'shish from the presence of the LORD. He went down to Jop'pa and found a ship going to Tar'shish; so he paid his fare and went on board, to go with them to Tar'shish, away from the presence of the LORD.

4 But the LORD hurled a great wind upon the sea, and such a mighty storm came upon the sea that the ship threatened to break up. 5 Then the mariners were afraid, and each cried to his god. They threw the cargo that was in the ship into the sea, to lighten it for them. Jonah, meanwhile, had gone down into the hold of the ship and had lain down, and was fast asleep. 6 The captain came and said to him, "What are you doing sound asleep? Get up, call on your god! Perhaps the god will spare us a thought so that we do not perish."

7 The sailors[a] said to one another, "Come, let us cast lots, so that we may know on whose account this calamity has come upon us." So they cast lots, and the lot fell on Jonah. 8 Then they said to him, "Tell us why this calamity has come upon us. What is your occupation? Where do you come from? What is your country? And of what people are you?" 9 "I am a Hebrew," he replied. "I worship the LORD, the God of heaven, who made the sea and the dry land." 10 Then the men were even more afraid, and said to him, "What is this that you have done!" For the men knew that he was fleeing from the presence of the LORD, because he had told them so.

11 Then they said to him, "What shall we do to you, that the sea may quiet down for us?" For the sea was growing more and more tempestuous. 12 He said to them, "Pick me up and throw me into the sea; then the sea will quiet down for you; for I know it is because of me that this great storm has come upon you." 13 Nevertheless the men rowed hard to bring the ship back to land, but they could not, for the sea grew more and more stormy against them. 14 Then they cried out to the LORD, "Please, O LORD, we pray, do not let us perish on account of this man's life. Do not make us guilty of innocent blood; for you, O LORD, have done as it pleased you." 15 So they picked Jonah up and threw him into the sea; and the sea ceased from its raging. 16 Then the men feared the LORD even more, and they offered a sacrifice to the LORD and made vows.

17[b] But the LORD provided a large fish to swallow up Jonah; and Jonah was in the belly of the fish three days and three nights.

---

a Heb *They* *b* Ch 2.1 in Heb

A Psalm of Thanksgiving

Then Jonah prayed to the LORD his God from the belly of the fish, ² saying,

"I called to the LORD out of my distress,
    and he answered me;
out of the belly of Shĕ′ōl I cried,
    and you heard my voice.
³ You cast me into the deep,
    into the heart of the seas,
    and the flood surrounded me;
all your waves and your billows
    passed over me.

yet you brought up my life from the Pit,
    O LORD my God.
⁷ As my life was ebbing away,
    I remembered the LORD;
and my prayer came to you,
    into your holy temple.
⁸ Those who worship vain idols
    forsake their true loyalty.
⁹ But I with the voice of thanksgiving
    will sacrifice to you;
what I have vowed I will pay.
    Deliverance belongs to the LORD!"
¹⁰ Then the LORD spoke to the fish, and it spewed Jonah out upon the dry land.

Conversion of Nineveh

The word of the LORD came to Jonah a second time, saying, ² "Get up, go to Nin′e•veh, that great city, and proclaim to it the message that I tell you." ³ So Jonah set out and went to Nin′e•veh, according to the word of the LORD. Now Nin′e•veh was an exceedingly large city, a three days' walk across. ⁴ Jonah began to go into the city, going a day's walk. And he cried out, "Forty days more, and Nin′e•veh shall be overthrown!" ⁵ And the people of Nin′e•veh believed God; they proclaimed a fast, and everyone, great and small, put on sackcloth.

6 When the news reached the king of Nin′e•veh, he rose from his throne, removed his robe, covered himself with sackcloth, and sat in ashes. ⁷ Then he had a proclamation made in Nin′e•veh: "By the decree of the king and his nobles: No human being or animal, no herd or flock, shall taste anything. They shall not feed, nor shall they drink water. ⁸ Human beings and animals shall be covered with sackcloth, and they shall cry mightily to God. All shall turn from their evil ways and from the violence that is in their hands. ⁹ Who knows? God may relent and change his mind; he may turn from his fierce anger, so that we do not perish."

10 When God saw what they did, how they turned from their evil ways, God changed his mind about the calamity that he had said he would bring upon them; and he did not do it.

PRAY IT!

Jesus and Jonah

Do you see any similarities between Jonah and Jesus? Jonah is in the darkness of a fish's belly for three days before the Lord commands the fish to spit him out. Jesus experiences the darkness of death for three days before he bursts from the tomb in resurrected glory. In Mt 16.4 and Lk 11.29, Jesus even refers to "the sign of Jonah" in relation to his own ministry.

Jonah's prayer in Jon 2.2–10 could well have been Jesus' prayer before his death. It reminds us that salvation comes from God when we are experiencing dark times. When you are going through a difficult time, use Jonah's prayer as a model for writing your own prayer of trust. Describe your difficulties and your situation, and end by expressing your ultimate trust in God. Then say your prayer until the difficulty passes. It could make a difference!

▸ Jon 2.2–10

Jonah's Anger

But this was very displeasing to Jonah, and he became angry. ² He prayed to the LORD and said, "O LORD! Is not this what I said while I was still in my own country? That is why I fled to Tar′shish at the beginning; for I knew that you are a gracious God and merciful, slow to anger, and abounding in steadfast love, and ready to relent from punishing. ³ And now, O LORD, please take my life from

4 Then I said, 'I am driven away
    from your sight;
how° shall I look again
    upon your holy temple?'
5 The waters closed in over me;
    the deep surrounded me;
weeds were wrapped around my head
6   at the roots of the mountains.
I went down to the land
    whose bars closed upon me forever;

---

c Theodotion: Heb surely

Mistaken Loyalties

When God spares Nineveh, Jonah is angry! He is so angry he is willing to let his anger destroy him. And all because of mistaken loyalty. Jonah thought he was loyal to God (which is funny because at first, he tried to run away from God), and he feels that God is being disloyal to him by not destroying Nineveh. Jonah does not—or will not—understand that God's loyalty is to the whole human race, not just to Jonah's desires.

Are you ever angry with God because things don't go your way? Maybe your anger is about mistaken loyalties. If you didn't get picked for the lead part, that doesn't mean God is being disloyal to you. God is God over everyone—which sometimes means you will not get what you want so that other people can receive what they need.

The next time you are angry at God, ask yourself: Am I willing to see things from a large enough perspective? Am I expecting to receive God's favor at someone else's expense?

▶ Jon 4.1–8

JON

me, for it is better for me to die than to live." ⁴And the LORD said, "Is it right for you to be angry?" ⁵Then Jonah went out of the city and sat down east of the city, and made a booth for himself there. He sat under it in the shade, waiting to see what would become of the city.

6 The LORD God appointed a bush,ᵈ and made it come up over Jonah, to give shade over his head, to save him from his discomfort; so Jonah was very happy about the bush. ⁷But when dawn came up the next day, God appointed a worm that attacked the bush, so that it withered. ⁸When the sun rose, God prepared a sultry east wind, and the sun beat down on the head of Jonah so that he was faint and asked that he might die. He said, "It is better for me to die than to live."

Jonah Is Reproved

9 But God said to Jonah, "Is it right for you to be angry about the bush?" And he said, "Yes, angry enough to die." ¹⁰Then the LORD said, "You are concerned about the bush, for which you did not labor and which you did not grow; it came into being in a night and perished in a night. ¹¹And should I not be concerned about Nin'e•veh, that great city, in which there are more than a hundred and twenty thousand persons who do not know their right hand from their left, and also many animals?"

---

d Heb *qiqayon*, possibly *the castor bean plant*

There is a story about a country mouse and a city mouse who visit each other on separate occasions. For each, the visit is a discovery of new experiences and a different way of life. Indeed, people who visit the places we live often see things that we have overlooked or taken for granted. The prophet Micah was like such a visitor. His home was a small village, but he prophesied in the big capital city of Jerusalem. God uses Micah's unique perspective to communicate warnings and promises to the people of Israel and to us.

At a Glance

- **Chapters 1–2.** a judgment against Israel and Judah, and promise

- **3.1—5.9.** a judgment against rulers, prophets, and priests, and promise

- **5.10—6.8.** a judgment against foreign religions, and a plea for justice

- **6.9—7.20.** a judgment against the people, and message of God's compassion

In-depth

The Book of Micah is a collection of oracles (poemlike prophetic messages) taking different forms. Some of the oracles are harsh judgments (see 1.8—2.11), some are comforting promises that God will not desert the people (see chapter 4), and some are the prophet's own confessions of faith (3.8; 7.7). The Book of Micah shows us a God who is passionate for justice and fairness (3.9).

Perhaps because of his rural background, the prophet Micah had a special connection to the land and the people who work it. He speaks against those who covet and seize fields and homes (2.2). He describes the destruction of Zion (Jerusalem) as plowing a field (3.12). He represents the Ideal Kingdom as a place where all the people have their own grapevines and fig trees (4.3–4).

The Book of Micah shows signs of being extensively edited and revised to keep the prophet's message relevant during changing times. This is particularly true in chapters 4 and 5, which were added after the Babylonian Exile to give hope following the nation's great tragedy. In 4.3, the prophet envisions a day when nations will "beat their swords into plowshares" and "nation shall not lift up sword against nation, / neither shall they learn war any more."

Micah prophesied at about the same time as First Isaiah (see the timeline at the back of this Bible), during the days of Kings Jotham, Ahaz, and Hezekiah (see 2 Chr 27.1—31.21). But whereas Isaiah was a member of the upper class, defending the rights of the poor, Micah was a poor person, suffering with the poor. That is why he speaks so passionately about their mistreatment (see Mic 3.2–3). Even though his message went unheeded at the time, he models for us trust in the Lord's saving power (7.7).

Quick Facts

Period Covered
the late eighth century B.C.

Authors
Micah and later editors

Themes
warnings against injustice and idolatry, promises of a new future

The Book of Micah

Micah

The word of the LORD that came to Mi′cah of Mō′-re•sheth in the days of Kings Jō′tham, Ā′haz, and Hez•e•kī′ah of Judah, which he saw concerning Sa-mār′i•a and Jerusalem.

Judgment Pronounced against Samaria

2 Hear, you peoples, all of you;
    listen, O earth, and all that is in it;
and let the Lord GOD be a witness
        against you,
    the Lord from his holy temple.
3 For lo, the LORD is coming out of his place,
    and will come down and tread upon the
        high places of the earth.
4 Then the mountains will melt under him
    and the valleys will burst open,
like wax near the fire,
    like waters poured down a steep place.
5 All this is for the transgression of Jacob
    and for the sins of the house of Israel.
What is the transgression of Jacob?
    Is it not Sa•mār′i•a?
And what is the high place*a* of Judah?
    Is it not Jerusalem?
6 Therefore I will make Sa•mār′i•a a heap in
        the open country,
    a place for planting vineyards.
I will pour down her stones into the valley,
    and uncover her foundations.

7 All her images shall be beaten to pieces,
    all her wages shall be burned with fire,
    and all her idols I will lay waste;
for as the wages of a prostitute she gathered
        them,
    and as the wages of a prostitute they
        shall again be used.

The Doom of the Cities of Judah

8 For this I will lament and wail;
    I will go barefoot and naked;
I will make lamentation like the jackals,
    and mourning like the ostriches.
9 For her wound*b* is incurable.
    It has come to Judah;
it has reached to the gate of my people,
    to Jerusalem.

10 Tell it not in Gath,
    weep not at all;
in Beth-le•aph′rah
    roll yourselves in the dust.
11 Pass on your way,
    inhabitants of Shā′phir,
    in nakedness and shame;
the inhabitants of Zā′a•nan
    do not come forth;
Beth-ē′zel is wailing
    and shall remove its support from you.

---

a Heb *what are the high places*   *b* Gk Syr Vg: Heb *wounds*

12 For the inhabitants of Mā′roth
    wait anxiously for good,
yet disaster has come down from the LORD
    to the gate of Jerusalem.
13 Harness the steeds to the chariots,
    inhabitants of Lā′chish;
it was the beginning of sin
    to daughter Zion,
for in you were found
    the transgressions of Israel.
14 Therefore you shall give parting gifts
    to Mō′re•sheth-gath;
the houses of Ach′zib shall be a deception
    to the kings of Israel.
15 I will again bring a conqueror upon you,
    inhabitants of Ma•rē′shah;
the glory of Israel
    shall come to A•dul′lam.
16 Make yourselves bald and cut off your hair
    for your pampered children;
make yourselves as bald as the eagle,
    for they have gone from you into exile.

Social Evils Denounced

Alas for those who devise wickedness
    and evil deeds*c* on their beds!
When the morning dawns, they perform it,
    because it is in their power.
2 They covet fields, and seize them;
    houses, and take them away;
they oppress householder and house,
    people and their inheritance.
3 Therefore thus says the LORD:
Now, I am devising against this family an
    evil
    from which you cannot remove your
    necks;
and you shall not walk haughtily,
    for it will be an evil time.
4 On that day they shall take up a taunt song
    against you,
    and wail with bitter lamentation,
and say, "We are utterly ruined;
    the LORD *d* alters the inheritance of my
    people;
how he removes it from me!
    Among our captors*e* he parcels out our
    fields."
5 Therefore you will have no one to cast the
    line by lot
    in the assembly of the LORD.

6 "Do not preach"—thus they preach—
    "one should not preach of such things;
    disgrace will not overtake us."
7 Should this be said, O house of Jacob?

Is the LORD's patience exhausted?
    Are these his doings?
Do not my words do good
    to one who walks uprightly?
8 But you rise up against my people*f* as an
    enemy;
    you strip the robe from the peaceful, *g*
from those who pass by trustingly
    with no thought of war.
9 The women of my people you drive out
    from their pleasant houses;
from their young children you take away
    my glory forever.
10 Arise and go;
    for this is no place to rest,
because of uncleanness that destroys
    with a grievous destruction.*h*
11 If someone were to go about uttering empty
    falsehoods,
    saying, "I will preach to you of wine and
    strong drink,"
    such a one would be the preacher for this
    people!

A Promise for the Remnant of Israel

12 I will surely gather all of you, O Jacob,
    I will gather the survivors of Israel;
I will set them together
    like sheep in a fold,
like a flock in its pasture;
    it will resound with people.
13 The one who breaks out will go up before
    them;
    they will break through and pass the gate,
    going out by it.
Their king will pass on before them,
    the LORD at their head.

Wicked Rulers and Prophets

And I said:
Listen, you heads of Jacob
    and rulers of the house of Israel!
Should you not know justice?—
2   you who hate the good and love the evil,
who tear the skin off my people,*i*
    and the flesh off their bones;
3 who eat the flesh of my people,
    flay their skin off them,
break their bones in pieces,
    and chop them up like meat*j* in a kettle,
    like flesh in a caldron.

---

c Cn: Heb *work evil*   *d* Heb *he*   *e* Cn: Heb *the rebellious*
f Cn: Heb *But yesterday my people rose*   *g* Cn: Heb *from
before a garment*   *h* Meaning of Heb uncertain
i Heb *from them*   *j* Gk: Heb *as*

4 Then they will cry to the LORD,
   but he will not answer them;
he will hide his face from them at that time,
   because they have acted wickedly.

5 Thus says the LORD concerning the prophets
      who lead my people astray,
who cry "Peace"
   when they have something to eat,
but declare war against those
   who put nothing into their mouths.

6 Therefore it shall be night to you, without
      vision,
   and darkness to you, without revelation.
The sun shall go down upon the prophets,
   and the day shall be black over them;

7 the seers shall be disgraced,
   and the diviners put to shame;
they shall all cover their lips,
   for there is no answer from God.

8 But as for me, I am filled with power,
   with the spirit of the LORD,
   and with justice and might,
to declare to Jacob his transgression
   and to Israel his sin.

9 Hear this, you rulers of the house of Jacob
   and chiefs of the house of Israel,
who abhor justice
   and pervert all equity,

10 who build Zion with blood
   and Jerusalem with wrong!

11 Its rulers give judgment for a bribe,
   its priests teach for a price,
   its prophets give oracles for money;
yet they lean upon the LORD and say,
   "Surely the LORD is with us!
   No harm shall come upon us."

12 Therefore because of you
   Zion shall be plowed as a field;
Jerusalem shall become a heap of ruins,
   and the mountain of the house a wooded
      height.

Peace and Security through Obedience
(Cp Isa 2.2–4)

In days to come
   the mountain of the LORD's house
shall be established as the highest of the
      mountains,
   and shall be raised up above the hills.
Peoples shall stream to it,

2   and many nations shall come and say:
"Come, let us go up to the mountain of the
      LORD,
   to the house of the God of Jacob;
that he may teach us his ways

and that we may walk in his paths."
For out of Zion shall go forth instruction,
   and the word of the LORD from Jerusalem.

3 He shall judge between many peoples,
   and shall arbitrate between strong nations
      far away;
they shall beat their swords into plowshares,
   and their spears into pruning hooks;
nation shall not lift up sword against
      nation,
   neither shall they learn war any more;

4 but they shall all sit under their own vines
      and under their own fig trees,
   and no one shall make them afraid;
for the mouth of the LORD of hosts has
      spoken.

5 For all the peoples walk,
   each in the name of its god,
but we will walk in the name of the LORD
      our God
   forever and ever.

Restoration Promised after Exile

6 In that day, says the LORD,
   I will assemble the lame
and gather those who have been driven
      away,
   and those whom I have afflicted.

7 The lame I will make the remnant,
   and those who were cast off, a strong
      nation;
and the LORD will reign over them in Mount
      Zion
   now and forevermore.

8 And you, O tower of the flock,
   hill of daughter Zion,
to you it shall come,
   the former dominion shall come,
   the sovereignty of daughter Jerusalem.

9 Now why do you cry aloud?
   Is there no king in you?
Has your counselor perished,
   that pangs have seized you like a woman
      in labor?

10 Writhe and groan,^{k} O daughter Zion,
   like a woman in labor;
for now you shall go forth from the city
   and camp in the open country;
   you shall go to Babylon.
There you shall be rescued,
   there the LORD will redeem you
   from the hands of your enemies.

_____
^{k} Meaning of Heb uncertain

11 Now many nations
  are assembled against you,
  saying, "Let her be profaned,
  and let our eyes gaze upon Zion."
12 But they do not know
  the thoughts of the LORD;
  they do not understand his plan,
    that he has gathered them as sheaves to
      the threshing floor.
13 Arise and thresh,
  O daughter Zion,
  for I will make your horn iron
  and your hoofs bronze;
  you shall beat in pieces many peoples,
  and shall[l] devote their gain to the LORD,
    their wealth to the Lord of the whole
      earth.

m Now you are walled around with a wall;[n]
  siege is laid against us;
  with a rod they strike the ruler of Israel
  upon the cheek.

The Ruler from Bethlehem

2o But you, O Bethlehem of Eph'ra·thah,
  who are one of the little clans of Judah,
  from you shall come forth for me
  one who is to rule in Israel,
  whose origin is from of old,
  from ancient days.
3 Therefore he shall give them up until the
    time
  when she who is in labor has brought
    forth;
  then the rest of his kindred shall return
  to the people of Israel.
4 And he shall stand and feed his flock in the
    strength of the LORD,
  in the majesty of the name of the LORD
    his God.
  And they shall live secure, for now he shall
    be great
  to the ends of the earth;
5 and he shall be the one of peace.

  If the Assyrians come into our land
  and tread upon our soil,[p]
  we will raise against them seven shepherds
  and eight installed as rulers.
6 They shall rule the land of Assyria with the
    sword,
  and the land of Nim'rod with the drawn
    sword;[q]
  they[r] shall rescue us from the Assyrians
  if they come into our land
  or tread within our border.

The Future Role of the Remnant

7 Then the remnant of Jacob,
  surrounded by many peoples,
  shall be like dew from the LORD,
  like showers on the grass,
  which do not depend upon people
  or wait for any mortal.
8 And among the nations the remnant of
    Jacob,
  surrounded by many peoples,
  shall be like a lion among the animals of
    the forest,
  like a young lion among the flocks of
    sheep,
  which, when it goes through, treads down
  and tears in pieces, with no one to
    deliver.

---

l Gk Syr Tg: Heb *and I will* m Ch 4.14 in Heb
n Cn Compare Gk: Meaning of Heb uncertain o Ch 5.1
in Heb p Gk: Heb *in our palaces* q Cn: Heb *in its
entrances* r Heb *he*

PRAY IT?
From Humble Beginnings

As a country boy, Micah has a different vision than do some of the other prophets. He doesn't see the Ideal Ruler coming out of a big city like Jerusalem. No, he sees this great person coming from Bethlehem—a tiny, insignificant city, but also a place free from political corruption. The Gospel of Matthew shows Micah's prophecy being fulfilled in the birth of Jesus (Mt 2.5–6).

Often in the Bible, we hear of God's accomplishing huge feats with small and humble people and things. In your prayer, reflect or journal on the following questions:

■ What famous people started from humble beginnings?
■ Why does God often use small and hidden people or things to accomplish God's purposes?
■ What small or hidden gifts do you have to offer God to work with?

▸ Mic 5.2–5

9 Your hand shall be lifted up over your
　　adversaries,
　and all your enemies shall be cut off.

10 In that day, says the LORD,
　I will cut off your horses from
　　among you
　and will destroy your chariots;
11 and I will cut off the cities of your land
　and throw down all your strongholds;
12 and I will cut off sorceries from your hand,
　and you shall have no more soothsayers;
13 and I will cut off your images
　and your pillars from among you,
　and you shall bow down no more
　　to the work of your hands;
14 and I will uproot your sacred poles[s] from
　　among you
　and destroy your towns.
15 And in anger and wrath I will execute
　　vengeance
　on the nations that did not obey.

God Challenges Israel

Hear what the LORD says:
　Rise, plead your case before
　　the mountains,
　and let the hills hear your voice.
2 Hear, you mountains, the controversy of the
　　LORD,
　and you enduring foundations of the
　　earth;
for the LORD has a controversy with his
　　people,
　and he will contend with Israel.

3 "O my people, what have I done to you?
　In what have I wearied you? Answer me!
4 For I brought you up from the land of
　　Egypt,
　and redeemed you from the house of
　　slavery;
and I sent before you Moses,
　Aaron, and Miriam.
5 O my people, remember now what King
　　Bāʹlak of Mōʹab devised,
　what Bāʹlaam son of Bēʹor answered him,
and what happened from Shitʹtim
　　to Gilʹgal,
　that you may know the saving acts of the
　　LORD."

What God Requires
(Cp Am 5.24)

6 "With what shall I come before the LORD,
　and bow myself before God on high?
Shall I come before him with
　　burnt offerings,
　with calves a year old?
7 Will the LORD be pleased with thousands of
　　rams,
　with ten thousands of rivers of oil?
Shall I give my firstborn for my
　　transgression,
　the fruit of my body for the sin of my
　　soul?"
8 He has told you, O mortal, what is good;
　and what does the LORD require of you
but to do justice, and to love kindness,
　and to walk humbly with your God?

Cheating and Violence to Be Punished

9 The voice of the LORD cries to the city
　(it is sound wisdom to fear your name):
Hear, O tribe and assembly of the city![t]
10 Can I forget[u] the treasures of wickedness
　　in the house of the wicked,
　and the scant measure that is accursed?
11 Can I tolerate wicked scales
　and a bag of dishonest weights?
12 Your[v] wealthy are full of violence;
　your[w] inhabitants speak lies,
　with tongues of deceit in their mouths.
13 Therefore I have begun[x] to strike you down,
　making you desolate because of your
　　sins.
14 You shall eat, but not be satisfied,

---

s Heb Asherim　t Cn Compare Gk: Heb tribe, and who has
appointed it yet?　u Cn: Meaning of Heb uncertain
v Heb Whose　w Heb whose　x Gk Syr Vg: Heb have
made sick

M
I
C

"To Love Kindness"

Perhaps you have heard the expression Perform a random act of kindness. It is a wonderful antidote to the reality of random acts of violence. Imagine what our world would be like if each day, each of us performed a random act of kindness—something nice and unexpected for someone, anyone, whether we knew them or not. We could make someone's day. And in turn, someone could make ours. Just as violence leads to more violence, so also can kindness create more kindness. No wonder Micah includes kindness in his simple formula for doing God's will: "to do justice, and to love kindness, / and to walk humbly with your God" (Mic 6.8).

▸ Mic 6.8

and there shall be a gnawing hunger
 within you;
you shall put away, but not save,
 and what you save, I will hand over to
 the sword.
15 You shall sow, but not reap;
 you shall tread olives, but not anoint
 yourselves with oil;
 you shall tread grapes, but not drink
 wine.
16 For you have kept the statutes of Om′rī*y*
 and all the works of the house of Ā′hab,
 and you have followed their counsels.
Therefore I will make you a desolation, and
 your*z* inhabitants an object
 of hissing;
 so you shall bear the scorn of my people.

The Total Corruption of the People

Woe is me! For I have become like one who,
 after the summer fruit has been gathered,
 after the vintage has been gleaned,
finds no cluster to eat;
 there is no first-ripe fig for which I
 hunger.
2 The faithful have disappeared from the land,
 and there is no one left who is upright;
they all lie in wait for blood,
 and they hunt each other with nets.
3 Their hands are skilled to do evil;
 the official and the judge ask for a bribe,
and the powerful dictate what they desire;
 thus they pervert justice.*a*
4 The best of them is like a brier,
 the most upright of them a thorn hedge.
The day of their*b* sentinels, of their*b*
 punishment, has come;
 now their confusion is at hand.
5 Put no trust in a friend,
 have no confidence in a loved one;

guard the doors of your mouth
 from her who lies in your embrace;
6 for the son treats the father with contempt,
 the daughter rises up against her mother,
the daughter-in-law against her
 mother-in-law;
 your enemies are members of your own
 household.
7 But as for me, I will look to the LORD,
 I will wait for the God of my salvation;
 my God will hear me.

Penitence and Trust in God

8 Do not rejoice over me, O my enemy;
 when I fall, I shall rise;
when I sit in darkness,
 the LORD will be a light to me.
9 I must bear the indignation of the LORD,
 because I have sinned against him,
until he takes my side
 and executes judgment for me.
He will bring me out to the light;
 I shall see his vindication.
10 Then my enemy will see,
 and shame will cover her who said
 to me,
 "Where is the LORD your God?"
My eyes will see her downfall;*c*
 now she will be trodden down
 like the mire of the streets.

A Prophecy of Restoration

11 A day for the building of your walls!
 In that day the boundary shall be far
 extended.
12 In that day they will come to you
 from Assyria to*d* Egypt,

---

y Gk Syr Vg Tg: Heb *the statutes of Omri are kept*
z Heb *its*   *a* Cn: Heb *they weave it*   *b* Heb *your*
c Heb lacks *downfall*   *d* One Ms: MT *Assyria and cities of*

and from Egypt to the River,
    from sea to sea and from mountain to
        mountain.
13 But the earth will be desolate
    because of its inhabitants,
    for the fruit of their doings.

14 Shepherd your people with your staff,
    the flock that belongs to you,
which lives alone in a forest
    in the midst of a garden land;
let them feed in Bā'shan and Gil'e•ad
    as in the days of old.
15 As in the days when you came out of the
        land of Egypt,
    show us*e* marvelous things.
16 The nations shall see and be ashamed
    of all their might;
they shall lay their hands on their mouths;
    their ears shall be deaf;
17 they shall lick dust like a snake,
    like the crawling things of the earth;

they shall come trembling out of their
        fortresses;
they shall turn in dread to the LORD
    our God,
    and they shall stand in fear of you.

God's Compassion and Steadfast Love

18 Who is a God like you, pardoning iniquity
    and passing over the transgression
    of the remnant of your*f* possession?
He does not retain his anger forever,
    because he delights in showing clemency.
19 He will again have compassion upon us;
    he will tread our iniquities under foot.
You will cast all our*g* sins
    into the depths of the sea.
20 You will show faithfulness to Jacob
    and unswerving loyalty to Abraham,
as you have sworn to our ancestors
    from the days of old.

---

e Cn: Heb *I will show him*   *f* Heb *his*   *g* Gk Syr Vg Tg:
Heb *their*

The Book of Nahum

Devastation, desolation, and destruction! If the Book of Nahum were made into a movie, it would have to be rated R for graphic violence. You are about to read some angry words. They portray a vengeful God bringing destruction upon Israel's enemies. What could make the prophet Nahum so angry? What could make God so angry?

In-depth

At the time Nahum was written, the Assyrian Empire had been the terror of the Middle East for several centuries. In 721 B.C., it destroyed the northern part of Israel, called Israel. In 701 B.C., it invaded the southern part of Israel, called Judah, and laid siege to Jerusalem (see the timeline and map 4, "The Assyrian Empire," at the back of this Bible). The siege broke off, and Jerusalem did not fall, but the chosen people of God got a gruesome taste of Assyria's savage cruelty.

The sole concern of the prophet Nahum is the destruction of this evil world power. In the first chapter of his book, he declares the coming wrath of God, and in chapters 2–3, he describes the destruction of Nineveh (the Assyrian capital). We shouldn't be too surprised that when Assyria falls in 612 B.C., Nahum sees the justice of God being worked out: the Assyrians are finally getting a taste of their own medicine! Nahum seems almost to be gloating in 3.19:

> All who hear the news about you
> clap their hands over you.
> For who has ever escaped
> your endless cruelty?

Hidden among the threats and violence against Assyria, we also find words of comfort for God's chosen people: the awesome war God will avenge them, because their enemies are God's enemies (1.2); good news and peace are coming for Judah (1.15); the Lord will restore Israel to its original majesty (2.2). We even find some wonderful reminders of God's love and protection, which balance the image of the God of vengeance and destruction: "the LORD is slow to anger but great in power" (1.3); "the LORD is good" (1.7); God is "a stronghold in a day of trouble" (1.7); God "protects those who take refuge in him" (1.7). Nahum reminds us that God has many sides and is always more than we can imagine.

At a Glance

- **1.1–11.** the coming of the Lord in judgment
- **1.12–15.** good news for Judah
- **Chapters 2–3.** the destruction of Nineveh

Quick Facts

Period Covered
663–612 B.C.

Author
Nahum

Theme
God will avenge Israel and destroy its cruel enemies, the Assyrians.

1084

Nahum

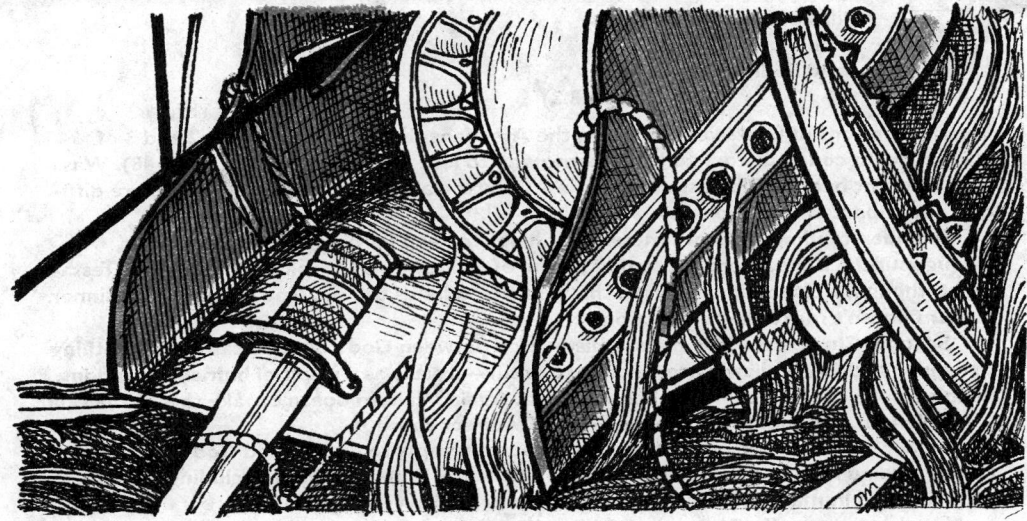

An oracle concerning Nin′e•veh. The book of the vision of Nā′hum of El′kosh.

The Consuming Wrath of God

2 A jealous and avenging God is the LORD,
    the LORD is avenging and wrathful;
the LORD takes vengeance on his adversaries
    and rages against his enemies.
3 The LORD is slow to anger but great in power,
    and the LORD will by no means clear the
        guilty.

His way is in whirlwind and storm,
    and the clouds are the dust of his feet.
4 He rebukes the sea and makes it dry,
    and he dries up all the rivers;
Bā′shan and Car′mel wither,
    and the bloom of Lebanon fades.
5 The mountains quake before him,
    and the hills melt;
the earth heaves before him,
    the world and all who live in it.
6 Who can stand before his indignation?
    Who can endure the heat of his anger?
His wrath is poured out like fire,
    and by him the rocks are broken in
        pieces.
7 The LORD is good,
    a stronghold in a day of trouble;
he protects those who take refuge in him,
8   even in a rushing flood.

He will make a full end of his adversaries,[a]
    and will pursue his enemies into
        darkness.
9 Why do you plot against the LORD?
    He will make an end;
    no adversary will rise up twice.
10 Like thorns they are entangled,
    like drunkards they are drunk;
    they are consumed like dry straw.
11 From you one has gone out
    who plots evil against the LORD,
    one who counsels wickedness.

Good News for Judah

12 Thus says the LORD,
    "Though they are at full strength and
        many,[b]
    they will be cut off and pass away.
Though I have afflicted you,
    I will afflict you no more.
13 And now I will break off his yoke from you
    and snap the bonds that bind you."

14 The LORD has commanded concerning you:
    "Your name shall be perpetuated no
        longer;
from the house of your gods I will cut off
    the carved image and the cast image.
I will make your grave, for you are worthless."

a Gk: Heb *of her place*   b Meaning of Heb uncertain

Images of God

LIVE IT!

> Piles of dead,
>   heaps of corpses,
>   dead bodies without end . . .
>   (Nah 3.3)

The descriptions of God's vengeance on the Assyrians throughout chapters 2 and 3 of Nahum seem contradictory to Jesus' command to love one's enemies (Mt 5.43–48). Was God different back in Old Testament times? Or was Nahum just mistaken? These are difficult but important questions!

In understanding Nahum's message, it helps to keep in mind three things. First, throughout the Bible, there is a strong theme of divine hatred for all sin. In the New Testament, though, a distinction emerges that while God hates the sin, God still loves the sinner. Nahum doesn't make that distinction.

Second, Christians today make a distinction between God's directly causing something to happen and God's allowing something to occur—usually as a result of human limitations, people's poor choices, or natural phenomena. Again, Nahum doesn't make this distinction —for Nahum, if something happens, God is its direct cause.

Finally, we have to keep in mind that all our attempts to understand God will fall short. God is beyond human understanding. That is why the Bible's authors, including Nahum, describe God in many different—and often contradictory—ways.

How do you see God? as a vengeful fire (Nah 1.6) or as a stronghold of protection (verse 7)? Are you comfortable imagining God in different—even opposite—ways?

▶ Nah 2.10—3.3

15c Look! On the mountains the feet of one
    who brings good tidings,
    who proclaims peace!
Celebrate your festivals, O Judah,
    fulfill your vows,
for never again shall the wicked invade you;
    they are utterly cut off.

The Destruction of the Wicked City

2 A shattererd has come up against you.
    Guard the ramparts;
    watch the road;
gird your loins;
    collect all your strength.
2 (For the LORD is restoring the majesty of
           Jacob,
    as well as the majesty of Israel,
though ravagers have ravaged them
    and ruined their branches.)

3 The shields of his warriors are red;
    his soldiers are clothed in crimson.
The metal on the chariots flashes
    on the day when he musters them;
    the chargerse prance.
4 The chariots race madly through the streets,
    they rush to and fro through the squares;

their appearance is like torches,
    they dart like lightning.
5 He calls his officers;
    they stumble as they come forward;
they hasten to the wall,
    and the manteletf is set up.
6 The river gates are opened,
    the palace trembles.
7 It is decreedf that the cityg be exiled,
    its slave women led away,
moaning like doves
    and beating their breasts.
8 Nin'e•veh is like a pool
    whose watersh run away.
"Halt! Halt!"—
    but no one turns back.
9 "Plunder the silver,
    plunder the gold!
There is no end of treasure!
    An abundance of every precious thing!"

10 Devastation, desolation, and destruction!
    Hearts faint and knees tremble,

---

c Ch 2.1 in Heb   d Cn: Heb *scatterer*   e Cn Compare
Gk Syr: Heb *cypresses*   f Meaning of Heb uncertain
g Heb *it*   h Cn Compare Gk: Heb *a pool, from the days*
that she has become, and they

all loins quake,
  all faces grow pale!
11 What became of the lions' den,
  the cave[i] of the young lions,
where the lion goes,
  and the lion's cubs, with no one to
    disturb them?
12 The lion has torn enough for his whelps
  and strangled prey for his lionesses;
he has filled his caves with prey
  and his dens with torn flesh.

13 See, I am against you, says the LORD of hosts, and I will burn your[j] chariots in smoke, and the sword shall devour your young lions; I will cut off your prey from the earth, and the voice of your messengers shall be heard no more.

Ruin Imminent and Inevitable

Ah! City of bloodshed,
  utterly deceitful, full of booty—
    no end to the plunder!
2 The crack of whip and rumble of wheel,
  galloping horse and bounding chariot!
3 Horsemen charging,
  flashing sword and glittering spear,
piles of dead,
  heaps of corpses,
dead bodies without end—
  they stumble over the bodies!
4 Because of the countless debaucheries of
    the prostitute,
  gracefully alluring, mistress of sorcery,
who enslaves[k] nations through her debaucheries,
  and peoples through her sorcery,
5 I am against you,
  says the LORD of hosts,
  and will lift up your skirts over your face;
and I will let nations look on your nakedness
  and kingdoms on your shame.
6 I will throw filth at you
  and treat you with contempt,
  and make you a spectacle.
7 Then all who see you will shrink from you
    and say,
"Nin'e•veh is devastated; who will
    bemoan her?"
  Where shall I seek comforters for you?

8 Are you better than Thēbes[l]
  that sat by the Nile,
with water around her,
  her rampart a sea,
  water her wall?
9 Ethiopia[m] was her strength,
  Egypt too, and that without limit;
  Put and the Libyans were her[n] helpers.

10 Yet she became an exile,
  she went into captivity;
even her infants were dashed in pieces
  at the head of every street;
lots were cast for her nobles,
  all her dignitaries were bound in fetters.
11 You also will be drunken,
  you will go into hiding;[o]
you will seek
  a refuge from the enemy.
12 All your fortresses are like fig trees
  with first-ripe figs—
if shaken they fall
  into the mouth of the eater.
13 Look at your troops:
  they are women in your midst.
The gates of your land
  are wide open to your foes;
  fire has devoured the bars of your gates.

14 Draw water for the siege,
  strengthen your forts;
trample the clay,
  tread the mortar,
  take hold of the brick mold!
15 There the fire will devour you,
  the sword will cut you off.
It will devour you like the locust.

Multiply yourselves like the locust,
  multiply like the grasshopper!
16 You increased your merchants
  more than the stars of the heavens.
  The locust sheds its skin and flies away.
17 Your guards are like grasshoppers,
  your scribes like swarms[o] of locusts
settling on the fences
  on a cold day—
when the sun rises, they fly away;
  no one knows where they have gone.

18 Your shepherds are asleep,
  O king of Assyria;
  your nobles slumber.
Your people are scattered on the mountains
  with no one to gather them.
19 There is no assuaging your hurt,
  your wound is mortal.
All who hear the news about you
  clap their hands over you.
For who has ever escaped
  your endless cruelty?

---

i Cn: Heb *pasture*   j Heb *her*   k Heb *sells*
l Heb *No-amon*   m Or *Nubia*; Heb *Cush*   n Gk: Heb *your*
o Meaning of Heb uncertain

The Book of Habakkuk

"God, why aren't you answering our cries for help? How long must we endure this trial?" Most people have wondered this at times. Why does our good, all-powerful God let suffering or injustice go on? The prophet Habakkuk struggled with these same painful and disturbing questions. His hope in God's justice is a model of faith amid doubt.

At a Glance

- **1.1—2.5.** Habakkuk's complaints and God's responses

- **2.6–20.** five warnings against wicked people

- **Chapter 3.** Habakkuk's prayer of confidence

In-depth

Habakkuk was the first prophet who dared to ask God about God's behavior. He looked around at all the terrible things that were happening to his people and cried out: "God, where are you? Do you even care about us? Why do you allow evil people to oppress us?"

We know little about Habakkuk except that he was a prophet in the southern kingdom of Judah in the late seventh century B.C. The Chaldeans (another name for the Babylonians) and the corrupt king of Judah, Jehoiakim, were causing so much trouble that Habakkuk was ready to despair. God answered him in a most surprising way, saying that the Chaldeans—as bad as they were—were chosen as God's instrument to punish the wicked all over the earth. Habakkuk was not satisfied. He asked why God was silent while the wicked destroyed the righteous. God then spoke to him in a vision (Hab 2.2), saying that justice would come to the wicked in its own time, but "the righteous live by their faith" (verse 4). Later, Paul would use these same words to describe the Christians (Rom 1.17; Gal 3.11). For Habakkuk, faith in God and hope in God's justice were the same thing.

The short Book of Habakkuk is unique among the prophetic books in the variety of its writings. Its reflections about the problem of evil in the world resemble the wisdom literature. Its dialogs with God (see 1.2) are similar to Jeremiah's confessions (see Jer 12.6). Chapter 3 is a canticle (song).

The prophet's concluding canticle is a prayer of confidence in God's power to save the people. We too can pray in confidence, because God is just and will save us in our time of need.

Quick Facts

Period Covered
probably the reign of King Jehoiakim, 609–597 B.C. (see 2 Kings 23.36—24.7)

Author
Habakkuk

Theme
The answer to evil is faith in God's justice.

Habakkuk

1.8

The oracle that the prophet Ha·bak′kuk saw.

The Prophet's First Complaint

2 O LORD, how long shall I cry for help,
  and you will not listen?
Or cry to you "Violence!"
  and you will not save?
3 Why do you make me see wrongdoing
  and look at trouble?
Destruction and violence are before me;
  strife and contention arise.
4 So the law becomes slack
  and justice never prevails.
The wicked surround the righteous—
  therefore judgment comes forth perverted.

God' Reply to the Prophet's Complaint

5 Look at the nations, and see!
  Be astonished! Be astounded!
For a work is being done in your days
  that you would not believe if you were
    told.
6 For I am rousing the Chal·dē′ans,
  that fierce and impetuous nation,
who march through the breadth of the earth
  to seize dwellings not their own.
7 Dread and fearsome are they;
  their justice and dignity proceed from
    themselves.
8 Their horses are swifter than leopards,
more menacing than wolves at dusk;
  their horses charge.
Their horsemen come from far away;
  they fly like an eagle swift to devour.
9 They all come for violence,
  with faces pressing*a* forward;
  they gather captives like sand.
10 At kings they scoff,
  and of rulers they make sport.
They laugh at every fortress,
  and heap up earth to take it.
11 Then they sweep by like the wind;
  they transgress and become guilty;
  their own might is their god!

The Prophet's Second Complaint

12 Are you not from of old,
  O LORD my God, my Holy One?
You*b* shall not die.
O LORD, you have marked them for
    judgment;
  and you, O Rock, have established them
    for punishment.
13 Your eyes are too pure to behold evil,
  and you cannot look on wrongdoing;
why do you look on the treacherous,
  and are silent when the wicked swallow

---

a Meaning of Heb uncertain   *b* Ancient Heb tradition:
MT *We*

those more righteous than they?

14 You have made people like the fish of
the sea,
like crawling things that have no ruler.

15 The enemy[c] brings all of them up with a
hook;
he drags them out with his net,
he gathers them in his seine;
so he rejoices and exults.

16 Therefore he sacrifices to his net
and makes offerings to his seine;
for by them his portion is lavish,
and his food is rich.

17 Is he then to keep on emptying his net,
and destroying nations without mercy?

4 Look at the proud!
Their spirit is not right in them,
but the righteous live by their faith.[e]

5 Moreover, wealth[f] is treacherous;
the arrogant do not endure.
They open their throats wide as Shĕʾōl;
like Death they never have enough.
They gather all nations for themselves,
and collect all peoples as their own.

The Woes of the Wicked

6 Shall not everyone taunt such people and,
with mocking riddles, say about them,
"Alas for you who heap up what is not
your own!"

Now!

"I want it all, and I want it now!"
That statement could sum up the ambitions of a lot of people. It is how they define success. The key word in their goal is *now*. They don't like to wait in lines; they want instant service and immediate gratification.
There is a temptation to apply this goal to our spiritual life. We want to grow closer to God—now! But the spiritual life does not work that way. Recall these words from the Book of Ecclesiastes: "For everything there is a season, and a time for every matter under heaven" (3.1). We have to remind ourselves that many valuable things take time. Our growth in faith will take time. We need to be open, patient, and trusting. As God reminds Habakkuk in his vision in Hab 2.3, "If it seems to tarry, wait for it; / it will surely come, it will not delay."
Consider these questions:

■ **What are your goals for your relationship with God?**
■ **How patient are you with your spiritual growth? How do you nurture it day by day?**

▶ Hab 2.3

God's Reply to the Prophet's Complaint

I will stand at my watchpost,
and station myself on the rampart;
I will keep watch to see what he will say
to me,
and what he[d] will answer concerning my
complaint.
2 Then the LORD answered me and said:
Write the vision;
make it plain on tablets,
so that a runner may read it.
3 For there is still a vision for the appointed
time;
it speaks of the end, and does not lie.
If it seems to tarry, wait for it;
it will surely come, it will not delay.

How long will you load yourselves with
goods taken in pledge?
7 Will not your own creditors suddenly rise,
and those who make you tremble wake up?
Then you will be booty for them.
8 Because you have plundered many nations,
all that survive of the peoples shall
plunder you—
because of human bloodshed, and violence
to the earth,
to cities and all who live in them.

9 "Alas for you who get evil gain for your houses,
setting your nest on high
to be safe from the reach of harm!"

---

[c] Heb *He*   [d] Syr: Heb *I*   [e] Or *faithfulness*   [f] Other Heb
Mss read *wine*

10 You have devised shame for your house
　　by cutting off many peoples;
　　you have forfeited your life.
11 The very stones will cry out from the wall,
　　and the plaster*g* will respond from the
　　　woodwork.

12 "Alas for you who build a town by
　　　bloodshed,
　　and found a city on iniquity!"
13 Is it not from the LORD of hosts
　　that peoples labor only to feed the
　　　flames,
　　and nations weary themselves for
　　　nothing?
14 But the earth will be filled
　　with the knowledge of the glory of the
　　　LORD,
　　as the waters cover the sea.

15 "Alas for you who make your neighbors
　　　drink,
　　pouring out your wrath*h* until they are
　　　drunk,
　　in order to gaze on their nakedness!"
16 You will be sated with contempt instead of
　　　glory.
　　Drink, you yourself, and stagger!*i*
　　The cup in the LORD's right hand
　　will come around to you,
　　and shame will come upon your glory!
17 For the violence done to Lebanon will
　　　overwhelm you;
　　the destruction of the animals will
　　　terrify you—*j*
　　because of human bloodshed and violence
　　　to the earth,
　　to cities and all who live in them.

18 What use is an idol
　　once its maker has shaped it—
　　a cast image, a teacher of lies?
　　For its maker trusts in what has been made,
　　　though the product is only an idol that
　　　cannot speak!
19 Alas for you who say to the wood,
　　　"Wake up!"
　　to silent stone, "Rouse yourself!"
　　Can it teach?
　　See, it is gold and silver plated,
　　　and there is no breath in it at all.

20 But the LORD is in his holy temple;
　　let all the earth keep silence before him!

A prayer of the prophet Ha·bak'kuk according to
Shig·i·ōn'oth.

The Prophet's Prayer

2 O LORD, I have heard of your renown,
　　and I stand in awe, O LORD, of your
　　　work.
　　In our own time revive it;
　　in our own time make it known;
　　in wrath may you remember mercy.
3 God came from Tē'man,
　　the Holy One from Mount Par'an.　　*Sē'lah*
　　His glory covered the heavens,
　　and the earth was full of his praise.
4 The brightness was like the sun;
　　rays came forth from his hand,
　　where his power lay hidden.
5 Before him went pestilence,
　　and plague followed close behind.
6 He stopped and shook the earth;
　　he looked and made the nations tremble.
　　The eternal mountains were shattered;
　　along his ancient pathways
　　the everlasting hills sank low.
7 I saw the tents of Cūsh'an under affliction;
　　the tent-curtains of the land of Mid'i·an
　　　trembled.
8 Was your wrath against the rivers,*k* O LORD?
　　Or your anger against the rivers,*k*
　　or your rage against the sea,*l*
　　when you drove your horses,
　　your chariots to victory?
9 You brandished your naked bow,
　　sated*m* were the arrows at your
　　　command.*n*　　　　　　　　*Sē'lah*
　　You split the earth with rivers.
10 The mountains saw you, and writhed;
　　a torrent of water swept by;
　　the deep gave forth its voice.
　　The sun*o* raised high its hands;
11 the moon*p* stood still in its exalted place,
　　at the light of your arrows speeding by,
　　at the gleam of your flashing spear.
12 In fury you trod the earth,
　　in anger you trampled nations.
13 You came forth to save your people,
　　to save your anointed.
　　You crushed the head of the wicked house,
　　laying it bare from foundation to roof.*n*
　　　　　　　　　　　　　　　　Sē'lah

---

g Or *beam*　　*h* Or *poison*　　*i* Q Ms Gk: MT *be uncircumcised*
j Gk Syr: Meaning of Heb uncertain　　*k* Or *against River*
l Or *against Sea*　　*m* Cn: Heb *oaths*　　*n* Meaning of Heb
uncertain　　*o* Heb *It*　　*p* Heb *sun, moon*

14 You pierced with their*q* own arrows the
  head*r* of his warriors,*s*
who came like a whirlwind to
  scatter us,*t*
gloating as if ready to devour the poor
  who were in hiding.
15 You trampled the sea with your
  horses,
churning the mighty waters.

16 I hear, and I tremble within;
  my lips quiver at the sound.
Rottenness enters into my bones,
  and my steps tremble*u* beneath
  me.
I wait quietly for the day of calamity
  to come upon the people who
  attack us.

Trust and Joy in the Midst of Trouble

17 Though the fig tree does not blossom,
  and no fruit is on the vines;
though the produce of the olive fails,
  and the fields yield no food;
though the flock is cut off from the fold,
  and there is no herd in the stalls,
18 yet I will rejoice in the LORD;
  I will exult in the God of my salvation.
19 GOD, the Lord, is my strength;
  he makes my feet like the feet of a deer,
  and makes me tread upon the heights.*v*

To the leader: with stringed*w* instruments.

q Heb *his*   *r* Or *leader*   *s* Vg Compare Gk Syr: Meaning
of Heb uncertain   *t* Heb *me*   *u* Cn Compare Gk:
Meaning of Heb uncertain   *v* Heb *my heights*
w Heb *my stringed*

During childhood, we usually have to clean up messes, take time-outs, or lose privileges as consequences for poor choices we have made. As we get older, we learn that our wrongdoing has more personal and painful consequences: perhaps a parent's refusal to trust us, a friend's anger, or pain after hurting someone we love. The prophet Zephaniah warned the people of Judah of the severe consequences of their sin against the Lord.

At a Glance

- **Chapter 1.** a warning about Judah's idolatry

- **2.1—3.7.** a discussion of the destruction of the nations and the corrupt nature of Jerusalem

- **3.8—20.** a message about the conversion of the nations and salvation for Jerusalem

In-depth

The Book of Zephaniah gives us few clues about the prophet Zephaniah's identity. We do know that he preached in the southern kingdom of Judah during the reign of King Josiah (see 2 Chronicles, chapters 34–35), around 630 B.C. He followed First Isaiah and Micah, and came a little before Habakkuk and during the time of Nahum.

Zephaniah follows the footsteps of the classical Old Testament prophets in denouncing the wrongdoing of society. His main contribution is considering pride (1.6; 2.10; 3.11) as the source of problems such as smugness (1.12), rebellion (3.2), and treachery (3.11). All these attitudes toward God lead to idolatry and social sin. Although all people sin, leaders have a greater responsibility, and their sins will provoke a harsh judgment during the coming day of the Lord (1.14). Only those who worship God humbly and who seek justice will be spared. Zephaniah calls them the remnant (3.12–13), meaning "a little piece that is left over." They are the ones who will stay faithful to God through both good times and bad.

The book ends with a song of joy reassuring the people of Jerusalem that God still loves them and will save them in the end. We are not sure if the song is from Zephaniah himself or is the addition of a later editor. It is as if the writer knows that when people are experiencing the negative results of sinful actions, they need to be reassured that they are still loved. God's punishment is to teach us, not to destroy us. Therefore, God's people should not despair but keep their trust in God.

Quick Facts

Period Covered
approximately 630 B.C.

Author
Zephaniah (and perhaps a later editor)

Theme
Judah and its neighbors will experience the consequences of their sinfulness.

The Book of *Zephaniah*

Zephaniah

The word of the LORD that came to Zeph•a•nī′ah son of Cū′shī son of Ged•a•lī′ah son of Am•a•rī′ah son of Hez•e•kī′ah, in the days of King Jō•sī′ah son of Ā′mon of Judah.

The Coming Judgment on Judah

2 I will utterly sweep away everything
   from the face of the earth, says the LORD.
3 I will sweep away humans and animals;
   I will sweep away the birds of the air
   and the fish of the sea.
   I will make the wicked stumble.*a*
   I will cut off humanity
   from the face of the earth, says the LORD.
4 I will stretch out my hand against Judah,
   and against all the inhabitants of
      Jerusalem;
   and I will cut off from this place every
      remnant of Bā′al
   and the name of the idolatrous priests;*b*
5 those who bow down on the roofs
   to the host of the heavens;
   those who bow down and swear to the
      LORD,
   but also swear by Mil′com;*c*
6 those who have turned back from following
      the LORD,
   who have not sought the LORD or
      inquired of him.

7 Be silent before the Lord GOD!
   For the day of the LORD is at hand;
   the LORD has prepared a sacrifice,
   he has consecrated his guests.
8 And on the day of the LORD's sacrifice
   I will punish the officials and the king's
      sons
   and all who dress themselves in foreign
      attire.
9 On that day I will punish
   all who leap over the threshold,
   who fill their master's house
   with violence and fraud.
10 On that day, says the LORD,
   a cry will be heard from the Fish Gate,
   a wail from the Second Quarter,
   a loud crash from the hills.
11 The inhabitants of the Mortar wail,
   for all the traders have perished;
   all who weigh out silver are cut off.
12 At that time I will search Jerusalem with
      lamps,
   and I will punish the people
   who rest complacently*d* on their dregs,
   those who say in their hearts,

---

a Cn: Heb *sea, and those who cause the wicked to stumble*
b Compare Gk: Heb *the idolatrous priests with the priests*
c Gk Mss Syr Vg: Heb *Malcam* (or, *their king*)   *d* Heb *who thicken*

"The LORD will not do good,
    nor will he do harm."
13 Their wealth shall be plundered,
    and their houses laid waste.
Though they build houses,
    they shall not inhabit them;
though they plant vineyards,
    they shall not drink wine from them.

The Great Day of the LORD

(Cp Am 5.18–20)

14 The great day of the LORD is near,
    near and hastening fast;
the sound of the day of the LORD is bitter,
    the warrior cries aloud there.
15 That day will be a day of wrath,
    a day of distress and anguish,
a day of ruin and devastation,
    a day of darkness and gloom,
a day of clouds and thick darkness,
16   a day of trumpet blast and battle cry
against the fortified cities
    and against the lofty battlements.

17 I will bring such distress upon people
    that they shall walk like the blind;
because they have sinned against the
    LORD,
their blood shall be poured out like dust,
    and their flesh like dung.
18 Neither their silver nor their gold
    will be able to save them
    on the day of the LORD's wrath;
in the fire of his passion
    the whole earth shall be consumed;
for a full, a terrible end
    he will make of all the inhabitants of the
    earth.

Judgment on Israel's Enemies

2 Gather together, gather,
    O shameless nation,
2 before you are driven away
    like the drifting chaff,*e*
before there comes upon you
    the fierce anger of the LORD,
before there comes upon you
    the day of the LORD's wrath.
3 Seek the LORD, all you humble of the land,
    who do his commands;
seek righteousness, seek humility;
    perhaps you may be hidden
    on the day of the LORD's wrath.
4 For Gā′za shall be deserted,
    and Ash′ke•lon shall become a desolation;

Ash′dod's people shall be driven out at
    noon,
    and Ek′ron shall be uprooted.
5 Ah, inhabitants of the seacoast,
    you nation of the Cher′e•thītes!
The word of the LORD is against you,
    O Cā′naan, land of the Phi•lis′tines;
and I will destroy you until no inhabitant
    is left.
6 And you, O seacoast, shall be pastures,
    meadows for shepherds
    and folds for flocks.
7 The seacoast shall become the possession
    of the remnant of the house of Judah,
    on which they shall pasture,
and in the houses of Ash′ke•lon
    they shall lie down at evening.
For the LORD their God will be mindful of
    them
    and restore their fortunes.

8 I have heard the taunts of Mō′ab
    and the revilings of the Am′mon•ītes,
how they have taunted my people
    and made boasts against their territory.
9 Therefore, as I live, says the LORD of hosts,
    the God of Israel,
Mō′ab shall become like Sod′om
    and the Am′mon•ītes like Go•mor′rah,
a land possessed by nettles and salt pits,
    and a waste forever.
The remnant of my people shall plunder
    them,
    and the survivors of my nation shall
    possess them.
10 This shall be their lot in return for their
    pride,
    because they scoffed and boasted
against the people of the LORD of hosts.
11 The LORD will be terrible against them;
    he will shrivel all the gods of the earth,
and to him shall bow down,
    each in its place,
    all the coasts and islands of the nations.

12 You also, O Ethiopians,*f*
    shall be killed by my sword.

13 And he will stretch out his hand against the
    north,
    and destroy Assyria;
and he will make Nin′e•veh a desolation,
    a dry waste like the desert.
14 Herds shall lie down in it,

---

e Cn Compare Gk Syr: Heb *before a decree is born; like chaff
a day has passed away*   *f* Or *Nubians;* Heb *Cushites*

every wild animal;[g]
the desert owl[h] and the screech owl[h]
   shall lodge on its capitals;
the owl[i] shall hoot at the window,
   the raven[j] croak on the threshold;
   for its cedar work will be laid bare.
15 Is this the exultant city
   that lived secure,
that said to itself,
   "I am, and there is no one else"?
What a desolation it has become,
   a lair for wild animals!
Everyone who passes by it
   hisses and shakes the fist.

The Wickedness of Jerusalem

Ah, soiled, defiled,
   oppressing city!
2 It has listened to no voice;
   it has accepted no correction.
It has not trusted in the LORD;
   it has not drawn near to its God.

3 The officials within it
   are roaring lions;
its judges are evening wolves
   that leave nothing until the morning.
4 Its prophets are reckless,
   faithless persons;
its priests have profaned what is sacred,
   they have done violence to the law.
5 The LORD within it is righteous;
   he does no wrong.
Every morning he renders his judgment,
   each dawn without fail;
   but the unjust knows no shame.

6 I have cut off nations;
   their battlements are in ruins;
I have laid waste their streets
   so that no one walks in them;
their cities have been made desolate,
   without people, without inhabitants.
7 I said, "Surely the city[k] will fear me,
   it will accept correction;
it will not lose sight[l]
   of all that I have brought upon it."
But they were the more eager
   to make all their deeds corrupt.

Punishment and Conversion
of the Nations
(Cp Gen 11.1–9; Acts 2.1–11)

8 Therefore wait for me, says the LORD,
   for the day when I arise as a witness.
For my decision is to gather nations,
   to assemble kingdoms,

to pour out upon them my indignation,
   all the heat of my anger;
for in the fire of my passion
   all the earth shall be consumed.

9 At that time I will change the speech of the
      peoples
   to a pure speech,
that all of them may call on the name of
      the LORD
   and serve him with one accord.
10 From beyond the rivers of Ethiopia[m]
   my suppliants, my scattered ones,
   shall bring my offering.

11 On that day you shall not be put to shame
   because of all the deeds by which you
      have rebelled against me;
for then I will remove from your midst
   your proudly exultant ones,
and you shall no longer be haughty
   in my holy mountain.
12 For I will leave in the midst of you
   a people humble and lowly.
They shall seek refuge in the name of the
      LORD—
13   the remnant of Israel;
they shall do no wrong
   and utter no lies,
nor shall a deceitful tongue
   be found in their mouths.
Then they will pasture and lie down,
   and no one shall make them afraid.

A Song of Joy

14 Sing aloud, O daughter Zion;
   shout, O Israel!
Rejoice and exult with all your heart,
   O daughter Jerusalem!
15 The LORD has taken away the judgments
      against you,
   he has turned away your enemies.
The king of Israel, the LORD, is in your
      midst;
   you shall fear disaster no more.
16 On that day it shall be said to Jerusalem:
Do not fear, O Zion;
   do not let your hands grow weak.
17 The LORD, your God, is in your midst,
   a warrior who gives victory;
he will rejoice over you with gladness,
   he will renew you[n] in his love;
he will exult over you with loud singing

---

g Tg Compare Gk: Heb *nation*   h Meaning of Heb
uncertain   i Cn: Heb *a voice*   j Gk Vg: Heb *desolation*
k Heb *it*   l Gk Syr: Heb *its dwelling will not be cut off*
m Or *Nubia*; Heb *Cush*   n Gk Syr: Heb *he will be silent*

MATERIAL POVERTY AND SPIRITUAL POVERTY!

In the Bible, God is always opposed to material poverty and misery. Over and over in the Old Testament, wealth is called a blessing and poverty a curse. The laws of the Covenant assert that poverty should not exist in Israel. Rich people are commanded to periodically forgive the debts of the poor and redistribute the land equally (see Lev 25.8). Selfishness leads to injustice, and injustice leads to tragedy, violence, and despair.

Zephaniah gives a spiritual connotation to the word *poor* (translated as "lowly" in Zeph 3.12). He relates poverty to humility. In this sense, to be poor is to be empty of egoism and pride, and therefore open to God's action in us. Zephaniah believes a small group of spiritually poor people, known as the remnant of Israel or the poor of God, will keep the Covenant alive.

Hispanic spirituality is deeply rooted in this concept of the poor, and the Virgin Mary is the culture's supreme example of it. To be spiritually poor is to be receptive to the Holy Spirit, to be generous with others, to trust in God's providence, and to accept suffering without losing hope.

- How will you live out the call to be spiritually poor, free of material goods beyond what is necessary to live?
- Ask God to give you the strength to respond to this call, which is so necessary in this world of pride, injustice, and materialism.

▶ Zeph 3.11–13

18 as on a day of festival.*o*
I will remove disaster from you,*p*
  so that you will not bear reproach for it.
19 I will deal with all your oppressors
    at that time.
And I will save the lame
    and gather the outcast,
and I will change their shame into praise
    and renown in all the earth.

20 At that time I will bring you home,
    at the time when I gather you;
for I will make you renowned and praised
    among all the peoples of the earth,
  when I restore your fortunes
    before your eyes, says the LORD.

---

o Gk Syr: Meaning of Heb uncertain   *p* Cn: Heb *I will remove from you; they were*

Z
E
P
H

I magine that you've been saving for months for a new stereo system. Just when you are about to purchase it, a good friend's family has a major house fire. Unfortunately, they were not insured—so the community is taking up a collection to help them rebuild. Now, you are faced with a decision: will you buy the new stereo or help your friend's family? The Jews at the time of the prophet Haggai faced an even more difficult decision: returning to Jerusalem after the Babylonian Exile, which would they rebuild first—their homes or God's Temple?

At a Glance

- **Chapter 1.** a command to rebuild the Temple
- **2.1–19.** a description of the future glory of God's Temple and the future prosperity of God's people
- **2.20–23.** a message about the future nation of Judah and its king

In-depth

When the people of ancient Judah lost their Temple in 587 B.C. and were deported to a strange land, they experienced a crisis in faith. Had God abandoned them? Were they no longer God's people? Was God punishing them for their sins? Some of them dreamed of a time when they could return to their land and rebuild God's Temple. However, when they finally were able to return in 538 B.C., things weren't as easy as they had hoped. Suffering from poverty, droughts, and crop failures (Hag 1.10–11), they put off rebuilding the Temple. Into this scene came the prophet Haggai. He told the people that God was still with them, and life was so difficult because they didn't seem to care that God's house was in ruins (verse 4). They had to get their priorities in order!

The people heard God's word spoken through Haggai, and immediately began working on the Temple. In their minds, they knew the new Temple would never be as beautiful as the original one (2.3). Haggai used this opportunity to prophesy about a future Temple that would be filled with God's splendor (verse 7), a time when God would again bless these people and make their offerings holy. God would establish Judah as a powerful nation, and Zerubbabel (a descendant of David's) would be its anointed king.

Quick Facts

Period Covered
approximately 520 B.C.
Author
Haggai
Theme
rebuilding God's Temple

Haggai

The Command to Rebuild the Temple
(Ezra 5.1)

In the second year of King Da·rī′us, in the sixth month, on the first day of the month, the word of the LORD came by the prophet Hag′gaī to Ze·rub′-ba·bel son of She·al′ti·el, governor of Judah, and to Joshua son of Je·hoz′a·dak, the high priest: 2 Thus says the LORD of hosts: These people say the time has not yet come to rebuild the LORD's house. 3 Then the word of the LORD came by the prophet Hag′gaī, saying: 4 Is it a time for you yourselves to live in your paneled houses, while this house lies in ruins? 5 Now therefore thus says the LORD of hosts: Consider how you have fared. 6 You have sown much, and harvested little; you eat, but you never have enough; you drink, but you never have your fill; you clothe yourselves, but no one is warm; and you that earn wages earn wages to put them into a bag with holes.

7 Thus says the LORD of hosts: Consider how you have fared. 8 Go up to the hills and bring wood and build the house, so that I may take pleasure in it and be honored, says the LORD. 9 You have looked for much, and, lo, it came to little; and when you brought it home, I blew it away. Why? says the LORD of hosts. Because my house lies in ruins, while all of you hurry off to your own houses. 10 Therefore the heavens above you have withheld the dew, and the earth has withheld its produce. 11 And I have called for a drought on the land and the hills, on the grain, the new wine, the oil, on what the soil produces, on human beings and animals, and on all their labors.

12 Then Ze·rub′ba·bel son of She·al′ti·el, and Joshua son of Je·hoz′a·dak, the high priest, with all the remnant of the people, obeyed the voice of the LORD their God, and the words of the prophet Hag′gaī, as the LORD their God had sent him; and the people feared the LORD. 13 Then Hag′gaī, the messenger of the LORD, spoke to the people with the LORD's message, saying, I am with you, says the LORD. 14 And the LORD stirred up the spirit of Ze·rub′ba·bel son of She·al′ti·el, governor of Judah, and the spirit of Joshua son of Je·hoz′a·dak, the high priest, and the spirit of all the remnant of the people; and they came and worked on the house of the LORD of hosts, their God, 15 on the twenty-fourth day of the month, in the sixth month.

The Future Glory of the Temple

In the second year of King Da·rī′us, 1 in the seventh month, on the twenty-first day of the month, the word of the LORD came by the prophet Hag′gaī, saying: 2 Speak now to Ze·rub′ba·bel son of She·al′-ti·el, governor of Judah, and to Joshua son of Je-hoz′a·dak, the high priest, and to the remnant of the people, and say, 3 Who is left among you that saw this house in its former glory? How does it

PRAY IT!

God at the Center

The people of Haggai's time felt that they did not have enough wealth to rebuild the Temple (Hag 1.2). God told them they were poor and unsuccessful because they had not rebuilt the Temple (verse 9). They needed to trust that if they put their priorities in the right order, God would provide.

Perhaps Haggai's people had forgotten what the true riches in life are. One of the first things many poor European immigrants settling in the United States did was to build a church (and often a school). They did this at a great sacrifice of time and materials. The church was more than a building; it was a symbol of their willingness to work together and of their common faith. It is in things like this that true wealth is found.

God, help me and my family, friends, and community to put you and the building of your Reign first in our lives. Give us the true wealth that comes from working with others for the good of all. Amen.

▸ **Haggai, chapter 1**

look to you now? Is it not in your sight as nothing? ⁴Yet now take courage, O Ze•rub′ba•bel, says the LORD; take courage, O Joshua, son of Je•hoz′a•dak, the high priest; take courage, all you people of the land, says the LORD; work, for I am with you, says the LORD of hosts, ⁵according to the promise that I made you when you came out of Egypt. My spirit abides among you; do not fear. ⁶For thus says the LORD of hosts: Once again, in a little while, I will shake the heavens and the earth and the sea and the dry land; ⁷and I will shake all the nations, so that the treasure of all nations shall come, and I will fill this house with splendor, says the LORD of hosts. ⁸The silver is mine, and the gold is mine, says the LORD of hosts. ⁹The latter splendor of this house shall be greater than the former, says the LORD of hosts; and in this place I will give prosperity, says the LORD of hosts.

A Rebuke and a Promise

10 On the twenty-fourth day of the ninth month, in the second year of Da•ri′us, the word of the LORD came by the prophet Hag′gai, saying: ¹¹Thus says the LORD of hosts: Ask the priests for a ruling: ¹²If one carries consecrated meat in the fold of one's garment, and with the fold touches bread, or stew, or wine, or oil, or any kind of food, does it become holy? The priests answered, "No." ¹³Then Hag′gai said, "If one who is unclean by contact with a dead body touches any of these, does it become unclean?" The priests answered, "Yes, it becomes unclean." ¹⁴Hag′gai then said, So is it with this people, and with this nation before me, says the LORD; and so with every work of their hands; and what they offer there is unclean. ¹⁵But now, consider what will come to pass from this day on. Before a stone was placed upon a stone in the LORD's temple, ¹⁶how did you fare?ᵃ When one came to a heap of twenty measures, there were but ten; when one came to the wine vat to draw fifty measures, there were but twenty. ¹⁷I struck you and all the products of your toil with blight and mildew and hail; yet you did not return to me, says the LORD. ¹⁸Consider from this day on, from the twenty-fourth day of the ninth month. Since the day that the foundation of the LORD's temple was laid, consider: ¹⁹Is there any seed left in the barn? Do the vine, the fig tree, the pomegranate, and the olive tree still yield nothing? From this day on I will bless you.

God's Promise to Zerubbabel

20 The word of the LORD came a second time to Hag′gai on the twenty-fourth day of the month: ²¹Speak to Ze•rub′ba•bel, governor of Judah, saying, I am about to shake the heavens and the earth, ²²and to overthrow the throne of kingdoms; I am about to destroy the strength of the kingdoms of the nations, and overthrow the chariots and their riders; and the horses and their riders shall fall, every one by the sword of a comrade. ²³On that day, says the LORD of hosts, I will take you, O Ze•rub′ba•bel my servant, son of She•al′ti•el, says the LORD, and make you like a signet ring; for I have chosen you, says the LORD of hosts.

———

ᵃ Gk: Heb *since they were*

What do you do when life is difficult and things only seem to be getting worse? Some people dream about the future. They imagine a time when all their troubles have ended and life is happy again. If their trouble is caused by certain people, they may imagine how these people eventually pay for their wrongdoing. The Book of Zechariah looks at Israel's future in exactly these two ways.

In-depth

Like the Book of Isaiah, the Book of Zechariah was written by at least two prophets. The original Zechariah—we'll call him First Zechariah—lived around the same time as Haggai, after the exiled Israelites returned to Jerusalem from Babylon (see the timeline at the back of this Bible). Second Zechariah, who may have been one or more prophets, wrote about two hundred years later.

The optimistic message of the first prophet in chapters 1–8 of Zechariah is centered on two concerns: the rebuilding of the Temple and the end of time. First Zechariah saw that a rebuilt Temple was needed to restore the people's unity, identity, and relationship with God. Through a series of visions (see "Apocalyptic Literature," Daniel, chapters 7–10), he announced his message: under the guidance of the priest Joshua and the prince Zerubbabel (a descendant of King David's), Israel would be restored. It would become a nation of justice, faith, love, mercy, and truth where the Lord would dwell. Even the Gentiles (non-Jews) would come from faraway lands to worship God.

Second Zechariah wrote later, when Israel was under Greek domination (see the timeline). He preached not through visions, but through oracles (prophetic speeches) of warning, violence, and also promise. He talked about a great battle that was about to take place between the forces of good and the forces of evil. This was the final war, which would bring an end to the present-day evil and corrupt world. But Second Zechariah also proclaimed the coming of a humble king who would bring peace to all nations. Jerusalem would be purified and would become victorious as the city where God reigns as the highest power for good.

Quick Facts

Period Covered
First Zechariah around 520 B.C., Second Zechariah sometime after 333 B.C.

Authors
the original Zechariah, and an unknown prophet or prophets writing much later

Themes
a command to rebuild the Temple, the message that God will win the final victory

Of Note
The prophecies of Zechariah are quoted in the New Testament as proof that Jesus was the promised Messiah.

The Book of Zechariah

Zechariah

Chap. 11

Israel Urged to Repent

In the eighth month, in the second year of Da·rī'us, the word of the LORD came to the prophet Zech·a·rī'ah son of Ber·e·chī'ah son of Id'dō, saying: 2 The LORD was very angry with your ancestors. 3 Therefore say to them, Thus says the LORD of hosts: Return to me, says the LORD of hosts, and I will return to you, says the LORD of hosts. 4 Do not be like your ancestors, to whom the former prophets proclaimed, "Thus says the LORD of hosts, Return from your evil ways and from your evil deeds." But they did not hear or heed me, says the LORD. 5 Your ancestors, where are they? And the prophets, do they live forever? 6 But my words and my statutes, which I commanded my servants the prophets, did they not overtake your ancestors? So they repented and said, "The LORD of hosts has dealt with us according to our ways and deeds, just as he planned to do."

First Vision: The Horsemen

7 On the twenty-fourth day of the eleventh month, the month of She·bat', in the second year of Da·rī'us, the word of the LORD came to the prophet Zech·a·rī'ah son of Ber·e·chī'ah son of Id'dō; and Zech·a·rī'ah*a* said, 8 In the night I saw a man riding on a red horse! He was standing among the myrtle trees in the glen; and behind him were red, sorrel, and white horses. 9 Then I said, "What are these, my lord?" The angel who talked with me said to me, "I will show you what they are." 10 So the man who was standing among the myrtle trees answered, "They are those whom the LORD has sent to patrol the earth." 11 Then they spoke to the angel of the LORD who was standing among the myrtle trees, "We have patrolled the earth, and lo, the whole earth remains at peace." 12 Then the angel of the LORD said, "O LORD of hosts, how long will you withhold mercy from Jerusalem and the cities of Judah, with which you have been angry these seventy years?" 13 Then the LORD replied with gracious and comforting words to the angel who talked with me. 14 So the angel who talked with me said to me, Proclaim this message: Thus says the LORD of hosts; I am very jealous for Jerusalem and for Zion. 15 And I am extremely angry with the nations that are at ease; for while I was only a little angry, they made the disaster worse. 16 Therefore, thus says the LORD, I have returned to Jerusalem with compassion; my house shall be built in it, says the LORD of hosts, and the measuring line shall be stretched out over Jerusalem. 17 Proclaim further: Thus says the LORD of hosts: My cities shall again overflow with prosperity; the LORD will again comfort Zion and again choose Jerusalem.

a Heb *and he*

1102

NATIVE AMERICAN

Four Winds, Four Directions

To many Native American peoples, the repeated emphasis on the number four in the visions of Zechariah could have a special meaning. In these visions are four horns representing the nations that oppressed Israel (Zech 1.18), four smiths to beat those horns down (verse 20), and four chariots sent out to the four directions of the world (6.1–8).

Native Americans see the number four as special because it is repeated often in nature. There are four compass directions, four chambers of the human heart, four seasons, four phases of human life (child, youth, adult, and elder), and four basic elements (fire, water, rock, and air).

When Native Americans offer a formal prayer, they often do so facing the four directions, each with its own traditional color and emphasis:

- east (yellow), where the sun rises; the direction of light and wisdom
- south (white), where the warmth is; the direction of life
- west (black), where the sun sets; the direction of water and cleansing
- north (red), where the cold is; the direction of strength in hardship

Sometimes, two more directions are added: up, toward Father Sky (blue), and down, toward Mother Earth (green).

▶ Zech 1.18–21

Second Vision: The Horns and the Smiths

18[b] And I looked up and saw four horns. 19 I asked the angel who talked with me, "What are these?" And he answered me, "These are the horns

that have scattered Judah, Israel, and Jerusalem." 20 Then the LORD showed me four blacksmiths. 21 And I asked, "What are they coming to do?" He answered, "These are the horns that scattered Judah, so that no head could be raised; but these have come to terrify them, to strike down the horns of the nations that lifted up their horns against the land of Judah to scatter its people."[c]

Third Vision: The Man with a Measuring Line

[d] I looked up and saw a man with a measuring line in his hand. 2 Then I asked, "Where are you going?" He answered me, "To measure Jerusalem, to see what is its width and what is its length." 3 Then the angel who talked with me came forward, and another angel came forward to meet him, 4 and said to him, "Run, say to that young man: Jerusalem shall be inhabited like villages without walls, because of the multitude of people and animals in it. 5 For I will be a wall of fire all around it, says the LORD, and I will be the glory within it."

Interlude: An Appeal to the Exiles

6 Up, up! Flee from the land of the north, says the LORD; for I have spread you abroad like the four winds of heaven, says the LORD. 7 Up! Escape to Zion, you that live with daughter Babylon. 8 For thus said the LORD of hosts (after his glory[e] sent me) regarding the nations that plundered you: Truly, one who touches you touches the apple of my eye.[f] 9 See now, I am going to raise[g] my hand against them, and they shall become plunder for their own slaves. Then you will know that the LORD of hosts has sent me. 10 Sing and rejoice, O daughter Zion! For lo, I will come and dwell in your midst, says the LORD. 11 Many nations shall join themselves to the LORD on that day, and shall be my people; and I will dwell in your midst. And you shall know that the LORD of hosts has sent me to you. 12 The LORD will inherit Judah as his portion in the holy land, and will again choose Jerusalem.

13 Be silent, all people, before the LORD; for he has roused himself from his holy dwelling.

Fourth Vision: Joshua and Satan

Then he showed me the high priest Joshua standing before the angel of the LORD, and Satan[h] standing at his right hand to accuse him. 2 And the LORD said to Satan,[h] "The LORD rebuke you, O Satan![h] The LORD who has chosen Jerusalem rebuke you! Is not this man a brand plucked from the fire?" 3 Now

b Ch 2.1 in Heb   c Heb *it*   d Ch 2.5 in Heb
e Cn: Heb *after glory he*   f Heb *his eye*   g Or *wave*
h Or *the Accuser*; Heb *the Adversary*

Joshua was dressed with filthy clothes as he stood before the angel. 4 The angel said to those who were standing before him, "Take off his filthy clothes." And to him he said, "See, I have taken your guilt away from you, and I will clothe you with festal apparel." 5 And I said, "Let them put a clean turban on his head." So they put a clean turban on his head and clothed him with the apparel; and the angel of the LORD was standing by.

6 Then the angel of the LORD assured Joshua, saying 7 "Thus says the LORD of hosts: If you will walk in my ways and keep my requirements, then you shall rule my house and have charge of my courts, and I will give you the right of access among those who are standing here. 8 Now listen, Joshua, high priest, you and your colleagues who sit before you! For they are an omen of things to come: I am going to bring my servant the Branch. 9 For on the stone that I have set before Joshua, on a single stone with seven facets, I will engrave its inscription, says the LORD of hosts, and I will remove the guilt of this land in a single day. 10 On that day, says the LORD of hosts, you shall invite each other to come under your vine and fig tree."

Fifth Vision: The Lampstand and Olive Trees

The angel who talked with me came again, and wakened me, as one is wakened from sleep. 2 He said to me, "What do you see?" And I said, "I see a lampstand all of gold, with a bowl on the top of it; there are seven lamps on it, with seven lips on each of the lamps that are on the top of it. 3 And by it there are two olive trees, one on the right of the bowl and the other on its left." 4 I said to the angel who talked with me, "What are these, my lord?" 5 Then the angel who talked with me answered me, "Do you not know what these are?" I said, "No, my lord." 6 He said to me, "This is the word of the LORD to Ze•rub′ba•bel: Not by might, nor by power, but by my spirit, says the LORD of hosts. 7 What are you, O great mountain? Before Ze•rub′ba•bel you shall become a plain; and he shall bring out the top stone amid shouts of 'Grace, grace to it!' "

8 Moreover the word of the LORD came to me, saying, 9 "The hands of Ze•rub′ba•bel have laid the foundation of this house; his hands shall also complete it. Then you will know that the LORD of hosts has sent me to you. 10 For whoever has despised the day of small things shall rejoice, and shall see the plummet in the hand of Ze•rub′ba•bel.

"These seven are the eyes of the LORD, which range through the whole earth." 11 Then I said to him, "What are these two olive trees on the right and the left of the lampstand?" 12 And a second time I said to him, "What are these two branches

of the olive trees, which pour out the oil[i] through the two golden pipes?" 13 He said to me, "Do you not know what these are?" I said, "No, my lord." 14 Then he said, "These are the two anointed ones who stand by the Lord of the whole earth."

Sixth Vision: The Flying Scroll

Again I looked up and saw a flying scroll. 2 And he said to me, "What do you see?" I answered, "I see a flying scroll; its length is twenty cubits, and its width ten cubits." 3 Then he said to me, "This is the curse that goes out over the face of the whole land; for everyone who steals shall be cut off according to the writing on one side, and everyone who swears falsely[j] shall be cut off according to the writing on the other side. 4 I have sent it out, says the LORD of hosts, and it shall enter the house of the thief, and the house of anyone who swears falsely by my name; and it shall abide in that house and consume it, both timber and stones."

Seventh Vision: The Woman in a Basket

5 Then the angel who talked with me came forward and said to me, "Look up and see what this is that is coming out." 6 I said, "What is it?" He said, "This is a basket[k] coming out." And he said, "This is their iniquity[l] in all the land." 7 Then a leaden cover was lifted, and there was a woman sitting in the basket![k] 8 And he said, "This is Wickedness." So he thrust her back into the basket,[k] and pressed the leaden weight down on its mouth. 9 Then I looked up and saw two women coming forward. The wind was in their wings; they had wings like the wings of a stork, and they lifted up the basket[k] between earth and sky. 10 Then I said to the angel who talked with me, "Where are they taking the basket?"[k] 11 He said to me, "To the land of Shi′nar, to build a house for it; and when this is prepared, they will set the basket[k] down there on its base."

Eighth Vision: Four Chariots

And again I looked up and saw four chariots coming out from between two mountains—mountains of bronze. 2 The first chariot had red horses, the second chariot black horses, 3 the third chariot white horses, and the fourth chariot dappled gray[m] horses. 4 Then I said to the angel who talked with me, "What are these, my lord?" 5 The angel answered me, "These are the four winds[n] of heaven going out, after presenting themselves before the Lord of all the earth. 6 The chariot with the black horses goes toward the north country, the white

---

i Cn: Heb *gold*   *j* The word *falsely* added from verse 4
k Heb *ephah*   *l* Gk Compare Syr: Heb *their eye*
m Compare Gk: Meaning of Heb uncertain   *n* Or *spirits*

6.1

ones go toward the west country,*o* and the dappled ones go toward the south country." ⁷When the steeds came out, they were impatient to get off and patrol the earth. And he said, "Go, patrol the earth." So they patrolled the earth. ⁸Then he cried out to me, "Lo, those who go toward the north country have set my spirit at rest in the north country."

The Coronation of the Branch

9 The word of the LORD came to me: ¹⁰Collect silver and gold*p* from the exiles—from Hel'daī, Tō-bī'jah, and Je·daī'ah—who have arrived from Babylon; and go the same day to the house of Jō·sī'ah son of Zeph·a·nī'ah. ¹¹Take the silver and gold and make a crown,*q* and set it on the head of the high priest Joshua son of Je·hoz'a·dak; ¹²say to him: Thus says the LORD of hosts: Here is a man whose name is Branch: for he shall branch out in his place, and he shall build the temple of the LORD. ¹³It is he that shall build the temple of the LORD; he shall bear royal honor, and shall sit upon his throne and rule. There shall be a priest by his throne, with peaceful understanding between the two of them. ¹⁴And the crown*r* shall be in the care of Hel'daī,*s* Tō·bī'jah, Je·daī'ah, and Jō·sī'ah*t* son of Zeph·a·nī'ah, as a memorial in the temple of the LORD.

15 Those who are far off shall come and help to build the temple of the LORD; and you shall know that the LORD of hosts has sent me to you. This will happen if you diligently obey the voice of the LORD your God.

Hypocritical Fasting Condemned

In the fourth year of King Da·rī'us, the word of the LORD came to Zech·a·rī'ah on the fourth day of the ninth month, which is Chis'lev. ²Now the people of Beth'el had sent Sha·rē'zer and Reg'em-mel'ech and their men, to entreat the favor of the LORD, ³and to ask the priests of the house of the LORD of hosts and the prophets, "Should I mourn and practice abstinence in the fifth month, as I have done for so many years?" ⁴Then the word of the LORD of hosts came to me: ⁵Say to all the people of the land and the priests: When you fasted and lamented in the fifth month and in the seventh, for these seventy years, was it for me that you fasted? ⁶And when you eat and when you drink, do you not eat and drink only for yourselves? ⁷Were not these the words that the LORD proclaimed by the former prophets, when Jerusalem was inhabited and in prosperity, along with the towns around it, and when the Neg'eb and the She·phē'lah were inhabited?

Punishment for Rejecting God's Demands

8 The word of the LORD came to Zech·a·rī'ah, saying: ⁹Thus says the LORD of hosts: Render true judgments, show kindness and mercy to one another; ¹⁰do not oppress the widow, the orphan, the alien, or the poor; and do not devise evil in your hearts against one another. ¹¹But they refused to listen, and turned a stubborn shoulder, and stopped their ears in order not to hear. ¹²They made their hearts adamant in order not to hear the law and the words that the LORD of hosts had sent by his spirit through the former prophets. Therefore great wrath came from the LORD of hosts. ¹³Just as, when I*u* called, they would not hear, so, when they called, I would not hear, says the LORD of hosts, ¹⁴and I scattered them with a whirlwind among all the nations that they had not known. Thus the land they left was desolate, so that no one went to and fro, and a pleasant land was made desolate.

God's Promises to Zion

The word of the LORD of hosts came to me, saying: ²Thus says the LORD of hosts: I am jealous for Zion with great jealousy, and I am jealous for her with great wrath. ³Thus says the LORD: I will return to Zion, and will dwell in the midst of Jerusalem; Jerusalem shall be called the faithful city, and the mountain of the LORD of hosts shall be called the

---

o Cn: Heb *go after them*   *p* Cn Compare verse 11: Heb lacks *silver and gold*   *q* Gk Mss Syr Tg: Heb *crowns*
r Gk Syr: Heb *crowns*   *s* Syr Compare verse 10: Heb *Helem*   *t* Syr Compare verse 10: Heb *Hen*   *u* Heb *he*

ZECH

holy mountain. ⁴Thus says the LORD of hosts: Old men and old women shall again sit in the streets of Jerusalem, each with staff in hand because of their great age. ⁵And the streets of the city shall be full of boys and girls playing in its streets. ⁶Thus says the LORD of hosts: Even though it seems impossible to the remnant of this people in these days, should it also seem impossible to me, says the LORD of hosts? ⁷Thus says the LORD of hosts: I will save my people from the east country and from the west country; ⁸and I will bring them to live in Jerusalem. They shall be my people and I will be their God, in faithfulness and in righteousness.

9 Thus says the LORD of hosts: Let your hands be strong—you that have recently been hearing these words from the mouths of the prophets who were present when the foundation was laid for the rebuilding of the temple, the house of the LORD of hosts. ¹⁰For before those days there were no wages for people or for animals, nor was there any safety from the foe for those who went out or came in, and I set them all against one another. ¹¹But now I will not deal with the remnant of this people as in the former days, says the LORD of hosts. ¹²For there shall be a sowing of peace; the vine shall yield its fruit, the ground shall give its produce, and the skies shall give their dew; and I will cause the remnant of this people to possess all these things. ¹³Just as you have been a cursing among the nations, O house of Judah and house of Israel, so I will save you and you shall be a blessing. Do not be afraid, but let your hands be strong.

14 For thus says the LORD of hosts: Just as I purposed to bring disaster upon you, when your ancestors provoked me to wrath, and I did not relent, says the LORD of hosts, ¹⁵so again I have purposed in these days to do good to Jerusalem and to the house of Judah; do not be afraid. ¹⁶These are the things that you shall do: Speak the truth to one another, render in your gates judgments that are true and make for peace, ¹⁷do not devise evil in your hearts against one another, and love no false oath; for all these are things that I hate, says the LORD.

Joyful Fasting

18 The word of the LORD of hosts came to me, saying: ¹⁹Thus says the LORD of hosts: The fast of the fourth month, and the fast of the fifth, and the fast of the seventh, and the fast of the tenth, shall be seasons of joy and gladness, and cheerful festivals for the house of Judah: therefore love truth and peace.

Many Peoples Drawn to Jerusalem

20 Thus says the LORD of hosts: Peoples shall yet come, the inhabitants of many cities; ²¹the inhabitants of one city shall go to another, saying, "Come, let us go to entreat the favor of the LORD, and to seek the LORD of hosts; I myself am going." ²²Many peoples and strong nations shall come to seek the LORD of hosts in Jerusalem, and to entreat the favor of the LORD. ²³Thus says the LORD of hosts: In those days ten men from nations of every language shall take hold of a Jew, grasping his garment and saying, "Let us go with you, for we have heard that God is with you."

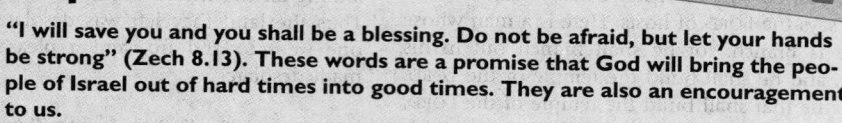

Thumbs Up!   LIVE IT!

"I will save you and you shall be a blessing. Do not be afraid, but let your hands be strong" (Zech 8.13). These words are a promise that God will bring the people of Israel out of hard times into good times. They are also an encouragement to us.

A young woman named Ana was in a car accident in which the driver lost control and three people were killed. Ana was severely hurt and faced months of rehabilitation. Ana, who once hoped to play college softball, now needed to learn to walk and talk again.

Ana knew that for some reason, God spared her life. She knew that it was not going to be easy and would take hard work. She was motivated by her faith and the feeling that God was there helping her. Her attitude and ambition came out every time she was asked how she was doing. She raised her hand and lifted her thumb and said faintly, "Thumbs up."

How might you say, "Thumbs up," when faced with a personal challenge?

▸ Zech 8.9–17

Judgment on Israel's Enemies

An Oracle.

The word of the LORD is against the land of
    Had'rach
    and will rest upon Damascus.
For to the LORD belongs the capital^v of
    Ar'am,^{w}
    as do all the tribes of Israel;
2 Hā'math also, which borders on it,
    Tȳre and Si'don, though they are very
        wise.
3 Tȳre has built itself a rampart,
    and heaped up silver like dust,
    and gold like the dirt of the streets.
4 But now, the Lord will strip it of its
        possessions
    and hurl its wealth into the sea,
    and it shall be devoured by fire.

5 Ash'ke•lon shall see it and be afraid;
    Gā'za too, and shall writhe in anguish;
    Ek'ron also, because its hopes
        are withered.
The king shall perish from Gā'za;
    Ash'ke•lon shall be uninhabited.
6 a mongrel people shall settle in Ash'dod,
    and I will make an end of the pride of
        Phi•lis'ti•a.
7 I will take away its blood from its mouth,
    and its abominations from between its
        teeth;
it too shall be a remnant for our God;
    it shall be like a clan in Judah,
    and Ek'ron shall be like the Jeb'u•sītes.
8 Then I will encamp at my house as a guard,
    so that no one shall march to and fro;
no oppressor shall again overrun them,
    for now I have seen with my own eyes.

The Coming Ruler of God's People
(Mt 21.5; Jn 12.14–15)

9 Rejoice greatly, O daughter Zion!
    Shout aloud, O daughter Jerusalem!
Lo, your king comes to you;
    triumphant and victorious is he,
humble and riding on a donkey,
    on a colt, the foal of a donkey.
10 He^x will cut off the chariot from Ē'phra•im
    and the war-horse from Jerusalem;
and the battle bow shall be cut off,
    and he shall command peace to the
        nations;
his dominion shall be from sea to sea,
    and from the River to the ends of the
        earth.

11 As for you also, because of the blood of my
        covenant with you,
    I will set your prisoners free from the
        waterless pit.
12 Return to your stronghold, O prisoners of
        hope;
    today I declare that I will restore to you
        double.
13 For I have bent Judah as my bow;
    I have made Ē'phra•im its arrow.
I will arouse your sons, O Zion,
    against your sons, O Greece,
    and wield you like a warrior's sword.

14 Then the LORD will appear over them,
    and his arrow go forth like lightning;
the Lord GOD will sound the trumpet
    and march forth in the whirlwinds of the
        south.
15 The LORD of hosts will protect them,
    and they shall devour and tread down
        the slingers;^{y}
they shall drink their blood^z like wine,
    and be full like a bowl,
    drenched like the corners of the altar.

16 On that day the LORD their God will save
        them
    for they are the flock of his people;
for like the jewels of a crown
    they shall shine on his land.
17 For what goodness and beauty are his!
    Grain shall make the young men flourish,
    and new wine the young women.

Restoration of Judah and Israel

Ask rain from the LORD
    in the season of the spring rain,
from the LORD who makes the storm clouds,
    who gives showers of rain to you,^{a}
    the vegetation in the field to everyone.
2 For the teraphim^b utter nonsense,
    and the diviners see lies;
the dreamers tell false dreams,
    and give empty consolation.
Therefore the people wander like sheep;
    they suffer for lack of a shepherd.

3 My anger is hot against the shepherds,
    and I will punish the leaders;^{c}
for the LORD of hosts cares for his flock, the
        house of Judah,

---

v Heb *eye* w Cn: Heb *of Adam* (or *of humankind*)
x Gk: Heb *I* y Cn: Heb *the slingstones* z Gk: Heb *shall
drink* a Heb *them* b Or *household gods* c Or *male
goats*

ZECH

and will make them like his proud
    war-horse.
4 Out of them shall come the cornerstone,
    out of them the tent peg,
out of them the battle bow,
    out of them every commander.
5 Together they shall be like warriors in
    battle,
    trampling the foe in the mud of the
      streets;
they shall fight, for the LORD is with them,
    and they shall put to shame the riders on
      horses.

6 I will strengthen the house of Judah,
    and I will save the house of Joseph.
I will bring them back because I have
      compassion on them,
    and they shall be as though I had not
      rejected them;
for I am the LORD their God and I will
      answer them.
7 Then the people of E′phra•im shall become
      like warriors,
and their hearts shall be glad as with
      wine.
Their children shall see it and rejoice,
    their hearts shall exult in the LORD.

8 I will signal for them and gather them in,
    for I have redeemed them,
    and they shall be as numerous as they
      were before.
9 Though I scattered them among the nations,
    yet in far countries they shall
      remember me,
and they shall rear their children and return.
10 I will bring them home from the land of
      Egypt,
    and gather them from Assyria;
I will bring them to the land of Gil′e•ad and
      to Lebanon,
until there is no room for them.
11 They*d* shall pass through the sea of distress,
    and the waves of the sea shall be struck
      down,
    and all the depths of the Nile dried up.
The pride of Assyria shall be laid low,
    and the scepter of Egypt shall depart.
12 I will make them strong in the LORD,
    and they shall walk in his name,
                says the LORD.

11 Open your doors, O Lebanon,
    so that fire may devour your cedars!
2 Wail, O cypress, for the cedar has fallen,
    for the glorious trees are ruined!

Wail, oaks of Bā′shan,
    for the thick forest has been felled!
3 Listen, the wail of the shepherds,
    for their glory is despoiled!
Listen, the roar of the lions,
    for the thickets of the Jordan
      are destroyed!

Two Kinds of Shepherds

4 Thus said the LORD my God: Be a shepherd of the flock doomed to slaughter. 5 Those who buy them kill them and go unpunished; and those who sell them say, "Blessed be the LORD, for I have become rich"; and their own shepherds have no pity on them. 6 For I will no longer have pity on the inhabitants of the earth, says the LORD. I will cause them, every one, to fall each into the hand of a neighbor, and each into the hand of the king; and they shall devastate the earth, and I will deliver no one from their hand.

7 So, on behalf of the sheep merchants, I became the shepherd of the flock doomed to slaughter. I took two staffs; one I named Favor, the other I named Unity, and I tended the sheep. 8 In one month I disposed of the three shepherds, for I had become impatient with them, and they also detested me. 9 So I said, "I will not be your shepherd. What is to die, let it die; what is to be destroyed, let it be destroyed; and let those that are left devour the flesh of one another!" 10 I took my staff Favor and broke it, annulling the covenant that I had made with all the peoples. 11 So it was annulled on that day, and the sheep merchants, who were watching me, knew that it was the word of the LORD. 12 I then said to them, "If it seems right to you, give me my wages; but if not, keep them." So they weighed out as my wages thirty shekels of silver. 13 Then the LORD said to me, "Throw it into the treasury"*e*—this lordly price at which I was valued by them. So I took the thirty shekels of silver and threw them into the treasury*e* in the house of the LORD. 14 Then I broke my second staff Unity, annulling the family ties between Judah and Israel.

15 Then the LORD said to me: Take once more the implements of a worthless shepherd. 16 For I am now raising up in the land a shepherd who does not care for the perishing, or seek the wandering,*f* or heal the maimed, or nourish the healthy,*g* but devours the flesh of the fat ones, tearing off even their hoofs.

---

d Gk: Heb *He*   *e* Syr: Heb *it to the potter*   *f* Syr Compare Gk Vg: Heb *the youth*   *g* Meaning of Heb uncertain

AFRICAN AMERICAN
The Principle of *Umoja*

Chapter 11 of Zechariah tells several parables that symbolize the breakdown of the Israelites' nation. In one, a shepherd's staff named Unity is broken—symbolizing that the people have lost the unity that bound them together.

Unity is vital to our success as a people. African Americans rely on the Kwanzaa principle of unity, called *umoja* (see "Kwanza as a Way of Life," Deut 10.12–22). It is unity in the family, community, nation, and race. It is the unity that will keep brothers from killing brothers and sisters from killing sisters. It is the unity that will keep families together even when the going gets rough.

Some people say that African Americans are not unified. This is not true. But they are sometimes unified in the wrong areas. People of all cultures can share a negative unity by drinking too much together, getting high together, going to jail for foolishness together, cheating on one another together, and dropping out of school together.

So, let's all just change our negative unity to positive unity. Let's be united in making the honor roll. Let's be united in starting businesses together. Let's be united in protecting one another. Let's be united in respecting and loving one another. Let's be united in stopping the flow of drugs, crime, and violence in our communities. Let's be united in being our best selves. *Umoja* is unity. We've got it; now, let's use it properly!

"How very good and pleasant it is / when kindred live together in unity!" (Ps 133.1).

▸ Zech 11.4–17

17 Oh, my worthless shepherd,
    who deserts the flock!
May the sword strike his arm
    and his right eye!
Let his arm be completely
    withered,
    his right eye utterly blinded!

Jerusalem's Victory

An Oracle.

The word of the LORD concerning Israel: Thus says the LORD, who stretched out the heavens and founded the earth and formed the human spirit within: 2 See, I am about to make Jerusalem a cup of reeling for all the surrounding peoples; it will be against Judah also in the siege against Jerusalem. 3 On that day I will make Jerusalem a heavy stone for all the peoples; all who lift it shall grievously hurt themselves. And all the nations of the earth shall come together against it. 4 On that day, says the LORD, I will strike every horse with panic, and its rider with madness. But on the house of Judah I will keep a watchful eye, when I strike every horse of the peoples with blindness. 5 Then the clans of Judah shall say to themselves, "The inhabitants of Jerusalem have strength through the LORD of hosts, their God."

6 On that day I will make the clans of Judah like a blazing pot on a pile of wood, like a flaming torch among sheaves; and they shall devour to the right and to the left all the surrounding peoples, while Jerusalem shall again be inhabited in its place, in Jerusalem.

7 And the LORD will give victory to the tents of Judah first, that the glory of the house of David and the glory of the inhabitants of Jerusalem may not be exalted over that of Judah. 8 On that day the LORD will shield the inhabitants of Jerusalem so that the feeblest among them on that day shall be like David, and the house of David shall be like God, like the angel of the LORD, at their head. 9 And on that day I will seek to destroy all the nations that come against Jerusalem.

Mourning for the Pierced One

10 And I will pour out a spirit of compassion and supplication on the house of David and the inhabitants of Jerusalem, so that, when they look on the one*h* whom they have pierced, they shall mourn for him, as one mourns for an only child, and weep bitterly over him, as one weeps over a firstborn. 11 On that day the mourning in Jerusalem will be as great as the mourning for Hā′dad-rim′mon in the plain of Me•gid′dō. 12 The land shall mourn, each family by itself; the family of the house of David by itself, and their wives by themselves; the family of the house of Nathan by itself, and their wives by themselves; 13 the family of the house of Levi by itself, and their wives by themselves; the family of the Shim′ē•ites by itself, and their wives by themselves; 14 and all the

---

h Heb *on me*

?did you KNOW?

Prophecies of God's Victory

Zechariah, chapters 12–14, has several of Second Zechariah's prophecies on the final judgment, the restoration of Israel, and the Reign of God. Many of these prophecies were applied to Jesus by the first Christians.

For example: Zechariah foretells a time of mourning for "one whom they have pierced" (Zech 12.10); the Gospel of John applies this verse to Jesus' death on the cross (Jn 19.37). Zechariah says the sheep will be scattered when the shepherd is struck (Zech 13.7); the Gospel of Matthew uses this verse to describe the disciples deserting Jesus (Mt 26.31). And passages from Zechariah's description of the day of the Lord (Zech 14.6–9) show up in the Book of Revelation's description of the new Jerusalem (Rev 11.15; 21.23)

These beautiful prophecies assured Israel's people of God's love and mercy. For Christians, they have additional meaning. They also describe Jesus Christ, whose death was our salvation and whose Resurrection was the promise of the fullness of God's Reign!

▸ Zechariah, chapters 12–14

families that are left, each by itself, and their wives by themselves.

On that day a fountain shall be opened for the house of David and the inhabitants of Jerusalem, to cleanse them from sin and impurity.

Idolatry Cut Off

2 On that day, says the LORD of hosts, I will cut off the names of the idols from the land, so that they shall be remembered no more; and also I will remove from the land the prophets and the unclean spirit. 3 And if any prophets appear again, their fathers and mothers who bore them will say to them, "You shall not live, for you speak lies in the name of the LORD"; and their fathers and their mothers who bore them shall pierce them through

when they prophesy. 4 On that day the prophets will be ashamed, every one, of their visions when they prophesy; they will not put on a hairy mantle in order to deceive, 5 but each of them will say, "I am no prophet, I am a tiller of the soil; for the land has been my possession[i] since my youth." 6 And if anyone asks them, "What are these wounds on your chest?"[j] the answer will be "The wounds I received in the house of my friends."

The Shepherd Struck, the Flock Scattered

7 "Awake, O sword, against my shepherd,
  against the man who is my associate,"
          says the LORD of hosts.
 Strike the shepherd, that the sheep may be
    scattered;
  I will turn my hand against
    the little ones.
8 In the whole land, says the LORD,
  two-thirds shall be cut off and perish,
  and one-third shall be left alive.
9 And I will put this third into the fire,
  refine them as one refines silver,
  and test them as gold is tested.
 They will call on my name,
  and I will answer them.
 I will say, "They are my people";
  and they will say, "The LORD is our God."

Future Warfare and Final Victory
(Cp Ezek 38—39; Mk 13; Rev 20—22)

See, a day is coming for the LORD, when the plunder taken from you will be divided in your midst. 2 For I will gather all the nations against Jerusalem to battle, and the city shall be taken and the houses looted and the women raped; half the city shall go into exile, but the rest of the people shall not be cut off from the city. 3 Then the LORD will go forth and fight against those nations as when he fights on a day of battle. 4 On that day his feet shall stand on the Mount of Olives, which lies before Jerusalem on the east; and the Mount of Olives shall be split in two from east to west by a very wide valley; so that one half of the Mount shall withdraw northward, and the other half southward. 5 And you shall flee by the valley of the LORD's mountain,[k] for the valley between the mountains shall reach to A′zal;[l] and you shall flee as you fled from the earthquake in the days of King Uz·zī′ah of Judah. Then the LORD my God will come, and all the holy ones with him.

---

i Cn: Heb for humankind has caused me to possess
j Heb wounds between your hands   k Heb my mountains
l Meaning of Heb uncertain

6 On that day there shall not be*m* either cold or frost.*n* 7 And there shall be continuous day (it is known to the LORD), not day and not night, for at evening time there shall be light.

8 On that day living waters shall flow out from Jerusalem, half of them to the eastern sea and half of them to the western sea; it shall continue in summer as in winter.

9 And the LORD will become king over all the earth; on that day the LORD will be one and his name one.

10 The whole land shall be turned into a plain from Gë′ba to Rim′mon south of Jerusalem. But Jerusalem shall remain aloft on its site from the Gate of Benjamin to the place of the former gate, to the Corner Gate, and from the Tower of Ha-nan′el to the king's wine presses. 11 And it shall be inhabited, for never again shall it be doomed to destruction; Jerusalem shall abide in security.

12 This shall be the plague with which the LORD will strike all the peoples that wage war against Jerusalem: their flesh shall rot while they are still on their feet; their eyes shall rot in their sockets, and their tongues shall rot in their mouths. 13 On that day a great panic from the LORD shall fall on them, so that each will seize the hand of a neighbor, and the hand of the one will be raised against the hand of the other; 14 even Judah will fight at Jerusalem. And the wealth of all the surrounding nations shall be collected—gold, sil-ver, and garments in great abundance. 15 And a plague like this plague shall fall on the horses, the mules, the camels, the donkeys, and whatever animals may be in those camps.

16 Then all who survive of the nations that have come against Jerusalem shall go up year after year to worship the King, the LORD of hosts, and to keep the festival of booths.*o* 17 If any of the families of the earth do not go up to Jerusalem to worship the King, the LORD of hosts, there will be no rain upon them. 18 And if the family of Egypt do not go up and present themselves, then on them shall*p* come the plague that the LORD inflicts on the nations that do not go up to keep the festival of booths.*o* 19 Such shall be the punishment of Egypt and the punishment of all the nations that do not go up to keep the festival of booths.*o*

20 On that day there shall be inscribed on the bells of the horses, "Holy to the LORD." And the cooking pots in the house of the LORD shall be as holy as*q* the bowls in front of the altar; 21 and every cooking pot in Jerusalem and Judah shall be sacred to the LORD of hosts, so that all who sacrifice may come and use them to boil the flesh of the sacrifice. And there shall no longer be traders*r* in the house of the LORD of hosts on that day.

m Cn: Heb *there shall not be light* Tg: Meaning of Heb uncertain *n* Compare Gk Syr Vg *o* Or *tabernacles*; Heb *succoth* *p* Gk Syr: Heb *shall not* *q* Heb *shall be like* *r* Or *Canaanites*

You promised me!" These three words speak volumes when they're used against us. A promise is a sacred thing, and breaking promises hurts and destroys relationships. The last book of the Old Testament, Malachi, focuses on promises with God that have been broken. At the time of its writing, priests had broken the Covenant by offering inferior sacrifices, and men had broken the Covenant by marrying foreign women and divorcing their Jewish wives. The prophet Malachi predicts that someone is coming who will purify the people, punishing the wicked and rewarding the righteous.

At a Glance

- **1.1—2.9.** a message of God's love for Israel and of the sins of the priests

- **2.10–16.** call for faithfulness in marriage

- **2.17—4.3.** prophecies about God's messenger and God's judgment

- **4.4–6.** God's promise to send the prophet Elijah

In-depth

The author of the Book of Malachi wrote just before the reforms of Ezra and Nehemiah, starting around 458 B.C. (see the timeline at the back of this Bible). The Temple had been rebuilt (see the Books of Haggai and Zechariah), and Temple worship had been restored, but serious violations of the covenantal law existed.

The Book of Malachi addresses two main problems. The first is the failure of Israel's priests to provide good leadership. Through a series of questions and answers, the prophet Malachi speaks harsh words against the priests of the Temple for failing to live up to their calling to honor God. They offer inferior sacrifices on the altar of the Temple, thinking that God won't notice. The prophet compares these priests with their ancestor Levi, who offered only the finest gifts to God. Levi was a good and honest man who kept God's Covenant; these priests are not.

The second problem has to do with marriage and divorce. Evidently, many men are marrying non-Jewish women and divorcing their Jewish wives. It's not clear why they are doing this, but maybe they are trying to climb the social ladder. The prophet challenges the people to be faithful to one another, because their marriages are a reminder of God's Covenant with the people of Judah.

The book ends with a prophecy that forms a bridge to the New Testament and the coming of Jesus. It says that God will send a messenger, the prophet Elijah, before the day of judgment. His job will be to prepare the way for God. Those who repent will enjoy God's blessings; those who do not will be punished by God. New Testament writers associated this prophecy with John the Baptist, who prepared the way for the coming of the Messiah, Jesus of Nazareth.

Quick Facts

Period Covered
around 500 to 450 B.C.

Author
unknown

Theme
calls for priestly reform and faithfulness in marriage

The Book of *Malachi*

Malachi

An oracle. The word of the LORD to Israel by Mal'-a•chī.ᵃ

Israel Preferred to Edom

2 I have loved you, says the LORD. But you say, "How have you loved us?" Is not Esau Jacob's brother? says the LORD. Yet I have loved Jacob ³ but I have hated Esau; I have made his hill country a desolation and his heritage a desert for jackals. ⁴ If Ē'dom says, "We are shattered but we will rebuild the ruins," the LORD of hosts says: They may build, but I will tear down, until they are called the wicked country, the people with whom the LORD is angry forever. ⁵ Your own eyes shall see this, and you shall say, "Great is the LORD beyond the borders of Israel!"

Corruption of the Priesthood

6 A son honors his father, and servants their master. If then I am a father, where is the honor due me? And if I am a master, where is the respect due me? says the LORD of hosts to you, O priests, who despise my name. You say, "How have we despised your name?" ⁷ By offering polluted food on my altar. And you say, "How have we polluted it?"ᵇ By thinking that the LORD's table may be despised. ⁸ When you offer blind animals in sacrifice, is that not wrong? And when you offer those that are lame or sick, is that not wrong? Try presenting that to your governor; will he be pleased with you or show you favor? says the LORD of hosts. ⁹ And now implore the favor of God, that he may be gracious to us. The fault is yours. Will he show favor to any of you? says the LORD of hosts. ¹⁰ Oh, that someone among you would shut the templeᶜ doors, so that you would not kindle fire on my altar in vain! I have no pleasure in you, says the LORD of hosts, and I will not accept an offering from your hands. ¹¹ For from the rising of the sun to its setting my name is great among the nations, and in every place incense is offered to my name, and a pure offering; for my name is great among the nations, says the LORD of hosts. ¹² But you profane it when you say that the Lord's table is polluted, and the food for itᵈ may be despised. ¹³ "What a weariness this is," you say, and you sniff at me,ᵉ says the LORD of hosts. You bring what has been taken by violence or is lame or sick, and this you bring as your offering! Shall I accept that from your hand? says the LORD. ¹⁴ Cursed be the cheat who has a male in the flock and vows to give it, and yet sacrifices to the Lord what is blemished; for I am a great King, says the LORD of hosts, and my name is reverenced among the nations.

ᵃ Or *by my messenger*   ᵇ Gk: Heb *you*   ᶜ Heb lacks *temple*   ᵈ Compare Syr Tg: Heb *its fruit, its food*   ᵉ Another reading is *at it*

M
A
L

And now, O priests, this command is for you. 2 If you will not listen, if you will not lay it to heart to give glory to my name, says the LORD of hosts, then I will send the curse on you and I will curse your blessings; indeed I have already cursed them,f because you do not lay it to heart. 3 I will rebuke your offspring, and spread dung on your faces, the dung of your offerings, and I will put you out of my presence.g

4 Know, then, that I have sent this command to you, that my covenant with Levi may hold, says the LORD of hosts. 5 My covenant with him was a covenant of life and well-being, which I gave him; this called for reverence, and he revered me and stood in awe of my name. 6 True instruction was in his mouth, and no wrong was found on his lips. He walked with me in integrity and uprightness, and he turned many from iniquity. 7 For the lips of a priest should guard knowledge, and people should seek instruction from his mouth, for he is the messenger of the LORD of hosts. 8 But you have turned aside from the way; you have caused many to stumble by your instruction; you have corrupted the covenant of Levi, says the LORD of hosts, 9 and so I make you despised and abased before all the people, inasmuch as you have not kept my ways but have shown partiality in your instruction.

The Covenant Profaned by Judah

10 Have we not all one father? Has not one God created us? Why then are we faithless to one another, profaning the covenant of our ancestors? 11 Judah has been faithless, and abomination has been committed in Israel and in Jerusalem; for Judah has profaned the sanctuary of the LORD, which he loves, and has married the daughter of a foreign god. 12 May the LORD cut off from the tents of Jacob anyone who does this—any to witnessh or answer, or to bring an offering to the LORD of hosts.

13 And this you do as well: You cover the LORD's altar with tears, with weeping and groaning because he no longer regards the offering or accepts it with favor at your hand. 14 You ask, "Why does he not?" Because the LORD was a witness between you and the wife of your youth, to whom you have been faithless, though she is your companion and your wife by covenant. 15 Did not one God make her?i Both flesh and spirit are his.j And what does the one Godk desire? Godly offspring. So look to yourselves, and do not let anyone be faithless to the wife of his youth. 16 For I hatel divorce, says the LORD, the God of Israel, and covering one's garment with violence, says the LORD of hosts. So take heed to yourselves and do not be faithless.

17 You have wearied the LORD with your words. Yet you say, "How have we wearied him?" By saying, "All who do evil are good in the sight of the LORD, and he delights in them." Or by asking, "Where is the God of justice?"

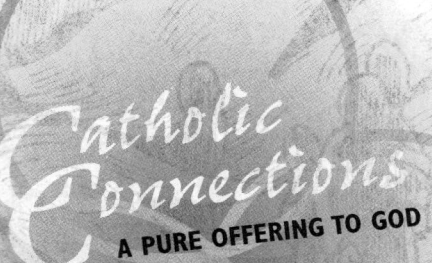

Catholic Connections
A PURE OFFERING TO GOD

The prophecy of a pure offering to God, from the sun's rising to its setting, in Mal 1.11, is a wonderful image. It is unclear what it meant to the writer of Malachi. However, with the spread of Catholicism across the globe, Catholics see this vision becoming reality: at any moment, somewhere in the world, people are celebrating the Mass.

Through the celebration of the Eucharist, Catholics are linked to their sisters and brothers in faith around the globe. At special times, like World Youth Day, this connection becomes a face-to-face reality. Such gatherings remind us of what a powerful experience it can be to gather together around the Lord's table.

▶ Mal 1.1–11

The Coming Messenger

See, I am sending my messenger to prepare the way before me, and the Lord whom you seek will suddenly come to his temple. The messenger of the covenant in whom you delight—indeed, he is coming, says the LORD of hosts. 2 But who can endure the day of his coming, and who can stand when he appears?

For he is like a refiner's fire and like fullers' soap; 3 he will sit as a refiner and purifier of silver, and he will purify the descendants of Levi and refine them like gold and silver, until they present

---

f Heb it   g Cn Compare Gk Syr: Heb and he shall bear you to it   h Cn Compare Gk: Heb arouse   i Or Has he not made one?   j Cn: Heb and a remnant of spirit was his   k Heb he   l Cn: Heb he hates

offerings to the LORD in righteousness.*m* [4] Then the offering of Judah and Jerusalem will be pleasing to the LORD as in the days of old and as in former years.

5 Then I will draw near to you for judgment; I will be swift to bear witness against the sorcerers, against the adulterers, against those who swear falsely, against those who oppress the hired workers in their wages, the widow and the orphan, against those who thrust aside the alien, and do not fear me, says the LORD of hosts.

6 For I the LORD do not change; therefore you, O children of Jacob, have not perished. [7] Ever since the days of your ancestors you have turned aside from my statutes and have not kept them. Return to me, and I will return to you, says the LORD of hosts. But you say, "How shall we return?"

Do Not Rob God

8 Will anyone rob God? Yet you are robbing me! But you say, "How are we robbing you?" In your tithes and offerings! [9] You are cursed with a curse, for you are robbing me—the whole nation of you! [10] Bring the full tithe into the storehouse, so that there may be food in my house, and thus put me to the test, says the LORD of hosts; see if I will not open the windows of heaven for you and pour down for you an overflowing blessing. [11] I will rebuke the locust*n* for you, so that it will not destroy the produce of your soil; and your vine in the field shall not be barren, says the LORD of hosts. [12] Then

all nations will count you happy, for you will be a land of delight, says the LORD of hosts.

13 You have spoken harsh words against me, says the LORD. Yet you say, "How have we spoken against you?" [14] You have said, "It is vain to serve God. What do we profit by keeping his command or by going about as mourners before the LORD of hosts? [15] Now we count the arrogant happy; evildoers not only prosper, but when they put God to the test they escape."

The Reward of the Faithful

16 Then those who revered the LORD spoke with one another. The LORD took note and listened, and a book of remembrance was written before him of those who revered the LORD and thought on his name. [17] They shall be mine, says the LORD of hosts, my special possession on the day when I act, and I will spare them as parents spare their children who serve them. [18] Then once more you shall see the difference between the righteous and the wicked, between one who serves God and one who does not serve him.

The Great Day of the LORD

o See, the day is coming, burning like an oven, when all the arrogant and all evildoers will be stubble; the day that comes shall burn them up, says the LORD of hosts, so that it will leave them

---

m Or *right offerings to the LORD*   *n* Heb *devourer*
o Ch 4.1-6 are Ch 3.19-24 in Heb

Prepare the Way

LIVE IT!

Malachi 3.1–2 talks about the sending of a messenger to prepare for God's coming. That arrival will mark a day of purification, when anything that isn't of value will be burnt away. What does that have to do with you? Take a few moments to reflect on the following dialog:

Prophet. **Prepare the way of the Lord!**

Listener. **Who, me?**

Prophet. **Yes, of course, you!**

Listener. **But that's John the Baptist's job.**

Prophet. ***Was.* That *was* John the Baptist's job. Now, it belongs to you, as a follower of Christ.**

Listener. **So, what do I do? Where do I start?**

Prophet. **Listen to Jesus. Nurture your relationship with God through prayer and the sacraments. Live a happy, holy, and healthy life in order to be a light for others. Share what you believe with others so that they can also find their way. By the way, you are not alone.**

Listener. **You mean there are a lot of us preparing the way?**

Prophet. **That's right.**

Listener. **Well, then, I'm on my way—or rather, we are on God's way.**

▶ **Mal 3.1–7**

neither root nor branch. ²But for you who revere my name the sun of righteousness shall rise, with healing in its wings. You shall go out leaping like calves from the stall. ³And you shall tread down the wicked, for they will be ashes under the soles of your feet, on the day when I act, says the Lord of hosts.

4 Remember the teaching of my servant Moses, the statutes and ordinances that I commanded him at Hō′reb for all Israel.

5 Lo, I will send you the prophet E•li′jah before the great and terrible day of the Lord comes. ⁶He will turn the hearts of parents to their children and the hearts of children to their parents, so that I will not come and strike the land with a curse. ᵖ

ᵖ Or *a ban of utter destruction*

See,
I am
sending
my
messenger...
WHO can endure the **day of his coming?**
3.1–2

THE New Testament

Introduction to the

Gospels

and the Acts of the Apostles

I f you have ever written a research paper for a class project, you know how important it is to have good sources. You want sources that have the most insight into your chosen topic, sources that provide inspiration. The books of the New Testament are those sources for the Christian faith. The Gospels of Matthew, Mark, Luke, and John lay the foundation for understanding the message and the mission of Jesus, the center of the Christian faith. The Acts of the Apostles continues with an inspiring account of how the earliest Christians continued Jesus' mission despite conflicts and persecution. The Good News in these books invites a response from us: to accept Jesus as the promised Messiah, the Son of God, the savior of the world.

In-depth

THE BOOKS OF THE NEW TESTAMENT CONTINUE the Old Testament's revelation of God's saving work in the world. Their focus is on Jesus Christ—the hoped-for Messiah, the savior. Jesus Christ is revealed as God's Son, being both fully human and fully divine. In Jesus, God's promises to Abraham, Moses, and David were fulfilled. In Jesus, a New Covenant is available to all people, not just the Jews. In Jesus lies the forgiveness of sins and a new life of love and freedom for anyone who believes.

The New Testament tells of this Good News through four different types of books: (1) four similar but unique views of Jesus' life and teaching in books called Gospels, (2) stories on how the Apostles spread the Good News of Jesus in the Acts of the Apostles, (3) letters from early Christian leaders to the first Christians and Christian communities, and (4) apocalyptic writings in the Book of Revelation. This introduction is on the four Gospels and the Acts of the Apostles; another introduction will give further background on the letters and Revelation.

The Gospels of Matthew, Mark, Luke, and John tell the story of Jesus from four different perspectives. They are not historical biographies or documentaries like you might read today. They grew out of the teaching and preaching about Jesus in different early Christian communities. They reflect these early Christian communities' beliefs about Jesus, but they do not tell us exactly what Jesus said and did in his life on earth. Inspired by God, the authors of the Gospels arranged the stories to bring out a particular understanding of Jesus that had great importance in their Christian communities.

The Gospels of Matthew, Mark, and Luke are similar in their style and share much of the same content. They are called synoptic (from a Greek word that means "seeing the whole together") Gospels. It is likely that Mark was written first and the authors of Matthew and Luke used Mark as a source in creating their own Gospels (Lk 1.1 mentions other accounts of Jesus). The Gospel of John is quite different from the synoptic Gospels. It was written later than them and is more symbolic in its expression of who Jesus is.

The Acts of the Apostles is a continuation of Luke's Gospel (see Acts 1.1). However, it is not itself a Gospel. It picks up where the Gospel of Luke ends, telling the story of the origins of Christianity after the death and Resurrection of Jesus, covering the period from about A.D. 30 to 64. Although Acts gives us a good deal of information about early church leaders like Peter and Paul, its purpose is not to tell us their biographies. Rather, it gives us an interpretation of the events of the beginnings of Christianity that emphasize God's saving purpose. The Book of Acts explains how Christianity, which began as an offshoot of the Jewish faith, gradually spread beyond Judaism into the Gentile, or non-Jewish, world.

The original Greek word for *gospel* is *euangelion*, which means "big or important news" (sometimes translated as "good news"). The authors of the Gospels wanted to share with others the important news of Jesus Christ. When you read these powerful stories of faith, let God use them to inspire and strengthen your faith in Jesus.

Other Background

- The Gospel of Matthew emphasizes Jesus as the promised Messiah of the Jewish people. Jesus is portrayed as the greatest prophet, teaching the New Law and calling people to be faithful to God.

- The Gospel of Mark was probably the first of the four Gospels to be written. It portrays Jesus as an active healer and miracle worker who accepts loneliness and suffering as the cost of obedience to God's will.

- The Gospel of Luke is a clear, orderly presentation of Jesus' mission to all people, Jews and Gentiles. This Gospel emphasizes Jesus' mercy, compassion, and concern for poor people.

- The Gospel of John was the last Gospel written and seeks to show Jesus as the fully divine Son of God. This Gospel portrays Jesus as noble and powerful, fully in control of his own destiny.

- The Acts of the Apostles was written by the author of the Gospel of Luke. It shows God at work in the growth of the early Christian communities, particularly through the efforts of Peter and Paul.

Does your family have a traditional way of celebrating a holiday? Family traditions are usually handed down from one generation to the next. They give meaning to our special celebrations and help us know where we came from. The author of the Gospel of Matthew presents Jesus as the promised Messiah and highlights Jesus' Jewish origins. The author wanted Jewish-Christian readers to know that believing in Jesus was not a break with their tradition but a continuation of it.

At a Glance

- **1.1—4.17.** the birth of Jesus and the beginning of Jesus' ministry
- **4.18—9.38.** the Sermon on the Mount and miracles in Galilee
- **10.1—12.50.** teaching on mission and rejection
- **13.1—17.27.** parables on the Kingdom of God, the disciples' acknowledging Jesus as the Messiah
- **18.1—20.34.** teaching about community and forgiveness
- **21.1—25.46.** teaching about coming destruction, conflicts with Jewish leaders in Jerusalem
- **26.1—28.20.** Jesus' death and Resurrection

In-depth

The author of Matthew was probably a Christian convert from Judaism in a community of Jewish Christians. This community was feeling the sting of being rejected by other Jews. In defense of the community's belief in Jesus, the Gospel of Matthew links Jesus to important Jewish traditions and gives them new meanings. The Gospel begins with a list of Jesus' Jewish ancestors, connecting Jesus to Abraham, the father of Judaism, and David, Israel's greatest king. Then it makes frequent references to Old Testament laws, prophecies, and events that Jesus fulfills or completes.

The author of Matthew also wanted to show how Jesus broke with certain Jewish beliefs—no doubt to help explain why his community of Jewish Christians was rejected by other Jews. So in the Sermon on the Mount (5.1—7.29), the Gospel has Jesus giving new interpretation to Jewish laws. And Jesus is frequently in conflict with the scribes and Pharisees over things like healing on the Sabbath (12.9–14). Such incidents probably reflect the experience of the author's community with Jewish leaders as much as Jesus' own conflicts.

Gradually, the Gospel of Matthew paints a picture of Jesus as the promised son of David who would reign as king forever. He is the Messiah, the fulfillment of all that the Jewish people have been waiting for, the one who will bring their liberation and salvation. This good news should be proclaimed to Jews and non-Jews alike. And so the Gospel ends with the risen Jesus telling his disciples, "Go therefore and make disciples of all nations" (28.19).

Quick Facts

Author
unknown; traditionally associated with the Apostle Matthew

Date Written
approximately A.D. 85

Audience
Christian Jews

Image of Jesus
the greatest prophet, who brings the New Law

Matthew

The Genealogy of Jesus the Messiah
(Ruth 4.18–22; 1 Chr 2.1–15; Lk 3.23–38)

An account of the genealogy*a* of Jesus the Messiah,*b* the son of David, the son of Abraham.

2 Abraham was the father of Isaac, and Isaac the father of Jacob, and Jacob the father of Judah and his brothers, 3 and Judah the father of Per′ez and Zē′rah by Tā′mar, and Per′ez the father of Hez′ron, and Hez′ron the father of Ar′am, 4 and Ar′am the father of A•min′a•dab, and A•min′a•dab the father of Nah′shon, and Nah′shon the father of Sal′mon, 5 and Sal′mon the father of Bō′az by Rā′hab, and Bō′az the father of O′bed by Ruth, and O′bed the father of Jesse, 6 and Jesse the father of King David.

And David was the father of Solomon by the wife of Ū•rī′ah, 7 and Solomon the father of Rē•ho•bō′am, and Rē•ho•bō′am the father of A•bī′jah, and A•bī′jah the father of Ā′saph,*c* 8 and Ā′saph*c* the father of Je•hosh′a•phat, and Je•hosh′a•phat the father of Jō′ram, and Jō′ram the father of Uz•zī′ah, 9 and Uz•zī′ah the father of Jō′tham, and Jō′tham the father of Ā′haz, and Ā′haz the father of Hez•e•kī′ah, 10 and Hez•e•kī′ah the father of Ma•nas′seh, and Ma•nas′seh the father of Ā′mos,*d* and Ā′mos*d* the father of Jō•sī′ah, 11 and Jō•sī′ah the father of Jech•o•nī′ah and his brothers, at the time of the deportation to Babylon.

12 And after the deportation to Babylon: Jech•o•nī′ah was the father of Sa•lā′thi•el, and Sa•lā′thi•el the father of Ze•rub′ba•bel, 13 and Ze•rub′ba•bel the father of A•bī′ud, and A•bī′ud the father of E•lī′a•kim, and E•lī′a•kim the father of Ā′zor, 14 and Ā′zor the father of Zā′dok, and Zā′dok the father of Ā′chim, and Ā′chim the father of E•lī′ud, 15 and E•lī′ud the father of El•e•ā′zar, and El•e•ā′zar the father of Mat′than, and Mat′than the father of Jacob, 16 and Jacob the father of Joseph the husband of Mary, of whom Jesus was born, who is called the Messiah.*e*

17 So all the generations from Abraham to David are fourteen generations; and from David to the deportation to Babylon, fourteen generations; and from the deportation to Babylon to the Messiah,*e* fourteen generations.

The Birth of Jesus the Messiah
(Lk 2.1–7)

18 Now the birth of Jesus the Messiah*b* took place in this way. When his mother Mary had been engaged to Joseph, but before they lived together, she was found to be with child from the Holy Spirit. 19 Her husband Joseph, being a righteous man and unwilling to expose her to public disgrace, planned to dismiss her quietly. 20 But just when he had resolved to do this, an angel of the Lord appeared to him in a dream and said, "Joseph, son of David, do not be afraid to take Mary as your wife, for the child conceived in her is from

a Or *birth* *b* Or *Jesus Christ* *c* Other ancient authorities read *Asa* *d* Other ancient authorities read *Amon* *e* Or *the Christ*

?did you KNOW?

Jesus' Family Tree

In the first two chapters of Matthew, the author begins to reveal the unique focus of the Gospel. He starts by tracing Jesus' family tree, making his case that Jesus was the Messiah who would restore the Covenant promised to Abraham, the father of the Jewish people. He also traces Jesus' ancestry back to David to show that Jesus is the fulfillment of the promises made to David (2 Samuel, chapter 7).

Things get even more interesting with a closer look at all the people mentioned in the list. There is a wide assortment of groups and social classes: patriarchs and slaves, kings and peasants, men and women, Jews and non-Jews. Matthew is planting the seed that Jesus has come for the salvation of all people.

▶ Mt 1.1–17

the Holy Spirit. 21 She will bear a son, and you are to name him Jesus, for he will save his people from their sins." 22 All this took place to fulfill what had been spoken by the Lord through the prophet:
23 "Look, the virgin shall conceive and bear
    a son,
    and they shall name him Em•man′u•el,"
which means, "God is with us." 24 When Joseph awoke from sleep, he did as the angel of the Lord commanded him; he took her as his wife, 25 but had no marital relations with her until she had borne a son;ᶠ and he named him Jesus.

The Visit of the Wise Men

In the time of King Her′od, after Jesus was born in Bethlehem of Judea, wise menᵍ from the East came to Jerusalem, 2 asking, "Where is the child who has been born king of the Jews? For we observed his star at its rising,ʰ and have come to pay him homage." 3 When King Her′od heard this, he was frightened, and all Jerusalem with him; 4 and calling together all the chief priests and scribes of the people, he inquired of them where the Messiahⁱ was to be born. 5 They told him, "In Bethlehem of Judea; for so it has been written by the prophet:
6 'And you, Bethlehem, in the land of Judah,
    are by no means least among the rulers
        of Judah;
    for from you shall come a ruler
        who is to shepherdʲ my people Israel.' "

---

f Other ancient authorities read *her firstborn son*
g Or *astrologers*; Gk *magi*   h Or *in the East*   i Or *the Christ*   j Or *rule*

JESUS BROUGHT THE GOOD NEWS OF SALVATION TO PEOPLE OF ALL RACES!

The Wise Men from another culture, who came to offer Jesus gifts for a royal messiah, symbolize that Jesus came as the savior of all races and cultures. Matthew 2.1–12 is the biblical basis for the religious feast day of Epiphany, which officially is 6 January but is celebrated on the first Sunday after the New Year.

In some Latin American traditions, children receive gifts on Epiphany, in remembrance of the gifts the Wise Men offered to Jesus. The evening before, at parties celebrated in homes and offices, a special bread is shared that has a figure of the baby Jesus baked inside of it. Whoever finds the figure of the baby Jesus in their piece of bread has to sponsor a party to celebrate Jesus' presentation in the Temple (Lk 2.22–24). This feast closes the Christmas season on 2 February.
■ How do you accept and celebrate people of different cultures?
■ Think of spiritual gifts that you have received from other people. Express your gratitude to God for those gifts.

▶ Mt 2.1–12

place where the child was. 10 When they saw that the star had stopped,m they were overwhelmed with joy. 11 On entering the house, they saw the child with Mary his mother; and they knelt down and paid him homage. Then, opening their treasure chests, they offered him gifts of gold, frankincense, and myrrh. 12 And having been warned in a dream not to return to Her'od, they left for their own country by another road.

The Escape to Egypt

13 Now after they had left, an angel of the Lord appeared to Joseph in a dream and said, "Get up, take the child and his mother, and flee to Egypt, and remain there until I tell you; for Her'od is about to search for the child, to destroy him." 14 Then Josephn got up, took the child and his mother by night, and went to Egypt, 15 and remained there until the death of Her'od. This was to fulfill what had been spoken by the Lord through the prophet, "Out of Egypt I have called my son."

The Massacre of the Infants

16 When Her'od saw that he had been tricked by the wise men,k he was infuriated, and he sent and killed all the children in and around Bethlehem who were two years old or under, according to the time that he had learned from the wise

7 Then Her'od secretly called for the wise menk and learned from them the exact time when the star had appeared. 8 Then he sent them to Bethlehem, saying, "Go and search diligently for the child; and when you have found him, bring me word so that I may also go and pay him homage." 9 When they had heard the king, they set out; and there, ahead of them, went the star that they had seen at its rising,l until it stopped over the

k Or astrologers; Gk magi   l Or in the East   m Gk saw the star   n Gk he

JESUS' FAMILY LIVES AS IMMIGRANTS!

Following an angel's order and facing the massacre of all boys under two years old, Joseph takes Mary and Jesus to Egypt to protect them from Herod's threats. They become immigrants to avoid persecution.

Every year, millions of people in the world become immigrants, fleeing their countries because of hunger, poverty, or persecution. Often, they find themselves unwelcomed strangers, not able to communicate in the language of their new land and even persecuted by its inhabitants. But Christians should have a special compassion for immigrants because Jesus told us to love everyone, especially those who suffer.

■ Imagine Jesus, Mary, and Joseph exiled in this country. How would you treat them?
■ What is your attitude toward refugees and immigrants in our country?
■ Ask God to bless legislators with the love and wisdom to welcome immigrants, and to give your generation a courageous heart to seek justice and peace in the world.

▶ Mt 2.13

The Slaughter of the Innocents

The event described in Mt 2.16–18 is often called the Slaughter of the Innocents. In many circumstances in history, innocent people, including infants and young children, have been massacred in the name of war or convenience (see "Rachel Weeps," Jer 31.15–17).

Today, abortion is one of those circumstances. To many people, it seems to be a simple solution to the inconvenience of an unwanted pregnancy. But what of the innocent lives that are destroyed? With abortion, "they are no more" (Mt 2.18). Our church teaching is clear: All human life is sacred, and abortion is wrong. How might we as individuals or communities support pregnant women to ensure they do not choose abortion?

▶ Mt 2.16–18

did you KNOW?

Pharisees, Sadducees, and Scribes

In Jesus' day, several groups of Jews held positions of status or leadership. The *Pharisees* were devoted laymen who believed that salvation was achieved by rigorously following the Jewish Law. People looked up to them for guidance about how they should live as good Jews. The *Sadducees* were associated with the Temple and the ruling class. They did not believe in life after death. They did believe that wealth was a sign of being blessed by God. The *scribes* were skilled at reading and writing, and performed those services for the majority of the population, who were unable to read and write for themselves. Scribes probably were involved in writing some of the Old Testament books.

The negative reaction of John the Baptist to the Pharisees and Sadducees is typical in Matthew. But in general, Pharisees, Sadducees, and scribes were respected leaders during Jesus' time. The persecution later experienced by the community in which the author of Matthew lived probably affected his portrayal of them. (See "Jewish Sects," near the end of 2 Maccabees, for more information on these groups.)

▶ Mt 3.7

men.*o* [17] Then was fulfilled what had been spoken through the prophet Jer•e•mī′ah:

18 "A voice was heard in Rā′mah,
  wailing and loud lamentation,
Rachel weeping for her children;
  she refused to be consoled, because they
    are no more."

The Return from Egypt
(Lk 2.39)

19 When Her′od died, an angel of the Lord suddenly appeared in a dream to Joseph in Egypt and said, 20 "Get up, take the child and his mother, and go to the land of Israel, for those who were seeking the child's life are dead." 21 Then Joseph*p* got up, took the child and his mother, and went to the land of Israel. 22 But when he heard that Ar•che•lā′us was ruling over Judea in place of his father Her′od, he was afraid to go there. And after being warned in a dream, he went away to the district of Galilee. 23 There he made his home in a town called Nazareth, so that what had been spoken through the prophets might be fulfilled, "He will be called a Naz•o•rē′an."

The Proclamation of John the Baptist
(Mk 1.2–8; Lk 3.1–20)

In those days John the Baptist appeared in the wilderness of Judea, proclaiming, 2 "Repent, for the kingdom of heaven has come near."*q* 3 This is the one of whom the prophet Ī•sāi′ah spoke when he said,

"The voice of one crying out in
  the wilderness:
'Prepare the way of the Lord,
  make his paths straight.' "

4 Now John wore clothing of camel's hair with a leather belt around his waist, and his food was

---

o Or *astrologers*; Gk *magi*   *p* Gk *he*   *q* Or *is at hand*

locusts and wild honey. 5 Then the people of Jerusalem and all Judea were going out to him, and all the region along the Jordan, 6 and they were baptized by him in the river Jordan, confessing their sins.

7 But when he saw many Phar'i•sees and Sad'du•cees coming for baptism, he said to them, "You brood of vipers! Who warned you to flee from the wrath to come? 8 Bear fruit worthy of repentance. 9 Do not presume to say to yourselves, 'We have Abraham as our ancestor'; for I tell you, God is able from these stones to raise up children to Abraham. 10 Even now the ax is lying at the root of the trees; every tree therefore that does not bear good fruit is cut down and thrown into the fire.

11 "I baptize you with*r* water for repentance, but one who is more powerful than I is coming after me; I am not worthy to carry his sandals. He will baptize you with*r* the Holy Spirit and fire. 12 His winnowing fork is in his hand, and he will clear his threshing floor and will gather his wheat into the granary; but the chaff he will burn with unquenchable fire."

The Baptism of Jesus
(Mk 1.9–11; Lk 3.21–22; Jn 1.29–34)

13 Then Jesus came from Galilee to John at the Jordan, to be baptized by him. 14 John would have prevented him, saying, "I need to be baptized by you, and do you come to me?" 15 But Jesus answered him, "Let it be so now; for it is proper for us in this way to fulfill all righteousness." Then he consented. 16 And when Jesus had been baptized, just as he came up from the water, suddenly the heavens were opened to him and he saw the Spirit of God descending like a dove and alighting on him. 17 And a voice from heaven said, "This is my Son, the Beloved,*s* with whom I am well pleased."

The Temptation of Jesus
(Mk 1.12–13; Lk 4.1–13)

Then Jesus was led up by the Spirit into the wilderness to be tempted by the devil. 2 He fasted forty days and forty nights, and afterwards he was famished. 3 The tempter came and said to him, "If you are the Son of God, command these stones to become loaves of bread." 4 But he answered, "It is written,

'One does not live by bread alone,
but by every word that comes from the
mouth of God.' "

5 Then the devil took him to the holy city and placed him on the pinnacle of the temple, 6 saying

Catholic Connections

BAPTISM

John the Baptist was the last great prophet before Jesus. John may have belonged to a religious group that initiated new members through a rite of immersion in water (baptism). The rite used by John symbolized the moral conversion—through repentance, confession of sins, and change of heart—required for receiving God's salvation. Although Jesus was without sin, his willingness to be baptized is a sign of how fully he embraced his humanity.

Baptism is also one of the seven sacraments that Catholics celebrate. Although many Catholics are baptized as infants, some young people and adults, called catechumens, are baptized at the Easter Vigil on Holy Saturday each year. During the Baptism ritual, the baptized person is marked with chrism, a special oil. (In the Old Testament, such an oil was used to anoint priests, prophets, and kings for service.) The person then has water poured over her or him or is immersed in water. This is a sign of dying to sin and rising anew in the presence of God. The Holy Trinity is called upon, baptizing her or him in the name of the Father, the Son, and the Holy Spirit. A candle is given to the newly baptized person to symbolize the light of Christ that now burns within her or him, and a white garment or stole is put on the person to signify her or his new life in Christ.

The sacraments of Baptism, Confirmation, and the Eucharist are a person's initiation into the Christian community. They ca[ll] Christians to continual conversion in follow[ing] Jesus.

▶ Mt 3.13–17

to him, "If you are the Son of God, throw yourself down; for it is written,

---

r Or *in*   *s* Or *my beloved Son*

PRAY IT!

Jesus' Temptations, My Temptations

Command these stones to become loaves of bread." (Mt 4.3)

Jesus, you trusted God to provide your material needs. Help me to avoid placing my priorities on material things.

"Throw yourself down; for it is written, . . .
'you will not dash your foot against a stone.'"

(Verse 6)

Jesus, you resisted using your power for vain and foolish reasons. Help me to resist doing foolish things only to impress others.

"All these I will give you, if you will fall down and worship me." (Verse 9)

Jesus, you refused to cooperate with the devil to achieve status and power. Help me to refuse to cooperate with evil and injustice in achieving my life's goals.

▸ Mt 4.1–11

'He will command his angels
concerning you,'
and 'On their hands they will bear
you up,
so that you will not dash your foot against a
stone.' "

7 Jesus said to him, "Again it is written, 'Do not put the Lord your God to the test.' "

8 Again, the devil took him to a very high mountain and showed him all the kingdoms of the world and their splendor; 9 and he said to him, "All these I will give you, if you will fall down and worship me." 10 Jesus said to him, "Away with you, Satan! for it is written,

'Worship the Lord your God,
and serve only him.' "

11 Then the devil left him, and suddenly angels came and waited on him.

Jesus Begins His Ministry in Galilee
(Mk 1.14–15; Lk 4.14–15)

12 Now when Jesus[s] heard that John had been arrested, he withdrew to Galilee. 13 He left Naza-

reth and made his home in Ca·per'na·um by the sea, in the territory of Zeb'ū·lun and Naph'ta·lī, 14 so that what had been spoken through the prophet I·sāi'ah might be fulfilled:

15 "Land of Zeb'ū·lun, land of Naph'ta·lī,
on the road by the sea, across the Jordan,
Galilee of the Gentiles—
16 the people who sat in darkness
have seen a great light,
and for those who sat in the region and
shadow of death
light has dawned."

17 From that time Jesus began to proclaim, "Repent, for the kingdom of heaven has come near."[t]

Jesus Calls the First Disciples
(Mk 1.16–20; Lk 5.1–11)

18 As he walked by the Sea of Galilee, he saw two brothers, Simon, who is called Peter, and Andrew his brother, casting a net into the sea—for they were fishermen. 19 And he said to them, "Follow me, and I will make you fish for people." 20 Immediately they left their nets and followed him. 21 As he went from there, he saw two other brothers, James son of Zeb'e·dee and his brother John, in the boat with their father Zeb'e·dee, mending their nets, and he called them. 22 Immediately they left the boat and their father, and followed him.

Follow Me

As the first disciples chose to follow Jesus, what did they leave behind? Nets, boats, even parents. The very things they depended on for life and security! Knowing what you know of Jesus, what are you ready to "leave behind" in order to follow him and continue his mission?

▸ Mt 4.18–22

Jesus Ministers to Crowds of People
(Mk 1.35–39; Lk 4.44; 6.17–19)

23 Jesus[u] went throughout Galilee, teaching in their synagogues and proclaiming the good news[v] of the kingdom and curing every disease and every sickness among the people. 24 So his fame spread throughout all Syria, and they brought to him all the sick, those who were afflicted with various diseases and pains, demoniacs, epileptics, and paralytics, and he cured them. 25 And great crowds

---

s Gk he   t Or is at hand   u Gk He   v Gk gospel

followed him from Galilee, the De•cap'o•lis, Jerusalem, Judea, and from beyond the Jordan.

The Sermon on the Mount

When Jesus[w] saw the crowds, he went up the mountain; and after he sat down, his disciples came to him. 2 Then he began to speak, and taught them, saying:

The Beatitudes
(Lk 6.20–26)

3 "Blessed are the poor in spirit, for theirs is the kingdom of heaven.

4 "Blessed are those who mourn, for they will be comforted.

5 "Blessed are the meek, for they will inherit the earth.

6 "Blessed are those who hunger and thirst for righteousness, for they will be filled.

7 "Blessed are the merciful, for they will receive mercy.

8 "Blessed are the pure in heart, for they will see God.

9 "Blessed are the peacemakers, for they will be called children of God.

10 "Blessed are those who are persecuted for righteousness' sake, for theirs is the kingdom of heaven.

11 "Blessed are you when people revile you and persecute you and utter all kinds of evil against you falsely[x] on my account. 12 Rejoice and be glad, for your reward is great in heaven, for in the same way they persecuted the prophets who were before you.

Salt and Light
(Mk 9.50; Lk 14.34–35)

13 "You are the salt of the earth; but if salt has lost its taste, how can its saltiness be restored? It is no longer good for anything, but is thrown out and trampled under foot.

14 "You are the light of the world. A city built on a hill cannot be hid. 15 No one after lighting a lamp puts it under the bushel basket, but on the lampstand, and it gives light to all in the house. 16 In the same way, let your light shine before others, so that they may see your good works and give glory to your Father in heaven.

The Law and the Prophets

17 "Do not think that I have come to abolish the law or the prophets; I have come not to abolish but to fulfill. 18 For truly I tell you, until heaven and earth pass away, not one letter,[y] not one stroke of a letter, will pass from the law until all is accomplished. 19 Therefore, whoever breaks[z] one of the least of these commandments, and teaches others to do the same, will be called least in the kingdom of heaven; but whoever does them and teaches them will be called great in the kingdom of heaven. 20 For I tell you, unless your righteousness exceeds that of the scribes and Phar'i•sees, you will never enter the kingdom of heaven.

Concerning Anger
(Lk 12.57–59)

21 "You have heard that it was said to those of ancient times, 'You shall not murder'; and 'whoever murders shall be liable to judgment.' 22 But I say to you that if you are angry with a brother or sister,[a] you will be liable to judgment; and if you insult[b] a brother or sister,[c] you will be liable to the council; and if you say, 'You fool,' you will be

---

w Gk *he*   x Other ancient authorities lack *falsely*
y Gk *one iota*   z Or *annuls*   a Gk *a brother*; other ancient authorities add *without cause*   b Gk *say Raca to* (an obscure term of abuse)   c Gk *a brother*

LIVE IT!

An Upside-Down Kingdom

Read Mt 5.1–12. These familiar words of Jesus, called the Beatitudes, begin what is called the Sermon on the Mount. In chapters 5–7, Jesus speaks about life in a way that startled his listeners. Many thought it was a sign of God's blessing to be rich, powerful, and content. They thought it was justified to respond to violence and oppression with violence and oppression.

Jesus' words continue to challenge us today. Pay attention to these hard words of Jesus. Christianity is not always easy, but it is the only way for all people to live as sons and daughters of God. The challenge for us is to see life more and more the way God does, and then to live that vision!

▸ Mt 5.1–12

liable to the hell[d] of fire. 23 So when you are offering your gift at the altar, if you remember that your brother or sister[e] has something against you, 24 leave your gift there before the altar and go; first be reconciled to your brother or sister,[e] and then come and offer your gift. 25 Come to terms quickly with your accuser while you are on the way to court[f] with him, or your accuser may hand you over to the judge, and the judge to the guard, and you will be thrown into prison. 26 Truly I tell you, you will never get out until you have paid the last penny.

Concerning Adultery

27 "You have heard that it was said, 'You shall not commit adultery.' 28 But I say to you that everyone who looks at a woman with lust has already committed adultery with her in his heart. 29 If your right eye causes you to sin, tear it out and throw it away; it is better for you to lose one of your members than for your whole body to be thrown into hell.[d] 30 And if your right hand causes you to sin, cut it off and throw it away; it is better for you to lose one of your members than for your whole body to go into hell.[d]

Concerning Divorce
(Mt 19.9; Mk 10.11–12; Lk 16.18)

31 "It was also said, 'Whoever divorces his wife, let him give her a certificate of divorce.' 32 But I say to you that anyone who divorces his wife, except on the ground of unchastity, causes her to commit adultery; and whoever marries a divorced woman commits adultery.

Concerning Oaths

33 "Again, you have heard that it was said to those of ancient times, 'You shall not swear falsely, but carry out the vows you have made to the Lord.' 34 But I say to you, Do not swear at all, either by heaven, for it is the throne of God, 35 or by the earth, for it is his footstool, or by Jerusalem, for it is the city of the great King. 36 And do not swear by your head, for you cannot make one hair white or black. 37 Let your word be 'Yes, Yes' or 'No, No'; anything more than this comes from the evil one.[g]

Concerning Retaliation
(Lk 6.29–31)

38 "You have heard that it was said, 'An eye for an eye and a tooth for a tooth.' 39 But I say to you, Do not resist an evildoer. But if anyone strikes you on the right cheek, turn the other also; 40 and if anyone wants to sue you and take your coat, give your cloak as well; 41 and if anyone forces you to go one mile, go also the second mile. 42 Give to everyone who begs from you, and do not refuse anyone who wants to borrow from you.

PRAY IT
Christians and Revenge

For Jesus, one way to love our enemies is to refuse to take revenge on those who have wronged us. Is this really possible to do?

Consider the case of a young woman named Julie Welch who was killed by a terrorist bombing in Oklahoma City. Julie's father worked unceasingly against the death penalty for the man responsible for the bombing. He knew that revenge would not bring his daughter back or make him feel better. He believed that Christians are obligated to always assume that for even the most heinous criminal, reconciliation and remorse are possible. Although his stance was not easy or popular, it illustrates what this passage teaches.

In your prayer, reflect or journal on the following questions:
- Who are your enemies?
- When they or someone else hurts you, what is your usual reaction?
- What is the greatest challenge for you in living out this teaching from Jesus?

▶ Mt 5.38–48

Love for Enemies
(Lk 6.27–28, 32–36)

43 "You have heard that it was said, 'You shall love your neighbor and hate your enemy.' 44 But I say to you, Love your enemies and pray for those who persecute you, 45 so that you may be children of your Father in heaven; for he makes his sun rise on the evil and on the good, and sends rain on the righteous and on the unrighteous. 46 For if you love those who love you, what reward do you have? Do not even the tax collectors do the same? 47 And if you greet only your brothers and sisters,[h]

---

d Gk Gehenna   e Gk your brother   f Gk lacks to court
g Or evil   h Gk your brothers

what more are you doing than others? Do not even the Gentiles do the same? 48 Be perfect, therefore, as your heavenly Father is perfect.

Concerning Almsgiving

"Beware of practicing your piety before others in order to be seen by them; for then you have no reward from your Father in heaven.

2 "So whenever you give alms, do not sound a trumpet before you, as the hypocrites do in the synagogues and in the streets, so that they may be praised by others. Truly I tell you, they have received their reward. 3 But when you give alms, do not let your left hand know what your right hand is doing, 4 so that your alms may be done in secret; and your Father who sees in secret will reward you.[i]

PRAY IT!
Ash Wednesday

Matthew 6.1–18 is read on Ash Wednesday, the beginning of Lent. Lent is traditionally a forty-day period to examine and renew our spiritual life. It is a time of prayer, service, and fasting. The forty days recall the forty years that the people of Israel wandered in the wilderness before arriving at the Promised Land and the forty days that Jesus spent in the wilderness after being baptized.

On Ash Wednesday, we receive ashes that remind us of our nature as created beings (Gen 3.19)—a tradition started by the first Christian communities to foster repentance for sins and the desire to follow Christ faithfully. As the ash cross is made on our forehead, we hear words that echo John the Baptist's call to conversion, "Turn away from sin and be faithful to the gospel" (*The Sacramentary,* p. 77). We respond "Amen," meaning "So be it."

When Lent begins again, how will you use the forty days to strengthen your spiritual life? Make a special commitment and ask God for the grace to grow from it.

▶ Mt 6.1–18

Concerning Prayer
(Lk 11.2–4)

5 "And whenever you pray, do not be like the hypocrites; for they love to stand and pray in the synagogues and at the street corners, so that they may be seen by others. Truly I tell you, they have received their reward. 6 But whenever you pray, go into your room and shut the door and pray to your Father who is in secret; and your Father who sees in secret will reward you.[i]

7 "When you are praying, do not heap up empty phrases as the Gentiles do; for they think that they will be heard because of their many words. 8 Do not be like them, for your Father knows what you need before you ask him.

9 "Pray then in this way:

Our Father in heaven,
    hallowed be your name.
10   Your kingdom come.
    Your will be done,
        on earth as it is in heaven.
11   Give us this day our daily bread.[j]
12   And forgive us our debts,
        as we also have forgiven our debtors.
13   And do not bring us to the time of trial,[k]
        but rescue us from the evil one.[l]

14 For if you forgive others their trespasses, your heavenly Father will also forgive you; 15 but if you do not forgive others, neither will your Father forgive your trespasses.

Concerning Fasting

16 "And whenever you fast, do not look dismal, like the hypocrites, for they disfigure their faces so as to show others that they are fasting. Truly I tell you, they have received their reward. 17 But when you fast, put oil on your head and wash your face, 18 so that your fasting may be seen not by others but by your Father who is in secret; and your Father who sees in secret will reward you.[i]

Concerning Treasures
(Lk 12.33–34)

19 "Do not store up for yourselves treasures on earth, where moth and rust[m] consume and where thieves break in and steal; 20 but store up for yourselves treasures in heaven, where neither moth nor rust[m] consumes and where thieves do not break in and steal. 21 For where your treasure is, there your heart will be also.

---

i Other ancient authorities add *openly*   j Or *our bread for tomorrow*   k Or *us into temptation*   l Or *from evil.* Other ancient authorities add, in some form, *For the kingdom and the power and the glory are yours forever. Amen.*
m Gk *eating*

PRAY IT!

A Lord's Prayer Reflection

In Matthew, Jesus teaches his followers the Lord's Prayer as an alternative to hypocritical and empty prayer. Most of us have memorized the Lord's Prayer. But although we know it by heart, we do not always pray it from the heart. It can easily become "empty phrases" (6.7). Let this reflection help you to pray the Lord's Prayer thoughtfully:

Our Father in heaven,
hallowed be your name.

(Verse 9)

How do I honor God as creator of all things? How do I honor God in my thoughts, my words, and my actions?

Your kingdom come.
Your will be done,
on earth as it is in heaven.

(Verse 10)

How does my life reflect God's reign of love, justice, and peace? Am I putting too much emphasis on the material things I have?

Give us this day our daily bread.

(Verse 11)

Can I trust God to provide for my daily physical, emotional, and spiritual needs?

And forgive us our debts,
as we also have forgiven our debtors.

(Verse 12)

When I have sinned, do I admit my wrong, ask God's forgiveness, and start anew? When someone has wronged me, do I hold a grudge? Am I able to forgive them as God forgives me?

And do not bring us to the time of trial,
but rescue us from the evil one.

(Verse 13)

What are the temptations I face in life? How do I rely on God for the strength to resist them?

▶ Mt 6.5–15

The Sound Eye
(Lk 11.34–36)

22 "The eye is the lamp of the body. So, if your eye is healthy, your whole body will be full of light; 23 but if your eye is unhealthy, your whole body will be full of darkness. If then the light in you is darkness, how great is the darkness!

Serving Two Masters

24 "No one can serve two masters; for a slave will either hate the one and love the other, or be devoted to the one and despise the other. You cannot serve God and wealth. *m*

Do Not Worry
(Lk 12.22–31)

25 "Therefore I tell you, do not worry about your life, what you will eat or what you will drink,*n* or about your body, what you will wear. Is not life more than food, and the body more than clothing? 26 Look at the birds of the air; they neither sow nor reap nor gather into barns, and yet your heavenly Father feeds them. Are you not of more value than they? 27 And can any of you by worrying add a single hour to your span of life?*o* 28 And why do you worry about clothing? Consider the lilies of the field, how they grow; they neither toil nor spin, 29 yet I tell you, even Solomon in all his glory was not clothed like one of these. 30 But if God so clothes the grass of the field, which is alive today and tomorrow is thrown into the oven, will he not much more clothe you—you of little faith? 31 Therefore do not worry, saying, 'What will we eat?' or 'What will we drink?' or 'What will we wear?' 32 For it is the Gentiles who strive for all these things; and indeed your heavenly Father knows that you need all these things. 33 But strive first for the kingdom of God*p* and his*q* righteousness, and all these things will be given to you as well.

34 "So do not worry about tomorrow, for tomorrow will bring worries of its own. Today's trouble is enough for today.

Judging Others
(Lk 6.37–42)

"Do not judge, so that you may not be judged. 2 For with the judgment you make you will be judged, and the measure you give will be the measure you get. 3 Why do you see the speck in your neighbor's*r* eye, but do not notice the log in your own eye? 4 Or how can you say to your neighbor,*s*

---

m Gk *mammon*   *n* Other ancient authorities lack *or what you will drink*   *o* Or *add one cubit to your height*   *p* Other ancient authorities lack *of God*   *q* Or *its*   *r* Gk *brother's*   *s* Gk *brother*

'Let me take the speck out of your eye,' while the log is in your own eye? ⁵ You hypocrite, first take the log out of your own eye, and then you will see clearly to take the speck out of your neighbor's*t* eye.

Profaning the Holy

6 "Do not give what is holy to dogs; and do not throw your pearls before swine, or they will trample them under foot and turn and maul you.

Ask, Search, Knock
(Lk 11.9–13)

7 "Ask, and it will be given you; search, and you will find; knock, and the door will be opened for you. ⁸ For everyone who asks receives, and everyone who searches finds, and for everyone who knocks, the door will be opened. ⁹ Is there anyone among you who, if your child asks for bread, will give a stone? ¹⁰ Or if the child asks for a fish, will give a snake? ¹¹ If you then, who are evil, know how to give good gifts to your children, how much more will your Father in heaven give good things to those who ask him!

The Golden Rule
(Lk 6.31)

12 "In everything do to others as you would have them do to you; for this is the law and the prophets.

The Narrow Gate
(Lk 13.24)

13 "Enter through the narrow gate; for the gate is wide and the road is easy*u* that leads to destruction, and there are many who take it. ¹⁴ For the gate is narrow and the road is hard that leads to life, and there are few who find it.

A Tree and Its Fruit
(Mt 12.33; Lk 6.43–45)

15 "Beware of false prophets, who come to you in sheep's clothing but inwardly are ravenous wolves. ¹⁶ You will know them by their fruits. Are grapes gathered from thorns, or figs from thistles? ¹⁷ In the same way, every good tree bears good fruit, but the bad tree bears bad fruit. ¹⁸ A good tree cannot bear bad fruit, nor can a bad tree bear good fruit. ¹⁹ Every tree that does not bear good fruit is cut down and thrown into the fire. ²⁰ Thus you will know them by their fruits.

Concerning Self-Deception
(Lk 6.46; 13.26–27)

21 "Not everyone who says to me, 'Lord, Lord,' will enter the kingdom of heaven, but only

the one who does the will of my Father in heaven. ²² On that day many will say to me, 'Lord, Lord, did we not prophesy in your name, and cast out demons in your name, and do many deeds of power in your name?' ²³ Then I will declare to them, 'I never knew you; go away from me, you evildoers.'

PRAY IT!
The Gospel Call to Conversion

In closing the Sermon on the Mount, Jesus calls people to conversion. It is not enough to talk the talk; you must also walk the walk. To make present the Reign of God, Jesus asks the following:
- Rich people need to share their wealth with poor people.
- Powerful people need to serve those without power.
- Priests need to serve all people, without prejudice.
- Politicians need to govern with justice, taking into account the needs of people, especially needy people.
- Wise people need to express their knowledge in ways everyone can understand.
- Pharisees need to leave their hypocrisy behind and remove the weight of the Law through which they oppressed the people.

In your prayer, reflect or journal on the following questions:
- In the above list, what are some of the most needed areas of conversion in society today? in your local community? in your life?
- List some concrete ways you can make those conversions real.

▶ Mt 7.21–27

Hearers and Doers
(Lk 6.47–49)

24 "Everyone then who hears these words of mine and acts on them will be like a wise man

t Gk *brother's*   u Other ancient authorities read *for the road is wide and easy*

who built his house on rock. 25The rain fell, the floods came, and the winds blew and beat on that house, but it did not fall, because it had been founded on rock. 26And everyone who hears these words of mine and does not act on them will be like a foolish man who built his house on sand. 27The rain fell, and the floods came, and the winds blew and beat against that house, and it fell—and great was its fall!"

28 Now when Jesus had finished saying these things, the crowds were astounded at his teaching, 29for he taught them as one having authority, and not as their scribes.

Jesus Cleanses a Leper
(Mk 1.40–45; Lk 5.12–16)

When Jesus[u] had come down from the mountain, great crowds followed him; 2and there was a leper[v] who came to him and knelt before him, saying, "Lord, if you choose, you can make me clean." 3He stretched out his hand and touched him, saying, "I do choose. Be made clean!" Immediately his leprosy[v] was cleansed. 4Then Jesus said to him, "See that you say nothing to anyone; but go, show yourself to the priest, and offer the gift that Moses commanded, as a testimony to them."

Jesus Heals a Centurion's Servant
(Lk 7.1–10)

5 When he entered Ca·per′na·um, a centurion came to him, appealing to him 6and saying, "Lord, my servant is lying at home paralyzed, in terrible distress." 7And he said to him, "I will come and cure him." 8The centurion answered, "Lord, I am not worthy to have you come under my roof; but only speak the word, and my servant will be healed. 9For I also am a man under authority, with soldiers under me; and I say to one, 'Go,' and he goes, and to another, 'Come,' and he comes, and to my slave, 'Do this,' and the slave does it." 10When Jesus heard him, he was amazed and said to those who followed him, "Truly I tell you, in no one[w] in Israel have I found such faith. 11I tell you, many will come from east and west and will eat with Abraham and Isaac and Jacob in the kingdom of heaven, 12while the heirs of the kingdom will be thrown into the outer darkness, where there will be weeping and gnashing of teeth." 13And to the centurion Jesus said, "Go; let it be done for you according to your faith." And the servant was healed in that hour.

Jesus Heals Many at Peter's House
(Mk 1.29–34; Lk 4.38–41)

14 When Jesus entered Peter's house, he saw his mother-in-law lying in bed with a fever; 15he touched her hand, and the fever left her, and she got up and began to serve him. 16That evening they brought to him many who were possessed with demons; and he cast out the spirits with a word, and cured all who were sick. 17This was to fulfill what had been spoken through the prophet I·sāi′ah, "He took our infirmities and bore our diseases."

Would-Be Followers of Jesus
(Lk 9.57–62)

18 Now when Jesus saw great crowds around him, he gave orders to go over to the other side. 19A scribe then approached and said, "Teacher, I will follow you wherever you go." 20And Jesus said to him, "Foxes have holes, and birds of the air have nests; but the Son of Man has nowhere to lay his head." 21Another of his disciples said to him, "Lord, first let me go and bury my father." 22But Jesus said to him, "Follow me, and let the dead bury their own dead."

---

u Gk *he*   *v* The terms *leper* and *leprosy* can refer to several diseases   *w* Other ancient authorities read *Truly I tell you, not even*

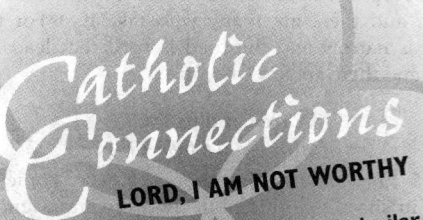

Catholic Connections
LORD, I AM NOT WORTHY

Those words of the centurion are similar to the ones Catholics say at Mass just before receiving the body and blood of Christ. We say these words not to emphasize our sinfulness but in humble recognition of God's awesome gift of Jesus, whom we are about to receive in the bread and wine of the Eucharist. The next time you receive the Eucharist, think about these words and pray for the faith it takes to believe in what you are saying.

▶ Mt 8.8

Jesus Stills the Storm
(Mk 4.35–41; Lk 8.22–25)

23 And when he got into the boat, his disciples followed him. 24 A windstorm arose on the sea, so great that the boat was being swamped by the waves; but he was asleep. 25 And they went and woke him up, saying, "Lord, save us! We are perishing!" 26 And he said to them, "Why are you afraid, you of little faith?" Then he got up and rebuked the winds and the sea; and there was a dead calm. 27 They were amazed, saying, "What sort of man is this, that even the winds and the sea obey him?"

Jesus Heals the Gadarene Demoniacs
(Mk 5.1–20; Lk 8.26–39)

28 When he came to the other side, to the country of the Gad′a•rēnes,ˣ two demoniacs coming out of the tombs met him. They were so fierce that no one could pass that way. 29 Suddenly they shouted, "What have you to do with us, Son of God? Have you come here to torment us before the time?" 30 Now a large herd of swine was feeding at some distance from them. 31 The demons begged him, "If you cast us out, send us into the herd of swine." 32 And he said to them, "Go!" So they came out and entered the swine; and suddenly, the whole herd rushed down the steep bank into the sea and perished in the water. 33 The swineherds ran off, and on going into the town, they told the whole story about what had happened to the demoniacs. 34 Then the whole town came out to meet Jesus; and when they saw him, they begged him to leave their neighborhood. 1 And after getting into a boat he crossed the sea and came to his own town.

Jesus Heals a Paralytic
(Mk 2.1–12; Lk 5.17–26)

2 And just then some people were carrying a paralyzed man lying on a bed. When Jesus saw their faith, he said to the paralytic, "Take heart, son; your sins are forgiven." 3 Then some of the scribes said to themselves, "This man is blaspheming." 4 But Jesus, perceiving their thoughts, said, "Why do you think evil in your hearts? 5 For which is easier, to say, 'Your sins are forgiven,' or to say, 'Stand up and walk'? 6 But so that you may know that the Son of Man has authority on earth to forgive sins"—he then said to the paralytic—"Stand up, take your bed and go to your home." 7 And he stood up and went to his home. 8 When the crowds saw it, they were filled with awe, and they glorified God, who had given such authority to human beings.

The Call of Matthew
(Mk 2.13–17; Lk 5.27–32)

9 As Jesus was walking along, he saw a man called Matthew sitting at the tax booth; and he said to him, "Follow me." And he got up and followed him.

10 And as he sat at dinnerʸ in the house, many tax collectors and sinners came and were sittingᶻ with him and his disciples. 11 When the Phar′i•sees saw this, they said to his disciples, "Why does your teacher eat with tax collectors and sinners?" 12 But when he heard this, he said, "Those who are well have no need of a physician, but those who are sick. 13 Go and learn what this means, 'I desire mercy, not sacrifice.' For I have come to call not the righteous but sinners."

The Question about Fasting
(Mk 2.18–22; Lk 5.33–39)

14 Then the disciples of John came to him, saying, "Why do we and the Phar′i•sees fast often,ᵃ

---

x Other ancient authorities read *Gergesenes*; others, *Gerasenes*
y Gk *reclined*   z Gk *were reclining*   a Other ancient authorities lack *often*

PRAY IT!
Spiritual Paralysis

*J*esus, healer, like the man you healed spiritually and physically, I too have experienced paralysis. Not a physical paralysis, but a spiritual paralysis that keeps me from walking with you.

This paralysis happens at times in school and in my neighborhood when I know what the right thing to do is, but I am afraid to do it. I see someone discriminating against or abusing another person, but I stand by and do nothing. By my silence, I give my approval, but I am afraid to risk ridicule and rejection.

Forgive me of my sin of silence, Lord. Help me to overcome my fears so that I can stand up for what is right. Heal me of my spiritual paralysis so that I may walk with you. Amen.

▶ Mt 9.1–8

but your disciples do not fast?" 15 And Jesus said to them, "The wedding guests cannot mourn as long as the bridegroom is with them, can they? The days will come when the bridegroom is taken away from them, and then they will fast. 16 No one sews a piece of unshrunk cloth on an old cloak, for the patch pulls away from the cloak, and a worse tear is made. 17 Neither is new wine put into old wineskins; otherwise, the skins burst, and the wine is spilled, and the skins are destroyed; but new wine is put into fresh wineskins, and so both are preserved."

did you KNOW?

Miracles and the Reign of God

Matthew, chapters 8–9, describe ten miracles of Jesus intended as signs of the coming of the Reign of God. Most of Jesus' miracles are healings, but some also show his power over demons and nature. The Gospel of Mark records the most miracles, twenty-one, and the Gospel of John, the least, eight.

People today tend to view reports of miracles with suspicion. That's because our scientific mind wants to believe everything has a rational explanation. Because of this, we miss the point. People in Jesus' time were more concerned about what the miracle revealed than in the miracle itself or even the miracle worker. Other people besides Jesus were known to perform miracles. In fact, Jesus' healing miracles were not taken as proof of his divinity (although this seemed to be the purpose of his nature miracles).

In curing people of their illnesses and driving out demons, Jesus was revealing that the Reign of God is a place where suffering and evil are banished. By curing sinners, women, and foreigners, he showed that the Reign of God is also open to all, especially outcasts.

Miracles—then and now—point to God. Whether they are easily explained or beyond reasonable explanation does not matter. What matters is that they make us aware of God's loving presence in our life. If we look at the events in our life and ask: "What do they point to? What do they tell us about God's presence in the world?" we might find ourselves utterly surrounded by miracles.

▶ **Mt 8.1—9.34**

A Girl Restored to Life and a Woman Healed
(Mk 5.21–43; Lk 8.40–56)

18 While he was saying these things to them, suddenly a leader of the synagogue[b] came in and knelt before him, saying, "My daughter has just died; but come and lay your hand on her, and she will live." 19 And Jesus got up and followed him, with his disciples. 20 Then suddenly a woman who had been suffering from hemorrhages for twelve years came up behind him and touched the fringe of his cloak, 21 for she said to herself, "If I only touch his cloak, I will be made well." 22 Jesus turned, and seeing her he said, "Take heart, daughter; your faith has made you well." And instantly the woman was made well. 23 When Jesus came to the leader's house and saw the flute players and the crowd making a commotion, 24 he said, "Go away; for the girl is not dead but sleeping." And they laughed at him. 25 But when the crowd had been put outside, he went in and took her by the hand, and the girl got up. 26 And the report of this spread throughout that district.

Jesus Heals Two Blind Men

27 As Jesus went on from there, two blind men followed him, crying loudly, "Have mercy on us, Son of David!" 28 When he entered the house, the blind men came to him; and Jesus said to them, "Do you believe that I am able to do this?" They said to him, "Yes, Lord." 29 Then he touched their eyes and said, "According to your faith let it be done to you." 30 And their eyes were opened. Then Jesus sternly ordered them, "See that no one knows of this." 31 But they went away and spread the news about him throughout that district.

Jesus Heals One Who Was Mute

32 After they had gone away, a demoniac who was mute was brought to him. 33 And when the demon had been cast out, the one who had been mute spoke; and the crowds were amazed and said, "Never has anything like this been seen in Israel." 34 But the Phar′i•sees said, "By the ruler of the demons he casts out the demons."[c]

---

b Gk lacks *of the synagogue*   c Other ancient authorities lack this verse

The Harvest Is Great,
the Laborers Few
(Lk 10.2–3)

35 Then Jesus went about all the cities and villages, teaching in their synagogues, and proclaiming the good news of the kingdom, and curing every disease and every sickness. 36When he saw the crowds, he had compassion for them, because they were harassed and helpless, like sheep without a shepherd. 37Then he said to his disciples, "The harvest is plentiful, but the laborers are few; 38therefore ask the Lord of the harvest to send out laborers into his harvest."

The Twelve Apostles
(Mk 3.13–19a; Lk 6.12–16)

Then Jesus*d* summoned his twelve disciples and gave them authority over unclean spirits, to cast them out, and to cure every disease and every sickness. 2These are the names of the twelve apostles: first, Simon, also known as Peter, and his brother Andrew; James son of Zeb'e•dee, and his brother John; 3 Philip and Bartholomew; Thomas and Matthew the tax collector; James son of Al•phae'us, and Thad•dae'us;*e* 4Simon the Cā•na•nae'an, and Judas Is•car'i•ot, the one who betrayed him.

9.25

The Mission of the Twelve
(Mk 6.6b–13; Lk 9.1–6)

5 These twelve Jesus sent out with the following instructions: "Go nowhere among the Gentiles, and enter no town of the Sa•mar'i•tans, 6but go rather to the lost sheep of the house of Israel. 7As you go, proclaim the good news, 'The kingdom of heaven has come near.'*f* 8Cure the sick,

raise the dead, cleanse the lepers,*g* cast out demons. You received without payment; give without payment. 9Take no gold, or silver, or copper in your belts, 10no bag for your journey, or two tunics, or sandals, or a staff; for laborers deserve their food. 11Whatever town or village you enter, find out who in it is worthy, and stay there until you leave. 12As you enter the house, greet it. 13If the house is worthy, let your peace come upon it; but if it is not worthy, let your peace return to you. 14If anyone will not welcome you or listen to your words, shake off the dust from your feet as you leave that house or town. 15Truly I tell you, it will be more tolerable for the land of Sod'om and Go-mor'rah on the day of judgment than for that town.

Coming Persecutions
(Mk 13.9–13; Lk 21.12–17)

16 "See, I am sending you out like sheep into the midst of wolves; so be wise as serpents and innocent as doves. 17Beware of them, for they will hand you over to councils and flog you in their synagogues; 18and you will be dragged before governors and kings because of me, as a testimony to them and the Gentiles. 19When they hand you over, do not worry about how you are to speak or what you are to say; for what you are to say will be given to you at that time; 20for it is not you who speak, but the Spirit of your Father speaking through you. 21Brother will betray brother to death, and a father his child, and children will rise against parents and have them put to death; 22and you will be hated by all because of my name. But the one who endures to the end will be saved. 23When they persecute you in one town, flee to the next; for truly I tell you, you will not have gone through all the towns of Israel before the Son of Man comes.

24 "A disciple is not above the teacher, nor a slave above the master; 25it is enough for the disciple to be like the teacher, and the slave like the master. If they have called the master of the house Be•el'ze•bul, how much more will they malign those of his household!

Whom to Fear
(Lk 12.2–7)

26 "So have no fear of them; for nothing is covered up that will not be uncovered, and nothing secret that will not become known. 27What I say to you in the dark, tell in the light; and what

---

d Gk *he*　　*e* Other ancient authorities read *Lebbaeus,* or *Lebbaeus called Thaddaeus*　　*f* Or *is at hand*　　*g* The terms *leper* and *leprosy* can refer to several diseases

you hear whispered, proclaim from the housetops. 28 Do not fear those who kill the body but cannot kill the soul; rather fear him who can destroy both soul and body in hell.[h] 29 Are not two sparrows sold for a penny? Yet not one of them will fall to the ground apart from your Father. 30 And even the hairs of your head are all counted. 31 So do not be afraid; you are of more value than many sparrows.

32 "Everyone therefore who acknowledges me before others, I also will acknowledge before my Father in heaven; 33 but whoever denies me before others, I also will deny before my Father in heaven.

sent me. 41 Whoever welcomes a prophet in the name of a prophet will receive a prophet's reward; and whoever welcomes a righteous person in the name of a righteous person will receive the reward of the righteous; 42 and whoever gives even a cup of cold water to one of these little ones in the name of a disciple—truly I tell you, none of these will lose their reward."

Now when Jesus had finished instructing his twelve disciples, he went on from there to teach and proclaim his message in their cities.

A Violent Jesus?

Jesus says a curious thing as he prepares the Twelve for their mission, "I have not come to bring peace, but a sword" (Mt 10.34). This is one of the many hard sayings attributed to Jesus in the Gospels. Jesus is speaking metaphorically to emphasize the extreme demands of discipleship. He is not advocating violence but simply predicting how people will react to the new values and way of life of his followers. The author of Matthew lived in a community that knew living as Jesus' disciples is not always simple or easy. The people wished for peace, but living by Jesus' words brought them hatred and conflict with people in power. At the time Matthew was written, Christians needed to be able to give up everything, including family attachments, in order to follow Jesus. Is it any different today? Are you up to the challenge?

▶ Mt 10.34–39

Not Peace, but a Sword
(Lk 12.51–53; 14.26–27)

34 "Do not think that I have come to bring peace to the earth; I have not come to bring peace, but a sword.

35 For I have come to set a man against his father,
and a daughter against her mother,
and a daughter-in-law against her
mother-in-law;

36 and one's foes will be members of one's
own household.

37 Whoever loves father or mother more than me is not worthy of me; and whoever loves son or daughter more than me is not worthy of me; 38 and whoever does not take up the cross and follow me is not worthy of me. 39 Those who find their life will lose it, and those who lose their life for my sake will find it.

Rewards
(Mk 9.41)

40 "Whoever welcomes you welcomes me, and whoever welcomes me welcomes the one who

Messengers from John the Baptist
(Lk 7.18–23)

2 When John heard in prison what the Messiah[i] was doing, he sent word by his[j] disciples 3 and said to him, "Are you the one who is to come, or are we to wait for another?" 4 Jesus answered them, "Go and tell John what you hear and see: 5 the blind receive their sight, the lame walk, the lepers[k] are cleansed, the deaf hear, the dead are raised, and the poor have good news brought to them. 6 And blessed is anyone who takes no offense at me."

Jesus Praises John the Baptist
(Lk 7.24–35)

7 As they went away, Jesus began to speak to the crowds about John: "What did you go out into the wilderness to look at? A reed shaken by the

---

[h] Gk *Gehenna*   [i] Or *the Christ*   [j] Other ancient authorities read *two of his*   [k] The terms *leper* and *leprosy* can refer to several diseases

wind? [8] What then did you go out to see? Someone[l] dressed in soft robes? Look, those who wear soft robes are in royal palaces. [9] What then did you go out to see? A prophet?[m] Yes, I tell you, and more than a prophet. [10] This is the one about whom it is written,

> 'See, I am sending my messenger ahead
>   of you,
> who will prepare your way before you.'

[11] Truly I tell you, among those born of women no one has arisen greater than John the Baptist; yet the least in the kingdom of heaven is greater than he. [12] From the days of John the Baptist until now the kingdom of heaven has suffered violence,[n] and the violent take it by force. [13] For all the prophets and the law prophesied until John came; [14] and if you are willing to accept it, he is E·li'jah who is to come. [15] Let anyone with ears[o] listen!

[16] "But to what will I compare this generation? It is like children sitting in the marketplaces and calling to one another,

[17]   'We played the flute for you, and you did
>   not dance;
> we wailed, and you did not mourn.'

[18] For John came neither eating nor drinking, and they say, 'He has a demon'; [19] the Son of Man came eating and drinking, and they say, 'Look, a glutton and a drunkard, a friend of tax collectors and sinners!' Yet wisdom is vindicated by her deeds."[p]

Woes to Unrepentant Cities
(Gen 19.12–14; Lk 10.13–15)

[20] Then he began to reproach the cities in which most of his deeds of power had been done, because they did not repent. [21] "Woe to you, Chō-ra'zin! Woe to you, Beth·sā'i·da! For if the deeds of power done in you had been done in Tyre and Si'don, they would have repented long ago in sackcloth and ashes. [22] But I tell you, on the day of judgment it will be more tolerable for Tyre and Si'don than for you. [23] And you, Ca·per'na·um,

> will you be exalted to heaven?

No, you will be brought down to Hades.
For if the deeds of power done in you had been done in Sod'om, it would have remained until this day. [24] But I tell you that on the day of judgment it will be more tolerable for the land of Sod'om than for you."

Jesus Thanks His Father
(Lk 10.21–22)

[25] At that time Jesus said, "I thank[q] you, Father, Lord of heaven and earth, because you have hidden these things from the wise and the intelligent and have revealed them to infants; [26] yes, Father, for such was your gracious will.[r] [27] All things have been handed over to me by my Father; and no one knows the Son except the Father, and no one knows the Father except the Son and anyone to whom the Son chooses to reveal him.

[28] "Come to me, all you that are weary and are carrying heavy burdens, and I will give you rest. [29] Take my yoke upon you, and learn from me; for I am gentle and humble in heart, and you will find rest for your souls. [30] For my yoke is easy, and my burden is light."

Plucking Grain on the Sabbath
(Mk 2.23–28; Lk 6.1–5)

At that time Jesus went through the grainfields on the sabbath; his disciples were hungry, and they began to pluck heads of grain and to eat. [2] When the Phar'i·sees saw it, they said to him, "Look, your disciples are doing what is not lawful to do on the sabbath." [3] He said to them, "Have you not read what David did when he and his companions were hungry? [4] He entered the house of God and ate the bread of the Presence, which it was not lawful for him or his companions to eat, but only for the priests. [5] Or have you not read in the law that on the sabbath the priests in the temple break the sabbath and yet are guiltless? [6] I tell you, something greater than the temple is here. [7] But if you had known what this means, 'I desire mercy and not sacrifice,' you would not have condemned the guiltless. [8] For the Son of Man is lord of the sabbath."

The Man with a Withered Hand
(Mk 3.1–6; Lk 6.6–11)

[9] He left that place and entered their synagogue; [10] a man was there with a withered hand, and they asked him, "Is it lawful to cure on the sabbath?" so that they might accuse him. [11] He said to them, "Suppose one of you has only one sheep and it falls into a pit on the sabbath; will you not lay hold of it and lift it out? [12] How much more valuable is a human being than a sheep! So it is lawful to do good on the sabbath." [13] Then he said to the man, "Stretch out your hand." He stretched it out, and it was restored, as sound as the other. [14] But the Phar'i·sees went out and conspired against him, how to destroy him.

---

[l] Or *Why then did you go out? To see someone*   [m] Other ancient authorities read *Why then did you go out? To see a prophet?*   [n] Or *has been coming violently*   [o] Other ancient authorities add *to hear*   [p] Other ancient authorities read *children*   [q] Or *praise*   [r] Or *for so it was well-pleasing in your sight*

MT

God's Chosen Servant

15 When Jesus became aware of this, he departed. Many crowds[s] followed him, and he cured all of them, 16 and he ordered them not to make him known. 17 This was to fulfill what had been spoken through the prophet I•sāi'ah:

18 "Here is my servant, whom I have chosen,
my beloved, with whom my soul is well
pleased.
I will put my Spirit upon him,
and he will proclaim justice to the
Gentiles.
19 He will not wrangle or cry aloud,
nor will anyone hear his voice in the
streets.
20 He will not break a bruised reed
or quench a smoldering wick
until he brings justice to victory.
21 And in his name the Gentiles will hope."

Jesus and Beelzebul
(Mk 3.19b–30; Lk 11.14–23)

22 Then they brought to him a demoniac who was blind and mute; and he cured him, so that the one who had been mute could speak and see. 23 All the crowds were amazed and said, "Can this be the Son of David?" 24 But when the Phar'i•sees heard it, they said, "It is only by Bē•el'ze•bul, the ruler of the demons, that this fellow casts out the demons." 25 He knew what they were thinking and said to them, "Every kingdom divided against itself is laid waste, and no city or house divided against itself will stand. 26 If Satan casts out Satan, he is divided against himself; how then will his kingdom stand? 27 If I cast out demons by Bē•el'ze•bul, by whom do your own exorcists[t] cast them out? Therefore they will be your judges. 28 But if it is by the Spirit of God that I cast out demons, then the kingdom of God has come to you. 29 Or how can one enter a strong man's house and plunder his property, without first tying up the strong man? Then indeed the house can be plundered. 30 Whoever is not with me is against me, and whoever does not gather with me scatters. 31 Therefore I tell you, people will be forgiven for every sin and blasphemy, but blasphemy against the Spirit will not be forgiven. 32 Whoever speaks a word against the Son of Man will be forgiven, but whoever speaks against the Holy Spirit will not be forgiven, either in this age or in the age to come.

A Tree and Its Fruit
(Mt 7.15–20)

33 "Either make the tree good, and its fruit good; or make the tree bad, and its fruit bad; for the tree is known by its fruit. 34 You brood of vipers! How can you speak good things, when you are evil? For out of the abundance of the heart the mouth speaks. 35 The good person brings good things out of a good treasure, and the evil person brings evil things out of an evil treasure. 36 I tell you, on the day of judgment you will have to give an account for every careless word you utter; 37 for by your words you will be justified, and by your words you will be condemned."

PRAY IT!
Tripping Over My Tongue

Watch what you say! Jesus is telling us that our words will ultimately reveal the intentions of our heart—just as a tree's fruit reveals whether the tree is good or bad. So let us tend to our heart as a gardener tends the trees in an orchard.

God, help me tend to the goodness of my heart. Let my words reflect my heart's goodness in building other people up—not tearing them down. Let me be careful in choosing my words so that they serve only to honor you. Amen.

▶ Mt 12.33–37

The Sign of Jonah
(Lk 11.29–32)

38 Then some of the scribes and Phar'i•sees said to him, "Teacher, we wish to see a sign from you." 39 But he answered them, "An evil and adulterous generation asks for a sign, but no sign will be given to it except the sign of the prophet Jonah. 40 For just as Jonah was three days and three nights in the belly of the sea monster, so for three days and three nights the Son of Man will be in the heart of the earth. 41 The people of Nin'e•veh will rise up at the judgment with this generation and condemn it, because they repented at the proclamation of Jonah, and see, something greater than Jonah is here! 42 The queen of the South will rise up at the judgment with this generation and condemn it, because she came from the ends of the

---

[s] Other ancient authorities lack *crowds*   [t] Gk *sons*

earth to listen to the wisdom of Solomon, and see, something greater than Solomon is here!

The Return of the Unclean Spirit
(Lk 11.24–26)

43 "When the unclean spirit has gone out of a person, it wanders through waterless regions looking for a resting place, but it finds none. 44 Then it says, 'I will return to my house from which I came.' When it comes, it finds it empty, swept, and put in order. 45 Then it goes and brings along seven other spirits more evil than itself, and they enter and live there; and the last state of that person is worse than the first. So will it be also with this evil generation."

did you KNOW?

Parables

The Gospels frequently describe Jesus teaching in parables. A parable is a literary form that uses a fictional story to make a point.

Many of Jesus' parables are like riddles. They have surprising or shocking endings designed to tease the people of his time into examining certain beliefs they took for granted. Unfortunately, the surprise of Jesus' parables is hard for some of us to understand today because we may be unfamiliar with the examples he used: baking bread, planting crops, herding sheep, or fishing for our supper.

Jesus also used parables to teach about God's Reign. These were often in the form of analogies comparing God's Reign to common things or events: "The Kingdom of God is like . . ." Using parables, Jesus challenged powerful and educated people but was also understood by common people.

▶ Mt 13.10

The True Kindred of Jesus
(Mk 3.31–35; Lk 8.19–21)

46 While he was still speaking to the crowds, his mother and his brothers were standing outside, wanting to speak to him. 47 Someone told him,

"Look, your mother and your brothers are standing outside, wanting to speak to you."*u* 48 But to the one who had told him this, Jesus*v* replied, "Who is my mother, and who are my brothers?" 49 And pointing to his disciples, he said, "Here are my mother and my brothers! 50 For whoever does the will of my Father in heaven is my brother and sister and mother."

The Parable of the Sower
(Mk 4.1–9, 13–20; Lk 8.4–8, 11–15)

That same day Jesus went out of the house and sat beside the sea. 2 Such great crowds gathered around him that he got into a boat and sat there, while the whole crowd stood on the beach. 3 And he told them many things in parables, saying: "Listen! A sower went out to sow. 4 And as he sowed, some seeds fell on the path, and the birds came and ate them up. 5 Other seeds fell on rocky ground, where they did not have much soil, and they sprang up quickly, since they had no depth of soil. 6 But when the sun rose, they were scorched; and since they had no root, they withered away. 7 Other seeds fell among thorns, and the thorns grew up and choked them. 8 Other seeds fell on good soil and brought forth grain, some a hundredfold, some sixty, some thirty. 9 Let anyone with ears*w* listen!"

The Purpose of the Parables
(Mk 4.10–12; Lk 8.9–10)

10 Then the disciples came and asked him, "Why do you speak to them in parables?" 11 He answered, "To you it has been given to know the secrets*x* of the kingdom of heaven, but to them it has not been given. 12 For to those who have, more will be given, and they will have an abundance; but from those who have nothing, even what they have will be taken away. 13 The reason I speak to them in parables is that 'seeing they do not perceive, and hearing they do not listen, nor do they understand.' 14 With them indeed is fulfilled the prophecy of I·sāi'ah that says:

'You will indeed listen, but never
        understand,
    and you will indeed look, but never
        perceive.
15 For this people's heart has grown dull,
        and their ears are hard of hearing,
        and they have shut their eyes;
            so that they might not look with their
                eyes,
            and listen with their ears,

---

u Other ancient authorities lack verse 47   v Gk *he*
w Other ancient authorities add *to hear*   x Or *mysteries*

and understand with their heart and turn—
and I would heal them.'
16 But blessed are your eyes, for they see, and your ears, for they hear. 17 Truly I tell you, many prophets and righteous people longed to see what you see, but did not see it, and to hear what you hear, but did not hear it.

The Parable of the Sower Explained

18 "Hear then the parable of the sower. 19 When anyone hears the word of the kingdom and does not understand it, the evil one comes and snatches away what is sown in the heart; this is what was sown on the path. 20 As for what was sown on rocky ground, this is the one who hears the word and immediately receives it with joy; 21 yet such a person has no root, but endures only for a while, and when trouble or persecution arises on account of the word, that person immediately falls away.y 22 As for what was sown among thorns, this is the one who hears the word, but the cares of the world and the lure of wealth choke the word, and it yields nothing. 23 But as for what was sown on good soil, this is the one who hears the word and understands it, who indeed bears fruit and yields, in one case a hundredfold, in another sixty, and in another thirty."

The Parable of Weeds among the Wheat

24 He put before them another parable: "The kingdom of heaven may be compared to someone who sowed good seed in his field; 25 but while everybody was asleep, an enemy came and sowed weeds among the wheat, and then went away. 26 So when the plants came up and bore grain, then the weeds appeared as well. 27 And the slaves of the householder came and said to him, 'Master, did you not sow good seed in your field? Where, then, did these weeds come from?' 28 He answered, 'An enemy has done this.' The slaves said to him, 'Then do you want us to go and gather them?' 29 But he replied, 'No; for in gathering the weeds you would uproot the wheat along with them. 30 Let both of them grow together until the harvest; and at harvest time I will tell the reapers, Collect the weeds first and bind them in bundles to be burned, but gather the wheat into my barn.' "

The Parable of the Mustard Seed
(Mk 4.30–32; Lk 13.18–19)

31 He put before them another parable: "The kingdom of heaven is like a mustard seed that someone took and sowed in his field; 32 it is the smallest of all the seeds, but when it has grown it is the greatest of shrubs and becomes a tree, so

that the birds of the air come and make nests in its branches."

The Parable of the Yeast
(Lk 13.20–21)

33 He told them another parable: "The kingdom of heaven is like yeast that a woman took and mixed in withz three measures of flour until all of it was leavened."

The Use of Parables

34 Jesus told the crowds all these things in parables; without a parable he told them nothing. 35 This was to fulfill what had been spoken through the prophet:a
"I will open my mouth to speak
in parables;
I will proclaim what has been hidden
from the foundation of the world."b

Jesus Explains the Parable of the Weeds

36 Then he left the crowds and went into the house. And his disciples approached him, saying, "Explain to us the parable of the weeds of the field." 37 He answered, "The one who sows the good seed is the Son of Man; 38 the field is the world, and the good seed are the children of the kingdom; the weeds are the children of the evil one, 39 and the enemy who sowed them is the devil; the harvest is the end of the age, and the reapers are angels. 40 Just as the weeds are collected and burned up with fire, so will it be at the end of the age. 41 The Son of Man will send his angels, and they will collect out of his kingdom all causes of sin and all evildoers, 42 and they will throw them into the furnace of fire, where there will be weeping and gnashing of teeth. 43 Then the righteous will shine like the sun in the kingdom of their Father. Let anyone with earsc listen!

Three Parables

44 "The kingdom of heaven is like treasure hidden in a field, which someone found and hid; then in his joy he goes and sells all that he has and buys that field.

45 "Again, the kingdom of heaven is like a merchant in search of fine pearls; 46 on finding one pearl of great value, he went and sold all that he had and bought it.

47 "Again, the kingdom of heaven is like a net that was thrown into the sea and caught fish of every kind; 48 when it was full, they drew it ashore,

---

y Gk stumbles   z Gk hid in   a Other ancient authorities read the prophet Isaiah   b Other ancient authorities lack of the world   c Other ancient authorities add to hear

sat down, and put the good into baskets but threw out the bad. ⁴⁹ So it will be at the end of the age. The angels will come out and separate the evil from the righteous ⁵⁰ and throw them into the furnace of fire, where there will be weeping and gnashing of teeth.

Treasures New and Old

51 "Have you understood all this?" They answered, "Yes." ⁵² And he said to them, "Therefore every scribe who has been trained for the kingdom of heaven is like the master of a household who brings out of his treasure what is new and what is old." ⁵³ When Jesus had finished these parables, he left that place.

PRAY IT!

The Kingdom Is Like . . .

In trying to get people to understand something as mystifying and overwhelming as the Reign (Kingdom) of God, Jesus used ordinary objects like seeds and light, salt and yeast. He chose everyday actions like farming, fishing, and baking. And in doing so, he helped the people of his time understand the new life that comes with the Reign of God.

What is this Reign like to you? Take a walk outside or look around the room you are in right now. Pick any object that catches your attention. Try to imagine how Jesus, the master teacher, would use that object to describe the Reign of God. For example, he might say: "The Kingdom of God is like this telephone. It connects you to everyone else in the world no matter who or where they are."

End your meditation with a prayer that your life will be a living sign to help others understand what the Reign of God is all about.

▶ Mt 13.10–53

The Rejection of Jesus at Nazareth
(Mk 6.1–6; Lk 4.16–30)

54 He came to his hometown and began to teach the people[d] in their synagogue, so that they were astounded and said, "Where did this man get

this wisdom and these deeds of power? ⁵⁵ Is not this the carpenter's son? Is not his mother called Mary? And are not his brothers James and Joseph and Simon and Judas? ⁵⁶ And are not all his sisters with us? Where then did this man get all this?" ⁵⁷ And they took offense at him. But Jesus said to them, "Prophets are not without honor except in their own country and in their own house." ⁵⁸ And he did not do many deeds of power there, because of their unbelief.

The Death of John the Baptist
(Lk 9.7–9; Mk 6.14–29)

At that time Her'od the ruler[e] heard reports about Jesus; ² and he said to his servants, "This is John the Baptist; he has been raised from the dead, and for this reason these powers are at work in him." ³ For Her'od had arrested John, bound him, and put him in prison on account of He•rō'di•as, his brother Philip's wife,[f] ⁴ because John had been telling him, "It is not lawful for you to have her." ⁵ Though Her'od[g] wanted to put him to death, he feared the crowd, because they regarded him as a prophet. ⁶ But when Her'od's birthday came, the daughter of He•rō'di•as danced before the company, and she pleased Her'od ⁷ so much that he promised on oath to grant her whatever she might ask. ⁸ Prompted by her mother, she said, "Give me the head of John the Baptist here on a platter." ⁹ The king was grieved, yet out of regard for his oaths and for the guests, he commanded it to be given; ¹⁰ he sent and had John beheaded in the prison. ¹¹ The head was brought on a platter and given to the girl, who brought it to her mother. ¹² His disciples came and took the body and buried it; then they went and told Jesus.

Feeding the Five Thousand
(Mk 6.30–44; Lk 9.10–17; Jn 6.1–14)

13 Now when Jesus heard this, he withdrew from there in a boat to a deserted place by himself. But when the crowds heard it, they followed him on foot from the towns. ¹⁴ When he went ashore, he saw a great crowd; and he had compassion for them and cured their sick. ¹⁵ When it was evening, the disciples came to him and said, "This is a deserted place, and the hour is now late; send the crowds away so that they may go into the villages and buy food for themselves." ¹⁶ Jesus said to them, "They need not go away; you give them something to eat." ¹⁷ They replied, "We have nothing here but five loaves and two fish." ¹⁸ And he said, "Bring them here to me." ¹⁹ Then he ordered the crowds to

---

d Gk *them*   *e* Gk *tetrarch*   *f* Other ancient authorities read *his brother's wife*   *g* Gk *he*

MT

sit down on the grass. Taking the five loaves and the two fish, he looked up to heaven, and blessed and broke the loaves, and gave them to the disciples, and the disciples gave them to the crowds. 20 And all ate and were filled; and they took up what was left over of the broken pieces, twelve baskets full. 21 And those who ate were about five thousand men, besides women and children.

Jesus Walks on the Water
(Mk 6.45–52; Jn 6.15–21)

22 Immediately he made the disciples get into the boat and go on ahead to the other side, while he dismissed the crowds. 23 And after he had dismissed the crowds, he went up the mountain by himself to pray. When evening came, he was there alone, 24 but by this time the boat, battered by the waves, was far from the land,*h* for the wind was against them. 25 And early in the morning he came walking toward them on the sea. 26 But when the disciples saw him walking on the sea, they were terrified, saying, "It is a ghost!" And they cried out in fear. 27 But immediately Jesus spoke to them and said, "Take heart, it is I; do not be afraid."

got into the boat, the wind ceased. 33 And those in the boat worshiped him, saying, "Truly you are the Son of God."

Jesus Heals the Sick in Gennesaret
(Mk 6.53–56)

34 When they had crossed over, they came to land at Gen·nes'a·ret. 35 After the people of that place recognized him, they sent word throughout the region and brought all who were sick to him, 36 and begged him that they might touch even the fringe of his cloak; and all who touched it were healed.

The Tradition of the Elders
(Mk 7.1–13)

Then Phar'i·sees and scribes came to Jesus from Jerusalem and said, 2 "Why do your disciples break the tradition of the elders? For they do not wash their hands before they eat." 3 He answered them, "And why do you break the commandment of God for the sake of your tradition? 4 For God said,*j* 'Honor your father and your mother,' and,

Do You Trust Jesus?

At this point in the Gospel of Matthew, different groups are beginning to line up for or against Jesus. The Pharisees, Sadducees, and scribes do not trust him. The disciples still follow Jesus, but they do not yet understand who he really is. In chapters 14–17, through several signs and wonders, the true identity of Jesus is revealed to the disciples. Peter in particular is being prepared for his role as leader.

Of the four Gospels, only Matthew includes the story of Peter walking on the water. If you have gotten acquainted with Peter (see "Peter the Rock," Mt 16.13–20), it will not surprise you that he was willing to take the risk. But why does Peter start to sink? When he is focused on Jesus, everything is fine. It is when he takes his eyes off Jesus, noticing the fierce wind, that he begins to sink.

Jesus invites you to risk a relationship with him. You have to step out in faith, maybe leaving some old ways of life behind. Learn from Peter to keep your focus on Jesus. As the disciples learned, this is no ordinary man but the Son of God! Following Jesus might get scary or difficult at times, but all great adventures involve some risks.

▶ **Mt 14.22–33**

28 Peter answered him, "Lord, if it is you, command me to come to you on the water." 29 He said, "Come." So Peter got out of the boat, started walking on the water, and came toward Jesus. 30 But when he noticed the strong wind,*i* he became frightened, and beginning to sink, he cried out, "Lord, save me!" 31 Jesus immediately reached out his hand and caught him, saying to him, "You of little faith, why did you doubt?" 32 When they

'Whoever speaks evil of father or mother must surely die.' 5 But you say that whoever tells father or mother, 'Whatever support you might have had from me is given to God,'*k* then that person need not honor the father.*l* 6 So, for the sake of your

---

h Other ancient authorities read *was out on the sea*
i Other ancient authorities read *the wind*   *j* Other ancient authorities read *commanded, saying*   *k* Or *is an offering*
l Other ancient authorities add *or the mother*

tradition, you make void the word[m] of God. 7 You hypocrites! I·sāi'ah prophesied rightly about you when he said:

8 'This people honors me with their lips,
     but their hearts are far from me;
9 in vain do they worship me,
     teaching human precepts as doctrines.' "

NATIVE AMERICAN

A Prayer for Healing Humankind

In Mt 15.1–20, Jesus addresses the hypocrisy of the Jewish leaders who manipulate the Law to their own good. They and the people who follow them are blind to the results. In this prayer, the Ojibwa (or Anishinabe) recognize the need for humans to overcome their blindness to the results of evil intentions:

> Grandfather,
> Look at our brokenness.
> We know that in all creation
> Only the human family
> Has strayed from the Sacred Way.
> We know that we are the ones
> Who must come back together
> To walk in the Sacred Way.
> Grandfather,
> Sacred One,
> Teach us love, compassion, and honor
> That we may heal the earth
> And heal each other.

> (David Schiller, editor, **The Little Book of Prayers**, pp. 328–329)

▶ Mt 15.1–20

Things That Defile
(Mk 7.14–23)

10 Then he called the crowd to him and said to them, "Listen and understand: 11 it is not what goes into the mouth that defiles a person, but it is what comes out of the mouth that defiles." 12 Then

the disciples approached and said to him, "Do you know that the Phar'i·sees took offense when they heard what you said?" 13 He answered, "Every plant that my heavenly Father has not planted will be uprooted. 14 Let them alone; they are blind guides of the blind.[n] And if one blind person guides another, both will fall into a pit." 15 But Peter said to him, "Explain this parable to us." 16 Then he said, "Are you also still without understanding? 17 Do you not see that whatever goes into the mouth enters the stomach, and goes out into the sewer? 18 But what comes out of the mouth proceeds from the heart, and this is what defiles. 19 For out of the heart come evil intentions, murder, adultery, fornication, theft, false witness, slander. 20 These are what defile a person, but to eat with unwashed hands does not defile."

The Canaanite Woman's Faith
(Mk 7.24–30)

21 Jesus left that place and went away to the district of Tȳre and Sī'don. 22 Just then a Ca'naan·ite woman from that region came out and started shouting, "Have mercy on me, Lord, Son of David; my daughter is tormented by a demon." 23 But he did not answer her at all. And his disciples came and urged him, saying, "Send her away, for she keeps shouting after us." 24 He answered, "I was sent only to the lost sheep of the house of Israel." 25 But she came and knelt before him, saying, "Lord, help me." 26 He answered, "It is not fair to take the children's food and throw it to the dogs." 27 She said, "Yes, Lord, yet even the dogs eat the crumbs that fall from their masters' table." 28 Then Jesus answered her, "Woman, great is your faith! Let it be done for you as you wish." And her daughter was healed instantly.

Jesus Cures Many People
(Mk 7.31–37)

29 After Jesus had left that place, he passed along the Sea of Galilee, and he went up the mountain, where he sat down. 30 Great crowds came to him, bringing with them the lame, the maimed, the blind, the mute, and many others. They put them at his feet, and he cured them, 31 so that the crowd was amazed when they saw the mute speaking, the maimed whole, the lame walking, and the blind seeing. And they praised the God of Israel.

m Other ancient authorities read *law*; others, *commandment*
n Other ancient authorities lack *of the blind*

M
T

Feeding the Four Thousand
(Mk 8.1–10)

32 Then Jesus called his disciples to him and said, "I have compassion for the crowd, because they have been with me now for three days and have nothing to eat; and I do not want to send them away hungry, for they might faint on the way." 33 The disciples said to him, "Where are we to get enough bread in the desert to feed so great a crowd?" 34 Jesus asked them, "How many loaves have you?" They said, "Seven, and a few small fish." 35 Then ordering the crowd to sit down on the ground, 36 he took the seven loaves and the fish; and after giving thanks he broke them and gave them to the disciples, and the disciples gave them to the crowds. 37 And all of them ate and were filled; and they took up the broken pieces left over, seven baskets full. 38 Those who had eaten were four thousand men, besides women and children. 39 After sending away the crowds, he got into the boat and went to the region of Mag'a•dan.*o*

The Demand for a Sign
(Mk 8.11–13; Lk 12.54–56)

The Phar'i•sees and Sad'du•cees came, and to test Jesus*p* they asked him to show them a sign from heaven. 2 He answered them, "When it is evening, you say, 'It will be fair weather, for the sky is red.' 3 And in the morning, 'It will be stormy today, for the sky is red and threatening.' You know how to interpret the appearance of the sky, but you cannot interpret the signs of the times.*q* 4 An evil and adulterous generation asks for a sign, but no sign will be given to it except the sign of Jonah." Then he left them and went away.

The Yeast of the Pharisees and Sadducees
(Mk 8.14–21)

5 When the disciples reached the other side, they had forgotten to bring any bread. 6 Jesus said to them, "Watch out, and beware of the yeast of the Phar'i•sees and Sad'du•cees." 7 They said to one another, "It is because we have brought no bread." 8 And becoming aware of it, Jesus said, "You of little faith, why are you talking about having no bread? 9 Do you still not perceive? Do you not remember the five loaves for the five thousand, and how many baskets you gathered? 10 Or the seven loaves for the four thousand, and how many baskets you gathered? 11 How could you fail to perceive that I was not speaking about bread? Beware of the yeast of the Phar'i•sees and Sad'du•cees!" 12 Then they understood that he had not told them

AFRICAN AMERICAN
The Principle of *Ujamaa*

A man who won't die for something is not fit to live. (Martin Luther King Jr.)

Jesus tells us that we need to leave behind our old life of selfishness, and embrace a new way of life marked by caring about the needs of others. Only then can the spirit of the Lord abound. Martin Luther King Jr. practiced this new way of life in his dream for a better day for African Americans—a dream he was willing to work and die for.

The Kwanzaa principle of *ujamaa*, or cooperative economics, requires this kind of selfless love for others. To practice *ujamaa* means sharing resources with our brothers and sisters, supporting one another's businesses, and living so that everybody receives what they need to prosper. Jesus' words challenge us to build up our communities, preserving the gains we have made and laying foundations for the success of those who come after us. The cost is our me-first attitudes, but the reward is a new life of justice and freedom.

Dear God, my humanness wants to hoard myself; my spirit wants to give!

▸ **Mt 16.25**

to beware of the yeast of bread, but of the teaching of the Phar'i•sees and Sad'du•cees.

Peter's Declaration about Jesus
(Mk 8.27–30; Lk 9.18–20)

13 Now when Jesus came into the district of Caes•a•re'a Phi•lip'pi, he asked his disciples, "Who do people say that the Son of Man is?" 14 And they said, "Some say John the Baptist, but others E•li'jah, and still others Jer•e•mi'ah or one of the prophets." 15 He said to them, "But who do you say that I am?" 16 Simon Peter answered, "You are the Messiah,*r* the Son of the living God." 17 And Jesus answered him, "Blessed are you, Simon son of Jonah! For flesh and blood has not revealed this to you, but my Father in heaven. 18 And I tell you,

---

o Other ancient authorities read *Magdala* or *Magdalan*
p Gk *him*   *q* Other ancient authorities lack *2When it is . . . of the times*   *r* Or *the Christ*

you are Peter,[s] and on this rock[t] I will build my church, and the gates of Hades will not prevail against it. [19] I will give you the keys of the kingdom of heaven, and whatever you bind on earth will be bound in heaven, and whatever you loose on earth will be loosed in heaven." [20] Then he sternly ordered the disciples not to tell anyone that he was[u] the Messiah.[v]

Jesus Foretells His Death and Resurrection
(Mk 8.31–33; Lk 9.21–22)

[21] From that time on, Jesus began to show his disciples that he must go to Jerusalem and undergo great suffering at the hands of the elders and chief priests and scribes, and be killed, and on the third day be raised. [22] And Peter took him aside and began to rebuke him, saying, "God forbid it, Lord! This must never happen to you." [23] But he turned and said to Peter, "Get behind me, Satan! You are a stumbling block to me; for you are setting your mind not on divine things but on human things."

The Cross and Self-Denial
(Mk 8.34—9.1; Lk 9.23–27)

[24] Then Jesus told his disciples, "If any want to become my followers, let them deny themselves and take up their cross and follow me. [25] For those who want to save their life will lose it, and those who lose their life for my sake will find it. [26] For

what will it profit them if they gain the whole world but forfeit their life? Or what will they give in return for their life?

[27] "For the Son of Man is to come with his angels in the glory of his Father, and then he will repay everyone for what has been done. [28] Truly I tell you, there are some standing here who will not taste death before they see the Son of Man coming in his kingdom."

The Transfiguration
(Mk 9.2–13; Lk 9.28–36; 2 Pet 1.16–18)

Six days later, Jesus took with him Peter and James and his brother John and led them up a high mountain, by themselves. [2] And he was transfigured before them, and his face shone like the sun, and his clothes became dazzling white. [3] Suddenly there appeared to them Moses and E•li′jah, talking with him. [4] Then Peter said to Jesus, "Lord, it is good for us to be here; if you wish, I[w] will make three dwellings[x] here, one for you, one for Moses, and one for E•li′jah." [5] While he was still speaking, suddenly a bright cloud overshadowed them, and from the cloud a voice said, "This is my Son, the Beloved;[y] with him I am well pleased; listen to him!" [6] When the disciples heard this, they fell to the ground and were overcome by fear. [7] But Jesus came and touched them, saying, "Get up and do

---

s Gk *Petros*   t Gk *petra*   u Other ancient authorities add *Jesus*   v Or *the Christ*   w Other ancient authorities read *we*   x Or *tents*   y Or *my beloved Son*

Introducing ▶ PETER THE ROCK

What images does the name Saint Peter bring to your mind? The simple fisherman named Simon who was among the first disciples called by Jesus (Mt 3.18, Mk 1.16, Lk 5.10)? The hopeful believer who first recognized Jesus as the Messiah (Mt 16.16, Mk 8.29, Lk 9.20)? The fearful friend who denied Jesus three times (Mt 26.69–74, Mk 14.66–72, Lk 22.54–61, Jn 18.15–17)? The leader of the early church whom we recognize as the first pope (Jn 21.15, Acts 2.14)? Peter is all these things and more. The Bible paints a picture of a very human leader with sins and weaknesses along with many gifts and great faith.

The author of Matthew uses a play on words to make a statement about Peter as the foundation of the church. The new name that Jesus gives him—Peter—means "rock." So Jesus is saying, "You are a rock, and on this rock I will build my church" (Mt 16.18). The Catholic church uses this Scripture passage as support for its teaching on the pope's position as the spiritual leader and highest authority of the church. Peter's primacy as the first of Jesus' Apostles is understood to be passed on to the current pope, through the succession of popes who go back to the beginnings of the church at Rome.

▶ Mt 16.13–20

MT

not be afraid." 8 And when they looked up, they saw no one except Jesus himself alone.

9 As they were coming down the mountain, Jesus ordered them, "Tell no one about the vision until after the Son of Man has been raised from the dead." 10 And the disciples asked him, "Why, then, do the scribes say that E·li'jah must come first?" 11 He replied, "E·li'jah is indeed coming and will restore all things; 12 but I tell you that E·li'jah has already come, and they did not recognize him, but they did to him whatever they pleased. So also the Son of Man is about to suffer at their hands." 13 Then the disciples understood that he was speaking to them about John the Baptist.

Jesus Cures a Boy with a Demon
(Mk 9.14–29; Lk 9.37–43a)

14 When they came to the crowd, a man came to him, knelt before him, 15 and said, "Lord, have mercy on my son, for he is an epileptic and he suffers terribly; he often falls into the fire and often into the water. 16 And I brought him to your disciples, but they could not cure him." 17 Jesus answered, "You faithless and perverse generation, how much longer must I be with you? How much longer must I put up with you? Bring him here to me." 18 And Jesus rebuked the demon,z and ita came out of him, and the boy was cured instantly. 19 Then the disciples came to Jesus privately and said, "Why could we not cast it out?" 20 He said to them, "Because of your little faith. For truly I tell you, if you have faith the size of ab mustard seed, you will say to this mountain, 'Move from here to there,' and it will move; and nothing will be impossible for you."c

Jesus Again Foretells His Death and Resurrection
(Mk 9.30–32; Lk 9.43b–45)

22 As they were gatheringd in Galilee, Jesus said to them, "The Son of Man is going to be betrayed into human hands, 23 and they will kill him, and on the third day he will be raised." And they were greatly distressed.

Jesus and the Temple Tax

24 When they reached Ca·per'na·um, the collectors of the temple taxe came to Peter and said, "Does your teacher not pay the temple tax?"e 25 He said, "Yes, he does." And when he came home, Jesus spoke of it first, asking, "What do you think, Simon? From whom do kings of the earth take toll or tribute? From their children or from others?" 26 When Peterf said, "From others," Jesus said to him, "Then the children are free. 27 However, so that we do not give offense to them, go to the sea and cast a hook; take the first fish that comes up; and when you open its mouth, you will find a coin;g take that and give it to them for you and me."

Catholic Connections
THE TRANSFIGURATION

The Gospels of Matthew, Mark, and Luke each include the story in Mt 17.1–13, called the Transfiguration. Jesus goes up a mountain with his select disciples, who get to see him in his full glory, as brilliant as the sun. In the Old Testament, mountains are sacred places where people encounter God. The same is true here. God's voice comes from a cloud overshadowing the mountain, and God reveals to the disciples that Jesus is God's beloved Son. Moses (see "Moses," near Ex 2.1), representing the Law, and Elijah (see "Elijah and Elisha," near 1 Kings 17.1), representing the prophets, also appear with Jesus. The appearance of these two Old Testament heroes confirms that Jesus is the fulfillment of both the Law and the prophets—a key point for the author of Matthew.

The Catholic church celebrates the Transfiguration of Jesus in its liturgical year on 6 August.

▶ Mt 17.1–13

True Greatness
(Mk 9.33–37; Lk 9.46–48)

At that time the disciples came to Jesus and asked, "Who is the greatest in the kingdom of heaven?" 2 He called a child, whom he put among them, 3 and said, "Truly I tell you, unless you change and become like children, you will never enter the kingdom of heaven. 4 Whoever becomes humble like this child is the greatest in the kingdom of

---

z Gk it or him   a Gk the demon   b Gk faith as a grain of
c Other ancient authorities add verse 21, But this kind does
not come out except by prayer and fasting   d Other ancient
authorities read living   e Gk didrachma   f Gk he
g Gk stater; the stater was worth two didrachmas

heaven. 5 Whoever welcomes one such child in my name welcomes me.

Temptations to Sin
(Mk 9.42–48; Lk 17.1–2)

6 "If any of you put a stumbling block before one of these little ones who believe in me, it would be better for you if a great millstone were fastened around your neck and you were drowned in the depth of the sea. 7 Woe to the world because of stumbling blocks! Occasions for stumbling are bound to come, but woe to the one by whom the stumbling block comes!

8 "If your hand or your foot causes you to stumble, cut it off and throw it away; it is better for you to enter life maimed or lame than to have two hands or two feet and to be thrown into the eternal fire. 9 And if your eye causes you to stumble, tear it out and throw it away; it is better for you to enter life with one eye than to have two eyes and to be thrown into the hell*h* of fire.

The Parable of the Lost Sheep
(Lk 15.1–7)

10 "Take care that you do not despise one of these little ones; for, I tell you, in heaven their angels continually see the face of my Father in heaven.*i* 12 What do you think? If a shepherd has a hundred sheep, and one of them has gone astray, does he not leave the ninety-nine on the mountains and go in search of the one that went astray? 13 And if he finds it, truly I tell you, he rejoices over it more than over the ninety-nine that never went astray. 14 So it is not the will of your*j* Father in heaven that one of these little ones should be lost.

Reproving Another Who Sins

15 "If another member of the church*k* sins against you,*l* go and point out the fault when the two of you are alone. If the member listens to you, you have regained that one.*m* 16 But if you are not listened to, take one or two others along with you, so that every word may be confirmed by the evidence of two or three witnesses. 17 If the member refuses to listen to them, tell it to the church; and if the offender refuses to listen even to the church, let such a one be to you as a Gentile and a tax collector. 18 Truly I tell you, whatever you bind on earth will be bound in heaven, and whatever you loose on earth will be loosed in heaven. 19 Again, truly I tell you, if two of you agree on earth about anything you ask, it will be done for you by my Father in heaven. 20 For where two or three are gathered in my name, I am there among them."

Forgiveness

21 Then Peter came and said to him, "Lord, if another member of the church*n* sins against me, how often should I forgive? As many as seven

---

h Gk *Gehenna*   *i* Other ancient authorities add verse 11, *For the Son of Man came to save the lost*   *j* Other ancient authorities read *my*   *k* Gk *If your brother*   *l* Other ancient authorities lack *against you*   *m* Gk *the brother*   *n* Gk *if my brother*

Santo Nino

The feast of Santo Nino, which means "Holy Child," is celebrated in the Philippines on the Sunday after the feast of the baptism of the Lord. The beginning of chapter 18 of Matthew is one of the readings you might hear at Mass that day. The feast of Santo Nino celebrates Jesus as a child and is associated with a special statue. The statue portrays the child Jesus wearing a crown, red pants, and a white robe with a large triangular red collar flaring out from the shoulders. The statue can be found in many Philippine churches and car windows.

The original Santo Nino statue was made in Belgium and sent to a girl in the Philippines as a gift for her Baptism. Then it was lost for twenty-four years, until, during a battle, a soldier found it unharmed in the flaming ruins of a house. Folklore says that the statue once hid the island of Cebu from English invaders and that when the statue was placed in the sea during a drought, it miraculously began to rain.

The devotion to Santo Nino can help us remember that Jesus was once a child, who was taught and cared for by loving parents. In the spirit of Santo Nino, why not surprise a parent or grandparent with a love letter thanking him or her for all he or she has done for you?

▶ Mt 18.1–11

MT

times?" 22 Jesus said to him, "Not seven times, but, I tell you, seventy-seven° times.

The Parable of the Unforgiving Servant

23 "For this reason the kingdom of heaven may be compared to a king who wished to settle accounts with his slaves. 24 When he began the reckoning, one who owed him ten thousand talents^p was brought to him; 25 and, as he could not pay, his lord ordered him to be sold, together with his wife and children and all his possessions, and payment to be made. 26 So the slave fell on his knees before him, saying, 'Have patience with me, and I will pay you everything.' 27 And out of pity for him, the lord of that slave released him and forgave him the debt. 28 But that same slave, as he went out, came upon one of his fellow slaves who owed him a hundred denarii;^q and seizing him by the throat, he said, 'Pay what you owe.' 29 Then his fellow slave fell down and pleaded with him, 'Have patience with me, and I will pay you.' 30 But he refused; then he went and threw him into prison until he would pay the debt. 31 When his fellow slaves saw what had happened, they were greatly distressed, and they went and reported to their lord all that had taken place. 32 Then his lord summoned him and said to him, 'You wicked

PRAY IT
Forgive Us Our Debts

The parable of the unforgiving servant spells out clearly (and a bit harshly) what it means to ask God to "forgive us our debts, / as we also have forgiven our debtors" (Mt 6.12).

Bring to mind a person who has hurt you or made you angry lately. Hold this person's image in your thoughts, and realize that Jesus is calling you to forgive her or him. Now, tell this person in your thoughts how she or he has hurt you. Finally, offer your forgiveness to the person so that you can let go of the burden of your hurt.

When you are done, imagine Jesus in your prayer and share with him something you have done that has hurt another person. Let Jesus forgive you in the same way you just forgave.

▶ Mt 18.21–35

Catholic Connections
MARRIAGE

When the Pharisees try to test Jesus with a question about divorce, Jesus speaks about marriage. Rather than focus on the negative, Jesus turns everyone's attention to the positive—the beauty of two people who "are no longer two, but one flesh" (Mt 19.6). Catholics celebrate Jesus' positive view in the sacrament of Marriage, one of the seven official sacraments of the church. The church believes that in a Christian marriage, God's love and grace are present in a special way (see Eph 5.21–33).

The wedding rings and the vows professed in front of the assembled guests are important symbols in the ceremony, but the primary sign of the sacrament is the spouses themselves. It is their love, commitment, and faith that make God's love real and present to the community.

▶ Mt 19.1–9

slave! I forgave you all that debt because you pleaded with me. 33 Should you not have had mercy on your fellow slave, as I had mercy on you?' 34 And in anger his lord handed him over to be tortured until he would pay his entire debt. 35 So my heavenly Father will also do to every one of you, if you do not forgive your brother or sister^r from your heart."

Teaching about Divorce
(Mk 10.1–12)

When Jesus had finished saying these things, he left Galilee and went to the region of Judea beyond the Jordan. 2 Large crowds followed him, and he cured them there.

3 Some Phar·i·sees came to him, and to test him they asked, "Is it lawful for a man to divorce his wife for any cause?" 4 He answered, "Have you

---

° Or *seventy times seven* ^p A talent was worth more than fifteen years' wages of a laborer ^q The denarius was the usual day's wage for a laborer ^r Gk *brother*

not read that the one who made them at the beginning 'made them male and female,' 5 and said, 'For this reason a man shall leave his father and mother and be joined to his wife, and the two shall become one flesh'? 6 So they are no longer two, but one flesh. Therefore what God has joined together, let no one separate." 7 They said to him, "Why then did Moses command us to give a certificate of dismissal and to divorce her?" 8 He said to them, "It was because you were so hard-hearted that Moses allowed you to divorce your wives, but from the beginning it was not so. 9 And I say to you, whoever divorces his wife, except for unchastity, and marries another commits adultery."s

10 His disciples said to him, "If such is the case of a man with his wife, it is better not to marry." 11 But he said to them, "Not everyone can accept this teaching, but only those to whom it is given. 12 For there are eunuchs who have been so from birth, and there are eunuchs who have been made eunuchs by others, and there are eunuchs who have made themselves eunuchs for the sake of the kingdom of heaven. Let anyone accept this who can."

Jesus Blesses Little Children
(Mk 10.13–16; Lk 18.15–17)

13 Then little children were being brought to him in order that he might lay his hands on them and pray. The disciples spoke sternly to those who brought them; 14 but Jesus said, "Let the little children come to me, and do not stop them; for it is to such as these that the kingdom of heaven belongs." 15 And he laid his hands on them and went on his way.

The Rich Young Man
(Mk 10.17–31; Lk 18.18–30)

16 Then someone came to him and said, "Teacher, what good deed must I do to have eternal life?" 17 And he said to him, "Why do you ask me about what is good? There is only one who is good. If you wish to enter into life, keep the commandments." 18 He said to him, "Which ones?" And Jesus said, "You shall not murder; You shall not commit adultery; You shall not steal; You shall not bear false witness; 19 Honor your father and mother; also, You shall love your neighbor as yourself." 20 The young man said to him, "I have kept all these;t what do I still lack?" 21 Jesus said to him, "If you wish to be perfect, go, sell your possessions, and give the moneyu to the poor, and you will have treasure in heaven; then come, follow me." 22 When the young man heard this word, he went away grieving, for he had many possessions.

23 Then Jesus said to his disciples, "Truly I tell you, it will be hard for a rich person to enter the kingdom of heaven. 24 Again I tell you, it is easier for a camel to go through the eye of a needle than for someone who is rich to enter the kingdom of God." 25 When the disciples heard this, they were greatly astounded and said, "Then who can be saved?" 26 But Jesus looked at them and said, "For mortals it is impossible, but for God all things are possible."

27 Then Peter said in reply, "Look, we have left everything and followed you. What then will we have?" 28 Jesus said to them, "Truly I tell you, at the renewal of all things, when the Son of Man is seated on the throne of his glory, you who have followed me will also sit on twelve thrones, judging the twelve tribes of Israel. 29 And everyone who has left houses or brothers or sisters or father or mother or children or fields, for my name's sake, will receive a hundredfold,v and will inherit eternal life. 30 But many who are first will be last, and the last will be first.

The Laborers in the Vineyard

"For the kingdom of heaven is like a landowner who went out early in the morning to hire laborers for his vineyard. 2 After agreeing with the laborers for the usual daily wage,w he sent them into his vineyard. 3 When he went out about nine o'clock, he saw others standing idle in the marketplace; 4 and he said to them, 'You also go into the vineyard, and I will pay you whatever is right.' So they went. 5 When he went out again about noon and about three o'clock, he did the same. 6 And about five o'clock he went out and found others standing around; and he said to them, 'Why are you standing here idle all day?' 7 They said to him, 'Because no one has hired us.' He said to them, 'You also go into the vineyard.' 8 When evening came, the owner of the vineyard said to his manager, 'Call the laborers and give them their pay, beginning with the last and then going to the first.' 9 When those hired about five o'clock came, each of them received the usual daily wage.w 10 Now when the first came, they thought they would receive more; but each of them also received the usual daily wage.w 11 And when they received it, they grumbled against the landowner, 12 saying, 'These last worked only one hour, and you have made them equal to us who have borne the burden of the day

---

s Other ancient authorities read *except on the ground of unchastity, causes her to commit adultery*; others add at the end of the verse *and he who marries a divorced woman commits adultery*　t Other ancient authorities add *from my youth*　u Gk lacks *the money*　v Other ancient authorities read *manifold*　w Gk *a denarius*

MT

and the scorching heat.' 13 But he replied to one of them, 'Friend, I am doing you no wrong; did you not agree with me for the usual daily wage?*x* 14 Take what belongs to you and go; I choose to give to this last the same as I give to you. 15 Am I not allowed to do what I choose with what belongs to me? Or are you envious because I am generous?'*y* 16 So the last will be first, and the first will be last."*z*

PRAY IT

Are You for Real?

Read Mt 20.1–16 as an introduction to this prayer:

Lord, could you really be such a generous God? I have heard that you offer the same welcome to the sinner as to the saint. That you walk with the angry as well as the joyful, and can embrace the hurtful as well as the helpful. That you even offer the exact same love for the last to turn to you as you do for the first.

That's just not the way it is done around here, God, so excuse me if I have a hard time believing. But then, I've heard it said that you are as patient with the doubtful as you are with the faithful.

If you are this type of God, then please be with me right now. I need to talk to someone who understands and loves me in spite of my doubts and sin. I need a God who breaks the rules to let me know how much I am loved.

If you are indeed this kind of God, thanks! Thanks for being so crazy with your love that you would allow someone like me to hang around you. Promise to stay with me as I learn to trust in you and your acceptance of all people. Amen.

▶ Mt 20.1–16

A Third Time Jesus Foretells His Death and Resurrection
(Mk 10.32–34; Lk 18.31–34)

17 While Jesus was going up to Jerusalem, he took the twelve disciples aside by themselves, and said to them on the way, 18 "See, we are going up to Jerusalem, and the Son of Man will be handed over to the chief priests and scribes, and they will condemn him to death; 19 then they will hand him over to the Gentiles to be mocked and flogged and crucified; and on the third day he will be raised."

The Request of the Mother of James and John
(Mk 10.35–45)

20 Then the mother of the sons of Zeb′e·dee came to him with her sons, and kneeling before him, she asked a favor of him. 21 And he said to her, "What do you want?" She said to him, "Declare that these two sons of mine will sit, one at your right hand and one at your left, in your kingdom." 22 But Jesus answered, "You do not know what you are asking. Are you able to drink the cup that I am about to drink?"*a* They said to him, "We are able." 23 He said to them, "You will indeed drink my cup, but to sit at my right hand and at my left, this is not mine to grant, but it is for those for whom it has been prepared by my Father."

24 When the ten heard it, they were angry with the two brothers. 25 But Jesus called them to him and said, "You know that the rulers of the Gentiles lord it over them, and their great ones are tyrants over them. 26 It will not be so among you; but whoever wishes to be great among you must be your servant, 27 and whoever wishes to be first among you must be your slave; 28 just as the Son of Man came not to be served but to serve, and to give his life a ransom for many."

Jesus Heals Two Blind Men
(Mk 10.46–52; Lk 18.35–43)

29 As they were leaving Jericho, a large crowd followed him. 30 There were two blind men sitting by the roadside. When they heard that Jesus was passing by, they shouted, "Lord,*b* have mercy on us, Son of David!" 31 The crowd sternly ordered them to be quiet; but they shouted even more loudly, "Have mercy on us, Lord, Son of David!" 32 Jesus stood still and called them, saying, "What do you want me to do for you?" 33 They said to him, "Lord, let our eyes be opened." 34 Moved with compassion, Jesus touched their eyes. Immediately they regained their sight and followed him.

---

x Gk *a denarius*   *y* Gk *is your eye evil because I am good?*
z Other ancient authorities add *for many are called but few are chosen*   *a* Other ancient authorities add *or to be baptized with the baptism that I am baptized with?*   *b* Other ancient authorities lack *Lord*

True Greatness

What good parent does not want his or her son or daughter to find success in life? Like most people at the time of Jesus, the mother of James and John is confused about the Kingdom that Jesus came to establish. She lobbies for her sons (Mt 20.21), hoping that they might be made "senior vice presidents" of the new "firm."

The resulting confusion and anger among the disciples allows Jesus the opportunity to remind them of how greatness is defined by God. Jesus turns the tables on them by asking in a veiled way, "Are you willing to suffer (drink the cup) as I will suffer?" He reminds them—and us—that true greatness is in serving others (verses 26–27).

Who do you know who is truly a servant to others? When you are in a position of leadership, do you see it as a chance to serve others? Why or why not?

▸ Mt 20.20–28

Jesus' Triumphal Entry into Jerusalem
(Mk 11.1–10; Lk 19.28–40; Jn 12.12–19)

When they had come near Jerusalem and had reached Beth′pha·gē, at the Mount of Olives, Jesus sent two disciples, 2 saying to them, "Go into the village ahead of you, and immediately you will find a donkey tied, and a colt with her; untie them and bring them to me. 3 If anyone says anything to you, just say this, 'The Lord needs them.' And he will send them immediately.c" 4 This took place to fulfill what had been spoken through the prophet, saying,

5 "Tell the daughter of Zion,
  Look, your king is coming to you,
    humble, and mounted on a donkey,
      and on a colt, the foal of a donkey."

6 The disciples went and did as Jesus had directed them; 7 they brought the donkey and the colt, and

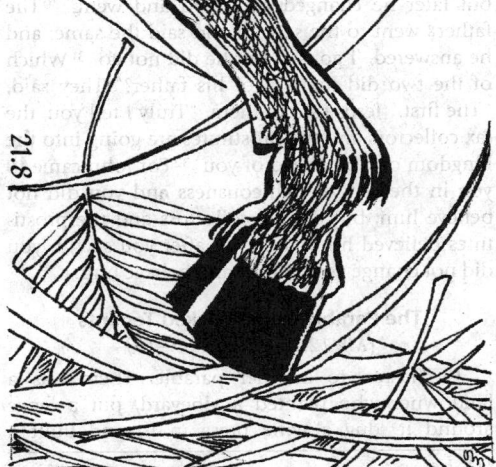

21.8

put their cloaks on them, and he sat on them. 8 A very large crowdd spread their cloaks on the road, and others cut branches from the trees and spread them on the road. 9 The crowds that went ahead of him and that followed were shouting,

"Hosanna to the Son of David!
  Blessed is the one who comes in the
    name of the Lord!
  Hosanna in the highest heaven!"

10 When he entered Jerusalem, the whole city was in turmoil, asking, "Who is this?" 11 The crowds were saying, "This is the prophet Jesus from Nazareth in Galilee."

Jesus Cleanses the Temple
(Mk 11.15–19; Lk 19.45–48; Jn 2.13–25)

12 Then Jesus entered the templee and drove out all who were selling and buying in the temple, and he overturned the tables of the money changers and the seats of those who sold doves. 13 He said to them, "It is written,

'My house shall be called a house of prayer';
  but you are making it a den of robbers."

14 The blind and the lame came to him in the temple, and he cured them. 15 But when the chief priests and the scribes saw the amazing things that he did, and heardf the children crying out in the temple, "Hosanna to the Son of David," they became angry 16 and said to him, "Do you hear what these are saying?" Jesus said to them, "Yes; have you never read,

'Out of the mouths of infants and nursing
    babies
  you have prepared praise for yourself'?"

---

c Or 'The Lord needs them and will send them back immediately.'   d Or Most of the crowd   e Other ancient authorities add of God   f Gk lacks heard

Jesus and Civil Disobedience

The cleansing of the Temple is one of the few stories that occurs in all four Gospels. To fully understand Jesus' anger in this situation, we need to remember that the Jews were required to offer sacrificial animals as part of their religious obligation. Herod the Great had turned the sale of sacrificial animals into a money-making enterprise. Money changers exchanged Roman coins (which were unsuitable for the purchase of sacrificial animals because they had images of pagan gods on them) for other coins. The Temple complex became the source of wealth for the religious and civil leaders of Jerusalem—something many people believed profaned the Temple.

Jesus' clearing of the Temple was an act of religious and civil disobedience challenging the highest members of Jewish society. The Gospels of Luke and Mark say it was immediately after this event that the Jewish leaders began looking for a way to kill Jesus. The only thing that prevented them from doing so immediately was his popularity with the people (Mk 11.18, Lk 19.47–48). Jesus knew that his actions and teachings challenging these corrupt leaders would lead to his death (see Mt 20.17–19).

If Jesus had been just a nice guy claiming to be God's Son, he probably would have been left alone. But he took an active stand against injustice, greed, and religious hypocrisy, outraging the leaders of his time. What is your response to Jesus when he challenges you to live justly and to protest the injustice of economic and political systems?

▶ Mt 21.12–13

---

17 He left them, went out of the city to Beth'a•ny, and spent the night there.

Jesus Curses the Fig Tree
(Mk 11.12–14, 20–25)

18 In the morning, when he returned to the city, he was hungry. 19 And seeing a fig tree by the side of the road, he went to it and found nothing at all on it but leaves. Then he said to it, "May no fruit ever come from you again!" And the fig tree withered at once. 20 When the disciples saw it, they were amazed, saying, "How did the fig tree wither at once?" 21 Jesus answered them, "Truly I tell you, if you have faith and do not doubt, not only will you do what has been done to the fig tree, but even if you say to this mountain, 'Be lifted up and thrown into the sea,' it will be done. 22 Whatever you ask for in prayer with faith, you will receive."

The Authority of Jesus Questioned
(Mk 11.27–33; Lk 20.1–8)

23 When he entered the temple, the chief priests and the elders of the people came to him as he was teaching, and said, "By what authority are you doing these things, and who gave you this authority?" 24 Jesus said to them, "I will also ask you one question; if you tell me the answer, then I will also tell you by what authority I do these things. 25 Did the baptism of John come from heaven, or was it of human origin?" And they argued with one another, "If we say, 'From heaven,' he will say to us, 'Why then did you not believe him?' 26 But if we say, 'Of human origin,' we are afraid of the crowd; for all regard John as a prophet." 27 So they answered Jesus, "We do not know." And he said to them, "Neither will I tell you by what authority I am doing these things.

The Parable of the Two Sons

28 "What do you think? A man had two sons; he went to the first and said, 'Son, go and work in the vineyard today.' 29 He answered, 'I will not'; but later he changed his mind and went. 30 The father^g went to the second and said the same; and he answered, 'I go, sir'; but he did not go. 31 Which of the two did the will of his father?" They said, "The first." Jesus said to them, "Truly I tell you, the tax collectors and the prostitutes are going into the kingdom of God ahead of you. 32 For John came to you in the way of righteousness and you did not believe him, but the tax collectors and the prostitutes believed him; and even after you saw it, you did not change your minds and believe him.

The Parable of the Wicked Tenants
(Mk 12.1–12; Lk 20.9–19)

33 "Listen to another parable. There was a landowner who planted a vineyard, put a fence around it, dug a wine press in it, and built a

g Gk He

watchtower. Then he leased it to tenants and went to another country. 34 When the harvest time had come, he sent his slaves to the tenants to collect his produce. 35 But the tenants seized his slaves and beat one, killed another, and stoned another. 36 Again he sent other slaves, more than the first; and they treated them in the same way. 37 Finally he sent his son to them, saying, 'They will respect my son.' 38 But when the tenants saw the son, they said to themselves, 'This is the heir; come, let us kill him and get his inheritance.' 39 So they seized him, threw him out of the vineyard, and killed him. 40 Now when the owner of the vineyard comes, what will he do to those tenants?" 41 They said to him, "He will put those wretches to a miserable death, and lease the vineyard to other tenants who will give him the produce at the harvest time."

42 Jesus said to them, "Have you never read in the scriptures:

'The stone that the builders rejected
  has become the cornerstone;[h]
this was the Lord's doing,
  and it is amazing in our eyes'?

43 Therefore I tell you, the kingdom of God will be taken away from you and given to a people that produces the fruits of the kingdom.[i] 44 The one who falls on this stone will be broken to pieces; and it will crush anyone on whom it falls."[j]

45 When the chief priests and the Phar'i·sees heard his parables, they realized that he was speaking about them. 46 They wanted to arrest him, but they feared the crowds, because they regarded him as a prophet.

The Parable of the Wedding Banquet
(Lk 14.15–24)

Once more Jesus spoke to them in parables, saying: 2 "The kingdom of heaven may be compared to a king who gave a wedding banquet for his son. 3 He sent his slaves to call those who had been invited to the wedding banquet, but they would not come. 4 Again he sent other slaves, saying, 'Tell those who have been invited: Look, I have prepared my dinner, my oxen and my fat calves have been slaughtered, and everything is ready; come to the wedding banquet.' 5 But they made light of it and went away, one to his farm, another to his business, 6 while the rest seized his slaves, mistreated them, and killed them. 7 The king was enraged. He sent his troops, destroyed those murderers, and burned their city. 8 Then he said to his slaves, 'The wedding is ready, but those invited were not worthy. 9 Go therefore into the main streets, and invite everyone you find to the wedding banquet.' 10 Those slaves went out into the

streets and gathered all whom they found, both good and bad; so the wedding hall was filled with guests.

11 "But when the king came in to see the guests, he noticed a man there who was not wearing a wedding robe, 12 and he said to him, 'Friend, how did you get in here without a wedding robe?' And he was speechless. 13 Then the king said to the attendants, 'Bind him hand and foot, and throw him into the outer darkness, where there will be weeping and gnashing of teeth.' 14 For many are called, but few are chosen."

The Question about Paying Taxes
(Mk 12.13–17; Lk 20.20–26)

15 Then the Phar'i·sees went and plotted to entrap him in what he said. 16 So they sent their disciples to him, along with the He·rō'di·ans, saying, "Teacher, we know that you are sincere, and teach the way of God in accordance with truth, and show deference to no one; for you do not regard people with partiality. 17 Tell us, then, what you think. Is it lawful to pay taxes to the emperor, or not?" 18 But Jesus, aware of their malice, said, "Why are you putting me to the test, you hypocrites? 19 Show me the coin used for the tax." And they brought him a denarius. 20 Then he said to them, "Whose head is this, and whose title?" 21 They answered, "The emperor's." Then he said to them, "Give therefore to the emperor the things that are the emperor's, and to God the things that are God's." 22 When they heard this, they were amazed; and they left him and went away.

The Question about the Resurrection
(Mk 12.18–27; Lk 20.27–40)

23 The same day some Sad'du·cees came to him, saying there is no resurrection;[k] and they asked him a question, saying, 24 "Teacher, Moses said, 'If a man dies childless, his brother shall marry the widow, and raise up children for his brother.' 25 Now there were seven brothers among us; the first married, and died childless, leaving the widow to his brother. 26 The second did the same, so also the third, down to the seventh. 27 Last of all, the woman herself died. 28 In the resurrection, then, whose wife of the seven will she be? For all of them had married her."

29 Jesus answered them, "You are wrong, because you know neither the scriptures nor the power of God. 30 For in the resurrection they neither marry nor are given in marriage, but are like

h Or keystone   i Gk the fruits of it   j Other ancient authorities lack verse 44   k Other ancient authorities read who say that there is no resurrection

MT

angels[l] in heaven. 31 And as for the resurrection of the dead, have you not read what was said to you by God, 32 'I am the God of Abraham, the God of Isaac, and the God of Jacob'? He is God not of the dead, but of the living." 33 And when the crowd heard it, they were astounded at his teaching.

The Greatest Commandment
(Mk 12.28–34; Lk 10.25–28)

34 When the Phar'i·sees heard that he had silenced the Sad'du·cees, they gathered together, 35 and one of them, a lawyer, asked him a question to test him. 36 "Teacher, which commandment in the law is the greatest?" 37 He said to him, " 'You shall love the Lord your God with all your heart, and with all your soul, and with all your mind.' 38 This is the greatest and first commandment. 39 And a second is like it: 'You shall love your neighbor as yourself.' 40 On these two commandments hang all the law and the prophets."

Jesus Denounces Scribes and Pharisees
(Mk 12.38–40; Lk 20.45–47)

Then Jesus said to the crowds and to his disciples, 2 "The scribes and the Phar'i·sees sit on Moses' seat; 3 therefore, do whatever they teach you and follow it; but do not do as they do, for they do not practice what they teach. 4 They tie up heavy burdens, hard to bear,[o] and lay them on the shoulders of others; but they themselves are unwilling to lift a finger to move them. 5 They do all their deeds to be seen by others; for they make their phylacteries broad and their fringes long. 6 They love to have the place of honor at banquets and the best seats in the synagogues, 7 and to be greeted with respect in the marketplaces, and to have people call them rabbi. 8 But you are not to be called rabbi, for you have one teacher, and you are all students.[p] 9 And call no one your father on earth, for you have one Father—the one in heaven. 10 Nor are you to be called instructors, for you have one instructor, the

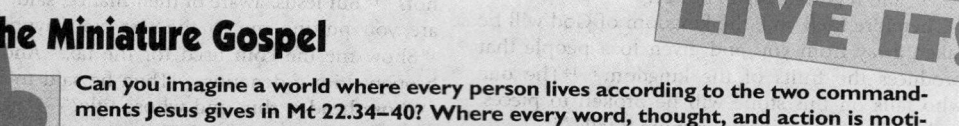

The Miniature Gospel   LIVE IT!

Can you imagine a world where every person lives according to the two commandments Jesus gives in Mt 22.34–40? Where every word, thought, and action is motivated by a deep love for God and by a desire for the well-being of others? Sounds a bit like the Garden of Eden! Libraries are filled with volumes describing philosophies for achieving the ideal human society, yet Jesus articulates the perfect plan in a few short sentences. These two great commands remain for us as a kind of miniature Gospel.

Why not take the time to memorize verses 37–39? Let this miniature Gospel become such a part of you that you become a living, breathing example for others.

▸ Mt 22.34–40

The Question about David's Son
(Mk 12.35–37; Lk 20.41–44)

41 Now while the Phar'i·sees were gathered together, Jesus asked them this question: 42 "What do you think of the Messiah?[m] Whose son is he?" They said to him, "The son of David." 43 He said to them, "How is it then that David by the Spirit[n] calls him Lord, saying,

44 'The Lord said to my Lord,
    "Sit at my right hand,
    until I put your enemies under your
        feet" '?
45 If David thus calls him Lord, how can he be his son?" 46 No one was able to give him an answer, nor from that day did anyone dare to ask him any more questions.

Messiah.[q] 11 The greatest among you will be your servant. 12 All who exalt themselves will be humbled, and all who humble themselves will be exalted.

13 "But woe to you, scribes and Phar'i·sees, hypocrites! For you lock people out of the kingdom of heaven. For you do not go in yourselves, and when others are going in, you stop them.[r] 15 Woe to you, scribes and Phar'i·sees, hypocrites!

---

[l] Other ancient authorities add *of God*   [m] Or *Christ*
[n] Gk *in spirit*   [o] Other ancient authorities lack *hard to bear*   [p] Gk *brothers*   [q] Or *the Christ*   [r] Other authorities add here (or after verse 12) verse 14, *Woe to you, scribes and Pharisees, hypocrites! For you devour widows' houses and for the sake of appearance you make long prayers; therefore you will receive the greater condemnation*

PRAY IT!

No Respect

The woe statements of Jesus in Mt 23.1–24 are his harshest words in all the Gospels. The community in which the author of Matthew lived had negative experiences with Jewish leaders (see "Pharisees, Sadducees, and Scribes," Mt 3.7), and their hard feelings are reflected in Jesus' words. We should take Mt 23.3–24 not as a condemnation of Jewish people but as a call to do the following:

- practice what we preach (verse 3)
- show compassion rather than burden others (verse 4)
- not use religious practices to look important (verses 5–7)
- be humble and respect the people who follow us (verses 8–15)
- be guided by mercy and justice in our understanding of law (verses 23–24)

In your prayer, reflect or journal on the following questions:

- How do I live out the faith I profess each week in both word and action?
- Do I ask of others what I am not ready to do myself?
- Will I use power, position, or influence humbly and at the service of others?

▶ Mt 23.1–36

For you cross sea and land to make a single convert, and you make the new convert twice as much a child of hell[s] as yourselves.

16 "Woe to you, blind guides, who say, 'Whoever swears by the sanctuary is bound by nothing, but whoever swears by the gold of the sanctuary is bound by the oath.' 17 You blind fools! For which is greater, the gold or the sanctuary that has made the gold sacred? 18 And you say, 'Whoever swears by the altar is bound by nothing, but whoever swears by the gift that is on the altar is bound by the oath.' 19 How blind you are! For which is greater, the gift or the altar that makes the gift sacred? 20 So whoever swears by the altar, swears by it and by everything on it; 21 and whoever swears by the sanctuary, swears by it and by the one who dwells in it; 22 and whoever swears by heaven, swears by the throne of God and by the one who is seated upon it.

23 "Woe to you, scribes and Phar'i•sees, hypocrites! For you tithe mint, dill, and cummin, and have neglected the weightier matters of the law: justice and mercy and faith. It is these you ought to have practiced without neglecting the others. 24 You blind guides! You strain out a gnat but swallow a camel!

25 "Woe to you, scribes and Phar'i•sees, hypocrites! For you clean the outside of the cup and of the plate, but inside they are full of greed and self-indulgence. 26 You blind Phar'i•see! First clean the inside of the cup,[t] so that the outside also may become clean.

27 "Woe to you, scribes and Phar'i•sees, hypocrites! For you are like whitewashed tombs, which on the outside look beautiful, but inside they are full of the bones of the dead and of all kinds of filth. 28 So you also on the outside look righteous to others, but inside you are full of hypocrisy and lawlessness.

29 "Woe to you, scribes and Phar'i•sees, hypocrites! For you build the tombs of the prophets and decorate the graves of the righteous, 30 and you say, 'If we had lived in the days of our ancestors, we would not have taken part with them in shedding the blood of the prophets.' 31 Thus you testify against yourselves that you are descendants of those who murdered the prophets. 32 Fill up, then, the measure of your ancestors. 33 You snakes, you brood of vipers! How can you escape being sentenced to hell?[s] 34 Therefore I send you prophets, sages, and scribes, some of whom you will kill and crucify, and some you will flog in your synagogues and pursue from town to town, 35 so that upon you may come all the righteous blood shed on earth, from the blood of righteous Abel to the blood of Zech•a•ri'ah son of Bar•a•chi'ah, whom you murdered between the sanctuary and the altar. 36 Truly I tell you, all this will come upon this generation.

The Lament over Jerusalem
(Lk 13.34–35)

37 "Jerusalem, Jerusalem, the city that kills the prophets and stones those who are sent to it! How often have I desired to gather your children together as a hen gathers her brood under her wings, and you were not willing! 38 See, your house is left to you, desolate.[u] 39 For I tell you, you will not see me again until you say, 'Blessed is the one who comes in the name of the Lord.' "

---

s Gk *Gehenna*   t Other ancient authorities add *and of the plate*   u Other ancient authorities lack *desolate*

The Destruction of the Temple Foretold
(Mk 13.1–2; Lk 21.5–6)

As Jesus came out of the temple and was going away, his disciples came to point out to him the buildings of the temple. 2 Then he asked them, "You see all these, do you not? Truly I tell you, not one stone will be left here upon another; all will be thrown down."

Signs of the End of the Age
(Mk 13.3–8; Lk 21.7–11)

3 When he was sitting on the Mount of Olives, the disciples came to him privately, saying, "Tell us, when will this be, and what will be the sign of your coming and of the end of the age?" 4 Jesus answered them, "Beware that no one leads you astray. 5 For many will come in my name, saying, 'I am the Messiah!'*v* and they will lead many astray. 6 And you will hear of wars and rumors of wars; see that you are not alarmed; for this must take place, but the end is not yet. 7 For nation will rise against nation, and kingdom against kingdom, and there will be famines*w* and earthquakes in various places: 8 all this is but the beginning of the birth pangs.

Persecutions Foretold
(Mk 13.9–13; Lk 21.12–19)

9 "Then they will hand you over to be tortured and will put you to death, and you will be hated by all nations because of my name. 10 Then many will fall away,*x* and they will betray one another and hate one another. 11 And many false prophets will arise and lead many astray. 12 And because of the increase of lawlessness, the love of many will grow cold. 13 But the one who endures to the end will be saved. 14 And this good news*y* of the kingdom will be proclaimed throughout the world, as a testimony to all the nations; and then the end will come.

The Desolating Sacrilege
(Mk 13.14–23; Lk 17.23–24, 37; 21.20–24)

15 "So when you see the desolating sacrilege standing in the holy place, as was spoken of by the prophet Daniel (let the reader understand), 16 then those in Judea must flee to the mountains; 17 the one on the housetop must not go down to take what is in the house; 18 the one in the field must not turn back to get a coat. 19 Woe to those who are pregnant and to those who are nursing infants in those days! 20 Pray that your flight may not be in winter or on a sabbath. 21 For at that time there will be great suffering, such as has not been from the beginning of the world until now, no, and never will be. 22 And if those days had not been cut short, no one would be saved; but for the sake of the elect those days will be cut short. 23 Then if anyone says to you, 'Look! Here is the Messiah!'*v* or 'There he is!'—do not believe it. 24 For false messiahs*z* and false prophets will appear and produce great signs and omens, to lead astray, if possible, even the elect. 25 Take note, I have told you beforehand. 26 So, if they say to you, 'Look! He is in the wilderness,' do not go out. If they say, 'Look! He is in the inner rooms,' do not believe it. 27 For as the lightning comes from the east and flashes as far as the west, so will be the coming of the Son of Man.

---

v Or *the Christ* *w* Other ancient authorities add *and pestilences* *x* Or *stumble* *y* Or *gospel* *z* Or *christs*

Be Ready

LIVE IT!

Have you ever been asked questions like these: If you knew you only had one week to live, what would you do in that time? If you knew you were going to see a loved one for the last time, what would you say to him or her? Faced with those scenarios, many people imagine themselves acting more lovingly and generously than they ordinarily do.

Jesus sets up a similar scenario when he warns his followers to keep awake (Mt 24.42). In this final teaching in Matthew, Jesus is speaking of the final coming of God. The Gospel reminds us that no one knows when Christ will come for us. It is foolish and dangerous to put off living a life committed to Christ.

If you knew you were to stand before God tomorrow, how would you live your life today?

▶ Mt 24.36–44

28 Wherever the corpse is, there the vultures will gather.

The Coming of the Son of Man
(Mk 13.24–27; Lk 21.25–28)

29 "Immediately after the suffering of those days

the sun will be darkened,
    and the moon will not give its light;
the stars will fall from heaven,
    and the powers of heaven will be shaken.

30 Then the sign of the Son of Man will appear in heaven, and then all the tribes of the earth will mourn, and they will see 'the Son of Man coming on the clouds of heaven' with power and great glory. 31 And he will send out his angels with a loud trumpet call, and they will gather his elect from the four winds, from one end of heaven to the other.

The Lesson of the Fig Tree
(Mk 13.28–31; Lk 21.29–33)

32 "From the fig tree learn its lesson: as soon as its branch becomes tender and puts forth its leaves, you know that summer is near. 33 So also, when you see all these things, you know that he*a* is near, at the very gates. 34 Truly I tell you, this generation will not pass away until all these things have taken place. 35 Heaven and earth will pass away, but my words will not pass away.

The Necessity for Watchfulness
(Mk 13.32–37; Lk 17.26–27, 34–35; 21.34–36)

36 "But about that day and hour no one knows, neither the angels of heaven, nor the Son,*b* but only the Father. 37 For as the days of Noah were, so will be the coming of the Son of Man. 38 For as in those days before the flood they were eating and drinking, marrying and giving in marriage, until the day Noah entered the ark, 39 and they knew nothing until the flood came and swept them all away, so too will be the coming of the Son of Man. 40 Then two will be in the field; one will be taken and one will be left. 41 Two women will be grinding meal together; one will be taken and one will be left. 42 Keep awake therefore, for you do not know on what day*c* your Lord is coming. 43 But understand this: if the owner of the house had known in what part of the night the thief was coming, he would have stayed awake and would not have let his house be broken into. 44 Therefore you also must be ready, for the Son of Man is coming at an unexpected hour.

The Faithful or the Unfaithful Slave
(Lk 12.41–48)

45 "Who then is the faithful and wise slave, whom his master has put in charge of his household, to give the other slaves*d* their allowance of food at the proper time? 46 Blessed is that slave whom his master will find at work when he arrives. 47 Truly I tell you, he will put that one in charge of all his possessions. 48 But if that wicked slave says to himself, 'My master is delayed,' 49 and he begins to beat his fellow slaves, and eats and drinks with drunkards, 50 the master of that slave will come on a day when he does not expect him and at an hour that he does not know. 51 He will cut him in pieces*e* and put him with the hypocrites, where there will be weeping and gnashing of teeth.

PRAY IT?

When Are You Coming?

I have accepted your invitation, Lord.
    But when are you coming?
I need to be ready, Lord.
    But when are you coming?
I want to share your love with others, Lord.
    But when are you coming?
I will be prepared, Lord.
    No matter when you are coming.

▶ Mt 25.1–13

The Parable of the Ten Bridesmaids

"Then the kingdom of heaven will be like this. Ten bridesmaids*f* took their lamps and went to meet the bridegroom.*g* 2 Five of them were foolish, and five were wise. 3 When the foolish took their lamps, they took no oil with them; 4 but the wise took flasks of oil with their lamps. 5 As the bridegroom was delayed, all of them became drowsy and slept. 6 But at midnight there was a shout, 'Look! Here is the bridegroom! Come out to meet him.' 7 Then all those bridesmaids*f* got up and trimmed their lamps. 8 The foolish said to the wise, 'Give us some of your oil, for our lamps are going out.' 9 But the wise replied, 'No! there will not be enough for you and for us; you had better go to the dealers and buy some for yourselves.'

---

a Or it   *b* Other ancient authorities lack *nor the Son*
c Other ancient authorities read *at what hour*   *d* Gk *to give them*   *e* Or *cut him off*   *f* Gk *virgins*   *g* Other ancient authorities add *and the bride*

10 And while they went to buy it, the bridegroom came, and those who were ready went with him into the wedding banquet; and the door was shut. 11 Later the other bridesmaids[h] came also, saying, 'Lord, lord, open to us.' 12 But he replied, 'Truly I tell you, I do not know you.' 13 Keep awake therefore, for you know neither the day nor the hour.[i]

AFRICAN AMERICAN

The Principle of *Kuumba*

I wish I had a great singing voice. I often daydream about belting out songs with the vocal power of the sister of soul, Aretha Franklin. Sure, I have other gifts, but more than anything else, I wish I could sing. Here I go, neglecting what I do have, as I yearn for what I lack.

This attitude sounds a bit like that of the ungrateful servant Jesus speaks of in Mt 25.14–30, the parable of the talents, doesn't it? In the parable, the servant is given a talent by his master, but he keeps it hidden. In the end, this timid servant loses the one talent he has.

Our talents and abilities have been given to us by God. The Kwanzaa principle of *kuumba* (creativity) calls us to use our talents creatively and boldly in the service of God. Don't second-guess the Lord by wanting something you do not have. Trust that God has blessed you with the gifts you need, and use them!

Dear God, thank you for what I have. Help me use it to your glory. Amen.

▶ **Mt 25.14–30**

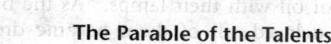

The Parable of the Talents
(Lk 19.11–27)

14 "For it is as if a man, going on a journey, summoned his slaves and entrusted his property to them; 15 to one he gave five talents,[j] to another two, to another one, to each according to his ability. Then he went away. 16 The one who had received the five talents went off at once and traded with them, and made five more talents. 17 In the same way, the one who had the two talents made two more talents. 18 But the one who had received the one talent went off and dug a hole in the ground and hid his master's money. 19 After a long time the master of those slaves came and settled accounts with them. 20 Then the one who had received the five talents came forward, bringing five more talents, saying, 'Master, you handed over to me five talents; see, I have made five more talents.' 21 His master said to him, 'Well done, good and trustworthy slave; you have been trustworthy in a few things, I will put you in charge of many things; enter into the joy of your master.' 22 And the one with the two talents also came forward, saying, 'Master, you handed over to me two talents; see, I have made two more talents.' 23 His master said to him, 'Well done, good and trustworthy slave; you have been trustworthy in a few things, I will put you in charge of many things; enter into the joy of your master.' 24 Then the one who had received the one talent also came forward, saying, 'Master, I knew that you were a harsh man, reaping where you did not sow, and gathering where you did not scatter seed; 25 so I was afraid, and I went and hid your talent in the ground. Here you have what is yours.' 26 But his master replied, 'You wicked and lazy slave! You knew, did you, that I reap where I did not sow, and gather where I did not scatter? 27 Then you ought to have invested my money with the bankers, and on my return I would have received what was my own with interest. 28 So take the talent from him, and give it to the one with the ten talents. 29 For to all those who have, more will be given, and they will have an abundance; but from those who have nothing, even what they have will be taken away. 30 As for this worthless slave, throw him into the outer darkness, where there will be weeping and gnashing of teeth.'

The Judgment of the Nations

31 "When the Son of Man comes in his glory, and all the angels with him, then he will sit on the throne of his glory. 32 All the nations will be gathered before him, and he will separate people one from another as a shepherd separates the sheep from the goats, 33 and he will put the sheep at his right hand and the goats at the left. 34 Then the king will say to those at his right hand, 'Come, you that are blessed by my Father, inherit the kingdom prepared for you from the foundation of the world; 35 for I was hungry and you gave me food, I was thirsty and you gave me something to drink, I was a stranger and you welcomed me, 36 I was naked and you gave me clothing, I was sick and you took care of me, I was in prison and you visited me.' 37 Then the righteous will answer him, 'Lord, when was it that we saw you hungry and gave you

---

h Gk *virgins*　　i Other ancient authorities add *in which the Son of Man is coming*　　j A talent was worth more than fifteen years' wages of a laborer

food, or thirsty and gave you something to drink? 38 And when was it that we saw you a stranger and welcomed you, or naked and gave you clothing? 39 And when was it that we saw you sick or in prison and visited you?' 40 And the king will answer them, 'Truly I tell you, just as you did it to one of the least of these who are members of my family,k you did it to me.' 41 Then he will say to those at his left hand, 'You that are accursed, depart from me into the eternal fire prepared for the devil and his angels; 42 for I was hungry and you gave me no food, I was thirsty and you gave me nothing to drink, 43 I was a stranger and you did not welcome me, naked and you did not give me clothing, sick and in prison and you did not visit me.' 44 Then they also will answer, 'Lord, when was it that we saw you hungry or thirsty or a stranger or naked or sick or in prison, and did not take care of you?' 45 Then he will answer them, 'Truly I tell you, just as you did not do it to one of the least of these, you did not do it to me.' 46 And these will go away into eternal punishment, but the righteous into eternal life."

The Plot to Kill Jesus
(Mk 14.1–2; Lk 22.1–2; Jn 11.45–53)

When Jesus had finished saying all these things, he said to his disciples, 2 "You know that after two days the Passover is coming, and the Son of Man will be handed over to be crucified."

3 Then the chief priests and the elders of the people gathered in the palace of the high priest, who was called Cā′i•a•phas, 4 and they conspired to arrest Jesus by stealth and kill him. 5 But they said, "Not during the festival, or there may be a riot among the people."

The Anointing at Bethany
(Mk 14.3–9; Jn 12.1–8)

6 Now while Jesus was at Beth′a•ny in the house of Simon the leper,l 7 a woman came to him with an alabaster jar of very costly ointment, and she poured it on his head as he sat at the table. 8 But when the disciples saw it, they were angry and said, "Why this waste? 9 For this ointment could have been sold for a large sum, and the money given to the poor." 10 But Jesus, aware of this, said to them, "Why do you trouble the woman? She has performed a good service for me. 11 For you always have the poor with you, but you will not always have me. 12 By pouring this ointment on my body she has prepared me for burial. 13 Truly I tell you, wherever this good newsm is proclaimed in the whole world, what she has done will be told in remembrance of her."

---

k Gk *these my brothers*   l The terms *leper* and *leprosy* can refer to several diseases   m Or *gospel*

"You Did It to Me"

LIVE IT!

"If the poor would only get out and find work, they would not be poor!" This common misconception pacifies the conscience of many people. Instead, Jesus says that we shouldn't let people suffer; we must reach out to them. He is neither suggesting that we respond nor encouraging us to; he is demanding that we do. He also states quite clearly that we will be judged by God as to how well we care for those who are disadvantaged.

How does your local community respond to Jesus' call? Can hungry people get a free meal somewhere? Does your school or parish have food or clothing drives? How are shut-ins and terminally ill people cared for? Who visits or writes to the prisoners in the county jail? How does your community, school, or parish respond to refugees or immigrants? Who are the hungry, the thirsty, the strangers, the naked, the sick, or the imprisoned in your neighborhood or community? What can you do to help minister to them?

Many opportunities exist for young people to do such ministry. For example, every spring break, young people from all over the country help build homes for poor people. Every weekend, teenagers in major cities serve food in soup kitchens. Many teenagers staff day-care centers for children of people who live in homeless shelters. Many young people are responding! Are you?

▶ Mt 25.31–46

M
T

Judas Agrees to Betray Jesus
(Mk 14.10–11; Lk 22.3–6)

14 Then one of the twelve, who was called Judas Is•car′i•ot, went to the chief priests 15 and said, "What will you give me if I betray him to you?" They paid him thirty pieces of silver. 16 And from that moment he began to look for an opportunity to betray him.

The Passover with the Disciples
(Mk 14.12–21; Lk 22.7–13)

17 On the first day of Unleavened Bread the disciples came to Jesus, saying, "Where do you want us to make the preparations for you to eat the Passover?" 18 He said, "Go into the city to a certain man, and say to him, 'The Teacher says, My time is near; I will keep the Passover at your house with my disciples.' " 19 So the disciples did as Jesus had directed them, and they prepared the Passover meal.

20 When it was evening, he took his place with the twelve;[n] 21 and while they were eating, he said, "Truly I tell you, one of you will betray me." 22 And they became greatly distressed and began to say to him one after another, "Surely not I, Lord?" 23 He answered, "The one who has dipped his hand into the bowl with me will betray me. 24 The Son of Man goes as it is written of him, but woe to that one by whom the Son of Man is betrayed! It would have been better for that one not to have been born." 25 Judas, who betrayed him, said, "Surely not I, Rabbi?" He replied, "You have said so."

Catholic Connections

THE NEW COVENANT

In the Old Testament, the word *covenant* is used to express the special relationship between God and the people of Israel. Covenant relationships are rooted in mutual and freely made promises. The laws and worship practices in the Old Testament were signs of this special relationship. But during the Last Supper, Jesus establishes a New Covenant, one sealed with his blood, his very life. (You will notice in the footnote for Mt 26.28 that some of the ancient authorities say New Covenant, and others just say Covenant.)

Christians believe that through the paschal mystery—Jesus' life, death, and Resurrection—the New Covenant is established and the Old Covenant is fulfilled. We enter into this new and eternal Covenant through our Baptism. We keep the Covenant by remaining faithful to Christ. The Holy Spirit, God's loving presence in our life, gives us power to live the New Covenant.

In the Eucharist, as we share in the consecrated bread and wine, it is the New Covenant that we celebrate and renew. So the next time you respond "Amen" at a eucharistic celebration, know that you are saying "Yes!" to a special and life-giving relationship with God.

For more on the Eucharist, see the articles for Mk 14.22–25, Lk 22.14–23, Jn 13.1–17.

▸ Mt 26.26–29

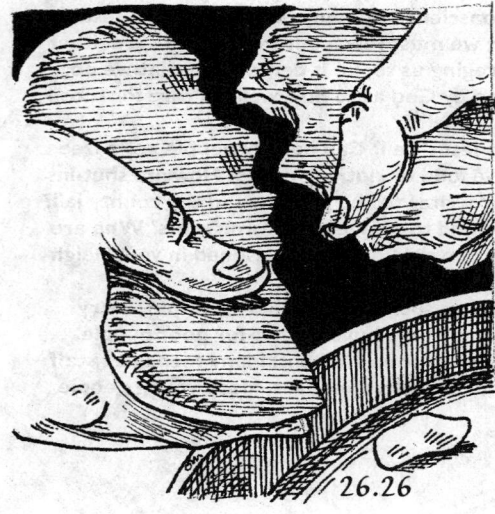

26.26

The Institution of the Lord's Supper
(Mk 14.22–26; Lk 22.14–23; 1 Cor 11.23–26)

26 While they were eating, Jesus took a loaf of bread, and after blessing it he broke it, gave it to the disciples, and said, "Take, eat; this is my body." 27 Then he took a cup, and after giving thanks he

---

[n] Other ancient authorities add *disciples*

Jesus' Imperfect Friends

Imagine that you are in the middle of a crisis and ask your best friends to stay with you while you prepare to face the situation. They all promise to be there for you. But one friend after another fails to come through, and you are left to face the trauma alone.

The friends of Jesus were no different. They were well intentioned and meant to stay awake with him. But in their tiredness, they let him down.

We usually think that the friends of Jesus, the Apostles in particular, were special and holy. But the friends of Jesus were human and had their own weaknesses. Even Peter, one of the greatest heroes of Christianity, lacked the courage to admit he knew Jesus, as we read in Mt 26.69–75. Yet Jesus loved them despite their failings and even when they were disloyal.

Is it easy for you to stay friends with those who let you down? Can you follow the example of Jesus?

▶ Mt 26.36–45

---

gave it to them, saying, "Drink from it, all of you; 28 for this is my blood of the⁰ covenant, which is poured out for many for the forgiveness of sins. 29 I tell you, I will never again drink of this fruit of the vine until that day when I drink it new with you in my Father's kingdom."

30 When they had sung the hymn, they went out to the Mount of Olives.

Peter's Denial Foretold
(Mk 14.27–31; Lk 22.31–34; Jn 13.36–38)

31 Then Jesus said to them, "You will all become deserters because of me this night; for it is written,

'I will strike the shepherd,
    and the sheep of the flock will
        be scattered.'

32 But after I am raised up, I will go ahead of you to Galilee." 33 Peter said to him, "Though all become deserters because of you, I will never desert you." 34 Jesus said to him, "Truly I tell you, this very night, before the cock crows, you will deny me three times." 35 Peter said to him, "Even though I must die with you, I will not deny you." And so said all the disciples.

Jesus Prays in Gethsemane
(Mk 14.32–42; Lk 22.39–46)

36 Then Jesus went with them to a place called Geth·sem′a·në; and he said to his disciples, "Sit here while I go over there and pray." 37 He took with him Peter and the two sons of Zeb′e·dee, and began to be grieved and agitated. 38 Then he said to them, "I am deeply grieved, even to death; remain here, and stay awake with me." 39 And going a little farther, he threw himself on the ground and prayed, "My Father, if it is possible, let this cup pass from me; yet not what I want but what you want." 40 Then he came to the disciples and found them sleeping; and he said to Peter, "So, could you not stay awake with me one hour? 41 Stay awake and pray that you may not come into the time of trial;ᵖ the spirit indeed is willing, but the flesh is weak." 42 Again he went away for the second time and prayed, "My Father, if this cannot pass unless I drink it, your will be done." 43 Again he came and found them sleeping, for their eyes were heavy. 44 So leaving them again, he went away and prayed for the third time, saying the same words. 45 Then he came to the disciples and said to them, "Are you still sleeping and taking your rest? See, the hour is at hand, and the Son of Man is betrayed into the hands of sinners. 46 Get up, let us be going. See, my betrayer is at hand."

The Betrayal and Arrest of Jesus
(Mk 14.43–52; Lk 22.47–53; Jn 18.1–11)

47 While he was still speaking, Judas, one of the twelve, arrived; with him was a large crowd with swords and clubs, from the chief priests and the elders of the people. 48 Now the betrayer had given them a sign, saying, "The one I will kiss is the man; arrest him." 49 At once he came up to Jesus and said, "Greetings, Rabbi!" and kissed him. 50 Jesus said to him, "Friend, do what you are here to do." Then they came and laid hands on Jesus and arrested him. 51 Suddenly, one of those with Jesus put his hand on his sword, drew it, and struck the slave of the high priest, cutting off his ear. 52 Then Jesus said to him, "Put your sword back into its place; for all who take the sword will

---

o Other ancient authorities add new   p Or into temptation

MT

perish by the sword. ⁵³ Do you think that I cannot appeal to my Father, and he will at once send me more than twelve legions of angels? ⁵⁴ But how then would the scriptures be fulfilled, which say it must happen in this way?" ⁵⁵ At that hour Jesus said to the crowds, "Have you come out with swords and clubs to arrest me as though I were a bandit? Day after day I sat in the temple teaching, and you did not arrest me. ⁵⁶ But all this has taken place, so that the scriptures of the prophets may be fulfilled." Then all the disciples deserted him and fled.

Jesus before the High Priest
(Mk 14.53–65; Lk 22.66–71;
Jn 18.12–14, 19–24)

57 Those who had arrested Jesus took him to Cā′i•a•phas the high priest, in whose house the scribes and the elders had gathered. ⁵⁸ But Peter was following him at a distance, as far as the courtyard of the high priest; and going inside, he sat with the guards in order to see how this would end. ⁵⁹ Now the chief priests and the whole council were looking for false testimony against Jesus so that they might put him to death, ⁶⁰ but they found none, though many false witnesses came forward. At last two came forward ⁶¹ and said, "This fellow said, 'I am able to destroy the temple of God and to build it in three days.' " ⁶² The high priest stood up and said, "Have you no answer? What is it that they testify against you?" ⁶³ But Jesus was silent. Then the high priest said to him, "I put you under oath before the living God, tell us if you are the Messiah,*q* the Son of God." ⁶⁴ Jesus said to him, "You have said so. But I tell you,

From now on you will see the Son of Man
seated at the right hand of Power
and coming on the clouds of heaven."

⁶⁵ Then the high priest tore his clothes and said, "He has blasphemed! Why do we still need witnesses? You have now heard his blasphemy. ⁶⁶ What is your verdict?" They answered, "He deserves death." ⁶⁷ Then they spat in his face and struck him; and some slapped him, ⁶⁸ saying, "Prophesy to us, you Messiah!*q* Who is it that struck you?"

Peter's Denial of Jesus
(Mk 14.66–72; Lk 22.54–62;
Jn 18.15–18, 25–27)

69 Now Peter was sitting outside in the courtyard. A servant-girl came to him and said, "You also were with Jesus the Galilean." ⁷⁰ But he denied it before all of them, saying, "I do not know what you are talking about." ⁷¹ When he went out to the porch, another servant-girl saw him, and she said to the bystanders, "This man was with Jesus of

did you KNOW?
Judas's Suicide

The Gospel of Matthew presents Judas's suicide as the fulfillment of an Old Testament prophecy from Jeremiah, but it does not tell us why Judas killed himself. Did he kill himself because he felt guilty and could not face the other disciples? Did he feel that the only way he could pay for his sin was with his own life? Whatever his reason, Judas did not believe that he could make up for his mistake—but suicide didn't solve his problem.

Some teenagers think suicide will end their pain, and use it as a way out. Unfortunately, suicide ends everything; not just the current pain but future possibilities for healing, for growth, for new relationships and good times. Consider that both Judas and Peter betrayed Jesus. But whereas Judas ended his life, Peter trusted in God's love and forgiveness and went on to become a great hero. Nothing you can do is so terrible that your only option is taking your life.

Do you ever have thoughts of suicide? If so, talk about them with someone you trust. Speak with a priest, a parent, a youth minister, a school counselor, a coach, or a trusted friend. Caring people will help you. Seeking their help is a better way out.

For more on suicide, see "Suicide Is Not an Option," 1 Sam 31.1–7.

▶ Mt 27.3–10

Nazareth."*r* ⁷² Again he denied it with an oath, "I do not know the man." ⁷³ After a little while the bystanders came up and said to Peter, "Certainly you are also one of them, for your accent betrays you." ⁷⁴ Then he began to curse, and he swore an oath, "I do not know the man!" At that moment the cock crowed. ⁷⁵ Then Peter remembered what Jesus had said: "Before the cock crows, you will deny me three times." And he went out and wept bitterly.

q Or *Christ*   *r* Gk *the Nazorean*

Jesus Brought before Pilate
(Mk 15.1; Lk 23.1; Jn 18.28)

When morning came, all the chief priests and the elders of the people conferred together against Jesus in order to bring about his death. 2 They bound him, led him away, and handed him over to Pilate the governor.

The Suicide of Judas
(Acts 1.18–19)

3 When Judas, his betrayer, saw that Jesus[s] was condemned, he repented and brought back the thirty pieces of silver to the chief priests and the elders. 4 He said, "I have sinned by betraying innocent[t] blood." But they said, "What is that to us? See to it yourself." 5 Throwing down the pieces of silver in the temple, he departed; and he went and hanged himself. 6 But the chief priests, taking the pieces of silver, said, "It is not lawful to put them into the treasury, since they are blood money." 7 After conferring together, they used them to buy the potter's field as a place to bury foreigners. 8 For this reason that field has been called the Field of Blood to this day. 9 Then was fulfilled what had been spoken through the prophet Jer•e•mi'ah,[u] "And they took[v] the thirty pieces of silver, the price of the one on whom a price had been set,[w] on whom some of the people of Israel had set a price, 10 and they gave[x] them for the potter's field, as the Lord commanded me."

Pilate Questions Jesus
(Mk 15.2–5; Lk 23.2–5; Jn 18.29–38a)

11 Now Jesus stood before the governor; and the governor asked him, "Are you the King of the Jews?" Jesus said, "You say so." 12 But when he was accused by the chief priests and elders, he did not answer. 13 Then Pilate said to him, "Do you not hear how many accusations they make against you?" 14 But he gave him no answer, not even to a single charge, so that the governor was greatly amazed.

Barabbas or Jesus?
(Mk 15.6–14; Lk 23.13–24; Jn 18.39–40)

15 Now at the festival the governor was accustomed to release a prisoner for the crowd, anyone whom they wanted. 16 At that time they had a notorious prisoner, called Jesus[y] Ba•rab'bas. 17 So after they had gathered, Pilate said to them, "Whom do you want me to release for you, Jesus[y] Ba•rab'bas or Jesus who is called the Messiah?"[z] 18 For he realized that it was out of jealousy that they had handed him over. 19 While he was sitting on the judgment seat, his wife sent word to him, "Have nothing to do with that innocent man, for today I have suffered a great deal because of a dream about him." 20 Now the chief priests and the elders persuaded the crowds to ask for Ba•rab'bas and to have Jesus killed. 21 The governor again said to them, "Which of the two do you want me to release for you?" And they said, "Ba•rab'bas." 22 Pilate said to them, "Then what should I do with Jesus who is called the Messiah?"[z] All of them said, "Let him be crucified!" 23 Then he asked, "Why, what evil has he done?" But they shouted all the more, "Let him be crucified!"

Pilate Hands Jesus over to Be Crucified
(Mk 15.15; Lk 23.25; Jn 19.16)

24 So when Pilate saw that he could do nothing, but rather that a riot was beginning, he took some water and washed his hands before the crowd, saying, "I am innocent of this man's blood;[a] see to it yourselves." 25 Then the people as a whole answered, "His blood be on us and on our children!" 26 So he released Ba•rab'bas for them; and after flogging Jesus, he handed him over to be crucified.

The Soldiers Mock Jesus
(Mk 15.16–20)

27 Then the soldiers of the governor took Jesus into the governor's headquarters,[b] and they gathered the whole cohort around him. 28 They stripped him and put a scarlet robe on him, 29 and after twisting some thorns into a crown, they put it on his head. They put a reed in his right hand and knelt before him and mocked him, saying, "Hail, King of the Jews!" 30 They spat on him, and took the reed and struck him on the head. 31 After mocking him, they stripped him of the robe and put his own clothes on him. Then they led him away to crucify him.

The Crucifixion of Jesus
(Mk 15.21–32; Lk 23.26–43; Jn 19.16b–27)

32 As they went out, they came upon a man from Cy•re'ne named Simon; they compelled this man to carry his cross. 33 And when they came to a place called Gol'go•tha (which means Place of a Skull), 34 they offered him wine to drink, mixed with gall; but when he tasted it, he would not drink it. 35 And when they had crucified him, they

---

[s] Gk *he*   [t] Other ancient authorities read *righteous*
[u] Other ancient authorities read *Zechariah* or *Isaiah*
[v] Or *I took*   [w] Or *the price of the precious One*   [x] Other ancient authorities read *I gave*   [y] Other ancient authorities lack *Jesus*   [z] Or *the Christ*   [a] Other ancient authorities read *this righteous blood*, or *this righteous man's blood*   [b] Gk *the praetorium*

divided his clothes among themselves by casting lots;c 36 then they sat down there and kept watch over him. 37 Over his head they put the charge against him, which read, "This is Jesus, the King of the Jews."

38 Then two bandits were crucified with him, one on his right and one on his left. 39 Those who passed by derivedd him, shaking their heads 40 and saying, "You who would destroy the temple and build it in three days, save yourself! If you are the Son of God, come down from the cross." 41 In the same way the chief priests also, along with the scribes and elders, were mocking him, saying, 42 "He saved others; he cannot save himself.e He is the King of Israel; let him come down from the cross now, and we will believe in him. 43 He trusts in God; let God deliver him now, if he wants to; for he said, 'I am God's Son.' " 44 The bandits who were crucified with him also taunted him in the same way.

PRAY IT!
Suffering Prayer

*J*esus, anointed one, everyone endures *some suffering in their life. Some suffer in silence. Some loudly complain, making it known to all. Some bitterly blame everyone around them. You suffered ridicule, betrayal, persecution, crucifixion, and death. Your burden was so great, yet you endured. Glorifying God, your sacrifice gives us the hope of eternal life.*

Strengthen me to withstand the suffering I must face in my life. When I feel that I have more than I can take, fortify me with the endurance of Job. Give me the patience to suffer injustices without lashing out at others. Fill me with mercy to forgive those who persecute me. Fill me with your loving presence to be a faithful witness to the glory of God and to the promise of eternal life. Amen.

▸ Mt 27.27–44

The Death of Jesus
(Mk 15.33–41; Lk 23.44–49; Jn 19.28–30)

45 From noon on, darkness came over the whole landf until three in the afternoon. 46 And about three o'clock Jesus cried with a loud voice,

did you KNOW?
The Dawn of a New Age

According to the Gospel of Matthew, some strange things happened when Jesus died. Each event tells us something about Jesus. The darkness that covered the land (27.45) and the earthquake (verse 51) show that all creation was aware that something significant had happened, a new age was dawning. The splitting of the Temple veil (verse 51), which is the barrier that separated the holiest part of the Temple (where God was thought to dwell) from the rest of the Temple area, symbolizes that now God would be directly accessible to the people. And what do the dead saints who came out of their tombs to walk in the city symbolize? They are the fulfillment of Ezekiel's vision (Ezekiel, chapter 37). The dried bones had come to life—God had triumphed over death!

▸ Mt 27.45–54

"Ē'lī, Ē'lī, le•ma' sa•bach'tha•nī?" that is, "My God, my God, why have you forsaken me?" 47 When some of the bystanders heard it, they said, "This man is calling for E•lī'jah." 48 At once one of them ran and got a sponge, filled it with sour wine, put it on a stick, and gave it to him to drink. 49 But the others said, "Wait, let us see whether E•lī'jah will come to save him."g 50 Then Jesus cried again with a loud voice and breathed his last.h 51 At that moment the curtain of the temple was torn in two, from top to bottom. The earth shook, and the rocks were split. 52 The tombs also were opened, and many bodies of the saints who had fallen asleep were raised. 53 After his resurrection they came out of the tombs and entered the holy city and appeared to many. 54 Now when the centurion and those with him, who were keeping watch over Jesus, saw the earthquake and what took place,

---

c Other ancient authorities add *in order that what had been spoken through the prophet might be fulfilled, "They divided my clothes among themselves, and for my clothing they cast lots."*   d Or *blasphemed*   e Or *is he unable to save himself?* f Or *earth*   g Other ancient authorities add *And another took a spear and pierced his side, and out came water and blood*   h Or *gave up his spirit*

they were terrified and said, "Truly this man was God's Son!"[i]

55 Many women were also there, looking on from a distance; they had followed Jesus from Galilee and had provided for him. [56]Among them were Mary Mag'da•lēne, and Mary the mother of James and Joseph, and the mother of the sons of Zeb'e•dee.

The Burial of Jesus
(Mk 15.42–47; Lk 23.50–56; Jn 19.38–42)

57 When it was evening, there came a rich man from Ar•i•ma•thē'a, named Joseph, who was also a disciple of Jesus. [58]He went to Pilate and asked for the body of Jesus; then Pilate ordered it to be given to him. [59]So Joseph took the body and wrapped it in a clean linen cloth [60]and laid it in his own new tomb, which he had hewn in the rock. He then rolled a great stone to the door of the tomb and went away. [61]Mary Mag'da•lēne and the other Mary were there, sitting opposite the tomb.

The Guard at the Tomb

62 The next day, that is, after the day of Preparation, the chief priests and the Phar'i•sees gathered before Pilate [63]and said, "Sir, we remember what that impostor said while he was still alive, 'After three days I will rise again.' [64]Therefore command the tomb to be made secure until the third day; otherwise his disciples may go and steal him away, and tell the people, 'He has been raised from the dead,' and the last deception would be worse than the first." [65]Pilate said to them, "You have a guard[j] of soldiers; go, make it as secure as you can."[k] [66]So they went with the guard and made the tomb secure by sealing the stone.

The Resurrection of Jesus
(Mk 16.1–8; Lk 24.1–12; Jn 20.1–10)

After the sabbath, as the first day of the week was dawning, Mary Mag'da•lēne and the other Mary went to see the tomb. [2]And suddenly there was a great earthquake; for an angel of the Lord, descending from heaven, came and rolled back the stone and sat on it. [3]His appearance was like lightning, and his clothing white as snow. [4]For fear of him the guards shook and became like dead men. [5]But the angel said to the women, "Do not be afraid; I know that you are looking for Jesus who was crucified. [6]He is not here; for he has been raised, as he said. Come, see the place where he[l] lay. [7]Then go quickly and tell his disciples, 'He

---

[i] Or *a son of God*   [j] Or *Take a guard*   [k] Gk *you know how*
[l] Other ancient authorities read *the Lord*

JESUS DIED ON THE CROSS BECAUSE HE LOVES US!

¡Jesus murió en la cruz porque nos ama! **HISPANIC**

Hispanics often identify more with the suffering and crucified Christ than with the risen Christ. In the cross, Hispanics find God's immense love for them. It is a redemptive love, one that brings peace and the strength to accept what cannot be changed and to continue the struggle out of poverty and oppression.

Hispanic young people learn from their families and culture that there is always suffering in life. When this suffering is not accepted, it is even worse. In contrast, when we accept suffering, it is bearable, and we have the inner peace needed to continue living and working for a better life. Suffering achieves its highest meaning when it is accepted out of love. That Jesus is capable of suffering gives witness to God's special love for those who suffer.

Finding God's life in the midst of suffering leads to generous sacrifices that are a source of life for those we love. Let's pray:

Jesus, help us to always remember that your commitment to your mission led to your death. Help us to understand that true life is always achieved through love. Help us to have love at the core of all we think and do. And help us to share your love, especially with those who need it the most, the poor and the marginalized. Amen.

▶ Mt 27.24–56

has been raised from the dead,^m and indeed he is going ahead of you to Galilee; there you will see him.' This is my message for you." [8] So they left the tomb quickly with fear and great joy, and ran to tell his disciples. [9] Suddenly Jesus met them and said, "Greetings!" And they came to him, took hold of his feet, and worshiped him. [10] Then Jesus said to them, "Do not be afraid; go and tell my brothers to go to Galilee; there they will see me."

The Report of the Guard

[11] While they were going, some of the guard went into the city and told the chief priests everything that had happened. [12] After the priestsⁿ had assembled with the elders, they devised a plan to give a large sum of money to the soldiers, [13] telling them, "You must say, 'His disciples came by night and stole him away while we were asleep.' [14] If this comes to the governor's ears, we will satisfy him and keep you out of trouble." [15] So they took the money and did as they were directed. And this story is still told among the Jews to this day.

PRAY IT!

I Will Follow

If you lead me to travel to other nations,
I will follow, Lord.
If you lead me to write to glorify your name,
I will follow, Lord.
If you lead me to preach of your heavenly
Kingdom,
I will follow, Lord.
If you lead me to show others your way,
I will follow, Lord.
If you lead me to use my actions to declare
your Gospel,
I will follow, Lord.
Because you are always with me,
so I will follow, Lord.

▶ Mt 28.16–20

Catholic Connections

TRINITY SUNDAY

On the first Sunday after Pentecost Sunday, the Catholic church celebrates Trinity Sunday. The Gospel of Matthew ends with Jesus' only specific reference to the Holy Trinity that appears in all four Gospels, instructing the disciples to go out and baptize "in the name of the Father and of the Son and of the Holy Spirit" (28.19).

▶ Mt 28.16–20

The Commissioning of the Disciples
(Mk 16.14–18; Lk 24.36–49; Jn 20.19–23;
Acts 1.6–8)

[16] Now the eleven disciples went to Galilee, to the mountain to which Jesus had directed them. [17] When they saw him, they worshiped him; but some doubted. [18] And Jesus came and said to them, "All authority in heaven and on earth has been given to me. [19] Go therefore and make disciples of all nations, baptizing them in the name of the Father and of the Son and of the Holy Spirit, [20] and teaching them to obey everything that I have commanded you. And remember, I am with you always, to the end of the age."^o

---

^m Other ancient authorities lack *from the dead*   ⁿ Gk *they*
^o Other ancient authorities add *Amen*

Have you ever been ridiculed or rejected by others—maybe even your friends—for trying to do something good? Jesus would understand your feelings. In the Gospel of Mark, Jesus is misunderstood and abandoned by those closest to him. This Gospel was written for early Christians experiencing persecution or death for their faith. The author is reminding them and us to put our total trust in God as Jesus did, despite whatever difficulties we encounter in being a Christian.

At a Glance

- **1.1–15.** John the Baptist's announcement of Jesus' ministry

- **1.16—8.21.** Jesus' preaching and miracles in Galilee

- **8.22—10.52.** Jesus' teaching and healing on the way to Jerusalem

- **Chapters 11–13.** Jesus' teaching in Jerusalem

- **Chapters 14–16.** Jesus' death and Resurrection

In-depth

The Gospel of Mark is the shortest of the four Gospels and can be easily read in one sitting. It portrays Jesus as a man of action—human in his feelings, and always on the move fulfilling his mission. This Gospel answers two fundamental questions: Who is this Jesus called the Christ? and What does it mean to be his disciple? Because the people hearing this Gospel were in danger of losing their life for what they believed, those questions were a matter of life and death.

To answer the first question, the Gospel of Mark tells stories about Jesus' power to heal and about his compassion for suffering people. It tells about his conflicts with demons and with religious and civil authorities and how he was misunderstood by his own disciples. Through these stories comes the realization that Jesus is the Messiah, the promised savior. But he did not come as the victorious king many Jews expected. Instead, he accepted the suffering that comes with doing God's will. His painful and shameful death was needed before his glory could be seen. Can we believe in a very human, suffering Messiah?

Mark answers the second question in surprising ways. The disciples Jesus called were initially fearful and hard-hearted. They wanted to be powerful and important, and they wanted the approval of their peers. But gradually, they came to believe that Jesus was the Messiah, and to understand his mission. The Gospel of Mark also tells stories about a blind man, a leper, and Gentiles (non-Jews), all of whom were Jesus' disciples because they placed their total trust in him. Whether gradually or quickly, can we place our complete faith in Jesus, becoming his disciples?

Quick Facts

Author
a Gentile Christian, possibly a disciple of Peter's

Date Written
approximately A.D. 65 to 70; this was the first written Gospel

Audience
non-Jewish Christians (in Rome?) who were experiencing persecution because of their belief in Jesus

Image of Jesus
healer and miracle worker who accepts suffering as the cost for following God's will

1167

Mark

1.9

The Proclamation of John the Baptist
(Mt 3.1–12; Lk 3.1–20; Jn 1.19–28)

The beginning of the good news[a] of Jesus Christ, the Son of God.[b]
2 As it is written in the prophet I•sāi′ah,[c]
"See, I am sending my messenger ahead
of you,[d]
who will prepare your way;
3 the voice of one crying out in the
wilderness:
'Prepare the way of the Lord,
make his paths straight,' "

4 John the baptizer appeared[e] in the wilderness, proclaiming a baptism of repentance for the forgiveness of sins. 5 And people from the whole Judean countryside and all the people of Jerusalem were going out to him, and were baptized by him in the river Jordan, confessing their sins. 6 Now John was clothed with camel's hair, with a leather belt around his waist, and he ate locusts and wild honey. 7 He proclaimed, "The one who is more powerful than I is coming after me; I am not worthy to stoop down and untie the thong of his sandals. 8 I have baptized you with[f] water; but he will baptize you with[f] the Holy Spirit."

The Baptism of Jesus
(Mt 3.13–17; Lk 3.21–22; Jn 1.29–34)

9 In those days Jesus came from Nazareth of Galilee and was baptized by John in the Jordan. 10 And just as he was coming up out of the water, he saw the heavens torn apart and the Spirit descending like a dove on him. 11 And a voice came from heaven, "You are my Son, the Beloved;[g] with you I am well pleased."

The Temptation of Jesus
(Mt 4.1–11; Lk 4.1–13)

12 And the Spirit immediately drove him out into the wilderness. 13 He was in the wilderness forty days, tempted by Satan; and he was with the wild beasts; and the angels waited on him.

The Beginning of the Galilean Ministry
(Mt 4.12–17; Lk 4.14–15)

14 Now after John was arrested, Jesus came to Galilee, proclaiming the good news[a] of God,[h] 15 and saying, "The time is fulfilled, and the kingdom of God has come near;[i] repent, and believe in the good news."[a]

Jesus Calls the First Disciples
(Mt 4.18–22; Lk 5.1–11)

16 As Jesus passed along the Sea of Galilee, he saw Simon and his brother Andrew casting a net into the sea—for they were fishermen. 17 And Jesus said to them, "Follow me and I will make you fish

---

a Or gospel   b Other ancient authorities lack the Son of God   c Other ancient authorities read in the prophets   d Gk before your face   e Other ancient authorities read John was baptizing   f Or in   g Or my beloved Son   h Other ancient authorities read of the kingdom   i Or is at hand

for people." [18] And immediately they left their nets and followed him. [19] As he went a little farther, he saw James son of Zeb'e•dee and his brother John, who were in their boat mending the nets. [20] Immediately he called them; and they left their father Zeb'e•dee in the boat with the hired men, and followed him.

The Man with an Unclean Spirit
(Lk 4.31–37)

[21] They went to Ca•per'na•um; and when the sabbath came, he entered the synagogue and taught. [22] They were astounded at his teaching, for he taught them as one having authority, and not as the scribes. [23] Just then there was in their synagogue a man with an unclean spirit, [24] and he cried out, "What have you to do with us, Jesus of Nazareth? Have you come to destroy us? I know who you are, the Holy One of God." [25] But Jesus rebuked him, saying, "Be silent, and come out of him!" [26] And the unclean spirit, convulsing him and crying with a loud voice, came out of him. [27] They were all amazed, and they kept on asking one another, "What is this? A new teaching—with authority! He[j] commands even the unclean spirits, and they obey him." [28] At once his fame began to spread throughout the surrounding region of Galilee.

Jesus Heals Many at Simon's House
(Mt. 8.14–17; Lk 4.38–41)

[29] As soon as they[k] left the synagogue, they entered the house of Simon and Andrew, with James and John. [30] Now Simon's mother-in-law was in bed with a fever, and they told him about her at once. [31] He came and took her by the hand and lifted her up. Then the fever left her, and she began to serve them.

[32] That evening, at sunset, they brought to him all who were sick or possessed with demons. [33] And the whole city was gathered around the door. [34] And he cured many who were sick with various diseases, and cast out many demons; and he would not permit the demons to speak, because they knew him.

A Preaching Tour in Galilee
(Mt 4.23–25; Lk 4.42–44)

[35] In the morning, while it was still very dark, he got up and went out to a deserted place, and there he prayed. [36] And Simon and his companions hunted for him. [37] When they found him, they said to him, "Everyone is searching for you." [38] He answered, "Let us go on to the neighboring towns, so that I may proclaim the message there also; for that is what I came out to do." [39] And he went throughout Galilee, proclaiming the message in their synagogues and casting out demons.

Jesus Cleanses a Leper
(Mt 8.1–4; Lk 5.12–16)

[40] A leper[l] came to him begging him, and kneeling[m] he said to him, "If you choose, you

---

[j] Or *A new teaching! With authority he*   [k] Other ancient authorities read *he*   [l] The terms *leper* and *leprosy* can refer to several diseases   [m] Other ancient authorities lack *kneeling*

LIVE IT!

Called to Follow Jesus

The response of Peter, Andrew, James, and John to Jesus is an example of obedience to God's call. Jesus calls them because he loves them and trusts them to share in his mission.

The Catholic church believes that through Baptism, all Christians are called to be Jesus' disciples (followers) in whatever path their life takes. Most people are called to mission as a layperson. A few are called to serve through the priesthood, diaconate, or religious life. So whether you end up a priest or a plumber, married or single, poor or rich, faithfulness to God's call is the most important loyalty you can have.

It might be hard to imagine how school or a fast-food job is part of your call to follow Jesus. But attitude is everything! Do you see school as a necessary evil to get a job that makes lots of money? Or do you see it as preparation for a career that will allow you to serve others and contribute to society? If you work, do you approach your job halfheartedly, or are you enthusiastic, always giving your best effort? Do you treat coworkers and customers with warmth and respect? Jesus is calling you to be his disciple wherever you are and whatever you might be doing.

▶ Mk 1.16–20

▶ ▶ ▶ ▶ ▶ ▶ ▶ ▶ ▶ ▶

NATIVE AMERICAN

Spirits

Most Native American peoples would not be surprised by all the angels and spirits in the first chapter of Mark. Many Native American cultures believe in the presence of good and bad spirits in the world. They view good spirits as personal helpers and message bearers, like the angels who attend Jesus in verse 13. They believe that spirits often appear as animals, much as the Holy Spirit appears as a dove in verse 10. And many believe bad spirits influence and control people, just as the unclean spirit does in verse 23.

Isn't it interesting that different cultures can develop such parallel religious beliefs? Whether we call them angels and demons or good and bad spirits, we share a common understanding about unseen powers influencing our life. It is an understanding of the world that is often rejected in our scientific, technology-filled culture.

▶ Mk 1.9–39

▶ ▶ ▶ ▶ ▶ ▶ ▶ ▶ ▶ ▶

can make me clean." [41] Moved with pity,[n] Jesus[o] stretched out his hand and touched him, and said to him, "I do choose. Be made clean!" [42] Immediately the leprosy[p] left him, and he was made clean. [43] After sternly warning him he sent him away at once, [44] saying to him, "See that you say nothing to anyone; but go, show yourself to the priest, and offer for your cleansing what Moses commanded, as a testimony to them." [45] But he went out and began to proclaim it freely, and to spread the word, so that Jesus[o] could no longer go into a town openly, but stayed out in the country; and people came to him from every quarter.

Jesus Heals a Paralytic
(Mt 9.2–8; Lk 5.17–26)

When he returned to Ca·per'na·um after some days, it was reported that he was at home. [2] So many gathered around that there was no longer room for them, not even in front of the door; and he was speaking the word to them. [3] Then some people[q] came, bringing to him a paralyzed man, carried by four of them. [4] And when they could not bring him to Jesus because of the crowd, they removed the roof above him; and after having dug through it, they let down the mat on which the paralytic lay. [5] When Jesus saw their faith, he said to the paralytic, "Son, your sins are forgiven." [6] Now some of the scribes were sitting there, questioning in their hearts, [7] "Why does this fellow speak in this way? It is blasphemy! Who can forgive sins but God alone?" [8] At once Jesus perceived in his spirit that they were discussing these questions among themselves; and he said to them, "Why do you

---

[n] Other ancient authorities read *anger*   [o] Gk *he*
[p] The terms *leper* and *leprosy* can refer to several diseases
[q] Gk *they*

Faithful Friends

LIVE IT!

We are not given many details about the paralyzed man in the story in Mk 2.1–12, but we might conclude one thing: he had at least four good friends! The main point of this story is that Jesus has the authority to forgive sins, a power that belongs only to God. But what can be said about the four friends who carried the paralyzed man to Jesus?

First, their actions show they were convinced that Jesus could do something for their paralyzed friend. Second, they were committed to their friend. And last, they didn't let a seemingly insurmountable obstacle—the crowded doorway—prevent them from getting their friend to the feet of Jesus.

What faithful people in your life have helped you come to know Jesus? For whom might you currently have the opportunity to be that kind of faithful friend?

▶ Mk 2.1–12

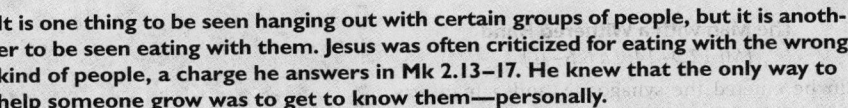

Getting Personal

It is one thing to be seen hanging out with certain groups of people, but it is another to be seen eating with them. Jesus was often criticized for eating with the wrong kind of people, a charge he answers in Mk 2.13–17. He knew that the only way to help someone grow was to get to know them—personally.

It did not matter to Jesus whether the person was rich or poor, well known or unknown, regarded as a saint or as a sinner. It did not matter to him whether the person was black or white, male or female, young or old. What did matter to Jesus was whether the person he approached was interested in getting to know him—and his heavenly Father—personally.

Are you ready to get to know Jesus personally? If so, take a few minutes to close your eyes and think about what it says in this passage. Talk to Jesus about what is going on in your life and in your family's life. When you are done talking, spend some time quietly listening for what Jesus has to say to you—personally.

▸ **Mk 2.13–17**

raise such questions in your hearts? 9 Which is easier, to say to the paralytic, 'Your sins are forgiven,' or to say, 'Stand up and take your mat and walk'? 10 But so that you may know that the Son of Man has authority on earth to forgive sins"—he said to the paralytic— 11 "I say to you, stand up, take your mat and go to your home." 12 And he stood up, and immediately took the mat and went out before all of them; so that they were all amazed and glorified God, saying, "We have never seen anything like this!"

Jesus Calls Levi
(Mt 9.9–13; Lk 5.27–32)

13 Jesus[r] went out again beside the sea; the whole crowd gathered around him, and he taught them. 14 As he was walking along, he saw Levi son of Al·phae'us sitting at the tax booth, and he said to him, "Follow me." And he got up and followed him.

15 And as he sat at dinner[s] in Levi's[t] house, many tax collectors and sinners were also sitting[u] with Jesus and his disciples—for there were many who followed him. 16 When the scribes of[v] the Phar'i·sees saw that he was eating with sinners and tax collectors, they said to his disciples, "Why does he eat[w] with tax collectors and sinners?" 17 When Jesus heard this, he said to them, "Those who are well have no need of a physician, but those who are sick; I have come to call not the righteous but sinners."

The Question about Fasting
(Mt 9.14–17; Lk 5.33–39)

18 Now John's disciples and the Phar'i·sees were fasting; and people[x] came and said to him,

"Why do John's disciples and the disciples of the Phar'i·sees fast, but your disciples do not fast?" 19 Jesus said to them, "The wedding guests cannot fast while the bridegroom is with them, can they? As long as they have the bridegroom with them, they cannot fast. 20 The days will come when the bridegroom is taken away from them, and then they will fast on that day.

21 "No one sews a piece of unshrunk cloth on an old cloak; otherwise, the patch pulls away from it, the new from the old, and a worse tear is made. 22 And no one puts new wine into old wineskins; otherwise, the wine will burst the skins, and the wine is lost, and so are the skins; but one puts new wine into fresh wineskins."[y]

Pronouncement about the Sabbath
(Mt 12.1–8; Lk 6.1–5)

23 One sabbath he was going through the grainfields; and as they made their way his disciples began to pluck heads of grain. 24 The Phar'i·sees said to him, "Look, why are they doing what is not lawful on the sabbath?" 25 And he said to them, "Have you never read what David did when he and his companions were hungry and in need of food? 26 He entered the house of God, when A·bi'a·thar was high priest, and ate the bread of the Presence, which it is not lawful for any but the priests to eat, and he gave some to his companions." 27 Then he said to them, "The sabbath was made for humankind, and not humankind for the

---

r Gk He   s Gk reclined   t Gk his   u Gk reclining
v Other ancient authorities read and   w Other ancient authorities add and drink   x Gk they   y Other ancient authorities lack but one puts new wine into fresh wineskins

MK

sabbath; ²⁸ so the Son of Man is lord even of the sabbath."

The Man with a Withered Hand
(Mt 12.9–14; Lk 6.6–11)

Again he entered the synagogue, and a man was there who had a withered hand. ²They watched him to see whether he would cure him on the sabbath, so that they might accuse him. ³And he said to the man who had the withered hand, "Come forward." ⁴Then he said to them, "Is it lawful to do good or to do harm on the sabbath, to save life or to kill?" But they were silent. ⁵He looked around at them with anger; he was grieved at their hardness of heart and said to the man, "Stretch out your hand." He stretched it out, and his hand was restored. ⁶The Phar′i•sees went out and immediately conspired with the He•rō′di•ans against him, how to destroy him.

A Multitude at the Seaside
(Mt 12.15–21)

7 Jesus departed with his disciples to the sea, and a great multitude from Galilee followed him; ⁸ hearing all that he was doing, they came to him in great numbers from Judea, Jerusalem, Id•ŭ•mē′a, beyond the Jordan, and the region around Tyre and Sī′don. ⁹He told his disciples to have a boat ready for him because of the crowd, so that they would not crush him; ¹⁰for he had cured many, so that all who had diseases pressed upon him to touch him. ¹¹Whenever the unclean spirits saw him, they fell down before him and shouted, "You are the Son of God!" ¹²But he sternly ordered them not to make him known.

Jesus Appoints the Twelve
(Mt 10.1–4; Lk 6.12–16)

13 He went up the mountain and called to him those whom he wanted, and they came to him. ¹⁴And he appointed twelve, whom he also named apostles,ᶻ to be with him, and to be sent out to proclaim the message, ¹⁵and to have authority to cast out demons. ¹⁶So he appointed the twelve:ᵃ Simon (to whom he gave the name Peter); ¹⁷James son of Zeb′e•dee and John the brother of James (to whom he gave the name Bō•a•ner′gēs, that is, Sons of Thunder); ¹⁸and Andrew, and Philip, and Bartholomew, and Matthew, and Thomas, and James son of Al•phae′us, and Thaddae′us, and Simon the Cā•na•nae′an, ¹⁹and Judas Is•car′i•ot, who betrayed him.

Catholic Connections
HOLY ORDERS

Jesus appoints twelve men as the Apostles (the word *apostle* means "sent out"). Their mission—to preach the Good News, drive out demons, and cure the sick—is an extension of Jesus' mission. The Catholic church considers bishops as the successors of the Apostles. Bishops are responsible for the church's mission, for its organization, and for seeing that Jesus' message is taught and lived faithfully from generation to generation.

Bishops are ordained by other bishops as a sign of their unbroken connection with the first Apostles. Bishops also ordain priests and deacons for service in the church, especially for sacramental ministry. These ordinations happen in the sacrament of Holy Orders, one of the seven sacraments of the church. In the sacrament of Holy Orders, the bishop places his hands on the head of the man being ordained and prays for a special outpouring of the Holy Spirit.

▶ Mk 3.13–19

Jesus and Beelzebul
(Mt 12.22–32; Lk 11.14–23)

Then he went home; ²⁰and the crowd came together again, so that they could not even eat. ²¹When his family heard it, they went out to restrain him, for people were saying, "He has gone out of his mind." ²²And the scribes who came down from Jerusalem said, "He has Bē•el′ze•bul, and by the ruler of the demons he casts out demons." ²³And he called them to him, and spoke to them in parables, "How can Satan cast out Satan? ²⁴If a kingdom is divided against itself, that kingdom cannot stand. ²⁵And if a house is divided against itself, that house will not be able to stand.

ᶻ Other ancient authorities lack *whom he also named apostles*   ᵃ Other ancient authorities lack *So he appointed the twelve*

26 And if Satan has risen up against himself and is divided, he cannot stand, but his end has come. 27 But no one can enter a strong man's house and plunder his property without first tying up the strong man; then indeed the house can be plundered.

28 "Truly I tell you, people will be forgiven for their sins and whatever blasphemies they utter; 29 but whoever blasphemes against the Holy Spirit can never have forgiveness, but is guilty of an eternal sin"— 30 for they had said, "He has an unclean spirit."

The True Kindred of Jesus
(Mt 12.46–50; Lk 8.19–21)

31 Then his mother and his brothers came; and standing outside, they sent to him and called him. 32 A crowd was sitting around him; and they said to him, "Your mother and your brothers and sisters[b] are outside, asking for you." 33 And he replied, "Who are my mother and my brothers?" 34 And looking at those who sat around him, he said, "Here are my mother and my brothers! 35 Whoever does the will of God is my brother and sister and mother."

The Parable of the Sower
(Mt 13.1–23; Lk 8.4–15)

Again he began to teach beside the sea. Such a very large crowd gathered around him that he got into a boat on the sea and sat there, while the whole crowd was beside the sea on the land. 2 He began to teach them many things in parables, and in his teaching he said to them: 3 "Listen! A sower went out to sow. 4 And as he sowed, some seed fell on the path, and the birds came and ate it up. 5 Other seed fell on rocky ground, where it did not have much soil, and it sprang up quickly, since it had no depth of soil. 6 And when the sun rose, it was scorched; and since it had no root, it withered away. 7 Other seed fell among thorns, and the thorns grew up and choked it, and it yielded no grain. 8 Other seed fell into good soil and brought forth grain, growing up and increasing and yielding thirty and sixty and a hundredfold." 9 And he said, "Let anyone with ears to hear listen!"

The Purpose of the Parables
(Mt 13.10–17; Lk 8.9–10)

10 When he was alone, those who were around him along with the twelve asked him about the parables. 11 And he said to them, "To you has been given the secret[c] of the kingdom of God, but for those outside, everything comes in parables; 12 in order that

'they may indeed look, but not perceive,
    and may indeed listen, but not
        understand;
so that they may not turn again and be
        forgiven.' "

13 And he said to them, "Do you not understand this parable? Then how will you understand all the parables? 14 The sower sows the word. 15 These are the ones on the path where the word

---

b Other ancient authorities lack *and sisters*   *c* Or *mystery*

LIVE IT!

Trusting God

Have you ever read the book *Johnny Tremain*? Its main character is a boy whose hand is severely burned, and the story is about how he learns to live with a disfigured limb. At many points in the story, Johnny hides his hand from others to avoid feeling embarrassed.

In Mk 3.1–6, among those gathered in the synagogue is a man with a "withered hand." There is no indication that he is seeking out Jesus, or that he commands any special attention. Jesus notices him and invites him to come forward. Jesus then asks the man to stretch out his disfigured hand for all to see.

Like Johnny Tremain, the man, we might guess, probably did not feel proud of his hand. It certainly would be understandable if, when invited by Jesus to stretch out his hand for all to see, the man had stormed out of the synagogue in anger and shame. Instead, he did what Jesus asked, and through his trust in Jesus, his hand was restored to wholeness.

Whether physically, emotionally, or spiritually, we are all "disfigured" in some ways. What source of pain or shame in your own life might Jesus be inviting you to share with him? Can you risk becoming vulnerable and trusting him with it?

▶ Mk 3.1–6

M
K

JESUS TEACHES US THROUGH STORIES!

In Mark, chapter 4, Jesus teaches about God's Reign through parables (see "Parables," Mt 13.10). In some Hispanic families, it is customary for young people to hear their *abuelita* (grandmother) tell stories about their family history, traditions, and faith. Many of the stories are true, others may be created to give a moral teaching, like the parables. Here is a true story:

A little girl's father died, leaving her family in extreme poverty. Her mother never lost faith in God, daily prayed to the Divine Providence, and asked other people to pray with her. Her prayers were always answered: food appeared miraculously in front of the family's door, and her six children were accepted free in Catholic schools.

Eventually, the mother married a creative businessman. When the business prospered, she remembered the way God had moved the hearts of people so that her family could have food and education, and with great confidence in God, she started a boarding school for boys. Whenever there was not enough food, she prayed and invited other people to pray. The Divine Providence always responded. The school has sheltered and educated two hundred boys each year for the last seventy years.

■ Which stories of faith, love, and service have marked the history of your family?
■ How are you honoring your family's tradition of bringing the Gospel to people in need?

▶ Mk 4.1–34

is sown: when they hear, Satan immediately comes and takes away the word that is sown in them. 16 And these are the ones sown on rocky ground: when they hear the word, they immediately receive it with joy. 17 But they have no root, and endure only for a while; then, when trouble or persecution arises on account of the word, immediately they fall away.*d* 18 And others are those sown among the thorns: these are the ones who hear the word, 19 but the cares of the world, and the lure of wealth, and the desire for other things come in and choke the word, and it yields nothing. 20 And these are the ones sown on the good soil: they hear the word and accept it and bear fruit, thirty and sixty and a hundredfold."

A Lamp under a Bushel Basket
(Lk 8.16–18)

21 He said to them, "Is a lamp brought in to be put under the bushel basket, or under the bed, and not on the lampstand? 22 For there is nothing hidden, except to be disclosed; nor is anything secret, except to come to light. 23 Let anyone with ears to hear listen!" 24 And he said to them, "Pay attention to what you hear; the measure you give will be the measure you get, and still more will be given you. 25 For to those who have, more will be given; and from those who have nothing, even what they have will be taken away."

The Parable of the Growing Seed

26 He also said, "The kingdom of God is as if someone would scatter seed on the ground, 27 and would sleep and rise night and day, and the seed would sprout and grow, he does not know how. 28 The earth produces of itself, first the stalk, then the head, then the full grain in the head. 29 But when the grain is ripe, at once he goes in with his sickle, because the harvest has come."

The Parable of the Mustard Seed
(Mt 13.31–32; Lk 13.18–19)

30 He also said, "With what can we compare the kingdom of God, or what parable will we use for it? 31 It is like a mustard seed, which, when sown upon the ground, is the smallest of all the seeds on earth; 32 yet when it is sown it grows up and becomes the greatest of all shrubs, and puts

d Or *stumble*

forth large branches, so that the birds of the air can make nests in its shade."

The Use of Parables

33 With many such parables he spoke the word to them, as they were able to hear it; 34 he did not speak to them except in parables, but he explained everything in private to his disciples.

Jesus Stills a Storm
(Mt 8.23–27; Lk 8.22–25)

35 On that day, when evening had come, he said to them, "Let us go across to the other side." 36 And leaving the crowd behind, they took him with them in the boat, just as he was. Other boats were with him. 37 A great windstorm arose, and the waves beat into the boat, so that the boat was already being swamped. 38 But he was in the stern, asleep on the cushion; and they woke him up and said to him, "Teacher, do you not care that we are perishing?" 39 He woke up and rebuked the wind, and said to the sea, "Peace! Be still!" Then the wind ceased, and there was a dead calm. 40 He said to them, "Why are you afraid? Have you still no faith?" 41 And they were filled with great awe and said to one another, "Who then is this, that even the wind and the sea obey him?"

PRAY IT!
Life's Storms

Storms on the Sea of Galilee are a common occurrence. They are a fisher's nightmare, and the one described in Mk 4.35–41 was really bad! It is no wonder the Apostles felt fearful and powerless. As part of your prayer, try this meditation:

Begin by closing your eyes and relaxing. Then visualize yourself standing on the beach with Jesus and the disciples. Join them as they board the boat. When the squall comes, experience the rocking of the boat, the waves crashing on deck, and the winds blowing. Feel the disciples' anxiety and fear as the boat is tossed and water pours into the boat. Go with the disciples to wake Jesus, and watch as Jesus calms the storm. Now, experience the peacefulness and tranquility of the miracle you have witnessed.

All of us have storms we must face, that is, parts of our life that are filled with anxiety or fear. Think about your life. What are the storms that batter and rock your world? Who in your family or in your community can calm your fears? How would you respond to Jesus' question, "Have you still no faith?" (Mk 4.40).

▸ Mk 4.35–41

PRAY IT!
Everyone's Welcome!

In Mark, chapters 5–8, Jesus expands his mission into Gentile territory, the region on the eastern side of the Sea of Galilee. Three miraculous healings of Gentiles—the Gerasene demoniac (5.1–6), the Syrophoenician's daughter (7.24–30), and the deaf man from Tyre (7.31–37)—extend the promises of the Reign of God to all who have faith in Jesus. In arranging these stories, the author of the Gospel emphasizes that God's salvation is available to everyone, not just to the Jews.

In your prayer, reflect or journal on the following questions:

■ How do you treat people from a different race, culture, or religion?
■ How could you be more welcoming toward them, more like Jesus?

Write a prayer expressing your desire.

▸ Mk 5.1—8.30

Jesus Heals the Gerasene Demoniac
(Mt 8.28—9.1; Lk 8.26–39)

They came to the other side of the sea, to the country of the Ger′a·senes.^e 2 And when he had stepped out of the boat, immediately a man out of the tombs with an unclean spirit met him. 3 He lived among the tombs; and no one could restrain him any more, even with a chain; 4 for he had often been restrained with shackles and chains, but the chains he wrenched apart, and the shackles he broke in pieces; and no one had the strength to subdue him. 5 Night and day among the tombs and on the mountains he was always howling and bruising himself with stones. 6 When he saw Jesus

---

e Other ancient authorities read *Gergesenes*; others, *Gadarenes*

from a distance, he ran and bowed down before him; 7 and he shouted at the top of his voice, "What have you to do with me, Jesus, Son of the Most High God? I adjure you by God, do not torment me." 8 For he had said to him, "Come out of the man, you unclean spirit!" 9 Then Jesus*f* asked him, "What is your name?" He replied, "My name is Legion; for we are many." 10 He begged him earnestly not to send them out of the country. 11 Now there on the hillside a great herd of swine was feeding; 12 and the unclean spirits*g* begged him, "Send us into the swine; let us enter them." 13 So he gave them permission. And the unclean spirits came out and entered the swine; and the herd, numbering about two thousand, rushed down the steep bank into the sea, and were drowned in the sea.

14 The swineherds ran off and told it in the city and in the country. Then people came to see what it was that had happened. 15 They came to Jesus and saw the demoniac sitting there, clothed and in his right mind, the very man who had had the legion; and they were afraid. 16 Those who had seen what had happened to the demoniac and to the swine reported it. 17 Then they began to beg Jesus*h* to leave their neighborhood. 18 As he was getting into the boat, the man who had been possessed by demons begged him that he might be with him. 19 But Jesus*f* refused, and said to him, "Go home to your friends, and tell them how much the Lord has done for you, and what mercy he has shown you." 20 And he went away and began to proclaim in the De·cap'o·lis how much Jesus had done for him; and everyone was amazed.

A Girl Restored to Life and a Woman Healed
(Mt 9.18–26; Lk 8.40–56)

21 When Jesus had crossed again in the boat*i* to the other side, a great crowd gathered around him; and he was by the sea. 22 Then one of the leaders of the synagogue named Jā·i'rus came and, when he saw him, fell at his feet 23 and begged him repeatedly, "My little daughter is at the point of death. Come and lay your hands on her, so that she may be made well, and live." 24 So he went with him.

And a large crowd followed him and pressed in on him. 25 Now there was a woman who had been suffering from hemorrhages for twelve years. 26 She had endured much under many physicians, and had spent all that she had; and she was no better, but rather grew worse. 27 She had heard about Jesus, and came up behind him in the crowd and touched his cloak, 28 for she said, "If I but touch his clothes, I will be made well." 29 Immediately her hemorrhage stopped; and she felt in her body that

did you KNOW?
Demon Possession

The Gospels of Matthew, Mark, and Luke all have stories about Jesus curing people of unclean spirits, or demons. Many cultures believe in spirits, both good and bad (see "Spirits," Mk 1.9–39), which can influence or even control people's decisions and actions. In the Bible, a demon is first mentioned in the Book of Tobit, which was written about two hundred years before Jesus' birth. Demons represented evil—mysterious powers hostile to God, health, and goodness. Jesus' ability to free people of demonic influence was a sign of the arrival of the Reign of God (see "Miracles and the Reign of God," Mt 8.1—9.34).

Over time, the explanation for evil or illness shifted from unclean spirits to Satan (see "Satan," Job 1.6—2.10), the leader of all demonic forces. The Gospel of John does not mention unclean spirits at all but instead refers to Satan's influence in the evil leading to Jesus' death (see Jn 13.2).

What the Bible calls demon possession, Western culture might call mental or physical illness. But many people are becoming aware of what the ancient people already knew: that illness and evil are part of the spiritual reality that can affect our life.

▶ Mk 1.23–34; 5.1–20

she was healed of her disease. 30 Immediately aware that power had gone forth from him, Jesus turned about in the crowd and said, "Who touched my clothes?" 31 And his disciples said to him, "You see the crowd pressing in on you; how can you say, 'Who touched me?'" 32 He looked all around to see who had done it. 33 But the woman, knowing what had happened to her, came in fear and trembling, fell down before him, and told him the whole truth. 34 He said to her, "Daughter, your faith has made you well; go in peace, and be healed of your disease."

---

f Gk *he*   *g* Gk *they*   *h* Gk *him*   *i* Other ancient authorities lack *in the boat*

35 While he was still speaking, some people came from the leader's house to say, "Your daughter is dead. Why trouble the teacher any further?" 36 But overhearing[j] what they said, Jesus said to the leader of the synagogue, "Do not fear, only believe." 37 He allowed no one to follow him except Peter, James, and John, the brother of James. 38 When they came to the house of the leader of the synagogue, he saw a commotion, people weeping and wailing loudly. 39 When he had entered, he said to them, "Why do you make a commotion and weep? The child is not dead but sleeping." 40 And they laughed at him. Then he put them all outside, and took the child's father and mother and those who were with him, and went in where the child was. 41 He took her by the hand and said to her, "Tal'i•tha cūm," which means, "Little girl, get up!" 42 And immediately the girl got up and began to walk about (she was twelve years of age). At this they were overcome with amazement. 43 He strictly ordered them that no one should know this, and told them to give her something to eat.

The Rejection of Jesus at Nazareth
(Mt 13.54–58; Lk 4.16–30)

He left that place and came to his hometown, and his disciples followed him. 2 On the sabbath he began to teach in the synagogue, and many who heard him were astounded. They said, "Where did this man get all this? What is this wisdom that has been given to him? What deeds of power are being done by his hands! 3 Is not this the carpenter, the son of Mary[k] and brother of James and Jō'sēs and Judas and Simon, and are not his sisters here with us?" And they took offense[l] at him. 4 Then Jesus said to them, "Prophets are not without honor, except in their hometown, and among their own kin, and in their own house." 5 And he could do no deed of power there, except that he laid his hands on a few sick people and cured them. 6 And he was amazed at their unbelief.

The Mission of the Twelve
(Mt 10.5–15; Lk 9.1–6)

Then he went about among the villages teaching. 7 He called the twelve and began to send them out two by two, and gave them authority over the unclean spirits. 8 He ordered them to take nothing for their journey except a staff; no bread, no bag, no money in their belts; 9 but to wear sandals and not to put on two tunics. 10 He said to them, "Wherever you enter a house, stay there until you leave the place. 11 If any place will not welcome you and they refuse to hear you, as you leave, shake off the dust that is on your feet as a testimony against them." 12 So they went out and proclaimed that all should repent. 13 They cast out many demons, and anointed with oil many who were sick and cured them.

PRAY IT?

When the Good News Comes Calling

We often can choose whether to allow into our life the people bearing the Good News of Jesus, just as the people to whom the disciples were sent in Mk 6.6–13 could. Why might we turn away such guests? Perhaps their message is too challenging or upsetting to our lifestyle. Maybe we are not ready to accept what God is offering to us through them. Maybe we are too busy to realize that they have something to offer us.

Open your hands as if to receive a gift, and offer a prayer to God for the openness to welcome God's messengers and to receive the Good News they bring.

▶ Mk 6.6–13

The Death of John the Baptist
(Mt 14.1–12; Lk 9.7–9)

14 King Her'od heard of it, for Jesus'[m] name had become known. Some were[n] saying, "John the baptizer has been raised from the dead; and for this reason these powers are at work in him." 15 But others said, "It is E•lī'jah." And others said, "It is a prophet, like one of the prophets of old." 16 But when Her'od heard of it, he said, "John, whom I beheaded, has been raised."

17 For Her'od himself had sent men who arrested John, bound him, and put him in prison on account of He•rō'di•as, his brother Philip's wife, because Her'od[o] had married her. 18 For John had been telling Her'od, "It is not lawful for you to have your brother's wife." 19 And He•rō'di•as had a grudge against him, and wanted to kill him. But she could not, 20 for Her'od feared John, knowing that he was a righteous and holy man, and he protected him. When he heard him, he was greatly

MK

perplexed;*p* and yet he liked to listen to him. 21 But an opportunity came when Her'od on his birthday gave a banquet for his courtiers and officers and for the leaders of Galilee. 22 When his daughter He·rō'di·as*q* came in and danced, she pleased Her'od and his guests; and the king said to the girl, "Ask me for whatever you wish, and I will give it." 23 And he solemnly swore to her, "Whatever you ask me, I will give you, even half of my kingdom." 24 She went out and said to her mother, "What should I ask for?" She replied, "The head of John the baptizer." 25 Immediately she rushed back to the king and requested, "I want you to give me at once the head of John the Baptist on a platter." 26 The king was deeply grieved; yet out of regard for his oaths and for the guests, he did not want to refuse her. 27 Immediately the king sent a soldier of the guard with orders to bring John's*r* head. He went and beheaded him in the prison, 28 brought his head on a platter, and gave it to the girl. Then the girl gave it to her mother. 29 When his disciples heard about it, they came and took his body, and laid it in a tomb.

Feeding the Five Thousand
(Mt 14.13–21; Lk 9.10–17; Jn 6.1–14)

30 The apostles gathered around Jesus, and told him all that they had done and taught. 31 He said to them, "Come away to a deserted place all by yourselves and rest a while." For many were coming and going, and they had no leisure even to eat. 32 And they went away in the boat to a deserted place by themselves. 33 Now many saw them going and recognized them, and they hurried there on foot from all the towns and arrived ahead of them. 34 As he went ashore, he saw a great crowd; and he had compassion for them, because they were like sheep without a shepherd; and he began to teach them many things. 35 When it grew late, his disciples came to him and said, "This is a deserted place, and the hour is now very late; 36 send them away so that they may go into the surrounding country and villages and buy something for themselves to eat." 37 But he answered them, "You give them something to eat." They said to him, "Are we to go and buy two hundred denarii*s* worth of bread, and give it to them to eat?" 38 And he said to them, "How many loaves have you? Go and see." When they had found out, they said, "Five, and two fish." 39 Then he ordered them to get all the people to sit down in groups on the green grass. 40 So they sat down in groups of hundreds and of fifties. 41 Taking the five loaves and the two fish, he looked up to heaven, and blessed and broke the loaves, and gave them to his disciples to set before the people; and he divided the two fish

did you KNOW?

Those Thickheaded Disciples

The disciples in the Gospel of Mark seem unable to do anything right. During a storm at sea, they fail to put their trust in Jesus (4.35–41). Then they cannot understand about the miracle of the bread because their hearts are hardened (6.52). When Jesus gives them private tutoring sessions, they still fail to understand his teachings. Later, Peter proclaims that Jesus is the Messiah, but ends up arguing with him after Jesus predicts he will be a suffering Messiah (8.27–33). Finally, when Jesus is arrested, the disciples all desert him (14.50).

The author of Mark intentionally emphasizes the lack of faith of the original disciples, in order to contrast it with the unexpected faith of people like the Syrophoenician woman in 7.24–30. The Gospel makes the point that Jesus' true disciples are the ones who hear Jesus and place their faith in him. But don't count out the original disciples. Their journey is like most of ours, a lifelong experience of growing in faith and understanding. The Acts of the Apostles tells how they fearlessly preached the news about the risen Christ. Despite their human weakness, God works through them. That goes for us too!

▶ Mk 6.30–52

among them all. 42 And all ate and were filled; 43 and they took up twelve baskets full of broken pieces and of the fish. 44 Those who had eaten the loaves numbered five thousand men.

Jesus Walks on the Water
(Mt 14.22–33; Jn 6.15–21)

45 Immediately he made his disciples get into the boat and go on ahead to the other side, to

---

p Other ancient authorities read *he did many things*
q Other ancient authorities read *the daughter of Herodias herself*   *r* Gk *his*   *s* The denarius was the usual day's wage for a laborer

Beth•sā'i•da, while he dismissed the crowd. 46 After saying farewell to them, he went up on the mountain to pray.

47 When evening came, the boat was out on the sea, and he was alone on the land. 48 When he saw that they were straining at the oars against an adverse wind, he came towards them early in the morning, walking on the sea. He intended to pass them by. 49 But when they saw him walking on the sea, they thought it was a ghost and cried out; 50 for they all saw him and were terrified. But immediately he spoke to them and said, "Take heart, it is I; do not be afraid." 51 Then he got into the boat with them and the wind ceased. And they were utterly astounded, 52 for they did not understand about the loaves, but their hearts were hardened.

Healing the Sick in Gennesaret
(Mt 14.34–36)

53 When they had crossed over, they came to land at Gen•nes'a•ret and moored the boat. 54 When they got out of the boat, people at once recognized him, 55 and rushed about that whole region and began to bring the sick on mats to wherever they heard he was. 56 And wherever he went, into villages or cities or farms, they laid the sick in the marketplaces, and begged him that they might touch even the fringe of his cloak; and all who touched it were healed.

The Tradition of the Elders
(Mt 15.1–20)

Now when the Phar'i•sees and some of the scribes who had come from Jerusalem gathered around him, 2 they noticed that some of his disciples were eating with defiled hands, that is, without washing them. 3 (For the Phar'i•sees, and all the Jews, do not eat unless they thoroughly wash their hands,^{t} thus observing the tradition of the elders; 4 and they do not eat anything from the market unless they wash it;^{u} and there are also many other traditions that they observe, the washing of cups, pots, and bronze kettles.^{v}) 5 So the Phar'i•sees and the scribes asked him, "Why do your disciples not live^w according to the tradition of the elders, but eat with defiled hands?" 6 He said to them, "Ī•sāi'ah prophesied rightly about you hypocrites, as it is written,

'This people honors me with their lips,
    but their hearts are far from me;
7   in vain do they worship me,
    teaching human precepts as doctrines.'

8 You abandon the commandment of God and hold to human tradition."

9 Then he said to them, "You have a fine way of rejecting the commandment of God in order to keep your tradition! 10 For Moses said, 'Honor your father and your mother'; and, 'Whoever speaks evil of father or mother must surely die.' 11 But you say that if anyone tells father or mother, 'Whatever support you might have had from me is Cor'ban' (that is, an offering to God^x)— 12 then you no longer permit doing anything for a father or mother, 13 thus making void the word of God through your tradition that you have handed on. And you do many things like this."

14 Then he called the crowd again and said to them, "Listen to me, all of you, and understand: 15 there is nothing outside a person that by going in can defile, but the things that come out are what defile."^{y}

17 When he had left the crowd and entered the house, his disciples asked him about the parable. 18 He said to them, "Then do you also fail to understand? Do you not see that whatever goes into a person from outside cannot defile, 19 since it enters, not the heart but the stomach, and goes out into the sewer?" (Thus he declared all foods clean.) 20 And he said, "It is what comes out of a person that defiles. 21 For it is from within, from the human heart, that evil intentions come: fornication,

---

^{t} Meaning of Gk uncertain ^{u} Other ancient authorities read *and when they come from the marketplace, they do not eat unless they purify themselves* ^{v} Other ancient authorities add *and beds* ^{w} Gk *walk* ^{x} Gk lacks *to God* ^{y} Other ancient authorities add verse 16, *"Let anyone with ears to hear listen"*

M
K

Sin's Source

LIVE IT!

Some people believe that spiritual depth is measured by how well certain rules or religious practices are followed. Jesus reminds us in Mk 7.14–15 that our greater concern ought to be with what is in our heart. What is in our heart should have a greater effect on our spiritual life than do outside sources.

▶ Mk 7.14–23

theft, murder, 22 adultery, avarice, wickedness, deceit, licentiousness, envy, slander, pride, folly. 23 All these evil things come from within, and they defile a person."

The Syrophoenician Woman's Faith
(Mt 15.21–28)

24 From there he set out and went away to the region of Tyre.z He entered a house and did not want anyone to know he was there. Yet he could not escape notice, 25 but a woman whose little daughter had an unclean spirit immediately heard about him, and she came and bowed down at his feet. 26 Now the woman was a Gentile, of Sy·ro·phoe·ni′ci·an origin. She begged him to cast the demon out of her daughter. 27 He said to her, "Let the children be fed first, for it is not fair to take the children's food and throw it to the dogs." 28 But she answered him, "Sir,a even the dogs under the table eat the children's crumbs." 29 Then he said to her, "For saying that, you may go—the demon has left your daughter." 30 So she went home, found the child lying on the bed, and the demon gone.

Jesus Cures a Deaf Man
(Mt 15.29–31)

31 Then he returned from the region of Tyre, and went by way of Si′don towards the Sea of Galilee, in the region of the De·cap′o·lis. 32 They brought to him a deaf man who had an impediment in his speech; and they begged him to lay his hand on him. 33 He took him aside in private, away from the crowd, and put his fingers into his ears, and he spat and touched his tongue. 34 Then looking up to heaven, he sighed and said to him,

"Eph′pha·tha," that is, "Be opened." 35 And immediately his ears were opened, his tongue was released, and he spoke plainly. 36 Then Jesusb ordered them to tell no one; but the more he ordered them, the more zealously they proclaimed it. 37 They were astounded beyond measure, saying, "He has done everything well; he even makes the deaf to hear and the mute to speak."

Feeding the Four Thousand
(Mt 15.32–39)

In those days when there was again a great crowd without anything to eat, he called his disciples and said to them, 2 "I have compassion for the crowd, because they have been with me now for three days and have nothing to eat. 3 If I send them away hungry to their homes, they will faint on the way—and some of them have come from a great distance." 4 His disciples replied, "How can one feed these people with bread here in the desert?" 5 He asked them, "How many loaves do you have?" They said, "Seven." 6 Then he ordered the crowd to sit down on the ground; and he took the seven loaves, and after giving thanks he broke them and gave them to his disciples to distribute; and they distributed them to the crowd. 7 They had also a few small fish; and after blessing them, he ordered that these too should be distributed. 8 They ate and were filled; and they took up the broken pieces left over, seven baskets full. 9 Now there were about four thousand people. And he sent them away. 10 And immediately he got into the boat with his disciples and went to the district of Dal·ma·nu′tha.c

The Demand for a Sign
(Mt 16.1–4)

11 The Phar′i·sees came and began to argue with him, asking him for a sign from heaven, to test him. 12 And he sighed deeply in his spirit and said, "Why does this generation ask for a sign? Truly I tell you, no sign will be given to this generation." 13 And he left them, and getting into the boat again, he went across to the other side.

The Yeast of the Pharisees and of Herod
(Mt 16.5–12)

14 Now the disciplesd had forgotten to bring any bread; and they had only one loaf with them in the boat. 15 And he cautioned them, saying, "Watch out—beware of the yeast of the Phar′i·sees and the yeast of Her′od."e 16 They said to one an-

---

z Other ancient authorities add *and Sidon*   a Or *Lord*; other ancient authorities prefix *Yes*   b Gk *he*   c Other ancient authorities read *Mageda* or *Magdala*   d Gk *they*   e Other ancient authorities read *the Herodians*

other, "It is because we have no bread." 17 And becoming aware of it, Jesus said to them, "Why are you talking about having no bread? Do you still not perceive or understand? Are your hearts hardened? 18 Do you have eyes, and fail to see? Do you have ears, and fail to hear? And do you not remember? 19 When I broke the five loaves for the five thousand, how many baskets full of broken pieces did you collect?" They said to him, "Twelve." 20 "And the seven for the four thousand, how many baskets full of broken pieces did you collect?" And they said to him, "Seven." 21 Then he said to them, "Do you not yet understand?"

Jesus Cures a Blind Man at Bethsaida

22 They came to Beth•sā′i•da. Some people*f* brought a blind man to him and begged him to touch him. 23 He took the blind man by the hand and led him out of the village; and when he had put saliva on his eyes and laid his hands on him, he asked him, "Can you see anything?" 24 And the man*g* looked up and said, "I can see people, but they look like trees, walking." 25 Then Jesus*g* laid his hands on his eyes again; and he looked intently and his sight was restored, and he saw everything clearly. 26 Then he sent him away to his home, saying, "Do not even go into the village."*h*

Peter's Declaration about Jesus
(Mt 16.13–20; Lk 9.18–20)

27 Jesus went on with his disciples to the villages of Caes•a•rē′a Phi•lip′pī; and on the way he asked his disciples, "Who do people say that I am?" 28 And they answered him, "John the Baptist; and others, E•lī′jah; and still others, one of the prophets." 29 He asked them, "But who do you say that I am?" Peter answered him, "You are the Messiah."*i*

30 And he sternly ordered them not to tell anyone about him.

Jesus Foretells His Death and Resurrection
(Mt 16.21–28; Lk 9.21–27)

31 Then he began to teach them that the Son of Man must undergo great suffering, and be rejected by the elders, the chief priests, and the scribes, and be killed, and after three days rise again. 32 He said all this quite openly. And Peter took him aside and began to rebuke him. 33 But turning and looking at his disciples, he rebuked Peter and said, "Get behind me, Satan! For you are setting your mind not on divine things but on human things."

34 He called the crowd with his disciples, and said to them, "If any want to become my followers, let them deny themselves and take up their cross and follow me. 35 For those who want to save their life will lose it, and those who lose their life for my sake, and for the sake of the gospel,*j* will save it. 36 For what will it profit them to gain the whole world and forfeit their life? 37 Indeed, what can they give in return for their life? 38 Those who are ashamed of me and of my words*k* in this adulterous and sinful generation, of them the Son of Man will also be ashamed when he comes in the glory of his Father with the holy angels." 1 And he said to them, "Truly I tell you, there are some standing here who will not taste death until they see that the kingdom of God has come with*l* power."

---

f Gk *They*   *g* Gk *he*   *h* Other ancient authorities add *or tell anyone in the village*   *i* Or *the Christ*   *j* Other ancient authorities read *lose their life for the sake of the gospel*   *k* Other ancient authorities read *and of mine*   *l* Or *in*

Total Commitment

LIVE IT!

In Mk 8.34–38, Jesus calls for a total commitment that requires great sacrifice. He tells the disciples that to be truly alive, they must be willing to deny themselves and take up their own crosses. The cross symbolizes denying the way of the world and embracing the way of Jesus. It means tough self-sacrifice and at times a willingness to suffer for what is right.

Why have so many people through the centuries been willing to say yes to this commitment we also call discipleship? Because it is the way to ultimate life! Whenever we try to make life more meaningful through wealth, power, prestige, or selfish pleasure, we can actually end up being less alive. But commitment to Jesus and the cross leads to true freedom, joy, and everlasting life! The path to resurrection is the way of the cross.

▶ Mk 8.34–38

The Transfiguration: On Top of the World

The story of the Transfiguration takes place after Jesus tells his disciples about his coming suffering, death, and Resurrection (Mk 8.31). They need hope and a boost of faith. Jesus takes three disciples to a mountaintop to see the Kingdom of God coming in power. The three disciples see Jesus in a glorious state talking with Moses and Elijah.

God revealed the secret about Jesus to three of his disciples. The two Old Testament figures are key symbols: Moses represents the Law, and Elijah, the prophets. The message is clear: Jesus is the person who fulfills the Law and who realizes God's promises to the prophets. It was a profound religious experience. The disciples glimpsed Jesus' glory, but they could not understand it. Understanding came only after Jesus' Resurrection.

It is understandable to want to found our faith on mountaintop experiences (see "Spiritual Highs," Lk 9.28–36). But though profound religious experiences enliven our faith, listening and following Jesus' words daily are what really fortify our faith and give us a new life.

▶ Mk 9.2–8

The Transfiguration
(Mt 17.1–8; Lk 9.28–36; 2 Pet 1.16–18)

2 Six days later, Jesus took with him Peter and James and John, and led them up a high mountain apart, by themselves. And he was transfigured before them, 3 and his clothes became dazzling white, such as no one^m on earth could bleach them. 4 And there appeared to them E·li'jah with Moses, who were talking with Jesus. 5 Then Peter said to Jesus, "Rabbi, it is good for us to be here; let us make three dwellings,^n one for you, one for Moses, and one for E·li'jah." 6 He did not know what to say, for they were terrified. 7 Then a cloud overshadowed them, and from the cloud there came a voice, "This is my Son, the Beloved;^o listen to him!" 8 Suddenly when they looked around, they saw no one with them any more, but only Jesus.

The Coming of Elijah
(Mt 17.9–13)

9 As they were coming down the mountain, he ordered them to tell no one about what they had seen, until after the Son of Man had risen from the dead. 10 So they kept the matter to themselves, questioning what this rising from the dead could mean. 11 Then they asked him, "Why do the scribes say that E·li'jah must come first?" 12 He said to them, "E·li'jah is indeed coming first to restore all things. How then is it written about the Son of Man, that he is to go through many sufferings and be treated with contempt? 13 But I tell you that E·li'jah has come, and they did to him whatever they pleased, as it is written about him."

The Healing of a Boy with a Spirit
(Mt 17.14–21; Lk 9.37–43a)

14 When they came to the disciples, they saw a great crowd around them, and some scribes arguing with them. 15 When the whole crowd saw him, they were immediately overcome with awe, and they ran forward to greet him. 16 He asked them, "What are you arguing about with them?" 17 Someone from the crowd answered him, "Teacher, I brought you my son; he has a spirit that makes him unable to speak; 18 and whenever it seizes him, it dashes him down; and he foams and grinds his teeth and becomes rigid; and I asked your disciples to cast it out, but they could not do so." 19 He answered them, "You faithless generation, how much longer must I be among you? How much longer must I put up with you? Bring him to me." 20 And they brought the boy^p to him. When the spirit saw him, immediately it convulsed the boy,^p and he fell on the ground and rolled about, foaming at the mouth. 21 Jesus^q asked the father, "How long has this been happening to him?" And he said, "From childhood. 22 It has often cast him into the fire and into the water, to destroy him; but if you are able to do anything, have pity on us and help us." 23 Jesus said to him, "If you are able!—All things can be done for the one who believes." 24 Immediately the father of the child cried out,^r "I believe; help my unbelief!" 25 When Jesus saw that a crowd came running

---

m Gk *no fuller*   n Or *tents*   o Or *my beloved Son*
p Gk *him*   q Gk *He*   r Other ancient authorities add *with tears*

together, he rebuked the unclean spirit, saying to it, "You spirit that keeps this boy from speaking and hearing, I command you, come out of him, and never enter him again!" 26 After crying out and convulsing him terribly, it came out, and the boy was like a corpse, so that most of them said, "He is dead." 27 But Jesus took him by the hand and lifted him up, and he was able to stand. 28 When he had entered the house, his disciples asked him privately, "Why could we not cast it out?" 29 He said to them, "This kind can come out only through prayer."[s]

PRAY IT?

I Believe; Help My Unbelief!

Saying we believe in something may not be enough to prove we truly believe. Faith in God means knowing that God is totally with us even when it doesn't seem that way!

When we have nagging doubts whether even God can help us in a particular situation—like the father in Mk 9.24—we can turn to God by praying for faith. We don't have to have our faith or our life perfectly together before we ask God for help. The test of faith is trusting that God cares for us and provides what we need, even when our prayers are not answered in the way we desire.

▸ Mk 9.14–29

Jesus Again Foretells His Death and Resurrection
(Mt 17.22–23; Lk 9.43b–45)

30 They went on from there and passed through Galilee. He did not want anyone to know it; 31 for he was teaching his disciples, saying to them, "The Son of Man is to be betrayed into human hands, and they will kill him, and three days after being killed, he will rise again." 32 But they did not understand what he was saying and were afraid to ask him.

Who Is the Greatest?
(Mt 18.1–5; Lk 9.46–48)

33 Then they came to Ca·per'na·um; and when he was in the house he asked them, "What were

you arguing about on the way?" 34 But they were silent, for on the way they had argued with one another who was the greatest. 35 He sat down, called the twelve, and said to them, "Whoever wants to be first must be last of all and servant of all." 36 Then he took a little child and put it among them; and taking it in his arms, he said to them, 37 "Whoever welcomes one such child in my name welcomes me, and whoever welcomes me welcomes not me but the one who sent me."

Another Exorcist
(Mt 10.40–42; Lk 9.49–50)

38 John said to him, "Teacher, we saw someone[t] casting out demons in your name, and we tried to stop him, because he was not following us." 39 But Jesus said, "Do not stop him; for no one who does a deed of power in my name will be able soon afterward to speak evil of me. 40 Whoever is not against us is for us. 41 For truly I tell you, whoever gives you a cup of water to drink because you bear the name of Christ will by no means lose the reward.

Temptations to Sin
(Mt 18.6–9; Lk 17.1–2)

42 "If any of you put a stumbling block before one of these little ones who believe in me,[u] it would be better for you if a great millstone were hung around your neck and you were thrown into the sea. 43 If your hand causes you to stumble, cut it off; it is better for you to enter life maimed than to have two hands and to go to hell,[v] to the unquenchable fire.[w] 45 And if your foot causes you to stumble, cut it off; it is better for you to enter life lame than to have two feet and to be thrown into hell.[v,w] 47 And if your eye causes you to stumble, tear it out; it is better for you to enter the kingdom of God with one eye than to have two eyes and to be thrown into hell,[v] 48 where their worm never dies, and the fire is never quenched.

49 "For everyone will be salted with fire.[x] 50 Salt is good; but if salt has lost its saltiness, how can you season it?[y] Have salt in yourselves, and be at peace with one another."

---

s Other ancient authorities add *and fasting*   t Other ancient authorities add *who does not follow us*   u Other ancient authorities lack *in me*   v Gk *Gehenna*   w Verses 44 and 46 (which are identical with verse 48) are lacking in the best ancient authorities   x Other ancient authorities either add or substitute *and every sacrifice will be salted with salt*   y Or *how can you restore its saltiness?*

Teaching about Divorce
(Mt 19.1–9)

He left that place and went to the region of Judea and[z] beyond the Jordan. And crowds again gathered around him; and, as was his custom, he again taught them.

2 Some Phar'i•sees came, and to test him they asked, "Is it lawful for a man to divorce his wife?" 3 He answered them, "What did Moses command you?" 4 They said, "Moses allowed a man to write a certificate of dismissal and to divorce her." 5 But Jesus said to them, "Because of your hardness of heart he wrote this commandment for you. 6 But from the beginning of creation, 'God made them male and female.' 7 'For this reason a man shall leave his father and mother and be joined to his wife,[a] 8 and the two shall become one flesh.' So they are no longer two, but one flesh. 9 Therefore what God has joined together, let no one separate."

10 Then in the house the disciples asked him again about this matter. 11 He said to them, "Whoever divorces his wife and marries another commits adultery against her; 12 and if she divorces her husband and marries another, she commits adultery."

Jesus Blesses Little Children
(Mt 19.13–15; Lk 18.15–17)

13 People were bringing little children to him in order that he might touch them; and the disciples spoke sternly to them. 14 But when Jesus saw this, he was indignant and said to them, "Let the little children come to me; do not stop them; for it is to such as these that the kingdom of God belongs. 15 Truly I tell you, whoever does not receive the kingdom of God as a little child will never enter it." 16 And he took them up in his arms, laid his hands on them, and blessed them.

The Rich Man
(Mt 19.16–30; Lk 18.18–30)

17 As he was setting out on a journey, a man ran up and knelt before him, and asked him, "Good Teacher, what must I do to inherit eternal life?" 18 Jesus said to him, "Why do you call me good? No one is good but God alone. 19 You know the commandments: 'You shall not murder; You shall not commit adultery; You shall not steal; You shall not bear false witness; You shall not defraud; Honor your father and mother.' " 20 He said to him, "Teacher, I have kept all these since my youth." 21 Jesus, looking at him, loved him and said, "You lack one thing; go, sell what you own, and give the money[b] to the poor, and you will have treasure in heaven; then come, follow me." 22 When he heard this, he was shocked and went away grieving, for he had many possessions.

23 Then Jesus looked around and said to his disciples, "How hard it will be for those who have wealth to enter the kingdom of God!" 24 And the disciples were perplexed at these words. But Jesus said to them again, "Children, how hard it is[c] to enter the kingdom of God! 25 It is easier for a camel to go through the eye of a needle than for someone who is rich to enter the kingdom of God." 26 They were greatly astounded and said to one another,[d] "Then who can be saved?" 27 Jesus looked at them and said, "For mortals it is impossible, but not for God; for God all things are possible."

28 Peter began to say to him, "Look, we have left everything and followed you." 29 Jesus said, "Truly I tell you, there is no one who has left house or brothers or sisters or mother or father or children or fields, for my sake and for the sake of the good news,[e] 30 who will not receive a hundredfold now in this age—houses, brothers and sisters, mothers and children, and fields, with persecutions—and in the age to come eternal life. 31 But many who are first will be last, and the last will be first."

A Third Time Jesus Foretells His Death and Resurrection
(Mt 20.17–19; Lk 18.31–34)

32 They were on the road, going up to Jerusalem, and Jesus was walking ahead of them; they were amazed, and those who followed were afraid. He took the twelve aside again and began to tell them what was to happen to him, 33 saying, "See, we are going up to Jerusalem, and the Son of Man will be handed over to the chief priests and the scribes, and they will condemn him to death; then they will hand him over to the Gentiles; 34 they will mock him, and spit upon him, and flog him, and kill him; and after three days he will rise again."

The Request of James and John
(Mt 20.20–28)

35 James and John, the sons of Zeb'e•dee, came forward to him and said to him, "Teacher, we want you to do for us whatever we ask of you." 36 And he said to them, "What is it you want me to do for you?" 37 And they said to him, "Grant us to sit, one at your right hand and one at your left, in your glory." 38 But Jesus said to them, "You do not

---

z Other ancient authorities lack *and*   a Other ancient authorities lack *and be joined to his wife*   b Gk lacks *the money*   c Other ancient authorities add *for those who trust in riches*   d Other ancient authorities read *to him*   e Or *gospel*

know what you are asking. Are you able to drink the cup that I drink, or be baptized with the baptism that I am baptized with?" [39] They replied, "We are able." Then Jesus said to them, "The cup that I drink you will drink; and with the baptism with which I am baptized, you will be baptized; [40] but to sit at my right hand or at my left is not mine to grant, but it is for those for whom it has been prepared."

41 When the ten heard this, they began to be angry with James and John. [42] So Jesus called them and said to them, "You know that among the Gentiles those whom they recognize as their rulers lord it over them, and their great ones are tyrants over them. [43] But it is not so among you; but whoever wishes to become great among you must be your servant, [44] and whoever wishes to be first among you must be slave of all. [45] For the Son of Man came not to be served but to serve, and to give his life a ransom for many."

The Healing of Blind Bartimaeus
(Mt 20.29–34; Lk 18.35–43)

46 They came to Jericho. As he and his disciples and a large crowd were leaving Jericho, Bar·ti·maḗus son of Ti·maḗus, a blind beggar, was sitting by the roadside. [47] When he heard that it was Jesus of Nazareth, he began to shout out and say, "Jesus, Son of David, have mercy on me!" [48] Many sternly ordered him to be quiet, but he cried out even more loudly, "Son of David, have mercy on me!" [49] Jesus stood still and said, "Call him here." And they called the blind man, saying to him, "Take heart; get up, he is calling you." [50] So throwing off his cloak, he sprang up and came to Jesus. [51] Then Jesus said to him, "What do you want me to do for you?" The blind man said to him, "My teacher,*f* let me see again." [52] Jesus said to him, "Go; your faith has made you well." Immediately he regained his sight and followed him on the way.

Jesus' Triumphal Entry into Jerusalem
(Mt 21.1–11; Lk 19.28–40; Jn 12.12–19)

When they were approaching Jerusalem, at Beth'-pha·gē and Beth'a·ny, near the Mount of Olives, he sent two of his disciples 2 and said to them, "Go into the village ahead of you, and immediately as you enter it, you will find tied there a colt that has never been ridden; untie it and bring it. [3] If anyone says to you, 'Why are you doing this?' just say this, 'The Lord needs it and will send it back here immediately.'" [4] They went away and found a colt tied near a door, outside in the street. As they were untying it, [5] some of the bystanders said to them, "What are you doing, untying the colt?" [6] They told

Catholic Connections

TRUE GREATNESS

The disciples think that Jesus is going to be a great king, and they want to share in his power and glory. Instead, Jesus tells them that they must be servants. Servanthood is the true mark of greatness. That is why the pope is sometimes called the servant of the servants of God. Jesus not only taught true servanthood but lived it by giving up his life as a ransom for all.

▶ Mk 10.35–45

them what Jesus had said; and they allowed them to take it. [7] Then they brought the colt to Jesus and threw their cloaks on it; and he sat on it. [8] Many people spread their cloaks on the road, and others spread leafy branches that they had cut in the fields. [9] Then those who went ahead and those who followed were shouting,

"Hosanna!
Blessed is the one who comes in the name of the Lord!
10 Blessed is the coming kingdom of our ancestor David!
Hosanna in the highest heaven!"

11 Then he entered Jerusalem and went into the temple; and when he had looked around at everything, as it was already late, he went out to Beth'a·ny with the twelve.

Jesus Curses the Fig Tree
(Mt 21.18–19)

12 On the following day, when they came from Beth'a·ny, he was hungry. [13] Seeing in the distance a fig tree in leaf, he went to see whether perhaps he would find anything on it. When he came to it, he found nothing but leaves, for it was not the season for figs. [14] He said to it, "May no one ever eat fruit from you again." And his disciples heard it.

---

f Aramaic *Rabbouni*

Jesus Cleanses the Temple
(Mt 21.12–17; Lk 19.45–48; Jn 2.13–22)

15 Then they came to Jerusalem. And he entered the temple and began to drive out those who were selling and those who were buying in the temple, and he overturned the tables of the money changers and the seats of those who sold doves; 16 and he would not allow anyone to carry anything through the temple. 17 He was teaching and saying, "Is it not written,

'My house shall be called a house of prayer
for all the nations'?
But you have made it a den of robbers."

18 And when the chief priests and the scribes heard it, they kept looking for a way to kill him; for they were afraid of him, because the whole crowd was spellbound by his teaching. 19 And when evening came, Jesus and his disciples*g* went out of the city.

The Lesson from the Withered Fig Tree
(Mt 21.20–22)

20 In the morning as they passed by, they saw the fig tree withered away to its roots. 21 Then Peter remembered and said to him, "Rabbi, look! The fig tree that you cursed has withered." 22 Jesus answered them, "Have*h* faith in God. 23 Truly I tell you, if you say to this mountain, 'Be taken up and thrown into the sea,' and if you do not doubt in your heart, but believe that what you say will come to pass, it will be done for you. 24 So I tell you, whatever you ask for in prayer, believe that you have received*i* it, and it will be yours.

PRAY IT
Unanswered Prayer

Did you ever want something so badly that you prayed for it? If so, how was your prayer answered? One dilemma of faith is that sometimes it seems that our prayers are not answered. But in Mk 11.24, Jesus tells us that when we ask for something in prayer, we will receive it. Could it be that we do not always recognize the answer? Maybe the answer is not exactly what we ask for but rather something that is better for us in the long run.

▶ Mk 11.24

25 "Whenever you stand praying, forgive, if you have anything against anyone; so that your Father in heaven may also forgive you your trespasses."*j*

Jesus' Authority Is Questioned
(Mt 21.23–27; Lk 20.1–8)

27 Again they came to Jerusalem. As he was walking in the temple, the chief priests, the scribes, and the elders came to him 28 and said, "By what authority are you doing these things? Who gave you this authority to do them?" 29 Jesus said to them, "I will ask you one question; answer me, and I will tell you by what authority I do these things. 30 Did the baptism of John come from heaven, or was it of human origin? Answer me." 31 They argued with one another, "If we say, 'From heaven,' he will say, 'Why then did you not believe him?' 32 But shall we say, 'Of human origin'?"—they were afraid of the crowd, for all regarded John as truly a prophet. 33 So they answered Jesus, "We do not know." And Jesus said to them, "Neither will I tell you by what authority I am doing these things."

The Parable of the Wicked Tenants
(Mt 21.33–46; Lk 20.9–19)

Then he began to speak to them in parables. "A man planted a vineyard, put a fence around it, dug a pit for the wine press, and built a watchtower; then he leased it to tenants and went to another country. 2 When the season came, he sent a slave to the tenants to collect from them his share of the produce of the vineyard. 3 But they seized him, and beat him, and sent him away empty-handed. 4 And again he sent another slave to them; this one they beat over the head and insulted. 5 Then he sent another, and that one they killed. And so it was with many others; some they beat, and others they killed. 6 He had still one other, a beloved son. Finally he sent him to them, saying, 'They will respect my son.' 7 But those tenants said to one another, 'This is the heir; come, let us kill him, and the inheritance will be ours.' 8 So they seized him, killed him, and threw him out of the vineyard. 9 What then will the owner of the vineyard do? He will come and destroy the tenants and give the vineyard to others. 10 Have you not read this scripture:

'The stone that the builders rejected
has become the cornerstone;*k*

---

g Gk *they*: other ancient authorities read *he*   h Other ancient authorities read *"If you have*   i Other ancient authorities read *are receiving*   j Other ancient authorities add verse 26, *"But if you do not forgive, neither will your Father in heaven forgive your trespasses."*   k Or *keystone*

11 this was the Lord's doing,
    and it is amazing in our eyes'?"

12 When they realized that he had told this parable against them, they wanted to arrest him, but they feared the crowd. So they left him and went away.

PRAY IT?

What Do You Want from Me?

Dear God, Jesus tells us to give to you what is yours. What do you want from me, God? What can I give to you?

As a young person still growing and developing, I don't have much to offer financially. I can make a small financial contribution to the church, to poor people, . . . but is it enough, Lord? What more can I give?

I can offer my time and talents to serve my faith community. I can sing, play an instrument, draw posters, greet visitors, clean, decorate, organize, cook, bake, and telephone. I can help teach children, lector, or usher, . . . but is it enough, Lord? What more can I give?

I can reach out to serve and share your love at home, in my neighborhood, my school, my community, . . . but is it enough, Lord? What more can I give?

I want to serve you better, Lord. Speak to me, and I will listen. Amen.

▶ Mk 12.13–17

The Question about Paying Taxes
(Mt 22.15–22; Lk 20.20–26)

13 Then they sent to him some Phar'i·sees and some He·rō'di·ans to trap him in what he said. 14 And they came and said to him, "Teacher, we know that you are sincere, and show deference to no one; for you do not regard people with partiality, but teach the way of God in accordance with truth. Is it lawful to pay taxes to the emperor, or not? 15 Should we pay them, or should we not?" But knowing their hypocrisy, he said to them, "Why are you putting me to the test? Bring me a denarius and let me see it." 16 And they brought one. Then he said to them, "Whose head is this, and whose title?" They answered, "The emperor's." 17 Jesus said

to them, "Give to the emperor the things that are the emperor's, and to God the things that are God's." And they were utterly amazed at him.

The Question about the Resurrection
(Mt 22.23–33; Lk 20.27–40)

18 Some Sad'dū·cees, who say there is no resurrection, came to him and asked him a question, saying, 19 "Teacher, Moses wrote for us that if a man's brother dies, leaving a wife but no child, the man[l] shall marry the widow and raise up children for his brother. 20 There were seven brothers; the first married and, when he died, left no children; 21 and the second married the widow[m] and died, leaving no children; and the third likewise; 22 none of the seven left children. Last of all the woman herself died. 23 In the resurrection[n] whose wife will she be? For the seven had married her."

24 Jesus said to them, "Is not this the reason you are wrong, that you know neither the scriptures nor the power of God? 25 For when they rise from the dead, they neither marry nor are given in marriage, but are like angels in heaven. 26 And as for the dead being raised, have you not read in the book of Moses, in the story about the bush, how God said to him, 'I am the God of Abraham, the God of Isaac, and the God of Jacob'? 27 He is God not of the dead, but of the living; you are quite wrong."

The First Commandment
(Mt 22.34–40; Lk 10.25–28)

28 One of the scribes came near and heard them disputing with one another, and seeing that he answered them well, he asked him, "Which commandment is the first of all?" 29 Jesus answered, "The first is, 'Hear, O Israel: the Lord our God, the Lord is one; 30 you shall love the Lord your God with all your heart, and with all your soul, and with all your mind, and with all your strength.' 31 The second is this, 'You shall love your neighbor as yourself.' There is no other commandment greater than these." 32 Then the scribe said to him, "You are right, Teacher; you have truly said that 'he is one, and besides him there is no other'; 33 and 'to love him with all the heart, and with all the understanding, and with all the strength,' and 'to love one's neighbor as oneself,'—this is much more important than all whole burnt offerings and sacrifices." 34 When Jesus saw that he answered wisely, he said to him, "You are not far from the kingdom of God." After that no one dared to ask him any question.

---

l Gk *his brother*   *m* Gk *her*   *n* Other ancient authorities add *when they rise*

The Question about David's Son
(Mt 22.41–46; Lk 20.41–44)

35 While Jesus was teaching in the temple, he said, "How can the scribes say that the Messiah[o] is the son of David? 36 David himself, by the Holy Spirit, declared,

'The Lord said to my Lord,
　"Sit at my right hand,
　　until I put your enemies under your
　　　feet." '

37 David himself calls him Lord; so how can he be his son?" And the large crowd was listening to him with delight.

NATIVE AMERICAN

Sacrificial Giving

Native Americans can appreciate the widow's offering in Mk 12.41–44. For example, the Lakota tribe has a custom called *otuhan,* or "giveaway." During important occasions, a person honors the other members of the tribe by giving away much of what he or she has. Sometimes, everything is given away. To be called stingy is the worst insult.

Think about your own circumstances. How easy would it be to share or give away your favorite possessions? Could you give away something you really value? Why or why not?

Many Native Americans believe that all we have belongs to the Great Spirit and is a gift to be shared with others. Make a decision! Follow the example of the widow and be generous to others to the point of sacrifice.

▸ Mk 12.41–44

Jesus Denounces the Scribes
(Mt 23.1–7; Lk 20.45–47)

38 As he taught, he said, "Beware of the scribes, who like to walk around in long robes, and to be greeted with respect in the marketplaces, 39 and to have the best seats in the synagogues and places of honor at banquets! 40 They devour widows' houses and for the sake of appearance say long prayers. They will receive the greater condemnation."

The Widow's Offering
(Lk 21.1–4)

41 He sat down opposite the treasury, and watched the crowd putting money into the treasury. Many rich people put in large sums. 42 A poor widow came and put in two small copper coins, which are worth a penny. 43 Then he called his disciples and said to them, "Truly I tell you, this poor widow has put in more than all those who are contributing to the treasury. 44 For all of them have contributed out of their abundance; but she out of her poverty has put in everything she had, all she had to live on."

The Destruction of the Temple Foretold
(Mt 24.1–8; Lk 21.5–11)

As he came out of the temple, one of his disciples said to him, "Look, Teacher, what large stones and what large buildings!" 2 Then Jesus asked him, "Do you see these great buildings? Not one stone will be left here upon another; all will be thrown down."

3 When he was sitting on the Mount of Olives opposite the temple, Peter, James, John, and Andrew asked him privately, 4 "Tell us, when will this be, and what will be the sign that all these things are about to be accomplished?" 5 Then Jesus began to say to them, "Beware that no one leads you astray. 6 Many will come in my name and say, 'I am he!'[p] and they will lead many astray. 7 When you hear of wars and rumors of wars, do not be alarmed; this must take place, but the end is still to come. 8 For nation will rise against nation, and kingdom against kingdom; there will be earthquakes in various places; there will be famines. This is but the beginning of the birth pangs.

Persecution Foretold
(Mt 24.9–14; Lk 21.12–19)

9 "As for yourselves, beware; for they will hand you over to councils; and you will be beaten in synagogues; and you will stand before governors and kings because of me, as a testimony to them. 10 And the good news[q] must first be proclaimed to all nations. 11 When they bring you to trial and hand you over, do not worry beforehand about what you are to say; but say whatever is

---

o Or *the Christ*　　*p* Gk *I am*　　*q* Gk *gospel*

given you at that time, for it is not you who speak, but the Holy Spirit. 12 Brother will betray brother to death, and a father his child, and children will rise against parents and have them put to death; 13 and you will be hated by all because of my name. But the one who endures to the end will be saved.

The Desolating Sacrilege
(Mt 24.15–28; Lk 21.20–24)

14 "But when you see the desolating sacrilege set up where it ought not to be (let the reader understand), then those in Judea must flee to the mountains; 15 the one on the housetop must not go down or enter the house to take anything away; 16 the one in the field must not turn back to get a coat. 17 Woe to those who are pregnant and to those who are nursing infants in those days! 18 Pray that it may not be in winter. 19 For in those days there will be suffering, such as has not been from the beginning of the creation that God created until now, no, and never will be. 20 And if the Lord had not cut short those days, no one would be saved; but for the sake of the elect, whom he chose, he has cut short those days. 21 And if anyone says to you at that time, 'Look! Here is the Messiah!'r or 'Look! There he is!'—do not believe it. 22 False messiahss and false prophets will appear and produce signs and omens, to lead astray, if possible, the elect. 23 But be alert; I have already told you everything.

The Coming of the Son of Man
(Mt 24.29–31; Lk 21.25–28)

24 "But in those days, after that suffering,
 the sun will be darkened,
 and the moon will not give its light,
25 and the stars will be falling from heaven,
 and the powers in the heavens will be shaken.

26 Then they will see 'the Son of Man coming in clouds' with great power and glory. 27 Then he will send out the angels, and gather his elect from the four winds, from the ends of the earth to the ends of heaven.

The Lesson of the Fig Tree
(Mt 24.32–35; Lk 21.29–33)

28 "From the fig tree learn its lesson: as soon as its branch becomes tender and puts forth its leaves, you know that summer is near. 29 So also, when you see these things taking place, you know that het is near, at the very gates. 30 Truly I tell you, this generation will not pass away until all these things have taken place. 31 Heaven and earth will pass away, but my words will not pass away.

The Necessity for Watchfulness
(Mt 24.36–44; Lk 21.34–36)

32 "But about that day or hour no one knows, neither the angels in heaven, nor the Son, but only the Father. 33 Beware, keep alert;u for you do not know when the time will come. 34 It is like a man going on a journey, when he leaves home and puts his slaves in charge, each with his work, and commands the doorkeeper to be on the watch. 35 Therefore, keep awake—for you do not know when the master of the house will come, in the evening, or at midnight, or at cockcrow, or at dawn, 36 or else he may find you asleep when he comes suddenly. 37 And what I say to you I say to all: Keep awake."

r Or *the Christ* s Or *christs* t Or *it* u Other ancient authorities add *and pray*

Signs and Omens
did you KNOW?

The community for which the author of Mark's Gospel wrote saw its sufferings as part of the troubles that would come with the end time. However, the author didn't intend that his readers take Jesus' signs and omens of wars and earthquakes literally to mean the end of the world was at hand. Rather, these descriptions were used symbolically (see "Apocalyptic Literature," Daniel, chapters 7–10) to help the community make sense of its persecutions. The message of this Gospel is that Christians who were getting beaten up and thrown in jail would be saved by God. And ultimately, human history would climax in the perfect Reign of God. It was their job to hang on and endure to the end. All they had to worry about was spreading the Good News of Jesus Christ, and God would take care of the rest.

▶ Mark, chapter 13

The Plot to Kill Jesus
(Mt 26.1–5; Lk 22.1–2; Jn 11.45–53)

It was two days before the Passover and the festival of Unleavened Bread. The chief priests and the scribes were looking for a way to arrest Jesus*v* by stealth and kill him; 2 for they said, "Not during the festival, or there may be a riot among the people."

The Anointing at Bethany
(Mt 26.6–13; Jn 12.1–8)

3 While he was at Beth'a•ny in the house of Simon the leper,*w* as he sat at the table, a woman came with an alabaster jar of very costly ointment of nard, and she broke open the jar and poured the ointment on his head. 4 But some were there who said to one another in anger, "Why was the ointment wasted in this way? 5 For this ointment could have been sold for more than three hundred denarii,*x* and the money given to the poor." And they scolded her. 6 But Jesus said, "Let her alone; why do you trouble her? She has performed a good service for me. 7 For you always have the poor with you, and you can show kindness to them whenever you wish; but you will not always have me. 8 She has done what she could; she has anointed my body beforehand for its burial. 9 Truly I tell you, wherever the good news*y* is proclaimed in the whole world, what she has done will be told in remembrance of her."

Judas Agrees to Betray Jesus
(Mt 26.14–16; Lk 22.3–6)

10 Then Judas Is•car'i•ot, who was one of the twelve, went to the chief priests in order to betray him to them. 11 When they heard it, they were greatly pleased, and promised to give him money. So he began to look for an opportunity to betray him.

The Passover with the Disciples
(Mt 26.17–25; Lk 22.7–13; Jn 13.21–30)

12 On the first day of Unleavened Bread, when the Passover lamb is sacrificed, his disciples said to him, "Where do you want us to go and make the preparations for you to eat the Passover?" 13 So he sent two of his disciples, saying to them, "Go into the city, and a man carrying a jar of water will meet you; follow him, 14 and wherever he enters, say to the owner of the house, 'The Teacher asks, Where is my guest room where I may eat the Passover with my disciples?' 15 He will show you a large room upstairs, furnished and ready. Make preparations for us there." 16 So the disciples set out

and went to the city, and found everything as he had told them; and they prepared the Passover meal.

17 When it was evening, he came with the twelve. 18 And when they had taken their places and were eating, Jesus said, "Truly I tell you, one of you will betray me, one who is eating with me." 19 They began to be distressed and to say to him one after another, "Surely, not I?" 20 He said to them, "It is one of the twelve, one who is dipping bread*z* into the bowl*a* with me. 21 For the Son of Man goes as it is written of him, but woe to that one by whom the Son of Man is betrayed! It would have been better for that one not to have been born."

---

v Gk *him* *w* The terms *leper* and *leprosy* can refer to several diseases *x* The denarius was the usual day's wage for a laborer *y* Or *gospel* *z* Gk lacks *bread* *a* Other ancient authorities read *same bowl*

The Institution of the Lord's Supper
(Mt 26.26–29; Lk 22.14–23; 1 Cor 11.23–26)

22 While they were eating, he took a loaf of bread, and after blessing it he broke it, gave it to them, and said, "Take; this is my body." 23 Then he took a cup, and after giving thanks he gave it to them, and all of them drank from it. 24 He said to them, "This is my blood of the*b* covenant, which is poured out for many. 25 Truly I tell you, I will never again drink of the fruit of the vine until that day when I drink it new in the kingdom of God."

Peter's Denial Foretold
(Mt 26.30–35; Lk 22.31–34; Jn 13.36–38)

26 When they had sung the hymn, they went out to the Mount of Olives. 27 And Jesus said to them, "You will all become deserters; for it is written,

'I will strike the shepherd,
   and the sheep will be scattered.'

28 But after I am raised up, I will go before you to Galilee." 29 Peter said to him, "Even though all become deserters, I will not." 30 Jesus said to him, "Truly I tell you, this day, this very night, before the cock crows twice, you will deny me three times." 31 But he said vehemently, "Even though I must die with you, I will not deny you." And all of them said the same.

Jesus Prays in Gethsemane
(Mt 26.36–46; Lk 22.39–46)

32 They went to a place called Geth·sem′a·nē; and he said to his disciples, "Sit here while I pray." 33 He took with him Peter and James and John, and began to be distressed and agitated. 34 And he said to them, "I am deeply grieved, even to death; remain here, and keep awake." 35 And going a little farther, he threw himself on the ground and prayed that, if it were possible, the hour might pass from him. 36 He said, "Abba,*c* Father, for you all things are possible; remove this cup from me; yet, not what I want, but what you want." 37 He came and found them sleeping; and he said to Peter, "Simon, are you asleep? Could you not keep awake one hour? 38 Keep awake and pray that you may not come into the time of trial;*d* the spirit indeed is willing, but the flesh is weak." 39 And again he went away and prayed, saying the same words. 40 And once more he came and found them sleeping, for their eyes were very heavy; and they did not know what to say to him. 41 He came a third time and said to them, "Are you still sleeping and taking your rest? Enough! The hour has come; the Son of Man is betrayed into the hands of sinners. 42 Get up, let us be going. See, my betrayer is at hand."

The Betrayal and Arrest of Jesus
(Mt 26.47–56; Lk 22.47–53; Jn 18.1–11)

43 Immediately, while he was still speaking, Judas, one of the twelve, arrived; and with him there was a crowd with swords and clubs, from the chief priests, the scribes, and the elders. 44 Now the betrayer had given them a sign, saying, "The one I will kiss is the man; arrest him and lead him away under guard." 45 So when he came, he went up to him at once and said, "Rabbi!" and kissed him. 46 Then they laid hands on him and arrested him. 47 But one of those who stood near drew his sword and struck the slave of the high priest, cutting off his ear. 48 Then Jesus said to them, "Have you come out with swords and clubs to arrest me as though I were a bandit? 49 Day after day I was with you in the temple teaching, and you did not arrest me. But let the scriptures be fulfilled." 50 All of them deserted him and fled.

51 A certain young man was following him, wearing nothing but a linen cloth. They caught hold of him, 52 but he left the linen cloth and ran off naked.

Jesus before the Council
*(Mt 26.57–68; Lk 22.66–71;
   Jn 18.12–14, 19–24)*

53 They took Jesus to the high priest; and all the chief priests, the elders, and the scribes were assembled. 54 Peter had followed him at a distance, right into the courtyard of the high priest; and he was sitting with the guards, warming himself at the fire. 55 Now the chief priests and the whole council were looking for testimony against Jesus to put him to death; but they found none. 56 For many gave false testimony against him, and their testimony did not agree. 57 Some stood up and gave false testimony against him, saying, 58 "We heard him say, 'I will destroy this temple that is made with hands, and in three days I will build another, not made with hands.' " 59 But even on this point their testimony did not agree. 60 Then the high priest stood up before them and asked Jesus, "Have you no answer? What is it that they testify against you?" 61 But he was silent and did not answer. Again the high priest asked him, "Are you the Messiah,*e* the Son of the Blessed One?" 62 Jesus said, "I am; and

---

b Other ancient authorities add *new*   *c* Aramaic for *Father*   *d* Or *into temptation*   *e* Or *the Christ*

'you will see the Son of Man
seated at the right hand of the Power,'
and 'coming with the clouds
    of heaven.' "

63 Then the high priest tore his clothes and said, "Why do we still need witnesses? 64 You have heard his blasphemy! What is your decision?" All of them condemned him as deserving death. 65 Some began to spit on him, to blindfold him, and to strike him, saying to him, "Prophesy!" The guards also took him over and beat him.

Peter Denies Jesus
(Mt 26.69–75; Lk 22.54–62;
Jn 18.15–18, 25–27)

66 While Peter was below in the courtyard, one of the servant-girls of the high priest came by. 67 When she saw Peter warming himself, she stared at him and said, "You also were with Jesus, the man from Nazareth." 68 But he denied it, saying, "I do not know or understand what you are talking about." And he went out into the forecourt. *f* Then the cock crowed. *g* 69 And the servant-girl, on seeing him, began again to say to the bystanders, "This man is one of them." 70 But again he denied it. Then after a little while the bystanders again said to Peter, "Certainly you are one of them; for you are a Galilean." 71 But he began to curse, and he swore an oath, "I do not know this man you are talking about." 72 At that moment the cock crowed for the second time. Then Peter remembered that Jesus had said to him, "Before the cock crows twice, you will deny me three times." And he broke down and wept.

Jesus before Pilate
(Mt 27.1–2, 11–14; Lk 23.1–5, 13–16;
Jn 18.28–38a)

As soon as it was morning, the chief priests held a consultation with the elders and scribes and the whole council. They bound Jesus, led him away, and handed him over to Pilate. 2 Pilate asked him, "Are you the King of the Jews?" He answered him, "You say so." 3 Then the chief priests accused him of many things. 4 Pilate asked him again, "Have you no answer? See how many charges they bring against you." 5 But Jesus made no further reply, so that Pilate was amazed.

Pilate Hands Jesus over to Be Crucified
(Mt 27.15–26; Lk 23.18–25; Jn 18.38b—19.16)

6 Now at the festival he used to release a prisoner for them, anyone for whom they asked. 7 Now a man called Ba·rab'bas was in prison with the rebels who had committed murder during the insurrection. 8 So the crowd came and began to ask Pilate to do for them according to his custom. 9 Then he answered them, "Do you want me to release for you the King of the Jews?" 10 For he realized that it was out of jealousy that the chief priests had handed him over. 11 But the chief priests stirred up the crowd to have him release Ba·rab'bas for them instead. 12 Pilate spoke to them again, "Then what do you wish me to do*h* with the man you call*i* the King of the Jews?" 13 They shouted back, "Crucify him!" 14 Pilate asked them, "Why, what evil has he done?" But they shouted all

---

f Or *gateway*   *g* Other ancient authorities lack *Then the*
cock crowed   *h* Other ancient authorities read *what should*
I do   *i* Other ancient authorities lack *the man you call*

A Friend's Betrayal

LIVE IT!

Imagine that you are facing a difficult time. Your best friend promises to be with you no matter what. This is the one person you rely on, who has been there for you and has been the most loyal and faithful of all your friends. You have spent the last three years together . . . working, studying, enjoying holidays, traveling, and sharing countless meals and discussions. Now, imagine that this friend completely lets you down.

Peter was one of Jesus' best friends. As the story is told in the Gospel of Mark, the relationship has its difficult times, but Jesus continuously tries to reach Peter. Knowing Peter is going to deny him, Jesus even tries warning Peter that things would happen this way (14.30).

Probably just like some of your friends, Peter had good intentions but could not follow through with his assurances to Jesus (verses 66–72). But Jesus did not give up on Peter (Jn 21.15–19), and Peter became one of the greatest heroes of our church. Don't give up on your friends either.

▶ Mk 14.66–72

the more, "Crucify him!" 15 So Pilate, wishing to satisfy the crowd, released Ba·rab′bas for them; and after flogging Jesus, he handed him over to be crucified.

PRAY IT!

Facing the Hard Times

Lord, you really do know what it is like to be beaten, teased, pushed around, and rejected.

If you could put up with this torment, then maybe there is hope for others who feel the same way at times. Like when we are made fun of or rejected because of the way we look or act or for what we believe in. Or when we feel all alone or that no one understands what we are feeling.

But now, I know that you understand, Lord. You took these difficult steps even before we did. You have been there. You show us a way through these tough times.

Teach me to pray as you did: "Abba, Father, for you all things are possible; remove this cup [suffering] from me; yet, not what I want, but what you want" (Mk 14.36). Give me the strength to overcome my despair. Give me faith to abandon myself in God's hands as you did. Give me hope to see a new life beyond these moments of pain and hopelessness. Amen.

▶ Mk 15.16–20

The Soldiers Mock Jesus
(Mt 27.27–31)

16 Then the soldiers led him into the courtyard of the palace (that is, the governor's headquartersⱼ); and they called together the whole cohort. 17 And they clothed him in a purple cloak; and after twisting some thorns into a crown, they put it on him. 18 And they began saluting him, "Hail, King of the Jews!" 19 They struck his head with a reed, spat upon him, and knelt down in homage to him. 20 After mocking him, they stripped him of the purple cloak and put his own clothes on him. Then they led him out to crucify him.

The Crucifixion of Jesus
(Mt 27.32–44; Lk 23.26–43; Jn 19.16b–27)

21 They compelled a passer-by, who was com-

ing in from the country, to carry his cross; it was Simon of Cy·re′ne, the father of Alexander and Rufus. 22 Then they brought Jesusᵏ to the place called Gol′go·tha (which means the place of a skull). 23 And they offered him wine mixed with myrrh; but he did not take it. 24 And they crucified him, and divided his clothes among them, casting lots to decide what each should take.

---

j Gk the praetorium   k Gk him

M
K

AFRICAN AMERICAN
We Were There

According to Mk 15.21, the Roman soldiers compelled a North African black man from Cyrene by the name of Simon, a passerby, to carry the cross of Jesus. We do not know anything more about Simon of Cyrene, except that Mark identifies him as the father of Alexander and Rufus. The reference to Simon's sons by name and the possibility that Rufus is the same person Paul greets in Rom 16.13 indicate that they were known among the early Christians. This is significant for African Americans because it is evidence of the prominence and influence of African people in the early Christian church.

African people were there from the beginning of Christianity (see also Acts 8.26–40). They were not latecomers to the Christian faith. Thank God, somebody always remembers! African Americans and other people who have experienced oppression are in danger of forgetting who they are and where they come from. Not because they are forgetful peoples, but because the oppressors have tried to erase their culture and identity in order to cripple and control them. Yet despite all of this, somebody always remembers.

We praise you, God, for having African people there from the beginning of your plan of salvation. We praise you in knowing that people of all races will be with you at the end. Hallelujah. Amen!

▶ Mk 15.21

25 It was nine o'clock in the morning when they crucified him. ²⁶ The inscription of the charge against him read, "The King of the Jews." ²⁷ And with him they crucified two bandits, one on his right and one on his left.*l* ²⁹ Those who passed by derided*m* him, shaking their heads and saying, "Aha! You who would destroy the temple and build it in three days, ³⁰ save yourself, and come down from the cross!" ³¹ In the same way the chief priests, along with the scribes, were also mocking him among themselves and saying, "He saved others; he cannot save himself. ³² Let the Messiah,*n* the King of Israel, come down from the cross now, so that we may see and believe." Those who were crucified with him also taunted him.

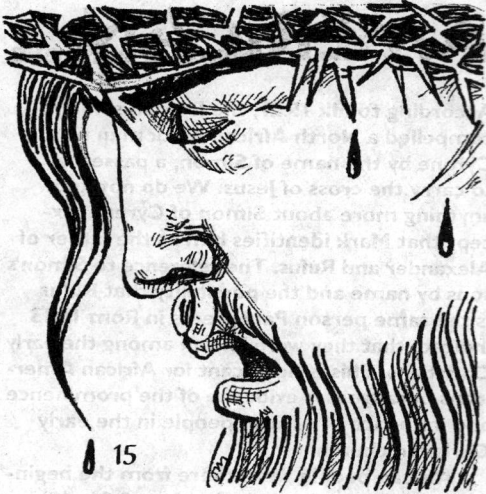

The Death of Jesus
(Mt 27.45–56; Lk 23.44–49; Jn 19.28–30)

33 When it was noon, darkness came over the whole land*o* until three in the afternoon. ³⁴ At three o'clock Jesus cried out with a loud voice, "E'lo·i, E'lo·i, le·ma' sa·bach'tha·ni?" which means, "My God, my God, why have you forsaken me?"*p* ³⁵ When some of the bystanders heard it, they said, "Listen, he is calling for E·li'jah." ³⁶ And someone ran, filled a sponge with sour wine, put it on a stick, and gave it to him to drink, saying, "Wait, let us see whether E·li'jah will come to take him down." ³⁷ Then Jesus gave a loud cry and breathed his last. ³⁸ And the curtain of the temple was torn in two, from top to bottom. ³⁹ Now when the centurion, who stood facing him, saw that in this way he*q* breathed his last, he said, "Truly this man was God's Son!"*r*

40 There were also women looking on from a distance; among them were Mary Mag'da·lene, and Mary the mother of James the younger and of Jo'ses, and Sa·lo'me. ⁴¹ These used to follow him and provided for him when he was in Galilee; and there were many other women who had come up with him to Jerusalem.

The Burial of Jesus
(Mt 27.57–61; Lk 23.50–56; Jn 19.38–42)

42 When evening had come, and since it was the day of Preparation, that is, the day before the sabbath, ⁴³ Joseph of Ar·i·ma·the'a, a respected member of the council, who was also himself waiting expectantly for the kingdom of God, went boldly to Pilate and asked for the body of Jesus. ⁴⁴ Then Pilate wondered if he were already dead; and summoning the centurion, he asked him whether he had been dead for some time. ⁴⁵ When he learned from the centurion that he was dead, he granted the body to Joseph. ⁴⁶ Then Joseph*s* bought a linen cloth, and taking down the body,*t* wrapped it in the linen cloth, and laid it in a tomb that had been hewn out of the rock. He then rolled a stone against the door of the tomb. ⁴⁷ Mary Mag'da·lene and Mary the mother of Jo'ses saw where the body*t* was laid.

The Resurrection of Jesus
(Mt 28.1–10; Lk 24.1–12; Jn 20.1–10)

When the sabbath was over, Mary Mag'da·lene, and Mary the mother of James, and Sa·lo'me bought spices, so that they might go and anoint him. ² And very early on the first day of the week, when the sun had risen, they went to the tomb. ³ They had been saying to one another, "Who will roll away the stone for us from the entrance to the tomb?" ⁴ When they looked up, they saw that the stone, which was very large, had already been rolled back. ⁵ As they entered the tomb, they saw a young man, dressed in a white robe, sitting on the right side; and they were alarmed. ⁶ But he said to them, "Do not be alarmed; you are looking for Jesus of Nazareth, who was crucified. He has been raised; he is not here. Look, there is the place they

---

laid him. 7 But go, tell his disciples and Peter that he is going ahead of you to Galilee; there you will see him, just as he told you." 8 So they went out and fled from the tomb, for terror and amazement had seized them; and they said nothing to anyone, for they were afraid.ᵘ

THE SHORTER ENDING OF MARK

⟦And all that had been commanded them they told briefly to those around Peter. And afterward Jesus himself sent out through them, from east to west, the sacred and imperishable proclamation of eternal salvation.ᵛ⟧

THE LONGER ENDING OF MARK

Jesus Appears to Mary Magdalene
(Jn 20.11–18)

9 ⟦Now after he rose early on the first day of the week, he appeared first to Mary Mag′da·lēne, from whom he had cast out seven demons. 10 She went out and told those who had been with him, while they were mourning and weeping. 11 But when they heard that he was alive and had been seen by her, they would not believe it.

Jesus Appears to Two Disciples
(Lk 24.13–43; Jn 20.19–23)

12 After this he appeared in another form to two of them, as they were walking into the country. 13 And they went back and told the rest, but they did not believe them.

Jesus Commissions the Disciples
(Mt 28.16–20; Lk 24.44–49; Jn 20.19–23; Acts 1.6–8)

14 Later he appeared to the eleven themselves as they were sitting at the table; and he upbraided them for their lack of faith and stubbornness, because they had not believed those who saw him after he had risen.ʷ 15 And he said to them, "Go into all the world and proclaim the good newsˣ to the whole creation. 16 The one who believes and is baptized will be saved; but the one who does not believe will be condemned. 17 And these signs will accompany those who believe: by using my name

---

ᵘ Some of the most ancient authorities bring the book to a close at the end of verse 8. One authority concludes the book with the shorter ending; others include the shorter ending and then continue with verses 9-20. In most authorities verses 9-20 follow immediately after verse 8, though in some of these authorities the passage is marked as being doubtful.   ᵛ Other ancient authorities add *Amen*   ʷ Other ancient authorities add, in whole or in part, *And they excused themselves, saying, "This age of lawlessness and unbelief is under Satan, who does not allow the truth and power of God to prevail over the unclean things of the spirits. Therefore reveal your righteousness now"—thus they spoke to Christ. And Christ replied to them, "The term of years of Satan's power has been fulfilled, but other terrible things draw near. And for those who have sinned I was handed over to death, that they may return to the truth and sin no more, that they may inherit the spiritual and imperishable glory of righteousness that is in heaven."*   ˣ Or *gospel*

LIVE IT!

Alone!

One summer weekend several years ago, eight teenagers went on a hiking trip to the high country in the mountains of New Mexico. After an argument, one of the girls wandered off by herself and became separated from the group. When her absence was discovered, a search party quickly formed. Everyone was worried and anxious.

Afraid! Vulnerable! Lost and alone! She later described her feelings as the worst she had ever had in her life. She had no way of changing the situation. She even screamed at the sky and begged God to save her! All she could do was just pray and wait and hope.

Jesus had similar feelings. He wasn't just lost, but felt completely abandoned by his friends and even by God. He had to face his death alone. Can you imagine anything more lonely? His prayers did not change his circumstances but gave him a way to lament, to cry out to God to express his distress.

What makes you the most lonely and afraid? Have you ever felt abandoned? It is always okay to lament. When do you most feel the need to do so? Crying out does not always change our circumstances, but it can help remind us that we are not truly alone—God is with us.

▶ Mk 15.33–34

Jesus Strengthens Our Faith

A group of faithful women accompany Jesus from afar when he dies on the cross, and look to see where he is buried (Mk 15.40–47). They are witnesses to the terrible violence of Jesus' death. Two days later, after the Sabbath, three of the women go to the tomb to anoint Jesus' body, giving him a proper burial. When they receive the good news that Jesus is alive, they flee from the tomb terrified and amazed.

This is where the original Gospel of Mark ends. Immediately, we want to ask lots of questions. What happened to the disciples? Did they go to Galilee? How did the word get out that Jesus had risen from the dead? Apparently, early Christians found this abrupt ending troublesome, and so they added other endings similar to those of the other Gospels.

These additions, starting at Mk 16.9, emphasize the surprise of the disciples. It seems as if they are paralyzed. Only a strong scolding by Jesus and being commissioned to proclaim the Good News to the whole creation brings them around.

How do doubts and confusion paralyze you in living your faith? Pay attention to Jesus! Hear his voice! He is telling you to carry his message of love to other people. By doing so, you will strengthen your faith, and your life will be full of joy!

▶ Mk 16.1–20

they will cast out demons; they will speak in new tongues; 18 they will pick up snakes in their hands,^{y} and if they drink any deadly thing, it will not hurt them; they will lay their hands on the sick, and they will recover."

The Ascension of Jesus
(Lk 24.50–53)

19 So then the Lord Jesus, after he had spoken to them, was taken up into heaven and sat down at the right hand of God. 20 And they went out and proclaimed the good news everywhere, while the Lord worked with them and confirmed the message by the signs that accompanied it.^{z}⟧

---

y Other ancient authorities lack *in their hands* z Other ancient authorities add *Amen*

Perhaps one of the most discouraging moments in life is the first time you realize that you are in the "out"-group. Children, youth, and adults all have ways of marking who's "in" and who's "out." For people who find themselves frequently in the out-group, life can be painful. The good news in the Gospel of Luke is that there is no out-group anymore. In the Reign of God, everyone is part of the in-group.

In-depth

The author of the Gospel of Luke was a Gentile (non-Jewish) convert to Christianity. So one of Luke's important concerns is to show that both Gentiles and Jews are seen as part of Jesus' in-group. In Luke, Jesus praises the faith of a centurion (7.1–10), who is a Gentile and a hated symbol of the Roman occupation. Jesus also makes a Samaritan (Samaritans were considered foreigners by other Jews) the hero of a parable (10.25–37).

At a Glance

- **Chapters 1–2.** introduction; stories about Jesus' birth and early childhood
- **3.1—9.50.** Jesus' ministry in Galilee
- **9.51—19.27.** parables and miracles on the way to Jerusalem
- **19.28—21.38.** Jesus in Jerusalem: conflict with the religious authorities
- **Chapters 22–24.** stories about Jesus' death, Resurrection, and Ascension

Other in-groups for Jesus in Luke's Gospel are women and poor people. Women had little status in society at the time. But Luke includes many stories about women, including Mary's visit to her cousin Elizabeth before the births of their sons, Jesus and John the Baptist (1.39–66). This Gospel also shows how Jesus loved the poor and scolded the rich for their lack of concern for the poor. For example, it includes a story about a poor man named Lazarus who begged for food at a rich man's door. God honored Lazarus with a special place in Abraham's bosom (heaven) when he died (16.19–31), whereas the rich man suffered in Hades.

Finally, Luke's Gospel shows Jesus' compassion and forgiveness for outcasts and sinners. It includes stories about the tax collector Zacchaeus who climbs a tree to see Jesus (19.1–10), the good Samaritan (10.25–37), and the penitent sinner who was crucified beside Jesus (23.39–43). The Gospel presents a vivid picture of how Jesus made the Reign of God present, inspiring his disciples to take the Gospel message to other lands and cultures.

Quick Facts

Author
a Gentile Christian named Luke, who may have been a disciple of Paul's (Col 4.14)

Date Written
approximately A.D. 80 to 85

Audience
Gentile (Greek) Christians represented by Theophilus (see Lk 1.3)

Of Note
Luke also wrote the Acts of the Apostles.

Image of Jesus
merciful, compassionate, with a special concern for poor people, women, and non-Jews

Dedication to Theophilus

Since many have undertaken to set down an orderly account of the events that have been fulfilled among us, ²just as they were handed on to us by those who from the beginning were eyewitnesses and servants of the word, ³I too decided, after investigating everything carefully from the very first,ᵃ to write an orderly account for you, most excellent Thē·oph'i·lus, ⁴so that you may know the truth concerning the things about which you have been instructed.

The Birth of John the Baptist Foretold

5 In the days of King Her'od of Judea, there was a priest named Zech·a·ri'ah, who belonged to the priestly order of A·bi'jah. His wife was a descendant of Aaron, and her name was Elizabeth. ⁶Both of them were righteous before God, living blamelessly according to all the commandments and regulations of the Lord. ⁷But they had no children, because Elizabeth was barren, and both were getting on in years.

8 Once when he was serving as priest before God and his section was on duty, ⁹he was chosen by lot, according to the custom of the priesthood, to enter the sanctuary of the Lord and offer incense. ¹⁰Now at the time of the incense offering, the whole assembly of the people was praying outside. ¹¹Then there appeared to him an angel of the Lord, standing at the right side of the altar of incense. ¹²When Zech·a·ri'ah saw him, he was terri-

fied; and fear overwhelmed him. ¹³But the angel said to him, "Do not be afraid, Zech·a·ri'ah, for your prayer has been heard. Your wife Elizabeth will bear you a son, and you will name him John. ¹⁴You will have joy and gladness, and many will rejoice at his birth, ¹⁵for he will be great in the sight of the Lord. He must never drink wine or strong drink; even before his birth he will be filled with the Holy Spirit. ¹⁶He will turn many of the people of Israel to the Lord their God. ¹⁷With the spirit and power of E·li'jah he will go before him, to turn the hearts of parents to their children, and the disobedient to the wisdom of the righteous, to make ready a people prepared for the Lord." ¹⁸Zech·a·ri'ah said to the angel, "How will I know that this is so? For I am an old man, and my wife is getting on in years." ¹⁹The angel replied, "I am Gabriel. I stand in the presence of God, and I have been sent to speak to you and to bring you this good news. ²⁰But now, because you did not believe my words, which will be fulfilled in their time, you will become mute, unable to speak, until the day these things occur."

21 Meanwhile the people were waiting for Zech·a·ri'ah, and wondered at his delay in the sanctuary. ²²When he did come out, he could not speak to them, and they realized that he had seen a vision in the sanctuary. He kept motioning to

---

ᵃ Or *for a long time*

them and remained unable to speak. 23 When his time of service was ended, he went to his home.

24 After those days his wife Elizabeth conceived, and for five months she remained in seclusion. She said, 25 "This is what the Lord has done for me when he looked favorably on me and took away the disgrace I have endured among my people."

The Birth of Jesus Foretold

26 In the sixth month the angel Gabriel was sent by God to a town in Galilee called Nazareth, 27 to a virgin engaged to a man whose name was Joseph, of the house of David. The virgin's name was Mary. 28 And he came to her and said, "Greetings, favored one! The Lord is with you."b 29 But she was much perplexed by his words and pondered what sort of greeting this might be. 30 The angel said to her, "Do not be afraid, Mary, for you have found favor with God. 31 And now, you will conceive in your womb and bear a son, and you will name him Jesus. 32 He will be great, and will be called the Son of the Most High, and the Lord God will give to him the throne of his ancestor David. 33 He will reign over the house of Jacob forever, and of his kingdom there will be no end." 34 Mary said to the angel, "How can this be, since

I am a virgin?"c 35 The angel said to her, "The Holy Spirit will come upon you, and the power of the Most High will overshadow you; therefore the child to be bornd will be holy; he will be called Son of God. 36 And now, your relative Elizabeth in her old age has also conceived a son; and this is the sixth month for her who was said to be barren. 37 For nothing will be impossible with God." 38 Then Mary said, "Here am I, the servant of the Lord; let it be with me according to your word." Then the angel departed from her.

Mary Visits Elizabeth

39 In those days Mary set out and went with haste to a Judean town in the hill country, 40 where she entered the house of Zech·a·ri'ah and greeted Elizabeth. 41 When Elizabeth heard Mary's greeting, the child leaped in her womb. And Elizabeth was filled with the Holy Spirit 42 and exclaimed with a loud cry, "Blessed are you among women, and blessed is the fruit of your womb. 43 And why has this happened to me, that the mother of my Lord comes to me? 44 For as soon as I heard the

b Other ancient authorities add *Blessed are you among women*　c Gk *I do not know a man*　d Other ancient authorities add *of you*

Introducing ▶ MARY OF NAZARETH

Luke's Gospel makes it clear that Mary of Nazareth has a special place in God's plan of salvation. Beginning with Mary's humble acceptance of God's will revealed by the angel Gabriel (1.26–38), Mary is presented as the true, first disciple who does the will of God. Her yes to God leads to Jesus' presence among us. She follows Jesus to the cross and is with the disciples in the upper room during the coming of the Holy Spirit (Acts 1.14). Mary reveals to us the meaning of true faith—a willingness to accept God's call and to gradually discover the full meaning of God's will.

In choosing Mary to be the mother of Jesus, God selected not a rich queen, but a poor young girl open to the action of the Holy Spirit in her life. In Mary, Luke emphasizes God's preference for the poor and the little ones (see "The Magnificat, the Prayer of the Poor!" Lk 1.39–56).

Besides being the mother of Jesus, Mary is presented in the Bible as the mother of the church (Jn 19.25–27). For this reason, Catholic Christians have a special devotion to Mary. They celebrate her virginal conception of Jesus on the feast of the Annunciation (25 March). They believe that Mary was born free from original sin, and celebrate this on the feast of the Immaculate Conception (8 December). They also believe she was taken into heaven, body and soul, at the end of her life, and celebrate this on the feast of the Assumption (15 August). Catholics also have a special prayer form honoring Mary, called the rosary.

▶ Lk 1.26–46

THE MAGNIFICAT, THE PRAYER OF THE POOR!

Mary gives a testimony of her faith right after she receives the news that she will be the mother of God. During her visit to her cousin Elizabeth, she sings of God's salvation in a song known as the Magnificat, which means "it praises." This prayer is mainly made up of verses taken from the Psalms and the Prophets. Mary first sings of her salvation; then she sings of God's salvation brought to the humble, the poor, and the hungry; and she finishes by singing of the salvation brought to all the people of God as promised to Abraham.

The Magnificat is an important prayer for Hispanic people. It is the song of the poor of God, those who expected salvation from God, not from people in power or through wars and conquests. The social consequences of God's salvation are clearly revealed in Mary's song. The Magnificat is like a summary of Jesus' life on earth, which raised up the lowly and brought down the powerful to build the Reign of God.

■ In a world marked by huge gaps between rich people and poor people, is it clear that Christians are in solidarity with the poor?

■ How are you helping the poor now, and how are you planning to do so as an adult?

■ Pray the Magnificat slowly, savoring what it says, letting it move to the core of your heart.

▶ Lk 1.39–56

sound of your greeting, the child in my womb leaped for joy. ⁴⁵ And blessed is she who believed that there would be^e a fulfillment of what was spoken to her by the Lord."

Mary's Magnificat

⁴⁶ And Mary^f said,
"My soul magnifies the Lord,
⁴⁷   and my spirit rejoices in God my Savior,
⁴⁸ for he has looked with favor on the
            lowliness of his servant.
        Surely, from now on all generations will
            call me blessed;
⁴⁹ for the Mighty One has done great things
            for me,
        and holy is his name.
⁵⁰ His mercy is for those who fear him
        from generation to generation.
⁵¹ He has shown strength with his arm;
        he has scattered the proud in the
            thoughts of their hearts.
⁵² He has brought down the powerful from
            their thrones,
        and lifted up the lowly;
⁵³ he has filled the hungry with good things,
        and sent the rich away empty.

⁵⁴ He has helped his servant Israel,
        in remembrance of his mercy,
⁵⁵ according to the promise he made to our
            ancestors,
        to Abraham and to his descendants
            forever."

⁵⁶ And Mary remained with her about three months and then returned to her home.

The Birth of John the Baptist

⁵⁷ Now the time came for Elizabeth to give birth, and she bore a son. ⁵⁸ Her neighbors and relatives heard that the Lord had shown his great mercy to her, and they rejoiced with her.

⁵⁹ On the eighth day they came to circumcise the child, and they were going to name him Zech-a•ri′ah after his father. ⁶⁰ But his mother said, "No; he is to be called John." ⁶¹ They said to her, "None of your relatives has this name." ⁶² Then they began motioning to his father to find out what name he wanted to give him. ⁶³ He asked for a writing tablet and wrote, "His name is John." And all of them were amazed. ⁶⁴ Immediately his mouth was opened and his tongue freed, and he began to

---

^e Or believed, for there will be   ^f Other ancient authorities read Elizabeth

speak, praising God. 65 Fear came over all their neighbors, and all these things were talked about throughout the entire hill country of Judea. 66 All who heard them pondered them and said, "What then will this child become?" For, indeed, the hand of the Lord was with him.

The Canticle of Zechariah

67 Then his father Zech•a•ri′ah was filled with the Holy Spirit and spoke this prophecy:
68 "Blessed be the Lord God of Israel,
　　for he has looked favorably on his people
　　　　and redeemed them.
69 He has raised up a mighty savior*g* for us
　　in the house of his servant David,
70 as he spoke through the mouth of his holy
　　　　prophets from of old,
71 that we would be saved from our
　　　　enemies and from the hand of all
　　　　who hate us.
72 Thus he has shown the mercy promised to
　　　　our ancestors,
　　and has remembered his holy covenant,
73 the oath that he swore to our ancestor
　　　　Abraham,
　　to grant us 74 that we, being rescued from
　　　　the hands of our enemies,
　　might serve him without fear, 75 in holiness
　　　　and righteousness
　　before him all our days.
76 And you, child, will be called the prophet of
　　　　the Most High;
　　for you will go before the Lord to prepare
　　　　his ways,
77 to give knowledge of salvation to his people
　　　　by the forgiveness of their sins.
78 By the tender mercy of our God,
　　the dawn from on high will break
　　　　upon*h* us,
79 to give light to those who sit in darkness
　　　　and in the shadow of death,
　　to guide our feet into the way of peace."

80 The child grew and became strong in spirit, and he was in the wilderness until the day he appeared publicly to Israel.

The Birth of Jesus
(Mt 1.18–25)

In those days a decree went out from Emperor Augustus that all the world should be registered. 2 This was the first registration and was taken while Qui•rin′i•us was governor of Syria. 3 All went to their own towns to be registered. 4 Joseph also went from the town of Nazareth in Galilee to Judea, to the city of David called Bethlehem, because he was descended from the house and family of David. 5 He went to be registered with Mary, to whom he was engaged and who was expecting a child. 6 While they were there, the time came for her to deliver her child. 7 And she gave birth to her firstborn son and wrapped him in bands of cloth, and laid him in a manger, because there was no place for them in the inn.

The Shepherds and the Angels

8 In that region there were shepherds living in the fields, keeping watch over their flock by night. 9 Then an angel of the Lord stood before them, and the glory of the Lord shone around them, and they were terrified. 10 But the angel said to them, "Do not be afraid; for see—I am bringing you good news of great joy for all the people: 11 to you is born this day in the city of David a Savior, who is the Messiah,*i* the Lord. 12 This will be a sign for you: you will find a child wrapped in bands of cloth and lying in a manger." 13 And suddenly there

---

Catholic Connections

THE BENEDICTUS

Zechariah's prayer in Lk 1.68–79 is called the Benedictus (which means "blessed") or the Canticle of Zechariah. After Zechariah regains his voice, he praises God for sending a savior from the line of David. The savior he sings of is not a warrior king but someone bringing salvation through the forgiveness of sins and leading people into the way of peace.

The Benedictus is recited during morning prayer, and the Magnificat (see Lk 1.46–55) is recited during evening prayer in the liturgy of the hours. Why not make the Magnificat and the Benedictus part of your prayer life too? Place a bookmark in this chapter and turn to it when you want to praise God and express your faith in God's saving power.

▸ Lk 1.46–80

---

g Gk a horn of salvation　　h Other ancient authorities read has broken upon　　i Or the Christ

was with the angel a multitude of the heavenly host,[j] praising God and saying,

14 "Glory to God in the highest heaven,
 and on earth peace among those whom
  he favors!"[k]

15 When the angels had left them and gone into heaven, the shepherds said to one another, "Let us go now to Bethlehem and see this thing that has taken place, which the Lord has made known to us." 16 So they went with haste and found Mary and Joseph, and the child lying in the manger. 17 When they saw this, they made known what had been told them about this child; 18 and all who heard it were amazed at what the shepherds told them. 19 But Mary treasured all these words and pondered them in her heart. 20 The shepherds returned, glorifying and praising God for all they had heard and seen, as it had been told them.

stated in the law of the Lord, "a pair of turtledoves or two young pigeons."

25 Now there was a man in Jerusalem whose name was Sim′e•on;[l] this man was righteous and devout, looking forward to the consolation of Israel, and the Holy Spirit rested on him. 26 It had been revealed to him by the Holy Spirit that he would not see death before he had seen the Lord's Messiah.[m] 27 Guided by the Spirit, Sim′e•on[n] came into the temple; and when the parents brought in the child Jesus, to do for him what was customary under the law, 28 Sim′e•on[o] took him in his arms and praised God, saying,

29 "Master, now you are dismissing your
  servant[p] in peace,
 according to your word;
30 for my eyes have seen your
  salvation,

Jesus' Birth: Good News to the Poor

On 25 December, we celebrate Christmas, the birth of Jesus. We recall the moment of God entering our world—a defining moment in the history of salvation. As Luke records the moment of the birth of the Messiah, who are the stars of the show? To whom do the angels appear to announce this remarkable event, this "good news of great joy for all the people"? the high priest? the rich and important residents of Bethlehem? No. The announcement is made to shepherds, poor workers living in the fields nearby.

Like Mary, the shepherds are people of little power and significance. Luke makes the point that sometimes what the world sees as unimportant, God honors. This is the justice of God. It is the same today. The poorest in our world, the most hidden people who have no power, hold a special place in the heart of God. And, like the shepherds, poor people often know God better than those who are rich or powerful by this world's standards.

This truth is a challenge but also good news for all of us, rich and poor alike. How do your attitudes and actions—even the way you celebrate Christmas—reflect God's special attention to poor people?

▶ Lk 2.8–20

Jesus Is Named

21 After eight days had passed, it was time to circumcise the child; and he was called Jesus, the name given by the angel before he was conceived in the womb.

Jesus Is Presented in the Temple

22 When the time came for their purification according to the law of Moses, they brought him up to Jerusalem to present him to the Lord 23 (as it is written in the law of the Lord, "Every firstborn male shall be designated as holy to the Lord"), 24 and they offered a sacrifice according to what is

31 which you have prepared in the presence
   of all peoples,
32 a light for revelation to the Gentiles
  and for glory to your people Israel."

33 And the child's father and mother were amazed at what was being said about him. 34 Then Sim′e•on[l] blessed them and said to his mother Mary, "This child is destined for the falling and the rising of many in Israel, and to be a sign that will be opposed 35 so that the inner thoughts of

---

j Gk *army*   *k* Other ancient authorities read *peace, goodwill among people*   *l* Gk *Symeon*   *m* Or *the Lord's Christ*   *n* Gk *In the Spirit, he*   *o* Gk *he*   *p* Gk *slave*

many will be revealed—and a sword will pierce your own soul too."

36 There was also a prophet, Anna^q the daughter of Phan'ū·el, of the tribe of Ash'er. She was of a great age, having lived with her husband seven years after her marriage, 37 then as a widow to the age of eighty-four. She never left the temple but worshiped there with fasting and prayer night and day. 38 At that moment she came, and began to praise God and to speak about the child^r to all who were looking for the redemption of Jerusalem.

The Return to Nazareth

39 When they had finished everything required by the law of the Lord, they returned to Galilee, to their own town of Nazareth. 40 The

to search for him. 46 After three days they found him in the temple, sitting among the teachers, listening to them and asking them questions. 47 And all who heard him were amazed at his understanding and his answers. 48 When his parents^s saw him they were astonished; and his mother said to him, "Child, why have you treated us like this? Look, your father and I have been searching for you in great anxiety." 49 He said to them, "Why were you searching for me? Did you not know that I must be in my Father's house?"^t 50 But they did not understand what he said to them. 51 Then he went down with them and came to Nazareth, and was obedient to them. His mother treasured all these things in her heart.

52 And Jesus increased in wisdom and in years,^u and in divine and human favor.

Introducing ▶ THE HOLY FAMILY

On the first Sunday after Christmas, the Catholic church celebrates the feast of the Holy Family: Jesus, Mary, and Joseph. The Bible does not tell us a lot about the Holy Family. We know that Joseph was a kind and compassionate man, eager to do God's will. He raised Jesus as his own son, even though he was not Jesus' biological father. Jesus was raised in a home in which love and faith were the norm.

We can be sure the Holy Family had their moments of conflict and crisis—all families do. Luke's story of Jesus getting separated from his parents demonstrates that. But we can also be sure that their love and faith helped them to survive such conflicts and grow stronger because of them. The church holds the Holy Family up as a model of respect, compassion, love, and faith in family life.

How does your family express love and respect for one another? What crises and conflicts have you and your family survived? What can you do to bring the qualities of the Holy Family more fully into your family's life?

▶ Lk 2.41–52

child grew and became strong, filled with wisdom; and the favor of God was upon him.

The Boy Jesus in the Temple

41 Now every year his parents went to Jerusalem for the festival of the Passover. 42 And when he was twelve years old, they went up as usual for the festival. 43 When the festival was ended and they started to return, the boy Jesus stayed behind in Jerusalem, but his parents did not know it. 44 Assuming that he was in the group of travelers, they went a day's journey. Then they started to look for him among their relatives and friends. 45 When they did not find him, they returned to Jerusalem

The Proclamation of John the Baptist
(Mt 3.1–12; Mk 1.1–8; Jn 1.19–28)

In the fifteenth year of the reign of Emperor Ti·bē'-ri·us, when Pon'ti·us Pilate was governor of Judea, and Her'od was ruler^v of Galilee, and his brother Philip ruler^v of the region of I·tu·rae'a and Trach·o·nī'tis, and Lÿ·sā'ni·as ruler^v of Ab·i·lē'nē, 2 during the high priesthood of An'nas and Cā'i·a·phas, the word of God came to John son of Zech·a·rī'ah in the wilderness. 3 He went into all the region around the Jordan, proclaiming a baptism of

---

^q Gk *Hanna*   ^r Gk *him*   ^s Gk *they*   ^t Or *be about my Father's interests?*   ^u Or *in stature*   ^v Gk *tetrarch*

L
K

Jesus Grows in Age and Wisdom

Luke is the only Gospel that has any stories of Jesus' childhood. When Jesus was twelve, he left his family to stay in the Temple in Jerusalem. At the Temple, Jesus listened to and questioned the teachers, trying to understand his faith better. His questions and his understanding—and we can presume his sincerity—amazed all who heard him.

Adolescence is an important time for exploring life's questions—including life's religious questions. Sometimes, young people are led to believe that they shouldn't have any questions—which is a sad statement about adult leaders and teachers. Wise teachers—like those the boy Jesus met in the Temple—welcome and encourage your questions, even your religious questions. So ask yourself: How well do I know my faith? What are my main questions? Who are the wise teachers I can go to for help in searching out the answers?

▸ Lk 2.41–52

repentance for the forgiveness of sins, 4 as it is written in the book of the words of the prophet I•sāi′ah,

"The voice of one crying out in the wilderness:
'Prepare the way of the Lord,
    make his paths straight.
5 Every valley shall be filled,
        and every mountain and hill shall be
            made low,
and the crooked shall be made straight,

and the rough ways made smooth;
6 and all flesh shall see the salvation of God.' "

7 John said to the crowds that came out to be baptized by him, "You brood of vipers! Who warned you to flee from the wrath to come? 8 Bear fruits worthy of repentance. Do not begin to say to yourselves, 'We have Abraham as our ancestor'; for I tell you, God is able from these stones to raise up children to Abraham. 9 Even now the ax is lying at the root of the trees; every tree therefore that does

Introducing
▶ JOHN THE BAPTIST

Picture a man living in the desert eating grasshoppers and wild honey and wearing a camel hair coat. Does this sound like the person Jesus described as "among those born of women no one is greater than John" (Lk 7.28)? The person Jesus is talking about is John the Baptist, and he plays an important role in all four Gospels. John is portrayed like an Old Testament prophet, calling people to repentance for their sins. Indeed, his ministry was so similar to Jesus' ministry that after Herod had John killed (Mt 14.1–12), he thought that Jesus might have been John raised from the dead (Lk 9.7–9). The power of John's preaching is demonstrated by Jesus' disciples still encountering John's followers years after John's death (Acts 19.1–6).

John the Baptist was Jesus' cousin, and the Gospel of Luke presents many parallels between the two men. John's preaching gives us a preview into Jesus' message. John was preparing the way for Jesus. He was a humble servant "not worthy to untie the thong of [Jesus'] sandals" (Lk 3.16). He described his baptism as a baptism of water in contrast with Jesus' baptism with "the Holy Spirit and fire" (verse 16).

John the Baptist is the model of how Christians should perform their prophetic mission, pointing others toward Jesus with passion and humility.

▸ Lk 3.1–20

not bear good fruit is cut down and thrown into the fire."

10 And the crowds asked him, "What then should we do?" 11 In reply he said to them, "Whoever has two coats must share with anyone who has none; and whoever has food must do likewise." 12 Even tax collectors came to be baptized, and they asked him, "Teacher, what should we do?" 13 He said to them, "Collect no more than the amount prescribed for you." 14 Soldiers also asked him, "And we, what should we do?" He said to them, "Do not extort money from anyone by threats or false accusation, and be satisfied with your wages."

15 As the people were filled with expectation, and all were questioning in their hearts concerning John, whether he might be the Messiah,[w] 16 John answered all of them by saying, "I baptize you with water; but one who is more powerful than I is coming; I am not worthy to untie the thong of his sandals. He will baptize you with[x] the Holy Spirit and fire. 17 His winnowing fork is in his hand, to clear his threshing floor and to gather the wheat into his granary; but the chaff he will burn with unquenchable fire."

18 So, with many other exhortations, he proclaimed the good news to the people. 19 But Her'od the ruler,[y] who had been rebuked by him because of He·rō'di·as, his brother's wife, and because of all the evil things that Her'od had done, 20 added to them all by shutting up John in prison.

The Baptism of Jesus
(Mt 3.13–17; Mk 1.9–11; Jn 1.29–34)

21 Now when all the people were baptized, and when Jesus also had been baptized and was praying, the heaven was opened, 22 and the Holy Spirit descended upon him in bodily form like a dove. And a voice came from heaven, "You are my Son, the Beloved;[z] with you I am well pleased."[a]

The Ancestors of Jesus
(Gen 5.1–32; 11.10–26; Ruth 4.18–22; 1 Chr 1.1–4, 24–27, 34; 2.1–15; Mt 1.2–16)

23 Jesus was about thirty years old when he began his work. He was the son (as was thought) of Joseph son of Hē'lī, 24 son of Mat'that, son of Levi, son of Mel'chī, son of Jan'naī, son of Joseph, 25 son of Mat·ta·thī'as, son of Ā'mos, son of Nā'hum, son of Es'lī, son of Nag'ga·ī, 26 son of Mā'ath, son of Mat·ta·thī'as, son of Sem'e·in, son of Jō'sech, son of Jō'da, 27 son of Jō·an'an, son of Rhē'sa, son of Ze·rub'ba·bel, son of She·al'ti·el,[b] son of Nē'rī, 28 son of Mel'chī, son of Ad'dī, son of Cō'sam, son of El·mā'dam, son of Er, 29 son of Joshua, son of

?did you KNOW?

The Liturgical Year

The story of Jesus' baptism is one of the readings for the feast of the baptism of the Lord. The feast days and holy days celebrated by Catholics and other Christians follow a yearly pattern. This pattern is called the liturgical year and is not the same as the calendar year. Here is a description of the major seasons in the liturgical year.

- *Advent* begins the liturgical year four Sundays before Christmas. It is a time of preparation for the coming of Christ.
- The *Christmas season* goes for twelve days, beginning with Christmas Day and concluding with the feast of the baptism of the Lord.
- *Lent* begins with Ash Wednesday and lasts for forty days. It is a solemn time of fasting and prayer in preparation for Easter.
- The *Easter Triduum* is the celebration of Holy Thursday, Good Friday, and the Easter Vigil on Holy Saturday. At these liturgies, Christians remember the Lord's Supper, Christ's Passion and death, and his Resurrection. They are the heart of the liturgical year.
- The *Easter season* lasts for fifty days, beginning with Easter day and ending with the feast of Pentecost.
- *Ordinary Time* is made up of the days between these special seasons. The weeks of Ordinary Time begin after the Christmas Season, stop at the beginning of Lent, and resume after the Easter Season.

▶ Lk 3.15–22

El·i·ē'zer, son of Jō'rim, son of Mat'that, son of Levi, 30 son of Sim'e·on, son of Judah, son of Joseph, son of Jō'nam, son of E·li'a·kim, 31 son of Mē'le·a, son of Men'na, son of Mat'ta·tha, son of Nathan, son of David, 32 son of Jesse, son

---

w Or *the Christ*   *x* Or *in*   *y* Gk *tetrarch*   *z* Or *my beloved Son*   *a* Other ancient authorities read *You are my Son, today I have begotten you*   *b* Gk *Salathiel*

of O'bed, son of Bō'az, son of Sā'la,[c] son of Nah'-shon, 33 son of Am•min'a•dab, son of Ad•min, son of Ar'nī,[d] son of Hez'ron, son of Per'ez, son of Ju-dah, 34 son of Jacob, son of Isaac, son of Abraham, son of Tē'rah, son of Nā'hor, 35 son of Sē'rug, son of Rē'ū, son of Pē'leg, son of Ē'ber, son of Shē'lah, 36 son of Cā•i'nan, son of Ar•phā'xad, son of Shem, son of Noah, son of Lā'mech, 37 son of Me•thū'se-lah, son of Ē'noch, son of Jar'ed, son of Ma•hā'la-lē•el, son of Cā•i'nan, 38 son of Ē'nos, son of Seth, son of Adam, son of God.

The Temptation of Jesus
(Mt 4.1–11; Mk 1.12–13)

Jesus, full of the Holy Spirit, returned from the Jordan and was led by the Spirit in the wilderness, 2 where for forty days he was tempted by the devil. He ate nothing at all during those days, and when they were over, he was famished. 3 The devil said to him, "If you are the Son of God, command this stone to become a loaf of bread." 4 Jesus answered him, "It is written, 'One does not live by bread alone.'"

5 Then the devil[e] led him up and showed him in an instant all the kingdoms of the world. 6 And the devil[e] said to him, "To you I will give their glory and all this authority; for it has been given over to me, and I give it to anyone I please. 7 If you, then, will worship me, it will all be yours." 8 Jesus answered him, "It is written,

'Worship the Lord your God,
   and serve only him.'"

9 Then the devil[e] took him to Jerusalem, and placed him on the pinnacle of the temple, saying to him, "If you are the Son of God, throw yourself down from here, 10 for it is written,

'He will command his angels concerning you,
   to protect you,'

11 and

'On their hands they will bear you up,
   so that you will not dash your foot
      against a stone.'"

12 Jesus answered him, "It is said, 'Do not put the Lord your God to the test.'" 13 When the devil had finished every test, he departed from him until an opportune time.

The Beginning of the Galilean Ministry
(Mt 4.17; Mk 1.14–15)

14 Then Jesus, filled with the power of the Spirit, returned to Galilee, and a report about him spread through all the surrounding country. 15 He began to teach in their synagogues and was praised by everyone.

Catholic Connections

THE BIBLE, TRADITION, AND THE MAGISTERIUM

Notice that each time Jesus is tempted, he uses phrases from the Bible as a defense against the devil (Lk 4.4,8,12). But also notice that the devil knows the Scriptures and uses them to try to tempt Jesus (verses 10–11)!

We should always be careful about mis-interpreting the Bible. That is why the Catholic church teaches that our faith is based on both the Bible and the sacred Tradition handed down by the Apostles. The apostolic Tradition provides direction for understanding the Bible, and the Bible provides background for understanding the Tradition. The magisterium—the pope and bishops—ensure that the Bible and Tradition are correctly taught and misinterpretations are corrected. That is why the Bible, Tradition, and the magisterium are considered the three pillars of the Catholic church.

The Bible is a reliable guide and companion as long as we take care not to misuse it!

▶ Lk 4.1–13

The Rejection of Jesus at Nazareth
(Mt 13.54–58; Mk 6.1–6)

16 When he came to Nazareth, where he had been brought up, he went to the synagogue on the sabbath day, as was his custom. He stood up to read, 17 and the scroll of the prophet I•sāi'ah was given to him. He unrolled the scroll and found the place where it was written:

18 "The Spirit of the Lord is upon me,
  because he has anointed me
    to bring good news to the poor.
He has sent me to proclaim release to the
    captives

---

[c] Other ancient authorities read *Salmon*   [d] Other ancient authorities read *Amminadab, son of Aram*; others vary widely   [e] Gk *he*

AFRICAN AMERICAN
Free . . . to Be Tempted

Black people have been struggling for freedom for a long time. They have sung about freedom. They have written poems about it. And they have had demonstrations over it. For most black people, freedom is the promised land, a place overflowing with milk and honey, a place like heaven where everything is pleasant.

After Jesus' baptism, he went out into the wilderness to be alone in order to plan his life. While he was out there, he realized that he could still be tempted to make selfish choices. Read Lk 4.1–13. Imagine how tempting it might have been for Jesus to use his power to prove to the world how great he was, instead of how great and loving God is.

Many people throughout history have faced the choice of using their newly won freedom for their own selfish interests or for the good of others. After securing their freedom, some slaves, like Harriet Tubman, decided to spend their lives helping others become free—often at great risk and sacrifice to themselves. You can be sure that they were tempted to choose an easier and safer life.

If we want to be free, we must face temptation. And if we want to remain free, we must resist the temptation to choose selfishly. Because once we give in to selfishness, we become less free to resist it the next time around. And before long, we will become slaves again—slaves to our own desires.

▶ Lk 4.1–13

and recovery of sight to the blind,
to let the oppressed go free,
19 to proclaim the year of the Lord's favor."
20 And he rolled up the scroll, gave it back to the attendant, and sat down. The eyes of all in the synagogue were fixed on him. 21 Then he began to say to them, "Today this scripture has been fulfilled in your hearing." 22 All spoke well of him and were amazed at the gracious words that came from his mouth. They said, "Is not this Joseph's son?" 23 He said to them, "Doubtless you will quote to me this proverb, 'Doctor, cure yourself!' And you will say, 'Do here also in your hometown the things that we have heard you did at Ca·per'na·um.' " 24 And he said, "Truly I tell you, no prophet is accepted in the prophet's hometown. 25 But the truth is, there were many widows in Israel in the time of E·li'jah, when the heaven was shut up three years and six months, and there was a severe famine over all the land; 26 yet E·li'jah was sent to none of them except to a widow at Zar'e·phath in Si'don. 27 There were also many lepersf in Israel in the time of the prophet E·li'sha, and none of them was cleansed except Na'a·man the Syrian." 28 When they heard this, all in the synagogue were filled with rage. 29 They got up, drove him out of the town, and led him to the brow of the hill on which their town was built, so that they might hurl him off the cliff. 30 But he passed through the midst of them and went on his way.

The Man with an Unclean Spirit
(Mk 1.21–28)

31 He went down to Ca·per'na·um, a city in Galilee, and was teaching them on the sabbath. 32 They were astounded at his teaching, because he spoke with authority. 33 In the synagogue there was a man who had the spirit of an unclean demon, and he cried out with a loud voice, 34 "Let us alone! What have you to do with us, Jesus of Nazareth? Have you come to destroy us? I know who you are, the Holy One of God." 35 But Jesus rebuked him, saying, "Be silent, and come out of him!" When the demon had thrown him down before them, he came out of him without having done him any harm. 36 They were all amazed and kept saying to one another, "What kind of utterance is this? For with authority and power he commands the unclean spirits, and out they come!" 37 And a report about him began to reach every place in the region.

Healings at Simon's House
(Mt 8.14–17; Mk 1.29–34)

38 After leaving the synagogue he entered Simon's house. Now Simon's mother-in-law was suffering from a high fever, and they asked him about her. 39 Then he stood over her and rebuked the fever, and it left her. Immediately she got up and began to serve them.

40 As the sun was setting, all those who had any who were sick with various kinds of diseases brought them to him; and he laid his hands on each of them and cured them. 41 Demons also came out of many, shouting, "You are the Son of

---

f The terms leper and leprosy can refer to several diseases

JESUS LIBERATES PEOPLE FROM OPPRESSION!

In Luke, Jesus begins his mission by referring to Isaiah's prophecy (Isa 61.1). In the Gospel, we see Jesus fulfilling this prophecy by acting in the following ways:

- healing the sick, whose sickness is viewed as God's punishment for their sinfulness
- touching and curing lepers, who are separated from the rest of society
- speaking and spending time with Samaritans, who are looked down upon and rejected by the Jews
- accepting as disciples women, who are generally not accepted as equals, socially and religiously
- responding to the request of the Roman centurion, a foreigner who represents social domination
- forgiving and eating with sinners, who are put down and discriminated against by leaders of the Temple
- liberating those possessed by demons, whom all avoid because they are believed to be under the power of Satan

    Consider these questions:

- What types of oppression in society do Christians need to respond to today?
- Are you suffering from oppression? If so, how and from whom?

Ask God for help in responding to oppression in your life and in society with truth and love.

▶ Lk 4.14–30

God!" But he rebuked them and would not allow them to speak, because they knew that he was the Messiah.*g*

Jesus Preaches in the Synagogues
(Mt 4.23–25; Mk 1.35–39)

42 At daybreak he departed and went into a deserted place. And the crowds were looking for him; and when they reached him, they wanted to prevent him from leaving them. 43 But he said to them, "I must proclaim the good news of the kingdom of God to the other cities also; for I was sent for this purpose." 44 So he continued proclaiming the message in the synagogues of Judea.*h*

Jesus Calls the First Disciples
(Mt 4.18–22; Mk 1.16–20)

Once while Jesus*i* was standing beside the lake of Gen·nes'a·ret, and the crowd was pressing in on him to hear the word of God, 2 he saw two boats there at the shore of the lake; the fishermen had gone out of them and were washing their nets. 3 He got into one of the boats, the one belonging to Simon, and asked him to put out a little way

from the shore. Then he sat down and taught the crowds from the boat. 4 When he had finished speaking, he said to Simon, "Put out into the deep water and let down your nets for a catch." 5 Simon answered, "Master, we have worked all night long but have caught nothing. Yet if you say so, I will let down the nets." 6 When they had done this, they caught so many fish that their nets were beginning to break. 7 So they signaled their partners in the other boat to come and help them. And they came and filled both boats, so that they began to sink. 8 But when Simon Peter saw it, he fell down at Jesus' knees, saying, "Go away from me, Lord, for I am a sinful man!" 9 For he and all who were with him were amazed at the catch of fish that they had taken; 10 and so also were James and John, sons of Zeb'e·dee, who were partners with Simon. Then Jesus said to Simon, "Do not be afraid; from now on you will be catching people." 11 When they had brought their boats to shore, they left everything and followed him.

---

g Or *the Christ*   *h* Other ancient authorities read *Galilee*
i Gk *he*

Jesus Cleanses a Leper
(Mt 8.1–4; Mk 1.40–45)

12 Once, when he was in one of the cities, there was a man covered with leprosy.*j* When he saw Jesus, he bowed with his face to the ground and begged him, "Lord, if you choose, you can make me clean." ¹³Then Jesus*k* stretched out his hand, touched him, and said, "I do choose. Be made clean." Immediately the leprosy*j* left him. ¹⁴And he ordered him to tell no one. "Go," he said, "and show yourself to the priest, and, as Moses commanded, make an offering for your cleansing, for a testimony to them." ¹⁵But now more than ever the word about Jesus*l* spread abroad; many crowds would gather to hear him and to be cured of their diseases. ¹⁶But he would withdraw to deserted places and pray.

Jesus Heals a Paralytic
(Mt 9.2–8; Mk 2.1–12)

17 One day, while he was teaching, Phar′i•sees and teachers of the law were sitting near by (they had come from every village of Galilee and Judea and from Jerusalem); and the power of the Lord was with him to heal.*m* ¹⁸Just then some men came, carrying a paralyzed man on a bed. They were trying to bring him in and lay him before Jesus;*l* ¹⁹but finding no way to bring him in because of the crowd, they went up on the roof and let him down with his bed through the tiles into the middle of the crowd*n* in front of Jesus. ²⁰When he saw their faith, he said, "Friend,*o* your sins are forgiven you." ²¹Then the scribes and the Phar′i•sees began to question, "Who is this who is speaking blasphemies? Who can forgive sins but God alone?" ²²When Jesus perceived their questionings, he answered them, "Why do you raise such questions in your hearts? ²³Which is easier, to say, 'Your sins are forgiven you,' or to say, 'Stand up and walk'? ²⁴But so that you may know that the Son of Man has authority on earth to forgive sins"—he said to the one who was paralyzed—"I say to you, stand up and take your bed and go to your home." ²⁵Immediately he stood up before them, took what he had been lying on, and went to his home, glorifying God. ²⁶Amazement seized all of them, and they glorified God and were filled with awe, saying, "We have seen strange things today."

Jesus Calls Levi
(Mt 9.9–13; Mk 2.13–17)

27 After this he went out and saw a tax collector named Levi, sitting at the tax booth; and he said to him, "Follow me." ²⁸And he got up, left everything, and followed him.

29 Then Levi gave a great banquet for him in his house; and there was a large crowd of tax collectors and others sitting at the table*p* with them. ³⁰The Phar′i•sees and their scribes were complaining to his disciples, saying, "Why do you eat and drink with tax collectors and sinners?" ³¹Jesus answered, "Those who are well have no need of a physician, but those who are sick; ³²I have come to call not the righteous but sinners to repentance."

---

j The terms *leper* and *leprosy* can refer to several diseases *k* Gk *he* *l* Gk *him* *m* Other ancient authorities read *was present to heal them* *n* Gk *into the midst* *o* Gk *Man* *p* Gk *reclining*

LIVE IT!

Do Not Be Afraid

How would you respond if someone walked into the room right now and announced that God wanted to see you in the next room in five minutes? As astonishing as that would be, few of us would probably be anxious to run right in to see God. We would probably want a little more time to get some things in our life "straightened out"!

The Gospel of Luke reveals something interesting when it describes a miraculous catch of fish and the call of the first disciples. Upon seeing the miraculous catch, Peter knows he is in the presence of a holy person and asks Jesus to leave because he is overwhelmed by his own sinfulness and feels unworthy in Jesus' presence (5.8).

If we found ourselves in a boat with God, we might respond the same way. Jesus reassures Peter, uttering words so important that they are repeated six times in Luke: "Do not be afraid." God knows we are sinners too. Jesus came not to condemn us but to save us and to make God's love known to us. Jesus is also saying to us: "Do not be afraid. Come, follow me!"

▸ Lk 5.1–11

The Man with a Withered Hand
(Mt 12.9–14; Mk 3.1–6)

6 On another sabbath he entered the synagogue and taught, and there was a man there whose right hand was withered. 7 The scribes and the Phar'i•sees watched him to see whether he would cure on the sabbath, so that they might find an accusation against him. 8 Even though he knew what they were thinking, he said to the man who had the withered hand, "Come and stand here." He got up and stood there. 9 Then Jesus said to them, "I ask you, is it lawful to do good or to do harm on the sabbath, to save life or to destroy it?" 10 After looking around at all of them, he said to him, "Stretch out your hand." He did so, and his hand was restored. 11 But they were filled with fury and discussed with one another what they might do to Jesus.

Jesus Chooses the Twelve Apostles
(Mt 10.1–4; Mk 3.13–19a)

12 Now during those days he went out to the mountain to pray; and he spent the night in prayer to God. 13 And when day came, he called his disciples and chose twelve of them, whom he also named apostles: 14 Simon, whom he named Peter, and his brother Andrew, and James, and John, and Philip, and Bartholomew, 15 and Matthew, and Thomas, and James son of Al•phae'us, and Simon, who was called the Zealot, 16 and Judas son of James, and Judas Is•car'i•ot, who became a traitor.

Sermon on the Plain
(Mt 4.23–25; Mk 1.35–39; Lk 4.44)

17 He came down with them and stood on a level place, with a great crowd of his disciples and a great multitude of people from all Judea, Jerusalem, and the coast of Tyre and Si'don. 18 They had come to hear him and to be healed of their diseases; and those who were troubled with unclean spirits were cured. 19 And all in the crowd were trying to touch him, for power came out from him and healed all of them.

The Question about Fasting
(Mt 9.14–17; Mk 2.18–22)

33 Then they said to him, "John's disciples, like the disciples of the Phar'i•sees, frequently fast and pray, but your disciples eat and drink." 34 Jesus said to them, "You cannot make wedding guests fast while the bridegroom is with them, can you? 35 The days will come when the bridegroom will be taken away from them, and then they will fast in those days." 36 He also told them a parable: "No one tears a piece from a new garment and sews it on an old garment; otherwise the new will be torn, and the piece from the new will not match the old. 37 And no one puts new wine into old wineskins; otherwise the new wine will burst the skins and will be spilled, and the skins will be destroyed. 38 But new wine must be put into fresh wineskins. 39 And no one after drinking old wine desires new wine, but says, 'The old is good.' "q

The Question about the Sabbath
(Mt 12.1–8; Mk 2.23–28)

One sabbathr while Jesuss was going through the grainfields, his disciples plucked some heads of grain, rubbed them in their hands, and ate them. 2 But some of the Phar'i•sees said, "Why are you doing what is not lawfult on the sabbath?" 3 Jesus answered, "Have you not read what David did when he and his companions were hungry? 4 He entered the house of God and took and ate the bread of the Presence, which it is not lawful for any but the priests to eat, and gave some to his companions?" 5 Then he said to them, "The Son of Man is lord of the sabbath."

Blessings and Woes
(Mt 5.1–12)

20 Then he looked up at his disciples and said:
"Blessed are you who are poor,
    for yours is the kingdom of God.

---

q Other ancient authorities read *better*; others lack verse 39
r Other ancient authorities read *On the second first sabbath*
s Gk *he*   t Other ancient authorities add *to do*

21 "Blessed are you who are hungry now,
        for you will be filled.
    "Blessed are you who weep now,
        for you will laugh.

22 "Blessed are you when people hate you, and when they exclude you, revile you, and defame you[u] on account of the Son of Man. 23 Rejoice in that day and leap for joy, for surely your reward is great in heaven; for that is what their ancestors did to the prophets.

24 "But woe to you who are rich,
        for you have received your consolation.

25 "Woe to you who are full now,
        for you will be hungry.
    "Woe to you who are laughing now,
        for you will mourn and weep.

PRAY IT!
Jesus' Preference for the Poor

In the Gospel of Luke, Jesus gives the Sermon on the Plain, which parallels the Sermon on the Mount in Matthew. Even more clearly than Matthew, Luke makes the point that God's justice has a preference for the poor and the little ones. So it's not surprising that the four beatitudes (blessings) in Luke are balanced by four woes ("Woe!" is like saying, "Trouble ahead!"). For example, "Blessed are you who are poor" (6.20) is countered by "Woe to you who are rich" (verse 24). Jesus shows his care for both rich people and poor people by calling the rich to practice justice and the poor to have hope.

Unlike Matthew, Luke does not "spiritualize" the Beatitudes. Matthew says, "Blessed are the poor in spirit" (5.3), but Luke simply says, "Blessed are you who are poor" (6.20), meaning materially poor. Matthew is concerned for people's salvation; Luke is concerned about their salvation and their material needs.

How do you show special concern for poor people? Pray that God helps us to share God's love with those caught in the struggles of life.

▶ Lk 6.17–49

26 "Woe to you when all speak well of you, for that is what their ancestors did to the false prophets.

Love for Enemies
(Mt 5.33–48)

27 "But I say to you that listen, Love your enemies, do good to those who hate you, 28 bless those who curse you, pray for those who abuse you. 29 If anyone strikes you on the cheek, offer the other also; and from anyone who takes away your coat do not withhold even your shirt. 30 Give to everyone who begs from you; and if anyone takes away your goods, do not ask for them again. 31 Do to others as you would have them do to you.

32 "If you love those who love you, what credit is that to you? For even sinners love those who love them. 33 If you do good to those who do good to you, what credit is that to you? For even sinners do the same. 34 If you lend to those from whom you hope to receive, what credit is that to you? Even sinners lend to sinners, to receive as much again. 35 But love your enemies, do good, and lend, expecting nothing in return.[v] Your reward will be great, and you will be children of the Most High; for he is kind to the ungrateful and the wicked. 36 Be merciful, just as your Father is merciful.

Judging Others
(Mt 7.1–5)

37 "Do not judge, and you will not be judged; do not condemn, and you will not be condemned. Forgive, and you will be forgiven; 38 give, and it will be given to you. A good measure, pressed down, shaken together, running over, will be put into your lap; for the measure you give will be the measure you get back."

39 He also told them a parable: "Can a blind person guide a blind person? Will not both fall into a pit? 40 A disciple is not above the teacher, but everyone who is fully qualified will be like the teacher. 41 Why do you see the speck in your neighbor's[w] eye, but do not notice the log in your own eye? 42 Or how can you say to your neighbor,[x] 'Friend,[x] let me take out the speck in your eye,' when you yourself do not see the log in your own eye? You hypocrite, first take the log out of your own eye, and then you will see clearly to take the speck out of your neighbor's[w] eye.

---

u Gk cast out your name as evil   v Other ancient
authorities read despairing of no one   w Gk brother's
x Gk brother

A Tree and Its Fruit
(Mt 7.15–20)

43 "No good tree bears bad fruit, nor again does a bad tree bear good fruit; 44 for each tree is

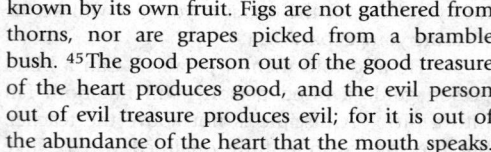

Asian American
The Reunion Dinner

The words of the centurion in Lk 7.6–7 are the basis for the words Catholics say before receiving the Holy Eucharist, "Lord, I am not worthy to receive you, but only say the word and I shall be healed." These words indicate our humility and our willingness to accept God's forgiveness and healing in our life. They remind us to receive Jesus in a state of peace with God and one another, especially by seeking reconciliation with family and friends.

The Chinese New Year's celebration includes a "reunion dinner." The whole family gathers at the home of the eldest family member. People travel from faraway cities, and even from other countries, to be together. The meal is not eaten until everyone is present, and no one eats until any disagreement or hurt is forgiven, and the family is at peace.

▸ Lk 7.1–10

known by its own fruit. Figs are not gathered from thorns, nor are grapes picked from a bramble bush. 45 The good person out of the good treasure of the heart produces good, and the evil person out of evil treasure produces evil; for it is out of the abundance of the heart that the mouth speaks.

The Two Foundations
(Mt 7.21–27)

46 "Why do you call me 'Lord, Lord,' and do not do what I tell you? 47 I will show you what someone is like who comes to me, hears my words, and acts on them. 48 That one is like a man building a house, who dug deeply and laid the foundation on rock; when a flood arose, the river burst against that house but could not shake it, because it had been well built.*y* 49 But the one who

hears and does not act is like a man who built a house on the ground without a foundation. When the river burst against it, immediately it fell, and great was the ruin of that house."

Jesus Heals a Centurion's Servant
(Mt 8.5–13)

After Jesus*z* had finished all his sayings in the hearing of the people, he entered Ca·per′na·um. 2 A centurion there had a slave whom he valued highly, and who was ill and close to death. 3 When he heard about Jesus, he sent some Jewish elders to him, asking him to come and heal his slave. 4 When they came to Jesus, they appealed to him earnestly, saying, "He is worthy of having you do this for him, 5 for he loves our people, and it is he who built our synagogue for us." 6 And Jesus went with them, but when he was not far from the house, the centurion sent friends to say to him, "Lord, do not trouble yourself, for I am not worthy to have you come under my roof; 7 therefore I did not presume to come to you. But only speak the word, and let my servant be healed. 8 For I also am a man set under authority, with soldiers under me; and I say to one, 'Go,' and he goes, and to another, 'Come,' and he comes, and to my slave, 'Do this,' and the slave does it." 9 When Jesus heard this he was amazed at him, and turning to the crowd that followed him, he said, "I tell you, not even in Israel have I found such faith." 10 When those who had been sent returned to the house, they found the slave in good health.

Jesus Raises the Widow's Son at Nain

11 Soon afterwards*a* he went to a town called Na′in, and his disciples and a large crowd went with him. 12 As he approached the gate of the town, a man who had died was being carried out. He was his mother's only son, and she was a widow; and with her was a large crowd from the town. 13 When the Lord saw her, he had compassion for her and said to her, "Do not weep." 14 Then he came forward and touched the bier, and the bearers stood still. And he said, "Young man, I say to you, rise!" 15 The dead man sat up and began to speak, and Jesus*z* gave him to his mother. 16 Fear seized all of them; and they glorified God, saying, "A great prophet has risen among us!" and "God has looked favorably on his people!" 17 This word about him spread throughout Judea and all the surrounding country.

---

y Other ancient authorities read *founded upon the rock*
z Gk *he*   *a* Other ancient authorities read *Next day*

Messengers from John the Baptist
(Mt 11.2–19)

18 The disciples of John reported all these things to him. So John summoned two of his disciples [19] and sent them to the Lord to ask, "Are you the one who is to come, or are we to wait for another?" [20] When the men had come to him, they said, "John the Baptist has sent us to you to ask, 'Are you the one who is to come, or are we to wait for another?' " [21] Jesus[b] had just then cured many people of diseases, plagues, and evil spirits, and had given sight to many who were blind. [22] And he answered them, "Go and tell John what you have seen and heard: the blind receive their sight, the lame walk, the lepers[c] are cleansed, the deaf hear, the dead are raised, the poor have good news brought to them. [23] And blessed is anyone who takes no offense at me."

24 When John's messengers had gone, Jesus[d] began to speak to the crowds about John:[e] "What did you go out into the wilderness to look at? A reed shaken by the wind? [25] What then did you go out to see? Someone[f] dressed in soft robes? Look, those who put on fine clothing and live in luxury are in royal palaces. [26] What then did you go out to see? A prophet? Yes, I tell you, and more than a prophet. [27] This is the one about whom it is written,

'See, I am sending my messenger ahead
of you,
who will prepare your way before
you.'

[28] I tell you, among those born of women no one is greater than John; yet the least in the kingdom of God is greater than he." [29] (And all the people who heard this, including the tax collectors, acknowledged the justice of God,[g] because they had been baptized with John's baptism. [30] But by refusing to be baptized by him, the Phar·i·sees and the lawyers rejected God's purpose for themselves.)

31 "To what then will I compare the people of this generation, and what are they like? [32] They are like children sitting in the marketplace and calling to one another,

'We played the flute for you, and you did
not dance;
we wailed, and you did not weep.'

[33] For John the Baptist has come eating no bread and drinking no wine, and you say, 'He has a demon'; [34] the Son of Man has come eating and drinking, and you say, 'Look, a glutton and a drunkard, a friend of tax collectors and sinners!' [35] Nevertheless, wisdom is vindicated by all her children."

A Sinful Woman Forgiven

36 One of the Phar·i·sees asked Jesus[e] to eat with him, and he went into the Phar·i·see's house and took his place at the table. [37] And a woman in the city, who was a sinner, having learned that he was eating in the Phar·i·see's house, brought an alabaster jar of ointment. [38] She stood behind him at his feet, weeping, and began to bathe his feet with her tears and to dry them with her hair. Then she continued kissing his feet and anointing them with the ointment. [39] Now when the Phar·i·see who had invited him saw it, he said to himself, "If this man were a prophet, he would have known who and what kind of woman this is who is touching him—that she is a sinner." [40] Jesus spoke up and said to him, "Simon, I have something to say to you." "Teacher," he replied, "speak." [41] "A certain creditor had two debtors; one owed five hundred denarii,[h] and the other fifty. [42] When they could not pay, he canceled the debts for both of them. Now which of them will love him more?" [43] Simon answered, "I suppose the one for whom he canceled the greater debt." And Jesus[d] said to him, "You have judged rightly." [44] Then turning toward the woman, he said to Simon, "Do you see this woman? I entered your house; you gave me no water for my feet, but she has bathed my feet with her tears and dried them with her hair. [45] You gave me no kiss, but from the time I came in she has not stopped kissing my feet. [46] You did not anoint my head with oil, but she has anointed my feet with ointment. [47] Therefore, I tell you, her sins, which were many, have been forgiven; hence she has shown great love. But the one to whom little is forgiven, loves little." [48] Then he said to her, "Your sins are forgiven." [49] But those who were at the table with him began to say among themselves, "Who is this who even forgives sins?" [50] And he said to the woman, "Your faith has saved you; go in peace."

Some Women Accompany Jesus

8 Soon afterwards he went on through cities and villages, proclaiming and bringing the good news of the kingdom of God. The twelve were with him, [2] as well as some women who had been cured of evil spirits and infirmities: Mary, called Mag·da·lēne, from whom seven demons had gone out, [3] and Jō·an'na, the wife of Her'od's steward

---

b Gk He   *c* The terms *leper* and *leprosy* can refer to several diseases   *d* Gk he   *e* Gk him   *f* Or *Why then did you go out? To see someone*   *g* Or *praised God*   *h* The denarius was the usual day's wage for a laborer

Chū′za, and Susanna, and many others, who provided for them[i] out of their resources.

The Parable of the Sower
(Mt 13.1–9; Mk 4.1–9)

4 When a great crowd gathered and people from town after town came to him, he said in a parable: 5 "A sower went out to sow his seed; and as he sowed, some fell on the path and was trampled on, and the birds of the air ate it up. 6 Some fell on the rock; and as it grew up, it withered for lack of moisture. 7 Some fell among thorns, and the thorns grew with it and choked it. 8 Some fell into good soil, and when it grew, it produced a hundredfold." As he said this, he called out, "Let anyone with ears to hear listen!"

PRAY IT!
Prayer for Roots and Fruit

God, master gardener, extend your hands to help me plant this tiny seed of faith. Provide me with fertile ground— the rich, moist soil of an open heart. Help me cultivate this seed as your word within me begins to take root and grow.

Lord, this seed needs the light of Christ to warm it, and your Holy Spirit to quench its thirst. Gather a faith community to help me tend my garden and remove any rocks and weeds that might prevent your word from taking root in me.

A tiny seed is a wondrous creation because it does not give much indication of the life within it. Master Gardener, only you know what kind of plant will sprout from this humble beginning. Let the seed of my faith blossom and bear much fruit for your Reign. Amen.

▶ Lk 8.4–15

The Purpose of the Parables
(Mt 13.10–17; Mk 4.10–12)

9 Then his disciples asked him what this parable meant. 10 He said, "To you it has been given to know the secrets[j] of the kingdom of God; but to others I speak[k] in parables, so that

'looking they may not perceive,
and listening they may not understand.'

The Parable of the Sower Explained
(Mt 13.18–23; Mk 4.13–20)

11 "Now the parable is this: The seed is the word of God. 12 The ones on the path are those who have heard; then the devil comes and takes away the word from their hearts, so that they may not believe and be saved. 13 The ones on the rock are those who, when they hear the word, receive it with joy. But these have no root; they believe only for a while and in a time of testing fall away. 14 As for what fell among the thorns, these are the ones who hear; but as they go on their way, they are choked by the cares and riches and pleasures of life, and their fruit does not mature. 15 But as for that in the good soil, these are the ones who, when they hear the word, hold it fast in an honest and good heart, and bear fruit with patient endurance.

A Lamp under a Jar
(Mt 4.21–25)

16 "No one after lighting a lamp hides it under a jar, or puts it under a bed, but puts it on a lampstand, so that those who enter may see the light. 17 For nothing is hidden that will not be disclosed, nor is anything secret that will not become known and come to light. 18 Then pay attention to how you listen; for to those who have, more will be given; and from those who do not have, even what they seem to have will be taken away."

The True Kindred of Jesus
(Mt 12.46–50; Mk 3.31–35)

19 Then his mother and his brothers came to him, but they could not reach him because of the crowd. 20 And he was told, "Your mother and your brothers are standing outside, wanting to see you." 21 But he said to them, "My mother and my brothers are those who hear the word of God and do it."

Jesus Calms a Storm
(Mt 8.23–27; Mk 4.35–41)

22 One day he got into a boat with his disciples, and he said to them, "Let us go across to the other side of the lake." So they put out, 23 and while they were sailing he fell asleep. A windstorm swept down on the lake, and the boat was filling with water, and they were in danger. 24 They went to him and woke him up, shouting, "Master, Master, we are perishing!" And he woke up and rebuked the wind and the raging waves; they ceased, and there was a calm. 25 He said to them, "Where is your faith?" They were afraid and amazed, and said to one another, "Who then is this, that he com-

---

i Other ancient authorities read *him*   *j* Or *mysteries*
k Gk lacks *I speak*

mands even the winds and the water, and they obey him?"

Jesus Heals the Gerasene Demoniac
(Mt 8.28 — 9.1; Mk 5.1–20)

26 Then they arrived at the country of the Ger'a•senes,*l* which is opposite Galilee. 27 As he stepped out on land, a man of the city who had demons met him. For a long time he had worn*m* no clothes, and he did not live in a house but in the tombs. 28 When he saw Jesus, he fell down before him and shouted at the top of his voice, "What have you to do with me, Jesus, Son of the Most High God? I beg you, do not torment me"— 29 for Jesus*n* had commanded the unclean spirit to come out of the man. (For many times it had seized him; he was kept under guard and bound with chains and shackles, but he would break the bonds and be driven by the demon into the wilds.) 30 Jesus then asked him, "What is your name?" He said, "Legion"; for many demons had entered him. 31 They begged him not to order them to go back into the abyss.

32 Now there on the hillside a large herd of swine was feeding; and the demons*o* begged Jesus*p* to let them enter these. So he gave them permission. 33 Then the demons came out of the man and entered the swine, and the herd rushed down the steep bank into the lake and was drowned.

34 When the swineherds saw what had happened, they ran off and told it in the city and in the country. 35 Then people came out to see what had happened, and when they came to Jesus, they found the man from whom the demons had gone sitting at the feet of Jesus, clothed and in his right mind. And they were afraid. 36 Those who had seen it told them how the one who had been possessed by demons had been healed. 37 Then all the people of the surrounding country of the Ger'a-senes*l* asked Jesus*p* to leave them; for they were seized with great fear. So he got into the boat and returned. 38 The man from whom the demons had gone begged that he might be with him; but Jesus*n* sent him away, saying, 39 "Return to your home, and declare how much God has done for you." So he went away, proclaiming throughout the city how much Jesus had done for him.

A Girl Restored to Life and a Woman Healed
(Mt 9.18–26; Mk 5.21–43)

40 Now when Jesus returned, the crowd welcomed him, for they were all waiting for him. 41 Just then there came a man named Jā•i'rus, a leader of the synagogue. He fell at Jesus' feet and begged him to come to his house, 42 for he had an only daughter, about twelve years old, who was dying.

As he went, the crowds pressed in on him. 43 Now there was a woman who had been suffering from hemorrhages for twelve years; and though she had spent all she had on physicians,*q* no one could cure her. 44 She came up behind him and touched the fringe of his clothes, and immediately her hemorrhage stopped. 45 Then Jesus asked, "Who touched me?" When all denied it, Peter*r* said, "Master, the crowds surround you and press in on you." 46 But Jesus said, "Someone touched me; for I noticed that power had gone out from me." 47 When the woman saw that she could not remain hidden, she came trembling; and falling down before him, she declared in the presence of all the people why she had touched him, and how she had been immediately healed. 48 He said to her, "Daughter, your faith has made you well; go in peace."

49 While he was still speaking, someone came from the leader's house to say, "Your daughter is dead; do not trouble the teacher any longer." 50 When Jesus heard this, he replied, "Do not fear. Only believe, and she will be saved." 51 When he came to the house, he did not allow anyone to enter with him, except Peter, John, and James, and the child's father and mother. 52 They were all weeping and wailing for her; but he said, "Do not weep; for she is not dead but sleeping." 53 And they laughed at him, knowing that she was dead. 54 But he took her by the hand and called out, "Child, get up!" 55 Her spirit returned, and she got up at once. Then he directed them to give her something to eat. 56 Her parents were astounded; but he ordered them to tell no one what had happened.

The Mission of the Twelve
(Mt 10.5–15)

Then Jesus*n* called the twelve together and gave them power and authority over all demons and to cure diseases, 2 and he sent them out to proclaim the kingdom of God and to heal. 3 He said to them, "Take nothing for your journey, no staff, nor bag, nor bread, nor money—not even an extra tunic. 4 Whatever house you enter, stay there, and leave from there. 5 Wherever they do not welcome you, as you are leaving that town shake the dust off your feet as a testimony against them." 6 They

---

l Other ancient authorities read *Gadarenes*; others, *Gergesenes*   *m* Other ancient authorities read *a man of the city who had had demons for a long time met him. He wore*   *n* Gk *he*   *o* Gk *they*   *p* Gk *him*   *q* Other ancient authorities lack *and though she had spent all she had on physicians*   *r* Other ancient authorities add *and those who were with him*

Mission Possible

Just like the director of operations from the classic television show *Mission Impossible*, Jesus in Lk 9.1–6 seems to say to the disciples, "Your mission, should you choose to accept it . . ." But whereas the director in the television show labeled his missions as impossible, Jesus knew his missions were possible—though not always popular.

We too are asked to share in Jesus' mission. Sound easy? We know it is not. Doing what Jesus would do may mean sticking our neck out rather than following the crowd. The hardest part? Letting people know that the reason for our actions is our faith in Jesus Christ. It's not impossible, but it's certainly a challenge! Are you up to it? If you trust in God, you will be!

▶ Lk 9.1–6

---

departed and went through the villages, bringing the good news and curing diseases everywhere.

Herod's Perplexity
(Mt 14.1–12; Mk 6.14–29)

7 Now Her'od the ruler[s] heard about all that had taken place, and he was perplexed, because it was said by some that John had been raised from the dead, [8] by some that E·li'jah had appeared, and by others that one of the ancient prophets had arisen. [9] Her'od said, "John I beheaded; but who is this about whom I hear such things?" And he tried to see him.

Feeding the Five Thousand
(Mt 14.13–21; Mk 6.30–44; Jn 6.1–15)

10 On their return the apostles told Jesus[t] all they had done. He took them with him and withdrew privately to a city called Beth·sa'i·da. [11] When the crowds found out about it, they followed him; and he welcomed them, and spoke to them about the kingdom of God, and healed those who needed to be cured. 12 The day was drawing to a close, and the twelve came to him and said, "Send the crowd away, so that they may go into the surrounding villages and countryside, to lodge and get provisions; for we are here in a deserted place." [13] But he said to them, "You give them something to eat." They said, "We have no more than five loaves and two fish—unless we are to go and buy food for all these people." [14] For there were about five thousand men. And he said to his disciples, "Make them sit down in groups of about fifty each." [15] They did so and made them all sit down. [16] And taking the five loaves and the two fish, he looked up to heaven, and blessed and broke them, and gave them to the disciples to set before the crowd. [17] And all ate and

were filled. What was left over was gathered up, twelve baskets of broken pieces.

Peter's Declaration about Jesus
(Mt 16.13–20; Mk 8.27–30)

18 Once when Jesus[u] was praying alone, with only the disciples near him, he asked them, "Who do the crowds say that I am?" [19] They answered, "John the Baptist; but others, E·li'jah; and still others, that one of the ancient prophets has arisen." [20] He said to them, "But who do you say that I am?" Peter answered, "The Messiah[v] of God."

Jesus Foretells His Death and Resurrection
(Mt 16.24–28; Mk 8.31—9.1)

21 He sternly ordered and commanded them not to tell anyone, [22] saying, "The Son of Man must undergo great suffering, and be rejected by the elders, chief priests, and scribes, and be killed, and on the third day be raised."

23 Then he said to them all, "If any want to become my followers, let them deny themselves and take up their cross daily and follow me. [24] For those who want to save their life will lose it, and those who lose their life for my sake will save it. [25] What does it profit them if they gain the whole world, but lose or forfeit themselves? [26] Those who are ashamed of me and of my words, of them the Son of Man will be ashamed when he comes in his glory and the glory of the Father and of the holy angels. [27] But truly I tell you, there are some standing here who will not taste death before they see the kingdom of God."

---

[s] Gk *tetrarch*   [t] Gk *him*   [u] Gk *he*   [v] Or *The Christ*

The Transfiguration
(Mt 17.1–8; Mk 9.2–8; 2 Pet 1.16–18)

28 Now about eight days after these sayings Jesus[w] took with him Peter and John and James, and went up on the mountain to pray. 29 And while he was praying, the appearance of his face changed, and his clothes became dazzling white. 30 Suddenly they saw two men, Moses and E·li′jah, talking to him. 31 They appeared in glory and were speaking of his departure, which he was about to accomplish at Jerusalem. 32 Now Peter and his companions were weighed down with sleep; but since they had stayed awake,[x] they saw his glory and the two men who stood with him. 33 Just as they were leaving him, Peter said to Jesus, "Master, it is good for us to be here; let us make three dwellings,[y] one for you, one for Moses, and one for E·li′jah"—not knowing what he said. 34 While he was saying this, a cloud came and overshadowed them; and they were terrified as they entered the cloud. 35 Then from the cloud came a voice that said, "This is my Son, my Chosen;[z] listen to him!" 36 When the voice had spoken, Jesus was found alone. And they kept silent and in those days told no one any of the things they had seen.

Jesus Heals a Boy with a Demon
(Mt 17.14–21; Mk 9.14–29)

37 On the next day, when they had come down from the mountain, a great crowd met him. 38 Just then a man from the crowd shouted, "Teacher, I beg you to look at my son; he is my only child. 39 Suddenly a spirit seizes him, and all at once he[a] shrieks. It convulses him until he foams at the mouth; it mauls him and will scarcely leave him. 40 I begged your disciples to cast it out, but they could not." 41 Jesus answered, "You faithless and perverse generation, how much longer must I be with you and bear with you? Bring your son here." 42 While he was coming, the demon dashed him to the ground in convulsions. But Jesus rebuked the unclean spirit, healed the boy, and gave him back to his father. 43 And all were astounded at the greatness of God.

Jesus Again Foretells His Death
(Mt 17.22–23; Mk 9.30–32)

While everyone was amazed at all that he was doing, he said to his disciples, 44 "Let these words sink into your ears: The Son of Man is going to be betrayed into human hands." 45 But they did not understand this saying; its meaning was concealed from them, so that they could not perceive it. And they were afraid to ask him about this saying.

True Greatness
(Mt 18.1–5; Mk 9.33–37)

46 An argument arose among them as to which one of them was the greatest. 47 But Jesus, aware of their inner thoughts, took a little child and put it by his side, 48 and said to them, "Whoever welcomes this child in my name welcomes

---

[w] Gk *he*   [x] Or *but when they were fully awake*   [y] Or *tents*
[z] Other ancient authorities read *my Beloved*   [a] Or *it*

Spiritual Highs

LIVE IT!

Have you ever been on a great retreat, camp, or service trip? If so, you may have felt really close to God and to others who shared that experience with you. You may have even wished the experience did not have to end.

Peter, James, and John must have felt that way when they saw Jesus in his glory talking with Moses and Elijah on the mountaintop. Peter wanted to stay up on the mountain, but it quickly became clear that he could not do so.

Faith has its high moments as well as its low moments. It is unrealistic to think that we can maintain some kind of spiritual high all the time—doing so may even be dangerous. The faith of those who depend on mountaintop experiences often fizzles out. The better challenge is to learn what it means to live as a Christian down in the thick of life. Remember: Our faith is more than feelings. God's love and mercy do not depend on our ability to feel "warm fuzzies," as nice as those can be.

Recall a special time in your life when you felt on top of the world. Relive the moment in your mind, this time looking for how God was present in that experience. What direction was God inviting you to go after it was over? Are you there yet?

▶ Lk 9.28–36

me, and whoever welcomes me welcomes the one who sent me; for the least among all of you is the greatest."

Another Exorcist
(Mk 9.38–41)

49 John answered, "Master, we saw someone casting out demons in your name, and we tried to stop him, because he does not follow with us." 50 But Jesus said to him, "Do not stop him; for whoever is not against you is for you."

A Samaritan Village Refuses to Receive Jesus

51 When the days drew near for him to be taken up, he set his face to go to Jerusalem. 52 And he sent messengers ahead of him. On their way they entered a village of the Sa·mar'i·tans to make ready for him; 53 but they did not receive him, because his face was set toward Jerusalem. 54 When his disciples James and John saw it, they said, "Lord, do you want us to command fire to come down from heaven and consume them?"[b] 55 But he turned and rebuked them. 56 Then[c] they went on to another village.

Would-Be Followers of Jesus
(Mt 8.18–22)

57 As they were going along the road, someone said to him, "I will follow you wherever you go." 58 And Jesus said to him, "Foxes have holes, and birds of the air have nests; but the Son of Man has nowhere to lay his head." 59 To another he said, "Follow me." But he said, "Lord, first let me go and bury my father." 60 But Jesus[d] said to him, "Let the dead bury their own dead; but as for you, go and proclaim the kingdom of God." 61 Another said, "I will follow you, Lord; but let me first say farewell to those at my home." 62 Jesus said to him, "No one who puts a hand to the plow and looks back is fit for the kingdom of God."

The Mission of the Seventy

After this the Lord appointed seventy[e] others and sent them on ahead of him in pairs to every town and place where he himself intended to go. 2 He said to them, "The harvest is plentiful, but the laborers are few; therefore ask the Lord of the harvest to send out laborers into his harvest. 3 Go on your way. See, I am sending you out like lambs into the midst of wolves. 4 Carry no purse, no bag, no sandals; and greet no one on the road. 5 Whatever house you enter, first say, 'Peace to this house!' 6 And if anyone is there who shares in peace, your peace will rest on that person; but if not, it will return to you. 7 Remain in the same house, eating and drinking whatever they provide,

for the laborer deserves to be paid. Do not move about from house to house. 8 Whenever you enter a town and its people welcome you, eat what is set before you; 9 cure the sick who are there, and say to them, 'The kingdom of God has come near to you.'[f] 10 But whenever you enter a town and they do not welcome you, go out into its streets and say, 11 'Even the dust of your town that clings to our feet, we wipe off in protest against you. Yet know this: the kingdom of God has come near.'[g] 12 I tell you, on that day it will be more tolerable for Sod'om than for that town.

Woes to Unrepentant Cities
(Mt 11.20–24)

13 "Woe to you, Chō·ra'zin! Woe to you, Beth-sā'i·da! For if the deeds of power done in you had been done in Tyre and Si'don, they would have repented long ago, sitting in sackcloth and ashes. 14 But at the judgment it will be more tolerable for Tyre and Si'don than for you. 15 And you, Ca·per'-na·um,

will you be exalted to heaven?

No, you will be brought down to Hades.

16 "Whoever listens to you listens to me, and whoever rejects you rejects me, and whoever rejects me rejects the one who sent me."

The Return of the Seventy

17 The seventy[e] returned with joy, saying, "Lord, in your name even the demons submit to us!" 18 He said to them, "I watched Satan fall from heaven like a flash of lightning. 19 See, I have given you authority to tread on snakes and scorpions, and over all the power of the enemy; and nothing will hurt you. 20 Nevertheless, do not rejoice at this, that the spirits submit to you, but rejoice that your names are written in heaven."

Jesus Rejoices
(Mt 11.25–27)

21 At that same hour Jesus[d] rejoiced in the Holy Spirit[h] and said, "I thank[i] you, Father, Lord of heaven and earth, because you have hidden these things from the wise and the intelligent and have revealed them to infants; yes, Father, for such was your gracious will.[j] 22 All things have been handed over to me by my Father; and no one

---

b Other ancient authorities add *as Elijah did*   c Other ancient authorities read *rebuked them, and said, "You do not know what spirit you are of, 56for the Son of Man has not come to destroy the lives of human beings but to save them."* Then   d Gk *he*   e Other ancient authorities read *seventy-two*   f Or *is at hand for you*   g Or *is at hand* h Other authorities read *in the spirit*   i Or *praise* j Or *for so it was well-pleasing in your sight*

knows who the Son is except the Father, or who the Father is except the Son and anyone to whom the Son chooses to reveal him."

23 Then turning to the disciples, Jesus[k] said to them privately, "Blessed are the eyes that see what you see! 24 For I tell you that many prophets and kings desired to see what you see, but did not see it, and to hear what you hear, but did not hear it."

The Parable of the Good Samaritan
(Mt 22.34–40; Mk 12.28–34)

25 Just then a lawyer stood up to test Jesus.[l] "Teacher," he said, "what must I do to inherit eternal life?" 26 He said to him, "What is written in the law? What do you read there?" 27 He answered, "You shall love the Lord your God with all your heart, and with all your soul, and with all your strength, and with all your mind; and your neighbor as yourself." 28 And he said to him, "You have given the right answer; do this, and you will live."

29 But wanting to justify himself, he asked Jesus, "And who is my neighbor?" 30 Jesus replied, "A man was going down from Jerusalem to Jericho, and fell into the hands of robbers, who stripped him, beat him, and went away, leaving him half dead. 31 Now by chance a priest was going down that road; and when he saw him, he passed by on the other side. 32 So likewise a Lē'-vite, when he came to the place and saw him, passed by on the other side. 33 But a Sa•mār'i•tan while traveling came near him; and when he saw him, he was moved with pity. 34 He went to him and bandaged his wounds, having poured oil and wine on them. Then he put him on his own animal, brought him to an inn, and took care of him. 35 The next day he took out two denarii,[m] gave them to the innkeeper, and said, 'Take care of him; and when I come back, I will repay you whatever more you spend.' 36 Which of these three, do you think, was a neighbor to the man who fell into the hands of the robbers?" 37 He said, "The one who showed him mercy." Jesus said to him, "Go and do likewise."

Jesus Visits Martha and Mary

38 Now as they went on their way, he entered a certain village, where a woman named Martha welcomed him into her home. 39 She had a sister named Mary, who sat at the Lord's feet and

---

k Gk *he*   l Gk *him*   m The denarius was the usual day's wage for a laborer

listened to what he was saying. 40 But Martha was distracted by her many tasks; so she came to him and asked, "Lord, do you not care that my sister has left me to do all the work by myself? Tell her then to help me." 41 But the Lord answered her, "Martha, Martha, you are worried and distracted by many things; 42 there is need of only one thing.*n* Mary has chosen the better part, which will not be taken away from her."

The Lord's Prayer
(Mt 6.9–15)

He was praying in a certain place, and after he had finished, one of his disciples said to him, "Lord, teach us to pray, as John taught his disciples." 2 He said to them, "When you pray, say:

Father,*o* hallowed be your name.
    Your kingdom come.*p*
3   Give us each day our daily bread.*q*
4   And forgive us our sins,
        for we ourselves forgive everyone
          indebted to us.
    And do not bring us to the time of
        trial."*r*

door will be opened for you. 10 For everyone who asks receives, and everyone who searches finds, and for everyone who knocks, the door will be opened. 11 Is there anyone among you who, if your child asks for*s* a fish, will give a snake instead of a fish? 12 Or if the child asks for an egg, will give a scorpion? 13 If you then, who are evil, know how to give good gifts to your children, how much more will the heavenly Father give the Holy Spirit*t* to those who ask him!"

Jesus and Beelzebul
(Mt 12.22–32; Mk 3.19b–30)

14 Now he was casting out a demon that was mute; when the demon had gone out, the one who had been mute spoke, and the crowds were amazed. 15 But some of them said, "He casts out demons by Bē·el'ze·bul, the ruler of the demons." 16 Others, to test him, kept demanding from him a sign from heaven. 17 But he knew what they were thinking and said to them, "Every kingdom divided against itself becomes a desert, and house falls on house. 18 If Satan also is divided against himself, how will his kingdom stand? —for you say

Nagging God

Did you ever think that nagging could get you somewhere with God? Nagging is certainly not valued in our friendships or family relationships. But in Lk 11.5–13, Jesus advises us to nag God for the things we really need. Of course, what we nag for makes the difference. So don't ever give up on God. Be persistent in praying for your needs and the needs of others!

▶ Lk 11.5–13

Perseverance in Prayer
(Mt 7.7–11)

5 And he said to them, "Suppose one of you has a friend, and you go to him at midnight and say to him, 'Friend, lend me three loaves of bread; 6 for a friend of mine has arrived, and I have nothing to set before him.' 7 And he answers from within, 'Do not bother me; the door has already been locked, and my children are with me in bed; I cannot get up and give you anything.' 8 I tell you, even though he will not get up and give him anything because he is his friend, at least because of his persistence he will get up and give him whatever he needs.

9 "So I say to you, Ask, and it will be given you; search, and you will find; knock, and the

that I cast out the demons by Bē·el'ze·bul. 19 Now if I cast out the demons by Bē·el'ze·bul, by whom do your exorcists*u* cast them out? Therefore they will be your judges. 20 But if it is by the finger of God that I cast out the demons, then the kingdom of God has come to you. 21 When a strong man, fully

---

n Other ancient authorities read *few things are necessary, or only one*   *o* Other ancient authorities read *Our Father in heaven*   *p* A few ancient authorities read *Your Holy Spirit come upon us and cleanse us.* Other ancient authorities add *Your will be done, on earth as in heaven*   *q* Or *our bread for tomorrow*   *r* Or *us into temptation.* Other ancient authorities add *but rescue us from the evil one* (or *from evil*)   *s* Other ancient authorities add *bread, will give a stone; or if your child asks for*   *t* Other ancient authorities read *the Father give the Holy Spirit from heaven*   *u* Gk *sons*

armed, guards his castle, his property is safe. 22 But when one stronger than he attacks him and overpowers him, he takes away his armor in which he trusted and divides his plunder. 23 Whoever is not with me is against me, and whoever does not gather with me scatters.

The Return of the Unclean Spirit
(Mt 12.43–45)

24 "When the unclean spirit has gone out of a person, it wanders through waterless regions looking for a resting place, but not finding any, it says, 'I will return to my house from which I came.' 25 When it comes, it finds it swept and put in order. 26 Then it goes and brings seven other spirits more evil than itself, and they enter and live there; and the last state of that person is worse than the first."

True Blessedness

27 While he was saying this, a woman in the crowd raised her voice and said to him, "Blessed is the womb that bore you and the breasts that nursed you!" 28 But he said, "Blessed rather are those who hear the word of God and obey it!"

The Sign of Jonah
(Mt 12.38–42)

29 When the crowds were increasing, he began to say, "This generation is an evil generation; it asks for a sign, but no sign will be given to it except the sign of Jonah. 30 For just as Jonah became a sign to the people of Nin′e•veh, so the Son of Man will be to this generation. 31 The queen of the South will rise at the judgment with the people of this generation and condemn them, because she came from the ends of the earth to listen to the wisdom of Solomon, and see, something greater than Solomon is here! 32 The people of Nin′e•veh will rise up at the judgment with this generation and condemn it, because they repented at the proclamation of Jonah, and see, something greater than Jonah is here!

The Light of the Body
(Mt 6.22–23)

33 "No one after lighting a lamp puts it in a cellar,ᵛ but on the lampstand so that those who enter may see the light. 34 Your eye is the lamp of your body. If your eye is healthy, your whole body is full of light; but if it is not healthy, your body is full of darkness. 35 Therefore consider whether the light in you is not darkness. 36 If then your whole body is full of light, with no part of it in darkness, it will be as full of light as when a lamp gives you light with its rays."

Jesus Denounces Pharisees and Lawyers

37 While he was speaking, a Phar′i•see invited him to dine with him; so he went in and took his place at the table. 38 The Phar′i•see was amazed to see that he did not first wash before dinner. 39 Then the Lord said to him, "Now you Phar′i•sees clean the outside of the cup and of the dish, but inside you are full of greed and wickedness. 40 You fools! Did not the one who made the outside make the inside also? 41 So give for alms those things that are within; and see, everything will be clean for you.

42 "But woe to you Phar′i•sees! For you tithe mint and rue and herbs of all kinds, and neglect justice and the love of God; it is these you ought to have practiced, without neglecting the others. 43 Woe to you Phar′i•sees! For you love to have the seat of honor in the synagogues and to be greeted with respect in the marketplaces. 44 Woe to you! For you are like unmarked graves, and people walk over them without realizing it."

45 One of the lawyers answered him, "Teacher, when you say these things, you insult us too." 46 And he said, "Woe also to you lawyers! For you load people with burdens hard to bear, and you yourselves do not lift a finger to ease them. 47 Woe to you! For you build the tombs of the prophets whom your ancestors killed. 48 So you are witnesses and approve of the deeds of your ancestors; for they killed them, and you build their tombs. 49 Therefore also the Wisdom of God said, 'I will send them prophets and apostles, some of whom they will kill and persecute,' 50 so that this generation may be charged with the blood of all the prophets shed since the foundation of the world, 51 from the blood of Abel to the blood of Zech•a•ri′ah, who perished between the altar and the sanctuary. Yes, I tell you, it will be charged against this generation. 52 Woe to you lawyers! For you have taken away the key of knowledge; you did not enter yourselves, and you hindered those who were entering."

53 When he went outside, the scribes and the Phar′i•sees began to be very hostile toward him and to cross-examine him about many things, 54 lying in wait for him, to catch him in something he might say.

ᵛ Other ancient authorities add *or under the bushel basket*

A Warning against Hypocrisy

Meanwhile, when the crowd gathered by the thousands, so that they trampled on one another, he began to speak first to his disciples, "Beware of the yeast of the Phar·i·sees, that is, their hypocrisy. ²Nothing is covered up that will not be uncovered, and nothing secret that will not become known. ³Therefore whatever you have said in the dark will be heard in the light, and what you have whispered behind closed doors will be proclaimed from the housetops.

Exhortation to Fearless Confession
(Mt 10.26–33)

4 "I tell you, my friends, do not fear those who kill the body, and after that can do nothing more. ⁵But I will warn you whom to fear: fear him who, after he has killed, has authority[w] to cast into hell.[x] Yes, I tell you, fear him! ⁶Are not five sparrows sold for two pennies? Yet not one of them is forgotten in God's sight. ⁷But even the hairs of your head are all counted. Do not be afraid; you are of more value than many sparrows.

8 "And I tell you, everyone who acknowledges me before others, the Son of Man also will acknowledge before the angels of God; ⁹but whoever denies me before others will be denied before the angels of God. ¹⁰And everyone who speaks a word against the Son of Man will be forgiven; but whoever blasphemes against the Holy Spirit will not be forgiven. ¹¹When they bring you before the synagogues, the rulers, and the authorities, do not worry about how[y] you are to defend yourselves or what you are to say; ¹²for the Holy Spirit will teach you at that very hour what you ought to say."

The Parable of the Rich Fool

13 Someone in the crowd said to him, "Teacher, tell my brother to divide the family inheritance with me." ¹⁴But he said to him, "Friend, who set me to be a judge or arbitrator over you?" ¹⁵And he said to them, "Take care! Be on your guard against all kinds of greed; for one's life does not consist in the abundance of possessions." ¹⁶Then he told them a parable: "The land of a rich man produced abundantly. ¹⁷And he thought to himself, 'What should I do, for I have no place to store my crops?' ¹⁸Then he said, 'I will do this: I will pull down my barns and build larger ones, and there I will store all my grain and my goods. ¹⁹And I will say to my soul, Soul, you have ample goods laid up for many years; relax, eat, drink, be merry.' ²⁰But God said to him, 'You fool! This very night your life is being demanded of you. And the things you have prepared, whose will they be?' ²¹So it is with those who store up treasures for themselves but are not rich toward God."

Do Not Worry
(Mt 6.19–21, 25–34)

22 He said to his disciples, "Therefore I tell you, do not worry about your life, what you will eat, or about your body, what you will wear. ²³For life is more than food, and the body more than clothing. ²⁴Consider the ravens: they neither sow nor reap, they have neither storehouse nor barn, and yet God feeds them. Of how much more value are you than the birds! ²⁵And can any of you by worrying add a single hour to your span of life?[z]

---

w Or *power*   x Gk *Gehenna*   y Other ancient authorities add *or what*   z Or *add a cubit to your stature*

The Greed Trap

LIVE IT!

It is easy to regard possessions as treasures and to find so much pleasure in them that we want more and more. This is the greed trap Jesus warns against in Lk 12.13–21. How do we let ourselves fall into this trap? Certainly, advertisements play a role in convincing us that we need to own everything that is new and improved (see "New and Improved!" Eccl 1.1–11). Our own insecurities also play a role—the more we possess, the more important we tend to think we are. But as Lk 12.18 indicates, greed is a sin that is addictive. Instead of feeling fulfilled by attaining the thing we crave, we feel that what we have still isn't enough. It is a vicious cycle.

The solution to greed is simple. It's sharing—that value that we learned when we were very small. Sharing our time and possessions makes us "rich toward God" (verse 21). Where do you see the sin of greed at work in your world? Where and when could you, your friends, and your family share more? Don't fall into the greed trap. Share!

▶ Lk 12.13–21

26 If then you are not able to do so small a thing as that, why do you worry about the rest? 27 Consider the lilies, how they grow: they neither toil nor spin;*a* yet I tell you, even Solomon in all his glory was not clothed like one of these. 28 But if God so clothes the grass of the field, which is alive today and tomorrow is thrown into the oven, how much more will he clothe you—you of little faith! 29 And do not keep striving for what you are to eat and what you are to drink, and do not keep worrying. 30 For it is the nations of the world that strive after all these things, and your Father knows that you need them. 31 Instead, strive for his*b* kingdom, and these things will be given to you as well.

32 "Do not be afraid, little flock, for it is your Father's good pleasure to give you the kingdom. 33 Sell your possessions, and give alms. Make purses for yourselves that do not wear out, an unfailing treasure in heaven, where no thief comes near and no moth destroys. 34 For where your treasure is, there your heart will be also.

Watchful Slaves

35 "Be dressed for action and have your lamps lit; 36 be like those who are waiting for their master to return from the wedding banquet, so that they may open the door for him as soon as he comes and knocks. 37 Blessed are those slaves whom the master finds alert when he comes; truly I tell you,

he will fasten his belt and have them sit down to eat, and he will come and serve them. 38 If he comes during the middle of the night, or near dawn, and finds them so, blessed are those slaves.

39 "But know this: if the owner of the house had known at what hour the thief was coming, he*c* would not have let his house be broken into. 40 You also must be ready, for the Son of Man is coming at an unexpected hour."

The Faithful or the Unfaithful Slave
(Mt 24.45–51)

41 Peter said, "Lord, are you telling this parable for us or for everyone?" 42 And the Lord said, "Who then is the faithful and prudent manager whom his master will put in charge of his slaves, to give them their allowance of food at the proper time? 43 Blessed is that slave whom his master will find at work when he arrives. 44 Truly I tell you, he will put that one in charge of all his possessions. 45 But if that slave says to himself, 'My master is delayed in coming,' and if he begins to beat the other slaves, men and women, and to eat and drink and get drunk, 46 the master of that slave will come on a day when he does not expect him and

---

a Other ancient authorities read *Consider the lilies; they neither spin nor weave*   *b* Other ancient authorities read *God's*   *c* Other ancient authorities add *would have watched and*

The Anxiety Trap

LIVE IT!

Doesn't it seem a little naive to assume that if we just trust God, we will get what we need; that we shouldn't worry about the everyday things like clothing, food, and shelter? Seems pretty risky and yet . . .

Lakeesha and Miguel were best friends. Miguel had a big problem. He worried all the time. He sometimes made himself sick with worrying. He worried that his parents would lose their jobs. He worried that he wouldn't find a job. He worried about doing poorly in school. When it was stormy out, he worried about tornadoes. He drove his friends crazy with his worrying.

Lakeesha, on the other hand, never worried. One day, Miguel asked her for her secret to staying calm. She told him: "Miguel, if you keep focused on the negative things that could happen and worry about them, you will not see all the good things happening around you. Did you know that your mom just got a raise? You didn't notice that our band teacher said you had the best fingering technique he had ever seen. And I bet you didn't even look at the want ads for new summer jobs. Right? You spend too much time worrying and not enough time noticing."

Jesus says the same thing. Don't worry so much about everyday needs. Look for the simple signs that God cares for you. Some people even keep a journal of the good things that happen to them every day. Life will be so much calmer and less stressful if you heed Jesus' message. Try it!

▶ Lk 12.22–34

at an hour that he does not know, and will cut him in pieces,[d] and put him with the unfaithful. [47] That slave who knew what his master wanted, but did not prepare himself or do what was wanted, will receive a severe beating. [48] But the one who did not know and did what deserved a beating will receive a light beating. From everyone to whom much has been given, much will be required; and from the one to whom much has been entrusted, even more will be demanded.

Jesus the Cause of Division
(Mt 10.34–39)

[49] "I came to bring fire to the earth, and how I wish it were already kindled! [50] I have a baptism with which to be baptized, and what stress I am under until it is completed! [51] Do you think that I have come to bring peace to the earth? No, I tell you, but rather division! [52] From now on five in one household will be divided, three against two and two against three; [53] they will be divided:

father against son
    and son against father,
mother against daughter
    and daughter against mother,
mother-in-law against her daughter-in-law
    and daughter-in-law against
        mother-in-law."

Interpreting the Time
(Mt 16.1–4)

[54] He also said to the crowds, "When you see a cloud rising in the west, you immediately say, 'It is going to rain'; and so it happens. [55] And when you see the south wind blowing, you say, 'There will be scorching heat'; and it happens. [56] You hypocrites! You know how to interpret the appearance of earth and sky, but why do you not know how to interpret the present time?

Settling with Your Opponent

[57] "And why do you not judge for yourselves what is right? [58] Thus, when you go with your accuser before a magistrate, on the way make an effort to settle the case,[e] or you may be dragged before the judge, and the judge hand you over to the officer, and the officer throw you in prison. [59] I tell you, you will never get out until you have paid the very last penny."

Repent or Perish

At that very time there were some present who told him about the Galileans whose blood Pilate had mingled with their sacrifices. [2] He asked them, "Do you think that because these Galileans suffered in this way they were worse sinners than all

Catholic Connections

ANOINTING OF THE SICK

The crippled woman in Lk 13.10–17 is just one of many people Jesus heals in Luke. Much of Jesus' ministry was spent healing people with physical, emotional, or spiritual illnesses. Through the sacrament of Anointing, one of the seven official sacraments of the Catholic church, Jesus' ministry of extending God's healing love is continued.

In this sacrament, people young and old are anointed with sacred oil, called chrism, and prayed over by a priest or deacon. The sacrament is often given to people who are struggling with a serious illness, going into surgery, or dying. The sacrament is not a guarantee of physical healing, but a way of receiving in a special way God's love and strength during those times of trial.

▶ Lk 13.10–17

other Galileans? [3] No, I tell you; but unless you repent, you will all perish as they did. [4] Or those eighteen who were killed when the tower of Si·lo'am fell on them—do you think that they were worse offenders than all the others living in Jerusalem? [5] No, I tell you; but unless you repent, you will all perish just as they did."

The Parable of the Barren Fig Tree

[6] Then he told this parable: "A man had a fig tree planted in his vineyard; and he came looking for fruit on it and found none. [7] So he said to the gardener, 'See here! For three years I have come looking for fruit on this fig tree, and still I find none. Cut it down! Why should it be wasting the soil?' [8] He replied, 'Sir, let it alone for one more year, until I dig around it and put manure on it. [9] If it bears fruit next year, well and good; but if not, you can cut it down.' "

---

[d] Or *cut him off*   [e] Gk *settle with him*

Jesus Heals a Crippled Woman

10 Now he was teaching in one of the synagogues on the sabbath. 11 And just then there appeared a woman with a spirit that had crippled her for eighteen years. She was bent over and was quite unable to stand up straight. 12 When Jesus saw her, he called her over and said, "Woman, you are set free from your ailment." 13 When he laid his hands on her, immediately she stood up straight and began praising God. 14 But the leader of the synagogue, indignant because Jesus had cured on the sabbath, kept saying to the crowd, "There are six days on which work ought to be done; come on those days and be cured, and not on the sabbath day." 15 But the Lord answered him and said, "You hypocrites! Does not each of you on the sabbath untie his ox or his donkey from the manger, and lead it away to give it water? 16 And ought not this woman, a daughter of Abraham whom Satan bound for eighteen long years, be set free from this bondage on the sabbath day?" 17 When he said this, all his opponents were put to shame; and the entire crowd was rejoicing at all the wonderful things that he was doing.

The Parable of the Mustard Seed
(Mt 13.31–32; Mk 4.30–32)

18 He said therefore, "What is the kingdom of God like? And to what should I compare it? 19 It is like a mustard seed that someone took and sowed in the garden; it grew and became a tree, and the birds of the air made nests in its branches."

The Parable of the Yeast
(Mt 13.33)

20 And again he said, "To what should I compare the kingdom of God? 21 It is like yeast that a woman took and mixed in with[f] three measures of flour until all of it was leavened."

The Narrow Door
(Mt 7.13–14)

22 Jesus[g] went through one town and village after another, teaching as he made his way to Jerusalem. 23 Someone asked him, "Lord, will only a few be saved?" He said to them, 24 "Strive to enter through the narrow door; for many, I tell you, will try to enter and will not be able. 25 When once the owner of the house has got up and shut the door, and you begin to stand outside and to knock at the door, saying, 'Lord, open to us,' then in reply he will say to you, 'I do not know where you come from.' 26 Then you will begin to say, 'We ate and drank with you, and you taught in our streets.' 27 But he will say, 'I do not know where you come from; go away from me, all you evildoers!' 28 There will be weeping and gnashing of teeth when you see Abraham and Isaac and Jacob and all the prophets in the kingdom of God, and you yourselves thrown out. 29 Then people will come from east and west, from north and south, and will eat in the kingdom of God. 30 Indeed, some are last who will be first, and some are first who will be last."

The Lament over Jerusalem
(Mt 23.37–39)

31 At that very hour some Phar′i•sees came and said to him, "Get away from here, for Her′od wants to kill you." 32 He said to them, "Go and tell that fox for me,[h] 'Listen, I am casting out demons and performing cures today and tomorrow, and on the third day I finish my work. 33 Yet today, tomorrow, and the next day I must be on my way, because it is impossible for a prophet to be killed outside of Jerusalem.' 34 Jerusalem, Jerusalem, the city that kills the prophets and stones those who are sent to it! How often have I desired to gather your children together as a hen gathers her brood under her wings, and you were not willing! 35 See, your house is left to you. And I tell you, you will not see me until the time comes when[i] you say, 'Blessed is the one who comes in the name of the Lord.' "

Jesus Heals the Man with Dropsy

On one occasion when Jesus[j] was going to the house of a leader of the Phar′i•sees to eat a meal on the sabbath, they were watching him closely. 2 Just then, in front of him, there was a man who had dropsy. 3 And Jesus asked the lawyers and Phar′i•sees, "Is it lawful to cure people on the sabbath, or not?" 4 But they were silent. So Jesus[j] took him and healed him, and sent him away. 5 Then he said to them, "If one of you has a child[k] or an ox that has fallen into a well, will you not immediately pull it out on a sabbath day?" 6 And they could not reply to this.

Humility and Hospitality

7 When he noticed how the guests chose the places of honor, he told them a parable. 8 "When you are invited by someone to a wedding banquet, do not sit down at the place of honor, in case someone more distinguished than you has been invited by your host; 9 and the host who invited both of you may come and say to you, 'Give this

---

f Gk *hid in*　　*g* Gk *He*　　*h* Gk lacks *for me*　　*i* Other ancient authorities lack *the time comes when*　　*j* Gk *he*　　*k* Other ancient authorities read *a donkey*

person your place,' and then in disgrace you would start to take the lowest place. 10 But when you are invited, go and sit down at the lowest place, so that when your host comes, he may say to you, 'Friend, move up higher'; then you will be honored in the presence of all who sit at the table with you. 11 For all who exalt themselves will be humbled, and those who humble themselves will be exalted."

12 He said also to the one who had invited him, "When you give a luncheon or a dinner, do not invite your friends or your brothers or your relatives or rich neighbors, in case they may invite you in return, and you would be repaid. 13 But when you give a banquet, invite the poor, the crippled, the lame, and the blind. 14 And you will be blessed, because they cannot repay you, for you will be repaid at the resurrection of the righteous."

The Parable of the Great Dinner
(Mt 22.1–14)

15 One of the dinner guests, on hearing this, said to him, "Blessed is anyone who will eat bread in the kingdom of God!" 16 Then Jesus[l] said to him, "Someone gave a great dinner and invited many. 17 At the time for the dinner he sent his slave to say to those who had been invited, 'Come; for everything is ready now.' 18 But they all alike began to make excuses. The first said to him, 'I have bought a piece of land, and I must go out and see it; please accept my regrets.' 19 Another said, 'I have bought five yoke of oxen, and I am going to try them out; please accept my regrets.' 20 Another said, 'I have just been married, and therefore I cannot come.' 21 So the slave returned and reported this to his master. Then the owner of the house became angry and said to his slave, 'Go out at once into the streets and lanes of the town and bring in the poor, the crippled, the blind, and the lame.' 22 And the slave said, 'Sir, what you ordered has been done, and there is still room.' 23 Then the master said to the slave, 'Go out into the roads and lanes, and compel people to come in, so that my house may be filled. 24 For I tell you,[m] none of those who were invited will taste my dinner.' "

The Cost of Discipleship
(Mt 10.34–39)

25 Now large crowds were traveling with him; and he turned and said to them, 26 "Whoever comes to me and does not hate father and mother, wife and children, brothers and sisters, yes, and even life itself, cannot be my disciple. 27 Whoever

God's Invitation List

Jesus uses the image of a banquet to describe the Reign of God. Jesus' point is not about what is on the menu but who is on the invitation list: the weak, the poor, and the little ones. Who is on your "invitation list"—who are the people you reach out to and serve?

▶ Lk 14.7–24

does not carry the cross and follow me cannot be my disciple. 28 For which of you, intending to build a tower, does not first sit down and estimate the cost, to see whether he has enough to complete it? 29 Otherwise, when he has laid a foundation and is not able to finish, all who see it will begin to ridicule him, 30 saying, 'This fellow began to build and was not able to finish.' 31 Or what king, going out to wage war against another king, will not sit down first and consider whether he is able with ten thousand to oppose the one who comes against him with twenty thousand? 32 If he cannot, then, while the other is still far away, he sends a delegation and asks for the terms of peace. 33 So therefore, none of you can become my disciple if you do not give up all your possessions.

---

[l] Gk he   [m] The Greek word for you here is plural

PRAY IT!

Spice Me Up, Lord

Lord, I want to be where I can make a difference, where I can spice up another person's life by bringing him or her the good news of your love and justice.

Help me discover all the gifts you have graced me with so that I can help turn this world around—starting with my own life! Show me how to keep fresh in my commitment to serve you each day. Amen.

▶ Lk 14.34–35

Lost and Found

Who hasn't been lost at some point in life? Everyone can identify with the frustration, fear, and loneliness that come with being lost. Which means that everyone can also identify with being found! What a wonderful feeling it is to finally see the familiar landmark or to make the right turn to the main road or to have someone help you get your life back on track.

If you identify with that lone sheep who strayed from the flock (Lk 15.1–7), remember that God never stops looking for you. Maybe all you need to do is stop and listen for God's call so that God can embrace you and celebrate your return.

Talk to God now about the recent experiences that have led you astray and have made you feel lost. Let God hold you tight and lift you high as the divine shepherd celebrates your return.

▶ Lk 15.1–7

L
K

About Salt
(Mt 5.13; Mk 9.50)

34 "Salt is good; but if salt has lost its taste, how can its saltiness be restored?[n] 35 It is fit neither for the soil nor for the manure pile; they throw it away. Let anyone with ears to hear listen!"

The Parable of the Lost Sheep
(Mt 18.10–14)

Now all the tax collectors and sinners were coming near to listen to him. 2 And the Phar′i•sees and the scribes were grumbling and saying, "This fellow welcomes sinners and eats with them."

3 So he told them this parable: 4 "Which one of you, having a hundred sheep and losing one of them, does not leave the ninety-nine in the wilderness and go after the one that is lost until he finds it? 5 When he has found it, he lays it on his shoulders and rejoices. 6 And when he comes home, he calls together his friends and neighbors, saying to them, 'Rejoice with me, for I have found my sheep that was lost.' 7 Just so, I tell you, there will be more joy in heaven over one sinner who repents than over ninety-nine righteous persons who need no repentance.

The Parable of the Lost Coin

8 "Or what woman having ten silver coins,[o] if she loses one of them, does not light a lamp, sweep the house, and search carefully until she finds it? 9 When she has found it, she calls together her friends and neighbors, saying, 'Rejoice with me, for I have found the coin that I had lost.' 10 Just so, I tell you, there is joy in the presence of the angels of God over one sinner who repents."

The Parable of the Prodigal and His Brother

11 Then Jesus[p] said, "There was a man who had two sons. 12 The younger of them said to his father, 'Father, give me the share of the property that will belong to me.' So he divided his property between them. 13 A few days later the younger son gathered all he had and traveled to a distant country, and there he squandered his property in dissolute living. 14 When he had spent everything, a severe famine took place throughout that country, and he began to be in need. 15 So he went and hired himself out to one of the citizens of that country, who sent him to his fields to feed the pigs. 16 He would gladly have filled himself with[q] the pods that the pigs were eating; and no one gave him anything. 17 But when he came to himself he said, 'How many of my father's hired hands have bread enough and to spare, but here I am dying of hunger! 18 I will get up and go to my father, and I will say to him, "Father, I have sinned against heaven and before you; 19 I am no longer worthy to be called your son; treat me like one of your hired hands." ' 20 So he set off and went to his father. But while he was still far off, his father saw him and was filled with compassion; he ran and put his arms around him and kissed him. 21 Then the son said to him, 'Father, I have sinned against heaven and before you; I am no longer worthy to be called your son.'[r] 22 But the father said to his slaves, 'Quickly, bring out a robe—the best one—and put it on him; put a ring on his finger and

n Or how can it be used for seasoning?   o Gk drachmas, each worth about a day's wage for a laborer   p Gk he q Other ancient authorities read filled his stomach with r Other ancient authorities add Treat me like one of your hired servants

15.20

sandals on his feet. 23 And get the fatted calf and kill it, and let us eat and celebrate; 24 for this son of mine was dead and is alive again; he was lost and is found!' And they began to celebrate.

25 "Now his elder son was in the field; and when he came and approached the house, he heard music and dancing. 26 He called one of the slaves and asked what was going on. 27 He replied, 'Your brother has come, and your father has killed the fatted calf, because he has got him back safe and sound.' 28 Then he became angry and refused to go in. His father came out and began to plead with him. 29 But he answered his father, 'Listen! For all these years I have been working like a slave for you, and I have never disobeyed your command; yet you have never given me even a young goat so that I might celebrate with my friends. 30 But when this son of yours came back, who has devoured your property with prostitutes, you killed the fatted calf for him!' 31 Then the father[s] said to him, 'Son, you are always with me, and all that is mine is yours. 32 But we had to celebrate and rejoice, because this brother of yours was dead and has come to life; he was lost and has been found.' "

The Parable of the Dishonest Manager

Then Jesus[s] said to the disciples, "There was a rich man who had a manager, and charges were brought to him that this man was squandering his property. 2 So he summoned him and said to him, 'What is this that I hear about you? Give me an accounting of your management, because you cannot be my manager any longer.' 3 Then the manager said to himself, 'What will I do, now that my master is taking the position away from me? I am not strong enough to dig, and I am ashamed to beg. 4 I have decided what to do so that, when I am dismissed as manager, people may welcome me into their homes.' 5 So, summoning his mas-

---

[s] Gk he

God's Limitless Love

The parable of the prodigal son in Lk 15.11–32 is one of the best-known stories told by Jesus. It contains many experiences and feelings that we can relate to: rebellion, independence, regret, jealousy, love, and forgiveness.

It also has characters that we can relate to strongly: The father who knows he must let his son go to make his own life but cannot help worrying about his safety. The younger son whose only goal is to have a good time—until he hits hard reality and recognizes that he must depend on the love of his father. The angry, conservative older son who is jealous of the special treatment his lazy and greedy younger brother gets from his father, not realizing there is no limit to his father's love for both of them.

What about you and me? Doesn't our relationship with God sometimes mean coming back after a period of ignoring or avoiding God? At times, don't we have to look honestly at our situation and admit that we have been trying to make it on our own, without God's help? It takes courage to trust in the love of God, who, like the father in this story, is always enthusiastically looking for us to come home. Jesus used the prodigal son image and others—like the shepherd searching for his lost sheep (verses 1–7) and the woman carefully combing her house in search of a lost coin (verses 8–10)—to demonstrate how eagerly God wants to be in a good relationship with us. Amen. Alleluia!

▶ Lk 15.11–32

ter's debtors one by one, he asked the first, 'How much do you owe my master?' 6 He answered, 'A hundred jugs of olive oil.' He said to him, 'Take your bill, sit down quickly, and make it fifty.' 7 Then he asked another, 'And how much do you owe?' He replied, 'A hundred containers of wheat.' He said to him, 'Take your bill and make it eighty.' 8 And his master commended the dishonest manager because he had acted shrewdly; for the children of this age are more shrewd in dealing with their own generation than are the children of light. 9 And I tell you, make friends for yourselves by means of dishonest wealth[t] so that when it is gone, they may welcome you into the eternal homes.[u]

10 "Whoever is faithful in a very little is faithful also in much; and whoever is dishonest in a very little is dishonest also in much. 11 If then you have not been faithful with the dishonest wealth,[t] who will entrust to you the true riches? 12 And if you have not been faithful with what belongs to another, who will give you what is your own? 13 No slave can serve two masters; for a slave will either hate the one and love the other, or be devoted to the one and despise the other. You cannot serve God and wealth."[t]

The Law and the Kingdom of God

14 The Phar'i·sees, who were lovers of money, heard all this, and they ridiculed him. 15 So he said to them, "You are those who justify yourselves in the sight of others; but God knows your hearts; for what is prized by human beings is an abomination in the sight of God.

16 "The law and the prophets were in effect until John came; since then the good news of the kingdom of God is proclaimed, and everyone tries to enter it by force.[v] 17 But it is easier for heaven and earth to pass away, than for one stroke of a letter in the law to be dropped.

18 "Anyone who divorces his wife and marries another commits adultery, and whoever marries a woman divorced from her husband commits adultery.

The Rich Man and Lazarus

19 "There was a rich man who was dressed in purple and fine linen and who feasted sumptuously every day. 20 And at his gate lay a poor man named Laz'a·rus, covered with sores, 21 who longed to satisfy his hunger with what fell from the rich man's table; even the dogs would come and lick his sores. 22 The poor man died and was carried away by the angels to be with Abraham.[w] The rich man also died and was buried. 23 In Hades, where he was being tormented, he looked up and saw

did you KNOW?

Understanding Parables

In some of Jesus' parables, the characters represent someone else. For example, in the parable of the prodigal son (Lk 15.11–32), the forgiving father represents God. In other parables, the characters are examples for us to follow, as in the parable of the good Samaritan (10.25–37). However, in some parables, the characters neither represent God nor are role models for us.

For example, in the parable of the dishonest manager (16.1–13), the master doesn't represent God. And Jesus is not encouraging us to be dishonest like the manager. Jesus is simply saying we need to be even more clever than dishonest people in using our money and talents for the sake of the Gospel.

For more on understanding the parables, see "Parables," Mt 13.10.

▶ Lk 16.1–13

Abraham far away with Laz'a·rus by his side.[x] 24 He called out, 'Father Abraham, have mercy on me, and send Laz'a·rus to dip the tip of his finger in water and cool my tongue; for I am in agony in these flames.' 25 But Abraham said, 'Child, remember that during your lifetime you received your good things, and Laz'a·rus in like manner evil things; but now he is comforted here, and you are in agony. 26 Besides all this, between you and us a great chasm has been fixed, so that those who might want to pass from here to you cannot do so, and no one can cross from there to us.' 27 He said, 'Then, father, I beg you to send him to my father's house— 28 for I have five brothers—that he may warn them, so that they will not also come into this place of torment.' 29 Abraham replied, 'They have Moses and the prophets; they should listen to them.' 30 He said, 'No, father Abraham; but if someone goes to them from the dead, they will repent.' 31 He said to him, 'If they do not listen to Moses and the prophets, neither will they be convinced even if someone rises from the dead.' "

---

t Gk mammon   u Gk tents   v Or everyone is strongly urged to enter it   w Gk to Abraham's bosom   x Gk in his bosom

Some Sayings of Jesus
(Mt 18.6–9; Mk 9.42–48)

Jesus[y] said to his disciples, "Occasions for stumbling are bound to come, but woe to anyone by whom they come! [2] It would be better for you if a millstone were hung around your neck and you were thrown into the sea than for you to cause one of these little ones to stumble. [3] Be on your guard! If another disciple[z] sins, you must rebuke the offender, and if there is repentance, you must forgive. [4] And if the same person sins against you seven times a day, and turns back to you seven times and says, 'I repent,' you must forgive."

[5] The apostles said to the Lord, "Increase our faith!" [6] The Lord replied, "If you had faith the size of a[a] mustard seed, you could say to this mulberry tree, 'Be uprooted and planted in the sea,' and it would obey you.

[7] "Who among you would say to your slave who has just come in from plowing or tending sheep in the field, 'Come here at once and take your place at the table'? [8] Would you not rather say to him, 'Prepare supper for me, put on your apron and serve me while I eat and drink; later you may eat and drink'? [9] Do you thank the slave for doing what was commanded? [10] So you also, when you have done all that you were ordered to do, say, 'We are worthless slaves; we have done only what we ought to have done!' "

Jesus Cleanses Ten Lepers

[11] On the way to Jerusalem Jesus[b] was going through the region between Sa·mār'i·a and Galilee. [12] As he entered a village, ten lepers[c] approached him. Keeping their distance, [13] they called out, saying, "Jesus, Master, have mercy on us!" [14] When he saw them, he said to them, "Go and show yourselves to the priests." And as they went, they were made clean. [15] Then one of them, when he saw that he was healed, turned back, praising God with a loud voice. [16] He prostrated himself at Jesus'[d] feet and thanked him. And he was a Sa·mar'i·tan. [17] Then Jesus asked, "Were not ten made clean? But the other nine, where are they? [18] Was none of them found to return and give praise to God except this foreigner?" [19] Then he said to him, "Get up and go on your way; your faith has made you well."

The Coming of the Kingdom
(Gen 6.5–8.22; 19.12–14)

[20] Once Jesus[b] was asked by the Phar'i·sees when the kingdom of God was coming, and he answered, "The kingdom of God is not coming with things that can be observed; [21] nor will they

say, 'Look, here it is!' or 'There it is!' For, in fact, the kingdom of God is among[e] you."

[22] Then he said to the disciples, "The days are coming when you will long to see one of the days of the Son of Man, and you will not see it. [23] They will say to you, 'Look there!' or 'Look here!' Do not go, do not set off in pursuit. [24] For as the lightning flashes and lights up the sky from one side to the other, so will the Son of Man be in his day.[f] [25] But first he must endure much suffering and be rejected by this generation. [26] Just as it was in the days of Noah, so too it will be in the days of the Son of Man. [27] They were eating and drinking, and marrying and being given in marriage, until the day Noah entered the ark, and the flood came and destroyed all of them. [28] Likewise, just as it was in the days of Lot: they were eating and drinking, buying and selling, planting and building, [29] but on the day that Lot left Sod'om, it rained fire and sulfur from heaven and destroyed all of them [30] —it will be like that on the day that the Son of Man is revealed. [31] On that day, anyone on the housetop who has belongings in the house must not come down to take them away; and likewise anyone in the field must not turn back. [32] Remember Lot's wife. [33] Those who try to make their life secure will lose it, but those who lose their life will keep it. [34] I tell you, on that night there will be two in one bed; one will be taken and the other left. [35] There will be two women grinding meal together; one

---

[y] Gk *He*   [z] Gk *your brother*   [a] Gk *faith as a grain of*   [b] Gk *he*   [c] The terms *leper* and *leprosy* can refer to several diseases   [d] Gk *his*   [e] Or *within*   [f] Other ancient authorities lack *in his day*

PRAY IT?
Can You Hear Me, Lord?

Dear God, Jesus had to remind people to pray always and not to lose hope when faced with injustice. I need to hear that too. Sometimes it seems like I pray and pray, but you are not answering.

I know that I have to be willing to look and listen for your response. I know that I have to pray always, not just in times of need. I know I need to share my daily life with you. Help me to do these things I know I need to do. Help me to pray, Lord. Amen.

▶ Lk 18.1–8

will be taken and the other left."[g] 37 Then they asked him, "Where, Lord?" He said to them, "Where the corpse is, there the vultures will gather."

The Parable of the Widow and the Unjust Judge

Then Jesus[h] told them a parable about their need to pray always and not to lose heart. 2 He said, "In a certain city there was a judge who neither feared God nor had respect for people. 3 In that city there was a widow who kept coming to him and saying, 'Grant me justice against my opponent.' 4 For a while he refused; but later he said to himself, 'Though I have no fear of God and no respect for anyone, 5 yet because this widow keeps bothering me, I will grant her justice, so that she may not wear me out by continually coming.'"[i] 6 And the Lord said, "Listen to what the unjust judge says. 7 And will not God grant justice to his chosen ones who cry to him day and night? Will he delay long in helping them? 8 I tell you, he will quickly grant justice to them. And yet, when the Son of Man comes, will he find faith on earth?"

The Parable of the Pharisee and the Tax Collector

9 He also told this parable to some who trusted in themselves that they were righteous and regarded others with contempt: 10 "Two men went up to the temple to pray, one a Phar′i•see and the other a tax collector. 11 The Phar′i•see, standing by himself, was praying thus, 'God, I thank you that I am not like other people: thieves, rogues, adulterers, or even like this tax collector. 12 I fast twice a week; I give a tenth of all my income.' 13 But the tax collector, standing far off, would not even look up to heaven, but was beating his breast and saying, 'God, be merciful to me, a sinner!' 14 I tell you, this man went down to his home justified rather than the other; for all who exalt themselves will be humbled, but all who humble themselves will be exalted."

Jesus Blesses Little Children
(Mt 19.13–15; Mk 10.13–16)

15 People were bringing even infants to him that he might touch them; and when the disciples saw it, they sternly ordered them not to do it. 16 But Jesus called for them and said, "Let the little children come to me, and do not stop them; for it is to such as these that the kingdom of God belongs. 17 Truly I tell you, whoever does not receive the kingdom of God as a little child will never enter it."

The Rich Ruler
(Mt 19.16–30; Mk 10.17–31)

18 A certain ruler asked him, "Good Teacher, what must I do to inherit eternal life?" 19 Jesus said to him, "Why do you call me good? No one is good but God alone. 20 You know the commandments: 'You shall not commit adultery; You shall not murder; You shall not steal; You shall not bear false witness; Honor your father and mother.' " 21 He replied, "I have kept all these since my

---

g Other ancient authorities add verse 36, "Two will be in the field; one will be taken and the other left."　　h Gk he　　i Or so that she may not finally come and slap me in the face

The Loaded Question

LIVE IT!

If you ask a loaded question, you should expect a loaded answer, especially if you're asking God! Picture the rich ruler in Lk 18.18–30, proud that he has closely and devoutly followed the Commandments all his life. Is it eagerness or conceit that makes him ask Jesus, "What must I do?"

Jesus' answer, "Sell all that you own and distribute the money to the poor," must have been like a blow. Jesus asked a radical commitment from this rich ruler, just as Jesus asks a radical commitment from us. As often happens in Luke's portrayal of Jesus, that radical commitment has something to do with wealth and the poor (verse 22). If we dare to ask the loaded question, "What must I do?" we must be prepared to unload something too. Our human tendency is to hoard our money and our material goods. But with God's help (verse 27), we can become generous with those in need.

▶ Lk 18.18–30

Noticed by Jesus

Why would Jesus choose Zacchaeus, who was hated and despised as a tax collector, to become a disciple? Besides that, he was pretty short and did not stand out in a crowd. Perhaps Luke is trying to tell us that our physical attributes, our past history, and other people's perceptions do not figure into God's equation. This is good news to the 98 percent of us who do not qualify as Ms. or Mr. Popularity.

When Jesus notices Zacchaeus, Zacchaeus ends up not only believing in Jesus but also doing something surprising. He gives away half of his money and possessions, perhaps to make up for all the times he cheated people. This is what conversion is—a change of heart and behavior. Conversion calls us to act in ways we would not have acted before.

Jesus has been with you from the moment of your conception. How have you tried to know him better? How do you feel knowing that he sees past externals and loves you for who you truly are?

▶ Lk 19.1–10

youth." 22 When Jesus heard this, he said to him, "There is still one thing lacking. Sell all that you own and distribute the money[j] to the poor, and you will have treasure in heaven; then come, follow me." 23 But when he heard this, he became sad; for he was very rich. 24 Jesus looked at him and said, "How hard it is for those who have wealth to enter the kingdom of God! 25 Indeed, it is easier for a camel to go through the eye of a needle than for someone who is rich to enter the kingdom of God."

26 Those who heard it said, "Then who can be saved?" 27 He replied, "What is impossible for mortals is possible for God."

28 Then Peter said, "Look, we have left our homes and followed you." 29 And he said to them, "Truly I tell you, there is no one who has left house or wife or brothers or parents or children, for the sake of the kingdom of God, 30 who will not get back very much more in this age, and in the age to come eternal life."

A Third Time Jesus Foretells His Death and Resurrection
(Mt 20.17–19; Mk 10.32–34)

31 Then he took the twelve aside and said to them, "See, we are going up to Jerusalem, and everything that is written about the Son of Man by the prophets will be accomplished. 32 For he will be handed over to the Gentiles; and he will be mocked and insulted and spat upon. 33 After they have flogged him, they will kill him, and on the third day he will rise again." 34 But they understood nothing about all these things; in fact, what he said was hidden from them, and they did not grasp what was said.

Jesus Heals a Blind Beggar Near Jericho
(Mt 20.29–34; Mk 10.46–52)

35 As he approached Jericho, a blind man was sitting by the roadside begging. 36 When he heard a crowd going by, he asked what was happening. 37 They told him, "Jesus of Nazareth[k] is passing by." 38 Then he shouted, "Jesus, Son of David, have mercy on me!" 39 Those who were in front sternly ordered him to be quiet; but he shouted even more loudly, "Son of David, have mercy on me!" 40 Jesus stood still and ordered the man to be brought to him; and when he came near, he asked him, 41 "What do you want me to do for you?" He said, "Lord, let me see again." 42 Jesus said to him, "Receive your sight; your faith has saved you." 43 Immediately he regained his sight and followed him, glorifying God; and all the people, when they saw it, praised God.

Jesus and Zacchaeus

He entered Jericho and was passing through it. 2 A man was there named Zac·chae'us; he was a chief tax collector and was rich. 3 He was trying to see who Jesus was, but on account of the crowd he could not, because he was short in stature. 4 So he ran ahead and climbed a sycamore tree to see him, because he was going to pass that way. 5 When Jesus came to the place, he looked up and said to him, "Zac·chae'us, hurry and come down; for I must stay at your house today." 6 So he hurried down and was happy to welcome him. 7 All who saw it began to grumble and said, "He has gone to be the guest of one who is a sinner." 8 Zac·chae'us stood there and said to the Lord, "Look, half of

---

j Gk lacks *the money*   k Gk *the Nazorean*

my possessions, Lord, I will give to the poor; and if I have defrauded anyone of anything, I will pay back four times as much." 9 Then Jesus said to him, "Today salvation has come to this house, because he too is a son of Abraham. 10 For the Son of Man came to seek out and to save the lost."

The Parable of the Ten Pounds
(Mt 25.14–30)

11 As they were listening to this, he went on to tell a parable, because he was near Jerusalem, and because they supposed that the kingdom of God was to appear immediately. 12 So he said, "A no-bleman went to a distant country to get royal power for himself and then return. 13 He sum-moned ten of his slaves, and gave them ten pounds,^{l} and said to them, 'Do business with these until I come back.' 14 But the citizens of his country hated him and sent a delegation after him, saying, 'We do not want this man to rule over us.' 15 When he returned, having received royal power, he ordered these slaves, to whom he had given the money, to be summoned so that he might find out what they had gained by trading. 16 The first came forward and said, 'Lord, your pound has made ten more pounds.' 17 He said to him, 'Well done, good slave! Because you have been trustworthy in a very small thing, take charge of ten cities.' 18 Then the second came, saying, 'Lord, your pound has made five pounds.' 19 He said to him, 'And you, rule over five cities.' 20 Then the other came, saying, 'Lord, here is your pound. I wrapped it up in a piece of cloth, 21 for I was afraid of you, because you are a harsh man; you take what you did not deposit, and reap what you did not sow.' 22 He said to him, 'I will judge you by your own words, you wicked slave! You knew, did you, that I was a harsh man, taking what I did not deposit and reaping what I did not sow? 23 Why then did you not put my money into the bank? Then when I returned, I could have collected it with interest.' 24 He said to the bystanders, 'Take the pound from him and give it to the one who has ten pounds.' 25 (And they said to him, 'Lord, he has ten pounds!') 26 'I tell you, to all those who have, more will be given; but from those who have nothing, even what they have will be taken away. 27 But as for these enemies of mine who did not want me to be king over them—bring them here and slaughter them in my presence.' "

Jesus' Triumphal Entry into Jerusalem
(Mt 21.1–11; Mk 11.1–11; Jn 12.12–19)

28 After he had said this, he went on ahead, going up to Jerusalem.

29 When he had come near Beth′pha•gē and Beth′a•ny, at the place called the Mount of Olives, he sent two of the disciples, 30 saying, "Go into the

---

l The mina, rendered here by *pound*, was about three months' wages for a laborer

JESUS GOES TO JERUSALEM AS THE MESSIAH!

As Jesus enters Jerusalem to celebrate the Passover, the crowd joyfully hails him as the king and Messiah returning to the City of David. He is the prophet who brings new hope and calls people to conversion.

On Palm Sunday—also known as Passion Sunday—we begin our preparation for Holy Week. At Mass, we receive blessed branches of palms to symbolize our profession of Jesus as the Messiah, king of peace. In some Hispanic communities, the palms are woven into beautiful braids, crosses, and flowers. In others, people receive a small donkey made of palm leaves, as a remembrance of Jesus' riding the donkey into Jerusalem. Often, his entrance into Jerusalem is re-enacted. Hispanics use art, song, and drama to celebrate and express their faith.

■ **Picture yourself in the crowd welcoming Jesus. Does Jesus' coming fill you with joy and hope?**

■ **Next Palm Sunday, find a special place for your palm. Think of a concrete way you will live out your calling as a disciple of Jesus in the coming year. Each time you see the palm, remember your call and pray for help to respond to it.**

▶ Lk 19.29–38

village ahead of you, and as you enter it you will find tied there a colt that has never been ridden. Untie it and bring it here. 31 If anyone asks you, 'Why are you untying it?' just say this, 'The Lord needs it.' " 32 So those who were sent departed and

did you KNOW?

The Human Jesus

Have you ever been so disappointed in something that you just sat down and wept? That's what happened to Jesus. In Lk 19.41–42, we hear of his great disappointment and frustration that he cannot help Jerusalem and its people. The people of Jerusalem do not accept his message of justice and peace, so the Temple and Jerusalem are to be destroyed again. Jesus is so upset that he weeps.

We often forget that although Jesus is fully God, he is also fully human and experienced all the things that normal people experience. He enjoyed excitement, laughter, and fun times with friends. He also experienced fear, sadness, and frustration. He was completely human in all things but sin.

What does it mean to you that Jesus shares our humanity? Why is Jesus' humanity an important part of the Christian message?

▶ Lk 19.41–42

found it as he had told them. 33 As they were untying the colt, its owners asked them, "Why are you untying the colt?" 34 They said, "The Lord needs it." 35 Then they brought it to Jesus; and after throwing their cloaks on the colt, they set Jesus on it. 36 As he rode along, people kept spreading their cloaks on the road. 37 As he was now approaching the path down from the Mount of Olives, the whole multitude of the disciples began to praise God joyfully with a loud voice for all the deeds of power that they had seen, 38 saying,

"Blessed is the king
 who comes in the name of the Lord!
Peace in heaven,
 and glory in the highest heaven!"

39 Some of the Phar'i·sees in the crowd said to him, "Teacher, order your disciples to stop." 40 He an-

swered, "I tell you, if these were silent, the stones would shout out."

Jesus Weeps over Jerusalem

41 As he came near and saw the city, he wept over it, 42 saying, "If you, even you, had only recognized on this day the things that make for peace! But now they are hidden from your eyes. 43 Indeed, the days will come upon you, when your enemies will set up ramparts around you and surround you, and hem you in on every side. 44 They will crush you to the ground, you and your children within you, and they will not leave within you one stone upon another; because you did not recognize the time of your visitation from God."m

Jesus Cleanses the Temple
(Mt 21.12–17; Mk 11.15–19; Jn 2.12–25)

45 Then he entered the temple and began to drive out those who were selling things there; 46 and he said, "It is written,

'My house shall be a house of prayer';

 but you have made it a den of robbers."

47 Every day he was teaching in the temple. The chief priests, the scribes, and the leaders of the people kept looking for a way to kill him; 48 but they did not find anything they could do, for all the people were spellbound by what they heard.

The Authority of Jesus Questioned
(Mt 21.23–27; Mk 11.27–33)

One day, as he was teaching the people in the temple and telling the good news, the chief priests and the scribes came with the elders 2 and said to him, "Tell us, by what authority are you doing these things? Who is it who gave you this authority?" 3 He answered them, "I will also ask you a question, and you tell me: 4 Did the baptism of John come from heaven, or was it of human origin?" 5 They discussed it with one another, saying, "If we say, 'From heaven,' he will say, 'Why did you not believe him?' 6 But if we say, 'Of human origin,' all the people will stone us; for they are convinced that John was a prophet." 7 So they answered that they did not know where it came from. 8 Then Jesus said to them, "Neither will I tell you by what authority I am doing these things."

The Parable of the Wicked Tenants
(Mt 21.33–46; Mk 12.1–12)

9 He began to tell the people this parable: "A man planted a vineyard, and leased it to tenants, and went to another country for a long time. 10 When the season came, he sent a slave to the

m Gk lacks from God

tenants in order that they might give him his share of the produce of the vineyard; but the tenants beat him and sent him away empty-handed. 11 Next he sent another slave; that one also they beat and insulted and sent away empty-handed. 12 And he sent still a third; this one also they wounded and threw out. 13 Then the owner of the vineyard said, 'What shall I do? I will send my beloved son; perhaps they will respect him.' 14 But when the tenants saw him, they discussed it among themselves and said, 'This is the heir; let us kill him so that the inheritance may be ours.' 15 So they threw him out of the vineyard and killed him. What then will the owner of the vineyard do to them? 16 He will come and destroy those tenants and give the vineyard to others." When they heard this, they said, "Heaven forbid!" 17 But he looked at them and said, "What then does this text mean:

'The stone that the builders rejected
    has become the cornerstone'?n

18 Everyone who falls on that stone will be broken to pieces; and it will crush anyone on whom it falls." 19 When the scribes and chief priests realized that he had told this parable against them, they wanted to lay hands on him at that very hour, but they feared the people.

The Question about Paying Taxes
(Mt 22.15–22; Mk 12.13–17)

20 So they watched him and sent spies who pretended to be honest, in order to trap him by what he said, so as to hand him over to the jurisdiction and authority of the governor. 21 So they asked him, "Teacher, we know that you are right in what you say and teach, and you show deference to no one, but teach the way of God in accordance with truth. 22 Is it lawful for us to pay taxes to the emperor, or not?" 23 But he perceived their craftiness and said to them, 24 "Show me a denarius. Whose head and whose title does it bear?" They said, "The emperor's." 25 He said to them, "Then give to the emperor the things that are the emperor's, and to God the things that are God's." 26 And they were not able in the presence of the people to trap him by what he said; and being amazed by his answer, they became silent.

The Question about the Resurrection
(Mt 22.23–33; Mk 12.18–27)

27 Some Sad'du·cees, those who say there is no resurrection, came to him 28 and asked him a question, "Teacher, Moses wrote for us that if a man's brother dies, leaving a wife but no children, the mano shall marry the widow and raise up children for his brother. 29 Now there were seven brothers; the first married, and died childless; 30 then the

second 31 and the third married her, and so in the same way all seven died childless. 32 Finally the woman also died. 33 In the resurrection, therefore, whose wife will the woman be? For the seven had married her."

34 Jesus said to them, "Those who belong to this age marry and are given in marriage; 35 but those who are considered worthy of a place in that age and in the resurrection from the dead neither marry nor are given in marriage. 36 Indeed they cannot die anymore, because they are like angels and are children of God, being children of the resurrection. 37 And the fact that the dead are raised Moses himself showed, in the story about the bush, where he speaks of the Lord as the God of Abraham, the God of Isaac, and the God of Jacob. 38 Now he is God not of the dead, but of the living; for to him all of them are alive." 39 Then some of the scribes answered, "Teacher, you have spoken well." 40 For they no longer dared to ask him another question.

The Question about David's Son
(Mt 22.41–46; Mk 12.35–37)

41 Then he said to them, "How can they say that the Messiahp is David's son? 42 For David himself says in the book of Psalms,

'The Lord said to my Lord,
    "Sit at my right hand,
43   until I make your enemies your
            footstool."'

44 David thus calls him Lord; so how can he be his son?"

Jesus Denounces the Scribes
(Mt 23.1–7; Mk 12.38–40)

45 In the hearing of all the people he said to theq disciples, 46 "Beware of the scribes, who like to walk around in long robes, and love to be greeted with respect in the marketplaces, and to have the best seats in the synagogues and places of honor at banquets. 47 They devour widows' houses and for the sake of appearance say long prayers. They will receive the greater condemnation."

The Widow's Offering
(Mk 12.41–44)

He looked up and saw rich people putting their gifts into the treasury; 2 he also saw a poor widow put in two small copper coins. 3 He said, "Truly I tell you, this poor widow has put in more than all of them; 4 for all of them have contributed out of

---

n Or keystone   o Gk his brother   p Or the Christ
q Other ancient authorities read his

Stewardship: Making a Contribution

In Lk 21.1–4, Jesus notices that the rich people gave from their excess wealth, but the widow gave from her limited budget. She actually contributed more meaningfully because she gave from what little she had.

God calls us to be contributing members of the faith community and the human family—even to the point of sacrifice. We are called to stewardship, which means giving our time, talents, and treasure to support the church's mission to spread the Good News of Jesus Christ. We should also support other organizations that contribute to the positive welfare of all people in need.

How are you responding to God's call to give? Pray for the generosity of the poor widow as you discern how much of your time, talents, and treasure you are being called to give.

▸ Lk 21.1–4

L
K

their abundance, but she out of her poverty has put in all she had to live on."

The Destruction of the Temple Foretold
(Mt 24.1–2; Mk 13.1–2)

5 When some were speaking about the temple, how it was adorned with beautiful stones and gifts dedicated to God, he said, 6 "As for these things that you see, the days will come when not one stone will be left upon another; all will be thrown down."

Signs and Persecutions
(Mt 24.3–14; Mk 13.3–13)

7 They asked him, "Teacher, when will this be, and what will be the sign that this is about to take place?" 8 And he said, "Beware that you are not led astray; for many will come in my name and say, 'I am he!'ʳ and, 'The time is near!'ˢ Do not go after them.

9 "When you hear of wars and insurrections, do not be terrified; for these things must take place first, but the end will not follow immediately." 10 Then he said to them, "Nation will rise against nation, and kingdom against kingdom; 11 there will be great earthquakes, and in various places famines and plagues; and there will be dreadful portents and great signs from heaven.

12 "But before all this occurs, they will arrest you and persecute you; they will hand you over to synagogues and prisons, and you will be brought before kings and governors because of my name. 13 This will give you an opportunity to testify. 14 So make up your minds not to prepare your defense in advance; 15 for I will give you wordsᵗ and a wisdom that none of your opponents will be able to withstand or contradict. 16 You will be betrayed

even by parents and brothers, by relatives and friends; and they will put some of you to death. 17 You will be hated by all because of my name. 18 But not a hair of your head will perish. 19 By your endurance you will gain your souls.

The Destruction of Jerusalem Foretold
(Mt 24.15–28; Mk 13.14–23)

20 "When you see Jerusalem surrounded by armies, then know that its desolation has come near.ᵘ 21 Then those in Judea must flee to the mountains, and those inside the city must leave it, and those out in the country must not enter it; 22 for these are days of vengeance, as a fulfillment of all that is written. 23 Woe to those who are pregnant and to those who are nursing infants in those days! For there will be great distress on the earth and wrath against this people; 24 they will fall by the edge of the sword and be taken away as captives among all nations; and Jerusalem will be trampled on by the Gentiles, until the times of the Gentiles are fulfilled.

The Coming of the Son of Man
(Mt 24.29–31; Mk 13.24–27)

25 "There will be signs in the sun, the moon, and the stars, and on the earth distress among nations confused by the roaring of the sea and the waves. 26 People will faint from fear and foreboding of what is coming upon the world, for the powers of the heavens will be shaken. 27 Then they will see 'the Son of Man coming in a cloud' with power and great glory. 28 Now when these things begin to take place, stand up and raise your heads, because your redemption is drawing near."

ʳ Gk I am   ˢ Or at hand   ᵗ Gk a mouth   ᵘ Or is at hand

The Lesson of the Fig Tree
(Mt 24.32–35; Mk 13.28–31)

29 Then he told them a parable: "Look at the fig tree and all the trees; 30 as soon as they sprout leaves you can see for yourselves and know that summer is already near. 31 So also, when you see these things taking place, you know that the kingdom of God is near. 32 Truly I tell you, this generation will not pass away until all things have taken place. 33 Heaven and earth will pass away, but my words will not pass away.

Exhortation to Watch
(Mt 24.36–44; Mk 13.32–37)

34 "Be on guard so that your hearts are not weighed down with dissipation and drunkenness and the worries of this life, and that day does not catch you unexpectedly, 35 like a trap. For it will come upon all who live on the face of the whole earth. 36 Be alert at all times, praying that you may have the strength to escape all these things that will take place, and to stand before the Son of Man."

37 Every day he was teaching in the temple, and at night he would go out and spend the night on the Mount of Olives, as it was called. 38 And all the people would get up early in the morning to listen to him in the temple.

The Plot to Kill Jesus
(Mt 26.1–5, 14–16; Mk 14.1–2, 10–11; Jn 11.45–53)

22 Now the festival of Unleavened Bread, which is called the Passover, was near. 2 The chief priests and the scribes were looking for a way to put Jesus*ᵛ* to death, for they were afraid of the people.

3 Then Satan entered into Judas called Is·car'i·ot, who was one of the twelve; 4 he went away and conferred with the chief priests and officers of the temple police about how he might betray him to them. 5 They were greatly pleased and agreed to give him money. 6 So he consented and began to look for an opportunity to betray him to them when no crowd was present.

The Preparation of the Passover
(Mt 26.17–19; Mk 14.12–16)

7 Then came the day of Unleavened Bread, on which the Passover lamb had to be sacrificed. 8 So Jesus*ʷ* sent Peter and John, saying, "Go and prepare the Passover meal for us that we may eat it." 9 They asked him, "Where do you want us to make preparations for it?" 10 "Listen," he said to them, "when you have entered the city, a man carrying a jar of water will meet you; follow him into the

Catholic Connections

THE EUCHARIST

In Luke's account of the Last Supper, Jesus asks his disciples to remember him and all that he did, as they share the loaf of bread that he identified as his body given for us and the cup of wine that he identified with the New Covenant sealed by his blood. The celebration of this great mystery, along with its awesome meaning, is at the center of the eucharistic celebration.

The Eucharist is one of the seven Catholic sacraments, and it is the heart and soul of what it means to be Catholic. It serves as the common celebration of our faith, and it brings together all Catholics—young and old, rich and poor, male and female, and people of all colors, nationalities, and walks of life—to participate in the death and Resurrection of Jesus. In the Eucharist, we are all members of the one Body of Christ. No matter where you go in the world, you can join in celebrating the Eucharist as a member of the Catholic church.

For more on the Eucharist, see the articles for Mt 26.26–29, Mk 14.22–25, Jn 13.1–17.

▶ Lk 22.14–23

house he enters 11 and say to the owner of the house, 'The teacher asks you, "Where is the guest room, where I may eat the Passover with my disciples?"' 12 He will show you a large room upstairs, already furnished. Make preparations for us there." 13 So they went and found everything as he had told them; and they prepared the Passover meal.

The Institution of the Lord's Supper
(Mt 26.20–30; Mk 14.17–26; Jn 13.21–30)

14 When the hour came, he took his place at the table, and the apostles with him. 15 He said to them, "I have eagerly desired to eat this Passover

---

ᵛ Gk *him*   *ʷ* Gk *he*

with you before I suffer; [16] for I tell you, I will not eat it[x] until it is fulfilled in the kingdom of God." [17] Then he took a cup, and after giving thanks he said, "Take this and divide it among yourselves; [18] for I tell you that from now on I will not drink of the fruit of the vine until the kingdom of God comes." [19] Then he took a loaf of bread, and when he had given thanks, he broke it and gave it to them, saying, "This is my body, which is given for you. Do this in remembrance of me." [20] And he did the same with the cup after supper, saying, "This cup that is poured out for you is the new covenant in my blood.[y] [21] But see, the one who betrays me is with me, and his hand is on the table. [22] For the Son of Man is going as it has been determined, but woe to that one by whom he is betrayed!" [23] Then they began to ask one another which one of them it could be who would do this.

The Dispute about Greatness

[24] A dispute also arose among them as to which one of them was to be regarded as the greatest. [25] But he said to them, "The kings of the Gentiles lord it over them; and those in authority over them are called benefactors. [26] But not so with you; rather the greatest among you must become like the youngest, and the leader like one who serves. [27] For who is greater, the one who is at the table or the one who serves? Is it not the one at the table? But I am among you as one who serves.

PRAY IT!
Prayer of a Servant Leader

Dear Jesus, you made it clear that those who are greatest are the ones who serve, not the ones who have fame, fortune, or authority. Help me adjust my priorities to put others first. Place within me a genuine desire to serve. Enable me to recognize the daily opportunities I have to reach out to those in need in my family, in my school, and in my community. Guide me as I strive to follow your example to become a servant leader. Amen.

▶ Lk 22.24–27

[28] "You are those who have stood by me in my trials; [29] and I confer on you, just as my Father has conferred on me, a kingdom, [30] so that you may eat and drink at my table in my kingdom, and you will sit on thrones judging the twelve tribes of Israel.

Jesus Predicts Peter's Denial
(Mt 26.31–35; Mk 14.27–31; Jn 13.36–38)

[31] "Simon, Simon, listen! Satan has demanded[z] to sift all of you like wheat, [32] but I have prayed for you that your own faith may not fail; and you, when once you have turned back, strengthen your brothers." [33] And he said to him, "Lord, I am ready to go with you to prison and to death!" [34] Jesus[a] said, "I tell you, Peter, the cock will not crow this day, until you have denied three times that you know me."

Purse, Bag, and Sword

[35] He said to them, "When I sent you out without a purse, bag, or sandals, did you lack anything?" They said, "No, not a thing." [36] He said to them, "But now, the one who has a purse must take it, and likewise a bag. And the one who has no sword must sell his cloak and buy one. [37] For I tell you, this scripture must be fulfilled in me, 'And he was counted among the lawless'; and indeed what is written about me is being fulfilled." [38] They said, "Lord, look, here are two swords." He replied, "It is enough."

Jesus Prays on the Mount of Olives
(Mt 26.36–46; Mk 14.32–42; Jn 18.1)

[39] He came out and went, as was his custom, to the Mount of Olives; and the disciples followed him. [40] When he reached the place, he said to them, "Pray that you may not come into the time of trial."[b] [41] Then he withdrew from them about a stone's throw, knelt down, and prayed, [42] "Father if you are willing, remove this cup from me; yet, not my will but yours be done." [[43] Then an angel from heaven appeared to him and gave him strength. [44] In his anguish he prayed more earnestly, and his sweat became like great drops of blood falling down on the ground.]][c] [45] When he got up from prayer, he came to the disciples and found them sleeping because of grief, [46] and he said to them, "Why are you sleeping? Get up and pray that you may not come into the time of trial."[b]

---

[x] Other ancient authorities read *never eat it again*   [y] Other ancient authorities lack, in whole or in part, verses 19b-20 (*which is given . . . in my blood*)   [z] Or *has obtained permission*   [a] Gk *He*   [b] Or *into temptation*   [c] Other ancient authorities lack verses 43 and 44

The Betrayal and Arrest of Jesus
(Mt 26.47–56; Mk 14.43–52; Jn 18.1–11)

47 While he was still speaking, suddenly a crowd came, and the one called Judas, one of the twelve, was leading them. He approached Jesus to kiss him; 48 but Jesus said to him, "Judas, is it with a kiss that you are betraying the Son of Man?" 49 When those who were around him saw what was coming, they asked, "Lord, should we strike with the sword?" 50 Then one of them struck the slave of the high priest and cut off his right ear. 51 But Jesus said, "No more of this!" And he touched his ear and healed him. 52 Then Jesus said to the chief priests, the officers of the temple police, and the elders who had come for him, "Have you come out with swords and clubs as if I were a bandit? 53 When I was with you day after day in the temple, you did not lay hands on me. But this is your hour, and the power of darkness!"

22.39

Peter Denies Jesus
(Mt 25.69–75; Mk 14.66–72; Jn 18.15–18, 25–27)

54 Then they seized him and led him away, bringing him into the high priest's house. But Peter was following at a distance. 55 When they had kindled a fire in the middle of the courtyard and sat down together, Peter sat among them. 56 Then a servant-girl, seeing him in the firelight, stared at him and said, "This man also was with him." 57 But he denied it, saying, "Woman, I do not know him." 58 A little later someone else, on seeing him, said, "You also are one of them." But Peter said, "Man, I am not!" 59 Then about an hour later still another kept insisting, "Surely this man also was with him; for he is a Galilean." 60 But Peter said, "Man, I do not know what you are talking about!" At that moment, while he was still speaking, the cock crowed. 61 The Lord turned and looked at Peter. Then Peter remembered the word of the Lord, how he had said to him, "Before the cock crows today, you will deny me three times." 62 And he went out and wept bitterly.

The Mocking and Beating of Jesus
(Mt 26.67–68; Mk 14.65)

63 Now the men who were holding Jesus began to mock him and beat him; 64 they also blindfolded him and kept asking him, "Prophesy! Who is it that struck you?" 65 They kept heaping many other insults on him.

Jesus before the Council
(Mt 26.57–68; Mk 14.61–64; Jn 18.12–14, 19–24)

66 When day came, the assembly of the elders of the people, both chief priests and scribes, gathered together, and they brought him to their council. 67 They said, "If you are the Messiah,*d* tell us." He replied, "If I tell you, you will not believe; 68 and if I question you, you will not answer. 69 But from now on the Son of Man will be seated at the right hand of the power of God." 70 All of them asked, "Are you, then, the Son of God?" He said to them, "You say that I am." 71 Then they said, "What further testimony do we need? We have heard it ourselves from his own lips!"

Jesus before Pilate
(Mt 27.1–2, 11–14; Mk 15.1–5; Jn 18.28–38)

Then the assembly rose as a body and brought Jesus*e* before Pilate. 2 They began to accuse him, saying, "We found this man perverting our nation, forbidding us to pay taxes to the emperor, and saying that he himself is the Messiah, a king."*f* 3 Then Pilate asked him, "Are you the king of the Jews?" He answered, "You say so." 4 Then Pilate said to the chief priests and the crowds, "I find no basis for an accusation against this man." 5 But they were insistent and said, "He stirs up the people by teaching throughout all Judea, from Galilee where he began even to this place."

Jesus before Herod

6 When Pilate heard this, he asked whether the man was a Galilean. 7 And when he learned that he was under Her'od's jurisdiction, he sent him off to Her'od, who was himself in Jerusalem at that time. 8 When Her'od saw Jesus, he was very glad, for he

---

d Or *the Christ*   *e* Gk *him*   *f* Or *is an anointed king*

L
K

did you KNOW?

Luke's Account of Jesus' Death

The stories of Jesus' Passion—the name Christians use to describe his suffering and death—differ in all four Gospels. By comparing these stories, we get insight into the authors' portrayal of Jesus. Let's take a closer look at the perspective in the Gospel of Luke.

First, in Jesus' Passion, Luke describes the openness of Gentiles to Jesus' message of salvation. For example, Pilate finds Jesus innocent three times in Luke (23.4,14,22) and hands him over to be crucified only at the insistence of the Jewish leaders (verse 24). Later, it is a Roman centurion who praises God at the moment of Jesus' death (verse 47).

Second, Luke emphasizes Jesus' compassion and forgiveness, even during his greatest suffering. While carrying the cross, Jesus shows his concern for the women who are following him (verses 28–31). As he is nailed to the cross, he forgives those responsible (verse 34). And when one of the criminals asks for Jesus to remember him, Jesus goes beyond that to promise him the first place in Paradise (verse 43).

Third, Luke emphasizes Jesus' glory and divinity. Whereas Mark portrays Jesus abandoned in his Passion (Mk 15.34), Luke surrounds Jesus with sympathetic people: a crowd including the women of Jerusalem (Lk 23.27), the good thief (verses 40–41), and the centurion (verse 47). In Mark, Jesus feels God's absence (Mk 15.34), but Luke presents Jesus in control even at his death, handing his spirit over to God (Lk 23.46). Luke is making it clear in his portrayal of Jesus' Passion that Jesus is the loving, forgiving savior of all humankind.

▸ Lk 22.47—23.56

at some length, but Jesus[g] gave him no answer. [10]The chief priests and the scribes stood by, vehemently accusing him. [11]Even Her′od with his soldiers treated him with contempt and mocked him; then he put an elegant robe on him, and sent him back to Pilate. [12]That same day Her′od and Pilate became friends with each other; before this they had been enemies.

Jesus Sentenced to Death
(Mt 27.15–26; Mk 15.6–15;
Jn 18.38b—19.16a)

13 Pilate then called together the chief priests, the leaders, and the people, [14]and said to them, "You brought me this man as one who was perverting the people; and here I have examined him in your presence and have not found this man guilty of any of your charges against him. [15]Neither has Her′od, for he sent him back to us. Indeed, he has done nothing to deserve death. [16]I will therefore have him flogged and release him."[h]

18 Then they all shouted out together, "Away with this fellow! Release Ba·rab′bas for us!" [19](This was a man who had been put in prison for an insurrection that had taken place in the city, and for murder.) [20]Pilate, wanting to release Jesus, addressed them again; [21]but they kept shouting, "Crucify, crucify him!" [22]A third time he said to them, "Why, what evil has he done? I have found in him no ground for the sentence of death; I will therefore have him flogged and then release him." [23]But they kept urgently demanding with loud shouts that he should be crucified; and their voices prevailed. [24]So Pilate gave his verdict that their demand should be granted. [25]He released the man they asked for, the one who had been put in prison for insurrection and murder, and he handed Jesus over as they wished.

The Crucifixion of Jesus
(Mt 27.32–44; Mk 15.21–32; Jn 19.16b–24)

26 As they led him away, they seized a man, Simon of Cy·re′ne, who was coming from the country, and they laid the cross on him, and made him carry it behind Jesus. [27]A great number of the people followed him, and among them were women who were beating their breasts and wailing for him. [28]But Jesus turned to them and said, "Daughters of Jerusalem, do not weep for me, but weep for yourselves and for your children. [29]For the days are surely coming when they will say, 'Blessed are the barren, and the wombs that never

had been wanting to see him for a long time, because he had heard about him and was hoping to see him perform some sign. [9]He questioned him

---

[g] Gk he   [h] Here, or after verse 19, other ancient authorities add verse 17, *Now he was obliged to release someone for them at the festival*

bore, and the breasts that never nursed.' 30 Then they will begin to say to the mountains, 'Fall on us'; and to the hills, 'Cover us.' 31 For if they do this when the wood is green, what will happen when it is dry?"

the Messiah?[k] Save yourself and us!" 40 But the other rebuked him, saying, "Do you not fear God, since you are under the same sentence of condemnation? 41 And we indeed have been condemned justly, for we are getting what we deserve for our deeds, but this man has done nothing wrong." 42 Then he said, "Jesus, remember me when you come into[n] your kingdom." 43 He replied, "Truly I tell you, today you will be with me in Paradise."

Asian American

Salubong

In the Philippines, Catholics celebrate the Salubong—meaning the encounter between the risen Jesus and his sorrowful mother on Easter morning. This is based on a tradition that Mary was with the women mentioned in Lk 23.27.

On the day of Salubong, at dawn, two groups of worshipers begin walking in two different directions. One group carries a statue of Jesus, and the other group, a statue of Mary. Both statues are draped in black capes. The people walk through the town and meet on a main street, usually under an arch. A little robed "angel" (a small girl or boy) then removes the sorrowful black capes to reveal joyful white or golden robes on each statue, symbolizing the joy and glory of the Resurrection. Then the entire assembly returns to the church, and Easter Mass begins.

▶ Lk 23.26–31

NATIVE AMERICAN

Waiting in Darkness

The darkness before Jesus died symbolizes the coming of the day of the Lord (see the introduction to Joel). This Iroquois prayer expresses the feeling of that moment:

> *We wait in the darkness!*
> *Come, all ye who listen,*
> *Help in our night journey:*
> *Now no sun is shining;*
> *Now no star is glowing;*
> *Come show us the pathway:*
> *The night is not friendly;*
> *The moon has forgot us,*
> *We wait in the darkness!*
> *(David Schiller, editor, The Little Book of Prayers, p. 322)*

▶ Lk 23.44–46

32 Two others also, who were criminals, were led away to be put to death with him. 33 When they came to the place that is called The Skull, they crucified Jesus[i] there with the criminals, one on his right and one on his left. [[34 Then Jesus said, "Father, forgive them; for they do not know what they are doing."]][j] And they cast lots to divide his clothing. 35 And the people stood by, watching; but the leaders scoffed at him, saying, "He saved others; let him save himself if he is the Messiah[k] of God, his chosen one!" 36 The soldiers also mocked him, coming up and offering him sour wine, 37 and saying, "If you are the King of the Jews, save yourself!" 38 There was also an inscription over him,[l] "This is the King of the Jews."

39 One of the criminals who were hanged there kept deriding[m] him and saying, "Are you not

The Death of Jesus
(Mt 27.45–56; Mk 15.33–41; Jn 19.25–30)

44 It was now about noon, and darkness came over the whole land[o] until three in the afternoon, 45 while the sun's light failed;[p] and the curtain of

---

[i] Gk *him*   [j] Other ancient authorities lack the sentence *Then Jesus . . . what they are doing*   [k] Or *the Christ*
[l] Other ancient authorities add *written in Greek and Latin and Hebrew* (that is, *Aramaic*)   [m] Or *blaspheming*
[n] Other ancient authorities read *in*   [o] Or *earth*   [p] Or *the sun was eclipsed.* Other ancient authorities read *the sun was darkened*

Resurrection Stories, Resurrection Hope

Think about the most hopeless time in your life. Did you feel depressed? lonely? angry? afraid? These were probably some of the feelings of the women who approached Jesus' tomb on the Sunday morning after his death (Lk 24.1–2). Their leader, their teacher, and their Lord had just been horribly executed before a huge crowd, and his wonderful vision of love, justice, and forgiveness had been shattered.

But what they encountered in that tomb changed their lives forever! The tomb was empty; two dazzling men appeared and spoke to them—Jesus had indeed risen!

There are fourteen stories about Jesus' Resurrection in the four Gospels. None of the stories describe the actual Resurrection or the physical appearance of the resurrected Christ. Matthew emphasizes God's power with dramatic symbols like earthquakes and lightning (Mt 28.2–3). Mark, in its original ending, focuses on the empty tomb (Mk 16.1–8). Luke emphasizes the living presence of Jesus in the Scriptures and the Eucharist (see the Emmaus story, Lk 34.13–35). John brings out the authority of the leaders of the early church (Jn 20.19–23; 21.15–17).

Taken together, all the stories convey the faith of the disciples that Jesus is alive. Through God's power, life has triumphed over death. The disciples are given the mission to communicate this good news.

When you think that a situation is hopeless, that no end is in sight, that evil is winning out, remember the Resurrection stories. They are the proof that despair and death do not win—that God is at work in the most hopeless of human situations!

▶ Lk 24.1–12

his last. 47 When the centurion saw what had taken place, he praised God and said, "Certainly this man was innocent."*q* 48 And when all the crowds who had gathered there for this spectacle saw what had taken place, they returned home, beating their breasts. 49 But all his acquaintances, including the women who had followed him from Galilee, stood at a distance, watching these things.

The Burial of Jesus
(Mt 27.57–61; Mk 15.42–47; Jn 19.38–42)

50 Now there was a good and righteous man named Joseph, who, though a member of the council, 51 had not agreed to their plan and action. He came from the Jewish town of Ar·i·ma·the′a, and he was waiting expectantly for the kingdom of God. 52 This man went to Pilate and asked for the body of Jesus. 53 Then he took it down, wrapped it in a linen cloth, and laid it in a rock-hewn tomb where no one had ever been laid. 54 It was the day of Preparation, and the sabbath was beginning.*r* 55 The women who had come with him from Galilee followed, and they saw the tomb and how his body was laid. 56 Then they returned, and prepared spices and ointments.

On the sabbath they rested according to the commandment.

The Resurrection of Jesus
(Mt 28.1–10; Mk 16.1–8; Jn 20.1–10)

But on the first day of the week, at early dawn, they came to the tomb, taking the spices that they had prepared. 2 They found the stone rolled away from the tomb, 3 but when they went in, they did not find the body.*s* 4 While they were perplexed about this, suddenly two men in dazzling clothes stood beside them. 5 The women*t* were terrified and bowed their faces to the ground, but the men*u* said to them, "Why do you look for the living among the dead? He is not here, but has risen.*v* 6 Remember how he told you, while he was still in Galilee, 7 that the Son of Man must be handed over to sinners, and be crucified, and on the third day rise again." 8 Then they remembered his words, 9 and returning from the tomb, they told all this to the eleven and to all the rest. 10 Now it was Mary Mag′da·lene, Jo·an′na, Mary the mother of James, and the other women with them who told this to the apostles. 11 But these words seemed to them an idle tale, and they did not believe them. 12 But Peter got up and ran to the tomb; stooping and look-

the temple was torn in two. 46 Then Jesus, crying with a loud voice, said, "Father, into your hands I commend my spirit." Having said this, he breathed

q Or *righteous*　　*r* Gk *was dawning*　　*s* Other ancient authorities add *of the Lord Jesus*　　*t* Gk *They*　　*u* Gk *but they*　　*v* Other ancient authorities lack *He is not here, but has risen*

Jesus Is with Us!

Tim was at Mass when he heard Lk 24.13–35. "Pretty strange!" he thought. "Those two guys did not recognize Jesus after they had been with him for three years. I wonder if he looked different after the Resurrection. If I had been walking on the road to Emmaus, I wonder if I would have recognized him. I wonder if people would recognize him today if he came among us." Tim continued to ponder these thoughts as the Mass continued. He remembered his mother saying that Jesus is present among us every day—in the people we meet, when we gather to pray, and in the Eucharist.

Suddenly, Tim was aware of what the priest was saying: "This is my body which will be given up for you. This is the cup of my blood . . . it will be shed for you and for all. Do this in memory of me."

Tim looked around the church, noticing people he had not paid attention to before: the Amouri family, who were refugees from a war-torn country; the little Tucker baby, who had been born with severe disabilities; Mrs. Murphy, who lived alone at ninety-six years old; some other teenagers who were sitting together in the front of church. Somehow, all these different people found love and acceptance in the parish family. "I think I understand now," Tim thought. "Jesus does look different, but he is here!"

When Jesus joined the disciples at their table and broke the bread, they recognized him. It was at the Eucharist that Tim recognized the presence of Jesus alive today. How about you? When and where do you recognize Jesus? Who in your community reminds you of him the most? Why?

▶ Lk 24.13–35

---

ing in, he saw the linen cloths by themselves; then he went home, amazed at what had happened.[w]

The Walk to Emmaus
(Mt 16.12–13)

13 Now on that same day two of them were going to a village called Em·mā′us, about seven miles[x] from Jerusalem, 14 and talking with each other about all these things that had happened. 15 While they were talking and discussing, Jesus himself came near and went with them, 16 but their eyes were kept from recognizing him. 17 And he said to them, "What are you discussing with each other while you walk along?" They stood still, looking sad.[y] 18 Then one of them, whose name was Clē′o·pas, answered him, "Are you the only stranger in Jerusalem who does not know the things that have taken place there in these days?" 19 He asked them, "What things?" They replied, "The things about Jesus of Nazareth,[z] who was a prophet mighty in deed and word before God and all the people, 20 and how our chief priests and leaders handed him over to be condemned to death and crucified him. 21 But we had hoped that he was the one to redeem Israel.[a] Yes, and besides all this, it is now the third day since these things took place. 22 Moreover, some women of our group astounded us. They were at the tomb early

this morning, 23 and when they did not find his body there, they came back and told us that they had indeed seen a vision of angels who said that he was alive. 24 Some of those who were with us went to the tomb and found it just as the women had said; but they did not see him." 25 Then he said to them, "Oh, how foolish you are, and how slow of heart to believe all that the prophets have declared! 26 Was it not necessary that the Messiah[b] should suffer these things and then enter into his glory?" 27 Then beginning with Moses and all the prophets, he interpreted to them the things about himself in all the scriptures.

28 As they came near the village to which they were going, he walked ahead as if he were going on. 29 But they urged him strongly, saying, "Stay with us, because it is almost evening and the day is now nearly over." So he went in to stay with them. 30 When he was at the table with them, he took bread, blessed and broke it, and gave it to them. 31 Then their eyes were opened, and they recognized him; and he vanished from their sight. 32 They said to each other, "Were not our hearts

w Other ancient authorities lack verse 12   x Gk sixty
stadia; other ancient authorities read *a hundred sixty stadia*
y Other ancient authorities read *walk along, looking sad?"*
z Other ancient authorities read *Jesus the Nazorean*
a Or *to set Israel free*   b Or *the Christ*

burning within us*c* while he was talking to us on the road, while he was opening the scriptures to us?" 33 That same hour they got up and returned to Jerusalem; and they found the eleven and their companions gathered together. 34 They were saying, "The Lord has risen indeed, and he has appeared to Simon!" 35 Then they told what had happened on the road, and how he had been made known to them in the breaking of the bread.

Jesus Appears to His Disciples
(Jn 20.19–23; Acts 1.3–5; 1 Cor 15.5)

36 While they were talking about this, Jesus himself stood among them and said to them, "Peace be with you."*d* 37 They were startled and terrified, and thought that they were seeing a ghost. 38 He said to them, "Why are you frightened, and why do doubts arise in your hearts? 39 Look at my hands and my feet; see that it is I myself. Touch me and see; for a ghost does not have flesh and bones as you see that I have." 40 And when he had said this, he showed them his hands and his feet.*e* 41 While in their joy they were disbelieving and still wondering, he said to them, "Have you anything here to eat?" 42 They gave him a piece of broiled fish, 43 and he took it and ate in their presence.

44 Then he said to them, "These are my words that I spoke to you while I was still with you—that everything written about me in the law of Moses, the prophets, and the psalms must be fulfilled." 45 Then he opened their minds to understand the scriptures, 46 and he said to them, "Thus it is written, that the Messiah*f* is to suffer and to rise from the dead on the third day, 47 and that repentance and forgiveness of sins is to be proclaimed in his name to all nations, beginning from Jerusalem. 48 You are witnesses*g* of these things. 49 And see, I am sending upon you what my Father promised; so stay here in the city until you have been clothed with power from on high."

The Ascension of Jesus
(Mk 16.19–20; Acts 1.9)

50 Then he led them out as far as Beth′a·ny, and, lifting up his hands, he blessed them. 51 While he was blessing them, he withdrew from them and was carried up into heaven.*h* 52 And they worshiped him, and*i* returned to Jerusalem with great joy; 53 and they were continually in the temple blessing God.*j*

---

c Other ancient authorities lack *within us*   *d* Other ancient authorities lack *and said to them, "Peace be with you."*   *e* Other ancient authorities lack verse 40   *f* Or *the Christ*   *g* Or *nations. Beginning from Jerusalem 48 you are witnesses*   *h* Other ancient authorities lack *and was carried up into heaven*   *i* Other ancient authorities lack *worshiped him, and*   *j* Other ancient authorities add *Amen*

We're both cut from the same cloth." "Lately, it seems like we're two ships passing in the night." People often use analogies or symbolic images in describing their closest relationships. The author of the Gospel of John does this. Throughout the Gospel, symbolic imagery is used to describe the Christian believer's relationship with Jesus. Very different in style from the other Gospels, John also gives us the clearest picture of the divinity of Jesus.

At a Glance

- **1.1–18.** prologue: a poem about the Word of God
- **1.19—12.50.** the Book of Signs: Jesus' miracles and teachings, disputes with "the Jews"
- **Chapters 13–20.** the Book of Glory: the Last Supper, and Jesus' suffering, death, and Resurrection
- **Chapter 21.** epilogue: the appearance of the risen Jesus

In-depth

The Gospel of John begins with symbolic language describing Jesus as the Word, who was with God in the beginning of creation and who took on flesh to live among us. The author goes on to describe Jesus as the light that overcomes darkness. Those who believe in Jesus walk in the light—their lives have meaning and direction. Those who do not believe stumble in the darkness of confusion and sin. John is clear that Jesus is the divine Son of God and that to belong to God, we have to follow Jesus.

In addition to its symbolic language and stress on Jesus' divinity, John's Gospel differs from the synoptic Gospels—Matthew, Mark, and Luke—in other ways:

- In the synoptic Gospels, Jesus' teaching focuses on the Kingdom (or Reign) of God. In John, Jesus' teaching stresses relationships: Jesus' relationship with God the Father and our relationship with Jesus.
- In the synoptic Gospels, Jesus teaches with parables and performs many healings and miracles. In John, Jesus does not teach by parables. Instead, Jesus performs seven miraculous signs and explains their meaning.
- John has several passages about the role of the Holy Spirit. The synoptic Gospels hardly mention the Holy Spirit.

John's story of Jesus climaxes with the coming of Jesus' "hour," a symbol for Jesus' death. But in John, Jesus' death is not tragic at all—it is his glorious return to the Father. This Gospel assures us that trust in God will pay off in the end. "I will come again and will take you to myself," says Jesus, "so that where I am, there you may be also" (14.3).

Quick Facts

Author
a member of a Christian community possibly founded by the Beloved Disciple

Date Written
most likely from A.D. 90 to 100

Audience
all the Christians of the world

Image of Jesus
noble, powerful, and divine; fully in control of his destiny

The Gospel According to John

John

The Word Became Flesh
(Gen 1.1—2.4a)

In the beginning was the Word, and the Word was with God, and the Word was God. ²He was in the beginning with God. ³All things came into being through him, and without him not one thing came into being. What has come into being ⁴in him was life,ᵃ and the life was the light of all people. ⁵The light shines in the darkness, and the darkness did not overcome it.

6 There was a man sent from God, whose name was John. ⁷He came as a witness to testify to the light, so that all might believe through him. ⁸He himself was not the light, but he came to testify to the light. ⁹The true light, which enlightens everyone, was coming into the world.ᵇ

10 He was in the world, and the world came into being through him; yet the world did not know him. ¹¹He came to what was his own,ᶜ and his own people did not accept him. ¹²But to all who received him, who believed in his name, he gave power to become children of God, ¹³who were born, not of blood or of the will of the flesh or of the will of man, but of God.

14 And the Word became flesh and lived among us, and we have seen his glory, the glory as of a father's only son,ᵈ full of grace and truth. ¹⁵(John testified to him and cried out, "This was he of whom I said, 'He who comes after me ranks ahead of me because he was before me.' ") ¹⁶From his fullness we have all received, grace upon grace.

¹⁷The law indeed was given through Moses; grace and truth came through Jesus Christ. ¹⁸No one has ever seen God. It is God the only Son,ᵉ who is close to the Father's heart,ᶠ who has made him known.

The Testimony of John the Baptist
(Mt 3.1–12; Mk 1.1–8; Lk 3.1–20)

19 This is the testimony given by John when the Jews sent priests and Lēʹvītes from Jerusalem to ask him, "Who are you?" ²⁰He confessed and did not deny it, but confessed, "I am not the Messiah."ᵍ ²¹And they asked him, "What then? Are you Eˑlīʹjah?" He said, "I am not." "Are you the prophet?" He answered, "No." ²²Then they said to him, "Who are you? Let us have an answer for those who sent us. What do you say about yourself?" ²³He said,

"I am the voice of one crying out in the
    wilderness,
'Make straight the way of the Lord,' "
as the prophet Iˑsāiʹah said.

24 Now they had been sent from the Pharʹisees. ²⁵They asked him, "Why then are you baptizing if you are neither the Messiah,ᵍ nor Eˑlīʹjah, nor the prophet?" ²⁶John answered them, "I bap-

---

ᵃ Or ³through him. And without him not one thing came into being that has come into being. ⁴In him was life ᵇ Or He was the true light that enlightens everyone coming into the world ᶜ Or to his own home ᵈ Or the Father's only Son ᵉ Other ancient authorities read It is an only Son, God, or It is the only Son ᶠ Gk bosom ᵍ Or the Christ

The "Cosmic Christ"

Science fiction or fantasy movies and books often include important eternal beings or powers. The *Star Wars* series has "the Force." The Chronicles of Narnia, a fantasy series by C. S. Lewis, has Aslan, the noble lion who is the creator and savior of Narnia.

The poem that begins the Gospel of John reads like something from a great science fiction classic. Only, in this case, the story is not fiction but God's revelation! The poem presents Jesus as the Word, who has existed from all time, the one through whom all things came into being. The Scriptures tell us a great mystery here: the man named Jesus, who lived in Nazareth some two thousand years ago, is the eternal God, who "became flesh and lived among us" (Jn 1.14). No one has ever seen God. But Jesus, the perfect image of God, "has made him known" (verse 18) in flesh and blood.

Many people in the Gospel of John do not recognize or accept Jesus, and many people still do not today. What does it mean for you to accept Jesus?

▶ Jn 1.1–18

---

tize with water. Among you stands one whom you do not know, 27 the one who is coming after me; I am not worthy to untie the thong of his sandal." 28 This took place in Beth′a•ny across the Jordan where John was baptizing.

The Lamb of God
(Mt 3.13–17; Mk 1.9–11; Lk 3.21–22)

29 The next day he saw Jesus coming toward him and declared, "Here is the Lamb of God who takes away the sin of the world! 30 This is he of whom I said, 'After me comes a man who ranks ahead of me because he was before me.' 31 I myself did not know him; but I came baptizing with water for this reason, that he might be revealed to Israel." 32 And John testified, "I saw the Spirit descending from heaven like a dove, and it remained on him. 33 I myself did not know him, but the one who sent me to baptize with water said to me, 'He on whom you see the Spirit descend and remain is the one who baptizes with the Holy Spirit.' 34 And I myself have seen and have testified that this is the Son of God."[h]

The First Disciples of Jesus

35 The next day John again was standing with two of his disciples, 36 and as he watched Jesus walk by, he exclaimed, "Look, here is the Lamb of God!" 37 The two disciples heard him say this, and they followed Jesus. 38 When Jesus turned and saw them following, he said to them, "What are you looking for?" They said to him, "Rabbi" (which translated means Teacher), "where are you staying?" 39 He said to them, "Come and see." They came and saw where he was staying, and they re-

mained with him that day. It was about four o'clock in the afternoon. 40 One of the two who heard John speak and followed him was Andrew, Simon Peter's brother. 41 He first found his brother Simon and said to him, "We have found the Messiah" (which is translated Anointed[i]). 42 He brought Simon[j] to Jesus, who looked at him and said, "You are Simon son of John. You are to be called Ce′phas" (which is translated Peter[k]).

Jesus Calls Philip and Nathanael

43 The next day Jesus decided to go to Galilee. He found Philip and said to him, "Follow me." 44 Now Philip was from Beth•sa′i•da, the city of Andrew and Peter. 45 Philip found Na•than′a•el and said to him, "We have found him about whom Moses in the law and also the prophets wrote, Jesus son of Joseph from Nazareth." 46 Na•than′a•el said to him, "Can anything good come out of Nazareth?" Philip said to him, "Come and see." 47 When Jesus saw Na•than′a•el coming toward him, he said of him, "Here is truly an Israelite in whom there is no deceit!" 48 Na•than′a•el asked him, "Where did you get to know me?" Jesus answered, "I saw you under the fig tree before Philip called you." 49 Na•than′a•el replied, "Rabbi, you are the Son of God! You are the King of Israel!" 50 Jesus answered, "Do you believe because I told you that I saw you under the fig tree? You will see greater things than these." 51 And he said to him, "Very truly, I tell you,[l] you will see heaven opened and

---

h Other ancient authorities read *is God's chosen one*
i Or *Christ*   j Gk *him*   k From the word for *rock* in Aramaic (*kepha*) and Greek (*petra*), respectively   l Both instances of the Greek word for *you* in this verse are plural

J
N

the angels of God ascending and descending upon the Son of Man."

The Wedding at Cana

On the third day there was a wedding in Cā'na of Galilee, and the mother of Jesus was there. 2 Jesus and his disciples had also been invited to the wedding. 3 When the wine gave out, the mother of Jesus said to him, "They have no wine." 4 And Jesus said to her, "Woman, what concern is that to you

? did you KNOW?

Righteous Anger

Shouting! Tipping over tables! These are signs of anger. Some people might even label this behavior as out of control. But Jesus does not strike anyone with the whip; he only drives out the animals. He is not out of control, but he certainly is angry!

Even though we are often told that we should not show anger, sometimes, it is appropriate to do so. Righteous anger is a reaction to an injustice or something that is not right. Jesus is upset because the greedy merchants and Temple officials have made the Temple a marketplace and have defiled the sacred space. He controls his righteous anger and channels it in a civil and religious challenge against the corrupt and greedy leaders (see "Jesus and Civil Disobedience," Mt 21.12–13). Righteous anger should be expressed in ways that challenge evil and unjust situations but never in ways that cause violence or injury to another person.

What situations in your life or in the world might call for a response of righteous anger? How might you express your anger without going out of control?

▶ Jn 2.13–17

and to me? My hour has not yet come." 5 His mother said to the servants, "Do whatever he tells you." 6 Now standing there were six stone water jars for the Jewish rites of purification, each holding twenty or thirty gallons. 7 Jesus said to them, "Fill the jars with water." And they filled them up to the

brim. 8 He said to them, "Now draw some out, and take it to the chief steward." So they took it. 9 When the steward tasted the water that had become wine, and did not know where it came from (though the servants who had drawn the water knew), the steward called the bridegroom 10 and said to him, "Everyone serves the good wine first, and then the inferior wine after the guests have become drunk. But you have kept the good wine until now." 11 Jesus did this, the first of his signs, in Cā'na of Galilee, and revealed his glory; and his disciples believed in him.

12 After this he went down to Ca·per'na·um with his mother, his brothers, and his disciples; and they remained there a few days.

Jesus Cleanses the Temple
(Mt 21.12–17; Mk 11.15–19; Lk 19.45–48)

13 The Passover of the Jews was near, and Jesus went up to Jerusalem. 14 In the temple he found people selling cattle, sheep, and doves, and the money changers seated at their tables. 15 Making a whip of cords, he drove all of them out of the temple, both the sheep and the cattle. He also poured out the coins of the money changers and overturned their tables. 16 He told those who were selling the doves, "Take these things out of here! Stop making my Father's house a marketplace!" 17 His disciples remembered that it was written, "Zeal for your house will consume me." 18 The Jews then said to him, "What sign can you show us for doing this?" 19 Jesus answered them, "Destroy this temple, and in three days I will raise it up." 20 The Jews then said, "This temple has been under construction for forty-six years, and will you raise it up in three days?" 21 But he was speaking of the temple of his body. 22 After he was raised from the dead, his disciples remembered that he had said this; and they believed the scripture and the word that Jesus had spoken.

23 When he was in Jerusalem during the Passover festival, many believed in his name because they saw the signs that he was doing. 24 But Jesus on his part would not entrust himself to them, because he knew all people 25 and needed no one to testify about anyone; for he himself knew what was in everyone.

Nicodemus Visits Jesus

Now there was a Phar'i·see named Nic·o·dē'mus, a leader of the Jews. 2 He came to Jesus[m] by night and said to him, "Rabbi, we know that you are a teacher who has come from God; for no one can do these signs that you do apart from the presence

---

m Gk *him*

of God." ³Jesus answered him, "Very truly, I tell you, no one can see the kingdom of God without being born from above."ⁿ ⁴Nic•o•dē′mus said to him, "How can anyone be born after having

did you KNOW?

"The Jews" in the Gospel of John

When you read the Gospel of John, you may notice that the Gospel writer often makes negative references to "the Jews." They are often portrayed questioning (2.18) or challenging Jesus. When the Gospel was being written, many Jews were persecuting Christian Jews who still worshiped in the synagogues. As a result, the Gospel writer lumps all Jews together, portraying them as the "bad guys." Christian churches teach that we should not take John's references to "the Jews" as a basis for prejudice or anger against Jewish people.

▶ Jn 2.18–20

grown old? Can one enter a second time into the mother's womb and be born?" ⁵Jesus answered, "Very truly, I tell you, no one can enter the kingdom of God without being born of water and

Spirit. ⁶What is born of the flesh is flesh, and what is born of the Spirit is spirit.ᵒ ⁷Do not be astonished that I said to you, 'Youᵖ must be born from above.'ᑫ ⁸The windᵒ blows where it chooses, and you hear the sound of it, but you do not know where it comes from or where it goes. So it is with everyone who is born of the Spirit." ⁹Nic•o•dē′mus said to him, "How can these things be?" ¹⁰Jesus answered him, "Are you a teacher of Israel, and yet you do not understand these things?

11 "Very truly, I tell you, we speak of what we know and testify to what we have seen; yet youʳ do not receive our testimony. ¹²If I have told you about earthly things and you do not believe, how can you believe if I tell you about heavenly things? ¹³No one has ascended into heaven except the one who descended from heaven, the Son of Man.ˢ ¹⁴And just as Moses lifted up the serpent in the wilderness, so must the Son of Man be lifted up, ¹⁵that whoever believes in him may have eternal life.ᵗ

16 "For God so loved the world that he gave his only Son, so that everyone who believes in him may not perish but may have eternal life. ¹⁷Indeed, God did not send the Son into the world to condemn the world, but in order that the world might be saved through him. ¹⁸Those who believe in him are not condemned; but those who do not believe are condemned already, because they have not believed in the name of the only Son of God. ¹⁹And this is the judgment, that the

ⁿ Or *born anew*   ᵒ The same Greek word means both *wind* and *spirit*   ᵖ The Greek word for *you* here is plural   ᑫ Or *anew*   ʳ The Greek word for *you* here and in verse 12 is plural   ˢ Other ancient authorities add *who is in heaven*   ᵗ Some interpreters hold that the quotation concludes with verse 15

LIVE IT!

Nic at Night

Nicodemus, a Jewish teacher with a high position of leadership, is meeting secretly with Jesus. Nicodemus has been waiting for a sign that God's promise of salvation through a savior will happen in his lifetime. He senses that maybe Jesus is this savior. But he does not yet believe in Jesus, as is emphasized by his coming to Jesus "by night" (Jn 3.2). Speaking symbolically, Jesus outlines what it takes for salvation: to believe in Jesus as the one sent by God and to be born again through baptism and the Holy Spirit. The same is true for people today.

Nicodemus knew that to publicly accept Jesus would put him in bad standing with the other Jewish leaders. Sometimes, we must make choices that might make us look foolish to others. How hard would it be for you to publicly express belief in Jesus? Will you be a believer in the night or in the light?

▶ Jn 3.1–21

light has come into the world, and people loved darkness rather than light because their deeds were evil. 20 For all who do evil hate the light and do not come to the light, so that their deeds may not be exposed. 21 But those who do what is true come to the light, so that it may be clearly seen that their deeds have been done in God."*u*

Jesus and John the Baptist

22 After this Jesus and his disciples went into the Judean countryside, and he spent some time there with them and baptized. 23 John also was baptizing at Aē'non near Sā'lim because water was abundant there; and people kept coming and were being baptized 24 —John, of course, had not yet been thrown into prison.

How Deep Is Your Well?

In Jn 4.1–42, Jesus engages a Samaritan woman in conversation. She has no idea who Jesus is and what living water he is referring to, but she stands and listens. She is changed as a result. She comes to believe in Jesus and goes to tell others about the Messiah. John uses her as a role model for those who believe.

Look inside the well of faith within you. How deep is that well? Do you thirst for a deeper relationship with Jesus? Are you ready to share the Good News with others? Jesus invites each of us to join with him in a personal relationship. All we have to do is ask. Begin your relationship with Jesus by praying:

Jesus, you are the Messiah, the anointed one. I am thirsty. . . . Quench my thirst.

▸ Jn 4.1–42

25 Now a discussion about purification arose between John's disciples and a Jew.*v* 26 They came to John and said to him, "Rabbi, the one who was with you across the Jordan, to whom you testified, here he is baptizing, and all are going to him." 27 John answered, "No one can receive anything except what has been given from heaven. 28 You yourselves are my witnesses that I said, 'I am not the Messiah,*w* but I have been sent ahead of him.' 29 He who has the bride is the bridegroom. The friend of the bridegroom, who stands and hears him, rejoices greatly at the bridegroom's voice. For this reason my joy has been fulfilled. 30 He must increase, but I must decrease."*x*

The One Who Comes from Heaven

31 The one who comes from above is above all; the one who is of the earth belongs to the earth and speaks about earthly things. The one who comes from heaven is above all. 32 He testifies to what he has seen and heard, yet no one accepts his testimony. 33 Whoever has accepted his testimony has certified*y* this, that God is true. 34 He whom God has sent speaks the words of God, for he gives the Spirit without measure. 35 The Father loves the Son and has placed all things in his hands. 36 Whoever believes in the Son has eternal life; whoever disobeys the Son will not see life, but must endure God's wrath.

Jesus and the Woman of Samaria

Now when Jesus*z* learned that the Phar'i·sees had heard, "Jesus is making and baptizing more disciples than John" 2 — although it was not Jesus himself but his disciples who baptized— 3 he left Judea and started back to Galilee. 4 But he had to go through Sa·mār'i·a. 5 So he came to a Sa·mār'i·tan city called Sȳ'char, near the plot of ground that Jacob had given to his son Joseph. 6 Jacob's well was there, and Jesus, tired out by his journey, was sitting by the well. It was about noon.

7 A Sa·mār'i·tan woman came to draw water, and Jesus said to her, "Give me a drink." 8 (His disciples had gone to the city to buy food.) 9 The Sa·mār'i·tan woman said to him, "How is it that you, a Jew, ask a drink of me, a woman of Sa·mār'i·a?" (Jews do not share things in common with Sa·mār'i·tans.)*a* 10 Jesus answered her, "If you knew the gift of God, and who it is that is saying to you, 'Give me a drink,' you would have asked him, and he would have given you living water." 11 The woman said to him, "Sir, you have no bucket, and the well is deep. Where do you get that living water? 12 Are you greater than our ancestor Jacob, who gave us the well, and with his sons and his flocks drank from it?" 13 Jesus said to her, "Everyone who drinks of this water will be thirsty again, 14 but those who drink of the water that I will give them will never be thirsty. The water that I will give will become in them a spring of water gushing

---

u Some interpreters hold that the quotation concludes with verse 15   *v* Other ancient authorities read *the Jews*   *w* Or *the Christ*   *x* Some interpreters hold that the quotation continues through verse 36   *y* Gk *set a seal to*   *z* Other ancient authorities read *the Lord*   *a* Other ancient authorities lack this sentence

up to eternal life." 15 The woman said to him, "Sir, give me this water, so that I may never be thirsty or have to keep coming here to draw water."

Asian American

This Is Christmas

This poem, by Masao and Fumiko Takenaka of Japan, is a reflection on Jesus as "living water" (Jn 4.10):

One who said I am the eternal water
Dwelt among us
Living with us
Sustaining us
This is Christmas.

To receive a cup of living water
Is not only to cleanse ourselves
But also to cleanse all the waters.
River and well, lake and ocean,
And to share them with all.
This is Christmas.

(From Maren C. Tirabassi and Kathy Wonson Eddy, editors, *Gifts of Many Cultures*, p. 144)

▸ Jn 4.1–15

16 Jesus said to her, "Go, call your husband, and come back." 17 The woman answered him, "I have no husband." Jesus said to her, "You are right in saying, 'I have no husband'; 18 for you have had five husbands, and the one you have now is not your husband. What you have said is true!" 19 The woman said to him, "Sir, I see that you are a prophet. 20 Our ancestors worshiped on this mountain, but you*b* say that the place where people must worship is in Jerusalem." 21 Jesus said to her, "Woman, believe me, the hour is coming when you will worship the Father neither on this mountain nor in Jerusalem. 22 You worship what you do not know; we worship what we know, for salvation is from the Jews. 23 But the hour is coming, and is now here, when the true worshipers will worship the Father in spirit and truth, for the Father seeks such as these to worship him. 24 God is spirit, and those who worship him must worship in spirit and truth." 25 The woman said to him, "I know that Messiah is coming" (who is called Christ). "When he comes, he will proclaim all

things to us." 26 Jesus said to her, "I am he,*c* the one who is speaking to you."

27 Just then his disciples came. They were astonished that he was speaking with a woman, but no one said, "What do you want?" or, "Why are you speaking with her?" 28 Then the woman left her water jar and went back to the city. She said to the people, 29 "Come and see a man who told me everything I have ever done! He cannot be the Messiah,*d* can he?" 30 They left the city and were on their way to him.

did you KNOW?

Why Are the Disciples Surprised?

The disciples "were astonished that he [Jesus] was speaking with a woman" (Jn 4.27). For several reasons, it was unusual for Jesus to be talking to her. First, in first-century Israel, men did not talk to women, especially strangers, in public places. Second, Jews did not talk to Samaritans (see "Who Belongs, and Who Does Not?" Ezra, chapters 9–10, and "Discrimination in Jesus' Time," Lk 10.25–37), who were considered guilty of false worship (Jn 4.20). And finally, the woman with whom Jesus was speaking was a known sinner, having married far too many times.

This episode is one more example in the Gospel of John that shows Jesus is not bound by customs and stereotypes when the message of the Gospel is at stake.

▸ Jn 4.1–42

31 Meanwhile the disciples were urging him, "Rabbi, eat something." 32 But he said to them, "I have food to eat that you do not know about." 33 So the disciples said to one another, "Surely no one has brought him something to eat?" 34 Jesus said to them, "My food is to do the will of him who sent me and to complete his work. 35 Do you not say, 'Four months more, then comes the harvest'? But I tell you, look around you, and see how the fields

b The Greek word for *you* here and in verses 21 and 22 is plural *c* Gk I am *d* Or *the Christ*

are ripe for harvesting. 36 The reaper is already re-ceiving*e* wages and is gathering fruit for eternal life, so that sower and reaper may rejoice together. 37 For here the saying holds true, 'One sows and another reaps.' 38 I sent you to reap that for which you did not labor. Others have labored, and you have entered into their labor."

39 Many Sa•mār'i•tans from that city believed in him because of the woman's testimony, "He told me everything I have ever done." 40 So when the Sa•mār'i•tans came to him, they asked him to stay with them; and he stayed there two days. 41 And many more believed because of his word. 42 They said to the woman, "It is no longer because of what you said that we believe, for we have heard for ourselves, and we know that this is truly the Savior of the world."

Jesus Returns to Galilee

43 When the two days were over, he went from that place to Galilee 44 (for Jesus himself had testi-fied that a prophet has no honor in the prophet's own country). 45 When he came to Galilee, the Galileans welcomed him, since they had seen all that he had done in Jerusalem at the festival; for they too had gone to the festival.

Jesus Heals an Official's Son

46 Then he came again to Cā'na in Galilee where he had changed the water into wine. Now there was a royal official whose son lay ill in Ca-per'na•um. 47 When he heard that Jesus had come from Judea to Galilee, he went and begged him to come down and heal his son, for he was at the point of death. 48 Then Jesus said to him, "Unless you*f* see signs and wonders you will not believe." 49 The official said to him, "Sir, come down before my little boy dies." 50 Jesus said to him, "Go; your son will live." The man believed the word that Jesus spoke to him and started on his way. 51 As he was going down, his slaves met him and told him that his child was alive. 52 So he asked them the hour when he began to recover, and they said to him, "Yesterday at one in the afternoon the fever left him." 53 The father realized that this was the hour when Jesus had said to him, "Your son will live." So he himself believed, along with his whole household. 54 Now this was the second sign that Jesus did after coming from Judea to Galilee.

Jesus Heals on the Sabbath

After this there was a festival of the Jews, and Jesus went up to Jerusalem.

2 Now in Jerusalem by the Sheep Gate there is a pool, called in Hebrew*g* Beth-zā'tha,*h* which has five porticoes. 3 In these lay many invalids—blind,

lame, and paralyzed.*i* 5 One man was there who had been ill for thirty-eight years. 6 When Jesus saw him lying there and knew that he had been there a long time, he said to him, "Do you want to be

"I Am" Sayings of Jesus

The Gospel of John contains a whole series of "I am" sayings as a way for Jesus to explain his role as the Messiah. For example:

- **"I am the bread of life" (6.35).**
- **"I am the light of the world" (8.12).**
- **"I am the gate for the sheep" (10.7).**
- **"I am the good shepherd" (10.11).**
- **"I am the resurrection and the life" (11.25).**
- **"I am the way, and the truth, and the life" (14.6).**
- **"I am the vine, you are the branches" (15.5).**

The "I am" sayings are also a means of establishing the divine nature of Jesus. Jesus' use of "I am" is similar to the rev-elation of God's name to Moses at the burning bush (Ex 3.14). Ironically, in John, the Jewish leaders are correct in thinking that Jesus is equating himself with God (5.18). But they are wrong in not recogniz-ing that Jesus is right!

▶ **Jn 5.16–18**

made well?" 7 The sick man answered him, "Sir, I have no one to put me into the pool when the water is stirred up; and while I am making my way, someone else steps down ahead of me." 8 Jesus said to him, "Stand up, take your mat and walk." 9 At once the man was made well, and he took up his mat and began to walk.

---

e Or 35. . . the fields are already ripe for harvesting. 36 The reaper is receiving   *f* Both instances of the Greek word for you in this verse are plural   *g* That is, Aramaic   *h* Other ancient authorities read Bethesda, others Bethsaida *i* Other ancient authorities add, wholly or in part, waiting for the stirring of the water; 4 for an angel of the Lord went down at certain seasons into the pool, and stirred up the water; whoever stepped in first after the stirring of the water was made well from whatever disease that person had.

Now that day was a sabbath. 10 So the Jews said to the man who had been cured, "It is the sabbath; it is not lawful for you to carry your mat." 11 But he answered them, "The man who made me well said to me, 'Take up your mat and walk.' " 12 They asked him, "Who is the man who said to you, 'Take it up and walk'?" 13 Now the man who had been healed did not know who it was, for Jesus had disappeared inʲ the crowd that was there. 14 Later Jesus found him in the temple and said to him, "See, you have been made well! Do not sin any more, so that nothing worse happens to you." 15 The man went away and told the Jews that it was Jesus who had made him well. 16 Therefore the Jews started persecuting Jesus, because he was doing such things on the sabbath. 17 But Jesus answered them, "My Father is still working, and I also am working." 18 For this reason the Jews were seeking all the more to kill him, because he was not only breaking the sabbath, but was also calling God his own Father, thereby making himself equal to God.

The Authority of the Son

19 Jesus said to them, "Very truly, I tell you, the Son can do nothing on his own, but only what he sees the Father doing; for whatever the Fatherᵏ does, the Son does likewise. 20 The Father loves the Son and shows him all that he himself is doing; and he will show him greater works than these, so that you will be astonished. 21 Indeed, just as the Father raises the dead and gives them life, so also the Son gives life to whomever he wishes. 22 The Father judges no one but has given all judgment to the Son, 23 so that all may honor the Son just as they honor the Father. Anyone who does not honor the Son does not honor the Father who sent him. 24 Very truly, I tell you, anyone who hears my word and believes him who sent me has eternal life, and does not come under judgment, but has passed from death to life.

25 "Very truly, I tell you, the hour is coming, and is now here, when the dead will hear the voice of the Son of God, and those who hear will live. 26 For just as the Father has life in himself, so he has granted the Son also to have life in himself; 27 and he has given him authority to execute judgment, because he is the Son of Man. 28 Do not be astonished at this; for the hour is coming when all who are in their graves will hear his voice 29 and will come out—those who have done good, to the resurrection of life, and those who have done evil, to the resurrection of condemnation.

Witnesses to Jesus

30 "I can do nothing on my own. As I hear, I judge; and my judgment is just, because I seek to do not my own will but the will of him who sent me. 31 "If I testify about myself, my testimony is not true. 32 There is another who testifies on my behalf, and I know that his testimony to me is true. 33 You sent messengers to John, and he testified to the truth. 34 Not that I accept such human testimony, but I say these things so that you may be saved. 35 He was a burning and shining lamp, and you were willing to rejoice for a while in his light. 36 But I have a testimony greater than John's. The works that the Father has given me to complete, the very works that I am doing, testify on my behalf that the Father has sent me. 37 And the Father who sent me has himself testified on my behalf. You have never heard his voice or seen his form, 38 and you do not have his word abiding in you, because you do not believe him whom he has sent.

39 "You search the scriptures because you think that in them you have eternal life; and it is they that testify on my behalf. 40 Yet you refuse to come to me to have life. 41 I do not accept glory from human beings. 42 But I know that you do not have the love of God inˡ you. 43 I have come in my Father's name, and you do not accept me; if another comes in his own name, you will accept him. 44 How can you believe when you accept glory from one another and do not seek the glory that comes from the one who alone is God? 45 Do not think that I will accuse you before the Father; your accuser is Moses, on whom you have set your hope. 46 If you believed Moses, you would believe me, for he wrote about me. 47 But if you do not believe what he wrote, how will you believe what I say?"

Feeding the Five Thousand
(Mt 14.13–21; Mk 6.30–44; Lk 9.10–17)

After this Jesus went to the other side of the Sea of Galilee, also called the Sea of Tĭ·bē′ri·as.ᵐ 2 A large crowd kept following him, because they saw the signs that he was doing for the sick. 3 Jesus went up the mountain and sat down there with his disciples. 4 Now the Passover, the festival of the Jews, was near. 5 When he looked up and saw a large crowd coming toward him, Jesus said to Philip, "Where are we to buy bread for these people to eat?" 6 He said this to test him, for he himself knew what he was going to do. 7 Philip answered him,

---

ʲ Or had left because of   ᵏ Gk that one   ˡ Or among
ᵐ Gk of Galilee of Tiberias

"Six months' wages[n] would not buy enough bread for each of them to get a little." [8] One of his disciples, Andrew, Simon Peter's brother, said to him, [9] "There is a boy here who has five barley loaves and two fish. But what are they among so many people?" [10] Jesus said, "Make the people sit down." Now there was a great deal of grass in the place; so they[o] sat down, about five thousand in all. [11] Then Jesus took the loaves, and when he had given thanks, he distributed them to those who were seated; so also the fish, as much as they wanted. [12] When they were satisfied, he told his disciples, "Gather up the fragments left over, so that nothing may be lost." [13] So they gathered them up, and from the fragments of the five barley loaves, left by those who had eaten, they filled twelve baskets. [14] When the people saw the sign that he had done, they began to say, "This is indeed the prophet who is to come into the world."

PRAY IT!

A Little Gift Goes a Long Way

God, could you use me like the boy who helped feed the five thousand? Out of the thousands of people gathered to see you, you chose a young person, took his five loaves and two fish, and made sure thousands had more than their fill to eat (Jn 6.1–13).

I wonder how those people felt when that little bit of food was offered by a youth? Were they embarrassed by the boy's foolishness? Or did they feel guilty that they had not offered their own food? Regardless, you accepted the gift and did fantastic things with it.

Could you do the same with me? Could you take my simple gifts and do wondrous things with them? I'm just afraid that my gifts will be rejected. It is risky, Lord, and I do not do well with risks, remember?

Help me to take the risk and let you use the gifts I have, trusting that it doesn't matter what other people think. Even if things don't work out as I plan, I'll trust that you are in charge and know better than I. Thanks, God—and wish me luck! Amen.

▶ Jn 6.1–14

[15] When Jesus realized that they were about to come and take him by force to make him king, he withdrew again to the mountain by himself.

Jesus Walks on the Water
(Mt 14.22–33; Mk 6.45–52)

[16] When evening came, his disciples went down to the sea, [17] got into a boat, and started across the sea to Ca·per'na·um. It was now dark, and Jesus had not yet come to them. [18] The sea became rough because a strong wind was blowing. [19] When they had rowed about three or four miles,[p] they saw Jesus walking on the sea and coming near the boat, and they were terrified. [20] But he said to them, "It is I;[q] do not be afraid." [21] Then they wanted to take him into the boat, and immediately the boat reached the land toward which they were going.

The Bread from Heaven

[22] The next day the crowd that had stayed on the other side of the sea saw that there had been only one boat there. They also saw that Jesus had not got into the boat with his disciples, but that his disciples had gone away alone. [23] Then some boats from Ti·be'ri·as came near the place where they had eaten the bread after the Lord had given thanks.[r] [24] So when the crowd saw that neither Jesus nor his disciples were there, they themselves got into the boats and went to Ca·per'na·um looking for Jesus.

[25] When they found him on the other side of the sea, they said to him, "Rabbi, when did you come here?" [26] Jesus answered them, "Very truly, I tell you, you are looking for me, not because you saw signs, but because you ate your fill of the loaves. [27] Do not work for the food that perishes, but for the food that endures for eternal life, which the Son of Man will give you. For it is on him that God the Father has set his seal." [28] Then they said to him, "What must we do to perform the works of God?" [29] Jesus answered them, "This is the work of God, that you believe in him whom he has sent." [30] So they said to him, "What sign are you going to give us then, so that we may see it and believe you? What work are you performing? [31] Our ancestors ate the manna in the wilderness; as it is written, 'He gave them bread from heaven to eat.' [32] Then Jesus said to them, "Very truly, I tell you, it was not Moses who gave you the bread from heaven, but it is my Father who gives you the true bread from heaven. [33] For the bread of God is that

---

[n] Gk *Two hundred denarii*; the denarius was the usual day's wage for a laborer   [o] Gk *the men*   [p] Gk *about twenty-five or thirty stadia*   [q] Gk *I am*   [r] Other ancient authorities lack *after the Lord had given thanks*

PRAY IT!

The Eucharist

Jesus calls himself the "bread of life" (Jn 6.35). Some type of bread is part of the basic diet of almost every culture. Thus, in a symbolic way, Jesus is telling us that he is part of the basic diet for spiritual life. And just as bread is shared and valued in every culture, Jesus shares himself with all people who are willing to believe.

Many of Jesus' early followers were troubled when he taught that they must eat his flesh and drink his blood in order to have true life (verses 56–60). The confusion and arguing among his listeners is understandable; his words must have sounded strange. Yet this teaching about the body and blood of Christ (which is portrayed in the Last Supper in Matthew, Mark, and Luke) is central to the Catholic faith. Catholics believe that Jesus is really present with us and nourishes us when we celebrate the Eucharist together, the bread and wine being changed into the body and blood of Christ.

In your prayer, reflect or journal on the following questions:

- How is Jesus a source of nourishment for you?
- How does celebrating the Eucharist help you recognize more clearly Jesus' presence?
- How are you called to be the body and blood of Christ to the world around you?

▶ John, chapter 6

which⁵ comes down from heaven and gives life to the world." ³⁴They said to him, "Sir, give us this bread always."

35 Jesus said to them, "I am the bread of life. Whoever comes to me will never be hungry, and whoever believes in me will never be thirsty. ³⁶But I said to you that you have seen me and yet do not believe. ³⁷Everything that the Father gives me will come to me, and anyone who comes to me I will never drive away; ³⁸for I have come down from heaven, not to do my own will, but the will of him who sent me. ³⁹And this is the will of him who sent me, that I should lose nothing of all that he

has given me, but raise it up on the last day. ⁴⁰This is indeed the will of my Father, that all who see the Son and believe in him may have eternal life; and I will raise them up on the last day."

41 Then the Jews began to complain about him because he said, "I am the bread that came down from heaven." ⁴²They were saying, "Is not this Jesus, the son of Joseph, whose father and mother we know? How can he now say, 'I have come down from heaven'?" ⁴³Jesus answered them, "Do not complain among yourselves. ⁴⁴No one can come to me unless drawn by the Father who sent me; and I will raise that person up on the last day. ⁴⁵It is written in the prophets, 'And they shall all be taught by God.' Everyone who has heard and learned from the Father comes to me. ⁴⁶Not that anyone has seen the Father except the one who is from God; he has seen the Father. ⁴⁷Very truly, I tell you, whoever believes has eternal life. ⁴⁸I am the bread of life. ⁴⁹Your ancestors ate the manna in the wilderness, and they died. ⁵⁰This is the bread that comes down from heaven, so that one may eat of it and not die. ⁵¹I am the living bread that came down from heaven. Whoever eats of this bread will live forever; and the bread that I will give for the life of the world is my flesh."

52 The Jews then disputed among themselves, saying, "How can this man give us his flesh to eat?" ⁵³So Jesus said to them, "Very truly, I tell you, unless you eat the flesh of the Son of Man and drink his blood, you have no life in you. ⁵⁴Those who eat my flesh and drink my blood have eternal life, and I will raise them up on the last day; ⁵⁵for my flesh is true food and my blood is true drink. ⁵⁶Those who eat my flesh and drink my blood abide in me, and I in them. ⁵⁷Just as the living Father sent me, and I live because of the Father, so whoever eats me will live because of me. ⁵⁸This is the bread that came down from heaven, not like that which your ancestors ate, and they died. But the one who eats this bread will live forever." ⁵⁹He said these things while he was teaching in the synagogue at Ca·per'na·um.

The Words of Eternal Life

60 When many of his disciples heard it, they said, "This teaching is difficult; who can accept it?" ⁶¹But Jesus, being aware that his disciples were complaining about it, said to them, "Does this offend you? ⁶²Then what if you were to see the Son of Man ascending to where he was before? ⁶³It is the spirit that gives life; the flesh is useless. The words that I have spoken to you are spirit and life.

⁵ Or he who

64 But among you there are some who do not believe." For Jesus knew from the first who were the ones that did not believe, and who was the one that would betray him. 65 And he said, "For this reason I have told you that no one can come to me unless it is granted by the Father."

66 Because of this many of his disciples turned back and no longer went about with him. 67 So Jesus asked the twelve, "Do you also wish to go away?" 68 Simon Peter answered him, "Lord, to whom can we go? You have the words of eternal life. 69 We have come to believe and know that you are the Holy One of God."t 70 Jesus answered them, "Did I not choose you, the twelve? Yet one of you is a devil." 71 He was speaking of Judas son of Simon Is·car'i·ot,u for he, though one of the twelve, was going to betray him.

The Unbelief of Jesus' Brothers

After this Jesus went about in Galilee. He did not wishv to go about in Judea because the Jews were looking for an opportunity to kill him. 2 Now the Jewish festival of Boothsw was near. 3 So his brothers said to him, "Leave here and go to Judea so that your disciples also may see the works you are doing; 4 for no one who wantsx to be widely known acts in secret. If you do these things, show yourself to the world." 5 (For not even his brothers believed in him.) 6 Jesus said to them, "My time has not yet come, but your time is always here. 7 The world cannot hate you, but it hates me because I testify against it that its works are evil. 8 Go to the festival yourselves. I am noty going to this festival, for my time has not yet fully come." 9 After saying this, he remained in Galilee.

Jesus at the Festival of Booths

10 But after his brothers had gone to the festival, then he also went, not publicly but as it werez in secret. 11 The Jews were looking for him at the festival and saying, "Where is he?" 12 And there was considerable complaining about him among the crowds. While some were saying, "He is a good man," others were saying, "No, he is deceiving the crowd." 13 Yet no one would speak openly about him for fear of the Jews.

14 About the middle of the festival Jesus went up into the temple and began to teach. 15 The Jews were astonished at it, saying, "How does this man have such learning,a when he has never been taught?" 16 Then Jesus answered them, "My teaching is not mine but his who sent me. 17 Anyone who resolves to do the will of God will know whether the teaching is from God or whether I am speaking on my own. 18 Those who speak on their own seek their own glory; but the one who seeks the glory of him who sent him is true, and there is nothing false in him.

19 "Did not Moses give you the law? Yet none of you keeps the law. Why are you looking for an opportunity to kill me?" 20 The crowd answered, "You have a demon! Who is trying to kill you?" 21 Jesus answered them, "I performed one work, and all of you are astonished. 22 Moses gave you circumcision (it is, of course, not from Moses, but from the patriarchs), and you circumcise a man on the sabbath. 23 If a man receives circumcision on the sabbath in order that the law of Moses may not be broken, are you angry with me because I healed a man's whole body on the sabbath? 24 Do not judge by appearances, but judge with right judgment."

Is This the Christ?

25 Now some of the people of Jerusalem were saying, "Is not this the man whom they are trying to kill? 26 And here he is, speaking openly, but they say nothing to him! Can it be that the authorities really know that this is the Messiah?b 27 Yet we know where this man is from; but when the Messiahb comes, no one will know where he is from." 28 Then Jesus cried out as he was teaching in the temple, "You know me, and you know where I am from. I have not come on my own. But the one who sent me is true, and you do not know him. 29 I know him, because I am from him, and he sent me." 30 Then they tried to arrest him, but no one laid hands on him, because his hour had not yet come. 31 Yet many in the crowd believed in him and were saying, "When the Messiahb comes, will he do more signs than this man has done?"c

Officers Are Sent to Arrest Jesus

32 The Phar'i·sees heard the crowd muttering such things about him, and the chief priests and Phar'i·sees sent temple police to arrest him. 33 Jesus then said, "I will be with you a little while longer, and then I am going to him who sent me. 34 You will search for me, but you will not find me; and where I am, you cannot come." 35 The Jews said to one another, "Where does this man intend to go that we will not find him? Does he intend to go to the Dispersion among the Greeks and teach the

---

t Other ancient authorities read *the Christ, the Son of the living God* u Other ancient authorities read *Judas Iscariot son of Simon*; others, *Judas son of Simon from Karyot (Kerioth)* v Other ancient authorities read *was not at liberty* w Or *Tabernacles* x Other ancient authorities read *wants it* y Other ancient authorities add *yet* z Other ancient authorities lack *as it were* a Or *this man know his letters* b Or *the Christ* c Other ancient authorities read *is doing*

?did you KNOW?

Jesus Fulfills Jewish Feasts

In John, chapters 5–10, several references are made to four Old Testament feasts, which are also called festivals. On each feast, the author of John has Jesus say or do something that cleverly indicates he is the fulfillment of the feast's intent.

In chapter 5, after healing on the *Sabbath*, Jesus says, "My Father is still working, and I also am working" (verse 17). Essentially, he is declaring himself equal to God. In chapter 6, near the feast of the *Passover* (see "The Passover," Ex 12.14–28), Jesus feeds five thousand people and teaches that he is the bread of life. The implication is that the Eucharist, symbolizing Jesus' own sacrifice, has taken over the Passover meal and the sacrifice of the lamb.

Chapters 7–9 of John refer to the *feast of booths*, also called tabernacles. This is a harvest festival that lasts for a whole week. Two of the main symbols of the feast of booths are water and light. Jesus proclaims himself living water (7.38) and the light of the world (8.12).

Finally, the *feast of the dedication*, sometimes called Hanukkah (see "Hanukkah," 1 Macc 4.52–59), is mentioned in chapter 10. During this festival, which celebrates the dedication of the Temple, Jesus claims to be the one who is consecrated and sent into the world (verse 26). In fulfilling these feasts, Jesus' divinity and his saving mission is made clear. But his actions also lead to continued conflicts with the Jewish leaders.

▶ John, chapters 5–10

one who believes in me drink. As[d] the scripture has said, 'Out of the believer's heart[e] shall flow rivers of living water.' " 39 Now he said this about the Spirit, which believers in him were to receive; for as yet there was no Spirit,[f] because Jesus was not yet glorified.

Division among the People

40 When they heard these words, some in the crowd said, "This is really the prophet." 41 Others said, "This is the Messiah."[g] But some asked, "Surely the Messiah[g] does not come from Galilee, does he? 42 Has not the scripture said that the Messiah[g] is descended from David and comes from Bethlehem, the village where David lived?" 43 So there was a division in the crowd because of him. 44 Some of them wanted to arrest him, but no one laid hands on him.

The Unbelief of Those in Authority

45 Then the temple police went back to the chief priests and Phar'i·sees, who asked them, "Why did you not arrest him?" 46 The police answered, "Never has anyone spoken like this!" 47 Then the Phar'i·sees replied, "Surely you have not been deceived too, have you? 48 Has any one of the authorities or of the Phar'i·sees believed in him? 49 But this crowd, which does not know the law—they are accursed." 50 Nic·o·de'mus, who had gone to Jesus[h] before, and who was one of them, asked, 51 "Our law does not judge people without first giving them a hearing to find out what they are doing, does it?" 52 They replied, "Surely you are not also from Galilee, are you? Search and you will see that no prophet is to arise from Galilee."

The Woman Caught in Adultery

〚53 Then each of them went home, 1 while Jesus went to the Mount of Olives. 2 Early in the morning he came again to the temple. All the people came to him and he sat down and began to teach them. 3 The scribes and the Phar'i·sees brought a woman who had been caught in adultery; and making her stand before all of them, 4 they said to him, "Teacher, this woman was caught in the very act of committing adultery. 5 Now in the law Moses commanded us to stone such women. Now what do you say?" 6 They said this to test him, so that they might have some charge to bring against him. Jesus bent down and wrote with his finger on the ground. 7 When they kept on questioning him, he straightened up and said to them, "Let anyone

Greeks? 36 What does he mean by saying, 'You will search for me and you will not find me' and 'Where I am, you cannot come'?"

Rivers of Living Water

37 On the last day of the festival, the great day, while Jesus was standing there, he cried out, "Let anyone who is thirsty come to me, 38 and let the

---

d Or *come to me and drink.* 38 *The one who believes in me, as*
e Gk *out of his belly*　f Other ancient authorities read *for as yet the Spirit* (others, *Holy Spirit*) *had not been given*
g Or *the Christ*　h Gk *him*

Divine Compassion

Jesus was great at turning the tables on his enemies. In Jn 8.2–11, the scribes and Pharisees think they have come up with a perfect trap. He will have to either abandon his teaching on forgiveness and have a woman caught in adultery stoned to death according to the Law of Moses, or set himself up as being above the law. Either way, it will make him unpopular with the people. They know they have him!

With one amazing sentence, Jesus redefines the game. The focus moves away from the woman and onto the accusers, who cannot deny that they too are guilty of sin. The trap fails miserably, and the humbled religious leaders leave in silence.

We are often quick to notice the sinfulness of others while minimizing our own guilt. Jesus reminds us to be compassionate toward the sins of others. And notice how tenderly Christ dealt with the woman, whose dignity and reputation had been trampled upon. When you recognize your own guilt and stand exposed and shamed before God and others, remember that God is just as tender and compassionate toward you.

▶ Jn 8.2–11

NATIVE AMERICAN

The Sun Gives Life

The Sun, the Light of the world,
I hear Him coming,
I see His Face as He comes.
He makes the beings on earth happy,
And they rejoice.
O Wakan-Tanka, I offer to You this world of
light . . .
I offer all to You. . . .
May all be attentive and behold! . . . that
they may live.

                         (Black Elk, "The Sun Dance")

For many Native Americans, the sun is a symbol of the Great Spirit, or Wakan-Tanka. Black Elk's poem prayer has a strong parallel in the Gospel of John, when Jesus reveals his divinity by saying, "I am the light of the world" (8.12). In Christian spirituality, Jesus is sometimes called the Sun (or Son) of Righteousness.

▶ Jn 8.12–20

among you who is without sin be the first to throw a stone at her." [8] And once again he bent down and wrote on the ground.[i] [9] When they heard it, they went away, one by one, beginning with the elders; and Jesus was left alone with the woman standing before him. [10] Jesus straightened up and said to her, "Woman, where are they? Has no one condemned you?" [11] She said, "No one, sir."[j] And Jesus said, "Neither do I condemn you. Go your way, and from now on do not sin again."[k]

Jesus the Light of the World

[12] Again Jesus spoke to them, saying, "I am the light of the world. Whoever follows me will never walk in darkness but will have the light of life." [13] Then the Phar′i·sees said to him, "You are testifying on your own behalf; your testimony is not valid." [14] Jesus answered, "Even if I testify on my own behalf, my testimony is valid because I know where I have come from and where I am going, but you do not know where I come from or where I am going. [15] You judge by human standards;[l] I judge no one. [16] Yet even if I do judge, my judgment is valid; for it is not I alone who judge, but I and the Father[m] who sent me. [17] In your law it is written that the testimony of two witnesses is valid. [18] I testify on my own behalf, and the Father who sent me testifies on my behalf." [19] Then they said to him, "Where is your Father?" Jesus an-

---

i Other ancient authorities add *the sins of each of them*
j Or *Lord*   k The most ancient authorities lack 7.53—8.11; other authorities add the passage here or after 7.36 or after 21.25 or after Luke 21.38, with variations of text; some mark the passage as doubtful.   l Gk *according to the flesh*   m Other ancient authorities read *he*

swered, "You know neither me nor my Father. If you knew me, you would know my Father also." 20 He spoke these words while he was teaching in the treasury of the temple, but no one arrested him, because his hour had not yet come.

Jesus Foretells His Death

21 Again he said to them, "I am going away, and you will search for me, but you will die in your sin. Where I am going, you cannot come." 22 Then the Jews said, "Is he going to kill himself? Is that what he means by saying, 'Where I am going, you cannot come'?" 23 He said to them, "You

one who sent me is with me; he has not left me alone, for I always do what is pleasing to him." 30 As he was saying these things, many believed in him.

True Disciples

31 Then Jesus said to the Jews who had believed in him, "If you continue in my word, you are truly my disciples; 32 and you will know the truth, and the truth will make you free." 33 They answered him, "We are descendants of Abraham and have never been slaves to anyone. What do you mean by saying, 'You will be made free'?"

JESUS IS THE LIGHT OF LIFE!

Once again, the Gospel of John creates a sharp distinction between light and darkness, good and evil. Those who follow Jesus will never walk in darkness but will have the light of life. Light is a symbol of life, happiness, justice, and the joy of salvation and liberation in Christ. Darkness is a symbol of death, disgrace, tears, and imprisonment.

Hispanics have a long tradition of lighting candles in church, at home, and at their job site. The candles symbolize the light that comes from Christ and guides us to true life.

We need the light of Christ to live with wholeness and integrity, and to give a proper value and place to material things and human activities. The light of Christ can direct us in our journey to God. Religious symbols and rituals are privileged means to help us remember the Gospel, give witness of the Gospel with our own life, and radiate God's love to those around us.

■ How do you transmit the light of Christ to others today?
■ Where in your life do you need the light of Christ?
■ Give thanks to Jesus for inviting you to share in the life of God.

▶ Jn 8.12–59

are from below, I am from above; you are of this world, I am not of this world. 24 I told you that you would die in your sins, for you will die in your sins unless you believe that I am he."n 25 They said to him, "Who are you?" Jesus said to them, "Why do I speak to you at all?o 26 I have much to say about you and much to condemn; but the one who sent me is true, and I declare to the world what I have heard from him." 27 They did not understand that he was speaking to them about the Father. 28 So Jesus said, "When you have lifted up the Son of Man, then you will realize that I am he,n and that I do nothing on my own, but I speak these things as the Father instructed me. 29 And the

34 Jesus answered them, "Very truly, I tell you, everyone who commits sin is a slave to sin. 35 The slave does not have a permanent place in the household; the son has a place there forever. 36 So if the Son makes you free, you will be free indeed. 37 I know that you are descendants of Abraham; yet you look for an opportunity to kill me, because there is no place in you for my word. 38 I declare what I have seen in the Father's presence; as for you, you should do what you have heard from the Father."p

---

n Gk I am   o Or What I have told you from the beginning
p Other ancient authorities read you do what you have heard from your father

Jesus and Abraham

39 They answered him, "Abraham is our father." Jesus said to them, "If you were Abraham's children, you would be doing*q* what Abraham did, 40 but now you are trying to kill me, a man who has told you the truth that I heard from God. This is not what Abraham did. 41 You are indeed doing what your father does." They said to him, "We are not illegitimate children; we have one father, God himself." 42 Jesus said to them, "If God were your Father, you would love me, for I came from God and now I am here. I did not come on my own, but he sent me. 43 Why do you not understand what I say? It is because you cannot accept my word. 44 You are from your father the devil, and you choose to do your father's desires. He was a murderer from the beginning and does not stand in the truth, because there is no truth in him. When he lies, he speaks according to his own nature, for he is a liar and the father of lies. 45 But because I tell the truth, you do not believe me.

46 Which of you convicts me of sin? If I tell the truth, why do you not believe me? 47 Whoever is from God hears the words of God. The reason you do not hear them is that you are not from God."

48 The Jews answered him, "Are we not right in saying that you are a Sa•mār'i•tan and have a demon?" 49 Jesus answered, "I do not have a demon; but I honor my Father, and you dishonor me. 50 Yet I do not seek my own glory; there is one who seeks it and he is the judge. 51 Very truly, I tell you, whoever keeps my word will never see death." 52 The Jews said to him, "Now we know that you have a demon. Abraham died, and so did the prophets; yet you say, 'Whoever keeps my word will never taste death.' 53 Are you greater than our father Abraham, who died? The prophets also died. Who do you claim to be?" 54 Jesus answered, "If I glorify myself, my glory is nothing. It is my Father who glorifies me, he of whom you say, 'He is our God,' 55 though you do not know him. But I know him; if I would say that I do not know him, I would be a liar like you. But I do know him and I keep his word. 56 Your ancestor Abraham rejoiced that he would see my day; he saw it and was glad." 57 Then the Jews said to him, "You are not yet fifty years old, and have you seen Abraham?"*r* 58 Jesus said to them, "Very truly, I tell you, before Abraham was, I am." 59 So they picked up stones to throw at him, but Jesus hid himself and went out of the temple.

A Man Born Blind Receives Sight

As he walked along, he saw a man blind from birth. 2 His disciples asked him, "Rabbi, who sinned, this man or his parents, that he was born blind?" 3 Jesus answered, "Neither this man nor his parents sinned; he was born blind so that God's works might be revealed in him. 4 We*s* must work the works of him who sent me*t* while it is day; night is coming when no one can work. 5 As long as I am in the world, I am the light of the world." 6 When he had said this, he spat on the ground and made mud with the saliva and spread the mud on the man's eyes, 7 saying to him, "Go, wash in the pool of Sī•lō'am" (which means Sent). Then he went and washed and came back able to see. 8 The neighbors and those who had seen him before as a beggar began to ask, "Is this not the man who used to sit and beg?" 9 Some were saying, "It is he." Others were saying, "No, but it is someone like him." He kept saying, "I am the man." 10 But they kept asking him, "Then how were your

---

PRAY IT

Seeing with God's Eyes

Lord, can you fix my eyesight like you did for the blind man?

I want to see with your eyes those who are teased for being different at school.

I want to see with your eyes the homeless person on a park bench.

I want to see with your eyes people from other races and cultures.

I want to see more than people who think that being thinner or stronger makes you more lovable.

I want to see more than people who look at wealth and think that's what life is all about.

Help me to see with your eyes, Lord! Blind me to the way the world sees so that I won't give in to judging people on their looks or skin color or possessions or personality.

Help me to see, and to love, as you love, Lord—with eyes so wide open that they see past the outside and right into the heart of another.

▸ John, chapter 9

---

q Other ancient authorities read *If you are Abraham's children, then do* *r* Other ancient authorities read *has Abraham seen you?* *s* Other ancient authorities read *I* *t* Other ancient authorities read *us*

eyes opened?" [11] He answered, "The man called Jesus made mud, spread it on my eyes, and said to me, 'Go to Sĭ·lō'am and wash.' Then I went and washed and received my sight." [12] They said to him, "Where is he?" He said, "I do not know."

The Pharisees Investigate the Healing

13 They brought to the Phar'i·sees the man who had formerly been blind. [14] Now it was a sabbath day when Jesus made the mud and opened his eyes. [15] Then the Phar'i·sees also began to ask him how he had received his sight. He said to them, "He put mud on my eyes. Then I washed, and now I see." [16] Some of the Phar'i·sees said, "This man is not from God, for he does not observe the sabbath." But others said, "How can a man who is a sinner perform such signs?" And they were divided. [17] So they said again to the blind man, "What do you say about him? It was your eyes he opened." He said, "He is a prophet."

18 The Jews did not believe that he had been blind and had received his sight until they called the parents of the man who had received his sight [19] and asked them, "Is this your son, who you say was born blind? How then does he now see?" [20] His parents answered, "We know that this is our son, and that he was born blind; [21] but we do not know how it is that now he sees, nor do we know who opened his eyes. Ask him; he is of age. He will speak for himself." [22] His parents said this because they were afraid of the Jews; for the Jews had already agreed that anyone who confessed Jesus[u] to be the Messiah[v] would be put out of the synagogue. [23] Therefore his parents said, "He is of age; ask him."

24 So for the second time they called the man who had been blind, and they said to him, "Give glory to God! We know that this man is a sinner." [25] He answered, "I do not know whether he is a sinner. One thing I do know, that though I was blind, now I see." [26] They said to him, "What did he do to you? How did he open your eyes?" [27] He answered them, "I have told you already, and you would not listen. Why do you want to hear it again? Do you also want to become his disciples?" [28] Then they reviled him, saying, "You are his disciple, but we are disciples of Moses. [29] We know that God has spoken to Moses, but as for this man, we do not know where he comes from." [30] The man answered, "Here is an astonishing thing! You do not know where he comes from, and yet he opened my eyes. [31] We know that God does not listen to sinners, but he does listen to one who worships him and obeys his will. [32] Never since the world began has it been heard that anyone opened the eyes of a person born blind. [33] If this man were not from God, he could do nothing." [34] They answered him, "You were born entirely in sins, and are you trying to teach us?" And they drove him out.

Spiritual Blindness

35 Jesus heard that they had driven him out, and when he found him, he said, "Do you believe in the Son of Man?"[w] [36] He answered, "And who is he, sir?[x] Tell me, so that I may believe in him." [37] Jesus said to him, "You have seen him, and the one speaking with you is he." [38] He said, "Lord,[x] I believe." And he worshiped him. [39] Jesus said, "I came into this world for judgment so that those who do not see may see, and those who do see may become blind." [40] Some of the Phar'i·sees near him heard this and said to him, "Surely we are not blind, are we?" [41] Jesus said to them, "If you were blind, you would not have sin. But now that you say, 'We see,' your sin remains.

Jesus the Good Shepherd

"Very truly, I tell you, anyone who does not enter the sheepfold by the gate but climbs in by another way is a thief and a bandit. [2] The one who enters by the gate is the shepherd of the sheep. [3] The gatekeeper opens the gate for him, and the sheep hear his voice. He calls his own sheep by name and leads them out. [4] When he has brought out all his own, he goes ahead of them, and the sheep follow him because they know his voice. [5] They will not follow a stranger, but they will run from him because they do not know the voice of strangers." [6] Jesus used this figure of speech with them, but they did not understand what he was saying to them.

7 So again Jesus said to them, "Very truly, I tell you, I am the gate for the sheep. [8] All who came before me are thieves and bandits; but the sheep did not listen to them. [9] I am the gate. Whoever enters by me will be saved, and will come in and go out and find pasture. [10] The thief comes only to steal and kill and destroy. I came that they may have life, and have it abundantly.

11 "I am the good shepherd. The good shepherd lays down his life for the sheep. [12] The hired hand, who is not the shepherd and does not own the sheep, sees the wolf coming and leaves the sheep and runs away—and the wolf snatches them and scatters them. [13] The hired hand runs away because a hired hand does not care for the sheep. [14] I am the good shepherd. I know my own and my

---

u Gk *him*   v Or *the Christ*   w Other ancient authorities read *the Son of God*   x *Sir* and *Lord* translate the same Greek word

own know me, 15 just as the Father knows me and I know the Father. And I lay down my life for the sheep. 16 I have other sheep that do not belong to this fold. I must bring them also, and they will listen to my voice. So there will be one flock, one shepherd. 17 For this reason the Father loves me, because I lay down my life in order to take it up again. 18 No one takes[y] it from me, but I lay it down of my own accord. I have power to lay it down, and I have power to take it up again. I have received this command from my Father."

19 Again the Jews were divided because of these words. 20 Many of them were saying, "He has a demon and is out of his mind. Why listen to him?" 21 Others were saying, "These are not the words of one who has a demon. Can a demon open the eyes of the blind?"

Jesus Is Rejected by the Jews

22 At that time the festival of the Dedication took place in Jerusalem. It was winter, 23 and Jesus was walking in the temple, in the portico of Solomon. 24 So the Jews gathered around him and said to him, "How long will you keep us in suspense? If you are the Messiah,[z] tell us plainly." 25 Jesus answered, "I have told you, and you do not believe. The works that I do in my Father's name testify to me; 26 but you do not believe, because you do not belong to my sheep. 27 My sheep hear my voice. I know them, and they follow me. 28 I give them eternal life, and they will never perish. No one will snatch them out of my hand. 29 What my Father has given me is greater than all else, and no one can snatch it out of the Father's hand.[a] 30 The Father and I are one."

31 The Jews took up stones again to stone him. 32 Jesus replied, "I have shown you many good works from the Father. For which of these are you going to stone me?" 33 The Jews answered, "It is not for a good work that we are going to stone you, but for blasphemy, because you, though only a human being, are making yourself God." 34 Jesus answered, "Is it not written in your law,[b] 'I said, you are gods'? 35 If those to whom the word of God came were called 'gods'—and the scripture cannot be annulled— 36 can you say that the one whom the Father has sanctified and sent into the world is blaspheming because I said, 'I am God's Son'? 37 If I am not doing the works of my Father, then do not believe me. 38 But if I do them, even though you do not believe me, believe the works, so that you may know and understand[c] that the Father is in me and I am in the Father." 39 Then they tried to arrest him again, but he escaped from their hands.

PRAY IT!

Jesus, the Good Shepherd

The theme of shepherds and sheep is a recurring one in the Bible. In the Old Testament, God is often portrayed as a shepherd. For example, see Psalm 23 and Ezekiel, chapter 34. David, the greatest king of Israel, is also portrayed as a shepherd in Ps 78.70–72. In passages like Jer 23.1–6, God promises to raise up new shepherds who will follow in David's legacy. So it is natural that Jesus compares himself to a shepherd in Jn 10.1–18.

Being a shepherd is not an easy job. Sheep are pretty defenseless creatures, and shepherds have to protect them from predators like lions and wolves. Sheep also have a tendency to stray from the flock, making them especially vulnerable. Shepherds endure the hardships of being away from their homes and putting up with simple food and harsh weather while pasturing sheep. Their lives can be endangered when confronted by desperate predators. Sheep learn to recognize their shepherd's voice, which makes it easier to separate different flocks when flocks are mixed together for grazing or protection.

In your prayer, reflect or journal on the following questions:

- How do you relate to Jesus as the good shepherd?
- When is it reassuring to know that Jesus is watching out for you? How do you see yourself helping to "shepherd" other people as a follower of Jesus?

▸ Jn 10.1–18

40 He went away again across the Jordan to the place where John had been baptizing earlier, and he remained there. 41 Many came to him, and

---

y Other ancient authorities read *has taken*   z Or *the Christ*
a Other ancient authorities read *My Father who has given them to me is greater than all, and no one can snatch them out of the Father's hand*   b Other ancient authorities read *in the law*   c Other ancient authorities lack *and understand*; others read *and believe*

they were saying, "John performed no sign, but everything that John said about this man was true." [42] And many believed in him there.

The Death of Lazarus

Now a certain man was ill, Laz'a•rus of Beth'a•ny, the village of Mary and her sister Martha. [2] Mary was the one who anointed the Lord with perfume and wiped his feet with her hair; her brother Laz'a-rus was ill. [3] So the sisters sent a message to Jesus,[d] "Lord, he whom you love is ill." [4] But when Jesus heard it, he said, "This illness does not lead to death; rather it is for God's glory, so that the Son of God may be glorified through it." [5] Accordingly, though Jesus loved Martha and her sister and Laz'-a•rus, [6] after having heard that Laz'a•rus[e] was ill, he stayed two days longer in the place where he was.

[7] Then after this he said to the disciples, "Let us go to Judea again." [8] The disciples said to him, "Rabbi, the Jews were just now trying to stone you, and are you going there again?" [9] Jesus answered, "Are there not twelve hours of daylight? Those who walk during the day do not stumble, because they see the light of this world. [10] But those who walk at night stumble, because the light is not in them." [11] After saying this, he told them, "Our friend Laz'a•rus has fallen asleep, but I am going there to awaken him." [12] The disciples said to him, "Lord, if he has fallen asleep, he will be all right." [13] Jesus, however, had been speaking about his death, but they thought that he was referring merely to sleep. [14] Then Jesus told them plainly, "Laz'a•rus is dead. [15] For your sake I am glad I was not there, so that you may believe. But let us go to him." [16] Thomas, who was called the Twin,[f] said to his fellow disciples, "Let us also go, that we may die with him."

Jesus the Resurrection and the Life

[17] When Jesus arrived, he found that Laz'a•rus[e] had already been in the tomb four days. [18] Now Beth'a•ny was near Jerusalem, some two miles[g] away, [19] and many of the Jews had come to Martha and Mary to console them about their brother. [20] When Martha heard that Jesus was coming, she went and met him, while Mary stayed at home. [21] Martha said to Jesus, "Lord, if you had been here, my brother would not have died. [22] But even now I know that God will give you whatever you ask of him." [23] Jesus said to her, "Your brother will rise again." [24] Martha said to him, "I know that he will rise again in the resurrection on the last day." [25] Jesus said to her, "I am the resurrection and the life.[h] Those who believe in me, even though they

die, will live, [26] and everyone who lives and believes in me will never die. Do you believe this?" [27] She said to him, "Yes, Lord, I believe that you are the Messiah,[i] the Son of God, the one coming into the world."

Jesus Weeps

[28] When she had said this, she went back and called her sister Mary, and told her privately, "The Teacher is here and is calling for you." [29] And when she heard it, she got up quickly and went to him. [30] Now Jesus had not yet come to the village, but was still at the place where Martha had met him. [31] The Jews who were with her in the house, consoling her, saw Mary get up quickly and go out. They followed her because they thought that she was going to the tomb to weep there. [32] When Mary came where Jesus was and saw him, she knelt at his feet and said to him, "Lord, if you had been here, my brother would not have died." [33] When Jesus saw her weeping, and the Jews who came with her also weeping, he was greatly disturbed in spirit and deeply moved. [34] He said, "Where have you laid him?" They said to him,

PRAY IT?
A God Who Cries

*L*ord, have I ever made you cry? angry enough to yell? tickled enough to laugh? proud enough to burst? I hope so. I hope you know me so well that my every movement, my every breath is noticed by you. I want to believe that about you, Jesus, because that is the image of you I can talk to, a God who can relate to me and accept me in all that I do. Amen.

▶ Jn 11.35

"Lord, come and see." [35] Jesus began to weep. [36] So the Jews said, "See how he loved him!" [37] But some of them said, "Could not he who opened the eyes of the blind man have kept this man from dying?"

---

d Gk him   e Gk he   f Gk Didymus   g Gk fifteen stadia
h Other ancient authorities lack *and the life*   i Or *the Christ*

Jesus Raises Lazarus to Life

38 Then Jesus, again greatly disturbed, came to the tomb. It was a cave, and a stone was lying against it. 39 Jesus said, "Take away the stone." Martha, the sister of the dead man, said to him, "Lord, already there is a stench because he has been dead four days." 40 Jesus said to her, "Did I not tell you that if you believed, you would see the glory of God?" 41 So they took away the stone. And Jesus looked upward and said, "Father, I thank you for having heard me. 42 I knew that you always hear me, but I have said this for the sake of the crowd standing here, so that they may believe that you sent me." 43 When he had said this, he cried with a loud voice, "Laz'a•rus, come out!" 44 The dead man came out, his hands and feet bound with strips of cloth, and his face wrapped in a cloth. Jesus said to them, "Unbind him, and let him go."

The Plot to Kill Jesus
(Mt 26.1–5; Mk 14.1–2; Lk 22.1–2)

45 Many of the Jews therefore, who had come with Mary and had seen what Jesus did, believed in him. 46 But some of them went to the Phar'i•sees and told them what he had done. 47 So the chief priests and the Phar'i•sees called a meeting of the council, and said, "What are we to do? This man is performing many signs. 48 If we let him go on like this, everyone will believe in him, and the Romans will come and destroy both our holy place[j] and our nation." 49 But one of them, Ca'i•a•phas, who was high priest that year, said to them, "You know nothing at all! 50 You do not understand that it is better for you to have one man die for the people than to have the whole nation destroyed." 51 He did not say this on his own, but being high priest that year he prophesied that Jesus was about to die for the nation, 52 and not for the nation only, but to gather into one the dispersed children of God. 53 So from that day on they planned to put him to death.

54 Jesus therefore no longer walked about openly among the Jews, but went from there to a town called E'phra•im in the region near the wilderness; and he remained there with the disciples.

55 Now the Passover of the Jews was near, and many went up from the country to Jerusalem before the Passover to purify themselves. 56 They were looking for Jesus and were asking one another as they stood in the temple, "What do you think? Surely he will not come to the festival, will he?" 57 Now the chief priests and the Phar'i•sees had given orders that anyone who knew where Jesus[k] was should let them know, so that they might arrest him.

Mary Anoints Jesus
(Mt 26.6–13; Mk 14.3–9)

Six days before the Passover Jesus came to Beth'a•ny, the home of Laz'a•rus, whom he had raised from the dead. 2 There they gave a dinner for him. Martha served, and Laz'a•rus was one of those at the table with him. 3 Mary took a pound of costly perfume made of pure nard, anointed Jesus' feet, and wiped them[l] with her hair. The house was filled with the fragrance of the perfume. 4 But Judas Is•car'i•ot, one of his disciples (the one who was about to betray him), said, 5 "Why was this perfume not sold for three hundred denarii[m] and the money given to the poor?" 6 (He said this not because he cared about the poor, but because he was a thief; he kept the common purse and used to steal what was put into it.) 7 Jesus said, "Leave her alone. She bought it[n] so that she might keep it for the day of my burial. 8 You always have the poor with you, but you do not always have me."

The Plot to Kill Lazarus

9 When the great crowd of the Jews learned that he was there, they came not only because of Jesus but also to see Laz'a•rus, whom he had raised from the dead. 10 So the chief priests planned to put Laz'a•rus to death as well, 11 since it was on account of him that many of the Jews were deserting and were believing in Jesus.

Jesus' Triumphal Entry into Jerusalem
(Mt 21.1–11; Mk 11.1–11; Lk 19.28–40)

12 The next day the great crowd that had come to the festival heard that Jesus was coming to Jerusalem. 13 So they took branches of palm trees and went out to meet him, shouting,

"Hosanna!
Blessed is the one who comes in the name
of the Lord—
the King of Israel!"

14 Jesus found a young donkey and sat on it; as it is written:

15 "Do not be afraid, daughter of Zion.
Look, your king is coming,
sitting on a donkey's colt!"

16 His disciples did not understand these things at first; but when Jesus was glorified, then they remembered that these things had been written of him and had been done to him. 17 So the crowd that had been with him when he called Laz'a•rus out of the tomb and raised him from the dead

---

j Or our temple; Greek our place   k Gk he   l Gk his feet
m Three hundred denarii would be nearly a year's wages
for a laborer   n Gk lacks She bought it

continued to testify.*ᵒ* ¹⁸It was also because they heard that he had performed this sign that the crowd went to meet him. ¹⁹The Phar'i•sees then said to one another, "You see, you can do nothing. Look, the world has gone after him!"

Some Greeks Wish to See Jesus

20 Now among those who went up to worship at the festival were some Greeks. ²¹They came to Philip, who was from Beth•sa'i•da in Galilee, and said to him, "Sir, we wish to see Jesus." ²²Philip went and told Andrew; then Andrew and Philip went and told Jesus. ²³Jesus answered them, "The hour has come for the Son of Man to be glorified. ²⁴Very truly, I tell you, unless a grain of wheat falls into the earth and dies, it remains just a single grain; but if it dies, it bears much fruit. ²⁵Those who love their life lose it, and those who hate their life in this world will keep it for eternal life. ²⁶Whoever serves me must follow me, and where I am, there will my servant be also. Whoever serves me, the Father will honor.

Jesus Speaks about His Death

27 "Now my soul is troubled. And what should I say—'Father, save me from this hour'? No, it is for this reason that I have come to this hour. ²⁸Father, glorify your name." Then a voice came from heaven, "I have glorified it, and I will glorify it again." ²⁹The crowd standing there heard it and said that it was thunder. Others said, "An angel has spoken to him." ³⁰Jesus answered, "This voice has come for your sake, not for mine. ³¹Now is the judgment of this world; now the ruler of this world will be driven out. ³²And I, when I am lifted up from the earth, will draw all people*ᵖ* to myself." ³³He said this to indicate the kind of death he was to die. ³⁴The crowd answered him, "We have heard from the law that the Messiah*q* remains forever. How can you say that the Son of Man must be lifted up? Who is this Son of Man?" ³⁵Jesus said to them, "The light is with you for a little longer. Walk while you have the light, so that the darkness may not overtake you. If you walk in the darkness, you do not know where you are going. ³⁶While you have the light, believe in the light, so that you may become children of light."

The Unbelief of the People

After Jesus had said this, he departed and hid from them. ³⁷Although he had performed so many signs in their presence, they did not believe in him. ³⁸This was to fulfill the word spoken by the prophet I•sai'ah:

PRAY IT
Dying for New Life

In Jn 12.24–26, Jesus is describing what Christians call the *paschal mystery*. It is the belief that God brings new life out of suffering and death. The first and ultimate expression of the paschal mystery is Jesus' own death and Resurrection. God used Christ's sacrifice to free us from the bonds of sin, and Christ's Resurrection to open the path to new life. It is a mystery that no one can fully explain, but the Gospels and experience tell us it is so.

Like the grain of wheat in this Gospel passage, in death, we bear the fruit of new life. The path to new life is through sacrifice and death. By dying to our selfishness and focusing on loving others, we experience the fullness of life in Christ Jesus.

In your prayer, reflect or journal on the following questions:
- What does the paschal mystery mean to you?
- What kinds of attitudes, desires, or actions must you "die to"?

Write a prayer asking God to give you the courage to let go of the things that keep you from fullness of life.

▶ Jn 12.24–26

"Lord, who has believed our message,
  and to whom has the arm of the Lord
    been revealed?"
³⁹And so they could not believe, because I•sai'ah also said,
40 "He has blinded their eyes
  and hardened their heart,
so that they might not look with their eyes,
  and understand with their heart and
    turn—
  and I would heal them."
⁴¹I•sai'ah said this because*r* he saw his glory and spoke about him. ⁴²Nevertheless many, even of the authorities, believed in him. But because of the Phar'i•sees they did not confess it, for fear that they would be put out of the synagogue; ⁴³for they

ᵒ Other ancient authorities read *with him began to testify that he had called. . .from the dead* *ᵖ* Other ancient authorities read *all things* *q* Or *the Christ* *r* Other ancient witnesses read *when*

loved human glory more than the glory that comes from God.

Summary of Jesus' Teaching

44 Then Jesus cried aloud: "Whoever believes in me believes not in me but in him who sent me. 45 And whoever sees me sees him who sent me. 46 I have come as light into the world, so that everyone who believes in me should not remain in the darkness. 47 I do not judge anyone who hears my words and does not keep them, for I came not to judge the world, but to save the world. 48 The one who rejects me and does not receive my word has a judge; on the last day the word that I have spoken will serve as judge, 49 for I have not spoken on my own, but the Father who sent me has himself given me a commandment about what to say and what to speak. 50 And I know that his commandment is eternal life. What I speak, therefore, I speak just as the Father has told me."

Jesus Washes the Disciples' Feet

Now before the festival of the Passover, Jesus knew that his hour had come to depart from this world and go to the Father. Having loved his own who were in the world, he loved them to the end. 2 The devil had already put it into the heart of Judas son of Simon Is•car'i•ot to betray him. And during supper 3 Jesus, knowing that the Father had given all things into his hands, and that he had come from God and was going to God, 4 got up from the table, s took off his outer robe, and tied a towel around himself. 5 Then he poured water into a basin and began to wash the disciples' feet and to wipe them with the towel that was tied around him. 6 He came to Simon Peter, who said to him, "Lord, are you going to wash my feet?" 7 Jesus answered, "You do not know now what I am doing,

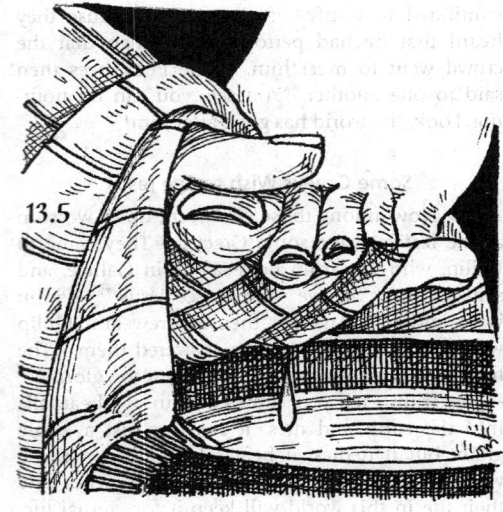

13.5

but later you will understand." 8 Peter said to him, "You will never wash my feet." Jesus answered, "Unless I wash you, you have no share with me." 9 Simon Peter said to him, "Lord, not my feet only but also my hands and my head!" 10 Jesus said to him, "One who has bathed does not need to wash, except for the feet, t but is entirely clean. And you u are clean, though not all of you." 11 For he knew who was to betray him; for this reason he said, "Not all of you are clean."

12 After he had washed their feet, had put on his robe, and had returned to the table, he said to them, "Do you know what I have done to you? 13 You call me Teacher and Lord—and you are right, for that is what I am. 14 So if I, your Lord and

---

s Gk *from supper*   t Other ancient authorities lack *except for the feet*   u The Greek word for *you* here is plural

---

Jesus Models Service to Others

LIVE IT!

In Matthew, Mark, and Luke, the focus of the Last Supper is on the institution of the Eucharist. But in John, the focus is on Jesus' cleaning his disciples' feet (13.1–17). John makes the point that serving others is at the heart of being a follower of Jesus. In Holy Thursday Mass, we celebrate both traditions, indicating that service is a necessary part of living the paschal mystery that we celebrate in the Eucharist.

- The washing of the feet is a symbol of service, humility, and purification. Have you ever felt honored and humbled at the same time?
- Read Jn 13.1–17. Reflect on and listen to Jesus' message to you.

   For more on the Eucharist, see the articles for Mt 26.26–29, Mk 14.22–25, Lk 22.14–23.

▸ Jn 13.1–17

KNOW?

Feast of the Passover

Chapter 13 is the beginning of the second part of the Gospel of John, sometimes called the Book of Glory. Its central theme is how Jesus is glorified through his Passion, death, and Resurrection. It begins with Jesus' washing the disciples' feet at the Last Supper, before the Passover.

The Jewish feast of Passover, also called the feast of unleavened bread, reminds us of how God rescued the Israelites from slavery in Egypt by killing the firstborn Egyptians and "passing over" the homes of the Israelites (about 1250 B.C.). The feast was traditionally celebrated with a meal of lamb, bitter herbs, and unleavened bread (see "The Passover," Ex 12.14–28). It was the blood of a lamb, smeared on the doorposts of the Israelites' houses, that signaled the angel of death to spare the firstborn of God's people.

In the other Gospels, the last meal that Jesus shares with his disciples is the Passover meal. However, in the Gospel of John, Jesus is arrested before Passover. He is crucified on the preparation day of the feast of unleavened bread, at the same time that the lambs are being sacrificed in the Temple. The symbolism would not be missed by the readers of John: Jesus is the new and perfect Passover lamb.

▶ Jn 13.1–20

Teacher, have washed your feet, you also ought to wash one another's feet. 15 For I have set you an example, that you also should do as I have done to you. 16 Very truly, I tell you, servants[v] are not greater than their master, nor are messengers greater than the one who sent them. 17 If you know these things, you are blessed if you do them. 18 I am not speaking of all of you; I know whom I have chosen. But it is to fulfill the scripture, 'The one who ate my bread[w] has lifted his heel against me.' 19 I tell you this now, before it occurs, so that when it does occur, you may believe that I am he.[x]

20 Very truly, I tell you, whoever receives one whom I send receives me; and whoever receives me receives him who sent me."

Jesus Foretells His Betrayal
(Mt 26.21–25; Mk 14.18–19; Lk 22.21–23)

21 After saying this Jesus was troubled in spirit, and declared, "Very truly, I tell you, one of you will betray me." 22 The disciples looked at one another, uncertain of whom he was speaking. 23 One of his disciples—the one whom Jesus loved—was reclining next to him; 24 Simon Peter therefore motioned to him to ask Jesus of whom he was speaking. 25 So while reclining next to Jesus, he asked him, "Lord, who is it?" 26 Jesus answered, "It is the one to whom I give this piece of bread when I have dipped it in the dish."[y] So when he had dipped the piece of bread, he gave it to Judas son of Simon Is•car'i•ot.[z] 27 After he received the piece of bread,[a] Satan entered into him. Jesus said to him, "Do quickly what you are going to do." 28 Now no one at the table knew why he said this to him. 29 Some thought that, because Judas had the common purse, Jesus was telling him, "Buy what we need for the festival"; or, that he should give something to the poor. 30 So, after receiving the piece of bread, he immediately went out. And it was night.

The New Commandment

31 When he had gone out, Jesus said, "Now the Son of Man has been glorified, and God has been glorified in him. 32 If God has been glorified in him,[b] God will also glorify him in himself and will glorify him at once. 33 Little children, I am with you only a little longer. You will look for me; and as I said to the Jews so now I say to you, 'Where I am going, you cannot come.' 34 I give you a new commandment, that you love one another. Just as I have loved you, you also should love one another. 35 By this everyone will know that you are my disciples, if you have love for one another."

Jesus Foretells Peter's Denial

36 Simon Peter said to him, "Lord, where are you going?" Jesus answered, "Where I am going, you cannot follow me now; but you will follow afterward." 37 Peter said to him, "Lord, why can I not follow you now? I will lay down my life for you." 38 Jesus answered, "Will you lay down your

---

v Gk slaves   w Other ancient authorities read ate bread with me   x Gk I am   y Gk dipped it   z Other ancient authorities read Judas Iscariot son of Simon; others, Judas son of Simon from Karyot (Kerioth)   a Gk After the piece of bread   b Other ancient authorities lack If God has been glorified in him

life for me? Very truly, I tell you, before the cock crows, you will have denied me three times.

Jesus the Way to the Father

"Do not let your hearts be troubled. Believe[c] in God, believe also in me. [2] In my Father's house there are many dwelling places. If it were not so, would I have told you that I go to prepare a place for you?[d] [3] And if I go and prepare a place for you, I will come again and will take you to myself, so that where I am, there you may be also. [4] And you know the way to the place where I am going."[e] [5] Thomas said to him, "Lord, we do not know where you are going. How can we know the way?" [6] Jesus said to him, "I am the way, and the truth, and the life. No one comes to the Father except through me. [7] If you know me, you will know[f] my Father also. From now on you do know him and have seen him."

[8] Philip said to him, "Lord, show us the Father, and we will be satisfied." [9] Jesus said to him, "Have I been with you all this time, Philip, and you still do not know me? Whoever has seen me has seen the Father. How can you say, 'Show us the Father'? [10] Do you not believe that I am in the Father and the Father is in me? The words that I say to you I do not speak on my own; but the Father who dwells in me does his works. [11] Believe me that I am in the Father and the Father is in me; but if you do not, then believe me because of the works themselves. [12] Very truly, I tell you, the one who believes in me will also do the works that I do and, in fact, will do greater works than these,

because I am going to the Father. [13] I will do whatever you ask in my name, so that the Father may be glorified in the Son. [14] If in my name you ask me[g] for anything, I will do it.

---

[c] Or *You believe*   [d] Or *If it were not so, I would have told you; for I go to prepare a place for you*   [e] Other ancient authorities read *Where I am going you know, and the way you know*   [f] Other ancient authorities read *If you had known me, you would have known*   [g] Other ancient authorities lack *me*

Asian American

The Way, and the Truth, and the Life

Laotian Catholics often point to Jn 14.6 as a significant connection between the Buddhist faith and their Catholic faith. There is a Buddhist tradition of honoring the way and the truth. Becoming a Catholic and knowing the risen Christ brings a deeper appreciation of everlasting life. This completes the triangle of "the way, and the truth, and the life."

▶ Jn 14.6–7

Introducing ▶ THE BELOVED DISCIPLE

In the Last Supper scene, we are introduced to a mysterious character found only in the Gospel of John, described as the disciple Jesus loved. He is mentioned several more times in John: at the foot of the cross with Jesus' mother (19.25–27), on Easter morning when he enters the empty tomb with Peter (20.2–12), and after the Resurrection when he identifies Jesus from the boat (21.7,20). He is always with Peter or where Peter should be (at the cross).

So who is the mystery man? Traditionally, he has been identified as John, the son of Zebedee and one of the twelve Apostles, and as the writer of the Gospel of John. But if that is true, why does he refer to himself so strangely? Many scholars today believe that the Beloved Disciple was a lesser-known follower of Jesus who was the founder of the Christian community that ultimately produced the Gospel of John. They think his eyewitness accounts (see 21.24) were passed on and are the basis for the Gospel we have today.

▶ Jn 13.23–25

The Promise of the Holy Spirit

15 "If you love me, you will keep[h] my commandments. 16 And I will ask the Father, and he will give you another Advocate,[i] to be with you forever. 17 This is the Spirit of truth, whom the world cannot receive, because it neither sees him nor knows him. You know him, because he abides with you, and he will be in[j] you.

18 "I will not leave you orphaned; I am coming to you. 19 In a little while the world will no longer see me, but you will see me; because I live, you also will live. 20 On that day you will know that I am in my Father, and you in me, and I in you. 21 They who have my commandments and keep them are those who love me; and those who love me will be loved by my Father, and I will love them and reveal myself to them." 22 Judas (not Iscar'i•ot) said to him, "Lord, how is it that you will reveal yourself to us, and not to the world?" 23 Jesus answered him, "Those who love me will keep my

Catholic Connections

THE PEACE OF CHRIST

John 14.27 is the passage the priest recites during Mass just before he invites the community to share a sign of peace. This is no ordinary peace, however. It is the peace of Christ. It is a peace that is not of this world. It has allowed Christians to endure hardships, oppression, war, sickness, and death, with dignity and hope. The next time you are at Mass, think about the awesome power in the peace of Christ that you are extending to the people around you.

▸ Jn 14.27

J
N

THE HOLY SPIRIT GUIDES US INTO ALL TRUTH!

¡El Espíritu santo nos guía en la verdad?

HISPANIC

Jesus told his disciples that after his death, God would send the Spirit of Truth to be with them forever. Jesus calls the Holy Spirit the Advocate (Jn 16.7), the one who defends us from evil and sin. The Holy Spirit also guides us into all Truth, by helping us to grasp the meaning of Jesus' words, actions, and miracles.

■ Jesus promises his followers that the Holy Spirit will abide in us (14.17). How are you aware of the Holy Spirit's presence in your life?

■ Place yourself in the hands of the Most Holy Trinity and call upon the Holy Spirit to protect you from all sin and evil and to bring you peace.

▸ Jn 14.15–31; 16.5–15

word, and my Father will love them, and we will come to them and make our home with them. 24 Whoever does not love me does not keep my words; and the word that you hear is not mine, but is from the Father who sent me.

25 "I have said these things to you while I am still with you. 26 But the Advocate,[i] the Holy Spirit, whom the Father will send in my name, will teach you everything, and remind you of all that I have said to you. 27 Peace I leave with you; my peace I give to you. I do not give to you as the world gives. Do not let your hearts be troubled, and do not let them be afraid. 28 You heard me say to you, 'I am going away, and I am coming to you.' If you loved me, you would rejoice that I am going to the Father, because the Father is greater than I. 29 And now I have told you this before it occurs, so that when it does occur, you may believe. 30 I will no longer talk much with you, for the ruler of this world is coming. He has no power over me; 31 but I do as the Father has commanded me, so that the world may know that I love the Father. Rise, let us be on our way.

_____

h Other ancient authorities read me, keep   i Or Helper
j Or among

Jesus the True Vine

"I am the true vine, and my Father is the vine-grower. [2] He removes every branch in me that bears no fruit. Every branch that bears fruit he prunes[k] to make it bear more fruit. [3] You have already been cleansed[k] by the word that I have spoken to you. [4] Abide in me as I abide in you. Just as the branch cannot bear fruit by itself unless it abides in the vine, neither can you unless you abide in me. [5] I am the vine, you are the branches. Those who abide in me and I in them bear much fruit, because apart from me you can do nothing. [6] Whoever does not abide in me is thrown away like a branch and withers; such branches are gathered, thrown into the fire, and burned. [7] If you abide in me, and my words abide in you, ask for whatever you wish, and it will be done for you. [8] My Father is glorified by this, that you bear much

MAKE YOUR HOME WITH JESUS

Jesus calls himself the true vine, and us the branches (Jn 15.5). What does this mean for us? First, it means that apart from Jesus, we can produce no fruit. That is, we have nothing of ultimate value to offer others. It also means that to stay alive, we must "abide" in Jesus (verse 4). To abide means to stay with or make our home with. How at home are you with Jesus?

▶ Jn 15.1–11

PRAY IT
Not of This World

It is easy to get caught up in the pressures put on us by our society. It seems that we have to dress a certain way, have certain possessions, and live in a certain kind of house just to be considered average. People who resist those pressures are often labeled weird or different. They often feel out of place, not of this world.

The community from which the Gospel of John emerged did not feel at home in the world either. Their message of the divine Jesus had been rejected by Jews, Gentiles, and perhaps even other early Christians. No wonder the author has Jesus emphasize, "Because you do not belong to the world, . . . therefore the world hates you" (15.19).

In your prayer, reflect or journal on the following questions:

- How might Christians today be considered not of this world?
- What societal pressures do you need to resist?
- How does Jesus' warning to his disciples about the world's hatred (verses 18–25) apply to Christians today?

▶ Jn 15.18–25

fruit and become[l] my disciples. [9] As the Father has loved me, so I have loved you; abide in my love. [10] If you keep my commandments, you will abide in my love, just as I have kept my Father's commandments and abide in his love. [11] I have said these things to you so that my joy may be in you, and that your joy may be complete.

12 "This is my commandment, that you love one another as I have loved you. [13] No one has greater love than this, to lay down one's life for one's friends. [14] You are my friends if you do what I command you. [15] I do not call you servants[m] any longer, because the servant[n] does not know what the master is doing; but I have called you friends, because I have made known to you everything that I have heard from my Father. [16] You did not choose me but I chose you. And I appointed you to go and bear fruit, fruit that will last, so that the Father will give you whatever you ask him in my name. [17] I am giving you these commands so that you may love one another.

The World's Hatred

18 "If the world hates you, be aware that it hated me before it hated you. [19] If you belonged to the world,[o] the world would love you as its own. Because you do not belong to the world, but I have chosen you out of the world—therefore the world hates you. [20] Remember the word that I said to you, 'Servants[p] are not greater than their mas-

---

k The same Greek root refers to pruning and cleansing
l Or be   m Gk slaves   n Gk slave   o Gk were of the world
p Gk Slaves

ter.' If they persecuted me, they will persecute you; if they kept my word, they will keep yours also. 21 But they will do all these things to you on account of my name, because they do not know him who sent me. 22 If I had not come and spoken to them, they would not have sin; but now they have no excuse for their sin. 23 Whoever hates me hates my Father also. 24 If I had not done among them the works that no one else did, they would not have sin. But now they have seen and hated both me and my Father. 25 It was to fulfill the word that is written in their law, 'They hated me without a cause.'

26 "When the Advocate*q* comes, whom I will send to you from the Father, the Spirit of truth who comes from the Father, he will testify on my behalf. 27 You also are to testify because you have been with me from the beginning.

"I have said these things to you to keep you from stumbling. 2 They will put you out of the synagogues. Indeed, an hour is coming when those who kill you will think that by doing so they are offering worship to God. 3 And they will do this because they have not known the Father or me. 4 But I have said these things to you so that when their hour comes you may remember that I told you about them.

The Work of the Spirit

"I did not say these things to you from the beginning, because I was with you. 5 But now I am going to him who sent me; yet none of you asks me, 'Where are you going?' 6 But because I have said these things to you, sorrow has filled your hearts. 7 Nevertheless I tell you the truth: it is to your advantage that I go away, for if I do not go away, the Advocate*q* will not come to you; but if I go, I will send him to you. 8 And when he comes, he will prove the world wrong about*r* sin and righteousness and judgment: 9 about sin, because they do not believe in me; 10 about righteousness, because I am going to the Father and you will see me no longer; 11 about judgment, because the ruler of this world has been condemned.

12 "I still have many things to say to you, but you cannot bear them now. 13 When the Spirit of truth comes, he will guide you into all the truth; for he will not speak on his own, but will speak whatever he hears, and he will declare to you the things that are to come. 14 He will glorify me,

---

q Or *Helper*   *r* Or *convict the world of*

CHRIST LIVES IN US THROUGH THE HOLY SPIRIT!

In his farewell speech to his Apostles, Jesus tells them that he will return to the Father, but will not leave them orphaned (Jn 14.18). The Father will give them another advocate—the Holy Spirit. We also receive the Holy Spirit, through our Baptism. Hispanic spirituality emphasizes the Spirit's gifts of love, freedom, truth, life, and hope.

- *Love* lets us find joy in the midst of suffering and pain. Christ did not end human suffering; instead, he showed how suffering for those we love can bring new life to them.
- *Freedom* from material goods, false gratification, and addictions nurtures the lifestyle we adopt as disciples of Jesus.
- *Truth* about God, us, and history can be achieved only through God's revelation. The Spirit gives us the light to discover this truth and the strength to direct our life by it.
- *God's life* in us helps us overcome prejudices, promote reconciliation, foster unity in diversity, and work for justice and peace.
- *Hope* in being forever with God and the people we love is continuously nourished by the Spirit, who gives us a glimpse of the glory to come despite our earthly limitations.

▶ Jn 14.12–21; 16.12–15

because he will take what is mine and declare it to you. 15 All that the Father has is mine. For this reason I said that he will take what is mine and declare it to you.

Sorrow Will Turn into Joy

16 "A little while, and you will no longer see me, and again a little while, and you will see me." 17 Then some of his disciples said to one another, "What does he mean by saying to us, 'A little while, and you will no longer see me, and again a little while, and you will see me'; and 'Because I am going to the Father'?" 18 They said, "What does he mean by this 'a little while'? We do not know what he is talking about." 19 Jesus knew that they wanted to ask him, so he said to them, "Are you discussing among yourselves what I meant when I said, 'A little while, and you will no longer see me, and again a little while, and you will see me'? 20 Very truly, I tell you, you will weep and mourn, but the world will rejoice; you will have pain, but your pain will turn into joy. 21 When a woman is in labor, she has pain, because her hour has come. But when her child is born, she no longer remembers the anguish because of the joy of having brought a human being into the world. 22 So you have pain now; but I will see you again, and your hearts will rejoice, and no one will take your joy from you. 23 On that day you will ask nothing of me.^{s} Very truly, I tell you, if you ask anything of the Father in my name, he will give it to you.^{t} 24 Until now you have not asked for anything in my name. Ask and you will receive, so that your joy may be complete.

Peace for the Disciples

25 "I have said these things to you in figures of speech. The hour is coming when I will no longer speak to you in figures, but will tell you plainly of the Father. 26 On that day you will ask in my name. I do not say to you that I will ask the Father on your behalf; 27 for the Father himself loves you, because you have loved me and have believed that I came from God.^{u} 28 I came from the Father and have come into the world; again, I am leaving the world and am going to the Father." 29 His disciples said, "Yes, now you are speaking plainly, not in any figure of speech! 30 Now we know that you know all things, and do not need to have anyone question you; by this we believe that you came from God." 31 Jesus answered them, "Do you now believe? 32 The hour is coming, indeed it has come, when you will be scattered, each one to his home, and you will leave me alone. Yet I am not alone because the Father is with me. 33 I have

said this to you, so that in me you may have peace. In the world you face persecution. But take courage; I have conquered the world!"

Jesus Prays for His Disciples

After Jesus had spoken these words, he looked up to heaven and said, "Father, the hour has come; glorify your Son so that the Son may glorify you, 2 since you have given him authority over all people,^{v} to give eternal life to all whom you have given him. 3 And this is eternal life, that they may know you, the only true God, and Jesus Christ whom you have sent. 4 I glorified you on earth by finishing the work that you gave me to do. 5 So now, Father, glorify me in your own presence with

---

^{s} Or *will ask me no question* ^{t} Other ancient authorities read *Father, he will give it to you in my name* ^{u} Other ancient authorities read *the Father* ^{v} Gk *flesh*

---

did you KNOW?

The Hour and the Glory of God

In the Gospel of John, Jesus makes several references to his "hour." In the Gospel's first miracle, at the wedding in Cana, when Mary asks Jesus to help, he responds, "My hour has not yet come" (2.4). In 4.23 and 5.25, he talks about a coming hour when there will be true worship and the dead will hear his voice. In 7.30 and 8.20, the authorities are unable to arrest him because his hour has not yet arrived. Finally, just before his arrest and Crucifixion, he prays, "Father, the hour has come; glorify your Son" (17.1).

Jesus is talking not about an actual hour but about the time when God's glory will be revealed. Read Jn 17.1–10. Jesus' death and Resurrection are the glorification of God, and the glory of God is the salvation of humankind. The hour of God is the time of our salvation, the reason God became a human being. It is the time of joy due to the triumph of good over evil.

▶ Jn 17.1–10

the glory that I had in your presence before the world existed.

6 "I have made your name known to those whom you gave me from the world. They were yours, and you gave them to me, and they have kept your word. ⁷Now they know that everything you have given me is from you; ⁸for the words that you gave to me I have given to them, and they have received them and know in truth that I came from you; and they have believed that you sent me. ⁹I am asking on their behalf; I am not asking on behalf of the world, but on behalf of those whom you gave me, because they are yours. ¹⁰All mine are yours, and yours are mine; and I have been glorified in them. ¹¹And now I am no longer in the world, but they are in the world, and I am coming to you. Holy Father, protect them in your name that you have given me, so that they may be one, as we are one. ¹²While I was with them, I protected them in your name that*w* you have given me. I guarded them, and not one of them was lost except the one destined to be lost,*x* so that the scripture might be fulfilled. ¹³But now I am coming to you, and I speak these things in the world so that they may have my joy made complete in themselves.*y* ¹⁴I have given them your word, and the world has hated them because they do not belong to the world, just as I do not belong to the world. ¹⁵I am not asking you to take them out of the world, but I ask you to protect them from the evil one.*z* ¹⁶They do not belong to the world, just as I do not belong to the world. ¹⁷Sanctify them in the truth; your word is truth. ¹⁸As you have sent me into the world, so I have sent them into the world. ¹⁹And for their sakes I sanctify myself, so that they also may be sanctified in truth.

20 "I ask not only on behalf of these, but also on behalf of those who will believe in me through their word, ²¹that they may all be one. As you, Father, are in me and I am in you, may they also be in us,*a* so that the world may believe that you have sent me. ²²The glory that you have given me I have given them, so that they may be one, as we are one, ²³I in them and you in me, that they may become completely one, so that the world may know that you have sent me and have loved them even as you have loved me. ²⁴Father, I desire that those also, whom you have given me, may be with me where I am, to see my glory, which you have given me because you loved me before the foundation of the world.

25 "Righteous Father, the world does not know you, but I know you; and these know that you have sent me. ²⁶I made your name known to them, and I will make it known, so that the love

PRAY IT!
A Prayer for Friends

In John, chapter 17, Jesus prays for his friends, the disciples. And he also prays for us, his future disciples (verse 20)! Here is a prayer you can say for your friends:

Dear Jesus, thank you for my true friends. They accept me for who I am. With them, I don't have to pretend to be someone else. They support me when I feel that the world is crumbling around me. They are honest with me even if what they say is not what I want to hear. They offer their sense of humor so that we can laugh together.

Spirit of Jesus, watch over these friends just as you watch over me. Show them your loving acceptance and support. Help them to honestly look at themselves and the decisions they are making. If they experience pain, frustration, or failure, give them strength to lean on you. Fill their days with laughter and love. Protect them and keep them safe all the days of their lives. Amen.

▶ John, chapter 17

with which you have loved me may be in them, and I in them."

The Betrayal and Arrest of Jesus
(Mt 26.47–56; Mk 14.43–52; Lk 22.47–53)

18 After Jesus had spoken these words, he went out with his disciples across the Kid'ron valley to a place where there was a garden, which he and his disciples entered. ²Now Judas, who betrayed him, also knew the place, because Jesus often met there with his disciples. ³So Judas brought a detachment of soldiers together with police from the chief priests and the Phar'i•sees, and they came there with lanterns and torches and weapons. ⁴Then Jesus, knowing all that was to happen to him, came forward and asked them, "Whom are you looking for?" ⁵They answered, "Jesus of Nazareth."*b* Jesus replied, "I am he."*c* Judas, who betrayed him, was standing with them. ⁶When Jesus*d* said to them, "I am he,"*c* they stepped back and fell to the

w Other ancient authorities read protected in your name those whom   x Gk except the son of destruction   y Or among themselves   z Or from evil   a Other ancient authorities read be one in us   b Gk the Nazorean   c Gk I am d Gk he

did you KNOW?

The Triumph of Jesus

The Gospel of John most closely resembles the other three Gospels in its stories of Jesus' trial, death, and Resurrection. But even here, John's unique portrayal of Jesus is seen. The most obvious difference is that in John, Jesus is clearly in charge and in his glory from the moment he is arrested. There is no agony in the garden. When the soldiers and police come to arrest Jesus, they fall to the ground as he speaks (18.6). He teaches Pilate about his identity and mission, in essence putting Pilate on trial (verses 33–38). Jesus brings together his mother and the Beloved Disciple (19.26–27). Jesus is not killed, but decides the moment of his death when he gives up his spirit (verse 30).

John is also careful to show in detail the ways Jesus' Crucifixion fulfills Old Testament prophecies of the Messiah. He identifies Jesus with the just man who was persecuted in Psalms 22 and 69. He does this by connecting the gambling for Jesus' seamless tunic (Jn 19.24) with Ps 22.18, and the offering of sour wine (Jn 19.29) with Ps 69.21. Jesus' unbroken legs (Jn 19.33) are a reference to the paschal lamb in Ex 12.46, and his pierced side (Jn 19.34) is seen as the fulfillment of Zech 12.10.

John wants us to know that these events are the central "Hour" in the world's history and the time of Jesus' triumph. For the author of John, Jesus is clearly the divine Son of God, and by Jesus' self-sacrifice, God brings salvation to the entire world. The author of John wants to focus us not on the tragedy but on God's power at work in Jesus.

▶ John, chapters 18–19

struck the high priest's slave, and cut off his right ear. The slave's name was Mal'chus. [11] Jesus said to Peter, "Put your sword back into its sheath. Am I not to drink the cup that the Father has given me?"

Jesus before the High Priest

12 So the soldiers, their officer, and the Jewish police arrested Jesus and bound him. [13] First they took him to An'nas, who was the father-in-law of Cā′i·a·phas, the high priest that year. [14] Cā′i·a·phas was the one who had advised the Jews that it was better to have one person die for the people.

Peter Denies Jesus
(Mt 26.69–75; Mk 14.66–72; Lk 22.54–62)

15 Simon Peter and another disciple followed Jesus. Since that disciple was known to the high priest, he went with Jesus into the courtyard of the high priest, [16] but Peter was standing outside at the gate. So the other disciple, who was known to the high priest, went out, spoke to the woman who guarded the gate, and brought Peter in. [17] The woman said to Peter, "You are not also one of this man's disciples, are you?" He said, "I am not." [18] Now the slaves and the police had made a charcoal fire because it was cold, and they were standing around it and warming themselves. Peter also was standing with them and warming himself.

The High Priest Questions Jesus

19 Then the high priest questioned Jesus about his disciples and about his teaching. [20] Jesus answered, "I have spoken openly to the world; I have always taught in synagogues and in the temple, where all the Jews come together. I have said nothing in secret. [21] Why do you ask me? Ask those who heard what I said to them; they know what I said." [22] When he had said this, one of the police standing nearby struck Jesus on the face, saying, "Is that how you answer the high priest?" [23] Jesus answered, "If I have spoken wrongly, testify to the wrong. But if I have spoken rightly, why do you strike me?" [24] Then An'nas sent him bound to Cā′i·a·phas the high priest.

Peter Denies Jesus Again

25 Now Simon Peter was standing and warming himself. They asked him, "You are not also one of his disciples, are you?" He denied it and said, "I am not." [26] One of the slaves of the high priest, a relative of the man whose ear Peter had cut off, asked, "Did I not see you in the garden with him?" [27] Again Peter denied it, and at that moment the cock crowed.

ground. [7] Again he asked them, "Whom are you looking for?" And they said, "Jesus of Nazareth."[e] [8] Jesus answered, "I told you that I am he.[f] So if you are looking for me, let these men go." [9] This was to fulfill the word that he had spoken, "I did not lose a single one of those whom you gave me." [10] Then Simon Peter, who had a sword, drew it,

[e] Gk the Nazorean   [f] Gk I am

Jesus before Pilate
(Mt 27.1–2, 11–14; Mk 15.1–5; Lk 23.1–5)

28 Then they took Jesus from Cā′i•a•phas to Pilate's headquarters.⁸ It was early in the morning. They themselves did not enter the headquarters,⁸ so as to avoid ritual defilement and to be able to eat the Passover. 29 So Pilate went out to them and said, "What accusation do you bring against this man?" 30 They answered, "If this man were not a criminal, we would not have handed him over to you." 31 Pilate said to them, "Take him yourselves and judge him according to your law." The Jews replied, "We are not permitted to put anyone to death." 32 (This was to fulfill what Jesus had said when he indicated the kind of death he was to die.)

33 Then Pilate entered the headquarters⁸ again, summoned Jesus, and asked him, "Are you the King of the Jews?" 34 Jesus answered, "Do you ask this on your own, or did others tell you about me?" 35 Pilate replied, "I am not a Jew, am I? Your own nation and the chief priests have handed you over to me. What have you done?" 36 Jesus answered, "My kingdom is not from this world. If my kingdom were from this world, my followers would be fighting to keep me from being handed over to the Jews. But as it is, my kingdom is not from here." 37 Pilate asked him, "So you are a king?" Jesus answered, "You say that I am a king. For this I was born, and for this I came into the world, to testify to the truth. Everyone who belongs to the truth listens to my voice." 38 Pilate asked him, "What is truth?"

Jesus Sentenced to Death
(Mt 27.15–31; Mk 15.6–20; Lk 23.13–25)

After he had said this, he went out to the Jews again and told them, "I find no case against him. 39 But you have a custom that I release someone for you at the Passover. Do you want me to release for you the King of the Jews?" 40 They shouted in reply, "Not this man, but Ba•rab′bas!" Now Ba•rab′bas was a bandit.

Then Pilate took Jesus and had him flogged. 2 And the soldiers wove a crown of thorns and put it on his head, and they dressed him in a purple robe. 3 They kept coming up to him, saying, "Hail, King of the Jews!" and striking him on the face. 4 Pilate went out again and said to them, "Look, I am bringing him out to you to let you know that I find no case against him." 5 So Jesus came out, wearing the crown of thorns and the purple robe. Pilate said to them, "Here is the man!" 6 When the chief priests and the police saw him, they shouted,

Catholic Connections
EASTER TRIDUUM

For Catholics, the center of the liturgical year is the Easter Triduum, the three holy days that celebrate Jesus' death and Resurrection. The Triduum begins on Holy Thursday, the Thursday before Easter. The reading for the day, Jn 13.1–15, recounts the Last Supper and Christ's humility when washing the feet of the disciples.

Holy Thursday is followed by Good Friday, during which John's account of Jesus' Passion (chapters 18–19) is read. During the service, Catholics venerate (honor) the cross, recalling Jesus' painful sacrifice that God used for our salvation.

The climax to the Triduum is the Easter Vigil held on Saturday evening, beginning at nightfall. This celebration incorporates a dramatic ceremony of light in which the Easter fire is lit, followed by the lighting of the paschal (Jesus) candle, and the lighting of a candle for every person in the church. Then those who have been preparing to join the church are baptized, confirmed, and welcomed to receive the Eucharist.

The Easter Triduum, though celebrated over three days, is actually one celebration, from the opening song on Holy Thursday to the closing song of the Easter Vigil.

▶ Jn 13.1—20.18

"Crucify him! Crucify him!" Pilate said to them, "Take him yourselves and crucify him; I find no case against him." 7 The Jews answered him, "We have a law, and according to that law he ought to die because he has claimed to be the Son of God."

8 Now when Pilate heard this, he was more afraid than ever. 9 He entered his headquarters⁸ again and asked Jesus, "Where are you from?" But Jesus gave him no answer. 10 Pilate therefore said

⁸ Gk *the praetorium*

did you KNOW?

The Words on the Cross

In the Gospel of John, Pontius Pilate acts as a mediator between two worlds—the outside world of darkness and unbelief and the inner world of light and truth. During Jesus' trial, Pilate goes back and forth between the Jewish religious authorities who are outside (in the dark) and Jesus who is inside Pilate's headquarters (in the light).

Does Pilate know the truth about Jesus? When he writes out the charges to be placed on the cross, "the Jews" (see "'The Jews' in the Gospel of John," Jn 2.18–20) argue with him about the wording. He answers by saying, "What I have written I have written" (19.22), that is, "These words are the truth about Jesus." The words he writes are "Jesus of Nazareth, the King of the Jews" (verse 19). In Latin, they read, *"Iesus Nazarenus Rex Iudaeorum."* When artists draw or sculpt the Crucifixion scene, they often include this Latin phrase in abbreviated form above the cross—*INRI.*

In another of the Gospel's ironies, Pilate recognizes what the Jewish leaders rejected—Jesus Christ is a king. Christians believe a deeper truth—Christ is king not only of the Jews but of all creation! On the last Sunday of the liturgical year, the Catholic church celebrates this in the feast of Christ the King.

▶ Jn 19.19–22

to him, "Do you refuse to speak to me? Do you not know that I have power to release you, and power to crucify you?" [11] Jesus answered him, "You would have no power over me unless it had been given you from above; therefore the one who handed me over to you is guilty of a greater sin." [12] From then on Pilate tried to release him, but the Jews cried out, "If you release this man, you are no friend of the emperor. Everyone who claims to be a king sets himself against the emperor."

[13] When Pilate heard these words, he brought Jesus outside and sat[h] on the judge's bench at a place called The Stone Pavement, or in Hebrew[i]

Gab'ba•tha. [14] Now it was the day of Preparation for the Passover; and it was about noon. He said to the Jews, "Here is your King!" [15] They cried out, "Away with him! Away with him! Crucify him!" Pilate asked them, "Shall I crucify your King?" The chief priests answered, "We have no king but the emperor." [16] Then he handed him over to them to be crucified.

The Crucifixion of Jesus
(Mt 27.32–56; Mk 15.21–41; Lk 23.26–49)

So they took Jesus; [17] and carrying the cross by himself, he went out to what is called The Place of the Skull, which in Hebrew[i] is called Gol'go•tha. [18] There they crucified him, and with him two others, one on either side, with Jesus between them. [19] Pilate also had an inscription written and put on the cross. It read, "Jesus of Nazareth,[j] the King of the Jews." [20] Many of the Jews read this inscription, because the place where Jesus was crucified was near the city; and it was written in Hebrew,[i] in Latin, and in Greek. [21] Then the chief priests of the Jews said to Pilate, "Do not write, 'The King of the Jews,' but, 'This man said, I am King of the Jews.' " [22] Pilate answered, "What I have written I have written." [23] When the soldiers had crucified Jesus, they took his clothes and divided them into four parts, one for each soldier. They also took his tunic; now the tunic was seamless, woven in one piece from the top. [24] So they said to one another, "Let us not tear it, but cast lots for it to see who will get it." This was to fulfill what the scripture says,

"They divided my clothes among
themselves,
and for my clothing they cast lots."

[25] And that is what the soldiers did.

Meanwhile, standing near the cross of Jesus were his mother, and his mother's sister, Mary the wife of Clo'pas, and Mary Mag'da•lene. [26] When Jesus saw his mother and the disciple whom he loved standing beside her, he said to his mother, "Woman, here is your son." [27] Then he said to the disciple, "Here is your mother." And from that hour the disciple took her into his own home.

[28] After this, when Jesus knew that all was now finished, he said (in order to fulfill the scripture), "I am thirsty." [29] A jar full of sour wine was standing there. So they put a sponge full of the wine on a branch of hyssop and held it to his mouth. [30] When Jesus had received the wine, he said, "It is finished." Then he bowed his head and gave up his spirit.

---

h Or *seated him*   *i* That is, *Aramaic*   *j* Gk *the Nazorean*

Jesus' Side Is Pierced

31 Since it was the day of Preparation, the Jews did not want the bodies left on the cross during the sabbath, especially because that sabbath was a day of great solemnity. So they asked Pilate to have the legs of the crucified men broken and the bodies removed. 32 Then the soldiers came and broke the legs of the first and of the other who had been crucified with him. 33 But when they came to Jesus and saw that he was already dead, they did not break his legs. 34 Instead, one of the soldiers pierced his side with a spear, and at once blood and water came out. 35 (He who saw this has testified so that you also may believe. His testimony is true, and he knows[k] that he tells the truth.) 36 These things occurred so that the scripture might be fulfilled, "None of his bones shall be broken." 37 And again another passage of scripture says, "They will look on the one whom they have pierced."

The Burial of Jesus
(Mt 27.57–61; Mk 15.42–47; Lk 23.50–56)

38 After these things, Joseph of Ar·i·ma·thē′a, who was a disciple of Jesus, though a secret one because of his fear of the Jews, asked Pilate to let him take away the body of Jesus. Pilate gave him permission; so he came and removed his body. 39 Nic·o·dē′mus, who had at first come to Jesus by night, also came, bringing a mixture of myrrh and aloes, weighing about a hundred pounds. 40 They took the body of Jesus and wrapped it with the spices in linen cloths, according to the burial custom of the Jews. 41 Now there was a garden in the place where he was crucified, and in the garden there was a new tomb in which no one had ever been laid. 42 And so, because it was the Jewish day of Preparation, and the tomb was nearby, they laid Jesus there.

---

k Or there is one who knows

OUR MOTHER OF GUADALUPE, A GIFT FROM GOD!

Devotion to Mary as mother of God and mother of the church has been a consistent dimension of Christian faith. From Jesus' words on the cross in Jn 19.25–27, Christians have identified with the Beloved Disciple and seen Mary as their mother. This experience has led Catholics of many countries to name Mary as their patroness (advocate, protector, supporter, mother): for instance, they call her Virgin of the Immaculate Conception in the United States and Chile, Virgin of Lourdes in France, and Virgin of Fátima in Portugal. The strong devotion of Latin American countries to Mary as a mother who protects and assists her children is revealed in their titles for her: Our Lady of Mercy in the Dominican Republic, Our Lady of Caridad del Cobre (charity) in Cuba, Our Lady of Divine Providence in Puerto Rico, and Our Lady of Help in Guatemala, to name a few.

But Mexico developed the strongest devotion to Mary as mother of a nation. The Virgin of Guadalupe appeared to Juan Diego, a humble native from Tenochtitlán, near Mexico City. She had the face of the mestizo people (the descendants of native and Spanish peoples), and her words to Juan Diego were those of a caring mother, especially for her children who are suffering, poor, or oppressed:

Here I wish to hear and help you, and all who dwell in this land and all those who love me, and invoke and place their confidence in me; and to hear your complaints and remedy all your sorrows, hardships, and suffering. . . .

Listen and understand well my son, smallest of all, that you have no cause to be frightened. . . . Is this not your mother here next to you? Are you not here in the shelter of my loving shadow? . . . Let nothing worry or afflict you further. . . . (Office of Religious Education, *A Handbook on Guadalupe*, pp. 148, 152)

▶ Jn 19.25–27

The Resurrection of Jesus
(Mt 28.1–10; Mk 16.1–8; Lk 24.1–12)

Early on the first day of the week, while it was still dark, Mary Mag′da•lēne came to the tomb and saw that the stone had been removed from the tomb. ²So she ran and went to Simon Peter and the other disciple, the one whom Jesus loved, and said to them, "They have taken the Lord out of the tomb, and we do not know where they have laid him." ³Then Peter and the other disciple set out and went toward the tomb. ⁴The two were running together, but the other disciple outran Peter and reached the tomb first. ⁵He bent down to look in and saw the linen wrappings lying there, but he did not go in. ⁶Then Simon Peter came, following him, and went into the tomb. He saw the linen wrappings lying there, ⁷and the cloth that had been on Jesus' head, not lying with the linen wrappings but rolled up in a place by itself. ⁸Then the other disciple, who reached the tomb first, also went in, and he saw and believed; ⁹for as yet they did not understand the scripture, that he must rise from the dead. ¹⁰Then the disciples returned to their homes.

Jesus Appears to Mary Magdalene

11 But Mary stood weeping outside the tomb. As she wept, she bent over to look*ˡ* into the tomb; ¹²and she saw two angels in white, sitting where the body of Jesus had been lying, one at the head and the other at the feet. ¹³They said to her, "Woman, why are you weeping?" She said to them, "They have taken away my Lord, and I do not know where they have laid him." ¹⁴When she had said this, she turned around and saw Jesus standing there, but she did not know that it was Jesus. ¹⁵Jesus said to her, "Woman, why are you weeping? Whom are you looking for?" Supposing him to be the gardener, she said to him, "Sir, if you have carried him away, tell me where you have laid him, and I will take him away." ¹⁶Jesus said to her, "Mary!" She turned and said to him in Hebrew,*ᵐ* "Rab•bou′ni!" (which means Teacher). ¹⁷Jesus said to her, "Do not hold on to me, because I have not yet ascended to the Father. But go to my brothers and say to them, 'I am ascending to my Father and your Father, to my God and your God.'" ¹⁸Mary Mag′da•lēne went and announced to the disciples, "I have seen the Lord"; and she told them that he had said these things to her.

Jesus Appears to the Disciples
(Lk 24.36–43; 1 Cor 15.5)

19 When it was evening on that day, the first day of the week, and the doors of the house where the disciples had met were locked for fear of the Jews, Jesus came and stood among them and said, "Peace be with you." ²⁰After he said this, he showed them his hands and his side. Then the disciples rejoiced when they saw the Lord. ²¹Jesus said to them again, "Peace be with you. As the Father has sent me, so I send you." ²²When he had said this, he breathed on them and said to them, "Receive the Holy Spirit. ²³If you forgive the sins

---

ˡ Gk lacks *to look*   *ᵐ* That is, *Aramaic*

Introducing ▶ MARY MAGDALENE

Like the Samaritan woman who is the first to spread the word that Jesus is the Messiah (Jn 4.1–42), Mary Magdalene is the first to announce that Jesus has been raised from the dead. She comes to the tomb while it is still dark (symbolizing unbelief). Later, she encounters the risen Jesus, and begins to see with eyes of faith. Belief prompts her to action, and so she goes to tell the others, "I have seen the Lord."

Mary Magdalene is first in every listing of Jesus' female disciples (Mt 27.55–56, Mk 15.40–41, Lk 8.2–3). She seems to have been the leader of a group of women who followed Jesus from the beginning of his ministry, through his death and beyond. Luke indicates that Jesus cured her of seven evil spirits (8.2). All four Gospels name her as one of the first eyewitnesses of Jesus' Resurrection. From all this, we can presume that she was a special friend and disciple of Jesus' and an important leader among the first Christians.

▶ Jn 20.1–18

of any, they are forgiven them; if you retain the sins of any, they are retained."

Jesus and Thomas

24 But Thomas (who was called the Twin[n]), one of the twelve, was not with them when Jesus came. 25 So the other disciples told him, "We have seen the Lord." But he said to them, "Unless I see the mark of the nails in his hands, and put my finger in the mark of the nails and my hand in his side, I will not believe."

26 A week later his disciples were again in the house, and Thomas was with them. Although the doors were shut, Jesus came and stood among them and said, "Peace be with you." 27 Then he said to Thomas, "Put your finger here and see my hands. Reach out your hand and put it in my side. Do not doubt but believe." 28 Thomas answered him, "My Lord and my God!" 29 Jesus said to him, "Have you believed because you have seen me? Blessed are those who have not seen and yet have come to believe."

The Purpose of This Book

30 Now Jesus did many other signs in the presence of his disciples, which are not written in this book. 31 But these are written so that you may come to believe[o] that Jesus is the Messiah,[p] the Son of God, and that through believing you may have life in his name.

Jesus Appears to Seven Disciples

21 After these things Jesus showed himself again to the disciples by the Sea of Ti·be'ri·as; and he showed himself in this way. 2 Gathered there together were Simon Peter, Thomas called the Twin,[n] Na·than'a·el of Ca'na in Galilee, the sons of Zeb'e·dee, and two others of his disciples. 3 Simon Peter said to them, "I am going fishing." They said to him, "We will go with you." They went out and got into the boat, but that night they caught nothing.

4 Just after daybreak, Jesus stood on the beach; but the disciples did not know that it was Jesus. 5 Jesus said to them, "Children, you have no fish, have you?" They answered him, "No." 6 He said to them, "Cast the net to the right side of the boat, and you will find some." So they cast it, and now they were not able to haul it in because there were so many fish. 7 That disciple whom Jesus loved said to Peter, "It is the Lord!" When Simon Peter heard that it was the Lord, he put on some clothes, for he was naked, and jumped into the sea. 8 But the other disciples came in the boat, dragging the

net full of fish, for they were not far from the land, only about a hundred yards[q] off.

9 When they had gone ashore, they saw a charcoal fire there, with fish on it, and bread. 10 Jesus said to them, "Bring some of the fish that you have just caught." 11 So Simon Peter went aboard and hauled the net ashore, full of large fish, a hundred fifty-three of them; and though there were so many, the net was not torn. 12 Jesus said to them, "Come and have breakfast." Now none of the disciples dared to ask him, "Who are you?" because they knew it was the Lord. 13 Jesus came and took the bread and gave it to them, and did the same with the fish. 14 This was now the third time that Jesus appeared to the disciples after he was raised from the dead.

Jesus and Peter

15 When they had finished breakfast, Jesus said to Simon Peter, "Simon son of John, do you

---

Catholic Connections

RECONCILIATION

In Jn 20.21–23, Jesus empowers his disciples to forgive the sins of others in his name. This is one of the Bible passages that the Catholic church teaches is the basis for the sacrament of Reconciliation (or Penance). Some may know this sacrament by the term confession, because we confess our sins to a priest. The priest serves as a representative of both God and the community in the sacrament. But confessing our sins is only one step in the reconciliation process. We must also be truly sorry and attempt to repair the damage our sin has done. By seeking true reconciliation through the sacrament, we restore the peace of the risen Christ.

▸ Jn 20.21–23

J N

---

n Gk *Didymus*　o Other ancient authorities read *may continue to believe*　p Or *the Christ*　q Gk *two hundred cubits*

had reclined next to Jesus at the supper and had said, "Lord, who is it that is going to betray you?" 21 When Peter saw him, he said to Jesus, "Lord, what about him?" 22 Jesus said to him, "If it is my will that he remain until I come, what is that to you? Follow me!" 23 So the rumor spread in the community[r] that this disciple would not die. Yet Jesus did not say to him that he would not die, but, "If it is my will that he remain until I come, what is that to you?"[s]

24 This is the disciple who is testifying to these things and has written them, and we know that his testimony is true. 25 But there are also many other things that Jesus did; if every one of them were written down, I suppose that the world itself could not contain the books that would be written.

r Gk among the brothers   s Other ancient authorities lack what is that to you

Catholic Connections
THE HUMBLE CHURCH

Peter must have felt terribly guilty about denying Jesus three times. When the risen Jesus appears to Peter, Jesus offers him three opportunities to reaffirm his love and be reconciled.

The Catholic church also believes that this passage establishes Peter as the leader of the early church and as the first pope, indicated by Jesus' commands to Peter to "feed my lambs" and "tend my sheep." By linking Peter's reconciliation to Peter's authority, John seems to be reminding the church to be humble and forgiving.

▸ Jn 21.15–19

love me more than these?" He said to him, "Yes, Lord; you know that I love you." Jesus said to him, "Feed my lambs." 16 A second time he said to him, "Simon son of John, do you love me?" He said to him, "Yes, Lord; you know that I love you." Jesus said to him, "Tend my sheep." 17 He said to him the third time, "Simon son of John, do you love me?" Peter felt hurt because he said to him the third time, "Do you love me?" And he said to him, "Lord, you know everything; you know that I love you." Jesus said to him, "Feed my sheep. 18 Very truly, I tell you, when you were younger, you used to fasten your own belt and to go wherever you wished. But when you grow old, you will stretch out your hands, and someone else will fasten a belt around you and take you where you do not wish to go." 19 (He said this to indicate the kind of death by which he would glorify God.) After this he said to him, "Follow me."

Jesus and the Beloved Disciple
20 Peter turned and saw the disciple whom Jesus loved following them; he was the one who

THE GOSPEL ACCORDING TO . . .

The Gospel of John ends by saying that if everything Jesus did were to be written down, the entire world could not contain it. Sounds like a challenge, doesn't it? Perhaps the author was thinking of all the things the risen Christ continues to do in the lives of believers. If you were to write your own Gospel story, one based on the risen Jesus at work in your life, what marvelous stories would it hold? What messages and teachings would you offer to the people of today? How has your life revealed and reflected the Good News of Jesus?

As you think about these things, why not take out some paper and a pen and begin to write your Gospel story. Keep your paper near this Bible so that you can add more good news each time you read it and reflect on where the risen Christ is alive in your life and in the world.

▸ Jn 21.24–25

n your history classes in school, you probably studied stories about the heroic men and women who helped create the United States: George Washington, Benjamin Franklin, Harriet Tubman, Susan B. Anthony, and Harry S. Truman to name a few. The stories about these famous people are an important part of our national identity. The Acts of the Apostles is a book containing stories like these. It continues the account of salvation history by telling about the beginnings of the Christian movement, primarily through stories about two of its most important missionaries, Peter and Paul.

In-depth

The Acts of the Apostles—sometimes simply called Acts—was written by the same author as the Gospel of Luke. So Acts is really the second volume of a two-volume history. Like the Gospels, it is not a history in the sense of an eyewitness account of the beginnings of Christianity. Rather, it is an interpretation of this history, explaining how Christianity spread outside of Judaism to the Gentile world under the direction of the Holy Spirit.

Lots of great stories are in the Acts of the Apostles. We read about the descent of the Holy Spirit on the Apostles (2.1–42), Paul's conversion to the Christian way (9.1–19), and some miraculous escapes from prisons and riots (12.6–11; 16.16–40). We learn about the first church council in Jerusalem, where a decision was made to accept Gentiles (non-Jews) as Christians without requiring that they also become practicing Jews (15.1–35). Acts continuously emphasizes how faith in Christ is shared and supported through Christian community.

The Acts of the Apostles gives us information about how Christians lived in the years after Jesus' Resurrection and Ascension. We learn how the believers celebrated the Eucharist together and shared their belongings (2.43–47). We learn how the Gospel message was preached, first to Jews in the synagogues and later to Gentiles. We learn how traveling missionaries like Paul went on long journeys and suffered many hardships to form new groups of believers across the Roman Empire. Under the guidance of the Holy Spirit, the church miraculously went from a small group of disciples in Jerusalem to a movement spreading across the entire Roman Empire, even to Rome itself.

Quick Facts

Author
often identified as Luke, who also wrote the Gospel of Luke

Date Written
approximately A.D. 80

Audience
Gentile (Greek) Christians represented by Theophilus (see Acts 1.1)

The Acts of the Apostles

Acts

The Promise of the Holy Spirit

In the first book, Thē·oph′i·lus, I wrote about all that Jesus did and taught from the beginning ²until the day when he was taken up to heaven, after giving instructions through the Holy Spirit to the apostles whom he had chosen. ³After his suffering he presented himself alive to them by many convincing proofs, appearing to them during forty days and speaking about the kingdom of God. ⁴While staying*a* with them, he ordered them not to leave Jerusalem, but to wait there for the promise of the Father. "This," he said, "is what you have heard from me; ⁵for John baptized with water, but you will be baptized with*b* the Holy Spirit not many days from now."

The Ascension of Jesus
(Mk 16.19–20; Lk 24.50–53)

6 So when they had come together, they asked him, "Lord, is this the time when you will restore the kingdom to Israel?" ⁷He replied, "It is not for you to know the times or periods that the Father has set by his own authority. ⁸But you will receive power when the Holy Spirit has come upon you; and you will be my witnesses in Jerusalem, in all Judea and Sa·mār′i·a, and to the ends of the earth." ⁹When he had said this, as they were watching, he was lifted up, and a cloud took him out of their sight. ¹⁰While he was going and they were gazing up toward heaven, suddenly two men in white robes stood by them. ¹¹They said, "Men of Gali-lee, why do you stand looking up toward heaven? This Jesus, who has been taken up from you into heaven, will come in the same way as you saw him go into heaven."

Matthias Chosen to Replace Judas
(Cp Ps 109.8)

12 Then they returned to Jerusalem from the mount called Ol′i·vet, which is near Jerusalem, a sabbath day's journey away. ¹³When they had entered the city, they went to the room upstairs where they were staying, Peter, and John, and James, and Andrew, Philip and Thomas, Bartholomew and Matthew, James son of Al·phae′us, and Simon the Zealot, and Judas son of*c* James. ¹⁴All these were constantly devoting themselves to prayer, together with certain women, including Mary the mother of Jesus, as well as his brothers.

15 In those days Peter stood up among the believers*d* (together the crowd numbered about one hundred twenty persons) and said, ¹⁶"Friends,*e* the scripture had to be fulfilled, which the Holy Spirit through David foretold concerning Judas, who became a guide for those who arrested Jesus— ¹⁷for he was numbered among us and was allotted his share in this ministry." ¹⁸(Now this man acquired a field with the reward of his wickedness; and falling headlong,*f* he burst open in the middle and all his bowels gushed out. ¹⁹This became

---

a Or *eating*   *b* Or *by*   *c* Or *the brother of*   *d* Gk *brothers*
e Gk *Men, brothers*   *f* Or *swelling up*

known to all the residents of Jerusalem, so that the field was called in their language Ha·kel'da·ma, that is, Field of Blood.) 20 "For it is written in the book of Psalms,

> 'Let his homestead become desolate,
> and let there be no one to live in it';

and

> 'Let another take his position of overseer.'

21 So one of the men who have accompanied us during all the time that the Lord Jesus went in and out among us, 22 beginning from the baptism of John until the day when he was taken up from us—one of these must become a witness with us to his resurrection." 23 So they proposed two, Joseph called Bar·sab'bas, who was also known as Justus, and Mat·thi'as. 24 Then they prayed and said,

SEND US YOUR SPIRIT!

After Jesus was taken up to heaven, the Apostles, Mary, and other women and men gathered to pray together. They knew that they needed the Holy Spirit, promised by Jesus, to begin the difficult task of giving witness to the Reign of God. Today, we continue to pray:

Jesus, send us your spirit and renew the face of the earth. You know our strengths and weaknesses. Transform us into messengers of your Gospel for those who yearn for you.

Jesus, send us your spirit and renew the face of the earth. You know our history, with its beautiful and painful experiences. Help us to be untiring promoters of a society based on love, justice, and peace.

Jesus, send us your spirit and renew the face of the earth. You know our longing for love and community. Make us instruments of unity and service, especially for those who are weak and those who are lonely. Amen.

▶ Acts 1.1–11

HISPANIC ¡Envíanos tu Espíritu!

Catholic Connections

CONFIRMATION

The first verses of the Acts of the Apostles, chapter 2, are a biblical story associated with the sacrament of Confirmation, one of the seven sacraments celebrated within the Catholic church. As one of the three sacraments of initiation—along with Baptism and the Eucharist—Confirmation celebrates a person's membership in the church. But in a special way, Confirmation is associated with the gift of the Holy Spirit.

During the Confirmation ceremony, the bishop anoints with oil the heads of those being confirmed and signs them with the gift of the Holy Spirit. We pray that the Holy Spirit strengthen those who have been confirmed to live the Gospel and share the Good News of Jesus Christ, just as the Apostles did at the first Pentecost.

If you have been confirmed, what was your experience of receiving the sacrament? How are you aware of the presence and guidance of the Holy Spirit? How do you participate in the life of your church community? If you have not been confirmed, what would you hope for in Confirmation?

▶ Acts 2.1–13

"Lord, you know everyone's heart. Show us which one of these two you have chosen 25 to take the place𝑔 in this ministry and apostleship from which Judas turned aside to go to his own place." 26 And they cast lots for them, and the lot fell on Mat·thi'as; and he was added to the eleven apostles.

The Coming of the Holy Spirit

When the day of Pentecost had come, they were all together in one place. 2 And suddenly from heaven there came a sound like the rush of a violent wind, and it filled the entire house where they were sitting. 3 Divided tongues, as of fire, appeared

---

𝑔 Other ancient authorities read *the share*

among them, and a tongue rested on each of them. 4 All of them were filled with the Holy Spirit and began to speak in other languages, as the Spirit gave them ability.

5 Now there were devout Jews from every nation under heaven living in Jerusalem. 6 And at this sound the crowd gathered and was bewildered, because each one heard them speaking in the native language of each. 7 Amazed and astonished, they asked, "Are not all these who are speaking Galileans? 8 And how is it that we hear, each of us, in our own native language? 9 Par′thi•ans, Mēdes, Ē′lam•ītes, and residents of Mes•o•po•tā′mi•a, Judea and Cap•pa•dō′ci•a, Pon′tus and Asia, 10 Phryg′i•a and Pam•phyl′i•a, Egypt and the parts of Lib′ya belonging to Cȳ•rē′nē, and visitors from Rome, both Jews and proselytes, 11 Crē′tans and Arabs—in our own languages we hear them speaking about God's deeds of power." 12 All were amazed and perplexed, saying to one another, "What does this mean?" 13 But others sneered and said, "They are filled with new wine."

Peter Addresses the Crowd
(Joel 2.28–32)

14 But Peter, standing with the eleven, raised his voice and addressed them, "Men of Judea and all who live in Jerusalem, let this be known to you, and listen to what I say. 15 Indeed, these are not drunk, as you suppose, for it is only nine o'clock in the morning. 16 No, this is what was spoken through the prophet Jō′el:

17 'In the last days it will be, God declares,
　　that I will pour out my Spirit upon all flesh,
　　　　and your sons and your daughters shall
　　　　　　prophesy,
　　and your young men shall see visions,
　　　　and your old men shall dream dreams.
18 Even upon my slaves, both men and
　　　　women,
　　in those days I will pour out my Spirit;
　　　　and they shall prophesy.
19 And I will show portents in the heaven
　　　　above
　　　　and signs on the earth below,
　　　　　　blood, and fire, and smoky mist.
20 The sun shall be turned to darkness
　　　　and the moon to blood,
　　　　before the coming of the Lord's great
　　　　　　and glorious day.
21 Then everyone who calls on the name of
　　　　the Lord shall be saved.'

22 "You that are Israelites,^{h} listen to what I have to say: Jesus of Nazareth,^{i} a man attested to

Catholic Connections
PENTECOST

Genesis, chapter 11, is the story of arrogant workers who tried to build the tower of Babel to reach up to heaven. God confused their languages so they couldn't understand one another. Building was impossible.

Pentecost was just the reverse! Heaven came down as the Holy Spirit descended upon the Apostles. The Jewish feast of Pentecost had celebrated the wheat harvest. Now the Apostles received the harvest of the Holy Spirit: the courage, confidence, and zeal to go out into the world and proclaim God's salvation in Jesus Christ. No matter what their language, everyone present could understand the Apostles' message. It was a holy day. It was a day to build God's people up.

Pentecost is considered the birthday of the Christian church. The Catholic church celebrates the feast of Pentecost on the second Sunday after Ascension Thursday, which is approximately fifty days after Easter (the term *pente* means "fifty"). It continues to be an important feast to celebrate the unity of all Christians. In the United States alone the Gospel is preached in more than a hundred languages to people of many different cultures.

▶ Acts 2.1–13

you by God with deeds of power, wonders, and signs that God did through him among you, as you yourselves know— 23 this man, handed over to you according to the definite plan and foreknowledge of God, you crucified and killed by the hands of those outside the law. 24 But God raised him up, having freed him from death,^{j} because it was im-

---

^{h} Gk Men, Israelites ^{i} Gk the Nazorean ^{j} Gk the pains of death

possible for him to be held in its power. 25 For David says concerning him,

'I saw the Lord always before me,
　for he is at my right hand so that I will not be shaken;

26 therefore my heart was glad, and my tongue rejoiced;
　moreover my flesh will live in hope.

27 For you will not abandon my soul to Hades,
　or let your Holy One experience corruption.

28 You have made known to me the ways of life;
　you will make me full of gladness with your presence.'

29 "Fellow Israelites,[k] I may say to you confidently of our ancestor David that he both died and was buried, and his tomb is with us to this day. 30 Since he was a prophet, he knew that God had sworn with an oath to him that he would put one of his descendants on his throne. 31 Foreseeing this, David[l] spoke of the resurrection of the Messiah,[m] saying,

'He was not abandoned to Hades,
　nor did his flesh experience corruption.'

32 This Jesus God raised up, and of that all of us are witnesses. 33 Being therefore exalted at[n] the right hand of God, and having received from the Father the promise of the Holy Spirit, he has poured out this that you both see and hear. 34 For David did not ascend into the heavens, but he himself says,

'The Lord said to my Lord,
"Sit at my right hand,
35　until I make your enemies your footstool." '

36 Therefore let the entire house of Israel know with certainty that God has made him both Lord and Messiah,[o] this Jesus whom you crucified."

The First Converts

37 Now when they heard this, they were cut to the heart and said to Peter and to the other apostles, "Brothers,[k] what should we do?" 38 Peter said to them, "Repent, and be baptized every one of you in the name of Jesus Christ so that your sins may be forgiven; and you will receive the gift of the Holy Spirit. 39 For the promise is for you, for your children, and for all who are far away, everyone whom the Lord our God calls to him." 40 And he testified with many other arguments and exhorted them, saying, "Save yourselves from this corrupt generation." 41 So those who welcomed his message were baptized, and that day about three thousand persons were added. 42 They devoted themselves to the apostles' teaching and fellowship, to the breaking of bread and the prayers.

Life among the Believers

43 Awe came upon everyone, because many wonders and signs were being done by the apostles. 44 All who believed were together and had all things in common; 45 they would sell their possessions and goods and distribute the proceeds[p] to all, as any had need. 46 Day by day, as they spent

[k] Gk *Men, brothers*　　[l] Gk *he*　　[m] Or *the Christ*　　[n] Or *by*　　[o] Or *Christ*　　[p] Gk *them*

ACTS

Christian Community

LIVE IT!

In the famous passage of Acts 2.43–47, the ideal Christian community is portrayed as open to the Holy Spirit. They shared everything in common, including prayer, meals, and possessions. No one went in need. Sound impossible?

　　Across the world, groups of people live together in intentional Christian communities similar to that among the believers described in Acts. Some of them pool their finances and possessions to provide for their food and housing. They commit themselves to building caring relationships of trust and respect with one another. They spend time praying together. They perform works of service together in the community. Many Christian families strive for this vision in their life together.

　　Is living like this attractive to you? What would be hard for you in living like this? What do you think society would be like today if this were everyone's lifestyle? Intentional Christian communities are attractive to many Christians today. As you grow older, you might look for such a community when you leave home—or even start one yourself. It is a wonderful experience of the Christian way of life.

▶ Acts 2.43–47

Share Christ

As is true in our own cities today, in Jerusalem during the first century, it was not uncommon to encounter beggars on the streets. And probably, like today, some people averted their eyes and walked by while others stopped to offer a few coins.

When Peter and John encounter a beggar in Acts 3.3, they don't have a whole lot of money to share with him, but they stop just the same. Looking him in the eye, Peter offers the lame man the one thing of value he does have: the powerful gift of healing found in the name of Jesus Christ.

You may not have the gift of healing or lots of extra money to give to those in need. But Peter and John remind us that knowing Jesus is the greatest treasure one can acquire in life, and that this treasure has been given to us freely. Don't forget to share it with others!

▶ Acts 3.1–10

much time together in the temple, they broke bread at home*q* and ate their food with glad and generous*r* hearts, 47 praising God and having the goodwill of all the people. And day by day the Lord added to their number those who were being saved.

Peter Heals a Crippled Beggar

One day Peter and John were going up to the temple at the hour of prayer, at three o'clock in the afternoon. 2 And a man lame from birth was being carried in. People would lay him daily at the gate of the temple called the Beautiful Gate so that he could ask for alms from those entering the temple. 3 When he saw Peter and John about to go into the temple, he asked them for alms. 4 Peter looked intently at him, as did John, and said, "Look at us." 5 And he fixed his attention on them, expecting to receive something from them. 6 But Peter said, "I have no silver or gold, but what I have I give you; in the name of Jesus Christ of Nazareth,*s* stand up and walk." 7 And he took him by the right hand and raised him up; and immediately his feet and ankles were made strong. 8 Jumping up, he stood and began to walk, and he entered the temple with them, walking and leaping and praising God. 9 All the people saw him walking and praising God, 10 and they recognized him as the one who used to sit and ask for alms at the Beautiful Gate of the temple; and they were filled with wonder and amazement at what had happened to him.

Peter Speaks in Solomon's Portico

11 While he clung to Peter and John, all the people ran together to them in the portico called Solomon's Portico, utterly astonished. 12 When Peter saw it, he addressed the people, "You Israel-

ites,*t* why do you wonder at this, or why do you stare at us, as though by our own power or piety we had made him walk? 13 The God of Abraham, the God of Isaac, and the God of Jacob, the God of our ancestors has glorified his servant*u* Jesus, whom you handed over and rejected in the presence of Pilate, though he had decided to release him. 14 But you rejected the Holy and Righteous One and asked to have a murderer given to you, 15 and you killed the Author of life, whom God raised from the dead. To this we are witnesses. 16 And by faith in his name, his name itself has made this man strong, whom you see and know; and the faith that is through Jesus*v* has given him this perfect health in the presence of all of you.

17 "And now, friends,*w* I know that you acted in ignorance, as did also your rulers. 18 In this way God fulfilled what he had foretold through all the prophets, that his Messiah*x* would suffer. 19 Repent therefore, and turn to God so that your sins may be wiped out, 20 so that times of refreshing may come from the presence of the Lord, and that he may send the Messiah*y* appointed for you, that is, Jesus, 21 who must remain in heaven until the time of universal restoration that God announced long ago through his holy prophets. 22 Moses said, 'The Lord your God will raise up for you from your own people*w* a prophet like me. You must listen to whatever he tells you. 23 And it will be that everyone who does not listen to that prophet will be utterly rooted out of the people.' 24 And all the prophets, as many as have spoken, from Samuel and those after him, also predicted these days. 25 You are the descendants of the prophets and of

q Or from house to house   r Or sincere   s Gk the Nazorean
t Gk Men, Israelites   u Or child   v Gk him
w Gk brothers   x Or his Christ   y Or the Christ

the covenant that God gave to your ancestors, saying to Abraham, 'And in your descendants all the families of the earth shall be blessed.' 26 When God raised up his servant,[z] he sent him first to you, to bless you by turning each of you from your wicked ways."

Peter and John before the Council

While Peter and John[a] were speaking to the people, the priests, the captain of the temple, and the Sad'du·cees came to them, 2 much annoyed because they were teaching the people and proclaiming that in Jesus there is the resurrection of the dead. 3 So they arrested them and put them in custody until the next day, for it was already evening. 4 But many of those who heard the word believed; and they numbered about five thousand.

5 The next day their rulers, elders, and scribes assembled in Jerusalem, 6 with An'nas the high priest, Ca'i·a·phas, John,[b] and Alexander, and all who were of the high-priestly family. 7 When they had made the prisoners[c] stand in their midst, they inquired, "By what power or by what name did you do this?" 8 Then Peter, filled with the Holy Spirit, said to them, "Rulers of the people and elders, 9 if we are questioned today because of a good deed done to someone who was sick and are asked how this man has been healed, 10 let it be known to all of you, and to all the people of Israel, that this man is standing before you in good health by the name of Jesus Christ of Nazareth,[d] whom you crucified, whom God raised from the dead. 11 This Jesus[e] is

'the stone that was rejected by you, the
    builders;
it has become the cornerstone.'[f]

12 There is salvation in no one else, for there is no other name under heaven given among mortals by which we must be saved."

13 Now when they saw the boldness of Peter and John and realized that they were uneducated and ordinary men, they were amazed and recognized them as companions of Jesus. 14 When they saw the man who had been cured standing beside them, they had nothing to say in opposition. 15 So they ordered them to leave the council while they discussed the matter with one another. 16 They said, "What will we do with them? For it is obvious to all who live in Jerusalem that a notable sign has been done through them; we cannot deny it. 17 But to keep it from spreading further among the people, let us warn them to speak no more to anyone in this name." 18 So they called them and ordered them not to speak or teach at all in the name of Jesus. 19 But Peter and John answered them, "Whether it is right in God's sight to listen

PRAY IT!

I Believe!
The Apostles' Creed

In Acts 4.5–12, Peter stands up before the unbelieving rulers and elders and boldly proclaims his faith in Jesus as healer and Messiah. Every Sunday at Mass, Catholic Christians profess the same faith when they pray the Nicene Creed. (A creed is a type of prayer that expresses faith beliefs.) Did you know there is also a shorter creed called the Apostles' Creed? The Apostles' Creed is based on the teachings and beliefs of the earliest Christians.

Take a moment to pray the Apostles' Creed:

I believe in God, the Father almighty, creator of heaven and earth. I believe in Jesus Christ, his only Son, our Lord. He was conceived by the power of the Holy Spirit and born of the Virgin Mary. He suffered under Pontius Pilate, was crucified, died, and was buried. He descended into hell. On the third day he rose again. He ascended into heaven and is seated at the right hand of the Father. He will come again to judge the living and the dead. I believe in the Holy Spirit, the holy catholic Church, the communion of saints, the forgiveness of sins, the resurrection of the body, and the life everlasting. Amen. (Catechism of the Catholic Church, pp. 49–50)

Then reflect or journal on the following questions:
- Which statements of the creed do you have questions about?
- How hard would it be for you to express your faith beliefs to people who don't believe in Jesus?

▸ Acts 4.5–12

to you rather than to God, you must judge; 20 for we cannot keep from speaking about what we

---

z Or *child*   a Gk *While they*   b Other ancient authorities read *Jonathan*   c Gk *them*   d Gk *the Nazorean*   e Gk *This*   f Or *keystone*

have seen and heard." 21 After threatening them again, they let them go, finding no way to punish them because of the people, for all of them praised God for what had happened. 22 For the man on whom this sign of healing had been performed was more than forty years old.

The Believers Pray for Boldness
(Cp Ps 2.1–2)

23 After they were released, they went to their friends*g* and reported what the chief priests and the elders had said to them. 24 When they heard it, they raised their voices together to God and said, "Sovereign Lord, who made the heaven and the earth, the sea, and everything in them, 25 it is you who said by the Holy Spirit through our ancestor David, your servant:*h*

'Why did the Gentiles rage,
　and the peoples imagine vain things?
26　The kings of the earth took their stand,
　　and the rulers have gathered together
　　　against the Lord and against his
　　　　Messiah.'*i*

27 For in this city, in fact, both Her'od and Pon'-ti·us Pilate, with the Gentiles and the peoples of Israel, gathered together against your holy servant*h* Jesus, whom you anointed, 28 to do whatever your hand and your plan had predestined to take place. 29 And now, Lord, look at their threats, and grant to your servants*j* to speak your word with all boldness, 30 while you stretch out your hand to heal, and signs and wonders are performed through the name of your holy servant*h* Jesus." 31 When they had prayed, the place in which they were gathered together was shaken; and they were all filled with the Holy Spirit and spoke the word of God with boldness.

The Believers Share Their Possessions

32 Now the whole group of those who believed were of one heart and soul, and no one claimed private ownership of any possessions, but everything they owned was held in common. 33 With great power the apostles gave their testimony to the resurrection of the Lord Jesus, and great grace was upon them all. 34 There was not a needy person among them, for as many as owned lands or houses sold them and brought the proceeds of what was sold. 35 They laid it at the apostles' feet, and it was distributed to each as any had need. 36 There was a Le'vīte, a native of Cyprus, Joseph, to whom the apostles gave the name Bar'-na·bas (which means "son of encouragement"). 37 He sold a field that belonged to him, then brought the money, and laid it at the apostles' feet.

Ananias and Sapphira

But a man named An·a·ni'as, with the consent of his wife Sap·phi'ra, sold a piece of property; 2 with his wife's knowledge, he kept back some of the proceeds, and brought only a part and laid it at the apostles' feet. 3 "An·a·ni'as," Peter asked, "why has

did you KNOW?
Stewardship

Acts 4.32–37 describes a Christian behavior called stewardship. Stewardship involves sharing the gifts of time, talent, and treasure that God has placed in your care (see "Stewardship: Making a Contribution," Lk 21.1–4). It is key to the life of any Christian community.

Sharing our treasure and giving money are the most obvious ways of sharing. Consider the disciple named in the passage, Joseph Barnabas. How did he share? Can you think of things you spend money on—a CD, new jeans, a movie—and make a commitment to give some of that money to a charitable organization?

But giving money isn't the only way to share with others. Think about your own gifts. What are you good at that you could share with your parish, school, or community? Do not discount even the simplest ability. For example, maybe you are persistent; this talent can help any project to be successful. Or perhaps you love children and can baby-sit for overwhelmed parents.

How are you a good steward of your time, talent, and treasure? Think about it!

▶ **Acts 4.32–37**

Satan filled your heart to lie to the Holy Spirit and to keep back part of the proceeds of the land? 4 While it remained unsold, did it not remain your own? And after it was sold, were not the proceeds at your disposal? How is it that you have contrived this deed in your heart? You did not lie to us*k* but

---

g Gk *their own*　　*h* Or *child*　　*i* Or *his Christ*　　*j* Gk *slaves*
k Gk *to men*

to God!" ⁵ Now when An•a•ni′as heard these words, he fell down and died. And great fear seized all who heard of it. ⁶ The young men came and wrapped up his body,¹ then carried him out and buried him.

7 After an interval of about three hours his wife came in, not knowing what had happened. ⁸ Peter said to her, "Tell me whether you and your husband sold the land for such and such a price." And she said, "Yes, that was the price." ⁹ Then Peter said to her, "How is it that you have agreed together to put the Spirit of the Lord to the test? Look, the feet of those who have buried your husband are at the door, and they will carry you out." ¹⁰ Immediately she fell down at his feet and died. When the young men came in they found her dead, so they carried her out and buried her beside her husband. ¹¹ And great fear seized the whole church and all who heard of these things.

The Apostles Heal Many

12 Now many signs and wonders were done among the people through the apostles. And they were all together in Solomon's Portico. ¹³ None of the rest dared to join them, but the people held them in high esteem. ¹⁴ Yet more than ever believers were added to the Lord, great numbers of both men and women, ¹⁵ so that they even carried out the sick into the streets, and laid them on cots and mats, in order that Peter's shadow might fall on some of them as he came by. ¹⁶ A great number of people would also gather from the towns around Jerusalem, bringing the sick and those tormented by unclean spirits, and they were all cured.

The Apostles Are Persecuted

17 Then the high priest took action; he and all who were with him (that is, the sect of the Sad′du·cees), being filled with jealousy, ¹⁸ arrested the apostles and put them in the public prison. ¹⁹ But during the night an angel of the Lord opened the prison doors, brought them out, and said, ²⁰ "Go, stand in the temple and tell the people the whole message about this life." ²¹ When they heard this, they entered the temple at daybreak and went on with their teaching.

When the high priest and those with him arrived, they called together the council and the whole body of the elders of Israel, and sent to the prison to have them brought. ²² But when the temple police went there, they did not find them in the prison; so they returned and reported, ²³ "We found the prison securely locked and the guards standing at the doors, but when we opened them, we found no one inside." ²⁴ Now when the captain of the temple and the chief priests heard these words, they were perplexed about them, wondering what might be going on. ²⁵ Then someone arrived and announced, "Look, the men whom you put in prison are standing in the temple and teaching the people!" ²⁶ Then the captain went with the temple police and brought them, but without violence, for they were afraid of being stoned by the people.

27 When they had brought them, they had them stand before the council. The high priest questioned them, ²⁸ saying, "We gave you strict orders

¹ Meaning of Gk uncertain

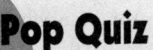

Pop Quiz

The scene. The disciples, who are spreading the Good News of Jesus Christ, are taken before the Jewish council to explain their motives and reasons for this work.

The test. Gamaliel, a wise Jewish leader, talks the rest of the council out of killing the disciples, by using the following reasoning: If the disciples' mission is from God, it will succeed despite anything the council does. But if it is not of God's design, it will fail and the Christians will eventually disappear anyway.

The question. If you were brought before a similar council, would your life's mission pass or fail this test? That is, would your words and actions in the past week reflect Jesus' attitudes, actions, and mission?

Your answer.

▶ Acts 5.27–39

not to teach in this name,^m yet here you have filled Jerusalem with your teaching and you are determined to bring this man's blood on us." ²⁹But Peter and the apostles answered, "We must obey God rather than any human authority.ⁿ ³⁰The God of our ancestors raised up Jesus, whom you had killed by hanging him on a tree. ³¹God exalted him at his right hand as Leader and Savior that he might give repentance to Israel and forgiveness of sins. ³²And we are witnesses to these things, and so is the Holy Spirit whom God has given to those who obey him."

33 When they heard this, they were enraged and wanted to kill them. ³⁴But a Phar·i·see in the council named Ga·ma'li·el, a teacher of the law, respected by all the people, stood up and ordered the men to be put outside for a short time. ³⁵Then he said to them, "Fellow Israelites,^o consider carefully what you propose to do to these men. ³⁶For some time ago Theu'das rose up, claiming to be somebody, and a number of men, about four hundred, joined him; but he was killed, and all who followed him were dispersed and disappeared. ³⁷After him Judas the Galilean rose up at the time of the census and got people to follow him; he also perished, and all who followed him were scattered. ³⁸So in the present case, I tell you, keep away from these men and let them alone; because if this plan or this undertaking is of human origin, it will fail; ³⁹but if it is of God, you will not be able to overthrow them—in that case you may even be found fighting against God!"

They were convinced by him, ⁴⁰and when they had called in the apostles, they had them flogged. Then they ordered them not to speak in the name of Jesus, and let them go. ⁴¹As they left the council, they rejoiced that they were considered worthy to suffer dishonor for the sake of the name. ⁴²And every day in the temple and at home^p they did not cease to teach and proclaim Jesus as the Messiah.^q

Seven Chosen to Serve

Now during those days, when the disciples were increasing in number, the Hellenists complained against the Hebrews because their widows were being neglected in the daily distribution of food. ²And the twelve called together the whole community of the disciples and said, "It is not right that we should neglect the word of God in order to wait on tables.^r ³Therefore, friends,^s select from among yourselves seven men of good standing, full of the Spirit and of wisdom, whom we may appoint to this task, ⁴while we, for our part, will devote ourselves to prayer and to serving the word." ⁵What they said pleased the whole community, and they chose Stephen, a man full of faith and

the Holy Spirit, together with Philip, Proch'o·rus, Ni·ca'nor, Ti'mon, Par'me·nas, and Nic·o·la'us, a proselyte of An'ti·och. ⁶They had these men stand before the apostles, who prayed and laid their hands on them.

7 The word of God continued to spread; the number of the disciples increased greatly in Jerusalem, and a great many of the priests became obedient to the faith.

The Arrest of Stephen

8 Stephen, full of grace and power, did great wonders and signs among the people. ⁹Then some of those who belonged to the synagogue of the Freedmen (as it was called), Cy·re'ni·ans, Alexandrians, and others of those from Ci·li'ci·a and Asia, stood up and argued with Stephen. ¹⁰But they could not withstand the wisdom and the Spirit^t with which he spoke. ¹¹Then they secretly instigated some men to say, "We have heard him speak blasphemous words against Moses and God." ¹²They stirred up the people as well as the elders and the scribes; then they suddenly confronted him, seized him, and brought him before the council. ¹³They set up false witnesses who said, "This man never stops saying things against this holy place and the law; ¹⁴for we have heard him say that this Jesus of Nazareth^u will destroy this place and will change the customs that Moses handed on to us." ¹⁵And all who sat in the council looked intently at him, and they saw that his face was like the face of an angel.

Stephen's Speech to the Council
(Gen 12.1—50.26)

Then the high priest asked him, "Are these things so?" ²And Stephen replied:

"Brothers^v and fathers, listen to me. The God of glory appeared to our ancestor Abraham when he was in Mes·o·po·ta'mi·a, before he lived in Har'an, ³and said to him, 'Leave your country and your relatives and go to the land that I will show you.' ⁴Then he left the country of the Chal·de'ans and settled in Har'an. After his father died, God had him move from there to this country in which you are now living. ⁵He did not give him any of it as a heritage, not even a foot's length, but promised to give it to him as his possession and to his descendants after him, even though he had no child. ⁶And God spoke in these terms, that his descendants would be resident aliens in a country

---

^m Other ancient authorities read *Did we not give you strict orders not to teach in this name?*   ⁿ Gk *than men*   ^o Gk *Men, Israelites*   ^p Or *from house to house*   ^q Or *the Christ*   ^r Or *keep accounts*   ^s Gk *brothers*   ^t Or *spirit*   ^u Gk *the Nazorean*   ^v Gk *Men, brothers*

Martyrs

The stoning of Stephen is a turning point in Luke's account of the first Christians. Stephen was the first Christian martyr— someone who dies for their faith. His death marked the beginning of a period of persecution of the early Christians. Up to then, Christians had been imprisoned but not put to death. Would the Christian movement fall apart now that the stakes were higher? Luke makes it clear that Stephen's death actually strengthened the church. His heroic sacrifice is even presented as a model for Christians—notice all the similarities between his death and Jesus'.

It is easy for North Americans to assume that religious persecution does not exist today. We do not normally hear stories of people being killed for their beliefs in Jesus or Christianity. Not so for people on other continents. All around the world, including places close to home, people are mistreated, and even killed, because of their religious beliefs.

For example, Archbishop Oscar Romero of El Salvador was shot to death because he challenged the wealthy and powerful people in his country to change their ways so the poor people could have a better quality of life. Archbishop Romero, like Stephen, was killed for being a faithful Christian.

Stephen was young just like you. He was convinced that following the teachings of Jesus was the most important way to live. He died for his beliefs, and the church became stronger because of his faith and heroism. What would you die for?

▶ **Acts 6.8—8.1**

belonging to others, who would enslave them and mistreat them during four hundred years. 7 'But I will judge the nation that they serve,' said God, 'and after that they shall come out and worship me in this place.' 8 Then he gave him the covenant of circumcision. And so Abraham^w became the father of Isaac and circumcised him on the eighth

day; and Isaac became the father of Jacob, and Jacob of the twelve patriarchs.

9 "The patriarchs, jealous of Joseph, sold him into Egypt; but God was with him, 10 and rescued him from all his afflictions, and enabled him to win favor and to show wisdom when he stood before Pharaoh, king of Egypt, who appointed him ruler over Egypt and over all his household. 11 Now there came a famine throughout Egypt and Cā'naan, and great suffering, and our ancestors could find no food. 12 But when Jacob heard that there was grain in Egypt, he sent our ancestors there on their first visit. 13 On the second visit Joseph made himself known to his brothers, and Joseph's family became known to Pharaoh. 14 Then Joseph sent and invited his father Jacob and all his relatives to come to him, seventy-five in all; 15 so Jacob went down to Egypt. He himself died there as well as our ancestors, 16 and their bodies^x were brought back to Shē'chem and laid in the tomb that Abraham had bought for a sum of silver from the sons of Hā'mor in Shē'chem.

17 "But as the time drew near for the fulfillment of the promise that God had made to Abraham, our people in Egypt increased and multiplied 18 until another king who had not known Joseph ruled over Egypt. 19 He dealt craftily with our race and forced our ancestors to abandon their infants so that they would die. 20 At this time Moses was born, and he was beautiful before God. For three months he was brought up in his father's house; 21 and when he was abandoned, Pharaoh's daughter adopted him and brought him up as her own son. 22 So Moses was instructed in all the wisdom of the Egyptians and was powerful in his words and deeds.

23 "When he was forty years old, it came into his heart to visit his relatives, the Israelites.^y 24 When he saw one of them being wronged, he defended the oppressed man and avenged him by striking down the Egyptian. 25 He supposed that his kinsfolk would understand that God through him was rescuing them, but they did not understand. 26 The next day he came to some of them as they were quarreling and tried to reconcile them, saying, 'Men, you are brothers; why do you wrong each other?' 27 But the man who was wronging his neighbor pushed Moses^z aside, saying, 'Who made you a ruler and a judge over us? 28 Do you want to kill me as you killed the Egyptian yesterday?' 29 When he heard this, Moses fled and became a resident alien in the land of Mid'i•an. There he became the father of two sons.

---

w Gk he   x Gk they   y Gk his brothers, the sons of Israel
z Gk him

30 "Now when forty years had passed, an angel appeared to him in the wilderness of Mount Sinai, in the flame of a burning bush. 31 When Moses saw it, he was amazed at the sight; and as he approached to look, there came the voice of the Lord: 32 'I am the God of your ancestors, the God of Abraham, Isaac, and Jacob.' Moses began to tremble and did not dare to look. 33 Then the Lord said to him, 'Take off the sandals from your feet, for the place where you are standing is holy ground. 34 I have surely seen the mistreatment of my people who are in Egypt and have heard their groaning, and I have come down to rescue them. Come now, I will send you to Egypt.'

35 "It was this Moses whom they rejected when they said, 'Who made you a ruler and a judge?' and whom God now sent as both ruler and liberator through the angel who appeared to him in the bush. 36 He led them out, having performed wonders and signs in Egypt, at the Red Sea, and in the wilderness for forty years. 37 This is the Moses who said to the Israelites, 'God will raise up a prophet for you from your own people*a* as he raised me up.' 38 He is the one who was in the congregation in the wilderness with the angel who spoke to him at Mount Sinai, and with our ancestors; and he received living oracles to give to us. 39 Our ancestors were unwilling to obey him; instead, they pushed him aside, and in their hearts they turned back to Egypt, 40 saying to Aaron, 'Make gods for us who will lead the way for us; as for this Moses who led us out from the land of Egypt, we do not know what has happened to him.' 41 At that time they made a calf, offered a sacrifice to the idol, and reveled in the works of their hands. 42 But God turned away from them and handed them over to worship the host of heaven, as it is written in the book of the prophets:

'Did you offer to me slain victims and
    sacrifices
forty years in the wilderness, O house of
    Israel?
43 No; you took along the tent of Mō'loch,
    and the star of your god Rē'phan,
    the images that you made to worship;
so I will remove you beyond Babylon.'

44 "Our ancestors had the tent of testimony in the wilderness, as God*b* directed when he spoke to Moses, ordering him to make it according to the pattern he had seen. 45 Our ancestors in turn brought it in with Joshua when they dispossessed the nations that God drove out before our ancestors. And it was there until the time of David, 46 who found favor with God and asked that he might find a dwelling place for the house of Jacob.*c* 47 But it was Solomon who built a house

AFRICAN AMERICAN
Don't Forget the Shoulders You Stand On

Take a few minutes to read about the martyrdom of Stephen, Acts 6.8—7.60. There is perhaps no more touching story in the New Testament than this young man's brave defense of his faith as he followed in his Lord's footsteps. He knew his history and his ancestors, and they gave him divine courage in the face of death.

People of all ages and cultures need to respect and honor the faith and sacrifices of their ancestors. For example, the video series *Eyes on the Prize* is a reminder for all Americans of the debt owed to African Americans of a previous generation. This documentation of the civil rights movement immortalizes the faith of countless people who were brave enough to protest the injustice of racism.

Today is a gift from them. Somebody died so that all Americans might live freely. Somebody suffered so that all Americans could enjoy civil rights. Somebody accepted persecution to call all Americans to respect God's justice.

How many youth today would be willing to make similar sacrifices in the struggle for freedom and equality—signs of the Reign of God?

Dear God, help me treasure my ancestors' sacrifice and bravery. Help me to follow their example in working for justice with love and courage. Amen.

▶ Acts 6.8—7.60

for him. 48 Yet the Most High does not dwell in houses made with human hands;*d* as the prophet says,
49 'Heaven is my throne,
    and the earth is my footstool.
What kind of house will you build for me,
    says the Lord,
    or what is the place of my rest?
50 Did not my hand make all these things?'

---

a Gk *your brothers*   *b* Gk *he*   *c* Other ancient authorities read *for the God of Jacob*   *d* Gk *with hands*

ACTS

51 "You stiff-necked people, uncircumcised in heart and ears, you are forever opposing the Holy Spirit, just as your ancestors used to do. 52 Which of the prophets did your ancestors not persecute? They killed those who foretold the coming of the Righteous One, and now you have become his betrayers and murderers. 53 You are the ones that received the law as ordained by angels, and yet you have not kept it."

The Stoning of Stephen

54 When they heard these things, they became enraged and ground their teeth at Stephen.*e* 55 But filled with the Holy Spirit, he gazed into heaven and saw the glory of God and Jesus standing at the right hand of God. 56 "Look," he said, "I see the heavens opened and the Son of Man standing at the right hand of God!" 57 But they covered their ears, and with a loud shout all rushed together against him. 58 Then they dragged him out of the city and began to stone him; and the witnesses laid their coats at the feet of a young man named Saul. 59 While they were stoning Stephen, he prayed, "Lord Jesus, receive my spirit." 60 Then he knelt down and cried out in a loud voice, "Lord, do not hold this sin against them." When he had said this, he died.*f* 1 And Saul approved of their killing him.

Saul Persecutes the Church

That day a severe persecution began against the church in Jerusalem, and all except the apostles were scattered throughout the countryside of Judea and Sa•mār'i•a. 2 Devout men buried Stephen and made loud lamentation over him. 3 But Saul was ravaging the church by entering house after house; dragging off both men and women, he committed them to prison.

Philip Preaches in Samaria

4 Now those who were scattered went from place to place, proclaiming the word. 5 Philip went down to the city*g* of Sa•mār'i•a and proclaimed the Messiah*h* to them. 6 The crowds with one accord listened eagerly to what was said by Philip, hearing and seeing the signs that he did, 7 for unclean

e Gk *him*   *f* Gk *fell asleep*   *g* Other ancient authorities read *a city*   *h* Or *the Christ*

Introducing ▶ SAINT PAUL

A
C
T
S

As Stephen is stoned to death, Acts introduces a person who will become the major character in the second half of the book, Saul of Tarsus, also known as Paul. Paul begins as a persecutor of the early Christians. He is a member of the Pharisees, a group that holds to a rigid interpretation of Jewish Law (26.4–5). He probably sees the Christians as a threat to the Jewish faith. But after a profound experience of the risen Christ, Paul is converted to the Christian faith. Paul is initially distrusted by other Christians who remember his persecution of them. However, another early Christian leader, Barnabas, becomes Paul's companion and advocate (9.27).

Paul's major insight is that God has made salvation available to everyone, Jews and Gentiles alike. He also knows that God's offer of salvation is a free gift, that no one could do anything to actually earn it. But many of the early Christians, who are former Jews, disagree with him. This conflict comes to a head at the Council of Jerusalem (Acts of the Apostles, chapter 15), where Paul stands toe-to-toe with Peter and James (Gal 2.1–10) and argued that the Gentiles can become Christians without following Jewish laws and customs, including circumcision.

Paul took it upon himself to spread the good news of God's salvation in Jesus to the Gentiles. During three different missionary journeys, he was instrumental in founding new Christian communities in what is now the Middle East and western Europe. He stayed in touch with those communities through letters, some of which are included as books in the New Testament. Paul's impact in spreading Christianity was so great that he is sometimes called the second founder of Christianity.

▶ Acts 8.1–3

spirits, crying with loud shrieks, came out of many who were possessed; and many others who were paralyzed or lame were cured. ⁸So there was great joy in that city.

9 Now a certain man named Simon had previously practiced magic in the city and amazed the people of Sa•mār′i•a, saying that he was someone great. ¹⁰All of them, from the least to the greatest, listened to him eagerly, saying, "This man is the power of God that is called Great." ¹¹And they listened eagerly to him because for a long time he had amazed them with his magic. ¹²But when they believed Philip, who was proclaiming the good news about the kingdom of God and the name of Jesus Christ, they were baptized, both men and women. ¹³Even Simon himself believed. After being baptized, he stayed constantly with Philip and was amazed when he saw the signs and great miracles that took place.

14 Now when the apostles at Jerusalem heard that Sa•mār′i•a had accepted the word of God, they sent Peter and John to them. ¹⁵The two went down and prayed for them that they might receive the Holy Spirit ¹⁶(for as yet the Spirit had not come*ⁱ* upon any of them; they had only been baptized in the name of the Lord Jesus). ¹⁷Then Peter and John*ʲ* laid their hands on them, and they received the Holy Spirit. ¹⁸Now when Simon saw that the Spirit was given through the laying on of the apostles' hands, he offered them money, ¹⁹saying, "Give me also this power so that anyone on whom I lay my hands may receive the Holy Spirit."

²⁰But Peter said to him, "May your silver perish with you, because you thought you could obtain God's gift with money! ²¹You have no part or share in this, for your heart is not right before God. ²²Repent therefore of this wickedness of yours, and pray to the Lord that, if possible, the intent of your heart may be forgiven you. ²³For I see that you are in the gall of bitterness and the chains of wickedness." ²⁴Simon answered, "Pray for me to the Lord, that nothing of what you*ᵏ* have said may happen to me."

25 Now after Peter and John*ˡ* had testified and spoken the word of the Lord, they returned to Jerusalem, proclaiming the good news to many villages of the Sa•mār′i•tans.

Philip and the Ethiopian Eunuch
(Cp Isa 53.7–8)

26 Then an angel of the Lord said to Philip, "Get up and go toward the south*ᵐ* to the road that goes down from Jerusalem to Gā′za." (This is a wilderness road.) ²⁷So he got up and went. Now there was an Ethiopian eunuch, a court official of the Can•dā′cē, queen of the Ethiopians, in charge of her entire treasury. He had come to Jerusalem to worship ²⁸and was returning home; seated in his chariot, he was reading the prophet Ī•sāi′ah. ²⁹Then the Spirit said to Philip, "Go over to this chariot and join it." ³⁰So Philip ran up to it and heard him reading the prophet Ī•sāi′ah. He asked,

ⁱ Gk *fallen*   *ʲ* Gk *they*   *ᵏ* The Greek word for *you* and the verb *pray* are plural   *ˡ* Gk *after they*   *ᵐ* Or *go at noon*

Bearing Good News

LIVE IT!

Acts 8.26–40 tells the story of an Ethiopian (African) eunuch. A eunuch is a man who has been castrated, either by accident or by design. Eunuchs often served as guards of the harems of kings. This eunuch was reading a text from Isaiah while returning from a visit to Jerusalem. The Holy Spirit moved the missionary Philip to explain to him how Isaiah's prophecies pointed to Jesus. And the eunuch believed and was baptized. His baptism signals the beginning acceptance of Gentile believers.

The eunuch's faith was dependent on the interaction of three characters: himself, the searching eunuch; Philip, bearing the Good News; and the Holy Spirit, who brought them together. Reflect for a moment on the following questions:

■ How are you like the Ethiopian? What are you searching for in your faith?
■ How are you like Philip? How do you share the Good News with others?
■ How can you share in the work of the Holy Spirit? How can you motivate other young people to become bearers of the Good News?

As Philip baptized the eunuch, geographical, ethnic, and legal barriers were washed away. Praise God for the salvation brought by Jesus to all people!

▶ Acts 8.26–40

"Do you understand what you are reading?" ³¹ He replied, "How can I, unless someone guides me?" And he invited Philip to get in and sit beside him. ³² Now the passage of the scripture that he was reading was this:

> "Like a sheep he was led to the slaughter,
>   and like a lamb silent before its shearer,
>   so he does not open his mouth.
> ³³ In his humiliation justice was denied him.
>   Who can describe his generation?
>   For his life is taken away from the
>   earth."

³⁴ The eunuch asked Philip, "About whom, may I ask you, does the prophet say this, about himself or about someone else?" ³⁵ Then Philip began to speak, and starting with this scripture, he proclaimed to him the good news about Jesus. ³⁶ As they were going along the road, they came to some water; and the eunuch said, "Look, here is water! What is to prevent me from being baptized?"ⁿ ³⁸ He commanded the chariot to stop, and both of them, Philip and the eunuch, went down into the water, and Philipᵒ baptized him. ³⁹ When they came up out of the water, the Spirit of the Lord snatched Philip away; the eunuch saw him no more, and went on his way rejoicing. ⁴⁰ But Philip found himself at A·zoʹtus, and as he was passing through the region, he proclaimed the good news to all the towns until he came to Caes·a·reʹa.

The Conversion of Saul
(Acts 22.6–16; 26.12–18)

Meanwhile Saul, still breathing threats and murder against the disciples of the Lord, went to the high priest ² and asked him for letters to the synagogues at Damascus, so that if he found any who belonged to the Way, men or women, he might bring them bound to Jerusalem. ³ Now as he was going along and approaching Damascus, suddenly a light from heaven flashed around him. ⁴ He fell to the ground and heard a voice saying to him, "Saul, Saul, why do you persecute me?" ⁵ He asked, "Who are you, Lord?" The reply came, "I am Jesus, whom you are persecuting. ⁶ But get up and enter the city, and you will be told what you are to do." ⁷ The men who were traveling with him stood speechless because they heard the voice but saw no one. ⁸ Saul got up from the ground, and though his eyes were open, he could see nothing; so they led him by the hand and brought him into Damascus. ⁹ For three days he was without sight, and neither ate nor drank.

10 Now there was a disciple in Damascus named An·a·niʹas. The Lord said to him in a vision, "An·a·niʹas." He answered, "Here I am, Lord." ¹¹ The Lord said to him, "Get up and go to the street called Straight, and at the house of Judas look for a man of Tarʹsus named Saul. At this moment he is praying, ¹² and he has seen in a visionᵖ a man named An·a·niʹas come in and lay his hands on him so that he might regain his sight." ¹³ But An·a·niʹas answered, "Lord, I have heard from many about this man, how much evil he has done to your saints in Jerusalem; ¹⁴ and here he has authority from the chief priests to bind all who invoke your name." ¹⁵ But the Lord said to him, "Go, for he is an instrument whom I have chosen to bring my name before Gentiles and kings and before the people of Israel; ¹⁶ I myself will show him how much he must suffer for the sake of my name." ¹⁷ So An·a·niʹas went and entered the house. He laid his hands on Saulᑫ and said, "Brother Saul, the Lord Jesus, who appeared to you on your way here, has sent me so that you may regain your sight and be filled with the Holy Spirit." ¹⁸ And immediately something like scales fell from his eyes, and his sight was restored. Then he got up and was baptized, ¹⁹ and after taking some food, he regained his strength.

Saul Preaches in Damascus

For several days he was with the disciples in Damascus, ²⁰ and immediately he began to proclaim Jesus in the synagogues, saying, "He is the Son of God." ²¹ All who heard him were amazed and said, "Is not this the man who made havoc in

---

ⁿ Other ancient authorities add all or most of verse 37,
And Philip said, "If you believe with all your heart, you may."
And he replied, "I believe that Jesus Christ is the Son of God."
ᵒ Gk *he*   ᵖ Other ancient authorities lack *in a vision*
ᑫ Gk *him*

9.4

PRAY IT!

Conversion

Saul (or Paul) experienced some dramatic events that converted him from a persecutor of Christians to a believer in Jesus Christ. He had a powerful experience of the risen Christ during which he was blinded. His physical blindness is symbolic of his previous spiritual blindness. For three days, Paul was practically lifeless—not seeing, not eating, not drinking. This period reminds us of Jesus' three days in the tomb. In many ways, going through a conversion is like dying—dying to old ways of thinking and acting. But after three days, Paul's blindness was lifted, and he was filled with the Holy Spirit, as the other Apostles were at Pentecost.

No longer a persecutor of Christians, Paul was a new person. He now felt compelled to learn more about Jesus and to share the Good News with other people. Paul's conversion told the early Christians that even the most hard-hearted person can be called by God and radically changed.

In your prayer, reflect or journal on the following questions:

■ Have you ever been suddenly aware of God's presence and calling in your life?
■ What mission is God calling you for?
■ How will you respond?

Then close with these words:

Dear Jesus, following you is an unending journey in which we must turn our back to sin and focus on living out Christ's message. Sometimes, it is an easy journey; sometimes, it is a struggle. Help me to find your light in the Scriptures, in others, and within myself. Amen.

▶ Acts 9.1–19

Saul Escapes from the Jews

23 After some time had passed, the Jews plotted to kill him, 24 but their plot became known to Saul. They were watching the gates day and night so that they might kill him; 25 but his disciples took him by night and let him down through an opening in the wall,^{t} lowering him in a basket.

Saul in Jerusalem

26 When he had come to Jerusalem, he attempted to join the disciples; and they were all afraid of him, for they did not believe that he was a disciple. 27 But Bar·na·bas took him, brought him to the apostles, and described for them how on the road he had seen the Lord, who had spoken to him, and how in Damascus he had spoken boldly in the name of Jesus. 28 So he went in and out among them in Jerusalem, speaking boldly in the name of the Lord. 29 He spoke and argued with the Hellenists; but they were attempting to kill him. 30 When the believers^u learned of it, they brought him down to Caes·a·re′a and sent him off to Tar′sus.

31 Meanwhile the church throughout Judea, Galilee, and Sa·mār′i·a had peace and was built up. Living in the fear of the Lord and in the comfort of the Holy Spirit, it increased in numbers.

The Healing of Aeneas

32 Now as Peter went here and there among all the believers,^{v} he came down also to the saints living in Lyd′da. 33 There he found a man named Ae·ne′as, who had been bedridden for eight years, for he was paralyzed. 34 Peter said to him, "Ae·ne′as, Jesus Christ heals you; get up and make your bed!" And immediately he got up. 35 And all the residents of Lyd′da and Sharon saw him and turned to the Lord.

Peter in Lydda and Joppa

36 Now in Jop′pa there was a disciple whose name was Tab′i·tha, which in Greek is Dor′cas.^{w} She was devoted to good works and acts of charity. 37 At that time she became ill and died. When they had washed her, they laid her in a room upstairs. 38 Since Lyd′da was near Jop′pa, the disciples, who heard that Peter was there, sent two men to him with the request, "Please come to us without delay." 39 So Peter got up and went with them; and when he arrived, they took him to the room upstairs. All the widows stood beside him, weeping

Jerusalem among those who invoked this name? And has he not come here for the purpose of bringing them bound before the chief priests?" 22 Saul became increasingly more powerful and confounded the Jews who lived in Damascus by proving that Jesus^r was the Messiah.^{s}

---

^{r} Gk *that this* ^{s} Or *the Christ* ^{t} Gk *through the wall*
^{u} Gk *brothers* ^{v} Gk *all of them* ^{w} The name Tabitha in Aramaic and the name Dorcas in Greek mean *a gazelle*

and showing tunics and other clothing that Dor'-cas had made while she was with them. 40 Peter put all of them outside, and then he knelt down and prayed. He turned to the body and said, "Tab'i•tha, get up." Then she opened her eyes, and seeing Peter, she sat up. 41 He gave her his hand and helped her up. Then calling the saints and widows, he showed her to be alive. 42 This became known throughout Jop'pa, and many believed in the Lord. 43 Meanwhile he stayed in Jop'pa for some time with a certain Simon, a tanner.

Peter and Cornelius

In Caes•a•re'a there was a man named Cornelius, a centurion of the Italian Cohort, as it was called. 2 He was a devout man who feared God with all his household; he gave alms generously to the people and prayed constantly to God. 3 One afternoon at about three o'clock he had a vision in which he clearly saw an angel of God coming in and saying to him, "Cornelius." 4 He stared at him in terror and said, "What is it, Lord?" He answered, "Your prayers and your alms have ascended as a memorial before God. 5 Now send men to Jop'pa for a certain Simon who is called Peter; 6 he is lodging with Simon, a tanner, whose house is by the seaside." 7 When the angel who spoke to him had left, he called two of his slaves and a devout soldier from the ranks of those who served him, 8 and after telling them everything, he sent them to Jop'pa.

9 About noon the next day, as they were on their journey and approaching the city, Peter went up on the roof to pray. 10 He became hungry and wanted something to eat; and while it was being prepared, he fell into a trance. 11 He saw the heaven opened and something like a large sheet coming down, being lowered to the ground by its four corners. 12 In it were all kinds of four-footed creatures and reptiles and birds of the air. 13 Then he heard a voice saying, "Get up, Peter; kill and eat." 14 But Peter said, "By no means, Lord; for I have never eaten anything that is profane or unclean." 15 The voice said to him again, a second time, "What God has made clean, you must not call profane." 16 This happened three times, and the thing was suddenly taken up to heaven.

17 Now while Peter was greatly puzzled about what to make of the vision that he had seen, suddenly the men sent by Cornelius appeared. They were asking for Simon's house and were standing by the gate. 18 They called out to ask whether Simon, who was called Peter, was staying there. 19 While Peter was still thinking about the vision, the Spirit said to him, "Look, three[x] men are

searching for you. 20 Now get up, go down, and go with them without hesitation; for I have sent them." 21 So Peter went down to the men and said, "I am the one you are looking for; what is the reason for your coming?" 22 They answered, "Cornelius, a centurion, an upright and God-fearing man, who is well spoken of by the whole Jewish nation, was directed by a holy angel to send for you to come to his house and to hear what you have to say." 23 So Peter[y] invited them in and gave them lodging.

---

[x] One ancient authority reads *two*; others lack the word
[y] Gk *he*

NATIVE AMERICAN

Here Comes Everybody

The word *catholic* means "universal." Someone once described being Catholic as, "Here comes everybody!"

In Acts 10.34–36, we hear that because God shows no partiality, neither should we. Even so, it is sometimes easier to stick with people who are similar to us. They understand us and know where we are coming from. There's less explaining to do. Right?

But being catholic means reaching out of our familiar circle of friends and including in our group people of different cultures and religions.

Have you ever seen a Native American blanket? Threads of various colors are woven together to form an intricate, new pattern. Each blanket is completely different from every other blanket. By building relationships with people of different cultures and embracing their diversity, we become like one of the threads in such a blanket, weaving our uniquenesses in a new and beautiful pattern. The result is different and enriching, and then we become truly catholic.

▶ Acts 10.34–36

A
C
T
S

The next day he got up and went with them, and some of the believers[z] from Jop'pa accompanied him. 24 The following day they came to Caes-a·rē'a. Cornelius was expecting them and had called together his relatives and close friends. 25 On Peter's arrival Cornelius met him, and falling at his feet, worshiped him. 26 But Peter made him get up, saying, "Stand up; I am only a mortal." 27 And as he talked with him, he went in and found that many had assembled; 28 and he said to them, "You yourselves know that it is unlawful for a Jew to associate with or to visit a Gentile; but God has shown me that I should not call anyone profane or unclean. 29 So when I was sent for, I came without objection. Now may I ask why you sent for me?"

30 Cornelius replied, "Four days ago at this very hour, at three o'clock, I was praying in my house when suddenly a man in dazzling clothes stood before me. 31 He said, 'Cornelius, your prayer has been heard and your alms have been remembered before God. 32 Send therefore to Jop'pa and ask for Simon, who is called Peter; he is staying in the home of Simon, a tanner, by the sea.' 33 Therefore I sent for you immediately, and you have been kind enough to come. So now all of us are here in the presence of God to listen to all that the Lord has commanded you to say."

Gentiles Hear the Good News

34 Then Peter began to speak to them: "I truly understand that God shows no partiality, 35 but in every nation anyone who fears him and does what is right is acceptable to him. 36 You know the message he sent to the people of Israel, preaching peace by Jesus Christ—he is Lord of all. 37 That message spread throughout Judea, beginning in Galilee after the baptism that John announced: 38 how God anointed Jesus of Nazareth with the Holy Spirit and with power; how he went about doing good and healing all who were oppressed by the devil, for God was with him. 39 We are witnesses to all that he did both in Judea and in Jerusalem. They put him to death by hanging him on a tree; 40 but God raised him on the third day and allowed him to appear, 41 not to all the people but to us who were chosen by God as witnesses, and who ate and drank with him after he rose from the dead. 42 He commanded us to preach to the people and to testify that he is the one ordained by God as judge of the living and the dead. 43 All the prophets testify about him that everyone who believes in him receives forgiveness of sins through his name."

Gentiles Receive the Holy Spirit

44 While Peter was still speaking, the Holy Spirit fell upon all who heard the word. 45 The circumcised believers who had come with Peter were astounded that the gift of the Holy Spirit had been poured out even on the Gentiles, 46 for they heard them speaking in tongues and extolling God. Then Peter said, 47 "Can anyone withhold the water for baptizing these people who have received the Holy Spirit just as we have?" 48 So he ordered them to be baptized in the name of Jesus Christ. Then they invited him to stay for several days.

PRAY IT!

Stretch Me, Lord

The conversion of Cornelius and his household was an important event. His conversion and acceptance by Peter was the result of God's direct intervention—confirming that both Jews and Gentiles were welcome in the growing Christian community.

God, just as you did with Peter, you ask me to s-t-r-e-t-c-h my comfort zone and widen the circle of people I call friends. You challenge me to embrace as my brothers and sisters those who are different in skin color or looks or speech or belief. I recognize that I have a long way to go, and I am not always in a hurry to get there.

So I ask you to help me to be more accepting of others. Let the Holy Spirit's wisdom help me see my own prejudices and rash judgments, and let the Holy Spirit's power give me the strength to stretch beyond them. Amen.

▸ Acts 11.1–18

Peter's Report to the Church at Jerusalem

Now the apostles and the believers[z] who were in Judea heard that the Gentiles had also accepted the word of God. 2 So when Peter went up to Jerusalem, the circumcised believers[a] criticized him, 3 saying, "Why did you go to uncircumcised men and eat with them?" 4 Then Peter began to explain it

---

z Gk *brothers*   a Gk lacks *believers*

to them, step by step, saying, 5 "I was in the city of Jop'pa praying, and in a trance I saw a vision. There was something like a large sheet coming down from heaven, being lowered by its four corners; and it came close to me. 6 As I looked at it closely I saw four-footed animals, beasts of prey, reptiles, and birds of the air. 7 I also heard a voice saying to me, 'Get up, Peter; kill and eat.' 8 But I replied, 'By no means, Lord; for nothing profane or unclean has ever entered my mouth.' 9 But a second time the voice answered from heaven, 'What God has made clean, you must not call profane.' 10 This happened three times; then everything was pulled up again to heaven. 11 At that very moment three men, sent to me from Caes·a·rē'a, arrived at the house where we were. 12 The Spirit told me to go with them and not to make a distinction between them and us.*b* These six brothers also accompanied me, and we entered the man's house. 13 He told us how he had seen the angel standing in his house and saying, 'Send to Jop'pa and bring Simon, who is called Peter; 14 he will give you a message by which you and your entire household will be saved.' 15 And as I began to speak, the Holy Spirit fell upon them just as it had upon us at the beginning. 16 And I remembered the word of the Lord, how he had said, 'John baptized with water, but you will be baptized with the Holy Spirit.' 17 If then God gave them the same gift that he gave us when we believed in the Lord Jesus Christ, who was I that I could hinder God?" 18 When they heard this, they were silenced. And they praised God, saying, "Then God has given even to the Gentiles the repentance that leads to life."

The Church in Antioch

19 Now those who were scattered because of the persecution that took place over Stephen traveled as far as Phoe·ni'ci·a, Cyprus, and An'ti·och, and they spoke the word to no one except Jews. 20 But among them were some men of Cyprus and Cy·rē'nē who, on coming to An'ti·och, spoke to the Hellenists*c* also, proclaiming the Lord Jesus. 21 The hand of the Lord was with them, and a great number became believers and turned to the Lord. 22 News of this came to the ears of the church in Jerusalem, and they sent Bar'na·bas to An'ti·och. 23 When he came and saw the grace of God, he rejoiced, and he exhorted them all to remain faithful to the Lord with steadfast devotion; 24 for he was a good man, full of the Holy Spirit and of faith. And a great many people were brought to the Lord. 25 Then Bar'na·bas went to Tar'sus to look for Saul, 26 and when he had found him, he brought him to An'ti·och. So it was that for an entire year they met with*d* the church and taught a great many people, and it was in An'ti·och that the disciples were first called "Christians."

27 At that time prophets came down from Jerusalem to An'ti·och. 28 One of them named Ag'a·bus stood up and predicted by the Spirit that there would be a severe famine over all the world; and this took place during the reign of Clau'di·us. 29 The disciples determined that according to their ability, each would send relief to the believers*e* living in Judea; 30 this they did, sending it to the elders by Bar'na·bas and Saul.

---

b Or *not to hesitate*   *c* Other ancient authorities read *Greeks*   *d* Or *were guests of*   *e* Gk *brothers*

A
C
T
S

Introducing ▶ BARNABAS

We first met Barnabas defending Paul after Paul's conversion in Acts of the Apostles, chapter 9. Now, in chapter 11, we are told that Barnabas "was a good man, full of the Holy Spirit and of faith." Barnabas's name literally means "son of encouragement." And encouraging others seemed to be Barnabas's gift. He recognized Paul's gifts and brought Paul to Antioch to minister to the new Christians there when no one else trusted Paul. Later, Barnabas reached out to Mark, disagreeing with Paul on whether to give Mark a second chance to travel with them (15.36–39). Barnabas sounds like the friend we would all like to have, someone who would believe in us through good times and bad.

Have you had a Barnabas in your life, someone who encouraged you and believed in you even after you made mistakes? Can you be that kind of encouraging friend to others?

▶ Acts 11.19–26

James Killed and Peter Imprisoned

About that time King Her'od laid violent hands upon some who belonged to the church. 2 He had James, the brother of John, killed with the sword. 3 After he saw that it pleased the Jews, he proceeded to arrest Peter also. (This was during the festival of Unleavened Bread.) 4 When he had seized him, he put him in prison and handed him over to four squads of soldiers to guard him, intending to bring him out to the people after the Passover. 5 While Peter was kept in prison, the church prayed fervently to God for him.

Peter Delivered from Prison

6 The very night before Her'od was going to bring him out, Peter, bound with two chains, was sleeping between two soldiers, while guards in front of the door were keeping watch over the prison. 7 Suddenly an angel of the Lord appeared and a light shone in the cell. He tapped Peter on the side and woke him, saying, "Get up quickly." And the chains fell off his wrists. 8 The angel said to him, "Fasten your belt and put on your sandals." He did so. Then he said to him, "Wrap your cloak around you and follow me." 9 Peter*f* went out and followed him; he did not realize that what was happening with the angel's help was real; he thought he was seeing a vision. 10 After they had passed the first and the second guard, they came before the iron gate leading into the city. It opened for them of its own accord, and they went outside and walked along a lane, when suddenly the angel left him. 11 Then Peter came to himself and said, "Now I am sure that the Lord has sent his angel and rescued me from the hands of Her'od and from all that the Jewish people were expecting."

12 As soon as he realized this, he went to the house of Mary, the mother of John whose other name was Mark, where many had gathered and were praying. 13 When he knocked at the outer gate, a maid named Rho'da came to answer. 14 On recognizing Peter's voice, she was so overjoyed that, instead of opening the gate, she ran in and announced that Peter was standing at the gate. 15 They said to her, "You are out of your mind!" But she insisted that it was so. They said, "It is his angel." 16 Meanwhile Peter continued knocking; and when they opened the gate, they saw him and were amazed. 17 He motioned to them with his hand to be silent, and described for them how the Lord had brought him out of the prison. And he added, "Tell this to James and to the believers."*g* Then he left and went to another place.

18 When morning came, there was no small commotion among the soldiers over what had become of Peter. 19 When Her'od had searched for him and could not find him, he examined the guards and ordered them to be put to death. Then he went down from Judea to Caes·a·re'a and stayed there.

PRAY IT!

What Imprisons You?

Holy Spirit, come! Open my mind to seek the truth. Break down the barriers that imprison me. Empower me to overcome any guilt by asking for forgiveness. Enable me to forgive others and release my past hurt and anger. Open my eyes to vices, habits, and attitudes that are destructive to me and to others. Guide me to true freedom with your Word. Amen.

▸ Acts 12.6–18

The Death of Herod

20 Now Her'od*h* was angry with the people of Tyre and Si'don. So they came to him in a body; and after winning over Blas'tus, the king's chamberlain, they asked for a reconciliation, because their country depended on the king's country for food. 21 On an appointed day Her'od put on his royal robes, took his seat on the platform, and delivered a public address to them. 22 The people kept shouting, "The voice of a god, and not of a mortal!" 23 And immediately, because he had not given the glory to God, an angel of the Lord struck him down, and he was eaten by worms and died.

24 But the word of God continued to advance and gain adherents. 25 Then after completing their mission Bar'na·bas and Saul returned to*i* Jerusalem and brought with them John, whose other name was Mark.

Barnabas and Saul Commissioned

Now in the church at An'ti·och there were prophets and teachers: Bar'na·bas, Sim'e·on who was called Ni'ger, Lucius of Cy·re'ne, Man'a·en a member of the court of Her'od the ruler,*j* and Saul. 2 While they were worshiping the Lord and fasting, the Holy Spirit said, "Set apart for me Bar'na·bas and Saul for the work to which I have called them."

f Gk *He*   *g* Gk *brothers*   *h* Gk *he*   *i* Other ancient authorities read *from*   *j* Gk *tetrarch*

3 Then after fasting and praying they laid their hands on them and sent them off.

The Apostles Preach in Cyprus

4 So, being sent out by the Holy Spirit, they went down to Se•leŭ′ci•a; and from there they sailed to Cyprus. 5 When they arrived at Sal′a•mis, they proclaimed the word of God in the synagogues of the Jews. And they had John also to assist them. 6 When they had gone through the whole island as far as Pā′phos, they met a certain magician, a Jewish false prophet, named Bar-Jesus. 7 He was with the proconsul, Ser′gi•us Paul′us, an intelligent man, who summoned Bar′na•bas and Saul and wanted to hear the word of God. 8 But the magician El′y•mas (for that is the translation of his name) opposed them and tried to turn the proconsul away from the faith. 9 But Saul, also known as Paul, filled with the Holy Spirit, looked intently at him 10 and said, "You son of the devil, you enemy of all righteousness, full of all deceit and villainy, will you not stop making crooked the straight paths of the Lord? 11 And now listen—the hand of the Lord is against you, and you will be blind for a while, unable to see the sun." Immediately mist and darkness came over him, and he went about groping for someone to lead him by the hand. 12 When the proconsul saw what had happened, he believed, for he was astonished at the teaching about the Lord.

Paul and Barnabas in Antioch of Pisidia

13 Then Paul and his companions set sail from Pā′phos and came to Per′ga in Pam•phyl′i•a. John, however, left them and returned to Jerusalem; 14 but they went on from Per′ga and came to An′ti-och in Pi•sid′i•a. And on the sabbath day they went into the synagogue and sat down. 15 After the reading of the law and the prophets, the officials of the synagogue sent them a message, saying, "Brothers, if you have any word of exhortation for the people, give it." 16 So Paul stood up and with a gesture began to speak:

"You Israelites,[k] and others who fear God, listen. 17 The God of this people Israel chose our ancestors and made the people great during their stay in the land of Egypt, and with uplifted arm he led them out of it. 18 For about forty years he put up with[l] them in the wilderness. 19 After he had destroyed seven nations in the land of Cā′naan, he gave them their land as an inheritance 20 for about four hundred fifty years. After that he gave them judges until the time of the prophet Samuel. 21 Then they asked for a king; and God gave them Saul son of Kish, a man of the tribe of Benjamin,

did you KNOW?

The Journeys of Paul

According to most interpretations of Acts, Paul made three missionary journeys over a ten-year period to spread the Gospel message. The details of his first journey are covered in chapters 13–14. The second journey is reported in chapters 16–18. The third journey is described in chapters 19–21. Paul himself may have seen these not as three separate journeys but as one continuous missionary activity. On these journeys, Paul made converts and started Christian communities. On the second and third journeys, he also visited established communities to give them guidance and support. See maps 7 and 8 for the routes of Paul's journeys.

Paul's third journey landed him back in Jerusalem, where some Jews had him arrested. On the basis of his Roman citizenship, Paul appealed to the emperor. So he was transported to Rome (this trip is referred to as his fourth journey). He probably died there as a martyr around A.D. 65. Some traditions say that Paul wasn't martyred there but went on to evangelize in Spain.

▶ Acts of the Apostles, chapters 13–21

A
C
T
S

who reigned for forty years. 22 When he had removed him, he made David their king. In his testimony about him he said, 'I have found David, son of Jesse, to be a man after my heart, who will carry out all my wishes.' 23 Of this man's posterity God has brought to Israel a Savior, Jesus, as he promised; 24 before his coming John had already proclaimed a baptism of repentance to all the people of Israel. 25 And as John was finishing his work, he said, 'What do you suppose that I am? I am not he. No, but one is coming after me; I am not worthy to untie the thong of the sandals[m] on his feet.'

26 "My brothers, you descendants of Abraham's family, and others who fear God, to us[n] the message of this salvation has been sent. 27 Because the residents of Jerusalem and their leaders did not

---

k Gk Men, Israelites　　l Other ancient authorities read cared for　　m Gk untie the sandals　　n Other ancient authorities read you

recognize him or understand the words of the prophets that are read every sabbath, they fulfilled those words by condemning him. 28 Even though they found no cause for a sentence of death, they asked Pilate to have him killed. 29 When they had carried out everything that was written about him, they took him down from the tree and laid him in a tomb. 30 But God raised him from the dead; 31 and for many days he appeared to those who came up with him from Galilee to Jerusalem, and they are now his witnesses to the people. 32 And we bring you the good news that what God promised to our ancestors 33 he has fulfilled for us, their children, by raising Jesus; as also it is written in the second psalm,

'You are my Son;
    today I have begotten you.'

34 As to his raising him from the dead, no more to return to corruption, he has spoken in this way,

'I will give you the holy promises made to
    David.'

35 Therefore he has also said in another psalm,

'You will not let your Holy One experience
    corruption.'

36 For David, after he had served the purpose of God in his own generation, died,ᵒ was laid beside his ancestors, and experienced corruption; 37 but he whom God raised up experienced no corruption. 38 Let it be known to you therefore, my brothers, that through this man forgiveness of sins is proclaimed to you; 39 by this Jesusᵖ everyone who believes is set free from all those sinsᵠ from which you could not be freed by the law of Moses. 40 Beware, therefore, that what the prophets said does not happen to you:

41 'Look, you scoffers!
    Be amazed and perish,
for in your days I am doing a work,
    a work that you will never believe, even
        if someone tells you.' "

42 As Paul and Bar′na•basʳ were going out, the people urged them to speak about these things again the next sabbath. 43 When the meeting of the synagogue broke up, many Jews and devout converts to Jū′da•ism followed Paul and Bar′na•bas, who spoke to them and urged them to continue in the grace of God.

44 The next sabbath almost the whole city gathered to hear the word of the Lord.ˢ 45 But when the Jews saw the crowds, they were filled with jealousy; and blaspheming, they contradicted what was spoken by Paul. 46 Then both Paul and Bar′na•bas spoke out boldly, saying, "It was necessary that the word of God should be spoken first to you. Since you reject it and judge yourselves to be unworthy of eternal life, we are now turning to the Gentiles. 47 For so the Lord has commanded us, saying,

'I have set you to be a light for the Gentiles,
    so that you may bring salvation to the
        ends of the earth.' "

48 When the Gentiles heard this, they were glad and praised the word of the Lord; and as many as had been destined for eternal life became believers. 49 Thus the word of the Lord spread throughout the region. 50 But the Jews incited the devout women of high standing and the leading men of the city, and stirred up persecution against Paul and Bar′na•bas, and drove them out of their region. 51 So they shook the dust off their feet in protest against them, and went to I•cō′ni•um. 52 And the disciples were filled with joy and with the Holy Spirit.

Paul and Barnabas in Iconium

The same thing occurred in I•cō′ni•um, where Paul and Bar′na•basʳ went into the Jewish synagogue and spoke in such a way that a great number of both Jews and Greeks became believers. 2 But the unbelieving Jews stirred up the Gentiles and poisoned their minds against the brothers. 3 So they remained for a long time, speaking boldly for the Lord, who testified to the word of his grace by granting signs and wonders to be done through them. 4 But the residents of the city were divided; some sided with the Jews, and some with the apostles. 5 And when an attempt was made by both Gentiles and Jews, with their rulers, to mistreat them and to stone them, 6 the apostlesʳ learned of it and fled to Lys′tra and Der′bē, cities of Lyc•ā•ō′-ni•a, and to the surrounding country; 7 and there they continued proclaiming the good news.

Paul and Barnabas in Lystra and Derbe

8 In Lys′tra there was a man sitting who could not use his feet and had never walked, for he had been crippled from birth. 9 He listened to Paul as he was speaking. And Paul, looking at him intently and seeing that he had faith to be healed, 10 said in a loud voice, "Stand upright on your feet." And the manᵗ sprang up and began to walk. 11 When the crowds saw what Paul had done, they shouted in the Lyc•ā•ō′ni•an language, "The gods have come down to us in human form!" 12 Bar′na•bas they called Zeūs, and Paul they called Her′mēs, because he was the chief speaker. 13 The priest of Zeūs, whose temple was just outside the city,ᵘ brought oxen and garlands to the gates; he and the crowds

ᵒ Gk fell asleep   ᵖ Gk this   ᵠ Gk all   ʳ Gk they
ˢ Other ancient authorities read God   ᵗ Gk he   ᵘ Or The priest of Zeus-Outside-the-City

A Courageous Stance

One thing is clear about taking a stand and spreading the Gospel—it takes great courage. The story of Paul and Barnabas in Iconium is further evidence of how the early disciples risked their own lives in order to preach the Good News. It seems the Good News is not easy for some people to hear or accept.

In your prayer, reflect or journal on the following questions:

- In what ways is God inviting you to live a little more courageously in order to spread the Good News in your school? your home? your neighborhood and community?
- What keeps you from responding?

▶ Acts 14.1–7

---

wanted to offer sacrifice. ¹⁴ When the apostles Bar′na·bas and Paul heard of it, they tore their clothes and rushed out into the crowd, shouting, ¹⁵ "Friends,ᵛ why are you doing this? We are mortals just like you, and we bring you good news, that you should turn from these worthless things to the living God, who made the heaven and the earth and the sea and all that is in them. ¹⁶ In past generations he allowed all the nations to follow their own ways; ¹⁷ yet he has not left himself without a witness in doing good—giving you rains from heaven and fruitful seasons, and filling you with food and your hearts with joy." ¹⁸ Even with these words, they scarcely restrained the crowds from offering sacrifice to them.

19 But Jews came there from An′ti·och and I·co′ni·um and won over the crowds. Then they stoned Paul and dragged him out of the city, supposing that he was dead. ²⁰ But when the disciples surrounded him, he got up and went into the city. The next day he went on with Bar′na·bas to Der′bē.

The Return to Antioch in Syria

21 After they had proclaimed the good news to that city and had made many disciples, they returned to Lys′tra, then on to I·co′ni·um and An′ti·och. ²² There they strengthened the souls of the disciples and encouraged them to continue in the faith, saying, "It is through many persecutions that we must enter the kingdom of God." ²³ And after they had appointed elders for them in each church, with prayer and fasting they entrusted them to the Lord in whom they had come to believe.

24 Then they passed through Pi·sid′i·a and came to Pam·phyl′i·a. ²⁵ When they had spoken the word in Per′ga, they went down to At·ta·li′a. ²⁶ From there they sailed back to An′ti·och, where they had been commended to the grace of God for the workʷ that they had completed. ²⁷ When they

arrived, they called the church together and related all that God had done with them, and how he had opened a door of faith for the Gentiles. ²⁸ And they stayed there with the disciples for some time.

The Council at Jerusalem

Then certain individuals came down from Judea and were teaching the brothers, "Unless you are circumcised according to the custom of Moses, you cannot be saved." ² And after Paul and Bar′na·bas had no small dissension and debate with them, Paul and Bar′na·bas and some of the others were appointed to go up to Jerusalem to discuss this question with the apostles and the elders. ³ So they were sent on their way by the church, and as they passed through both Phoe·ni′ci·a and Sa·mar′i·a, they reported the conversion of the Gentiles, and brought great joy to all the believers.ˣ ⁴ When they came to Jerusalem, they were welcomed by the church and the apostles and the elders, and they reported all that God had done with them. ⁵ But some believers who belonged to the sect of the Phar′i·sees stood up and said, "It is necessary for them to be circumcised and ordered to keep the law of Moses."

6 The apostles and the elders met together to consider this matter. ⁷ After there had been much debate, Peter stood up and said to them, "My brothers,ʸ you know that in the early days God made a choice among you, that I should be the one through whom the Gentiles would hear the message of the good news and become believers. ⁸ And God, who knows the human heart, testified to them by giving them the Holy Spirit, just as he did to us; ⁹ and in cleansing their hearts by faith he has made no distinction between us and them. ¹⁰ Now therefore why are you putting God to the test by placing on the neck of the disciples a yoke

ᵛ Gk Men   ʷ Or committed in the grace of God to the work
ˣ Gk brothers   ʸ Gk Men, brothers

that neither our ancestors nor we have been able to bear? [11] On the contrary, we believe that we will be saved through the grace of the Lord Jesus, just as they will."

12 The whole assembly kept silence, and listened to Bar'na·bas and Paul as they told of all the signs and wonders that God had done through them among the Gentiles. [13] After they finished speaking, James replied, "My brothers,[z] listen to me. [14] Sim'e·on has related how God first looked favorably on the Gentiles, to take from among them a people for his name. [15] This agrees with the words of the prophets, as it is written,

[16] 'After this I will return,
    and I will rebuild the dwelling of David,
        which has fallen;
    from its ruins I will rebuild it,
        and I will set it up,
[17] so that all other peoples may seek the
        Lord—
    even all the Gentiles over whom my
        name has been called.
    Thus says the Lord, who has been
        making these things [18] known from
        long ago.'[a]

[19] Therefore I have reached the decision that we should not trouble those Gentiles who are turning to God, [20] but we should write to them to abstain only from things polluted by idols and from fornication and from whatever has been strangled[b] and from blood. [21] For in every city, for generations past, Moses has had those who proclaim him, for he has been read aloud every sabbath in the synagogues."

The Council's Letter to Gentile Believers

22 Then the apostles and the elders, with the consent of the whole church, decided to choose men from among their members[c] and to send them to An'ti·och with Paul and Bar'na·bas. They sent Judas called Bar·sab'bas, and Silas, leaders among the brothers, [23] with the following letter: "The brothers, both the apostles and the elders, to the believers[d] of Gentile origin in An'ti·och and Syria and Ci·li'ci·a, greetings. [24] Since we have heard that certain persons who have gone out from us, though with no instructions from us, have said things to disturb you and have unsettled your minds,[e] [25] we have decided unanimously to choose representatives[f] and send them to you, along with our beloved Bar'na·bas and Paul, [26] who have risked their lives for the sake of our Lord Jesus Christ. [27] We have therefore sent Judas and Silas, who themselves will tell you the same things by word of mouth. [28] For it has seemed

Catholic Connections

MINISTRY IN THE CHURCH

The Acts of the Apostles gives us some clues about how positions of ministry developed in the first Christian communities. One of the first ministries that developed was the ministry of service. Acts 6.1–7 tells how seven people were chosen for a special ministry of service. Eventually, people with special roles of service were called deacons or deaconesses (see 1 Tim 3.8–13). Today, deacons continue to have service to the community as their primary goal.

Acts 14.21–28 tells how Paul and Barnabas appointed elders as leaders in the communities they formed. These elders watched over the community and guarded against those who would distort the true faith (20.28–32). Over time, the chief leaders in this role became known as bishops (see 1 Tim 3.1–7), and were recognized as the successors of the Apostles. Other elders who assisted the bishops became known as presbyters, or priests.

Many other ministries are listed in the New Testament, including the ministries of evangelization, of teaching, of interpreting the Scriptures, of prophecy, and of healing (see 1 Cor 12.7–11 for one list). Many of these ministries required no special office. Today, parish ministers such as youth ministers, religious educators, liturgical ministers, outreach ministers, and many others, continue this practice of sharing their gifts with the Christian community.

good to the Holy Spirit and to us to impose on you no further burden than these essentials: [29] that you abstain from what has been sacrificed to idols

---

[z] Gk Men, brothers   [a] Other ancient authorities read *things.* [18] *Known to God from of old are all his works.'*   [b] Other ancient authorities lack *and from whatever has been strangled*   [c] Gk *from among them*   [d] Gk *brothers*   [e] Other ancient authorities add *saying, 'You must be circumcised and keep the law,'*   [f] Gk *men*

and from blood and from what is strangled^g and from fornication. If you keep yourselves from these, you will do well. Farewell."

30 So they were sent off and went down to An'ti•och. When they gathered the congregation together, they delivered the letter. 31 When its members^h read it, they rejoiced at the exhortation. 32 Judas and Silas, who were themselves prophets, said much to encourage and strengthen the believers.^{i} 33 After they had been there for some time, they were sent off in peace by the believers^i to those who had sent them.^{j} 35 But Paul and Bar'na•bas remained in An'ti•och, and there, with many others, they taught and proclaimed the word of the Lord.

Timothy Joins Paul and Silas

Paul^k went on also to Der'bē and to Lys'tra, where there was a disciple named Timothy, the son of a Jewish woman who was a believer; but his father was a Greek. 2 He was well spoken of by the believers^i in Lys'tra and I•cō'ni•um. 3 Paul wanted Timothy to accompany him; and he took him and had him circumcised because of the Jews who were in those places, for they all knew that his father was a Greek. 4 As they went from town to town, they delivered to them for observance the decisions that had been reached by the apostles and elders who were in Jerusalem. 5 So the churches were strengthened in the faith and increased in numbers daily.

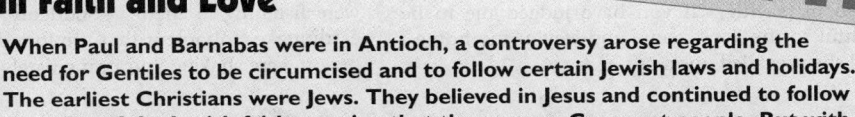

Unity in Faith and Love

When Paul and Barnabas were in Antioch, a controversy arose regarding the need for Gentiles to be circumcised and to follow certain Jewish laws and holidays. The earliest Christians were Jews. They believed in Jesus and continued to follow the rules of the Jewish faith as a sign that they were a Covenant people. But with Gentiles becoming Christians, new questions were raised, like: Do Gentiles have to follow all the Jewish rules? Do Gentiles need to be circumcised as a sign of the Covenant? Circumcision is the surgical removal of the foreskin from a penis, and the Gentile converts did not see the need for it.

Paul and Barnabas insisted that Christians were free from such Jewish laws; they went to Jerusalem to meet with the other Apostles to defend their position. With Peter's support, Paul and Barnabas's view won the day. This meeting of the Apostles is called the Council of Jerusalem and was a pivotal point in the history of the church. At it the Apostles decided that the center of the Christian faith was believing in the risen Christ not conforming to a Jewish ritual.

How does your youth group or parish handle conflict? Does it handle it better when members remind themselves that they are united by their faith in Jesus?

▸ Acts 15.1–35

ACTS

Paul and Barnabas Separate

36 After some days Paul said to Bar'na•bas, "Come, let us return and visit the believers^i in every city where we proclaimed the word of the Lord and see how they are doing." 37 Bar'na•bas wanted to take with them John called Mark. 38 But Paul decided not to take with them one who had deserted them in Pam•phyl'i•a and had not accompanied them in the work. 39 The disagreement became so sharp that they parted company; Bar'na•bas took Mark with him and sailed away to Cyprus. 40 But Paul chose Silas and set out, the believers^i commending him to the grace of the Lord. 41 He went through Syria and Ci•li'ci•a, strengthening the churches.

Paul's Vision of the Man of Macedonia

6 They went through the region of Phryg'i•a and Galatia, having been forbidden by the Holy Spirit to speak the word in Asia. 7 When they had come opposite My'si•a, they attempted to go into Bi•thyn'i•a, but the Spirit of Jesus did not allow them; 8 so, passing by My'si•a, they went down to Trō'as. 9 During the night Paul had a vision: there stood a man of Mac•e•dō'ni•a pleading with him and saying, "Come over to Mac•e•dō'ni•a and help us." 10 When he had seen the vision, we

g Other ancient authorities lack *and from what is strangled* h Gk *When they* i Gk *brothers* j Other ancient authorities add verse 34, *But it seemed good to Silas to remain there* k Gk *He*

immediately tried to cross over to Mac·e·dō'ni·a, being convinced that God had called us to proclaim the good news to them.

The Conversion of Lydia

11 We set sail from Trō'as and took a straight course to Sam'o·thrāce, the following day to Nē·ap'o·lis, 12 and from there to Phi·lip'pī, which is a leading city of the district[l] of Mac·e·dō'ni·a and a Roman colony. We remained in this city for some days. 13 On the sabbath day we went outside the gate by the river, where we supposed there was a place of prayer; and we sat down and spoke to the women who had gathered there. 14 A certain woman named Lyd'i·a, a worshiper of God, was listening to us; she was from the city of Thȳ·a·tī'ra and a dealer in purple cloth. The Lord opened her heart to listen eagerly to what was said by Paul. 15 When she and her household were baptized, she urged us, saying, "If you have judged me to be faithful to the Lord, come and stay at my home." And she prevailed upon us.

Jesus Christ to come out of her." And it came out that very hour.

19 But when her owners saw that their hope of making money was gone, they seized Paul and Silas and dragged them into the marketplace before the authorities. 20 When they had brought them before the magistrates, they said, "These men are disturbing our city; they are Jews 21 and are advocating customs that are not lawful for us as Romans to adopt or observe." 22 The crowd joined in attacking them, and the magistrates had them stripped of their clothing and ordered them to be beaten with rods. 23 After they had given them a severe flogging, they threw them into prison and ordered the jailer to keep them securely. 24 Following these instructions, he put them in the innermost cell and fastened their feet in the stocks.

25 About midnight Paul and Silas were praying and singing hymns to God, and the prisoners were listening to them. 26 Suddenly there was an earthquake, so violent that the foundations of the prison were shaken; and immediately all the doors

Introducing
▶ LYDIA AND PRISCILLA

Women were a crucial part of Christianity from its beginnings. The Acts of the Apostles names two women who were instrumental in Paul's missionary journeys: Lydia and Priscilla. Lydia (16.11–14) was Paul's first convert in Philippi, which is part of modern-day Europe. She was a textile merchant and was wealthy enough to support a household and open her home to Paul and Silas to stay for an extended time.

In chapter 18, we meet Priscilla and her husband, Aquila. This family hosted Paul in Corinth. Later, they accompanied him from Corinth to Antioch. While there, they instructed Apollos in the "Way of God" (18.26). Luke's inclusion of these women indicates that women were active in the early church, not only supporting the missionary work of Paul but also leading and teaching. For more on the women in the Bible, see the chapter titled "Suggested Reading Plans," near the beginning of this Bible.

▶ **Acts 16.14–15; 18.1–26**

Paul and Silas in Prison

16 One day, as we were going to the place of prayer, we met a slave-girl who had a spirit of divination and brought her owners a great deal of money by fortune-telling. 17 While she followed Paul and us, she would cry out, "These men are slaves of the Most High God, who proclaim to you[m] a way of salvation." 18 She kept doing this for many days. But Paul, very much annoyed, turned and said to the spirit, "I order you in the name of

were opened and everyone's chains were unfastened. 27 When the jailer woke up and saw the prison doors wide open, he drew his sword and was about to kill himself, since he supposed that the prisoners had escaped. 28 But Paul shouted in a loud voice, "Do not harm yourself, for we are all here." 29 The jailer[n] called for lights, and rushing in, he fell down trembling before Paul and Silas.

---

[l] Other authorities read *a city of the first district*   [m] Other ancient authorities read *to us*   [n] Gk *He*

30 Then he brought them outside and said, "Sirs, what must I do to be saved?" 31 They answered, "Believe on the Lord Jesus, and you will be saved, you and your household." 32 They spoke the word of the Lord*o* to him and to all who were in his house. 33 At the same hour of the night he took them and washed their wounds; then he and his entire family were baptized without delay. 34 He brought them up into the house and set food before them; and he and his entire household rejoiced that he had become a believer in God.

35 When morning came, the magistrates sent the police, saying, "Let those men go." 36 And the jailer reported the message to Paul, saying, "The magistrates sent word to let you go; therefore come out now and go in peace." 37 But Paul replied, "They have beaten us in public, uncondemned, men who are Roman citizens, and have thrown us into prison; and now are they going to discharge us in secret? Certainly not! Let them come and take us out themselves." 38 The police reported these words to the magistrates, and they were afraid when they heard that they were Roman citizens; 39 so they came and apologized to them. And they took them out and asked them to leave the city. 40 After leaving the prison they went to Lyd'i•a's home; and when they had seen and encouraged the brothers and sisters*p* there, they departed.

The Uproar in Thessalonica

After Paul and Silas*q* had passed through Am•phip'o•lis and Ap•ol•lō'ni•a, they came to Thes•sa•lo•ni'ca, where there was a synagogue of the Jews. 2 And Paul went in, as was his custom, and on three sabbath days argued with them from the scriptures, 3 explaining and proving that it was necessary for the Messiah*r* to suffer and to rise from the dead, and saying, "This is the Messiah,*r* Jesus whom I am proclaiming to you." 4 Some of them were persuaded and joined Paul and Silas, as did a great many of the devout Greeks and not a few of the leading women. 5 But the Jews became jealous, and with the help of some ruffians in the marketplaces they formed a mob and set the city in an uproar. While they were searching for Paul and Silas to bring them out to the assembly, they attacked Jason's house. 6 When they could not find them, they dragged Jason and some believers*p* before the city authorities,*s* shouting, "These people who have been turning the world upside down have come here also, 7 and Jason has entertained them as guests. They are all acting contrary to the decrees of the emperor, saying that there is another king named Jesus." 8 The people and the city officials were disturbed when they heard this, 9 and after they had taken bail from Jason and the others, they let them go.

Paul and Silas in Beroea

10 That very night the believers*p* sent Paul and Silas off to Be•roē'a; and when they arrived, they went to the Jewish synagogue. 11 These Jews were more receptive than those in Thes•sa•lo•ni'ca, for they welcomed the message very eagerly and examined the scriptures every day to see whether these things were so. 12 Many of them therefore believed, including not a few Greek women and men of high standing. 13 But when the Jews of Thes•sa•lo•ni'ca learned that the word of God had been proclaimed by Paul in Be•roē'a as well, they came there too, to stir up and incite the crowds. 14 Then the believers*p* immediately sent Paul away to the coast, but Silas and Timothy remained behind. 15 Those who conducted Paul brought him as far as Athens; and after receiving instructions to have Silas and Timothy join him as soon as possible, they left him.

Paul in Athens

16 While Paul was waiting for them in Athens, he was deeply distressed to see that the city was full of idols. 17 So he argued in the synagogue with the Jews and the devout persons, and also in the marketplace*t* every day with those who happened to be there. 18 Also some Ep•i•cū•rē'an and Stoic philosophers debated with him. Some said, "What does this babbler want to say?" Others said, "He seems to be a proclaimer of foreign divinities." (This was because he was telling the good news about Jesus and the resurrection.) 19 So they took him and brought him to the Ar•e•op'a•gus and asked him, "May we know what this new teaching is that you are presenting? 20 It sounds rather strange to us, so we would like to know what it means." 21 Now all the Athenians and the foreigners living there would spend their time in nothing but telling or hearing something new.

22 Then Paul stood in front of the Ar•e•op'a•gus and said, "Athenians, I see how extremely religious you are in every way. 23 For as I went through the city and looked carefully at the objects of your worship, I found among them an altar with the inscription, 'To an unknown god.' What therefore you worship as unknown, this I proclaim to you. 24 The God who made the world and everything in it, he who is Lord of heaven and earth, does not live in shrines made by human hands, 25 nor is he served by human hands, as though he needed anything, since he himself gives to all

---

o Other ancient authorities read *word of God*
p Gk *brothers*   *q* Gk *they*   *r* Or *the Christ*
s Gk *politarchs*   *t* Or *civic center;* Gk *agora*

PRAY IT!

Help Us Evangelize

Paul was wonderfully gifted for his work as an evangelist. He had the ability to communicate with both common people and intellectuals. He was familiar with three cultures—Jewish, Greek, and Roman—and proclaimed the Gospel message in ways all three could understand. He was skilled at building Christian communities. And he was absolutely fearless in preaching about Jesus Christ. Let's pray for these gifts in ourselves so that we can continue the church's mission of evangelization, particularly to young people.

O God, how I admire Paul! I too want to share your Good News with my generation. So let your Holy Spirit bless me with the gift of evangelization. Help me reach out to other young people no matter what clique or group they belong to. Help me to bring out the best in our culture and to challenge that which is wrong or misleading. Give me courage to speak fearlessly about my faith in Jesus when it is right to do so. And let me be your instrument in building communities of faith, hope, and love. Amen.

▸ Acts of the Apostles, chapter 17

mortals life and breath and all things. 26 From one ancestor[u] he made all nations to inhabit the whole earth, and he allotted the times of their existence and the boundaries of the places where they would live, 27 so that they would search for God[v] and perhaps grope for him and find him—though indeed he is not far from each one of us. 28 For 'In him we live and move and have our being'; as even some of your own poets have said,

'For we too are his offspring.'

29 Since we are God's offspring, we ought not to think that the deity is like gold, or silver, or stone, an image formed by the art and imagination of mortals. 30 While God has overlooked the times of human ignorance, now he commands all people everywhere to repent, 31 because he has fixed a day on which he will have the world judged in righteousness by a man whom he has appointed, and of this he has given assurance to all by raising him from the dead."

32 When they heard of the resurrection of the dead, some scoffed; but others said, "We will hear you again about this." 33 At that point Paul left them. 34 But some of them joined him and became believers, including Di•o•nys'i•us the Ar•e•op'a•gite and a woman named Dam'a•ris, and others with them.

Paul in Corinth

After this Paul[w] left Athens and went to Corinth. 2 There he found a Jew named A•qui'la, a native of Pon'tus, who had recently come from Italy with his wife Priscilla, because Clau'di•us had ordered all Jews to leave Rome. Paul[x] went to see them, 3 and, because he was of the same trade, he stayed with them, and they worked together—by trade they were tentmakers. 4 Every sabbath he would argue in the synagogue and would try to convince Jews and Greeks.

5 When Silas and Timothy arrived from Mac•e•dō'ni•a, Paul was occupied with proclaiming the word,[y] testifying to the Jews that the Messiah[z] was Jesus. 6 When they opposed and reviled him, in protest he shook the dust from his clothes[a] and said to them, "Your blood be on your own heads! I am innocent. From now on I will go to the Gentiles." 7 Then he left the synagogue[b] and went to the house of a man named Tit'i•us[c] Justus, a worshiper of God; his house was next door to the synagogue. 8 Cris'pus, the official of the synagogue, became a believer in the Lord, together with all his household; and many of the Corinthians who heard Paul became believers and were baptized. 9 One night the Lord said to Paul in a vision, "Do not be afraid, but speak and do not be silent; 10 for I am with you, and no one will lay a hand on you to harm you, for there are many in this city who are my people." 11 He stayed there a year and six months, teaching the word of God among them.

12 But when Gal'li•ō was proconsul of A•chā'i•a, the Jews made a united attack on Paul and brought him before the tribunal. 13 They said, "This man is persuading people to worship God in ways that are contrary to the law." 14 Just as Paul was about to speak, Gal'li•ō said to the Jews, "If it were a matter of crime or serious villainy, I would be justified in accepting the complaint of you Jews; 15 but since it is a matter of questions about words and names and your own law, see to it yourselves; I do not wish to be a judge of these matters." 16 And he dismissed them from the

---

u Gk *From one*; other ancient authorities read *From one blood*   *v* Other ancient authorities read *the Lord*   *w* Gk *he*   *x* Gk *He*   *y* Gk *with the word*   *z* Or *the Christ*   *a* Gk *reviled him, he shook out his clothes*   *b* Gk *left there*   *c* Other ancient authorities read *Titus*

ACTS

tribunal. [17] Then all of them[d] seized Sos'the•nēs, the official of the synagogue, and beat him in front of the tribunal. But Gal'li•ō paid no attention to any of these things.

18.18

Paul's Return to Antioch

18 After staying there for a considerable time, Paul said farewell to the believers[e] and sailed for Syria, accompanied by Priscilla and A•qui'la. At Cen'chrē•ae he had his hair cut, for he was under a vow. [19] When they reached Eph'e•sus, he left them there, but first he himself went into the synagogue and had a discussion with the Jews. [20] When they asked him to stay longer, he declined; [21] but on taking leave of them, he said, "I[f] will return to you, if God wills." Then he set sail from Eph'e•sus.

22 When he had landed at Caes•a•rē'a, he went up to Jerusalem[g] and greeted the church, and then went down to An'ti•och. [23] After spending some time there he departed and went from place to place through the region of Galatia[h] and Phryg'i•a, strengthening all the disciples.

Ministry of Apollos

24 Now there came to Eph'e•sus a Jew named A•pol'los, a native of Alexandria. He was an eloquent man, well-versed in the scriptures. [25] He had been instructed in the Way of the Lord; and he spoke with burning enthusiasm and taught accurately the things concerning Jesus, though he knew only the baptism of John. [26] He began to speak boldly in the synagogue; but when Priscilla and A•qui'la heard him, they took him aside and explained the Way of God to him more accurately. [27] And when he wished to cross over to A•chā'i•a,

the believers[e] encouraged him and wrote to the disciples to welcome him. On his arrival he greatly helped those who through grace had become believers, [28] for he powerfully refuted the Jews in public, showing by the scriptures that the Messiah[i] is Jesus.

Paul in Ephesus

While A•pol'los was in Corinth, Paul passed through the interior regions and came to Eph'e•sus, where he found some disciples. [2] He said to them, "Did you receive the Holy Spirit when you became believers?" They replied, "No, we have not even heard that there is a Holy Spirit." [3] Then he said, "Into what then were you baptized?" They answered, "Into John's baptism." [4] Paul said, "John baptized with the baptism of repentance, telling the people to believe in the one who was to come after him, that is, in Jesus." [5] On hearing this, they were baptized in the name of the Lord Jesus. [6] When Paul had laid his hands on them, the Holy Spirit came upon them, and they spoke in tongues and prophesied— [7] altogether there were about twelve of them.

8 He entered the synagogue and for three months spoke out boldly, and argued persuasively about the kingdom of God. [9] When some stubbornly refused to believe and spoke evil of the Way before the congregation, he left them, taking the disciples with him, and argued daily in the lecture hall of Ty•ran'nus.[j] [10] This continued for two years, so that all the residents of Asia, both Jews and Greeks, heard the word of the Lord.

The Sons of Sceva

11 God did extraordinary miracles through Paul, [12] so that when the handkerchiefs or aprons that had touched his skin were brought to the sick, their diseases left them, and the evil spirits came out of them. [13] Then some itinerant Jewish exorcists tried to use the name of the Lord Jesus over those who had evil spirits, saying, "I adjure you by the Jesus whom Paul proclaims." [14] Seven sons of a Jewish high priest named Scē'va were doing this. [15] But the evil spirit said to them in reply, "Jesus I know, and Paul I know; but who are you?" [16] Then the man with the evil spirit leaped on them, mastered them all, and so overpowered them that they fled out of the house naked and wounded. [17] When this became known to all residents of

---

d Other ancient authorities read *all the Greeks*
e Gk *brothers*   *f* Other ancient authorities read *I must at all costs keep the approaching festival in Jerusalem, but I*
g Gk *went up*   *h* Gk *the Galatian region*   *i* Or *the Christ*
j Other ancient authorities read *of a certain Tyrannus, from eleven o'clock in the morning to four in the afternoon*

Eph'e•sus, both Jews and Greeks, everyone was awestruck; and the name of the Lord Jesus was praised. [18]Also many of those who became believers confessed and disclosed their practices. [19]A number of those who practiced magic collected their books and burned them publicly; when the value of these books[k] was calculated, it was found to come to fifty thousand silver coins. [20]So the word of the Lord grew mightily and prevailed.

The Riot in Ephesus

[21] Now after these things had been accomplished, Paul resolved in the Spirit to go through Mac•e•dō'ni•a and A•chā'i•a, and then to go on to Jerusalem. He said, "After I have gone there, I must also see Rome." [22]So he sent two of his helpers, Timothy and E•ras'tus, to Mac•e•dō'ni•a, while he himself stayed for some time longer in Asia.

[23] About that time no little disturbance broke out concerning the Way. [24]A man named De•mē'tri•us, a silversmith who made silver shrines of Ar'te•mis, brought no little business to the artisans. [25]These he gathered together, with the workers of the same trade, and said, "Men, you know that we get our wealth from this business. [26]You also see and hear that not only in Eph'e•sus but in almost the whole of Asia this Paul has persuaded and drawn away a considerable number of people by saying that gods made with hands are not gods. [27]And there is danger not only that this trade of ours may come into disrepute but also that the temple of the great goddess Ar'te•mis will be scorned, and she will be deprived of her majesty that brought all Asia and the world to worship her."

[28] When they heard this, they were enraged and shouted, "Great is Ar'te•mis of the E•phē'si•ans!" [29]The city was filled with the confusion; and people[l] rushed together to the theater, dragging with them Gā'i•us and Ar•is•tar'chus, Mac•e•dō'ni•ans who were Paul's travel companions. [30]Paul wished to go into the crowd, but the disciples would not let him; [31]even some officials of the province of Asia,[m] who were friendly to him, sent him a message urging him not to venture into the theater. [32]Meanwhile, some were shouting one thing, some another; for the assembly was in confusion, and most of them did not know why they had come together. [33]Some of the crowd gave instructions to Alexander, whom the Jews had pushed forward. And Alexander motioned for silence and tried to make a defense before the people. [34]But when they recognized that he was a Jew, for about two hours all of them shouted in unison, "Great is Ar'te•mis of the E•phē'si•ans!" [35]But when the town clerk had quieted the crowd, he said, "Citizens of Eph'e•sus, who is there that does not know that the

city of the E•phē'si•ans is the temple keeper of the great Ar'te•mis and of the statue that fell from heaven?[n] [36]Since these things cannot be denied, you ought to be quiet and do nothing rash. [37]You have brought these men here who are neither temple robbers nor blasphemers of our[o] goddess. [38]If therefore De•mē'tri•us and the artisans with him have a complaint against anyone, the courts are open, and there are proconsuls; let them bring charges there against one another. [39]If there is anything further[p] you want to know, it must be settled in the regular assembly. [40]For we are in danger of being charged with rioting today, since there is no cause that we can give to justify this commotion." [41]When he had said this, he dismissed the assembly.

Paul Goes to Macedonia and Greece

After the uproar had ceased, Paul sent for the disciples; and after encouraging them and saying farewell, he left for Mac•e•dō'ni•a. [2]When he had gone through those regions and had given the believers[q] much encouragement, he came to Greece, [3]where he stayed for three months. He was about to set sail for Syria when a plot was made against him by the Jews, and so he decided to return through Mac•e•dō'ni•a. [4]He was accompanied by Sop'a•ter son of Pyr'rhus from Be•roē'a, by Ar•is•tar'chus and Se•cun'dus from Thes•sa•lo•nī'ca, by Gā'i•us from Der'bē, and by Timothy, as well as by Tych'i•cus and Troph'i•mus from Asia. [5]They went ahead and were waiting for us in Trō'as; [6]but we sailed from Phi•lip'pī after the days of Unleavened Bread, and in five days we joined them in Trō'as, where we stayed for seven days.

Paul's Farewell Visit to Troas

[7] On the first day of the week, when we met to break bread, Paul was holding a discussion with them; since he intended to leave the next day, he continued speaking until midnight. [8]There were many lamps in the room upstairs where we were meeting. [9]A young man named Eū'ty•chus, who was sitting in the window, began to sink off into a deep sleep while Paul talked still longer. Overcome by sleep, he fell to the ground three floors below and was picked up dead. [10]But Paul went down, and bending over him took him in his arms, and said, "Do not be alarmed, for his life is in him." [11]Then Paul went upstairs, and after he had broken bread and eaten, he continued to converse with them until dawn; then he left.

---

k Gk *them*   *l* Gk *they*   *m* Gk *some of the Asiarchs*
n Meaning of Gk uncertain   *o* Other ancient authorities read *your*   *p* Other ancient authorities read *about other matters*   *q* Gk *given them*

12 Meanwhile they had taken the boy away alive and were not a little comforted.

The Voyage from Troas to Miletus

13 We went ahead to the ship and set sail for As'sos, intending to take Paul on board there; for he had made this arrangement, intending to go by land himself. 14 When he met us in As'sos, we took him on board and went to Mit•y•lē'nē. 15 We sailed from there, and on the following day we arrived opposite Chi'os. The next day we touched at Sā'mos, and[r] the day after that we came to Mi•lē'tus. 16 For Paul had decided to sail past Eph'e•sus, so that he might not have to spend time in Asia; he was eager to be in Jerusalem, if possible, on the day of Pentecost.

Paul Speaks to the Ephesian Elders

17 From Mi•lē'tus he sent a message to Eph'e•sus, asking the elders of the church to meet him. 18 When they came to him, he said to them:

"You yourselves know how I lived among you the entire time from the first day that I set foot in Asia, 19 serving the Lord with all humility and with tears, enduring the trials that came to me through the plots of the Jews. 20 I did not shrink from doing anything helpful, proclaiming the message to you and teaching you publicly and from house to house, 21 as I testified to both Jews and Greeks about repentance toward God and faith toward our Lord Jesus. 22 And now, as a captive to the Spirit,[s] I am on my way to Jerusalem, not knowing what will happen to me there, 23 except that the Holy Spirit testifies to me in every city that imprisonment and persecutions are waiting for me. 24 But I do not count my life of any value to myself, if only I may finish my course and the ministry that I received from the Lord Jesus, to testify to the good news of God's grace.

25 "And now I know that none of you, among whom I have gone about proclaiming the kingdom, will ever see my face again. 26 Therefore I declare to you this day that I am not responsible for the blood of any of you, 27 for I did not shrink from declaring to you the whole purpose of God. 28 Keep watch over yourselves and over all the flock, of which the Holy Spirit has made you overseers, to shepherd the church of God[t] that he obtained with the blood of his own Son.[u] 29 I know that after I have gone, savage wolves will come in among you, not sparing the flock. 30 Some even from your own group will come distorting the truth in order to entice the disciples to follow them. 31 Therefore be alert, remembering that for three years I did not cease night or day to warn everyone with tears. 32 And now I commend you to God and to the message of his grace, a message that is able to build you up and to give you the inheritance among all who are sanctified. 33 I coveted no one's silver or gold or clothing. 34 You know for yourselves that I worked with my own hands to support myself and my companions. 35 In all this I have given you an example that by such work we must support the weak, remembering the words of the Lord Jesus, for he himself said, 'It is more blessed to give than to receive.' "

PRAY IT
Good-bye to a Friend

As Paul sadly says good-bye in Acts 20.36–38, we hear that the Christian community is experiencing similar feelings as they prepare to say good-bye to Paul. He has been an important person in their lives, and they have come to depend on him. Their grief overwhelms them, and they all experience great pain over his departure.

When we have to say good-bye to someone we care for deeply, we go through a grieving process. We feel sad and mad at the same time. Even after our friend has been gone for a long time, our heart has an empty space that our friend used to fill.

Lord, it is so difficult to say good-bye to my friend. We have shared so much together. I thank you for blessing me with this friendship. As we depart in separate directions, be our constant guardian and companion. Guide each of us safely to our destination. And until our paths cross again, surround my dear friend in your loving and protective embrace. Amen.

▸ **Acts 20.36–38**

36 When he had finished speaking, he knelt down with them all and prayed. 37 There was much weeping among them all; they embraced

---

r Other ancient authorities add *after remaining at Trogyllium* s Or *And now, bound in the spirit* t Other ancient authorities read *of the Lord* u Or *with his own blood*; Gk *with the blood of his Own*

Paul and kissed him, 38 grieving especially because of what he had said, that they would not see him again. Then they brought him to the ship.

Paul's Journey to Jerusalem

21 When we had parted from them and set sail, we came by a straight course to Cōs, and the next day to Rhōdes, and from there to Pat'a•ra.ᵛ 2 When we found a ship bound for Phoe•ni'ci•a, we went on board and set sail. 3 We came in sight of Cyprus; and leaving it on our left, we sailed to Syria and landed at Tȳre, because the ship was to unload its cargo there. 4 We looked up the disciples and stayed there for seven days. Through the Spirit they told Paul not to go on to Jerusalem. 5 When our days there were ended, we left and proceeded on our journey; and all of them, with wives and children, escorted us outside the city. There we knelt down on the beach and prayed 6 and said farewell to one another. Then we went on board the ship, and they returned home.

7 When we had finishedʷ the voyage from Tȳre, we arrived at Ptol•e•mä'is; and we greeted the believersˣ and stayed with them for one day. 8 The next day we left and came to Caes•a•rē'a; and we went into the house of Philip the evangelist, one of the seven, and stayed with him. 9 He had four unmarried daughtersʸ who had the gift of prophecy. 10 While we were staying there for several days, a prophet named Ag'a•bus came down from Judea. 11 He came to us and took Paul's belt, bound his own feet and hands with it, and said, "Thus says the Holy Spirit, 'This is the way the Jews in Jerusalem will bind the man who owns this belt and will hand him over to the Gentiles.' " 12 When we heard this, we and the people there urged him not to go up to Jerusalem. 13 Then Paul answered, "What are you doing, weeping and breaking my heart? For I am ready not only to be bound but even to die in Jerusalem for the name of the Lord Jesus." 14 Since he would not be persuaded, we remained silent except to say, "The Lord's will be done."

15 After these days we got ready and started to go up to Jerusalem. 16 Some of the disciples from Caes•a•rē'a also came along and brought us to the house of Mnā'son of Cyprus, an early disciple, with whom we were to stay.

Paul Visits James at Jerusalem

17 When we arrived in Jerusalem, the brothers welcomed us warmly. 18 The next day Paul went with us to visit James; and all the elders were present. 19 After greeting them, he related one by one the things that God had done among the Gentiles through his ministry. 20 When they heard it,

they praised God. Then they said to him, "You see, brother, how many thousands of believers

ᵛ Other ancient authorities add *and Myra*   ʷ Or *continued*
ˣ Gk *brothers*   ʸ Gk *four daughters, virgins,*

did you KNOW?

Who Are Paul's Opponents?

As you read about Paul's return to Jerusalem, it may become confusing keeping track of the main characters. To help you keep it straight, here are some clues:

- **One group is the Jewish Christians, represented by James and the elders (Acts 21.17–26). Although the Jewish Christians might be suspicious of Paul's defense of the Gentile Christians, they support Paul and come up with a plan for him to try to prove his Jewish loyalty.**

- **Another group is the Jews who don't believe in Jesus. These Jews see the rise of the Christian faith as a threat to Judaism, and Paul as the most well-known representative of Christians. They attempt to arrest him and have him killed in a mob scene (verses 27–36).**

- **The third group is the Roman rulers. The Romans probably have no interest in this conflict except to keep the peace. The Roman tribune (governor) thinks he can keep the Jews happy by having Paul flogged (22.22–29). But surprise! Paul is a Roman citizen and has civil rights that the tribune must honor.**

So who are Paul's—and Christianity's—opponents? Luke tells us that at first they are the Jewish Christians. Later, they are the Jews who don't believe in Jesus. Still later—after this story occurs—they will be the Romans. Luke knows all this in hindsight and brings all three opponents into play in describing Paul's arrest and imprisonment.

▶ **Acts 21.17–26**

A
C
T
S

there are among the Jews, and they are all zealous for the law. 21 They have been told about you that you teach all the Jews living among the Gentiles to forsake Moses, and that you tell them not to circumcise their children or observe the customs. 22 What then is to be done? They will certainly hear that you have come. 23 So do what we tell you. We have four men who are under a vow. 24 Join these men, go through the rite of purification with them, and pay for the shaving of their heads. Thus all will know that there is nothing in what they have been told about you, but that you yourself observe and guard the law. 25 But as for the Gentiles who have become believers, we have sent a letter with our judgment that they should abstain from what has been sacrificed to idols and from blood and from what is strangled*z* and from fornication." 26 Then Paul took the men, and the next day, having purified himself, he entered the temple with them, making public the completion of the days of purification when the sacrifice would be made for each of them.

Paul Arrested in the Temple

27 When the seven days were almost completed, the Jews from Asia, who had seen him in the temple, stirred up the whole crowd. They seized him, 28 shouting, "Fellow Israelites, help! This is the man who is teaching everyone everywhere against our people, our law, and this place; more than that, he has actually brought Greeks into the temple and has defiled this holy place." 29 For they had previously seen Troph'i•mus the E•phe'si•an with him in the city, and they supposed that Paul had brought him into the temple. 30 Then all the city was aroused, and the people rushed together. They seized Paul and dragged him out of the temple, and immediately the doors were shut. 31 While they were trying to kill him, word came to the tribune of the cohort that all Jerusalem was in an uproar. 32 Immediately he took soldiers and centurions and ran down to them. When they saw the tribune and the soldiers, they stopped beating Paul. 33 Then the tribune came, arrested him, and ordered him to be bound with two chains; he inquired who he was and what he had done. 34 Some in the crowd shouted one thing, some another; and as he could not learn the facts because of the uproar, he ordered him to be brought into the barracks. 35 When Paul*a* came to the steps, the violence of the mob was so great that he had to be carried by the soldiers. 36 The crowd that followed kept shouting, "Away with him!"

Paul Defends Himself

37 Just as Paul was about to be brought into the barracks, he said to the tribune, "May I say something to you?" The tribune*b* replied, "Do you know Greek? 38 Then you are not the Egyptian who recently stirred up a revolt and led the four thousand assassins out into the wilderness?" 39 Paul replied, "I am a Jew, from Tar'sus in Ci•li'ci•a, a citizen of an important city; I beg you, let me speak to the people." 40 When he had given him permission, Paul stood on the steps and motioned to the people for silence; and when there was a great hush, he addressed them in the Hebrew*c* language, saying:

"Brothers and fathers, listen to the defense that I now make before you."

2 When they heard him addressing them in Hebrew,*c* they became even more quiet. Then he said:

3 "I am a Jew, born in Tar'sus in Ci•li'ci•a, but brought up in this city at the feet of Ga•ma'li•el, educated strictly according to our ancestral law, being zealous for God, just as all of you are today. 4 I persecuted this Way up to the point of death by binding both men and women and putting them in prison, 5 as the high priest and the whole council of elders can testify about me. From them I also received letters to the brothers in Damascus, and I went there in order to bind those who were there and to bring them back to Jerusalem for punishment.

Paul Tells of His Conversion
(Acts 9.1–19a; 26.12–18)

6 "While I was on my way and approaching Damascus, about noon a great light from heaven suddenly shone about me. 7 I fell to the ground and heard a voice saying to me, 'Saul, Saul, why are you persecuting me?' 8 I answered, 'Who are you, Lord?' Then he said to me, 'I am Jesus of Nazareth*d* whom you are persecuting.' 9 Now those who were with me saw the light but did not hear the voice of the one who was speaking to me. 10 I asked, 'What am I to do, Lord?' The Lord said to me, 'Get up and go to Damascus; there you will be told everything that has been assigned to you to do.' 11 Since I could not see because of the brightness of that light, those who were with me took my hand and led me to Damascus.

12 "A certain An•a•ni'as, who was a devout man according to the law and well spoken of by all the Jews living there, 13 came to me; and standing

---

z Other ancient authorities lack *and from what is strangled*
a Gk *he*   *b* Gk *He*   *c* That is, *Aramaic*   *d* Gk *the Nazorean*

beside me, he said, 'Brother Saul, regain your sight!' In that very hour I regained my sight and saw him. 14 Then he said, 'The God of our ancestors has chosen you to know his will, to see the Righteous One and to hear his own voice; 15 for you will be his witness to all the world of what you have seen and heard. 16 And now why do you delay? Get up, be baptized, and have your sins washed away, calling on his name.'

citizen who is uncondemned?" 26 When the centurion heard that, he went to the tribune and said to him, "What are you about to do? This man is a Roman citizen." 27 The tribune came and asked Paul,*e* "Tell me, are you a Roman citizen?" And he said, "Yes." 28 The tribune answered, "It cost me a large sum of money to get my citizenship." Paul said, "But I was born a citizen." 29 Immediately those who were about to examine him drew back

Sharing Your Story

Have you ever heard a dramatic conversion story? Sometimes on religious television programs or at large youth rallies, individuals share personal stories of overcoming addictions, terrible problems, or a great sin by believing in God. Or they tell of how they came to recognize and accept God in their life as a result of a serious illness or the death of a close friend or family member. Listening to these dramatic stories may make us feel that our own journey as a follower of Jesus—our own story—does not quite measure up. Nothing could be further from the truth in God's eyes.

We all have our own conversion stories—those moments of turning to God, of receiving a special call to serve others. And though our personal story might not be as dramatic as other people's stories, God will use it to encourage others to put their faith in Christ and dedicate their life to his mission. Are you willing to share your story of faith with others?

▶ Acts 22.6–16

Paul Sent to the Gentiles

17 "After I had returned to Jerusalem and while I was praying in the temple, I fell into a trance 18 and saw Jesus*e* saying to me, 'Hurry and get out of Jerusalem quickly, because they will not accept your testimony about me.' 19 And I said, 'Lord, they themselves know that in every synagogue I imprisoned and beat those who believed in you. 20 And while the blood of your witness Stephen was shed, I myself was standing by, approving and keeping the coats of those who killed him.' 21 Then he said to me, 'Go, for I will send you far away to the Gentiles.' "

Paul and the Roman Tribune

22 Up to this point they listened to him, but then they shouted, "Away with such a fellow from the earth! For he should not be allowed to live." 23 And while they were shouting, throwing off their cloaks, and tossing dust into the air, 24 the tribune directed that he was to be brought into the barracks, and ordered him to be examined by flogging, to find out the reason for this outcry against him. 25 But when they had tied him up with thongs,*f* Paul said to the centurion who was standing by, "Is it legal for you to flog a Roman

from him; and the tribune also was afraid, for he realized that Paul was a Roman citizen and that he had bound him.

Paul before the Council

30 Since he wanted to find out what Paul*g* was being accused of by the Jews, the next day he released him and ordered the chief priests and the entire council to meet. He brought Paul down and had him stand before them.

While Paul was looking intently at the council he said, "Brothers,*h* up to this day I have lived my life with a clear conscience before God." 2 Then the high priest An•a•ni´as ordered those standing near him to strike him on the mouth. 3 At this Paul said to him, "God will strike you, you whitewashed wall! Are you sitting there to judge me according to the law, and yet in violation of the law you order me to be struck?" 4 Those standing nearby said, "Do you dare to insult God's high priest?" 5 And Paul said, "I did not realize, brothers, that he was high priest; for it is written, 'You shall not speak evil of a leader of your people.' "

---

e Gk *him*   *f* Or *up for the lashes*   *g* Gk *he*   *h* Gk *Men, brothers*

A
C
T
S

6 When Paul noticed that some were Sad'du-
cees and others were Phar'i•sees, he called out in
the council, "Brothers, I am a Phar'i•see, a son of
Phar'i•sees. I am on trial concerning the hope of
the resurrection[i] of the dead." 7 When he said this,
a dissension began between the Phar'i•sees and the
Sad'du•cees, and the assembly was divided. 8 (The
Sad'du•cees say that there is no resurrection, or angel, or spirit; but the Phar'i•sees acknowledge all
three.) 9 Then a great clamor arose, and certain
scribes of the Phar'i•sees' group stood up and contended, "We find nothing wrong with this man.
What if a spirit or an angel has spoken to him?"
10 When the dissension became violent, the tribune, fearing that they would tear Paul to pieces,
ordered the soldiers to go down, take him by
force, and bring him into the barracks.

11 That night the Lord stood near him and
said, "Keep up your courage! For just as you have
testified for me in Jerusalem, so you must bear witness also in Rome."

The Plot to Kill Paul

12 In the morning the Jews joined in a conspiracy and bound themselves by an oath neither
to eat nor drink until they had killed Paul. 13 There
were more than forty who joined in this conspiracy. 14 They went to the chief priests and elders
and said, "We have strictly bound ourselves by an
oath to taste no food until we have killed Paul.
15 Now then, you and the council must notify the
tribune to bring him down to you, on the pretext
that you want to make a more thorough examination of his case. And we are ready to do away with
him before he arrives."

16 Now the son of Paul's sister heard about
the ambush; so he went and gained entrance to
the barracks and told Paul. 17 Paul called one of the
centurions and said, "Take this young man to the
tribune, for he has something to report to him."
18 So he took him, brought him to the tribune, and
said, "The prisoner Paul called me and asked me
to bring this young man to you; he has something
to tell you." 19 The tribune took him by the hand,
drew him aside privately, and asked, "What is it
that you have to report to me?" 20 He answered,
"The Jews have agreed to ask you to bring Paul
down to the council tomorrow, as though they
were going to inquire more thoroughly into his
case. 21 But do not be persuaded by them, for more
than forty of their men are lying in ambush for
him. They have bound themselves by an oath neither to eat nor drink until they kill him. They are
ready now and are waiting for your consent." 22 So
the tribune dismissed the young man, ordering

him, "Tell no one that you have informed me of
this."

Paul Sent to Felix the Governor

23 Then he summoned two of the centurions
and said, "Get ready to leave by nine o'clock tonight for Caes•a•re̅'a with two hundred soldiers, seventy horsemen, and two hundred spearmen.
24 Also provide mounts for Paul to ride, and take
him safely to Felix the governor." 25 He wrote a letter to this effect:

26 "Clau'di•us Lys'i•as to his Excellency the
governor Felix, greetings. 27 This man was seized
by the Jews and was about to be killed by them,
but when I had learned that he was a Roman
citizen, I came with the guard and rescued him.
28 Since I wanted to know the charge for which
they accused him, I had him brought to their
council. 29 I found that he was accused concerning
questions of their law, but was charged with nothing deserving death or imprisonment. 30 When I
was informed that there would be a plot against
the man, I sent him to you at once, ordering his
accusers also to state before you what they have
against him.[j]"

31 So the soldiers, according to their instructions, took Paul and brought him during the night
to An•tip'a•tris. 32 The next day they let the horsemen go on with him, while they returned to the
barracks. 33 When they came to Caes•a•re̅'a and delivered the letter to the governor, they presented
Paul also before him. 34 On reading the letter, he
asked what province he belonged to, and when he
learned that he was from Ci•li'ci•a, 35 he said, "I will
give you a hearing when your accusers arrive." Then
he ordered that he be kept under guard in Her'od's
headquarters.[k]

Paul before Felix at Caesarea

Five days later the high priest An•a•ni'as came down
with some elders and an attorney, a certain Ter-
tul'lus, and they reported their case against Paul to
the governor. 2 When Paul[l] had been summoned,
Ter•tul'lus began to accuse him, saying:

"Your Excellency,[m] because of you we have long
enjoyed peace, and reforms have been made for
this people because of your foresight. 3 We welcome this in every way and everywhere with utmost gratitude. 4 But, to detain you no further, I
beg you to hear us briefly with your customary
graciousness. 5 We have, in fact, found this man a
pestilent fellow, an agitator among all the Jews

---

i Gk *concerning hope and resurrection*   j Other ancient
authorities add *Farewell*   k Gk *praetorium*   l Gk *he*
m Gk lacks *Your Excellency*

throughout the world, and a ringleader of the sect of the Naz′a•rēnes.*n* 6 He even tried to profane the temple, and so we seized him.*o* 8 By examining him yourself you will be able to learn from him concerning everything of which we accuse him."

9 The Jews also joined in the charge by asserting that all this was true.

Paul's Defense before Felix

10 When the governor motioned to him to speak, Paul replied:

"I cheerfully make my defense, knowing that for many years you have been a judge over this nation. 11 As you can find out, it is not more than twelve days since I went up to worship in Jerusalem. 12 They did not find me disputing with anyone in the temple or stirring up a crowd either in the synagogues or throughout the city. 13 Neither can they prove to you the charge that they now bring against me. 14 But this I admit to you, that according to the Way, which they call a sect, I worship the God of our ancestors, believing everything laid down according to the law or written in the prophets. 15 I have a hope in God—a hope that they themselves also accept—that there will be a resurrection of both*p* the righteous and the unrighteous. 16 Therefore I do my best always to have a clear conscience toward God and all people. 17 Now after some years I came to bring alms to my nation and to offer sacrifices. 18 While I was doing this, they found me in the temple, completing the rite of purification, without any crowd or disturbance. 19 But there were some Jews from Asia—they ought to be here before you to make an accusation, if they have anything against me. 20 Or let these men here tell what crime they had found when I stood before the council, 21 unless it was this one sentence that I called out while standing before them, 'It is about the resurrection of the dead that I am on trial before you today.' "

22 But Felix, who was rather well informed about the Way, adjourned the hearing with the comment, "When Lys′i•as the tribune comes down, I will decide your case." 23 Then he ordered the centurion to keep him in custody, but to let him have some liberty and not to prevent any of his friends from taking care of his needs.

Paul Held in Custody

24 Some days later when Felix came with his wife Drū•sil′la, who was Jewish, he sent for Paul and heard him speak concerning faith in Christ Jesus. 25 And as he discussed justice, self-control, and the coming judgment, Felix became frightened and said, "Go away for the present; when I have an opportunity, I will send for you." 26 At the same time he hoped that money would be given him by Paul, and for that reason he used to send for him very often and converse with him.

27 After two years had passed, Felix was succeeded by Por′ci•us Fes′tus; and since he wanted to grant the Jews a favor, Felix left Paul in prison.

Paul Appeals to the Emperor

Three days after Fes′tus had arrived in the province, he went up from Caes•a•rē′a to Jerusalem 2 where the chief priests and the leaders of the Jews gave him a report against Paul. They appealed to him 3 and requested, as a favor to them against Paul,*q* to have him transferred to Jerusalem. They were, in fact, planning an ambush to kill him along the way. 4 Fes′tus replied that Paul was being kept at Caes•a•rē′a, and that he himself intended to go there shortly. 5 "So," he said, "let those of you who have the authority come down with me, and if there is anything wrong about the man, let them accuse him."

6 After he had stayed among them not more than eight or ten days, he went down to Caes•a•rē′a; the next day he took his seat on the tribunal and ordered Paul to be brought. 7 When he arrived, the Jews who had gone down from Jerusalem surrounded him, bringing many serious charges against him, which they could not prove. 8 Paul said in his defense, "I have in no way committed an offense against the law of the Jews, or against the temple, or against the emperor." 9 But Fes′tus, wishing to do the Jews a favor, asked Paul, "Do you wish to go up to Jerusalem and be tried there before me on these charges?" 10 Paul said, "I am appealing to the emperor's tribunal; this is where I should be tried. I have done no wrong to the Jews, as you very well know. 11 Now if I am in the wrong and have committed something for which I deserve to die, I am not trying to escape death; but if there is nothing to their charges against me, no one can turn me over to them. I appeal to the emperor." 12 Then Fes′tus, after he had conferred with his council, replied, "You have appealed to the emperor; to the emperor you will go."

Festus Consults King Agrippa

13 After several days had passed, King A•grip′pa and Ber•nī′cē arrived at Caes•a•rē′a to welcome Fes′tus. 14 Since they were staying there several days, Fes′tus laid Paul's case before the king, saying,

---

n Gk *Nazoreans*   *o* Other ancient authorities add *and we would have judged him according to our law.* 7 *But the chief captain Lysias came and with great violence took him out of our hands,* 8 *commanding his accusers to come before you.*
p Other ancient authorities read *of the dead, both of*
q Gk *him*

"There is a man here who was left in prison by Felix. 15 When I was in Jerusalem, the chief priests and the elders of the Jews informed me about him and asked for a sentence against him. 16 I told them that it was not the custom of the Romans to hand over anyone before the accused had met the accusers face to face and had been given an opportunity to make a defense against the charge. 17 So when they met here, I lost no time, but on the next day took my seat on the tribunal and ordered the man to be brought. 18 When the accusers stood up, they did not charge him with any of the crimes[r] that I was expecting. 19 Instead they had certain points of disagreement with him about their own religion and about a certain Jesus, who had died, but whom Paul asserted to be alive. 20 Since I was at a loss how to investigate these questions, I asked whether he wished to go to Jerusalem and be tried there on these charges.[s] 21 But when Paul had appealed to be kept in custody for the decision of his Imperial Majesty, I ordered him to be held until I could send him to the emperor." 22 A·grip′pa said to Fes′tus, "I would like to hear the man myself." "Tomorrow," he said, "you will hear him."

Paul Brought before Agrippa

23 So on the next day A·grip′pa and Ber·ni′ce came with great pomp, and they entered the audience hall with the military tribunes and the prominent men of the city. Then Fes′tus gave the order and Paul was brought in. 24 And Fes′tus said, "King A·grip′pa and all here present with us, you see this man about whom the whole Jewish community petitioned me, both in Jerusalem and here, shouting that he ought not to live any longer. 25 But I found that he had done nothing deserving death; and when he appealed to his Imperial Majesty, I decided to send him. 26 But I have nothing definite to write to our sovereign about him. Therefore I have brought him before all of you, and especially before you, King A·grip′pa, so that, after we have examined him, I may have something to write— 27 for it seems to me unreasonable to send a prisoner without indicating the charges against him."

Paul Defends Himself before Agrippa

A·grip′pa said to Paul, "You have permission to speak for yourself." Then Paul stretched out his hand and began to defend himself:
2 "I consider myself fortunate that it is before you, King A·grip′pa, I am to make my defense today against all the accusations of the Jews, 3 because you are especially familiar with all the customs and controversies of the Jews; therefore I beg of you to listen to me patiently.

4 "All the Jews know my way of life from my youth, a life spent from the beginning among my own people and in Jerusalem. 5 They have known for a long time, if they are willing to testify, that I have belonged to the strictest sect of our religion and lived as a Phar′i·see. 6 And now I stand here on trial on account of my hope in the promise made by God to our ancestors, 7 a promise that our twelve tribes hope to attain, as they earnestly worship day and night. It is for this hope, your Excellency,[t] that I am accused by Jews! 8 Why is it thought incredible by any of you that God raises the dead?

did you KNOW?

What About the Jews?

The earliest Christians were Jews. It was agonizing to them that so many of their Jewish friends wouldn't believe in Jesus. Indeed, not only did those friends not believe in Jesus, but many tried to stop the spread of Christianity. Acts of the Apostles, chapters 22–28, tells of Jewish attacks against Paul, which ultimately end with Paul traveling to Rome to make his case before the emperor.

But the questions remain: If the Jews are God's people, why don't they believe? Couldn't God make it easier for them to believe? Does God cause their lack of faith in Jesus? Who is ultimately responsible for anyone's faith? If you are interested, read Romans, chapter 9, where Paul tries to answer those questions.

▶ Acts 22.30—28.31

9 "Indeed, I myself was convinced that I ought to do many things against the name of Jesus of Nazareth.[u] 10 And that is what I did in Jerusalem; with authority received from the chief priests, I not only locked up many of the saints in prison, but I also cast my vote against them when they were being condemned to death. 11 By punishing them often in all the synagogues I tried to force them to

A C T S

r Other ancient authorities read *with anything*   s Gk *on them*   t Gk *O king*   u Gk *the Nazorean*

blaspheme; and since I was so furiously enraged at them, I pursued them even to foreign cities.

Paul Tells of His Conversion
(Acts 9.1–19; 22.6–16)

12 "With this in mind, I was traveling to Damascus with the authority and commission of the chief priests, [13]when at midday along the road, your Excellency,[v] I saw a light from heaven, brighter than the sun, shining around me and my companions. [14]When we had all fallen to the ground, I heard a voice saying to me in the Hebrew[w] language, 'Saul, Saul, why are you persecuting me? It hurts you to kick against the goads.' [15]I asked, 'Who are you, Lord?' The Lord answered, 'I am Jesus whom you are persecuting. [16]But get up and stand on your feet; for I have appeared to you for this purpose, to appoint you to serve and testify to the things in which you have seen me[x] and to those in which I will appear to you. [17]I will rescue you from your people and from the Gen-

tiles—to whom I am sending you [18]to open their eyes so that they may turn from darkness to light and from the power of Satan to God, so that they may receive forgiveness of sins and a place among those who are sanctified by faith in me.'

Paul Tells of His Preaching

19 "After that, King A•grip'pa, I was not disobedient to the heavenly vision, [20]but declared first to those in Damascus, then in Jerusalem and throughout the countryside of Judea, and also to the Gentiles, that they should repent and turn to God and do deeds consistent with repentance. [21]For this reason the Jews seized me in the temple and tried to kill me. [22]To this day I have had help from God, and so I stand here, testifying to both small and great, saying nothing but what the prophets and Moses said would take place: [23]that

v Gk *O king*   *w* That is, *Aramaic*   *x* Other ancient authorities read *the things that you have seen*

PAUL TEACHES US HOW TO LIVE OUR FAITH!

Reporters Marisa and Ricardo. [Speaking into their microphones] **We're here, live, in Caesarea, where Paul of Tarsus has just spoken with King Agrippa and Governor Festus. Here comes Paul now. Let's see what he has to say. Paul, why has your message caused so much controversy?**

Paul. **It was never my intention to cause strife or conflict. But I must speak the truth, and the truth is that God has revealed his salvation for us in Jesus Christ. In Jesus, salvation is available to everyone—Jews and Gentiles, slaves and free people, men and women—and we are all equal as sons and daughters of God. Unfortunately, this truth is upsetting to some people, and they have gone to great lengths to try to get rid of me.**

Marisa and Ricardo. **But hasn't your message been well received by many people—including many different types of people?**

Paul. **Yes it has. I think this is because Jesus taught us always to respect every person as a son or daughter of God regardless of his or her culture or social class. Under the guidance of the Holy Spirit, Christian communities allow for diversity while keeping a common unity in Jesus Christ. I think people are hungry for this.**

Marisa and Ricardo. **Soon you will be heading for Rome, where you will be on trial for alleged crimes against the empire. Are you worried?**

Paul. [Smiling] **Why be worried? No one has ultimate power over me except my Lord Jesus Christ. I only need to be faithful to my calling, and I will receive my prize—eternal life with God. Plus I have the prayers and support of many close friends. But thank you for your concern. God's grace and peace be with you.**

Marisa and Ricardo. **And thank you, Paul.**

▶ Acts of the Apostles, chapter 26

the Messiah[y] must suffer, and that, by being the first to rise from the dead, he would proclaim light both to our people and to the Gentiles."

Paul Appeals to Agrippa to Believe

24 While he was making this defense, Fes'tus exclaimed, "You are out of your mind, Paul! Too much learning is driving you insane!" 25 But Paul said, "I am not out of my mind, most excellent Fes'tus, but I am speaking the sober truth. 26 Indeed the king knows about these things, and to him I speak freely; for I am certain that none of these things has escaped his notice, for this was not done in a corner. 27 King A•grip'pa, do you believe the prophets? I know that you believe." 28 A•grip'pa said to Paul, "Are you so quickly persuading me to become a Christian?"[z] 29 Paul replied, "Whether quickly or not, I pray to God that not only you but also all who are listening to me today might become such as I am—except for these chains."

30 Then the king got up, and with him the governor and Ber•ni'cē and those who had been seated with them; 31 and as they were leaving, they said to one another, "This man is doing nothing to deserve death or imprisonment." 32 A•grip'pa said to Fes'tus, "This man could have been set free if he had not appealed to the emperor."

Paul Sails for Rome

When it was decided that we were to sail for Italy, they transferred Paul and some other prisoners to a centurion of the Augustan Cohort, named Julius. 2 Embarking on a ship of Ad•ra•myt'ti•um that was about to set sail to the ports along the coast of Asia, we put to sea, accompanied by Ar•is•tar'chus, a Mac•e•dō'ni•an from Thes•sa•lo•ni'ca. 3 The next day we put in at Si'don; and Julius treated Paul kindly, and allowed him to go to his friends to be cared for. 4 Putting out to sea from there, we sailed under the lee of Cyprus, because the winds were against us. 5 After we had sailed across the sea that is off Ci•li'ci•a and Pam•phyl'i•a, we came to Mÿ'ra in Ly'-ci•a. 6 There the centurion found an Alexandrian ship bound for Italy and put us on board. 7 We sailed slowly for a number of days and arrived with difficulty off Cni'dus, and as the wind was against us, we sailed under the lee of Crete off Sal-mō'nē. 8 Sailing past it with difficulty, we came to a place called Fair Havens, near the city of La•sē'a.

9 Since much time had been lost and sailing was now dangerous, because even the Fast had already gone by, Paul advised them, 10 saying, "Sirs, I can see that the voyage will be with danger and much heavy loss, not only of the cargo and the ship, but also of our lives." 11 But the centurion paid more attention to the pilot and to the owner of the ship than to what Paul said. 12 Since the harbor was not suitable for spending the winter, the majority was in favor of putting to sea from there, on the chance that somehow they could reach Phoenix, where they could spend the winter. It was a harbor of Crete, facing southwest and northwest.

The Storm at Sea

13 When a moderate south wind began to blow, they thought they could achieve their purpose; so they weighed anchor and began to sail past Crete, close to the shore. 14 But soon a violent wind, called the northeaster, rushed down from Crete.[a] 15 Since the ship was caught and could not be turned head-on into the wind, we gave way to it and were driven. 16 By running under the lee of a small island called Cau'da[b] we were scarcely able to get the ship's boat under control. 17 After hoisting it up they took measures[c] to undergird the ship; then, fearing that they would run on the Syr'-tis, they lowered the sea anchor and so were driven. 18 We were being pounded by the storm so violently that on the next day they began to throw the cargo overboard, 19 and on the third day with their own hands they threw the ship's tackle overboard. 20 When neither sun nor stars appeared for many days, and no small tempest raged, all hope of our being saved was at last abandoned.

21 Since they had been without food for a long time, Paul then stood up among them and said, "Men, you should have listened to me and not have set sail from Crete and thereby avoided this damage and loss. 22 I urge you now to keep up your courage, for there will be no loss of life among you, but only of the ship. 23 For last night there stood by me an angel of the God to whom I belong and whom I worship, 24 and he said, 'Do not be afraid, Paul; you must stand before the emperor; and indeed, God has granted safety to all those who are sailing with you.' 25 So keep up your courage, men, for I have faith in God that it will be exactly as I have been told. 26 But we will have to run aground on some island."

27 When the fourteenth night had come, as we were drifting across the sea of Ā'dri•a, about midnight the sailors suspected that they were nearing land. 28 So they took soundings and found twenty fathoms; a little farther on they took soundings again and found fifteen fathoms. 29 Fearing that we might run on the rocks, they let down four

---

[y] Or *the Christ*   [z] Or *Quickly you will persuade me to play the Christian*   [a] Gk *it*   [b] Other ancient authorities read *Clauda*   [c] Gk *helps*

anchors from the stern and prayed for day to come. 30 But when the sailors tried to escape from the ship and had lowered the boat into the sea, on the pretext of putting out anchors from the bow, 31 Paul said to the centurion and the soldiers, "Unless these men stay in the ship, you cannot be saved." 32 Then the soldiers cut away the ropes of the boat and set it adrift.

When the Waves Get Too Rough

I t is not easy to be courageous when you face danger. When you find yourself in situations where things are beyond your control, like the storm that endangered the ship Paul was on, turn to God. After all, isn't faith for the times when you feel the most helpless and out of control?

Help, Lord, I'm lost at sea! When I started this journey of life, I thought I knew where I was headed, but then a few waves started to rock the boat, and I became frightened.

Next, the wind picked up, and my fear turned into confusion. Then the night fell, and my confusion turned into despair. And now, I am lost and need you to help calm the waves in my life and stand beside me until the night turns into day.

Help me to find my bearings again, Lord. And when this storm is over, gift me with the wisdom to learn from this experience—to go back and make right what was wrong, to not lose hope at the first sign of trouble, and to hang on to you, my anchor, when life gets rough. Amen.

▸ Acts 27.21–25

33 Just before daybreak, Paul urged all of them to take some food, saying, "Today is the fourteenth day that you have been in suspense and remaining without food, having eaten nothing. 34 Therefore I urge you to take some food, for it will help you survive; for none of you will lose a hair from your heads." 35 After he had said this, he took bread; and giving thanks to God in the presence of all, he broke it and began to eat. 36 Then all of them were encouraged and took food for themselves. 37 (We were in all two hundred seventy-six[d] persons in the ship.) 38 After they had satisfied their hunger, they lightened the ship by throwing the wheat into the sea.

The Shipwreck

39 In the morning they did not recognize the land, but they noticed a bay with a beach, on which they planned to run the ship ashore, if they could. 40 So they cast off the anchors and left them in the sea. At the same time they loosened the ropes that tied the steering-oars; then hoisting the foresail to the wind, they made for the beach. 41 But striking a reef,[e] they ran the ship aground; the bow stuck and remained immovable, but the stern was being broken up by the force of the waves. 42 The soldiers' plan was to kill the prisoners, so that none might swim away and escape; 43 but the centurion, wishing to save Paul, kept them from carrying out their plan. He ordered those who could swim to jump overboard first and make for the land, 44 and the rest to follow, some on planks and others on pieces of the ship. And so it was that all were brought safely to land.

Paul on the Island of Malta

After we had reached safety, we then learned that the island was called Malta. 2 The natives showed us unusual kindness. Since it had begun to rain and was cold, they kindled a fire and welcomed all of us around it. 3 Paul had gathered a bundle of brushwood and was putting it on the fire, when a viper, driven out by the heat, fastened itself on his hand. 4 When the natives saw the creature hanging from his hand, they said to one another, "This man must be a murderer; though he has escaped from the sea, justice has not allowed him to live." 5 He, however, shook off the creature into the fire and suffered no harm. 6 They were expecting him to swell up or drop dead, but after they had waited a long time and saw that nothing unusual had happened to him, they changed their minds and began to say that he was a god.

7 Now in the neighborhood of that place were lands belonging to the leading man of the island, named Pub'li•us, who received us and entertained us hospitably for three days. 8 It so happened that the father of Pub'li•us lay sick in bed with fever and dysentery. Paul visited him and cured him by praying and putting his hands on him. 9 After this happened, the rest of the people on the island who had diseases also came and were cured. 10 They bestowed many honors on us, and when we were

---

d Other ancient authorities read *seventy-six*; others, *about seventy-six*   e Gk *place of two seas*

A
C
T
S

about to sail, they put on board all the provisions we needed.

Paul Arrives at Rome

11 Three months later we set sail on a ship that had wintered at the island, an Alexandrian ship with the Twin Brothers as its figurehead. 12 We put in at Syracuse and stayed there for three days; 13 then we weighed anchor and came to Rhḗ'gi•um. After one day there a south wind sprang up, and on the second day we came to Pŭ•tḗ'o•lī. 14 There we found believers*f* and were invited to stay with them for seven days. And so we came to Rome. 15 The believers*f* from there, when they heard of us, came as far as the Forum of Ap'pi•us and Three Taverns to meet us. On seeing them, Paul thanked God and took courage.

16 When we came into Rome, Paul was allowed to live by himself, with the soldier who was guarding him.

Paul and Jewish Leaders in Rome

17 Three days later he called together the local leaders of the Jews. When they had assembled, he said to them, "Brothers, though I had done nothing against our people or the customs of our ancestors, yet I was arrested in Jerusalem and handed over to the Romans. 18 When they had examined me, the Romans*g* wanted to release me, because there was no reason for the death penalty in my case. 19 But when the Jews objected, I was compelled to appeal to the emperor—even though I had no charge to bring against my nation. 20 For this reason therefore I have asked to see you and speak with you,*h* since it is for the sake of the hope of Israel that I am bound with this chain." 21 They replied, "We have received no letters from Judea about you, and none of the brothers coming here has reported or spoken anything evil about you. 22 But we would like to hear from you what you think, for with regard to this sect we know that everywhere it is spoken against."

Paul Preaches in Rome
(Isa 6.9–10)

23 After they had set a day to meet with him, they came to him at his lodgings in great numbers. From morning until evening he explained the matter to them, testifying to the kingdom of God and trying to convince them about Jesus both from the law of Moses and from the prophets. 24 Some were convinced by what he had said, while others refused to believe. 25 So they disagreed with each other; and as they were leaving, Paul made one further statement: "The Holy Spirit was right in

saying to your ancestors through the prophet Ī•sāi'ah,

26 'Go to this people and say,
    You will indeed listen, but never
        understand,
      and you will indeed look, but never
        perceive.
27 For this people's heart has grown dull,
    and their ears are hard of hearing,
      and they have shut their eyes;
      so that they might not look with their
        eyes,
    and listen with their ears,
and understand with their heart and turn—
    and I would heal them.'

28 Let it be known to you then that this salvation of God has been sent to the Gentiles; they will listen."*i*

30 He lived there two whole years at his own expense*j* and welcomed all who came to him, 31 proclaiming the kingdom of God and teaching about the Lord Jesus Christ with all boldness and without hindrance.

---

f Gk *brothers*   *g* Gk *they*   *h* Or *I have asked you to see me and speak with me*   *i* Other ancient authorities add verse 29, *And when he had said these words, the Jews departed, arguing vigorously among themselves*   *j* Or *in his own hired dwelling*

did you KNOW?

To Rome and Beyond!

Does the Acts of the Apostles seem to end abruptly? Luke probably had a reason for this. He ended Acts with Paul "teaching about the Lord Jesus Christ with all boldness and without hindrance." But Paul was doing it in Rome! The whole Book of Acts follows the spread of Christianity from Jerusalem—a relatively minor city in the Roman Empire—to Rome, the center of the Roman Empire and of the world known to Luke. Luke is saying to his readers: "Look at how Christianity has spread. Instead of stopping it, opposition just helps it grow. Surely this must be from God."

Letters

and Revelation

Despite the popularity of e-mailing, writing letters with pen and paper is still alive today. In letters, people often express themselves more clearly than they do in person, and say things that are difficult to say face-to-face. Perhaps you've been lucky enough to receive some special letters. Letters between parents and children, engaged couples, and even pen pals are often saved to be read again and again. They are treasured for their stories, their advice, and their expressions of love. The next twenty-one books of the New Testament are also treasured letters. Their stories, their advice, and their confidence in God's loving guidance have inspired generations of Christians.

In-depth

WHEN YOU READ SOMEONE ELSE'S MAIL, YOU see only one side of the conversation. So you have to do some reading between the lines to understand the issues being addressed. This is also true of the New Testament letters. But when you do this, they give you a firsthand look at the first Christian communities and what they believed. In fact, the letters written by Paul are the oldest Christian documents that we have, written even before the four Gospels. Paul's earliest letter, 1 Thessalonians, was probably written around A.D. 50. That's just a little over twenty years after the death and Resurrection of Jesus!

These letters follow a common pattern. They usually begin with (1) a greeting from the sender to the receiver or receivers. Next is (2) a prayer, most often of thanksgiving. This is followed by (3) the body of the letter, which addresses whatever issues the author wants to discuss; often, it includes general advice about Christian living. The letters close with (4) greetings and instructions to specific people and a final blessing.

There are exceptions to this pattern. Hebrews and 1 John do not have all four of these features, and are more like essays about faith. James has more of the features, but reads like a good sermon rather than a letter.

Saint Paul was the most prolific writer of the letters. At one time, it was thought that he produced thirteen of the twenty-one. However, modern scholars believe that some of the letters traditionally attributed to Paul were actually written by associates or later followers. Scholars have reached this conclusion because of differences in writing style, vocabulary, and thought. Those associates or followers of Paul's applied his teaching to new situations faced by the early Christian communities. Similarly, the letters bearing the names of James, Peter, and John were probably written by associates or later followers of those men.

To a modern person, that might seem like forgery. But in the ancient world, it was not uncommon for followers of an important person to write in the person's name after her or his death. It was a way of honoring the person and keeping her or his traditions alive.

Although the Book of Revelation is grouped together with the letters in this introduction, it really is not a letter at all. Revelation was written as a series of visions to a disciple named John. The visions are filled with dramatic imagery and events. Some people interpret them as prophecies about the way the world will end, but for the most part they are really coded messages about events happening in John's own time. Ultimately, the Book of Revelation is a hopeful message to persecuted Christians that God is in control and that goodness and justice will triumph.

As you explore these letters and the Book of Revelation, you'll see the church at its best: the miraculous growth, the Spirit-filled enthusiasm, and the deep love the early Christians had for one another and for Jesus. You'll also see how the early church was threatened by intense disagreements, jealousy, and scandals. Through it all, the authors reveal a deep faith and missionary spirit. They focus again and again on the death and Resurrection of Jesus and on the mystery of the church as the living Body of Christ acting in the world through the power of the Holy Spirit. These letters had a specific audience in the first century A.D., but because God inspired them, their words are for you too!

Other Background

- There are nine letters by Paul or his followers named for the communities in which the recipient churches were located: Romans, 1 and 2 Corinthians, Galatians, Ephesians (called a captivity letter because it is attributed to Paul writing from jail), Philippians (also a captivity letter), Colossians (also a captivity letter), and 1 and 2 Thessalonians.

- There are four letters by Paul or his followers named for the individuals to whom they were sent: 1 and 2 Timothy and Titus (called pastoral letters), and Philemon (a captivity letter).

- Hebrews is named for the Christian Jews for whom it was intended.

- There are seven catholic letters named after their stated authors: James; 1 and 2 Peter; 1, 2, and 3 John; and Jude. They are called catholic because they are general letters to all Christians.

- The Book of Revelation is not a letter. It is a collection of the prophecies and visions of John of Patmos, a Christian prophet.

Have you ever wondered if you're good enough to deserve someone's unconditional love? Has it ever puzzled you that sometimes it is easier to do the wrong thing than the right thing? If you have, you're not alone. Saint Paul felt the same way. In his Letter to the Romans, he addresses some important questions of life and faith. But at its core, the message of the letter is simple: We are justified—made right with God—by faith in Jesus Christ.

At a Glance

- **1.1–15.** a greeting and thanks
- **1.16—7.25.** the lesson that humanity is lost, but saved through faith in Christ
- **Chapter 8.** a description of our life in the spirit of Christ
- **Chapters 9–11.** a discussion of Judaism and Christianity
- **Chapters 12–16.** moral advice, personal notes, and blessings

In-depth

Many people consider the Letter to the Romans to be the deepest expression of Paul's thinking. This was the only letter Paul wrote to a community he had not yet visited. At the time, he was planning to go to Rome and was trying to prepare the way by explaining his teaching on salvation and faith. His ideas are summed up in a verse from the first chapter: "I am not ashamed of the gospel; it is the power of God for salvation to everyone who has faith" (verse 16).

Romans is not easy reading. Paul often makes his case by using arguments that might seem strange to us today. Some of his main points are these:

- Salvation is available to both Jews and Gentiles (non-Jews).
- Because all people have sinned, no one has "earned" salvation.
- Salvation comes through faith in Jesus Christ, not through following the Jewish religious Law.
- Even though salvation has come to the Gentiles, God has not abandoned the Jews.

The Letter to the Romans contains many wonderfully comforting words. It tells us that when we don't know how to pray, God prays for us "with sighs too deep for words" (8.26)! And it says that "all things work together for good for those who love God" (verse 28). And it asks, "If God is for us, who is against us?" (verse 31).

So as you read this powerful letter, let go of your fears. Even though you're not perfect, God will never leave you. As Paul says, "I am convinced that neither death, nor life . . . nor anything else in all creation, will be able to separate us from the love of God in Christ Jesus our Lord" (verses 38–39).

Quick Facts

Author
Paul

Date Written
A.D. 56–58

Audience
Jewish and Gentile Christians in Rome

Romans

The Letter to the

Romans

6.4

Salutation

Paul, a servant[a] of Jesus Christ, called to be an apostle, set apart for the gospel of God, [2] which he promised beforehand through his prophets in the holy scriptures, [3] the gospel concerning his Son, who was descended from David according to the flesh [4] and was declared to be Son of God with power according to the spirit[b] of holiness by resurrection from the dead, Jesus Christ our Lord, [5] through whom we have received grace and apostleship to bring about the obedience of faith among all the Gentiles for the sake of his name, [6] including yourselves who are called to belong to Jesus Christ,

[7] To all God's beloved in Rome, who are called to be saints:

Grace to you and peace from God our Father and the Lord Jesus Christ.

Prayer of Thanksgiving

[8] First, I thank my God through Jesus Christ for all of you, because your faith is proclaimed throughout the world. [9] For God, whom I serve with my spirit by announcing the gospel[c] of his Son, is my witness that without ceasing I remember you always in my prayers, [10] asking that by God's will I may somehow at last succeed in coming to you. [11] For I am longing to see you so that I may share with you some spiritual gift to strengthen you— [12] or rather so that we may be mutually encouraged by each other's faith, both yours and mine. [13] I want you to know, brothers and sisters,[d] that I have often intended to come to you (but thus far have been prevented), in order that I may reap some harvest among you as I have among the rest of the Gentiles. [14] I am a debtor both to Greeks and to barbarians, both to the wise and to the foolish [15] — hence my eagerness to proclaim the gospel to you also who are in Rome.

The Power of the Gospel

16 For I am not ashamed of the gospel; it is the power of God for salvation to everyone who has faith, to the Jew first and also to the Greek. [17] For in it the righteousness of God is revealed through faith for faith; as it is written, "The one who is righteous will live by faith."[e]

The Guilt of Humankind

18 For the wrath of God is revealed from heaven against all ungodliness and wickedness of those who by their wickedness suppress the truth. [19] For what can be known about God is plain to them, because God has shown it to them. [20] Ever since the creation of the world his eternal power and divine nature, invisible though they are, have been understood and seen through the things he

---

a Gk slave   b Or Spirit   c Gk my spirit in the gospel
d Gk brothers   e Or The one who is righteous through faith will live

?did you KNOW?

The Many Meanings of Gospel

The word *gospel* is the best translation of the Greek word *euangelion*, which was used in Rom 1.16. *Gospel* comes from the old English word *godspel*, which means "good news." From *euangelion*, we get the word *evangelize*, which means "to share the good news."

In the New Testament, the meaning of the word *Gospel* goes through an evolution. For Paul, whose writings are the earliest in the New Testament, *Gospel* referred to the good news of salvation for all who believe. Paul associated the Gospel directly with Jesus himself, centering on his death and Resurrection.

As Christian faith developed, the understanding of *Gospel* expanded to include the Reign (Kingdom) of God that Jesus preached. The Gospel was not just associated with Jesus' saving death and Resurrection, but included all his teachings, miracles, promises, and demands. After the original Apostles died or were killed, Christian communities desired a record of their teachings about Jesus, and the Gospel message was written down. So *Gospel* came also to refer to the writings named for Matthew, Mark, Luke, and John.

▶ Rom 1.16

has made. So they are without excuse; 21 for though they knew God, they did not honor him as God or give thanks to him, but they became futile in their thinking, and their senseless minds were darkened. 22 Claiming to be wise, they became fools; 23 and they exchanged the glory of the immortal God for images resembling a mortal human being or birds or four-footed animals or reptiles.

24 Therefore God gave them up in the lusts of their hearts to impurity, to the degrading of their bodies among themselves, 25 because they exchanged the truth about God for a lie and worshiped and served the creature rather than the Creator, who is blessed forever! Amen.

26 For this reason God gave them up to degrading passions. Their women exchanged natural intercourse for unnatural, 27 and in the same way also the men, giving up natural intercourse with women, were consumed with passion for one another. Men committed shameless acts with men and received in their own persons the due penalty for their error.

?did you KNOW?

Homosexuality and AIDS

In making his case that all people are in need of salvation, Paul talks about the sinfulness of humankind in Rom 1.18–32. As a specific example of what happens when people turn from God's truth, he discusses homosexual activity in verses 26–27.

Some people interpret these verses to mean Paul is condemning homosexual persons. But this is a serious misinterpretation of Paul's words. Why? First, look at the context. After this specific example in verses 26–27, Paul lists all kinds of sinful behaviors in verses 28–32. He is not picking on homosexuals—rather, he is showing that all people are guilty of sin.

Most important, notice that Paul never condemns people; he condemns sinful behavior. The Catholic church does the same. The church teaches that homosexual orientation is not sinful, but it also states that any sexual activity outside of marriage is wrong.

Romans 1.18–32 has also been used wrongly against AIDS victims. Some of them have been told that their horrible disease is a result of God's vengeance against homosexual behavior. Our loving God would never use AIDS, or any other disease, to punish people.

▶ Rom 1.18–32

28 And since they did not see fit to acknowledge God, God gave them up to a debased mind and to things that should not be done. 29 They were filled with every kind of wickedness, evil, covetousness, malice. Full of envy, murder, strife,

deceit, craftiness, they are gossips, [30] slanderers, God-haters,[f] insolent, haughty, boastful, inventors of evil, rebellious toward parents, [31] foolish, faithless, heartless, ruthless. [32] They know God's decree, that those who practice such things deserve to die— yet they not only do them but even applaud others who practice them.

Examination of Conscience

Lord, knock me off my pedestal whenever I begin to think I've earned the right to judge others. Paul reminds us that we are all guilty of sin. I have no right to judge others.

Direct me to turn my attention to examining my own conscience:

Have I been patient with those around me?

Have I offered forgiveness to those who have hurt me?

Have I had the courage to admit when I am wrong?

Have I treated my parents and siblings with respect?

Have I been sensitive to the feelings and needs of those around me?

Forgive me, God, for I have sinned. Bathe me in your mercy and love. Deliver me from evil as I continue to grow in Christ. Amen.

▶ Rom 2.1–4

The Righteous Judgment of God

Therefore you have no excuse, whoever you are, when you judge others; for in passing judgment on another you condemn yourself, because you, the judge, are doing the very same things. [2] You say,[g] "We know that God's judgment on those who do such things is in accordance with truth." [3] Do you imagine, whoever you are, that when you judge those who do such things and yet do them yourself, you will escape the judgment of God? [4] Or do you despise the riches of his kindness and forbearance and patience? Do you not realize that God's kindness is meant to lead you to repentance? [5] But by your hard and impenitent heart you are storing up wrath for yourself on the day of wrath, when God's righteous judgment will be re-

vealed. [6] For he will repay according to each one's deeds: [7] to those who by patiently doing good seek for glory and honor and immortality, he will give eternal life; [8] while for those who are self-seeking and who obey not the truth but wickedness, there will be wrath and fury. [9] There will be anguish and distress for everyone who does evil, the Jew first and also the Greek, [10] but glory and honor and peace for everyone who does good, the Jew first and also the Greek. [11] For God shows no partiality.

12 All who have sinned apart from the law will also perish apart from the law, and all who have sinned under the law will be judged by the law. [13] For it is not the hearers of the law who are righteous in God's sight, but the doers of the law who will be justified. [14] When Gentiles, who do not possess the law, do instinctively what the law requires, these, though not having the law, are a law to themselves. [15] They show that what the law requires is written on their hearts, to which their own conscience also bears witness; and their conflicting thoughts will accuse or perhaps excuse them [16] on the day when, according to my gospel, God, through Jesus Christ, will judge the secret thoughts of all.

The Jews and the Law

17 But if you call yourself a Jew and rely on the law and boast of your relation to God [18] and know his will and determine what is best because you are instructed in the law, [19] and if you are sure that you are a guide to the blind, a light to those who are in darkness, [20] a corrector of the foolish, a teacher of children, having in the law the embodiment of knowledge and truth, [21] you, then, that teach others, will you not teach yourself? While you preach against stealing, do you steal? [22] You that forbid adultery, do you commit adultery? You that abhor idols, do you rob temples? [23] You that boast in the law, do you dishonor God by breaking the law? [24] For, as it is written, "The name of God is blasphemed among the Gentiles because of you."

25 Circumcision indeed is of value if you obey the law; but if you break the law, your circumcision has become uncircumcision. [26] So, if those who are uncircumcised keep the requirements of the law, will not their uncircumcision be regarded as circumcision? [27] Then those who are physically uncircumcised but keep the law will condemn you that have the written code and circumcision but break the law. [28] For a person is not a Jew who is one outwardly, nor is true circumcision something external and physical. [29] Rather, a person is a Jew

R
O
M

f Or *God-hated*   g Gk lacks *You say*

who is one inwardly, and real circumcision is a matter of the heart—it is spiritual and not literal. Such a person receives praise not from others but from God.

? did you KNOW?

Circumcision, the Law, and Faith

Circumcision is the surgical removal of the foreskin from a male's penis. It was the sign of the covenant (agreement) between Israel and God (Gen 17.2). As Gentiles became Christians, many Jewish Christians claimed they had to live by Jewish religious laws, including circumcision.

Paul consistently insists that such rituals are not necessary. He says that "real circumcision is a matter of the heart" (Rom 2.29), which leads to "faith working through love" (Gal 5.6). In Romans, chapter 4, Paul sheds further light on this by considering the case of Abraham. Abraham was considered the father of the Jewish faith. He was made righteous by God before he was circumcised (verse 10). Why? Because of his strong and heroic faith in God. Christians are called to this kind of faith in God, whose plan of salvation is now fully revealed in Jesus Christ.

▶ Rom 2.25–29

Then what advantage has the Jew? Or what is the value of circumcision? 2 Much, in every way. For in the first place the Jews[h] were entrusted with the oracles of God. 3 What if some were unfaithful? Will their faithlessness nullify the faithfulness of God? 4 By no means! Although everyone is a liar, let God be proved true, as it is written,

"So that you may be justified in your
words,
and prevail in your judging."[i]

5 But if our injustice serves to confirm the justice of God, what should we say? That God is unjust to inflict wrath on us? (I speak in a human way.) 6 By no means! For then how could God judge the world? 7 But if through my falsehood God's truthfulness abounds to his glory, why am I still being condemned as a sinner? 8 And why not say (as some people slander us by saying that we say), "Let us do evil so that good may come"? Their condemnation is deserved!

None Is Righteous
(Ps 14.1–3; 53.1–4)

9 What then? Are we any better off?[j] No, not at all; for we have already charged that all, both Jews and Greeks, are under the power of sin, 10 as it is written:

"There is no one who is righteous, not
even one;
11   there is no one who has understanding,
there is no one who seeks God.
12 All have turned aside, together they have
become worthless;
there is no one who shows kindness,
there is not even one."
13 "Their throats are opened graves;
they use their tongues to deceive."
"The venom of vipers is under their lips."
14   "Their mouths are full of cursing and
bitterness."
15 "Their feet are swift to shed blood;
16   ruin and misery are in their paths,
17 and the way of peace they have not known."
18 "There is no fear of God before their
eyes."

19 Now we know that whatever the law says, it speaks to those who are under the law, so that every mouth may be silenced, and the whole world may be held accountable to God. 20 For "no human being will be justified in his sight" by deeds prescribed by the law, for through the law comes the knowledge of sin.

Righteousness through Faith

21 But now, apart from law, the righteousness of God has been disclosed, and is attested by the law and the prophets, 22 the righteousness of God through faith in Jesus Christ[k] for all who believe. For there is no distinction, 23 since all have sinned and fall short of the glory of God; 24 they are now justified by his grace as a gift, through the redemption that is in Christ Jesus, 25 whom God put forward as a sacrifice of atonement[l] by his blood, effective through faith. He did this to show his righteousness, because in his divine forbearance he had passed over the sins previously committed;

---

h Gk they   i Gk when you are being judged   j Or at any disadvantage?   k Or through the faith of Jesus Christ
l Or a place of atonement

26 it was to prove at the present time that he himself is righteous and that he justifies the one who has faith in Jesus.[m]

27 Then what becomes of boasting? It is excluded. By what law? By that of works? No, but by the law of faith. 28 For we hold that a person is justified by faith apart from works prescribed by the law. 29 Or is God the God of Jews only? Is he not the God of Gentiles also? Yes, of Gentiles also, 30 since God is one; and he will justify the circumcised on the ground of faith and the uncircumcised through that same faith. 31 Do we then overthrow the law by this faith? By no means! On the contrary, we uphold the law.

faith is reckoned as righteousness. 6 So also David speaks of the blessedness of those to whom God reckons righteousness apart from works:

7 "Blessed are those whose iniquities are forgiven,
   and whose sins are covered;
8 blessed is the one against whom the Lord
      will not reckon sin."

9 Is this blessedness, then, pronounced only on the circumcised, or also on the uncircumcised? We say, "Faith was reckoned to Abraham as righteousness." 10 How then was it reckoned to him? Was it before or after he had been circumcised? It was not after, but before he was circumcised. 11 He received the sign of circumcision as a seal of the

LIVE IT!

The Law, Faith, and Salvation

Throughout much of Romans, Paul is explaining the relationship between the Law, faith, and salvation. At the end of chapter 2 and the beginning of chapter 3, he shows that the Jewish Law of the Old Testament cannot save us from the effect of sin. But he recognizes the value of the Law (see 3.31). The Law was the expression of the Jewish people's response of faith to God's Covenant. It protected their relationships with God and one another.

We often think of sin as breaking God's law. But at its core, sin is really breaking our relationship with God and distancing ourselves from God. Remember what Adam and Eve did after their first sin? They hid from God, ashamed of their action. Paul is clear that we are all guilty of sin. Separated from God, the source of all life, we would eventually perish without God's help. But God is always seeking us out. In the ultimate act of love, God sent Jesus to restore the break in our relationship caused by sin. Jesus' death and Resurrection show us that God's great love is far more powerful than any sin we can commit.

Paul uses two key words to explain all of this. He talks about *justification*, which is the process that brings us back into a good relationship with God. And he talks about *righteousness* as the state of being right with God, of not being separated from God.

How are we justified? How are we considered righteous? Not by our ability to keep any laws but by our faith in Jesus Christ. And the effect of faith is opposite that of sin. Where sin creates distance, faith draws us close. Where sin kills, faith gives life. Where sin shrivels in hate, faith is active in love.

▶ Rom 3.21–31

The Example of Abraham
(Gen 17.10)

What then are we to say was gained by[n] Abraham, our ancestor according to the flesh? 2 For if Abraham was justified by works, he has something to boast about, but not before God. 3 For what does the scripture say? "Abraham believed God, and it was reckoned to him as righteousness." 4 Now to one who works, wages are not reckoned as a gift but as something due. 5 But to one who without works trusts him who justifies the ungodly, such

righteousness that he had by faith while he was still uncircumcised. The purpose was to make him the ancestor of all who believe without being circumcised and who thus have righteousness reckoned to them, 12 and likewise the ancestor of the circumcised who are not only circumcised but who also follow the example of the faith that our ancestor Abraham had before he was circumcised.

---

m Or *who has the faith of Jesus*   n Other ancient authorities read *say about*

God's Promise Realized through Faith

13 For the promise that he would inherit the world did not come to Abraham or to his descendants through the law but through the righteousness of faith. [14] If it is the adherents of the law who are to be the heirs, faith is null and the promise is void. [15] For the law brings wrath; but where there is no law, neither is there violation.

16 For this reason it depends on faith, in order that the promise may rest on grace and be guaranteed to all his descendants, not only to the adherents of the law but also to those who share the faith of Abraham (for he is the father of all of us, [17] as it is written, "I have made you the father of many nations") — in the presence of the God in whom he believed, who gives life to the dead and calls into existence the things that do not exist. [18] Hoping against hope, he believed that he would become "the father of many nations," according to what was said, "So numerous shall your descendants be." [19] He did not weaken in faith when he considered his own body, which was already[o] as good as dead (for he was about a hundred years old), or when he considered the barrenness of Sarah's womb. [20] No distrust made him waver concerning the promise of God, but he grew strong in his faith as he gave glory to God, [21] being fully convinced that God was able to do what he had promised. [22] Therefore his faith[p] "was reckoned to him as righteousness." [23] Now the words, "it was reckoned to him," were written not for his sake alone, [24] but for ours also. It will be reckoned to us who believe in him who raised Jesus our Lord from the dead, [25] who was handed over to death for our trespasses and was raised for our justification.

Results of Justification

Therefore, since we are justified by faith, we[q] have peace with God through our Lord Jesus Christ, [2] through whom we have obtained access[r] to this grace in which we stand; and we[s] boast in our hope of sharing the glory of God. [3] And not only that, but we[s] also boast in our sufferings, knowing that suffering produces endurance, [4] and endurance produces character, and character produces hope, [5] and hope does not disappoint us, because God's love has been poured into our hearts through the Holy Spirit that has been given to us.

6 For while we were still weak, at the right time Christ died for the ungodly. [7] Indeed, rarely will anyone die for a righteous person — though perhaps for a good person someone might actually dare to die. [8] But God proves his love for us in that while we still were sinners Christ died for us. [9] Much more surely then, now that we have been justified by his blood, will we be saved through him from the wrath of God.[t] [10] For if while we were enemies, we were reconciled to God through the death of his Son, much more surely, having been reconciled, will we be saved by his life. [11] But more than that, we even boast in God through our Lord Jesus Christ, through whom we have now received reconciliation.

Adam and Christ
(Gen 3.1–19)

12 Therefore, just as sin came into the world through one man, and death came through sin, and so death spread to all because all have

---

[o] Other ancient authorities lack *already* [p] Gk *Therefore it*
[q] Other ancient authorities read *let us* [r] Other ancient
authorities add *by faith* [s] Or *let us* [t] Gk *the wrath*

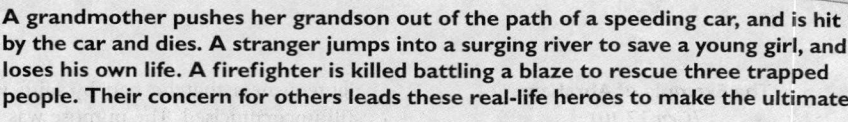

Trusting the Grace of God

A grandmother pushes her grandson out of the path of a speeding car, and is hit by the car and dies. A stranger jumps into a surging river to save a young girl, and loses his own life. A firefighter is killed battling a blaze to rescue three trapped people. Their concern for others leads these real-life heroes to make the ultimate sacrifice.

Like the grandson, the young girl, and the three trapped people, we too have been saved from death at a great cost—Jesus' loving sacrifice in obedience to God's will. Paul reminds us that our justification—our reconciliation and peace with God—is not a reward we deserve for being good. It is God's free gift of love and salvation despite our weakness and sin. And that is grace. Put your faith not in your own ability to please God, but in God's abundant grace.

▶ Rom 5.1–11

sinned— [13] sin was indeed in the world before the law, but sin is not reckoned when there is no law. [14] Yet death exercised dominion from Adam to Moses, even over those whose sins were not like the transgression of Adam, who is a type of the one who was to come.

15 But the free gift is not like the trespass. For if the many died through the one man's trespass, much more surely have the grace of God and the free gift in the grace of the one man, Jesus Christ, abounded for the many. [16] And the free gift is not like the effect of the one man's sin. For the judgment following one trespass brought condemnation, but the free gift following many trespasses brings justification. [17] If, because of the one man's trespass, death exercised dominion through that one, much more surely will those who receive the abundance of grace and the free gift of righteousness exercise dominion in life through the one man, Jesus Christ.

18 Therefore just as one man's trespass led to condemnation for all, so one man's act of righteousness leads to justification and life for all. [19] For just as by the one man's disobedience the many were made sinners, so by the one man's obedience the many will be made righteous. [20] But law came in, with the result that the trespass multiplied; but where sin increased, grace abounded all the more, [21] so that, just as sin exercised dominion in death, so grace might also exercise dominion through justification[u] leading to eternal life through Jesus Christ our Lord.

Dying and Rising with Christ

What then are we to say? Should we continue in sin in order that grace may abound? [2] By no means! How can we who died to sin go on living in it? [3] Do you not know that all of us who have been baptized into Christ Jesus were baptized into his death? [4] Therefore we have been buried with him by baptism into death, so that, just as Christ was raised from the dead by the glory of the Father, so we too might walk in newness of life.

5 For if we have been united with him in a death like his, we will certainly be united with him in a resurrection like his. [6] We know that our old self was crucified with him so that the body of sin might be destroyed, and we might no longer be enslaved to sin. [7] For whoever has died is freed from sin. [8] But if we have died with Christ, we believe that we will also live with him. [9] We know that Christ, being raised from the dead, will never die again; death no longer has dominion over him. [10] The death he died, he died to sin, once for all; but the life he lives, he lives to God. [11] So you also must consider yourselves dead to sin and alive to God in Christ Jesus.

12 Therefore, do not let sin exercise dominion in your mortal bodies, to make you obey their passions. [13] No longer present your members to sin as instruments[v] of wickedness, but present yourselves to God as those who have been brought from death to life, and present your members to God as instruments[v] of righteousness. [14] For sin will have no dominion over you, since you are not under law but under grace.

PRAY IT!

In Christ, We Receive New Life!

In chapter 6 of Romans, Paul tells us that we die to sin and receive a new life in Jesus Christ—who died for the forgiveness of all sin and overcame death with his Resurrection. By participating in the paschal mystery (see "Dying for New Life," Jn 12.24–26) through Baptism, we are no longer enslaved to sin.

"The end is eternal life. For the wages of sin is death, but the free gift of God is eternal life in Christ Jesus our Lord" (Rom 6.22–23). Let the message of this passage fill you. Feel God's liberating grace in you. Never forget that Christ has already saved you, and God's mercy is there for you as soon as you repent, pray for forgiveness, and are willing to sin no more.

▸ Rom 6.1–23

Slaves of Righteousness

15 What then? Should we sin because we are not under law but under grace? By no means! [16] Do you not know that if you present yourselves to anyone as obedient slaves, you are slaves of the one whom you obey, either of sin, which leads to death, or of obedience, which leads to righteousness? [17] But thanks be to God that you, having once been slaves of sin, have become obedient from the heart to the form of teaching to which you were entrusted, [18] and that you, having been

u Or *righteousness*   v Or *weapons*

set free from sin, have become slaves of righteousness. [19] I am speaking in human terms because of your natural limitations.[w] For just as you once presented your members as slaves to impurity and to greater and greater iniquity, so now present your members as slaves to righteousness for sanctification.

20 When you were slaves of sin, you were free in regard to righteousness. [21] So what advantage did you then get from the things of which you now are ashamed? The end of those things is death. [22] But now that you have been freed from sin and enslaved to God, the advantage you get is sanctification. The end is eternal life. [23] For the wages of sin is death, but the free gift of God is eternal life in Christ Jesus our Lord.

PRAY IT!

I'm Not Perfect

Some people today think, "If God is always willing to forgive me, why should I be concerned about sinning?" Evidently, some people in Paul's time thought that too (see Rom 6.15). Paul reminds them, and us, that faith in Christ should be a matter of the heart, not simply a mechanical commitment. Like a married couple's love calls them to commit to each other (7.2), so our love for Christ should make us want to live in the light, free from sin. Why would we want to return to the things that bring death to the soul (6.21)?

But even when we commit to follow Christ, sin is a constant challenge. Paul encourages us, in the face of temptation, to maintain our focus on God and refrain from sin.

Jesus, you experienced temptation throughout your ministry. Yet you always made the decision to avoid sin and live in the light.

I have made the commitment to follow you. Give me the strength to overcome temptations and avoid sin. If in my weaknesses I allow my sin and passions to steer me in the wrong direction, please forgive me and help me regain control. Amen.

▶ Rom 6.15—7.6

An Analogy from Marriage

Do you not know, brothers and sisters[x]—for I am speaking to those who know the law—that the law is binding on a person only during that person's lifetime? [2] Thus a married woman is bound by the law to her husband as long as he lives; but if her husband dies, she is discharged from the law concerning the husband. [3] Accordingly, she will be called an adulteress if she lives with another man while her husband is alive. But if her husband dies, she is free from that law, and if she marries another man, she is not an adulteress.

4 In the same way, my friends,[x] you have died to the law through the body of Christ, so that you may belong to another, to him who has been raised from the dead in order that we may bear fruit for God. [5] While we were living in the flesh, our sinful passions, aroused by the law, were at work in our members to bear fruit for death. [6] But now we are discharged from the law, dead to that which held us captive, so that we are slaves not under the old written code but in the new life of the Spirit.

The Law and Sin

7 What then should we say? That the law is sin? By no means! Yet, if it had not been for the law, I would not have known sin. I would not have known what it is to covet if the law had not said, "You shall not covet." [8] But sin, seizing an opportunity in the commandment, produced in me all kinds of covetousness. Apart from the law sin lies dead. [9] I was once alive apart from the law, but when the commandment came, sin revived [10] and I died, and the very commandment that promised life proved to be death to me. [11] For sin, seizing an opportunity in the commandment, deceived me and through it killed me. [12] So the law is holy, and the commandment is holy and just and good.

13 Did what is good, then, bring death to me? By no means! It was sin, working death in me through what is good, in order that sin might be shown to be sin, and through the commandment might become sinful beyond measure.

The Inner Conflict

14 For we know that the law is spiritual; but I am of the flesh, sold into slavery under sin.[y] [15] I do not understand my own actions. For I do not do what I want, but I do the very thing I hate. [16] Now if I do what I do not want, I agree that the law is good. [17] But in fact it is no longer I that do it, but sin that dwells within me. [18] For I know that

---

w Gk *the weakness of your flesh*   x Gk *brothers*   y Gk *sold under sin*

LIVE IT!

Our Inner Struggle

In Rom 7.15–16, Paul reveals his own struggle to do what is right. It seems there's a part of us that wants to do right, and another part that wants to do wrong. Even when we try to be good, "evil lies close at hand" (verse 21), ready to have its way.

Paul uses the words *spirit* and *flesh* to describe this struggle. In his time, people thought passions and strong emotions originated in the body. So Paul says our flesh tempts us to do wrong, and our spirit wants us to do right. Paul does not mean that our physical bodies are evil and the source of sin. He means that we are all at war with ourselves.

Sin is hard to resist at times. To do what is right requires us to stop and think clearly about our choices and actively select good over sin. The good news is that God, the understanding forgiver, is on our side in the struggle. Thanks be to God!

▶ Rom 7.14–25

nothing good dwells within me, that is, in my flesh. I can will what is right, but I cannot do it. 19 For I do not do the good I want, but the evil I do not want is what I do. 20 Now if I do what I do not want, it is no longer I that do it, but sin that dwells within me.

21 So I find it to be a law that when I want to do what is good, evil lies close at hand. 22 For I delight in the law of God in my inmost self, 23 but I see in my members another law at war with the law of my mind, making me captive to the law of sin that dwells in my members. 24 Wretched man that I am! Who will rescue me from this body of death? 25 Thanks be to God through Jesus Christ our Lord!

So then, with my mind I am a slave to the law of God, but with my flesh I am a slave to the law of sin.

Life in the Spirit

There is therefore now no condemnation for those who are in Christ Jesus. 2 For the law of the Spirit*z* of life in Christ Jesus has set you*a* free from the law of sin and of death. 3 For God has done what the law, weakened by the flesh, could not do: by sending his own Son in the likeness of sinful flesh, and to deal with sin,*b* he condemned sin in the flesh, 4 so that the just requirement of the law might be fulfilled in us, who walk not according to the flesh but according to the Spirit.*z* 5 For those who live according to the flesh set their minds on the things of the flesh, but those who live according to the Spirit*z* set their minds on the things of the Spirit.*z* 6 To set the mind on the flesh is death, but to set the mind on the Spirit*z* is life and peace.

7 For this reason the mind that is set on the flesh is hostile to God; it does not submit to God's law—indeed it cannot, 8 and those who are in the flesh cannot please God.

9 But you are not in the flesh; you are in the Spirit,*z* since the Spirit of God dwells in you. Anyone who does not have the Spirit of Christ does not belong to him. 10 But if Christ is in you, though the body is dead because of sin, the Spirit*z* is life because of righteousness. 11 If the Spirit of him who raised Jesus from the dead dwells in you, he who raised Christ*c* from the dead will give life to your mortal bodies also through*d* his Spirit that dwells in you.

12 So then, brothers and sisters,*e* we are debtors, not to the flesh, to live according to the flesh—13 for if you live according to the flesh, you will die; but if by the Spirit you put to death the deeds of the body, you will live. 14 For all who are led by the Spirit of God are children of God. 15 For you did not receive a spirit of slavery to fall back into fear, but you have received a spirit of adoption. When we cry, "Abba!*f* Father!" 16 it is that very Spirit bearing witness*g* with our spirit that we are children of God, 17 and if children, then heirs, heirs of God and joint heirs with Christ—if, in fact, we suffer with him so that we may also be glorified with him.

R
O
M

---

z Or *spirit*   *a* Here the Greek word *you* is singular number; other ancient authorities read *me* or *us*   *b* Or *and as a sin offering*   *c* Other ancient authorities read *the Christ* or *Christ Jesus* or *Jesus Christ*   *d* Other ancient authorities read *on account of*   *e* Gk *brothers*   *f* Aramaic for *Father*   *g* Or 15*a spirit of adoption, by which we cry, "Abba! Father!"* 16*The Spirit itself bears witness*

Future Glory

18 I consider that the sufferings of this present time are not worth comparing with the glory about to be revealed to us. 19 For the creation waits with eager longing for the revealing of the children

We know that
all things work together
for good for those who

love
God,

who are called
according to his purpose

8.28

of God; 20 for the creation was subjected to futility, not of its own will but by the will of the one who subjected it, in hope 21 that the creation itself will be set free from its bondage to decay and will obtain the freedom of the glory of the children of God. 22 We know that the whole creation has been groaning in labor pains until now; 23 and not only the creation, but we ourselves, who have the first fruits of the Spirit, groan inwardly while we wait

for adoption, the redemption of our bodies. 24 For in^h hope we were saved. Now hope that is seen is not hope. For who hopes^i for what is seen? 25 But if we hope for what we do not see, we wait for it with patience.

26 Likewise the Spirit helps us in our weakness; for we do not know how to pray as we ought, but that very Spirit intercedes^j with sighs too deep for words. 27 And God,^{k} who searches the heart, knows what is the mind of the Spirit, because the Spirit^l intercedes for the saints according to the will of God.^{m}

28 We know that all things work together for good^n for those who love God, who are called according to his purpose. 29 For those whom he foreknew he also predestined to be conformed to the image of his Son, in order that he might be the firstborn within a large family.^{o} 30 And those whom he predestined he also called; and those whom he called he also justified; and those whom he justified he also glorified.

God's Love in Christ Jesus

31 What then are we to say about these things? If God is for us, who is against us? 32 He who did not withhold his own Son, but gave him up for all

---

^{h} Or *by* ^{i} Other ancient authorities read *awaits*
^{j} Other ancient authorities add *for us* ^{k} Gk *the one*
^{l} Gk *he* or *it* ^{m} Gk *according to God* ^{n} Other ancient authorities read *God makes all things work together for good,* or *in all things God works for good* ^{o} Gk *among many brothers*

Hope

LIVE IT!

Life is something of a mixed bag. There are days of joy, when all seems complete and we are perfectly contented. Then there are days when we feel lost, confused about our purpose, and alone in facing our difficulties. We enjoy happy moments: a new birth, a deep friendship, a marriage celebration. We also go through periods of pain: the death of a loved one, divorce, physical suffering. All are part of life.

While embracing the fullness of this human experience, Paul reminds us that our hope is in something more. There is a longing deep within us—deep within all of creation—for another home. This present world, in all its beauty and wonder, cannot compare with the glory that awaits us in heaven.

Does that mean we should avoid the real issues of suffering in this life and focus only on the hope of heaven? Hardly! Life, in all its moments, is a gift meant to be lived fully. The suffering we endure now can form us into a faithful people—a family able to offer hope to others who feel lost.

▸ **Rom 8.18–30**

PRAY IT!

Absolutely Nothing!

God, what could separate me from your
love?
Not a failed test, or a broken promise, or a
hurtful word.
What could tear you from me?
Not the lure of power, or immediate
gratification, or unnatural highs.
If you, God, are on my side, who could be
against me?
Not a vengeful peer, or an uncaring date, or
someone whose relationship with me has
gone sour.
What situation could divide you and me,
God?
Not depression over a loss, or anger over
being laughed at, or guilt from being
caught red-handed.

No, in all these things, I know that I am
never alone, because you, God, conquered
sin, despair, and even death itself through
your endless love, a love that showed itself
through your Son. I am convinced, Lord,
that nothing, absolutely nothing, will ever
separate me from your love . . . ever!
Amen.

▶ Rom 8.31–35

of us, will he not with him also give us everything
else? 33 Who will bring any charge against God's
elect? It is God who justifies. 34 Who is to condemn? It is Christ Jesus, who died, yes, who was
raised, who is at the right hand of God, who indeed intercedes for us.*p* 35 Who will separate us
from the love of Christ? Will hardship, or distress,
or persecution, or famine, or nakedness, or peril,
or sword? 36 As it is written,
"For your sake we are being killed all day
long;
we are accounted as sheep to be
slaughtered."
37 No, in all these things we are more than conquerors through him who loved us. 38 For I am
convinced that neither death, nor life, nor angels,
nor rulers, nor things present, nor things to come,
nor powers, 39 nor height, nor depth, nor anything
else in all creation, will be able to separate us from
the love of God in Christ Jesus our Lord.

God's Election of Israel
(Gen 25.19–23)

I am speaking the truth in Christ—I am not lying;
my conscience confirms it by the Holy Spirit— 2 I
have great sorrow and unceasing anguish in my
heart. 3 For I could wish that I myself were accursed and cut off from Christ for the sake of my
own people,*q* my kindred according to the flesh.
4 They are Israelites, and to them belong the adoption, the glory, the covenants, the giving of the
law, the worship, and the promises; 5 to them belong the patriarchs, and from them, according to
the flesh, comes the Messiah,*r* who is over all,
God blessed forever.*s* Amen.

6 It is not as though the word of God had
failed. For not all Israelites truly belong to Israel,
7 and not all of Abraham's children are his true
descendants; but "It is through Isaac that descendants shall be named for you." 8 This means that it
is not the children of the flesh who are the children of God, but the children of the promise are
counted as descendants. 9 For this is what the
promise said, "About this time I will return and
Sarah shall have a son." 10 Nor is that all; something similar happened to Rebecca when she had
conceived children by one husband, our ancestor
Isaac. 11 Even before they had been born or had
done anything good or bad (so that God's purpose
of election might continue, 12 not by works but by
his call) she was told, "The elder shall serve the
younger." 13 As it is written,
"I have loved Jacob,
but I have hated Esau."

14 What then are we to say? Is there injustice
on God's part? By no means! 15 For he says to
Moses,
"I will have mercy on whom I have mercy,
and I will have compassion on whom I
have compassion."
16 So it depends not on human will or exertion,
but on God who shows mercy. 17 For the scripture
says to Pharaoh, "I have raised you up for the very
purpose of showing my power in you, so that my
name may be proclaimed in all the earth." 18 So
then he has mercy on whomever he chooses, and
he hardens the heart of whomever he chooses.

God's Wrath and Mercy

19 You will say to me then, "Why then does
he still find fault? For who can resist his will?"

R
O
M

---

p Or Is it Christ Jesus . . . for us?   *q* Gk my brothers
r Or the Christ   *s* Or Messiah, who is God over all, blessed
forever; or Messiah. May he who is God over all be blessed
forever

did you KNOW?

The Fate of Israel

In Romans, chapters 9–11, Paul takes on a difficult question: What will happen to Israel (the Jews), God's chosen people, if they reject Jesus? For the early Jewish Christians, who probably had friends and maybe had family members who didn't believe in Jesus, this was an important question.

To respond, Paul makes several points. In the beginning of chapter 9, he affirms Israel's special place in God's plan of salvation. But the people's righteousness (see "The Law, Faith, and Salvation," Rom 3.21–31) is based on faith, not on fulfilling the Law. In chapter 10, Paul notes that salvation is available for all. The Jewish people are not left out if they call on the name of the Lord. But Israel's rejection of Jesus is good news for the Gentiles, who have come to believe.

In chapter 11, Paul uses the analogy of grafting branches onto a tree. The Gentiles were grafted onto the original tree, which is Israel. Paul says the Jews can be grafted back onto that tree (verse 23). In fact, he ends with the hopeful promise that after the salvation of the Gentiles, all Israel will be saved (verse 26)!

Christians recognize Jewish people as their spiritual ancestors. Christians have inherited from the Jews part of their Scriptures and a rich spiritual tradition. They respect the Jews' faith and their relationship with God. They pray for the Jews' salvation and their own, in the hope that Paul's promise will come to pass.

▶ Romans, chapters 9–11

ROM

20 But who indeed are you, a human being, to argue with God? Will what is molded say to the one who molds it, "Why have you made me like this?" 21 Has the potter no right over the clay, to make out of the same lump one object for special use and another for ordinary use? 22 What if God, desiring to show his wrath and to make known his power, has endured with much patience the objects of wrath that are made for destruction; 23 and what if he has done so in order to make known the riches of his glory for the objects of mercy, which he has prepared beforehand for glory— 24 including us whom he has called, not from the Jews only but also from the Gentiles? 25 As indeed he says in Hō•sē'a,

> "Those who were not my people I will call
> 'my people,'
> and her who was not beloved I will call
> 'beloved.' "
> 26 "And in the very place where it was said to
> them, 'You are not my people,'
> there they shall be called children of the
> living God."

27 And Ī•sāi'ah cries out concerning Israel, "Though the number of the children of Israel were like the sand of the sea, only a remnant of them will be saved; 28 for the Lord will execute his sentence on the earth quickly and decisively."[t] 29 And as Ī•sāi'ah predicted,

> "If the Lord of hosts had not left survivors[u]
> to us,
> we would have fared like Sod'om
> and been made like Go•mor'rah."

Israel's Unbelief

30 What then are we to say? Gentiles, who did not strive for righteousness, have attained it, that is, righteousness through faith; 31 but Israel, who did strive for the righteousness that is based on the law, did not succeed in fulfilling that law. 32 Why not? Because they did not strive for it on the basis of faith, but as if it were based on works. They have stumbled over the stumbling stone, 33 as it is written,

> "See, I am laying in Zion a stone that will
> make people stumble, a rock that
> will make them fall,
> and whoever believes in him[v] will not be
> put to shame."

Brothers and sisters,[w] my heart's desire and prayer to God for them is that they may be saved. 2 I can testify that they have a zeal for God, but it is not enlightened. 3 For, being ignorant of the righteousness that comes from God, and seeking to establish their own, they have not submitted to God's righteousness. 4 For Christ is the end of the law so that there may be righteousness for everyone who believes.

---

t Other ancient authorities read *for he will finish his work and cut it short in righteousness, because the Lord will make the sentence shortened on the earth*   u Or *descendants*; Gk *seed*   v Or *trusts in it*   w Gk *Brothers*

Salvation Is for All

5 Moses writes concerning the righteousness that comes from the law, that "the person who does these things will live by them." 6 But the righteousness that comes from faith says, "Do not say in your heart, 'Who will ascend into heaven?'" (that is, to bring Christ down) 7 "or 'Who will descend into the abyss?'" (that is, to bring Christ up from the dead). 8 But what does it say?

"The word is near you,
    on your lips and in your heart"

(that is, the word of faith that we proclaim); 9 because*x* if you confess with your lips that Jesus is Lord and believe in your heart that God raised him from the dead, you will be saved. 10 For one believes with the heart and so is justified, and one

PRAY IT

Are Your Feet Beautiful?

Spread the word!" "Attention all shoppers!" "Special announcement!" Companies trying to sell a product, and organizations trying to attract new members go to great lengths and expense to get their message out. Without this effort, they will reach few people and fail in their mission.

The church has undoubtedly the most important mission of all—to share with others the saving power that comes from faith in Jesus Christ. The promise in Rom 10.11–15 is that all who know and call on the name of Jesus will be saved. God is great!

How do others hear about this Good News? Paul says only through us. And he adds, "How beautiful are the feet of those who bring good news!" (verse 15). In your prayer, reflect or journal on the following questions:

■ Who brought the Good News to you? What made you trust what they had to tell you about Jesus?
■ Which of your friends need to hear this Good News about Jesus? How can you share your faith with them, perhaps through a message of hope, forgiveness, healing, or encouragement?

▶ Rom 10.11–15

confesses with the mouth and so is saved. 11 The scripture says, "No one who believes in him will be put to shame." 12 For there is no distinction between Jew and Greek; the same Lord is Lord of all and is generous to all who call on him. 13 For, "Everyone who calls on the name of the Lord shall be saved."

14 But how are they to call on one in whom they have not believed? And how are they to believe in one of whom they have never heard? And how are they to hear without someone to proclaim him? 15 And how are they to proclaim him unless they are sent? As it is written, "How beautiful are the feet of those who bring good news!" 16 But not all have obeyed the good news;*y* for I•sāi'ah says, "Lord, who has believed our message?" 17 So faith comes from what is heard, and what is heard comes through the word of Christ.*z*

18 But I ask, have they not heard? Indeed they have; for

"Their voice has gone out to all the earth,
    and their words to the ends of the world."

19 Again I ask, did Israel not understand? First Moses says,

"I will make you jealous of those who are
        not a nation;
    with a foolish nation I will make you
        angry."

20 Then I•sāi'ah is so bold as to say,

"I have been found by those who did not
        seek me;
    I have shown myself to those who did
        not ask for me."

21 But of Israel he says, "All day long I have held out my hands to a disobedient and contrary people."

Israel's Rejection Is Not Final
(Cp Ps 69.22–23; Isa 29.10)

I ask, then, has God rejected his people? By no means! I myself am an Israelite, a descendant of Abraham, a member of the tribe of Benjamin. 2 God has not rejected his people whom he foreknew. Do you not know what the scripture says of E•li'jah, how he pleads with God against Israel? 3 "Lord, they have killed your prophets, they have demolished your altars; I alone am left, and they are seeking my life." 4 But what is the divine reply to him? "I have kept for myself seven thousand who have not bowed the knee to Bā'al." 5 So too at the present time there is a remnant, chosen by grace.

---

x Or *namely, that*   *y* Or *gospel*   *z* Or *about Christ*; other ancient authorities read *of God*

6 But if it is by grace, it is no longer on the basis of works, otherwise grace would no longer be grace.*a*

7 What then? Israel failed to obtain what it was seeking. The elect obtained it, but the rest were hardened, 8 as it is written,

"God gave them a sluggish spirit,
     eyes that would not see
     and ears that would not hear,
   down to this very day."

9 And David says,

"Let their table become a snare and a trap,
     a stumbling block and a retribution for
       them;
10 let their eyes be darkened so that they
       cannot see,
   and keep their backs forever bent."

The Salvation of the Gentiles

11 So I ask, have they stumbled so as to fall? By no means! But through their stumbling*b* salvation has come to the Gentiles, so as to make Israel*c* jealous. 12 Now if their stumbling*b* means riches for the world, and if their defeat means riches for Gentiles, how much more will their full inclusion mean!

13 Now I am speaking to you Gentiles. Inasmuch then as I am an apostle to the Gentiles, I glorify my ministry 14 in order to make my own people*d* jealous, and thus save some of them. 15 For if their rejection is the reconciliation of the world, what will their acceptance be but life from the dead! 16 If the part of the dough offered as first fruits is holy, then the whole batch is holy; and if the root is holy, then the branches also are holy.

17 But if some of the branches were broken off, and you, a wild olive shoot, were grafted in their place to share the rich root*e* of the olive tree, 18 do not boast over the branches. If you do boast, remember that it is not you that support the root, but the root that supports you. 19 You will say, "Branches were broken off so that I might be grafted in." 20 That is true. They were broken off because of their unbelief, but you stand only through faith. So do not become proud, but stand in awe. 21 For if God did not spare the natural branches, perhaps he will not spare you.*f* 22 Note then the kindness and the severity of God: severity toward those who have fallen, but God's kindness toward you, provided you continue in his kindness; otherwise you also will be cut off. 23 And even those of Israel,*g* if they do not persist in unbelief, will be grafted in, for God has the power to graft them in again. 24 For if you have been cut from what is by nature a wild olive tree and grafted, contrary to nature, into a cultivated olive tree, how much more will these natural branches be grafted back into their own olive tree.

All Israel Will Be Saved

25 So that you may not claim to be wiser than you are, brothers and sisters,*h* I want you to under-

---

a Other ancient authorities add *But if it is by works, it is no longer on the basis of grace, otherwise work would no longer be work*   *b* Gk *transgression*   *c* Gk *them*   *d* Gk *my flesh*   *e* Other ancient authorities read *the richness*   *f* Other ancient authorities read *neither will he spare you*   *g* Gk lacks *of Israel*   *h* Gk *brothers*

A Great Team

LIVE IT!

Tracy comes up to the mound and tries to ignore the banter of the players on the opposing bench. This is it! One more out, and her team will be the new state champions!

The batter taps the dirt beside the box and glares at Tracy. Tracy focuses on her catcher's signals and hurls her best pitch. A hit! It bounces toward third, and Tracy holds her breath as Ginny twists sideways to scoop it up. Ginny turns and throws to first. Everyone can see that the ball is high. But Carrie jumps, catches it, and stretches to tag the base before the runner gets there. A cheer erupts as the fans realize that Tracy's team has won! It is the best team in the state!

A good team has talented players. A great team has players who work together so well that they respond automatically. In Rom 12.1-8, Paul is challenging the Romans to work together to become a great team. (See also 1 Cor 12.12.) What kind of teamwork do you find in your family, your parish, or your school?

▶ Rom 12.1–8

stand this mystery: a hardening has come upon part of Israel, until the full number of the Gentiles has come in. 26 And so all Israel will be saved; as it is written,

> "Out of Zion will come the Deliverer;
>> he will banish ungodliness from Jacob."
> 27 "And this is my covenant with them,
>> when I take away their sins."

28 As regards the gospel they are enemies of God*i*

The New Life in Christ

I appeal to you therefore, brothers and sisters,*k* by the mercies of God, to present your bodies as a living sacrifice, holy and acceptable to God, which is your spiritual*l* worship. 2 Do not be conformed to this world,*m* but be transformed by the renewing of your minds, so that you may discern what is the will of God—what is good and acceptable and perfect.*n*

WE ARE THE BODY OF CHRIST!

According to Rom 12.1–8, we are the Body of Christ! Just thinking about this beautiful and powerful belief fills us with energy. Imagine the power if all Christians really behaved as the living Body of Christ in their home, church, neighborhood, country, and planet.

In verse 1, Paul calls us to present our body to God as a living, holy, and acceptable sacrifice. The best thing that we can offer to God is our whole life—all we are and all we do. When we worship God by doing this, our prayer and rituals are real and meaningful.

In verse 2, Paul calls us not to be conformed to this world but to be transformed. We are transformed by renewing our mind. We are intelligent people. God gave us the power to discern what is good and evil, true and false, in agreement with or against God's loving plan for humanity.

We must think and act according to the measure of faith and the different gifts that we have received for the service of others (charisms). So we, who are many, may become one Body in Christ and be better collaborators in Jesus' mission.

▸ Rom 12.1–8

for your sake; but as regards election they are beloved, for the sake of their ancestors; 29 for the gifts and the calling of God are irrevocable. 30 Just as you were once disobedient to God but have now received mercy because of their disobedience, 31 so they have now been disobedient in order that, by the mercy shown to you, they too may now*j* receive mercy. 32 For God has imprisoned all in disobedience so that he may be merciful to all.

33 O the depth of the riches and wisdom and knowledge of God! How unsearchable are his judgments and how inscrutable his ways!
34 "For who has known the mind of the Lord?
Or who has been his counselor?"
35 "Or who has given a gift to him,
to receive a gift in return?"
36 For from him and through him and to him are all things. To him be the glory forever. Amen.

3 For by the grace given to me I say to everyone among you not to think of yourself more highly than you ought to think, but to think with sober judgment, each according to the measure of faith that God has assigned. 4 For as in one body we have many members, and not all the members have the same function, 5 so we, who are many, are one body in Christ, and individually we are members one of another. 6 We have gifts that differ according to the grace given to us: prophecy, in proportion to faith; 7 ministry, in ministering; the teacher, in teaching; 8 the exhorter, in exhortation; the giver, in generosity; the leader, in diligence; the compassionate, in cheerfulness.

---

i Gk lacks *of God*   *j* Other ancient authorities lack *now*
k Gk *brothers*   *l* Or *reasonable*   *m* Gk *age*   *n* Or *what is the good and acceptable and perfect will of God*

Becoming a Peacemaker

A common response when someone mistreats us is to seek revenge. But in Rom 12.17–19, Paul tells us that only God should be the avenger. He goes on to remind us of Jesus' teaching to treat our enemies with kindness. That is certainly easier said than done! It is difficult to respond with goodwill when we are hurt.

Nevertheless, real people have tried to live by this teaching—Martin Luther King Jr., Mohandas Gandhi, Mother Teresa, and Dorothy Day, to name a few. Perhaps you know people who have made similar commitments in your own community.

Think of the people you know. Who is a peacemaker in your life? What can you do to be a peacemaker in your family, school, or community?

▶ Rom 12.17–19

Marks of the True Christian

9 Let love be genuine; hate what is evil, hold fast to what is good; [10] love one another with mutual affection; outdo one another in showing honor. [11] Do not lag in zeal, be ardent in spirit, serve the Lord.[o] [12] Rejoice in hope, be patient in suffering, persevere in prayer. [13] Contribute to the needs of the saints; extend hospitality to strangers.

14 Bless those who persecute you; bless and do not curse them. [15] Rejoice with those who rejoice, weep with those who weep. [16] Live in harmony with one another; do not be haughty, but associate with the lowly;[p] do not claim to be wiser than you are. [17] Do not repay anyone evil for evil, but take thought for what is noble in the sight of all. [18] If it is possible, so far as it depends on you, live peaceably with all. [19] Beloved, never avenge yourselves, but leave room for the wrath of God;[q] for it is written, "Vengeance is mine, I will repay, says the Lord." [20] No, "if your enemies are hungry, feed them; if they are thirsty, give them something to drink; for by doing this you will heap burning coals on their heads." [21] Do not be overcome by evil, but overcome evil with good.

Being Subject to Authorities

Let every person be subject to the governing authorities; for there is no authority except from God, and those authorities that exist have been instituted by God. [2] Therefore whoever resists authority resists what God has appointed, and those who resist will incur judgment. [3] For rulers are not a terror to good conduct, but to bad. Do you wish to have no fear of the authority? Then do what is good, and you will receive its approval; [4] for it is God's servant for your good. But if you do what is wrong, you should be afraid, for the authority[r] does not bear the sword in vain! It is the servant of God to execute wrath on the wrongdoer. [5] Therefore one must be subject, not only because of wrath but also because of conscience. [6] For the same reason you also pay taxes, for the authorities are God's servants, busy with this very thing. [7] Pay to all what is due them—taxes to whom taxes are due, revenue to whom revenue is due, respect to whom respect is due, honor to whom honor is due.

Love for One Another
(Cp Mk 12.31; Jas 2.8)

8 Owe no one anything, except to love one another; for the one who loves another has fulfilled

A Real Love

Lord, why is it so hard to love? Love is mentioned so much in the Bible that it makes me wonder why we don't get it. It seems that we do a good job of talking love and a poor job of doing love. We can point out where there is no love, but it sure is hard to bring love to where it is needed.

Jesus, fill me with your love to share with others. The kind of love that changes people forever. The kind of love that breaks down barriers and overcomes fears. The love that gives without counting the costs. Amen.

▶ Rom 13.8–10

---

o Other ancient authorities read *serve the opportune time*
p Or *give yourselves to humble tasks*   q Gk *the wrath*
r Gk *it*

ROM

the law. 9 The commandments, "You shall not commit adultery; You shall not murder; You shall not steal; You shall not covet"; and any other commandment, are summed up in this word, "Love your neighbor as yourself." 10 Love does no wrong to a neighbor; therefore, love is the fulfilling of the law.

An Urgent Appeal

11 Besides this, you know what time it is, how it is now the moment for you to wake from sleep. For salvation is nearer to us now than when we became believers; 12 the night is far gone, the day is near. Let us then lay aside the works of darkness and put on the armor of light; 13 let us live honorably as in the day, not in reveling and drunkenness, not in debauchery and licentiousness, not in quarreling and jealousy. 14 Instead, put on the Lord Jesus Christ, and make no provision for the flesh, to gratify its desires.

Do Not Judge Another

Welcome those who are weak in faith,*s* but not for the purpose of quarreling over opinions. 2 Some believe in eating anything, while the weak eat only vegetables. 3 Those who eat must not despise those who abstain, and those who abstain must not pass judgment on those who eat; for God has welcomed them. 4 Who are you to pass judgment on servants of another? It is before their own lord that they stand or fall. And they will be upheld, for the Lord*t* is able to make them stand.

5 Some judge one day to be better than another, while others judge all days to be alike. Let all be fully convinced in their own minds. 6 Those who observe the day, observe it in honor of the Lord. Also those who eat, eat in honor of the Lord, since they give thanks to God; while those who abstain, abstain in honor of the Lord and give thanks to God.

7 We do not live to ourselves, and we do not die to ourselves. 8 If we live, we live to the Lord, and if we die, we die to the Lord; so then, whether we live or whether we die, we are the Lord's. 9 For to this end Christ died and lived again, so that he might be Lord of both the dead and the living.

10 Why do you pass judgment on your brother or sister?*u* Or you, why do you despise your brother or sister?*u* For we will all stand before the judgment seat of God.*v* 11 For it is written,

> "As I live, says the Lord, every knee shall
>   bow to me,
> and every tongue shall give praise
>   to*w* God."

12 So then, each of us will be accountable to God.*x*

Do Not Make Another Stumble

13 Let us therefore no longer pass judgment on one another, but resolve instead never to put a stumbling block or hindrance in the way of another.*y* 14 I know and am persuaded in the Lord Jesus that nothing is unclean in itself; but it is

---

s Or *conviction*   *t* Other ancient authorities read *for God*
u Gk *brother*   *v* Other ancient authorities read *of Christ*
w Or *confess*   *x* Other ancient authorities lack *to God*
y Gk *of a brother*

Respecting Differences   LIVE IT!

What is a regular coffee in your part of the country? In the Boston area, it has sugar and cream in it. In many other parts of the country, it comes without cream and sugar.

In the same way that people from different parts of the United States have different ideas about coffee, Christians have different ideas about what to believe and how to act. It seems Paul has heard that the Christians in Rome disagree about what to eat (Rom 14.2) and what days to hold holy (verse 5). He tells them not to quarrel over these differences. Whatever they do, they should do it "in honor of the Lord" (verse 6). The church would be shamed if these minor differences became a stumbling block to someone's faith.

A healthy respect for differences pulls together Christians from various religious denominations or traditions. Christians of all denominations should rejoice in their common faith, respect and learn from their differences, and work together "in honor of the Lord."

▶ Rom 14.1–23

unclean for anyone who thinks it unclean. [15] If your brother or sister[z] is being injured by what you eat, you are no longer walking in love. Do not let what you eat cause the ruin of one for whom Christ died. [16] So do not let your good be spoken of as evil. [17] For the kingdom of God is not food and drink but righteousness and peace and joy in the Holy Spirit. [18] The one who thus serves Christ is acceptable to God and has human approval. [19] Let us then pursue what makes for peace and for mutual upbuilding. [20] Do not, for the sake of food, destroy the work of God. Everything is indeed clean, but it is wrong for you to make others fall by what you eat; [21] it is good not to eat meat or drink wine or do anything that makes your brother or sister[z] stumble.[a] [22] The faith that you have, have as your own conviction before God. Blessed are those who have no reason to condemn themselves because of what they approve. [23] But those who have doubts are condemned if they eat, because they do not act from faith;[b] for whatever does not proceed from faith[b] is sin.[c]

Please Others, Not Yourselves

We who are strong ought to put up with the failings of the weak, and not to please ourselves. [2] Each of us must please our neighbor for the good purpose of building up the neighbor. [3] For Christ did not please himself; but, as it is written, "The insults of those who insult you have fallen on me." [4] For whatever was written in former days was written for our instruction, so that by steadfastness and by the encouragement of the scriptures we might have hope. [5] May the God of steadfastness and encouragement grant you to live in harmony with one another, in accordance with Christ Jesus, [6] so that together you may with one voice glorify the God and Father of our Lord Jesus Christ.

The Gospel for Jews and Gentiles Alike

[7] Welcome one another, therefore, just as Christ has welcomed you, for the glory of God. [8] For I tell you that Christ has become a servant of the circumcised on behalf of the truth of God in order that he might confirm the promises given to the patriarchs, [9] and in order that the Gentiles might glorify God for his mercy. As it is written,

"Therefore I will confess[d] you among the
　　　Gentiles,
　and sing praises to your name";
[10] and again he says,

"Rejoice, O Gentiles, with his people";
[11] and again,

"Praise the Lord, all you Gentiles,
　and let all the peoples praise him";
[12] and again Ī•sāi′ah says,

"The root of Jesse shall come,
　the one who rises to rule the Gentiles;
　in him the Gentiles shall hope."
[13] May the God of hope fill you with all joy and peace in believing, so that you may abound in hope by the power of the Holy Spirit.

Paul's Reason for Writing So Boldly

14 I myself feel confident about you, my brothers and sisters,[e] that you yourselves are full of goodness, filled with all knowledge, and able to instruct one another. [15] Nevertheless on some points I have written to you rather boldly by way of reminder, because of the grace given me by God [16] to be a minister of Christ Jesus to the Gentiles in the priestly service of the gospel of God, so that the offering of the Gentiles may be acceptable, sanctified by the Holy Spirit. [17] In Christ Jesus, then, I have reason to boast of my work for God. [18] For I will not venture to speak of anything except what Christ has accomplished[f] through me to win obedience from the Gentiles, by word and deed, [19] by the power of signs and wonders, by the power of the Spirit of God,[g] so that from Jerusalem and as far around as Il•lyr′i•cum I have fully proclaimed the good news[h] of Christ. [20] Thus I make it my ambition to proclaim the good news,[h] not where Christ has already been named, so that I do not build on someone else's foundation, [21] but as it is written,

"Those who have never been told of him
　　　shall see,
　and those who have never heard of him
　　　shall understand."

Paul's Plan to Visit Rome

22 This is the reason that I have so often been hindered from coming to you. [23] But now, with no further place for me in these regions, I desire, as I have for many years, to come to you [24] when I go to Spain. For I do hope to see you on my journey and to be sent on by you, once I have enjoyed your company for a little while. [25] At present, however, I am going to Jerusalem in a ministry to the saints; [26] for Mac•e•dō′ni•a and A•chā′i•a have been pleased to share their resources with the poor among the saints at Jerusalem. [27] They were pleased to do this, and indeed they owe it to them; for if the Gentiles have come to share in their spiritual blessings, they ought also to be of service to

---

[z] Gk *brother*　　[a] Other ancient authorities add *or be upset or be weakened*　　[b] Or *conviction*　　[c] Other authorities, some ancient, add here 16.25-27　　[d] Or *thank* [e] Gk *brothers*　　[f] Gk *speak of those things that Christ has not accomplished*　　[g] Other ancient authorities read *of the Spirit* or *of the Holy Spirit*　　[h] Or *gospel*

them in material things. 28 So, when I have completed this, and have delivered to them what has been collected,[i] I will set out by way of you to Spain; 29 and I know that when I come to you, I will come in the fullness of the blessing[j] of Christ.

30 I appeal to you, brothers and sisters,[k] by our Lord Jesus Christ and by the love of the Spirit, to join me in earnest prayer to God on my behalf, 31 that I may be rescued from the unbelievers in Judea, and that my ministry[l] to Jerusalem may be

9 Greet Ur·bā'nus, our co-worker in Christ, and my beloved Stā'chys. 10 Greet A·pel'lēs, who is approved in Christ. Greet those who belong to the family of Ar·is·tob'ū·lus. 11 Greet my relative[r] He·rō'di·on. Greet those in the Lord who belong to the family of Nar·cis'sus. 12 Greet those workers in the Lord, Trȳ·phae'na and Trȳ·phō'sa. Greet the beloved Per'sis, who has worked hard in the Lord. 13 Greet Rufus, chosen in the Lord; and greet his mother—a mother to me also. 14 Greet A·syn'cri·tus,

Introducing
▶ PHOEBE AND JUNIA

In Rom 16.1–16, Paul greets almost thirty people and their families in Rome—more people than he greets in any of his other letters. It is thought that perhaps he is trying to establish a connection among the Christians in Rome by mentioning mutual acquaintances. About a third of the people he greets are women, highlighting the important role women played in Paul's ministry and in the leadership of the early church.

Of particular interest are Paul's comments about Phoebe, whom he calls a deacon, and Junia (also called Julia), whom he declares "prominent among the apostles" (verse 7). In Paul's time, deacons were usually associated with a ministry of service, and apostles with a ministry of leadership. Even though women were not allowed to fill official positions in government or society, the early church recognized them as being as important as men in service, leadership, and bringing the Gospel to others.

▶ Rom 16.1–16

acceptable to the saints, 32 so that by God's will I may come to you with joy and be refreshed in your company. 33 The God of peace be with all of you.[m] Amen.

Personal Greetings

I commend to you our sister Phoē'bē, a deacon[n] of the church at Cen'chrē·ae, 2 so that you may welcome her in the Lord as is fitting for the saints, and help her in whatever she may require from you, for she has been a benefactor of many and of myself as well.

3 Greet Pris'ca and A·qui'la, who work with me in Christ Jesus, 4 and who risked their necks for my life, to whom not only I give thanks, but also all the churches of the Gentiles. 5 Greet also the church in their house. Greet my beloved E·pae'netus, who was the first convert[o] in Asia for Christ. 6 Greet Mary, who has worked very hard among you. 7 Greet An·dron'i·cus and Jū'ni·a,[p] my relatives[q] who were in prison with me; they are prominent among the apostles, and they were in Christ before I was. 8 Greet Am·pli·ā'tus, my beloved in the Lord.

Phlē'gon, Her'mēs, Pat'ro·bas, Her'mas, and the brothers and sisters[k] who are with them. 15 Greet Phi·lol'o·gus, Julia, Nē're·us and his sister, and Ō·lym'pas, and all the saints who are with them. 16 Greet one another with a holy kiss. All the churches of Christ greet you.

Final Instructions

17 I urge you, brothers and sisters,[k] to keep an eye on those who cause dissensions and offenses, in opposition to the teaching that you have learned; avoid them. 18 For such people do not serve our Lord Christ, but their own appetites,[s] and by smooth talk and flattery they deceive the hearts of the simple-minded. 19 For while your obedience is known to all, so that I rejoice over

---

i Gk *have sealed to them this fruit*   j Other ancient authorities add *of the gospel*   k Gk *brothers*   l Other ancient authorities read *my bringing of a gift*   m One ancient authority adds 16.25-27 here   n Or *minister*   o Gk *first fruits*   p Or *Junias*; other ancient authorities read *Julia*   q Or *compatriots*   r Or *compatriot*   s Gk *their own belly*

you, I want you to be wise in what is good and guileless in what is evil. [20] The God of peace will shortly crush Satan under your feet. The grace of our Lord Jesus Christ be with you.[t]

21 Timothy, my co-worker, greets you; so do Lucius and Jason and Sō·sip'a·ter, my relatives.[u]

22 I Ter'ti·us, the writer of this letter, greet you in the Lord.[v]

23 Gā'i·us, who is host to me and to the whole church, greets you. E·ras'tus, the city treasurer, and our brother Quar'tus, greet you.[w]

Final Doxology

25 Now to God[x] who is able to strengthen you according to my gospel and the proclamation of Jesus Christ, according to the revelation of the mystery that was kept secret for long ages [26] but is now disclosed, and through the prophetic writings is made known to all the Gentiles, according to the command of the eternal God, to bring about the obedience of faith— [27] to the only wise God, through Jesus Christ, to whom[y] be the glory forever! Amen.[z]

[t] Other ancient authorities lack this sentence
[u] Or *compatriots*   [v] Or *I Tertius, writing this letter in the Lord, greet you*   [w] Other ancient authorities add verse 24, *The grace of our Lord Jesus Christ be with all of you. Amen.*
[x] Gk *the one*   [y] Other ancient authorities lack *to whom*. The verse then reads, *to the only wise God be the glory through Jesus Christ forever. Amen.*   [z] Other ancient authorities lack 16.25-27 or include it after 14.23 or 15.33; others put verse 24 after verse 27

C hurches have problems. Sometimes, parishes harbor power struggles, sex scandals, troubled marriages, bitter disagreements, alcohol abuse, and even disorderly worship. Maybe you know Christian communities that have had some of these difficulties. The early church in Corinth had them all. In his first letter to the Corinthians, Paul gave them guidance and encouragement. This letter can teach churches in all times to more faithfully follow Christ.

At a Glance

- **1.1–9.** a greeting and thanks

- **1.10—4.21.** a discussion of divisions in the church

- **Chapters 5–11.** advice and answers to some questions

- **Chapters 12–14.** an explanation of spiritual gifts and the primacy of love

- **Chapter 15.** Paul's teaching about the Resurrection

- **Chapter 16.** Paul's plans and final blessing

In-depth

Corinth was an important seaport city in what is now southern Greece. It was a center of commerce for people from many cultures. It also had quite a reputation for sexual immorality. Paul established the Christian church there around A.D. 51 and spent about eighteen months with its converts. After Paul left, a man named Apollos came to help the young church grow.

Later, when Paul was in Ephesus, he got a letter (1 Cor 7.1) and visitors (1.11; 16.17) from Corinth. The church there was having problems. The problems were natural in a young Christian community whose members included both Jewish Christians and Gentile (non-Jewish) converts. The community was divided into groups with different leaders. There were some disagreements on how to worship properly. And there were different opinions about eating meat that had been sacrificed to pagan idols. In addition, some of the wealthy Christians were ignoring those who were poorer. And those with certain spiritual gifts were claiming to be more important than other people.

In response to all these divisions and various questions, Paul gives the Corinthians good, practical advice. At the same time, he reminds them of what is truly important for Christian believers: the Resurrection is central to faith; human wisdom is foolish when measured against God's wisdom; others' needs and concerns must always be put before their own; and love should be the primary focus in everything they do and say.

To this divided, confused community, Paul offers a picture of unity: we are all different parts of the same Body of Christ (12.12–27). Paul celebrates our diversity and insists on our unity. The advice and teaching he gives in this letter are good for Christians of any time or place to take to heart.

Quick Facts

Author
Paul

Date Written
A.D. 56

Audience
the mainly Gentile church at Corinth

1 Corinthians

Salutation

Paul, called to be an apostle of Christ Jesus by the will of God, and our brother Sos'the•nēs,

2 To the church of God that is in Corinth, to those who are sanctified in Christ Jesus, called to be saints, together with all those who in every place call on the name of our Lord Jesus Christ, both their Lord*a* and ours:

3 Grace to you and peace from God our Father and the Lord Jesus Christ.

4 I give thanks to my*b* God always for you because of the grace of God that has been given you in Christ Jesus, 5 for in every way you have been enriched in him, in speech and knowledge of every kind— 6 just as the testimony of*c* Christ has been strengthened among you— 7 so that you are not lacking in any spiritual gift as you wait for the revealing of our Lord Jesus Christ. 8 He will also strengthen you to the end, so that you may be blameless on the day of our Lord Jesus Christ. 9 God is faithful; by him you were called into the fellowship of his Son, Jesus Christ our Lord.

Divisions in the Church

10 Now I appeal to you, brothers and sisters,*d* by the name of our Lord Jesus Christ, that all of you be in agreement and that there be no divisions among you, but that you be united in the same mind and the same purpose. 11 For it has been reported to me by Chlō'ē's people that there are quarrels among you, my brothers and sisters.*e* 12 What I mean is that each of you says, "I belong to Paul," or "I belong to A•pol'los," or "I belong to Cē'phas," or "I belong to Christ." 13 Has Christ been divided? Was Paul crucified for you? Or were you baptized in the name of Paul? 14 I thank God*f* that I baptized none of you except Cris'pus and Gā'i•us, 15 so that no one can say that you were baptized in my name. 16 (I did baptize also the household of Steph'a•nas; beyond that, I do not know whether I baptized anyone else.) 17 For Christ did not send me to baptize but to proclaim the gospel, and not with eloquent wisdom, so that the cross of Christ might not be emptied of its power.

Christ the Power and Wisdom of God
(Cp Isa 29.14)

18 For the message about the cross is foolishness to those who are perishing, but to us who are being saved it is the power of God. 19 For it is written,

"I will destroy the wisdom of the wise,
 and the discernment of the discerning I
  will thwart."

20 Where is the one who is wise? Where is the scribe? Where is the debater of this age? Has not God made foolish the wisdom of the world? 21 For

---

a Gk *theirs* *b* Other ancient authorities lack *my* *c* Or *to*
d Gk *brothers* *e* Gk *my brothers* *f* Other ancient
authorities read *I am thankful*

Divisions in the Church

At a family reunion to honor his grandfather's eighty-fifth birthday, Tyrone brags about his school's victory over his cousin Martin's school in a recent football game, and how he sacked Martin on a critical play. Martin counters that the referees overlooked Tyrone's holding his face mask on the play. The families of the boys take sides. Before long, the entire gathering is fighting about which team was the best. The birthday party is ruined.

This is what happened to the Christians in Corinth. They held a common belief in Jesus, but spent useless energy arguing over which leaders to follow. Paul challenges them to get over this foolish division and focus on the important thing they share—the love of God and their salvation through the cross of Christ.

Today, Christians face similar challenges. Strong divisions in the past have created different Christian churches. Even within the Catholic church, divisions distract people from their central mission.

What causes division in your family, your school, and your church? How can you help people focus on the important things you hold in common?

▶ I Cor 1.10–17

---

since, in the wisdom of God, the world did not know God through wisdom, God decided, through the foolishness of our proclamation, to save those who believe. 22 For Jews demand signs and Greeks desire wisdom, 23 but we proclaim Christ crucified, a stumbling block to Jews and foolishness to Gentiles, 24 but to those who are the called, both Jews and Greeks, Christ the power of God and the wisdom of God. 25 For God's foolish-

ness is wiser than human wisdom, and God's weakness is stronger than human strength.

26 Consider your own call, brothers and sisters:*g* not many of you were wise by human standards,*h* not many were powerful, not many were of noble birth. 27 But God chose what is foolish in the world to shame the wise; God chose what is

---

g Gk brothers   h Gk according to the flesh

God's Wisdom and Ours

What is the difference between a smart person and a wise person? Many smart people excel in a subject in school or a skill at work. You have to be very smart to run an illegal drug ring or to make a nuclear bomb. But being smart in these ways does not make a person wise in the ways of God.

Paul reminds the Corinthians that the central Christian message—that Christ was crucified for our salvation—seems foolish to many wise people of their time. The Jews and Greeks of this period pride themselves on their wisdom. But the Jews hope for a kingly messiah who will make the nation strong. And the Greeks believe that their gods are strong. Both Jews and Greeks think the idea of a crucified messiah, or a god who can suffer and die, is foolish.

There is great mystery here: the foolishness of God is wiser than the greatest wisdom of the world. Our ways are not God's ways. Christ hanging on a cross turns upside down the world's ideas of success and failure, of victory and defeat, of power and weakness. Many people in Paul's time—and many people in our time—are not able to accept this "foolish" way of seeing the world as God sees it.

▶ I Cor 1.18–31

1

C
O
R

weak in the world to shame the strong; 28 God chose what is low and despised in the world, things that are not, to reduce to nothing things that are, 29 so that no one[i] might boast in the presence of God. 30 He is the source of your life in Christ Jesus, who became for us wisdom from God, and righteousness and sanctification and redemption, 31 in order that, as it is written, "Let the one who boasts, boast in[j] the Lord."

Proclaiming Christ Crucified

When I came to you, brothers and sisters,[k] I did not come proclaiming the mystery[l] of God to you in lofty words or wisdom. 2 For I decided to know nothing among you except Jesus Christ, and him crucified. 3 And I came to you in weakness and in fear and in much trembling. 4 My speech and my proclamation were not with plausible words of wisdom,[m] but with a demonstration of the Spirit and of power, 5 so that your faith might rest not on human wisdom but on the power of God.

The True Wisdom of God

6 Yet among the mature we do speak wisdom, though it is not a wisdom of this age or of the rulers of this age, who are doomed to perish. 7 But we speak God's wisdom, secret and hidden, which God decreed before the ages for our glory. 8 None of the rulers of this age understood this; for if they had, they would not have crucified the Lord of glory. 9 But, as it is written,

"What no eye has seen, nor ear heard,
    nor the human heart conceived,
what God has prepared for those who
        love him"—

10 these things God has revealed to us through the Spirit; for the Spirit searches everything, even the depths of God. 11 For what human being knows what is truly human except the human spirit that is within? So also no one comprehends what is truly God's except the Spirit of God. 12 Now we have received not the spirit of the world, but the Spirit that is from God, so that we may understand the gifts bestowed on us by God. 13 And we speak of these things in words not taught by human wisdom but taught by the Spirit, interpreting spiritual things to those who are spiritual.[n]

14 Those who are unspiritual[o] do not receive the gifts of God's Spirit, for they are foolishness to them, and they are unable to understand them because they are spiritually discerned. 15 Those who are spiritual discern all things, and they are themselves subject to no one else's scrutiny.

16 "For who has known the mind of the Lord
        so as to instruct him?"
But we have the mind of Christ.

On Divisions in the Corinthian Church

And so, brothers and sisters,[k] I could not speak to you as spiritual people, but rather as people of the flesh, as infants in Christ. 2 I fed you with milk, not solid food, for you were not ready for solid

---

i Gk *no flesh*   j Or *of*   k Gk *brothers*   l Other ancient authorities read *testimony*   m Other ancient authorities read *the persuasiveness of wisdom*   n Or *interpreting spiritual things in spiritual language,* or *comparing spiritual things with spiritual*   o Or *natural*

WE ARE GOD'S SERVANTS, WHO SHARE A COMMON MISSION!

Sometimes, Christians engage in destructive competition or are motivated by personal pride. Paul says clearly that all Christians are God's servants, and should work together, and have a common purpose. Whatever we do for the Gospel is part of Jesus' mission and has the same value for God. Paul uses two images to tell us this: "So neither the one who plants nor the one who waters is anything, but only God who gives the growth" (3.7) and "Like a skilled master builder I laid a foundation, and someone else is building on it. . . . That foundation is Jesus Christ" (verses 10–11).

■ As a young person, how can you work cooperatively with other young people and with the adult community?

■ Express your gratitude for the building of the church done by previous generations of Christians. Pray that young Christians will embrace Jesus' mission with passion and with the global perspective needed at this time in history.

▶ 1 Cor 3.1–15

food. Even now you are still not ready, ³ for you are still of the flesh. For as long as there is jealousy and quarreling among you, are you not of the flesh, and behaving according to human inclinations? ⁴ For when one says, "I belong to Paul," and another, "I belong to A·pol′los," are you not merely human?

5 What then is A·pol′los? What is Paul? Servants through whom you came to believe, as the Lord assigned to each. ⁶ I planted, A·pol′los watered, but God gave the growth. ⁷ So neither the one who plants nor the one who waters is anything, but only God who gives the growth. ⁸ The one who plants and the one who waters have a common purpose, and each will receive wages according to the labor of each. ⁹ For we are God's servants, working together; you are God's field, God's building.

10 According to the grace of God given to me, like a skilled master builder I laid a foundation, and someone else is building on it. Each builder must choose with care how to build on it. ¹¹ For no one can lay any foundation other than the one that has been laid; that foundation is Jesus Christ. ¹² Now if anyone builds on the foundation with gold, silver, precious stones, wood, hay, straw— ¹³ the work of each builder will become visible, for the Day will disclose it, because it will be revealed with fire, and the fire will test what sort of work each has done. ¹⁴ If what has been built on the foundation survives, the builder will receive a reward. ¹⁵ If the work is burned up, the builder will suffer loss; the builder will be saved, but only as through fire.

16 Do you not know that you are God's temple and that God's Spirit dwells in you? *p* ¹⁷ If anyone destroys God's temple, God will destroy that person. For God's temple is holy, and you are that temple.

18 Do not deceive yourselves. If you think that you are wise in this age, you should become fools so that you may become wise. ¹⁹ For the wisdom of this world is foolishness with God. For it is written,

"He catches the wise in their craftiness,"
²⁰ and again,

"The Lord knows the thoughts of the wise,
    that they are futile."

²¹ So let no one boast about human leaders. For all things are yours, ²² whether Paul or A·pol′los or Ce′phas or the world or life or death or the present or the future—all belong to you, ²³ and you belong to Christ, and Christ belongs to God.

PRAY IT?

From the Bottom Up

The most important part of a building is its foundation. If the foundation is built well and with care, then, what is placed on it will last. And so it is with people. We all have before us a wide variety of construction materials—values, beliefs, and principles—to use in building the foundation of our life. Initially, our foundation is built through our family, using the values taught in schools and churches. In our adolescent years, most of us discover that other materials are available and that we must choose which ones to add to our foundation.

In 1 Cor 3.10–17, Paul tells the people of Corinth that whatever they choose to use in building their foundation will show itself in the end. A poor foundation will lead to a poor end. He also reminds them that they are living temples of God, to be filled with the Holy Spirit.

In your prayer, reflect or journal on the following questions:

■ On what foundation do you want to build your life?

■ What kind of person do you want to be remembered as when you are gone?

■ What qualities, values, and virtues do you want to have? How can these be a sign of the Holy Spirit living within you?

▶ 1 Cor 3.10–17

The Ministry of the Apostles

Think of us in this way, as servants of Christ and stewards of God's mysteries. ² Moreover, it is required of stewards that they be found trustworthy. ³ But with me it is a very small thing that I should be judged by you or by any human court. I do not even judge myself. ⁴ I am not aware of anything against myself, but I am not thereby acquitted. It is the Lord who judges me. ⁵ Therefore do not pronounce judgment before the time, before the Lord comes, who will bring to light the things now hidden in darkness and will disclose the purposes of the heart. Then each one will receive commendation from God.

p In verses 16 and 17 the Greek word for *you* is plural

1
C
O
R

PRAY IT

We Are God's Temple

We are God's temple.
  We are rich, we are poor,
We are young, we are old,
We are male, we are female,
We are disabled, we are sick, we are healthy,
We are unborn,
We are all races and cultures.
O God,
Fill us with your spirit of unity.
Abolish the destructive forces of hate:
  prejudice, racism, physical and verbal
  abuse, abortion, murder, and euthanasia.
Break down the barriers that divide us.
Fill us with your loving spirit and an
  appreciation for the value of each and
  every life. Amen.

▶ I Cor 3.16–17

6 I have applied all this to A·pol'los and myself for your benefit, brothers and sisters,*q* so that you may learn through us the meaning of the saying, "Nothing beyond what is written," so that none of you will be puffed up in favor of one against another. 7 For who sees anything different in you?*r* What do you have that you did not receive? And if you received it, why do you boast as if it were not a gift?

8 Already you have all you want! Already you have become rich! Quite apart from us you have become kings! Indeed, I wish that you had become kings, so that we might be kings with you! 9 For I think that God has exhibited us apostles as last of all, as though sentenced to death, because we have become a spectacle to the world, to angels and to mortals. 10 We are fools for the sake of Christ, but you are wise in Christ. We are weak, but you are strong. You are held in honor, but we in disrepute. 11 To the present hour we are hungry and thirsty, we are poorly clothed and beaten and homeless, 12 and we grow weary from the work of our own hands. When reviled, we bless; when persecuted, we endure; 13 when slandered, we speak kindly. We have become like the rubbish of the world, the dregs of all things, to this very day.

Fatherly Admonition

14 I am not writing this to make you ashamed, but to admonish you as my beloved children.

15 For though you might have ten thousand guardians in Christ, you do not have many fathers. Indeed, in Christ Jesus I became your father through the gospel. 16 I appeal to you, then, be imitators of me. 17 For this reason I sent*s* you Timothy, who is my beloved and faithful child in the Lord, to remind you of my ways in Christ Jesus, as I teach them everywhere in every church. 18 But some of you, thinking that I am not coming to you, have become arrogant. 19 But I will come to you soon, if the Lord wills, and I will find out not the talk of these arrogant people but their power. 20 For the kingdom of God depends not on talk but on power. 21 What would you prefer? Am I to come to you with a stick, or with love in a spirit of gentleness?

Sexual Immorality Defiles the Church

It is actually reported that there is sexual immorality among you, and of a kind that is not found even among pagans; for a man is living with his father's wife. 2 And you are arrogant! Should you not rather have mourned, so that he who has done this would have been removed from among you?

3 For though absent in body, I am present in spirit; and as if present I have already pronounced judgment 4 in the name of the Lord Jesus on the man who has done such a thing.*t* When you are assembled, and my spirit is present with the power of our Lord Jesus, 5 you are to hand this man over to Satan for the destruction of the flesh, so that his spirit may be saved in the day of the Lord.*u*

6 Your boasting is not a good thing. Do you not know that a little yeast leavens the whole batch of dough? 7 Clean out the old yeast so that you may be a new batch, as you really are unleavened. For our paschal lamb, Christ, has been sacrificed. 8 Therefore, let us celebrate the festival, not with the old yeast, the yeast of malice and evil, but with the unleavened bread of sincerity and truth.

Sexual Immorality Must Be Judged

9 I wrote to you in my letter not to associate with sexually immoral persons— 10 not at all meaning the immoral of this world, or the greedy and robbers, or idolaters, since you would then need to go out of the world. 11 But now I am writing to you not to associate with anyone who bears the name of brother or sister*v* who is sexually immoral or greedy, or is an idolater, reviler, drunkard, or robber. Do not even eat with such a one. 12 For what have I to do with judging those outside? Is it not

q Gk brothers   *r* Or Who makes you different from another?
s Or am sending   *t* Or on the man who has done such a
thing in the name of the Lord Jesus   *u* Other ancient
authorities add Jesus   *v* Gk brother

Living Well

Some people think that God or the Christian religion is primarily interested in preventing us from doing fun things. They imagine the Bible as a book of thou-shalt-nots, and the church as a place where they are told to avoid enjoying themselves!

Paul helps us understand that God's desire is for us to live well. All good gifts from God, including food and sexuality, are meant to be enjoyed to the fullest. But they also can be misused, and if they are, we miss out on the joy and purpose intended by God.

For example, in 1 Cor 6.12–20, Paul affirms that sexual intercourse is meant to bond two people for life. Fornication—sexual intercourse between people who are not married—defeats its true purpose. Fornication diminishes the full joy and beauty of sexual intimacy as intended by God.

God created our sexuality. Our sexual desires—felt keenly during adolescence!—are not sinful but a normal part of being human. As the author of our sexuality, God wants us not to be hurt by this gift but instead to experience its fullness in marriage.

▶ **1 Cor 6.12–20**

those who are inside that you are to judge? ¹³God will judge those outside. "Drive out the wicked person from among you."

Lawsuits among Believers

When any of you has a grievance against another, do you dare to take it to court before the unrighteous, instead of taking it before the saints? ²Do you not know that the saints will judge the world? And if the world is to be judged by you, are you incompetent to try trivial cases? ³Do you not know that we are to judge angels—to say nothing of ordinary matters? ⁴If you have ordinary cases, then, do you appoint as judges those who have no standing in the church? ⁵I say this to your shame. Can it be that there is no one among you wise enough to decide between one believer*w* and another, ⁶but a believer*w* goes to court against a believer*w*—and before unbelievers at that?

7 In fact, to have lawsuits at all with one another is already a defeat for you. Why not rather be wronged? Why not rather be defrauded? ⁸But you yourselves wrong and defraud—and believers*x* at that.

9 Do you not know that wrongdoers will not inherit the kingdom of God? Do not be deceived! Fornicators, idolaters, adulterers, male prostitutes, sodomites, ¹⁰thieves, the greedy, drunkards, revilers, robbers—none of these will inherit the kingdom of God. ¹¹And this is what some of you used to be. But you were washed, you were sanctified, you were justified in the name of the Lord Jesus Christ and in the Spirit of our God.

Glorify God in Body and Spirit

12 "All things are lawful for me," but not all things are beneficial. "All things are lawful for me," but I will not be dominated by anything. ¹³"Food is meant for the stomach and the stomach for food,"*y* and God will destroy both one and the other. The body is meant not for fornication but for the Lord, and the Lord for the body. ¹⁴And God raised the Lord and will also raise us by his power. ¹⁵Do you not know that your bodies are members of Christ? Should I therefore take the members of Christ and make them members of a prostitute? Never! ¹⁶Do you not know that whoever is united to a prostitute becomes one body with her? For it is said, "The two shall be one flesh." ¹⁷But anyone united to the Lord becomes one spirit with him. ¹⁸Shun fornication! Every sin that a person commits is outside the body; but the fornicator sins against the body itself. ¹⁹Or do you not know that your body is a temple*z* of the Holy Spirit within you, which you have from God, and that you are not your own? ²⁰For you were bought with a price; therefore glorify God in your body.

Directions concerning Marriage

Now concerning the matters about which you wrote: "It is well for a man not to touch a woman." ²But because of cases of sexual immorality, each man should have his own wife and each woman her own husband. ³The husband should give to his wife her conjugal rights, and likewise the wife

---

w Gk *brother*   *x* Gk *brothers*   *y* The quotation may extend to the word *other*   *z* Or *sanctuary*

to her husband. 4 For the wife does not have authority over her own body, but the husband does; likewise the husband does not have authority over his own body, but the wife does. 5 Do not deprive one another except perhaps by agreement for a set time, to devote yourselves to prayer, and then come together again, so that Satan may not tempt you because of your lack of self-control. 6 This I say by way of concession, not of command. 7 I wish that all were as I myself am. But each has a particular gift from God, one having one kind and another a different kind.

8 To the unmarried and the widows I say that it is well for them to remain unmarried as I am. 9 But if they are not practicing self-control, they should marry. For it is better to marry than to be aflame with passion.

10 To the married I give this command—not I but the Lord—that the wife should not separate from her husband 11 (but if she does separate, let her remain unmarried or else be reconciled to her husband), and that the husband should not divorce his wife.

12 To the rest I say—I and not the Lord—that if any believer[a] has a wife who is an unbeliever, and she consents to live with him, he should not divorce her. 13 And if any woman has a husband who is an unbeliever, and he consents to live with her, she should not divorce him. 14 For the unbelieving husband is made holy through his wife, and the unbelieving wife is made holy through her husband. Otherwise, your children would be unclean, but as it is, they are holy. 15 But if the unbelieving partner separates, let it be so; in such a case the brother or sister is not bound. It is to peace that God has called you.[b] 16 Wife, for all you know, you might save your husband. Husband, for all you know, you might save your wife.

The Life That the Lord Has Assigned

17 However that may be, let each of you lead the life that the Lord has assigned, to which God called you. This is my rule in all the churches. 18 Was anyone at the time of his call already circumcised? Let him not seek to remove the marks of circumcision. Was anyone at the time of his call uncircumcised? Let him not seek circumcision. 19 Circumcision is nothing, and uncircumcision is nothing; but obeying the commandments of God is everything. 20 Let each of you remain in the condition in which you were called. 21 Were you a slave when called? Do not be concerned about it. Even if you can gain your freedom, make use of your present condition now more than ever.[c] 22 For whoever was called in the Lord as a slave is a freed person belonging to the

Lord, just as whoever was free when called is a slave of Christ. 23 You were bought with a price; do not become slaves of human masters. 24 In whatever condition you were called, brothers and sisters,[d] there remain with God.

did you KNOW?

Strange Advice!?

First Corinthians, chapter 7, says people shouldn't marry, uncircumcised people shouldn't get circumcised, and slaves should remain slaves.

Why is Paul giving such strange advice? Because Paul thinks that Jesus will be returning soon to establish God's Reign for all time (verse 31). So he advises the Corinthians to remain in whatever condition they were called, in order to avoid the confusion that comes when making big life changes.

But Jesus didn't come back during Paul's time. In fact, we are still waiting for his return. When is Jesus going to come again? Don't try to figure it out. Jesus told us we will never know (Mt 24.36–44). But whatever our state of life is or will become, we would be wise to follow Paul's intent "to promote good order and unhindered devotion to the Lord" (1 Cor 7.35).

▸ 1 Corinthians, chapter 7

The Unmarried and the Widows

25 Now concerning virgins, I have no command of the Lord, but I give my opinion as one who by the Lord's mercy is trustworthy. 26 I think that, in view of the impending[e] crisis, it is well for you to remain as you are. 27 Are you bound to a wife? Do not seek to be free. Are you free from a wife? Do not seek a wife. 28 But if you marry, you do not sin, and if a virgin marries, she does not sin. Yet those who marry will experience distress in this life,[f] and I would spare you that. 29 I mean, brothers and sisters,[d] the appointed time has grown short; from now on, let even those who

---

a Gk brother   b Other ancient authorities read us
c Or avail yourself of the opportunity   d Gk brothers
e Or present   f Gk in the flesh

have wives be as though they had none, ³⁰ and those who mourn as though they were not mourning, and those who rejoice as though they were not rejoicing, and those who buy as though they had no possessions, ³¹ and those who deal with the world as though they had no dealings with it. For the present form of this world is passing away.

32 I want you to be free from anxieties. The unmarried man is anxious about the affairs of the Lord, how to please the Lord; ³³ but the married man is anxious about the affairs of the world, how to please his wife, ³⁴ and his interests are divided. And the unmarried woman and the virgin are anxious about the affairs of the Lord, so that they may be holy in body and spirit; but the married woman is anxious about the affairs of the world, how to please her husband. ³⁵ I say this for your own benefit, not to put any restraint upon you, but to promote good order and unhindered devotion to the Lord.

36 If anyone thinks that he is not behaving properly toward his fiancée,ᵍ if his passions are strong, and so it has to be, let him marry as he wishes; it is no sin. Let them marry. ³⁷ But if someone stands firm in his resolve, being under no necessity but having his own desire under control, and has determined in his own mind to keep her as his fiancée,ᵍ he will do well. ³⁸ So then, he who marries his fiancéeᵍ does well; and he who refrains from marriage will do better.

39 A wife is bound as long as her husband lives. But if the husband dies,ʰ she is free to marry anyone she wishes, only in the Lord. ⁴⁰ But in my judgment she is more blessed if she remains as she is. And I think that I too have the Spirit of God.

Food Offered to Idols

Now concerning food sacrificed to idols: we know that "all of us possess knowledge." Knowledge puffs up, but love builds up. ² Anyone who claims to know something does not yet have the necessary knowledge; ³ but anyone who loves God is known by him.

4 Hence, as to the eating of food offered to idols, we know that "no idol in the world really exists," and that "there is no God but one." ⁵ Indeed, even though there may be so-called gods in heaven or on earth—as in fact there are many gods and many lords— ⁶ yet for us there is one God, the Father, from whom are all things and for whom we exist, and one Lord, Jesus Christ, through whom are all things and through whom we exist.

7 It is not everyone, however, who has this knowledge. Since some have become so accustomed to idols until now, they still think of the food they eat as food offered to an idol; and their conscience, being weak, is defiled. ⁸ "Food will not bring us close to God."ⁱ We are no worse off if we do not eat, and no better off if we do. ⁹ But take care that this liberty of yours does not somehow become a stumbling block to the weak. ¹⁰ For if others see you, who possess knowledge, eating in

ᵍ Gk *virgin*   ʰ Gk *falls asleep*   ⁱ The quotation may extend to the end of the verse

LIVE IT!

Restrain Your Ego!

Maria's parents have stopped drinking alcohol. Not that they ever drank to excess. But for months, Maria bugged them, "If I can't drink, then why do you?" Because she accepted none of their arguments, they agreed that they would stop until she reached legal age.

Crazy? Not according to Paul. He recommends something similar. Paul recognizes that it is not necessarily wrong for the community of Christians in Corinth to eat meat sacrificed to idols, or pagan gods, because they don't believe in those gods. Still, he recommends that they not do it, because some members of the community find it upsetting. For Paul, keeping unity is more important than always "being right."

Do you ever do things that aren't necessarily wrong just because it's your right? like whistle around a sibling who cannot stand it? or pick a sweater for the family picture that doesn't match anyone else's? or, when your younger brothers and sisters are around, watch a television show that's okay for you but not for them? When you find yourself doing something like this, think about Paul's advice. Are you making your ego more important than other people's feelings?

▶ 1 Cor 8.1–13

the temple of an idol, might they not, since their conscience is weak, be encouraged to the point of eating food sacrificed to idols? 11 So by your knowledge those weak believers for whom Christ died are destroyed.*j* 12 But when you thus sin against members of your family,*k* and wound their conscience when it is weak, you sin against Christ. 13 Therefore, if food is a cause of their falling,*l* I will never eat meat, so that I may not cause one of them*m* to fall.

The Rights of an Apostle

Am I not free? Am I not an apostle? Have I not seen Jesus our Lord? Are you not my work in the Lord? 2 If I am not an apostle to others, at least I am to you; for you are the seal of my apostleship in the Lord.

3 This is my defense to those who would examine me. 4 Do we not have the right to our food and drink? 5 Do we not have the right to be accompanied by a believing wife,*n* as do the other apostles and the brothers of the Lord and Cē′phas? 6 Or is it only Bar′na·bas and I who have no right to refrain from working for a living? 7 Who at any time pays the expenses for doing military service? Who plants a vineyard and does not eat any of its fruit? Or who tends a flock and does not get any of its milk?

8 Do I say this on human authority? Does not the law also say the same? 9 For it is written in the law of Moses, "You shall not muzzle an ox while it is treading out the grain." Is it for oxen that God is concerned? 10 Or does he not speak entirely for our sake? It was indeed written for our sake, for whoever plows should plow in hope and whoever threshes should thresh in hope of a share in the crop. 11 If we have sown spiritual good among you, is it too much if we reap your material benefits? 12 If others share this rightful claim on you, do not we still more?

Nevertheless, we have not made use of this right, but we endure anything rather than put an obstacle in the way of the gospel of Christ. 13 Do you not know that those who are employed in the temple service get their food from the temple, and those who serve at the altar share in what is sacrificed on the altar? 14 In the same way, the Lord commanded that those who proclaim the gospel should get their living by the gospel.

15 But I have made no use of any of these rights, nor am I writing this so that they may be applied in my case. Indeed, I would rather die than that—no one will deprive me of my ground for boasting! 16 If I proclaim the gospel, this gives me no ground for boasting, for an obligation is laid on me, and woe to me if I do not proclaim the gospel! 17 For if I do this of my own will, I have a reward; but if not of my own will, I am entrusted with a commission. 18 What then is my reward? Just this: that in my proclamation I may make the gospel free of charge, so as not to make full use of my rights in the gospel.

19 For though I am free with respect to all, I have made myself a slave to all, so that I might win more of them. 20 To the Jews I became as a Jew, in order to win Jews. To those under the law I became as one under the law (though I myself am not under the law) so that I might win those under the law. 21 To those outside the law I be-

---

j Gk the weak brother . . . is destroyed   *k* Gk against the brothers   *l* Gk my brother's falling   *m* Gk cause my brother   *n* Gk a sister as wife

Spiritual Perseverance

LIVE IT!

Did you know that Michael Jordan—once the points leader of the record-setting Chicago Bulls—had difficulty making his high school varsity basketball team the first year he tried out? He could have quit trying, but he set a goal for himself and made practicing over and over a priority for his daily life. Not only did he finally make the team, he broke state scoring records and was named all-state. And that was just the beginning!

Persevering means setting priorities, sticking to them even when you get discouraged, and trying over and over to accomplish your goals. For the next six months, set yourself a goal that will help you grow closer to God. What will you have to do to accomplish it? What priorities must you establish? As 1 Cor 9.24–27 says, run your race by staying focused on your goal!

▸ 1 Cor 9.24–27

LIVE IT!

Addictive Behavior

How do you spend the bulk of your free time? talking with your friends on the phone? playing video games? listening to your favorite music? If you discover that you have become obsessed with that activity, maybe it has become addictive. Although perhaps your obsession is not a true addiction—like those caused by drugs, alcohol, gambling, or eating disorders—it still might have more control over your life than it should have.

Paul reminds the Corinthians that they should put God at the center of their life. He points out that they will always be tempted to replace God with something else—which is called idolatry—like the ancient Israelites were tempted.

How about us today? We may not worship foreign gods or eat meat sacrificed to idols. But in many ways, our addictive behaviors are like idolatry. They consume our thoughts and time and can even lead us away from God.

Addictive behaviors are hard to break. And true addictions are very difficult to control. But you have the promise that God "will not let you be tested beyond your strength" (1 Cor. 10.13). If you think you may have an addiction, talk to a parent or school counselor or minister.

▸ **1 Cor 10.6–14**

came as one outside the law (though I am not free
from God's law but am under Christ's law) so that
I might win those outside the law. 22 To the weak I
became weak, so that I might win the weak. I have
become all things to all people, that I might by all
means save some. 23 I do it all for the sake of the
gospel, so that I may share in its blessings.

24 Do you not know that in a race the runners
all compete, but only one receives the prize? Run
in such a way that you may win it. 25 Athletes exercise self-control in all things; they do it to receive a
perishable wreath, but we an imperishable one.
26 So I do not run aimlessly, nor do I box as
though beating the air; 27 but I punish my body
and enslave it, so that after proclaiming to others I
myself should not be disqualified.

Warnings from Israel's History

10 I do not want you to be unaware, brothers and
sisters,[o] that our ancestors were all under the
cloud, and all passed through the sea, 2 and all
were baptized into Moses in the cloud and in the
sea, 3 and all ate the same spiritual food, 4 and all
drank the same spiritual drink. For they drank
from the spiritual rock that followed them, and
the rock was Christ. 5 Nevertheless, God was not
pleased with most of them, and they were struck
down in the wilderness.

6 Now these things occurred as examples for
us, so that we might not desire evil as they did.
7 Do not become idolaters as some of them did; as
it is written, "The people sat down to eat and
drink, and they rose up to play." 8 We must not
indulge in sexual immorality as some of them did,
and twenty-three thousand fell in a single day.
9 We must not put Christ[p] to the test, as some of
them did, and were destroyed by serpents. 10 And
do not complain as some of them did, and were
destroyed by the destroyer. 11 These things happened to them to serve as an example, and they
were written down to instruct us, on whom the
ends of the ages have come. 12 So if you think you
are standing, watch out that you do not fall. 13 No
testing has overtaken you that is not common to
everyone. God is faithful, and he will not let you
be tested beyond your strength, but with the testing he will also provide the way out so that you
may be able to endure it.

14 Therefore, my dear friends,[q] flee from the
worship of idols. 15 I speak as to sensible people;
judge for yourselves what I say. 16 The cup of blessing that we bless, is it not a sharing in the blood of
Christ? The bread that we break, is it not a sharing
in the body of Christ? 17 Because there is one
bread, we who are many are one body, for we all
partake of the one bread. 18 Consider the people of
Israel;[r] are not those who eat the sacrifices partners in the altar? 19 What do I imply then? That
food sacrificed to idols is anything, or that an idol
is anything? 20 No, I imply that what pagans sacrifice, they sacrifice to demons and not to God. I do

[o] Gk *brothers* [p] Other ancient authorities read *the Lord*
[q] Gk *my beloved* [r] Gk *Israel according to the flesh*

not want you to be partners with demons. 21 You cannot drink the cup of the Lord and the cup of demons. You cannot partake of the table of the Lord and the table of demons. 22 Or are we provoking the Lord to jealousy? Are we stronger than he?

Do All to the Glory of God
(Cp Ps 24.1)

23 "All things are lawful," but not all things are beneficial. "All things are lawful," but not all things build up. 24 Do not seek your own advantage, but that of the other. 25 Eat whatever is sold in the meat market without raising any question on the ground of conscience, 26 for "the earth and its fullness are the Lord's." 27 If an unbeliever invites you to a meal and you are disposed to go, eat whatever is set before you without raising any question on the ground of conscience. 28 But if someone says to you, "This has been offered in sacrifice," then do not eat it, out of consideration for the one who informed you, and for the sake of conscience— 29 I mean the other's conscience, not your own. For why should my liberty be subject to the judgment of someone else's conscience? 30 If I partake with thankfulness, why should I be denounced because of that for which I give thanks?

Whatever you do, do everything

for the glory of God

10.31

31 So, whether you eat or drink, or whatever you do, do everything for the glory of God. 32 Give no offense to Jews or to Greeks or to the church of God, 33 just as I try to please everyone in everything I do, not seeking my own advantage, but that of many, so that they may be saved. 1 Be imitators of me, as I am of Christ.

NATIVE AMERICAN

Food and Gratitude

Have you ever considered eating and drinking for the glory of God? Paul tells the Corinthians that it is more important to respect the conscience of their dining partners than to worry about where the meat came from. By appreciating what they have been given to eat, they show respect for the people who have prepared the food.

Native Americans have that same sense of appreciation—not just for the people they share meals with but for the animals and plants that provide the food. When they kill an animal to eat, they pray to its spirit for forgiveness. Everything from the animal is put to good use because wasting any part of it would be an insult to its honor.

This Native American meal blessing is an expression of thanks:

Now that I am about to eat, O great Spirit, give my thanks to the beasts and birds whom You have provided for my hunger, and pray deliver my sorrow that living things must make a sacrifice for my comfort and well-being. Let the feather of corn spring up in its time and let it not wither but make full grains for the fires of our cooking pots, now that I am about to eat. (From the Lama Foundation, San Cristobal, New Mexico)

▶ 1 Cor 10.23–33

Head Coverings

2 I commend you because you remember me in everything and maintain the traditions just as I handed them on to you. 3 But I want you to understand that Christ is the head of every man, and the husband[s] is the head of his wife,[t] and God is the head of Christ. 4 Any man who prays or prophesies

---

s The same Greek word means man or husband   *t Or head of the woman* with something on his head disgraces his head, [5] but any woman who prays or prophesies with her head unveiled disgraces her head—it is one and the same thing as having her head shaved. [6] For if a woman will not veil herself, then she should cut off her hair; but if it is disgraceful for a woman to have her hair cut off or to be shaved, she should wear a veil. [7] For a man ought not to have his head veiled, since he is the image and reflection[u] of God; but woman is the reflection[u] of man. [8] Indeed, man was not made from woman, but woman from man. [9] Neither was man created for the sake of woman, but woman for the sake of man. [10] For this reason a woman ought to have a symbol of[v] authority on her head,[w] because of the angels. [11] Nevertheless, in the Lord woman is not independent of man or man independent of woman. [12] For just as woman came from man, so man comes through woman; but all things come from God. [13] Judge for yourselves: is it proper for a woman to pray to God with her head unveiled? [14] Does not nature itself teach you that if a man wears long hair, it is degrading to him, [15] but if a woman has long hair, it is her glory? For her hair is given to her for a covering. [16] But if anyone is disposed to be contentious—we have no such custom, nor do the churches of God.

Abuses at the Lord's Supper

17 Now in the following instructions I do not commend you, because when you come together it is not for the better but for the worse. [18] For, to begin with, when you come together as a church, I hear that there are divisions among you; and to some extent I believe it. [19] Indeed, there have to be factions among you, for only so will it become clear who among you are genuine. [20] When you come together, it is not really to eat the Lord's supper. [21] For when the time comes to eat, each of you goes ahead with your own supper, and one goes hungry and another becomes drunk. [22] What! Do you not have homes to eat and drink in? Or do you show contempt for the church of God and humiliate those who have nothing? What should I say to you? Should I commend you? In this matter I do not commend you!

The Institution of the Lord's Supper
(Mt 26.26–29; Mk 14.22–25; Lk 22.14–23)

23 For I received from the Lord what I also handed on to you, that the Lord Jesus on the night when he was betrayed took a loaf of bread, [24] and when he had given thanks, he broke it and said, "This is my body that is for[x] you. Do this in remembrance of me." [25] In the same way he took the cup also, after supper, saying, "This cup is the new

covenant in my blood. Do this, as often as you drink it, in remembrance of me." [26] For as often as you eat this bread and drink the cup, you proclaim the Lord's death until he comes.

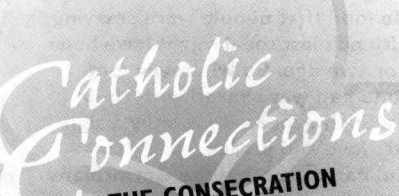

Catholic Connections

THE CONSECRATION

First Corinthians 11.23–26 contains the earliest recorded words of the Christian celebration of the Last Supper. These words are at the heart of the celebration of the Catholic Mass, or Eucharist. They are known as the words of consecration and are said by the priest just before he holds up the bread and wine. Catholics believe that the bread and wine are changed (or transubstantiated) into the real body and blood of Jesus Christ.

▸ 1 Cor 11.23–26

Partaking of the Supper Unworthily

27 Whoever, therefore, eats the bread or drinks the cup of the Lord in an unworthy manner will be answerable for the body and blood of the Lord. [28] Examine yourselves, and only then eat of the bread and drink of the cup. [29] For all who eat and drink[y] without discerning the body,[z] eat and drink judgment against themselves. [30] For this reason many of you are weak and ill, and some have died.[a] [31] But if we judged ourselves, we would not be judged. [32] But when we are judged by the Lord, we are disciplined[b] so that we may not be condemned along with the world.

33 So then, my brothers and sisters,[c] when you come together to eat, wait for one another. [34] If you are hungry, eat at home, so that when you

---

[u] Or *glory*   [v] Gk lacks *a symbol of*   [w] Or *have freedom of choice regarding her head*   [x] Other ancient authorities read *is broken for*   [y] Other ancient authorities add *in an unworthy manner,*   [z] Other ancient authorities read *the Lord's body*   [a] Gk *fallen asleep*   [b] Or *When we are judged, we are being disciplined by the Lord*   [c] Gk *brothers*

American

Called to Share

In China and Singapore, when people meet up with friends, they ask whether the friends have eaten a meal yet. This custom dates back to the great famine of China in the 1950s, when there was so little food that people were starving and a friend's last meal might have been a day or two ago. So whatever food someone had was shared with their friends. Such generosity is truly a sign of God's love and justice.

Paul had to remind the Corinthians about God's love and justice when they gathered in their homes to talk about their faith, share a meal, and celebrate the Eucharist. In 1 Cor 11.17–22, Paul tells the Corinthians that when the wealthy humiliate the poor by not inviting them to share the meal, they are abusing the purpose of the Lord's Supper. To celebrate the Lord's Supper is to partake in the body and blood of Christ, and it is impossible to do this if they do not live out the values of Christ.

In your prayer, journal or reflect on the following questions:

- What might Paul say to your church community if he sat with you during Sunday Mass?
- How do you share with people who have little or nothing?
- What can you do in your community so that the celebration of the Lord's Supper is more truly a sign of generosity, justice, and love?

▶ 1 Cor 11.17–33

come together, it will not be for your condemnation. About the other things I will give instructions when I come.

Spiritual Gifts

Now concerning spiritual gifts,[d] brothers and sisters,[e] I do not want you to be uninformed. 2 You know that when you were pagans, you were enticed and led astray to idols that could not speak.

3 Therefore I want you to understand that no one speaking by the Spirit of God ever says "Let Jesus be cursed!" and no one can say "Jesus is Lord" except by the Holy Spirit.

4 Now there are varieties of gifts, but the same Spirit; 5 and there are varieties of services, but the same Lord; 6 and there are varieties of activities, but it is the same God who activates all of them in everyone. 7 To each is given the manifestation of the Spirit for the common good. 8 To one is given through the Spirit the utterance of wisdom, and to another the utterance of knowledge according to the same Spirit, 9 to another faith by the same Spirit, to another gifts of healing by the one Spirit, 10 to another the working of miracles, to another prophecy, to another the discernment of spirits, to another various kinds of tongues, to another the interpretation of tongues. 11 All these are activated by one and the same Spirit, who allots to each one individually just as the Spirit chooses.

One Body with Many Members
(Cp Eph 4.1–16)

12 For just as the body is one and has many members, and all the members of the body, though many, are one body, so it is with Christ. 13 For in the one Spirit we were all baptized into one body—Jews or Greeks, slaves or free—and we were all made to drink of one Spirit.

14 Indeed, the body does not consist of one member but of many. 15 If the foot would say, "Because I am not a hand, I do not belong to the body," that would not make it any less a part of the body. 16 And if the ear would say, "Because I am not an eye, I do not belong to the body," that would not make it any less a part of the body. 17 If the whole body were an eye, where would the hearing be? If the whole body were hearing, where would the sense of smell be? 18 But as it is, God arranged the members in the body, each one of them, as he chose. 19 If all were a single member, where would the body be? 20 As it is, there are many members, yet one body. 21 The eye cannot say to the hand, "I have no need of you," nor again the head to the feet, "I have no need of you." 22 On the contrary, the members of the body that seem to be weaker are indispensable, 23 and those members of the body that we think less honorable we clothe with greater honor, and our less respectable members are treated with greater respect; 24 whereas our more respectable members do not need this. But God has so arranged the body, giving the greater honor to the inferior member,

---

d Or spiritual persons   e Gk brothers

25 that there may be no dissension within the body, but the members may have the same care for one another. 26 If one member suffers, all suffer together with it; if one member is honored, all rejoice together with it.

27 Now you are the body of Christ and individually members of it. 28 And God has appointed in the church first apostles, second prophets, third teachers; then deeds of power, then gifts of healing, forms of assistance, forms of leadership, various kinds of tongues. 29 Are all apostles? Are all prophets? Are all teachers? Do all work miracles? 30 Do all possess gifts of healing? Do all speak in tongues? Do all interpret? 31 But strive for the greater gifts. And I will show you a still more excellent way.

AFRICAN AMERICAN
The Body of Christ

As Christians, we are called to work together within the Body of Christ. Read 1 Cor 12.12–31. Here, Paul says that God has given us different gifts precisely so that we need one another.

A long time ago, Booker T. Washington realized that everyone can make a contribution to the world, regardless of their status or possessions. He wrote, "No race can prosper till it learns that there is as much dignity in tilling a field as in writing a poem." This is the Kwanzaa principle of *umoja*, or unity (see "Kwanzaa as a Way of Life," Deut 10.12–22).

Paul proclaims that each part of the Body of Christ—not only each person, but each diverse culture and race—is needed for the church to function properly. Many look at the most visible people in the church and conclude that they are more important than others. Remember that God sees differently. Often, important things are done by quiet people with little fanfare, but God always notices.

Can you focus on the success of the whole, rather than on what you have or do not have?

Dear God, free me from excessive worry about what someone else has or is able to do. Place my mind on unity and community. Amen.

▶ 1 Cor 12.12–31

did you KNOW?
God's Love

Greek, the language of the New Testament, has several words for love. There are words for parental love, romantic love, and love between friends or relatives. The rare Greek word Paul uses in First Corinthians, chapter 13—*agape*—is reserved for a special kind of love.

Agape (ah-GAH-pay) is love without conditions or motivations. It is there no matter who you are or what you do. It willingly chooses to serve without expectation of service in return. The Bible tells us that God is agape (1 Jn 4.16). The source of agape is the unconditional love of God. God's agape is revealed to us in Jesus Christ. Through our faith in Christ, we become a channel for communicating this wonderful love to others.

We are created in God's image. God wants us to love one another with the agape that Paul describes in chapter 13. It's a wonderful challenge!

▶ 1 Corinthians, chapter 13

The Gift of Love

If I speak in the tongues of mortals and of angels, but do not have love, I am a noisy gong or a clanging cymbal. 2 And if I have prophetic powers, and understand all mysteries and all knowledge, and if I have all faith, so as to remove mountains, but do not have love, I am nothing. 3 If I give away all my possessions, and if I hand over my body so that I may boast,f but do not have love, I gain nothing.

4 Love is patient; love is kind; love is not envious or boastful or arrogant 5 or rude. It does not insist on its own way; it is not irritable or resentful; 6 it does not rejoice in wrongdoing, but rejoices in the truth. 7 It bears all things, believes all things, hopes all things, endures all things.

8 Love never ends. But as for prophecies, they will come to an end; as for tongues, they will cease; as for knowledge, it will come to an end. 9 For we know only in part, and we prophesy only in part; 10 but when the complete comes, the partial will come to an end. 11 When I was a child, I

---

f Other ancient authorities read *body to be burned*

PRAY IT!

Loving Others

Read 1 Cor 13.1–13. It is a beautiful description of how the love we receive from God translates into multiple and delicate details for the people we love.

The following statements can help you see how to express God's love to others. Think about that love as you complete the statements. Repeat each statement as many times as necessary to include all the people and situations it applies to in your life. You might want to record your responses on a sheet of paper or in your journal.

1. I show love to _____ by being patient when _____.
2. I need to show kindness to _____, especially when _____.
3. I should not envy _____, especially about _____.
4. I should not act arrogantly with _____ when _____.
5. I should not be rude with _____, especially when _____.
6. I must not force my way on _____, particularly in regard to _____.
7. When _____ does _____ to me, I should not become irritated or resentful.
8. When _____ does _____ to me, I should forgive and seek reconciliation.
9. When _____ suffers or experiences something bad, I should show empathy.
10. I should rejoice in the truth whenever _____.
11. I must bear the behaviors that bother me, especially _____.
12. I must believe when I am told _____.
13. I must hope that my relationship with _____ will be _____.
14. I would endure hard times with _____ even though _____.

Now, pray to God to give you enough love to share in the ways you have described.

▶ 1 Corinthians, chapter 13

spoke like a child, I thought like a child, I reasoned like a child; when I became an adult, I put an end to childish ways. 12 For now we see in a mirror, dimly,g but then we will see face to face. Now I know only in part; then I will know fully, even as I have been fully known. 13 And now faith, hope, and love abide, these three; and the greatest of these is love.

Gifts of Prophecy and Tongues

Pursue love and strive for the spiritual gifts, and especially that you may prophesy. 2 For those who speak in a tongue do not speak to other people but to God; for nobody understands them, since they are speaking mysteries in the Spirit. 3 On the other hand, those who prophesy speak to other people for their upbuilding and encouragement and consolation. 4 Those who speak in a tongue build up themselves, but those who prophesy build up the church. 5 Now I would like all of you to speak in tongues, but even more to prophesy. One who prophesies is greater than one who speaks in tongues, unless someone interprets, so that the church may be built up.

6 Now, brothers and sisters,h if I come to you speaking in tongues, how will I benefit you unless I speak to you in some revelation or knowledge or prophecy or teaching? 7 It is the same way with lifeless instruments that produce sound, such as the flute or the harp. If they do not give distinct notes, how will anyone know what is being played? 8 And if the bugle gives an indistinct sound, who will get ready for battle? 9 So with yourselves; if in a tongue you utter speech that is not intelligible, how will anyone know what is being said? For you will be speaking into the air. 10 There are doubtless many different kinds of sounds in the world, and nothing is without sound. 11 If then I do not know the meaning of a sound, I will be a foreigner to the speaker and the speaker a foreigner to me. 12 So with yourselves; since you are eager for spiritual gifts, strive to excel in them for building up the church.

13 Therefore, one who speaks in a tongue should pray for the power to interpret. 14 For if I pray in a tongue, my spirit prays but my mind is unproductive. 15 What should I do then? I will pray with the spirit, but I will pray with the mind also; I will sing praise with the spirit, but I will sing praise with the mind also. 16 Otherwise, if you say a blessing with the spirit, how can anyone in the position of an outsider say the "Amen" to your thanksgiving, since the outsider does not know

---

g Gk *in a riddle* h Gk *brothers*

what you are saying? 17 For you may give thanks well enough, but the other person is not built up. 18 I thank God that I speak in tongues more than all of you; 19 nevertheless, in church I would rather speak five words with my mind, in order to instruct others also, than ten thousand words in a tongue.

20 Brothers and sisters,*i* do not be children in your thinking; rather, be infants in evil, but in thinking be adults. 21 In the law it is written,

"By people of strange tongues
and by the lips of foreigners
I will speak to this people;
yet even then they will not listen to me,"

says the Lord. 22 Tongues, then, are a sign not for believers but for unbelievers, while prophecy is not for unbelievers but for believers. 23 If, therefore, the whole church comes together and all speak in tongues, and outsiders or unbelievers enter, will they not say that you are out of your mind? 24 But if all prophesy, an unbeliever or outsider who enters is reproved by all and called to account by all. 25 After the secrets of the unbeliever's heart are disclosed, that person will bow down before God and worship him, declaring, "God is really among you."

Orderly Worship

26 What should be done then, my friends?*i* When you come together, each one has a hymn, a lesson, a revelation, a tongue, or an interpretation. Let all things be done for building up. 27 If anyone speaks in a tongue, let there be only two or at most three, and each in turn; and let one interpret. 28 But if there is no one to interpret, let them be silent in church and speak to themselves and to God. 29 Let two or three prophets speak, and let the others weigh what is said. 30 If a revelation is made to someone else sitting nearby, let the first person be silent. 31 For you can all prophesy one by one, so that all may learn and all be encouraged. 32 And the spirits of prophets are subject to the prophets, 33 for God is a God not of disorder but of peace.

(As in all the churches of the saints, 34 women should be silent in the churches. For they are not permitted to speak, but should be subordinate, as the law also says. 35 If there is anything they desire to know, let them ask their husbands at home. For it is shameful for a woman to speak in church.*j* 36 Or did the word of God originate with you? Or are you the only ones it has reached?)

37 Anyone who claims to be a prophet, or to have spiritual powers, must acknowledge that what I am writing to you is a command of the

did you KNOW?

What's Going On?

In 1 Cor 14.34, Paul says women should be silent in church. Yet, in 11.5, he implies that women can pray and prophesy in church, and throughout his life, he supported and worked closely with many different women (see "Lydia and Priscilla," Acts 16.14–15; 18.1–26 and "Phoebe and Junia," Rom 16.1–16).

What explains Paul's turnaround? It appears that 1 Cor 14.34–36, which is set in parentheses, was added to Paul's original letter by a later writer. Perhaps someone copying Paul's letters needed to show that Christianity was not a movement that would disrupt the social order by allowing women to speak in public.

Like Paul, the Catholic church today values women's participation in worship. Women are cantors, musicians, lectors, and eucharistic ministers. But like the later editor of 1 Corinthians, chapter 14, the church insists on a certain order in worship. Only those who are ordained can read the Gospel, preach, and say the words of consecration.

▶ 1 Cor 14.34–36

Lord. 38 Anyone who does not recognize this is not to be recognized. 39 So, my friends,*k* be eager to prophesy, and do not forbid speaking in tongues; 40 but all things should be done decently and in order.

The Resurrection of Christ
(Cp Mk 16.9–20)

Now I would remind you, brothers and sisters,*i* of the good news*l* that I proclaimed to you, which you in turn received, in which also you stand, 2 through which also you are being saved, if you hold firmly to the message that I proclaimed to you—unless you have come to believe in vain.

3 For I handed on to you as of first importance what I in turn had received: that Christ died for our sins in accordance with the scriptures, 4 and

---

i Gk brothers   *j* Other ancient authorities put verses 34-35 after verse 40   *k* Gk my brothers   *l* Or gospel

that he was buried, and that he was raised on the third day in accordance with the scriptures, 5 and that he appeared to Ce'phas, then to the twelve. 6 Then he appeared to more than five hundred brothers and sisters[m] at one time, most of whom are still alive, though some have died.[n] 7 Then he appeared to James, then to all the apostles. 8 Last of all, as to one untimely born, he appeared also to me. 9 For I am the least of the apostles, unfit to be called an apostle, because I persecuted the church of God. 10 But by the grace of God I am what I am, and his grace toward me has not been in vain. On the contrary, I worked harder than any of them—though it was not I, but the grace of God that is with me. 11 Whether then it was I or they, so we proclaim and so you have come to believe.

The Resurrection of the Dead
(Cp 1 Thess 4.13–18)

12 Now if Christ is proclaimed as raised from the dead, how can some of you say there is no resurrection of the dead? 13 If there is no resurrection of the dead, then Christ has not been raised;

---

[m] Gk brothers   [n] Gk fallen asleep

THE FIRST CREED AND A CONTEMPORARY CREED!

First Corinthians 15.3–11 contains the first creed written in the Scriptures. It expresses the fundamental aspects of the Christian faith and is made up of historic facts and faith statements such as the following. (See also "I Believe! The Apostles' Creed," Acts 4.5–12.)

- **Christ died for our sins, according to the Scriptures (see Isaiah, chapter 53). (fact)**
- **Christ was buried. (fact)**
- **Christ rose on the third day. (faith statement based on the experience of Jesus' disciples)**

All Christian communities can create their own creed, based on the foundations of the Christian faith and their experience of God. Here are some extracts from a credo created by Hispanics during their Third Encuentro Nacional de Pastoral, in 1985:

We believe in the most holy Trinity, **God the Father, Son, and Holy Spirit. We sense [her] powerful work in our people, and we see it as a model to be followed. . . .**

We believe in our identification with Christ, **as the suffering people we are. We believe, . . . as he did, in the dignity of all human beings and in their liberation through love. . . .**

We believe in the Catholic Church, **which is integrated in Christ by means of the communion we, as laity, share with bishops, priests, and men and women religious. . . .**

We have faith in our people **because we know that God, who abides in a special manner and forever among us, has raised it [our people] up. . . .**

We believe in the gift of being a prophetic voice **as something given by God to our people and as a means of promoting the unity and love that are necessary for the building of the Kingdom. . . .**

We believe in Mary, our Mother, **who has taken our Hispanic culture under her protection, and who has accompanied us and will accompany us always in our journey as she works to carry the message of Jesus to the whole world. . . . Amen. (Secretariat for Hispanic Affairs, *Prophetic Voices*, pp. 17–18)**

▶ 1 Cor 15.3–11

14 and if Christ has not been raised, then our proclamation has been in vain and your faith has been in vain. 15 We are even found to be misrepresenting God, because we testified of God that he raised Christ—whom he did not raise if it is true that the dead are not raised. 16 For if the dead are not raised, then Christ has not been raised. 17 If Christ has not been raised, your faith is futile and you are still in your sins. 18 Then those also who have died*o* in Christ have perished. 19 If for this life only we have hoped in Christ, we are of all people most to be pitied.

20 But in fact Christ has been raised from the dead, the first fruits of those who have died.*o* 21 For since death came through a human being, the resurrection of the dead has also come through a human being; 22 for as all die in Adam, so all will be made alive in Christ. 23 But each in his own order: Christ the first fruits, then at his coming those who belong to Christ. 24 Then comes the end,*p* when he hands over the kingdom to God the Father, after he has destroyed every ruler and every authority and power. 25 For he must reign until he has put all his enemies under his feet. 26 The last enemy to be destroyed is death. 27 For "God*q* has put all things in subjection under his feet." But when it says, "All things are put in subjection," it is plain that this does not include the one who put all things in subjection under him. 28 When all things are subjected to him, then the Son himself will also be subjected to the one who put all things in subjection under him, so that God may be all in all.

29 Otherwise, what will those people do who receive baptism on behalf of the dead? If the dead are not raised at all, why are people baptized on their behalf?

30 And why are we putting ourselves in danger every hour? 31 I die every day! That is as certain, brothers and sisters,*r* as my boasting of you—a boast that I make in Christ Jesus our Lord. 32 If with merely human hopes I fought with wild animals at Eph·e·sus, what would I have gained by it? If the dead are not raised,

"Let us eat and drink,
    for tomorrow we die."

33 Do not be deceived:

"Bad company ruins good morals."

34 Come to a sober and right mind, and sin no more; for some people have no knowledge of God. I say this to your shame.

The Resurrection Body

35 But someone will ask, "How are the dead raised? With what kind of body do they come?" 36 Fool! What you sow does not come to life unless it dies. 37 And as for what you sow, you do not sow the body that is to be, but a bare seed, perhaps of wheat or of some other grain. 38 But God gives it a body as he has chosen, and to each kind of seed its own body. 39 Not all flesh is alike, but there is one flesh for human beings, another for animals, another for birds, and another for fish. 40 There are both heavenly bodies and earthly bodies, but the glory of the heavenly is one thing, and that of the earthly is another. 41 There is one glory of the sun, and another glory of the moon, and another glory of the stars; indeed, star differs from star in glory.

42 So it is with the resurrection of the dead. What is sown is perishable, what is raised is imperishable. 43 It is sown in dishonor, it is raised in glory. It is sown in weakness, it is raised in power. 44 It is sown a physical body, it is raised a spiritual body. If there is a physical body, there is also a spiritual body. 45 Thus it is written, "The first man, Adam, became a living being"; the last Adam became a life-giving spirit. 46 But it is not the spiritual that is first, but the physical, and then the spiritual. 47 The first man was from the earth, a man of dust; the second man is*s* from heaven. 48 As was the man of dust, so are those who are of the dust; and as is the man of heaven, so are those who are of heaven. 49 Just as we have borne the image of the man of dust, we will*t* also bear the image of the man of heaven.

50 What I am saying, brothers and sisters,*r* is this: flesh and blood cannot inherit the kingdom of God, nor does the perishable inherit the imperishable. 51 Listen, I will tell you a mystery! We will not all die,*u* but we will all be changed, 52 in a moment, in the twinkling of an eye, at the last trumpet. For the trumpet will sound, and the dead will be raised imperishable, and we will be changed. 53 For this perishable body must put on imperishability, and this mortal body must put on immortality. 54 When this perishable body puts on imperishability, and this mortal body puts on immortality, then the saying that is written will be fulfilled:

"Death has been swallowed up in victory."
55 "Where, O death, is your victory?
        Where, O death, is your sting?"

56 The sting of death is sin, and the power of sin is the law. 57 But thanks be to God, who gives us the victory through our Lord Jesus Christ.

58 Therefore, my beloved,*v* be steadfast, immovable, always excelling in the work of the Lord,

---

o Gk *fallen asleep*   *p* Or *Then come the rest*   *q* Gk *he*
r Gk *brothers*   *s* Other ancient authorities add *the Lord*
t Other ancient authorities read *let us*   *u* Gk *fall asleep*
v Gk *beloved brothers*

Life After Death

During childhood, reality and fantasy are often confused. We might believe in Santa Claus, the Easter Bunny, the Tooth Fairy, even a monster living under our bed. We may imagine heaven as having pearly gates, golden streets, and angels flying with harps. As we grow older, some of us exchange this fantastic image for a more mature belief in the mystery of the Resurrection. But many adult Christians simply do not know what to believe about life after death.

Christians from Corinth also had problems with the concept of human resurrection. Their philosophical system did not allow them to image a body that returned to life after death. For them, the body and soul were separate. The soul was immortal and continued living after the body died.

In contrast, the Hebrews believed that the whole person, both body and soul, died. Their experience of God coming to life as a human being led them to believe in a resurrected body. Several prophets had spoken directly of a bodily resurrection. (See "Resurrection," Dan 12.1–3.)

Believing in the Resurrection is essential in the Christian faith. The Gospel writers describe the risen Jesus as different from the Jesus who died on the cross; the disciples did not recognize him at first sight, they knew him only through their faith.

Paul gets right to the point: our faith depends on the fact that Christ was raised from death. He explains the resurrected body as different from our earthly body—a glorious, imperishable, and immortal body. We will not be disembodied spirits or souls when we have eternal life in communion with God. And we will be made alive in Christ, whether our mind can comprehend that idea or not. Our end is not death, but eternal life with Christ!

▶ 1 Cor 15.35–58

---

because you know that in the Lord your labor is not in vain.

The Collection for the Saints

Now concerning the collection for the saints: you should follow the directions I gave to the churches of Galatia. 2 On the first day of every week, each of you is to put aside and save whatever extra you earn, so that collections need not be taken when I come. 3 And when I arrive, I will send any whom you approve with letters to take your gift to Jerusalem. 4 If it seems advisable that I should go also, they will accompany me.

Plans for Travel
(Cp Acts 19.21)

5 I will visit you after passing through Mac·e·dō′ni·a—for I intend to pass through Mac·e·dō′ni·a— 6 and perhaps I will stay with you or even spend the winter, so that you may send me on my way, wherever I go. 7 I do not want to see you now just in passing, for I hope to spend some time with you, if the Lord permits. 8 But I will stay in Eph′e·sus until Pentecost, 9 for a wide door for effective work has opened to me, and there are many adversaries.

10 If Timothy comes, see that he has nothing to fear among you, for he is doing the work of the Lord just as I am; 11 therefore let no one despise him. Send him on his way in peace, so that he may come to me; for I am expecting him with the brothers.

12 Now concerning our brother A·pol′los, I strongly urged him to visit you with the other brothers, but he was not at all willing^w to come now. He will come when he has the opportunity.

Final Messages and Greetings

13 Keep alert, stand firm in your faith, be courageous, be strong. 14 Let all that you do be done in love.

15 Now, brothers and sisters,^{x} you know that members of the household of Steph′a·nas were the first converts in A·chā′i·a, and they have devoted themselves to the service of the saints; 16 I urge you to put yourselves at the service of such people, and of everyone who works and toils with them. 17 I rejoice at the coming of Steph′a·nas and For·tu·nā′tus and A·chā′i·cus, because they have made up for your absence; 18 for they refreshed my spirit as well as yours. So give recognition to such persons.

---

w Or *it was not at all God's will for him*   *x* Gk *brothers*

19 The churches of Asia send greetings. A·qui'la and Pris'ca, together with the church in their house, greet you warmly in the Lord. 20 All the brothers and sisters*y* send greetings. Greet one another with a holy kiss.

21 I, Paul, write this greeting with my own hand. 22 Let anyone be accursed who has no love for the Lord. Our Lord, come!*z* 23 The grace of the Lord Jesus be with you. 24 My love be with all of you in Christ Jesus.*a*

---

y Gk *brothers*   *z* Gk *Marana tha.* These Aramaic words can also be read *Maran atha,* meaning *Our Lord has come*   *a* Other ancient authorities add *Amen*

Corinthians

Unfortunately, you probably know all too well what it's like to be criticized. It's no fun to be under attack. Our instinct is to get defensive and strike back. But in his Second Letter to the Corinthians, Paul shows us how God helps us rise above our instincts. Paul responds to personal attacks with directness and honesty. He demonstrates how to witness to Jesus—even when we are in the middle of conflict.

At a Glance

- **1.1–11.** greetings
- **1.12—7.16.** a description of how Paul and the Corinthians resolve their conflict
- **Chapters 8–9.** a discussion of a collection for the church at Jerusalem
- **10.1—13.10.** a defense of Paul's ministry as an Apostle
- **13.11–13.** a final greeting and a blessing

In-depth

The relationship between Paul and the Corinthians deteriorated after he wrote 1 Corinthians. Apparently, some other traveling missionaries came to Corinth and undermined Paul's credibility. They attacked him as a person (2 Cor 10.10), implied that he was mentally imbalanced (5.13), and criticized him as a speaker (10.10). They even suggested that Paul was not trustworthy about money (8.20–21).

As part of these attacks, some people claimed that Paul couldn't make up his mind about returning to visit Corinth; they said he kept changing between yes and no. In defending himself, Paul skillfully changes the focus and says that in Jesus, we always find a yes. For in Jesus, every one of God's promises is a yes (1.19–20). And whereas Paul's opponents make boastful claims for themselves, Paul realizes that God's grace is all he needs. In fact, he says, "I will boast . . . of my weaknesses, so that the power of Christ may dwell in me" (12.9).

With breathtaking insight, Paul puts all the conflict into perspective. "From now on, . . . we regard no one from a human point of view. . . . So if anyone is in Christ, there is a new creation" (5.16–17). Knowing Christ changes everything! Through Christ, we are reconciled with God—meaning, God overcomes the sin and weakness that separate us from God's love. We should also become ambassadors for Christ, reconciling with one another and announcing to all that they are reconciled with God.

Scholars see evidence that several original letters were combined to form 2 Corinthians. For example, Paul's concerns seem to be resolved in chapter 7, but then, chapters 10–13 pick up those concerns again. And chapters 8 and 9 each describe a collection being taken up for the Christians in Jerusalem without making any connection between the two collections. Despite its uneven flow, the letter reveals a very personal look into Paul's life and ministry.

Quick Facts

Author
Paul

Date Written
around A.D. 57

Audience
the mainly Gentile (non-Jewish) church in Corinth

2 Corinthians

Salutation

Paul, an apostle of Christ Jesus by the will of God, and Timothy our brother,

To the church of God that is in Corinth, including all the saints throughout A·chā′i·a:

2 Grace to you and peace from God our Father and the Lord Jesus Christ.

Paul's Thanksgiving after Affliction

3 Blessed be the God and Father of our Lord Jesus Christ, the Father of mercies and the God of all consolation, 4 who consoles us in all our affliction, so that we may be able to console those who are in any affliction with the consolation with which we ourselves are consoled by God. 5 For just as the sufferings of Christ are abundant for us, so also our consolation is abundant through Christ. 6 If we are being afflicted, it is for your consolation and salvation; if we are being consoled, it is for your consolation, which you experience when you patiently endure the same sufferings that we are also suffering. 7 Our hope for you is unshaken; for we know that as you share in our sufferings, so also you share in our consolation.

8 We do not want you to be unaware, brothers and sisters,*a* of the affliction we experienced in Asia; for we were so utterly, unbearably crushed that we despaired of life itself. 9 Indeed, we felt that we had received the sentence of death so that we would rely not on ourselves but on God who

raises the dead. 10 He who rescued us from so deadly a peril will continue to rescue us; on him we have set our hope that he will rescue us again, 11 as you also join in helping us by your prayers, so that many will give thanks on our*b* behalf for the blessing granted us through the prayers of many.

The Postponement of Paul's Visit

12 Indeed, this is our boast, the testimony of our conscience: we have behaved in the world with frankness*c* and godly sincerity, not by earthly wisdom but by the grace of God—and all the more toward you. 13 For we write you nothing other than what you can read and also understand; I hope you will understand until the end— 14 as you have already understood us in part—that on the day of the Lord Jesus we are your boast even as you are our boast.

15 Since I was sure of this, I wanted to come to you first, so that you might have a double favor;*d* 16 I wanted to visit you on my way to Mac·e·dō′ni·a, and to come back to you from Mac·e·dō′ni·a and have you send me on to Judea. 17 Was I vacillating when I wanted to do this? Do I make my plans according to ordinary human standards,*e* ready to say "Yes, yes" and "No, no" at the same time? 18 As surely as God is faithful, our word to you has not

---

a Gk *brothers*   *b* Other ancient authorities read *your*
c Other ancient authorities read *holiness*   *d* Other ancient
authorities read *pleasure*   *e* Gk *according to the flesh*

Asian American

Yes, Yes, May We Not Fail

This prayer from Hong Kong could have been written as a response to Paul's assurance that he is not wavering in his commitment to the Corinthians (2 Cor 1.17–22). By staying faithful to our commitment to be Jesus' disciples, we imitate Christ, who is the yes of all God's promises.

Pray for us, brothers and sisters in Christ, that we may not fail in the oil of comfort, the wine of justice, the involvement of the patient mule, and the generosity which, having given, promises more, until recovery is complete. (From Maren C. Tirabassi and Kathy Wonson Eddy, editors, Gifts of Many Cultures, p. 37)

▶ 2 Cor 1.17–22

been "Yes and No." ¹⁹ For the Son of God, Jesus Christ, whom we proclaimed among you, Sil•vā′-

nus and Timothy and I, was not "Yes and No"; but in him it is always "Yes." ²⁰ For in him every one of God's promises is a "Yes." For this reason it is through him that we say the "Amen," to the glory of God. ²¹ But it is God who establishes us with you in Christ and has anointed us, ²² by putting his seal on us and giving us his Spirit in our hearts as a first installment.

23 But I call on God as witness against me: it was to spare you that I did not come again to Corinth. ²⁴ I do not mean to imply that we lord it over your faith; rather, we are workers with you for your joy, because you stand firm in the faith. ¹ So I made up my mind not to make you another painful visit. ² For if I cause you pain, who is there to make me glad but the one whom I have pained? ³ And I wrote as I did, so that when I came, I might not suffer pain from those who should have made me rejoice; for I am confident about all of you, that my joy would be the joy of all of you. ⁴ For I wrote you out of much distress and anguish of heart and with many tears, not to cause you pain, but to let you know the abundant love that I have for you.

Forgiveness for the Offender

5 But if anyone has caused pain, he has caused it not to me, but to some extent—not to exaggerate it—to all of you. ⁶ This punishment by the majority is enough for such a person; ⁷ so now instead you should forgive and console him, so that he may not be overwhelmed by excessive sorrow. ⁸ So I

The Presence of God

The POWs (prisoners of war) are cold, and it takes every bit of their energy to stay warm. The conversation this night centers on the discouragement the men feel and their frustration about being abandoned and being left alone. Captain Valdez listens to the conversation for a long time, and then he interrupts: "We are not alone, and we have not been abandoned. God has been with us every minute through this ordeal. I pray every morning and every night in thanksgiving for that presence. It is on the worst days that I most strongly feel the presence of God."

When we are suffering, we often feel alone and abandoned—sometimes even by God. But Paul indicates that God is present, consoling us in our affliction. It is sometimes difficult to feel this presence because we are caught up in the pain and hurt of the situation, as are the POWs in this story. How do you experience God's presence or absence during times of pain and suffering?

Paul also says that the support of the Christian community can help us get through our pain. The comfort of friends and relatives during difficult times can help us recognize the action of God. Is there someone you can comfort who is going through a hard time?

▶ 2 Cor 1.3–11

urge you to reaffirm your love for him. 9 I wrote for this reason: to test you and to know whether you are obedient in everything. 10 Anyone whom you forgive, I also forgive. What I have forgiven, if I have forgiven anything, has been for your sake in the presence of Christ. 11 And we do this so that we may not be outwitted by Satan; for we are not ignorant of his designs.

Paul's Anxiety in Troas

12 When I came to Trō′as to proclaim the good news of Christ, a door was opened for me in the Lord; 13 but my mind could not rest because I did not find my brother Titus there. So I said farewell to them and went on to Mac•e•dō′ni•a.

14 But thanks be to God, who in Christ always leads us in triumphal procession, and through us spreads in every place the fragrance that comes from knowing him. 15 For we are the aroma of Christ to God among those who are being saved and among those who are perishing; 16 to the one a fragrance from death to death, to the other a fragrance from life to life. Who is sufficient for these things? 17 For we are not peddlers of God's word like so many;f but in Christ we speak as persons of sincerity, as persons sent from God and standing in his presence.

Ministers of the New Covenant
(Cp Jer 31.31–34)

Are we beginning to commend ourselves again? Surely we do not need, as some do, letters of recommendation to you or from you, do we? 2 You yourselves are our letter, written on ourg hearts, to be known and read by all; 3 and you show that you are a letter of Christ, prepared by us, written not with ink but with the Spirit of the living God, not on tablets of stone but on tablets of human hearts.

4 Such is the confidence that we have through Christ toward God. 5 Not that we are competent of ourselves to claim anything as coming from us; our competence is from God, 6 who has made us competent to be ministers of a new covenant, not of letter but of spirit; for the letter kills, but the Spirit gives life.

7 Now if the ministry of death, chiseled in letters on stone tablets,h came in glory so that the people of Israel could not gaze at Moses' face because of the glory of his face, a glory now set aside, 8 how much more will the ministry of the Spirit come in glory? 9 For if there was glory in the ministry of condemnation, much more does the ministry of justification abound in glory! 10 Indeed, what once had glory has lost its glory because of the greater glory; 11 for if what was set aside came through glory, much more has the permanent come in glory!

12 Since, then, we have such a hope, we act with great boldness, 13 not like Moses, who put a veil over his face to keep the people of Israel from gazing at the end of the glory thati was being set aside. 14 But their minds were hardened. Indeed, to this very day, when they hear the reading of the old covenant, that same veil is still there, since only in Christ is it set aside. 15 Indeed, to this very day whenever Moses is read, a veil lies over their

f Other ancient authorities read *like the others*   g Other ancient authorities read *your*   h Gk *on stones*   i Gk *of what*

Ministers of the New Covenant

LIVE IT!

In the face of accusations against himself and his ministry, and of insecurity experienced by the community at Corinth, Paul presents himself as a minister of the New Covenant. Recalling God's words, "I will put my law within them, and I will write it on their hearts" (Jer 31.33), Paul emphasizes that Christ enables us to be ministers of this New Covenant, not of the old written Law, "for the letter [of the Law] kills, but the Spirit gives life" (2 Cor 3.6). Because Paul's ministry comes from the Spirit, it is the only letter of recommendation he needs.

The same is true for us. With the law of the New Covenant written on our heart, we give witness to it in our lifestyle. In promoting reconciliation, fostering peace and hope, and passing Christ to others, we are a living letter of recommendation for the Gospel, to be known and read by all people.

Think of the great honor of having been called by God to be a minister of the New Covenant. How are you doing your job? How can you do it better?

▶ 2 Cor 3.1–11

Christin Us

It is sometimes tempting to take ourselves a bit too seriously, to feel too self-important. When given a particular responsibility at school, home, or church, we may begin to act as though *we* are what is important, rather than the task.

The same is true when we accept our calling as a disciple of Christ. Feelings of self-righteousness or pride can creep in, leading to what friends might call a holier-than-thou attitude. Paul reminds us that "we do not proclaim ourselves; we proclaim Jesus Christ as Lord" (2 Cor 4.5). We are simply ordinary clay jars that hold a great treasure to be shared with all. What a wonderful and awesome responsibility we have been given: to share, with our life and our words, what Jesus has done in us, giving him the glory and not seeking it for ourselves.

▸ 2 Cor 4.5–10

minds; 16 but when one turns to the Lord, the veil is removed. 17 Now the Lord is the Spirit, and where the Spirit of the Lord is, there is freedom. 18 And all of us, with unveiled faces, seeing the glory of the Lord as though reflected in a mirror, are being transformed into the same image from one degree of glory to another; for this comes from the Lord, the Spirit.

Treasure in Clay Jars

Therefore, since it is by God's mercy that we are engaged in this ministry, we do not lose heart. 2 We have renounced the shameful things that one hides; we refuse to practice cunning or to falsify God's word; but by the open statement of the truth we commend ourselves to the conscience of everyone in the sight of God. 3 And even if our gospel is veiled, it is veiled to those who are perishing. 4 In their case the god of this world has blinded the minds of the unbelievers, to keep them from seeing the light of the gospel of the glory of Christ, who is the image of God. 5 For we do not proclaim ourselves; we proclaim Jesus Christ as Lord and ourselves as your slaves for Jesus' sake. 6 For it is the God who said, "Let light shine out of darkness," who has shone in our hearts to give the light of the knowledge of the glory of God in the face of Jesus Christ.

7 But we have this treasure in clay jars, so that it may be made clear that this extraordinary power belongs to God and does not come from us. 8 We are afflicted in every way, but not crushed; perplexed, but not driven to despair; 9 persecuted, but not forsaken; struck down, but not destroyed; 10 always carrying in the body the death of Jesus, so that the life of Jesus may also be made visible in our bodies. 11 For while we live, we are always being given up to death for Jesus' sake, so that the

life of Jesus may be made visible in our mortal flesh. 12 So death is at work in us, but life in you.

13 But just as we have the same spirit of faith that is in accordance with scripture—"I believed, and so I spoke"—we also believe, and so we speak, 14 because we know that the one who raised the Lord Jesus will raise us also with Jesus, and will bring us with you into his presence. 15 Yes, everything is for your sake, so that grace, as it extends to

Hopeless and Hurting

Lord, I am losing hope. It all seemed to be going okay. Things were flowing along, and life seemed good. Then, it all fell apart. I am not even sure why it happened, it just did, and then despair and hopelessness followed. I don't feel like I used to anymore. I don't have the energy or the desire to do much. I feel kind of numb.

I am trying to find a way out of this mess. Saint Paul says we should not lose heart, but what if I already have? I'm having a hard time seeing beyond today's gloom. Talk to me, God, and help me to climb out of the hole I am in. Rekindle in me a passion for life and for my dreams. Bring someone into my life that I can lean on for a little while until I regain my strength and rediscover my path, the path that leads to hope. Amen.

▸ 2 Cor 4.16–18

2
C
O
R

more and more people, may increase thanksgiving, to the glory of God.

Living by Faith

16 So we do not lose heart. Even though our outer nature is wasting away, our inner nature is being renewed day by day. 17 For this slight momentary affliction is preparing us for an eternal weight of glory beyond all measure, 18 because we look not at what can be seen but at what cannot be seen; for what can be seen is temporary, but what cannot be seen is eternal.

PRAY IT

It's What's Inside That Counts

Television, magazines, and advertising show the ideal person as skinny, well developed, muscular, clear complexioned, tall, and with perfect features. Very few people fit that image. Many of those who don't fit that image feel insecure and inadequate. Some people try desperately to measure up to that standard with crash diets, workouts at fitness centers, weight training, steroids, or plastic surgery. Some people even end up with eating disorders like bulimia and anorexia.

In 2 Cor 5.1–5, Paul reminds us that our earthly body is a temporary dwelling. It is important for us to take care of this earthly "tent" with a healthy diet and regular exercise. But our desire for our heavenly dwelling should cause us to focus on our inner appearance more than our outer appearance.

In your prayer, reflect on the following questions:

■ Are you satisfied with your physical appearance? Why or why not?
■ Do you spend as much time working on your inner appearance—by developing virtues like compassion, generosity, mercy, and patience—as you do on your outer appearance?

Write a prayer asking God for the grace (gift) to feel secure in your outward appearance. Listen for God's response.

▶ 2 Cor 5.1–5

For we know that if the earthly tent we live in is destroyed, we have a building from God, a house not made with hands, eternal in the heavens. 2 For in this tent we groan, longing to be clothed with our heavenly dwelling— 3 if indeed, when we have taken it off [j] we will not be found naked. 4 For while we are still in this tent, we groan under our burden, because we wish not to be unclothed but to be further clothed, so that what is mortal may be swallowed up by life. 5 He who has prepared us for this very thing is God, who has given us the Spirit as a guarantee.

6 So we are always confident; even though we know that while we are at home in the body we are away from the Lord— 7 for we walk by faith, not by sight. 8 Yes, we do have confidence, and we would rather be away from the body and at home with the Lord. 9 So whether we are at home or away, we make it our aim to please him. 10 For all of us must appear before the judgment seat of Christ, so that each may receive recompense for what has been done in the body, whether good or evil.

The Ministry of Reconciliation

11 Therefore, knowing the fear of the Lord, we try to persuade others; but we ourselves are well known to God, and I hope that we are also well known to your consciences. 12 We are not commending ourselves to you again, but giving you an opportunity to boast about us, so that you may be able to answer those who boast in outward appearance and not in the heart. 13 For if we are beside ourselves, it is for God; if we are in our right mind, it is for you. 14 For the love of Christ urges us on, because we are convinced that one has died for all; therefore all have died. 15 And he died for all, so that those who live might live no longer for themselves, but for him who died and was raised for them.

16 From now on, therefore, we regard no one from a human point of view; [k] even though we once knew Christ from a human point of view, [k] we know him no longer in that way. 17 So if anyone is in Christ, there is a new creation: everything old has passed away; see, everything has become new! 18 All this is from God, who reconciled us to himself through Christ, and has given us the ministry of reconciliation; 19 that is, in Christ God was reconciling the world to himself, [l] not counting their trespasses against them, and entrusting the message of reconciliation to us. 20 So we are

---

j Other ancient authorities read *put it on*   k Gk *according to the flesh*   l Or *God was in Christ reconciling the world to himself*

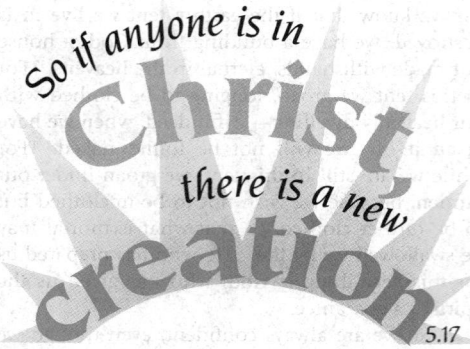

So if anyone is in **Christ,** there is a new **creation.**

5.17

ambassadors for Christ, since God is making his appeal through us; we entreat you on behalf of Christ, be reconciled to God. 21 For our sake he made him to be sin who knew no sin, so that in him we might become the righteousness of God.

As we work together with him,*m* we urge you also not to accept the grace of God in vain. 2 For he says,

"At an acceptable time I have listened to you,
    and on a day of salvation I have
        helped you."

See, now is the acceptable time; see, now is the day of salvation! 3 We are putting no obstacle in anyone's way, so that no fault may be found with our ministry, 4 but as servants of God we have commended ourselves in every way: through great endurance, in afflictions, hardships, calamities, 5 beatings, imprisonments, riots, labors, sleepless

nights, hunger; 6 by purity, knowledge, patience, kindness, holiness of spirit, genuine love, 7 truthful speech, and the power of God; with the weapons of righteousness for the right hand and for the left; 8 in honor and dishonor, in ill repute and good repute. We are treated as impostors, and yet are true; 9 as unknown, and yet are well known; as dying, and see—we are alive; as punished, and yet not killed; 10 as sorrowful, yet always rejoicing; as poor, yet making many rich; as having nothing, and yet possessing everything.

11 We have spoken frankly to you Corinthians; our heart is wide open to you. 12 There is no restriction in our affections, but only in yours. 13 In return—I speak as to children—open wide your hearts also.

The Temple of the Living God

14 Do not be mismatched with unbelievers. For what partnership is there between righteousness and lawlessness? Or what fellowship is there between light and darkness? 15 What agreement does Christ have with Bē'li•ar? Or what does a believer share with an unbeliever? 16 What agreement has the temple of God with idols? For we*n* are the temple of the living God; as God said,

"I will live in them and walk among them,
    and I will be their God,
    and they shall be my people.
17   Therefore come out from them,

---

m Gk *As we work together*   *n* Other ancient authorities read *you*

Ambassadors for Christ

The title ambassador is usually used by people who are authorized to represent their country while living as a resident in a foreign nation. For example, the U.S. ambassador to Mexico is an official representative of the United States who lives in Mexico and speaks for the U.S. government in Mexico.

Paul tells us that we are reconciled—that is, united—with God through Christ, and that God has now entrusted us with the ministry of helping others to be reconciled through Christ. Imagine that; we are called ambassadors for Christ! Of all the ways God could be made known in the world, God chooses to use us. We are "authorized representatives." We are God's messengers.

That might sound a bit intimidating! We might naturally wonder how we, broken and imperfect people, are supposed to represent God, who is completely holy and just. The reality is that God wants to use us, flaws and all. God does not need perfect people—just willing people! Spend some time in prayer and share with God your thoughts, feelings, and fears about being invited to take on this great role of ambassador for Christ.

▶ 2 Cor 5.17–21

AFRICAN AMERICAN
An "Anyway" God

We serve an "anyway" God. Impediments, hurdles, and obstacles are part of our inheritance, yet we excel anyway. Some of us were kidnapped from Africa, enslaved and shackled, stripped of our culture, robbed of our native language, and torn from our family, yet today, we thrive anyway.

Surely, the Lord was in the midst of the African Americans' past, ushering them on to a better day. The evidence that the Lord walked with them through horrific conditions is simply too great to deny. Yet, as a people, they can identify with Paul's words in 2 Cor 6.1–10—their struggles have only made them stronger.

Even today, life for most of us is no cakewalk, but our ability to walk at all comes from God, who conquers all. Can you recognize God's grace and mercy and celebrate the presence of God in your good and bad times?

Dear God, no matter how high the odds are stacked against me, I can overcome them with your grace and mercy, and survive. Amen.

▶ 2 Cor 6.1–10

and be separate from them, says the Lord,
and touch nothing unclean;
then I will welcome you,
18 and I will be your father,
and you shall be my sons and daughters,
says the Lord Almighty."
Since we have these promises, beloved, let us cleanse ourselves from every defilement of body and of spirit, making holiness perfect in the fear of God.

Paul's Joy at the Church's Repentance

2 Make room in your hearts⁰ for us; we have wronged no one, we have corrupted no one, we have taken advantage of no one. 3 I do not say this to condemn you, for I said before that you are in our hearts, to die together and to live together. 4 I often boast about you; I have great pride in you; I am filled with consolation; I am overjoyed in all our affliction.

5 For even when we came into Mac•e•do′ni•a, our bodies had no rest, but we were afflicted in every way—disputes without and fears within. 6 But God, who consoles the downcast, consoled us by the arrival of Titus, 7 and not only by his coming, but also by the consolation with which he was consoled about you, as he told us of your longing, your mourning, your zeal for me, so that I rejoiced still more. 8 For even if I made you sorry with my letter, I do not regret it (though I did regret it, for I see that I grieved you with that letter, though only briefly). 9 Now I rejoice, not because you were

---
⁰ Gk lacks *in your hearts*

Shine Like a Star

LIVE IT!

Second Corinthians 6.14 makes a sudden transition; 6.14—7.1 may even be a fragment from another letter. We are not sure what kind of behavior or problem Paul is talking about here. But it does seem clear that Paul is cautioning the Corinthians against being too closely influenced by non-Christians—unbelievers. Paul doesn't want the Corinthians to return to sinful behaviors.

Christians in the United States are also surrounded by many unhealthy and unholy choices. Our words and behaviors should show that "we are the temple of the living God" (6.16). We must be careful of friendships and media influences that might tempt us to start thinking that wrong is right. This doesn't mean we should be arrogant and separate ourselves from others. Remember that Jesus sometimes hung around with sinners. But he didn't share in their sins. He was a light for them.

As Paul says in Phil 2.15, we are "children of God" in a "perverse generation," where we shine "like stars in the world."

▶ 2 Cor 6.14–18

2 COR

grieved, but because your grief led to repentance;
for you felt a godly grief, so that you were not
harmed in any way by us. 10 For godly grief produces a repentance that leads to salvation and
brings no regret, but worldly grief produces death.
11 For see what earnestness this godly grief has produced in you, what eagerness to clear yourselves,
what indignation, what alarm, what longing, what
zeal, what punishment! At every point you have
proved yourselves guiltless in the matter. 12 So although I wrote to you, it was not on account of
the one who did the wrong, nor on account of the
one who was wronged, but in order that your zeal
for us might be made known to you before God.
13 In this we find comfort.
In addition to our own consolation, we rejoiced
still more at the joy of Titus, because his mind has
been set at rest by all of you. 14 For if I have been
somewhat boastful about you to him, I was not
disgraced; but just as everything we said to you
was true, so our boasting to Titus has proved true
as well. 15 And his heart goes out all the more to
you, as he remembers the obedience of all of you,
and how you welcomed him with fear and trembling. 16 I rejoice, because I have complete confidence in you.

Encouragement to Be Generous

8 We want you to know, brothers and sisters,[p] about
the grace of God that has been granted to the
churches of Mac•e•dō'ni•a; 2 for during a severe ordeal of affliction, their abundant joy and their extreme poverty have overflowed in a wealth of
generosity on their part. 3 For, as I can testify, they
voluntarily gave according to their means, and
even beyond their means, 4 begging us earnestly
for the privilege[q] of sharing in this ministry to the
saints— 5 and this, not merely as we expected; they
gave themselves first to the Lord and, by the will of
God, to us, 6 so that we might urge Titus that, as he
had already made a beginning, so he should also
complete this generous undertaking[r] among you.
7 Now as you excel in everything—in faith, in
speech, in knowledge, in utmost eagerness, and in
our love for you[s]—so we want you to excel also
in this generous undertaking.[r]
8 I do not say this as a command, but I am
testing the genuineness of your love against the
earnestness of others. 9 For you know the generous
act[t] of our Lord Jesus Christ, that though he was
rich, yet for your sakes he became poor, so that by
his poverty you might become rich. 10 And in this
matter I am giving my advice: it is appropriate for
you who began last year not only to do something
but even to desire to do something— 11 now finish
doing it, so that your eagerness may be matched
by completing it according to your means. 12 For if
the eagerness is there, the gift is acceptable according to what one has—not according to what one
does not have. 13 I do not mean that there should
be relief for others and pressure on you, but it is a
question of a fair balance between 14 your present
abundance and their need, so that their abundance
may be for your need, in order that there may be a
fair balance. 15 As it is written,

HISPANIC

¡Los cristianos compartimos nuestro dinero por solidaridad!

CHRISTIANS SHARE THEIR MONEY OUT OF SOLIDARITY!

In chapters 8–9 of 2 Corinthians, Paul encourages the Corinthians to be generous in a collection for poor Christians in Jerusalem. Such voluntary generosity provides much-needed financial support. In addition, particularly when it is a sacrifice, it shows that the givers are following the Holy Spirit's guidance. And it is also a sign of solidarity and unity among different church communities. Paul explains that this type of generosity follows the example of Jesus, who, "though he was rich, yet for your sakes . . . became poor, so that by his poverty you might become rich" (8.9).

- **How are you generous with your money? What sacrifice can you make this week for the sake of others who are as poor as or poorer than you?**
- **Ask the Holy Spirit for the gift of generosity, for yourself and for other young Catholics. Pray that a willingness to share the resources God has blessed you with will become a lifelong habit.**

► 2 Corinthians, chapters 8–9

p Gk *brothers* q Gk *grace* r Gk *this grace* s Other ancient authorities read *your love for us* t Gk *the grace*

"The one who had much did not have too
much,
and the one who had little did not have
too little."

Commendation of Titus

16 But thanks be to God who put in the heart of Titus the same eagerness for you that I myself have. 17 For he not only accepted our appeal, but since he is more eager than ever, he is going to you of his own accord. 18 With him we are sending the brother who is famous among all the churches for his proclaiming the good news;*u* 19 and not only that, but he has also been appointed by the churches to travel with us while we are administering this generous undertaking*v* for the glory of the Lord himself*w* and to show our goodwill. 20 We intend that no one should blame us about this generous gift that we are administering, 21 for we intend to do what is right not only in the Lord's sight but also in the sight of others. 22 And with them we are sending our brother whom we have often tested and found eager in many matters, but who is now more eager than ever because of his great confidence in you. 23 As for Titus, he is my partner and co-worker in your service; as for our brothers, they are messengers*x* of the churches, the glory of Christ. 24 Therefore openly before the churches, show them the proof of your love and of our reason for boasting about you.

The Collection for Christians at Jerusalem

Now it is not necessary for me to write you about the ministry to the saints, 2 for I know your eagerness, which is the subject of my boasting about you to the people of Mac·e·dō'ni·a, saying that A·chā'i·a has been ready since last year; and your zeal has stirred up most of them. 3 But I am sending the brothers in order that our boasting about you may not prove to have been empty in this case, so that you may be ready, as I said you would be; 4 otherwise, if some Mac·e·dō'ni·ans come with me and find that you are not ready, we would be humiliated—to say nothing of you—in this undertaking.*y* 5 So I thought it necessary to urge the brothers to go on ahead to you, and arrange in advance for this bountiful gift that you have promised, so that it may be ready as a voluntary gift and not as an extortion.

6 The point is this: the one who sows sparingly will also reap sparingly, and the one who sows bountifully will also reap bountifully. 7 Each of you must give as you have made up your mind, not reluctantly or under compulsion, for God loves a cheerful giver. 8 And God is able to provide you with every blessing in abundance, so that by always having enough of everything, you may share abundantly in every good work. 9 As it is written,

"He scatters abroad, he gives to the poor;
his righteousness*z* endures forever."

10 He who supplies seed to the sower and bread for food will supply and multiply your seed for sowing and increase the harvest of your righteousness.*z* 11 You will be enriched in every way for your great generosity, which will produce thanksgiving to God through us; 12 for the rendering of this ministry not only supplies the needs of the saints but also overflows with many thanksgivings to God. 13 Through the testing of this ministry you glorify God by your obedience to the confession of the gospel of Christ and by the generosity of your sharing with them and with all others, 14 while they long for you and pray for you because of the surpassing grace of God that he has given you. 15 Thanks be to God for his indescribable gift!

Paul Defends His Ministry

I myself, Paul, appeal to you by the meekness and gentleness of Christ—I who am humble when face to face with you, but bold toward you when I am away!— 2 I ask that when I am present I need not show boldness by daring to oppose those who think we are acting according to human standards.*a* 3 Indeed, we live as human beings,*b* but we do not wage war according to human standards;*a* 4 for the weapons of our warfare are not merely human,*c* but they have divine power to destroy strongholds. We destroy arguments 5 and every proud obstacle raised up against the knowledge of God, and we take every thought captive to obey Christ. 6 We are ready to punish every disobedience when your obedience is complete.

7 Look at what is before your eyes. If you are confident that you belong to Christ, remind yourself of this, that just as you belong to Christ, so also do we. 8 Now, even if I boast a little too much of our authority, which the Lord gave for building you up and not for tearing you down, I will not be ashamed of it. 9 I do not want to seem as though I am trying to frighten you with my letters. 10 For they say, "His letters are weighty and strong, but his bodily presence is weak, and his speech contemptible." 11 Let such people understand that what we say by letter when absent, we will also do when present.

---

u Or *the gospel*   *v* Gk *this grace*   *w* Other ancient authorities lack *himself*   *x* Gk *apostles*   *y* Other ancient authorities add *of boasting*   *z* Or *benevolence*   *a* Gk *according to the flesh*   *b* Gk *in the flesh*   *c* Gk *fleshly*

12 We do not dare to classify or compare ourselves with some of those who commend themselves. But when they measure themselves by one another, and compare themselves with one another, they do not show good sense. 13 We, however, will not boast beyond limits, but will keep within the field that God has assigned to us, to reach out even as far as you. 14 For we were not overstepping our limits when we reached you; we were the first to come all the way to you with the good news*d* of Christ. 15 We do not boast beyond limits, that is, in the labors of others; but our hope is that, as your faith increases, our sphere of action among you may be greatly enlarged, 16 so that we may proclaim the good news*d* in lands beyond you, without boasting of work already done in someone else's sphere of action. 17 "Let the one who boasts, boast in the Lord." 18 For it is not those who commend themselves that are approved, but those whom the Lord commends.

Paul and the False Apostles

I wish you would bear with me in a little foolishness. Do bear with me! 2 I feel a divine jealousy for you, for I promised you in marriage to one husband, to present you as a chaste virgin to Christ. 3 But I am afraid that as the serpent deceived Eve by its cunning, your thoughts will be led astray from a sincere and pure*e* devotion to Christ. 4 For if someone comes and proclaims another Jesus than the one we proclaimed, or if you receive a different spirit from the one you received, or a different gospel from the one you accepted, you submit to it readily enough. 5 I think that I am not in the least inferior to these super-apostles. 6 I may be untrained in speech, but not in knowledge; certainly in every way and in all things we have made this evident to you.

7 Did I commit a sin by humbling myself so that you might be exalted, because I proclaimed God's good news*f* to you free of charge? 8 I robbed other churches by accepting support from them in order to serve you. 9 And when I was with you and was in need, I did not burden anyone, for my needs were supplied by the friends*g* who came from Mac·e·dó'ni·a. So I refrained and will continue to refrain from burdening you in any way. 10 As the truth of Christ is in me, this boast of mine will not be silenced in the regions of A·chā'i·a. 11 And why? Because I do not love you? God knows I do! 12 And what I do I will also continue to do, in order to deny an opportunity to those who want an opportunity to be recognized as our equals in what they boast about. 13 For such boasters are false apostles, deceitful workers, disguising themselves as apostles of Christ. 14 And no wonder!

Even Satan disguises himself as an angel of light. 15 So it is not strange if his ministers also disguise themselves as ministers of righteousness. Their end will match their deeds.

Paul's Sufferings as an Apostle

16 I repeat, let no one think that I am a fool; but if you do, then accept me as a fool, so that I too may boast a little. 17 What I am saying in regard to this boastful confidence, I am saying not with the Lord's authority, but as a fool; 18 since many boast according to human standards,*h* I will also boast. 19 For you gladly put up with fools, being wise yourselves! 20 For you put up with it when someone makes slaves of you, or preys upon you, or takes advantage of you, or puts on airs, or gives you a slap in the face. 21 To my shame, I must say, we were too weak for that!

But whatever anyone dares to boast of—I am speaking as a fool—I also dare to boast of that. 22 Are they Hebrews? So am I. Are they Israelites? So am I. Are they descendants of Abraham? So am I. 23 Are they ministers of Christ? I am talking like a madman—I am a better one: with far greater labors, far more imprisonments, with countless floggings, and often near death. 24 Five times I have received from the Jews the forty lashes minus one. 25 Three times I was beaten with rods. Once I received a stoning. Three times I was shipwrecked; for a night and a day I was adrift at sea; 26 on frequent journeys, in danger from rivers, danger from bandits, danger from my own people, danger from Gentiles, danger in the city, danger in the wilderness, danger at sea, danger from false brothers and sisters;*g* 27 in toil and hardship, through many a sleepless night, hungry and thirsty, often without food, cold and naked. 28 And, besides other things, I am under daily pressure because of my anxiety for all the churches. 29 Who is weak, and I am not weak? Who is made to stumble, and I am not indignant?

30 If I must boast, I will boast of the things that show my weakness. 31 The God and Father of the Lord Jesus (blessed be he forever!) knows that I do not lie. 32 In Damascus, the governor*i* under King Ar'e·tas guarded the city of Damascus in order to*j* seize me, 33 but I was let down in a basket through a window in the wall,*k* and escaped from his hands.

---

d Or *the gospel*   *e* Other ancient authorities lack *and pure*
f Gk *the gospel of God*   *g* Gk *brothers*   *h* Gk *according to the flesh*   *i* Gk *ethnarch*   *j* Other ancient authorities read *and wanted to*   *k* Gk *through the wall*

Paul's Visions and Revelations

It is necessary to boast; nothing is to be gained by it, but I will go on to visions and revelations of the Lord. 2 I know a person in Christ who fourteen years ago was caught up to the third heaven—whether in the body or out of the body I do not know; God knows. 3 And I know that such a person—whether in the body or out of the body I do not know; God knows— 4 was caught up into Paradise and heard things that are not to be told, that no mortal is permitted to repeat. 5 On behalf of such a one I will boast, but on my own behalf I will not boast, except of my weaknesses. 6 But if I wish to boast, I will not be a fool, for I will be speaking the truth. But I refrain from it, so that no one may think better of me than what is seen in me or heard from me, 7 even considering the exceptional character of the revelations. Therefore, to keep*l* me from being too elated, a thorn was given me in the flesh, a messenger of Satan to torment me, to keep me from being too elated.*m* 8 Three times I appealed to the Lord about this, that it would leave me, 9 but he said to me, "My grace is sufficient for you, for power*n* is made perfect in weakness." So, I will boast all the more gladly of my weaknesses, so that the power of Christ may dwell in me. 10 Therefore I am content with weaknesses, insults, hardships, persecutions, and calamities for the sake of Christ; for whenever I am weak, then I am strong.

Paul's Concern for the Corinthian Church

11 I have been a fool! You forced me to it. Indeed you should have been the ones commending me, for I am not at all inferior to these super-apostles, even though I am nothing. 12 The signs of a true apostle were performed among you with utmost patience, signs and wonders and mighty works. 13 How have you been worse off than the other churches, except that I myself did not burden you? Forgive me this wrong!

14 Here I am, ready to come to you this third time. And I will not be a burden, because I do not want what is yours but you; for children ought not to lay up for their parents, but parents for their children. 15 I will most gladly spend and be spent for you. If I love you more, am I to be loved less? 16 Let it be assumed that I did not burden you. Nevertheless (you say) since I was crafty, I took you in by deceit. 17 Did I take advantage of you through any of those whom I sent to you? 18 I urged Titus to go, and sent the brother with him. Titus did not take advantage of you, did he? Did we not conduct ourselves with the same spirit? Did we not take the same steps?

19 Have you been thinking all along that we have been defending ourselves before you? We are speaking in Christ before God. Everything we do, beloved, is for the sake of building you up. 20 For I fear that when I come, I may find you not as I wish, and that you may find me not as you wish; I fear that there may perhaps be quarreling, jealousy, anger, selfishness, slander, gossip, conceit, and disorder. 21 I fear that when I come again, my God may humble me before you, and that I may have to mourn over many who previously sinned and have not repented of the impurity, sexual

---

l Other ancient authorities read *To keep*　　*m* Other ancient authorities lack *to keep me from being too elated*　　*n* Other ancient authorities read *my power*

When I Am Weak, Then I Am Strong!

LIVE IT!

Sensible people go to a physician when they are suffering from an illness or injury. Smart students seek help from a teacher when they are stumped by an assigned project. Honest people admit when they have failed. Humble people are not afraid to apologize. Admitting that we are sick, or need help with a problem, or have failed or been wrong is a sign not of weakness but of wisdom and maturity.

Paul mentions a mysterious affliction he had to suffer—a "thorn . . . in the flesh" (2 Cor 12.7)—and how desperately he wanted to be rid of it. When he asked God to remove the "thorn," God chose to let it remain in Paul's life.

Paul wanted to be strong on his own, but his experience of struggling with this thorn reminded him that he needed to depend completely on the grace of God. Recognizing that we need God, admitting that we cannot make it on our own—that is a sign of true strength!

▶ 2 Cor 12.1–10

A Spiritual Checkup

STOP!

How often do you take a break from all the activities in your life to do a spiritual checkup on your relationships with God, other people, and yourself? In 2 Cor 13.5–7, Paul suggests that the Corinthians give themselves a spiritual self-check. This is good advice for us today as well.

A STOP sign is a good guiding image for a spiritual checkup. It signals you to interrupt the motion of life and look at what's going on around you. Each letter of the sign can be a reminder to check a different area of your spiritual life:

- *S* can stand for "seek." Do you seek information, counsel, and help when facing difficult or confusing situations and choices?
- *T* can stand for "think." Do you honestly think about how your actions and behaviors affect you, others, and your relationship with God?
- *O* can stand for "others." Do you make it a priority to reach out and support others—particularly those in great need? Are you there for your family and friends?
- *P* can stand for "pray." Do you turn to God for guidance in your life? for the strength to do what is right? Do you thank God for your blessings and the struggles that make you stronger?

▶ 2 Cor 13.5–7

---

immorality, and licentiousness that they have practiced.

Further Warning

This is the third time I am coming to you. "Any charge must be sustained by the evidence of two or three witnesses." 2 I warned those who sinned previously and all the others, and I warn them now while absent, as I did when present on my second visit, that if I come again, I will not be lenient— 3 since you desire proof that Christ is speaking in me. He is not weak in dealing with you, but is powerful in you. 4 For he was crucified in weakness, but lives by the power of God. For we are weak in him,*o* but in dealing with you we will live with him by the power of God.

5 Examine yourselves to see whether you are living in the faith. Test yourselves. Do you not realize that Jesus Christ is in you?—unless, indeed, you fail to meet the test! 6 I hope you will find out that we have not failed. 7 But we pray to God that you may not do anything wrong—not that we may appear to have met the test, but that you may do

what is right, though we may seem to have failed. 8 For we cannot do anything against the truth, but only for the truth. 9 For we rejoice when we are weak and you are strong. This is what we pray for, that you may become perfect. 10 So I write these things while I am away from you, so that when I come, I may not have to be severe in using the authority that the Lord has given me for building up and not for tearing down.

Final Greetings and Benediction

11 Finally, brothers and sisters,*p* farewell.*q* Put things in order, listen to my appeal,*r* agree with one another, live in peace; and the God of love and peace will be with you. 12 Greet one another with a holy kiss. All the saints greet you.

13 The grace of the Lord Jesus Christ, the love of God, and the communion of*s* the Holy Spirit be with all of you.

---

o Other ancient authorities read *with him*   *p* Gk *brothers*
q Or *rejoice*   *r* Or *encourage one another*   *s* Or *and the sharing in*

Do you ever scan a letter before you start to read, to see what mood the writer was in? Try it with Galatians. Notice that Paul is angry and upset. He was weak and sick when he founded the church in Galatia. Now, everything is falling apart. He feels like a mother who has to give birth to her children all over again (4.12–20). Why? Paul is afraid the Galatians are trading in the true Gospel, based on faith in Jesus, for a false gospel based on Jewish rules and customs.

At a Glance

- **1.1–5.** a greeting
- **1.6—2.21.** the work of Paul and the other Apostles
- **3.1—5.1.** the message that salvation is by faith, not works
- **5.2—6.10.** advice on Christian living
- **6.11–18.** final words and a blessing

In-depth

Jesus, the disciples, and most of the first Christians were Jewish. When Gentiles (non-Jews) started to become Christians, a question came up that almost split the early Christian community: Do Gentiles have to become Jewish before they can become Christian? The whole debate soon centered around the Jewish law of circumcision. (Circumcision is the surgical removal of the foreskin of a male's penis.)

Paul insisted that circumcision—and all the other Jewish ceremonial laws— had nothing to do with faith in Jesus and was unnecessary for Gentile Christians. At the Council of Jerusalem (see Acts of the Apostles, chapter 15), the other Apostles reluctantly agreed with Paul. But the argument wasn't over. Other Christian missionaries came to Galatia after Paul left the Christian community there. They implied that faith in Christ wasn't enough and insisted that Gentile Christians must be circumcised. They attacked Paul's credibility by saying he wasn't a true Apostle.

When Paul heard of this, he was mad! In his Letter to the Galatians, he doesn't even include his typical thanksgiving at the end of his greeting but launches right into his concern. He starts by defending his apostlehood. He goes on to tell how the other Apostles at the Council of Jerusalem had agreed with him that the Gentiles do not need to be circumcised. He states how he later challenged Peter personally when Peter allowed himself to be influenced by missionaries preaching something else.

In his passion, Paul confronts the Galatians: "I am afraid that my work for you may have been wasted" (4.11). He condemns the false missionaries: "If anyone proclaims to you a gospel contrary to what you received, let that one be accursed!" (1.9). Paul is defending the freedom of Christians from the old Jewish religious laws. He is writing the Christians' declaration of independence: "Christ has set us free" (5.1).

Quick Facts

Author
Paul

Date
A.D. 54–55

Audience
Gentile Christian churches in northern Galatia

Galatians

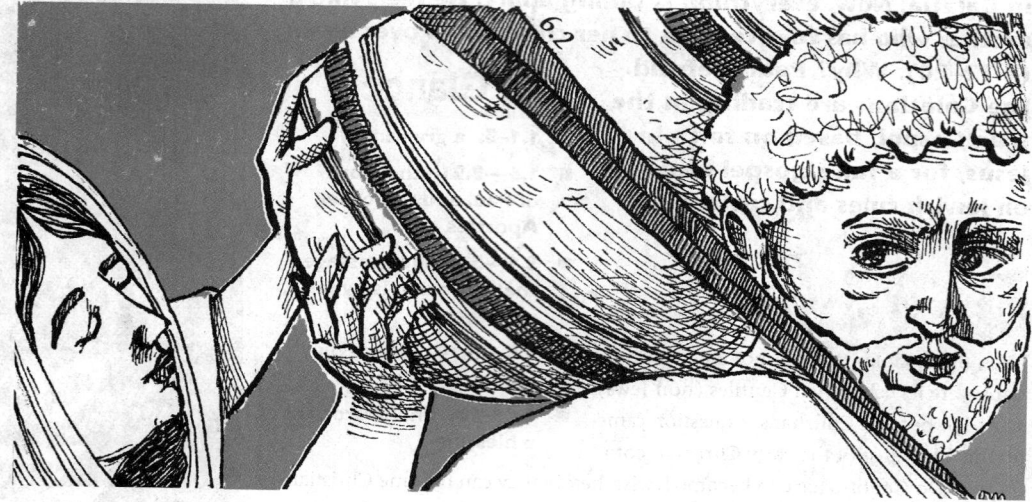

Salutation

Paul an apostle—sent neither by human commission nor from human authorities, but through Jesus Christ and God the Father, who raised him from the dead— 2 and all the members of God's family*a* who are with me,

To the churches of Galatia:

3 Grace to you and peace from God our Father and the Lord Jesus Christ, 4 who gave himself for our sins to set us free from the present evil age, according to the will of our God and Father, 5 to whom be the glory forever and ever. Amen.

There Is No Other Gospel

6 I am astonished that you are so quickly deserting the one who called you in the grace of Christ and are turning to a different gospel— 7 not that there is another gospel, but there are some who are confusing you and want to pervert the gospel of Christ. 8 But even if we or an angel*b* from heaven should proclaim to you a gospel contrary to what we proclaimed to you, let that one be accursed! 9 As we have said before, so now I repeat, if anyone proclaims to you a gospel contrary to what you received, let that one be accursed!

10 Am I now seeking human approval, or God's approval? Or am I trying to please people? If I were still pleasing people, I would not be a servant*c* of Christ.

Paul's Vindication of His Apostleship
(Cp Acts 9)

11 For I want you to know, brothers and sisters,*d* that the gospel that was proclaimed by me is not of human origin; 12 for I did not receive it from a human source, nor was I taught it, but I received it through a revelation of Jesus Christ.

13 You have heard, no doubt, of my earlier life in Jŭ′da•ism. I was violently persecuting the church of God and was trying to destroy it. 14 I advanced in Jŭ′da•ism beyond many among my people of the same age, for I was far more zealous for the traditions of my ancestors. 15 But when God, who had set me apart before I was born and called me through his grace, was pleased 16 to reveal his Son to me,*e* so that I might proclaim him among the Gentiles, I did not confer with any human being, 17 nor did I go up to Jerusalem to those who were already apostles before me, but I went away at once into Arabia, and afterwards I returned to Damascus.

18 Then after three years I did go up to Jerusalem to visit Cĕ′phas and stayed with him fifteen days; 19 but I did not see any other apostle except James the Lord's brother. 20 In what I am writing to you, before God, I do not lie! 21 Then I went into the regions of Syria and Ci•li′ci•a, 22 and I was still unknown by sight to the churches of Judea that are

a Gk all the brothers   *b* Or a messenger   *c* Gk slave
d Gk brothers   *e* Gk in me

in Christ; 23 they only heard it said, "The one who formerly was persecuting us is now proclaiming the faith he once tried to destroy." 24 And they glorified God because of me.

Paul and the Other Apostles
(Cp Acts 15.1–21)

Then after fourteen years I went up again to Jerusalem with Bar′na•bas, taking Titus along with me. 2 I went up in response to a revelation. Then I laid before them (though only in a private meeting with the acknowledged leaders) the gospel that I proclaim among the Gentiles, in order to make sure that I was not running, or had not run, in vain. 3 But even Titus, who was with me, was not compelled to be circumcised, though he was a Greek. 4 But because of false believers*f* secretly brought in, who slipped in to spy on the freedom we have in Christ Jesus, so that they might enslave us— 5 we did not submit to them even for a moment, so that the truth of the gospel might always remain with you. 6 And from those who were supposed to be acknowledged leaders (what they actually were makes no difference to me; God shows no partiality)—those leaders contributed nothing to me. 7 On the contrary, when they saw that I had been entrusted with the gospel for the uncircumcised, just as Peter had been entrusted with the gospel for the circumcised 8 (for he who worked through Peter making him an apostle to the circumcised also worked through me in sending me

to the Gentiles), 9 and when James and Cē′phas and John, who were acknowledged pillars, recognized the grace that had been given to me, they gave to Bar′na•bas and me the right hand of fellowship, agreeing that we should go to the Gentiles and they to the circumcised. 10 They asked only one thing, that we remember the poor, which was actually what I was*g* eager to do.

Paul Rebukes Peter at Antioch

11 But when Cē′phas came to An′ti•och, I opposed him to his face, because he stood self-condemned; 12 for until certain people came from James, he used to eat with the Gentiles. But after they came, he drew back and kept himself separate for fear of the circumcision faction. 13 And the other Jews joined him in this hypocrisy, so that even Bar′na•bas was led astray by their hypocrisy. 14 But when I saw that they were not acting consistently with the truth of the gospel, I said to Cē′phas before them all, "If you, though a Jew, live like a Gentile and not like a Jew, how can you compel the Gentiles to live like Jews?"*h*

Jews and Gentiles Are Saved by Faith

15 We ourselves are Jews by birth and not Gentile sinners; 16 yet we know that a person is justified*i* not by the works of the law but through

---

f Gk *false brothers*   *g* Or *had been*   *h* Some interpreters hold that the quotation extends into the following paragraph   *i* Or *reckoned as righteous*; and so elsewhere

LIVE IT!

Consistent and Trustworthy

At the beginning of Galatians, chapter 2, Paul describes what went on at the Council of Jerusalem. The council established that freedom from the Jewish Law is at the core of Christian beliefs and identity. Faith in Christ is enough to save people from sin and human weakness. Paul pleads with the Galatians not to fall back into the legalism and empty rituals being taught by some Jewish Christian leaders.

So when Peter stops eating with Gentile Christians under pressure from some Jewish Christians, Paul challenges him. He points out that Peter's behavior is not consistent with the truth of the Gospel and that this inconsistency is misleading and confusing to the Christian community.

To be a credible Christian demands that you stay consistent in your words and actions. Remember, your actions speak louder than your words. Furthermore, when your actions do not match your words, people lose their trust in you. And you begin to feel like a hypocrite and lose your self-esteem.

Take some time to reflect on how consistently your actions reflect your words. Consider ways you can improve. When your actions match your words, people will recognize you as a person of integrity and place their trust in you.

▶ Gal 2.11–14

faith in Jesus Christ.*j* And we have come to believe in Christ Jesus, so that we might be justified by faith in Christ,*k* and not by doing the works of the law, because no one will be justified by the works of the law. 17 But if, in our effort to be justified in Christ, we ourselves have been found to be sinners, is Christ then a servant of sin? Certainly not! 18 But if I build up again the very things that I once tore down, then I demonstrate that I am a transgressor. 19 For through the law I died to the law, so that I might live to God. I have been crucified with Christ; 20 and it is no longer I who live, but it is Christ who lives in me. And the life I now live in the flesh I live by faith in the Son of God,*l* who loved me and gave himself for me. 21 I do not nullify the grace of God; for if justification*m* comes through the law, then Christ died for nothing.

Saved by Christ

Throughout Galatians, Paul speaks about the difference between being saved by faith and being saved through the Law. Christians believe that they are justified—made right with God—not through a perfect keeping of religious laws, but through faith in Christ. Christ's saving sacrifice alone will set them free from their sin. Their trust must be in him and not in their own ability to please God.

▶ **Gal 3.1—4.7**

Law or Faith
(Cp Rom 4.1–25)

You foolish Galatians! Who has bewitched you? It was before your eyes that Jesus Christ was publicly exhibited as crucified! 2 The only thing I want to learn from you is this: Did you receive the Spirit by doing the works of the law or by believing what you heard? 3 Are you so foolish? Having started with the Spirit, are you now ending with the flesh? 4 Did you experience so much for nothing?—if it really was for nothing. 5 Well then, does God*n* supply you with the Spirit and work miracles among you by your doing the works of the law, or by your believing what you heard?

6 Just as Abraham "believed God, and it was reckoned to him as righteousness," 7 so, you see,

those who believe are the descendants of Abraham. 8 And the scripture, foreseeing that God would justify the Gentiles by faith, declared the gospel beforehand to Abraham, saying, "All the Gentiles shall be blessed in you." 9 For this reason, those who believe are blessed with Abraham who believed.

10 For all who rely on the works of the law are under a curse; for it is written, "Cursed is everyone who does not observe and obey all the things written in the book of the law." 11 Now it is evident that no one is justified before God by the law; for "The one who is righteous will live by faith."*o* 12 But the law does not rest on faith; on the contrary, "Whoever does the works of the law*p* will live by them." 13 Christ redeemed us from the curse of the law by becoming a curse for us—for it is written, "Cursed is everyone who hangs on a tree"— 14 in order that in Christ Jesus the blessing of Abraham might come to the Gentiles, so that we might receive the promise of the Spirit through faith.

The Promise to Abraham
(Cp Gen 12.1–3)

15 Brothers and sisters,*q* I give an example from daily life: once a person's will*r* has been ratified, no one adds to it or annuls it. 16 Now the promises were made to Abraham and to his offspring;*s* it does not say, "And to offsprings,"*t* as of many; but it says, "And to your offspring,"*s* that is, to one person, who is Christ. 17 My point is this: the law, which came four hundred thirty years later, does not annul a covenant previously ratified by God, so as to nullify the promise. 18 For if the inheritance comes from the law, it no longer comes from the promise; but God granted it to Abraham through the promise.

The Purpose of the Law

19 Why then the law? It was added because of transgressions, until the offspring*s* would come to whom the promise had been made; and it was ordained through angels by a mediator. 20 Now a mediator involves more than one party; but God is one.

21 Is the law then opposed to the promises of God? Certainly not! For if a law had been given that could make alive, then righteousness would indeed come through the law. 22 But the scripture has imprisoned all things under the power of sin,

---

j Or *the faith of Jesus Christ*   *k* Or *the faith of Christ*
l Or *by the faith of the Son of God*   *m* Or *righteousness*
n Gk *he*   *o* Or *The one who is righteous through faith will live*   *p* Gk *does them*   *q* Gk *Brothers*   *r* Or *covenant* (as in verse 17)   *s* Gk *seed*   *t* Gk *seeds*

so that what was promised through faith in Jesus Christ[u] might be given to those who believe.

23 Now before faith came, we were imprisoned and guarded under the law until faith would be revealed. 24 Therefore the law was our disciplinarian until Christ came, so that we might be justified by faith. 25 But now that faith has come, we are no longer subject to a disciplinarian, 26 for in Christ Jesus you are all children of God through faith. 27 As many of you as were baptized into Christ have clothed yourselves with Christ.

There is no longer
Jew or Greek,
there is no longer
slave *or free,*
there is no longer
male and **female;**
for all of you are one in
Christ Jesus
3.28

28 There is no longer Jew or Greek, there is no longer slave or free, there is no longer male and female; for all of you are one in Christ Jesus. 29 And if you belong to Christ, then you are Abraham's offspring,[v] heirs according to the promise.

My point is this: heirs, as long as they are minors, are no better than slaves, though they are the owners of all the property; 2 but they remain under guardians and trustees until the date set by the father. 3 So with us; while we were minors, we were enslaved to the elemental spirits[w] of the world. 4 But when the fullness of time had come, God sent his Son, born of a woman, born under the law, 5 in order to redeem those who were under the law, so that we might receive adoption as children. 6 And because you are children, God has sent the Spirit of his Son into our[x] hearts, crying, "Abba![y] Father!" 7 So you are no longer a slave but a child, and if a child then also an heir, through God.[z]

Paul Reproves the Galatians

8 Formerly, when you did not know God, you were enslaved to beings that by nature are not gods. 9 Now, however, that you have come to know God, or rather to be known by God, how can you turn back again to the weak and beggarly elemental spirits?[a] How can you want to be enslaved to them again? 10 You are observing special days, and months, and seasons, and years. 11 I am afraid that my work for you may have been wasted.

12 Friends,[b] I beg you, become as I am, for I also have become as you are. You have done me no wrong. 13 You know that it was because of a physical infirmity that I first announced the gospel to you; 14 though my condition put you to the test, you did not scorn or despise me, but welcomed me as an angel of God, as Christ Jesus. 15 What has become of the goodwill you felt? For I testify that, had it been possible, you would have torn out your eyes and given them to me. 16 Have I now become your enemy by telling you the truth? 17 They make much of you, but for no good purpose; they want to exclude you, so that you may

u Or *through the faith of Jesus Christ*   v Gk *seed*   w Or *the rudiments*   x Other ancient authorities read *your*   y Aramaic for *Father*   z Other ancient authorities read *an heir of God through Christ*   a Or *beggarly rudiments*   b Gk *Brothers*

LIVE IT!

Radical Equality

Galatians 3.28 may have been an early baptismal formula. In it, Paul makes a radical statement: The source of our equality as humans is Jesus Christ! (Note that the word *radical* means both "root" and "extreme"—and that Paul's statement is both fundamental to Christian belief and a great expression of that belief.)

Think about what Paul says: Everyone is equal! But is this the reality in the world around you? Are all the people in your school regarded as equally valuable? Consider the equality of women in work, church, and society. What about those who are poor, how are they regarded? It is clear that we still need to work toward Paul's vision!

▶ Gal 3.28

make much of them. [18] It is good to be made much of for a good purpose at all times, and not only when I am present with you. [19] My little children, for whom I am again in the pain of childbirth until Christ is formed in you, [20] I wish I were present with you now and could change my tone, for I am perplexed about you.

The Allegory of Hagar and Sarah
(Gen 21.8–21; Isa 54.1)

[21] Tell me, you who desire to be subject to the law, will you not listen to the law? [22] For it is written that Abraham had two sons, one by a slave woman and the other by a free woman. [23] One, the child of the slave, was born according to the flesh; the other, the child of the free woman, was born through the promise. [24] Now this is an allegory: these women are two covenants. One woman, in fact, is Hāʾgar, from Mount Sinai, bearing children for slavery. [25] Now Hāʾgar is Mount Sinai in Arabia[c] and corresponds to the present Jerusalem, for she is in slavery with her children. [26] But the other woman corresponds to the Jerusalem above; she is free, and she is our mother. [27] For it is written,

"Rejoice, you childless one, you who bear
     no children,
burst into song and shout, you who
     endure no birth pangs;
for the children of the desolate woman are
     more numerous
than the children of the one who is
     married."

[28] Now you,[d] my friends,[e] are children of the promise, like Isaac. [29] But just as at that time the child who was born according to the flesh persecuted the child who was born according to the Spirit, so it is now also. [30] But what does the scripture say? "Drive out the slave and her child; for the child of the slave will not share the inheritance with the child of the free woman." [31] So then, friends,[e] we are children, not of the slave but of the free woman. [1] For freedom Christ has set us free. Stand firm, therefore, and do not submit again to a yoke of slavery.

The Nature of Christian Freedom

[2] Listen! I, Paul, am telling you that if you let yourselves be circumcised, Christ will be of no benefit to you. [3] Once again I testify to every man who lets himself be circumcised that he is obliged to obey the entire law. [4] You who want to be justified by the law have cut yourselves off from Christ; you have fallen away from grace. [5] For through the Spirit, by faith, we eagerly wait for the hope of righteousness. [6] For in Christ Jesus neither circumcision nor uncircumcision counts for anything; the only thing that counts is faith working[f] through love.

[7] You were running well; who prevented you from obeying the truth? [8] Such persuasion does not come from the one who calls you. [9] A little yeast leavens the whole batch of dough. [10] I am confident about you in the Lord that you will not

PRAY IT!

Fill Me, Lord

Fill me with the fruits of your Spirit, Lord.

Fill me with love, so that I seek to understand and appreciate the rich variety and diversity of life that surrounds me.

Fill me with joy, so that I celebrate your presence in each and every moment I am on this earth.

Fill me with peace, so that I know how to ease those angry and sometimes violent urges that well up inside of me.

Fill me with patience, so that I stop rushing long enough to witness your miraculous work taking place all around me (and within me!).

Fill me with kindness, so that I take the extra time to help the one in need, even when it isn't convenient for me.

Fill me with faithfulness, so that I place my mind, heart, and all that I do in the service of your Gospel.

Fill me with gentleness, so that others know that I believe in a God who loves and cares for all people.

Fill me with self-control, so that I act not on my impulses and urges, but rather on my beliefs and values, which are rooted in you.

Fill me with these fruits of your spirit, Lord! Amen.

▸ **Gal 5.22–26**

think otherwise. But whoever it is that is confusing you will pay the penalty. [11] But my friends,[e] why am I still being persecuted if I am still preaching circumcision? In that case the offense of the cross

---

[c] Other ancient authorities read *For Sinai is a mountain in Arabia*   [d] Other ancient authorities read *we*   [e] Gk *brothers*   [f] Or *made effective*

has been removed. ¹²I wish those who unsettle you would castrate themselves!

13 For you were called to freedom, brothers and sisters;*g* only do not use your freedom as an opportunity for self-indulgence,*h* but through love become slaves to one another. ¹⁴For the whole law is summed up in a single commandment, "You shall love your neighbor as yourself." ¹⁵If, however, you bite and devour one another, take care that you are not consumed by one another.

The Works of the Flesh

16 Live by the Spirit, I say, and do not gratify the desires of the flesh. ¹⁷For what the flesh desires is opposed to the Spirit, and what the Spirit desires is opposed to the flesh; for these are opposed to each other, to prevent you from doing what you want. ¹⁸But if you are led by the Spirit, you are not subject to the law. ¹⁹Now the works of the flesh are obvious: fornication, impurity, licentiousness, ²⁰idolatry, sorcery, enmities, strife, jealousy, anger, quarrels, dissensions, factions, ²¹envy,*i* drunkenness, carousing, and things like these. I am warning you, as I warned you before: those who do such things will not inherit the kingdom of God.

The Fruit of the Spirit
(Cp Col 3.12–13)

22 By contrast, the fruit of the Spirit is love, joy, peace, patience, kindness, generosity, faithfulness, ²³gentleness, and self-control. There is no law against such things. ²⁴And those who belong to Christ Jesus have crucified the flesh with its passions and desires. ²⁵If we live by the Spirit, let us also be guided by the Spirit. ²⁶Let us not become conceited, competing against one another, envying one another.

Bear One Another's Burdens

My friends,*j* if anyone is detected in a transgression, you who have received the Spirit should restore such a one in a spirit of gentleness. Take care that you yourselves are not tempted. ²Bear one another's burdens, and in this way you will fulfill*k* the law of Christ. ³For if those who are nothing think they are something, they deceive themselves. ⁴All must test their own work; then that work, rather than their neighbor's work, will become a cause for pride. ⁵For all must carry their own loads.

6 Those who are taught the word must share in all good things with their teacher.

7 Do not be deceived; God is not mocked, for you reap whatever you sow. ⁸If you sow to your own flesh, you will reap corruption from the flesh; but if you sow to the Spirit, you will reap eternal

AFRICAN AMERICAN
The Principle of *Imani*

Be not discouraged. There is a future for you. . . . The resistance encountered now predicates hope. . . . Only as we rise . . . do we encounter opposition.

These words by Frederick Douglass in 1892 encouraged African Americans not to abandon their struggle for equality. It seemed that the more they struggled, the more pain was inflicted on them. In the face of certain suffering, Douglass urged them to look toward the promise of living as equals under the law.

They knew that God was their liberator and justice giver. God made them brave in the face of danger and capable of dying for the cause they embraced. They looked to God and saw their future. They took the words of Gal 6.9 seriously: "Let us not grow weary in doing what is right."

Today, we don't face slave masters and live on plantations as servants in fetters, but we do endure other situations equally as perilous. Let us not grow weary or lose heart. We must practice the Kwanzaa principle of *imani*, or "faith" (see "Kwanzaa as a Way of Life," Deut 10.12–22). Our God is still in the saving business.

Dear God, my future is in your hands. Lead me to it with your power. Amen.

▶ **Gal 6.9**

life from the Spirit. ⁹So let us not grow weary in doing what is right, for we will reap at harvest time, if we do not give up. ¹⁰So then, whenever we have an opportunity, let us work for the good of all, and especially for those of the family of faith.

---

g Gk brothers   *h* Gk the flesh   *i* Other ancient authorities add *murder*   *j* Gk Brothers   *k* Other ancient authorities read *in this way fulfill*

Final Admonitions and Benediction

11 See what large letters I make when I am writing in my own hand! [12] It is those who want to make a good showing in the flesh that try to compel you to be circumcised—only that they may not be persecuted for the cross of Christ. [13] Even the circumcised do not themselves obey the law, but they want you to be circumcised so that they may boast about your flesh. [14] May I never boast of anything except the cross of our Lord Jesus Christ, by which[l] the world has been crucified to me, and I to the world. [15] For[m] neither circumcision nor un-circumcision is anything; but a new creation is everything! [16] As for those who will follow this rule—peace be upon them, and mercy, and upon the Israel of God.

17 From now on, let no one make trouble for me; for I carry the marks of Jesus branded on my body.

18 May the grace of our Lord Jesus Christ be with your spirit, brothers and sisters.[n] Amen.

---

[l] Or through whom   [m] Other ancient authorities add in Christ Jesus   [n] Gk brothers

What's the purpose to life? Why am I alive? What's the point of it all anyway? You may have asked questions like these out of simple curiosity, or during a time when life wasn't going so well. In either case, God has an answer for you tucked away inside the Letter to the Ephesians. This letter talks about God's plan to save us for a life in union with God and one another, both now and for all eternity!

At a Glance

- **1.1–2.** a greeting
- **1.3–23.** a benediction, and thanksgiving for salvation
- **Chapters 2–3.** a discussion of unity in Christ
- **4.1—6.20.** advice for Christian living
- **6.21–24.** a final message and a blessing

In-depth

Three times in the poetic opening chapter, the writer of Ephesians tells us that we are here because we have been chosen by God! In this beautiful trinity of praise for the Father (verses 3–6), the Son (verse 12), and the Holy Spirit (verses 13–14), we are told that that's why we're alive!

This letter has hardly any of the personal greeting you'd expect in a communication to a specific group of people. Also, the reference to the saints in the first verse doesn't appear in many of the earliest copies we have of the letter. For these reasons, most scholars believe that this letter was intended to be read by several Christian communities and has a universal message for the early church.

Ephesians emphasizes unity among Christians. It especially emphasizes that Gentile (non-Jewish) Christians are one with Jewish Christians, for Christ "has made both groups into one" (2.14). It explains that it is the early Christians' job—as it is our job—to treat one another with love, "making every effort to maintain the unity" (4.3). The image of the body is used here, as it is in 1 Corinthians, chapter 12, to emphasize our unity (4.15–16).

Ephesians also talks about the place of good works in the life of a Christian. Good works can be thought of as living a moral life, or as following moral rules, such as the Jewish Law. Paul has made clear that we are not saved by the Law. So, what is the point of living a moral life? The letter explains that we are saved not *by doing* good works but *in order to do* good works.

The letter ends with some practical advice for living out the faith on a daily basis. There are rules for moral living. There are instructions for Christian family life. There is an analogy for putting on the "armor of God" to resist evil in all its forms. If we keep in mind that this letter is written for a culture that was different from ours, the advice will serve us well too!

Quick Facts

Author
a follower of Paul's (see "Introduction to the Letters and Revelation")

Date Written
after Paul's death, A.D. 70–95

Audience
Gentile churches, possibly in Asia Minor

The Letter to the **Ephesians**

Ephesians

Salutation

Paul, an apostle of Christ Jesus by the will of God,
  To the saints who are in Eph′e•sus and are faithful[a] in Christ Jesus:
  2 Grace to you and peace from God our Father and the Lord Jesus Christ.

Spiritual Blessings in Christ

3 Blessed be the God and Father of our Lord Jesus Christ, who has blessed us in Christ with every spiritual blessing in the heavenly places, 4 just as he chose us in Christ[b] before the foundation of the world to be holy and blameless before him in love. 5 He destined us for adoption as his children through Jesus Christ, according to the good pleasure of his will, 6 to the praise of his glorious grace that he freely bestowed on us in the Beloved. 7 In him we have redemption through his blood, the forgiveness of our trespasses, according to the riches of his grace 8 that he lavished on us. With all wisdom and insight 9 he has made known to us the mystery of his will, according to his good pleasure that he set forth in Christ, 10 as a plan for the fullness of time, to gather up all things in him, things in heaven and things on earth. 11 In Christ we have also obtained an inheritance,[c] having been destined according to the purpose of him who accomplishes all things according to his counsel and will, 12 so that we, who were the first

to set our hope on Christ, might live for the praise of his glory. 13 In him you also, when you had heard the word of truth, the gospel of your salvation, and had believed in him, were marked with the seal of the promised Holy Spirit; 14 this[d] is the pledge of our inheritance toward redemption as God's own people, to the praise of his glory.

Paul's Prayer

15 I have heard of your faith in the Lord Jesus and your love[e] toward all the saints, and for this reason 16 I do not cease to give thanks for you as I remember you in my prayers. 17 I pray that the God of our Lord Jesus Christ, the Father of glory, may give you a spirit of wisdom and revelation as you come to know him, 18 so that, with the eyes of your heart enlightened, you may know what is the hope to which he has called you, what are the riches of his glorious inheritance among the saints, 19 and what is the immeasurable greatness of his power for us who believe, according to the working of his great power. 20 God[f] put this power to work in Christ when he raised him from the dead and seated him at his right hand in the heavenly places, 21 far above all rule and authority and power and dominion, and above every name that

---

a Other ancient authorities lack *in Ephesus*, reading *saints who are also faithful*   *b* Gk *in him*   *c* Or *been made a heritage*   *d* Other ancient authorities read *who*   *e* Other ancient authorities lack *and your love*   *f* Gk *He*

is named, not only in this age but also in the age to come. 22 And he has put all things under his feet and has made him the head over all things for the church, 23 which is his body, the fullness of him who fills all in all.

PRAY IT?

I Give God Thanks for You!

Think of people in your family, community, school, and church who are living out the Gospel message. Who is honestly striving to live her or his Christian faith? a parent or guardian? a friend? a neighbor? a teacher? a minister?

Hold this person in your heart as you read Eph 1.15–23. Meditate on how this person has influenced you as a Christian. How has he or she helped you on your faith journey? Consider writing your own prayer of thanks to God for this person's example. If it seems appropriate, share your prayer with this person.

▸ Eph 1.15–23

From Death to Life

You were dead through the trespasses and sins 2 in which you once lived, following the course of this world, following the ruler of the power of the air, the spirit that is now at work among those who are disobedient. 3 All of us once lived among them in the passions of our flesh, following the desires of flesh and senses, and we were by nature children of wrath, like everyone else. 4 But God, who is rich in mercy, out of the great love with which he loved us 5 even when we were dead through our trespasses, made us alive together with Christ g—by grace you have been saved— 6 and raised us up with him and seated us with him in the heavenly places in Christ Jesus, 7 so that in the ages to come he might show the immeasurable riches of his grace in kindness toward us in Christ Jesus. 8 For by grace you have been saved through faith, and this is not your own doing; it is the gift of God— 9 not the result of works, so that no one may boast. 10 For we are what he has made us, created in Christ Jesus for good works, which God prepared beforehand to be our way of life.

One in Christ

11 So then, remember that at one time you Gentiles by birth, h called "the uncircumcision" by those who are called "the circumcision"—a physical circumcision made in the flesh by human hands— 12 remember that you were at that time without Christ, being aliens from the commonwealth of Israel, and strangers to the covenants of promise, having no hope and without God in the world. 13 But now in Christ Jesus you who once were far off have been brought near by the blood of Christ. 14 For he is our peace; in his flesh he has made both groups into one and has broken down the dividing wall, that is, the hostility between us. 15 He has abolished the law with its commandments and ordinances, that he might create in himself one new humanity in place of the two, thus making peace, 16 and might reconcile both groups to God in one body i through the cross, thus putting to death that hostility through it. j 17 So he came and proclaimed peace to you who

g Other ancient authorities read in Christ　h Gk in the flesh　i Or reconcile both of us in one body for God　j Or in him, or in himself

did you KNOW?

Faith Versus Good Works

Ephesians 2.1–10 deals with the question of faith versus good works (good works are moral living and Gospel-motivated works of service, justice, courage, and so on). This issue has divided Christians since the early church and was a major issue at the time of the Protestant Reformation. Some say that we are saved by our good works. Others say good works are irrelevant, and we are saved only through our faith in Christ.

The writer of Ephesians makes it clear that both those statements are wrong. The core Christian belief is this: We are saved by God's grace through faith in Jesus Christ. We are saved not by doing good works but in order to do good works. Our salvation is God's gift to us; how we live is our gift to God.

▸ Eph 2.1–10

were far off and peace to those who were near; [18] for through him both of us have access in one Spirit to the Father. [19] So then you are no longer strangers and aliens, but you are citizens with the saints and also members of the household of God, [20] built upon the foundation of the apostles and prophets, with Christ Jesus himself as the cornerstone.[k] [21] In him the whole structure is joined together and grows into a holy temple in the Lord; [22] in whom you also are built together spiritually[l] into a dwelling place for God.

Paul's Ministry to the Gentiles

This is the reason that I Paul am a prisoner for[m] Christ Jesus for the sake of you Gentiles— [2] for surely you have already heard of the commission of God's grace that was given me for you, [3] and how the mystery was made known to me by revelation, as I wrote above in a few words, [4] a reading of which will enable you to perceive my understanding of the mystery of Christ. [5] In former generations this mystery[n] was not made known to humankind, as it has now been revealed to his holy apostles and prophets by the Spirit: [6] that is, the Gentiles have become fellow heirs, members of the same body, and sharers in the promise in Christ Jesus through the gospel.

[7] Of this gospel I have become a servant according to the gift of God's grace that was given me by the working of his power. [8] Although I am the very least of all the saints, this grace was given to me to bring to the Gentiles the news of the boundless riches of Christ, [9] and to make everyone see[o] what is the plan of the mystery hidden for ages in[p] God who created all things; [10] so that through the church the wisdom of God in its rich variety might now be made known to the rulers and authorities in the heavenly places. [11] This was in accordance with the eternal purpose that he has carried out in Christ Jesus our Lord, [12] in whom we have access to God in boldness and confidence through faith in him.[q] [13] I pray therefore that you[r] may not lose heart over my sufferings for you; they are your glory.

Prayer for the Readers

[14] For this reason I bow my knees before the Father,[s] [15] from whom every family[t] in heaven and on earth takes its name. [16] I pray that, according to the riches of his glory, he may grant that you may be strengthened in your inner being with power through his Spirit, [17] and that Christ may dwell in your hearts through faith, as you are being rooted and grounded in love. [18] I pray that you

may have the power to comprehend, with all the saints, what is the breadth and length and height and depth, [19] and to know the love of Christ that surpasses knowledge, so that you may be filled with all the fullness of God.

[20] Now to him who by the power at work within us is able to accomplish abundantly far more than all we can ask or imagine, [21] to him be glory in the church and in Christ Jesus to all generations, forever and ever. Amen.

---

k Or *keystone*   l Gk *in the Spirit*   m Or *of*   n Gk *it*
o Other ancient authorities read *to bring to light*   p Or *by*
q Or *the faith of him*   r Or *I*   s Other ancient authorities add *of our Lord Jesus Christ*   t Gk *fatherhood*

Asian American

Rooted in Love

Read the prayer in Eph 3.14–21. Then reflect on the prayer below from the Philippines, which also talks about roots and love.

Lord,
make us realise that our Christianity is
    like a rice field:
when it is newly planted the paddies are
    prominent,
but as the plants take root and grow
    taller,
these divided paddies gradually vanish,
and soon there appears only one vast
    continuous field.
So give us roots that love,
and help us grow in Christian fellowship
    and service,
that thy will be done in our lives,
through our Savior, Jesus Christ.
                (From Maren C. Tirabassi and
                    Kathy Wonson Eddy, editors,
                Gifts of Many Cultures, p. 30)

Finally, personalize the prayer in 3.14–21 by changing you to I or we, and your to my or our. Kneel and pray this prayer, knowing that God is indeed listening to you at this very moment.

▸ **Eph 3.14–17**

Unity in the Body of Christ

I therefore, the prisoner in the Lord, beg you to lead a life worthy of the calling to which you have been called, ²with all humility and gentleness, with patience, bearing with one another in love, ³making every effort to maintain the unity of the

There is *one* body and *one* Spirit, just as you were called to the *one* hope of your calling, *one* Lord, *one* faith, *one* baptism, *one* God and Father of all

4.4–6

Spirit in the bond of peace. ⁴There is one body and one Spirit, just as you were called to the one hope of your calling, ⁵one Lord, one faith, one baptism, ⁶one God and Father of all, who is above all and through all and in all.

7 But each of us was given grace according to the measure of Christ's gift. ⁸Therefore it is said,
"When he ascended on high he made
captivity itself a captive;
he gave gifts to his people."
⁹(When it says, "He ascended," what does it mean but that he had also descended ᵘ into the lower parts of the earth? ¹⁰He who descended is the same one who ascended far above all the heavens, so that he might fill all things.) ¹¹The gifts he gave were that some would be apostles, some prophets, some evangelists, some pastors and teachers, ¹²to equip the saints for the work of ministry, for building up the body of Christ, ¹³until all of us

NATIVE AMERICAN

Weave for Us a Garment

Paul's prayer in Eph 4.1–6 is a prayer of unity, a prayer for us to live as one—one faith, one Baptism, one God, one Body, one Spirit, one hope. This Native American prayer is also a prayer of unity, a prayer for us to live in a world where all people, all creation, are woven into one garment. May we walk in such a world. May we be part of creating such a world.

Weave for us a garment of brightness;
May the warp be the white light of morning,
May the weft be the red light of evening,
May the fringes be the falling rain,
May the border be the standing rainbow.
Thus weave for us a garment of brightness,
That we may walk fittingly where birds sing,
That we may walk fittingly where grass is
    green,
O our Mother the Earth, O our Father the Sky.
        (From Suzanne Slesin and Emily
        Gwathmey, compilers, Amen, n.p.)

▶ **Eph 4.1–6**

come to the unity of the faith and of the knowledge of the Son of God, to maturity, to the measure of the full stature of Christ. ¹⁴We must no longer be children, tossed to and fro and blown about by every wind of doctrine, by people's trickery, by their craftiness in deceitful scheming. ¹⁵But speaking the truth in love, we must grow up in every way into him who is the head, into Christ, ¹⁶from whom the whole body, joined and knit together by every ligament with which it is equipped, as each part is working properly, promotes the body's growth in building itself up in love.

ᵘ Other ancient authorities add *first*

The Old Life and the New

17 Now this I affirm and insist on in the Lord: you must no longer live as the Gentiles live, in the futility of their minds. 18 They are darkened in their understanding, alienated from the life of God because of their ignorance and hardness of heart. 19 They have lost all sensitivity and have abandoned themselves to licentiousness, greedy to practice every kind of impurity. 20 That is not the way you learned Christ! 21 For surely you have heard about him and were taught in him, as truth is in Jesus. 22 You were taught to put away your former way of life, your old self, corrupt and deluded by its lusts, 23 and to be renewed in the spirit of your minds, 24 and to clothe yourselves with the new self, created according to the likeness of God in true righteousness and holiness.

Rules for the New Life

25 So then, putting away falsehood, let all of us speak the truth to our neighbors, for we are members of one another. 26 Be angry but do not sin; do not let the sun go down on your anger, 27 and do not make room for the devil. 28 Thieves must give up stealing; rather let them labor and work honestly with their own hands, so as to have something to share with the needy. 29 Let no evil talk come out of your mouths, but only what is useful for building up,[v] as there is need, so that

---

v Other ancient authorities read *building up faith*

PROPHETS OF HOPE, YOUTH ON A MISSION!

Ephesians 4.17–32 has some teachings that were probably used in the preparation for Baptism. Most Hispanic young people have been baptized as Catholics but have not had an opportunity to live their faith in a vital church community. Those who are trying to follow Jesus want to be prophets of hope, as expressed in this song:

We're Prophets of Hope, youth on a mission,
spreading the Gospel of Christ.
We're Prophets of Hope, issuing the challenge:
to build the Reign of God.

Pilgrims on a journey, marching towards our goal.
Led by the Spirit, strengthened by the Lord.
We bear each other's burdens and give each other hope.
Following our savior we press on towards our goal.

We come from towns and cities.
We are immigrants and natives,
laborers and students who want a better life.
We want to be successful, but not at any cost.
Unless we work for justice humanity is lost.

We face discrimination, poverty and drugs.
The values of our culture are all under attack.
But we have faith in Jesus; he will give us strength.
Together we will struggle to build a better world.

The Gospel is our road map, the Church is our guide.
We're Catholic Latinos, youth who take a stand.
Leaders in our churches, reflecting as we go.
Learning from our set-backs, we never give up hope.

(Jose Antonio Rubio)

▶ Eph 4.17–32

Alcohol

The author of Eph 5.10–20 does not mince words. This passage encourages the early Christians to wake up and find out what pleases God. It calls them and us to avoid participating in things that we would be ashamed of if they were exposed in the light. Its tone is not of scolding but rather of passionate encouragement, wanting the best for each of us.

The abuse of alcohol is singled out in this passage as something Christians should avoid. Drinking is an issue virtually everyone confronts during adolescence. The author of Ephesians is saying not that wine is evil in itself, but that getting drunk prevents us from being filled with the Spirit.

Making wise choices about alcohol is important. What temptations do you face in this regard? What choices do you need to make to please God and to enjoy the fullness of life in the Spirit?

▶ Eph 5.10–20

EPH

your words may give grace to those who hear. 30 And do not grieve the Holy Spirit of God, with which you were marked with a seal for the day of redemption. 31 Put away from you all bitterness and wrath and anger and wrangling and slander, together with all malice, 32 and be kind to one another, tenderhearted, forgiving one another, as God in Christ has forgiven you.^w 1 Therefore be imitators of God, as beloved children, 2 and live in love, as Christ loved us^x and gave himself up for us, a fragrant offering and sacrifice to God.

Renounce Pagan Ways

3 But fornication and impurity of any kind, or greed, must not even be mentioned among you, as is proper among saints. 4 Entirely out of place is obscene, silly, and vulgar talk; but instead, let there be thanksgiving. 5 Be sure of this, that no fornicator or impure person, or one who is greedy (that is, an idolater), has any inheritance in the kingdom of Christ and of God.

6 Let no one deceive you with empty words, for because of these things the wrath of God comes on those who are disobedient. 7 Therefore do not be associated with them. 8 For once you were darkness, but now in the Lord you are light. Live as children of light— 9 for the fruit of the light is found in all that is good and right and true. 10 Try to find out what is pleasing to the Lord. 11 Take no part in the unfruitful works of darkness, but instead expose them. 12 For it is shameful even to mention what such people do secretly; 13 but everything exposed by the light becomes visible, 14 for everything that becomes visible is light. Therefore it says,

"Sleeper, awake!
    Rise from the dead,
    and Christ will shine on you."

15 Be careful then how you live, not as unwise people but as wise, 16 making the most of the time, because the days are evil. 17 So do not be foolish, but understand what the will of the Lord is. 18 Do not get drunk with wine, for that is debauchery; but be filled with the Spirit, 19 as you sing psalms and hymns and spiritual songs among yourselves, singing and making melody to the Lord in your hearts, 20 giving thanks to God the Father at all times and for everything in the name of our Lord Jesus Christ.

The Christian Household
(Cp Col 3.18–19)

21 Be subject to one another out of reverence for Christ.

22 Wives, be subject to your husbands as you are to the Lord. 23 For the husband is the head of the wife just as Christ is the head of the church, the body of which he is the Savior. 24 Just as the church is subject to Christ, so also wives ought to be, in everything, to their husbands.

25 Husbands, love your wives, just as Christ loved the church and gave himself up for her, 26 in order to make her holy by cleansing her with the washing of water by the word, 27 so as to present the church to himself in splendor, without a spot or wrinkle or anything of the kind—yes, so that she may be holy and without blemish. 28 In the same way, husbands should love their wives as they do

w Other ancient authorities read *us*   x Other ancient authorities read *you*

Family Relationships

When Eph 5.21—6.4 comes up in the Sunday readings, it sometimes causes confusion. People ask, "How can the Bible teach that a wife should be subject to her husband?" This is another case where we must take into account the cultural context in order to properly interpret the passage. At the time the Letter to the Ephesians was written, the male gender was dominant in society. Wives and children were considered men's property. The letter's challenge to a man to love his wife and to treat his children respectfully was probably viewed as a radical statement by people at the time.

Our culture is different. Just as we should not interpret 6.5–9 as giving permission to own slaves, we should not interpret 5.21—6.4 as commanding submissive behavior of married women today. Understanding this, we can appreciate the passage as it was intended: a practical guide for a family life where love is the rule (see "The Christian Family," Col 3.18—4.1).

Read Eph 5.21—6.4 and then reflect on these questions:

■ How does 6.1–4 indicate that honoring is a two-way street?
■ What does it mean to live in a family where love is the rule?
■ How do you love and honor your parents and siblings?

▶ Eph 5.21—6.4

---

their own bodies. He who loves his wife loves himself. 29 For no one ever hates his own body, but he nourishes and tenderly cares for it, just as Christ does for the church, 30 because we are members of his body.^{y} 31 "For this reason a man will leave his father and mother and be joined to his wife, and the two will become one flesh." 32 This is a great mystery, and I am applying it to Christ and the church. 33 Each of you, however, should love his wife as himself, and a wife should respect her husband.

Children and Parents
(Ex 20.12; Deut 5.16)

Children, obey your parents in the Lord,^{z} for this is right. 2 "Honor your father and mother"—this is the first commandment with a promise: 3 "so that it may be well with you and you may live long on the earth."

4 And, fathers, do not provoke your children to anger, but bring them up in the discipline and instruction of the Lord.

Slaves and Masters

5 Slaves, obey your earthly masters with fear and trembling, in singleness of heart, as you obey Christ; 6 not only while being watched, and in order to please them, but as slaves of Christ, doing the will of God from the heart. 7 Render service with enthusiasm, as to the Lord and not to men and women, 8 knowing that whatever good we do, we will receive the same again from the Lord, whether we are slaves or free.

9 And, masters, do the same to them. Stop threatening them, for you know that both of you have the same Master in heaven, and with him there is no partiality.

The Whole Armor of God

10 Finally, be strong in the Lord and in the strength of his power. 11 Put on the whole armor of God, so that you may be able to stand against the wiles of the devil. 12 For our^a struggle is not against enemies of blood and flesh, but against the rulers, against the authorities, against the cosmic powers of this present darkness, against the spiritual forces of evil in the heavenly places. 13 Therefore take up the whole armor of God, so that you may be able to withstand on that evil day, and having done everything, to stand firm. 14 Stand therefore, and fasten the belt of truth around your waist, and put on the breastplate of righteousness. 15 As shoes for your feet put on whatever will make you ready to proclaim the gospel of peace. 16 With all of these,^{b} take the shield of faith, with which you will be able to quench all the flaming arrows of the evil one. 17 Take the helmet of salvation, and the sword of the Spirit, which is the word of God.

---

^{y} Other ancient authorities add *of his flesh and of his bones*
^{z} Other ancient authorities lack *in the Lord* ^{a} Other ancient authorities read *your* ^{b} Or *In all circumstances*

PRAY IT!

The Peace Prayer of Saint Francis of Assisi

Ephesians 6.10–17 is a poetic passage encouraging us to resist evil. The Peace Prayer of Saint Francis of Assisi tells us how to do this—without using the imagery of warfare. After you read each line of this powerful prayer, close your eyes to meditate on its meaning for your life. What is one way you can live out each line of this prayer?

Lord, make me an instrument of your peace;
where there is hatred, let me sow love;
where there is injury, pardon;
where there is doubt, faith;
where there is despair, hope;
where there is darkness, light;
and where there is sadness, joy.
Grant that I may not so much seek
to be consoled as to console;
to be understood, as to understand,
to be loved as to love;
for it is in giving that we receive,
it is in pardoning that we are pardoned,
and it is in dying that we are born to eternal life.

▸ Eph 6.10–17

18 Pray in the Spirit at all times in every prayer and supplication. To that end keep alert and always persevere in supplication for all the saints. [19] Pray also for me, so that when I speak, a message may be given to me to make known with boldness the mystery of the gospel,[c] [20] for which I am an ambassador in chains. Pray that I may declare it boldly, as I must speak.

Personal Matters and Benediction

21 So that you also may know how I am and what I am doing, Tych'i•cus will tell you everything. He is a dear brother and a faithful minister in the Lord. [22] I am sending him to you for this very purpose, to let you know how we are, and to encourage your hearts.

23 Peace be to the whole community,[d] and love with faith, from God the Father and the Lord Jesus Christ. [24] Grace be with all who have an undying love for our Lord Jesus Christ.[e]

---

[c] Other ancient authorities lack *of the gospel*   [d] Gk *to the brothers*   [e] Other ancient authorities add *Amen*

Philippians

To be, or not to be: that is the question." In this line from Shakespeare's play *Hamlet,* Hamlet wonders which is better for him—to live or to die. He doesn't want to live and suffer, but he's afraid the "sleep of death" may be worse. Either way, he loses. In the Letter to the Philippians, Paul struggles with a similar question.

At a Glance

- **1.1–26.** a greeting, thanks, and a discussion of Paul's imprisonment
- **1.27—2.18.** advice to imitate Christ
- **2.19—3.1.** plans for Timothy and Epaphroditus
- **3.2—4.9.** advice for Christian living
- **4.10–23.** thanks, a final greeting, and a blessing

In-depth

When Paul wrote this letter, he was imprisoned facing a charge that might end in his death. He wrote it either near the end of his life when he was under house arrest in Rome or, more likely, during an earlier imprisonment in Ephesus (see 1 Cor 15.32, 2 Cor 1.8).

Like Hamlet, Paul is torn: "I am hard pressed between" life and death (Phil 1.23). But unlike Hamlet, Paul feels he'll win either way: "For to me, living is Christ and dying is gain" (verse 21). In addition, Paul believes that this imprisonment will not end with his death, because he is still needed to support the new churches he helped start.

Incredibly, even in prison, Paul exhibits a spirit of hope and encouragement. In this short letter, he uses the words *joy, rejoice, be glad,* and *be cheered* seventeen times! Living in Christ doesn't mean everything will always go wonderfully. But it does mean that God can get you through the good times and the difficult times with joy.

In this letter, Paul asks the Philippians—and us—to imitate Christ. Imitating Christ is the way to keep a positive attitude even when things aren't going our way. Paul quotes an early Christian song (2.6–11) to the Philippians to show what imitating Christ means. The song praises our Lord Jesus, who chose to humble himself, chose to become a servant, and was "obedient to the point of death" (verse 8).

It is clear from this letter that Paul had a close relationship with the Philippians. No doubt, they were upset for him. Paul wanted them to rejoice and stop worrying (4.4–6). He encouraged them to present their concerns—all of them— to God in prayer. And he pointed out that if they did so, "the peace of God, which surpasses all understanding, will guard your hearts and your minds in Christ Jesus" (verse 7). What marvelous advice and comfort for people of all times and ages.

Quick Facts

Author
Paul

Date Written
A.D. 52–56 if from Ephesus, A.D. 60–62 if from Rome

Audience
the church in Philippi

Philippians

Salutation

Paul and Timothy, servants*a* of Christ Jesus,

To all the saints in Christ Jesus who are in Phi-lip′pī, with the bishops*b* and deacons:*c*

2 Grace to you and peace from God our Father and the Lord Jesus Christ.

Paul's Prayer for the Philippians

3 I thank my God every time I remember you, 4 constantly praying with joy in every one of my prayers for all of you, 5 because of your sharing in the gospel from the first day until now. 6 I am con-fident of this, that the one who began a good work among you will bring it to completion by the day of Jesus Christ. 7 It is right for me to think this way about all of you, because you hold me in your heart,*d* for all of you share in God's grace*e* with me, both in my imprisonment and in the defense and confirmation of the gospel. 8 For God is my witness, how I long for all of you with the compas-sion of Christ Jesus. 9 And this is my prayer, that your love may overflow more and more with knowledge and full insight 10 to help you to deter-mine what is best, so that in the day of Christ you may be pure and blameless, 11 having produced the harvest of righteousness that comes through Jesus Christ for the glory and praise of God.

Paul's Present Circumstances

12 I want you to know, beloved,*f* that what has happened to me has actually helped to spread the gospel, 13 so that it has become known throughout the whole imperial guard*g* and to ev-eryone else that my imprisonment is for Christ; 14 and most of the brothers and sisters,*f* having been made confident in the Lord by my imprison-ment, dare to speak the word*h* with greater bold-ness and without fear.

15 Some proclaim Christ from envy and ri-valry, but others from goodwill. 16 These proclaim Christ out of love, knowing that I have been put here for the defense of the gospel; 17 the others proclaim Christ out of selfish ambition, not sin-cerely but intending to increase my suffering in my imprisonment. 18 What does it matter? Just this, that Christ is proclaimed in every way, whether out of false motives or true; and in that I rejoice.

Yes, and I will continue to rejoice, 19 for I know that through your prayers and the help of the Spirit of Jesus Christ this will turn out for my de-liverance. 20 It is my eager expectation and hope that I will not be put to shame in any way, but that

---

a Gk *slaves*   *b* Or *overseers*   *c* Or *overseers and helpers*
d Or *because I hold you in my heart*   *e* Gk *in grace*
f Gk *brothers*   *g* Gk *whole praetorium*   *h* Other ancient
authorities read *word of God*

by my speaking with all boldness, Christ will be exalted now as always in my body, whether by life or by death. 21 For to me, living is Christ and dying is gain. 22 If I am to live in the flesh, that means fruitful labor for me; and I do not know which I prefer. 23 I am hard pressed between the two: my desire is to depart and be with Christ, for that is far better; 24 but to remain in the flesh is more necessary for you. 25 Since I am convinced of this, I know that I will remain and continue with all of you for your progress and joy in faith, 26 so that I may share abundantly in your boasting in Christ Jesus when I come to you again.

27 Only, live your life in a manner worthy of the gospel of Christ, so that, whether I come and see you or am absent and hear about you, I will know that you are standing firm in one spirit, striving side by side with one mind for the faith of the gospel, 28 and are in no way intimidated by your opponents. For them this is evidence of their destruction, but of your salvation. And this is God's doing. 29 For he has graciously granted you the privilege not only of believing in Christ, but of suffering for him as well— 30 since you are having the same struggle that you saw I had and now hear that I still have.

Imitating Christ's Humility

If then there is any encouragement in Christ, any consolation from love, any sharing in the Spirit, any compassion and sympathy, 2 make my joy complete: be of the same mind, having the same love, being in full accord and of one mind. 3 Do

FRIENDSHIP

In Phil 1.3–11, Paul writes beautifully of his love for and friendship with the people living in Philippi. We need to remember that Paul— and the other people who wrote the inspired words of the Scriptures—was a real person with problems and needs. He had some dear friends in Philippi, and his words to them provide a great model of true friendship: sharing the ups and downs, being committed to one another, being thankful for one another, and wanting the best for one another. Friendship in Christ is like that!

Who are true friends for you? How can you keep Christ at the center of your friendships?

▶ Phil 1.3–11

nothing from selfish ambition or conceit, but in humility regard others as better than yourselves. 4 Let each of you look not to your own interests, but to the interests of others. 5 Let the same mind be in you that was[i] in Christ Jesus,

6 who, though he was in the form of God,
      did not regard equality with God
         as something to be exploited,
7 but emptied himself,
      taking the form of a slave,
         being born in human likeness.

---

i Or that you have

Divine Humility, Cosmic Glory

LIVE IT!

Mention the name Jesus, or the title Christ, and many images spring to mind. That is good, because no single image can capture Jesus' true nature completely.

In Phil 2.6–11, borrowing from a hymn sung in the earliest days of the church, Paul describes the mystery of Jesus Christ. Jesus willingly gave up the right to remain "in the form of God" (verse 6) and entered our world as a human being. He lived in utter humility, from his simple birth to his Crucifixion. Because of his humility and obedience, Jesus' name is exalted by God so that Jesus Christ is now Lord of all creation. Because of Jesus' humility, creation achieves cosmic harmony!

To be the loving people God calls us to be, we must imitate Christ's humility in our love for one another. Most of us are used to seeing those who are "powerful" in this world being served by others. But Paul reminds us it is the nature of Jesus to serve. Christians are called to be powerful in a radically different way—to see humble service as their basic call and the path to true glory—with the "same mind . . . that was in Christ Jesus" (verse 5).

▶ Phil 2.1–11

And being found in human form,
8 he humbled himself
and became obedient to the point of
death—
even death on a cross.

9 Therefore God also highly exalted him
and gave him the name
that is above every name,
10 so that at the name of Jesus
every knee should bend,
in heaven and on earth and under the
earth,
11 and every tongue should confess
that Jesus Christ is Lord,
to the glory of God the Father.

Shining as Lights in the World

12 Therefore, my beloved, just as you have always obeyed me, not only in my presence, but much more now in my absence, work out your own salvation with fear and trembling; 13 for it is God who is at work in you, enabling you both to will and to work for his good pleasure.

14 Do all things without murmuring and arguing, 15 so that you may be blameless and innocent, children of God without blemish in the midst of a crooked and perverse generation, in which you shine like stars in the world. 16 It is by your holding fast to the word of life that I can boast on the day of Christ that I did not run in vain or labor in vain. 17 But even if I am being poured out as a libation over the sacrifice and the offering of your faith, I am glad and rejoice with all of you— 18 and in the same way you also must be glad and rejoice with me.

Timothy and Epaphroditus

19 I hope in the Lord Jesus to send Timothy to you soon, so that I may be cheered by news of you. 20 I have no one like him who will be genuinely concerned for your welfare. 21 All of them are seeking their own interests, not those of Jesus Christ. 22 But Timothy's[j] worth you know, how like a son with a father he has served with me in the work of the gospel. 23 I hope therefore to send him as soon as I see how things go with me; 24 and I trust in the Lord that I will also come soon.

25 Still, I think it necessary to send to you E•paph•ro•di′tus—my brother and co-worker and fellow soldier, your messenger[k] and minister to my need; 26 for he has been longing for[l] all of you, and has been distressed because you heard that he was ill. 27 He was indeed so ill that he nearly died. But God had mercy on him, and not only on him but on me also, so that I would not have one sor-

row after another. 28 I am the more eager to send him, therefore, in order that you may rejoice at seeing him again, and that I may be less anxious. 29 Welcome him then in the Lord with all joy, and honor such people, 30 because he came close to death for the work of Christ,[m] risking his life to make up for those services that you could not give me.

Finally, my brothers and sisters,[n] rejoice[o] in the Lord.

Breaking with the Past

To write the same things to you is not troublesome to me, and for you it is a safeguard.

2 Beware of the dogs, beware of the evil workers, beware of those who mutilate the flesh![p] 3 For it is we who are the circumcision, who worship in the Spirit of God[q] and boast in Christ Jesus and have no confidence in the flesh— 4 even though I, too, have reason for confidence in the flesh.

If anyone else has reason to be confident in the flesh, I have more: 5 circumcised on the eighth day, a member of the people of Israel, of the tribe of Benjamin, a Hebrew born of Hebrews; as to the law, a Phar′i•see; 6 as to zeal, a persecutor of the church; as to righteousness under the law, blameless.

7 Yet whatever gains I had, these I have come to regard as loss because of Christ. 8 More than that, I regard everything as loss because of the surpassing value of knowing Christ Jesus my Lord. For his sake I have suffered the loss of all things, and I regard them as rubbish, in order that I may gain Christ 9 and be found in him, not having a righteousness of my own that comes from the law, but one that comes through faith in Christ,[r] the righteousness from God based on faith. 10 I want to know Christ[s] and the power of his resurrection and the sharing of his sufferings by becoming like him in his death, 11 if somehow I may attain the resurrection from the dead.

Pressing toward the Goal

12 Not that I have already obtained this or have already reached the goal;[t] but I press on to make it my own, because Christ Jesus has made me his own. 13 Beloved,[u] I do not consider that I have made it my own;[v] but this one thing I do:

j Gk his   k Gk apostle   l Other ancient authorities read longing to see   m Other ancient authorities read of the Lord   n Gk my brothers   o Or farewell   p Gk the mutilation   q Other ancient authorities read worship God in spirit   r Or through the faith of Christ   s Gk him   t Or have already been made perfect   u Gk Brothers   v Other ancient authorities read my own yet

forgetting what lies behind and straining forward to what lies ahead, 14 I press on toward the goal for the prize of the heavenly*w* call of God in Christ Jesus. 15 Let those of us then who are mature be of the same mind; and if you think differently about anything, this too God will reveal to you. 16 Only let us hold fast to what we have attained.

17 Brothers and sisters,*x* join in imitating me, and observe those who live according to the example you have in us. 18 For many live as enemies of the cross of Christ; I have often told you of them, and now I tell you even with tears. 19 Their end is destruction; their god is the belly; and their glory is in their shame; their minds are set on earthly things. 20 But our citizenship*y* is in heaven, and it is from there that we are expecting a Savior, the Lord Jesus Christ. 21 He will transform the body of our humiliation*z* that it may be conformed to the body of his glory,*a* by the power that also enables him to make all things subject to himself. 1 Therefore, my brothers and sisters,*b* whom I love and long for, my joy and crown, stand firm in the Lord in this way, my beloved.

Exhortations

2 I urge Eū·ō'di·a and I urge Syn'ty·chē to be of the same mind in the Lord. 3 Yes, and I ask you also, my loyal companion,*c* help these women, for they have struggled beside me in the work of the gospel, together with Clement and the rest of my co-workers, whose names are in the book of life.

4 Rejoice*d* in the Lord always; again I will say, Rejoice.*d* 5 Let your gentleness be known to everyone. The Lord is near. 6 Do not worry about anything, but in everything by prayer and supplication with thanksgiving let your requests be made known to God. 7 And the peace of God, which surpasses all understanding, will guard your hearts and your minds in Christ Jesus.

8 Finally, beloved,*e* whatever is true, whatever is honorable, whatever is just, whatever is pure, whatever is pleasing, whatever is commendable, if there is any excellence and if there is anything worthy of praise, think about*f* these things. 9 Keep on doing the things that you have learned and received and heard and seen in me, and the God of peace will be with you.

Acknowledgment of the Philippians' Gift

10 I rejoice*g* in the Lord greatly that now at last you have revived your concern for me; indeed, you were concerned for me, but had no opportunity to

---

w Gk *upward*　　*x* Gk *Brothers*　　*y* Or *commonwealth* *z* Or *our humble bodies*　　*a* Or *his glorious body*　　*b* Gk *my brothers*　　*c* Or *loyal Syzygus*　　*d* Or *Farewell* *e* Gk *brothers*　　*f* Gk *take account of*　　*g* Gk *I rejoiced*

Commitment to Your Goal

In what ways have you become more mature in the last five years? How do other people recognize that you are maturing?

In Phil 3.13–16, Paul describes one measure of maturity—the ability to keep a commitment to an ultimate goal. Mature people—whether sixteen or sixty—are always striving to perfect themselves in pursuit of their goals.

Paul says the goal that guides his life is "to know Christ and the power of his resurrection" (verse 10). What is the goal that guides your life? How hard is it for you to stay focused on your goal?

▸ Phil 3.13–16

NATIVE AMERICAN

The Beauty of Creation

Paul ends his message to the Philippians by encouraging them to keep their minds on anything that is of excellence and worthy of praise. This would certainly include the wonder and beauty of creation, something Native Americans are deeply aware of. Let this Navaho prayer in praise of creation inspire you to keep focused on the beauty God has provided in the world around us:

> *I walk with beauty before me*
> *I walk with beauty behind me*
> *I walk with beauty above me*
> *I walk with beauty below me*
> *Beauty has been restored from the East*
> *Beauty has been restored from the South*
> *Beauty has been restored from the West*
> *Beauty has been restored from the North*
> *Beauty has been restored from the sky-top*
> *Beauty has been restored from the*
> *   earth-bottom*
> *Beauty has been restored from all around me*
> *(From Michael F. Steltenkamp,*
> *   The Sacred Vision, p. 92)*

▶ Phil 4.8–9

show it.*h* ¹¹ Not that I am referring to being in need; for I have learned to be content with whatever I have. ¹² I know what it is to have little, and I know what it is to have plenty. In any and all circumstances I have learned the secret of being well-fed and of going hungry, of having plenty and of being in need. ¹³ I can do all things through him who strengthens me. ¹⁴ In any case, it was kind of you to share my distress.

15 You Phi·lip′pi·ans indeed know that in the early days of the gospel, when I left Mac·e·dō′ni·a, no church shared with me in the matter of giving and receiving, except you alone. ¹⁶ For even when I was in Thes·sa·lo·ni′ca, you sent me help for my needs more than once. ¹⁷ Not that I seek the gift, but I seek the profit that accumulates to your account. ¹⁸ I have been paid in full and have more than enough; I am fully satisfied, now that I have received from E·paph·ro·dī′tus the gifts you sent, a fragrant offering, a sacrifice acceptable and pleasing to God. ¹⁹ And my God will fully satisfy every need of yours according to his riches in glory in Christ Jesus. ²⁰ To our God and Father be glory forever and ever. Amen.

Final Greetings and Benediction

21 Greet every saint in Christ Jesus. The friends*i* who are with me greet you. ²² All the saints greet you, especially those of the emperor's household.

23 The grace of the Lord Jesus Christ be with your spirit.*j*

---

h Gk lacks *to show it*   *i* Gk *brothers*   *j* Other ancient authorities add *Amen*

P H I L

Every now and then, we hear about some cult on the news. All cults tend to have the same characteristics: strict rules, strange ideas, and total obedience to the leader. Cults have been around a long time. In fact, some strange things that sounded pretty cultish were going on in the early Christian community at Colossae. The author's advice in the Letter to the Colossians is pretty direct: Let Christ be the one and only ruler in your heart!

At a Glance

- **1.1–14.** a greeting
- **1.15—2.3.** a description of Christ as the First, the Creator, the One
- **2.4–23.** warnings against false teachers
- **3.1–4.6.** advice for Christian living
- **4.7–18.** final greetings

In-depth

This letter attacks a group that was teaching a weird mixture of ideas. It insisted on rituals (2.16), plenty of regulations (verse 22), severe treatment of one's own body (verse 23), special festivals (verse 16), and a fancy philosophy that included "the elemental spirits of the universe" (verse 8). This strange group might have had Jewish roots, because it observed the Sabbath (verse 16). The biggest concern was that it was teaching that faith in Christ's death and Resurrection was not enough for salvation.

Against the backdrop of all this mysterious thinking, the author—who probably wasn't Paul but a disciple of Paul's—declares the supreme mystery of Christ. Quoting a Christian hymn (1.15–20), the writer says Christ is lifted up not only as the firstborn of creation, but also as the one through whom everything was created and who holds everything together. Christ is all we need!

Christians believe that Jesus is more than just a great teacher; they believe Jesus is God, who chose to become human and live with us. This letter gives us an early statement of that belief: "In [Christ] the whole fullness of deity dwells bodily" (2.9).

The Letter to the Colossians also offers comforting words about our God. God has given us life and forgiveness. God erased the record of our sins, and set it aside, "nailing it to the cross" (verse 14). Unlike cults that burden their followers with guilt and impossible rules, our God frees us from guilt and gives us life! As you read this letter, you will find these and many other words to live by: "God's chosen ones . . . forgive each other . . . clothe yourselves with love . . . And let the peace of Christ rule in your hearts" (3.12–15).

Quick Facts

Author
most likely a follower of Paul's (see "Introduction to the Letters and Revelation")

Date Written
around A.D. 61 if by Paul, after A.D. 61 if by a follower

Audience
the Christian community at Colossae

Colossians

Salutation

Paul, an apostle of Christ Jesus by the will of God, and Timothy our brother,

2 To the saints and faithful brothers and sisters[a] in Christ in Co·los'saē:

Grace to you and peace from God our Father.

Paul Thanks God for the Colossians

3 In our prayers for you we always thank God, the Father of our Lord Jesus Christ, 4 for we have heard of your faith in Christ Jesus and of the love that you have for all the saints, 5 because of the hope laid up for you in heaven. You have heard of this hope before in the word of the truth, the gospel 6 that has come to you. Just as it is bearing fruit and growing in the whole world, so it has been bearing fruit among yourselves from the day you heard it and truly comprehended the grace of God. 7 This you learned from Ep'a·phras, our beloved fellow servant.[b] He is a faithful minister of Christ on your[c] behalf, 8 and he has made known to us your love in the Spirit.

9 For this reason, since the day we heard it, we have not ceased praying for you and asking that you may be filled with the knowledge of God's[d] will in all spiritual wisdom and understanding, 10 so that you may lead lives worthy of the Lord, fully pleasing to him, as you bear fruit in every good work and as you grow in the knowledge of God. 11 May you be made strong with all the strength that comes from his glorious power, and may you be prepared to endure everything with patience, while joyfully 12 giving thanks to the Father, who has enabled[e] you[f] to share in the inheritance of the saints in the light. 13 He has rescued us from the power of darkness and transferred us into the kingdom of his beloved Son, 14 in whom we have redemption, the forgiveness of sins.[g]

The Supremacy of Christ
(Cp Jn 1.1–5)

15 He is the image of the invisible God, the firstborn of all creation; 16 for in[h] him all things in heaven and on earth were created, things visible and invisible, whether thrones or dominions or rulers or powers—all things have been created through him and for him. 17 He himself is before all things, and in[h] him all things hold together. 18 He is the head of the body, the church; he is the beginning, the firstborn from the dead, so that he might come to have first place in everything. 19 For in him all the fullness of God was pleased to dwell, 20 and through him God was pleased to reconcile to himself all things, whether on earth or in heaven, by making peace through the blood of his cross.

21 And you who were once estranged and

---

a Gk *brothers*   *b* Gk *slave*   *c* Other ancient authorities read *our*   *d* Gk *his*   *e* Other ancient authorities read *called*   *f* Other ancient authorities read *us*   *g* Other ancient authorities add *through his blood*   *h* Or *by*

The Image of God

It is possible to describe God by naming certain characteristics. We can say God is all-powerful, all-knowing, and eternal. But knowing about God is not the same as knowing God. So how can we really understand the mysterious, invisible, eternal God?

The author of Colossians gives us a clue. This writer calls Jesus "the image of the invisible God" (Col 1.15). If we want to know about God, who is hidden from us in mystery, we look at Christ. God has existed for all eternity; through God, all things were created; and in God, all things continue to "hold together." But God also appeared on our earth as a real human being, Jesus.

Is there still mystery? Yes. We still cannot comprehend God completely. But we can understand more about God by getting to know more about Jesus Christ.

► Col 1.15–20

---

hostile in mind, doing evil deeds, [22] he has now reconciled[i] in his fleshly body[j] through death, so as to present you holy and blameless and irreproachable before him— [23] provided that you continue securely established and steadfast in the faith, without shifting from the hope promised by the gospel that you heard, which has been proclaimed to every creature under heaven. I, Paul, became a servant of this gospel.

Paul's Interest in the Colossians

[24] I am now rejoicing in my sufferings for your sake, and in my flesh I am completing what is lacking in Christ's afflictions for the sake of his body, that is, the church. [25] I became its servant according to God's commission that was given to me for you, to make the word of God fully known, [26] the mystery that has been hidden throughout the ages and generations but has now been revealed to his saints. [27] To them God chose to make known how great among the Gentiles are the riches of the glory of this mystery, which is Christ in you, the hope of glory. [28] It is he whom we proclaim, warning everyone and teaching everyone in all wisdom, so that we may present everyone mature in Christ. [29] For this I toil and struggle with all the energy that he powerfully inspires within me.

For I want you to know how much I am struggling for you, and for those in Lā•o•di•cē′a, and for all who have not seen me face to face. [2] I want their hearts to be encouraged and united in love, so that they may have all the riches of assured understanding and have the knowledge of God's mystery, that is, Christ himself,[k] [3] in whom are hidden all the treasures of wisdom and knowledge. [4] I am saying this so that no one may deceive you with

plausible arguments. [5] For though I am absent in body, yet I am with you in spirit, and I rejoice to see your morale and the firmness of your faith in Christ.

Fullness of Life in Christ

[6] As you therefore have received Christ Jesus the Lord, continue to live your lives[l] in him, [7] rooted and built up in him and established in the faith, just as you were taught, abounding in thanksgiving.

[8] See to it that no one takes you captive through philosophy and empty deceit, according to human tradition, according to the elemental spirits of the universe,[m] and not according to Christ. [9] For in him the whole fullness of deity dwells bodily, [10] and you have come to fullness in him, who is the head of every ruler and authority. [11] In him also you were circumcised with a spiritual circumcision,[n] by putting off the body of the flesh in the circumcision of Christ; [12] when you were buried with him in baptism, you were also raised with him through faith in the power of God, who raised him from the dead. [13] And when you were dead in trespasses and the uncircumcision of your flesh, God[o] made you[p] alive together with him, when he forgave us all our trespasses, [14] erasing the record that stood against us with its legal demands. He set this aside, nailing it to the cross. [15] He disarmed[q] the rulers and authorities

---

[i] Other ancient authorities read *you have now been reconciled*   [j] Gk *in the body of his flesh*   [k] Other ancient authorities read *of the mystery of God, both of the Father and of Christ*   [l] Gk *to walk*   [m] Or *the rudiments of the world*   [n] Gk *a circumcision made without hands*   [o] Gk *he*   [p] Other ancient authorities read *made us*; others, *made*   [q] Or *divested himself of*

and made a public example of them, triumphing over them in it.

16 Therefore do not let anyone condemn you in matters of food and drink or of observing festivals, new moons, or sabbaths. 17 These are only a shadow of what is to come, but the substance belongs to Christ. 18 Do not let anyone disqualify you, insisting on self-abasement and worship of angels, dwelling^r on visions,^{s} puffed up without cause by a human way of thinking,^{t} 19 and not holding fast to the head, from whom the whole body, nourished and held together by its ligaments and sinews, grows with a growth that is from God.

Warnings against False Teachers

20 If with Christ you died to the elemental spirits of the universe,^{u} why do you live as if you still belonged to the world? Why do you submit to regulations, 21 "Do not handle, Do not taste, Do not touch"? 22 All these regulations refer to things that perish with use; they are simply human commands and teachings. 23 These have indeed an appearance of wisdom in promoting self-imposed piety, humility, and severe treatment of the body, but they are of no value in checking self-indulgence.^{v}

PRAY IT?

Where Are Your Roots?

What is one thing that motivates you, that keeps you going? Is it a special friendship or a close family? the drive to succeed or to be the best? Maybe it's having a car or holding down a job.

Colossians 2.7 says that we should be "rooted and built up in [Christ]." Where you have your roots is where you get your nourishment to keep going. Think again about what motivates you. Is it enough to nourish a full, rich life?

In your prayer, journal or reflect on the following questions:

- What things are most important in your life right now? Where is God in each of those things?
- What do you need to reorder so that God "might come to have first place" in your life (1.18)?

▸ Col 2.6–7

The New Life in Christ

So if you have been raised with Christ, seek the things that are above, where Christ is, seated at the right hand of God. 2 Set your minds on things that are above, not on things that are on earth, 3 for you have died, and your life is hidden with Christ in God. 4 When Christ who is your^w life is revealed, then you also will be revealed with him in glory.

5 Put to death, therefore, whatever in you is earthly: fornication, impurity, passion, evil desire, and greed (which is idolatry). 6 On account of these the wrath of God is coming on those who are disobedient.^{x} 7 These are the ways you also once followed, when you were living that life.^{y} 8 But now you must get rid of all such things—anger, wrath, malice, slander, and abusive^z language from your mouth. 9 Do not lie to one another, seeing that you have stripped off the old self with its practices 10 and have clothed yourselves with the new self, which is being renewed in knowledge according to the image of its creator. 11 In that renewal^a there is no longer Greek and Jew, circumcised and uncircumcised, barbarian, Scyth'i•an, slave and free; but Christ is all and in all!

12 As God's chosen ones, holy and beloved, clothe yourselves with compassion, kindness, humility, meekness, and patience. 13 Bear with one another and, if anyone has a complaint against another, forgive each other; just as the Lord^b has forgiven you, so you also must forgive. 14 Above all, clothe yourselves with love, which binds everything together in perfect harmony. 15 And let the peace of Christ rule in your hearts, to which indeed you were called in the one body. And be thankful. 16 Let the word of Christ^c dwell in you richly; teach and admonish one another in all wisdom; and with gratitude in your hearts sing psalms, hymns, and spiritual songs to God.^{d} 17 And whatever you do, in word or deed, do everything in the name of the Lord Jesus, giving thanks to God the Father through him.

COL

^{r} Other ancient authorities read *not dwelling*　^{s} Meaning of Gk uncertain　^{t} Gk *by the mind of his flesh*　^{u} Or *the rudiments of the world*　^{v} Or *are of no value, serving only to indulge the flesh*　^{w} Other authorities read *our*　^{x} Other ancient authorities lack *on those who are disobedient* (Gk *the children of disobedience*)　^{y} Or *living among such people*　^{z} Or *filthy*　^{a} Gk *its creator,* ^{11}*where*　^{b} Other ancient authorities read *just as Christ*　^{c} Other ancient authorities read *of God,* or *of the Lord*　^{d} Other ancient authorities read *to the Lord*

A Top-Shelf Life

In stores, the best product is often put on the top shelf, for all to see. It is also usually priced higher than other products, and therefore is not purchased by everyone. Colossians 3.1 calls us to "seek the things that are above, where Christ is"—in other words, a top-shelf life.

Living a top-shelf life means living a moral life, free from sin. It means ridding ourselves of "anger, wrath, malice, slander, and abusive language" (verse 8). It means avoiding "fornication, impurity, . . . strife, jealousy, anger, quarrels, dissensions, factions, envy, drunkenness, carousing" (Gal 5.19–21). It also means living with "compassion, kindness, humility, meekness, and patience," and forgiving one another and clothing ourselves with love (Col 3.12–14). Paul and the other authors of the letters focus on moral living because it is what God wants for us. How could we claim to have faith in Jesus Christ and choose to live in sin?

Living a moral life, a top-shelf life, isn't always easy. But it is the way to true happiness, holiness, and health. This is the witness of the church and generations of Christian believers. Why settle for less?

▶ Col 3.1–4

Rules for Christian Households
(Cp Eph 5.21 — 6.9)

18 Wives, be subject to your husbands, as is fitting in the Lord. 19 Husbands, love your wives and never treat them harshly.

20 Children, obey your parents in everything, for this is your acceptable duty in the Lord. 21 Fathers, do not provoke your children, or they may lose heart. 22 Slaves, obey your earthly masters*e* in everything, not only while being watched and in order to please them, but wholeheartedly, fearing the Lord.*e* 23 Whatever your task, put yourselves into it, as done for the Lord and not for your masters,*f* 24 since you know that from the Lord you will receive the inheritance as your reward; you serve*g* the Lord Christ. 25 For the wrongdoer will be paid back for whatever wrong has been done, and there is no partiality. 1 Masters, treat your slaves justly and fairly, for you know that you also have a Master in heaven.

Further Instructions

2 Devote yourselves to prayer, keeping alert in it with thanksgiving. 3 At the same time pray for us as well that God will open to us a door for the word, that we may declare the mystery of Christ, for which I am in prison, 4 so that I may reveal it clearly, as I should.

5 Conduct yourselves wisely toward outsiders, making the most of the time.*h* 6 Let your speech always be gracious, seasoned with salt, so that you may know how you ought to answer everyone.

Final Greetings and Benediction
(Cp Eph 6.21–22)

7 Tych'i•cus will tell you all the news about me; he is a beloved brother, a faithful minister, and a fellow servant*i* in the Lord. 8 I have sent him to you for this very purpose, so that you may know how we are*j* and that he may encourage your hearts; 9 he is coming with Ō•nes'i•mus, the faithful and beloved brother, who is one of you. They will tell you about everything here.

10 Ar•is•tar'chus my fellow prisoner greets you, as does Mark the cousin of Bar'na•bas, concerning whom you have received instructions—if he comes to you, welcome him. 11 And Jesus who is called Justus greets you. These are the only ones of the circumcision among my co-workers for the kingdom of God, and they have been a comfort to me. 12 Ep'a•phras, who is one of you, a servant*i* of Christ Jesus, greets you. He is always wrestling in his prayers on your behalf, so that you may stand mature and fully assured in everything that God wills. 13 For I testify for him that he has worked hard for you and for those in Lā•o•di•cē'a and in Hī•er•ap'o•lis. 14 Luke, the beloved physician, and Dē'mas greet you. 15 Give my greetings to the brothers and sisters*k* in Lā•o•di•cē'a, and to Nym'-pha and the church in her house. 16 And when this letter has been read among you, have it read also

---

e In Greek the same word is used for *master* and *Lord*
f Gk *not for men*   *g* Or *you are slaves of*, or *be slaves of*
h Or *opportunity*   *i* Gk *slave*   *j* Other authorities read *that I may know how you are*   *k* Gk *brothers*

LIVE IT!

The Christian Family

The rules for Christian families in chapter 3 of Colossians seem a little strange in our culture. But Colossians is simply calling families to be rooted in loving relationships (see also "Family Relationships," Eph 5.21—6.4). A family is God's gift. It is a community where we are loved and accepted simply for who we are, and where we can freely love in return, a community we can turn to for comfort and support. The Catholic church calls families the domestic church, meaning that they are the primary place where people learn about God and God's love.

Being the domestic church doesn't just happen. Every member of a family must make an effort. That means taking time to listen to one another, to help one another out, and to respect each person in the family. Sometimes, selfishness gets in the way of making God's love real. At those times, family members must try even harder. Taking time to pray together, and to read and talk about the Bible together, can help a family focus on God's presence in its life.

How is your family life? Is love the guiding rule? Does everyone take time to pray together? Do you support family activities willingly? Are you generous in helping with family chores? Are you your best self around your family?

▶ Col 3.18—4.1

in the church of the Lā·o·di·cē'ans; and see that you read also the letter from Lā·o·di·cē'a. [17] And say to Ar·chip'pus, "See that you complete the task that you have received in the Lord."

18 I, Paul, write this greeting with my own hand. Remember my chains. Grace be with you.[1]

---

[1] Other ancient authorities add *Amen*

COL

You're about to read what is probably the oldest book in the New Testament. It was written a little over twenty years after Jesus' death and Resurrection, by a man named Paul. It is the very first Christian letter that we still have! In it, Paul answers some questions that were on people's minds back then. Even though it was written so long ago, you might have some of the same questions.

At a Glance

- **Chapter 1.** a greeting
- **Chapters 2–3.** a discussion of Paul's ministry and Timothy's trip
- **4.1—5.11.** advice about life now and the life to come
- **5.12–28.** final advice and a blessing

In-depth

Thessalonica was the capital of a Roman province called Macedonia. Today, that area is in northern Greece (see map 7, "Paul's First and Second Journeys"). Acts of the Apostles, chapter 17, tells us that Paul spent three weeks in Thessalonica preaching about Jesus Christ. Because of his preaching, many people, mainly Gentiles (non-Jews), became Christians. Paul was forced to leave the city by the non-Christians there. After he left, he worried about the new Christian community, so he sent his coworker Timothy back to check things out. When Timothy rejoined Paul, he had some great news. Even though the Thessalonians were being persecuted, they were staying strong in their "faith and love" (1 Thess 3.6).

When you read this letter, you can tell that Paul is thankful that the church is thriving! Four different times he expresses his gratitude. But he also apparently feels the need to defend himself against some critics. So he reminds everyone that he has been genuine and "like a nurse tenderly caring for her own children" (2.7).

After reassuring the Thessalonians that the persecution they are suffering is to be expected (3.3–4), Paul takes the time to answer some questions about the coming of the Lord at the end of time. Apparently, some of the Thessalonians are concerned about their friends who have already died. Will they join the living when Christ returns again?

Paul tells them that they don't have to worry about those who die before Jesus returns; the dead will be raised first and join the living, to "be with the Lord forever" (4.17). When will that happen? they ask. No one knows, Paul says, but Christians don't have to be afraid of that day. Their job is to stay alert and clothe themselves with "faith and love, and . . . hope" (5.8).

Quick Facts

Author
Paul

Date Written
A.D. 50–51

Audience
the mainly Gentile church in Thessalonica

1 Thessalonians

5.4–6

Salutation

Paul, Sil•vā'nus, and Timothy,
  To the church of the Thes•sa•lō'ni•ans in God the Father and the Lord Jesus Christ:
  Grace to you and peace.

The Thessalonians' Faith and Example

2 We always give thanks to God for all of you and mention you in our prayers, constantly ³ remembering before our God and Father your work of faith and labor of love and steadfastness of hope in our Lord Jesus Christ. ⁴ For we know, brothers and sisters*a* beloved by God, that he has chosen you, ⁵ because our message of the gospel came to you not in word only, but also in power and in the Holy Spirit and with full conviction; just as you know what kind of persons we proved to be among you for your sake. ⁶ And you became imitators of us and of the Lord, for in spite of persecution you received the word with joy inspired by the Holy Spirit, ⁷ so that you became an example to all the believers in Mac•e•dō'ni•a and in A•chā'i•a. ⁸ For the word of the Lord has sounded forth from you not only in Mac•e•dō'ni•a and A•chā'i•a, but in every place your faith in God has become known, so that we have no need to speak about it. ⁹ For the people of those regions*b* report about us what kind of welcome we had among you, and how you turned to God from idols, to serve a living and true God, ¹⁰ and to wait for his Son from heaven, whom he raised from the dead— Jesus, who rescues us from the wrath that is coming.

Paul's Ministry in Thessalonica
(Cp Acts 17.1–9)

You yourselves know, brothers and sisters,*a* that our coming to you was not in vain, ² but though we had already suffered and been shamefully mistreated at Phi•lip'pī, as you know, we had courage in our God to declare to you the gospel of God in spite of great opposition. ³ For our appeal does not spring from deceit or impure motives or trickery, ⁴ but just as we have been approved by God to be entrusted with the message of the gospel, even so we speak, not to please mortals, but to please God who tests our hearts. ⁵ As you know and as God is our witness, we never came with words of flattery or with a pretext for greed; ⁶ nor did we seek praise from mortals, whether from you or from others, ⁷ though we might have made demands as apostles of Christ. But we were gentle*c* among you, like a nurse tenderly caring for her own children. ⁸ So deeply do we care for you that we are determined

---

a Gk *brothers* *b* Gk *For they* *c* Other ancient authorities read *infants*

PRAY IT!
Doing the Right Thing

Angela normally keeps to herself. But the three girls teasing Nicole have her almost in tears. Angela hesitates to say anything. But then, she looks at her WWJD ("What would Jesus do?") bracelet and speaks up: "Stop it, you guys. Can't you see you are hurting Nicole's feelings?" The three girls are quiet for a second. Then, they start in on Angela. "Hey, this isn't your business. Who do you think you are telling us what to do?" The comments sting, but despite them, Angela experiences a growing sense of peace, almost as if she can feel Jesus smiling at her.

Lord, make me stronger. Stronger to do the right thing—the Christlike thing—the next time I'm in a hurtful situation. Stronger to declare my faith in you as the reason for my actions. Stronger to even forgive those who insult me.

Jesus, give me the courage to live out what I believe in my heart, and allow me the wisdom to know that it comes from you. Amen.

▶ 1 Thess 2.1–2

to share with you not only the gospel of God but also our own selves, because you have become very dear to us.

9 You remember our labor and toil, brothers and sisters;*d* we worked night and day, so that we might not burden any of you while we proclaimed to you the gospel of God. 10 You are witnesses, and God also, how pure, upright, and blameless our conduct was toward you believers. 11 As you know, we dealt with each one of you like a father with his children, 12 urging and encouraging you and pleading that you lead a life worthy of God, who calls you into his own kingdom and glory.

13 We also constantly give thanks to God for this, that when you received the word of God that you heard from us, you accepted it not as a human word but as what it really is, God's word, which is also at work in you believers. 14 For you, brothers and sisters,*d* became imitators of the churches of

God in Christ Jesus that are in Judea, for you suffered the same things from your own compatriots as they did from the Jews, 15 who killed both the Lord Jesus and the prophets,*e* and drove us out; they displease God and oppose everyone 16 by hindering us from speaking to the Gentiles so that they may be saved. Thus they have constantly been filling up the measure of their sins; but God's wrath has overtaken them at last.*f*

PRAY IT!
Encouragement

Sometimes, we feel alone in our faith. We wonder if anyone feels, thinks, or prays the way we do. As a first missionary of the faith, Paul must have experienced his share of dark days when he wondered if the people would really accept the Good News. He must have been so encouraged when Timothy returned to tell him of the "faith and love" of the Thessalonians (1 Thess 3.6).

The Christian faith is never meant to be held privately. We don't grow in our faith, hope, and love by being isolated from other people. Like Paul, we need the encouragement and challenge of other people: our family, friends, and the entire Christian community.

In your prayer, reflect or journal on the following questions:
- How do you encourage others to grow in Christ?
- How do others encourage or challenge you to grow in faith, hope, and love?

▶ 1 Thess 3.6–13

Paul's Desire to Visit the Thessalonians Again

17 As for us, brothers and sisters,*d* when, for a short time, we were made orphans by being separated from you—in person, not in heart—we longed with great eagerness to see you face to face. 18 For we wanted to come to you—certainly I, Paul, wanted to again and again—but Satan blocked our way. 19 For what is our hope or joy or crown of

d Gk *brothers*   *e* Other ancient authorities read *their own prophets*   *f* Or *completely* or *forever*

LIVE IT!

True Love Waits

The church has taught from its beginning that fornication, including premarital sex, is wrong. Paul's teaching in 1 Thess 4.1–8 clearly explains why. If we get involved in a sexual relationship outside of marriage, we are exploiting another person (verse 6)—even if that person is a willing partner. God intends sexual intercourse to create a lifelong bond between two people for the creation of a family. Sexual expression outside of marriage diminishes the beautiful purpose of sexual intimacy.

Paul reminds the Thessalonians to live in ways pleasing to God. To behave contrary to God's purpose is to say no to the gift of the Holy Spirit and to the holiness God wants for us. In our culture, sex is often portrayed as a recreational activity, violating the gift of sexuality God created within us! God's message in the Bible and the church calls us to take a stand that is unpopular with some people—to support sexual abstinence until marriage.

Valuing our gift of sexuality and expressing it as God intended is not always easy. However, this old idea has a new slogan and campaign today: True love waits. Think about it!

▶ 1 Thess 4.1–8

boasting before our Lord Jesus at his coming? Is it not you? 20 Yes, you are our glory and joy! Therefore when we could bear it no longer, we decided to be left alone in Athens; 2 and we sent Timothy, our brother and co-worker for God in proclaiming*g* the gospel of Christ, to strengthen and encourage you for the sake of your faith, 3 so that no one would be shaken by these persecutions. Indeed, you yourselves know that this is what we are destined for. 4 In fact, when we were with you, we told you beforehand that we were to suffer persecution; so it turned out, as you know. 5 For this reason, when I could bear it no longer, I sent to find out about your faith; I was afraid that somehow the tempter had tempted you and that our labor had been in vain.

Timothy's Encouraging Report

6 But Timothy has just now come to us from you, and has brought us the good news of your faith and love. He has told us also that you always remember us kindly and long to see us—just as we long to see you. 7 For this reason, brothers and sisters,*h* during all our distress and persecution we have been encouraged about you through your faith. 8 For we now live, if you continue to stand firm in the Lord. 9 How can we thank God enough for you in return for all the joy that we feel before our God because of you? 10 Night and day we pray most earnestly that we may see you face to face and restore whatever is lacking in your faith.

11 Now may our God and Father himself and our Lord Jesus direct our way to you. 12 And may the Lord make you increase and abound/ in love

for one another and for all, just as we abound in love for you. 13 And may he so strengthen our hearts in holiness that you may be blameless before our God and Father at the coming of our Lord Jesus with all his saints.

A Life Pleasing to God

Finally, brothers and sisters,*h* we ask and urge you in the Lord Jesus that, as you learned from us how you ought to live and to please God (as, in fact, you are doing), you should do so more and more. 2 For you know what instructions we gave you through the Lord Jesus. 3 For this is the will of God, your sanctification: that you abstain from fornication; 4 that each one of you know how to control your own body*i* in holiness and honor, 5 not with lustful passion, like the Gentiles who do not know God; 6 that no one wrong or exploit a brother or sister*j* in this matter, because the Lord is an avenger in all these things, just as we have already told you beforehand and solemnly warned you. 7 For God did not call us to impurity but in holiness. 8 Therefore whoever rejects this rejects not human authority but God, who also gives his Holy Spirit to you.

9 Now concerning love of the brothers and sisters,*h* you do not need to have anyone write to you, for you yourselves have been taught by God to love one another; 10 and indeed you do love all the brothers and sisters*h* throughout Mac•e•do'ni•a. But we urge you, beloved,*h* to do so more and more, 11 to aspire to live quietly, to mind your

g Gk lacks *proclaiming*   *h* Gk *brothers*   *i* Or *how to take a wife for himself*   *j* Gk *brother*

own affairs, and to work with your hands, as we directed you, ¹²so that you may behave properly toward outsiders and be dependent on no one.

NATIVE AMERICAN

Iroquois Prayer of Thanksgiving

In 1 Thess 5.16–24, Paul instructs the Thessalonians to give thanks without ceasing. Using this Iroquois prayer of thanksgiving, offer your thanks to God:

We return thanks to our mother,
the earth, which sustains us.
We return thanks to the rivers and streams,
which supply us with water.
We return thanks to all herbs,
which furnish medicines for the cure to our
diseases.
We return thanks to the corn, and to her
sisters,
the beans and squashes,
which give us life.
We return thanks to the bushes and trees,
which provide us with fruit.
We return thanks to the wind,
which, moving in the air, has banished
diseases.
We return thanks to the moon and stars,
which have given to us their light
when the sun was gone.
We return thanks to our grandfather Hé-no,
that he has protected his grandchildren
from witches and reptiles,
and has given to us his rain.
We return thanks to the sun,
that he has looked upon the earth
with a beneficent eye.
Lastly, we return thanks to the Great Spirit,
in whom is embodied all goodness,
and who directs all things
for the good of his children.

(From David Schiller, editor,
The Little Book of Prayers, pp. 154–155)

▶ 1 Thess 5.16–24

Catholic Connections

THE COMMUNION OF SAINTS

Many early Christians thought the world would end during their lifetime. So when people started to die before Jesus returned and the world was made new, they were concerned. Paul didn't want his Thessalonian friends to worry about their dead friends and family. He assured them that just as Jesus died and rose again, so the "dead in Christ will rise" (1 Thess 4.16). A time would come when those who were alive would meet the Lord along with the risen dead.

Grief always comes with the death of someone we love. But for Christians, there is also the joy of knowing that the person will rise again to be with God. Those who believe have God's promise that they will someday be together again in the communion of saints—which is the whole church, including the Christians who are alive and those who have died.

▶ 1 Thess 4.13–18

The Coming of the Lord

13 But we do not want you to be uninformed, brothers and sisters,*k* about those who have died,*l* so that you may not grieve as others do who have no hope. ¹⁴For since we believe that Jesus died and rose again, even so, through Jesus, God will bring with him those who have died.*l* ¹⁵For this we declare to you by the word of the Lord, that we who are alive, who are left until the coming of the Lord, will by no means precede those who have died.*l* ¹⁶For the Lord himself, with a cry of command, with the archangel's call and with the

k Gk *brothers*   *l* Gk *fallen asleep*

sound of God's trumpet, will descend from heaven, and the dead in Christ will rise first. [17] Then we who are alive, who are left, will be caught up in the clouds together with them to meet the Lord in the air; and so we will be with the Lord forever. [18] Therefore encourage one another with these words.

Now concerning the times and the seasons, brothers and sisters,[m] you do not need to have anything written to you. [2] For you yourselves know very well that the day of the Lord will come like a thief in the night. [3] When they say, "There is peace and security," then sudden destruction will come upon them, as labor pains come upon a pregnant woman, and there will be no escape! [4] But you, beloved,[m] are not in darkness, for that day to surprise you like a thief; [5] for you are all children of light and children of the day; we are not of the night or of darkness. [6] So then let us not fall asleep as others do, but let us keep awake and be sober; [7] for those who sleep sleep at night, and those who are drunk get drunk at night. [8] But since we belong to the day, let us be sober, and put on the breastplate of faith and love, and for a helmet the hope of salvation. [9] For God has destined us not for wrath but for obtaining salvation through our Lord Jesus Christ, [10] who died for us, so that whether we are awake or asleep we may live with

him. [11] Therefore encourage one another and build up each other, as indeed you are doing.

Final Exhortations, Greetings, and Benediction

12 But we appeal to you, brothers and sisters,[m] to respect those who labor among you, and have charge of you in the Lord and admonish you; [13] esteem them very highly in love because of their work. Be at peace among yourselves. [14] And we urge you,

---

[m] Gk *brothers*

> ## Test everything;
>
> ☑ hold fast   ☑ abstain from
> to what is   every form
> good;   of evil
>
> 5.21–22

GIVE THANKS AT ALL TIMES!

Gratitude is an essential element of the Christian faith for Hispanic people. Paul continuously promoted gratitude among the first Christians. Mary personified this gratitude when she accepted the responsibility of bearing the Son of God in her womb.

- **To be grateful is to respond to God's gifts by loving God and our neighbor.**
- **To be grateful, we need to be humble, open to receiving God's gifts and willing to recognize them.**
- **Gratitude leads us into prayer and union with God, responding from the deepness of our heart to God's generosity.**
- **To be grateful is to value our relationship with God more than anything else.**
- **To be grateful is to share in Jesus' gratitude to the Father and celebrate with him God's love.**

   From our gratitude to God springs our gratitude to our brothers and sisters. This gratitude allows us to receive with humility the love, service, and gifts of others. Christian gratitude finds its highest expression in the Eucharist, where we offer our whole life to God in union with Christ. It helps us to be constructive and to build community, and it provides us with enthusiasm for doing God's work.

▶ 1 Thess 5.18

beloved,[m] to admonish the idlers, encourage the fainthearted, help the weak, be patient with all of them. 15 See that none of you repays evil for evil, but always seek to do good to one another and to all. 16 Rejoice always, 17 pray without ceasing, 18 give thanks in all circumstances; for this is the will of God in Christ Jesus for you. 19 Do not quench the Spirit. 20 Do not despise the words of prophets,[n] 21 but test everything; hold fast to what is good; 22 abstain from every form of evil.

23 May the God of peace himself sanctify you entirely; and may your spirit and soul and body be kept sound[o] and blameless at the coming of our Lord Jesus Christ. 24 The one who calls you is faithful, and he will do this.

25 Beloved,[p] pray for us.

26 Greet all the brothers and sisters[m] with a holy kiss. 27 I solemnly command you by the Lord that this letter be read to all of them.[q]

28 The grace of our Lord Jesus Christ be with you.[r]

---

m Gk brothers   n Gk despise prophecies   o Or complete
p Gk Brothers   q Gk to all the brothers   r Other ancient authorities add Amen

Has a parent or another adult ever said to you, "You know, when I was your age," and launched into some story about how hard it was in the "good old days"? It seems all past generations, including those who lived in biblical times, had their struggles and challenges. When the Thessalonians were going through some really tough times, Paul's second letter to them promised that if they continued to trust God, everything would come out right.

At a Glance

- **Chapter 1.** a greeting
- **Chapter 2.** information about the day of the Lord
- **3.1–14.** a prayer request, and warning against idleness
- **3.16–18.** a final blessing

In-depth

From the short Second Letter to the Thessalonians, it appears the Thessalonians were experiencing two problems. First, they were being persecuted by non-Christians. Second, some of them were becoming confused over "the coming of our Lord Jesus Christ" (2.1), sometimes called the Second Coming. Word was being spread that Jesus had already come again (verse 2)! And some believers may have been using that as an excuse not to work and earn their keep (3.6).

This letter speaks to the Thessalonians using apocalyptic language (see "Apocalyptic Literature," Daniel, chapters 7–10; and the introduction to Revelation). It tells the Thessalonians to have peace and not let themselves be deceived, "for that day will not come unless the rebellion comes first and the lawless one is revealed, the one destined for destruction" (2.3). It also tells them to have hope, because at the end time, Christ will overcome all evil and will destroy the lawless one.

This letter is not as warm and personal as 1 Thessalonians. Perhaps that's because it's filled with the sobering awareness that persecution is here to stay, and that evil and deception are all around. In such an environment, the letter advises the Thessalonians—and us—to "stand firm and hold fast to the traditions that you were taught" (verse 15).

Quick Facts

Author
possibly Paul, but more likely a disciple of Paul's

Date Written
around A.D. 51 if by Paul, A.D. 70–90 if by a disciple

Audience
the mainly Gentile (non-Jewish) church in Thessalonica

2 Thessalonians

Salutation

Paul, Sil·va′nus, and Timothy,

To the church of the Thes·sa·lo′ni·ans in God our Father and the Lord Jesus Christ:

2 Grace to you and peace from God our[a] Father and the Lord Jesus Christ.

Thanksgiving

3 We must always give thanks to God for you, brothers and sisters,[b] as is right, because your faith is growing abundantly, and the love of everyone of you for one another is increasing. 4 Therefore we ourselves boast of you among the churches of God for your steadfastness and faith during all your persecutions and the afflictions that you are enduring.

The Judgment at Christ's Coming

5 This is evidence of the righteous judgment of God, and is intended to make you worthy of the kingdom of God, for which you are also suffering. 6 For it is indeed just of God to repay with affliction those who afflict you, 7 and to give relief to the afflicted as well as to us, when the Lord Jesus is revealed from heaven with his mighty angels 8 in flaming fire, inflicting vengeance on those who do not know God and on those who do not obey the gospel of our Lord Jesus. 9 These will suffer the

punishment of eternal destruction, separated from the presence of the Lord and from the glory of his might, 10 when he comes to be glorified by his saints and to be marveled at on that day among all who have believed, because our testimony to you was believed. 11 To this end we always pray for you, asking that our God will make you worthy of his call and will fulfill by his power every good resolve and work of faith, 12 so that the name of our Lord Jesus may be glorified in you, and you in him, according to the grace of our God and the Lord Jesus Christ.

The Man of Lawlessness

As to the coming of our Lord Jesus Christ and our being gathered together to him, we beg you, brothers and sisters,[b] 2 not to be quickly shaken in mind or alarmed, either by spirit or by word or by letter, as though from us, to the effect that the day of the Lord is already here. 3 Let no one deceive you in any way; for that day will not come unless the rebellion comes first and the lawless one[c] is revealed, the one destined for destruction.[d] 4 He opposes and exalts himself above every so-called god or object of worship, so that he takes his seat

---

a Other ancient authorities read *the*   b Gk *brothers*
c Gk *the man of lawlessness*; other ancient authorities read *the man of sin*   d Gk *the son of destruction*

did you **KNOW?**

The Parousia

After Jesus' death and Resurrection, the early Christians start to wait for his Second Coming, also called the Parousia. They think Jesus will return soon in glory to judge the living and the dead and to bring to complete fulfillment the Reign of God. They even see some signs of his imminent arrival and express an urgent call to be prepared. Paul seems to expect Christ's return in the near future but insists that nobody can predict when. He emphasizes the importance of living the Gospel and always being prepared for "our being gathered together to him" (2 Thess 2.1).

The important message for us today is that our history has meaning and purpose and that Christ ultimately triumphs over sin and death. The various descriptions of the signs preceding the end time are intended not to predict the future but rather to encourage us to live the Gospel as we wait in hope for Christ's glorious return.

▶ 2 Thess 1.5—2.17

in the temple of God, declaring himself to be God. [5] Do you not remember that I told you these things when I was still with you? [6] And you know what is now restraining him, so that he may be revealed when his time comes. [7] For the mystery of lawlessness is already at work, but only until the one who now restrains it is removed. [8] And then the lawless one will be revealed, whom the Lord Jesus[e] will destroy[f] with the breath of his mouth, annihilating him by the manifestation of his coming. [9] The coming of the lawless one is apparent in the working of Satan, who uses all power, signs, lying wonders, [10] and every kind of wicked deception for those who are perishing, because they refused to love the truth and so be saved. [11] For this reason God sends them a powerful delusion, leading them to believe what is false, [12] so that all who have not believed the truth but took pleasure in unrighteousness will be condemned.

Chosen for Salvation

13 But we must always give thanks to God for you, brothers and sisters[g] beloved by the Lord, because God chose you as the first fruits[h] for salvation through sanctification by the Spirit and through belief in the truth. [14] For this purpose he called you through our proclamation of the good news,[i] so that you may obtain the glory of our Lord Jesus Christ. [15] So then, brothers and sisters,[g] stand firm and hold fast to the traditions that you were taught by us, either by word of mouth or by our letter.

---

e Other ancient authorities lack *Jesus*   *f* Other ancient authorities read *consume*   *g* Gk *brothers*   *h* Other ancient authorities read *from the beginning*   *i* Or *through our gospel*

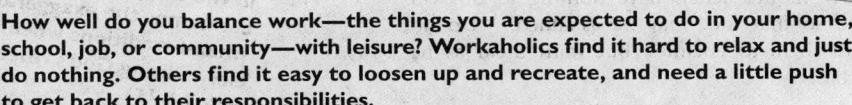

LIVE IT!

Laziness

How well do you balance work—the things you are expected to do in your home, school, job, or community—with leisure? Workaholics find it hard to relax and just do nothing. Others find it easy to loosen up and recreate, and need a little push to get back to their responsibilities.

Evidently, some of the early Thessalonians are determined to avoid work altogether (2 Thess 3.6), presuming they can depend on the Christian community to feed and take care of them. Perhaps they feel that if the Second Coming is close, there is no need to work. The author of 2 Thessalonians sees this idleness as destructive for the church. His answer is simple: no work, no food (verse 10).

Christ invites us not to a life of laziness, where we take advantage of the kindness of others, but to an active life. Our work ought to be an expression of who we are and should contribute something meaningful and positive to the world.

▶ 2 Thess 3.6–13

16 Now may our Lord Jesus Christ himself and God our Father, who loved us and through grace gave us eternal comfort and good hope, [17] comfort your hearts and strengthen them in every good work and word.

Request for Prayer

Finally, brothers and sisters,*j* pray for us, so that the word of the Lord may spread rapidly and be glorified everywhere, just as it is among you, [2] and that we may be rescued from wicked and evil people; for not all have faith. [3] But the Lord is faithful; he will strengthen you and guard you from the evil one.*k* [4] And we have confidence in the Lord concerning you, that you are doing and will go on doing the things that we command. [5] May the Lord direct your hearts to the love of God and to the steadfastness of Christ.

Warning against Idleness

6 Now we command you, beloved,*j* in the name of our Lord Jesus Christ, to keep away from believers who are*l* living in idleness and not according to the tradition that they*m* received from us. [7] For you yourselves know how you ought to imitate us; we were not idle when we were with you, [8] and we did not eat anyone's bread without paying for it; but with toil and labor we worked night and day, so that we might not burden any of you. [9] This was not because we do not have that right, but in order to give you an example to imitate. [10] For even when we were with you, we gave you this command: Anyone unwilling to work should not eat. [11] For we hear that some of you are living in idleness, mere busybodies, not doing any work. [12] Now such persons we command and exhort in the Lord Jesus Christ to do their work quietly and to earn their own living. [13] Brothers and sisters,*n* do not be weary in doing what is right.

14 Take note of those who do not obey what we say in this letter; have nothing to do with them, so that they may be ashamed. [15] Do not regard them as enemies, but warn them as believers.*o*

Final Greetings and Benediction

16 Now may the Lord of peace himself give you peace at all times in all ways. The Lord be with all of you.

17 I, Paul, write this greeting with my own hand. This is the mark in every letter of mine; it is the way I write. [18] The grace of our Lord Jesus Christ be with all of you.*p*

---

j Gk *brothers*   *k* Or *from evil*   *l* Gk *from every brother who is*   *m* Other ancient authorities read *you*   *n* Gk *Brothers*
o Gk *a brother*   *p* Other ancient authorities add *Amen*

Catholic Connections

TRADITIONS

Second Thessalonians 2.15 directs the Thessalonians to "stand firm and hold fast to the traditions that" they were taught (this message is repeated somewhat differently in 3.6). Traditions are an important part of the Catholic church. They give Catholics their identity and also keep them faithful to the mission and teachings of Jesus Christ.

It's important to understand the difference between traditions with a small t and Tradition with a large T. Large-T Tradition is the core truths of the Christian faith as taught by the Apostles (see "The Bible, Tradition, and the Magisterium," Lk 4.1–13). Like the Bible, it is a primary source of God's revelation for us. The truths of Tradition are unchanging and the same for every age.

Small-t traditions are the customs and rituals that help Catholics and other Christians live out their faith. These traditions are influenced by history and culture. They can differ between cultures and times, and they account for the rich variety of faith expressions in the universal church. These traditions are also important, and they are good as long as they help us live out the mission and teachings of Jesus embodied in the Scriptures and Tradition. But Jesu condemns the exaggerated importance o small-t traditions when they present obst cles to living God's revealed commandme (Mk 7.1–15).

Answer this question: What from th Tradition or traditions of the church ha been important to you? Then ask the sa question of a parent, a grandparent, or other person from a previous generatio and compare the answers.

▶ 2 Thess 2.15

Imagine you are a bishop writing a letter to the new priests, deacons, and lay ministers in your diocese. How do you encourage them? What do you warn them about? The two Letters to Timothy and the Letter to Titus are such letters, written to give good, practical advice to the leaders of the early church.

In-depth

The Letters to Timothy and Titus are called the pastoral letters because they were written to church leaders, or pastors. These letters sound as if they were written by Paul. But a great deal of evidence suggests they may have been written by later disciples of Paul's, adapting Paul's teaching and advice to the situation of the churches a generation later.

The First Letter to Timothy addresses practical issues the churches needed to deal with in order to achieve stability and respond to new challenges as Christianity became more visible in society: How should the churches deal with people teaching false beliefs? What qualities should church leaders have? Who deserves financial help from the community? How should Christians view success?

The Second Letter to Timothy presents Paul as being close to his execution. As you read this letter, you will experience his sadness at death, hear his reflections on his life and ministry, and see a man who feels deserted by many. This letter tells Timothy—who stands for all faithful Christians—that he needs to endure suffering. Doing the right thing often means more pain than popularity. But even when other people desert us, God "remains faithful— / for he cannot deny himself" (2.13).

The Letter to Titus gives advice for elders, bishops, older men, older women, slaves, younger men, and younger women. It also offers repeated warnings to guard against temptations and false teachings and to be self-controlled.

The pastoral letters give us a picture of the church moving into a new phase. The church seems to have more structure, leadership roles are becoming more defined, and the people are more concerned about its public appearance. Like Christians today, the early Christians struggled to be faithful in applying the Gospel of Jesus Christ to their culture and time.

At a Glance

- **1 Tim 1.1–2.** a greeting
- **1 Tim 1.3—2.15.** advice for Timothy
- **1 Tim 3.1—6.21.** rules for God's people, final advice, and a blessing
- **2 Tim 1.1–5.** a greeting and thanks
- **2 Tim 1.6—4.8.** advice to Timothy
- **2 Tim 4.9–22.** final instructions, greetings, and a blessing
- **Titus 1.1–4.** a greeting
- **Titus 1.5—3.15.** advice for the community of faith and a final blessing

Quick Facts

Author
probably followers of Paul's (see "Introduction to the Letters and Revelation")

Date Written
around A.D. 65 if by Paul, A.D. 90–100 if by followers

Audience
leaders of the early churches

The Pastoral Letters

1 Timothy

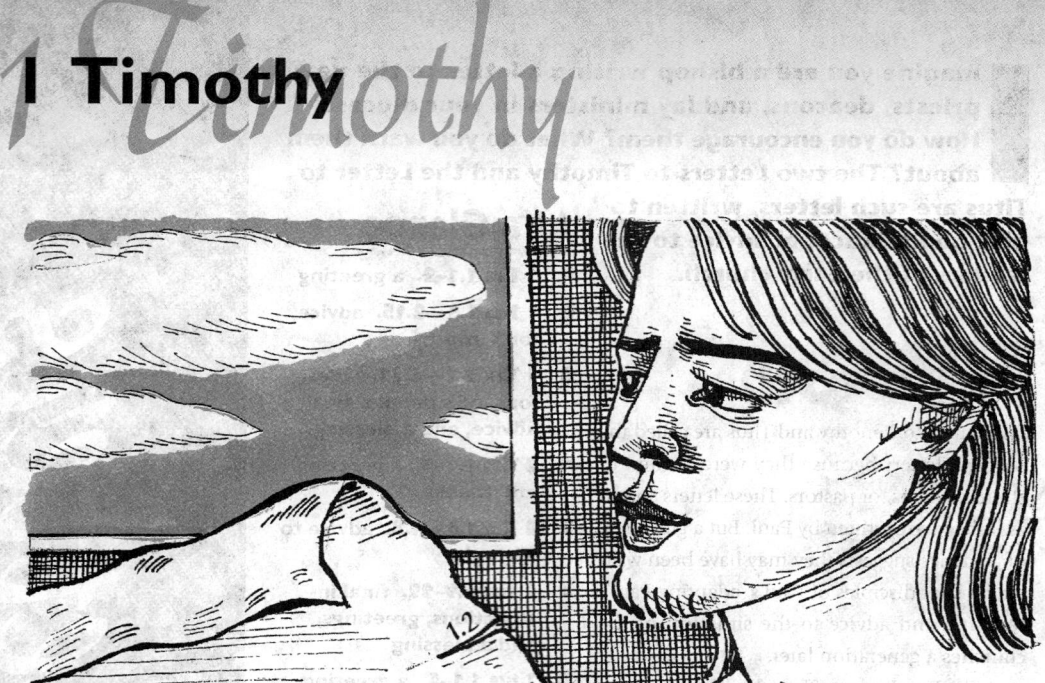

Salutation

Paul, an apostle of Christ Jesus by the command of God our Savior and of Christ Jesus our hope,

2 To Timothy, my loyal child in the faith:

Grace, mercy, and peace from God the Father and Christ Jesus our Lord.

Warning against False Teachers

3 I urge you, as I did when I was on my way to Mac·e·dō′ni·a, to remain in Eph′e·sus so that you may instruct certain people not to teach any different doctrine, 4 and not to occupy themselves with myths and endless genealogies that promote speculations rather than the divine training[a] that is known by faith. 5 But the aim of such instruction is love that comes from a pure heart, a good conscience, and sincere faith. 6 Some people have deviated from these and turned to meaningless talk, 7 desiring to be teachers of the law, without understanding either what they are saying or the things about which they make assertions.

8 Now we know that the law is good, if one uses it legitimately. 9 This means understanding that the law is laid down not for the innocent but for the lawless and disobedient, for the godless and sinful, for the unholy and profane, for those who kill their father or mother, for murderers, 10 fornicators, sodomites, slave traders, liars, perjurers, and whatever else is contrary to the sound teaching 11 that conforms to the glorious gospel of the blessed God, which he entrusted to me.

Gratitude for Mercy
(Cp Acts 8.1–3; 9.1–19)

12 I am grateful to Christ Jesus our Lord, who has strengthened me, because he judged me faithful and appointed me to his service, 13 even though I was formerly a blasphemer, a persecutor, and a man of violence. But I received mercy because I had acted ignorantly in unbelief, 14 and the grace of our Lord overflowed for me with the faith and love that are in Christ Jesus. 15 The saying is sure and worthy of full acceptance, that Christ Jesus came into the world to save sinners—of whom I am the foremost. 16 But for that very reason I received mercy, so that in me, as the foremost, Jesus Christ might display the utmost patience, making me an example to those who would come to believe in him for eternal life. 17 To the King of the ages, immortal, invisible, the only God, be honor and glory forever and ever.[b] Amen.

18 I am giving you these instructions, Timothy, my child, in accordance with the prophecies made earlier about you, so that by following them you may fight the good fight, 19 having faith and a good conscience. By rejecting conscience, certain persons have suffered shipwreck in the faith; 20 among them are Hȳ·me·naē′us and Alexander,

a Or plan   b Gk to the ages of the ages

1420

Conscience: God in the Gut

Do you ever wonder where God is during those really difficult moments of decision? Like when you're with some friends and someone proposes you all do something exciting but dangerous, and you feel caught in the middle. Or when an entire group is taking advantage of a teacher who has left the room during a test, or when a new kid trips and falls in the cafeteria and no one makes a move to help.

One of the best places to look for God's direction is that feeling in the center of your stomach when you are faced with life's dilemmas. That feeling may be a sign of your conscience prompting you to act.

In I Tim 1.19, Timothy is told to have "faith and a good conscience." A good conscience is based on reason and love and is developed through a commitment to make good and thoughtful moral decisions. Take time to develop your conscience by studying moral issues and the church's teaching on them. The more you develop your conscience, the more you will experience God speaking to you through those gut feelings.

▶ I Tim 1.18–19

---

whom I have turned over to Satan, so that they may learn not to blaspheme.

Instructions concerning Prayer

First of all, then, I urge that supplications, prayers, intercessions, and thanksgivings be made for everyone, 2 for kings and all who are in high positions, so that we may lead a quiet and peaceable life in all godliness and dignity. 3 This is right and is acceptable in the sight of God our Savior, 4 who desires everyone to be saved and to come to the knowledge of the truth. 5 For

there is one God;
there is also one mediator between God
and humankind,
Christ Jesus, himself human,
6 who gave himself a ransom for all

—this was attested at the right time. 7 For this I was appointed a herald and an apostle (I am telling the truth,c I am not lying), a teacher of the Gentiles in faith and truth.

8 I desire, then, that in every place the men should pray, lifting up holy hands without anger or argument; 9 also that the women should dress themselves modestly and decently in suitable clothing, not with their hair braided, or with gold, pearls, or expensive clothes, 10 but with good works, as is proper for women who profess reverence for God. 11 Let a womand learn in silence with full submission. 12 I permit no womand to teach or to have authority over a man;e she is to keep silent. 13 For Adam was formed first, then Eve; 14 and Adam was not deceived, but the woman was deceived and became a transgressor. 15 Yet she will be saved through childbearing, pro-

vided they continue in faith and love and holiness, with modesty.

Qualifications of Bishops

The saying is sure:f whoever aspires to the office of bishopg desires a noble task. 2 Now a bishoph must be above reproach, married only once,i temperate, sensible, respectable, hospitable, an apt teacher, 3 not a drunkard, not violent but gentle, not quarrelsome, and not a lover of money. 4 He must manage his own household well, keeping his children submissive and respectful in every way— 5 for if someone does not know how to manage his own household, how can he take care of God's church? 6 He must not be a recent convert, or he may be puffed up with conceit and fall into the condemnation of the devil. 7 Moreover, he must be well thought of by outsiders, so that he may not fall into disgrace and the snare of the devil.

Qualifications of Deacons

8 Deacons likewise must be serious, not double-tongued, not indulging in much wine, not greedy for money; 9 they must hold fast to the mystery of the faith with a clear conscience. 10 And let them first be tested; then, if they prove themselves blameless, let them serve as deacons. 11 Womenj likewise must be serious, not slanderers, but temperate, faithful in all things. 12 Let

c Other ancient authorities add in Christ   d Or wife
e Or her husband   f Some interpreters place these words at the end of the previous paragraph. Other ancient authorities read The saying is commonly accepted
g Or overseer   h Or an overseer   i Gk the husband of one wife   j Or Their wives, or Women deacons

?did you KNOW?

Women and Cultural Roles

A modern person reading 1 Tim 2.8–15 may be shocked by the teaching there. A passage like this can be easily misunderstood and even misused against women. It is very important to realize that it is a reflection of women's roles in the ancient world. Whatever her religious background—Jewish, Christian, or pagan—a woman's place was in the home. Women generally married young, had no education, and were not allowed to hold a position of public authority.

The earliest Christian communities gathered in members' homes. In this less public arena, women taught and performed other ministries. As Christianity became more widely accepted, concern for how the church appeared to outsiders grew—including concern about drunken bishops, immodest dress, and women teaching in public. That is probably why the author of First Timothy says, "I permit no woman to teach" (2.12).

Are things different for women in contemporary Christianity? Yes! Society has changed. Today, people in the United States are not scandalized if a woman manages a business, runs for public office, or leads a private foundation. Today, if you ask people to name influential church leaders, Mother Teresa almost always comes up. Think of other women you know who are involved in church life. In your own parish or community, for example, there are probably women who are religious education directors, coordinators of youth ministry, or pastoral ministers.

▶ 1 Tim 2.8–15

The Mystery of Our Religion

14 I hope to come to you soon, but I am writing these instructions to you so that, 15 if I am delayed, you may know how one ought to behave in the household of God, which is the church of the living God, the pillar and bulwark of the truth. 16 Without any doubt, the mystery of our religion is great:

> He^l was revealed in flesh,
> vindicated^m in spirit,^{n}
> seen by angels,
> proclaimed among Gentiles,
> believed in throughout the world,
> taken up in glory.

False Asceticism

Now the Spirit expressly says that in later^o times some will renounce the faith by paying attention to deceitful spirits and teachings of demons, 2 through the hypocrisy of liars whose consciences are seared with a hot iron. 3 They forbid marriage and demand abstinence from foods, which God created to be received with thanksgiving by those who believe and know the truth. 4 For everything created by God is good, and nothing is to be rejected, provided it is received with thanksgiving; 5 for it is sanctified by God's word and by prayer.

A Good Minister of Jesus Christ

6 If you put these instructions before the brothers and sisters,^{p} you will be a good servant^q of Christ Jesus, nourished on the words of the faith and of the sound teaching that you have followed. 7 Have nothing to do with profane myths and old wives' tales. Train yourself in godliness, 8 for, while physical training is of some value, godliness is valuable in every way, holding promise for both the present life and the life to come. 9 The saying is sure and worthy of full acceptance. 10 For to this end we toil and struggle,^{r} because we have our hope set on the living God, who is the Savior of all people, especially of those who believe.

11 These are the things you must insist on and teach. 12 Let no one despise your youth, but set the believers an example in speech and conduct, in love, in faith, in purity. 13 Until I arrive, give attention to the public reading of scripture,^{s} to exhorting, to teaching. 14 Do not neglect the gift that is in you, which was given to you through prophecy with the laying on of hands by the council of el-

deacons be married only once,^{k} and let them manage their children and their households well; 13 for those who serve well as deacons gain a good standing for themselves and great boldness in the faith that is in Christ Jesus.

^{k} Gk be husbands of one wife ^{l} Gk Who; other ancient authorities read God; others, Which ^{m} Or justified ^{n} Or by the Spirit ^{o} Or the last ^{p} Gk brothers ^{q} Or deacon ^{r} Other ancient authorities read suffer reproach ^{s} Gk to the reading

ders.[t] [15] Put these things into practice, devote yourself to them, so that all may see your progress. [16] Pay close attention to yourself and to your teaching; continue in these things, for in doing this you will save both yourself and your hearers.

Duties toward Believers

Do not speak harshly to an older man,[u] but speak to him as to a father, to younger men as brothers, [2] to older women as mothers, to younger women as sisters—with absolute purity.

3 Honor widows who are really widows. [4] If a widow has children or grandchildren, they should first learn their religious duty to their own family and make some repayment to their parents; for this is pleasing in God's sight. [5] The real widow, left alone, has set her hope on God and continues in supplications and prayers night and day; [6] but the widow[v] who lives for pleasure is dead even while she lives. [7] Give these commands as well, so that they may be above reproach. [8] And whoever does not provide for relatives, and especially for family members, has denied the faith and is worse than an unbeliever.

9 Let a widow be put on the list if she is not less than sixty years old and has been married only once;[w] [10] she must be well attested for her good works, as one who has brought up children, shown hospitality, washed the saints' feet, helped the afflicted, and devoted herself to doing good in every way. [11] But refuse to put younger widows on the list; for when their sensual desires alienate them from Christ, they want to marry, [12] and so they incur condemnation for having violated their first pledge. [13] Besides that, they learn to be idle, gadding about from house to house; and they are not merely idle, but also gossips and busybodies,

TRAINING FOR CHRIST

Jesus, Son of God,
Train me to be merciful,
extending my hands in forgiveness.
Train me to be compassionate,
extending my heart to those in need.
Train me to be generous,
extending my gifts and talents and resources to
　　others.
Train me to be courageous,
extending my voice to eliminate injustices.
Train me to be committed to love,
stretching my faith to unlimited possibilities.
Amen.

▶ I Tim 4.7–10

saying what they should not say. [14] So I would have younger widows marry, bear children, and manage their households, so as to give the adversary no occasion to revile us. [15] For some have already turned away to follow Satan. [16] If any believing woman[x] has relatives who are really widows, let her assist them; let the church not be burdened, so that it can assist those who are real widows.

17 Let the elders who rule well be considered worthy of double honor,[y] especially those who labor in preaching and teaching; [18] for the scripture says, "You shall not muzzle an ox while it is treading out the grain," and, "The laborer deserves to be paid." [19] Never accept any accusation against an elder except on the evidence of two or three witnesses. [20] As for those who persist in sin, rebuke them in the presence of all, so that the rest also may stand in fear. [21] In the presence of God and of Christ Jesus and of the elect angels, I warn you to keep these instructions without prejudice, doing nothing on the basis of partiality. [22] Do not ordain[z] anyone hastily, and do not participate in the sins of others; keep yourself pure.

Let no one despise your youth, but set the believers an example in speech and conduct

4.12

1
T
I
M

---

[t] Gk by the presbytery　　[u] Or an elder, or a presbyter
[v] Gk she　　[w] Gk the wife of one husband　　[x] Other ancient authorities read believing man or woman; others, believing man　　[y] Or compensation　　[z] Gk Do not lay hands on

23 No longer drink only water, but take a little wine for the sake of your stomach and your frequent ailments.

24 The sins of some people are conspicuous and precede them to judgment, while the sins of others follow them there. 25 So also good works are conspicuous; and even when they are not, they cannot remain hidden.

Let all who are under the yoke of slavery regard their masters as worthy of all honor, so that the name of God and the teaching may not be blasphemed. 2 Those who have believing masters must not be disrespectful to them on the ground that they are members of the church;*a* rather they must serve them all the more, since those who benefit by their service are believers and beloved.*b*

False Teaching and True Riches

Teach and urge these duties. 3 Whoever teaches otherwise and does not agree with the sound words of our Lord Jesus Christ and the teaching that is in accordance with godliness, 4 is conceited, understanding nothing, and has a morbid craving for controversy and for disputes about words. From these come envy, dissension, slander, base suspicions, 5 and wrangling among those who are depraved in mind and bereft of the truth, imagining that godliness is a means of gain.*c* 6 Of course, there is great gain in godliness combined with contentment; 7 for we brought nothing into the world, so that*d* we can take nothing out of it; 8 but if we have food and clothing, we will be content

with these. 9 But those who want to be rich fall into temptation and are trapped by many senseless and harmful desires that plunge people into ruin and destruction. 10 For the love of money is a root of all kinds of evil, and in their eagerness to be rich some have wandered away from the faith and pierced themselves with many pains.

The Good Fight of Faith

11 But as for you, man of God, shun all this; pursue righteousness, godliness, faith, love, endurance, gentleness. 12 Fight the good fight of the faith; take hold of the eternal life, to which you were called and for which you made*e* the good confession in the presence of many witnesses. 13 In the presence of God, who gives life to all things, and of Christ Jesus, who in his testimony before Pon'ti·us Pilate made the good confession, I charge you 14 to keep the commandment without spot or blame until the manifestation of our Lord Jesus Christ, 15 which he will bring about at the right time—he who is the blessed and only Sovereign, the King of kings and Lord of lords. 16 It is he alone who has immortality and dwells in unapproachable light, whom no one has ever seen or can see; to him be honor and eternal dominion. Amen.

---

a Gk *are brothers*   *b* Or *since they are believers and beloved, who devote themselves to good deeds*   *c* Other ancient authorities add *Withdraw yourself from such people*   *d* Other ancient authorities read *world—it is certain that*   *e* Gk *confessed*

Dangers of Money

LIVE IT!

We live in a culture that glorifies material things, money, and consumption. People are generally thought to be successful if they have great riches and all the luxury items to prove it to their neighbors. There is a bumper sticker that reads, The one who dies with the most toys wins! Even when individuals or families have the essential things to live comfortably, many are driven to acquire more.

An important truth found many places in the Scriptures (see, for example, Lk 12.20) is repeated here: You can't take it with you. The Scriptures warn about something that most of us know deep down but often ignore: "The love of money is a root of all kinds of evil," and in our eagerness to become financially rich, we usually lose sight of God and become entangled in all kinds of senseless distractions (1 Tim 6.10).

All of us need the basic stuff of life: food, clothing, and shelter. God wants us to have these things—and more! Ultimately, real riches or success will not be measured by bank accounts or material things, but by the love and generosity with which we have lived. How rich are you becoming in these things?

▶ 1 Tim 6.6–10

17 As for those who in the present age are rich, command them not to be haughty, or to set their hopes on the uncertainty of riches, but rather on God who richly provides us with everything for our enjoyment. 18 They are to do good, to be rich in good works, generous, and ready to share, 19 thus storing up for themselves the treasure of a good foundation for the future, so that they may take hold of the life that really is life.

Personal Instructions and Benediction

20 Timothy, guard what has been entrusted to you. Avoid the profane chatter and contradictions of what is falsely called knowledge; 21 by professing it some have missed the mark as regards the faith.

Grace be with you.*f*

---

f The Greek word for *you* here is plural; in other ancient authorities it is singular. Other ancient authorities add *Amen*

2 Timothy

For background on this letter, see the introduction to the pastoral letters, before I Timothy.

Salutation

Paul, an apostle of Christ Jesus by the will of God, for the sake of the promise of life that is in Christ Jesus,

2 To Timothy, my beloved child:

Grace, mercy, and peace from God the Father and Christ Jesus our Lord.

Thanksgiving and Encouragement

3 I am grateful to God—whom I worship with a clear conscience, as my ancestors did—when I remember you constantly in my prayers night and day. ⁴Recalling your tears, I long to see you so that I may be filled with joy. ⁵I am reminded of your sincere faith, a faith that lived first in your grandmother Lō′is and your mother Eū′nice and now, I am sure, lives in you. ⁶For this reason I remind you to rekindle the gift of God that is within you through the laying on of my hands; ⁷for God did not give us a spirit of cowardice, but rather a spirit of power and of love and of self-discipline.

8 Do not be ashamed, then, of the testimony about our Lord or of me his prisoner, but join with me in suffering for the gospel, relying on the power of God, ⁹who saved us and called us with a holy calling, not according to our works but according to his own purpose and grace. This grace was given to us in Christ Jesus before the ages be-

gan, ¹⁰but it has now been revealed through the appearing of our Savior Christ Jesus, who abolished death and brought life and immortality to light through the gospel. ¹¹For this gospel I was appointed a herald and an apostle and a teacher,ᵃ ¹²and for this reason I suffer as I do. But I am not ashamed, for I know the one in whom I have put my trust, and I am sure that he is able to guard until that day what I have entrusted to him.ᵇ ¹³Hold to the standard of sound teaching that you have heard from me, in the faith and love that are in Christ Jesus. ¹⁴Guard the good treasure entrusted to you, with the help of the Holy Spirit living in us.

15 You are aware that all who are in Asia have turned away from me, including Phȳ′ge•lus and Her•mog′e•nēs. ¹⁶May the Lord grant mercy to the household of On•e•siph′o•rus, because he often refreshed me and was not ashamed of my chain; ¹⁷when he arrived in Rome, he eagerlyᶜ searched for me and found me ¹⁸—may the Lord grant that he will find mercy from the Lord on that day! And you know very well how much service he rendered in Eph′e•sus.

ᵃ Other ancient authorities add *of the Gentiles*   ᵇ Or *what has been entrusted to me*   ᶜ Or *promptly*

Do Not Be Ashamed

LIVE IT!

Terry is a popular guy in the senior class. He is on the basketball and track teams and served on student council. He is extremely friendly and never says anything bad about anyone. Everyone likes him.

Terry is also very active in his church's youth group. He is not afraid to let others know that church is important to him. He never preaches religion, but he lets people know that church and Jesus are central to his life.

The author of 2 Timothy encourages readers, "Do not be ashamed, then, of the testimony about our Lord" (1.8). You do not have to announce your faith from mountaintops or from street corners, but like Terry, you should not be afraid to admit that God is important to you. You will likely discover that others admire you for your faith and commitment.

▸ 2 Tim 1.6–18

A Good Soldier of Christ Jesus

You then, my child, be strong in the grace that is in Christ Jesus; 2 and what you have heard from me through many witnesses entrust to faithful people who will be able to teach others as well. 3 Share in suffering like a good soldier of Christ Jesus. 4 No one serving in the army gets entangled in everyday affairs; the soldier's aim is to please the enlisting officer. 5 And in the case of an athlete, no one is crowned without competing according to the rules. 6 It is the farmer who does the work who ought to have the first share of the crops. 7 Think over what I say, for the Lord will give you understanding in all things.

8 Remember Jesus Christ, raised from the dead, a descendant of David—that is my gospel, 9 for which I suffer hardship, even to the point of being chained like a criminal. But the word of God is not chained. 10 Therefore I endure everything for the sake of the elect, so that they may also obtain the salvation that is in Christ Jesus, with eternal glory. 11 The saying is sure:
If we have died with him, we will also live
        with him;
12 if we endure, we will also reign with him;
    if we deny him, he will also deny us;
13 if we are faithless, he remains faithful—
    for he cannot deny himself.

A Worker Approved by God

14 Remind them of this, and warn them before God[d] that they are to avoid wrangling over words, which does no good but only ruins those who are listening. 15 Do your best to present yourself to God as one approved by him, a worker who has no need to be ashamed, rightly explaining the word of truth. 16 Avoid profane chatter, for it will lead people into more and more impiety, 17 and

their talk will spread like gangrene. Among them are Hy·me·nae′us and Phi·le′tus, 18 who have swerved from the truth by claiming that the resurrection has already taken place. They are upsetting the faith of some. 19 But God's firm foundation stands, bearing this inscription: "The Lord knows those who are his," and, "Let everyone who calls on the name of the Lord turn away from wickedness."

20 In a large house there are utensils not only of gold and silver but also of wood and clay, some for special use, some for ordinary. 21 All who cleanse themselves of the things I have mentioned[e] will become special utensils, dedicated and useful to the owner of the house, ready for every good work. 22 Shun youthful passions and pursue righteousness, faith, love, and peace, along with those who call on the Lord from a pure heart. 23 Have nothing to do with stupid and senseless controversies; you know that they breed quarrels. 24 And the Lord's servant[f] must not be quarrelsome but kindly to everyone, an apt teacher, patient, 25 correcting opponents with gentleness. God may perhaps grant that they will repent and come to know the truth, 26 and that they may escape from the snare of the devil, having been held captive by him to do his will.[g]

Godlessness in the Last Days

You must understand this, that in the last days distressing times will come. 2 For people will be lovers of themselves, lovers of money, boasters, arrogant, abusive, disobedient to their parents, ungrateful, unholy, 3 inhuman, implacable, slanderers, profligates, brutes, haters of good,

---

d Other ancient authorities read *the Lord*   e Gk *of these things*   f Gk *slave*   g Or *by him, to do his* (that is, God's) *will*

Teaching Others

Have you ever tried to explain to someone something about your faith? That can be challenging. Second Timothy 2.22–26 contains some tips on sharing faith with others: Avoid senseless controversies. Be kind, patient, and gentle. And be an apt teacher, that is, someone who is qualified or prepared.

Imagine that you are helping to teach a group of younger people about their faith. What do you want to say about God? How do you explain Jesus' love? How do you show your patience and gentleness? If you can answer these questions, maybe you should volunteer to help with your church's religious education program!

▶ 2 Tim 2.22–26

PRAY IT!

For Those Who Walk with Us

We pray, Lord, for those who formed us in our faith.
We pray for our families who first spoke your name to us and shared our journey of faith from the beginning.
We pray for our friends who shared their faith and continue to walk with us in our journey.
We pray for the teachers, priests, youth ministers, and other members of our church who took the time to recognize us as individuals and who showed us that faith can be both fun and challenging.
Thank you, God, for sending these people into our lives and for their gifts of faith, love, and patience. May we honor them by sharing our faith with a new generation of believers. We pray this in Jesus' name. Amen.

▶ 2 Tim 3.12–14

4 treacherous, reckless, swollen with conceit, lovers of pleasure rather than lovers of God, 5 holding to the outward form of godliness but denying its power. Avoid them! 6 For among them are those who make their way into households and captivate silly women, overwhelmed by their sins and swayed by all kinds of desires, 7 who are always being instructed and can never arrive at a knowledge of the truth. 8 As Jan′nēs and Jam′brēs opposed Moses, so these people, of corrupt mind and counterfeit faith, also oppose the truth. 9 But they will not make much progress, because, as in the case of those two men,*h* their folly will become plain to everyone.

Paul's Charge to Timothy

10 Now you have observed my teaching, my conduct, my aim in life, my faith, my patience, my love, my steadfastness, 11 my persecutions, and my suffering the things that happened to me in An′ti·och, I·cō′ni·um, and Lys′tra. What persecutions I endured! Yet the Lord rescued me from all of them. 12 Indeed, all who want to live a godly life in Christ Jesus will be persecuted. 13 But wicked people and impostors will go from bad to worse, deceiving others and being deceived. 14 But as for you, continue in what you have learned and firmly believed, knowing from whom you learned it, 15 and how from childhood you have known the sacred writings that are able to instruct you for salvation through faith in Christ Jesus. 16 All scripture is inspired by God and is*i* useful for teaching, for reproof, for correction, and for training in righteousness, 17 so that everyone who belongs to God may be proficient, equipped for every good work.

In the presence of God and of Christ Jesus, who is to judge the living and the dead, and in view of his appearing and his kingdom, I solemnly urge you: 2 proclaim the message; be persistent whether the time is favorable or unfavorable; convince, rebuke, and encourage, with the utmost patience in teaching. 3 For the time is coming when people will not put up with sound doctrine, but having itching ears, they will accumulate for themselves teachers to suit their own desires, 4 and will turn away from listening to the truth and wander away to myths.

h Gk lacks *two men*   *i* Or *Every scripture inspired by God is also*

Misleading Messages

Sticking with something can be difficult. When things get tough, many people are tempted to quit or walk away. If swim practice is boring, they drop off the team. If personalities on a committee are difficult, they drop out. If marriage loses its spark, they leave. We are surrounded by messages like "If it feels good, do it," and "You should have whatever your heart desires," and "Life will be great if you wear these clothes" or "drink this beverage" or "hang out with these people."

But reaching a worthy goal often requires hard choices and hard work. Second Timothy 4.1–5 warns us against being taken in by deceptive teachers or messages—like cultural teachings that life should always be easy and pleasurable. Such teachings water down the real challenge of living as a follower of Jesus Christ! If we are not finding life to be challenging, maybe we have tuned in to these misleading messages.

▸ 2 Tim 4.1–5

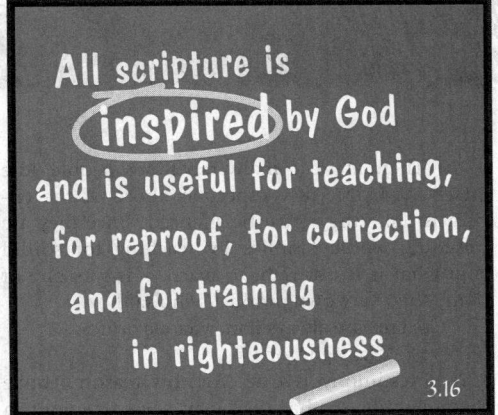

All scripture is ⟨inspired⟩ by God and is useful for teaching, for reproof, for correction, and for training in righteousness

3.16

5 As for you, always be sober, endure suffering, do the work of an evangelist, carry out your ministry fully.

6 As for me, I am already being poured out as a libation, and the time of my departure has come. 7 I have fought the good fight, I have finished the race, I have kept the faith. 8 From now on there is reserved for me the crown of righteousness, which the Lord, the righteous judge, will give me on that day, and not only to me but also to all who have longed for his appearing.

Personal Instructions

9 Do your best to come to me soon, 10 for De'-mas, in love with this present world, has deserted

me and gone to Thes·sa·lo·ni'ca; Cres'cens has gone to Galatia,[j] Titus to Dal·ma'tia. 11 Only Luke is with me. Get Mark and bring him with you, for he is useful in my ministry. 12 I have sent Tych'i·cus to Eph'e·sus. 13 When you come, bring the cloak that I left with Car'pus at Tro'as, also the books, and above all the parchments. 14 Alexander the copper-smith did me great harm; the Lord will pay him back for his deeds. 15 You also must beware of him, for he strongly opposed our message.

16 At my first defense no one came to my support, but all deserted me. May it not be counted against them! 17 But the Lord stood by me and gave me strength, so that through me the message might be fully proclaimed and all the Gentiles might hear it. So I was rescued from the lion's mouth. 18 The Lord will rescue me from every evil attack and save me for his heavenly kingdom. To him be the glory forever and ever. Amen.

Final Greetings and Benediction

19 Greet Pris'ca and A·qui'la, and the household of On·e·siph'o·rus. 20 E·ras'tus remained in Corinth; Troph'i·mus I left ill in Mi·le'tus. 21 Do your best to come before winter. Eu·bu'lus sends greetings to you, as do Pu'dens and Li'nus and Clau'-di·a and all the brothers and sisters.[k]

22 The Lord be with your spirit. Grace be with you.[l]

---

[j] Other ancient authorities read *Gaul*   [k] Gk *all the brothers*   [l] The Greek word for *you* here is plural. Other ancient authorities add *Amen*

2 TIM

Titus

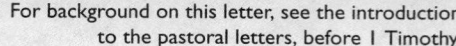

Salutation

Paul, a servant[a] of God and an apostle of Jesus Christ, for the sake of the faith of God's elect and the knowledge of the truth that is in accordance with godliness, 2 in the hope of eternal life that God, who never lies, promised before the ages began— 3 in due time he revealed his word through the proclamation with which I have been entrusted by the command of God our Savior,

4 To Titus, my loyal child in the faith we share:

Grace[b] and peace from God the Father and Christ Jesus our Savior.

Titus in Crete

5 I left you behind in Crete for this reason, so that you should put in order what remained to be done, and should appoint elders in every town, as I directed you: 6 someone who is blameless, married only once,[c] whose children are believers, not accused of debauchery and not rebellious. 7 For a bishop,[d] as God's steward, must be blameless; he must not be arrogant or quick-tempered or addicted to wine or violent or greedy for gain; 8 but he must be hospitable, a lover of goodness, prudent, upright, devout, and self-controlled. 9 He must have a firm grasp of the word that is trustworthy in accordance with the teaching, so that he may be able both to preach with sound doctrine and to refute those who contradict it.

10 There are also many rebellious people, idle talkers and deceivers, especially those of the circumcision; 11 they must be silenced, since they are upsetting whole families by teaching for sordid gain what it is not right to teach. 12 It was one of them, their very own prophet, who said,

"Cre̅'tans are always liars, vicious brutes,
lazy gluttons."

13 That testimony is true. For this reason rebuke them sharply, so that they may become sound in the faith, 14 not paying attention to Jewish myths or to commandments of those who reject the truth. 15 To the pure all things are pure, but to the corrupt and unbelieving nothing is pure. Their very minds and consciences are corrupted. 16 They profess to know God, but they deny him by their actions. They are detestable, disobedient, unfit for any good work.

Teach Sound Doctrine

But as for you, teach what is consistent with sound doctrine. 2 Tell the older men to be temperate, serious, prudent, and sound in faith, in love, and in endurance.

3 Likewise, tell the older women to be reverent in behavior, not to be slanderers or slaves to drink; they are to teach what is good, 4 so that they may encourage the young women to love their hus-

---

a Gk slave   b Other ancient authorities read Grace, mercy,
c Gk husband of one wife   d Or an overseer

Christian Leadership

Leadership is an awesome task. A good leader knows how to motivate people to grow and to serve society. Church leaders in particular must earn the respect of others through the integrity of their lifestyle and their commitment to the values of Jesus Christ. Look at the qualifications for bishops that are given in Titus 1.5–9. These make a great checklist for any leader to use.

Which leaders in your school or youth program do you admire the most? What qualities make them good leaders? How do these leaders stack up against the list in verses 5–9? How do you?

▶ Titus 1.5–9

NATIVE AMERICAN

Sioux Prayer for Transformation

I come before thee as one of thy many children.
   See, I am small and weak; I need thy
   strength and wisdom.
Grant me to walk in beauty and that my eyes
   may ever behold the crimson sunset. May my
   hands treat with respect the things which
   thou hast created, may my ears hear thy
   voice!
Make me wise, that I may understand the
   things which thou hast taught my people,
   which thou hast hidden in every leaf and
   every rock.
I long for strength, not in order that I may
   overreach my brother but to fight my
   greatest enemy—myself.
Make me ever ready to come to thee with pure
   hands and candid eyes, so that my spirit,
   when life disappears like the setting sun, may
   stand unashamed before thee.
                        (From David Schiller, editor,
           The Little Book of Prayers, pp. 280–281)

▶ Titus 3.3–7

bands, to love their children, 5 to be self-controlled, chaste, good managers of the household, kind, being submissive to their husbands, so that the word of God may not be discredited.

6 Likewise, urge the younger men to be self-controlled. 7 Show yourself in all respects a model of good works, and in your teaching show integrity, gravity, 8 and sound speech that cannot be censured; then any opponent will be put to shame, having nothing evil to say of us.

9 Tell slaves to be submissive to their masters and to give satisfaction in every respect; they are not to talk back, 10 not to pilfer, but to show complete and perfect fidelity, so that in everything they may be an ornament to the doctrine of God our Savior.

11 For the grace of God has appeared, bringing salvation to all,*e* 12 training us to renounce impiety and worldly passions, and in the present age to live lives that are self-controlled, upright, and godly, 13 while we wait for the blessed hope and the manifestation of the glory of our great God and Savior,*f* Jesus Christ. 14 He it is who gave himself for us that he might redeem us from all iniquity and purify for himself a people of his own who are zealous for good deeds.

15 Declare these things; exhort and reprove with all authority.*g* Let no one look down on you.

Maintain Good Deeds

Remind them to be subject to rulers and authorities, to be obedient, to be ready for every good work, 2 to speak evil of no one, to avoid quarreling, to be gentle, and to show every courtesy to everyone. 3 For we ourselves were once foolish, disobedient, led astray, slaves to various passions and pleasures, passing our days in malice and envy,

---

e Or *has appeared to all, bringing salvation*   *f* Or *of the great God and our Savior*   *g* Gk *commandment*

despicable, hating one another. ⁴ But when the goodness and loving kindness of God our Savior appeared, ⁵ he saved us, not because of any works of righteousness that we had done, but according to his mercy, through the water*ʰ* of rebirth and renewal by the Holy Spirit. ⁶ This Spirit he poured out on us richly through Jesus Christ our Savior, ⁷ so that, having been justified by his grace, we might become heirs according to the hope of eternal life. ⁸ The saying is sure.

I desire that you insist on these things, so that those who have come to believe in God may be careful to devote themselves to good works; these things are excellent and profitable to everyone. ⁹ But avoid stupid controversies, genealogies, dissensions, and quarrels about the law, for they are unprofitable and worthless. ¹⁰ After a first and second admonition, have nothing more to do with anyone who causes divisions, ¹¹ since you know that such a person is perverted and sinful, being self-condemned.

Final Messages and Benediction

12 When I send Ar'te•mas to you, or Tych'i•cus, do your best to come to me at Ni•cop'o•lis, for I have decided to spend the winter there. ¹³ Make every effort to send Zē'nas the lawyer and A•pol'los on their way, and see that they lack nothing. ¹⁴ And let people learn to devote themselves to good works in order to meet urgent needs, so that they may not be unproductive.

15 All who are with me send greetings to you. Greet those who love us in the faith.

Grace be with all of you.*ⁱ*

ʰ Gk *washing*   *ⁱ* Other ancient authorities add *Amen*

The brief Letter to Philemon is about slavery. It may surprise you that it doesn't condemn slavery outright. In fact, other parts of the Bible take the idea of human slavery for granted! How can the Bible not challenge something we think is wrong? Seeking to understand this puzzling question gives us a key to understanding God's revelation in the Bible.

At a Glance

- **Verses 1–7.** a greeting and gratitude for Philemon

- **Verses 8–22.** Paul's request

- **Verses 23–25.** final greetings and a blessing

In-depth

One key to understanding God's message in the Bible is to understand the beliefs of the authors and the first readers. The Letter to Philemon is addressed to a slave owner named Philemon, a woman named Apphia, and a soldier named Archippus, who all lived in Colossae. Philemon's slave, Onesimus, ran away, wound up in prison with Paul, and became a Christian. Now, Paul is sending him back to Philemon, as the law requires. That same law gives Philemon the right to punish Onesimus for escaping. But Paul asks—indirectly, but clearly enough—for Onesimus's freedom. Paul also asks for something far more challenging—that Philemon, Apphia, and Archippus accept Onesimus as "a beloved brother" (verse 16) in Christ.

It is safe to believe that Paul did not agree with slavery. Recall his basic statement on Christian freedom in Gal 3.28: "There is no longer slave or free, there is no longer male and female; for all of you are one in Christ Jesus." However, Paul expected slavery would pass away very soon with the Second Coming of Jesus Christ (see "Strange Advice!?" 1 Corinthians, chapter 7). This is probably why he never directly challenged the institution of slavery.

Although Paul may not have been a social revolutionary by our standards, he consistently challenged social institutions to reflect Gospel values. This letter is a masterpiece of persuasion as it urges the church community in Colossae to accept Onesimus as a beloved brother in Christ. It uses flattery (verses 4–7), a veiled reference to Paul's authority (verses 8–9), Paul's personal relationship with everyone involved (verses 12–17), and maybe even a little guilt in Paul's offer to pay for anything Onesimus stole (verses 18–19). Paul's message to the household of Philemon and to us is this: We must get beyond whatever cultural boundaries prevent us from treating one another as equals in Christ!

Quick Facts

Author
Paul

Date Written
A.D. 54–56 if from Ephesus, A.D. 60–63 if from Rome

Audience
Philemon and his household

The Letter to Philemon

Philemon

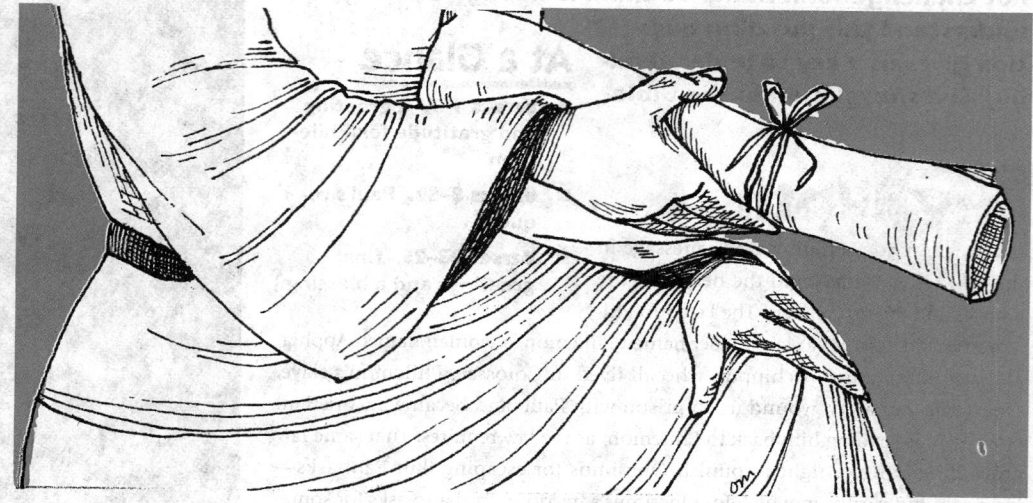

Salutation

1 Paul, a prisoner of Christ Jesus, and Timothy our brother,*a*

To Phi·le'mon our dear friend and co-worker, [2] to Ap'phi·a our sister,*b* to Ar·chip'pus our fellow soldier, and to the church in your house:

3 Grace to you and peace from God our Father and the Lord Jesus Christ.

Philemon's Love and Faith

4 When I remember you*c* in my prayers, I always thank my God [5] because I hear of your love for all the saints and your faith toward the Lord Jesus. [6] I pray that the sharing of your faith may become effective when you perceive all the good that we*d* may do for Christ. [7] I have indeed received much joy and encouragement from your love, because the hearts of the saints have been refreshed through you, my brother.

Paul's Plea for Onesimus

8 For this reason, though I am bold enough in Christ to command you to do your duty, [9] yet I would rather appeal to you on the basis of love—and I, Paul, do this as an old man, and now also as a prisoner of Christ Jesus.*e* [10] I am appealing to you for my child, O·nes'i·mus, whose father I have become during my imprisonment. [11] Formerly he was useless to you, but now he is indeed useful*f*

both to you and to me. [12] I am sending him, that is, my own heart, back to you. [13] I wanted to keep him with me, so that he might be of service to me in your place during my imprisonment for the gospel; [14] but I preferred to do nothing without your consent, in order that your good deed might be voluntary and not something forced. [15] Perhaps this is the reason he was separated from you for a while, so that you might have him back forever, [16] no longer as a slave but more than a slave, a beloved brother—especially to me but how much more to you, both in the flesh and in the Lord.

17 So if you consider me your partner, welcome him as you would welcome me. [18] If he has wronged you in any way, or owes you anything, charge that to my account. [19] I, Paul, am writing this with my own hand: I will repay it. I say nothing about your owing me even your own self. [20] Yes, brother, let me have this benefit from you in the Lord! Refresh my heart in Christ. [21] Confident of your obedience, I am writing to you, knowing that you will do even more than I say.

22 One thing more—prepare a guest room for me, for I am hoping through your prayers to be restored to you.

---

a Gk *the brother*   *b* Gk *the sister*   *c* From verse 4 through verse 21, *you* is singular   *d* Other ancient authorities read *you* (plural)   *e* Or *as an ambassador of Christ Jesus, and now also his prisoner*   *f* The name Onesimus means *useful* or (compare verse 20) *beneficial*

Rethinking Social Structures

In sending Onesimus back to Philemon, Paul asked Philemon not only to forgive his runaway slave but to rethink his relationship with him. Paul's plea to Philemon and the church in Colossae to look on Onesimus as a brother in Christ was radical for the time. People expected runaway slaves to be punished severely. Accepting Onesimus as a Christian would be a sign that the church truly believed in baptismal forgiveness and new life.

What commonly accepted social structures in our day might need a fresh look? Might any privileges that we take for granted actually prevent true equality in Christ?

▶ Philemon, verses 8–21

Final Greetings and Benediction

23 Ep′a•phras, my fellow prisoner in Christ Jesus, sends greetings to you,*g* 24 and so do Mark, Ar•is•tar′chus, De̅′mas, and Luke, my fellow workers.

25 The grace of the Lord Jesus Christ be with your spirit.*h*

---

g Here *you* is singular   *h* Other ancient authorities add *Amen*

Have you ever wondered why it makes sense to believe that Jesus is the savior of all humanity? It's an honest question. Evidently, some early Christians asked it. The Letter to the Hebrews is a sermon—to them and to us—to strengthen our faith and belief in Jesus Christ, the Son of God and our "great high priest" (4.14).

In-depth

The Letter to the Hebrews gives us almost no information about its author and the community it is addressed to. But it appears that some members of the community are in danger of giving up their faith—and this is happening after the group has already survived a period of persecution. The letter encourages them to be strong in their faith and seeks to give a sound foundation for believing in Jesus Christ. It is a statement on Christ's divinity and the saving power of Christ's sacrificial death.

At a Glance

- **Chapters 1–2.** an introduction, and a message that Christ is greater than the angels

- **Chapters 3–7.** a message that Christ is greater than Moses, and a discussion of Melchizedek and the priests of the Temple

- **8.1—10.18.** a message that Christ offers the sacrifice of the New Covenant

- **10.19—12.29.** exhortations and warnings, and a list of the heroes of the Christian faith

- **Chapter 13.** a conclusion

The letter presents Christ as the divine Son of God, through whom the world was created, superior to any angel, and the culmination of all the promises and expectations of the Old Testament. In explaining Christ's importance, the letter uses a type of argument called "from the lesser to the greater." This type of argument is based on the idea that if you accept something as true in a lesser situation, then it is certainly true in a greater situation. The author uses it to show that Christ's sacrifice is far greater than the sacrifices offered by the priests in the Temple. As the perfect high priest, Christ offers the perfect sacrifice—his death on the cross—through which God saves us once and for all from sin.

This letter reads like one long sermon made up of interconnecting parts. Begin by reading the whole thing out loud to truly appreciate its power and wording. Then, look up some of its references to people and events in the Old Testament to better appreciate its inspired explanation of Christ's nature and mission.

Quick Facts

Author
unknown

Date Written
approximately A.D. 80–90

Audience
Hellenistic (Greek-speaking) Christians and possibly Jewish Christians

Hebrews

God Has Spoken by His Son
(Cp Jn 1.1–4)

Long ago God spoke to our ancestors in many and various ways by the prophets, 2 but in these last days he has spoken to us by a Son,*a* whom he appointed heir of all things, through whom he also created the worlds. 3 He is the reflection of God's glory and the exact imprint of God's very being, and he sustains*b* all things by his powerful word. When he had made purification for sins, he sat down at the right hand of the Majesty on high, 4 having become as much superior to angels as the name he has inherited is more excellent than theirs.

The Son Is Superior to Angels

5 For to which of the angels did God ever say,
"You are my Son;
today I have begotten you"?
Or again,
"I will be his Father,
and he will be my Son"?
6 And again, when he brings the firstborn into the world, he says,
"Let all God's angels worship him."
7 Of the angels he says,
"He makes his angels winds,
and his servants flames of fire."

8 But of the Son he says,
"Your throne, O God, is*c* forever and ever,
and the righteous scepter is the scepter of
your*d* kingdom.
9 You have loved righteousness and hated
wickedness;
therefore God, your God, has anointed you
with the oil of gladness beyond your
companions."
10 And,
"In the beginning, Lord, you founded the
earth,
and the heavens are the work of your
hands;
11 they will perish, but you remain;
they will all wear out like clothing;
12 like a cloak you will roll them up,
and like clothing*e* they will be changed.
But you are the same,
and your years will never end."
13 But to which of the angels has he ever said,
"Sit at my right hand
until I make your enemies a footstool for
your feet"?

---

a Or *the Son*   *b* Or *bears along*   *c* Or *God is your throne*
d Other ancient authorities read *his*   *e* Other ancient
authorities lack *like clothing*

"The Exact Imprint"

Throughout history, there have been many opinions about who Jesus of Nazareth was. Some have called him a great teacher, some a prophet, some a charismatic preacher, and others a worker of miracles. Christians believe Jesus was all of these and more—much more.

The New Testament makes a bold claim about Jesus. It says the historical human being from Nazareth named Jesus is the perfect human image of God. Jesus reflects God's glory and is "the exact imprint of God's very being" (1.3). In other words, although a human being like us, Jesus is God.

This astonishing claim is central to the Christian faith. If you accept it as true, it will change your life. And if you are to believe it, you need to know the whole story behind it and all the evidence that supports it. The best place to start is with the book in your hands right now. Read on!

▶ Heb 1.1–14

14 Are not all angels^f spirits in the divine service, sent to serve for the sake of those who are to inherit salvation?

So Great a Salvation!

I t is easy for us humans to rationalize why we do certain things. Even if our actions hurt other people and separate us from God, we can come up with a way to justify them. Though this way of thinking may seem to work for us, Heb 2.1–4 says quite clearly that it never works with God.

We cannot hide from our "just penalty" (verse 2). But the good news is that God offers us salvation from our sins through Jesus Christ. In your prayer, journal or reflect on the following questions:

- Do you believe that you will receive a just penalty for the things you have done wrong?
- If we can be saved from our just penalty by placing our faith in Jesus Christ, why would anyone want to "neglect so great a salvation" (verse 3)?
- How can you avoid drifting away (verse 1) from the good news of salvation?

▶ Heb 2.1–4

Warning to Pay Attention

Therefore we must pay greater attention to what we have heard, so that we do not drift away from it. 2 For if the message declared through angels was valid, and every transgression or disobedience received a just penalty, 3 how can we escape if we neglect so great a salvation? It was declared at first through the Lord, and it was attested to us by those who heard him, 4 while God added his testimony by signs and wonders and various miracles, and by gifts of the Holy Spirit, distributed according to his will.

Exaltation through Abasement
(Cp Ps 8.1–9)

5 Now God^g did not subject the coming world, about which we are speaking, to angels. 6 But someone has testified somewhere,

"What are human beings that you are
      mindful of them,^{h}
   or mortals, that you care for them?^{i}
7 You have made them for a little while
      lower^j than the angels;
   you have crowned them with glory and
      honor,^{k}
8   subjecting all things under their feet."

Now in subjecting all things to them, God^g left nothing outside their control. As it is, we do not yet see everything in subjection to them, 9 but we do see Jesus, who for a little while was made

---

^{f} Gk all of them ^{g} Gk he ^{h} Gk What is man that you are mindful of him? ^{i} Gk or the son of man that you care for him? In the Hebrew of Psalm 8.4-6 both man and son of man refer to all humankind ^{j} Or them only a little lower ^{k} Other ancient authorities add and set them over the works of your hands

lower[l] than the angels, now crowned with glory and honor because of the suffering of death, so that by the grace of God[m] he might taste death for everyone.

10 It was fitting that God,[n] for whom and through whom all things exist, in bringing many children to glory, should make the pioneer of their salvation perfect through sufferings. 11 For the one who sanctifies and those who are sanctified all have one Father.[o] For this reason Jesus[n] is not ashamed to call them brothers and sisters,[p] 12 saying,

"I will proclaim your name to my brothers
and sisters,[p]
in the midst of the congregation I will
praise you."

13 And again,

"I will put my trust in him."

And again,

"Here am I and the children whom God
has given me."

14 Since, therefore, the children share flesh and blood, he himself likewise shared the same things, so that through death he might destroy the one who has the power of death, that is, the devil, 15 and free those who all their lives were held in slavery by the fear of death. 16 For it is clear that he did not come to help angels, but the descendants of Abraham. 17 Therefore he had to become like his brothers and sisters[p] in every respect, so that he might be a merciful and faithful high priest in the service of God, to make a sacrifice of atonement for the sins of the people. 18 Because he himself was tested by what he suffered, he is able to help those who are being tested.

Moses a Servant, Christ a Son

Therefore, brothers and sisters,[p] holy partners in a heavenly calling, consider that Jesus, the apostle and high priest of our confession, 2 was faithful to the one who appointed him, just as Moses also "was faithful in all[q] God's[r] house." 3 Yet Jesus[s] is worthy of more glory than Moses, just as the builder of a house has more honor than the house itself. 4 (For every house is built by someone, but the builder of all things is God.) 5 Now Moses was faithful in all God's[r] house as a servant, to testify to the things that would be spoken later. 6 Christ, however, was faithful over God's[r] house as a son, and we are his house if we hold firm[t] the confidence and the pride that belong to hope.

Warning against Unbelief
(Ps 95.7b–11)

7 Therefore, as the Holy Spirit says,

"Today, if you hear his voice,

8 do not harden your hearts as in
the rebellion,
as on the day of testing in the wilderness,
9 where your ancestors put me to the test,
though they had seen my works 10 for
forty years.
Therefore I was angry with that generation,
and I said, 'They always go astray in their
hearts,
and they have not known my ways.'
11 As in my anger I swore,
'They will not enter my rest.' "

12 Take care, brothers and sisters,[p] that none of you may have an evil, unbelieving heart that turns away from the living God. 13 But exhort one another every day, as long as it is called "today," so that none of you may be hardened by the deceitfulness of sin. 14 For we have become partners of Christ, if only we hold our first confidence firm to the end. 15 As it is said,

"Today, if you hear his voice,
do not harden your hearts as in
the rebellion."

16 Now who were they who heard and yet were rebellious? Was it not all those who left Egypt under the leadership of Moses? 17 But with whom was he angry forty years? Was it not those who sinned, whose bodies fell in the wilderness? 18 And to whom did he swear that they would not enter his rest, if not to those who were disobedient? 19 So we see that they were unable to enter because of unbelief.

The Rest That God Promised

Therefore, while the promise of entering his rest is still open, let us take care that none of you should seem to have failed to reach it. 2 For indeed the good news came to us just as to them; but the message they heard did not benefit them, because they were not united by faith with those who listened.[u] 3 For we who have believed enter that rest, just as God[n] has said,

"As in my anger I swore,
'They shall not enter my rest,' "

though his works were finished at the foundation of the world. 4 For in one place it speaks about the seventh day as follows, "And God rested on the seventh day from all his works." 5 And again in this place it says, "They shall not enter my rest." 6 Since therefore it remains open for some to enter it, and

---

l Or who was made a little lower   *m Other ancient authorities read apart from God*   *n Gk he*   *o Gk are all of one*   *p Gk brothers*   *q Other ancient authorities lack all*   *r Gk his*   *s Gk this one*   *t Other ancient authorities add to the end*   *u Other ancient authorities read it did not meet with faith in those who listened*

H
E
B

those who formerly received the good news failed to enter because of disobedience, 7 again he sets a certain day—"today"—saying through David much later, in the words already quoted,

"Today, if you hear his voice,
do not harden your hearts."

8 For if Joshua had given them rest, God^v would not speak later about another day. 9 So then, a sabbath rest still remains for the people of God; 10 for those who enter God's rest also cease from their labors as God did from his. 11 Let us therefore make every effort to enter that rest, so that no one may fall through such disobedience as theirs.

The **word**
of **God** is
living and *active,*
**sharper than
any two-edged**
s**word**

4.12

12 Indeed, the word of God is living and active, sharper than any two-edged sword, piercing until it divides soul from spirit, joints from marrow; it is able to judge the thoughts and intentions of the heart. 13 And before him no creature is hidden, but all are naked and laid bare to the eyes of the one to whom we must render an account.

Jesus the Great High Priest

14 Since, then, we have a great high priest who has passed through the heavens, Jesus, the Son of God, let us hold fast to our confession. 15 For we do not have a high priest who is unable to sympathize with our weaknesses, but we have one who in every respect has been tested^w as we are, yet without sin. 16 Let us therefore approach the throne of grace with boldness, so that we may receive mercy and find grace to help in time of need.

Every high priest chosen from among mortals is put in charge of things pertaining to God on their behalf, to offer gifts and sacrifices for sins. 2 He is able to deal gently with the ignorant and wayward, since he himself is subject to weakness; 3 and because of this he must offer sacrifice for his own sins as well as for those of the people. 4 And one does not presume to take this honor, but takes it only when called by God, just as Aaron was.

5 So also Christ did not glorify himself in becoming a high priest, but was appointed by the one who said to him,

"You are my Son,
today I have begotten you";
6 as he says also in another place,

"You are a priest forever,
according to the order of Mel•chiz•e•dek."

7 In the days of his flesh, Jesus^v offered up prayers and supplications, with loud cries and tears, to the one who was able to save him from death, and he was heard because of his reverent

v Gk *he*   *w* Or *tempted*

Approach God Boldly!

Have you ever believed that you did something that God could never forgive? Or do you ever have thoughts that make you feel so ashamed that you do not dare talk with God about them?

Hebrews 4.14–16 reminds us of a remarkable truth: Jesus, while fully divine, was also fully human. And though he never sinned, this Scripture passage tells us that he was tempted as we are in every respect. Think about that! Jesus was once fourteen years old. He was once seventeen. He was once twenty-two. There is no temptation that you have considered that Jesus cannot understand. And that is why you can approach him in any circumstance—even your deepest trouble—and find compassion and grace.

Remember: (1) you cannot hide from God, and (2) you don't have to!

▸ Heb 4.14–16

?did you KNOW?

The Priesthood and Christ's Sacrifice

In the Old Testament, the priesthood evolved after Israel became a nation, and it underwent a long process of development. Priests were not ordained; the priesthood was considered hereditary within the tribe of Levi. After the Exile, three classes of clergy emerged: high priests, priests, and Levites. Priestly functions included maintaining religion as the center of Israel's life, taking care of the Temple of Jerusalem, and interpreting and teaching the Scriptures. In a special way, the priests of Israel represented the people before God by offering prayer and sacrifices for the forgiveness of sin. Their sacrifices foreshadowed the sacrifice of Jesus, the only sacrifice truly capable of reconciling a broken relationship with God caused by sin.

In the New Testament, Christ made the Apostles co-ministers in his saving mission, including a special participation in his high priesthood—the high priesthood described in Heb 4.14—5.10. Today, the bishops, as successors of the Apostles, continue the apostolic tradition. They ordain priests to assist in their responsibilities as pastors of the faithful, preachers of God's word, and celebrants of Christian worship (see "Holy Orders," Mk 3.13–19).

Catholic bishops and priests exercise their special participation in Christ's priesthood while presiding at the Eucharist. Acting in Christ's name and in communion with the assembly, they celebrate a memorial of Jesus' life, death, and Resurrection. In the celebration of the Eucharist, Christ's sacrifice on the cross is "re-presented," that is, Jesus' sacrifice for the forgiveness of sins is made real and present.

▸ Heb 4.14—5.10

submission. [8] Although he was a Son, he learned obedience through what he suffered; [9] and having been made perfect, he became the source of eternal salvation for all who obey him, [10] having been designated by God a high priest according to the order of Mel·chiz'e·dek.

Warning against Falling Away

[11] About this[x] we have much to say that is hard to explain, since you have become dull in understanding. [12] For though by this time you ought to be teachers, you need someone to teach you again the basic elements of the oracles of God. You need milk, not solid food; [13] for everyone who lives on milk, being still an infant, is unskilled in the word of righteousness. [14] But solid food is for the mature, for those whose faculties have been trained by practice to distinguish good from evil.

The Peril of Falling Away

Therefore let us go on toward perfection,[y] leaving behind the basic teaching about Christ, and not laying again the foundation: repentance from dead works and faith toward God, [2] instruction about baptisms, laying on of hands, resurrection of the dead, and eternal judgment. [3] And we will do[z] this, if God permits. [4] For it is impossible to restore again to repentance those who have once been enlightened, and have tasted the heavenly gift, and have shared in the Holy Spirit, [5] and have tasted the goodness of the word of God and the powers of the age to come, [6] and then have fallen away, since on their own they are crucifying again the Son of God and are holding him up to contempt. [7] Ground that drinks up the rain falling on it repeatedly, and that produces a crop useful to those for whom it is cultivated, receives a blessing from God. [8] But if it produces thorns and thistles, it is worthless and on the verge of being cursed; its end is to be burned over.

[9] Even though we speak in this way, beloved, we are confident of better things in your case, things that belong to salvation. [10] For God is not unjust; he will not overlook your work and the love that you showed for his sake[a] in serving the saints, as you still do. [11] And we want each one of you to show the same diligence so as to realize the full assurance of hope to the very end, [12] so that you may not become sluggish, but imitators of those who through faith and patience inherit the promises.

---

x Or him   y Or *toward maturity*   z Other ancient authorities read *let us do*   a Gk *for his name*

The Certainty of God's Promise
(Cp Gen 12.1–3)

13 When God made a promise to Abraham, because he had no one greater by whom to swear, he swore by himself, [14] saying, "I will surely bless you and multiply you." [15] And thus Abraham,[b] having patiently endured, obtained the promise. [16] Human beings, of course, swear by someone greater than themselves, and an oath given as confirmation puts an end to all dispute. [17] In the same way, when God desired to show even more clearly to the heirs of the promise the unchangeable character of his purpose, he guaranteed it by an oath, [18] so that through two unchangeable things, in which it is impossible that God would prove false, we who have taken refuge might be strongly encouraged to seize the hope set before us. [19] We

H
E
B

AFRICAN AMERICAN
Anchor of the Soul

Something mighty powerful kept a smile on my mother's face every day when I was a little girl. I never knew she was in pain. All I saw was a woman with a demeanor of hope and a purpose in life.

I did not know it back then, but she was enduring racial harassment on her job. There was unceasing verbal hate toward African Americans. As I have matured, I have learned that her harassment was not unique. It was a common experience for many African Americans in this country.

When faced with oppressive situations, let us be thankful for a God who continuously fills us with hope. Without hope, oppression is lethal. Hope keeps us moving forward when we'd just as soon give up. Hope makes us smile at tomorrow, even though today is a bitter pill.

Hope is "a sure and steadfast anchor of the soul" (Heb 6.19). A hopeless soul is a major threat to the body. Is your hope anchored in the Lord?

Dear God, give me hope when I face oppression. Amen.

▶ Heb 6.19–20

Catholic Connections
MELCHIZEDEK

Look with favor on these offerings and accept them as once you accepted the gifts of your servant Abel, the sacrifice of Abraham, our father in faith, and the bread and wine offered by your priest Melchisedech.
(The Sacramentary, p. 546)

This quote is from the first eucharistic prayer in the Catholic Mass. Who is Melchisedech (also spelled Melchizedek)? In the Book of Genesis, after Abraham successfully conquers the enemies of his nephew Lot, Melchizedek, a priest and king, offers a sacrifice of bread and wine to God on Abraham's behalf (14.17–20). In this way, he becomes Abraham's priest. Early Christians saw parallels to Jesus in the story of Melchizedek, and even in his name, which means "king of righteousness." Thus, Melchizedek's life came to be viewed as an early but incomplete example of Jesus' high priesthood.

▶ Heb 7.1–10

have this hope, a sure and steadfast anchor of the soul, a hope that enters the inner shrine behind the curtain, [20] where Jesus, a forerunner on our behalf, has entered, having become a high priest forever according to the order of Mel·chiz'e·dek.

The Priestly Order of Melchizedek
(Gen 14.17–20)

This "King Mel·chiz'e·dek of Salem, priest of the Most High God, met Abraham as he was returning from defeating the kings and blessed him"; [2] and to him Abraham apportioned "one-tenth of everything." His name, in the first place, means "king of righteousness"; next he is also king of Salem, that

---
b Gk *he*

is, "king of peace." ³Without father, without mother, without genealogy, having neither beginning of days nor end of life, but resembling the Son of God, he remains a priest forever.

4 See how great he is! Even*c* Abraham the patriarch gave him a tenth of the spoils. ⁵And those descendants of Levi who receive the priestly office have a commandment in the law to collect tithes*d* from the people, that is, from their kindred,*e* though these also are descended from Abraham. ⁶But this man, who does not belong to their ancestry, collected tithes*d* from Abraham and blessed him who had received the promises. ⁷It is beyond dispute that the inferior is blessed by the superior. ⁸In the one case, tithes are received by those who are mortal; in the other, by one of whom it is testified that he lives. ⁹One might even say that Levi himself, who receives tithes, paid tithes through Abraham, ¹⁰for he was still in the loins of his ancestor when Mel•chiz'e•dek met him.

Another Priest, Like Melchizedek
(Ps 110.4)

11 Now if perfection had been attainable through the levitical priesthood—for the people received the law under this priesthood—what further need would there have been to speak of another priest arising according to the order of Mel•chiz'e•dek, rather than one according to the order of Aaron? ¹²For when there is a change in the priesthood, there is necessarily a change in the law as well. ¹³Now the one of whom these things are spoken belonged to another tribe, from which no one has ever served at the altar. ¹⁴For it is evident that our Lord was descended from Judah, and in connection with that tribe Moses said nothing about priests.

15 It is even more obvious when another priest arises, resembling Mel•chiz'e•dek, ¹⁶one who has become a priest, not through a legal requirement concerning physical descent, but through the power of an indestructible life. ¹⁷For it is attested of him,

"You are a priest forever,
     according to the order of Mel•chiz'e•dek."
¹⁸There is, on the one hand, the abrogation of an earlier commandment because it was weak and ineffectual ¹⁹(for the law made nothing perfect); there is, on the other hand, the introduction of a better hope, through which we approach God.

20 This was confirmed with an oath; for others who became priests took their office without an oath, ²¹but this one became a priest with an oath, because of the one who said to him,

"The Lord has sworn

and will not change his mind,
'You are a priest forever' "—
²²accordingly Jesus has also become the guarantee of a better covenant.

23 Furthermore, the former priests were many in number, because they were prevented by death from continuing in office; ²⁴but he holds his priesthood permanently, because he continues forever. ²⁵Consequently he is able for all time to save*f* those who approach God through him, since he always lives to make intercession for them.

26 For it was fitting that we should have such a high priest, holy, blameless, undefiled, separated from sinners, and exalted above the heavens. ²⁷Unlike the other*g* high priests, he has no need to offer sacrifices day after day, first for his own sins, and then for those of the people; this he did once for all when he offered himself. ²⁸For the law appoints as high priests those who are subject to weakness, but the word of the oath, which came later than the law, appoints a Son who has been made perfect forever.

Mediator of a Better Covenant
(Jer 31.31–34)

Now the main point in what we are saying is this: we have such a high priest, one who is seated at the right hand of the throne of the Majesty in the heavens, ²a minister in the sanctuary and the true tent*h* that the Lord, and not any mortal, has set up. ³For every high priest is appointed to offer gifts and sacrifices; hence it is necessary for this priest also to have something to offer. ⁴Now if he were on earth, he would not be a priest at all, since there are priests who offer gifts according to the law. ⁵They offer worship in a sanctuary that is a sketch and shadow of the heavenly one; for Moses, when he was about to erect the tent,*h* was warned, "See that you make everything according to the pattern that was shown you on the mountain." ⁶But Jesus*i* has now obtained a more excellent ministry, and to that degree he is the mediator of a better covenant, which has been enacted through better promises. ⁷For if that first covenant had been faultless, there would have been no need to look for a second one.

8 God*j* finds fault with them when he says:
"The days are surely coming, says the Lord,
     when I will establish a new covenant
          with the house of Israel
          and with the house of Judah;

c Other ancient authorities lack *Even*   *d* Or *a tenth*
e Gk *brothers*   *f* Or *able to save completely*   *g* Gk lacks
other   *h* Or *tabernacle*   *i* Gk *he*   *j* Gk *He*

HEB

9 not like the covenant that I made with their
  ancestors,
  on the day when I took them by the
      hand to lead them out of the land
      of Egypt;
  for they did not continue in my covenant,
      and so I had no concern for them, says
      the Lord.
10 This is the covenant that I will make with
      the house of Israel
  after those days, says the Lord:
  I will put my laws in their minds,
  and write them on their hearts,
  and I will be their God,
  and they shall be my people.
11 And they shall not teach one another
      or say to each other, 'Know the Lord,'
  for they shall all know me,
  from the least of them to the greatest.
12 For I will be merciful toward their
      iniquities,
  and I will remember their sins no more."

13 In speaking of "a new covenant," he has made the first one obsolete. And what is obsolete and growing old will soon disappear.

The Earthly and the Heavenly Sanctuaries
(Cp Ex 25.10–40)

Now even the first covenant had regulations for worship and an earthly sanctuary. 2 For a tent[k] was constructed, the first one, in which were the lampstand, the table, and the bread of the Presence;[l] this is called the Holy Place. 3 Behind the second curtain was a tent[k] called the Holy of Holies. 4 In it stood the golden altar of incense and the ark of the covenant overlaid on all sides with gold, in which there were a golden urn holding the manna, and Aaron's rod that budded, and the tablets of the covenant; 5 above it were the cherubim of glory overshadowing the mercy seat.[m] Of these things we cannot speak now in detail.

6 Such preparations having been made, the priests go continually into the first tent[k] to carry out their ritual duties; 7 but only the high priest goes into the second, and he but once a year, and not without taking the blood that he offers for himself and for the sins committed unintentionally by the people. 8 By this the Holy Spirit indicates that the way into the sanctuary has not yet been disclosed as long as the first tent[k] is still standing. 9 This is a symbol[n] of the present time, during which gifts and sacrifices are offered that cannot perfect the conscience of the worshiper, 10 but deal only with food and drink and various

baptisms, regulations for the body imposed until the time comes to set things right.

11 But when Christ came as a high priest of the good things that have come,[o] then through the greater and perfect[p] tent[k] (not made with hands, that is, not of this creation), 12 he entered once for all into the Holy Place, not with the blood of goats and calves, but with his own blood, thus obtaining eternal redemption. 13 For if the blood of goats and bulls, with the sprinkling of the ashes of a heifer, sanctifies those who have been defiled so that their flesh is purified, 14 how much more will the blood of Christ, who through the eternal Spirit[q] offered himself without blemish to God, purify our[r] conscience from dead works to worship the living God!

15 For this reason he is the mediator of a new covenant, so that those who are called may receive the promised eternal inheritance, because a death has occurred that redeems them from the transgressions under the first covenant.[s] 16 Where a will[s] is involved, the death of the one who made it must be established. 17 For a will[s] takes effect only at death, since it is not in force as long as the one who made it is alive. 18 Hence not even the first covenant was inaugurated without blood. 19 For when every commandment had been told to all the people by Moses in accordance with the law, he took the blood of calves and goats,[t] with water and scarlet wool and hyssop, and sprinkled both the scroll itself and all the people, 20 saying, "This is the blood of the covenant that God has ordained for you." 21 And in the same way he sprinkled with the blood both the tent[k] and all the vessels used in worship. 22 Indeed, under the law almost everything is purified with blood, and without the shedding of blood there is no forgiveness of sins.

Christ's Sacrifice Takes Away Sin

23 Thus it was necessary for the sketches of the heavenly things to be purified with these rites, but the heavenly things themselves need better sacrifices than these. 24 For Christ did not enter a sanctuary made by human hands, a mere copy of the true one, but he entered into heaven itself, now to appear in the presence of God on our behalf. 25 Nor was it to offer himself again and again, as the high priest enters the Holy Place year after year

---

k Or *tabernacle*   l Gk *the presentation of the loaves*
m Or *the place of atonement*   n Gk *parable*   o Other ancient authorities read *good things to come*   p Gk *more perfect*   q Other ancient authorities read *Holy Spirit*
r Other ancient authorities read *your*   s The Greek word used here means both *covenant* and *will*   t Other ancient authorities lack *and goats*

with blood that is not his own; 26 for then he would have had to suffer again and again since the foundation of the world. But as it is, he has appeared once for all at the end of the age to remove sin by the sacrifice of himself. 27 And just as it is appointed for mortals to die once, and after that the judgment, 28 so Christ, having been offered once to bear the sins of many, will appear a second time, not to deal with sin, but to save those who are eagerly waiting for him.

Christ's Sacrifice Once for All
(Cp Ps 40.6–8)

Since the law has only a shadow of the good things to come and not the true form of these realities, it*u* can never, by the same sacrifices that are continually offered year after year, make perfect those who approach. 2 Otherwise, would they not have ceased being offered, since the worshipers, cleansed once for all, would no longer have any consciousness of sin? 3 But in these sacrifices there is a reminder of sin year after year. 4 For it is impossible for the blood of bulls and goats to take away sins. 5 Consequently, when Christ*v* came into the world, he said,

"Sacrifices and offerings you have not
        desired,
    but a body you have prepared for me;
6 in burnt offerings and sin offerings
        you have taken no pleasure.
7 Then I said, 'See, God, I have come to do
        your will, O God'
    (in the scroll of the book*w* it is written
        of me)."

8 When he said above, "You have neither desired nor taken pleasure in sacrifices and offerings and burnt offerings and sin offerings" (these are offered according to the law), 9 then he added, "See, I have come to do your will." He abolishes the first in order to establish the second. 10 And it is by God's will*x* that we have been sanctified through the offering of the body of Jesus Christ once for all.

11 And every priest stands day after day at his service, offering again and again the same sacrifices that can never take away sins. 12 But when Christ*y* had offered for all time a single sacrifice for sins, "he sat down at the right hand of God," 13 and since then has been waiting "until his enemies would be made a footstool for his feet." 14 For by a single offering he has perfected for all time those who are sanctified. 15 And the Holy Spirit also testifies to us, for after saying,

16 "This is the covenant that I will make with
        them
    after those days, says the Lord:

I will put my laws in their hearts,
    and I will write them on their minds,"
17 he also adds,

"I will remember*z* their sins and their
        lawless deeds no more."
18 Where there is forgiveness of these, there is no longer any offering for sin.

?did you KNOW?
The Perfect Sacrifice

The author of the Letter to the Hebrews uses the "from the lesser to the greater" argument again to explain that Christ's sacrifice on the cross is greater than any sacrifice that could ever be offered in the Temple. Even though perfect animals are offered over and over, they never take away sins (10.1–4). The sacrifice of Christ takes away sins because it is the perfect sacrifice, offered only once for the sins of all (verses 12–14). After Christ's death, there is no longer any need for anyone else to offer a sacrifice for the forgiveness of sins.

▶ **Heb 10.1–18**

A Call to Persevere

19 Therefore, my friends,*a* since we have confidence to enter the sanctuary by the blood of Jesus, 20 by the new and living way that he opened for us through the curtain (that is, through his flesh), 21 and since we have a great priest over the house of God, 22 let us approach with a true heart in full assurance of faith, with our hearts sprinkled clean from an evil conscience and our bodies washed with pure water. 23 Let us hold fast to the confession of our hope without wavering, for he who has promised is faithful. 24 And let us consider how to provoke one another to love and good deeds, 25 not neglecting to meet together, as is the habit of some, but encouraging one another, and all the more as you see the Day approaching.

26 For if we willfully persist in sin after having received the knowledge of the truth, there no

---

u Other ancient authorities read *they*   *v* Gk *he*
w Meaning of Gk uncertain   *x* Gk *by that will*   *y* Gk *this*
one   *z* Gk *on their minds and I will remember*
a Gk *Therefore, brothers*

longer remains a sacrifice for sins, 27 but a fearful prospect of judgment, and a fury of fire that will consume the adversaries. 28 Anyone who has violated the law of Moses dies without mercy "on the testimony of two or three witnesses." 29 How much worse punishment do you think will be deserved by those who have spurned the Son of God, profaned the blood of the covenant by which they were sanctified, and outraged the Spirit of grace? 30 For we know the one who said, "Vengeance is mine, I will repay." And again, "The Lord will judge his people." 31 It is a fearful thing to fall into the hands of the living God.

32 But recall those earlier days when, after you had been enlightened, you endured a hard struggle with sufferings, 33 sometimes being publicly exposed to abuse and persecution, and sometimes being partners with those so treated. 34 For you had compassion for those who were in prison, and you cheerfully accepted the plundering of your possessions, knowing that you yourselves possessed something better and more lasting. 35 Do not, therefore, abandon that confidence of yours; it brings a great reward. 36 For you need endurance, so that when you have done the will of God, you may receive what was promised.

37 For yet "in a very little while,
　the one who is coming will come and
　　will not delay;
38 but my righteous one will live by faith.
　My soul takes no pleasure in anyone who
　　shrinks back."

39 But we are not among those who shrink back and so are lost, but among those who have faith and so are saved.

The Meaning of Faith

Now faith is the assurance of things hoped for, the conviction of things not seen. 2 Indeed, by faith[b] our ancestors received approval. 3 By faith we understand that the worlds were prepared by the word of God, so that what is seen was made from things that are not visible.[c]

The Examples of Abel, Enoch, and Noah
(Gen 4.1–16; 6.5—8.22)

4 By faith Abel offered to God a more acceptable[d] sacrifice than Cain's. Through this he received approval as righteous, God himself giving approval to his gifts; he died, but through his faith[e] he still speaks. 5 By faith Ē´noch was taken so that he did not experience death; and "he was not found, because God had taken him." For it was attested before he was taken away that "he had pleased God." 6 And without faith it is impossible

to please God, for whoever would approach him must believe that he exists and that he rewards those who seek him. 7 By faith Noah, warned by God about events as yet unseen, respected the warning and built an ark to save his household; by this he condemned the world and became an heir to the righteousness that is in accordance with faith.

The Faith of Abraham
(Gen 15.1–6; 21.1–7; 22.1–14; 48.8–16; 50.22–25)

8 By faith Abraham obeyed when he was called to set out for a place that he was to receive as an inheritance; and he set out, not knowing where he was going. 9 By faith he stayed for a time in the land he had been promised, as in a foreign land, living in tents, as did Isaac and Jacob, who were

How Do You Spell Faith?

In Heb 11.1–3, the author spells out what he means by the word *faith*. Here is another way to spell its meaning:
F orever knowing God loves me totally and unconditionally
A bly meeting any problem with hope and confidence
I n truth believing in the life, death, and Resurrection of Jesus Christ
T otally trusting in God
H aving eyes that see the God that cannot be seen

　How do you spell the meaning of faith?
F
A
I
T
H

▶ Heb 11.1–3

heirs with him of the same promise. 10 For he looked forward to the city that has foundations, whose architect and builder is God. 11 By faith he received power of procreation, even though he was

b Gk by this　c Or was not made out of visible things
d Gk greater　e Gk through it

too old—and Sarah herself was barren—because he considered him faithful who had promised.*f* 12 Therefore from one person, and this one as good as dead, descendants were born, "as many as the stars of heaven and as the innumerable grains of sand by the seashore."

13 All of these died in faith without having received the promises, but from a distance they saw and greeted them. They confessed that they were strangers and foreigners on the earth, 14 for people who speak in this way make it clear that they are seeking a homeland. 15 If they had been thinking of the land that they had left behind, they would have had opportunity to return. 16 But as it is, they desire a better country, that is, a heavenly one. Therefore God is not ashamed to be called their God; indeed, he has prepared a city for them.

17 By faith Abraham, when put to the test, offered up Isaac. He who had received the promises was ready to offer up his only son, 18 of whom he had been told, "It is through Isaac that descendants shall be named for you." 19 He considered the fact that God is able even to raise someone from the dead—and figuratively speaking, he did receive him back. 20 By faith Isaac invoked blessings for the future on Jacob and Esau. 21 By faith Jacob, when dying, blessed each of the sons of Joseph, "bowing in worship over the top of his staff." 22 By faith Joseph, at the end of his life, made mention of the exodus of the Israelites and gave instructions about his burial.*g*

The Faith of Moses
(Ex 2.1–10; 12.31–51)

23 By faith Moses was hidden by his parents for three months after his birth, because they saw that the child was beautiful; and they were not afraid of the king's edict.*h* 24 By faith Moses, when he was grown up, refused to be called a son of Pharaoh's daughter, 25 choosing rather to share illtreatment with the people of God than to enjoy the fleeting pleasures of sin. 26 He considered abuse suffered for the Christ*i* to be greater wealth than the treasures of Egypt, for he was looking ahead to the reward. 27 By faith he left Egypt, unafraid of the king's anger; for he persevered as though*j* he saw him who is invisible. 28 By faith he kept the Passover and the sprinkling of blood, so that the destroyer of the firstborn would not touch the firstborn of Israel.*k*

The Faith of Other Israelite Heroes

29 By faith the people passed through the Red Sea as if it were dry land, but when the Egyptians attempted to do so they were drowned. 30 By faith the walls of Jericho fell after they had been encir-

cled for seven days. 31 By faith Rā'hab the prostitute did not perish with those who were disobedient,*l* because she had received the spies in peace.

32 And what more should I say? For time would fail me to tell of Gideon, Bar'ak, Samson, Jeph'thah, of David and Samuel and the prophets— 33 who through faith conquered kingdoms, administered justice, obtained promises, shut the mouths of lions, 34 quenched raging fire, escaped the edge of the sword, won strength out of weakness, became mighty in war, put foreign armies to flight. 35 Women received their dead by resurrection. Others were tortured, refusing to accept release, in order to obtain a better resurrection. 36 Others suffered mocking and flogging, and even chains and imprisonment. 37 They were stoned to death, they were sawn in two,*m* they were killed by the sword; they went about in skins of sheep and goats, destitute, persecuted, tormented— 38 of whom the world was not worthy. They wandered in deserts and mountains, and in caves and holes in the ground.

39 Yet all these, though they were commended for their faith, did not receive what was promised, 40 since God had provided something better so that they would not, apart from us, be made perfect.

The Example of Jesus
(Prov 3.11–12)

Therefore, since we are surrounded by so great a cloud of witnesses, let us also lay aside every weight and the sin that clings so closely,*n* and let us run with perseverance the race that is set before us, 2 looking to Jesus the pioneer and perfecter of our faith, who for the sake of*o* the joy that was set before him endured the cross, disregarding its shame, and has taken his seat at the right hand of the throne of God.

3 Consider him who endured such hostility against himself from sinners,*p* so that you may not grow weary or lose heart. 4 In your struggle against sin you have not yet resisted to the point of

---

f Or By faith Sarah herself, though barren, received power to conceive, even when she was too old, because she considered him faithful who had promised.   g Gk his bones   h Other ancient authorities add By faith Moses, when he was grown up, killed the Egyptian, because he observed the humiliation of his people (Gk brothers)   i Or the Messiah   j Or because k Gk would not touch them   l Or unbelieving   m Other ancient authorities add they were tempted   n Other ancient authorities read sin that easily distracts   o Or who instead of   p Other ancient authorities read such hostility from sinners against themselves

shedding your blood. ⁵And you have forgotten the exhortation that addresses you as children—

"My child, do not regard lightly the
discipline of the Lord,
or lose heart when you are punished
by him;
⁶ for the Lord disciplines those whom he
loves,
and chastises every child whom he
accepts."

⁷Endure trials for the sake of discipline. God is treating you as children; for what child is there whom a parent does not discipline? ⁸If you do not have that discipline in which all children share, then you are illegitimate and not his children. ⁹Moreover, we had human parents to discipline us, and we respected them. Should we not be even more willing to be subject to the Father of spirits and live? ¹⁰For they disciplined us for a short time as seemed best to them, but he disciplines us for our good, in order that we may share his holiness. ¹¹Now, discipline always seems painful rather than pleasant at the time, but later it yields the peaceful fruit of righteousness to those who have been trained by it.

12 Therefore lift your drooping hands and strengthen your weak knees, ¹³and make straight paths for your feet, so that what is lame may not be put out of joint, but rather be healed.

Warnings against Rejecting
God's Grace
(Gen 25.29–34; 27.30–40)

14 Pursue peace with everyone, and the holiness without which no one will see the Lord. ¹⁵See to it that no one fails to obtain the grace of God; that no root of bitterness springs up and causes trouble, and through it many become defiled. ¹⁶See to it that no one becomes like Esau, an immoral and godless person, who sold his birthright for a single meal. ¹⁷You know that later, when he wanted to inherit the blessing, he was rejected, for he found no chance to repent,*q* even though he sought the blessing*r* with tears.

18 You have not come to something*s* that can be touched, a blazing fire, and darkness, and gloom, and a tempest, ¹⁹and the sound of a trumpet, and a voice whose words made the hearers beg that not another word be spoken to them. ²⁰(For they could not endure the order that was given, "If even an animal touches the mountain, it shall be stoned to death." ²¹Indeed, so terrifying was the sight that Moses said, "I tremble with fear.") ²²But you have come to Mount Zion and to the city of the living God, the heavenly Jerusalem,

and to innumerable angels in festal gathering, ²³and to the assembly*t* of the firstborn who are enrolled in heaven, and to God the judge of all, and to the spirits of the righteous made perfect, ²⁴and to Jesus, the mediator of a new covenant, and to the sprinkled blood that speaks a better word than the blood of Abel.

25 See that you do not refuse the one who is speaking; for if they did not escape when they refused the one who warned them on earth, how much less will we escape if we reject the one who warns from heaven! ²⁶At that time his voice shook the earth; but now he has promised, "Yet once more I will shake not only the earth but also the heaven." ²⁷This phrase, "Yet once more," indicates the removal of what is shaken—that is, created things—so that what cannot be shaken may remain. ²⁸Therefore, since we are receiving a kingdom that cannot be shaken, let us give thanks, by which we offer to God an acceptable worship with reverence and awe; ²⁹for indeed our God is a consuming fire.

Service Well-Pleasing to God

Let mutual love continue. ²Do not neglect to show hospitality to strangers, for by doing that some have entertained angels without knowing it. ³Remember those who are in prison, as though you were in prison with them; those who are being tortured, as though you yourselves were being tortured.*u* ⁴Let marriage be held in honor by all, and let the marriage bed be kept undefiled; for God will judge fornicators and adulterers. ⁵Keep your lives free from the love of money, and be content with what you have; for he has said, "I will never leave you or forsake you." ⁶So we can say with confidence,

"The Lord is my helper;
I will not be afraid.
What can anyone do to me?"

7 Remember your leaders, those who spoke the word of God to you; consider the outcome of their way of life, and imitate their faith. ⁸Jesus Christ is the same yesterday and today and forever. ⁹Do not be carried away by all kinds of strange teachings; for it is well for the heart to be strengthened by grace, not by regulations about food,*v* which have not benefited those who observe them. ¹⁰We have an altar from which those who officiate in the tent*w* have no right to eat. ¹¹For the bodies of those animals whose blood is brought

---

q Or *no chance to change his father's mind*   *r* Gk *it*
s Other ancient authorities read *a mountain*   *t* Or *angels,
and to the festal gathering* ²³*and assembly*   *u* Gk *were in the
body*   *v* Gk *not by foods*   *w* Or *tabernacle*

Entertaining Angels

The media, especially movies and television, have always been fascinated by the subject of angels. They often adopt this fantastic idea from the Letter to the Hebrews: that we may actually encounter angels in the form of strangers we meet.

Does God really send angels to roam this world in the form of people? How would we treat that other driver, that other person waiting in line, that person who is racially different from ourselves—if we believed he or she might be an angel sent by God? How would this possibility change the way we look at prisoners, at those who suffer under an oppressive government, at members of the other sex?

How will you treat the strangers you meet today? You might encounter an angel . . .

▶ Heb 13.1–5

into the sanctuary by the high priest as a sacrifice for sin are burned outside the camp. 12 Therefore Jesus also suffered outside the city gate in order to sanctify the people by his own blood. 13 Let us then go to him outside the camp and bear the abuse he endured. 14 For here we have no lasting city, but we are looking for the city that is to come. 15 Through him, then, let us continually offer a sacrifice of praise to God, that is, the fruit of lips that confess his name. 16 Do not neglect to do good and to share what you have, for such sacrifices are pleasing to God.

17 Obey your leaders and submit to them, for they are keeping watch over your souls and will give an account. Let them do this with joy and not with sighing—for that would be harmful to you.

18 Pray for us; we are sure that we have a clear conscience, desiring to act honorably in all things. 19 I urge you all the more to do this, so that I may be restored to you very soon.

Benediction

20 Now may the God of peace, who brought back from the dead our Lord Jesus, the great shepherd of the sheep, by the blood of the eternal covenant, 21 make you complete in everything good so that you may do his will, working among us[x] that which is pleasing in his sight, through Jesus Christ, to whom be the glory forever and ever. Amen.

Final Exhortation and Greetings

22 I appeal to you, brothers and sisters,[y] bear with my word of exhortation, for I have written to you briefly. 23 I want you to know that our brother Timothy has been set free; and if he comes in time, he will be with me when I see you. 24 Greet all your leaders and all the saints. Those from Italy send you greetings. 25 Grace be with all of you.[z]

---

x Other ancient authorities read *you*   y Gk *brothers*
z Other ancient authorities add *Amen*

Have you ever noticed how a kite strains at the string as it soars in the sky? It seems to want to be free of the string that ties it down, free to fly on its own. But if that string does break, the kite flounders and crashes. The kite only has the freedom to fly as long as it's tied to something. That's the way we are under the New Covenant in Christ. We may think we're free to do whatever we want. But if we break from a faithful response to God's love for us, we flounder and crash. The Letter of James provides guidance for living "the law of liberty" (1.25), which leads to real freedom.

At a Glance

- **Chapter 1.** proverbs for Christian living
- **2.1–13.** a discussion of discrimination within the Christian community
- **2.14–26.** a message that faith without works is dead
- **3.1–12.** warnings about controlling the tongue
- **3.13—5.19.** more advice for Christian living

In-depth

Defining the literary style of James is a little difficult. It opens like the other letters but lacks the typical closing. In ways, it is similar to the wisdom literature of the Old Testament. It provides practical advice for how wise people ought to live. It is also similar to Greek moral teaching, which used famous people as models for how we ought to live. This has led scholars to think the book might have been written by an educated Jewish Christian, possibly living in Jerusalem. The author could have been an admirer of James's, the first leader of the early church in Jerusalem.

The letter addresses several issues in Christian living. It warns that rich people should not discriminate against poor people. It insists that Christians' actions must reflect their beliefs. It cautions against careless speech and a poorly controlled tongue. It encourages believers to patiently endure suffering.

James also addresses a misunderstanding of Paul's teaching that "a person is justified by faith apart from works prescribed by the law" (Rom 3.28). Using Abraham and Rahab as examples, the author of James declares, "A person is justified by works and not by faith alone" (Jas 2.24). After all, "faith by itself, if it has no works, is dead" (verse 17). To say you love Jesus, and then do unloving things, makes no sense; it's just plain hypocritical.

So here is God's message of freedom for you: Soar like a kite by staying connected to the law of liberty!

Quick Facts

Author
possibly James the relative of Jesus, but more likely a later admirer of James's

Date Written
A.D. 57–67 if by James, A.D. 70–150 if by a later admirer

Audience
Christians in Palestine or Rome

The Letter of James

James

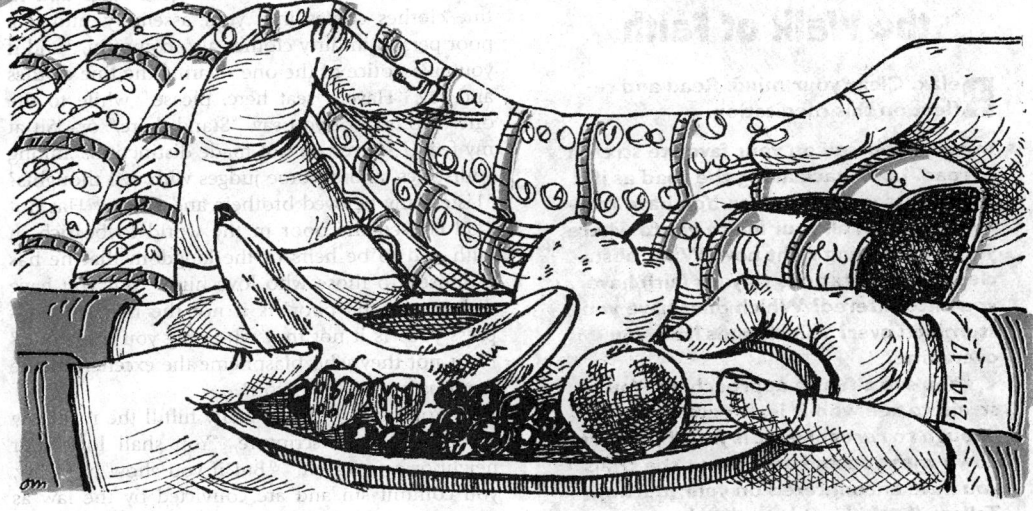

Salutation

James, a servant*a* of God and of the Lord Jesus Christ,

To the twelve tribes in the Dispersion:

Greetings.

Faith and Wisdom

2 My brothers and sisters,*b* whenever you face trials of any kind, consider it nothing but joy, 3 because you know that the testing of your faith produces endurance; 4 and let endurance have its full effect, so that you may be mature and complete, lacking in nothing.

5 If any of you is lacking in wisdom, ask God, who gives to all generously and ungrudgingly, and it will be given you. 6 But ask in faith, never doubting, for the one who doubts is like a wave of the sea, driven and tossed by the wind; 7, 8 for the doubter, being double-minded and unstable in every way, must not expect to receive anything from the Lord.

Poverty and Riches

9 Let the believer*c* who is lowly boast in being raised up, 10 and the rich in being brought low, because the rich will disappear like a flower in the field. 11 For the sun rises with its scorching heat and withers the field; its flower falls, and its beauty perishes. It is the same way with the rich; in the midst of a busy life, they will wither away.

Trial and Temptation

12 Blessed is anyone who endures temptation. Such a one has stood the test and will receive the crown of life that the Lord*d* has promised to those who love him. 13 No one, when tempted, should say, "I am being tempted by God"; for God cannot be tempted by evil and he himself tempts no one. 14 But one is tempted by one's own desire, being lured and enticed by it; 15 then, when that desire has conceived, it gives birth to sin, and that sin, when it is fully grown, gives birth to death. 16 Do not be deceived, my beloved.*e*

17 Every generous act of giving, with every perfect gift, is from above, coming down from the Father of lights, with whom there is no variation or shadow due to change.*f* 18 In fulfillment of his own purpose he gave us birth by the word of truth, so that we would become a kind of first fruits of his creatures.

Hearing and Doing the Word

19 You must understand this, my beloved:*e* let everyone be quick to listen, slow to speak, slow to anger; 20 for your anger does not produce God's righteousness. 21 Therefore rid yourselves of all sordidness and rank growth of wickedness, and

---

a Gk *slave*   *b* Gk *brothers*   *c* Gk *brother*   *d* Gk *he*; other ancient authorities read *God*   *e* Gk *my beloved brothers*   *f* Other ancient authorities read *variation due to a shadow of turning*

PRAY IT!

Meditation on the Walk of Faith

Relax. Clear your mind. Read and reflect on this meditation:

Imagine yourself on your favorite stretch of road. Look back along the road as if it represents your life so far. You have traveled this road all your life to get to where you are standing right now. What obstacles and temptations to your faith have you encountered? Which ones have you stumbled over? Which ones have you overcome?

You see a figure approaching. You strain to see who it is. It gets close enough to recognize. It is Jesus! Jesus sits down with you and asks about the trials you have encountered on your journey. Talk to Jesus about how they have given you the opportunity to grow. Talk to him about the many choices you have made, the good and the bad.

Leave with Jesus to continue forward on the journey. With Jesus, you can joyfully accept the tests of faith that lie ahead, knowing that each is an opportunity to build endurance "so that you may be mature and complete, lacking in nothing" (Jas 1.4).

▸ Jas 1.2–17

welcome with meekness the implanted word that has the power to save your souls.

22 But be doers of the word, and not merely hearers who deceive themselves. 23 For if any are hearers of the word and not doers, they are like those who look at themselves*g* in a mirror; 24 for they look at themselves and, on going away, immediately forget what they were like. 25 But those who look into the perfect law, the law of liberty, and persevere, being not hearers who forget but doers who act—they will be blessed in their doing.

26 If any think they are religious, and do not bridle their tongues but deceive their hearts, their religion is worthless. 27 Religion that is pure and undefiled before God, the Father, is this: to care for orphans and widows in their distress, and to keep oneself unstained by the world.

Warning against Partiality

My brothers and sisters,*h* do you with your acts of favoritism really believe in our glorious Lord Jesus Christ?*i* 2 For if a person with gold rings and in fine clothes comes into your assembly, and if a poor person in dirty clothes also comes in, 3 and if you take notice of the one wearing the fine clothes and say, "Have a seat here, please," while to the one who is poor you say, "Stand there," or, "Sit at my feet,"*j* 4 have you not made distinctions among yourselves, and become judges with evil thoughts? 5 Listen, my beloved brothers and sisters.*k* Has not God chosen the poor in the world to be rich in faith and to be heirs of the kingdom that he has promised to those who love him? 6 But you have dishonored the poor. Is it not the rich who oppress you? Is it not they who drag you into court? 7 Is it not they who blaspheme the excellent name that was invoked over you?

8 You do well if you really fulfill the royal law according to the scripture, "You shall love your neighbor as yourself." 9 But if you show partiality, you commit sin and are convicted by the law as transgressors. 10 For whoever keeps the whole law but fails in one point has become accountable for all of it. 11 For the one who said, "You shall not commit adultery," also said, "You shall not murder." Now if you do not commit adultery but if you murder, you have become a transgressor of the law. 12 So speak and so act as those who are to be judged by the law of liberty. 13 For judgment will be without mercy to anyone who has shown no mercy; mercy triumphs over judgment.

Faith without Works Is Dead
(Cp Gen 22; Josh 2)

14 What good is it, my brothers and sisters,*k* if you say you have faith but do not have works? Can faith save you? 15 If a brother or sister is naked and lacks daily food, 16 and one of you says to them, "Go in peace; keep warm and eat your fill," and yet you do not supply their bodily needs, what is the good of that? 17 So faith by itself, if it has no works, is dead.

18 But someone will say, "You have faith and I have works." Show me your faith apart from your works, and I by my works will show you my faith. 19 You believe that God is one; you do well. Even the demons believe—and shudder. 20 Do you want to be shown, you senseless person, that faith apart from works is barren? 21 Was not our ancestor Abraham justified by works when he offered his

---

g Gk at the face of his birth   *h* Gk My brothers   *i* Or hold the faith of our glorious Lord Jesus Christ without acts of favoritism   *j* Gk Sit under my footstool   *k* Gk brothers

The Favorite

We all know people who are the favorite. Teacher's pet or golden child—whatever the name used, when some person or some group is raised up above others because of money, personality, or power, it seems unfair.

This is the situation in Jas 2.1–13. The author clearly spells out where God stands on the issue of favoritism and partiality. God's response is to turn things upside down by raising up the poor and the lowly (verse 5). The Catholic church refers to this response as the preferential option for the poor, which means always keeping in mind the needs of those who are poor, when setting policies, providing benefits, and so on.

In our world, there is a big difference between rich and poor, top and bottom, the included and the excluded. God needs us to carry out the divine response to this injustice. If we do not give poor people real opportunities to rise up, and if we do not challenge the people in power to live according to God's justice, then, who will?

▶ Jas 2.1–13

---

son Isaac on the altar? ²²You see that faith was active along with his works, and faith was brought to completion by the works. ²³Thus the scripture was fulfilled that says, "Abraham believed God, and it was reckoned to him as righteousness," and he was called the friend of God. ²⁴You see that a person is justified by works and not by faith alone. ²⁵Likewise, was not Raʹhab the prostitute also justified by works when she welcomed the messengers and sent them out by another road? ²⁶For just as the body without the spirit is dead, so faith without works is also dead.

Taming the Tongue

Not many of you should become teachers, my brothers and sisters,[1] for you know that we who teach will be judged with greater strictness. ²For all of us make many mistakes. Anyone who makes no mistakes in speaking is perfect, able to keep the whole body in check with a bridle. ³If we put bits into the mouths of horses to make them obey us, we guide their whole bodies. ⁴Or look at ships: though they are so large that it takes strong winds

[1] Gk brothers

The Tongue: Friend or Foe?

Sometimes, we are advised to hold it. Other times, we are ordered to bite it. Try as we may to keep this counsel, our tongue often proves to be much stronger than our will to control it.

All of us have said things that we later regretted. Frequently against our better judgment, we find ourselves speaking in ways that hurt or offend others and God. People are injured by what others say to—or about—them far more often than by physical attack. The scars left by hurtful words can last a lifetime, destroying families and ruining friendships.

How have you used your tongue lately? Have you spoken words that are hurtful to another person, directly or behind the person's back? How might you use your tongue to begin to heal someone's hurts? Apologies, compliments, and affirmations—the tongue can utter these things too! It is a mark of maturity and confidence when we are able to ask forgiveness or affirm others. Christians are called to this kind of courage and maturity.

Put your tongue to good use today!

▶ Jas 3.1–12

Justice for Those Who Are Poor

Warnings to the rich are common in the Bible, and should be of concern for Christians living in a wealthy nation like the United States. Here are two tough questions to consider: First, in what do we put our trust—the comfort and plea-sure that can be had in wealth and material possessions, or God? And second, how does our lifestyle—including the way we spend money, the choices we make about our future work, and the way we use our time—affect the poor people of this world?

God's justice requires that Christians care about the abuse of poor people for the ben-efit of rich people. God does not want us to become paralyzed with guilt because we are wealthy compared with the poorest of the earth. But the Scriptures remind us that the life choices we make matter, and that those choices may either contribute to a more just world, or support a status quo that keeps rich people comfortable and poor people down. To make good life choices, we must educate ourselves about the situations that cause poverty, and examine how our own lifestyle or beliefs might unintentionally contribute to the misery of those who are poor. That is hard work—perhaps work we would rather avoid. But ignoring the plight of poor people is exactly what the Scriptures warn us against!

▶ Jas 5.1–6

to drive them, yet they are guided by a very small rudder wherever the will of the pilot directs. ⁵ So also the tongue is a small member, yet it boasts of great exploits.

How great a forest is set ablaze by a small fire! ⁶ And the tongue is a fire. The tongue is placed among our members as a world of iniquity; it stains the whole body, sets on fire the cycle of na-ture,ᵐ and is itself set on fire by hell.ⁿ ⁷ For every species of beast and bird, of reptile and sea crea-ture, can be tamed and has been tamed by the human species, ⁸ but no one can tame the tongue—a restless evil, full of deadly poison. ⁹ With it we bless the Lord and Father, and with it we curse those who are made in the likeness of God. ¹⁰ From the same mouth come blessing and curs-ing. My brothers and sisters,ᵒ this ought not to be so. ¹¹ Does a spring pour forth from the same opening both fresh and brackish water? ¹² Can a fig tree, my brothers and sisters,ᵖ yield olives, or a grapevine figs? No more can salt water yield fresh.

Two Kinds of Wisdom

13 Who is wise and understanding among you? Show by your good life that your works are done with gentleness born of wisdom. ¹⁴ But if you have bitter envy and selfish ambition in your hearts, do not be boastful and false to the truth. ¹⁵ Such wisdom does not come down from above, but is earthly, unspiritual, devilish. ¹⁶ For where there is envy and selfish ambition, there will also be disorder and wickedness of every kind. ¹⁷ But

the wisdom from above is first pure, then peace-able, gentle, willing to yield, full of mercy and good fruits, without a trace of partiality or hypoc-risy. ¹⁸ And a harvest of righteousness is sown in peace forᵍ those who make peace.

Friendship with the World

Those conflicts and disputes among you, where do they come from? Do they not come from your cravings that are at war within you? ² You want something and do not have it; so you commit murder. And you covetʳ something and cannot obtain it; so you engage in disputes and conflicts. You do not have, because you do not ask. ³ You ask and do not receive, because you ask wrongly, in order to spend what you get on your pleasures. ⁴ Adulterers! Do you not know that friendship with the world is enmity with God? Therefore whoever wishes to be a friend of the world be-comes an enemy of God. ⁵ Or do you suppose that it is for nothing that the scripture says, "Godˢ yearns jealously for the spirit that he has made to dwell in us"? ⁶ But he gives all the more grace; therefore it says,

"God opposes the proud,
    but gives grace to the humble."

⁷ Submit yourselves therefore to God. Resist the devil, and he will flee from you. ⁸ Draw near to

---

ᵐ Or *wheel of birth*   ⁿ Gk *Gehenna*   ᵒ Gk *My brothers*
ᵖ Gk *my brothers*   ᵍ Or *by*   ʳ Or *you murder and you covet*
ˢ Gk *He*

God, and he will draw near to you. Cleanse your hands, you sinners, and purify your hearts, you double-minded. ⁹Lament and mourn and weep. Let your laughter be turned into mourning and your joy into dejection. ¹⁰Humble yourselves before the Lord, and he will exalt you.

Draw near to God, and he will draw near to you 4.8

Warning against Judging Another

11 Do not speak evil against one another, brothers and sisters.ᵗ Whoever speaks evil against another or judges another, speaks evil against the law and judges the law; but if you judge the law, you are not a doer of the law but a judge. ¹²There is one lawgiver and judge who is able to save and to destroy. So who, then, are you to judge your neighbor?

Boasting about Tomorrow

13 Come now, you who say, "Today or tomorrow we will go to such and such a town and spend a year there, doing business and making money." ¹⁴Yet you do not even know what tomorrow will bring. What is your life? For you are a mist that appears for a little while and then vanishes. ¹⁵Instead you ought to say, "If the Lord wishes, we will live and do this or that." ¹⁶As it is, you boast in your arrogance; all such boasting is evil. ¹⁷Anyone, then, who knows the right thing to do and fails to do it, commits sin.

Warning to Rich Oppressors

Come now, you rich people, weep and wail for the miseries that are coming to you. ²Your riches have rotted, and your clothes are moth-eaten. ³Your gold and silver have rusted, and their rust will be evidence against you, and it will eat your flesh like fire. You have laid up treasureᵘ for the last days. ⁴Listen! The wages of the laborers who mowed your fields, which you kept back by fraud, cry out, and the cries of the harvesters have reached the ears of the Lord of hosts. ⁵You have lived on the earth in luxury and in pleasure; you have fattened your hearts in a day of slaughter. ⁶You have condemned and murdered the righteous one, who does not resist you.

ᵗ Gk brothers   ᵘ Or will eat your flesh, since you have stored up fire

PRAY IT!

The Making of a Prayer

Have you ever been in a prayer rut? It happens when you get stuck on saying the same prayer every time, no matter what the situation. It becomes a habit, and like all habits, after a while, you may stop thinking about why you are even doing it.

James offers some advice in 5.13 that can help you to get out of such a rut and back on track with your prayer life. This passage says to think about the needs and feelings you have at any given moment of the day and turn them into a prayer. Feeling down? Tell God about it. Just had the best day of your life? Share it with God. Want to get even with a person who hurt you? Let God know about it. In fact, there is nothing you can't tell God—even if you are mad and God is the one you are mad at.

Get in touch with what is occupying your mind the most right now—good, bad, or ordinary—and turn it into a prayer by sharing it with the God who is always ready to hear what you have to say.

▶ Jas 5.13

JAS

Patience in Suffering

7 Be patient, therefore, beloved,[v] until the coming of the Lord. The farmer waits for the precious crop from the earth, being patient with it until it receives the early and the late rains. 8 You also must be patient. Strengthen your hearts, for the coming of the Lord is near.[w] 9 Beloved,[x] do not grumble against one another, so that you may not be judged. See, the Judge is standing at the doors! 10 As an example of suffering and patience, beloved,[v] take the prophets who spoke in the name of the Lord. 11 Indeed we call blessed those who showed endurance. You have heard of the endurance of Jōb, and you have seen the purpose of the Lord, how the Lord is compassionate and merciful.

12 Above all, my beloved,[v] do not swear, either by heaven or by earth or by any other oath, but let your "Yes" be yes and your "No" be no, so that you may not fall under condemnation.

The Prayer of Faith
(Cp 1 Kings 18.41–46)

13 Are any among you suffering? They should pray. Are any cheerful? They should sing songs of praise. 14 Are any among you sick? They should call for the elders of the church and have them pray over them, anointing them with oil in the name of the Lord. 15 The prayer of faith will save the sick, and the Lord will raise them up; and anyone who has committed sins will be forgiven. 16 Therefore confess your sins to one another, and pray for one another, so that you may be healed. The prayer of the righteous is powerful and effective. 17 E•li′jah was a human being like us, and he prayed fervently that it might not rain, and for three years and six months it did not rain on the earth. 18 Then he prayed again, and the heaven gave rain and the earth yielded its harvest.

19 My brothers and sisters,[y] if anyone among you wanders from the truth and is brought back by another, 20 you should know that whoever brings back a sinner from wandering will save the sinner's[z] soul from death and will cover a multitude of sins.

---

[v] Gk brothers [w] Or is at hand [x] Gk Brothers [y] Gk My brothers [z] Gk his

Close friends refuse to speak to you after you challenge them about shoplifting. Students make fun of classmates who are trying to start a prayer group before school. Citizens break windows in the homes of Christian leaders who have spoken out publicly against racist attitudes. It's enough to make some Christians ask, Is living our faith worth this persecution and separation? This is a major concern addressed by the First Letter of Peter.

At a Glance

- **1.1–2.** a greeting and thanksgiving

- **1.3—2.10.** the message that Christians are called to be a chosen race and a royal priesthood

- **2.11—3.12.** a description of the Christian way of life

- **3.13—5.11.** a discussion of Christian suffering

- **5.12–14.** a closing

In-depth

The First Letter of Peter was written to a Christian community that was alienated and persecuted because of its Christian lifestyle. Its members were ridiculed, treated as evildoers, and insulted by unbelieving neighbors who did not understand their faith or their moral code of behavior. The author—who may have been Peter but was more likely a later disciple of his—wants to console them and help them make sense of what they're going through.

The author of Peter says that Christ suffered, and therefore we should expect to suffer too. The writer also says that suffering purifies our faith and makes it more genuine (1 Pet 1.7). When we suffer, we are united with all the world's people who are suffering (5.9). And no matter how great our suffering is, we should be hopeful, and we should be willing to witness to our hope. Then, our persecutors will be ashamed and will repent of their wrongdoing (3.14–16). We cannot avoid suffering, but when we follow in the footsteps of Jesus, we can make it result in something good.

Despite all this attention to suffering, 1 Peter is a hope-filled letter. It offers constant reminders of the wonderful things God has done—and will do—for us. When you are going through a hard time, turn to this letter for hope and encouragement. "And after you have suffered for a little while, the God of all grace, who has called you to his eternal glory in Christ, will himself restore, support, strengthen, and establish you" (5.10).

Quick Facts

Author
possibly Peter, but most likely a later disciple of Peter's

Date Written
A.D. 60–63 if by Peter, A.D. 70–90 if by a later disciple

Audience
a Gentile (non-Jewish) Christian community

1 Peter

Salutation

Peter, an apostle of Jesus Christ,

To the exiles of the Dispersion in Pon'tus, Gala-tia, Cap·pa·do'ci·a, Asia, and Bi·thyn'i·a, 2 who have been chosen and destined by God the Father and sanctified by the Spirit to be obedient to Jesus Christ and to be sprinkled with his blood:

May grace and peace be yours in abundance.

A Living Hope

3 Blessed be the God and Father of our Lord Jesus Christ! By his great mercy he has given us a new birth into a living hope through the resurrection of Jesus Christ from the dead, 4 and into an inheritance that is imperishable, undefiled, and unfading, kept in heaven for you, 5 who are being protected by the power of God through faith for a salvation ready to be revealed in the last time. 6 In this you rejoice,[a] even if now for a little while you have had to suffer various trials, 7 so that the genuineness of your faith—being more precious than gold that, though perishable, is tested by fire—may be found to result in praise and glory and honor when Jesus Christ is revealed. 8 Although you have not seen[b] him, you love him; and even though you do not see him now, you believe in him and rejoice with an indescribable and glorious joy, 9 for you are receiving the outcome of your faith, the salvation of your souls.

10 Concerning this salvation, the prophets who prophesied of the grace that was to be yours made careful search and inquiry, 11 inquiring about the person or time that the Spirit of Christ within them indicated when it testified in advance to the sufferings destined for Christ and the subsequent glory. 12 It was revealed to them that they were serving not themselves but you, in regard to the things that have now been announced to you through those who brought you good news by the Holy Spirit sent from heaven—things into which angels long to look!

A Call to Holy Living

13 Therefore prepare your minds for action;[c] discipline yourselves; set all your hope on the grace that Jesus Christ will bring you when he is revealed. 14 Like obedient children, do not be conformed to the desires that you formerly had in ignorance. 15 Instead, as he who called you is holy, be holy yourselves in all your conduct; 16 for it is written, "You shall be holy, for I am holy."

17 If you invoke as Father the one who judges all people impartially according to their deeds, live in reverent fear during the time of your exile. 18 You know that you were ransomed from the futile ways inherited from your ancestors, not with

---

a Or *Rejoice in this*   *b* Other ancient authorities read *known*   *c* Gk *gird up the loins of your mind*

4 Come to him, a living stone, though rejected by mortals yet chosen and precious in God's sight, and 5 like living stones, let yourselves be built[h] into a spiritual house, to be a holy priesthood, to offer spiritual sacrifices acceptable to God through Jesus Christ. 6 For it stands in scripture:

"See, I am laying in Zion a stone,
a cornerstone chosen and precious;
and whoever believes in him[i] will not be
put to shame."

7 To you then who believe, he is precious; but for those who do not believe,

"The stone that the builders rejected
has become the very head of the corner,"

8 and

"A stone that makes them stumble,
and a rock that makes them fall."

They stumble because they disobey the word, as they were destined to do.

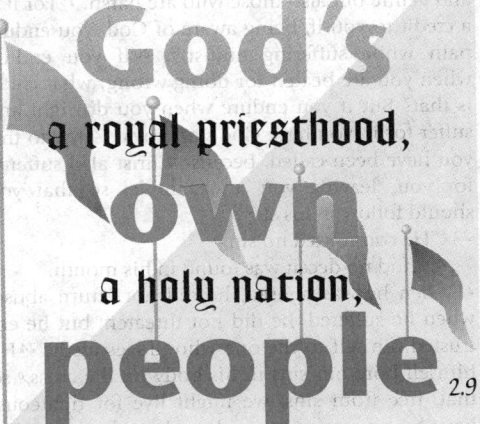

You are a chosen race, a royal priesthood, a holy nation, God's own people 2.9

perishable things like silver or gold, 19 but with the precious blood of Christ, like that of a lamb without defect or blemish. 20 He was destined before the foundation of the world, but was revealed at the end of the ages for your sake. 21 Through him you have come to trust in God, who raised him from the dead and gave him glory, so that your faith and hope are set on God.

22 Now that you have purified your souls by your obedience to the truth[d] so that you have genuine mutual love, love one another deeply[e] from the heart.[f] 23 You have been born anew, not of perishable but of imperishable seed, through the living and enduring word of God.[g] 24 For

"All flesh is like grass
and all its glory like the flower of grass.
The grass withers,
and the flower falls,
25 but the word of the Lord endures forever."

That word is the good news that was announced to you.

The Living Stone and a Chosen People
(Ps 118.22; Isa 28.16)

Rid yourselves, therefore, of all malice, and all guile, insincerity, envy, and all slander. 2 Like newborn infants, long for the pure, spiritual milk, so that by it you may grow into salvation— 3 if indeed you have tasted that the Lord is good.

9 But you are a chosen race, a royal priesthood, a holy nation, God's own people,[j] in order that you may proclaim the mighty acts of him who called you out of darkness into his marvelous light.

10 Once you were not a people,
but now you are God's people;
once you had not received mercy,
but now you have received mercy.

---

d Other ancient authorities add *through the Spirit*
e Or *constantly*   f Other ancient authorities read *a pure heart*   g Or *through the word of the living and enduring God*
h Or *you yourselves are built*   i Or *it*   j Gk *a people for his possession*

Live as Servants of God
(Cp Rom 13.1–5)

11 Beloved, I urge you as aliens and exiles to abstain from the desires of the flesh that wage war against the soul. 12 Conduct yourselves honorably among the Gentiles, so that, though they malign you as evildoers, they may see your honorable deeds and glorify God when he comes to judge.[k]

13 For the Lord's sake accept the authority of every human institution,[l] whether of the emperor as supreme, 14 or of governors, as sent by him to punish those who do wrong and to praise those who do right. 15 For it is God's will that by doing right you should silence the ignorance of the foolish. 16 As servants[m] of God, live as free people, yet do not use your freedom as a pretext for evil. 17 Honor everyone. Love the family of believers.[n] Fear God. Honor the emperor.

Advice for Slaves
(Isa 53.7–9)

18 Slaves, accept the authority of your masters with all deference, not only those who are kind and gentle but also those who are harsh. 19 For it is a credit to you if, being aware of God, you endure pain while suffering unjustly. 20 If you endure when you are beaten for doing wrong, what credit is that? But if you endure when you do right and suffer for it, you have God's approval. 21 For to this you have been called, because Christ also suffered for you, leaving you an example, so that you should follow in his steps.

22 "He committed no sin,
    and no deceit was found in his mouth."

23 When he was abused, he did not return abuse; when he suffered, he did not threaten; but he entrusted himself to the one who judges justly. 24 He himself bore our sins in his body on the cross,[o] so that, free from sins, we might live for righteousness; by his wounds[p] you have been healed. 25 For you were going astray like sheep, but now you have returned to the shepherd and guardian of your souls.

Advice for Wives and Husbands

Wives, in the same way, accept the authority of your husbands, so that, even if some of them do not obey the word, they may be won over without a word by their wives' conduct, 2 when they see the purity and reverence of your lives. 3 Do not adorn yourselves outwardly by braiding your hair, and by wearing gold ornaments or fine clothing; 4 rather, let your adornment be the inner self with the lasting beauty of a gentle and quiet spirit, which is very precious in God's sight. 5 It was in this way

long ago that the holy women who hoped in God used to adorn themselves by accepting the authority of their husbands. 6 Thus Sarah obeyed Abraham and called him lord. You have become her daughters as long as you do what is good and never let fears alarm you.

7 Husbands, in the same way, show consideration for your wives in your life together, paying honor to the woman as the weaker sex,[q] since they too are also heirs of the gracious gift of life—so that nothing may hinder your prayers.

PRAY IT
Part of the Family

All of us come from and belong to a family. Some families are large and some small, some have two parents and others one, and some include aunts, uncles, or grandparents. Every family is unique.

Christians belong to a family that extends well beyond the relationships of blood or adoption. As followers of Christ, they make up a "royal priesthood" and a "holy nation," and are called "God's own people" (1 Pet 2.9). That is pretty lofty language! What does it mean?

First, it means that our faith is not just between us and God but also shared with others. Yes, there is something personal about our relationship with the Lord, but in addition, we are called by God into a community of disciples who share a common faith. Second, God has chosen us to live together in such a way that others who see our example will see something so good that they want to be a part of it.

In your prayer, reflect or journal on the following questions:

- How connected do you feel to the Christian family?
- What kind of support would you like to receive from other believers? What kind of support can you give?

▸ 1 Pet 2.9–17

---

k Gk God on the day of visitation   l Or every institution ordained for human beings   m Gk slaves   n Gk Love the brotherhood   o Or carried up our sins in his body to the tree   p Gk bruise   q Gk vessel

Advice for All

8 Finally, all of you, have unity of spirit, sympathy, love for one another, a tender heart, and a humble mind. 9 Do not repay evil for evil or abuse for abuse; but, on the contrary, repay with a blessing. It is for this that you were called—that you might inherit a blessing. 10 For

"Those who desire life
    and desire to see good days,
let them keep their tongues from evil
    and their lips from speaking deceit;
11 let them turn away from evil and do good;
    let them seek peace and pursue it.
12 For the eyes of the Lord are on
        the righteous,
    and his ears are open to their prayer.
But the face of the Lord is against those
    who do evil."

Suffering for Doing Right

13 Now who will harm you if you are eager to do what is good? 14 But even if you do suffer for doing what is right, you are blessed. Do not fear what they fear,[r] and do not be intimidated, 15 but in your hearts sanctify Christ as Lord. Always be ready to make your defense to anyone who demands from you an accounting for the hope that is in you; 16 yet do it with gentleness and reverence.[s] Keep your conscience clear, so that, when you are maligned, those who abuse you for your good conduct in Christ may be put to shame. 17 For it is better to suffer for doing good, if suffering should be God's will, than to suffer for doing evil. 18 For Christ also suffered[t] for sins once for all, the righteous for the unrighteous, in order to bring you[u] to God. He was put to death in the flesh, but made alive in the spirit, 19 in which also he went and made a proclamation to the spirits in prison, 20 who in former times did not obey, when God waited patiently in the days of Noah, during the building of the ark, in which a few, that is, eight persons, were saved through water. 21 And baptism, which this prefigured, now saves you—not as a removal of dirt from the body, but as an appeal to God for[v] a good conscience, through the resurrection of Jesus Christ, 22 who has gone into

---

r Gk *their fear*   s Or *respect*   t Other ancient authorities read *died*   u Other ancient authorities read *us*   v Or *a pledge to God from*

LIVING GOSPEL VALUES EVEN IF IT DEMANDS SUFFERING!

HISPANIC

¡Viviendo los valores del Evangelio aunque exijan sufrir!

Many Hispanic teenagers and young adults in the United States send money to parents in Latin America. Others work to sustain the education of younger brothers and sisters here. Many times, they are criticized because they are unable to continue their own studies and advance in society.

Other young people, of any culture, also suffer for living the Gospel. Those who want to leave a gang are harassed by gang members. Young women and men who want to maintain their virginity are made fun of. Young people who start participating in church programs are not understood by their friends. The commitment of young leaders sometimes is misinterpreted by their parents as a way of escaping their duties at home.

These behaviors cause suffering because Gospel values are conflicting with society's values. In today's First World, particularly in the United States, to blend into the surrounding society is pushed by the media and is almost an ideal set by society.

■ How does a true Christian lifestyle cause conflict with mainstream society? How can young Hispanics keep their values of love, generosity, and solidarity with their family, while continuing their own personal development?

■ Think of Peter's advice to the early Christian communities. Remember Jesus' suffering, and offer yours together with his so that you and all young people may share Christ's new life.

▶ 1 Pet 3.13–22

heaven and is at the right hand of God, with angels, authorities, and powers made subject to him.

Good Stewards of God's Grace

Since therefore Christ suffered in the flesh,[w] arm yourselves also with the same intention (for whoever has suffered in the flesh has finished with sin), [2] so as to live for the rest of your earthly life[x] no longer by human desires but by the will of God. [3] You have already spent enough time in doing what the Gentiles like to do, living in licentiousness, passions, drunkenness, revels, carousing, and lawless idolatry. [4] They are surprised that you no longer join them in the same excesses of dissipation, and so they blaspheme.[y] [5] But they will have to give an accounting to him who stands ready to judge the living and the dead. [6] For this is the reason the gospel was proclaimed even to the dead, so that, though they had been judged in the flesh as everyone is judged, they might live in the spirit as God does.

7 The end of all things is near;[z] therefore be serious and discipline yourselves for the sake of your prayers. [8] Above all, maintain constant love for one another, for love covers a multitude of sins. [9] Be hospitable to one another without complaining. [10] Like good stewards of the manifold grace of God, serve one another with whatever gift each of you has received. [11] Whoever speaks must do so as one speaking the very words of God; whoever serves must do so with the strength that God supplies, so that God may be glorified in all things through Jesus Christ. To him belong the glory and the power forever and ever. Amen.

Suffering as a Christian

12 Beloved, do not be surprised at the fiery ordeal that is taking place among you to test you, as though something strange were happening to you. [13] But rejoice insofar as you are sharing Christ's sufferings, so that you may also be glad and shout for joy when his glory is revealed. [14] If you are reviled for the name of Christ, you are blessed, because the spirit of glory,[a] which is the Spirit of God, is resting on you.[b] [15] But let none of you suffer as a murderer, a thief, a criminal, or even as a mischief maker. [16] Yet if any of you suffers as a Christian, do not consider it a disgrace, but glorify God because you bear this name. [17] For the time has come for judgment to begin with the household of God; if it begins with us, what will be the end for those who do not obey the gospel of God? [18] And

"If it is hard for the righteous to be saved,
　　what will become of the ungodly and the
　　　　sinners?"

[19] Therefore, let those suffering in accordance with God's will entrust themselves to a faithful Creator, while continuing to do good.

SHOUT FOR JOY!

No healthy person likes to suffer. Yet, when we suffer for something good—like being identified as a follower of Christ or defending someone who is under attack by others—First Peter calls us blessed. God notices when we are mocked or ridiculed for our faith. We are challenged to rejoice when we experience such treatment, rather than take it as a sign of failure. For didn't Christ suffer for doing good? And won't he be with us when we suffer for his name? The Gospel has a strange way of turning things upside down—it says that what would cause others sorrow should cause us joy!

The Bible has a lot of other things to say on the topic of suffering. You can use reading plan 7, "Why Do We Suffer?" to locate other passages.

▶ 1 Pet 4.12–19

Tending the Flock of God

Now as an elder myself and a witness of the sufferings of Christ, as well as one who shares in the glory to be revealed, I exhort the elders among you [2] to tend the flock of God that is in your charge, exercising the oversight,[c] not under compulsion but willingly, as God would have you do it[d]—not for sordid gain but eagerly. [3] Do not lord it over those in your charge, but be examples to the flock. [4] And when the chief shepherd appears, you will win the crown of glory that never fades away. [5] In the same way, you who are younger must accept the authority of the elders.[e] And all of you must clothe yourselves with humility in your dealings with one another, for

"God opposes the proud,
　　but gives grace to the humble."

---

w Other ancient authorities add *for us*; others, *for you*
x Gk *rest of the time in the flesh*　y Or *they malign you*
z Or *is at hand*　a Other ancient authorities add *and of power*　b Other ancient authorities add *On their part he is blasphemed, but on your part he is glorified*　c Other ancient authorities lack *exercising the oversight*　d Other ancient authorities lack *as God would have you do it*
e Or *of those who are older*

6 Humble yourselves therefore under the mighty hand of God, so that he may exalt you in due time. [7] Cast all your anxiety on him, because he cares for you. [8] Discipline yourselves, keep alert.*f* Like a roaring lion your adversary the devil prowls around, looking for someone to devour. [9] Resist him, steadfast in your faith, for you know that your brothers and sisters*g* in all the world are undergoing the same kinds of suffering. [10] And after you have suffered for a little while, the God of all grace, who has called you to his eternal glory in Christ, will himself restore, support, strengthen, and establish you. [11] To him be the power forever and ever. Amen.

Final Greetings and Benediction

12 Through Sil•vā′nus, whom I consider a faithful brother, I have written this short letter to encourage you and to testify that this is the true grace of God. Stand fast in it. [13] Your sister church*h* in Babylon, chosen together with you, sends you greetings; and so does my son Mark. [14] Greet one another with a kiss of love.

Peace to all of you who are in Christ.*i*

---

f Or *be vigilant*   *g* Gk *your brotherhood*   *h* Gk *She who is*
i Other ancient authorities add *Amen*

What happens to us when we die? What is heaven like? Does God even care what happens to us? Many people believe there is no heaven, no hell, and no God. Some say that when we die, our bodies simply decay and we no longer exist in any form. They say that there is no life after death, no punishment, and no reward. But the Bible tells us differently. Second Peter was written to reassure believers that God does indeed care, and that they will be rewarded for leading a faithful and virtuous life.

At a Glance

- **Chapter 1.** a greeting, and encouragement to lead a holy life

- **Chapter 2.** a warning to beware of false teachers

- **Chapter 3.** a message that the day of God's judgment is coming

In-depth

Bible scholars have convincing evidence that 2 Peter is one of the latest books in the New Testament. The letter appears to have been written by someone who is appealing to the authority of the dead Apostle Peter (see "Introduction to the Letters and Revelation"). At the time of its writing—perhaps as much as one hundred years after Jesus' death and Resurrection—some Christians were starting to wonder if what they believed was true. People were even teaching that there would be no reward or punishment after death. So why not live any way you wanted to?

The author of the Second Letter of Peter is arguing against these false teachers. This writer uses famous examples from the Old Testament to remind readers how God has acted through history. And the author promises that those who have chosen to separate themselves from God in their lifetime will experience the fullness of separation from God in death—a separation that Christians call hell. Those who have stayed faithful to God's calling will enjoy eternal life in union with God—a life that Christians call heaven. Why? Because God is good and just.

Tied in to this argument is another concern. Many of the earliest Christians believed that Christ would return soon after his Resurrection, probably within their lifetime, to establish God's Reign once and for all (see "The Parousia," 2 Thess 1.5—2.17). When generations had passed and Christ had not yet returned, false teachers claimed that he would never return. The author of 2 Peter reminds readers that God's time is not our time—Christ is simply waiting so that more people have a chance to repent of their sins before he comes for judgment (2 Pet 3.9).

Quick Facts

Author
an unknown person writing in Peter's name

Date Written
approximately A.D. 130

Audience
a community of both Jewish and Gentile (non-Jewish) Christians

1464

2 Peter

We wait for New Heavens and a new earth
3.13

Salutation

Sim′ē·on[a] Peter, a servant[b] and apostle of Jesus Christ,

To those who have received a faith as precious as ours through the righteousness of our God and Savior Jesus Christ:[c]

2 May grace and peace be yours in abundance in the knowledge of God and of Jesus our Lord.

The Christian's Call and Election

3 His divine power has given us everything needed for life and godliness, through the knowledge of him who called us by[d] his own glory and goodness. 4 Thus he has given us, through these things, his precious and very great promises, so that through them you may escape from the corruption that is in the world because of lust, and may become participants of the divine nature. 5 For this very reason, you must make every effort to support your faith with goodness, and goodness with knowledge, 6 and knowledge with self-control, and self-control with endurance, and endurance with godliness, 7 and godliness with mutual[e] affection, and mutual[e] affection with love. 8 For if these things are yours and are increasing among you, they keep you from being ineffective and unfruitful in the knowledge of our Lord Jesus Christ. 9 For anyone who lacks these things is short-sighted and blind, and is forgetful of the cleansing of past sins. 10 Therefore, brothers and sisters,[f] be all the more eager to confirm your call and election, for if you do this, you will never stumble. 11 For in this way, entry into the eternal kingdom of our Lord and Savior Jesus Christ will be richly provided for you.

12 Therefore I intend to keep on reminding you of these things, though you know them already and are established in the truth that has come to you. 13 I think it right, as long as I am in this body,[g] to refresh your memory, 14 since I know that my death[h] will come soon, as indeed our Lord Jesus Christ has made clear to me. 15 And I will make every effort so that after my departure you may be able at any time to recall these things.

Eyewitnesses of Christ's Glory
(Mt 17.5; Mk 9.7; Lk 9.35)

16 For we did not follow cleverly devised myths when we made known to you the power and coming of our Lord Jesus Christ, but we had been eyewitnesses of his majesty. 17 For he received honor and glory from God the Father when that voice was conveyed to him by the Majestic Glory, saying, "This is my Son, my Beloved,[i] with whom I am well pleased." 18 We ourselves heard this voice

---

a Other ancient authorities read *Simon*   b Gk *slave*
c Or *of our God and the Savior Jesus Christ*   d Other ancient authorities read *through*   e Gk *brotherly*
f Gk *brothers*   g Gk *tent*   h Gk *the putting off of my tent*
i Other ancient authorities read *my beloved Son*

come from heaven, while we were with him on the holy mountain.

19 So we have the prophetic message more fully confirmed. You will do well to be attentive to this as to a lamp shining in a dark place, until the day dawns and the morning star rises in your hearts. 20 First of all you must understand this, that no prophecy of scripture is a matter of one's own interpretation, 21 because no prophecy ever came by human will, but men and women moved by the Holy Spirit spoke from God.*j*

False Prophets and Their Punishment

But false prophets also arose among the people, just as there will be false teachers among you, who will secretly bring in destructive opinions. They will even deny the Master who bought them— bringing swift destruction on themselves. 2 Even so, many will follow their licentious ways, and because of these teachers*k* the way of truth will be maligned. 3 And in their greed they will exploit you with deceptive words. Their condemnation, pronounced against them long ago, has not been idle, and their destruction is not asleep.

4 For if God did not spare the angels when they sinned, but cast them into hell*l* and committed them to chains*m* of deepest darkness to be kept until the judgment; 5 and if he did not spare the ancient world, even though he saved Noah, a herald of righteousness, with seven others, when he brought a flood on a world of the ungodly; 6 and if by turning the cities of Sod'om and Go•mor'rah to ashes he condemned them to extinction*n* and made them an example of what is coming to the ungodly;*o* 7 and if he rescued Lot, a righteous man greatly distressed by the licentiousness of the lawless 8 (for that righteous man, living among them day after day, was tormented in his righteous soul by their lawless deeds that he saw and heard), 9 then the Lord knows how to rescue the godly from trial, and to keep the unrighteous under punishment until the day of judgment 10 —especially those who indulge their flesh in depraved lust, and who despise authority.

Bold and willful, they are not afraid to slander the glorious ones,*p* 11 whereas angels, though greater in might and power, do not bring against them a slanderous judgment from the Lord.*q* 12 These people, however, are like irrational animals, mere creatures of instinct, born to be caught and killed. They slander what they do not understand, and when those creatures are destroyed,*r* they also will be destroyed, 13 suffering*s* the penalty for doing wrong. They count it a pleasure to revel in the daytime. They are blots and blemishes, reveling in their dissipation*t* while they feast with

?did you KNOW?

Identifying False Prophets

Many times throughout history, people have misled others in the name of God. Adolf Hitler is probably the best-known such leader in the twentieth century. Some of these leaders have even convinced their followers to commit mass suicide as part of their beliefs. These extreme examples show how people can be misguided by false prophets.

Second Peter 2.1–3 gives guidelines for identifying false prophets. The author says false prophets use secrets, propose destructive opinions, deny God's teachings, twist the truth to their needs, and exploit their followers. Beware of any leader, religious or nonreligious, who uses these techniques. As 2 Peter says, they malign the way of truth.

▶ **2 Pet 2.1–3**

you. 14 They have eyes full of adultery, insatiable for sin. They entice unsteady souls. They have hearts trained in greed. Accursed children! 15 They have left the straight road and have gone astray, following the road of Ba'laam son of Bo'sor,*u* who loved the wages of doing wrong, 16 but was rebuked for his own transgression; a speechless donkey spoke with a human voice and restrained the prophet's madness.

17 These are waterless springs and mists driven by a storm; for them the deepest darkness has been reserved. 18 For they speak bombastic nonsense, and with licentious desires of the flesh they entice people who have just*v* escaped from those who live in error. 19 They promise them freedom, but they themselves are slaves of corruption; for

---

j Other ancient authorities read *but moved by the Holy Spirit saints of God spoke*   *k* Gk *because of them*   *l* Gk *Tartaros*   *m* Other ancient authorities read *pits*   *n* Other ancient authorities lack *to extinction*   *o* Other ancient authorities read *an example to those who were to be ungodly*   *p* Or *angels;* Gk *glories*   *q* Other ancient authorities read *before the Lord;* others lack the phrase   *r* Gk *in their destruction*   *s* Other ancient authorities read *receiving*   *t* Other ancient authorities read *love-feasts*   *u* Other ancient authorities read *Beor*   *v* Other ancient authorities read *actually*

people are slaves to whatever masters them. 20 For if, after they have escaped the defilements of the world through the knowledge of our Lord and Savior Jesus Christ, they are again entangled in them and overpowered, the last state has become worse for them than the first. 21 For it would have been better for them never to have known the way of righteousness than, after knowing it, to turn back from the holy commandment that was passed on to them. 22 It has happened to them according to the true proverb,

"The dog turns back to its own vomit,"

and,

"The sow is washed only to wallow in
    the mud."

The Promise of the Lord's Coming
(Gen 6.5—8.22)

This is now, beloved, the second letter I am writing to you; in them I am trying to arouse your sincere intention by reminding you 2 that you should remember the words spoken in the past by the holy prophets, and the commandment of the Lord and Savior spoken through your apostles. 3 First of all you must understand this, that in the last days scoffers will come, scoffing and indulging their own lusts 4 and saying, "Where is the promise of his coming? For ever since our ancestors died,[w] all things continue as they were from the beginning of creation!" 5 They deliberately ignore this fact, that by the word of God heavens existed long ago and an earth was formed out of water and by means of water, 6 through which the world of that time was deluged with water and perished. 7 But by the same word the present heavens and earth have been reserved for fire, being kept until the day of judgment and destruction of the godless.

8 But do not ignore this one fact, beloved, that with the Lord one day is like a thousand years, and a thousand years are like one day. 9 The Lord is not slow about his promise, as some think of slowness, but is patient with you,[x] not wanting any to perish, but all to come to repentance. 10 But the day of the Lord will come like a thief, and then the heavens will pass away with a loud noise, and the elements will be dissolved with fire, and the earth and everything that is done on it will be disclosed.[y]

11 Since all these things are to be dissolved in this way, what sort of persons ought you to be in leading lives of holiness and godliness, 12 waiting for and hastening[z] the coming of the day of God, because of which the heavens will be set ablaze and dissolved, and the elements will melt with fire? 13 But, in accordance with his promise, we wait for new heavens and a new earth, where righteousness is at home.

Final Exhortation and Doxology

14 Therefore, beloved, while you are waiting for these things, strive to be found by him at peace, without spot or blemish; 15 and regard the patience of our Lord as salvation. So also our beloved brother Paul wrote to you according to the wisdom given him, 16 speaking of this as he does

---

w Gk *our fathers fell asleep*   x Other ancient authorities read *on your account*   y Other ancient authorities read *will be burned up*   z Or *earnestly desiring*

LIVE IT!

Where Is God?

A frustrated and frazzled New York City tour guide is trying to get her group through a maze of homeless people and panhandlers outside the great Saint Patrick's Cathedral. After the group has safely entered the cathedral, she exclaims, with arms outstretched, "God is definitely here!" A young girl whose gaze lingers on the people outside asks, with all seriousness, "Why won't they let him out?"

The early readers of 2 Peter were confused that Jesus Christ had not yet returned again (see "The Parousia," 2 Thess 1.5—2.17). They wondered, "Where is God?" The author reminds them not to apply human limits to God's response.

Sometimes, when we pray for something, it seems like God keeps us waiting for an eternity. We want something to happen quickly—but God is on a different schedule. You might say the only limits we have in seeing God's actions are the ones we establish. Where are you not seeing God these days?

▶ 2 Pet 3.9

in all his letters. There are some things in them hard to understand, which the ignorant and unstable twist to their own destruction, as they do the other scriptures. 17 You therefore, beloved, since you are forewarned, beware that you are not carried away with the error of the lawless and lose your own stability. 18 But grow in the grace and knowledge of our Lord and Savior Jesus Christ. To him be the glory both now and to the day of eternity. Amen.[a]

---

[a] Other ancient authorities lack *Amen*

Betrayal is painful. Unfortunately, most of us have experienced it at one time or another. It often begins with a misunderstanding. Sometimes, harsh words are exchanged, and people part ways feeling sad and bitter. The community addressed by the three Letters of John had experienced sharp division and conflict. It is impossible to avoid the author's feeling of betrayal as you read these letters.

In-depth

All three Letters of John were probably written by the same person, the elder referred to in the second and third letters. This writer had, perhaps a decade earlier, belonged to the community for which the Gospel of John was written. He saw himself and his community as being faithful to the true meaning of John's Gospel. Now, others who had once belonged to this community had abandoned it in its time of need. They too read the Gospel of John, but they interpreted it very differently. The disagreement between these two groups resulted in a bitter conflict.

The First Letter of John really isn't a letter at all but is more like a teaching homily. The second letter tells the community not to associate with the "deceivers" who have broken off from the group. The third letter asks the community to welcome a representative or missionary sent by the elder.

Even after careful study of the first letter, it is difficult to determine exactly what the disagreement was about. One issue seems to have been the proper understanding of Jesus' humanity. Apparently, the deceivers did not fully believe in Jesus' humanity and its connection to salvation through Jesus' death and Resurrection. To emphasize Jesus' humanity, the author several times mentions that Jesus came "in the flesh" and comments on the saving power of the "blood of Jesus."

The author also challenges the deceivers' claims that they were free to do anything they wanted and still love God. If they truly loved God, they would also love their brothers and sisters and would not have abandoned the community.

Through this letter, God reminds today's Christians that believers can have profoundly different understandings about what they believe. Conflict and disagreement will occur even within the Christian community. Can Christians handle such discord with love and respect?

At a Glance

- **1 Jn 1.1–4.** an introduction
- **1 Jn 1.5—3.10.** a message that God is light, and we must walk in the light
- **1 Jn 3.11—5.12.** a message that those who are God's children show it by their love
- **1 Jn 5.13–21.** a conclusion

Quick Facts

Author
an unknown person associated with the community that produced the Gospel of John

Date Written
approximately A.D. 100

Audience
Christians who were suffering from a split in their community

1 John

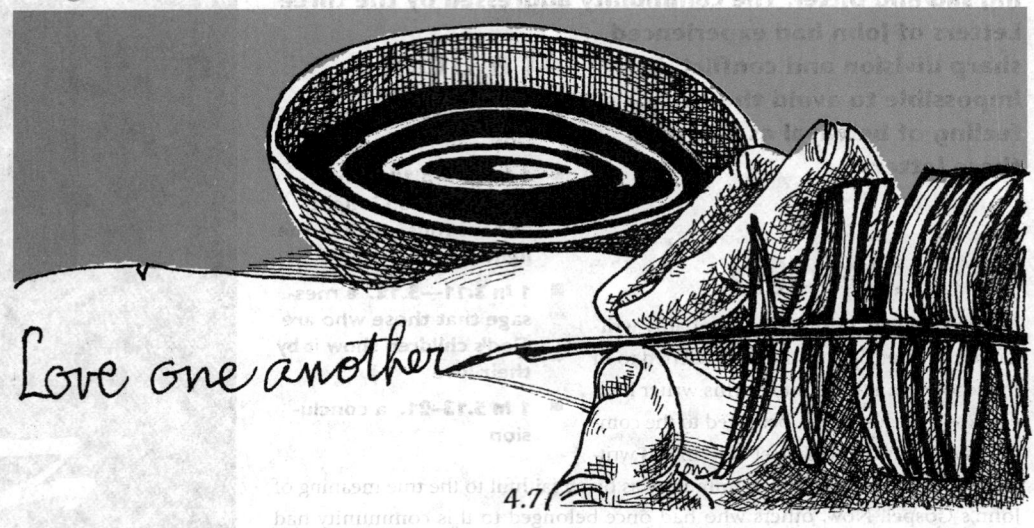

Love one another

4.7

The Word of Life
(Jn 1.1–5)

We declare to you what was from the beginning, what we have heard, what we have seen with our eyes, what we have looked at and touched with our hands, concerning the word of life— 2 this life was revealed, and we have seen it and testify to it, and declare to you the eternal life that was with the Father and was revealed to us— 3 we declare to you what we have seen and heard so that you also may have fellowship with us; and truly our fellowship is with the Father and with his Son Jesus Christ. 4 We are writing these things so that our[a] joy may be complete.

God Is Light

5 This is the message we have heard from him and proclaim to you, that God is light and in him there is no darkness at all. 6 If we say that we have fellowship with him while we are walking in darkness, we lie and do not do what is true; 7 but if we walk in the light as he himself is in the light, we have fellowship with one another, and the blood of Jesus his Son cleanses us from all sin. 8 If we say that we have no sin, we deceive ourselves, and the truth is not in us. 9 If we confess our sins, he who is faithful and just will forgive us our sins and cleanse us from all unrighteousness. 10 If we say that we have not sinned, we make him a liar, and his word is not in us.

Christ Our Advocate

My little children, I am writing these things to you so that you may not sin. But if anyone does sin, we have an advocate with the Father, Jesus Christ the righteous; 2 and he is the atoning sacrifice for our sins, and not for ours only but also for the sins of the whole world.

3 Now by this we may be sure that we know him, if we obey his commandments. 4 Whoever says, "I have come to know him," but does not obey his commandments, is a liar, and in such a person the truth does not exist; 5 but whoever obeys his word, truly in this person the love of God has reached perfection. By this we may be sure that we are in him: 6 whoever says, "I abide in him," ought to walk just as he walked.

A New Commandment

7 Beloved, I am writing you no new commandment, but an old commandment that you have had from the beginning; the old commandment is the word that you have heard. 8 Yet I am writing you a new commandment that is true in him and in you, because[b] the darkness is passing away and the true light is already shining. 9 Whoever says, "I am in the light," while hating a brother or sister,[c] is still in the darkness. 10 Whoever loves a brother or sister[d] lives in the light, and in such a person[e]

---

a Other ancient authorities read *your*   b Or *that*   c Gk *hating a brother*   d Gk *loves a brother*   e Or *in it*

LIVE IT!

Live in the Light

Do you ever find it hard to decide whether something is right or wrong? Instead of the sharp distinction between light and darkness described in 1 John, you might see a lot of shades of gray. But be careful; you might simply be seeing what you want to see! Remember, "If we say that we have no sin, we deceive ourselves" (1 Jn 1.8). There are times when our choices aren't clear—but usually, they are. Listen to your inner voice of honesty and integrity, and courageously choose to live in the light!

▸ 1 Jn 1.5–10

there is no cause for stumbling. 11 But whoever hates another believer*f* is in the darkness, walks in the darkness, and does not know the way to go, because the darkness has brought on blindness.

Asian American

Be Reconciled

Sometimes, it's hardest to show your love to the people you are closest to. Maybe, you get along great with all your friends but are always arguing with your brother or sister. Or in your youth group, you are always tense around that one person with whom you had angry words several months ago.

The author of 1 John tells us that we cannot ignore a relationship with a brother or sister in the Lord who has been upset. The Hmong culture has the same tradition. If you frighten or hurt or offend someone, you have created an imbalance of spirits. It is your responsibility to go back and seek to re-establish harmony. It is the Hmong custom to go to a shaman (an elder of the community, a holy person) for advice and to perform a ritual for reconciliation.

The Catholic Tradition has the sacrament of Reconciliation for the same purpose: to admit the imbalance in a relationship caused by sin, discuss ways to make things right, express sorrow, and celebrate God's forgiveness and love.

▸ 1 Jn 2.7–11

12 I am writing to you, little children,
      because your sins are forgiven on account
            of his name.
13 I am writing to you, fathers,
      because you know him who is from the
            beginning.
   I am writing to you, young people,
      because you have conquered the evil one.
14 I write to you, children,
      because you know the Father.
   I write to you, fathers,
      because you know him who is from the
            beginning.
   I write to you, young people,
      because you are strong
      and the word of God abides in you,
            and you have overcome the evil one.

15 Do not love the world or the things in the world. The love of the Father is not in those who love the world; 16 for all that is in the world—the desire of the flesh, the desire of the eyes, the pride in riches—comes not from the Father but from the world. 17 And the world and its desire*g* are passing away, but those who do the will of God live forever.

Warning against Antichrists

18 Children, it is the last hour! As you have heard that antichrist is coming, so now many antichrists have come. From this we know that it is the last hour. 19 They went out from us, but they did not belong to us; for if they had belonged to us, they would have remained with us. But by going out they made it plain that none of them belongs to us. 20 But you have been anointed by the Holy One, and all of you have knowledge.*h* 21 I write to you, not because you do not know the truth, but because you know it, and you know that no lie comes from the truth. 22 Who is the liar but the

---

f Gk *hates a brother*   *g* Or *the desire for it*   *h* Other ancient authorities read *you know all things*

one who denies that Jesus is the Christ?[i] This is the antichrist, the one who denies the Father and the Son. 23 No one who denies the Son has the Father; everyone who confesses the Son has the Father also. 24 Let what you heard from the beginning abide in you. If what you heard from the beginning abides in you, then you will abide in the Son and in the Father. 25 And this is what he has promised us,[j] eternal life.

26 I write these things to you concerning those who would deceive you. 27 As for you, the anointing that you received from him abides in you, and so you do not need anyone to teach you. But as his anointing teaches you about all things, and is true and is not a lie, and just as it has taught you, abide in him.[k]

28 And now, little children, abide in him, so that when he is revealed we may have confidence and not be put to shame before him at his coming.

Children of God

29 If you know that he is righteous, you may be sure that everyone who does right has been born of him. 1 See what love the Father has given us, that we should be called children of God; and that is what we are. The reason the world does not know us is that it did not know him. 2 Beloved, we are God's children now; what we will be has not yet been revealed. What we do know is this: when he[k] is revealed, we will be like him, for we will see him as he is. 3 And all who have this hope in him purify themselves, just as he is pure.

4 Everyone who commits sin is guilty of lawlessness; sin is lawlessness. 5 You know that he was revealed to take away sins, and in him there is no sin. 6 No one who abides in him sins; no one who sins has either seen him or known him. 7 Little children, let no one deceive you. Everyone who does what is right is righteous, just as he is righteous. 8 Everyone who commits sin is a child of the devil; for the devil has been sinning from the beginning. The Son of God was revealed for this purpose, to destroy the works of the devil. 9 Those who have been born of God do not sin, because God's seed abides in them;[l] they cannot sin, because they have been born of God. 10 The children of God and the children of the devil are revealed in this way: all who do not do what is right are not from God, nor are those who do not love their brothers and sisters.[m]

Love One Another
(Mt 22.39)

11 For this is the message you have heard from the beginning, that we should love one another. 12 We must not be like Cain who was from the evil one and murdered his brother. And why did he murder him? Because his own deeds were evil and his brother's righteous. 13 Do not be astonished, brothers and sisters,[n] that the world hates you. 14 We know that we have passed from death to life because we love one another. Whoever does not love abides in death. 15 All who hate a brother or sister[m] are murderers, and you know that murderers do not have eternal life abiding in them. 16 We know love by this, that he laid down his life for us—and we ought to lay down our lives for one another. 17 How does God's love abide in anyone who has the world's goods and sees a brother or sister[o] in need and yet refuses help?

PRAY IT!

Love in Action

Clear your mind of all thoughts and concerns. Help your body and mind relax with some deep breaths. Now, read 1 Jn 3.18 several times until you can say it by heart. Reflect on its meaning. Think about how you have lived and acted during this past week. Have you shown love in truth and action? by word or speech?

Ask God to forgive you for any situations in which you failed to act lovingly. Pray for the gift of being able to put your love in action in your daily life. Throughout the remainder of this day, remind yourself of this prayer by calling to mind verse 18.

▸ 1 Jn 3.18

18 Little children, let us love, not in word or speech, but in truth and action. 19 And by this we will know that we are from the truth and will reassure our hearts before him 20 whenever our hearts condemn us; for God is greater than our hearts, and he knows everything. 21 Beloved, if our hearts do not condemn us, we have boldness before God; 22 and we receive from him whatever we ask, because we obey his commandments and do what pleases him.

---

i Or *the Messiah*   j Other ancient authorities read *you*
k Or *it*   l Or *because the children of God abide in him*
m Gk *his brother*   n Gk *brothers*   o Gk *brother*

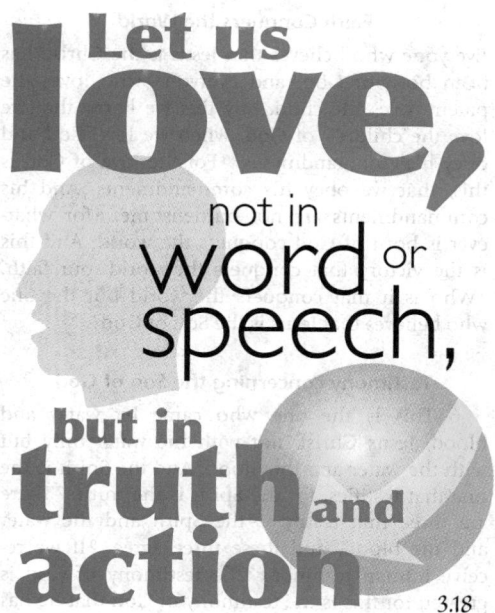

Let us love,
not in word or speech,
but in truth and action
3.18

23 And this is his commandment, that we should believe in the name of his Son Jesus Christ and love one another, just as he has commanded us. 24 All who obey his commandments abide in him, and he abides in them. And by this we know that he abides in us, by the Spirit that he has given us.

Testing the Spirits

Beloved, do not believe every spirit, but test the spirits to see whether they are from God; for many false prophets have gone out into the world. 2 By this you know the Spirit of God: every spirit that confesses that Jesus Christ has come in the flesh is from God, 3 and every spirit that does not confess Jesus*p* is not from God. And this is the spirit of the antichrist, of which you have heard that it is coming; and now it is already in the world. 4 Little children, you are from God, and have conquered them; for the one who is in you is greater than the one who is in the world. 5 They are from the world; therefore what they say is from the world, and the world listens to them. 6 We are from God. Whoever knows God listens to us, and whoever is not from God does not listen to us. From this we know the spirit of truth and the spirit of error.

---

p Other ancient authorities read *does away with Jesus* (Gk *dissolves Jesus*)

LIVE IT!

Testing Spirits

The spirit is the primary essence of a person or a belief. The First Letter of John talks about two kinds of spirit: that which comes from God and that which does not come from God. This letter gives us two ways for testing whether our spirit comes from God: The first has to do with whether our actions reflect love for God and love for our brothers and sisters (3.18). The second has to do with our beliefs about Jesus Christ. To understand this, let's look closer at the controversy that prompted the author of this letter to offer these two tests.

The controversy in the community addressed by 1 John seems to revolve around what Christians call the Incarnation—the belief that Jesus Christ was both fully God and fully human. The "false prophets" deny Christ's humanity, saying Jesus only appeared to be human. The author insists that the spirits who come from God will confess, "Jesus Christ has come in the flesh" (4.2)—that is, he was fully human. Believing in the Incarnation is the foundation for understanding "that the Father has sent his Son as the Savior of the world" (verse 14).

You can apply this letter's two tests to just about any spiritual idea or practice you come across, whether it has to do with different religious traditions, New Age spirituality, or magic or the occult. Ask yourself: Does this help me love God and other people? Does this support the Christian belief that Jesus Christ was fully God and fully human, and that faith in him is necessary for salvation? If you cannot answer yes to both these questions, then stay away!

▶ 1 Jn 4.1–21

1
J
N

God Is Love
(Cp Jn 3.16)

7 Beloved, let us love one another, because love is from God; everyone who loves is born of God and knows God. [8] Whoever does not love does not know God, for God is love. [9] God's love was revealed among us in this way: God sent his only Son into the world so that we might live through him. [10] In this is love, not that we loved God but that he loved us and sent his Son to be the atoning sacrifice for our sins. [11] Beloved, since God loved us so much, we also ought to love one another. [12] No one has ever seen God; if we love one another, God lives in us, and his love is perfected in us.

13 By this we know that we abide in him and he in us, because he has given us of his Spirit. [14] And we have seen and do testify that the Father has sent his Son as the Savior of the world. [15] God abides in those who confess that Jesus is the Son of God, and they abide in God. [16] So we have known and believe the love that God has for us.

God is love, and those who abide in love abide in God, and God abides in them. [17] Love has been perfected among us in this: that we may have boldness on the day of judgment, because as he is, so are we in this world. [18] There is no fear in love, but perfect love casts out fear; for fear has to do with punishment, and whoever fears has not reached perfection in love. [19] We love[q] because he first loved us. [20] Those who say, "I love God," and hate their brothers or sisters,[r] are liars; for those who do not love a brother or sister[s] whom they have seen, cannot love God whom they have not seen. [21] The commandment we have from him is this: those who love God must love their brothers and sisters[r] also.

Faith Conquers the World

Everyone who believes that Jesus is the Christ[t] has been born of God, and everyone who loves the parent loves the child. [2] By this we know that we love the children of God, when we love God and obey his commandments. [3] For the love of God is this, that we obey his commandments. And his commandments are not burdensome, [4] for whatever is born of God conquers the world. And this is the victory that conquers the world, our faith. [5] Who is it that conquers the world but the one who believes that Jesus is the Son of God?

Testimony concerning the Son of God

6 This is the one who came by water and blood, Jesus Christ, not with the water only but with the water and the blood. And the Spirit is the one that testifies, for the Spirit is the truth. [7] There are three that testify:[u] [8] the Spirit and the water and the blood, and these three agree. [9] If we receive human testimony, the testimony of God is greater; for this is the testimony of God that he has testified to his Son. [10] Those who believe in the Son of God have the testimony in their hearts. Those who do not believe in God[v] have made him a liar by not believing in the testimony that God has given concerning his Son. [11] And this is the testimony: God gave us eternal life, and this life is in his Son. [12] Whoever has the Son has life; whoever does not have the Son of God does not have life.

---

[q] Other ancient authorities add *him*; others add *God*   [r] Gk *brothers*   [s] Gk *brother*   [t] Or *the Messiah*   [u] A few other authorities read (with variations) [7]*There are three that testify in heaven, the Father, the Word, and the Holy Spirit, and these three are one.* [8]*And there are three that testify on earth:*   [v] Other ancient authorities read *in the Son*

Understanding Love

LIVE IT!

Some of the most beautiful prose and poetry about love are contained in the Bible. First John 4.7–21 is a particularly eloquent piece that captures the heart of the Good News: God has loved us in Christ Jesus, who came as the savior of the world. Now, we have been given God and Jesus' spirit, and we are commanded to love others as we have been loved by God.

It is easy to say, "I love God." But 1 John tells us that our love for God is shown in our love for one another. Loving one another is much harder than simply saying, "I love God." What does this love for God look like? It is not the romantic love or sentimental affection the world usually presents to us. Read Mt 25.31–36 or 1 Corinthians, chapter 13, for some ideas.

▸ 1 Jn 4.7–21

1
J
N

Epilogue

13 I write these things to you who believe in the name of the Son of God, so that you may know that you have eternal life.

14 And this is the boldness we have in him, that if we ask anything according to his will, he hears us. 15 And if we know that he hears us in whatever we ask, we know that we have obtained the requests made of him. 16 If you see your brother or sister[w] committing what is not a mortal sin, you will ask, and God[x] will give life to such a one—to those whose sin is not mortal. There is sin that is mortal; I do not say that you should pray about that. 17 All wrongdoing is sin, but there is sin that is not mortal.

18 We know that those who are born of God do not sin, but the one who was born of God protects them, and the evil one does not touch them. 19 We know that we are God's children, and that the whole world lies under the power of the evil one. 20 And we know that the Son of God has come and has given us understanding so that we may know him who is true;[y] and we are in him who is true, in his Son Jesus Christ. He is the true God and eternal life.

21 Little children, keep yourselves from idols.[z]

---

w Gk *your brother*   x Gk *he*   y Other ancient authorities read *know the true God*   z Other ancient authorities add *Amen*

2 John

For background on this letter, see the introduction to 1, 2, and 3 John, before 1 John.

For background on this letter, see the introduction to 1, 2, and 3 John, before 1 John.

Salutation

1 The elder to the elect lady and her children, whom I love in the truth, and not only I but also all who know the truth, 2 because of the truth that abides in us and will be with us forever:

3 Grace, mercy, and peace will be with us from God the Father and from*a* Jesus Christ, the Father's Son, in truth and love.

Truth and Love

4 I was overjoyed to find some of your children walking in the truth, just as we have been commanded by the Father. 5 But now, dear lady, I ask you, not as though I were writing you a new commandment, but one we have had from the be-

---

a Other ancient authorities add *the Lord*

Unwelcome Guests

The author of 2 John is warning a Christian community—called elect lady and dear lady—about the false message of some "deceivers" (see the introduction to 1, 2, and 3 John, before 1 John). The author cautions the community not to have anything to do with such people, not even to let them into their homes (verses 10–11). Although the words sound harsh, the reasoning is sound.

Every day, we could be letting people with false messages into our home "virtually" through television, books, music, the Internet, and even magazines. Their false messages promote values and behaviors that are contrary to a healthy and holy way of life. Can these "guests" affect our attitudes and choices? They sure can, especially if we welcome them blindly without thinking about the impact of their messages.

On a piece of paper or in your journal, identify the television shows, magazines, radio stations, and Internet sites that regularly visit your home. List the positive values and behaviors these guests display. Now, list the negative ones. How do the lists compare? How can you manage your media exposure wisely in order to resist its negative influence?

ginning, let us love one another. 6 And this is love, that we walk according to his commandments; this is the commandment just as you have heard it from the beginning—you must walk in it.

7 Many deceivers have gone out into the world, those who do not confess that Jesus Christ has come in the flesh; any such person is the deceiver and the antichrist! 8 Be on your guard, so that you do not lose what we*b* have worked for, but may receive a full reward. 9 Everyone who does not abide in the teaching of Christ, but goes beyond it, does not have God; whoever abides in the teaching has both the Father and the Son. 10 Do not receive into the house or welcome anyone who comes to you and does not bring this teaching; 11 for to welcome is to participate in the evil deeds of such a person.

Final Greetings

12 Although I have much to write to you, I would rather not use paper and ink; instead I hope to come to you and talk with you face to face, so that our joy may be complete.

13 The children of your elect sister send you their greetings.*c*

---

b Other ancient authorities read *you*   *c* Other ancient authorities add *Amen*

3 John

For background on this letter, see the introduction to 1, 2, and 3 John, before 1 John.

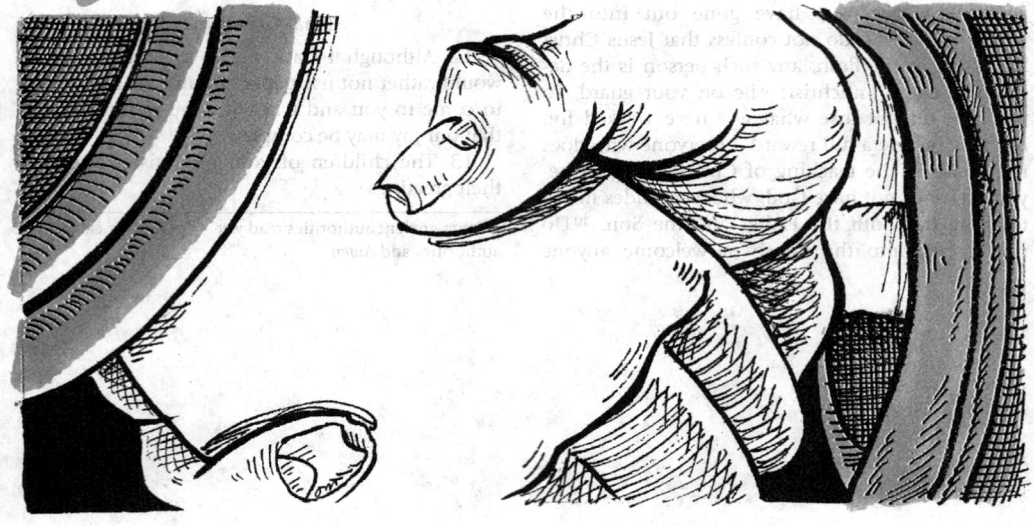

Salutation

1 The elder to the beloved Gā′i•us, whom I love in truth.

Gaius Commended for His Hospitality

2 Beloved, I pray that all may go well with you and that you may be in good health, just as it is well with your soul. 3 I was overjoyed when some of the friends*a* arrived and testified to your faithfulness to the truth, namely how you walk in the truth. 4 I have no greater joy than this, to hear that my children are walking in the truth.

5 Beloved, you do faithfully whatever you do for the friends,*a* even though they are strangers to you; 6 they have testified to your love before the church. You will do well to send them on in a manner worthy of God; 7 for they began their journey for the sake of Christ,*b* accepting no support from non-believers.*c* 8 Therefore we ought to support such people, so that we may become co-workers with the truth.

---

a Gk brothers   *b* Gk for the sake of the name   *c* Gk the Gentiles

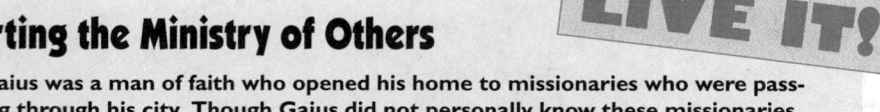

Supporting the Ministry of Others

Gaius was a man of faith who opened his home to missionaries who were passing through his city. Though Gaius did not personally know these missionaries, he provided hospitality for them because he knew that they were helping spread the Good News. In 3 John, the elder appeals to him to welcome his messenger, Demetrius, even when others refuse to do so.

Christians find many needs that they cannot respond to by themselves. The story of Gaius shows how you can become a co-missionary with Christians who are ministering in some way that you cannot. These may be ministers in your own parish or diocese, or a religious group that sends missionaries to other countries. You can offer them your hospitality, support them financially, or promote their work in your parish or community. Consider talking with your family about a specific ministry or missionary activity you can support together.

Diotrephes and Demetrius

9 I have written something to the church; but Di·ot′re·phēs, who likes to put himself first, does not acknowledge our authority. [10] So if I come, I will call attention to what he is doing in spreading false charges against us. And not content with those charges, he refuses to welcome the friends,[d] and even prevents those who want to do so and expels them from the church.

11 Beloved, do not imitate what is evil but imitate what is good. Whoever does good is from God; whoever does evil has not seen God. [12] Every-one has testified favorably about De·mē′tri·us, and so has the truth itself. We also testify for him,[e] and you know that our testimony is true.

Final Greetings

13 I have much to write to you, but I would rather not write with pen and ink; [14] instead I hope to see you soon, and we will talk together face to face.

15 Peace to you. The friends send you their greetings. Greet the friends there, each by name.

d Gk brothers   e Gk lacks for him

They pretend to be part of your group, but all they really do is cause trouble. They claim to have all the right answers, but they won't listen to other people's opinions. They flatter people to get what they want, but then they grumble and complain behind people's backs. They cause division wherever they go. Do you know people like this? Maybe you even find yourself acting like them sometimes. The Letter of Jude has some things to say about "these people."

At a Glance

- **Verses 1–2.** an opening
- **Verses 3–23.** warnings about judgment
- **Verses 24–25.** a closing

In-depth

The purpose of the Letter of Jude is to warn churches about false teachers who come into the Christian community with lies and tricks, making trouble wherever they go. The author recalls stories from the past in which God punished such people: stories about the Egyptians who opposed God's plan to bring the Hebrew people to the Promised Land; the immoral people of Sodom and Gomorrah; the angels who revolted against God; and Cain, who killed his brother. The author also encourages people to build themselves in the faith. Finally, the author cautions Christians to ignore ungodly people—unless those people truly want to change, in which case, Christians should be examples of the mercy of Jesus Christ.

Notice that this letter includes some words that are unfamiliar to modern Christians or that have different meanings today. For instance, the word *saints* refers to the members of the Christian community, and a *love feast* is a celebration of the Eucharist.

The message of the Letter of Jude is difficult to understand for many reasons. We know almost nothing about who wrote it, who it was written to, when it was written, and what it is really addressing—except from hints in the letter itself.

Tradition says the author is Jude the brother of James and Jesus (see Mk 6.3; the name Jude is a form of Judas). Modern readers often find the letter's message too negative and its examples too strange to provide direction for life today.

Quick Facts

Author
unknown

Date Written
maybe A.D. 90

Audience
unknown

The Letter of Jude

Jude

Salutation

1 Jude,[a] a servant[b] of Jesus Christ and brother of James,

To those who are called, who are beloved[c] in[d] God the Father and kept safe for[d] Jesus Christ:

2 May mercy, peace, and love be yours in abundance.

Occasion of the Letter

3 Beloved, while eagerly preparing to write to you about the salvation we share, I find it necessary to write and appeal to you to contend for the faith that was once for all entrusted to the saints. 4 For certain intruders have stolen in among you, people who long ago were designated for this condemnation as ungodly, who pervert the grace of our God into licentiousness and deny our only Master and Lord, Jesus Christ.[e]

Judgment on False Teachers

5 Now I desire to remind you, though you are fully informed, that the Lord, who once for all saved[f] a people out of the land of Egypt, afterward destroyed those who did not believe. 6 And the angels who did not keep their own position, but left their proper dwelling, he has kept in eternal chains in deepest darkness for the judgment of the great day. 7 Likewise, Sod'om and Go·mor'rah and the surrounding cities, which, in the same manner as they, indulged in sexual immorality and pursued unnatural lust,[g] serve as an example by undergoing a punishment of eternal fire.

8 Yet in the same way these dreamers also defile the flesh, reject authority, and slander the glorious ones.[h] 9 But when the archangel Michael contended with the devil and disputed about the body of Moses, he did not dare to bring a condemnation of slander[i] against him, but said, "The Lord rebuke you!" 10 But these people slander whatever they do not understand, and they are destroyed by those things that, like irrational animals, they know by instinct. 11 Woe to them! For they go the way of Cain, and abandon themselves to Bā'laam's error for the sake of gain, and perish in Kō'rah's rebellion. 12 These are blemishes[j] on your love-feasts, while they feast with you without fear, feeding themselves.[k] They are waterless clouds carried along by the winds; autumn trees without fruit, twice dead, uprooted; 13 wild waves of the sea, casting up the foam of their own shame; wandering stars, for whom the deepest darkness has been reserved forever.

14 It was also about these that Ē'noch, in the seventh generation from Adam, prophesied,

---

a Gk *Judas*   b Gk *slave*   c Other ancient authorities read *sanctified*   d Or *by*   e Or *the only Master and our Lord Jesus Christ*   f Other ancient authorities read *though you were once for all fully informed, that Jesus* (or *Joshua*) *who saved*   g Gk *went after other flesh*   h Or *angels; Gk glories*   i Or *condemnation for blasphemy*   j Or *reefs*   k Or *without fear. They are shepherds who care only for themselves*

1481

saying, "See, the Lord is coming[l] with ten thousands of his holy ones, 15 to execute judgment on all, and to convict everyone of all the deeds of ungodliness that they have committed in such an ungodly way, and of all the harsh things that ungodly sinners have spoken against him." 16 These are grumblers and malcontents; they indulge their own lusts; they are bombastic in speech, flattering people to their own advantage.

Warnings and Exhortations

17 But you, beloved, must remember the predictions of the apostles of our Lord Jesus Christ; 18 for they said to you, "In the last time there will be scoffers, indulging their own ungodly lusts." 19 It is these worldly people, devoid of the Spirit, who are causing divisions. 20 But you, beloved, build yourselves up on your most holy faith; pray in the Holy Spirit; 21 keep yourselves in the love of God; look forward to the mercy of our Lord Jesus Christ that leads to[m] eternal life. 22 And have mercy on some who are wavering; 23 save others by snatching them out of the fire; and have mercy on still others with fear, hating even the tunic defiled by their bodies.[n]

Benediction

24 Now to him who is able to keep you from falling, and to make you stand without blemish in the presence of his glory with rejoicing, 25 to the only God our Savior, through Jesus Christ our Lord, be glory, majesty, power, and authority, before all time and now and forever. Amen.

---

[l] Gk *came*   [m] Gk *Christ to*   [n] Gk *by the flesh*. The Greek text of verses 22-23 is uncertain at several points

What do you think about when someone mentions the Book of Revelation? Many people immediately think of its bizarre descriptions of monstrous beasts and its warnings about the terrible things that will happen at the end of the world. Some people believe it proves that the end of the world is about to take place very soon. In fact, the Book of Revelation does not predict when the world will end, but brings us hope in proclaiming God's ultimate triumph over evil in history.

In-depth

This book is unique in that the author—who calls himself John—received a series of visions from God that form most of the content. The recorded visions take the form of apocalyptic literature (see "Apocalyptic Literature," Daniel, chapters 7–10) and are full of symbols. These symbols are like the language of a secret club. You use it when you want to keep people who do not belong to your club from understanding what you are saying.

Why was it important that the meaning of the visions be known only to the Christian communities addressed by the letter? Because the Christians still remembered their persecution under the Roman emperor Nero Caesar (A.D. 54–68), and were suffering a new persecution under the Roman emperor Domitian (A.D. 81–96). This "coded language" allowed John to criticize the Roman emperor and empire without necessarily putting his readers at risk of persecution or even death. John himself was exiled to an island off Asia Minor for preaching the Gospel (Rev 1.9).

Once the symbols are understood, it is clear that the Book of Revelation offers hope to a church under persecution. It expresses belief in God's justice and God's victory over evil—an evil that at John's time was embodied in the Roman Empire. But it also expresses the great Christian belief that God will ultimately be victorious, at the end of time, when Christ will come again in his full glory and power. It is a mistake for Christians to try to decipher Revelation as a prediction as to when and how that final coming will occur. But they can take great joy and hope in the promise of a new world where God will wipe away every tear, and suffering and death will be no more (21.4).

At a Glance

- **Chapters 1–3.** an introduction, and letters to the seven churches
- **Chapters 4–11.** visions of God's throne, the Lamb, the seven seals, and the seven trumpets
- **Chapters 12–14.** visions of the dragon and the two beasts
- **Chapters 15–18.** visions of the seven plagues, and the fall of Babylon (Rome)
- **Chapters 19–22.** visions of the victory of Christ and the end of history

Quick Facts

Author
a Jewish-Christian prophet named John

Date
probably A.D. 92–96

Audience
Christian churches in Asia Minor during a time of Roman persecution

The Revelation to John

Revelation

Introduction and Salutation

The revelation of Jesus Christ, which God gave him to show his servants[a] what must soon take place; he made[b] it known by sending his angel to his servant[c] John, 2 who testified to the word of God and to the testimony of Jesus Christ, even to all that he saw.

3 Blessed is the one who reads aloud the words of the prophecy, and blessed are those who hear and who keep what is written in it; for the time is near.

4 John to the seven churches that are in Asia:

Grace to you and peace from him who is and who was and who is to come, and from the seven spirits who are before his throne, 5 and from Jesus Christ, the faithful witness, the firstborn of the dead, and the ruler of the kings of the earth.

To him who loves us and freed[d] us from our sins by his blood, 6 and made[b] us to be a kingdom, priests serving[e] his God and Father, to him be glory and dominion forever and ever. Amen.

7 Look! He is coming with the clouds;
    every eye will see him,
  even those who pierced him;
    and on his account all the tribes of the
        earth will wail.
So it is to be. Amen.

8 "I am the Alpha and the Omega," says the Lord God, who is and who was and who is to come, the Almighty.

A Vision of Christ

9 I, John, your brother who share with you in Jesus the persecution and the kingdom and the patient endurance, was on the island called Pat'mos because of the word of God and the testimony of Jesus.[f] 10 I was in the spirit[g] on the Lord's day, and I heard behind me a loud voice like a trumpet 11 saying, "Write in a book what you see and send it to the seven churches, to Eph'e•sus, to Smyrna, to Per'ga•mum, to Thÿ•a•ti'ra, to Sar'dis, to Philadel-phia, and to Lā•o•di•cē'a."

12 Then I turned to see whose voice it was that spoke to me, and on turning I saw seven golden lampstands, 13 and in the midst of the lampstands I saw one like the Son of Man, clothed with a long robe and with a golden sash across his chest. 14 His head and his hair were white as white wool, white as snow; his eyes were like a flame of fire, 15 his feet were like burnished bronze, refined as in a furnace, and his voice was like the sound of many waters. 16 In his right hand he held seven stars, and from his mouth came a sharp, two-edged sword, and his face was like the sun shining with full force.

---

a Gk slaves   b Gk and he made   c Gk slave   d Other ancient authorities read washed   e Gk priests to   f Or testimony to Jesus   g Or in the Spirit

17 When I saw him, I fell at his feet as though dead. But he placed his right hand on me, saying, "Do not be afraid; I am the first and the last, 18 and the living one. I was dead, and see, I am alive forever and ever; and I have the keys of Death and of Hades. 19 Now write what you have seen, what is, and what is to take place after this. 20 As for the mystery of the seven stars that you saw in my right hand, and the seven golden lampstands: the seven stars are the angels of the seven churches, and the seven lampstands are the seven churches.

PRAY IT!
The Alpha and the Omega

In the first chapter of Revelation, John introduces God's message to the seven churches in Asia. After explaining that he received the message through a vision and that an angel instructed him to communicate it to them, John describes a vision of Christ.

A vision is like a dream. It cannot be interpreted literally; we must seek its deep meaning and be open to its message. For example, in the vision of Rev 1.12–16, a magnificently robed Jesus stands amid seven lampstands. The deeper meaning is that the resurrected Jesus in all his glory and power is watching over the seven churches. Here's another example: Rev 1.8 has Jesus (or God) saying, "I am the Alpha and the Omega." In the Greek alphabet, *alpha* is the first letter and *omega* is the last letter. This passage is telling us that God and Jesus are in control of all history, from its beginning to its end.

In your prayer, think of any current event that frightens you or harassments that you experience because of your faith or moral principles. See the image of the risen Christ described by John. Feel Jesus lovingly touching your head. Hear Jesus telling you that history is always in God's hands. Let God strengthen your faith and renew your hope with this wonderful revelation of God's love.

▶ Rev 1.7–20

did you KNOW?
The Seven Churches

The messages addressed to the seven churches in Asia Minor (modern Greece and Turkey) are not predictions of the future. Like the prophets of the Old Testament who called Israel to return to the Covenant, John calls these communities to deeper faith. Two churches (Smyrna and Philadelphia) are praised, two (Sardis and Laodicea) are scolded, and the remaining three receive both praise and criticism. The churches are scolded because they have tolerated leaders whose teaching contradicts the true Gospel message and because their faith has become "lukewarm," lacking the devotion it had when they first became Christians.

If the author of Revelation wrote such a prophecy to your local church, what would he praise and what would he criticize? Is your community on fire in living the Gospel, or is it lukewarm in its commitment?

▶ Rev 2.1—3.22

The Message to Ephesus

"To the angel of the church in Eph'e•sus write: These are the words of him who holds the seven stars in his right hand, who walks among the seven golden lampstands:

2 "I know your works, your toil and your patient endurance. I know that you cannot tolerate evildoers; you have tested those who claim to be apostles but are not, and have found them to be false. 3 I also know that you are enduring patiently and bearing up for the sake of my name, and that you have not grown weary. 4 But I have this against you, that you have abandoned the love you had at first. 5 Remember then from what you have fallen; repent, and do the works you did at first. If not, I will come to you and remove your lampstand from its place, unless you repent. 6 Yet this is to your credit: you hate the works of the Nic•ō•lā'i•tans, which I also hate. 7 Let anyone who has an ear listen to what the Spirit is saying to the churches. To everyone who conquers, I will give permission

to eat from the tree of life that is in the paradise of God.

The Message to Smyrna

8 "And to the angel of the church in Smyrna write: These are the words of the first and the last, who was dead and came to life:

9 "I know your affliction and your poverty, even though you are rich. I know the slander on the part of those who say that they are Jews and are not, but are a synagogue of Satan. ¹⁰ Do not fear what you are about to suffer. Beware, the devil is about to throw some of you into prison so that you may be tested, and for ten days you will have affliction. Be faithful until death, and I will give you the crown of life. ¹¹ Let anyone who has an ear listen to what the Spirit is saying to the churches. Whoever conquers will not be harmed by the second death.

The Message to Pergamum

12 "And to the angel of the church in Per'ga-mum write: These are the words of him who has the sharp two-edged sword:

13 "I know where you are living, where Satan's throne is. Yet you are holding fast to my name, and you did not deny your faith in me^h even in the days of An'ti•pas my witness, my faithful one, who was killed among you, where Satan lives. ¹⁴ But I have a few things against you: you have some there who hold to the teaching of Bā'laam, who taught Bā'lak to put a stumbling block before the people of Israel, so that they would eat food sacrificed to idols and practice fornication. ¹⁵ So you also have some who hold to the teaching of the Nic•ō•lā'i•tans. ¹⁶ Repent then. If not, I will come to you soon and make war against them with the sword of my mouth. ¹⁷ Let anyone who has an ear

listen to what the Spirit is saying to the churches. To everyone who conquers I will give some of the hidden manna, and I will give a white stone, and on the white stone is written a new name that no one knows except the one who receives it.

The Message to Thyatira

18 "And to the angel of the church in Thȳ•a-ti'ra write: These are the words of the Son of God, who has eyes like a flame of fire, and whose feet are like burnished bronze:

19 "I know your works—your love, faith, service, and patient endurance. I know that your last works are greater than the first. ²⁰ But I have this against you: you tolerate that woman Jez'e•bel, who calls herself a prophet and is teaching and beguiling my servants^i to practice fornication and to eat food sacrificed to idols. ²¹ I gave her time to repent, but she refuses to repent of her fornication. ²² Beware, I am throwing her on a bed, and those who commit adultery with her I am throwing into great distress, unless they repent of her doings; ²³ and I will strike her children dead. And all the churches will know that I am the one who searches minds and hearts, and I will give to each of you as your works deserve. ²⁴ But to the rest of you in Thȳ•a•ti'ra, who do not hold this teaching, who have not learned what some call 'the deep things of Satan,' to you I say, I do not lay on you any other burden; ²⁵ only hold fast to what you have until I come. ²⁶ To everyone who conquers and continues to do my works to the end,

I will give authority over the nations;
²⁷   to rule^j them with an iron rod,
     as when clay pots are shattered—

---

^{h} Or *deny my faith* ^{i} Gk *slaves* ^{j} Or *to shepherd*

Opening the Door

LIVE IT!

The image in Rev 3.20 inspired an artist to depict our relationship with Christ in a popular painting. The painting shows a door overgrown with vines. The door obviously has not been opened in a long time. As you examine it, you realize that it has no outside latch or knob—it can be opened only from the inside. At the door stands Jesus, knocking—not pounding, just knocking patiently.

What is your relationship with Christ like right now? Is the door of your life open to let Christ in? Or has it been closed for a while? Jesus will not force his way into your life. Jesus seeks a close friendship with you, and real friendship—real love—always involves a free choice. No one can choose to open the door but you.

▸ **Rev 3.14–22**

28 even as I also received authority from my Father. To the one who conquers I will also give the morning star. 29 Let anyone who has an ear listen to what the Spirit is saying to the churches.

The Message to Sardis

"And to the angel of the church in Sar′dis write: These are the words of him who has the seven spirits of God and the seven stars:

"I know your works; you have a name of being alive, but you are dead. 2 Wake up, and strengthen what remains and is on the point of death, for I have not found your works perfect in the sight of my God. 3 Remember then what you received and heard; obey it, and repent. If you do not wake up, I will come like a thief, and you will not know at what hour I will come to you. 4 Yet you have still a few persons in Sar′dis who have not soiled their clothes; they will walk with me, dressed in white, for they are worthy. 5 If you conquer, you will be clothed like them in white robes, and I will not blot your name out of the book of life; I will confess your name before my Father and before his angels. 6 Let anyone who has an ear listen to what the Spirit is saying to the churches.

The Message to Philadelphia

7 "And to the angel of the church in Philadelphia write:

These are the words of the holy one, the
     true one,
who has the key of David,
who opens and no one will shut,
     who shuts and no one opens:

8 "I know your works. Look, I have set before you an open door, which no one is able to shut. I know that you have but little power, and yet you have kept my word and have not denied my name. 9 I will make those of the synagogue of Satan who say that they are Jews and are not, but are lying—I will make them come and bow down before your feet, and they will learn that I have loved you. 10 Because you have kept my word of patient endurance, I will keep you from the hour of trial that is coming on the whole world to test the inhabitants of the earth. 11 I am coming soon; hold fast to what you have, so that no one may seize your crown. 12 If you conquer, I will make you a pillar in the temple of my God; you will never go out of it. I will write on you the name of my God, and the name of the city of my God, the new Jerusalem that comes down from my God out of heaven, and my own new name. 13 Let anyone who has an ear listen to what the Spirit is saying to the churches.

The Message to Laodicea

14 "And to the angel of the church in Lā•o•di•cē′a write: The words of the Amen, the faithful and true witness, the origin[k] of God's creation:

15 "I know your works; you are neither cold nor hot. I wish that you were either cold or hot. 16 So, because you are lukewarm, and neither cold nor hot, I am about to spit you out of my mouth. 17 For you say, 'I am rich, I have prospered, and I need nothing.' You do not realize that you are wretched, pitiable, poor, blind, and naked. 18 Therefore I counsel you to buy from me gold refined by fire so that you may be rich; and white robes to clothe you and to keep the shame of your nakedness from being seen; and salve to anoint your eyes so that you may see. 19 I reprove and discipline those whom I love. Be earnest, therefore, and repent. 20 Listen! I am standing at the door, knocking; if you hear my voice and open the door, I will come in to you and eat with you, and you with me. 21 To the one who conquers I will give a place with me on my throne, just as I myself conquered and sat down with my Father on his throne. 22 Let anyone who has an ear listen to what the Spirit is saying to the churches."

The Heavenly Worship

(Isa 6.1–3)

After this I looked, and there in heaven a door stood open! And the first voice, which I had heard speaking to me like a trumpet, said, "Come up here, and I will show you what must take place after this." 2 At once I was in the spirit,[l] and there in heaven stood a throne, with one seated on the throne! 3 And the one seated there looks like jasper and carnelian, and around the throne is a rainbow that looks like an emerald. 4 Around the throne are twenty-four thrones, and seated on the thrones are twenty-four elders, dressed in white robes, with golden crowns on their heads. 5 Coming from the throne are flashes of lightning, and rumblings and peals of thunder, and in front of the throne burn seven flaming torches, which are the seven spirits of God; 6 and in front of the throne there is something like a sea of glass, like crystal.

Around the throne, and on each side of the throne, are four living creatures, full of eyes in front and behind: 7 the first living creature like a lion, the second living creature like an ox, the third living creature with a face like a human face, and the fourth living creature like a flying eagle. 8 And the four living creatures, each of them with six wings, are full of eyes all around and inside. Day and night without ceasing they sing,

---

k Or *beginning*   l Or *in the Spirit*

"Holy, holy, holy,
the Lord God the Almighty,
who was and is and is to come."
[9] And whenever the living creatures give glory and honor and thanks to the one who is seated on the throne, who lives forever and ever, [10] the twenty-four elders fall before the one who is seated on the throne and worship the one who lives forever and ever; they cast their crowns before the throne, singing,

[11] "You are worthy, our Lord and God,
to receive glory and honor and power,
for you created all things,
and by your will they existed and were
created."

The Scroll and the Lamb

Then I saw in the right hand of the one seated on the throne a scroll written on the inside and on the back, sealed[m] with seven seals; [2] and I saw a mighty angel proclaiming with a loud voice, "Who is worthy to open the scroll and break its seals?" [3] And no one in heaven or on earth or under the earth was able to open the scroll or to look into it. [4] And I began to weep bitterly because no one was found worthy to open the scroll or to look into it. [5] Then one of the elders said to me, "Do not weep. See, the Lion of the tribe of Judah,

the Root of David, has conquered, so that he can open the scroll and its seven seals."

[6] Then I saw between the throne and the four living creatures and among the elders a Lamb standing as if it had been slaughtered, having seven horns and seven eyes, which are the seven spirits of God sent out into all the earth. [7] He went and took the scroll from the right hand of the one who was seated on the throne. [8] When he had taken the scroll, the four living creatures and the twenty-four elders fell before the Lamb, each holding a harp and golden bowls full of incense, which are the prayers of the saints. [9] They sing a new song:

"You are worthy to take the scroll
and to open its seals,
for you were slaughtered and by your blood
you ransomed for God
saints from[n] every tribe and language and
people and nation;
[10] you have made them to be a kingdom and
priests serving[o] our God,
and they will reign on earth."

---

m Or *written on the inside, and sealed on the back*
n Gk *ransomed for God from*   o Gk *priests to*

Jesus Christ Is the Lord of History

After the messages to the churches in Asia, John presents several visions that reveal God's action in history. Read Rev 4.1–11. The vision of God's throne is the background of the whole Book of Revelation. It symbolizes God's authority over history. The vision is enhanced by a heavenly liturgy proclaiming and praising God's name:

"Holy, holy, holy,
the Lord God the Almighty,
who was and is and is to come."
(4.8)

Read 5.1–14. The vision continues. Two symbols stand out: a sealed scroll and a lamb. God holds a scroll containing the history of Israel, whose meaning was hidden to the Christian communities in their persecution. A slain lamb appears. It's the risen Jesus, carrying in his body the signs of his Passion. He receives the scroll from God. He is the only one who can open the scroll and reveal the mystery of death and life.

Read both passages again and experience the honor, glory, and power of Christ. Let these visions reinforce your faith and renew your hope every time that you wonder about the meaning of an event you cannot make sense of.

▶ Revelation, chapters 4–5

did you KNOW?

Symbolic Numbers and Colors

To understand the Book of Revelation, we need to understand the symbolism of its numbers and colors. The numbers seven and twelve symbolize fullness or perfection. The number four symbolizes universalism (as in the four compass directions). The number one thousand symbolizes a multitude or a quantity too big to count. Thus, the twenty-four elders (4.4) represent the perfection of the twelve tribes of Israel and the twelve Apostles. The Lamb with horns and eyes (5.6) represents the risen Christ, who has the fullness of power (seven horns) and perfect knowledge (seven eyes). The 144,000 who will be saved (7.4) represent a chosen multitude from the twelve tribes of Israel, because 144,000 equals 12 times 12 times 1,000.

The color white symbolizes victory, and red symbolizes bloodshed. Thus, the people who are slaughtered and given white robes (6.9–11) are the martyrs who gave up their life for their faith. They are victorious in martyrdom because God raised them to eternal life.

▶ Rev 4.1—7.17

11 Then I looked, and I heard the voice of many angels surrounding the throne and the living creatures and the elders; they numbered myriads of myriads and thousands of thousands, 12 singing with full voice,

"Worthy is the Lamb that was slaughtered
  to receive power and wealth and wisdom
    and might
  and honor and glory and blessing!"
13 Then I heard every creature in heaven and on earth and under the earth and in the sea, and all that is in them, singing,

"To the one seated on the throne and to
    the Lamb
  be blessing and honor and glory and might
  forever and ever!"
14 And the four living creatures said, "Amen!" And the elders fell down and worshiped.

The Seven Seals

Then I saw the Lamb open one of the seven seals, and I heard one of the four living creatures call out, as with a voice of thunder, "Come!"[p] 2 I looked, and there was a white horse! Its rider had a bow; a crown was given to him, and he came out conquering and to conquer.

PRAY IT

Enthusiastic Praise!

Over and over in John's vision of heaven, we find enthusiastic praise being offered to God, or to the Lamb of God, who is Christ Jesus. There are angels, incense, fantastic creatures, jewels, gold, elders, white-robed martyrs, and a crowd too great to number. The scenes of this vision inspire us to add our voice to theirs, to praise the majesty of God and the saving sacrifice of Jesus Christ.

In some Christian traditions, particularly the charismatic and Pentecostal traditions, loud, spontaneous praise of God is common. Most Catholics and Christians from other denominations usually express their praise through softer types of songs and common prayers in worship services. Whatever our expression, we should be enthusiastic with our praise!

How does the vision of the "thousands of thousands, singing with full voice" in Rev 5.11–12 encourage you to be more bold in your praise of God? Can you sing out more loudly in Mass? Can you participate more from your heart in saying common prayers with others? In your private prayer, can you praise God without asking for anything or using memorized prayers?

▶ Rev 4.1—5.14

3 When he opened the second seal, I heard the second living creature call out, "Come!"[p] 4 And out came[q] another horse, bright red; its rider was permitted to take peace from the earth, so that people would slaughter one another; and he was given a great sword.

p Or "Go!"   q Or went

5 When he opened the third seal, I heard the third living creature call out, "Come!"[r] I looked, and there was a black horse! Its rider held a pair of scales in his hand, 6 and I heard what seemed to be a voice in the midst of the four living creatures saying, "A quart of wheat for a day's pay,[s] and three quarts of barley for a day's pay,[s] but do not damage the olive oil and the wine!"

7 When he opened the fourth seal, I heard the voice of the fourth living creature call out, "Come!"[r] 8 I looked and there was a pale green horse! Its rider's name was Death, and Hades followed with him; they were given authority over a fourth of the earth, to kill with sword, famine, and pestilence, and by the wild animals of the earth.

9 When he opened the fifth seal, I saw under the altar the souls of those who had been slaughtered for the word of God and for the testimony they had given; 10 they cried out with a loud voice, "Sovereign Lord, holy and true, how long will it be before you judge and avenge our blood on the inhabitants of the earth?" 11 They were each given a white robe and told to rest a little longer, until the number would be complete both of their fellow servants[t] and of their brothers and sisters,[u] who were soon to be killed as they themselves had been killed.

12 When he opened the sixth seal, I looked, and there came a great earthquake; the sun became black as sackcloth, the full moon became like blood, 13 and the stars of the sky fell to the earth as the fig tree drops its winter fruit when shaken by a gale. 14 The sky vanished like a scroll rolling itself up, and every mountain and island was removed from its place. 15 Then the kings of the earth and the magnates and the generals and the rich and the powerful, and everyone, slave and free, hid in the caves and among the rocks of the mountains, 16 calling to the mountains and rocks, "Fall on us and hide us from the face of the one seated on the throne and from the wrath of the Lamb; 17 for the great day of their wrath has come, and who is able to stand?"

The 144,000 of Israel Sealed

After this I saw four angels standing at the four corners of the earth, holding back the four winds of the earth so that no wind could blow on earth or sea or against any tree. 2 I saw another angel ascending from the rising of the sun, having the seal of the living God, and he called with a loud voice to the four angels who had been given power to damage earth and sea, 3 saying, "Do not damage the earth or the sea or the trees, until we have marked the servants[t] of our God with a seal on their foreheads."

---

did you KNOW?

The Seven Seals and Seven Trumpets

The vision continues. In chapters 6–8 of Revelation, the Lamb opens the seven seals on the scroll and thus reveals the great forces in salvation history. The opening of the first four seals reveals the four horses of the apocalypse that bring conquest, strife, famine, and plagues. These are the things that throughout history have made people yearn for God's salvation.

The opening of the fifth seal reveals the souls of the martyrs who demand justice. Their white robes indicate that they are already with the risen Christ. They are waiting for other martyrs, but this stage will end soon.

The opening of the sixth seal reveals the future. History will change, and all people, even the powerful, will suffer. The visions of the census and of the great crowd in 7.1–19 reveal the destiny of Christians. As in the Exodus, 144,000 people from all the tribes of Israel will be saved. After this, a multitude that cannot be counted, from all nations, tribes, peoples, and languages, will experience God's salvation and sing of God's glory.

Finally, the Lamb opens the last seal. Seven more trumpets are revealed. When they are played by angels, a new series of plagues is released (8.6—9.21). One-third of the people are destroyed by these plagues so that those remaining might repent. But in spite of these warnings, many people do not change.

This vision tells us that no matter what evil besets us, God saves the faithful.

▶ Revelation, chapters 6–9

---

r Or "Go!"   s Gk a denarius   t Gk slaves   u Gk brothers

4 And I heard the number of those who were sealed, one hundred forty-four thousand, sealed out of every tribe of the people of Israel:

5 From the tribe of Judah twelve thousand sealed,

from the tribe of Reuben twelve thousand,

from the tribe of Gad twelve thousand,

6 from the tribe of Ash′er twelve thousand,

from the tribe of Naph′ta•lī twelve thousand,

from the tribe of Ma•nas′seh twelve thousand,

7 from the tribe of Sim′ē•on twelve thousand,

from the tribe of Levi twelve thousand,

from the tribe of Is′sa•char twelve thousand,

8 from the tribe of Zeb′ū•lun twelve thousand,

from the tribe of Joseph twelve thousand,

from the tribe of Benjamin twelve thousand sealed.

The Multitude from Every Nation

9 After this I looked, and there was a great multitude that no one could count, from every nation, from all tribes and peoples and languages, standing before the throne and before the Lamb, robed in white, with palm branches in their hands. 10 They cried out in a loud voice, saying,

"Salvation belongs to our God who is
        seated on the throne, and to the
        Lamb!"

11 And all the angels stood around the throne and around the elders and the four living creatures, and they fell on their faces before the throne and worshiped God, 12 singing,

"Amen! Blessing and glory and wisdom
    and thanksgiving and honor
    and power and might
be to our God forever and ever!
    Amen."

13 Then one of the elders addressed me, saying, "Who are these, robed in white, and where have they come from?" 14 I said to him, "Sir, you are the one that knows." Then he said to me, "These are they who have come out of the great ordeal; they have washed their robes and made them white in the blood of the Lamb.

15   For this reason they are before the throne
        of God,
    and worship him day and night within
        his temple,
    and the one who is seated on the throne
        will shelter them.

16   They will hunger no more, and thirst no
        more;
    the sun will not strike them,
    nor any scorching heat;

17   for the Lamb at the center of the throne will
        be their shepherd,
    and he will guide them to springs of the
        water of life,
and God will wipe away every tear from
        their eyes."

PRAY IT!
Sing God's Glory

The Book of Revelation contains beautiful prayers of praise. Among them are the hymn to the Lamb (5.9–14), the hymn of the multitude from every nation (7.10–17), the song of the Lamb (15.3–4), and the victory song (19.1–8).

In your prayer, read these prayers slowly and carefully. Imagine the awe-inspiring scenes of God's glory they describe. Quietly reflect on how you have experienced the glory and power of God in your life. Look at the events you experience day to day; can you find the extraordinary in the ordinary? End your reflection by letting these songs inspire your own prayer of praise to God.

▶ Rev 7.10–17

The Seventh Seal and the Golden Censer

When the Lamb opened the seventh seal, there was silence in heaven for about half an hour. 2 And I saw the seven angels who stand before God, and seven trumpets were given to them.

3 Another angel with a golden censer came and stood at the altar; he was given a great quantity of incense to offer with the prayers of all the saints on the golden altar that is before the throne. 4 And the smoke of the incense, with the prayers of the saints, rose before God from the hand of the angel. 5 Then the angel took the censer and filled it with fire from the altar and threw it on the earth; and there were peals of thunder, rumblings, flashes of lightning, and an earthquake.

The Seven Trumpets

6 Now the seven angels who had the seven trumpets made ready to blow them.

7 The first angel blew his trumpet, and there came hail and fire, mixed with blood, and they were hurled to the earth; and a third of the earth

was burned up, and a third of the trees were burned up, and all green grass was burned up.

8 The second angel blew his trumpet, and something like a great mountain, burning with fire, was thrown into the sea. 9 A third of the sea became blood, a third of the living creatures in the sea died, and a third of the ships were destroyed.

10 The third angel blew his trumpet, and a great star fell from heaven, blazing like a torch, and it fell on a third of the rivers and on the springs of water. 11 The name of the star is Wormwood. A third of the waters became wormwood, and many died from the water, because it was made bitter.

12 The fourth angel blew his trumpet, and a third of the sun was struck, and a third of the moon, and a third of the stars, so that a third of their light was darkened; a third of the day was kept from shining, and likewise the night.

13 Then I looked, and I heard an eagle crying with a loud voice as it flew in midheaven, "Woe, woe, woe to the inhabitants of the earth, at the blasts of the other trumpets that the three angels are about to blow!"

And the fifth angel blew his trumpet, and I saw a star that had fallen from heaven to earth, and he was given the key to the shaft of the bottomless pit; 2 he opened the shaft of the bottomless pit, and from the shaft rose smoke like the smoke of a great furnace, and the sun and the air were darkened with the smoke from the shaft. 3 Then from the smoke came locusts on the earth, and they were given authority like the authority of scorpions of the earth. 4 They were told not to damage the grass of the earth or any green growth or any tree, but only those people who do not have the seal of God on their foreheads. 5 They were allowed to torture them for five months, but not to kill them, and their torture was like the torture of a scorpion when it stings someone. 6 And in those days people will seek death but will not find it; they will long to die, but death will flee from them.

7 In appearance the locusts were like horses equipped for battle. On their heads were what looked like crowns of gold; their faces were like human faces, 8 their hair like women's hair, and their teeth like lions' teeth; 9 they had scales like iron breastplates, and the noise of their wings was like the noise of many chariots with horses rushing into battle. 10 They have tails like scorpions, with stingers, and in their tails is their power to harm people for five months. 11 They have as king over them the angel of the bottomless pit; his name in Hebrew is A•bad′don,v and in Greek he is called A•pol′lyon.w

12 The first woe has passed. There are still two woes to come.

13 Then the sixth angel blew his trumpet, and I heard a voice from the fourx horns of the golden altar before God, 14 saying to the sixth angel who had the trumpet, "Release the four angels who are bound at the great river Euphrates." 15 So the four angels were released, who had been held ready for the hour, the day, the month, and the year, to kill a third of humankind. 16 The number of the troops of cavalry was two hundred million; I heard their number. 17 And this was how I saw the horses in my vision: the riders wore breastplates the color of fire and of sapphirey and of sulfur; the heads of the horses were like lions' heads, and fire and smoke and sulfur came out of their mouths. 18 By these three plagues a third of humankind was killed, by the fire and smoke and sulfur coming out of their mouths. 19 For the power of the horses is in their mouths and in their tails; their tails are like serpents, having heads; and with them they inflict harm.

20 The rest of humankind, who were not killed by these plagues, did not repent of the works of their hands or give up worshiping demons and idols of gold and silver and bronze and stone and wood, which cannot see or hear or walk. 21 And they did not repent of their murders or their sorceries or their fornication or their thefts.

The Angel with the Little Scroll

And I saw another mighty angel coming down from heaven, wrapped in a cloud, with a rainbow over his head; his face was like the sun, and his legs like pillars of fire. 2 He held a little scroll open in his hand. Setting his right foot on the sea and his left foot on the land, 3 he gave a great shout, like a lion roaring. And when he shouted, the seven thunders sounded. 4 And when the seven thunders had sounded, I was about to write, but I heard a voice from heaven saying, "Seal up what the seven thunders have said, and do not write it down." 5 Then the angel whom I saw standing on the sea and the land

raised his right hand to heaven

6   and swore by him who lives forever and
            ever,

who created heaven and what is in it, the earth and what is in it, and the sea and what is in it: "There will be no more delay, 7 but in the days when the seventh angel is to blow his trumpet, the mystery of God will be fulfilled, as he announced to his servantsz the prophets."

---

v That is, *Destruction*   w That is, *Destroyer*   x Other ancient authorities lack *four*   y Gk *hyacinth*   z Gk *slaves*

8 Then the voice that I had heard from heaven spoke to me again, saying, "Go, take the scroll that is open in the hand of the angel who is standing on the sea and on the land." 9 So I went to the angel and told him to give me the little scroll; and he said to me, "Take it, and eat; it will be bitter to your stomach, but sweet as honey in your mouth." 10 So I took the little scroll from the hand of the angel and ate it; it was sweet as honey in my mouth, but when I had eaten it, my stomach was made bitter.

11 Then they said to me, "You must prophesy again about many peoples and nations and languages and kings."

The Two Witnesses

Then I was given a measuring rod like a staff, and I was told, "Come and measure the temple of God and the altar and those who worship there, 2 but do not measure the court outside the temple; leave that out, for it is given over to the nations, and they will trample over the holy city for forty-two months. 3 And I will grant my two witnesses authority to prophesy for one thousand two hundred sixty days, wearing sackcloth."

4 These are the two olive trees and the two lampstands that stand before the Lord of the earth. 5 And if anyone wants to harm them, fire pours from their mouth and consumes their foes; anyone who wants to harm them must be killed in this manner. 6 They have authority to shut the sky, so that no rain may fall during the days of their prophesying, and they have authority over the waters to turn them into blood, and to strike the earth with every kind of plague, as often as they desire.

7 When they have finished their testimony, the beast that comes up from the bottomless pit will make war on them and conquer them and kill them, 8 and their dead bodies will lie in the street of the great city that is prophetically*a* called Sod'om and Egypt, where also their Lord was crucified. 9 For three and a half days members of the peoples and tribes and languages and nations will gaze at their dead bodies and refuse to let them be placed in a tomb; 10 and the inhabitants of the earth will gloat over them and celebrate and exchange presents, because these two prophets had been a torment to the inhabitants of the earth.

11 But after the three and a half days, the breath*b* of life from God entered them, and they stood on their feet, and those who saw them were terrified. 12 Then they*c* heard a loud voice from heaven saying to them, "Come up here!" And they went up to heaven in a cloud while their enemies watched them. 13 At that moment there was a great earthquake, and a tenth of the city fell; seven thousand people were killed in the earthquake, and the rest were terrified and gave glory to the God of heaven.

14 The second woe has passed. The third woe is coming very soon.

The Seventh Trumpet

15 Then the seventh angel blew his trumpet, and there were loud voices in heaven, saying,
> "The kingdom of the world has become the
>   kingdom of our Lord
>   and of his Messiah,*d*
>   and he will reign forever and ever."

a Or *allegorically*; Gk *spiritually*   *b* Or *the spirit*   *c* Other ancient authorities read *I*   *d* Gk *Christ*

R
E
V

God in Control

LIVE IT!

The world is a wonderful place, full of life and hope. At the same time, it is full of pain and suffering, illness and death. It can seem frightening and out of control. Wars break out, a drought threatens the lives of millions, a friend dies in a senseless car accident, terrorists attack and kill innocent people; we can be left wondering why God allows such things.

The Book of Revelation was written to encourage the people of John's time that despite the evil that happens, God is in control. It can do the same for us too. The song in 11.15–18 reminds us that there will come a time when the just will be rewarded and the wicked punished. And although God's Reign is not yet fully realized, as members of that Reign, we are called to be people of justice, peace, and hope to a world desperately seeking these things.

▸ Rev 11.15–18

16 Then the twenty-four elders who sit on their thrones before God fell on their faces and worshiped God, 17 singing,

"We give you thanks, Lord God Almighty,
　　who are and who were,
for you have taken your great power
　　and begun to reign.
18 The nations raged,
　　but your wrath has come,
　　and the time for judging the dead,
for rewarding your servants,ᵉ the prophets
　　and saints and all who fear your name,
　　both small and great,
and for destroying those who destroy the
　　earth."

19 Then God's temple in heaven was opened, and the ark of his covenant was seen within his temple; and there were flashes of lightning, rumblings, peals of thunder, an earthquake, and heavy hail.

The Woman and the Dragon

A great portent appeared in heaven: a woman clothed with the sun, with the moon under her feet, and on her head a crown of twelve stars. 2 She was pregnant and was crying out in birth pangs, in the agony of giving birth. 3 Then another portent appeared in heaven: a great red dragon, with seven heads and ten horns, and seven diadems on his heads. 4 His tail swept down a third of the stars of heaven and threw them to the earth. Then the dragon stood before the woman who was about to bear a child, so that he might devour her child as soon as it was born. 5 And she gave birth to a son, a male child, who is to ruleᶠ all the nations with a rod of iron. But her child was snatched away and

taken to God and to his throne; 6 and the woman fled into the wilderness, where she has a place prepared by God, so that there she can be nourished for one thousand two hundred sixty days.

Michael Defeats the Dragon

7 And war broke out in heaven; Michael and his angels fought against the dragon. The dragon and his angels fought back, 8 but they were defeated, and there was no longer any place for them in heaven. 9 The great dragon was thrown down, that ancient serpent, who is called the Devil and Satan, the deceiver of the whole world—he was thrown down to the earth, and his angels were thrown down with him.

10 Then I heard a loud voice in heaven, proclaiming,

"Now have come the salvation and the
　　power

ᵉ Gk *slaves*　　ᶠ Or *to shepherd*

and the kingdom of our God
   and the authority of his Messiah,*g*
for the accuser of our comrades*h* has been
      thrown down,
   who accuses them day and night before
      our God.
11 But they have conquered him by the blood
      of the Lamb
   and by the word of their testimony,
for they did not cling to life even in the face
      of death.
12 Rejoice then, you heavens
   and those who dwell in them!
But woe to the earth and the sea,
   for the devil has come down to you
      with great wrath,
   because he knows that his time is short!"

The Dragon Fights Again on Earth

13 So when the dragon saw that he had been thrown down to the earth, he pursued*i* the woman who had given birth to the male child. 14 But the woman was given the two wings of the great eagle, so that she could fly from the serpent into the wilderness, to her place where she is nourished for a time, and times, and half a time. 15 Then from his mouth the serpent poured water like a river after the woman, to sweep her away with the flood. 16 But the earth came to the help of the woman; it opened its mouth and swallowed the river that the dragon had poured from his mouth. 17 Then the dragon was angry with the woman, and went off to make war on the rest of her children, those who keep the commandments of God and hold the testimony of Jesus.

The First Beast

18 Then the dragon*j* took his stand on the sand of the seashore. 1 And I saw a beast rising out of the sea, having ten horns and seven heads; and on its horns were ten diadems, and on its heads were blasphemous names. 2 And the beast that I saw was like a leopard, its feet were like a bear's, and its mouth was like a lion's mouth. And the dragon gave it his power and his throne and great authority. 3 One of its heads seemed to have received a death-blow, but its mortal wound*k* had been healed. In amazement the whole earth followed the beast. 4 They worshiped the dragon, for he had given his authority to the beast, and they

---

g Gk *Christ*   *h* Gk *brothers*   *i* Or *persecuted*   *j* Gk *Then he*; other ancient authorities read *Then I stood*   *k* Gk *the plague of its death*

MARY HAS A VITAL MISSION IN SALVATION HISTORY!

The New Testament links Mary's mission intimately to the mystery of Christ. In Lk 1.38, Mary's yes to the angel Gabriel allows God to enter the world as a human person. At a wedding in Canaan (Jn 2.1–11), Mary is a model for the church as she intercedes before Jesus, has faith in him, points to him as the source of life, and leads others to follow his words. Jesus' words to Mary and the Beloved Disciple at the cross (Jn 19.26–27) name Mary mother of the universal church, which is symbolized by the Beloved Disciple.

   The Catholic church teaches that in chapter 12 of Revelation, the unnamed woman represents Mary and the church, who both share in Jesus' messianic mission. In the feast of the Assumption, this passage is one of the readings that celebrate Mary's entrance into heaven as the first disciple. Mary is a symbol of the triumphant church that awaits and intercedes for us, the pilgrim church.

   Catholics of Latino origin have a long tradition of linking Mary to their history of salvation. She is their companion in their journey of faith and a very dear member of their community. Hispanic popular piety draws strength from Mary's example in daily life, in situations of need and suffering, and in times of celebration.

   Reflect on the ways Mary teaches us to be servants of the Reign of God. Pray that we are as willing to fulfill our mission in salvation history as she is.

▶ Revelation, chapter 12

3 The second angel poured his bowl into the sea, and it became like the blood of a corpse, and every living thing in the sea died.

A Young Person's Song of Praise

D*ear God,*
Thank you for the sun.
Thank you for the Son.
Both are vital to life.
Without each, we could not exist.
The sun gives us the light.
The Son is the light.
From the light plants grow.
From the Light grow the plants of your
Kingdom.
We devour the plants and other creatures
that devour the plants.
We devour the fruits of his knowledge for
they are eternal food.
The sun is our life.
The Son is our life.
Thank you, gracious God.
(Robert Traxler)

4 The third angel poured his bowl into the rivers and the springs of water, and they became blood. 5 And I heard the angel of the waters say,
"You are just, O Holy One, who are and were,
for you have judged these things;
6 because they shed the blood of saints and prophets,
you have given them blood to drink.
It is what they deserve!"
7 And I heard the altar respond,
"Yes, O Lord God, the Almighty,
your judgments are true and just!"
8 The fourth angel poured his bowl on the sun, and it was allowed to scorch people with fire; 9 they were scorched by the fierce heat, but they cursed the name of God, who had authority over these plagues, and they did not repent and give him glory.
10 The fifth angel poured his bowl on the throne of the beast, and its kingdom was plunged into darkness; people gnawed their tongues in agony, 11 and cursed the God of heaven because of

their pains and sores, and they did not repent of their deeds.

12 The sixth angel poured his bowl on the great river Euphrates, and its water was dried up in order to prepare the way for the kings from the east. 13 And I saw three foul spirits like frogs coming from the mouth of the dragon, from the mouth of the beast, and from the mouth of the false prophet. 14 These are demonic spirits, performing signs, who go abroad to the kings of the whole world, to assemble them for battle on the great day of God the Almighty. 15 ("See, I am coming like a thief! Blessed is the one who stays awake and is clothed,*y* not going about naked and exposed to shame.") 16 And they assembled them at the place that in Hebrew is called Har·ma·ged'on.

17 The seventh angel poured his bowl into the air, and a loud voice came out of the temple, from the throne, saying, "It is done!" 18 And there came flashes of lightning, rumblings, peals of thunder, and a violent earthquake, such as had not occurred since people were upon the earth, so violent was that earthquake. 19 The great city was split into three parts, and the cities of the nations fell. God remembered great Babylon and gave her the winecup of the fury of his wrath. 20 And every island fled away, and no mountains were to be found; 21 and huge hailstones, each weighing about a hundred pounds,*z* dropped from heaven on people, until they cursed God for the plague of the hail, so fearful was that plague.

The Great Whore and the Beast

Then one of the seven angels who had the seven bowls came and said to me, "Come, I will show you the judgment of the great whore who is seated on many waters, 2 with whom the kings of the earth have committed fornication, and with the wine of whose fornication the inhabitants of the earth have become drunk." 3 So he carried me away in the spirit*a* into a wilderness, and I saw a woman sitting on a scarlet beast that was full of blasphemous names, and it had seven heads and ten horns. 4 The woman was clothed in purple and scarlet, and adorned with gold and jewels and pearls, holding in her hand a golden cup full of abominations and the impurities of her fornication; 5 and on her forehead was written a name, a mystery: "Babylon the great, mother of whores and of earth's abominations." 6 And I saw that the woman was drunk with the blood of the saints and the blood of the witnesses to Jesus.

y Gk *and keeps his robes*   *z* Gk *weighing about a talent*
a Or *in the Spirit*

When I saw her, I was greatly amazed. 7 But the angel said to me, "Why are you so amazed? I will tell you the mystery of the woman, and of the beast with seven heads and ten horns that carries her. 8 The beast that you saw was, and is not, and is about to ascend from the bottomless pit and go to destruction. And the inhabitants of the earth, whose names have not been written in the book of life from the foundation of the world, will be amazed when they see the beast, because it was and is not and is to come.

9 "This calls for a mind that has wisdom: the seven heads are seven mountains on which the woman is seated; also, they are seven kings, 10 of whom five have fallen, one is living, and the other has not yet come; and when he comes, he must remain only a little while. 11 As for the beast that was and is not, it is an eighth but it belongs to the seven, and it goes to destruction. 12 And the ten horns that you saw are ten kings who have not yet received a kingdom, but they are to receive authority as kings for one hour, together with the beast. 13 These are united in yielding their power and authority to the beast; 14 they will make war on the Lamb, and the Lamb will conquer them, for he is Lord of lords and King of kings, and those with him are called and chosen and faithful."

15 And he said to me, "The waters that you saw, where the whore is seated, are peoples and multitudes and nations and languages. 16 And the ten horns that you saw, they and the beast will hate the whore; they will make her desolate and naked; they will devour her flesh and burn her up with fire. 17 For God has put it into their hearts to carry out his purpose by agreeing to give their kingdom to the beast, until the words of God will be fulfilled. 18 The woman you saw is the great city that rules over the kings of the earth."

The Fall of Babylon

After this I saw another angel coming down from heaven, having great authority; and the earth was made bright with his splendor. 2 He called out with a mighty voice,

"Fallen, fallen is Babylon the great!
 It has become a dwelling place
  of demons,
 a haunt of every foul spirit,
  a haunt of every foul bird,
  a haunt of every foul and hateful beast.[b]
3 For all the nations have drunk[c]
  of the wine of the wrath of her
   fornication,

---

b Other ancient authorities lack the words *a haunt of every foul beast* and attach the words *and hateful* to the previous line so as to read *a haunt of every foul and hateful bird*
c Other ancient authorities read *She has made all nations drink*

The Sins of Empires

LIVE IT!

In John's coded language, the whore called Babylon in chapter 17 is Rome, a city built on seven hills. She is dressed in colors that symbolize her royalty (purple) and her obscene and immoral behavior (scarlet). Her gold and pearls are signs of her wealth and excessive luxury. The blasphemous names on her forehead are the titles that should be given to God but are given to the emperor instead. By calling her Babylon, John is creating a tie with the capital of another evil empire from the Old Testament (see "The Fall of Jerusalem," 2 Kings 25.1–21).

The whore is drunk on the blood of the saints who have been killed for their faith. John indicates that her evil is caused by her unrestrained desire for wealth and luxury and her abuse of power (Rev 18.3–19). He tells his Christian readers that they can be hopeful even amid so much suffering, because in the end, the Lamb (Christ) will conquer the beast (17.14).

Since Revelation was written, many other empires have abused their power, including the United States. Consider, for example, its treatment of Native Americans, practice of slavery, and lack of care for the environment.

Reflect for a moment. In what areas does your country need to take more responsibility to ensure justice for all people? Where has the desire for wealth and luxury gone too far? What can you do locally to take greater responsibility in these areas?

▶ Revelation, chapter 17

the thousand years were ended. After that he must be let out for a little while.

4 Then I saw thrones, and those seated on them were given authority to judge. I also saw the souls of those who had been beheaded for their testimony to Jesus[n] and for the word of God. They had not worshiped the beast or its image and had not received its mark on their foreheads or their hands. They came to life and reigned with Christ a thousand years. 5 (The rest of the dead did not come to life until the thousand years were ended.) This is the first resurrection. 6 Blessed and holy are those who share in the first resurrection. Over these the second death has no power, but they will be priests of God and of Christ, and they will reign with him a thousand years.

Satan's Doom
(Cp Ezek 38—39)

7 When the thousand years are ended, Satan will be released from his prison 8 and will come out to deceive the nations at the four corners of the earth, Gog and Mā'gog, in order to gather them for battle; they are as numerous as the sands of the sea. 9 They marched up over the breadth of the earth and surrounded the camp of the saints and the beloved city. And fire came down from heaven[o] and consumed them. 10 And the devil who had deceived them was thrown into the lake of fire and sulfur, where the beast and the false prophet were, and they will be tormented day and night forever and ever.

The Dead Are Judged

11 Then I saw a great white throne and the one who sat on it; the earth and the heaven fled from his presence, and no place was found for them. 12 And I saw the dead, great and small, standing before the throne, and books were opened. Also another book was opened, the book of life. And the dead were judged according to their works, as recorded in the books. 13 And the sea gave up the dead that were in it, Death and Hades gave up the dead that were in them, and all were judged according to what they had done. 14 Then Death and Hades were thrown into the lake of fire. This is the second death, the lake of fire; 15 and anyone whose name was not found written in the book of life was thrown into the lake of fire.

---

[n] Or *for the testimony of Jesus*　　[o] Other ancient authorities read *from God, out of heaven,* or *out of heaven from God*

The New Jerusalem

The last three chapters of Revelation contain John's visions of the Reign of God, the end of history, and eternal life. In chapter 20, Satan is alive but has limited power. This is symbolized by the dragon's thousand-year imprisonment, during which the martyrs reign with Christ. The thousand-year reign has been interpreted in many different ways over the centuries, but no one knows its true significance. At the end of the thousand years, Satan is defeated, and Christ sits in final judgment over all the dead.

In chapter 21, John describes a new heaven and a new earth. The Bible begins in Genesis with the story of the creation of a world in which everything is good. It ends in Revelation with a new creation where God's goodness again overflows. A holy city, the new Jerusalem, comes down out of heaven. The new Jerusalem is described as a beautiful bride who is preparing to marry Jesus Christ. John tells his Christian readers that they should look forward to the time of this new city with joy, because when it comes, God and Christ will live in their midst. The whole city will be God's temple. The sun will always shine, a river of living water will flow from God's throne, and the trees will produce fruit year-round. The new Jerusalem is a symbol for the new world that God will establish when evil is destroyed and suffering is banished.

These visions helped Christians at the end of the first century to maintain their hope by focusing on the glorious victory of God in history. They can also help us to renew our commitment to Christ and keep our hope alive, especially when we are misunderstood or harassed because of our faith.

▶ Rev 20.1—22.5

The New Heaven and the New Earth

Then I saw a new heaven and a new earth; for the first heaven and the first earth had passed away, and the sea was no more. 2 And I saw the holy city, the new Jerusalem, coming down out of heaven from God, prepared as a bride adorned for her husband. 3 And I heard a loud voice from the throne saying,

"See, the home*p* of God is among mortals.
He will dwell*q* with them;
they will be his peoples,*r*
and God himself will be with them;*s*
4 he will wipe every tear from their eyes.
Death will be no more;
mourning and crying and pain will be no
      more,
for the first things have passed away."

5 And the one who was seated on the throne said, "See, I am making all things new." Also he said, "Write this, for these words are trustworthy and true." 6 Then he said to me, "It is done! I am the Alpha and the Omega, the beginning and the end. To the thirsty I will give water as a gift from the spring of the water of life. 7 Those who conquer will inherit these things, and I will be their God and they will be my children. 8 But as for the cowardly, the faithless,*t* the polluted, the murderers, the fornicators, the sorcerers, the idolaters, and all liars, their place will be in the lake that burns with fire and sulfur, which is the second death."

Vision of the New Jerusalem
(Cp Ezek 48.30–35)

9 Then one of the seven angels who had the seven bowls full of the seven last plagues came and said to me, "Come, I will show you the bride, the wife of the Lamb." 10 And in the spirit*u* he carried me away to a great, high mountain and showed me the holy city Jerusalem coming down out of heaven from God. 11 It has the glory of God and a radiance like a very rare jewel, like jasper, clear as crystal. 12 It has a great, high wall with twelve gates, and at the gates twelve angels, and on the gates are inscribed the names of the twelve tribes of the Israelites; 13 on the east three gates, on the north three gates, on the south three gates, and on the west three gates. 14 And the wall of the city has twelve foundations, and on them are the twelve names of the twelve apostles of the Lamb.

15 The angel*v* who talked to me had a measuring rod of gold to measure the city and its gates and walls. 16 The city lies foursquare, its length the same as its width; and he measured the city with his rod, fifteen hundred miles;*w* its length and width and height are equal. 17 He also measured its wall, one hundred forty-four cubits*x* by human measurement, which the angel was using. 18 The wall is built of jasper, while the city is pure gold, clear as glass. 19 The foundations of the wall of the city are adorned with every jewel; the first was jasper, the second sapphire, the third agate, the fourth emerald, 20 the fifth onyx, the sixth carnelian, the seventh chrysolite, the eighth beryl, the ninth topaz, the tenth chrysoprase, the eleventh jacinth, the twelfth amethyst. 21 And the twelve gates are twelve pearls, each of the gates is a single pearl, and the street of the city is pure gold, transparent as glass.

22 I saw no temple in the city, for its temple is the Lord God the Almighty and the Lamb. 23 And the city has no need of sun or moon to shine on it, for the glory of God is its light, and its lamp is the Lamb. 24 The nations will walk by its light, and the kings of the earth will bring their glory into it. 25 Its gates will never be shut by day—and there will be no night there. 26 People will bring into it the glory and the honor of the nations. 27 But nothing unclean will enter it, nor anyone who practices abomination or falsehood, but only those who are written in the Lamb's book of life.

The River of Life

Then the angel*y* showed me the river of the water of life, bright as crystal, flowing from the throne of God and of the Lamb 2 through the middle of the street of the city. On either side of the river is the tree of life*z* with its twelve kinds of fruit, producing its fruit each month; and the leaves of the tree are for the healing of the nations. 3 Nothing accursed will be found there any more. But the throne of God and of the Lamb will be in it, and his servants*a* will worship him; 4 they will see his face, and his name will be on their foreheads. 5 And there will be no more night; they need no light of lamp or sun, for the Lord God will be their light, and they will reign forever and ever.

Epilogue and Benediction

6 And he said to me, "These words are trustworthy and true, for the Lord, the God of the spirits of the prophets, has sent his angel to show his servants*a* what must soon take place."

7 "See, I am coming soon! Blessed is the one who keeps the words of the prophecy of this book."

---

p Gk *the tabernacle*   *q* Gk *will tabernacle*   *r* Other ancient authorities read *people*   *s* Other ancient authorities add *and be their God*   *t* Or *the unbelieving*   *u* Or *in the Spirit*   *v* Gk *He*   *w* Gk *twelve thousand stadia*   *x* That is, almost seventy-five yards   *y* Gk *he*   *z* Or *the Lamb.* 2 *In the middle of the street of the city, and on either side of the river, is the tree of life*   *a* Gk *slaves*

8 I, John, am the one who heard and saw these things. And when I heard and saw them, I fell down to worship at the feet of the angel who showed them to me; 9 but he said to me, "You must not do that! I am a fellow servant[b] with you and your comrades[c] the prophets, and with those who keep the words of this book. Worship God!"

10 And he said to me, "Do not seal up the words of the prophecy of this book, for the time is near. 11 Let the evildoer still do evil, and the filthy still be filthy, and the righteous still do right, and the holy still be holy."

12 "See, I am coming soon; my reward is with me, to repay according to everyone's work. 13 I am the Alpha and the Omega, the first and the last, the beginning and the end."

14 Blessed are those who wash their robes,[d] so that they will have the right to the tree of life and may enter the city by the gates. 15 Outside are the dogs and sorcerers and fornicators and murderers and idolaters, and everyone who loves and practices falsehood.

16 "It is I, Jesus, who sent my angel to you with this testimony for the churches. I am the root and the descendant of David, the bright morning star."

17 The Spirit and the bride say, "Come."
And let everyone who hears say, "Come."
And let everyone who is thirsty come.
Let anyone who wishes take the water of life
     as a gift.

AMEN!

In Hebrew, *amen* means "so be it" or "yes, it is true." So saying "Amen" in your prayers is the same as saying, "Yes, I believe!" It is an appropriate way to conclude the last book of the Bible, and it should not be said lightly. Are you able to say "Amen" to all that you have read, prayed, and reflected on in this Bible? Have the stories and the poems, the teachings and the parables, the songs and the sayings led you to believe in a God who is with you every step of your journey, every minute of the day and night?

Each of us is invited to join the great Amen, to say: "Yes, I believe in a loving God who is father and mother to us all! Yes, I believe in God's Son, Jesus Christ, who is my lord and savior! Yes, I believe in the Holy Spirit, who will help me continue Jesus' mission of justice, reconciliation, and love!" But these words remain just words until people with courage and conviction take the risk to live them out in their own corner of the world. Take the risk; heaven awaits you! Amen!

▶ Rev 22.21

---

b Gk *slave*   *c* Gk *brothers*   *d* Other ancient authorities read *do his commandments*

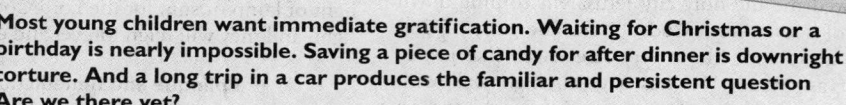

Come, Lord Jesus!

Most young children want immediate gratification. Waiting for Christmas or a birthday is nearly impossible. Saving a piece of candy for after dinner is downright torture. And a long trip in a car produces the familiar and persistent question Are we there yet?

The Bible tells us that Jesus will return. In the creed, Christians proclaim, "He will come again in glory to judge the living and the dead, / and his kingdom will have no end" (*The Sacramentary*, p. 368). When will this happen? Like impatient children, some people have tried to predict the Lord's Second Coming. "But about that day and hour no one knows . . . only the Father" (Mt 24.36).

Can we say, with John, "Amen. Come, Lord Jesus!" (Rev 22.20) and really hope that Jesus will come today? We may hesitate, wanting to hang on to the life we know here and now. Yet, the coming of Christ will be the most glorious event imaginable for those who have put their trust in God. So keep preparing and praying for the return of Christ!

▶ Rev 22.7–21

18 I warn everyone who hears the words of the prophecy of this book: if anyone adds to them, God will add to that person the plagues described in this book; 19 if anyone takes away from the words of the book of this prophecy, God will take away that person's share in the tree of life and in the holy city, which are described in this book.

20 The one who testifies to these things says, "Surely I am coming soon."

Amen. Come, Lord Jesus!

21 The grace of the Lord Jesus be with all the saints. Amen.*e*

---

e Other ancient authorities lack *all*; others lack *the saints*; others lack *Amen*

Where Do I Find It?

EVENTS, PEOPLE, AND TEACHINGS ?

OLD TESTAMENT STORIES

These stories are listed in the order in which they first appear in the Bible.

Creation, *Gen, chs 1–2*
original sin and its punishment, *Gen, ch 3*
Cain and Abel, *Gen 4.1–16*
Noah and the Great Flood, *Gen, chs 6–9*
God's covenant with Abraham,
      Gen 17.1—18.15
God's command to sacrifice Isaac,
      Gen 22.1–19
Isaac's blessing of Jacob, *Gen 27.1–29*
Jacob's dream, *Gen 28.10–22*
Joseph and his brothers, *Gen, chs 37–46*
birth and youth of Moses, *Ex 2.1–10*
Moses at the burning bush, *Ex 3.1–12*
plagues on Egypt, *Ex, chs 7–12*
Passover and the Exodus, *Ex, chs 12–14*
Ten Commandments, *Ex 20.1–17*
destruction of Jericho, *Josh 5.13—6.27*
Gideon and the sign of the fleece,
      Judg 6.36–40
Samson, *Judg, chs 13–16*
Samuel's birth and calling, *1 Sam, chs 1–3*
David and Goliath, *1 Sam, ch 17*
David and Bathsheba, *2 Sam, ch 11*
Solomon's wisdom, *1 Kings, ch 3*
Elijah's triumph over the priests of Baal,
      1 Kings 18.20–40
miracles of Elisha, *2 Kings 4.1—6.23*
end of the Babylonian captivity, *Ezra, ch 1*
battles of Judas Maccabeus, *1 Macc, chs 3–5*
Ezekiel and the valley of dry bones,
      Ezek 37.1–14
Daniel, *Dan, chs 1–6*
Jonah and the Ninevites, *Jon, chs 1–3*

NEW TESTAMENT STORIES

These stories are listed in the order in which they first appear in the Bible.

birth of Jesus, *Mt 1.18—2.12; Lk, chs 1–2*
baptism of Jesus, *Mt 3.13–17; Mk 1.9–11;*
      Lk 3.21–22
temptation of Jesus, *Mt 4.1–11; Mk 1.12–13;*
      Lk 4.1–13
Peter's declaration about Jesus, *Mt 16.13–20;*
      Mk 8.27–30; Lk 9.18–20
Transfiguration of Jesus, *Mt 17.1–13;*
      Mk 9.2–13; Lk 9.28–36
Jesus' triumphal entry into Jerusalem,
      Mt 21.1–11; Mk 11.1–11; Lk 19.28–40;
      Jn 12.12–19
Jesus in the Temple, *Mt 21.12–17;*
      Mk 11.15–19; Lk 19.45–48; Jn 2.13–16
Judas's betrayal of Jesus, *Mt 26.14–16,47–56;*
      Mk 14.10–11,43–52; Lk 22.1–53;
      Jn 13.21–30; Jn 18.1–5
Last Supper, *Mt 26.17–30; Mk 14.12–25;*
      Lk 22.7–38; 1 Cor 11.23–26
Jesus at Gethsemane, *Mt 26.36–56;*
      Mk 14.32–51; Lk 22.39–53
Peter's denial of Christ, *Mt 26.69–75; Mk*
      14.66–72; Lk 22.54–62; Jn 18.15–18,25–27
Crucifixion, *Mt 27.32–56; Mk 15.21–41;*
      Lk 23.26–49; Jn 19.16–30
Resurrection and appearances, *Mt, ch 28; Mk,*
      ch 16; Lk, ch 24; Jn, chs 20–21; Acts 1.1–11
Jesus washing his disciples' feet, *Jn 13.1–17*
Holy Spirit at Pentecost, *Acts 2.1–42*
stoning of Stephen, *Acts, chs 6–7*
conversion of Saul, *Acts 9.1–31*
Peter's escape from prison, *Acts 12.1–19*
Paul and Silas's escape from prison,
      Acts 16.16–40
Paul's journey to Rome for his trial,
      Acts, chs 27–28

PEOPLE

Each person entry is followed by a page number or numbers that lead you to an "Introducing . . ." article or other articles in which the person is featured.

Abraham, *18, 23, 28*
Barnabas, *1299*
Beloved Disciple, *1268*
David, *285, 287, 302, 310, 311*
Elijah, *350, 359*
Elisha, *350*
Ezekiel, *973*
First Isaiah, *830*
Holy Family, *1123*
Jacob, *34, 35, 36, 37, 40, 41*
Jeremiah, *894, 907*
John the Baptist, *1125, 1204*
Joseph, *45*
Junia, *1343*
Lady Wisdom, *699*
Lydia, *1306*
Mary, the mother of Jesus, *1199, 1200, 1277, 1495*
Mary Magdalene, *1278*
Moses, *62, 66, 81, 97, 210*
Nicodemus, *1249*
Paul, *1293, 1296, 1301, 1308, 1312, 1317, 1318, 1366, 1379, 1396*
Peter, *1145, 1161, 1192, 1209, 1268, 1280*
Phoebe, *1343*
Priscilla, *1306*
Samson, *254, 257*
Sarah, *18*
Satan, *570, 1176, 1494, 1502*
Solomon, *329, 332, 342, 414*
Stephen, *1291, 1292*

PRAYERS

These prayers are listed in the order in which they first appear in the Bible.

The Lord bless you and keep you, *Num 6.24–27*
Hannah's prayer, *1 Sam 2.1–10*
Speak, Lord, for your servant is listening, *1 Sam 3.9–10*
Blessed be the Lord, *1 Kings 8.56–61*
Tobit's thanksgiving, *Tob, ch 13*
Judith's hymn of praise, *Jdt 16.1–17*

The Lord is my shepherd, *Ps 23*
Have mercy on me, O God, *Ps 51*
O Lord, you have searched me and known me, *Ps 139*
Holy, Holy, Holy (Hosanna), *Isa 6.3; Mt 21.9; Mk 11.9–10; Lk 19.38; Jn 12.13; Rev 4.8*
Lord's Prayer, *Mt 6.9–15; Lk 11.2–4*
Lord, I am not worthy, *Mt 8.8*
Jesus' prayer for deliverance, *Mt 26.39; Mk 14.36; Lk 22.42*
Mary's song of praise, *Lk 1.46–55*
Zechariah's prophecy, *Lk 1.68–79*
Glory to God in the highest, *Lk 2.14*
Simeon's prayer, *Lk 2.29–32*
God, be merciful to me, a sinner!, *Lk 18.13*
Lamb of God, *Jn 1.29*
Jesus' prayer for his disciples, *Jn, ch 17*
Paul's prayer for the Ephesians, *Eph 3.14–21*
Amen, *1 Pet 5.11; Jude, v 25; Rev 1.6–7; 3.14*

MIRACLES OF JESUS

These miracle stories are listed in the order in which they first appear in the Bible.

Healing Individuals

leper, *Mt 8.1–4; Mk 1.40–45; Lk 5.12–16*
centurion's servant, *Mt 8.5–13; Lk 7.1–10*
many at Peter's house, *Mt 8.14–17; Mk 1.29–34; Lk 4.38–41*
Gadarene (Gerasene) demoniacs, *Mt 8.28–34; Mk 5.1–20; Lk 8.26–39*
paralytic, *Mt 9.1–8; Mk 2.1–12; Lk 5.17–26*
woman with bleeding, *Mt 9.20–22; Mk 5.25–34; Lk 8.43–48*
two blind men, *Mt 9.27–31*
mute man, *Mt 9.32–34*
man with a withered hand, *Mt 12.9–13; Mk 3.1–5; Lk 6.6–11*
blind, mute, and possessed man, *Mt 12.22*
Canaanite woman's daughter, *Mt 15.21–28; Mk 7.24–30*
boy with a demon, *Mt 17.14–21; Mk 9.14–29; Lk 9.37–43*
blind Bartimaeus, *Mt 20.29–34; Mk 10.46–52; Lk 18.35–43*
man with an unclean spirit, *Mk 1.21–28; Lk 4.31–37*
deaf man, *Mk 7.31–37*
blind man at Bethsaida, *Mk 8.22–26*
crippled woman, *Lk 13.11–13*

MIRACLES OF JESUS (continued)

man with dropsy, Lk 14.1–4
ten lepers, Lk 17.11–19
high priest's servant, Lk 22.50–51
official's son, Jn 4.46–54
man at the pool of Bethzatha, Jn 5.1–9

Controlling Nature

stilling the storm, Mt 8.23–27; Mk 4.35–41;
   Lk 8.22–25
feeding five thousand, Mt 14.13–21;
   Mk 6.30–44; Lk 9.10–17; Jn 6.1–15
walking on water, Mt 14.22–33; Mk 6.45–52;
   Jn 6.16–21
feeding four thousand, Mt 15.32–39;
   Mk 8.1–10
fish with a coin, Mt 17.24–27
fig tree withers, Mt 21.18–22;
   Mk 11.12–14,20–25
huge catch of fish, Lk 5.1–11; Jn 21.1–11
turning water into wine, Jn 2.1–11

Raising the Dead

Jairus's daughter, Mt 9.18–19,23–26;
   Mk 5.21–24,35–43; Lk 8.40–42,49–56
widow's son at Nain, Lk 7.11–17
Lazarus, Jn 11.1–44

PARABLES OF JESUS

These parables are listed in alphabetical order.

barren fig tree, Lk 13.6–9
canceled debts, Lk 7.41–43
cost of discipleship, Lk 14.25–33
dishonest manager, Lk 16.1–8
faithful or unfaithful slave, Mt 24.45–51;
   Lk 12.42–48
fig tree, Mt 24.32–35; Mk 13.28–31;
   Lk 21.29–33
good Samaritan, Lk 10.30–37
great dinner, Lk 14.16–24
growing seed, Mk 4.26–29
hidden treasure and pearl, Mt 13.44–46
honor at a banquet, Lk 14.7–14
laborers in the vineyard, Mt, ch 20
light of the world, Mt 5.14–16
lost coin, Lk 15.8–10
lost sheep, Mt 18.12–14; Lk 15.3–7
mustard seed, Mt 13.31–32; Mk 4.30–32;
   Lk 13.18–19
net, Mt 13.47–50

new wine in old wineskins, Mt 9.16–17;
   Mk 2.21–22; Lk 5.36–39
persistent friend, Lk 11.5–8
persistent widow, Lk 18.2–8
Pharisee and the tax collector, Lk 18.10–14
prodigal son, Lk 15.11–32
rich fool, Lk 12.16–21
rich man and Lazarus, Lk 16.19–31
salt, Mt 5.13; Mk 9.50; Lk 14.34–35
sheep and the goats, Mt 25.31–46
sower, Mt 13.3–8,18–23; Mk 4.3–9,14–20;
   Lk 8.5–8,11–15
talents, Mt 25.14–30
ten bridesmaids, Mt 25.1–13
ten pounds, Lk 19.1–10
two sons, Mt 21.28–31
unforgiving servant, Mt 18.23–35
watchful slaves, Lk 12.35–40
wedding banquet, Mt 22.1–14
weeds among the wheat, Mt 13.24–30,36–43
wicked tenants, Mt 21.33–44; Mk 12.1–12;
   Lk 20.9–18
wise and foolish builders, Mt 7.24–27;
   Lk 6.47–49
worthless slaves, Lk 17.7–10
yeast, Mt 13.33; Lk 13.20–21

TEACHINGS OF JESUS

These teachings are listed in alphabetical order.

Beatitudes, Mt 5.1–12; Lk 6.20–26
born from above, Jn 3.1–21
bread of life, Jn 6.25–59
children, Mk 10.13–16
discipleship, Lk 14.25–33
do not worry, Mt 6.19–21,25–34; Lk 12.22–34
golden rule, Mt 7.12; Lk 6.31
good shepherd, Jn 10.1–21
greatest commandment, Mt 22.34–40;
   Mk 12.28–34; Lk 10.25–28
living water, Jn 4.1–26
Lord's Prayer, Mt 6.9–13; Lk 11.2–4
mission of the twelve Apostles, Mt 10.1–15
paying taxes, Mt 22.15–22; Mk 12.13–17;
   Lk 20.20–26
rich young man, Mt 19.16–30; Mk 10.17–31;
   Lk 18.18–30
Sermon on the Mount, Mt, chs 5–7
Sermon on the Plain, Lk 6.17–49
vine and branches, Jn 15.1–17
"the way, the truth, and the life," Jn 14.1–14
"where two or three are gathered," Mt 18.20

SACRAMENT CONNECTIONS

BAPTISM

Isa 43.1
Mt 3.13–17; 28.19–20
Mk 1.9–11
Lk 3.21–22
Jn 1.29–34; 3.5
Acts 2.37–41
Rom 6.3–4

CONFIRMATION

Isa 11.2; 61.1
Mt 3.13–17
Jn 1.33–34; 14.15–31;
    16.5–15
Acts 2.1–4; 8.14–17
2 Cor 1.21–22
Gal 5.22–23

EUCHARIST

Gen 14.17–20
Ex 12.1–28; 24.1–8
Mt 14.13–21; 26.17–29
Mk 6.30–44; 14.12–25
Lk 9.10–17; 22.7–20;
    24.13–35
Jn 6.1–13,25–59
1 Cor 11.17–34

RECONCILIATION (PENANCE)

Gen 45.1–15
Joel 2.12–13
Mt 5.21–26,38–48; 18.23–35
Mk 2.1–12
Lk 15.11–32
Jn 20.19–23
Rom, ch 6

ANOINTING

Ps 23
Mk 6.7–13
Lk 13.10–13
2 Tim 2.11–12
Jas 5.14–16

HOLY ORDERS

Deut 18.1–5
Ps 110.1–4
Mt 10.1–4
Mk 3.14–19
Lk 6.12–16
Jn 13.1–14
Rom 12.1–8
1 Tim 3.1–13
Titus 1.5–9
Heb 4.14—5.10

MARRIAGE

Gen 2.18–25
Song 8.6–7
Mt 19.1–12
Mk 10.2–12
Jn 2.1–11
1 Cor, ch 13
Eph 5.21–33
1 Jn 4.4–16

LIFE AND FAITH ISSUES

PROMISES OF GOD
Ex 6.1–9
Jer 29.11
Lk 4.14–30

REPENTANCE
1 Chr 21.1–17
Joel 2.12–18
Lk 15.11–32

RESPONSIBILITY
Sir 15.11–20
Ezek, ch 18

SERVICE
Isa 42.1–6
Mt 20.20–28;
    25.31–46
Mk 10.35–45
Jn 13.1–17

SEXUALITY
Gen 1.26–31
Tob 8.4–9
Song
Eph 5.1–14
1 Thess 4.3–8

SUFFERING
Job 1.13–21
Ps 22
Mt 5.1–12
1 Pet 3.13–18

TEMPTATION
Gen, ch 3
Mt 4.1–11
Mk 1.12–13;
    7.14–23
Lk 4.1–13

TRUST IN GOD
Ps 62
Isa 43.1–5
Mt 11.28–30
Mk 10.46–52

VOCATION (*See*
call; discipleship)

WISDOM
2 Chr 1.7–13
Prov 8.1–21
Wis, ch 7

ANGER
Mt 5.21–24
Jn 2.13–17
Eph 4.25–27,31–32
Jas 1.19–21

CALL
Gen 12.1–9
1 Sam, chs 1–3
Isa 6.1–8
Jer 1.4–10
Mt 4.18–22;
    28.16–20
Mk 1.16–20
Lk 5.1–11

COMMITMENT
Num 30.2–4
Deut 6.1–9; 11.8–9
Josh 24.14–15
Mk 8.34–38

COURAGE
Josh 1.9
1 Sam, ch 17
Ps 31

DISCIPLESHIP
Mk 8.34–38
Lk 9.1–6
Jn 4.1–42

FAMILY
Gen 4.9; 12.10–20
Sir 3.1–16
Eph 5.21—6.4

FEAR
Ps 27, 91
Zeph 3.14–20
Mt 14.22–33
Mk 4.35–41
Lk 22.54–62

FORGIVENESS
Gen 33.1–17
Ps 51
Mt 18.21–35
Lk 6.27–36; 23.34
Jn 8.2–11

FRIENDSHIP
Ruth 1.1–19
1 Sam, ch 20
Sir 6.5–17
Jn 15.12–17

FRIENDSHIP
WITH GOD
Gen 28.10–22
Mic 6.8
Jn 15.12–17

GIVING
2 Chr 31.2–10
Ezra 1.6–11
Mk 12.41–44
Lk 21.1–4

HAPPINESS
Sir 25.1–11
Lk 12.22–34
Phil 4.4–9

HONESTY
WITH GOD
Gen 18.22–33
Jer 12.1–16
Mk 14.32–42

HOPE
Eccl 3.1–8
Lam 3.22–26
Rom 8.18–30

HYPOCRISY
Mt 6.1–6; 23.1–36
Lk 18.9–14
Jas 1.22—2.4

IMAGES OF GOD
Gen 1.26–27;
    32.22–32
Ps 23
Jer 18.1–11

JUDGMENT
OF OTHERS
Mt 7.1–5
Rom 14.1–12
Gal 3.26–28

LONELINESS AND
ABANDONMENT
Ps 22.1–12
Mk 15.33–34
2 Tim 4.9–18

LOVE
Song 8.6–7
Mt 5.43–48
Mk 12.28–34
1 Cor, ch 13

PEACE
Isa 11.1–9
Mic 4.1–5
Jn 14.25–31

PERSISTENCE
Lk 11.5–8; 18.1–8

POPULARITY
Mk 9.33–37
1 Cor 3.1–9
Phil 2.1–11

PRESENCE OF GOD
Gen 15.7
Ex 3.1–6; 33.17–23
Mt 18.20

ARTICLE SUBJECT INDEX ?

This subject index is not an index to the Bible itself (sometimes called a concordance). Rather, it is an index to the subjects covered in the various articles in The Catholic Youth Bible. But because most articles are based on a Bible passage, this index will also help you find Bible passages related to these topics.

A

abandonment
1195. *See also* despair; loneliness

abortion
62, 684, 926, 1124

Abraham
18, 23, 28

abuse
21, 27

acceptance
1150

addiction
1222, 1355

Advent
857

advertising
724

Advocate
1269

African American articles
7, 75, 185, 187, 334, 492, 641, 644, 735, 936, 1109, 1144, 1158, 1193, 1207, 1292, 1359, 1373, 1385, 1442

afterlife
729, 1037, 1364. *See also* Resurrection

agape
1359

aging
732

AIDS
652, 1326

alcohol
496, 799, 1393

altars
222

ancestors
22, 59, 131, 1292

angels
479, 1449

anger
570, 627, 663, 708, 712, 1075, 1248

Anointing, sacrament of
1224

anxiety
731, 933, 1219, 1223

apocalyptic literature
1031, 1483

apocryphal books
472

Apostles
1161, 1169, 1172, 1175, 1178

Apostles' Creed
1287

ark of the Covenant
102, 105, 928

arrogance
548

Ash Wednesday
1056, 1129

Asian American articles
57, 63, 80, 105, 131, 411, 475, 553, 666, 725, 769, 882, 1050, 1147, 1212, 1241, 1251, 1268, 1358, 1368, 1390, 1471

Assyrian Empire
375, 1084

atheism
608

authority
241

awe
63, 612, 618, 710, 996

B

baals
226, 350

Babylon
951, 1499

Babylonian Exile
384

balance
725

Baptism, sacrament of
1125, 1331

Barnabas
1299

Beatitudes
1127, 1211

beauty
735, 1401

beliefs
1287

Beloved Disciple
1268

Benedictus
1201

Bethlehem
1080

betrayal
257, 634, 1192

Bible
vi–vii, xii–xv, 2–3, 193, 212–213, 362, 472, 504, 568, 1118–1119, 1206, 1245, 1322–1323, 1326, 1419, 1483. *See also* literary devices and genres

bishops
See ministry in the church

blessing
145, 340

body of Christ
1339, 1359

boldness
492, 1158

bread and wine
19, 1132, 1255

breath
1006

brothers and sisters
10, 32, 609, 1298

C

call
831, 866, 893, 973, 974, 1115, 1169, 1232. *See also* discipleship

Canaan
214, 226

canon
472

caretakers
8, 913

celebration
306, 499, 726, 769. *See also* praise

childbirth
118

children
687, 769, 913, 926, 991, 1124

choices
128, 637, 780, 967, 1023, 1047, 1249, 1333, 1373, 1421, 1471, 1476

Christmas
834, 1122, 1202, 1251. *See also* liturgical year

church
1280, 1392, 1407, 1495

circumcision
23, 1305, 1328, 1379

civil disobedience
62, 1152

commitment
169, 696, 1050, 1181, 1231, 1400

communion
See Eucharist, sacrament of

communion of saints
1412

community
1114, 1285, 1304, 1410

compassion of God
27, 652, 822–823, 873, 1258, 1440

complaining
79, 907

confession
See Reconciliation, sacrament of

confidence
967

Confirmation, sacrament of
1125, 1283

conflict
16, 195, 234, 290, 1345, 1347

conscience
1421

consciousness raising
975

consecration
1132, 1357

contentment
724

contrition
896. *See also* Reconciliation, sacrament of

conversion
424, 444, 967, 1027, 1125, 1129, 1131, 1232, 1247, 1294, 1296, 1298

cooperation
1144, 1348

corruption
283, 1248

Council of Jerusalem
1293, 1305, 1381

courage
66, 216, 287, 529, 552, 553, 620, 933, 1303, 1410

covenant
4–5, 8, 13, 15, 18, 22, 34, 49, 1160. *See also* New Covenant; Sinai Covenant

creation
6, 8, 596, 609, 1401, 1502

creativity
1158

creeds
1287, 1362

crucifixion
1165, 1181, 1275, 1276

cults
1402, 1466

culture
693, 967, 1270, 1373, 1422,
1461

D

dancing
306

darkness
1074, 1241, 1259

daughters
754

David
285, 287, 302, 310, 311

Day of Atonement
167

deacons
See ministry in the church

death
319, 729, 1330. See also
crucifixion; suffering

death penalty
10

deception
37, 54

demons
1176

despair
613, 1164, 1193, 1242, 1320,
1370

Diaspora
504

disappointment
1161

discernment
694, 1473

disciples
1199, 1428. See also Apostles

discipleship
66, 671, 687, 707, 866, 1126,
1136, 1142, 1151, 1166, 1177,
1178, 1181, 1182, 1185, 1209,
1216, 1226, 1231, 1232, 1251,
1270, 1280, 1289, 1303,
1368, 1406, 1410, 1423,
1429, 1460, 1504

disobedience
9, 62, 1152

diversity
863, 1260, 1297, 1318

doubts
608, 893, 1150, 1183, 1204

dreams
49

E

Easter
1241, 1275. See also liturgical
year

eating disorders
1371

ecumenism
1341

elders
714, 732

Elijah
350, 359

Elisha
350

embarrassment
See humiliation

Emmanuel (Immanuel)
832, 834, 1123, 1243

encouragement
75, 1299, 1410

end time
1189, 1502

enemies, love of
1128

Epiphany
1122

equality
810, 1383, 1433, 1435

Essenes
565

Eucharist, sacrament of
19, 80, 88, 1114, 1132, 1160,
1190, 1237, 1245, 1255, 1266,
1269, 1357, 1358, 1441

evangelization
1166, 1293, 1294, 1308, 1318,
1326, 1337, 1427

evil
12, 1176, 1476, 1493, 1494.
See also Satan

examination of conscience
786, 1327, 1378

Exile
See Babylonian Exile

Exodus
69, 760

Ezekiel
973

Ezra
445

F

failure
872

faith
18, 28, 363, 459, 482, 570,
603, 608, 838, 1142, 1175,
1178, 1183, 1196, 1200, 1214,
1250, 1291, 1320, 1328,
1329, 1335, 1362, 1364,
1382, 1384, 1385, 1389,
1428, 1446, 1452

faith sharing
1286, 1314, 1372, 1428

false prophets
910, 1466

families
131, 666, 720, 768, 769,
1203, 1212, 1353, 1394, 1407

fasting
457

fatalism
986

fear
216, 710, 838, 866, 933, 1175,
1193, 1320

festivals (feasts)
73, 99, 131, 167, 512, 522,
1122, 1147, 1199, 1212, 1257,
1267. *See also* individual
names of

fidelity
885

fighting
708

fire
20

First Isaiah
830

flood
12, 13, 14

food
73, 80, 117, 475, 1356

forgiveness
41, 45, 251, 632, 663, 1044,
1129, 1148, 1212, 1227, 1240.
See also Reconciliation,
sacrament of

fornication
1351, 1411

foundation, God as life's
323, 1349

freedom
1207, 1292

friendship
267, 290, 704, 712, 771, 775,
934, 1044, 1161, 1170, 1192,
1273, 1311, 1398. *See also*
God, closeness with

fruits of the Spirit
1384, 1459

G

genealogies
59, 389, 1122

generosity
438, 447, 475, 670, 1187,
1188, 1374

genocide
505

Gentiles
1175, 1240, 1294, 1328, 1336

gifts
447, 699, 726, 958, 1158,
1187, 1226, 1236, 1254, 1271,
1359, 1413

giving, sacrificial
438, 615, 1188, 1236, 1288,
1374

God
598, 600; closeness with, 24,
36, 98, 574, 738, 743, 832,
873, 1150, 1219, 1335; glory
of, 971, 1272, 1491; help of,
27; 614, 678, 685, 764, 1106;
holiness of, 20; name of, 64,
411, 832, 1247; need for, 353;
power of, 612, 618, 966;
struggling with, 40, 894; will
of, 35, 54, 67, 193, 694, 1075,
1488. *See also* compassion of
God; images of God; presence
of God; Reign of God; trust in
God

gods
13, 226, 350

golden calf
97

Good Friday
613, 1275

goodness
6, 8, 54, 482. *See also* right
living

Good News
1118–1119, 1177, 1294, 1326,
1337

good shepherd
614, 1003, 1262

good works
826, 1387, 1389, 1431

gospel, **meaning of term**
1119, 1326

gossip
702, 795, 1138, 1453

grace
764, 1330, 1389

gratitude
See thanksgiving

greatness, true
1151

greed
727, 1152, 1222

grief
319, 571, 926, 960, 1263,
1311

H

Hail Mary
202, 1199

Hanukkah
522

harassment
21

hard times
764, 1193

healing
319, 672, 805, 960, 1143,
1170, 1173

heart
743, 980

pleasure
726

politics
845

poor people
86, 161, 199, 266, 359, 460,
895, 1066, 1097, 1159, 1202,
1211, 1226, 1277, 1286, 1358,
1374. *See also* oppressed
people; preferential option for
the poor

pope
1145, 1206, 1280

pornography
736

positive attitude
75, 79

power
283, 618, 1499

praise
78, 307, 499, 601, 641, 690,
1489, 1491, 1498. *See also*
celebration

prayer
80, 161, 183, 271, 273, 401,
435, 457, 463, 474, 482, 493,
574, 603, 694, 707, 738, 764,
1007, 1033, 1037, 1129, 1183,
1186, 1211, 1220, 1230, 1455

**preferential option
for the poor**
852, 895, 1066, 1202, 1211,
1226, 1453

prejudice
217, 453, 505, 1219, 1249,
1260, 1298

preparedness
See readiness

presence of God
20, 36, 63, 98, 338, 353, 402,
479, 612, 618, 648, 971, 1013,
1368, 1467

pride
16, 342, 1097, 1370

priests
See ministry in the church

priorities
1100, 1354

Priscilla
1306

prodigal son
1228

profanity
789

promiscuity
126

promises of God
67. *See also* covenant; New
Covenant; Sinai Covenant

prophetic themes
962, 971, 1110, 1485

prophets
49, 62, 65, 161, 359, 429,
822–823, 824, 874, 975,
1040, 1392

protection
1003; 1262

Purim, feast of
512

purity
109, 1005, 1115

R

race
266

Rachel
926

racism
1219, 1292, 1442. *See also*
prejudice

rainbow
15

rape
43

readiness
1115, 1156, 1157, 1352, 1417

reading plans
xvi–xix

Reconciliation, sacrament of
404, 1279, 1471

redeemer
110, 1165. *See* Jesus Christ;
Messiah

reflection time
307, 648, 786, 1452

reforms, religious
381

Reign of God
837, 1131, 1134, 1141, 1226,
1493, 1502

remnant
1062, 1097

repentance
404, 1129, 1204. *See also*
Reconciliation, sacrament of

respect
655, 710, 1341

responsibility
10, 81, 97, 124, 185, 311, 780,
917, 971, 986, 991, 1047

Resurrection
1037, 1074, 1196, 1242, 1275,
1364

revenge
841, 940, 1086, 1128

rice
80

ridicule
627

right living
128, 414, 617, 620, 671, 691,
699, 752, 754, 967, 1023,
1050, 1071, 1154, 1351, 1387,
1406, 1459, 1461. *See also*
values

risk taking
936, 1133

role models
1389

Romans
1312, 1496, 1499

Rome
1321, 1499

S

Sabbath
7, 463

sabbatical year
133

sacraments
See individual names of

sacrifice
28, 88, 553, 1291, 1445

Sadducees
565, 1124

saints
216, 332, 1412

salvation
110, 877, 1122, 1175, 1240,
1249, 1272, 1324, 1329,
1330, 1331, 1336, 1382,
1389, 1438

salvation history
8, 206, 1488, 1490, 1495

Samaritans
1219, 1250

Samson
254, 257

Sarah
18

Satan
570, 1176, 1494, 1502

scapegoats
124, 167

scribes
1124

Second Coming
1352, 1415, 1417, 1502

security
680, 695

self-control
784, 1393

self-deception
910, 1471

self-determination
492

self-image
6, 7, 735, 1371

Sermon on the Mount
1127, 1211

Sermon on the Plain
1211

service
866, 1151, 1159, 1169, 1174,
1185, 1187, 1226, 1238, 1266,
1343, 1398

sexism
507, 810

sexuality
126, 310, 632, 733, 735, 736,
739, 1351, 1411

shalom
855

Shema
183

sibling rivalry
32

Simon of Cyrene
1193

sin
9, 12, 13, 97, 110, 251, 310,
342, 457, 632, 786, 917, 991,
1258, 1279, 1329, 1332,
1333, 1406, 1499

Sinai Covenant
2–3, 83, 85, 109, 236,
822–823, 902, 928, 1097,
1328

sin offering
110

slavery
76, 1433

social action
457, 460

social justice
See justice

Solomon
329, 332, 342, 414

songs
78, 499, 657, 690, 865

sons
752

speaking
789, 1138, 1453. See also
gossip; language

spirits
1170, 1176, 1473

spiritual growth
363, 1090, 1179, 1203, 1214,
1217, 1270, 1349, 1378

spiritual poverty
1377

spiritual writings
381

status
1359

Stephen
1291, 1292

stereotypes
1251

stewardship
1236, 1288, 1374

stories
311, 1174. See also parables

strangers
25, 86, 199, 1449

street theater
975

strength
874, 1410

strength in God
459, 1373, 1377

submissiveness
1422

success
872

suffering
474, 568, 570, 571, 574, 586, 600, 604, 1164, 1165, 1193, 1334, 1368, 1457, 1461, 1462

suffering servant
110, 865, 872, 874, 877

suicide
299, 474, 1162

superstition
969

symbols, biblical
6, 14, 15, 20, 102, 567, 885, 920, 971, 973, 975, 1006, 1031, 1047, 1125, 1141, 1189, 1233, 1245, 1258, 1483, 1489

symbols, Native American
863, 944, 1103, 1258

T

teaching
1428

teamwork
1338

temper
97, 708, 712

Temple
450, 522, 615, 902, 971, 1013, 1152

temptation
9, 310, 784, 1126, 1206, 1207, 1332, 1333, 1373, 1440

Ten Commandments
83, 85, 181, 928. See also Sinai Covenant

testing God
247

thanksgiving
666, 672, 726, 1356, 1412, 1413

tithing
438

Torah
193, 414

Tradition
1206, 1418

Transfiguration
1146, 1182

transformation
98, 1431

treasure
420, 644, 1236

Trinity
See Holy Trinity

trust
257, 637, 701, 702, 757, 1381

trust in God
7, 18, 28, 76, 195, 247, 459, 598, 608, 634, 637, 685, 757, 832, 838, 1074, 1100, 1209, 1254, 1330, 1382, 1385, 1504

Truth
1269

Truth, Sojourner
492

twelve tribes
34, 236, 238, 344

U

understanding
234, 332, 1150, 1178

unity
16, 222, 236, 1109, 1284, 1304, 1345, 1347, 1353, 1358, 1359, 1374, 1387, 1391

V

values
187, 422, 617, 967. See also right living

violence
10, 43, 226, 243, 244, 497, 505, 926, 957, 1124

virginity, secondary
632

visions
951, 973, 1031, 1057, 1485, 1490, 1494, 1496, 1502

vocation
See call; discipleship

vows
169

W

war
140, 195, 243, 244, 497, 525. See also violence

water
13, 14, 240, 1250, 1251

the way, the truth, and the life
1268

weakness
9, 1178, 1377

wealth
420, 1100, 1231, 1424

weeping
448, 926

welcoming others
25, 265, 453, 627, 1123, 1175, 1177, 1298, 1449

widows
86, 199

wind
1006, 1103

wisdom
332, 334, 414, 645, 648, 699, 714, 747, 748, 749, 752, 754, 1347

witnesses
1283, 1370, 1427

women
78, 243, 244, 271, 492, 499, 507, 739, 810, 1251, 1278, 1306, 1343, 1361, 1422,

work
185, 805, 1169, 1417

worship
338, 340, 463, 615, 1064, 1361, 1489. *See also* Eucharist, sacrament of; praise

Y

Yahweh
See God

young people
687, 1204, 1308, 1392

youth
731, 893

Z

Zion
681

Acknowledgments *(continued)*

Consultants: Barbara Allaire, Mary Lee Becker, Brian K. Johnson, Carl Koch, Stephan Nagel, Pheme Perkins, and Kevin Schneider

Publishing team: Brian Singer-Towns, general editor; Carmen María Cervantes, Shirley Kelter, and Robert P. Stamschror, consulting editors; Lynn Riska Dahdal, production editor; Cheryl Drivdahl and Mary Duerson, copy editors; Hollace Storkel, article typesetter; Auto-Graphics, Scripture typesetters; Peachtree Editorial and Proofreading Service, Scripture proofreaders; Maurine R. Twait, art director; Stephan Nagel, art director and cover designer; Sue Campbell, Carol Evans-Smith, Kent Linder, and Cindi Ramm, designers; Alan S. Hanson, pre-press specialist; Gary J. Boisvert and Alan S. Hanson, illustration colorizers; Michael O. McGrath, illustrator

A special thank-you to the members of the original *Catholic Youth Bible* focus group: Catherine Cory; Carole Goodwin; Maryann Hakowski; Shirley Kelter; Marilyn Kielbasa; Joseph A. Morris, CM; Daniel Ponsetto; Pat Rinker; Virginia Smith; Carleen Suttman; and especially Robert P. Stamschror for his work in starting this project.

Finally, we are very grateful for the many young people, youth leaders, and teachers who helped as reviewers and consultants through the duration of this project.

The Old Testament

The poem from Japan on page 1251, the prayer from Hong Kong on page 1368, and the prayer from the Philippines on page 1390 are quoted from *Gifts of Many Cultures*, edited by Maren C. Tirabassi and Kathy Wonson Eddy, pages 144, 37, and 30, respectively. Used by permission. The quotation on page 1390 is reprinted from *Your Will Be Done* (Hong Kong: Christian Conferences of Asia, 1986). Copyright © 1986 CCA Youth, Christian Conference of Asia. Used by permission.

The prayer by Black Elk on page 1258 and the Navaho prayer on page 1401 are quoted from *The Sacred Vision: Native American Religion and Its Practice Today*, by Michael F. Steltenkamp (New York: Paulist Press, 1982), pages 82 and 92. Copyright © 1982 by Michael Steltenkamp. Used by permission.

The quotation on page 1277 is from *A Handbook on Guadalupe: Our Lady Patroness of the Americas* (Stockton, CA: Office of Religious Education, Department of Catechesis, 1974), pages 148, 152. Copyright © 1974 by Franciscan Marytown Press, Kenosha, Wisconsin.

The Apostles' Creed on page 1289 is from the *Catechism of the Catholic Church*, by the Libreria Editrice Vaticana, translated by the USCC (Washington, DC: USCC, 1994), pages 49–50. English translation copyright © 1994 by the USCC—Libreria, Editrice Vaticana.

The Native American meal blessing on page 1356 is from *One Hundred Graces*, selected by Marcia Kelly and Jack Kelly (New York: Bell Tower, 1992), page 85. Copyright © 1992 by Marcia Kelly and Jack Kelly. Used by permission of Lama Foundation, New Mexico.

The quotation on page 1362 is from *Prophetic Voices: The Document on the Process of the Ill Encuentro Nacional Hispano de Pastoral*, by the Secretariat for Hispanic Affairs, pages 17–18. Copyright © 1986 by the USCC, Washington, DC. Used by permission. All rights reserved.

The Native American prayer on page 1391 is quoted from *Amen*, compiled by Suzanne Slesin and Emily Gwathmey.

The Peace Prayer on page 1395 is quoted from the *Catholic Source Book*, third edition, edited by the Reverend Peter Klein, page 25.

The line from Shakespeare's play *Hamlet* on page 1396 is quoted from *The Standard Book of Shakespeare Quotations*, compiled and arranged by Burton Stevenson (New York: Funk and Wagnalls Co., 1953), page 149. Copyright © 1953 by Funk and Wagnalls Co.

The prayer by Robert Traxler on page 1498 is quoted from *More Dreams Alive: Prayers by Teenagers*, edited by Carl Koch, FSC (Winona, MN: Saint Mary's Press, 1995), page 87. Copyright © 1995 by Saint Mary's Press. All rights reserved.

Photo Credits

Art Resource, NY, copyright © 1999 Artists Rights Society (ARS), New York/ADAGP, Paris: page 1549 (middle left)

Copyright © John Giuliani. Used with permission of Bridge Building Images, P.O. Box 1048, Burlington, VT 05402: page 1549 (bottom right)

Rick Bowmer, AP Photo: page 1548 (lower-middle left)

Paul Chesley, Tony Stone Images: page 1548 (lower-middle right)

David Cimino, International Stock Photo: page 1546 (top left)

Sylvain Grandadam, Tony Stone Images: page 1548 (bottom)

The Laughing Christ, by Frances Hook, on page 1549 (top left) is used by permission of John Brandi, JB Co.

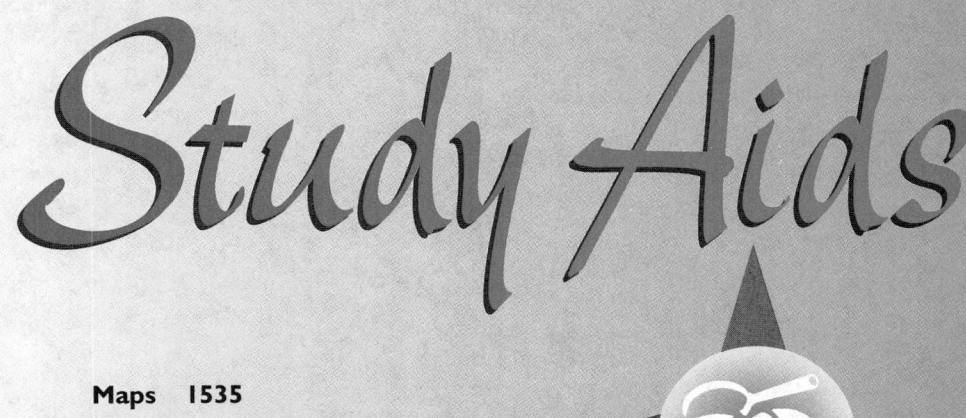

Study Aids

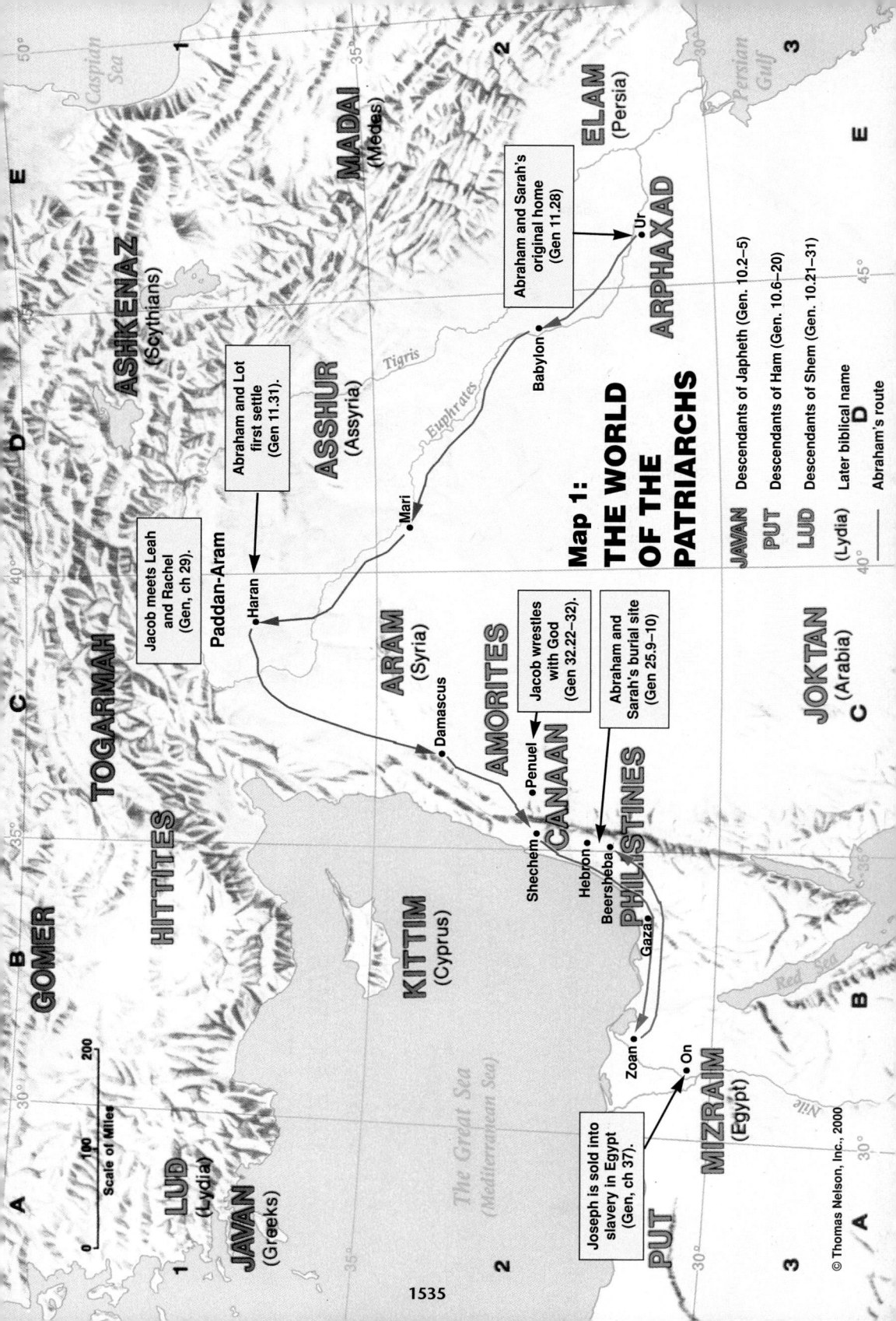

Map 1:
THE WORLD
OF THE PATRIARCHS

JAVAN Descendants of Japheth (Gen. 10.2–5)
(Greeks)
PUT Descendants of Ham (Gen. 10.6–20)
LUD Descendants of Shem (Gen. 10.21–31)
(Lydia)
D Later biblical name
          Abraham's route

Abraham and Sarah's original home (Gen 11.28)

Abraham and Lot first settle (Gen 11.31).

Jacob meets Leah and Rachel (Gen, ch 29).

Jacob wrestles with God (Gen 32.22–32).

Abraham and Sarah's burial site (Gen 25.9–10)

Joseph is sold into slavery in Egypt (Gen, ch 37).

Paddan-Aram

GOMER
LUD
(Lydia)
JAVAN
(Greeks)
TOGARMAH
HITTITES
ASHKENAZ
(Scythians)
MADAI
(Medes)
ELAM
(Persia)
ARPHAXAD
ASSHUR
(Assyria)
ARAM
(Syria)
AMORITES
CANAAN
KITTIM
(Cyprus)
PHILISTINES
JOKTAN
(Arabia)
MIZRAIM
(Egypt)
PUT

Ur
Babylon
Mari
Haran
Damascus
Penuel
Shechem
Hebron
Beersheba
Gaza
Zoan
On

Caspian Sea
Persian Gulf
Tigris
Euphrates
The Great Sea
(Mediterranean Sea)
Red Sea
Nile

Scale of Miles
0   100   200

1535

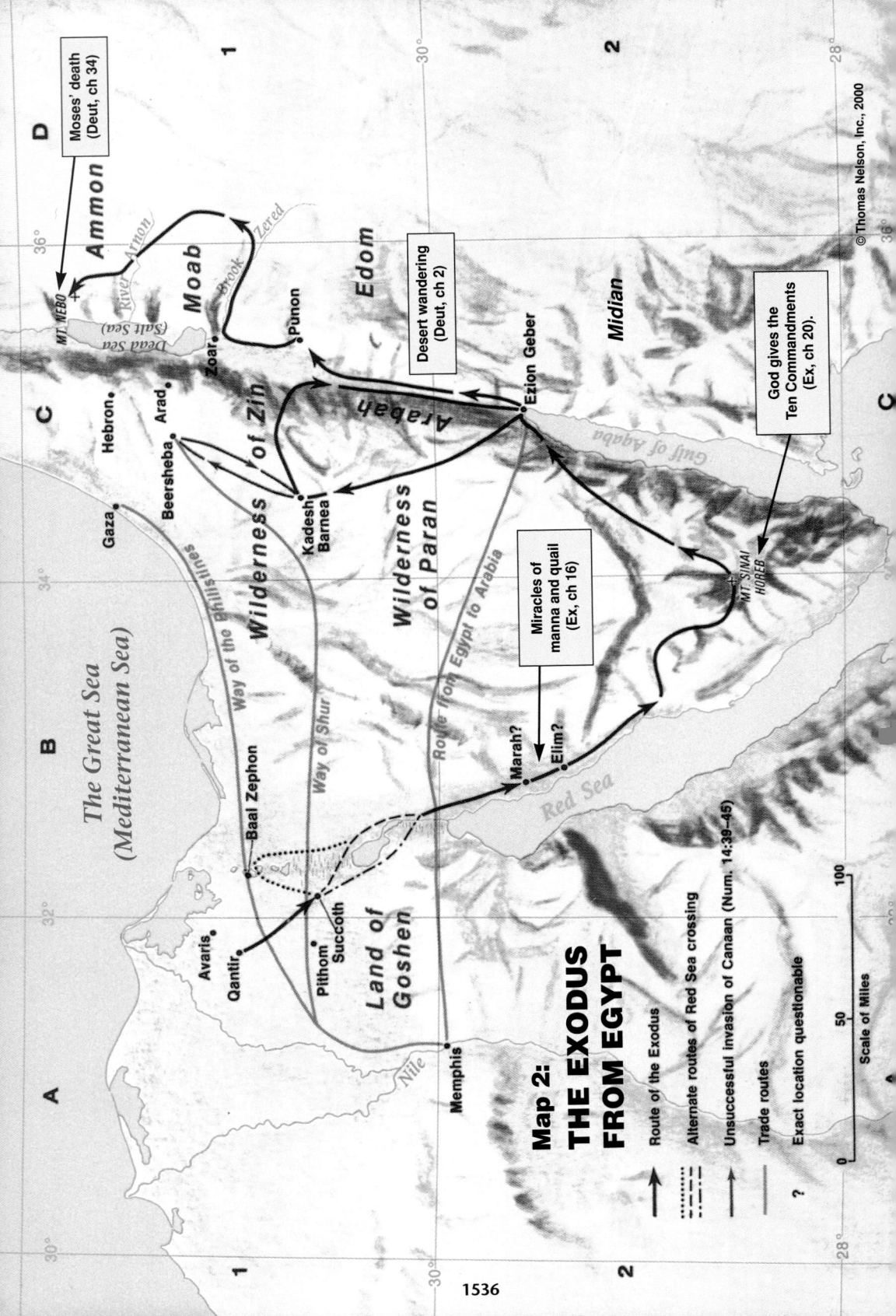

Map 2:
THE EXODUS
FROM EGYPT

Route of the Exodus
Alternate routes of Red Sea crossing
Unsuccessful invasion of Canaan (Num. 14:39–45)
Trade routes
? Exact location questionable

Scale of Miles
0   50   100

Moses' death
(Deut, ch 34)

Desert wandering
(Deut, ch 2)

God gives the
Ten Commandments
(Ex, ch 20).

Miracles of manna and quail
(Ex, ch 16)

The Great Sea
(Mediterranean Sea)

Ammon

Moab

Edom

Midian

River Arnon

Brook Zered

MT. NEBO

Dead Sea
(Salt Sea)

Zoar

Punon

Hebron

Arad

Beersheba

Gaza

Kadesh
Barnea

Wilderness of Zin

Wilderness
of Paran

Arabah

Ezion Geber

Gulf of Aqaba

MT. SINAI
HOREB

Way of the Philistines

Way of Shur

Route from Egypt to Arabia

Baal Zephon

Pithom
Succoth

Avaris

Qantir

Land of
Goshen

Memphis

Nile

Marah?

Elim?

Red Sea

© Thomas Nelson, Inc., 2000

1536

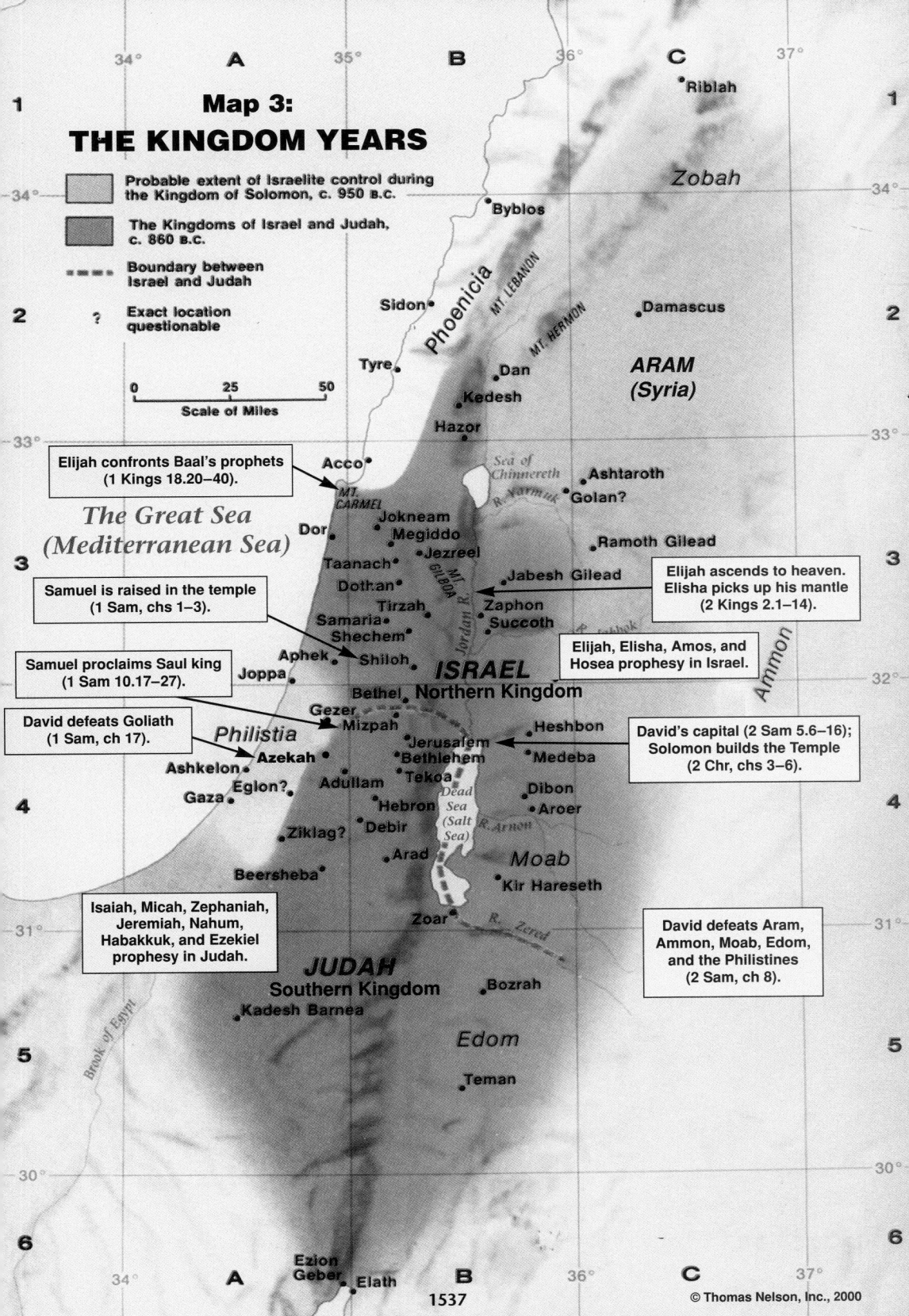

Map 3:
THE KINGDOM YEARS

Probable extent of Israelite control during the Kingdom of Solomon, c. 950 B.C.

The Kingdoms of Israel and Judah, c. 860 B.C.

Boundary between Israel and Judah

? Exact location questionable

0   25   50
Scale of Miles

Elijah confronts Baal's prophets (1 Kings 18.20–40).

The Great Sea (Mediterranean Sea)

Samuel is raised in the temple (1 Sam, chs 1–3).

Samuel proclaims Saul king (1 Sam 10.17–27).

David defeats Goliath (1 Sam, ch 17).

Elijah ascends to heaven. Elisha picks up his mantle (2 Kings 2.1–14).

Elijah, Elisha, Amos, and Hosea prophesy in Israel.

David's capital (2 Sam 5.6–16); Solomon builds the Temple (2 Chr, chs 3–6).

Isaiah, Micah, Zephaniah, Jeremiah, Nahum, Habakkuk, and Ezekiel prophesy in Judah.

David defeats Aram, Ammon, Moab, Edom, and the Philistines (2 Sam, ch 8).

Riblah

Zobah

Byblos

Sidon

MT. LEBANON

MT. HERMON

Damascus

Tyre

Phoenicia

Dan

Kedesh

Hazor

ARAM (Syria)

Acco

MT. CARMEL

Sea of Chinnereth

R. Yarmuk

Ashtaroth

Golan?

Dor

Jokneam

Megiddo

Jezreel

Taanach

MT. GILBOA

Jabesh Gilead

Ramoth Gilead

Dothan

Tirzah

Samaria

Shechem

Zaphon

Succoth

R. Jabbok

Jordan R.

Aphek

Shiloh

Joppa

ISRAEL
Northern Kingdom

Ammon

Bethel

Gezer

Mizpah

Jerusalem

Bethlehem

Tekoa

Heshbon

Medeba

Philistia

Azekah

Ashkelon

Eglon?

Adullam

Hebron

Debir

Dead Sea (Salt Sea)

Dibon

Aroer

R. Arnon

Gaza

Ziklag?

Arad

Moab

Beersheba

Kir Hareseth

Zoar

R. Zered

JUDAH
Southern Kingdom

Bozrah

Brook of Egypt

Kadesh Barnea

Edom

Teman

Ezion Geber

Elath

1537

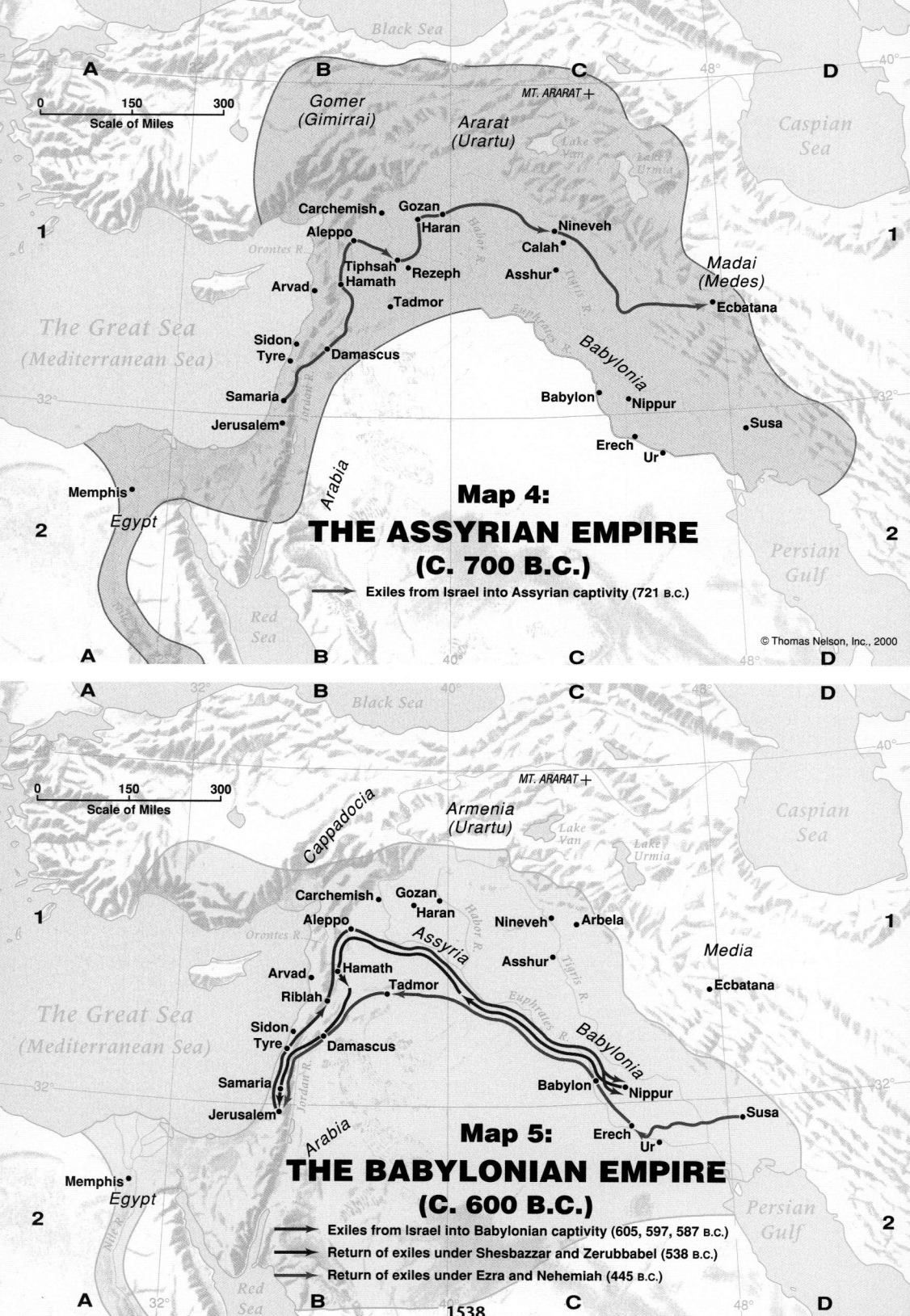

Map 4:
THE ASSYRIAN EMPIRE
(C. 700 B.C.)

→ Exiles from Israel into Assyrian captivity (721 B.C.)

© Thomas Nelson, Inc., 2000

Black Sea

Caspian Sea

Gomer (Gimirrai)

Ararat (Urartu)

MT. ARARAT +

Lake Van

Lake Urmia

Carchemish

Gozan

Haran

Aleppo

Nineveh

Calah

Asshur

Madai (Medes)

Tiphsah

Hamath

Rezeph

Orontes R.

Arvad

Tadmor

Ecbatana

Euphrates R.

Tigris R.

Habor R.

Babylonia

The Great Sea (Mediterranean Sea)

Sidon

Tyre

Damascus

Samaria

Babylon

Nippur

Jerusalem

Susa

Erech

Ur

Arabia

Memphis

Egypt

Red Sea

Persian Gulf

Scale of Miles
0   150   300

A   B   C   D

1   1

2   2

Map 5:
THE BABYLONIAN EMPIRE
(C. 600 B.C.)

→ Exiles from Israel into Babylonian captivity (605, 597, 587 B.C.)
→ Return of exiles under Shesbazzar and Zerubbabel (538 B.C.)
→ Return of exiles under Ezra and Nehemiah (445 B.C.)

© Thomas Nelson, Inc., 2000

Black Sea

Caspian Sea

Cappadocia

Armenia (Urartu)

MT. ARARAT +

Lake Van

Lake Urmia

Carchemish

Gozan

Haran

Aleppo

Assyria

Nineveh

Arbela

Asshur

Media

Orontes R.

Arvad

Hamath

Riblah

Tadmor

Ecbatana

Habor R.

Tigris R.

Euphrates R.

Babylonia

The Great Sea (Mediterranean Sea)

Sidon

Tyre

Damascus

Samaria

Babylon

Nippur

Jerusalem

Erech

Ur

Susa

Jordan R.

Arabia

Memphis

Egypt

Nile R.

Red Sea

Persian Gulf

Scale of Miles
0   150   300

A   B   C   D

1   1

2   2

1538

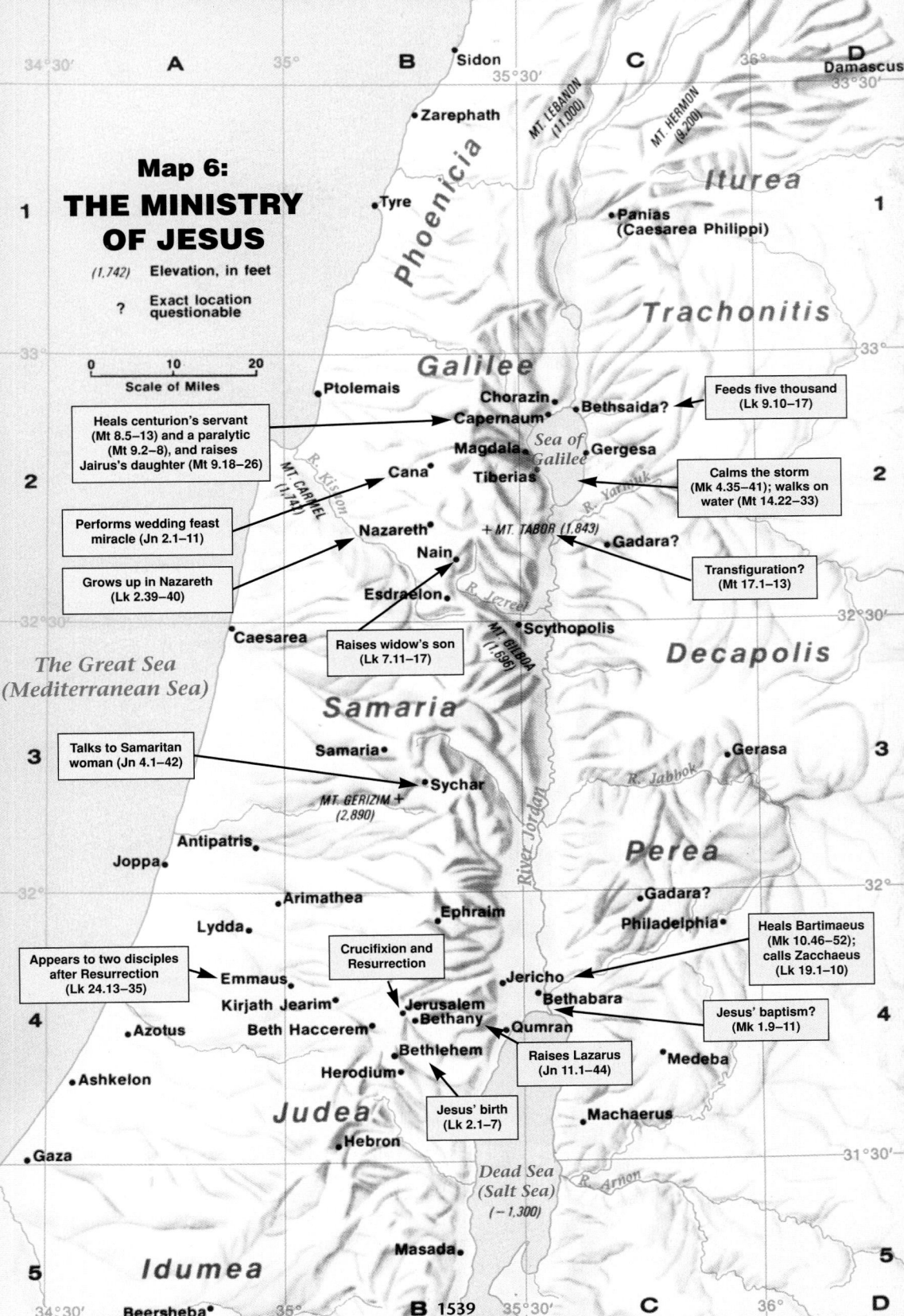

Map 6:
THE MINISTRY OF JESUS

(1,742)   Elevation, in feet

?   Exact location questionable

0   10   20
Scale of Miles

Sidon

Damascus

Zarephath

MT. LEBANON (11,000)

MT. HERMON (9,200)

Phoenicia

Tyre

Iturea

Panias (Caesarea Philippi)

Trachonitis

Galilee

Ptolemais

Chorazin

Bethsaida?

Feeds five thousand (Lk 9.10–17)

Capernaum

Heals centurion's servant (Mt 8.5–13) and a paralytic (Mt 9.2–8), and raises Jairus's daughter (Mt 9.18–26)

Magdala

Sea of Galilee

Gergesa

MT. CARMEL (1,742)

R. Kishon

Cana

Tiberias

Calms the storm (Mk 4.35–41); walks on water (Mt 14.22–33)

R. Yarmuk

Performs wedding feast miracle (Jn 2.1–11)

Nazareth

+ MT. TABOR (1,843)

Gadara?

Grows up in Nazareth (Lk 2.39–40)

Nain

Transfiguration? (Mt 17.1–13)

Esdraelon

R. Jezreel

Caesarea

Raises widow's son (Lk 7.11–17)

MT. GILBOA (1,696)

Scythopolis

Decapolis

The Great Sea (Mediterranean Sea)

Samaria

Talks to Samaritan woman (Jn 4.1–42)

Samaria

Gerasa

Sychar

R. Jabbok

MT. GERIZIM + (2,890)

Antipatris

Joppa

Perea

Arimathea

Ephraim

Gadara?

Lydda

Philadelphia

Heals Bartimaeus (Mk 10.46–52); calls Zacchaeus (Lk 19.1–10)

Appears to two disciples after Resurrection (Lk 24.13–35)

Emmaus

Crucifixion and Resurrection

Jericho

Kirjath Jearim

Jerusalem

Bethabara

Bethany

Jesus' baptism? (Mk 1.9–11)

Azotus

Beth Haccerem

Qumran

Bethlehem

Raises Lazarus (Jn 11.1–44)

Medeba

Ashkelon

Herodium

Jesus' birth (Lk 2.1–7)

Judea

Machaerus

Hebron

Gaza

Dead Sea (Salt Sea) (– 1,300)

R. Arnon

Idumea

Masada

Beersheba

B   1539

C

D

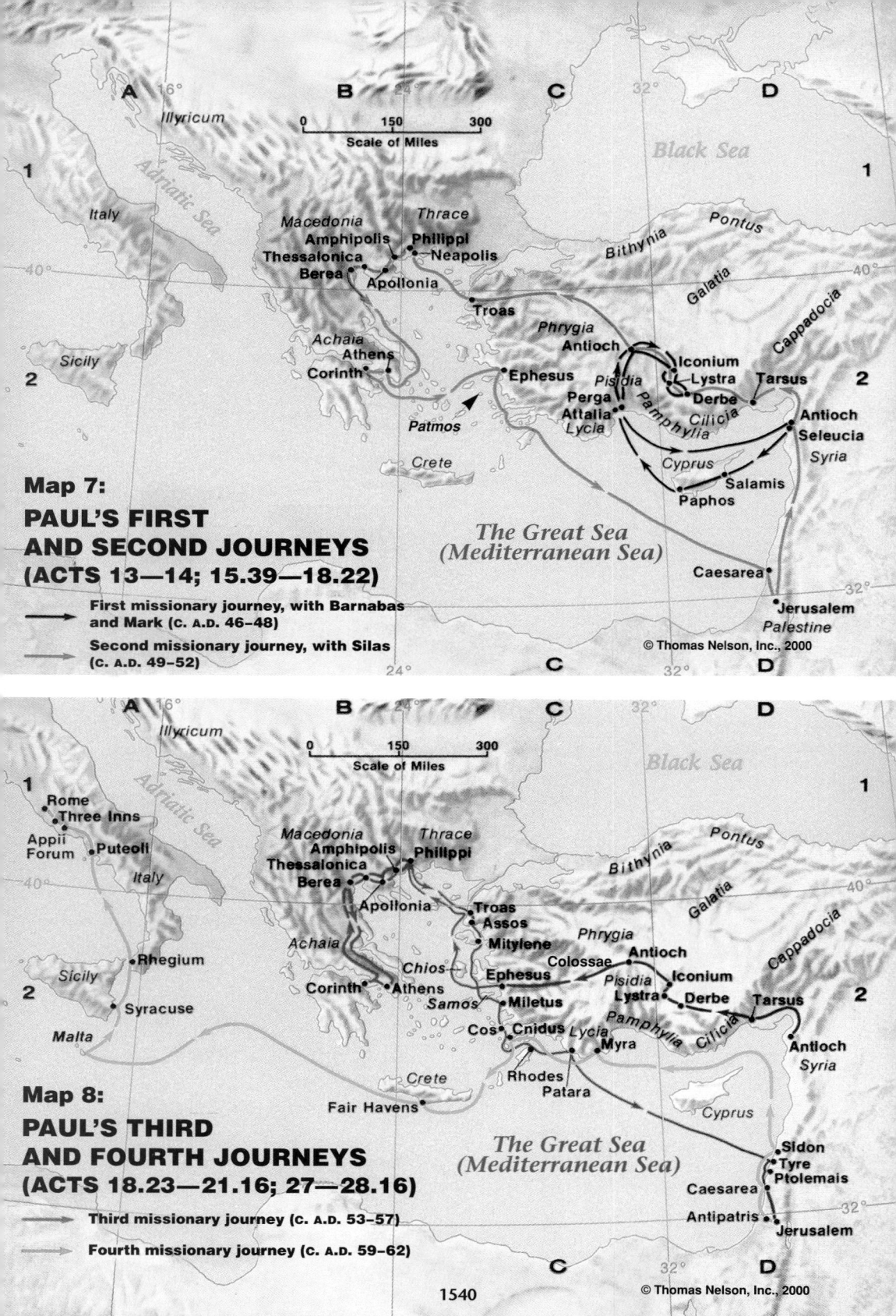

Map 7:
PAUL'S FIRST AND SECOND JOURNEYS
(ACTS 13—14; 15.39—18.22)

→ First missionary journey, with Barnabas and Mark (c. A.D. 46–48)

→ Second missionary journey, with Silas (c. A.D. 49–52)

© Thomas Nelson, Inc., 2000

Illyricum
Italy
Adriatic Sea
Sicily
0   150   300
Scale of Miles
Black Sea
Macedonia
Amphipolis
Thessalonica
Berea
Apollonia
Thrace
Philippi
Neapolis
Bithynia
Pontus
Galatia
Cappadocia
Troas
Achaia
Athens
Corinth
Phrygia
Antioch
Ephesus
Pisidia
Perga
Attalia
Lycia
Iconium
Lystra
Derbe
Tarsus
Cilicia
Pamphylia
Antioch
Seleucia
Syria
Patmos
Crete
Cyprus
Salamis
Paphos
The Great Sea
(Mediterranean Sea)
Caesarea
Jerusalem
Palestine

Map 8:
PAUL'S THIRD AND FOURTH JOURNEYS
(ACTS 18.23—21.16; 27—28.16)

→ Third missionary journey (c. A.D. 53–57)

→ Fourth missionary journey (c. A.D. 59–62)

© Thomas Nelson, Inc., 2000

Illyricum
Adriatic Sea
Rome
Three Inns
Appii Forum
Puteoli
Italy
Sicily
Rhegium
Syracuse
Malta
0   150   300
Scale of Miles
Black Sea
Macedonia
Amphipolis
Thessalonica
Berea
Apollonia
Thrace
Philippi
Troas
Assos
Mitylene
Bithynia
Pontus
Galatia
Cappadocia
Achaia
Chios
Corinth
Athens
Samos
Phrygia
Colossae
Ephesus
Miletus
Cos
Cnidus
Pisidia
Lystra
Antioch
Iconium
Derbe
Tarsus
Cilicia
Pamphylia
Lycia
Myra
Rhodes
Patara
Antioch
Syria
Crete
Fair Havens
Cyprus
The Great Sea
(Mediterranean Sea)
Sidon
Tyre
Ptolemais
Caesarea
Antipatris
Jerusalem

1540

Map 9:
THE HOLY LAND IN MODERN TIMES

Area occupied by Israel since June, 1967

Scale of Miles
0   25   50

A B C D E

LEBANON

Tripoli

Beirut

LEBANON MTS.   BEKAA VALLEY   ANTI-LEBANON MTS.

Sidon

Damascus

Tyre

Dan

U.N. Buffer Zone
1973 Line

SYRIA

Qiryat Shemona

Quneitra
1967 Cease-Fire Line

Nahariyya

Safad

Golan Heights

Akko

Sea of Galilee

Haifa

Tiberias

Dera

Nazareth

Ramtha

Afula

The Great Sea (Mediterranean Sea)

Beth Shean

Hadera

Tulkarm

Jarash

Netanya

Nablus

Herzliyya

Jordan River

Tel Aviv

West Bank

Yafo

Petah Tiqwa

Amman

Rishon le Zion

Lod

Ramla

Ramalah

Ashdod

Jericho

Jerusalem

Ashqelon

Bethlehem

Madaba

Gaza

Qiryat Gat

Hebron

Dhiban

En Gedi

Dead Sea (Salt Sea)

Al-Arish

Beersheba

Karak

JORDAN

ISRAEL

EGYPT

Negev

Arabah

Sinai

Elat   Aqaba

1541

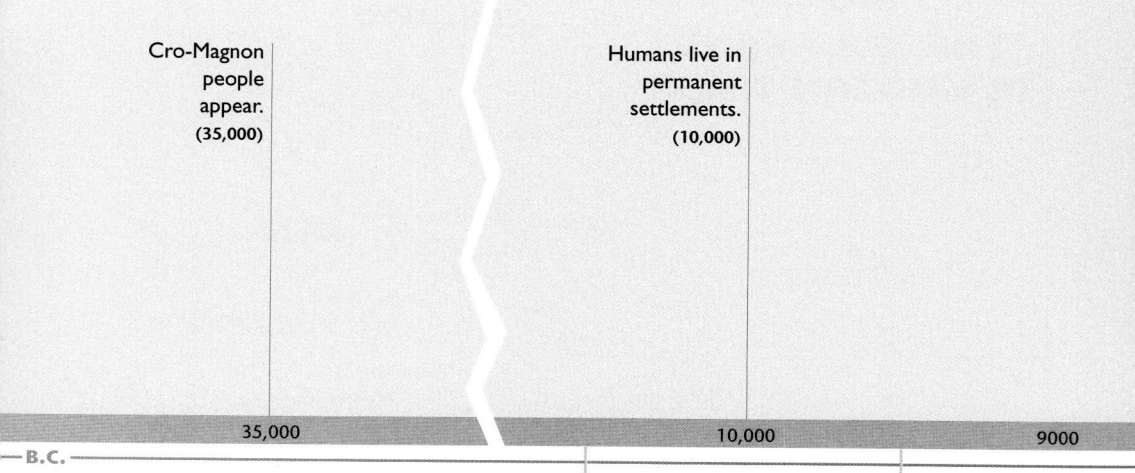

Cro-Magnon people appear. (35,000)		Humans live in permanent settlements. (10,000)	
35,000		10,000	9000

— B.C. ——

Timeline of Human History

Timeline of Biblical History

— B.C. ——

PREHISTORY	2000	1900	1800	1700

Jacob's
descendants
settle in Egypt.
(1750)

Abraham and Sarah
arrive in Canaan.
(1850)

BIBLICAL PREHISTORY

Important Biblical Figures
Adam and Eve
Cain and Abel
Noah

TIME OF THE PATRIARCHS
AND MATRIARCHS

Important Biblical Figures
Abraham and Sarah
Isaac and Rebekah
Jacob, Leah, and Rachel
Joseph and Asenath

1542

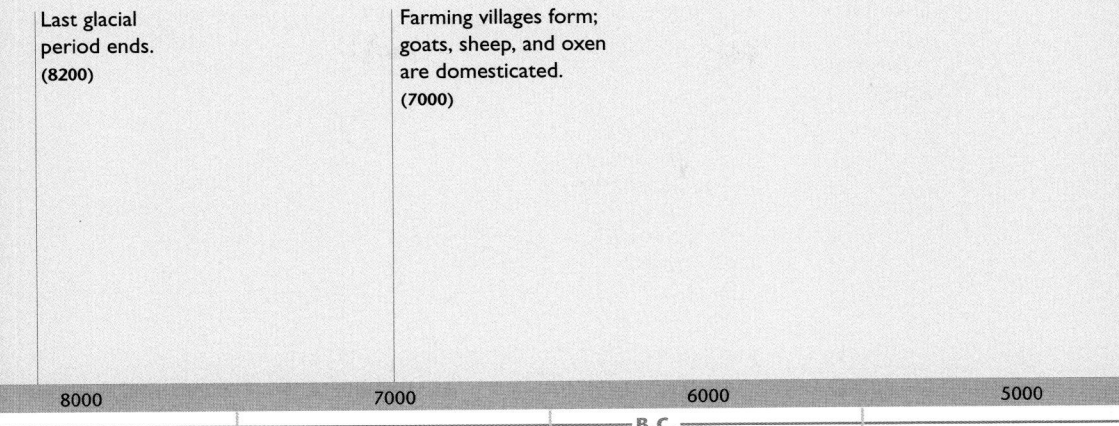

Last glacial
period ends.
(8200)

Farming villages form;
goats, sheep, and oxen
are domesticated.
(7000)

8000	7000	6000	5000

B.C.

Timeline of Human History

Timeline of Biblical History

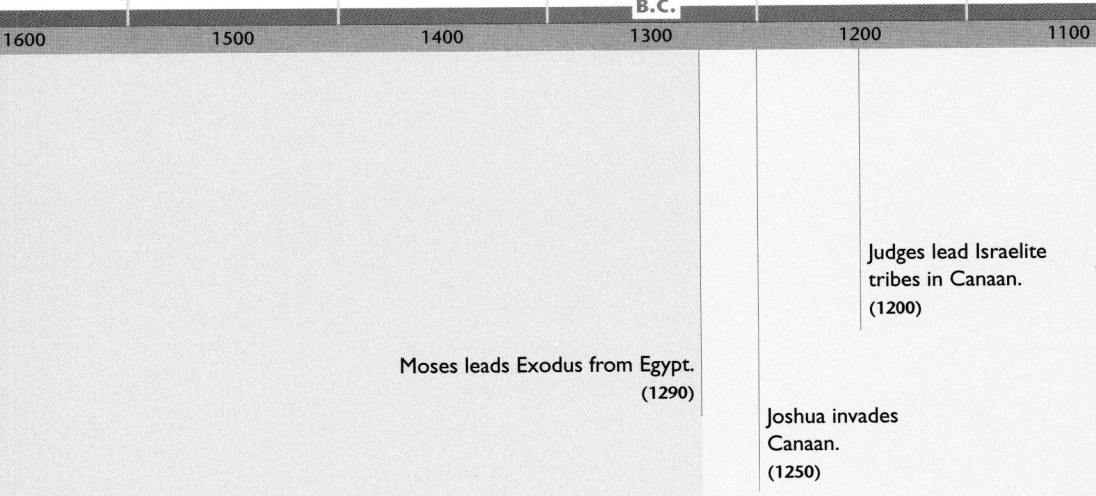

B.C.

1600	1500	1400	1300	1200	1100

Judges lead Israelite
tribes in Canaan.
(1200)

Moses leads Exodus from Egypt.
(1290)

Joshua invades
Canaan.
(1250)

TIME IN EGYPT AND THE EXODUS

Important Biblical Figures
Moses
Aaron
Miriam

TIME OF THE JUDGES

Important Biblical Figures
Deborah
Gideon
Samson
Samuel

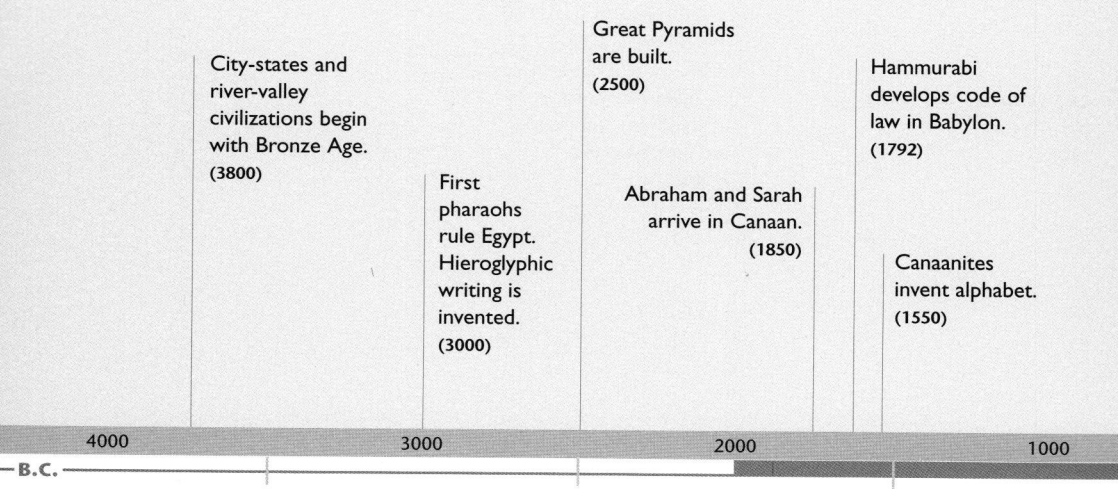

Timeline of Human History

City-states and river-valley civilizations begin with Bronze Age. (3800)	First pharaohs rule Egypt. Hieroglyphic writing is invented. (3000)	Great Pyramids are built. (2500) Abraham and Sarah arrive in Canaan. (1850)	Hammurabi develops code of law in Babylon. (1792) Canaanites invent alphabet. (1550)

B.C. — 4000 — 3000 — 2000 — 1000

Timeline of Biblical History   PROPHETS   Prominent Kings of Israel   Prominent Kings of Judah

B.C.

1000   900   800   700   600   500

Kingdom divides into Israel and Judah. (922)

Solomon rules kingdom, builds Temple. (961)

David unites kingdom, takes Jerusalem as capital. (1000)

Saul is named first king of Israel. (1020)

Assyrians capture Samaria, ending the kingdom of Israel. (721)

Babylonians take Jerusalem. Exile of Judah begins. (587)

Cyrus of Persia frees Jews to return to Judah. (538)

People of Judah rebuild Temple. (515)

ELIJAH (865)
ELISHA (850)
AMOS (783)
HOSEA (755)
FIRST ISAIAH (740)
MICAH (720)
NAHUM (663)
ZEPHANIAH (630)
JEREMIAH (626)
HABAKKUK (609)
EZEKIEL (593)
ZECHARIAH (520)
HAGGAI (520)
SECOND ISAIAH (540)

TIME OF THE KINGS AND PROPHETS

UNITED KINGDOM	DIVIDED KINGDOM	PERSIAN DOMINATION

	Jeroboam I (922)	Ahab (869)	Ahaziah (850)	Jeroboam II (786)	Hoshea (732)			
Saul David Solomon	Rehoboam (922)	Ahaziah (842)	Jehoash (837)	Uzziah (783)	Hezekiah (715)	Josiah (640)	Jehoiachin (598)	Zedekiah (597)

1544

Timeline of Human History

Buddha is born in India.
(563)

Confucius is born in China.
(551)

Greece has golden age.
(400)

Roman Empire is established.
(43 B.C.)

Jesus is crucified in Palestine.
(A.D. 30)

Roman Empire falls.
(476)

Muhammad founds Islam in Arabia.
(622)

Crusades begin.
(1096)

Gutenberg invents printing press.
(1450)

Columbus sails to America.
(1492)

Luther starts Protestant Reformation.
(1517)

Declaration of Independence is signed.
(1776)

Dominion of Canada is created.
(1867)

Personal computers become available.
(1972)

World War II begins.
(1939)

| 0 | 1000 | 2000 |

— A.D. —

Timeline of Biblical History

New Testament Books

B.C. — A.D.

| 400 | 300 | 200 | 100 | 0 | 100 |

Revolt against Greeks by Maccabees begins.
(166)

Temple is rededicated.
(165)

Greeks conquer Holy Land.
(332)

Romans conquer Holy Land.
(63)

Jesus is born.
(5 B.C.)

Ezra brings Torah to Jerusalem.
(398)

Jesus is crucified.
(A.D. 30)

Saul is converted.
(31)

Nehemiah becomes governor of Judah, starts renewal.
(445)

James is martyred.
(61)

Nero persecutes Christians. Peter and Paul are martyred.
(64–68)

MALACHI (458)

Romans destroy Jerusalem Temple.
(70)

1 Thess (51), Paul's major letters (mid- to late 50s)

Colossians, Philemon (early 60s)

Gospel of Mark (mid-60s)

Gospels of Matthew and Luke, Acts of the Apostles, Hebrews (70s to 80s)

Gospel of John; 1, 2, and 3 John; and Revelation (90s); 2 Peter (after 100)

TIME OF FOREIGN DOMINATION

TIME OF NEW TESTAMENT

| GREEK DOMINATION | ROMAN CONTROL | ROMAN DOMINATION |

Nehemiah   Ezra   The Maccabees

Domitian persecutes Christians.
(95)

The Holy Land: Old Testament Places

◀ **Mount Sinai, Egypt**
A trail leads down Mount Sinai, where Moses received the Ten Commandments from God.

▼ **Canaan**
The Promised Land of Canaan offered the Israelites the chance to settle down into agricultural life, planting vineyards and raising crops.

◀ **Gleaning**
Jewish law required the gleanings of crops (grain left over from reaping or cutting stalks) to be left for the poor.

◀ **Baal**
The Canaanite fertility god, Baal; when the Jews were exiled in Babylon, some of them fell into worshiping Baal so their crops would flourish.

◀ **Herod's Temple**
The Temple in Jerusalem was the center of Jewish life. This is a model of the Temple Herod rebuilt shortly before Jesus' time.

The Holy Land: New Testament Places

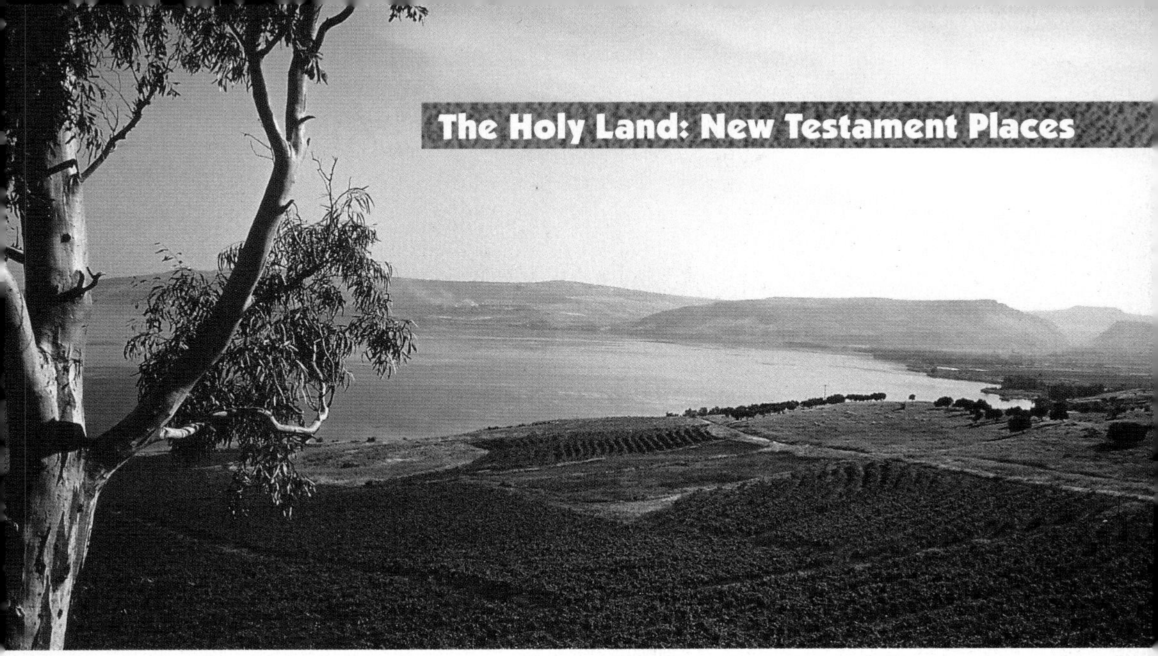

▲ Mount of Beatitudes, Sea of Galilee
The Mount of Beatitudes, overlooking the Sea of Galilee, is where Jesus preached the Sermon on the Mount.

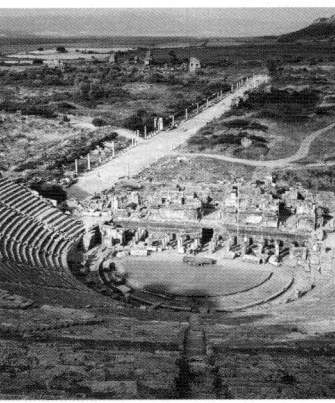

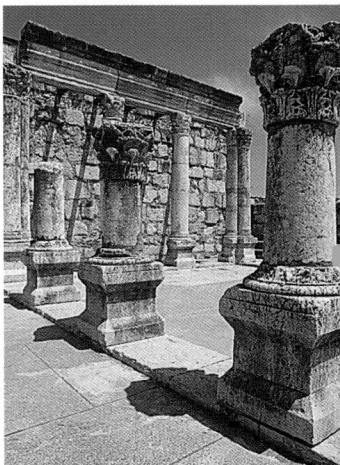

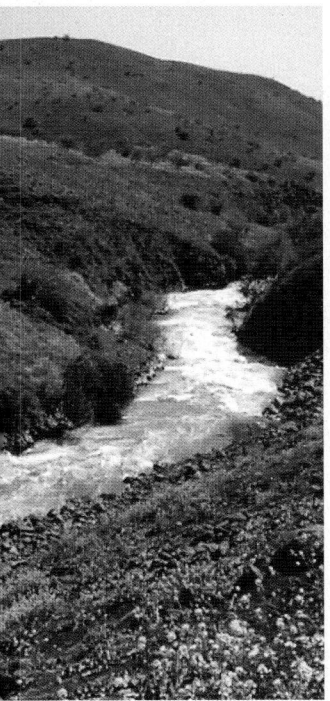

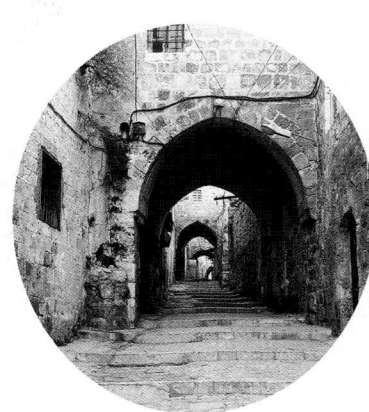

▲ Jordan River
Jesus began his mission by being baptized in the Jordan River by John the Baptist.

▲ Ephesus, Turkey
Ruins of the great amphitheater where Paul preached in Ephesus, Turkey.

▼ Capernum
Ruins of a synagogue in Capernaum, where Jesus based his ministry. Jesus often taught in the synagogues, referring to the Hebrew Scriptures frequently.

◄ Via Dolorosa
A street in Jerusalem, leading off the Via Dolorosa, the path believed to have been taken by Jesus on the way to the Crucifixion.

▲ Bedouins
A bedouin girl returning from the water hole in a desert oasis in Israel.

▶ Western Wall
The Western Wall is the only portion of Herod's Temple that survived destruction by the Romans in A.D. 70. Today, the Wall is a central place of prayer for Jews and pilgrims to the Holy Land.

▶ Peace now
An Israeli woman holds a sign reading "Peace now," written in Hebrew, Arabic, and English, during a demonstration for an end to conflict between the Jews and Arabs.

◀ Man praying at the Western Wall
An Orthodox Jewish man prays at the Western Wall. In the cracks of the Wall are slips of paper with prayer intentions that the Jews and pilgrims write.

◀ Jerusalem
A view of Jerusalem from the Mount of Olives. The Old City is surrounded by a high brick wall and divided into quadrants: Jewish, Christian, Armenian, and Muslim.

▲ The joyful Jesus

▲ Jesus prays in the Garden of Gethsemane
(Mt 26.36–46, Mk 14.32–42, Lk 22.39–46)

▲ Jesus united with those
who suffer

▲ Jesus and the Beloved
Disciple (Jn 13.23)

▲ The glorified Christ
"His face was like the sun shining
with full force" (Rev 1.16).

▲ The Sacred Heart of Jesus
"By his wounds you have been
healed" (1 Pet 2.24).

▲ Jesus' crucifixion
"But God proves his love for
us in that while we still were
sinners Christ died for us"
(Rom 5.8).

▼ Jesus and the
children
(Mt 19.13–15,
Mk 10.13–16,
Lk 18.15–17)

1549

Alphabetical List of Bible Books and Abbreviations

Book	Abbreviation	Page	Book	Abbreviation	Page
Acts	Acts	1281	1 Kings	1 Kings	327
Amos	Am	1059	2 Kings	2 Kings	358
Baruch	Bar	962	Lamentations	Lam	953
1 Chronicles	1 Chr	386	Leviticus	Lev	107
2 Chronicles	2 Chr	413	Luke	Lk	1197
Colossians	Col	1402	1 Maccabees	1 Macc	514
1 Corinthians	1 Cor	1345	2 Maccabees	2 Macc	543
2 Corinthians	2 Cor	1366	Malachi	Mal	1112
Daniel	Dan	1019	Mark	Mk	1167
Deuteronomy	Deut	175	Matthew	Mt	1120
Ecclesiastes	Eccl	722	Micah	Mic	1076
Ephesians	Eph	1387	Nahum	Nah	1084
Esther	Esth	501	Nehemiah	Neh	456
Exodus	Ex	60	Numbers	Num	137
Ezekiel	Ezek	971	Obadiah	Ob	1069
Ezra	Ezra	445	1 Peter	1 Pet	1457
Galatians	Gal	1379	2 Peter	2 Pet	1464
Genesis	Gen	4	Philemon	Philem	1433
Habakkuk	Hab	1088	Philippians	Phil	1396
Haggai	Hag	1098	Proverbs	Prov	691
Hebrews	Heb	1436	Psalms	Ps	601
Hosea	Hos	1041	Revelation	Rev	1483
Isaiah	Isa	824	Romans	Rom	1324
James	Jas	1450	Ruth	Ruth	263
Jeremiah	Jer	891	1 Samuel	1 Sam	269
Job	Job	568	2 Samuel	2 Sam	300
Joel	Joel	1053	Sirach	Sir	765
1 John	1 Jn	1469	Song of Solomon	Song	733
2 John	2 Jn	1476	1 Thessalonians	1 Thess	1408
3 John	3 Jn	1478	2 Thessalonians	2 Thess	1415
John	Jn	1245	1 Timothy	1 Tim	1419
Jonah	Jon	1072	2 Timothy	2 Tim	1426
Joshua	Josh	214	Titus	Titus	1430
Jude	Jude	1480	Tobit	Tob	470
Judges	Judg	238	Wisdom of Solomon	Wis	741
Judith	Jdt	485	Zechariah	Zech	1101
			Zephaniah	Zeph	1093

All scripture is inspired by God and is useful for teaching, for reproof, for correction, and for training in righteousness, so that everyone who belongs to God may be proficient, equipped for every good work.

(2 Tim 3.16–17)